Williams on Wills

Editors of previous editions

First edition	1952	W J Williams
Second edition	1961	W J Williams
Third edition	1967	W J Williams
Fourth edition	1974	C H Sherrin and R F D Barlow
Fifth edition	1980	C H Sherrin, R F D Barlow and R A Wallington
Sixth edition	1987	C H Sherrin, R F D Barlow and R A Wallington
Seventh edition	1995	C H Sherrin, R F D Barlow and R A Wallington
Eighth edition	2002	C H Sherrin, R F D Barlow, R A Wallington, S L Meadway and M C Waterworth

Williams on Wills

Ninth Edition

Consultant Editor

FRANCIS BARLOW
MA (OXON)
One of Her Majesty's Counsel, a Bencher of Lincoln's Inn
10 Old Square, Lincoln's Inn, London WC2A 3SU

Editors

CHRISTOPHER SHERRIN
LLM PHD
Professor of Law, Department of Professional Legal Education, University of Hong Kong

RICHARD WALLINGTON
MA (CANTAB)
Barrister, a Bencher of Lincoln's Inn
10 Old Square, Lincoln's Inn, London WC2A 3SU

SUSANNAH MEADWAY
MA (OXON)
of the Middle Temple and Lincoln's Inn, Barrister
10 Old Square, Lincoln's Inn, London WC2A 3SU

MICHAEL WATERWORTH
MA (CANTAB)
of Lincoln's Inn, Barrister
10 Old Square, Lincoln's Inn, London WC2A 3SU

Volume 2
Precedents and Statutes

LexisNexis®
® Butterworths

Members of the LexisNexis Group worldwide

United Kingdom	LexisNexis Butterworths, a Division of Reed Elsevier (UK) Ltd, Halsbury House, 35 Chancery Lane, London, WC2A 1EL, and RSH, 1–3 Baxter's Place, Leith Walk Edinburgh EH1 3AF
Argentina	LexisNexis Argentina, BUENOS AIRES
Australia	LexisNexis Butterworths, CHATSWOOD, New South Wales
Austria	LexisNexis Verlag ARD Orac GmbH & Co KG, VIENNA
Canada	LexisNexis Butterworths, MARKHAM, Ontario
Chile	LexisNexis Chile Ltda, SANTIAGO DE CHILE
Czech Republic	Nakladatelství Orac sro, PRAGUE
France	Editions du Juris-Classeur SA, PARIS
Germany	LexisNexis Deutschland GmbH, FRANKFURT and MUNSTER
Hong Kong	LexisNexis Butterworths, HONG KONG
Hungary	HVG-Orac, BUDAPEST
India	LexisNexis Butterworths, NEW DELHI
Italy	Giuffrè Editore, MILAN
Malaysia	Malayan Law Journal Sdn Bhd, KUALA LUMPUR
New Zealand	LexisNexis Butterworths, WELLINGTON
Poland	Wydawnictwo Prawnicze LexisNexis, WARSAW
Singapore	LexisNexis Butterworths, SINGAPORE
South Africa	LexisNexis Butterworths, Durban
Switzerland	Stämpfli Verlag AG, BERNE
USA	LexisNexis, DAYTON, Ohio

Published by LexisNexis Butterworths

A CIP Catalogue record for this book is available from the British Library.

Volume 2 ISBN: 9781405725859

Set ISBN: 9781405725835

ISBN 978-1-4057-2585-9

9 781405 725859

ISBN 978-1-4057-2583-5

9 781405 725835

Typeset by Columns Design Ltd, Reading, England

Printed and bound by William Clowes Limited, Beccles, Suffolk

Visit LexisNexis Butterworths at www.lexisnexis.co.uk

Contents

VOLUME 2 – PRECEDENTS AND STATUTES

Form Finder .... *xxxvii*

Table of Abbreviations .... *lxxi*

Cumulative Table of Statutes .... *lxxiii*

Cumulative Table of Cases .... *ciii*

PART A – INTRODUCTORY NOTE

PARA

I. GENERAL .... **[200.1]**
- (a) Capacity and freedom from influence .... **[200.2]**
- (b) Form of will .... **[200.9]**
- (c) Other points .... **[200.27]**
- (d) The Trusts of Land and Appointment of Trustees Act 1996 and the Trustee Act 2000 .... **[200.48]**

II. INHERITANCE TAX .... **[200.68]**
- (a) Main characteristics .... **[200.69]**
- (b) Exemptions and reliefs relevant to testamentary dispositions .... **[200.84]**
- (c) Will trusts .... **[200.92]**
- (d) Incidence of IHT .... **[200.111]**
- (e) Partially exempt estates .... **[200.112]**
- (f) The consequences of IHT for dispositions by will (other than the creation of will trusts) .... **[200.119]**
- (g) Trusts in dispositions by will – usefulness, the alternatives, and tax consequences .... **[200.125]**
- (h) Review of existing wills after FA 2006 and the Pre-Budget Report of 9 October 2007 .... **[200.134]**

PART B – CLAUSES IN WILLS

B1 Commencement of will .... **[201.1]**

PRELIMINARY NOTE .... **[201.1]**
- B1.1 Ordinary commencement .... **[201.6]**
- B1.2 Commencement of will made in expectation of marriage .... **[201.7]**
- B1.3 Commencement of will made in expectation of forming a civil partnership .... **[201.8]**
- B1.4 Commencement of will made in expectation of marriage—conditional form .... **[201.9]**

B1.5 Commencement of will made in expectation of civil partnership – conditional form ..... **[201.10]**

B1.6 Commencement of will of testator with UK and foreign property confining the will to UK property ..... **[201.11]**

B1.7 Commencement of concurrent will of testator with UK and foreign property confining the will to UK property ..... **[201.12]**

B1.8 Commencement of mutual will made in pursuance of an agreement that it shall not be revoked ..... **[201.13]**

B1.9 Commencement of mirror but not mutual wills ..... **[201.14]**

B1.10 Commencement of will made on behalf of a mentally disordered person pursuant to an order of the Court of Protection ..... **[201.15]**

B2 Miscellaneous declarations and desires sometimes included in wills ..... **[202.1]**

GENERAL NOTE ..... **[202.1]**

Disposal of body ..... **[202.2]**

B2.1 Direction as to place of burial and tombstone ..... **[202.3]**

B2.2 Expressions of desire as to cremation ..... **[202.4]**

B2.3 Direction that only necessary expense shall be incurred ..... **[202.5]**

B2.4 Direction as to the ascertainment of the testator's death in order to prevent his being buried alive ..... **[202.6]**

B2.5 Power for executor to incur expense in respect of directions ..... **[202.7]**

Anatomical research and organ transplantation ..... **[202.8]**

B2.6 Direction for anatomical examination and corneal grafting ..... **[202.16]**

B2.7 Clause providing for the use of the testator's body for therapeutic purposes, but not for medical education or research ..... **[202.17]**

Maintenance of graves ..... **[202.18]**

B2.8 Gift for the upkeep of a particular grave during a perpetuity period ..... **[202.31]**

B2.9 Perpetual gift for the upkeep of a churchyard with a request to maintain a particular grave ..... **[202.32]**

B2.10 Gift for the upkeep of a particular grave in a churchyard during a perpetuity period followed by a perpetual gift for the upkeep of the churchyard with a request to maintain the particular grave ..... **[202.33]**

B2.11 Direction to executors to enter into an agreement for the maintenance of a grave in a local authority cemetery ..... **[202.34]**

B2.12 Gift to a charity conditional upon the maintenance of a particular grave with a gift over on breach of the condition to another charity ..... **[202.35]**

Maintenance of animals ..... **[202.36]**

B2.13 Gift for the maintenance and upkeep of an animal ..... **[202.37]**

B2.14 Combined gift of legacy and pet animal coupled with a non-binding expression of hope that the legatee will look after the animal ..... **[202.38]**

Declarations under the Inheritance (Provision for Family and Dependants) Act 1975 .... **[202.39]**

B2.15 Declarations under the Inheritance (Provision for Family and Dependants) Act 1975—Alternative forms .... **[202.40]**

Clause headings or marginal notes .... **[202.41]**

B2.16 Direction regarding clause headings or marginal notes .... **[202.42]**

B3 Appointment of executors, trustees and guardians .... [203.1]

Preliminary Note on Executors and Trustees .... **[203.1]**

Individuals .... **[203.7]**

B3.1 Appointment of wife as sole executrix and trustee with alternative appointment .... **[203.7]**

B3.2 Appointment of civil partner as sole executor and trustee with alternative appointment .... **[203.8]**

B3.3 Appointment of executors .... **[203.9]**

B3.4 Appointment of same persons as executors and trustees .... **[203.10]**

B3.5 Appointment of executors and of different persons as trustees .... **[203.11]**

B3.6 Appointment of wife / civil partner during widowhood/until formation of a civil partnership adult son and infant son when he attains majority to be executors and trustees .... **[203.12]**

B3.7 Appointment of three persons, one of whom is abroad, to be executors and trustees, and also trustees for the purposes of the Settled Land Act 1925 .... **[203.13]**

B3.8 Appointment of executors and trustees with provisions for substitution in case of vacancy .... **[203.14]**

Solicitors .... **[203.15]**

B3.9 Appointment of future partners in a solicitors' firm as executors and trustees .... **[203.24]**

B3.10 Appointment of members of solicitors' incorporated practice including a limited liability partnership .... **[203.25]**

B3.11 Appointment of members and employees held out as partners of solicitors' incorporated practice including a limited liability partnership .... **[203.26]**

B3.12 Appointment of future partners in a solicitors' firm or future members of the body or limited liability partnership in the event of incorporation .... **[203.27]**

Corporations .... **[203.28]**

B3.13 Appointment of a bank together with individuals as executors and trustees .... **[203.32]**

B3.14 Appointment of bank as sole executor and trustee .... **[203.33]**

B3.15 Appointment of insurance company as executor and trustee .... **[203.34]**

B3.16 Remuneration clause for bank appointed as executor and trustee .... **[203.35]**

The Public Trustee .... **[203.36]**

B3.17 Application by an intending testator to the Public Trustee to act as executor and trustee under a will .... **[203.36]**

B3.18 Clause in will appointing the Public Trustee as sole executor and trustee or jointly with others .... **[203.37]**

B3.19 Clauses in will appointing executors and trustees, the Public Trustee being only a trustee or custodian trustee .... **[203.38]**

B3.20 Clauses in will of a person domiciled elsewhere than in England and Wales appointing an individual executor and providing for transfer of the residuary estate or of a legacy to the Public Trustee to be held upon English trusts . **[203.39]**

B3.21 Codicil revoking appointment of executors and trustees and appointing the Public Trustee sole executor and trustee in their place .... **[203.40]**

B3.22 Codicil appointing the Public Trustee as executor and trustee jointly with executors and trustees previously appointed or in place of one who has died .... **[203.41]**

B3.23 Clause in will prohibiting appointment of the Public Trustee as a trustee .... **[203.42]**

Separate executors for particular assets .... **[203.43]**

B3.24 Appointment of literary executors .... **[203.43]**

B3.25 Appointment of separate executors for testator's business .... **[203.44]**

B3.26 Appointment of separate executors for UK property and foreign property .... **[203.45]**

B3.27 Appointment of special executors of settled land ...... **[203.46]**

Guardians .... **[203.47]**

B3.28 Appointment of guardian to take effect only if the other parent predeceases the appointor, with optional wording making it also take effect if the other parent does not make an effective appointment .... **[203.60]**

B3.29 Appointment of guardian which takes effect if the other parent predeceases the appointor or if there is a residence order in favour of the testator at his or her death, with optional wording making it also take effect if the other parent does not make an effective appointment .... **[203.61]**

B3.30 Appointment of two guardians with expression of wishes about religious education .... **[203.62]**

B3.31 Appointment of a guardian with an alternative appointment if the first choice predeceases the testator or disclaims .... **[203.63]**

B3.32 Appointment by the mother of illegitimate children, appointing the father as guardian with alternative appointment in the event of him predeceasing her .... **[203.64]**

B3.33 Appointment of wife to be the guardian of children by a former marriage with general revocation of previous appointments .... **[203.65]**

B3.34 Appointment of a guardian by a guardian .... **[203.66]**

B4 Specific gifts... [204.1]

NOTE ON THE INCIDENCE OF INHERITANCE TAX .... **[204.1]**

Personal chattels .... **[204.2]**

B4.1 Gift of personal chattels by incorporation of Statutory Will Forms 1925, Form 2 .... **[204.15]**

B4.2 Gift of personal chattels by incorporation of definition in the Administration of Estates Act 1925 .... **[204.16]**

B4.3 Gift of personal chattels to wife....[204.17]
B4.4 Gift of personal chattels to wife—alternative form....[204.18]
B4.5 Gift of personal chattels—short form....[204.19]
B4.6 Gift to wife of such articles as she may select....[204.20]
B4.7 Gift to wife of such articles as she may select up to a stated amount and of the residue to testator's daughters....[204.21]
B4.8 Gift of articles of personal adornment to daughters as trustees shall determine....[204.22]
B4.9 Gift of articles with request to distribute them in accordance with testator's wishes....[204.23]
B4.10 Gift of chattels selected by trustees on life interest trusts....[204.24]
B4.11 Gift to trustees of chattels upon a short-term discretionary trust....[204.25]
B4.12 Gift of chattels in specific dwellinghouse....[204.26]
B4.13 Gift of chattel with residuary estate paying costs of preservation, transport, packing and insurance....[204.27]
B4.14 Gift of item which might be conditionally exempt from inheritance tax....[204.28]
B4.15 Gift to a public collection or the nation of a work of art....[204.29]
B4.16 Gift of a library....[204.30]
B4.17 Gift of sporting implements....[204.31]
B4.18 Gift of wearing apparel to servants....[204.32]
B4.19 Gift of letters and papers....[204.33]
B4.20 Gift by reference to a document already in existence.[204.34]
Consumable stores....[204.35]
B4.21 Gift of consumable stores....[204.36]
Furniture....[204.37]
B4.22 Gift of furniture to wife....[204.40]
B4.23 Gift of furniture in a certain house....[204.41]
B4.24 Gift of furniture to such of testator's children as survive him....[204.42]
B4.25 Gift to a daughter of furniture and effects in her bedroom....[204.43]
B4.26 Gifts of furniture and effects to daughters contingently on their attaining eighteen or twenty-one or marrying ...[204.44]
B4.27 Gift of furniture and effects to wife for life or during widowhood; no inventory....[204.45]
B4.28 Gift of furniture and effects to civil partner for life or until marriage or formation of civil partnership; no inventory....[204.46]
B4.29 Gift of furniture to wife during widowhood; repairs and insurance to be provided for by her, and an inventory made....[204.47]
B4.30 Gift of furniture to civil partner until marriage or formation of civil partnership; repairs and insurance to be provided for by him, and an inventory made....[204.48]
B4.31 Gift of furniture to wife or civil partner during life and thereafter for children directions for inventory, and for repairs and insurance out of income during life....[204.49]

B4.32 Gift of furniture to widow for life and then to son, incorporation of Statutory Will Form as to inventory .... **[204.50]**

Stocks and shares .... **[204.51]**

B4.33 Gift of stock as a general legacy .... **[204.55]**

B4.34 Specific gift of stock .... **[204.56]**

B4.35 Gift of shares held by testator at death and of shares to which he will be entitled at death .... **[204.57]**

B4.36 Gift of shares in public company .... **[204.58]**

B4.37 Gift of shares in public or private company—provision for only a lesser number of shares being available .... **[204.59]**

B4.38 Gift of shares with provision for amalgamation, reconstruction, reorganisation or demerger .... **[204.60]**

B4.39 Specific legacy of shares with added words negativing apportionment .... **[204.61]**

Debts .... **[204.62]**

B4.40 Gift of a debt .... **[204.62]**

B4.41 Gift of principal of a debt but not of arrears of interest .... **[204.63]**

B4.42 Release to a debtor of debts present or future .... **[204.64]**

B4.43 Release of children's debts with optional provision for hotchpot .... **[204.65]**

B4.44 Gift of debt to a legatee of a share of residue with provision for hotchpot .... **[204.66]**

B4.45 Gift of mortgage debt to the mortgagor .... **[204.67]**

B4.46 Declaration that sums advanced were by way of gifts .... **[204.68]**

Undivided shares and clause dealing with joint property .... **[204.69]**

B4.47 Gift of undivided share in equity of real property .... **[204.69]**

B4.48 Gift of undivided share in personal property .... **[204.70]**

B4.49 Clause dealing with property held in joint tenancy .... **[204.71]**

Intellectual property .... **[204.72]**

B4.50 Absolute gift of copyrights and unpublished works to literary executor .... **[204.72]**

B4.51 Same—proceeds to be transferred to general executors .... **[204.73]**

B4.52 Gift of patents .... **[204.74]**

Miscellaneous gifts .... **[204.75]**

B4.53 Gift of entailed personalty .... **[204.75]**

B4.54 Gift of a reversionary interest .... **[204.76]**

B4.55 Gift of money secured by an insurance policy on testator's life .... **[204.77]**

B4.56 Clause exonerating specific gifts from charges .... **[204.78]**

B4.57 Gift of live and dead stock .... **[204.79]**

B4.58 Gift of farming stock .... **[204.80]**

B4.59 Gift of ready money .... **[204.81]**

B4.60 Gift of proceeds of premium savings bonds and prizes received or awarded since the testator's death .... **[204.82]**

B5 Gifts and other provisions relating to business property ....[205.1]

PRELIMINARY NOTE ....[205.1]

Business assets and inheritance tax—general points ....[205.4]

Payment of inheritance tax by instalments.................................[205.17]

Sole traders...[205.21]

Partnership interests ....[205.26]

Private company shares ....[205.29]

Land, buildings, plant and machinery ....[205.41]

Implications of inheritance tax business relief and instalment payment for what dispositions to make...[205.46]

B5.1 Bequest of a sole trader's business ....[205.58]

B5.2 Bequest to trustees of a business carried on on leasehold premises upon trust to carry on for a limited period .[205.59]

B5.3 Trusts of net profits and proceeds of sale of a business ....[205.60]

B5.4 Gift of Lloyd's underwriting business ....[205.61]

B5.5 Clause providing that inheritance tax on business premises be paid by trustees and repaid to them by son...........[205.62]

B5.6 Nomination of a son to succeed testator in partnership and gift to him of partnership share if he becomes a partner...[205.63]

B5.7 Clause giving effect to provision in partnership deed and granting widow a share of the profits during the joint lives of the widow and the surviving partner ....[205.64]

B5.8 Clauses giving assistance to son in acquiring partnership share, with alternative provision for realisation of the share ....[205.65]

B5.9 Gift of such of unquoted shares as shall have been owned for two years by the time of testator's death, subject to inheritance tax..[205.66]

B5.10 Gift of unquoted shares or any substitute shares on condition that they qualify for business relief, subject to inheritance tax, and with power to disclaim part of the gift ....[205.67]

B5.11 Bequest of an annuity to widow of principal director from shares in a family company, the shares being given to sons on the widow's death ....[205.68]

B5.12 Appointment by will of permanent director of private company ....[205.69]

Trustees' powers ....[205.70]

B5.13 Power to carry on business.......................................[205.70]

B5.14 Power to turn business into limited or unlimited company ....[205.71]

B5.15 Indemnity to trustees carrying on business ....[205.72]

B5.16 Power to trustees to carry on business where the will contains a general trust for conversion.......................[205.73]

B5.17 Power for some of the trustees only to carry on testator's business ....[205.74]

B5.18 Provision for exercise of powers though trustees interested in business ....[205.75]

B5.19 Power to lend money to legatee of business...............[205.76]

B5.20 Power to employ a manager ..... [205.77]
B5.21 Powers relating to sale of a business ..... [205.78]
B5.22 Powers to give warranties etc on the sale of a business or private company shares ..... [205.79]

B6 Gifts of freehold land ..... [206.1]

B6.1 Absolute general gift of freeholds or lands generally ..... [206.10]
B6.2 General gift of lands in a particular place ..... [206.11]
B6.3 Gift of freehold lands purchased in a certain year ..... [206.12]
B6.4 Specific gift of freeholds ..... [206.13]
B6.5 Specific gift of property with provision against apportionment ..... [206.14]
B6.6 Specific gift of registered land ..... [206.15]
B6.7 Gift to joint tenants or tenants in common ..... [206.16]
B6.8 Gift to minor ..... [206.17]
B6.9 Gift of land of which the testator is tenant in tail ..... [206.18]
B6.10 Gift of entailed property generally ..... [206.19]
B6.11 Gift of freeholds subject to the payment of a legacy ..... [206.20]
B6.12 Gift subject to the payment of debts, funeral, and testamentary expenses ..... [206.21]
B6.13 Gift subject to a mortgage ..... [206.22]
B6.14 Gift freed from a mortgage debt ..... [206.23]
B6.15 Gift of lands, and in the event of such lands being sold during testator's lifetime, bequest of the proceeds of sale of such lands ..... [206.24]
B6.16 Gift of lands which the testator has contracted to purchase ..... [206.25]
B6.17 Gift of certain freehold lands to a charity ..... [206.26]
B6.18 Gift subject to a condition as to taking a name ..... [206.27]
B6.19 Gift to a person with a gift over on death without issue ..... [206.28]
B6.20 Gift in exercise of a special power of appointment ..... [206.29]
B6.21 Expression of testator's intention not to exercise a general power of appointment over land ..... [206.30]
B6.22 Gift of lands upon the trusts of a settlement ..... [206.31]
B6.23 Gift by reference to a settlement on trust for sale ..... [206.32]
B6.24 Gift of lands to testator's sons, with successive gifts over if sons predecease testator without issue [male] ..... [206.33]
B6.25 Gift for the benefit of testator's children and the issue of deceased children at eighteen or marriage ..... [206.34]
B6.26 Gift with provision against lapse ..... [206.35]
B6.27 Clause creating an easement over land given to one person in favour of devisee of other land ..... [206.36]
B6.28 Gift of part of land to one person and the other part to another by reference to a plan, with cross easements ..... [206.37]
B6.29 Declaration as to payment of inheritance tax on specific gifts ..... [206.38]

B6.30 Specific gift subject to inheritance tax....................... [206.39]
B6.31 Specific gift of land which may qualify for agricultural property relief subject to inheritance tax .... [206.40]

B7 Gifts of leasehold land... [207.1]

B7.1 Gift of leaseholds.. [207.15]
B7.2 Gift of leasehold flat and devise of any interest in freehold of premises in which flat is contained .... [207.16]
B7.3 Gift of leasehold house free from mortgage .... [207.17]
B7.4 Gift of leaseholds with a direction that the legatee is to pay all arrears of rent and cost of dilapidations.............. [207.18]
B7.5 Gift of leaseholds to trustees upon trust to pay rents and profits to a person for life, and after his death to assign to another .... [207.19]
B7.6 Declaration that gift of lease includes the freehold reversion or any renewal if subsequently acquired .... [207.20]
B7.7 Contingent gift of leaseholds .... [207.21]
B7.8 Gift of undivided share in leaseholds......................... [207.22]
B7.9 Gift of sinking fund policies in respect of leasehold properties... [207.23]
B7.10 Declaration as to inheritance tax on settled leaseholds .... [207.24]
B7.11 Gift of leaseholds upon trust out of the rents and profits to form sinking fund... [207.25]
B7.12 Alternative provision for sinking fund to replace leasehold value .... [207.26]

B8 Rights of residence .... [208.1]

The statutory right of occupation under a trust of land.............. [208.5]
Giving rights of residence by will.. [208.19]
Other aspects .... [208.29]
Trusts of land .... [208.38]

B8.1 Interest of beneficiary limited to a right of residence with provision for changing residences.............................. [208.38]
B8.2 Interest of beneficiary limited to right of residence, with the beneficiary's consent to a sale being required generally, with provision for changing residences.............................. [208.39]
B8.3 Trust to permit residence and use of furniture etc by the testator's wife and children....................................... [208.40]
B8.4 Trust for wife for life or until she remarries and then for son, with power to permit residence.......................... [208.41]
B8.5 Trust for civil partner for life or until marriage or the formation of another civil partnership and then for son, with power to permit residence .... [208.42]
B8.6 Gift of residence for wife for life with the intention that she reside there—fuller form, providing for the possibility of a change of house by the testator before his death or by the trustees after his death .... [208.43]
B8.7 Clause in will of widow or widower providing residence and furniture for children .... [208.44]

Miscellaneous.. [208.45]

B8.8 Gift with the object of ensuring personal residence, giving the right to a series of short leases .... **[208.45]**

B8.9 The like—in the form of a lease determinable on death with rentcharge to support residence .... **[208.46]**

B8.10 Gift with the object of ensuring personal residence by the devisee—alternative form using a periodic tenancy .... **[208.47]**

B8.11 Gift of the testator's interest as tenant in common in a house, the gift being postponed to allow the other tenants in common to continue to reside in the house .... **[208.48]**

B9 Testamentary options .... [209.1]

B9.1 Clause giving option to purchase land .... **[209.6]**

B9.2 Direction to trustees to offer farm and farming assets to the testator's sons successively at a valuation before selling under a trust .... **[209.7]**

B9.3 Devise of freehold property conditional upon the donee conferring a right of pre-emption on another person .. **[209.8]**

B9.4 Clause giving option to testator's wife to purchase retail business .... **[209.9]**

B9.5 Clause giving option to son to take lease or purchase freehold of business premises .... **[209.10]**

B9.6 Clause giving option to purchase shares in family company .... **[209.11]**

B9.7 Clause giving option to purchase shares in private company (longer form) .... **[209.12]**

B10 Pecuniary legacies .... [210.1]

Absolute gifts .... **[210.9]**

B10.1 Legacy to one individual .... **[210.9]**

B10.2 Gift of a number of legacies .... **[210.10]**

B10.3 Legacies given by reference to a schedule .... **[210.11]**

B10.4 Legacy to husband and wife or survivor .... **[210.12]**

B10.5 Direction as to payment of interest at a variable rate .... **[210.13]**

B10.6 Legacy uprated by reference to Index of Retail Prices .... **[210.14]**

Provision for immediate needs .... **[210.15]**

B10.7 Immediate legacy to wife or civil partner or other person in charge of testator's household .... **[210.19]**

Deferred and prior legacies .... **[210.20]**

B10.8 Legacy payable six months after the death of the survivor of testator and his wife .... **[210.20]**

B10.9 Legacy with priority .... **[210.21]**

B10.10 Declaration as to time of payment and priority of legacies .... **[210.22]**

B10.11 Legacy payable on death of life tenant .... **[210.23]**

B10.12 Power to trustees to postpone payment of legacies .... **[210.24]**

Legacies with substitutional provisions .... **[210.25]**

B10.13 Legacy with a clause of substitution in the case of an individual legatee .... **[210.25]**

B10.14 Legacy to nieces, and the children of deceased nieces ..... [210.26]
Legacies to debtors and creditors ..... [210.27]
B10.15 Legacy to a creditor ..... [210.28]
B10.16 Declaration as to legacies to creditors ..... [210.29]
B10.17 Legacy to debtor without forgiveness of debt ..... [210.30]
B10.18 Legacy to debtor with forgiveness of debt ..... [210.31]
B10.19 Legacy to a son subject to deduction of sums owing ..... [210.32]
Minors and children ..... [210.33]
B10.20 Legacy to minor ..... [210.34]
B10.21 Small legacy to minor with provision for opening National Savings Bank account ..... [210.35]
B10.22 Legacy to a minor who is married ..... [210.36]
B10.23 Legacy to minor to be applied in maintenance ..... [210.37]
B10.24 Legacy to minor to provide an allowance for him ..... [210.38]
B10.25 Legacy of a capital sum for the education of children ..... [210.39]
B10.26 Legacy to grandchildren ..... [210.40]
B10.27 Legacy to an adopted child ..... [210.41]
B10.28 Legacy to children and an illegitimate child ..... [210.42]
B10.29 Legacy to illegitimate children of the testator, including one en ventre sa mère ..... [210.43]
B10.30 Legacy to legitimate and illegitimate children of a brother of the testator ..... [210.44]
B10.31 Legacy to married daughters to become subject to the trusts of their respective marriage settlements, the amount of the legacies varying in order to equalise the provisions made by the testator for all his daughters ..... [210.45]
Contingent and conditional legacies ..... [210.46]
B10.32 Legacy contingent on attaining eighteen or twenty-one ..... [210.46]
B10.33 Legacy contingent on attaining eighteen or twenty-one carrying interest ..... [210.47]
B10.34 Legacies to two persons contingently on their attaining eighteen or twenty-one years of age with survivorship ..... [210.48]
B10.35 Legacy contingent on attaining twenty-five or marrying, relying on the statutory powers of maintenance ..... [210.49]
B10.36 Legacy subject to discharge of guarantee ..... [210.50]
Legacies to executors and trustees ..... [210.51]
B10.37 Legacies to executors ..... [210.52]
B10.38 Legacies to executors and annuities to trustees ..... [210.53]
Legacies for improvident persons ..... [210.54]
B10.39 Legacy with provision for forfeiture on alienation ..... [210.55]
B10.40 Legacy to improvident person payable by instalments ..... [210.56]

Legacies to employees ..... [210.57]

B10.41 Legacy to a servant, if not under notice to leave at testator's death .... [210.58]
B10.42 Legacy to chauffeur with alternative gift if he shall have left the testator's service .... [210.59]
B10.43 Legacies to indoor servants .... [210.60]
B10.44 Legacies to servants—longer form .... [210.61]
B10.45 Legacy to clerks .... [210.62]
B10.46 Adjustment of legacies to servants or employees occasioned by redundancy payments under the Employment Rights Act 1996 .... [210.63]
Inheritance tax and foreign death duties .... [210.64]
B10.47 Legacies free of inheritance tax and duties payable outside Great Britain .... [210.68]
B10.48 Clause dealing with inheritance tax on lifetime gifts made by the testator .... [210.69]
B10.49 Clause providing for payment out of residue of inheritance tax on property not passing under the will .... [210.70]
B10.50 Clause providing for payment by the donee of the inheritance tax on a testamentary gift which would otherwise be free of inheritance tax .... [210.71]
Nil-rate band legacies .... [210.72]
B10.51 Nil-rate band legacy .... [210.72]
Miscellaneous .... [210.73]
B10.52 Legacies with provision for some of the legatees not being able to be found .... [210.73]
B10.53 Demonstrative legacy .... [210.74]
B10.54 Bequest of legacies payable exclusively out of a particular property with provision for abatement and interest ... [210.75]
B10.55 Clause providing for reduction of legacies where the testator's estate proves to have decreased in value...... [210.76]
B10.56 Declaration as to currency in which legacies payable. [210.77]
B10.57 Direction as to rate of exchange for payment of legacies in a foreign currency .... [210.78]
B10.58 Legacy for purchase of customary mourning .... [210.79]

B11 Annuities .... [211.1]
B11.1 Gift of simple annuity .... [211.8]
B11.2 Gift of annuity tax-free .... [211.9]
B11.3 Gift of annuity with reference to liability of annuitant to account for reliefs and repayments—alternative forms .... [211.10]
B11.4 Gifts of annuity of such sum as after deduction of income tax at the basic rate for the time being will amount to a stated sum to be varied with reference to the Index of Retail Prices .... [211.11]
B11.5 Gift of several annuities .... [211.12]
B11.6 Gift of annuities charged on land .... [211.13]
B11.7 Power to purchase annuities, the capital cost being recouped out of income .... [211.14]
B11.8 Power to trustees to appropriate investments to answer annuities1—separate fund for each annuity .... [211.15]

B11.9 Power to trustees to appropriate investments to answer annuities—aggregate fund for all annuities ....[211.16]
B11.10 Gift of annuity with direction to purchase ....[211.17]
B11.11 Annuity provisions designed to mitigate inheritance tax and income tax ....[211.18]
B11.12 Gift of annuity and direction to trustees to purchase; the annuity to cease on alienation, and the annuitant not to be entitled to purchase-money in lieu of the annuity......[211.19]
B11.13 Proviso for cesser of annuities on alienation..............[211.20]
B11.14 Declaration that annuities are to be paid clear of all deductions ....[211.21]
B11.15 Gift of several annuities to same person, being annuities to widow with reduction on remarriage and provision for minor children residing with widow...........................[211.22]
B11.16 Gift of an annuity to a trustee in trust for a mentally disabled daughter ....[211.23]
B11.17 Gift of an annuity upon trust for a spendthrift son and his wife and children..[211.24]
B11.18 Direction as to payment of an annuity not created by the will for insertion where the residue is settled..............[211.25]

B12 Charitable gifts...[212.1]

B12.1 Gifts to several charitable institutions..........................[212.3]
B12.2 Gifts of shares of residue to individual and charitable institutions ....[212.4]
B12.3 Gift of a share of residue upon trust for charitable objects to be selected by trustees...[212.5]
B12.4 Gift of residue upon a charitable trust ....[212.6]
B12.5 Gift to a Church of England Board of Finance..........[212.7]
B12.6 Gift to vicar for poor of a parish.................................[212.8]
B12.7 Bequest coupled with a request to effectuate a purpose which the law will not enforce.....................................[212.9]
B12.8 Bequest for religious purposes in a particular parish .[212.10]
B12.9 Bequest of legacy to provide Sunday school prizes....[212.11]
B12.10 Legacy to a religious community ....[212.12]
B12.11 Bequests for masses..[212.13]
B12.12 Gift to the representative body of the Church in Wales...[212.14]
B12.13 Gift to the Salvation Army ....[212.15]
B12.14 Bequest to the Trustees for Methodist Church Purposes on the model trusts of the Methodist Church Act 1976 .[212.16]
B12.15 Bequest to the Baptist Union....................................[212.17]
B12.16 Gift to the United Reformed Church.........................[212.18]
B12.17 Bequest to the Congregational Federation................[212.19]
B12.18 Bequest to the Presbyterian Church of Wales (Calvinistic Methodists) ....[212.20]
B12.19 Devise for the Presbyterian Church of Wales (Calvinistic Methodists) ....[212.21]
B12.20 Bequest to the Unitarian and Free Christian Churches ....[212.22]

B12.21 Gift of land or houses to the Unitarian and Free Christian Churches ....[212.23]

B12.22 Gift to the United Synagogue ....[212.24]

B12.23 Gift to a hospital supported by public funds ....[212.25]

B12.24 Bequest to school for provision of playing fields ....[212.26]

B12.25 Bequest to school to be applied for the encouragement of sport ....[212.27]

B12.26 Gift of residue to found college fellowships ....[212.28]

B12.27 Legacies in favour of the Scout Association ....[212.29]

B12.28 Legacies in favour of the Guide Association ....[212.30]

B12.29 General provision against lapse of charitable gifts ....[212.31]

B13 Exercises of special powers of appointment ....[213.1]

Objects of Power ....[213.4]

Delegation ....[213.7]

Perpetuities ....[213.8]

Accumulations ....[213.9]

Some Tax Considerations ....[213.10]

B13.1 Appointment by widow of her husband's residuary estate among children and issue ....[213.12]

B13.2 Appointment by woman of fund in which she has a life interest in unequal shares, one child's share appointed direct to his own children, another's settled on him for life, the others appointed absolutely ....[213.13]

B13.3 Exercise by married woman of powers of appointment contained in her marriage settlement in favour of her husband for life and if she has no children in favour of her husband absolutely ....[213.14]

B14 Residue ....[214.1]

Note ....[214.2]

B14.1 Administration trust without a trust for sale ....[214.10]

B14.2 Administration trust without a trust for sale, concise form ....[214.11]

B14.3 Residuary disposition to trustees on trust for sale, with administration trusts, directions as to inheritance tax, and exclusion of equitable and statutory apportionment ....[214.12]

B14.4 Residuary disposition with power of sale with respect to personalty so as to prevent the rules in Howe v Dartmouth and Re Chesterfield's Trusts from applying, with administration trusts and exclusion of statutory apportionment and the rule in Allhusen v Whittell ....[214.13]

B14.5 Residuary gift with no trust for sale and a power of sale which is to be used only if appropriation in specie not practicable ....[214.14]

B14.6 General residuary gift to trustees—direction to pay inheritance tax on specific gifts, pecuniary legacies, and lifetime gifts ....[214.15]

B14.7 Trust for conversion ....[214.16]

B14.8 Trust to pay debts and invest residue—directions as to inheritance tax ....[214.17]

B14.9 Gift of residue to trustees who are different persons from the executors ....[214.18]
B14.10 Gift of residue on trust for sale—exclusion of equitable apportionment rules ....[214.19]
B14.11 The same by incorporation of Statutory Will Forms 1925, Form 8....[214.20]
B14.12 Definition of residuary estate....[214.21]
B14.13 Declaration negativing the exercise of the statutory power to dispose of entailed property or the exercise of a general power of appointment....[214.22]
B14.14 Devise and bequest of residue charged with payment of debts ....[214.23]
B14.15 Bequest of residuary personal estate only....[214.24]
B14.16 Devise of residuary real estate only ....[214.25]
B14.17 Trusts of proceeds of sale of residue with general direction to pay inheritance tax on free estate out of residue ...[214.26]
B14.18 Power to trustees to sell or mortgage for payment of incumbrances....[214.29]
B14.19 Power to trustees to postpone conversion except as to certain property....[214.30]
B14.20 Power to trustees to defer the calling in of certain debts ....[214.31]
B14.21 Direction to determine tenancy of a house....[214.32]
B14.22 Direction to trustees to convert foreign property, with powers of management ....[214.33]
B14.23 Direction to foreign trustees to remit proceeds of sale to English trustees ....[214.34]
B14.24 Exclusion of rule in Howe v Earl of Dartmouth....[214.39]
B14.25 Exclusion of rule in Re Chesterfield's Trusts....[214.40]
B14.26 Exclusion of rules in Howe v Earl of Dartmouth and Re Chesterfield's Trusts—short form naming case ....[214.41]
B14.27 Exclusion of rules in Howe v Earl of Dartmouth and Re Chesterfield's Trusts—alternative form....[214.42]
B14.28 Trustees given a discretion as to allocation ....[214.45]
B14.29 Liabilities to be paid out of capital....[214.46]
B14.30 Liabilities to be paid out of capital, but interest on them payable for periods after the testator's death to be paid out of income as far as possible ....[214.47]
B14.31 Exclusion of Apportionment Acts as between before and after testator's death....[214.53]
B14.32 Exclusion of Apportionment Acts generally....[214.54]
B14.33 General declaration making all inheritance tax and foreign death duties on free estate payable out of residue......[214.76]
B14.34 Declaration that inheritance tax and foreign death duties on pecuniary legacies and personal chattels shall be paid out of residue ....[214.77]
B14.35 Declaration concerning partially exempt residue – Re Ratcliffe direction....[214.78]
B14.36 Alternative declaration concerning fractional shares of partially exempt residue – Re Benham direction........[214.79]
B14.37 Alternative declaration concerning equal shares of partially

exempt residue – Re Benham direction .... [214.80]
A – Widow or civil partner and child .... [214.80]
B – Charity and non-exempt individual
B14.38 Specific gift subject to inheritance tax where the estate may turn out to be partially exempt and include business or agricultural property .... [214.81]
B14.39 Declaration that free of inheritance tax provisions relate only to tax on the testator's death .... [214.82]

B15 Absolute and simple contingent gifts .... [215.1]

B15.1 Residuary bequest to one person .... [215.1]
B15.2 Trusts of residue, as two persons jointly or the survivor of them shall appoint .... [215.2]
B15.3 Gift of residuary estate to three named persons .... [215.3]
B15.4 Gift of residue to named children making provision for death in testator's lifetime or after his death in the latter case without leaving issue.. [215.4]
B15.5 Clause disposing of residue in unequal shares, the interest of one of the beneficiaries being contingent, and with substitutional gifts to spouses and children and accruer provisions .... [215.5]
B15.6 Clause disposing of residue in percentage shares .... [215.6]
B15.7 Residuary gift without administration trusts .... [215.7]
B15.8 Absolute residuary gift to three children of the testator land to be sold .... [215.8]

B16 Life interests.. [216.1]

B16.1 Statutory protective trusts, varied by allowing accumulation for a period of years after a forfeiture has occurred .... [216.8]
Form .... [216.8]
B16.2 Protective income trusts for woman for life .... [216.9]
B16.3 Determinable life interest .... [216.10]
B16.4 Life or widowhood interest to wife .... [216.11]
B16.5 Life interest to wife reducible on remarriage.............. [216.12]
B16.6 Trust for wife during widowhood subject to an obligation to maintain children .... [216.13]
B16.7 Same where no legal obligation imposed .... [216.14]
B16.8 Gift of income of residuary estate to a reputed wife as long as she is unmarried.. [216.15]
B16.9 Trust of income for several persons for life giving a general testamentary power of disposition to the survivor ..... [216.16]
B16.10 Trust for wife for life and then to children in equal shares .... [216.17]
B16.11 Trust for wife for life and then to children in equal shares by incorporation of Statutory Will Forms 1925, Form 10.. [216.18]
B16.12 Trust for wife for life and then to unmarried daughters for life .... [216.19]
B16.13 Trust for wife for life and then to children as she shall appoint, with hotchpot provision .... [216.20]
B16.14 Trust for wife for life and then to issue upon such trusts as she shall appoint .... [216.21]

B16.15 Trust for wife during widowhood, then to son for life with remainder to his children .... **[216.22]**

B16.16 Trust for wife for life and then to children for life with substitution of their issue .... **[216.23]**

B16.17 Trust for wife for life and then to children as she shall appoint incorporating Statutory Will Forms 1925, Form 9 .... **[216.24]**

B16.18 Clause directing trustees to resort to the capital of residue in order to make up income to a minimum amount .... **[216.25]**

B16.19 Clause empowering trustees to resort to capital .... **[216.26]**

B16.20 Clause empowering trustees to lend capital money to make up income of a share of residue to a stated amount .... **[216.27]**

B16.21 Gift of residue to children incorporating Statutory Will Forms 1925, Form 7, with modification .... **[216.28]**

B16.22 Gift of residue incorporating intestacy provisions .... **[216.29]**

B16.23 Settlement of child's share of residuary estate .... **[216.30]**

B16.24 Provision directing payment of capital to a female life tenant having no likelihood of children, where she has herself a general power of appointment in default of children .... **[216.31]**

B16.25 Settled legacy—concise form .... **[216.32]**

B16.26 Settled legacy—full form .... **[216.33]**

B16.27 Trust for accumulation of income .... **[216.34]**

B16.28 Payment of income to banker .... **[216.35]**

B16.29 Clause as to annual sums payable under an insurance policy .... **[216.36]**

B16.30 No apportionment on death of life tenant .... **[216.37]**

B17 Trusts for children .... [217.1]

B17.1 Trust for the minor children of the testator at age 18 falling within Inheritance Tax Act 1984, s 71A (trusts for bereaved minors) and Finance Act 2005, ss 23–45 (special income tax and capital gains tax treatment for trusts for the vulnerable) .... **[217.9]**

B17.2 Trust for children of the testator at twenty-five falling within Inheritance Tax Act 1984, s 71D (age 18 to 25 trusts) with substitutional trusts for those who die in testator's lifetime or after testator's death .... **[217.10]**

B17.3 Trust for the children of the testator falling within Inheritance Tax Act 1984, s 71A (trusts for bereaved minors) or s 71D (age 18-to-25 trusts), in variable shares .... **[217.11]**

B17.4 Trust for children or issue as life tenant shall appoint variation where there is a joint power of appointment .... **[217.12]**

B17.5 Trust for children at eighteen, with alternative contingency of previous marriage with consent of guardians .... **[217.13]**

B17.6 Trust for children; sons at twenty-five or on marriage after twenty-one, and daughters at twenty-one or on previous marriage .... **[217.14]**

B17.7 Trust for children at twenty-one by settling each child's share and giving trustees power to pay or apply capital in favour of life tenant .... **[217.15]**

B17.8 Trust for children of a person who takes no life interest ....[217.16]

B17.9 Trust for children of testator, including children dying in testator's lifetime leaving issue ....[217.17]

B17.10 Trust for children of another, including children dying in testator's lifetime leaving issue ....[217.18]

B17.11 Trust for children of testator living at his decease and issue of deceased children then living at eighteen or twenty-one or on previous marriage ....[217.19]

B17.12 The same by reference to the statutory trusts for issue ....[217.20]

B17.13 Trust for children at discretion of trustees until the youngest attains eighteen or twenty-one years of age ....[217.21]

B17.14 Remainder trust for children and issue of deceased children of life tenant at eighteen or twenty-one or on previous marriage ....[217.22]

B17.15 The same by reference to the statutory trusts for issue ....[217.23]

B17.16 Trust for children of another person who attain twenty-five within the limits of the rule against perpetuities ....[217.24]

B17.17 Trust for children with entitlement to income during minority ....[217.25]

B17.18 Gift to children absolutely ....[217.26]

B17.19 Trusts for children, sons taking double shares ....[217.27]

B17.20 Trusts for various persons unequally ....[217.28]

B17.21 Trust for children in unequal shares ....[217.29]

B17.22 Gift to class of children with one child having the option to have assets appropriated in satisfaction of his share ....[217.30]

B17.23 Trust for children, in definite sums ....[217.31]

B17.24 Trust for children other than a child who becomes entitled to settled estates ....[217.32]

B17.25 Trust for two persons as tenants in common on attaining twenty-five, with a gift over on the death of either to the other of them ....[217.33]

B17.26 Trust for wife and children equally ....[217.34]

B17.27 Trust after life interest to a wife for nephews and nieces as wife shall appoint, and in default of appointment equally ....[217.35]

B17.28 Trust for brothers and sisters and children of deceased brothers and sisters ....[217.36]

B17.29 Trust of child's share by reference ....[217.37]

B17.30 Trust of child's share by reference—another form ....[217.38]

B17.31 Declaration excluding s 33 of the Wills Act 1837 ....[217.39]

B17.32 Clause providing for forfeiture of gift on marriage to person not professing a certain religion ....[217.40]

B17.33 Child en ventre—general clause ....[217.41]

B17.34 Gift of land for the benefit of testator's children and issue of deceased children, sons taking at eighteen or twenty-one, and in either case with the alternative of taking on previous marriage—variation for children of a person other than testator ....[217.42]

B17.35 Gift of land to minor with provision for his death under eighteen or twenty-one leaving issue ....[217.43]
B17.36 Declaration that provisions made by will for testator's wife and children are in addition to and not in substitution for provisions made for them in his lifetime ....[217.44]
B17.37 Declaration that provisions made by will for children are not to be in addition to provisions made for them by the testator's marriage settlement ....[217.45]
B17.38 Declaration that certain children are to bring specified sums into hotchpot..[217.46]
B17.39 Declaration negativing ademption of a gift by will by subsequent gift ....[217.47]
B17.40 Declaration that certain future gifts are to be brought into hotchpot...[217.48]
B17.41 Express provision against satisfaction and ademption ....[217.49]

B18 Discretionary trusts and powers..[218.1]

B18.1 Discretionary trust for the testator's family................[218.33]
B18.2 Legacy equal to inheritance tax threshold to be held on discretionary trusts...[218.34]
B18.3 Devise to beneficiary on discretionary trusts ....[218.35]
B18.4 Trusts for a disabled person ....[218.36]
B18.5 Power to daughter to appoint life interest in a settled share to her husband ....[218.37]
B18.6 Power to trustees to settle child's share ....[218.38]
B18.7 Protective life interest with a power to raise and pay capital...[218.39]
B18.8 Life interest subject to trustees' power to pay or apply capital to or for the benefit of the life tenant, with remainders to the life tenant's children subject to powers of the life tenant to appoint a life interest to his spouse and to appoint capital among his issue ....[218.40]
B18.9 Power to pay, to children who have life interests, increasing proportions of capital as they grow older..................[218.41]
B18.10 Power to trustees to vary trusts of child's settled share...[218.42]
B18.11 Variation of the statutory provision for maintenance and accumulation to maximise the trustees' discretion .....[218.79]
B18.12 Statutory maintenance and accumulation to continue to the age of twenty-one...[218.80]
B18.13 Statutory maintenance and accumulation to continue to maximum possible age ....[218.81]
B18.14 Variation of the statutory provision for maintenance and accumulation—on the birth of a new member of the class existing accumulations are shared with the new member ....[218.82]
B18.15 Variation of the statutory provision for maintenance and accumulation—accumulations vesting absolutely.......[218.83]
B18.16 Maintenance of a class; applicable to shares in income as well as in capital...[218.84]
B18.17 Another clause providing for maintenance out of a common fund..[218.85]

B18.18 Maintenance clause; simple express trusts .... **[218.86]**
B18.19 Statutory advancement clause restricted .... **[218.104]**
B18.20 Statutory advancement clause varied to apply to the whole of a presumptive share .... **[218.105]**
B18.21 Express Advancement clause; ordinary form .... **[218.106]**
B18.22 Variation for advancement to life tenant .... **[218.107]**
B18.23 Expressions of desire for the guidance of trustees in exercising powers of advancement and of lending capital to the testator's spouse .... **[218.108]**
B18.24 Powers to permit enjoyment in kind—restricted to prevent prejudice to inheritance tax status of beneficial trusts .... **[218.110]**
B18.25 Clause where trustees are to have power to purchase property for use of beneficiary .... **[218.111]**
B18.26 Power where wife is given residence for life or house is bought for beneficiary to invest trust money in purchase of furniture .... **[218.112]**
B18.27 Loans to a life tenant .... **[218.113]**
B18.28 Loans to individuals without security .... **[218.114]**
B18.29 Loans to beneficiary to whom a business is bequeathed .... **[218.115]**
B18.30 Power for trustees to make loans to guardians .... **[218.116]**
B18.31 Testator's wishes as to the exercise of powers of maintenance and advancement [and power to make loans to guardians] during period of guardianship .... **[218.117]**
B18.32 Powers and discretions exercisable in favour of a beneficiary trustee .... **[218.118]**
B18.33 Power to release powers .... **[218.119]**

B19 Provisions for failure of primary trusts .... [219.1]

B19.1 Contingent gift of property which does carry intermediate income during the commorientes period .... **[219.14]**
B19.2 'Omnibus' commorientes provision extending to all gifts in the will .... **[219.15]**
B19.3 Spouse or civil partner survivorship clause for will of older spouse or civil partner only .... **[219.16]**
B19.4 Proviso for will of older spouse or civil partner only to be added at the end of a general survivorship clause .... **[219.17]**
B19.5 Substitution clause limited to children of deceased children .... **[219.18]**
B19.6 Trust for testator's children at twenty-five with substitution of issue of a child who predeceases the testator and further substitution of children on death after the testator's death without attaining a vested interest .... **[219.19]**
B19.7 Accruer of share .... **[219.20]**
B19.8 Accruer of settled share .... **[219.21]**
B19.9 Accruer where shares given to named children .... **[219.22]**
B19.10 Declaration against lapse in the case of a gift to a named person .... **[219.23]**
B19.11 Clause providing against lapse in the case of a gift to a named person and that the clause shall operate as a direct gift to the substituted persons .... **[219.24]**

B19.12 Declaration against lapse in the case of a class gift of residue .... [219.25]
B19.13 Declaration against lapse of settled share .... [219.26]
B19.14 Clause as to application of lapsed share of residue ... [219.27]
B19.15 General form of gift over on failure of the trusts of residue .... [219.28]
B19.16 Gift to testator's wife with alternative gift to take on the failure for any reason of the primary gift .... [219.29]
B19.17 Clause allowing for a partial disclaimer, the property disclaimed devolving as if the person disclaiming had predeceased the testator .... [219.30]
B19.18 Forfeiture on contesting the will or attempting to intermeddle .... [219.31]

B20 Administrative powers and provisions .... [220.1]

B20.1 Power of investment confined to fixed interest investments quoted shares and legal estates in land .... [220.40]
B20.2 Full discretion—long form .... [220.41]
B20.3 Full discretion—short form .... [220.42]
B20.4 Statutory power subject to an ethical investment policy .... [220.43]
B20.5 Retention of shares in family company .... [220.44]
B20.6 Powers of sale and transposing assets .... [220.45]
B20.7 Power to give warranties on the sale of private company shares .... [220.46]
B20.8 Power to delegate investment powers and vest assets in nominees .... [220.47]
B20.9 Clause as to bonus shares .... [220.48]
B20.10 Power of management in relation to land in any location .... [220.59]
B20.11 Power to apply other capital in improving land .... [220.60]
B20.12 Treatment of mining rent and royalties and proceeds of timber .... [220.61]
B20.13 Exercise of powers to be subject to beneficiary's consent .... [220.62]
B20.14 Powers of management of foreign land .... [220.63]
B20.15 Declaration that statutory provisions shall apply to foreign property .... [220.64]
B20.16 Power to pay foreign tax .... [220.65]
B20.17 Power to carry on business .... [220.66]
B20.18 Power to carry on farming business .... [220.67]
B20.19 Power to incorporate business .... [220.68]
B20.20 Power to borrow .... [220.69]
B20.21 Power for trustees to appropriate .... [220.74]
B20.22 Another power for trustees to appropriate .... [220.75]
B20.23 Short form of power of appropriation, by reference to the statutory power .... [220.76]
B20.24 Clause allowing appropriation without the beneficiary's consent and where trustees are beneficially interested—alternative form .... [220.77]

B20.25 Clause as to appropriation incorporating Statutory Will Forms 1925, Form 6 ..... [220.78]
B20.26 Power of appropriation with consent of beneficiaries of full age ..... [220.79]
B20.27 Power for trustees to partition and appropriate land . [220.80]
B20.28 General restriction to prevent administrative powers prejudicing inheritance tax status of beneficial trusts ..... [220.81]
B20.29 Power to give guarantees for loans to companies wholly or substantially owned by trustees ..... [220.82]

B21 Trustees and executors ..... [221.1]

B21.1 Definition of 'my trustees' ..... [221.1]
B21.2 Short definition 'my trustees' ..... [221.2]
B21.3 Powers conferred on trustees and executors ..... [221.3]
B21.4 Clause giving named trustee power to purchase part of testator's estate with safeguard against improper purchase ..... [221.5]
B21.5 Power to trustees to purchase the trust property—no safeguards ..... [221.6]
B21.6 Power to trustees to purchase with safeguard against improper purchase ..... [221.7]
B21.7 Power to a trustee to enter into any transaction provided there is at least one other trustee ..... [221.8]
B21.8 Power to trustees to enter into transactions in two capacities ..... [221.9]
B21.9 Power for trustees to become directors and to retain remuneration1—short form ..... [221.10]
B21.10 Power for trustees to become directors, retain remuneration and to hold shares as qualifying shares ..... [221.11]
B21.11 Retention of benefits—fuller form including benefits from subsidiary companies ..... [221.12]
B21.12 General indemnity clause—proviso excluding professional and corporate trustees ..... [221.16]
B21.13 Clause excluding the statutory duty of care ..... [221.17]
B21.14 Indemnity to trustees acting on counsel's opinion ..... [221.18]
B21.15 Liability for acts of an agent, nominee or custodian appointed under the Trustee Act 2000 ..... [221.19]
B21.16 Liability for attorney's acts ..... [221.20]
B21.17 No duty to intervene in the affairs of a private company ..... [221.21]
B21.18 Power to life tenants of settled shares to give releases to trustees ..... [221.22]
B21.19 Power to insure against liability for inheritance tax on lifetime dispositions ..... [221.23]
B21.20 Receipts by or on behalf of minors ..... [221.24]
B21.21 Receipts on behalf of charities and unincorporated associations ..... [221.25]
B21.22 Missing beneficiaries ..... [221.26]
B21.23 Clause excluding trustees' duty to consult with beneficiaries as to land ..... [221.27]

B21.24 Direction as to order of names of trustees in the registers of companies to secure voting rights .... **[221.28]**
B21.25 Direction that opinion of majority of trustees is to prevail .... **[221.29]**
B21.26 Power authorising an audit .... **[221.30]**
B21.27 Direction to employ a named solicitor .... **[221.31]**
B21.28 Nomination of trust corporation to receive notices ... **[221.32]**
B21.29 Power to vest assets in nominees .... **[221.33]**
B21.30 Power to distribute on assumption that no further children .... **[221.34]**
B21.31 Power to appoint new trustees conferred by the Trustee Act 1925 .... **[221.36]**
B21.32 Power to appoint separate trustees of parts of trust property .... **[221.37]**
B21.33 Power to remove trustees .... **[221.38]**
B21.34 Clause excluding beneficiaries' statutory right to direct retirement and appointment of trustees .... **[221.39]**
B21.35 Direction as to keeping up the number of trustees .... **[221.40]**
B21.36 Variation of statutory power to facilitate appointment of foreign trustees, and a sole trustee .... **[221.41]**
B21.37 Power to professional trustee to charge—concise form .... **[221.49]**
B21.38 Power to professional trustee to charge—full form .... **[221.50]**
B21.39 Proviso enabling professional trustee to elect not to charge .... **[221.51]**
B21.40 Provision for appointment of trust corporation .... **[221.52]**

B22 Testimonium and attestation clauses .... [222.1]

B22.1 Usual form of testimonium and attestation .... **[222.3]**
B22.2 Short form of testimonium and attestation .... **[222.4]**
B22.3 Alternative form of attestation clause .... **[222.5]**
B22.4 Further alternative form of attestation clause .... **[222.6]**
B22.5 Form where testator signs with his mark .... **[222.7]**
B22.6 Form where another signs on behalf of the testator .... **[222.8]**
B22.7 Form where the testator is blind .... **[222.9]**
B22.8 Form of attestation where the testator is deaf and dumb but is able to read .... **[222.10]**
B22.9 Form of testimonium and attestation clause to a codicil .... **[222.11]**
B22.10 Form of attestation where the testator acknowledges a signature which he or another has made previously... **[222.12]**
B22.11 Form of attestation where the testator acknowledges a signature which he has made previously—short form .... **[222.13]**
B22.12 Form of attestation where the will has been altered .. **[222.14]**
B22.13 Attestation clause where the testator has an imperfect knowledge of English .... **[222.15]**
B22.14 Forms of testimonium and attestation clause for will made on behalf of a mentally disordered person pursuant to an order of the Court of Protection .... **[222.16]**

PART C – COMPLETE WILLS

C1 Wills for use in emergency .... [223.1]

C1.1 Gift of entire estate to one person .... [223.2]

C1.2 Gift of entire estate to children .... [223.3]

C1.3 Will incorporating gift of residue on discretionary charitable trusts .... [223.4]

C1.4 Will incorporating instructions for will .... [223.5]

C1.5 Settled gift of residue on trusts for spouse and children by reference to Statutory Will Forms .... [223.6]

C1.6 Will expressly incorporating intestacy rules .... [223.7]

C1.7 Adoption of intestacy rules by revocation of former wills .... [223.8]

C1.8 Settled gift of residue on express trusts for spouse and children .... [223.9]

C1.9 Gift of estate on discretionary trusts for family .... [223.10]

C1.10 Codicil reviving a former will and codicils which have been revoked .... [223.11]

C1.11 Codicil reviving a will which has been revoked by marriage or civil partnership .... [223.12]

C1.12 Codicil adding legacy and increasing the share of residue of one of the testator's children .... [223.13]

C2 Wills for married couples (or civil partners) with young children .... [224.1]

C2.1 Reciprocal wills giving entire estate to spouse absolutely, with alternative gift to issue .... [224.27]

C2.2 Reciprocal wills giving entire estate to spouse absolutely with alternative gift of IPDIs to issue .... [224.42]

C2.3 Reciprocal wills leaving entire estate to spouse for life with power to resort to capital and with remainder to children .... [224.58]

C2.4 Reciprocal wills giving spouse life interest with power of appointment amongst issue, incorporating Statutory Will Forms .... [224.73]

C2.5 Will of husband who owns matrimonial home giving wife income of residue and right of residence for life or until remarriage .... [224.86]

C2.6 Will of husband settling residue on wife for life with remainder on discretionary trusts .... [224.102]

C3 Wills for married couples (or civil partners) with adult children.. [225.1]

C3.1 Reciprocal wills giving nil-rate band legacy to children and residue to spouse with default gift to children in equal/unequal shares .... [225.9]

C3.2 Reciprocal wills with nil-rate band legacy on trust for the children, residue on trust for spouse for life and then on trust for the children, son taking a life interest and daughter a protected life interest .... [225.23]

C3.3 Will dividing residue between spouse and issue .... [225.42]

C3.4 Reciprocal wills containing nil-rate band legacy on discretionary trusts with gift of residue to spouse ..... [225.57]

C3.5 Reciprocal wills giving nil-rate band legacy on discretionary trusts and settling residue on protective trusts for spouse for life, with overriding trustees' powers over capital, and discretionary trusts for issue after the surviving spouse's death .... **[225.68]**

C3.6 Will providing two-year discretionary trust .... **[225.92]**

C3.7 Reciprocal wills giving entire estate to spouse absolutely, with alternative gift to issue .... **[225.110]**

C4 Wills providing for someone with a disability .... [226.1]

C4.1 Reciprocal wills for husband and wife with a disabled child and other children; gift by first to die of entire estate to survivor subject to a nil-rate band discretionary trust, and a discretionary trust of residue on the death of the survivor .... **[226.13]**

C4.2 Reciprocal wills for husband and wife with grown-up children of whom one is disabled; gift by first to die of entire estate to survivor subject to a nil-rate band discretionary trust; on the death of the survivor a trust of residue for the children in equal shares with the disabled child's share settled on a 'trust for the vulnerable' within the Finance Act 2005, ss 23–45 .... **[226.40]**

C4.3 Will providing for spouse suffering from mental disorder .... **[226.57]**

C5 Wills where there is more than one family .... [227.1]

C5.1 Will of twice-married testator who has adult children from his first marriage and minor children from his second and who owns the matrimonial home; nil-rate band discretionary trust, and gift of residue on trust for second wife for life with remainder to all the testator's children .... **[227.7]**

C5.2 Reciprocal wills of spouses both having adult children by previous marriages (but none by their own), the first to die making a nil-rate band gift to his or her own children and giving the survivor a life interest in residue with remainder to his or her own children, and the survivor leaving his or her estate to his or her own children .... **[227.25]**

C5.3 Reciprocal wills of spouses both having adult children by previous marriages (but none by their own), the first to die giving the survivor his or her estate absolutely and the survivor dividing his or her estate between children and stepchildren .... **[227.39]**

C5.4 Will of married man with adult children making provision for an illegitimate child who is a minor by means of a settled legacy .... **[227.50]**

C6 Wills for unmarried couples with children .... [228.1]

C6.1 Reciprocal wills of couple living together who have young children and who are planning to marry .... **[228.5]**

C6.2 Reciprocal wills of couple living together who have children, leaving residue on discretionary trusts .... **[228.19]**

C6.3 Will of man separated (but not judicially separated) from wife and living with another woman, where divorce proceedings are contemplated .... **[228.33]**

C7 Wills for sole parents with young children ....[229.1]

C7.1 Will of mother giving entire estate to her minor child.**[229.2]**

C7.2 Will of mother appointing sister sole executrix and guardian of children and giving entire estate to her if accepting office, with alternative gift to children ....**[229.13]**

C7.3 Will of widow or widower in favour of children........[229.26]

C7.4 Will of widow or widower settling residue on children equally for life with remainder to their children.........**[229.37]**

C8 Wills for sole parents with adult children...................................[230.1]

C8.1 Will of widow or widower leaving residue to children absolutely ....**[230.2]**

C8.2 Will of widow or widower dividing residue between son and daughter, son's share being settled on protective trusts for his benefit and daughter's share being either given to her absolutely or settled on trusts for her benefit.............**[230.16]**

C8.3 Will of widow or widower leaving one share of residue on trust for the children absolutely and the other share subjected to immediate post-death interests for the grandchildren ....**[230.30]**

C8.4 Will of grandparent incorporating discretionary trusts of residue for grandchildren ....**[230.45]**

C8.5 Will of widow leaving her house to a daughter who is looking after her and residue to grandchildren on bare trusts ....**[230.62]**

C8.6 Will of widow or widower settling residue on trusts for children with progressive powers to pay them capital at different ages ....**[230.73]**

C9 Wills for members of childless households.................................[231.1]

C9.1 Reciprocal wills for a childless couple, each giving his or her entire estate to the other absolutely............................**[231.10]**

C9.2 Reciprocal wills for husband and wife or civil partners, each giving his or her entire estate to the other contingently on surviving him or her by a specified period, and providing in the alternative pecuniary legacies, a specific gift and a gift of residue in favour of the nephews and nieces of both testators in equal or other specified proportions........**[231.14]**

C9.3 Reciprocal wills for a childless couple, the first to die giving entire estate to the survivor, and the survivor giving a legacy equal in value to the estate of the first to die to the latter's relatives and leaving residue to the survivor's own relatives ....**[231.30]**

C9.4 Reciprocal wills for couple each giving the other a life interest in residue with legacies payable on the death of the survivor and different ultimate trusts of their respective estates...**[231.42]**

C9.5 Reciprocal wills for unmarried sisters leaving residue to survivor(s) with alternative gift to charity..................**[231.53]**

C9.6 Will of unmarried and childless testatrix giving her unmarried and childless sister a right of residence in her house and dividing residue between her nephews and nieces and charity ....**[231.62]**

C10 Wills for childless individuals..[232.1]

C10.1 Will of young person dividing his or her estate equally between his or her siblings but making a gift of the share of a sibling with living children direct to such children....**[232.2]**

C10.2 Will of young person creating discretionary trust of residue for his or her parents and brothers and sisters and their issue..**[232.15]**

C10.3 Will of older person in favour of brothers and sisters, with substitution of issue of those who predecease the testator ....**[232.27]**

C10.4 Will of older childless person settling residue in equal shares on brothers and sisters (or nephews and nieces) for life with remainders for their children.....................................**[232.39]**

C10.5 Will of unmarried childless person in favour of unmarried sister for life with remainders over to brothers and sisters or their issue ....**[232.52]**

C10.6 Will of childless individual giving charitable and other legacies, with a specific gift of a house and residue given on trust for nephews and nieces for life with remainders for their children ....**[232.64]**

C11 Wills disposing of business property ....[233.1]

C11.1 Will settling private company shares entitled to business relief and optional 'top up' legacy on a nil-rate band discretionary trust, with residue given to wife with alternative gift to issue ....**[233.13]**

C11.2 Reciprocal wills for husband and wife who have recently acquired share capital of private trading company, the first to die making a direct gift of the shares to the children and otherwise leaving estate to the survivor......................**[233.26]**

C11.3 Will giving business carried on as sole trader or in partnership to sons, and legacies to daughters, with residue to wife for life with remainder to children with substitution clause and hotchpot of specific gifts..........................**[233.36]**

C12 Wills disposing of farms and farming businesses ....[234.1]

C12.1 Will of widower giving estate equally between his children, one son being given an option to purchase the farming assets ....**[234.17]**

C12.2 Will of farmer leaving legacies to his daughters, a right of residence in a farm cottage to his wife, and residue to his son if farming at his death, with residue given to the children in equal shares if he is not...........................[234.31]

C12.3 Will of tenant farmer leaving his farming business either to his wife or his son with residue held on trust for wife for life with remainders to children with substitution of issue..**[234.45]**

C13 Wills for owners of substantial property ....[235.1]

C13.1 Will of owner of substantial property with no immediate family containing specific gift of controlling shareholding in family company on trusts for the employees and leaving residue on charitable trusts ....**[235.2]**

C13.2 Will of a bachelor landowner settling the principal family estate together with a share of residue on one nephew and his issue, creating a maintenance fund for the upkeep of the mansion house and settled chattels and settling substantial legacies on two nieces and their issue .... [235.18]

C14 Wills with a foreign element .... [236.1]

C14.1 Will of English-domiciled testator/testatrix owning property in England and in foreign country, appointing separate executors to administer foreign property with direction to remit the proceeds of the foreign estate to the English executors .... [236.9]

C14.2 Reciprocal wills of English-domiciled couple who own foreign holiday home and who intend to execute foreign wills giving the home to their son on the death of the survivor, leaving their estates to each other with the survivor making a tax-free gift of holiday home to the son (with a tax-free legacy equal to the amount of the IHT on the home in the event that the foreign wills are executed), giving the daughter a compensating legacy and leaving residue to the son and daughter equally .... [236.24]

C14.3 Reciprocal wills of English-domiciled couple who own foreign holiday home and who have already executed foreign wills giving the home to their son on the death of the survivor, leaving their estates to each other with the survivor leaving a tax-free legacy to the son equal to the amount of the IHT on the holiday home, giving the daughter a compensating legacy and leaving residue to the son and daughter equally .... [236.39]

PART D CODICILS

D Codicils .... [237.1]

D1 Codicil appointing an executor and trustee in substitution for an executor and trustee who has died; revocation of a gift of a one-fifth share of residue to a son by name, where such son has died without children, and gift of such share of residue to other children of testator .... [237.11]

D2 Codicil revoking settlement of a one-third share of testator's residuary estate on his sister, and giving such one-third share to a niece on the same trusts by reference .... [237.12]

D3 Codicil on a gift or advance being made to a child.... [237.13]

D4 Codicil directing sums given to daughters on marriage to be brought into hotchpot .... [237.14]

D5 Codicil altering the trusts of a settled share............... [237.15]

D6 Codicil on the occasion of testator's second marriage, reviving his will, substituting the name of his second wife for that of his first, and including any children by his second wife in the gift of residue contained in his will .... [237.16]

D7 Codicil where specifically devised realty has been sold after the execution of the will .... [237.17]

D8 Codicil after divorce .... [237.18]

D9 Codicil reducing benefits owing to reduction of estate .... [237.19]

D10 Codicil increasing an annuity .... [237.20]

D11 Codicil altering legacies .... [237.21]

D12 Codicil imposing protective trusts on share of a child who might become insolvent ..... [237.22]
D13 Codicil appointing a guardian, the testator having acquired parental responsibility for his illegitimate children since making his will ..... [237.23]
D14 Codicil revoking a nil-rate band legacy ..... [237.24]
D15 Codicil ensuring that a trust for the testator's children is a trust for bereaved minors ..... [237.25]
D16 Codicil substituting absolute gifts for a settled gift ..... [237.26]
D17 Codicil making revisions consequent upon the Trusts of Land and Appointment of Trustees Act 1996 ..... [237.27]
D18 Codicil excluding or restricting provisions of the Trustee Act 2000 ..... [237.28]
D19 Codicil varying appointment of guardian ..... [237.29]
D20 Codicil increasing the amount of a legacy to the current inheritance tax nil-rate band ..... [237.30]
D21 Codicil imposing an actual value limit on a formula nil-rate band legacy to the testator's children ..... [237.31]
D22 Codicil correcting a clerical error in a will ..... [237.32]
D23 Codicil to render valid alterations made in will ..... [237.33]
D24 Codicil reviving a former will and codicils thereto which have been revoked ..... [237.34]
D25 Revocation of a will ..... [237.35]

PART E – STATUTORY WILL FORMS 1925

E Statutory Will Forms 1925 ..... [238.1]
E1 Statutory Will Forms 1925, Form 1 Confirmation of settlements ..... [238.7]
E2 Statutory Will Forms 1925, Form 2 Meaning of 'personal chattels' ..... [238.8]
E3 Statutory Will Forms 1925, Form 3 Inventories and provisions respecting chattels ..... [238.9]
E4 Statutory Will Forms 1925, Form 4 Legacies to charities ..... [238.10]
E5 Statutory Will Forms 1925, Form 5 Directions\respecting annuities ..... [238.11]
E6 Statutory Will Forms 1925, Form 6 Power of appropriation ..... [238.12]
E7 Statutory Will Forms 1925, Form 7 Trusts of a settled legacy ..... [238.13]
E8 Statutory Will Forms 1925, Form 8 Administration trusts ..... [238.14]
E9 Statutory Will Forms 1925, Form 9 Trusts for spouse for life, with power to appoint to issue and gift over to them ..... [238.15]
E10 Statutory Will Forms 1925, Form 10 Trusts for spouse and issue, without a power of appointment ..... [238.16]

PART F – NON-TESTAMENTARY INSTRUMENTS

F1 Renunciation of probate and disclaimer of trusteeships ....[239.1]

F1.1 Renunciation of probate ....[239.2]

F1.2 Deed of disclaimer of the trusteeship of a will by an executor and trustee who has renounced probate ....[239.3]

F1.3 Deed of disclaimer of the trusteeship of a will—short form ....[239.4]

F1.4 Appointment of new trustees by disclaiming trustee who has proved testator's will ....[239.5]

F2 Executors and trustees ....[240.1]

F2.1 Notice to the Public Trustee of death of a testator who has appointed the Public Trustee as an executor of his will ....[240.1]

F2.2 Notice to the Public Trustee of death of a testator who has appointed the Public Trustee as a trustee or as custodian trustee under his will ....[240.2]

F2.3 Words to be included in executors' oath where partners in a solicitors' firm have been appointed executors ....[240.3]

F2.4 Application for an advance from a bank by executors and undertaking to repay ....[240.4]

F2.5 Declaration of trust of property devised or bequeathed by will on a secret trust ....[240.5]

F3 Disclaimers and variations of beneficial interests ....[241.1]

F3.1 Disclaimer by devisee of a gift under a will—short form...[241.22]

F3.2 Disclaimer—longer form ....[241.23]

F3.3 Disclaimer of a life interest ....[241.24]

F3.4 Deed of variation of dispositions effected by a will...[241.25]

F3.5 Deed of variation of disposition of property held by deceased and spouse on a joint tenancy....................[241.26]

F3.6 Deed of variation creating a nil-rate band non-exempt legacy where entire estate given to the deceased's widow ....[241.27]

F3.7 Deed of variation conferring a short-term interest in possession on a surviving spouse ....[241.28]

F3.8 Deed of variation where spouses have died within two years of each other varying the disposition of the estate of the first to die..[241.29]

F3.9 Deed of variation of trusts of a will settling a life interest on discretionary trusts without disturbing remainders...[241.30]

F3.10 Deed of variation of trusts of a will settling a life interest on the same trusts as contingent remainders from time to time ....[241.31]

F4 Exercises of dispositive powers created by wills ....[242.1]

F4.1 Appointment from discretionary trust within two years of testator's death ....[242.7]

F4.2 Appointment to spouse from nil-rate band discretionary trust within two years of testator's death ....[242.8]

F4.3 Appointment from discretionary trust of money to beneficiaries who are sui juris ....[242.9]
F4.4 Appointment from discretionary trust of investments ....[242.10]
F4.5 Appointment of immediate post-death interests in residue for the testator's grandchildren....................[242.12]
F4.6 Appointment from discretionary trust of investments to a bereaved minor trust or age 18–25 trust....................[242.13]
F4.7 Appointment of a trust for bereaved minors terminating an immediate post-death interest....................[242.15]
F4.8 Exercise of power of advancement ....[242.17]
F4.9 Exercise of power of advancement for the benefit of someone by creating a trust for his minor children....[242.19]

F5 Miscellaneous documents giving effect to legacies....................[243.1]
F5.1 Resolution of appropriation ....[243.2]
F5.2 Assent ....[243.3]
F5.3 Deed of promise to give effect to a nil-rate band debt scheme....................[243.4]
F5.4 Deed of charge to give effect to a nil-rate band charge scheme....................[243.5]
F5.5 Assent of property subject to a charge as part of a nil-rate band charge scheme ....[243.6]

PART G – STATUTES

Section 1 – Wills and intestacy....................[244.1]
WILLS ACT 1837....................[244.2]
WILLS ACT AMENDMENT ACT 1852....................[244.39]
WILLS ACT 1861....................[244.43]
WILLS (SOLDIERS AND SAILORS) ACT 1918 ....[244.48]
LAW OF PROPERTY ACT 1925 ....[244.53]
ADMINISTRATION OF ESTATES ACT 1925....................[244.59]
INTESTATES' ESTATES ACT 1952....................[244.71]
WILLS ACT 1963....................[244.77]
WILLS ACT 1968....................[244.84]
FAMILY LAW REFORM ACT 1969....................[244.86]
MATRIMONIAL CAUSES ACT 1973 ....[244.88]
INTESTATE SUCCESSION (INTEREST AND CAPITALISATION) ORDER 1977....................[244.90]
ADMINISTRATION OF JUSTICE ACT 1982....................[244.94]
CHILDREN ACT 1989 ....[244.112]
LAW REFORM (SUCCESSION) ACT 1995 ....[244.124]
CIVIL PARTNERSHIP ACT 2004....................[244.130]
MENTAL CAPACITY ACT 2005....................[244.135]

Section 2 – Succession rights and adoption, legitimation, illegitimacy and change of gender ....[245.1]
ADOPTION OF CHILDREN ACT 1926 ....[245.2]
LEGITIMACY ACT 1926 ....[245.6]
ADOPTION ACT 1950 ....[245.16]
ADOPTION ACT 1958 ....[245.24]
LEGITIMACY ACT 1959 ....[245.31]
ADOPTION ACT 1960 ....[245.35]
FAMILY LAW REFORM ACT 1969 ....[245.37]
LEGITIMACY ACT 1976 ....[245.43]
ADOPTION ACT 1976 ....[245.55]
FAMILY LAW REFORM ACT 1987 ....[245.69]
HUMAN FERTILISATION AND EMBRYOLOGY ACT 1990 ....[245.82]
ADOPTION AND CHILDREN ACT 2002 ....[245.92]
GENDER RECOGNITION ACT 2004 ....[245.103]

Section 3 – Miscellaneous provisions relevant to the drafting of wills ....[246.1]
APPORTIONMENT ACT 1870 ....[246.2]
TRUSTEE ACT 1925 ....[246.9]
LAW OF PROPERTY ACT 1925 ....[246.41]
ADMINISTRATION OF ESTATES ACT 1925 ....[246.60]
LAW OF PROPERTY (AMENDMENT) ACT 1926 ....[246.70]
PUBLIC TRUSTEE RULES 1912 ....[246.72]
PERPETUITIES AND ACCUMULATIONS ACT 1964 ....[246.74]
FAMILY LAW REFORM ACT 1969 ....[246.89]
INTERPRETATION ACT 1978 ....[246.95]
INHERITANCE TAX ACT 1984 ....[246.99]
CHARITIES ACT 1993 ....[246.101]
TRUSTS OF LAND AND APPOINTMENT OF TRUSTEES ACT 1996 ....[246.102]
TRUSTEE ACT 2000 ....[246.132]

Section 4 – Family provision and relief from forfeiture ....[247.1]
INHERITANCE (PROVISION FOR FAMILY AND DEPENDANTS) ACT 1975 ....[247.1]
FORFEITURE ACT 1982 ....[247.34]

PAGE

Cumulative Index 1387

FORM FINDER

ACCRUER CLAUSES

Accruer of settled share – B19.8 **[219.21]**

Accruer of share – B19.7 **[219.20]**

Accruer where shares given to named children – B19.9 **[219.22]**

ACCUMULATION AND MAINTENANCE

See also CHILDREN

Statutory provisions for maintenance

Accumulation and maintenance trust of investment property – B17.35 **[217.40]**

Clause providing for maintenance out of a common fund – B18.17 **[218.85]**

Maintenance clause; simple express trusts – B18.18 **[218.86]**

Maintenance of a class; applicable to shares in income as well as in capital – B18.16 **[218.84]**

Statutory maintenance and accumulation to continue to maximum possible age – B18.13 **[218.81]**

Statutory maintenance and accumulation to continue to the age of twenty-one – B18.12 **[218.78]**

Trust for accumulation of income – B16.27 **[216.32]**

Variation of the statutory provision for maintenance and accumulation—accumulations vesting absolutely – B18.15 **[218.83]**

Variation of the statutory provision for maintenance and accumulation—on the birth of a new member of the class existing accumulations are shared with the new member – B18.14 **[218.82]**

Variation of the statutory provision for maintenance and accumulation to maximise the trustees' discretion – B18.11 **[218.79]**

Trust for,

Share of residue on accumulation and maintenance trusts for grandchild – C8.3 **[230.38]**

ADMINISTRATIVE POWERS *see* POWERS OF TRUSTEES

ADVANCEMENT

Exercise of power of advancement – F4.8 **[242.17]**

Exercise of power of advancement for the benefit of someone by creating a trust for his minor children – F4.9 **[242.19]**

Express Advancement clause; ordinary form – B18.21 **[218.106]**

Expressions of desire for the guidance of trustees in exercising powers of advancement and of lending capital to the testator's spouse – B18.23 **[218.108]**

Statutory advancement clause restricted – B18.19 **[218.104]**

Statutory advancement clause varied to apply to the whole of a presumptive share – B18.20 **[218.105]**

Variation for advancement to life tenant – B18.22 **[218.107]**

AGRICULTURAL PROPERTY *see* – BUSINESS PROPERTY

ANATOMICAL RESEARCH AND ORGAN TRANSPLANTATION

Clause providing for the use of the testator's body for therapeutic purposes, but not for medical education and research – B2.7 **[202.17]**

Direction for anatomical examination and corneal grafting – B2.6 **[202.16]**

ANIMALS, MAINTENANCE OF

Combined gift of legacy and pet animal coupled with a non-binding expression of hope that the legatee will look after the animal – B2.14 **[202.38]**

Gift for the maintenance and upkeep of an animal – B2.13 **[202.37]**

ANNUITIES

Declaration that annuities are to be paid clear of all deductions – B11.14 **[211.21]**

Direction as to payment of an annuity not created by the will for insertion where the residue is settled – B11.18 **[211.25]**

Gift of an annuity upon trust for a spendthrift son and his wife and children – B11.17 **[211.24]**

Gift of annuity and direction to trustees to purchase; the annuity to cease on alienation, and the annuitant not to be entitled to purchase-money in lieu of the annuity – B11.12 **[211.19]**

Gift of annuity of such sum as after deduction of income tax at the basic rate for the time being will amount to a stated sum to be varied with reference to the Index of Retail Prices – B11.4 **[211.11]**

Gift of annuity with direction to purchase – B11.10 **[211.17]**

Gift of annuity with reference to liability of annuitant to account for reliefs and repayments — alternative forms – B11.3 **[211.10]**

Gift of several annuities – B11.5 **[211.12]**

Gift of several annuities to same person, being annuities to widow with reduction on remarriage and provision for minor children residing with widow – B11.15 **[211.22]**

Gift of simple annuity – B11.1 **[211.8]**

Power to purchase annuities, the capital cost being recouped out of income – B11.7 **[211.14]**

Power to trustees to appropriate investments to answer annuities -aggregate fund for all annuities – B11.9 **[211.16]**

Power to trustees to appropriate investments to answer annuities—separate fund for each annuity – B11.8 **[211.15]**

Proviso for cesser of annuities on alienation – B11.13 **[211.20]**

APPOINTMENT, POWER OF

Appointment by widow of her husband's residuary estate among children and issue – B13.1 **[213.12]**

Appointment by woman of fund in which she has a life interest in unequal shares, one child's share appointed direct to his own children, another's settled on him for life, the others appointed absolutely – B13.2 **[213.13]**

Appointment from discretionary trust of investments – F4.4 **[242.10]**

Appointment from discretionary trust of money to beneficiaries who are sui juris – F4.3 **[242.9]**

Appointment from discretionary trust within two years of testator's death – F4.1 **[242.7]**

Appointment from discretionary trust of investments to a bereaved minor trust or age 18–25 trust – F4.6 **[242.13]**

Appointment of immediate post-death interests in residue for the testator's grandchildren – F4.5 **[242.12]**

Appointment of a trust for bereaved minors terminating an immediate post-death interest – F4.7 **[242.15]**

Appointment to spouse from nil-rate band discretionary trust within two years of testator's death – F4.2 **[242.8]**

Declaration negativing the exercise of the statutory power to dispose of entailed property or the exercise of a general power of appointment – B14.13 **[214.22]**

Exercise by married woman of powers of appointment contained in her marriage settlement in favour of her husband for life and if she has no children in favour of her husband absolutely – B13.3 **[213.14]**

Expression of testator's intention not to exercise a general power of appointment over land – B6.21 **[206.30]**
Gift in exercise of a special power of appointment – B6.20 **[206.29]**

APPORTIONMENT
No apportionment on death of life tenant – B16.30 **[216.37]**
Exclusion of apportionment between capital and income (Rules in *Howe v Earl Of Dartmouth* and *Re Chesterfield's Trusts*)
Exclusion of rule in *Howe v Earl of Dartmouth* – B14.24 **[214.39]**
Exclusion of rule in *Re Chesterfield's Trusts* – B14.25 **[214.40]**
Exclusion of rules in *Howe v Earl of Dartmouth and Re Chesterfield's Trusts*—alternative form – B14.27 **[214.42]**
Exclusion of rules in *Howe v Earl of Dartmouth* and *Re Chesterfield's Trusts*—short form naming case – B14.26 **[214.41]**
Gift of residue on trust for sale—exclusion of equitable apportionment rules – B14.10 **[214.19]**
Residuary disposition to trustees on trust for sale, with administration trusts, directions as to inheritance tax, and exclusion of equitable and statutory apportionment – B14.3 **[214.12]**
Specific gift of property with provision against apportionment – B6.5 **[206.14]**
Exclusion of rule for apportionment of liabilities between capital and income (Rule in *Allhusen v Whittell*)
Liabilities to be paid out of capital – B14.29 **[214.46]**
Liabilities to be paid out of capital, but interest on them payable for periods after the testator's death to be paid out of income as far as possible – B14.30 **[214.47]**
Trustees given a discretion as to allocation – B14.28 **[214.45]**
Exclusion of time apportionment
Exclusion of Apportionment Acts as between before and after testator's death – B14.31 **[214.53]**
Exclusion of Apportionment Acts generally – B14.32 **[214.54]**
Residuary disposition with power of sale with respect to personalty so as to prevent the rules in *Howe v Dartmouth* and *Re Chesterfield's Trusts* from applying, with administration trusts and exclusion of statutory apportionment and the rule in *Allhusen v Whittell* – B14.4 **[214.13]**

APPROPRIATION, POWERS OF
Another power for trustees to appropriate – B20.22 **[220.75]**
Clause allowing appropriation without the beneficiary's consent and where trustees are beneficially interested—alternative form – B20.24 **[220.77]**
Clause as to appropriation incorporating Statutory Will Forms 1925, Form 6 – B20.25 **[220.78]**
Power for trustees to appropriate – B20.21 **[220.74]**
Power for trustees to partition and appropriate land – B20.27 **[220.80]**
Power of appropriation with consent of beneficiaries of full age – B20.26 **[220.79]**
Power to trustees to appropriate investments to answer annuities—aggregate fund for all annuities – B11.9 **[211.16]**
Power to trustees to appropriate investments to answer annuities—separate fund for each annuity – B11.8 **[211.15]**
Resolution of appropriation – F5.1 **[243.2]**
Short form of power of appropriation, by reference to the statutory power – B20.23 **[220.76]**

ASSENT
Assent – F5.2 **[243.3]**

ATTESTATION *see* TESTIMONIUM AND ATTESTATION

BURIAL *see* FUNERAL

BUSINESS PROPERTY
Appointment by will of permanent director of private company – B5.12 **[205.69]**
Appointment of separate executors for testator's business – B3.25 **[203.44]**
Clause giving effect to provision in partnership deed and granting widow a share of the profits during the joint lives of the widow and the surviving partner – B5.7 **[205.64]**
Clause providing that inheritance tax on business premises be paid by trustees and repaid to them by son – B5.5 **[205.62]**
Clauses giving assistance to son in acquiring partnership share, with alternative provision for realisation of the share – B5.8 **[205.65]**
Gifts of,
Annuity to widow of principal director from shares in a family company, the shares being given to sons on the widow's death – B5.11 **[205.68]**
Bequest of farming business and nomination of successor to tenancy – C12.3(3) **[234.48]**
Bequest to trustees of a business carried on on leasehold premises upon trust to carry on for a limited period – B5.2 **[205.59]**
Farming stock – B4.58 **[204.80]**
Live and dead stock – B4.57 **[204.79]**
Lloyd's underwriting business – B5.4 **[205.61]**
Trusts of net profits and proceeds of sale of a business – B5.3 **[205.60]**
Sole trader's business – B5.1 **[205.58]**
Such of unquoted shares as shall have been owned for two years by the time of testator's death, subject to inheritance tax – B5.9 **[205.66]**
Unquoted shares or any substitute shares on condition that they qualify for business relief, subject to inheritance tax, and with power to disclaim part of the gift – B5.10 **[205.67]**
Indemnity to trustees carrying on business – B5.15 **[205.72]**
Nomination of a son to succeed testator in partnership and gift to him of partnership share if he becomes a partner – B5.6 **[205.63]**
Powers of Trustees *see* POWERS OF TRUSTEES
Wills disposing of, complete,
Reciprocal wills for husband and wife who have recently acquired share capital of private trading company, the first to die making na direct gift of the shares to the children and otherwise leaving estate to the survivor – C11.2 **[233.26]**
Will giving business carried on as sole trader or in partnership to sons, and legacies to daughters, with residue to wife for life with remainder to children with substitution clause and hotchpot of specific gifts – C11.3 **[233.36]**
Will of farmer leaving legacies to his daughters, a right of residence in a farm cottage to his wife, and residue to his son if farming at his death, with residue given to the children in equal shares if he is not – C12.2 **[234.31]**
Will of owner of substantial property with no immediate family containing specific gift of controlling shareholding in family company on trusts for the employees and leaving residue on charitable trusts – C13.1 **[235.2]**

Will of tenant farmer leaving his farming business either to his wife or his son with residue held on trust for wife for life with remainders to children with substitution of issue – C12.3 **[234.45]**
Will of widower giving estate equally between his children, one son being given an option to purchase the farming assets – C12.1 **[234.17]**
Will settling private company shares entitled to business relief and 'top up' legacy on a nil-rate band discretionary trust, with residue given to wife with alternative gift to issue – C11.1 **[233.13]**

CHARITY
Bequest coupled with a request to effectuate a purpose which the law will not enforce – B12.7 **[212.9]**
Bequests for masses – B12.11 **[212.13]**
Bequest for religious purposes in a particular parish – B12.8 **[212.10]**
Bequest of legacy to provide Sunday school prizes – B12.9 **[212.11]**
Bequest to school for provision of playing fields – B12.24 **[212.26]**
Bequest to school to be applied for the encouragement of sport – B12.25 **[212.27]**
Bequest to the Baptist Union – B12.15 **[212.17]**
Bequest to the Congregational Federation – B12.17 **[212.19]**
Bequest to the Presbyterian Church of Wales (Calvinistic Methodists) – B12.18 **[212.20]**
Bequest to the Trustees for Methodist Church Purposes on the model trusts of the Methodist Church Act 1976 – B12.14 **[212.16]**
Bequest to the Unitarian and Free Christian Churches – B12.20 **[212.22]**
Devise for the Presbyterian Church of Wales (Calvinistic Methodists) – B12.19 **[212.21]**
General provision against lapse of charitable gifts – B12.29 **[212.31]**
Gift of certain freehold lands to a charity – B6.17 **[206.26]**
Gift of land or houses to the Unitarian and Free Christian Churches – B12.21 **[212.23]**
Gift of a share of residue upon trust for charitable objects to be selected by trustees – B12.3 **[212.5]**
Gift of residue to found college fellowships – B12.26 **[212.28]**
Gift of residue upon a charitable trust – B12.4 **[212.6]**
Gifts of shares of residue to individual and charitable institutions – B12.2 **[212.4]**
Gift to a charity conditional upon the maintenance of a particular grave with a gift over on breach of the condition to another charity – B2.12 **[202.35]**
Gift to a Church of England Board of Finance – B12.5 **[212.7]**
Gift to a hospital supported by public funds – B12.23 **[212.25]**
Gift to the representative body of the Church in Wales – B12.12 **[212.14]**
Gift to the Salvation Army – B12.13 **[212.15]**
Gift to the United Reformed Church – B12.16 **[212.18]**
Gift to the United Synagogue – B12.22 **[212.24]**
Gift to vicar for poor of a parish – B12.6 **[212.8]**
Gifts to several charitable institutions – B12.1 **[212.3]**
Legacies in favour of the Guide Association – B12.28 **[212.30]**
Legacies in favour of the Scout Association – B12.27 **[212.29]**
Legacy to a religious community – B12.10 **[212.12]**
Provision against lapse of charitable gifts – C10.6(4) **[232.68]**
Receipts on behalf of charities and unincorporated associations – B21.21 **[221.25]**
Residuary gift to charities – C13.1(8) **[235.11]**

CHILDLESS HOUSEHOLDS, COMPLETE WILLS

Reciprocal wills for a childless couple, each giving his or her entire estate to the other absolutely – C9.1 **[231.10]**

Reciprocal wills for childless couple, the first to die giving entire estate to the survivor, and the survivor giving a legacy equal in value to the estate of the first to die to the latter's relatives and leaving residue to the survivor's own relatives – C9.3 **[231.30]**

Reciprocal wills for couple each giving the other a life interest in residue with legacies payable on the death of the survivor and different ultimate trusts of their respective estates – C9.4 **[231.42]**

Reciprocal wills for husband and wife or civil partner, each giving his or her entire estate to the other contingently on surviving him or her by a specified period, and providing in the alternative pecuniary legacies, a specific gift and a gift of residue in favour of the nephews and nieces of both testators in equal or other specified proportions – C9.2 **[231.14]**

Reciprocal wills for unmarried sisters leaving residue to survivor(s) with alternative gift to charity – C9.5 **[231.53]**

Will of unmarried and childless testatrix giving her unmarried and childless sister a right of residence in her house and dividing residue between her nephews and nieces and charity – C9.6 **[231.62]**

CHILDREN

Child en ventre—general clause – B17.33 **[217.41]**

Clause providing for forfeiture of gift on marriage to person not professing a certain religion – B17.32 **[217.40]**

Declaration excluding s 33 of the Wills Act 1837 – B17.31 **[217.39]**

Gift to children absolutely – B17.18 **[217.26]**

Gift to class of children with one child having the option to have assets appropriated in satisfaction of his share – B17.22 **[217.30]**

Legacies to,

Legacy of a capital sum for the education of children – B10.25 **[210.39]**

Legacy to a minor who is married – B10.22 **[210.36]**

Legacy to an adopted child – B10.27 **[210.41]**

Legacy to children and an illegitimate child – B10.28 **[210.42]**

Legacy to grandchildren – B10.26 **[210.40]**

Legacy to illegitimate children of the testator, including one en ventre sa mère – B10.29 **[210.43]**

Legacy to legitimate and illegitimate children of a brother of the testator – B10.30 **[210.44]**

Legacy to married daughters to become subject to the trusts of their respective marriage settlements, the amount of the legacies varying in order to equalise the provisions made by the testator for all his daughters – B10.31 **[210.45]**

Legacy to minor – B10.20 **[210.34]**

Legacy to minor to be applied in maintenance – B10.23 **[210.37]**

Legacy to minor to provide an allowance for him – B10.24 **[210.38]**

Small legacy to minor with provision for opening National Savings Bank account – B10.21 **[210.35]**

Trusts for,

Remainder trust for children and issue of deceased children of life tenant at eighteen or twenty-one or on previous marriage – B17.14 **[217.22]**

Remainder trust for children and issue of deceased children of life tenant by reference to the statutory trusts for issue – B17.15 **[217.23]**

Trust after life interest to a wife for nephews and nieces as wife shall appoint, and in default of appointment equally – B17.27 **[217.35]**

Trust of child's share by reference – B17.29 **[217.37]**
Trust of child's share by reference—another form – B17.29 **[217.34]**
Trust for brothers and sisters and children of deceased brothers and sisters – B17.28 **[217.36]**
Trust for children at discretion of trustees until the youngest attains eighteen or twenty-one years of age – B17.13 **[217.21]**
Trust for children at eighteen, with alternative contigency of previous marriage with consent of guardians – B17.5 **[217.13]**
Trust for children at twenty-one by settling each child's share and giving trustees power to pay or apply capital in favour of life tenant – B17.7 **[217.15]**
Trust for children, in definite sums – B17.23 **[217.31]**
Trust for children of a person who takes no life interest – B17.8 **[217.16]**
Trust for children of another, including children dying in testator's lifetime leaving issue – B17.10 **[217.18]**
Trust for children of another person who attain twenty-five within the limits of the rule against perpetuities – B17.16 **[217.24]**
Trust for children of the testator at twenty-five falling within Inheritance Tax Act 1984, s 71D (age 18 to 25 trusts) with substitutional trusts for those who die in testator's lifetime or after testator's death – B17.2 **[217.10]**
Trust for the children of the testator falling within Inheritance Tax Act 1984, s 71A (trusts for bereaved minors) or s 71D (age 18-to-25 trusts), in variable shares – B17.3 **[217.11]**
Trust for children of testator, including children dying in testator's lifetime leaving issue – B17.9 **[217.17]**
Trust for children of testator living at his decease and issue of deceased children by reference to the statutory trusts for issue – B17.12 **[217.20]**
Trust for children of testator living at his decease and issue of deceased children then living at eighteen or twenty-one or on previous marriage – B17.11 **[217.19]**
Trust for children or issue as life tenant shall appoint: variation where there is a joint power of appointment – B17.4 **[217.12]**
Trust for children other than a child who becomes entitled to settled estates – B17.24 **[217.32]**
Trust for children; sons at twenty-five or on marriage after twenty-one, and daughters at twenty-one or on previous marriage – B17.6 **[217.14]**
Trust for children with entitlement to income during minority – B17.17 **[217.25]**
Trust for children in unequal shares – B17.21 **[217.29]**
Trust for the minor children of the testator at age 18 falling within Inheritance Tax Act 1984, s 71A (trusts for bereaved minors) and Finance Act 2005, ss 23–45 (special income tax and capital gains tax treatment for trusts for the vulnerable – B17.1 **[217.9]**
Trust for two persons as tenants in common on attaining twenty-five, with a gift over on the death of either to the other of them – B17.25 **[217.33]**
Trust for wife and children equally – B17.26 **[217.34]**
Trusts for children, sons taking double shares – B17.19 **[217.27]**
Trusts for various persons unequally – B17.20 **[217.28]**

CLAUSE HEADINGS
Direction regarding clause headings or marginal notes – B2.16 **[202.42]**

CODICILS
Adding legacy and increasing the share of residue of one of the testator's children – C1.12 **[223.13]**

Alterations made in will, validating – D23 **[237.33]**
Altering trusts of a settled share – D5 **[237.15]**
Annuity, increasing – D10 **[237.20]**
Appointment of the Public Trustee as executor and trustee jointly with executors and trustees previously appointed or in place of one who has died – B3.22 **[203.41]**
Clerical error in a will, correcting – D22 **[237.32]**
Complete codicil appointing an executor and trustee in substitution for an executor and trustee who has died; revocation of a gift of a one-fifth share of residue to a son by name, where such son has died without children, and gift of such share of residue to other children of testator – D1 **[237.11]**
Complete codicil revoking settlement of a one-third share of testator's residuary estate on his sister, and giving such one-third share to a niece on the same trusts by reference – D12 **[237.9]**
Divorce after execution of the will – D8 **[237.18]**
Ensuring that a trust for the testator's children is a trust for bereaved minors – D15 **[237.25]**
Gift or advance being made to a child – D3 **[237.13]**
Guardian, appointing, the testator having acquired parental responsibility for his illegitimate children since making his will – D13 **[237.20]**
Guardian, varying appointment of, – D19 **[237.29]**
Hotchpot, directing sums given to daughters on marriage to be brought into, – D4 **[237.14]**
Imposing life interests with powers to pay or apply capital on the shares of beneficiaries under an accumulation and maintenance trust – D17 **[237.24]**
Legacies, altering – D11 **[237.21]**
Legacy increased to the current inheritance tax nil-rate band – D20 **[237.30]**
Nil-rate band legacy to children, imposing actual value limit on formula for – D21 **[237.31]**
Protective trusts imposed on share of a child who might become insolvent – D12 **[237.22]**
Reducing benefits owing to reduction of estate – D9 **[237.19]**
Reviving a will which has been revoked by marriage – C1.11 **[223.12]**
Reviving a former will and codicils thereto which have been revoked – C1.10, D24 **[223.11]**, **[237.34]**
Revocation a nil-rate band legacy – D14 **[237.24]**
Revocation of a will – D25 **[237.35]**
Revocation of appointment of executors and trustees and appointing the Public Trustee sole executor and trustee in their place – B3.21 **[203.40]**
Second marriage, reviving will, substituting the name of second wife for that of first, and including any children by second wife in the gift of residue contained in will – D6 **[237.16]**
Specifically devised realty sold after execution of the will – D7 **[237.17]**
Substituting absolute gifts for a settled gift – D16 **[237.26]**
Trustee Act 2000, excluding or restricting provisions of, – D18 **[237.28]**
Trusts of Land and Appointment of Trustees Act 1996, revisions consequent upon, – D17 **[237.27]**

COMMENCEMENT
Concurrent will of testator with UK and foreign property confining the will to UK property – B1.7 **[201.12]**
Mentally disordered person, will made pursuant to an order of the Court of Protection – B1.10 **[201.15]**
Mirror but not mutual wills – B1.9 **[201.14]**

Mutual will made in pursuance of an agreement that it shall not be revoked – B1.8 **[201.13]**
Ordinary commencement – B1.1 **[201.6]**
Testator with UK and foreign property confining the will to UK property – B1.6 **[201.11]**
Will made in expectation of forming a civil partnership – B1.3 **[201.8]**
Will made in expectation of forming a civil partnership – B1.5 **[201.10]**
Will made in expectation of marriage – B1.2 **[201.7]**
Will made in expectation of marriage—conditional form – B1.4 **[201.9]**

COMMORIENTES
Contingent gift of property which does carry intermediate income during the commorientes period – B19.1 **[219.14]**
'Omnibus' commorientes provision extending to all gifts in the will – B19.2 **[219.15]**
Proviso for will of older spouse or civil partner only to be added at the end of a general survivorship clause – B19.4 **[219.17]**
Spouse or civil partner survivorship clause for will of older spouse or civil partner only – B19.3 **[219.16]**

CONSUMABLES
Gift of consumable stores – B4.21 **[204.36]**

CORPORATIONS
Executors and Trustees, Appointment of *see* EXECUTORS, Appointment of

CREMATION *see* FUNERAL

DEBTS
Declaration as to legacies to creditors – B10.16 **[210.29]**
Gifts of,
Gift of a debt – B4.40 **[204.62]**
Gift of debt to a legatee of a share of residue with provision for hotchpot – B4.44 **[204.66]**
Gift of leasehold house free from mortgage – B7.3 **[207.17]**
Gift of mortgage debt to the mortgagor – B4.45 **[204.67]**
Gift of principal of a debt but not of arrears of interest – B4.41 **[204.63]**
Gifts subject to,
Devise and bequest of residue charged with payment of debts – B14.14 **[214.23]**
Gift of leaseholds with a direction that the legatee is to pay all arrears of rent and cost of dilapidations – B7.4 **[207.18]**
Gift subject to a mortgage – B6.13 **[206.22]**
Legacy to a son subject to deduction of sums owing – B10.19 **[210.32]**
Legacy to debtor without forgiveness of debt – B10.17 **[210.30]**
Legacy to a creditor – B10.15 **[210.28]**
Release of,
Declaration that sums advanced were by way of gifts – B4.46 **[204.68]**
Gift freed from a mortgage debt – B6.14 **[206.23]**
Legacy to debtor with forgiveness of debt – B10.18 **[210.31]**
Release of children's debts with optional provision for hotchpot – B4.43 **[204.65]**
Release to a debtor of debts present or future – B4.42 **[204.64]**

DEPENDANTS
Declarations under the Inheritance (Provision for Family and Dependants) Act 1975—Alternative forms – B2.15 **[202.40]**

DISABLED PERSON
Commencement of will for mentally disordered person made pursuant to an order of the Court of Protection – B1.10 **[201.15]**
Forms of testimonium and attestation clause for will made on behalf of a mentally disordered person pursuant to an order of the Court of Protection – B22.14 **[222.16]**
Gift of an annuity to a trustee in trust for a mentally disabled daughter – B11.16 **[211.23]**
Reciprocal wills for husband and wife with a disabled child and other children; gift by first to die of entire estate to survivor subject to a nil-rate band discretionary trust, and a discretionary trust of residue on the death of the survivor – C4.2 **[226.40]**
Trusts for a disabled person – B18.4 **[218.36]**
Will providing for spouse suffering from mental disorder – C4.3 **[226.57]**

DISCLAIMER
See also VARIATION OF BENEFICIAL INTERESTS
Appointment of new trustees by disclaiming trustee who has proved testator's will – F1.4 **[239.5]**
Clause allowing for a partial disclaimer, the property disclaimed devolving as if the person disclaiming had predeceased the testator – B19.17 **[219.30]**
Deed of disclaimer of the trusteeship of a will by an executor and trustee who has renounced probate – F1.2 **[239.3]**
Deed of disclaimer of the trusteeship of a will—short form – F1.3 **[239.4]**
Disclaimer by devisee of a gift under a will—short form – F3.1 **[241.22]**
Disclaimer—longer form – F3.2 **[241.23]**
Disclaimer of a life interest – F3.3 **[241.24]**

DISCRETIONARY TRUSTS AND POWERS
Appointment from discretionary trust of investments to a bereaved minor trust or age 18–25 trust – F4.6 **[242.13]**
Appointment from discretionary trust of investments upon trusts – F4.4 **[242.10]**
Appointment from discretionary trust of money to beneficiaries who are sui juris – F4.3 **[242.9]**
Appointment from discretionary trust within two years of testator's death – F4.1 **[242.7]**
Appointment to spouse from nil-rate band discretionary trust within two years of testator's death – F4.2 **[242.8]**
Devise to beneficiary on discretionary trusts – B18.3 **[218.35]**
Discretionary trust of chattels – C9.2(5) **[231.20]**
Discretionary trust of residue – C6.2(7), C10.2(6) **[228.28]**, **[232.22]**
Discretionary trust of residue in will for disabled person on the death of the survivor of husband and wife – C4.2 **[226.13]**
Discretionary trust of shares – C11.1(2) **[233.17]**
Discretionary trust for the testator's family – B18.1 **[218.33]**
Gift of chattels to trustees to, upon a short-term discretionary trust – B4.11 **[204.25]**
Gift of estate on discretionary trusts for family – C1.9 **[223.10]**
Legacy equal to inheritance tax threshold to be held on discretionary trusts – B18.2 **[218.34]**
Life interest subject to trustees' power to pay or apply capital to or for the benefit of the life tenant, with remainders to the life tenant's children subject to powers of the life tenant to appoint a life interest to his spouse and to appoint capital among his issue – B18.8 **[218.40]**

Nil-rate band legacy *see also* NIL-RATE BAND LEGACIES
Power to daughter to appoint life interest in a settled share to her husband – B18.5 **[218.37]**
Power to pay, to children who have life interests, increasing proportions of capital as they grow older – B18.9 **[218.41]**
Power to trustees to settle child's share – B18.6 **[218.36]**
Power to trustees to vary trusts of child's settled share – B18.10 **[218.42]**
Protective life interest with a power to raise and pay capital – B18.7 **[218.37]**
Reciprocal wills containing nil-rate band legacy on discretionary trusts with gift of residue to spouse – C3.4 **[225.57]**
Reciprocal wills giving nil-rate band legacy to children and residue to spouse with default gift to children in equal/unequal shares – C3.1 **[225.9]**
Reciprocal wills with nil-rate band legacy on trust for the children, residue on trust for spouse for life and then on trust for the children, son taking a life interest and daughter a protected life interest – C3.2 **[225.23]**
Trusts for a disabled person – B18.4 **[218.34]**
Will giving nil-rate band legacy on discretionary trusts and settling residue on protective trusts for spouse for life, with overriding trustees' powers over capital – C3.5 **[225.68]**
Will providing two-year discretionary trust – C3.6 **[225.92]**

EMERGENCY, WILLS FOR USE IN
Adoption of intestacy rules by revocation of former wills – C1.7 **[223.8]**
Gift of estate on discretionary trusts for family – C1.9 **[223.10]**
Gift of entire estate to children – C1.2 **[223.3]**
Gift of entire estate to one person – C1.1 **[223.2]**
Settled gift of residue on express trusts for spouse and children – C1.8 **[223.9]**
Settled gift of residue on trusts for spouse and children by reference to Statutory Will Forms – C1.5 **[223.6]**
Will expressly incorporating intestacy rules – C1.6 **[223.7]**
Will incorporating instructions for will – C1.4 **[223.5]**
Will incorporating gift of residue on discretionary charitable trusts – C1.3 **[223.4]**

EMPLOYEES
Legacies to,
Adjustment of legacies to servants or employees occasioned by redundancy payments under the Employment Rights Act 1996 – B10.46 **[210.63]**
Legacy to chauffeur with alternative gift if he shall have left the testator's service – B10.42 **[210.59]**
Legacy to clerks – B10.45 **[210.62]**
Legacies to indoor servants – B10.43 **[210.60]**
Legacies to servants—longer form – B10.44 **[210.61]**
Legacy to a servant, if not under notice to leave at testator's death – B10.41 **[210.58]**

ENJOYMENT IN KIND *see* RIGHTS OF RESIDENCE

ENTAILS
See also SETTLED LAND
Declaration negativing the exercise of the statutory power to dispose of entailed property or the exercise of a general power of appointment – B14.13 **[214.22]**
Gift of entailed personalty – B4.53 **[204.75]**
Gift of entailed property generally – B6.10 **[206.19]**
Gift of land of which the testator is tenant in tail – B6.9 **[206.18]**

EXCLUSION OF APPORTIONMENT *see* APPORTIONMENT

EXECUTORS
Application by an intending testator to the Public Trustee to act as executor and trustee under a will – B3.17 **[203.36]**
Application for an advance from a bank by executors and undertaking to repay – F2.4 **[240.4]**
Appointment of,
Appointment of bank as sole executor and trustee – B3.14 **[203.33]**
Appointment of a bank together with individuals as executors and trustees – B3.13 **[203.32]**
Appointment of civil partner as sole executor and trustee with alternative appointment – B3.2 **[203.8]**
Appointment of executors and trustees with provisions for substitution in case of vacancy – B3.7 **[203.13]**
Appointment of future partners in a solicitors' firm as executors and trustees – B3.9 **[203.24]**
Appointment of future partners in a solicitors' firm or future members of the body in the event of incorporation – B3.12 **[203.27]**
Appointment of individuals as executors – B3.3 **[203.9]**
Appointment of insurance company as executor and trustee – B3.15 **[203.34]**
Appointment of members and employees held out as partners of solicitors' incorporated practice including a limited liability partnership – B3.11 **[203.26]**
Appointment of members of solicitors' incorporated practice iincluding a limited liability partnership – B3.10 **[203.25]**
Appointment of new trustees by disclaiming trustee who has proved testator's will – F1.4 **[239.5]**
Appointment of same persons as executors and trustees – B3.4 **[203.10]**
Appointment of same persons as executors and of different persons as trustees – B3.5 **[203.11]**
Appointment of separate executors for testator's business – B3.25 **[203.44]**
Appointment of separate executors for UK property and foreign property – B3.26 **[203.45]**
Appointment of special executors of settled land – B3.27 **[203.46]**
Appointment of three persons, one of whom is abroad, to be executors and trustees, and also trustees for the purposes of the Settled Land Act 1925 – B3.7 **[203.13]**
Appointment of wife as sole executrix and trustee with alternative appointment – B3.1 **[203.7]**
Appointment of wife / civil partner during widowhood/until formation of a civil partnership adult son and infant son when he attains majority to be executors and trustees – B3.6 **[203.12]**
Clause in will prohibiting appointment of the Public Trustee as a trustee – B3.23 **[203.42]**
Clauses in will appointing executors and trustees, the Public Trustee being only a trustee or custodian trustee – B3.19 **[203.38]**
Clause in will appointing the Public Trustee as sole executor and trustee or jointly with others – B3.18 **[203.37]**
Clauses in will of a person domiciled elsewhere than in England and Wales appointing an individual executor and providing for transfer of the residuary estate or of a legacy to Public Trustee to be held upon English trusts – B3.20 **[203.39]**

Codicil appointing the Public Trustee as executor and trustee jointly with executors and trustees previously appointed or in place of one who has died – B3.22 **[203.41]**
Notice to the Public Trustee of death of a testator who has appointed the Public Trustee as an executor of his will – F2.1 **[240.1]**
Notice to the Public Trustee of death of a testator who has appointed the Public Trustee as a trustee or as a custodian trustee under his will – F2.2 **[240.2]**
Codicil revoking appointment of executors and trustees and appointing the Public Trustee sole executor and trustee in their place – B3.21 **[203.40]**
Provision for appointment of trust corporation – B21.40 **[221.52]**
Words to be included in executors' oath where partners in a solicitors' firm have been appointed executors – F2.3 **[240.3]**
Declaration of trust of property devised or bequeathed by will on a secret trust – F2.5 **[240.5]**

Gifts to,
Legacies to executors – B10.37 **[210.52]**
Legacies to executors and annuities to trustees – B10.38 **[210.53]**

Remuneration of,
Power to professional trustee to charge—concise form – B21.37 **[221.49]**
Power to professional trustee to charge—full form – B21.38 **[221.50]**
Proviso enabling professional trustee to elect not to charge – B21.39 **[221.51]**
Provision for appointment of trust corporation – B21.40 **[221.52]**
Remuneration clause for bank appointed as executor and trustee – B3.16 **[203.35]**

EXERCISE OF POWERS *see* POWERS OF TRUSTEES

FARMING *see* BUSINESS PROPERTY

FOREIGN PROPERTY
Appointment of separate executors for UK property and foreign property – B3.26 **[203.45]**
Commencement of concurrent will of testator with UK and foreign property confining the will to UK property – B1.7 **[201.12]**
Commencement of will of testator with UK and foreign property confining the will to UK property – B1.6 **[201.11]**
Declaration that statutory provisions shall apply to foreign property – B20.15 **[220.64]**
Direction to foreign trustees to remit proceeds of sale to English trustees – B14.23 **[214.34]**
Direction to trustees to convert foreign property, with powers of management – B14.22 **[214.33]**
Legacies free of inheritance tax and duties payable outside Great Britain – B10.47 **[210.68]**
Powers of management of foreign land – B20.14 **[220.63]**
Power to pay foreign tax – B20.16 **[220.65]**

Wills disposing of, complete
Reciprocal wills of English-domiciled couple who own foreign holiday home and who have already executed foreign wills giving the home to their son on the death of the survivor, leaving their estates to each other with the survivor leaving a tax-free legacy to the son equal to the amount of the inheritance tax on the holiday home, giving the daughter a compensating legacy and leaving residue to the son and daughter equally – C14.3 **[236.39]**

Reciprocal wills of English-domiciled couple who own foreign holiday home and who intend to execute foreign wills giving the home to their son on the death of the survivor, leaving their estates to each other with the survivor making a tax-free gift of holiday home to the son (with a tax-free legacy equal to the inheritance tax on the home in the event that the foreign wills are executed), giving the daughter a compensating legacy and leaving residue to the son and daughter equally – C14.2 **[236.24]**
Will of English-domiciled testator/testatrix owning property in England and in foreign country, appointing separate executors to administer foreign property with direction to remit the proceeds of the foreign estate to the English executors – C14.1 **[236.9]**

FORFEITURE
Forfeiture on contesting the will or attempting to intermeddle – B19.18 **[219.31]**

FREEHOLDS *see* LAND

FUNERAL
Direction as to place of burial and tombstone – B2.1 **[202.3]**
Direction that only necessary expense shall be incurred – B2.3 **[202.5]**
Directions as to the ascertainment of the testator's death in order to prevent his being buried alive – B2.4 **[202.6]**
Expressions of desire as to cremation – B2.2 **[202.4]**
Power for executor to incur expense in respect of directions – B2.5 **[202.7]**

FURNITURE, GIFT OF
Bedroom effects, daughter, to – B4.25 **[204.43]**
Civil partner to, for life or until marriage or formation of civil partnership; no inventory – B4.28 **[204.46]**
Civil partner to, until marriage or formation of civil partnership; repairs and insurance to be provided for by him, and an inventory made – B4.30 **[204.48]**
Daughters to, contingently on their attaining eighteen or twenty-one or marrying – B4.26 **[204.44]**
Located in a certain house – B4.23 **[204.41]**
Surviving children, to – B4.24 **[204.42]**
Wife to, for life and then to son, incorporation of Statutory Will Form as to inventory – B4.32 **[204.50]**
Wife, to – B4.22 **[204.40]**
Wife or civil partner to, during life and thereafter for children: directions for inventory, and for repairs and insurance out of wife's income during her life – B4.31 **[204.49]**
Wife to, for life or during widowhood; no inventory – B4.27 **[204.45]**
Wife to, during widowhood; repairs and insurance to be provided for by her, and an inventory made – B4.29 **[204.47]**

GRAVES, MAINTENANCE OF
Direction to executors to enter into an agreement for the maintenance of a grave in a local authority cemetery – B2.11 **[202.34]**
Gift for the upkeep of a particular grave during a perpetuity period – B2.8 **[202.31]**
Gift for the upkeep of a particular grave in a churchyard during a perpetuity period followed by a perpetual gift for the upkeep of the churchyard with a request to maintain the particular grave – B2.10 **[202.33]**
Gift to a charity conditional upon the maintenance of a particular grave with a gift over on breach of the condition to another charity – B2.12 **[202.35]**
Perpetual gift for the upkeep of a churchyard with a request to maintain a particular grave – B2.9 **[202.32]**

GUARDIANS
Appointment by the mother of illegitimate children, appointing the father as guardian with alternative appointment in the event of him predeceasing her – B3.32 **[203.64]**
Appointment of a guardian by a guardian – B3.34 **[203.66]**
Appointment of a guardian with an alternative appointment if the first choice predeceases the testator or disclaims – B3.31 **[203.63]**
Appointment of guardian to take effect only if the other parent predeceases the appointor, with optional wording making it also take effect if the other parent does not make an effective appointment – B3.28 **[203.60]**
Appointment of guardian which takes effect if the other parent predeceases the appointor or if there is a residence order in favour of the testator at his or her death, with optional wording-making it also take effect if the other parent does not make an effective appointment – B3.29 **[203.61]**
Appointment of two guardians with expression of wishes about religious education – B3.30 **[203.62]**
Appointment of wife to be the guardian of children by a former marriage with general revocation of previous appointments – B3.33 **[203.65]**
Power for trustees to make loans to guardians – B18.30 **[218.116]**
Testator's wishes as to the exercise of powers of maintenance and advancement [and power to make loans to guardians] during period of guardianship – B18.31 **[218.117]**

HOTCHPOT PROVISIONS
Declaration negativing ademption of a gift by will by subsequent gift – B17.39 **[217.47]**
Declaration that certain children are to bring specified sums into hotchpot – B17.38 **[217.46]**
Declaration that certain future gifts are to be brought into hotchpot – B17.40 **[217.48]**
Declaration that provisions made by will for children are not to be in addition to provisions made for them by the testator's marriage settlement – B17.37 **[217.45]**
Declaration that provisions made by will for testator's wife and children are in addition to and not in substitution for provisions made for them in his lifetime – B17.36 **[217.44]**
Express provision against satisfaction and ademption – B17.41 **[217.49]**
Gift of debt to a legatee of a share of residue with provision for hotchpot – B4.44 **[204.66]**
Release of children's debts with optional provision for hotchpot – B4.43 **[204.65]**
Trust for wife for life and then to children as she shall appoint, with hotchpot provision – B16.13 **[216.20]**

HOUSE *see* LAND and RIGHTS OF RESIDENCE

HUSBAND AND WIFE *see* MARRIED COUPLES

INDIVIDUALS, COMPLETE WILLS FOR
With adult children
Will of grandparent incorporating fixed or flexible accumulation and maintenance trusts of residue for grandchildren – C8.4 **[230.45]**
Will of widow leaving her house to a daughter who is looking after her and residue to grandchildren on bare trusts – C8.5 **[230.62]**

Will of widow or widower dividing residue between son and daughter, son's share being settled on protective trusts for his benefit and daughter's share being either given to her absolutely or settled on trusts for her benefit – C8.2 **[230.16]**

Will of widow or widower leaving one share of residue on trust for the children absolutely and the other share subjected to immediate post-death interests for the grandchildren – C8.3 **[230.30]**

Will of widow or widower leaving residue to children absolutely – C8.1 **[230.2]**

Will of widow or widower settling residue on trusts for children with progressive powers to pay them capital at different ages – C8.6 **[230.73]**

Will of widower giving estate equally between his children, one son being given an option to purchase the farming assets – C12.1 **[234.17]**

With young children

Will of mother appointing sister sole executrix and guardian of children and giving entire estate to her if accepting office, with alternative gift to children – C7.2 **[229.13]**

Will of mother giving entire estate to her minor child – C7.1 **[229.2]**

Will of widow or widower in favour of children – C7.3 **[229.26]**

Will of widow or widower settling residue on children equally for life with remainder to their children – C7.4 **[229.37]**

Without children

Will of a bachelor landowner settling the principal family estate together with a share of residue on one nephew and his issue, creating a maintenance fund for the upkeep of the mansion house and settled chattels and settling substantial legacies on two nieces and their issue – C13.2 **[235.18]**

Will of childless individual giving charitable and other legacies, with a specific gift of a house and residue given on trust for nephews and nieces for life with remainders for their children – C10.6 **[232.64]**

Will of older childless person settling residue in equal shares on brothers and sisters (or nephews and nieces) for life with remainders for their children – C10.4 **[232.39]**

Will of older person in favour of brothers and sisters, with substitution of issue of those who predecease the testator – C10.3 **[232.27]**

Will of owner of substantial property with no immediate family containing specific gift of controlling shareholding in family company on trusts for the employees and leaving residue on charitable trusts – C13.1 **[235.2]**

Will of unmarried childless person in favour of unmarried sister for life with remainders over to brothers and sisters or their issue – C10.5 **[232.52]**

Will of young person creating discretionary trust of residue for his or her parents and brothers and sisters and their issue – C10.2 **[232.15]**

Will of young person dividing his or her estate equally between his or her siblings but making a gift of the share of a sibling with living children direct to such children – C10.1 **[232.2]**

INHERITANCE (PROVISION FOR FAMILY AND DEPENDANTS) ACT 1975

Declarations under the Inheritance (Provision for Family and Dependants) Act 1975—Alternative forms – B2.15 **[202.40]**

INHERITANCE TAX

Alternative declaration concerning equal shares of partially exempt residue – *Re Benham* direction – B14.37 **[214.80]**

Alternative declaration concerning fractional shares of partially exempt residue – *Re Benham* direction – B14.36 **[214.79]**

Annuity provisions designed to mitigate inheritance tax and income tax – B11.11 **[211.18]**
Clause dealing with inheritance tax on lifetime gifts made by the testator – B10.48 **[210.69]**
Clause providing for payment by the donee of the inheritance tax on a testamentary gift which would otherwise be free of inheritance tax – B10.50 **[210.71]**
Clause providing for payment out of residue of inheritance tax on property not passing under the will – B10.49 **[210.70]**
Clause providing that inheritance tax on business premises be paid by trustees and repaid to them by son – B5.5 **[205.62]**
Declaration as to inheritance tax on settled leaseholds – B7.10 **[207.24]**
Declaration as to payment of inheritance tax on specific gifts – B6.29 **[206.38]**
Declaration concerning partially exempt residue – B14.35 **[214.78]**
Declaration that free of inheritance tax provisions relate only to tax on the testator's death – B14.39 **[214.82]**
Declaration that inheritance tax and foreign death duties on pecuniary legacies and personal chattels shall be paid out of residue – B14.34 **[214.77]**
General declaration making all inheritance tax and foreign death duties on free estate payable out of residue – B14.33 **[214.76]**
General residuary gift to trustees—direction to pay inheritance tax on specific gifts, pecuniary legacies, and lifetime gifts – B14.6 **[214.15]**
General restriction to prevent administrative powers prejudicing inheritance tax status of beneficial trusts – B20.28 **[220.81]**
Gift of annuity tax-free – B11.2 **[211.9]**
Gift of item which might be conditionally exempt from inheritance tax – B4.14 **[204.28]**
Gift of such of unquoted shares as shall have been owned for two years by the time of testator's death, subject to inheritance tax – B5.9 **[205.66]**
Gift of unquoted shares or any substitute shares on condition that they qualify for business relief, subject to inheritance tax, and with power to disclaim part of the gift – B5.10 **[205.67]**
Legacy equal to inheritance tax threshold to be held on discretionary trusts – B18.2 **[218.34]**
Legacies free of inheritance tax and duties payable outside Great Britain – B10.47 **[210.68]**
Nil-rate band *see* NIL-RATE BAND LEGACIES
Power to insure against liability for inheritance tax on lifetime dispositions – B21.19 **[221.23]**
Powers to permit enjoyment in kind—restricted to prevent prejudice to inheritance tax status of beneficial trusts – B18.24 **[218.110]**
Specific gift of land which may qualify for agricultural property relief subject to inheritance tax – B6.31 **[206.40]**
Specific gift subject to inheritance tax – B6.30 **[206.39]**
Specific gift subject to inheritance tax where the estate may turn out to be partially exempt and include business or agricultural property – B14.38 **[214.81]**
Trusts of proceeds of sale of residue with general direction to pay inheritance tax on free estate out of residue – B14.17 **[214.26]**
Trust to pay debts and invest residue—directions as to inheritance tax – B14.8 **[214.17]**
Two-year discretionary trusts *see* DISCRETIONARY TRUSTS

INTELLECTUAL PROPERTY
Absolute gift of copyrights and unpublished works to literary executor – B4.50 **[204.72]**
Absolute gift of copyrights—proceeds to be transferred to general executors – B4.51 **[204.73]**
Appointment of literary executors – B3.24 **[203.43]**
Gift of letters and papers – B4.19 **[204.33]**
Gift of patents – B4.52 **[204.74]**

JOINT PROPERTY
Clause dealing with property held in joint tenancy – B4.49 **[204.71]**

LAND
Absolute general gift of freeholds or lands generally – B6.1 **[206.10]**
Accumulation and maintenance trust of investment property – B17.35 **[217.40]**
Clause creating an easement over land given to one person in favour of devisee of other land – B6.27 **[206.36]**
Contingent gift of leaseholds – B7.7 **[207.21]**
Declaration as to inheritance tax on settled leaseholds – B7.10 **[207.24]**
Declaration as to payment of inheritance tax on specific gifts – B6.29 **[206.38]**
Declaration that gift of lease includes the freehold reversion or any renewal if subsequently acquired – B7.6 **[207.20]**
Devise and bequest of residue charged with payment of debts – B14.14 **[214.23]**
Devise of residuary real estate only – B14.16 **[214.25]**
Expression of testator's intention not to exercise a general power of appointment over land – B6.21 **[206.30]**
General gift of lands in a particular place – B6.2 **[206.11]**
Gift by reference to a settlement on trust for sale – B6.23 **[206.32]**
Gift for the benefit of testator's children and the issue of deceased children at eighteen or marriage – B6.25 **[206.34]**
Gift freed from a mortgage debt – B6.14 **[206.23]**
Gift in exercise of a special power of appointment – B6.20 **[206.29]**
Gift of annuities charged on land – B11.6 **[211.13]**
Gift of certain freehold lands to a charity – B6.17 **[206.26]**
Gift of entailed property generally – B6.10 **[206.19]**
Gift of freehold lands purchased in a certain year – B6.3 **[206.12]**
Gift of freeholds subject to the payment of a legacy – B6.11 **[206.20]**
Gift of land for the benefit of testator's children and issue of deceased children, sons taking at eighteen or twenty-one, daughters taking at eighteen or twenty-one or on marriage—variation for children of a person other than testator – B17.34 **[217.42]**
Gift of land of which the testator is tenant in tail – B6.9 **[206.18]**
Gift of land to minor with trust for sale and provision for his death under eighteen or twenty-one leaving issue – B17.35 **[217.43]**
Gift of lands, and in the event of such lands being sold during testator's lifetime, bequest of the proceeds of sale of such lands – B6.15 **[206.24]**
Gift of lands to testator's sons, with successive gifts over if sons predecease testator without issue [male] – B6.24 **[206.33]**
Gift of lands upon the trusts of a settlement – B6.22 **[206.31]**
Gift of lands which the testator has contracted to purchase – B6.16 **[206.25]**
Gift of leasehold flat and devise of any interest in freehold of premises in which flat is contained – B7.2 **[207.16]**
Gift of leasehold house free from mortgage – B7.3 **[207.17]**
Gift of leaseholds – B7.1 **[207.15]**

Gift of leaseholds to trustees upon trust to pay rents and profits to a person for life, and after his death to assign to another – B7.5 **[207.19]**
Gift of leaseholds upon trust out of the rents and profits to form sinking fund – B7.11 **[207.25]**
Gift of leaseholds with alternative provision for sinking fund to replace leasehold value – B7.12 **[207.26]**
Gift of leaseholds with a direction that the legatee is to pay all arrears of rent and cost of dilapidations – B7.4 **[207.18]**
Gift of part of land to one person and the other part to another by reference to a plan, with cross easements – B6.28 **[206.37]**
Gift of sinking fund policies in respect of leasehold properties – B7.9 **[207.23]**
Gift subject to a condition as to taking a name – B6.18 **[206.27]**
Gift subject to a mortgage – B6.13 **[206.22]**
Gift subject to the payment of debts, funeral, and testamentary expenses – B6.12 **[206.21]**
Gift to a person with a gift over on death without issue – B6.19 **[206.28]**
Gift to joint tenants or tenants in common – B6.7 **[206.16]**
Gift to minor – B6.8 **[206.17]**
Gift of undivided share in leaseholds – B7.8 **[207.22]**
Gift with provision against lapse – B6.26 **[206.35]**
Specific gift of freeholds – B6.4 **[206.13]**
Specific gift of property with provision against apportionment – B6.5 **[206.14]**
Specific gift of registered land – B6.6 **[206.15]**
Specific gift subject to inheritance tax – B6.30 **[206.39]**
Specific gift of land which may qualify for agricultural property relief subject to inheritance tax – B6.31 **[206.40]**

LAPSE, PROVISIONS CONCERNING
Clause as to application of lapsed share of residue – B19.14 **[219.27]**
Clause providing against lapse in the case of a gift to a named person and that the clause shall operate as a direct gift to the substituted persons – B19.11 **[219.24]**
Declaration against lapse in the case of a class gift of residue – B19.12 **[219.25]**
Declaration against lapse in the case of a gift to a named person – B19.10 **[219.23]**
Declaration against lapse of settled share – B19.13 **[219.26]**
General form of gift over on failure of the trusts of residue – B19.15 **[219.28]**
General provision against lapse of charitable gifts – B12.29 **[212.31]**
Gift to testator's wife with alternative gift to take on the failure for any reason of the primary gift – B19.16 **[219.29]**
Gift of land with provision against lapse – B6.26 **[206.35]**
Provision against lapse of charitable gifts – C10.6(4) **[232.68]**

LEASEHOLDS *see* LAND

LEGACIES
See DISCRETIONARY TRUSTS, NIL RATE BAND LEGACIES, PECUNIARY LEGACIES, PERSONAL CHATTELS *and* SETTLED LEGACIES
Miscellaneous documents giving effect to legacies
Assent – F5.2 **[243.3]**
Deed of charge to give effect to a nil-rate band charge scheme – F5.4 **[243.5]**
Deed of promise to give effect to a nil-rate band debt scheme – F5.3 **[243.4]**
Resolution of appropriation – F5.1 **[243.2]**

LIFE INTERESTS
Clause as to annual sums payable under an insurance policy – B16.29 **[216.36]**
Clause directing trustees to resort to the capital of residue in order to make up income to a minimum amount – B16.18 **[216.25]**
Clause empowering trustees to resort to capital – B16.19 **[216.26]**
Clause empowering trustees to lend capital money to make up income of a share of residue to a stated amount – B16.20 **[216.27]**
Determinable life interest – B16.3 **[216.10]**
Gift of income of residuary estate to a reputed wife as long as she is unmarried – B16.8 **[216.15]**
Gift of residue incorporating intestacy provisions – B16.22 **[216.29]**
Gift of residue to children incorporating Statutory Will Forms 1925, Form 7, with modification – B16.21 **[216.28]**
Life interest to wife reducible on remarriage – B16.5 **[216.12]**
Life or widowhood interest to wife – B16.4 **[216.11]**
Payment of income to banker – B16.28 **[216.35]**
Power to life tenants of settled shares to give releases to trustees – B21.18 **[221.22]**
Protective income trusts for woman for life – B16.2 **[216.9]**
Provision directing payment of capital to a female life tenant having no likelihood of children, where she has herself a general power of appointment in default of children – B16.24 **[216.31]**
Settlement of child's share of residuary estate – B16.23 **[216.30]**
Statutory protective trusts, varied by allowing accumulation for a period of years after a forfeiture has occurred – B16.1 **[216.8]**
Trust for wife during widowhood subject to an obligation to maintain children – B16.6 **[216.13]**
Trust for wife during widowhood, then to son for life with remainder to his children – B16.15 **[216.22]**
Trust for wife during widowhood where no legal obligation imposed – B16.7 **[216.14]**
Trust for wife for life and then to children as she shall appoint incorporating Statutory Will Forms 1925, Form 9 – B16.17 **[216.24]**
Trust for wife for life and then to children as she shall appoint, with hotchpot provision – B16.13 **[216.20]**
Trust for wife for life and then to children for life with substitution of their issue – B16.16 **[216.23]**
Trust for wife for life and then to children in equal shares – B16.10 **[216.17]**
Trust for wife for life and then to children in equal shares by incorporation of Statutory Will Forms 1925. Form 10 – B16.11 **[216.18]**
Trust for wife for life and then to issue upon such trusts as she shall appoint – B16.14 **[216.21]**
Trust for wife for life and then to unmarried daughters for life – B16.12 **[216.19]**
Trust of income for several persons for life giving a general testamentary power of disposition to the survivor – B16.9 **[216.16]**

LITERARY ASSETS *see* INTELLECTUAL PROPERTY

LOANS TO BENEFICIARIES
Loans to a life tenant – B18.27 **[218.113]**
Loans to beneficiary to whom a business is bequeathed – B18.29 **[218.115]**
Loans to individuals without security – B18.28 **[218.114]**
Power for trustees to make loans to guardians – B18.30 **[218.116]**

MAINTENANCE *see* ACCUMULATION AND MAINTENANCE

MARRIAGE/CIVIL PARTNERSHIP
Commencement of will made in expectation of marriage – B1.2 **[201.7]**
Commencement of will made in expectation of marriage—conditional form – B1.3 **[201.9]**

MARRIED COUPLES, COMPLETE WILLS FOR
With adult children
Reciprocal wills containing nil-rate band legacy on discretionary trusts with gift of residue to spouse – C3.4 **[225.57]**
Reciprocal wills giving nil-rate band legacy to children and residue to spouse with default gift to children in equal/unequal shares – C3.1 **[225.9]**
Reciprocal wills with nil-rate band legacy on trust for the children, residue on trust for spouse for life and then on trust for the children, son taking a life interest and daughter a protected life interest – C3.2 **[225.23]**
Will dividing residue between spouse and issue – C3.3 **[225.42]**
Reciprocal wills giving nil-rate band legacy on discretionary trusts and settling residue on protective trusts for spouse for life, with overriding trustees' powers over capital, and discretionary trusts for issue after the surviving spouse's death – C3.5 **[225.68]**
Will providing two-year discretionary trust – C3.6 **[225.92]**
With young children
Reciprocal wills giving entire estate to spouse absolutely with alternative gift of IPDIs to issue – C2.2 **[224.42]**
Reciprocal wills giving entire estate to spouse absolutely, with alternative gift to issue – C2.1 **[224.27]**
Reciprocal wills giving spouse life interest with power of appointment amongst issue, incorporating Statutory Wills Forms – C2.4 **[224.73]**
Reciprocal wills leaving entire estate to spouse for life with power to resort to capital and with remainder to children – C2.3 **[224.58]**
Will of husband who owns matrimonial home giving wife income of residue and right of residence for life or until remarriage – C2.5 **[224.86]**
Will of husband settling residue on wife for life with remainder on discretionary trusts – C2.6 **[224.102]**
See also CHILDLESS HOUSEHOLDS

MENTAL DISORDER *see* DISABLED PERSON

MONEY
Gift of money secured by an insurance policy on testator's life – B4.55 **[204.77]**
Gift of ready money – B4.59 **[204.81]**

MOURNING *see* FUNERAL

MULTIPLE FAMILIES, COMPLETE WILLS FOR,
Reciprocal wills of spouses both having adult children by previous marriages (but none by their own), the first to die giving the survivor his or her estate absolutely and the survivor dividing his or her estate between children and stepchildren – C5.3 **[227.39]**
Reciprocal wills of spouses both having adult children by previous marriages (but none by their own), the first to die making a nil-rate band gift to his or her own children and giving the survivor a life interest in residue with remainder to his or her own children, and the survivor leaving his or her estate to his or her own children – C5.2 **[227.25]**
Will of married man with adult children making provision for an illegitimate child who is a minor by means of a settled legacy – C5.4 **[227.50]**

Will of twice-married testator who has adult children from his first marriage and minor children from his second and who owns the matrimonial home; nil-rate band discretionary trust, and gift of matrimonial home and residue on trust for second wife for life with remainder to all the testator's children – C5.1 **[227.7]**

MUTUAL WILLS
Commencement of mirror but not mutual wills – B1.7 **[201.11]**
Commencement of mutual will made in pursuance of an agreement that it shall not be revoked – B1.8 **[201.13]**

NAME
Gift subject to a condition as to taking a name – B6.18 **[206.27]**

NIL-RATE BAND LEGACIES
Deed of charge to give effect to a nil-rate band charge scheme – F5.4 **[243.5]**
Deed of promise to give effect to a nil-rate band debt scheme – F5.3 **[243.4]**
Gift of shares on nil-rate band discretionary trusts – C11.1(2) **[233.17]**
Legacy equal to inheritance tax threshold to be held on discretionary trusts – B18.2 **[218.34]**
Nil-rate band gift to children including private company shares – C11.2(2) **[233.29]**
Nil-rate band legacy – B10.51 **[210.72]**
Reciprocal wills containing nil-rate band legacy on discretionary trusts with gift of residue to spouse – C3.4 **[225.57]**
Reciprocal wills for husband and wife with a disabled child and other children; gift by first to die of entire estate to survivor subject to a nil-rate band discretionary trust, and a discretionary trust of residue on the death of the survivor – C4.1 **[226.13]**
Reciprocal wills giving nil-rate band legacy to children and residue to spouse with default gift to children in equal/unequal shares – C3.1 **[225.9]**
Reciprocal wills of spouses both having adult children by previous marriages (but none by their own), the first to die making a nil-rate band gift to his or her own children and giving the survivor a life interest in residue with remainder to his or her own children, and the survivor leaving his or her estate to his or her own children – C5.2 **[227.25]**
Reciprocal wills with nil-rate band legacy on trust for the children, residue on trust for spouse for life and then on trust for the children, son taking a life interest and daughter a protected life interest – C3.2 **[225.23]**
Reciprocal wills giving nil-rate band legacy on discretionary trusts and settling residue on protective trusts for spouse for life, with overriding trustees' powers over capital, and discretionary trusts for issue after the surviving spouse's death – C3.5 **[225.68]**
Will of twice-married testator who has adult children from his first marriage and minor children from his second and who owns the matrimonial home; nil-rate band discretionary trust, and gift of matrimonial home and residue on trust for second wife for life with remainder to all the testator's children – C5.1 **[227.7]**

OCCUPATION OF PROPERTY *see* RIGHTS OF RESIDENCE

OPTIONS
Clause giving option to purchase land – B9.1 **[209.6]**
Clause giving option to purchase shares in family company – B9.6 **[209.11]**
Clause giving option to purchase shares in private company (longer form) – B9.7 **[209.12]**

Clause giving option to son to take lease or purchase freehold of business premises – B9.5 **[209.10]**
Clause giving option to testator's wife to purchase retail business – B9.4 **[209.9]**
Clause granting son option to purchase farming assets – C12.1(3) **[234.21]**
Devise of freehold property conditional upon the donee conferring a right of pre-emption on another person – B9.3 **[209.8]**
Direction to trustees to offer farm and farming assets to the testator's sons successively at a valuation before selling under a trust – B9.2 **[209.7]**

PARTNERSHIP *see* BUSINESS PROPERTY

PECUNIARY LEGACIES

Absolute gifts

Direction as to payment of interest at a variable rate – B10.5 **[210.13]**
Gift of a number of legacies – B10.2 **[210.10]**
Legacy to husband and wife or survivor – B10.4 **[210.12]**
Legacy to one individual – B10.1 **[210.9]**
Legacy uprated by reference to Index of Retail Prices – B10.6 **[210.14]**
Legacies given by reference to a schedule – B10.3 **[210.11]**

Children to,

Legacy of a capital sum for the education of children – B10.25 **[210.39]**
Legacy to a minor who is married – B10.22 **[210.36]**
Legacy to an adopted child – B10.27 **[210.41]**
Legacy to children and an illegitimate child – B10.28 **[210.42]**
Legacy to grandchildren – B10.26 **[210.40]**
Legacy to illegitimate children of the testator, including one en ventre sa mère – B10.29 **[210.43]**
Legacy to legitimate and illegitimate children of a brother of the testator – B10.30 **[210.44]**
Legacy to married daughters to become subject to the trusts of their respective marriage settlements, the amount of the legacies varying in order to equalise the provisions made by the testator for all his daughters – B10.31 **[210.45]**
Legacy to minor – B10.20 **[210.34]**
Legacy to minor to be applied in maintenance – B10.23 **[210.37]**
Legacy to minor to provide an allowance for him – B10.24 **[210.38]**
Small legacy to minor with provision for opening National Savings – Bank account – B10.21 **[210.35]**

Contingent and conditional legacies

Legacy contingent on attaining eighteen or twenty-one – B10.32 **[210.46]**
Legacy contingent on attaining eighteen or twenty-one carrying interest – B10.33 **[210.47]**
Legacy contingent on attaining twenty-five or marrying, relying on the statutory powers of maintenance – B10.35 **[210.49]**
Legacy subject to discharge of guarantee – B10.36 **[210.50]**
Legacies to two persons contingently on their attaining eighteen or twenty-one years of age with survivorship – B10.34 **[210.48]**

Debtors and creditors, to

Declaration as to legacies to creditors – B10.16 **[210.29]**
Legacy to a creditor – B10.15 **[210.28]**
Legacy to a son subject to deduction of sums owing – B10.19 **[210.32]**
Legacy to debtor with forgiveness of debt – B10.18 **[210.31]**
Legacy to debtor without forgiveness of debt – B10.17 **[210.30]**

Deferred and prior legacies

Declaration as to time of payment and priority of legacies – B10.10 **[210.22]**

Legacy payable on death of life tenant – B10.11 **[210.23]**
Legacy payable six months after the death of the survivor of testator and his wife – B10.8 **[210.20]**
Legacy with priority – B10.9 **[210.21]**
Power to trustees to postpone payment of legacies – B10.12 **[210.24]**

Employees to,
Adjustment of legacies to servants or employees occasioned by redundancy payments under the Employment Rights Act 1996 – B10.46 **[210.63]**
Legacy to chauffeur with alternative gift if he shall have left the testator's service – B10.42 **[210.59]**
Legacy to clerks – B10.45 **[210.62]**
Legacies to indoor servants – B10.43 **[210.60]**
Legacies to servants—longer form – B10.44 **[210.61]**
Legacy to a servant, if not under notice to leave at testator's death – B10.41 **[210.58]**

Executors and trustees to,
Legacies to executors – B10.37 **[210.52]**
Legacies to executors and annuities to trustees – B10.38 **[210.53]**

Improvident persons for,
Legacy to improvident person payable by instalments – B10.40 **[210.56]**
Legacy with provision for forfeiture on alienation – B10.39 **[210.55]**

Inheritance tax and foreign death duties
Clause dealing with inheritance tax on lifetime gifts made by the testator – B10.48 **[210.69]**
Clause providing for payment by the donee of the inheritance tax on a testamentary gift which would otherwise be free of inheritance tax – B10.50 **[210.71]**
Clause providing for payment out of residue of inheritance tax on property not passing under the will – B10.49 **[210.70]**
Legacies free of inheritance tax and duties payable outside Great Britain – B10.47 **[210.68]**

Miscellaneous
Bequest of legacies payable exclusively out of a particular property with provision for abatement and interest – B10.54 **[210.75]**
Clause providing for reduction of legacies where the testator's estate proves to have decreased in value – B10.55 **[210.76]**
Declaration as to currency in which legacies payable – B10.56 **[210.77]**
Demonstrative legacy – B10.53 **[210.74]**
Direction as to rate of exchange for payment of legacies in a foreign currency – B10.57 **[210.78]**
Legacies with provision for some of the legatees not being able to be found – B10.52 **[210.73]**
Legacy for purchase of customary mourning – B10.58 **[210.79]**

Nil-rate band legacy *see* NIL-RATE BAND LEGACIES

Provision for immediate needs
Immediate legacy to wife or civil partner or other person in charge of testator's household – B10.7 **[210.19]**

Substitutional provisions with,
Legacy to nieces, and the children of deceased nieces – B10.14 **[210.26]**
Legacy with a clause of substitution in the case of an individual legatee – B10.13 **[210.25]**

PERSONAL CHATTELS, GIFTS OF
Articles of personal adornment to daughters as trustees shall determine – B4.8 **[204.22]**

Articles with request to distribute them in accordance with testator's wishes – B4.9 **[204.23]**
By reference to a document already in existence – B4.20 **[204.34]**
Consumable stores – B4.21 **[204.36]**
Furniture *see* FURNITURE
Incorporation of definition in the Administration of Estates Act 1925 – B4.2 **[204.16]**
Incorporation of Statutory Will Forms 1925, Form 2 – B4.1 **[204.15]**
Item which might be conditionally exempt from inheritance tax – B4.14 **[204.28]**
Letters and papers – B4.19 **[204.33]**
Library – B4.16 **[204.30]**
Located in specific dwellinghouse – B4.12 **[204.26]**
Public collection or the nation of a work of art – B4.15 **[204.29]**
Residuary estate paying costs of preservation, transport, packing and insurance – B4.13 **[204.27]**
Selected by trustees on life interest trusts – B4.10 **[204.24]**
Short form – B4.5 **[204.19]**
Sporting implements – B4.17 **[204.31]**
Statutory Will Forms 1925, Form 2: Meaning of 'personal chattels' – E3 **[238.8]**
Stocks and Shares *see* STOCKS AND SHARES
Trustees to, upon a short-term discretionary trust – B4.11 **[204.25]**
Wearing apparel to servants – B4.18 **[204.32]**
Wife, to – B4.3 **[204.17]**
Wife to, —alternative form – B4.4 **[204.18]**
Wife to, of such articles as she may select – B4.6 **[204.20]**
Wife to, of such articles as she may select up to a stated amount and of the residue to daughters – B4.7 **[204.21]**

POWERS OF TRUSTEES
Administrative powers, set for complete wills – C2.1(9) **[224.30]**
Appropriation *see* APPROPRIATION
Borrowing
Power to borrow – B20.20 **[220.69]**
Business property, over
No duty to intervene in the affairs of a private company – B21.17 **[221.21]**
Power to carry on business – B5.13, B20.17 **[205.70]**, **[220.66]**
Power to carry on farming business – B20.18 **[220.67]**
Provision for exercise of powers though trustees interested in business – B5.18 **[205.75]**
Power for some of the trustees only to carry on testator's business – B5.17 **[205.74]**
Power to give guarantees for loans to companies wholly or substantially owned by trustees – B20.29 **[220.82]**
Power to incorporate business – B20.19 **[220.68]**
Power to trustees to carry on business where the will contains a general trust for conversion – B5.16 **[205.73]**
Power to turn business into limited or unlimited company – B5.14 **[205.71]**
Powers relating to sale of a business – B5.21 **[205.78]**
Powers to give warranties etc on the sale of a business or private company shares – B5.22 **[205.79]**
Retention of shares in family company – B20.5 **[220.44]**
Set for complete wills – C11.1(6) **[233.21]**
Exercise and release of powers
Powers and discretions exercisable in favour of a beneficiary trustee – B18.32 **[218.118]**

Power to release powers – B18.33 **[218.119]**
Testator's wishes as to the exercise of powers of maintenance and advancement [and power to make loans to guardians] during period of guardianship – B18.31 **[218.117]**

Foreign property, over *see* FOREIGN PROPERTY

Investment and general powers

Clause as to bonus shares – B20.9 **[220.48]**
Clause excluding the statutory duty of care – B21.13 **[221.17]**
General restriction to prevent administrative powers prejudicing inheritance tax status of beneficial trusts – B20.28 **[220.81]**
Investment, full discretion—long form – B20.2 **[220.41]**
Investment, full discretion—short form – B20.3 **[220.42]**
Power authorising an audit – B21.26 **[221.30]**
Power for trustees to make loans to guardians – B18.30 **[218.116]**
Power of investment confined to fixed interest investments quoted shares and legal estates in land – B20.1 **[220.40]**
Power to delegate investment powers and vest assets in nominees – B20.8 **[220.47]**
Power to distribute on assumption that no further children – B21.30 **[221.34]**
Power to employ a manager – B5.20 **[205.77]**
Power to give warranties on the sale of private company shares – B20.7 **[220.46]**
Power to insure against liability for inheritance tax on lifetime dispositions – B21.19 **[221.23]**
Power to lend money to legatee of business – B5.19 **[205.76]**
Power to vest assets in nominees – B21.29 **[221.33]**
Powers of sale and transposing assets – B20.6 **[220.45]**
Statutory power subject to an ethical investment policy – B20.4 **[220.43]**

Management of land

See also LAND
Clause excluding trustees' duty to consult with beneficiaries as to land – B21.23 **[221.27]**
Exercise of powers to be subject to beneficiary's consent – B20.13 **[220.62]**
Power of management in relation to land in any location – B20.10 **[220.59]**
Power to apply other capital in improving land – B20.11 **[220.60]**
Treatment of mining rent and royalties and proceeds of timber – B20.12 **[220.61]**

Retention of directors' remuneration etc

Power for trustees to become directors and to retain remuneration—short form – B21.9 **[221.10]**
Power for trustees to become directors, retain remuneration and to hold shares as qualifying shares – B21.10 **[221.11]**
Retention of benefits—fuller form including benefits from subsidiary companies – B21.11 **[221.12]**

Self-dealing

Clause giving named trustee power to purchase part of testator's estate with safeguard against improper purchase – B21.4 **[221.5]**
Power to a trustee to enter into any transaction provided there is at least one other trustee – B21.7 **[221.8]**
Power to trustees to enter into transactions in two capacities – B21.8 **[221.9]**
Power to trustees to purchase the trust property—no safeguards – B21.5 **[221.6]**
Power to trustees to purchase with safeguard against improper purchase – B21.6 **[221.7]**

PREMIUM BONDS
Gift of proceeds of premium savings bonds and prizes received or awarded since the testator's death – B4.60 **[204.82]**

PUBLIC TRUSTEE
Application by an intending testator to the Public Trustee to act as executor and trustee under a will – B3.17 **[203.36]**
Clause in will prohibiting appointment of the Public Trustee as a trustee – B3.23 **[203.42]**
Clauses in will appointing executors and trustees, the Public Trustee being only a trustee or custodian trustee – B3.19 **[203.38]**
Clause in will appointing the Public Trustee as sole executor and trustee or jointly with others – B3.18 **[203.37]**
Clauses in will of a person domiciled elsewhere than in England and Wales appointing an individual executor and providing for transfer of the residuary estate or of a legacy to Public Trustee to be held upon English trusts – B3.20 **[203.39]**
Codicil appointing the Public Trustee as executor and trustee jointly with executors and trustees previously appointed or in place of one who has died – B3.22 **[203.41]**
Codicil revoking appointment of executors and trustees and appointing the Public Trustee sole executor and trustee in their place – B3.21 **[203.40]**

RECEIPTS
Receipts by or on behalf of minors – B21.20 **[221.24]**
Receipts on behalf of charities and unincorporated associations – B21.21 **[221.25]**

RENUNCIATION
Renunciation of probate – F1.1 **[239.2]**

RESIDUE
Absolute and simple contingent gifts of,
Absolute residuary gift to three children of the testator: land to be sold – B15.8 **[215.8]**
Clause disposing of residue in percentage shares – B15.6 **[215.6]**
Clause disposing of residue in unequal shares, the interest of one of the beneficiaries being contingent, and with substitutional gifts to spouses and children and accruer provisions – B15.5 **[215.5]**
Gift of residuary estate to three named persons – B15.3 **[215.3]**
Gift of residue to named children making provision for death in testator's lifetime or after his death in the latter case without leaving issue – B15.4 **[215.4]**
Residuary bequest to one person – B15.1 **[215.1]**
Residuary gift without administration trusts – B15.7 **[215.7]**
Trusts of residue, as two persons jointly or the survivor of them shall appoint – B15.2 **[215.2]**
Administration trusts
Administration trust without a trust for sale – B14.1 **[214.10]**
Administration trust without a trust for sale, concise form – B14.2 **[214.11]**
Bequest of residuary personal estate only – B14.15 **[214.24]**
Declaration negativing the exercise of the statutory power to dispose of entailed property or the exercise of a general power of appointment – B14.13 **[214.22]**
Definition of residuary estate – B14.12 **[214.21]**

Devise and bequest of residue charged with payment of debts – B14.14 **[214.23]**
Devise of residuary real estate only – B14.16 **[214.25]**
General residuary gift to trustees—direction to pay inheritance tax on specific gifts, pecuniary legacies, and lifetime gifts – B14.6 **[214.15]**
Gift of residue on trust for sale by incorporation of Statutory Will Forms 1925, Form 8 – B14.11 **[214.20]**
Gift of residue on trust for sale—exclusion of equitable apportionment rules – B14.10 **[214.19]**
Gift of residue to trustees who are different persons from the executors – B14.9 **[214.18]**
Residuary disposition to trustees on trust for sale, with administration trusts, directions as to inheritance tax, and exclusion of equitable and statutory apportionment – B14.3 **[214.12]**
Residuary disposition with power of sale with respect to personalty so as to prevent the rules in *Howe v Dartmouth* and *Re Chesterfield's Trusts* from applying, with administration trusts and exclusion of statutory apportionment and the rule in *Allhusen v Whittell* – B14.4 **[214.13]**
Residuary gift with no trust for sale and a power of sale which is to be used only if appropriation in specie not practicable – B14.5 **[214.14]**
Trust for conversion – B14.7 **[214.16]**
Trusts of proceeds of sale of residue with general direction to pay inheritance tax on free estate out of residue – B14.17 **[214.26]**
Trust to pay debts and invest residue—directions as to inheritance tax – B14.8 **[214.17]**
Discretionary trust of residue – C6.2(7) **[228.28]**

Powers and directions for administration

Direction to determine tenancy of a house – B14.21 **[214.32]**
Direction to foreign trustees to remit proceeds of sale to English trustees – B14.23 **[214.34]**
Direction to trustees to convert foreign property, with powers of management – B14.22 **[214.33]**
Power to trustees to defer the calling in of certain debts – B14.20 **[214.31]**
Power to trustees to postpone conversion except as to certain property – B14.19 **[214.30]**
Power to trustees to sell or mortgage for payment of incumbrances – B14.18 **[214.29]**

RIGHTS OF RESIDENCE

Clause in will giving right to sister to occupy home – C9.6(4) **[231.67]**
Clause in will giving right to wife to occupy matrimonial home – C2.5(5) **[224.92]**
Clause in will of widow or widower providing residence and furniture for children – B8.6 **[208.44]**
Clause where trustees are to have power to purchase property for use of beneficiary – B18.25 **[218.111]**
Gift of interest in dwellinghouse on trusts permitting wife to occupy dwellinghouse for life or during widowhood – C6.3(3) **[228.37]**
Gift of residence for wife for life with the intention that she reside there—fuller form, providing for the possibility of a change of house by the testator before his death or by the trustees after his death – B8.6 **[208.43]**
Gift of the testator's interest as tenant in common in a house, the gift being postponed to allow the other tenants in common to continue to reside in the house – B8.11 **[208.48]**

Gift with the object of ensuring personal residence, giving the right to a series of short leases – B8.8 **[208.45]**
Gift with the object of ensuring personal residence by the devisee—alternative form using a periodic tenancy – B8.10 **[208.47]**
Gift with the object of ensuring personal residence in the form of a lease determinable on death with rentcharge to support residence – B8.9 **[208.46]**
Interest of beneficiary limited to right of residence, with the beneficiary's consent to a sale being required generally, with provision for changing residences – B8.2 **[208.39]**
Interest of beneficiary limited to a right of residence with provision for changing residences – B8.1 **[208.38]**
Powers to permit enjoyment in kind—restricted to prevent prejudice to inheritance tax status of beneficial trusts – B18.24 **[218.110]**
Power where wife is given residence for life or house is bought for beneficiary to invest trust money in purchase of furniture – B18.26 **[218.112]**
Trust for civil partner for life or until marriage or the formation of another civil partnership and then for son, with power to permit residence – B8.5 **[208.42]**
Trust for wife for life or until she remarries and then for son, with power to permit residence – B8.4 **[208.41]**
Trust to permit residence and use of furniture etc by the testator's wife and children – B8.3 **[208.40]**

SECRET TRUST
Declaration of trust of property devised or bequeathed by will on a secret trust – F2.5 **[240.5]**

SETTLED LAND
See also ENTAILS *and* LAND
Appointment of special executors of settled land – B3.27 **[203.46]**
Appointment of three persons, one of whom is abroad, to be executors and trustees, and also trustees for the purposes of the settled Land Act 1925 – B3.7 **[203.13]**
Gift of entailed property generally – B6.10 **[206.19]**
Gift of land of which the testator is tenant in tail – B6.9 **[206.18]**

SETTLED LEGACIES
Settled legacy—concise form – B16.25 **[216.32]**
Settled legacy—full form – B16.26 **[216.33]**

SOLICITORS
Executors and Trustees, appointment of ***see*** EXECUTORS, Appointment of

SPECIFIC GIFTS
See also BUSINESS PROPERTY, CONSUMABLES,DEBTS, FURNITURE, INTELLECTUAL PROPERTY, PERSONAL CHATTELS *and* STOCKS AND SHARES,
Clause exonerating specific gifts from charges – B4.56 **[204.78]**
Gift of a reversionary interest – B4.54 **[204.76]**

STATUTORY FORMS
Clauses incorporating,
Gift of furniture to wife for life and then to son, incorporating of Statutory Will Form as to inventory – B4.32 **[204.50]**
Gift of personal chattels by incorporation of Statutory Will Forms 1925, Form 2 – B4.1 **[204.15]**
Gift of residue on trust for sale by incorporation of Statutory Will Forms 1925, Form 8 – B14.11 **[214.20]**

Gift of residue to children incorporating Statutory Will Forms 1925, Form 7, with modification – B16.21 **[216.28]**
Trust for wife for life and then to children as she shall appoint incorporating Statutory Will Forms 1925, Form 9 – B16.17 **[216.24]**
Trust for wife for life and then to children in equal shares by incorporation of Statutory Will Forms 1925. Form 10 – B16.11 **[216.18]**

Forms,
Statutory Will Forms 1925, Form 1: Confirmation of settlements – E1 **[238.7]**
Statutory Will Forms 1925, Form 2: Meaning of 'personal chattels' – E2 **[238.8]**
Statutory Will Forms 1925, Form 3: Inventories and provisions respecting chattels – E3 **[238.9]**
Statutory Will Forms 1925, Form 4: Legacies to charities – E4 **[238.10]**
Statutory Will Forms 1925, Form 5: Directions respecting annuities – E5 **[238.11]**
Statutory Will Forms 1925, Form 6: Power of appropriation – E6 **[238.12]**
Statutory Will Forms 1925, Form 7: Trusts of a settled legacy – E7 **[238.13]**
Statutory Will Forms 1925, Form 8: Administration trusts – E8 **[238.14]**
Statutory Will Forms 1925, Form 9: Trusts for spouse for life, with power to appoint to issue and gift over to them – E9 **[238.15]**
Statutory Will Forms 1925, Form 10: Trusts for spouse and issue, without a power of appointment – E10 **[238.16]**

STOCKS AND SHARES
Gift of shares held by testator at death and of shares to which he will be entitled at death – B4.35 **[204.57]**
Gift of shares in public company – B4.36 **[204.58]**
Gift of shares in public or private company—provision for only a lesser number of shares being available – B4.36 **[204.59]**
Gift of shares with provision for amalgamation, reconstruction, reorganisation or demerger – B4.38 **[204.60]**
Gift of stock as a general legacy – B4.33 **[204.55]**
Specific gift of stock – B4.34 **[204.56]**
Specific legacy of shares with added words negativing apportionment – B4.39 **[204.61]**

SUBSTANTIAL PROPERTY OWNERS, WILLS FOR
Will of a bachelor landowner settling the principal family estate together with a share of residue on one nephew and his issue, creating a maintenance fund for the upkeep of the mansion house and settled chattels and settling substantial legacies on two nieces and their issue – C13.2 **[235.18]**
Will of owner of substantial property with no immediate family containing specific gift of controlling shareholding in family company on trusts for the employees and leaving residue on charitable trusts – C13.1 **[235.2]**

SUBSTITUTION CLAUSES
Substitution clause limited to children of deceased children – B19.5 **[219.18]**
Trust for testator's children at twenty-five with substitution of issue of a child who predeceases the testator and further substitution of children on death after the testator's death without attaining a vested interest – B19.6 **[219.19]**

TESTIMONIUM AND ATTESTATION
Alternative form of attestation clause – B22.3 **[222.5]**
Attestation clause where the testator has an imperfect knowledge of English – B22.13 **[222.15]**

Form of attestation where the testator acknowledges a signature which he has made previously—short form – B22.11 **[222.13]**
Form of attestation where the testator acknowledges a signature which he or another has made previously – B22.10 **[222.12]**
Form of attestation where the testator is deaf and dumb but is able to read – B22.8 **[222.10]**
Form of attestation where the will has been altered – B22.12 **[222.14]**
Form of testimonium and attestation clause to a codicil – B22.9 **[222.11]**
Form where another signs on behalf of the testator – B22.6 **[222.8]**
Form where testator signs with his mark – B22.5 **[222.7]**
Form where the testator is blind – B22.7 **[222.9]**
Forms of testimonium and attestation clause for will made on behalf of a mentally disordered person pursuant to an order of the Court of Protection – B22.14 **[222.16]**
Further alternative form of attestation clause – B22.4 **[222.6]**
Short form of testimonium and attestation – B22.2 **[222.4]**
Usual form of testimonium and attestation – B22.1 **[222.3]**

TRUSTEES
See also EXECUTORS
Appointment and retirement of,
Appointment of executors and of different persons as trustees – B3.4 **[203.10]**
Appointment of new trustees by disclaiming trustee who has proved testator's will – F1.4 **[239.5]**
Clause excluding beneficiaries' statutory right to direct retirement and appointment of trustees – B21.34 **[221.39]**
Direction as to keeping up the number of trustees – B21.35 **[221.40]**
Deed of disclaimer of the trusteeship of a will by an executor and trustee who has renounced probate – F1.2 **[239.3]**
Deed of disclaimer of the trusteeship of a will—short form – F1.3 **[239.4]**
Renunciation of probate – F1.1 **[239.2]**
Power to appoint new trustees conferred by the Trustee Act 1925 – B21.31 **[221.36]**
Power to appoint separate trustees of parts of trust property – B21.32 **[221.37]**
Power to remove trustees – B21.33 **[221.38]**
Variation of statutory power to facilitate appointment of foreign trustees, and a sole trustee – B21.36 **[221.41]**
Conduct of trusteeship
Clause excluding the statutory duty of care – B21.13 **[221.17]**
Clause excluding trustees' duty to consult with beneficiaries as to land – B21.23 **[221.27]**
Direction as to order of names of trustees in the registers of companies to secure voting rights – B21.24 **[221.28]**
Direction that opinion of majority of trustees is to prevail – B21.25 **[221.29]**
Direction to employ a named solicitor – B21.27 **[221.31]**
No duty to intervene in the affairs of a private company – B21.17 **[221.21]**
Nomination of trust corporation to receive notices – B21.28 **[221.32]**
Power authorising an audit – B21.26 **[221.30]**
Power to distribute on assumption that no further children – B21.30 **[221.34]**
Power to vest assets in nominees – B21.29 **[221.33]**
Indemnities
General indemnity clause—proviso excluding professional and corporate trustees – B21.12 **[221.16]**

Indemnity to trustees acting on counsel's opinion – B21.14 **[221.18]**
Liability for acts of an agent, nominee or custodian appointed under the Trustee Act 2000 – B21.15 **[221.19]**
Liability for attorney's acts – B21.16 **[221.20]**
Missing beneficiaries – B21.22 **[221.26]**

Meaning of 'my trustees'
Definition of 'my trustees' – B21.1 **[221.1]**
Powers conferred on trustees and executors – B21.3 **[221.3]**
Short definition of 'my trustees' – B21.2 **[221.2]**

Powers of *see* POWERS OF TRUSTEES

Releases
Power to life tenants of settled shares to give releases to trustees – B21.18 **[221.22]**

Remuneration
Power to professional trustee to charge—concise form – B21.37 **[221.49]**
Power to professional trustee to charge—full form – B21.38 **[221.50]**
Proviso enabling professional trustee to elect not to charge – B21.39 **[221.51]**
Provision for appointment of trust corporation – B21.40 **[221.52]**

Retention of directors' remuneration etc
Power for trustees to become directors and to retain remuneration—short form – B21.9 **[221.10]**
Power for trustees to become directors, retain remuneration and to hold shares as qualifying shares – B21.10 **[221.11]**
Retention of benefits—fuller form including benefits from subsidiary companies – B21.11 **[21.12]**

Self-dealing
Clause giving named trustee power to purchase part of testator's estate with safeguard against improper purchase – B21.4 **[221.5]**
Clause in will permitting trustee self-dealing – C11.1(8) **[233.23]**
Power to a trustee to enter into any transaction provided there is at least one other trustee – B21.7 **[221.8]**
Power to trustees to enter into transactions in two capacities – B21.8 **[221.9]**
Power to trustees to purchase the trust property—no safeguards – B21.5 **[221.6]**
Power to trustees to purchase with safeguard against improper purchase – B21.6 **[221.7]**

UNDIVIDED SHARES
Gift of undivided share in equity of real property – B4.47 **[204.69]**
Gift of undivided share in personal property – B4.48 **[204.70]**

UNMARRIED COUPLES WITH CHILDREN, COMPLETE WILLS FOR,
Reciprocal wills of couple living together who have children, leaving residue on discretionary trusts – C6.2 **[228.19]**
Reciprocal wills of couple living together who have young children and who are planning to marry – C6.1 **[228.5]**
Will of man separated (but not judicially separated) from wife and living with another woman, where divorce proceedings are contemplated – C6.3 **[228.33]**

VARIATION OF BENEFICIAL INTERESTS
See also DISCLAIMER
Deed of variation conferring a short-term interest in possession on a surviving spouse – F3.7 **[241.28]**
Deed of variation creating a nil-rate band non-exempt legacy where entire estate given to the deceased's widow – F3.6 **[241.27]**
Deed of variation of dispositions effected by a will – F3.4 **[241.25]**

Deed of variation of disposition of property held by deceased and spouse on a joint tenancy – F3.5 **[241.26]**
Deed of variation of trusts of a will settling a life interest on discretionary trusts without disturbing remainders – F3.9 **[241.30]**
Deed of variation of trusts of a will settling a life interest on the same trusts as contingent remainders from time to time – F3.10 **[241.31]**
Deed of variation where spouses have died within two years of each other varying the disposition of the estate of the first to die – F3.8 **[241.29]**

Table of abbreviations

Abbreviation	Full Title
AA 1976	Adoption Act 1976
AA 1984	Anatomy Act 1984
ACA 2002	Adoption and Children Act 2002
AEA 1925	Administration of Estates Act 1925
AJA 1982	Administration of Justice Act 1982
CA 1985	Companies Act 1985
CCA 1984	County Courts Act 1984
CDPA 1988	Copyright, Designs and Patents Act 1988
ChA 1989	Children Act 1989
CLSA 1990	Courts and Legal Services Act 1990
CPA 2004	Civil Partnership Act 2004
FA 1984	Finance Act 1984
FA 2002	Finance Act 2002
FA 2003	Finance Act 2003
FA 2004	Finance Act 2004
FA 2005	Finance Act 2005
FA 2006	Finance Act 2006
FAA 1976	Fatal Accidents Act 1976
FoA 1982	Forfeiture Act 1982
FLRA 1969	Family Law Reform Act 1969
FLRA 1987	Family Law Reform Act 1987
FPA 1966	Family Provision Act 1966
GRA 2004	Gender Recognition Act 2004
HA 1996	Housing Act 1996
HFEA 1990	Human Fertilisation and Embryology Act 1990
HRA 1998	Human Rights Act 1998
HTA 1961	Human Tissue Act 1961
HTA 2004	Human Tissue Act 2004
IA 1978	Interpretation Act 1978
ICTA 1988	Income and Corporation Taxes Act 1988
IEA 1952	Intestates' Estates Act 1952
IHTA 1984	Inheritance Tax Act 1984
I(PFD)A 1975	Inheritance (Provision for Family and Dependants) Act 1975
ITA 2007	Income Tax Act 2007
ITTOIA 2005	Income Tax (Trading and Other Income) Act 2005
LA 1976	Legitimacy Act 1976

LLPA 2000	Limited Liability Partnerships Act 2000.
LP(MP)A 1989	Law of Property (Miscellaneous Provisions) Act 1989
LRA 2002	Land Registration Act 2002
LR(S)A 1995	Law Reform (Succession) Act 1995
MCA 2005	Mental Capacity Act 2005
MeHA 1983	Mental Health Act 1983
MFPA 1984	Matrimonial and Family Proceedings Act 1984
MGACA 1972	Museums and Galleries Admissions Charges Act 1972
MGA 1992	Museum and Galleries Act 1992
MHA 1959	Mental Health Act 1959
PLMA 1964	Public Libraries and Museums Act 1964
RA 1977	Rent Act 1977
SL(R)A 1981	Statute Law (Repeals) Act 1981
TA 1925	Trustee Act 1925
TCGA 1992	Taxation of Chargeable Gains Act 1992
TLATA 1996	Trusts of Land and Appointment of Trustees Act 1996
TrA 2000	Trustee Act 2000
WA 1837	Wills Act 1837
WA 1968	Wills Act 1968

Cumulative Table of Statutes

[Entries up to and including (prefix) 105 are to Volume 1. Entries from (prefix) 200 onward are to Volume 2.]

References printed in **bold** type indicate where an Act is set out in part or in full.

A

Accumulations Act 1800 .... 95.3
Act of Uniformity 1662 .... 35.32
Administration of Estates Act 1925 .... 64.35, 238.12
s 1 .... 7.16, 7.18, 25.18
(1) 1.7
(2) 104.5, 221.1
2(2) 27.15, 203.13
3 .... 7.16, 7.18
(1) 203.13
(2) 39.5
(4) 7.3, 26.2
5 .... 25.11, 25.13
(ii) 239.2
6 .... 25.13
(1) 203.12
7(3)(a) 25.10
9 .... 1.7
15 .... 25.15
22 .... 26.4, 203.4, 203.46
23 .... 26.6
(1) 26.4
(3) 26.7
24 .... 26.9

Administration of Estates Act 1925 – *contd*
s 27 .... 25.16
32 .... 39.1, 214.4
(2) 31.18
33 ...... 27.15, 30.11, 38.22, 38.23, 101.5, 104.11, 200.54, 216.29, 223.7, 233.40, 237.5, 241.29, **244.60**
(1) 38.24, 38.25, 214.2, 214.10, 214.38, 224.34, 225.33, 230.9
(5) 38.25, 104.14, 214.37
(7) 38.25
34 .... **246.61**
(3) 9.11, 27.10, 31.1, 214.4
35 ... 41.8, 200.13, 204.4, 204.58, 204.77, 204.78, 205.58, 206.22, 207.17, 208.29, 209.6, 214.4, 214.26, 232.69, 234.35, **246.62**
36 .... 8.5, 25.9
(4) 25.18, 46.1, 243.3
(7) 25.18, 46.1, 203.16
(10) 31.19
37 .... 25.15, 25.16
39 .... 200.63, 214.2, 214.10, 215.1, 220.23, 220.24, **246.63**
(1)(I), (ii) 27.15
(1A) 27.15

Administration of Estates Act 1925 – *contd*
s 40 .... 214.2, **246.64**
41 .... 29.11, 29.17, 29.19, 104.6, 214.14, 215.7, 220.70, 220.74, 220.77, 220.79, 230.11, 243.1, 243.2, **246.65**
(1)(iii) 29.1
(3) 29.18
(4) 29.1, 29.19
(5) 29.21
(6) 29.22
(7) 29.23
(9) 29.24
42 .... 29.1, 210.34, **246.66**
(1) 9.40
(6)(a) 9.1, 9.40, 29.1
44 .... 30.31
45 .... 79.1
(1)(a) 78.1
46 .... 9.17, 17.5, 77.1, 101.5, 104.1, 104.3, 104.11, 223.7, 235.22, **244.62**
(1)(I) 104.2, 104.5, 104.7, 104.9, 206.34
(ii) 104.7
(vi) 48.4
(2) 104.2, 104.7
(2A) 70.3, 104.2
(3) 70.3, 104.9, 219.2, 224.5
(a) 104.2
(b)(I), (ii) 104.2
47 .... 9.17, 17.5, 77.1, 94.12, 101.5, 104.1, 104.3, 104.11, 216.29, 223.7, 235.22, **244.63**
(1) 216.23, 217.13
(i) 104.8, 206.34, 224.95, 230.9, 234.24, 241.16
(ii) 104.8
(iii) 7.11, 100.1, 104.8, 104.14
(v) 241.16
(vi) 104.10
(2)(c) 104.7
47A 104.1, 104.3, 104.6, **244.64**
(3) 104.14
48 .... 104.1, 235.22, **244.65**
49 .... 61.1, 104.11, 104.12, 235.22, **244.66**
(1)(a) 100.1
(aa) 104.14, 104.16
(b) 104.13
(2), (3) 100.1
50 .... 17.5, 235.22, **244.67**

Administration of Estates Act 1925 – *contd*
s 50(1), (2) 77.2
51 .... 104.1, 104.3, **244.68**
(3) 9.39, 206.5, 231.10
52 .... **244.69**
54 .... **244.70**
55 .... 104.1, 104.3, **246.67**
(1)(vi) 1.10
(ix) 30.2, 55.4, 214.65
(x) 64.8, 64.44, 104.4, 204.3, 204.16, 204.17, 204.25, 214.77, 223.7, 223.9, 224.62, 224.77, 224.90, 225.31, 226.60, 227.12, 227.28, 228.25, 230.6, 230.21, 230.64, 231.20, 231.45, 231.65, 232.5, 232.54, 233.41, 234.20, 234.34, 236.13, 236.29, 238.8
(xvii) 206.22
(2) 73.1, 104.7
Sch 1
Pt I 214.2, 214.4, 214.6, **246.68**
Pt II 214.2, 214.4, 214.6, **246.69**
para 2 .... 30.3
Administration of Justice Act 1969
s 17 .... 4.22
Administration of Justice Act 1970
s 1(4) 49.6
Administration of Justice Act 1982 ...... 11.23, 11.24, 12.2, 12.7, 12.9, 39.4, 66.6, 80.3, 200.47, 223.3
s 2 .... 57.1
3 .... 105.14
17 .... 10.13, 10.18, 11.1, 11.9, 11.21, 11.25, 12.1, 12.3, 12.5, 12.13, 14.6, 15.1, 36.2, 222.1, **244.95**
18 .... 2.9, 16.4, 201.4, 201.6, 224.17, 225.46, 231.44, 233.16, 233.28, 233.39, **244.96**
(1) 17.1, 17.6, 17.8
(2) 17.1, 25.7, 25.11, 47.2, 48.14, 105.13, 200.25, 219.29
(3), (4) 17.6
18A 2.9
19 ...... 38.2, 47.11, 47.15, 47.29, 47.33, 47.38, 47.39, 73.2, 87.1, 206.33, 210.26, 215.7, 219.15, 219.23, 233.43, 234.20, 234.34, **244.97**
20 ..... 1.5, 2.4, 5.1, 5.6, 5.7, 6.1, 6.2, 6.4, 18.15, 28.5, 52.2, 57.3, 57.25, 200.46, **244.98**

Administration of Justice Act 1982 – *contd*
s 20(1) 6.3, 57.29
(2)–(4) 6.5
21 .... 5.8, 6.3, 18.14, 25.1, 44.14, 57.1, 57.2, 57.23, 57.27, 69.1, 204.80, **244.99**
(1) 57.23, 57.24
(a), (b) 57.25
22 .... 51.13, 83.10, **244.100**
23 .... 23.21, **244.101**
(2), (3) 10.20
(4)(a), (b) 10.20
24 .... **244.102**
(1) 10.20
25 .... 10.20, 23.21, **244.103**
26 .... 10.20, **244.104**
27 .... 23.21, **244.105**
(3) 10.3
28 .... 10.3, **244.106**
(3)–(6) 23.21
49 .... 4.24
73 .... 17.8, **244.107**
(6) 11.1, 11.2, 11.9, 12.1, 12.13, 17.1, 47.11, 47.15, 47.16, 51.13, 52.2, 57.1, 57.23, 73.2, 87.1, 215.7
(c) 6.1
(7) 17.2, 17.4, 17.6
75(1) 11.2, 11.9, 17.4, 17.6, 47.16
76 .... **244.108**
(5), (6) 10.3, 10.20, 23.21
(11) 6.1, 11.1, 11.2, 11.9, 12.1, 12.13, 17.1, 17.2, 17.4, 17.6, 17.8, 47.11, 47.15, 51.13, 52.2, 57.1, 57.23, 73.2, 87.1
77 .... **244.109**
(1) 6.1, 12.1
(5) 11.9
78 .... **244.110**
Sch 2 .... 10.3, 23.21, **244.111**
Sch 9
Pt I 11.1, 11.2, 11.9, 17.6
Administration of Justice Act 1985
s 9 .... 203.20
17 .... 10.1
48 .... 221.18
49 .... 10.1
50 .... 25.17, 239.1
Adoption Act 1950
s 1 .... **245.17**
13 .... 75.1, **245.18**
Adoption Act 1950 – *contd*
s 14 .... 75.1, **245.19**
45 .... **245.20**
46 .... **245.21**
47 .... **245.22**
Sch 5 .... **245.23**
para 4 .... 75.1
Adoption Act 1958 .... 75.7
s 1 .... **245.25**
16 .... 75.1, **245.26**
17 .... 75.1, **245.27**
59 .... **245.28**
60 .... **245.29**
Sch 5 .... **245.30**
Adoption Act 1960
s 1 .... **245.36**
Adoption Act 1976 .... 72.10, 72.11, 75.1, 200.28, 235.20
s 12 .... **245.56**
38 .... 75.2, **245.57**
39 .... 206.17, 206.28, 217.8, 217.42, 217.43, **245.58**
(1) 224.14
41 .... **245.59**
42 .... 206.17, 206.28, 217.8, 217.42, 217.43, **245.60**
(4) 75.3
(5) 221.34
43 .... **245.61**
44 .... 75.3, **245.62**
45 .... 75.9, **245.63**
46 .... 75.4, 75.8, **245.64**
(4) 104.7
47(1)(iii) 217.20
72 .... **245.65**
73 .... **245.66**
74 .... **245.67**
Sch 2 .... **245.68**
Adoption and Children Act 2002 .... 200.28, 203.50
Pt 1 Ch 4 (ss 66–76) 237.10
s 66 .... 217.8, **245.93**
(1)(a)–(d) 75.1
(6)(e) 75.2
67 .... 217.8, 224.14, **245.94**
(1) 75.4
(2)(a), (b) 75.3
(3), (4) 75.3
(6)(a) 75.2, 75.6
(6)(b) 75.2

Adoption and Children Act 2002 – *contd*
s 68 .... 217.8, 245.95
69 .... 217.8, 245.96
(1) 75.7
(2) 75.4
(b) 75.5
(3) 75.4
(4) 75.3
(5) 75.9
70 .... 217.8, **245.97**
(2) 75.5
71 .... 217.8, **245.98**
(1), (2) 75.3
72 .... 217.8, **245.99**
(1)–(3) 75.9
73 .... 217.8, **245.100**
(1), (2) 75.6
(4) 75.4, **237.10**
(5) 75.8
111 .... 28.2, 210.33
(7) 28.2
112 .... 28.2, 210.33
139 .... **245.101**
Sch 4 .... **245.102**
para 17 .... 75.4
18
Pt H 237.10
Adoption of Children Act 1926
s 1 .... **245.3**
5 .... **245.4**
(2), (4) 75.1
12 .... **245.5**
13(1) 75.1
Adoption of Children Act 1949
s 9, 10 .... 75.1
Agricultural Holdings Act 1984 .... 7.5
Agricultural Holdings Act 1986 ..... 234.7, 234.15, 234.21, 234.48
s 34 .... 7.5
(1) 234.12, 234.48
35–39 .... 7.5
40 .... 7.5
(1), (2) 234.48
41–48 .... 7.5
Agricultural (Miscellaneous Provisions) Act 1976
s 18–23 .... 7.5
Agricultural Tenancies Act 1995
s 4 .... 7.5, 234.7, 234.15, 234.21
Anatomy Act 1984 .... 202.16
s 4(1)–(3) 7.34
Apportionment Act 1870 ...... 32.2, 38.23, 200.36, 204.61, 214.19, 214.50, 214.52, 214.54, 216.35
s 1 .... 214.48, **246.2**
2 .... 206.14, **246.3**
3 .... **246.4**
4 .... **246.5**
5 .... 214.49, **246.6**
6 .... **246.7**
7 .... 214.51, **246.8**
Apportionment Act 1834 .... 214.52, 214.54
s 3 .... 214.51

B

British Nationality Act 1981 .... 9.37
Building Societies Act 1986 .... 220.40

C

Calvinistic Methodist ir Presbyterian Church of Wales Act 1933
s 7(2) 212.21
Charitable Trusts (Validation) Act 1954
s 2(1)–(3) 102.24
Charities Act 1960
s 5(1) 102.2
13(2)–(5) 103.19
14(1)–(5) 103.20
18 .... 103.18
30 .... 103.4
38 .... 9.32, 36.2, 206.26
Charities Act 1992
s 15 .... 103.20
Charities Act 1993 .... 9.28, 9.32
s 4(1) 102.2
13(1)(e)(iii) 103.19
(1A) 103.19
(5) 103.18
14 .... 103.20
14A(2) 103.21
14B 103.21
16 .... 103.18
35 .... **246.101**
45 .... 103.4

Charities Act 1993 – *contd*
s 63 .... 103.4
74(1), (2) 103.23
74B 103.23
74C 103.23
82 .... 221.29
96 .... 212.6
(1) 102.2, 226.26
97 .... 212.6
Charities Act 2006 .... 102.2, 212.1, 212.4, 212.6, 212.26
s 1(1) 102.3, 226.26, 235.11
(3) 102.3
2(1) 102.3
(b) 102.10, 102.14, 102.15, 102.16
(2) 102.3
(a) 102.7
(b) 102.8
(c) 102.9
(d) 102.6
(g) 102.12
(j) 102.5
(k) 102.13
(3) 102.3
(a) 102.9
(4) 102.3, 102.4
(6), (7) 102.3, 235.11
3 .... 102.10, 235.11
(2), (3) 102.3
4 .... 102.3, 235.11
5 .... 235.11
15 .... 103.19
16 .... 103.20
17 .... 103.21
18 .... 103.22
38 .... 103.23
Children Act 1948
s 15 .... 102.7
Children Act 1975 .... 75.1, 75.8, 235.20
Sch 1 .... 72.11, 72.15
para 3, 5 .... 206.17, 206.28, 217.5
Children Act 1988
s 5(8) 237.29
Children Act 1989 .... 203.58, 224.11
s 2 .... 210.33, **244.113**
(1) 28.2, 203.48, 203.49, 228.1
(2)(a) 28.2
(3) 28.2, 203.48, 203.49, 228.1
(4)–(5) 28.2
3 .... **244.114**

Children Act 1989 – *contd*
s 3(1), (2) 28.2
(3) 9.42, 200.27, 203.46, 210.33, 210.34, 217.7, 217.26, 218.54, 224.36, 224.52, 224.66, 224.80, 224.96, 225.17, 225.52, 225.63, 227.18, 229.7, 229.8, 230.10, 231.25, 232.10, 232.67, 233.20, 235.33, 236.19
4 .... 28.2, 203.50, 210.33, 228.1; **244.115**
(1), (2) 28.2
(3) 28.2, 28.4
4A 28.1, 203.50, 227.6, **244.116**
5 .... 1.11, **244.116A**
(1) 28.2, 28.3
(2) 28.2
(3) 28.2, 28.3, 28.4, 200.45
(4) 28.2, 28.3, 28.4, 28.8, 200.45, 203.66
(5) 10.2, 28.5, 200.44, 200.45
(6) 28.2
(7) 28.7, 28.8, 203.52
(a), (b) 28.4
(8) 28.2, 28.4, 28.7, 28.8, 203.51, 203.52
(9) 28.4, 203.52
(10) 28.4
(13) 28.1, 28.4
6 .... **244.117**
(1) 28.4, 28.6, 28.8, 200.45, 201.3, 203.57, 203.59
(2) 28.6, 28.8, 200.45
(3) 28.6, 28.8
(3A) 28.6, 203.65, 227.6
(3B) 28.6, 227.6
(4) 28.6, 28.8, 203.59
(5), (6) 28.7
8 .... **244.118**
(1) 28.4
12(2) 28.2
(3)(c) 28.2
105 .... **244.119**
(1) 28.1
108 .... **244.120**
Sch 13 .... **244.120**
Sch 14 .... **244.121**, **244.122**
para 4 .... 28.2
6(2), (4) 28.2
8(2) 28.4
12 .... 28.1

Children Act 1989 – *contd*
Sch 14 – *contd*
para 12(1) 28.8
13 .... 28.1, 28.8
Sch 15 .... **244.123**
Civil Evidence Act 1968
s 1 .... 18.12
2 .... 105.25
Civil Evidence Act 1995
s 1 .... 202.39
Civil Partnership Act 2004 .... 7.3, 17.1, 80.2, 80.3, 104.1, 104.3, 105.1, 105.8, 201.5, 201.13, 201.14, 203.60, 203.61, 203.62, 203.65, 208.38, 208.39, 208.40, 208.41, 208.43, 208.45, 208.46, 208.47, 209.09, 210.12, 210.20, 210.36, 210.45, 210.50, 210.57, 210.79, 211.11, 211.22, 213.12, 213.14, 215.3, 215.4, 215.5, 215.6, 215.7, 237.18, 238.6
s 1 .... 80.9, **244.131**
55 .... 9.2
71 .... 1.10, 2.9, 9.3, 9.8, 12.8, 17.3, 25.7, 25.11, 47.3, 51.13, 80.9, 80.9, 83.10, 104.2, 105.10, 105.11, 105.12, 105.15, 105.17, 105.30, 105.35, 105.39, 105.40, 105.50, **244.132**
75(1), (2) 210.33
76 .... 28.6
246 .... 224.35
263(2) 104.2
Sch 4 .... 9.8, 25.7, 25.11, 80.9, 104.3, 105.8, 105.35
Pt I **244.133**
para 2 .... 2.9, 17.3, 47.3
3 .... 9.3, 12.8
5 .... 51.13, 83.10
Pt II **244.134**
para 7 .... 104.2
13 .... 104.6
15 .... 1.10, 105.10, 105.15, 105.17
16 .... 105.10, 105.30
17 .... 105.10
18 .... 105.10, 105.27
19 .... 105.10, 105.39
20 .... 105.10, 105.11
21 .... 105.10, 105.12, 105.50
22–26 .... 105.10
27 .... 105.10, 105.11
Companies Act 1948 .... 221.11
Sch 1 .... 221.28
Companies Act 1985
s 143(3) 9.33
303 .... 205.69
Consular Conventions Act 1949
s 1 .... 30.42
6 .... 30.42
Contingent Remainders Act 1877 .... 93.10
s 1 .... 94.33
Conveyancing Act 1881
s 42 .... 203.10, 203.13
43 .... 218.44
70 .... 25.16
Conveyancing Act 1882
s 10 .... 97.11
Copyright, Designs and Patents Act 1988
s 93 .... 61.1, 203.43, 204.72
County Courts Act 1984
s 25 .... 105.4
32, 33 .... 49.6
40–42 .... 105.4
Courts and Legal Services Act 1990
s 71 .... 221.18
Criminal Justice Act 1948
s 70 .... 4.6, 9.44
Criminal Law Act 1967
s 1 .... 9.44
12 .... 9.44

D

Domestic Violence and Matrimonial Proceedings Act 1976
s 1(2) 105.14
Domicile and Matrimonial Proceedings Act 1973 .... 200.7
s 1 .... 236.4
3–5 .... 23.2

E

Education Act 1944 .... 102.8
Employment Protection (Consolidation) Act 1978
Pt VI 232.67
Employment Rights Act 1996 .... 210.63

Enduring Powers of Attorney Act 1985
s 2(8) 1.11, 27.9
3(3) 1.11, 27.9
4 .... 1.11
6 .... 1.11
Enterprise Act 2002
s 251(1) 221.44
Sch 26 .... 221.44
Evidence Act 1938
s 3, 4 .... 25.15

F

Family Law Act 1996 .... 105.1
Family Law Reform Act 1969 .... 7.12, 9.40, 9.43, 72.10, 72.11, 72.16, 74.6, 74.8, 104.2, 200.28, 218.79, 238.6, 238.15
s 1 .... 27.3, 29.17, 32.18, 56.1, 200.27, 206.4, 210.33, 210.34, 217.40, 218.80, 221.24, 223.6, 238.9, **246.89**
(2) 9.39, 55.5, 95.4
(a) 32.24
(3) ... 32.20, 32.24, 93.25, 97.11, 207.21
(4) 32.24, 95.4, 218.43
(7) 4.7, 22.3
2 .... 35.9
(1) 217.13
3 .... **244.87**
(1) 16.1, 94.44
(2) 104.8
(3) 16.10
9(1) 4.7
14 .... 104.7, **245.38**
15 .... 57.18, 57.20, 57.22, 72.14, 74.1, 200.30, 217.42, 235.20, **245.39**
(1) 206.17, 206.28, 217.8, 217.43, 237.11
(2) 72.10, 72.14, 78.1, 200.32
(5) 72.10
(7) 9.25, 9.26, 72.10
(8) 9.25, 9.26, 72.1, 72.10, 200.29, 237.8
16 .... **245.40**
(1), (2) 47.16
17 .... 72.14, 200.31, **245.41**
28 .... **245.42**

Family Law Reform Act 1969 – *contd*
Sch 1 .... **246.90**
Pt I 25.4, 32.24, 97.11, 207.21
Sch 3
para 1 .... **246.91**
5(1)(a) **246.92**, 2178.43
(2) **246.92**, 32.24
7 .... 95.4, **246.93**
9 .... **246.94**
Family Law Reform Act 1987 .... 7.12, 9.40, 9.43, 22.3, 28.4, 72.1, 72.10, 72.15, 74.8, 200.28, 200.30, 217.42, 235.20, 237.11
s 1 .... 57.18, 57.20, 57.22, 74.6, 77.2, 99.4, 104.7, 200.32, 206.17, 206.28, 210.42, 217.8, 217.43, 219.24, 237.8, **245.70**
(2) 28.2, 203.49, 228.1
(3) 28.2, 72.14, 203.49, 228.1
4 .... 28.9
(1) 28.2
6 .... 28.9
18 .... 72.14, 77.2, 104.7, **245.71**
(2) 104.9
19 ... 57.18, 57.20, 57.22, 200.32, 206.17, 206.28, 217.8, 217.43, 219.24, **245.72**
(1) 72.14, 210.42
(2) 72.14, 78.1
(4) 72.14
(7) 72.14, 200.29, 237.8
20 .... 72.14, 200.31, **245.73**
21 .... 72.14
27 .... 74.6, **245.74**
(1) 74.4
28 .... 72.15, **245.75**
30 .... **245.76**
33 .... **245.77**
34 .... **245.78**
Sch 2 .... **245.79**
Sch 3 .... **245.80**
para 9 .... 237.8
Sch 4 .... **245.81**
Family Provision Act 1966 .... 104.2
s 1 .... 104.5
Fatal Accidents Act 1976
s 1(3)(b) 105.14
Finance Act 1894
s 14(1) 214.62
Finance Act 1965
s 29(9) 200.95

Finance Act 1969 .... 218.6
Finance Act 1975 .... 200.18
s 19(1) 105.51
28 .... 55.7, 214.55
Sch 4
para 20 .... 55.7
Sch 5
para 15(1) 95.14
Sch 6
para 10–15 .... 102.1
Sch 8 .... 234.7
Sch 13 .... 55.7
Finance Act 1976
s 122(7A) 105.51
Finance Act 1980
s 92 .... 105.51
Finance Act 1982 .... 218.6
s 92(2), (3) 102.1
Finance Act 1985
s 82(1) 241.18
84(1) 241.18
(4) 29.16, 220.72, 238.12
95 .... 235.28
Finance Act 1986
s 100(1)(b) 200.37, 238.6, 238.14
102 .... 204.45, 205.60, 208.14, 209.6, 210.67, 210.69, 216.2, 216.8, 216.9, 216.10, 216.11, 216.12, 216.14, 216.15, 224.23, 224.64, 225.35, 225.76, 227.17, 241.9, 242.15, 242.19
(3) 200.82, 210.69, 210.70, 214.60
(4) 210.69, 210.70, 214.60
(5)–(5C) 200.76
102A, 102B 200.76, 210.69, 241.9
102C 200.76, 210.69
102ZA 200.76, 200.131, 204.45, 208.14, 209.6, 210.66, 210.69, 216.2, 216.8, 216.9, 216.10, 216.11, 216.12, 216.14, 216.15, 224.23, 224.64, 224.65, 224.95, 224.111, 225.35, 225.76, 227.17, 230.16, 241.9, 242.15, 242.19
103 .... 218.23
(1) 200.78, 214.60, 214.61, 218.21
(2), (3) 200.78, 214.60, 214.61
(4) 200.78, 218.19, 214.60, 214.61
(5), (6) 200.78, 214.60, 214.61
(7) 200.78
105 .... 214.73, 234.9
106(3), (4) 210.69

Finance Act 1986 – *contd*
s 114(5) 241.9
Sch 19
para 40 .... 210.66
Sch 20 .... 200.76, 241.9
Finance Act 1988 .... 211.6
Finance Act 1989 .... 105.51, 218.27
Finance Act 1995
s 145 .... 234.2
146 .... 234.7
Sch 18 .... 241.19
Finance Act 1996
s 185 .... 234.7
Finance Act 1999 .... 200.76
Finance Act 2003 .... 200.27
s 23–45 .... 224.95
s 123 .... 241.18
Sch 3
para 3A(1) 220.72, 238.12
(2) 220.72
(4) 220.72
4(3) 241.18
Sch 16
para 7 .... 242.6
8 .... 220.72, 238.12
Finance Act 2004 .... 200.27
Sch 15
para 3 .... 241.19
6 .... 241.19
8(2) 241.19
Finance Act 2005
s 23, 24 ..... 200.40, 200.41, 200.99, 217.2, 217.4, 217.9, 217.13, 217.20, 223.7, 223.8, 223.9, 224.26, 224.35, 224.65, 224.95, 226.7, 226.8, 226.9, 226.10, 226.40
25–33 ..... 200.40, 200.41, 200.99, 217.2, 217.4, 217.9, 217.13, 217.20, 218.89, 223.7, 223.8, 223.9, 224.26, 224.35, 224.65, 224.95, 226.7, 226.8, 226.9, 226.10, 226.40
34 .... 200.40, 200.41, 200.99, 217.2, 217.4, 217.9, 217.13, 217.20, 223.7, 223.8, 223.9, 224.26, 224.35, 224.65, 224.95, 226.7, 226.8, 226.9, 226.40
(1)(b) 226.10
(2)(a) 226.11
(3) 226.11
(4) 226.10, 226.12

Finance Act 2005 – *contd*
s 35 .... 200.40, 200.41, 200.99, 217.2, 217.9, 217.13, 223.8, 223.9, 224.26, 224.35, 224.65, 224.95, 226.7, 226.8, 226.9, 226.10, 226.40
(1)(a) 217.4, 217.20, 223.7
(b) 217.20, 223.7
(2)(a) 217.4
(3)(a)–(c) 217.4
(4) 217.4
36, 37 ..... 200.40, 200.41, 200.99, 217.2, 217.4, 217.9, 217.13, 217.20, 223.7, 223.8, 223.9, 224.26, 224.65, 224.95, 226.7, 226.8, 226.9, 226.10, 226.40
38 .... 200.40, 200.41, 200.99, 217.2, 217.4, 217.9, 217.13, 217.20, 223.7, 223.8, 223.9, 224.26, 224.65, 224.95, 226.4, 226.7, 226.8, 226.9, 226.10, 226.40, 226.49
39–43 ..... 200.40, 200.41, 200.99, 217.2, 217.4, 217.9, 217.13, 217.20, 223.7, 223.8, 223.9, 224.26, 224.65, 224.95, 226.7, 226.8, 226.9, 226.10, 226.40
44, 45 .... 200.99, 217.2, 217.4, 217.9, 217.13, 217.20, 223.7, 223.8, 223.9, 224.35, 224.26, 224.65, 224.95, 226.7, 226.8, 226.9, 226.10, 226.40
98 .... 208.34, 210.72, 237.30, 237.31
Finance Act 2006 ... 200.11, 200.18, 200.19, 200.27, 200.68, 200.92, 200.119, 200.134, 200.136, 204.25, 204.49, 208.13, 214.28, 217.2
s 155 ...... 208.34, 210.72, 218.34, 225.13, 226.3, 237.30, 237.31, 242.7
Sch 20 .... 237.2
Finance Act 2007
s 4 .... 208.34, 210.72, 218.34, 225.13
Finance Act (No 2) 1983
s 13 .... 55.7, 214.55
19 .... 102.1
Financial Services Act 1986 .... 220.40
Financial Services and Markets Act 2000 .... 220.40
Forfeiture Act 1870 .... 4.6
s 9, 10 .... 9.44
Forfeiture Act 1982 .... 9.15, 9.18, 9.19
s 1 .... **247.35**
(1) 9.13, 9.20
2 .... 105.8, **247.36**
(1)–(3) 9.20

Forfeiture Act 1982 – *contd*
s 2(5), (7) 9.20
3 .... 9.18, **247.37**
(1) 9.22
(2) 9.22
(a) 105.8
4 .... **247.38**
5 .... 9.20, 9.21, **247.39**
6 .... **247.40**
7 .... **247.41**
(2) 9.20
31(6) 9.22
36(1) 9.22
Friendly Societies Act 1974
s 66 .... 7.9
(4) 7.10
(6), (7) 7.10
68, 69 .... 7.10

G

Gender Recognition Act 2004 .... 74.9, 76.5, 200.28, 202.39, 203.12, 203.62, 204.22, 204.24, 204.27, 204.28, 204.43, 204.44, 204.50, 204.59, 205.60, 205.62, 205.63, 205.65, 205.68, 205.76, 206.16, 206.29, 206.33, 206.35, 206.37, 206.38, 208.41, 208.42, 209.6, 209.7, 209.10, 209.11, 209.12, 210.24, 210.26, 210.32, 210.39, 210.41, 210.45, 210.73, 210.79, 212.4,
s 1 .... **245.104**
9 .... 81.1, **245.105**
12 .... **245.106**
15 .... 81.1, **245.107**
16 .... **245.108**
17 .... **245.109**
(1)–(3) 81.1
18 .... 81.1, **245.110**
Guardianship Act 1973
s 7 .... 9.42
Guardianship of Minors Act 1971
s 3 .... 28.8
(4) 28.9
4 .... 28.8
(1)–(4) 28.9
(7) 28.9
(b) 28.4

Guardianship of Minors Act 1971 – *contd*
s 5 .... 28.8
14(3) 28.9
20(5) 28.9

H

Housing Act 1980 .... 207.9
Housing Act 1985
s 87–90 .... 7.4
113(1) 105.14
Housing Act 1988
s 17(1) 7.4
39 .... 7.4
Housing Act 1996 ..... 207.9, 207.11, 207.13
Human Fertilisation and Embryology Act 1990 ...... 9.27, 74.3, 74.7, 200.28, 200.29, 206.17, 206.28, 217.8, 217.42, 219.24, 227.5, 235.20
s 1 .... **245.83**
2 .... **245.84**
27 ... 72.18, 74.6, 203.48, 221.34, 237.10, **245.85**
(5) 74.5
28 .... 72.18, 74.6, 203.48, 237.10, **245.86**
(2) 224.14
29 .... 72.18, 203.48, 221.34, **245.87**
(1) 74.5, 74.6, 224.14
(3) 74.6, 224.14, 237.10
30 .... 72.18, **245.88**
47 .... **245.89**
48 .... **245.90**
49 .... **245.91**
Human Rights Act 1998 .... 72.1, 75.1
3 .... 7.4, 9.22, 105.8
Human Tissue Act 1961
s 1 .... 7.34
2(1) 7.34
3 .... 7.34
Human Tissue Act 2004 .... 7.34, 202.13, 202.16
s 1(1) 7.34
s 1(3) 7.34
s 1(4)–(6) 7.34
s 2(a) 7.34
s 3(a) 7.34
s 3(2) 7.34
s 3(3) 7.34, 202.10
(5) 7.34, 202.10

Human Tissue Act 2004 – *contd*
s 3(6) 7.34
4 .... 7.34, 202.10
(6) 7.34
12 .... 202.10
54(1) 7.34, 202.9
(2), (3), (9) 7.34

I

Income and Corporation Taxes Act 1988 .... 217.20
s 9(4) 102.1
347A 211.6
347B 211.6
414–417 .... 235.7
505 .... 102.1, 235.11
686 .... 32.24
656 .... 211.6
657(2)(c) 211.6
660A 46.6
660B 46.6
686 ...... 218.27, 218.29, 218.31, 218.67, 226.7
(1) 218.30
(3) 218.32
686D 218.32
687 ...... 218.29, 218.30, 218.31, 218.67, 226.7
695–701 .... 241.19
Income Tax Act 2007
s 9 .... 200.40, 217.2, 226.7, 228.19
(1) 218.27
(2) 218.31
Pt 7 Ch 4(ss 350–353) 211.6
s 453, 454 .... 211.6
472 .... 241.19
479 .... 200.126, 200.131, 218.29, 218.67, 224.36, 226.7, 228.19
(3) 218.31
(4) 218.30
480 .... 200.126, 200.131, 218.29, 224.36, 228.19
(1),(2) 218.30
481–483 ...... 200.126, 200.131, 218.29, 224.36, 228.19
491(3) 218.32
493, 494 .... 218.30, 218.31, 218.67, 228.19

Income Tax Act 2007 – *contd*
s 495–498 .... 228.19
521 .... 102.1
Income Tax (Trading and Other Income) Act 2005
s 624 .... 216.2, 241.19
629 .... 200.42, 216.2, 241.19
Industrial and Provident Societies Act 1965
s 23, 24 .... 7.10
Inheritance Act 1933 .... 78.3
Inheritance (Family Provision) Act 1938 .... 1.11, 105.1, 105.9, 105.10, 105.16, 105.22, 105.23, 105.24, 105.30, 105.31, 105.36, 105.41
s 1(7) 105.25
2(1A) 105.5
3(1), (2) 105.38
Inheritance (Provision for Family and Dependants) Act 1975 .... 1.11, 4.23, 4.24, 9.18, 17.2, 34.25, 35.38, 47.3, 51.7, 78.1, 80.3, 105.1, 105.3, 105.4, 105.6, 105.13, 105.20, 200.34, 201.14, 208.43, 226.1, 227.54, 228.37, 233.9, 241.20
s 1 .... 225.91, **247.2**
(1) 24.3, 79.3, 105.2, 105.6, 105.16, 105.40
(a) 105.9, 200.34
(b) 105.11
(ba) 105.14, 105.18, 105.19, 105.27
(c) 105.16
(d) 105.15
(e) 105.14, 105.18, 105.19
(1A) 105.14, 105.18, 105.19, 105.27
(1B) 105.15
(2) 105.23
(a) 1.1, 105.9
(b) 47.2, 105.14, 105.16
(3) 79.3, 105.18, 105.19
2 .... 105.8, 105.18, 105.21, 105.30, 105.36, 105.40, **247.3**
(1) 9.22
(a) 105.31
(b) 105.32
(c), (d) 105.33
(e) 105.34
(f) 105.35
(g) 105.10
Inheritance (Provision for Family and Dependants) Act 1975 – *contd*
s 2(2) 105.31
(3) 105.31, 105.37
(4) 105.36
3 .... **247.4**
(1) 105.21
(g) 105.9, 105.25
(2) 105.10, 105.26
(2A) 105.10, 105.14, 105.27
(3) 105.28
(4) 105.18, 105.29
(5) 105.23
4 ..... 30.31, 105.5, 105.40, 225.91, **247.5**
5 .... **247.6**
(1) 105.36
6 .... 105.31, 105.37, **247.7**
(1) 105.39
(2) 105.40
(3) 105.39
(6)–(8) 105.39
(9) 105.33, 105.34, 105.35
(10) 105.40
7 .... **247.8**
(1), (2) 105.31
8 .... **247.9**
8(1) 105.40, 105.41, 105.47, 105.51
(2) 1.15, 105.40, 105.41, 105.51
9 .... 105.41, **247.10**
(2) 105.51
10 .... 105.41, 105.42, 105.45, 105.48, 105.49, **247.11**
(1) 105.44
(3), (4) 105.44, 105.51
(5) 105.45
(6) 105.46
(7) 105.47
(8) 105.43
11 .... 105.41, 105.42, 105.48, 105.49, **247.12**
(1) 3.12
(2) 105.49
(a)–(d) 3.12
(4) 105.49
12 .... 105.43, **247.13**
(1) 105.48
(2) 105.48, 105.49
(3) 105.46
(4) 105.45
13 .... 105.43, **247.14**

Inheritance (Provision for Family and Dependants) Act 1975 – *contd*
s 13(3) 105.45, 105.49
14 .... **247.15**
(1) 105.11
14A **247.16**
15 .... 202.39, 227.1, **247.17**
(1) 105.12, 105.50
15ZA 105.12, 105.50, 202.39, 227.1, **247.18**
15A 105.11, 105.50, **247.19**
15B 105.12, 105.50, **247.20**
16 .... 105.50, **247.21**
17 .... 105.50, **247.22**
18 .... 105.50, **247.23**
18A **247.24**
19 .... 105.50, 200.83, **247.25**
(2) 105.31
20 .... 7.18, 210.15, **247.26**
(1) 30.31
(2) 105.36
21 .... 105.25, **247.27**
22 .... **247.28**
23 .... **247.29**
24 .... **247.30**
25 .... **247.31**
(1) 3.12, 105.11, 105.16, 105.41, 105.42, 105.43
(4) 105.9
(4A) 105.11
(5) 105.11
(5A) 105.11
(6A) 105.11
26 .... **247.32**
27 .... **247.33**
Inheritance Tax Act 1984 .... 200.18, 208.12, 208.17
s 2 .... 217.32
(1) 216.8, 216.9
3(4) 200.102
3A 200.70, 208.31, 217.28
(1) 200.102
(1A) 200.102, 210.66
(a), (b) 242.15
(c)(ii) 200.108
(iii) 200.128, 242.15
(3A) 210.66
(3B) 200.102, 200.108, 224.24, 224.65, 242.15
(e)(i) 200.128

Inheritance Tax Act 1984 – *contd*
s 3a(7) 200.102, 242.15
4 .... 214.59
(1) 200.72, 200.81, 200.82, 200.102, 205.37, 208.31, 214.60, 219.9, 224.9
(2) 200.72, 219.5, 219.9, 224.5, 224.9
5(1) 200.72, 200.82, 200.89, 200.102, 204.76, 205.37, 208.31, 214.60, 241.5
(3) 3.7
(5) 3.7, 200.77, 214.61
6 .... 200.72
(1) 200.89, 236.3
(2), (3) 200.90
7(1) 200.74
(2) 200.73, 218.11
(4), (5) 200.73
8A 227.14, 233.17
(2)–(6) 200.75
(5) 200.75, 200.130
(6) 200.75
8B 200.75
8C 200.75
11 .... 218.21
13 .... 235.2
(5) 235.7
16 .... 234.13
17 .... 204.9, 241.9, 241.19
(a) 46.6, 241.1
18 .... 80.8, 208.32, 218.18, 218.19, 219.7, 224.9, 237.24
(2) 200.85, 200.113, 236.4
19–22 .... 200.70
23 .... 102.1, 200.87, 212.2
(1) 206.26
(2)–(5) 200.88
24 .... 102.1, 212.2
(2) 200.87
(3) 200.88
24A 212.2
25 .... 102.1, 204.29, 212.2
(1) 200.87
(2) 200.88
26 .... 102.1
27 .... 102.1, 200.87
(1A) 235.28
28(1) 235.7
(4), (5) 235.2, 235.7
(6), (7) 235.7
29A 105.51, 241.20

Inheritance Tax Act 1984 – *contd*
s 30 .... 200.72, 200.91, 206.39, 214.76, 214.77, 234.14, 235.28
(1)(b) 214.67
31 .... 200.72, 234.14, 235.28
(2)–(4) 214.67
32–34 .... 200.72, 234.14
Pt II Ch III (ss 36–42) 200.112, 200.113, 200.114, 214.81, 242.4
s 36 .... 213.9
37 .... 213.9
(2) 233.9
38 .... 213.9
(2) 200.113
(3) 214.74
(6) 200.116
39 .... 200.116, 213.9
39A 200.117, 205.7, 205.23, 209.5, 214.73, 214.78, 214.79, 214.80, 214.81, 233.2, 233.5, 233.42, 234.9
(2) 233.3, 233.6
(3)–(4) 233.3
(6) 233.4
40 .... 213.9
41 .... 200.112, 213.9, 214.62, 214.72
42 .... 213.9
(1) 233.6
Pt III (ss 43–93) 200.92, 218.40, 224.51, 230.38, 242.12, 242.16
s 43 .... 213.9, 230.68
(2) 206.3, 209.13, 210.46
(a) 208.48
(c) 33.32, 234.36
(3) 208.4, 208.46
44 .... 213.9, 218.15
45–46 .... 213.9
48(1) 200.72, 204.76
(c) 208.4
(3) 200.89, 236.3
(a) 213.10
(4)–(7) 200.90
49 .... 200.72, 208.13
(1) ... 200.82, 200.92, 200.102, 205.37, 208.14, 208.31, 210.66, 210.69, 210.70, 211.6, 211.18, 214.60, 216.2, 216.3, 216.10, 216.11, 216.12, 216.14, 216.15, 216.17, 218.34, 218.40, 224.24, 225.32, 225.88, 231.49, 241.31, 242.2, 242.3

Inheritance Tax Act 1984 – *contd*
s 49(1A) ... 200.92, 200.99, 220.81, 224.37, 225.18, 226.31, 227.19, 228.15, 229.9, 230.26, 232.48, 233.21, 235.12, 236.20
(a) 224.24, 242.15
(b) 218.40, 225.32, 226.3
49A 204.45, 208.14, 208.29, 208.30, 210.69, 210.70, 211.18, 214.28, 216.18, 216.30, 218.83, 223.7, 223.8, 223.9, 224.111, 224.1, 224.24, 224.42, 224.51, 224.58, 224.64, 224.95, 225.24, 225.32, 225.35, 227.17, 227.46, 230.38, 231.47, 231.67, 232.1, 232.46, 232.58, 232.73, 237.2, 237.26, 238.13, 238.15, 238.16, 241.8, 241.28, 241.31, 242.12, 242.15
(3) 200.98
(4) 224.26
(A) 200.108
49B 208.14, 210.69, 210.70, 211.18, 241.9
49C, 49D 200.100, 200.134
49E 200.100
50(2) 33.32, 211.3
(3) 211.3
(5) 200.95, 208.14
51 .... 200.102
(1) 200.98
52 .... 242.15
(1) 200.96, 200.98, 200.102, 200.104, 210.69, 211.18, 211.19, 211.22, 211.24, 216.8, 216.9, 216.10, 216.11, 216.12, 216.13, 216.14, 216.15, 216.22, 217.28, 217.32, 231.67
(2) 211.6
(2A) 211.18
(3) 208.38, 218.109
(4)(b) 211.6
53 .... 200.102, 210.69
(1) 200.98
(2) 200.96, 200.98, 217.10, 217.11, 217.14, 217.17, 217.19, 217.27, 217.29, 217.31, 217.33, 217.42, 218.39, 218.74, 224.24, 226.5, 242.17
(2A) 200.98, 218.39
54 .... 200.72
(4) 219.5

Inheritance Tax Act 1984 – *contd*
s 58 .... 200.92
(1)(b) 235.2
(1B), (1C) 235.2
60 .... 218.9, 218.14
61(2) 213.10
62 .... 218.9, 218.14
64 .... 218.9, 225.84, 242.4
65 .... 200.39, 218.27, 242.7, 242.10, 242.13
(1)(b) 218.109
(4) 225.85, 242.4
(8) 213.10
66(1), (2) 218.11
(3)(b) 218.15
(4)–(6) 218.12
67 .... 218.12
68(1)–(3) 218.11
(4)(b) 218.13, 218.15
(5) 218.13
(b) 218.18
69 .... 218.13
(1), (4) 218.11
71 .... 32.24, 95.14, 200.19, 200.39, 200.107, 200.108, 200.136, 204.44, 206.17, 207.21, 208.15, 208.18, 210.38, 210.39, 210.46, 214.28, 217.1, 217.2, 217.16, 217.25, 218.40, 218.79, 220.4, 220.53, 224.3, 224.25, 224.95, 229.36, 230.1, 237.2, 237.26, 241.9, 241.31, 242.3, 242.4
(1) 204.44
(a) 217.1, 218.68
(b) 220.8
71A 200.19, 200.68, 200.69, 200.71, 200.98, 200.101, 200.107, 200.110, 200.126, 200.128, 200.132, 200.133, 200.136, 208.14, 208.15, 208.18, 208.31, 210.38, 210.66, 210.70, 214.28, 216.2, 216.29, 217.1, 217.2, 217.5, 217.9, 217.11, 217.13, 217.20, 217.22, 217.23, 217.32, 218.38, 218.79, 218.83, 218.84, 218.85, 218.86, 218.89, 218.109, 218.116, 218.117, 220.4, 220.10, 220.61, 220.81, 223.7, 223.8, 223.9, 224.3,

Inheritance Tax Act 1984 – *contd*
s 71A 224.23, 224.27, 224.35, 224.36, 224.37, 224.65, 224.66, 224.79, 224.95, 224.96, 225.18, 225.87, 226.31, 227.5, 227.17, 227.18, 227.19, 227.54, 228.2, 228.4, 228.13, 228.15, 229.7, 229.8, 229.9, 229.36, 230.1, 233.21, 235.12, 236.20, 237.2, 237.26, 238.13, 238.15, 238.16, 241.9, 242.3, 242.15
(1) 200.108
(c)(i) 224.26
(2) 200.109
(3) 220.9
(a) 217.4, 220.8
(c) 218.69, 218.70, 220.8
(4) 200.109, 217.4, 224.24
(b) 242.14, 242.16
(5) 200.109, 218.101, 218.104, 218.106
(7) 200.108, 200.109
71B(1)(b) 218.109
(2)(b) 217.5
(c) 200.108, 218.101, 224.24
71D ... 200.68, 200.69, 200.107, 200.126, 200.128, 200.132, 200.133, 200.136, 208.15, 208.18, 214.28, 216.2, 216.18, 217.1, 217.2, 217.5, 217.22, 217.23, 217.32, 218.38, 218.79, 218.80, 218.81, 218.84, 218.85, 218.86, 218.89, 218.116, 218.117, 220.4, 220.10, 220.61, 220.81, 223.9, 224.3, 224.23, 224.24, 224.25, 224.27, 224.35, 224.36, 224.37, 224.65, 224.66, 224.79, 224.80, 224.96, 225.18, 225.84, 225.87, 226.31, 227.5, 227.17, 227.18, 227.19, 227.54, 228.2, 228.4, 228.13, 228.15, 229.7, 229.8, 229.9, 230.1, 233.21, 235.12, 236.20, 237.2, 237.26, 238.13, 238.15, 238.16, 241.9, 242.3
(1)(b) 218.109
(5)(c) 200.109, 217.10, 217.11, 217.14, 217.17, 217.19, 217.27, 217.29, 217.31, 217.33, 217.42
(ii) 218.74, 218.83
(6) 220.9
(a) 220.8

Inheritance Tax Act 1984 – *contd*
s 71d(6)(c) 218.69, 218.70, 218.74, 220.8
(7) 200.109, 218.101, 218.104, 218.106
(b) 242.14
71E(1) ... 217.10, 217.11, 217.14, 217.17, 217.19, 217.27, 217.29, 217.31, 217.33, 217.42, 224.24, 242.17
(a) 218.74, 218.101, 242.4
(2) 224.24
(a) 242.4
(b) 217.5, 217.10
(d) 218.101, 242.17
71F 200.109
(5) 242.4
71H 200.107, 217.1, 227.5
75 .... 225.85, 242.4
76 .... 218.9, 225.85, 242.4
80 .... 213.10, 218.14, 218.15, 218.18, 224.102, 225.75, 236.3
82 .... 213.10, 236.3
83 .... 218.15, 242.4
84(4) 218.36
86(1) 235.2
(b) 235.7
(2) 235.2
(3)(a) 235.2, 235.7
88 .... 200.102, 211.19, 211.24, 216.7, 225.32, 225.75, 230.16, 230.24
(4)(b)(i) 216.8, 216.9, 216.33, 218.39, 237.22
89 ... 211.23, 226.1, 226.5, 226.8, 226.11, 226.14, 226.16, 226.17, 226.19, 226.21, 226.26, 226.29, 226.30, 226.31, 226.32, 226.40, 226.57
(1) 226.4, 226.64
(a) 226.3, 226.6
(b) 218.36, 226.3, 226.6, 226.15, 226.33, 226.67
(2) 226.3, 226.5, 226.64
(3) 217.4, 226.4, 226.65
(4) ... 200.84, 200.95, 200.99, 200.105, 200.126, 208.30, 218.21, 218.36, 225.60, 226.4, 226.64, 227.14

Inheritance Tax Act 1984 – *contd*
s 89(5), (6) 200.84, 200.95, 200.99, 200.105, 200.126, 208.30, 218.36, 226.4, 226.64
89B 200.99, 200.119, 200.126, 208.14, 208.29, 210.69, 210.70, 211.18, 216.30, 216.33, 218.34, 225.60, 226.3, 227.14, 237.2, 242.2
(1)(c) 226.40
90 .... 210.53
91 .... 200.97, 200.98, 205.12, 208.13, 225.87, 234.5, 241.8
92 .... 200.97, 200.98, 204.24, 205.60, 216.8, 216.9, 216.10, 216.11, 216.12, 216.14, 216.15, 216.16, 216.17, 216.19, 216.20, 216.21, 216.22, 216.23, 216.30, 216.32, 216.33, 218.34, 218.40, 219.6, 219.8, 219.11, 224.6, 224.10, 224.24, 224.32, 225.104, 225.115, 228.9, 228.39, 238.13, 238.15, 238.16
93 .... 241.5
102 .... 235.7
103 .... 200.91
104(1) 205.1, 205.7
(a) 235.2
(b), (bb) 205.30
105(1) 205.7
(b) 235.2
(1A) 233.29
(1ZA) 205.29
(3) 205.8, 235.2
(4) 205.8
(5) 205.14
(6) 205.6, 205.41
(7) 205.8
106 .... 205.11
107 .... 233.26
108 .... 205.11, 205.50, 233.7, 233.26, 233.29
109 .... 205.11, 233.7, 233.26
109A 233.29
110 .... 205.24
112 .... 205.51, 235.2
(3) 205.9, 205.41
113 .... 205.14, 205.28, 233.40
113A 200.73
113B 200.73
114 .... 205.15
(1) 234.1, 234.8

Inheritance Tax Act 1984 – *contd*
s 115 .... 200.91
(2) 233.5, 234.2, 234.3
(4), (5) 234.2
116(1)(c) 234.7
(2)(a), (b) 234.7
(3) 234.7
(5A)–(5E) 234.7
117 .... 234.4, 234.5, 234.9
118 .... 234.4
120(1)(b) 234.5
120, 121 .... 234.5
122, 123 .... 234.6
124A 200.73
124B 200.73
125 .... 200.72, 200.91
(1) 234.14
(2) 214.67
126 .... 200.72
(1)(a) 234.14
127–129 .... 200.72
130 .... 200.72
(1)(a) 234.14
141 .... 200.72, 218.24, 219.5, 224.10
142 .... 105.51, 200.42, 200.83, 200.97, 205.67, 225.52, 225.90, 225.91, 241.2, 241.6, 241.15, 241.16, 241.18, 241.19, 241.20, 242.4
(1) 46.6, 241.1, 241.3, 241.4, 241.6, 241.7, 241.8, 241.9, 241.11, 241.13, 241.14, 241.16, 241.17, 241.19, 241.24, 241.25, 241.26, 241.27, 241.29, 241.30, 241.31
(2) 241.3, 241.13, 241.16
(b) 241.26
(2A) 241.3
(3) 241.7, 241.14, 241.20
(4) 241.4, 241.8
(5) 225.88, 241.5
143 .... 36.1, 82.6, 200.83, 204.8, 204.9, 204.10, 204.23, 224.62, 225.85, 226.60, 227.12, 230.6, 231.20, 232.5, 234.20, 234.34, 241.20

Inheritance Tax Act 1984 – *contd*
s 144 .... 36.1, 200.83, 200.98, 200.126, 200.130, 200.131, 200.133, 200.135, 200.136, 203.19, 204.10, 204.20, 208.15, 208.30, 208.33, 209.7, 217.2, 217.10, 217.11, 217.14, 217.17, 217.19, 217.27, 217.29, 217.31, 217.33, 217.42, 218.7, 218.18, 218.19, 218.21, 218.26, 218.34, 219.6, 221.3, 223.10, 225.3, 225.52, 225.57, 225.60, **225.83**, 225.87, 225.88, 225.90, 225.91, 225.93, 225.94, 225.100, 225.101, 225.103, 225.104, 226.5, 226.15, 226.18, 226.33, 226.57, 226.67, 227.14, 228.20, 228.28, 230.45, 231.20, 232.15, 233.10, 233.14, 237.3, 242.5, 242.10
(1) 200.133, 225.89, 242.4, 242.7, 242.8
(a) 217.5, 225.84, 242.4
(b) 225.85
(1A) 242.4, 242.7, 242.8
(2) 200.133, 225.89, 242.4, 242.7, 242.8
(3) 217.28, 225.87, 242.13
(c) 200.133, 225.89, 242.4
(4) 200.133, 217.28, 225.87, 242.12, 242.13, 242.14
(a) 242.4
(5) 217.28, 225.87, 242.4, 242.12, 242.13
(d), (e) 225.89
(6) 217.28, 225.87, 242.4, 242.12, 242.13
146 .... 200.83, 241.20
(1), (2) 105.51
(4), (5), (8) 105.51
151BA 200.75
154 .... 200.72
157–159 .... 200.72
160 .... 200.81
161 .... 234.7
(2) 200.82
(a) 234.13
162(1) 200.77
(4) 200.77, 205.10, 205.24, 234.10
(5) 200.77, 236.7
163(1)(a) 3.7
171 .... 200.81

Inheritance Tax Act 1984 – *contd*
s 172 .... 200.77, 202.3
173 .... 200.77, 236.7
178–198 .... 200.72, 200.82
199(1), (2) 200.79
200(1) 241.26
(a) 200.79, 200.80, 203.5
(b)–(d) 200.80
204(1) 200.80
(8) 200.79, 200.124
(9) 200.79, 200.124, 214.60
207, 208 .... 214.60
211 .... 55.7, 200.111, 204.54, 205.39, 205.52, 206.3, 206.20, 206.39, 208.29, 209.3, 209.6, 210.3, 211.13, 214.9, 214.17, 214.55, 214.56, 214.57, 214.58, 214.60, 214.64, 231.35, 232.69, 235.5, **246.100**
(1) ... 214.59, 214.62, 214.63, 214.70, 214.76, 224.34, 225.33, 230.7, 231.65, 236.17
(b) 210.4
(3) 200.80
213 .... 205.62
218A 241.3
226(2) 200.123
(3A) 200.74
227 .... 205.62, 214.68
(1) 205.38
(2)(a) 205.17, 205.19
(b), (c) 205.17
(4), (6) 205.20
228 .... 214.68
(1)(a) 205.17, 205.35
(b) 205.17, 205.39
(c) 205.17, 205.36
(d) 205.17, 205.37
(2) 205.17, 205.39
(3) 205.17, 205.37
(4) 205.37
229 .... 214.68
230 .... 204.14, 204.29
231 .... 204.14
234 .... 205.34
(1)(a) 205.17
(3) 205.17
237 .... 214.62
239(2), (2A) 227.5
267 .... 200.89, 236.2, 236.3
(2) 200.90

Inheritance Tax Act 1984 – *contd*
s 269 .... 205.41
(2), (3) 205.17
272 .... 224.35, 227.5
Sch 2
para 1A 200.74
3 .... 218.15
Sch 3 .... 200.87, 204.14, 204.29, 212.2, 218.9
Sch 4
para 1 .... 235.28
2(1)(b) 235.28
3(1)(a), (c) 35.28
(3) 235.28
16(1) 225.85, 242.4
Sch 6
para 1 .... 200.37, 238.6
2 .... 200.72
Insolvency Act 1986
s 421 .... 202.5, 240.4
Sch 6 .... 221.44
Interpretation Act 1978 .... 234.3
s 5 .... **246.95**
6(c) 28.4
17 .... **246.96**
(2)(a) 200.38
23 .... **246.97**
(3) 200.38
Sch 1 .... 7.10, 10.14, 205.19, 220.16, 220.17, 220.24, 220.52, 246.98
Intestates' Estates Act 1952 ... 104.2, 104.5, 104.16
s 1 .... **244.72**
2(b) 104.6
3 .... 104.1, 104.14
5 .... 104.6, **244.73**
6 .... **244.74**
9 .... **244.75**
Sch 2 .... 29.20, 104.6, **244.76**
Irish Church Act 1869 .... 41.2, 41.13

J

Judicial Trustees Act 1896
s 1 .... 25.17

L

Landlord and Tenant Act 1954 .... 205.58

Land Charges Act 1972 .... 209.8
Land Registration Act 1925 .... 209.8
s 123 .... 243.3
Land Registration Act 1997
s 1 .... 243.3
Land Transfer Act 1897 .... 1.7, 94.33
s 1 .... 25.18
Law of Property Act 1925 ...... 27.1, 41.13, 238.4
s 1 .... 93.10, 94.33
(1) 26.2
3(1)(b) 37.8, 86.1
16(6) 55.7
20 .... 9.43, 27.3
21 .... 9.40, 210.36, 218.54, **246.42**
23 .... 37.8, 246.43
24 .... **246.44**
25 .... 27.3, 200.58, 246.45
(1) 200.54, 214.3
(2) 214.3
(3) 214.2
(4) 200.60
26 .... 27.3, 27.16, 27.17, 246.45
(3) 220.58
27 .... 200.61, **246.46**
(2) 27.16, 203.38
28(1) 200.60;208.38, 208.43, 220.19, 220.49, 220.50, 224.92, 231.67, 237.5, 246.47
(2) 38.22, 38.25, 200.60, 200.67, 214.35, 220.61, 220.62
(3) 220.71, 220.80
29 .... 38.22, 220.54, 246.47
30 .... 38.22, 200.59, 200.62, 246.47
31 .... **246.48**
32 .... 200.60, 246.49
(1) 220.19
33 .... **246.50**
34 .... 7.3, 41.18, 86.1, 200.54, 200.67, 206.29, 237.5, **246.51**
(2), (3) 206.16
35 .... 86.1, **246.52**
36 .... 7.16, 41.18, 86.1, 200.54, 237.5, **246.53**
(1) 206.16
(2) 7.3, 204.71
37 .... 86.2
40 .... 3.4
(1) 3.1
52(2) 46.1

Law of Property Act 1925 – *contd*
s 52(2)(b) 239.3
55(1) 7.4
60 .... 83.1
61 .... 200.38, 203.10, 210.9, 210.55, 216.9, 221.1, **246.54**
(c) 67.2
72(1)–(4) 218.23
82 .... 218.23
90 .... 8.2
121 .... 8.2, 94.39
122 .... 94.39
130 .... 7.2, 33.12, 76.5, 78.1, 101.12
(1) 73.2, 76.1, 84.2, 89.2
(2) 76.1, 84.2, 101.11
(3) 84.2
(6), (7) 84.2
131 .... 84.4
132 .... 78.1, 78.4, 84.3
134 .... 97.11, 98.1
138 .... 221.32
155 .... 40.10
156(2) 40.12
157(1), (3) 40.19
158 .... 39.2, 40.1
159(2) 40.6
160 .... 40.10
163 .... 55.5, 94.19, 94.45, **246.55**
164 .... 32.16, 32.28, 95.3, 95.4, 95.7, 205.73, 207.21, 207.25, 213.8, 216.34, 218.57, 218.71, 218.75, **246.56**
(1)(b) 33.30, 216.8, 218.33, 218.34, 218.73, 218.80, 218.81, 226.6, 227.54, 228.28, 229.7, 235.7, 241.30
(d) 218.72, 218.85
(2) 95.9
(iii) 220.61
165 .... 95.6, 213.8, 218.57, 218.71, **246.57**
(1)(b) 218.73
166 .... 207.21, 218.57, **246.58**
(1), (2) 95.5
172 .... 105.48
175 ...... 32.3, 32.16, 32.28, 33.25, 93.16, 207.21, 208.44, 210.46, 217.29, 218.44, 218.57, 235.29, **244.54**

Law of Property Act 1925 – *contd*
s 176 .... 84.1, 204.75, 206.3, 206.10, 206.19, 210.33, 210.70, 214.12, 214.15, 214.60, 214.76, **244.55**
(1) 7.2, 206.18, 210.4, 214.10, 215.8, 224.32, 224.34, 225.33, 225.115, 228.9, 230.7, 231.12
(3) 7.2
177 .... 16.4, 17.1, 17.4, 17.6, 201.7, **244.56**
179 ..... 238.1, **244.57**
184 .... 70.2, 75.5, 104.2, 219.2, 19.4, 219.9, 224.5, 224.9, **244.58**
188 ..... 204.21, 204.42
196 ..... 234.21
204 ..... 25.16, 26.2
205 ..... **246.59**
(1)(ix) 38.25, 200.51, 218.23, 220.24, 220.52, 228.37
(xxvii) 27.4
(xxviii) 203.28
Law of Property (Amendment) Act 1924
Sch 9 ..... 1.7, 7.18
para 3 ..... 9.39
Law of Property (Amendment) Act 1926 ..... 203.38, 221.47
s 3 ..... **246.71**
Schedule 26.2
Law of Property (Miscellaneous Provisions) Act 1989
s 1 ...... 239.3, 239.4, 239.5, 240.5, 241.22, 241.24, 242.7, 242.8, 243.4, 243.5
2 ..... 209.2
Law of Property (Miscellaneous Provisions) Act 1994
s 14 ..... 7.4
16(1) 27.15
Law Reform (Married Women and Tortfeasors) Act 1935 ..... 46.3
s 1 ..... 4.8
2(1) 4.8
Law Reform (Miscellaneous Provisions) Act 1989 ..... 3.1
s 2 ..... 2.6, 3.4
Law Reform (Succession) Act 1995
s 1 ..... 77.1, 104.1, **244.124**
(1) 70.3, 104.2
(2) 100.1
(a) 104.8
Law Reform (Succession) Act 1995 – *contd*
s 1(2)(b) 104.15
(4) 77.2
2 ..... 1.10, 105.1, 105.14, 105.17, 105.27
3 ...... 25.11, 48.14, 80.3, 105.13, 200.25, **244.125**
(1), (2) 47.2
4 ..... 28.6, 203.65, **244.126**
5 ..... **244.127**
6 ..... **244.128**
46, 47 ..... 104.1
49 ..... 104.1
Schedule 47.3, 48.14, 104.15, **244.129**
Leasehold Reform Act 1967 .... 207.1, 207.5
s 1(1ZB)(a), (b) 207.9
(2) 207.9
3(4) 208.45
7(2)(b) 207.10
(7) 207.10
Leasehold Reform, Housing and Urban Development Act 1993 ..... 207.5, 207.9
s 7(4) 208.45
14(2) 207.12
(5), (6) 207.12
Pt I Ch II (ss 39–62) 208.45
s 39(2), (2A) 207.13
(3A) 207.13
43 ..... 207.13
93A 207.11
Legitimacy Act 1926 ..... 72.11, 72.15
s 1 ..... **245.7**
3 ..... **245.8**
4 ..... **245.9**
5 ..... **245.10**
8 ..... **245.11**
9 ..... **245.12**
10 ..... **245.13**
11 ..... **245.14**
12 ..... **245.15**
Legitimacy Act 1959
s 1 ..... **245.32**
2 ..... **245.33**
6 ..... **245.34**
Legitimacy Act 1976 ..... 200.28, 235.20
s 1 ..... 72.9, **245.44**
(1), (2) 72.15
2 ..... 47.16, **245.45**
3 ..... **245.46**

Legitimacy Act 1976 – *contd*
s 4 .... **245.47**
5 .... **245.48**
(1) 72.16
(2) 72.16, 104.7
(3) 72.16, 224.14
(4) 72.11
(a), (b) 72.16
(5) 72.16
6 .... **245.49**
(1) 72.11, 72.16
(2)–(3) 72.11
7 .... **245.50**
(1), (2) 72.17
10 .... 228.1, **245.51**
(1) 72.16
(3) 72.16, 237.10
11 .... 47.16, **245.52**
12 .... **245.53**
76(4) 72.15
Sch 1 .... **245.54**
Sch 2 .... 47.16
Limitation Act 1939
s 19 .... 30.38
20 .... 30.3, 30.38
Limitation Act 1980
s 15(1) 30.39
20 .... 32.30
21(1)(b) 30.37
22 .... 30.3, 30.37, 30.38, 32.30
23 .... 30.37
38(1) 30.39
Limted Liability Partnerships Act 2000
s 1 .... 203.22
Local Government Act 1972
s 214(3) 202.26
Local Government Finance Act 1988
s 47 .... 102.1
51 .... 102.1

M

Marriage Act 1949
s 2 .... 35.9
3 .... 35.9, 217.13
78(1) 217.13
Married Women (Restraint Upon Anticipation) Act 1949 ...... 46.3, 99.3
Married Women's Property Act 1882
s 11 .... 7.12
Married Women's Property Act 1893
s 2 .... 4.8
Matrimonial and Family Proceedings Act 1984 .... 105.50
s 8 .... 105.12
17 .... 105.12
25(2)(a), (b) 105.11
(3) 105.12
Matrimonial Causes Act 1965
s 26–28A 105.1
Matrimonial Causes Act 1973 .... 9.22, 105.10
s 11 .... 17.2
12 .... 17.2
16 .... 17.2, 35.8, 72.9, 80.4, 80.6, 224.86
17 .... 105.50
18 .... **244.89**
23 .... 105.9, 105.17
24 .... 105.9, 105.33
25 .... 105.9, 105.20
31 .... 105.50
36 .... 105.50
37 .... 105.48
s 52(1) 105.17
Mental Capacity Act 2005 ...... 17.2, 226.1
s 1 .... **244.136**
(2) 4.9
2 .... 4.9, **244.137**
3 .... **244.138**
(1) 4.9
4 .... **244.139**
16 .... 4.12, 201.15, 208.23, 221.39, **244.140**
(2)(a) 4.22
17 .... 4.12
18 .... 208.23, **244.141**
(1) 4.12
(i) 4.22, 201.15, 221.39
(ii) 4.22
(2) 201.15
42 .... **244.142**
64 .... **244.143**
69 .... **244.144**

Mental Capacity Act 2005 – *contd*
Sch 2 .... **244.145**
para 1 .... 4.12, 4.22
2 .... 4.12, 4.22
3 .... 4.12, 4.22, 201.15, 222.2, 222.16
4 .... 4.12
(1) 4.22
(3)–(5) 4.22
Sch 6
para 20 .... 244.146
Mental Health Act 1959 .... 4.23, 17.2
s 102 .... 4.22
103(1) 4.22
(1)(dd) 4.24
107 .... 41.12
Mental Health Act 1983 ... 4.23, 17.2, 226.1
s 1(2) 4.12, 226.4
(3) 4.12
94(2) 201.15
95 .... 4.24
96 .... 4.12
(1)(k) 221.39
97 .... 4.12 222.2, 222.16
99 .... 9.45, 34.24, 42.13
100 .... 9.45, 34.24
101 .... 9.45, 34.24, 41.12
102 .... 34.24
103 .... 4.24
112 .... 201.12
Mental Health Act 2007
s 1(4) 4.12
Mental Health (Amendment) Act 1982
s 1, 2 .... 4.12
Methodist Church Act 1976
s 15(2) 212.6
Sch 2 .... 212.6
Mortmain and Charitable Uses Act 1891 .... 1.10
s 5 .... 206.26
Museums and Galleries Act 1992 .... 35.53
Museums and Galleries Admissions Charges Act 1972 .... 35.53

N

National Health Service Act 1946 ... 103.4, 103.10
National Health Service Act 1977
s 91(3) 212.25
National Savings Bank Act 1971
s 8 .... 7.11
Naturalization Act 1870 .... 9.37
s 2(3) 4.5
Navy and Marines (Wills) Act 1953 .... 16.11
Nullity Act 1971 .... 17.2

P

Parish Councils and Burial Authorities (Miscellaneous Provisions) Act 1970 ... 202.22, 202.34
s 1 .... 9.30
Partnership Act 1890
s 2(3)(c) 205.64
Perpetuities and Accumulations Act 1964 ...... 35.52, 75.9, 94.16, 94.49
s 1 ..... 94.17, 94.41, 216.4, 218.33, 223.10, 228.28, 235.7, **246.74**
(1) 94.6, 202.31, 213.7
(2) 94.6, 94.51
2 .... 66.3, 95.12, **246.75**
(1)(a) 216.31
(4) 94.18
3 ... 213.7, 216.16, 216.23, 218.33, **246.76**
(1) 94.17, 94.53
(2) 94.53
(3) 92.6, 94.53
(4) 94.17, 94.53
(a) 75.4
(5) 94.17, 94.53, 216.5
4 .... 94.45, **246.77**
(1)–(3) 94.19
(4) 94.19, 94.22
(5) 94.19
(6) 55.5
5 .... 80.5, 94.17, **246.78**
6 .... 48.13, 48.15, 94.32, **246.79**
7 .... 39.2, 94.52, **246.80**
8 .... **246.81**
9 .... 209.8, **246.82**
(2) 209.5
10 .... **246.83**
11 .... 94.39, **246.84**
12 .... 9.29, **246.85**
(1) 94.40, 202.29

Perpetuities and Accumulations Act 1964 – *contd*
s 12(2) 94.40
13 ... 95.4, 207.21, 207.25, 213.8, 216.34, 218.57, 218.71, **246.86**
(1)(a) 218.73, 241.30
14 .... 95.12, **246.87**
15 .... 94.40, **246.88**
(2) 94.50
(4) 202.19
(5) 55.5, 94.42, 213.7
Powers of Attorney Act 1971
s 9 .... 27.9
Public Libraries and Museums Act 1964
s 13 .... 35.53
Public Trustee Act 1906 .... 203.39
s 2(2) 25.8, 203.37
(3)–(4) 25.8
4(3) 27.4
5(1) 25.8, 203.38
(3) 25.8, 203.42, 221.48
6 .... 25.8
Public Trustee (Law Reform Miscellaneous) Provisions Act 1994
s 14 .... 1.7

R

Race Relations Act 1968 .... 34.12, 35.30
Race Relations Act 1976 .... 9.38, 35.30
s 1 .... 103.12
34(1) 103.12
(2)(a), (b) 103.12
(4) 103.12
Railways Act 1921 .... 41.13
Recognition of Trusts Act 1987 .... 24.5
Recreational Charities Act 1958
s 1(1) 102.12
(2)(b)(ii) 102.12
(3) 102.12
Redundancy Payments Act 1965 .... 210.63
Rent Act 1977
Sch 1
para 2 .... 7.4
3(1) 7.4

S

Settled Land Act 1925 .... 23.7, 26.1, 27.1, 27.13, 35.18, 35.21, 83.6, 200.51, 200.55, 200.66, 203.4, 203.10, 203.11, 203.14, 203.24, 203.33, 203.34, 203.37, 203.38, 203.40, 203.41, 206.4, 206.6, 206.31, 207.6, 207.9, 207.11, 207.13, 208.7, 214.1, 214.2, 218.93, 220.49, 220.54, 237.5, 237.27
s 1(7) 26.2
3 .... 26.3
4, 5 .... 26.2
7(1) 26.2
8(3) 203.5
(5), (6) 203.5
19 .... 26.2
20 .... 26.2
(1)(v) 7.19
22, 23 .... 26.2
25(1) 200.54
27 .... 9.39, 9.40
28(1) 200.60
29 .... 9.40
30 .... 27.18
(3) ... 26.4, 27.7, 203.10, 203.12, 221.1
47 .... 207.6, 220.61
66 .... 220.61
67(1) 200.52
73(1)(iii) 220.52
79 .... 207.6
94 .... 27.7, 27.16, 27.18
102 .... 203.13
106 .... 35.28, 99.3
117(1)(xxxi) 7.19
Sch 3 .... 95.5
Settled Land Act 1996 .... 35.21
Sex Discrimination Act 1975 .... 9.38
s 43 .... 103.12
Sexual Offences Act 1956
s 38(3) 28.8
Social Security Contributions and Benefits Act 1992
s 64 .... 218.34, 226.4
71 .... 218.34, 226.4
72 .... 226.4
137 .... 105.14

Social Security Contributions and Benefits (Northern Ireland) Act 1992
s 64 .... 218.34
71 .... 218.34
Statute Law Revision Act 1950 .... 218.44
Supreme Court Act 1981
s 25 .... 49.6
62 .... 49.6
109(1) 200.124
114 .... 25.1, 26.4
(1) 203.9, 221.40, 233.39
(2) 203.1
115 .... 203.2, 203.28, 236.12
116 .... 9.14, 25.1, 26.4
(2) 26.8
118 .... 25.4, 203.12, 231.10
119 .... 25.4
126 .... 10.20
Sch 1 .... 49.6
Supreme Court of Judicature (Consolidation) Act 1925
s 160(1) 26.4
162(1) 9.14
172 .... 10.20

T

Taxation of Chargeable Gains Act 1992
s 4 .... 32.24, 200.40, 230.45
(1AA) 217.3
(a) 218.27, 226.7
5 .... 32.24, 242.5
62(1) 200.39
(3) 220.72
(4) 209.4, 219.11, 220.72, 234.21, 241.17, 242.5
(6) 46.6, 241.1, 241.3, 241.6, 241.17, 241.19, 241.25, 241.26, 241.27, 241.29, 241.30
(7) 46.6, 241.1, 241.3, 241.17, 241.25
(8)–(10) 46.6, 241.1, 241.17
64 .... 219.11
(1) 209.4
(2) 220.72, 242.5
68C(2) 225.90, 241.17, 241.30
(3), (4) 241.17

Taxation of Chargeable Gains Act 1992 – *contd*
s 68C(5) 241.17, 241.30
(6) 241.30
71 .... 200.39, 217.10, 217.11, 217.14, 217.17, 217.19, 217.27, 217.29, 217.31, 217.33, 217.42, 217.43, 218.74, 218.103, 219.11, 220.72, 242.5, 242.13, 242.15, 242.17, 242.19
(1) 242.3
72 .... 200.39, 213.11
73 .... 200.39
(1)(b) 213.11
74 .... 200.39
77 .... 46.6, 241.17, 241.30
79(2) 241.30
87 .... 236.3
88, 89 .... 200.39
126–136 .... 205.67
165 .... 200.39, 200.108, 200.127, 200.131, 217.40, 218.28, 242.3, 242.5
168 .... 242.10
222 .... 200.127, 208.35
223, 224 .... 200.127
225 .... 200.95, 200.127, 208.35
225A 208.35
260 .... 200.119, 218.28, 242.3, 242.5, 242.10
(1) 200.39
(2)(a) 200.39, 200.109, 218.74, 242.3, 242.17
(d) 200.39, 217.10, 217.11, 217.14, 217.17, 217.19, 217.27, 217.29, 217.31, 217.32, 217.42, 218.36, 218.103, 224.24, 242.3
(da) 200.39, 200.108, 217.25, 218.103, 224.24, 242.3
(db) 200.39, 200.109, 218.103, 224.24, 242.3, 242.17
262 .... 204.23
263 .... 102.1
272 .... 209.12
Sch 1
para 1 .... 226.4, 226.6, 226.40
(1)(b) 226.65
Sch 7 .... 217.40, 218.28
Tenures Abolition Act 1660 .... 28.9
Trade Union and Labour Relations (Consolidation) Act 1992
s 17(1) 7.10

Trading with the Enemy
Act 1939 .... 9.37, 99.4, 99.7

Trustee Act 1925 .... 25.17, 226.37
s 1 .... 220.23
(1)(b) 64.53
8 .... 220.16
10 .... 220.16
(3) 220.20, 233.21
(4) 220.20
12 .... 220.24, **246.10**
13 .... 220.24, **246.11**
14 .... **246.12**
(2) 7.6, 27.7, 27.16
15 .... 221.15, **246.13**
(3) 72.12
(8) 72.13
16 .... 220.23, **246.14**
(2) 220.69
17 .... 220.69, **246.15**
18 .... 246.16
(1) 27.7
(2) 7.6, 27.7, 27.16, 203.1, 203.12, 221.1
19 .... 27.14, 204.38, 204.44, 220.51, 221.15, 224.37, 230.11, **246.17**
20 .... 204.44, 204.45, 204.47, **246.18**
21 .... **246.19**
22 .... **246.20**
(1) 221.15
(3) 220.75, 221.15
(4) 221.30
23 .... 27.9, **246.21**
24 .... 208.48, **246.22**
25 .... **246.23**
(7) 221.20
(8) 27.9
(10) 27.1
26 .... **246.24**
27 .... 9.2, 72.14, 200.31, 200.123, **246.25**
28 .... **246.26**
(3) 9.11
29 .... **246.27**
30 .... 27.9, **246.28**

Trustee Act 1925 – *contd*
s 31 ...... 32.20, 32.21, 32.26, 32.28, 66.14, 93.16, 200.108, 200.109, 200.110, 200.132, 200.136, 206.17, 207.21, 208.9, 210.37, 210.38, 210.40, 210.47, 210.48, 210.49, 213.8, 213.12, 214.50, 215.8, 216.30, 217.9, 217.20, 217.24, 217.25, 218.29, 218.44, 218.46, 218.48, 218.49, 218.64, 218.68, 218.69, 218.71, 218.72, 218.73, 218.74, 218.75, 218.78, 218.79, 218.80, 218.81, 218.83, 218.84, 218.86, 218.93, 221.24, 224.24, 224.25, 224.36, 224.51, 224.52, 224.66, 224.80, 224.96, 225.13, 225.17, 225.32, 225.51, 225.52, 225.62, 225.63, 227.17, 227.18, 227.29, 227.31, 227.32, 227.54, 227.57, 227.58, 228.13, 228.14, 228.37, 228.39, 228.40, 229.7, 229.8, 229.21, 229.45, 229.46, 229.47, 230.9, 230.10, 230.24, 230.37, 230.38, 230.80, 230.81, 231.24, 231.25, 231.35, 231.37, 232.9, 232.10, 232.46, 232.58, 232.72, 232.73, 233.19, 233.20, 233.29, 233.31, 233.45, 234.24, 234.36, 234.51, 235.22, 235.29, 235.33, 236.19, 236.34, 237.25, 242.12, 242.16, 242.20, **246.29**
(1) 33.25, 218.50
(c) 217.4
(i) 218.63, 241.31
(ii) ... 32.16, 32.24, 217.10, 217.11, 217.14, 217.17, 217.19, 217.27, 217.29, 217.31, 217.33, 217.42, 217.43, 223.9, 224.79, 230.68, 238.13, 238.15, 238.16, 241.31, 242.4, 242.14, 242.17
(2) 93.25, 218.56, 218.82, 238.14, 242.4
(i)(a), (b) 32.24
(ii) 32.24, 218.55
(3) 32.25, 210.46, 218.59
(4) 218.53, 218.62
(5) 218.43

Trustee Act 1925 – *contd*
s 32 .... 66.14, 200.108, 200.109, 200.1102, 200.1, 215.8, 217.4, 217.9, 218.4, 218.36, 218.87, 218.91, 218.92, 218.94, 218.95, 218.96, 218.98, 218.99, 218.100, 218.101, 218.102, 218.103, 218.104, 218.106, 218.107, 224.36, 224.51, 224.52, 224.66, 224.80, 224.96, 225.17, 225.32, 225.51, 225.52, 225.62, 225.63, 226.49, 226.65, 227.18, 227.29, 227.31, 227.54, 227.58, 228.13, 228.14, 228.37, 228.39, 229.7, 229.21, 229.45, 229.46, 229.47, 230.9, 230.10, 230.24, 230.37, 230.38, 230.68, 230.80, 230.81, 231.24, 231.25, 231.35, 231.37, 232.9, 232.10, 232.46, 232.58, 232.72, 232.73, 233.19, 233.20, 233.29, 233.31, 233.45, 234.24, 234.51, 235.22, 235.33, 236.19, 236.34, 242.1, 242.10, 242.12, 242.14, 242.16, 242.18, 242.20, **246.30**
32(1) 218.88, 218.105, 226.4
(b) 226.11
(c) 218.90, 226.11
(2) 218.93
33 .... 9.11, 40.5, 99.4, 200.20, 200.104, 211.24, 216.8, 216.10, 218.90, 225.32, 225.75, 230.16, 230.24, 237.22, **246.31**
(1)(ii) 216.18
(b) 216.9
(3) 72.12
34 .... 27.16, **246.32**
(2) 27.17, 203.1
35 .... **246.33**
36 .... 203.24, 206.4, 221.35, 221.36, 221.39, 221.41, 239.1, **246.34**
(1) 25.14, 27.3, 27.5, 27.6, 239.5
(b) 27.15
(5) 25.12, 27.6
(6) 27.3, 27.5, 27.7
(b) 27.2
(6B), (6C), (6D) 27.2
(7) 27.7
(9) 27.5
37 .... 221.35, **246.35**
(1)(b) 221.37

Trustee Act 1925 – *contd*
s 37(1)(c) 221.41
38 .... **246.36**
39 .... **246.37**
(1) 221.41
40 .... 239.5, **246.38**
42 .... 203.30, 221.48
53 .... 218.66, 218.94
57 .... 220.25
63 .... 9.1, 9.40, 9.45, 29.1, 210.34
68 .... **246.39**
(13) 64.53
(17) 32.26
(18) 203.28, 221.41, 221.47
(20) 221.41
69 .... **246.40**
(1) 220.51
(2) 32.16, 33.25, 218.47, 218.52, 218.78, 218.91, 218.92, 218.93, 221.14, 221.35

Trustee Act 2000 .... 25.5, 30.15, 102.1, 103.19, 200.65, 200.66, 200.67, 214.10, 214.33, 220.15, 223.6, 237.4, 237.6
s 1 .... 27.11, 27.14, 206.7, 220.57, 221.15, 221.17, 237.28, **246.133**
(1)(a), (b) 27.8
2 .... 27.8, 221.33, **246.134**
3 .... 27.11, 204.38, 206.7, 208.36, 208.43, 212.5, 214.35, 220.16, 220.18, 220.20, 220.21, 220.40, 220.43, 220.71, 221.15, 224.37, 230.11, 237.28, **246.135**
(1) 220.12, 220.22, 220.23, 220.32
(2) 220.12
(3) 220.12, 220.16
(4), (5) 220.16
4 .... 27.11, 220.13, 220.37, 220.40, 220.41, 220.42, 221.15, 224.37, 230.11, 237.28, **246.136**
(3)(b) 220.44
5 .... 27.9, 27.11, 220.14, 220.37, 220.40, 220.41, 220.42, 224.37, 221.15, 230.11, 237.28, **246.137**
6 .... 27.11, **246.138**
(1) 220.12, 220.18, 220.40
(b) 237.28
(2)–(4) 220.14
7 .... **246.139**
(1) 220.12

Trustee Act 2000 – *contd*
s 8 .... 27.11, 208.36, 220.13, 220.14, 220.30, 220.40, 220.43, 220.71, 221.15, 230.11, **246.140**
(1) 27.12, 208.43, 220.17, 220.22, 220.24, 220.49, 2200.52
(b) 218.109
(2) 218.109, 220.17
(3) 27.12, 208.43, 220.24, 220.49, 220.52, 220.69, 224.37, 230.11
9 .... 220.18, 220.25, 220.40, 220.50, **246.141**
10 .... **246.142**
11 .... 220.37, 220.38, 220.39, 221.14, 221.15, **246.143**
(1), (2) 220.36
12 .... **246.144**
(1) 220.37
(3) 220.47, 224.37, 230.11
13 .... **246.145**
14 .... 220.36, 220.37, **246.146**
(2) 220.47, 224.37, 230.11
15 .... 220.36, 220.37, 220.47, 224.37, 230.11, **246.147**
16 .... 220.36, 220.38, 221.14, 221.15, **246.148**
17 .... 221.14, 221.15, **246.149**
18 .... 220.21, 221.14, 221.15, **246.150**
19 .... **246.151**
(1) 220.36, 220.37
(2) 220.21, 220.36, 220.47, 224.37, 230.11
(5)(a) 221.33
20 .... 220.21, 220.36, **246.152**
(1) 220.37
(2) 220.47, 224.37, 230.11
(3) 221.33
21 .... **246.153**
(2) 221.33
(3) 220.37, 221.33
22 .... 27.9, 220.21, 220.36, 220.37, 220.38, 220.47, 221.19, 221.33, 224.37, 225.18, 226.31, 227.19, 228.15, 229.9, 230.11, 230.26, 231.26, 231.49, 232.11, 232.48, 233.21, 235.12, 236.20, **246.154**
23 .... 221.33, **246.155**
(1) 220.38, 225.19, 226.35, 227.20, 228.16
24 .... **246.156**

Trustee Act 2000 – *contd*
s 25 .... 220.39, 221.14, **246.157**
26 .... 27.8, 27.9, 220.37, **246.158**
27 .... 27.10, **246.159**
28 .... 221.47, **246.160**
(1) 221.43, 221.44
(a), (b) 27.10
(2) 27.10, 221.43, 221.46, 221.49, 221.50, 221.52
(3) 27.10, 221.43, 223.9
(4) 25.16, 31.1
(a) 200.2, 221.44, 222.2
(b) 221.44
(5) 221.43, 221.44, 221.45, 221.46, 221.50
(6) 221.43
29 .... 203.30, 221.47, 221.52, 223.1, 225.60, 226.37, **246.161**
(1) 27.10, 221.42, 221.51
(2) 27.10, 221.16, 221.42, 221.44, 225.20, 225.67, 226.36, 227.22, 228.17
(3) 27.10, 221.48, 224.42
(4) 27.10, 221.42, 221.46
(5) 221.44
30 .... 27.10, 221.42, **246.162**
31 .... 27.10, **246.163**
32 .... 27.10, 220.36, **246.164**
(2), (3) 221.33
33 .... 27.10, **246.165**
(1) 221.16, 221.42, 221.43
(2) 31.1, 221.44
(a) 222.2
34 .... 220.51, 224.37, **246.166**
(1) 204.38, 204.44
(a), (b) 27.14
(2) 204.44, 204.45, 204.46, 212.5
35 .... 220.1, 220.12, 220.24, 220.49, 220.51, 221.42, 221.46, 223.1, 223.9, **246.167**
(1) 27.1, 31.1, 200.2
(2)(a)–(c) 27.1
(3) 25.16
(a), (b) 221.44
(4) 221.44
39 .... **246.168**
(1) 221.47
40 .... **246.169**
(1) 233.21
41 .... **246.170**

Trustee Act 2000 – *contd*
s 42 .... **246.171**
43 .... **246.172**
Sch 1 .... 221.17, **246.173**
para 2 .... 220.16, 220.17
3(1)(a), (b) 220.38
(d), (e) 220.38, 221.33
(2) 220.38
5 .... 27.8
7 ... 220.38, 221.15, 221.33, 237.28
Sch 2 .... 27.1, 27.11
para 18 .... 220.16, 220.20
21 .... 32.24, 93.25
22 .... 72.12
23 .... 27.15
37 .... 9.1, 9.40, 29.1
38 .... 27.8
40 .... 27.8
Sch 3 .... 27.11
Sch 4 .... 27.1, 27.11
Trustee Act (Northern Ireland) 1958
s 33 .... 226.4, 226.11
Trustee Delegation Act 1999 ... 1.2, 220.39, 221.14
s 1(1) 27.9
(3) 27.9
(5) 27.9
5 .... 27.1
(1), (2) 221.20
8 .... 27.2
Schedule 27.1
Trustee Investments Act 1961 .... 27.11, 204.38, 220.1, 220.12, 237.6
s 6(1) 220.13
Trustee Savings Banks Act 1985 ...... 7.11
Trusts of Land and Appointment of Trustees Act 1996 .... 26.3, 38.18, 38.24, 38.25, 47.11, 64.32, 64.45, 76.5, 89.2, 200.16, 200.22, 200.49, 200.50, 200.55, 200.64, 200.66, 200.95, 200.101, 204.69, 206.6, 206.27, 206.28, 206.31, 207.6, 208.3, 210.5, 214.1, 214.14, 214.38, 220.19, 224.37, 237.4, 238.6
s 1 .... 23.7, 27.13, 27.18, 38.22, 94.37, 206.26, 220.1, **246.103**
(1)(a), (b) 26.1, 27.17, 200.51
(2)(a), (b) 200.51
(3) 200.51

Trusts of Land and Appointment of Trustees Act 1996 – *contd*
s 2 .... 9.39, 23.7, 27.7, 27.18, 30.11, 38.22, 47.20, 56.5, 76.1, 101.11, 206.4, 211.13, 223.6, **246.104**
(1) ... 7.19, 8.2, 26.1, 35.18, 35.28, 83.6, 95.5, 99.3, 200.52
(2) 7.19, 8.2, 26.1, 35.18, 35.28, 200.52
(4) 26.1, 200.52
(5) 26.1, 206.26
(6) 7.2, 27.15, 78.1, 84.1, 200.53
3 .... 8.2, 23.7, 26.2, 38.22, 41.5, 41.7, 200.54, 220.1, 237.5, **246.105**
(1) 37.1
(2) 37.1, 41.18
(3) 37.1
4 .... 8.2, 23.7, 26.2, 38.22, 94.37, 200.56, 200.58, 217.40, 220.25, **246.106**
(1) 200.54, 214.3, 214.12, 14.30, 220.28, 241.26
5 ... 8.2, 23.7, 26.2, 38.22, 104.1, **246.107**
(1) 84.1, 86.1
6 .... 200.60, 200.67, 237.27, **246.108**
(1) 27.13, 200.66, 206.26, 207.2, 208.36, 208.38, 208.43, 214.2, 214.29, 220.24, 220.25, 220.49, 220.52, 220.61, 220.69, 224.37, 224.92, 230.11, 237.5
(2) 86.1, 200.57, 206.16, 206.29
(3) 27.12, 224.92
(4) 27.12
(5) 27.13, 200.61
(6) 102.1
(9) 27.8
7 .... 200.57, 200.67, 220.71, 220.74, 220.80, 224.37, 230.11, **246.109**
(3) 200.61
8 .... **246.110**
(1) 27.13, 208.38,, 220.25, 220.50, 237.5
(2) 27.13, 208.19, 208.38, 208.43, 220.25, 220.50, 220.62, 224.92, 231.67, 237.5
(3) 206.26, 9 208.12, 208.19, 208.38, 211.13, 220.39, 220.54, 220.57, **246.111**
(1) 221.14, 221.16
9 .... 208.38, **246.111**
9A 221.14, 221.16, **246.112**

Trusts of Land and Appointment of Trustees Act 1996 – *contd*
s 10 .... 27.1, 27.17, **246.113**
11 .... 35.18, 200.56, 200.63, 200.67, 208.12, 208.19, 211.13, 217.40, 220.57, 220.62, **246.114**
(1) 200.61, 221.27, 224.38, 225.19, 225.78, 226.29, 226.35, 227.34, 228.16, 229.10, 230.12, 231.27, 232.12, 233.23, 235.13, 235.26, 236.21, 237.11
(2)(a) 200.59, 215.8, 220.58, 237.9
(b) 200.66, 220.58, 237.9
11A 200.61
12 .... 35.18, 207.2, 208.13, 208.15, 208.17, 208.26, 208.33, 208.44, 211.13, 217.1, 217.40, 218.2, 218.35, 218.109, 218.110, 224.37, 225.33, 230.11, 231.67, **246.115**
1) 208.5, 208.10, 208.12
(a) 208.7, 208.8, 208.9, 208.18, 208.19, 208.43, 224.92
(b) 208.7, 208.8, 208.9, 208.18
2) 208.5, 208.7, 208.8, 208.9
13 .... 208.13, 208.14, 208.15, 208.33, 230.11, **246.116**
(1) 208.9
(2) 208.5
(3) 207.2, 208.5, 208.9, 208.10, 208.11, 208.18, 208.19, 208.26, 208.27, 234.35
(4) 208.18, 208.26
(5) 207.2, 208.5, 208.9, 208.19, 208.27, 234.35
(b) 208.9
(6) 208.5, 208.9
(7) 208.10, 208.11, 208.18
14 .... 200.56, 200.58, 200.59, 200.62, 200.63, 208.11, 208.21, 208.23, 208.27, 208.38, 214.3, 220.57, **246.117**
(2)(a) 208.19
15 .... 200.62, 208.18, 220.57, **246.118**
(1) 208.26
(2) 208.9
(3) 200.59
16 .... 37.8, **246.119**
(1), (2) 200.61
17 .... 200.52, **246.120**
18 .... 220.1, 220.24, 220.49, **246.121**

Trusts of Land and Appointment of Trustees Act 1996 – *contd*
s 18(1) 200.63, 214.3, 225.78
(2)–(3) 200.63
19 .... 7.6, 27.2, 27.3, 27.7, 35.18, 200.66, 221.39, 225.40, 227.37, 237.5, 237.27, **246.122**
20 .... 7.6, 27.2, 27.3, 27.7, 200.66, 221.39, 237.5, 237.27, **246.123**
21 .... 7.6, **246.124**
(2), (3) 221.14
(5) 27.2, 221.39, 237.5
22 .... 27.2, 211.13, **246.125**
(1), (2) 208.10
(3) 208.12, 208.13
23 .... 27.2, 221.14, **246.126**
(2) 200.51, 220.24, 220.52, 228.37
24 .... 27.2, **246.127**
25 .... 27.2, 38.22, 38.23, **246.128**
25(1) 9.40, 27.3, 27.5, 27.7, 27.16, 27.17, 29.17, 29.22, 55.7, 66.14, 72.14, 78.1, 206.5
(2) 9.39, 9.40, 37.8, 47.20, 75.6
(4) 75.6, 218.87, 218.93
26 .... 27.2, **246.129**
27 .... **246.130**
(3) 200.48, 208.38, 208.43
33 .... 104.1
35 .... 238.14
41 .... 238.12
Sch 1 .... 27.1, **246.131**
para 1(2), (3) 9.39
2 .... 9.39, 206.4
4 .... 102.1
5 .... 47.20, 56.5, 76.1, 78.1, 84.1, 101.11, 200.53, 204.75, 206.10, 206.18
(1) 7.2
7 .... 221.14
Sch 2 .... 27.1, 200.54, 237.5
para 3 .... 41.18, 86.1
4 .... 7.3, 86.1
5 .... 27.15, 30.11, 38.22, 38.23, 104.1, 224.34, 225.33, 230.7
(2) 214.2, 214.10
Sch 3 .... 27.1
para 2 .... 9.40
(9) 26.4
3 .... 7.6, 27.7
(7) 72.14

Trusts of Land and Appointment of Trustees Act 1996 – *contd*
Sch 3 – *contd*
para 3(8) 66.14
(9) 27.16
(11) 27.3, 27.5
4 .... 9.39, 27.2, 27.17
(4) 55.7
6 .... 206.7, 220.24
(1) 206.5
(3) 29.17, 29.22
(4)(a) 206.5
25 .... 72.14, 78.1
Sch 4 ... 9.40, 27.1, 27.3, 37.8, 47.20, 75.6, 84.1, 84.2, 200.60, 214.2
para 4 .... 27.16

V

Variation of Trusts Act 1958 .... 241.11, 241.31
s 1(1) 40.16
(2) 200.104

W

War Loan Act 1919 .... 64.58
Wills Act 1837 ... 1.2, 6.1, 9.8, 10.11, 11.19, 11.25, 16.8, 24.12, 28.6, 36.13, 57.24
s 1 .... 7.26, **244.3**
(1) 1.7
3 .... 1.7, 7.18, 7.19, 7.20, 7.21, 25.18, **244.4**
7 .... 4.7, **244.5**
9 .... 1.5, 1.6, 4.22, 10.1, 10.3, 10.13, 10.18, 10.19, 11.1, 11.2, 11.10, 11.11, 11.12, 11.21, 11.23, 11.24, 12.3, 12.5, 12.7, 12.9, 12.11, 12.13, 13.3, 14.6, 14.12, 15.1, 16.4, 18.12, 28.5, 36.2, 202.10, 222.1, **244.6**, **244.7**
(a) 11.9
(b) 11.9, 14.1
(c) 11.9, 12.1
(d) 12.1, 14.1
(ii) 222.13
10 .... 24.11, **244.8**
11 .... 9.10, 16.1, 16.3, 28.5, **244.9**
13 .... **244.10**
14 .... 12.16, **244.11**

Wills Act 1837 – *contd*
s 15 ...... 9.3, 9.10, 9.11, 12.1, 12.8, 12.16, 19.1, 19.4, 27.10, 30.15, 31.1, 38.14, 48.6, 209.2, 221.44, **244.12**
16 .... 9.3, 12.16, **244.13**
17 .... 12.16, **244.14**
18 ...... 2.9, 16.4, 17.1, 17.2, 17.5, 18.15, 77.2, 77.2, 201.4, 201.7, 223.12, 228.7, **244.15**, **244.16**
(1) 17.2, 17.3, 232.15
(2) 17.3, 17.8, 17.8
(3) 17.3, 17.6
(4)–(6) 17.3
18A ... 9.17, 17.1, 47.1, 47.3, 48.14, 93.9, 200.25, 203.7, 219.29, 224.17, 224.18, 224.20, 224.60, 225.11, 225.46, 225.59, 225.101, 227.27, 227.43, 228.33, 228.37, 231.44, 231.47, 233.16, 233.28, 233.39, 237.18, **244.17**, **244.18**
(1) ... 25.7, 47.2, 47.4, 105.13, 224.16
(a) 25.11, 80.3, 224.21, 224.29, 231.16
(b) 80.3, 224.21, 224.22, 224.23, 224.33, 228.11
(2) 47.2, 105.13
(3) 47.4, 48.14, 80.3
18B 17.1, 17.3, 201.8, 223.12, 228.7, 232.15, **244.19**
(1) 201.5
(3) 201.5
18C 17.3, 25.7, 200.25, 203.8, 224.16, 224.17, 224.20, 225.11, 225.59, 231.44, 237.18, **244.20**
(1)(a) 224.21
(b) 224.21, 224.22, 224.23
(2)(a), (b) 25.11, 47.3
19 .... **244.21**
20 ...... 18.5, 18.16, 18.17, 18.21, 18.25, 18.32, 223.8, 237.20, 237.35, **244.22**
21 .... 14.1, **244.23**
22 .... 21.1, 21.6, 21.8, 237.16, **244.24**
23 .... 41.5, 207.3, **244.25**
24 ..... 7.3, 39.20, 41.2, 54.1, 54.2, 59.1, 64.8, 65.2, 207.3, **244.26**
25 .... 47.6, **244.27**
26 .... 64.32, 206.10, 214.25, **244.28**

Wills Act 1837 – *contd*
s 27 ..... 24.16, 38.2, 39.1, 39.2, 39.3, 39.9, 39.11, 39.13, 39.31, 47.38, 47.39, 59.1, 206.10, 206.30, 214.10, 215.8, 224.32, 224.34, 225.33, 225.115, 228.9, 230.7, 231.12, **244.29**
28 .... 83.1, **244.30**
29 .... 54.5, 78.5, 98.1, 98.12, **244.31**
30 .... **244.32**
31 .... **244.33**
32 .... 47.11, 47.19, **244.34**
33 .... 38.2, 39.4, 47.10, 47.11, 47.12, 47.13, 47.15, 47.16, 47.19, 47.29, 47.33, 47.38, 47.39, 66.8, 75.4, 87.1, 206.33, 210.26, 213.4, 217.5, 217.14, 217.39, 219.15, 219.23, 223.3, 223.9, 233.43, 234.20, 234.34, 236.13, 236.29, **244.35**, **244.36**
(1), (2) 47.15, 47.18
(3) 47.15, 87.1
(4) 73.2
(a) 47.16
(b) 47.17
34 .... 20.4, 21.1, 22.3, **244.37**
35 .... **244.38**
70 .... 18.5

Wills Act 1861 .... 24.16
s 1 .... 23.6, 23.7, **244.43**
2 .... 23.7, 23.8, **244.44**
3 .... **244.45**
4 .... **244.46**
5 .... **244.47**

Wills Act 1952 .... 11.2

Wills Act 1963 ...... 10.3, 23.10, 23.15, 24.1
s 1 .... 23.8, 23.9, 23.12, 23.13, 24.12, **244.77**
2 .... **244.78**
(1)(a) 23.9
(b) 23.12
(c) 23.13
(d) 24.12
(2) 24.12
3 .... 23.9, **244.79**
4 .... 23.9, 24.6, 24.8, **244.80**
5 .... **244.81**
6 .... 23.13, **244.82**
(1) 23.9
7 .... **244.83**
(2) 23.9
(3) 23.6
(4) 23.6, 24.12

Wills Act 1968 .... 200.44, 222.2
s 1 .... 9.8, **244.84**
(1) 12.8
2 .... **244.85**

Wills Act Amendment Act 1852 ...... 11.1, 11.2, 11.9
s 1 .... **244.40**
2 .... **244.41**
3 .... **244.42**

Wills (Soldiers and Sailors) Act 1918
s 1 .... 16.1, **244.48**
2 .... 16.1, **244.49**
3 .... 16.1, **244.50**
4 .... 16.1, 28.5, **244.51**
5 .... **244.52**
(2) 16.1

Cumulative Table of Cases

[Entries up to and including (prefix) 105 are to Volume 1. Entries from (prefix) 200 onward are to Volume 2.]

A

A (child of the family), Re [1998] 1 FCR 458, [1998] 1 FLR 347, [1998] Fam Law 14, CA 105.17
AN v Barclays Private Bank & Trust (Cayman) Limited [2007] WTLR 565 ...... [34.11], [34.12], [34.25]
ARMS (Multiple Sclerosis Research) Ltd, Re, Alleyne v A-G [1997] 2 All ER 679, [1997] 1 WLR 877, [1997] 1 BCLC 157 .... 103.4
Abadam v Abadam (1864) 33 Beav 475, 33 LJ Ch 593, 10 Jur NS 505, 12 WR 615, 10 LT 53 .... 33.47
Abbay v Howe (1847) 1 De G & Sm 470, 11 Jur 765, 9 LTOS 392, sub nom Abbey v Howe 16 LJ Ch 437 .... 87.1, 87.2
Abbey Malvern Wells Ltd v Ministry of Local Government and Planning [1951] Ch 728, [1951] 2 All ER 154, 49 LGR 776, 1 P & CR 467, 115 JP 389, 95 Sol Jo 381, [1951] 1 TLR 1050 .... 102.5
Abbiss v Burney, Re Finch (1880) 17 Ch D 211, 28 WR 903, 43 LT 20; on appeal (1881) 17 Ch D 211, 50 LJ Ch 348, 29 WR 449, 44 LT 267, CA 35.39, 55.3, 94.33
Abbot v Massie (1796) 3 Ves 148 .... 30.15
Abbott, Re (1974) 45 DLR (3d) 478 .... 103.3
Abbott, Re, Peacock v Frigout [1893] 1 Ch 54, 62 LJ Ch 46, 3 R 72, 41 WR 154, 67 LT 794 .... 94.30, 94.43, 94.44, 94.48, 216.23
Abbott, Re, Public Trustee v St Dunstan's British Home and Hospital for Incurables and Trustees of Western Ophthalmic Hospital and Lady Dugan [1944] 2 All ER 457, 88 Sol Jo 406, CA 38.3, 63.1, 64.28
Abbott v Fraser (1874) LR 6 PC 96, 44 LJPC 26, 23 WR 422, 31 LT 596 .... 103.11
Abbott v Middleton (1858) 7 HL Cas 68, 28 LJ Ch 110, 5 Jur NS 717, 33 LTOS 66 .... 51.7, 51.9, 51.10, 52.2, 52.3, 82.2
Abbott v Service. See Westminster Bank Ltd's Declaration of Trust, Re
Abbott and Bearman v Willstead (1885) 2 TLR 23 .... 18.27
Aberconway's Settlement Trusts, Re, McLaren v Aberconway [1953] Ch 647, [1953] 2 All ER 350, 97 Sol Jo 454, CA 35.28
Aberdeen University v Irvine (1868) LR 1 Sc & Div 289, 40 Sc Jur 459, 6 M 29, HL 102.8

Abergavenny's (Marquess) Estate Act Trusts, Re, Marquess of Abergavenny v Ram [1981] 2 All ER 643, [1981] 1 WLR 843, 125 Sol Jo 291 .... 242.17
Abney v Miller (1743) 2 Atk 593 .... 61.1
Abraham v Joseph (1859) 5 Jur NS 179 .... 18.22
Abrahams, Re, Abrahams v Abrahams [1908] 2 Ch 69, 77 LJ Ch 578, 99 LT 240 .... 30.12
Abrahams, Re, Abrahams v Bendon [1911] 1 Ch 108, 80 LJ Ch 83, 55 Sol Jo 46, 103 LT 532 .... 32.20, 218.59
Abrahams' Will Trusts, Re, Caplan v Abrahams [1969] 1 Ch 463, [1967] 2 All ER 1175, [1967] 3 WLR 1198, 111 Sol Jo 794 .... 1.6, 8.7, 34.11, 35.31, 39.31, 40.5, 53.2, 94.48, 218.95
Abram, Re [1997] 2 FCR 85, [1996] 2 FLR 379, [1996] Fam Law 666, [1997] BPIR 1 .... 105.5, 105.16
Abrey v Newman (1853) 16 Beav 431, 22 LJ Ch 627, 17 Jur 153, 1 WR 156 .... 87.1
Acherley v Vernon (1739) 2 Com 513, Fortes Rep 186, Willes 153 .... 34.2
Acheson v Fair (1843) 2 Con & Law 208, 3 Dr & War 512 .... 101.3
Acheson v Russell [1951] Ch 67, 66 (pt 2) TLR 279, sub nom Re Manor Farm, Kytes Hardwick, Acheson v Russell [1950] 2 All ER 572 .... 7.2, 204.75
Ackerley, Re, Chapman v Andrew [1913] 1 Ch 510, 82 LJ Ch 260, 108 LT 712 .... 39.10, 39.16, 39.24
Ackers v Phipps (1835) 9 Bli NS 430, 3 Cl & Fin 665, HL 34.2, 60.2
Ackland Trust, Re (1944) 22 Man R 29, [1944] 2 WWR 56 .... 50.2
Acklom, Re, Oakeshott v Hawkins [1929] 1 Ch 195, 98 LJ Ch 44, 72 Sol Jo 810, 140 LT 192 .... 35.28, 83.6
Ackroyd v Smithson. See Akeroid v Smithson
Adair, Re [1909] 1 IR 311 .... 34.24, 35.28, 83.6
Adair v Maitland. See Maitland v Adair
Adam & Co International Trustees Ltd v Theodore Goddard (a firm) [2000] WTLR 349, [2000] 13 LS Gaz R 44, 144 Sol Jo LB 150 .... 221.41
Adam's Policy Trusts, Re (1883) 23 Ch D 525, 52 LJ Ch 642, 31 WR 810, 48 LT 727 .... 85.3
Adam's Trusts, Re (1865) 11 Jur NS 961, 14 WR 18, 13 LT 347 .... 97.3, 99.1
Adams, Re [1990] Ch 601, [1990] 2 All ER 97, [1990] 2 WLR 924, [1990] 2 FLR 519, [1990] Fam Law 403, 134 Sol Jo 518 ... 14.2, 14.13, 18.17, 18.22, 18.25, 18.27
Adams, Re, Adams v Adams (1906) 94 LT 720, CA 76.1
Adams, Re, Bank of Ireland Trustee Co Ltd v Adams, Hutchings and Parker [1967] IR 424 .... 24.1, 24.2
Adams, Re, Gee v Barnet Group Hospital Management Committee [1968] Ch 80, [1967] 3 All ER 285, [1967] 3 WLR 1088, 111 Sol Jo 587, CA 102.10, 103.11, 212.25
Adams, Re, Harle v Adams (1888) 4 TLR 757 .... 103.9
Adams, Re, Sursham v Farquharson [1951] Ch 716, [1951] 1 All ER 1037, 95 Sol Jo 353, [1951] 1 TLR 841 .... 72.9
Adams, Re, Verrier v Haskins [1906] WN 220, 51 Sol Jo 113 .... 32.26
Adams v Adams (1842) 1 Hare 537, 11 LJ Ch 305, 6 Jur 681 .... 52.11
Adams v Adams [1892] 1 Ch 369, 61 LJ Ch 237, 40 WR 261, 36 Sol Jo 215, 66 LT 98, 8 TLR 236, CA 34.11, 35.38, 221.18
Adams v Adams (12 November 1993, unreported), CA 105.5

Adams v Austen (1829) 3 Russ 461 .... 39.12
Adams v Barry (1845) 2 Coll 285 .... 30.37
Adams v Jones (1852) 9 Hare 485, 21 LJ Ch 352, 16 Jur 159, 18 LTOS 326 .... 53.1, 53.2, 58.10
Adams v Lopdell (1890) 25 LR Ir 311 .... 82.7
Adams v Robarts (1858) 25 Beav 658 .... 93.28, 93.29
Adams and Kensington Vestry, Re (1884) 27 Ch D 394, 54 LJ Ch 87, 32 WR 883, 51 LT 382, CA 82.5
Adams Estate, Re [1957] OWN 568 .... 87.1
Adams' Goods, Re (1872) LR 2 P & D 367, 36 JP 407, 41 LJP & M 31, 20 WR 400, 26 LT 526 .... 10.14
Adams' Trustees' and Frost's Contract, Re [1907] 1 Ch 695, 76 LJ Ch 408, 51 Sol Jo 427, 96 LT 833 .... 40.9
Adamson, Re (1875) LR 3 P & D 253 .... 14.11, 25.2
Adamson, Re, Public Trustee v Billing (1913) 108 LT 179 .... 99.5
Adeoso (otherwise Ametepe) v Adeoso [1981] 1 All ER 107, [1980] 1 WLR 1535, 124 Sol Jo 847, CA 105.14
Adkins, Re, Solomon v Catchpole (1908) 98 LT 667 .... 64.35, 64.36
Adnam v Cole (1843) 6 Beav 353 .... 33.10
Adney v Greatrex (1869) 38 LJ Ch 414, 17 WR 637, 20 LT 647 .... 71.1
Adshead v Willetts (1861) 29 Beav 358, 9 WR 405 .... 50.8, 62.1, 82.2
Advocate (Lord) v Bogie [1894] AC 83, 63 LJPC 85, 6 R 98, 70 LT 533, HL 47.24
Advocate (HM) v Routledge's Trustees (1907) 44 SLR 305 .... 46.4
Affleck v Affleck (1857) 26 LJ Ch 358, 3 Jur NS 326, 3 Sm & G 394, 5 WR 425, 29 LTOS 37 .... 40.7
Agar v Chatham Public General Hospital [1955] 1 DLR 401 .... 4.14
Agnew, Re, Brown v Agnew [1941] 4 DLR 653, 3 WWR 723 .... 25.4
Agulian v Cyganik [2006] WTLR 565, CA 105.7
Ahchay, Re (1997) 6 Tas R 369 .... 74.1
Ahearne v Ahearne (1881) 9 LR Ir 144 .... 101.9
Aiken, Re, Bolon v Gilliland [1898] 1 IR 335 .... 30.3, 38.3
Aimers v Taylor (1897) 15 NZLR 530 .... 5.9
Ainsworth, Re, Finch v Smith [1915] 2 Ch 96, 84 LJ Ch 701, 113 LT 368, 31 TLR 392 .... 31.8
Ainsworth, Re, Millington v Ainsworth [1922] 1 Ch 22, 91 LJ Ch 51, [1922] B & CR 21, 66 Sol Jo 107, 126 LT 247 .... 100.6
Ainsworth's Goods, Re (1870) LR 2 P & D 151, 34 JP 664, 23 LT 324 .... 11.2, 11.3
Aird Estate, Re, Webber v Aird [1954] 2 DLR 473, 12 WWR (NS) 13 .... 58.8
Aird's Estate, Re, Aird v Quick (1879) 12 Ch D 291, 48 LJ Ch 631, 27 WR 882, 41 LT 180 .... 43.6
Airey, Re, Airey v Stapleton [1897] 1 Ch 164, 66 LJ Ch 152, 45 WR 286, 41 Sol Jo 128, 76 LT 151 .... 40.5
Airey v Bower (1887) 12 App Cas 263, 56 LJ Ch 742, 35 WR 637, 56 LT 409, HL 39.14
Aislabie v Rice (1818) 3 Madd 256, 8 Taunt 459, 2 Moore CP 358 .... 35.12
Akerman, Re, Akerman v Akerman [1891] 3 Ch 212, 61 LJ Ch 34, 40 WR 12, [1891–4] All ER Rep 196, 65 LT 194 .... 30.10, 30.11, 30.12
Akeroid v Smithson (1780) 2 Dick 566, 3 P Wms 22n, sub nom Ackroyd v Smithson 1 Bro CC 503, [1775–1802] All ER Rep 227, 1 Wh & T 68 .... 37.7

Akeroyd's Settlement, Re, Roberts v Akeroyd [1893] 3 Ch 363, 63 LJ Ch 32, 7 R 405, 69 LT 474, CA ... 93.21
Aktiebolaget Volvo v Heritage (Leicester) Ltd [2000] FSR 253 ... 21.25
Alberti's Estate, Re [1955] 3 All ER 730n, [1955] 1 WLR 1240, 99 Sol Jo 817 ... 23.13
Albery, Re (1946) 42 DLR (2d) 201, [1946] 1 OR 342 ... 41.20
Alchin's Trusts, Re, ex p Furley, ex p Earl Romney (1872) LR 14 Eq 230, 20 WR 763, 26 LT 824 ... 103.7
Alcock, Re, Bonser v Alcock (or Seville) [1945] Ch 264, [1945] 1 All ER 613, 114 LJ Ch 161, 89 Sol Jo 246, 173 LT 4, 61 TLR 351 ... 87.1
Alcock v Ellen (1692) 2 Eq Cas Abr 290, Freem Ch 186 ... 85.3
Alcock v Sloper (1833) 2 My & K 699, 39 RR 334 ... 38.23
Alder v Lawless (1863) 32 Beav 72 ... 33.14
Aldersey, Re, Gibson v Hall [1905] 2 Ch 181, 74 LJ Ch 548, [1904–7] All ER Rep 644, 92 LT 826 ... 9.2
Alderton, Re, Hughes v Vanderspar [1913] WN 129 ... 68.13
Aldhous, Re, Noble v Treasury Solicitor [1955] 2 All ER 80, [1955] 1 WLR 459, 99 Sol Jo 276 ... 200.31
Aldwell v Aldwell (1875) 21 Gr 627 ... 73.1
Alexander, Re, Alexander v Alexander [1919] 1 Ch 371, 88 LJ Ch 242, 120 LT 692 ... 47.31, 87.4
Alexander, Re, Bathurst v Greenwood [1910] WN 94, CA ... 59.3
Alexander, Re, Courtauld-Thomson v Tilney. See Alexander's Will Trust
Alexander v Alexander (1755) 2 Ves Sen 640 ... 40.21
Alexander v Alexander (1842) 5 Beav 518 ... 91.6
Alexander v Alexander (1855) 16 CB 59, 24 LJCP 150, 1 Jur NS 598, 3 WR 450, 3 CLR 801, 25 LTOS 99 ... 93.13
Alexander v Alexander (1856) 6 De GM & G 593, 3 Jur NS 28, 5 WR 28, 28 LTOS 112 ... 83.2
Alexander v IRC [1991] STC 112, 23 HLR 236, [1991] 2 EGLR 179, [1991] 26 EG 141, CA ... 200.81
Alexander v Kirkpatrick (1874) LR 2 Sc & Div 397, HL ... 18.10
Alexander v M'Cullock (1787) 1 Cox Eq Cas 391, 2 Ves 192, 197, 29 ER 1216 ... 33.18
Alexander's Will Trust, Re [1948] 2 All ER 111, sub nom Re Alexander, Courtauld-Thomson v Tilney [1948] LJR 1373, 92 Sol Jo 350, 64 TLR 308 ... 52.7, 52.10, 57.22
Alexandra Park and Palace Acts, Re, Alexandra Park Trustees v Haringey London Borough Council (1967) 66 LGR 306, 111 Sol Jo 515, 203 Estates Gazette 601 ... 102.10
Aleyn v Belchier (1758) 1 Eden 132, 28 ER 634 ... 40.14, 40.15
Alford's Case. See Goring v Bickerstaff
Alford's Estate, Re (1939) 83 Sol Jo 566 ... 18.10, 21.6
Alfreton's Trust Estates, Re (1883) 52 LJ Ch 745, 31 WR 702 ... 100.2
Alger v Parrott (1866) LR 3 Eq 328 ... 83.16
Algermann v Ford. See Angermann v Ford
Alker v Barton (1842) 12 LJ Ch 16 ... 87.2
Allan, Re [1939] 1 DLR 766 ... 78.2
Allan, Re (1950) ALR 822, [1950] VLR 405 ... 52.4

Allan, Re, Allan v Midland Bank Executor and Trustee Co Ltd [1954] Ch 295, [1954] 1 All ER 646, [1954] 2 WLR 512, 98 Sol Jo 193, CA 80.3, 216.30

Allan, Re, Dow v Cassaigne [1903] 1 Ch 276, 72 LJ Ch 159, 51 WR 403, 88 LT 246, CA 20.5, 38.13, 90.1

Allan, Re, Roberts v Robinson (1933) 77 Sol Jo 448 .... 64.35

Allan v Gott (1872) 7 Ch App 439, 41 LJ Ch 571, 20 WR 427, 26 LT 412 .... 210.7, 214.2, 214.6

Allan v Morrison [1900] AC 604, 69 LJPC 141, PC 18.7, 18.12, 18.28, 18.30, 18.31

Allan's Executors v Allan 1908 SC 807 .... 102.9, 103.17

Allan's Will Trusts, Re, Curtis v Nalder [1958] 1 All ER 401, [1958] 1 WLR 220, 102 Sol Jo 140 .... 48.15, 94.30

Allen, Re [1933] SASR 122 .... 79.1

Allen, Re [1988] 1 Qd R 1 .... 57.12

Allen, Re, Faith v Allen [1953] Ch 810, [1953] 2 All ER 898, [1953] 3 WLR 637, 97 Sol Jo 606, CA 34.9, 35.29, 35.32

Allen, Re, Hargreaves v Taylor [1905] 2 Ch 400, 74 LJ Ch 593, 54 WR 91, 49 Sol Jo 671, 93 LT 597, 21 TLR 662 .... 102.25

Allen, Re, Hincks v Allen (1880) 49 LJ Ch 553, 28 WR 533 .... 3.3

Allen, Re, Wilson v Atter (1881) 29 WR 480, 44 LT 240 .... 47.32

Allen v Allen (1729) Mos 112 .... 64.27, 64.31, 64.47

Allen v Anderson (1846) 5 Hare 163, 15 LJ Ch 178, 10 Jur 196, 6 LTOS 430 .... 23.4

Allen v Callow (1796) 3 Ves 289 .... 88.4

Allen v Crane (1953) 89 CLR 152, [1953] ALR 959, 27 ALJ 538 (Aust HC) 76.5, 216.31, 218.86

Allen v Dundas (1789) 3 Term Rep 125 .... 25.14, 49.7

Allen v Edmonds (1886) 12 VLR 789 .... 31.1

Allen v Jackson (1875) 1 Ch D 399, 40 JP 262, 45 LJ Ch 310, 24 WR 306, 33 LT 713, CA 35.8

Allen v M'Pherson (1847) 1 HL Cas 191, 11 Jur 785 .... 25.15

Allen v Maddock (1858) 11 Moo PCC 427, 6 WR 825, [1843–60] All ER Rep 285, 31 LTOS 359 .... 15.1

Allen v Webster (1860) 2 Giff 177, 6 Jur NS 574, 2 LT 206 .... 72.6

Allen v Wood (1834) 1 Bing NC 8, 3 LJCP 219, 4 Moo & S 510, 131 ER 1020 .... 35.6, 35.8

Allen Estate, Re [1935] 1 WWR 584, 5 FLJ (Can) 51 .... 18.10

Allen-Meyrick's Will Trusts, Re, Mangnall v Allen-Meyrick [1966] 1 All ER 740, [1966] 1 WLR 499, 109 Sol Jo 957 .... 99.4

Allen's Estate, Re, Prescott v Allen and Beaumont [1945] 2 All ER 264, 114 LJ Ch 298, 89 Sol Jo 316, 173 LT 198 .... 24.6, 24.10, 42.2, 42.5, 42.15

Allen's Goods, Re (1839) 2 Curt 331 .... 12.3

Allen's Trusts, Re [1909] WN 181 .... 47.13

Alleyn, Re [1965] SALR 22 .... 58.10, 64.5

Allgood v Blake (1873) LR 8 Exch 160, 42 LJ Ex 101, 21 WR 599, 29 LT 331 .... 89.1

Allhusen v Whittell (1867) LR 4 Eq 295, [1861–73] All ER Rep 149, 36 LJ Ch 929, 16 LT 695 .... 33.23, 38.26, 200.36, 214.39, 224.34, 225.33, 230.7

Allied Finance and Investments Ltd v Haddow & Co [1983] NZLR 22, NZ CA 1.14

Alliston v Chapple (1860) 6 Jur NS 288, 2 LT 110 .... 60.1
Allott, Re, Hanmer v Allott [1924] 2 Ch 498, 94 LJ Ch 91, [1911–13] All ER Rep 810, 132 LT 141, CA 94.37
Alloway v Alloway (1843) 2 Con & Law 517, 4 Dr & War 380 .... 100.2
Allsop, Re, Cardinal v Warr [1968] Ch 39, [1967] 3 WLR 793, 111 Sol Jo 415, sub nom Re Alsopp, Cardinal v Warr [1967] 2 All ER 1056, CA 50.9, 51.8, 67.1
Allsop, Re, Gell v Carver (1884) 1 TLR 4 .... 102.8
Almack v Horn (1863) 1 Hem & M 630, 32 LJ Ch 304, 1 New Rep 535, 11 WR 505, 8 LT 415 .... 66.20, 81.2
Alsopp, Re, Cardinal v Warr. See Allsop, Re, Cardinal v Warr
Alston, Re [1955] VLR 281 .... 36.1, 53.5
Alt v Gregory (1856) 8 De GM & G 221, 2 Jur NS 577, 4 WR 436 .... 101.6
Ambrose v Hodgson. See Hodgson v Ambrose
Ames v Cadogan (1879) 12 Ch D 868, 48 LJ Ch 762, 27 WR 905, 41 LT 211 .... 39.18
Ames v Parkinson (1844) 7 Beav 379, 64 RR 100, 3 LTOS 199 .... 29.8
Amherst (Lord) v Duchess of Leeds (1842) 12 Sim 476, 6 Jur 141 .... 82.7
Amherst v Lytton (1729) Mos 131, 211, 5 Bro Parl Cas 254, Fitz-G 99 .... 93.23
Amiss's Goods, Re (1849) 2 Rob Eccl 116, 7 Notes of Cases 274 .... 12.12
Amodeo, Re [1958] NZLR 787 .... 33.27, 93.29
Amodeo, Re (1962) 33 DLR (3d) 24, [1962] OR 548 .... 33.25
Amos, Re [1954] 2 DLR 574, OWN 545 .... 13.1
Amos, Re, Carrier v Price [1891] 3 Ch 159, 60 LJ Ch 570, 39 WR 550, [1891–4] All ER Rep 320, 65 LT 69, 7 TLR 559 .... 9.35
Amos v Horner (1699) 1 Eq Cas Abr 112 .... 34.15
Amson v Harris (1854) 19 Beav 210 .... 87.1, 87.3
Amyot v Dwarris [1904] AC 268, 73 LJPC 40, 53 WR 16, 90 LT 102, 20 TLR 268, PC 47.6, 54.1, 65.2, 81.3
Anderson, Re [1908] VLR 593 .... 35.35
Anderson, Re [1916] 12 Tas LR 71 .... 63.4
Anderson, Re (1933) 1 DLR 581, [1933] OR 131 .... 18.23
Anderson, Re [1943] 4 DLR 268, [1943] OWN 303 .... 102.9
Anderson, Re, Halligey v Kirkley [1920] 1 Ch 175, 89 LJ Ch 81, 122 LT 261 .... 35.19, 83.6
Anderson, Re, Pegler v Gillatt [1905] 2 Ch 70, 74 LJ Ch 433, 53 WR 510, 92 LT 725 .... 42.2, 43.3
Anderson, Re, Public Trustee v Bielby (1928) 44 TLR 295 .... 41.13, 58.4
Anderson v Abbott (1857) 23 Beav 457, 3 Jur NS 833, 5 WR 381, 29 LTOS 223 .... 42.16
Anderson v Anderson (1872) LR 13 Eq 381, 41 LJ Ch 247, 20 WR 313, [1861–73] All ER Rep 161, 26 LT 12 .... 9.5
Anderson v Bell (1883) 8 AR 531, 29 Gr 452 .... 87.1
Anderson v Berkley [1902] 1 Ch 936, 71 LJ Ch 444, 50 WR 684, 46 Sol Jo 450, 86 LT 443, 18 TLR 531 .... 58.5, 58.10, 80.1, 80.6
Anderson v Dawson (1808) 15 Ves 532 .... 83.16
Anderson v Dougall (1868) 15 Gr 405 .... 31.1
Anderson's Estate, Re, Anderson v Anderson [1944] P 1, [1943] 2 All ER 609, 113 LJP 25, 87 Sol Jo 431, 169 LT 345, 60 TLR 40 .... 16.2
Anderson's Will, Re (1953) 75 WNNSW 334 .... 16.2

Andree v Ward (1826) 1 Russ 260, 4 LJOS Ch 98 .... 98.4
Andrew, Re, Andrew v Andrew [1934] NZLR 526, GLR 529 .... 38.3
Andrew v Andrew (1845) 1 Coll 686 .... 8.4
Andrew v Andrew (1875) 1 Ch D 410, 45 LJ Ch 232, 24 WR 349, 34 LT 82, CA 93.6, 93.13
Andrew v Master and Wardens of Merchant Taylors' Co. See A-G v Andrew
Andrew v Motley (1862) 12 CBNS 514 .... 18.17
Andrew v Trinity Hall, Cambridge (1804) 9 Ves 525 .... 27.6, 46.3
Andrew v Wrigley (1792) 4 Bro CC 125 .... 25.18
Andrew's Estate, Re, Creasey v Graves (1902) 50 WR 471, 46 Sol Jo 450 ... 38.4, 38.11, 64.45
Andrew's Will, Re (1859) 27 Beav 608, 29 LJ Ch 291, 5 Jur NS 114, 1 LT 319 .... 84.4, 85.5
Andrewes v George (1830) 3 Sim 393 .... 100.5
Andrews, Re [1980] Qd R 317 .... 93.9
Andrews, Re [1985] 2 Qd R 161 .... 67.2
Andrews, Re, Dunedin Corpn v Smyth (1910) 29 NZLR 43 .... 58.11
Andrews, Re, Public Trustee v Vincent [1922] WN 34, 66 Sol Jo 284 .... 39.14
Andrews v Andrews (1885) 15 LR Ir 199, 211, Ir CA 57.18, 58.9
Andrews v Partington (1791) 3 Bro CC 401, [1775–1802] All ER Rep 209 .... 66.12, 66.13, 66.18, 66.21, 217.16
Andrews' Will, Re, Andrews v O'Mara (1899) 25 VLR 408 .... 64.40
Andros, Re, Andros v Andros (1883) 24 Ch D 637, 52 LJ Ch 793, 32 WR 30, [1881–5] All ER Rep 467, 49 LT 163 .... 72.7
Angell Estate, Re (1955) 63 Man R 401, 16 WWR 342 .... 102.7
Angermann v Ford (1861) 29 Beav 349, sub nom Algermann v Ford 7 Jur NS 668, 9 WR 512, 4 LT 230 .... 30.15, 32.6
Angerstein v Martin (1823) 2 LJOS Ch 88 .... 30.31
Angus's Executrix v Batchan's Trustees 1949 SC 335 .... 103.17
Angus's Will Trusts, Re, Hall v Angus [1960] 3 All ER 835, [1960] 1 WLR 1296, 104 Sol Jo 1034 .... 52.11
Annesley, Re, Davidson v Annesley [1926] Ch 692, 95 LJ Ch 404, 135 LT 508, 42 TLR 584 .... 23.13, 24.1, 24.2
Anon (1550) Bro NC 69 .... 64.25
Anon (1574) Jenk 243 .... 35.2
Anon (1588) 1 And 181, Gouldsb 109, sub nom Forse and Hembling's Case 4 Co Rep 60b 4.3, 4.9
Anon (1599) Gouldsb 139. See Wild's Case
Anon (1617). See Webb v Hearing
Anon (1699) 1 Ld Raym 480, sub nom Sir Robert Howard's Case 2 Salk 625, Holt KB 195 .... 4.7
Anon (1703) 2 Eq Cas Abr 212, sub nom Ashton v Ashton Prec Ch 226, sub nom Aston v Aston 2 Vern 452 .... 34.14, 34.23
Anon (1847). See Cunningham v Murray
Anon (1862) 31 Beav 310 .... 30.42
Ansley v Cotton (1846) 16 LJ Ch 55, 8 LTOS 209 .... 30.1
Anstee v Nelms (1856) 1 H & N 225, 26 LJ Ex 5, 4 WR 612, 27 LTOS 190 .... 43.2, 57.12, 57.14, 63.3
Anstee's Goods, Re [1893] P 283, 63 LJP 61, 1 R 487, 42 WR 16 .... 11.3, 14.12
Anstice, Re (1856) 23 Beav 135 .... 97.6

Anstruther v Chalmer (1826) 2 Sim 1, 4 LJOS Ch 123 .... 84.4
Anziani, Re, Herbert v Christopherson [1930] 1 Ch 407, 99 LJ Ch 215, 142 LT 570 .... 1.3, 10.5
Aplin v Stone [1904] 1 Ch 543, 73 LJ Ch 456, 90 LT 284 .... 9.9, 48.7, 50.3, 51.4
Aplin's Trust, Re (1865) 13 WR 1062 .... 42.7
Applebee, Re, Leveson v Beales [1891] 3 Ch 422, 60 LJ Ch 793, 40 WR 90, 65 LT 406 .... 36.1, 57.32
Applebee's Trusts, Re (1873) 21 WR 290, 28 LT 102 .... 93.8
Appleby, Re, Walker v Lever, Walker v Nisbet [1903] 1 Ch 565, 72 LJ Ch 332, 51 WR 455, 47 Sol Jo 334, 88 LT 219, CA 94.37
Appleton, Re, Barber v Tebbit (1885) 29 Ch D 893, 54 LJ Ch 594, 49 JP 708, 53 LT 906, CA 30.14, 210.51
Apreece v Apreece (1813) 1 Ves & B 364 .... 82.7
Arbery v Ashe (1828) 1 Hag Ecc 214 .... 4.18, 4.20
Arbib and Class's Contract, Re [1891] 1 Ch 601, 60 LJ Ch 263, 39 WR 305, 64 LT 217, CA 34.21, 45.1, 203.13
Arbuthnot, Re, Arbuthnot v Arbuthnot [1915] 1 Ch 422, 84 LJ Ch 424, 59 Sol Jo 398, 112 LT 987 .... 100.4
Archbold, Re (1855) 3 WR 582. See Dunn v Bownas
Archbold, Re, McKee v Archbold [1933] NI 47 .... 34.1
Archbold v Austin Gourlay (1880) 5 LR Ir 214 .... 91.1
Archer, Re [1907] 14 OLR 374, 9 OWR 652 .... 48.15
Archer v Jegon (1837) 8 Sim 446, 6 LJ Ch 340, Coop Pr Cas 172, 1 Jur 792 .... 66.1
Archer v Legg (1862) 31 Beav 187, 10 WR 703 .... 87.2
Archer's Goods, Re (1871) LR 2 P & D 252, 35 JP 712, 40 LJP & M 80, 19 WR 785, 25 LT 274 .... 11.12
Archibald, Re [1992] 2 NZLR 109 .... 18.8, 21.5
Archibald v Hartley (1852) 21 LJ Ch 399 .... 64.30
Archibald v Wright (1838) 9 Sim 161, 7 LJ Ch 120, 2 Jur 759 .... 83.12
Ards v Walkin (1598) Cro Eliz 637, sub nom Ardes v Watkins Moore KB 549 .... 7.24
Arkell v Fletcher (1839) 10 Sim 299, 3 Jur 1099 .... 63.1, 64.33, 64.45
Arkitt, Re. See Rickit's Trusts, Re
Armenian Patriarch of Jerusalem v Sonsino [2002] EWHC 1304 (Ch), [2002] All ER (D) 98 (Jul) 102.8
Armitage, Re, Ellam v Norwich Corpn [1972] Ch 438, [1972] 2 WLR 503, 70 LGR 305, 116 Sol Jo 62, sub nom Re Armitage's Will Trusts, Ellam v City and County of Norwich [1972] 1 All ER 708 .... 9.34, 102.7, 103.17
Armitage v Armitage (1868) 16 WR 643 .... 35.4
Armitage v Nurse [1998] Ch 241, [1997] 2 All ER 705, [1997] 3 WLR 1046, [1997] PLR 51, 74 P & CR D13, CA 221.13, 221.16
Armitage v Williams (1859) 27 Beav 346, 7 WR 650 .... 66.5, 66.14, 87.1
Armstrong, Re (1970) 7 DLR (3d) 36 .... 36.1
Armstrong, Re, ex p Gilchrist (1886) 17 QBD 521, 51 JP 292, 55 LJQB 578, 34 WR 709, 55 LT 538, 2 TLR 745, CA 83.2
Armstrong, Re, Ayne v Woodward (1893) 31 LR Ir 154 .... 88.3, 88.4
Armstrong v Armstrong (1871) LR 12 Eq 614, 19 WR 971, 25 LT 199 .... 30.13
Armstrong v Armstrong (1888) 21 LR Ir 114 .... 79.2, 96.4
Armstrong v Buckland (1854) 18 Beav 204 .... 58.10, 63.4

Armstrong v Clavering (1859) 27 Beav 226 .... 30.24
Armstrong v Eldridge (1791) 3 Bro CC 215 .... 101.6
Armstrong v Lynn (1875) IR 9 Eq 186 .... 42.8, 100.2
Armstrong v Reeves (1890) 25 LR Ir 325 .... 9.31
Armstrong v Stockham (1843) 7 Jur 230 .... 87.3
Armstrong's Will Trusts, Re, Graham v Armstrong [1943] Ch 400, [1943] 2 All ER 537, 112 LJ Ch 335, 87 Sol Jo 310, 169 LT 268, 59 TLR 420 .... 92.5
Armytage v Wilkinson (1878) 3 App Cas 355, 47 LJPC 31, 26 WR 559, sub nom Armytage v Master in Equity of Supreme Court of Victoria 38 LT 185, PC 93.1
Arnal Estate, Re (1967) 60 WWR 317 .... 58.2
Arnald v Arnald (1784) 1 Bro CC 401 .... 41.5
Arnander v Customs and Excise Comrs [2006] STC (SCD) 800 .... 234.3
Arndt's Will, Re [1990] WAR 5 .... 67.1
Arning v James [1936] Ch 158, 105 LJ Ch 27, 154 LT 252 .... 203.38
Arnold v Arnold (1834) 2 My & K 365, 4 LJ Ch 79, 123 .... 24.9, 38.10
Arnold v Ennis (1853) 2 I Ch R 601 .... 38.18, 61.1
Arnold's Estate, Re (1863) 33 Beav 163, 9 Jur NS 1186, 12 WR 4, 9 LT 530 .... 52.11, 93.1
Arnold's Trusts, Re (1870) LR 10 Eq 252, 39 LJ Ch 875, 18 WR 912, 23 LT 337 .... 67.6
Arnould, Re, Arnould v Lloyd [1955] 2 All ER 316, [1955] 1 WLR 539, 99 Sol Jo 338 .... 101.8
Arnould v Grinstead (1872) 21 WR 155 .... 64.30
Arrowsmith's Trust, Re (1860) 29 LJ Ch 774, 6 Jur NS 1231, 8 WR 555; on appeal (1860) 2 De GF & J 474, 30 LJ Ch 148, 7 Jur NS 9, 9 WR 258, 3 LT 635 .... 97.7
Arthur v Bokenham (1708) 11 Mod Rep 148, Fitz-G 233 .... 4.10
Arthur v Mackinnon (1879) 11 Ch D 385, 48 LJ Ch 534, 27 WR 704, 41 LT 275 .... 8.7, 204.20
Arthur's Goods, Re (1871) LR 2 P & D 273, 36 JP 168, 19 WR 1016, 25 LT 274 .... 11.2
Ashburner v Macguire (1786) 2 Bro CC 108 .... 30.3, 30.8, 41.11, 41.19
Ashburner v Wilson (1850) 17 Sim 204, 19 LJ Ch 330, 14 Jur 497 .... 53.5, 65.2, 98.3
Ashburnham, Re, Gaby v Ashburnham (1912) 107 LT 601, 57 Sol Jo 28 .... 59.3, 204.41
Ashburnham v Ashburnham (1848) 16 Sim 186, 12 Jur 299 .... 33.34
Ashby v Hayden (1931) 48 WN 61, 31 SRNSW 324 .... 64.39
Ashdown, Re [1943] 4 DLR 517, [1943] OWN 425 .... 41.9
Ashe v Berry (1829) Beat 255 .... 41.19
Asher v Whitlock (1865) LR 1 QB 1, 30 JP 6, 35 LJQB 17, 11 Jur NS 925, 14 WR 26, 13 LT 254 .... 7.30, 43.2
Ashforth, Re, Sibley v Ashforth [1905] 1 Ch 535, [1904–7] All ER Rep 275, sub nom Re Ashforth's Trusts, Ashforth v Sibley 74 LJ Ch 361, 53 WR 328, 49 Sol Jo 350, 92 LT 534, 21 TLR 329 .... 86.7, 94.8, 94.12, 94.33
Ashley v Ashley (1833) 6 Sim 358, 3 LJ Ch 61 .... 93.13
Ashley v Waugh (1839) 9 LJ Ch 31, 4 Jur 572 .... 20.4
Ashling v Knowles (1856) 3 Drew 593 .... 68.4, 210.25
Ashmore's Trusts, Re (1869) LR 9 Eq 99, 39 LJ Ch 202 .... 93.36

Ashton, Re, Ballard v Ashton [1920] 2 Ch 481, 89 LJ Ch 583, 65 Sol Jo 44, 124 LT 374 .... 34.6, 83.8
Ashton, Re, Gordon v Siddall [1950] NZLR 42 .... 102.23
Ashton, Re, Ingram v Papillon [1897] 2 Ch 574, 66 LJ Ch 731, 46 WR 138, 41 Sol Jo 677, 77 LT 49; revsd [1898] 1 Ch 142, 67 LJ Ch 84, 46 WR 231, 77 LT 582, CA 44.1, 44.4, 44.8
Ashton, Re, Siddall v Gordon [1955] NZLR 192 .... 102.17
Ashton v Adamson (1841) 1 Dr & War 198 .... 33.12, 50.21, 62.4, 64.2
Ashton v Ashton (1703). See Anon 2 Eq Cas Abr 212
Ashton v Ashton (1735) 2 Eq Cas Abr 558, Cas temp Talb 152, 3 P Wms 384 .... 30.8, 64.32
Ashton v Lord Langdale (1851) 4 De G & Sm 402, 20 LJ Ch 234, 15 Jur 868, 17 LTOS 175 .... 102.10
Ashton's Charity, Re (1859) 23 JP 469, 27 Beav 115, 5 Jur NS 665, 7 WR 659, 33 LTOS 195 .... 103.14
Ashton's Goods, Re [1892] P 83, 61 LJP 85, 67 LT 325 .... 25.1, 57.22
Ashwell v Lomi (1850) LR 2 P & D 477 .... 4.17, 5.9
Askew v Askew (1888) 57 LJ Ch 629, 36 WR 620, 58 LT 472 .... 83.12
Askew v Woodhead (1880) 14 Ch D 27, 44 JP 570, 49 LJ Ch 320, 28 WR 874, [1874–80] All ER Rep 644, 42 LT 567, CA 38.28
Askham v Barker (1850) 12 Beav 499 .... 40.15, 40.20
Aspinall v Duckworth (1866) 35 Beav 307, 14 WR 527 .... 47.1, 47.30, 47.32, 47.33
Aspinall's Settlement Trusts, Re (1861) 30 LJ Ch 321, 9 WR 269, 4 LT 176 ... 77.1, 79.4
Associated Artists Ltd v IRC [1956] 2 All ER 583, [1956] 1 WLR 752, 36 TC 499, 32 ATC 118, 49 R & IT 434, [1956] TR 127, 100 Sol Jo 450 .... 102.10
Astbury v Astbury [1898] 2 Ch 111, 67 LJ Ch 471, 46 WR 536, 78 LT 494 .... 221.29
Asten v Asten [1894] 3 Ch 260, 63 LJ Ch 834, 8 R 496, 71 LT 228 .... 8.7, 53.1, 53.2, 57.9, 89.1
Astley v Earl of Essex (1871) 6 Ch App 898, 25 LT 470 .... 93.4
Astley v Earl of Essex (1874) LR 18 Eq 290, 43 LJ Ch 817, 22 WR 620, 30 LT 485 .... 35.27, 35.39
Aston v Aston. See Anon (1703)
Aston v Wood (1874) 43 LJ Ch 715, 22 WR 893, 31 LT 293 .... 46.3
Aston's Goods, Re (1881) 6 PD 203, 46 JP 104, 50 LJP 77, 30 WR 92 .... 38.3, 64.35
Astor, Re, Astor v Astor [1922] 1 Ch 364, 91 LJ Ch 277, CA 93.5, 93.6, 93.16, 93.17, 210.49
Atcherley (or Acherley) v Vernon (1723) 10 Mod Rep 518; affd (1725) 1 Com 382, 3 Bro Parl Cas 85, HL 60.1
Atherton v Crowther (1854) 19 Beav 448, 2 WR 639, 24 LTOS 64 .... 79.7
Athill, Re, Athill v Athill (1880) 16 Ch D 211, 50 LJ Ch 123, 29 WR 309, 43 LT 581, CA 50.11
Atkin's Will Trusts, Re, National Westminster Bank Ltd v Atkins [1974] 2 All ER 1, [1974] 1 WLR 761, 118 Sol Jo 391 .... 94.5, 94.11, 94.13
Atkins, Re (1912) 3 DLR 180, 3 OWN 665, 21 OWR 238 .... 30.6
Atkins v Hiccocks (1737) 1 Atk 500, West temp Hard 114 .... 93.27
Atkinson, Re, Atkinson v Weightman [1925] WN 30, CA 20.3
Atkinson, Re, Proctor v Atkinson [1908] 2 Ch 307, 77 LJ Ch 766, 99 LT 174, CA 31.18
Atkinson, Re, Pybus v Boyd [1918] 2 Ch 138, 87 LJ Ch 505, [1918–19] All ER Rep 1043, 119 LT 235 .... 74.1

Atkinson, Re, Webster v Walter [1930] 1 Ch 47, [1929] All ER Rep 491, 99 LJ Ch 35, 142 LT 129 .... 214.7

Atkinson, Re, Wilson v Atkinson [1892] 3 Ch 52, 61 LJ Ch 504, 40 WR 666, 36 Sol Jo 503, 66 LT 717 .... 86.3

Atkinson v Atkinson (1872) IR 6 Eq 184, 189 .... 68.6

Atkinson v Bartrum (1860) 28 Beav 219 .... 87.2

Atkinson v Holtby (1863) 10 HL Cas 313, 32 LJ Ch 735, 9 Jur NS 503, 11 WR 544, 8 LT 583 .... 51.8, 101.13

Atkinson v Hutchinson (1734) 2 Eq Cas Abr 294, 3 P Wms 258 .... 53.2

Atkinson v L'Estrange (1885) 15 LR Ir 340 .... 84.4

Atkinson v Littlewood (1874) LR 18 Eq 595, [1874–80] All ER Rep 203, 31 LT 225 .... 44.15

Atkinson v Morris [1897] P 40, 66 LJP 17, 45 WR 293, 41 Sol Jo 110, 75 LT 440, 13 TLR 83, CA 18.12, 18.29

Atkinson v Paice (1781) 1 Bro CC 91 .... 101.7

Atkinson v Webb (1704) 1 Eq Cas Abr 203, Prec Ch 236, 2 Vern 478 .... 44.15

Atkinson's Goods, Re (1883) 8 PD 165, 47 JP 440, 52 LJP 80, 31 WR 660 .... 12.9, 18.8

Atkinson's Will Trust, Re, Prescott v Child [1957] Ch 117, [1956] 3 All ER 738, [1956] 3 WLR 900, 100 Sol Jo 859 .... 90.5, 219.21

Atkinson's Will Trusts, Re, Atkinson v Hall [1978] 1 All ER 1275, [1978] 1 WLR 586, 122 Sol Jo 148 .... 50.9, 50.11, 53.1, 57.18, 102.23

Attenborough v Attenborough (1855) 1 K & J 296, 25 LTOS 155 .... 94.43

Attenborough (George) & Son v Solomon [1913] AC 76, 82 LJ Ch 178, [1911–13] All ER Rep 155, 57 Sol Jo 76, 107 LT 833, 29 TLR 79, HL 25.9, 25.18

Atter v Atkinson (1869) LR 1 P & D 665, 33 JP 440, 20 LT 404 .... 5.1

A-G v Andrew (1798) 3 Ves 633; affd sub nom Andrew v Master and Wardens of Merchant Taylors' Co (1800) 7 Ves 223, HL 45.1

A-G v Becher [1910] 2 IR 251, 44 ILT 67 .... 102.9

A-G v Bishop of Chester (1785) 1 Bro CC 444 .... 103.11

A-G v Blizard (1855) 20 JP 3, 21 Beav 233, 25 LJ Ch 171, 1 Jur NS 1195, 26 LTOS 181 .... 102.7, 102.9

A-G v Bovill (1840) 1 Ph 762, 4 Jur 548 .... 102.7

A-G v Brackenbury (1863) 1 H & C 782, 32 LJ Ex 108, 9 Jur NS 257, 1 New Rep 334, 11 WR 380, 8 LT 22 .... 46.3, 46.4

A-G v Bristol Corpn (1820) 2 Jac & W 294 .... 103.16

A-G v Buckland (or Bucknall) (1742) 2 Atk 328, cited in Amb 71 .... 103.17

A-G v Buller (1822) Jac 407 .... 103.17

A-G v Bushby (1857) 24 Beav 299 .... 102.10

A-G v Caius College (1837) 2 Keen 150, 6 LJ Ch 282, [1835–42] All ER Rep 701 .... 103.13

A-G v Cast-Plate Glass Co (1792) 1 Anst 39 .... 50.13

A-G v Christ's Hospital (1790) 3 Bro CC 165 .... 45.2

A-G v Coopers' Co (1812) 19 Ves 187, [1803–13] All ER Rep 622 .... 103.18

A-G v Cordwainers' Co (1833) 3 My & K 534 .... 102.20

A-G v Crispin (1784) 1 Bro CC 386 .... 65.3

A-G v Dartmouth Corpn (1883) 48 LT 933 .... 102.9, 102.10, 102.23

A-G v Davies (1802) 9 Ves 535 .... 102.19

A-G v Day [1900] 1 Ch 31, 64 JP 88, 69 LJ Ch 8, 81 LT 806 .... 102.10

A-G v Dean and Canons of Windsor (1860) 24 JP 467, 8 HL Cas 369, 30 LJ Ch 529, 6 Jur NS 833, 8 WR 477, 2 LT 578 .... 103.13, 103.14, 103.15, 103.16
A-G v Dillon (1862) 13 I Ch R 127, 14 Ir Jur 251 .... 52.11
A-G v Doyley. See Doyley v A-G
A-G v Drapers' Co (1840) 2 Beav 508 .... 103.16
A-G v Drapers' Co, Kendrick's Charity (1841) 4 Beav 67 .... 103.14
A-G v Duke of Northumberland (1877) 7 Ch D 745, 47 LJ Ch 569, 26 WR 586; varied (1878) 38 LT 245, CA 102.14
A-G v Earl of Lonsdale (1827) 1 Sim 105, 5 LJOS Ch 99, [1824–34] All ER Rep 666 .... 102.10, 103.11
A-G v Eastlake (1853) 18 JP 262, 11 Hare 205, 2 Eq Rep 145, 17 Jur 801, 1 WR 323, 22 LTOS 20 .... 102.10
A-G v Exeter Corpn (1826) 2 Russ 45 .... 102.7
A-G v Exeter Corpn (1827) 3 Russ 395, 6 LJOS Ch 50 .... 102.7
A-G v Fletcher (1835) 5 LJ Ch 75 .... 103.17
A-G v Fletcher (1871) LR 13 Eq 128, 41 LJ Ch 167, 25 LT 892 .... 68.13, 86.5
A-G v Flood (1816) Hayes & Jo App xxi; affd (1817) Hayes 611 .... 102.8
A-G v Gascoigne (1833) 2 My & K 647, 1 LJ Ch 122 .... 103.16
A-G v George (1836) 8 Sim 138 .... 33.10
A-G v Gill (1726) 2 P Wms 369 .... 84.2
A-G v Gladstone (1842) 6 JP 375, 13 Sim 7, 11 LJ Ch 361, 6 Jur 498 .... 103.1
A-G v Grote (1827) 2 Russ & M 699 .... 30.8, 50.4
A-G v Haberdashers' Co (1834) 1 My & K 420 .... 102.5
A-G v Hird (1782) 1 Bro CC 170 .... 98.12
A-G v Holbrook (1823) 3 Y & J 114, 12 Price 407 .... 30.4, 47.22
A-G v Hollingworth (1857) 2 H & N 416, 27 LJ Ex 102, 5 WR 684, 29 LTOS 184 .... 30.4
A-G v Jefferys [1908] AC 411, 77 LJ Ch 685, 52 Sol Jo 660, 99 LT 737, 24 TLR 793, HL 49.5
A-G v Jesus College, Oxford (1861) 29 Beav 163, 30 LJ Ch 675, 7 Jur NS 592, 9 WR 449, 4 LT 728 .... 102.22
A-G v Jones and Bartlett (1817) 3 Price 368 .... 1.2, 15.3
A-G v Lawes (1849) 8 Hare 32, 19 LJ Ch 300, 14 Jur 77 .... 29.14, 102.7
A-G v Lloyd (1747) 3 Atk 551, 1 Ves Sen 32 .... 19.2, 102.22
A-G v M'Carthy (1885) 12 VLR 535 .... 102.7
A-G v Marchant (1866) LR 3 Eq 424, 36 LJ Ch 47, 12 Jur NS 957, 15 WR 144 .... 102.8, 103.15
A-G v Margaret and Regius Professors in Cambridge (1682) 1 Vern 55, 1 Eq Cas Abr 99 pl 5 .... 102.8
A-G v Mathieson, Re Wilkinson and Fell's Contract [1907] 2 Ch 383, 76 LJ Ch 682, 97 LT 450, 23 TLR 754, CA 102.7
A-G v Matthews. See A-G v Peacock
A-G v Minshull (1798) 4 Ves 11 .... 102.7
A-G v National Provincial and Union Bank of England [1924] AC 262, [1923] All ER Rep 123, 68 Sol Jo 235, 40 TLR 191, sub nom Re Tetley, A-G v National Provincial and Union Bank of England 93 LJ Ch 231, 131 LT 34, HL 1.6, 8.7, 103.17, 212.5
A-G v Painter-Stainers' Co (1788) 2 Cox Eq Cas 51 .... 103.15
A-G v Parker (1747) 3 Atk 576, 1 Ves Sen 43 .... 102.9
A-G v Parnther (1792) 3 Bro CC 441 .... 4.14

A-G v Partington (1864) 3 H & C 193, 33 LJ Ex 281, 10 Jur NS 825, 13 WR 54, 10 LT 751, Ex Ch; on appeal sub nom Partington v A-G (1869) LR 4 HL 100, 38 LJ Ex 205, 21 LT 370 .... 25.15
A-G v Peacock (1676) Cas temp Finch 245, sub nom A-G v Matthews 2 Lev 167 .... 102.7
A-G v Pearce (1740) 2 Atk 87, Barn Ch 208 .... 102.7
A-G v Plowden. See Grove-Grady, Re, Plowden v Lawrence
A-G v Poulden (1844) 3 Hare 555, 8 Jur 611, 3 LTOS 99 .... 33.23, 33.28
A-G v Power (1809) 1 Ball & B 145 .... 102.7
A-G v Price (1810) 17 Ves 371, [1803–13] All ER Rep 467 .... 79.4, 101.9, 102.14
A-G v Rance (1728) cited in (1762) Amb 422 .... 103.1
A-G v Ross [1985] 3 All ER 334, [1986] 1 WLR 252, 130 Sol Jo 184, [1985] LS Gaz R 869 .... 102.8, 102.23
A-G v Rowsell (1844) 36 Ch D 67n, 56 LJ Ch 942n, 36 WR 378n, sub nom Re Rowsell 3 LTOS 105 .... 7.9
A-G v Rye Corpn (1817) 7 Taunt 546, 1 Moore CP 267 .... 58.4
A-G v Shore (1843) 7 JP 302, 11 Sim 592, 7 Jur 781, 1 LTOS 166 .... 102.7
A-G v Sidney Sussex College, Cambridge (1865) 34 Beav 654; on appeal (1866) 21 Ch D 514n, 15 WR 162, 15 LT 518 .... 79.4, 102.8
A-G v Skinners' Co (1833) 5 Sim 596 .... 103.13
A-G v Stepney (1804) 10 Ves 22 .... 102.8, 103.11, 212.11
A-G v Sutton (1721) 3 Bro Parl Cas 75, 1 P Wms 754, HL 98.4
A-G v Trinity College, Cambridge (1856) 24 Beav 383 .... 102.20, 103.16
A-G v Vigor (1803) 8 Ves 256 .... 60.1
A-G v Vint (1850) 3 De G & Sm 704, 19 LJ Ch 150, 14 Jur 824, 15 LTOS 83 .... 102.7, 103.11
A-G v Wansay (1808) 15 Ves 231 .... 102.7
A-G v Ward (1797) 3 Ves 327 .... 102.22
A-G v Wax Chandlers' Co (1873) LR 6 HL 1, 37 JP 532, 42 LJ Ch 425, 21 WR 361, 28 LT 681 .... 91.2, 102.20, 103.13
A-G v Webster (1875) LR 20 Eq 483, 44 LJ Ch 766 .... 102.26
A-G v Wilkinson (1839) 1 Beav 370, 3 Jur 358 .... 103.1
A-G v Wilson (1834) 3 My & K 362, 3 LJ Ch 126 .... 103.13
A-G for New South Wales v Perpetual Trustee Co Ltd (1940) 63 CLR 209, 46 ALR 209 (Aust HC), 14 ALJ 122 .... 103.1
A-G for New Zealand v Brown [1917] AC 393, [1916–17] All ER Rep 245, 86 LJPC 132, 116 LT 624, 33 TLR 294, [1917] NZPCC 698 .... 102.23
A-G for New Zealand v New Zealand Insurance Co Ltd [1936] 3 All ER 888, 80 Sol Jo 912, 53 TLR 37, PC 1.6
A-G for Northern Ireland v Forde [1932] NI 1, CA 102.7
A-G of New South Wales v Henry George Foundation Ltd (2002–03) 5 ITELR 568, SC NSW 102.8
A-G of the Bahamas v Royal Trust Co [1986] 3 All ER 423, [1986] 1 WLR 1001, 130 Sol Jo 526, [1986] LS Gaz R 2487, PC 102.23
A-G of the Cayman Islands v Wahr-Hansen [2001] 1 AC 75, [2000] 3 All ER 642, [2000] 3 WLR 869, PC 102.23
Attree v Attree (1871) LR 11 Eq 280, 40 LJ Ch 192, 19 WR 464, 24 LT 121 .... 38.3, 38.4
Attwater v Attwater (1853) 18 Beav 330, 23 LJ Ch 692, 18 Jur 50, 2 WR 81, 22 LTOS 150 .... 58.6, 63.3, 93.14, 93.17, 99.2, 101.14

Attwood v Alford (1866) LR 2 Eq 479, 14 WR 956 .... 33.18, 68.2

Atwell v Atwell (1871) LR 13 Eq 23, 41 LJ Ch 23, 20 WR 108, 25 LT 526 ... 37.2, 37.3

Aubin v Daly (1820) 4 B & Ald 59 .... 33.12

Audsley v Horn (1858) 26 Beav 195, 1 F & F 135, 28 LJ Ch 293, 4 Jur NS 1267, 7 WR 125, 32 LTOS 203; affd (1859) 1 De GF & J 226, 29 LJ Ch 201, 6 Jur NS 205, 8 WR 150, 1 LT 317 .... 84.4, 85.3

Auerbach's Estate, Re, Union Fidelity Trustee Co of Australia Ltd v Proctor [1974] NSWLR 57 .... 68.8

Auger v Beaudry [1920] AC 1010, 89 LJPC 251, 124 LT 106, PC 67.1, 67.5, 98.7

Augustine v Schrier (1889) 18 OR 192 .... 30.3

Auldjo v Wallace (1862) 31 Beav 193 .... 91.5

Austen v Collins (1886) 54 LT 903 .... 35.42

Austen v Graham (1854) 8 Moo PCC 493, 1 Ecc & Ad 357, 24 LTOS 37 .... 4.18

Auster v Powell (1863) 1 De GJ & Sm 99, 9 Jur NS 421, 8 LT 73 .... 100.6

Austin's Estate, Re (1929) 73 Sol Jo 545, P, D and Admlty 5.1

Austin, Re, Austin v Trotter [1962] NZLR 516 .... 76.3

Austin v Beddoe (1893) 3 R 580, 41 WR 619, 37 Sol Jo 456 .... 38.16

Austin v Tawney (1867) 2 Ch App 143, 36 LJ Ch 339, 15 WR 463 ...... 34.22, 92.3, 92.4

Austin's Estate, Re, Sullivan and Lee v Cameron [1949] 1 WWR 1041 .... 10.8

Auther v Auther (1843) 13 Sim 422, 7 Jur 410, 1 LTOS 106 .... 30.8

Avard, Re, Hook v Parker [1948] Ch 43, [1947] 2 All ER 548, [1948] LJR 354, 91 Sol Jo 613, 63 TLR 567 .... 34.21, 92.1, 92.4, 209.2, 209.5

Avelyn v Ward (1750) 1 Ves Sen 420 .... 93.19

Avenon's Charity, Re, A-G v Pelly (1912) 56 Sol Jo 241, 106 LT 295 ..... 103.13, 103.18

Avenon's Charity, Re, A-G v Pelly [1913] 2 Ch 261, 82 LJ Ch 398, 57 Sol Jo 626, 109 LT 98 .... 103.13

Averill, Re, Salsbury v Buckle [1898] 1 Ch 523, 67 LJ Ch 233, 46 WR 460, 78 LT 320 .... 32.28

Avery, Re, Pinsent v Avery [1913] 1 Ch 208, 82 LJ Ch 434, 57 Sol Jo 112, 108 LT 1, CA 55.7

Avison v Holmes (1861) 1 John & H 530, 30 LJ Ch 564, 7 Jur NS 722, 9 WR 550, 4 LT 617 .... 30.12, 99.8

Avison v Simpson (1859) John 43, 5 Jur NS 594, 7 WR 277, 33 LTOS 27 .... 64.25, 77.1

Axford, Re (1860) 1 Sw & Tr 540, 8 WR 340, 2 LT 86 .... 5.2

Aydit's Estate, Re, Bergermann v Aydit (1965) 54 DLR (2d) 771, [1965] 55 WWR 315 .... 102.23, 103.17

Ayer v Benton (1967) 204 Estates Gazette 359 .... 38.3

Ayles' Trusts, Re (1875) 1 Ch D 282, 40 JP 181, 45 LJ Ch 223, 24 WR 202 .... 72.2

Aylwin's Trusts, Re (1873) LR 16 Eq 585, 42 LJ Ch 745, 21 WR 864, 28 LT 865 .... 66.9

Aynsley, Re, Kyrle v Turner [1914] 2 Ch 422, 83 LJ Ch 807, 50 Sol Jo 754, 111 LT 525, 30 TLR 664; on appeal [1915] 1 Ch 172, 84 LJ Ch 211, 59 Sol Jo 128, 112 LT 433, 31 TLR 101, CA 20.4, 22.4, 41.3, 44.2, 44.11

Ayrey v Hill (1824) 2 Add 206 .... 4.19

Ayscough v Savage (1865) 13 WR 373 .... 87.2

Ayton v Ayton (1787) 1 Cox Eq Cas 327, 1 Bro CC 542n 66.8

B

B, Re [1999] Ch 206, [1999] 2 All ER 425, [1999] 2 WLR 1114, [1999] 2 FCR 145, sub nom Bouette v Rose [1999] 2 FLR 466, [1999] Fam Law 303; revsd sub nom B, Re [2000] Ch 662, [2000] 1 All ER 665, [2000] 2 WLR 929, [2000] 1 FCR 385, sub nom Bouette v Rose [2000] 1 FLR 363, [2000] Fam Law 316, [2000] NLJR 20, CA 105.3, 105.5, 105.18, 105.29
B, Re, O v D [1916] 1 IR 364 .... 72.3
Babcock, Re (1892) 9 Gr 427 .... 34.6
Bacchus v Gilbee (1863) 3 De GJ & Sm 577, 9 Jur NS 838, 2 New Rep 502, 11 WR 1049, 8 LT 714 .... 64.53
Bacharach's Will Trusts, Re, Minden v Bacharach [1959] Ch 245, [1958] 3 All ER 618, [1959] 2 WLR 1, 103 Sol Jo 16 .... 52.5
Backhouse, Re, Findlay v Backhouse [1921] 2 Ch 51, 90 LJ Ch 443, 65 Sol Jo 580, 125 LT 218 .... 94.2, 94.30
Backhouse, Re, Salmon v Backhouse [1916] 1 Ch 65, 85 LJ Ch 146, 60 Sol Jo 121, 114 LT 39 .... 91.6, 237.11
Backhouse, Re, Westminster Bank Ltd v Shaftesbury School and Ragged School Union [1931] WN 168, 172 LT Jo 10, 71 L Jo 79 .... 48.4
Backwell v Child (1755) Amb 260 .... 41.15
Bacon, Re, Grissel v Leathes (1893) 62 LJ Ch 445, 3 R 459, 41 WR 478, 37 Sol Jo 340, 68 LT 522 .... 38.27
Bacon v Cosby (1851) 4 De G & Sm 261, 20 LJ Ch 213, 15 Jur 695, 17 LTOS 239 .... 98.13
Bacon v Pianta (1965) 40 ALJR 187 .... 9.35
Bacon v Pianta (1966) 114 CLR 634, [1966] ALR 1044, HC of A 102.11
Bacon v Proctor (1822) Turn & R 31 .... 93.4
Bacon's Goods, Re (1859) 23 JP 712 .... 18.21
Bacon's Will, Re, Camp v Coe (1886) 31 Ch D 460, 55 LJ Ch 368, 34 WR 319, 54 LT 150, 2 TLR 278, DC 57.31
Baddeley v IRC [1953] Ch 504, [1953] 2 All ER 233, [1953] 3 WLR 135, 31 ATC 524, 46 R & IT 44, [1953] TR 485, 97 Sol Jo 436, CA; revsd sub nom IRC v Baddeley [1955] AC 572, [1955] 1 All ER 525, [1955] 2 WLR 552, 35 TC 661, 34 ATC 22, 48 R & IT 157, 99 Sol Jo 166, HL 102.7, 102.8, 102.10, 102.12
Baddeley v Leppingwell (1764) 3 Burr 1533, Wilm 228 .... 50.2
Baden's Deed Trusts (No 2), Re [1973] Ch 9, [1972] 2 All ER 1304, [1972] 3 WLR 250, 116 Sol Jo 356, CA 34.10, 39.31, 53.6
Badenach's Goods, Re (1864) 28 JP 711, 33 LJPM & A 179, 10 Jur NS 521, 3 Sw & Tr 465, 11 LT 275 .... 25.12
Badge v Floyd (1699) 1 Com 62, sub nom Badger v Lloyd 1 Ld Raym 523, 1 Salk 232; affd sub nom Badge v Floyd (1701) 1 Ld Raym 523, HL 98.9
Badger v Lloyd. See Badge v Floyd
Bagge v Bagge [1921] 1 IR 213 .... 38.1
Bagnall, Re, Scale v Willett [1948] WN 324, [1949] LJR 1, 92 Sol Jo 485 .... 88.3, 88.4
Bagot, Re, Paton v Ormerod [1893] 3 Ch 348, 62 LJ Ch 1006, 37 Sol Jo 730, 69 LT 399, CA 38.1, 52.11
Bagot v Legge (1864) 34 LJ Ch 156, 10 Jur NS 994, 4 New Rep 492, 12 WR 1097, 10 LT 898 .... 35.39

Bagot's Settlement, Re (1862) 31 LJ Ch 772, 10 WR 607, 6 LT 774 .... 41.5
Bagots Executors and Trustees Co Ltd v Bathern (1982) 15 NTR 3 .... 20.3
Bagshaw, Re, Westminster Bank Ltd v Taylor [1954] 1 All ER 227, [1954] 1 WLR 238, 98 Sol Jo 78 .... 103.10
Bagshaw's Trusts, Re (1877) 46 LJ Ch 567, 25 WR 659, 36 LT 749, CA 8.4, 52.1, 52.10, 82.3
Bagwell v Dry (1721) 2 Eq Cas Abr 344, 1 P Wms 700 .... 47.6
Bailey, Re (1974) 47 DLR (3d) 670 .... 5.9
Bailey, Re, Bailey v Working Ladies Guild (1931) 75 Sol Jo 415 .... 103.3
Bailey, Re, Barclay's Bank Ltd v James [1945] Ch 191, [1945] 1 All ER 616, 114 LJ Ch 147, 89 Sol Jo 130, 172 LT 333, 61 TLR 256 .... 38.9, 38.12
Bailey, Re, Barrett v Hyder [1951] Ch 407, [1951] 1 All ER 391, 95 Sol Jo 155, CA 93.9
Bailey v Frowan (1871) 19 WR 511 .... 13.1
Bailey v Hammond (1802) 7 Ves 590 .... 31.19
Bailey's Goods, Re (1838) 1 Curt 914 .... 11.21
Baillie, Re, Faithful v Sydney Industrial Blind Institution (1907) 7 SRNSW 265 .... 94.30
Baillie v Butterfield (1787) 1 Cox Eq Cas 392 .... 25.15, 88.2
Bain, Re, Public Trustee v Ross [1930] 1 Ch 224, [1929] All ER Rep 387, 99 LJ Ch 171, 142 LT 344, 45 TLR 617, CA 102.17
Bain v Lescher (1840) 11 Sim 397 .... 47.32, 85.3
Bainbridge, Re, Darell v Bainbridge [1948] Ch 717, [1948] 2 All ER 657, [1949] LJR 625, 92 Sol Jo 485 .... 218.90
Bainbridge v Bainbridge (1838) 9 Sim 16, 7 LJ Ch 4, 2 Jur 63 .... 64.39
Bainbridge v Cream (1852) 16 Beav 25, 19 LTOS 151 .... 66.10, 93.20
Baines v Ottey (1832) 1 My & K 465, 1 LJ Ch 210 .... 83.16
Baird v Baird [1990] 2 AC 548, [1990] 2 All ER 300, [1990] 2 WLR 1412, [1990] ICR 525, [1991] Fam Law 96, 134 Sol Jo 725, [1990] 23 LS Gaz R 28, PC 1.3, 1.9, 7.13, 10.11
Baird's Trustees v Crombie 1926 SC 518 .... 87.2
Baker, Re, Baker v Baker [1904] 1 Ch 157, 73 LJ Ch 172, 52 WR 213, 48 Sol Jo 101, 89 LT 742 .... 99.10
Baker, Re, Baker v Baker [1929] 1 Ch 668, 98 LJ Ch 174, 141 LT 29 ... 18.10, 21.6, 21.8
Baker, Re, Steadman v Dicksee [1934] WN 94, 78 Sol Jo 336, CA 38.2, 39.4, 47.36
Baker v Baker (1847) 6 Hare 269, 11 Jur 585 .... 52.8, 87.1
Baker v Baker (1858) 6 HL Cas 616, 4 Jur NS 491, 6 WR 410, 31 LTOS 62 .... 33.23
Baker v Bayldon (1862) 31 Beav 209 .... 76.3
Baker v Blount [1917] 1 IR 316 .... 62.1
Baker v Dening (1838) 8 Ad & El 94, 7 LJQB 137, 1 Will Woll & H 148, sub nom Taylor v Dening 2 Jur 775, 3 Nev & PKB 228 .... 11.13
Baker v Farmer (1867) LR 4 Eq 382, 36 LJ Ch 819, 15 WR 917, 17 LT 46; on appeal (1868) 3 Ch App 537, 37 LJ Ch 820, 16 WR 923 .... 29.1, 29.14
Baker v Martin (1836) 8 Sim 25, 5 LJ Ch 205 .... 30.15, 33.17
Baker v Merckel [1960] 1 QB 657, [1960] 1 All ER 668, [1960] 2 WLR 492, 104 Sol Jo 231, CA 41.20
Baker v Newton (1839) 2 Beav 112, 8 LJ Ch 306, 3 Jur 649, 48 ER 1122 ...... 53.5, 57.9
Baker v Simes (1902) 21 NZLR 184 .... 10.8
Baker v Smith (1853) 1 WR 490 .... 62.1
Baker v Tucker (1850) 3 HL Cas 106, 14 Jur 771 .... 98.3

Baker Estate v Myhre [1995] 6 WWR 410 .... 4.10, 5.9
Baker's Estate, Re, Baker v Baker (1858) 6 HL Cas 616, 27 LJ Ch 417, 4 Jur NS 491, 6 WR 410, 31 LTOS 62 .... 33.27, 49.1
Baker's Settlement Trusts, Re, Hunt v Baker [1908] WN 161 .... 50.19
Baker's Will, Re, ex p Cochrane [1964–5] NSWR 1805 .... 14.1
Baker's Will, Re, Baker v Hutchinson [1905] VLR 416 .... 62.1
Balakian, Re [1952] Argus LR 781 .... 38.3
Balchin, Re, Havenhand v Perugia (1922) 67 Sol Jo 12, 38 TLR 868 .... 64.58
Bald, Re, Bald v Bald (1897) 66 LJ Ch 524, 45 WR 499, 41 Sol Jo 490, 76 LT 462 .... 39.5
Baldry v Feintuck [1972] 2 All ER 81, [1972] 1 WLR 552, 115 Sol Jo 965 .... 102.8, 102.11, 102.23
Baldwin v Rogers (1853) 3 De GM & G 649, 22 LJ Ch 665, 17 Jur 267, 21 LTOS 70, 22 LTOS 29 .... 66.6, 66.19, 68.10, 68.15
Balfour v Cooper (1883) 23 Ch D 472, 52 LJ Ch 495, 31 WR 569, 48 LT 323, CA 32.33
Balfour v Scott (1793) 6 Bro Parl Cas 550, HL 23.16, 23.17
Balkind, Re [1969] NZLR 669 .... 34.11
Balkwill v Smith (1957) 65 Man R 55, 21 WWR 474 .... 3.3, 3.6
Ball, Re [1899] 2 IR 313, 33 ILT 42, CA 30.40
Ball, Re, Jones v Jones [1930] WN 111, 74 Sol Jo 298 .... 200.58, 214.3
Ball, Re, Lucas v Ball [1940] 4 All ER 245 .... 33.36, 33.39
Ball, Re, Slattery v Ball (1888) 40 Ch D 11, 58 LJ Ch 232, 37 WR 37, 59 LT 800, CA 96.4
Ball v Church of Ascension (Rector and Churchwardens) (1883) 5 OR 386 .... 88.2
Ballantyne v Evans (1886) 13 R 652, 23 SLR 449, Ct of Sess 4.15
Ballard v Marsden (1880) 14 Ch D 374, [1874–80] All ER Rep 999, 49 LJ Ch 614, 28 WR 914, 42 LT 763 .... 29.14, 30.11
Balls, Re, Trewby v Balls [1909] 1 Ch 791, 78 LJ Ch 341, 100 LT 780 .... 214.26
Balm v Balm (1830) 3 Sim 492 .... 66.18
Balme's Goods, Re [1897] P 261, 66 LJP 161, 77 LT 219, 13 TLR 365 .... 15.1
Bamfield v Popham. See Popham v Bamfield
Bamford v Chadwick. See Bamford v Lord
Bamford v Lord (1854) 14 CB 708, sub nom Bamford v Chadwick 23 LJCP 172, 1 Jur NS 139, 2 WR 531, 2 CLR 1757 .... 98.7
Bamgbose v Daniel [1955] AC 107, [1954] 3 All ER 263, [1954] 3 WLR 561, 98 Sol Jo 732, PC 72.7, 74.1
Bancroft, Re, Bancroft v Bancroft [1928] Ch 577, 97 LJ Ch 245, 139 LT 372, 43 TLR 591 .... 41.4, 59.3, 61.1
Bancroft, Re, Eastern Trust Co v Calder [1936] 4 DLR 571 .... 86.2
Bandon (Earl) v Moreland [1910] 1 IR 220 .... 8.7, 94.28
Banfield, Re, Lloyds Bank Ltd v Smith [1968] 2 All ER 276, [1968] 1 WLR 846, 112 Sol Jo 396 .... 102.9
Bangham's Goods, Re (1876) 1 PD 429, 24 WR 712, sub nom Re Baugham's Goods 40 JP 487, 45 LJP 80 .... 21.2, 21.6
Bangs Estate, Re, Royal Trust Co and Bangs (Bangs Estate) v Bangs (1962) 38 DLR (2d) 99, 39 WWR 623 .... 64.35
Banham, Re, Westminster Bank Ltd v A-G (1931) 75 Sol Jo 311, 47 TLR 376 .... 64.45

Bank of Credit and Commerce International SA (in liquidation) v Ali [2001] UKHL 8, [2002] 1 AC 251, [2001] 1 All ER 961, [2001] 2 WLR 735, [2001] ICR 337, [2001] IRLR 292, 151 NLJ 351, (2001) Times, 6 March, 145 Sol Jo LB 67, [2001] All ER (D) 06 (Mar) 50.1
Bank of Ireland v McCarthy [1898] AC 181, 67 LJPC 13, 77 LT 777, HL 82.1
Bankes v Holme (1821) 1 Russ 304n 98.9
Bankes v Holme (1821) 1 Russ 394n, HL 98.9
Bankes v Le Despencer (1840) 10 Sim 576, 9 LJ Ch 185, 4 Jur 601 .... 94.15
Banko Estate, Re [1958] 12 DLR (2d) 515, [1958] OR 213, [1958] OWN 160 .... 83.15
Banks v Braithwaite (1863) 32 LJ Ch 198, 9 Jur NS 294, 1 New Rep 306, 11 WR 298, 8 LT 80 .... 83.7, 99.1
Banks v Goodfellow (1870) LR 5 QB 549, [1861–73] All ER Rep 47, 39 LJQB 237, 22 LT 813 .... 4.9, 4.10, 4.11, 4.13, 4.17, 244.145
Banks v National Westminster Bank plc [2006] WTLR 1693 .... 41.1
Banks' Trustees v Banks' Trustees 1907 SC 125 .... 68.8
Banks' Trusts, Re, ex p Hovill (1855) 2 K & J 387 .... 83.9, 84.4, 99.1
Banks' Will, Re, Public Trustee v Eaves (1901) 20 NZLR 436 .... 47.29
Bannatyne and Bannatyne v Bannatyne (1852) 2 Rob Eccl 472, 16 Jur 864 .... 4.14, 4.20
Bannerman's Estate, Re, Bannerman v Young (1882) 21 Ch D 105, 51 LJ Ch 449 .... 33.47
Bannister, Re [1985] 2 Qd R 246 .... 64.10, 64.40
Bannister, Re, Heys-Jones v Bannister (1921) 90 LJ Ch 415, 125 LT 54 .... 83.9
Bannister v Lang (1867) 17 LT 137 .... 84.4
Banton v Banton (1998) 164 DLR (4th) 176 .... 4.11, 5.9
Barber, Re, Burgess v Vinnicome (1886) 31 Ch D 665, 55 LJ Ch 373, 34 WR 395, 54 LT 375 .... 9.11
Barber v Barber (1838) 3 My & Cr 688, 8 LJ Ch 36, 2 Jur 1029 .... 47.32
Barber v Wood (1877) 4 Ch D 885, 46 LJ Ch 728, 36 LT 373 .... 58.12, 63.3
Barclay, Re, Gardner v Barclay [1929] 2 Ch 173, [1929] All ER Rep 272, 98 LJ Ch 410, 141 LT 447, 45 TLR 406, CA 81.5
Barclay v Barclay [1970] 2 QB 677, [1970] 2 All ER 676, [1970] 3 WLR 82, 21 P & CR 908, 215 Estates Gazette 439, 114 Sol Jo 456, CA 215.8
Barclay v Collett (1838) 4 Bing NC 658, 7 LJCP 235, 1 Arn 287, 6 Scott 408 .... 60.2
Barclay v Maskelyne (1858) 22 JP 786, John 124, 28 LJ Ch 15, 4 Jur NS 1293, 1294, 5 Jur NS 12, 7 WR 43, 32 LTOS 205 .... 18.8, 102.7
Barclay v Owen (1889) 60 LT 220 .... 29.1, 29.2, 29.9, 29.13, 29.15, 29.19
Barclay v Wainwright (1797) 3 Ves 462 .... 33.10, 88.4
Barden v Meagher (1867) 1 IR Eq 246 .... 33.12
Barfield, Re, Goodman v Child (1901) 84 LT 28 .... 64.7
Barfoot v Lee (1905) 50 Sol Jo 44 .... 64.26
Baring v Ashburton (1886) 54 LT 463 .... 42.15, 50.19, 58.2
Baring's Settlement Trusts, Re, Baring Bros & Co Ltd v Liddell [1940] Ch 737, [1940] 3 All ER 20, 109 LJ Ch 337, 84 Sol Jo 382, 163 LT 403, 56 TLR 777 .... 99.8
Barke's Goods, Re (1845) 4 Notes of Cases 44 .... 22.1, 22.3
Barker, Re [1964] NZLR 299 .... 31.1
Barker, Re [1995] 2 VR 439 .... 18.5, 18.26, 23.13
Barker, Re, Asquith v Saville (1882) 51 LJ Ch 835, 47 LT 38 .... 68.6

Barker, Re, Buxton v Campbell [1892] 2 Ch 491, 62 LJ Ch 76, 66 LT 848 .... 30.38
Barker, Re, Gilbey v Barker [1918] 1 Ch 128, 87 LJ Ch 166, 62 Sol Jo 142, 118 LT 206 .... 100.4
Barker, Re, Sherrington v Dean and Chapter of St Paul's Cathedral (1909) 25 TLR 753 .... 102.10, 102.22
Barker v Barker (1852) 5 De G & Sm 753, 21 LJ Ch 794, 17 Jur 125, 19 LTOS 268 .... 68.11
Barker v Barker (1870) LR 10 Eq 438, 39 LJ Ch 825 .... 45.2
Barker v Cocks (1843) 6 Beav 82 .... 97.6
Barker v Gyles (1727) 3 Bro Parl Cas 104 .... 86.3
Barker v Lea (1814) 3 Ves & B 113 .... 66.1
Barker v Lea (1823) Turn & R 413 .... 90.1
Barker v Rayner (1826) 2 Russ 122 .... 30.6, 41.11
Barker v Young (1864) 33 Beav 353, 33 LJ Ch 279, 10 Jur NS 163, 3 New Rep 350, 12 WR 659, 9 LT 704; affd sub nom Earle v Barker (1865) 11 HL Cas 280, 13 LT 29 .... 40.7, 56.7
Barker's Settlement, Re, Knocker v Vernon Jones [1920] 1 Ch 527, 89 LJ Ch 209, 123 LT 41 .... 39.28
Barker's Trusts, Re (1883) 52 LJ Ch 565, 48 LT 573 .... 84.4
Barker's Will Trusts, Re, Barker v Crouch [1948] WN 155, 92 Sol Jo 323, 64 TLR 273 .... 102.9
Barklie, Re, McClamont v Barklie [1917] 1 IR 1 .... 33.20, 62.3, 83.7
Barksdale v Gilliat (1818) 1 Swan 562 .... 50.4, 57.20
Barksdale v Morgan (1693) 4 Mod Rep 185 .... 50.12
Barkwell v Barkwell [1928] P 91, [1927] All ER Rep 138, 72 Sol Jo 69, 44 TLR 207, sub nom Re Barkwell's Estate, Barkwell v Barkwell 97 LJP 53, 138 LT 526 .... 18.12, 21.4
Barkworth v Barkworth (1906) 75 LJ Ch 754 .... 96.2, 96.4
Barlow v Bateman (1735) 2 Bro Parl Cas 272 .... 58.11
Barlow v Grant (1684) 1 Vern 255, [1558–1774] All ER Rep 198 .... 82.7
Barlow v Salter (1810) 17 Ves 479 .... 98.10
Barlow's Will Trusts, Re [1979] 1 All ER 296, [1979] 1 WLR 278, 122 Sol Jo 646 .... 8.7, 34.9, 35.29, 53.6, 79.2
Barnaby v Tassell (1871) LR 11 Eq 363, 19 WR 323, 24 LT 221 ... 38.11, 66.8, 87.2, 87.3
Barnard v Birch [1919] 2 IR 404 .... 16.3
Barnard Estate, Re [1948] 2 WWR 879 .... 41.5
Barnardiston v Fane (1699) 2 Vern 366 .... 34.25
Barnardo's Homes v Special Income Tax Comrs. See R v Income Tax Special Purposes Comrs, ex p Dr Barnardo's Homes National Incorporated Association
Barnes, Re [1954] NZLR 714 .... 10.7
Barnes, Re, Ashenden v Heath [1940] Ch 267, 109 LJ Ch 102, 84 Sol Jo 151, 162 LT 263, 56 TLR 356 .... 7.9, 10.11
Barnes, Re, Simpson v Barnes [1930] 2 Ch 80n, 99 LJ Ch 380n, 143 LT 332n 212.7
Barnes v Crowe (1792) 1 Ves 485, 4 Bro CC 2 .... 22.2
Barnes v Cunningham [1933] 3 DLR 653 .... 3.3
Barnes v Grant (1856) 26 LJ Ch 92, 2 Jur NS 1127, 5 WR 14, 28 LTOS 78 .... 82.5
Barnes v Jennings (1866) LR 2 Eq 448, 35 LJ Ch 675, 14 WR 831 .... 93.19
Barnes v Patch (1803) 8 Ves 604 .... 79.1, 87.1

Barnes v Rowley (1797) 3 Ves 305 .... 33.6
Barnes v Whittaker (1893) 14 NSW Eq 148 .... 97.7
Barnes Estate v Wilson (1992) 91 DLR (4th) 22 .... 74.1
Barnes Goods, Re, Hodson v Barnes (1926) 96 LJP 26, 136 LT 380, 43 TLR 71 .... 10.14, 16.3
Barnes' Will Trusts, Re, Prior v Barnes [1972] 2 All ER 639, [1972] 1 WLR 587, 116 Sol Jo 336 .... 38.3, 50.12, 50.14, 64.35, 64.36, 64.37, 64.40
Barnesly v Powel (1748) 1 Ves Sen 119 .... 25.15
Barnesly v Powel (1749) 1 Ves Sen 284 .... 25.15, 49.7
Barnet v Barnet (1861) 29 Beav 239 .... 93.1, 101.4
Barnett, Re, Dawes v Ixer [1908] 1 Ch 402, 77 LJ Ch 267, 52 Sol Jo 224, 98 LT 346 .... 39.2
Barnett, Re, Waring v Painter Stainers' Co (1908) 24 TLR 788 .... 102.26
Barnett v Sheffield (1852) 1 De GM & G 371, 21 LJ Ch 692, 16 Jur 942, 91 RR 122 .... 29.15, 30.17
Barnett's Trusts, Re [1902] 1 Ch 847, 71 LJ Ch 408, 50 WR 681, 86 LT 346, 18 TLR 454 .... 23.16
Barnett's Will, Re, Bradbury v Barnett [1919] VLR 524 .... 52.6
Barns v Barns [2005] WTLR 1093, Aust HC 2.3, 3.12, 105.42. 105.49
Barnshaw's Trusts, Re (1867) 15 WR 378 .... 93.37
Barr, Re [1947] 3 DLR 784, [1947] OR 557, OWN 574 .... 32.4
Barraclough, Re, Barraclough v Young [1967] P 1, [1965] 2 All ER 311, [1965] 3 WLR 1023, 109 Sol Jo 134 .... 25.16
Barraclough v Cooper [1908] 2 Ch 121n, 77 LJ Ch 555n, 98 LT 852, HL 49.5, 50.18, 51.8, 68.9
Barralet v A-G [1980] 3 All ER 918, sub nom Re South Place Ethical Society, Barralet v A-G [1980] 1 WLR 1565, 54 TC 446, [1980] TR 217, 124 Sol Jo 744 .... 102.8, 102.9, 102.10
Barrance, Re, Barrance v Ellis [1910] 2 Ch 419, 79 LJ Ch 544, 54 Sol Jo 651, 103 LT 104 .... 25.15, 49.7
Barrass v Harding [2001] 1 FCR 297, [2001] 1 FLR 138, [2000] Fam Law 878, CA 105.9
Barrat, Re, Body v Barrat [1929] 1 Ch 336, 98 LJ Ch 74, 140 LT 328 .... 67.3
Barratt, Re, Barratt v Coates (1915) 31 TLR 502, CA 64.6
Barratt, Re, National Provincial Bank Ltd v Barratt [1925] Ch 550, 94 LJ Ch 345, [1925] All ER Rep 193, 133 LT 133 .... 38.23
Barret v Beckford (1750) 1 Ves Sen 519 .... 44.15
Barrett, Re, Beard v Barrett [1955] SCR 93, [1953] OR 897 .... 33.30
Barrett v White (1855) 24 LJ Ch 724, 1 Jur NS 652, 3 WR 578 .... 38.3, 64.35
Barrett's Will, Re (1876) 2 VLR 98 .... 18.25
Barretto v Young [1900] 2 Ch 339, 69 LJ Ch 605, 83 LT 154 .... 24.12
Barrington (Viscount) v Liddell (1852) 2 De GM & G 480, 22 LJ Ch 1, 17 Jur 241, 1 WR 41, 20 LTOS 133 .... 95.11
Barrington v Tristram (1801) 6 Ves 345 .... 32.2, 66.12, 66.18, 74.1
Barrow v Methold (1855) 1 Jur NS 994, 3 WR 629, 26 LT 56 .... 57.6
Barrs v Fewkes (1864) 2 Hem & M 60, 33 LJ Ch 484, 10 Jur NS 466, 3 New Rep 704, 12 WR 66, 10 LT 232 .... 82.5
Barrs v Fewkes (1865) 34 LJ Ch 522, 11 Jur NS 669, 6 New Rep 355, 13 WR 987, 12 LT 727 .... 57.31
Barrs v Jackson (1845) 1 Ph 582, 14 LJ Ch 433, 9 Jur 609, 5 LTOS 365 .... 49.7

Barry, Re (1911) 30 NZLR 1192 .... 20.2
Barry v Butlin. See Butlin v Barry
Barry v Crundall (1835) 7 Sim 430, 4 LJ Ch 264 .... 91.6
Barry v Harding (1844) 7 I Eq R 313, 1 Jo & Lat 475 .... 44.4, 64.53
Bartholomew and Brown v Henley (1820) 3 Phillim 317 .... 88.3
Bartholomew's Trust, Re (1849) 19 LJ Ch 237, 1 H & Tw 565, 14 Jur 181, 1 Mac & G 354 .... 93.27
Bartholomew's Trustees v Bartholomew (1904) 41 SLR 259, 6 F 322, 11 SLT 608 .... 90.1
Bartleman v Murchison (1831) 2 Russ & M 136, 9 LJOS Ch 60 .... 65.1, 66.4
Bartlett v Barclays Bank Trust Co Ltd [1980] Ch 515, [1980] 1 All ER 139, [1980] 2 WLR 430, 124 Sol Jo 85 .... 221.15, 221.17, 221.21, 237.28
Bartlett v Gillard (1827) 3 Russ 149, 6 LJOS 19, 38 ER 532 .... 44.15
Barton, Re, Barton v Bourne (1932) 48 TLR 205 .... 15.5
Barton v Barton (1857) 3 K & J 512, 3 Jur NS 808 .... 34.6
Barton v Cooke (1800) 5 Ves 461 .... 82.7
Barwick's Estate, Re (1957) 11 DLR (2d) 341, [1957] OWN 512 .... 102.26
Basan v Brandon (1836) 8 Sim 171 .... 41.1
Basham, Re [1987] 1 All ER 405, [1986] 1 WLR 1498, [1987] 2 FLR 264, [1987] Fam Law 310, 130 Sol Jo 986, [1987] LS Gaz R 112 .... 3.1, 43.1, 104.1, 105.17
Basioli, Re, Re Depaoli, McGahey v Depaoli [1953] Ch 367, [1953] 1 All ER 301, [1953] 2 WLR 251, 97 Sol Jo 80 .... 47.13, 47.15
Baskin, Re, Canada Trust Co v Baskin [1954] 2 DLR 748 .... 83.2
Basset v St Levan (1894) 13 R 235, 43 WR 165, 39 Sol Jo 80, 71 LT 718 .... 64.19
Bassett, Re [1961] VR 51 .... 63.3, 80.1, 101.6
Bassett's Estate, Re, Perkins v Fladgate (1872) LR 14 Eq 54, 41 LJ Ch 681, 20 WR 589 .... 53.3, 69.2
Bastin v Watts (1840) 3 Beav 97, 4 Jur 791 .... 91.1
Batchelor, Re (1915) 34 NZLR 379 .... 64.45
Batchelor, Re, Sloper v Oliver (1873) LR 16 Eq 481, 43 LJ Ch 101, 21 WR 901 .... 30.13
Bate, Re, Chillingworth v Bate [1947] 2 All ER 418, [1947] LJR 1409, 91 Sol Jo 560 .... 70.2
Bate, Re, Public Trustee v Bate [1938] 4 All ER 218 .... 32.2, 38.23
Bate v Amherst and Norton (1663) 1 Eq Cas Abr 212, T Raym 82 .... 53.5
Bate v Hooper (1855) 5 De GM & G 338, 104 RR 146, 3 WR 639 .... 214.3
Bateman, Re 1972 SLT (Notes) 78 .... 103.9
Bateman, Re, Wallace v Mawdsley (1911) 27 TLR 313 .... 57.19
Bateman v Bateman [1941] 3 DLR 762 .... 101.2
Bateman v Butler (1843) 1 LTOS 167 .... 25.15
Bateman v Foster (1844) 1 Coll 118, 3 LTOS 3 .... 66.14
Bateman v Gray (1868) LR 6 Eq 215, 37 LJ Ch 592, 16 WR 962 .... 66.14
Bateman v Pennington (1840) 3 Moo PCC 223 .... 11.17
Bateman v Roach (1724) 9 Mod Rep 104 .... 93.25
Bateman's Trusts, Re (1873) LR 15 Eq 355, 37 JP 484, 42 LJ Ch 553, 12 Cox CC 447, 21 WR 435, 28 LT 395 .... 93.22
Bateman's Will Trusts, Re, Brierley v Perry [1970] 3 All ER 817, [1970] 1 WLR 1463, 114 Sol Jo 707 .... 15.1, 36.11, 57.5

Bates, Re, Hodgson v Bates [1907] 1 Ch 22, [1906] WN 191, 76 LJ Ch 29, [1904–7] All ER Rep 450, 51 Sol Jo 27, 95 LT 753, 23 TLR 15 .... 38.18, 38.23
Bath and North East Somerset Council v A-G [2002] EWCA 1623 (Ch), [2002] WTLR 1257, 5 ITELR 274, [2002] NPC 111, [2002] All ER (D) 518 (Jul) 102.12
Bath and Wells Diocesan Board of Finance v Jenkinson [2002] EWHC 218 (Ch), [2003] Ch 89, [2002] 4 All ER 245, [2002] 3 WLR 202, [2002] P & CR 350, (2002) Times, 29 March, [2002] All ER (D) 355 (Feb) 7.21
Bathe, Re, Bathe v Public Trustee [1925] Ch 377, 133 LT 132, sub nom Re Bathe, Public Trustee v Bathe 95 LJ Ch 37 .... 34.11, 35.6
Bathern, Re [1941] SASR 266 .... 10.8
Bathurst v Burke [1946] IR 214 .... 33.26
Bathurst v Errington (1877) 2 App Cas 698, 46 LJ Ch 748, 25 WR 908, 37 LT 338, HL 51.7, 51.8, 81.3
Batley, Re, Public Trustee v Hert [1951] Ch 558, 30 ATC 182, [1951] 1 TLR 935, CA 33.47
Batsford v Kebbell (1797) 3 Ves 363 .... 93.31, 93.32, 93.39
Battan Singh v Amirchand [1948] AC 161, [1948] 1 All ER 152, [1948] LJR 827, PC 4.10, 4.17
Batten's Will Trusts, Re (1961) 105 Sol Jo 529 .... 9.14
Battersbee's Goods, Re (1852) 2 Rob Eccl 439 .... 15.1
Battersby's Trusts [1896] 1 IR 600 .... 68.11, 68.13, 79.1
Batthyany v Walford (1887) 36 Ch D 269, 56 LJ Ch 881, 35 WR 814, 57 LT 206, CA 45.2
Battie-Wrightson, Re, Cecil v Battie-Wrightson [1920] 2 Ch 330, 89 LJ Ch 550, [1920] All ER Rep 597, 64 Sol Jo 585, 124 LT 84, 36 TLR 693 .... 57.5, 57.11, 57.22
Batty, Re, Public Trustee v Bell [1952] Ch 280, [1952] 1 All ER 425, 96 Sol Jo 120, [1952] 1 TLR 412 .... 218.93
Battyll v Lyles and Phillips (1858) 4 Jur NS 718 .... 18.29
Baugh v Reed (1790) 1 Ves 257, 3 Bro CC 192 .... 44.13
Baugham's Goods, Re. See Bangham's Goods, Re
Baulderstone, Re [1928] SALR 262 .... 87.1
Bawden, Re, Bawden v Cresswell [1894] 1 Ch 693, 63 LJ Ch 412, 8 R 76, 42 WR 235, 70 LT 526 .... 50.18, 50.21
Bawden, Re, National Provincial Bank of England v Cresswell [1894] 1 Ch 693, 63 LJ Ch 412, 8 R 76, 42 WR 235, 70 LT 526 .... 50.18, 50.21
Bawden's Settlement, Re, Besant v London Hospital Board of Governors [1953] 2 All ER 1235, [1954] 1 WLR 33n, 98 Sol Jo 11 .... 102.26, 103.10
Baxendale, Re, Baxendale v Baxendale (1919) 148 LT Jo 139 .... 63.1
Baxter v Losh (1851) 14 Beav 612, 21 LJ Ch 55, 18 LTOS 181 .... 101.6, 101.13
Baxter's Goods, Re [1903] P 12, 72 LJP 2, 51 WR 302, 87 LT 748 .... 7.9, 10.11
Baxter's Trusts, Re (1864) 10 Jur NS 845, 4 New Rep 131, 10 LT 487 .... 93.1, 93.42
Bayard's Goods, Re (1849) 1 Rob Eccl 768, 13 Jur 664, 13 LTOS 448, 7 Notes of Cases 117 .... 25.10
Bayer v Montreal Trust Co [1953] Que SC 89 .... 24.6
Bayerische Motorenwerke AG (BMW) and BMW Nederland BV v Deenik: C-63/97 [1999] ECR I-905, [1999] All ER (EC) 235, [1999] 1 CMLR 1099, [1999] ETMR 339, ECJ 21.25

Baylee v Quin (1842) 2 Dr & War 116 .... 33.10
Bayley v Bishop (1803) 9 Ves 6 .... 33.6, 93.44
Baylis v A-G (1741) 2 Atk 239 .... 57.10, 103.17
Baylis' Goods, Re (1862) 31 LJPM & A 119, 26 JP 599, 8 Jur NS 546, 2 Sw & Tr 613, 7 LT 251 .... 25.1, 203.15
Baylis's Goods, Re (1865) LR 1 P & D 21, 35 LJP & M 15, 11 Jur NS 1028, 13 LT 446 .... 25.2
Bayliss' Trust, Re (1849) 17 Sim 178, 13 Jur 1090 .... 54.1
Bayne v Crowther (1855) 20 Beav 400, 3 WR 395 .... 33.18
Bayne's Goods, Re (1858) 1 Sw & Tr 132, 6 WR 815, 31 LTOS 172 .... 25.10
Baynham, Re, Hart v Mackenzie (1891) 7 TLR 587 .... 57.5, 74.1
Beachcroft v Beachcroft (1816) 1 Madd 430 .... 72.2
Beachcroft v Broome (1791) 4 Term Rep 441 .... 56.1
Beadle, Re, Mayes v Beadle [1974] 1 All ER 493, [1974] 1 WLR 417, 118 Sol Jo 170 .... 11.2, 11.4, 11.7, 11.9, 11.11, 12.14
Beak's Estate, Re, Beak v Beak (1872) LR 13 Eq 489, 36 JP 436, 41 LJ Ch 470, 26 LT 281 .... 1.15
Beal v Eastern Trust Co (1914) 14 ELR 432 .... 33.26
Beal v Henri [1951] 1 DLR 260, [1950] OR 780, [1950] OWN 760 .... 4.15
Beal v Wyman (1650) Sty 240 .... 53.5
Beale, Re, Beale v Royal Hospital for Incurables (1890) 6 TLR 308, CA 57.15
Beale v Beale (1713) 1 P Wms 244 .... 81.3
Beales v Crisford (1843) 13 Sim 592, 13 LJ Ch 26, 7 Jur 1076, 2 LTOS 146 .... 64.35, 64.38, 79.1, 85.3
Beales' Settlement, Re, Barrett v Beales [1905] 1 Ch 256, 74 LJ Ch 67, 53 WR 216, 49 Sol Jo 101, 92 LT 268, 21 TLR 101 .... 42.4, 94.10
Bean v Griffiths (1855) 1 Jur NS 1045, sub nom Benn v Griffiths 3 WR 640, 26 LTOS 56 .... 35.35
Bean's Estate, Re [1944] P 83, [1944] 2 All ER 348, 113 LJP 65, 60 TLR 418 .... 11.4, 11.7, 11.9, 11.11
Beard, Re, Reversionary and General Securities Co Ltd v Hall [1908] 1 Ch 383, 77 LJ Ch 265, 98 LT 315, 24 TLR 225 .... 35.46
Beard, Re, Simpson v Beard (1888) 57 LJ Ch 887, 36 WR 519, 58 LT 629 .... 64.7
Beard v Westcott (1813) 5 Taunt 393 .... 94.3
Beardsley v Beardsley [1899] 1 QB 746, 68 LJQB 270, 47 WR 284, 43 Sol Jo 225, 80 LT 51, 15 TLR 173, DC 43.4
Beardsley v Beynon (1865) 13 WR 831, 12 LT 698 .... 93.19, 97.10
Beardsley v Lacey (1897) 67 LJP 35, 78 LT 25, 14 TLR 140 .... 18.5, 18.15, 18.17, 19.5
Beattie Estate, Re [1944] WWR 727 .... 18.5, 18.31
Beatty's Will Trusts, Re, Hinves v Brooke [1990] 3 All ER 844, sub nom Re Beatty, Hinves v Brooke [1990] 1 WLR 1503 .... 1.6, 39.2, 40.5, 204.5, 218.3, 218.4, 225.91, 225.100
Beatty, Re, Hinves v Brooke. See Beatty's Will Trusts, Re, Hinves v Brooke
Beauchamp, Re (1975) 56 DLR (3d) 644 .... 42.2, 58.3
Beaudry v Barbeau [1900] AC 569, 69 LJPC 131, 83 LT 236, PC 50.2, 51.11, 57.3
Beaufort (Duke) v Lord Dundonald (1716) 2 Vern 739 .... 63.1
Beaulieu (Lord) v Lord Cardigan (1767) Amb 533, sub nom Montagu (Duke) v Duke of Beaulieu 3 Bro Parl Cas 277, HL 35.50
Beaumont, Re, Beaumont v Ewbank [1902] 1 Ch 889, 71 LJ Ch 478, 50 WR 389, [1900–3] All ER Rep 273, 46 Sol Jo 317, 86 LT 410 .... 1.15

Beaumont, Re, Bradshaw v Packer [1913] 1 Ch 325, 82 LJ Ch 183, 57 Sol Jo 283, 108 LT 181 .... 210.45
Beaumont, Re, Martin v Midland Bank Trust Co Ltd [1980] Ch 444, [1980] 1 All ER 266, [1979] 3 WLR 818, 123 Sol Jo 803 ..... 105.18, 105.22, 105.29
Beaumont, Re, Woods v Beaumont [1910] WN 181, 79 LJ Ch 744, 103 LT 124 .... 99.8
Beaumont v Fell (1723) 2 P Wms 141 .... 57.15, 58.4
Beaumont v Oliveira (1868) LR 6 Eq 534; on appeal (1869) 4 Ch App 309, 33 JP 391, 38 LJ Ch 239, 17 WR 269, 20 LT 53 .... 23.4, 102.8
Beaumont v Squire (1852) 17 QB 905, 21 LJQB 123, 16 Jur 591, 19 LTOS 44 .... 34.22, 35.11
Beaumont's Will Trusts, Re, Walker v Lawson [1950] Ch 462, [1950] 1 All ER 802, 94 Sol Jo 239, 66 (pt 1) TLR 712 .... 55.7, 214.9
Beavan, Re, Beavan v Beavan (1885) 53 LT 245 .... 64.11, 64.35, 64.53
Beavan v M'Donnell (1854) 23 LJ Ex 326, 10 Exch 184, 2 CLR 1292 .... 4.20
Beavan's Goods, Re (1840) 2 Curt 369 .... 14.1
Beaver v Nowell (1858) 25 Beav 551 .... 84.4, 85.5, 101.13
Bebb v Beckwith (1839) 2 Beav 308 .... 68.10
Beckett's Settlement, Re, Re Beckett, Eden v Von Stutterheim [1940] Ch 279, 109 LJ Ch 81, 84 Sol Jo 133, 163 LT 78, 56 TLR 342 .... 218.90, 226.4
Beckley v Newland (1723) 2 P Wms 182 .... 30.1, 55.4
Beckton v Barton (1859) 27 Beav 99, 28 LJ Ch 673, 5 Jur NS 349, 33 LTOS 231 .... 93.30, 97.5
Beckwith v Beckwith (1876) 46 LJ Ch 97, 25 WR 282, 36 LT 128, CA 67.6
Bective v Hodgson. See Hodgson v Bective
Bedborough v Bedborough (No 2) (1865) 34 Beav 286 .... 34.21
Beddington, Re, Micholls v Samuel [1900] 1 Ch 771, 69 LJ Ch 374, 48 WR 552, 82 LT 557, 16 TLR 291 .... 44.6, 100.5
Beddington v Baumann. See Moses, Re, Beddington v Beddington
Beddy v Smith (1843) 1 LTOS 390 .... 30.31
Bedford, Re, National Provincial Bank Ltd v Aulton [1951] Ch 905, [1951] 1 All ER 1093, 95 Sol Jo 368, [1951] 2 TLR 216 .... 30.26
Bedford v Bedford (1865) 35 Beav 584 .... 214.5
Bedford's Goods, Re (1847) 5 Notes of Cases 188 .... 14.13
Bedson's Trusts, Re (1885) 28 Ch D 523, 54 LJ Ch 644, 33 WR 386, 52 LT 554, CA 49.4, 49.5, 50.5, 50.18, 66.9, 66.12
Beech v Lord St Vincent (1850) 3 De G & Sm 678, 19 LJ Ch 130, 14 Jur 731, 14 LTOS 503 .... 95.9, 95.10
Beech's Estate, Re, Beech v Public Trustee [1923] P 46, 92 LJP 33, 67 Sol Jo 145, 128 LT 616, 39 TLR 88, CA 5.7, 10.18, 16.4
Beecham, Re, Woolley v Beecham (1919) 63 Sol Jo 430 .... 64.7, 82.1
Beer's Goods, Re (1851) 2 Rob Eccl 349, 15 Jur 160, 16 LTOS 512 .... 25.10
Beere v Hoffmister (1856) 23 Beav 101, 26 LJ Ch 177, 3 Jur NS 78, 28 LTOS 155 .... 40.15
Beesty's Will Trusts, Re, Farrar v Royal Alfred Merchant Seamen's Society [1966] Ch 223, [1964] 3 All ER 82, [1964] 3 WLR 689, 108 Sol Jo 481 .... 39.28, 62.1, 102.26
Beevor v Partridge (1840) 11 Sim 229, 10 LJ Ch 89 .... 82.8
Begbie v Crook (1835) 2 Bing NC 70, 44 LJCP 264, 2 Scott 128 .... 27.6, 46.1

Begg-MacBrearty (Inspector of Taxes) v Stilwell [1996] 4 All ER 205, [1996] 1 WLR 951, [1996] STC 413, 68 TC 426, [1996] 15 LS Gaz R 31, 140 Sol Jo LB 110 .... 218.43, 218.46
Begin v Bilodeau [1951] SCR 699 .... 18.8
Beiers, Re [1953] QWN 9 .... 9.18
Beirnstein, Re, Barnett v Beirnstein [1925] Ch 12, 94 LJ Ch 62, 69 Sol Jo 88, 132 LT 251 .... 20.4
Belaney v Belaney (1867) 2 Ch App 138, 36 LJ Ch 265, 15 WR 369, 16 LT 269 .... 57.8, 64.45
Belfast Town Council, Re, ex p Sayers (1884) 13 LR Ir 169 .... 67.2
Belk v Slack (1836) 1 Keen 238, 44 RR 71 .... 67.7
Bell, Re [1969] VR 597 .... 58.2
Bell, Re, Ballarat Trustees, Executors and Agency Co Ltd [1943] ALR 192, [1943] VLR 103 .... 102.10
Bell, Re, Bell v Agnew (1931) 47 TLR 401 .... 35.30
Bell, Re, Wright v Scrivener (1914) 58 Sol Jo 517 .... 30.23
Bell v Cade (1861) 2 John & H 122, 31 LJ Ch 383, 10 WR 38, 5 LT 528 .... 93.36
Bell v Clarke (1858) 25 Beav 437, 27 LJ Ch 674, 4 Jur NS 499, 6 WR 476, 31 LTOS 324 .... 3.2
Bell v Fothergill (1870) LR 2 P & D 148, 34 JP 679, 18 WR 1040, 23 LT 323 .... 18.18, 18.20, 21.5
Bell v Park [1914] 1 IR 158 .... 88.4
Bell v Phyn (1802) 7 Ves 453 .... 56.8, 98.13
Bell's Goods, Re, Hunt v Hunt. See Hunt v Hunt (1866) LR 1 P & D 209
Bellairs v Bellairs (1874) LR 18 Eq 510, 43 LJ Ch 669, 22 WR 942 .... 34.13, 35.2, 93.24
Bellamy, Re, Pickard v Holroyd (1883) 48 LT 212 .... 35.2
Bellamy's Goods, Re (1866) 14 WR 501 .... 10.14
Bellamy's Trust, Re (1862) 1 New Rep 191 .... 52.8
Bellasis v Ermine (1663) 1 Cas in Ch 22, Freem Ch 171 .... 34.13, 34.14
Bellasis v Uthwatt (1737) 1 Atk 426, West temp Hard 273 .... 44.11
Bellew, Re, O'Reilly v Bellew [1924] 1 IR 1 .... 35.28
Belling v Ellise. See Bulling v Ellice
Belliss, Re, Polson v Parrott (1929) 73 Sol Jo 628, 141 LT 245, 45 TLR 452 .... 4.15
Belshaw v Rollins (1904) 38 LT 90, [1904] 1 IR 284, 289 .... 92.1
Bence, Re, Smith v Bence [1891] 3 Ch 242, 60 LJ Ch 636, 65 LT 530, 7 TLR 593, CA 94.21, 98.3
Bence v Gilpin (1868) LR 3 Exch 76, 37 LJ Ex 36, 16 WR 705, 17 LT 655 .... 45.1
Bengough v Walker (1808) 15 Ves 507 .... 44.11
Benham, Re [1939] SASR 450 .... 102.10
Benham's Will Trusts, Re, Lockhart v Harker, Read and the Royal National Lifeboat Institution [1995] STC 210 .... 38.15, 200.118, 214.72, 214.79
Benjamin, Re, Mason v Benjamin [1926] VLR 378, 48 ALT 9 .... 93.37
Benjamin, Re, Neville v Benjamin [1902] 1 Ch 723, 71 LJ Ch 319, 46 Sol Jo 266, 86 LT 387, 18 TLR 283 .... 9.2
Benjamin v Bennett [2007] All ER (D) 243 (Feb) 18.6
Benjamin's Estate, Re [1934] All ER Rep 359, 150 LT 417 .... 12.3
Benjamins v Chartered Trust Co [1965] SCR 251, 49 DLR (2d) 1 .... 2.2
Benn, Re, Benn v Benn (1885) 29 Ch D 839, 34 WR 6, 53 LT 240, CA 50.6, 51.1, 67.1, 67.2, 67.5
Benn v Griffiths. See Bean v Griffiths

Benn v Hawthorne [1925] 4 DLR 400 .... 3.13
Bennet v Bennet (1879) 10 Ch D 474, 27 WR 573, 40 LT 378 .... 44.8
Bennet v Davis (1725) 2 P Wms 316 .... 57.10
Bennet v Duke of Manchester (1854) 2 WR 644, 23 LTOS 331 .... 4.14
Bennett, Re [1955] OWN 211 .... 30.3, 64.38
Bennett, Re, ex p Kirk (1877) 5 Ch D 800, 46 LJ Bcy 101, 25 WR 598, 36 LT 431, CA 58.6
Bennett, Re, ex p Official Receiver [1907] 1 KB 149, 76 LJKB 134, 14 Mans 6, 51 Sol Jo 83, 95 LT 887, 23 TLR 99 .... 31.17
Bennett v Aburrow (1803) 8 Ves 609 .... 39.19
Bennett v Batchelor (1789) 1 Ves 63, 3 Bro CC 28 .... 38.3
Bennett v Bennett (1864) 2 Drew & Sm 266, 34 LJ Ch 34, 10 Jur NS 1170, 13 WR 66, 11 LT 362 .... 35.39, 35.41, 35.43, 35.52, 81.3
Bennett v Colley (1833) 2 My & K 225, Coop temp Brough 248 .... 45.2
Bennett v Honywood (1772) Amb 708 .... 79.4
Bennett v Houldsworth (1877) 6 Ch D 671, 46 LJ Ch 646, 36 LT 648 .... 3.2, 42.14, 44.9
Bennett v Houldsworth [1911] WN 47, 55 Sol Jo 270, 104 LT 304 .... 76.3, 86.2
Bennett v Marshall (1856) 2 K & J 740 .... 57.22, 71.4
Bennett v Slater [1899] 1 QB 45, 68 LJQB 45, 47 WR 82, 43 Sol Jo 26, 79 LT 324, 15 TLR 25, CA 7.9, 7.10, 7.13
Bennett's Trust, Re (1857) 3 K & J 280 .... 87.3, 93.28, 93.29
Benor, Re (1963) 39 DLR (2d) 122, [1963] 2 OR 248 .... 95.13
Benson v Benson (1870) LR 2 P & D 172, 34 JP 807, 40 LJP & M 1, 19 WR 190, 23 LT 709 .... 18.7, 18.25, 18.31
Benson v Maude (1821) 6 Madd 15 .... 30.31, 32.5
Benson v Whittam (1831) 5 Sim 22, 1 LJ Ch 94, 35 RR 113 .... 82.5
Bensusan v Nehemias (1851) 4 De G & Sm 381 .... 44.15
Bent v Cullen (1871) 6 Ch App 235, 40 LJ Ch 250, 19 WR 368 .... 33.9
Bentham, Re, Pearce v Bentham (1906) 94 LT 307 .... 38.18, 38.23
Bentinck v Duke of Portland (1877) 7 Ch D 693, 47 LJ Ch 235, 26 WR 278, 38 LT 58 .... 94.23
Bentley, Re, Podmore v Smith (1914) 58 Sol Jo 362, 110 LT 623 ...... 38.13, 47.28, 47.32
Bentley v Meech (1858) 25 Beav 197 .... 56.4
Bentley v Oldfield (1854) 19 Beav 225 .... 53.1
Bentley's Trusts, Re (1935) 9 MPR 271 .... 68.2
Benton's Will, Re (1959) 20 DLR (2d) 737, 29 WWR 657 .... 10.1
Benyon, Re, Benyon v Grieve (1884) 53 LJ Ch 1165, 32 WR 871, 51 LT 116 .... 30.24, 91.6
Benyon v Benyon (1810) 17 Ves 34 .... 44.1, 88.4
Benzon, Re, Bower v Chetwynd [1914] 2 Ch 68, 83 LJ Ch 658, 21 Mans 8, 58 Sol Jo 430, 110 LT 926, 30 TLR 435, CA 39.6
Berchtold, Re, Berchtold v Capron [1923] 1 Ch 192, 92 LJ Ch 185, 67 Sol Jo 212, 128 LT 591 .... 23.4
Bercovitz, Re, Canning v Enever [1962] 1 All ER 552, [1962] 1 WLR 321, 106 Sol Jo 110, CA 11.2, 13.1
Berens, Re (1888) 5 TLR 473 .... 35.31
Berens, Re, Re Dowdeswell, Berens-Dowdeswell v Holland-Martin [1926] Ch 596, 95 LJ Ch 370, 70 Sol Jo 405, 135 LT 298, 42 TLR 267, 314 .... 34.8, 35.41, 35.42, 35.43
Beresford, Re (1966) 57 DLR (2d) 380 .... 102.9

Beresford v Preston (1920) 54 ILT 48 .... 8.4, 64.27
Beresford Estate, Re [1966] 56 WWR 248 .... 34.5
Beresford's Will Trusts, Re, Sturges v Beresford [1938] 3 All ER 566, 82 Sol Jo 664 .... 39.25
Beresford-Hope, Re, Aldenham v Beresford-Hope [1917] 1 Ch 287, 86 LJ Ch 182, 116 LT 79 .... 94.15
Berger, Re [1990] Ch 118, [1989] 1 All ER 591, [1989] 2 WLR 147, 133 Sol Jo 122, [1989] 15 LS Gaz R 41, CA 1.2, 10.1, 10.4, 10.12, 15.1, 24.2, 49.6, 57.4, 57.7
Berkeley (Earl), Re, Inglis v Countess of Berkeley [1968] Ch 744, [1968] 3 All ER 364, [1968] 3 WLR 253, 112 Sol Jo 601, CA ... 33.23, 33.25, 33.26, 33.30, 33.31, 38.27, 95.1, 95.7, 211.11
Berkeley v Berkeley [1946] AC 555, [1946] 2 All ER 154, 25 ATC 209, 115 LJ Ch 281, 90 Sol Jo 345, 175 LT 153, 62 TLR 478, HL 22.3
Berkeley v Swinburne (1848) 16 Sim 275, 17 LJ Ch 416, 12 Jur 571 ... 66.17, 93.1, 93.42
Berkenshaw v Gilbert. See Burtenshaw v Gilbert
Berkheiser v Berkheiser and Glaisler [1957] SCR 387, 7 DLR (2d) 721; revsd [1955] 5 DLR 183, 16 WWR 459 .... 41.5
Bernal v Bernal (1838) 3 My & Cr 559, 7 LJ Ch 115, Coop Pr Cas 55, 2 Jur 273 .... 24.6, 74.9, 102.14
Bernard v Minshull (1859) John 276, 28 LJ Ch 649, 5 Jur NS 931, 70 ER 427 .... 38.1, 39.14
Bernard v Mountague (1816) 1 Mer 422 .... 93.4
Bernard v Walker (1921) 55 ILT 73 .... 93.2
Bernard's Settlement, Re, Bernard v Jones [1916] 1 Ch 552, 85 LJ Ch 414, 60 Sol Jo 458, 114 LT 654 .... 19.3
Bernasconi v Atkinson (1853) 10 Hare 345, 23 LJ Ch 184, 17 Jur 128, 1 WR 125, 20 LTOS 217 .... 57.19, 57.22, 58.7, 58.10
Bernstein's Will Trusts, Re, National Westminster Bank Ltd v Board of Governors of United Liverpool Hospitals (1971) 115 Sol Jo 808 .... 102.7
Berrey's Will Trusts, Re, Greening v Warner (or Waters) [1959] 1 All ER 15, [1959] 1 WLR 30, 103 Sol Jo 34 .... 214.7, 214.9
Berridge, Re, Berridge v Turner (1890) 63 LT 470, CA 102.8
Berry, Re, Lloyds Bank Ltd v Berry [1962] Ch 97, [1961] 1 All ER 529, [1961] 1 WLR 329, 105 Sol Jo 256 .... 38.19, 38.23, 214.30, 214.35, 220.34
Berry v Berry (1861) 3 Giff 134, 7 Jur NS 752, 9 WR 889, 4 LT 635 .... 74.1
Berry v Fisher [1903] 1 IR 484 .... 76.3, 76.4
Berry v Geen [1938] AC 575, 159 LT 122, sub nom Re Blake, Berry v Geen [1938] 2 All ER 362, 107 LJ Ch 173, 82 Sol Jo 491, 54 TLR 703, HL 66.3, 66.13, 95.13
Berryman, Re, Berryman v Berryman [1913] 1 IR 21 .... 83.13
Bertie v Faulkland (1698) 1 Eq Cas Abr 110, 3 Cas in Ch 129, Freem Ch 220, 12 Mod Rep 182, 1 Salk 231, sub nom Falkland (Lord Viscount) v Bertie Holt KB 230, 2 Vern 333, [1558–1774] All ER Rep 396; on appeal sub nom Bertie v Viscount Falkland (1698) Colles 10, HL 34.23, 34.25, 57.10
Berton, Re, Vandyk v Berton [1939] Ch 200, [1938] 4 All ER 286, 108 LJ Ch 139, 82 Sol Jo 890, 159 LT 566, 55 TLR 40 .... 38.25
Berwick Estate, Re, Canada Trust Co v Berwick [1948] SCR 151, 3 DLR 81 .... 83.12
Besant v Cox (1877) 6 Ch D 604, 25 WR 789 .... 97.6

Bescoby v Pack (1823) 1 Sim & St 500, 2 LJOS Ch 17 ..... 64.53
Bessette v Toronto General Trusts Corpn (No 3) (1953) 2 DLR 311, 7 WWRNS 673 ..... 10.5
Best, Re, Belk v Best [1942] Ch 77, [1941] 3 All ER 315, 111 LJ Ch 30, 85 Sol Jo 474, 58 TLR 31 ..... 33.47
Best, Re, Jarvis v Birmingham Corpn [1904] 2 Ch 354, 73 LJ Ch 808, 53 WR 21, 48 Sol Jo 620 ..... 102.23, 212.5
Best v Stonehewer (1864) 34 Beav 66, 34 LJ Ch 26, 10 Jur NS 1140, 13 WR 126, 11 LT 468; affd (1865) 2 De GJ & Sm 537, 34 LJ Ch 349, 11 Jur NS 315, 5 New Rep 500, 13 WR 566, 12 LT 195 ..... 47.31, 50.16, 74.8
Best's Settlement Trusts, Re (1874) LR 18 Eq 686, 43 LJ Ch 545, 22 WR 599 ..... 83.16
Besterman, Re, Besterman v Grusin [1984] Ch 458, [1984] 2 All ER 656, [1984] 3 WLR 280, [1984] FLR 503, [1984] Fam Law 203, 128 Sol Jo 515, CA 105.9, 105.22, 105.26, 105.32
Bethell v Abraham (1874) 3 Ch D 590n, 22 WR 745, 31 LT 112 ..... 44.13
Bethune v Bethune [1944] Que SC 14 ..... 56.8
Betts, Re, Burrell v Betts [1949] 1 All ER 568, 93 Sol Jo 164;, sub nom Betts, Re, Burnell v Betts [1949] WN 91 ..... 64.7
Betts v Gannell (1903) 19 TLR 304 ..... 12.3, 12.6
Betts's Goods, Re (1861) 25 JP 392, 30 LJPM & A 167 ..... 25.3
Betty, Re, Betty v A-G [1899] 1 Ch 821, 68 LJ Ch 435, 80 LT 675 ..... 207.2
Bevan v A-G (1863) 4 Giff 361, 9 Jur NS 1099, 2 New Rep 52, 9 LT 221 ..... 30.6, 64.7
Bevan v Bevan (1880) 5 LR Ir 57, Ir CA 64.40
Bevan v Mahon-Hagan (1892) 27 LR Ir 399; affd (1893) 31 LR Ir 342, Ir CA 34.24, 35.39, 35.42
Bevan's Trusts, Re (1887) 34 Ch D 716, 56 LJ Ch 652, 35 WR 400, [1886–90] All ER Rep 706, 56 LT 277 ..... 51.2, 93.43
Beveridge's Will, Re (1905) 22 WN 224, 6 SRNSW 125 ..... 15.1
Beverley Corpn v A-G (1857) 21 JP 675, 6 HL Cas 310, 27 LJ Ch 66, 3 Jur NS 871, 5 WR 840, 30 LTOS 13 ..... 103.1, 103.13, 103.14, 103.15, 103.16
Beverly, Re, Watson v Watson [1901] 1 Ch 681, 70 LJ Ch 295, 49 WR 343, 45 Sol Jo 259, 84 LT 296, 17 TLR 228 ..... 29.2, 29.9, 29.12, 29.16, 214.14
Bewick, Re, Ryle v Ryle [1911] 1 Ch 116, 80 LJ Ch 47, 55 Sol Jo 109, 103 LT 634 ..... 93.4, 94.13, 94.37
Beyer v Beyer [1960] VLR 126 ..... 10.5
Beyfus v Lawley. See Lawley, Re, Zaiser v Lawley (or Perkins)
Bezpalko, Re (1980) 106 DLR (3d) 290 ..... 103.3
Bheekhun v Williams [1999] 2 FLR 229, [1999] Fam Law 379, CA 105.9, 105.22
Bibbens v Potter (1879) 10 Ch D 733, 27 WR 304 ..... 83.9, 97.3, 99.1
Bibin v Walker (1768) Amb 661 ..... 52.11
Bick, Re, Edwards v Bush [1920] 1 Ch 488, 89 LJ Ch 335, 64 Sol Jo 359, 123 LT 49 ..... 41.5
Bickenden v Williams. See Brickenden v Williams
Bickerdike's Will, Re, Bickerdike v Hill [1918] VLR 191 ..... 34.5
Bickersteth v Shanu [1936] AC 290, [1936] 1 All ER 227, 105 LJPC 53, 80 Sol Jo 164, 154 LT 360, 52 TLR 290, PC 34.2, 93.2, 93.3, 93.6
Bickerton's Settlement, Re, Shaw v Bickerton [1942] Ch 84, [1942] 1 All ER 217, 111 LJ Ch 132, 85 Sol Jo 481, 166 LT 38 ..... 101.13
Bickford v Chalker (1854) 2 Drew 327, 2 WR 502 ..... 52.1, 52.8

Biddles v Biddles (1843) 3 Curt 458, 7 Jur 777 .... 18.11
Biddulph v Biddulph (1806) 12 Ves 161 .... 37.5
Biddulph v Lees (1859) EB & E 289, 308, 28 LJQB 211, 5 Jur NS 818, 7 WR 309, 32 LTOS 392, Ex Ch 84.2, 98.3
Biddulph's Trusts, Re, Re Poole's Trusts (1852) 5 De G & Sm 469 .... 5.2
Bide v Harrison (1873) LR 17 Eq 76, 43 LJ Ch 86, 29 LT 451 .... 64.39
Biden, Re (1906) 4 WLR 477 .... 38.3
Bidie, Re, Bidie v General Accident Fire and Life Assurance Corpn Ltd [1949] Ch 121, [1948] 2 All ER 995, 47 LGR 465, 113 JP 22, [1949] LJR 386, 92 Sol Jo 705, 65 TLR 25, CA 105.5
Bidwell's Settlement Trusts, Re (1862) 32 LJ Ch 71, 9 Jur NS 37, 1 New Rep 176, 11 WR 161, 8 LT 107 .... 42.5
Bifield's Case. See Milliner v Robinson
Biggar, Re, Biggar v Stinson (1884) 8 OR 372 .... 74.2
Bigge, Re, Granville v Moore [1907] 1 Ch 714, 76 LJ Ch 413, 51 Sol Jo 410, 96 LT 903 .... 33.26, 33.30
Biggs' Estate, Re [1966] P 118, [1966] 1 All ER 358, [1966] 2 WLR 536, 110 Sol Jo 173 .... 25.13
Bignall v Rose (1854) 24 LJ Ch 27, 3 WR 77 .... 62.1
Bignold v Giles (1859) 4 Drew 343, 28 LJ Ch 358, 5 Jur NS 84, 7 WR 195, 32 LTOS 308 .... 33.1
Bilham, Re, Buchanan v Hill [1901] 2 Ch 169, 70 LJ Ch 518, 49 WR 483, 45 Sol Jo 537, 84 LT 499 .... 67.5
Billinghurst v Vickers (formerly Leonard) (1810) 1 Phillim 187, 199 .... 4.11
Billingsley v Wills (1745) 3 Atk 219 .... 93.29
Biln Estate, Re (1967) 61 DLR (2d) 535, 59 WWR 229 .... 51.1
Bingham, Re, Public Trustee v New Plymouth Council for Social Service Inc [1951] NZLR 491, [1951] GLR 223 .... 102.5
Bingham v Lord Clanmorris (1828) 2 Mol 253 .... 27.6
Bingley Estate, Re (1953) 7 WWRNS 507, 61 Maw R 25 .... 58.8
Binning (or Billing) v Binning (or Billing) [1895] WN 116, 13 R 654, 39 Sol Jo 622, 11 TLR 502 .... 86.2, 86.4, 86.5
Binns, Re, Lee v Binns [1896] 2 Ch 584, 65 LJ Ch 830, 40 Sol Jo 654, 75 LT 99 .... 30.12, 30.13
Binns, Re, Public Trustee v Ingle [1929] 1 Ch 677, [1929] All ER Rep 542, 98 LJ Ch 307, 141 LT 91 .... 44.2, 100.4, 217.17
Birch, Re (1853) 17 Beav 358 .... 35.16, 35.17
Birch v Birch (1848) 1 Rob Eccl 675, 12 Jur 1057, 12 LTOS 334, 6 Notes of Cases 581 .... 14.10
Birch v Birch [1902] P 130, 71 LJP 58, 50 WR 437, 46 Sol Jo 393, 80 LT 364, 18 TLR 485, CA 25.16
Birch v Curtis [2002] EWHC 1158 (Ch), [2002] 2 FLR 847, [2002] Fam Law 815, [2002] 29 EG 139, [2002] All ER (D) 77 (Jun) 2.6
Birch v Dawson (1834) 2 Ad & El 37, 6 C & P 658, 4 LJKB 49, 4 Nev & MKB 22 .... 64.27
Birch v Sherratt (1867) 2 Ch App 644, 36 LJ Ch 925, 16 WR 30, 17 LT 153 .... 33.24
Birch v Treasury Solicitor [1951] Ch 298, [1950] 2 All ER 1198, 94 Sol Jo 838, [1951] 1 TLR 225, CA 1.15
Birch v Wade (1814) 3 Ves & B 198 .... 79.4
Birch's Estate, Re [1929] P 164, 98 LJP 66, 73 Sol Jo 221, 141 LT 32 .... 26.5

Birchall, Re, Birchall v Ashton (1889) 40 Ch D 436, 37 WR 387, 60 LT 369, CA 27.5, 27.6, 46.1
Birchall, Re, Kennedy v Birchall [1940] Ch 424, [1940] 1 All ER 545, 109 LJ Ch 129, 162 LT 261, TLR 408, CA 68.9
Bird, Re, Bird v Cross (1894) 8 R 326 .... 34.8
Bird, Re, Pitman v Pitman [1892] 1 Ch 279, 61 LJ Ch 288, 40 WR 359, 66 LT 274 .... 37.2
Bird, Re, Watson v Nunes [1927] 1 Ch 210, 96 LJ Ch 127, 70 Sol Jo 1139, 136 LT 346 .... 32.28
Bird, Re, Re Evans, Dodd v Evans [1901] 1 Ch 916, 70 LJ Ch 514, 49 WR 599, 45 Sol Jo 327, 84 LT 294 .... 38.28
Bird v Bird (1842) 11 LJ Ch 390, 6 Jur 1030 .... 93.12
Bird v Christopher (1653) Sty 389 .... 40.10
Bird v Harris (1870) LR 9 Eq 204, 39 LJ Ch 226, 18 WR 374, 23 LT 213 .... 91.2
Bird v Hunsdon (1818) 1 Wils Ch 456, 3 Swan 342 .... 101.4
Bird v Luckie (1850) 8 Hare 301, 14 Jur 1015 .... 51.7, 77.3
Bird v Webster (1853) 1 Drew 338, 22 LJ Ch 483, 1 WR 121 .... 82.3
Birds v Askey (1857) 24 Beav 615 .... 93.4
Birdsall v York (1859) 5 Jur NS 1237 .... 87.3
Birkett, Re (1878) 9 Ch D 576, 43 JP 111, 47 LJ Ch 846, 27 WR 164, 39 LT 418 .... 9.29, 102.22
Birkett, Re, Holland v Duncan [1950] Ch 330, [1950] 1 All ER 316, 94 Sol Jo 131, 66 (pt 1) TLR 411 .... 74.2, 87.1
Birkin, Re, Heald v Millership [1949] 1 All ER 1045, [1949] LJR 1252, 93 Sol Jo 338 .... 50.2, 71.5
Birks, Re, Kenyon v Birks [1900] 1 Ch 417, 69 LJ Ch 723, 50 WR 695, 46 Sol Jo 632, 87 LT 316, 18 TLR 710, CA 50.3, 54.5, 76.1, 76.3
Birks v Birks (1865) 29 JP 360, 34 LJPM & A 90, 4 Sw & Tr 23, 13 WR 638, 13 LT 193 .... 18.8, 18.14
Birley v Birley (1858) 25 Beav 299, 27 LJ Ch 569, 4 Jur NS 315, 6 WR 400, 31 LTOS 160 .... 40.15
Birmingham, Re, Savage v Stannard [1959] Ch 523, [1958] 2 All ER 397, [1958] 3 WLR 10, 102 Sol Jo 454 .... 204.77, 204.78, 206.25
Birmingham v Renfrew (1936) 57 CLR 666, 43 ALR 520, [1937] VLR 327, 11 ALJ 188, Aus HC 2.6, 2.8
Birmingham, Dudley and District Banking Co v Ross (1888) 38 Ch D 295, 57 LJ Ch 601, 36 WR 914, 59 LT 609, 4 TLR 437, CA 61.1
Birt's Goods, Re (1871) LR 2 P & D 214, 35 JP 296, 19 WR 511, 24 LT 142, sub nom Re Burt's Goods 40 LJP & M 26 .... 11.3, 14.12
Birtwhistle v Myers (1899) 25 VLR 306 .... 35.30
Bischoffsheim, Re, Cassel v Grant [1948] Ch 79, [1947] 2 All ER 830, [1948] LJR 213, 92 Sol Jo 26, 64 TLR 36 .... 72.7
Biscoe v Jackson (1887) 35 Ch D 460, 56 LJ Ch 540, 35 WR 554, 56 LT 753, 3 TLR 577, CA 102.7, 103.1, 103.11, 103.18
Bishop v Cappel (1847) 1 De G & Sm 411, 11 Jur 939, 9 LTOS 371 .... 79.6
Bishop v Curtis (1852) 18 QB 878, 21 LJQB 391, 17 Jur 23, 19 LTOS 217 .... 7.28
Bishop v Plumley [1991] 1 All ER 236, [1991] 1 WLR 582, [1991] 1 FLR 121, [1991] Fam Law 61, [1990] NLJR 1153, CA 105.18, 105.19, 105.29
Bishop's Goods, Re (1882) 46 JP 392, 30 WR 567 .... 11.26

Biss, Re, Heasman v Biss [1956] Ch 243, [1956] 1 All ER 89, [1956] 2 WLR 94, 100 Sol Jo 35 .... 206.22, 209.6
Biss v Smith (1857) 2 H & N 105, 26 LJ Ex 295 .... 98.7
Blachford, Re, Blachford v Worsley (1884) 27 Ch D 676, 54 LJ Ch 215, 33 WR 11 .... 32.11, 32.30
Black, Re, Falls v Alford [1907] 1 IR 486 .... 82.7
Black v Campbell (1864) 14 I Ch R 92 .... 76.3
Black v Jobling (1869) LR 1 P & D 685, 33 JP 727, 38 LJP & M 74, 17 WR 1108, 21 LT 298 .... 18.15, 18.28, 20.2
Blackborn v Edgley (1719) 1 P Wms 600, [1558–1774] All ER Rep 486 .... 64.2, 64.26
Blackburn, Re, Smiles v Blackburn (1889) 43 Ch D 75, 59 LJ Ch 208, 38 WR 140 .... 39.22, 40.7
Blackburn v McCallum (1903) 33 SCR 65 .... 99.1
Blackburn v Stables (1814) 13 RR 120, 2 Ves & B 367 .... 53.5, 73.1, 82.1, 94.15
Blacket v Blizard (1829) 9 B & C 851, 2 Man & Ry MC 369, 4 Man & Ry KB 641, sub nom Freeman v Meymott 8 LJOSKB 85 .... 221.29
Blacket v Lamb (1851) 14 Beav 482, 21 LJ Ch 46, 16 Jur 142, 18 LTOS 115 .... 42.4, 42.7
Blackham's Case (1709) 1 Salk 290 .... 49.7
Blackler v Webb (1726) 2 P Wms 383 .... 87.1
Blackman, Re (1852) 16 Beav 377 .... 58.11, 74.1
Blackman v Fysh [1892] 3 Ch 209, 2 R 1, 67 LT 802, CA 66.23, 99.8
Blackmore v Snee (1857) 1 De G & J 455 .... 67.2
Blackmore v White [1899] 1 QB 293, 68 LJQB 180, 47 WR 448, 80 LT 79 .... 45.2
Blackstock Estate, Re (1957) 10 DLR (2d) 192, 21 WWR 241 .... 83.8
Blackwell, Re, Blackwell v Blackwell [1926] Ch 223, 95 LJ Ch 172, [1925] All ER Rep 498, 70 Sol Jo 366, 134 LT 367, CA; affd [1929] AC 318, 98 LJ Ch 251, 73 Sol Jo 92, 140 LT 444, 45 TLR 208, HL 34.2, 36.1, 36.9, 36.10, 36.12, 61.1, 93.2, 93.3, 93.6, 93.12
Blackwell v Blackwell [1929] AC 318, sub nom Blackwell, Re, Blackwell v Blackwell 98 LJ Ch 251, [1929] All ER Rep 71, 73 Sol Jo 92, 140 LT 444, 45 TLR 208, HL 103.1
Blackwell v Bull (1836) 1 Keen 176, Donnelly 54, 5 LJ Ch 251 .... 79.2, 101.4
Blackwell v Pennant (1852) 9 Hare 551, 22 LJ Ch 155, 16 Jur 420, 19 LTOS 336 .... 30.24, 30.25
Blackwell's Goods, Re (1877) 2 PD 72, 46 LJP 29, 41 JP 392, 25 WR 305, 36 LT 413 .... 25.1, 203.15
Bladen, Re [1952] ALR 326, [1952] VLR 82 .... 13.3
Blagrove v Bradshaw (1858) 4 Drew 230, 27 LJ Ch 440, 4 Jur NS 107, 6 WR 266, 30 LTOS 363 .... 35.40, 96.1
Blagrove v Coore (1859) 27 Beav 138 .... 63.1, 66.5
Blaiberg, Re, Blaiberg and Public Trustee v De Andia Yrarrazaval and Blaiberg [1940] Ch 385, [1940] 1 All ER 632, 109 LJ Ch 166, 84 Sol Jo 287, 162 LT 418, 56 TLR 487 .... 34.11, 35.31
Blaiklock v Grindle (1868) LR 7 Eq 215, 38 LJ Ch 247, 17 WR 114 .... 42.2
Blair v Duncan [1902] AC 37, 71 LJPC 22, 50 WR 369, 86 LT 157, 18 TLR 194, HL 1.6, 102.4, 102.23, 103.17
Blair's Goods, Re (1848) 6 Notes of Cases 528 .... 11.21
Blake, Re, Berry v Green. See Berry v Green

Blake, Re, Gawthorne v Blake [1917] 1 Ch 18, 86 LJ Ch 160, 61 Sol Jo 71, 115 LT 663 .... 41.20
Blake v Blake (1880) 15 Ch D 481, 49 LJ Ch 393, 28 WR 647, 42 LT 724 ... 41.5, 41.21
Blake v Blake [1923] 1 IR 88 .... 59.3
Blake v Bunbury (1792) 1 Ves 514, 4 Bro CC 21 .... 42.1, 42.5
Blake v Gale (1886) 32 Ch D 571, 55 LJ Ch 559, 34 WR 555, 55 LT 234, CA 31.12
Blake v Gibbs (1825) 5 Russ 13n 64.20
Blake v Jones (1811) 1 Hud & B 227 .... 35.6, 35.7
Blake v Knight (1843) 3 Curt 547, 7 Jur 633, 1 LTOS 208, 2 Notes of Cases 337 .... 11.25, 11.26, 13.1
Blake v O'Reily [1895] 1 IR 479 .... 38.28
Blake v Shaw (1860) John 732, 8 WR 410, [1843–60] All ER Rep 504, 2 LT 84 .... 64.7
Blake's Estate, Re (1871) 19 WR 765 .... 81.3
Blake's Trust, Re (1867) LR 3 Eq 799, 36 LJ Ch 747, 16 LT 279 .... 101.4
Blake's Trusts, Re [1904] 1 IR 98 .... 58.10
Blakemore's Settlement, Re (1855) 20 Beav 214 .... 93.2
Blakeney v Blakeney (1833) 6 Sim 52 .... 82.5
Blanch, Re, Blanch v Honhold [1967] 2 All ER 468, [1967] 1 WLR 987, 111 Sol Jo 258 .... 105.24
Bland, Re, Miller v Bland [1899] 2 Ch 336, 68 LJ Ch 745 .... 38.23, 214.35
Bland v Lamb (1820) 2 Jac & W 399 .... 38.1
Bland v Williams (1834) 3 My & K 411, 3 LJ Ch 218 .... 93.22, 93.42
Bland-Sutton's Will Trusts, Re, National Provincial Bank Ltd v Middlesex Hospital [1951] Ch 70, [1950] 2 All ER 466, 66 (pt 2) TLR 519; affd [1951] Ch 485, [1951] 1 All ER 494, 95 Sol Jo 121, [1951] 1 TLR 629, CA; on appeal sub nom Royal College of Surgeons of England v National Provincial Bank Ltd [1952] AC 631, [1952] 1 All ER 984, 45 R & IT 615, 96 Sol Jo 280, [1952] 1 TLR 978, HL 9.35, 102.8, 102.10, 102.18, 102.26, 103.10
Blandford v Thackerell (1793) 2 Ves 238, 4 Bro CC 394 .... 94.33, 103.11
Blandy v Widmore (1715) 1 P Wms 324, 2 Vern 709 .... 3.11
Blann v Bell (1852) 2 De GM & G 775, 22 LJ Ch 236, 16 Jur 1103, 20 LTOS 162 .... 38.23, 62.1
Blantern, Re, Lowe v Cooke [1891] WN 54, CA 50.21
Blasson v Blasson (1864) 2 De GJ & Sm 665, 36 LJ Ch 18, 10 Jur NS 1113, 5 New Rep 65, 13 WR 113, 46 ER 534, 11 LT 353 .... 73.1
Blathwayt v Baron Cawley [1976] AC 397, [1975] 3 All ER 625, [1975] 3 WLR 684, 119 Sol Jo 795, HL 34.9, 34.12, 35.29, 35.30, 35.31, 35.36, 35.40, 35.41, 48.5, 48.11, 50.2, 51.8, 217.40
Blathwayt's Will Trusts, Re, Blathwayt v Blathwayt [1950] 1 All ER 582, 94 Sol Jo 254, 66 (pt 1) TLR 669 .... 48.5, 48.11
Blausten v IRC [1972] Ch 256, [1972] 1 All ER 41, [1972] 2 WLR 376, 47 TC 542, [1971] TR 363, 115 Sol Jo 871, CA 40.14, 53.6, 225.91, 225.100
Blayney's (Lord) Trust, Re (1875) IR 9 Eq 413 .... 58.10
Blech v Blech [2002] WTLR 483 .... 50.1, 67.1, 200.35
Blease v Burgh (1840) 2 Beav 221, 9 LJ Ch 226 .... 93.27, 95.8
Bleckley's Goods, Re (1883) 8 PD 169, 47 JP 663, 52 LJP 102, 32 WR 171 .... 18.15

Bleckly, Re, Bleckly v Bleckly [1951] Ch 740, [1951] 1 All ER 1064, 95 Sol Jo 335, [1951] 1 TLR 902, CA 66.12, 66.13
Bleckly, Re, Sidebotham v Bleckly [1920] 1 Ch 450, 89 LJ Ch 290, 64 Sol Jo 306, 122 LT 754, 36 TLR 246, CA 72.2
Blew, Re, Blew v Gunner [1906] 1 Ch 624, 75 LJ Ch 373, 54 WR 481, [1904–7] All ER Rep 264, 95 LT 382 .... 94.38
Blewitt v Roberts (1841) Cr & Ph 274, 10 LJ Ch 342, 5 Jur 979 .... 33.12
Blewitt's Goods, Re (1880) 5 PD 116, 44 JP 768, 49 LJP 31, 28 WR 520, 42 LT 329 .... 14.6
Blight, Re, Blight v Hartnall (1880) 13 Ch D 858, 49 LJ Ch 255, 28 WR 302, 41 LT 730 .... 93.8
Blight v Hartnoll (1881) 19 Ch D 294, 51 LJ Ch 162, 30 WR 513, 45 LT 524; on appeal (1883) 23 Ch D 218, [1881–5] All ER Rep 660, 52 LJ Ch 672, 31 WR 535, 48 LT 543, CA 33.9, 33.12, 38.1, 38.3, 47.8, 47.9, 93.4, 94.44, 94.46, 211.8
Blisset's Goods, Re (1881) 44 LT 816 .... 25.10
Blockley, Re, Blockley v Blockley (1885) 29 Ch D 250, 54 LJ Ch 722, 33 WR 777 .... 44.4
Bloomfield's Goods, Re (1861) 31 LJPM & A 119 .... 38.3
Blount v Crozier [1917] 1 IR 461 .... 80.1, 80.7
Blount v Viditz [1895] 1 IR 42 .... 103.17
Blow, Re, St Bartholomew's Hospital (Governors) v Cambden [1914] 1 Ch 233, 83 LJ Ch 185, 58 Sol Jo 136, 109 LT 913, 30 TLR 117, CA 30.38
Blower v Morret (1752) 2 Ves Sen 420 .... 31.1, 33.33
Blower's Trusts, Re (1871) 6 Ch App 351, 42 LJ Ch 24, 19 WR 666, 25 LT 181 .... 71.1, 71.5
Blundell, Re, Blundell v Blundell [1906] 2 Ch 222, 75 LJ Ch 561, 94 LT 818, 22 TLR 570 .... 44.13, 47.13
Blundell v Chapman (1864) 33 Beav 648, 33 LJ Ch 660, 10 Jur NS 332, 12 WR 540, sub nom Bundell v Chapman 10 LT 152 .... 56.5
Blundell v Gladstone (1844) 14 Sim 83, 8 Jur 301, 3 LTOS 118 .... 53.1, 57.9
Blunt's Trusts, Re, Wigan v Clinch [1904] 2 Ch 767, 2 LGR 1295, 68 JP 571, 74 LJ Ch 33, 53 WR 152, 48 Sol Jo 687, 91 LT 687, 20 TLR 754 ... 102.26, 102.27, 103.6
Blyth, Re, Trustees, Executors and Agency Co Ltd v Malcolm [1925] VLR 633, 47 ALT 69, 31 Argus LR 454 .... 77.3
Blyth v Lord Advocate [1945] AC 32, [1944] 2 All ER 375, 113 LJPC 78, 88 Sol Jo 359, 171 LT 319, 61 TLR 1, HL 16.2
Boam, Re, Shorthouse v Annibal (1911) 56 Sol Jo 142 .... 47.26, 93.27
Board v Board (1873) LR 9 QB 48, 43 LJQB 4, 22 WR 206, [1861–73] All ER Rep 803, 29 LT 459 .... 43.2
Boardman v Stanley (1873) 21 WR 644 .... 64.35, 64.36
Boards, Re, Knight v Knight [1895] 1 Ch 499, [1895–9] All ER Rep 994, 64 LJ Ch 305, 13 R 278, 43 WR 472, 72 LT 220 .... 210.6
Bobier, Re [1949] 4 DLR 288, [1949] OWN 593 .... 102.10
Boddington, Re, Boddington v Clairat (1884) 25 Ch D 685, 53 LJ Ch 475, 32 WR 448, 50 LT 761, CA 8.7, 33.20, 35.6, 62.3, 80.2, 80.4, 83.7, 91.6
Boddy v Carpenter [1931] 4 DLR 927, [1931] OR 694 .... 18.27

Boden, Re, Boden v Boden [1907] 1 Ch 132, 76 LJ Ch 100, 95 LT 741, CA 33.23, 33.26, 33.30, 50.4, 50.9, 50.17, 91.6
Bodman, Re, Bodman v Bodman [1891] 3 Ch 135, 61 LJ Ch 31, 40 WR 60, 65 LT 522 .... 64.11, 64.54, 64.57
Boehm v Clarke [1804] 9 Ves 580 .... 98.10
Boehm's Goods, Re [1891] P 247, 60 LJP 80, 39 WR 576, 64 LT 806, 7 TLR 368, [1891–4] All ER Rep Ext 2044 .... 5.7, 6.1
Bogg, Re, Allison v Paice [1917] 2 Ch 239, 86 LJ Ch 536, 116 LT 714 .... 37.8
Bogg v Raper [1998] CLY 4592, (1998) Times, 22 April, CA 221.13
Bogle, Re, Bogle v Yorstoun (1898) 78 LT 457 .... 83.2, 96.4
Bogstie Estate, Re [1963] 42 WWR 702 .... 48.5
Bohachewski Estate, Re (1967) 60 WWR 635 .... 2.4
Bohrmann's Estate, Re, Caesar and Watmough v Bohrmann [1938] 1 All ER 271, 82 Sol Jo 176, 158 LT 180 .... 4.11, 4.15
Boidell v Golightly. See Boydell v Golightly
Boileau's Will Trusts, Re [1921] WN 222 .... 40.15
Boland, Re [1950] QSR 45 .... 102.25
Bold, Re, Banks v Hartland (1926) 95 LJ Ch 201, 70 Sol Jo 526, 134 LT 595 .... 48.15
Bolger v Mackell (1800) 5 Ves 509 .... 93.27
Bolitho v Hillyar (1865) 34 Beav 180, 11 Jur NS 556, 13 WR 600 .... 97.1
Bolton, Re, Brown v Bolton (1886) 31 Ch D 542, 50 JP 532, 55 LJ Ch 398, 34 WR 325, 54 LT 396, 2 TLR 303, CA 9.25
Bolton v Bolton (1861) 12 I Ch R 233 .... 93.44
Bolton v Bolton (1879) 11 Ch D 968, 43 JP 764, 48 LJ Ch 467, sub nom Bolton v London School Board 40 LT 582 .... 7.26
Bolton Estate, Re, Bolton and Hess v Toronto General Trusts Corpn (1961) 29 DLR (2d) 173, 35 WWR 621 .... 19.4
Bon v Smith (1596) Cro Eliz 532 .... 58.11
Bonar Law Memorial Trust v IRC (1933) 17 TC 508, 12 ATC 164, 77 Sol Jo 101, 49 TLR 220 .... 102.11
Bond v Graham (1842) 1 Hare 482, 11 LJ Ch 306, 6 Jur 620 .... 25.15
Bond (Inspector of Taxes) v Pickford [1983] STC 517, 57 TC 301, CA 218.102
Bone v Cook (1824) M'Cle 168, 13 Price 332, 28 RR 697 .... 47.24
Bone, Re, Bone v Midland Bank Ltd [1955] 2 All ER 555, [1955] 1 WLR 703, 99 Sol Jo 434 .... 105.5
Bonefant v Greinfield. See Bonifaut v Greenfield
Bones, Re, Goltz v Ballart Trustees, Executors and Agency Co Ltd (1930) 36 ALR 279, [1930] VLR 346 .... 102.10
Bonifaut v Greenfield (1587) Cro Eliz 80, 1 Leon 60, sub nom Bonefant v Greinfield Godb 77 .... 27.6
Bonnefoi, Re, Surrey v Perrin [1912] P 233, 82 LJP 17, 57 Sol Jo 62, 107 LT 512, CA 49.8, 50.19
Bonner, Re, Tucker v Good (1881) 19 Ch D 201, 51 LJ Ch 83, 30 WR 58, 45 LT 470 .... 71.4
Bonython v Commonwealth [1948] 1 ALR 185 .... 30.43
Booker v Allen (1831) 2 Russ & M 270, 9 LJOS Ch 130 .... 44.8, 44.14
Boorer, Re, Boorer v Boorer [1908] WN 189 .... 64.38
Boosey v Gardener (1854) 5 De GM & G 122 .... 51.7, 91.4, 93.8

Booth, Re, Booth v Booth [1894] 2 Ch 282, 63 LJ Ch 560, 8 R 256, 42 WR 613 .... 33.18, 50.21, 82.5, 216.13
Booth, Re, Booth v Booth [1926] P 118, 95 LJP 64, 134 LT 229, 42 TLR 454 .... 16.2, 16.4, 18.5, 18.17
Booth, Re, Booth v Robinson [1906] 2 Ch 321, 75 LJ Ch 610, 95 LT 524 .... 42.10
Booth, Re, Hattersley v Cowgill (1917) 86 LJ Ch 270, 116 LT 465 .... 83.2
Booth, Re, Pickard v Booth [1900] 1 Ch 768, 69 LJ Ch 474, 48 WR 566, 44 Sol Jo 348 .... 97.11, 98.13
Booth v Alington (1857) 27 LJ Ch 117, 3 Jur NS 835, 5 WR 811 .... 86.2
Booth v Booth (1799) 4 Ves 399 .... 51.2, 93.27, 93.33
Booth v Coulton (1870) 5 Ch App 684, 39 LJ Ch 622, 18 WR 877 .... 33.26, 33.28, 33.30
Booth v Meyer (1877) 38 LT 125 .... 35.12
Booth v Vicars (1844) 13 LJ Ch 147, 1 Coll 6, 8 Jur 76, 2 LTOS 307 .... 79.7
Booth's Will Trusts, Re, Robbins v King (1940) 84 Sol Jo 256, 163 LT 77, 56 TLR 507; affd [1940] WN 293, CA 54.2, 68.4, 68.6
Bootle v Blundell (1815) Coop G 136, 1 Mer 193, 15 RR 93, 19 Ves 494 .... 4.20, 206.21
Bor v Bor (1756) 3 Bro Parl Cas 167 .... 44.15
Boraston's Case (1587) 3 Co Rep 16a, 19a 93.11, 93.12, 93.14, 93.15
Bordass' Estate, Re [1929] P 107, 98 LJP 65, 72 Sol Jo 826, 140 LT 120, 45 TLR 52 .... 26.3, 26.5
Boreham v Bignall (1850) 8 Hare 131 .... 80.1, 93.38
Boreham v Prince Henry Hospital (1955) 29 ALJ 179 .... 4.9
Borlase v Borlase (1845) 4 Notes of Cases 106 .... 4.14, 18.5
Borne, Re, Bailey v Bailey [1944] Ch 190, [1944] 1 All ER 382, 113 LJ Ch 159, 88 Sol Jo 120, 171 LT 63, 60 TLR 221 .... 30.8, 41.11
Borrows v Ellison (1871) LR 6 Exch 128, 40 LJ Ex 131, 19 WR 850, 24 LT 365 .... 64.26, 64.34
Borthwick, Re, Borthwick v Beauvais (No 2) [1949] Ch 395, [1949] 1 All ER 472, [1949] LJR 752, 93 Sol Jo 147 .... 105.25
Bortoft v Wadsworth (1864) 12 WR 523 .... 66.8
Borton v Borton (1849) 16 Sim 552, 18 LJ Ch 219, 13 Jur 247, 13 LTOS 5 .... 83.9
Borton v Dunbar (1860) 2 De GF & J 338, 30 LJ Ch 8, 6 Jur NS 1128, 9 WR 41, 3 LT 519 .... 38.10
Borwick, Re, Borwick v Borwick [1933] Ch 657, [1933] All ER Rep 737, 102 LJ Ch 199, 77 Sol Jo 197, 149 LT 116, 49 TLR 288 .... 35.30, 35.36, 217.40
Bosanquet, Re, Unwin v Petre (1915) 85 LJ Ch 14, 113 LT 152 .... 47.24
Bossi, Re [1897] 5 BCR 446 .... 87.1
Bosworthick v Clegg [1929] WN 133, 45 TLR 438 .... 80.3, 80.4, 80.7, 83.7
Bothamley v Sherson (1875) LR 20 Eq 304, 44 LJ Ch 589, 23 WR 848, 33 LT 150 .... 30.3, 30.8
Botting's Estate, Re, Botting v Botting [1951] 2 All ER 997, [1951] 2 TLR 1089 .... 19.4
Bouette v Rose. See B, Re
Boughen v Farrer (1855) 3 WR 495 .... 87.1
Boughton v Boughton (1848) 1 HL Cas 406, 10 LTOS 497 .... 35.52, 52.1, 66.1, 93.34, 214.5, 214.6
Boughton v James (1844) 1 Coll 26, 8 Jur 329; varied (1848) 1 HL Cas 406, 10 LTOS 497 .... 93.22
Boughton v Knight (1873) LR 3 P & D 64, 37 JP 598, 647, 42 LJP & M 25, 41, [1861–73] All ER Rep 40, 28 LT 562 .... 4.11, 4.15, 4.20

Boughton-Knight v Wilson (1915) 32 TLR 146 .... 10.1
Boulcott v Boulcott (1853) 2 Drew 25, 23 LJ Ch 57, 2 Eq Rep 457, 18 Jur 231, 2 WR 52, 22 LTOS 130 .... 21.1
Boulcott's Settlement, Re, Wood v Boulcott (1911) 55 Sol Jo 313, 104 LT 205 .... 33.26, 33.30
Boulter, Re, Capital and Counties Bank v Boulter [1918] 2 Ch 40, [1918–19] All ER Rep 350, 87 LJ Ch 385, 118 LT 783 .... 32.20, 218.59
Boulter, Re, Capital and Counties Bank v Boulter [1922] 1 Ch 75, [1921] All ER Rep 167, 91 LJ Ch 250, 126 LT 653, 66 Sol Jo (WR) 14 .... 34.2, 34.11, 35.22, 35.24, 35.25, 35.36
Boulton v Beard (1853) 3 De GM & G 608, 98 RR 252 .... 66.2, 93.16
Boulton v Pilcher (1861) 29 Beav 633, 7 Jur NS 767, 9 WR 626 .... 93.30
Boulton's Settlement Trust, Re, Stewart v Boulton [1928] Ch 703, 97 LJ Ch 243, 139 LT 288 .... 40.5, 94.29, 213.6
Bourk's Will, Re, Cunningham v Rubenach [1907] VLR 171 .... 83.2
Bourke, Re [1923] VLR 480, 45 ALT 44, 29 Argus LR 344 .... 19.4
Bourke, Re [1952] VLR 216 .... 67.7
Bourke v Ricketts (1804) 10 Ves 330 .... 32.4, 32.33
Bourke's Trusts, Re (1891) 27 LR Ir 573 .... 82.3
Bourke's Will Trusts, Re, Barclays Bank Trust Co Ltd v Canada Permanent Trust Co [1980] 1 All ER 219, [1980] 1 WLR 539, 124 Sol Jo 362 .... 50.3, 67.2, 68.2, 76.3, 77.3, 78.1, 78.4, 78.6
Bourne, Re, Bourne v Brandreth (1888) 58 LT 537 .... 64.27
Bourne v Buckton (1851) 2 Sim NS 91, 21 LJ Ch 193, 19 LTOS 372 .... 95.9
Bourne v Keane [1919] AC 815, [1918–19] All ER Rep 167, 89 LJ Ch 17, 63 Sol Jo 606, 121 LT 426, 35 TLR 560, HL 9.36, 102.9, 102.26, 212.13
Bourne's Settlement Trusts, Re, Bourne v Mackay [1946] 1 All ER 411, 115 LJ Ch 152, 90 Sol Jo 200, 174 LT 281, 62 TLR 269, CA 95.3, 95.9
Bousfield v Lawford (1863) 1 De GJ & Sm 459, 33 LJ Ch 26, 2 New Rep 293, 11 WR 842, 8 LT 619 .... 30.12, 30.13
Bouverie, Re, Bouverie v Marshall [1952] Ch 400, [1952] 1 All ER 408, 96 Sol Jo 90, [1952] 1 TLR 355 .... 35.40, 206.27, 235.27
Bouverie v Bouverie (1847) 2 Ph 349, 16 LJ Ch 411, 11 Jur 661, 9 LTOS 469 .... 51.10
Bowden's Goods, Re (1904) 21 TLR 13 .... 9.2
Bowen, Re [1965] VR 113 .... 57.17
Bowen, Re, Lloyd Phillips v Davis [1893] 2 Ch 491, 62 LJ Ch 681, 3 R 529, 41 WR 535, [1891–4] All ER Rep 238, 37 Sol Jo 386, 68 LT 789, 9 TLR 380 .... 94.13, 102.26
Bowen, Re, Treasury Solicitor v Bowen [1949] Ch 67, [1948] 2 All ER 979, [1949] LJR 413, 92 Sol Jo 689 .... 93.9
Bowen v Barlow (1872) 8 Ch App 171, 42 LJ Ch 82, 21 WR 149, 27 LT 733 .... 64.32
Bowen v Lewis (1884) 9 App Cas 890, 54 LJQB 55, 52 LT 189, HL 50.2, 57.3, 74.1, 98.3
Bowen v Scowcroft (1837) 2 Y & C Ex 640, 7 LJ Ex Eq 25 .... 85.2
Bowen-Buscarlet's Will Trusts, Re, Nathan v Bowen-Buscarlet [1972] Ch 463, [1971] 3 All ER 636, [1971] 3 WLR 742, 115 Sol Jo 872 .... 104.1, 104.16
Bower, Re, Bower v Mercer [1930] 2 Ch 82, 99 LJ Ch 17, 141 LT 639, 143 LT 674 .... 39.20

Bower's Settlement Trusts, Re, Bower v Ridley-Thompson [1942] Ch 197, [1942] 1 All ER 278, 111 LJ Ch 225, 86 Sol Jo 48, 58 TLR 137 .... 90.6
Bowers v Bowers (1870) 5 Ch App 244, 39 LJ Ch 351, 18 WR 301, 23 LT 35 .... 97.5, 97.6
Bowes, Re, Earl Strathmore v Vane [1896] 1 Ch 507, 65 LJ Ch 298, 44 WR 441, 74 LT 16 .... 82.9
Bowes v Goslett (1857) 27 LJ Ch 249, 4 Jur NS 17, 6 WR 8, 30 LTOS 268 .... 83.9
Bowick, Re [1926] NZLR 79 .... 64.20
Bowlby, Re, Bowlby v Bowlby [1904] 2 Ch 685, 73 LJ Ch 810, 53 WR 270, 48 Sol Jo 698, 91 LT 573, CA 32.20, 32.24
Bowles (decd), Re; Hayward v Jackson [2003] EWHC 253 (Ch), [2003] Ch 422, [2003] 2 All ER 387, [2003] 2 WLR 1274, [2003] 13 LS Gaz R 27, (2003) Times, 27 February, [2003] All ER (D) 240 (Feb) 34.21, 92.1, 92.4, 209.5
Bowles, Re, Page v Page [1905] 1 Ch 371, 74 LJ Ch 338, 92 LT 556 .... 94.12, 94.28, 94.29, 94.44, 94.46, 94.48
Bowles' Will, Re, Keam v Bowles [1921] VLR 506 .... 35.8
Bowman, Re, Re Lay, Whytehead v Boulton (1889) 41 Ch D 525, 37 WR 583, 60 LT 888 .... 67.4
Bowman v Bowman [1899] AC 518, HL 51.8, 68.1
Bowman v Secular Society Ltd [1917] AC 406, 86 LJ Ch 568, [1916–17] All ER Rep 1, 61 Sol Jo 478, 117 LT 161, 33 TLR 376, HL 102.9, 102.11
Bowyer v West (1871) 19 WR 598, 24 LT 414 .... 93.6
Box v Barrett (1866) LR 3 Eq 244, 15 WR 217 .... 42.5
Box Estate, Re (1957) 7 DLR (2d) 478 .... 83.12
Box's Settlement, Re, Box v Plaut [1945] 1 All ER 547, 114 LJ Ch 177, 89 Sol Jo 225, 172 LT 312, 61 TLR 286 .... 39.14
Boyce v Boyce (1849) 16 Sim 476, 80 RR 123 .... 8.7, 34.8, 204.21
Boyce v Corbally (1834) L & G temp Plunk 102 .... 35.13
Boycot v Cotton (1738) 1 Atk 552, West temp Hard 520, [1558–1774] All ER Rep 313 .... 93.44
Boyd, Re (1969) 6 DLR (3d) 110 .... 86.2, 103.3
Boyd, Re, Kelly v Boyd [1897] 2 Ch 232, 66 LJ Ch 614, 45 WR 648, 77 LT 76 .... 39.7
Boyd, Re, Nield v Boyd (1890) 63 LT 92 .... 39.22, 82.4, 94.25, 94.31, 94.48
Boyd v Boyd (1867) LR 4 Eq 305, 36 LJ Ch 877, 15 WR 1071, 16 LT 660 .... 44.4
Boyd v Cowell [1952] ALR 523, [1952] VLR 288 .... 64.53
Boyd v Martin (1840) 2 Dr & Wal 355 .... 74.1
Boyd Estate, Re, Boyd v Boyd [1928] NI 14 .... 31.1
Boyd's Will, Re, ex p Whelan [1959] SRNSW 369 .... 18.29
Boyd's Will, Re, Miller v Farr (1872) 3 VR 46 .... 5.9
Boydell v Golightly (1844) 14 Sim 327, 9 Jur 2, sub nom Boidell v Golightly 14 LJ Ch 109 .... 98.3
Boyes, Re, Boyes v Carritt (1884) 26 Ch D 531, 53 LJ Ch 654, 32 WR 630, 50 LT 581 .... 36.4, 36.7, 36.10, 36.11, 36.13
Boyes v Bedale (1863) 1 Hem & M 798, 33 LJ Ch 283, 10 Jur NS 196, 3 New Rep 290, 12 WR 232, 10 LT 131 .... 72.7
Boyes v Cook (1880) 14 Ch D 53, 49 LJ Ch 350, 28 WR 754, 42 LT 556, CA 38.2, 39.4, 39.14, 57.15

Boyington Estate, Re (1953) 8 WWRNS 206 .... 71.3
Boyko v Jendzyjowsky (1958) 14 DLR (2d) 584, 24 WWR 608, [1958] Can Abr 976; affd (1958) 16 DLR (2d) 464, 27 WWR 144 .... 10.5
Boyle v Bishop of Peterborough (1791) 1 Ves 299, 3 Bro CC 243 .... 40.2, 47.37
Boyle's Goods, Re (1864) 28 JP 424, 33 LJPM & A 109, 4 New Rep 120, 3 Sw & Tr 426, 10 LT 541 .... 25.13
Boynton v Boynton (1785) 1 Bro CC 445 .... 42.9
Boys v Boys (1860) 28 Beav 436 .... 38.23
Boys v Morgan (1838) 3 My & Cr 661, 2 Jur 608 .... 38.3
Boys v Williams (1831) 2 Russ & M 689 .... 57.20
Boyse v Coleclough (1857) 6 HL Cas 2, 3 Jur NS 373, 5 WR 414, 29 LTOS 27 .... 5.9
Boyse v Rossborough (1857) 6 HL Cas 2, 3 Jur NS 373, 5 WR 414, [1843–60] All ER Rep 610, 29 LTOS 27 .... 5.9
Brace, Re, Gurton v Clements [1954] 2 All ER 354, [1954] 1 WLR 955, 98 Sol Jo 456 .... 35.21, 38.3, 64.48
Brace, Re, Welch v Colt [1891] 2 Ch 671, 60 LJ Ch 505, 29 WR 508, 64 LT 525 .... 39.15
Bradberry, Re, National Provincial Bank Ltd v Bradberry [1943] Ch 35, [1942] 2 All ER 629, 112 LJ Ch 49, 86 Sol Jo 349, 167 LT 396, 59 TLR 131 .... 33.35, 33.36, 33.37, 33.38, 33.40
Bradbury, Re, Needham v Reekie [1950] 2 All ER 1150n, 94 Sol Jo 839, [1951] 1 TLR 130 .... 102.5
Bradbury, Re, Wing v Bradbury (1904) 73 LJ Ch 591, 48 Sol Jo 524, 90 LT 824, CA 68.11, 96.2
Braddock's Goods, Re (1876) 1 PD 433, 40 JP 792, 45 LJP 96, 24 WR 1017 .... 12.11
Bradfield, Re, Bradfield v Bradfield [1914] WN 423 .... 64.4, 64.35, 64.45
Bradfield, Re, Bradfield v Hancock (1892) 36 Sol Jo 646, 8 TLR 696 .... 103.3, 103.8
Bradford v Foley (1779) 1 Doug KB 63 .... 93.23
Bradford v Young (1884) 26 Ch D 656, 54 LJ Ch 96, 32 WR 901, 50 LT 707; on appeal (1885) 29 Ch D 617, 33 WR 860, 53 LT 407, CA 24.6, 24.8, 25.15, 49.7, 50.19, 236.10
Bradish v Ellames (1864) 10 Jur NS 1170, 13 WR 128, 11 LT 470 .... 64.27
Bradley v Cartwright (1867) LR 2 CP 511, 36 LJCP 218, 15 WR 922, 16 LT 587 .... 101.9
Bradley v Saunders (1906) Cout 380 .... 25.1
Bradley's Goods, Re (1846) 5 Notes of Cases 187 .... 14.8
Bradly v Westcott (1807) 13 Ves 445 .... 83.11, 83.12
Bradshaw, Re, Bradshaw v Bradshaw [1902] 1 Ch 436, 71 LJ Ch 230, 86 LT 253 .... 3.14
Bradshaw v Bradshaw (1756) 2 Lee 270 .... 38.3
Bradshaw v Bradshaw (1836) 2 Y & C Ex 72, 6 LJ Ex Eq 1 .... 57.15, 58.7, 58.10
Bradshaw v Bradshaw [1908] 1 IR 288, 42 ILT 80 .... 76.6, 85.3
Bradshaw v Jackman (1887) 21 LR Ir 12 .... 9.35, 9.36
Bradshaw v Melling (1853) 19 Beav 417, 23 LJ Ch 603 .... 87.2
Bradshaw v Thompson (1843) 2 Y & C Ch Cas 295, 7 Jur 386, 1 LTOS 143 .... 103.7
Bradwell, Re, Goode v Board of Trustees for Methodist Church Purposes [1952] Ch 575, [1952] 2 All ER 286, 96 Sol Jo 462, [1952] 2 TLR 96 .... 102.28
Bradwin v Harpur (1759) Amb 374 .... 58.4

Brady v Cubitt (1778) 1 Doug KB 31 .... 30.1, 55.4
Bragger, Re, Bragger v Bragger (1887) 56 LJ Ch 490, 56 LT 521 .... 93.27
Brailsford, Re, Holmes v Crompton and Evans' Union Bank [1916] 2 Ch 536, 85 LJ Ch 709, 115 LT 343 .... 97.6
Brain v Brain (1821) 6 Madd 221 .... 41.8
Brake's Goods, Re (1881) 6 PD 217, 50 LJP 48, 29 WR 744, 45 LT 191 .... 25.1, 57.15, 58.10
Bramley's Goods, Re [1902] P 106, 71 LJP 32, 85 LT 645 .... 64.35
Bramwell, Re, Campbell v Tobin [1988] 2 FLR 263, [1988] Fam Law 391 .... 105.6
Brand, Re (1957) 7 DLR (2d) 579, [1957] OWN 26 .... 72.2
Brand v Chaddock (1871) 19 WR 378, 24 LT 347 .... 30.14
Brander Estates, Re (1952) 4 DLR 688, 6 WWRNS 702 .... 2.4
Brandon, Re, Samuels v Brandon (1932) 49 TLR 48 .... 38.26, 38.28
Brandon v Aston (1843) 2 Y & C Ch Cas 24, 7 Jur 10 .... 66.9
Brandon v Brandon (1819) 2 Wils Ch 14, 3 Swan 312 .... 79.4
Brandon v Robinson (1811) 11 RR 226, 1 Rose 197, 18 Ves 429, [1803–13] All ER Rep 290 .... 99.2, 99.3, 99.4
Brannan, Re (1991) 83 DLR (4th) 106 .... 48.5
Brannigan v Murphy [1896] 1 IR 418 .... 57.6
Bransbury's Will Trusts, Re, Grece v Bransbury [1954] 1 All ER 605, [1954] 1 WLR 496, 98 Sol Jo 179 .... 218.93
Branson, Re (1911) 31 NZLR 79 .... 25.2
Branton, Re (1910) 15 SRNSW 287 .... 101.7
Brasier v Hudson. See Brazier v Hudson
Brasier's Goods, Re [1899] P 36, 79 LT 476, sub nom Brazier's Goods, Re 68 LJP 2, 47 WR 272 .... 14.2
Brassington's Goods, Re [1902] P 1, 71 LJP 9, 85 LT 644, 18 TLR 15 .... 18.5, 18.17
Brathwaite v Brathwaite (1685) 1 Vern 334 .... 74.1
Bravda's Estate, Re [1968] 2 All ER 217, [1968] 1 WLR 479, 112 Sol Jo 137, CA 9.8, 12.14
Bray v Bree. See Bray v Hammersley
Bray v Hammersley (1830) 3 Sim 513; affd sub nom Bray v Bree (1834) 8 Bli NS 568, 2 Cl & Fin 453, HL 40.2, 40.5, 94.43, 94.44, 94.48
Braybrook (Lord) v A-G (1861) 25 JP 531, 9 HL Cas 150, 31 LJ Ex 177, 7 Jur NS 741, 9 WR 601, 4 LT 218 .... 40.3
Brazier v Hudson (1836) 8 Sim 67, sub nom Brasier v Hudson 5 LJ Ch 296 .... 25.18
Brazier Cregh's Trusts, Re, Holmes v Langley [1913] 1 IR 232 .... 41.9
Brazier's Goods, Re. See Brasier's Goods, Re
Brechin, Re (1973) 38 DLR (3d) 305 .... 80.1
Bree v Perfect (1844) 1 Coll 128, 8 Jur 282, 2 LTOS 476 .... 93.43
Breedon v Tugman (1834) 3 My & K 289, 2 LJ Ch 169 .... 93.31
Breeds' Will, Re (1875) 1 Ch D 226, 45 LJ Ch 191, 24 WR 200 .... 32.20
Breidenbach Estate, Re, Yaerger v Breidenbach (1956) 19 WWRNS 109 .... 4.13
Bremer v Freeman (1857) 10 Moo PCC 306, 5 WR 618, 29 LTOS 251 .... 24.12
Brems, Re (1963) 36 DLR (2d) 218, [1963] 1 OR 122 .... 38.7, 63.1
Brenchley v Lynn. See Brenchley v Still
Brenchley v Still (1850) 2 Rob Eccl 162, sub nom Brenchley v Lynn 16 Jur 226; affd (1850) 16 Jur 228n 13.1, 13.3, 18.16
Brennan v Brennan (1868) IR 2 Eq 321 .... 64.35
Brennan v Brennan [1894] 1 IR 69, 73 .... 93.31, 93.35, 93.40

Brennan v Moran (1866) 16 I Ch R 126 .... 88.2
Brennan v Permanent Trustee Co [1945] ALR 411, 19 ALJ 200 .... 67.1
Brennan's Will, Re [1952] QWN 1 .... 14.9
Brentano's Goods, Re. See Von Brentano's Estate, Re
Breslin v Waldron (1855) 4 I Ch R 333, 14 Ir Jur 135 .... 30.25
Breton v Mockett (1878) 9 Ch D 95, 47 LJ Ch 754, 26 WR 850 .... 8.4
Brett v A-G [1945] IR 526 .... 102.7
Brett v Horton (1841) 4 Beav 239, 10 LJ Ch 371, 5 Jur 696 .... 87.2
Brett v Rigden (1568) 1 Plowd 340, 341, 1 Co Rep 105a, 155b 68.2
Bretton v Lethulier (1710) 2 Vern 653 .... 97.4
Brewer v McCauley [1954] SCR 645, [1955] 1 DLR 415 .... 102.23
Brewer's Settlement, Re, Morton v Blackmore [1896] 2 Ch 503, 65 LJ Ch 821, 45 WR 8, 75 LT 177 .... 99.8
Brewster, Re, Butler v Southam [1908] 2 Ch 365, 77 LJ Ch 605, 99 LT 517 .... 30.34
Brewster v Foreign Mission Board of Baptist Convention of Maritime Provinces (1900) 2 NB Eq Rep 172, 21 CLT 131 .... 102.23
Brewster's Goods, Re (1859) 24 JP 87, Sea & Sm 108, 29 LJPM & A 69, 6 Jur NS 56 .... 18.17, 18.25
Brian's Estate, Re [1974] 2 NSWLR 231 .... 18.14, 21.5, 21.6
Briant v Edrick (1870) 1 VLR 35 .... 52.7
Brice v Brice (1828) 2 Mol 21 .... 42.11
Brickenden v Williams (1869) LR 7 Eq 310, 17 WR 441, sub nom Bickenden v Williams 38 LJ Ch 222 .... 39.7
Bridge v Abbot (1791) 3 Bro CC 224 .... 79.7
Bridgen, Re, Chaytor v Edwin [1938] Ch 205, [1937] 4 All ER 342, 107 LJ Ch 124, 81 Sol Jo 922, 158 LT 238, 54 TLR 100 .... 17.5, 77.4, 77.5, 79.4
Bridger, Re, Brompton Hospital for Consumption v Lewis [1894] 1 Ch 297, 63 LJ Ch 186, 42 WR 179, 38 Sol Jo 111, 70 LT 204, 10 TLR 153, CA 51.5, 54.4, 59.1, 59.2
Bridger v Ramsey (1853) 10 Hare 320 .... 98.3
Bridger's Goods, Re (1878) 4 PD 77, 42 JP 520, 47 LJP 46, 26 WR 535, 39 LT 123 .... 25.10
Bridges v Bridges (1729) 2 Eq Cas Abr 330 .... 38.10
Bridgett and Hayes' Contract, Re [1928] Ch 163, 97 LJ Ch 33, [1927] All ER Rep 191, 71 Sol Jo 910, 138 LT 106, 44 TLR 222 .... 25.16, 26.2, 26.3, 26.4, 26.5
Bridgewater (Countess) v Duke of Bolton (1704) 1 Eq Cas Abr 177, 6 Mod Rep 106, 1 Salk 236, Holt KB 281 .... 64.19
Bridgewater's Estate, Re [1965] 1 All ER 717, [1965] 1 WLR 416, 109 Sol Jo 13 .... 19.3
Bridgman v Dove (1744) 3 Atk 201 .... 64.27
Bridgnorth Corpn v Collins (1847) 15 Sim 538 .... 71.4
Bridle, Re (1879) 4 CPD 336, 41 LT 343 .... 30.3, 41.2, 41.4
Brierley, Re, Brierley v Brierley (1894) 12 R 55, 43 WR 36, 38 Sol Jo 647, CA 83.18, 101.9
Briese v Dugard (No 2) [1936] 1 DLR 723, 43 Man LR 489, [1936] 1 WWR 193 .... 3.3
Briggs v Penny (1849) 3 De G & Sm 525, 21 LJ Ch 265, 13 Jur 905, 13 LTOS 443; on appeal (1851) 16 Jur 93, 3 Mac & G 546, 87 RR 192, 18 LTOS 101 .... 57.10
Briggs v Upton (1872) 7 Ch App 376, 41 LJ Ch 519, 21 WR 30, 26 LT 485 .... 83.16

Bright v Rowe (1834) 3 My & K 316 .... 51.10, 90.1
Bright v Tyndall (1876) 4 Ch D 189, 25 WR 109 .... 49.9
Bright's Trusts, Re (1855) 21 Beav 67, 3 WR 544 .... 93.29
Bright-Smith, Re, Bright-Smith v Bright-Smith (1886) 31 Ch D 314, 55 LJ Ch 365, 34 WR 252, 54 LT 47, 2 TLR 230 .... 50.21, 58.1, 58.2, 58.6, 64.22
Brighton College v Marriott (Inspector of Taxes) [1926] AC 192, 10 TC 213, 5 ATC 32, 95 LJKB 356, [1925] All ER Rep 600, 70 Sol Jo 245, 134 LT 417, 42 TLR 228, HL 102.8
Brill v Proud [1984] Fam Law 59, CA 105.11
Brimble, Re, Brimble v Brimble (1918) 144 LT Jo 217 .... 63.1
Brine v Ferrier (1835) 7 Sim 549 .... 33.10, 88.2
Brinkley's Will Trusts, Re, Westminster Bank Ltd v Brinkley [1968] Ch 407, [1967] 3 All ER 805, [1968] 2 WLR 217, 111 Sol Jo 852 .... 213.3
Brisco v Baillie and Hamilton [1902] P 234, 71 LJP 121, 87 LT 746 .... 5.7
Briscoe v Green [2006] All ER (D) 182 (Jul) 13.1, 13.2
Bristol (Marquis), Re, Earl Grey v Grey [1897] 1 Ch 946, 66 LJ Ch 446, 45 WR 552, 41 Sol Jo 451, 76 LT 757 .... 100.3
Bristow v Bristow (1842) 5 Beav 289 .... 32.2, 53.1, 58.4, 91.6, 102.7
Bristow v Masefield (1882) 52 LJ Ch 27, 31 WR 88 .... 52.9
Bristow v Skirrow (1870) 39 LJ Ch 840, 18 WR 719, 22 LT 642, IR 10 Eq 1 .... 39.7
British Home and Hospital for Incurables v Royal Hospital for Incurables (1904) 90 LT 601, CA 103.7
British School of Egyptian Archaeology, Re, Murray v Public Trustee [1954] 1 All ER 887, [1954] 1 WLR 546, 98 Sol Jo 216 .... 102.8
Britt, Re [1968] 2 OR 12 .... 41.8
Brittlebank, Re, Coates v Brittlebank (1881) 30 WR 99 .... 218.107
Britton v Twining (1817) 3 Mer 176 .... 83.9, 84.4, 99.1
Broad, Re [1953] ALR 128, [1953] VLR 49 .... 64.7, 64.37
Broad, Re, Smith v Draeger [1901] 2 Ch 86, 70 LJ Ch 601, 84 LT 577 .... 39.2
Broad v Bevan (1823) 1 Russ 511n, 1 LJOS Ch 69 .... 53.2
Broadbent, Re [2001] 28 LS Gaz R 44, Times, 27 June, CA 103.3
Broadway Cottages Trust v IRC. See IRC v Broadway Cottages Trust
Broadwood, Re, Edwards v Broadwood (No 2) (1912) 56 Sol Jo 703, CA 3.3
Brockbank, Re, Ward v Bates [1948] Ch 206, [1948] 1 All ER 287, [1948] LJR 952, 92 Sol Jo 141 .... 27.2, 27.7, 221.39, 246.102
Brocket, Re, Dawes v Miller [1908] 1 Ch 185, 77 LJ Ch 245, 52 Sol Jo 159, 97 LT 780 .... 58.3, 58.6, 58.8
Brocklebank v Johnson (1855) 20 Beav 205, 24 LJ Ch 505, 1 Jur NS 318, 3 WR 341, 25 LTOS 56 .... 52.7, 93.30, 93.35
Brocklehurst v Flint (1852) 16 Beav 100 .... 100.4
Broderick, Re (1913) 32 NZLR 1193 .... 25.2
Brodie, Re, Barclays Bank Ltd v Dallas [1967] Ch 818, [1967] 2 All ER 97, [1967] 2 WLR 1379, 111 Sol Jo 356 .... 47.13
Brodribb, Re, Queensland Trustees Ltd v Brodribb (1942) QSR 263 .... 34.5, 99.1
Bromham's Estate, Re, Wass v Treasury Solicitor (or Solicitor-General) [1952] 1 All ER 110n, 95 Sol Jo 804, [1951] 2 TLR 1149 .... 19.3
Bromhead v Hunt (1821) 2 Jac & W 459 .... 96.1
Bromhead's Trusts, Re [1922] 1 IR 75 .... 76.3
Bromitt v Moor (1851) 9 Hare 374, 22 LJ Ch 129 .... 83.6

Bromley, Re, Wilson v Bromley (1900) 44 Sol Jo 675, 83 LT 315 .... 79.7
Bromley v Fettiplace (1700) 1 Eq Cas Abr 18, Freem Ch 245, Prec Ch 138 .... 3.2
Bromley v Wright (1849) 7 Hare 334 .... 58.10, 93.27, 93.28
Bromson, Re (1958) 14 DLR (2d) 51, [1958] OR 367, [1958] OWN 220 ..... 49.8, 202.7, 221.18
Bronsdon v Winter (1738) Amb 57 .... 41.13
Brook, Re, Brook v Hirst (1914) 58 Sol Jo 399, 111 LT 36 .... 35.50
Brook v Brook (1856) 3 Sm & G 280 .... 83.9, 101.9
Brook's Settlement, Re, Brook v Brook [1968] 3 All ER 416, [1968] 1 WLR 1661, 112 Sol Jo 845 .... 40.16
Brooke, Re, Brooke v Dickson [1923] 2 Ch 265, 92 LJ Ch 504, 67 Sol Jo 594, 129 LT 379, CA 48.5
Brooke (Lord) v Earl of Warwick (1848) 2 De G & Sm 425, 12 Jur 912, 12 LTOS 41; on appeal (1849) 18 LJ Ch 137, 1 H & Tw 142, 13 Jur 547, 13 LTOS 5 .... 63.1, 64.31
Brooke v Garrod (1857) 2 De G & J 62, 27 LJ Ch 226, 6 WR 121, 30 LTOS 194 .... 34.22, 34.25, 92.2, 92.4, 209.2
Brooke v Haymes (1868) LR 6 Eq 25 .... 25.12
Brooke v Kent (1841) 3 Moo PCC 334, 1 Notes of Cases 93 .... 14.13
Brooke v Turner (1836) 7 Sim 671, Donnelly 20, 5 LJ Ch 175, 1 Hodg 440 .... 63.1
Brooke's Will Trusts, Re, Jubber v Brooke [1953] 1 All ER 668, [1953] 1 WLR 439, 97 Sol Jo 151 .... 68.8, 68.13, 86.2, 93.29
Brooker, Re, Brooker v Brooker [1926] WN 93, 70 Sol Jo 526 .... 38.22, 38.25
Brooker, Re, Public Trustee v Young [1934] Ch 610, [1934] All ER Rep 703, 151 LT 345, sub nom Re Brooker, Young v Public Trustee 103 LJ Ch 247, 78 Sol Jo 447 .... 220.80
Brookes, Re, Brookes v Taylor [1914] 1 Ch 558, 83 LJ Ch 424, 58 Sol Jo 286, 110 LT 691 .... 29.11
Brookman v Smith (1872) LR 7 Exch 271, 41 LJ Ex 114, 20 WR 906, 26 LT 974 .... 93.9
Brookman's Trust, Re (1869) 5 Ch App 182, 39 LJ Ch 138, 18 WR 199, 22 LT 891 .... 3.10, 47.21, 47.38
Brooks, Re (1969) 4 DLR (3d) 694, 68 WWR 132 .... 64.36, 102.9
Brooks, Re, Coles v Davis (1897) 76 LT 771 .... 29.6, 29.9, 29.11
Brooks, Re, Public Trustee v White [1928] Ch 214, 97 LJ Ch 88, 72 Sol Jo 17, 138 LT 437, CA 79.7, 82.3, 83.16
Brooks' Will, Re (1865) 2 Drew & Sm 362, 34 LJ Ch 616, 13 WR 573, 12 LT 172 .... 38.1, 83.9
Brooksbank, Re, Beauclerk v James (1886) 34 Ch D 160, 56 LJ Ch 82, 35 WR 101, 55 LT 593 .... 42.1, 42.4
Brooksbank v Wentworth (1743) 3 Atk 64 .... 64.57
Broome, Re, King and Ewens v Broome (1961) 29 DLR (2d) 631, 35 WWR 590 .... 18.31
Broomfield v Summerfield (1876) 2 VLR (Eq) 174 .... 54.1
Brosseau v Dore (1904) 35 SCR 205 .... 53.2
Brotherton v Bury (1853) 18 Beav 65, 2 WR 46, 22 LTOS 140 .... 97.6
Brougham (Lord) v Lord Poulett (1855) 19 Beav 119, 24 LJ Ch 233, 1 Jur NS 151, 105 RR 85, 24 LTOS 248 .... 55.7
Broughton, Re, Peat v Broughton (1887) 57 LT 8 .... 99.10

Brouncker v Bagot (1816) 1 Mer 271, sub nom Browncker v Bagot 19 Ves 574 .... 84.4
Brouncker v Brouncker (1812) 2 Phillim 57 .... 4.10, 4.20
Brown, Re [1953] SASR 341 .... 53.5
Brown, Re (1962) 31 DLR (2d) 477, [1962] OR 237 .... 101.2
Brown, Re, Brown v Brown [1933] NZLR 115 .... 73.1
Brown, Re, Cavanagh v Cronin [1940] QSR 154 .... 30.31
Brown, Re, District Bank Ltd v Brown [1954] Ch 39, [1953] 2 All ER 1342, [1953] 3 WLR 877, 97 Sol Jo 796 .... 99.2
Brown, Re, Golding v Brady (1910) 54 Sol Jo 251, 26 TLR 257 .... 80.1
Brown, Re, Ingall v Brown [1904] 1 Ch 120, 73 LJ Ch 130, 52 WR 173, 90 LT 220 .... 35.16
Brown, Re, Leeds v Spencer [1917] 2 Ch 232, 86 LJ Ch 561, 61 Sol Jo 546, 117 LT 268 .... 54.2, 68.6
Brown, Re, Penrose v Manning (1890) 63 LT 159 .... 72.2
Brown, Re, Wace v Smith [1918] WN 118, 62 Sol Jo 487 .... 31.1
Brown v Brown (1858) 4 K & J 704, 6 WR 613, 31 LTOS 297 .... 64.23, 64.39
Brown v Brown (1858) 8 E & B 876, 27 LJQB 173, 4 Jur NS 163, 30 LTOS 273 .... 18.12, 18.13
Brown v Brown (1864) 33 Beav 399, 10 Jur NS 461, 12 WR 506, 10 LT 83 .... 37.8
Brown v Brown (1866) LR 2 Eq 481, 14 LT 694 .... 42.16
Brown v Cutler. See Luxford v Cheeke
Brown v Deacy [2002] WTLR 781 .... 4.13
Brown v Davies [1958] 1 QB 117, [1957] 3 All ER 401, [1957] 3 WLR 818, 101 Sol Jo 885, CA 204.47
Brown v Gellatly (1867) 2 Ch App 751, [1861–73] All ER Rep Ext 2080, 15 WR 1188, 17 LT 131 .... 214.35
Brown v Gregg [1945] IR 224 .... 79.4
Brown v Gregson [1920] AC 860, 89 LJPC 195, [1920] All ER Rep 730, 123 LT 465, HL 24.10, 42.1, 42.6, 42.15
Brown v Higgs (1799) 4 RR 323, 4 Ves 708; re-heard (1800) 5 Ves 495; affd (1803) 8 Ves 561; on appeal (1813) 18 Ves 192, HL 53.6, 101.9
Brown v Jarvis (1860) 2 De GF & J 168, 29 LJ Ch 595, 6 Jur NS 789, 8 WR 644, 2 LT 708 .... 93.20
Brown v Langley (1731) 2 Barn KB 118 .... 57.10
Brown v Oakshot (1857) 24 Beav 254 .... 86.5
Brown v Peck (1758) 1 Eden 140 .... 35.35
Brown v Peys (1594) 1 And 306, Cro Eliz 357 .... 34.21
Brown v Pocock (1833) 6 Sim 257 .... 101.9
Brown v Pourau [1995] 1 NZLR 352 .... 4.11
Brown v Skirrow [1902] P 3, 71 LJP 19, 85 LT 645, 18 TLR 59 .... 11.24, 12.3, 12.7
Brown v Walker (1824) 2 LJOS Ch 82 .... 56.7
Brown v Wooler (1843) 2 Y & C Ch Cas 134, 7 Jur 103 .... 93.44
Brown v Woolley (1959) 27 WWR 425 .... 18.29
Brown and Sibly's Contract, Re (1876) 3 Ch D 156, 24 WR 782, 35 LT 305 .... 40.21
Brown and Slater, Re (1903) 5 OLR 386, 2 OWR 101, 23 CTL 172 .... 89.1
Brown Estate, Re [1920] 2 WWR 226 .... 51.3
Brown Estate, Re (1953) 10 WWRNS 163 .... 10.18, 11.3
Brown Estate, Re (1953) 3 DLR 767, 9 WWRNS 27 .... 18.16

Brown's Goods, Re (1858) 27 LJP & M 20, 4 Jur NS 244, 1 Sw & Tr 32, 30 LTOS 353 .... 21.1, 21.8
Brown's Goods, Re (1877) 2 PD 110, 41 JP 601, 46 LJP 31, WR 431, 36 LT 519 .... 25.2
Brown's Goods, Re (1910) 54 Sol Jo 478 .... 25.2
Brown's Goods, Re (1912) 31 NZLR 272 .... 25.2
Brown's Goods, Re [1942] 2 All ER 176. See Hope Brown's Goods, Re
Brown's Settlement, Re, Public Trustee v Brown [1939] Ch 944, [1939] 3 All ER 391, 83 Sol Jo 524, 161 LT 56, 55 TLR 864 .... 3.15, 40.10, 40.11
Brown's Trust, Re (1865) LR 1 Eq 74 .... 40.21
Brown's Trust, Re (1873) LR 16 Eq 239, 38 JP 4, 43 LJ Ch 84, 21 WR 721, 28 LT 616 .... 96.2
Brown's Trusts, Re (1855) 1 K & J 522, 3 WR 542 .... 47.7
Brown's Will, Re (1895) 13 NZLR 645 .... 14.6
Brown's Will, Re [1948] QWN 425 .... 38.3
Brown's Will, Re, Re Brown's Settlement (1881) 18 Ch D 61, 50 LJ Ch 724, 30 WR 171, 44 LT 757, CA 35.13
Brown-Séquard's Goods, Re (1894) 6 R 565, 70 LT 811 .... 23.7
Browncker v Bagot. See Brouncker v Bagot
Browne v Browne [1912] 1 IR 272 .... 34.21
Browne v Browne [1919] 1 IR 251 .... 31.13
Browne v Collins (1871) LR 12 Eq 586 .... 32.2
Browne v Groombridge (1819) 4 Madd 495 .... 81.2
Browne v Hammond (1858) John 210 .... 47.12, 47.33, 66.5, 66.6, 66.23
Browne v Hope (1872) LR 14 Eq 343, 41 LJ Ch 475, 20 WR 667, 26 LT 688 .... 9.2, 47.23, 47.39, 93.2
Browne v King (1885) 17 LR Ir 488 .... 102.7
Browne v Lord Kenyon (1818) 3 Madd 410, 18 RR 261 .... 67.7
Browne v Moody [1936] AC 635, [1936] 2 All ER 1695, 105 LJPC 140, 80 Sol Jo 814, 155 LT 469, 53 TLR 5, PC 93.28, 93.29
Browne v Paull (1850) 1 Sim NS 92, 20 LJ Ch 75, 15 Jur 5, 16 LTOS 550 .... 82.5
Browne's Will, Re (1859) 27 Beav 324, 122 RR 142 .... 33.7
Browne's Will Trusts, Re, Landon v Brown [1915] 1 Ch 690, 84 LJ Ch 623, 113 LT 39 .... 87.2, 101.14
Brownell, Re (1858) 41 MPR 171 .... 64.28
Browning v Budd (1849) 6 Moo PCC 430, 13 LTOS 1, PC 5.9
Brownlie, Re, Brownlie v Muaux [1938] 4 All ER 54 .... 74.8
Brownlow (Earl), Re, Tower v Sedgwick (1924) 69 Sol Jo 176 .... 30.24
Brownsword v Edwards (1751) 2 Ves Sen 243, 28 ER 157, [1558–74] All ER Rep 369 .... 56.2
Bruce (an infant), Re (1882) 30 WR 922 .... 218.66
Bruce, Re, Lawford v Bruce [1908] 2 Ch 682, 78 LJ Ch 56, 99 LT 704, CA 30.12
Bruce, Re, Tasmanian Permanent Executors and Trustees Association v MacFarlane [1979] Tas SR 110 .... 66.12
Bruce v Bruce (1871) LR 11 Eq 371, 40 LJ Ch 141, 24 LT 212 .... 39.19, 40.21
Bruce v Bruce's Trustees (1875) 2 R 775, 12 SLR 485 .... 58.4
Bruce v Charlton (1842) 13 Sim 65, 6 Jur 594; affd (1843) 13 LJ Ch 97 .... 47.26, 93.26
Bruce v Curzon Howe (1870) 19 WR 116, sub nom Cardigan v Curzon-Howe 23 LT 642 .... 63.1
Bruce v Deer Presbytery (1867) LR 1 Sc & Div 96, HL 102.7

Bruce and Bruce's Estates, Re (1910) 26 TLR 381 .... 70.1
Bruce's Judicial Factor v Lord Advocate 1969 SC 296, 1969 SLT 337 .... 18.18, 18.28
Brunel v Brunel (1871) LR 12 Eq 298, 19 WR 970, 25 LT 378 .... 236.10
Brunning, Re, Gammon v Dale [1909] 1 Ch 276, 78 LJ Ch 75, 99 LT 918 ... 33.5, 33.11, 211.17
Brunt v Brunt (1873) LR 3 P & D 37, 37 JP 312, 21 WR 392, 28 LT 368 ..... 4.19, 18.5, 18.17
Brush, Re [1943] 1 DLR 74, [1942] OR 647 .... 9.8
Bruyn v Perpetual Trustee [1974] 131 CLR 387 .... 74.2
Bryan v Mansion (1852) 5 De G & Sm 737, 22 LJ Ch 233, 17 Jur 202, 19 LTOS 362 .... 98.4
Bryan v Twigg (1867) 3 Ch App 183, 37 LJ Ch 249, 16 WR 298 .... 33.14
Bryan v White (1850) 2 Rob Eccl 315, 14 Jur 919 .... 12.9
Bryan's Estate, Re [1907] P 125, 76 LJP 30, 96 LT 584 .... 18.8, 18.10, 18.14
Bryan's Trust, Re, ex p Darnborough (1851) 2 Sim NS 103, 18 LTOS 269, sub nom ex p Bryan's Trust 21 LJ Ch 7 .... 80.7
Bryant, Re, Bryant v Hickley [1894] 1 Ch 324, 63 LJ Ch 197, 8 R 32, 42 WR 183, 38 Sol Jo 79, 70 LT 301 .... 218.66
Bryant v Easterson (1859) 5 Jur NS 166, 7 WR 298, 32 LTOS 352 .... 8.4
Bryce's Goods, Re (1839) 2 Curt 325 .... 11.13
Bryce's Trustee (1878) 5 R 722, 15 SLR 412 .... 69.1, 88.3
Bryden v Willett (1869) LR 7 Eq 472, 20 LT 518 .... 76.3, 96.2
Brydges v King (1828) 1 Hag Ecc 256 .... 4.20
Brynelsen's Estate v Verdeck (2001–02) 4 ITELR 857, BC CA 2.6
Bryon, Re, Drummond v Leigh (1885) 30 Ch D 110, 55 LJ Ch 30 .... 72.2, 72.3
Bubb v Padwick (1880) 13 Ch D 517, 49 LJ Ch 178, 28 WR 382, 42 LT 116 .... 97.7
Bubb v Yelverton (1871) LR 13 Eq 131, 20 WR 164 .... 30.14
Bubnich, Marcan v Bubnich [1965] WAR 138 .... 64.43
Buccleuch (Duchess Dowager) v Hoare (1819) 4 Madd 467 .... 64.53
Buchan v Porteous (1879) 7 R 211, 17 SLR 90 .... 74.1
Buchanan, Re, Stephens v Draper [1915] 1 IR 95, Ir CA 33.28
Buchanan v Angus (1862) 4 Macq 374 .... 37.2
Buchanan v Harrison (1861) 1 John & H 662, 31 LJ Ch 74, 8 Jur NS 965, 10 WR 118 .... 62.1, 64.45, 94.12
Buck, Re [1964] VR 284 .... 204.61
Buck, Re, Bruty v Mackey [1896] 2 Ch 727, 60 JP 775, 65 LJ Ch 881, 45 WR 106, [1895–9] All ER Rep 366, 40 Sol Jo 729, 75 LT 312 .... 102.16
Buck d Whalley v Nurton (1797) 1 Bos & P 53 .... 64.2
Buckenham v Dickinson [1997] CLY 4733 .... 4.17, 4.21, 200.2
Buckinghamshire Rly Co, Re, Tookey's Trust, Re, ex p Hooper (1852) 1 Drew 264, 21 LJ Ch 402 .... 96.2
Buckland, Re, Buckland v Bennett (1887) 22 LJNC 7 .... 102.8
Buckle, Re, Williams v Marson [1894] 1 Ch 286, 63 LJ Ch 330, 7 R 72, 42 WR 229, 38 Sol Jo 112, 70 LT 115, CA 33.47, 54.5
Buckle v Bristow (1864) 10 Jur NS 1095, 5 New Rep 7, 13 WR 68, 11 LT 265 .... 8.7, 53.2, 102.22, 102.25
Buckle v Fawcett (1845) 4 Hare 536, 9 Jur 891, 5 LTOS 236 .... 67.2
Buckley, Re [1952] VLR 107 .... 18.10
Buckley v Buckley (1888) 19 LR Ir 544 .... 44.15, 51.3

Buckley's Trust, Re (1853) 17 Beav 110, 22 LJ Ch 934, 1 Eq Rep 18, 17 Jur 678, 21 LTOS 71 .... 61.1
Buckley's Trusts, Re (1883) 22 Ch D 583, 52 LJ Ch 439, 31 WR 376, 48 LT 109 .... 32.14, 32.23
Buckman v Ives (1837) 6 LJ Ch 197, sub nom Rickman v Ives 1 Jur 234 .... 64.53
Buckmaster's Estate, Re (1882) 47 LT 514 .... 85.2
Buckton's Settlement Trusts, Re, Public Trustee v Midland Bank Executor and Trustee Co Ltd [1964] Ch 497, [1964] 2 All ER 487, [1964] 2 WLR 1318, 108 Sol Jo 378 .... 48.13, 94.30
Budd's Goods, Re (1862) 3 Sw & Tr 196 .... 18.14
Buffar v Bradford (1741) 2 Atk 220 .... 85.3
Buick v Equity Trustees, Executors and Agency Co Ltd (1957) 97 CLR 599, 31 ALJ 839 .... 62.1, 76.2
Bukowski, Re [1954] QSR 286 .... 32.28, 66.13
Bulcock, Re, Ingham v Ingham [1916] 2 Ch 495, 86 LJ Ch 82, 115 LT 299 .... 66.1, 77.1
Bull v Bull [1955] 1 QB 234, [1955] 1 All ER 253, [1955] 2 WLR 78, 99 Sol Jo 60, CA 208.6
Bull v Comberbach (1858) 25 Beav 540, 4 Jur NS 526, 31 LTOS 324 .... 78.4, 84.4
Bull v Johns (1830) Taml 513 .... 93.27
Bull v Jones (1862) 31 LJ Ch 858, 10 WR 820 .... 97.10
Bull v Kingston (1816) 1 Mer 314 .... 34.6, 83.2, 83.20
Bull v Pritchard (1847) 5 Hare 567, 16 LJ Ch 185, 11 Jur 34, 8 LTOS 337 .... 93.1, 93.16
Bullen, Re, Bowman v Bowman (1915) 17 WALR 73 .... 66.21
Buller, Re, Buller v Giberne (1896) 74 LT 406 .... 64.35, 64.36, 101.6
Bulley's Trust Estate, Re (1865) 11 Jur NS 847, 13 LT 264 .... 93.31
Bulling v Ellice (1845) 9 Jur 936, sub nom Belling v Ellise 5 LTOS 475 .... 30.24
Bullmore v Wynter (1883) 22 Ch D 619, 47 JP 373, 31 WR 396, sub nom Bullmore, Re, Bullmore v Wynter 52 LJ Ch 456, 48 LT 309 .... 80.3, 80.7
Bullmore, Re, Bullmore v Wynter. See Bullmore v Wynter
Bulloch's Estate, Re [1968] NI 96 .... 12.12
Bullock v Bennett (1855) 7 De GM & G 283, 24 LJ Ch 512, 3 Eq Rep 779, 1 Jur NS 567, 3 WR 545, 25 LTOS 230 .... 1.2, 54.1, 54.2, 54.3, 65.2
Bullock v Downes (1860) 9 HL Cas 1, [1843–60] All ER Rep 706, 3 LT 194 .... 77.2, 77.4
Bullock v Thomas (1839) 9 Sim 634, 3 Jur 312 .... 41.21
Bullock's Goods, Re (1845) 1 Rob Eccl 275, 4 Notes of Cases 645 .... 25.10
Bulwilowicz, Re [1957] SASR 252 .... 9.37
Bunbury v Doran (1874) IR 8 CL 516; affd (1875) IR 9 CL 284 .... 34.7, 34.8, 57.14
Bunbury's Trusts, Re (1876) 10 IR Eq 408 .... 30.14
Bund, Re, Cruikshank v Willis [1929] 2 Ch 455, 99 LJ Ch 4, 142 LT 39 .... 18.10, 20.3
Bund v Green (1879) 12 Ch D 819, 28 WR 275 .... 101.2
Bundell v Chapman. See Blundell v Chapman
Bunn, Re, Durber v Bunn [1926] All ER Rep 626, 134 LT 669 .... 19.4
Bunn, Re, Isaacson v Webster (1880) 16 Ch D 47, 29 WR 348 .... 93.31, 93.35
Bunn v Pettinger (1866) LR 1 Eq 510, 35 Beav 321, 35 LJ Ch 389, 14 LT 118 .... 1.6
Bunning, Re, Bunning v Salmon [1984] Ch 480, [1984] 3 All ER 1, [1984] 3 WLR 265, [1985] FLR 1, [1985] Fam Law 21, 128 Sol Jo 516 .... 105.9, 105.22, 105.32, 105.38
Bunny v Bunny (1840) 3 Beav 109, 9 LJ Ch 335, 4 Jur 716 .... 18.15

Bunter v Coke (1707) 1 Salk 237 .... 4.4
Bunting, Re [1974] 2 NZLR 219 .... 9.11
Bunting v Marriott (1854) 19 Beav 163 .... 103.11
Burbey v Burbey (1862) 9 Jur NS 96, 6 LT 573 .... 71.4
Burbey v Burbey (1867) 15 WR 479, 15 LT 501 .... 58.10
Burbidge v Burbidge (1867) 37 LJ Ch 47, 16 WR 76, 17 LT 138 .... 64.20
Burchett v Woolward (1823) Turn & R 442 .... 30.24
Burden, Re, Mitchell v St Luke's Hostel Trustees [1948] Ch 160, [1948] 1 All ER 31, [1948] LJR 631, 92 Sol Jo 72 .... 35.28, 51.1
Burdet v Hopegood (1718) 1 P Wms 486 .... 73.1
Burdett v Thompson (1873) LR 3 P & D 72n 4.11
Burdus v Dixon (1858) 4 Jur NS 967, 6 WR 427 .... 64.32
Burger Estate, Re [1949] 1 WWR 280 .... 34.5
Burgess, Re (1968) 67 DLR (2d) 526, 64 WWR 44 .... 69.2
Burgess v Burgess (1844) 1 Coll 367, 8 Jur 660, 3 LTOS 452 .... 30.14
Burgess v Rawnsley [1975] Ch 429, [1975] 3 All ER 142, [1975] 3 WLR 99, 30 P & CR 221, 119 Sol Jo 406, 235 Estates Gazette 371, CA 7.3
Burgess v Robinson (1817) 3 Mer 7 .... 29.14, 35.48
Burgin's Will, Re [1922] VLR 686 .... 61.1
Burgoyne v Showler (1844) 1 Rob Eccl 5, 8 Jur 814, 3 Notes of Cases 201 .... 13.1, 14.9
Burke, Re (1959) 20 DLR 396, [1960] OR 26, [1960] OWN 4 .... 83.9
Burke, Re, Wood v Taylor [1914] 1 IR 81 .... 64.39
Burke v Burke (1899) 18 NZLR 216 .... 9.9, 48.7
Burke v Moore, Re Moore's Goods (1875) IR 9 Eq 609 .... 11.9, 11.24
Burke and O'Reilly v Burke and Quail [1951] IR 216, 84 ILTR 70 .... 35.30
Burke Irwin's Trusts, Barrett v Barrett [1918] 1 IR 350 .... 48.4
Burkinshaw v Hodge (1874) 22 WR 484 .... 88.1
Burkitt, Re, Handcock v Studdert [1915] 1 IR 205 .... 83.11, 83.12
Burkitt v Tozer (1889) 17 OR 587 .... 79.7
Burleigh v Pearson (1749) 1 Ves Sen 281 .... 56.9
Burleton v Humfrey (1755) Amb 256 .... 35.16
Burls v Burls (1868) LR 1 P & D 472, 36 LJP & M 125, 15 WR 1090, 16 LT 677 .... 18.12
Burne v Knowles (1892) 11 NZLR 98 .... 44.15
Burnett's Goods, Re (1844) 2 LTOS 317 .... 10.15
Burney v Macdonald (1845) 15 Sim 6, 9 Jur 588, 6 LTOS 1 .... 36.4, 36.8, 36.13
Burnham, Re (1958) 17 DLR (2d) 298 .... 62.1
Burnham, Re, Carrick v Carrick [1918] 2 Ch 196, 87 LJ Ch 617, [1918–19] All ER Rep 1194, 119 LT 299 .... 76.1, 76.2
Burnie v Getting (1845) 2 Coll 324, 9 Jur 937, 63 ER 754, 6 LTOS 97 .... 64.23
Burns Estate, Re (1960) 25 DLR (2d) 427, 32 WWR 689 .... 102.28
Burns Philp Trust Co Ltd v Stott (1955) 72 WNNSW 322 .... 58.4
Burns Philp Trustee Co Ltd v Elliott [1976] 1 NSWR 14 .... 9.3
Burns' Will, Re (1903) 4 SRNSW 257 .... 25.2
Burnside v Burnside (1921) 56 ILT 20 .... 64.27
Burnyeat v Van de Loeff [1924] AC 653, [1924] All ER Rep 524, 93 LJ Ch 397, 68 Sol Jo 517, 131 LT 292, 40 TLR 493, HL 19.4, 237.11
Burrage, Re, Burningham v Burrage (1890) 62 LT 752 .... 38.23, 214.3
Burrell v Baskerfield (1849) 11 Beav 525, 18 LJ Ch 422, 13 Jur 311, sub nom Burrell v Maberley 14 LTOS 61 .... 37.4, 47.32

Burrell v Maberley. See Burrell v Baskerfield
Burridge v Row (1842) 1 Y & C Ch Cas 183, 11 LJ Ch 369, 6 Jur 121; affd (1844) 13 LJ Ch 173, 8 Jur 299, 3 LTOS 1 .... 30.11
Burrow's Trusts, Re (1864) 10 LT 184 .... 80.1
Burrowes v Lord Clonbrock (1891) 27 LR Ir 538 .... 43.6
Burrows, Re, Cleghorn v Burrows [1895] 2 Ch 497, 65 LJ Ch 52, 13 R 689, 43 WR 683, 39 Sol Jo 656, 73 LT 148, 11 TLR 527 .... 73.1
Burt v Hellyar (1872) LR 14 Eq 160, 41 LJ Ch 430, 26 LT 833 .... 68.2, 79.1
Burtenshaw v Gilbert (1774) 1 Cowp 49, sub nom Berkenshaw v Gilbert Lofft 465 .... 18.5, 18.17
Burton, Re, Public Trustee v Burton [1965] NZLR 712 .... 83.9
Burton v Collingwood (1832) 4 Hag Ecc 176 .... 1.5
Burton v Gowell (1593) Cro Eliz 306 .... 18.6
Burton v McGregor [1953] NZLR 487 .... 17.4
Burton v Mount (1848) 2 De G & Sm 383, 12 Jur 934, 11 LTOS 492 .... 38.23
Burton v Newbery (1875) 1 Ch D 234, 45 LJ Ch 202, 24 WR 388, 34 LT 15 .... 9.5, 20.4, 21.7, 22.3
Burton's Settlement Trusts, Re, Public Trustee v Montefiore [1955] Ch 348, [1955] 1 All ER 433, [1955] 2 WLR 452, 99 Sol Jo 148, CA 82.4, 210.45
Burton's Settlements, Re, Scott v National Provincial Bank Ltd [1955] Ch 82, [1954] 3 All ER 193, [1954] 3 WLR 581, 98 Sol Jo 734 .... 34.10, 40.15
Burton's Will, Re, Banks v Heaven [1892] 2 Ch 38, 61 LJ Ch 702, 67 LT 221 .... 32.16
Busch v Eastern Trust Co [1928] SCR 479, [1928] 3 DLR 834 .... 93.29
Bush v Cowan (1863) 32 Beav 228, 9 Jur NS 429, 11 WR 395, 9 LT 161 ... 39.14, 47.39
Bushell v Faith [1970] AC 1099, [1970] 1 All ER 53, [1970] 2 WLR 272, 114 Sol Jo 54, HL 205.69
Bushnell, Re, Lloyds Bank Ltd v Murray [1975] 1 All ER 721, [1975] 1 WLR 1596, 119 Sol Jo 189 .... 102.10, 102.11
Busk v Aldam (1874) LR 19 Eq 16, 44 LJ Ch 119, 23 WR 21, 31 LT 370 .... 213.12
Bustard v Saunders (1843) 7 Beav 92, 7 Jur 986 .... 85.3
Busteed v Eager (1834) Milw 345, 348 .... 18.10, 18.14
Butcher, Re [1920] VLR 166 .... 16.4
Butcher v Butcher (1812) 1 Ves & B 79 .... 47.38
Butcher v Jackson (1845) 14 Sim 444 .... 40.15
Butcher v Leach (1843) 5 Beav 392, 7 Jur 74 .... 93.35
Bute (Marquess), Re, Marquess of Bute v Ryder (1884) 27 Ch D 196, 53 LJ Ch 1090, 32 WR 996 .... 58.10
Bute (Marquis) v Harman (1846) 9 Beav 320 .... 93.39
Butler, Re (1965) 50 DLR (2d) 210, [1965] 2 OR 236 .... 77.3
Butler, Re, Joyce v Brew [1918] 1 IR 394 .... 47.12
Butler v Borton (1820) 5 Madd 40 .... 61.1
Butler v Butler (1884) 28 Ch D 66, 54 LJ Ch 197, 33 WR 192, 52 LT 90 .... 64.32, 214.25
Butler v Gray (1869) 5 Ch App 26, 39 LJ Ch 291, 18 WR 193, 25 LT 227 .... 39.21, 101.9
Butler v Lowe (1839) 10 Sim 317, 3 Jur 1143 .... 65.3, 66.20
Butler v Stratton (1791) 3 Bro CC 367 .... 87.1
Butler v Trustees, Executors and Agency Co Ltd (1906) 3 CLR 435 .... 56.3

Butler's Settlement Trusts, Re [1942] Ch 403, [1942] 2 All ER 191, 111 LJ Ch 280, 86 Sol Jo 268, 167 LT 238, 58 TLR 323 .... 39.27
Butler's Trusts, Re, Hughes v Anderson (1888) 38 Ch D 286, 57 LJ Ch 643, 36 WR 817, 59 LT 386, CA 7.3
Butlin v Barry (1837) 1 Curt 614; affd sub nom Barry v Butlin (1838) 2 Moo PCC 480 .... 4.20, 5.1, 5.2, 5.3, 5.4, 5.9
Butlin's Settlement Trusts, Re, Butlin v Butlin [1976] Ch 251, [1976] 2 All ER 483, [1976] 2 WLR 547, 119 Sol Jo 794 .... 6.1, 6.3, 200.46
Butricke v Broadhurst (1790) 1 Ves 171, 3 Bro CC 88 .... 42.9, 42.11
Butter v Ommaney (1827) 4 Russ 70, 6 LJOS Ch 54 .... 85.5
Butter v Ommaney (1828) 4 Russ 73 .... 68.6
Buxton, Re, Buxton v Buxton [1930] 1 Ch 648, 99 LJ Ch 334, [1930] All ER Rep 396, 143 LT 37 .... 32.3, 61.1
Buxton v Blakiston (1886) 2 TLR 293 .... 103.7
Buzzacott, Re, Munday v King's College Hospital [1953] Ch 28, [1952] 2 All ER 1011, 96 Sol Jo 850, [1952] 2 TLR 884 .... 103.10
Byde v Byde (1761) 2 Eden 19, 1 Cox Eq Cas 44 .... 44.15
Byles v Cox (1896) 74 LT 222 .... 12.11, 13.1
Byne v Blackburn (1858) 26 Beav 41, 27 LJ Ch 788, 4 Jur NS 803, 6 WR 861, 32 LTOS 34 .... 82.5
Byng v Byng. See Webb v Byng
Byng v Lord Strafford (1843) 5 Beav 558, 12 LJ Ch 169, 7 Jur 98; affd sub nom Hoare v Byng (1844) 10 Cl & Fin 508, 8 Jur 563, HL 34.13, 82.2
Byrne, Re, Byrne v Kenny (1889) 23 LR Ir 260 .... 93.35
Byrne v Cullinan [1904] 1 IR 42 .... 39.22
Byrne v Healy (1828) 2 Mol 94 .... 33.11
Byrne's Goods (No 2), Re (1910) 44 ILT 192 .... 25.16
Byrne's Will, Re, Byrne v Byrne (1898) 24 VLR 832 .... 53.3, 57.15
Byrom v Brandreth (1873) LR 16 Eq 475, 42 LJ Ch 824 .... 64.35, 64.38
Byron's Settlement, Re, Williams v Mitchell [1891] 3 Ch 474, 60 LJ Ch 807, 40 WR 11, 65 LT 218 .... 39.3, 39.13, 39.31, 40.3
Bythsea v Bythsea (1854) 23 LJ Ch 1004, 2 WR 677, 24 LTOS 17 .... 51.10, 96.2
Bythway, Re, Gough v Dames (1911) 80 LJ Ch 246, 55 Sol Jo 235, 104 LT 411 .... 29.1, 29.13, 29.19
Bywater, Re, Bywater v Clarke (1881) 18 Ch D 17, 30 WR 94, CA 5.8, 52.7, 57.10

C

C (a patient), Re [1991] 3 All ER 866, [1992] 1 FLR 51, [1991] Fam Law 521, 8 BMLR 1, [1991] NLJR 671 .... 4.24, 4.25
C (leave to apply for provision), Re [1995] 2 FLR 24. See W (a minor) (claim from deceased's estate), Re [1995] 2 FCR 689
CIBC Trust Corpn v Peebles (1999) 180 DLR (4th) 720 .... 71.5
Cabburn, Re, Gage v Rutland (1882) 46 LT 848 .... 82.3
Cable (Lord), Re, Garratt v Waters [1976] 3 All ER 417, [1977] 1 WLR 7, 120 Sol Jo 317 .... 24.6
Caborne, Re, Hodge and Nabarro v Smith [1943] Ch 224, [1943] 2 All ER 7, 112 LJ Ch 210, 87 Sol Jo 201, 169 LT 109, 59 TLR 309 .... 35.35

Cadell v Palmer (1833) 10 Bing 140, 7 Bli NS 202, 1 Cl & Fin 372, 3 Moo & S 571, HL 73.1, 94.2, 94.3, 94.4, 94.8, 94.13, 94.33
Cadell v Wilcocks [1898] P 21, 67 LJP 8, 46 WR 394, 78 LT 83, 14 TLR 100 .... 18.10
Cadett v Earle (1877) 5 Ch D 710, 46 LJ Ch 798 .... 64.23
Cadge's Goods, Re (1868) LR 1 P & D 543, 32 JP 198, 37 LJP & M 15, 16 WR 406, 17 LT 484 .... 14.10
Cadman v Cadman (1872) LR 13 Eq 470, 41 LJ Ch 468, 20 WR 356 .... 64.45
Cadogan, Re, Cadogan v Palagi (1883) 25 Ch D 154, 53 LJ Ch 207, 32 WR 57, 49 LT 666 .... 64.35, 64.36
Cafe v Bent (1845) 5 Hare 24, 9 Jur 653 .... 38.23
Caffary v Caffary (1844) 8 Jur 329, 3 LTOS 70 .... 85.3
Cain v Watson [1910] VLR 256 .... 95.9
Cairnes, Re, Howard v Cairnes (1982) 4 FLR 225, 12 Fam Law 177 .... 105.41
Caithness (Earl), Re (1891) 7 TLR 354 .... 21.6
Caithness (Earl) v Sinclair 1912 SC 79 .... 34.12
Caldbeck v Caldbeck [1911] 1 IR 144 .... 81.3
Calder v Alexander (1900) 16 TLR 294 .... 7.30
Caldwell v Caldwell (1921) 91 LJPC 95, 65 Sol Jo 765, 37 TLR 953, HL 56.7, 56.9, 102.23
Caldwell v Cresswell (1871) 6 Ch App 278, 24 LT 564 .... 34.21
Caldwell v Fleming [1927] NZLR 145 .... 99.1, 103.11
Caledonian Rly Co v North British Rly Co (1881) 6 App Cas 114, 29 WR 685, HL 50.6
Callaghan, Re [1985] Fam 1, [1984] 3 All ER 790, [1984] 3 WLR 1076, [1985] FLR 116, [1985] Fam Law 28, 128 Sol Jo 705 .... 105.3, 105.16, 105.17, 105.22, 105.28, 105.32
Callaway, Re, Callaway v Treasury Solicitor [1956] Ch 559, [1956] 2 All ER 451, [1956] 3 WLR 257, 100 Sol Jo 452 .... 9.17, 9.18
Callicott's Goods, Re [1899] P 189, 68 LJP 67, 80 LT 421 .... 9.2
Callow v Callow (1889) 42 Ch D 550, 58 LJ Ch 698, 38 WR 104, 5 TLR 705 .... 64.53
Calow, Re, Calow v Calow [1928] Ch 710, 97 LJ Ch 253, [1928] All ER Rep 518, 72 Sol Jo 437, 139 LT 235 .... 7.27, 41.20
Calt, Re [1957] 12 DLR 140 .... 52.7
Calvert v Sebbon (1841) 4 Beav 222 .... 30.14
Cambridge v Rous (1802) 6 RR 199, 8 Ves 12 .... 47.6
Cambridge v Rous (1858) 25 Beav 409 .... 67.3, 94.28
Camden v Fletcher (1838) 8 LJ Ex 17, 1 Horn & H 361, 4 M & W 378 .... 25.12
Camden (Marquis) v IRC [1914] 1 KB 641, 83 LJKB 509, 58 Sol Jo 219, 110 LT 173, 30 TLR 225, CA; affd sub nom IRC v Marquess Camden [1915] AC 241, 84 LJKB 145, 58 Sol Jo 782, 111 LT 1033, 30 TLR 681, HL 50.13, 57.6
Cameron, Re (1967) 62 DLR (2d) 389, MPR 214 .... 38.3, 83.11
Cameron, Re [1999] Ch 386, [1999] 2 All ER 924, [1999] 3 WLR 394, [1999] 16 LS Gaz R 35 .... 44.1, 44.2, 44.3, 44.4, 44.5, 44.7, 44.8, 44.12, 44.13, 95.9, 100.1, 100.6, 237.10, 237.14
Cameron, Re, Currie v Milligan [1955] 1 All ER 424, [1955] 1 WLR 140, 99 Sol Jo 130, CA 33.30

Cameron, Re, Nixon v Cameron (1884) 26 Ch D 19, 53 LJ Ch 1139, 32 WR 834, 50 LT 339, CA 205.73
Cameron v Cuddy [1914] AC 651, 83 LJPC 70, 110 LT 89, PC 92.3
Cameron v Harper (1892) 21 SCR 273 .... 64.19, 64.51
Cameron v Treasury Solicitor [1997] 1 FCR 188, [1996] 2 FLR 716, [1996] Fam Law 723, CA 105.11
Camfield v Gilbert (1803) 3 East 516 .... 64.16
Camoys (Lord) v Blundell (1848) 1 HL Cas 778 .... 57.15, 57.18, 58.4, 58.10
Campbell, Re [1928] 4 DLR 797, 63 OLR 36 .... 77.3
Campbell, Re (1963) 40 DLR (2d) 681, [1963] 2 OR 633 .... 51.2
Campbell, Re, Campbell v Campbell [1893] 3 Ch 468, 62 LJ Ch 878, 37 Sol Jo 582, 69 LT 134 .... 29.1, 32.31
Campbell, Re, Cooper v Campbell (1919) 88 LJ Ch 239, 63 Sol Jo 286, 120 LT 562 .... 93.6, 93.36, 93.38, 93.41, 93.43
Campbell, Re, M'Cabe v Campbell [1918] 1 IR 429 .... 50.2, 50.15, 82.5
Campbell, Re, Peacock v Ewen [1930] NZLR 713 .... 102.7
Campbell, Re, Public Trustee v Campbell [1952] NZLR 214 .... 76.3
Campbell v Beaufoy (1859) John 320, 28 LJ Ch 645, 7 WR 513, 33 LTOS 199 .... 24.1, 24.2
Campbell v Bouskell (1859) 27 Beav 325 .... 71.5, 85.4
Campbell v Brownrigg (1843) 1 Ph 301, 13 LJ Ch 7 .... 82.4
Campbell v Campbell (1866) LR 1 Eq 383, 35 LJ Ch 241, 12 Jur NS 118, 14 WR 327, 13 LT 667 .... 24.9
Campbell v Campbell (1906) 5 WLR 59, 6 Terr LR 378 .... 4.19
Campbell v Campbell and Davis (1895) 72 LT 294 .... 99.6
Campbell v French (1797) 3 Ves 321 .... 18.5
Campbell v Graham (1831) 1 Russ & M 453, 9 LJOS Ch 234; on appeal sub nom Campbell and Hay v Graham, Campbell and Hay v Sandford (1834) 8 Bli NS 622, 2 Cl & Fin 429, HL 30.43
Campbell v Harding (1831) 2 Russ & M 390; on appeal sub nom Candy v Campbell (1834) 8 Bli NS 469, 2 Cl & Fin 421, HL 84.4, 98.4
Campbell v Home (1842) 1 Y & C Ch Cas 664, 7 Jur 635, 57 RR 510 .... 40.15
Campbell v IRC [1970] AC 77, [1968] 3 All ER 588, [1968] 3 WLR 1025, 45 TC 427, 47 ATC 341, [1968] TR 327, 112 Sol Jo 864, HL 102.1
Campbell v M'Grain (1875) IR 9 Eq 397 .... 38.10, 64.17
Campbell v Sandys (1803) 1 Sch & Lef 281 .... 40.2
Campbell and Hay v Graham, Campbell and Hay v Sandford. See Campbell v Graham
Campbell's Estate, Re [1954] 1 All ER 448, [1954] 1 WLR 516, 98 Sol Jo 197 .... 203.31, 221.48
Campbell's Trustee v Dick 1915 SC 100 .... 68.11
Campbell's Trustee v Welsh 1952 SC 343, 1952 SLT 352 .... 86.5, 87.1
Campbell's Trustees v Campbell (1921) 58 SLR 69, 1921 SC (HL) 12 .... 102.23
Campbell's Trusts, Re (1886) 31 Ch D 685, 55 LJ Ch 389, 34 WR 396, 54 LT 419; affd (1886) 33 Ch D 98, 55 LJ Ch 911, 34 WR 629, 55 LT 463, CA 87.2
Campbell's Trusts, Re, Public Trustee v Campbell [1922] 1 Ch 551, 91 LJ Ch 433, [1922] All ER Rep 79, 127 LT 236 .... 39.5
Campden Charities, Re (1881) 18 Ch D 310, 50 LJ Ch 646, 30 WR 496, 45 LT 152, CA 103.18

Canada Permanent Trust Co v Bowman [1962] SCR 711 .... 10.18
Canada Permanent Trust Co v MacFarlane (1972) 27 DLR (3d) 480 .... 102.7
Canada Permanent Trust Co v Share (1958) 25 WWR 638 .... 74.2, 87.1
Canada Permanent Trust Co and McGregor, Re (1980) 115 DLR (3d) 697 .... 38.23
Cancellor v Cancellor (1862) 2 Drew & Sm 194, 32 LJ Ch 17, 8 Jur NS 1146, 1 New Rep 12, 11 WR 16, 7 LT 307 .... 87.1
Candy v Campbell. See Campbell v Harding
Cane, Re, Ruff v Sivers (1890) 60 LJ Ch 36, 63 LT 746 .... 93.20
Canney's Trusts, Re, Mayers v Strover (1910) 54 Sol Jo 214, 101 LT 905 ... 66.13, 66.23
Canning's Will Trusts, Re, Skues v Lyon [1936] Ch 309, 105 LJ Ch 241, 154 LT 693 .... 48.15, 94.30
Cannon, Re, Cannon v Cannon (1915) 60 Sol Jo 43, 114 LT 231, 32 TLR 51 .... 33.13
Cant's Estate, Re (1859) 4 De G & J 503, 28 LJ Ch 641, 5 Jur NS 829, 7 WR 624, [1843–60] All ER Rep 542, 33 LTOS 280 .... 92.5
Cantillon's Minors, Re (1864) 16 I Ch R 301 .... 56.3, 93.27
Caparo Industries plc v Dickman [1990] 2 AC 605, [1990] 1 All ER 568, [1990] 2 WLR 358, [1990] BCLC 273, [1990] BCC 164, 134 Sol Jo 494, [1990] 12 LS Gaz R 42, [1990] NLJR 248, HL 1.14
Cape v Cape (1837) 2 Y & C Ex 543, 1 Jur 307 .... 85.3
Capel, Re, Arbuthnot v Capel (1914) 59 Sol Jo 177 .... 38.3, 60.1, 64.35, 64.36
Capel v Girdler (1804) 9 Ves 509 .... 60.1
Caplin's Will, Re (1865) 2 Drew & Sm 527, 34 LJ Ch 578, 11 Jur NS 383, 6 New Rep 17, 143 RR 273, 13 WR 646, 12 LT 526 .... 39.3, 79.4, 101.9
Capron v Capron (1874) LR 17 Eq 288, 43 LJ Ch 677, 22 WR 347, 29 LT 826 .... 20.4
Carberry v M'Carthy (1881) 7 LR Ir 328 .... 101.9
Carbery v Cox (1852) 3 I Ch R 231n, 4 Ir Jur 274 .... 102.8, 102.9
Carden v Tuck (1588) Cro Eliz 89, sub nom Chard and Tuck's Case 3 Leon 214 .... 64.34
Cardigan v Curzon-Howe. See Bruce v Curzon Howe
Careless v Careless (1816) 1 Mer 384, 19 Ves 601 .... 51.11, 57.15, 57.22
Carew, Re, Carew v Carew [1896] 1 Ch 527; affd [1896] 2 Ch 311, 65 LJ Ch 686, 44 WR 700, 74 LT 501, CA 30.17
Carew, Re, Channer v Francklyn [1939] Ch 794, [1939] 3 All ER 200, 108 LJ Ch 291, 83 Sol Jo 545, 161 LT 139, 55 TLR 875 .... 33.45
Carey, Re (1977) 121 Sol Jo 173 .... 19.1
Carey, Re, Wardle v Carey [1950] 1 All ER 726, 66 (pt 1) TLR 802 .... 33.23, 33.30
Carey v Carey (1857) 6 I Ch R 255 .... 68.1
Carfrae, Re [1905] VLR 641 .... 32.21
Cargill, Re (1977) 79 DLR (3d) 726 .... 57.20
Carile, Re, Dakin v Trustees, Executors and Agency Co Ltd [1920] VLR 263 .... 10.5
Carleton, Re (1909) 28 NZLR 1066 .... 93.20
Carleton's Goods, Re [1915] 2 IR 9 .... 21.7
Carlson, Re (1975) 55 DLR (3d) 616 .... 93.39
Carmichael v Gee (1880) 5 App Cas 588, 49 LJ Ch 829, 29 WR 293, 43 LT 227, HL 33.24, 33.27
Carne v Long (1860) 24 JP 676, 2 De GF & J 75, 29 LJ Ch 503, 6 Jur NS 639, 8 WR 570, 2 LT 552 .... 9.35, 102.8

Carne's Settled Estates, Re [1899] 1 Ch 324, 68 LJ Ch 120, 47 WR 352, sub nom Re St Donats Settled Estate 79 LT 542 .... 27.18
Carolin v Carolin (1881) 17 LR Ir 25n 55.6, 56.8
Carr v Atkinson (1872) LR 14 Eq 397, 41 LJ Ch 785, 20 WR 620, 26 LT 680 .... 40.5
Carr v Bedford (1678) 2 Rep Ch 146 .... 79.4, 102.14
Carr v Carr (1811) 1 Mer 541n 64.37, 64.39
Carr v Carr (23 June 1997, unreported) 105.17
Carr v Eastabrooke (1797) 3 Ves 561 .... 44.15
Carr v Ingleby (1831) 1 De G & Sm 362 .... 33.41
Carr-Glynn v Frearsons (a firm) [1997] 2 All ER 614; revsd [1999] Ch 326, [1998] 4 All ER 225, [1999] 2 WLR 1046, [1998] 3 FCR 487, [1999] 1 FLR 8, [1998] Fam Law 739, [1998] NLJR 1487, [1998] EGCS 128, CA 1.14, 200.46, 204.69
Carrington, Re, Ralphs v Swithenbank [1932] 1 Ch 1, 100 LJ Ch 299, [1931] All ER Rep 658, 145 LT 284, CA 41.20
Carritt's Goods, Re (1892) 66 LT 379 .... 21.7
Carrodus v Carrodus [1913] VLR 1 .... 35.2
Carroll v Perpetual Trustee Co Ltd (1916) 22 CLR 423 .... 95.9
Carson, Re (1963) 37 DLR (2d) 292, [1963] 1 OR 373 .... 64.14
Carson, Re, Carson v Carson [1915] 1 IR 321 .... 61.1
Carson, Re, Carson v Presbyterian Church of Queensland [1956] St R Qd 466 .... 57.22
Carson v Wilson (1961) 26 DLR (2d) 307, [1961] OR 113 .... 10.5
Carson Estate, Re (1921) 62 DLR 263, [1921] 2 WWR 273 .... 52.1
Carter, Re (1892) 41 WR 140 .... 38.19, 38.23
Carter, Re (1909) 20 OLR 127 .... 87.2
Carter, Re, Dodds v Pearson [1900] 1 Ch 801, 69 LJ Ch 426, 48 WR 555, 82 LT 526 .... 64.32
Carter, Re, Harding v Carter (1903) 21 NZLR 227 .... 34.5
Carter, Re, Walker v Litchfield (1911) 30 NZLR 707 .... 66.5, 66.21
Carter v Bentall (1840) 2 Beav 551, 9 LJ Ch 303, 4 Jur 691 .... 54.5, 76.2
Carter v Carter (1857) 3 K & J 617, 27 LJ Ch 74, 4 Jur NS 63, 112 RR 308, 30 LTOS 349 .... 34.24, 99.4
Carter v Green (1857) 21 JP 626, 3 K & J 591, 26 LJ Ch 845, 3 Jur NS 905, 5 WR 856, 29 LTOS 342 .... 34.6, 36.5, 102.25
Carter v Haswell (1857) 26 LJ Ch 576, 3 Jur NS 788, 5 WR 388, 29 LTOS 398 .... 47.6
Carter v Seaton (1901) 45 Sol Jo 673, 85 LT 76, 17 TLR 671 .... 12.6
Carter v Silber [1891] 3 Ch 553, 60 LJ Ch 716, 39 WR 552, 65 LT 51, 7 TLR 561; revsd [1892] 2 Ch 278, 61 LJ Ch 401, 66 LT 473, CA; affd sub nom Edwards v Carter [1893] AC 360, [1891–4] All ER Rep 1259, 63 LJ Ch 100, 58 JP 4, 1 R 218, 69 LT 153, HL 42.6, 42.16
Carthew v Enraght (1872) 20 WR 743, 26 LT 834 .... 101.9
Cartwright, Re, Cartwright v Smith [1939] Ch 90, [1938] 4 All ER 209, 108 LJ Ch 51, 82 Sol Jo 930, 159 LT 538, 55 TLR 69, CA 23.7
Cartwright v Cartwright (1793) 1 Phillim 90 .... 4.13, 4.14, 4.20
Cartwright v Cartwright [1903] 2 Ch 306, sub nom Re Cartwright, Cartwright v Cartwright 72 LJ Ch 622, 51 WR 666, 47 Sol Jo 618, 88 LT 854 .... 44.1, 44.9
Cartwright v Shepheard (1853) 17 Beav 301 .... 18.15

Cartwright v Vawdry (1800) 5 Ves 530 .... 72.2
Carvell Estate, Re (1977) 21 NBR (2d) 642 .... 4.21
Carver v Bowles (1831) 2 Russ & M 301, 9 LJOS Ch 91 .... 42.4
Carver v Burgess (1853) 18 Beav 541 .... 90.2
Carver v Duncan (Inspector of Taxes) [1985] AC 1082, [1985] 2 All ER 645, [1985] 2 WLR 1010, [1985] STC 356, 59 TC 125, 129 Sol Jo 381, HL 218.30, 220.5
Carver v Richards (1859) 27 Beav 488, 29 LJ Ch 169, 8 WR 157, 1 LT 257; affd (1860) 1 De GF & J 548 .... 39.18
Carvill, Re (1913) 26 WLR 189, 15 DLR 206 .... 58.5
Carville, Re, Shone v Walthamstow Borough Council [1937] 4 All ER 464 ... 77.7, 104.1
Casamajor v Strode (1843) 8 Jur 14 .... 96.2, 96.4
Casborne v Scarfe. See Casburne v Inglis
Casburne v Inglis (1738) 2 Jac & W 194, Lee temp Hard 399, West temp Hard 221, sub nom Casborne v Scarfe 2 Eq Cas Abr 728, 1 Atk 603 .... 64.32
Casmore's Goods, Re (1869) LR 1 P & D 653, 33 JP 392, 38 LJP & M 54, 17 WR 627, 20 LT 497 .... 11.6
Cassel, Re, Public Trustee v Ashley (1922) 39 TLR 75 .... 30.24
Cassidy, Re [1979] VR 369 .... 221.34
Casson v Dade (1781) 2 Dick 586, 1 Bro CC 99 .... 11.24
Castiglione's Will Trusts, Re, Hunter v Mackenzie [1958] Ch 549, [1958] 1 All ER 480, [1958] 2 WLR 400, 102 Sol Jo 176 .... 9.33, 30.8
Castle, Re, Nesbitt v Baugh [1916] WN 195 .... 33.5
Castle, Re, Public Trustee v Floud [1949] Ch 46, [1948] 2 All ER 927, [1949] LJR 610, 64 TLR 599 .... 67.1
Castle v Eate (1844) 7 Beav 296, 8 Jur 280, 3 LTOS 2 .... 93.30
Castle v Fox (1871) LR 11 Eq 542, 40 LJ Ch 302, 19 WR 840, 24 LT 536 .... 57.18
Castle v Torre. See Torre v Castle
Castledon v Turner (1745) 3 Atk 257 .... 50.8, 57.8
Castlehow, Re, Lamonby v Carter [1903] 1 Ch 352, 72 LJ Ch 211, 88 LT 455 .... 38.10
Cater's Trusts (No 2), Re (1858) 25 Beav 366, 119 RR 453 .... 30.42
Cathcart (Earl), Re (1912) 56 Sol Jo 271 .... 65.2, 78.4
Catling, Re, Public Trustee v Catling [1931] 2 Ch 359, 100 LJ Ch 390, [1931] All ER Rep 677, 145 LT 613 .... 83.6
Cator v Cator (1851) 14 Beav 463 .... 85.3
Catt's Trusts, Re (1864) 2 Hem & M 46, 33 LJ Ch 495, 10 Jur NS 536, 4 New Rep 88, 12 WR 739, 10 LT 409 .... 34.13
Cattell, Re, Cattell v Cattell [1907] 1 Ch 567, 76 LJ Ch 242, 96 LT 612, 23 TLR 331; affd [1914] 1 Ch 177, 83 LJ Ch 322, 58 Sol Jo 67, 110 LT 137, CA 95.3
Cattermole v Prisk [2006] 1 FLR 693, [2006] Fam Law 98 .... 4.17, 4.21
Cattley v Vincent (1852) 15 Beav 198 .... 93.8
Cattlin v Brown (1853) 11 Hare 372, 1 Eq Rep 550, 1 WR 533 .... 93.7, 94.21, 94.27
Caulfield v Maguire (1845) 2 Jo & Lat 141 .... 76.3
Caus, Re, Lindeboom v Camille [1934] Ch 162, [1933] All ER Rep 818, 103 LJ Ch 49, 77 Sol Jo 816, 150 LT 131, 50 TLR 80 .... 9.36, 102.9, 212.13
Cavan (Lady) v Pulteney (1795) 2 Ves 544 .... 42.8
Cavanagh, Re [1938] 2 DLR 761 .... 27.15
Cave v Cave (1762) 2 Eden 139 .... 50.2

Cave v Harris (1887) 57 LJ Ch 62, 36 WR 182, 57 LT 768 .... 58.6, 58.12, 59.3
Cave v Horsell [1912] 3 KB 533, 81 LJKB 981, 107 LT 186, 28 TLR 543, CA 50.6, 50.10, 50.14, 55.2
Cavendish v Cavendish (1784) 1 Cox Eq Cas 77, 1 Bro CC 467 .... 64.3
Cavendish (Lord) v Lowther. See Lowther v Cavendish
Cavendish's Settlement, Re, Grosvenor v Butler [1912] 1 Ch 794, 81 LJ Ch 400, 56 Sol Jo 399, 106 LT 510 .... 100.3
Cawthron's Goods, Re (1863) 28 JP 201, 33 LJPM & A 23, 10 Jur NS 51, 3 New Rep 93, 3 Sw & Tr 417, 12 WR 443 .... 1.5
Cazenove v Cazenove (1889) 61 LT 115 .... 31.1
Central and Nova Scotia Trust Co v Freeman (1975) 58 DLR (3d) 541 .... 52.3
Central Employment Bureau for Women and Students' Careers Association Inc, Re [1942] 1 All ER 232 .... 102.7
Central Trust and Safe Deposit Co v Snider [1916] 1 AC 266, 85 LJPC 87, 114 LT 250, PC 42.5
Chadock v Cowley (1624) Cro Jac 695 .... 98.10
Chadwick v Doleman (1705) 1 Eq Cas Abr 344, 2 Vern 528 .... 81.3
Chadwick v Heatley (1845) 2 Coll 137, 9 Jur 504, 5 LTOS 303 .... 30.42
Chadwick's Trusts, Re, Shaw v Woodward [1939] 1 All ER 850, 83 Sol Jo 358 .... 40.15
Chadwin, Re, ex p Chadwin (1818) 3 Swan 380 .... 29.1
Chaffers and Abell v Abell (1839) 3 Jur 578 .... 93.27
Chalcraft, Re, Chalcraft v Giles [1948] P 222, [1948] 1 All ER 700, [1948] LJR 1111, 92 Sol Jo 181, 64 TLR 246 .... 11.14, 12.6
Chalmers v Storil (1813) 2 Ves & B 222 .... 38.10
Chamberlain's Goods, Re (1867) LR 1 P & D 316, 31 JP 247, 36 LJP & M 52, 15 WR 680, 16 LT 97, [1861–73] All ER Rep Ext 2106 .... 25.16
Chamberlayne v Brockett (1872) 8 Ch App 206, 37 JP 261, 42 LJ Ch 368, 21 WR 299, [1861–73] All ER Rep 271, 28 LT 248 .... 94.13, 102.26, 103.11, 103.18
Chambers, Re (1847) 11 I Eq R 518 .... 40.10
Chambers, Re [1971] NZLR 703 .... 33.26
Chambers v Atkins (1823) 1 Sim & St 382, 1 LJOS Ch 208 .... 82.5
Chambers v Brailsford (1816) 2 Mer 25, 19 Ves 652 .... 52.5
Chambers v Chambers (1846) 15 Sim 183, 15 LJ Ch 318, 10 Jur 326, 7 LTOS 385 .... 30.3
Chambers v Goldwin (1805) 11 Ves 1 .... 32.22
Chambers v Jeoffery (1709) 2 Eq Cas Abr 541 .... 30.3
Chambers and Yatman v Queen's Proctor (1840) 2 Curt 415 .... 4.13, 4.14
Chamney's Goods, Re (1849) 1 Rob Eccl 757, 14 LTOS 89, 7 Notes of Cases 70 .... 12.11
Champ v Champ (1892) 30 LR Ir 72 .... 101.10
Champion, Re, Dudley v Champion [1893] 1 Ch 101, 62 LJ Ch 372, 2 R 162, 67 LT 694, CA 20.4, 22.2, 22.3, 59.3
Champion v Pickax (1737) 1 Atk 472 .... 74.1
Champney v Davy (1879) 11 Ch D 949, 48 LJ Ch 268, 27 WR 390, 40 LT 189 .... 47.7
Chan Chun Wah v Chan Chun Wai [1987] 2 HKC 397 .... 1.8
Chana v Chana [2001] WTLR 205 .... 4.19
Chance, Re, Westminster Bank Ltd v Chance [1962] Ch 593, [1962] 1 All ER 942, [1962] 1 WLR 409, 106 Sol Jo 285 .... 33.30

Chance v Chance (1853) 16 Beav 572 .... 93.6, 93.26
Chancellor, Re, Chancellor v Brown (1884) 26 Ch D 42, 53 LJ Ch 443, 32 WR 465, 51 LT 33, CA 38.23
Chancey's Case (1725) 1 P Wms 408, 2 Eq Cas Abr 354 pl 18, sub nom Chancy v Wootton Cas temp King 44 .... 44.15
Chancy v Wootton. See Chancey's Case
Chandler v Pocock (1880) 15 Ch D 491, 49 LJ Ch 442, 28 WR 806, 43 LT 112; affd (1881) 16 Ch D 648, 50 LJ Ch 380, 29 WR 877, [1881–5] All ER Rep 296, 44 LT 115, CA 37.5, 39.12
Chandos (Duke) (or Chandois (Dux)) v Talbot (or Talbott) (1731) Kel W 25, 2 P Wms 601 .... 93.44, 93.45
Channon v Perkins (a firm) [2006] WTLR 425 .... 13.2
Chant, Re, Chant v Lemon [1900] 2 Ch 345, 69 LJ Ch 601, 48 WR 646, 83 LT 341 .... 55.6, 56.8
Chaplin, Re, Neame v A-G [1933] Ch 115, 102 LJ Ch 56, 76 Sol Jo 576, 148 LT 190 .... 102.6, 102.7
Chaplin, Re, Royal Bank of Scotland v Chaplin [1950] Ch 507, [1950] 2 All ER 155, 94 Sol Jo 369, 66 (pt 1) TLR 1166 .... 64.44, 104.4, 204.16
Chaplin and Staffordshire Potteries Waterworks Co's Contract, Re [1922] 2 Ch 824, 92 LJ Ch 34, 67 Sol Jo 46, 128 LT 186, 38 TLR 857, CA 25.18
Chaplin's Trusts, Re (1863) 33 LJ Ch 183, 3 New Rep 192, 12 WR 147, 9 LT 475 .... 47.31, 47.32
Chapman, Re, Charley v Lewis (1922) 56 ILT 32 .... 66.23, 74.1
Chapman, Re, Ellick v Cox (1883) 32 WR 424, 49 LT 673 .... 77.1
Chapman, Re, Hales v A-G [1922] 2 Ch 479, 91 LJ Ch 527, 66 Sol Jo 522, 127 LT 616, CA 83.3, 102.23
Chapman, Re, Perkins v Chapman [1904] 1 Ch 431, 73 LJ Ch 291, 52 WR 467, 90 LT 339, CA; affd sub nom Chapman v Perkins [1905] AC 106, 74 LJ Ch 331, 53 WR 485, 92 LT 372, HL 50.21, 50.21, 54.1, 54.2, 93.9, 97.4
Chapman v Chapman (1876) 4 Ch D 800, 46 LJ Ch 104 .... 38.3, 38.11
Chapman v Gilbert (1853) 4 De GM & G 366 .... 52.8
Chapman v Hart (1749) 1 Ves Sen 271 .... 63.1
Chapman v Perkins. See Chapman, Re, Perkins v Chapman
Chapman v Reynolds (1860) 28 Beav 221, 29 LJ Ch 594, 6 Jur NS 440, 8 WR 403, 2 LT 319 .... 64.35
Chapman's Goods, Re (1844) 1 Rob Eccl 1, 8 Jur 902, 3 Notes of Cases 198 .... 21.7
Chapman's Settlement Trusts, Re, Jones v Chapman [1978] 1 All ER 1122, [1977] 1 WLR 1163, 121 Sol Jo 619, CA 66.12, 66.13, 66.14, 66.20
Chapman's Will, Re (1863) 32 Beav 382, 9 Jur NS 657, 11 WR 578 .... 68.9
Chappell's Goods, Re [1894] P 98, 63 LJP 95, 6 R 576, 70 LT 245 .... 25.1, 57.15, 57.22, 58.10
Chappell's Trusts, Re (1862) 10 WR 573, 6 LT 643 .... 93.9
Chapple, Re, Newton v Chapman (1884) 27 Ch D 584, 33 WR 336, 51 LT 748 .... 221.43
Chard and Tuck's Case. See Carden v Tuck
Chardon, Re, Johnston v Davies [1928] Ch 464, [1927] All ER Rep 483, 97 LJ Ch 289, 139 LT 261 .... 9.29, 202.29
Charge v Goodyer (1826) 3 Russ 140 .... 71.4

Charitable Donations and Bequests Comrs v Cotter (1841) 1 Dr & War 498 .... 97.9
Charitable Donations and Bequests Comrs v De Clifford (1841) 1 Dr & War 245 .... 103.16
Charitable Donations and Bequests Comrs v Deey (1891) 27 LR Ir 289 .... 79.2
Charitable Donations and Bequests Comrs v Wybrants (1845) 2 Jo & Lat 182 .... 102.20
Charles v Barzey [2002] UKPC 68, [2003] 1 WLR 437, [2002] All ER (D) 328 (Dec) 34.5
Charleson, Re [1968] VR 252 .... 58.1
Charleton, Re, Bracey v Sherwin [1911] WN 54, 55 Sol Jo 330 .... 35.35
Charlton v West (1861) 30 Beav 124, 7 Jur NS 905, 9 WR 884, 5 LT 16 .... 44.15
Charlton Estate, Re [1919] 1 WWR 134 .... 74.1
Charter v Charter (1874) LR 7 HL 364, 43 LJP & M 73 .... 57.12, 57.22, 58.10
Charteris, Re, Charteris v Biddulph [1917] 2 Ch 379, 86 LJ Ch 658, 61 Sol Jo 591, 117 LT 391, CA 29.11, 30.31, 243.2
Charteris, Re, Charteris v Kenyon [1917] 2 Ch 257, 87 LJ Ch 78, 61 Sol Jo 415, 116 LT 718 .... 214.3
Chartres, Re, Farman v Barrett [1927] 1 Ch 466, 96 LJ Ch 241, [1927] All ER Rep 408, 137 LT 52 .... 48.6, 66.4, 66.13, 66.15
Chase, Re [1951] VLR 477 .... 17.4
Chaston, Re, Chaston v Seago (1881) 18 Ch D 218, 50 LJ Ch 716, 29 WR 778, 45 LT 20 .... 67.6, 90.1, 97.7
Chatard's Settlement, Re [1899] 1 Ch 712, 68 LJ Ch 350, 47 WR 515, 80 LT 645 .... 9.41
Chatfield v Berchtoldt (1872) 7 Ch App 192, 41 LJ Ch 255, 20 WR 401, 26 LT 267 .... 23.4
Chatham (Earl) v Tothill. See Tothill v Pitt
Chatteris v Young (1827) 2 Russ 183 .... 91.6
Chauncy v Graydon (1743) 2 Atk 616 .... 34.24
Chave v Farrant (1810) 18 Ves 8 .... 44.17
Chaworth v Beech (1799) 4 Ves 555 .... 30.3, 30.34
Chaytor, Re, Chaytor v Horn [1905] 1 Ch 233, 74 LJ Ch 106, 53 WR 251, [1904–7] All ER Rep 230, 92 LT 290 .... 38.19
Cheadle, Re, Bishop v Holt [1900] 2 Ch 620, 69 LJ Ch 753, 49 WR 88, 44 Sol Jo 673, 83 LT 297, CA 8.7, 57.19, 57.22, 57.23
Cheese v Lovejoy (1877) 2 PD 251, 25 WR 853, 37 LT 295, sub nom Re Harris, Cheese v Lovejoy 46 LJP 66, CA 18.5, 18.17, 18.25
Chellew v Martin (1873) 21 WR 671, 28 LT 662 .... 93.15
Chennells v Bruce [1939] WN 75, 83 Sol Jo 136, 55 TLR 422 .... 5.9
Cherrington, Re [1984] 2 All ER 285, [1984] 1 WLR 772, [1984] FLR 559, [1984] Fam Law 181, 128 Sol Jo 302, [1984] CLY 3660 .... 47.2
Cherry v Boultbee (1839) 2 Keen 319, 4 My & Cr 442, 9 LJ Ch 118, 3 Jur 1116 .... 30.10, 30.13
Cherry v Mott (1836) 1 My & Cr 123, 5 LJ Ch 65 .... 102.22
Chesham (Lord), Re, Cavendish v Dacre (1886) 31 Ch D 466, 55 LJ Ch 401, 34 WR 321, 54 LT 154, 2 TLR 265 .... 42.1, 42.6
Chesline v Hermiston [1928] 4 DLR 786, 62 OLR 575 .... 12.5
Chester, Re, Servant v Hills [1914] 2 Ch 580, 84 LJ Ch 78 .... 71.4
Chester v Baston (1980) 118 DLR (3d) 323 .... 13.1
Chester v Painter (1725) 2 Eq Cas Abr 314, 2 P Wms 335, PC 64.19, 93.27

Chester v Urwick (1856) 23 Beav 404 .... 32.2
Chesterfield's (Earl) Trusts, Re (1883) 24 Ch D 643, [1881–5] All ER Rep 737, 52 LJ Ch 958, 32 WR 361, 49 LT 261 .... 38.17, 38.22, 104.16, 200.36, 224.34, 225.33, 230.7
Chevaux v Aislabie (1842) 13 Sim 71 .... 93.27
Cheyney's (Lord) Case (1591) 5 Co Rep 68a 57.10
Chia Khwee Eng v Chia Poh Choon [1923] AC 424, 92 LJPC 70, 128 LT 556, PC 93.18
Chichester (Lord) v Coventry (1867) LR 2 HL 71, 36 LJ Ch 673, 15 WR 849, 17 LT 35 .... 44.1, 44.2, 44.3, 44.7, 44.9, 44.11, 44.12, 44.13, 44.15
Chichester v Quatrefages [1895] P 186, 64 LJP 79, 11 R 605, 43 WR 667, 72 LT 475, 11 TLR 328 .... 18.10
Chichester Diocesan Fund and Board of Finance Inc v Simpson [1944] AC 341, [1944] 2 All ER 60, 113 LJ Ch 225, 88 Sol Jo 246, 171 LT 141, 60 TLR 492, HL 1.6, 56.7, 102.23, 102.24, 212.5
Chichester's (Earl) Will Trusts, Re, Pelham v Countess of Chichester [1946] Ch 289, [1946] 1 All ER 722, 115 LJ Ch 217, 90 Sol Jo 223, 175 LT 45, 62 TLR 442 .... 16.6
Chilcot v Bromley (1806) 12 Ves 114 .... 30.24
Chilcott's Goods, Re [1897] P 223, 66 LJP 108, 46 WR 32, 77 LT 372, 13 TLR 378 .... 21.7, 22.5
Child v Elsworth (1852) 2 De GM & G 679 .... 57.5, 91.4
Child v Giblett (1834) 3 My & K 71, 3 LJ Ch 124 .... 97.5
Childes's Goods, Re (1845) 4 Notes of Cases 36 .... 12.11
Childs v A-G [1973] 2 All ER 108, [1973] 1 WLR 497, 117 Sol Jo 283 .... 102.2
Chinery, Re, Chinery v Hill (1888) 39 Ch D 614, 57 LJ Ch 804, 59 LT 303 .... 68.6
Chinnery's Estate, Re (1877) 1 LR Ir 296 .... 94.21
Chipchase v Simpson (1849) 16 Sim 485, 18 LJ Ch 145, 13 Jur 90 .... 68.1
Chirnside, Re (1903) 29 VLR 4 .... 44.11
Chirnside, Re, Lewis v Forrest [1956] VLR 295 .... 221.3
Chittenden, Re, Chittenden v Doe [1970] 3 All ER 562, [1970] 1 WLR 1618, 114 Sol Jo 954 .... 105.5
Chitty's Will Trust, Re, Re Thomas's Will Trusts, Ransford (or Ransferd) v Lloyds Bank Ltd [1970] Ch 254, [1969] 3 WLR 643, 113 Sol Jo 798, sub nom Re Thomas's Will Trust [1969] 3 All ER 1492 .... 102.24
Choa Eng Wan v Choa Giang Tee [1923] AC 469, 92 LJPC 145, 129 LT 226, PC 18.8, 237.11
Chorley v Loveband (1863) 33 Beav 189, 12 WR 187, 9 LT 596 .... 35.39, 55.3
Chow Siu Po v Wong Ming Fund [2004] 1 HKC 120 .... 10.1
Christ's Hospital v Grainger (1849) 13 JP 778, 19 LJ Ch 33, 1 H & Tw 533, 14 Jur 339, 1 Mac & G 460, 84 RR 128, [1843–60] All ER Rep 204, 15 LTOS 497 .... 9.29, 102.26
Christian v Taylor [1926] AC 773, 96 LJPC 6, 136 LT 168, 42 TLR 699, PC 97.6
Christian's Goods, Re (1849) 2 Rob Eccl 110, 7 Notes of Cases 265 .... 12.12
Christie, Re, Christie v Keeble [1979] Ch 168, [1979] 1 All ER 546, [1979] 2 WLR 105, 122 Sol Jo 663 .... 105.16
Christie v Gosling (1866) LR 1 HL 279, 35 LJ Ch 667, 15 LT 40 .... 94.15
Christie v Saunders (1856) 5 Gr 464 .... 40.7
Christie's Will, Re (1883) 9 VLR 46 .... 18.9

Christmas and Christmas v Whinyates (1863) 27 JP 327, 32 LJPM & A 73, 9 Jur NS 283, 1 New Rep 336, 3 Sw & Tr 81, 11 WR 371, 7 LT 801 ...... 14.8, 18.18, 18.27
Christopherson v Naylor (1816) 1 Mer 320 ...... 66.6, 68.6
Chunilal Parvatishankar v Bai Samrath (1914) 30 TLR 407, PC 96.2, 98.13
Church v Hill [1923] SCR 642, [1923] 3 DLR 1045, [1923] 3 WWR 405 ...... 59.3
Church Estate Charity, Wandsworth, Re (1871) 6 Ch App 296, 35 JP 484, 19 WR 456, 24 LT 243, sub nom Re Wandsworth Church Estate Charity 40 LJ Ch 159 ...... 102.9
Church of Scientology's Application for Registration as a Charity [2005] WTLR 1151 ...... 102.9
Church Property Trustees v Public Trustee (1907) 27 NZLR 354 ...... 50.6, 63.2
Churchhill, Re [1919] 3 WWR 557 ...... 62.1
Churchill, Re, Hiscock v Lodder [1909] 2 Ch 431, 79 LJ Ch 10, 53 Sol Jo 697, 101 LT 380 ...... 32.20, 32.22
Churchill, Re, Taylor v Manchester University [1917] 1 Ch 206, 86 LJ Ch 209, 61 Sol Jo 131, 115 LT 769 ...... 19.2
Churchill v Churchill (1867) LR 5 Eq 44, 37 LJ Ch 92, 16 WR 182 ...... 42.4
Churchill v Marks (1844) 14 LJ Ch 65, 1 Coll 441, 4 LTOS 452, sub nom Marks v Churchill 9 Jur 155 ...... 99.3
Churchill v Roach [2002] EWHC 3230 (Ch), [2004] 3 FCR 744, [2004] 2 FLR 989, [2004] Fam Law 720, [2003] WTLR 779, [2003] All ER (D) 348 (Apr) 105.14
Churston Settled Estates, Re [1954] Ch 334, [1954] 2 WLR 386, 98 Sol Jo 178, sub nom Re Churston Settled Estates, Freemantle v Baron Churston [1954] 1 All ER 725 ...... 39.2
Circuitt v Perry (1856) 23 Beav 275, 2 Jur NS 1157, 5 WR 15, 28 LTOS 115 ...... 38.1
City of London Building Society v Flegg [1988] AC 54, [1987] 3 All ER 435, [1987] 2 WLR 1266, [1988] 1 FLR 98, [1988] Fam Law 17, 54 P & CR 337, 19 HLR 484, 131 Sol Jo 806, [1987] LS Gaz R 1966, [1987] NLJ Rep 475, HL 208.6
Claman Estate, Re (1963) 42 DLR (2d) 670, 45 WWR 193 ...... 83.14
Clancarty v Clancarty (1892) 31 LR Ir 530 ...... 38.6
Clanchy's Will Trusts, Re, Lynch v Edwards [1970] 2 All ER 489, CA 77.3
Clancy, Re [1953] OWN 741 ...... 101.6
Clancy v Clancy [2003] EWHC 1885 (Ch), [2003] 37 LS Gaz R 32, [2003] All ER (D) 536 (Jul) 4.10
Clapham, Re, Barraclough v Mell [2006] WTLR 203 ...... 44.3
Clarges v Albemarle (1691) Nels 174, 2 Vern 245 ...... 8.3
Claringbull's Goods, Re (1844) 3 Notes of Cases 1 ...... 12.5
Clark, Re (1932) 101 LJP 27, 76 Sol Jo 461, 147 LT 240, 48 TLR 544 ...... 5.7
Clark, Re, Clark v Clark [1926] Ch 833, 95 LJ Ch 325, [1926] B & CR 77, [1925] All ER Rep 219, 70 Sol Jo 344, 135 LT 666 ...... 99.8
Clark, Re, Clark v Randall (1885) 31 Ch D 72, 55 LJ Ch 89, 34 WR 70, 53 LT 591, 2 TLR 53 ...... 9.9, 48.7
Clark, Re, Cross v Hillis [1924] WN 75, 59 L Jo 150 ...... 100.4
Clark, Re, Horwell v Dent [1961] NZLR 635 ...... 62.1, 99.1, 102.9, 103.11
Clark, Re, McKecknie v Clark [1904] 1 Ch 294, 73 LJ Ch 188, 52 WR 212, 48 Sol Jo 130, 89 LT 736, 20 TLR 101 ...... 63.1

Clark v Browne (1854) 18 Jur 903, 2 Sm & G 524, 2 WR 665, 24 LTOS 3 .... 41.16
Clark v Henry (1871) 6 Ch App 588, 40 LJ Ch 377, 19 WR 706, CA 97.6
Clark v Phillips (1853) 17 Jur 886 .... 20.5, 38.13
Clark v Phillips (1854) 2 WR 331 .... 25.12
Clark v Sewell (1744) 3 Atk 96 .... 32.7, 44.15, 210.27
Clark v Taylor (1853) 1 Drew 642, 1 Eq Rep 435, 1 WR 476, 21 LTOS 287 .... 103.1, 103.3
Clark (Mary) Home Trustees v Anderson (Surveyor of Taxes) [1904] 2 KB 645, 5 TC 48, 73 LJKB 806, 91 LT 457, 20 TLR 626 .... 102.7
Clark's Estate, Re (1864) 3 De GJ & Sm 111, 13 WR 115 .... 67.1
Clark's Estate, Re (1954) 13 WWRNS 79 .... 64.37
Clark's Estate, Re, Maddick v Marks (1880) 14 Ch D 422, 49 LJ Ch 586, 28 WR 753, 43 LT 40, CA 39.14
Clark's Goods, Re (1839) 2 Curt 239 .... 11.21
Clark's Trusts, Re (1863) 32 LJ Ch 525, 2 New Rep 386, 11 WR 871, 8 LT 571 .... 101.13
Clarke, Re [1966] VR 321 .... 31.1
Clarke, Re, Bracey v Royal National Lifeboat Institution [1923] 2 Ch 407, 92 LJ Ch 629, [1923] All ER Rep 607, 67 Sol Jo 680, 129 LT 310, 39 TLR 433 .... 102.6, 102.7, 102.22
Clarke, Re, Clarke v Clarke [1901] 2 Ch 110, 70 LJ Ch 631, 49 WR 628, 45 Sol Jo 484, 84 LT 811, 17 TLR 479 .... 9.35, 102.26
Clarke, Re, Clarke v Roberts [1968] 1 All ER 451, [1968] 1 WLR 415, 112 Sol Jo 97 .... 105.25
Clarke, Re, Clarke v Sturt [1929] VLR 249 .... 100.6
Clarke, Re, Sheldon v Redrup [1942] Ch 434, [1942] 2 All ER 294, 111 LJ Ch 261, 86 Sol Jo 282, 167 LT 220, 58 TLR 366 .... 33.21, 47.8, 48.10, 237.7
Clarke v Blake (1788) 2 Bro CC 319; on appeal (1795) 2 Ves 673 .... 73.1
Clarke v Brothwood [2006] EWHC 2939 (Ch), [2006] All ER (D) 207 (Nov) 6.2
Clarke v Bruce Lance & Co (a firm) [1988] 1 All ER 364, [1988] 1 WLR 881, 131 Sol Jo 1698, [1988] 2 LS Gaz R 37, [1987] NLJ Rep 1064, CA 1.14
Clarke v Clarke (1836) 8 Sim 59, 5 LJ Ch 286 .... 66.17, 66.20
Clarke v Clarke (1868) IR 2 CL 395 .... 7.30
Clarke v Clarke (1879) 5 LR Ir 47 .... 13.2
Clarke v Clarke 1925 SC 431 .... 18.10
Clarke v Clemmans (1866) 36 LJ Ch 171, 15 WR 250 .... 47.1, 47.28
Clarke v Colls (1861) 9 HL Cas 601 .... 50.17
Clarke v Earl of Ormonde (1821) Jac 108, [1814–23] All ER Rep 329 .... 30.34
Clarke v Leare and Scarwell (1791) 1 Phillim 119 .... 4.13, 4.20
Clarke v Lubbock (1842) 1 Y & C Ch Cas 492, 6 Jur 548 .... 97.1
Clarke v Parker (1812) 19 Ves 1, [1803–13] All ER Rep 301 .... 34.25, 35.13, 35.16, 35.17
Clarke v Portland Burying Ground Association 151 Conn 527 (1964) 202.30
Clarke v Scripps (1852) 2 Rob Eccl 563, 16 Jur 783, 20 LTOS 83 ...... 18.6, 18.18, 18.23
Clarke's Goods, Re (1858) 27 LJP & M 18, 4 Jur NS 234, 1 Sw & Tr 22, 6 WR 307, 30 LTOS 340 .... 11.13, 11.20
Clarkson, Re, Public Trustee v Clarkson [1915] 2 Ch 216, 84 LJ Ch 881, 59 Sol Jo 630, 113 LT 917 .... 86.2

Clarkson v Clarkson (1862) 26 JP 631, 31 LJPM & A 143, 2 Sw & Tr 497, 10 WR 781, 6 LT 506 .... 18.5, 18.17, 19.5
Clarkson v Robinson [1900] 2 Ch 722, 69 LJ Ch 859, 48 WR 698, 83 LT 164 .... 221.43, 221.46
Clausen v Denson [1958] NZLR 572 .... 3.13
Clavering v Ellison (1859) 7 HL Cas 707, 29 LJ Ch 761 .... 34.10, 34.21, 35.32, 35.33
Clay v Coles [1880] WN 145 .... 33.17
Clay v Coles (1887) 57 LT 682 .... 96.4
Clay v Pennington (1835) 7 Sim 370, 6 LJ Ch 183, sub nom Clayton v Pennington Donnelly 165 .... 56.5, 68.1, 76.4
Clayton v Gregson (1836) 5 Ad & El 302, 4 LJKB 161, 1 Har & W 159, 6 Nev & MKB 694, 4 Nev & MKB 159, [1835–42] All ER Rep 626 .... 50.11
Clayton v Lord Nugent (1844) 13 LJ Ex 363, 13 M & W 200 .... 57.6
Clayton v Lowe (1822) 5 B & Ald 636 .... 97.6
Clayton v Pennington. See Clay v Pennington
Clayton v Ramsden. See Samuel, Re, Jacobs v Ramsden
Clayton v Roe. See Roe d Wren v Clayton
Cleare and Forster v Cleare (1869) LR 1 P & D 655, 38 LJP & M 81, 17 WR 687, 20 LT 497 .... 4.14
Cleaver, Re, Cleaver v Insley [1981] 2 All ER 1018, [1981] 1 WLR 939, 125 Sol Jo 445 .... 2.3, 2.4, 2.6, 2.8
Cleaver v Mutual Reserve Fund Life Association [1892] 1 QB 147, 56 JP 180, 61 LJQB 128, 40 WR 230, [1891–4] All ER Rep 335, 36 Sol Jo 106, 66 LT 220, 8 TLR 139, CA 9.14, 9.15, 9.17, 9.18
Clegg's Estate, Re, ex p Evans (1862) 15 Jur 27, 14 I Ch R 70 .... 56.3
Cleghorn, Re (1919) 48 DLR 511, 45 OLR 540, 15 OWN 444 .... 34.1
Cleghorn, Re [1931] 2 DLR 865 .... 25.1
Clement v Cheesman (1884) 27 Ch D 631, 54 LJ Ch 158, 33 WR 40 .... 1.15
Clements, Re, Clements v Pearsall [1894] 1 Ch 665, 63 LJ Ch 326, 42 WR 374, 38 Sol Jo 272, 70 LT 682 .... 32.3, 32.15, 32.21
Clements v Paske (1784) 2 Cl & Fin 230n, 3 Doug KB 384 .... 81.3
Clements' Goods, Re [1892] P 254, 61 LJP 130, 67 LT 356 .... 18.15, 18.28, 20.2
Clementson v Gandy (1836) 1 Keen 309, Donnelly 85, 5 LJ Ch 260 .... 42.5, 57.3, 57.10
Clemow, Re, Yeo v Clemow [1900] 2 Ch 182, 69 LJ Ch 522, 48 WR 541, 44 Sol Jo 428, 82 LT 550 .... 55.7
Cleoburey v Beckett (1851) 14 Beav 583 .... 18.6
Clergy Society, Re (1856) 2 K & J 615, 4 WR 664 .... 57.19, 103.3, 103.7
Clerke, Re, Clowes v Clerke [1915] 2 Ch 301, 84 LJ Ch 807, 59 Sol Jo 667, 113 LT 1105 .... 76.1, 78.4, 78.5, 85.4, 98.2
Clery v Barry (1887) 21 LR Ir 152, CA 11.24, 13.3, 13.4
Cleveland (Dowager Duchess) v Meyrick (1867) 37 LJ Ch 125, 16 WR 104, 17 LT 238 .... 64.54
Cleveland's (Duke) Settled Estates, Re [1893] 3 Ch 244, 37 Sol Jo 630, 69 LT 735, 9 TLR 573, sub nom Re Cleveland (Duke), Barnard v Wolmer 62 LJ Ch 955, CA 39.12
Clibborn v Clibborn (1857) 2 Ir Jur 386 .... 38.1
Cliff's Trusts, Re [1892] 2 Ch 229, 61 LJ Ch 397, 40 WR 439, 36 Sol Jo 398, 66 LT 483 .... 24.6, 25.15, 50.11, 57.5, 57.6
Clifford, Re, Mallam v McFie [1912] 1 Ch 29, 81 LJ Ch 220, 56 Sol Jo 91, 106 LT 14, 28 TLR 57 .... 41.14, 59.2, 64.54, 102.26

Clifford v Beaumont (1828) 4 Russ 325 .... 34.22
Clifford v Clifford (1852) 9 Hare 675 .... 39.12
Clifford v Koe (1880) 5 App Cas 447, 28 WR 633, 43 LT 322, HL 54.5, 57.15, 85.2
Clifford v Tanner [1987] CLY 3881 .... 105.43
Clifford's Estate, Re (1953) 9 WWRNS 454 .... 64.35
Clifford's Settlement Trusts, Re, Heaton v Westwater [1981] Ch 63, [1980] 1 All ER 1013, [1980] 2 WLR 749, 124 Sol Jo 362 .... 66.13, 66.20
Clift v Clift [1964–5] NSWR 1896 .... 9.15
Clifton v Crawford (1900) 27 AR 315 .... 90.1
Clifton v Goodbun (1868) LR 6 Eq 278 .... 72.2, 72.3
Clinton, Re [1988] ILRM 80 .... 57.12
Clissold's Settlement, Re (1864) 10 LT 642 .... 27.3
Clive v Clive (1854) Kay 600, 23 LJ Ch 981, 2 Eq Rep 913, 24 LTOS 33 .... 32.2, 83.6
Clogstoun v Walcott (1843) 13 Sim 523, 7 Jur 616 .... 39.26
Clore, Re [1982] Ch 456, [1982] 3 All ER 419, [1982] 3 WLR 228, [1982] STC 625, 126 Sol Jo 497, CA 25.1
Clore's Settlement Trusts, Re, Sainer v Clore [1966] 2 All ER 272, [1966] 1 WLR 955, 110 Sol Jo 252 .... 218.96, 218.98
Close v Coote (1880) 7 LR Ir 564, CA 100.2
Clothier, Re [1971] NZLR 745 .... 33.26
Cloudesley's Charity, Re (1900) 17 TLR 123 .... 103.8
Clough v Clough (1834) 3 My & K 296 .... 41.21, 41.22
Clough v Wynne (1817) 2 Madd 188 .... 62.1
Clout and Frewer's Contract, Re [1924] 2 Ch 230, 93 LJ Ch 624, [1924] All ER Rep 798, 68 Sol Jo 738, 132 LT 483 .... 27.5, 27.6, 46.1
Cloutte v Storey [1911] 1 Ch 18, 80 LJ Ch 193, 103 LT 617, [1908–10] All ER Rep Ext 1073, CA 40.19
Cloves v Awdry (1850) 12 Beav 604 .... 39.3
Clowes, Re [1893] 1 Ch 214, 2 R 115, 41 WR 69, 37 Sol Jo 25, 68 LT 395, CA 41.6, 64.32
Clowes v Hilliard (1876) 4 Ch D 413, 46 LJ Ch 271, 25 WR 224 .... 77.4
Clulow's Trust, Re (1859) 1 John & H 639, 28 LJ Ch 696, 5 Jur NS 1002, 7 WR 594, 33 LTOS 359 .... 47.8, 95.9, 95.10
Clune v Apjohn (1865) 17 I Ch R 25 .... 100.2
Clunies-Ross, Re, Stubbings v Clunies-Ross (1912) 56 Sol Jo 252, 106 LT 96 .... 47.23
Clutterbuck v Edwards (1832) 2 Russ & M 577 .... 93.27
Coake, Re, Winckley v Winterton [1922] 1 Ch 292, 91 LJ Ch 273, 66 Sol Jo 351, 126 LT 598 .... 3.14, 3.15, 40.11
Coard v Holderness (1855) 20 Beav 147, 24 LJ Ch 388, 1 Jur NS 316, 3 WR 311, 25 LTOS 27 .... 38.4, 50.4, 60.2
Coates, Re, Ramsden v Coates [1955] Ch 495, [1955] 1 All ER 26, [1954] 3 WLR 959, 98 Sol Jo 871 .... 53.6
Coates v Coates (1864) 33 Beav 249, 33 LJ Ch 448, 10 Jur NS 532, 3 New Rep 355, 12 WR 634, 9 LT 795 .... 30.12
Coates v Coates [1898] 1 IR 258, 32 ILT 7 .... 44.15
Coates v Hart (1863) 32 Beav 349; varied (1863) 3 De GJ & Sm 504 .... 56.7, 101.13
Cobban's Trustees v Cobban 1915 SC 82 .... 86.5, 87.1
Cobbold, Re, Cobbold v Lawton [1903] 2 Ch 299, [1915] 1 Ch 847n, 72 LJ Ch 588, 88 LT 745, CA 96.2, 96.4

Cochran v Graham (1811) 19 Ves 63 ... 3.8
Cochrane, Re, Shaw v Cochrane [1955] Ch 309, [1955] 1 All ER 222, [1955] 2 WLR 267, 99 Sol Jo 96 ... 52.2, 52.3
Cochrane v Cochrane [1922] 2 Ch 230, 91 LJ Ch 605, [1922] All ER Rep 614, 66 Sol Jo 522, 127 LT 737, 38 TLR 607 ... 40.15
Cochrane v Moore (1890) 25 QBD 57, [1886–90] All ER Rep 731, 59 LJQB 377, 54 JP 804, 38 WR 588, 63 LT 153, 6 TLR 296, CA ... 204.80
Cochrane v Wiltshire (1847) 16 LJ Ch 366, 11 Jur 426, sub nom Cockrane v Wiltshire 9 LTOS 310 ... 93.29
Cock v Cooke (1866) LR 1 P & D 241, 36 LJP & M 5, 15 WR 89, 15 LT 296 ... 1.3, 10.1, 10.4, 10.9
Cockayne v Harrison (1872) LR 13 Eq 432, 41 LJ Ch 509, 20 WR 504, 26 LT 385 ... 8.4
Cockayne's Goods, Re (1856) Dea & Sw 177, 2 Jur NS 454, 4 WR 555 ... 19.4
Cockburn v Chief Adjudication Officer [1997] 3 All ER 844, [1997] 1 WLR 799, [1997] 1 CMLR 794, [1997] 24 LS Gaz R 32, 141 Sol Jo LB 122, HL ... 226.4
Cockburn's Trustees v Dundas (1864) 36 Sc Jur 594, 4 M 1185 ... 66.6
Cockburn's Will Trusts, Re, Cockburn v Lewis [1957] Ch 438, [1957] 2 All ER 522, [1957] 3 WLR 212, 101 Sol Jo 534 ... 27.15, 239.1, 243.3
Cockcroft, Re, Broadbent v Groves (1883) 24 Ch D 94, 52 LJ Ch 811, 32 WR 223, 49 LT 497 ... 206.25
Cocke's Goods, Re [1960] 2 All ER 289, [1960] 1 WLR 491, 104 Sol Jo 389 ... 19.4
Cocker v Dingey [1963] Tas SR (NC) 20 ... 71.3
Cockerell v Barber (1810) 16 Ves 461 ... 30.43
Cockle's Will Trusts, Re [1967] Ch 690, [1967] 1 All ER 391, [1967] 2 WLR 637, 111 Sol Jo 37 ... 50.21, 51.8, 66.7, 66.12, 66.16, 66.19, 76.3, 87.1
Cockran v Cockran (1844) 14 Sim 248, 8 Jur 679, 41 LTOS 49 ... 38.23
Cockrane v Wiltshire. See Cochrane v Wiltshire
Cockrill v Pitchforth (1845) 1 Coll 626, 9 Jur 223, 4 LTOS 352 ... 91.4
Cocks v Manners (1871) LR 12 Eq 574, 36 JP 244, 40 LJ Ch 640, 19 WR 1055, 24 LT 869 ... 9.35, 66.19, 102.7, 102.9, 102.26
Cockshott v Cockshott (1846) 15 LJ Ch 131, 2 Coll 432, 10 Jur 41, 6 LTOS 389 ... 101.4
Cocquerel, Re [1918] P 4, 87 LJP 47, 118 LT 96 ... 23.8
Codrington v Lindsay (1873) 8 Ch App 578, 42 LJ Ch 526, 21 WR 182, 28 LT 177; affd sub nom Codrington v Codrington (1875) LR 7 HL 854, 45 LJ Ch 660, 24 WR 648, 34 LT 221 ... 42.16
Coe's Trust, Re (1858) 4 K & J 199, 4 Jur NS 158, 32 LTOS 239 ... 34.11, 35.45
Coffill v Stamp Duties Comr (1920) SRNSW 278 ... 3.6, 3.12
Cogan v Stephens (1835) 1 Beav 482n, 5 LJ Ch 17 ... 47.6
Coghill, Re, Drury v Burgess [1948] 1 All ER 254 ... 204.64
Coghlan v Coghlan (circa 1790) 1 Phillim 120, 19 Ves 508 ... 4.14
Cogswell v Armstrong (1855) 2 K & J 227, 1 Jur NS 1162 ... 38.3, 38.4
Cohen, Re, Brookes v Cohen [1911] 1 Ch 37, 80 LJ Ch 208, 55 Sol Jo 11, 103 LT 626 ... 40.15, 40.21
Cohen, Re, Cohen v Cohen [1915] WN 361, 60 Sol Jo 239 ... 82.4
Cohen, Re, Cowan v Cohen [1973] 1 All ER 889, [1973] 1 WLR 415, 117 Sol Jo 222 ... 102.14

Cohen, Re, National Provincial Bank Ltd v Katz [1960] Ch 179, [1959] 3 All ER 740, [1959] 3 WLR 916, 103 Sol Jo 961 .... 31.4, 206.22
Cohen's Executors and LCC, Re [1902] 1 Ch 187, 71 LJ Ch 164, 50 WR 117, 86 LT 73 .... 233.39
Cohen's Will Trusts, Re, Cullen v Westminster Bank Ltd [1936] 1 All ER 103 .... 82.3, 82.4
Cohn (or Cohen), Re [1945] Ch 5, 114 LJ Ch 97, 88 Sol Jo 430, 171 LT 377 .... 24.3
Cohn, Re, Keshen v Ferguson [1952] 3 DLR 833 .... 102.14
Cohn, Re, National Westminster Bank Ltd v Cohn [1974] 3 All ER 928, [1974] 1 WLR 1378, 118 Sol Jo 662, CA 93.29
Coke v Bullock (1604) 1 Eq Cas Abr 410, Cro Jac 49 .... 52.8
Colahan, Re, Molloy v Hara Hara Shrewbridge and Hara [1967] IR 29 .... 71.4
Coldicott v Best [1881] WN 150 .... 93.30
Coldwell v Holme (1854) 23 LJ Ch 594, 2 Eq Rep 390, 18 Jur 396, 2 Sm & G 31, 2 WR 150 .... 103.9
Cole, Re, Cole v Cole [1919] 1 Ch 218, 88 LJ Ch 82, 120 LT 374, 35 TLR 183 .... 30.24, 34.21, 34.24
Cole, Re, Westminster Bank Ltd v Moore [1958] Ch 877, [1958] 3 All ER 102, [1958] 3 WLR 447, 122 JP 433, 102 Sol Jo 618, CA 102.7
Cole v Fitzgerald (1827) 3 Russ 301 .... 64.27
Cole v Muddle (1852) 10 Hare 186, 22 LJ Ch 401, 16 Jur 853, 90 RR 332, 20 LTOS 107 .... 30.17
Cole v Scott (1849) 19 LJ Ch 63, 1 H & Tw 477, 14 Jur 25, 1 Mac & G 518, 14 LTOS 325 .... 59.1, 59.3
Cole v Sewell (1848) 2 HL Cas 186, 12 Jur 927 .... 67.4, 94.33
Cole v Willard (1858) 25 Beav 568, 4 Jur NS 988, 6 WR 712 .... 44.15
Coleman, Re, Coleman v Coleman [1976] Ch 1, [1975] 1 All ER 675, [1975] 2 WLR 213, 119 Sol Jo 86 .... 17.4, 17.6
Coleman, Re, Henry v Strong (1888) 39 Ch D 443, 58 LJ Ch 226, 60 LT 127, CA 93.35
Coleman, Re, Public Trustee v Coleman [1936] Ch 528, [1936] 2 All ER 225, 105 LJ Ch 244, 155 LT 402 .... 48.13, 48.15, 94.9, 94.30
Coleman v Bloomfield (1884) 2 NZLR 49 .... 49.9
Coleman and Jarrom, Re (1876) 4 Ch D 165, 46 LJ Ch 33, 25 WR 137, 35 LT 614 .... 47.29, 47.33, 66.5
Coleman's Goods, Re [1920] 2 IR 332 .... 16.4
Coles v Blakeley [1955] SCR 508 .... 77.3
Coles's Goods, Re (1871) LR 2 P & D 362, 36 JP 120, 41 LJP & M 21, 20 WR 214, 25 LT 852 .... 10.1, 10.9
Coley, Re, Gibson v Gibson [1901] 1 Ch 40, 70 LJ Ch 153, 49 WR 165, 45 Sol Jo 164, 83 LT 671 .... 68.13
Coley, Re, Hollinshead v Coley [1903] 2 Ch 102, 72 LJ Ch 502, 51 WR 563, 47 Sol Jo 491, 88 LT 517, CA 80.1
Colgan (infants), Re (1881) 19 Ch D 305, 51 LJ Ch 180, 30 WR 266, 46 LT 152 .... 218.66
Collard's Will Trusts, Re, Lloyds Bank Ltd v Rees [1961] Ch 293, [1961] 1 All ER 821, [1961] 2 WLR 415, [1961] TR 325, 105 Sol Jo 208 .... 218.99

Collens, Re, Royal Bank of Canada (London) Ltd v Krogh [1986] Ch 505, [1986] 1 All ER 611, [1986] 2 WLR 919, 130 Sol Jo 373, [1986] LS Gaz R 1901 .... 23.16, 23.17, 104.2, 104.5
Coller's Deed Trusts, Re, Coller v Coller [1939] Ch 277, [1937] 3 All ER 292, 106 LJ Ch 326, 81 Sol Jo 550, 157 LT 84, 53 TLR 859, CA 33.23, 33.24, 33.26, 33.30, 95.7
Colles' Estate, Re [1918] 1 IR 1 .... 97.6
Collet v Lawrence (1791) 1 Ves 268 .... 64.35
Colleton v Garth (1833) 6 Sim 19, 2 LJ Ch 75 .... 63.1
Collett v Collett (1866) 35 Beav 312, 12 Jur NS 180, 14 WR 446, 14 LT 94 .... 35.6, 35.12, 56.3
Collett's Goods, Re (1857) Dea & Sw 274, 3 Jur NS 72, 5 WR 251, 28 LTOS 276 .... 25.2
Colley's Goods, Re (1879) 3 LR Ir 243 .... 21.6
Collier v Rivaz (1841) 2 Curt 855 .... 23.7
Colling, Re, Lawson v von Winckler [1972] 3 All ER 729, [1972] 1 WLR 1440, 116 Sol Jo 547 .... 11.14, 11.24, 12.2, 12.3, 12.5, 12.13
Collings, Re, Jones v Collings [1933] Ch 920, 102 LJ Ch 337, [1933] All ER Rep 745, 150 LT 19 .... 64.35
Collingwood v Row (1857) 26 LJ Ch 649, 3 Jur NS 785, 5 WR 484, 29 LTOS 191 .... 7.27
Collingwood v Stanhope (1869) LR 4 HL 43, 38 LJ Ch 421, 17 WR 537 .... 81.3
Collins (an infant), Re [1950] Ch 498, [1950] 1 All ER 1057, 66 (pt 1) TLR 1107, 94 Sol Jo 352, CA 203.62
Collins, Re [1955] OWN 603 .... 13.1
Collins, Re [1990] Fam 56, [1990] 2 All ER 47, [1990] 2 WLR 161, [1990] FCR 433, [1990] 2 FLR 72, [1990] Fam Law 337, 134 Sol Jo 262 .... 105.16, 105.25, 105.31
Collins, Re, Collins v Collins (1886) 32 Ch D 229, [1886–90] All ER Rep 683, 55 LJ Ch 672, 50 JP 821, 34 WR 650, 55 LT 21, 2 TLR 423 .... 218.66
Collins, Re, Robinson v Collins. See Robinson v Collins
Collins v Collins (1833) 2 My & K 703, 39 RR 337 .... 38.23
Collins v Collins (1871) LR 12 Eq 455, 40 LJ Ch 541, 19 WR 971, 24 LT 780 .... 64.35
Collins v Doyle (1826) 1 Russ 135 .... 64.39
Collins v Elstone [1893] P 1, 62 LJP 26, 1 R 458, 41 WR 287, 67 LT 624, 9 TLR 16 .... 5.7, 18.8
Collins v Macpherson (1827) 2 Sim 87 .... 97.8
Collins' Settlement Trusts, Re, Donne v Hewetson [1971] 1 All ER 283, [1971] 1 WLR 37, 114 Sol Jo 936 .... 8.7, 30.34, 38.7, 64.18, 64.27, 64.44, 64.45, 64.56, 104.4, 204.16
Collins' Trust, Re [1877] WN 87 .... 77.2
Collishaw, Re [1953] 3 DLR 829 .... 24.6, 47.32, 78.5, 82.7
Collison, Re, Collison v Barber (1879) 12 Ch D 834, 48 LJ Ch 720, 28 WR 391, 41 LT 175 .... 97.7
Collyer, Re, Collyer v Back (1907) 24 TLR 117 .... 55.6
Colman's Estate, Re [1958] 2 All ER 35, [1958] 1 WLR 457, 102 Sol Jo 292 .... 16.2
Colpoys v Colpoys (1822) Jac 451 .... 57.20
Colquhoun's Trustees v Colquhoun 1907 SC 346 .... 95.9

Colson's Trusts, Re (1853) Kay 133, 23 LJ Ch 155, 2 Eq Rep 257, 2 WR 111, 22 LTOS 183 .... 82.9
Colston v Morris (1821) Jac 257n, 6 Madd 89 .... 34.23, 35.36
Colston v Pemberton (1836) Donnelly 19, 5 LJ Ch 181 .... 40.3
Coltman v Gregory (1870) 40 LJ Ch 352, 19 WR 122, 23 LT 583 .... 58.10
Coltsmann v Coltsmann (1868) LR 3 HL 121, 16 WR 943 .... 50.5, 98.12
Colvile, Re, Colvile v Martin (1911) 56 Sol Jo 33, [1911] 105 LT 622 .... 50.3
Colyer, Re, Millikin v Snelling (1886) 55 LT 344, 3 TLR 7 .... 8.4, 91.6, 99.1
Combe, Re, Combe v Combe [1925] Ch 210, 94 LJ Ch 267, [1925] All ER Rep 159, sub nom Re Coombe, Coombe v Coombe 69 Sol Jo 397, 133 LT 473 .... 1.6, 83.18, 101.9
Combe v Hughes (1872) LR 14 Eq 415, 41 LJ Ch 693, 20 WR 793, 27 LT 366 .... 85.3
Comber v Graham (1830) 1 Russ & M 450 .... 83.2, 83.9
Comber's Case (1721) 1 P Wms 766 .... 25.14
Comber's Settlement, Re (1865) 11 Jur NS 968, 14 WR 172, 13 LT 459 .... 39.18
Comfort v Brown (1878) 10 Ch D 146, 48 LJ Ch 318, 27 WR 226 .... 84.4
Comiskey v Bowring-Hanbury [1905] AC 84, 74 LJ Ch 263, 53 WR 402, 92 LT 241, 21 TLR 252, HL 34.6, 50.3, 50.21, 51.4, 83.9, 99.1, 200.22, 216.13
Commercial Railway Act, Re, ex p Harrison (1838) 3 Y & C Ex 275, 8 LJ Ex Eq 28, 2 Jur 1038 .... 84.4
Compton, Re, Powell v Compton [1945] Ch 123, [1945] 1 All ER 198, 114 LJ Ch 99, 89 Sol Jo 142, 172 LT 158, 61 TLR 167, CA 9.31, 102.8, 102.10, 102.14, 102.15
Compton, Re, Powell v Compton [1946] 1 All ER 117 .... 94.12
Compton, Re, Vaughan v Smith [1914] 2 Ch 119, 83 LJ Ch 862, 58 Sol Jo 580, 111 LT 245 .... 30.3, 30.8, 31.4, 204.55
Compton v Bloxham (1845) 14 LJ Ch 380, 2 Coll 201, 9 Jur 935, 5 LTOS 368 .... 30.14, 57.5
Comstock, Re [1949] 3 DLR 677, [1949] OR 537, OWN 494 .... 83.12
Conbay's Estate, Re [1916] 1 IR 51 .... 98.1
Concha v Concha (1886) 11 App Cas 541, 56 LJ Ch 257, 35 WR 477, 55 LT 522, HL 25.15, 43.4, 49.7
Conduitt v Soane (1844) 13 LJ Ch 390, 1 Coll 285 .... 8.3, 204.45
Congregational Union of New South Wales v Thistlethwayte (1952) 87 CLR 375, ALR 729, 26 ALJ 335 .... 62.1, 93.29, 94.30
Congreve v Palmer (1853) 16 Beav 435, 23 LJ Ch 54, 1 WR 156 .... 68.6, 87.2
Conmy v Cawley [1910] 2 IR 465, Ir CA 52.1
Conn, Re, Conn v Burns [1898] 1 IR 337 .... 53.2
Connell's Settlement, Re, Re Benett's Trusts, Fair v Connell [1915] 1 Ch 867, 84 LJ Ch 601, 113 LT 234 .... 82.4
Connington's Will, Re (1860) 2 LT 535, sub nom Re Conington's Will 24 JP 419, 6 Jur NS 992, 8 WR 444 .... 34.21, 35.39
Connolly, Re [1935] 2 DLR 465, 8 MPR 448 .... 74.1
Connolly, Re, Walton v Connolly (1914) 110 LT 688, CA 64.11, 64.54, 64.57
Connolly v Connolly (1887) 56 LT 304 .... 8.4
Connor's Estate, Re (1970) 10 DLR (3d) 5, 72 WWR 388 .... 53.5
Conolly v Brophy (1920) 54 ILT 41 .... 66.1
Conolly v Farrell (1846) 10 Beav 142 .... 31.16
Conron v Conron (1858) 7 HL Cas 168 .... 82.1

Conservative and Unionist Central Office v Burrell (Inspector of Taxes) [1980] 3 All ER 42, [1980] STC 400, 55 TC 671, [1980] TR 143, 124 Sol Jo 361; affd [1982] 2 All ER 1, [1982] 1 WLR 522, [1982] STC 317, 55 TC 671, [1981] TR 543, 126 Sol Jo 50, CA 9.35
Consett v Bell (1842) 1 Y & C Ch Cas 569, 11 LJ Ch 401, 6 Jur 869 .... 10.5
Constable v Bull (1849) 3 De G & Sm 411, 18 LJ Ch 302, 22 LJ Ch 182, 13 Jur 619 .... 83.9, 97.3, 99.1
Constantine v Constantine (1801) 6 Ves 100 .... 50.16
Construction Industry Training Board v A-G [1973] Ch 173, [1972] 2 All ER 1339, [1972] 3 WLR 187, [1972] RA 241, 116 Sol Jo 466, CA 102.2, 102.8
Conyers v Orr and Skelton (1944) 59 BCR 455, [1944] 1 DLR 201, [1943] WWR 418 .... 10.5
Conyngham, Re, Conyngham v Conyngham [1921] 1 Ch 491, 90 LJ Ch 364, 65 Sol Jo 342, 125 LT 300, 37 TLR 420, CA 48.5
Conyngham (Marchioness), Re, Ramsden v Conyngham (1908) 24 TLR 789 .... 64.46
Conyngham v Conyngham (1750) 1 Ves Sen 522 .... 27.5
Conyngham v Tripp [1925] 1 IR 27 .... 85.3
Cooch v Walden (1877) 46 LJ Ch 639 .... 58.12
Coode, Re, Coode v Foster (1913) 108 LT 94 .... 27.3
Coogan v Hayden (1879) 4 LR Ir 585 .... 79.4
Cook, Re, Beck v Grant [1948] Ch 212, [1948] 1 All ER 231, [1948] LJR 902, 92 Sol Jo 125, 64 TLR 97 .... 50.7
Cook v Cook (1706) 2 Vern 545 .... 66.23, 85.2, 85.3
Cook v Gerrard (1668) 2 Keb 206, 224, 1 Lev 212, 1 Saund 180 .... 83.6
Cook v Hutchinson (1836) 1 Keen 42, 44 RR 11 .... 57.31
Cook v IRC [2002] STC (SCD) 318, [2002] WTLR 1003 .... 208.34
Cook v Lambert (1863) 27 JP 376, 32 LJPM & A 93, 9 Jur NS 258, 3 Sw & Tr 46, 11 WR 401, 8 LT 211 .... 11.4
Cook v Saxlova (18 October 1988, unreported) 57.23
Cook's Estate, Re, Murison v Cook [1960] 1 All ER 689, [1960] 1 WLR 353, 104 Sol Jo 311 .... 11.20
Cook's Goods, Re [1902] P 114, 71 LJP 49, 46 Sol Jo 318, 86 LT 537 .... 25.2
Cooke, Re, Randall v Cooke [1916] 1 Ch 480, 85 LJ Ch 452, 60 Sol Jo 403, 114 LT 555 .... 100.5
Cooke v Bowen (1840) 4 Y & C Ex 244 .... 87.1
Cooke v Cholmondeley (1849) 19 LJ Ch 81, 2 H & Tw 162, 14 Jur 117, 2 Mac & G 18, 14 LTOS 413 .... 4.14
Cooke v Cooke (1865) 29 JP 692, 4 De GJ & Sm 704, 34 LJ Ch 459, 11 Jur NS 533, 6 New Rep 134, 13 WR 697, sub nom Cooke v Elmsall 12 LT 408 .... 35.6
Cooke v Cooke (1887) 38 Ch D 202, 36 WR 756, 59 LT 693 .... 82.4, 94.31, 94.44, 94.48
Cooke v Elmsall. See Cooke v Cooke
Cooke v Mirehouse (1864) 34 Beav 27 .... 56.2
Cooke v Stationers' Co (1831) 3 My & K 262 .... 47.8
Cooke v Turner (1846) 14 Sim 493, 17 LJ Ex 106, 15 M & W 727 .... 34.12, 35.38
Cooke v Wagster (1854) 23 LJ Ch 496, 2 Eq Rep 789, 18 Jur 849, 2 Sm & G 296, 2 WR 434, 23 LTOS 293 .... 64.40
Cooke's Goods, Re (1847) 5 Notes of Cases 390 .... 18.17, 18.23
Cooke's Settlement, Re, Tarry v Cooke [1913] 2 Ch 661, 83 LJ Ch 76, 58 Sol Jo 67, 109 LT 705 .... 29.6, 29.9

Cookson v Cookson. See Cookson v Reay
Cookson v Hancock (1836) 2 My & Cr 606 .... 91.6
Cookson v Reay (1842) 5 Beav 22; affd sub nom Cookson v Cookson (1845) 12 Cl & Fin 121, 9 Jur 499, HL 37.8
Coole, Re, Coole v Flight [1920] 2 Ch 536, 89 LJ Ch 519, 64 Sol Jo 739, 124 LT 61, 36 TLR 736 .... 43.3
Coombe, Re, Coombe v Coombe. See Combe, Re, Combe v Combe
Coombs's Goods, Re (1866) LR 1 P & D 302, 31 JP 9, 36 LJP & M 25, 15 LT 363 .... 11.2
Cooney v Nicholls (1881) 7 LR Ir 107, 115, Ir CA 62.1, 91.6
Cooper, Re, Townend v Townend (1917) 86 LJ Ch 507, [1917] HBR 186, 61 Sol Jo 444, 116 LT 760 .... 48.5, 48.11
Cooper (Colin), Re, Le Neve-Foster v National Provincial Bank Ltd [1939] Ch 580, [1939] 2 All ER 192, 160 LT 453; affd [1939] Ch 811, [1939] 3 All ER 586, 108 LJ Ch 388, 83 Sol Jo 671, 161 LT 127, CA 36.10, 36.13, 57.11, 221.48
Cooper v Bockett (1843) 3 Curt 648; revsd (1846) 4 Moo PCC 419, 10 Jur 931, 4 Notes of Cases 685 .... 12.3, 12.11, 13.3, 14.3, 14.9
Cooper v Cooper (1855) 1 K & J 658, 3 WR 470 .... 97.6
Cooper v Cooper (1856) 6 I Ch R 217 .... 22.3
Cooper v Cooper (1861) 29 Beav 229, 7 Jur NS 178, 9 WR 354, 3 LT 800 .... 93.30
Cooper v Cooper (1869) LR 8 Eq 312; on appeal (1869) 5 Ch App 203, 39 LJ Ch 240, 18 WR 299, 22 LT 1 .... 40.15
Cooper v Cooper (1870) 6 Ch App 15; on appeal (1874) LR 7 HL 53, 44 LJ Ch 6, 22 WR 713, [1874–80] All ER Rep 307, 30 LT 409 .... 1.8, 7.14, 24.10, 29.17, 42.2, 42.3, 42.4, 42.8, 104.13
Cooper v Cooper (1873) 8 Ch App 813, 43 LJ Ch 158, 21 WR 921, 29 LT 321 .... 44.1, 100.6
Cooper v Cooper (1874) LR 7 HL 53, [1874–80] All ER Rep 307, 44 LJ Ch 6, 22 WR 713, 30 LT 409 .... 214.14
Cooper v Day (1817) 3 Mer 154 .... 91.6
Cooper v Douglas (1787) 2 Bro CC 231 .... 29.15
Cooper v MacDonald (1873) LR 16 Eq 258, 42 LJ Ch 533, 21 WR 833, 28 LT 693 .... 44.1, 44.9, 44.13, 93.5
Cooper v Stuart (1889) 14 App Cas 286, 58 LJPC 93, 60 LT 875, 5 TLR 387 .... 94.1
Cooper v Thornton (1790) 3 Bro CC 96; on appeal (1790) 3 Bro CC 186 .... 9.40, 82.5
Cooper v Woolfitt (1857) 2 H & N 122, 26 LJ Ex 310, 3 Jur NS 870, 5 WR 790, 29 LTOS 212 .... 61.1, 82.1
Cooper's Conveyance Trusts, Re, Crewdson v Bagot [1956] 3 All ER 28, [1956] 1 WLR 1096, 100 Sol Jo 620 .... 103.18
Cooper's Estate, Re, Bendall v Cooper [1946] Ch 109, [1946] 1 All ER 28, 115 LJ Ch 47, 89 Sol Jo 591, 174 LT 79, 62 TLR 65 .... 50.12
Cooper's Goods, Re (1847) 11 Jur 1070, 10 LTOS 230, 5 Notes of Cases 618 .... 13.2
Cooper's Goods, Re (1855) Dea & Sw 9, 4 WR 182, 26 LTOS 138 .... 1.5
Cooper's Trusts, Re (1853) 4 De GM & G 757, 23 LJ Ch 25, 2 Eq Rep 65, 17 Jur 1087, 2 WR 601, 22 LTOS 162 .... 47.8
Coote v Boyd (1789) 2 Bro CC 521 .... 44.1, 57.8, 57.31, 88.3, 88.4

Cope, Re, Cross v Cross [1908] 2 Ch 1, 77 LJ Ch 558, [1908–10] All ER Rep 154, 99 LT 374, CA 50.9, 50.21, 54.2, 68.6
Cope v Henshaw (1866) 35 Beav 420, 14 WR 627 .... 53.5
Cope v Wilmot (1772) Amb 704, 1 Coll 396n 82.7
Cope's Estate, Re [1954] 1 All ER 698, [1954] 1 WLR 608, 98 Sol Jo 253 .... 25.16
Cope's Goods, Re (1850) 2 Rob Eccl 335 .... 12.12
Copland's Executors v Milne (1908) 45 SLR 314, 1908 SC 426, 15 SLT 733 .... 71.4
Coppard's Estate, Re, Howlett v Hodson (1887) 35 Ch D 350, 56 LJ Ch 606, 35 WR 473, 56 LT 359 .... 51.2, 66.16
Coppin v Coppin (1725) 2 P Wms 291, Cas temp King 28 .... 23.12, 31.2, 47.21
Coppley, Re [1940] 3 DLR 535, [1940] OR 314 .... 101.9
Corballis v Corballis (1882) 9 LR Ir 309 .... 38.3, 58.1
Corbett, Re (1921) 17 Tas LR 139 .... 102.11
Corbett, Re, Corbett v Lord Cobham [1903] 2 Ch 326, 72 LJ Ch 775, 52 WR 74, 88 LT 591 .... 44.2, 102.21
Corbett v Corbett (1888) 14 PD 7, 58 LJP 17, 37 WR 114, 60 LT 74, CA 34.5, 99.1
Corbett v IRC [1938] 1 KB 567, [1937] 4 All ER 700, 21 TC 449, 107 LJKB 276, 82 Sol Jo 34, 158 LT 98, 54 TLR 279, CA 1.8
Corbett v Newey [1994] Ch 388, [1995] 1 All ER 570, [1994] 3 WLR 548, [1994] 26 LS Gaz R 36; revsd [1998] Ch 57, [1996] 2 All ER 914, [1996] 3 WLR 729, [1996] 09 LS Gaz R 29, [1996] NLJR 333, 140 Sol Jo LB 65, CA 1.2, 1.5, 5.7, 10.1, 10.2, 10.4, 28.5, 57.30, 200.44
Corbett's Trusts, Re (1860) John 591, 29 LJ Ch 458, 6 Jur NS 339, 8 WR 257, 2 LT 147 .... 67.4
Corbyn, Re, Midland Bank Executor and Trustee Co Ltd v A-G [1941] Ch 400, [1941] 2 All ER 160, 110 LJ Ch 200, 85 Sol Jo 256, 165 LT 372, 57 TLR 483 .... 102.10
Corcoran, Re, Corcoran v O'Kane [1913] 1 IR 1 .... 81.5, 91.2
Corder's Goods Re (1848) 1 Rob Eccl 669, 12 Jur 966, 12 LTOS 249, 6 Notes of Cases 556 .... 10.15
Cordwell's Estate, Re, White v Cordwell (1875) LR 20 Eq 644, 44 LJ Ch 746, 23 WR 826 .... 30.11, 30.12
Corlass, Re (1875) 1 Ch D 460, 45 LJ Ch 118, 24 WR 204, 33 LT 630 .... 73.1, 76.4
Corley v Corley (1912) 31 NZLR 887 .... 64.54
Cormack v Copous (1853) 17 Beav 397 .... 85.2, 98.3
Corneby v Gibbons (1849) 1 Rob Eccl 705, 13 Jur 264, 13 LTOS 27, 6 Notes of Cases 679 .... 10.15
Cornewall v Cornewall (1841) 12 Sim 298, 10 LJ Ch 364, 5 Jur 744 .... 64.3
Cornfield v Wyndham (1845) 14 LJ Ch 375, 2 Coll 184, 9 Jur 651, 5 LTOS 494 .... 30.1, 55.4
Cornwallis, Re, Cornwallis v Wykeham-Martin (1886) 32 Ch D 388, 55 LJ Ch 716, 54 LT 844 .... 35.43
Corr v Corr (1873) IR 7 Eq 397 .... 93.27
Corsellis, Re, Freeborn v Napper [1906] 2 Ch 316, 75 LJ Ch 607, 54 WR 536, 50 Sol Jo 499, 95 LT 583 .... 57.20, 72.3
Cort v Winder (1844) 1 Coll 320, 3 LTOS 280 .... 97.8
Cory, Re, Cory v Morel [1955] 2 All ER 630, [1955] 1 WLR 725, 99 Sol Jo 435 .... 52.3
Cory's Goods, Re (1901) 84 LT 270 .... 16.2

Cosby v Lord Ashtown (1859) 10 I Ch R 219 .... 42.5
Cosby v Millington (1869) 38 LJCP 373, Ex Ch 63.7
Cosby's Estate, Re [1922] 1 IR 120, CA 76.1
Cosgrove's Estate, Re, Wills v Goddard (1909) Times, 3 April 64.40
Cosnahan's Goods, Re (1866) LR 1 P & D 183, 35 LJP & M 76, 14 WR 969, 14 LT 337 .... 23.8
Cossentine, Re, Philp v Wesleyan Methodist Local Preachers' Mutual Aid Association Trustees [1933] Ch 119, 102 LJ Ch 78, [1932] All ER Rep 785, 76 Sol Jo 512, 148 LT 261 .... 74.2, 87.1
Cossey v Cossey (1900) 64 JP 89, 69 LJP 17, 82 LT 203, 16 TLR 133 .... 19.1, 19.4
Costabadie v Costabadie (1847) 6 Hare 410, 16 LJ Ch 259, 11 Jur 345, 9 LTOS 20 .... 82.5
Cotgrave, Re, Mynors v Cotgrave [1903] 2 Ch 705, 710, 72 LJ Ch 777, 10 Mans 377, 52 WR 411, 89 LT 433 .... 99.6
Cottam's Will Trusts, Re, Midland Bank Executor and Trustee Co Ltd v Huddersfield Corpn [1955] 3 All ER 704, [1955] 1 WLR 1299, 99 Sol Jo 889 .... 102.5, 102.7
Cotter, Re (1915) 24 DLR 289, 34 OLR 24, 8 OWN 46, 354 .... 101.7
Cotter, Re (1918) 42 OLR 99, 13 OWN 421 .... 60.1
Cotton, Re (1923) 19 Tas LR 57 .... 9.9
Cotton v Cotton (1839) 2 Beav 67, 8 LJ Ch 349, 3 Jur 886 .... 79.7
Cotton, Re, Wood v Cotton (1888) 40 Ch D 41, 58 LJ Ch 174, 37 WR 232 ... 39.25, 40.2
Cotton v Cotton (1850) 14 Jur 950 .... 38.23
Cotton v Cotton (1854) 23 LJ Ch 489, 2 WR 207 .... 97.5
Cotton v Heath (1638) Poll 26, 1 Eq Cas Abr 191 pl 2 .... 8.3
Cotton v Scarancke (1815) 1 Madd 45 .... 77.1
Cotton's Goods, Re [1923] 2 IR 52 .... 22.2
Cottrell, Re, Buckland v Bedingfield [1910] 1 Ch 402, 79 LJ Ch 189, [1908–10] All ER Rep 70, 102 LT 157 .... 33.3, 33.35, 33.44
Cottrell v Cottrell (1872) LR 2 P & D 397, 36 JP 567, 41 LJP & M 57, 20 WR 590, 26 LT 527 .... 18.8, 23.13
Cottrell v Cottrell (1885) 28 Ch D 628, 54 LJ Ch 417, 33 WR 361, 52 LT 486 .... 38.28
Cottrell Estate, Re [1951] 4 DLR 600, 2 WWRNS 247 .... 14.6
Couch v Stratton (1799) 4 Ves 391 .... 3.11
Coughlan Estate, Re (1955) 16 WWRNS 14 .... 10.18
Coulden, Re, Coulden v Coulden [1908] 1 Ch 320, 77 LJ Ch 209, 52 Sol Jo 172, 98 LT 389 .... 56.8, 68.2, 85.4, 85.5, 87.2
Coull's Settled Estates, Re [1905] 1 Ch 712, 74 LJ Ch 378, 53 WR 504, 92 LT 616 .... 27.18
Coulman, Re, Munby v Ross (1885) 30 Ch D 186, 55 LJ Ch 34, 53 LT 560 .... 40.21, 94.30, 94.48
Coulson, Re (1977) 78 DLR (3d) 435, 16 OR (2d) 497 .... 46.3
Coulson's Trusts, Re, Prichard v Coulson (1907) 97 LT 754 .... 93.7
Coulthard's Goods, Re (1865) 11 Jur NS 184 .... 20.2
Coulthurst, Re, Coutts & Co v Coulthurst [1951] Ch 661, [1951] 1 All ER 774, 95 Sol Jo 188, [1951] 1 TLR 651, CA 102.7
Coulthurst v Carter (1852) 15 Beav 421, 21 LJ Ch 555, 16 Jur 532, 20 LTOS 20 .... 68.6

Councell's Goods, Re (1871) LR 2 P & D 314, 36 JP 89, 41 LJP & M 16, 25 LT 763 .... 47.13
Couper's Judicial Factor v Valentine 1976 SLT 83 .... 80.3
Courtenay, Re, Pearce v Foxwell (1905) 74 LJ Ch 654 .... 66.12, 66.14
Courtenay v Gallagher (1856) 5 I Ch R 154, 356 .... 33.12
Courtenay v Williams (1844) 3 Hare 539, 639, 13 LJ Ch 461, 8 Jur 844; affd (1846) 15 LJ Ch 204, [1843–60] All ER Rep 755, 6 LTOS 517 .... 30.12
Courtenay's Goods, Re (1891) 27 LR Ir 507 .... 21.5
Courtier v Oram (1855) 21 Beav 91 .... 94.8, 94.12
Cousen's Will Trusts, Re, Wright v Killick [1937] Ch 381, [1937] 2 All ER 276, 106 LJ Ch 261, 81 Sol Jo 317, 157 LT 32, 53 TLR 490 .... 47.24, 219.23
Couser v Couser [1996] 3 All ER 256, [1996] 1 WLR 1301, [1996] 3 FCR 745, [1996] 2 FLR 46, [1996] Fam Law 470, [1996] 12 LS Gaz R 29, [1996] NLJR 651, 140 Sol Jo LB 91 .... 11.24
Cousins, Re, Alexander v Cross (1885) 30 Ch D 203, CA 92.1
Cousins v Schroder (1830) 4 Sim 23 .... 93.29
Couturier, Re, Couturier v Shea [1907] 1 Ch 470, 76 LJ Ch 296, 51 Sol Jo 342, 96 LT 560, [1904–7] All ER Rep Ext 1191 .... 30.36, 34.5, 72.6, 93.27, 93.28
Coventry, Re, Coventry v Coventry [1980] Ch 461, [1979] 2 All ER 408, [1979] 2 WLR 853, 123 Sol Jo 406; affd [1980] Ch 461, [1979] 3 All ER 815, [1979] 3 WLR 802, 123 Sol Jo 606, CA 105.16, 105.17, 105.20, 105.22, 105.23, 105.28
Coventry v Coventry (1865) 34 Beav 572, 2 Drew & Sm 470, 13 WR 985, 13 LT 83 .... 66.8, 66.11, 66.13, 66.19
Coventry v Earl Lauderdale (1846) 10 Jur 793, 7 LTOS 467 .... 55.6
Coventry v Higgins (1844) 14 Sim 30, 8 Jur 182 .... 32.10, 35.13
Coventry's (Earl) Indentures, Re, Smith v Earl of Coventry [1974] Ch 77, [1973] 3 All ER 1, [1973] 3 WLR 122, 117 Sol Jo 547 .... 39.2, 94.15, 94.48, 94.52
Coverdale v Eastwood (1872) LR 15 Eq 121, 37 JP 212, 42 LJ Ch 118, 21 WR 216, 27 LT 646 .... 3.3, 3.6
Cowan and Barry, Re (1977) 82 DLR (3d) 419 .... 64.37
Cowan and Johnson v Ball [1933] NI 173 .... 98.2
Coward v Larkman. See Coward, Re, Coward v Larkman
Coward, Re, Coward v Larkman (1887) 57 LT 285, CA; affd sub nom Coward v Larkman [1886–90] All ER Rep 896, 60 LT 1, 4 TLR 759, HL 49.4, 50.21, 82.1, 83.6
Cowen v Truefitt Ltd [1899] 2 Ch 309, 68 LJ Ch 563, 47 WR 661, 43 Sol Jo 622, 81 LT 104, CA 58.3, 58.4, 58.5
Cowley, Re [1971] NZLR 468 .... 34.12, 35.32
Cowley, Re, Souch v Cowley (1885) 53 LT 494 .... 34.4, 45.2, 91.2
Cowley (Earl) v Countess of Cowley [1901] AC 450, 70 LJP 83, 50 WR 81, 85 LT 254, 17 TLR 725, HL 35.40
Cowley v Hartstonge (1813) 1 Dow 361 .... 37.3
Cowling, Re, Jinkin v Cowling [1924] P 113, 93 LJP 43, [1924] All ER Rep 469, 131 LT 157, 40 TLR 358 .... 18.20
Cowling v Cowling (1859) 26 Beav 449, 33 LTOS 5 .... 64.35
Cowlishaw, Re [1959] Qd R 67 .... 82.4
Cowlishaw, Re, Cowlishaw v Cowlishaw [1939] Ch 654, 108 LJ Ch 196, 83 Sol Jo 298, 160 LT 455, 55 TLR 537 .... 33.47

Cowman v Harrison (1852) 10 Hare 234, 22 LJ Ch 993, 17 Jur 313, 90 RR 334, 1 WR 96, 21 LTOS 148 .... 82.5
Cowper v Mantell (1856) 22 Beav 223, 2 Jur NS 745, 4 WR 500, 27 LTOS 130 .... 41.3, 47.8
Cowper v Mantell (No 2) (1856) 22 Beav 231, 2 Jur NS 745, 4 WR 500, 52 ER 1097, 27 LTOS 130 .... 20.4, 82.8
Cowper v Scott (1731) 3 P Wms 119 .... 84.2
Cowx v Foster (1860) 1 John & H 30, 29 LJ Ch 886, 6 Jur NS 1051, sub nom Cox v Forster 2 LT 797 .... 39.26
Cox, Re (1927) 60 OLR 426 .... 64.37
Cox, Re, Baker v National Trust Co Ltd [1955] AC 627, [1955] 2 All ER 550, [1955] 3 WLR 42, 99 Sol Jo 383, [1955] 3 DLR 497, 16 WWR 49, PC 102.15
Cox, Re, Public Trustee v Eve [1938] Ch 556, [1938] 1 All ER 661, 108 LJ Ch 67, 82 Sol Jo 233, 159 LT 13, 54 TLR 527 .... 33.36, 33.44
Cox v Archer (1964) 110 CLR 1, [1964] ALR 782 (Aust HC) 92.5
Cox v Bennett (1868) LR 6 Eq 422 .... 41.5, 58.12, 207.3
Cox v Bockett (1865) 35 Beav 48 .... 99.4, 99.9
Cox v Forster. See Cowx v Foster
Cox v Godsalve (1699) 6 East 604n 61.1
Cox v Parker (1856) 22 Beav 168, 25 LJ Ch 873, 2 Jur NS 842, 4 WR 453, 27 LTOS 179 .... 93.9, 96.1
Cox v Sutton (1856) 25 LJ Ch 845, 2 Jur NS 733, 28 LTOS 119 .... 82.9
Cox's Trustees v Cox 1950 SC 117 .... 73.1
Coxe v Basset (1796) 3 Ves 155 .... 102.25
Coxen, Re, McCallum v Coxen [1948] Ch 747, [1948] 2 All ER 492, [1948] LJR 1590, 92 Sol Jo 442 .... 34.10, 34.11, 35.19, 35.22, 35.29, 64.3, 64.8, 102.8, 204.4, 217.40
Coxen v Rowland [1894] 1 Ch 406, 63 LJ Ch 179, 8 R 525, 42 WR 568, 38 Sol Jo 98, 70 LT 89 .... 24.12
Coyne v Coyne (1876) IR 10 Eq 496 .... 41.20
Coyte, Re, Coyte v Coyte (1887) 56 LT 510, 3 TLR 352 .... 18.23, 51.4, 100.7
Cozens, Re, Miles v Wilson [1903] 1 Ch 138, 72 LJ Ch 39, 51 WR 220, 47 Sol Jo 50, 87 LT 581 .... 50.2, 71.1, 72.3
Cozens v Crout (1873) 42 LJ Ch 840, 21 WR 781 .... 9.8
Crabb v Arun District Council [1976] Ch 179, [1975] 3 All ER 865, [1975] 3 WLR 847, 119 Sol Jo 711, CA 43.1
Crabtree, Re [1954] ALR 779, [1954] VLR 492 .... 35.20, 76.3
Crabtree, Re, Thomas v Crabtree [1912] WN 24, 106 LT 49, CA 205.73
Cradock v Cradock (1858) 4 Jur NS 626, 6 WR 710, 32 LTOS 48 .... 53.1
Craig, Re [1955] VLR 196 .... 94.15
Craig, Re (1976) 74 DLR (3d) 442, 14 OR (2d) 589 .... 52.3
Craig v Lamoureux [1920] AC 349, 89 LJPC 22, 122 LT 208, 36 TLR 26, PC 5.9
Craig v Wheeler (1860) 29 LJ Ch 374, 9 WR 172, 3 LT 142 .... 64.32
Craik v Lamb (1844) 14 LJ Ch 84, 1 Coll 489, 9 Jur 6, 4 LTOS 152 .... 50.17, 74.8
Crake v Supplementary Benefits Commission [1982] 1 All ER 498, 2 FLR 264 .... 105.14
Cramp v Playfoot (1858) 4 K & J 479 .... 103.11
Crandon's Goods, Re (1901) 84 LT 330, 17 TLR 341 .... 4.10, 18.12

Crane, Re, Adams v Crane [1908] 1 Ch 379, [1904–7] All ER Rep 577, 77 LJ Ch 212, 98 LT 314 .... 32.22, 216.13
Crane v Crane (1949) 80 CLR 327 .... 66.12
Crane v Maritime Trust Co (1954) 33 UPR 15 .... 204.64
Cranfield, Re, Mosse v Cranfield [1895] 1 IR 80 .... 58.4, 64.35
Cranley (Lord) v Hale (1807) 14 Ves 307 .... 104.13
Cranley v Dixon (1857) 23 Beav 512, 26 LJ Ch 529, 3 Jur NS 531, 29 LTOS 119 .... 101.4
Cranmer's Case (1701) 2 Salk 508 .... 44.15
Crannis' Estate, Re, Mansell v Crannis (1978) 122 Sol Jo 489 .... 18.8, 19.4
Cranston, Re, Webb v Oldfield [1898] 1 IR 431 .... 9.31
Cranstoun's Will Trusts, Re, Gibbs v Home of Rest for Horses [1949] Ch 523, [1949] 1 All ER 871, [1949] LJR 1066, 93 Sol Jo 251 .... 46.4
Cranswick v Pearson (1862) 31 Beav 624, 9 Jur NS 397, 11 WR 229, 9 LT 215; affd (1863) 9 LT 275 .... 33.14
Crause v Cooper (1859) 1 John & H 207 .... 68.11
Craven, Re, Crewdson v Craven (1908) 99 LT 390, 24 TLR 750; affd (1909) 100 LT 284, CA 9.5, 38.3, 63.1, 64.46
Craven, Re, Watson v Craven [1914] 1 Ch 358, 83 LJ Ch 403, 58 Sol Jo 138, 109 LT 846 .... 29.6, 29.9, 31.6, 100.5
Craven v Brady (1867) LR 4 Eq 209; affd (1869) 4 Ch App 296, 38 LJ Ch 345, 17 WR 505, 23 LT 57 .... 40.21, 48.11
Craven's Estate, Re, Lloyds Bank v Cockburn [1937] Ch 423, [1937] 3 All ER 33, 106 LJ Ch 308, 81 Sol Jo 398, 157 LT 283, 53 TLR 694 .... 1.15
Crawford, Re (1982) 4 FLR 273 .... 105.11, 105.41
Crawford v Broddy (1896) 26 SCR 345 .... 50.6
Crawford v Trotter (1819) 4 Madd 361 .... 84.4, 85.3
Crawford's Trustees v Fleck (1910) 47 SLR 755, 1910 SC 998 .... 52.3
Crawford's Trusts, Re (1854) 2 Drew 230, 23 LJ Ch 625, 2 Eq Rep 553, 18 Jur 616, 2 WR 341 .... 50.6, 50.9, 79.7, 83.16
Crawhall's Trust, Re (1856) 8 De GM & G 480, 2 Jur NS 892, 27 LTOS 278 .... 74.1, 90.1
Crawley, Re (1976) 68 DLR (3d) 193 .... 67.1
Crawley v Crawley (1835) 7 Sim 427, 4 LJ Ch 265 .... 38.28
Crawshay, Re, Crawshay v Crawshay (1890) 43 Ch D 615, 59 LJ Ch 395, 38 WR 600, 62 LT 489 .... 40.15
Crawshay, Re, Crawshay v Crawshay (1915) 60 Sol Jo 275 .... 33.47
Creagh v Blood (1845) 8 I Eq R 434, 2 Jo & Lat 509 .... 4.14
Creagh v Creagh (1862) 13 I Ch R 28 .... 64.57
Creagh v Wilson (1706) 2 Vern 572 .... 34.15, 35.10
Creamer Estate, Re [1932] 3 WWR 621 .... 64.45
Creed, Re, Thomas v Hudson [1905] WN 94, 49 Sol Jo 566 .... 39.7
Creeth v Wilson (1882) 9 LR Ir 216, 223 .... 93.1
Cregeen v Willoughby (1860) 24 JP 408, 6 Jur NS 590 .... 13.3
Creighton Estate, Re [1950] 2 WWR 529 .... 54.1
Cremorne v Antrobus (1829) 5 Russ 312, 7 LJOS Ch 88 .... 64.27
Crerar v Crerar (1956) unreported 5.1, 5.7
Cresswell, Re, Lineham v Cresswell (1914) 58 Sol Jo 360, CA 30.36

Cresswell v Cresswell (1868) LR 6 Eq 69, 32 JP 564, 37 LJ Ch 521, 16 WR 699, 18 LT 392 .... 9.4, 88.3
Creswick v Gaskell (1853) 16 Beav 577 .... 97.8
Crewe v Dicken (1798) 4 Ves 97 .... 27.6
Crichton v Crichton [1895] 2 Ch 853, 59 JP 792, 65 LJ Ch 13, 44 WR 202, 73 LT 556; revsd [1896] 1 Ch 870, 65 LJ Ch 491, 74 LT 357, CA 44.4, 44.15, 44.17
Crichton v Symes (1743) 3 Atk 61 .... 64.25
Crichton's Settlement, Re, Sweetman v Batty (1912) 56 Sol Jo 398, 106 LT 588 .... 91.6, 94.8
Crichton's Trust, Re (1855) 24 LTOS 267 .... 9.40
Crigan v Baines (1834) 7 Sim 40 .... 97.1
Cringan's Goods, Re (1828) 1 Hag Ecc 548 .... 25.1
Crippen's Estate, Re [1911] P 108, 80 LJP 47, [1911–13] All ER Rep 207, 55 Sol Jo 273, 104 LT 224, 27 TLR 258 .... 9.14, 9.15
Crips, Re, Crips v Todd (1906) 95 LT 865 .... 37.3
Cripps v Wolcott (1819) 4 Madd 11 .... 67.2
Crispin's Will Trusts, Re, Arkwright v Thurley [1973] 2 All ER 141; revsd [1975] Ch 245, [1974] 3 All ER 772, [1974] 3 WLR 657, 118 Sol Jo 739, CA 64.44, 64.45, 104.4, 204.5, 204.16
Critchett v Taynton (1830) 1 Russ & M 541, 8 LJOS Ch 143 .... 74.1
Crocker, Re, Crocker v Crocker [1916] 1 Ch 25, 85 LJ Ch 179, 114 LT 61, [1914–15] All ER Rep Ext 1211 .... 44.5, 44.6, 100.5
Crockett v Crockett (1848) 2 Ph 553, 17 LJ Ch 230, 12 Jur 234, 78 RR 183, 10 LTOS 409 .... 82.5, 85.3
Crocombe, Re [1949] SASR 302 .... 50.2
Croft v Croft (1865) 29 JP 168, 34 LJPM & A 44, 11 Jur NS 183, 4 Sw & Tr 10, 13 WR 526, 11 LT 781 .... 13.3
Croft v Day (1838) 1 Curt 782 .... 5.9
Crofton's Goods, Re (1897) 13 TLR 374 .... 2.2
Crofts v Beamish [1905] 2 IR 349, CA 49.9, 81.3
Croker v Marquess of Hertford (1844) 4 Moo PCC 339, 8 Jur 863, 3 Notes of Cases 150, sub nom Re Marquis of Hertford's Will 3 LTOS 257 .... 15.1, 50.9
Crolla, Re 1942 SC 21 .... 25.4
Croly v Weld (1853) 3 De GM & G 993, 22 LJ Ch 916, 1 Eq Rep 134 .... 33.24
Cromek v Lumb (1839) 3 Y & C Ex 565 .... 67.4, 93.39
Crommelin v Crommelin (1796) 3 Ves 227 .... 35.13
Crompe v Barrow (1799) 4 Ves 681 .... 94.28
Crompton v Sale (1729) 1 Eq Cas Abr 205, 2 P Wms 553 .... 44.15
Crone, Re (1969) 5 DLR (3d) 317 .... 51.1
Crone v Odell (1811) 1 Ball & B 449; affd sub nom Odell v Crone (1815) 3 Dow 61, HL 66.4, 66.5, 66.22, 66.23
Crook v Hill (1871) 6 Ch App 311, 35 JP 564, 40 LJ Ch 216, 19 WR 649, 24 LT 488; on appeal sub nom Hill v Crook (1873) LR 6 HL 265, 42 LJ Ch 702, 22 WR 137, [1874–80] All ER Rep 62 .... 9.25, 50.3, 72.2, 72.3, 72.5, 101.1
Crook v Whitley (1857) 7 De GM & G 490, 26 LJ Ch 350, 3 Jur NS 703, 5 WR 383 .... 50.2, 50.6, 57.15, 71.5
Crooke v De Vandes (1803) 9 Ves 197 .... 84.4, 86.2, 98.7, 98.12
Crooke v De Vandes (1805) 11 Ves 330 .... 38.3, 94.5
Croome v Croome (1888) 59 LT 582, CA; affd (1889) 61 LT 814, HL 82.5

Cropton v Davies (1869) LR 4 CP 159, 38 LJCP 159, 17 WR 444, 20 LT 30 .... 101.7
Croskery v Ritchie [1901] 1 IR 437 .... 35.22
Crosland, Re, Craig v Midgley (1886) 54 LT 238 .... 97.9
Cross, Petitioner 1987 SLT 384 .... 9.20
Cross, Re, Law v Cross (1938) 44 ALR 449, [1938] VLR 221 .... 35.33
Cross v Lloyd-Greame (1909) 74 Sol Jo 152, 102 LT 163, 26 TLR 171 .... 102.7, 103.18
Cross v Wilks (1866) 35 Beav 562 .... 38.10, 64.16, 64.17
Cross Estate, Re (1965) 51 WWR 377 .... 100.2
Crosse, Re, Crosse v Crosse [1933] WN 36, 77 Sol Jo 116 .... 66.12, 67.6
Crosse v Eldridge (1918) 53 L Jo 52 .... 93.8
Crossman, Re, Re Paulin. See IRC v Crossman
Crosthwaite v Dean (1879) 40 LT 837, [1874–80] All ER Rep 714 .... 68.13, 86.2, 86.5
Crother's Trusts, Re [1915] 1 IR 53 .... 48.5, 48.6, 66.10, 66.15, 99.8
Crother's Trusts (No 2), Re [1917] 1 IR 356 .... 93.25, 93.29
Crowder v Clowes (1794) 2 Ves 449 .... 91.6
Crowder v Stone (1829) 3 Russ 217, 7 LJOS Ch 93 .... 67.3, 90.1, 97.8, 98.5
Crowe v Appleby (Inspector of Taxes) [1975] 3 All ER 529, [1975] 1 WLR 1539, [1975] STC 502, 51 TC 457, 54 ATC 177, [1975] TR 151, 119 Sol Jo 776; affd [1976] 2 All ER 914, [1976] 1 WLR 885, [1976] STC 301, 51 TC 457, [1976] TR 105, CA 220.73
Crowhurst Park, Re, Sims-Hilditch v Simmons [1974] 1 All ER 991, [1974] 1 WLR 583, 28 P & CR 14, 118 Sol Jo 331 .... 25.14
Crown Trust Co v McKenzie (1958) 66 Man R 294 .... 35.2
Crowther, Re, Midgley v Crowther [1895] 2 Ch 56, [1895–9] All ER Rep 1208, 64 LJ Ch 537, 13 R 496, 43 WR 571, 72 LT 762, 11 TLR 380 .... 205.25, 205.73
Croxon, Re, Croxon v Ferrers [1904] 1 Ch 252, 73 LJ Ch 170, 52 WR 343, 48 Sol Jo 191, 89 LT 733 .... 34.8, 35.42, 35.43, 50.16
Croxon, Re, Ferrers v Croxton [1915] 2 Ch 290, 84 LJ Ch 845, [1914–15] All ER Rep 816, 59 Sol Jo 693, 113 LT 1103 .... 33.26
Crozier v Crozier (1843) 3 Dr & War 353 .... 40.21
Crozier v Crozier (1873) LR 15 Eq 282, 21 WR 398 .... 82.2
Crumpe, Re, Orpen v Moriarty [1912] 1 IR 485 .... 34.21, 34.24, 35.19
Crumpe v Crumpe [1900] AC 127, 69 LJPC 7, 82 LT 130, HL 50.2, 83.1, 83.9, 99.1, 101.3
Cruse, Re, Gass v Ingham [1930] WN 206 .... 64.54
Cruse v Barley (1727) 2 Eq Cas Abr 543, 3 P Wms 19 .... 37.7
Cruse v Howell (1858) 4 Drew 215, 6 WR 271 .... 47.29
Crusoe d Blencowe v Bugby (1771) 3 Wils 234, 2 Wm Bl 766 .... 7.23
Crutchley, Re, Kidson v Marsden [1912] 2 Ch 335, 81 LJ Ch 644, 107 LT 194 .... 56.1
Cruwys v Colman (1804) 9 Ves 319 .... 79.2
Cudney v Cudney (1874) 21 Gr 153 .... 61.1
Cuffe, Re, Fooks v Cuffe [1908] 2 Ch 500, 77 LJ Ch 776, 52 Sol Jo 661, 99 LT 267, 24 TLR 781 .... 1.10, 104.1
Culbertson, Re (1966) 59 DLR (2d) 381 .... 30.6, 31.3
Cullen v A-G for Ireland (1866) LR 1 HL 190, 12 Jur NS 531, 14 WR 869, 14 LT 644 .... 9.4
Cullen v McNeil (1908) 42 NSR 346 .... 30.31

Cullen's Estate, Re [1907] 1 IR 73 .... 84.4
Cullimore's Trust, Re (1891) 27 LR Ir 18 .... 79.2
Cullum, Re, Mercer v Flood [1924] 1 Ch 540, 93 LJ Ch 281, 68 Sol Jo 369, 130 LT 601 .... 72.3
Culsha v Cheese (1849) 7 Hare 236 .... 47.1, 52.11
Culverhouse, Re, Cook v Culverhouse [1896] 2 Ch 251, 65 LJ Ch 484, 45 WR 10, 40 Sol Jo 374, 74 LT 347 .... 55.7
Cuming, Re [1943] SASR 336 .... 49.4
Cumming, Re (1963) 38 DLR (2d) 243, [1963] 1 OR 625 .... 9.3
Cunard's Trustees v IRC [1946] 1 All ER 159, 27 TC 122, 174 LT 133, CA 205.68, 210.39, 216.17, 216.25, 216.27
Cuninghame v Anstruther (1872) LR 2 Sc & Div 223 .... 40.3, 40.15
Cunliffe v Fielden [2005] EWCA Civ 1508, [2006] Ch 361, [2006] 2 All ER 115, [2006] 2 WLR 481, sub nom Fielden v Cunliffe [2005] 3 FCR 593, [2006] 1 FLR 745, [2006] Fam Law 263, 150 Sol Jo LB 96, [2005] All ER (D) 80 (Dec) 105.9
Cunliffe-Owen, Re, Mountain v Comber [1951] Ch 964, [1951] 2 All ER 220, 95 Sol Jo 285, [1951] 2 TLR 231, [1951] 1 TLR 1073 .... 210.68
Cunningham, Re, Dulcken v Cunningham [1914] 1 Ch 427, 83 LJ Ch 342, 110 LT 371 .... 33.12, 33.24, 103.18
Cunningham v Foot (1878) 3 App Cas 974, 26 WR 858, 38 LT 889, HL 91.2
Cunningham v Murray (1847) 1 De G & Sm 366, 16 LJ Ch 484, 11 Jur 814, sub nom Anon 10 LTOS 34; revsd sub nom Cunningham v Murray (1848) 17 LJ Ch 407 .... 85.3, 87.1
Cunningham's Goods, Re (1860) Sea & Sm 132, 29 LJPM & A 71, 4 Sw & Tr 194 .... 12.12, 14.6, 14.7, 22.2
Cunningham's Trustees v Blackwell 1909 SC 219 .... 87.1
Cunnington, Re, Healing v Webb [1924] 1 Ch 68, 93 LJ Ch 95, 68 Sol Jo 118, 130 LT 308 .... 24.6, 236.10
Curle's Trustees v Millar. See Lamont (or Chearnley) v Millar
Curlett Estate, Re [1996] 3 WWR 545 .... 1.8
Curling's Goods, Re [1928] IR 521 .... 38.10, 64.17
Curran v Corbet [1897] 1 IR 343 .... 35.12
Currie, Re (1978) 91 DLR (3d) 559 .... 15.1
Currie v Pye (1811) 17 Ves 462 .... 44.1
Currie's Settlement, Re, Re Rooper, Rooper v Williams [1910] 1 Ch 329, 70 LJ Ch 285, 54 Sol Jo 270, 101 LT 899 .... 1.2, 38.13, 47.1, 47.23, 210.45
Curry, Re, Curry v Curry (1908) 53 Sol Jo 117 .... 30.8
Curryer's Will Trusts, Re, Wyly v Curryer [1938] Ch 952, [1938] 3 All ER 574, 107 LJ Ch 417, 82 Sol Jo 625, 159 LT 599, 54 TLR 1055 .... 94.28
Cursham v Newland (1838) 7 LJ Ex 212, 1 Horn & H 296, 4 M & W 101 .... 76.3
Cursham v Newland (1839) 2 Beav 145 .... 90.2
Curtin v Evans (1875) IR 9 Eq 553 .... 44.14
Curtis v Curtis (1821) 6 Madd 14 .... 66.13
Curtis v Lukin (1842) 5 Beav 147, 11 LJ Ch 380, 6 Jur 721 .... 30.36, 94.7
Curzon, Re, Martin v Perry (1912) 56 Sol Jo 362 .... 66.9, 66.23
Curzon v Curzon (1859) 1 Giff 248, 5 Jur NS 907, 34 LTOS 14 .... 35.39
Cusack v Rood (1876) 24 WR 391 .... 77.3
Cushing, Re [1943] 2 WWR 606 .... 30.2
Cussen v Hynes [1906] 1 IR 539 .... 9.36

Cust, Re, Glasgow v Campbell [1919] VLR 221 .... 76.2
Cust v Goring (1854) 18 Beav 383, 24 LJ Ch 308, 18 Jur 884, 2 WR 370, 23 LTOS 338 .... 64.53
Custance's Settlements, Re, Keppel v Douglas [1946] Ch 42, [1945] 2 All ER 441, 114 LJ Ch 293, 89 Sol Jo 381, 173 LT 195, 61 TLR 541 .... 99.5
Cutcliffe's Will Trusts, Re, Brewer v Cutcliffe [1940] Ch 565, [1940] 2 All ER 297, 109 LJ Ch 192, 84 Sol Jo 303, 163 LT 284, 56 TLR 537 .... 23.4
Cuthbert v Lemprière (1814) 3 M & S 158 .... 62.4
Cuthbert v Purrier (1822) Jac 415 .... 56.1
Cuthbert v Robinson (1882) 51 LJ Ch 238, 30 WR 366, 46 LT 57 .... 64.2
Cuthbertson, Re, Cuthbertson v Cuthbertson [1979] Tas SR 93 .... 64.18, 64.27, 64.45
Cutto v Gilbert (1854) 9 Moo PCC 131, 1 Ecc & Ad 417, 18 Jur 560, 24 LTOS 193 .... 1.1, 18.8, 18.9, 18.13
Cyganik v Agulian [2005] EWHC 444 (Ch), [2005] All ER (D) 400 (Mar); revsd [2006] EWCA Civ 129, [2006] 1 FCR 406, [2006] All ER (D) 372 (Feb) 105.18

D

D (J), Re [1982] Ch 237, [1982] 2 All ER 37, [1982] 2 WLR 373 ... 4.22, 4.23, 4.24, 4.25
DWS, Re; Re EHS; TWGS (a child) v JMG [2000] 2 All ER 83; affd [2001] Ch 568, [2001] 1 All ER 97, [2000] 3 WLR 1910, [2001] 1 FCR 339, [2000] NLJR 1788, 150 NLJ 1788, (2000) Times, 22 November, CA 9.1, 9.13, 9.17, 46.1, 46.5, 48.4, 48.8, 104.9, 241.16
D'Abbadie v Bizoin (1871) IR 5 Eq 205 .... 40.15
Da Costa, Re, Clarke v Church of England Collegiate School of St Peter [1912] 1 Ch 337, 81 LJ Ch 293, 56 Sol Jo 240, 106 LT 458, 28 TLR 189 .... 45.2, 94.34
Dacre, Re, Whitaker v Dacre [1916] 1 Ch 344, 85 LJ Ch 274, 60 Sol Jo 306, 114 LT 387, CA 30.11, 30.17
Dacre (Dowager Lady) v Doe d Baroness Dacre. See Doe d Dacre (Baroness) v Dowager Lady Dacre
Dadds' Goods, Re (1857) Dea & Sw 290, 29 LTOS 99 .... 18.21
Dagley v Tolferry. See Doyley v Tollferry
D'Aglie v Fryer (1841) 12 Sim 1; affd (1841) 12 Sim 328n 38.23, 58.8
D'Aguilar v Drinkwater (1813) 2 Ves & B 225 .... 34.25, 35.16
Daintree v Butcher and Fasulo (1888) 13 PD 102, 57 LJP 76, 58 LT 661, 4 TLR 445, CA 11.24, 11.26
Dakin v Nicholson (1837) 6 LJ Ch 329 .... 84.4
Dale, Re, Mayer v Wood [1931] 1 Ch 357, 100 LJ Ch 237, [1930] All ER Rep 10, 145 LT 632 .... 74.2
Dale, Re, Proctor v Dale [1994] Ch 31, [1993] 4 All ER 129, [1993] 3 WLR 652, [1994] Fam Law 77, [1993] 14 LS Gaz R 43, [1993] NLJR 544, 137 Sol Jo LB 83 .... 1.2, 2.3, 2.4, 2.5, 2.8, 2.9, 2.10, 201.310
Dale's Estates, Re (1984) 32 SASR 215 .... 10.1
Daley v Desbouverie (1738) 2 Atk 261, sub nom Daly v Desbouverie West temp Hard 547 .... 34.14
Dall, Re [1918] NZLR 755 .... 71.5

Dalley, Re (1926) 70 Sol Jo 839, 136 LT 223 .... 26.5
Dallmeyer, Re, Dallmeyer v Dallmeyer [1896] 1 Ch 372, 65 LJ Ch 201, 44 WR 375, 40 Sol Jo 151, 73 LT 671, CA 100.5
Dallow's Goods, Re (1866) LR 1 P & D 189, 35 LJP & M 81, 12 Jur NS 492, 14 WR 902, 14 LT 573 .... 15.1, 25.1
Dallow's Goods, Re, Evans v Dallow (1862) 26 JP 631, 31 LJPM & A 128 .... 18.22
Dally v Dally [1954] Tas LR 12 .... 82.4
D'Almaine v Moseley (1853) 1 Drew 629, 22 LJ Ch 971, 1 Eq Rep 252, 17 Jur 872, 1 WR 475, 21 LTOS 297 .... 38.5, 60.2
Dalrymple, Re, Bircham v Springfield (1901) 49 WR 627, 45 Sol Jo 555 ..... 35.28, 83.6
Dalrymple v Hall (1881) 16 Ch D 715, 50 LJ Ch 302, 29 WR 421 .... 55.6
Dalton v Fitzgerald [1897] 2 Ch 86, 66 LJ Ch 604, 45 WR 685, 41 Sol Jo 560, 76 LT 700, 13 TLR 456, CA 43.2, 43.3
Dalton v Latham [2003] EWHC 796 (Ch), [2003] WTLR 687, 147 Sol Jo LB 537, [2003] NPC 54, [2003] All ER (D) 305 (Apr) 9.20
d'Altroy's Will Trusts, Re, Crane v Lowman [1968] 1 All ER 181, [1968] 1 WLR 120, 111 Sol Jo 870 .... 35.8, 80.4
Daly v Aldworth (1863) 15 I Ch R 69 .... 7.3
Daly v A-G (1860) 11 I Ch R 41 .... 103.3
Daly v Desbouverie. See Daley v Desbouverie
Dalzell, Re, McGivern v Dalzell (1958) 26 WWR 215 .... 64.18, 64.37
Dalzell v Welch (1828) 2 Sim 319 .... 54.5
Dalziel, Re, Midland Bank Executor and Trustee Co Ltd v St Bartholomew's Hospital [1943] Ch 277, [1943] 2 All ER 656, 112 LJ Ch 353, 87 Sol Jo 281, 169 LT 168, 59 TLR 408 .... 9.29
Damphousse v Damphousse [1943] OWN 349 .... 3.4
Dancer v Crabb (1873) LR 3 P & D 98, 37 JP 663, 42 LJP & M 53, [1861–73] All ER Rep 692, 28 LT 914 .... 19.4
Daniel, Re, Jones v Michael [1945] 2 All ER 101, 173 LT 315 .... 87.2
Daniel v Arkwright (1864) 2 Hem & M 95, 10 Jur NS 764, 4 New Rep 418, 11 LT 18 .... 40.15
Daniel v Dudley (1841) 1 Ph 1 .... 83.16
Daniel v Warren (1843) 2 Y & C Ch Cas 290, 7 Jur 462, 60 RR 148 .... 38.23, 98.7
Daniell v Daniell (1849) 3 De G & Sm 337, 18 LJ Ch 157, 13 Jur 164, 12 LTOS 492 .... 69.2
Daniels, Re, London City and Midland Executor and Trustee Co Ltd v Daniels (1918) 87 LJ Ch 661, 118 LT 435 .... 29.7, 31.1, 54.3, 65.2
Danish Bacon Co Ltd Staff Pension Fund, Re, Christensen v Arnett [1971] 1 All ER 486, [1971] 1 WLR 248, 115 Sol Jo 95 .... 1.3, 1.9, 7.13, 10.11
Dansereau v Berget [1954] AC 1, [1953] 2 All ER 1058, 97 Sol Jo 728, PC 49.7
Danvers v Manning (1786) 1 Cox Eq Cas 203, 2 Bro CC 18 .... 38.1
Daoust, Re, Dobell v Dobell [1944] 1 All ER 443, 113 LJ Ch 193, 171 LT 39 .... 71.5, 231.9
Darbon v Rickards (1845) 14 Sim 537, 14 LJ Ch 344, 9 Jur 364 .... 33.23, 33.28, 33.30
Darby, Re, Russell v MacGregor [1939] Ch 905, [1939] 3 All ER 6, 108 LJ Ch 347, 83 Sol Jo 436, 160 LT 602, 55 TLR 792, CA 38.26
Darley v Langworthy (1774) 3 Bro Parl Cas 359, HL 34.19, 35.26
Darley v Martin (1853) 13 CB 683, 22 LJCP 249, 17 Jur 1125, 1 CLR 729 .... 20.3, 52.11
Darley v Perceval [1900] 1 IR 129 .... 93.2

Darling, Re, Farquhar v Darling [1896] 1 Ch 50, 65 LJ Ch 62, 13 R 834, 44 WR 75, 40 Sol Jo 11, 73 LT 382 .... 102.7
Darlow v Edwards (1862) 1 H & C 547, 32 LJ Ex 51, 9 Jur NS 336, 10 WR 700, 6 LT 905, Ex Ch 30.24
Darnley (Earl) Re, Clifton v Darnley [1907] 1 Ch 159, 76 LJ Ch 58, 51 Sol Jo 82, 95 LT 706, 23 TLR 93 .... 38.25
Darrel v Molesworth (1700) 2 Vern 378 .... 97.4
Dash, Re, Darley v King (1887) 57 LT 219 .... 99.8
Dashwood v Jermyn (1879) 12 Ch D 776, 27 WR 868 .... 3.3
Dashwood v Lord of Bulkeley (1804) 10 Ves 230, 32 ER 832 .... 34.25, 35.16
Dashwood v Magniac [1891] 3 Ch 306, 60 LJ Ch 809, 36 Sol Jo 362, 65 LT 811, 7 TLR 629, [1891–4] All ER Rep Ext 1906, CA 57.14
Dashwood v Peyton (1811) 18 Ves 27 .... 52.11, 101.3
Da Silva's Goods, Re (1861) 25 JP 519, 30 LJPM & A 171, 2 Sw & Tr 315, 5 LT 140 .... 1.5, 21.6
Daubeny v Cockburn (1816) 1 Mer 626, 15 RR 174, [1814–23] All ER Rep 604 .... 40.15, 40.20
Daubeny v Coghlan (1842) 12 Sim 507, 11 LJ Ch 177, 6 Jur 230 .... 57.10, 57.20, 58.2
Davenport, Re, Turner v King [1895] 1 Ch 361, 64 LJ Ch 252, 13 R 167, 43 WR 217, 71 LT 875 .... 83.16
Davenport v Coltman (1842) 11 LJ Ex 114, 6 Jur 381, 9 M & W 481 .... 101.14
Davenport v Coltman (1842) 12 Sim 588, 11 LJ Ch 262, 6 Jur 381 .... 38.12, 50.18
Davenport v Hanbury (1796) 3 Ves 257 .... 68.1, 68.13, 76.4
Davenport's Trust, Re (1852) 17 Jur 314, 1 Sm & G 126, 1 WR 103, 20 LTOS 165 .... 80.1
Daveron, Re, Bowen v Churchill [1893] 3 Ch 421, 63 LJ Ch 54, 3 R 685, 42 WR 24, 37 Sol Jo 631, 69 LT 752, 9 TLR 570 .... 7.24, 94.37
Davey, Re [1980] 3 All ER 342, [1981] 1 WLR 164, 124 Sol Jo 810 .... 4.22, 4.23, 4.24, 4.25, 17.2
Davey, Re, Prisk v Mitchell [1915] 1 Ch 837, 84 LJ Ch 505, 113 LT 60, CA 94.28, 94.30
David v Frowd (1833) 1 My & K 200, 2 LJ Ch 68, [1824–34] All ER Rep 714 .... 31.11
David's Trusts, Re (1859) John 495, 29 LJ Ch 116, 6 Jur NS 94, 8 WR 39, 1 LT 130 .... 39.19, 83.11, 83.17, 99.1
Davidson, Re (1979) 101 DLR (3d) 372 .... 58.10
Davidson, Re, Martin v Trimmer (1879) 11 Ch D 341, 40 LT 726, CA 37.8
Davidson, Re, Minty v Bourne [1909] 1 Ch 567, 78 LJ Ch 437, [1908–10] All ER Rep 140, 52 Sol Jo 622, 99 LT 222, 24 TLR 760, CA 102.22, 102.23
Davidson, Re, National Provincial Bank Ltd v Davidson [1949] Ch 670, [1949] 2 All ER 551, 65 TLR 574 .... 71.3
Davidson v Dallas (1808) 14 Ves 576 .... 66.12, 67.4
Davidson v Kimpton (1881) 18 Ch D 213, 29 WR 912, 45 LT 132 .... 62.1, 83.12
Davidson v Proctor (1848) 19 LJ Ch 395, 14 Jur 31 .... 93.44
Davies, Re (1913) 10 DLR 164, 4 OWN 1013, 24 OWR 321 .... 87.1
Davies, Re, Davies v Davies [1892] 3 Ch 63, 61 LJ Ch 595, 41 WR 13, [1891–4] All ER Rep 498, 36 Sol Jo 627, 67 LT 548, 8 TLR 673 .... 7.12, 39.13
Davies, Re, Davies v Mackintosh [1957] 3 All ER 52, [1957] 1 WLR 922, 101 Sol Jo 611 .... 48.6, 66.15, 88.3

Davies, Re, Davies v Public Trustee [1954] NZLR 520 .... 35.2, 93.20
Davies, Re, Lloyd v Cardigan County Council [1915] 1 Ch 543, 84 LJ Ch 493, 79 JP 291, 13 LGR 437, 59 Sol Jo 413, 112 LT 1110 .... 9.29, 202.28
Davies, Re, Lloyds Bank Ltd v Mostyn (1932) 76 Sol Jo 474, 48 TLR 539; affd (1932) 49 TLR 5, CA 102.17
Davies, Re, Panton v Jones [1978] CLY 3095, (1978) Times, 23 May 18.12, 18.28
Davies, Re, Public Trustee v Davies [1950] 1 All ER 120, 94 Sol Jo 48, 66 (pt 1) TLR 171 .... 86.5, 86.6, 101.6
Davies, Re, Scourfield v Davies [1925] Ch 642, 94 LJ Ch 337, [1925] All ER Rep 494, 69 Sol Jo 744, 133 LT 460 .... 54.2, 59.2
Davies, Re, Thomas v Thomas-Davies [1928] Ch 24, 97 LJ Ch 141, 71 Sol Jo 880, 138 LT 262 .... 20.4, 47.7, 59.2
Davies v Bush (1831) You 341 .... 31.2
Davies v Davies (1858) 28 LJ Ch 102, 4 Jur NS 1291, 7 WR 85, 32 LTOS 156 .... 39.19
Davies v Fisher (1842) 5 Beav 201, 11 LJ Ch 338, 6 Jur 248 .... 39.21, 93.35, 93.41, 93.42
Davies v Fowler (1873) LR 16 Eq 308, 43 LJ Ch 90, 29 LT 285 .... 30.8
Davies v Lowndes (1835) 1 Bing NC 597, 4 LJCP 214, 1 Hodg 125, 2 Scott 71; on appeal (1838) 4 Bing NC 478, Ex Ch 34.22, 35.39, 35.40
Davies v Morgan (1839) 1 Beav 405, 3 Jur 284 .... 30.3
Davies v Nicolson (1858) 2 De G & J 693, 27 LJ Ch 719, 5 Jur NS 49, 6 WR 790, 31 LTOS 374 .... 31.15
Davies v Perpetual Trustee Co Ltd [1959] AC 439, [1959] 2 All ER 128, [1959] 2 WLR 673, 103 Sol Jo 370, PC 102.8, 102.10, 102.15
Davies v Thorns (1849) 3 De G & Sm 347, 18 LJ Ch 212, 13 Jur 383, 12 LTOS 551 .... 39.19
Davies v Wattier (1823) 1 Sim & St 463 .... 33.24
Davies and Kent's Contract, Re [1910] 2 Ch 35, 79 LJ Ch 689, 102 LT 622, CA 27.18, 94.28, 94.37, 94.44
Davies' Estate, Re, Russell v Delaney [1951] 1 All ER 920 .... 12.3, 19.4
Davies' Goods, Re (1850) 2 Rob Eccl 337 .... 11.24
Davies' Policy Trusts, Re [1892] 1 Ch 90, 61 LJ Ch 650, 66 LT 104 .... 85.3
Davies' Trusts, Re (1871) LR 13 Eq 163, 41 LJ Ch 97, 20 WR 165, 25 LT 785 .... 39.12, 47.39
Davies' Trusts, Re (1872) 21 WR 154 .... 103.7
Davies' Will, Re (1860) 29 Beav 93, 7 Jur NS 118, 9 WR 134 .... 74.2
Davis, Re (1963) 40 DLR (2d) 801, [1963] 2 OR 666 .... 4.13
Davis, Re [1993] 1 FCR 1002, [1993] 1 FLR 54, [1993] Fam Law 59, CA 105.9
Davis, Re, Evans v Moore [1891] 3 Ch 119, 61 LJ Ch 85, 39 WR 627, 35 Sol Jo 624, 65 LT 128, CA 30.3, 30.38
Davis, Re, Hannen v Hillyer [1902] 1 Ch 876, 71 LJ Ch 459, 50 WR 378, [1900–3] All ER Rep 336, 46 Sol Jo 317, 86 LT 292 .... 103.3
Davis, Re, Thomas v Davis [1923] 1 Ch 225, 92 LJ Ch 322, 67 Sol Jo 297, 128 LT 735, 39 TLR 201 .... 102.23
Davis, Re, Tuxford v Davis (1906) 23 WN 237, 7 SRNSW 71 .... 58.1
Davis, Re, Watts v Davis and Westralian Farmers Co-operative Ltd [1965] WAR 25 .... 102.10
Davis v Angel (1862) 4 De GF & J 524, 31 LJ Ch 613, 8 Jur NS 1024, 10 WR 722, 6 LT 880 .... 35.7

Davis v Bennett (1861) 30 Beav 226; on appeal (1862) 4 De GF & J 327, 31 LJ Ch 337, 8 Jur NS 269, 10 WR 275, 5 LT 815 .... 52.9, 87.2
Davis v Chambers (1857) 7 De GM & G 386, 3 Jur NS 297, 5 WR 245, 28 LTOS 348 .... 44.1
Davis v Davis (1830) 1 Russ & M 645, 1 LJ Ch 155 .... 101.8
Davis v Davis (1896) 27 OR 532 .... 42.11
Davis v Lister [1964] NSWR 1240 .... 67.2
Davis' Estate, Re [1952] P 279, [1952] 2 All ER 509, 96 Sol Jo 514, [1952] 2 TLR 541 .... 21.5, 21.6
Davis' Goods, Re (1843) 3 Curt 748, 2 Notes of Cases 350 .... 12.11
Davison, Re (1980) 99 DLR (3d) 80 .... 68.6
Davison, Re, Greenwell v Davison (1888) 58 LT 304 .... 64.32
Davison and Torrens, Re (1865) 17 I Ch R 7 .... 92.2
Davitt v Titcumb [1990] Ch 110, [1989] 3 All ER 417, [1990] 2 WLR 168, 134 Sol Jo 21, [1990] 1 LS Gaz R 30 .... 9.18
Davy v Clarke [1920] 1 IR 137 .... 94.47
Davy v Redington [1917] 1 IR 250, Ir CA 50.7, 50.11, 60.1, 64.32
Davys v Boucher (1839) 3 Y & C Ex 397, 3 Jur 674 .... 44.3, 44.11
Dawkins, Re, Dawkins v Judd [1986] 2 FLR 360, [1986] Fam Law 295 .... 105.5, 105.43
Dawley v Ballfrey. See Doyley v Tollferry
Dawson, Re [1968] NZLR 115 .... 101.13
Dawson, Re [1987] 1 NZLR 580 .... 41.20, 93.28
Dawson, Re, Arathoon v Dawson [1906] 2 Ch 211, 75 LJ Ch 604, 54 WR 556, 94 LT 817 .... 38.27
Dawson, Re, Johnston v Hill (1888) 39 Ch D 155, 57 LJ Ch 1061, 37 WR 51, 59 LT 725 .... 66.3, 94.11
Dawson, Re, Swainson v Dawson [1919] 1 Ch 102, [1918–19] All ER Rep 866, 88 LJ Ch 73, 63 Sol Jo 25, 120 LT 189 .... 44.8, 218.59
Dawson v Bourne (1852) 16 Beav 29, 19 LTOS 252 .... 85.3
Dawson v Dawson (1837) 8 Sim 346, Donnelly 212 .... 92.4, 209.5
Dawson v Dawson (1867) LR 4 Eq 504 .... 44.9, 44.15
Dawson v Gaskin (1837) 1 Jur 669 .... 38.3
Dawson v Hearn (1831) 1 Russ & M 606, 9 LJOS Ch 249 .... 33.5
Dawson v IRC [1905] 2 IR 69 .... 29.16
Dawson v Killet (1781) 1 Bro CC 119 .... 93.44
Dawson v Oliver-Massey (1876) 2 Ch D 753, 45 LJ Ch 519, 40 JP 676, 24 WR 993, 34 LT 551, CA 34.8, 34.21, 35.13, 66.12, 66.21, 217.13
Dawson v Reid (1915) 113 LT 52, HL 30.3, 30.6
Dawson v Small (1874) 9 Ch App 651 .... 98.1
Dawson v Small (1874) LR 18 Eq 114, 38 JP 646, 43 LJ Ch 406, 22 WR 514, 30 LT 252 .... 102.7, 102.22
Dawson's Estate, Re [1941] 1 WWR 177 .... 83.8
Dawson's Settlement, Re, Lloyds Bank Ltd v Dawson [1966] 3 All ER 68, [1966] 1 WLR 1456, 110 Sol Jo 689 .... 48.5, 48.14
Dawson's Will Trusts, Re, National Provincial Bank Ltd v National Council of YMCA Inc [1957] 1 All ER 177, [1957] 1 WLR 391, 50 R & IT 431, 101 Sol Jo 191 .... 58.11, 103.9, 210.9
Day v Barnard (1860) 1 Drew & Sm 351, 30 LJ Ch 220, 9 WR 136, 3 LT 537 .... 55.6
Day v Croft (1842) 4 Beav 561 .... 91.6

Day v Daveron (1841) 12 Sim 200, 10 LJ Ch 349 .... 38.12
Day v Day (1853) 1 Drew 569, 22 LJ Ch 878, 1 Eq Rep 195, 17 Jur 586, 1 WR 402 .... 33.8
Day v Day (1854) Kay 703, 18 Jur 1013, 2 WR 700, 24 LTOS 5 .... 56.8
Day v Harris (1882) 1 OR 147 .... 30.6
Day v Trig (1715) 2 Eq Cas Abr 323, 1 P Wms 286 .... 58.10, 64.22
Day's Will Trusts, Re, Lloyds Bank Ltd v Shafe [1962] 3 All ER 699, [1962] 1 WLR 1419, 106 Sol Jo 856 .... 206.8
Dayman v Dayman (1894) 71 LT 699 .... 13.1, 13.3
Dayrell, Re, Hastie v Dayrell [1904] 2 Ch 496, 73 LJ Ch 795, 91 LT 373 .... 50.2, 52.4
Deacon's Trusts, Re, Deacon v Deacon (1906) 95 LT 701 .... 67.7
Deacon's Trusts, Re, Hagger v Heath (1906) 95 LT 701 .... 48.15
Deakin, Re, Starkey v Eyres [1894] 3 Ch 565, 63 LJ Ch 779, 8 R 702, 43 WR 70, 71 LT 838 .... 72.2, 72.3, 79.4
Dean, Re, Cooper-Dean v Stevens (1889) 41 Ch D 552, 58 LJ Ch 693, 60 LT 813, 5 TLR 404 .... 7.33, 9.31, 33.16, 94.2, 102.13, 202.36
Dean, Re, Worland v Dickinson (1923) 67 Sol Jo 768 .... 76.3
Dean v Gibson (1867) LR 3 Eq 713, 36 LJ Ch 657, 15 WR 809 .... 38.10
Dean v Rees [1954] NZLR 877 .... 64.3
Dean's Will Trusts, Re, Cowan v Board of Governors of St Mary's Hospital, Paddington [1950] 1 All ER 882, 94 Sol Jo 239, 66 (pt 1) TLR 728 .... 102.7, 212.25
Deane, Re, Bridger v Deane (1889) 42 Ch D 9, 37 WR 786, 61 LT 492, CA 40.14
Dear, Re [1975] 2 NZLR 254 .... 18.8, 18.9, 18.13, 21.5, 21.7, 57.22
Dear, Re, Helby v Dear (1889) 58 LJ Ch 659, 38 WR 31, 61 LT 432 .... 66.10, 93.20
Dearle's Goods, Re (1878) 42 JP 664, 47 LJP 45, 39 LT 93 .... 12.11
Debac's Goods, Re, Sanger v Hart (1897) 77 LT 374 .... 18.13
De Beauvoir v De Beauvoir (1852) 3 HL Cas 524, 16 Jur 1147, 88 RR 191 .... 50.3, 51.4
Debenham, Re [1986] 1 FLR 404, [1986] Fam Law 101 .... 105.16, 105.31
Debeze v Mann (1789) 11 Ves 548, 2 Bro CC 519 .... 44.14
Debney v Eckett (1858) 4 Jur NS 805 .... 30.16
De Carteret, Re, Forster v De Carteret [1933] Ch 103, 102 LJ Ch 52, [1932] All ER Rep 355, 76 Sol Jo 474, 148 LT 188, 48 TLR 555 .... 102.7
de Chassiron, Re, Lloyds Bank Ltd v Sharpe [1939] Ch 934, [1939] 3 All ER 321, 108 LJ Ch 406, 83 Sol Jo 524, 161 LT 53, 55 TLR 841 .... 33.3, 33.44
De Crespigny, Re, De Crespigny v De Crespigny [1886] WN 24, CA 82.7
Deeley and Green, Re [1930] 1 DLR 603, 64 OLR 535 .... 11.21
Deeley's Settlement, Re, Batchelor v Russell [1974] Ch 454, [1973] 3 All ER 1127, [1974] 2 WLR 41, 117 Sol Jo 877 .... 66.16, 66.19, 94.14
Deerhurst (Lord) v Duke of St Albans (1820) 5 Madd 232; revsd sub nom Tollemache v Earl of Coventry (1834) 8 Bli NS 547, 2 Cl & Fin 611, HL 94.15
Deering v Hanbury (1687) 1 Vern 478 .... 8.4
D'Este's Settlement Trusts, Re, Poulter v D'Este [1903] 1 Ch 898, 72 LJ Ch 305, 51 WR 552, 47 Sol Jo 353, 88 LT 384 .... 24.12
D'Eyncourt v Gregory (1876) 1 Ch D 441, 45 LJ Ch 205, 24 WR 424 .... 35.41
Defflis v Goldschmidt (1816) 1 Mer 417, 19 Ves 566 .... 29.7, 65.3
De Fogassieras v Duport (1881) 11 LR Ir 123 .... 23.4, 23.11, 23.12
De Garagnol v Liardet (1863) 32 Beav 608, 2 New Rep 296 .... 67.4
Deglman v Guaranty Trust Co of Canada [1954] SCR 725, Can SC 3.4, 3.6
De Gruchy, Re (1941) 56 BCR 271 .... 11.4

Deichman's Goods, Re (1842) 3 Curt 123, 1 Notes of Cases 514 .... 25.1
Deighton's Settled Estates, Re (1876) 2 Ch D 783, 45 LJ Ch 825, 35 LT 81, CA 66.1, 93.2
Delacour's Goods, Re (1874) 9 IR Eq 86 .... 25.12
De La Hunty, Re, O'Connor v Butler [1907] 1 IR 507, 41 ILT 155 .... 82.5
Delamere's Settlement Trusts, Re, Kenny v Cunningham-Reid [1984] 1 All ER 584, [1984] 1 WLR 813, 128 Sol Jo 318, [1984] LS Gaz R 1597, CA 218.53
Delaney Estate, Re, Canada Trust Co v Roman Catholic Archiepiscopal Corpn of Winnipeg (1957) 12 DLR (2d) 23, 22 WWR 574, 26 WWR 69 .... 102.23
Delany, Re, Conoley v Quick [1902] 2 Ch 642, 71 LJ Ch 811, 51 WR 27, 87 LT 46, 18 TLR 741 .... 9.35, 102.7, 102.9
Delany, Re, Delany v Delany (1895) 39 Sol Jo 468 .... 67.1
Delany v Delany (1885) 15 LR Ir 55 .... 64.7
Delany's Estate, Re (1882) 9 LR Ir 226 .... 9.35, 66.19
De La Saussaye's Goods, Re (1873) LR 3 P & D 42, 37 JP 312, 42 LJP & M 47, 21 WR 549, 28 LT 368, [1861–73] All ER Rep Ext 1143 .... 1.1, 18.9
Delgoffe v Fader [1939] Ch 922, [1939] 3 All ER 682, 109 LJ Ch 6, 83 Sol Jo 689, 161 LT 166, 55 TLR 989 .... 1.15
De Lisle v Hodges (1874) LR 17 Eq 440, 43 LJ Ch 385, 22 WR 363, 30 LT 158 .... 31.4
De Lisle's Will Trusts, Re, White v De Lisle [1968] 1 All ER 492, [1968] 1 WLR 322, [1968] TR 221, 111 Sol Jo 999 .... 92.3, 204.30
Delius, Re, Emanuel v Rosen [1957] Ch 299, [1957] 2 WLR 548, 101 Sol Jo 286, sub nom Re Delius' Will Trusts, Emanuel v Rosen [1957] 1 All ER 854 .... 102.10
Dellar v Zivy [2007] EWHC 2266 (Ch), [2007] All ER (D) 121 (Oct) 24.6
Deller's Estate, Re, Warman v Greenwood [1888] WN 62 .... 64.7
Dellow's Will Trusts, Re, Lloyds Bank Ltd v Institute of Cancer Research [1964] 1 All ER 771, [1964] 1 WLR 451, 108 Sol Jo 156 .... 9.15, 9.18
Del Mare v Robello (1792) Cas temp Talb 296, 1 Ves 412, 3 Bro CC 446 ... 57.10, 57.20, 58.2
Deloitte, Re, Griffiths v Deloitte [1926] Ch 56, 95 LJ Ch 154, [1925] All ER Rep 118, 70 Sol Jo 161, 135 LT 150 .... 66.3, 66.13, 95.13
De Lusi's Trusts, Re (1879) 3 LR Ir 232 .... 39.7
Delves, Re (1875) 1 VLR 33 .... 14.6
Delves v Newington (1885) 52 LT 512 .... 33.38
Dempsey v Lawson (1877) 2 PD 98, 41 JP 696, 46 LJP 23, 25 WR 629, [1874–80] All ER Rep 296, 36 LT 515 .... 18.8, 18.9, 18.10, 18.14
Dempster, Re, Borthwick v Lovell [1915] 1 Ch 795, 84 LJ Ch 597, [1914–15] All ER Rep 998, 112 LT 1124 .... 33.2, 33.3, 33.40
Denby, Re (1861) 3 De GF & J 350, 31 LJ Ch 184, 10 WR 115, 5 LT 514, [1861–73] All ER Rep Ext 1592, sub nom Re Dendy 31 LJ Ch 184 .... 30.14
Dench v Dench (1877) 2 PD 60, 41 JP 328, 46 LJP 13, 25 WR 414 .... 14.10, 14.11
Dendy, Re. See Denby, Re
Denekin, Re, Peters v Tanchereau (1895) 13 R 294, 72 LT 220 .... 9.39, 210.36, 232.67
Denholm's Trustees v Denholm (1908) 45 SLR 32, 1908 SC 43, 15 SLT 429 .... 64.8

De Nicols, Re, De Nicols v Curlier [1898] 1 Ch 403, 67 LJ Ch 274, 46 WR 326, 78 LT 152, 14 TLR 206; on appeal [1898] 2 Ch 60, 67 LJ Ch 419, 46 WR 532, 78 LT 541, 14 TLR 428, CA; revsd sub nom De Nicols v Curlier [1900] AC 21, 69 LJ Ch 109, 48 WR 269, 81 LT 733, 16 TLR 101, HL 24.10
De Nicols, Re, De Nicols v Curlier [1900] 2 Ch 410, 69 LJ Ch 680, 48 WR 602, 44 Sol Jo 573, 82 LT 840, 16 TLR 461 .... 200.7
Denison, Re (1974) 42 DLR (3d) 652 .... 102.10
Denley's Trust Deed, Re, Holman v HH Martyn & Co Ltd [1969] 1 Ch 373, [1968] 3 All ER 65, [1968] 3 WLR 457, 112 Sol Jo 673 .... 9.35, 34.11, 53.5
Denn d Radclyffe v Bagshaw (1796) 6 Term Rep 512 .... 68.2
Denn d Wilkins v Kemeys (1808) 8 East 366 .... 56.1, 63.9
Denn d Franklin v Trout (1812) 15 East 394 .... 64.15
Denning, Re, Harnett v Elliott [1958] 2 All ER 1, [1958] 1 WLR 462, 102 Sol Jo 293 .... 12.11, 13.1, 13.2
Dennis, Re, Dennis v Dennis (1908) 24 TLR 499 .... 64.8
Dennis, Re, Dennis v Lloyds Bank Ltd [1981] 2 All ER 140, 124 Sol Jo 885, 131 NLJ 210 .... 105.5, 105.16, 105.22
Dennis v Frend (1863) 14 I Ch R 271 .... 93.4, 94.9
Dennis' Goods, Re [1891] P 326 .... 21.6
Denny v Denny (1866) 14 LT 854 .... 32.33
Dent v Pepys (1822) 6 Madd 350 .... 52.4
Denton, Re (1912) 4 DLR 626, 26 OLR 294, 3 OWN 1109, 21 OWR 954 .... 49.4
Denton, Re [1956] NZLR 104 .... 83.6
Denyssen v Mostert (1872) LR 4 PC 236, 8 Moo PCC 502, 41 LJPC 41, 20 WR 1017 .... 2.2
Deprez, Re, Henriques v Deprez [1917] 1 Ch 24, 86 LJ Ch 91, 61 Sol Jo 72, 115 LT 662 .... 57.5, 100.7, 217.48
De Quetteville v De Quetteville (1905) 93 LT 579, CA 47.7
Derbyshire, Re, Webb v Derbyshire [1906] 1 Ch 135, 75 LJ Ch 95, 54 WR 135, 94 LT 138 .... 64.36, 64.37, 64.39
De Reneville (otherwise Sheridan) v De Reneville [1948] P 100, [1948] 1 All ER 56, [1948] LJR 1761, 92 Sol Jo 83, 64 TLR 82, CA 17.2
Dering, Re, Neall v Beale (1911) 105 LT 404 .... 47.31, 87.4
De Robeck v Lord Cloncurry (1871) IR 5 Eq 588 .... 50.6, 64.35
De Rosaz's Goods, Re (1877) 2 PD 66, 41 JP 247, 46 LJP 6, 25 WR 352, 36 LT 263 .... 25.1, 57.15, 57.15
Derry v Peek (1889) 14 App Cas 337, 54 JP 148, 58 LJ Ch 864, 1 Meg 292, 38 WR 33, [1886–90] All ER Rep 1, 61 LT 265, 5 TLR 625, HL 36.2
Desbody v Boyville (1729) 2 Eq Cas Abr 365, 2 P Wms 547 .... 35.14
De Sommery, Re, Coelenbier v De Sommery [1912] 2 Ch 622, 82 LJ Ch 17, 57 Sol Jo 78, 107 LT 253, 823 .... 30.34, 94.43
De Themmines v De Bonneval (1828) 5 Russ 288, 7 LJOS Ch 35 .... 34.6
De Trafford v Tempest (1856) 21 Beav 564 .... 47.7, 48.4
Devall v Dickens (1845) 9 Jur 550 .... 83.16
Devese v Pontet (1785) Prec Ch 240n, 1 Cox Eq Cas 188 .... 44.15
De Virte, Re, Vaiani v De Virte [1915] 1 Ch 920, 84 LJ Ch 617, 112 LT 972 .... 42.15
Devitt v Kearney (1883) 13 LR Ir 45, Ir CA 64.7
Devling, Re [1955] ALR 700, [1955] VLR 238 .... 65.2, 80.1, 80.3
Devon (Duke) v Atkins (1726) 2 P Wms 381, Cas temp King 71 .... 31.4

Devon's (Earl) Settled Estates, Re, White v Earl of Devon [1896] 2 Ch 562, 65 LJ Ch 810, 45 WR 25, 40 Sol Jo 685, 75 LT 178 .... 39.5
Devorkin, Re [1951] OWN 913 .... 64.29
Dew v Clark and Clark (1826) 3 Add 79 .... 4.15
Dewar v Brooke (1880) 14 Ch D 529, 49 LJ Ch 374, 28 WR 613 .... 93.39
Dewar v Maitland (1866) LR 2 Eq 834, 12 Jur NS 699, 14 WR 958, 14 LT 853 .... 24.10, 42.2, 42.9, 42.12, 42.15
Dewell's Goods, Re (1853) 1 Ecc & Ad 103, 17 Jur 1130, 22 LTOS 124 .... 11.26, 14.6
Dewhirst, Re, Flower v Dewhirst [1948] Ch 198, [1948] 1 All ER 147, [1948] LJR 912, 92 Sol Jo 84, 64 TLR 74 .... 33.20, 35.6, 35.8, 80.4, 224.86
De Windt v De Windt (1866) LR 1 HL 87, 35 LJ Ch 332, 14 WR 545, 14 LT 529 .... 89.1
De Witte v De Witte (1840) 11 Sim 41, 9 LJ Ch 270, 4 Jur 625 .... 85.3
Dhaliwall v Dhaliwall (1986) 6 BCLR (2d) 62, [1986] 6 WWR 278, 30 DLR (4th) 420 .... 9.18
Dias v De Livera (1879) 5 App Cas 123, PC 2.2, 66.20, 66.23
Dibbs v Goren (1849) 11 Beav 483 .... 31.8
Dicey, Re, Julian v Dicey [1957] Ch 145, [1956] 3 All ER 696, [1956] 3 WLR 981, 100 Sol Jo 874, CA 42.2, 42.5
Dick, Re, Knight v Dick [1953] Ch 343, [1953] 1 All ER 559, 97 Sol Jo 149, CA 40.15
Dick v Audsley. See Dick's Trustees v Dick
Dick v Lacy (1845) 8 Beav 214, 14 LJ Ch 150, 9 Jur 221, 5 LTOS 70 .... 74.8, 85.5, 87.3
Dick's Trustees v Dick 1907 SC 953; affd sub nom Dick v Audsley [1908] AC 347, 77 LJPC 126, HL 103.17
Dick's Trustees v Dick 1911 48 SLR 325, 1911 SLT 95 .... 82.7
Dicken v Clarke (1837) 2 Y & C Ex 572 .... 93.23
Dickens, Re, Dickens v Hawksley [1935] Ch 267, 104 LJ Ch 174, 78 Sol Jo 898, 152 LT 375, 51 TLR 181, CA 204.33
Dickenson v Blisset (1754) 1 Dick 268 .... 5.2
Dicker, Re [1947] Ch 248, [1947] 1 All ER 317, [1948] LJR 544, 91 Sol Jo 148, 177 LT 274 .... 72.3
Dickinson v Stidolph (1861) 11 CBNS 341 .... 18.13
Dickinson's Settlements, Re, Bickersteth v Dickinson [1939] Ch 27, 108 LJ Ch 40, 82 Sol Jo 744, 159 LT 614 .... 218.43, 218.46
Dicks v Lambert (1799) 4 Ves 725 .... 64.53
Dickson, Re (1965) 49 DLR (2d) 289, [1965] 1 OR 661 .... 57.3, 71.5
Dickson, Re, Hill v Grant (1885) 29 Ch D 331, 54 LJ Ch 510, 33 WR 511, 52 LT 707, 1 TLR 331, CA 32.15
Dickson's Trust, Re, ex p Dickson (1850) 1 Sim NS 37, 20 LJ Ch 33, 15 Jur 282, sub nom Re Dixon's Trusts 16 LTOS 168 .... 34.13, 34.25, 35.30
Dieppe, Re, Millard v Dieppe (1915) 138 LT Jo 564 .... 72.2
Dietrich, Re (1963) 36 DLR (2d) 17, [1963] 1 OR 70 .... 80.2
Dilke, Re, Re Dilke's Settlement Trusts, Verey v Dilke [1921] 1 Ch 34, 90 LJ Ch 89, [1920] All ER Rep 200, 124 LT 229, 37 TLR 13, CA 39.2
Dilkes v Broadmead (1860) 2 Giff 113; on appeal (1860) 2 De GF & J 566 .... 31.18
Dilkes's Goods, Re (1874) LR 3 P & D 164, 38 JP 329, 43 LJP & M 38, 22 WR 456, 30 LT 305 .... 11.3, 12.5, 12.11
Dilley v Matthews (1865) 11 Jur NS 425, 13 WR 676, 12 LT 488 .... 72.2

Dillon, Re, Duffin v Duffin (1890) 44 Ch D 76, 59 LJ Ch 420, 38 WR 369, [1886–90] All ER Rep 407, 62 LT 614, 6 TLR 204, CA 1.15
Dillon v Arkins (1885) 17 LR Ir 636, Ir CA 64.11, 64.54
Dillon v Coppin (1839) 4 My & Cr 647, 9 LJ Ch 87, 4 Jur 427 .... 10.5
Dillon v Harris (1830) 4 Bli NS 321, HL 35.16, 56.8, 57.5, 57.11
Dillon v M'Donnell (1881) 7 LR Ir 335 .... 64.35
Dillon v Parker (1818) 1 Swan 359; on appeal (1822) Jac 505; affd (1833) 7 Bli NS 325, 1 Cl & Fin 303, HL 42.1, 42.12
Dillon v Public Trustee of New Zealand [1941] AC 294, [1941] 2 All ER 284, 165 LT 357, 57 TLR 425, PC 3.6, 3.12
Dillon v Reilly (1873) IR 10 Eq 152 .... 102.7
Dilnot v Hinkley (1888) 14 VLR 702 .... 97.1
Dimes v Dimes (1856) 10 Moo PCC 422 .... 4.14
Dimond v Bostock (1875) 10 Ch App 358, 23 WR 554, 33 LT 217 .... 47.29, 47.32, 66.19
Dingle v Coppen [1899] 1 Ch 726, 68 LJ Ch 337, 47 WR 279, 79 LT 693 .... 30.12, 45.2
Dingle v Turner [1972] AC 601, [1972] 1 All ER 878, [1972] 2 WLR 523, 116 Sol Jo 195, HL 102.1, 102.8, 102.10, 102.14, 102.15, 102.16
Dingmar v Dingmar [2006] EWCA Civ 942, [2007] Ch 109, [2007] 2 All ER 382, [2006] 3 WLR 1183, [2006] WTLR 1171, [2006] 2 FCR 595, [2007] 1 FLR 210, [2006] All ER (D) 160 (Jul) 105.32, 105.41
Dingwell v Askew (1788) 1 Cox Eq Cas 427 .... 41.21, 41.22
Dinmore's Goods, Re (1853) 2 Rob Eccl 641, 1 Ecc & Ad 2 .... 11.6
Diplock, Re, Diplock v Wintle [1948] Ch 465, [1948] 2 All ER 318, [1948] LJR 1670, 92 Sol Jo 409, 484, CA; affd sub nom Ministry of Health v Simpson [1951] AC 251, [1950] 2 All ER 1137, 94 Sol Jo 777, 66 (pt 2) TLR 1015, HL 30.38, 31.11, 31.12
Disney v Crosse (1866) LR 2 Eq 592 .... 39.18
Di Sora v Phillipps (1863) 10 HL Cas 624, 33 LJ Ch 129, 2 New Rep 553 ... 49.8, 50.19, 57.7
Ditchburn v Fearn (1842) 6 Jur 201 .... 4.15
Diver Estate, Re (1962) 34 DLR (2d) 667, 39 WWR 612 .... 64.36
Dix, Re. See Gully v Dix
Dix v Reed (1823) 1 Sim & St 237 .... 30.14
Dixon, Re [1892] P 386, 56 JP 841, 8 TLR 744 .... 7.33
Dixon, Re, Dixon v Charlesworth [1903] 2 Ch 458, 72 LJ Ch 642, 51 WR 652, 88 LT 862 .... 34.6, 83.8, 99.1
Dixon, Re, Dixon v Dixon (1912) 56 Sol Jo 445 .... 83.9, 99.1
Dixon v Treasury Solicitor [1905] P 42, 74 LJP 33, 92 LT 427, 21 TLR 145 .... 19.1, 19.4, 19.5
Dixon Hartland, Re, Banks v Hartland. See Hartland, Re, Banks v Hartland
Dixon's Estate, Re [1969] 2 NSWR 223, 90 (Pt 1) WNNSW 469 .... 70.2
Dixon's Trusts, Re (1850) 16 LTOS 168. See Dickson's Trust, Re, ex p Dickson
Dixon's Trusts, Re (1869) IR 4 Eq 1 .... 76.3
Dobbs v Brain [1892] 2 QB 207, 57 JP 22, 61 LJQB 749, 41 WR 7, [1891–4] All ER Rep 631, 67 LT 371, 8 TLR 630, CA 9.40
Dobson v Bowness (1868) LR 5 Eq 404, 37 LJ Ch 309, 16 WR 640 .... 60.2

Dobson v North Tyneside Health Authority [1996] 4 All ER 474, [1997] 1 WLR 596, [1997] 2 FCR 651, [1997] 1 FLR 598, [1997] Fam Law 326, [1996] 31 LS Gaz R 29, [1996] NLJR 1458, 140 Sol Jo LB 165, CA ... 202.3
Dobson's Goods, Re (1866) LR 1 P & D 88, 35 LJP & M 54, 14 WR 408, 13 LT 758 ... 1.10
Dodd v Wake (1837) 8 Sim 615 ... 66.1, 94.21
Dodds v Dodds (1860) 11 I Ch R 374, 13 Ir Jur 75, Ir. CA ... 84.4
Dodgson's Trust, Re (1853) 1 Drew 440 ... 97.7
Dodson v Hay (1791) 3 Bro CC 405 ... 93.35, 93.36
Dodsworth v Addy (1842) 11 LJ Ch 382, 6 Jur 700 ... 76.2
Doe d Borwell v Abey (1813) 1 M & S 428 ... 67.8, 86.7, 101.6
Doe d Phillips v Aldridge (1791) 4 Term Rep 264 ... 81.5
Doe d Allen v Allen (1840) 12 Ad & El 451, 9 LJQB 395, 4 Jur 985, 4 Per & Dav 220 ... 57.22
Doe d Angell v Angell (1846) 9 QB 328, 15 LJQB 193, 10 Jur 705, 6 LTOS 520 ... 53.1, 76.5
Doe d Blandford v Applin (1790) 4 Term Rep 82 ... 50.3
Doe d Turner v Ash (1852) 18 LTOS 239 ... 64.15
Doe d Renow v Ashley (1847) 10 QB 663, 16 LJQB 356, 11 Jur 905 ... 58.6, 64.2
Doe d Bainbrigge v Bainbrigge (1850) 4 Cox CC 454, 16 LTOS 245 ... 4.20
Doe d Ashby v Baines (1835) 2 Cr M & R 23, 4 LJ Ex 141, 1 Gale 135, 5 Tyr 655 ... 83.6
Doe d Jearrad v Bannister (1840) 10 LJ Ex 33, H & W 61, 5 Jur 102, 7 M & W 292 ... 84.2
Doe d Goodbehere v Bevan (1815) 3 M & S 353, 2 Rose 456, [1814–23] All ER Rep 706 ... 7.23
Doe d Thomas v Beynon (1840) 12 Ad & El 431, 9 LJQB 359, 4 Per & Dav 193 ... 57.15
Doe d Leicester v Biggs (1809) 2 Taunt 109 ... 52.7
Doe d Clift v Birkhead (1849) 18 LJ Ex 441, 4 Exch 110, 13 LTOS 529 ... 90.1, 101.12
Doe d Hatch v Bluck (1816) 6 Taunt 485, 2 Marsh 170 ... 84.2
Doe d Ashforth v Bower (1832) 3 B & Ad 453, 1 LJKB 156 ... 58.6, 63.4
Doe d Gigg v Bradley (1812) 16 East 399 ... 85.3
Doe d Annandale v Brazier (1821) 5 B & Ald 64 ... 101.14
Doe d Brown v Brown (1809) 11 East 441 ... 58.6
Doe d Spearing v Buckner (1796) 6 Term Rep 610 ... 60.2
Doe d Counsell v Caperton (1839) 9 C & P 112 ... 12.12
Doe d Campton v Carpenter (1850) 16 QB 181, 20 LJQB 70, 15 Jur 719, 16 LTOS 234 ... 63.7
Doe d Tatum v Catomore (1851) 16 QB 745, sub nom Doe d Tatham v Cattamore 15 JP 673, 20 LJQB 364, 15 Jur 728, 17 LTOS 74 ... 14.3
Doe d Evers v Challis (1852) 18 QB 224; affd sub nom Evers v Challis (1859) 7 HL Cas 531, 29 LJQB 121, 5 Jur NS 825, 115 RR 257, 7 WR 622, 33 LTOS 373 ... 93.19
Doe d Burkitt v Chapman (1789) 1 Hy Bl 223 ... 60.2
Doe d Oxenden v Chichester (1816) 4 Dow 65, HL ... 57.20
Doe d Clarke v Clarke (1795) 2 Hy Bl 399 ... 73.1
Doe d Clements v Collins (1788) 2 Term Rep 498 ... 63.7
Doe d Everett v Cooke (1806) 7 East 269, 3 Smith KB 236 ... 56.8

Doe d Dunning v Cranstoun (1840) 9 LJ Ex 294, 4 Jur 683, 7 M & W 1 .... 64.22
Doe d Cross v Cross (1846) 8 QB 714, 15 LJQB 217, 10 Jur 564, 7 LTOS 61 .... 1.3
Doe d Wright v Cundall (1808) 9 East 400 .... 101.7
Doe d Davies v Davies (1851) 16 QB 951, 20 LJQB 408, 15 Jur 1029, 17 LTOS 104 .... 92.1
Doe d Lloyd v Davies. See Lloyd v Davies
Doe d Dacre (Baroness) v Dowager Lady Dacre (1798) 1 Bos & P 250; affd sub nom Dacre (Dowager Lady) v Doe d Baroness Dacre (1799) 8 Term Rep 112 .... 93.13
Doe d Hick v Dring (1814) 2 M & S 448 .... 38.4, 51.3, 64.15, 64.16
Doe d Todd v Duesbury (1841) 10 LJ Ex 410, 8 M & W 514 .... 98.10
Doe d Beach v Earl of Jersey (1818) 1 B & Ald 550; on appeal (1825) 3 B & C 870, HL 57.18, 58.9, 58.10, 63.2, 63.5
Doe d Haw v Earles (1846) 16 LJ Ex 242, 15 M & W 450, 9 LTOS 538 ...... 38.7, 64.15
Doe d Gilman v Elvey (1803) 4 East 313, 1 Smith KB 94 .... 85.4
Doe d Evans v Evans (1839) 10 Ad & El 228, 8 LJQB 284, 3 Jur 844, 2 Per & Dav 378 .... 19.5
Doe d Cadogan v Ewart (1838) 7 Ad & El 636, 7 LJQB 177, 3 Nev & PKB 197, 1 Will Woll & H 246 .... 93.12, 98.7
Doe d Blomfield v Eyre (1848) 5 CB 713, 18 LJCP 284, 10 LTOS 525, Ex Ch 40.21, 48.15
Doe d Smith v Fleming (1835) 2 Cr M & R 638, 5 LJ Ex 74, 1 Gale 278, 5 Tyr 1013 .... 65.1, 79.2
Doe d Westminster (Dean) v Freeman (1786) 2 Chit 498, 1 Term Rep 389 ..... 82.3, 83.7
Doe d Nixon v French (1850) 15 LTOS 93 .... 64.15
Doe d Pottow v Fricker (1851) 20 LJ Ex 265, 6 Exch 510, 17 LTOS 81 .... 64.19
Doe d King v Frost (1820) 3 B & Ald 546 .... 78.2, 79.2
Doe d Smith v Galloway (1833) 5 B & Ad 43, 2 LJKB 182, 2 Nev & MKB 240 .... 58.3
Doe d Gillard v Gillard (1822) 5 B & Ald 785 .... 38.8, 84.2
Doe d Harris v Greathed (1806) 8 East 91 .... 58.1, 63.6
Doe d Littlewood v Green (1838) 8 LJ Ex 65, 1 Horn & H 314, 2 Jur 859, 4 M & W 229 .... 86.3
Doe d Browne v Greening (1814) 3 M & S 171 .... 57.20
Doe d Gwillim v Gwillim (1833) 5 B & Ad 122, 2 LJKB 194, 2 Nev & MKB 247 .... 49.2, 57.3
Doe d James v Hallett (1813) 1 M & S 124 .... 81.2
Doe d Reed v Harris (1837) 6 Ad & El 209, 6 LJKB 84, 1 Nev & PKB 405, Will Woll & Dav 106, sub nom Doe d Read v Harris 1 Jur 134 .... 18.17, 18.22
Doe d Chidgey v Harris (1847) 16 M & W 517 .... 27.5, 27.6, 45.1
Doe d Bosnall v Harvey (1825) 4 B & C 610, sub nom Doe d Bagnall v Harvey 4 LJOSKB 18, 7 Dow & Ry KB 78 .... 50.3
Doe d Hickman v Haslewood (1837) 6 Ad & El 167, 6 LJKB 96, 1 Nev & PKB 352, Will Woll & Dav 116 .... 49.1, 84.2
Doe d Blakiston v Haslewood (1851) 10 CB 544, 20 LJCP 89, 15 Jur 272 .... 101.2
Doe d Norfolk (Duke) v Hawke (1802) 2 East 481 .... 35.20, 35.39
Doe d Parsey v Hemming (1851) 17 LTOS 89 .... 64.22
Doe d Hearle v Hicks (1832) 8 Bing 475, 6 Bli NS 37, 1 Cl & Fin 20, 1 Moo & S 759, HL 18.6, 18.14, 20.3, 52.1, 82.2

Doe d Hiscocks v Hiscocks (1839) 9 LJ Ex 27, 2 Horn & H 54, 3 Jur 955, 5 M & W 363, [1835–42] All ER Rep 380 ...... 57.3, 57.12, 57.13, 57.18, 57.19, 57.22, 58.9
Doe d Biddulph v Hole (1850) 15 QB 848, 20 LJQB 57, 15 LTOS 392 .... 20.4, 22.3
Doe d Preedy v Holtom (1835) 4 Ad & El 76, 5 LJKB 10, 1 Har & W 528, 5 Nev & MKB 391 ...... 57.12, 57.20
Doe d Bills v Hopkinson (1843) 5 QB 223, 13 LJQB 85, 8 Jur 142, 2 LTOS 207 ...... 50.3
Doe d Hubbard v Hubbard (1850) 15 QB 227, 20 LJQB 61, 14 Jur 1110, 15 LTOS 411 ...... 58.3, 58.6, 63.7
Doe d Hurrell v Hurrell (1821) 5 B & Ald 18 ...... 60.2
Doe d Le Chevalier v Huthwaite (1820) 3 B & Ald 632 ...... 57.12, 57.14, 58.10
Doe d Usher v Jessep (1810) 12 East 288 ...... 56.7, 56.9
Doe d Wright v Jesson (1816) 5 M & S 95; affd sub nom Jesson v Wright (1820) 2 Bligh 1, HL 50.17, 50.21
Doe d Pell v Jeyes (1830) 1 B & Ad 593, 9 LJOSKB 82 ...... 60.1
Doe d Johnson v Johnson (1852) 22 LJ Ex 90, 8 Exch 81, 19 LTOS 313 ...... 98.11
Doe d Hayter v Joinville (1802) 3 East 172, 6 RR 585 ...... 57.19, 79.2
Doe d Turner v Kett (1792) 4 Term Rep 601 ...... 22.4, 68.2
Doe d Andrew v Lainchbury (1809) 11 East 290 ...... 50.10
Doe d Goldin v Lakeman (1831) 2 B & Ad 30, 9 LJOSKB 138 ...... 62.1
Doe d Long v Laming (1760) 2 Burr 1100, 1 Wm Bl 265 ...... 49.4
Doe d Lancashire v Lancashire (1792) 5 Term Rep 49 ...... 73.1
Doe d Wall v Langlands (1811) 14 East 370 ...... 38.3, 38.6, 51.3, 64.51
Doe d Gore v Langton (1831) 2 B & Ad 680 ...... 57.14
Doe d Wheedon v Lea (1789) 3 Term Rep 41 ...... 93.11
Doe d Caldwell v Lee (1852) 19 LTOS 49 ...... 12.5
Doe d Herbert v Lewis and Thomas. See Doe d Herbert v Thomas
Doe d Kenrick v Lord Beauclerk (1809) 11 East 657 ...... 35.39
Doe d Phipps v Lord Mulgrave (1793) 5 Term Rep 320 ...... 89.1
Doe d Rew v Lucraft (1832) 8 Bing 386, 1 LJCP 109, 1 Moo & S 573 ...... 98.4
Doe d Clarke v Ludlam (1831) 7 Bing 275, 9 LJOSCP 74, 5 Moo & P 48 .... 49.5, 50.21
Doe d Tyrrell v Lyford (1816) 4 M & S 550 ...... 57.20, 63.3, 63.8
Doe d Murch v Marchant (1843) 13 LJCP 59, 8 Jur 21, 6 Man & G 813, 7 Scott NR 644, 2 LTOS 209 ...... 20.4
Doe d Lempriere v Martin (1777) 2 Wm Bl 1148 ...... 64.2
Doe d Willis v Martin (1790) 4 Term Rep 39, [1775–1802] All ER Rep 343 ...... 101.9
Doe d Templeman v Martin (1833) 4 B & Ad 771, 1 Nev & MKB 512 ...... 57.20, 58.1
Doe d Biddulph v Meakin (1801) 1 East 456 ...... 64.26
Doe d Ashburnham v Michael (1851) 17 QB 276, 20 LJQB 480, 15 Jur 677, 17 LTOS 154 ...... 25.15
Doe d Leach v Micklem (1805) 6 East 486, sub nom Doe d Leech v Micklem 2 Smith KB 499 ...... 52.3, 91.3
Doe d Taylor v Mills (1833) 1 Mood & R 288 ...... 9.8
Doe d Morgan v Morgan (1832) 1 Cr & M 235, 2 LJ Ex 88, 3 Tyr 179 ...... 57.22
Doe d Gord v Needs (1836) 6 LJ Ex 59, 2 Gale 245, 2 M & W 129 ...... 57.22
Doe d Snape v Nevell. See Roe d Snape v Nevill
Doe d Hawthorn v Nickliss (1840) 4 Jur 660 ...... 63.8
Doe d Norton v Norton (1846) 8 LTOS 160 ...... 64.26

Doe d Roake v Nowell (1813) 1 M & S 327; affd sub nom Randoll v Doe d Roake (1817) 5 Dow 202, HL 93.16
Doe d Thwaites v Over (1808) 1 Taunt 263 .... 66.22
Doe d Jones v Owens (1830) 1 B & Ad 318, 8 LJOSKB 404 .... 98.10
Doe d Page v Page (1851) 17 LTOS 123 .... 64.7
Doe d Shallcross v Palmer (1851) 16 QB 747, 15 JP 689, 20 LJQB 367, 15 Jur 836, [1843–60] All ER Rep 139, 17 LTOS 252 .... 14.4, 14.11
Doe d Parkin v Parkin (1814) 5 Taunt 321, 1 Marsh 61 .... 58.6, 63.7
Doe d Gill v Pearson (1805) 6 East 173, 2 Smith KB 295 .... 99.2
Doe d Spencer v Pedley (1836) 5 LJ Ex 221, 2 Gale 106, 1 M & W 662, Tyr & Gr 882 .... 52.8
Doe d Winter v Perratt (1843) 9 Cl & Fin 606, 6 Man & G 314, 7 Scott NR 1, HL 51.12, 53.1, 78.2, 94.33
Doe d Phillips v Phillips (1786) 1 Term Rep 105 .... 60.1
Doe d Dell v Pigott (1817) 7 Taunt 553, 1 Moore CP 274 .... 63.3
Doe d Wright v Plumptre (1820) 3 B & Ald 474 .... 58.11
Doe d Roberts v Polgrean (1791) 1 Hy Bl 535 .... 8.3
Doe d Pratt v Pratt (1837) 6 Ad & El 180, 6 LJKB 101, 1 Nev & PKB 366, Will Woll & Dav 113 .... 84.2
Doe d Long v Prigg (1828) 8 B & C 231, 6 LJOSKB 296, 2 Man & Ry KB 338 .... 67.2, 97.9
Doe d Bailey v Pugh. See Goodtitle d Bailey v Pugh
Doe d Baldwin v Rawding (1819) 2 B & Ald 441 .... 50.16, 52.6, 56.8
Doe d Humphreys v Roberts (1822) 5 B & Ad 407 .... 58.2, 63.4
Doe d Gains v Rouse (1848) 5 CB 422, 17 LJCP 108, 12 Jur 99, 10 LTOS 327 .... 58.10, 80.6
Doe d Bunny v Rout (1816) 7 Taunt 79, 2 Marsh 397 .... 38.6, 64.51
Doe d Patrick v Royle (1849) 13 QB 100, 18 LJQB 145, 13 Jur 745, 12 LTOS 493 .... 101.6
Doe d Wells v Scott (1814) 3 M & S 300 .... 93.19
Doe d Planner v Scudamore (1800) 2 Bos & P 289 .... 34.2, 93.16
Doe d Herbert v Selby (1824) 2 B & C 926, 4 Dow & Ry KB 608 .... 56.1
Doe d Stewart v Sheffield (1811) 13 East 526 .... 47.32
Doe d Blesard v Simpson (1842) 3 Man & G 929, 3 Scott NR 774, Ex Ch 98.13
Doe d Bailey v Sloggett (1850) 19 LJ Ex 220, 5 Exch 107 .... 91.4
Doe d Chattaway v Smith (1816) 5 M & S 126 .... 54.5, 79.1
Doe d Smyth v Smyth (1826) 6 B & C 112, 5 LJOSKB 13, 9 Dow & Ry KB 136 .... 46.4
Doe d Pilkington v Spratt (1833) 5 B & Ad 731, 3 LJKB 53, 2 Nev & MKB 524 .... 78.2
Doe d Shaw v Steward (1834) 1 Ad & El 300, 3 LJKB 141, 3 Nev & MKB 372 .... 35.20
Doe d Stopford v Stopford (1804) 5 East 501, 2 Smith KB 92 .... 54.5
Doe d Strickland v Strickland (1849) 8 CB 724, 19 LJCP 89, 14 LTOS 270 .... 14.8
Doe d Newton v Taylor (1827) 7 B & C 384, 6 LJOSKB 149 .... 63.8
Doe d Herbert v Thomas (1835) 3 Ad & El 123, sub nom Doe d Herbert v Lewis and Thomas 1 Har & W 231, 4 Nev & MKB 697 .... 83.9, 83.13
Doe d Howell v Thomas (1840) 1 Man & G 335, 1 Scott NR 359 .... 60.1
Doe d Brodbelt v Thomson (1858) 12 Moo PCC 116, 32 LTOS 65 .... 50.4, 82.1
Doe d Thorley v Thorley (1809) 10 East 438 .... 83.17

Doe d Tofield v Tofield (1809) 11 East 246 .... 64.45
Doe d Liversage v Vaughan (1822) 5 B & Ald 464, 1 Dow & Ry KB 52 .... 85.2
Doe d Watts v Wainwright (1793) 5 Term Rep 427 .... 67.4
Doe d York v Walker (1844) 13 LJ Ex 153, 12 M & W 591, 2 LTOS 424 .... 59.2, 59.3
Doe d Dolley v Ward (1839) 9 Ad & El 582, 8 LJQB 154, 1 Per & Dav 568 .... 93.16, 93.17
Doe d Evers v Ward (1852) 18 QB 197, 21 LJQB 145, 16 Jur 709, 18 LTOS 317 .... 18.14
Doe d Lord and Lady Cholmondeley v Weatherby (1809) 11 East 322 .... 60.1
Doe d Smith v Webber (1818) 1 B & Ald 713 .... 74.1, 98.10, 98.13
Doe d Westlake v Westlake (1820) 4 B & Ald 57 .... 57.20, 57.22
Doe d Chillcott v White (1800) 1 East 33 .... 38.7, 64.16
Doe d Burton v White (1848) 18 LJ Ex 59, 2 Exch 797 .... 64.19
Doe d Mather v Whitefoot (1838) 8 C & P 270 .... 4.20
Doe d Vessey v Wilkinson (1788) 2 Term Rep 209 .... 93.23
Doe d Hemming v Willetts (1849) 7 CB 709, 18 LJCP 240 .... 64.26
Doe d Luscombe v Yates (1822) 5 B & Ald 544, 1 Dow & Ry KB 187 .... 35.40
Doering, Re [1949] 1 DLR 267, [1948] OR 923, OWN 840 .... 102.8
Doering v Doering (1889) 42 Ch D 203, 58 LJ Ch 553, 37 WR 796 .... 30.17
Doglioni v Crispin (1866) LR 1 HL 301, 35 LJP & M 129, 15 LT 44 .... 23.8
Doherty, Re, Quinn v Clarke [1950] NI 83, CA 34.2, 35.19
Doherty v Doherty [1936] 2 DLR 180, 5 FLJ (Can) 277, 10 MPR 286 .... 34.5, 99.1
Doherty v Dwyer (1890) 25 LR Ir 297 .... 14.5, 14.8
Doherty-Waterhouse, Re, Musgrave v De Chair [1918] 2 Ch 269, 87 LJ Ch 630, [1918–19] All ER Rep 944, 62 Sol Jo 636, 119 LT 298 .... 39.7, 39.12, 39.14
Doland's Will Trusts, Re, Westminster Bank Ltd v Phillips [1970] Ch 267, [1969] 3 All ER 713, [1969] 3 WLR 614, 113 Sol Jo 798 .... 9.3, 9.9, 38.14, 48.7, 50.4, 50.9, 51.8, 52.3
Dolamore, Re, Hammond v Dolamore (1897) 41 Sol Jo 623, 13 TLR 487 .... 22.4
Dolan v Macdermot (1868) 3 Ch App 676, 17 WR 3 .... 102.23
Dolebear, Re [1958] OWN 36 .... 35.21
Dolling, Re [1956] VLR 535 .... 9.2
Dominion Students' Hall Trust, Re, Dominion Students' Hall Trust v A-G [1947] Ch 183, [1947] LJR 371, 91 Sol Jo 100, 176 LT 224, 63 TLR 90 .... 9.38, 103.12, 103.18
Domvile v Taylor (1863) 32 Beav 604, 2 New Rep 258, 11 WR 796, 8 LT 624 .... 63.1
Domville v Lamb (1853) 1 WR 246 .... 40.15
Donald, Re, Moore v Somerset [1909] 2 Ch 410, 78 LJ Ch 761, 53 Sol Jo 673, 101 LT 377 .... 20.4, 58.11, 102.7, 102.10, 103.3, 103.10
Donald, Re, Royal Exchange Assurance v Donald [1947] 1 All ER 764, 91 Sol Jo 338, CA 50.8
Donaldson's Goods, Re (1840) 2 Curt 386 .... 16.2
Donn, Re, Donn v Moses [1944] Ch 8, [1943] 2 All ER 564, 113 LJ Ch 61, 87 Sol Jo 406, 169 LT 335, 60 TLR 30 .... 34.11, 35.29, 35.31
Donn v Penny (1815) 1 Mer 20, 19 Ves 545 .... 85.5
Donnellan v O'Neill (1870) IR 5 Eq 523 .... 81.5
Donnelly v Broughton [1891] AC 435, 60 LJPC 48, 40 WR 209, 65 LT 558, PC 5.9, 11.13
Donner's Estate, Re (1917) 62 Sol Jo 161, 34 TLR 138 .... 16.4

Donovan v Needham (1846) 9 Beav 164, 15 LJ Ch 193, 10 Jur 150, 7 LTOS 107 .... 32.10, 32.20
Doody v Higgins (1856) 2 K & J 729, 25 LJ Ch 773, 4 WR 737, 27 LTOS 281 .... 78.4
Dooley v Dooley [1927] IR 190, CA 43.4
Dooley v Mahon (1877) IR 11 Eq 299 .... 58.11
Door v Geary. See Dore v Geary
Dorchester (Lord) v Earl Effingham (1813) 3 Beav 180n, 10 Sim 587n 94.15
Dore v Geary (1749) 1 Wils 247, sub nom Door v Geary 1 Ves Sen 255 .... 58.10
Dorigan's Will, Re (1962) 40 WWR 505 .... 57.5
Dorin v Dorin (1875) LR 7 HL 568, 39 JP 790, 45 LJ Ch 652, 23 WR 570, [1874–80] All ER Rep 71, 33 LT 281 .... 72.2
Dorman, Re [1994] 1 All ER 804, [1994] 1 WLR 282, [1994] 2 FLR 52, [1994] Fam Law 569, [1994] 9 LS Gaz R 38 .... 41.2, 41.22
Dormer v Phillips (1855) 4 De GM & G 855, 3 WR 337, 25 LTOS 74 .... 49.9, 57.3, 78.2
Douce's Goods, Re (1862) 8 Jur NS 723, 2 Sw & Tr 593, 6 LT 789, sub nom Re Douse's Goods 31 LJPM & A 172, ... 11.13, 11.20
Doucet v Geoghegan (1878) 9 Ch D 441, 26 WR 825, CA 236.10
Dougal, Re [1981] STC 514, Ct of Sess 55.7, 200.111, 204.1, 204.54, 209.3, 210.3, 211.13, 214.56, 214.58, 214.76
Douglas, Re, Douglas v Simpson [1905] 1 Ch 279, 74 LJ Ch 196, 92 LT 78, 21 TLR 140 .... 102.9
Douglas, Re, Obert v Barrow (1886) 35 Ch D 472; affd (1887) 35 Ch D 472, 56 LJ Ch 913, 35 WR 740, [1886–90] All ER Rep 228, 56 LT 786, 3 TLR 589, CA 9.31, 102.23, 102.25, 103.11, 103.17
Douglas v Andrews (1851) 14 Beav 347 .... 90.1
Douglas (Lord) v Chalmer (1795) 2 Ves 501 .... 97.2
Douglas v Congreve (1838) 1 Beav 59, 8 LJ Ch 53, 3 Jur 120 .... 84.4
Douglas v Douglas (1854) Kay 400, 23 LJ Ch 732 .... 59.1, 59.3
Douglas v Douglas (1871) LR 12 Eq 617, 41 LJ Ch 74, 20 WR 55, 25 LT 530 .... 42.9
Douglas v Fellows (1853) Kay 114, 23 LJ Ch 167, 2 WR 654, 24 LTOS 21 .... 57.19, 57.22, 58.4
Douglas v Willes (1849) 7 Hare 318 .... 44.4, 100.4, 100.6
Douglas and Powell's Contract, Re [1902] 2 Ch 296, 71 LJ Ch 850 .... 37.8
Douglas's Will Trusts, Re, Lloyds Bank Ltd v Nelson [1959] 2 All ER 620, [1959] 1 WLR 744, 103 Sol Jo 657; affd [1959] 3 All ER 785, [1959] 1 WLR 1212, 104 Sol Jo 126, CA 64.53, 67.2, 67.7, 104.16
Douglas-Menzies v Umphelby [1908] AC 224, 77 LJPC 64, 98 LT 509, 24 TLR 344, PC 1.1, 42.2
Douse's Goods, Re. See Re Douce's Goods
Dowdle v Coppel [1987] VR 1024 .... 40.14
Dowglass v Waddell (1886) 17 LR Ir 384 .... 40.21
Dowley v Winfield (1844) 14 Sim 277, 8 Jur 972 .... 9.2
Dowling, Re, Thompson v Union Trustee Co of Australia Ltd [1961] VR 615 .... 94.47
Dowling v Dowling (1866) 1 Ch App 612, 12 Jur NS 720, 14 WR 1003, 15 LT 152 .... 101.10
Dowling v Dowling [1902] 1 IR 79, 83 .... 82.7
Down, Re (1968) 68 DLR (2d) 30, [1968] 2 OR 16 .... 35.19, 35.22

Down v Down (1817) 7 Taunt 343, 1 Moore CP 80 .... 58.1
Downer, Re [1957] SASR 207 .... 76.2
Downer's Goods, Re (1853) 1 Ecc & Ad 106, 18 Jur 66, 23 LTOS 11 .... 18.5, 18.17
Downing v Bagnall. See Downing (or Downes) v Townsend
Downing (or Downes) v Townsend (1755) Amb 280, sub nom Downing v Bagnall Amb App 818 .... 64.35
Downing's Residuary Estate, Re (1888) 60 LT 140 .... 36.7
Dowse, Re, Dowse v Dowse [1951] 1 All ER 558n, 95 Sol Jo 107, [1951] 1 TLR 444 .... 92.3
Dowse, Re, Dowse v Glass (1881) 50 LJ Ch 285, 29 WR 563 .... 44.15
Dowset v Sweet (1753) Amb 175 .... 53.5, 57.18, 58.9, 58.10, 58.11
Dowsett, Re, Dowsett v Meakin [1901] 1 Ch 398, 70 LJ Ch 149, 49 WR 268, 45 Sol Jo 119 .... 41.1, 41.21, 47.39
Dowson, Re, Dowson v Beadle [1909] WN 245, 101 LT 671 .... 71.1
Dowson v Gaskoin (1837) 2 Keen 14, 6 LJ Ch 295 .... 64.35
Doyle v Blake (1804) 9 RR 76, 2 Sch & Lef 231 .... 25.12
Doyle v Coyle [1895] 1 IR 205 .... 39.20, 59.1
D'Oyley, Re, Swayne v D'Oyley (1921) 152 LT Jo 259 .... 80.1
Doyley v A-G (1735) 2 Eq Cas Abr 194, 4 Vin Abr 485 pl 16, sub nom A-G v Doyley 7 Ves 58n, [1558–1774] All ER Rep 566 .... 101.9, 103.17
Doyley v Tollferry (1715) 1 Eq Cas Abr 300, sub nom Dawley v Ballfrey Gilb Ch 103, sub nom Dagley v Tolferry 1 P Wms 285 .... 9.40
Drake, Re, Drake v Green [1921] 2 Ch 99, 90 LJ Ch 381, [1921] All ER Rep 157, 65 Sol Jo 553, 125 LT 461 .... 30.24, 34.21
Drake v Collins (1869) 20 LT 970 .... 97.5
Drake v Drake (1860) 8 HL Cas 172, 29 LJ Ch 850, 3 LT 193 ..... 51.3, 53.1, 57.9, 57.10, 57.19, 58.10
Drake v Martin (1856) 23 Beav 89, 26 LJ Ch 786 .... 38.10, 58.10, 64.23
Drake's Will Trusts, Re, Drake v Drake [1971] Ch 179, [1970] 3 All ER 32, [1970] 3 WLR 228, 114 Sol Jo 399, CA 74.9, 76.5
Drant v Vause (1842) 1 Y & C Ch Cas 580, 11 LJ Ch 170, 6 Jur 313 .... 7.27, 41.20
Draper, Re (1888) 57 LJ Ch 942, 36 WR 783, 58 LT 942 .... 33.7, 33.8
Drax, Re, Dunsany v Sawbridge (1906) 75 LJ Ch 317, 54 WR 418, 50 Sol Jo 325, 94 LT 611, 22 TLR 343 .... 35.40, 235.27
Drax, Re, Savile v Yeatman (1887) 57 LT 475 .... 30.24
Draycott v Wood (1856) 5 WR 158, 28 LTOS 196 .... 93.1
Drayton, Re, Francis v Drayton (1912) 56 Sol Jo 253 .... 33.13
Dreger, Re (1976) 69 DLR (3d) 47 .... 9.18
Drew, Re, Drew v Drew [1899] 1 Ch 336, 68 LJ Ch 157, 47 WR 265, 43 Sol Jo 126, 79 LT 656 .... 79.2, 80.1
Drewett v Pollard (1859) 27 Beav 196 .... 95.9
Drexler (George) Ofrex Foundation (Trustees) v IRC [1966] Ch 675, [1965] 3 All ER 529, [1965] 3 WLR 1168, 42 TC 524, 44 ATC 295, [1965] TR 307, 109 Sol Jo 775 .... 102.1, 102.4, 102.8
Dreyfus (Camille and Henry) Foundation Inc v IRC [1956] AC 39, [1955] 3 All ER 97, [1955] 3 WLR 451, 36 TC 126, 34 ATC 208, 48 R & IT 551, [1955] TR 229, 99 Sol Jo 560, 1955 SLT 335, HL 212.2
Driffill, Re, Harvey v Chamberlain [1950] Ch 92, [1949] 2 All ER 933, 93 Sol Jo 803, 66 (pt 1) TLR 80 .... 102.10
Drinkwater v Falconer (1755) 2 Ves Sen 623 .... 22.4, 41.19, 47.1

Driver d Frank v Frank (1814) 3 M & S 25; affd (1818) 8 Taunt 468, 2 Moore CP 519, 6 Price 41, Ex Ch 51.7, 93.2
Druce v Denison (1801) 6 Ves 385 .... 57.20
Drumm's Goods, Re [1931] NI 12 .... 25.2
Drummond, Re (1912) 5 DLR 516, 3 OWN 1459, 22 OWR 554 .... 31.8
Drummond, Re, Ashworth v Drummond [1914] 2 Ch 90, 83 LJ Ch 817, [1914–15] All ER Rep 223, 58 Sol Jo 472, 111 LT 156, 30 TLR 429 .... 9.35, 102.7, 102.26
Drummond v Parish (1843) 3 Curt 522, 7 Jur 538, 1 LTOS 207, 2 Notes of Cases 318 .... 16.2, 16.4
Drummond's Settlement, Re, Foster v Foster [1988] 1 All ER 449, [1988] 1 WLR 234, 132 Sol Jo 192, [1988] 9 LS Gaz R 46, CA ... 66.13, 93.1, 94.21
Drury's Will, Re (1882) 22 NBR 318 .... 18.22
Drylie's Factor v Robertson etc (1882) 9 R 1178, 19 SLR 884 .... 71.4
Duane v Lee (1884) 14 LR Ir 56 .... 31.21
Du Bochet, Re, Mansell v Allen [1901] 2 Ch 441, 70 LJ Ch 647, 49 WR 588, 84 LT 710 .... 9.25
Dubourdieu v Patterson (1919) 54 ILT 23 .... 13.2
Duckmanton v Duckmanton (1860) 5 H & N 219, 29 LJ Ex 132 .... 8.7, 89.1
Duckworth, Re [1958] OWN 236 .... 71.3
Du Cros' Settlement, Re, Du Cros Family Trustee Co Ltd v Du Cros [1961] 3 All ER 193, [1961] 1 WLR 1252, 105 Sol Jo 630 .... 76.5
Duddell, Re, Roundway v Roundway [1932] 1 Ch 585, 101 LJ Ch 248, 146 LT 565 .... 2.1, 2.2, 39.8
Dudding v Gauss (1886) 2 TLR 465, HL 34.3
Duddy v Gresham (1878) 2 LR Ir 442, Ir CA 34.13, 34.16, 35.6, 35.8, 35.10
Dudgeon, Re, Truman v Pope (1896) 74 LT 613, 12 TLR 465 .... 102.5
Dudman, Re, Dudman v Dudman [1925] Ch 553, 95 LJ Ch 204, 133 LT 465 .... 1.15
Duffell, Re, Equity Trustees, Executors and Agency Co Ltd v Duffell [1926] VLR 489, 48 ALT 105 .... 38.10
Duffied, Re (1971) 16 DLR (3d) 7 .... 93.29
Duffield v Currie (1860) 29 Beav 284 .... 91.6
Duffield v Duffield (1829) 3 Bli NS 260, 1 Dow & Cl 268, HL 93.4, 93.5, 93.6, 93.17
Duffield v Elwes (1823) 1 Sim & St 239; on appeal (1827) 1 Bli NS 497, 1 Dow & CI 1, [1824–34] All ER Rep 247, HL 1.15, 35.16
Duffield v M'Master [1906] 1 IR 333, 353, Ir CA 51.10, 93.8
Duffill v Duffill [1903] AC 491, 72 LJPC 97, 89 LT 82, 19 TLR 600, PC 97.5
Duffy's Goods, Re (1871) IR 5 Eq 506 .... 14.4
Dufour v Pereira (1769) 1 Dick 419, sub nom Durour v Perraro 2 Hargrave Juridical Arguments 304 .... 2.3, 2.4, 2.6, 2.8, 2.10, 3.6
Dugdale, Re, Dugdale v Dugdale (1888) 38 Ch D 176, 57 LJ Ch 634, 36 WR 462, 58 LT 581, [1886–90] All ER Rep Ext 1505 .... 34.5, 94.34
Dugdale v Dugdale (1849) 11 Beav 402 .... 87.1
Duggan v Duggan (1880) 5 LR Ir 525; affd (1880) 7 LR Ir 152 .... 40.15
Duggan v Kelly (1848) 10 I Eq R 295, 473 .... 35.30
Duggins' Goods, Re (1870) 34 JP 265, 39 LJP & M 24, 22 LT 182 .... 12.12
Duguid v Fraser (1886) 31 Ch D 449, 55 LJ Ch 285, 34 WR 267, 54 LT 70 .... 18.10
Duhamel v Ardovin (1751) 2 Ves Sen 162 .... 38.3
Duke v Hinxman (1833) 2 LJ Ch 185 .... 38.3

Dulson, Re (1929) 140 LT 470, 45 TLR 228 .... 82.5
Dumaresq Will, Re (1967) 58 WWR 172 .... 62.1
Du Maurier, Re, Millar v Coles (1916) 32 TLR 579 .... 64.3
Dumble, Re, Williams v Murrell (1883) 23 Ch D 360, 52 LJ Ch 631, 31 WR 605, 48 LT 661 .... 32.16
Dummer v Pitcher (1833) 2 My & K 262, Coop temp Brough 257, 39 ER 944 .... 42.5
Dunally v Dunally (1857) 6 I Ch R 540 .... 64.35
Dunbar v Plant [1998] Ch 412, [1997] 4 All ER 289, [1997] 3 WLR 1261, [1998] 1 FLR 157, [1998] Fam Law 139, [1997] 36 LS Gaz R 44, CA ... 9.15, 9.18, 9.20
Duncan v Duncan (No 2) (1859) 27 Beav 392 .... 88.4, 91.6
Duncan v Equity Trustees etc Co Ltd (1958) 32 ALJR 238 .... 82.4
Duncan v Lawson (1889) 41 Ch D 394, 53 JP 532, 58 LJ Ch 502, 37 WR 524, 60 LT 732 .... 23.4, 23.12, 23.16, 23.17, 24.2
Duncan v Watts (1852) 16 Beav 204 .... 30.16, 31.1, 210.51
Duncan Estate, Re (1953) 10 WWRNS 289 .... 35.21
Dundas v Dundas (1830) 2 Dow & Cl 349, HL 24.10, 42.15
Dundas v Wolfe Murray (1863) 1 Hem & M 425, 32 LJ Ch 151, 1 New Rep 429, 11 WR 359 .... 32.3, 32.10, 32.21, 93.31, 93.40
Dundee General Hospitals Board of Management v Walker [1952] 1 All ER 896, sub nom Dundee General Hospitals v Bell's Trustees 1952 SC (HL) 78, 1952 SLT 270 .... 34.10, 35.38
Dundee Magistrates v Dundee Presbytery (1861) 4 Macq 228, HL 102.9
Dundee Magistrates v Morris. See Ewan v Morgan
Dungannon (Lord) v Smith (1846) 12 Cl & Fin 546, 10 Jur 721, 61 RR 137, HL 94.27
Dunk v Fenner (1831) 2 Russ & M 557 .... 84.4
Dunlevy's Trusts, Re (1882) 7 LR Ir 525 .... 67.4
Dunn, Re (1904) 70 LT 560, 3 OWR 311, 24 CLT 295 .... 31.1
Dunn, Re, Carter v Barrett [1916] 1 Ch 97, 85 LJ Ch 168, [1914–15] All ER Rep 566, 60 Sol Jo 175, 113 LT 1206 .... 86.2
Dunn, Re, Dunn v McCowan [1927] St R Qd 265 .... 99.1
Dunn v Bownas (1855) 19 JP 659, 1 K & J 596, sub nom Re Archbold 3 WR 582, 25 LTOS 245 .... 103.11
Dunn v Dunn (1866) LR 1 P & D 277, 15 WR 231, 15 LT 216 .... 11.9, 22.2
Dunn v Flood (1883) 25 Ch D 629, 53 LJ Ch 537, 32 WR 197, 49 LT 670; on appeal (1885) 28 Ch D 586, 54 LJ Ch 370, 33 WR 315, 52 LT 699, 1 TLR 206, CA 94.34
Dunn v Morgan (1915) 84 LJ Ch 812, 113 LT 444 .... 98.5
Dunnage v White (1820) 1 Jac & W 583, 37 ER 490 .... 60.2
Dunne v Byrne [1912] AC 407, 81 LJPC 202, [1911–13] All ER Rep 1105, 56 Sol Jo 324, 106 LT 394, 28 TLR 257, PC 102.22
Dunne v Duignan [1908] 1 IR 228 .... 102.9
Dunne v Dunne (1855) 7 De GM & G 207, 3 Eq Rep 760, 1 Jur NS 1056, 3 WR 380, 25 LTOS 60 .... 34.11, 35.22
Dunne's Trusts, Re (1878) 1 LR Ir 516; affd (1880) 5 LR Ir 76, CA 40.10
Dunstan, Re, Dunstan v Dunstan [1918] 2 Ch 304, 87 LJ Ch 597, [1918–19] All ER Rep 694, 63 Sol Jo 10, 119 LT 561 ... 47.26, 48.5, 48.10, 83.8, 83.9

Dunster, Re, Brown v Heywood [1909] 1 Ch 103, 78 LJ Ch 138, 99 LT 921 .... 20.5, 38.13, 47.29, 47.31
Dupree's Deed Trusts, Re, Daley v Lloyds Bank [1945] Ch 16, [1944] 2 All ER 443, 114 LJ Ch 1, 88 Sol Jo 407, 171 LT 384, 61 TLR 50 .... 102.8
Durance's Goods, Re (1872) LR 2 P & D 406, 36 JP 615, 41 LJP & M 60, 20 WR 759, 26 LT 983 .... 18.16
Durand v Durand Manor [1920] NZLR 489 .... 93.25
Durdin's Estate, Re [1957] SASR 199 .... 74.2
Durham v Northen [1895] P 66, 6 R 582, 69 LT 691, 10 TLR 49 .... 15.2
Durham (Earl) v Wharton (1836) 10 Bli NS 526, 3 Cl & Fin 146, sub nom Wharton v Earl of Durham 3 My & K 698, 6 LJ Ch 15, HL 44.12
Durling and Parker v Loveland (1839) 2 Curt 225 .... 4.20
Durnell v Corfield (1844) 1 Rob Eccl 51, 8 Jur 915, 3 LTOS 323, 3 Notes of Cases 225 .... 4.17
Durour v Perraro. See Dufour v Pereira
Durran v Durran (1904) 91 LT 819, CA 99.4, 99.9
Durrant v Friend (1852) 5 De G & Sm 343, 21 LJ Ch 353, 16 Jur 709, 19 LTOS 152 .... 41.1
Dutton, Re, ex p Peake (1878) 4 Ex D 54, 43 JP 6, 48 LJQB 350, 27 WR 398, 40 LT 430 .... 9.35, 102.26
Dutton, Re, Herbert v Harrison (1869) 17 WR 523, 20 LT 386 .... 38.3, 64.23, 64.35
Dutton, Re, Plunkett v Simeon [1893] WN 65 .... 69.2
Dutton v Crowdy (1863) 33 Beav 272, 33 LJ Ch 241, 10 Jur NS 28, 3 New Rep 234, 12 WR 222, 9 LT 630 .... 90.1
Dutton v Dutton [2001] WTLR 553 .... 209.5
Dutton v Hockenhull (1874) 22 WR 701 .... 38.10
Dwyer v Lysaght (1812) 2 Ball & B 156 .... 57.22
Dwyer's Will, Re [1916] VLR 114 .... 93.6
Dyer v Dyer (1816) 1 Mer 414, 19 Ves 612 .... 101.4
Dyke, Re, Dyke v Dyke (1881) 44 LT 568 .... 88.1
Dyson, Re, Challinor v Sykes [1910] 1 Ch 750, 79 LJ Ch 433, 102 LT 425 .... 37.2
Dytrych, Re [1928] VLR 144, [1928] Argur LR 88 .... 11.4

E

E, Re, E v E [1966] 2 All ER 44, [1966] 1 WLR 709, 110 Sol Jo 214 .... 105.16
EHS, Re, TWGS v JMG [2000] 2 All ER 83; affd [2001] Ch 568, [2001] 1 All ER 97, [2000] 3 WLR 1910, [2001] 1 FCR 339, [2000] NLJR 1788, CA 1.6, 9.13, 9.17, 46.1, 46.5, 48.8, 104.9
Eades, Re, Eades v Eades [1920] 2 Ch 353, 89 LJ Ch 604, 123 LT 777 .... 102.23
Eady v Waring (1974) 43 DLR (3d) 667, [1974] 2 OR (2d) 627, Ont CA 5.9
Eager, Re [1952] St R Qd 105 .... 8.7, 30.8
Eager v Furnivall (1881) 17 Ch D 115, 45 JP 603, 50 LJ Ch 537, 29 WR 649, 44 LT 464 .... 47.13
Eagles v Le Breton (1873) LR 15 Eq 148, 42 LJ Ch 362 .... 79.6
Eaglestone, Re [1950] SASR 257 .... 11.4
Eales v Drake (1875) 1 Ch 217, 45 LJ Ch 51, 24 WR 184 .... 100.2
Eales v Earl Cardigan (1838) 9 Sim 384, 8 LJ Ch 11 .... 33.15

Eames v Anstee (1863) 33 Beav 264 .... 91.5
Eardley's Will, Re, Simeon v Freemantle [1920] 1 Ch 397, 89 LJ Ch 234, 122 LT 769 .... 44.1, 44.8
Earl, Re, Tucker v Donne (1923) 68 Sol Jo 386, 131 LT 383 .... 33.30, 95.7
Earle v Barker. See Barker v Young
Earle v Bellingham (1857) 24 Beav 445 .... 33.23, 33.28
Earle v Bellingham (No 2) (1857) 24 Beav 448, 27 LJ Ch 545, 3 Jur NS 1237, 6 WR 45, 30 LTOS 162 .... 32.11
Earle's Settlement Trusts, Re, Reiss v Norrie [1971] 2 All ER 1188, [1971] 1 WLR 1118, 115 Sol Jo 529 .... 68.2, 68.8, 68.10, 68.11, 87.3, 232.9
East, Re [1964] Qd R 42 .... 64.45, 64.48
East v Cook (1750) 2 Ves Sen 30 .... 42.3
East v Twyford (1853) 4 HL Cas 517, 22 LTOS 173 .... 57.6
Eastbourne Mutual Building Society v Hastings Corpn [1965] 1 All ER 779, [1965] 1 WLR 861, 17 P & CR 121, 129 JP 300, 109 Sol Jo 156, [1965] RVR 220 .... 1.8
Eastern Trust Co v Stairs [1955] 1 DLR 280 .... 76.3
Eastes, Re, Pain v Paxon [1948] Ch 257, [1948] 1 All ER 536, [1948] LJR 917, 92 Sol Jo 206, 64 TLR 216 .... 102.17
Eastgood v Styles. See Eastwood v Vinke
Eastman v Baker (1808) 1 Taunt 174 .... 56.1
Eastwood v Avison (1869) LR 4 Exch 141, 38 LJ Ex 74, 19 LT 834 .... 98.4
Eastwood v Lockwood (1867) LR 3 Eq 487, 36 LJ Ch 573, 15 WR 611 .... 93.18
Eastwood v Vinke (1731) 2 P Wms 613; affd sub nom Eastgood v Styles (1732) Kel W 36 .... 44.15
Easum v Appleford (1840) 5 My & Cr 56, 10 LJ Ch 81, 4 Jur 981 .... 38.1
Eaton v A-G (1865) 13 WR 424 .... 64.35
Eaton v Hewitt (1862) 2 Drew & Sm 184, 8 Jur NS 1120, 1 New Rep 10, 11 WR 76, 7 LT 496 .... 93.8, 93.20
Eaton (Norris Estate) v Heyman (1946) 4 DLR 441, [1946] 3 WWR 98 .... 18.5, 18.29
Eaves, Re, Eaves v Eaves [1940] Ch 109, [1939] 4 All ER 260, 109 LJ Ch 97, 83 Sol Jo 942, 162 LT 8, 56 TLR 110, CA 33.20, 80.4, 224.86
Eavestaff v Austin (1854) 19 Beav 591 .... 48.5, 48.6, 48.9, 66.15
Ebbern v Fowler [1909] 1 Ch 578, 78 LJ Ch 497, [1908–10] All ER Rep 673, 53 Sol Jo 356, 100 LT 717, CA 9.25, 72.2, 72.5
Eccard v Brooke (1790) 2 Cox Eq Cas 213 .... 56.5, 68.1, 85.3
Eccles v Cheyne (1856) 2 K & J 676 .... 38.2, 39.4, 47.14, 47.39
Eccles v Mills [1898] AC 360, 67 LJPC 25, 46 WR 398, 78 LT 206, 14 TLR 270 .... 206.14
Eccles Provident Industrial Co-operative Society Ltd v Griffiths [1912] AC 483, 81 LJKB 594, 56 Sol Jo 359, 106 LT 465, 28 TLR 299, HL 7.9, 7.13
Eckersley v Platt (1866) LR 1 P & D 281, 36 LJP & M 7, 15 WR 232, sub nom Ekersley v Platt 15 LT 327 .... 18.29, 19.3
Eddowes, Re (1861) 1 Drew & Sm 395, 7 Jur NS 354, 5 LT 389 .... 101.9
Eddowes v Eddowes (1862) 30 Beav 603 .... 66.23
Eden, Re, Ellis v Crampton [1957] 2 All ER 430, [1957] 1 WLR 788, 101 Sol Jo 481 .... 53.6, 53.7
Eden v Wilson. See Wilson v Eden
Edgar, Re, Cohen v Edgar [1939] 1 All ER 635, 83 Sol Jo 154 .... 35.46

Edge v Pensions Ombudsman [1998] Ch 512, [1998] 2 All ER 547, [1998] 3 WLR 466, [1998] PLR 15; affd [2000] Ch 602, [1999] 4 All ER 546, [2000] 3 WLR 79, [2000] ICR 748, [1999] PLR 215, [1999] 35 LS Gaz R 39, [1999] NLJR 1442, CA 218.4, 223.9
Edge v Salisbury (1749) Amb 70, [1558–1774] All ER Rep 628 .... 57.18, 79.5
Edgeworth v Edgeworth (1869) LR 4 HL 35, 17 WR 714 ..... 34.2, 50.2, 51.1, 91.1, 93.15, 93.19
Edgeworth v Johnston (1878) IR 11 Eq 326 .... 44.5
Edmonds v Edmonds [1965] 1 All ER 379n, [1965] 1 WLR 58, 108 Sol Jo 1047 .... 99.4
Edmonds v Fessey. See Edmunds v Fessey
Edmonds v Millett (1855) 20 Beav 54, 109 RR 341 .... 92.3
Edmondson v Edmondson (1901) 45 Sol Jo 395, 17 TLR 397 .... 1.5
Edmondson's Estate, Re (1868) LR 5 Eq 389, 16 WR 890 .... 51.2, 93.1, 93.42
Edmondson's Will Trusts, Re, Baron Sandford of Banbury v Edmondson [1971] 3 All ER 1121, [1971] 1 WLR 1652, 115 Sol Jo 850; on appeal [1972] 1 All ER 444, [1972] 1 WLR 183, 116 Sol Jo 79, CA 49.4, 66.13, 66.14, 66.19, 66.20, 66.21, 66.23, 225.51
Edmunds v Bisson (1950) 50 SRNSW 28 .... 67.7
Edmunds v Fessey (1861) 29 Beav 233, 30 LJ Ch 279, 7 Jur NS 282, 9 WR 365, sub nom Edmonds v Fessey 3 LT 765 .... 72.2
Edmunds v Low (1857) 3 K & J 318, 26 LJ Ch 432, 3 Jur NS 598, 5 WR 444, 30 LTOS 31 .... 44.15
Edmunds v Waugh (1858) 4 Drew 275, 6 WR 589; on appeal (1863) 2 New Rep 408 .... 93.26
Edward, Re, Turner v Roberts [1981] VR 794 .... 58.10
Edwardes, Re, Midland Bank Exor and Trustee Co Ltd v Paul [1951] WN 263, 95 Sol Jo 382 .... 38.3, 79.2
Edwardes v Jones (No 2) (1866) 35 Beav 474, 14 WR 815 .... 53.2
Edwards, Re [1950] NZLR 516 .... 83.6
Edwards, Re [1952] SASR 67 .... 102.23
Edwards, Re (1959) 20 DLR (2d) 755, [1959] OWN 313 .... 94.48
Edwards, Re [1964] VR 551 .... 64.5
Edwards, Re, Edwards v Edwards [1894] 3 Ch 644, 64 LJ Ch 179, 8 R 618, 43 WR 169 .... 50.11, 98.1
Edwards (deceased), Re, Edwards v Edwards [2007] All ER (D) 46 (May) 5.9
Edwards, Re, Jones v Jones [1906] 1 Ch 570, 75 LJ Ch 321, 54 WR 446, 50 Sol Jo 324, 94 LT 593, CA 51.1, 93.6, 93.43, 98.3
Edwards, Re, Lloyd v Boyes [1910] 1 Ch 541, 79 LJ Ch 281, 54 Sol Jo 325, 102 LT 308, 26 TLR 308 .... 34.8, 35.39
Edwards, Re, Macadam v Wright [1958] Ch 168, [1957] 2 All ER 495, [1957] 3 WLR 131, 101 Sol Jo 515 .... 3.3, 41.5, 42.2, 42.5
Edwards, Re, Newbery v Edwards [1918] 1 Ch 142, 87 LJ Ch 248, [1916–17] All ER Rep 258, 62 Sol Jo 191, 118 LT 17, 34 TLR 135 .... 32.2
Edwards, Re, Rowland v Edwards (1890) 63 LT 481 .... 59.3
Edwards v Alliston (1827) 4 Russ 78, 6 LJOS Ch 30 .... 101.12
Edwards v Carter. See Carter v Silber
Edwards v Champion (1853) 3 De GM & G 202, 23 LJ Ch 123, 1 Eq Rep 419, 1 WR 497, 21 LTOS 293 .... 86.3
Edwards v Edwards (1834) 2 Cr & M 612, 3 LJ Ex 204, 4 Tyr 438 .... 202.5

Edwards v Edwards (1849) 12 Beav 97 .... 54.5, 76.3
Edwards v Edwards (1852) 15 Beav 357, 21 LJ Ch 324, 16 Jur 259, 19 LTOS 483 .... 97.5
Edwards v Edwards [1909] AC 275, 78 LJ Ch 504, 100 LT 84, HL 50.3, 94.14
Edwards v Fincham. See Fincham v Edwards
Edwards v Hall (1853) 11 Hare 1, 1 Eq Rep 145, 17 Jur 593, 1 WR 348; on appeal (1855) 6 De GM & G 74 .... 103.11
Edwards v Saloway (1848) 2 Ph 625, 17 LJ Ch 329, 12 Jur 487, 12 LTOS 101 .... 47.37, 77.2
Edwards v Thompson (1868) 38 LJ Ch 65 .... 38.10
Edwards v Tuck (1853) 3 De GM & G 40, 23 LJ Ch 204, 1 Eq Rep 470, 17 Jur 921, 1 WR 521, 22 LTOS 6 .... 95.9, 95.10
Edwards' Settlement, Re [1897] 2 Ch 412, 66 LJ Ch 658, 76 LT 774 .... 35.28, 83.6
Edwards' Will Trusts, Re, Dalgleish v Leighton [1947] 2 All ER 521, [1948] LJR 60, 91 Sol Jo 572; revsd [1948] Ch 440, [1948] 1 All ER 821, [1948] LJR 1364, 92 Sol Jo 297, CA 15.1, 15.3, 15.4, 57.5, 57.11, 218.4
Edwards' Will Trusts, Re, Edwards v Edwards [1982] Ch 30, [1981] 2 All ER 941, [1981] 3 WLR 15, 125 Sol Jo 258, CA 27.15
Edyvean v Archer, Re Brooke [1903] AC 379, 72 LJPC 85, 89 LT 4, 19 TLR 561, PC 54.5, 76.1
Eeles's Goods, Re (1862) 27 JP 9, 32 LJPM & A 4, 2 Sw & Tr 600, 11 WR 31, 7 LT 338 .... 18.20, 19.4
Egan, Re, Mills v Penton [1899] 1 Ch 688, 68 LJ Ch 307, 80 LT 153 .... 38.3, 60.1
Egerton v Earl Brownlow (1853) 4 HL Cas 1, 8 State Tr NS 193, 23 LJ Ch 348, 18 Jur 71, [1843–60] All ER Rep 970, 21 LTOS 306 ... 8.1, 34.2, 34.7, 34.8, 34.12, 34.17, 35.47, 51.4, 93.3
Egerton v Jones (1830) 3 Sim 409 .... 98.9
Egg v Devey (1847) 10 Beav 444, 16 LJ Ch 509, 11 Jur 1023, 76 RR 170, 10 LTOS 243 .... 45.2
Eichardt, Re, Brebrer v O'Meara (1905) 25 NZLR 374 .... 93.37, 93.38, 101.7
Eighmie, Re, Colbourne v Wilks [1935] Ch 524, 104 LJ Ch 254, 153 LT 295, 51 TLR 404 .... 9.29, 30.43
Eiser's Will Trusts, Re, Fogg v Eastwood [1937] 1 All ER 244 .... 30.12
Ekersley v Platt. See Eckersley v Platt
Elcock v Campbell [1931] NZLR 1060 .... 34.22
Elcock's Goods, Re (1869) 33 JP 535, 20 LT 757 .... 11.21
Elcom, Re, Layborn v Grover Wright [1894] 1 Ch 303, 63 LJ Ch 392, 7 R 87, 42 WR 279, [1891–4] All ER Rep 258, 38 Sol Jo 127, 70 LT 54, 10 TLR 162, CA 1.1, 9.5, 22.3, 30.3
Elders Trustees and Executor Co Ltd v Eastoe [1963] WAR 36 .... 44.8
Elen, Re, Thomas v McKechnie [1893] WN 90, 68 LT 816 .... 39.14
Elford, Re, Elford v Elford [1910] 1 Ch 814, 79 LJ Ch 385, 54 Sol Jo 542, 102 LT 488 .... 38.19, 38.23
Elgar, Re, Rhodes v Pharazyn [1957] NZLR 556; affd [1957] NZLR 1221 .... 102.10
Ellard v Phelan [1914] 1 IR 76 .... 44.15, 52.4
Ellice's Goods, Re (1863) 28 JP 248, 33 LJPM & A 27, 12 WR 353 .... 18.28
Elliot, Re, Kelly v Elliot [1896] 2 Ch 353, 65 LJ Ch 753, 44 WR 632, 40 Sol Jo 600, 75 LT 138, 12 TLR 497 .... 8.1, 50.4

Elliot v Joicey [1935] AC 209, [1935] All ER Rep 578, 104 LJ Ch 111, 79 Sol Jo 144, 51 TLR 261, 1935 SC (HL) 57, sub nom Re Joicey, Joicey v Elliot 152 LT 398, HL 47.17, 73.1, 73.2, 200.35
Elliott, Re, Elliott v Smith. See Elliott v Smith
Elliott, Re, Lloyds Bank Ltd v Burton-on-Trent Hospital Management Committee [1952] Ch 217, [1952] 1 All ER 145, 96 Sol Jo 73, [1952] 1 TLR 298 .... 9.29, 34.17, 34.18, 202.28
Elliott, Re, Public Trustee v Pinder [1918] 2 Ch 150, 87 LJ Ch 449, [1918–19] All ER Rep 1151, 62 Sol Jo 383, 118 LT 675 .... 95.9
Elliott, Re, Raven v Nicholson (1910) 54 Sol Jo 426, 102 LT 528 .... 102.6
Elliott v Davenport (1705) 1 P Wms 83, 2 Vern 521 .... 47.1, 47.22, 68.2
Elliott v Elliott (1841) 11 LJ Ex 3, 9 M & W 23 .... 64.57
Elliott v Elliott (1841) 12 Sim 276, 10 LJ Ch 363 .... 66.16
Elliott v Elliott (1846) 15 Sim 321, 15 LJ Ch 393, 10 Jur 730 .... 39.19, 39.21
Elliott v Elliott (1885) 54 LJ Ch 1142 .... 9.40, 210.35
Elliott v Kemp (1840) 10 LJ Ex 321, 7 M & W 306 .... 29.9, 29.13, 29.19
Elliott v Lord Minto (1821) 6 Madd 16 .... 23.4
Elliott v Smith (1882) 22 Ch D 236, 48 LT 27, sub nom Re Elliott, Elliott v Smith 52 LJ Ch 222, 31 WR 336 .... 97.1
Ellis, Re, Nettleton v Crimmins [1935] Ch 193, 104 LJ Ch 53, [1934] All ER Rep 58, 152 LT 370 .... 33.3, 33.28, 33.36
Ellis, Re, Owen v Bentley (1918) 53 ILT 6 .... 36.13
Ellis, Re, Perpetual Trustee Co Ltd v Ellis (1929) 46 WN 149, 29 SRNSW 470 .... 35.36
Ellis v Bartrum (No 2) (1857) 25 Beav 109 .... 58.4
Ellis v Eden (1857) 23 Beav 543, 26 LJ Ch 533, 3 Jur NS 950, 30 LTOS 60 .... 64.23
Ellis v Eden (No 2) (1858) 25 Beav 482 .... 58.10
Ellis v Ellis (1802) 1 Sch & Lef 1 .... 34.2, 44.8, 93.27
Ellis v Ellis [1905] 1 Ch 613, 74 LJ Ch 296, 53 WR 617, 92 LT 727 .... 25.15, 25.16
Ellis v Houston (1878) 10 Ch D 236, 27 WR 501 .... 57.18, 57.20, 72.2
Ellis v IRC (1949) 31 TC 178, 28 ATC 12, 42 R & IT 151, 93 Sol Jo 133; affd (1949) 31 TC 178, 28 ATC 267, 42 R & IT 372, [1949] TR 273, 93 Sol Jo 678, CA 102.23
Ellis v Maxwell (1841) 3 Beav 587, 10 LJ Ch 266, 52 RR 235 .... 93.1
Ellis v Rowbotham [1900] 1 QB 740, [1900–3] All ER Rep 299, 69 LJQB 379, 48 WR 423, 82 LT 191, 16 TLR 258, CA 206.14, 214.49
Ellis v Selby (1836) 1 My & Cr 286, 5 LJ Ch 214, 43 RR 188 .... 102.23
Ellis Estate, Re, Bond and Kirby (Ellis Estate) v Bond and Ellis (1961) 33 DLR (2d) 594, 37 WWR 440 .... 64.53
Ellison v Airey (1748) 1 Ves Sen 111 .... 66.12
Ellison v Thomas (1862) 1 De GJ & Sm 18, 32 LJ Ch 32, 8 Jur NS 1139, 1 New Rep 37, 11 WR 56, 7 LT 342 .... 81.3
Ellisons' Goods, Re [1907] 2 IR 480, 41 ILT 123 .... 12.11
Elms v Elms (1858) 27 LJP & M 96, 4 Jur NS 765, 1 Sw & Tr 155, 6 WR 864, 31 LTOS 332 .... 18.17, 18.20, 18.27
Elmsley v Young (1835) 2 My & K 780, 4 LJ Ch 200 .... 66.20, 77.1
Else v Else (1872) LR 13 Eq 196, 41 LJ Ch 213, 20 WR 286, 25 LT 927 .... 56.7
Elton, Re, Elton v Elton [1917] 2 Ch 413, 87 LJ Ch 49, 62 Sol Jo 71, 117 LT 533 .... 50.3
Elton v Eason (1812) 19 Ves 73 .... 98.7

Elton v Elton (1747) 3 Atk 504, 1 Wils 159, 1 Ves Sen 4 .... 34.15, 35.11
Elwin v Elwin (1803) 8 Ves 547 .... 93.4
Ely, Re, Tottenham v Ely (1891) 65 LT 452 .... 57.10, 57.19, 57.22, 58.11
Emanuel, Re [1981] VR 113 .... 5.4
Embleton's Will Trusts, Re, Sodeau v Nelson [1965] 1 All ER 771, [1965] 1 WLR 840, 44 ATC 69, [1965] TR 83, 109 Sol Jo 437 .... 214.66
Embury, Re, Bowyer v Page (No 2) [1914] WN 220, 58 Sol Jo 612, 111 LT 275 .... 72.2
Embury, Re, Page v Bowyer (1913) 58 Sol Jo 49, 109 LT 511 .... 68.11, 76.3, 216.17
Emerson, Re, Morrill v Nutty [1929] 1 Ch 128, 98 LJ Ch 145, [1928] All ER Rep 386, 140 LT 217 .... 64.35
Emerson's Goods, Re (1882) 9 LR Ir 443 .... 11.13, 11.15, 11.19
Emery's Estate, Re, Jones v Emery (1876) 3 Ch D 300, sub nom Emery's Estate, Re, Jones v Ratcliffe 24 WR 917, 34 LT 846 .... 69.1, 73.1
Emes v Emes (1865) 11 Gr 325 .... 4.17
Emes v Hancock (1743) 2 Atk 507 .... 8.2
Emmet's Estate, Re, Emmet v Emmet (1880) 13 Ch D 484, 49 LJ Ch 295, 28 WR 401, [1874–8] All ER Rep 576, 42 LT 4, CA 66.4, 66.7, 66.12, 66.13, 66.17, 66.21
Emuss v Smith (1848) 2 De G & Sm 722 .... 7.27, 41.20, 58.12, 59.3, 207.3
Endacott, Re, Corpe v Endacott [1960] Ch 232, [1959] 3 All ER 562, [1959] 3 WLR 799, 58 LGR 25, 103 Sol Jo 918, CA 102.10
Enever's Trusts, Re, Power v Power [1912] 1 IR 511 .... 40.21
Engelhardt v Engelhardt (1878) 26 WR 853 .... 33.12
Engels, Re, National Provincial Bank Ltd v Mayer [1943] 1 All ER 506, 87 Sol Jo 148, 168 LT 311 .... 94.5
England, Re, England v Bayles [1906] VLR 94 .... 64.7
England, Re, England v Garnett (1912) 134 LT Jo 29 .... 44.4
English's Goods, Re (1864) 29 JP 72, 34 LJPM & A 5, 3 Sw & Tr 586, 13 WR 503, sub nom Newcombe v English, Re English's Goods 11 LT 612 .... 10.1
Eno v Eno (1847) 6 Hare 171, 16 LJ Ch 358, 11 Jur 746 .... 98.9
Enohin v Wylie. See Wylie v Wylie
Epple v Stone (1906) 3 CLR 412 .... 62.1
Epstein, Re (1963) 39 DLR (2d) 228, [1963] 2 OR 276 .... 204.66
Equitable Trust Co v Doull (1958) 25 WWR 465 .... 14.6
Equity Trustees, Executors and Agency Co v Green (1895) 21 VLR 618 .... 87.1
Errington, Re, Errington-Turbutt v Errington (1897) 45 WR 573, 41 Sol Jo 468, 76 LT 616 .... 95.3, 95.8
Errington, Re, Gibbs v Lassam [1927] 1 Ch 421, 96 LJ Ch 345, 71 Sol Jo 309, 136 LT 764 .... 87.2
Erskine's Settlement Trusts, Re, Hollis v Pigott [1971] 1 All ER 572, [1971] 1 WLR 162, 115 Sol Jo 113 .... 95.13, 218.47
Escott's Goods, Re (1842) 1 Notes of Cases 571 .... 14.14
Esmonde, Re, Synnott v McGonigal [1946] IR 551 .... 33.45
Espie, Re, Maffey v Espie [1956] VLR 605 .... 37.2
Espinasse v Luffingham (1846) 3 Jo & Lat 186 .... 83.6
Espinosa v Bourke [1999] 3 FCR 76, [1999] 1 FLR 747, [1999] Fam Law 210, CA 105.16, 105.32
Essington v Vashon (1817) 3 Mer 434 .... 64.23

Esso Petroleum Co Ltd v Harper's Garage (Stourport) Ltd [1968] AC 269, [1967] 1 All ER 699, [1967] 2 WLR 871, 111 Sol Jo 174, 201 Estates Gazette 1043, HL 34.12
Esterhuizen v Allied Dunbar Assurance plc [1998] 2 FLR 668, [1998] Fam Law 527 .... 1.14
Estlin, Re, Prichard v Thomas (1903) 72 LJ Ch 687, 47 Sol Jo 691, 89 LT 88 .... 102.5, 102.6, 102.7
Etches v Etches (1856) 3 Drew 441, 4 WR 307 .... 68.10, 93.21
Eteson's Will, Re (1927) 45 WN 6, 27 SRNSW 119 .... 22.2
Eumorfopoulos, Re, Ralli v Eumorfopoulos [1944] Ch 133, [1943] 2 All ER 719, 113 LJ Ch 30, 87 Sol Jo 423, 170 LT 21 .... 64.28, 204.30
Eustace, Re, Lee v McMillan [1912] 1 Ch 561, 81 LJ Ch 529, 56 Sol Jo 468, 106 LT 789 .... 31.12
Euston (Earl) v Lord Seymour (1802) 2 Curt 339 .... 16.3
Evan's Charities, Re (1858) 10 I Ch R 271 .... 33.33
Evan's Will Trusts, Re, Pickering v Evans [1921] 2 Ch 309, 91 LJ Ch 29, 65 Sol Jo 753, 125 LT 822 .... 38.23
Evans, Re [1950] VLR 60 .... 57.22, 58.2, 58.4
Evans, Re [1957] SR Qd 345 .... 102.8
Evans, Re, Evans v Powell [1909] 1 Ch 784, 78 LJ Ch 441, 100 LT 779 .... 58.13, 59.3
Evans, Re, Evans v Westcombe [1999] 2 All ER 777, 143 Sol Jo LB 72 .... 9.2
Evans, Re, Hewitt v Edwards [1940] Ch 629, 109 LJ Ch 216, 84 Sol Jo 319, 162 LT 420, 56 TLR 630 .... 34.11, 35.29, 35.30, 217.40
Evans, Re, Public Trustee v Evans [1920] 2 Ch 304, 89 LJ Ch 525, 123 LT 735, 36 TLR 674, CA 50.5, 50.9
Evans, Re, Thomas v Thomas (1908) 77 LJ Ch 583, 99 LT 271 .... 33.15
Evans v Angell (1858) 26 Beav 202, 5 Jur NS 134, 32 LTOS 382 .... 57.20, 58.6, 63.3, 64.2
Evans v Crosbie (1847) 15 Sim 600, 16 LJ Ch 494, 11 Jur 510, 9 LTOS 291 .... 38.12
Evans v Davies (1849) 7 Hare 498, 18 LJ Ch 180 .... 72.2
Evans v Evans (1858) 25 Beav 81, 53 ER 566 .... 90.1
Evans v Evans (1865) 33 LJ Ch 662, 10 LT 59, CA 83.2
Evans v Evans [1892] 2 Ch 173, 61 LJ Ch 456, 40 WR 465, 36 Sol Jo 425, 67 LT 152, CA 78.1
Evans v Harris (1842) 5 Beav 45 .... 65.3
Evans v Hellier. See Shaw v Rhodes
Evans v John (1841) 4 Beav 35, 55 RR 7 .... 27.5
Evans v Jones (1846) 2 Coll 516 .... 76.3
Evans v Jones (1877) 41 JP 552, 46 LJQB 280, 36 LT 218 .... 38.4
Evans v Knight and Moore (1822) 1 Add 229 .... 4.13, 4.20
Evans v Massey (1819) 8 Price 22 .... 9.25
Evans v Pilkington (1839) 10 Sim 412 .... 93.30
Evans v Rosser (1864) 2 Hem & M 190, 10 Jur NS 385, 3 New Rep 685, 12 WR 570, sub nom Evans v Rossall 10 LT 159 .... 34.3, 35.2, 35.8
Evans v Scott (1847) 1 HL Cas 43, 11 Jur 291, 9 LTOS 509 .... 93.44
Evans v Stratford (1864) 2 Hem & M 142, 10 Jur NS 861, 10 LT 713 .... 45.1, 92.3
Evans v Tripp (1821) 6 Madd 91 .... 58.2, 58.4
Evans v Turner (1904) 23 NZLR 825 .... 87.1
Evans v Walker (1876) 3 Ch D 211, 25 WR 7 .... 86.5, 94.9

Evans and Bettell's Contract, Re [1910] 2 Ch 438, 79 LJ Ch 669, [1908–10] All ER Rep 202, 54 Sol Jo 680, 103 LT 181 .... 33.24
Evans d Brooke v Astley (1764) 3 Burr 1570, 1 Wm Bl 499, 521 .... 98.3
Evans' Contract, Re [1920] 2 Ch 469, 89 LJ Ch 626, 124 LT 188 .... 35.43, 235.27
Evans' Settlement, Re, Watkins v Whitworth-Jones [1967] 3 All ER 343, [1967] 1 WLR 1294, 111 Sol Jo 811 .... 218.92
Evanturel v Evanturel (1874) LR 6 PC 1, 43 LJPC 58, 23 WR 32, 31 LT 105 .... 34.11, 34.12, 35.38
Eve, Re, Belton v Thompson (1905) 93 LT 235 .... 47.26, 93.26, 93.27
Eve, Re, Edwards v Burns [1909] 1 Ch 796, 78 LJ Ch 388, [1908–10] All ER Rep 131, 100 LT 874 .... 57.15, 72.2
Eve, Re, Hall v Eve [1917] 1 Ch 562, 86 LJ Ch 396, 116 LT 682, 33 TLR 251 .... 235.22
Eve, Re, National Provincial Bank Ltd v Eve [1956] Ch 479, [1956] 2 All ER 321, [1956] 3 WLR 69, 100 Sol Jo 381 .... 30.3, 209.12
Everall v Browne (1853) 22 LJ Ch 376, 1 Sm & G 368, 1 WR 210 .... 38.3, 38.10
Evered, Re, Molineux v Evered [1910] 2 Ch 147, 79 LJ Ch 465, 54 Sol Jo 540, 102 LT 694, CA 3.15, 39.2, 40.7, 40.10, 40.11, 40.15
Everest, Re [1975] Fam 44, [1975] 1 All ER 672, [1975] 2 WLR 333, 119 Sol Jo 86 .... 18.23
Everett, Re, Prince v Hunt [1944] Ch 176, [1944] 2 All ER 19, 113 LJ Ch 81, 170 LT 178, 60 TLR 223 .... 64.54
Everett v Everett (1877) 7 Ch D 428, 47 LJ Ch 367, 26 WR 333, 38 LT 580, CA 59.1, 59.2
Evers v Challis. See Doe d Evers v Challis
Eversley, Re, Mildmay v Mildmay [1900] 1 Ch 96, 69 LJ Ch 14, 48 WR 249, 44 Sol Jo 11, 81 LT 600, 16 TLR 6 .... 35.41
Ewan v Morgan (1858) 22 JP 607, 6 WR 556, 32 LTOS 19, sub nom Dundee Magistrates v Morris 3 Macq 134, HL 53.2, 102.22
Ewart v Cochrane (1861) 25 JP 612, 7 Jur NS 925, 10 WR 3, 5 LT 1, 4 Macq 117, HL 61.1
Ewen v Bannerman (1830) 2 Dow & Cl 74, HL 102.22
Ewen v Franklin (1855) Dea & Sw 7, 1 Jur NS 1220, 4 WR 164, 26 LTOS 127 .... 11.3, 11.4, 12.11
Ewens v Addison (1858) 4 Jur NS 1034, 7 WR 23, 32 LTOS 103 .... 35.13
Ewer v Corbet (1723) 2 P Wms 148 .... 25.18
Ewing v Orr Ewing (1885) 10 App Cas 453, 53 LT 826, 1 TLR 645, HL 23.16
Exmouth (Viscount), Re, Viscount Exmouth v Praed (1883) 23 Ch D 158, 52 LJ Ch 420, 31 WR 545, 48 LT 422 .... 34.10, 51.3, 94.2, 94.15
Eynon's Goods, Re (1873) LR 3 P & D 92, 37 JP 616, 42 LJP & M 52, 21 WR 856, 29 LT 45 .... 12.12
Eyre, Re, Eyre v Eyre (1883) 49 LT 259 .... 40.5, 40.10
Eyre, Re, Johnson v Williams [1917] 1 Ch 351, 86 LJ Ch 257, 61 Sol Jo 336, 116 LT 469 .... 32.3, 32.15, 32.19, 44.8
Eyre v Eyre [1903] P 131, 72 LJP 45, 51 WR 701, 88 LT 567, 19 TLR 380 .... 15.1
Eyre v Marsden (1838) 2 Keen 564, 7 LJ Ch 220, 2 Jur 583, [1835–42] All ER Rep 675; affd (1839) 4 My & Cr 231, 3 Jur 450 .... 90.1, 95.9
Eyre v Monro (1857) 3 K & J 305, 26 LJ Ch 757, 3 Jur NS 584, 5 WR 870, 30 LTOS 61 .... 3.2
Eyre's Goods, Re [1905] 2 IR 540 .... 18.16

F

Fabrigas v Mostyn. See Mostyn v Fabrigas
Fabro's Estate, Re [1965] SASR 69 .... 58.10
Fairer v Park (1876) 3 Ch D 309, 45 LJ Ch 760, 35 LT 27 .... 44.15
Fairfield v Bushell (1863) 32 Beav 158 .... 76.3
Fairfield v Morgan (1805) 2 Bos & PNR 38, HL 56.1
Falconer's Trusts, Re, Property and Estates Co Ltd v Frost [1908] 1 Ch 410, 77 LJ Ch 303 .... 40.3
Falkiner, Re, Mead v Smith [1924] 1 Ch 88, 93 LJ Ch 76, [1923] All ER Rep 681, 68 Sol Jo 101, 130 LT 405 .... 15.6, 36.1, 36.6, 36.13, 82.5
Falkland (Lord Viscount) v Bertie. See Bertie v Faulkland
Falkland (Viscountess) v Lytton. See Strode (Sir Litton) v Lady Russel and Lady Falkland Falkner v Butler (1765) Amb 514 .... 71.5
Fane, Re, Fane v Fane (1886) 2 TLR 510 .... 57.11
Fane, Re, Fane v Fane [1913] 1 Ch 404, 82 LJ Ch 225, 57 Sol Jo 321, 108 LT 288, 29 TLR 306, CA 94.10
Fane v Duke of Devonshire (1718) 6 Bro Parl Cas 137, HL 4.20
Fanshawe's Trusts, Re (1904) 48 Sol Jo 525 .... 55.6
Far West Children's Health Scheme v Perpetual Trustee Co Ltd. See Resch's Will Trusts, Re, Far West Children's Health Scheme v Perpetual Trustee Co Ltd
Faraker, Re, Faraker v Durell [1912] 2 Ch 488, 81 LJ Ch 635, [1911–13] All ER Rep 488, 56 Sol Jo 668, 107 LT 36, CA 103.3, 103.4, 103.9
Faris, Re, Goddard v Overend (No 2) [1911] 1 IR 469 .... 18.5, 18.8, 19.1, 19.5
Farmer, Re, Nightingale v Whybrow [1939] Ch 573, [1939] 1 All ER 319, 108 LJ Ch 197, 2 Sol Jo 1050, 160 LT 59 .... 33.45
Farmer v Francis (1824) 2 Bing 151 .... 93.17
Farmer v Francis (1826) 2 Sim & St 505, 4 LJOS Ch 154 .... 93.16, 93.17, 93.24, 93.27
Farmer v Martin (1828) 2 Sim 502 .... 40.20
Farncombe's Trusts, Re (1878) 9 Ch D 652, 47 LJ Ch 328 .... 40.21, 47.29
Farquhar v Hadden (1871) 7 Ch App 1, 41 LJ Ch 260, 20 WR 46, 25 LT 717 .... 82.1
Farr v Hennis (1881) 44 LT 202, CA 33.18, 82.5
Farrant v Nichols (1846) 9 Beav 327, 15 LJ Ch 259 .... 51.10, 76.3
Farrar v Lord Winterton (1842) 5 Beav 1, 6 Jur 204 .... 7.27, 41.5, 64.32, 206.24
Farrell, Re [1953] NZLR 147 .... 97.5
Farrelly, Re, Howard v Shelley [1941] IR 261 .... 59.3
Farrer v Barker (1852) 9 Hare 737 .... 51.10
Farrer v St Catharine's College, Cambridge (1873) LR 16 Eq 19, 42 LJ Ch 809, 21 WR 643, 28 LT 800, [1861–73] All ER Rep Ext 1108 .... 18.14, 18.15, 31.1, 52.11, 58.10, 102.8
Farrer's Estate, Re (1858) 8 ICLR 370 .... 20.4
Farrow, Re [1987] 1 FLR 205, [1987] Fam Law 14 .... 105.11
Fast v Van Vliet (1965) 51 WWR 65 .... 93.6
Faucher v Tucker (1993) 109 DLR (4th) 699, Man CA 4.16
Faulding's Trust, Re (1858) 26 Beav 263, 28 LJ Ch 217, 4 Jur NS 1289, 7 WR 74, 32 LTOS 154 .... 68.4, 68.10
Faulkner v IRC [2001] STC (SCD) 112 .... 208.34

Faux, Re, Taylor v Faux [1915] WN 135, 84 LJ Ch 873, 59 Sol Jo 457, 113 LT 81, 31 TLR 289 .... 32.28, 66.13
Faversham Corpn v Ryder (1854) 18 JP 455, 5 De GM & G 350, 23 LJ Ch 905, 2 Eq Rep 749, 18 Jur 587, 2 WR 573, 23 LTOS 282 .... 103.11
Fawcett, Re, Public Trustee v Dugdale [1940] Ch 402, 109 LJ Ch 124, 84 Sol Jo 186, 162 LT 250, 56 TLR 468 .... 38.17, 38.18, 38.21, 38.27
Fawcett v Jones, Codrington and Pulteney (1810) 3 Phillim 434; on appeal (1820) 3 Phillim 490 .... 18.14
Fawkes v Gray (1811) 18 Ves 131 .... 34.23
Fay v Fay (1880) 5 LR Ir 274 .... 51.2, 98.2
Feake v Brandsby (1674) 2 Rep Ch 101 .... 30.24
Feakes v Standley (1857) 24 Beav 485, 30 LTOS 182 .... 98.7
Fearon v Desbrisay (1851) 14 Beav 635, 21 LJ Ch 505 .... 40.15
Feather, Re, Harrison v Tapsell [1945] Ch 343, [1945] 1 All ER 552, 115 LJ Ch 6, 89 Sol Jo 235, 172 LT 308 .... 30.24, 30.28, 55.4
Featherstone v Staples [1986] 2 All ER 461, [1986] 1 WLR 861, 52 P & CR 287, [1986] 1 EGLR 6, 278 Estates Gazette 867, 130 Sol Jo 482, [1986] LS Gaz R 1226, CA 234.15
Featherstone's Trusts, Re (1882) 22 Ch D 111, 52 LJ Ch 75, 31 WR 89, 47 LT 538 .... 47.31, 74.2, 93.1
Feis, Re, Guillaume v Ritz-Remorf [1964] Ch 106, [1963] 3 All ER 303, [1963] 3 WLR 451, 107 Sol Jo 555 .... 19.4
Fell v Biddolph (1875) LR 10 CP 701, 44 LJPC 402, 23 WR 913, 32 LT 864 .... 9.8, 9.9, 47.29, 66.5
Fell v Fell (1922) 40 WN 4, 31 CLR 268, 23 SRNSW 285, 29 Argus LR 31 .... 51.1, 51.2, 51.3, 53.4
Feltham's Will Trusts, Re (1855) 1 K & J 528 .... 57.15, 57.18, 58.10
Fenn v Death (1856) 23 Beav 73, 2 Jur NS 700, 4 WR 828 .... 74.1
Fenston's Settlement, Re, Max-Muller v Simonsen [1971] 3 All ER 1092, [1971] 1 WLR 1640, 115 Sol Jo 741 .... 24.16, 57.7
Fentem, Re, Cockerton v Fentem [1950] 2 All ER 1073, 94 Sol Jo 779 .... 35.2, 65.2
Fenton v Farington (1856) 2 Jur NS 1120 .... 91.6
Fenton (No 2), Re, ex p Fenton Textile Association Ltd [1932] 1 Ch 178, [1931] B & CR 59, [1930] All ER Rep 27, 146 LT 229, sub nom Re Fenton (No 2), ex p Trustee under Deed of Arrangement v Fenton Textile Association Ltd 101 LJ Ch 1 .... 30.13
Fenton's Goods, Re (1825) 3 Add 35 .... 239.2
Fenwick, Re [1972] VR 646 .... 5.1
Fenwick, Re, Burns v Fenwick [1957] NZLR 709 .... 33.9, 33.12, 53.2
Fenwick v Clarke (1862) 4 De GF & J 240, 31 LJ Ch 728, 10 WR 636, 6 LT 593 .... 29.11, 31.9
Fenwick v Schmalz (1868) LR 3 CP 313, 37 LJCP 78, 3 Mar LC 64, 16 WR 481, 18 LT 27 .... 38.10
Fenwick's Goods, Re (1867) LR 1 P & D 319, 31 JP 359, 36 LJP & M 54, 16 LT 124 .... 17.5, 18.14
Fenwick's Will Trusts, Re, Fenwick v Stewart [1936] Ch 720, [1936] 2 All ER 1096, 105 LJ Ch 351, 80 Sol Jo 553, 155 LT 199 .... 38.26, 38.28
Ferguson, Re [1942] 2 DLR 332, [1942] OWN 115 .... 35.8
Ferguson, Re [1957] VLR 635 .... 83.9
Ferguson, Re, Curry v Bell (1915) 49 ILT 110 .... 32.3

Ferguson v Borrett (1859) 1 F & F 613 .... 4.20
Ferguson v Ferguson (1872) IR 6 Eq 199 .... 59.3
Ferguson v Ferguson (1878) 2 SCR 497 .... 49.4
Ferguson v IRC [1970] AC 442, [1969] 1 All ER 1025, [1969] 2 WLR 1116, 46 TC 1, 48 ATC 50, [1969] TR 63, 113 Sol Jo 286, 1969 SC (HL) 103, 1969 SLT 201, HL 33.47
Ferguson v Ogilby (1842) 2 Dr & War 548 .... 64.53
Ferguson-Davie v Ferguson-Davie (1890) 15 PD 109, 59 LJP 70, 62 LT 703 .... 5.7, 10.1
Ferguson-Smith Estate, Re, Watch Tower Bible and Tract Society Inc v Innes-Kerr (1954) 13 WWRNS 387; on appeal (1955) 15 WWR 237, Sask CA 18.12
Fergusson, Re (1914) 34 NZLR 70 .... 78.4
Fergusson's Will, Re [1902] 1 Ch 483, 71 LJ Ch 360, 50 WR 312, 46 Sol Jo 247 .... 77.1
Fernie's Goods, Re (1849) 13 Jur 216, 12 LTOS 559, 6 Notes of Cases 657 .... 25.5
Ferrand v Wilson (1845) 4 Hare 344, 15 LJ Ch 41, 9 Jur 860 .... 94.7
Ferreira, Re [1927] VLR 90, 48 ALT 145, [1927] Argus LR 87 .... 13.1
Ferrier v Jay (1870) LR 10 Eq 550, 39 LJ Ch 686, 18 WR 1130, 23 LT 302 .... 39.22, 39.24
Fessi v Whitmore [1999] 1 FLR 767, [1999] Fam Law 221 .... 202.4
Festing v Allen (1843) 13 LJ Ex 74, 12 M & W 279, 2 LTOS 150 .... 93.17
Festing v Allen (1844) 5 Hare 573 .... 32.10
Festing v Taylor (1862) 27 JP 281, 3 B & S 217, 235, 32 LJQB 41, 9 Jur NS 44, 1 New Rep 32, 11 WR 70, 7 LT 429, Ex Ch 33.47
Fetcher's Goods, Re (1883) 11 LR Ir 359 .... 2.2
Fetherstonaugh v IRC. See Finch v IRC Fetherston-Haugh-Whitney's Estate, Re [1924] 1 IR 153, Ir CA 38.12, 39.12, 50.11, 64.51
Ffennell's Settlement, Re, Re Ffennell's Estate, Wright v Holton [1918] 1 Ch 91, 87 LJ Ch 54, 62 Sol Jo 103, 118 LT 171, 34 TLR 86 .... 37.4
Ffinch v Combe [1894] P 191, 63 LJP 113, 6 R 545, 70 LT 695, 10 TLR 358 .... 14.2, 14.13, 18.22
Fickus, Re, Farina v Fickus [1900] 1 Ch 331, 69 LJ Ch 161, 48 WR 250, 44 Sol Jo 157, 81 LT 749 .... 3.3
Fidelity Trust Co of Ontario v Purdom and Northern Life Association Co of Canada [1930] SCR 119, 1 DLR 1003 .... 42.12
Field, Re, Sanderson v Young [1925] Ch 636, 94 LJ Ch 322, 69 Sol Jo 661, 133 LT 463 .... 208.27
Field v Mostin (1778) 3 Anst 831n, 2 Dick 543 .... 44.15
Field v Peckett (No 2) (1861) 29 Beav 573, 30 LJ Ch 813, 7 Jur NS 983, 9 WR 526, 4 LT 459 .... 64.27, 64.47
Field v Seward (1877) 5 Ch D 538 .... 100.5
Field's Will Trusts, Re, Parry-Jones v Hillman [1950] Ch 520, [1950] 2 All ER 188, 66 (pt 1) TLR 1221 .... 35.22
Fielden v Ashworth (1875) LR 20 Eq 410, 33 LT 197 .... 77.5, 79.6
Fielden v Cunliffe. See Cunliffe v Fielden
Fielding v Preston (1857) 1 De G & J 438, 5 WR 851, 29 LTOS 337 .... 33.12
Fielding v Walshaw, Re Walshaw's Goods (1879) 43 JP 463, 48 LJP 27, 27 WR 492, 40 LT 103 .... 10.5
Fielding and Lord v Rochdale Equitable Pioneers Society (1892) 92 LT Jo 431 .... 7.9, 7.10

Figgis, Re, Roberts v MacLaren [1969] 1 Ch 123, [1968] 1 All ER 999, [1968] 2 WLR 1173, 112 Sol Jo 156 .... 34.22, 210.9, 210.70
Fillingham v Bromley (1823) Turn & R 530 .... 35.22
Filmer v Gott (1774) 4 Bro Parl Cas 230 .... 4.20
Filoon Estate, Re 71 D & C 506 (1950) 202.30
Finch v Finch (1867) LR 1 P & D 371, 31 JP 647, 36 LJP & M 78, 15 WR 797, 16 LT 268 .... 18.29
Finch v Finch (1876) 45 LJ Ch 816, 35 LT 235, [1874–80] All ER Rep Ext 1861 .... 64.2
Finch v Hollingsworth (1855) 21 Beav 112, 25 LJ Ch 55, 3 Eq Rep 993, 1 Jur NS 718, 3 WR 589, 25 LTOS 252 .... 79.4
Finch v IRC [1985] Ch 1, [1984] 3 WLR 212, 128 Sol Jo 302, sub nom Fetherstonaugh v IRC [1984] STC 261, CA 205.6, 205.22
Finch v Lane (1870) LR 10 Eq 501 .... 93.16
Finch v Poplar Borough Council (1967) 66 LGR 324, [1968] RA 208, 14 RRC 107, 204 Estates Gazette 1245 .... 102.2
Finch and Chew's Contract, Re [1903] 2 Ch 486, 72 LJ Ch 690, 89 LT 162 .... 40.5, 40.21, 94.15, 94.45
Fincham v Edwards (1842) 3 Curt 63; affd sub nom Edwards v Fincham (1842) 4 Moo PCC 198, 7 Jur 25, PC 5.2, 18.12
Findlater v Lowe [1904] 1 IR 519, 38 ILT 127 .... 57.17, 58.12
Fingal (Earl) v Blake (1828) 2 Mol 50, 80 .... 34.12, 35.47
Finger's Will Trusts, Re, Turner v Ministry of Health [1972] Ch 286, [1971] 3 All ER 1050, [1971] 3 WLR 775, 115 Sol Jo 790 .... 58.11, 103.3, 103.4, 103.5
Fingland Estates, Re [1920] 1 WWR 473 .... 52.7
Finkle, Re (1977) 82 DLR (3d) 445 .... 102.5
Finlason v Tatlock (1870) LR 9 Eq 258, 39 LJ Ch 422, 18 WR 332, 22 LT 3 .... 68.13, 78.5
Finlay, Re, Dinsmore v Finlay [1933] NI 89 .... 34.22
Finlay's Trustees v Finlay (1886) 13 R 1052, 23 SLR 774 .... 93.25
Finn's Estate, Re (1935) 105 LJP 36, [1935] All ER Rep 419, 80 Sol Jo 56, 154 LT 242, 52 TLR 153 .... 11.13
Finnemore, Re [1992] 1 All ER 800, [1991] 1 WLR 793 ... 9.6, 19.1, 19.2, 19.3, 19.4, 19.6
Finney v Grice (1878) 10 Ch D 13, 48 LJ Ch 247, 27 WR 147 .... 64.27
Firn, Re, Firn v Firn [1962] NZLR 668 .... 64.7
Firstpost Homes Ltd v Johnson [1995] 4 All ER 355, [1995] 1 WLR 1567, [1995] NPC 135, [1996] 1 EGLR 175, [1995] 28 LS Gaz R 30, [1996] 13 EG 125, 139 Sol Jo LB 187, CA; on appeal [1996] 1 WLR 67, HL 12.12
Firth, Re, Loveridge v Firth [1914] 2 Ch 386, 83 LJ Ch 901, 111 LT 332 .... 96.1
Firth, Re, Sykes v Ball [1938] Ch 517, [1938] 2 All ER 217, 107 LJ Ch 251, 82 Sol Jo 332, 158 LT 489, 54 TLR 633 .... 216.37
Firth v Fielden (1874) 22 WR 622 .... 80.1
Fischer v Popham (1875) LR 3 P & D 246, 39 JP 728, 44 LJP & M 47, 23 WR 683, 33 LT 231 .... 11.26
Fish, Re, Ingham v Rayner [1894] 2 Ch 83, 63 LJ Ch 437, 7 R 434, 42 WR 520, 38 Sol Jo 307, 70 LT 825, CA 53.3, 57.20, 57.22, 72.2
Fisher, Re, Canada Permanent Trust Co v Fisher (1976) 74 DLR (3d) 680 .... 64.10

Fisher, Re, Harris v Fisher [1943] Ch 377, [1943] 2 All ER 615, 113 LJ Ch 17, 87 Sol Jo 372, 169 LT 289, 59 TLR 446 ... 38.17, 38.19, 38.28, 214.38, 216.36
Fisher, Re, Robinson v Eardley [1915] 1 Ch 302, 84 LJ Ch 342, 59 Sol Jo 318, 112 LT 548 ... 68.1, 86.2, 97.1
Fisher v Anderson (1879) 4 SCR 406 ... 86.2
Fisher v Hepburn (1851) 14 Beav 626 ... 38.10
Fisher v Wentworth (1925) 36 CLR 310, 32 Argus LR 129 ... 82.4
Fisher's Goods, Re (1869) 33 JP 503, 20 LT 684 ... 64.35
Fisk v A-G (1867) LR 4 Eq 521, 32 JP 52, 15 WR 1200, 17 LT 27 ... 9.29, 102.22
Fison's Will Trusts, Re, Fison v Fison [1950] Ch 394, [1950] 1 All ER 501, 94 Sol Jo 238, 66 (pt 1) TLR 475 ... 60.1, 92.2, 92.3, 209.6, 209.12
Fiszhaut Estate, Re (1966) 56 DLR (2d) 381, 55 WWR 303 ... 11.21
Fitch v Weber (1848) 6 Hare 145, 17 LJ Ch 361, 12 Jur 645, 77 RR 56, 11 LTOS 83 ... 51.3
Fitch's Will Trusts, Re, Public Trustee v Nives (1928) 139 LT 556, CA; affd sub nom Shaw v Public Trustee (1929) 141 LT 465, HL ... 30.1, 64.1
Fitzgerald, Re (1889) 58 LJ Ch 662, 37 WR 552, 61 LT 221 ... 77.2
Fitzgerald, Re, Brereton v Day [1902] 1 IR 162 ... 35.28
Fitzgerald v National Bank Ltd [1929] 1 KB 394, 98 LJKB 382, [1928] All ER Rep 596, 140 LT 406 ... 44.15
Fitzgerald v Ryan [1899] 2 IR 637 ... 34.2, 34.22, 57.15
Fitzgerald v Smith (1889) 15 VLR 467 ... 64.51
Fitzhenry v Bonner (1853) 2 Drew 36, 2 Eq Rep 454, 2 WR 30, 22 LTOS 152 ... 101.7
Fitzpatrick, Re, Bennett v Bennett [1952] Ch 86, [1951] 2 All ER 949, 95 Sol Jo 744, [1951] 2 TLR 995 ... 30.34
Fitzpatrick, Re, Deane v De Valera (1934) 78 Sol Jo 735 ... 64.17
Fitzpatrick v Sterling Housing Association Ltd [1998] Ch 304, [1997] 4 All ER 991, [1998] 2 WLR 225, [1998] 1 FCR 417, [1998] 1 FLR 43, 30 HLR 576, [1997] NLJR 1275, CA; revsd [2001] 1 AC 27, [1999] 4 All ER 705, [1999] 3 WLR 1113, [2000] 1 FCR 21, [2000] 1 FLR 271, [2000] Fam Law 14, 32 HLR 178, [1999] 43 LS Gaz R 34, [1999] EGCS 125, 79 P & CR D4, [2000] 3 LRC 294, HL ... 7.4, 105.15
Fitzpatrick's Goods, Re (1892) 29 LR Ir 328 ... 25.12
Fitz Ray Estate, Re (1966) 57 WWR 77 ... 17.2
Fitz Roy v Duke of Richmond (1859) 27 Beav 186, 28 LJ Ch 750, 5 Jur NS 971, 33 LTOS 267 ... 47.29, 66.6
Fitzroy's Goods, Re (1858) 1 Sw & Tr 133, 6 WR 863, 31 LTOS 171 ... 17.5
Fitzsimmons, Re [1939] 2 DLR 50, 8 FLJ (Can) 228, 13 MPR 429 ... 18.10
Fitzwilliam v IRC [1993] 3 All ER 184, [1993] 1 WLR 1189, [1993] STC 502, 67 TC 614, [1993] 45 LS Gaz R 46, 137 Sol Jo LB 184, HL ... 241.13
Flannagan, Re, Bealty v A-G [1962] NZLR 480 ... 62.1
Flavel's Will Trusts, Re, Coleman v Flavel [1969] 2 All ER 232, [1969] 1 WLR 444, 113 Sol Jo 189 ... 8.7, 53.2, 94.15, 102.24
Flavell, Re, Murray v Flavell (1883) 25 Ch D 89, [1881–5] All ER Rep 267, 53 LJ Ch 185, 32 WR 102, 49 LT 690, CA ... 7.12, 205.64
Fleck, Re (1923) 55 OLR 441 ... 57.19
Fleetwood, Re, Sidgreaves v Brewer (1880) 15 Ch D 594, 49 LJ Ch 514, 29 WR 45 ... 9.4, 9.5, 9.9, 18.10, 19.3, 36.12, 38.10

Fleming, Re, McNamara v Fleming [1963] VR 17 .... 57.22
Fleming v Brook (1804) 1 Sch & Lef 318 .... 63.1, 64.51
Fleming v Burrows (1826) 1 Russ 276, 4 LJOS Ch 115 .... 38.3
Fleming v Fleming (1862) 1 H & C 242, 31 LJ Ex 419, 8 Jur NS 1042, 10 WR 778, 6 LT 896 .... 57.22
Fleming's Estate, Re [1987] 1 LRM 638 .... 17.2
Fleming's Trusts [1951] QSR 179 .... 68.6
Fleming's Will Trust, Re, Ennion v Hampstead Old People's Housing Trust Ltd [1974] 3 All ER 323, [1974] 1 WLR 1552, 118 Sol Jo 850 .... 41.5, 41.10, 58.12, 59.2, 63.9, 207.3
Fletcher, Re (1914) 19 DLR 624, 31 OLR 633, 6 OWN 235, 582 .... 38.10
Fletcher, Re, Barclays Bank Ltd v Ewing [1949] Ch 473, [1949] 1 All ER 732, [1949] LJR 1255, 93 Sol Jo 301 .... 75.7
Fletcher, Re, Doré v Fletcher (1885) 34 WR 29, 53 LT 813 .... 93.6
Fletcher, Re, Gillings v Fletcher (1888) 38 Ch D 373, 57 LJ Ch 1032, 36 WR 841, 59 LT 313, 4 TLR 486 .... 44.2, 44.15
Fletcher v Fletcher (1844) 4 Hare 67, 14 LJ Ch 66, 8 Jur 1040, 67 RR 6 .... 1.3, 10.6
Fletcher's Settlement Trusts, Re, Medley v Fletcher [1936] 2 All ER 236, 80 Sol Jo 486 .... 42.1
Fligelstone v Fligelstone (1902) 46 Sol Jo 451 .... 14.14
Flinn, Re, Public Trustee v Flinn [1948] Ch 241, sub nom Re Flinn, Public Trustee v Griffin [1948] 1 All ER 541, [1948] LJR 923, 92 Sol Jo 232, 64 TLR 203 .... 102.17, 103.17
Flint v Hughes (1843) 6 Beav 342, 7 Jur 523, 1 LTOS 311 .... 53.4
Flint v Warren (1847) 15 Sim 626, 16 LJ Ch 441, 11 Jur 665, 9 LTOS 351 .... 51.3, 56.5, 68.1
Flood v Flood [1902] 1 IR 538 .... 58.4, 58.12
Florence, Re, Lydall v Haberdashers' Co (1917) 87 LJ Ch 86, 62 Sol Jo 87, 117 LT 701 .... 20.3
Florent Estate, Re [1927] 3 DLR 946, [1927] 3 WWR 127 .... 62.1
Flower, Re, Edmonds v Edmonds (1885) 55 LJ Ch 200, 34 WR 149, 53 LT 717 .... 39.2, 94.48
Flower, Re, Matheson v Goodwyn (1890) 62 LT 216; revsd (1890) 63 LT 201, CA 38.17, 74.8
Flower's Settlement Trusts, Re, Flower v IRC [1957] 1 All ER 462, [1957] 1 WLR 401, 36 ATC 22, 50 R & IT 150, [1957] TR 29, 101 Sol Jo 189, CA 48.5
Flynn, Re, Flynn v Flynn [1982] 1 All ER 882, [1982] 1 WLR 310, 126 Sol Jo 189 .... 4.10, 4.13, 4.17, 5.1
Foakes v Jackson [1900] 1 Ch 807, 69 LJ Ch 352, 48 WR 616, 83 LT 26 .... 40.13
Foley, Re [1955] NZLR 535 .... 64.54
Foley, Re [1955] NZLR 702 .... 41.6
Foley, Re, Channell v Foley (1952) 70 WN 1, 53 SRNSW 31 .... 64.25
Foley v Burnell (1783) 1 Bro CC 274; affd (1785) 4 Bro Parl Cas 319, [1558–1774] All ER Rep 123, Rom 1, HL 8.3, 204.45
Foley v Burnell (1789) 4 Bro Parl Cas 34, HL 8.5
Foley's Goods, Re (1855) 2 Ecc & Ad 206, 25 LTOS 311 .... 14.11
Folkes v Western (1804) 9 Ves 456 .... 40.2
Follett, Re, Barclays Bank Ltd v Dovell [1955] 2 All ER 22, [1955] 1 WLR 429, 99 Sol Jo 275, CA 52.2, 52.3

Follett v Pettman (1883) 23 Ch D 337, 52 LJ Ch 521, 31 WR 779, 48 LT 865 .... 18.9, 18.14, 18.15, 22.3
Fong, Yee Charles, Re [1997] 1 HKC 348 .... 39.2
Fonnereau v Fonnereau (1745) 3 Atk 315 .... 8.3, 101.7
Fonnereau v Fonnereau (1748) 3 Atk 645, 1 Ves Sen 119 .... 93.27
Fontaine v Tyler (1821) 9 Price 94 .... 30.5, 30.8
Foord, Re, Foord v Conder [1922] 2 Ch 519, 92 LJ Ch 46, [1922] All ER Rep 166, 128 LT 501 .... 82.5
Foote and Purdon's Estate [1910] 1 IR 365 .... 40.15
Forbes, Re (1916) 33 WLR 605, 28 DLR 787, 26 Man LR 230, 9 WWR 1159 .... 47.28
Forbes, Re, Harrison v Commis [1928] 3 DLR 22, [1928] 1 WWR 230 .... 35.32
Forbes, Re, Public Trustee v Hadlow (1934) 78 Sol Jo 336 .... 30.24
Forbes v Adams (1839) 9 Sim 462, 8 LJ Ch 116 .... 23.4
Forbes v Ball (1817) 3 Mer 437 .... 39.19
Forbes v Forbes (1854) 18 Beav 552, 23 LJ Ch 422, 23 LTOS 108 .... 102.10
Forbes v Richardson (1853) 11 Hare 354, 1 WR 230, 21 LTOS 86 .... 33.23
Forbes v Steven (1870) LR 10 Eq 178, 39 LJ Ch 485, 18 WR 686, 22 LT 703 .... 23.4
Ford, Re, Ford v Ford [1902] 2 Ch 605, 71 LJ Ch 778, 51 WR 20, 46 Sol Jo 715, 87 LT 113, 18 TLR 809, CA 1.10, 104.1
Ford, Re, Myers v Molesworth [1911] 1 Ch 455, 80 LJ Ch 355, 104 LT 245 .... 204.62
Ford, Re, Patten v Sparks (1895) 72 LT 5, CA 77.3
Ford v Batley (1852) 17 Beav 303, 23 LJ Ch 225, 228 .... 33.5, 58.10
Ford v Ford (1848) 6 Hare 486 .... 60.1
Ford v Fowler (1840) 3 Beav 146, 9 LJ Ch 352, 4 Jur 958 .... 82.5
Ford v Rawlins (1823) 1 Sim & St 328, 1 LJOS Ch 170 .... 93.30
Forder, Re, Forder v Forder [1927] 2 Ch 291, 96 LJ Ch 314, [1927] B & CR 84, [1927] All ER Rep 324, 137 LT 538, CA 99.4, 99.10
Fordyce v Bridges (1848) 2 Ph 497, 17 LJ Ch 185, 2 Coop temp Cott 324 .... 94.1
Forest's Goods, Re (1861) 31 LJPM & A 200, 2 Sw & Tr 334, 5 LT 689 .... 9.8
Forester, Re, Jervis v Forester (1897) 41 Sol Jo 696, 13 TLR 555 .... 103.1
Formaniuk Estate, Re, Pitz v Kasjan (1963) 42 DLR (2d) 78, 44 WWR 686 .... 18.24
Forrest, Re, Bubb v Newcomb [1916] 2 Ch 386, 85 LJ Ch 784, [1916–17] All ER Rep 767, 60 Sol Jo 655, 115 LT 476, 32 TLR 656 .... 30.24
Forrest, Re, Carr v Forrest [1931] 1 Ch 162, 100 LJ Ch 122, 144 LT 297 .... 18.33, 20.5, 38.13, 47.28
Forrest v Whiteway (1849) 18 LJ Ex 207, 3 Exch 367, 12 LTOS 380 .... 86.3
Forrester v Cotton (1760) Amb 388, 1 Eden 531 .... 42.3
Forse and Hembling's Case. See Anon (1588) 1 And 181
Forshaw, Re, Wallace v Middlesex Hospital (1934) 78 Sol Jo 859, 51 TLR 97, CA 103.3
Forsight v Grant (1791) 1 Ves 298, 3 Bro CC 242 .... 44.15
Forster, Re (1841). See Hudson v Forster
Forster v Abraham (1874) LR 17 Eq 351, 43 LJ Ch 199, 22 WR 386 .... 27.3, 49.9
Forster v Williams Deacon's Bank Ltd [1935] Ch 359, [1935] All ER Rep 374, 104 LJ Ch 132, 79 Sol Jo 145, 152 LT 433, 51 TLR 254, CA 203.38
Forster's Estate, Re (1889) 23 LR Ir 269 .... 33.12
Forster-Brown, Re, Barry v Forster-Brown [1914] 2 Ch 584, 84 LJ Ch 361, 112 LT 681 .... 100.5

Forsyth, Re (1963) 37 DLR (2d) 379, [1963] 1 OR 425 .... 76.5, 96.3
Fortescue v Gregor (1800) 5 Ves 553 .... 100.2
Fortescue v Hennah (1812) 19 Ves 67 .... 3.8
Forth v Chapman (1720) 2 Eq Cas Abr 292, 359, 1 P Wms 663 ...... 50.2, 54.5, 84.4, 98.7
Fortlage, Re, Ross v Fortlage (1916) 60 Sol Jo 527 .... 64.6, 64.46
Foss Estate, Re [1940] 4 DLR 791, [1940] 3 WWR 61 .... 82.2
Foster, Re [1930] NZLR 60 .... 25.13
Foster, Re [1956] NZLR 44 .... 2.4
Foster, Re, Coomber v Hospital for the Maintenance and Education of Exposed and Deserted Young Children (Governors and Guardians) [1946] Ch 135, [1946] 1 All ER 333, 115 LJ Ch 251, 90 Sol Jo 116, 174 LT 392, 62 TLR 152 .... 87.1, 87.2, 101.6
Foster, Re, Hunt v Foster [1920] 1 Ch 391, 89 LJ Ch 206, 122 LT 585 .... 100.5
Foster v Cautley (1855) 6 De GM & G 55, 2 Jur NS 25, 26 LTOS 249 .... 39.18, 100.2
Foster v Cook (1791) 3 Bro CC 347 .... 93.19
Foster v Earl of Romney (1809) 11 East 594 .... 98.3
Foster v Hayes (1855) 4 E & B 717, 24 LJQB 161, 1 Jur NS 515, 3 WR 168, 119 ER 265, 3 CLR 576, 24 LTOS 312, Ex Ch 98.3
Foster v Royal Trust Co [1951] 1 DLR 147, [1950] OR 673, [1950] OWN 626 .... 3.4
Foster v Smith (1846) 1 Ph 629, 15 LJ Ch 183 .... 33.23, 33.28, 33.30
Foster v Wybrants (1874) IR 11 Eq 40 .... 84.4
Foster's Goods, Re (1871) LR 2 P & D 304, 36 JP 24, 41 LJP & M 18, 20 WR 302, 25 LT 763 .... 25.3
Foster's Will Trusts, Re, Smith v Foster (1967) 111 Sol Jo 685 .... 87.1
Fothergill, Re, Horwood v Fothergill (1916) 51 L Jo 169 .... 64.3
Found, Re, Semmens v Loveday [1924] SASR 301 .... 35.30
Fountain Forestry Ltd v Edwards [1975] Ch 1, [1974] 2 All ER 280, [1974] 2 WLR 767, 118 Sol Jo 367 .... 27.15
Fourdrin v Gowdey (1834) 3 My & K 383, 3 LJ Ch 171 .... 44.15
Foveaux, Re, Cross v London Anti-Vivisection Society [1895] 2 Ch 501, 64 LJ Ch 856, 13 R 730, 43 WR 661, 39 Sol Jo 671, 73 LT 202, 11 TLR 540 .... 9.31, 102.10
Fowkes v Pascoe (1875) 10 Ch App 343, [1874–80] All ER Rep 521, 44 LJ Ch 367, 23 WR 538, 32 LT 545, CA 44.8, 57.31
Fowler, Re [1963] VR 639 .... 35.2, 35.8, 57.15
Fowler, Re, Fowler v Booth (1914) 31 TLR 102, CA 81.5
Fowler, Re, Fowler v Wittingham (1915) 139 LT Jo 183 .... 59.3, 63.7
Fowler v Fowler (1735) 3 P Wms 353, [1558–1774] All ER Rep 579 .... 44.15, 44.16
Fowler v Fowler (1864) 28 JP 707, 33 Beav 616, 33 LJ Ch 674, 10 Jur NS 648, 12 WR 972, 10 LT 682 .... 9.29
Fowler v Fowler (1952) 69 WNNSW 283 .... 59.3
Fowler v Garlike (1830) 1 Russ & M 232, 8 LJOS Ch 66 .... 102.25
Fowler v Willoughby (1825) 2 Sim & St 354, 4 LJOS Ch 72 .... 30.6, 31.3
Fowler's Trust, Re (1859) 27 Beav 362 .... 42.7
Fowlis v Davidson (1848) 6 Notes of Cases 461 .... 4.15
Fox, Re (1865) 35 Beav 163, 11 Jur NS 735, 6 New Rep 374, 13 WR 1013 .... 87.1
Fox, Re [1951] 3 DLR 337, [1951] OR 378, OWN 375 .... 2.6
Fox, Re [1997] 1 Qd R 43 .... 79.4

Fox, Re, Wodehouse v Fox [1904] 1 Ch 480, 73 LJ Ch 314, 52 WR 229, 48 Sol Jo 223, 90 LT 477 .... 100.1
Fox v Collins (1761) 2 Eden 107 .... 57.22
Fox v Fox (1870) LR 11 Eq 142, 40 LJ Ch 182, 19 WR 151, 23 LT 584 .... 100.4
Fox v Fox (1875) LR 19 Eq 286, 23 WR 314 .... 93.34, 93.36, 93.38, 93.39, 93.42, 210.49
Fox v Swann (1655) Sty 482 .... 7.23
Fox's Estate, Re, Dawes v Druitt [1937] 4 All ER 664, 82 Sol Jo 74, CA 47.1, 48.15, 93.9, 93.19
Fox's Estate, Re, Phoenix Assurance Co Ltd v Fox [1937] 4 All ER 664, 82 Sol Jo 74, CA 93.9
Foxen v Foxen (1864) 10 Jur NS 1061, 5 New Rep 1, 13 WR 33, 11 LT 292 .... 38.3
Foy v Foy (1785) 1 Cox Eq Cas 163 .... 88.3
Fraenkel v Whitty [1948] Ch 55, [1947] 2 All ER 646, [1948] LJR 322, 91 Sol Jo 638, 63 TLR 580 .... 99.4
Frame, Re, Edwards v Taylor [1939] Ch 700, [1939] 2 All ER 865, 108 LJ Ch 217, 83 Sol Jo 438, 160 LT 620, 55 TLR 746 .... 34.4
Framlingham v Brand (1746) 3 Atk 390, 1 Wils 140 .... 56.8
Francis, Re, Francis v Francis [1905] 2 Ch 295, 74 LJ Ch 487, 53 WR 571, 49 Sol Jo 536, 93 LT 132 .... 93.6, 93.12, 210.49
Francis v Grover (1845) 5 Hare 39, 15 LJ Ch 99, 10 Jur 280, 6 LTOS 235 .... 14.8
Franco v Alvares (1746) 3 Atk 342 .... 34.7, 34.21
Franguesco v Shaw [1977] 1 NSWLR 660 .... 30.3
Frankcombe v Hayward (1845) 9 Jur 344 .... 39.12
Frankland v IRC [1996] STC 735; affd [1997] STC 1450, CA 225.85, 242.4
Franklin, Re, Franklin v Franklin (1907) 52 Sol Jo 12 .... 44.9, 44.12
Franks, Re, Franks v Franks [1948] Ch 62, [1947] 2 All ER 638, [1948] LJR 345, 91 Sol Jo 638, 63 TLR 583 .... 105.5
Franks v Brooker (1860) 27 Beav 635, 29 LJ Ch 292, 6 Jur NS 87, 8 WR 205, 1 LT 426 .... 80.7
Franks v Price (1838) 5 Bing NC 37, 1 LT 426 .... 98.4
Franks v Sinclair [2006] EWHC 3365 (Ch), [2006] All ER (D) 340 (Dec) 5.3
Fraser, Re (1986) 29 DLR (4th) 88 .... 47.31, 66.2, 93.28
Fraser, Re, Lowther v Fraser [1904] 1 Ch 726, 73 LJ Ch 481, 52 WR 516, [1904–7] All ER Rep 177, 48 Sol Jo 383, 91 LT 48, 20 TLR 414, CA 20.4, 22.3
Fraser, Re, Yeates v Fraser (1883) 22 Ch D 827, 52 LJ Ch 469, 31 WR 375, 48 LT 187 .... 102.6
Fraser v Croft (1898) 25 R 496 .... 64.27
Fraser v Fraser (1863) 1 New Rep 430, 8 LT 20 .... 55.5
Fraser v Fraser (1896) 26 SCR 316 .... 86.5
Fraser v Murdoch (1881) 6 App Cas 855, sub nom Robinson v Murdock 30 WR 162, 45 LT 417, HL 29.9, 29.14, 31.6
Free Church of Scotland Trustees v Maitland (1887) 14 R 333, 24 SLR 290 .... 57.15
Freeborn's Trustees v Bennett 1940 SC 517 .... 93.22
Freeland, Re, Jackson v Rodgers [1952] Ch 110, 95 Sol Jo 802, sub nom Jackson v Rodger [1952] 1 All ER 16, [1951] 2 TLR 1076 .... 30.18, 57.32
Freeland v Pearson (1867) LR 3 Eq 658, 36 LJ Ch 374, 15 WR 419 .... 47.14, 47.38, 83.17
Freeman, Re [1984] 3 All ER 906, [1984] 1 WLR 1419, [1985] FLR 543, [1985] Fam Law 256, 128 Sol Jo 769, [1984] LS Gaz R 3254 .... 105.5

Freeman, Re, Hope v Freeman [1910] 1 Ch 681, 79 LJ Ch 678, 54 Sol Jo 443, 102 LT 516, CA 18.6, 49.2, 82.2, 237.11
Freeman, Re, Shilton v Freeman [1908] 1 Ch 720, 77 LJ Ch 401, 52 Sol Jo 262, 98 LT 429, 24 TLR 300, CA 102.22, 102.26, 103.1
Freeman v Duke of Chandos (1775) 1 Cowp 363 .... 63.6
Freeman v Freeman (1854) 5 De GM & G 704, 23 LJ Ch 838, 2 Eq Rep 970, 2 WR 658, 23 LTOS 317 .... 1.1, 18.9
Freeman v Meymott. See Blacket v Blizard
Freeman's Estate, Re (1931) 75 Sol Jo 764, 146 LT 143, sub nom Re Freeman's Goods 48 TLR 1 .... 203.14
Freeman's Will Trusts, Re (10 July 1987, unreported) 57.23
Freer v Peacocke. See Frere v Peacocke
Freeston's Charity, Re, Sylvester v University College, Oxford [1978] 1 All ER 481, [1978] 1 WLR 120, 121 Sol Jo 527; affd [1979] 1 All ER 51, [1978] 1 WLR 741, 122 Sol Jo 294, CA 102.8, 211.4, 216.12, 220.71
Freke v Lord Carbery (1873) LR 16 Eq 461, 21 WR 835 .... 23.4, 23.11, 23.12, 23.16, 23.17, 24.2, 24.3
Freme, Re, Samuel v Freme (1912) 56 Sol Jo 362 .... 35.28
Freme v Clement (1881) 18 Ch D 499, 50 LJ Ch 801, 30 WR 1, 44 LT 339 .... 39.12, 39.14, 39.29
Freme's Contract, Re [1895] 2 Ch 256; affd [1895] 2 Ch 778, 64 LJ Ch 862, 44 WR 164, 73 LT 366, CA 49.9, 91.6
French v Caddell (1765) 3 Bro Parl Cas 257, HL 98.8
French v Craig (1858) 8 I Ch R 142 .... 61.1
French v French (1755) 1 Dick 268 .... 25.15, 49.7
French v French (1840) 11 Sim 257 .... 85.3
French v French [1902] 1 IR 172, HL 36.13
French v Hoey [1899] 2 IR 472 .... 9.5, 21.7, 22.3
Frere, Re, Kidd v Farnham Group Hospital Management Committee [1951] Ch 27, [1950] 2 All ER 513, 66 (pt 2) TLR 354 .... 103.10
Frere v Peacocke (1846) 1 Rob Eccl 442, sub nom Freer v Peacocke 11 Jur 247 .... 4.11, 4.15, 4.18
Frewen v Frewen (1875) 10 Ch App 610, 23 WR 864, 33 LT 43 .... 41.2, 41.13
Frewen v Law Life Assurance Society [1896] 2 Ch 511, 65 LJ Ch 787, 44 WR 682, 40 Sol Jo 621, 75 LT 17 .... 46.3
Friedman, Re, Friedman v Friedman (1908) 25 WN 49, 8 SRNSW 127 .... 64.35, 64.40
Friend, Re, Friend v Young (No 2) (1898) 78 LT 222 .... 33.11
Friend of the Clergy's Charters, Re, Friend of the Clergy v A-G [1921] 1 Ch 409, 90 LJ Ch 210, 124 LT 506 .... 102.7
Friend's Settlement, Re, Cole v Allcot [1906] 1 Ch 47, 75 LJ Ch 14, 54 WR 295, 93 LT 739 .... 67.4
Frith, Re, Hindson v Wood (1901) 46 Sol Jo 15, 85 LT 455 .... 78.2
Frith's Goods, Re (1858) 27 LJP & M 6, 4 Jur NS 288, 1 Sw & Tr 8, 6 WR 262, 30 LTOS 295 .... 12.12
Froggatt v Wardell (1850) 3 De G & Sm 685, 14 Jur 1101, 15 LTOS 21 .... 85.3
Frogley v Phillips (1861) 3 De GF & J 466, 7 Jur NS 349, 3 LT 718 .... 71.1
Frogley's Estate, Re [1905] P 137, 74 LJP 72, 54 WR 48, 92 LT 429, 21 TLR 341 .... 9.25, 72.2

Frost, Re, Frost v Frost (1889) 43 Ch D 246, 59 LJ Ch 118, 38 WR 264, 62 LT 25 .... 94.17, 94.33
Froy, Re, Froy v Froy [1938] Ch 566, [1938] 2 All ER 316, 107 LJ Ch 342, 82 Sol Jo 273, 158 LT 518, 54 TLR 613 .... 68.13, 86.2
Fry, Re, Reynolds v Denne [1945] Ch 348, [1945] 2 All ER 205, 115 LJ Ch 3, 89 Sol Jo 349, 173 LT 282, 61 TLR 449 .... 34.2, 34.11, 35.39, 35.40, 35.43, 35.52
Fry v Porter (1670) 1 Eq Cas Abr 111, 1 Cas in Ch 137, 1 Mod Rep 300, 2 Rep Ch 26 .... 34.3
Fry's Estate, Re (1957) 9 DLR (2d) 549, 40 MPR 71 .... 47.9
Fry's Estate, Re, Matthews v Greenman (1874) 22 WR 813, 31 LT 8, CA 58.10
Fryer v Morris (1804) 9 Ves 360 .... 41.19
Fryer v Ranken (1840) 11 Sim 55, 9 LJ Ch 337 .... 64.40
Fuld's Estate (No 2), Re, Hartley v Fuld [1965] P 405, [1965] 2 All ER 657, 109 Sol Jo 575 .... 12.17
Fuld's Estate (No 3), Re, Hartley v Fuld [1968] P 675, [1965] 3 All ER 776, [1966] 2 WLR 717, 110 Sol Jo 133 .... 4.2, 5.1, 5.3, 5.9, 23.2, 23.10, 24.7, 105.7
Fulford, Re, Fulford v Hyslop [1930] 1 Ch 71, 8 ATC 588, 99 LJ Ch 80, 142 LT 185 .... 61.1
Fullard, Re, Fullard v King [1982] Fam 42, [1981] 2 All ER 796, [1981] 3 WLR 743, 11 Fam Law 116, 125 Sol Jo 747, CA 105.11
Fullarton v Humble (1958) 42 MPR 118 .... 35.2
Fuller, Re, Arnold v Chandler (1915) 59 Sol Jo 304 .... 63.7, 64.26
Fuller v Fuller (1595) Cro Eliz 422, Moore KB 353 .... 48.10
Fuller v Strum [2001] EWCA Civ 1879, [2002] 2 All ER 87, [2002] 1 WLR 1097, [2002] 1 FCR 608, (2002) Times, 22 January, [2001] All ER (D) 92 (Dec) 5.1, 5.3, 5.4
Fuller v Taylor (1897) 15 NZLR 229 .... 59.3
Fuller's Goods, Re [1892] P 377, 56 JP 713, 62 LJP 40, 1 R 453, 67 LT 501 .... 11.12
Fullerton v Martin (1853) 22 LJ Ch 893, 1 Eq Rep 224, 17 Jur 778, 1 WR 379 .... 60.2, 64.19
Fullerton v Martin (1860) 1 Drew & Sm 31, 29 LJ Ch 469, 6 Jur NS 265, 8 WR 289, 1 LT 531 .... 38.28
Fulton, Re (1978) 85 DLR (3d) 291 .... 93.6
Fulton v Andrew (1875) LR 7 HL 448, 44 LJP 17, 23 WR 566, [1874–80] All ER Rep 1240, 32 LT 209 .... 4.17, 5.1, 5.2, 5.4, 5.7, 5.9, 51.4
Fulwood's Case (1591) 4 Co Rep 64b, [1558–1774] All ER Rep 277 .... 9.32
Funnell v Stewart. See Le Cren Clarke, Re, Funnell v Stewart
Furness, Re, Furness v Stalkartt [1901] 2 Ch 346, 70 LJ Ch 580, 45 Sol Jo 557, 84 LT 680 .... 44.2, 44.8, 44.12
Fyfe v Irwin [1939] 2 All ER 271, 83 Sol Jo 454, HL 82.4
Fytche v Fytche (1868) LR 7 Eq 494, 19 LT 343 .... 42.10

G

G (infants), Re [1899] 1 Ch 719, 68 LJ Ch 374, 47 WR 491, 80 LT 470 .... 33.18, 216.13
G's Estate, Re, M v L [1946] P 183, [1946] 1 All ER 579, 115 LJP 72, 174 LT 395, 62 TLR 279 .... 9.16
GE v KM [1995] 1 VR 471 .... 76.3

Gaffney v Hevey (1837) 1 Dr & Wal 12 .... 38.3
Gage, Re, Crozier v Gutheridge [1934] Ch 536, 103 LJ Ch 241, [1934] All ER Rep 610, 151 LT 240 .... 30.8, 41.11
Gage, Re, Hill v Gage [1898] 1 Ch 498, 67 LJ Ch 200, 46 WR 569, 78 LT 347 .... 94.8, 94.12
Gainsford v Dunn (1874) LR 17 Eq 405, 43 LJ Ch 403, 22 WR 499, 30 LT 283 .... 39.22
Gaite's Will Trusts, Re, Banks v Gaite [1949] 1 All ER 459, 93 Sol Jo 148, 65 TLR 194 .... 94.10, 94.21
Gaitskell's Trusts, Re (1873) LR 15 Eq 386, 21 WR 768, 28 LT 760 .... 93.9, 97.4
Galbraith Estate, Re [1919] 2 WWR 193 .... 93.6
Galbraith's Goods, Re [1951] P 422, [1951] 2 All ER 470n, 95 Sol Jo 548, [1951] 2 TLR 412 .... 25.16
Gale, Re, Gale v Gale [1941] Ch 209, [1941] 1 All ER 329, 110 LJ Ch 69, 85 Sol Jo 118, 165 LT 224, 57 TLR 320 .... 33.20, 80.1, 80.4, 83.7
Gale v Gale (1856) 21 Beav 349, 4 WR 277 .... 41.5, 41.21, 47.39
Gallagher v Adams (1887) 13 VLR 948 .... 58.1, 58.5
Galland v Leonard (1818) 1 Wils Ch 129, 1 Swan 161 .... 97.1, 97.6
Galligan, Re, Galligan v Galligan (1913) 30 WN 180, 13 SRNSW 291 .... 98.13
Galloway v Galloway (1877) 3 JRNS (CA) 29 .... 25.16
Galvin v Devereux [1903] 1 IR 185 .... 42.5
Galway Incorporated Cripples' Institute, People's Palace and Homes of Rest, Re [1944] NI 28 .... 64.23
Galway's Will Trusts, Re, Lowther v Viscount Galway [1950] Ch 1, [1949] 2 All ER 419, [1949] LJR 1531, 93 Sol Jo 525, 65 TLR 499 .... 41.3, 41.4, 41.5, 41.13
Galwey v Barden [1899] 1 IR 508 .... 34.21
Gamboa's Trusts, Re (1858) 4 K & J 756 .... 78.4
Game, Re, Game v Young [1897] 1 Ch 881, 66 LJ Ch 505, 45 WR 472, 41 Sol Jo 438, 76 LT 450 .... 38.23
Gammon, Re, Shelton v Williams [1986] CLY 3547 .... 64.35
Gangell, Re (1912) 8 Tas LR 120 .... 64.45
Gann v Gregory (1854) 3 De GM & G 777, 2 Eq Rep 605, 18 Jur 1063, 2 WR 484, 23 LTOS 136 .... 57.5
Gannon, Re, Spence v Martin [1914] 1 IR 86 .... 83.1
Ganong Estate, Re, Ganong v Belyea (1941) SCR 125, [1941] 1 DLR 433 .... 30.8
Gansloser's Will Trusts, Re, Chartered Bank of India, Australia and China v Chillingworth [1952] Ch 30, [1951] 2 All ER 936, CA 68.13, 77.1, 77.3, 79.4, 79.6
Gape, Re, Verey v Gape [1952] Ch 743, 96 Sol Jo 595, [1952] TLR 477, sub nom Gape's Will Trusts, Re, Verey v Gape [1952] 2 All ER 579, CA 35.22
Garbrand v Mayot (1689) 2 Vern 105 .... 65.3
Garbut v Hilton (1739) 1 Atk 381, 9 Mod Rep 210 .... 34.15, 35.11
Garden v Pulteney (1765) 2 Eden 323 .... 85.3
Gardiner, Re, Gardiner v Smith [1901] 1 Ch 697, 70 LJ Ch 407 .... 94.5, 95.1, 207.25, 207.26
Gardiner v Courthope (1886) 12 PD 14, 50 JP 791, 56 LJP 55, 35 WR 352, 57 LT 280 .... 18.15, 18.28, 20.2
Gardiner v Slater (1858) 25 Beav 509 .... 34.15, 35.10, 35.11, 93.26
Gardiner v Stevens (1860) 30 LJ Ch 199, 7 Jur NS 307, 9 WR 138 .... 101.7
Gardiner v Young (1876) 34 LT 348 .... 83.16

Gardiner (W) & Co Ltd v Dessaix [1915] AC 1096, 84 LJPC 231, 113 LT 933, PC 85.4, 99.1
Gardner, Re [1935] 1 DLR 308, OR 71 .... 18.10
Gardner, Re [1938] 2 DLR 772 .... 41.5
Gardner, Re, Huey v Cunnington [1920] 2 Ch 523, 89 LJ Ch 649, 64 Sol Jo 650, 124 LT 49, 36 TLR 784, CA 36.13, 82.5
Gardner, Re, Huey v Cunningham [1923] 2 Ch 230, 92 LJ Ch 569, 67 Sol Jo 517, 129 LT 206 .... 9.4, 36.9
Gardner, Re, Long v Gardner (1892) 3 R 96, 41 WR 203, 37 Sol Jo 67, 67 LT 552 .... 32.6
Gardner v Hatton (1833) 6 Sim 93 .... 30.3
Gardner v James (1843) 6 Beav 170 .... 66.14
Gardner v Parker (1818) 3 Madd 184 .... 1.15
Gardom, Re, Le Page v A-G [1914] 1 Ch 662, 83 LJ Ch 681, 108 LT 955, CA; revsd sub nom Le Page v Gardom [1915] WN 216, 84 LJ Ch 749, 59 Sol Jo 599, 113 LT 475, HL 36.5, 36.13, 102.7
Gare, Re, Filmer v Carter [1952] Ch 80, [1951] 2 All ER 863, 95 Sol Jo 744, [1951] 2 TLR 1003 .... 10.17, 38.1, 52.9, 102.17
Garioch's Trustees v Garioch's Executors 1917 SC 404 .... 2.5
Garland, Re, Eve v Garland [1934] Ch 620, 103 LJ Ch 287, [1934] All ER Rep 605, 78 Sol Jo 519, 151 LT 326 .... 64.32
Garland v Beverley (1878) 9 Ch D 213, 26 WR 718, 38 LT 911, sub nom Re Garland, Garland v Beverley 47 LJ Ch 711 .... 58.10
Garland v Brown (1864) 10 LT 292 .... 86.5, 94.8, 94.30
Garland v Morris [2007] EWHC 2 (Ch), [2007] 2 FLR 528, [2007] Fam Law 585, [2007] All ER (D) 11 (Jan) 105.16
Garner v Garner (1860) 29 Beav 114, 7 LT 182, 3 LT 396 .... 57.22, 58.10
Garner's Goods, Re (1861) 25 JP 183 .... 12.3
Garnett Estate, Re, Armstrong v Garnett (1954) 12 WWRNS 617 .... 33.5, 44.11
Garnett Orme and Hargreaves' Contract, Re (1883) 25 Ch D 595, 53 LJ Ch 196, 32 WR 313, 49 LT 655 .... 27.18
Garnett's Goods, Re [1894] P 90, 63 LJP 82, 6 R 579, 70 LT 37 .... 15.1
Garnett-Botfield v Garnett-Botfield [1901] P 335, 71 LJP 1, 85 LT 641 .... 51.4
Garnham, Re, Taylor v Baker [1916] 2 Ch 413, 85 LJ Ch 646, 115 LT 148 .... 37.2, 94.17, 94.37
Garnock, Re, Garnock v Garnock (1909) 27 WN 3, 10 SRNSW 51 .... 72.15
Garratt v Niblock (1830) 1 Russ & M 629 .... 80.1
Garret v Pritty (1693) 2 Vern 293 .... 34.14
Garrett, Re, Croft v Ruck [1934] Ch 477, [1934] All ER Rep 128, 103 LJ Ch 244, 151 LT 194 .... 218.88, 218.90
Garrett v Noble (1834) 6 Sim 504, 3 LJ Ch 159 .... 205.25
Garrett's Goods, Re (1872) 36 JP 615, 26 LT 984 .... 38.3
Garrick v Lord Camden (1807) 14 Ves 372 .... 77.2
Garside, Re, Wragg v Garside [1919] 1 Ch 132, 88 LJ Ch 116, [1918–19] All ER Rep 1139, 63 Sol Jo 156, 120 LT 339, 35 TLR 129 .... 95.13
Garth v Baldwin (1755) 2 Ves Sen 646 .... 84.4
Garth v Meyrick (1779) 1 Bro CC 30 .... 58.10, 88.2
Garthshore v Chalie (1804) 10 Ves 1, [1803–13] All ER Rep 239 .... 3.11, 30.31
Gartside, Re [1956] VLR 15 .... 64.43, 71.5
Gartside, Re, Coote and Eyre-Kaye v Lees [1949] 2 All ER 546 .... 103.10

Gartside v Sheffield, Young and Ellis [1983] NZLR 37, NZ CA 1.14, 200.46, 223.1
Garvey v Hibbert (1812) 19 Ves 125 .... 69.2
Gaskell v Harman (1805) 11 Ves 489 .... 93.4, 97.7
Gaskell v Holmes (1844) 3 Hare 438, 8 Jur 396, 3 LTOS 5 .... 66.1, 68.10
Gaskin v Rogers (1866) LR 2 Eq 284, 14 WR 707 .... 9.5, 30.1, 33.1, 55.4
Gassiot, Re, Brougham v Rose-Gassiot (1907) 51 Sol Jo 570 .... 34.11
Gassiot, Re, Fladgate v Vintners' Co (1901) 70 LJ Ch 242, 17 TLR 216 .... 34.17
Gate, Re [1923] NZLR 419 .... 83.9
Gates, Re (1895) 39 Sol Jo 331 .... 99.6
Gates, Re, Gates v Cabell [1929] 2 Ch 420, 98 LJ Ch 360, [1929] All ER Rep 379, 73 Sol Jo 429, 141 LT 392, 45 TLR 522, CA 64.35
Gates's Goods, Re [1928] P 128, 97 LJP 76, 72 Sol Jo 172, 138 LT 714, 44 TLR 353; varied [1928] P 178, CA 64.37
Gath v Burton (1839) 1 Beav 478, 3 Jur 817 .... 34.19
Gattward v Knee [1902] P 99, 71 LJP 34, [1900–03] All ER Rep 151, 18 TLR 163, sub nom Re Knee's Goods, Gattward v Knee 46 Sol Jo 123, 86 LT 119 .... 16.2
Gauntlett v Carter (1853) 17 Beav 586, 23 LJ Ch 219, 17 Jur 981, 1 WR 500 .... 50.2, 50.15, 63.4
Gausden's Goods, Re (1862) 26 JP 216, 31 LJPM & A 53, 8 Jur NS 180, 2 Sw & Tr 362, 5 LT 767 .... 11.4
Gauthier, Re [1944] OR 401 .... 23.5
Gawler v Cadby (1821) Jac 346 .... 85.3, 97.2
Gaynon v Wood. See Wood v Gaynon
Gaynor Will, Re [1960] VLR 640 .... 35.38
Gayre v Gayre (1705) 2 Vern 538 .... 63.1
Gaze v Gaze (1843) 3 Curt 451, 7 Jur 803, 2 Notes of Cases 224 .... 11.26
Geale's Goods, Re (1864) 28 JP 630, 33 LJPM & A 125, 4 New Rep 349, 3 Sw & Tr 431, 12 WR 1027 .... 5.2
Geary v Beaumont (1817) 3 Mer 431 .... 30.17
Geary's Trusts, Re (1890) 25 LR Ir 171 .... 103.3
Gebhardt, Re [1943] SASR 380 .... 64.45
Geddis v Semple [1903] 1 IR 73 .... 36.5, 36.8
Gee, Re [1928] 3 DLR 54, 62 OLR 184 .... 64.5
Gee, Re (1973) 41 DLR (3d) 317 .... 34.6
Gee, Re, Wood v Staples [1948] Ch 284, [1948] 1 All ER 498, [1948] LJR 1400, 92 Sol Jo 232 .... 221.10, 233.23
Gee v Liddell (1866) LR 2 Eq 341, 35 Beav 658, 35 LJ Ch 640, 12 Jur NS 541, 14 WR 853 .... 67.1
Gee v Liddell (No 2) (1866) 35 Beav 629 .... 30.12
Gee v Manchester Corpn (1852) 17 QB 737, 12 LJQB 242, 16 Jur 758, 18 LTOS 236 .... 97.1, 97.6
Gee's Goods, Re (1898) 78 LT 843 .... 11.2, 11.3, 14.12
Geering, Re, Gulliver v Geering [1964] Ch 136, [1962] 3 All ER 1043, [1962] 3 WLR 1541, 106 Sol Jo 919 .... 32.17, 33.25, 218.60
Gemmell v Gemmell (1892) 18 VLR 781 .... 50.11
General Accident Fire and Life Assurance Corpn Ltd v IRC [1963] 3 All ER 259, [1963] 1 WLR 1207, 42 ATC 313, 107 Sol Jo 870, sub nom Lacy's Settlement Trustee (General Accident, Fire and Life Assurance Corpn Ltd) v IRC [1963] TR 321, CA 99.4

General Nursing Council for England and Wales v St Marylebone Borough Council [1959] AC 540, [1959] 1 All ER 325, [1959] 2 WLR 308, 57 LGR 101, 52 R & IT 119, 4 RRC 53, 123 JP 169, 103 Sol Jo 154, HL 102.10
Gent and Eason's Contract, Re [1905] 1 Ch 386, 74 LJ Ch 333, 53 WR 330, 92 LT 356 .... 64.53
Gentili's Goods, Re (1875) IR 9 Eq 541 .... 23.17
Gentle v Faulkner [1900] 2 QB 267, 69 LJQB 777, 44 Sol Jo 483, 82 LT 708, 16 TLR 397, CA 7.23
Gentle's Trustees v Bunting 1908 16 SLT 437 .... 72.2
Gentry's Goods, Re (1873) LR 3 P & D 80, 37 JP 456, 42 LJP & M 49, 21 WR 888, 28 LT 480 .... 19.2
George, Re (1877) 5 Ch D 837, 47 LJ Ch 118, 26 WR 65, 37 LT 204, CA 32.15, 32.20, 218.61
George v Daily (1997) 143 DLR (4th) 273, Man CA 1.2, 10.7
George's Estate, Re, King v George. See King v George
George's Will Trusts, Re, Barclay's Bank Ltd v George [1949] Ch 154, [1948] 2 All ER 1004, 92 Sol Jo 689 .... 44.4, 44.11
Georgetti's Will, Re, Georgetti v Georgetti (1900) 18 NZLR 849 .... 59.3
Gerhardy v Bible Society [1982] 30 SASR 12 .... 1.6
German v Chapman (1877) 7 Ch D 271, 42 JP 358, 47 LJ Ch 250, 26 WR 149, 37 LT 685, CA 102.8
Gerrard v Butler (1855) 20 Beav 541 .... 40.21
Gertsman, Re [1966] VR 45 .... 32.15
Gertzbein v Winer (1971) 13 DLR 692 .... 3.13
Gestetner Settlement, Re, Barnett v Blumka [1953] Ch 672, [1953] 1 All ER 1150, [1953] 2 WLR 1033, 32 ATC 102, 46 R & IT 467, [1953] TR 113, 97 Sol Jo 332 .... 53.6
Gether v Capper (1855) 24 LJCP 69 .... 50.6
Ghaidan v Godin-Mendoza [2004] UKHL 30, [2004] 2 AC 557, [2004] 3 WLR 113, [2004] 2 FCR 481, [2004] 2 FLR 600, [2004] Fam Law 641, [2004] HLR 827, [2004] 2 EGLR 132, [2004] 27 LS Gaz R 30, [2004] NLJR 1013, (2004) Times, 24 June, 148 Sol Jo LB 792, [2004] All ER (D) 210 (Jun), sub nom Ghaidan v Mendoza [2004] 3 All ER 411, [2005] 1 LRC 449 .... 7.4, 105.15
Ghafoor v Cliff [2006] WTLR 1209 .... 25.16
Gibb, Re [1984] 1 NZLR 708 .... 50.3
Gibbard, Re, Public Trustee v Davis [1966] 1 All ER 273, [1967] 1 WLR 42, 110 Sol Jo 871 .... 53.6
Gibbings's Estates, Re [1928] P 28, 97 LJP 4, 71 Sol Jo 911, 138 LT 272, 44 TLR 230 .... 26.4
Gibbon v Gibbon (1853) 17 JP 151, 13 CB 205, 22 LJCP 131, 17 Jur 416, Saund & M 94, 20 LTOS 260 .... 64.39
Gibbons, Re, Gibbons v Gibbons [1920] 1 Ch 372, 89 LJ Ch 148, 64 Sol Jo 274, 122 LT 710, 36 TLR 203, CA 83.6
Gibbons v Gibbons (1881) 6 App Cas 471, 50 LJPC 45, 45 LT 177, PC 50.4, 50.7, 50.11
Gibbons v Langdon (1833) 6 Sim 260 .... 90.2
Gibbs, Re, Martin v Harding [1907] 1 Ch 465, 76 LJ Ch 238, 96 LT 423 .... 38.12, 57.15
Gibbs v Lawrence (1860) 30 LJ Ch 170, 7 Jur NS 137, 9 WR 93, sub nom Gibson v Lawrence 3 LT 367 .... 38.10, 64.17

Gibson, Re [1949] P 434, [1949] 2 All ER 90, [1949] LJR 1260, 93 Sol Jo 376, 65 TLR 395 ... 12.3, 12.16
Gibson, Re [1952] NZLR 875 ... 92.4
Gibson, Re [1953] NZLR 122 ... 11.26
Gibson, Re, Mathews v Foulsham (1866) LR 2 Eq 669, 35 LJ Ch 596, 14 WR 818 ... 59.3, 64.8
Gibson v Bott (1802) 7 Ves 89 ... 38.17
Gibson v Coleman (1868) 16 WR 892, 18 LT 236 ... 103.3
Gibson v Fisher (1867) LR 5 Eq 51, 37 LJ Ch 67, 16 WR 115 ... 87.3, 87.4
Gibson v Gibson (1698) 2 Eq Cas Abr 184, Freem Ch 223 ... 73.1
Gibson v Gibson (1852) 1 Drew 42, 22 LJ Ch 346 ... 65.2
Gibson v Lawrence. See Gibbs v Lawrence
Gibson v South American Stores (Gath and Chaves) Ltd [1950] Ch 177, [1949] 2 All ER 985, 93 Sol Jo 822, 66 (pt 1) TLR 83, CA ... 102.7, 102.10, 102.15
Gibson Estate v Ashbury College Inc (1999) 179 DLR (4th) 557 ... 50.2, 79.2
Gibson Will, Re, MacLellan v Howson [1922] VLR 165, 43 ALT 154, 28 Argus LR 66 ... 20.5, 47.31
Gibson's Estate, Re [1941] P 118n, [1941] 2 All ER 91, 110 LJP 73n ... 16.2
Gibson's Trusts, Re (1861) 2 John & H 656, 31 LJ Ch 231 ... 47.32, 91.6
Giesler v Jones (1858) 25 Beav 418 ... 91.6
Gifford, Re, Gifford v Seaman [1944] Ch 186, [1944] 1 All ER 268, 113 LJ Ch 94, 88 Sol Jo 76, 170 LT 267, 60 TLR 202 ... 58.4, 64.58
Gilbert, Re [1959] OWN 294 ... 35.8
Gilbert, Re, Daniel v Matthews (1886) 34 WR 577, 54 LT 752 ... 68.8, 68.13
Gilbert, Re, Gilbert v Gilbert [1908] WN 63 ... 100.5
Gilbert v Boorman (1805) 11 Ves 238 ... 66.20
Gilbert's Goods, Re [1895–9] All ER Rep 370, 78 LT 762 ... 11.3
Gilbertstone, Re [1975] 2 NZLR 298 ... 52.2
Gilchrist Educational Trust, Re [1895] 1 Ch 367, 64 LJ Ch 298, 13 R 228, 43 WR 234, 71 LT 875 ... 102.8
Gildersleeve, Re [1934] OWN 51 ... 33.5
Giles, Re (1878) 4 VLR 37 ... 32.21
Giles, Re, Giles v Giles [1972] Ch 544, [1971] 3 All ER 1141, [1971] 3 WLR 640, 115 Sol Jo 428 ... 9.14, 9.15, 9.18, 9.20
Giles v Giles (1836) 1 Keen 685, sub nom Penfold v Giles 6 LJ Ch 4 ... 58.10, 80.6
Giles v Giles (1837) 8 Sim 360, 6 LJ Ch 176, 1 Jur 234 ... 68.10
Giles v Melsom (1873) LR 6 HL 24, 42 LJCP 122, 21 WR 417, 28 LT 789 ... 50.4, 50.7, 50.17, 90.1, 90.2
Giles v Warren (1872) LR 2 P & D 401, 36 JP 663, 41 LJP & M 59, 20 WR 827, 26 LT 780 ... 18.5, 18.17, 19.5
Gilfoyle v Wood-Martin [1921] 1 IR 105 ... 41.5, 41.6
Gilham v Walker and Walker [1919] St R Qd 9 ... 83.6
Gill, Re (1920) CR Rep 63 ... 7.10
Gill, Re [1959] Qd R 373 ... 87.1
Gill v Bagshaw (1866) LR 2 Eq 746, 35 LJ Ch 842, 14 WR 1013 ... 72.3
Gill v Barrett (1860) 29 Beav 372 ... 54.5
Gill v Gill [1909] P 157, 78 LJP 60, 53 Sol Jo 359, 100 LT 861, 25 TLR 400 ... 18.21, 18.31
Gill v Gill (1921) 38 WN 130, 21 SRNSW 400 ... 35.21
Gill v Shelley (1831) 2 Russ & M 336, 9 LJOS Ch 68 ... 72.2

Gill's Goods, Re (1873) LR 3 P & D 113 .... 25.13
Gillaume v Adderley (1808) 15 Ves 384 .... 30.8
Gillespie, Re [1955] QSR 330 .... 47.32
Gillespie, Re [1965] VR 402 .... 102.10
Gillespie, Re (1969) 3 DLR (3d) 317, [1969] 1 OR 585 .... 2.2, 2.6, 2.8
Gillespie, Re, Gillespie v Gillespie (1902) 22 NZLR 74 .... 8.7
Gillespie v Alexander (1827) 3 Russ 130 .... 31.14
Gillet v Wray (1715) 1 P Wms 284 .... 34.15
Gillett v Gane (1870) LR 10 Eq 29, 39 LJ Ch 818, 18 WR 423, 22 LT 58 .... 58.10
Gillett v Holt [1998] 3 All ER 917, [1998] 2 FLR 470, [1998] Fam Law 596, [1998] 26 LS Gaz R 31; revsd [2001] Ch 210, [2000] 2 All ER 289, [2000] 3 WLR 815, [2000] 1 FCR 705, [2000] 2 FLR 266, [2000] Fam Law 714, [2000] 12 LS Gaz R 40, 144 Sol Jo LB 141, 80 P & CR D3, CA 3.1, 3.4, 43.1
Gillett's Will Trusts, Re, Barclays Bank Ltd v Gillett [1950] Ch 102, [1949] 2 All ER 893, 93 Sol Jo 742, 65 TLR 727 .... 32.17, 214.9, 218.60
Gilliat v Gilliat (1860) 28 Beav 481 .... 58.6
Gillies, Re [1991] 1 NZLR 760 .... 1.5, 20.4
Gillies v Longlands (1851) 4 De G & Sm 372, 20 LJ Ch 441, 15 Jur 570, 17 LTOS 250 .... 39.12
Gilligan, Re [1950] P 32, [1949] 2 All ER 401, [1949] LJR 1592, 93 Sol Jo 563, 65 TLR 651 .... 17.5, 77.2
Gillingham Bus Disaster Fund, Re, Bowman v Official Solicitor [1958] Ch 300, [1958] 1 All ER 37, [1957] 3 WLR 1069, 101 Sol Jo 974; affd [1959] Ch 62, [1958] 2 All ER 749, [1958] 3 WLR 325, 102 Sol Jo 581, CA 102.7, 102.23, 102.24, 103.6, 103.18, 103.20
Gillins, Re, Inglis v Gillins [1909] 1 Ch 345, 78 LJ Ch 244, 15 Mans 74, 100 LT 226 .... 59.1, 59.2
Gillis Estate, Re [1988] 6 WWR 726 .... 14.1, 47.1
Gillman v Daunt (1856) 3 K & J 48 .... 66.12
Gilmore v Gilmore (1930) 31 SRNSW 83 .... 33.1
Gilmour, Re [1948] NZLR 687 .... 10.7
Gilmour v Coats [1949] AC 426, [1949] 1 All ER 848, [1949] LJR 1034, 93 Sol Jo 355, 65 TLR 234, HL 9.36, 102.9, 212.13
Gilmour v Gilmour (1931) 48 WN 15, SRNSW 83 .... 33.1
Gilmour v MacPhillamy [1930] AC 712, 143 LT 606, sub nom MacPhillamy, Re, Gilmour v MacPhillamy 99 LJPC 199, PC 67.1, 67.5
Gilpin, Re, Hutchinson v Gilpin [1954] Ch 1, [1953] 2 All ER 1218, [1953] 3 WLR 746, 97 Sol Jo 763 .... 75.7
Gimblett v Purton (1871) LR 12 Eq 427, 40 LJ Ch 556, 24 LT 793 .... 65.1, 66.14, 66.18, 66.19
Gingell v Horne (1839) 9 Sim 539, 3 Jur 194 .... 25.15
Ginger, Re, Wood Roberts v Westminster Hospital Board of Governors [1951] Ch 458, 95 Sol Jo 76, [1951] 1 TLR 750, sub nom Re Ginger, Roberts v Westminster Hospital Governors [1951] 1 All ER 422 .... 212.25
Ginger d White v White (1742) Willes 348 .... 85.2
Girdlestone v Creed (1853) 10 Hare 480, 1 WR 228, 21 LTOS 124 .... 63.8, 103.11
Girdlestone v Doe (1828) 2 Sim 225 .... 68.1
Girvin Estate, Re (1932) 40 Man LR 481 .... 52.7

Gisborne v Gisborne (1877) 2 App Cas 300, [1874–80] All ER Rep Ext 1698, 46 LJ Ch 556, 25 WR 516, 36 LT 564, HL 214.3
Gittings v M'Dermott (1834) 2 My & K 69, 2 LJ Ch 212 .... 68.2
Gittins v Steele (1818) 1 Swan 199 .... 31.21
Givan, Re, Rees v Green [1966] 3 All ER 393, [1966] 1 WLR 1378, 110 Sol Jo 653 .... 64.9
Givan v Massey (1892) 31 LR Ir 126 .... 92.2
Glanville v Glanville (1863) 33 Beav 302, 33 LJ Ch 317, 9 Jur NS 1189, 3 New Rep 58, 12 WR 92, 9 LT 470 .... 58.8
Glass, Re, Public Trustee v South-West Middlesex Hospital Management Committee [1950] Ch 643n, [1950] 2 All ER 953n 41.13
Glassington, Re, Glassington v Follett [1906] 2 Ch 305, 75 LJ Ch 670, 95 LT 100 .... 57.3, 57.13, 58.4, 64.32
Gleadow v Leetham (1882) 22 Ch D 269, 52 LJ Ch 102, 31 WR 269, 48 LT 264 .... 33.47
Gleeson, Re, Gleeson v Gleeson [1910] VLR 181 .... 97.5
Gleeson, Re, Smyth v Gleeson [1911] 1 IR 113 .... 44.15
Glendinning, Re, Steel v Glendinning (1918) 88 LJ Ch 87, 63 Sol Jo 156, 120 LT 222 .... 64.35, 64.37
Gliddon, Re, Smith v Gliddon [1917] 1 Ch 174, 86 LJ Ch 253, 116 LT 13 .... 64.35
Glover v Hall (1849) 16 Sim 568, 18 LJ Ch 305 .... 83.2
Glover v Hartcup (1864) 34 Beav 74 .... 44.15
Glover v Heelis (1875) 23 WR 677, 32 LT 534 .... 37.2
Glover v Monckton (1825) 3 Bing 13, 3 LJOSCP 189, 10 Moore CP 453 .... 98.11
Glover v Smith (1886) 50 JP 456, 57 LT 60 .... 13.3
Glover v Spendlove (1793) 4 Bro CC 337 .... 60.1
Glover's Goods, Re (1847) 11 Jur 1022, 10 LTOS 118, 5 Notes of Cases 553 .... 11.20
Glubb, Re, Bamfield v Rogers [1900] 1 Ch 354, 69 LJ Ch 278, 82 LT 412, CA 34.22
Glubb, Re, Barnfield v Rogers (1897) 14 TLR 66 .... 103.7
Glyn v Glyn (1857) 26 LJ Ch 409, 3 Jur NS 179, 5 WR 241 .... 96.7
Glyn's Will Trusts, Re, Public Trustee v A-G [1950] 2 All ER 1150n, 66 (pt 2) TLR 510 .... 102.5
Glynn v Glynn [1987] ILRM 589 .... 1.3
Glynn v Oglander (1829) 2 Hag Ecc 428 .... 10.6
Goblet v Beechey (1829) 3 Sim 24; revsd (1831) 2 Russ & M 624 .... 50.11, 57.6
Godfree, Re, Godfree v Godfree [1914] 2 Ch 110, 83 LJ Ch 734 .... 38.19, 38.23
Godfrey v Davis (1901) 6 Ves 43 .... 72.3
Godfrey v Hughes (1847) 1 Rob Eccl 593, 5 Notes of Cases 499 .... 34.3, 35.2
Godfrey's Goods, Re (1893) 1 R 484, 69 LT 22 .... 18.22
Godkin v Murphy (1843) 2 Y & C Ch Cas 351, 7 Jur 505 .... 77.2
Godman v Godman [1920] P 261, 89 LJP 193, 123 LT 274, sub nom Re Godman, Godman v Godman 64 Sol Jo 424, 36 TLR 434, CA 10.1
Goetze, Re, National Provincial Bank Ltd v Mond [1953] Ch 96, [1953] 1 All ER 76, [1953] 2 WLR 26, 31 ATC 551, [1952] TR 511, 97 Sol Jo 28, CA 210.68
Goff, Re, Featherstonehaugh v Murphy (1914) 58 Sol Jo 535, 111 LT 34 .... 57.32
Goguen v Godwin (1978) 82 DLR (3d) 547 .... 93.29

Goilmere v Battison (1682) 1 Eq Cas Abr 17, 1 Vern 48, sub nom Goylmer v Paddiston 2 Vent 353 .... 3.6
Going, Re (1951) 2 DLR 136, [1951] OR 147, OWN 156 .... 34.2, 35.33
Golan Estate, Re [1996] 2 WWR 614 .... 50.2
Golay, Re, Morris v Bridgewater [1965] 2 All ER 660, [1965] 1 WLR 969, 109 Sol Jo 517 .... 53.4
Gold v Gold [2005] WTLR 673 .... 105.16
Gold v Hill [1999] 1 FLR 54, [1998] Fam Law 664, 142 Sol Jo LB 226 .... 7.12
Goldcorp Exchange Ltd (in receivership), Re [1995] 1 AC 74, [1994] 2 All ER 806, [1994] 3 WLR 199, [1994] 2 BCLC 578, [1994] NLJR 792, sub nom Kensington v Unrepresented Non-allocated Claimants [1994] 24 LS Gaz R 46, 138 Sol Jo LB 127, PC 8.8
Goldie, Re, Goldie v Goldie [1952] NZLR 928 .... 77.3
Goldie v Adam [1938] P 85, 107 LJP 106, 158 LT 359, 54 TLR 422, sub nom Re Taylor's Estate, Goldie v Adam [1938] 1 All ER 586, 82 Sol Jo 236 .... 18.10, 21.6, 21.7
Goldie v Greaves (1844) 14 Sim 348 .... 76.3
Goldney, Re, Re Dighton, Clarke v Dighton (1911) 130 LT Jo 484 .... 96.2
Goldney v Crabb (1854) 19 Beav 338, 2 WR 579 .... 84.4
Golds v Greenfield (1854) 23 LJ Ch 639, 2 Eq Rep 793, 2 Sm & G 476, 2 WR 583 .... 100.6
Goldsbrough Mort & Co Ltd v Hall (1948) 1 ALR 201, [1948] VLR 145; affd (1949) 78 CLR 1 .... 30.43
Goldschmidt, Re, Commercial Union Assurance Co Ltd v Central British Fund for Jewish Relief and Rehabilitation [1957] 1 All ER 513, [1957] 1 WLR 524, 101 Sol Jo 285 .... 103.3
Goldsmid v Goldsmid (1842) 2 Hare 187, 12 LJ Ch 113, 7 Jur 11 .... 40.15
Goldsmith v Goldsmith (1815) Coop G 225, 19 Ves 368 .... 35.13
Goldsmith's Will Trusts, Re, Brett v Bingham [1947] Ch 339, [1947] 1 All ER 451, [1947] LJR 775, 91 Sol Jo 131, 176 LT 321 .... 34.21, 92.4
Goldstein v Salvation Army Assurance Society [1917] 2 KB 291, 86 LJKB 793, 117 LT 63 .... 7.33
Goldsworthy v Thompson (1974) 46 DLR (3d) 237 .... 5.9
Gollin's Declaration of Trust, Re, Turner v Williams [1969] 3 All ER 1591, [1969] 1 WLR 1858, 113 Sol Jo 904 .... 29.14
Gompertz v Gompertz (1846) 2 Ph 107, 16 LJ Ch 23, 10 Jur 937, 78 RR 43 .... 82.4
Gompertz's Estate, Re, Parker v Gompertz (1910) 55 Sol Jo 76 .... 29.14
Gonin, Re [1979] Ch 16, [1977] 3 WLR 379, 121 Sol Jo 558, sub nom Re Gonin, Gonin v Garmeson [1977] 2 All ER 720 .... 30.18, 105.5
Gonne v Cook (1867) 15 WR 576 .... 55.6, 56.7, 56.8
Gooch v Gooch (1853) 3 De GM & G 366, 22 LJ Ch 1089, 1 WR 397, 21 LTOS 249 .... 66.23, 86.7, 94.2, 94.8, 94.12
Good, Re, Brennan v Good [2002] EWHC 640 (Ch), [2002] WTLR 801 .... 5.3
Good, Re, Carapeto v Good [2002] EWHC 640 (Ch), [2002] WTLR 801 .... 5.3
Good, Re, Harington v Watts [1905] 2 Ch 60, 74 LJ Ch 512, 53 WR 476, 49 Sol Jo 445, 92 LT 796, 21 TLR 450 .... 102.10
Good's Will Trusts, Re, Oliver v Batten [1950] 2 All ER 653, 66 (pt 2) TLR 465 .... 103.6, 103.18

Goodchild, Re, Goodchild v Goodchild [1996] 1 All ER 670, [1996] 1 WLR 694, [1997] 1 FCR 45, [1996] 1 FLR 591, [1996] Fam Law 209; affd [1997] 3 All ER 63, [1997] 1 WLR 1216, [1997] 2 FLR 644, sub nom Goodchild v Goodchild [1997] 3 FCR 601, [1997] NLJR 758, CA 2.3, 2.5, 2.6, 2.8, 2.9, 105.16, 201.411
Goode, Re, Spiller v Kennedy [1960] VR 117 .... 99.1
Goodenough v Tremamondo (1840) 2 Beav 512, 50 RR 262 .... 38.23
Goodfellow v Goodfellow (1854) 18 Beav 356, 2 WR 360, 23 LTOS 46 .... 101.2
Goodier v Edmunds [1893] 3 Ch 455, 62 LJ Ch 649, 37 Sol Jo 526 .... 37.2, 94.37
Goodier v Johnson (1881) 18 Ch D 441, 51 LJ Ch 369, 30 WR 449, 45 LT 515, CA 94.24, 94.30
Gooding v Read (1853) 4 De GM & G 510 .... 94.12, 94.30, 94.38
Goodinge v Goodinge (1749) 1 Ves Sen 231 .... 57.15, 57.18, 79.5
Goodisson v Goodisson [1913] 1 IR 31; on appeal [1913] 1 IR 218, CA 13.2
Goodlad v Burnett (1855) 1 K & J 341 .... 59.3, 64.8
Goodman v Drury (1852) 21 LJ Ch 680, 20 LTOS 6 .... 93.44
Goodman v Gallant [1986] Fam 106, [1986] 1 All ER 311, [1986] 2 WLR 236, 52 P & CR 180, [1986] 1 FLR 513, [1986] Fam Law 159, 129 Sol Jo 891, CA 7.3
Goodman v Goodman (1847) 1 De G & Sm 695, 17 LJ Ch 103, 12 Jur 258, 10 LTOS 322 .... 51.2, 90.1, 91.6
Goodman v Goodman [2006] EWHC 1757 (Ch), [2006] WTLR 1807, [2006] All ER (D) 193 (Jul) 6.3
Goodman v Saltash Corpn (1882) 7 App Cas 633, [1881–5] All ER Rep 1076, 52 LJQB 193, 47 JP 276, 31 WR 293, 48 LT 239, HL 102.10
Goodright v Dunham (1779) 1 Doug KB 264 .... 98.3
Goodright v Wright. See Woodright v Wright
Goodright d Drewry v Barron (1809) 11 East 220 .... 83.6
Goodright d Hoskins v Hoskins (1808) 9 East 306 .... 101.7
Goodright d Lloyd v Jones (1815) 4 M & S 88 .... 93.13
Goodright d Lamb v Pears (1809) 11 East 58 .... 58.5, 63.7
Goodtitle d Daniel v Miles (1805) 6 East 494, 2 Smith KB 467 .... 60.1
Goodtitle d Pearson v Otway (1753) 2 Wils 6 .... 83.11
Goodtitle d Bailey v Pugh (1787) 2 Jac & W 102, sub nom Pugh v Goodtitle 3 Bro Parl Cas 454, sub nom Doe d Bailey v Pugh 2 Mer 348, HL 78.1
Goodtitle d Radford v Southern (1813) 1 M & S 299 .... 63.7
Goodwin, Re (1905) 22 WN 215, 5 SRNSW 576 .... 42.5
Goodwin, Re, Ainslie v Goodwin [1924] 2 Ch 26, 93 LJ Ch 331, [1924] All ER Rep 180, 68 Sol Jo 478, 130 LT 822 .... 34.22, 92.1
Goodwin, Re, Goodwin v Goodwin [1969] 1 Ch 283, [1968] 3 All ER 12, [1968] 3 WLR 558, 112 Sol Jo 691 .... 105.23
Goodwin v Finlayson (1858) 25 Beav 65 .... 52.1, 90.1
Goodwyn v Goodwyn (1748–9) 1 Ves Sen 226 .... 64.19, 74.1
Goold v Teague (1858) 5 Jur NS 116, 7 WR 84, 32 LTOS 251 .... 64.53
Goold's Will Trusts, Re, Lloyd's Bank Ltd v Goold [1967] 3 All ER 652, 111 Sol Jo 812 .... 82.4
Gorbell v Davison (1854) 18 Beav 556 .... 77.3
Gordon, Re (1965) 52 DLR (2d) 197, [1965] 2 OR 805 .... 103.3
Gordon, Re, Public Trustee v Bland [1942] Ch 131, [1942] 1 All ER 59, 111 LJ Ch 114, 86 Sol Jo 21, 166 LT 102, 58 TLR 112 .... 100.2

Gordon, Re, Roberts v Gordon (1877) 6 Ch D 531, 46 LJ Ch 794, 37 LT 627 .... 27.5, 27.6, 37.8
Gordon, Re, Watts v Rationalist Press Association Ltd [1940] Ch 769, [1940] 3 All ER 205, 109 LJ Ch 289, 84 Sol Jo 415, 163 LT 308, 56 TLR 860 .... 214.7
Gordon v Anderson (1858) 4 Jur NS 1097, 32 LTOS 119 .... 88.2
Gordon v Beere [1962] NZLR 257 .... 18.28
Gordon v Bowden (1822) 6 Madd 342 .... 33.24
Gordon v Duff, Re Ward (1861) 3 De GF & J 662, 7 Jur NS 746, 9 WR 643, 4 LT 598 .... 30.8
Gordon v Gordon (1816) 1 Mer 141 .... 9.25
Gordon v Gordon (1871) LR 5 HL 254 .... 50.2, 50.6, 50.15, 51.8, 57.8, 91.4
Gordon v Hoffmann (1834) 7 Sim 29 .... 52.11
Gordon v Hope (1849) 3 De G & Sm 351, 18 LJ Ch 228, 13 Jur 382, 12 LTOS 551 .... 96.1
Gordon v Whieldon (1848) 11 Beav 170, 18 LJ Ch 5, 12 Jur 988, 12 LTOS 63 .... 85.3
Gordon's (Lady Isabella) Goods, Re [1892] P 228, 61 LJP 132, 67 LT 328 .... 21.7
Gordon's Will Trusts, Re, National Westminster Bank Ltd v Gordon [1978] Ch 145, [1978] 2 All ER 969, [1978] 2 WLR 754, 122 Sol Jo 148, CA 42.1, 42.6, 42.7, 42.16, 44.13
Gore's Goods, Re (1843) 3 Curt 758, 7 Jur 1094, 2 Notes of Cases 479 .... 10.15
Goring v Bickerstaff (1662) 1 Cas in Ch 4, Freem Ch 163, Poll 31, sub nom Alford's Case O Bridg 584 .... 94.2
Goring v Howard (1848) 16 Sim 395, 18 LJ Ch 105 .... 94.28
Gorringe v Mahlstedt [1907] AC 225, 76 LJ Ch 527, 51 Sol Jo 497, 97 LT 111, HL 50.2, 50.6, 50.21, 54.2, 68.6, 68.9
Gorringe and Braybons Ltd's Contract, Re [1934] Ch 614n, [1933] All ER Rep 401, 151 LT 347n 220.80
Gorst v Lowndes (1841) 11 Sim 434, 10 LJ Ch 161, 5 Jur 457 .... 34.22
Gorton's Will, Re (1910) 29 NZLR 733 .... 15.1
Gosden v Dotterill (1832) 1 My & K 56, 2 LJ Ch 15 .... 64.35
Gosling, Re, Gosling v Smith (1900) 48 WR 300, 44 Sol Jo 196, 16 TLR 152 .... 102.7, 102.15
Gosling v Gosling (1859) John 265, 5 Jur NS 910, 123 RR 107 .... 30.36, 34.5, 51.2
Gosling v Townsend (1853) 2 WR 23, 22 LTOS 125 .... 97.6
Gosling's Goods, Re (1886) 11 PD 79, 50 JP 263, 55 LJP 27, 34 WR 492, 2 TLR 476 .... 18.16
Gossage's Estate, Re, Wood v Gossage [1921] P 194, 90 LJP 201, [1921] All ER Rep 107, 65 Sol Jo 274, 124 LT 770, 37 TLR 302, CA 16.2, 16.4, 16.10
Gosselin, Re, Gosselin v Gosselin [1906] 1 Ch 120, 75 LJ Ch 88, 54 WR 193 .... 35.50, 64.32
Gosset's Settlement, Re, Gribble v Lloyds Bank Ltd [1943] Ch 351, [1943] 2 All ER 515, 112 LJ Ch 291, 87 Sol Jo 282, 169 LT 172, 59 TLR 386 .... 89.1
Gossling, Re, Gossling v Elcock [1903] 1 Ch 448, 72 LJ Ch 433, 88 LT 279, CA 93.37, 210.49
Goswell's Trusts, Re [1915] 2 Ch 106, 84 LJ Ch 719, 59 Sol Jo 579, 113 LT 319 .... 37.4

Gott, Re, Glazebrook v Leeds University [1944] Ch 193, [1944] 1 All ER 293, 113 LJ Ch 124, 88 Sol Jo 103, 170 LT 210, 60 TLR 214 .... 103.1
Gough, Re, Phillips v Simpson [1957] Ch 323, [1957] 2 All ER 193, [1957] 2 WLR 961, 101 Sol Jo 409 .... 38.25
Gough v Bult (1847) 16 Sim 45, 17 LJ Ch 10, 80 RR 19; affd (1848) 16 Sim 50, 17 LJ Ch 401, 12 Jur 859, 80 RR 80, 13 LTOS 86 .... 53.4, 82.7, 82.8, 102.22
Gough v Bult (1848) 16 Sim 323, 17 LJ Ch 486, 12 Jur 859 .... 32.9
Gouk, Re, Allen v Allen [1957] 1 All ER 469, [1957] 1 WLR 493, 101 Sol Jo 265 .... 76.1, 82.2
Goulbourn v Brooks (1837) 2 Y & C Ex 539, 7 LJ Ex Eq 33, 1 Jur 354 .... 93.44
Gould v Lakes (1880) 6 PD 1, 44 JP 698, 49 LJP 59, 29 WR 155, 43 LT 382 .... 11.5
Goulder, Re, Goulder v Goulder [1905] 2 Ch 100, 74 LJ Ch 552, 53 WR 531, 49 Sol Jo 481, 93 LT 163 .... 34.11, 97.7
Gourju's Will Trusts, Re, Starling v Custodian of Enemy Property [1943] Ch 24, [1942] 2 All ER 605, 112 LJ Ch 75, 86 Sol Jo 367, 168 LT 1, 59 TLR 47 .... 99.4, 216.8
Gover v Davis (1860) 29 Beav 222, 30 LJ Ch 505, 7 Jur NS 399, 9 WR 87 .... 37.5, 38.11
Governesses' Benevolent Institution v Rusbridger (1854) 18 Beav 467 .... 29.15
Govier, Re [1950] P 237, 66 (pt 1) TLR 1042 .... 1.5, 2.2, 57.30
Gower v Mainwaring (1750) 2 Ves Sen 87 .... 79.4, 101.9
Gower v Public Trustee. See Public Trustee v Gower
Gower v Towers (1858) 25 Beav 81 .... 91.4
Gower's Settlement, Re [1934] Ch 365, [1934] All ER Rep 796, 103 LJ Ch 164, 150 LT 449 .... 218.66
Gowling v Thompson (1868) 16 WR 1131, 19 LT 242, LR 11 Eq 366n ... 66.6, 87.2, 87.3
Goylmer v Paddiston. See Goilmere v Battison
Grace v Webb. See Webb v Grace
Graham, Re, Graham v Graham [1929] 2 Ch 127, 98 LJ Ch 291, [1929] All ER Rep 433, 141 LT 197 .... 47.23, 48.15, 93.9
Graham v Clarke (Dorland Estate) and Dorland [1949] 3 DLR 539, 1 WWR 751; affd [1949] 4 DLR 770, 2 WWR 1042 .... 42.5
Graham v Graham (1749) 1 Ves Sen 262 .... 44.15
Graham v Lee (1857) 23 Beav 388, 26 LJ Ch 395, 3 Jur NS 550, 4 WR 328, 29 LTOS 46 .... 99.5
Graham v Murphy [1997] 2 FCR 441, [1997] 1 FLR 860, [1997] Fam Law 393 .... 105.18
Graham v Wickham (1863) 1 De GJ & Sm 474 .... 3.2, 3.9
Graham's Estate, Re [1946] 1 DLR 357, [1945] 3 WWR 713 .... 96.1
Graham's Estate, Re (1949) 67 WNNSW 23 .... 16.2
Grainger, Re, Dawson v Higgins [1900] 2 Ch 756, 69 LJ Ch 789, 48 WR 673, 83 LT 209, CA; revsd sub nom Higgins v Dawson [1902] AC 1, 71 LJ Ch 132, 50 WR 337, 85 LT 763, HL 50.3, 50.6, 51.4, 57.3, 57.8, 57.20, 59.1
Gramp, Re [1952] SASR 12 .... 13.3
Grant v Bridger (1866) LR 3 Eq 347, 36 LJ Ch 377, 15 WR 610 .... 41.22
Grant v Dyer (1813) 2 Dow 73, HL 35.12, 35.13, 56.3
Grant v Edwards [1986] Ch 638, [1986] 2 All ER 426, [1986] 3 WLR 114, [1987] 1 FLR 87, [1986] Fam Law 300, 130 Sol Jo 408, [1986] LS Gaz R 1996, [1986] NLJ Rep 439, CA 43.1

Grant v Fuller (1902) 33 SCR 34 ... 85.2
Grant v Grant (1869) LR 2 P & D 8, 34 JP 23, 39 LJP & M 17, 18 WR 230, 21 LT 645 ... 25.1
Grant v Grant (1870) LR 5 CP 380; on appeal (1870) LR 5 CP 727, [1861–73] All ER Rep 308, 39 LJCP 272, 18 WR 951, 22 LT 829, Ex Ch ... 57.3, 57.15, 57.22, 71.1
Grant v Leslie (1819) 3 Phillim 116 ... 25.2
Grant v Lynam (1828) 4 Russ 292, 6 LJOS Ch 129 ... 79.1, 79.2, 79.4
Grant v McLennan (1866) 16 C & P 395 ... 35.21
Grant v Winbolt (1854) 23 LJ Ch 282, 2 Eq Rep 539, 2 WR 151, 22 LTOS 233 ... 33.14
Grant Estate, Re [1944] 1 WWR 71 ... 4.16
Grant's Will Trusts, Re, Harris v Anderson [1979] 3 All ER 359, [1980] 1 WLR 360, 124 Sol Jo 84 ... 9.35, 102.26
Grassett, Re (1969) 31 DLR (3d) 153 ... 68.2, 68.9
Grassi, Re, Stubberfield v Grassi [1905] 1 Ch 584, 74 LJ Ch 341, 53 WR 396, [1904–7] All ER Rep 845, 49 Sol Jo 366, 92 LT 455, 21 TLR 343 ... 23.7, 23.12, 94.1
Gratrix v Chambers (1860) 2 Giff 321, 7 Jur NS 960 ... 33.41
Grattan's Estate, Re, Grattan v McNaughton [2001] WTLR 1305 ... 6.3, 105.9
Grattan v Langdale (1883) 11 LR Ir 473 ... 81.3
Gratton's Trusts, Re (1857) 26 LJ Ch 648, 3 Jur NS 684, 5 WR 795, 29 LTOS 399 ... 55.6
Gratwick's Trusts, Re (1865) LR 1 Eq 177, 35 Beav 215, 11 Jur NS 919 ... 39.19
Grave v Earl of Salisbury (1784) 1 Bro CC 425 ... 44.8
Gravenor v Watkins (1871) LR 6 CP 500, 40 LJCP 220, 19 WR 978, 24 LT 802, Ex Ch ... 52.10, 83.1
Graves v Bainbrigge (1792) 1 Ves 562 ... 51.7
Graves v Hicks (1833) 6 Sim 391 ... 33.33
Graves v Waters (1847) 10 I Eq R 234 ... 101.13
Gray, Re (1990) 73 DLR (4th) 161 ... 51.1
Gray (decd), Re; Allardyce v Roebuck [2004] EWHC 1538 (Ch), [2004] 3 All ER 754, [2004] All ER (D) 34 (Jul) ... 92.4, 209.5
Gray, Re, Bennett v Toronto Gen Trusts Corpn [1958] SCR 392, 14 DLR (2d) 1 ... 10.1, 10.18
Gray, Re, Corkill v Gray [1956] NZLR 981 ... 20.3
Gray, Re, Gray v Gray [1896] 1 Ch 620, 65 LJ Ch 462, 60 JP 314, 44 WR 406, 74 LT 275, 12 TLR 270 ... 214.61
Gray, Re, Todd v Taylor [1925] Ch 362, [1925] All ER Rep 250, 94 LJ Ch 430, 69 Sol Jo 398, 133 LT 630, 41 TLR 335 ... 102.10, 103.3, 212.26
Gray v Barr [1970] 2 QB 626, [1970] 2 All ER 702, [1970] 3 WLR 108, [1970] 2 Lloyd's Rep 69, 114 Sol Jo 413; on appeal [1971] 2 QB 554, [1971] 2 All ER 949, [1971] 2 WLR 1334, [1971] 2 Lloyd's Rep 1, 115 Sol Jo 364, CA ... 9.15
Gray v Fidler [1943] KB 694, [1943] 2 All ER 289, 112 LJKB 627, 87 Sol Jo 362, 169 LT 193, 59 TLR 449, CA ... 204.18
Gray v Garman (1843) 2 Hare 268, 12 LJ Ch 259, 7 Jur 275 ... 68.6, 68.14
Gray v Golding (1860) 6 Jur NS 474, 8 WR 371, 2 LT 198, HL ... 93.8
Gray v Gray (1852) 2 Sim NS 273, 21 LJ Ch 745, 89 RR 297, 20 LTOS 23 ... 29.15
Gray v Gray (1889) 23 LR Ir 399 ... 34.15, 35.10, 35.11, 35.14

Gray v Perpetual Trustee Co Ltd [1928] AC 391, 97 LJPC 85, [1928] All ER Rep 758, 139 LT 469, 44 TLR 654 .... 2.3, 2.5, 2.6, 2.10, 40.13, 42.1
Gray v Richards Butler (a firm) (1996) [2001] WTLR 625, [1996] 29 LS Gaz R 29, 140 Sol Jo LB 194 .... 9.11, 12.3, 25.16, 221.45
Gray v Siggers (1880) 15 Ch D 74, 49 LJ Ch 819, 29 WR 13 .... 38.18, 38.23
Gray Estate, Re (1957) 22 WWR 241 .... 10.8
Gray Estate v Yule (1990) 73 DLR (4th) 162 .... 102.10
Gray's Estate, Re (1963) 107 Sol Jo 156 .... 17.4
Gray's Settlement, Re, Akers v Sears [1896] 2 Ch 802, 65 LJ Ch 858, 40 Sol Jo 702, 75 LT 407 .... 77.2
Gray's Trustees v Murray 1970 SLT 105 .... 1.3, 10.10, 15.1
Grayburn v Clarkson (1868) 3 Ch App 605, 37 LJ Ch 550, 16 WR 716, 18 LT 494 .... 38.15
Graydon v Hicks (1739) 2 Atk 16, 9 Mod Rep 215 .... 35.13
Grayson v Grayson [1922] St R Qd 155 .... 35.30
Grazebrook, Re, Chase v Layton [1928] VLR 75 .... 51.1
Grbic, Re [1969] NZLR 574 .... 9.19
Grealey v Sampson [1917] 1 IR 286, Ir CA 20.4, 22.2, 57.20, 88.4
Greally, Re, Travers v O'Donoghue [1910] 1 IR 239 .... 38.12
Greaves, Re, Greaves v Greaves [1954] 2 All ER 109, [1954] 1 WLR 760, 98 Sol Jo 337 .... 105.5
Greasley v Cooke [1980] 3 All ER 710, [1980] 1 WLR 1306, 124 Sol Jo 629, CA 43.1
Greated v Greated (1859) 26 Beav 621, 28 LJ Ch 756, 5 Jur NS 454, 7 WR 367, 33 LTOS 176 .... 56.1, 56.6
Greaves v Smith (1874) 22 WR 388, 29 LT 798 .... 38.23
Greaves' Settlement Trusts, Re (1883) 23 Ch D 313, 52 LJ Ch 753, 31 WR 807, 48 LT 414 .... 39.12
Greaves' Will Trusts, Re, Public Trustee v Ash [1954] Ch 434, [1954] 1 All ER 771, [1954] 2 WLR 557, 98 Sol Jo 214 .... 40.14, 40.17
Green, Re [1975] 1 NZLR 475 .... 47.31
Green, Re, Baldock v Green (1888) 40 Ch D 610, 58 LJ Ch 157, 37 WR 300, 60 LT 225 .... 30.3, 38.26, 62.2
Green, Re, Bath v Cannon [1914] 1 Ch 134, 83 LJ Ch 248, 58 Sol Jo 185, 110 LT 58 .... 71.1
Green, Re, Fitzwilliam v Green (1916) 50 ILT 179 .... 89.1
Green, Re, Lindner v Green [1951] Ch 148, [1950] 2 All ER 913, 94 Sol Jo 742, 66 (pt 2) TLR 819 .... 2.5, 2.6, 2.8, 2.9, 2.10, 201.310
Green, Re, McKenzie v Stringer [1963] NZLR 148 .... 67.2, 68.11, 76.1
Green, Re, Walsh v Green (1893) 31 LR Ir 338 .... 60.1
Green v Andrews (1877) 41 JP 105 .... 10.5
Green v Barrow (1853) 10 Hare 459, 1 WR 197, 21 LTOS 33 .... 97.1
Green v Belchier (1737) 1 Atk 505, West temp Hard 217 .... 32.20
Green v Britten (1872) 42 LJ Ch 187, 27 LT 811 .... 46.3
Green v Dunn (1855) 20 Beav 6, 24 LJ Ch 577, 3 WR 277, 25 LTOS 154 .... 38.3
Green v Gascoyne (1865) 4 De GJ & Sm 565, 34 LJ Ch 268, 11 Jur NS 145, 5 New Rep 227, 13 WR 371, 12 LT 35 .... 49.4, 50.3, 51.4
Green v Gaul [2006] WTLR 1391, CA 30.37
Green v Giles (1855) 5 I Ch R 25, 8 Ir Jur 90 .... 98.2
Green v Green (1845) 2 Jo & Lat 529 .... 35.12

Green v Green (1849) 3 De G & Sm 480, 18 LJ Ch 465, 14 Jur 74, 14 LTOS 3 .... 98.1, 98.2
Green v Harvey (1842) 1 Hare 428, 11 LJ Ch 290, 6 Jur 704 .... 56.1, 56.6
Green v Howard (1779) 1 Bro CC 31 .... 57.20
Green v IRC. See St Barbe Green v IRC
Green v Marsden (1853) 1 Drew 646, 22 LJ Ch 1092, 1 Eq Rep 437, 54 RR 789, 1 WR 511, 22 LTOS 17 .... 20.3, 79.2, 83.6
Green v Pertwee (1846) 5 Hare 249, 15 LJ Ch 372, 10 Jur 538, 7 LTOS 405 .... 38.14
Green v Pigot (1781) 2 Dick 585, 1 Bro CC 103 .... 29.3
Green v Symonds (1730) 1 Bro CC 129n 63.1
Green v Tribe (1878) 9 Ch D 231, 27 WR 39, 38 LT 914, sub nom Re Love, Green v Tribe 47 LJ Ch 783 .... 1.1, 18.15, 20.4, 21.7, 22.3, 48.5, 48.9
Green's Estate, Re (1860) 1 Drew & Sm 68, 29 LJ Ch 716, 6 Jur NS 479, 8 WR 403, 2 LT 791 .... 47.26, 93.19
Green's Will, Re, Crowson v Wild [1907] VLR 284 .... 91.5
Green's Will Trusts, Re, Fitzgerald-Hart v A-G [1985] 3 All ER 455 .... 9.2, 94.6, 102.13
Greenberry, Re, Hops v Daniell (1911) 55 Sol Jo 633 .... 41.14, 64.54
Greene, Re, Greene v Kirkwood [1895] 1 IR 130, 142 .... 35.2, 35.4
Greene v Potter (1843) 2 Y & C Ch Cas 517, 7 Jur 736 .... 93.12
Greenhill v Greenhill (1711) Gilb Ch 77, Prec Ch 320, 2 Vern 679, 1 Eq Cas Abr 174 pl 4 .... 60.1
Greenough v Martin (1824) 2 Add 239 .... 22.3
Greenslade, Re, Greenslade v McCowen [1915] 1 Ch 155, 84 LJ Ch 235, 59 Sol Jo 105, 112 LT 337 .... 40.5
Greenslade v Dare (1855) 20 Beav 284, 24 LJ Ch 490, 1 Jur NS 294, 3 WR 220 .... 4.20
Greenway v Greenway (1860) 2 De GF & J 128, 29 LJ Ch 601, 129 RR 41 .... 37.3, 78.5, 98.2, 98.7
Greenwich Hospital Improvement Act, Re (1855) 20 Beav 458 .... 38.4, 60.2, 64.51
Greenwood, Re, Goodhart v Woodhead [1902] 2 Ch 198, 71 LJ Ch 579, 86 LT 500, 18 TLR 530; revsd [1903] 1 Ch 749, 72 LJ Ch 281, 51 WR 358, 47 Sol Jo 238, 88 LT 212, 19 TLR 180, CA 34.2, 34.8, 34.22, 34.24, 35.6, 35.39, 35.43, 93.3
Greenwood, Re, Greenwood v Sutcliffe [1912] 1 Ch 392, 81 LJ Ch 298, 56 Sol Jo 443, 106 LT 424 .... 47.23, 47.33
Greenwood, Re, Sutcliffe v Gledhill [1901] 1 Ch 887, 70 LJ Ch 326, 49 WR 461, [1900–3] All ER Rep 97, 84 LT 118 .... 99.4, 99.9
Greenwood v Greenwood (1790) 3 Curt App 1 .... 4.15
Greenwood v Greenwood (1877) 5 Ch D 954, 47 LJ Ch 298, 26 WR 5, 21 Sol Jo 630, 37 LT 305, CA 101.3
Greenwood v Greenwood [1939] 2 All ER 150n, 55 TLR 607, {C 93.28
Greenwood v Penny (1850) 12 Beav 403 .... 42.6
Greenwood v Percy (1859) 26 Beav 572 .... 67.4
Greenwood v Verdon (1854) 1 K & J 74, 24 LJ Ch 65, 3 Eq Rep 181, 3 WR 124 .... 98.10
Greenwood's Goods, Re [1892] P 7, 61 LJP 56, 66 LT 61 .... 11.3, 14.12
Greenwood's Will, Re (1861) 3 Giff 390, 31 LJ Ch 119, 8 Jur NS 907, 10 WR 117, 5 LT 487 .... 79.4
Greet v Greet (1842) 5 Beav 123 .... 93.40
Gregg v Coates (1856) 23 Beav 33, 2 Jur NS 964, 4 WR 735 .... 45.2

Gregg v Perpetual Trustee Co (1918) 35 WN 82, 18 SRNSW 252 ..... 42.6
Gregor v Kemp (1722) 3 Swan 404 ..... 3.8
Gregory, Re, Gregory v Goodenough [1971] 1 All ER 497, [1970] 1 WLR 1455, 114 Sol Jo 532, CA 105.23, 105.25
Gregory, Re, How v Charrington (1935) 79 Sol Jo 880, 52 TLR 130 ..... 91.1
Gregory v Gregory (1849) 13 Jur 843 ..... 18.19
Gregory v Hudson (1998) 45 NSWLR 300 ..... 1.6
Gregory v Queen's Proctor (1846) 7 LTOS 470, 4 Notes of Cases 620 ..... 13.1
Gregory v Smith (1852) 9 Hare 708 ..... 57.15, 79.1, 79.2
Gregory's Settlement and Will, Re (1865) 34 Beav 600, 11 Jur NS 634, 6 New Rep 282, 13 WR 828 ..... 51.11, 57.15
Gregson v Taylor [1917] P 256, 86 LJP 124, sub nom Re Philpot, Gregson v Taylor 61 Sol Jo 578, 117 LT 318, 33 TLR 402 ..... 5.1, 5.7, 51.4
Gregson's Trusts, Re (1864) 2 Hem & M 504, 33 LJ Ch 531, 10 Jur NS 696, 4 New Rep 222, 12 WR 935, 10 LT 642; on appeal (1864) 2 De GJ & Sm 428, 34 LJ Ch 41, 10 Jur NS 1138, 5 New Rep 99, 13 WR 193, 11 LT 460 ..... 57.12, 57.15, 67.2, 97.9
Greig v Martin (1859) 5 Jur NS 329, 7 WR 315, 33 LTOS 41 ..... 53.5
Gresham Life Assurance Society v Crowther [1915] 1 Ch 214, 84 LJ Ch 312, [1914–15] All ER Rep 991, 59 Sol Jo 103, 111 LT 887, CA 37.3
Gresley v Mousley (1859) 4 De G & J 78, 28 LJ Ch 620, 5 Jur NS 583, 124 RR 164, 7 WR 427, 33 LTOS 154 ..... 7.8
Gresley's Settlement, Re, Willoughby v Drummond [1911] 1 Ch 358, 80 LJ Ch 255, 104 LT 244 ..... 47.12, 47.23
Gretton v Haward (1819) 1 Swan 409 ..... 42.1
Greville v Browne (1859) 7 HL Cas 689, [1843–60] All ER Rep 888, 5 Jur NS 849, 7 WR 673, 34 LTOS 8 ..... 50.18, 210.6
Greville v Tylee (1851) 7 Moo PCC 320 ..... 5.9, 14.1, 14.4, 14.6, 14.10
Grey v Pearson. See Pearson v Rutter
Grey's Trusts, Re, Grey v Stamford [1892] 3 Ch 88, 61 LJ Ch 622, 41 WR 60, 36 Sol Jo 523 ..... 72.7
Grieve v Grieve (1867) LR 4 Eq 180, 36 LJ Ch 932, 15 WR 577, 16 LT 201 ..... 85.2
Grieves v Rawley (1852) 10 Hare 63, 22 LJ Ch 625 ..... 70.1
Griffin v McCabe (1918) 52 ILT 134 ..... 8.4
Griffith, Re [1951] 1 DLR 551, 27 MPR 181 ..... 47.32
Griffith v Bourke (1888) 21 LR Ir 92 ..... 44.14
Griffith v Chomley (1868) 5 WW & A'B (Eq) 186 ..... 47.28
Griffith v Jones (1686) Freem Ch 96, 2 Rep Ch 394 ..... 79.4
Griffith v Pownall (1843) 13 Sim 393 ..... 94.47
Griffith's Goods, Re (1872) LR 2 P & D 457, 36 JP 424, 20 WR 495, 26 LT 780 ..... 18.14
Griffiths, Re [1955] NZLR 127 ..... 13.2
Griffiths, Re, Griffiths v Griffiths [1926] VLR 212, 47 ALT 171, [1926] Argus LR 107 ..... 79.4
Griffiths, Re, Haworth v Welton [1945] 1 All ER 610, CA 33.30
Griffiths, Re, Jones v Jenkins [1926] Ch 1007, 95 LJ Ch 429, [1926] B & CR 56, [1926] All ER Rep 639, 70 Sol Jo 735, 136 LT 57 ..... 99.6
Griffiths v Gale (1844) 12 Sim 327, 354, 13 LJ Ch 286, 8 Jur 235, 3 LTOS 17 ..... 47.14, 47.38
Griffiths v Pruen (1840) 11 Sim 202 ..... 30.14

Griffiths v Smith (1790) 1 Ves 97 .... 34.23
Griffiths v Vere (1803) 148 RR 317, Tudor LC Real Prop 618, 9 Ves 127 .... 95.8
Griffiths' Estate, Re, Morgan v Stephens [1917] P 59, 86 LJP 42, 116 LT 382 .... 93.20
Griffiths' Policy, Re [1903] 1 Ch 739, 72 LJ Ch 330, 88 LT 547 .... 80.1
Griffiths' Settlement, Re, Griffiths v Waghorne [1911] 1 Ch 246, 80 LJ Ch 176, 104 LT 125 .... 47.17, 73.2
Griffyn v Griffyn (1740) Barn Ch 391 .... 55.4
Griggs v Gibson, ex p Maynard (No 2) (1866) 35 LJ Ch 458, 14 WR 538 ... 47.14, 47.36
Grimond v Grimond [1905] AC 124, 74 LJPC 35, 92 LT 477, 21 TLR 323, HL 1.6
Grimshaw's Trusts, Re (1879) 11 Ch D 406, 48 LJ Ch 399, 27 WR 544 .... 93.36
Grimshawe v Pickup (1839) 9 Sim 591, 3 Jur 286 .... 56.3
Grimston v Lord Bruce (1707) 1 Salk 156, 2 Vern 594 .... 34.25
Grimwood, Re, Trewhella v Grimwood [1946] Ch 54, [1945] 2 All ER 686, 115 LJ Ch 21, 89 Sol Jo 579, 174 LT 76, 62 TLR 40 .... 64.47
Grisor, Re (1980) 101 DLR (3d) 728 .... 2.6
Grissell v Swinhoe (1869) LR 7 Eq 291, 17 WR 438 .... 42.8
Groffman, Re, Groffman and Block v Groffman [1969] 2 All ER 108, [1969] 1 WLR 733, 113 Sol Jo 58 .... 11.24, 12.3
Groom, Re, Booty v Groom [1897] 2 Ch 407, 66 LJ Ch 778, 77 LT 154 .... 55.7, 69.2
Groom v Thomas (1829) 2 Hag Ecc 433 .... 4.13, 4.14
Groos, Re, Groos v Groos [1915] 1 Ch 572, 84 LJ Ch 422, 59 Sol Jo 477, 112 LT 984 .... 24.2
Groos' Estate, Re [1904] P 269, 73 LJP 82, 91 LT 322 .... 23.15
Grosvenor, Re, Grosvenor v Grosvenor [1916] 2 Ch 375, 85 LJ Ch 735, 60 Sol Jo 681, 115 LT 298 .... 30.34, 206.15
Grosvenor v Durston (1858) 25 Beav 97 .... 42.5, 64.35
Grotrian, Re, Cox v Grotrian [1955] Ch 501, [1955] 1 All ER 788, [1955] 2 WLR 695, 99 Sol Jo 220 .... 94.2
Grove, Re, Public Trustee v Dixon [1919] 1 Ch 249, 88 LJ Ch 96, 63 Sol Jo 213, 120 LT 382 .... 34.8, 35.12, 93.2
Grove's Trusts, Re (1859) 1 Giff 74, 28 LJ Ch 536, 5 Jur NS 855, 7 WR 522, 33 LTOS 365 .... 33.12
Grove's Trusts, Re (1862) 3 Giff 575, 9 Jur NS 38, 6 LT 376 .... 93.30
Grove-Grady, Re, Plowden v Lawrence [1929] 1 Ch 557, 98 LJ Ch 261, [1929] All ER Rep 158, 73 Sol Jo 158, 140 LT 659, 45 TLR 261, CA; on appeal sub nom A-G v Plowden [1931] WN 89, 171 LT Jo 308, 71 L Jo 329, HL 9.31, 102.10, 102.13
Grovenor, Re [1965] NSWR 723 .... 102.26
Grover v Burningham (1850) 5 Exch 184 .... 49.2
Grover v Raper (1856) 5 WR 134, 28 LTOS 215 .... 52.11
Grover's Will Trusts, Re, National Provincial Bank Ltd v Clarke [1971] Ch 168, [1970] 1 All ER 1185, [1970] 2 WLR 574, 114 Sol Jo 207 .... 104.14
Groves v Wright (1856) 2 K & J 347, 2 Jur NS 277 .... 8.4
Grylls' Trusts, Re (1868) LR 6 Eq 589 .... 55.3
Guardhouse v Blackburn (1866) LR 1 P & D 109, 35 LJP & M 116, 12 Jur NS 278, 14 WR 463, [1861–73] All ER Rep 680, 14 LT 69 .... 5.1, 5.7, 10.7, 51.4
Guardian Trust and Executors Co Ltd v Smith [1923] NZLR 1284 .... 54.2

Guardian Trust and Executors Co of New Zealand Ltd v Public Trustee of New Zealand [1942] AC 115, [1942] 1 All ER 598, 111 LJPC 119, 167 LT 162, 58 TLR 132, [1942] NZLR 294, sub nom Public Trustee of New Zealand v Guardian Trust and Executors Co of New Zealand Ltd [1942] 2 WWR 289 .... 25.15
Guardian Trusts Executors Co of New Zealand Ltd v Inwood [1946] NZLR 614 .... 2.4
Gude v Worthington (1849) 3 De G & Sm 389, 18 LJ Ch 303, 13 Jur 847, 13 LTOS 88 .... 82.8
Gue, Re, Smith v Gue [1892] WN 88, 61 LJ Ch 510, 40 WR 552, 36 Sol Jo 503, 67 LT 823; affd [1892] WN 132, 36 Sol Jo 698, CA 71.1
Guedalla, Re, Lee v Guedalla's Trustee [1905] 2 Ch 331, [1904–7] All ER Rep 1012, 75 LJ Ch 52, 12 Mans 392, 54 WR 77, 94 LT 94 .... 39.6, 39.12
Guerin v Guerin [1962] SCR 550 .... 4.13
Guest v Webb [1965] VR 427 .... 36.11
Guild (Executor nominate of the late James Young Russell) v IRC [1992] 2 AC 310, [1992] 2 All ER 10, [1992] 2 WLR 397, [1992] STC 162, 1992 SLT 438, 136 Sol Jo LB 88, HL 102.1, 102.12
Guild v Mallory (1983) 144 DLR (3d) 603, 41 OR (2d) 21 .... 8.7
Guinness's Settlement, Re, Guinness v SG Warburg (Executor and Trustee) Ltd [1966] 2 All ER 497, [1966] 1 WLR 1355, 110 Sol Jo 636 .... 38.23, 38.25
Guiry v Condon [1918] 1 IR 23 .... 41.5
Gulbenkian's Settlement Trusts (No 2), Re, Stevens v Maun [1970] Ch 408, [1969] 2 All ER 1173, [1969] 3 WLR 450, 113 Sol Jo 758 .... 46.1
Gulbenkian's Settlements, Re, Hacobian v Maun [1968] Ch 126, [1967] 3 All ER 15, [1967] 3 WLR 1112, 111 Sol Jo 686, CA; affd sub nom Whishaw v Stephens [1970] AC 508, [1968] 3 WLR 1127, 112 Sol Jo 882, sub nom Re Gulbenkian's Settlement Trusts, Whishaw v Stephens [1968] 3 All ER 785, HL 1.6, 34.2, 34.9, 34.10, 39.31, 53.6, 105.47
Gullan v Grove (1858) 26 Beav 64 .... 18.23
Gullan's Goods, Re (1858) 27 LJP & M 15, 4 Jur NS 196, 1 Sw & Tr 23, 5 WR 307, 30 LTOS 326 .... 18.27
Gulliver v Vaux (1746) 8 De GM & G 167n, 114 RR 83 .... 83.8
Gulliver v Wickett (1745) 1 Wils 105 .... 93.19
Gulliver d Corrie v Ashby (1766) 4 Burr 1929, 1 Wm Bl 607 .... 34.2, 35.39, 35.40, 35.43
Gulliver d Jeffereys v Poyntz (1770) 3 Wils 141, 2 Wm Bl 726 .... 64.26
Gully v Dix [2004] EWCA Civ 139, [2004] 1 FCR 453, [2004] 1 FLR 918, [2004] Fam Law 334, [2004] 06 LS Gaz R 32, (2004) Times, 28 January, [2004] All ER (D) 162 (Jan), sub nom Dix, Re [2004] 1 WLR 1399 .... 105.14
Gun, Re, Sheehy v Nugent [1915] 1 IR 42 .... 79.4
Gundry v Pinniger (1852) 1 De GM & G 502, [1843–60] All ER Rep 403, 21 LJ Ch 405, 16 Jur 488, 18 LTOS 325 .... 77.3, 217.23
Gunn, Re (1912) 32 NZLR 153 .... 33.18
Gunning's Estate, Re (1884) 13 LR Ir 203 .... 93.41, 93.42
Gunning's Goods, Re (1846) 1 Rob Eccl 459, 5 Notes of Cases 75 .... 11.6
Gunstan's (or Gunston) Goods, Re, Blake v Blake (1882) 7 PD 102, 51 LJ Ch 377, 51 LJP 36, 30 WR 505, [1881–5] All ER Rep 870, 46 LT 641, CA 11.24, 12.3

Gunther's Will Trusts, Re, Alexander v Gunther [1939] Ch 985, [1939] 3 All ER 291, 108 LJ Ch 395, 83 Sol Jo 545, 161 LT 156, 55 TLR 890 ... 100.5
Gurney v Gurney (1855) 3 Drew 208, 24 LJ Ch 656, 3 Eq Rep 569, 1 Jur NS 298, 3 WR 353, 25 LTOS 30 ... 9.5
Gutheil v Ballarat Trustees, Executors and Agency Co Ltd (1922) 30 CLR 293, [1922] VLR 607, 28 Argus LR 223 ... 77.1
Guthrie, Re, Trustees, Executors and Agency Co of New Zealand Ltd v Guthrie [1925] NZLR 379 ... 38.6
Guthrie v Walrond (1883) 22 Ch D 573, 52 LJ Ch 165, 31 WR 285, 47 LT 614 ... 24.9, 32.2, 32.3, 46.3, 63.1, 207.18
Guy v Guy (1911) 30 NZLR 383 ... 82.4
Guy v Sharp (1833) 1 My & K 589, Coop temp Brough 80 ... 88.1
Guyton and Rosenberg's Contract, Re [1901] 2 Ch 591, 70 LJ Ch 751, 50 WR 38, 85 LT 66 ... 64.32
Gwillim v Gwillim (1859) 23 JP 825, Sea & Sm 26, 29 LJP & M 31, 3 Sw & Tr 200 ... 11.25
Gwilym, Re [1952] VLR 282 ... 103.6
Gwynne v Berry (1875) IR 9 CL 494 ... 98.11
Gyde, Re, Ward v Little (1898) 79 LT 261, 15 TLR 1, CA ... 102.26
Gyett v Williams (1862) 2 John & H 429, 6 LT 279 ... 30.1, 55.4
Gyles, Re, Gibbon v Chaytor [1907] 1 IR 65 ... 32.10
Gynes v Kemsley (1677) Freem KB 293 ... 58.9

H

H, Re [1990] 1 FLR 441, [1990] Fam Law 175 ... 9.15
H, Re, Smith v Public Trustee [1956] NZLR 48 ... 72.2
H v W (1857) 3 K & J 382, 112 RR 196, 69 ER 1157 ... 35.35
HMF, Re [1976] Ch 33, [1975] 2 All ER 795, [1975] 3 WLR 395, 119 Sol Jo 661 ... 4.22, 4.24
Habergham v Ridehalgh (1870) LR 9 Eq 395, 39 LJ Ch 545, 18 WR 427, 23 LT 214 ... 47.26, 47.32, 50.3, 68.9
Hack, Re, Beadman v Beadman [1925] Ch 633, 94 LJ Ch 343, 69 Sol Jo 662, 133 LT 134 ... 84.2
Hack v London Provident Building Society (1883) 23 Ch D 103, 52 LJ Ch 541, 31 WR 392, 48 LT 247, CA ... 50.21
Hacket, Re, Hacket v Gardiner [1907] 1 Ch 385, 76 LJ Ch 249, 96 LT 420 ... 214.62
Hackett's Goods, Re (1859) 28 LJP & M 42, 23 JP 152, 4 Sw & Tr 220 ... 16.8
Hadaway v Hadaway [1955] 1 WLR 16, 99 Sol Jo 27, PC ... 102.10
Haddelsey v Adams (1856) 22 Beav 266, 25 LJ Ch 826, 2 Jur NS 724, 27 LTOS 148 ... 67.8, 86.7
Hadden, Re, Public Trustee v More [1932] 1 Ch 133, [1931] All ER Rep 539, 75 Sol Jo 781, 146 LT 190, 48 TLR 9, sub nom Re Hadden, Public Trustee v Ware 101 LJ Ch 52 ... 102.10
Hadden's Will, Re (1879) 5 VLR 91 ... 25.1
Hadley, Re, Johnson v Hadley [1909] 1 Ch 20, 78 LJ Ch 254, 53 Sol Jo 46, 100 LT 54, 25 TLR 44, CA ... 24.12
Hadow v Hadow (1838) 9 Sim 438 ... 82.5

Hagen's Trusts, Re (1877) 46 LJ Ch 665 .... 67.6
Hagger, Re, Freeman v Arscott [1930] 2 Ch 190, [1930] All ER Rep 620, 99 LJ Ch 492, 143 LT 610 .... 2.2, 2.3, 2.6, 2.8
Hagger v Payne (1857) 23 Beav 474, 26 LJ Ch 617, 3 Jur NS 479, 29 LTOS 47 .... 66.11
Haidl v Sacher (1980) 106 DLR (3d) 360 .... 57.8, 87.1
Haig v Swiney (1823) 1 Sim & St 487, 2 LJOS Ch 26 .... 62.1
Haigh's Estate, Re, Haigh v Haigh (1907) 51 Sol Jo 343 .... 64.7
Hain's Settlement, Re, Tooth v Hain [1961] 1 All ER 848, [1961] 1 WLR 440, 105 Sol Jo 154, CA 53.6
Hains, Re, Hains v Elder's Trustee and Executor Co Ltd [1942] SASR 172 .... 34.10
Hains's Goods, Re (1847) 5 Notes of Cases 621 .... 18.19
Hair Estate, Re [1941] 2 WWR 159 .... 25.3
Halbert v Mynar [1981] 2 NSWLR 659 .... 70.2
Haldan v Beatty (1876) 40 UCR 110 .... 31.20
Haldorson Estate, Re (1953) 9 WWRNS 145 .... 44.15
Hale v Beck (1764) 2 Eden 229 .... 101.7
Hale v Hale (1692) Prec Ch 50 .... 73.1
Hale v Hale (1876) 3 Ch D 643, 24 WR 1065, 35 LT 933 .... 93.1, 93.7, 94.21
Hale's Goods, Re [1915] 2 IR 362 .... 16.3
Hales v Darell (1840) 3 Beav 324, 10 LJ Ch 10 .... 44.15
Hales v Margerum (1796) 3 Ves 299 .... 34.6
Haley v Bannister (1857) 23 Beav 336 .... 91.6
Halford v Halford [1897] P 36, 66 LJP 29, 75 LT 520, 13 TLR 69 .... 1.5
Halford v Stains (1849) 16 Sim 488, 13 Jur 73 .... 95.9
Hall, Re (1988) 50 DLR (4th) 51 .... 5.1, 5.2
Hall, Re, Barclays Bank Ltd v Hall [1951] 1 All ER 1073, 95 Sol Jo 300, [1951] 1 TLR 850 .... 30.8
Hall, Re, Branston v Weightman (1887) 35 Ch D 551, 56 LJ Ch 780, 35 WR 797, 57 LT 42 .... 72.2, 72.3
Hall, Re, Foster v Metcalfe [1903] 2 Ch 226, 72 LJ Ch 554, 51 WR 529, [1900–3] All ER Rep 371, 42 Sol Jo 514, 88 LT 619, CA 9.40, 29.1, 29.2, 29.3, 29.4, 30.33
Hall, Re, Hall v Hall [1932] 1 Ch 262, 101 LJ Ch 129, [1931] All ER Rep 88, 147 LT 33 .... 71.3, 72.2
Hall, Re, Hope v Hall [1918] 1 Ch 562, 87 LJ Ch 393, 62 Sol Jo 505, 118 LT 700 .... 44.15
Hall, Re, Parker v Knight [1948] Ch 437, [1948] LJR 1430, 92 Sol Jo 310, 64 TLR 243 .... 74.2, 87.1, 87.2
Hall, Re, Public Trustee v Montgomery [1944] Ch 46, [1943] 2 All ER 753, 113 LJ Ch 67, 87 Sol Jo 423, 169 LT 387, 60 TLR 84 .... 99.4, 99.7
Hall, Re, Sheil v Clark [1890] 1 IR 308 .... 101.9
Hall, Re, Watson v Hall (1912) 56 Sol Jo 615, 107 LT 196, 28 TLR 480 .... 64.8
Hall v Derby Borough Urban Sanitary Authority (1885) 16 QBD 163, 50 JP 278, 55 LJMC 21, 54 LT 175, 2 TLR 81 .... 102.7, 102.10
Hall v Fennell (1875) IR 9 Eq 615, 10 ILT 1 .... 64.7
Hall v Fisher (1844) 1 Coll 47, 8 Jur 119 .... 58.6, 64.22
Hall v Hall (1868) LR 1 P & D 481, 32 JP 503, 37 LJP & M 40, 16 WR 544, 18 LT 152 .... 5.9

Hall v Hall [1891] 3 Ch 389, 60 LJ Ch 802, 40 WR 138, 35 Sol Jo 695, 65 LT 643; affd [1892] 1 Ch 361, 61 LJ Ch 289, 40 WR 277, 36 Sol Jo 200, 66 LT 206, CA 38.7, 51.1, 51.3, 64.15, 64.16
Hall v Hill (1841) 4 I Eq R 27, 1 Con & Law 120, 1 Dr & War 94 ... 44.13, 44.14, 44.15, 44.16, 57.31
Hall v Lietch (1870) LR 9 Eq 376, 18 WR 423, 23 LT 298 .... 101.1
Hall v Robertson (1853) 22 LJ Ch 1054, 1 Eq Rep 245, 17 Jur 874, 1 WR 464, 21 LTOS 192; on appeal (1853) 4 De GM & G 781, 23 LJ Ch 241, 2 Eq Rep 15, 18 Jur 635 .... 55.6
Hall v Robertson (1853) 4 De GM & G 781, 23 LJ Ch 241, 2 Eq Rep 15, 18 Jur 635, 1 WR 464 .... 55.6, 66.5
Hall v Terry (1738) 1 Atk 502, West temp Hard 500 .... 93.44
Hall v Turner (1880) 14 Ch D 829, 44 JP 734, 28 WR 859, 42 LT 495, [1874–80] All ER Rep Ext 1448 .... 30.42
Hall v Warren (1804) 9 Ves 605 .... 4.14, 4.20
Hall v Warren (1861) 9 HL Cas 420, 7 Jur NS 1089, 10 WR 66, 5 LT 190 .... 50.2, 50.7, 51.3, 93.9
Hall's Estate, Re [1943] 2 All ER 159 .... 202.40
Hall's Estate, Re [1944] IR 54 .... 97.1
Hall's Estate, Re, Hall v Knight and Baxter [1914] P 1, 83 LJP 1, [1911–13] All ER Rep 381, 58 Sol Jo 30, 109 LT 587, 30 TLR 1, CA 9.13, 9.14, 9.15, 9.16
Hall's Goods, Re (1871) LR 2 P & D 256, 35 JP 808, 40 LJP & M 37, 19 WR 897, 25 LT 384 .... 10.14, 14.8
Hall's Settlement Trusts, Re, Samuel v Lamont [1937] Ch 227, [1937] 1 All ER 571, 106 LJ Ch 111, 81 Sol Jo 179, 156 LT 269, 53 TLR 382 .... 47.1
Hall's Will, Re (1855) 1 Jur NS 974 .... 8.4
Hall-Dare, Re, Le Marchant v Lee Warner [1916] 1 Ch 272, 85 LJ Ch 365, 114 LT 559 .... 29.14, 55.6, 55.7
Hallett, Re, Hallett v Hallett [1892] WN 148 .... 73.1
Hallett v Hallett (1898) 14 TLR 420, CA 58.6, 63.9, 64.22
Hallifax v Wilson (1809) 16 Ves 168; affd (1812) 16 Ves 168 .... 93.29, 97.8
Hallinan's Trusts, Re [1904] 1 IR 452, CA 94.48
Halpin's Goods, Re (1873) 8 IR Eq 567 .... 10.5
Halsted's Will Trusts, Re, Halsted v Halsted [1937] 2 All ER 570 .... 218.94
Halston, Re, Ewen v Halston [1912] 1 Ch 435, 81 LJ Ch 265, [1911–13] All ER Rep 667, 56 Sol Jo 311, 106 LT 182 .... 57.22, 58.11
Halton v Foster (1868) 3 Ch App 505, 37 LJ Ch 547, 16 WR 683, 18 LT 623 .... 77.1, 77.2
Hambleton, Re, Hamilton v Hambleton [1884] WN 157 .... 96.4
Hambro's Marriage Settlements, Re, Hambro v Hambro [1949] Ch 484, [1949] LJR 1062, CA 39.28
Hambrough's Estate, Re, Hambrough v Hambrough [1909] 2 Ch 620, 79 LJ Ch 19, 53 Sol Jo 770, 101 LT 521 .... 218.66
Hamer's Estate, Re (1943) 113 LJP 31, 60 TLR 168 .... 14.2
Hamilton, Re (1941) 47 ALR 52, [1941] VLR 60 .... 17.4
Hamilton, Re [1953] QSR 48 .... 56.8, 56.9, 93.29
Hamilton, Re, Bazeley v Royal National Hospital for Consumption (President and Governors) (1890) 6 TLR 173, CA 64.23

Hamilton, Re, Hamilton v Hamilton (1907) 25 NZLR 218 .... 35.21
Hamilton v Baldwin (1852) 15 Beav 232 .... 61.1
Hamilton v Buckmaster (1866) LR 3 Eq 323, 36 LJ Ch 58, 12 Jur NS 986, 15 WR 149, 15 LT 177 .... 49.9, 60.2
Hamilton v Carroll (1839) 1 I Eq R 175 .... 22.3
Hamilton v Hart (1919) 47 DLR 231, [1919] 2 WWR 164 .... 97.8
Hamilton v Kirwan (1845) 2 Jo & Lat 393 .... 40.15
Hamilton v Mills (1861) 29 Beav 193, 13 LT 766 .... 78.4, 78.5
Hamilton v Ritchie [1894] AC 310, HL 50.6, 93.2
Hamilton Corpn v Hodsdon (1847) 6 Moo PCC 76, 11 Jur 193 .... 38.5, 64.19
Hamilton's Trustees v Hamilton (1901) 39 SLR 159, 1901 4 F 266 .... 10.9
Hamlet, Re, Stephen v Cunningham (1888) 39 Ch D 426, 58 LJ Ch 242, 37 WR 245, 59 LT 745, 4 TLR 752, CA 50.21, 51.7, 51.10, 96.4
Hamley v Gilbert (1821) Jac 354 .... 82.5
Hammersley, Re, Foster v Hammersley [1965] Ch 481, [1965] 2 All ER 24, [1965] 2 WLR 938, 109 Sol Jo 198 .... 92.5
Hammersley, Re, Heasman v Hammersley (1899) 81 LT 150 .... 64.17
Hammersley, Re, Kitchen v Myers (1886) 2 TLR 459 .... 71.1
Hammersley v Baron de Biel (1845) 12 Cl & Fin 45, 69 RR 18, HL 3.2, 3.3, 3.6
Hammill v Hammill (1884) 9 OR 530 .... 64.16
Hammond, Re, Burniston v White [1911] 2 Ch 342, 80 LJ Ch 690, 55 Sol Jo 649, 105 LT 302, 27 TLR 522 .... 33.20, 80.2, 80.4, 80.6
Hammond, Re, Hammond v Treharne [1938] 3 All ER 308, 82 Sol Jo 523, 54 TLR 903 .... 52.7
Hammond, Re, Parry v Hammond [1924] 2 Ch 276, 93 LJ Ch 620, [1924] All ER Rep 183, 68 Sol Jo 706, 131 LT 632 .... 68.2, 85.4, 85.5
Hammond v Maule (1844) 13 LJ Ch 386, 1 Coll 281, 8 Jur 568, 3 LTOS 261 .... 93.31
Hammond v Neame (1818) 1 Wils Ch 9, 1 Swan 35 .... 82.7
Hammond v Osborn [2002] EWCA Civ 885, [2002] WTLR 1125, 146 Sol Jo LB 176, [2002] 34 LS Gaz R 29, [2002] 2 P & CR D41, (2001) Times, 18 July, [2002] All ER (D) 232 (Jun) 5.9
Hammond v Smith (1864) 33 Beav 452, 10 Jur NS 117, 12 WR 328, 9 LT 746, [1861–73] All ER Rep Ext 1525 .... 44.15
Hammond's Estate, Re [1935] SCR 550, [1935] 4 DLR 209 .... 33.25
Hammond's Goods, Re (1863) 27 JP 521, 32 LJPM & A 200, 9 Jur NS 581, 3 Sw & Tr 90, 11 WR 639, 8 LT 516 .... 11.3, 12.3
Hampden Settlement Trusts, Re [1977] TR 177 .... 218.96, 218.98, 242.19
Hampshire's Estate, Re [1951] WN 174 .... 18.8
Hampson v Guy (1891) 64 LT 778, CA 5.9
Hampton v Holman (1877) 5 Ch D 183, 46 LJ Ch 248, 25 WR 459, 36 LT 287 .... 50.3, 94.8
Hanbey's Will Trusts, Re, Cutlers' Co v President and Governors of Christ's Hospital, London (or London Corpn) [1956] Ch 264, [1955] 3 All ER 874, [1956] 2 WLR 23, 100 Sol Jo 15 .... 103.18
Hanbury, Re, Comiskey v Hanbury (1909) 53 Sol Jo 616, 101 LT 32, 25 TLR 654 .... 38.26
Hanbury v Bateman [1920] 1 Ch 313, 89 LJ Ch 134, 122 LT 765 .... 40.7
Hanbury v Hanbury (1788) 2 Bro CC 352 .... 44.11

Hanbury v Hanbury [1999] 3 FCR 217, [1999] 2 FLR 255, [1999] Fam Law 447 .... 105.41, 105.43
Hanbury v Spooner (1843) 5 Beav 630, 12 LJ Ch 434 .... 30.15
Hancock, Re [1999] 1 FCR 500, [1998] 2 FLR 346, [1998] Fam Law 520, CA 105.16
Hancock, Re, Hancock v Pawson [1905] 1 Ch 16, 74 LJ Ch 69, 53 WR 89, 91 LT 737 .... 42.6, 42.9
Hancock, Re, Malcolm v Burford-Hancock [1896] 2 Ch 173, 65 LJ Ch 690, 44 WR 545, 40 Sol Jo 498, 74 LT 658, CA 40.13
Hancock v Clavey (1871) 19 WR 1044, 25 LT 323 .... 84.2
Hancock v Podmore (1830) 1 B & Ad 260, 8 LJOSKB 403 .... 202.5
Hancock v Watson [1902] AC 14, 71 LJ Ch 149, 50 WR 321, [1900–3] All ER Rep 87, 85 LT 729, HL 82.4, 93.19, 94.21, 94.25, 94.31
Hand's Goods, Re (1849) 13 Jur 663, 13 LTOS 405, 7 Notes of Cases 59 .... 64.35
Handcock's Trusts, Re (1889) 23 LR Ir 34, 42 .... 42.4
Handley v Stacey (1858) 1 F & F 253, 574 .... 4.19
Hanlon, Re, Heads v Hanlon [1933] Ch 254, 102 LJ Ch 62, [1932] All ER Rep 851, 76 Sol Jo 868, 148 LT 448 .... 34.13
Hannah, Re [1954] NZLR 836 .... 18.12
Hannah's Will, Re, Shields v A-G (1939) 34 Tas LR 45 .... 79.4
Hannam, Re, Haddelsey v Hannam [1897] 2 Ch 39, 66 LJ Ch 471, 45 WR 613, 76 LT 681 .... 47.32, 68.8
Hannam v Sims (1858) 2 De G & J 151, 27 LJ Ch 251, 4 Jur NS 863, 6 WR 347, 30 LTOS 358 .... 68.4, 93.9
Hannam's Goods, Re (1850) 14 Jur 558, 15 LTOS 188, 7 Notes of Cases 437 .... 12.3
Hansen Estate, Re (1951) 4 WWRNS 358 .... 68.9
Hansley v Wills (1866) 14 LT 162 .... 86.5
Hanson v Graham (1801) 6 Ves 239 .... 93.27, 93.35
Haque v Haque (1962) 108 CLR 230 .... 24.2
Haque v Haque [1963] WALR 15; affd [1964] ALR 34 .... 3.5
Haque v Haque (No 2) (1965) 114 CLR 98, [1966] ALR 553, Aus HC 23.5
Harari's Settlement Trusts, Re, Wordsworth v Fanshawe [1949] 1 All ER 430, [1949] WN 79, [1949] LJR 675, 93 Sol Jo 102 .... 220.29
Harbin v Masterman (1871) LR 12 Eq 559 .... 102.7, 102.22
Harbin v Masterman [1894] 2 Ch 184, 63 LJ Ch 388, 7 R 159, 38 Sol Jo 306, 70 LT 357, 10 TLR 340, CA; affd sub nom Wharton v Masterman [1895] AC 186, [1895–9] All ER Rep 687, 64 LJ Ch 369, 11 R 169, 43 WR 449, 72 LT 431, 11 TLR 301, HL 30.36, 32.17, 33.25, 34.5, 93.27, 95.12, 102.28, 212.11
Harbin v Masterman [1896] 1 Ch 351, [1895–9] All ER Rep 695, 65 LJ Ch 195, 44 WR 421, 40 Sol Jo 129, 73 LT 591, 12 TLR 105, CA 33.2, 33.24
Harbison, Re, Morris v Larkin [1902] 1 IR 103 .... 82.7
Harby v Moore (1860) 6 Jur NS 883, 3 LT 209 .... 8.7
Harcourt, Re, Fitzwilliam v Portman [1920] 1 Ch 492, 89 LJ Ch 655, 123 LT 36 .... 89.1
Harcourt v Harcourt (1857) 26 LJ Ch 536, 5 WR 478, 29 LTOS 174 .... 86.5
Harcourt v Morgan (1838) 2 Keen 274 .... 61.1, 64.39
Harcourt v Seymour (1851) 2 Sim NS 12, 15 Jur 740, 18 LTOS 16, sub nom Seymour v Lord Vernon 20 LJ Ch 606 .... 37.8

Hardacre v Nash (1794) 5 Term Rep 716 .... 55.4
Hardcastle v Hardcastle (1862) 1 Hem & M 405, 1 New Rep 83, 7 LT 503 .... 93.41, 93.42
Hardcastle (Vernede's Executors) v IRC [2000] STC (SCD) 532 .... 205.61
Hardebol v Perpetual Trustee Co Ltd [1975] 1 NSWLR 221 .... 94.2
Harding, Re [1956] NZLR 482 .... 76.1, 93.38
Harding, Re, Drew v St Thomas's Hospital (1910) 55 Sol Jo 93, 27 TLR 102 .... 64.35, 64.36
Harding v Glyn (1739) 1 Atk 469, 5 Ves 501 .... 79.4
Harding (Loveday's Executors) v IRC [1997] STC (SCD) 321 .... 204.10, 225.85, 242.4
Hardingham v Thomas (1854) 2 Drew 353, 23 LJ Ch 910, 2 WR 547 .... 44.1, 44.17
Hardwick v Hardwick (1873) LR 16 Eq 168, 42 LJ Ch 636, 21 WR 719 .... 58.1, 58.2, 58.8, 63.3, 63.7
Hardwick v Thurston (1828) 4 Russ 380, 6 LJOS Ch 124 .... 47.37
Hardwicke (Earl) v Douglas (1840) 7 Cl & Fin 795, West 555, HL 18.33, 52.1, 52.9
Hardy, Re, Nelson v A-G [1933] NI 150 .... 103.6
Hardy, Re, Wells v Borwick (1881) 17 Ch D 798, 50 LJ Ch 241, 29 WR 834, 41 LT 49 .... 31.1
Hardy v Shaw [1976] Ch 82, [1975] 2 All ER 1052, [1975] 2 WLR 1002, 119 Sol Jo 408 .... 100.6
Hardy's Goods, Re (1861) 25 JP 407, 30 LJPM & A 142 .... 14.11
Hardyman, Re, Teesdale v McClintock [1925] Ch 287, 94 LJ Ch 204, [1925] All ER Rep 83, 133 LT 175 .... 20.3, 20.4, 80.1
Hare, Re (1959) 61 DLR 774 .... 74.2
Harford v Browning (1787) 1 Cox Eq Cas 302 .... 30.15
Hargreaves, Re, Hargreaves v Hargreaves (1902) 86 LT 43; varied [1900–3] All ER Rep 80, 88 LT 100, CA 100.5
Hargreaves, Re, Midgley v Tatley (1889) 43 Ch D 401, 59 LJ Ch 384, 38 WR 470, 62 LT 473, CA 94.8, 94.12, 94.43, 94.44
Hargreaves v Pennington (1864) 34 LJ Ch 180, 10 Jur NS 834, 12 WR 1047, 10 LT 857 .... 91.6
Hargrove's Trusts, Re (1873) IR 8 Eq 256 .... 101.9
Harington v Moffat (1853) 4 De GM & G 1, 22 LJ Ch 775, 1 Eq Rep 35, 1 WR 294 .... 61.1, 64.54
Harker's Will Trusts, Re, Kean v Harker [1969] 3 All ER 1, [1969] 1 WLR 1124, 113 Sol Jo 588 .... 47.4, 48.6, 66.13, 66.15, 66.19
Harland v Trigg (1782) 1 Bro CC 142 .... 79.2
Harland-Peck, Re, Hercy v Mayglothing [1941] Ch 182, [1940] 4 All ER 347, 110 LJ Ch 81, 84 Sol Jo 717, 164 LT 215, 57 TLR 118, CA 55.7, 214.7
Harlow v National Westminster Bank (3 January 1994, unreported) 105.16
Harman, Re, Lloyd v Tardy [1894] 3 Ch 607, 63 LJ Ch 822, 8 R 549, 71 LT 401 .... 24.16, 39.12, 50.8, 50.19
Harman v Anderson [1930] NZLR 67 .... 48.5
Harman v Gurner (1866) 35 Beav 478 .... 58.10, 63.4
Harmer, Re (1964) 42 DLR (2d) 321, [1964] 1 OR 367; affd sub nom Kilby v Meyers [1965] SCR 24 .... 52.3, 71.3
Harmes v Hinkson [1946] WN 118, 62 TLR 445, [1946] 3 DLR 497, PC 5.4
Harmore v Brook (1674) Cas temp Finch 183, 2 Rep Ch 92 .... 3.8
Harney v Towell. See Harvey v Towell
Harper, Re (1843) 6 Man & G 732, 7 Scott NR 431 .... 5.2

Harper, Re, Plowman v Harper [1914] 1 Ch 70, 83 LJ Ch 157, 58 Sol Jo 120, 109 LT 925 .... 74.2, 87.1
Harper's Goods, Re (1849) 7 Notes of Cases 44 .... 21.6
Harper's Trustee v Bain (1903) 40 SLR 476, 5 F 716, 10 SLT 758 .... 64.35
Harpur's Will Trusts, Re, Haller v A-G [1961] Ch 38, [1960] 3 All ER 237, [1960] 3 WLR 607, 104 Sol Jo 726; affd [1962] Ch 78, [1961] 3 All ER 588, [1961] 3 WLR 924, 105 Sol Jo 609, CA 102.23, 102.24
Harrington (Countess) v Atherton (1864) 2 De GJ & Sm 352, 10 Jur NS 1088, 5 New Rep 1, 13 WR 62, 11 LT 291 .... 38.17
Harrington v Gill (1983) 4 FLR 265, CA 105.18, 105.33
Harris, Re, Cope v Evans [1945] Ch 316, [1945] 1 All ER 702, 114 LJ Ch 302, 89 Sol Jo 282, 173 LT 284, 61 TLR 364 .... 99.4, 99.7
Harris, Re, Cheese v Lovejoy. See Cheese v Lovejoy
Harris, Re, Leacroft v Harris [1909] 2 Ch 206, 78 LJ Ch 448, 100 LT 805 .... 42.2
Harris, Re, Murray v Everard [1952] P 319, [1952] 2 All ER 409, 96 Sol Jo 563, [1952] 2 TLR 585 .... 11.2, 11.9
Harris v Berrall (1858) 1 Sw & Tr 153, 7 WR 19 .... 18.7, 18.31
Harris v Davis (1844) 1 Coll 416, 9 Jur 269 .... 18.15, 56.5, 78.5, 84.2, 98.1
Harris v Du Pasquier (1872) 20 WR 668, 26 LT 689 .... 102.25
Harris v Goddard [1983] 3 All ER 242, [1983] 1 WLR 1203, 46 P & CR 417, [1984] FLR 209, [1984] Fam Law 242, 127 Sol Jo 617, [1983] LS Gaz R 2517, 133 NLJ 958, CA 7.3
Harris v Harris (1861) 29 Beav 107, 7 Jur NS 955, 131 RR 475, 9 WR 444 .... 64.53
Harris v Harris (1869) 17 WR 790 .... 38.1, 52.11
Harris v James (1864) 12 WR 509 .... 38.10, 64.25
Harris v Knight (1890) 15 PD 170, 62 LT 507, 6 TLR 234, CA 13.2, 18.12
Harris v Lloyd (1823) Turn & R 310 .... 66.5
Harris v Loftus [1899] 1 IR 491 .... 76.3
Harris v Newton (1877) 46 LJ Ch 268, 25 WR 228, 36 LT 173 .... 77.1
Harris v Poyner (1852) 1 Drew 174, 21 LJ Ch 915, 16 Jur 880 .... 38.23, 207.2
Harris v Watkins (1856) 2 K & J 473 .... 46.1
Harris' Goods, Re (1860) 29 LJPM & A 79, 1 Sw & Tr 536, 8 WR 368, 2 LT 118 .... 14.1, 19.4
Harris's Goods, Re (1875) 23 WR 734 .... 11.6
Harrison, Re, Day v Harrison (1920) 90 LJ Ch 186 .... 210.17
Harrison, Re, Harrison v Higson [1894] 1 Ch 561, 63 LJ Ch 385, 70 LT 868 .... 72.3
Harrison, Re, Townson v Harrison (1889) 43 Ch D 55, 59 LJ Ch 169, 38 WR 265, 61 LT 762 .... 38.27
Harrison, Re; Harrison v Gibson [2005] EWHC 2957 (Ch), [2006] 1 All ER 858, (2006) Times, 25 January, [2005] All ER (D) 345 (Dec), sub nom Harrison v Gibson [2006] 1 WLR 1212 .... 51.13, 83.10
Harrison, Re, Turner v Hellard (1885) 30 Ch D 390, 55 LJ Ch 799, 34 WR 420, 53 LT 799, CA 25.15, 50.8, 51.1, 57.5
Harrison v Asher (1848) 2 De G & Sm 436, 17 LJ Ch 452, 12 Jur 833, 12 LTOS 25 .... 41.11
Harrison v Buckle (1719) 1 Stra 238 .... 93.27
Harrison v Elvin (1842) 3 QB 117, 11 LJQB 197, 2 Gal & Dav 769, 6 Jur 849 .... 12.12
Harrison v Foreman (1800) 5 Ves 207 .... 67.7

Harrison v Grimwood (1849) 12 Beav 192, 18 LJ Ch 485, 13 Jur 864, 14 LTOS 502 ... 93.22, 93.35, 93.42
Harrison v Harrison (1829) 1 Russ & M 71, Taml 273 ... 69.2
Harrison v Harrison (1873) 8 Ch App 342, 42 LJ Ch 495, 21 WR 490, 28 LT 545 ... 42.2
Harrison v Harrison (1876) IR 10 Eq 290 ... 81.2
Harrison v Harrison [1901] 2 Ch 136, 70 LJ Ch 551, 49 WR 613, 45 Sol Jo 484, 85 LT 39 ... 67.4, 67.6
Harrison v Jackson (1877) 47 Ch 142, 7 Ch D 339 ... 41.14, 41.16
Harrison v Kirk [1904] AC 1, 73 LJPC 35, [1900–3] All ER Rep 680, 89 LT 566, HL ... 31.12, 31.13
Harrison v Mitchell (1731) 2 Barn KB 20, Fitz-G 303, sub nom Harrison v Weldon 2 Stra 911 ... 25.16
Harrison v Randall (1851) 9 Hare 397, 21 LJ Ch 294, 16 Jur 72 ... 40.14, 40.15, 40.20
Harrison v Rhodes (1753) 1 Lee 197 ... 32.13
Harrison v Rowley (1798) 4 Ves 212 ... 25.12, 30.15
Harrison v Southampton Corpn (1854) 18 JP 488, 23 LJ Ch 919, 18 Jur 669, 2 Sm & G 387, 2 WR 659, 23 LTOS 330 ... 102.10
Harrison v Tucker [2003] EWHC 1168 (Ch), 147 Sol Jo LB 692, [2003] All ER (D) 341 (May) ... 93.39
Harrison v Weldon. See Harrison v Mitchell
Harrison's Estate, Re (1870) 5 Ch App 408 ... 101.7
Harrison's Estate, Re (1879) 3 LR Ir 114 ... 76.3
Harrold v IRC [1996] STC (SCD) 195 ... 234.3
Harrop's Estate, Re (1857) 21 JP 325, 3 Drew 726, 26 LJ Ch 516, 3 Jur NS 380, 5 WR 449, 29 LTOS 49 ... 37.8
Hart, Re, Hart v Arnold (1912) 107 LT 759 ... 100.5
Hart, Re, Smith v Clarke [1963] NSWR 627 ... 66.13, 95.13
Hart v Durand (1796) 3 Anst 684 ... 72.2
Hart v Griffiths-Jones [1948] 2 All ER 729 ... 7.33
Hart v Hernandez (1885) 52 LT 217 ... 64.35
Hart v Tribe (1853) 22 LJ Ch 890. See Hartley v Tribber
Hart v Tribe (1854) 18 Beav 215, 23 LJ Ch 462, 2 WR 289, 23 LTOS 124 ... 82.5
Hart v Tulk (1852) 2 De GM & G 300, 22 LJ Ch 649, 21 LTOS 174 ... 51.7, 51.8, 52.4
Hart's Trusts, Re, ex p Block (1858) 3 De G & J 195, 28 LJ Ch 7, 4 Jur NS 1264, 7 WR 28, 32 LTOS 98 ... 93.24, 93.32, 93.35
Hart's Will Trusts, Re, Public Trustee v Barclays Bank Ltd [1950] Ch 84, [1949] 2 All ER 898, 93 Sol Jo 791, 65 TLR 742 ... 94.12, 101.13
Harter v Harter (1873) LR 3 P & D 11, 37 JP 583, 42 LJP & M 1, 21 WR 341, 27 LT 858 ... 5.1, 5.7
Hartigan, Re [1989] 2 Qd R 401 ... 48.5
Hartland, Re, Banks v Hartland [1911] 1 Ch 459, sub nom Re Dixon Hartland, Banks v Hartland 80 LJ Ch 305, 55 Sol Jo 312, 104 LT 490 ... 214.62
Hartley, Re, Stedman v Dunster (1887) 34 Ch D 742, 56 LJ Ch 564, 35 WR 624, 56 LT 565 ... 34.21, 35.48
Hartley v Ostler (1856) 22 Beav 449, 2 Jur NS 1199 ... 33.10
Hartley v Tribber (1853) 16 Beav 510, sub nom Hart v Tribe 22 LJ Ch 890, 21 LTOS 29 ... 20.3
Hartley Colliery Accident Relief Fund, Re, Plummer v Jordan (1908) 102 LT 165n ... 102.7

Hartley's Goods, Re (1880) 50 LJP 1, 29 WR 356 .... 18.14
Hartley's Trusts, Re (1878) 47 LJ Ch 610, 26 WR 590 .... 30.24, 30.26
Hartopp v Hartopp (1810) 17 Ves 184 .... 44.10
Hartshorne v Nicholson (1858) 22 JP 671, 26 Beav 58, 27 LJ Ch 810, 4 Jur NS 864 .... 102.22
Harvey, Re, Banister v Thirtle [1950] 1 All ER 491, 66 (pt 1) TLR 609 .... 39.31
Harvey, Re, Jenkinson v McWatters [1962] NZLR 524 .... 63.1
Harvey, Re, Peek v Savory (1888) 39 Ch D 289, 60 LT 79, CA 94.21
Harvey, Re, Public Trustee v Hoskin [1947] Ch 285, [1947] 1 All ER 349, [1947] LJR 1015, 91 Sol Jo 148, 177 LT 133 .... 41.18
Harvey v Cooke (1827) 4 Russ 34, 6 LJOS Ch 84 .... 61.1
Harvey v Harvey (1842) 5 Beav 134, [1835–42] All ER Rep 544 .... 38.23, 83.6, 83.11
Harvey v Harvey (1863) 32 Beav 441 .... 64.20
Harvey v Harvey (1875) 23 WR 478, 32 LT 141 .... 39.16
Harvey v Harvey (1915) 50 ILT 12 .... 33.11
Harvey v Lady Aston (1737) 2 Eq Cas Abr 539, 1 Atk 361, 2 Com 726, sub nom Hervey v Aston West temp Hard 350 .... 34.13, 34.15, 35.10, 35.11, 35.16
Harvey v Stracey (1852) 1 Drew 73, 22 LJ Ch 13, 16 Jur 771, 20 LTOS 61 .... 39.18, 39.21, 40.21, 66.11
Harvey v Towell (1847) 7 Hare 231, 17 LJ Ch 217, 68 ER 94, sub nom Harney v Towell 12 Jur 241 .... 84.3, 84.4
Harvey's Estate, Re, Harvey v Gillow [1893] 1 Ch 567, 62 LJ Ch 328, 3 R 247, 41 WR 293, 37 Sol Jo 212, 68 LT 562, 9 TLR 187 .... 47.12, 47.33, 66.6
Harward, Re, Newton v Bankes [1938] Ch 632, [1938] 2 All ER 804, 107 LJ Ch 307, 159 LT 354, 54 TLR 784 .... 47.25, 219.26
Harwood, Re, Coleman v Innes [1936] Ch 285, 105 LJ Ch 142, [1935] All ER Rep 918, 154 LT 624 .... 103.3, 103.5
Harwood v Baker (1840) 3 Moo PCC 282 .... 4.10, 4.13, 4.17
Haseldine, Re, Grange v Sturdy (1886) 31 Ch D 511, 50 JP 390, 34 WR 327, 54 LT 322, 2 TLR 256, CA 72.2
Haselgrove, Re [1950] SASR 99 .... 11.4
Haskell v Marlow [1928] 2 KB 45, 97 LJKB 311, 138 LT 521, 44 TLR 171 .... 208.27
Hasker v Sutton (1824) 1 Bing 500, 2 LJOSCP 68, 9 Moore CP 2 .... 56.2
Hasluck v Pedley (1874) LR 19 Eq 271, 44 LJ Ch 143, 23 WR 155 .... 54.4
Hassell v Hawkins (1859) 4 Drew 468, sub nom Russel v Hawkins 7 WR 314 .... 44.15
Hastead v Searle (1679) 1 Ld Raym 728 .... 63.2
Hastie's Trusts, Re (1887) 35 Ch D 728, 56 LJ Ch 792, 35 WR 692, 57 LT 168 .... 72.3
Hastilow v Stobie (1865) LR 1 P & D 64, 35 LJP & M 18, 11 Jur NS 1039, 14 WR 211, 13 LT 473 .... 1.6
Hastings v Hane (1833) 6 Sim 67 .... 64.35
Hastings' Goods, Re (1872) 36 JP 614, 20 WR 616, 26 LT 715 .... 18.15
Hastings-Bass, Re, Hastings-Bass v IRC [1975] Ch 25, [1974] 2 All ER 193, [1974] 2 WLR 904, [1974] STC 211, 53 ATC 87, [1974] TR 87, 118 Sol Jo 422, CA 218.95
Hatch, Re, Public Trustee v Hatch [1948] Ch 592, [1948] 2 All ER 288, [1948] LJR 1393, 92 Sol Jo 456 .... 99.4, 99.8
Hatch v Hatch (1855) 20 Beav 105, 3 WR 354 .... 33.23, 68.1

Hatfeild v Minet (1878) 8 Ch D 136, 47 LJ Ch 612, 26 WR 701, 38 LT 629, CA 44.4
Hatfeild's Will Trusts, Re, Hatfeild v Hatfeild [1958] Ch 469, [1957] 2 All ER 261, [1957] 3 WLR 28, 101 Sol Jo 480 .... 48.5, 48.8
Hatton v Finch (1841) 4 Beav 186, 5 Jur 548 .... 33.15
Hatton v Hooley. See Hooley v Hatton
Hatton v May (1876) 3 Ch D 148, 24 WR 754 .... 33.7
Haughton v Haughton (1824) 1 Mol 611, 614 .... 35.6, 35.34
Havelock v Havelock, Re Allan (1881) 17 Ch D 807, 50 LJ Ch 778, 29 WR 859, 44 LT 168 .... 218.66
Havergal v Harrison (1843) 7 Beav 49, 13 LJ Ch 36, 7 Jur 1100 .... 47.32
Haverland, Re (1975) 55 DLR (3d) 122 .... 13.1
Haverty v Curtis [1895] 1 IR 23 .... 39.18, 93.44
Haves, Re, Haves v Haves [1951] 2 All ER 928, 95 Sol Jo 728, [1951] 2 TLR 892 .... 44.15
Hawes v Hawes (1747) 1 Wils 165. See Haws v Haws
Hawes v Hawes (1880) 14 Ch D 614, 43 LT 280 .... 74.2
Hawker, Re [1939] SASR 426 .... 61.1
Hawkes v Baldwin (1838) 9 Sim 355, 7 LJ Ch 297, 2 Jur 698 .... 30.32, 35.39, 35.48
Hawkin's Trusts, Re (1864) 33 Beav 570, 34 LJ Ch 80, 10 Jur NS 922, 12 WR 945, 10 LT 557 .... 30.15
Hawkins, ex p (1843) 13 Sim 569, 2 LTOS 94 .... 41.5
Hawkins, Re, Hawkins v Argent (1913) 109 LT 969 .... 64.7
Hawkins, Re, Public Trustee v Shaw [1922] 2 Ch 569, 91 LJ Ch 486, 66 Sol Jo 612, 127 LT 488 .... 30.8, 204.51
Hawkins, Re, Walrond v Newton (1906) 22 TLR 521 .... 102.8
Hawkins, Re, White v White [1916] 2 Ch 570, 86 LJ Ch 25, 61 Sol Jo 29, 115 LT 543 .... 95.13
Hawkins v Hamerton (1848) 16 Sim 410, 13 JR 2 .... 98.7, 101.6
Hawkins v Hawkins (1880) 13 Ch D 470 .... 46.3
Hawkins v Kemp (1803) 3 East 410 .... 40.5, 40.6
Hawkins Estate, Re, Carlson and Pendray v Hawkins and Ellery [1941] 2 WWR 469 .... 14.4
Hawkinson and Hawkinson, Re (1977) 80 DLR (3d) 390 .... 52.3
Hawks v Longridge (1873) 29 LT 449 .... 38.1
Hawksbee v Hawksbee (1853) 11 Hare 230, 23 LJ Ch 521 .... 43.2
Hawksley v Barrow (1866) LR 1 P & D 147, 35 LJP & M 67, 14 WR 822, 14 LT 672 .... 18.16
Hawksley's Settlement, Re, Black v Tidy [1934] Ch 384, [1934] All ER Rep 94, 50 TR 231, 151 LT 299 .... 18.9, 18.10, 19.2, 19.4, 49.6, 57.3
Hawksworth v Hawksworth (1858) 27 Beav 1 .... 64.19
Hawley v Cutts (1677) Freem Ch 24, 22 ER 1034 .... 64.39
Haws v Haws (1747) 3 Atk 524, 1 Ves Sen 13, sub nom Hawes v Hawes 1 Wils 165 .... 56.9
Hawthorn v Shedden (1856) 25 LJ Ch 833, 2 Jur NS 749, 3 Sm & G 293, 27 LTOS 304 .... 30.5, 39.12, 39.13
Hay, Re (1912) 2 DLR 152, 3 OWN 735, 21 OWR 546 .... 93.25
Hay, Re, Kerr v Stinnear [1904] 1 Ch 317, 73 LJ Ch 33, 52 WR 92, 48 Sol Jo 15 .... 14.8
Hay, Re, Leech v Hay [1932] NI 215 .... 48.15

Hay v Watkins (1843) 5 I Eq R 273, 2 Con & Law 157, 3 Dr & War 339 .... 40.15
Hay's Settlement Trusts, Re [1981] 3 All ER 786, [1982] 1 WLR 202, 125 Sol Jo 866 .... 1.6, 39.31, 40.5, 40.21, 53.6, 225.91, 225.100
Hay Drummond, Re, Halsey v Pechell (1922) 128 LT 621, [1922] All ER Rep 330, 67 Sol Jo 247, 39 TLR 144 .... 64.53
Hayden, Re, Pask v Perry [1931] 2 Ch 333, [1931] All ER Rep 139, 100 LJ Ch 381, 146 LT 303 .... 56.5, 68.1, 76.1, 78.5, 85.4
Haydon v Rose (1870) LR 10 Eq 224, 39 LJ Ch 688, 18 WR 1146, 23 LT 334 .... 97.8
Haydon v Wilshire (1789) 3 Term Rep 372 .... 76.3
Hayes, Re, Turnbull v Hayes [1900] 2 Ch 322, 69 LJ Ch 691, 49 WR 25, 83 LT 152, 16 TLR 448; on appeal [1901] 2 Ch 529, 70 LJ Ch 770, 49 WR 659, 45 Sol Jo 722, 85 LT 85, 17 TLR 740, CA 39.16, 39.20, 59.1
Hayes v Hayes (1674) 1 Eq Cas Abr 78, Cas temp Finch 231, 1 Cas in Ch 223, Freem Ch 138 .... 34.25
Hayes v Hayes (1836) 1 Keen 97, 5 LJ Ch 243 .... 41.11, 82.3
Hayes v Hayes [1917] 1 IR 194 .... 90.2
Hayes v National Heart Foundation of Australia [1976] 1 NSWLR 29 .... 50.3, 82.5
Hayes v Oatley (1872) LR 14 Eq 1, 41 LJ Ch 510, 26 LT 816 .... 39.5
Hayes v Williams [1918] 1 IR 6 .... 41.15
Hayes' Goods, Re (1839) 2 Curt 338 .... 16.2, 16.3
Hayes' Will Trusts, Re, Dobie v National Hospital Board of Governors [1953] 2 All ER 1242, [1954] 1 WLR 22, 98 Sol Jo 11 .... 103.10
Hayes' Will Trusts, Re, Pattinson v Hayes [1971] 2 All ER 341, [1971] 1 WLR 758, 115 Sol Jo 310, 219 Estates Gazette 1181 ...... 1.8, 92.3, 203.10
Haygarth, Re, Wickham v Haygarth [1913] 2 Ch 9, 82 LJ Ch 328, 108 LT 756 .... 50.2, 52.3, 100.4
Haylion v Trotter (1892) 10 NZLR 543 .... 44.15
Haynes, Re, Kemp v Haynes (1887) 37 Ch D 306, 57 LJ Ch 519, 36 WR 321, 58 LT 14, 4 TLR 168 .... 35.28, 83.6
Haynes v Haynes (1853) 3 De GM & G 590 .... 33.24, 33.33
Haynes v Mico (1781) Rom 41, 1 Bro CC 129 .... 44.15
Hayter, Re Hayter v Tranter [1937] 2 All ER 110 .... 38.3
Haythornwaite's Estate, Re (1930) 3 DLR 235, [1930] 1 WWR 38 .... 35.2
Hayton's Trusts, Re (1864) 4 New Rep 55, 10 LT 336 .... 101.10
Hayward, Re, Creery v Lingwood (1882) 19 Ch D 470, 51 LJ Ch 513, 30 WR 315, 45 LT 790 .... 68.7, 97.6
Hayward, Re, Kerrod v Hayward [1957] Ch 528, [1957] 2 All ER 474, [1957] 3 WLR 50, 101 Sol Jo 502, CA 7.11, 100.6, 104.14
Hayward v Angell (1683) 1 Vern 222 .... 34.25
Hayward v James (1860) 28 Beav 523, 29 LJ Ch 822, 6 Jur NS 689, 8 WR 676, 2 LT 452 .... 97.8
Hazeldine, Re, Public Trustee v Hazeldine [1918] 1 Ch 433, 87 LJ Ch 303, 62 Sol Jo 350, 118 LT 437 .... 38.20
Hazlette, Re [1915] 1 IR 285 .... 91.2
Heach v Prichard [1882] WN 140 .... 64.26
Head v Randall (1843) 2 Y & C Ch Cas 231, 7 Jur 298 .... 54.5
Healy Brown [2002] WTLR 849, 4 ITEL 894, [2002] 19 EG 147 (CS), [2002] NPC 59 .... 2.3, 2.8, 3.1
Healy v Donnery (1853) 3 ICLR 213 .... 83.18, 101.9

Healy v Healy (1875) IR 9 Eq 418 .... 53.3, 57.22
Heard, Re [1956] VLR 102 .... 56.6, 93.16, 93.29
Heard, Re, McDonald v Edney [1942] ALR 321, [1942] VLR 199 .... 76.3
Hearle v Greenbank (1749) 3 Atk 695, [1558–1774] All ER Rep 190, 1 Ves Sen 298 .... 32.20
Hearn v Baker (1856) 2 K & J 383 .... 67.2
Hearne v Wigginton (1821) 6 Madd 119 .... 38.3
Heasman v Pearse (1871) 7 Ch App 275, 41 LJ Ch 705, 20 WR 271, 26 LT 299 .... 50.16, 51.4, 51.11, 68.10, 68.11, 68.13, 76.3, 94.14
Heath, Re, Jackson v Norman (1904) 48 Sol Jo 416 .... 67.1
Heath, Re, Public Trustee v Heath [1936] Ch 259, [1935] All ER Rep 677, 105 LJ Ch 29, 154 LT 536, 52 TLR 54 .... 93.16, 93.22
Heath v Lewis (1853) 3 De GM & G 954, 22 LJ Ch 721, 1 Eq Rep 55, 17 Jur 443, 98 RR 386, 1 WR 314, 21 LTOS 135 .... 33.20, 34.3, 35.2
Heath v Nugent (1860) 29 Beav 226 .... 33.38
Heath v Perry (1744) 3 Atk 101 .... 93.27
Heath v Weston (1853) 3 De GM & G 601 .... 30.1, 55.4
Heath's Goods, Re [1892] P 253, 61 LJP 131, 67 LT 356 .... 14.8, 14.10
Heath's Will Trusts, Re, Hamilton v Lloyds Bank Ltd [1949] Ch 170, [1949] 1 All ER 199, [1949] LJR 641, 93 Sol Jo 59 .... 22.3
Heathcote, Re, Trench v Heathcote [1891] WN 10 .... 100.2
Heather, Re (1958) 13 DLR (2d) 587, [1958] OWN 231 .... 87.1
Heather, Re, Pumfrey v Fryer [1906] 2 Ch 230, 75 LJ Ch 568, 54 WR 625, 95 LT 352 .... 44.10
Heather v O'Neil (1858) 2 De G & J 399, 27 LJ Ch 512, 4 Jur NS 957, 6 WR 484, 31 LTOS 125 .... 40.3
Hedgedale Ltd v Hards (1990) 23 HLR 158, [1991] 1 EGLR 118, [1991] 15 EG 107, CA 7.4
Hedges v Aldworth (1851) 13 I Eq R 406 .... 57.12
Hedges v Harpur (1858) 3 De G & J 129, 27 LJ Ch 742, 4 Jur NS 1209, 6 WR 842, 32 LTOS 67 .... 33.12, 96.4
Hedley Byrne & Co Ltd v Heller & Partners Ltd [1964] AC 465, [1963] 2 All ER 575, [1963] 3 WLR 101, [1963] 1 Lloyd's Rep 485, 107 Sol Jo 454, HL 1.14
Hedley's Trusts, Re (1877) 25 WR 529 .... 101.7
Heenan v Heenan (1894) 12 NZLR 111 .... 99.4
Heidenreich, Re, Cole v Heidenreich [1981] 27 SASR 455 .... 57.12
Heilbronner, Re, Nathan v Kenny [1953] 2 All ER 1016, [1953] 1 WLR 1254, 97 Sol Jo 729 .... 63.1, 64.37
Heinbigner v Heinbigner (1972) 23 DLR (3d) 218, 5 WWR 282 .... 74.1
Hele v Gilbert (1752) 2 Ves Sen 430 .... 64.27
Hellier v Hellier (1884) 9 PD 237, 53 LJP 105, 49 JP 8, 33 WR 324 .... 18.13
Helliwell, Re, Pickles v Helliwell [1916] 2 Ch 580, 86 LJ Ch 45, 60 Sol Jo 619, 115 LT 478 .... 72.3
Hellmann's Will, Re (1866) LR 2 Eq 363, 14 WR 682 .... 9.39, 9.41, 24.4, 30.30
Helmcken Estate, Re, Helmcken v Bullen (1924) 34 BCR 184, [1924] 3 WWR 172 .... 67.2
Helsby, Re, Neate v Bozie (1914) 84 LJ Ch 682, 112 LT 539 .... 66.1, 77.4
Heming v Clutterbuck (1827) 1 Bli NS 479, sub nom Hemming v Gurrey 1 Dow & Cl 35, HL 88.2

Hemings v Munckley (1783) 1 Cox Eq Cas 38, sub nom Hemmings v Munckley 1 Bro CC 304 .... 34.15
Hemingway, Re, James v Dawson (1890) 45 Ch D 453, 60 LJ Ch 85, 39 WR 4, 63 LT 218 .... 96.4
Hemming v Gurrey. See Heming v Clutterbuck
Hemmings v Munckley. See Hemings v Munckley
Henderson, Re [1996] 1 Qd R 249 .... 18.9
Henderson, Re, Henderson v Henderson [1926] NZLR 766, Gaz LR 550 .... 61.1
Henderson, Re, Public Trustee v Reddie [1940] Ch 368, [1940] 1 All ER 623, 109 LJ Ch 169, 84 Sol Jo 255, 162 LT 376, 56 TLR 423 .... 216.37
Henderson v Constable (1842) 5 Beav 297, 11 LJ Ch 332 .... 39.20
Henderson v Cross (1861) 29 Beav 216, 7 Jur NS 177, 9 WR 263 .... 34.6, 83.11
Henderson v Fraser [1923] SCR 23, [1923] 1 DLR 636, [1923] 1 WWR 391 .... 88.3
Henderson v Henderson [1905] 1 IR 353 .... 57.22
Henderson v Kennicot (1848) 2 De G & Sm 492, 18 LJ Ch 40, 12 Jur 848, 12 LTOS 64 .... 97.9
Henderson's Trusts, Re, Schreiber v Baring [1969] 3 All ER 769, [1969] 1 WLR 651, 113 Sol Jo 328, CA 50.21, 66.14
Hendrie, Re (1969) 3 DLR (3d) 590, [1969] 1 OR 673 .... 38.23
Hendry v Perpetual Executors and Trustees Association of Australia Ltd (1962) 106 CLR 256, [1962] ALR 249 .... 7.31, 64.43
Hendy's Will, Re, Hayes v Hendy [1913] VLR 559 .... 34.5, 93.27
Heneage v Lord Andover (1829) 3 Y & J 360, 10 Price 316, Ex Ch 33.23
Henfrey v Henfrey (1842) 4 Moo PCC 29, 6 Jur 355, 1 Notes of Cases 356, PC 18.10
Henrion v Bonham (1844) Drury temp Sug 476 .... 9.35, 33.17
Henrique's Trusts, Re [1875] WN 187 .... 90.1
Henry, Re, Gordon v Gordon [1907] 1 Ch 30, 76 LJ Ch 74, 95 LT 776 .... 38.27
Henry v Henry (1872) 6 IR Eq 286 .... 42.5
Henry Will Trust, Re, Mussett v Smith (or Henry) [1953] 1 All ER 531, [1953] 1 WLR 376, 97 Sol Jo 133 .... 33.20, 62.3, 93.20, 216.32
Henshaw v Atkinson (1818) 3 Madd 306 .... 103.11
Hensler, Re, Jones v Hensler (1881) 19 Ch D 612, 51 LJ Ch 303, 30 WR 482, 45 LT 672 .... 47.13
Hensman v Fryer (1867) 3 Ch App 420, 37 LJ Ch 97, 16 WR 162, 17 LT 394 .... 30.3, 57.8, 57.20
Henton, Re, Henton v Henton (1882) 30 WR 702 .... 64.7
Hepburn v Skirving (1858) 4 Jur NS 651, 32 LTOS 26 .... 59.3
Hepplewhite's Will Trusts, Re (1977) Times 21 January 35.35
Heppner, Re, Heppner v Heppner (1913) 30 WN 220, 14 SRNSW 173 .... 35.8
Heptinstall v Gott (1862) 2 John & H 449, 31 LJ Ch 776, 8 Jur NS 1091, 10 WR 708, 7 LT 92 .... 47.8, 47.9
Hepworth v Taylor (1784) 1 Cox Eq Cas 112 .... 56.8
Heran v James [1982] 2 NSWLR 376, NSW CA 1.6
Herbert, Re, Herbert v Lord Bicester [1946] 1 All ER 421, 90 Sol Jo 210, 175 LT 227 .... 35.28
Herbert v Badgery (1894) 10 WN 128, 15 NSWLR 236 .... 31.6
Herbert v Reid (1810) 16 Ves 481 .... 30.24, 30.28, 57.9
Herbert v Turball (1663) 1 Keb 589, 1 Sid 162, sub nom Herbert v Tuckal T Raym 84 .... 4.7

Herbert's Trusts, Re (1860) 1 John & H 121, 29 LJ Ch 870, 6 Jur NS 1027, 8 WR 660, 2 LT 743 .... 57.15, 72.3
Herdman's Trusts, Re (1893) 31 LR Ir 87 .... 39.19
Herlichka, Re (1969) 3 DLR (3d) 700, [1969] 1 OR 724 .... 80.1
Hernando, Re, Hernando v Sawtell (1884) 27 Ch D 284, 53 LJ Ch 865, 33 WR 252, 51 LT 117 .... 23.12, 24.13
Heron v Stokes (1842) 2 Dr & War 89; revsd sub nom Stokes v Heron (1845) 12 Cl & Fin 161, 9 Jur 563, HL 85.3, 101.9
Heron v Ulster Bank Ltd [1974] NI 44 .... 67.6, 90.4
Herrick, Re, Colohan v A-G (1918) 52 ILT 213 .... 9.31
Herrick v Franklin (1868) LR 6 Eq 593, 37 LJ Ch 908 .... 84.4
Herring, Re, Murray v Herring [1908] 2 Ch 493, 77 LJ Ch 665, 99 LT 144, 24 TLR 747 .... 57.6, 64.11
Hertford (Marquis) v Lord Lowther (1843) 7 Beav 1, 13 LJ Ch 41, 7 Jur 1167 .... 38.11, 63.1
Hertford (Marquis) v Lord Lowther (1845) 4 LTOS 450 .... 88.4
Hertford (Marquis) v Lord Lowther (1846) 9 Beav 266, 15 LJ Ch 126, 6 LTOS 410 .... 32.4
Hertford's (Marquis) Will, Re. See Croker v Marquess of Hertford
Hervey v Aston. See Harvey v Lady Aston
Hervey v M'Laughlin (1815) 1 Price 264 .... 97.1
Hervey-Bathurst v Stanley (1876) 4 Ch D 251, 46 LJ Ch 162, 25 WR 482, 35 LT 709, CA 34.21
Heseltine v Heseltine (1818) 3 Madd 276 .... 63.1
Hess, Re [1992] 1 Qd R 176 .... 5.7, 6.1
Hester v Trustees, Executors and Agency Co Ltd (1892) 18 VLR 509 .... 64.32
Hetherington, Re [1990] Ch 1, [1989] 2 WLR 1094, sub nom Re Hetherington, Gibbs v McDonnell [1989] 2 All ER 129, 133 Sol Jo 457 .... 9.36, 102.9, 212.13
Hetherington v Oakman (1843) 2 Y & C Ch Cas 299, 7 Jur 570 .... 56.8
Hetley, Re, Hetley v Hetley [1902] 2 Ch 866, [1900–3] All ER Rep 292, 71 LJ Ch 769, 51 WR 202, 87 LT 265 .... 36.11
Heubner, Re (1974) 53 DLR (3d) 730 .... 1.5
Heward v Heward (1868) 15 Gr 516 .... 60.1
Hewet v Ireland (1718) Gilb Ch 145, 1 P Wms 426, sub nom Hewitt v Ireland Prec Ch 489, 2 Eq Cas Abr 139, pl 9 .... 81.2
Hewett, Re, Eldridge v Hewett (1920) 90 LJ Ch 126, 65 Sol Jo 116 .... 30.34
Hewett, Re, Eldridge v Iles [1918] 1 Ch 458, [1918–19] All ER Rep 530, 118 LT 524, sub nom Re Hewitt, Eldridge v Iles 87 LJ Ch 209 .... 33.20, 35.2
Hewett's Settlement, Re, Hewett v Eldridge [1915] 1 Ch 810, 84 LJ Ch 715, 59 Sol Jo 476, 113 LT 315 .... 94.30
Hewit v Bredin (1865) 17 Ir Jur 85; affd (1865) 17 Ir Jur 265 .... 64.35
Hewitson v Todhunter (1852) 22 LJ Ch 76, 1 WR 78, 20 LTOS 153 .... 47.24
Hewitt, Re [1945] SASR 102 .... 79.2
Hewitt, Re, Hewitt v Hewitt [1926] Ch 740, [1926] All ER Rep 628, 95 LJ Ch 300, 70 Sol Jo 607, 135 LT 319 .... 54.2
Hewitt v Ireland. See Hewet v Ireland
Hewitt v Jardine (1872) LR 14 Eq 58, 26 LT 546 .... 100.2, 100.4
Hewitt v Kaye (1868) LR 6 Eq 198, 32 JP 776, 37 LJ Ch 633, 16 WR 835 .... 1.15

Hewitt's Settlement, Re, Hewitt v Hewitt [1915] 1 Ch 228, 84 LJ Ch 358, 59 Sol Jo 177, 112 LT 287, 31 TLR 81 .... 25.8
Hewson v Shelley [1914] 2 Ch 13, 83 LJ Ch 607, 58 Sol Jo 397, 10 LT 785, 30 TLR 402, CA 25.15, 25.16, 49.7
Hey's Estate, Re, Walker v Gaskill [1914] P 192, 83 LJP 152, 59 Sol Jo 45, 111 LT 941, 30 TLR 637 .... 2.1, 2.2, 2.3, 2.4, 2.6, 2.8, 7.3, 225.27
Hey's Settlement Trusts and Will Trusts, Re, Hey v Nickell-Lean [1945] Ch 294, [1945] 1 All ER 618, 114 LJ Ch 278, 89 Sol Jo 269, 172 LT 396, 61 TLR 334 .... 38.19, 38.22, 38.23, 101.6, 214.37, 214.41
Heywood's Estate, Re [1916] P 47, 85 LJP 24, 60 Sol Jo 239, 114 LT 375 .... 16.9
Heyworth's Contingent Reversionary Interest, Re [1956] Ch 364, [1956] 2 WLR 1044, 100 Sol Jo 342, sub nom Re Heyworth's Settlements [1956] 2 All ER 21 .... 218.66
Hibbard v Lamb (1756) Amb 309 .... 103.17
Hibbert v Hibbert (1873) LR 15 Eq 372, 42 LJ Ch 383, 21 WR 506, 28 LT 397 .... 71.1, 79.4
Hibon v Hibon (1863) 32 LJ Ch 374, 9 Jur NS 511, 1 New Rep 532, 11 WR 455, 8 LT 195 .... 64.26
Hickey, Re, Beddoes v Hodgson [1917] 1 Ch 601, 86 LJ Ch 385, 61 Sol Jo 368, 116 LT 556 .... 54.5, 68.9, 74.8, 87.2
Hickey, Re, Hickey v Hickey [1913] 1 IR 390 .... 82.5
Hicklin, Re, Public Trustee v Hoare [1917] 2 Ch 278, [1916–17] All ER Rep 658, 86 LJ Ch 740, 61 Sol Jo 630, 117 LT 403, 33 TLR 478 .... 55.7
Hickling v Boyer (1851) 21 LJ Ch 388, 16 Jur 137, 3 Mac & G 635, 20 LTOS 33 .... 45.2, 207.2
Hickling v Fair [1899] AC 15, 68 LJPC 12, HL 34.2, 49.1, 50.21, 51.7, 66.2, 66.5, 93.2, 93.3, 93.29
Hickman v Peacey [1945] AC 304, [1945] 2 All ER 215, 114 LJ Ch 225, 89 Sol Jo 339, 173 LT 89, 61 TLR 489, HL 70.2
Hickman v Upsall (1860) 2 Giff 124, 6 Jur NS 367, 8 WR 359, 2 LT 80 .... 33.23
Hickman's Will Trusts, Re, Hickman v Hickman [1948] Ch 624, [1948] 2 All ER 303, [1948] LJR 1500, 64 TLR 420 .... 53.5, 65.2, 80.1, 80.7
Hickman's Will Trusts, Re, Re Playfair, Palmer v Playfair. See Playfair, Re, Palmer v Playfair
Hicks v Hirst (1907) 26 NZLR 1376 .... 39.17
Hicks v McClure (1922) 64 SCR 361 .... 41.6, 41.7
Hicks v Ross (1872) LR 14 Eq 141, 41 LJ Ch 677, 26 LT 470 .... 33.12
Hicks v Sallitt (1854) 3 De GM & G 782, 23 LJ Ch 571, 2 Eq Rep 818, 18 Jur 915, 2 WR 173, 22 LTOS 322 .... 50.9, 50.17
Hicks' Goods, Re (1869) LR 1 P & D 683, 38 LJP & M 65, 33 JP 711, 21 LT 300 .... 18.16
Hickson v Wolfe (1858) 9 I Ch R 144 .... 39.14
Hide v Parrat. See Hyde v Parrat
Higginbottom, Re [1892] 3 Ch 132, [1891–4] All ER Rep 1070, 62 LJ Ch 74, 3 R 23, 67 LT 190 .... 27.3
Higgins v Dawson. See Grainger, Re, Dawson v Higgins
Higham, Re, Higham v Higham [1937] 2 All ER 17 .... 78.3
Hill, Re [1951] OR 619 .... 51.2
Hill, Re [1958] SASR 269 .... 66.7

Hill, Re, Hill v Hill [1902] 1 Ch 807, 71 LJ Ch 417, 50 WR 434, 86 LT 336, 18 TLR 487, CA 94.15
Hill, Re, Public Trustee v O'Donnell [1923] 2 Ch 259, 93 LJ Ch 13, 129 LT 824 .... 79.2, 82.5
Hill, Re, Westminster Bank Ltd v Wilson [1944] Ch 270, [1944] 1 All ER 502, 113 LJ Ch 241, 88 Sol Jo 179, 170 LT 317, 60 TLR 358, CA 33.3, 33.35
Hill v Chapman (1791) 1 Ves 405, 3 Bro CC 391 .... 66.5, 66.8
Hill v Cock (1813) 1 Ves & B 173 .... 37.7
Hill v Crook. See Crook v Hill
Hill v Hill (1904) 8 OLR 710, 5 OWR 2, 25 CLT 41 .... 10.10
Hill v Jones (1868) 37 LJ Ch 465 .... 91.6
Hill v Mason (1820) 2 Jac & W 248 .... 64.35, 64.38
Hill v Potts. See Hill v Rattey
Hill v Rattey (1862) 2 John & H 634, sub nom Hill v Potts 31 LJ Ch 380, 8 Jur NS 555, 10 WR 439, 5 LT 787 .... 33.12
Hill v Walker (1858) 4 K & J 166, 32 LTOS 71 .... 18.33
Hill's Goods, Re (1845) 1 Rob Eccl 276, 4 Notes of Cases 174 .... 16.2
Hillas v Hillas (1847) 10 I Eq R 134 .... 38.12
Hillas-Drake, Re, National Provincial Bank Ltd v Liddell [1944] Ch 235, [1944] 1 All ER 375, 113 LJ Ch 137, 88 Sol Jo 103, 170 LT 240, 60 TLR 261 .... 100.5
Hillersdon v Lowe (1843) 2 Hare 355, 12 LJ Ch 321, 7 Jur 482 .... 51.8, 93.15
Hilliard v Fulford (1876) 4 Ch D 389, [1874–80] All ER Rep 247, 46 LJ Ch 43, 25 WR 161, 35 LT 750 .... 31.6, 31.19
Hillier, Re, Dauncey v Finch and A-G [1944] 1 All ER 480 .... 102.6
Hillier, Re, Hillier v A-G [1954] 2 All ER 59, [1954] 1 WLR 700, 98 Sol Jo 319, CA 103.6, 103.18, 103.20
Hilton v Hilton (1872) LR 14 Eq 468 .... 100.5, 100.6
Hinchcliffe v Hinchcliffe (1797) 3 Ves 516 .... 44.1, 44.7, 44.15
Hinckes, Re, Dashwood v Hinckes [1921] 1 Ch 475, [1921] All ER Rep 558, 90 LJ Ch 335, 65 Sol Jo 291, 124 LT 681, 37 TLR 308, CA 34.21, 35.39
Hind, Re, Bernstone v Montgomery [1933] Ch 208, 102 LJ Ch 91, 148 LT 281 .... 35.43
Hindle, Re, Megson v Hindle. See Megson v Hindle
Hindle v Taylor (1855) 20 Beav 109, 1 Jur NS 1031n, 26 LTOS 81; revsd (1855) 5 De GM & G 577, 25 LJ Ch 78, 1 Jur NS 1029, 4 WR 62, 26 LTOS 81 .... 33.28
Hindmarch's Goods, Re (1866) LR 1 P & D 307, 36 LJP & M 24, 31 JP 41, 15 LT 391 .... 14.10
Hindmarsh v Charlton (1861) 8 HL Cas 160, [1861–73] All ER Rep 63, 25 JP 339, 7 Jur NS 611, 9 WR 521, 4 LT 125 .... 11.13, 12.3, 12.12
Hinds's Goods, Re (1852) 16 Jur 1161, 20 LTOS 264 .... 14.6
Hine's Goods, Re [1893] P 282, 63 LJP 45, 6 R 573, 69 LT 458 .... 18.5, 18.7, 18.17, 18.31
Hinkson, Re [1959] VR 686 .... 78.5
Hinton, Re [1953] NZLR 607 .... 68.2
Hipwell, Re, Hipwell v Hewitt [1945] 2 All ER 476, 173 LT 192, 89 Sol Jo 487, CA 76.1, 76.3
Hirschhorn v Evans [1938] 2 KB 801, [1938] 3 All ER 491, 107 LJKB 756, 82 Sol Jo 664, 159 LT 405, 54 TLR 1069, CA 210.17

Hiscock's Goods, Re [1901] P 78, [1900–03] All ER Rep 63, 70 LJP 22, 84 LT 61, 17 TLR 110 .... 16.2
Hiscoe, Re, Hiscoe v Waite (1883) 48 LT 510 .... 66.8
Hiscoe, Re, Hiscoe v Waite [1902] WN 49, 71 LJ Ch 347 .... 33.11
Hixon v Oliver (1806) 13 Ves 108 .... 83.2
Hoare v Byng. See Byng v Lord Strafford
Hoare v Hoare (1886) 56 LT 147 .... 103.11
Hoare v Osborne (1866) LR 1 Eq 585, [1861–73] All ER Rep 675, 35 LJ Ch 345, 30 JP 309, 12 Jur NS 243, 14 WR 383, 14 LT 9 .... 9.29, 102.22
Hoare v Parker (1788) 2 Term Rep 376 .... 8.3
Hoare Trustees v Gardner (Inspector of Taxes) [1979] Ch 10, [1978] 1 All ER 791, [1978] 2 WLR 839, [1978] STC 89, 52 TC 53, [1977] TR 293, 121 Sol Jo 852 .... 218.102
Hobart v Merryfield (1844) 2 LTOS 518 .... 4.18
Hobart v Hobart (19 May 2006, unreported) 6.2
Hobbs, Re [1929] 4 DLR 433, 64 OLR 370 .... 79.1
Hobbs, Re, Hobbs v Hobbs [1917] 1 Ch 569, 86 LJ Ch 409, 116 LT 270; affd [1917] 1 Ch 569, CA 76.1, 76.3
Hobbs v Knight (1838) 1 Curt 768 .... 18.17, 18.22
Hobgen v Neale (1870) LR 11 Eq 48, 40 LJ Ch 36, 19 WR 144, 23 LT 681 .... 68.12, 76.4
Hobley, Re [2006] WTLR 467 .... 2.7
Hobourn Aero Components Ltd's Air Raid Distress Fund, Re, Ryan v Forrest [1946] Ch 194, [1946] 1 All ER 501, 115 LJ Ch 158, 90 Sol Jo 260, 174 LT 428, 62 TLR 313, CA 102.10, 102.15
Hobson, Re, Barwick v Holt [1912] 1 Ch 626, [1911–13] All ER Rep 257, 56 Sol Jo 400, 106 LT 507 .... 33.14, 51.3, 67.5, 86.6, 101.6
Hobson v Blackburn (1833) 1 My & K 571, 2 LJ Ch 168 .... 8.7, 60.2, 64.2, 64.33
Hobson v Blackburn and Blackburn (1822) 1 Add 274 .... 2.8
Hobson's Estate, Re, Hobson v Sharp [1907] VLR 724 .... 53.2, 94.21
Hobson's Goods, Re (1861) 7 Jur NS 1208 .... 1.5
Hockley v Mawbey (1790) 1 Ves 143, 3 Bro CC 82 .... 98.4
Hodge, Re, Hodge v Griffiths [1940] Ch 260, 109 LJ Ch 185, 84 Sol Jo 113, 162 LT 155, 56 TLR 327 .... 45.1, 46.2, 91.2
Hodge, Re, Midland Bank Executor and Trustee Co Ltd v Morrison [1943] Ch 300, [1943] 2 All ER 304, 112 LJ Ch 241, 87 Sol Jo 274, 169 LT 155, 59 TLR 373 .... 48.8
Hodge v Churchward (1847) 16 Sim 71 .... 91.2
Hodge v Foot (1865) 34 Beav 349 .... 67.1
Hodges v Grant (1867) LR 4 Eq 140, 36 LJ Ch 935, 15 WR 607 .... 68.13
Hodges' Legacy, Re (1873) LR 16 Eq 92, 42 LJ Ch 452, 21 WR 558, 28 LT 624 .... 34.24, 35.39
Hodgins, Re (1978) 85 DLR (3d) 705 .... 5.9, 11.13
Hodgkinson's Goods, Re [1893] P 339, 62 LJP 116, 37 Sol Jo 700, 69 LT 540, 9 TLR 650, CA 18.14, 21.1, 21.8
Hodgson, Re, Hodgson v Fox (1878) 9 Ch D 673, 48 LJ Ch 52, 27 WR 38 .... 30.13
Hodgson, Re, Hodgson v Gillett [1952] 1 All ER 769, 96 Sol Jo 262 .... 67.1
Hodgson, Re, Nowell v Flannery [1936] Ch 203, [1935] All ER Rep 161, 105 LJ Ch 51, 79 Sol Jo 880, 154 LT 338, 52 TLR 88 .... 57.3, 64.35, 64.58

Hodgson, Re, Taylor v Hodgson [1898] 2 Ch 545, 67 LJ Ch 591, 47 WR 44, 79 LT 345 .... 64.32
Hodgson, Re, Weston v Hodgson [1913] 1 Ch 34, 82 LJ Ch 31, 57 Sol Jo 112, 107 LT 607 .... 218.90
Hodgson v Ambrose (1780) 1 Doug KB 337; affd sub nom Ambrose v Hodgson (1781) 3 Bro Parl Cas 416, HL 49.4
Hodgson v Bective (1863) 1 Hem & M 376; varied sub nom Bective v Hodgson (1864) 10 HL Cas 656, 33 LJ Ch 601, 10 Jur NS 373, 3 New Rep 654, 138 RR 350, 12 WR 625, 10 LT 202 .... 32.16, 32.17, 37.7
Hodgson v Clarke (1860) 1 De GF & J 394 .... 57.15, 58.10
Hodgson v Green (1842) 11 LJ Ch 312, 6 Jur 819 .... 82.5
Hodgson v Halford (1879) 11 Ch D 959, 48 LJ Ch 548, 27 WR 545 .... 35.31, 94.26, 217.40
Hodgson v Hodgson (1876) 24 WR 575 .... 38.3
Hodgson v Jex (1876) 2 Ch D 122, 45 LJ Ch 388 .... 38.7, 38.10, 64.17, 64.18
Hodgson v Smithson (1856) 8 De GM & G 604, 26 LJ Ch 110, 2 Jur NS 1199, 111 RR 120, 5 WR 3, 28 LTOS 73 .... 68.4, 97.1
Hodson v Ball (1845) 14 Sim 558, 9 Jur 407 .... 94.12
Hodson v Micklethwaite (1854) 2 Drew 294, 23 LJ Ch 719, 2 Eq Rep 1157, 2 WR 440 .... 66.1, 66.20
Hodson's Will Trusts, Re, Hodson v Horth (1948) 92 Sol Jo 271 .... 35.20
Hoff, Re, Carnley v Hoff [1942] Ch 298, [1942] 1 All ER 547, 111 LJ Ch 163, 86 Sol Jo 105, 166 LT 241, 58 TLR 247 .... 213.3
Hoff v Atherton [2004] EWCA Civ 1554, [2005] WTLR 99, [2004] All ER (D) 314 (Nov) 5.3
Hogan v Byrne (1862) 13 ICLR 166, 14 Ir Jur 223 .... 9.35
Hogan v Jackson (1775) 1 Cowp 299; affd sub nom Jackson v Hogan (1776) 3 Bro Parl Cas 388, HL 38.4, 38.7, 64.16
Hogbin Estate, Re [1950] 3 DLR 843, [1950] 2 WWR 264 .... 72.2
Hogden v Hogden [1957] SRNSW 269 .... 34.3
Hogg, Re (11 July 1983, unreported) 214.43
Hogg v Cook (1863) 32 Beav 641 .... 71.1
Holburne, Re, Coates v Mackillop (1885) 53 LT 212, 1 TLR 517 .... 102.10
Holden, Re (1903) 5 OLR 156, 2 OWR 11, 23 CLT 52 .... 64.27
Holden, Re, Holden v Smith (1888) 57 LJ Ch 648, 59 LT 358 .... 83.9, 99.1
Holden v Ramsbottom (1863) 4 Giff 205, 9 Jur NS 350, 1 New Rep 307, 354, 11 WR 302, 7 LT 735 .... 64.27, 64.47
Holden Estate, Re [1945] 3 WWR 564 .... 14.3
Holder, Re, National Provincial Bank Ltd v Holder [1953] Ch 468, [1953] 2 All ER 1, [1953] 2 WLR 1079, 97 Sol Jo 353 .... 214.53
Holder v Holder [1968] Ch 353, [1968] 1 All ER 665, [1968] 2 WLR 237, 112 Sol Jo 17, 205 Estates Gazette 211, CA 7.7, 25.12, 221.4
Holder v Howell (1803) 8 Ves 97 .... 18.33
Holford, Re, Holford v Holford [1894] 3 Ch 30, 63 LJ Ch 637, 7 R 304, 42 WR 563, 38 Sol Jo 512, 70 LT 777, 10 TLR 496, CA 32.28
Holford v Wood (1798) 4 Ves 76 .... 33.10, 88.2
Holford's Settlement, Re, Lloyds Bank Ltd v Holford [1945] Ch 21, [1944] 2 All ER 462, 114 LJ Ch 71, 171 LT 379, 61 TLR 47 .... 39.25, 39.26
Holgate v Jennings (1857) 24 Beav 623 .... 38.23
Holland, Re, Brettell v Holland [1907] 2 Ch 88, 76 LJ Ch 449, 97 LT 49 .... 82.1

Holland, Re, Holland v Clapton [1914] 2 Ch 595, 84 LJ Ch 389, 112 LT 27 .... 40.15, 40.21
Holland v McKenzie [1932] NZLR 1153 .... 83.6
Holland v Wood (1870) LR 11 Eq 91 .... 66.23, 68.1
Holland's Estate, Re [1936] 3 All ER 13, 105 LJP 113, 80 Sol Jo 838, 155 LT 417, 53 TLR 3 .... 25.1, 203.9, 203.43, 221.40, 233.39
Holland's Estate, Re (1950) 2 DLR 135, 57 Man R 415, [1950] 1 WWR 209 .... 64.53
Hollebone, Re, Hollebone v Hollebone [1919] 2 Ch 93, [1918–19] All ER Rep 323, 88 LJ Ch 386, 63 Sol Jo 553, 121 LT 116 .... 38.17
Holliday, Re, Houghton v Adlard [1947] Ch 402, [1947] 1 All ER 695, [1947] LJR 1086, 91 Sol Jo 278, 76 LT 478, 63 TLR 255 .... 38.17
Hollinrake v Lister (1826) 1 Russ 500 .... 34.25
Hollins, Re, Hollins v Hollins [1918] 1 Ch 503, [1918–19] All ER Rep 301, 87 LJ Ch 326, 62 Sol Jo 403, 118 LT 672, 34 TLR 310, CA 33.6
Hollis' Hospital Trustees and Hague's Contract, Re [1899] 2 Ch 540, [1895–9] All ER Rep 643, 68 LJ Ch 673, 47 WR 691, 43 Sol Jo 644, 81 LT 90 .... 34.7
Hollis's Estate, Re (1968) 66 DLR (2d) 369, 62 WWR 681 .... 78.5
Holloway v Clarkson (1843) 2 Hare 521 .... 83.16
Holloway v Radcliffe (1857) 23 Beav 163, 26 LJ Ch 401, 5 WR 271, 28 LTOS 301 .... 77.5
Hollywood, Re, Smyth v A-G (1917) 52 ILT 51 .... 9.31
Holmes, Re, Holmes v Holmes (1890) 62 LT 383 .... 101.2
Holmes, Re, Villiers v Holmes [1917] 1 IR 165 .... 38.16, 59.3, 64.54
Holmes v A-G (1981) Times, 12 February 102.9
Holmes v Barker (1816) 2 Madd 462 .... 60.1
Holmes v Crispe (1849) 18 LJ Ch 439 .... 32.10, 32.11
Holmes v Custance (1806) 12 Ves 279 .... 57.20
Holmes v Godson (1856) 8 De GM & G 152, 25 LJ Ch 317, 2 Jur NS 383, 114 RR 73, 4 WR 415, 27 LTOS 8 .... 34.6
Holmes v Holmes (1783) 1 Cox Eq Cas 39, 1 Bro CC 555 .... 44.11
Holmes v Holmes (1830) 1 Russ & M 660, 8 LJOS Ch 157 .... 30.43
Holmes v Lysaght (1733) 2 Bro Parl Cas 261 .... 35.15
Holmes v Prescott (1864) 33 LJ Ch 264, 10 Jur NS 507, 3 New Rep 559, 12 WR 636, 11 LT 38 .... 93.17
Holmes v Taggart (1862) 1 NSWSCR (Eq) 27 .... 33.18
Holmes' Trusts, Re (1853) 1 Drew 321, 22 LJ Ch 393 .... 58.10
Holosko's Will, Re, Patrick and Patek v Hanewich (1968) 63 WWR 125 ..... 57.18, 57.22
Holt, Re [1952] 3 DLR 426, 29 MPR 60 .... 35.48, 97.5
Holt, Re, Holt v Holt [1921] 2 Ch 17, 90 LJ Ch 410, 65 Sol Jo 293, 125 LT 478 .... 64.32, 214.25
Holt v Sindrey (1868) LR 7 Eq 170, 38 LJ Ch 126, 33 JP 260, 17 WR 249, 19 LT 669 .... 72.2, 72.5
Holt's Estate, Re, Bolding v Strugnell (1876) 45 LJ Ch 208, 24 WR 339 .... 93.31, 93.35
Holtam's Estate, Re, Gillett v Rogers (1913) 108 LT 732 .... 4.17, 11.13, 11.21
Holton v Lloyd (1827) 1 Mol 30 .... 35.16
Holyland, ex p (1805) 11 Ves 10 .... 4.14
Holyland v Lewin (1884) 26 Ch D 266, 53 LJ Ch 530, 32 WR 443, 51 LT 14, CA 39.12, 39.14, 39.29, 47.14, 47.38, 213.4

Home v Pillans (1833) 2 My & K 15, 4 LJ Ch 2, Coop temp Brough 198 ...... 97.1, 97.5
Homer, Re, Cowlishaw v Rendell (1916) 86 LJ Ch 324, 115 LT 703 .... 9.25
Homer v Homer (1878) 8 Ch D 758, 47 LJ Ch 635, 27 WR 101, 39 LT 3, CA 57.20, 58.6, 58.10, 63.3, 63.7
Homerton v Hewett (1872) 36 JP 216, 25 LT 854 .... 19.4
Hone v Medcraft (1783) 1 Bro CC 261 .... 41.10
Hone's Trusts, Re (1883) 22 Ch D 663, 52 LJ Ch 295, 31 WR 379, 48 LT 266 .... 47.13
Honeyfield, Re, Honeyfield v Honeyfield [1961] NZLR 1049 .... 64.35
Honywood v Honywood (1874) LR 18 Eq 306, [1874–80] All ER Rep Ext 1946, 43 LJ Ch 652, 22 WR 749, 30 LT 671 .... 220.61
Honywood v Honywood (1905) 92 LT 814, HL 89.1
Hood, Re, Public Trustee v Hood [1931] 1 Ch 240, [1930] All ER Rep 215, 100 LJ Ch 115, 74 Sol Jo 549, 143 LT 691, 46 TLR 571, CA 102.10, 102.11, 102.25
Hood v Oglander (1865) 34 Beav 513, 34 LJ Ch 528, 11 Jur NS 498, 6 New Rep 57, 145 RR 639, 13 WR 705, 12 LT 626 .... 99.1
Hoof, Re, Picken v Matthews. See Picken v Matthews
Hooley v Hatton (1773) 2 Dick 461, 1 Bro CC 390n, sub nom Hatton v Hooley Lofft 122 .... 88.2, 88.3
Hooper, Re, Hooper v Carpenter [1936] Ch 442, [1936] 1 All ER 277, 105 LJ Ch 298, 80 Sol Jo 205, 154 LT 677, CA 78.2
Hooper, Re, Hooper v Warner (1902) 51 WR 153, 47 Sol Jo 30, 88 LT 160 .... 58.7, 58.10
Hooper, Re, Parker v Ward [1932] 1 Ch 38, [1931] All ER Rep 129, 101 LJ Ch 61, 146 LT 208 .... 9.29, 202.19
Hooper, Re, Phillips v Steel [1944] Ch 171, [1944] 1 All ER 227, 113 LJ Ch 89, 88 Sol Jo 58, 170 LT 90, 60 TLR 161 .... 33.47
Hooper v Fynmores [2001] 26 LS Gaz R 45, 145 Sol Jo LB 156 .... 200.46, 223.1
Hooper v Smart (1875) 1 Ch D 90, 45 LJ Ch 99, 24 WR 152, 33 LT 499 .... 31.18
Hooper's Settlement, Re, Phillips v Lake [1943] Ch 116, [1943] 1 All ER 173, 112 LJ Ch 135, 87 Sol Jo 83, 168 LT 165, 59 TLR 182, CA 77.2
Hooper's Settlement Trusts, Re, Bosman v Hooper [1948] Ch 586, [1948] 2 All ER 261, [1948] LJR 1455, 92 Sol Jo 362 .... 94.24
Hope v Campbell [1899] AC 1, HL 4.15, 4.16
Hope v d'Hedouville [1893] 2 Ch 361, 62 LJ Ch 589, 3 R 348, 41 WR 330, 68 LT 516 .... 38.25
Hope v Potter (1857) 3 K & J 206, 5 WR 389 .... 52.2, 91.3
Hope d Brown v Taylor (1757) 1 Burr 268, 2 Keny 9 .... 55.4
Hope's Will Trust, Re, Hope v Thorp [1929] 2 Ch 136, [1929] All ER Rep 561, 98 LJ Ch 249, 141 LT 509 .... 84.4
Hope Brown's Goods, Re [1942] P 136, 111 LJP 78, 58 TLR 338, sub nom Re Brown's Goods [1942] 2 All ER 176, 86 Sol Jo 260, 167 LT 95 .... 19.4, 19.5
Hope Johnstone, Re, Hope Johnstone v Hope Johnstone [1904] 1 Ch 470, 73 LJ Ch 321, 90 LT 253, 20 TLR 282 .... 35.35
Hope Johnstone v Sinclair's Trustees (1904) 7 F 25 .... 66.13
Hope-Scott v Earl Shrewsbury. See Shrewsbury (Earl) v Scott
Hopkins, Re (1982) 132 DLR (3d) 671 .... 53.1
Hopkins v Abbott (1875) LR 19 Eq 222, 44 LJ Ch 316, 23 WR 227, 31 LT 820 .... 64.53

Hopkins' Trusts, Re (1878) 9 Ch D 131, 47 LJ Ch 672, 26 WR 629 .... 76.3
Hopkins' Will Trusts, Re, Naish v Francis Bacon Society Inc [1965] Ch 669, [1964] 3 All ER 46, [1964] 3 WLR 840, 108 Sol Jo 601 .... 102.8
Hopkinson, Re, Dyson v Hopkinson [1922] 1 Ch 65, 91 LJ Ch 128, 126 LT 649, 66 Sol Jo 18 .... 37.7
Hopkinson, Re, Lloyds Bank Ltd v Baker [1949] 1 All ER 346, 93 Sol Jo 87, 65 TLR 108 .... 102.8, 102.11
Hopkinson v Ellis (1842) 5 Beav 34 .... 58.4, 103.7
Hopwood v Hopwood (1859) 7 HL Cas 728, 29 LJ Ch 747, 5 Jur NS 897, 34 LTOS 56 .... 20.4, 22.3, 22.4, 44.1, 44.12
Hordern v Hordern [1909] AC 210, 78 LJPC 49, 100 LT 52, 25 TLR 185, PC 51.8, 97.6
Horgan, Re [1971] P 50, [1969] 3 All ER 1570, [1970] 2 WLR 393, 113 Sol Jo 878 .... 25.5, 202.23, 203.15
Horlock, Re, Calham v Smith [1895] 1 Ch 516, 64 LJ Ch 325, 13 R 356, 43 WR 410, 39 Sol Jo 284, 72 LT 223 .... 44.15
Horlock v Wiggins (1888) 39 Ch D 142, [1886–90] All ER Rep 1125, 58 LJ Ch 46, 59 LT 710, CA 44.15
Horn, Re, Westminster Bank Ltd v Horn [1946] Ch 254, [1946] 2 All ER 118, 115 LJ Ch 271, 90 Sol Jo 307, 175 LT 194, 62 TLR 408, CA 100.4
Hornby, Re [1946] P 171, [1946] 2 All ER 150, 90 Sol Jo 249, 175 LT 161, 62 TLR 348 .... 11.2, 11.9
Hornby's Will, Re (1859) 7 WR 729, 34 LTOS 6 .... 47.32
Horne, Re, Wilson v Cox Sinclair [1905] 1 Ch 76, 74 LJ Ch 25, 53 WR 317, 92 LT 263 .... 31.8
Horne v Barton (1815) Coop G 257, 19 Ves 398 .... 101.13
Horner, Re [1965] VR 177 .... 10.1
Horner, Re, Eagleton v Horner (1887) 37 Ch D 695, 57 LJ Ch 211, 36 WR 348, 58 LT 103, 4 TLR 100 .... 50.3, 68.13, 72.3, 79.7
Horner's Estate, Re, Pomfret v Graham (1881) 19 Ch D 186, 51 LJ Ch 43, 45 LT 670 .... 67.4
Horridge v Ferguson (1822) Jac 583 .... 56.5, 68.1
Horrigan v Horrigan [1904] 1 IR 29; on appeal [1904] 1 IR 271, CA 34.2, 35.48
Horrocks, Re, Taylor v Kershaw [1939] P 198, [1939] 1 All ER 579, 108 LJP 86, 83 Sol Jo 214, 160 LT 324, 55 TLR 444, CA 5.7, 6.1, 212.5
Horsford's Goods, Re (1874) LR 3 P & D 211, [1874–80] All ER Rep 732, 44 LJP & M 9, 23 WR 211, 31 LT 553 .... 11.4, 14.2, 14.13, 19.4
Horsnaill, Re, Womersley v Horsnaill [1909] 1 Ch 631, 78 LJ Ch 331, 100 LT 603 .... 30.36
Horton, Re, Lloyd v Hatchett [1920] 2 Ch 1, 89 LJ Ch 297, 64 Sol Jo 425, 123 LT 262 .... 7.3, 59.3
Horton v Jones (1934) 51 WN 126, 34 SRNSW 356; affd (1934) 52 WN 138, 53 CLR 475, 35 SRNSW 397, 8 ALJ 470, 41 Argus LR 177 .... 3.4
Horwood v Griffith (1853) 4 De GM & G 700, 23 LJ Ch 465, 2 Eq Rep 158, 2 WR 71 .... 57.20
Horsfall v Haywards (a firm) [1999] 1 FLR 1182 .... 6.4
Hoskin's Trusts, Re (1877) 5 Ch D 229, 46 LJ Ch 274, 35 LT 935; on appeal (1877) 6 Ch D 281, 46 LJ Ch 817, 25 WR 779, CA 39.5
Hoskins's Goods, Re (1863) 32 LJPM & A 158, 1 New Rep 569 .... 12.5
Hoste v Pratt (1798) 3 Ves 730 .... 66.12, 66.21

Hotchkiss's Trusts, Re (1869) LR 8 Eq 643, 38 LJ Ch 631 .... 68.6
Hotchkys, Re, Freke v Calmady (1886) 32 Ch D 408, [1886–90] All ER Rep 1104, 55 LJ Ch 546, 34 WR 569, 55 LT 110, CA 37.2, 46.3
Hotham v Sutton (1808) 15 Ves 319 .... 38.10
Houghton, Re, Houghton v Brown (1884) 53 LJ Ch 1018, 50 LT 529 .... 82.3
Houghton, Re, Houghton v Houghton [1915] 2 Ch 173, 84 LJ Ch 726, 59 Sol Jo 562, 113 LT 422, 31 TLR 427 .... 9.14
Houghton v Bell (1892) 23 SCR 498, 508 .... 45.1, 87.1
Houghton v Franklin (1823) 1 Sim & St 390, 1 LJOS Ch 231 .... 33.11
Houghton's Goods, Re (1870) 18 WR 767 .... 25.13
Houlding v Cross (1855) 1 Jur NS 250, 3 WR 334, 25 LTOS 29 .... 63.1
House v Way (1848) 18 LJ Ch 22, 12 Jur 958, 12 LTOS 268 .... 38.23
Houston v Burns [1918] AC 337, 87 LJPC 99, 118 LT 462, 34 TLR 219, HL 1.6, 8.7, 50.15, 53.2, 102.23
How, Re, How v How [1930] 1 Ch 66, [1929] All ER Rep 354, 99 LJ Ch 1, 12 LT 86 .... 50.11, 50.12
Howard, Re, Howard v Treasury Solicitor [1944] P 39, 113 LJP 39, 171 LT 376, 60 TLR 248 .... 18.11, 70.2
Howard, Re, Oakley v Aldridge (1908) Times, 30 October 33.16
Howard, Re, Taylor v Howard [1901] 1 Ch 412, 70 LJ Ch 317, 84 LT 296 ... 33.20, 62.3, 83.7, 93.20
Howard v Braithwaite (1812) 1 Ves & B 202 .... 4.20
Howard v Collins (1868) LR 5 Eq 349 .... 67.2
Howard v Howard (1856) 21 Beav 550 .... 97.1
Howard v Wilson (1832) 4 Hag Ecc 107 .... 30.24
Howard's (Sir Robert) Case. See Anon (1699) 1 Ld Raym 480
Howard's Goods, Re (1869) LR 1 P & D 636, 38 LJP & M 32, 33 JP 280, 20 LT 230 .... 18.9
Howard's Will Trusts, Re, Levin v Bradley [1961] Ch 507, [1961] 2 All ER 413, [1961] 2 WLR 821, 105 Sol Jo 347 .... 35.39, 235.27
Howarth, Re, Howarth v Makinson [1909] 2 Ch 19, 78 LJ Ch 687, 53 Sol Jo 519, 100 LT 865, CA 33.24
Howe, Re, Ferniehough v Wilkinson [1908] WN 223 .... 64.27
Howe, Re, Wilkinson v Ferniehough (1910) 54 Sol Jo 704, 103 LT 185 .... 91.6
Howe v Earl of Dartmouth (1802) 6 RR 96, [1775–1802] All ER Rep 24, 7 Ves 137, 1 White & Tud LC 68 ... 8.4, 37.6, 38.17, 38.21, 104.16, 200.36, 200.65, 210.6, 224.34, 225.33, 230.7
Howe v Howe (1849) 14 Jur 359, 14 LTOS 290 .... 38.23
Howe's Goods, Re (1884) 48 JP 743, 33 WR 48 .... 58.10
Howell, Re [1955] OWN 85 .... 5.9
Howell, Re, Re Buckingham, Liggins v Buckingham [1915] 1 Ch 241, [1914–15] All ER Rep 211, 84 LJ Ch 209, 112 LT 188, CA 83.3
Howell, Re, Drury v Fletcher [1952] Ch 264, [1952] 1 All ER 363, 31 ATC 115, [1952] TR 65, 96 Sol Jo 104, [1952] 1 TLR 371 .... 214.66
Howell's Trusts, Re, Barclays Bank Ltd v Simmons [1937] 3 All ER 647 .... 30.26, 210.62
Howell-Shepherd, Re, Churchill v St George's Hospital [1894] 3 Ch 649, sub nom Re Shepherd, Churchill v St George's Hospital 64 LJ Ch 42, 8 R 735, 43 WR 95, 71 LT 516 .... 30.8

Howells v Jenkins (1863) 1 De GJ & Sm 617, 32 LJ Ch 788, 2 New Rep 539, 11 WR 1050, 9 LT 184 .... 42.5
Howley, Re, Naughton v Hegarty [1940] IR 109, 74 ILTR 197 .... 102.17
Howorth v Dewell (1860) 29 Beav 18, 6 Jur NS 1360, 9 WR 27 .... 83.9, 83.13
Howse v Seagoe (1854) 2 WR 597 .... 64.17
Hoy v Master (1834) 6 Sim 568, 3 LJ Ch 134, 38 RR 176 .... 83.11
Hoyles, Re, Row v Jagg [1911] 1 Ch 179, 80 LJ Ch 274, 55 Sol Jo 169, 103 LT 817, 27 TLR 131, CA 23.3, 23.4, 23.5, 24.2
Hubbard v Alexander (1876) 3 Ch D 738, 45 LJ Ch 740, 24 WR 1058, 35 LT 52 .... 88.4
Hubbard v Young (1847) 10 Beav 203, 16 LJ Ch 182, 11 Jur 177, 9 LTOS 263 .... 38.23
Hubbard's Goods, Re (1865) LR 1 P & D 53, 35 LJP & M 27 .... 15.1
Hubbard's Will Trusts, Re, Marston v Angier [1963] Ch 275, [1962] 2 All ER 917, [1962] 3 WLR 682, 106 Sol Jo 705 .... 48.13, 94.30
Hubbuck, Re, Hart v Stone [1896] 1 Ch 754, 65 LJ Ch 271, 44 WR 289, 40 Sol Jo 257, 73 LT 738, CA 38.23
Hubbuck's Estate, Re [1905] P 129, 74 LJP 58, 54 WR 16, 92 LT 665, 21 TLR 333 .... 25.1, 57.22
Huber's Goods, Re [1896] P 209, 65 LJP 119, 75 LT 453, 12 TLR 499 .... 24.17
Huckstep v Mathews (1685) 1 Vern 362 .... 34.22, 92.4
Huckvale's Goods, Re (1867) LR 1 P & D 375, 36 LJP & M 84, 16 WR 64, 16 LT 434 .... 11.6, 11.25
Huddleston, Re, Bruno v Eyston [1894] 3 Ch 595, 64 LJ Ch 157, 8 R 462, 43 WR 139 .... 39.19, 39.25
Hudleston v Gouldsbury (1847) 10 Beav 547, 11 Jur 464, 9 LTOS 531 .... 64.5, 64.53
Hudson, Re [1912] VLR 140 .... 34.11, 97.7
Hudson, Re (1971) 14 DLR (3d) 79 .... 56.1, 66.5, 76.3
Hudson, Re, Creed v Henderson (1885) 54 LJ Ch 811, 33 WR 319, 1 TLR 447 .... 3.3, 102.22
Hudson, Re, Hudson v Hudson (1882) 20 Ch D 406, 51 LJ Ch 455, 30 WR 487, 46 LT 93 .... 51.8, 101.13
Hudson, Re, Spencer v Turner [1911] 1 Ch 206, 80 LJ Ch 129, 103 LT 718 .... 55.7
Hudson v Bower (1968) 1 DLR (3d) 288, 67 WWR 564 .... 12.3
Hudson v Bryant (1845) 1 Coll 681 .... 52.5
Hudson v Forster (1841) 2 Mont D & De G 177, sub nom Re Forster 10 LJ Ch 340 .... 93.44
Hudson (deceased); Nicholls v Hudson [2006] EWHC 3006 (Ch), 150 Sol Jo LB 1333, [2006] All ER (D) 60 (Oct) 18.12
Hudson v Parker (1844) 1 Rob Eccl 14, 8 Jur 786, 3 Notes of Cases 236 .... 12.3
Hudson v Spencer [1910] 2 Ch 285, [1908–10] All ER Rep 232, 79 LJ Ch 506, 54 Sol Jo 601, 103 LT 276 .... 44.2
Hudson's Minors, Re (1843) Drury temp Sug 6 .... 93.24, 93.45
Huffman, Re (1979) 101 DLR (3d) 365 .... 50.2
Hughes, Re (1888) 36 WR 821, 59 LT 586, CA 12.3
Hughes, Re [1956] NZLR 892 .... 52.8
Hughes, Re [1968] VR 28 .... 87.1
Hughes, Re, Ellis v Hughes [1913] 2 Ch 491, 83 LJ Ch 31, 109 LT 509 .... 206.14
Hughes, Re, Loddiges v Jones [1916] 1 Ch 493, 85 LJ Ch 476, 60 Sol Jo 418, 114 LT 845 .... 77.2

Hughes, Re, Rea v Black [1943] Ch 296, [1943] 2 All ER 269, 112 LJ Ch 234, 87 Sol Jo 265, 169 LT 140, 59 TLR 375 .... 35.39
Hughes v Hardy (1885) Diprose & Gammon 402 .... 7.10
Hughes v Hughes (1807) 14 Ves 256 .... 66.1
Hughes v Kelly (1843) 61 RR 109, 5 I Eq R 286, 2 Con & Law 223, 3 Dr & War 482 .... 91.2
Hughes v McNaull [1923] 1 IR 78, Ir CA 48.4
Hughes v Pritchard (1877) 6 Ch D 24, 46 LJ Ch 840, 25 WR 761, 37 LT 259, CA 38.9, 38.12, 51.3
Hughes v Sayer (1718) 1 P Wms 534 .... 98.10, 98.13
Hughes v Turner (1835) 3 My & K 666, 4 LJ Ch 141 .... 20.4, 39.21
Hughson, Re [1955] SCR 498, [1955] OWN 541 .... 41.7
Hugo's Goods, Re (1877) 2 PD 73, 46 LJP 21, 41 JP 632, 25 WR 396, 36 LT 518 .... 1.5
Huguenin v Baseley (1807) 9 RR 276, [1803–13] All ER Rep 1, 14 Ves 273, 1 White & Tud LC 259 .... 5.9
Huish, Re, Bradshaw v Huish (1889) 43 Ch D 260, 59 LJ Ch 135, 38 WR 199, 62 LT 52 .... 44.15
Huish's Charity, Re (1870) LR 10 Eq 5, 39 LJ Ch 499, 18 WR 817, 22 LT 565 .... 40.15
Hulks v Wills (1949) 50 SRNSW 74 .... 57.20
Hull, Re, Melhuish v Fletcher (1896) 40 Sol Jo 257 .... 32.9
Hull v Carpenter [1920] NZLR 361 .... 50.2
Hull v Christian (1874) LR 17 Eq 546, 43 LJ Ch 861, 22 WR 611 .... 33.17
Hull v Hill (1876) 4 Ch D 97, 25 WR 223 .... 64.5
Hulme v Hulme (1839) 9 Sim 644 .... 82.4
Humberstone v Stanton (1813) 1 Ves & B 385 .... 97.8
Humble v Bowman (1877) 47 LJ Ch 62 .... 83.17
Humble v Shore (1847) 7 Hare 247, 1 Hem & M 550n, 33 LJ Ch 188n, 10 Jur NS 308n, 12 WR 149n; affd (1847) 7 Hare 249 .... 38.13
Humblestone v Martin Tolhurst Partnership (a firm) [2004] EWHC 151 (Ch), (2004) Times, 27 February, [2004] All ER (D) 67 (Feb) 1.14
Hume, Re, Public Trustee v Mabey [1912] 1 Ch 693, 81 LJ Ch 382, 56 Sol Jo 414, 106 LT 335 .... 51.4, 93.17, 93.36, 93.38, 93.39, 94.14
Humfrey, Re (1944) 60 BCR 146, [1944] 2 DLR 476 .... 64.37, 103.7
Hummeltenberg, Re, Beatty v London Spiritualistic Alliance Ltd [1923] 1 Ch 237, [1923] All ER Rep 49, 92 LJ Ch 326, 67 Sol Jo 313, 129 LT 124, 39 TLR 203 .... 102.10
Humphery v Humphery (1877) 36 LT 91 .... 39.19
Humphrey v Humphrey (1851) 1 Sim NS 536, 20 LJ Ch 425 .... 62.1
Humphrey v Tayleur (1752) Amb 136, 1 Dick 161 .... 20.5
Humphrey's Estate, Re [1916] 1 IR 21 .... 83.9
Humphreys, Re, Humphreys v Levett [1893] 3 Ch 1, 62 LJ Ch 498, 2 R 436, 41 WR 519, 37 Sol Jo 439, 68 LT 729, 9 TLR 417, CA 32.23
Humphreys, Re, Wren v Ward (1915) 60 Sol Jo 105, 114 LT 230 ...... 64.11, 64.54, 64.57
Humphreys v Green (1882) 10 QBD 148, 52 LJQB 140, 47 JP 244, 48 LT 60, CA 2.6, 3.4
Humphreys v Howes (1830) 1 Russ & M 639, Taml 497, 8 LJOS Ch 165 ...... 97.4, 97.8
Humphreys v Humphreys (1789) 2 Cox Eq Cas 184 .... 41.2, 41.11
Humphries, Re, Smith v Millidge (1883) 24 Ch D 691, 49 LT 594 .... 72.3

Hunloke v Gell (1830) 1 Russ & M 515 .... 39.18
Hunt, Re, Davies v Hetherington (1890) 62 LT 753 .... 52.3
Hunt v Dorsett (1855) 5 De GM & G 570, 1 Jur NS 1053, 26 LTOS 113 .... 87.2
Hunt v Hort (1791) 3 Bro CC 311 .... 57.10
Hunt v Hunt (1866) LR 1 P & D 209, 35 LJP & M 135, 30 JP 679, sub nom Re Bell's Goods, Hunt v Hunt 14 LT 859 .... 11.12
Hunt v Hunt (1902) 19 WN 96, 2 SRNSW (Eq) 72 .... 97.7, 97.8
Hunt v Scott (1847) 1 De G & Sm 219 .... 38.23
Hunt's Goods, Re (1875) LR 3 P & D 250, 44 LJP & M 43, 39 JP 744, 23 WR 553, 33 LT 321 .... 5.7
Hunt's Trusts, Re (1885) 31 Ch D 308, 55 LJ Ch 280, 34 WR 247, 54 LT 69 .... 39.23, 47.38
Hunt-Foulston v Furber (1876) 3 Ch D 285, 24 WR 756 .... 33.3, 33.7, 99.1
Hunter, Re (1973) 34 DLR (3d) 602 .... 103.3
Hunter, Re (1975) 58 DLR (3d) 175 .... 41.1
Hunter, Re, Lloyds Bank Ltd v Girton College, Cambridge (Mistress and Governors) [1951] Ch 190, [1951] 1 All ER 58, 95 Sol Jo 61, 66 (pt 2) TLR 1108 .... 41.13, 103.10
Hunter, Re, Northey v Northey (1908) 25 TLR 19 .... 63.1, 64.35, 64.37
Hunter v A-G [1899] AC 309, [1895–9] All ER Rep 558, 68 LJ Ch 449, 47 WR 673, 43 Sol Jo 530, 80 LT 732, 15 TLR 384, HL ... 50.5, 102.22, 102.25, 103.11, 212.5
Hunter v Bullock (1872) LR 14 Eq 45, 41 LJ Ch 637, 20 WR 460, 26 LT 349 .... 9.29, 102.22
Hunter v Hunter [1930] 4 DLR 255, 65 OLR 586 .... 7.33
Hunter v Judd (1833) 4 Sim 455 .... 93.6, 93.27
Hunter v Moss [1994] 3 All ER 215, [1994] 1 WLR 452, [1994] 8 LS Gaz R 38, 138 Sol Jo LB 25, CA 8.8
Hunter v Pugh (1839) 1 Hare 308n, 9 LJ Ch 62, 4 Jur 571 .... 60.2
Hunter (Sir G B) (1922) C Trust (Trustees) v IRC (1929) 14 TC 427, 73 Sol Jo 284, 45 TLR 344 .... 102.8
Hunter's Estate, Re [1957] SASR 194 .... 64.7
Hunter's Executors, Petitioners, Re 1992 SC 474, 1992 SLT 1141 .... 9.17, 9.18
Hunter's Settlement Trust, Re, Elliott v Hunter (1939) 83 Sol Jo 339 .... 53.2, 53.4
Hunter's Trusts, Re (1865) LR 1 Eq 295 .... 93.30
Hunter's Will Trusts, Re, Gilks v Harris [1963] Ch 372, [1962] 3 All ER 1050, [1962] 3 WLR 1442, 113 JP 25, 106 Sol Jo 938 .... 40.5, 213.6, 213.12
Huntingdon's Settlement Trusts, Re, Struthers v Mayne [1949] Ch 414, [1949] 1 All ER 674, [1949] LJR 1185, 93 Sol Jo 217, 65 TLR 249 .... 90.3
Hurd, Re, Stott v Stott [1941] Ch 196, [1941] 1 All ER 238, 110 LJ Ch 67, 85 Sol Jo 70, 164 LT 296, 57 TLR 287 .... 47.12, 47.13
Hurd's Will, Re (1883) 9 VLR 23 .... 11.20
Hurdle, Re, Blakeney v Hurdle [1936] 3 All ER 810 .... 15.3, 57.5, 57.10
Hurlbatt, Re, Hurlbatt v Hurlbatt [1910] 2 Ch 553, [1908–10] All ER Rep 439, 80 LJ Ch 29, 103 LT 585 .... 94.5, 95.1, 207.26
Hurley, Re, Nichols v Pargiter (1900) 17 TLR 115 .... 102.25
Hurlstone v Ashton (1865) 11 Jur NS 725 .... 39.12
Hurring, Re [1950] NZLR 948 .... 50.2, 57.20, 71.5
Hurry v Hurry (1870) LR 10 Eq 346, 39 LJ Ch 824, 18 WR 829 .... 56.8, 68.2
Hurshman, Re, Mindlin v Hurshman (1956) 6 DLR 615 .... 35.31

Hurst, Re, Addison v Topp (1892) 67 LT 96, 8 TLR 528, CA 29.11
Hurst v Beach (1821) 5 Madd 351, [1814–23] All ER Rep 523 .... 44.1, 57.31, 88.4
Hurst v Hurst (1882) 21 Ch D 278, [1881–5] All ER Rep 903, 51 LJ Ch 729, 31 WR 327, 46 LT 899, CA 48.15, 99.4, 99.10
Hurzin and Neumeyer Estate, Re (1990) 69 DLR (4th) 18 .... 41.20
Hussey v Berkeley. See Hussey v Lady Dillon
Hussey v Lady Dillon (1763) Amb 603, sub nom Hussey v Berkeley 2 Eden 194 .... 71.1, 71.3
Hussey and Green's Contract, Re, Re Hussey, Hussey v Simper [1921] 1 Ch 566, 90 LJ Ch 253, 65 Sol Jo 357, 124 LT 783, 37 TLR 407 .... 84.2
Hutcheon v Mannington (1791) 1 Ves 366, 4 Bro CC 491n 37.6, 97.7
Hutcheson v Hammond (1790) 3 Bro CC 128 .... 22.4, 29.15, 47.1
Hutchins v Hutchins (1876) IR 10 Eq 453 .... 40.18
Hutchins v Osborne (1858) 4 K & J 252, 27 LJ Ch 421, 4 Jur NS 830, 6 WR 426, 31 LTOS 281; affd (1858) 3 De G & J 142 .... 39.14
Hutchinson, Re, Crispin v Hadden (1919) 88 LJ Ch 352, [1918–19] All ER Rep 1174, 121 LT 239 .... 64.53
Hutchinson, Re, Holt v Hutchinson [1955] Ch 255, [1955] 1 All ER 689, [1955] 2 WLR 586, 99 Sol Jo 185 .... 104.4, 204.16
Hutchinson v Barrow (1861) 6 H & N 583, 30 LJ Ex 280, 9 WR 538, 4 LT 554 .... 59.3
Hutchinson v National Refuges for Homeless and Destitute Children [1920] AC 795, [1920] All ER Rep 701, 89 LJ Ch 469, 64 Sol Jo 496, 123 LT 439, HL 66.1, 77.4, 217.23, 236.18
Hutchinson v Rough (1879) 40 LT 289 .... 38.3, 38.10, 82.7
Hutchinson v Smith (1863) 1 New Rep 513, 11 WR 417, 8 LT 602 .... 64.27
Hutchinson v Tottenham [1898] 1 IR 403; affd [1899] 1 IR 344, CA 94.14, 94.44, 94.47, 98.4, 100.3
Hutchinson and Tenant, Re (1878) 8 Ch D 540, 26 WR 904, 39 LT 86 .... 79.1, 83.9
Hutchinson's Trusts, Re (1882) 21 Ch D 811, 51 LJ Ch 924, 47 LT 573 .... 87.2
Hutchinson's Will Trusts, Re, Gibbons v Nottingham Area No 1 Hospital Management Committee [1953] Ch 387, [1953] 1 All ER 996, [1953] 2 WLR 872, 97 Sol Jo 300 .... 103.3, 212.3
Hutchison v Skelton (1856) 2 Macq 492, HL 42.10
Hutchison's Goods, Re (1902) 18 TLR 706 .... 11.5
Hutchison's Settlement, Re, ex p Drum (1852) 5 De G & Sm 681, 17 Jur 59 .... 100.3
Hutley v Grimstone (1879) 5 PD 24, 48 LJP 68, 41 LT 531 .... 5.9
Hutton, Re, Allen v Hutton [1916] VLR 546 .... 41.1
Hutton v Simpson. See Sympson v Hutton
Huxtable, Re, Huxtable v Crawfurd [1902] 2 Ch 793, [1900–3] All ER Rep 799, 71 LJ Ch 876, 51 WR 282, 87 LT 415, CA 36.5, 36.13, 103.1
Huxtep v Brooman (1785) 1 Bro CC 437 .... 38.3
Hyde, Re, Smith v Jack [1932] 1 Ch 95, [1931] All ER Rep 52, 101 LJ Ch 95, 75 Sol Jo 781, 146 LT 255 .... 9.25
Hyde v Parrat (1696) 1 P Wms 1, sub nom Hide v Parrat 2 Vern 331 .... 8.3
Hyett v Mekin (1884) 25 Ch D 735, 53 LJ Ch 241, 32 WR 513, 50 LT 54 .... 37.2
Hyndman v Hyndman [1895] 1 IR 179 .... 82.2
Hyne, Re [1958] Qd R 431 .... 94.38

Hynes, Re, Knapp v Hynes [1950] 2 All ER 879, 94 Sol Jo 687, 66 (pt 2) TLR 795, CA 38.3, 64.45
Hyslop, Re, Hyslop v Chamberlain [1894] 3 Ch 522, 64 LJ Ch 168, 8 R 680, 43 WR 6, 38 Sol Jo 663, 71 LT 373 .... 57.11

I

Ibbetson, Re, Ibbetson v Ibbetson (1903) 88 LT 461 .... 68.8, 78.5
Ibbetson's Goods, Re (1839) 2 Curt 337 .... 14.1, 14.2
Ilchester (Earl), ex p (1803) 7 Ves 348, [1803–13] All ER Rep 310 .... 74.1
Ilott v Genge (1842) 3 Curt 160, 1 Notes of Cases 572; affd (1844) 4 Moo PCC 265, PC 11.26, 12.3
Imray v Imeson (1872) 26 LT 93 .... 56.1
Ince's Goods, Re (1877) 2 PD 111, 46 LJP 30, 41 JP 425, 25 WR 396, 36 LT 519 .... 18.6
Inchley v Robinson (1587) 3 Leon 165 .... 64.32
Inchley and Robinson's Case (1587) 2 Leon 41, sub nom Jelsey v Robinson Owen 88 .... 53.1
Income Tax Special Purposes Comrs v Pemsel [1891] AC 531, 3 TC 53, 55 JP 805, 61 LJQB 265, [1891–4] All ER Rep 28, 65 LT 621, 7 TLR 657, HL 102.4, 102.7, 102.8
Incorporated Council of Law Reporting for England and Wales v A-G [1972] Ch 73, [1971] 3 All ER 1029, [1971] 3 WLR 853, 47 TC 321, 115 Sol Jo 808, CA 102.4, 102.8, 102.10, 102.18
Incorporated Society in Dublin v Richards (1841) 4 I Eq R 177, 1 Con & Law 58, 1 Dr & War 258 .... 56.1, 60.1
Inderwick v Tatchell [1901] 2 Ch 738, CA; affd [1903] AC 120, 72 LJ Ch 393, 88 LT 399, HL 67.4, 67.6
Inderwick v Tatchell [1903] AC 120, 72 LJ Ch 393, 88 LT 399, HL...... 50.3, 50.4, 50.5, 50.21, 51.7, 67.1
Ingham v Daly (1882) 9 LR Ir 484 .... 33.11, 33.34
Ingilby v Amcotts (1856) 21 Beav 585, 25 LJ Ch 769, 2 Jur NS 556, 4 WR 433, 27 LTOS 94 .... 7.20, 60.1
Ingle's Trusts, Re (1871) LR 11 Eq 578, 40 LJ Ch 310, 19 WR 676, 24 LT 315 .... 57.12, 58.10, 74.2
Inglefield v Coghlan (1845) 2 Coll 247 .... 88.2
Ingleman v Worthington (1855) 25 LJ Ch 46, 1 Jur NS 1062, 4 WR 61, 26 LTOS 253 .... 33.27
Inglesant v Inglesant (1874) LR 3 P & D 172, 43 LJP & M 43, 38 JP 584, 22 WR 741, 30 LT 909 .... 11.26
Ingram v IRC [2000] 1 AC 293, [1999] 1 All ER 297, [1999] 2 WLR 90, [1999] STC 37, [1999] 03 LS Gaz R 32, [1998] EGCS 181, 143 Sol Jo LB 52, HL 200.76
Ingram v Soutten (1874) LR 7 HL 408, 44 LJ Ch 55, 23 WR 363, 31 LT 215 .... 97.5, 97.6
Ingram v Suckling (1859) 7 WR 386, 33 LTOS 89 .... 93.24, 93.43
Ingram v Wyatt. See Wyatt v Ingram
Ingram Estate, Re (1961) 32 DLR (2d) 152, 36 WWR 536 .... 82.2
IRC v Baddeley. See Baddeley v IRC

IRC v Bernstein [1960] Ch 444, [1960] 1 All ER 697, [1960] 2 WLR 554, 39 TC 391, 39 ATC 117, 53 R & IT 301, [1960] TR 21, 104 Sol Jo 250; affd [1961] Ch 399, [1961] 1 All ER 320, [1961] 2 WLR 143, 39 TC 391, 39 ATC 415, [1960] TR 369, 105 Sol Jo 128, CA 66.3, 218.90, 218.92

IRC v Broadway Cottages Trust [1955] Ch 20, [1954] 3 All ER 120, [1954] 3 WLR 438, 35 TC 577, 98 Sol Jo 588, sub nom Broadway Cottages Trust v IRC 33 ATC 305, 47 R & IT 574, [1954] TR 295, CA 53.6

IRC v Buchanan [1958] Ch 289, [1957] 2 All ER 400, [1957] 3 WLR 68, 37 TC 365, 36 ATC 36, 50 R & IT 223, [1957] TR 43, 100 Sol Jo 502, L(TC) 1823, CA 216.1

IRC v City of Glasgow Police Athletic Association [1953] AC 380, [1953] 1 All ER 747, [1953] 2 WLR 625, 34 TC 76, 32 ATC 62, 46 R & IT 207, [1953] TR 49, 117 JP 201, 97 Sol Jo 208, 1953 SC (HL) 13, 1953 SLT 105 .... 102.8, 102.10, 102.12

IRC v Cookson [1975] 3 All ER 590, [1975] STC 536, 50 TC 705, 54 ATC 204, [1975] TR 173; affd [1977] 2 All ER 331, [1977] 1 WLR 962, [1977] STC 140, 50 TC 705, 715, [1977] TR 17, 121 Sol Jo 544, CA 18.15, 224.23, 233.45

IRC v Crossman [1937] AC 26, [1936] 1 All ER 762, 80 Sol Jo 485, 52 TLR 415, sub nom Crossman, Re, Re Paulin 15 ATC 94, 105 LJKB 450, 154 LT 570, HL 200.81

IRC v Educational Grants Association Ltd [1967] Ch 993, [1967] 2 All ER 893, [1967] 3 WLR 41, 44 TC 93, 46 ATC 71, [1967] TR 79, 111 Sol Jo 194, CA 102.1

IRC v Falkirk Temperance Cafe Trust (1927) 11 TC 353, 1927 SC 261 .... 102.11

IRC v Glasgow Musical Festival Association (1926) 11 TC 154, 1926 SC 920 .... 102.8

IRC v Gray (Executor of Lady Fox) [1994] STC 360, [1994] RVR 129, CA 200.81, 205.27, 205.44

IRC v Hawley [1928] 1 KB 578, 13 TC 327, 6 ATC 1021, 97 LJKB 191, 138 LT 710 .... 1.8, 200.97

IRC v Helen Slater Charitable Trust Ltd [1982] Ch 49, [1981] 3 All ER 98, [1981] 3 WLR 377, [1981] STC 471, 55 TC 230, [1981] TR 225, 125 Sol Jo 414, CA 235.11

IRC v Lloyds Private Banking Ltd [1998] STC 559, [1998] 2 FCR 41, [1999] 1 FLR 147, [1999] Fam Law 309, [1998] 19 LS Gaz R 23, 142 Sol Jo LB 164 .... 208.34, 208.48

IRC v McMullen [1978] 1 All ER 230, [1978] 1 WLR 664, 54 TC 413, 122 Sol Jo 331; affd [1979] 1 All ER 588, [1979] 1 WLR 130, 54 TC 413, 123 Sol Jo 15, CA; revsd [1981] AC 1, [1980] 1 All ER 884, [1980] 2 WLR 416, 54 TC 413, [1980] TR 85, 124 Sol Jo 206, 130 NLJ 260, HL 102.4, 102.8, 102.12, 212.26

IRC v Mallender (Drury-Lowe's Executors) [2001] STC 514 .... 205.61

IRC v Marquess Camden. See Camden (Marquis) v IRC

IRC v National Anti-Vivisection Society. See National Anti-Vivisection Society v IRC

IRC v Peeblesshire Nursing Association (1927) 11 TC 335, 1927 SC 215 .... 102.7

IRC v Roberts Marine Mansions Trustees (1927) 11 TC 425, 43 TLR 270, CA 102.7

IRC v Sir Aubrey Smith [1930] 1 KB 713, 99 LJKB 361, 15 TC 661, 142 LT 517, CA 38.16
IRC v Society for Relief of Widows and Orphans of Medical Men (1926) 136 LT 60, 11 TC 1, 70 Sol Jo 837, 42 TLR 612 .... 102.7
IRC v Stannard [1984] 2 All ER 105, [1984] 1 WLR 1039, [1984] STC 245, 128 Sol Jo 400 .... 200.97, 200.123
IRC v Stype Investments (Jersey) Ltd [1982] Ch 456, [1982] 3 All ER 419, [1982] 3 WLR 228, [1982] STC 625, 126 Sol Jo 497, CA 25.1
IRC v Temperance Council of Christian Churches of England and Wales (1926) 10 TC 748, 5 ATC 679, 136 LT 27, 42 TLR 618 .... 102.11
IRC v Williams [1969] 3 All ER 614, [1969] 1 WLR 1197, 48 ATC 154, [1969] TR 153, 113 Sol Jo 587 .... 94.48
IRC v Yorkshire Agricultural Society [1928] 1 KB 611, [1927] All ER Rep 536, 97 LJKB 100, 13 TC 58, 72 Sol Jo 68, 138 LT 192, 44 TLR 59, CA 102.8, 102.10
Inman, Re [1965] VR 238 .... 62.1
Inman, Re, Inman v Inman [1915] 1 Ch 187, 84 LJ Ch 309, 59 Sol Jo 161, 112 LT 240 .... 38.19, 38.23, 64.57
Inman, Re, Inman v Rolls [1893] 3 Ch 518, 62 LJ Ch 940, 8 R 293, 42 WR 156, 69 LT 374 .... 32.3, 32.15, 32.21, 49.5
Inne's Trustees v Bowen 1920 SC 133 .... 95.8
Innes, Re, Barclay v Innes (1908) 125 LT Jo 60 .... 44.5, 44.12
Innes, Re, Innes v Innes [1910] 1 Ch 188, 79 LJ Ch 174, 101 LT 633 .... 30.18, 57.32
Innes (Inspector of Taxes) v Harrison [1954] 1 All ER 884, [1954] 1 WLR 668, 35 TC 594, 33 ATC 77, 47 R & IT 223, [1954] TR 81, 98 Sol Jo 269 .... 94.14
Innes v Johnson (1799) 4 Ves 568 .... 30.3
Innes v Mitchell (1846) 1 Ph 710 .... 33.42
Innes v Sayer (1851) 21 LJ Ch 190, 16 Jur 21, 3 Mac & G 606, 18 LTOS 129 .... 39.19
Investors' Compensation Scheme Ltd v West Bromwich Building Society [1998] 1 All ER 98, [1998] 1 WLR 896, [1998] 1 BCLC 493, [1997] NLJR 989, [1997] CLC 1243, [1997] PNLR 541, HL 50.1, 57.2
Ionides, Re, London County Westminster and Parr's Bank Ltd v Craies [1922] WN 46, 66 Sol Jo 315, 38 TLR 269 .... 58.4, 64.58
Irani v Irani [2006] EWHC 1811 (Ch), [2006] WTLR 1561, [2006] All ER (D) 335 (Jul) 3.1, 105.49
Irby v Irby (No 3) (1858) 25 Beav 632, 4 Jur NS 989, 119 RR 577, 6 WR 853, 32 LTOS 141 .... 30.12, 30.17
Iredell v Iredell (1858) 25 Beav 485 .... 66.14, 66.20
Ireland, Re (1963) 147 DLR (3d) 480 .... 5.1
Irvin v Ironmonger (1831) 2 Russ & M 531 .... 33.11
Irvin's Estate, Re (1908) 25 TLR 41 .... 19.4
Irvine v Sullivan (1869) LR 8 Eq 673, 38 LJ Ch 635, 17 WR 1083 .... 36.5, 36.7, 57.10
Irvine's Goods, Re [1919] 2 IR 485 .... 19.1, 19.4
Irwin, Re [1920] NZLR 440 .... 13.3
Irwin v Tyson [1966] ALR 117 .... 99.4
Irwin's Estate, Re (1910) 44 ILT 50 .... 42.2
Isaac, Re, Harrison v Isaac [1905] 1 Ch 427, 74 LJ Ch 277, 92 LT 227 .... 38.3, 47.6, 52.9

Isaacs, Re, Isaacs v Reginall [1894] 3 Ch 506, 63 LJ Ch 815, 8 R 660, 42 WR 685, 38 Sol Jo 662, 71 LT 386 .... 41.20
Isaacson v Van Goor (1872) 42 LJ Ch 193, 21 WR 156, 27 LT 752 .... 101.4
Isherwood v Payne (1800) 5 Ves 677 .... 82.7
Israell v Rodon (1839) 2 Moo PCC 51 .... 17.2
Itter, Re, Dedman v Godfrey [1950] P 130, [1950] 1 All ER 68, 93 Sol Jo 805, 66 (pt 1) TLR 45 .... 14.2, 14.13, 19.4
Ive v King (1852) 16 Beav 46, 21 LJ Ch 560, 16 Jur 489, 20 LTOS 5 .... 47.32, 68.3, 68.4, 68.5, 68.6, 68.12, 97.4, 210.25
Iversen Estate, Re, Nowee v Iversen (1956) 19 WWR 524 .... 83.9
Iverson's Estate, Re [1950] 2 WWR 1021 .... 52.9
Ives v Dodgson (1870) LR 9 Eq 401, 39 LJ Ch 693, 23 LT 215 .... 52.11
Ivory, Re, Hankin v Turner (1878) 10 Ch D 372 .... 49.7
Izard v Tamahau Mahupuku (1902) 22 NZLR 418 .... 7.20
Izon v Butler (1815) 2 Price 34 .... 30.4, 47.22

J

JH, Re (1911) 25 OLR 132 .... 64.53
Jack, Re, Jack v Jack [1899] 1 Ch 374, 68 LJ Ch 188, 80 LT 321 .... 39.18, 100.2
Jack d Westby v Fetherstone (1829) 2 Hud & B 320 .... 94.33
Jackson, Re, Beattie v Murphy [1933] Ch 237, [1932] All ER Rep 696, 102 LJ Ch 1, 76 Sol Jo 779, 148 LT 238, 49 TLR 5 .... 53.3, 57.20, 57.22, 57.26, 72.2
Jackson, Re, Bell v Adlam (1910) Times, 11 June 9.31
Jackson, Re, Day v Atkin [1946] 1 All ER 327, 90 Sol Jo 163 .... 33.12, 33.18, 211.8
Jackson, Re, Holliday v Jackson [1944] WN 26, 113 LJ Ch 78, 88 Sol Jo 17, 170 LT 244, 60 TLR 157 .... 77.2
Jackson, Re, Jackson v Hamilton [1923] 2 Ch 365, 92 LJ Ch 622, 67 Sol Jo 481, 129 LT 307, 39 TLR 400, CA 30.24
Jackson, Re, Midland Bank Executor and Trustee Co Ltd v Archbishop of Wales [1930] 2 Ch 389, 99 LJ Ch 450, 144 LT 102, 46 TLR 558 .... 102.17
Jackson, Re, Shiers v Ashworth (1883) 25 Ch D 162, 53 LJ Ch 180, 32 WR 194, 50 LT 18 .... 47.12, 47.29, 47.32
Jackson, Re, Wilson v Donald (1881) 44 LT 467 .... 63.8
Jackson v Calvert (1860) 1 John & H 235 .... 84.4
Jackson v Dover (1864) 2 Hem & M 209, 10 Jur NS 631, 4 New Rep 136, 12 WR 855, 10 LT 489 .... 51.10
Jackson v Hamilton (1846) 9 I Eq R 430, 3 Jo & Lat 702 .... 53.2
Jackson v Hillas (1869) 18 WR 216 .... 5.9
Jackson v Hogan. See Hogan v Jackson
Jackson v Jackson (1749) 1 Ves Sen 217 .... 56.9, 93.27
Jackson v Jackson (1840) 7 Cl & Fin 977, HL 40.15
Jackson v Kelly (1751) 2 Ves Sen 285 .... 38.3
Jackson v Marjoribanks (1841) 12 Sim 93, 5 Jur 885 .... 93.12, 93.14
Jackson v Noble (1838) 2 Keen 590, 7 LJ Ch 133, 2 Jur 251 .... 48.15
Jackson v Rodger. See Freeland, Re, Jackson v Rodgers
Jackson v Simons [1923] 1 Ch 373, [1922] All ER Rep 583, 92 LJ Ch 161, 67 Sol Jo 262, 128 LT 572, 39 TLR 147 .... 7.23
Jackson v Yates [1912] 1 IR 267 .... 30.12

Jackson and Gill v Paulet (1851) 2 Rob Eccl 344 .... 25.1
Jackson and Simcock v Johnson. See Johnson v Simcock
Jackson's Estates, Re, Houston v Western Trust Co (No 2) [1940] 1 WWR 65, 9 FLJ (Can) 261 .... 35.8
Jackson's Settled Estate, Re [1902] 1 Ch 258, 71 LJ Ch 154, 50 WR 235, 46 Sol Jo 136, 85 LT 625, 18 TLR 168 .... 27.18
Jackson's Will, Re (1879) 13 Ch D 189, 49 LJ Ch 82, 28 WR 209, 41 LT 499 .... 50.6, 50.21, 83.17, 96.2, 96.4
Jacob, Re, M'Coy v Jacob [1919] 1 IR 134 .... 32.2, 61.1, 64.14
Jacob, Re, Mortimer v Mortimer [1907] 1 Ch 445, 76 LJ Ch 217, 51 Sol Jo 249, 96 LT 362 .... 39.12, 39.14
Jacob v Catling [1881] WN 105 .... 47.32
Jacob's Goods, Re (1842) 1 Notes of Cases 401 .... 14.9
Jacob's Will, Re (1861) 29 Beav 402, 7 Jur NS 302, 9 WR 474, 4 LT 104 .... 93.31
Jacobs, Re, Westminster Bank Ltd v Chinn (1970) 114 Sol Jo 515 .... 102.10, 103.7
Jacobs v Jacobs (1853) 16 Beav 557, 22 LJ Ch 668, 17 Jur 293, 1 WR 238, 21 LTOS 97 .... 77.3
Jacobsen, Re (1977) 80 DLR (3d) 122 .... 103.3
Jacobson, Re [1970] VR 180 .... 64.7
Jacques, Re (1967) 63 DLR (2d) 673 .... 102.10
Jacques, Re (1985) 16 DLR (4th) 472 .... 48.8, 93.28, 101.2
Jacques v Chambers (1846) 4 Ry & Can Cas 205, 2 Coll 435, 10 Jur 151, 6 LTOS 429, sub nom Jaques v Chambers 4 Ry & Can Cas 499, 16 LJ Ch 243, 11 Jur 295 .... 8.7, 32.2
Jacquet v Jacquet (1859) 27 Beav 332, 7 WR 543 .... 91.2
Jacubs v Rylance (1874) LR 17 Eq 341, 43 LJ Ch 280 .... 30.17
Jagger v Jagger (1883) 25 Ch D 729, 53 LJ Ch 201, 32 WR 284, 49 LT 667 .... 95.3, 218.72
James, Re [1965] VR 569 .... 57.22
James, Re, Clutterbuck v James (1890) 62 LT 545, 6 TLR 240 .... 99.7, 99.8
James, Re, Grenfell v Hamilton [1932] 2 Ch 25, [1932] All ER Rep 452, 101 LJ Ch 265, 76 Sol Jo 146, 146 LT 528, 48 TLR 250 .... 102.6, 102.7
James, Re, James v James [1935] Ch 449, [1935] All ER Rep 235, 104 LJ Ch 247, 153 LT 277 .... 30.18
James, Re, Lloyds Bank Ltd v Atkins [1947] Ch 256, [1947] 1 All ER 402, [1947] LJR 735, 91 Sol Jo 236, 176 LT 370, 63 TLR 246 .... 214.7
James v Burdekin [1990] 3 WAR 299 .... 14.1
James v Castle (1875) 33 LT 665 .... 3.11
James v Gard (1887) 13 VLR 908 .... 99.1
James v Lord Wynford (1852) 22 LJ Ch 450, 17 Jur 17, 1 Sm & G 40, 1 WR 61, 20 LTOS 273 .... 93.12, 93.24
James v Lord Wynford (1854) 23 LJ Ch 767, 18 Jur 868, 2 Sm & G 350, 2 WR 607, 23 LTOS 320 .... 79.2
James v Richardson (1677) 3 Keb 832, 2 Lev 232, Poll 457, T Jo 99, 1 Vent 334, Freem KB 472, 1 Eq Cas Abr 214 pl 11; affd (1678) Freem KB 472n, HL 66.1
James v Shannon (1868) IR 2 Eq 118 .... 101.7
James v Shrimpton (1876) 1 PD 431, 45 LJP 85 .... 18.5, 19.5
James v Smith (1844) 14 Sim 214, 13 LJ Ch 376, 8 Jur 594, 3 LTOS 297 .... 71.1, 71.5

James v Williams [2000] Ch 1, [1999] 3 All ER 309, [1999] 3 WLR 451, 79 P & CR 421, [1999] 2 FCR 498, [1999] 15 LS Gaz R 30, 78 P & CR D17, CA 25.1
James' Estate, Re [1934] 3 WWR 364 .... 10.18
James' Goods, Re (1858) 1 Sw & Tr 238 .... 14.1
James' Settled Estates, Re (1884) 32 WR 898, 51 LT 596 .... 93.6, 93.13
James' Will Trusts, Re, Peard v James [1962] Ch 226, [1960] 3 All ER 744, [1960] 3 WLR 1031, 104 Sol Jo 1077 .... 49.2, 50.4, 51.7, 51.8, 67.1, 67.3
Jameson, Re, King v Winn [1908] 2 Ch 111, 77 LJ Ch 729, 98 LT 745 .... 41.2, 41.4, 58.12
Jamieson's Estate, Re (1959) 22 DLR (2d) 745, 29 WWR 650 .... 74.1
Janaway's Goods, Re (1874) 44 LJP & M 6, 39 JP 104, 23 WR 385, 31 LT 800 .... 11.25
Jane v Jane (1917) 33 TLR 389 .... 5.7, 21.7
Jankowski v Pelek Estate [1996] 2 WWR 457, 131 DLR (4th) 717 .... 51.1
Jaques, Re, Hodgson v Braisby [1903] 1 Ch 267, 72 LJ Ch 197, 51 WR 229, 47 Sol Jo 145, 88 LT 210, CA 44.11, 100.6
Jaques v Chambers. See Jacques v Chambers
Jarman v Vye (1866) LR 2 Eq 784, 35 LJ Ch 821, 14 WR 1011 .... 98.5
Jarman's Estate, Re, Leavers v Clayton (1878) 8 Ch D 584, 47 LJ Ch 675, 42 JP 662, 26 WR 907, 39 LT 89 .... 102.23
Jarman's Trusts, Re (1865) LR 1 Eq 71 .... 90.2
Jarmin (Inspector of Taxes) v Rawlings [1994] STC 1005, 67 TC 130, [1995] 02 LS Gaz R 37 .... 205.23
Jarrett, Re, Re Vrenegroor, Bird v Green [1919] 1 Ch 366, 88 LJ Ch 150, 63 Sol Jo 353, 121 LT 119 .... 39.14
Jarvis v Duke (1681) 1 Vern 19 .... 34.13, 35.6
Jarvis v Pond (1839) 9 Sim 549, 8 LJ Ch 167 .... 68.9
Jasmine Trustees Ltd v Wells & Hind (a firm) [2007] EWHC 38 (Ch), [2007] 1 All ER 1142, [2007] 3 WLR 810, [2007] STC 660, (2007) Times, 12 February, [2007] SWTI 261, [2007] All ER (D) 112 (Jan) 221.41
Jauncey v A-G (1861) 3 Giff 308, 8 Jur NS 6, 10 WR 129, 5 LT 374 ... 32.13, 38.6, 64.51
Jay v Jay [1924] 1 KB 826, 93 LJKB 280, 130 LT 667, DC 42.1, 208.27
Jeacock v Falkener (1783) 1 Cox Eq Cas 37, 1 Bro CC 295 .... 44.15
Jeaffreson's Trusts, Re (1866) LR 2 Eq 276, 35 LJ Ch 622, 12 Jur NS 660, 14 WR 759 .... 40.21, 78.4, 84.4
Jeans, Re, Upton v Jeans (1895) 13 R 627, 72 LT 835 .... 74.1
Jebb, Re, Ward-Smith v Jebb [1966] Ch 666, [1965] 3 All ER 358, [1965] 3 WLR 810, 109 Sol Jo 613, CA 75.7
Jee v Audley (1787) 1 Cox Eq Cas 324 .... 94.11, 94.12, 94.21
Jeeves, Re, Morris-Williams v Haylett [1949] Ch 49, [1948] 2 All ER 961, [1949] LJR 317, 92 Sol Jo 675 .... 87.2
Jefferies v Michell (1855) 20 Beav 15 .... 44.15
Jeffery, Re (1974) 53 DLR (3d) 650 .... 41.1
Jeffery, Re, Arnold v Burt [1895] 2 Ch 577, 64 LJ Ch 830, 13 R 857, 44 WR 61, 73 LT 332 .... 32.28
Jeffery, Re, Nussey v Jeffery [1914] 1 Ch 375, 83 LJ Ch 251, 58 Sol Jo 120, 110 LT 11 .... 30.6, 57.15, 57.22, 86.2, 93.27
Jeffery v De Vitre (1857) 24 Beav 296 .... 85.3
Jeffery v Honywood (1819) 4 Madd 398 .... 85.2

Jeffery's Trusts, Re (1866) LR 2 Eq 68, 35 LJ Ch 426 .... 32.2
Jefferys, Re, Finch v Martin [1939] Ch 205, [1938] 4 All ER 120, 108 LJ Ch 123, 82 Sol Jo 869, 159 LT 542, 55 TLR 44 .... 99.3
Jeffrey, Re, Welch v Jeffrey [1948] 2 All ER 131, 92 Sol Jo 377 .... 50.15, 87.1, 87.2
Jeffreys v Conner (1860) 28 Beav 328, 6 Jur NS 986, 8 WR 572, 3 LT 45 .... 98.13
Jeffreys v Jeffreys (1744) 3 Atk 120 .... 30.8
Jeffreys v Jeffreys (1901) 84 LT 417, 17 TLR 356 .... 34.11
Jeffries v Alexander (1860) 8 HL Cas 594, 31 LJ Ch 9, 24 JP 643, 7 Jur NS 221, 2 LT 748 .... 10.6
Jeffs, Re, Brown v Jeffs (1912) 31 NZLR 156 .... 20.4
Jeffs v Wood (1723) 2 P Wms 128, 2 Eq Cas Abr 10 pl 9 .... 30.11
Jelley v Iliffe [1981] Fam 128, [1981] 2 All ER 29, [1981] 2 WLR 801, 125 Sol Jo 355, CA 105.14, 105.18, 105.19, 105.22, 105.29
Jelsey v Robinson. See Inchley and Robinson's Case
Jenings v Baily (1853) 17 Beav 118, 22 LJ Ch 977, 17 Jur 433, 21 LTOS 112 .... 62.1
Jenkins, Re, Jenkins v Davies [1931] 2 Ch 218, [1931] All ER Rep 382, 100 LJ Ch 265, 145 LT 184, 47 TLR 379, CA 41.13, 59.2
Jenkins, Re, Jenkins v May (1954) 2 DLR 268 .... 62.1
Jenkins, Re, Tucker v Jenkins (1901) 46 Sol Jo 13 .... 64.35
Jenkins, Re, Williams v Jenkins [1915] 1 Ch 46, 84 LJ Ch 349 .... 99.8, 99.9, 214.50
Jenkins v Gaisford and Thring, Re Jenkins's Goods (1863) 32 LJPM & A 122, 27 JP 504, 9 Jur NS 630, 2 New Rep 401, 3 Sw & Tr 93, 11 WR 854, 8 LT 517 .... 11.16, 11.21
Jenkins v Gower (1846) 2 Coll 537, 10 Jur 702, 7 LTOS 449 .... 77.2
Jenkins v Herries (1819) 4 Madd 67; on appeal (1823) 55 Lords Journals 517, HL 84.2
Jenkins v Hughes (1860) 8 HL Cas 571, 30 LJ Ch 870, 6 Jur NS 1043, 8 WR 667, 3 LT 106 .... 50.3, 50.5, 51.7, 51.11, 84.2
Jenkins v Jones (1866) LR 2 Eq 323, sub nom Re Jones, Jenkins v Jones 35 LJ Ch 520, 12 Jur NS 368, 14 WR 665, 14 LT 540 .... 41.1
Jenkins v Morris (1880) 14 Ch D 674, 49 LJ Ch 392, 42 LT 817, CA 4.15, 4.20
Jenkins v Stewart (1906) 3 CLR 799 .... 20.3
Jenkins' Trusts, Re (1889) 23 LR Ir 162 .... 38.1
Jenner v Ffinch (1879) 5 PD 106, 49 LJP 25, 28 WR 520, 42 LT 327 .... 12.6, 18.8, 18.14
Jenner v Turner (1880) 16 Ch D 188, 50 LJ Ch 161, 45 JP 124, 29 WR 99, 43 LT 468 .... 34.16, 35.4, 35.10
Jennings, Re (1954) 33 UPR 230 .... 80.1, 99.1
Jennings, Re [1994] Ch 286, [1994] 3 All ER 27, [1994] 3 WLR 67, [1995] 1 FCR 257, sub nom Re Jennings, Harlow v National Westminster Bank plc [1994] 1 FLR 536, [1994] Fam Law 439, CA 105.16, 105.23
Jennings, Re, Caldbeck v Stafford and Lindemere [1930] 1 IR 196 .... 64.35
Jennings v Bond (1845) 2 Jo & Lat 720, 8 IR Eq 755 .... 31.18
Jennings v Cairns [2003] EWCA Civ 1935, [2004] WTLR 361, (2003) Times, 26 November, [2003] All ER (D) 249 (Nov) 5.9
Jennings v Hanna [1904] 1 IR 540 .... 101.6, 101.14
Jennings v Jennings (1877) 1 LR Ir 552 .... 57.18
Jennings v Newman (1839) 10 Sim 219, 3 Jur 748; varied (1839) 3 Jur 1068 .... 52.6, 66.1

Jennings v Rice [2001] WTLR 871; affd [2002] EWCA Civ 159, [2003] 1 P & CR 100, [2003] 1 FCR 501, [2002] WTLR 367, [2002] NPC 28, [2002] All ER (D) 324 (Feb), [2002] WTLR 367 .... 43.1
Jenour v Jenour (1805) 10 Ves 562 .... 29.14
Jensen, Re [1992] 2 NZLR 506 .... 6.1
Jermingham Trusts, Re, Gormanstown v Nicholl [1922] 1 IR 115 .... 48.9
Jermyn, Re [1965] VR 376 .... 77.3
Jerningham v Herbert (1829) 4 Russ 388, 6 LJOS Ch 134,Taml 103 .... 23.4, 53.3
Jersey Society for the Prevention of Cruelty to Animals v Rees (2001–02) 4 ITELR 294, Royal Ct Jersey 18.12
Jervis v Howle and Talke Colliery Co Ltd [1937] Ch 67, [1936] 3 All ER 193, 106 LJ Ch 34, 80 Sol Jo 875, 155 LT 572 .... 6.1
Jervis v Wolferstan (1874) LR 18 Eq 18, [1874–80] All ER Rep Ext 1933, 43 LJ Ch 809, 30 LT 452 .... 3.2, 3.8, 3.10, 31.7, 47.38
Jesson v Wright. See Doe d Wright v Jesson
Jessop, Re (1859) 11 I Ch R 424 .... 52.9
Jessop, Re [1924] P 221, [1924] All ER Rep 692, 93 LJP 135, 132 LT 31, 40 TLR 800 .... 14.11
Jessopp v Watson (1833) 1 My & K 665, 2 LJ Ch 197 .... 37.7
Jesus College Case (1615) Duke on Charitable Uses, ed Bridgman 363 .... 102.8
Jewis v Lawrence (1869) LR 8 Eq 345, 33 JP 776 .... 30.14
Jewish Home for Aged of British Columbia v Toronto General Trusts Corpn [1961] SCR 465, 28 DLR (2d) 48, 34 WWR 638 .... 102.26, 102.28
Jobson, Re, Jobson v Richardson (1889) 44 Ch D 154, 59 LJ Ch 245, 62 LT 148 .... 51.1, 93.13
Jobson's Case (1597) Cro Eliz 576 .... 58.11
Jodrell, Re, Jodrell v Seale (1890) 44 Ch D 590, 59 LJ Ch 538, 38 WR 721, 63 LT 15, CA; on appeal sub nom Seale-Hayne v Jodrell [1891] AC 304, [1891–4] All ER Rep 477, 61 LJ Ch 70, 65 LT 57, HL 50.3, 50.6, 50.18, 50.21, 51.9, 55.2, 58.10, 71.1, 72.2, 72.3
Joel, Re, Johnson v Joel [1936] 2 All ER 962 .... 32.2, 204.61
Joel, Re, Rogerson v Joel [1943] Ch 311, [1943] 2 All ER 263, 112 LJ Ch 282, 87 Sol Jo 353, 169 LT 247, 59 TLR 355, CA 46.3, 241.16
Joel's Will Trusts, Re, Rogerson v Brudenell-Bruce [1967] Ch 14, [1966] 2 All ER 482, [1966] 3 WLR 209, 110 Sol Jo 570 .... 32.28, 214.50, 214.52, 218.55, 218.68
Johns v Wilson [1900] 1 IR 342 .... 47.6, 52.9
Johnson, Re [1928] SASR 490 .... 8.7
Johnson, Re [1931] 2 DLR 987 .... 64.27
Johnson, Re [1950] 2 DLR 69, 57 Man R 488, 1 WWR 263 .... 9.14
Johnson, Re [1953] 4 DLR 777, 32 MPR 170 .... 13.3
Johnson, Re [1955] VLR 198 .... 35.28
Johnson, Re (1963) 37 DLR (2d) 185, [1963] 1 OR 366 .... 94.21
Johnson, Re [1987] CLY 3882 .... 105.5
Johnson, Re, Cockerell v Earl of Essex (1884) 26 Ch D 538, 53 LJ Ch 645, 32 WR 634, 52 LT 44 .... 63.1
Johnson, Re, Cowley v Public Trustee [1915] 1 Ch 435, 84 LJ Ch 393, 59 Sol Jo 333, 112 LT 935 .... 37.3
Johnson, Re, Danily v Johnson (1893) 3 R 308, 68 LT 20 .... 48.5, 48.6, 66.15, 66.22

Johnson, Re, Greenwood v Greenwood and Robinson (1903) 89 LT 520, CA 64.53
Johnson, Re, Pitt v Johnson (1913) 30 TLR 200, 58 Sol Jo 219; affd (1914) 111 LT 130, 30 TLR 505, CA 50.3, 76.3
Johnson, Re, Public Trustee v Calvert [1939] 2 All ER 458 .... 82.2
Johnson, Re, Sandy v Reilly (1905) 92 LT 357, [1904–7] All ER Rep 539, 49 Sol Jo 314 .... 1.15, 64.27
Johnson v Ball (1851) 5 De G & Sm 85, 16 Jur 538, 18 LTOS 182 .... 36.11, 57.11
Johnson v Blane (1848) 6 Notes of Cases 442 .... 4.15, 4.17
Johnson v Clarke [1928] Ch 847, 97 LJ Ch 337, 72 Sol Jo 556, 139 LT 552 .... 49.9
Johnson v Crook (1879) 12 Ch D 639, 48 LJ Ch 777, 28 WR 12, 41 LT 400 .... 97.7
Johnson v Digby (1829) 8 LJOS Ch 38 .... 64.23
Johnson v Foulds (1868) LR 5 Eq 268, 37 LJ Ch 260 .... 93.6
Johnson v Johnson (1841) 4 Beav 318 .... 47.23
Johnson v Johnson (1843) 3 Hare 157, 13 LJ Ch 79, 8 Jur 77, 2 LTOS 118 .... 7.22, 47.12, 47.13
Johnson v Johnson (1846) 2 Coll 441, 10 Jur 279, 7 LTOS 3 .... 38.3
Johnson v Mills (1749) 1 Ves Sen 282 .... 29.2
Johnson v Routh (1857) 27 LJ Ch 305, 3 Jur NS 1048, 6 WR 6, 30 LTOS 111 .... 38.17
Johnson v Simcock (1861) 7 H & N 344, 31 LJ Ex 38, 8 Jur NS 284, 9 WR 895, sub nom Jackson and Simcock v Johnson 4 LT 836, Ex Ch 56.1
Johnson v Smith (1749) 1 Ves Sen 314 .... 34.22
Johnson v Telford (1830) 1 Russ & M 244, 8 LJOS Ch 94 .... 42.15
Johnson's Estate, Re [1946] 3 WWR 424 .... 4.20
Johnson's Estate, Re (1957) 8 DLR (2d) 221, 21 WWR 289; affd sub nom Pratt v Johnson [1959] SCR 102, 16 DLR (2d) 385 .... 2.2
Johnson's Estate, Re [2006] EWHC 2568 (Ch), [2006] All ER (D) 146 (Oct) 5.3
Johnson's Goods, Re (1858) 27 LJP & M 9, 1 Sw & Tr 17, 6 WR 275, 30 LTOS 295 .... 25.3
Johnson's Goods, Re (1897) 78 LT 85 .... 70.1
Johnson's Settlement Trusts, Re, McClure v Johnson [1943] Ch 341, [1943] 2 All ER 499, 112 LJ Ch 297, 87 Sol Jo 291, 169 LT 220, 59 TLR 434 .... 94.13, 94.48
Johnson's Trusts, Re (1866) LR 2 Eq 716, 12 Jur NS 616 .... 102.26
Johnson's Will Trusts, Re, National Provincial Bank Ltd v Jeffrey [1967] Ch 387, [1967] 1 All ER 553, [1967] 2 WLR 152, 110 Sol Jo 811 .... 35.35
Johnston, Re (1970) 7 DLR (3d) 256 .... 38.10
Johnston, Re (1982) 138 DLR (3d) 392 .... 51.1, 77.3
Johnston, Re (1985) 1 Qd R 516 .... 10.1
Johnston, Re, Mills v Johnston [1894] 3 Ch 204, 63 LJ Ch 753, 8 R 563, 42 WR 616, 38 Sol Jo 564, 71 LT 392 .... 30.36, 34.6, 82.8
Johnston v Antrobus (1856) 21 Beav 556 .... 82.3, 97.5, 97.6
Johnston v Doak [1953] VLR 678 .... 64.27
Johnston v Moore (1858) 27 LJ Ch 453, 4 Jur NS 356, 6 WR 490, 31 LTOS 353 .... 38.23
Johnston v O'Neill (1879) 3 LR Ir 476 .... 93.26

Johnston v Rowlands (1848) 2 De G & Sm 356, 17 LJ Ch 438, 12 Jur 769, 11 LTOS 511 .... 83.2
Johnstone v Earl of Harrowby (1859) 1 De GF & J 183, 29 LJ Ch 145, 6 Jur NS 153, 8 WR 105, 1 LT 390 .... 88.3, 91.6
Johnstone v Haviland [1896] AC 95, 22 R 396, HL 44.2
Johnstone's Estate, Re, Royal Trust Co v Vogler and Lawson (1966) 55 WWR 167 .... 51.3
Johnstone's Settlement, Re (1880) 14 Ch D 162, 49 LJ Ch 596, 28 WR 593 .... 41.11, 41.21
Johnstone's Trustee v Johnstone 1936 SC 706 .... 73.1
Joicey, Re, Joicey v Elliot [1915] 2 Ch 115, 84 LJ Ch 613, 113 LT 437, CA 40.5
Joicey, Re, Joicey v Elliot (1935) 152 LT 398. See Elliot v Joicey Joliffe v Twyford (1858) 28 LJ Ch 93, 26 Beav 227, 4 Jur NS 1165, 32 LTOS 141 .... 45.2
Joliffe, ex p. See Jolliffe, ex p
Jolley, Re (1985) 36 SASR 204 .... 52.1, 93.9
Jolley, Re, Jolley v Jarvis [1964] P 262, [1964] 1 All ER 596, [1964] 2 WLR 556, 108 Sol Jo 115, CA 25.16
Jolley, Re, Neal v Jolley (1901) 17 TLR 244 .... 55.7
Jolliffe, ex p (1845) 8 Beav 168, 10 Jur 813, 4 LTOS 309, sub nom Joliffe, ex p 14 LJ Ch 134 .... 25.15
Jolliffe v East (1789) 3 Bro CC 25 .... 86.2
Jolly, Re, Gathercole v Norfolk [1900] 2 Ch 616, [1900–3] All ER Rep 286, 69 LJ Ch 661, 48 WR 657, 44 Sol Jo 642, 83 LT 118, 16 TLR 521, CA 100.6
Jonathan, Re, Jonathan v Ward [1962] NZLR 536 .... 39.19
Jones, Re [1927] 2 DLR 113, 60 OLR 136 .... 62.1
Jones, Re [1955] NZLR 917 .... 30.2, 52.3
Jones, Re [1971] NZLR 796 .... 50.9, 57.22
Jones, Re (1973) 34 DLR (3d) 479 .... 63.1
Jones, Re [1981] Fam 7, [1981] 1 All ER 1, [1981] 1 WLR 106, 124 Sol Jo 545 .... 16.2, 16.4
Jones, Re, Evans v Harries [1976] Ch 200, [1976] 1 All ER 593, [1976] 2 WLR 437, 120 Sol Jo 10, CA 18.22, 19.1, 19.3, 19.4
Jones, Re, Greene v Gordon (1886) 34 Ch D 65, 56 LJ Ch 58, 35 WR 74, 31 Sol Jo 28, 55 LT 597 .... 39.3, 39.13
Jones, Re, Harris v Jones [1910] VLR 306 .... 87.1
Jones, Re, Jenkins v Jones. See Jenkins v Jones
Jones, Re, Jones v McConkey [1962] NZLR 460 .... 82.4
Jones, Re, Jones v Midland Bank Trust Co Ltd [1997] 3 FCR 697, [1998] 1 FLR 246, [1997] Fam Law 660, 141 Sol Jo LB 107, CA ... 9.15, 9.17, 9.18, 48.4, 48.14
Jones, Re, Last v Dobson [1915] 1 Ch 246, 84 LJ Ch 222, 59 Sol Jo 218, 112 LT 409 .... 40.21, 55.6, 56.8
Jones, Re, Lewis v Lewis [1910] 1 Ch 167, 79 LJ Ch 34, 101 LT 549 .... 51.8, 85.2, 85.3
Jones, Re, Meacock v Jones [1932] 1 Ch 642, [1932] All ER Rep 804, 101 LJ Ch 307, 147 LT 137 .... 32.20, 218.52
Jones, Re, Midland Bank Executor and Trustee Co Ltd v Jones [1953] Ch 125, [1953] 1 All ER 357, [1953] 2 WLR 283, 97 Sol Jo 96 .... 33.22, 34.9, 34.10, 35.29, 35.45

Jones, Re, Midland Bank Executor and Trustee Co Ltd v League of Welldoers [1950] 2 All ER 239, 94 Sol Jo 405, 66 (pt 2) TLR 51 .... 33.9, 94.13, 94.38
Jones, Re, Public Trustee v Jones [1934] Ch 315, [1933] All ER Rep 841, 103 LJ Ch 102, 78 Sol Jo 82, 150 LT 400 .... 84.2
Jones, Re, Public Trustee v Jones [1945] Ch 105, 115 LJ Ch 33, 89 Sol Jo 22, 173 LT 357, 61 TLR 120 .... 1.6, 39.31
Jones, Re, Richards v Jones [1898] 1 Ch 438, 67 LJ Ch 211, 46 WR 313, 42 Sol Jo 269, 78 LT 74 .... 82.2, 83.8, 83.9, 83.13, 99.1
Jones, Re, Royal Trust Co v Jones (No 2) (1934) 49 BCR 204 .... 35.35
Jones, Re, Williams v Rowlands [1948] Ch 67, [1947] 2 All ER 716, [1948] LJR 431, 91 Sol Jo 678 .... 34.7, 34.22, 34.24
Jones v Badley (1866) LR 3 Eq 635; revsd (1868) 3 Ch App 362, 16 WR 713, 19 LT 106, CA 36.2, 36.4, 36.5, 36.7, 36.8, 36.13
Jones v Bromley (1821) 6 Madd 137 .... 35.45, 35.49
Jones v Challenger [1961] 1 QB 176, [1960] 1 All ER 785, [1960] 2 WLR 695, 104 Sol Jo 328, 175 Estates Gazette 695, CA 200.62
Jones v Davies (1878) 8 Ch D 205, 47 LJ Ch 654, 26 WR 554, 38 LT 710 .... 40.15
Jones v Davies (1880) 28 WR 455 .... 48.15
Jones v Executive Officers of T Eaton Co Ltd (1973) 35 DLR (3d) 97 .... 102.7
Jones v Frewin (1864) 3 New Rep 415, 12 WR 369, 10 LT 330 .... 47.32, 68.4
Jones v Hall (1849) 16 Sim 500 .... 90.1, 90.2
Jones v Harding (1887) 52 JP 71, 58 LT 60 .... 18.7, 18.19
Jones v Henley (1685) 2 Rep Ch 361 .... 30.23
Jones v How (1850) 9 CB 1 .... 3.10
Jones v Jones (1843) 13 Sim 561, 13 LJ Ch 16, 7 Jur 986 .... 93.29
Jones v Jones (1876) 1 QBD 279, 45 LJQB 166, 24 WR 274, 34 LT 243 .... 34.3, 35.2
Jones v Jones (1881) 29 WR 786, 44 LT 642, DC 86.5
Jones v Lord Sefton (1798) 4 Ves 166 .... 63.1
Jones v Mackilwain (1826) 1 Russ 220 .... 93.32, 93.36
Jones v Martin (1798) 3 Anst 882 .... 3.8
Jones v Morgan (1774) 3 Bro Parl Cas 323, HL 98.9
Jones v Morris (1922) 91 LJ Ch 495, 127 LT 94 .... 97.2
Jones v Nicolay (1850) 2 Rob Eccl 288, 14 Jur 675, 15 LTOS 328, 7 Notes of Cases 564 .... 10.10
Jones v Ogle (1872) 8 Ch App 192, 42 LJ Ch 334, 21 WR 236, 28 LT 245 .... 51.5, 54.4
Jones v Price (1841) 10 LJ Ch 195, 11 Sim 557, 5 Jur 719 .... 50.2, 52.6
Jones v Randall (1819) 1 Jac & W 100 .... 33.14
Jones v Roberts [1995] 2 FLR 422, [1995] Fam Law 673 .... 9.14, 9.15
Jones v Robinson (1878) 3 CPD 344, 47 LJQB 673, 27 WR 48, 38 LT 945 .... 38.4, 38.10
Jones v Roe (1789) 3 Term Rep 88 .... 7.20
Jones v Selby (1710) 2 Eq Cas Abr 573, Prec Ch 300 .... 1.15
Jones v Skinner (1835) 5 LJ Ch 87 .... 60.1, 64.51
Jones v Southall (No 2) (1862) 32 Beav 31, 32 LJ Ch 130, 9 Jur NS 93, 1 New Rep 152, 11 WR 247, 8 LT 103 .... 38.2, 39.4, 41.11, 47.36, 47.37
Jones v Torin (1833) 6 Sim 255 .... 68.1, 74.8
Jones v Treasury Solicitor (1932) 147 LT 340, 76 Sol Jo 690, 48 TLR 615; affd (1932) 49 TLR 75, CA 18.9
Jones v Tucker (1817) 2 Mer 533 .... 39.19
Jones v Watkins [1987] CA Transcript 1200, CA 43.1

Jones v Westcomb (1711) 1 Eq Cas Abr 245, Gilb Ch 74, Prec Ch 316 .... 34.21, 47.1, 92.5, 93.9, 93.19
Jones v Williams (1767) Amb 651 .... 102.10
Jones' Estate, Re, Hume v Lloyd (1878) 47 LJ Ch 775, 26 WR 828 .... 68.12
Jones Estate, Re, Shaw and Brooks v Stromme (1955) 16 WWR 78 .... 18.31
Jones' Estate, Re, Thomas v Jones. See Thomas v Jones [1928] P 162
Jones' Goods, Re (1842) 1 Notes of Cases 396 .... 12.11
Jones' Goods, Re (1920) 123 LT 202, 36 TLR 294 .... 15.1
Jones' Settlement, Re, Stunt v Jones [1915] 1 Ch 373, 84 LJ Ch 406, 59 Sol Jo 364, 112 LT 1067 .... 40.14, 40.15, 40.17
Jones' Trusts, Re (1857) 23 Beav 242 .... 76.2, 76.4
Jones' Will, Re (1870) 23 LT 211 .... 99.1
Jones' Will Trusts, Re, Jones v Hawtin Squire [1965] Ch 1124, [1965] 2 All ER 828, [1965] 3 WLR 506, 109 Sol Jo 476 .... 75.7
Jones' Will Trusts, Re, Jones v Jones [1942] Ch 328, [1942] 1 All ER 642, 111 LJ Ch 193, 86 Sol Jo 174, 167 LT 84, 58 TLR 403 ...... 15.1, 36.11, 36.13, 57.5, 57.11, 204.34, 217.48, 240.5
Jopling v IRC [1940] 2 KB 282, [1940] 3 All ER 279, 109 LJKB 734, 84 Sol Jo 525, 163 LT 361, 56 TLR 877 .... 29.16, 220.72
Jordan v Dunn (1887) 13 OR 267, 15 AR 744 .... 35.45
Jordan v Fortescue (1847) 16 LJ Ch 332, 10 Beav 259, 11 Jur 549, 9 LTOS 290 .... 52.11
Jordan v Jordan (1965) 109 Sol Jo 353 .... 105.48
Jordan's Trusts, Re (1863) 2 New Rep 57, 8 LT 307 .... 68.10
Jorden v Jorden (1843) 2 Notes of Cases 388 .... 21.2
Jordison, Re, Raine v Jordison [1922] 1 Ch 440, 91 LJ Ch 497, 66 Sol Jo 282, 126 LT 490, CA 32.30
Joscelyne v Nissen [1970] 2 QB 86, [1970] 1 All ER 1213, [1970] 2 WLR 509, 114 Sol Jo 55, CA 6.1
Joseph, Re, Pain v Joseph [1908] 2 Ch 507, 77 LJ Ch 832, 99 LT 539, 24 TLR 770, CA 91.6, 237.11
Joseph v Phillips [1934] AC 348, [1934] All ER Rep 685, 103 LJPC 79, 78 Sol Jo 317, 151 LT 51, 50 TLR 385 .... 63.1, 64.17, 64.18, 64.48
Josiak v Setler (1971) 16 DLR (3d) 490 .... 57.20
Joslin v Hammond (1834) 3 My & K 110, 3 LJ Ch 148 .... 82.3, 97.3
Josselyn v Josselyn (1837) 9 Sim 63 .... 30.36, 93.27
Joy, Re, Purday v Johnson (1888) 60 LT 175, [1886–90] All ER Rep 1111, 5 TLR 117 .... 58.11, 102.13, 103.3, 103.9
Joynt v Richards (1882) 11 LR Ir 278 .... 33.12
Jubber v Jubber (1839) 9 Sim 503 .... 30.14, 53.4, 55.6, 66.5, 82.5
Judd v Judd (1830) 3 Sim 525, sub nom Judd v Hobbs 8 LJOS Ch 119 .... 93.6, 93.27
Judd v Wyatt (1805) 11 Ves 483 .... 91.5
Judd's Trusts, Re [1884] WN 206 .... 76.3
Judge v Revenue and Customs Comrs [2005] STC (SCD) 863 .... 208.33, 208.34
Judge v Revenue and Customs Comrs [2005] STC (SCD) 874, [2005] WTLR 1311 .... 225.94
Judkin's Trusts, Re (1884) 25 Ch D 743, [1881–5] All ER Rep 979, 53 LJ Ch 496, 32 WR 407, 50 LT 200 .... 32.15, 32.21, 38.14
Juler v Juler (1860) 29 Beav 34, 30 LJ Ch 142, 6 Jur NS 1320, 9 WR 61, 3 LT 395 .... 83.3

Jull v Jacobs (1876) 3 Ch D 703, 24 WR 947, 35 LT 153 .... 9.9, 48.5, 48.6, 48.7, 57.5, 66.15
Jump, Re, Galloway v Hope [1903] 1 Ch 129, 72 LJ Ch 16, 51 WR 266, 87 LT 502 .... 37.8
Jung, Re (1979) 99 DLR (3d) 65 .... 46.5
Jupp, Re, Gladman v Jupp (1903) 87 LT 739 .... 47.9
Jupp, Re, Harris v Grierson [1922] 2 Ch 359, 91 LJ Ch 572, 66 Sol Jo 539, 127 LT 360 .... 44.2, 44.5
Jupp's Goods, Re [1891] P 300, 60 LJP 92, 55 JP 456, 40 WR 176, 65 LT 166 .... 38.3
Jury v Jury (1882) 9 LR Ir 207 .... 51.6

K

KPMG LLP v Network Rail Infrastructure Ltd [2007] EWCA Civ 363, 151 Sol Jo LB 611, [2007] All ER (D) 245 (Apr) 52.3
K, Re [1985] Ch 85, [1985] 1 All ER 403, [1985] 2 WLR 262, [1985] FLR 558, [1985] Fam Law 129, 129 Sol Jo 132, [1985] LS Gaz R 1335; affd [1986] Ch 180, [1985] 2 All ER 833, [1985] 3 WLR 234, [1986] 1 FLR 79, [1985] Fam Law 19, 129 Sol Jo 364, [1985] LS Gaz R 2242, [1985] NLJ Rep 655, CA 1.8, 9.15, 9.19, 9.20, 9.21, 9.22
K's Estate, Re (1996) 5 Tas R 365 .... 74.4
K's Settlement Trusts, Re [1969] 2 Ch 1, [1969] 1 All ER 194, [1969] 2 WLR 219, 112 Sol Jo 968 .... 9.45
Kagan, Re [1966] VR 538 .... 102.26
Kallil, Re [1957] NZLR 10 .... 98.13
Kampf v Jones (1837) 2 Keen 756, 7 LJ Ch 63, Coop Pr Cas 13, 1 Jur 814, 47 ER 378 .... 30.8, 94.47
Kane v Radley-Kane [1999] Ch 274, [1998] 3 All ER 753, [1998] 3 WLR 617, [1998] 3 FCR 502, [1998] 24 LS Gaz R 33, 142 Sol Jo LB 189, sub nom Radley-Kane, Re [1998] 2 FLR 585, [1998] Fam Law 525 .... 29.1, 29.9, 29.11, 29.14, 29.18, 29.19, 29.20, 220.70, 221.4, 243.1, 243.2
Kappele, Re [1954] OR 456; affd [1955] 1 DLR 29, [1954] OWN 912 .... 20.3, 33.11, 103.9
Karch, Re (1921) 64 DLR 541, [1921] 50 OLR 509 .... 54.2
Karkalatos Estate, Re [1962] SCR 390, 34 DLR (2d) 7 .... 87.4
Karsten, Re, Edwards v Moore [1953] NZLR 456 .... 36.1, 36.10, 36.13
Kaufman, Re, Anderson and Houge v Walkey and Mason (1961) 27 DLR (2d) 178, [1961] OR 289 .... 5.9
Kavanagh, Re, Murphy v Doyle (1892) 29 LR Ir 333, Ir CA 64.53
Kavanagh v Best [1971] NI 89 .... 1.8
Kavanagh v Kelly (1903) 37 ILT 71 .... 30.3
Kavanagh v Morland (1853) Kay 16, 23 LJ Ch 41, 2 Eq Rep 771, 18 Jur 185, 2 WR 8, 22 LTOS 143 .... 76.1
Kay v Crook (1857) 3 Jur NS 104, 3 Sm & G 407, 5 WR 220, 29 LTOS 10 .... 3.2
Kaye v Laxon (1780) 1 Bro CC 76 .... 62.4, 64.2
Keane's (Baron) Estate, Re [1903] 1 IR 215 .... 50.7
Kearins v Kearins [1957] 74 WN 63, [1957] SRNSW 286 .... 102.10
Kearney, Re [1957] VLR 56 .... 35.30, 67.2

Kearney v Kearney [1911] 1 IR 137, CA 48.5
Keating v Brooks (1845) 9 Jur 216, 4 Notes of Cases 253 .... 13.1, 13.3
Keating v O'Hagan (1922) 56 ILT 157 .... 64.26
Keay v Boulton (1883) 25 Ch D 212, 54 LJ Ch 48, 32 WR 591, 49 LT 631 .... 78.4
Kebty-Fletcher's Will Trusts, Re, Public Trustee v Swan and Snowden [1969] 1 Ch 339, [1967] 3 All ER 1076, [1968] 2 WLR 34, 111 Sol Jo 892 .... 47.4, 48.5, 48.6, 66.13, 66.15, 66.19
Kecskemeti v Rubens Rabin & Co (1992) Times, 31 December 1.14, 200.46, 204.69
Keen, Re, Evershed v Griffiths [1937] Ch 236, [1937] 1 All ER 452, 106 LJ Ch 177, 81 Sol Jo 97, 156 LT 207, 53 TLR 320, CA 15.1, 36.4, 36.10, 36.11, 36.13, 57.11
Keen v Keen (1873) LR 3 P & D 105, 42 LJP & M 61, 37 JP 696, 29 LT 247 .... 18.26, 18.29
Keep's Will, Re (1863) 32 Beav 122 .... 67.1
Kehoe's Goods, Re (1883) 13 LR Ir 13 .... 15.1
Kehr, Re, Martin v Foges [1952] Ch 26, [1951] 2 All ER 812, 95 Sol Jo 711, [1951] 2 TLR 788 .... 9.40
Keighley, Re, Keighley v Keighley [1919] 2 Ch 388, 88 LJ Ch 445, 63 Sol Jo 643, 121 LT 465, 35 TLR 491 .... 79.2, 83.12
Keigwin v Keigwin (1843) 3 Curt 607, 7 Jur 840 .... 11.26, 14.11
Keily v Monck (1795) 3 Ridg Parl Rep 205 .... 35.2, 35.4
Kekewich v Barker (1903) 88 LT 130, HL 47.31, 47.32, 87.1
Kell v Charmer (1856) 23 Beav 195, 4 WR 787 .... 10.16, 14.10, 57.6, 57.24
Kellett v Kellett (1815) 3 Dow 248, HL 38.12
Kellett v Kellett (1868) LR 3 HL 160 .... 18.6, 83.2
Kellett v Kellett (1871) IR 5 Eq 298 .... 47.37, 93.9
Kellick's Goods, Re (1864) 28 JP 760, 34 LJPM & A 2, sub nom Killick's Goods, Re 10 Jur NS 1083, 3 Sw & Tr 578 .... 12.6
Kellner's Will Trusts, Re, Blundell v Royal Cancer Hospital [1950] Ch 46, [1949] 2 All ER 774, 93 Sol Jo 710, 65 TLR 695, CA 103.10
Kelly, Re (1964) 43 DLR (2d) 23, [1964] 1 OR 500 .... 33.24
Kelly, Re, Cleary v Dillon [1932] IR 255 .... 9.31, 202.36
Kelly v A-G [1917] 1 IR 183 .... 48.4
Kelly v Hammond (1858) 26 Beav 36 .... 72.3
Kelly v Keatinge (1871) IR 5 Eq 174 .... 11.24
Kelly v Powlet (1763) Amb 605, 1 Dick 359 .... 64.27
Kelly's Settlement, Re, West v Turner (1888) 59 LT 494 .... 99.6
Kelsey v Ellis (1878) 38 LT 471 .... 68.6
Kelsey, Re, Woolley v Kelsey [1905] 2 Ch 465, 74 LJ Ch 701, 54 WR 136, 49 Sol Jo 701, 93 LT 662 .... 43.6, 100.7
Keluga Estate, Re (1956) 64 Man R 138 .... 18.29
Kemaghan v M'Nally (1861) 12 I Ch R 89 .... 43.2
Kemnal and Still's Contract, Re [1923] 1 Ch 293, [1923] All ER Rep Ext 723, 92 LJ Ch 298, 67 Sol Jo 364, 129 LT 12, 39 TLR 285, CA 25.18
Kemp Estate, Re (1954) 2 DLR 451, 11 WWRNS 624 .... 10.4
Kempthorne, Re, Charles v Kempthorne [1930] 1 Ch 268, [1929] All ER Rep 495, 99 LJ Ch 177, 142 LT 111, 46 TLR 15, CA 41.18, 204.69, 214.5, 214.7
Kendall v Kendall (1828) 4 Russ 360, 6 LJOS Ch 111 .... 38.11, 64.25
Kendall v Russell (1830) 3 Sim 424, 8 LJOS Ch 108 .... 33.24
Kendall's Trust, Re (1851) 14 Beav 608, 18 LTOS 116 .... 38.10

Kendrew, Re, Hird v Kendrew [1953] Ch 291, [1953] 1 All ER 551, [1953] 2 WLR 550, 97 Sol Jo 169, CA 30.24
Kennedy, Re, Corbould v Kennedy [1917] 1 Ch 9, 86 LJ Ch 40, 61 Sol Jo 55, 115 LT 690, 33 TLR 44, CA 235.22
Kennedy, Re, Kennedy v Official Solicitor to the Supreme Court [1980] CLY 2820 .... 105.48
Kennedy v Keily (1860) 28 Beav 223 .... 64.26
Kennedy v Kelly (1862) 14 Ir Jur 326 .... 57.22
Kennedy v Kennedy (1853) 10 Hare 438, 1 WR 177 .... 8.7
Kennedy v Kennedy [1914] AC 215, 83 LJPC 63, 51 SLR 581, 109 LT 833, PC 82.9
Kennedy v Kingston (1821) 2 Jac & W 431 .... 47.38, 101.9
Kennedy v Peikoff (1966) 56 WWR 381 .... 18.5
Kennedy v Sedgwick (1857) 3 K & J 540 .... 93.6, 93.30, 96.2
Kennedy Estate, Re, Kennedy Estate Executors v Jickling [1936] 1 WWR 204 .... 64.54
Kennedy's Will, Re [1954] Tas LR 64 .... 52.6
Kennett's Goods, Re (1863) 2 New Rep 461 .... 18.20
Kenny, Re, Clode v Andrews (1907) 97 LT 130 .... 102.22
Kenny, Re, Read v Isaacs (1921) LS Gaz R 518, [1921] NZLR 537 .... 97.7
Kenny v Wilson (1911) 28 WN 124, 11 SRNSW 460 .... 4.10
Kensington (Baron), Re, Earl of Longford v Baron Kensington [1902] 1 Ch 203, 71 LJ Ch 170, 50 WR 201, 46 Sol Jo 176, 85 LT 577, 18 TLR 89 .... 46.3, 207.2
Kensington v Unrepresented Non-allocated Claimants. See Goldcorp Exchange Ltd (in receivership), Re
Kent, Re (1982) 139 DLR (3d) 318 .... 34.13, 35.38
Kent v Kent [1902] P 108, 71 LJP 50, 46 Sol Jo 247, 86 LT 536, 18 TLR 293 .... 39.25
Kent v Tapley (1847) 17 LJ Ch 99, 11 Jur 940 .... 61.1
Kenward v Adams [1975] CLY 3591 .... 4.17, 4.21, 200.2
Kenworthy v Bate (1802) 6 Ves 793 .... 40.9
Kenworthy v Ward (1853) 11 Hare 196, 1 Eq Rep 389, 17 Jur 1047, 1 WR 493, 22 LTOS 92 .... 86.4
Kenyon's Estate, Re, Mann v Knap (1887) 56 LT 626 .... 41.16
K'Eogh v K'Eogh [1911] 1 IR 396 .... 82.5
Keogh v Keogh (1874) IR 8 Eq 179 .... 58.4, 58.6, 58.10, 63.3
Keogh's Estate, Re (1889) 23 LR Ir 257 .... 44.15
Keown's Estate, Re (1867) IR 1 Eq 372 .... 39.7
Keren Kayemeth Le Jisroel Ltd v IRC [1931] 2 KB 465, 100 LJKB 596, 145 LT 320, 47 TLR 461, CA; affd [1932] AC 650, [1932] All ER Rep 971, 101 LJKB 459, 17 TC 27, 76 Sol Jo 377, 147 LT 161, 48 TLR 459, HL 102.9, 102.10
Kernahan, Re [1990] 4 WWR 68, 68 DLR (4th) 150; on appeal sub nom Kernahan v Hanson (1990) 73 DLR (4th) 286 .... 57.12, 76.1, 76.3
Kernahan v Hanson. See Kernahan, Re
Keroak Estate, Re (1957) 24 WWR 145 .... 82.2, 83.8
Kerr, Re [1894] P 284, 10 TLR 522 .... 7.33
Kerr, Re [1948] 3 DLR 668, [1948] OR 543, [1948] OWN 511; affd [1949] 1 DLR 736, [1949] OWN 711 .... 2.2

Kerr, Re [1957] QSR 292 .... 103.3
Kerr v Baroness Clinton (1869) LR 8 Eq 462, 17 WR 980 .... 52.1, 52.8
Kerr v Middlesex Hospital (1852) 2 De GM & G 576, 22 LJ Ch 355, 17 Jur 49, 1 WR 92, 42 ER 996, 20 LTOS 160 .... 33.12, 64.23
Kerr's Estate, Re [1913] 1 IR 214 .... 97.1
Kerr's Trusts, Re (1877) 4 Ch D 600, 46 LJ Ch 287, 25 WR 390, 36 LT 356 .... 40.21
Kerrich v Bransby (1727) 7 Bro Parl Cas 437, HL 49.7
Kerrigan, Re, National Trustees, Executors and Agency Co of Australasia Ltd v Kerrigan [1916] VLR 516 .... 38.21
Kerry, Re, Bocock v Kerry, Arnull v Kerry [1889] WN 3, 5 TLR 178 .... 92.5
Kersey, Re, Alington v Alington [1952] WN 541, 96 Sol Jo 851 .... 35.40
Kershaw, Re, Whittaker v Kershaw. See Whittaker v Kershaw
Kershaw's Trusts, Re (1868) LR 6 Eq 322, 37 LJ Ch 751, 16 WR 963, 18 LT 899 .... 218.40, 218.97
Kettlewell, Re, Jones v Kettlewell (1907) 98 LT 23 .... 80.2, 216.30
Kevern v Williams (1832) 5 Sim 171 .... 66.17
Kevil v Lynch (1874) IR 9 Eq 249 .... 11.18
Kevil's Goods, Re (1873) IR 8 Eq 244 .... 11.21
Key v Key (1853) 4 De GM & G 73, 22 LJ Ch 641, 1 Eq Rep 82, 17 Jur 769, 22 LTOS 67 .... 50.4, 50.10, 93.15, 98.4
Key v Key (1855) 1 Jur NS 372 .... 52.5, 56.7, 56.8, 56.9
Khan's Settlement, Re, Coutts & Co v Senior Dowager Begum of Bhopal [1966] Ch 567, [1966] 1 All ER 160, [1965] 3 WLR 1291, 109 Sol Jo 997 .... 24.12, 24.16
Kiallmark v Kiallmark (1856) 26 LJ Ch 1 .... 96.1
Kidd v North (1846) 2 Ph 91, 16 LJ Ch 116, 10 Jur 995, sub nom Tidd v North 8 LTOS 289 .... 88.4
Kiddle, Re [1951] VLR 415 .... 93.29
Kiddle, Re, Gent v Kiddle (1905) 53 WR 616, 49 Sol Jo 481, 92 LT 724 .... 50.3, 72.3, 72.6
Kidman, Re [1953] SASR 28 .... 59.3, 64.54
Kidman v Kidman (1871) 40 LJ Ch 359 .... 29.8, 32.15, 93.43, 98.3
Kidney v Coussmaker (1806) 12 Ves 136 .... 42.9
Kiel v Berghofer (1949) 6 WN 206, 49 SRNSW 363 .... 39.3
Kieran, Re [1933] IR 222 .... 11.13
Kiersey v Flahavan [1905] 1 IR 45 .... 32.3, 34.2, 35.7
Kilby v Meyers. See Harmer, Re
Kileher's Goods, Re (1848) 12 Jur 163, 10 LTOS 482, 6 Notes of Cases 15 .... 12.12
Kilkelly v Powell [1897] 1 IR 457, 31 ILT 6 .... 61.1, 64.32
Killick's Goods, Re. See Kellick's Goods, Re
Killick's Will, Re (1960) VLR 98 .... 21.6
Kilpatrick's Policies Trusts, Re, Kilpatrick v IRC [1966] Ch 730, [1965] 2 All ER 673, [1966] 2 WLR 1346, 44 ATC 170, [1965] TR 173, 109 Sol Jo 417; affd [1966] Ch 730, [1966] 2 All ER 149, [1966] 2 WLR 1346, 110 Sol Jo 232, CA 93.16
Kilroy and Callan v Parker and McGauran [1966] IR 309 .... 53.5, 79.4
Kilvert, Re, Midland Bank Executor and Trustee Co Ltd v Kilvert [1957] Ch 388, [1957] 2 All ER 196, [1957] 2 WLR 854, 101 Sol Jo 372 .... 67.2, 68.13, 77.1, 78.4, 78.6, 79.4

Kilvert's Trusts, Re (1871) 7 Ch App 170, 41 LJ Ch 351, 20 WR 225, 26 LT 221 .... 103.3, 103.7
Kilvington v Gray (1825) 2 Sim & St 396, 4 LJOS Ch 80 .... 38.25
Kilvington v Parker (1872) 21 WR 121 .... 52.9
Kimberley v Tew (1843) 4 Dr & War 139 .... 29.14
Kimpton's Goods, Re (1864) 33 LJPM & A 153, 28 JP 552, 3 New Rep 691, 3 Sw & Tr 427, 10 LT 137 .... 11.3
Kinchington, Re [1958] Qd R 136 .... 64.7
Kindl, Re (1982) 140 DLR (3d) 92 .... 80.3
King, Re, Barclays Bank Ltd v King [1942] Ch 413, [1942] 2 All ER 182, 111 LJ Ch 289, 86 Sol Jo 252, 167 LT 129, CA 210.9, 210.10, 210.20, 210.28
King, Re, Jackson v A-G [1917] 2 Ch 420, [1916–17] All ER Rep 786, 87 LJ Ch 3, 62 Sol Jo 9, 117 LT 529, 33 TLR 535 .... 30.24, 30.26, 43.4
King, Re, Public Trustee v Aldridge [1928] Ch 330, 97 LJ Ch 172, 138 LT 641 .... 32.28, 218.55
King, Re, Salisbury v Ridley (1890) 62 LT 789, 6 TLR 320 .... 55.6, 56.8
King v Badeley (1834) 3 My & K 417, 3 LJ Ch 206 .... 57.6
King v Bennett (1838) 7 LJ Ex 242, 1 Horn & H 289, 4 M & W 36 .... 81.3
King v Cleaveland (1858) 26 Beav 26, 4 Jur NS 702; affd (1859) 4 De G & J 477, 28 LJ Ch 835, 7 WR 602, 33 LTOS 340 .... 47.32, 68.8, 79.7
King v Cullen (1848) 2 De G & Sm 252 .... 97.10
King v Denison (1813) 12 RR 227, 1 Ves & B 260 .... 82.5
King v Evans (1895) 24 SCR 356 .... 84.2
King v Farley (1828) 1 Hag Ecc 502 .... 4.20
King v Frost (1890) 15 App Cas 548, 60 LJPC 15, 63 LT 422, 6 TLR 443, PC 67.4, 67.5
King v George (1877) 5 Ch D 627, 36 LT 759, sub nom Re George's Estate, King v George 46 LJ Ch 670, 25 WR 638, CA 38.10
King v King (1864) 15 I Ch R 479 .... 42.4
King v King (1885) 13 LR Ir 531 .... 42.4, 57.20
King v King [1942] P 1, [1941] 2 All ER 103, 111 LJP 90, 167 LT 241, 57 TLR 529 .... 35.23
King v Malcott (1852) 9 Hare 692, 22 LJ Ch 157, 16 Jur 237, 19 LTOS 19 ... 29.4, 30.33
King v Melling (1671) 1 Vent 225; on appeal (1671) 1 Vent 232, Ex Ch 76.1
King v Mullins (1852) 1 Drew 308, 20 LTOS 178 .... 30.42
King v Perpetual Trustee Co Ltd (1955) 94 CLR 70 .... 87.1
King v Rymill (1898) 67 LJPC 107, 78 LT 696 .... 50.3
King v Tootel (1858) 25 Beav 23 .... 66.20, 91.6
King v Withers (1735) Cas temp Talb 117, 3 P Wms 414; affd sub nom Wither v King (1735) 3 Bro Parl Cas 135, HL 93.44
King's College Hospital v Wheildon (1854) 18 Beav 30, 23 LJ Ch 537, 2 WR 202 .... 57.15
King's Estate, Re (1888) 21 LR Ir 273 .... 36.3
King's Goods, Re (1875) 23 WR 552 .... 14.10, 14.11
King's Proctor v Daines (1830) 3 Hag Ecc 218 .... 10.1
King's Trusts, Re (1892) 29 LR Ir 401 .... 33.20, 34.3
King's Will Trusts, Re, Assheton v Boyne [1964] Ch 542, [1964] 1 All ER 833, [1964] 2 WLR 913, 108 Sol Jo 335, 189 Estates Gazette 879 .... 27.15, 239.5, 243.3
King-Harman v Cayley [1899] 1 IR 39 .... 32.21

Kingcome, Re, Hickley v Kingcome [1936] Ch 566, [1936] 1 All ER 173, 105 LJ Ch 209, 80 Sol Jo 112, 154 LT 462, 52 TLR 268 .... 211.9, 211.10
Kingdon, Re, Wilkins v Pryer (1886) 32 Ch D 604, 55 LJ Ch 598, 34 WR 634, 54 LT 753 .... 18.8
Kingham, Re, Kingham v Kingham [1897] 1 IR 170 .... 94.13
Kingsbury v Walter [1901] AC 187, 70 LJ Ch 546, 84 LT 697, HL 47.31, 47.32, 47.35, 50.21, 57.15
Kingston (Earl) v Lady Elizabeth Pierepont (1681) 1 Vern 5 .... 34.12, 35.47
Kinleside v Harrison (1818) 2 Phillim 449 .... 4.14, 4.20
Kinnaird v Allen (1898) 24 VLR 609 .... 72.6
Kinnear, Re, Kinnear v Barnett (1904) 90 LT 537 .... 66.6
Kinsella v Caffrey (1860) 11 I Ch R 154; affd (1860) 13 Ir Jur 277 .... 101.10
Kipping, Re, Kipping v Kipping [1914] 1 Ch 62, 83 LJ Ch 218, 109 LT 919, CA 30.36, 66.13
Kirby, Re (1982) 3 FLR 249, 11 Fam Law 210 .... 105.18
Kirby v Potter (1799) 4 Ves 748 .... 30.8
Kirby's Goods, Re [1902] P 188, 71 LJP 116, 87 LT 141 .... 25.2
Kirby-Smith v Parnell [1903] 1 Ch 483, 72 LJ Ch 468, 51 WR 493, 47 Sol Jo 279 .... 49.5, 50.18, 51.1, 60.2
Kirk, Re, Kirk v Kirk (1882) 21 Ch D 431, 31 WR 94, 47 LT 36, CA 34.4, 47.8, 91.2
Kirk, Re, Nicholson v Kirk (1885) 52 LT 346 .... 74.1
Kirk, Re, Wethey v Kirk (1915) 85 LJ Ch 182, 113 LT 1204 .... 54.2, 68.9
Kirk v Eddowes (1844) 3 Hare 509, 13 LJ Ch 402, 8 Jur 530 ..... 44.5, 44.14, 57.31, 100.7
Kirk v Eustace [1937] AC 491, [1937] 2 All ER 715, 106 LJKB 617, 81 Sol Jo 376, 157 LT 171, 53 TLR 748, HL 202.40
Kirk v Kirk (1896) 40 NSR 147 .... 42.6
Kirkbank v Hudson (1819) Dan 259, 7 Price 212 .... 102.19
Kirkbride's Trusts, Re (1866) LR 2 Eq 400, 14 WR 728, 15 LT 51 .... 50.17, 56.8, 96.1
Kirkby v Phillips [1948] Ch 109, [1947] 2 All ER 777, 92 Sol Jo 11, 63 TLR 631 .... 33.12
Kirkley, Re, Halligey v Kirkley (1918) 87 LJ Ch 247, 62 Sol Jo 364, 119 LT 304 .... 93.4, 93.6, 93.31
Kirkman v Booth (1848) 11 Beav 273, 18 LJ Ch 25, 13 Jur 525, 83 RR 158, 13 LTOS 482 .... 205.25
Kirkman v Miles (1807) 13 Ves 338 .... 37.8
Kirkman's Trust, Re (1859) 3 De G & J 558 .... 68.11
Kirkpatrick, Re, Ferguson v Kirkpatrick (1912) 29 WN 56, 12 SRNSW 282 .... 68.6
Kirkpatrick v Bedford (1878) 4 App Cas 96, HL 88.2
Kirs Estate, Re (1990) 55 SASR 61 .... 14.2
Kitcat v King [1930] P 266, 99 LJP 126, 74 Sol Jo 488, 143 LT 408, 46 TLR 617 .... 9.8, 18.9
Kiver v Oldfield (1859) 4 De G & J 30 .... 82.2
Kleinwort Benson (Hong Kong) Trustees Ltd v Wong Foon Hang [1993] 1 HKC 649 .... 27.15
Knaggs, Re, Knaggs v Knaggs (1905) 49 Sol Jo 314 .... 64.54
Knapman, Re, Knapman v Wreford (1881) 18 Ch D 300, [1881–5] All ER Rep Ext 1758, 50 LJ Ch 629, 30 WR 395, 45 LT 102, CA 30.11
Knapp, Re, Spreckley v A-G [1929] 1 Ch 341, 98 LJ Ch 95, 140 LT 533 ... 95.12, 102.28
Knapp v Noyes (1768) Amb 662 .... 35.14

Knapp's Settlement, Re, Knapp v Vassall [1895] 1 Ch 91, 64 LJ Ch 112, 13 R 147, 43 WR 279, 71 LT 625 .... 66.8, 66.12, 66.13
Knapping v Tomlinson (1864) 34 LJ Ch 3, 10 Jur NS 626, 12 WR 784, 10 LT 558 .... 94.21
Knapton, Re, Knapton v Hindle [1941] Ch 428, [1941] 2 All ER 573, 110 LJ Ch 177, 85 Sol Jo 322, 166 LT 37 .... 8.7, 89.1, 204.21
Knee's Goods, Re, Gattward v Knee. See Gattward v Knee
Knibbs' Estate, Re, Flay v Trueman (Hoskins cited) [1962] 2 All ER 829, [1962] 1 WLR 852, 106 Sol Jo 454 .... 16.4
Knight, Re (1944) unreported 17.4
Knight, Re, Knight v Burgess (1887) 34 Ch D 518, 56 LJ Ch 770, 35 WR 536, 56 LT 630, 3 TLR 387 .... 58.12, 63.7
Knight, Re, Re Wynn, Midland Bank Executor and Trustee Co Ltd v Parker [1957] Ch 441, [1957] 2 All ER 252, [1957] 2 WLR 987, 101 Sol Jo 429, CA 39.16, 39.18, 39.20, 39.25, 39.26
Knight v Cameron (1807) 14 Ves 389 .... 93.27
Knight v Davis (1833) 3 My & K 358, 3 LJ Ch 81 .... 30.10
Knight v Gould (1833) 2 My & K 295, Coop temp Brough 240 .... 47.32
Knight v Knight (1826) 2 Sim & St 490 .... 32.22, 93.31
Knight v Knight (1846) 15 LJ Ch 363 .... 31.1, 31.6
Knight v Knight (1861) 2 Giff 616, 30 LJ Ch 644, 7 Jur NS 893, 5 LT 72 .... 64.35
Knight v Knight (1912) 14 CLR 86 .... 67.1
Knotsford v Gardiner (1742) 2 Atk 450 .... 64.32
Knott's Estate, Re (1959) 27 WWR 382 .... 2.4
Knott's Goods, Re [1920] 2 IR 397 .... 25.16
Knowles, Re [1938] 3 DLR 178, [1938] OR 369 .... 102.10
Knowles, Re, Nottage v Buxton (1882) 21 Ch D 806, 51 LJ Ch 851, 31 WR 182, 47 LT 161 .... 51.10, 65.1
Knowles, Re, Rainford v Knowles (1888) 59 LT 359 .... 79.7
Knowles v Knowles [1962] P 161, [1962] 1 All ER 659, [1962] 2 WLR 742, 105 Sol Jo 1011 .... 72.8
Knowles v Morgan (1909) 54 Sol Jo 117 .... 40.15
Knox, Re (1910) 29 NZLR 1179 .... 79.4
Knox, Re, Fleming v Carmichael [1937] Ch 109, [1936] 3 All ER 623, 106 LJ Ch 97, 80 Sol Jo 915, 156 LT 189 .... 103.2
Knox, Re, Von Scheffler v Shuldham [1912] 1 IR 288 .... 34.7, 34.22
Knox v Lord Hotham (1845) 15 Sim 82 .... 30.35, 82.7
Knox v Wells (1864) 2 Hem & M 674, 34 LJ Ch 150, 10 Jur NS 1252, 13 WR 228, 11 LT 666 .... 93.30
Knox v Wells (1883) 31 WR 559, 48 LT 655 .... 33.20, 35.6
Knox Estate, Re (1963) 40 DLR (2d) 397, 44 WWR 694 .... 25.4
Knox's Goods, Re (1889) 23 LR Ir 542 .... 35.33
Koch, Re, Koch v Koch [1931] VLR 263, 37 Argus LR 274 .... 9.3
Koeppler Will Trusts, Re, Barclays Bank Trust Co Ltd v Slack [1984] Ch 243, [1984] 2 All ER 111, [1984] 2 WLR 973, 128 Sol Jo 398, [1984] LS Gaz R 1843; revsd [1986] Ch 423, [1985] 2 All ER 869, [1985] 3 WLR 765, 129 Sol Jo 670, [1985] NLJ Rep 531, CA 34.21, 93.9, 102.8, 102.11, 102.23

Koettgen's Will Trusts, Re, Westminster Bank Ltd v Family Welfare Association Trustees Ltd [1954] Ch 252, [1954] 1 All ER 581, [1954] 2 WLR 166, 98 Sol Jo 78 .... 102.8, 102.10
Kornatzki v Oppenheimer [1937] 4 All ER 133 .... 30.43
Kotke v Saffarini [2005] EWCA Civ 221, [2005] 1 FCR 642, [2005] 2 FLR 517, [2005] Fam Law 535, [2005] NLJR 414, [2005] All ER (D) 145 (Mar) 105.14
Kotsar v Shattock [1981] VR 13 .... 93.16
Kourkgy v Lusher (1981) 4 FLR 65, 12 Fam Law 86 .... 105.18, 105.41
Kozminsky, Re [1966] VR 299 .... 34.11, 34.14
Krause, Re (1985) 18 DLR (4th) 631 .... 67.2
Krawitz's Will Trusts, Re, Krawitz v Crawford [1959] 3 All ER 793, [1959] 1 WLR 1192, 103 Sol Jo 1004 .... 34.10, 35.31, 77.4
Kreh v Moses (1892) 22 OR 307 .... 10.9
Krubert, Re [1997] Ch 97, [1996] 3 WLR 959, [1996] 3 FCR 281, [1997] 1 FLR 42, [1997] Fam Law 165, [1996] 27 LS Gaz R 28, 140 Sol Jo LB 167, CA 105.9, 105.22, 105.28
Krull v Bradey (1885) 4 NZLR 369 .... 86.5
Kryskiw, Re [1954] OWN 717 .... 13.2
Kuypers, Re, Kuypers v Kuypers [1925] Ch 244, 94 LJ Ch 253, 69 Sol Jo 366, 133 LT 468 .... 41.1, 41.14
Kytherian Association of Queensland v Sklavos (1958) 101 CLR 56, [1959] ALR 5, [1959] Qd R 282, 32 ALJR 275 .... 102.7

L

L (WJG), Re [1966] Ch 135, [1966] 2 WLR 233, 110 Sol Jo 74, sub nom Re WJGL [1965] 3 All ER 865 .... 1.9, 4.22, 4.23
Labron, Re, Johnson v Johnson (1885) 1 TLR 248 .... 64.27
Lachlan v Reynolds (1852) 9 Hare 796 .... 56.5, 78.4, 94.21
Lackersteen v Lackersteen (1860) 30 LJ Ch 5, 6 Jur NS 1111, 3 LT 581 .... 6.1
Lacon, Re, Lacon v Lacon [1891] 2 Ch 482, 60 LJ Ch 403, 39 WR 514, 64 LT 429, 7 TLR 457, CA 44.2, 44.4
Lacroix's Goods, Re (1877) 2 PD 94, 46 LJP 40, 41 JP 664 .... 23.7
Lacy, Re, Royal General Theatrical Fund Association v Kydd [1899] 2 Ch 149, 68 LJ Ch 488, 47 WR 664, 80 LT 706 .... 102.7
Lacy's Settlement Trustee (General Accident, Fire and Life Assurance Corpn Ltd) v IRC. See General Accident Fire and Life Assurance Corpn Ltd v IRC
Ladd, Re, Henderson v Porter [1932] 2 Ch 219, 101 LJ Ch 392, 147 LT 433 .... 47.23, 47.36, 47.38, 219.23
Laffan and Downes Contract, Re [1897] 1 IR 469 .... 65.2, 66.19
Lahay v Brown (1958) 8 DLR (2d) 728, [1957] OWN 210; affd [1958] SCR 240, 12 DLR (2d) 785 (Can SC) 3.3, 44.15
Laing, Re, Laing v Morrison [1912] 2 Ch 386, 81 LJ Ch 686, 57 Sol Jo 80, 107 LT 822 .... 47.26, 93.5
Laing v Cowan (1857) 24 Beav 112 .... 39.7, 39.12

Laing (JW) Trust, Re, Stewards' Co Ltd v A-G [1984] Ch 143, [1984] 1 All ER 50, [1983] 3 WLR 886, 127 Sol Jo 839, [1984] LS Gaz R 358 .... 103.11, 103.18, 103.19
Lainson v Lainson (1854) 5 De GM & G 754, 24 LJ Ch 46, 3 Eq Rep 43, 1 Jur NS 49, 3 WR 31, 24 LTOS 85 .... 48.5, 48.9
Laird, Re [1982] NZLR 325 .... 57.8
Laird v Tobin (1830) 1 Mol 543 .... 35.14
Lake v Currie [1852] 2 De GM & G 536, 16 Jur 1027, 21 LTOS 26 .... 38.2, 39.14
Laker v Hordern (1876) 1 Ch D 644, 45 LJ Ch 315, 24 WR 543, 34 LT 88 .... 57.18, 72.2, 72.4
Lal Chand Marwari v Mahant Ramrup Gir (1925) 42 TLR 159, PC 9.2
Lall v Lall [1965] 3 All ER 330, [1965] 1 WLR 1249, 109 Sol Jo 815 .... 1.8
Lamb, Re [1954] OWN 31 .... 82.1
Lamb, Re, Marston v Chauvet (1933) 77 Sol Jo 503, 49 TLR 541 .... 58.4, 64.58
Lamb, Re, Vipond v Lamb [1929] 1 Ch 722, [1929] All ER Rep 82, 98 LJ Ch 305, 73 Sol Jo 77, 141 LT 60, 45 TLR 190 .... 214.7
Lambe v Eames (1871) 6 Ch App 597, 40 LJ Ch 447, 19 WR 659, 25 LT 174 .... 79.2, 82.5, 83.9
Lambert, Re, Corns v Harrison [1908] 2 Ch 117, [1908–10] All ER Rep 521, 77 LJ Ch 553, 98 LT 851 .... 54.2, 68.9
Lambert, Re, Lambert v Lambert [1910] 1 IR 280 .... 40.21
Lambert, Re, Middleton v Moore [1897] 2 Ch 169, 66 LJ Ch 624, 45 WR 661, 41 Sol Jo 560, 76 LT 752 .... 100.5
Lambert v Lambert (1873) LR 16 Eq 320, 43 LJ Ch 106, 21 WR 748 .... 38.26
Lambert v Overton (1864) 13 WR 227, 11 LT 503 .... 58.6, 63.4
Lambert v Peyton (1860) 8 HL Cas 1, 125 RR 1 .... 76.5
Lambert v Thwaites (1866) LR 2 Eq 151, 35 LJ Ch 406, 14 WR 532, 14 LT 159 .... 94.48, 101.9
Lambert's Goods, Re (1841) 1 Notes of Cases 131 .... 18.23
Lambeth Charities, Re (1853) 22 LJ Ch 959 .... 102.7
Lambourn v McLellan [1903] 2 Ch 268, 72 LJ Ch 617, 51 WR 594, 47 Sol Jo 582, 88 LT 748, 19 TLR 529, CA 38.10
Lamont v Glasgow Magistrates (1887) 14 R 603, 24 SLR 426 .... 14.8
Lamont (or Chearnley) v Millar [1921] WN 334, 152 LT Jo 417, sub nom Curle's Trustees v Millar 59 SLR 21, 1922 SC (HL) 15 .... 67.5
Lamont's Will, Re (1881) 7 VLR 87 .... 25.16
Lamothe v Lamothe [2006] WTLR 1431 .... 18.6, 18.7
Lamphier v Buck. See Lanphier v Buck
Lamphier v Despard (1842) 2 Dr & War 59 .... 38.10, 64.25
Lampley v Blower (1746) 3 Atk 396 .... 85.1
Lancaster v Varty (1826) 5 LJOS Ch 41 .... 82.3
Lancefield v Iggulden (1874) 10 Ch App 136, [1874–80] All ER Rep 910, 44 LJ Ch 203, 23 WR 223, 31 LT 813 .... 30.3
Land v Land's Estate [2006] WTLR 1447 .... 9.22, 105.8
Land (decd), Re; Land v Land [2006] EWHC 2069 (Ch), [2007] 1 All ER 324, [2007] 1 WLR 1009, [2006] All ER (D) 71 (Oct) 9.15, 9.18
Lander, Re, Lander v Lander [1951] Ch 546, [1951] 1 All ER 622, 30 ATC 93, [1951] TR 93, [1951] 1 TLR 456 .... 92.2, 209.3, 209.4, 209.6, 209.12
Landry and Steinhoff, Re [1941] 1 DLR 699, [1941] OR 67 .... 23.5
Lane, Re, Belli v Lane [1908] 2 Ch 581, 77 LJ Ch 774, 99 LT 693 .... 39.10

Lane, Re, Luard v Lane (1880) 14 Ch D 856, 49 LJ Ch 768, 28 WR 764, 43 LT 87 .... 41.2, 41.14, 64.11
Lane v Brown (1871) 25 LT 152 .... 38.23
Lane v Earl of Stanhope (1795) 6 Term Rep 345 .... 60.2
Lane v Goudge (1803) 9 Ves 225 .... 93.29
Lane v Green (1851) 4 De G & Sm 239, 15 Jur 763, 17 LTOS 1 .... 69.1
Lane v Sewell (1874) 43 LJ Ch 378 .... 63.1
Lane's Estate, Re, Meagher v National Gallery of Ireland (Governors and Guardians) and Heaven [1946] 1 All ER 735, 115 LJ Ch 195, 175 LT 50 .... 101.8
Lane's Goods, Re (1864) 33 LJPM & A 185, 4 New Rep 253 .... 25.3
Lanesborough (Lady) v Fox (1733) Cas temp Talb 262, 3 Bro Parl Cas 130, HL 98.9
Lang v Pugh (1842) 1 Y & C Ch Cas 718, 6 Jur 939 .... 50.2
Langan v Bergin [1896] 1 IR 331 .... 52.11
Langdale (Lady) v Briggs (1855) 25 LJ Ch 100, 2 Jur NS 35, 3 Sm & G 246, 4 WR 144, 26 LTOS 306; on appeal (1856) 8 De GM & G 391 .... 20.4, 34.2, 35.39, 50.4, 59.1, 59.2, 93.3, 96.1
Langdale v Whitfeld (1858) 4 K & J 426, 27 LJ Ch 795, 4 Jur NS 706, 6 WR 862, 32 LTOS 18 .... 64.37
Langdon v Rooke. See Thorne v Rooke
Langford's Goods, Re (1867) LR 1 P & D 458, 37 LJP & M 20, 32 JP 104, 17 LT 415 .... 25.3
Langham v Peterson (1903) 67 JP 75, 87 LT 744, 19 TLR 157 .... 102.23
Langham v Sanford (1816) 2 Mer 6, 19 Ves 641 .... 57.22
Langhorn's Goods, Re (1847) 5 Notes of Cases 512 .... 20.2
Langlais v Langley [1952] 1 SCR 28 .... 4.11, 5.4
Langlands, Re, Langlands v Langlands (1917) 87 LJ Ch 1, 117 LT 11 .... 68.11, 76.3
Langley, Re, Sissons v Public Trustee [1972] NZLR 218 .... 57.15, 72.2
Langley v Baldwin (1707) 1 Eq Cas Abr 185 .... 98.4
Langley v Thomas (1856) 6 De GM & G 645, 3 Jur NS 345, 5 WR 219, 28 LTOS 298 .... 52.6
Langley's Goods, Re (1851) 2 Rob Eccl 407 .... 25.16
Langslow v Langslow (1856) 21 Beav 552, 25 LJ Ch 610, 2 Jur NS 1057 .... 39.18, 42.4, 42.5, 100.2
Langston v Langston (1834) 8 Bli NS 167, [1824–34] All ER Rep 598, 2 Cl & Fin 194, HL 51.6, 52.3, 57.10, 81.3
Langston's Estate, Re [1953] P 100, [1953] 1 All ER 928, [1953] 1 WLR 581, 97 Sol Jo 249 .... 17.4
Langton's Estate, Re [1964] P 163, [1964] 2 WLR 585, sub nom Re Langton, Langton v Lloyds Bank Ltd [1964] 1 All ER 749, 108 Sol Jo 96, CA 25.16
Lanphier v Buck (1865) 2 Drew & Sm 484, 34 LJ Ch 650, 11 Jur NS 837, 112 LT 660, sub nom Lamphier v Buck 6 New Rep 196, 13 WR 767 ... 68.2, 68.11, 76.3, 93.19
Lansdowne (Marquis) v Dowager Marchioness of Lansdowne (1820) 2 Bli NS 60, HL 30.43, 32.33
Lansdowne's (Marquis) Goods, Re (1863) 32 LJPM & A 121, 3 Sw & Tr 194, 11 WR 749, 9 LT 22 .... 15.1
Lanyon, Re [1957] SASR 135 .... 64.43

Lanyon, Re, Lanyon v Lanyon [1927] 2 Ch 264, [1927] All ER Rep 61, 96 LJ Ch 487, 71 Sol Jo 865, 137 LT 806, 43 TLR 714 .... 34.10, 35.4
Lappin, Re [1945] 1 DLR 241, [1944] OWN 756 .... 64.27
Laramée v Ferron (1909) 41 SCR 391 .... 5.9
Larence v Larence (1911) 17 WLR 197, 21 Man LR 145 .... 25.10
Larke v Nugus (1979) 123 Sol Jo 337, sub nom Re Moss, Larke v Nugus [2000] WTLR 1033, CA 200.4
Larking, Re, Larking v Larking (1887) 37 Ch D 310, 57 LJ Ch 282 .... 41.1, 47.7
Larner v Larner (1857) 3 Drew 704, 26 LJ Ch 668, 5 WR 513, 29 LTOS 208 .... 64.35
Larsen's Will, Re (1968) 66 WWR 358 .... 218.86
Lart, Re, Wilkinson v Blades [1896] 2 Ch 788, 65 LJ Ch 846, 45 WR 27, 40 Sol Jo 653, 75 LT 175 .... 43.4
Lashbrook v Cock (1816) 2 Mer 70 .... 86.5
Lassence v Tierney (1849) 2 H & Tw 115, [1843–60] All ER Rep 47, 14 Jur 182, 1 Mac & G 551, 84 RR 158, 15 LTOS 557 .... 30.35, 82.4, 94.25, 94.31, 210.45
Lasseur v Tyrconnel (1846) 10 Beav 28, 8 LTOS 153 .... 25.15
Last, Re [1958] P 137, [1958] 1 All ER 316, [1958] 2 WLR 186, 102 Sol Jo 89 .... 83.9
Latham v Travers [1912] 1 IR 140 .... 64.32
Latta's Marriage Settlement Trusts, Re, Public Trustee v Latta [1949] Ch 490, [1949] 1 All ER 665, [1949] LJR 892, 93 Sol Jo 182 .... 39.25
Lau Hau Chu v Ip Kam [2006] HKLR 100 .... 5.1
Laudry's Estate, Re [1941] 1 WWR 280 .... 35.29
Laurie, Re [1970] NZLR 710 .... 67.7
Lavelle, Re, Concannon v A-G [1914] 1 IR 194 .... 102.8
Laver v Fielder (1862) 32 Beav 1, 32 LJ Ch 365, 9 Jur NS 190, 1 New Rep 188, 11 WR 245, 7 LT 602 .... 3.3
Lavin v Howley (1897) 102 LT Jo 560 .... 7.10
Law v Law (1989) 33 ETR 183 .... 14.3
Law v Thompson (1827) 4 Russ 92, 6 LJOS Ch 56 .... 97.7
Law v Thorp (1858) 27 LJ Ch 649, 4 Jur NS 447, 6 WR 480, 31 LTOS 378 .... 76.4, 85.5
Law Ip Po (a bankrupt) (Trustee of the Property of) v Yuen Yip Kan [1994] 3 HKC 493 .... 1.8
Law Union and Crown Insurance Co v Hill [1902] AC 263, 71 LJ Ch 602, 86 LT 773, HL 50.5
Law's Trustees v Gray 1921 SC 455 .... 101.1
Lawes v Bennett (1785) 1 Cox Eq Cas 167 .... 41.20, 233.7, 233.40
Lawes, Re, Lawes v Lawes (1881) 20 Ch D 81, 30 WR 33, 45 LT 453, CA 44.8, 44.11
Lawes-Wittewronge, Re, Maurice v Bennett [1915] 1 Ch 408, [1914–15] All ER Rep 502, 84 LJ Ch 472, 112 LT 931 .... 62.1, 64.7
Lawley, Re, Zaiser v Lawley (or Perkins) [1902] 2 Ch 799, 71 LJ Ch 895, 51 WR 150, 47 Sol Jo 29, 87 LT 536, 19 TLR 8, CA; affd sub nom Beyfus v Lawley [1903] AC 411, [1900–3] All ER Rep 796, 72 LJ Ch 781, 89 LT 309, HL 3.14, 31.2, 39.5, 40.15
Lawlor v Henderson (1877) IR 10 Eq 150 .... 79.4
Lawrance v Galsworthy (1857) 3 Jur NS 1049, 30 LTOS 112 .... 64.53
Lawrence, Re [1943] Tas LR 33 .... 67.1

Lawrence (Lord), Re, Lawrence v Lawrence [1915] 1 Ch 129, 84 LJ Ch 273, 59 Sol Jo 127, 112 LT 195, CA 85.4
Lawrence v Dodwell (1699) 1 Ld Raym 438, Lut 734 .... 57.10
Lawrence's Will Trusts, Re, Public Trustee v Lawrence [1972] Ch 418, [1971] 3 All ER 433, [1971] 3 WLR 188, 115 Sol Jo 550 .... 18.15, 20.1, 39.1, 39.10, 39.12, 39.13, 39.16, 39.18, 39.20, 39.31
Lawrie v Bankes (1858) 4 K & J 142, 27 LJ Ch 265, 4 Jur NS 299, 6 WR 244, 32 LTOS 18 .... 40.14
Lawry, Re, Andrew v Coad [1938] Ch 318, [1937] 4 All ER 1, 107 LJ Ch 170, 158 LT 493 .... 83.12
Lawson, Re, Wardley v Bringloe [1914] 1 Ch 682, [1914–15] All ER Rep 206, 83 LJ Ch 519, 58 Sol Jo 320, 110 LT 573, 30 TLR 335 .... 30.24
Lawson v Stitch (1738) 1 Atk 507, West temp Hard 325 .... 30.3, 41.19
Lawson's Goods, Re (1842) 6 Jur 349 .... 10.14
Lawton, Re, Gartside v A-G [1936] 3 All ER 378 .... 103.17
Lawton, Re, Lloyds Bank Ltd v Longfleet St Mary's Parochial Church Council [1940] Ch 984, 110 LJ Ch 47, 84 Sol Jo 536, 164 LT 297, 56 TLR 1002 .... 102.17
Laxer, Re (1963) 37 DLR (2d) 192, [1963] 1 OR 343 .... 13.2
Lay's Goods, Re (1840) 2 Curt 375 .... 16.3
Laye, Re, Turnbull v Laye [1913] 1 Ch 298, 82 LJ Ch 218, 20 Mans 124, 57 Sol Jo 284, 108 LT 324 .... 99.7
Layer v Burn Philip Trustee Co Ltd (1986) 6 NSWLR 60 .... 17.4, 57.12
Layton v Martin [1986] 2 FLR 227, [1986] Fam Law 212 .... 43.1, 105.18
Lazarewicz (otherwise Fadanelli) v Lazarewicz [1962] P 171, [1962] 2 All ER 5, [1962] 2 WLR 933, 106 Sol Jo 38 .... 72.9
Lazarus v Lazarus (1919) 88 LJ Ch 525, sub nom Re Lazarus, Lazarus v Lazarus 121 LT 491, CA 63.1
Lea, Re, Lea v Cooke (1887) 34 Ch D 528, 56 LJ Ch 671, 35 WR 572, 56 LT 482, 3 TLR 360 .... 103.17
Lea, Re, Wells v Holt (1911) 104 LT 253 .... 63.1
Lea v Grundy (1855) 1 Jur NS 951, 25 LTOS 287 .... 38.12
Leach, Re, Leach v Leach [1912] 2 Ch 422, 81 LJ Ch 683, 56 Sol Jo 649, 106 LT 1003 .... 98.1, 98.12
Leach, Re, Leach v Lindeman [1986] Ch 226, [1985] 2 All ER 754, [1985] 3 WLR 413, [1985] FLR 1120, [1985] Fam Law 319, 129 Sol Jo 318, CA 105.3, 105.16, 105.17, 105.22, 105.32
Leach, Re, Milne v Daubeny [1923] 1 Ch 161, [1922] All ER Rep 714, 92 LJ Ch 225, 67 Sol Jo 198, 128 LT 525 .... 30.34, 31.1
Leach v Jay (1878) 9 Ch D 42, 47 LJ Ch 876, 27 WR 99, 39 LT 242, CA 50.11
Leach v Leach (1843) 13 Sim 304, 7 Jur 273 .... 82.5
Leach v Leach (1843) 2 Y & C Ch Cas 495 .... 47.32, 51.4
Leach v Leach (1866) 35 Beav 185 .... 47.24
Leach v Leach [1878] WN 79 .... 64.2
Leach v Smith (1859) 23 JP 168 .... 5.9
Leach v Thompson. See Thompson v Leach
Leach's Goods, Re (1890) 63 LT 111 .... 18.23
Leach's Will Trusts, Re, Chatterton v Leach [1948] Ch 232, [1948] 1 All ER 383, [1948] LJR 990, 92 Sol Jo 167, 64 TLR 175 .... 47.21, 204.64
Leacroft v Maynard (1791) 1 Ves 279, 3 Bro CC 233 .... 91.6

Leadbeater v Cross (1876) 2 QBD 18, 46 LJQB 31, 25 WR 96, LT 803 ...... 93.13, 93.15
Leader v Duffey (1888) 13 App Cas 294, 58 LJPC 13, 59 LT 9, HL 50.2, 50.21
Leahy, Re, Leahy v Payne [1920] 1 IR 260 .... 40.21
Leahy v A-G for New South Wales [1959] AC 457, [1959] 2 All ER 300, [1959] 2 WLR 722, 103 Sol Jo 391, 33 ALJR 105, PC 9.35, 102.24, 102.26
Leak v Macdowall (No 2) (1863) 33 Beav 238, 3 New Rep 185 .... 83.3
Leake v Robinson (1817) 2 Mer 363 ... 66.4, 66.5, 67.4, 93.5, 93.6, 93.34, 93.39, 94.21, 94.28
Lean v Lean (1875) 23 WR 484, 32 LT 305 .... 38.23
Lear v Leggett (1830) 1 Russ & M 690 .... 99.6
Le Blanc Estate, Re (1955) 16 WWR 389 .... 52.3
Leche v Lord Kilmorey (1823) Turn & R 207 .... 82.7
Lechmere v Curtler (1855) 24 LJ Ch 647, 19 JP 709, 3 Eq Rep 938 .... 103.7
Le Cras v Perpetual Trustee Co Ltd. See Resch's Will Trusts, Re, Le Cras v Perpetual Trustee Co Ltd
Le Cren Clarke, Re, Funnell v Stewart [1996] 1 All ER 715, sub nom Funnell v Stewart [1996] 1 WLR 288 .... 102.9
Ledger, Re [1983] Qd R 176 .... 64.30
Ledsome v Hickman (1708) 2 Vern 611 .... 97.4
Ledward v Hassells (1856) 2 K & J 370, 25 LJ Ch 311, 2 Jur NS 277, 4 WR 315 .... 9.39, 34.21, 34.24
Lee, Re [1955] 1 DLR (2d) 48, [1955] OWN 984 .... 82.7
Lee, Re, Gibbon v Peele (1910) 103 LT 103 .... 38.1, 52.11
Lee, Re, Sinclair v Lee. See Sinclair v Lee
Lee v Fernie (1839) 1 Beav 483 .... 40.15, 40.18
Lee v Lee (1858) 27 LJ Ch 824, 6 WR 846, 32 LTOS 59 .... 41.1, 41.4, 41.11, 41.22
Lee v Lee (1860) 1 Drew & Sm 85, 29 LJ Ch 788, 6 Jur NS 621, 8 WR 443, 2 LT 532 .... 51.10, 66.5, 77.2, 77.3, 77.6
Lee v Lee (1864) 10 Jur NS 1041 .... 69.2
Lee v Pain (1844) 4 Hare 201, 8 Jur 705 ..... 44.1, 50.21, 51.6, 57.18, 58.4, 66.19, 69.2, 88.3
Leech v Bates (1849) 1 Rob Eccl 714, 6 Notes of Cases 699 .... 11.26, 13.1
Leech's Case. See Thompson v Leach
Leeds (Duke) v Lord Amherst (1844) 13 Sim 459, 14 LJ Ch 73, 9 Jur 359 .... 64.46
Leek, Re, Darwen v Leek [1967] Ch 1061, [1967] 2 All ER 1160, [1967] 3 WLR 576, 47 ATC 28, 111 Sol Jo 500; on appeal [1969] 1 Ch 563, [1968] 1 All ER 793, [1968] 2 WLR 1385, 47 ATC 28, [1967] TR 375, 112 Sol Jo 444, CA 53.6
Leeming, Re, Turner v Leeming [1912] 1 Ch 828, 81 LJ Ch 453, 106 LT 793 .... 41.14
Leeming v Sherratt (1842) 2 Hare 14, [1835–42] All ER Rep 458, 11 LJ Ch 423, 6 Jur 663 .... 54.5, 67.4, 90.1, 93.25, 93.30, 98.4
Lees v Lees (1871) IR 5 Eq 549 .... 39.18
Lees' Trustees v Lees 1927 SC 886 .... 93.2
Leese's Goods, Re (1853) 17 Jur 216, 21 LTOS 24 .... 16.4
Leeson's Goods, Re [1928] IR 168 .... 25.8
Le Farrant v Spencer (1748) 24 LJ Ch 526n, 1 Ves Sen 97 .... 64.27
L'Fit v L'Batt (1718) 1 P Wms 526, 2 Eq Cas Abr 777 pl 1 .... 57.5, 57.6
Legard v Haworth (1800) 1 East 120 .... 74.8
Legeas v Trusts and Guarantee Co (1912) 20 WLR 172, 5 DLR 389, 4 Alta LR 190, 1 WWR 802 .... 3.3, 3.8
Leggatt, Re, Griffith v Calder [1908] VLR 385 .... 44.14

Legge v Asgill (1818) 3 Hare 194n; affd (1818) Turn & R 265n 64.35
Legh's Settlement Trusts, Re, Public Trustee v Legh [1938] Ch 39, [1937] 3 All ER 823, 107 LJ Ch 6, 81 Sol Jo 701, 157 LT 270, 53 TLR 1036, CA 67.8, 93.5, 94.8, 94.43, 94.48, 216.16
Leguia's Estate, Re (1936) 105 LJP 72, 155 LT 270, CA 25.16
L'Herminier, Re, Mounsey v Buston [1894] 1 Ch 675, 63 LJ Ch 496, 8 R 598, 70 LT 727 .... 62.1, 83.13
Leigh v Byron (1853) 22 LJ Ch 1064, 1 Eq Rep 519, 17 Jur 822, 1 Sm & G 486, 1 WR 407, 22 LTOS 32 .... 72.2
Leigh v Leigh (1808) 15 Ves 92 .... 58.11
Leigh v Leigh (1854) 17 Beav 605, 23 LJ Ch 287, 18 Jur 115, 2 WR 205, 22 LTOS 279 .... 47.29, 66.19
Leigh v Mosley (1851) 14 Beav 605, 18 LTOS 84 .... 90.2
Leigh's Goods, Re [1892] P 82, 61 LJP 124, 66 LT 379, 8 TLR 210 .... 18.21
Leigh's Marriage Settlement, Re, Rollo v Leigh [1952] 2 All ER 57, 96 Sol Jo 412, [1952] 1 TLR 1463 .... 218.93
Leigh's Will Trusts, Re, Handyside v Durbridge [1970] Ch 277, [1969] 3 All ER 432, [1969] 3 WLR 649, 113 Sol Jo 758 .... 1.8, 7.14, 7.22, 7.28, 42.2, 64.53, 241.10, 241.17, 241.25
Leighton v Bailie (1834) 3 My & K 267, 3 LJ Ch 133 .... 38.3
Leighton v Leighton (1874) LR 18 Eq 458, 43 LJ Ch 594, 22 WR 727 .... 44.4
Leitch, Re [1965] VR 204 .... 102.8
Leitch, Re [1997] 1 NZLR 38 .... 47.5
Le Jeune v Budd (1834) 6 Sim 441 .... 35.16
Le Jeune v Le Jeune (1837) 2 Keen 701, 1 Jur 235 .... 68.4
Lemage v Goodban (1865) LR 1 P & D 57, 35 LJP & M 28, 12 Jur NS 32, 13 LT 508 .... 1.1, 18.9, 18.10, 18.14
Lemaine v Staneley (1681) Freem KB 538, 3 Lev 1 .... 11.13
Lenden v Blackmore (1840) 10 Sim 626 .... 85.3
Leneham v Wall [1922] 1 IR 59 .... 44.1, 44.11
Leng, Re, Dodsworth v Leng [1938] Ch 821, [1938] 3 All ER 181, 108 LJ Ch 65, 82 Sol Jo 545, 159 LT 355, 54 TLR 988 .... 32.16, 32.21, 218.47
Lennox's Estate, Re [1949] SCR 446, [1949] 3 DLR 9 .... 38.20
Lenox v Lenox (1839) 10 Sim 400, 9 LJ Ch 83, 4 Jur 5 .... 93.9
Leonard, Re, Theobald v King (1880) 29 WR 234, 43 LT 664 .... 38.23
Leonard v Leonard [1902] P 243, 71 LJP 117, 46 Sol Jo 666, 87 LT 145, 18 TLR 747 .... 14.12, 18.23, 18.27, 18.33
Leong v Lim Beng Chye [1955] AC 648, [1955] 2 All ER 903, [1955] 3 WLR 303, 99 Sol Jo 524, PC 34.14, 35.8
Le Page v Gardom. See Gardom, Re, Le Page v A-G
Lepine, Re, Dowsett v Culver [1892] 1 Ch 210, [1891–4] All ER Rep 945, 61 LJ Ch 153, 66 LT 360, CA 29.1, 29.2, 29.9, 29.11, 29.14, 29.15, 29.16
Lepine v Bean (1870) LR 10 Eq 160, 39 LJ Ch 847, 18 WR 797, 22 LT 833 .... 72.3
Lepine v Ferard (1831) 2 Russ & M 378, 1 LJ Ch 150 .... 98.10
Lepton's Charity, Re, Ambler v Thomas [1972] Ch 276, [1971] 2 WLR 659, 114 Sol Jo 970, sub nom Re Lepton's Will Trusts, Re Lepton's Charity, Ambler v Thomas [1971] 1 All ER 799 .... 103.19
Lesingham's Trusts, Re (1883) 24 Ch D 703, 53 LJ Ch 333, 32 WR 116, 49 LT 235 .... 55.6
Leslie, Re [1954] OWN 472 .... 35.39, 63.1

Leslie v Earl of Rothes [1894] 2 Ch 499, 63 LJ Ch 617, 7 R 600, 71 LT 134, CA ... 35.39, 57.8, 82.2
Leslie v Leslie (1835) L & G temp Sugd 1 ... 32.22
Leslie v Leslie (1872) IR 6 Eq 332 ... 18.9
Lester, Re, Burton v Lester (1906) 23 WN 240, 7 SRNSW 58 ... 34.23
Lester, Re, Lester v Lester [1942] Ch 324, [1942] 1 All ER 646, 111 LJ Ch 197, 86 Sol Jo 168, 58 TLR 250 ... 45.1, 91.2, 206.20
Lester v Garland (1808) 15 Ves 248, [1803–13] All ER Rep 436 ... 34.22, 35.6
L'Estrange v L'Estrange (1890) 25 LR Ir 399 ... 39.18, 93.17
Lethbridge v Lethbridge (1862) 4 De GF & J 35, 31 LJ Ch 737, 8 Jur NS 836, 10 WR 449, 6 LT 727 ... 64.26
Lethbridge v Thurlow (1851) 15 Beav 334, 21 LJ Ch 538 ... 44.9, 44.10
Lett v Randall (1855) 24 LJ Ch 708, 3 Eq Rep 1034, 1 Jur NS 747, 3 Sm & G 83, 3 WR 564, 25 LTOS 244; affd (1860) 2 De GF & J 388, 30 LJ Ch 110, 6 Jur NS 1359, 9 WR 130, 3 LT 455 ... 94.12
Lett v Randall (1860) 2 De GF & J 388 ... 33.12
Letterstedt v Broers (1884) 9 App Cas 371, 53 LJPC 44, [1881–5] All ER Rep 882, 51 LT 169, PC ... 25.17
Leung Wai Jing [2004] 1 KHC 453 ... 1.2, 1.3
Leury, Re [1975] VR 601 ... 64.48
Leven and Melville's (Earl) Goods, Re (1889) 15 PD 22, 59 LJP 35 ... 25.2
Leventhorpe v Ashbie (1635) 1 Roll Abr 831 ... 84.4
Leverhulme, Re, Cooper v Leverhulme [1943] 2 All ER 143 ... 102.8
Leverhulme, Re, Cooper v Leverhulme (No 2) [1943] 2 All ER 274, 169 LT 294 ... 53.3, 94.2
Leverington's Goods, Re (1886) 11 PD 80, 55 LJP 62 ... 12.12
Levick's Will Trusts, Re, ffennell v IRC [1963] 1 All ER 95, [1963] 1 WLR 311, 41 ATC 313, [1962] TR 333, 107 Sol Jo 235 ... 24.2, 24.6
Levien, Re, Lloyds Bank Ltd v Worshipful Co of Musicians [1955] 3 All ER 35, [1955] 1 WLR 964, 99 Sol Jo 542 ... 102.10
Levien, Re, Trustees, Executors and Agency Co Ltd v Levien [1937] VLR 80, 43 Argus LR 39 ... 38.23
Levy, Re, ex p Walton (1881) 17 Ch D 746, [1881–5] All ER Rep 548, 50 LJ Ch 657, 30 WR 395, 45 LT 1, CA ... 50.6
Levy, Re, Barclays Bank Ltd v Board of Guardians and Trustees for the Relief of the Jewish Poor [1960] Ch 346, [1960] 1 All ER 42, [1960] 2 WLR 278, 104 Sol Jo 86, CA ... 62.1, 102.26, 212.12, 235.11
Levy, Re, Cohen v Cohen (1907) 24 WN 211, 7 SRNSW 885 ... 93.38
Levy v Lindo (1817) 3 Mer 81 ... 4.13, 4.14, 4.20
Levy Estate Trust, Re [2000] CLY 5263 ... 221.34
Lewal's Settlement Trusts, Re, Gould v Lewal [1918] 2 Ch 391, 87 LJ Ch 588, 62 Sol Jo 702, 119 LT 520, 34 TLR 538 ... 24.6, 24.15, 24.16
Lewes v Lewes (1848) 16 Sim 266, 17 LJ Ch 425 ... 33.18, 82.7
Lewes' Trusts, Re (1871) 6 Ch App 356, 40 LJ Ch 602, 35 JP 357, 19 WR 617, 24 LT 533 ... 9.2
Lewin v Killey (1888) 13 App Cas 783, 59 LT 675, PC ... 97.6
Lewis, Re [1964] VR 537 ... 41.20
Lewis, Re, Foxwell v Lewis (1885) 30 Ch D 654, 55 LJ Ch 232, 34 WR 150, 53 LT 387 ... 37.8

Lewis, Re, Goronwy v Richards [1942] Ch 424, [1942] 2 All ER 364, 111 LJ Ch 256, 86 Sol Jo 253, 167 LT 235 .... 68.1, 86.2
Lewis, Re, Lewis v Lewis [1904] 2 Ch 656, 73 LJ Ch 748, 53 WR 393, 91 LT 242, CA 30.32, 34.24
Lewis, Re, Prothero v Lewis (1909) 26 TLR 145 .... 64.47
Lewis, Re, Public Trustee v Allen [1955] Ch 104, [1954] 3 All ER 257, [1954] 3 WLR 610, 98 Sol Jo 748 .... 102.5, 102.6
Lewis v Cotton [2001] WTLR 1117, 3 ITELR 447, NZCA 2.6
Lewis v Lewis (1861) 26 JP 88, 2 Sw & Tr 153, 4 LT 583, sub nom Lewis's Goods, Re 31 LJPM & A 153, 7 Jur NS 688 .... 12.12
Lewis v Lewis [1908] P 1, 77 LJP 7, 52 Sol Jo 31, 98 LT 58, 24 TLR 45 .... 11.4, 11.9, 11.18, 11.24
Lewis v Madocks (1803) 8 Ves 150 .... 3.8
Lewis v Mathews (1869) LR 8 Eq 277, 38 LJ Ch 510, 33 JP 775, 17 WR 841, 20 LT 905 .... 27.6, 30.15
Lewis v Moore (1896) 24 AR 393 .... 30.31
Lewis v Morris (1854) 19 Beav 34 .... 87.2
Lewis v Rees (1856) 3 K & J 132, 26 LJ Ch 101, 3 Jur NS 12, 5 WR 96, 28 LTOS 229 .... 50.7
Lewis v Templer (1864) 33 Beav 625, 12 WR 928, 10 LT 638 .... 98.9
Lewis & Sons Ltd v Dawson [1934] SCR 676, 4 DLR 753 .... 63.7
Lewis d Ormond v Waters (1805) 6 East 336 .... 89.1, 93.13, 98.3
Lewis' Estate, Re [1974] 2 NSWLR 323 .... 16.2
Lewis' Goods, Re (1850) 14 Jur 514, 15 LTOS 165, 7 Notes of Cases 436 .... 18.8
Lewis' Goods, Re (1858) 27 LJP & M 31, 4 Jur NS 243, 1 Sw & Tr 31, 30 LTOS 353 .... 18.27
Lewis' Goods, Re (1861) 31 LJPM & A 153. See Lewis v Lewis (1861) 26 JP 88
Lewis' Will Trust, Re, Whitelaw v Beaumont [1951] WN 591, 95 Sol Jo 789, [1951] 2 TLR 1032 .... 35.40, 206.27, 235.27
Lewis' Will Trusts, Re, Lewis v Williams [1984] 3 All ER 930, [1985] 1 WLR 102, 128 Sol Jo 385 .... 58.2, 58.4, 64.7, 64.20, 204.70, 204.80, 233.37, 234.15
Lewis' Will Trusts, Re, O'Sullivan v Robbins [1937] Ch 118, [1937] 1 All ER 227, 106 LJ Ch 90, 80 Sol Jo 1035, 156 LT 235, 53 TLR 132 .... 41.4, 64.30
Lewis' Will Trusts, Re, Phillips v Bowkett [1937] 1 All ER 556, 81 Sol Jo 179 .... 74.1, 74.2
Liddell-Grainger's Will Trusts, Re, Dormer v Liddell-Grainger [1936] 3 All ER 173, 80 Sol Jo 836, 53 TLR 12 .... 236.10
Liddle, Re, Shrewsbury v McGuffie (1915) 34 NZLR 962 .... 88.2
Liddle v Kebbells (1915) 34 NZLR 593 .... 64.37
Lightbody's Trusts, Re (1884) 33 WR 452, 52 LT 40 .... 27.3
Lightfoot, Re [1948] 2 DLR 418, [1948] OWN 332 .... 30.32
Lightfoot v Burstall (1863) 1 Hem & M 546, 33 LJ Ch 188, 10 Jur NS 308, 3 New Rep 112, 12 WR 148, 9 LT 711 .... 50.21
Lightfoot v Maybery. See Watkins, Re, Maybery v Lightfoot
Lilford (Lord) v Keck (1862) 30 Beav 295 .... 92.1, 92.3, 92.4
Lill v Lill (1857) 104.16, 5 WR 390 .... 33.15, 101.14
Lillcott v Compton (1708) 2 Vern 638 .... 64.28
Lillicrap v Sinclair [1919] NZLR 194 .... 101.1

Lillingston, Re, Pembery v Pembery [1952] 2 All ER 184, [1952] WN 358, 96 Sol Jo 462, [1952] 1 TLR 1622 .... 1.15
Lilly's Will Trusts, Re, Public Trustee v Johnstone [1948] 2 All ER 906, [1949] LJR 270, 92 Sol Jo 705 .... 64.30, 64.53
Limbrey v Gurr (1819) 6 Madd 151 .... 102.22
Limond, Re, Limond v Cunliffe [1915] 2 Ch 240, 84 LJ Ch 833, 59 Sol Jo 613, 113 LT 815 .... 9.10, 16.7
Limpus v Arnold (1884) 15 QBD 300, 54 LJQB 85, 33 WR 537, CA 49.4, 49.5, 50.21
Lincoln (Countess) v Duke of Newcastle (1806) 12 Ves 218, HL 94.15
Lincoln (Lady) v Pelham (1804) 10 Ves 166 .... 87.1
Lindgren v Lindgren (1846) 9 Beav 358, 15 LJ Ch 428, 10 Jur 674 .... 57.17, 58.12
Lindley, Re, Lindley v Lindley and Union Trustee Co of Australia Ltd [1911] SR Qd 96 .... 101.4
Lindop, Re, Lee-Barber v Reynolds [1942] Ch 377, [1942] 2 All ER 46, 111 LJ Ch 226, 86 Sol Jo 242, 167 LT 235, 58 TLR 291 .... 70.2
Lindrea, Re [1953] VLR 168 .... 19.4
Lindsay, Re (1852) 5 Ir Jur 97 .... 101.2
Lindsay v Ellicott (1876) 46 LJ Ch 878 .... 77.6
Line v Hall (1873) 43 LJ Ch 107, 22 WR 124, 29 LT 568 .... 40.21
Lines v Lines (1869) 17 WR 1004, 22 LT 400 .... 38.4, 64.45
Ling v Ling [2002] WTLR 553 .... 47.15
Linklater, Re, Trustees and Executors Agency Co Ltd v Laidlaw [1926] VLR 456, 48 ALT 80, 32 Argus LR 334 .... 57.22
Linklater's Estate, Re (1967) 66 DLR (2d) 30, 62 WWR 163 .... 76.1
Linley, Re, McDonnell v Linley (1949) 207 LT Jo 372, CA 12.3
Lipinski's Will Trusts, Re, Gosschalk v Levy [1976] Ch 235, [1977] 1 All ER 33, [1976] 3 WLR 522, 120 Sol Jo 473 .... 9.35, 102.10, 102.23
Lissenden v CAV Bosch Ltd [1940] AC 412, [1940] 1 All ER 425, 109 LJKB 350, 84 Sol Jo 357, 162 LT 195, 56 TLR 347, 33 BWCC 21, HL 42.1
List, Re, List v Prime [1949] NZLR 78 .... 102.10
Lister v Bradley (1841) 1 Hare 10, 11 LJ Ch 49, 5 Jur 1034 .... 93.35, 93.40
Lister v Gilbert (1938) 12 MPR 566 .... 83.12
Lister v Pickford (1865) 34 Beav 576, [1861–73] All ER Rep 374, 34 LJ Ch 582, 11 Jur NS 649, 6 New Rep 243, 13 WR 827, 12 LT 587 .... 64.2
Lister v Smith (1863) 28 JP 40, 33 LJPM & A 29, 10 Jur NS 107, 3 Sw & Tr 282, 12 WR 319, 9 LT 578 .... 5.7, 10.1
Lister v Tidd (1861) 29 Beav 618 .... 76.6
Litchfield, Re, Horton v Jones (1911) 104 LT 631 .... 91.3
Litt's Will Trusts, Re, Parry v Cooper [1946] Ch 154, [1946] 1 All ER 314, 115 LJ Ch 114, 90 Sol Jo 116, 174 LT 184, 62 TLR 303, CA 82.4, 90.4
Little, Re [1953] 1 DLR 78, [1952] OWN 732 .... 78.5
Little, Re, Barclays Bank Ltd v Bournemouth and East Dorset Hospital Management Committee [1953] 2 All ER 852, [1953] 1 WLR 1132, 97 Sol Jo 574 .... 41.13, 103.10
Little, Re, Foster v Cooper [1960] 1 All ER 387, [1960] 1 WLR 495, 104 Sol Jo 369 .... 11.2, 11.4, 11.12
Little, Re, Harrison v Harrison (1889) 40 Ch D 418, 58 LJ Ch 233, 37 WR 289, 60 LT 246, 5 TLR 236, CA 40.15
Littledale v Bickersteth (1876) 24 WR 507 .... 8.7

Littlewood, Re, Clark v Littlewood [1931] 1 Ch 443, [1930] All ER Rep 151, 100 LJ Ch 243, 144 LT 718, 47 TLR 79 .... 214.7
Littras v Littras [1995] 2 VR 283 .... 35.40
Liverpool and District Hospital for Diseases of the Heart v A-G [1981] Ch 193, [1981] 1 All ER 994, [1981] 2 WLR 379, 125 Sol Jo 79, 131 NLJ 142 .... 103.4
Liverpool Dock Acts, Re, Re Colshead's Will Trusts (1852) 2 De G & J 690 .... 91.5
Liverton, Re [1951] NZLR 351 .... 39.22, 94.48
Liverton, Re, Liverton v Liverton [1954] NZLR 612 .... 64.27
Livesey v Livesey (1827) 3 Russ 287, 6 LJOS Ch 13 .... 31.8
Livesey v Livesey (1830) 3 Russ 542 .... 93.34
Livesey v Livesey (1849) 2 HL Cas 419, 13 Jur 371, 13 LTOS 153 .... 49.2, 81.3
Livesey's Settlement Trusts, Re, Livesey v Livesey [1953] 2 All ER 723, [1953] 1 WLR 1114, 97 Sol Jo 572 .... 44.4
Livingston, Re, Irving v Irving [1923] SASR 387 .... 57.19, 57.20
Livingston's Estate, Re (1922) 66 DLR 776, [1922] 2 WWR 408 .... 30.31
Livingston's Estate (No 2), Re (1923) 32 Man LR 465, [1923] 1 WWR 358 .... 93.25
Livingstone, Re [1951] 3 DLR 848, [1951] OWN 385 .... 58.3
Livingstone, Re, Livingstone v Durell (1917) 61 Sol Jo 384 .... 61.1
Livock's Goods, Re (1838) 1 Curt 906 .... 14.1
Llangattock (Lord), Re, Johnson v Central Board of Finance of Church of England (1918) 34 TLR 341 .... 30.31, 82.5
Llangattock, Re, Shelley v Harding (1917) 33 TLR 250 .... 35.41
Llanover (Baroness), Re, Herbert v Freshfield (No 2) [1903] 2 Ch 330, 72 LJ Ch 729, 51 WR 615, 88 LT 856, 19 TLR 524 .... 1.2, 51.5
Llanover's (Baroness) Will, Re, Herbert v Freshfield [1903] 2 Ch 16, 72 LJ Ch 406, 51 WR 418, 47 Sol Jo 385, 88 LT 648, 19 TLR 338, CA 83.6
Llewellin's Will Trusts, Re, Griffiths v Wilcox [1949] Ch 225, [1949] 1 All ER 487, [1949] LJR 724, 93 Sol Jo 148 .... 221.10
Lloyd, Re [1958] VLR 523 .... 102.9
Lloyd, Re [1960] VLR 63 .... 41.14
Lloyd, Re, Greame v A-G (1893) 10 TLR 66 .... 102.23
Lloyd, Re, Lloyd v Chambers (1894) 38 Sol Jo 235 .... 64.37
Lloyd v Branton (1817) 3 Mer 108 .... 34.14, 35.14
Lloyd v Davies (1854) 15 CB 76, 18 Jur 1056, 2 WR 495, 2 CLR 1788, 23 LTOS 160, sub nom Doe d Lloyd v Davies 23 LJCP 169 .... 96.7
Lloyd v Jackson (1867) LR 2 QB 269, 36 LJQB 169, 7 B & S 683, 15 WR 408, Ex Ch 83.6
Lloyd v Lloyd (1841) 4 Beav 231, 10 LJ Ch 327, 5 Jur 673 .... 38.14
Lloyd v Lloyd (1852) 2 Sim NS 255, 21 LJ Ch 596, 16 Jur 306, 19 LTOS 84 .... 35.2, 35.8
Lloyd v Lloyd (1856) 3 K & J 20 .... 93.30, 93.36
Lloyd v Lloyd (1866) LR 2 Eq 722 .... 99.10
Lloyd v Lloyd (1869) LR 7 Eq 458, 38 LJ Ch 458, 17 WR 702, 20 LT 898 ... 60.2, 64.51
Lloyd v Lloyd (1886) 34 WR 608, 54 LT 841 .... 64.35
Lloyd v Roberts (1858) 12 Moo PCC 158, PC 13.2
Lloyd v Tweedy [1898] 1 IR 5 .... 83.8, 99.1
Lloyd v Williams (1740) 2 Atk 108, Barn Ch 224 .... 32.12
Lloyd and Jobson v Spillet (1741) 2 Atk 148, Barn Ch 384 .... 35.38
Lloyd's Estate, Re, Baker v Mason. See Mason v Baker

Lloyds Bank Ltd v Marcan [1973] 2 All ER 359, [1973] 1 WLR 339, 25 P & CR 65, 117 Sol Jo 187; affd [1973] 3 All ER 754, [1973] 1 WLR 1387, 117 Sol Jo 761, 228 Estates Gazette 1919, CA 105.48
Lloyds Bank plc v Duker [1987] 3 All ER 193, [1987] 1 WLR 1324, 131 Sol Jo 1358, [1987] LS Gaz R 3254 .... 30.9, 30.36, 200.57
Lloyds Bank plc v Rosset [1991] 1 AC 107, [1990] 1 All ER 1111, [1990] 2 WLR 867, 60 P & CR 311, [1990] 2 FLR 155, [1990] Fam Law 395, 22 HLR 349, [1990] 16 LS Gaz R 41, [1990] NLJR 478, HL 2.8
Lloyds TSB Private Banking plc v Twiddy (Inland Revenue Capital Taxes) (10 October 2005, unreported) 234.3
Lloyds TSB (personal representative of Antrobus dec'd) v IRC [2002] STC (SCD) 468 .... 234.3
Lock v Lock (1915) 32 WN 84, 15 SRNSW 287 .... 101.7
Lock v Venables (1859) 27 Beav 598, sub nom Loch v Venables 29 LJ Ch 179, 6 Jur NS 238, 8 WR 121, 1 LT 506 .... 61.1
Locke v Dunlop (1888) 39 Ch D 387, 57 LJ Ch 1010, 59 LT 683, 4 TLR 712, CA 81.2, 81.3
Locke v James (1843) 13 LJ Ex 186, 11 M & W 901, 1 LTOS 387 .... 14.7
Locke v Lamb (1867) LR 4 Eq 372, 15 WR 1010, 16 LT 616 ... 66.18, 93.26, 93.27, 93.31
Locker's Settlement Trusts, Re, Meachem v Sachs [1978] 1 All ER 216, [1977] 1 WLR 1323, 121 Sol Jo 796 .... 53.6
Lockhart v Hardy (1846) 9 Beav 379, 10 Jur 728 .... 82.7
Lockhart v Harker, Read and the Royal National Lifeboat Institution [1995] STC 210 .... 57.25
Lockhart v Ray (1880) 20 NBR 129 .... 38.3
Lockwood v Sikes (1884) 51 LT 562 .... 99.8
Lodwig, Re, Lodwig v Evans [1916] 2 Ch 26, 85 LJ Ch 585, 60 Sol Jo 494, 114 LT 881, 32 TLR 491, CA 93.30
Loffus v Maw (1862) 3 Giff 592, 32 LJ Ch 49, 8 Jur NS 607, 10 WR 513, 6 LT 346 .... 3.3
Lofthouse, Re (1885) 29 Ch D 921, 54 LJ Ch 1087, 33 WR 668, 53 LT 174, CA 218.66
Loftus v Harris (1914) 19 DLR 670, 30 OLR 479, 5 OWN 770 .... 13.3
Loftus v Stoney (1867) 15 WR 550, 17 I Ch R 178 .... 18.11, 38.5
Loftus-Otway (or Otway), Re, Otway v Otway [1895] 2 Ch 235, 64 LJ Ch 529, 13 R 536, 43 WR 501, 39 Sol Jo 449, 72 LT 656 .... 99.10
Logan v Wienholt (1833) 7 Bli NS 1, 1 Cl & Fin 611, sub nom Wienholt v Logan 3 Sim 141, HL 3.8
Lomax v Holmden (1749) 1 Ves Sen 290 .... 65.2
Lomax v Ripley (1855) 24 LJ Ch 254, 3 Eq Rep 301, 1 Jur NS 272, 3 Sm & G 48, 3 WR 269, 24 LTOS 323 .... 36.3, 36.5
Lombe v Stoughton (1849) 17 Sim 84, 18 LJ Ch 400, 13 LTOS 398 .... 64.26
Londesborough, Re, Bridgeman v Fitzgerald (1880) 50 LJ Ch 9, 43 LT 408 .... 64.27
Londesborough (Lord) v Somerville (1854) 19 Beav 295, 23 LJ Ch 646, 23 LTOS 291 .... 32.13
London and North Western Railway (New Works and Additional Powers) Act 1869, Re, Re Sewell's Trusts. See Sewell's Estate, Re

London and South Western Rly Co v Gomm (1881) 20 Ch D 562, 51 LJ Ch 193, 30 WR 321, 45 LT 505; revsd (1882) 20 Ch D 562, [1881–5] All ER Rep 1190, 51 LJ Ch 530, 30 WR 620, 46 LT 449, CA 94.13, 94.36
London, Brighton and South Coast Rly Co, Re, ex p Wilkinson (1849) 3 De G & Sm 633, 19 LJ Ch 257, 14 Jur 301, 14 LTOS 171 .... 33.28
London Hospital Medical College v IRC [1976] 2 All ER 113, [1976] 1 WLR 613, [1976] TR 29, 120 Sol Jo 250 .... 102.8, 102.12
London Regional Transport Pension Fund Trustee Co Ltd v Hatt [1993] PLR 227 .... 221.35
London University v Yarrow (1857) 21 JP 596, 1 De G & J 72, 26 LJ Ch 430, 3 Jur NS 421, 5 WR 543, 29 LTOS 172 .... 102.10
London Wine Co (Shippers) Ltd, Re [1986] PCC 121 .... 8.8
Long, Re [1938] 1 DLR 344, [1938] OR 28 .... 66.12
Long, Re, Lovegrove v Long [1901] WN 166 .... 9.40
Long v Blackall (1797) 7 Term Rep 100 .... 94.12
Long v Dennis (1767) 4 Burr 2052, 1 Wm Bl 630 .... 35.2, 35.4
Long v Hughes (1831) 1 De G & Sm 364, 7 LJOS Ch 105 .... 33.35
Long v Kent (1865) 11 Jur NS 724, 6 New Rep 354, 13 WR 961, 12 LT 794 .... 46.3
Long v Lane (1885) 17 LR Ir 11; on appeal (1885) 17 LR Ir 24, CA 56.8
Long v Ovenden (1881) 16 Ch D 691, 50 LJ Ch 314, 29 WR 709, 44 LT 462 .... 32.2, 40.21
Long v Watkinson (1852) 17 Beav 471, 21 LJ Ch 844, 16 Jur 235, 19 LTOS 309 .... 47.24, 83.3
Long and Feaver v Symes and Hannam (1832) 3 Hag Ecc 771 .... 25.12
Long's Estate, Re [1936] P 166, [1936] 1 All ER 435, 105 LJP 44, 80 Sol Jo 248, 154 LT 469, 52 TLR 323 .... 11.2, 11.3
Longley, Re, Longley and Longley v Longley [1981] CLY 2885 .... 105.5
Longley v Longley (1871) LR 13 Eq 133, 41 LJ Ch 168, 20 WR 227, 25 LT 736 .... 60.2
Longman, Re, Westminster Bank Ltd v Hatton [1955] 1 All ER 455, [1955] 1 WLR 197, 99 Sol Jo 169 .... 99.4, 99.8
Longmore v Broom (1802) 7 Ves 124 .... 56.5, 68.1, 101.9
Longmore v Elcum (1843) 2 Y & C Ch Cas 363, 12 LJ Ch 469, 1 LTOS 311 .... 33.18, 82.5
Longmuir v Holland (2000) 192 DLR (4th) 62, BC CA 4.10
Longworth, Re, Longworth v Campbell [1910] 1 IR 23 .... 84.4, 85.5
Longworth v Bellamy (1871) 40 LJ Ch 513 .... 80.1
Lonsdale (Earl) v Countess of Berchtoldt (1854) Kay 646, 23 LJ Ch 816, 18 Jur 811, 24 LTOS 51 .... 82.3
Lonsdale (Earl) v Countess of Berchtoldt (1857) 3 K & J 185, 3 Jur NS 328 .... 46.4, 82.9
Loom, Re, Fulford v Reversionary Interest Society Ltd [1910] 2 Ch 230, 79 LJ Ch 704, 54 Sol Jo 583, 102 LT 907 .... 45.2, 46.3, 207.18
Lopes, Re, Bence-Jones v Zoological Society of London [1931] 2 Ch 130, [1930] All ER Rep 45, 100 LJ Ch 295, 74 Sol Jo 581, 146 LT 8, 46 TLR 577 .... 102.8
Lord and Fullerton's Contract, Re [1896] 1 Ch 228, 65 LJ Ch 184, 44 WR 195, 40 Sol Jo 113, 73 LT 689, CA 27.5, 27.6

Lord's Estate, Re, Lord v Lord (1867) 2 Ch App 782, 36 LJ Ch 533, 15 WR 1118, 17 LT 105 .... 30.32, 32.4, 32.10, 32.11
Lord's Settlement, Re, Martins Bank Ltd v Lord [1947] 2 All ER 685, [1948] LJR 207, 91 Sol Jo 654 .... 94.24
Loring v Thomas (1861) 1 Drew & Sm 497, 30 LJ Ch 789, 7 Jur NS 1116, 9 WR 919, [1861–73] All ER Rep 620, 5 LT 269 .... 54.2, 68.9, 74.1
Lory, Re (1891) 7 TLR 419 .... 80.1
Lory's Will Trusts, Re, Lambrick v Public Trustee of Colony and Protectorate of Kenya [1950] 1 All ER 349, 94 Sol Jo 98, 66 (pt 1) TLR 330 .... 64.32
Loscombe v Wintringham (1849) 12 Beav 46 .... 61.1
Loscombe v Wintringham (1850) 13 Beav 87 .... 102.7, 103.3
Lothian's Trustees v Back 1918 SC 401 .... 21.2
Lottman v Stanford (1980) 107 DLR (3d) 28 .... 38.17, 38.22, 38.25
Loughhead, Re, Hamilton v Loughhead [1918] 1 IR 227 .... 40.21
Louis v Louis (1863) 9 Jur NS 244, 7 LT 666 .... 76.2
Louis, Re, Louis v Treloar (1916) 32 TLR 313 .... 15.6, 36.6, 57.5, 57.10
Lousada, Re, Bacon v Bacon (1887) 82 LT Jo 358 .... 102.7
Lovat (Lord) v Duchess of Leeds (1862) 2 Drew & Sm 62, 31 LJ Ch 503, 10 WR 397, 6 LT 307; on appeal sub nom Lovet (Lord) v Duchess of Leeds (1862) 7 LT 36 .... 33.47
Lovatt v Tribe (1862) 3 F & F 9 .... 4.20
Love, Re, Green v Tribe. See Green v Tribe
Love v Gaze (1845) 8 Beav 472, 9 Jur 910, 5 LTOS 453 .... 57.31, 83.3
Love v Love (1881) 7 LR Ir 306 .... 93.6
Love's Goods, Re (1881) 7 LR Ir 178 .... 25.2
Loveacres d Mudge v Blight (1775) 1 Cowp 352 .... 83.6
Loveday v Hopkins (1755) Amb 273 .... 78.4
Lovegrove's Goods, Re (1862) 26 JP 375, 31 LJPM & A 87, 8 Jur NS 442, 2 Sw & Tr 453, 6 LT 131 .... 2.2
Lovejoy v Crafter (1865) 35 Beav 149 .... 74.1
Lovelace v Lovelace (1585) 1 And 132, Cro Eliz 40, sub nom Lovelace's Case 2 Leon 35, Sav 75 .... 76.1
Loveland, Re, Loveland v Loveland [1906] 1 Ch 542, 75 LJ Ch 314, 94 LT 336, 22 TLR 321 .... 9.25
Loveless, Re, Farrer v Loveless [1918] 2 Ch 1, [1918–19] All ER Rep 403, 87 LJ Ch 461, 62 Sol Jo 470, 119 LT 24, 34 TLR 356, CA 33.47
Lovell, Re, Sparks v Southall [1920] 1 Ch 122, 88 LJ Ch 540, 64 Sol Jo 35, 122 LT 26, 35 TLR 715 .... 8.2, 34.3, 35.35
Loveman, Re, Watson v Watson (1879) 48 LJ Ch 565 .... 41.13, 64.54
Lovet (Lord) v Duchess of Leeds. See Lovat (Lord) v Duchess of Leeds
Lovett v Lovett (1857) 1 F & F 581 .... 5.9
Lovett v Lovett [1898] 1 Ch 82, [1895–9] All ER Rep 474, 67 LJ Ch 20, 46 WR 105, 42 Sol Jo 81, 77 LT 650 .... 39.5
Low v Burron (1734) 3 P Wms 262 .... 94.2
Low v Carter (1839) 1 Beav 426 .... 7.3, 83.6
Low v Guthrie [1909] AC 278, 78 LJPC 126, HL 5.4, 5.9
Low v Smith (1856) 25 LJ Ch 503, 2 Jur NS 344, 4 WR 429 .... 78.4
Lowe, Re, Danily v Platt (1892) 61 LJ Ch 415, 40 WR 475, 36 Sol Jo 413, 8 TLR 491 .... 72.3, 80.1
Lowe, Re, Westminster Bank Ltd v Lowe (1939) 83 Sol Jo 421 .... 34.11

Lowe v Manners (1822) 5 B & Ald 917 .... 35.15
Lowe v Thomas (1854) Kay 369; on appeal (1854) 5 De GM & G 315, 23 LJ Ch 616, 2 Eq Rep 742, 18 Jur 563, 2 WR 499, 23 LTOS 238 .... 64.35, 64.36
Lowe's Estate, Re, Swann v Rockley [1938] 2 All ER 774, 82 Sol Jo 454 .... 64.35
Lowen v Cocks (1627) Het 63 .... 50.2
Lowfield v Stoneham (1746) 2 Stra 1261 .... 57.10
Lowit, Re [1967] NZLR 883 .... 64.55
Lowman, Re, Devenish v Pester [1895] 2 Ch 348, 64 LJ Ch 567, 12 R 362, 72 LT 816, 11 TLR 396, CA 47.26, 48.10, 64.32, 84.4
Lowndes v Stone (1799) 4 Ves 649 .... 56.5, 68.1
Lowry v Fulton (1839) 9 Sim 104, 47 RR 188 .... 27.6
Lowry v Patterson (1874) IR 8 Eq 372, 8 LR Ir 372 .... 35.13, 64.27
Lowry's Will Trusts, Re, Barclays Bank Ltd v United Newcastle-upon-Tyne Hospitals Board of Governors [1967] Ch 638, [1966] 3 All ER 955, 110 Sol Jo 871 .... 34.9, 103.10
Lowther v Bentinck (1874) LR 19 Eq 166, [1874–80] All ER Rep 362, 44 LJ Ch 197, 23 WR 156, 31 LT 719 .... 50.6, 218.97, 218.107
Lowther v Cavendish (1758) 1 Eden 99, Amb 356; affd sub nom Cavendish (Lord) v Lowther (1759) 3 Bro Parl Cas 186, HL 34.7, 34.8
Lowthorpe-Lutwidge v Lowthorpe-Lutwidge [1935] P 151, [1935] All ER Rep 338, 104 LJKB 71, 153 LT 103 .... 18.8
Loxton, Re [2006] WTLR 1567 .... 4.11, 5.2, 5.9
Loy, Re [1984] 1 Qd R 396 .... 70.2
Loyd v Finlayson (1797) 2 Esp 564 .... 25.15, 49.7
Lucas, Re [1966] VR 267 .... 13.1
Lucas, Re, Rhys v A-G [1922] 2 Ch 52, [1922] All ER Rep 317, 91 LJ Ch 480, 66 Sol Jo 368, 127 LT 272 .... 102.5, 102.7
Lucas, Re, Sheard v Mellor [1948] Ch 175, [1947] 2 All ER 773, [1948] LJR 712, 92 Sol Jo 26, 64 TLR 32; revsd [1948] Ch 424, [1948] 2 All ER 22, [1948] LJR 1914, 92 Sol Jo 336, 64 TLR 343, CA 103.3, 103.4
Lucas v Carline (1840) 2 Beav 367 .... 93.27
Lucas v Cuday (1876) IR 10 Eq 514 .... 71.5
Lucas v Goldie [1920] NZLR 28 .... 34.5
Lucas v Goldsmid (1861) 29 Beav 657, 30 LJ Ch 935, 7 Jur NS 719, 9 WR 759, 4 LT 632 .... 79.2
Lucas's Will, Re (1881) 17 Ch D 788, 29 WR 860 .... 9.2
Lucas-Tooth, Re, Lucas-Tooth v Public Trustee (1923) 156 LT Jo 382 .... 60.1
Lucas-Tooth v Lucas-Tooth [1921] 1 AC 594, 90 LJ Ch 347, 65 Sol Jo 377, 125 LT 225, HL 78.2
Lucena v Lucena (1876) 7 Ch D 255, 36 LT 87; on appeal (1877) 7 Ch D 266, 47 LJ Ch 203, 26 WR 254, 37 LT 420, CA 67.5
Luck, Re [1977] WAR 148 .... 5.7
Lucking's Will Trusts, Re, Renwick v Lucking [1967] 3 All ER 726, [1968] 1 WLR 866, 112 Sol Jo 444 .... 221.21
Luddy, Re, Peard v Morton (1883) 25 Ch D 394, 53 LJ Ch 21, 32 WR 272, 49 LT 706 .... 96.7, 97.6
Ludlam, Re, Ludlam v Ludlam (1890) 63 LT 330 .... 30.37
Ludlow, Re, Bence-Jones v A-G (1923) 93 LJ Ch 30, CA 102.23
Ludlow v Bunbury (1865) 35 Beav 36 .... 99.1
Ludlow v Stevenson (1857) 1 De G & J 496, 5 WR 828, 29 LTOS 371 .... 64.35

Ludlow's Goods, Re (1858) 1 Sw & Tr 29, 6 WR 409, 30 LTOS 340 .... 38.3
Luffman's Goods, Re (1847) 11 Jur 211, 8 LTOS 478, 5 Notes of Cases 183 .... 20.2
Lugar v Harman (1786) 1 Cox Eq Cas 250 .... 74.2
Luke v South Kensington Hotel Co (1879) 11 Ch D 121, [1874–80] All ER Rep 1293, 48 LJ Ch 361, 27 WR 514, 40 LT 638, CA 221.29
Luke's Goods, Re (1865) 34 LJPM & A 105, 11 Jur NS 397 .... 15.1
Lumley v Robbins (1853) 10 Hare 621, 22 LJ Ch 869, 1 Eq Rep 129, 17 Jur 410, 1 WR 285, 22 LTOS 40 .... 91.5
Lundy v Lundy (1895) 24 SCR 650 .... 9.15, 34.2
Lunn v Osborne (1834) 7 Sim 56, 3 LJ Ch 233 .... 57.5, 91.3
Lupton's Estate, Re [1905] P 321, 74 LJP 162, 94 LT 100 .... 82.3
Lush's Goods, Re (1887) 13 PD 20, 57 LJP 23, 52 JP 199, 36 WR 847, 58 LT 684 .... 25.2
Lusher, Re, Lusher v Lusher [1928] NZLR 73 .... 68.9
Lushington, Re [1964] NZLR 161, NZ CA 61.1, 95.13
Lushington v Onslow (1848) 12 Jur 465, 11 LTOS 206, 6 Notes of Cases 183 .... 14.2, 14.8
Lushington v Penrice (1868) 16 WR 836, 18 LT 597 .... 93.1
Lutheran Church of Australia etc v Farmers Co-operative Executors and Trustees Ltd (1969–70) (1970) 121 CLR 628, [1970] ALR 545, Aus HC 1.6, 40.5, 53.2
Luty v Magill (2005) 246 DLR (4th) 762 .... 14.3
Luxford v Cheeke (1683) 3 Lev 125, sub nom Brown v Cutler 2 Show 152, T Raym 427 .... 34.3
Luxmoore v Chambers (circa 1885) 58 LT 61 .... 18.19
Lybbe's Will Trusts, Re, Kildahl v Bowker [1954] 1 All ER 487, [1954] 1 WLR 573, 98 Sol Jo 215 .... 38.13, 90.1
Lycett, Re, Riley v King's College Hospital (1897) 13 TLR 373 .... 103.7
Lyddon v Ellison (1854) 19 Beav 565, 18 Jur 1006, 2 WR 690, 24 LTOS 123 .... 44.8, 81.3, 94.15
Lynch, Re, Lynch v Lynch [1943] 1 All ER 168, 87 Sol Jo 48, 168 LT 189, 59 TLR 130 .... 33.20, 50.3, 80.1, 80.4, 83.7
Lynch v Johnson (1878) 4 VLR 263 .... 50.6
Lynch's Estate, Re [1986] SASR 131 .... 10.1
Lyndon v Lyndon [1930] NZLR 76 .... 62.1
Lyne v De La Ferté and Dunn (1910) 102 LT 143 .... 23.7
Lyne's Settlement Trusts, Re, Re Gibbs, Lyne v Gibbs [1919] 1 Ch 80, [1918–19] All ER Rep 419, 88 LJ Ch 1, 63 Sol Jo 53, 120 LT 81, 35 TLR 44, CA 23.7
Lyne's Trust, Re (1869) LR 8 Eq 65, 38 LJ Ch 471, 20 LT 735 .... 80.1
Lynn v Beaver (1823) 23 RR 185 .... 57.4
Lynneberg v Kildahl [1948] NZLR 207 .... 71.1
Lyon v Coward (1846) 15 Sim 287, 15 LJ Ch 460, 10 Jur 486, 7 LTOS 385 .... 68.11, 68.13
Lyon v Mitchell (1816) 1 Madd 467 .... 85.5
Lyon's Trusts, Re (1879) 48 LJ Ch 245 .... 58.10
Lyons Corpn v Advocate-General of Bengal (1876) 1 App Cas 91, 45 LJPC 17, 24 WR 679, 34 LT 77 .... 102.27, 103.1, 103.18

Lysaght, Re, Hill v Royal College of Surgeons [1966] Ch 191, [1965] 2 All ER 888, [1965] 3 WLR 391, 109 Sol Jo 577 .... 9.38, 102.10, 103.1, 103.12, 103.17, 103.18
Lysaght, Re, Lysaght v Lysaght [1898] 1 Ch 115, 67 LJ Ch 65, 77 LT 637, CA 204.61
Lysaght v Edwards (1876) 2 Ch D 499, 45 LJ Ch 554, 3 Char Pr Cas 243, 24 WR 778, 34 LT 787 .... 7.27, 59.2
Lysiak, Re (1975) 55 DLR (3d) 161 .... 1.6, 34.2, 82.5
Lysons, Re, Beck v Lysons (1912) 107 LT 146, 56 Sol Jo 705 .... 46.3, 207.2, 207.15, 207.18
Lytton v Lytton (1793) 4 Bro CC 441 .... 98.8, 98.9
Lywood v Kimber (1860) 29 Beav 38, sub nom Lywood v Warwick 30 LJ Ch 507, 7 Jur NS 507, 9 WR 88 .... 76.5

M

Ma Shiu-lim's Estate, Re, Ma Po-chim v Ma Lok-shan [1992] 2 HKLR 286 .... 5.9
Mabank v Brooks (1780) 2 Dick 577, sub nom Maybank v Brooks 1 Bro CC 84 .... 9.2, 47.1
Mabbett, Re, Pitman v Holborrow [1891] 1 Ch 707, 60 LJ Ch 279, 39 WR 537, 64 LT 447 .... 33.3, 33.4, 33.7
Maber, Re, Armsby v Maber (1896) 12 TLR 267 .... 38.1, 52.11
Maber, Re, Ward v Maber [1928] Ch 88, 97 LJ Ch 101, 138 LT 318 .... 32.28, 95.6, 218.73
Maberley v Strode (1797) 3 Ves 450 .... 56.8, 56.9
Maberly's Settlement Trusts, Re (1871) 19 WR 522, 24 LT 262 .... 38.10, 64.39
Macadam, Re, Dallow and Moscrop v Codd [1946] Ch 73, [1945] 2 All ER 664, 115 LJ Ch 14, 89 Sol Jo 531, 173 LT 395, 62 TLR 48 .... 221.10
M'Adam v Walker (1813) 1 Dow 148, HL 4.20
McAfee v Kerr (1918) 52 ILT 178 .... 63.1
M'Afee, Re, Mack v Quirey [1909] 1 IR 124 .... 64.54
Macandrew's Will Trusts, Re, Stephens v Barclays Bank Ltd [1964] Ch 704, [1963] 2 All ER 919, [1963] 3 WLR 822, 107 Sol Jo 910 .... 52.6
M'Ara v M'Cay (1889) 23 LR Ir 138 .... 18.10, 18.13
MacArthur Estate, Re [1953] 1 DLR 380, 7 WWR 182 .... 38.1, 38.3
Macartney, Re, Brookhouse v Barman (1920) 36 TLR 394 .... 41.13
Macartney, Re, Macfarlane v Macartney [1918] 1 Ch 300, 87 LJ Ch 143, 118 LT 174 .... 42.1
MacAulay, Re (1971) 18 DLR (3d) 726 .... 103.3
Macaulay's Estate, Re, Macaulay v O'Donnell [1943] Ch 435n, HL 9.35
McBroom, Re [1992] 2 FLR 49, [1992] Fam Law 376 .... 105.5
McC's Estate, Re (1978) 9 Fam Law 26 .... 105.19
M'Cabe's Goods, Re (1862) 31 LJPM & A 190, 26 JP 744, 2 Sw & Tr 474, 10 WR 848, 6 LT 474 .... 21.7
McCabe's Goods, Re (1873) LR 3 P & D 94, 42 LJP & M 79, 38 JP 9, 29 LT 250 .... 14.2, 19.4
McCalmont, Re, Rooper v McCalmont (1903) 19 TLR 490 .... 63.1, 64.2
M'Cann, Re, Donnelly v Moore [1916] 1 IR 255 .... 79.1

McCarogher v Whieldon (1867) LR 3 Eq 236, sub nom Whieldon v McCarogher 36 LJ Ch 196, 15 WR 296 .... 42.7, 44.13
M'Carthy v M'Carthy (1878) 3 LR Ir 317, 1 LR Ir 189 .... 48.5, 93.18
McCaughey v Stamp Duties Comrs (1945) 46 NSWR 192 .... 1.8
McCaul, Re, McCaul v Mason (1909) 27 NZLR 65 .... 52.7
McCauley v McCauley (1910) 10 CLR 434 .... 18.28
M'Cleary, Re, Moffatt v M'Cleary [1923] 1 IR 16 .... 35.22
McClintock, Re (1976) 70 DLR (3d) 175 .... 47.22
McClintock v Calderwood [2005] EWHC 836 (Ch), [2005] All ER (D) 356 (Apr) 4.11
M'Clure v Evans (or Dawson) (1861) 29 Beav 422, 30 LJ Ch 295, 7 Jur NS 204, 9 WR 428, 3 LT 870 .... 100.4
McClymont v Hooper (1973) 47 ALJR 222, HC of A 101.8
McColgan, Re (1969) 4 DLR (3d) 572, [1969] 2 OR 152 .... 34.11, 35.19
McColl-Frontenac Oil Co Ltd v Hamilton [1953] 1 SCR 127, [1953] 1 DLR 721 .... 41.5
McCormick, Re, Hazlewood v Foot [1915] 1 IR 315, 49 ILT 174 .... 42.4
McCormick v Grogan (1869) 4 App Cas 82, LR 4 HL 82, 17 WR 961 ... 36.1, 36.2, 36.7, 36.12, 36.13
McCormick v Simpson [1907] AC 494, 77 LJPC 12, 97 LT 616, PC 97.6
M'Creight v M'Creight (1849) 13 I Eq R 314, 2 Ir Jur 17 .... 9.40
Macculloch v Anderson [1904] AC 55, HL 50.21, 66.13
M'Culloch v M'Culloch (1862) 3 Giff 606, 10 WR 515, 6 LT 489 .... 83.7
M'Cutcheon v Allen (1880) 5 LR Ir 268 .... 93.27
McCutcheon's Will, Re [1960] VLR 289 .... 32.2, 204.61
M'Dermot v O'Conor (1876) 10 IR Eq 352 .... 33.17
M'Dermott v A-G (No 2) [1923] 1 IR 142, 148 .... 37.7
McDonald, Re (1911) 30 NZLR 896 .... 10.5
Macdonald, Re [1931] 4 DLR 920, [1931] OR 659 .... 62.1
Macdonald, Re (1971) 18 DLR (3d) 521, [1971] 2 OR 577 .... 34.8, 102.8
Macdonald v Irvine (1878) 8 Ch D 101, 47 LJ Ch 494, 26 WR 381, 38 LT 155, CA 38.23, 41.11
Macdonald v Macdonald (1872) LR 14 Eq 60, 41 LJ Ch 566, 20 WR 739, 26 LT 685 .... 24.2, 24.3
McDonald v McDonald (No 2) (1935) 52 WN 145, 35 SRNSW 463 .... 3.10
McDonald v McLeod (1921) 54 NSR 379 .... 35.21
McDonald v Moran (1938) 12 MPR 424 .... 36.2
McDonald v Trustees, Executors and Agency Co Ltd (1902) 28 VLR 442 ... 35.24, 35.36
McDonald Estate (NS), Re (1914) 14 ELR 109, 15 DLR 558 .... 4.16
Macdonald's Estate, Re (1956) 5 DLR (2d) 175, 19 WWR 468 .... 101.10
M'Donald's Trustees v M'Donald's Executors 1940 SC 433 .... 33.13
Macdonell v Purcell (1896) 23 SCR 101 .... 21.5
MacDonnell, Re (1982) 133 DLR (3d) 128 .... 51.1
MacDonnell, Re, Colgan v Macdonnell [1927] 1 IR 213 .... 47.1
McDonnell v Morrow (1889) 23 LR Ir 591 .... 64.53
McDonnell v Neil [1951] AC 342, 95 Sol Jo 298, [1951] 1 TLR 642, PC 87.2
MacDougall, Re [1927] 3 DLR 464, [1927] 1 WWR 612, 21 Sask LR 397 ..... 41.5, 85.3
Macduff, Re, Macduff v Macduff [1896] 2 Ch 451, [1895–9] All ER Rep 154, 65 LJ Ch 700, 45 WR 154, 40 Sol Jo 651, 74 LT 706, 12 TLR 452, CA 102.23

McElligott, Re, Grant v McElligott [1944] Ch 216, [1944] 1 All ER 441, 113 LJ Ch 277, 88 Sol Jo 170, 171 LT 10, 60 TLR 246 .... 78.5, 83.1
McEnery, Re, O'Connell v A-G [1941] IR 323 .... 102.14
McEuen, Re, McEuen v Phelps [1913] 2 Ch 704, 83 LJ Ch 66, 30 TLR 44, sub nom Re McEwen, McEwen v Phelps 109 LT 701, [1911–13] All ER Rep 176, 58 Sol Jo 82, CA 38.26
McEwan, Re, McEwan v Day [1955] NZLR 575 .... 53.5
MacEwen, Re (1963) 40 DLR (2d) 152, [1963] 2 OR 490 .... 71.5, 73.1
McEwen, Re, McEwen v Phelps. See McEuen, Re, McEuen v Phelps
McEwen Estate, Re (1967) 62 WWR 277 .... 51.1
McFadden v Public Trustee for Victoria [1981] 1 NSWLR 15 .... 10.11
McFadden, Re, Wright v Dowds [1963] NZLR 289 .... 67.4
McFarland, Re (1963) 36 DLR (2d) 689, [1963] 1 OR 273 .... 83.15
McFarlane, Re [1934] 3 DLR 457, [1934] OR 383 .... 93.29
McFee, Re, McFee v Toner (1910) 79 LJ Ch 676, 103 LT 210 .... 77.4
McFetridge, Re, Speakman v McFetridge [1950] NZLR 176 .... 64.45
McGarrity, Re, Ballance and Benson v McGarrity (1912) 46 ILT 175 .... 93.41
McGeachy v Russ (1955) 3 DLR 349, 15 WWRNS 178 .... 2.7
McGeorge, Re, Ratcliff v McGeorge [1963] Ch 544, [1963] 1 All ER 519, [1963] 2 WLR 767, 107 Sol Jo 253 .... 33.25
McGibbon v Abbott (1885) 10 App Cas 653, 34 LJPC 39, 54 LT 138, PC 50.19
MacGillivray's Estate, Re [1946] 2 All ER 301, 90 Sol Jo 488, 175 LT 383, 62 TLR 538, CA 16.4, 16.5, 18.12
McGinn Estate, Re (1969) 70 WWR 159 .... 18.5, 18.20
McGovern v A-G [1982] Ch 321, [1981] 3 All ER 493, [1982] 2 WLR 222, [1981] TR 157, 125 Sol Jo 255 .... 102.4, 102.5, 102.10, 102.11
McGowan v Hamblett (2005–06) 8 ITELR 943 .... 200.112
McGrath Estate, Re (1952) 60 Man R 365, 5 WWRNS 637 .... 62.1
McGrath's Will, Re (1899) 16 WN 160, 20 NSWLR (B & P) 55 .... 79.1
McGredy v IRC [1951] NI 155 .... 93.16
McGregor (Inspector of Taxes) v Adcock [1977] 3 All ER 65, [1977] 1 WLR 864, [1977] STC 206, 51 TC 692, [1977] TR 23, 121 Sol Jo 240, 242 Estates Gazette 289 .... 205.23
Macgregor v Macgregor (1845) 2 Coll 192 .... 68.11
M'Gregor v M'Gregor (1859) 1 De GF & J 63 .... 76.1, 76.3, 86.4
MacGregor's Goods, Re (1889) 53 JP 231, 60 LT 840 .... 15.2
Macgregor's Will, Re (1901) 18 WN 17, 1 SRNSW 50 .... 25.1
Machin, Re (1980) 101 DLR (3d) 438 .... 103.1, 103.3
M'Hugh v M'Hugh [1908] 1 IR 155 .... 50.12, 57.19, 71.5
McIlrath, Re [1959] ALR 1297, [1959] VR 720 .... 78.3
McInerney, Re [1966] VR 263 .... 80.2
MacInnes, Re (1958) 15 DLR (2d) 684, [1958] OR 592, [1958] OWN 354 .... 93.29
McIntosh, Re [1933] IR 69 .... 83.15
Macintosh v Pogose. See Mackintosh v Pogose
McIntyre Estate, Re [1950] 2 WWR 682 .... 54.1
McIsaac v Beaton (1905) 37 SCR 143, 38 NSR 60 .... 82.5
M'Kane's Goods, Re (1887) 21 LR Ir 1 .... 25.2
McKay, Re [1968] NZLR 131 .... 101.6
Mackay, Re, Mackay v Gould [1906] 1 Ch 25, 75 LJ Ch 47, 54 WR 88, 50 Sol Jo 43, 93 LT 694 .... 30.32, 34.24

McKay, Re, McKay v McKay (1904) 22 NZLR 121 .... 34.5
M'Kay v M'Alister (1912) 46 ILT 88 .... 98.13
M'Kay v M'Kay [1900] 1 IR 213 .... 20.5, 47.28, 47.29
M'Kay v M'Kay [1901] 1 IR 109, 120 .... 93.15
MacKay Estate, Re, St Andrew's-Wesley Church v Toronto General Trusts Corpn and Stobie [1948] SCR 500 .... 102.23
MacKay's Estate, Re (1935) 8 MPR 526 .... 5.4
Mackay's Trustees v Mackay 1909 SC 139, 143 .... 95.9
Mackechnie v Marjoribanks (1870) 39 LJ Ch 604, 18 WR 993, 22 LT 841 .... 40.15
Mckechnie v Vaughan (1873) LR 15 Eq 289, 21 WR 399, 28 LT 263 .... 69.2
McKee, Re, Public Trustee v McKee [1931] 2 Ch 145, 100 LJ Ch 325, 75 Sol Jo 442, 145 LT 605, 47 TLR 424, CA 38.24, 104.1, 104.11, 104.12, 104.13, 104.16
M'Kee v Meikle (1893) 27 ILT 100 .... 7.9, 7.10
Mackell v Winter (1797) 3 Ves 536 .... 93.27
McKendrick v Winter (1889) 15 VLR 450 .... 92.1
McKenna v McCarten [1915] 1 IR 282 .... 82.4, 83.9, 83.13
McKenna's Will Trusts, Re, Higgins v Bank of Ireland and McKenna [1947] IR 277 .... 35.30
Mackenzie, Re (1958) 15 DLR (2d) 113, [1958] OWN 183 .... 78.2
McKenzie, Re (1968) 67 DLR (2d) 105, [1968] 1 OR 567 .... 51.2
Mackenzie, Re, Bain v Mackenzie [1916] 1 Ch 125, 85 LJ Ch 197, 114 LT 283 .... 213.12
McKenzie, Re, McKenzie v Thomas [1968] NZLR 493 .... 19.4
Mackenzie, Re, Moir v Angus County Council [1962] 2 All ER 890, [1962] 1 WLR 880, 60 LGR 388, 106 Sol Jo 688 .... 102.8
Mackenzie, Re, Thornton v Huddleston [1917] 2 Ch 58, 86 LJ Ch 543, 117 LT 114 .... 39.19, 39.20, 39.26
Mackenzie v Bradbury (1865) 35 Beav 617, 34 LJ Ch 627, 11 Jur NS 650, 6 New Rep 283 .... 52.11
Mackenzie v Handasyde (1829) 2 Hag Ecc 211 .... 4.17
Mackenzie v King (1848) 17 LJ Ch 448, 12 Jur 787, 12 LTOS 4 .... 56.8
Mackenzie v Mackenzie (1826) 2 Russ 262 .... 88.4
McKenzie v McKenzie [1925] 1 DLR 373, 36 OLR 247 .... 62.1
Mackenzie's Estate, Re [1909] P 305, 79 LJP 4, 26 TLR 39 .... 18.29, 25.2
Mackenzie's Trustees v Mackenzie's Executors 1947 SC 161 .... 67.5
Mackesy v Mackesy [1896] 1 IR 511 .... 64.32
Mackett v Mackett (1872) LR 14 Eq 49, 41 LJ Ch 704, 20 WR 860 .... 82.5
M'Key's Goods, Re (1876) 11 IR Eq 220 .... 11.4
Mackie v Mackie (1845) 5 Hare 70, 9 Jur 753 .... 38.19
Mackinlay, Re, Scrimgeour v Mackinlay (1911) 56 Sol Jo 142 .... 97.6
Mackinley v Sison (1837) 8 Sim 561, 1 Jur 558 .... 39.19, 58.10
McKinnon, Re (1966) 55 DLR (2d) 20, [1966] 1 OR 663 .... 78.6, 78.7, 87.1
Mackinnon v Peach (1838) 2 Keen 555, 7 LJ Ch 211 .... 88.2, 97.4
McKinnon v Voight [1998] 3 VR 543, Vic CA 5.4
M'Kinnon's Trustees v Brownlie. See Mackintosh (or Miller) v Gerrard
Mackintosh (or Miller) v Gerrard [1947] AC 461, [1948] LJR 692, 176 LT 262, 63 TLR 265, sub nom M'Kinnon's Trustees v Brownlie 1947 SC 27, HL 66.1, 68.6
Mackintosh v Pogose [1895] 1 Ch 505, 2 Mans 27, 13 R 254, 43 WR 247, 39 Sol Jo 218, 72 LT 251, sub nom Macintosh v Pogose 64 LJ Ch 274 .... 99.4

Mackintosh v Townsend (1809) 16 Ves 330 .... 23.4
McKittrick Estate, Re [1934] 1 DLR 422, 41 Man LR 454, [1933] 3 WWR 536 .... 5.7
Macklem v Macklem (1890) 19 OR 482 .... 35.19
Mackreth v Fox (1791) 4 Bro Parl Cas 258, HL 221.4
M'Lachlan v Taitt (1860) 28 Beav 407, 30 LJ Ch 276, 2 De GF & J 449, 6 Jur NS 1269, 9 WR 152, 3 LT 492 .... 50.17, 66.2, 93.2, 93.4
MacLaren v MacLaren (1907) 15 OLR 142, 10 OWR 835 .... 64.53
Maclaren v Stainton (1858) 27 LJ Ch 442, 4 Jur NS 199, 30 LTOS 331 .... 35.19, 83.6
McLean, Re [1929] Argus LR 216 .... 40.5
McLean, Re (1957) 6 DLR (2d) 519, [1957] OWN 11 .... 35.8
McLean, Re, Bullen v Paton [1926] VLR 21, 47 ALT 107 .... 94.48
McLean, Re, Larlee v Earle (1969) 4 DLR (3d) 617 .... 30.8
Maclean, Re, Williams v Nelson (1894) 11 TLR 82 .... 64.36
M'Lean v Simpson (1887) 19 LR Ir 528 .... 101.10
Maclean's Trustees v M'Nair (1969) 48 ATC 228, [1969] TR 229, 1969 SC 65, 1969 SLT 146 .... 210.68
Macleay, Re (1875) LR 20 Eq 186, 44 LJ Ch 441, 23 WR 718, 32 LT 682 .... 79.2, 99.2
Macleay v Treadwell [1937] AC 626, [1937] 2 All ER 38, 106 LJPC 91, 81 Sol Jo 356, 157 LT 1, 53 TLR 434, PC 78.1
M'Leod v Drummond (1810) 17 Ves 152 .... 25.18
McLeod v McNab [1891] AC 471, 60 LJP 70, 65 LT 266, PC 20.4, 21.5, 21.6, 21.7, 22.3
McLeod's Will, Re [1923] VLR 218, 44 ALT 156 .... 47.32
M'Loughlin's Estate, Re (1878) 1 LR Ir 421, Ir CA 33.20
McLuckie, Re, Perpetual Executors and Trustees Association of Australia Ltd v Honeycombe [1943] ALR 334, [1943] VLR 137 .... 64.27
M'Mahon, Re, M'Mahon v M'Mahon [1901] 1 IR 489, CA 30.32, 45.2
McMillan, Re [1925] 3 WWR 584 .... 25.2
MacMillan, Re (1977) 80 DLR (3d) 54 .... 50.18
MacMillan v Kennedy [1942] 3 DLR 170, 2 WWR 497 .... 36.2
M'Murdo's Goods, Re (1868) LR 1 P & D 540, 37 LJP & M 14, 32 JP 72, 3 Mar LC 37, 16 WR 283, 17 LT 393 .... 16.3
McMurray v Dilworth, Re Dilworth [1904] 22 NZLR 125 .... 57.22
McMurty v Scarrow and Scarrow (1938) 20 DLR 270, 46 Man LR 86, [1938] 2 WWR 39 .... 10.4
McMylor v Lynch (1894) 24 OR 632 .... 32.12
Macnamara, Re, Hewitt v Jeans (1911) 104 LT 771 .... 102.9
McNamee, Re (1912) 31 NZLR 1007 .... 11.13
McNare, Re, McNare v McNare [1964] 3 All ER 373, [1964] 1 WLR 1255, 108 Sol Jo 839 .... 105.5
McNaughten, Re [1955] NZLR 45 .... 38.19
McNeil Estate, Re (1959) 43 MPR 357 .... 87.1, 87.2
McNeill, Re (1980) 109 DLR (3d) 109 .... 47.12
McNeill, Re, Wright v Johnstone (1909) 26 WN 45, 9 SRNSW 220 .... 69.1
M'Neillie v Acton (1853) 4 De GM & G 744, 23 LJ Ch 11, 2 Eq Rep 21, 17 Jur 1041, 22 LTOS 111 .... 205.25

MacNiven (Inspector of Taxes) v Westmoreland Investments Ltd [2001] UKHL 6, [2003] 1 AC 311, [2001] 1 All ER 865, [2001] 2 WLR 377, [2001] STC 237, 73 TC 1, [2001] NLJR 223, 145 Sol Jo LB 55, [2001] All ER (D) 93 (Feb) 241.13
McParland v Coulson [1930] NI 138 .... 25.16
McPhail v Doulton [1971] AC 424, [1970] 2 All ER 228, [1970] 2 WLR 1110, 114 Sol Jo 375, HL 34.9, 34.10, 39.31, 53.6
McPhail v McIntosh (1887) 14 OR 312 .... 74.1
MacPhail v Phillips [1904] 1 IR 155 .... 38.10, 64.17
Macphail v Torrance (1909) 25 TLR 810 .... 3.2
McPhee Estate, Re [1948] 1 WWR 65 .... 58.1
McPhee's Trustees v McPhee (1912) 49 SLR 33, 1912 SC 75 .... 102.23
McPherson, Re [1968] VR 368 .... 68.6
Macpherson v Macpherson (1852) 16 Jur 847, 1 WR 8, 19 LTOS 221, 1 Macq 243, HL 38.25
Macpherson v Stewart (1858) 28 LJ Ch 177, 7 WR 34, 32 LTOS 143 .... 50.3
MacPhillamy, Re, Gilmour v MacPhillamy. See Gilmour v MacPhillamy
McRae, Re, McDonald v Creer (1928) 45 WN 93, 28 SRNSW 447 .... 77.3
McVay Estate, Re (1955) 16 WWR 200 .... 14.6
McVicar's Goods, Re (1869) LR 1 P & D 671, 38 LJP & M 84, 33 JP 678, 17 WR 832, 20 LT 1013 .... 17.5
Madden's Goods, Re [1905] 2 IR 612, 39 ILT Jo 205 .... 11.4
Maddison v Alderson (1883) 8 App Cas 467, 52 LJQB 737, [1881–5] All ER Rep 742, 47 JP 821, 31 WR 820, 49 LT 303, HL 3.2, 3.3, 3.4
Maddison v Andrew (1747) 1 Ves Sen 57 .... 47.38, 93.25, 93.27
Maddison v Chapman (1858) 4 K & J 709; affd (1859) 3 De G & J 536 .... 55.5, 90.1, 93.15, 96.1
Maddison v Chapman (1861) 1 John & H 470 .... 67.7
Maddock, Re, Llewelyn v Washington [1902] 2 Ch 220, 71 LJ Ch 567, 50 WR 598, 86 LT 644, CA 30.3, 36.7, 36.9, 36.13
Maddock v Legg (1858) 25 Beav 531 .... 76.3
Maddock v Victoria Registrar of Titles (1915) 19 CLR 681, [1915] VLR 152 .... 25.10
Maddock's Goods, Re (1874) LR 3 P & D 169, [1874–80] All ER Rep 367, 43 LJP & M 29, 38 JP 631, 22 WR 741, 30 LT 696 .... 11.14, 11.18, 12.12
Maddox v Staines (1727) 2 P Wms 421; affd sub nom Staines v Maddock (1728) 3 Bro Parl Cas 108, HL 94.3, 94.35
Maddy's Estate, Re, Maddy v Maddy [1901] 2 Ch 820, 71 LJ Ch 18, 45 Sol Jo 673, 85 LT 341 .... 50.11
Maden v Taylor (1876) 45 LJ Ch 569 .... 67.4
Madge, Re, Pridie v Bellamy (1928) 44 TLR 372, 72 Sol Jo 284 .... 8.7, 53.2, 204.20
Madill v Madill (1907) 26 NZLR 737 .... 34.23
Madore Estate, Re [1936] NLR 215 .... 35.30
Magee v Magee [1936] 3 All ER 15, PC 53.5
Magee v Martin [1902] 1 IR 367, 36 ILT 62, 110 .... 83.9, 99.1
Magnesi v Hazelton (1881) 45 JP 816, 44 LT 586 .... 18.20, 18.27
Magrath, Re, Histed v Queen's University of Belfast [1913] 2 Ch 331, 82 LJ Ch 532, 108 LT 1015, 29 TLR 622 .... 103.3, 103.9
Maguire, Re (1870) LR 9 Eq 632, 39 LJ Ch 710, 18 WR 623 .... 102.9
Maguire v A-G [1943] IR 238 .... 102.9

Maguire v Boylan (1870) 5 IR Eq 90 .... 35.30
Mahaffy v Rooney (1853) 5 Ir Jur 245 .... 56.1
Maher, Re Maher v Toppin [1909] 1 IR 70, 76, 41 ILT 232, Ir CA 77.3, 78.2
Maher v Maher (1877) 1 LR Ir 22 .... 93.27
Mahon v Savage (1803) 1 Sch & Lef 111 .... 79.4, 101.9, 102.14
Mahony v Donovan (1863) 14 I Ch R 388, Ir CA 63.1
Main, Re (1953) 30 MPR 313 .... 47.23, 68.4
Main, Re, Official Solicitor v Main [1947] 1 All ER 255, [1947] LJR 548, 91 Sol Jo 160, 176 LT 191 .... 93.20
Maine, Re, Union Trustee Co of Australia v Maine [1927] VLR 82, 48 ALT 118 .... 77.3
Mainwaring v Baxter (1800) 5 Ves 458 .... 94.38
Mainwaring v Beevor (1849) 8 Hare 44, 19 LJ Ch 396, 14 Jur 58 .... 51.4, 66.14, 66.19
Mainwaring v Mainwaring (1923) 40 WN 102, 23 SRNSW 531 .... 35.33
Mair, Re, Public Trustee v Mair [1925] NZLR 436 .... 66.21
Mair, Re, Williamson v French [1909] 2 Ch 280, 78 LJ Ch 711, 101 LT 70 .... 99.4
Mair v Quilter (1843) 2 Y & C Ch Cas 465 .... 93.6
Maitland, Re, Chitty v Maitland (1896) 74 LT 274 .... 64.53
Maitland v Adair (1796) 3 Ves 231; affd sub nom Adair v Maitland (1798) 7 Bro Parl Cas 587 .... 47.22
Maitland v Chalie (1822) 6 Madd 243 .... 96.2
Major and Mundy v Williams and Iles (1843) 3 Curt 432, 7 Jur 219, 2 Notes of Cases 196 .... 21.8
Makeown v Ardagh (1876) IR 10 Eq 445 .... 102.21, 103.3, 103.7
Malcolm, Re [1947] 4 DLR 756, [1947] OWN 871 .... 99.1
Malcolm v Malcolm (1856) 21 Beav 225 .... 56.7
Malcolm v Martin (1790) 3 Bro CC 50 .... 30.43, 32.33, 101.6
Malcolm v O'Callaghan (1817) 2 Madd 349 .... 34.15, 35.10, 35.11, 35.16
Malcolm v O'Callaghan (1833) Coop temp Brough 73 .... 35.11, 56.3, 93.41
Malcolm v Taylor (1832) 2 Russ & M 416 .... 48.4, 98.3
Malcolmson v Malcolmson (1851) 17 LTOS 44 .... 62.1
Malcomson v Malcomson (1885) 17 LR Ir 69, CA 32.22
Malden v Maine (1855) 2 Jur NS 206 .... 56.7
Maldonado, Re, State of Spain v Treasury Solicitor [1954] P 223, [1953] 2 All ER 300, [1953] 3 WLR 204, 97 Sol Jo 457; affd [1954] P 223, [1953] 2 All ER 1579, [1954] 2 WLR 64, 98 Sol Jo 27, CA 23.16
Malen's Goods, Re (1885) 50 JP 262, 54 LJP 91, 33 WR 825 .... 12.11, 14.12
Maley's Goods, Re (1887) 12 PD 134, 56 LJP 112, 51 JP 423, 35 WR 764, 57 LT 500 .... 18.18, 18.23, 18.26
Malin's Will and Estate, Re [1905] VLR 270 .... 81.3
Malins's Goods, Re (1887) 19 LR Ir 231 .... 13.2
Mallinson v Siddle (1870) 39 LJ Ch 426, 18 WR 569 .... 79.7
Mallinson Consolidated Trusts, Re, Mallinson v Gooley [1974] 2 All ER 530, [1974] 1 WLR 1120, 118 Sol Jo 549 .... 93.16
Mallott v Wilson [1903] 2 Ch 494, [1900–3] All ER Rep 326, 72 LJ Ch 664, 89 LT 522 .... 46.1
Malmesbury v Malmesbury (1862) 31 Beav 407 .... 56.8
Malone v Harrison [1979] 1 WLR 1353, 123 Sol Jo 804 .... 105.18
Malone v Malone [1925] 1 IR 140, Ir CA 64.17

Malpass, Re, Lloyds Bank plc v Malpass [1985] Ch 42, [1984] 2 All ER 313, [1984] 3 WLR 372, 128 Sol Jo 334, [1984] LS Gaz R 1916 .... 92.3, 209.5
Malzy v Edge (1856) 2 Jur NS 80, 4 WR 213, 27 LTOS 12 .... 27.5
Man v Ricketts (1844) 7 Beav 93, 13 LJ Ch 194, 8 Jur 159, 2 LTOS 456; on appeal sub nom Ricketts v Turquand (1848) 1 HL Cas 472 .... 25.15, 57.18, 57.24, 63.5
Manchester and Southport Rly Co, Re (1854) 19 Beav 365 .... 41.5
Mander, Re, Westminster Bank Ltd v Mander [1950] Ch 547, [1950] 2 All ER 191, 94 Sol Jo 370, 66 (pt 1) TLR 1164 .... 94.38
Mandeville's Case (1328) Co Litt 26b 78.1
Mangin v Mangin (1852) 16 Beav 300 .... 64.23
Manifold, Re, Slater v Chryssaffinis [1962] Ch 1, [1961] 1 All ER 710, [1961] 2 WLR 456, 105 Sol Jo 321 .... 23.7
Manisty's Settlement, Re, Manisty v Manisty [1974] Ch 17, [1973] 2 All ER 1203, [1973] 3 WLR 341, 117 Sol Jo 665 .... 1.6, 39.31, 40.5, 53.2, 53.6, 105.47, 225.91, 225.100
Manly's Will Trusts, Re (or Re Manly), Burton v Williams [1969] 3 All ER 1011, [1969] 1 WLR 1818, 113 Sol Jo 941 .... 68.8, 76.3, 93.22
Manly's Will Trusts (No 2), Re, Tickle v Manly [1976] 1 All ER 673 .... 76.3
Mann, Re, Ford v Ward (or Mann) [1912] 1 Ch 388, 81 LJ Ch 217, 56 Sol Jo 272, 106 LT 64 .... 64.35, 64.36
Mann, Re, Hardy v A-G [1903] 1 Ch 232, [1900–3] All ER Rep 93, 72 LJ Ch 150, 51 WR 165, 87 LT 734 .... 103.3
Mann v Copland (1817) 2 Madd 223 .... 30.6, 31.3
Mann v Fuller (1854) Kay 624, 23 LJ Ch 543, 2 Eq Rep 1085, 2 WR 510, 24 LTOS 34 .... 52.11, 91.6
Mann v Thompson (1854) Kay 628, 18 Jur 826, 2 WR 582, 23 LTOS 345 ... 65.3, 66.13, 67.4
Mann's Goods, Re (1858) 28 LJP & M 19 .... 11.6
Mann's Goods, Re [1942] P 146, [1942] 2 All ER 193, 111 JP 86, 86 Sol Jo 254, 167 LT 189, 58 TLR 400 .... 11.4, 11.9, 11.11
Mannai Investment Co Ltd v Eagle Star Life Assurance Co Ltd [1997] AC 749, [1997] 3 All ER 352, [1997] 2 WLR 945, [1997] 1 EGLR 57, [1997] 30 LS Gaz R 30, [1997] NLJR 846, [1997] 24 EG 122, 141 Sol Jo LB 130, HL 50.1, 57.2, 67.1
Manners, Re, Manners v Manners [1923] 1 Ch 220, 92 LJ Ch 249, 67 Sol Jo 262, 128 LT 564 .... 50.11, 57.5, 57.6, 64.5
Manners, Re, Public Trustee v Manners [1949] Ch 613, [1949] 2 All ER 201, [1949] LJR 1574, CA 44.15
Manners, Re, Public Trustee v Manners [1955] 3 All ER 83, [1955] 1 WLR 1096, 99 Sol Jo 726 .... 66.13, 66.14
Manning, Re (1976) 84 DLR (3d) 715 .... 101.9
Manning v Purcell (1855) 7 De GM & G 55, 24 LJ Ch 522, 3 Eq Rep 387, 3 WR 273, 24 LTOS 317 .... 8.4, 50.15, 57.5, 64.27, 64.35, 64.37
Manning v Robinson (1898) 29 OR 483 .... 103.17
Manning v Thesiger (1835) 3 My & K 29, 4 LJ Ch 285 .... 88.2
Manning Estate, Re [1947] 2 WWR 487 .... 103.7
Mannox v Greener (1872) LR 14 Eq 456, 27 LT 408 .... 35.19, 62.1, 83.6
Manor Farm, Kytes Hardwick, Re, Acheson v Russell. See Acheson v Russell

Mansel, Re, Smith v Mansel [1930] 1 Ch 352, [1929] All ER Rep 189, 99 LJ Ch 128, 142 LT 281 .... 100.5
Mansell v Grove (1843) 2 Y & C Ch Cas 484, 7 Jur 666, 1 LTOS 410 .... 98.7
Mansen v Nash [1954] 3 DLR 496 .... 82.8, 83.12
Manser, Re, A-G v Lucas [1905] 1 Ch 68, 74 LJ Ch 95, 53 WR 261, 92 LT 79 .... 102.9, 202.20, 202.22
Mansergh v Campbell (1858) 3 De G & J 232, 28 LJ Ch 61, 4 Jur NS 1207, 7 WR 72, 32 LTOS 168 .... 33.12
Mansey v Mansey [1940] P 139, [1940] 2 All ER 424, 109 LJP 83, 84 Sol Jo 370, 163 LT 157, 56 TLR 676 .... 35.23
Manson v Ross (1884) 1 BCR (pt 2) 49 .... 46.1
Manton v Tabois (1885) 30 Ch D 92, 54 LJ Ch 1008, 33 WR 832, 53 LT 289 .... 41.4, 41.5, 41.16, 64.25
Manuel, Re [1958] OWN 194 .... 102.9
Mapleton v Mapleton (1859) 4 Drew 515, 28 LJ Ch 785, 7 WR 468 .... 40.3
March, Re, Mander v Harris (1884) 27 Ch D 166, 54 LJ Ch 143, 32 WR 941, 51 LT 380, CA 51.5, 54.4
March v Russell (1837) 3 My & Cr 31, [1835–42] All ER Rep 501, 6 LJ Ch 303, 1 Jur 588, 45 RR 196 .... 31.15
Marchant, Re, Weaver v Royal Society for the Prevention of Cruelty to Animals (1910) 54 Sol Jo 425 .... 103.9
Marchuk v Marchuk (1965) 52 WWR 652 .... 50.2, 57.10, 64.13, 64.45
Marcus, Re, Marcus v Marcus (1887) 56 LJ Ch 830, 57 LT 399, 3 TLR 816 ... 9.5, 30.23
Mardon's Estate, Re [1944] P 109, [1944] 2 All ER 397, 113 LJP 67, 171 LT 276, 60 TLR 539 .... 15.1, 21.8
Mardulyn v Lee Yee Hung [1992] 2 HKC 164 .... 49.2, 50.2
Margary v Robinson (1886) 12 PD 8, 56 LJP 42, 51 JP 407, 35 WR 350, 57 LT 281 .... 18.22
Margitson, Re, Haggard v Haggard (1882) 31 WR 257, 48 LT 172, CA 52.11
Margitson v Hall (1864) 10 Jur NS 89, 12 WR 334, 9 LT 755 .... 68.1
Marie of Roumania (Queen), Re [1950] WN 457, 94 Sol Jo 673 .... 18.12
Mariette, Re, Mariette v Aldenham School Governing Body [1915] 2 Ch 284, [1914–15] All ER Rep 794, 84 LJ Ch 825, 59 Sol Jo 630, 113 LT 920, 31 TLR 536 .... 102.8, 212.26
Marjoribanks, Re, Marjoribanks v Dansey [1923] 2 Ch 307, 92 LJ Ch 609, 67 Sol Jo 659, 129 LT 669 .... 61.1, 204.61
Marjoribanks v Hovenden (1843) Drury temp Sug 11 .... 1.3
Marjoribanks' Indenture, Re, Frankland v Ministry of Health [1952] Ch 181, [1952] 1 All ER 191, 96 Sol Jo 72, [1952] 1 TLR 224, CA 103.10
Mark, Re (1921) 64 DLR 516, 50 OLR 473 .... 44.1
Marklew v Turner (1900) 17 TLR 10 .... 5.7, 18.8
Marks v Churchill. See Churchill v Marks
Marks v Marks (1833) 2 LJ Ch 110 .... 60.2
Marks v Marks (1908) 40 SCR 210 .... 80.1
Marks v Solomons (1850) 19 LJ Ch 555, 2 H & Tw 323 .... 38.10
Marlay, Re, Duke of Rutland v Bury [1915] 2 Ch 264, 84 LJ Ch 706, 59 Sol Jo 494, 113 LT 433, 31 TLR 422, CA 41.20
Marlborough (Duke) v Earl Godolphin (1759) 1 Eden 404; affd sub nom Spencer (Lord) v Duke of Marlborough (1763) 3 Bro Parl Cas 232 .... 94.15
Marlborough (Duke) v Lord Godolphin (1750) 2 Ves Sen 61 .... 47.38

Marples v Bainbridge (1816) 1 Madd 590, 16 RR 271 .... 35.2, 35.6, 35.8
Marriott, Re (1808) 2 Mol 516 .... 46.3
Marriott v Abell (1869) LR 7 Eq 478, 38 LJ Ch 451, 17 WR 569, 20 LT 690 .... 67.7
Marryat, Re, Wesminster Bank Ltd v Hobcroft [1948] Ch 298, [1948] 1 All ER 796, [1918] LJR 1237, 92 Sol Jo 283, 64 TLR 125 .... 30.24, 30.26, 30.27
Marsden, Re, Bowden v Layland (1884) 26 Ch D 783, [1881–5] All ER Rep 993, 54 LJ Ch 640, 33 WR 28, 51 LT 417 .... 25.12
Marsden's Goods, Re (1860) 6 Jur NS 405, 1 Sw & Tr 542, 2 LT 87 .... 10.10
Marsden's Trust, Re (1859) 4 Drew 594, 28 LJ Ch 906, 5 Jur NS 590, 7 WR 520, 33 LTOS 217 .... 40.15
Marsh, Re [1960] NZLR 294 .... 76.2, 93.27
Marsh, Re, Mason v Thorne (1888) 38 Ch D 630, 57 LJ Ch 639, 37 WR 10, 59 LT 595 .... 39.14
Marsh, Re, Rhys v Needham [1917] WN 373, 62 Sol Jo 141 .... 33.6
Marsh v A-G (1860) 30 LJ Ch 233, 25 JP 180, 2 John & H 61, 7 Jur NS 184, 9 WR 179, 3 LT 615 .... 103.3
Marsh v Kirby (1634) 1 Rep Ch 76 .... 73.1
Marsh v Marsh (1860) 30 LJPM & A 77, 24 JP 311, 6 Jur NS 380, 1 Sw & Tr 528, 1 LT 523 .... 11.4, 21.5, 21.6
Marsh v Means (1857) 21 JP 725, 3 Jur NS 790, 5 WR 815, 30 LTOS 89 .... 9.31
Marshall, Re, Graham v Marshall [1928] Ch 661, [1928] All ER Rep 694, 97 LJ Ch 415, 139 LT 189 .... 82.4
Marshall, Re, Marshall v Marshall [1914] 1 Ch 192, [1911–13] All ER Rep 671, 83 LJ Ch 307, 58 Sol Jo 118, 109 LT 835, CA 30.9, 30.36, 200.57
Marshall, Re, Marshall v Whateley [1920] 1 Ch 284, [1920] All ER Rep 190, 89 LJ Ch 204, 64 Sol Jo 241, 122 LT 673 .... 99.4
Marshall v Bremner (1854) 2 Sm & G 237, 2 WR 320 .... 38.23
Marshall v Crowther (1874) 2 Ch D 199, 23 WR 210 .... 38.26
Marshall v Hill (1814) 2 M & S 608 .... 96.2
Marshall v Hill [2003] All ER (D) 304 (Mar) 67.1, 200.35
Marshall v Holloway (1820) 19 RR 94, [1814–23] All ER Rep 395, 2 Swan 432 .... 93.4, 95.8
Marshall v Hopkins (1812) 15 East 309 .... 63.7
Marshall (Inspector of Taxes) v Kerr [1995] 1 AC 148, [1994] 3 All ER 106, [1994] 3 WLR 299, [1994] STC 638, 67 TC 56, 138 Sol Jo LB 155, HL 241.17
Marshall v Marshall (1912) 31 NZLR 1120 .... 86.5
Marshall Estate, Re [1944] 3 DLR 178 .... 78.5
Marshall Estate, Re (1963) 38 DLR (2d) 181, 42 WWR 40 .... 30.12
Marshall's Goods, Re (1866) 13 LT 643 .... 11.21
Marshall's Goods, Re (1869) 17 WR 687 .... 18.22
Marsland, Re, Lloyds Bank Ltd v Marsland [1939] Ch 820, [1939] 3 All ER 148, 108 LJ Ch 344, 83 Sol Jo 564, 161 LT 1, 55 TLR 819, CA 2.9, 2.10, 3.13
Marston v Roe d Fox (1838) 8 Ad & El 14, 8 LJ Ex 293, 2 Nev & PKB 504, Will Woll & Dav 712, Ex Ch 17.2
Martell v Consett Iron Co Ltd [1955] Ch 363, [1955] 1 All ER 481, [1955] 2 WLR 463, 99 Sol Jo 148, CA 5.1
Martelli v Holloway (1872) LR 5 HL 532, 42 LJ Ch 26 .... 51.4, 94.14

Marten, Re, Shaw v Marten [1901] 1 Ch 370, 70 LJ Ch 354, 85 LT 704; revsd [1902] 1 Ch 314, 71 LJ Ch 203, 50 WR 209, 46 Sol Jo 163, 85 LT 704, CA 24.12, 32.2, 39.7
Martin, Re (1977) 121 Sol Jo 828 .... 102.5
Martin, Re, Barclays Bank Ltd v St Bartholomew's Hospital Board of Governors [1952] WN 339, 96 Sol Jo 462 .... 9.29
Martin, Re, Loustalan v Loustalan [1900] P 211, 69 LJP 75, 48 WR 509, 44 Sol Jo 449, 82 LT 806, 16 TLR 354, CA 23.13
Martin, Re, MacGregor v Ryan [1965] SCR 757, 53 DLR (2d) 126 .... 4.17
Martin, Re, Martin v Martin [1892] WN 120 .... 62.1
Martin, Re, Midland Bank Executor and Trustee Co Ltd v Marfleet [1955] Ch 698, [1955] 1 All ER 865, [1955] 2 WLR 1029, 99 Sol Jo 318 .... 214.7, 214.9
Martin, Re, Smith v Martin (1885) 54 LJ Ch 1071, 53 LT 34 .... 93.15
Martin, Re, Tuke v Gilbert (1887) 57 LT 471 .... 93.36
Martin v Drinkwater (1840) 2 Beav 215, 9 LJ Ch 247 .... 57.19, 91.6
Martin v Fear (1832) 2 LJ Ch 21 .... 30.34
Martin v Glover (1844) 1 Coll 269, 8 Jur 640 .... 38.3, 77.2, 77.5
Martin v Hobson (1873) 8 Ch App 401, 42 LJ Ch 342, 21 WR 376, 28 LT 427 .... 64.39
Martin v Holgate (1866) LR 1 HL 175, 35 LJ Ch 789, 15 WR 135 .... 50.5, 50.17, 51.7, 68.2, 68.11, 76.3
Martin v Johnston (1858) 1 F & F 122 .... 4.20
Martin v Lee (1861) 14 Moo PCC 142, 9 WR 522, 4 LT 657 .... 50.2
Martin v Long (1690) 1 Eq Cas Abr 193, Prec Ch 15, 2 Vern 151 .... 98.11
Martin v Martin (1866) LR 1 Eq 369, 35 LJ Ch 281, 14 WR 421, 14 LT 129 .... 32.22
Martin v Martin (1866) LR 2 Eq 404, 35 LJ Ch 679, 12 Jur NS 889, 14 WR 986, 15 LT 99 .... 50.3, 97.7
Martin v Martin (1904) 8 OLR 462, 3 OWR 930, 24 CLT 367 .... 42.12
Martin v Martin [1953] QSR 54 .... 68.9
Martin v Maugham (1844) 13 LJ Ch 392, [1843–60] All ER Rep 717, 8 JP 532, 14 Sim 230, 8 Jur 609, 3 LTOS 433 .... 102.28
Martin v Swannell (1840) 2 Beav 249, 9 LJ Ch 174 .... 85.4, 101.9
Martin v Welstead (1848) 18 LJ Ch 1, 12 LTOS 286 .... 51.6
Martin's Estate, Re [1958] SASR 365 .... 33.6
Martin's Goods, Re (1849) 1 Rob Eccl 712, 6 Notes of Cases 694 .... 12.4, 14.6, 14.7
Martin's Goods, Re (1867) LR 1 P & D 380, 36 LJP & M 116, 31 JP 727, 17 LT 32 .... 1.5
Martin's Will, Re (1899) 17 NZLR 418 .... 14.12
Martineau v Briggs (1875) 45 LJ Ch 674, 23 WR 889, HL 51.7
Martineau v Rogers (1856) 8 De GM & G 328, 25 LJ Ch 398, 4 WR 502, 27 LTOS 129 .... 29.14, 96.7
Martinez' Trusts, Re (1870) 22 LT 403 .... 27.6
Martley, Re, Simpson v Cardinal Bourne (1931) 75 Sol Jo 279, 47 TLR 392 .... 102.17
Mason, Re [1971] NZLR 714 .... 102.8
Mason, Re, Mason v Mason [1891] 3 Ch 467, 61 LJ Ch 25 .... 95.7
Mason, Re, Mason v Mason [1910] 1 Ch 695, 79 LJ Ch 605, 54 Sol Jo 425, 102 LT 514, CA 33.20, 34.3, 62.1, 62.3, 83.7, 93.20

Mason, Re, Mason v Robinson (1878) 8 Ch D 411, 47 LJ Ch 660, 26 WR 734 .... 33.23, 33.24
Mason v Baker (1856) 2 K & J 567, sub nom Re Lloyd's Estate, Baker v Mason 2 Jur NS 539 .... 52.3, 74.2, 87.1
Mason v Bishop (1883) 1 Cab & El 21 .... 12.15
Mason v Clarke (1853) 17 Beav 126, 22 LJ Ch 956, 17 Jur 479, 1 WR 297, 21 LTOS 122 .... 85.3
Mason v Mason (1816) 1 Mer 308 .... 9.2
Mason v Robinson (1825) 2 Sim & St 295 .... 51.7, 53.1
Mason's Will, Re (1865) 34 Beav 494, 34 LJ Ch 603, 11 Jur NS 835, 6 New Rep 193, 13 WR 799 .... 47.12, 64.35, 64.53
Masoud, Re (1961) 28 DLR (2d) 646, [1961] OR 583 .... 102.4
Massenburgh v Ash (1684) 2 Rep Ch 275, 1 Vern 234, 304 .... 94.3
Massey v Barton (1844) 7 I Eq R 95 .... 94.45
Massey v Hudson (1817) 2 Mer 130 .... 93.15, 93.27, 98.10
Masson, Re, Morton v Masson (1917) 86 LJ Ch 753, 61 Sol Jo 676, 117 LT 548, 33 TLR 527, CA 50.21, 64.6, 64.27, 64.46
Masson v Smellie (1903) 41 SLR 104, 6 F 148, 11 SLT 450 .... 64.37
Massy v Rogers (1883) 11 LR Ir 409 .... 49.8
Massy v Rowen (1869) LR 4 HL 288 .... 50.16, 55.6
Mastaka v Midland Bank Executor and Trustee Co Ltd [1941] Ch 192, sub nom White, Re, Mastaka v Midland Bank Executor and Trustee Co Ltd [1941] 1 All ER 236, 110 LJ Ch 49, 85 Sol Jo 56, 164 LT 282, 57 TLR 279 .... 24.3, 105.7
Master v Willoughby (1705) 2 Bro Parl Cas 244, HL 92.4, 209.5
Master's Settlement, Re, Master v Master [1911] 1 Ch 321, 80 LJ Ch 190, 55 Sol Jo 170, 103 LT 899 .... 94.48, 101.9
Masterman v Maberly (1829) 2 Hag Ecc 235 .... 10.1
Masters, Re, Coutts & Co v Masters [1953] 1 All ER 19, [1953] 1 WLR 81, 97 Sol Jo 10 .... 203.30
Masters v Masters (1718) 1 P Wms 421, 2 Eq Cas Abr 352 pl 12, 8 Vin Abr 312 pl 29 .... 57.6, 58.4
Masters v Scales (1850) 13 Beav 60, 15 LTOS 452 .... 68.11
Masterson, Re, Trevanion v Dumas [1902] WN 192, CA 47.24
Mather, Re, Mather v Mather [1927] WN 13, 163 LT Jo 52, 71 Sol Jo 142, 63 L Jo 82 .... 60.1
Mathew, Re [1984] 2 All ER 396, [1984] 1 WLR 1011, [1984] FLR 676, [1984] Fam Law 246, 128 Sol Jo 533, [1984] LS Gaz R 1361 .... 25.1
Mathews, Re, Ballarat Trustees, Executors and Agency Co Ltd v Mathews [1917] VLR 1 .... 58.4
Mathews v Keble (1868) 3 Ch App 691, 37 LJ Ch 657, 16 WR 1213, 19 LT 246 .... 95.7, 95.9
Mathews v Mathews (1755) 2 Ves Sen 635 .... 44.15
Mathews v Mathews (1867) LR 4 Eq 278, 15 WR 761 .... 58.6, 64.22, 64.32
Matt Estate, Re, Collins v Lamb and Toronto General Trusts Corpn (1954) 11 WWRNS 28 .... 18.29
Matthews, Re [1920] NZLR 135 .... 8.7, 53.2
Matthews, Re [1958] VR 194 .... 47.24
Matthews, Re [1960] VLR 3 .... 76.1

Matthews v Foulsham (or Foulshaw) (1864) 4 New Rep 500, 12 WR 1141, 11 LT 82 .... 69.1
Matthews v Gardiner (1853) 17 Beav 254, 21 LTOS 236 .... 98.13
Matthews v Maude (1830) 1 Russ & M 397, 8 LJOS Ch 106 .... 58.8, 61.1
Matthews v Paul (1819) 2 Wils Ch 64, 3 Swan 328 .... 81.3
Matthews's Will Trusts, Re, Bristow v Matthews [1961] 3 All ER 869, [1961] 1 WLR 1415, [1961] TR 345, 105 Sol Jo 888 .... 236.6
Mattingley's Trusts, Re (1862) 2 John & H 426 .... 39.19
Mattison v Tanfield (1840) 3 Beav 131, 4 Jur 933 .... 87.1, 87.2
Maud v Maud (1860) 27 Beav 615, 29 LJ Ch 312 .... 34.11, 35.45
Maude v Maude (1856) 22 Beav 290 .... 56.6
Maule v Maule (1890) 62 LT 702 .... 14.1
Maunder, Re, Maunder v Maunder [1902] 2 Ch 875, 71 LJ Ch 815, 51 WR 31, 87 LT 262; affd [1903] 1 Ch 451, 72 LJ Ch 367, 51 WR 549, 88 LT 280, CA 97.9
Maunsell v White (1854) 4 HL Cas 1039, 22 LTOS 293 .... 3.3
Maurice, Re, Brown v Maurice (1896) 75 LT 415, 13 TLR 36 .... 30.34
Mavromatis, Re [1964] VR 612 .... 99.2
Maw v Dickey (1974) 52 DLR (3d) 178 .... 4.21, 5.9
Maw Estate, Re (1952) 6 WWRNS 609 .... 62.1
Maxton, Re (1858) 4 Jur NS 407 .... 79.1
Maxwell, Re, Eivers v Curry [1906] 1 IR 386, CA 30.14, 47.32
Maxwell v Hyslop (1867) LR 4 Eq 407, 16 LT 660; affd sub nom Maxwell v Maxwell (1870) LR 4 HL 506, 39 LJ Ch 698, 19 WR 15, 23 LT 325, HL 24.10, 42.15
Maxwell v Maxwell (1852) 16 Beav 106, 22 LJ Ch 43, 2 De GM & G 705, 16 Jur 982, 1 WR 2, 20 LTOS 86 .... 24.10, 42.2, 42.15, 58.2, 60.1
Maxwell v Maxwell (1868) IR 2 Eq 478 .... 47.24
Maxwell v Maxwell (1870) LR 4 HL 506. See Maxwell v Hyslop
Maxwell's Will, Re (1857) 24 Beav 246, 26 LJ Ch 854, 3 Jur NS 902, 30 LTOS 49 .... 83.2, 83.11, 83.18, 83.19
May, Re, Eggar v May [1917] 2 Ch 126, 86 LJ Ch 698, 61 Sol Jo 577, 117 LT 401, 33 TLR 419 .... 35.30
May, Re, Eggar v May [1932] 1 Ch 99, [1931] All ER Rep 558, 101 LJ Ch 12, 75 Sol Jo 741, 146 LT 56, 48 TLR 3, CA 33.19, 35.30
May v Bennett (1826) 1 Russ 370 .... 33.27
May v Grave (1849) 3 De G & Sm 462, 18 LJ Ch 401, 13 Jur 1021, 13 LTOS 463 .... 64.40
May v May (1881) 44 LT 412 .... 35.19, 83.6
May v May [1902] P 103n, 71 LJP 35, 18 TLR 184, sub nom May's Goods, Re, May v May 86 LT 120 .... 16.2
May v Potter (1877) 25 WR 507 .... 32.20
May v Wood (1792) 3 Bro CC 471 .... 93.25, 93.27
May's Goods, Re, May v May. See May v May
May's Settlement, Re, Public Trustee v Meredith [1926] Ch 136, [1925] All ER Rep 444, 95 LJ Ch 230, 134 LT 696 .... 40.5
May's Will Trusts, Re, Cockerton v Jones [1944] Ch 1, [1943] 2 All ER 604, 113 LJ Ch 73, 87 Sol Jo 399, 169 LT 386, 60 TLR 43 .... 93.9
Maybank v Brooks. See Mabank v Brooks

Mayd v Field (1876) 3 Ch D 587, 45 LJ Ch 699, 41 JP 20, 24 WR 660, 34 LT 614 .... 44.13
Mayell, Re, Foley v Wood [1913] 2 Ch 488, 83 LJ Ch 40, 109 LT 40 .... 58.10, 63.4
Mayer v Townsend (1841) 3 Beav 443, 10 LJ Ch 216, 5 Jur 91 .... 82.4
Mayer Estate, Re [1950] 2 WWR 858 .... 83.15
Mayhew, Re (1989) 63 DLR (4th) 198 .... 51.4
Mayhew, Re, Spencer v Cutbush [1901] 1 Ch 677, 70 LJ Ch 428, 49 WR 330, 45 Sol Jo 326, 84 LT 761 .... 39.22, 39.25
Maynard v Gibson [1876] WN 204 .... 8.4
Maynard v Wright (1858) 26 Beav 285 .... 56.8, 56.9, 76.3
Mayne, Re, Stoneham v Woods [1914] 2 Ch 115, 83 LJ Ch 815, [1914] WN 202, 58 Sol Jo 579 .... 64.53
Mayne v Mayne [1897] 1 IR 324, 35 ILT 35 .... 64.40
Mayo, Re, Chester v Keirl [1901] 1 Ch 404, 70 LJ Ch 261, 45 Sol Jo 219, 84 LT 117 .... 57.3, 57.22, 58.11, 69.1
Mayo, Re, Mayo v Mayo [1943] Ch 302, [1943] 2 All ER 440, 59 TLR 395, sub nom Re Mayo's Will Trusts 112 LJ Ch 257, 169 LT 205 .... 200.58, 214.3
Mayott v Mayott (1786) 2 Bro CC 125 .... 71.4
Mead, Re, Austin v Mead (1880) 15 Ch D 651, 50 LJ Ch 30, 28 WR 891, 43 LT 117 .... 1.15
Mead v Lord Orrery (1745) 3 Atk 235 .... 25.18
Mead's Goods, Re (1842) 6 Jur 351, 1 Notes of Cases 456 .... 12.12
Mead's Trust Deed, Re, Briginshaw v National Society of Operative Printers and Assistants [1961] 2 All ER 836, [1961] 1 WLR 1244, 105 Sol Jo 569 .... 102.7, 102.8, 102.24
Meadows v Duchess of Kingston (1775) Amb 756 .... 25.15
Meadows v Parry (1812) 1 Ves & B 124 .... 93.19
Meagher, Re, Trustees, Executors and Agency Co Ltd v Meagher [1910] VLR 407 .... 34.1, 34.13
Mears, Re, Parkers v Mears [1914] 1 Ch 694, 83 LJ Ch 450, 110 LT 686 .... 101.13
Medaini Estate, Re (1927) 38 BCR 319, [1927] 4 DLR 1137, [1927] 2 WWR 38 .... 9.14
Medlock, Re, Ruffle v Medlock (1886) 55 LJ Ch 738, 54 LT 828 .... 32.15, 32.20, 32.21
Meeds v Wood (1854) 19 Beav 215 .... 34.3, 64.19, 82.3
Meek v Devenish (1877) 6 Ch D 566, 47 LJ Ch 57, 25 WR 688, 36 LT 911 .... 37.8
Mégret, Re, Tweedie v Maunder [1901] 1 Ch 547, 70 LJ Ch 451, 84 LT 192 .... 24.12
Megson v Hindle (1880) 15 Ch D 198, sub nom Hindle, Re, Megson v Hindle 28 WR 866, 43 LT 551, CA 72.3
Meikle Estate, Re [1943] 3 DLR 668 .... 103.7
Meinertzagen v Walters (1872) 7 Ch App 670, 41 LJ Ch 801, 20 WR 918, 27 LT 326, CA 44.10
Meldrum, Re, Swinson v Meldrum [1952] Ch 208, [1952] 1 All ER 274, [1952] 1 TLR 92 .... 214.7
Mellish, Re [1927] 164 LT Jo 23 .... 41.18
Mellish, Re, Day v Withers [1916] 1 Ch 562, [1916–17] All ER Rep 634, 85 LJ Ch 433, 114 LT 991 .... 66.1, 77.4
Mellish v Mellish (1798) 4 Ves 45 .... 5.8
Mellody, Re, Brandwood v Haden [1918] 1 Ch 228, [1916–17] All ER Rep 324, 87 LJ Ch 185, 82 JP 128, 62 Sol Jo 121, 118 LT 155, 34 TLR 122 .... 102.10

Mellor, Re, ex p Butcher (1880) 13 Ch D 465, 28 WR 484, 42 LT 299, CA 205.74
Mellor, Re, Alvarez v Dodgson [1922] 1 Ch 312, [1922] All ER Rep 735, 91 LJ Ch 393, 66 Sol Jo 249, 126 LT 562, CA 32.16, 32.24, 61.1, 216.8
Mellor, Re, Dodgson v Ashworth (1912) 28 TLR 473, 56 Sol Jo 596 .... 30.15, 49.2, 237.11
Mellor, Re, Porter v Hindsley [1929] 1 Ch 446, 98 LJ Ch 209, 140 LT 469 .... 64.35, 64.36
Mellor v Daintree (1886) 33 Ch D 198, [1886–90] All ER Rep 343, 56 LJ Ch 33, 55 LT 175 .... 67.1, 101.1, 101.3
Melnik v Sawycky (1977) 80 DLR (3d) 371 .... 93.2
Melnyk Estate, Re, Lazaruk v Zelenko [1936] 1 WWR 666 .... 38.3
Melton, Re, Milk v Towers [1918] 1 Ch 37, [1916–17] All ER Rep 672, 87 LJ Ch 18, [1917] HBR 246, 117 LT 679, 34 TLR 20, CA 30.11, 30.12, 30.13
Meluish v Milton (1876) 3 Ch D 27, 45 LJ Ch 836, 24 WR 892, 35 LT 82, CA 25.15
Melville v Ancketill (1909) 25 TLR 655, CA 25.13
Melvin, Re (1972) 24 DLR (3d) 240 .... 83.3
Mendham v Williams (1866) LR 2 Eq 396, 15 LT 130 .... 93.29
Mengel's Will Trusts, Re, Westminster Bank Ltd v Mengel [1962] Ch 791, [1962] 2 All ER 490, [1962] 3 WLR 311, 106 Sol Jo 510 .... 24.10, 42.2, 64.18
Mercer, Re [1954] 1 DLR 295, [1953] OWN 765 .... 34.9, 35.33, 60.1, 61.1
Mercer, Re, Drewe-Mercer v Drewe-Mercer (1889) 6 TLR 95 .... 35.44
Mercer v Hall (1793) 4 Bro CC 326 .... 35.12, 35.13, 35.16
Mercer, Re, Tanner v Bulmer [1944] 1 All ER 759, 113 LJ Ch 257, 88 Sol Jo 298, 171 LT 254, 60 TLR 487 .... 70.2
Merceron's Trusts, Re, Davies v Merceron (1876) 4 Ch D 182, 35 LT 701 ..... 98.3, 98.4
Merchant Taylors' Co v A-G (1871) 6 Ch App 512, 40 LJ Ch 545, 35 JP 774, 19 WR 641, 25 LT 109 .... 57.8, 102.19, 102.20, 103.13, 103.16
Merchants Bank of Canada v Keefer (1885) 13 SCR 515 .... 93.15
Meredith, Re, Davies v Davies [1924] 2 Ch 552, 94 LJ Ch 87, 131 LT 800 .... 47.12
Meredith v Farr (1843) 2 Y & C Ch Cas 525, 7 Jur 797 .... 72.3
Meredith v Treffry (1879) 12 Ch D 170, 48 LJ Ch 337, 27 WR 406 .... 81.3
Meredith v Webber (1666) O Bridg 560 .... 64.32
Meredith, Re, Stone v Meredith (1898) 67 LJ Ch 409, 78 LT 492 .... 61.1
Meredith's Trusts, Re (1876) 3 Ch D 757, 25 WR 107 .... 94.44
Merlin v Blagrave (1858) 25 Beav 125, 119 RR 356 .... 93.6, 93.32
Merrall, Re, Greener v Merrall [1924] 1 Ch 45, 93 LJ Ch 162, 68 Sol Jo 209, 130 LT 312 .... 44.4
Merrick's Trusts, Re (1866) LR 1 Eq 551, 35 LJ Ch 418, 12 Jur NS 245, 14 WR 473, 14 LT 130 .... 68.2, 68.11, 93.2, 94.9
Merrill v Morton (1881) 17 Ch D 382, 50 LJ Ch 249, 29 WR 394, 43 LT 750 .... 57.22, 71.1
Merry v Hill (1869) LR 8 Eq 619, 17 WR 985 .... 93.27, 93.39
Merry v Ryves (1757) 1 Eden 1, 28 ER 584 .... 35.16
Merton's Settlement, Re, Public Trustee v Wilson [1953] 2 All ER 707, [1953] 1 WLR 1096, 97 Sol Jo 572 .... 40.15
Mervin, Re, Mervin v Crossman [1891] 3 Ch 197, 60 LJ Ch 671, 39 WR 697, 65 LT 186 .... 47.32, 66.12, 66.16, 66.18, 66.21, 93.36, 93.38, 94.14
Messenger v Andrews (1828) 4 Russ 478, [1824–34] All ER Rep 651 .... 45.2

Messenger's Estate, Re, Chaplin v Ruane [1937] 1 All ER 355, 81 Sol Jo 138 .... 51.1, 51.2, 51.3, 53.4, 57.5
Metcalf, Re, Metcalf v Blencowe [1903] 2 Ch 424, [1900–03] All ER Rep 986, 72 LJ Ch 786, 51 WR 650, 88 LT 727 .... 33.42, 33.43
Metcalfe, Re (1973) 29 DLR (3d) 60 .... 9.35, 46.3
Metcalfe, Re, Metcalfe v Earle [1909] 1 Ch 424, 78 LJ Ch 303, 100 LT 222 .... 68.9
Metcalfe v Hutchinson (1875) 1 Ch D 591, 45 LJ Ch 210 .... 62.2
Metcalfe v Metcalfe (1889) 43 Ch D 633, sub nom Re Metcalfe, Metcalfe v Metcalfe 59 LJ Ch 159, 38 WR 397, 61 LT 767, 6 TLR 92; affd sub nom Metcalfe v Metcalfe [1891] 3 Ch 1, sub nom Re Metcalfe, Metcalfe v Metcalfe 60 LJ Ch 647, 35 Sol Jo 528, 65 LT 426, 7 TLR 558, CA 99.3, 99.4, 99.10
Metcalfe v O'Kennedy (1904) 1 CLR 421, 4 SRNSW 175 .... 83.2
Metcalfe's Trusts, Re (1864) 28 JP 260, 33 LJ Ch 308, 2 De GJ & Sm 122, 10 Jur NS 287, 3 New Rep 657, 12 WR 538, 10 LT 78 .... 9.36, 40.15
Methuen and Blore's Contract, Re (1881) 16 Ch D 696, 50 LJ Ch 464, 29 WR 656, 44 LT 332 .... 38.9, 38.12, 51.1
Mette v Mette (1859) 28 LJP & M 117, 1 Sw & Tr 416, 7 WR 543, 33 LTOS 139 .... 17.2
Mette's Estate, Re (1868) LR 7 Eq 72, 38 LJ Ch 445 .... 38.28
Meux, Re, Gilmour v Gilmour [1958] Ch 154, [1957] 2 All ER 630, [1957] 3 WLR 377, 55 LGR 456, 107 Sol Jo 611 .... 218.66, 218.94
Mewburn's Settlement, Re, Perks v Wood [1934] Ch 112, [1933] All ER Rep 663, 103 LJ Ch 37, 77 Sol Jo 467, 150 LT 76 .... 40.5
Mexborough (Earl) v Savile (1903) 88 LT 131, 19 TLR 287, HL 82.7
Meyer's Estate, Re [1908] P 353, 77 LJP 150, 52 Sol Jo 716, 99 LT 881 .... 5.7
Meyers, Re, London Life Association v St George's Hospital [1951] Ch 534, [1951] 1 All ER 538, [1951] 1 TLR 435 .... 41.13, 103.5, 103.10, 212.3
Meynell, Re [1949] WN 273, 93 Sol Jo 466 .... 10.7
Michaels, Re [1958] NZLR 476 .... 93.38
Michel's Trust, Re (1860) 24 JP 581, 29 LJ Ch 547, 28 Beav 39, 6 Jur NS 573, 8 WR 299, 2 LT 46 .... 102.8
Michell, Re, Thomas v Hoskins [1929] 1 Ch 552, 98 LJ Ch 197, 140 LT 686, 45 TLR 243 .... 20.4, 33.10, 88.2, 88.3, 88.4
Michell v Michell (1820) 5 Madd 69 .... 38.7, 64.15
Michell v Thomas. See Mitchell v Thomas
Michell v Wilton (1875) LR 20 Eq 269, 44 LJ Ch 490, 23 WR 789 .... 33.23, 33.27
Michnik Estate, Re (1945) 4 DLR 521, [1945] 2 WWR 570 .... 13.3
Middleton v Messenger (1799) 5 Ves 136 .... 66.5, 66.8
Middleton v Sherburne (1841) 4 Y & C Ex 358, 10 LJ Ex Eq 75; on appeal sub nom Sherburne v Middleton (1842) 9 Cl & Fin 72, HL 4.16
Middleton v Windross (1873) LR 16 Eq 212, 42 LJ Ch 555, 21 WR 822 .... 34.24
Middleton's Goods, Re (1864) 34 LJPM & A 16, 10 Jur NS 1109, 3 Sw & Tr 583, 11 LT 684 .... 19.5
Midgley, Re, Barclays Bank Ltd v Midgley [1955] Ch 576, [1955] 2 All ER 625, [1955] 3 WLR 119, 99 Sol Jo 434 .... 47.28, 47.32, 214.9
Midland Bank Executor and Trustee Co Ltd v Yarners Coffee Ltd [1937] 2 All ER 54, 81 Sol Jo 237, 156 LT 274, 53 TLR 403 .... 30.12, 204.64
Midland Counties Rly Co v Oswin (1844) 3 Ry & Can Cas 497, 13 LJ Ch 209, 1 Coll 74, 8 Jur 138, 2 LTOS 399 .... 38.4, 64.19

Midland Rly Co, Re, Re Otley and Ilkey Branch (1865) 34 Beav 525, 34 LJ Ch 596, 11 Jur NS 818, 6 New Rep 244, 13 WR 851, 12 LT 659 .... 59.3
Midleton's Will Trusts, Re, Whitehead v Earl of Midleton [1969] 1 Ch 600, [1967] 2 All ER 834, [1967] 3 WLR 965, 111 Sol Jo 637 .... 7.20, 35.40, 53.5
Mihalopulos Estate, Re (1956) 19 WWR 118 .... 15.1
Milbank v Vane [1893] 3 Ch 79, 62 LJ Ch 629, 2 R 443, 68 LT 735, 9 TLR 362, CA 35.43
Miles, Re, Miles v Miles (1889) 61 LT 359 .... 66.6, 68.13
Miles v Dyer (1832) 5 Sim 435 .... 56.4
Miles v Harford (1879) 12 Ch D 691, 41 LT 378 .... 50.21, 94.15
Miles v Harrison (1874) 9 Ch App 316, 43 LJ Ch 585, 22 WR 441, 30 LT 190 .... 55.7
Miles v Miles (1866) LR 1 Eq 462, 35 LJ Ch 315, 35 Beav 191, 12 Jur NS 116, 14 WR 272, 13 LT 697 .... 58.12, 63.9, 207.3
Miley v Carty and Miley [1927] 1 IR 541 .... 41.5
Mill's Declaration of Trust, Re, Midland Bank Executor and Trustee Co Ltd v Mill [1950] 2 All ER 292, CA 94.30
Millar, Re [1927] 3 DLR 270, 60 OLR 434 .... 30.8
Millar, Re [1938] 2 DLR 164, [1938] OR 188 .... 34.12
Millar, Re, Barnard v Mahoney (1898) 17 NZLR 160 .... 57.19, 57.22
Millar v Turner (1748) 1 Ves Sen 85 .... 73.1
Millar v Woodside (1872) IR 6 Eq 546 .... 58.2, 58.6
Millard v Bailey (1866) LR 1 Eq 378, 35 LJ Ch 312, 14 WR 385, 13 LT 751 .... 8.7, 57.20
Miller, Re [1938] 2 DLR 765 .... 94.5
Miller, Re (1957) 8 DLR (2d) 170, [1957] OWN 84 .... 32.10
Miller, Re [1991] 1 Qd R 359 .... 7.15, 41.20, 64.43
Miller, Re, Bailie v Miller [1914] 1 Ch 511, 83 LJ Ch 457, 58 Sol Jo 415, 110 LT 505 .... 24.2, 50.19
Miller, Re, Daniel v Daniel (1889) 61 LT 365, 5 TLR 711 .... 38.10, 64.17
Miller, Re, Galloway v Miller (1913) 135 LT Jo 10 .... 30.23, 30.27
Miller, Re, Miller v de Courcey [1968] 3 All ER 844, [1969] 1 WLR 583, 113 Sol Jo 246 .... 105.5
Miller v Huddlestone (1851) 21 LJ Ch 1, 15 Jur 1043, 3 Mac & G 513, 87 RR 171, 18 LTOS 147 .... 31.1, 33.23, 33.26, 33.34, 33.35
Miller v IRC [1987] STC 108, Ct of Sess 207.8, 207.25, 214.36, 220.48, 220.61
Miller v Miller (1872) LR 13 Eq 263, 41 LJ Ch 291, 20 WR 324 .... 38.23
Miller v Rowan (1837) 5 Cl & Fin 99, 2 Sh & Macl 866, HL 103.1
Miller v Thurgood (1864) 33 Beav 496, 33 LJ Ch 511, 10 Jur NS 304, 12 WR 660, 10 LT 255 .... 42.5
Miller v Travers (1832) 8 Bing 244, 1 LJ Ch 157, 1 Moo & S 342 .... 57.20
Miller v Wheatley (1891) 28 LR Ir 144 .... 34.22, 35.39
Miller's Trustees v Miller (1907) 44 SLR 543, 1907 SC 833, 14 SLT 904 .... 64.27
Milliner v Robinson (1600) Moore KB 682, sub nom Bifield's Case 1 Vent 231 .... 98.13
Milling's Settlement, Re, Peake v Thom [1944] Ch 263, [1944] 1 All ER 541, 113 LJ Ch 167, 88 Sol Jo 179, 171 LT 92, 60 TLR 317 .... 96.2
Mills, Re [1952] SASR 274 .... 44.8
Mills, Re [1968] 2 NSWLR 393, 70 SRNSW 36 .... 19.4
Mills, Re (1981) 27 SASR 200 .... 102.14

Mills, Re, Midland Bank Executor and Trustee Co Ltd v United Birmingham Hospitals Board of Governors [1953] 1 All ER 835, [1953] 1 WLR 554, 97 Sol Jo 229 .... 102.22, 212.25

Mills, Re, Mills v Lawrence [1930] 1 Ch 654, [1930] All ER Rep 355, 99 LJ Ch 396, 74 Sol Jo 437, 143 LT 409, 46 TLR 328, CA 40.10

Mills, Re, Mills v Mills (1886) 34 Ch D 186, 56 LJ Ch 118, 35 WR 133, 55 LT 665 .... 39.16, 39.20

Mills, Re, Mills v Mills (1902) 22 NZLR 425 .... 85.3

Mills v Anderson [1984] QB 704, [1984] 2 All ER 538, [1984] 3 WLR 481, 128 Sol Jo 550 .... 25.14

Mills v Drewitt (1855) 20 Beav 632, 1 Jur NS 816, 3 WR 626, 25 LTOS 293 .... 33.27

Mills v Farmer (1815) 1 Mer 55, [1814–23] All ER Rep 53, 19 Ves 483, 488n 51.12, 102.22, 103.1

Mills v Fox (1887) 37 Ch D 153, 57 LJ Ch 56, 36 WR 219, 57 LT 792 .... 206.29

Mills v Mills (1835) 7 Sim 501, 4 LJ Ch 266 .... 64.23

Mills v Millward (1889) 15 PD 20, 59 LJP 23, 61 LT 651 .... 18.21

Mills v Norris (1800) 5 Ves 335 .... 32.28

Mills v Robarts (1830) 1 Russ & M 555, Taml 476, 8 LJOS 141 .... 32.23, 93.31

Mills' Goods, Re (1847) 11 Jur 1070, 10 LTOS 230 .... 14.8

Mills' Will Trusts, Re, Marriott v Mills [1937] 1 All ER 142, 106 LJ Ch 159, 80 Sol Jo 975, 156 LT 190, 53 TLR 139 .... 64.4, 64.45

Mills' Will Trusts, Re, Yorkshire Insurance Co Ltd v Coward [1967] 2 All ER 193, [1967] 1 WLR 837, 111 Sol Jo 522 .... 35.32

Millward v Buswell (1904) 20 TLR 714 .... 11.3

Millward v Shenton [1972] 2 All ER 1025, [1972] 1 WLR 711, 116 Sol Jo 355, CA 105.23, 105.25

Milne, Re, Grant v Heysham (1887) 56 LJ Ch 543, 56 LT 852; affd (1887) 57 LT 828, CA 66.1

Milne v Gilbart (1852) 2 De GM & G 715 .... 77.2

Milne's Executors v Aberdeen University Court (1905) 42 SLR 533, 7 F 642, 13 SLT 45 .... 102.7

Milne's Trustees v Davidson 1956 SC 81, 1956 SLT 34 .... 38.11

Milner, Re, Bray v Milner [1899] 1 Ch 563, 68 LJ Ch 255, 47 WR 369, 80 LT 151 .... 39.22, 39.24, 39.25, 39.26

Milner v Milner (1748) 1 Ves Sen 106 .... 82.7

Milner's Safe Co Ltd v Great Northern and City Rly Co [1907] 1 Ch 208, 75 LJ Ch 807, 50 Sol Jo 668, 95 LT 321, 22 TLR 706; on appeal [1907] 1 Ch 229, 76 LJ Ch 99, 23 TLR 88, CA 61.1

Milner-Gibson-Cullum, Re, Cust v A-G [1924] 1 Ch 456, 93 LJ Ch 196, 68 Sol Jo 383, 131 LT 555, 40 TLR 298 .... 58.1

Milnes, Re, Milnes v Sherwin (1885) 33 WR 927, 53 LT 534 .... 30.11, 30.12

Milnes v Foden (1890) 15 PD 105, 59 LJP 62, 62 LT 498 .... 10.1, 10.4, 10.5

Milroy v Milroy (1844) 14 Sim 48, 13 LJ Ch 266, 8 Jur 234, 2 LTOS 456 ... 55.5, 93.12, 93.35

Milsome v Long (1857) 3 Jur NS 1073 .... 51.3, 57.5

Milson v Awdry (1800) 5 Ves 465 .... 51.2, 90.1, 90.2

Milward's Estate, Re, ex p Midland Rly Co [1940] Ch 698, 109 LJ Ch 274, 84 Sol Jo 393, 163 LT 108, 56 TLR 849 .... 74.1, 98.13

Minchell's Will Trusts, Re [1964] 2 All ER 47 .... 83.11

Minchin v Gabbett [1896] 1 IR 1, 30 ILT 71 .... 42.5
Miner v Baldwin (1853) 17 Jur 823, 1 Sm & G 522 .... 33.24
Minifie v Hall (1867) 1 CA 421 .... 41.10
Ministry of Health v Fox [1950] Ch 369, [1950] 1 All ER 1050, 66 (pt 1) TLR 997 .... 103.10
Ministry of Health v Simpson. See Diplock, Re, Diplock v Wintle
Minors v Battison (1876) 1 App Cas 428, 46 LJ Ch 2, 25 WR 27, 35 LT 1, HL 96.1, 97.7
Minter v Wraith (1842) 13 Sim 52 .... 94.28
Minton v Minton (1853) 21 LTOS 40 .... 64.27
Mirrel v Nicholls (1611) 1 Bulst 117 .... 63.7
Miskelly's Goods, Re (1869) 4 IR Eq 62 .... 2.2
Mitchel v Reynolds (1711) 1 P Wms 181 .... 34.12
Mitchell, Re, Ballarat Trustees, Executors and Agency Co Ltd v National Trustees, Executors and Agency Co of Australasia Ltd [1929] VLR 95, Argus LR 108 .... 72.3
Mitchell, Re, Freelove v Mitchell [1913] 1 Ch 201, [1911–13] All ER Rep 187, 82 LJ Ch 121, 57 Sol Jo 213, 108 LT 34 .... 30.12, 31.4, 59.1
Mitchell, Re, Hatton v Jones [1954] Ch 525, [1954] 2 All ER 246, [1954] 2 WLR 1114, 98 Sol Jo 373 .... 23.16
Mitchell, Re, Mitchell v Mitchell (1913) 57 Sol Jo 339, 108 LT 180 .... 52.2, 82.2, 97.6
Mitchell v Arblaster [1964–5] NSWR 119 .... 83.3
Mitchell v Thomas (1847) 6 Moo PCC 137, sub nom Michell v Thomas 12 Jur 967, 11 LTOS 90, 5 Notes of Cases 600, PC 4.17
Mitchell Estate (Man), Re [1924] 1 DLR 1039, [1924] 1 WWR 484 .... 4.15, 10.8
Mitchell Estate, Re, Bradshaw v Pidgeon (1954) 33 MPR 359 .... 18.10, 18.11, 20.2
Mitchell's Estate, Re, National Trust Co Ltd v Carson [1936] 3 WWR 249, [1937] 1 WWR 165 .... 38.18
Mitchell's Goods, Re (1841) 2 Curt 916 .... 9.8
Mitcheson's Goods, Re (1863) 32 LJPM & A 202, 9 Jur NS 360 .... 19.4
Mitchison v Buckton (1875) 23 WR 480, 32 LT 11 .... 87.1
Mitchner, Re [1922] St R Qd 39 .... 103.18
Mitford v Reynolds (1842) 1 Ph 185, [1835–42] All ER Rep 331, 12 LJ Ch 40, 7 Jur 3 .... 102.10, 102.22
Moase v White (1876) 3 Ch D 763, 24 WR 1038 .... 64.32, 214.25
Mobbs's Goods, Re (1854) 2 Ecc & Ad 59 .... 12.12
Mocatta v Mocatta (1883) 32 WR 477, 49 LT 629 .... 64.26
Mocatta v Mocatta (1915) 19 CLR 515 .... 79.7
Moffatt v Burnie (1853) 18 Beav 211, 23 LJ Ch 591, 18 Jur 32, 2 WR 83, 22 LTOS 218 .... 33.14, 101.6
Moffett v Bates (1857) 26 LJ Ch 465, 3 Jur NS 200, 3 Sm & G 468, 5 WR 338, 28 LTOS 352 .... 46.3
Mogg v Mogg (1815) 1 Mer 654, [1814–23] All ER Rep 314 .... 66.23, 73.1, 217.16
Moggridge v Thackwell (1792) 1 Ves 464, [1775–1802] All ER Rep 218, 3 Bro CC 517; on appeal (1803) 7 Ves 36; affd (1807) 13 Ves 416, [1803–13] All ER Rep 754, HL 88.4, 103.1, 103.17, 103.18
Mohan v Broughton [1900] P 56, 69 LJP 20, 48 WR 371, 44 Sol Jo 210, 82 LT 29, CA 49.7
Mohun v Mohun (1818) 1 Wils Ch 151, 1 Swan 201 .... 53.3

Moir, Re, Warner v Moir (1884) 25 Ch D 605, 53 LJ Ch 474, 32 WR 377, 50 LT 10 .... 34.21, 35.19
Moir v Graham (1894) 12 NZLR 42 .... 67.2
Moir Estate, Re (1942) 1 DLR 337, [1942] 1 WWR 241 .... 11.4
Moir's Estate, Re, Moir v Warner [1882] WN 139 .... 8.4
Molinari v Winfrey [1961] SCR 91 .... 10.8
Molyneux v Rowe (1856) 8 De GM & G 368, 25 LJ Ch 570, 2 Jur NS 769, 4 WR 539, 27 LTOS 179 .... 64.19
Monck v Lord Monck (1810) 1 Ball & B 298 .... 44.2, 44.14
Monck's (Lady) Will, Re, Monck v Croker [1900] 1 IR 56, Ir CA 51.1, 82.3, 97.2
Monk, Re, Giffen v Wedd [1927] 2 Ch 197, [1927] All ER Rep 157, 96 LJ Ch 296, 137 LT 4, 43 TLR 256, CA 102.7, 102.28, 103.11, 103.13, 103.18
Monk v Mawdsley (1827) 1 Sim 286, 5 LJOS Ch 149 .... 50.17
Monkhouse v Holme (1783) 1 Bro CC 298 .... 93.25
Monkhouse v Monkhouse (1829) 3 Sim 119 .... 56.2
Monroe Estate, Re (1995) 9 WWR 372 .... 93.6
Montagu, Re, Faber v Montagu [1896] 1 Ch 549, 65 LJ Ch 372, 44 WR 583, 74 LT 346 .... 42.14
Montagu (Duke) v Duke of Beaulieu. See Beaulieu (Lord) v Lord Cardigan
Montagu v Earl of Sandwich (1863) 33 Beav 324, 10 Jur NS 61, 3 New Rep 186, 12 WR 236, 9 LT 632 .... 64.35
Montagu v Earl of Sandwich (1886) 32 Ch D 525, 55 LJ Ch 925, 54 LT 502, 2 TLR 392, CA 44.2, 44.12, 44.14
Montagu v Nucella (1826) 1 Russ 165 .... 68.1
Montague v Montague (1852) 15 Beav 565 .... 20.4, 22.4, 44.4, 100.3
Montefiore v Guedalla (1859) 1 De GF & J 93, 29 LJ Ch 65, 6 Jur NS 329, 8 WR 53, 1 LT 251 .... 44.1, 44.3, 44.10
Montefiore v Guedalla [1903] 2 Ch 723, [1900–3] All ER Rep 384, 73 LJ Ch 13, 52 WR 151, 47 Sol Jo 877, 89 LT 472 .... 27.3
Monteith v Monteith's Trustees 1882 9 R 982 .... 23.4, 23.5
Montgomerie v Woodley (1800) 5 Ves 522 .... 94.9
Montgomery's Goods, Re (1846) 10 Jur 1063, 8 LTOS 294, 5 Notes of Cases 99 .... 10.5
Montone, Re [1955] OWN 799 .... 5.9
Montreal Trust Co v McKay (1957) 21 WWR 611 .... 4.11
Montreal Trust Co's Application (Cleveland Estate), Re, Re Trustee Act (1962) 41 WWR 193 .... 64.52
Montresor v Montresor (1845) 1 Coll 693 .... 8.4, 64.23, 83.6
Monypenny v Bristow (1832) 2 Russ & M 117, 1 LJ Ch 88 .... 20.4
Monypenny v Dering (1852) 2 De GM & G 145, [1843–60] All ER Rep 1098, 22 LJ Ch 313, 17 Jur 467, 19 LTOS 320 .... 35.39, 50.3, 94.28, 94.30, 101.1
Moodie v Commins (1904) 22 NZLR 510 .... 64.17
Moody, Re, Woodroffe v Moody [1895] 1 Ch 101, 64 LJ Ch 174, 13 R 13, 43 WR 462, 72 LT 190 .... 32.20, 218.59
Moody v Stevenson [1992] Ch 486, [1992] 2 WLR 640, [1992] 1 FCR 107, [1992] 1 FLR 494, [1992] Fam Law 284, 135 Sol Jo LB 84, sub nom Re Moody, Moody v Stevenson [1992] 2 All ER 524, CA 105.9, 105.23, 105.25, 105.28, 105.33
Moon, Re, ex p Dawes (1886) 17 QBD 275, [1886–90] All ER Rep 479, 3 Morr 105, 34 WR 752, 55 LT 114, 2 TLR 506, CA 99.6, 99.7

Moon's Will Trusts, Re, Foale v Gillians [1948] 1 All ER 300, [1948] LJR 778, 92 Sol Jo 141, 64 TLR 123 .... 102.17
Moons v De Bernales (1826) 1 Russ 301 .... 49.7
Moor v Raisbeck (1841) 12 Sim 123 .... 41.5, 41.6, 64.32, 74.1
Moore, Re (1885) 17 LR Ir 549 .... 99.7
Moore, Re [1931] 4 DLR 668, [1931] OR 454 .... 93.4
Moore, Re [1941] 2 DLR 112, 15 MPR 357 .... 18.6
Moore, Re, Long v Moore [1907] 1 IR 315, 41 ILT 150 .... 20.4, 22.3
Moore, Re, Moore v His Holiness Pope Benedict XV (1919) 53 ILR 217, [1919] 1 IR 443 .... 102.22
Moore, Re, Moore v Johnson (1885) 54 LJ Ch 432, 33 WR 447, 52 LT 510 .... 38.28
Moore, Re, Moore v Moore (1881) 45 LT 466 .... 30.11, 31.19
Moore, Re, Prior v Moore [1901] 1 Ch 936, [1900–3] All ER Rep 140, 70 LJ Ch 358, 49 WR 484, 84 LT 501, 17 TLR 356 .... 9.29, 51.3, 53.3, 53.7, 94.2
Moore, Re, Trafford v Maconochie (1888) 39 Ch D 116, [1886–90] All ER Rep 187, 57 LJ Ch 936, 52 JP 596, 37 WR 83, 59 LT 681, 4 TLR 591, CA 8.2, 34.2, 34.3, 34.17, 35.35
Moore v Darton (1851) 4 De G & Sm 517, [1843–60] All ER Rep 814, 20 LJ Ch 626, 87 RR 464, 18 LTOS 24 .... 1.15
Moore v Ffolliot (1887) 19 LR Ir 499 .... 101.9
Moore v King (1842) 3 Curt 243, 7 Jur 205, 2 Notes of Cases 45 .... 12.3, 12.5
Moore v Moore (1781) 1 Bro CC 127 .... 63.1
Moore v Moore (1860) 29 Beav 496 .... 41.16
Moore v Moore (1872) IR 6 Eq 166 .... 14.10
Moore v Phelan [1920] 1 IR 232 .... 58.4
Moore v Royal Trust Co [1956] SCR 880 .... 83.6
Moore and Osborne v IRC. See Trafford's Settlement, Re, Moore v IRC
Moore Estate, Re, Cooke v Walsh (1965) 52 WWR 449 .... 5.4
Moore's Goods, Re (1845) 3 Notes of Cases 601 .... 25.16
Moore's Goods, Re [1892] P 378, 62 LJP 9, 1 R 454 .... 5.7, 10.14, 18.8
Moore's Goods, Re [1901] P 44, 70 LJP 16, 84 LT 60 .... 11.6, 13.3
Moore's Rents, Re [1917] 1 IR 244 .... 44.1, 44.5
Moore's Trusts, Re, Lewis v Moore (1906) 96 LT 44 .... 34.11, 35.2
Moore's Will, Re [1963] VR 168 .... 87.2
Moorhouse v Colvin (1851) 15 Beav 341, 21 LJ Ch 177, 18 LTOS 296; affd (1852) 21 LJ Ch 782, 19 LTOS 370 .... 3.2
Moorhouse v Lord (1863) 10 HL Cas 272, 32 LJ Ch 295, 9 Jur NS 677, 1 New Rep 555, 11 WR 637, 8 LT 212 .... 18.9
Morant's Goods, Re (1874) LR 3 P & D 151, 43 LJP & M 16, 38 JP 168, 22 WR 267, 30 LT 74 .... 25.13, 239.2
Mordaunt, Re, Mordaunt v Mordaunt (1914) 49 L Jo 225 .... 99.8
Moreland (formerly Pittaway) v Draffen [1967] Ch 690, [1967] 1 All ER 391, [1967] 2 WLR 637, 111 Sol Jo 37 .... 50.21, 51.8, 76.3
Moren, Re [1953] 4 DLR 138 .... 83.9
Mores' Trust, Re (1851) 10 Hare 171 .... 47.12, 91.6
Morgan, Re (1857) 7 I Ch R 18 .... 39.20
Morgan, Re (1883) 24 Ch D 114, 53 LJ Ch 85, 31 WR 948, 48 LT 964 .... 98.11
Morgan, Re, Cecil-Williams v A-G [1955] 2 All ER 632, [1955] 1 WLR 738, 99 Sol Jo 453 .... 102.10
Morgan, Re, Dowson v Davey (1910) 26 TLR 398 .... 35.24, 35.25, 35.36

Morgan, Re, Marriott v Society for Abolition of Vivisection (1909) 25 TLR 303 .... 103.7
Morgan, Re, Morgan v Morgan [1893] 3 Ch 222, 62 LJ Ch 789, 37 Sol Jo 581, 69 LT 407, CA 33.9, 33.12, 50.21, 50.21, 62.1, 74.8
Morgan, Re, Morgan v Morgan [1942] Ch 345, [1942] 2 All ER 30, 111 LJ Ch 231, 86 Sol Jo 195, 167 LT 9, CA; revsd sub nom Perrin v Morgan [1943] AC 399, [1943] 1 All ER 187, 112 LJ Ch 81, 87 Sol Jo 47, 168 LT 177, 59 TLR 134, HL 49.5, 50.6, 50.12, 50.14, 50.18, 50.21, 64.35, 64.36, 93.23
Morgan v Britten (1871) LR 13 Eq 28, 41 LJ Ch 70 .... 86.4
Morgan v Gronow (1873) LR 16 Eq 1, 42 LJ Ch 410, 28 LT 434 .... 94.45, 94.48
Morgan v Holford (1852) 17 Jur 225, 1 Sm & G 101, 1 WR 101, 20 LTOS 177 .... 7.27
Morgan v Morgan (1851) 14 Beav 72 .... 38.23
Morgan v Morgan (1851) 4 De G & Sm 164, 20 LJ Ch 109, 15 Jur 319, 17 LTOS 114 .... 93.26, 93.27, 93.31, 95.9
Morgan v Morgan (1853) 4 I Ch R 606 .... 42.12
Morgan v Thomas (1877) 6 Ch D 176, 46 LJ Ch 775, 25 WR 750, 36 LT 689 .... 41.16
Morgan v Thomas (1882) 9 QBD 643, 51 LJQB 556, 31 WR 106, 47 LT 281, CA 5.8, 50.21
Morgan d. Surman v Surman (1808) 1 Taunt 289 .... 60.2
Morgan's Goods, Re (1866) LR 1 P & D 214, 35 LJP & M 98, 30 JP 679, 14 WR 1022, 14 LT 894 .... 10.5
Morgan's Will, Re [1950] VLR 335 .... 12.3
Morgan's Will Trusts, Re, Lewarne v Ministry of Health or Minister of Health [1950] Ch 637, [1950] 1 All ER 1097, 94 Sol Jo 368, 66 (pt 1) TLR 1037 .... 41.13, 103.10
Moriarty's Will, Re [1956] VLR 400 .... 13.1
Morley, Re, Morley v Saunders (1869) LR 8 Eq 594, 38 LJ Ch 552, 17 WR 959, 21 LT 132 .... 30.12
Morley, Re, Morley v Williams (1935) 35 SRNSW 102 .... 66.21
Morley v Bird (1798) 3 Ves 628 .... 47.27, 47.32, 86.2
Morley v Rennoldson (1843) 2 Hare 570, 12 LJ Ch 372, 7 Jur 938, 62 RR 236, 1 LTOS 12 .... 33.20, 34.2, 35.2
Morley v Rennoldson [1895] 1 Ch 449, 64 LJ Ch 485, 12 R 158, 43 WR 518, 39 Sol Jo 283, 72 LT 308, CA 18.10, 20.3
Morley's Estate, Re, Hollenden v Morley [1937] Ch 491, [1937] 3 All ER 204, 107 LJ Ch 18, 81 Sol Jo 458, 157 LT 547, 53 TLR 768 .... 32.29
Morpeth v Williamson [1926] NZLR 39 .... 32.10
Morrall v Sutton (1842) 5 Beav 100, 14 LJ Ch 266; on appeal (1845) 1 Ph 533, 14 LJ Ch 266, 9 Jur 697, 5 LTOS 1 .... 50.21, 52.7, 82.3
Morrell v Fisher (1849) 19 LJ Ex 273, 4 Exch 591, 14 LTOS 398 ... 58.3, 58.4, 58.5, 58.6, 64.22
Morrell v Fisher (1851) 4 De G & Sm 422 .... 55.7
Morrell v Morrell (1882) 7 PD 68, [1881–5] All ER Rep 642, 51 LJP 49, 46 JP 328, 30 WR 491, 46 LT 485 .... 5.7
Morrice v Aylmer (1875) LR 7 HL 717, [1874–80] All ER Rep 914, 45 LJ Ch 614, 24 WR 587, 34 LT 218 .... 64.54
Morrieson, Re, Hitchins v Morrieson (1888) 40 Ch D 30, 58 LJ Ch 80, 37 WR 91, 59 LT 847 .... 80.3, 80.7

Morris, Re (1857) 26 LJ Ch 688, 5 WR 423 .... 97.10
Morris, Re, Corfield v Waller (1916) 86 LJ Ch 456, 115 LT 915 .... 47.12, 47.33, 90.1
Morris, Re, Lloyds Bank Ltd v Peake (Hurdwell cited) [1971] P 62, [1970] 1 All ER 1057, [1970] 2 WLR 865, 113 Sol Jo 923, P, D and Admlty 1.5, 5.1, 5.4, 5.7, 6.1, 6.2, 49.6, 51.4, 52.2, 52.3, 57.22, 200.46
Morris, Re, Morris v Atherden (1894) 71 LT 179 .... 38.12
Morris, Re, Salter v A-G (1885) 33 WR 895, 52 LT 840 .... 93.36
Morris, Re, Special Trustees for Great Ormond Street Hospital for Children v Rushin [2001] WTLR 1137 .... 5.9
Morris v Burroughs (1737) 1 Atk 399, West temp Hard 242, 2 Eq Cas Abr 272 pl 39 .... 35.38
Morris v Howes (1845) 4 Hare 599; on appeal (1846) 16 LJ Ch 121, 10 Jur 955, 8 LTOS 229 .... 40.7
Morris v Livie (1842) 1 Y & C Ch Cas 380, [1835–42] All ER Rep 77, 11 LJ Ch 172, 57 RR 391 .... 30.17
Morris v Morris (1853) 17 Beav 198, 1 Eq Rep 167, 17 Jur 966, 1 WR 377, 21 LTOS 190 .... 56.1, 98.1, 98.11
Morris' Settlement Trusts, Re, Adams v Napier [1951] 2 All ER 528, 95 Sol Jo 609, CA 40.5
Morris's Will Trusts, Re, Public Trustee v Morris [1960] 3 All ER 548, [1960] 1 WLR 1210, 104 Sol Jo 934 .... 38.28
Morrison, Re [1942] 1 DLR 273, [1941] OR 313 .... 18.28
Morrison, Re, Morrison v Morrison (1910) 102 LT 530, 26 TLR 395 .... 55.7
Morrison, Re, Wakefield v Falmouth (1967) 111 Sol Jo 758 .... 102.7, 103.3, 103.5
Morrison v Bell (1843) 5 I Eq R 354 .... 42.14
Morrison v Hoppe (1851) 4 De G & Sm 234, 15 Jur 737, 17 LTOS 1 .... 38.6, 60.2, 64.51
Morrison v M'Ferran [1901] 1 IR 360 .... 36.13
Morrison v Martin (1846) 5 Hare 507, 7 LTOS 320 .... 69.2
Morrison v Mills and Mills (1961) 31 DLR (2d) 159, 36 WWR 673 .... 82.7
Morrison Estate, Re [1953] 3 DLR 274 .... 4.17
Morrison's Goods, Re (1861) 2 Sw & Tr 129, 9 WR 518, 3 LT 786 .... 25.10
Morrison's Will Trusts, Re, Walsingham v Blathwayt [1940] Ch 102, [1939] 4 All ER 332, 109 LJ Ch 25, 83 Sol Jo 908, 162 LT 45, 56 TLR 99 .... 34.11, 35.30, 94.23
Morrissey's Trusts, Re [1952] SR Qd 98 .... 93.1
Morritt v Douglas (1872) LR 3 P & D 1, 42 LJP & M 10, 37 JP 24, 21 WR 162, 27 LT 591 .... 11.26
Morrow v McConville (1883) 11 LR Ir 236 .... 9.35
Morse v Lord Ormonde (1826) 1 Russ 382, 4 LJOS Ch 158 .... 98.9
Morse v Martin (1865) 34 Beav 500 .... 94.44
Morse v Morse (1829) 2 Sim 485 .... 85.3
Morse's Settlement, Re (1855) 21 Beav 174, 25 LJ Ch 192, 2 Jur NS 6, 4 WR 148, 26 LTOS 163 .... 93.1
Mort, Re, Perpetual Trustee Co Ltd v Bisdee (1904) 21 WN 259, 4 SRNSW 760 .... 64.53
Mortimer, Re, Gray v Gray [1905] 2 Ch 502, 74 LJ Ch 745, 93 LT 459, CA 51.4, 94.14, 101.1
Mortimer, Re, Griffiths v Mortimer (1885) 54 LJ Ch 414, 33 WR 441, 52 LT 383 .... 67.4

Mortimer v Hartley (1851) 3 De G & Sm 328n, 20 LJ Ex 129, 6 Exch 47, 16 LTOS 551 .... 56.2, 83.9, 99.1
Mortimer v West (1827) 3 Russ 370, 5 LJOS Ch 181 .... 72.2, 72.3
Mortimore v Mortimore (1879) 4 App Cas 448, 48 LJ Ch 470, 27 WR 601, 40 LT 696, HL 77.4
Mortlock's Trusts, Re (1857) 3 K & J 456, 26 LJ Ch 671, 112 RR 230, 5 WR 748, 30 LTOS 90 .... 34.6, 83.9, 83.20
Morton, Re [1963] VR 40 .... 41.5
Morton, Re, M'Auley v Harvey (1919) 53 ILT 105 .... 101.1
Morton, Re, Morton v Warham [1956] Ch 644, [1956] 3 All ER 259, [1956] 3 WLR 663, 100 Sol Jo 650 .... 104.14
Morton v French (1908) 45 SLR 126, 1908 SC 171, 15 SLT 517 .... 7.10
Morton v Tewart (1842) 2 Y & C Ch Cas 67, 60 RR 35 .... 79.2
Morton Estate, Re, Summerfield and London and Western Trusts Co Ltd v Phillips [1941] WWR 310 .... 102.9
Morton's Goods, Re (1887) 12 PD 141, 56 LJP 96, 51 JP 680, 35 WR 735, 57 LT 501, 3 TLR 577 .... 18.22
Moryoseph v Moryoseph [1920] 2 Ch 33, [1920] All ER Rep 216, 89 LJ Ch 376, 64 Sol Jo 497, 123 LT 569 .... 82.4
Moseley's Trusts, Re (1879) 11 Ch D 555, CA; affd sub nom Pearks v Moseley (1880) 5 App Cas 714, 50 LJ Ch 57, 21 WR 1, 43 LT 449, HL 47.31, 51.4, 93.16, 94.14, 94.21, 94.24
Moser v Platt (1844) 14 Sim 95, 8 Jur 389, 3 LTOS 217 .... 58.6, 63.2
Moses, Re, Beddington v Beddington [1902] 1 Ch 100, 71 LJ Ch 101, 85 LT 596, 18 TLR 147, CA; affd sub nom Beddington v Baumann [1903] AC 13, 72 LJ Ch 155, 51 WR 383, 47 Sol Jo 90, 87 LT 658, 19 TLR 58, HL 41.4, 41.11, 41.21
Moses, Re, Moses v Valentine [1908] 2 Ch 235, 77 LJ Ch 783, 99 LT 519 ... 23.4, 23.12, 24.2, 24.3
Mosley v Massey (1806) 8 East 149 .... 63.2
Moss, Re (1977) 77 DLR (3d) 314 .... 46.1
Moss, Re, Fox v Moss [1919] VLR 192 .... 35.31
Moss, Re, Hobrough v Harvey [1949] 1 All ER 495, 93 Sol Jo 164, 65 TLR 299 .... 9.31, 102.13
Moss, Re, Larke v Nugus. See Larke v Nugus
Moss v Cooper (1861) 1 John & H 352, 128 RR 410, 4 LT 790 .... 36.2, 36.8, 36.13
Moss v Harter (1854) 18 Jur 973, 2 Sm & G 458, 2 WR 540, 24 LTOS 19 .... 39.14
Moss's Trusts, Re, Moss v Allen [1945] 1 All ER 207, 114 LJ Ch 152, 89 Sol Jo 69, 172 LT 196, 61 TLR 147 .... 34.11, 35.29, 35.31
Mostyn v Fabrigas (1775) 1 Cowp 161, [1775–1802] All ER Rep 266, sub nom Fabrigas v Mostyn 20 State Tr 81, 226, Ex Ch 57.7
Mostyn v Mostyn (1854) 5 HL Cas 155, 23 LJ Ch 925, 24 LTOS 175 .... 57.18, 58.10
Motan, Re [1950] SASR 209 .... 101.6
Motherwell, Re, Keane v Motherwell [1910] 1 IR 249, 44 ILT 148 .... 101.14
Mottram, Re (1864) 10 Jur NS 915, 10 LT 866 .... 93.12
Mountcashell (Earl) v Smyth [1895] 1 IR 346 .... 20.4, 22.3
Mousley v Rigby [1955] Ch 139, [1954] 3 All ER 553, [1954] 3 WLR 891, 98 Sol Jo 820 .... 68.11, 216.17
Mower v Orr (1849) 7 Hare 473, 13 Jur 421, 82 RR 191, 13 LTOS 184, sub nom Mower v Orr, Mower v Mower 18 LJ Ch 361 .... 37.3, 47.12

Moyle, Re, Howie v Moyle [1920] VLR 147 ..... 74.1
Moyles' Estate, Re (1878) 1 LR Ir 155 ..... 85.2
Muckleston v Brown (1801) 6 Ves 52 ..... 36.2, 36.4, 104.1
Mucklow v Fuller (1821) Jac 198, 23 RR 186 ..... 25.12
Muddle v Fry (1822) 6 Madd 270 ..... 64.19
Mudie's Will, Re, Beattie v Mudie [1916] VLR 265 ..... 93.1
Mudway v Croft (1843) 3 Curt 671, 7 Jur 979, 1 LTOS 479, 2 Notes of Cases 438 ..... 4.18, 4.20
Muffett, Re, Jones v Mason (1886) 55 LT 671, 3 TLR 126; on appeal (1887) 56 LJ Ch 600, CA 33.17, 35.49, 79.1
Mugford, Re, Breene v Bangs (1975) 56 DLR 758 ..... 64.37
Muir v IRC [1966] 3 All ER 38, [1966] 1 WLR 1269, 43 TC 367, 45 ATC 185, [1966] TR 165, 110 Sol Jo 448, CA 40.10, 40.14
Muir v Open Brethren (1956) 96 CLR 166 ..... 102.6
Muir's Trustees (1869) 42 Sc Jur 25, 8 M 53 ..... 10.14
Muirhead v Muirhead and Crellin (1890) 15 App Cas 289, HL 48.8
Muirhead Estate, Re (1919) 12 Sask LR 123, [1919] 2 WWR 454 ..... 35.8
Mulcahy, Re, Butler v Meagher [1931] IR 239 ..... 103.18
Mulder, Re, Westminster Bank Ltd v Mulder [1943] 2 All ER 150, CA 58.2, 64.7
Muller, Re [1950] QWN 33 ..... 101.8
Mullins v Smith (1860) 1 Drew & Sm 204, 8 WR 739 ... 30.1, 30.6, 30.8, 31.3, 33.1, 38.10, 55.4
Mulock's Goods, Re [1933] IR 171 ..... 21.5, 21.7
Mulqueen's Trusts, Re (1881) 7 LR Ir 127 ..... 79.1
Mundy's Goods, Re (1860) 25 JP 151, 30 LJPM & A 85, 7 Jur NS 52, 2 Sw & Tr 119, 9 WR 171, 3 LT 380 ..... 10.8
Munn, Re, Hopkins v Warren [1943] SASR 304 ..... 4.17
Munro v Fitzgerald (1844) 3 LTOS 3 ..... 30.42
Munro v Henderson [1907] 1 IR 440; affd [1908] 1 IR 260, Ir CA 52.8, 57.5
Munster & Leinster Bank Ltd v A-G [1940] IR 19 ..... 102.9
Murawski's Will Trusts, Re, Lloyds Bank Ltd v Royal Society for the Prevention of Cruelty to Animals [1971] 2 All ER 328, [1971] 1 WLR 707, 115 Sol Jo 189 ..... 102.2, 102.13
Murfett v Smith (1887) 12 PD 116, 51 JP 374, 57 LT 498 ..... 4.11, 4.15
Murguia's Goods, Re (1884) 9 PD 236, 53 LJP 47, 48 JP 711, 2 WR 799 ..... 25.10
Murkin v Phillipson (1834) 3 My & K 257, 3 LJ Ch 143 ..... 93.44
Murphy, Re [1953] QWN 36 ..... 16.5
Murphy v Brentwood District Council [1991] 1 AC 398, [1990] 2 All ER 908, [1990] 3 WLR 414, 89 LGR 24, [1990] 2 Lloyd's Rep 467, 22 HLR 502, 21 Con LR 1, 134 Sol Jo 1076, [1990] NLJR 1111, 50 BLR 1, HL 1.14
Murphy v Deichler [1909] AC 446, 78 LJPC 159, 53 Sol Jo 671, 101 LT 143, 25 TLR 719, HL 24.17
Murphy v Donnelly (1870) IR 4 Eq 111 ..... 38.8, 84.2
Murphy v Donnelly (1871) IR 6 Eq 203 ..... 51.11
Murphy v Lamphier (1914) 31 OLR 287; affd (1914) 20 DLR 906, 32 OLR 19 ..... 4.17, 4.21
Murphy v Murphy [2003] EWCA Civ 1862, [2004] Lloyd's Rep IR 744, [2004] 1 FCR 1, [2003] All ER (D) 410 (Dec) 105.41
Murphy v Paxton (1930) 4 ALJ 236, Argus LR 389 ..... 90.3
Murphy's Goods, Re (1868) 18 LT 63 ..... 25.2

Murphy's Goods, Re (1873) 8 IR Eq 300 .... 9.8
Murray, Re [1958] VR 4 .... 83.2
Murray, Re, Brownrigg v Murray [1951] Tas SR 38 .... 101.10
Murray, Re, Clarke v Wakem [1964] NZLR 627 .... 58.8, 64.21, 69.1
Murray, Re, Martins Bank Ltd v Dill [1955] Ch 69, [1954] 3 All ER 129, [1954] 3 WLR 521, 98 Sol Jo 716, CA 35.43, 52.2
Murray, Re, Murray v Murray [1956] 2 All ER 353, [1956] 1 WLR 605, 100 Sol Jo 420 .... 19.2, 19.3, 20.4
Murray, Re, Perpetual Trustees (Canberra) Ltd v Lathom [1963] ALR 68 .... 66.12, 74.2
Murray v Addenbrook (1830) 4 Russ 407, 8 LJOS Ch 79 .... 98.10
Murray v Champernowne [1901] 2 IR 232, 35 ILT 68 .... 23.4
Murray v Haylow [1927] 3 DLR 1036, 60 OLR 629 .... 10.16
Murray's Goods, Re [1896] P 65, 65 LJP 49, 44 WR 414, 12 TLR 143 .... 201.11
Murray's Trust, Re (1868) 18 LT 747 .... 29.10
Murray's Trustee v Murray (1919) 56 SLR 503, 1919 SC 552, 1919 SLT 47 .... 73.1
Murthwaite v Jenkinson (1824) 2 B & C 357, 3 Dow & Ry KB 764 .... 62.1
Muschamp v Bluet (1617) J Bridg 132 .... 99.2
Musgrave, Re, Machell v Parry [1916] 2 Ch 417, 85 LJ Ch 639, 60 Sol Jo 694, 115 LT 149 .... 33.47
Musgrove's Estate, Re, Davis v Mayhew [1927] P 264, 96 LJP 140, 71 Sol Jo 542, 137 LT 612, 43 TLR 648, CA 13.1
Musther, Re, Groves v Musther (1890) 43 Ch D 569, 59 LJ Ch 296, CA 68.6
Musurus's Estate, Re [1936] 2 All ER 1666, 80 Sol Jo 637 .... 23.16
Myers v Myers [204] EWHC 1944 (Fam), [2005] WTLR 851 .... 105.16
Myers v Washbrook [1901] 1 KB 360, 70 LJKB 357, 83 LT 633, DC 8.4
Mytton v Boodle (1834) 6 Sim 457 .... 56.1, 93.22
Mytton v Mytton (1874) LR 19 Eq 30, 44 LJ Ch 18, 23 WR 477, 31 LT 328 .... 30.8

N

N v M (1885) 1 TLR 523 .... 80.3
Naidoo v Naidu (2000) Times, 1 November 5.9
Naismith v Boyes [1899] AC 495 .... 37.7
Nakauchi Estate, Re (1927) 3 DLR 1087, 21 Sask LR 673, [1927] 2 WWR 607 .... 9.40
Nannock v Horton (1802) 7 Ves 391 .... 38.3, 83.12
Napier's Goods, Re (1809) 1 Phillim 83 .... 25.16
Nash, Re, Cook v Frederick [1910] 1 Ch 1, 79 LJ Ch 1, 54 Sol Jo 48, 101 LT 837, 26 TLR 57, CA 42.4, 94.48
Nash, Re, Miller v Allen [1965] 1 All ER 51, [1965] 1 WLR 221, 109 Sol Jo 94 .... 33.25, 33.30, 93.15, 95.7
Nash, Re, Prall v Bevan (1894) 38 Sol Jo 513, 71 LT 5, CA 77.3
Nash v Allen (1889) 42 Ch D 54, 58 LJ Ch 754, 37 WR 646, 61 LT 193 .... 74.1
Nash v Morley (1842) 5 Beav 177, 11 LJ Ch 336, 6 Jur 520 .... 102.7
Natal Bank Ltd v Rood [1910] AC 570, 80 LJPC 22, 103 LT 229, 26 TLR 622, PC 2.2

Nathan v Leonard [2002] EWHC 1701 (Ch), [2003] 4 All ER 198, [2003] 1 WLR 827, [2002] 28 LS Gaz R 32, (2002) Times, 4 June, 146 Sol Jo LB 160, [2002] All ER (D) 432 (May) 34.25, 35.38
National Anti-Vivisection Society v IRC [1948] AC 31, [1947] 2 All ER 217, 26 ATC 309, 41 R & IT 99, [1947] LJR 1112, 177 LT 226, 63 TLR 424, 311, sub nom IRC v National Anti-Vivisection Society 28 TC 311, HL 9.31, 102.4, 102.10, 102.11, 102.13
National Association of Local Government Officers v Bolton Corpn [1943] AC 166, [1942] 2 All ER 425, 40 LGR 273, 106 JP 255, 111 LJKB 974, 167 LT 312, 59 TLR 1, HL 38.10
National Assurance Co v Scott [1909] 1 IR 325 .... 31.12
National Mutual Trustees Ltd v Gooding [1990] VR 791 .... 34.10, 35.21
National Society for the Prevention of Cruelty to Children v Scottish National Society for the Prevention of Cruelty to Children [1915] AC 207, 84 LJPC 29, 58 Sol Jo 720, 111 LT 869, 30 TLR 657, HL 58.1
National Trust Co v Mendelson [1942] 1 DLR 438, [1941] OWN 435 .... 23.12, 25.14
National Trust Co Ltd and Bond v Crafts [1939] 2 WWR 487 .... 30.32
National Trustee Co Ltd v Fleury [1965] SCR 817 .... 30.43, 77.3
National Trustees, Executors and Agency Co Ltd v Keast (1896) 22 VLR 447 .... 35.30, 83.6
National Trustees, Executors and Agency Co of Australasia Ltd v Doyle (1898) 24 VLR 626 .... 30.14
Natusch, Re, Pettit v Natusch [1963] NZLR 273 .... 17.4
Neal, Re, Barclays Bank Ltd v Neal (1966) 110 Sol Jo 549 .... 102.5
Neal v Denston (1932) 76 Sol Jo 691, 147 LT 460, 48 TLR 637 .... 13.3
Neale v Davies (1854) 5 De GM & G 258, 23 LJ Ch 744, 2 Eq Rep 530, 2 WR 358 .... 29.15
Neary's Estate, Re (1881) 7 LR Ir 311 .... 97.1
Neate v Pickard (1843) 2 Notes of Cases 406 .... 21.1, 21.6
Neathway v Reed (1853) 3 De GM & G 18, 22 LJ Ch 809, 17 Jur 169 .... 54.5
Needham, Re (1844) 6 I Eq R 537, 1 Jo & Lat 34 .... 27.5
Needham v Kirkman (1820) 3 B & Ald 531 .... 3.8
Needham v Smith (1828) 4 Russ 318, 6 LJOS Ch 107 .... 3.8, 3.10
Neeld, Re, Carpenter v Inigo-Jones [1962] Ch 643, [1962] 2 All ER 335, [1962] 2 WLR 1097, 106 Sol Jo 449, CA 1.8, 35.39, 35.40, 35.43, 206.22, 206.27, 235.27
Neeld, Re, Carpenter v Inigo-Jones [1964] 2 All ER 952n, [1965] 1 WLR 73n, 43 ATC 397, [1964] TR 437, CA 214.70
Neeld, Re, Inigo-Jones v Inigo-Jones (No 3) [1969] 2 All ER 1025, [1969] 1 WLR 988, 113 Sol Jo 527 .... 35.42, 235.27
Neighbour v Thurlow (1860) 28 Beav 33 .... 101.10
Neilson, Re, Cumming v Clyde (1929) 73 Sol Jo 765 .... 63.1
Neilson v Monro (1879) 27 WR 936, 41 LT 209 .... 68.8
Nelson v Carter (1832) 5 Sim 530 .... 30.3
Nelson v Hopkins (1851) 21 LJ Ch 410 .... 63.9
Nelson (Earl) v Lord Bridport (1846) 8 Beav 547, 10 Jur 1043, 68 RR 174, 9 LTOS 471 .... 24.2
Nelson's Goods, Re (1872) IR 6 Eq 569 .... 18.23, 19.4
Nelthrop v Hill (1669) 1 Cas in Ch 135 .... 31.19

Nesbitt's Will Trusts, Re, Dr Barnardo's Homes National Inc Association v Board of Governors of United Newcastle-upon-Tyne Hospitals [1953] 1 All ER 936, [1953] 1 WLR 595, 32 ATC 101, 46 R & IT 332, [1953] TR 111, 97 Sol Jo 264 .... 57.22, 103.3
Nettleton v Stephenson (1849) 3 De G & Sm 366, 18 LJ Ch 191, 13 Jur 618, 13 LTOS 42 .... 87.2
Nevill v Boddam (1860) 28 Beav 554, 29 LJ Ch 738, 6 Jur NS 573, 8 WR 490, 2 LT 273 .... 19.2, 67.4
Nevill v Nevill (1701) 2 Vern 431 .... 82.7
Neville, Re, Neville v First Garden City Ltd [1925] Ch 44, [1924] All ER Rep 377, 94 LJ Ch 130, 69 Sol Jo 125, 132 LT 602, 41 TLR 2 .... 30.12, 204.64
Neville v Thacker (1888) 23 LR Ir 344, 359 .... 98.1, 98.2
Neville Estates Ltd v Madden [1962] Ch 832, [1961] 3 All ER 769, [1961] 3 WLR 999, 105 Sol Jo 806 .... 9.35, 102.8, 102.9
Neville's Goods, Re (1859) 28 LJP & M 52, 4 Sw & Tr 218 .... 16.8
Newbolt v Pryce (1844) 14 Sim 354, 8 Jur 1112, 4 LTOS 272 .... 58.10
Newbould, Re, Carter v Newbould (1913) 110 LT 6, CA 37.2
Newburgh v Newburgh (1820) 5 Madd 364 .... 57.10
Newcombe, Re (1918) 42 OLR 590, 14 OWN 103 .... 30.3
Newcombe, Re, Cresswell v Newcombe [1938] NZLR 98, 14 NZLJ 47 .... 80.3
Newcombe v English, Re English's Goods. See English's Goods, Re
Newill v Newill (1872) 7 Ch App 253, 41 LJ Ch 432, 20 WR 308, 26 LT 175 .... 85.3
Newis v Lark. See News v Lark
Newland v A-G (1809) 3 Mer 684 .... 102.10
Newland v Marjoribanks (1813) 5 Taunt 268, 1 Marsh 44 .... 60.2
Newland v Shephard (1723) 9 Mod Rep 57, 2 P Wms 194, 2 Eq Cas Abr 329 pl 4 .... 101.7
Newland's Goods, Re [1952] P 71, [1952] 1 All ER 841, [1952] 1 Lloyd's Rep 280, 96 Sol Jo 230, [1952] 1 TLR 896 .... 16.3, 16.10
Newman, Re [1967] VR 201 .... 57.22
Newman, Re, Slater v Newman [1930] 2 Ch 409, [1930] All ER Rep 617, 99 LJ Ch 427, 143 LT 676 .... 41.18, 200.66, 204.69
Newman v Barton (1690) 2 Vern 205 .... 31.6
Newman v Newman (1783) 1 Bro CC 186 .... 42.2
Newman v Newman (1839) 10 Sim 51, 8 LJ Ch 354 .... 93.6, 94.37
Newman v Newman (1858) 26 Beav 218, 4 Jur NS 1030, 7 WR 6, 32 LTOS 83 .... 64.35
Newman v Newman (No 2) (1858) 26 Beav 220, 4 Jur NS 1030, 32 LTOS 83 .... 38.11
Newman v Nightingale (1787) 1 Cox Eq Cas 341 .... 85.3
Newman v Piercey (1876) 4 Ch D 41, 46 LJ Ch 36, 25 WR 37, 35 LT 461 .... 69.1
News v Lark (1571) Benl 196, sub nom Newis v Lark 2 Plowd 408 .... 34.3
Newson-Smith's Settlement, Re, Grice v Newson-Smith [1962] 3 All ER 963n, [1962] 1 WLR 1478 .... 9.2
Newton v Lucas (1836) 1 My & Cr 391 .... 58.10, 63.4
Newton v Marsden (1862) 2 John & H 356, 31 LJ Ch 690, 8 Jur NS 1034, 10 WR 438, 6 LT 155 .... 35.8
Newton v Newton (1861) 12 I Ch R 118 .... 18.5, 19.2, 19.5
Newton King, Re [1953] NZLR 245 .... 44.4, 44.10, 44.12

Newton's Trusts, Re (1867) LR 4 Eq 171, 37 LJ Ch 23 .... 47.24, 78.4
Ng Chi-fong v Hui Ho Pui-fong [1987] HKLR 462 ...... 49.2, 50.2, 51.1, 52.1, 57.15, 62.1, 66.5, 78.4
Nicholas's Will, Re [1923] VLR 461, 45 ALT 33 .... 64.37
Nicholl, Re, Re Perkins, Nicholl v Perkins (1920) 65 Sol Jo 8, 125 LT 62 .... 39.19, 39.21, 57.17, 58.4
Nicholls, Re (1973) 32 DLR (3d) 683, [1973] 2 OR 33 .... 72.2
Nicholls, Re (1987) 34 DLR (4th) 321, Ont CA 1.6
Nicholls, Re, Hunter v Nicholls [1921] 2 Ch 11, 90 LJ Ch 379, 65 Sol Jo 533, 125 LT 55 .... 11.4
Nicholls v Judson (1742) 2 Atk 300 .... 44.15
Nichols v Haviland (1855) 1 K & J 504, 1 Jur NS 891, 26 LTOS 52 .... 47.37, 77.2
Nichols v Hawkes (1853) 10 Hare 342, 22 LJ Ch 255, 1 WR 124, 20 LTOS 257 .... 83.1
Nichols v Hooper (1712) 1 P Wms 198, 2 Vern 686; revsd (1712) 1 P Wms 200n, HL 98.10
Nichols v Nichols (1814) 2 Phillim 180 .... 10.1
Nichols v Tolley (1700) 2 Vern 388 .... 56.6
Nichols and Freeman v Binns (1858) 1 Sw & Tr 239, 32 LTOS 50 .... 4.13 4.14
Nicholson, Re, Chadwyck-Healey v Crawford [1938] 3 All ER 270, 82 Sol Jo 624 .... 33.45
Nicholson, Re, Eade v Nicholson [1909] 2 Ch 111, 78 LJ Ch 516, [1908–10] All ER Rep 669, 100 LT 877 .... 38.18, 38.19, 38.20, 38.23
Nicholson, Re, Stace v Nicholson (1904) 24 NZLR 633 .... 93.30
Nicholson v Field [1893] 2 Ch 511, 62 LJ Ch 1015, 3 R 528, 42 WR 48, 69 LT 299 .... 27.7
Nicholson v Patrickson (1861) 3 Giff 209, 7 Jur NS 987, 5 LT 202 .... 38.3, 47.32
Nicholson's Settlement, Re, Molony v Nicholson [1939] Ch 11, [1938] 3 All ER 532, 107 LJ Ch 338, 82 Sol Jo 603, 159 LT 314, 54 TLR 1060, CA 40.15
Nickels, Re, Nickels v Nickels [1898] 1 Ch 630, 67 LJ Ch 406, 46 WR 422, [1895–9] All ER Rep 783, 42 Sol Jo 414, 78 LT 379 ... 29.6, 29.9, 29.11, 29.14, 29.15
Nickisson v Cockill (1863) 3 De GJ & Sm 622, 32 LJ Ch 753, 9 Jur NS 975, 2 New Rep 557, 142 RR 189, 11 WR 1082, 8 LT 778 .... 33.34
Nicloson v Wordsworth (1818) 19 RR 86, 2 Swan 365 .... 27.6
Nielson-Jones v Fedden [1975] Ch 222, [1974] 3 All ER 38, [1974] 3 WLR 583, 118 Sol Jo 776 .... 7.3
Nightingale, Re, Green v Nightingale (No 2) (1974) 119 Sol Jo 189 .... 4.17
Nightingale v Goulbourn (1848) 2 Ph 594, 17 LJ Ch 296, 12 Jur 317, [1843–60] All ER Rep 420, 11 LTOS 169 .... 102.10
Nightingall v Smith (1848) 1 Exch 879 .... 58.6
Nilen's Will, Re, Kidd v Nilen [1908] VLR 332 .... 34.3, 103.17
Nina Kung (alias Nina TH Wang) v Wang Din Shin 2006, FACV No 12 of 2004, Hong Kong Ct of Final Appeal 5.9
Nisbett v Murray (1799) 5 Ves 149 .... 24.6, 63.1
Nixon v Prince (1918) 34 TLR 444 .... 16.4
Niyazi's Will Trusts, Re [1978] 3 All ER 785, [1978] 1 WLR 910, 122 Sol Jo 129 .... 102.7
Noad, Re, Noad v Noad [1951] Ch 553, [1951] 1 All ER 467, 95 Sol Jo 188, [1951] 1 TLR 703 .... 76.2, 76.3

Noble, Re [1927] 1 DLR 1078, [1927] 1 WWR 442 .... 64.45
Noble, Re [1955] SASR 92 .... 92.5
Noble v Brett (1858) 24 Beav 499, 27 LJ Ch 516, 4 Jur NS 623, 6 WR 219, 31 LTOS 228 .... 31.18
Noble's Trusts, Re (1870) IR 5 Eq 140 .... 57.15
Nockolds v Locke (1856) 3 K & J 6, 2 Jur NS 1064, 5 WR 3 .... 50.9, 87.2
Noding v Alliston (1850) 14 Jur 904 .... 13.3
Noel v Jones (1848) 16 Sim 309, 17 LJ Ch 470, 12 Jur 906 .... 82.7
Noel v Lord Henley, ex p Schwench and Mann (1825) M'Cle & Yo 302, Ex Ch 40.10
Noel v Lord Walsingham (1824) 2 Sim & St 99, 3 LJOS Ch 12 .... 40.2
Noel v Noel (1859) 4 Drew 624, 7 WR 572 .... 39.19
Noel v Weston (1813) 2 Ves & B 269 .... 82.1
Noell v Wells and Page (1668) 2 Keb 337, 343, 1 Lev 235, 1 Sid 359 .... 49.7
Nolan, Re, Sheridan v Nolan [1912] 1 IR 416 .... 82.5
Noone v Lyons (1862) 1 W & W (Eq) 235 .... 59.3
Norman, Re, Andrew v Vine [1947] Ch 349, [1947] 1 All ER 400, [1947] LJR 780, 91 Sol Jo 221, 177 LT 125 .... 102.17
Norman v Norman (1830) Beat 430 .... 66.5
Norman v Norman [1919] 1 Ch 297, 88 LJ Ch 109, 120 LT 379, 35 TLR 181 .... 58.6, 58.10, 63.8
Norman's Goods, Re (1847) 5 Notes of Cases 550 .... 15.1
Norman's Trust, Re (1853) 3 De GM & G 965, 22 LJ Ch 720, 1 Eq Rep 53, 17 Jur 444, 1 WR 220, 21 LTOS 97 .... 50.2
Norreys v Franks (1875) IR 9 Eq 18 .... 63.1
Norrington, Re, Brindley v Partridge (1879) 13 Ch D 654, 44 JP 474, 28 WR 711, CA 38.17
Norrington, Re, Norrington v Norrington (1923) 40 TLR 96 .... 84.2
Norris, Re (1866) 14 WR 348 .... 15.1
Norris, Re, Allen v Norris (1884) 27 Ch D 333, 53 LJ Ch 913, 32 WR 955, 51 LT 593 .... 27.3
Norris v Norris (1839) 2 D 220 .... 71.1
Norris v Norris (1846) 15 LJ Ch 420, 2 Coll 719, 10 Jur 629, 7 LTOS 508 .... 63.1
North, Re, North v Cusden [1952] Ch 397, [1952] 1 All ER 609, 96 Sol Jo 181, [1952] 1 TLR 674 .... 86.5
North v North (1909) 25 TLR 322 .... 18.6, 18.26, 18.27
North Devon and West Somerset Relief Fund Trusts, Re, Baron Hylton v Wright [1953] 2 All ER 1032, [1953] 1 WLR 1260, 97 Sol Jo 728 .... 102.7, 103.20
North Settled Estates, Re, Public Trustee v Graham [1946] Ch 13, 115 LJ Ch 138, 174 LT 303 .... 100.2
North's Goods, Re (1842) 6 Jur 564 .... 14.14
Northcliffe, Re, Arnholz v Hudson [1925] Ch 651, 95 LJ Ch 41, 133 LT 466 .... 20.4
Northcliffe's Settlements, Re [1937] 3 All ER 804, 81 Sol Jo 716, CA 27.3
Northcote's Will Trusts, Re, Northcote v Northcote [1949] 1 All ER 442, [1949] WN 69 .... 236.12
Northen's Estate, Re, Salt v Pym (1884) 28 Ch D 153, 54 LJ Ch 273, 33 WR 336, 52 LT 173 .... 52.4
Northey v Paxton (1888) 60 LT 30 .... 38.10, 64.27
Northey v Strange (1716) 1 P Wms 340 .... 73.1, 87.1

Northumberland (Earl) v Earl of Aylsford (1760) Amb 540, sub nom Northumberland (Earl) v Marquis of Gransby 1 Eden 489; affd sub nom Northumberland (Duke) v Lord Egremont (1768) Amb 657 .... 34.4, 45.2
Norton, Re, Norton v Norton [1911] 2 Ch 27, 80 LJ Ch 119, 55 Sol Jo 169, 103 LT 821 .... 94.9, 94.29, 94.30, 94.45, 94.46
Norton v Bazett (1856) Dea & Sw 259, 3 Jur NS 1084, 4 WR 830, 27 LTOS 289 .... 12.6
Norton v Johnstone (1885) 30 Ch D 649, 55 LJ Ch 222, 34 WR 13 .... 38.26, 38.28
Norwich Town Close Estate Charity, Re (1888) 40 Ch D 298, 37 WR 362, 60 LT 202, 5 TLR 197, CA 102.10, 102.26
Nosworthy's Goods, Re (1865) 34 LJPM & A 145, 11 Jur NS 570, 4 Sw & Tr 44 .... 10.1
Nottage, Re, Jones v Palmer [1895] 2 Ch 649, [1895–9] All ER Rep 1203, 64 LJ Ch 695, 12 R 571, 44 WR 22, 39 Sol Jo 655, 73 LT 269, 11 TLR 519, CA 102.8, 212.26
Nottage, Re, Jones v Palmer (No 2) [1895] 2 Ch 657, 64 LJ Ch 695, 12 R 571, 44 WR 22, sub nom Re Nottage, Nottage v Palmer 73 LT 265, CA 64.11
Nottidge v Dering [1910] 1 Ch 297, 79 LJ Ch 439, 102 LT 145, CA 40.10, 40.13
Nottingham v Jennings (1700) 2 Eq Cas Abr 308, 1 Com 82, 1 Ld Raym 568, 1 P Wms 23, 1 Salk 233, Willes 166n 84.2, 98.12
Nourse, Re, Hampton v Nourse [1899] 1 Ch 63, 68 LJ Ch 15, 47 WR 116, 43 Sol Jo 29, 79 LT 376 .... 34.15, 35.10, 35.15
Nowlan v Nelligan (1785) 1 Bro CC 489 .... 97.2
Nowlan v Walsh (1851) 4 De G & Sm 584, 17 LTOS 292 .... 83.2, 83.11, 83.19
Noyce, Re, Brown v Rigg (1885) 31 Ch D 75, 55 LJ Ch 114, 34 WR 147, 53 LT 688 .... 97.9
Nugee v Chapman (1860) 29 Beav 288 .... 100.4
Nugee v Chapman (No 2) (1860) 29 Beav 290 .... 38.10
Nunburnholme (Lord), Re, Wilson v Nunburnholme [1912] 1 Ch 489, 81 LJ Ch 347, 56 Sol Jo 343, 106 LT 361, CA 93.39, 93.40
Nunn v Hancock (1868) 16 WR 818 .... 51.4
Nunn's Estate, Re [1936] 1 All ER 555, 105 LJP 57, 80 Sol Jo 267, 154 LT 498, 52 TLR 322 .... 18.23
Nunn's Trusts, Re (1875) LR 19 Eq 331, 44 LJ Ch 255, 23 WR 376 .... 33.7, 58.10
Nussey's Goods, Re (1898) 78 LT 169 .... 25.2
Nutt v Burrell (1724) Cas temp King 1 .... 35.38
Nutting v Southern Housing Group Ltd [2004] EWHC 2982 (Ch), [2005] 2 P & CR 14, [2005] HLR 25, [2005] 1 FLR 1066, [2005] Fam Law 210, [2005] 6 LS Gaz R 32, [2005] 1 P & CR D63, (2005) Times, 5 January, [2004] All ER (D) 347 (Dec) 105.14
Nye v Sewell (1894) 15 NSWLR 18 .... 5.9

O

Oakes v Oakes (1852) 9 Hare 666 .... 41.2, 41.8, 41.13, 64.54
Oakes v Strachey (1843) 13 Sim 414, 7 Jur 433 .... 38.23
Oakes v Uzzell [1932] P 19, 100 LJP 99, 75 Sol Jo 543, 146 LT 95, 47 TLR 573, P, D and Admlty 10.1

Oakes Will Trusts, Re, Lloyds Bank Ltd v Barker [1948] WN 110, 92 Sol Jo 167 .... 41.21
Oakley v IRC [2005] STC (SCD) 343 .... 208.34
Oates d Hatterley v Jackson (1742) 7 Mod Rep 439, 2 Stra 1172 .... 85.2, 86.4
Oates's Estate, Re, Callow v Sutton [1946] 2 All ER 735, 63 TLR 83 .... 14.10, 14.11
Oberg, Re [1952] QWN 38 .... 9.11
O'Bierne, Re [1844] 1 Jo & Lat 352 .... 98.2
O'Brien, Re (1977) 77 DLR (3d) 397 .... 50.13
O'Brien, Re, Little v O'Brien (1946) 115 LJ Ch 340, 90 Sol Jo 528, 175 LT 406, 62 TLR 594 .... 41.14, 64.54
O'Brien, Re, O'Brien v O'Brien [1906] 1 IR 649, 40 ILT 93, Ir CA 38.10, 63.1
O'Brien, Re, Prytz v Trustees, Executors and Agency Co Ltd (1898) 24 VLR 360 .... 94.30, 94.45
O'Brien v Condon [1905] 1 IR 51, 38 ILT 252 .... 9.4, 36.9, 36.13
O'Brien v O'Brien [1896] 2 IR 459, Ir CA 67.4
O'Brien's Goods, Re [1900] P 208, 69 LJP 55 .... 11.4
O'Callaghan v Coady (1912) 11 ELR 63 .... 44.8
Occleston v Fullalove (1874) 9 Ch App 147, 38 JP 196, 43 LJ Ch 297, 22 WR 305, 29 LT 785 .... 9.25, 51.7, 72.4
Ockley Estate, Re (1953) 10 WWRNS 282 .... 18.33
O'Connell v Shortland (1989) 51 SASR 337 .... 4.11, 4.12, 4.13, 4.15, 4.20
O'Connor, Re, Westminster Bank Ltd v O'Connor [1948] Ch 628, [1948] 2 All ER 270, [1948] LJR 1606, 92 Sol Jo 441 .... 30.2, 30.8
O'Connor v Minister of National Revenue [1943] 4 DLR 160, C Tax C 257, Ex CR 168 .... 33.1
O'Connor v O'Connor (1870) IR 4 Eq 483 .... 58.6, 64.26
O'Connor's Estate, Re [1942] 1 All ER 546, 86 Sol Jo 106, 166 LT 222 .... 1.5, 2.2, 2.8
O'Connor's Goods, Re (1884) 13 LR Ir 406 .... 18.9
Oddie v Brown (1859) 4 De G & J 179, 28 LJ Ch 542, 5 Jur NS 635, 7 WR 472, 33 LTOS 174 .... 53.2, 53.4, 93.2, 94.7
Oddie v Woodford (1821) 3 My & Cr 584; on appeal (1825) 3 My & Cr 625, HL 50.16, 53.1, 74.8, 74.9
Oddy, Re, Connell v Oddy (1910) 104 LT 128 .... 214.3
Odell v Crone. See Crone v Odell
O'Donnell v O'Donnell (1878) 1 LR Ir 284 .... 57.6
O'Donnell v Welsh [1903] 1 IR 115 .... 8.7
O'Donoghue v O'Donoghue [1906] 1 IR 482 .... 93.20
Offen v Harman (1859) 1 De GF & J 253, 29 LJ Ch 307, 6 Jur NS 487, 8 WR 129, 1 LT 315 .... 40.6
Offiler, Re, Offiler v Offiler (1901) 83 LT 758 .... 68.6
Ofner, Re, Samuel v Ofner [1909] 1 Ch 60, 78 LJ Ch 50, [1908–10] All ER Rep 851, 99 LT 813, CA 57.18, 57.22, 58.2, 58.11
Ogden, Re, Brydon v Samuel [1933] Ch 678, [1933] All ER Rep 720, 102 LJ Ch 226, 77 Sol Jo 216, 149 LT 162, 49 TLR 341 .... 9.35, 53.6, 102.11
Ogilby, Re, Cochrane v Ogilby [1903] 1 IR 525 .... 30.24
Ogilby, Re, Ogilby v Wentworth-Stanley [1942] Ch 288, [1942] 1 All ER 524, 111 LJ Ch 169, 86 Sol Jo 132, 167 LT 65, 58 TLR 209 .... 64.44, 104.4
Ogilvie, Re, Ogilvie v Ogilvie [1918] 1 Ch 492, 87 LJ Ch 363, 118 LT 749 .... 24.9, 24.10, 42.4, 42.15

Ogle v Knipe (1869) LR 8 Eq 434, 38 LJ Ch 692, 17 WR 1090, 20 LT 867 .... 64.35, 64.53
Ogle v Morgan (1852) 1 De GM & G 359 .... 30.24, 30.25
O'Grady v Wilmot [1916] 2 AC 231, 85 LJ Ch 386, 60 Sol Jo 456, 32 TLR 456, sub nom Re O'Grady, O'Grady v Wilmot 114 LT 1097, [1916–17] All ER Rep Ext 1385, HL 24.12, 39.5, 55.7
O'Hanlon v Unthank (1872) IR 7 Eq 68 .... 84.2
O'Higgins v Walsh [1918] 1 IR 126 .... 31.1, 35.39
Ohorodnyk, Re (1979) 97 DLR (3d) 502, 24 OR (2d) 228; affd (1980) 102 DLR (3d) 576, 26 OR (2d) 704 .... 2.6, 57.3, 83.9
Oke v Heath (1748) 1 Ves Sen 135 .... 47.8, 47.38
Old's Trusts, Re, Pengelley v Herbert (1886) 54 LT 677 .... 38.2
Oldham, Re, Hadwen v Myles [1925] Ch 75, 95 LJ Ch 148, [1924] All ER Rep 288, 69 Sol Jo 193, 132 LT 658 .... 2.3, 2.5, 2.6, 2.9, 2.10, 3.13
Oldham, Re, Oldham v Myles [1927] WN 113, 71 Sol Jo 491 .... 38.26
Oldham v Oldham (1867) LR 3 Eq 404, 36 LJ Ch 205, 15 WR 300 .... 99.8
Olding's Goods, Re (1814) 2 Curt 865, 1 Notes of Cases 169 .... 12.5
Oldroyd v Harvey [1907] P 326, 76 LJP 161, 98 LT 56, 23 TLR 729 .... 1.2, 10.1, 14.8
O'Leary v Douglass (1878) 1 LR Ir 45; revsd (1879) 3 LR Ir 323, CA ... 5.7, 18.8, 18.10, 57.30
Oliphant's Goods, Re (1860) 24 JP 231, 30 LJPM & A 82, 6 Jur NS 256, 1 Sw & Tr 525, 1 LT 446 .... 25.2
Oliphant's Trusts, Re, Re Dixon's Will, Phillips v Phelps (1916) 86 LJ Ch 452, 116 LT 115 .... 40.21, 94.48
Olivant v Wright (1875) 1 Ch D 346, 45 LJ Ch 1, 24 WR 84, 33 LT 457, CA 97.6
Olive, Re, Olive v Westerman (1884) 53 LJ Ch 525, 32 WR 608, 50 LT 355 .... 32.12
Oliver, Re, Newbald v Beckitt (1890) 62 LT 533 .... 34.4, 91.2
Oliver, Re, Theobald v Oliver [1927] 2 Ch 323, 96 LJ Ch 496, 71 Sol Jo 710, 137 LT 788 .... 30.37, 30.38
Oliver, Re, Wilson v Oliver [1908] 2 Ch 74, 77 LJ Ch 547, 99 LT 241 .... 38.25
Oliver v Oliver (1871) LR 11 Eq 506, 40 LJ Ch 189, 19 WR 432, 24 LT 350 .... 30.8, 41.16
Oliver v Oliver [1958] ALR 609, 32 ALJR 198, HC of A 92.4
Oliver's Settlement, Re, Evered v Leigh [1905] 1 Ch 191, 74 LJ Ch 62, 53 WR 215, 21 TLR 61 .... 42.4
Olliver's Goods, Re (1854) 2 Ecc & Ad 57 .... 12.12
Olney v Bates (1855) 3 Drew 319, 3 WR 606, 26 LTOS 35 .... 47.12, 47.33, 66.6
O'Loughlin v Bellew [1906] 1 IR 487 .... 72.2
O'Loughlin's Goods, Re (1870) LR 2 P & D 102, 39 LJP & M 53, 18 WR 902 .... 64.17
Olson v Olson [1988] 6 WWR 631 .... 14.1
Olszanecki v Hillocks [2002] EWHC 1997 (Ch), [2004] WTLR 975, [2002] All ER (D) 68 (Aug) 34.4, 35.21
O'Mahoney v Burdett (1874) LR 7 HL 388, 44 LJ Ch 56n, 23 WR 361, 31 LT 705 .... 48.15, 96.7, 97.1, 97.5, 97.6
O'Meagher v O'Meagher (1883) 11 LR Ir 117 .... 11.24, 12.7, 13.2, 14.9
Ommanney v Butcher (1823) Turn & R 260, [1814–23] All ER Rep 154 ..... 64.35, 64.36
O'Mullane, Re, Davidson v O'Mullane [1955] ALR 736, [1955] VLR 217 ... 64.58, 82.7, 86.5, 99.2

O'Neil v Royal Trust Co and McClure [1946] SCR 622, 4 DLR 545 .... 4.15, 4.20
O'Neill v M'Grorty [1915] 1 IR 1 .... 31.14
O'Neill's Goods, Re (1916) 50 ILT 180 .... 12.5, 12.11
Ongley v Chambers (1824) 1 Bing 483, 2 LJOSCP 49, 8 Moore CP 665 .... 64.2
Ongley v Peale. See Ungly v Peale
Onions v Tyrer. See Onyons v Tryers
Onofrichuk, Re, Onofrichuk v Onofrichuk [1974] 2 WWR 469 .... 4.15
Onslow, Re, Plowden v Gayford (1888) 39 Ch D 622, 57 LJ Ch 940, 36 WR 883, 59 LT 308 .... 83.16
Onyons v Tryers (1716) Gilb Ch 130, Prec Ch 459, sub nom Onions v Tyrer 1 P Wms 343, 2 Vern 741 .... 18.5, 18.17, 19.3
Oppenheim, Re, Oppenheim v Oppenheim (1914) 58 Sol Jo 723, 111 LT 937 .... 63.1
Oppenheim v Henry (1853) 9 Hare 802n, 1 WR 126, 20 LTOS 291 .... 25.15, 57.5
Oppenheim v Henry (1853) 9 Hare 803n, 10 Hare 441, 1 WR 126, 20 LTOS 291 .... 50.15, 66.5, 93.27
Oppenheim v Tobacco Securities Trust Co Ltd [1951] AC 297, [1951] 1 All ER 31, [1951] 1 TLR 118, HL 102.8, 102.10, 102.15
Oppenheim's Will Trusts, Re, Westminster Bank Ltd v Oppenheim [1950] Ch 633, [1950] 2 All ER 86, 66 (pt 1) TLR 1040 .... 9.45, 99.4
Oram, Re, Oram v Oram [1940] Ch 1001, [1940] 4 All ER 161, 109 LJ Ch 427, 84 Sol Jo 549, 164 LT 264 .... 100.5
Orchard, Re, Carpenter v Lauer [1948] 1 All ER 203, 92 Sol Jo 97, 64 TLR 144 .... 34.21
Ord, Re, Dickinson v Dickinson (1879) 12 Ch D 22, 28 WR 141, 41 LT 13, CA 33.13, 59.1, 59.2, 59.3
Ord v Ord (1866) LR 2 Eq 393, 15 LT 51 .... 91.5
O'Reilly v Smith (1851) 17 LTOS 280 .... 60.1
O'Reilly v Walsh (1872) 6 IR Eq 555; affd (1872) 7 IR Eq 167 .... 93.22
Orford v Orford [1903] 1 IR 121, 37 ILT 119 .... 47.32
Orlebar, Re, Orlebar v Orlebar [1936] Ch 147, 105 LJ Ch 92, [1935] All ER Rep 502, 154 LT 293 .... 35.28
Orles and Kruger v R (1958) 38 Sask LR 38 .... 4.21
Ormiston's Executor v Laws 1966 SC 47, 1966 SLT 110 .... 34.1
Orpen, Re, Beswick v Orpen (1880) 16 Ch D 202, 50 LJ Ch 25, 29 WR 467, 43 LT 728 .... 30.13
Orr, Re [1940] SASR 395 .... 35.30
Orr, Re, M'Dermott v Anderson [1915] 1 IR 191 .... 62.1, 82.4
Orr v Kaines (1750) 2 Ves Sen 194 .... 31.9
Orrell v Orrell (1871) 6 Ch App 302, 40 LJ Ch 539, 19 WR 370, 24 LT 245 .... 24.10, 42.2, 42.15
Orton's Trust, Re (1866) LR 3 Eq 375, 36 LJ Ch 279, 15 WR 251, 16 LT 146 .... 68.11, 87.3
Orwell's Will Trusts, Re, Dixon v Blair [1982] 3 All ER 177, [1982] 1 WLR 1337, 126 Sol Jo 593 .... 25.5
Osborne v Estate of Osborne (2001–02) 4 ITELR 804, Vic CA 2.4, 2.6
Osborne v Rowlett (1880) 13 Ch D 774, 49 LJ Ch 310, 28 WR 365, 42 LT 650 .... 49.9
Osborne v Smith (1960) 105 CLR 153, [1961] ALR 831, 34 ALJR 368 (Aust HC) 5.7

Osburn, Re (1969) 113 Sol Jo 387, CA 64.50
Oseland v Oseland (1795) 3 Anst 628 .... 93.27
O'Shea, Re [1953] VLR 43 .... 64.18, 64.39
Osmond, Re, Cummings v Gallaway (1911) 30 NZLR 65 .... 93.6, 93.30
Osoba, Re, Osoba v Osoba [1978] 2 All ER 1099, [1978] 1 WLR 791, 122 Sol Jo 402; varied [1979] 2 All ER 393, [1979] 1 WLR 247, 123 Sol Jo 35, CA 23.17, 23.18, 82.7, 104.14
Ostrom v Bendall and Ostrom (1956) 5 DLR (2d) 419, 19 WWR 535 .... 83.9
Oswald, Re, Oswald v Oswald (1919) 64 Sol Jo 242 .... 29.4, 30.33
Oswald's Goods, Re (1874) LR 3 P & D 162, 38 JP 425, 43 LJP & M 24, 30 LT 344 .... 5.7, 18.8
Oswell, Re (1982) 136 DLR (3d) 672 .... 93.28
O'Toole v Browne (1854) 3 E & B 572, 23 LJQB 282, 18 Jur 1113, 2 WR 430, 2 CLR 1701, 23 LTOS 111 .... 60.2, 64.19
Ott, Re (1972) 24 DLR (3d) 517 .... 19.3
Ottaway v Norman [1972] Ch 698, [1971] 3 All ER 1325, [1972] 2 WLR 50, 116 Sol Jo 38, 220 Estates Gazette 1434 .... 2.8, 36.2
Ottewell, Re. See Tottrup v Patterson
Ottey v Grundy [2002] EWCA Civ 1176, [2003] WTLR 1253 .... 43.1
Ousby v Harvey (1848) 17 LJ Ch 160 .... 84.4
Ouseley v Anstruther (1847) 10 Beav 453 .... 64.27
Outerbridge v Hollis [1951] WN 318, PC 67.2
Overand (otherwise Overend) Estate, Re (1963) 42 WWR 625 .... 20.3
Overbury, Re, Sheppard v Matthews [1955] Ch 122, [1954] 3 All ER 308, [1954] 3 WLR 644, 98 Sol Jo 768 .... 72.8
Overend v Gurney (1834) 7 Sim 128 .... 91.6
Overhill's Trusts, Re, Re Trustee Relief Act (1853) 22 LJ Ch 485, 17 Jur 342, 1 Sm & G 362, 1 WR 208, 20 LTOS 290 .... 57.3, 57.15, 57.20
Overton v Banister (1841) 4 Beav 205 .... 87.2
Ovey, Re, Broadbent v Barrow (1882) 51 LJ Ch 665, CA 38.3
Ovey, Re, Broadbent v Barrow (1885) 29 Ch D 560, 54 LJ Ch 752, 33 WR 821, 52 LT 849, 1 TLR 401 .... 103.3, 103.5
Owen, Re [1894] 3 Ch 220, 63 LJ Ch 749, 8 R 566, 43 WR 55, 38 Sol Jo 617, 71 LT 181 .... 30.39
Owen, Re, Hodgson v Clare [2002] WTLR 619 .... 57.23
Owen, Re, Peat v Owen (1898) 78 LT 643 .... 64.3
Owen, Re, Slater v Owen [1912] 1 Ch 519, 81 LJ Ch 337, 56 Sol Jo 381, 106 LT 671 .... 38.21
Owen v Bryant (1852) 2 De GM & G 697, 21 LJ Ch 860, 16 Jur 877, 20 LTOS 45 .... 72.2
Owen v Peacock. See Peacock's Estate, Re
Owen v Penny (1850) 14 Jur 359 .... 79.1
Owen's Trusts, Re (1871) LR 12 Eq 316, 25 LT 489 .... 85.3
Owens Estate, Re (1956) 2 DLR (2d) 144, 18 WWR 43 .... 18.10, 19.4
Owers, Re, Public Trustee v Death [1941] Ch 17, [1940] 4 All ER 225, 110 LJ Ch 22, 84 Sol Jo 633, 164 LT 337, 57 TLR 80, CA 55.7, 210.3, 214.17, 214.64
Owston's Goods, Re (1862) 26 JP 728, 31 LJPM & A 177, 2 Sw & Tr 461, 10 WR 410, 6 LT 368 .... 5.2, 11.24

Oxford Group v IRC [1949] 2 All ER 537, 31 TC 221, 28 ATC 204, 42 R & IT 438, [1949] TR 281, 93 Sol Jo 525, L(TC) 1495, CA 102.9, 102.24

P

Packard, Re, Packard v Waters [1920] 1 Ch 596, 89 LJ Ch 301, 123 LT 401 .... 34.22
Packe, Re, Campion v A-G. See Packe, Re, Sanders v A-G
Packe, Re, Sanders v A-G [1918] 1 Ch 437, 87 LJ Ch 300, 62 Sol Jo 488, 118 LT 693; on appeal sub nom Re Packe, Campion v A-G (1918) 145 LT Jo 111, CA 103.6, 103.11
Packer v Scott (1864) 33 Beav 511 .... 94.3
Packham v Gregory (1845) 4 Hare 396, 14 LJ Ch 191, 9 Jur 175 .... 93.28
Padbury v Clark (1850) 19 LJ Ch 533, 2 H & Tw 341, 2 Mac & G 298 .... 42.12
Padgham v Rochelle [2002] WTLR 1483, [2002] 38 LS Gaz R 36 .... 5.9
Page, Re, Jones v Morgan [1893] 1 Ch 304, 62 LJ Ch 592, 3 R 171, 41 WR 357 .... 30.38
Page v Hayward (1705) 2 Eq Cas Abr 362, 11 Mod Rep 61, 2 Salk 570, Holt KB 618 .... 34.1, 34.3, 35.6
Page v Leapingwell (1812) 18 Ves 463 .... 30.3, 31.4
Page v Soper (1853) 11 Hare 321, 22 LJ Ch 1044, 1 Eq Rep 540, 17 Jur 851, 1 WR 518 .... 83.16
Page v Young (1875) LR 19 Eq 501, 23 WR 479 .... 38.1
Paget, Re, Mellor v Mellor [1898] 1 Ch 290, 67 LJ Ch 151, 46 WR 328, 78 LT 72 .... 40.9
Paget's Goods, Re (1913) 47 ILT 284 .... 18.28
Paget's Settled Estates, Re (1885) 30 Ch D 161, 55 LJ Ch 42, 33 WR 898, 53 LT 90, 1 TLR 567 .... 35.28, 83.6
Paice v Archbishop of Canterbury (1807) 14 Ves 364 .... 82.7, 202.5
Paige v Brooks (1896) 75 LT 455 .... 18.15, 18.19
Paine v Countess of Warwick [1914] 2 KB 486, sub nom White v Paine 83 LJKB 895, 58 Sol Jo 381, 30 TLR 347 .... 8.4
Paine v Hall (1812) 18 Ves 475 .... 36.3
Paine v Hyde (1841) 4 Beav 468 .... 34.25
Paine v Jones (1874) LR 18 Eq 320, 43 LJ Ch 787, 22 WR 837, 30 LT 779 .... 43.3
Paine v Wagner (1841) 12 Sim 184 .... 85.3, 87.1
Painton v Berry, etc (Administrators of Thornton). See Peyton v Bury
Paithouski, Re (1976) 71 DLR (3d) 60 .... 83.9
Palfreeman, Re, Public Trustee v Palfreeman [1914] 1 Ch 877, [1914–15] All ER Rep Ext 1541, 83 LJ Ch 702, 58 Sol Jo 456, 110 LT 972 .... 32.5, 32.10, 210.23
Palin v Brooks (1878) 48 LJ Ch 191, 26 WR 877 .... 30.8
Palin v Ponting [1930] P 185, 99 LJP 121, 74 Sol Jo 234, 46 TLR 310, sub nom Paling v Ponting 143 LT 23 .... 11.3
Paling v Ponting. See Palin v Ponting
Palmer, ex p (1852) 5 De G & Sm 649, 17 Jur 108 .... 34.23
Palmer (a debtor), Re [1994] Ch 316, [1994] 3 All ER 835, [1994] 3 WLR 420, [1995] 1 FCR 320, [1994] 2 FLR 609, [1994] Fam Law 566, 138 Sol Jo LB 72, CA 241.26

Palmer, Re, National Provincial Bank Ltd v Barwell [1945] Ch 8, [1944] 2 All ER 406, 114 LJ Ch 17, 88 Sol Jo 398, 171 LT 316, 61 TLR 34, CA 64.53
Palmer, Re, Palmer v Answorth [1893] 3 Ch 369, 62 LJ Ch 988, 2 R 619, 42 WR 151, 37 Sol Jo 701, 69 LT 477, CA 20.5, 38.13, 50.21
Palmer, Re, Palmer v Clarke (1894) 13 R 220 ..... 30.11
Palmer, Re, Palmer v Palmer [1916] 2 Ch 391, 85 LJ Ch 577, 60 Sol Jo 565, 115 LT 57, CA 30.31
Palmer v Bank of New South Wales (1975) 133 CLR 150, 7 ALR 671 (Aust HC) 3.8
Palmer v Craufurd (1819) 2 Wils Ch 79, 3 Swan 483 ..... 33.6
Palmer v Crutwell (1862) 8 Jur NS 479 ..... 87.2, 87.3
Palmer v Fleshees (1663) 1 Keb 625, 1 Sid 167, sub nom Palmer v Fletcher 1 Lev 122 ..... 61.1
Palmer v Fletcher. See Palmer v Fleshees
Palmer v Flower (1871) LR 13 Eq 250, 41 LJ Ch 193, 20 WR 174, 25 LT 816 ..... 82.7
Palmer v Holford (1828) 4 Russ 403, 6 LJOS Ch 104 ..... 94.5, 94.21
Palmer v Locke (1880) 15 Ch D 294, 50 LJ Ch 113, 28 WR 926, 43 LT 454, CA 3.14, 40.10
Palmer v Newell (1855) 20 Beav 32, 24 LJ Ch 424, 1 Jur NS 924, 3 WR 333, 25 LTOS 41; affd (1856) 8 De GM & G 74, 25 LJ Ch 461, 2 Jur NS 268, 4 WR 346, 27 LTOS 7 ..... 44.9
Palmer v Orpen [1894] 1 IR 32 ..... 50.9, 66.1
Palmer v Palmer (1886) 18 LR Ir 192 ..... 81.2
Palmer and Brown v Dent (1850) 2 Rob Eccl 284, 7 Notes of Cases 555 ..... 4.10
Palmer's Goods, Re, Palmer v Peat (1889) 58 LJP 44 ..... 18.10
Pankhurst v Howell (1870) 6 Ch App 136, 19 WR 312 ..... 44.2, 44.8
Panter, Re, Panter-Downes v Bally (1906) 22 TLR 431 ..... 93.4
Pape Estate, Re (1946) 4 DLR 700, [1946] 3 WWR 8 ..... 35.46
Papijans v Gudowski [1963] Tas SR 183 ..... 4.20
Papillon v Voice (1728) 1 Eq Cas Abr 185, Kel W 27, 2 P Wms 471, Fitz-G 38; affd (1728) Kel W 34, 2 P Wms 478 ..... 49.1
Papillon (decd), Re; Murrin v Matthews [2006] EWHC 3419 (Ch), [2006] All ER (D) 297 (Dec) 5.4, 13.1
Paramour v Yardley (1579) 2 Plowd 539 ..... 52.7
Pare v Cusson (1921) 60 DLR 105, 31 Man R 197, [1921] 2 WWR 8 ..... 4.15
Parfitt v Lawless (1872) LR 2 P & D 462, 36 JP 822, 41 LJP & M 68, 21 WR 200, 27 LT 215 ..... 5.9
Parfitt's Goods, Re (1842) 1 Notes of Cases 533 ..... 14.9
Parish, Re (1964) 42 DLR (2d) 212, [1964] 1 OR 353 ..... 64.8, 87.2
Parish v Sharman [2001] WTLR 593 ..... 105.9
Park, Re, Bott v Chester [1910] 2 Ch 322, 79 LJ Ch 502, 54 Sol Jo 563, 102 LT 725 ..... 20.4, 22.3, 34.19, 35.6, 35.12, 35.13
Park, Re, Public Trustee v Armstrong [1932] 1 Ch 580, 101 LJ Ch 295, [1931] All ER Rep 633, 147 LT 118 ..... 1.6, 39.31, 40.5
Parker, Re (1982) 139 DLR (3d) 292 ..... 9.9, 64.38
Parker, Re, Ballarat Trustees, Executors and Agency Co Ltd v Parker [1949] ALR 545, [1949] VLR 133 ..... 102.23
Parker, Re, Barker v Barker (1880) 16 Ch D 44 ..... 93.36, 93.37, 210.47, 210.49

Parker, Re, Bentham v Wilson (1881) 17 Ch D 262, 50 LJ Ch 639, 29 WR 855, 44 LT 885, CA 57.20, 71.4
Parker, Re, Parker v Osborne [1897] 2 Ch 208, 66 LJ Ch 509, 45 WR 536, 76 LT 421 .... 50.3, 51.4
Parker, Re, Stephenson v Parker [1901] 1 Ch 408, 70 LJ Ch 170, 49 WR 215, 45 Sol Jo 219, 84 LT 116 .... 38.14
Parker v Birks (1854) 1 K & J 156, 24 LJ Ch 117, 3 WR 102 .... 98.13
Parker v Clark [1960] 1 All ER 93, [1960] 1 WLR 286, 104 Sol Jo 251 .... 3.3, 3.4
Parker v Dowling (1916) 16 SRNSW 234, 33 WNNSW 75 .... 44.11
Parker v Felgate (1883) 8 PD 171, 47 JP 808, 52 LJP 95, 32 WR 186 ..... 4.9, 4.10, 4.17, 5.1, 11.21
Parker v Golding (1843) 13 Sim 418 .... 93.36
Parker v Hodgson (1861) 1 Drew & Sm 568, 30 LJ Ch 590, 7 Jur NS 750, 9 WR 607, 4 LT 762 .... 93.44, 93.45
Parker v Marchant (1842) 1 Y & C Ch Cas 290, 11 LJ Ch 223, 6 Jur 292, [1843–60] All ER Rep 1061; affd (1843) 1 Ph 356, 12 LJ Ch 385, [1843–60] All ER Rep 1061 .... 30.23, 38.3, 38.10, 50.12, 64.15, 64.25, 64.40
Parker v Nickson (1863) 1 De GJ & Sm 177, 32 LJ Ch 397, 9 Jur NS 451, 1 New Rep 298, 11 WR 533, 7 LT 813 .... 84.2
Parker v Parker (1841) Milw 541 .... 11.21, 11.24
Parker v Parker (1863) 1 New Rep 508 .... 83.6
Parker v Sowerby (1853) 1 Drew 488, 22 LJ Ch 942, 1 Eq Rep 217, 17 Jur 752, 1 WR 404; affd (1854) 4 De GM & G 321, 23 LJ Ch 623, 2 Eq Rep 664, 18 Jur 523, 2 WR 547 .... 93.4, 93.30
Parker v Tootal (1865) 11 HL Cas 143, 34 LJ Ex 198, 11 Jur NS 185, 5 New Rep 378, 13 WR 442, 12 LT 89 .... 50.16, 52.3, 98.3, 101.1
Parker's Goods, Re (1860) 24 JP 199, 31 LJPM & A 8, 6 Jur NS 354, 1 Sw & Tr 523, 1 LT 447 .... 47.12
Parker's Will, Re (1888) 39 Ch D 303, 58 LJ Ch 23, 37 WR 313, 60 LT 83, 4 TLR 740, CA 30.41
Parker-Jervis, Re, Salt v Locker [1898] 2 Ch 643, 67 LJ Ch 682, 47 WR 147, 79 LT 403 .... 33.47, 211.13
Parkes (or Keswick) v Parkes (or Keswick) [1936] 3 All ER 653, HL 93.1, 93.2
Parkes, Re, Cottrell v Parkes (1909) 25 TLR 523 .... 103.3
Parkin, Re, Hill v Schwarz [1892] 3 Ch 510, 62 LJ Ch 55, 3 R 9, 41 WR 120, 36 Sol Jo 647, 67 LT 77 .... 3.14, 40.15
Parkin v Hodgkinson (1846) 15 Sim 293 .... 97.10
Parkin v Knight (1846) 15 Sim 83, 15 LJ Ch 209, 10 Jur 23, 6 LTOS 450 ..... 56.5, 68.1, 93.12
Parkinson's Trust, Re, ex p Thompson (1851) 1 Sim NS 242, 20 LJ Ch 224, 15 Jur 165 .... 79.1, 79.2
Parnell, Re, Ranks v Holmes [1944] Ch 107, 113 LJ Ch 92, 88 Sol Jo 25, 170 LT 40, 60 TLR 154 .... 38.14, 47.9
Parnell v Boyd [1896] 2 IR 571 .... 46.3, 82.3, 83.2
Parnell Estate, Re [1924] 1 DLR 15, 34 Man LR 41, [1924] 1 WWR 1 .... 53.2
Parnell's Goods, Re (1872) LR 2 P & D 379, 36 JP 376, 41 LJP & M 35, 20 WR 494, 26 LT 744 .... 28.9
Parnham's Trusts, Re (1876) 46 LJ Ch 80 .... 99.4, 99.10
Parr v Parr (1833) 1 My & K 647, 2 LJ Ch 167 .... 50.11, 50.13, 66.6
Parr v Swindels (1828) 4 Russ 283, 6 LJOS Ch 99 .... 98.4

Parr's Goods, Re (1859) Sea & Sm 146, 29 LJPM & A 70, 6 Jur NS 56 .... 14.6, 19.4
Parr's Trusts, Re (1871) 41 LJ Ch 170 .... 93.1
Parrott, Re, Cox v Parrott [1946] Ch 183, [1946] 1 All ER 321, 115 LJ Ch 211, 90 Sol Jo 139, 175 LT 190, 62 TLR 189 .... 34.7, 34.11, 35.40
Parrott, Re, Parrott v Parrott (1885) 53 LT 12 .... 38.10, 64.23
Parrott, Re, Walter v Parrott (1886) 33 Ch D 274, 34 WR 553, 55 LT 132, CA 74.1
Parrott v Worsford (1820) 1 Jac & W 594 .... 30.8
Parry, Re, Brown v Parry [1947] Ch 23, [1946] 2 All ER 412, [1947] LJR 81, 90 Sol Jo 478, 175 LT 395, 62 TLR 543 .... 38.21
Parry, Re, Dalton v Cooke [1969] 2 All ER 512, [1969] 1 WLR 614, 113 Sol Jo 228 .... 30.15, 35.49, 210.52, 232.67, 237.11
Parry, Re, Leak v Scott [1888] WN 179, 4 TLR 696 .... 77.2
Parry, Re, Powell v Parry (1889) 60 LT 489 .... 95.13
Parry, Re, Scott v Leak (1889) 42 Ch D 570, 38 WR 226, 61 LT 380 .... 33.24
Parry v Roberts (1871) 19 WR 1000, 25 LT 371 .... 34.24, 35.19, 35.25
Parry and Daggs, Re (1885) 31 Ch D 130, 55 LJ Ch 237, 34 WR 353, 54 LT 229, CA 97.5
Parson, Re (1968) 67 DLR (2d) 685, [1968] 1 OR 785 .... 62.1
Parsons, Re, Borman v Lel [2002] WTLR 237 .... 11.13
Parsons, Re, Parsons v A-G [1942] Ch 335, [1942] 1 All ER 631, 86 Sol Jo 202, 166 LT 357, 58 TLR 28; affd [1943] Ch 12, [1942] 2 All ER 496, 86 Sol Jo 359, 167 LT 384, 59 TLR 19, CA 46.5
Parsons, Re, Stockley v Parsons (1890) 45 Ch D 51, 59 LJ Ch 666, 38 WR 712, 62 LT 929 .... 7.20
Parsons v Coke (1858) 27 LJ Ch 828, 6 WR 715 .... 41.5, 82.7
Parsons v Coke (1858) 4 Drew 296 .... 85.3, 85.5
Parsons v Lanoe (1748) Amb 557, 1 Wils 243, 1 Ves Sen 189 .... 1.5
Parsons v Parsons (1869) LR 8 Eq 260, 17 WR 1005 .... 33.1, 33.12
Parsons v Saffery (1821) 9 Price 578 .... 47.32
Parsons' Estates, Borman v Lel [2002] WTLR 237 .... 4.13
Partington v A-G. See A-G v Partington
Parton, Re, Parton v Parton (1911) 131 LT Jo 106 .... 9.40
Partriche v Powlet (1740) 2 Atk 54, West temp Hard 4 .... 7.3
Partridge v Baylis (1881) 17 Ch D 835, 29 WR 820, 44 LT 737 .... 97.8
Partridge v Foster (No 2) (1866) 35 Beav 545 .... 93.8
Partridge v Partridge (1736) 2 Eq Cas Abr 570, Cas temp Talb 226, 9 Mod Rep 269 .... 41.13
Partridge v Partridge [1894] 1 Ch 351, 63 LJ Ch 122, 70 LT 261 .... 34.24, 35.19, 35.25, 35.39
Pashak Estate, Re [1923] 1 DLR 1130, [1923] 1 WWR 873 .... 34.13
Paskins' Will Trusts, Re, Paskins v Underwood [1948] 2 All ER 156, 92 Sol Jo 377 .... 35.19
Pasmore v Huggins (1855) 21 Beav 103, 25 LJ Ch 251, 1 Jur NS 1060, 4 WR 33, 26 LTOS 66 .... 74.1
Passant v Jackson [1985] STC 133, 59 TC 230, [1985] LS Gaz R 124; affd [1986] STC 164, 59 TC 230, [1986] LS Gaz R 876, CA 209.4, 220.72
Passingham v Sherborn (1846) 9 Beav 424 .... 27.3
Passmore Estate, Re (1964) 49 WWR 588 .... 33.25
Patane, Re [1957] QSR 529 .... 83.11

Patch v Graves (1855) 3 Drew 347 .... 18.15
Patch v Shore (1862) 2 Drew & Sm 589, 32 LJ Ch 185, 9 Jur NS 63, 1 New Rep 157, 11 WR 142, 7 LT 554 .... 10.6, 38.2
Patching v Barnett [1907] 2 Ch 154n, 51 LJ Ch 74, 45 LT 292, [1881–5] All ER Rep Ext 1761, CA 34.22
Paton v Ormerod [1892] P 247, 61 LJP 120, 66 LT 381 .... 15.1, 18.14, 21.2, 21.7
Paton's Trustees v Paton 1947 SC 250 .... 78.1
Patrick v Yeathered (1864) 33 LJ Ch 286, 3 New Rep 367, 12 WR 304, 10 LT 92 .... 64.35
Patrick's Estate, Re, Patrick v De Zeeuw [2000] NI 506 .... 104.9
Patten, Re, Westminster Bank v Carlyon [1929] 2 Ch 276, 98 LJ Ch 419, [1929] All ER Rep 416, 141 LT 295, 45 TLR 504 .... 35.28, 83.6
Patten v Poulton (1858) 22 JP 180, 27 LJP & M 41, 4 Jur NS 341, 1 Sw & Tr 55, 6 WR 458, 31 LTOS 40 .... 18.27, 18.29
Pattenden v Hobson (1853) 22 LJ Ch 697, 1 Eq Rep 28, 17 Jur 406, 1 WR 282, 21 LTOS 84 .... 78.4
Patterson, Re [1940] 1 DLR 802 .... 64.37
Patterson, Re, Dunlop v Greer [1899] 1 IR 324 .... 50.2, 79.4, 101.9
Patterson v Benbow (1889) 7 NZLR 673 .... 11.26
Patterson v Huddart (1853) 17 Beav 210, 1 WR 423 .... 64.19
Patterson Estate, Re (1958) 66 Man R 416 .... 76.1, 98.7
Patterson's Estate, Re, Mitchell v Smith (1864) 4 De GJ & Sm 422, 33 LJ Ch 596, 4 New Rep 310, 12 WR 941, 10 LT 801 .... 10.10
Patterson's Goods, Re (1898) 79 LT 123 .... 16.3
Pattie v Fry (1911) 30 NZLR 581 .... 13.3
Pattison v Pattison (1832) 1 My & K 12, 2 LJ Ch 15 .... 20.4, 41.11
Pattison v Pattison (1855) 19 Beav 638 .... 66.5, 87.1, 101.9
Pattison's Goods, Re, Henderson v Priestman [1918] 2 IR 90 .... 11.27
Patton, Re [1929] 3 DLR 459, 63 OLR 655 .... 54.2
Patton, Re (1971) 19 DLR (3d) 497, [1971] 3 OR 85 .... 50.15
Patton v Toronto General Trusts Corpn [1930] AC 629, 143 LT 572, sub nom Re Patton, Patton v Toronto General Trusts Corpn 99 LJPC 213, PC 35.30
Patulla Estate, Re (1955) 17 WWR 666 .... 14.6
Paul, Re, Public Trustee v Pearce [1921] 2 Ch 1, 90 LJ Ch 446, 125 LT 566 .... 17.5, 94.48, 94.49
Paul v Children (1871) LR 12 Eq 16, 19 WR 941, 25 LT 82 .... 72.2
Paul v Hewetson (1833) 2 My & K 434 .... 83.17
Paul's Settlement Trusts, Re, Paul v Nelson [1920] 1 Ch 99, 88 LJ Ch 530, 63 Sol Jo 724, 121 LT 544 .... 39.5, 66.13
Pauling's Settlement Trusts, Re, Younghusband v Coutts & Co [1964] Ch 303, [1963] 3 All ER 1, [1963] 3 WLR 742, 107 Sol Jo 492, CA 218.100
Pawlet v Dogget (1688) 2 Vern 86 .... 98.11
Pawson v Pawson (1854) 19 Beav 146, 23 LJ Ch 954, 2 WR 321 .... 33.12
Paxton's Trustees v Cowie (1886) 13 R 1191, 23 SLR 830 .... 86.5
Paykel v Guardian Trust and Executors Co of New Zealand Ltd [1963] NZLR 168 .... 39.22, 39.25, 57.22
Payling's Will Trusts, Re, Armstrong v Payling [1969] 3 All ER 698, [1969] 1 WLR 1595, 113 Sol Jo 776 .... 102.7
Paylor v Pegg (1857) 24 Beav 105 .... 91.4, 93.8
Payne, Re (1858) 25 Beav 556 .... 65.1, 99.3

Payne, Re, Poplett v A-G [1940] Ch 576, [1940] 2 All ER 115, 109 LJ Ch 369, 84 Sol Jo 287, 163 LT 100, 56 TLR 525 .... 55.7
Payne, Re, Westminster Bank Ltd v Payne [1943] 2 All ER 675, 113 LJ Ch 46, 87 Sol Jo 406, 169 LT 365, 60 TLR 49 .... 38.17, 216.36
Payne v Federal Comr of Taxation (1935) 51 CLR 197 .... 30.43
Payne v Webb (1874) LR 19 Eq 26, 23 WR 43, 31 LT 637 .... 87.1
Payne and Meredith v Trappes (1847) 1 Rob Eccl 583, 11 Jur 854, 10 LTOS 36, 5 Notes of Cases 478 .... 21.7
Payne's Estate, Re [1935] 1 DLR 474, [1934] 3 WWR 631 .... 25.15
Peace v Hains (1853) 11 Hare 151, 17 Jur 1091 .... 45.2
Peacock, Re [1958] NZLR 374 .... 52.6
Peacock, Re, Midland Bank Executor and Trustee Co Ltd v Peacock [1957] Ch 310, [1957] 2 All ER 98, [1957] 2 WLR 793, 101 Sol Jo 339 .... 9.17, 9.18, 47.29, 47.32
Peacock, Re, Public Trustee v Birchenough [1929] WN 76, 73 Sol Jo 220, 45 TLR 301 .... 30.25, 210.61
Peacock v Stockford (1853) 3 De GM & G 73 .... 52.2, 74.2
Peacock's Estate, Re (1872) LR 14 Eq 236, sub nom Owen v Peacock 27 LT 472 .... 44.4
Pearce, Re [1926] NZLR 698 .... 46.3
Pearce, Re [1946] SASR 118 .... 7.33
Pearce, Re, Alliance Assurance Co Ltd v Francis [1913] 2 Ch 674, 109 LT 514; affd [1914] 1 Ch 254, 83 LJ Ch 266, [1911–13] All ER Rep 1067, 58 Sol Jo 197, 110 LT 168, CA 9.25, 72.2, 72.3
Pearce, Re, Crutchley v Wells [1909] 1 Ch 819, 78 LJ Ch 484, 53 Sol Jo 419, 100 LT 699, 25 TLR 497, [1908–10] All ER Rep Ext 1323 .... 30.34
Pearce, Re, Eastwood v Pearce (1912) 56 Sol Jo 686, CA 68.1
Pearce, Re, Pearce v Davis Pearce [1999] 2 FCR 179, [1998] 2 FLR 705, [1998] Fam Law 588, CA 105.16
Pearce, Re, Roberts v Stephens (1894) 8 R 805 .... 41.5
Pearce v Carrington (1873) 8 Ch App 969, 42 LJ Ch 900, 22 WR 41, 29 LT 706 .... 73.1
Pearce v Edmeades (1838) 3 Y & C Ex 246, 8 LJ Ex Eq 61, 3 Jur 245 ... 86.5, 87.1, 87.2
Pearce v Graham (1863) 32 LJ Ch 359, 9 Jur NS 568, 1 New Rep 507, 11 WR 415, 8 LT 378 .... 47.13
Pearce v Vincent (1836) 2 Keen 230, Donnelly 128, 7 LJ Ch 285 .... 79.6
Peard v Kekewich (1852) 15 Beav 166, 21 LJ Ch 456, 19 LTOS 360 .... 93.4
Pearks v Moseley. See Moseley's Trusts, Re
Pearman v Pearman (1864) 33 Beav 394 .... 93.2, 93.35
Pearn's Goods, Re (1875) 1 PD 70, 39 JP 824, 45 LJP 31, 24 WR 143, 33 LT 705 .... 11.6
Pearsall v Simpson (1808) 15 Ves 29 .... 93.15
Pearse, Re, Genn v Pearse [1955] 1 DLR 801 .... 103.11
Pearse's Goods, Re (1867) LR 1 P & D 382, 31 JP 728, 36 LJP & M 117, 16 LT 853 .... 12.11
Pearson, Re, Rowling v Crowther [1963] 3 All ER 763, [1963] 1 WLR 1358, 107 Sol Jo 872 .... 18.10, 21.6
Pearson, Re, Smith v Pearson [1920] 1 Ch 247, 89 LJ Ch 123, [1920] B & CR 38, [1918–19] All ER Rep 390, 64 Sol Jo 83, 122 LT 515 .... 47.12, 47.13
Pearson v Dolman (1866) LR 3 Eq 315, 36 LJ Ch 258, 15 WR 120 .... 93.35

Pearson v Helliwell (1874) LR 18 Eq 411, 22 WR 839, 31 LT 159 .... 33.29
Pearson v IRC [1981] AC 753, [1980] 2 All ER 479, [1980] 2 WLR 872, [1980] STC 318, [1980] TR 177, 124 Sol Jo 377, HL ... 95.1, 200.94, 208.17, 218.33, 220.5
Pearson v Pearson (1802) 1 Sch & Lef 10 .... 30.31, 32.8
Pearson v Pearson (1871) LR 2 P & D 451, 40 LJP & M 53, 19 WR 1014, 24 LT 917 .... 11.26
Pearson v Rutter (1853) 3 De GM & G 398; affd sub nom Grey v Pearson (1857) 6 HL Cas 61, 26 LJ Ch 473, 3 Jur NS 823, 5 WR 454, 29 LTOS 67 .... 49.2, 50.8, 50.18, 50.21, 50.21, 56.1, 56.2, 56.7, 93.8
Pearson v Spencer (1863) 3 B & S 761, 11 WR 471, 8 LT 166, sub nom R v Pearson 1 New Rep 373, Ex Ch 7.26, 61.1
Pearson v Stephen (1831) 5 Bli NS 203, 2 Dow & Cl 328 .... 85.5, 87.3
Pearson Fund Trusts, Re (21 October 1977, unreported) 2.8
Pearsons's Goods, Re (1864) 33 LJPM & A 177, 10 Jur NS 372 .... 12.3
Pease v Pattinson (1886) 32 Ch D 154, 55 LJ Ch 617, 34 WR 361, [1886–90] All ER Rep 507, 54 LT 209, 2 TLR 306 .... 102.7, 102.16
Peat v Powell (1760) Amb 387, 1 Eden 479 .... 101.7, 101.8
Pechar, Re [1969] NZLR 574 .... 9.19
Pechell's Goods, Re. See Petchell's Goods, Re
Peck v Halsey (1726) 2 P Wms 387 .... 53.4
Peczenik's Settlement (or Settlement Trusts), Re, Cole v Ingram [1964] 2 All ER 339, [1964] 1 WLR 720, 108 Sol Jo 462 ..... 220.29, 220.30, 220.32
Pedley v Dodds (1866) LR 2 Eq 819, 12 Jur NS 759, 14 WR 884, 14 LT 823 .... 58.6, 63.3
Pedrotti's Will, Re (1859) 27 Beav 583, 29 LJ Ch 92, 6 Jur NS 187, 1 LT 390 .... 83.15
Peek's Trusts, Re (1873) LR 16 Eq 221, 42 LJ Ch 422, 21 WR 820 .... 93.31
Peel, Re, Tattersall v Peel [1936] Ch 161, [1935] All ER Rep 179, 105 LJ Ch 65, 80 Sol Jo 54, 154 LT 373 .... 216.8, 218.47
Peel v Catlow (1838) 9 Sim 372, 7 LJ Ch 273, 2 Jur 759 .... 76.3
Peel's Goods, Re (1870) LR 2 P & D 46, 34 JP 392, 39 LJP & M 36, 22 LT 417 .... 25.1
Peel's Release, Re [1921] 2 Ch 218, 90 LJ Ch 369, [1921] All ER Rep 103, 65 Sol Jo 580, 127 LT 123 .... 94.13, 94.34, 102.26
Peel's Settlement, Re, Biddulph v Peel [1911] 2 Ch 165, 80 LJ Ch 574, 55 Sol Jo 580, 105 LT 330 .... 44.4
Peerless, Re, Peerless v Smith [1901] WN 151, 45 Sol Jo 670 .... 31.16, 47.12
Peggs v Lamb [1994] Ch 172, [1994] 2 All ER 15, [1994] 2 WLR 1 .... 102.10, 103.19
Peirce v M'Neale [1894] 1 IR 118 .... 39.18, 39.19
Pelham-Clinton v Duke of Newcastle [1902] 1 Ch 34, 69 LJ Ch 875, 49 WR 12, 83 LT 627, 16 TLR 543; on appeal [1902] 1 Ch 34, 71 LJ Ch 53, 50 WR 83, 18 TLR 7, CA; affd [1903] AC 111, 72 LJ Ch 424, 51 WR 608, 88 LT 273, 19 TLR 275, HL 34.3, 35.7, 76.1, 83.1
Pellew v Horsford (1856) 25 LJ Ch 352, 2 Jur NS 514, 4 WR 442, 27 LTOS 134 .... 64.28
Pemberton v Barnes [1899] 1 Ch 544, 68 LJ Ch 192, 47 WR 444, 80 LT 181 .... 7.21
Pembroke's (Dowager Countess) Goods, Re (1856) Dea & Sw 182, 2 Jur NS 526 .... 15.1

Penfold v Giles. See Giles v Giles
Penley v Penley (1850) 12 Beav 547 .... 56.5, 68.1
Pennant v Kingscote (1843) 3 Curt 642, 7 Jur 754, 2 Notes of Cases 405n, sub nom Pennant v Sedgwick 1 LTOS 412 .... 4.20, 13.3
Pennant v Sedgwick. See Pennant v Kingscote
Pennefather, Re, Savile v Savile [1896] 1 IR 249 .... 83.1
Pennefather v Lloyd [1917] 1 IR 337 .... 18.31, 20.3, 52.9
Pennefather v Pennefather (1873) IR 7 Eq 300 .... 39.18
Pennington, Re, Penninton v Pennington [1914] 1 Ch 203, 83 LJ Ch 54, 20 Mans 411, 109 LT 814, 30 TLR 106, CA 38.28
Pennington v Buckley (1848) 6 Hare 451, 11 Jur 468 .... 102.9
Pennington v Waine (No 2) [2003] WTLR 1011 .... 41.20
Pennock v Pennock (1871) LR 13 Eq 144, LJ Ch 141, 20 WR 141, 25 LT 691 .... 83.11, 83.12, 99.1
Penny v Penny (1879) 11 Ch D 440, 48 LJ Ch 691, 40 LT 393, [1874–80] All ER Rep Ext 1516 .... 55.7
Penny v Railways Comr [1900] AC 628, 69 LJPC 113, 83 LT 182, PC 67.7, 97.1, 97.2
Penny v Turner (1848) 2 Ph 493, 17 LJ Ch 133 .... 56.5, 101.9
Penrose, Re, Penrose v Penrose [1933] Ch 793, 102 LJ Ch 321, 149 LT 325, 49 TLR 285 .... 40.14
Penton's Settlements, Re, Humphreys v Birch-Reynardson [1968] 1 All ER 36, [1968] 1 WLR 248, 112 Sol Jo 114 .... 48.8, 93.16
Pepin v Bruyère [1902] 1 Ch 24, 71 LJ Ch 39, 50 WR 34, 46 Sol Jo 29, 85 LT 461, CA 23.4, 23.11, 23.12
Pepper (Inspector of Taxes) v Daffurn [1993] STC 466, 66 TC 68, [1993] 2 EGLR 199, [1993] 41 EG 184, [1993] 32 LS Gaz R 40 .... 205.23
Pepper v Pepper (1870) IR 5 Eq 85 .... 18.9
Peppin v Bickford (1797) 3 Ves 570 .... 80.1
Percival, Re, Boote v Dutton (1888) 59 LT 21, CA 237.11
Percy, Re, Percy v Percy (1883) 24 Ch D 616, 53 LJ Ch 143, 49 LT 554 .... 82.2
Perdue, Re [1943] 1 DLR 46, 50 Man R 267, 1 WWR 515 .... 21.8
Pereira, Re, Worsley v Society for Propagation of Gospel in Foreign Parts (1912) 56 Sol Jo 614, 28 TLR 479 .... 18.33, 38.12
Perera v Perera [1901] AC 354, 70 LJPC 46, 84 LT 371, 17 TLR 389, PC 4.10, 4.17, 5.1
Perkins, Re, Brown v Perkins [1907] 2 Ch 596, 77 LJ Ch 16, [1904–7] All ER Rep 273, 97 LT 706 .... 33.23, 38.26, 38.27
Perkins, Re, Brown v Perkins (1909) 53 Sol Jo 698, 101 LT 345 .... 37.7
Perkins, Re, Perkins v Bagot [1893] 1 Ch 283, 62 LJ Ch 531, 3 R 40, 41 WR 170, 37 Sol Jo 26, 67 LT 743 .... 40.15, 100.3
Perkins v Goodwin [1877] WN 111 .... 72.3
Perkins v Micklethwaite (1714) 1 P Wms 274 .... 20.4, 22.4, 90.1, 97.4
Permanent Trustee Co v Dougall (1931) 34 SRNSW 83 .... 34.12
Permanent Trustee Co v Freedom from Hunger Campaign (1991) 25 NSWLR 140 .... 9.14
Permanent Trustee Co v Milton (1995) 39 NSWLR 330 .... 10.8
Permanent Trustee Co of New South Wales Ltd v D'Apice (1967–1968) (1968) 118 CLR 105 .... 93.15
Permanent Trustee Co of New South Wales Ltd v R (1929) 30 SRNSW 318, 47 WNNSW 116 .... 66.14

Perowne, Re, Perowne v Moss [1951] Ch 785, [1951] 2 All ER 201, [1951] 1 TLR 1135 .... 79.2, 101.9
Perpetual Executors and Trustee Association of Australia v Adams [1975] VR 462 .... 39.13
Perpetual Executors and Trustees Association of Australia Ltd v Probate Duties Comr [1981] VR 91 .... 46.1
Perpetual Trustee Co v Hogg (1936) 36 SRNSW 61, 53 WNNSW 67 .... 35.33
Perpetual Trustee Co Ltd v Waddell (1949) 66 WN 203, 49 SRNSW 266 .... 34.25
Perpetual Trustee Co Ltd v Wansey (1945) 63 WN 119, 46 SRNSW 226 .... 35.31
Perpetual Trustee Co Ltd v Wright, Re Cox's Will (1987) 9 NSWLR 18 .... 76.3
Perpetual Trustees Executors and Agency Co Ltd v Walker [1953] ALR 397 .... 35.22
Perpetual Trustees WA Ltd v Darvell [2002] WTLR 1349, SC WA 83,6
Perreyman (or Perryman), Re, National Provincial Bank Ltd v Perreyman (or Perryman) [1953] 1 All ER 223, 96 Sol Jo 851 .... 103.10
Perrin v Lyon (1807) 9 East 170 .... 35.4, 91.3
Perrin v Morgan. See Morgan, Re, Morgan v Morgan [1942] Ch 345
Perrott v Davies (1877) 38 LT 52 .... 93.36
Perry, Re [1925] 1 DLR 930, 56 OLR 278 .... 18.28
Perry, Re [1941] 2 DLR 690, [1941] OR 153 .... 57.15, 57.17
Perry v Meddowcroft (1841) 4 Beav 197; affd (1842) 12 LJ Ch 104 .... 30.34
Perry v Merritt (1874) LR 18 Eq 152, 43 LJ Ch 608, 22 WR 600 .... 83.8, 99.1
Perry v Whitehead (1801) 6 Ves 544 .... 44.8
Perry's Goods, Re (1840) 2 Curt 655 .... 25.12
Petchell's Goods, Re (1874) LR 3 P & D 153, 38 JP 824, 43 LJP & M 22, 22 WR 353, sub nom Re Pechell's Goods 30 LT 74 .... 18.9, 18.10, 18.14
Peter v Stirling (1878) 10 Ch D 279, 27 WR 469 .... 30.34, 236.6
Peter's Estate, Re [1952] 4 DLR 259, 5 WWRNS 193 .... 93.2
Peters Will, Re (1967) 63 WWR 180 .... 86.2
Peterson v Peterson (1866) LR 3 Eq 111, 36 LJ Ch 101, 15 WR 164 .... 29.11, 29.14, 31.10
Petre v Petre (1851) 14 Beav 197, 15 Jur 693, 18 LTOS 14 .... 31.4
Petre's Settlement Trusts, Re, Legh v Petre [1910] 1 Ch 290, 79 LJ Ch 145, 54 Sol Jo 199, 101 LT 847 .... 35.39
Petrie, Re, Lloyds Bank Ltd v Royal National Institute for the Blind [1962] Ch 355, [1961] 3 All ER 1067, [1961] 3 WLR 1348, 105 Sol Jo 966, CA 94.5
Pettifer, Re, Pettifer v Pettifer [1900] WN 182, 44 Sol Jo 698 .... 34.13, 35.8, 35.10
Pettifor's Will Trusts, Re, Roberts v Roberts [1966] Ch 257, [1966] 1 All ER 913, [1966] 2 WLR 778, 110 Sol Jo 191 .... 216.31
Pettingall v Pettingall (1842) 11 LJ Ch 176 .... 9.31, 33.16
Pettinger v Ambler (1866) LR 1 Eq 510, 35 Beav 321, 35 LJ Ch 389, 14 LT 118 .... 1.1
Pettitt, Re, Flaxman v Pettitt (1894) 38 Sol Jo 531 .... 64.27
Petts, Re (1859) 27 Beav 576, sub nom Re Pitts 29 LJ Ch 168, 5 Jur NS 1235, 8 WR 157, 1 LT 153 .... 58.10, 80.6
Petty, Re, Holliday v Petty [1929] 1 Ch 726, [1929] All ER Rep 493, 98 LJ Ch 207, 141 LT 31 .... 214.5
Peverett's Goods, Re [1902] P 205, 71 LJP 114, 87 LT 143 .... 13.2
Pewterers Co v Governors of Christ's Hospital (1683) 1 Vern 161 .... 102.26

Pexton (Inspector of Taxes) v Bell [1975] 1 All ER 498, [1975] 1 WLR 707, [1975] STC 84, 119 Sol Jo 323; affd [1976] 2 All ER 914, [1976] 1 WLR 885, [1976] STC 301, 120 Sol Jo 368, CA 220.73
Peyton v Bury (1731) 2 P Wms 626; on appeal sub nom Painton v Berry, etc (Administrators of Thornton) (1732) Kel W 37 .... 34.2, 35.12, 35.13
Peyton v Hughes (1842) 7 Jur 311 .... 65.3
Pfrimmer's Estate, Re (1945) 3 DLR 518, [1945] 2 WWR 142 .... 93.6
Pharazyn, Re (1897) 15 NZLR 709 .... 31.4, 32.2
Phelan, Re [1972] Fam 33, [1971] 3 All ER 1256, [1971] 3 WLR 888, 115 Sol Jo 710 .... 5.7, 18.8, 19.5
Phelan v Slattery (1887) 19 LR Ir 177 .... 57.15, 57.22
Phelps, Re, Wells v Phelps [1980] Ch 275, [1979] 3 All ER 373, [1980] 2 WLR 277, 124 Sol Jo 85, CA 29.11, 29.18, 104.6
Phené's Trusts, Re (1870) 5 Ch App 139, 39 LJ Ch 316, 18 WR 303, [1861–73] All ER Rep 514, 22 LT 111, CA 9.2
Pheysey v Vicary (1847) 16 M & W 484, 8 LTOS 451 .... 61.1, 64.2
Phibbs' Estate, Re [1917] P 93, 86 LJP 81, 116 LT 575, 33 TLR 214 .... 18.12
Philbrick's Settlement, Re (1865) 34 LJ Ch 368, 11 Jur NS 558, 5 New Rep 502, 13 WR 570, 12 LT 261 .... 39.5
Philby v Philby (1866) 15 WR 98 .... 35.51
Philipps v Chamberlaine (1798) 4 Ves 51 .... 51.2, 57.5
Philips v Paget (1740) 2 Atk 80 .... 9.39
Philips v Philips (1844) 3 Hare 281, 13 LJ Ch 445 .... 44.15, 47.21
Philipson-Stow v IRC [1961] AC 727, [1960] 3 All ER 814, [1960] 3 WLR 1008, 39 ATC 394, [1960] TR 333, 104 Sol Jo 1055, HL 24.2, 24.8
Phillip's Estate, Re, Boyle v Thompson (1918) 34 TLR 256 .... 15.1, 15.2
Phillips, Re, Lawrence v Huxtable [1931] 1 Ch 347, 100 LJ Ch 65, [1930] All ER Rep 165, 144 LT 178 .... 39.2
Phillips v Beal (1858) 25 Beav 25 .... 38.4, 64.16
Phillips v Beal (1862) 32 Beav 25 .... 8.4
Phillips v Cayley (1889) 43 Ch D 222, 59 LJ Ch 177, 38 WR 241, 62 LT 86, 6 TLR 128, CA 39.13, 39.14
Phillips v Eastwood (1835) L & G temp Sugd 270 .... 64.11
Phillips v Garth (1790) 3 Bro CC 64; on appeal (1790) 3 Bro CC 69 .... 87.1
Phillips v Gutteridge (1862) 3 De GJ & Sm 332, 32 LJ Ch 1, 8 Jur NS 1196, 1 New Rep 3, 11 WR 12, 7 LT 402 .... 33.28, 62.2
Phillips v Low [1892] 1 Ch 47, 61 LJ Ch 44, 65 LT 552, 8 TLR 23 .... 7.26, 61.1
Phillips v Phillips [1877] WN 260 .... 35.38
Phillips v Rail (1906) 54 WR 517 .... 52.3, 101.3
Phillips v Turner (1853) 17 Beav 194, 1 Eq Rep 143, 1 WR 376, 21 LTOS 215 .... 41.9
Phillips' Insurance, Re (1883) 23 Ch D 235, 52 LJ Ch 441, 31 WR 511, 48 LT 81, CA 7.9, 7.12
Phillips' Trusts, Re (1868) LR 6 Eq 250 .... 38.28
Philp, Re [1952] OWN 783 .... 53.5
Philpot, Re, Gregson v Taylor. See Gregson v Taylor
Philps v Evans (1850) 4 De G & Sm 188, 15 Jur 809, 17 LTOS 87 .... 77.3
Philps' Will, Re (1868) LR 7 Eq 151, 19 LT 713 .... 68.8, 68.12, 77.3, 78.4
Phipps v Ackers (1835) 3 Cl & Fin 702, HL 93.16

Phipps v Ackers (1842) 9 Cl & Fin 583, 6 Jur 745, 4 Man & G 1107, 5 Scott NR 955, HL 93.6, 93.11, 93.16, 93.22
Phipps v Earl of Anglesea (1721) 1 P Wms 696, 2 Eq Cas Abr 220 pl 1, 5 Vin Abr 209 pl 8 .... 32.33
Phipps v Earl of Anglesey (1751) 7 Bro Parl Cas 443, HL 52.7
Phipps v Hale (1874) LR 3 P & D 166, 22 WR 742 .... 11.3, 12.11
Phipson v Turner (1838) 9 Sim 227, 2 Jur 414 .... 94.44
Phizackerley v Revenue and Customs Comrs [2005] WTLR 745 .... 218.20
Phuler's Will Trusts, Re, Midland Bank Executor and Trustee Co Ltd v Logan [1964] 2 All ER 948, [1965] 1 WLR 68, 43 ATC 400, [1964] TR 441, 108 Sol Jo 710 .... 214.70, 235.6
Piazzi-Smyth's Goods, Re [1898] P 7, 46 WR 426, 77 LT 375, sub nom Re Smyth's Goods 67 LJP 4 .... 2.2
Picard v Mitchell (1851) 14 Beav 103 .... 33.24
Picken v Matthews (1878) 10 Ch D 264, 39 LT 531, sub nom Re Hoof, Picken v Matthews 48 LJ Ch 150 .... 66.12
Pickering v Lord Stamford (1797) 3 Ves 492 .... 47.23
Pickersgill v Rodger (1876) 5 Ch D 163 .... 42.1, 42.5, 42.6, 47.13
Pickford v Brown (1856) 2 K & J 426, 25 LJ Ch 702, 2 Jur NS 781, 4 WR 473, 27 LTOS 259 .... 93.1, 93.39
Pickles v Pickles (1861) 31 LJ Ch 146, 7 Jur NS 1065, 9 WR 763, 4 LT 755 .... 40.15
Pickup's Trusts, Re (1861) 1 John & H 389, 30 LJ Ch 278, 9 WR 251, 4 LT 85 .... 74.1
Pickwick v Gibbes (1839) 1 Beav 271, 3 Jur 101 .... 32.10
Pickworth, Re, Snaith v Parkinson [1899] 1 Ch 642, 68 LJ Ch 324, 80 LT 212, CA 67.3, 67.7, 96.1
Picton, Re, Porter v Jones [1944] Ch 303, 113 LJ Ch 177, 88 Sol Jo 224, 171 LT 27, 60 TLR 378 .... 88.4
Pidgely v Pidgely (1844) 1 Coll 255, 8 Jur 529, 3 LTOS 200 .... 39.25
Piercy, Re, Whitwham v Piercy [1895] 1 Ch 83, 64 LJ Ch 249, 13 R 106, 43 WR 134, 39 Sol Jo 43, 71 LT 745, 11 TLR 21 .... 23.4, 23.12
Piercy's Goods, Re (1845) 1 Rob Eccl 278, 4 Notes of Cases 250 .... 12.6
Pierson v Garnet (1786) 2 Bro CC 38; on appeal (1787) 2 Bro CC 226 .... 30.43, 81.3
Pieschel v Paris (1825) 2 Sim & St 384, 4 LJOS Ch 77 .... 57.10
Pigg v Clarke (1876) 3 Ch D 672, 45 LJ Ch 849, 24 WR 1014 .... 50.14, 79.1, 79.2
Piggott v Green (1833) 6 Sim 72 .... 30.14
Pigott v Waller (1802) 7 Ves 98 .... 22.2
Pigott v Wilder (1858) 26 Beav 90 .... 91.5
Pile v Salter (1832) 5 Sim 411 .... 93.20
Pilkington, Re, Pilkington v Pilkington (1892) 29 LR Ir 370 .... 66.1, 66.13, 66.16
Pilkington v Boughey (1841) 12 Sim 114, 5 Jur 1149 .... 102.19
Pilkington v Gray [1899] AC 401, 68 LJPC 63, PC 4.18, 13.3
Pilkington v IRC. See Pilkington's Will Trusts, Re, Pilkington v Pilkington
Pilkington's Trusts, Re (1865) 6 New Rep 246, 13 LT 35 .... 41.2, 41.13, 41.14
Pilkington's Will Trusts, Re, Pilkington v Harrison [1937] Ch 574, [1937] 3 All ER 213, 106 LJ Ch 360, 81 Sol Jo 459, 157 LT 132, 53 TLR 745 .... 216.7

Pilkington's Will Trusts, Re, Pilkington v Pilkington [1961] Ch 466, [1961] 2 All ER 330, [1961] 2 WLR 776, 40 TC 416, 105 Sol Jo 422, CA; on appeal sub nom Pilkington v IRC [1964] AC 612, [1962] 3 All ER 622, [1962] 3 WLR 1051, 40 TC 416, 41 ATC 285, [1962] TR 265, 106 Sol Jo 834, HL 40.5, 218.95, 218.96, 218.99, 242.1
Pilot v Gainfort [1931] P 103, 100 LJP 60, 75 Sol Jo 490, 145 LT 22, 47 TLR 376 .... 17.2, 17.4
Pilsworth v Mosse (1862) 14 I Ch R 163 .... 18.10
Pimm, Re, Sharpe v Hodgson [1904] 2 Ch 345, 73 LJ Ch 627, 52 WR 648, 48 Sol Jo 588, 91 LT 190 .... 214.70
Pinchin v Simms (1861) 30 Beav 119 .... 44.15
Pinckard's Trust, Re (1858) 27 LJ Ch 422, 4 Jur NS 1041, 31 LTOS 67 .... 10.8
Pinder v Pinder (1870) 18 WR 309 .... 64.7
Pinede's Settlement, Re (1879) 12 Ch D 667, 48 LJ Ch 741, 28 WR 178, 41 LT 579 .... 24.12, 39.7
Pinhorne, Re, Moreton v Hughes [1894] 2 Ch 276, 63 LJ Ch 607, 8 R 264, 42 WR 438, 38 Sol Jo 400, 70 LT 901 .... 47.25, 50.3, 219.26
Pinion, Re, Westminster Bank Ltd v Pinion [1965] Ch 85, [1964] 1 All ER 890, [1964] 2 WLR 919, 108 Sol Jo 296, CA 102.10
Pink, Re, Pink v Pink [1912] 1 Ch 498, 81 LJ Ch 353, [1911–13] All ER Rep 1037, 56 Sol Jo 274, 106 LT 338; varied [1912] 2 Ch 528, 81 LJ Ch 753, [1911–13] All ER Rep 1037, 56 Sol Jo 668, 107 LT 338, 28 TLR 528, CA 30.13, 30.18, 57.32
Pinnel v Annison [2005] EWHC 1421 (Ch), [2006] WTLR 1047 .... 57.23, 58.10
Pinney v Hunt (1877) 6 Ch D 98, 26 WR 69 .... 25.14
Pinney v Marriott (1863) 32 Beav 643 .... 63.6
Pinney v Pinney (1828) 8 B & C 335, 6 LJOSKB 353, 2 Man & Ry KB 436 .... 25.14
Piper, Re, Dodd v Piper [1946] 2 All ER 503, 90 Sol Jo 528, 175 LT 426, 62 TLR 618 .... 34.12, 34.18, 35.36
Piper v Piper (1886) 5 NZLR 135 .... 52.7
Pipon v Pipon (1744) 9 Mod Rep 431, Amb 25, 799, sub nom Pippon v Pippon Ridg temp H 165 .... 23.16
Pirbright v Salwey [1896] WN 86 .... 9.29, 202.19
Pirie's Will, Re (1884) 10 VLR 43 .... 25.12
Pistol d Randal v Riccardson (1784) 3 Doug KB 361, 1 Hy Bl 26n 64.33
Pitcairn, Re, Brandreth v Colvin [1896] 2 Ch 199, [1895–9] All ER Rep 1244, 65 LJ Ch 120, 44 WR 200, 73 LT 430 .... 38.18, 38.23, 214.9, 214.38, 224.34, 225.33, 230.7
Pitcairn v Pitcairn (1870) 42 Sc Jur 306, 8 M 604 .... 64.16
Pitcairne v Brase (1679) Cas temp Finch 403 .... 58.10
Pitman v Crum Ewing [1911] AC 217, 80 LJPC 175, 104 LT 611, HL 45.2
Pitman v Stevens (1812) 15 East 505 .... 38.12
Pitt, Re, Pitt v Mann (1928) 44 TLR 371 .... 27.15
Pitt v Jackson (1786) 2 Bro CC 51 .... 40.21
Pitt Rivers, Re, Scott v Pitt Rivers [1902] 1 Ch 403, 66 JP 275, 71 LJ Ch 225, 50 WR 342, 46 Sol Jo 246, 86 LT 6, 18 TLR 272, CA 36.7, 36.13
Pittaway, Re [1967] Ch 690, [1967] 1 All ER 391, [1967] 2 WLR 637, 111 Sol Jo 37 .... 51.8, 76.3
Pitts, Re (1859) 29 LJ Ch 168. See Petts, Re

Pitts, Re, Cox v Kilsby [1931] 1 Ch 546, 100 LJ Ch 284, 145 LT 116, 47 TLR 293 .... 9.14
Pla v Andorra (Application 69498/01) [2004] 2 FCR 630, 18 BHRC 120, [2004] ECHR 69498/01, ECtHR 72.1, 75.1
Plaister, Re, Perpetual Trustee Co v Crawshaw (1934) 34 SRNSW 547, 51 NSWWN 141 .... 9.14
Plant, Re [1974] Qd R 203 .... 64.37
Plant, Re, Griffith v Hill (1898) 47 WR 183, 43 Sol Jo 63 .... 72.3
Plant, Re, Johnson v Hardwicke [1952] Ch 298, [1952] 1 All ER 78n, [1952] 1 TLR 1 .... 88.4
Planta v Greenshields [1931] 2 DLR 189, [1931] 1 WWR 401 .... 102.23, 103.17
Planta v Greenshields (No 2) (1932) 45 BCR 228, 3 DLR 423, [1932] 2 WWR 60 .... 32.10
Plato, Re, AMP Perpetual Trustee Co Ltd v Shalders [1990] NZLJ 3 .... 9.2
Platt, Re, Sykes v Dawson [1916] 2 Ch 563, 86 LJ Ch 114, [1916–17] All ER Rep 570, 61 Sol Jo 10, 115 LT 524 .... 33.26, 33.30
Playfair, Re, Palmer v Playfair [1951] Ch 4, 66 (pt 1) TLR 1203, sub nom Re Hickman's Will Trusts, Re Playfair, Palmer v Playfair [1950] 2 All ER 285 .... 47.24
Playne v Scriven (1849) 1 Rob Eccl 772, 13 Jur 712, 13 LTOS 405, 7 Notes of Cases 122 .... 11.18, 12.12
Pleasants, Re, Pleasants v A-G (1923) 39 TLR 675 .... 102.10
Plenty v West (1848) 6 CB 201 .... 62.1
Plenty v West and Budd (1845) 1 Rob Eccl 264, 9 Jur 458, 4 Notes of Cases 103 .... 18.9
Pleydell v Pleydell (1721) 1 P Wms 748 .... 98.13
Plimmer v City of Wellington Corpn (1884) 9 App Cas 699, 53 LJPC 105, 51 LT 475, PC 43.1
Plowden, Re, Plowden v Plowden (1908) 24 TLR 883 .... 64.6
Plowden v Hyde (1852) 2 De GM & G 684, 21 LJ Ch 796, 16 Jur 823, 20 LTOS 18 .... 41.8
Plowman, Re, Westminster Bank Ltd v Plowman [1943] Ch 269, [1943] 2 All ER 532, 112 LJ Ch 229, 87 Sol Jo 248, 169 LT 118, 59 TLR 335 .... 104.11
Plumb's Estate, Re [1947] 1 WWR 666 .... 64.19
Plunkett v Lewis (1844) 3 Hare 316, 13 LJ Ch 295, 8 Jur 682, 2 LTOS 457 .... 44.15, 44.16, 44.17
Pocock v A-G (1876) 3 Ch D 342, 46 LJ Ch 495, 25 WR 277, 35 LT 575, CA 102.25, 103.1
Pocock v Bishop of Lincoln (1821) 3 Brod & Bing 27, 6 Moore CP 159 .... 51.3
Pocock v Pocock [1952] OR 155, [1952] OWN 23 .... 5.9
Podger's Will, Re [1957] VLR 275 .... 18.28
Podmore v Gunning (1836) 7 Sim 644, Donnelly 74, 5 LJ Ch 266 .... 36.5, 36.13
Pogson v Thomas (1840) 6 Bing NC 337, 8 Scott 621 .... 60.2, 63.3
Poirier Estate, Re, Leger v Poirier [1944] SCR 152, 3 DLR 1 .... 4.11
Pole v Lord Somers (1801) 6 Ves 309 .... 44.7
Pole v Pole [1924] 1 Ch 156, 93 LJ Ch 145, 68 Sol Jo 184, 130 LT 333, CA 94.15
Pollard v Jackson (1993) 67 P & CR 327, CA 25.1

Pollard's Estate, Re (1863) 3 De GJ & Sm 541, 32 LJ Ch 657, 2 New Rep 404, 11 WR 1083, 8 LT 710 .... 7.3, 51.7
Pollexfen v Moore (1745) 3 Atk 272 .... 27.6
Polley v Polley (1861) 29 Beav 134 .... 56.5, 98.12
Pollock, Re [1964] VR 554 .... 210.7
Pollock, Re, Pollock v Pollock [1941] Ch 219, [1941] 1 All ER 360, 110 LJ Ch 97, 85 Sol Jo 130, 165 LT 152, 57 TLR 359 .... 9.14, 9.16, 9.18
Pollock, Re, Pollock v Worrall (1885) 28 Ch D 552, 54 LJ Ch 489, 52 LT 718, CA 44.2, 44.3, 44.5, 44.8, 67.4
Pollock, Re, Pugsley v Pollock [1943] Ch 338, [1943] 2 All ER 443, 112 LJ Ch 345, 87 Sol Jo 373, 169 LT 282, 59 TLR 456 .... 30.30, 32.5, 32.13, 32.20, 210.15, 210.19, 224.91
Pollock v Croft (1816) 1 Mer 181 .... 35.16
Pollock v Pollock (1874) LR 18 Eq 329, 44 LJ Ch 168, 22 WR 724, 30 LT 779 .... 61.1
Polson v Polson (1900) 21 NSWLR Eq 90 .... 34.23
Pomfret v Perring (1854) 5 De GM & G 775, 24 LJ Ch 187, 3 Eq Rep 145, 1 Jur NS 173, 3 WR 81, 24 LTOS 123 .... 39.28
Ponder, Re, Ponder v Ponder [1921] 2 Ch 59, [1921] All ER Rep 164, 90 LJ Ch 426, 65 Sol Jo 455, 125 LT 568 .... 27.15, 203.9
Poole, Re, Stewart v Poole (PEI) [1929] 1 DLR 418 .... 15.1
Poole v Bott (1853) 11 Hare 33, 22 LJ Ch 1042, 1 Eq Rep 21, 17 Jur 688, 1 WR 276, 21 LTOS 262 .... 35.4, 93.1
Poole v Odling (1862) 10 WR 591 .... 64.23
Poole v Poole (1871) 7 Ch App 17, 20 WR 133, 25 LT 771 .... 100.6
Poole v Terry (1831) 4 Sim 294 .... 93.44
Poole's Estate, Re, Poole v Poole [1919] P 10, 88 LJP 77, 63 Sol Jo 179, 35 TLR 143 .... 17.5
Pooley, Re (1888) 40 Ch D 1, 58 LJ Ch 1, 37 WR 17, [1886–90] All ER Rep 157, 60 LT 73, 5 TLR 21, CA 9.11
Pope, Re, Sharp v Marshall [1901] 1 Ch 64, 70 LJ Ch 26, 49 WR 122, 45 Sol Jo 45 .... 95.13
Pope v Pope (1851) 14 Beav 591, 21 LJ Ch 276, 18 LTOS 83 .... 76.3
Pope v Whitcombe (1810) 3 Mer 689 .... 79.4
Pope v Whitcombe (1827) 3 Russ 124, 6 LJOS Ch 53 .... 66.6
Pope's Contract, Re [1911] 2 Ch 442, 80 LJ Ch 692, 105 LT 370 .... 220.27
Popham, Re, Butler v Popham [1914] WN 257, 58 Sol Jo 673, 111 LT 524 .... 38.26
Popham v Bamfield (1703) 2 Eq Cas Abr 308, Freem Ch 269, 1 Salk 236, sub nom Bamfield v Popham 1 Eq Cas Abr 183, Freem Ch 266, 1 P Wms 54, 2 Vern 449, Holt KB 233 .... 98.3
Popham v Bampfield (1682) 1 Eq Cas Abr 108, 1 Vern 167 .... 34.2
Popham v Lady Aylesbury (1748) Amb 68 .... 63.1
Portal and Lamb, Re (1885) 30 Ch D 50, 54 LJ Ch 1012, 33 WR 859, 53 LT 650, CA 58.12, 59.1, 59.3
Porter, Re, Coulson v Capper [1892] 3 Ch 481, 61 LJ Ch 688, 3 R 19, 41 WR 38, 36 Sol Jo 626, 67 LT 823 .... 99.3, 99.5
Porter, Re, Logan v Northern Bank Ltd [1975] NI 157 .... 34.2, 34.10, 34.25, 91.2
Porter, Re, Porter v Porter [1925] Ch 746, 95 LJ Ch 46, [1925] All ER Rep 179, 133 LT 812 .... 53.3, 102.22
Porter v Baddeley (1877) 5 Ch D 542 .... 38.23

Porter v Bradley (1789) 3 Term Rep 143 .... 98.7
Porter v Tournay (1797) 3 Ves 311 .... 8.4, 64.27
Porter's Goods, Re (1869) LR 2 P & D 22, 34 JP 247, 39 LJP & M 12, 18 WR 231, 21 LT 680 .... 1.5
Porter's Trust, Re (1857) 4 K & J 188, 27 LJ Ch 196, 4 Jur NS 20, 6 WR 187, 32 LTOS 86 .... 47.23, 47.24, 68.1, 68.2, 68.8
Portland (Duke of) v Lady Topham. See Topham v Duke of Portland
Portman v Viscount Portman [1922] 2 AC 473, 91 LJ Ch 708, 128 LT 129, 38 TLR 887, HL 94.15
Portman v Willis (1593) Cro Eliz 386, Moore KB 352 .... 64.25
Posner, Re, Posner v Miller [1953] P 277, [1953] 1 All ER 1123, [1953] 2 WLR 1149, 97 Sol Jo 390 .... 58.10, 80.6
Pothecary v Pothecary (1848) 2 De G & Sm 738, 18 LJ Ch 48, 12 Jur 1016, 12 LTOS 240 .... 9.45, 30.41
Potter, Re, Stevens v Potter (1900) 83 LT 405 .... 58.12
Potter v Dudeney (1887) 56 LT 395, 3 TLR 420 .... 37.8
Potter v Potter (1750) 1 Ves Sen 437 .... 21.3, 22.2, 60.1
Potter v Richards (1855) 24 LJ Ch 488, 1 Jur NS 462, 3 WR 266 .... 33.20, 34.3, 35.2
Potter's Will Trusts, Re [1944] Ch 70, [1943] 2 All ER 805, 113 LJ Ch 173, 170 LT 26, 60 TLR 155, CA 74.1
Pottruff, Re (1972) 27 DLR (3d) 405 .... 44.15
Potts v Atherton (1859) 28 LJ Ch 486, 7 WR 331 .... 93.32, 96.1
Potts v Britton (1871) LR 11 Eq 433, 19 WR 651, 24 LT 409 .... 40.7, 40.8
Potts v Smith (1869) LR 8 Eq 683, 39 LJ Ch 131, 17 WR 1083, 21 LT 54 .... 33.36, 33.38, 33.42
Pouey v Hordern [1900] 1 Ch 492, 69 LJ Ch 231, 82 LT 51, 16 TLR 191 .... 24.12
Poulett (Earl) v Hood (1866) 35 Beav 234, 12 Jur NS 85, 14 WR 298, 13 LT 783; affd (1868) LR 5 Eq 115, 37 LJ Ch 224, 16 WR 323, 17 LT 486 .... 64.39
Poultney, Re, Poultney v Poultney [1912] 2 Ch 541, 81 LJ Ch 748, 56 Sol Jo 667, 107 LT 1, CA 67.2
Poulton's Will Trusts, Re, Smail v Litchfield [1987] 1 All ER 1068, [1987] 1 WLR 795, 131 Sol Jo 412, [1987] LS Gaz R 981 .... 79.4
Pounder, Re, Williams v Pounder (1886) 56 LJ Ch 113, 56 LT 104 .... 51.4, 53.2, 83.9, 83.12, 99.1
Powel v Cleaver (1789) 2 Bro CC 499 .... 44.2, 44.8
Powell, Re (1956) 5 DLR (2d) 67, [1956] OR 522, [1956] OWN 493 .... 71.4
Powell, Re, Bodvel-Roberts v Poole [1918] 1 Ch 407, 87 LJ Ch 237, 65 Sol Jo 330, 118 LT 567 .... 38.13, 51.1, 210.45
Powell, Re, Campbell v Campbell [1900] 2 Ch 525, 69 LJ Ch 788, 83 LT 24 .... 47.25, 219.26
Powell, Re, Crosland v Holliday [1898] 1 Ch 227, 67 LJ Ch 148, 46 WR 231, 42 Sol Jo 150, 77 LT 649 .... 66.4, 66.21, 94.21
Powell, Re, Dodd v Williams [1921] 1 Ch 178, 90 LJ Ch 161, 125 LT 603 .... 8.4, 204.45
Powell v A-G (1817) 3 Mer 48 .... 102.7
Powell v Boggis (1866) 35 Beav 535, 35 LJ Ch 472, 14 WR 670 .... 78.4
Powell v Davies (1839) 1 Beav 532, 3 Jur 839 .... 53.5
Powell v Hellicar [1919] 1 Ch 138, 88 LJ Ch 68, 63 Sol Jo 116, 120 LT 218 .... 67.4, 67.5
Powell v Morgan (1688) 2 Vern 90 .... 35.38

Powell v Powell (1866) LR 1 P & D 209, 35 LJP & M 100, [1861–73] All ER Rep 362, 14 LT 800 ... 18.5, 18.17, 19.1, 19.3, 19.4, 21.8
Powell v Rawle (1874) LR 18 Eq 243, 22 WR 629 ... 30.32, 34.24, 35.48
Powell v Riley (1871) LR 12 Eq 175, 40 LJ Ch 533, 19 WR 869 ... 38.3
Powell's Goods, Re (1848) 6 Notes of Cases 557 ... 12.12
Powell's Trust, Re (1858) John 49, 5 Jur NS 331, 7 WR 138, 32 LTOS 252 ... 64.40
Powell's Trusts, Re (1869) 39 LJ Ch 188, 18 WR 228 ... 39.13
Power, Re, O'Leary v Power [1904] St R Qd 93 ... 35.8
Power, Re, Public Trustee v Hastings [1947] Ch 572, [1947] 2 All ER 282, 91 Sol Jo 409, 177 LT 245 ... 220.30
Power v Hayne (1869) LR 8 Eq 262, 17 WR 783 ... 33.7, 33.8
Power v Lencham (1838) 2 Jo Ex Ir 728 ... 58.10
Power v Quealy (1878) 2 LR Ir 227; affd (1878) 4 LR Ir 20, Ir CA ... 51.12
Power's Estate, Re (1964) 48 WWR 250 ... 32.17, 33.25
Power's Settlement Trusts, Re, Power v Power [1951] Ch 1074, [1951] 2 All ER 513, 95 Sol Jo 467, [1951] 2 TLR 355, CA ... 27.3
Powis v Burdett (1804) 9 Ves 428 ... 97.8
Powles, Re, Little v Powles [1954] 1 All ER 516, [1954] 1 WLR 336, 98 Sol Jo 111 ... 83.15, 216.26
Powys v Mansfield (1837) 3 My & Cr 359, 7 LJ Ch 9, 1 Jur 861 ... 20.4, 22.4, 41.3, 44.8, 44.11
Poyser, Re [1918] 1 Ch 573n ... 44.9
Poyser, Re, Landon v Poyser [1908] 1 Ch 828, 77 LJ Ch 482, 99 LT 50 ... 100.5
Poyser, Re, Landon v Poyser [1910] 2 Ch 444, 79 LJ Ch 748, [1908–10] All ER Rep 374, 103 LT 134 ... 38.26, 38.27
Pozot's Settlement Trusts, Re, Westminster Bank Ltd v Guerbois [1952] Ch 427, [1952] 1 All ER 1107, [1952] 1 TLR 1042, CA ... 99.4
Practice Direction [1953] 1 WLR 689 ... 11.3
Practice Direction (incapacity: evidence of) [1969] 1 All ER 494, [1969] 1 WLR 301 ... 25.4
Practice Direction [1970] 1 All ER 15, 113 Sol Jo 948, sub nom Practice Note [1970] 1 WLR 228 ... 4.25
Practice Direction [1983] 3 All ER 255, sub nom Practice Note [1983] 1 WLR 1077 ... 4.25
Practice Direction [1988] 1 All ER 192, [1988] 1 WLR 195, [1988] 1 FLR 184, [1988] Fam Law 50, 132 Sol Jo 46, [1988] 6 LS Gaz R 38 ... 25.1
Practice Direction [1988] 2 All ER 308, [1988] 1 WLR 610, [1988] 2 FLR 93, [1988] Fam Law 359, 132 Sol Jo 648, [1988] NLJR 154 ... 72.14
Practice Direction [1990] 2 All ER 576, [1990] 2 FLR 91, [1990] 27 LS Gaz R 42 ... 25.5
Practice Direction [1990] 3 All ER 734, [1990] 1 WLR 1510, [1990] 2 FLR 533, [1990] Fam Law 466 ... 10.1
Practice Note [1915] WN 134. See Pritt, Re, Morton v National Church League
Practice Note [1945] WN 210 ... 105.24
Practice Note [1970] 1 WLR 228. See Practice Direction [1970] 1 All ER 15
Practice Note [1976] 1 WLR 418. See Practice Direction [1976] 2 All ER 447
Prater, Re, Desinge v Beare (1888) 37 Ch D 481, 57 LJ Ch 342, 36 WR 561, 58 LT 784, 4 TLR 249, CA ... 63.1
Pratt, Re, Pratt v Pratt [1894] 1 Ch 491, 63 LJ Ch 484, 8 R 601, 70 LT 489 ... 30.8

Pratt v Church (1830) 4 Beav 177 .... 83.13
Pratt v Johnson. See Johnson's Estate, Re
Pratt v Mathew (1856) 22 Beav 328, 25 LJ Ch 409, 2 Jur NS 364, 4 WR 418, 27 LTOS 74; on appeal (1856) 8 De GM & G 522, 25 LJ Ch 686, 2 Jur NS 1055, 4 WR 772, 27 LTOS 267, CA 58.10, 80.6
Pratt v Pratt (1844) 14 Sim 129, 8 Jur 507, 3 LTOS 466 .... 18.15
Pratt's Settlement Trusts, Re, McCullum v Phipps-Hornby [1943] Ch 356, [1943] 2 All ER 458, 112 LJ Ch 251, 87 Sol Jo 265, 169 LT 181, 59 TLR 352 .... 48.15
Pratt's Will Trusts, Re, Barrow v McCarthy [1943] Ch 326, [1943] 2 All ER 375, 112 LJ Ch 269, 87 Sol Jo 319, 169 LT 263, 59 TLR 371 .... 220.23
Prendergast v Prendergast (1850) 3 HL Cas 195, 14 Jur 989, HL 29.7
Prescott v Barker (1874) 9 Ch App 174, 43 LJ Ch 498, 22 WR 423, 30 LT 149 .... 50.4, 60.2, 64.32
Prescott v Long (1795) 2 Ves 690 .... 66.13
Press v Parker (1825) 2 Bing 456, 3 LJOSCP 96, 10 Moore CP 158 .... 52.8
Preston, Re, Preston v Hoggarth [1969] 2 All ER 961, [1969] 1 WLR 317, 113 Sol Jo 208 .... 105.25, 105.38, 202.39
Preston v Funnell (1739) 7 Mod Rep 296, Willes 164 .... 84.2
Preston v Preston (1869) 21 LT 346 .... 40.14
Preston's Trusts, Re (1863) 1 New Rep 470, 8 LT 20 .... 78.4
Prestwidge v Groombridge (1833) 6 Sim 171 .... 93.9
Previté, Re, Sturges v Previté [1931] 1 Ch 447, 100 LJ Ch 286, 145 LT 40 .... 238.14
Price, Re [1928] Ch 579, 97 LJ Ch 423, 139 LT 339 .... 41.18
Price, Re, Midland Bank Executor and Trustee Co Ltd v Harwood [1943] Ch 422, [1943] 2 All ER 505, 112 LJ Ch 273, 87 Sol Jo 282, 169 LT 121, 59 TLR 367 .... 9.35, 102.10
Price, Re, Price v Newton [1905] 2 Ch 55, 74 LJ Ch 437, 53 WR 600, [1904–7] All ER Rep 448, 93 LT 44 .... 51.3, 51.11, 57.15, 64.30, 64.40
Price, Re, Tomlin v Latter [1900] 1 Ch 442, 69 LJ Ch 225, 48 WR 373, 44 Sol Jo 242, 82 LT 79, 16 TLR 189 .... 24.6, 24.12, 49.7, 50.19
Price, Re, Trumper v Price [1932] 2 Ch 54, 101 LJ Ch 278, 76 Sol Jo 217, 147 LT 351, 48 TLR 318 .... 58.4, 64.58
Price, Re, Wasley v Price [1950] Ch 242, [1950] 1 All ER 338, 94 Sol Jo 146, 66 (pt 1) TLR 291 .... 64.4, 64.45
Price v Boustead (1863) 8 LT 565 .... 83.7
Price v Craig [2006] EWHC 2561 (Ch), [2006] All ER (D) 249 (Oct) 6.2
Price v Dewhurst (1837) 8 Sim 279, Donnelly 264, 6 LJ Ch 226; affd (1838) 4 My & Cr 76, 8 LJ Ch 57, 2 Jur 1006, [1835–42] All ER Rep 442 .... 49.7, 49.8
Price v Hall (1868) LR 5 Eq 399, 37 LJ Ch 191, 16 WR 642 .... 93.17
Price v Page (1799) 4 Ves 680 .... 57.22
Price v Powell (1858) 3 H & N 341, sub nom Price v Price 27 LJ Ex 409, 6 WR 597, 31 LTOS 204 .... 18.22
Price v St Hill (1914) 33 NZLR 1096 .... 93.38
Price Estate, Re, Shultz v Price (1965) 55 DLR (2d) 458, 55 WWR 26 .... 34.5
Prichard v Prichard (1870) LR 11 Eq 232, 40 LJ Ch 92, 19 WR 226, 24 LT 259 .... 64.35
Pride v Fooks (1840) 2 Beav 430, 9 LJ Ch 234, 4 Jur 213, 50 RR 227 .... 95.9
Pride v Fooks (1858) 3 De G & J 252, 28 LJ Ch 81, 5 Jur NS 158, 7 WR 109, 32 LTOS 358 .... 50.10, 74.1, 93.18, 98.3, 98.4

Pridham, Re [1953] 1 DLR 782, [1953] OWN 190 .... 64.27
Priest, Re, Belfield v Duncan [1944] Ch 58, [1944] 1 All ER 51, 113 LJ Ch 145, 88 Sol Jo 43, 170 LT 159, 60 TLR 145 .... 9.12, 23.8, 24.2, 24.3
Priestley v Holgate (1857) 3 K & J 286, 26 LJ Ch 448, 3 Jur NS 486, 5 WR 445, 30 LTOS 30 .... 34.8, 34.21, 34.25
Priestley's Will Trusts, Re, Hambros Bank Executor and Trustee Co Ltd v Rabagliati [1971] Ch 562, [1970] 3 All ER 1025, [1970] 3 WLR 1054, 114 Sol Jo 881; affd [1971] Ch 858, [1971] 2 All ER 817, [1971] 2 WLR 1119, 115 Sol Jo 350, CA 39.10, 39.12, 39.13, 39.14, 39.16, 39.18, 39.20, 50.9, 50.13
Priestman v Thomas (1884) 9 PD 210, 53 LJP 109, 32 WR 842, 51 LT 843, CA 25.15, 25.16, 43.4
Prince, Re, Hardman v Willis (1935) 51 TLR 526 .... 32.29
Pringle, Re, Baker v Matheson [1946] Ch 124, [1946] 1 All ER 88, 115 LJ Ch 92, 90 Sol Jo 9, 174 LT 115, 62 TLR 147 .... 70.2, 101.6
Pringle, Re, Walker v Stewart (1881) 17 Ch D 819, 50 LJ Ch 689, 30 WR 44, 45 LT 11 .... 64.35, 64.36
Prinsep and East India Co v Dyce Sombre, Troup and Solaroli (1856) 10 Moo PCC 232, 4 WR 714 .... 4.14, 4.20
Pritchard, Re, Hamblin v Pritchard (1906) 6 SRNSW 353, 23 WNNSW 105 .... 101.6
Pritt, Re, Morton v National Church League (1915) 85 LJ Ch 166, 113 LT 136, 31 TLR 299, sub nom Practice Note [1915] WN 134 .... 103.9
Prittie, Re [1940] 1 DLR 795 .... 100.6
Proctor v Bishop of Bath and Wells (1794) 2 Hy Bl 358 .... 93.5, 94.2, 94.30
Property Holding Co Ltd v Mischeff [1946] KB 645, [1946] 2 All ER 294, 115 LJKB 484, 90 Sol Jo 454, 175 LT 192, 62 TLR 568, CA; affd [1948] AC 291, [1948] 1 All ER 1, [1948] LJR 600, 92 Sol Jo 53, 64 TLR 2, HL 204.18
Prosser, Re, Prosser v Griffith [1929] WN 85, 167 LT Jo 307, 67 L Jo 346 ... 51.11, 74.2
Proud v Proud (1862) 32 Beav 234, 32 LJ Ch 125, 11 WR 101, 7 LT 553 .... 30.39, 91.2
Prout, Re [1943] 2 DLR 125, [1943] OWN 156 .... 38.3
Prowse v Abingdon (1738) 2 Eq Cas Abr 464n, 1 Atk 482, West temp Hard 312 .... 93.45
Prowse v Spurgin (1868) LR 5 Eq 99, 37 LJ Ch 251, 16 WR 413, 17 LT 590 .... 31.9
Pryce, Re, Lawford v Pryce [1911] 2 Ch 286, 80 LJ Ch 525, 105 LT 51, CA 24.12, 24.13
Pryor, Re, Woods v Pryor [1923] SASR 199 .... 86.5
Pryor v Pryor (1860) 23 JP 712, 29 LJPM & A 114 .... 12.12
Pryor v Pryor (1864) 2 De GJ & Sm 205, 33 LJ Ch 441, 10 Jur NS 603, 4 New Rep 82, 12 WR 781, 10 LT 360 .... 40.15
Pryse's Goods, Re [1904] P 301, 73 LJP 84, 48 Sol Jo 474, 90 LT 747, CA 25.2
Public Trustee v Beckman (1914) 15 SRNSW 6, 32 WNNSW 6 .... 42.6
Public Trustee v Bolton [1918] NZLR 908 .... 68.6
Public Trustee v Bowyer [1929] NZLR 438 .... 93.30
Public Trustee v Edmond (1912) 32 NZLR 202 .... 83.6
Public Trustee v Fraser (1987) 9 NSWLR 433 .... 9.18
Public Trustee v Gower [1924] NZLR 1233; revsd sub nom Gower v Public Trustee [1924] NZLR 1233, CA 35.29
Public Trustee v Kells (1904) 23 NZLR 605 .... 18.29
Public Trustee v Leslie [1917] NZLR 841 .... 72.6

Public Trustee v Nolan (1943) 60 WN 84, 43 SRNSW 169 .... 102.10
Public Trustee v Prisk (1896) 14 NZLR 306 .... 4.10
Public Trustee v Smith (1944) 61 WN 206, 44 SRNSW 348 .... 102.22
Public Trustee v Wilson [1916] NZLR 798 .... 62.1
Public Trustee for Saskatchewan v Montreal Trust Co of Canada (1989) 57 DLR (4th) 742 .... 41.20
Public Trustee of New Zealand v Guardian Trust and Executors Co of New Zealand Ltd. See Guardian Trust and Executors Co of New Zealand Ltd v Public Trustee of New Zealand
Puczka, Re (1970) 10 DLR (3d) 339, 63 WWR 56 .... 41.2, 64.38
Pugh, Re (1889) 15 VLR 833 .... 14.6
Pugh, Re, Pugh v Pugh [1943] Ch 387, [1943] 2 All ER 361, 112 LJ Ch 311, 87 Sol Jo 363, 169 LT 284, 59 TLR 430 .... 105.25
Pugh v Goodtitle. See Goodtitle d Bailey v Pugh
Pugh's Will Trusts, Re, Marten v Pugh [1967] 3 All ER 337, [1967] 1 WLR 1262, 111 Sol Jo 480 .... 36.2, 36.10, 53.5, 83.3
Pulbrook v Richmond Consolidated Mining Co (1878) 9 Ch D 610, 48 LJ Ch 65, 27 WR 377 .... 221.11
Pullen v Ready (1743) 2 Atk 587, 1 Wils 21, [1558–1774] All ER Rep 502 .... 34.14, 34.16, 35.10, 35.14
Pulley, Re, Midland Bank v Carter (1948) 92 Sol Jo 181 .... 64.31
Pullin v Pullin (1825) 3 Bing 47, 3 LJOSCP 193, 10 Moore CP 464 .... 58.1, 63.9
Pulsford v Hunter (1792) 3 Bro CC 416 .... 93.34
Pulteney v Earl of Darlington (1783) 1 Bro CC 223; affd (1796) 7 Bro Parl Cas 530, HL 37.8
Purcell v Bergin (1893) 20 AR 535 .... 21.5
Purchase v Shallis (1850) 19 LJ Ch 518, 2 H & Tw 354, 14 Jur 403 .... 63.8
Purfry v Rogers (1671) 3 Keb 11, sub nom Purefoy v Rogers 2 Lev 39, 2 Wms Saund 380 .... 93.10
Purnchard's Will Trusts, Re, Public Trustee v Pelly [1948] Ch 312, [1948] 1 All ER 790, [1948] LJR 1274, 92 Sol Jo 245 .... 64.54
Purse v Snaplin (1738) 1 Atk 414, West temp Hard 470 .... 41.1
Pursell v Elder (1865) 13 LT 203, 4 Macq 992, HL 61.1
Purssglove's Goods, Re (1872) 26 LT 405 .... 9.8
Purvis's Will, Re (1877) 3 VLR 37 .... 14.10
Pusey v Desbouvrie (1734) 2 Eq Cas Abr 270, 3 P Wms 315, [1558–1774] All ER Rep 425 .... 42.9
Putner, Re, Putner v Brooke (1929) 45 TLR 325 .... 64.35
Puxley v Puxley (1863) 1 New Rep 509, 8 LT 570 .... 64.53
Pycroft v Gregory (1829) 4 Russ 526, 6 LJOS Ch 121 .... 77.1
Pye, ex p, ex p Dubost (1811) 18 Ves 140, [1803–13] All ER Rep 96 .... 44.1, 44.2, 44.5, 44.8
Pyle, Re, Pyle v Pyle [1895] 1 Ch 724, 64 LJ Ch 477, 13 R 396, 43 WR 420, 39 Sol Jo 346, 72 LT 327 .... 7.27, 20.4, 41.20
Pym v Lockyer (1841) 5 My & Cr 29, 10 LJ Ch 153, 5 Jur 620 .... 44.1, 44.5, 44.8
Pym v Lockyer (1841) 12 Sim 394, 11 LJ Ch 8 .... 99.6
Pyne, Re, Lilley v A-G [1903] 1 Ch 83, 72 LJ Ch 72, 51 WR 283, 87 LT 730 .... 103.1
Pyne v Franklin (1832) 5 Sim 458, 2 LJ Ch 41 .... 85.3
Pyot v Pyot (1749) 1 Ves Sen 335, Belt's Sup 161 .... 58.11, 79.4

Pyrke v Waddingham (1852) 10 Hare 1 .... 49.9
Pytt v Fendall (1754) 1 Lee 553 .... 25.12

Q

Quarm v Quarm [1892] 1 QB 184, 61 LJQB 154, 40 WR 302, 66 LT 418, DC 50.16, 67.8, 83.1
Quay, Re (1907) 14 OLR 471, 9 OWR 823 .... 35.45
Queen's College, Oxford v Sutton (1842) 12 Sim 521, 11 LJ Ch 198, 6 Jur 906 .... 30.8
Queensland Trustees Ltd v Gray [1927] St R Qd 68 .... 85.3
Queensland Trustees Ltd v Robertson [1911] St R Qd 172 .... 77.2
Quennell v Turner (1851) 13 Beav 240, 20 LJ Ch 237, 15 Jur 547, 17 LTOS 101 .... 58.6, 58.10
Quibell's Will Trusts, Re, White v Reichert [1956] 3 All ER 679, [1957] 1 WLR 186, 101 Sol Jo 131 .... 64.7
Quicke v Leach (1844) 13 LJ Ex 348, 13 M & W 218 .... 93.8
Quihampton v Going (1876) 24 WR 917 .... 57.5, 100.7
Quilter v Quilter [2003] EWHC 2986 (Ch), [2004] 01 EG 94, [2004] 1 EGLR 79, [2003] All ER (D) 70 (Jun) 105.21
Quin v Armstrong (1876) IR 11 Eq 161 .... 39.28
Quinn v Butler (1868) LR 6 Eq 225 .... 19.2, 237.11
Quintin Dick, Re, Lord Cloncurry v Fenton [1926] Ch 992, [1926] All ER Rep 644, 96 LJ Ch 9, 70 Sol Jo 876, 136 LT 23, 42 TLR 681 .... 35.39

R

R, Re [1951] P 10, [1950] 2 All ER 117, 94 Sol Jo 386, 66 (pt 2) TLR 26 .... 5.3, 5.9
R (execution of statutory will), Re [2003] WTLR 1051 .... 4.22, 4.24
R, Re, R v O [1986] Fam Law 58 .... 105.6
R v Chief National Insurance Comr, ex p Connor [1981] QB 758, [1981] 1 All ER 769, [1981] 2 WLR 412, [1980] Crim LR 579, 124 Sol Jo 478 .... 9.15
R v Garland (1870) LR 5 QB 269, 39 LJQB 86, 18 WR 429, 22 LT 160 .... 27.5
R v Income Tax Acts Special Purposes Comr, ex p Dr Barnardo's Homes National Incorporated Association. See R v Income Tax Special Purposes Comrs, ex p Dr Barnardo's Homes National Incorporated Association
R v Income Tax Special Purposes Comrs, ex p Dr Barnardo's Homes National Incorporated Association [1920] 1 KB 468, CA; revsd sub nom Barnardo's Homes v Special Income Tax Comrs [1921] 2 AC 1, 90 LJKB 545, 65 Sol Jo 433, 125 LT 250, 37 TLR 540, sub nom R v Income Tax Acts Special Purposes Comr, ex p Dr Barnardo's Homes National Incorporated Association 7 TC 646, HL 1.8, 38.16
R v Pearson. See Pearson v Spencer
R v Price (1884) 12 QBD 247, 53 LJMC 51, 15 Cox CC 389, 33 WR 45n 7.33
R v Ringstead Inhabitants (1829) 9 B & C 218, 7 LJOSMC 103, 2 Man & Ry MC 71, 4 Man & Ry KB 67 .... 101.14
R v Stephenson (1884) 13 QBD 331, 49 JP 486, 53 LJMC 176, 15 Cox CC 679, 33 WR 44, 52 LT 267, CCR 7.33

R v Vincent (1721) 1 Stra 481 .... 49.7
Rabbeth v Squire (1859) 4 De G & J 406, 28 LJ Ch 565, 7 WR 657, 34 LTOS 40 .... 83.6, 101.13
Racal Group Services Ltd v Ashmore [1994] STC 416; affd [1995] STC 1151, 68 TC 86, CA 6.3
Race v Race [2002] EWHC 1868 (Ch), [2002] WTLR 1193 .... 44.3
Rackham v De La Mare (1864) 2 De GJ & Sm 74, 10 Jur NS 190, 3 New Rep 398, 12 WR 363, 9 LT 699 .... 47.26, 97.4
Rackstraw v Douglas 1917 SC 284 .... 94.11
Radburn v Jervis (1841) 3 Beav 450 .... 33.10, 33.12
Radcliffe, Re, Radcliffe v Bewes, [1892] 1 Ch 227, 61 LJ Ch 186, 40 WR 323, 36 Sol Jo 151, 66 LT 363, CA 40.10, 40.15
Radcliffe, Re, Young v Beale (1903) 51 WR 409 .... 20.5, 47.28
Radcliffe v Buckley (1804) 10 Ves 195 .... 74.1
Radford, Re, Jones v Radford (1918) 62 Sol Jo 604 .... 93.12, 93.30
Radford v Radford (1836) 1 Keen 486, 6 LJ Ch 138 .... 98.7
Radford v Risdon (1912) 56 Sol Jo 416, 28 TLR 342 .... 5.9
Radford v Willis (1871) 7 Ch App 7, 41 LJ Ch 19, 20 WR 132, 25 LT 720 .... 49.9, 53.5, 54.3, 65.1, 65.2, 80.1, 80.7
Radley-Kane, Re. See Kane v Radley-Kane
Radnor (Earl) v Shafto (1805) 11 Ves 448 .... 92.1, 92.3
Ragdale, Re, Public Trustee v Tuffill [1934] Ch 352, 103 LJ Ch 181, [1933] All ER Rep 284, 78 Sol Jo 48, 150 LT 459, 50 TLR 159 ... 51.2, 101.1, 101.6
Raikes v Ward (1842) 1 Hare 445, 11 LJ Ch 276, 6 Jur 530 .... 82.5
Raine, Re, Tyerman v Stansfield [1929] 1 Ch 716, 98 LJ Ch 244, 141 LT 25 ...... 32.16, 32.20, 32.22, 210.46, 210.47, 218.43, 218.57, 218.59
Raine, Re, Walton v A-G [1956] Ch 417, [1956] 1 All ER 355, [1956] 2 WLR 449, 100 Sol Jo 111 .... 103.13
Raine's Goods, Re (1865) 34 LJPM & A 125, 11 Jur NS 587 .... 9.8
Rajabally v Rajabally [1987] 2 FLR 390, [1987] Fam Law 314, CA 105.9
Rajendra v Mrinalini (1921) ILR 48 Calc 1100 .... 34.24
Ralli's Will Trusts, Re, Ralli's Marriage Settlement [1964] Ch 288, [1963] 3 All ER 940, [1964] 2 WLR 144, 108 Sol Jo 74 .... 30.18
Ralph v Carrick (1877) 5 Ch D 984, 46 LJ Ch 530, 25 WR 530, 37 LT 112; on appeal (1879) 11 Ch D 873, 48 LJ Ch 801, 28 WR 67, [1874–80] All ER Rep 1054, 40 LT 505, CA 50.2, 50.18, 74.8, 76.1, 76.3, 93.22, 101.4
Ralph v Watson (1840) 9 LJ Ch 328 .... 52.11
Ralphs, Re, Ralphs v District Bank Ltd [1968] 3 All ER 285, [1968] 1 WLR 1522, 112 Sol Jo 787 .... 30.31, 105.36
Ralston, Re [1906] VLR 689 .... 23.16, 104.5
Ramadge, Re [1969] NI 71 .... 47.32
Ramadge's Settlement, Re, Hamilton v Ramadge [1919] 1 IR 205 .... 94.12, 94.14, 94.33, 94.48
Rammell v Gillow (1845) 15 LJ Ch 35, 9 Jur 704 .... 97.7
Ramsay, Re [1948] VLR 347 .... 35.35
Ramsay, Re, Thorpe v Ramsay [1917] 2 Ch 64, 86 LJ Ch 514, 117 LT 117 .... 32.22, 216.13
Ramsay v Lowther (1912) 16 CLR 1 .... 62.2

Ramsay v Shelmerdine (1865) LR 1 Eq 129, 11 Jur NS 903, 14 WR 46, 13 LT 393 .... 20.5, 47.28
Ramsay (W T) Ltd v IRC [1982] AC 300, [1981] 1 All ER 865, [1981] 2 WLR 449, [1981] STC 174, 54 TC 101, [1982] TR 123, 125 Sol Jo 220, HL 241.13
Ramsden, Re (1974) 46 DLR (3d) 758 .... 97.7
Ramsden v Hassard (1791) 3 Bro CC 236 .... 101.3
Rancliffe (Lord) v Lady Parkyns (1818) 6 Dow 149 .... 42.5
Randal v Payne (1779) 1 Bro CC 55 .... 34.22, 35.6, 35.11
Randall v Russell (1817) 3 Mer 190, 17 RR 56 .... 8.4, 64.57
Randell, Re, Randell v Dixon (1888) 38 Ch D 213, 57 LJ Ch 899, 36 WR 543, [1886–90] All ER Rep 159, 58 LT 626, 4 TLR 307 .... 102.26, 102.27
Randfield v Randfield (1860) 8 HL Cas 225, 30 LJ Ch 177 .... 8.4, 9.8, 18.6, 82.2, 97.5
Randfield v Randfield (1863) 32 LJ Ch 668, 9 Jur NS 842, 2 New Rep 309, 11 WR 847 .... 9.8
Randoll v Doe d Roake. See Doe d Roake v Nowell
Ranelagh v Ranelagh (1834) 2 My & K 441 .... 98.10
Ranelagh v Ranelagh (1841) 4 Beav 419 .... 90.2
Rank's Settlement Trusts, Re, Newton v Rollo [1979] 1 WLR 1242, 123 Sol Jo 720 .... 40.4, 213.6, 213.13
Rankin v Weguelin (1832) 27 Beav 309, 29 LJ Ch 323n 1.15
Ranking v Barnes (1864) 33 LJ Ch 539, 10 Jur NS 463, 3 New Rep 660, 12 WR 565, 10 LT 124 .... 40.20
Ransome, Re, Moberley v Ransome [1957] Ch 348, [1957] 2 WLR 556, 101 Sol Jo 302, sub nom Re Ransome's Will Trusts [1957] 1 All ER 690 ... 32.16, 32.28, 66.13, 66.16, 66.21, 93.2, 93.30, 95.3, 218.72
Raphael, Re, Permanent Trustee Co of NSW Ltd v Lee (1903) 3 SRNSW 196, 20 WNNSW 84 .... 98.13
Raphael v Boehm (1852) 22 LJ Ch 299 .... 50.19
Rapley's Estate, Re, Rapley v Rapley [1983] 3 All ER 248, [1983] 1 WLR 1069, [1984] FLR 173, 127 Sol Jo 394 .... 16.3
Ratcliffe, Re, Holmes v McMullan [1999] STC 262, [1999] 11 LS Gaz R 70, 143 Sol Jo LB 82, [1999] All ER (D) 167 .... 38.15, 200.18, 214.72, 214.79
Rathborne v Lord Aldborough (1831) Hayes 207 .... 42.12
Rattenberry, Re, Ray v Grant [1906] 1 Ch 667, 75 LJ Ch 304, 54 WR 311, 50 Sol Jo 240, 94 LT 475, 22 TLR 249 .... 44.15, 210.27
Rauckman, Re (1970) 8 DLR (3d) 494, 71 WWR 73 .... 82.4, 93.28
Raven, Re, Spencer v National Association for the Prevention of Consumption and Other Forms of Tuberculosis [1915] 1 Ch 673, [1914–15] All ER Rep 353, 84 LJ Ch 489, 113 LT 131 .... 34.11, 35.38, 49.8, 221.18
Raven, Re, Spencer v Raven (1914) 111 LT 938 .... 64.14, 204.61
Raven v Waite (1818) 1 Wils Ch 204, 1 Swan 553 .... 32.5, 32.22
Ravensworth, Re, Ravensworth v Tindale [1905] 2 Ch 1, 74 LJ Ch 353, 92 LT 490, 21 TLR 357, CA 30.25, 210.58, 210.59, 210.61
Raw, Re, Morris v Griffiths (1884) 26 Ch D 601, 53 LJ Ch 1051, 32 WR 986, 51 LT 283 .... 37.2, 93.4
Rawlings v Jennings (1806) 13 Ves 39 .... 38.10, 64.17
Rawlins v Burgis (1814) 2 Ves & B 382 .... 41.22
Rawlins v Powel (1718) 1 P Wms 297 .... 44.15
Rawlins v Rawlins (1796) 2 Cox Eq Cas 425 .... 32.15, 32.20, 73.1

Rawlins' Goods, Re (1879) 44 JP 60, 48 LJP 64, 28 WR 139, 41 LT 559 .... 22.5
Rawlins' Trusts, Re (1890) 45 Ch D 299, CA; affd sub nom Scalé v Rawlins [1892] AC 342, 61 LJ Ch 421, 66 LT 542, 8 TLR 558, HL 49.2, 62.1, 101.1, 101.10
Rawlinson, Re, Hill v Withall [1909] 2 Ch 36, 78 LJ Ch 443, 100 LT 509 ..... 74.8, 87.3, 93.22
Rawlinson v Rawlinson (1876) 3 Ch D 302, 24 WR 946, 34 LT 848 .... 63.1
Rawlinson v Wass (1852) 9 Hare 673, 16 Jur 282 .... 78.2
Rawson, Re, Rigby v Rawson (1920) 90 LJ Ch 304, 65 Sol Jo 204, 124 LT 498 .... 93.22
Ray, Re, Cant v Johnstone [1916] 1 Ch 461, 85 LJ Ch 781, 114 LT 688 ..... 57.13, 57.17, 57.22, 71.5
Ray's Will Trusts, Re, Public Trustee v Barry [1936] Ch 520, [1936] 2 All ER 93, 105 LJ Ch 257, 80 Sol Jo 406, 155 LT 405, 52 TLR 446 .... 9.4, 81.5, 212.12
Rayer, Re, Rayer v Rayer [1903] 1 Ch 685, 72 LJ Ch 230, 51 WR 538, 87 LT 712 .... 20.4, 51.5, 54.4, 58.3, 58.4
Raymond v Brodbelt (1800) 5 Ves 199 .... 30.43, 32.33
Rayner, Re [1907] SALR 129 .... 64.20
Rayner, Re, Cloutman v Regnart (1920) 84 JP 61, 89 LJ Ch 369, 122 LT 577 .... 102.7, 102.8
Rayner, Re, Couch v Warner [1925] All ER Rep 484, 134 LT 141 .... 54.2, 66.12
Rayner, Re, Rayner v Rayner [1904] 1 Ch 176, 73 LJ Ch 111, 52 WR 273, [1900–3] All ER Rep 107, 48 Sol Jo 178, 89 LT 681, CA 50.13, 57.6, 64.53
Rayner's Goods, Re (1908) 52 Sol Jo 226 .... 25.10
Rayner's Will, Re (1929) 23 Tas LR 41 .... 64.26, 64.27
Rea, Re, Rea v Rea [1902] 1 IR 451 .... 23.4, 23.17, 104.5
Read, Re, Galloway v Harris (1892) 36 Sol Jo 626 .... 7.33
Read v Backhouse (1831) 2 Russ & M 546 .... 50.7
Read v Read (1866) 15 WR 165 .... 64.26
Read v Snell (1743) 2 Atk 642 .... 56.5, 56.6, 78.5
Read v Wills (1844) 1 Coll 86, 8 Jur 165, 2 LTOS 438 .... 85.3
Reade v Reade (1801) 5 Ves 744 .... 47.37
Reade v Reade (1881) 9 LR Ir 409 .... 44.17
Reade's Goods, Re [1902] P 75, 71 LJP 45, 86 LT 258 .... 5.7, 21.3
Reade-Revell, Re, Crellin v Melling [1930] 1 Ch 52, [1929] All ER Rep 506, 99 LJ Ch 136, 142 LT 177 .... 32.21, 218.47
Reading, Re, Edmonds v Reading [1916] WN 262, 60 Sol Jo 655 .... 31.8
Real, Re, McDowell v Real (1914) 33 NZLR 1342 .... 27.15
Reay v Rawlinson (1860) 29 Beav 88, 30 LJ Ch 330, 7 Jur NS 118, 9 WR 134 .... 66.20, 79.1
Recher's Will Trusts, Re, National Westminster Bank Ltd v National Anti-Vivisection Society Ltd [1972] Ch 526, [1971] 3 All ER 401, [1971] 3 WLR 321, 115 Sol Jo 448 .... 9.31, 9.35, 58.11, 102.26
Recknell, Re, White v Carter [1936] 2 All ER 36, 80 Sol Jo 406 .... 38.10, 64.35
Reddel v Dobree (1839) 10 Sim 244, 3 Jur 722 .... 1.15
Redding's (otherwise Higgins') Goods, Re (1850) 2 Rob Eccl 339, 14 Jur 1052, 16 LTOS 177 .... 11.20
Redfern v Hall. See Redfern, Re, Redfern v Bryning
Redfern, Re, Redfern v Bryning (1877) 6 Ch D 133, 47 LJ Ch 17, 25 WR 902, sub nom Redfern v Hall 37 LT 241 .... 51.1, 52.3, 101.1

Redgate, Re, Marsh v Redgate [1903] 1 Ch 356, 72 LJ Ch 204, 51 WR 216 .... 40.9, 213.12
Redington v Browne (1893) 32 LR Ir 347 .... 93.7, 94.7
Reece v Pressey (1856) 2 Jur NS 380 .... 4.17
Reed, Re (1888) 57 LJ Ch 790, 36 WR 682 .... 71.1
Reed, Re, Reed v Reed [1911] VLR 232 .... 64.35
Reed v Braithwaite (1871) LR 11 Eq 514, 40 LJ Ch 355, 19 WR 697, 24 LT 351 .... 56.7
Rees, Re, Jones v Evans [1920] 2 Ch 59, 89 LJ Ch 382, [1920] All ER Rep 138, 123 LT 567 .... 102.9, 102.22
Rees, Re, Lloyds Bank Ltd v Rees [1954] Ch 202, [1954] 2 WLR 59, 98 Sol Jo 28, sub nom Re Rees' Will Trusts, Lloyds Bank Ltd v Rees [1954] 1 All ER 7 .... 218.90, 218.91
Rees, Re, Rees v George (1881) 17 Ch D 701, 50 LJ Ch 328, 29 WR 301, 44 LT 241 .... 100.5
Rees, Re, Rees v Rees (1889) 60 LT 260 .... 30.12, 30.13
Rees, Re, Williams v Davies (1890) 44 Ch D 484, 59 LJ Ch 305, 38 WR 523, 62 LT 362 .... 77.3
Rees, Re, Williams v Hopkins [1950] Ch 204, [1949] 2 All ER 1003, 66 (pt 1) TLR 23, CA 36.10, 36.13, 82.5
Rees v Engelback (1871) LR 12 Eq 225, 40 LJ Ch 382, 19 WR 809, 24 LT 417 .... 45.2, 91.2
Rees v Fraser (1879) 26 Gr 233 .... 77.3
Rees v Hughes [1946] KB 517, [1946] 2 All ER 47, 115 LJKB 389, 90 Sol Jo 394, 175 LT 379, 62 TLR 394, CA 202.5
Rees v Newbery and Institute of Cancer Research [1998] 1 FLR 1041, [1998] Fam Law 320 .... 105.18
Rees v Rees (1873) LR 3 P & D 84, 37 JP 760, 29 LT 375 .... 11.4
Rees's Goods, Re (1865) 29 JP 296, 34 LJPM & A 56 .... 11.26, 13.2
Reeve v A-G (1843) 3 Hare 191, 7 Jur 1168, 1 LTOS 432 .... 102.7
Reeve's Trusts, Re (1877) 4 Ch D 841, 46 LJ Ch 412, 25 WR 628, 36 LT 906 .... 30.14
Reeves, Re, Edwards v Reeves-Hughes (1907) 51 Sol Jo 325 .... 97.1
Reeves, Re, Reeves v Pawson [1928] Ch 351, [1928] All ER Rep 342, 97 LJ Ch 211, 72 Sol Jo 121, 139 LT 66 .... 20.4, 41.3, 41.10, 207.4
Reeves v Baker (1854) 18 Beav 372, 23 LJ Ch 599, 2 Eq Rep 476, 18 Jur 588, 2 WR 354, 23 LTOS 54 .... 58.8
Reeves v Brymer (1799) 4 Ves 692 .... 74.1
Reeves v Grainger (1908) 52 Sol Jo 355 .... 11.18, 11.24, 13.3
Reeves v Reeves [1909] 2 IR 521 .... 18.10, 18.14
Reffell v Reffell (1866) LR 1 P & D 139, 35 LJP & M 121, 12 Jur NS 910, 14 WR 647, 14 LT 705 .... 57.3
Regan, Re, Phinney and Rand v Moore (1957) 8 DLR (2d) 541 .... 35.30
Regan's Goods, Re (1838) 1 Curt 908 .... 11.24
Regis Property Co Ltd v Dudley [1959] AC 370, [1958] 3 All ER 491, [1958] 3 WLR 647, 102 Sol Jo 844, HL 204.47
Reich, Re, Public Trustee v Guthrie (1924) 40 TLR 398 .... 34.11
Reid v Atkinson (1871) IR 5 Eq 373 .... 83.12, 99.1
Reid v Carleton [1905] 1 IR 147 .... 83.2, 83.11

Reid v Coggans or Reid [1944] AC 91, [1944] 1 All ER 134, 113 LJPC 20, 88 Sol Jo 16, 170 LT 97, 60 TLR 134, HL 33.13
Reid v Reid (1858) 25 Beav 469 .... 39.19, 40.21
Reid v Swan [1911] 1 IR 405, 45 ILT 224 .... 79.4
Reid v Wishart (1898) 16 NZLR 218 .... 97.10
Reid's Goods, Re (1866) LR 1 P & D 74, 35 LJP & M 43, 12 Jur NS 300, 14 WR 316, 13 LT 681 .... 23.13, 23.15
Reid's Goods, Re (1868) 33 JP 7, 38 LJP & M 1, 19 LT 265 .... 15.2
Reigh v Kearney [1936] 1 IR 138 .... 83.2
Reith v Seymour (1828) 4 Russ 263, 6 LJOS Ch 97 .... 83.11, 83.12
Remnant v Hood (1860) 2 De GF & J 396, 30 LJ Ch 71, 6 Jur NS 1173, 3 LT 485 .... 93.44
Renaud v Lamothe (1902) 32 SCR 357 .... 35.34
Rendle's Goods, Re (1899) 68 LJP 125 .... 15.2
Rendlesham v Woodford (1813) 1 Dow 249. See Thellusson v Woodford (1806) 13 Ves 209
Renouf's Trustees v Haining 1919 2 SLT 15 .... 7.3
Rentoul v Rentoul (1944) ALR 372, [1944] VLR 205 .... 86.2
Resch's Will Trusts, Re, Far West Children's Health Scheme v Perpetual Trustee Co Ltd [1969] 1 AC 514, [1968] 3 WLR 1153, [1968] ALR 161, [1967] 2 NSWR 706, sub nom Far West Children's Health Scheme v Perpetual Trustee Co Ltd [1967] 3 All ER 915, PC 38.10, 64.31
Resch's Will Trusts, Re, Le Cras v Perpetual Trustee Co Ltd [1969] 1 AC 514, [1968] 3 WLR 1153, [1968] ALR 161, [1967] 2 NSWR 706, sub nom Le Cras v Perpetual Trustee Co Ltd [1967] 3 All ER 915, PC 18.10, 18.14, 18.15, 20.3, 20.4, 38.10, 64.31, 88.4, 102.5, 102.10, 102.23
Revel v Watkinson (1748) 1 Ves Sen 93, [1558–1774] All ER Rep 284 .... 218.66
Reynard v Spence (1841) 4 Beav 103 .... 42.12
Reynette-James, Re, Wightman v Reynette-James [1975] 3 All ER 1037, [1976] 1 WLR 161, 119 Sol Jo 682 .... 5.7, 6.1, 52.2
Reynish v Martin (1746) 3 Atk 330, sub nom Rhenish v Martin 1 Wils 130 .... 34.2, 34.13, 34.16, 34.17, 35.8, 35.10, 35.16
Reynolds v Kortright (1854) 18 Beav 417, 2 Eq Rep 784, 2 WR 445, 24 LTOS 40 .... 50.19, 57.6
Reynolds v Reynolds [2005] EWHC 6 (Ch), [2005] All ER (D) 70 (Jan) 5.3
Reynolds' Goods, Re (1873) LR 3 P & D 35, 37 JP 215, 42 LJP & M 20, 21 WR 512, 28 LT 144 .... 21.6, 21.7, 21.8
Reynolds' Will Trusts, Re, Dove v Reynolds [1965] 3 All ER 686, [1966] 1 WLR 19, 109 Sol Jo 903 .... 64.44, 104.4, 204.5
Rhagg, Re, Easten v Boyd [1938] Ch 828, [1938] 3 All ER 314, 107 LJ Ch 436, 82 Sol Jo 546, 159 LT 434, 54 TLR 990 .... 32.2, 41.15, 64.7, 205.58, 205.59, 233.40
Rheeder v Ower (1791) 3 Bro CC 240 .... 97.4
Rhenish v Martin. See Reynish v Martin
Rhodes, Re (1914) 34 NZLR 190 .... 21.7
Rhodes, Re [1959] NZLR 458 .... 94.30
Rhodes, Re, Vennell v Godby [1961] NZLR 65, NZ CA 66.8, 76.2, 94.14
Rhodes v Muswell Hill Land Co (1861) 29 Beav 560, 30 LJ Ch 509, 7 Jur NS 178, 9 WR 472, 4 LT 229 .... 35.38, 49.8
Rhodes v Rhodes (1859) 27 Beav 413 .... 54.5

Rhodes v Rhodes (1874) 22 WR 835 .... 63.1
Rhodes v Rhodes (1882) 7 App Cas 192, [1881–5] All ER Rep Ext 1675, 51 LJPC 53, 30 WR 709, 46 LT 463, PC 5.1, 5.7, 50.9, 50.10, 50.21, 93.2, 101.14
Rhodesia Goldfields Ltd, Re, Partridge v Rhodesia Goldfields Ltd [1910] 1 Ch 239, 79 LJ Ch 133, 17 Mans 23, 54 Sol Jo 135, 102 LT 126 .... 30.12
Riach v Ferris [1934] SCR 725, [1935] 1 DLR 118 .... 5.9
Riall, Re, Westminster Bank Ltd v Harrison [1939] 3 All ER 657 .... 101.13
Ricabe v Garwood. See Rickabe v Garwood
Rice, Re, Turner v Rice [1920] VLR 44 .... 35.32
Rich, Re [1947] SASR 98 .... 19.4
Rich v Whitfield (1866) LR 2 Eq 583, 14 WR 907 .... 37.8
Richards, Re (1869) LR 8 Eq 119 .... 32.22
Richards, Re, Cawley v Dacey (1940) 84 Sol Jo 43, 162 LT 47 .... 79.4
Richards, Re, Davies v Edwards [1910] 2 Ch 74, 79 LJ Ch 500, 103 LT 130 .... 77.5, 87.1
Richards, Re, Jones v Rebbeck (1921) 90 LJ Ch 298, 65 Sol Jo 342, 124 LT 597 .... 20.4, 22.4, 41.6
Richards, Re, Uglow v Richards [1902] 1 Ch 76, 71 LJ Ch 66, 50 WR 90, [1900–3] All ER Rep 146, 46 Sol Jo 50, 85 LT 452 .... 83.11, 83.12, 83.15, 99.1
Richards, Re, Williams v Gorvin (1883) 50 LT 22 .... 82.4
Richards v Allan [2002] WTLR 1031 .... 4.11
Richards v Davies (1862) 13 CBNS 69, 32 LJCP 3, 1 New Rep 62, 11 WR 38, 7 LT 357; affd (1863) 13 CBNS 861, Ex Ch 50.2, 98.7, 98.13
Richards v Queen's Proctor (1854) 1 Ecc & Ad 235, 18 Jur 540, 23 LTOS 248 .... 18.9
Richardson, Re [1951] 2 DLR 162, [1951] OR 130, [1951] OWN 152 .... 83.6
Richardson, Re [1956] QSR 485 .... 77.2, 77.3
Richardson, Re, Mahoney v Treacy [1915] 1 IR 39 .... 33.41
Richardson, Re, Morgan v Richardson [1896] 1 Ch 512, 65 LJ Ch 512, 44 WR 279, 40 Sol Jo 225, 74 LT 12 .... 29.1, 29.6, 29.9, 29.13, 29.14, 29.20
Richardson, Re, Pole v Pattenden [1920] 1 Ch 423, 89 LJ Ch 258, 64 Sol Jo 290, 122 LT 714, 36 TLR 205, CA 30.37, 30.38
Richardson, Re, Richardson v Richardson [1904] 2 Ch 777, 73 LJ Ch 783, 53 WR 11, 48 Sol Jo 688, 91 LT 775 .... 35.21
Richardson, Re, Richardson v Richardson [1915] 1 Ch 353, 84 LJ Ch 438, [1914–15] All ER Rep 484, 112 LT 554 .... 33.3, 33.24, 33.28, 33.45
Richardson, Re, Shuldham v Royal National Lifeboat Institution (1887) 56 LJ Ch 784, 35 WR 710, 57 LT 17 .... 102.19
Richardson v Brown (1798) 4 Ves 177 .... 30.8
Richardson v Elphinstone (1794) 2 Ves 463 .... 44.15
Richardson v Greese (1743) 3 Atk 65 .... 44.15, 93.45
Richardson v Harrison (1885) 16 QBD 85, 55 LJQB 58, 54 LT 456, CA 101.9
Richardson v Power (1865) 19 CBNS 780, 35 LJCP 44, 11 Jur NS 739, 13 WR 1104, Ex Ch 93.1, 97.10
Richardson v Richardson (1845) 14 Sim 526, 9 Jur 322, 5 LTOS 142 .... 86.5
Richardson v Richardson (1867) LR 3 Eq 686, 36 LJ Ch 653, 15 WR 690 .... 30.12
Richardson v Smith (1870) 5 Ch App 648, 39 LJ Ch 877, 19 WR 81 .... 92.3
Richardson v Spraag (1718) 1 P Wms 434, 2 Eq Cas Abr 368 pl 1 .... 56.5, 68.1

Richardson v Watson (1833) 4 B & Ad 787, 2 LJKB 134, 1 Nev & MKB 567 .... 53.1, 57.9, 57.19
Richardson v Yardley. See Wild's Case
Richardson's Estate, Re (1935) 29 Tas LR 149 .... 3.6, 3.12
Richardson's Goods, Re (1859) 6 Jur NS 326, 1 Sw & Tr 515, 1 LT 448 .... 25.10
Richardson's Trusts, Re (1886) 17 LR Ir 436 .... 39.22, 39.25
Richardson's Trusts, Re [1896] 1 IR 295 .... 97.5
Richardson's Will Trusts, Re, Public Trustee v Llewellyn-Evans' Trustee [1958] Ch 504, [1958] 1 All ER 538, [1958] 2 WLR 414, 102 Sol Jo 176 .... 99.4
Richer, Re (1920) 50 DLR 614, 46 OLR 367 .... 83.6
Richerson, Re, Scales v Heyhoe [1892] 1 Ch 379, 61 LJ Ch 202, 40 WR 233, 36 Sol Jo 200, 66 LT 174 .... 37.7
Richerson, Re, Scales v Heyhoe (No 2) [1893] 3 Ch 146, 62 LJ Ch 708, 41 WR 583, 69 LT 590 .... 86.6, 101.6
Richmond v Savill [1926] 2 KB 530, [1926] All ER Rep 362, 95 LJKB 1042, 70 Sol Jo 875, 136 LT 15, CA 214.32
Rickabe v Garwood (1845) 8 Beav 579, sub nom Ricabe v Garwood 5 LTOS 515 .... 87.1
Rickerby v Nicolson [1912] 1 IR 343 .... 50.16
Rickett v Guillemard (1841) 12 Sim 88, 5 Jur 818 .... 90.1
Ricketts, Re, Ricketts v Ricketts (1910) 103 LT 278 .... 93.38, 93.39
Ricketts v Harling (1870) 23 LT 760 .... 64.14
Ricketts v Loftus (1841) 4 Y & C Ex 519 .... 40.9, 47.37
Ricketts v Turquand. See Man v Ricketts
Rickit's Trusts, Re (1853) 11 Hare 299, 22 LJ Ch 1044, 1 Eq Rep 251, 17 Jur 664, 1 WR 492, 21 LTOS 334, sub nom Arkitt, Re 21 LTOS 219 .... 58.10, 71.5
Rickless v United Artists Corpn [1988] QB 40, [1987] 1 All ER 679, [1987] 2 WLR 945, [1987] FSR 362, 131 Sol Jo 362, [1987] LS Gaz R 654, CA 25.1
Rickman, Re, Stokes v Rickman (1899) 80 LT 518 .... 39.19, 39.24
Rickman v Ives. See Buckman v Ives
Riddell, Re, Public Trustee v Riddell [1936] Ch 747, [1936] 2 All ER 1600, 105 LJ Ch 378, 80 Sol Jo 595, 155 LT 247, 52 TLR 675 .... 30.30, 32.5, 206.25, 210.15
Riddell's Will, Re (1880) 6 VLR 5 .... 14.10
Rider v Wager (1725) 2 Eq Cas Abr 569, 2 P Wms 328 .... 41.19
Ridge, Re, Hancock v Dutton (1933) 149 LT 266, [1933] All ER Rep 449 .... 54.5, 71.1, 71.5
Ridge, Re, Hellard v Moody (1885) 31 Ch D 504, 55 LJ Ch 265, 34 WR 159, 54 LT 549, CA 220.61
Ridge v Newton (1842) 4 I Eq R 389, 1 Con & Law 381, 2 Dr & War 239 .... 58.6
Ridge's Trusts, Re (1872) 7 Ch App 665, 41 LJ Ch 787, 20 WR 878, 27 LT 141 .... 90.2, 101.13
Ridges v Morrison (1784) 1 Bro CC 389 .... 44.1
Ridgeway v Munkittrick (1841) 1 Dr & War 84 .... 54.5, 76.3
Ridgway v Newstead (1860) 2 Giff 492, 6 Jur NS 1185, 9 WR 31, 3 LT 360; on appeal (1861) 3 De GF & J 474, 30 LJ Ch 889, 7 Jur NS 451, 9 WR 401, 4 LT 6492 .... 31.12
Ridgway v Woodhouse (1844) 7 Beav 437, 3 LTOS 19 .... 35.23, 35.35

Ridley, Re, Nicholson v Nicholson [1950] Ch 415, [1950] 2 All ER 1, 94 Sol Jo 338, 66 (pt 1) TLR 981 .... 30.3, 38.3, 210.5, 210.6, 210.7, 214.7
Ridout v Pain (or Payne) (1747) 3 Atk 486, 1 Ves Sen 10 .... 49.8, 52.10, 60.1
Rigetti Estate, Re [1950] 1 WWR 529 .... 38.4
Riggall, Re, Wildash v Riggall [1949] WN 491 .... 48.15, 93.19
Right v Price (1779) 1 Doug KB 241 .... 12.6
Right d Compton v Compton (1808) 9 East 267 .... 54.5
Right d Day v Day (1812) 16 East 67 .... 56.1, 98.11
Rigley's Trusts, Re (1866) 36 LJ Ch 147, 15 WR 190, 15 LT 499 .... 9.29, 102.22
Rigney Estate, Re (1954) 12 WWRNS 171 .... 61.1
Riland's Estate, Re, Phillips v Robinson [1881] WN 173 .... 102.23
Riley v Garnett (1849) 3 De G & Sm 629, 19 LJ Ch 146, 14 Jur 236, 14 LTOS 289 .... 93.24
Riley's Will Trusts, Re, Riley v Riley [1962] 1 All ER 513, [1962] 1 WLR 344, 106 Sol Jo 285 .... 52.3
Rimell v Simpson (1848) 18 LJ Ch 55 .... 9.40, 29.1
Ring v Hardwick (1840) 2 Beav 352, 4 Jur 242 .... 82.4
Rintoul's Trustees v Rintoul 1949 SC 297 .... 102.23
Riordan, Re [1961] VR 271 .... 18.28
Riordan v Banon (1876) IR 10 Eq 469 .... 36.11
Rippon's Estate, Re [1943] P 61, [1943] 1 All ER 676, 112 LJP 65, 87 Sol Jo 175, 168 LT 357, 59 TLR 285 .... 16.2
Rippon's Goods, Re (1863) 32 LJPM & A 141, 3 Sw & Tr 177, 9 LT 117 ..... 23.7, 23.8
Risdon v Public Trustee [1967] Ch 690, [1967] 1 All ER 391, [1967] 2 WLR 637, 111 Sol Jo 37 .... 51.8, 76.3
Rishton v Cobb (1839) 5 My & Cr 145, 9 LJ Ch 110, 4 Jur 2, [1835–42] All ER Rep 398 .... 33.20, 35.8, 62.3, 83.7, 93.20
Rising, Re, Rising v Rising [1904] 1 Ch 533, 73 LJ Ch 455, 90 LT 504 .... 101.1
Ritch v Sanders (1651) Sty 261 .... 64.32
Ritchie v Magree (1964) 114 CLR 173, [1964] ALR 649 .... 82.2, 83.9
Ritchie v Malcolm [1902] 2 IR 403 .... 43.4
Ritchie's Trustees v M'Donald 1915 SC 501 .... 86.2
River's Case (1737) 1 Atk 410 .... 58.9
Rivers, Re, Pullen v Rivers [1920] 1 Ch 320, 88 LJ Ch 462, [1918–19] All ER Rep 273, 63 Sol Jo 534, 121 LT 57 .... 29.4, 31.10
Rivett-Carnac's Will, Re (1885) 30 Ch D 136, 54 LJ Ch 1074, 33 WR 837, 53 LT 81, 1 TLR 582 .... 33.12
Rix, Re, Steward v Lonsdale (1921) 90 LJ Ch 474, 65 Sol Jo 513, 125 LT 216 .... 7.27, 41.5, 206.25
Roach v Trood (1876) 3 Ch D 429, 24 WR 803, 34 LT 105, CA 40.15
Roadley, Re, Iveson v Wakefield [1930] 1 Ch 524, 99 LJ Ch 232, 144 LT 64, 46 TLR 215 .... 102.6, 102.7
Robb, Re, Marshall v Marshall [1953] Ch 459, [1953] 2 WLR 819, 97 Sol Jo 263, sub nom Re Robb's Will Trusts, Marshall v Marshall [1953] 1 All ER 920 .... 33.30, 95.4, 95.7, 95.13
Robbins, Re, Robbins v Legge [1906] 2 Ch 648, 75 LJ Ch 751, 95 LT 779; affd [1907] 2 Ch 8, 76 LJ Ch 531, 51 Sol Jo 445, 96 LT 755, CA 33.5, 33.11, 211.17
Robe, Re, Slade v Walpole (1889) 61 LT 497 .... 41.9
Roberts, Re (1978) 82 DLR (3d) 591 .... 66.5

Roberts, Re, Kiff v Roberts (1886) 33 Ch D 265, 35 WR 176, 55 LT 498, CA 38.10
Roberts, Re, Percival v Roberts [1903] 2 Ch 200, 72 LJ Ch 597, 88 LT 505 .... 51.10, 56.5, 57.8, 66.6, 68.1, 82.2, 96.1
Roberts, Re, Repington v Roberts-Gawen (1881) 19 Ch D 520, 45 LT 450, CA 66.4, 66.5, 74.8, 89.1, 94.8, 94.12, 94.21, 102.26
Roberts, Re, Roberts v Morgan [1916] 2 Ch 42, 85 LJ Ch 713, 114 LT 1119 .... 97.6
Roberts, Re, Roberts v Parry (1902) 50 WR 469, 46 Sol Jo 359 .... 44.15
Roberts, Re, Roberts v Roberts [1978] 3 All ER 225, [1978] 1 WLR 653; affd [1978] 3 All ER 225, [1978] 1 WLR 653, 122 Sol Jo 264, CA 4.24, 17.2, 35.8
Roberts, Re, Stenton v Hardy [1963] 1 All ER 674, [1963] 1 WLR 406, 107 Sol Jo 175 .... 103.3, 103.9
Roberts, Re, Tarleton v Bruton (1885) 30 Ch D 234, 53 LT 432, CA 47.25, 219.26
Roberts v Bishop Kilmore [1902] 1 IR 333 .... 50.17, 55.6, 56.8
Roberts v Edwards (1863) 33 Beav 259, 33 LJ Ch 369, 9 Jur NS 1219, 12 WR 33, 9 LT 360 .... 61.1
Roberts v Kuffin (1741) 2 Atk 112, Barn Ch 259 .... 63.1, 64.39
Roberts v Phillips (1855) 4 E & B 450, 24 LJQB 171, 1 Jur NS 444, 3 CLR 513, 24 LTOS 337 .... 12.11, 12.15
Roberts v Pocock (1798) 4 Ves 150 .... 30.6, 31.3
Roberts v Roberts (1613) 2 Bulst 123 .... 50.2
Roberts v Roberts (1862) 26 JP 168, 31 LJPM & A 46, 8 Jur NS 220, 2 Sw & Tr 337, 5 LT 689 .... 1.5
Roberts v Round (1830) 3 Hag Ecc 548 .... 18.19
Roberts v Thorp (1911) 56 Sol Jo 13 .... 58.8, 83.9, 99.1
Roberts v Walker (1830) 1 Russ & M 752, [1824–34] All ER Rep 723 .... 210.6, 210.7
Roberts v Youle (1880) 49 LJ Ch 744 .... 97.7
Roberts' Estate, Re [1934] P 102, 103 LJP 61, [1934] All ER Rep 62, 78 Sol Jo 319, 51 LT 79, 50 TLR 321 .... 11.2, 11.9
Roberts' Estate, Re (1985) 38 SASR 324 .... 10.1
Roberts' Trusts, Re (1869) 38 LJ Ch 708, 17 WR 639 .... 30.42
Roberts' Will, Re (1929) 29 SRNSW 562, 46 WNNSW 188 .... 78.5
Robertson, Re (1908) 17 OLR 568, 13 OWR 208 .... 9.39, 210.36
Robertson, Re [1948] 4 DLR 606, [1948] OR 764, [1948] OWN 659 .... 33.24
Robertson, Re [1953] 2 SCR 1 .... 95.1, 205.73
Robertson, Re [1966] VR 196 .... 52.9
Robertson v Broadbent (1883) 8 App Cas 812, 53 LJ Ch 266, 32 WR 205, 50 LT 243, HL 30.3, 38.3, 210.6
Robertson v Flynn [1920] 1 IR 78, Ir CA 57.3, 57.13, 57.15, 58.1
Robertson v Fraser (1871) 6 Ch App 696, 40 LJ Ch 776, 19 WR 989 .... 86.2, 86.5, 86.8
Robertson v Junkin (1896) 26 SCR 192 .... 45.2
Robertson v Quiddington (1860) 28 Beav 529 .... 7.31
Robertson v Richardson (1885) 30 Ch D 623, 55 LJ Ch 275, 33 WR 897 .... 99.10
Robertson v Smith (1870) LR 2 P & D 43, 34 JP 377, 39 LJP & M 41, 22 LT 417 .... 10.4, 10.5
Robertson v Smith [1998] 4 VR 144, Vic CA 5.9
Robertson's Estate, Re [1964] NSWR 1087 .... 13.1
Robertson's Estate, Re, Marsden v Marsden (1963) 107 Sol Jo 318 .... 9.17
Robertson's Judicial Factor v Robertson 1968 SLT 32 .... 79.3
Robertson's Trust, Re (1858) 6 WR 405 .... 82.5

Robertson's Trustees v Robertson's Trustees 1933 SC 639 .... 95.5
Robins v National Trust Co [1927] AC 515, 96 LJPC 84, [1927] All ER Rep 73, 71 Sol Jo 158, 137 LT 1, 43 TLR 243, PC 4.13
Robinson, Re (1976) 75 DLR (3d) 532 .... 102.26
Robinson, Re, Besant v German Reich [1931] 2 Ch 122, 100 LJ Ch 321, 145 LT 254, 47 TLR 264 .... 102.4, 102.6
Robinson, Re, Davis v Robinson [1951] Ch 198, [1950] 2 All ER 1148, 94 Sol Jo 839, [1951] 1 TLR 132 .... 27.15, 102.5, 102.7
Robinson, Re, Lamb v Robinson [1930] 2 Ch 332, 99 LJ Ch 431, [1930] All ER Rep 658, 143 LT 593, 46 TLR 542 .... 18.10
Robinson, Re, McDonell v Robinson (1892) 22 OR 438 .... 32.12
Robinson, Re, Wright v Tugwell [1892] 1 Ch 95, 40 WR 137, 66 LT 81; on appeal [1897] 1 Ch 85, 61 JP 132, 66 LJ Ch 97, 45 WR 181, 41 Sol Jo 96, 76 LT 95, 13 TLR 72, CA 34.7, 45.2
Robinson, Re, Wright v Tugwell [1923] 2 Ch 332, 92 LJ Ch 340, 67 Sol Jo 619, 129 LT 527, 39 TLR 509 .... 103.18
Robinson v Clarke (1877) 2 PD 269, 42 JP 217, 47 LJP 17, 39 LT 43 .... 18.8
Robinson v Collins [1975] 1 All ER 321, sub nom Re Collins, Robinson v Collins [1975] 1 WLR 309, 119 Sol Jo 66 .... 29.11, 29.18, 104.6
Robinson v Comyns (1736) Cas temp Talb 164 .... 34.2
Robinson v Hardcastle (1786) 2 Bro CC 22 .... 94.43
Robinson v Hunt (1841) 4 Beav 450 .... 33.12
Robinson v Jenkins (1890) 24 QBD 275, 59 LJQB 147, 38 WR 360, 62 LT 439, 6 TLR 158, CA 64.9
Robinson v Murdock. See Fraser v Murdoch
Robinson v Ommanney (1882) 21 Ch D 780, 51 LJ Ch 894, 30 WR 939, 47 LT 78; affd (1883) 23 Ch D 285, 52 LJ Ch 440, 31 WR 525, [1881–5] All ER Rep 265, 49 LT 19, CA 2.9, 3.13, 3.14, 40.15
Robinson v Robinson (1854) 19 Beav 494 .... 37.2, 37.8
Robinson v Shepherd (1863) 4 De GJ & Sm 129, 10 Jur NS 53, 12 WR 234, 9 LT 527 .... 87.4
Robinson v Stuart (1891) 12 NSW Eq 47 .... 64.19
Robinson v Tickell (1803) 8 Ves 142 .... 9.40, 82.5
Robinson v Waddelow (1836) 8 Sim 134, Donnelly 108, 5 LJ Ch 350 .... 79.2
Robinson v Wheelwright (1856) 21 Beav 214, De GM & G 535 .... 53.2
Robinson v Wood (1858) 27 LJ Ch 726, 4 Jur NS 625, 6 WR 728, 31 LTOS 311 .... 48.15
Robinson Estate, Re [1930] 2 WWR 673 .... 18.28
Robinson Estate, Re [1931] 1 DLR 289, 39 Man LR 93, [1930] 2 WWR 609 .... 82.2
Robinson's Goods, Re (1867) LR 1 P & D 384, 31 JP 743, 36 LJP & M 93, 17 LT 19 .... 10.6
Robinson's Goods, Re (1870) LR 2 P & D 171, 34 JP 775, 40 LJP & M 16, 19 WR 135, 23 LT 397 .... 1.5
Robinson's Will Trusts, Re, Public Trustee v Gotto [1963] 1 All ER 777, [1963] 1 WLR 628, 107 Sol Jo 476 .... 94.30
Robotham v Dunnett. See Rowbotham v Dunnett
Robson, Re, Douglass v Douglass [1916] 1 Ch 116, 85 LJ Ch 137, 60 Sol Jo 222, 114 LT 134 .... 94.33

Robson, Re, Robson v Hamilton [1891] 2 Ch 559, 60 LJ Ch 851, 65 LT 173, 7 TLR 512 .... 63.1, 64.18
Robson v Flight (1865) 4 De GJ & Sm 608, 34 LJ Ch 226, 11 Jur NS 147, 5 New Rep 344, 146 RR 478, 13 WR 393, 11 LT 725 .... 27.7
Robson v Ibbs (1837) Donnelly 226, 6 LJ Ch 213 .... 77.1
Roby, Re, Howlett v Newington [1908] 1 Ch 71, 77 LJ Ch 169, 97 LT 773, CA 1.10
Roch v Callen (1848) 6 Hare 531, 17 LJ Ch 144, 12 Jur 112 .... 33.10, 44.1
Roche v Harding (1858) 7 I Ch R 338, 10 Ir Jur 253 .... 31.1, 33.34
Roche v M'Dermott [1901] 1 IR 394, 35 ILT 238 .... 9.36, 34.23
Rocke v Rocke (1845) 9 Beav 66 .... 30.36
Rodd v Lewis (1755) 2 Lee 176 .... 4.14, 4.20
Roddy v Fitzgerald (1858) 6 HL Cas 823 .... 49.2, 50.2, 50.7, 50.8, 50.9, 50.17, 50.21, 50.21, 57.3, 57.8, 76.1, 85.4, 101.9
Roden v Smith (1744) Amb 588 .... 93.27
Rodger, Re (1966) 60 DLR (2d) 666, [1967] 1 OR 379 .... 41.5, 41.20, 63.1
Rodger Estate, Re [1943] 2 WWR 700 .... 10.1
Rodmell, Re, Safford v Safford (1913) 57 Sol Jo 284, 108 LT 184 .... 64.40
Rodwell, Re, Midgley v Rumbold [1970] Ch 726, [1969] 3 All ER 1363, [1969] 3 WLR 1115, 113 Sol Jo 904 .... 80.4
Rodziszewski's Estate, Re (1982) 29 SASR 256 .... 4.10
Roe d James v Avis (1792) 4 Term Rep 605 .... 84.2
Roe d Wren v Clayton (1805) 6 East 628; affd sub nom Clayton v Roe (1813) 1 Dow 384, HL 101.13
Roe d Sampson v Down (1787) 2 Chit 529 .... 35.19
Roe d Buxton v Dunt (1767) 2 Wils 336 .... 40.2
Roe d Dodson v Grew (1767) 2 Wils 322, Wilm 272 .... 49.4
Roe d Urry v Harvey (1770) 5 Burr 2638 .... 64.19
Roe d Sheers v Jeffrey (1798) 7 Term Rep 589 .... 98.7, 98.10
Roe d Snape v Nevill (1848) 11 QB 466, sub nom Doe d Snape v Nevell 17 LJQB 119, 12 Jur 181, 10 LTOS 391 .... 52.8
Roe d Bendall v Summerset (1770) 2 Wm Bl 692, 5 Burr 2608 .... 101.4
Roe d Conolly v Vernon and Vyse (1804) 5 East 51, 1 Smith KB 318 .... 58.6
Roe d Walker v Walker (1803) 3 Bos & P 375 .... 64.26
Roffey v Bent (1867) LR 3 Eq 759 .... 99.7
Rogers, Re [1955] SASR 211 .... 51.2, 83.11
Rogers, Re [2006] EWHC 753 (Ch), [2006] 2 All ER 792, [2006] 1 WLR 1577, [2006] WTLR 691, [2006] NLJR 644, (2006) Times, 3 May, [2006] All ER (D) 68 (Apr) 25.5, 202.23
Rogers, Re, Lloyds Bank Ltd v Lory [1944] Ch 297, [1944] 2 All ER 1, 113 LJ Ch 287, 88 Sol Jo 246, 171 LT 65, 60 TLR 406, CA 93.35, 93.39, 218.86
Rogers, Re, Public Trustee v Rogers [1915] 2 Ch 437, 84 LJ Ch 837, 60 Sol Jo 27, 113 LT 916 .... 38.19, 38.23
Rogers v Frank (1827) 1 Y & J 409 .... 25.12
Rogers v Jones (1876) 3 Ch D 688, 24 WR 1039 .... 42.6, 42.12
Rogers v Jones (1877) 7 Ch D 345, 38 LT 17 .... 42.6
Rogers v Mutch (1878) 10 Ch D 25, 48 LJ Ch 133, 27 WR 131 .... 65.3
Rogers v Rogers (1855) 25 LTOS 262 .... 29.15
Rogers v Rogers (1910) 11 SRNSW 38, 28 WNNSW 38 .... 64.7
Rogers v Thomas (1837) 2 Keen 8 .... 38.3

Rogers v Towsey (1845) 9 Jur 575, 2 Holt Eq 270 .... 67.2
Rogers and Andrews v Goodenough and Rogers (1862) 26 JP 119, 31 LJPM & A 49, 8 Jur NS 391, 2 Sw & Tr 342, 5 LT 719 .... 21.3
Rogerson, Re, Bird v Lee [1901] 1 Ch 715, 70 LJ Ch 444, 84 LT 200 .... 9.29, 47.8, 102.22
Rohatynski Estate, Re [1948] 2 WWR 618 .... 83.12
Rolfe v Perry (1863) 3 De GJ & Sm 481, 32 LJ Ch 471, 9 Jur NS 853, 11 WR 674, 8 LT 441 .... 22.3
Rolfe's Goods, Re (1846) 4 Notes of Cases 406 .... 14.14
Rolleston v Sinclair [1924] 2 IR 157, CA 13.1
Rolls v Miller (1884) 27 Ch D 71, 53 LJ Ch 682, 32 WR 806, [1881–5] All ER Rep 915, 50 LT 597, CA 102.7
Rolt, Re, Rolt v Burdett [1908] WN 76 .... 39.10
Rook v A-G (1862) 31 Beav 313, 31 LJ Ch 791, 9 Jur NS 9, 10 WR 745 .... 87.1
Rooke, Re, Jeans v Gatehouse [1933] Ch 970, 102 LJ Ch 371, [1933] All ER Rep 978, 149 LT 445 .... 30.34
Rooke v Langdon (1844) 2 LTOS 495 .... 18.21
Rooke's Will Trusts, Re, Taylor v Rooke [1953] Ch 716, [1953] 2 All ER 110, [1953] 2 WLR 1176, 97 Sol Jo 388 .... 40.21, 48.15, 68.10, 97.6, 214.3, 214.30
Roome v Roome (1744) 3 Atk 181 .... 44.2, 44.8
Rooney, Re [1950] SASR 67 .... 50.7, 54.2
Roos v Karpenkow (1998) 71 SASR 497 .... 5.4
Roose, Re, Evans v Williamson (1880) 17 Ch D 696, 45 JP 343, 50 LJ Ch 197, 29 WR 230, 43 LT 719 .... 7.25, 64.20
Roper v Roper (1867) LR 3 CP 32, 37 LJCP 7, 16 WR 253, 17 LT 286, Ex Ch 73.1, 85.2
Roper v Roper (1876) 3 Ch D 714, 24 WR 1013, 35 LT 155 .... 33.7
Roper's Estate, Re, Morrell v Gissing (1889) 41 Ch D 409, 58 LJ Ch 439, 37 WR 731, 61 LT 42, 5 TLR 364 .... 67.4
Roper-Curzon v Roper-Curzon (1871) LR 11 Eq 452, 19 WR 519, 24 LT 406 .... 218.94, 218.95
Ropner's Settlements Trusts, Re, Ropner v Ropner [1956] 3 All ER 332n, [1956] 1 WLR 902, 100 Sol Jo 530 .... 218.94
Rosar, Re (1975) 60 DLR (3d) 615 .... 83.6
Rose, Re, Midland Bank Executor and Trustee Co Ltd v Rose [1949] Ch 78, [1948] 2 All ER 971, [1949] LJR 208, 92 Sol Jo 661 .... 30.8
Rose, Re, Rose v Rose (1915) 85 LJ Ch 22, 113 LT 142 .... 33.30
Rose v Bartlett (1633) Cro Car 292 .... 64.32
Rose v Gould (1852) 15 Beav 189, 21 LJ Ch 360, 19 LTOS 42 .... 30.12
Rose v Sowerby (1830) Taml 376 .... 93.35
Rosenberg v Scraggs (1900) 19 NZLR 196 .... 99.1
Rosenthal, Re, Schwarz v Bernstein [1972] 3 All ER 552, [1972] 1 WLR 1273, 51 ATC 371, [1972] TR 329, 116 Sol Jo 666 .... 55.7
Rosher, Re, Rosher v Rosher (1884) 26 Ch D 801, 53 LJ Ch 722, 32 WR 821, 51 LT 785 .... 34.5, 99.2
Ross, Re (1901) 1 SRNSW 1, 18 NSWWN 40 .... 84.2
Ross, Re (1904) 7 OLR 493, 3 OWR 405, 24 CLT 231 .... 35.22
Ross, Re, Ashton v Ross [1900] 1 Ch 162, 69 LJ Ch 192, 48 WR 264, 81 LT 578 .... 33.2, 33.15
Ross, Re, Carrail v Tilley [1963] SASR 32 .... 64.35

Ross, Re, Piddington v Presbyterian Church of Queensland [1964] Qd R 132 ... 9.29
Ross, Re, Ross v Waterfield [1930] 1 Ch 377, 99 LJ Ch 67, [1929] All ER Rep 456, 142 LT 189, 46 TLR 61 ... 24.2
Ross v Borer (1862) 2 John & H 469, 31 LJ Ch 709, 8 Jur NS 1058, 10 WR 644, 6 LT 514 ... 33.12
Ross v Caunters [1980] Ch 297, [1979] 3 All ER 580, [1979] 3 WLR 605, 123 Sol Jo 605 ... 1.14, 4.21, 9.3
Ross v Dunlop (1878) 5 R 833, 15 SLR 580 ... 66.21
Ross v National Trust Co [1939] SCR 276, 4 DLR 653 ... 93.29
Ross v Perrin-Hughes [2004] EWHC 2559 (Ch), [2004] All ER (D) 159 (Nov) ... 41.8, 41.10, 207.3
Ross v Ross (1845) 2 Coll 269, 9 Jur 795, 5 LTOS 430 ... 91.5
Ross v Ross (1855) 20 Beav 645 ... 76.3, 87.3
Ross v Ross (1894) 25 SCR 307 ... 79.4
Ross v Ross (1930) 42 BCR 272, 2 DLR 42, [1930] 1 WWR 375 ... 44.15
Ross v Veal (1855) 1 Jur NS 751, 3 WR 652 ... 64.26
Ross Estate, Re (1967) 59 WWR 572 ... 34.2
Rosse (Countess), Re, Parsons v Earl of Rosse (1923) 93 LJ Ch 8, [1923] All ER Rep 634, 67 Sol Jo 638, 129 LT 592, CA ... 30.24
Rosslyn's (Lady) Trust, Re (1848) 16 Sim 391, 18 LJ Ch 98, 13 Jur 27, 12 LTOS 267 ... 95.3, 95.8
Roth, Re, Goldberger v Roth (189) 74 LT 50, [1895–9] All ER Rep 455 ... 214.3, 221.29
Rotherham v Fanshaw (1748) 3 Atk 628 ... 9.40
Rothermere (Viscount), Re, Mellors Basden & Co v Coutts & Co [1945] Ch 72, [1944] 2 All ER 593, 115 LJ Ch 34, 88 Sol Jo 437, 172 LT 98, 61 TLR 69 ... 33.41
Round v Pickett (1878) 47 LJ Ch 631, 26 WR 493 ... 101.4, 101.6, 101.14
Roundel v Currer (1786) 2 Bro CC 67 ... 34.8, 34.21, 42.12
Rous v Jackson (1885) 29 Ch D 521, 54 LJ Ch 732, 33 WR 773, 52 LT 733 ... 94.48
Routledge's Trusts, Re, Routledge v Saul [1909] 1 Ch 280, 99 LT 919, sub nom Re Routledge, Saul v Routledge 78 LJ Ch 136 ... 7.6, 27.7
Rowbotham v Dunnett (1878) 8 Ch D 430, sub nom Robotham v Dunnett 47 LJ Ch 449, 26 WR 529, 38 LT 278 ... 36.2, 36.3, 36.4, 36.8
Rowe, Re, Bennetts v Eddy [1941] Ch 343, [1941] 2 All ER 330, 110 LJ Ch 145, 85 Sol Jo 264, 165 LT 76, 57 TLR 592 ... 30.3, 38.3, 210.5, 210.6, 210.7
Rowe, Re, Merchant Taylors' Co v London Corpn (1914) 30 TLR 528 ... 103.14
Rowe, Re, Pike v Hamlyn [1898] 1 Ch 153, 67 LJ Ch 87, 46 WR 357, 42 Sol Jo 96, 77 LT 475, CA ... 52.11, 58.4
Rowe v Clarke [2006] EWHC 1292 (Ch), [2006] WTLR 347, [2006] All ER (D) 124 (May) ... 18.12
Rowe v Rowe (1848) 2 De G & Sm 294, 17 LJ Ch 357, 12 Jur 909, 64 ER 132, 11 LTOS 392 ... 44.15
Rowe v Rowe (1861) 29 Beav 276 ... 38.23
Rowe and Brown v Public Trustee [1928] NZLR 51 ... 68.13
Rowell, Re, Public Trustee v Bailey (1982) 31 SASR 36 ... 103.3
Rowinska, Re, Wyniczenko v Plucinska-Surowka [2006] WTLR 487 ... 5.3
Rowland, Re, Jones v Rowland (1902) 86 LT 78 ... 83.7, 83.11, 99.1
Rowland, Re, Smith v Russell [1963] Ch 1, [1962] 2 All ER 837, [1962] 3 WLR 637, 106 Sol Jo 450, CA ... 49.2, 50.6, 50.13, 70.2, 219.2

Rowland v Gorsuch (1789) 2 Cox Eq Cas 187 .... 74.8
Rowland v Tawney (1858) 26 Beav 67 .... 93.1
Rowland v Vancouver College Ltd (2000–03) 3 ITELR 182, SC BC 102.8
Rowlands, Re [1984] FLR 813; affd [1984] FLR 813, [1984] Fam Law 280, CA 105.9
Rowlatt v Easton (1863) 2 New Rep 262, 11 WR 767 .... 58.10
Rowley v Merlin (1860) 24 JP 824, 6 Jur NS 1165 .... 14.8
Rowley v Rowley (1854) Kay 242, 23 LJ Ch 275, 2 Eq Rep 241, 18 Jur 306, 23 LTOS 55 .... 40.15
Rowlls, Re, Walters v Treasury Solicitor [1900] 2 Ch 107, [1900–3] All ER Rep 756, 69 LJ Ch 562, 48 WR 562, 44 Sol Jo 448, 82 LT 633, CA ... 38.23, 214.37
Rowlls v Bebb [1900] 2 Ch 107, [1900–3] All ER Rep 756, 69 LJ Ch 562, 48 WR 562, 44 Sol Jo 448, 82 LT 633, CA 38.17, 38.19, 214.3
Rowntree (Joseph) Memorial Trust Housing Association Ltd v A-G [1983] Ch 159, [1983] 1 All ER 288, [1983] 2 WLR 284, 127 Sol Jo 137 .... 102.5, 102.7, 102.18
Rowsell, Re. See A-G v Rowsell
Rowson's Estate, Re [1944] 2 All ER 36, 88 Sol Jo 232, 171 LT 70 .... 16.2
Royal Choral Society v IRC [1943] 2 All ER 101, 25 TC 263, 112 LJKB 648, 87 Sol Jo 336, 169 LT 100, CA 102.10
Royal College of Nursing v St Marylebone Corpn [1959] 3 All ER 663, [1959] 1 WLR 1077, 57 LGR 347, 52 R & IT 722, 124 JP 49, 103 Sol Jo 873, 174 Estates Gazette 799, CA 102.10, 102.18
Royal College of Surgeons of England v National Provincial Bank Ltd. See Bland-Sutton's Will Trusts, Re, National Provincial Bank Ltd v Middlesex Hospital
Royal North Shore Hospital of Sydney v A-G for New South Wales (1938) 60 CLR 396, 38 SRNSW 405, 55 WNNSW 116, 12 ALJ 182, 44 ALN 434 .... 102.8
RSPCA of New South Wales v Benevolent Society of New South Wales (1960) 102 CLR 629 (Aust HC) 202.28
Royal Society of London and Thompson (1881) 17 Ch D 407, 50 LJ Ch 344, 29 WR 838, 44 LT 274 .... 102.8
Royal Trust Co v Ford (1971) 20 DLR (3d) 348, [1971] 3 WWR 517 .... 4.13, 4.15
Royal Trust Co v Moore (1955) 16 WWR 204 .... 35.21, 35.22, 62.1
Royal Trust Co v Shimmin (1933) 47 BCR 138, [1933] 3 DLR 718 .... 54.1
Royal Trust Co and MacMurray v Crawford [1955] SCR 184 .... 38.19
Royce, Re, Turner v Wormald [1940] Ch 514, [1940] 2 All ER 291, 109 LJ Ch 327, 84 Sol Jo 288, 163 LT 172, 56 TLR 540 .... 102.9
Royce's Will Trusts, Re, Tildesley v Tildesley [1959] Ch 626, [1959] 3 All ER 278, [1959] 3 WLR 254, 103 Sol Jo 675, CA 9.3, 9.11
Royle v Hamilton (1799) 4 Ves 437 .... 74.1
Royle v Harris [1895] P 163, 64 LJP 65, 11 R 601, 43 WR 352, 72 LT 474, 11 TLR 268 .... 11.2, 11.3
Royse, Re, Royse v Royse [1985] Ch 22, [1984] 3 All ER 339, [1984] 3 WLR 784, [1985] FLR 196, [1984] Fam Law 156, 128 Sol Jo 665, [1984] LS Gaz R 2543, CA 9.14, 9.18, 9.22, 105.8
Rubbins, Re, Gill v Worrall (1898) 79 LT 313, CA 83.12
Rücker v Scholefield (1862) 1 Hem & M 36, 32 LJ Ch 46, 9 Jur NS 17, 1 New Rep 48, 136 RR 18, 11 WR 137 .... 40.21, 100.2

Rudd, Re, Rudd v Leitch (1914) 33 NZLR 1446 .... 59.3
Rudd v Harper (1888) 16 OR 422 .... 30.3
Rudderham, Re (1971) 21 DLR (3d) 457 .... 100.5
Ruddock, Re, Newberry v Mansfield [1908–10] All ER Rep 725, 102 LT 89, CA 29.9
Rudge v Winnall (1849) 12 Beav 357, 18 LJ Ch 469, 13 Jur 737, 14 LTOS 325 .... 7.25, 64.20, 93.34
Rufenack v Hope Mission {2003) 6 ITELR 1, QB (Alt) 36.1
Rumball, Re, Sherlock v Allan [1956] Ch 105, [1955] 3 All ER 71, [1955] 1 WLR 1037, 48 R & IT 672, 99 Sol Jo 579, CA 102.17
Rumsey v Sterne (1967) 111 Sol Jo 113 .... 17.2
Ruscombe v Hare (1828) 2 Bli NS 192, 6 Dow 1, 4 ER 1103, HL 40.3
Rushbrook v Pearman (1913) 32 NZLR 680 .... 78.1
Rushout's Goods, Re (1849) 13 Jur 458, 13 LTOS 264 .... 14.10
Russel v Buchanan (1836) 7 Sim 628, 5 LJ Ch 122 .... 93.16
Russel v Hawkins. See Hassell v Hawkins
Russell, Re (1885) 52 LT 559, CA 82.3, 97.3
Russell, Re, Dorrell v Dorrell [1895] 2 Ch 698, 64 LJ Ch 891, 12 R 499, 44 WR 100, [1895–9] All ER Rep 793, 73 LT 195, CA 94.23, 94.25
Russell, Re, Public Trustee v Campbell (1912) 56 Sol Jo 651 .... 30.14, 30.15
Russell, Re, Russell v Chell (1882) 19 Ch D 432, 51 LJ Ch 401, 30 WR 454, 46 LT 336 .... 7.3, 59.2, 59.3
Russell v Dickson (1842) 2 Dr & War 133; affd (1853) 4 HL Cas 293, 17 Jur 307, 21 LTOS 161 .... 88.4
Russell v Durie [1920] 39 NZLR 91 .... 35.8
Russell v Fraser (1980) 118 DLR (3d) 733 (BCCA) 5.4
Russell v IRC [1988] 2 All ER 405, [1988] 1 WLR 834, [1988] STC 195, 132 Sol Jo 659, [1988] 16 LS Gaz R 44 .... 241.15
Russell v Jackson (1852) 10 Hare 204, 90 RR 336 .... 36.2, 36.4, 36.5, 36.8, 36.13, 102.11
Russell v Kellett (1855) 20 JP 131, 2 Jur NS 132, 3 Sm & G 264, 26 LTOS 193 .... 102.7
Russell v Perpetual Trustee Co Ltd [1956] ALR 952 .... 82.4
Russell v Russell [1903] 1 IR 168, 36 ILT 207 .... 93.39
Russell v White (1895) 16 NSW Eq 158 .... 44.15
Russell's Goods, Re (1890) 15 PD 111, 59 LJP 80, 62 LT 644 .... 17.5
Russell's Goods, Re [1892] P 380, 62 LJP 15, 1 R 456, 67 LT 504 .... 25.2
Russell's Will Trusts, Re [1955] 2 DLR 721 .... 40.18
Rust v Baker (1837) 8 Sim 443 .... 68.10
Rutherford v IRC [1965] NZLR 444 .... 205.25
Rutherford v Maule (1832) 4 Hag Ecc 213 .... 4.13, 4.20
Rutherford's Trustee v Dickie (1907) 44 SLR 960, 1907 SC 1280, 15 SLT 296 .... 77.1
Rutland v Rutland [2007] All ER (D) 326 (Mar) 4.11
Rutter, Re, Donaldson v Rutter [1907] 2 Ch 592, 77 LJ Ch 34, 97 LT 883, 24 TLR 12 .... 33.20
Ruttie, Re, Ruttie v Saul [1969] 3 All ER 1633, [1970] 1 WLR 89, 113 Sol Jo 903 .... 105.5
Ryall v Hannam (1847) 10 Beav 536, 16 LJ Ch 491, 11 Jur 761, 10 LTOS 126 .... 58.10
Ryan, Re (1887) 19 LR Ir 24 .... 99.7

Ryan v Cowley (1835) L & G temp Sugd 7 .... 98.3, 98.4
Ryan v Public Trustee [2000] 1 NZLR 700 .... 1.14
Ryan v Smith (1972) 22 DLR (3d) 1 .... 30.26
Ryan's Estate, Re [1955] VLR 316 .... 11.4
Ryder, Re, Burton v Kearsley [1914] 1 Ch 865, 83 LJ Ch 653, [1914–15] All ER Rep 144, 58 Sol Jo 556, 110 LT 970, CA 83.11, 83.15
Ryder's Goods, Re (1843) 2 Notes of Cases 462 .... 9.4
Ryder's Goods, Re (1861) 31 LJPM & A 215, 7 Jur NS 196, 2 Sw & Tr 127, 3 LT 756 .... 25.1
Rymer, Re, Rymer v Stanfield [1895] 1 Ch 19, 64 LJ Ch 86, 12 R 22, 43 WR 87, [1891–4] All ER Rep 328, 39 Sol Jo 26, 71 LT 590, CA 103.1, 103.3
Rymes v Clarkson (1809) 1 Phillim 22 .... 10.14

S

S (gifts by mental patient), Re [1997] 2 FCR 320, [1997] 1 FLR 96, [1997] Fam Law 92 .... 4.24
S's Estate, Re [1968] P 302, [1967] 2 All ER 150, [1967] 3 WLR 325, 110 Sol Jo 911 .... 9.14, 25.1
Sabatini, Re (1969) 114 Sol Jo 35 .... 18.17
Sacks v Gridiger (1990) 22 NSWLR 502 .... 19.4
Sackville-West v Viscount Holmesdale (1870) LR 4 HL 543, 39 LJ Ch 505 ... 50.4, 57.8, 94.15
Sadler, Re, Furniss v Cooper (1915) 60 Sol Jo 89 .... 67.5
Sadlier v Butler (1867) IR 1 Eq 415 .... 42.5
Safford's Settlement, Re, Davies v Burgess [1915] 2 Ch 211, 84 LJ Ch 766, [1914–15] All ER Rep 939, 59 Sol Jo 666, 113 LT 723, 31 TLR 529 .... 40.7
Saillard, Re, Pratt v Gamble [1917] 2 Ch 401, 86 LJ Ch 749, 117 LT 545, CA 33.47
St Albans (Duke) v Beauclerk (1743) 2 Atk 636 .... 88.3, 88.4
St Alphage, London Wall, Re (1888) 59 LT 614, 4 TLR 756 .... 102.7, 102.9
St Barbe Green v IRC [2005] EWHC 14 (Ch), [2005] STC 288, [2005] SWTI 106, [2005] All ER (D) 17 (Jan), sub nom Green v IRC [2005] 1 WLR 1722, (2005) Times, 14 January 200.77
St Donats Settled Estate, Re. See Carne's Settled Estates, Re
St Dunstan's University v Canada Permanent Trust Co (1976) 67 DLR (3d) 480 .... 103.3
St George (AT) Re, Perpetual Trustee Co Ltd v St George [1964] NSWR 587 .... 35.30
St Hill v St Hill (1906) 26 NZLR 1105 .... 57.15
St Nicholas Acons (Parish), Re (1889) 60 LT 532 .... 102.10
St Thomas More Collegiate Ltd v Burnett (2000–03) 3 ITELR 182, SC BC 102.8
St Vincent Estate, Re (1953) 9 WWRNS 274 .... 82.5, 82.7
Sakzewski's Will and Codicil, Re [1943] QWN 38 .... 18.25
Salaman, Re, De Pass v Sonnenthal [1907] 2 Ch 46, 76 LJ Ch 419, 96 LT 809; revsd [1908] 1 Ch 4, 77 LJ Ch 60, 98 LT 255, CA 29.1, 29.2, 73.1
Salisbury v Petty (1843) 3 Hare 86, 7 Jur 1011 .... 68.1, 68.14
Salisbury v Salisbury (1848) 6 Hare 526, 17 LJ Ch 480, 12 Jur 671 .... 3.11
Salkeld v Vernon (1758) 1 Eden 64 .... 98.3

Sallery, Re (1861) 11 I Ch R 236 .... 84.4, 98.1
Sallis v Jones [1936] P 43, [1935] All ER Rep 872, 105 LJP 17, 79 Sol Jo 880, 154 LT 112, 52 TLR 113 .... 17.4
Salmen, Re, Salmen v Bernstein (1912) 56 Sol Jo 632, 107 LT 108, CA 205.74
Salmon, Re, Coard v National Westminster Bank Ltd [1981] Ch 167, [1980] 3 All ER 532, [1980] 3 WLR 748, 124 Sol Jo 813 .... 105.5
Salmon v Gibbs (1849) 3 De G & Sm 343, 18 LJ Ch 177, 13 Jur 355, 12 LTOS 470 .... 40.15
Salmon v Tidmarsh (1859) 5 Jur NS 1380 .... 85.3
Salomons, Re, Public Trustee v Wortley [1920] 1 Ch 290, [1920] All ER Rep 768, 89 LJ Ch 222, 64 Sol Jo 241, 122 LT 670, 36 TLR 212 .... 9.40, 29.1
Salter, Re, Farrant v Carter (1881) 44 LT 603 .... 38.12
Salter, Re, Rea v Crozier [1911] 1 IR 289, 45 ILT 174 .... 102.23
Salusbury v Denton (1857) 21 JP 726, 3 K & J 529, 26 LJ Ch 851, 3 Jur NS 740, 5 WR 865, 30 LTOS 63 .... 79.4, 101.9, 102.22
Salvesen's Trustees v Wye 1954 SC 440 .... 53.5
Salvin, Re, Marshall v Wolseley [1906] 2 Ch 459, 75 LJ Ch 825, 50 Sol Jo 594, 95 LT 289 .... 39.3, 39.13
Salvin v Weston (1866) 35 LJ Ch 552, 12 Jur NS 700, 14 WR 757 .... 33.23
Sample Estate, Re (1955) 3 DLR 199, 15 WWR 193, CA 4.13
Sampson, Re, Sampson v Sampson [1896] 1 Ch 630, 65 LJ Ch 406, 44 WR 557, 40 Sol Jo 353, 74 LT 246 .... 97.7, 99.8
Sampson v Sampson (1869) LR 8 Eq 479 .... 63.9
Samson, Re (1966) 59 DLR (2d) 132 .... 14.3, 14.12, 64.35
Samuda's Settlement Trusts, Re, Horne v Courtenay [1924] 1 Ch 61, 93 LJ Ch 141, 68 Sol Jo 101, 130 LT 286 .... 94.8, 94.12, 94.48
Samuel, Re, Jacobs v Ramsden [1941] Ch 1, [1941] 3 All ER 196, CA; on appeal sub nom Clayton v Ramsden [1943] AC 320, [1943] 1 All ER 16, 112 LJ Ch 22, 86 Sol Jo 384, 168 LT 113, 59 TLR 75, HL 34.9, 34.10, 34.11, 35.29, 35.30, 35.31, 35.33, 217.40
Samuel v Samuel (1845) 14 LJ Ch 222, 2 Coop temp Cott 119, 9 Jur 222, 5 LTOS 34 .... 85.5
Samuel v Samuel (1879) 12 Ch D 152, 47 LJ Ch 716, 26 WR 750, 41 LT 462 .... 99.4, 99.10
Samuel v Ward (1856) 22 Beav 347, 2 Jur NS 962, 4 WR 540, 27 LTOS 164 .... 44.1
Sandbrook, Re, Noel v Sandbrook [1912] 2 Ch 471, 81 LJ Ch 800, [1911–13] All ER Rep 559, 56 Sol Jo 721, 107 LT 148 .... 34.11, 34.24, 35.36
Sandeman's Will Trusts, Re, Sandeman v Hayne [1937] 1 All ER 368, 81 Sol Jo 137 .... 30.9, 30.36
Sanders v Ashford (1860) 28 Beav 609 .... 47.32, 98.4
Sanders v Franks (1817) 2 Madd 147 .... 83.3
Sanders' Trusts, Re (1866) LR 1 Eq 675, 12 Jur NS 351, 14 WR 576 .... 55.6, 56.7, 56.8, 56.9, 98.3
Sanders' Will Trusts, Re, Public Trustee v McLaren [1954] Ch 265, [1954] 1 All ER 667, [1954] 2 WLR 487, 98 Sol Jo 196; on appeal (1954) Times, 22 July, CA 102.7, 103.1
Sanderson, Re, Sanderson v Sanderson (1912) 56 Sol Jo 291, 106 LT 26 .... 39.25
Sanderson, Re, Wright v Sanderson. See Wright v Sanderson

Sanderson v Bayley (1838) 4 My & Cr 56, sub nom Saunderson v Bailey 8 LJ Ch 18, 2 Jur 958 .... 71.4
Sanderson v Dobson. See Saunderson v Dobson
Sanderson's Trust, Re (1857) 3 K & J 497, 26 LJ Ch 804, 3 Jur NS 658, 112 RR 357, 5 WR 864, 30 LTOS 140 .... 82.7, 82.8, 93.37
Sandes v Cooke (1888) 21 LR Ir 445 .... 76.2
Sandys' Will Trust, Re, Sandys v Kirton [1947] 2 All ER 302, CA 236.12
Sanford, Re, Sanford v Sanford [1901] 1 Ch 939, 70 LJ Ch 591, 84 LT 456 .... 50.16, 50.21, 51.4, 53.2, 82.3, 83.1, 83.9, 99.1
Sanford v Irby (1820) 3 B & Ald 654 .... 98.8, 98.9
Sanford v Irby (1825) 4 LJOS Ch 23 .... 64.26
Sanford v Raikes (1816) 1 Mer 646 .... 50.15, 57.12
Sanforth's Will, Re [1901] WN 152 .... 93.15
Sanger, Re, Taylor v North [1939] Ch 238, [1938] 4 All ER 417, 108 LJ Ch 165, 82 Sol Jo 950, 159 LT 603, 55 TLR 109 .... 214.7, 214.9
Sansom v Peay (Inspector of Taxes) [1976] 3 All ER 375, [1976] 1 WLR 1073, [1976] STC 494, 52 TC 1, 120 Sol Jo 571, sub nom Sansom and Bridge v Peay (Inspector of Taxes) [1976] TR 205 .... 200.95, 208.35, 218.18
Sapusak, Re (1984) 8 DLR (4th) 158 .... 8.7
Sarel v Sarel (1856) 23 Beav 87 .... 101.14
Sargeant v National Westminster Bank plc. See Sergeant v National Westminster Bank
Sargent v Roberts (1848) 17 LJ Ch 117, 12 Jur 429, 11 LTOS 170 .... 38.3
Sartoris' Estate, Re, Sartoris v Sartoris [1892] 1 Ch 11, 60 LJ Ch 634, 64 LT 730; on appeal [1892] 1 Ch 11, 61 LJ Ch 1, 40 WR 82, [1891–4] All ER Rep 193, 36 Sol Jo 41, 65 LT 544, 8 TLR 51, CA 99.7
Satterthwaite's Will Trusts, Re, Midland Bank Executor and Trustee Co Ltd v Royal Veterinary College [1966] 1 All ER 919, [1966] 1 WLR 277, 110 Sol Jo 92, CA 102.13, 103.2
Saul v Pattinson (1886) 55 LJ Ch 831, 34 WR 561, 45 LT 670 .... 40.10
Saumarez v Saumarez (1839) 4 My & Cr 331 .... 64.51
Saumarez v Saumarez (1865) 34 Beav 432 .... 93.27
Saunders v Carden (1891) 27 LR Ir 43 .... 39.18
Saunders v Drake (1742) 2 Atk 465 .... 30.43, 32.33
Saunders v Garrett [2005] WTLR 749 .... 105.15
Saunders v Lowe (1775) 2 Wm Bl 1014 .... 101.1
Saunders v Vautier (1841) 4 Beav 115; affd (1841) Cr & Ph 240, [1835–42] All ER Rep 58, 10 LJ Ch 354, 54 RR 286 .... 30.36, 34.5, 93.27, 93.31, 93.40, 95.4, 218.77
Saunders and Halom, Re (1986) 32 DLR (4th) 503 (BC CA) 83.11
Saunders' Goods, Re (1865) LR 1 P & D 16, 35 LJP & M 26, 11 Jur NS 1027, 14 WR 148, 13 LT 411 .... 16.3
Saunderson v Bailey. See Sanderson v Bayley
Saunderson v Dobson (1847) 16 LJ Ex 249, sub nom Sanderson v Dobson 1 Exch 141, 9 LTOS 269 .... 60.2
Savage v Robertson (1868) LR 7 Eq 176 .... 72.2, 72.3
Savage v Tyers (1872) 7 Ch App 356, 41 LJ Ch 815, 20 WR 817 .... 82.4, 101.7
Savage's Goods, Re (1870) LR 2 P & D 78, 34 JP 359, 39 LJP & M 25, 17 WR 766, 22 LT 375 .... 18.15
Savery v Dyer (1752) Amb 139, 1 Dick 162 .... 33.1, 33.12, 33.13

Savile v Kinnaird (1865) 11 Jur NS 195, 13 WR 308, 11 LT 687 .... 52.11
Savill Bros Ltd v Bethell [1902] 2 Ch 523, 71 LJ Ch 652, 50 WR 580, 87 LT 191, CA 94.33
Savory's Goods, Re (1851) 15 Jur 1042, 18 LTOS 280 .... 11.15, 12.12
Sawrey v Rumney (1852) 5 De G & Sm 698, 17 Jur 83, 19 LTOS 337 .... 30.8, 88.4
Sawyer v Birchmore (1837) 1 Keen 825, 2 My & Cr 611, 6 LJ Ch 277 .... 31.11
Sax, Re, Barned v Sax [1893] WN 104, 62 LJ Ch 688, 3 R 638, 41 WR 584, 37 Sol Jo 560, 68 LT 849 .... 34.21, 35.49
Saxby, Re, Saxby v Kiddell [1890] WN 171 .... 64.53
Saxby v Saxby Executors 1952 SC 352 .... 2.5
Saxone Shoe Co Ltd's Trust Deed, Re, Re Abbott's Will Trusts, Abbott v Pearson [1962] 2 All ER 904, [1962] 1 WLR 943, 106 Sol Jo 687 .... 53.6, 102.24
Saxton v Saxton (1879) 13 Ch D 359, 49 LJ Ch 128, 28 WR 294, 41 LT 648 .... 41.5, 58.12, 59.2, 63.9, 207.3
Saxton's Estate, Re, Barclays Bank Ltd v Treasury Solicitor [1939] 2 All ER 418, 83 Sol Jo 341 .... 15.1
Sayer, Re, McClellan v Clark (1884) 53 LJ Ch 832, 50 LT 616 .... 41.11
Sayer v Bradly (1856) 5 HL Cas 873, 2 Jur NS 887, 4 WR 808, 28 LTOS 59, sub nom Sayer v Boys 25 LJ Ch 593 .... 50.17, 76.5, 77.1
Sayer v Masterman (1757) Amb 344, Wilm 386 .... 49.4
Sayer v Sayer (1714) Gilb Ch 87, Prec Ch 392, 2 Vern 688 .... 30.3, 63.1
Sayer Trust, Re, MacGregor v Sayer [1957] Ch 423, [1956] 3 All ER 600, [1957] 2 WLR 261, 101 Sol Jo 130 .... 53.6, 102.15
Saywell v Saywell (1932) 32 SRNSW 155, 49 WNNSW 33 .... 35.30
Scadding, Re (1902) 4 OLR 632 .... 32.10
Scaife, Re, ex p West (1784) 1 P Wms 275n, 1 Bro CC 575 .... 90.1
Scalé v Rawlins. See Rawlins' Trusts, Re
Scarborough (Earl) v Doe d Savile (1836) 3 Ad & El 897, 6 LJ Ex 270, 6 Nev & MKB 884, Ex Ch 35.43, 49.1, 50.3, 57.3
Scarborough v Scarborough (1888) 58 LT 851 .... 93.20
Scarborough's Goods, Re (1860) 30 LJPM & A 85, 6 Jur NS 1166, 9 WR 149 .... 38.3
Scarff v Scarff [1927] 1 IR 13, CA 13.2
Scarisbrick, Re, Cockshott v Public Trustee [1951] Ch 622, [1951] 1 All ER 822, 95 Sol Jo 299, [1951] 1 TLR 989, CA 79.4, 101.9, 102.10, 102.14, 102.15
Scarlett v Lord Abinger (1865) Beav 338 .... 35.50
Scatterwood (or Scattergood) v Edge (1697) 1 Eq Cas Abr 190, 12 Mod Rep 278, 1 Salk 229 .... 93.19, 94.2
Scawin v Watson (1847) 10 Beav 200, 16 LJ Ch 404, 11 Jur 576 .... 82.4
Schaefer v Schuhmann [1972] AC 572, [1972] 1 All ER 621, [1972] 2 WLR 481, 116 Sol Jo 121, [1972–73] ALR 501, PC 2.3, 3.2, 3.3, 3.6, 3.8, 3.9, 3.10, 3.12, 105.42, 105.49
Schar, Re, Midland Bank Executor and Trustee Co Ltd v Damer [1951] Ch 280, [1950] 2 All ER 1069, 94 Sol Jo 804, 66 (pt 2) TLR 1131 .... 46.1
Schellenberger v Trustees Executors and Agency Co Ltd (1953) 86 CLR 454, 26 ALJ 496, sub nom Re Shelley, Schellenberger v Trustees Executors and Agency Co Ltd [1953] ALR 39 .... 102.10
Schenck v Legh (1803) 9 Ves 300 .... 97.8

Schintz's Will Trusts, Re, Lloyds Bank Ltd v Moreton [1951] Ch 870, [1951] 1 All ER 1095, 95 Sol Jo 369 .... 15.4
Schloss v Stiebel (1833) 6 Sim 1 .... 80.1
Schmidt Estate, Re [1949] 2 WWR 513 .... 34.13, 35.8
Schnadhorst, Re, Sandkuhl v Schnadhorst [1901] 2 Ch 338, 70 LJ Ch 583, 84 LT 587; affd [1902] 2 Ch 234, 71 LJ Ch 454, 50 WR 485, 46 Sol Jo 431, 86 LT 426, CA 97.5
Schnapper, Re [1928] Ch 420, 97 LJ Ch 237, [1928] All ER Rep 528, 72 Sol Jo 137, 139 LT 42 .... 9.41, 24.4, 30.30
Schnapper, Re, Westminster Bank Ltd v Schnapper [1936] 1 All ER 322 .... 30.43
Schneider, Re, Kirby v Schneider (1906) 22 TLR 223 .... 38.23, 214.3
Schnell v Tyrrell (1834) 7 Sim 86 .... 34.21, 34.24, 35.19
Schobelt v Barber (1966) 60 DLR (2d) 519, [1967] 1 OR 349 .... 9.18, 9.19
Schofield, Re, Baker v Cheffins [1918] 2 Ch 64, 87 LJ Ch 510, 62 Sol Jo 488, 118 LT 755 .... 67.8
Schofield v Heap (1858) 27 Beav 93, 28 LJ Ch 104, 4 Jur NS 1067, 32 LTOS 114 .... 44.4, 44.10
Scholefield, Re, Scholefield v St John [1905] 2 Ch 408, 74 LJ Ch 610, 54 WR 56, 93 LT 122, 21 TLR 675; on appeal [1907] 1 Ch 664, 75 LJ Ch 720, 22 TLR 764, CA 24.18, 57.3
Scholefield v Redfern (1863) 2 Drew & Sm 173, 32 LJ Ch 627, 9 Jur NS 485, 1 New Rep 465, 143 RR 74, 11 WR 453, 8 LT 487 .... 33.1
Schott's Goods, Re [1901] P 190, 70 LJP 46, 84 LT 571, 17 TLR 476 .... 5.7, 6.1
Schott's Will Trust, Re, Prause v Malmcrantz (1968) 112 Sol Jo 335, 206 Estates Gazette 538 .... 38.3, 64.4
Schultz, Re (1984) 8 DLR (4th) 147 .... 11.15
Schulze's Case 1917 SC 400 .... 25.4
Schwann v Cotton [1916] 2 Ch 459, 85 LJ Ch 689, [1916–17] All ER Rep 368, 60 Sol Jo 654, 115 LT 168, CA 7.26
Schwartz, Re (1970) 10 DLR (3d) 15; on appeal (1971) 20 DLR (3d) 313 .... 4.13, 4.17, 4.20, 5.1
Schwartz, Re (1975) 59 DLR (3d) 161 .... 94.14
Schweder's Estate, Re, Oppenheim v Schweder [1891] 3 Ch 44, [1891–4] All ER Rep Ext 1972, 60 LJ Ch 656, 39 WR 588, 65 LT 64 .... 30.31, 31.1, 210.19, 210.21, 224.91, 232.67
Score, Re, Tolman v Score (1887) 57 LT 40 .... 84.4
Scorer, Re, Burtt v Harrison (1924) 94 LJ Ch 196, [1924] All ER Rep 330, 132 LT 529 .... 47.32, 64.53
Scorey v Harrison (1852) 16 Jur 1130, 1 WR 99, 20 LTOS 302 .... 63.1
Scotney v Lomer (1886) 31 Ch D 380, 55 LJ Ch 443, 34 WR 407, 54 LT 194, CA 40.8, 93.31, 213.12
Scott (Scott's Trustees) 1912 50 SLR 299 .... 44.1
Scott, Re [1901] 1 KB 228, 65 JP 84, 70 LJQB 66, 49 WR 178, 83 LT 613, 17 TLR 148, CA 7.22, 47.12, 47.23
Scott, Re [1919] SALR 134 .... 93.6
Scott, Re, Langton v Scott [1903] 1 Ch 1, 72 LJ Ch 20, 51 WR 182, 47 Sol Jo 70, 87 LT 574, CA 44.4, 44.14
Scott, Re, Scott v Scott [1911] 2 Ch 374, 80 LJ Ch 750, 105 LT 577 .... 48.5, 48.8

Scott, Re, Scott v Scott [1914] 1 Ch 847, 83 LJ Ch 694, 110 LT 809, 30 TLR 345; on appeal [1915] 1 Ch 592, 84 LJ Ch 366, 112 LT 1057, 31 TLR 227, CA 30.34, 58.4
Scott, Re, Scott v Scott (No 2) (1915) 31 TLR 505 .... 91.2
Scott, Re, Widdows v Friends of the Clergy Corpn [1975] 2 All ER 1033, [1975] 1 WLR 1260, 119 Sol Jo 508 .... 9.17, 46.1, 46.5, 48.5, 48.8, 104.9, 241.16
Scott v Bargeman (1722) 2 Eq Cas Abr 542, 2 P Wms 69 .... 101.13
Scott v Brownrigg (1881) 9 LR Ir 246 .... 102.9
Scott v Earl Scarborough (1838) 1 Beav 154, 8 LJ Ch 65 .... 32.28, 66.1, 66.20
Scott v Harwood (1821) 5 Madd 332 .... 66.22
Scott v Josselyn (1859) 26 Beav 174, 28 LJ Ch 297, 32 LJOS 250, 5 Jur NS 560 .... 83.11, 83.12, 99.1
Scott v Moore (1844) 14 Sim 35, 13 LJ Ch 283, 8 Jur 281, 2 LTOS 474 .... 38.1
Scott v Salmond (1833) 1 My & K 363, Coop temp Brough 46 .... 47.8
Scott v Scott (1845) 15 Sim 47, 14 LJ Ch 439, 9 Jur 589 .... 85.3
Scott v Scott (1859) 5 Jur NS 228, 1 Sw & Tr 258 .... 18.5, 18.17, 19.5
Scott v Tyler (1788) 2 Dick 712, 2 Bro CC 431, [1775–1802] All ER Rep 237 .... 33.20, 34.15, 35.2
Scott Estate, Re (1957) 11 DLR (2d) 223 .... 103.3
Scott Trustees v Smart 1954 SC 12 .... 72.2
Scott's Estate, Re (1938) 4 DLR 786, 46 Man LR 241, [1938] 3 WWR 278, 8 FLJ (Can) 196 .... 10.18
Scottish Burial Reform and Cremation Society Ltd v Glasgow Corpn [1968] AC 138, [1967] 3 All ER 215, [1967] 3 WLR 1132, [1967] RA 272, 132 JP 30, 111 Sol Jo 654, 1967 SC (HL) 116, 1967 SLT 265, HL 102.1, 102.4, 102.10, 102.18
Scottish Woollen Technical College v IRC (1926) 11 TC 139, 1926 SC 934 .... 102.8
Scowcroft, Re, Ormrod v Wilkinson [1898] 2 Ch 638, 67 LJ Ch 697, [1895–9] All ER Rep 274, 43 Sol Jo 11, 79 LT 342, 15 TLR 4 .... 102.10, 102.23
Scriven v Sandom (1862) 2 John & H 743 .... 39.14
Scruby and Finch v Fordham (1822) 1 Add 74 .... 18.5
Scurfield v Howes (1790) 3 Bro CC 90 .... 67.7
Seabrook, Re, Gray v Baddeley [1911] 1 Ch 151, 80 LJ Ch 61, 103 LT 587 .... 30.5, 39.12
Seaford, Re, Seaford v Seifert [1968] P 53, [1968] 1 All ER 482, [1968] 2 WLR 155, 111 Sol Jo 981, CA 80.3, 80.4
Seal, Re, Seal v Taylor [1894] 1 Ch 316, 63 LJ Ch 275, 70 LT 329, CA 51.7, 57.12, 57.20, 58.1, 58.6, 63.7
Seale v Barter (1801) 2 Bos & P 485 .... 85.2
Seale v Lowndes (1868) 17 LT 555 .... 7.8
Seale v Perry [1982] VR 193, Vic Full Ct 1.14
Seale v Seale (1715) Gilb Ch 105, 1 P Wms 290, Prec Ch 421 .... 53.4, 84.4
Seale-Hayne v Jodrell. See Jodrell, Re, Jodrell v Seale
Sealy v Stawell (1868) IR 2 Eq 326 .... 98.7
Sealy v Stawell (1876) IR 2 Eq 499 .... 44.15
Seaman v Wood (1856) 22 Beav 591 .... 94.21
Searey's Trustees v Allbuary (1907) 44 SLR 536, 1907 SC 823, 14 SLT 898 .... 79.1
Searle, Re, Searle v Baker [1900] 2 Ch 829, 69 LJ Ch 712, 49 WR 44, 44 Sol Jo 716, 83 LT 364 .... 37.6, 38.25
Searle, Re, Searle v Searle [1905] WN 86 .... 96.1

Searle, Re, Searle v Siems [1949] Ch 73, [1948] 2 All ER 426, [1948] LJR 1843, 92 Sol Jo 456, 64 TLR 397 .... 105.5
Searle's Estate, Re [1963] SASR 303 .... 72.2
Sears, Re (1951) 53 WALR 57 .... 64.14
Seaton, Re, Ellis v Seaton [1913] 2 Ch 614, 83 LJ Ch 124, 107 LT 192 .... 93.21
Sebag-Montefiore, Re, Sebag-Montefiore v Alliance Assurance Co Ltd [1944] Ch 331, [1944] 1 All ER 672, 113 LJ Ch 280, 88 Sol Jo 238, 170 LT 395, 60 TLR 401, CA 22.3
Sebba, Re, Lloyds Bank Ltd v Hutson [1959] Ch 166, [1958] 3 All ER 393, [1958] 3 WLR 605, 37 ATC 325, [1958] TR 329, 102 Sol Jo 810 .... 210.3, 210.68, 214.17, 214.64
Seccombe v Edwards (1860) 28 Beav 440, 6 Jur NS 642, 8 WR 595, 2 LT 622 .... 56.8
Secretary of State for Social Security v Fairey (also known as Halliday) [1997] 3 All ER 844, [1997] 1 WLR 799, sub nom Secretary of State for Social Security v Fairey [1997] 24 LS Gaz R 32, 141 Sol Jo LB 122, HL 226.4
Sedgeley, Re [1961] NZLR 394 .... 101.13
Seed v Bradford (1750) 1 Ves Sen 501 .... 44.17
Seers v Hind (1791) 1 Hov Supp 128, 1 Ves 294 .... 208.45
Sefton (Earl), Re [1898] 2 Ch 378, 67 LJ Ch 518, 47 WR 49, 42 Sol Jo 570, 78 LT 765, 14 TLR 466, CA 34.24
Sefton (Earl) v Hopwood (1855) 1 F & F 578 .... 4.18, 5.9
Segelcke, Re, Ziegler v Nicol [1906] 2 Ch 301, 75 LJ Ch 494, 54 WR 624, 95 LT 708 .... 82.7, 88.1
Segelman, Re [1996] Ch 171, [1995] 3 All ER 676, [1996] 2 WLR 173 .... 6.2, 50.9, 102.14
Sehota, Re, Surjit Kaur v Gian Kaur [1978] 3 All ER 385, [1978] 1 WLR 1506, 122 Sol Jo 844 .... 105.9
Selby, Re [1952] VLR 273 .... 47.32
Selby, Re, Church v Tancred [1903] 1 Ch 715, 72 LJ Ch 324, 51 WR 510, 47 Sol Jo 319, 88 LT 164 .... 99.8
Selby v Whittaker (1877) 6 Ch D 239, 47 LJ Ch 121, 26 WR 117, 37 LT 514, CA 51.7, 51.11, 66.2, 93.2
Selby's Will Trusts, Re, Donn v Selby [1965] 3 All ER 386, [1966] 1 WLR 43, 110 Sol Jo 74 .... 34.9, 35.29, 35.31
Selby-Bigge, Re [1950] 1 All ER 1009, 94 Sol Jo 287, 66 (pt 1) TLR 993 .... 12.9, 222.6
Selby-Walker, Re, Public Trustee v Selby-Walker [1949] 2 All ER 178 .... 32.22, 210.37
Seldon, Re (1970) 10 DLR (3d) 306, [1970] 2 OR 201 .... 92.1
Seley v Wood (1804) 10 Ves 71 .... 30.14
Selinger's Will Trusts, Re, Midland Bank Executor and Trustee Co Ltd v Levy [1959] 1 All ER 407, [1959] 1 WLR 217, 103 Sol Jo 178 .... 34.22
Sellwood's Estate, Re, Heynes v Sellwood (1964) 108 Sol Jo 523 .... 5.2, 11.22
Selman Estate, Re (1957) 23 WWR 349 .... 83.3
Selsey (Lord) v Lord Lake (1839) 1 Beav 146, 8 LJ Ch 233 .... 69.1
Selwin v Brown (1735) 3 Bro Parl Cas 607, HL 57.10, 57.32
Selwood v Selwood [1920] All ER Rep 413, 125 LT 26 .... 16.4
Sembaliuk v Sembaliuk (1985) 15 DLR (4th) 303 .... 46.5
Semphill v Bayly (1721) 2 Eq Cas Abr 213, Prec Ch 562 .... 34.13

Sen v Headley [1990] Ch 728, [1990] 1 All ER 898, [1990] 2 WLR 620, [1990] 1 FLR 449, [1990] Fam Law 394, 134 Sol Jo 342, [1990] NLJR 133; revsd [1991] Ch 425, [1991] 2 All ER 636, [1991] 2 WLR 1308, 62 P & CR 277, [1996] 1 FCR 692, [1991] 2 FLR 449, [1991] Fam Law 373, 135 Sol Jo 384, [1991] NLJR 384, CA 1.15
Sergeant, Re, Mertens v Walley (1884) 26 Ch D 575, 54 LJ Ch 159, 32 WR 987 .... 55.6
Sergeant v National Westminster Bank (1988) 59 P & CR 182; affd sub nom Sargeant v National Westminster Bank plc (1990) 61 P & CR 518, CA 218.4, 223.9, 234.15
Serocold v Hemming (1758) 2 Lee 490 .... 22.2
Serres's Estate, Re, Venes v Marriott (1862) 26 JP 709, 31 LJ Ch 519, 8 Jur NS 882, 10 WR 751, 6 LT 892 .... 30.24
Service, Re [1964] 1 OR 197 .... 19.4
Seton-Smith, Re, Burnand v Waite [1902] 1 Ch 717, 71 LJ Ch 386, 50 WR 456, [1900–3] All ER Rep 144, 86 LT 322 .... 64.27
Sever's Will, Re (1887) 13 VLR 572 .... 4.10
Sewell, Re, White v Sewell [1909] 1 Ch 806, 78 LJ Ch 432, 16 Mans 113, 100 LT 883 .... 30.17
Sewell's Estate, Re (1870) LR 11 Eq 80, 40 LJ Ch 135, sub nom Re London and North Western Railway (New Works and Additional Powers) Act 1869, Re Sewell's Trusts 19 WR 220, 23 LT 835 .... 38.23, 214.3
Seymour v Kilbee (1879) 3 LR Ir 33 .... 101.10
Seymour v Lord Vernon. See Harcourt v Seymour
Seymour's Trusts, Re (1859) John 472, 28 LJ Ch 765, 5 Jur NS 1049, 7 WR 609, 33 LTOS 314 .... 47.24
Seyton, Re, Seyton v Satterthwaite (1887) 34 Ch D 511, 56 LJ Ch 775, 35 WR 373, 56 LT 479, 3 TLR 377 .... 85.3
Shadbolt v Vanderplank (1861) 29 Beav 405 .... 44.15
Shaftesbury (Earl) v Duke of Marlborough (1835) 7 Sim 237 .... 91.6
Shaftsbury (Earl) v Countess of Shaftsbury (1716) 1 Eq Cas Abr 201, 2 Vern 747 .... 63.1
Shakespeare Memorial Trust, Re, Lytton (Earl) v A-G [1923] 2 Ch 398, 92 LJ Ch 551, [1923] All ER Rep 106, 67 Sol Jo 809, 130 LT 56, 39 TLR 610, 676 .... 102.8
Shand v Kidd (1854) 19 Beav 310 .... 56.5, 87.2
Shand v Robinson (1898) 19 NSW Eq 85, 14 WNNSW 214 .... 98.1
Shand Kydd's Settlement Trusts, Re, Shand Kydd v Shand Kydd (1970) 114 Sol Jo 789 .... 48.5
Shanley v Baker (1799) 4 Ves 732 .... 91.5
Shannon, Re [1968] NZLR 852 .... 7.20, 93.27
Sharland, Re, Kemp v Rozey [1896] 1 Ch 517, 65 LJ Ch 280, 74 LT 20 ... 30.23, 210.59, 210.60, 232.67
Sharland, Re, Kemp v Rozey (No 2) (1896) 74 LT 664, 40 Sol Jo 514, CA ... 8.7, 204.20
Sharland, Re, Re Rew, Rew v Wippell [1899] 2 Ch 536, 68 LJ Ch 747, 81 LT 384 .... 39.24
Sharman, Re, Wright v Sharman [1901] 2 Ch 280, 70 LJ Ch 671, 49 WR 555, 45 Sol Jo 576, 84 LT 859 .... 55.7
Sharman's Goods, Re (1869) LR 1 P & D 661, 33 JP 695, 38 LJP & M 47, 17 WR 687, 20 LT 683 .... 9.8, 12.14, 12.15, 38.3

Sharman's Will Trusts, Re, Public Trustee v Sharman [1942] Ch 311, [1942] 2 All ER 74, 111 LJ Ch 257, 86 Sol Jo 174, 167 LT 285 .... 27.5, 27.6, 30.15, 34.21, 35.49, 210.52, 232.67, 237.11, 239.3, 239.4
Sharp, Re, Canty v Sharp (1904) 4 SRNSW 155, 21 WNNSW 57 .... 35.6
Sharp, Re, Maddison v Gill [1908] 1 Ch 372, 77 LJ Ch 251, 98 LT 234; on appeal [1908] 2 Ch 190, 77 LJ Ch 724, 99 LT 129, CA 47.28, 50.3, 69.1, 69.2
Sharp, Re, Sharp v Sharp (1887) 3 TLR 806 .... 10.9
Sharp v Adam [2005] EWHC 1806 (Ch), [2005] All ER (D) 398 (Jul); affd [2006] EWCA Civ 449, [2006] WTLR 1059, [2006] All ER (D) 277 (Apr) 4.11
Sharp v Eastern Trust Co [1949] 1 DLR 557 .... 39.17
Sharp v Lush (1879) 10 Ch D 468, 48 LJ Ch 231, 27 WR 528 .... 30.34, 55.7
Sharp v St Sauveur (1871) 7 Ch App 343, 41 LJ Ch 576, 20 WR 269, 26 LT 142 .... 37.8
Sharp v Sharp (1819) 2 B & Ald 405 .... 27.6
Sharp's Settlement Trusts, Re, Ibbotson v Bliss [1973] Ch 331, [1972] 3 All ER 151, [1972] 3 WLR 765, 116 Sol Jo 666 .... 218.56
Sharpe, Re [1946] Tas SR 13 .... 56.7, 56.8
Sharpe, Re (1985) 18 DLR (4th) 421 .... 101.2
Sharpe v M'Call [1903] 1 IR 179 .... 39.4, 47.36
Shaw, ex p (1836) 8 Sim 159, 5 LJ Ch 378 .... 83.13
Shaw, Re, Mountain v Mountain [1929] WN 246, 168 LT Jo 371, 68 L Jo 334 .... 64.35
Shaw, Re, Public Trustee v Day [1957] 1 All ER 745, [1957] 1 WLR 729, 101 Sol Jo 408; on appeal [1958] 1 All ER 245n, CA 102.10
Shaw, Re, Public Trustee v Little [1914] WN 141, 58 Sol Jo 414, 110 LT 924, 30 TLR 418, CA 25.8, 240.2
Shaw, Re, Robinson v Shaw [1894] 2 Ch 573, 63 LJ Ch 770, 8 R 421, 43 WR 43, 38 Sol Jo 513, 71 LT 79 .... 9.25, 72.5
Shaw, Re, Shaw v Shaw [1955] QSR 284 .... 50.2
Shaw, Re, Williams v Pledger (1912) 56 Sol Jo 380 .... 66.6
Shaw v Ford (1877) 7 Ch D 669, 47 LJ Ch 531, 26 WR 235, 37 LT 749 .... 83.8, 86.5
Shaw v Halifax Corpn [1915] 2 KB 170, 13 LGR 316, 79 JP 257, 84 LJKB 761, 59 Sol Jo 315, 112 LT 921, CA 102.7, 102.10
Shaw v M'Mahon (1843) 4 Dr & War 431 .... 20.5, 47.32
Shaw v Neville (1855) 2 Ecc & Ad 203, 1 Jur NS 408, 24 LTOS 339 .... 12.3
Shaw v Public Trustee. See Fitch's Will Trusts, Re, Public Trustee v Nives
Shaw v Rhodes (1835) 1 My & Cr 135; affd sub nom Evans v Hellier (1837) 5 Cl & Fin 114, HL 94.3
Shaw's Estate, Re [1905] P 92, 74 LJP 39, 92 LT 428 .... 25.4
Shaw's Goods, Re (1838) 1 Curt 905 .... 18.5
Shaw's Goods, Re (1895) 73 LT 192 .... 25.2
Shaw's Settlement, Re, Shaw v Shaw [1951] Ch 833, [1951] 1 All ER 656, [1951] 1 TLR 470 .... 218.90
Shaw's Will Trusts, Re, National Provincial Bank Ltd v National City Bank Ltd [1952] Ch 163, [1952] 1 All ER 49, 95 Sol Jo 803, [1951] 2 TLR 1249 .... 102.8
Shea v Boschetti (1854) 18 Beav 321, 23 LJ Ch 652, 2 Eq Rep 608, 18 Jur 614, 2 WR 281, 23 LTOS 137 .... 25.15, 57.5
Shearer v Hogg (1912) 46 SCR 492 .... 83.9, 99.1

Shearn's Goods, Re (1880) 45 JP 303, 50 LJP 15, 29 WR 445, 43 LT 736 ..... 12.4, 14.6
Sheffield (Earl), Re, Ryde v Bristow [1911] 2 Ch 267, 80 LJ Ch 521, 105 LT 236, CA 30.25, 210.58, 210.59, 210.61
Sheffield v Earl of Coventry (1852) 2 De GM & G 551, 22 LJ Ch 498, 17 Jur 289, 20 LTOS 193 .... 93.8
Sheffield v Kennett (1859) 4 De G & J 593 .... 66.2, 93.1, 96.2
Sheffield v Lord Orrery (1745) 3 Atk 282 .... 93.21, 93.23, 98.7
Sheldon, Re, Nixon v Sheldon (1888) 39 Ch D 50, 58 LJ Ch 25, 37 WR 26, 59 LT 133 .... 38.18, 38.23
Sheldon v Sheldon (1739) 9 Mod Rep 211 .... 93.27
Sheldon and Kemble, Re (1885) 53 LT 527 .... 83.9, 99.1
Shelley, Re, Schellenberger v Trustees Executors and Agency Co Ltd. See Schellenberger v Trustees Executors and Agency Co Ltd
Shelley v Bryer (1821) Jac 207 .... 71.5
Shelley v Shelley (1868) LR 6 Eq 540, 37 LJ Ch 357, 16 WR 1036 .... 94.15
Shelley's Case, Wolfe v Shelley (1581) 1 And 69, 3 Dyer 373b, Moore KB 136, Jenk 249, 1 Co Rep 93b 84.2, 84.4
Shelton v Watson (1849) 16 Sim 543, 18 LJ Ch 223, 13 Jur 203 .... 84.2
Shenton v Tyler [1939] Ch 620, [1939] 1 All ER 827, 108 LJ Ch 256, 83 Sol Jo 194, 160 LT 314, 55 TLR 522, CA 36.2
Shephard's Estate, Re (1982) 29 SASR 247 .... 18.25
Shepheard's Goods, Re (1879) 44 JP 24, 48 LJP 62, 41 LT 530 .... 38.3
Shepherd, Re, Churchill v St George's Hospital. See Howell-Shepherd, Re, Churchill v St George's Hospital
Shepherd, Re, Harris v Shepherd [1943] Ch 8, [1942] 2 All ER 584, 112 LJ Ch 133, 86 Sol Jo 385, 168 LT 187, 59 TLR 50 .... 42.12
Shepherd, Re, Mitchell v Loram [1914] WN 65, 58 Sol Jo 304 .... 30.1, 55.4, 64.35
Shepherd v Ingram (1764) Amb 448 .... 32.28, 66.5, 66.23
Shepherd v Nottidge (1862) 2 John & H 766, 1 New Rep 15, 7 LT 399 .... 38.10
Shepherd v Wheeler [2000] WTLR 1175 .... 25.16
Shepp Estate, Re 29 D & C 2d 385 (1962) 202.30
Sheppard v Sheppard (1863) 32 Beav 194 .... 33.23, 33.28
Sheppard's Trust, Re (1855) 1 K & J 269 .... 93.19
Sherburne v Middleton. See Middleton v Sherburne
Sheridan v O'Reilly [1900] 1 IR 386 .... 62.1, 67.6, 76.1
Sherman, Re, Re Walters, Trevenen v Pearce [1954] Ch 653, sub nom Re Sherman, Trevenen v Pearce [1954] 1 All ER 893, [1954] 2 WLR 903, 98 Sol Jo 302 .... 7.7, 41.5
Sherman v Collins (1745) 3 Atk 319, 1 Ves Sen 45 .... 8.2
Sherratt v Bentley (1834) 2 My & K 149 .... 52.6, 52.7, 52.10, 82.3
Sherratt v Mountford (1873) 8 Ch App 928, 42 LJ Ch 688, 21 WR 818, 29 LT 284, CA 57.12, 57.19, 57.21, 71.1
Sherrington v Sherrington [2005] EWCA Civ 326, [2005] 3 FCR 538, [2005] WTLR 587, 7 ITELR 711, [2005] 19 LS Gaz R 34, 149 Sol Jo LB 392, (2005) Times, 24 March, [2005] All ER (D) 359 (Mar) 5.3, 12.4, 12.14, 13.1, 13.2
Sherry, Re, Sherry v Sherry [1913] 2 Ch 508, 83 LJ Ch 126, 109 LT 474 .... 38.19, 38.23
Sheward, Re, Sheward v Brown [1893] 3 Ch 502, 3 R 667, 41 WR 685, 69 LT 302 .... 99.4, 99.5
Sheward v A-G [1964] 2 All ER 324, [1964] 1 WLR 724, 108 Sol Jo 159 .... 72.9
Shewchuk, Re (1968) 1 DLR (3d) 288 .... 11.24

Shewell v Dwarris (1858) John 172 .... 35.35
Shield's Will Trusts, Re, Bache v Shield [1974] Ch 373, [1974] 2 All ER 274, [1974] 2 WLR 885, 118 Sol Jo 406 .... 79.4, 79.6
Shields, Re, Corbould-Ellis v Dales [1912] 1 Ch 591, 81 LJ Ch 370, 106 LT 748 .... 44.2, 44.14, 57.31
Shields v Shields [1910] 1 IR 116 .... 50.5, 82.2
Shillington v Portadown Urban Council [1911] 1 IR 247 .... 102.10
Shirley's Trusts (1863) 32 Beav 394 .... 91.5
Shirt v Westby (1808) 16 Ves 393 .... 32.8
Shore v Weekly (1849) 3 De G & Sm 467, 18 LJ Ch 403, 13 Jur 1022, 13 LTOS 463 .... 64.14
Shore v Wilson, Lady Hewley's Charities (1842) 9 Cl & Fin 355, 11 Sim 615n, 7 Jur 787n, 5 Scott NR 958, 4 State Tr NS App A 1370, HL 50.9, 50.11, 50.12, 50.13, 57.6, 57.20
Short, Re [1929] 1 DLR 454 .... 58.8
Shortts, Re [1954] 2 DLR 817, OWN 481 .... 41.19
Shrewsbury (Earl) v Scott (1859) 6 CBNS 1, 29 LJCP 34, 6 Jur NS 452, 33 LTOS 368; affd (1860) 6 CBNS 221, 29 LJCP 190, sub nom Hope-Scott v Earl Shrewsbury 6 Jur NS 472, Ex Ch 34.8, 34.12
Shrewsbury Estate Acts, Re, Shrewsbury v Shrewsbury [1924] 1 Ch 315, 93 LJ Ch 171, [1923] All ER Rep 666, 68 Sol Jo 79, 130 LT 238, 40 TLR 16, CA 33.47
Shrewsbury's (Earl) Estate, Re, McLeod v Earl of Shrewsbury [1922] P 112, 91 LJP 46, 126 LT 415, 38 TLR 203 .... 5.9
Shrimpton v Shrimpton (1862) 31 Beav 425, 11 WR 61 .... 93.27, 93.35
Shuck v Loveridge [2005] EWHC 72 (Ch), [2005] All ER (D) 306 (Jan) 5.3
Shuckburgh's Settlement, Re, Robertson v Shuckburgh [1901] 2 Ch 794, 71 LJ Ch 32, 50 WR 133, [1900–3] All ER Rep 101, 46 Sol Jo 13, 85 LT 406 .... 51.1, 93.15
Shudal v Jekyll (1743) 2 Atk 516 .... 44.8
Shuker's Estate, Re, Bromley v Reed [1937] 3 All ER 25, 81 Sol Jo 498 .... 83.2
Shuldham v Smith (1818) 6 Dow 22, HL 93.23
Shum v Hobbs (1855) 3 Drew 93, 24 LJ Ch 377, 3 WR 221 .... 93.27
Shurey, Re, Savory v Shurey [1918] 1 Ch 263, 87 LJ Ch 245, 62 Sol Jo 246, 118 LT 355, 34 TLR 171 .... 4.7, 93.6
Shuttleworth v Greaves (1838) 4 My & Cr 35, 8 LJ Ch 7, 2 Jur 957 .... 47.32
Shuttleworth v Howarth (1841) Cr & Ph 228, 5 Jur 499 .... 38.1
Sibley v Cook (1747) 3 Atk 572 .... 47.23, 47.24
Sibley v Perry (1802) 7 Ves 522 .... 30.1, 55.4, 76.3
Sibley's Trusts, Re (1877) 5 Ch D 494, 46 LJ Ch 387, [1874–80] All ER Rep 250, 37 LT 180 .... 56.5, 68.1, 68.2, 68.9, 68.12, 87.3
Sibthorp v Moxom (1747) 3 Atk 580, 1 Wils 178, 1 Ves Sen 49 .... 47.22
Sidebotham v Watson (1853) 11 Hare 170, 1 WR 303 .... 30.3, 41.4
Sidey v Perpetual Trustees Estate and Agency Co of New Zealand Ltd [1944] AC 194, [1944] 2 All ER 225, 113 LJPC 91, 171 LT 309, 60 TLR 507, PC 87.4
Sidney, Re, Hingeston v Sidney [1908] 1 Ch 488, 77 LJ Ch 296, 52 Sol Jo 262, 98 LT 625, CA 102.23
Sidney v Miller (1815) Coop G 206, sub nom Sidney v Shelley 19 Ves 352 .... 47.8
Sidney v Shelley. See Sidney v Miller

Sidney v Sidney (1873) LR 17 Eq 65, 43 LJ Ch 15, 22 WR 101, 29 LT 569 .... 20.4, 22.4, 30.3, 30.4
Sidney v Wilmer (1858) 25 Beav 260 .... 48.5
Sifton v Sifton [1938] AC 656, [1938] 3 All ER 435, 107 LJPC 97, 82 Sol Jo 680, 159 LT 289, 54 TLR 969 .... 34.2, 34.10, 34.11, 35.22, 93.3
Sigsworth, Re, Bedford v Bedford [1935] Ch 89, 104 LJ Ch 46, 78 Sol Jo 735, 152 LT 329, 51 TLR 9 .... 9.14, 9.17, 9.18
Sikes, Re, Moxon v Crossley [1927] 1 Ch 364, 96 LJ Ch 263, 70 Sol Jo 1197, 136 LT 666, 43 TLR 57 .... 41.2, 59.3, 64.8
Silcock v Roynon (1834) 2 Y & C Ch Cas 376, 7 Jur 548 .... 46.1
Silcocks v Silcocks [1916] 2 Ch 161, 85 LJ Ch 464, 60 Sol Jo 445, 114 LT 843 .... 78.3
Silcox v Bell (1823) 1 Sim & St 301, 1 LJOS Ch 137 .... 71.4
Sillick v Booth (1841) 1 Y & C Ch Cas 117, 6 Jur 142 .... 97.10
Sillick v Booth (1842) 1 Y & C Ch Cas 117, 11 LJ Ch 41, 123, 5 Jur 1151, 6 Jur 142 .... 90.1
Sills v Warner (1896) 27 OR 266 .... 102.8
Silverside v Silverside (1858) 25 Beav 340 .... 100.4
Silverston, Re, Westminster Bank Ltd v Kohler [1949] Ch 270, [1949] 1 All ER 641, [1949] LJR 961, 93 Sol Jo 250 .... 30.24, 30.26
Silvester's Case (1619) Poph 148, 79 ER 1248 .... 3.2
Sim, Re [1917] NZLR 169 .... 64.27
Simcoe, Re, Vowler-Simcoe v Vowler [1913] 1 Ch 552, 82 LJ Ch 270, 57 Sol Jo 533, 108 LT 891 .... 50.7, 50.11, 76.1
Sime v Hume (1901) 20 NZLR 191 .... 9.40
Simkin, Re [1950] VLR 341 .... 18.21
Simmonds, Re, Public Trustee v Stone [1933] NZLR Supp 172 .... 102.6
Simmonds v Cock (1861) 29 Beav 455, 7 Jur NS 718, 9 WR 517 .... 93.13
Simmons, Re, Dennison v Orman (1902) 87 LT 594 .... 96.2
Simmons v Pitt (1873) 8 Ch App 978, 43 LJ Ch 267, 21 WR 860, 29 LT 320 .... 47.9
Simmons v Rose (1856) 6 De GM & G 411, 25 LJ Ch 615, 2 Jur NS 73, 4 WR 225, 26 LTOS 265 .... 214.5
Simmons v Simmons (1836) 8 Sim 22, 5 LJ Ch 198 .... 84.4
Simmons v Vallance (1793) 4 Bro CC 345 .... 30.8
Simmons Estate, Re (1990) 56 SASR 1 .... 46.1
Simpson, Re [1945] 1 DLR 478, [1945] OR 169 .... 93.29
Simpson, Re, Chadderton v Simpson [1952] Ch 412, [1952] 1 All ER 963, 96 Sol Jo 262, [1952] 1 TLR 868 .... 40.15
Simpson, Re, Clarke v Simpson [1913] 1 Ch 277, 82 LJ Ch 169, 57 Sol Jo 302, 108 LT 317 .... 35.28, 207.7
Simpson, Re, Coutts & Co v Church Missionary Society [1916] 1 Ch 502, 85 LJ Ch 329, 114 LT 835 .... 24.12, 24.16
Simpson, Re, Schaniel v Simpson (1977) 121 Sol Jo 224, [1977] LS Gaz R 187, 127 NLJ 487 .... 4.17, 4.21, 200.2
Simpson v Ashworth (1843) 6 Beav 412, 7 Jur 410 .... 84.2
Simpson v Foxon [1907] P 54, 76 LJP 7, 96 LT 473, 23 TLR 150 ... 1.1, 18.9, 18.10, 49.2
Simpson v Hornby. See Sympson v Hutton
Simpson v Lester (1858) 4 Jur NS 1269, [1843–60] All ER Rep 690, 33 LTOS 6 .... 38.18, 38.23

Simpson v Margitson (1847) 11 QB 23, 17 LJQB 81, 12 Jur 155 .... 50.12
Simpson v Mountain (1835) 4 LJ Ch 221 .... 61.1
Simpson v Peach (1873) LR 16 Eq 208, 42 LJ Ch 816, 21 WR 728, 28 LT 731 .... 93.1
Simpson v Vickers (1807) 14 Ves 341 .... 34.22, 34.23, 34.25, 35.51
Simpson's Goods, Re (1859) 5 Jur NS 1366 .... 18.22
Sims, Re, Sims v Faulkner (1972) 116 Sol Jo 356 .... 13.1
Sims v Doughty (1800) 5 Ves 243 .... 52.6
Simson, Re, Fowler v Tinley [1946] Ch 299, [1946] 2 All ER 220, [1947] LJR 183, 90 Sol Jo 418, 175 LT 314, 62 TLR 498 .... 102.17
Simson, Re, Simson v National Provincial Bank Ltd [1950] Ch 38, [1949] 2 All ER 826, 93 Sol Jo 822, 65 TLR 721 .... 30.31
Simson v Simson (1883) 10 R 1247, 20 SLR 831 .... 10.14
Sinclair, Re (1963) 37 DLR (2d) 103, [1963] 1 OR 335 .... 76.3
Sinclair, Re, Allen v Sinclair [1897] 1 Ch 921, 66 LJ Ch 514, 45 WR 596, 76 LT 452 .... 33.41
Sinclair, Re, Lloyds Bank plc v Imperial Cancer Research Fund [1984] 3 All ER 362, [1984] 1 WLR 1240, [1985] FLR 229, [1985] Fam Law 94, 128 Sol Jo 753, [1984] LS Gaz R 3254; affd [1985] Ch 446, [1985] 1 All ER 1066, [1985] 2 WLR 795, [1985] FLR 965, [1985] Fam Law 227, 129 Sol Jo 206, [1985] LS Gaz R 1567, CA 9.17, 9.18, 47.1, 47.5, 47.15, 48.4, 48.14, 80.3, 93.9, 219.29, 224.17
Sinclair v Lee [1993] Ch 497, [1993] 3 WLR 498, [1994] 1 BCLC 286, sub nom Re Lee, Sinclair v Lee [1993] 3 All ER 926 .... 220.48
Sinclair Estate, Re (1996) 136 DLR (4th) 427 .... 87.4
Sinclair's Trust, Re (1884) 13 LR Ir 150 .... 102.23
Sing, Re, Sing v Mills [1914] WN 90 .... 67.1
Singer v Singer [1932] SCR 44, 1 DLR 284 .... 93.6
Singh, Re (1974) 50 DLR (3d) 628 .... 66.5
Singh, Re [1995] 2 NZLR 487 .... 91.1
Singleton v Gilbert (1784) 1 Cox Eq Cas 68 .... 66.8, 66.13, 66.22
Singleton v Tomlinson (1878) 3 App Cas 404, 26 WR 722, 38 LT 653, HL 15.1, 38.12, 39.12, 49.5, 50.3, 50.21, 57.3, 57.5
Sinnett v Herbert (1871) LR 12 Eq 201, 24 LT 778; on appeal (1872) 7 Ch App 232, 36 JP 516, 41 LJ Ch 388, 20 WR 270, 26 LT 7 .... 3.3, 103.11
Sinnott v Walsh (1880) 5 LR Ir 27, CA 101.9
Sitwell, Re, Worsley v Sitwell [1913] WN 261, 57 Sol Jo 730, 135 Sol Jo 323 .... 46.3
Sitwell v Bernard (1801) 5 RR 374, 6 Ves 520, [1775–1802] All ER Rep 308 .... 29.2, 38.25, 93.4
Sivewright, Re, Law v Fenwick [1922] WN 338, 67 Sol Jo 168, 128 LT 416 .... 30.34, 64.8
Sivewright v Sivewright's Trustees 1920 SC (HL) 63, 1919 2 SLT 261 .... 4.15
Skeats, Re, Thain v Gibbs [1936] Ch 683, [1936] 2 All ER 298, 105 LJ Ch 262, 80 Sol Jo 406, 155 LT 451, 52 TLR 558 .... 104.1
Skeats' Settlement, Re, Skeats v Evans (1889) 42 Ch D 522, 58 LJ Ch 656, 37 WR 778, 61 LT 500 .... 27.3
Skelton v Flanagan (1867) IR 1 Eq 362 .... 40.14
Skelton v Younghouse [1942] AC 571, [1942] 1 All ER 650, 111 LJ Ch 185, 86 Sol Jo 273, 167 LT 325, 58 TLR 258, HL 8.7, 92.1, 204.20, 209.7

Skey v Barnes (1816) 3 Mer 335 .... 93.27, 93.41, 101.13
Skillen, Re, Charles v Charles [1916] 1 Ch 518, 85 LJ Ch 383, 60 Sol Jo 387, 114 LT 692 .... 57.20, 64.35
Skingley, Re (1851) 20 LJ Ch 142, 15 Jur 958, 3 Mac & G 221, 16 LTOS 405 .... 45.2
Skinner, Re [1965] VR 660 .... 57.17, 93.29
Skinner, Re (1970) 12 DLR (3d) 227 .... 46.3
Skinner, Re, Milbourne v Skinner [1942] Ch 82, [1942] 1 All ER 32, 111 LJ Ch 73, 86 Sol Jo 13, 58 TLR 77 .... 33.47, 211.8
Skinner v Gumbleton [1903] 1 IR 36, 37 ILT 126 .... 78.1, 78.4
Skinner v Ogle (1845) 1 Rob Eccl 363, 9 Jur 432, 4 Notes of Cases 74 .... 21.1, 22.1, 47.12
Skinner's Trusts, Re (1860) 1 John & H 102, 8 WR 605, 3 LT 177 .... 30.35, 82.7
Skippen, Re, Hodgson v Armstrong and MacInnes (1947) 63 BCR 75, [1947] 1 DLR 858 .... 2.6
Skirving v Williams (1857) 24 Beav 275, 3 Jur NS 927, 30 LTOS 49 .... 38.23
Skottowe v Young (1871) LR 11 Eq 474, 40 LJ Ch 366, 19 WR 583, 24 LT 220 .... 72.7
Skude's Estate, Re [1950] 3 DLR 494, 1 WWR 1066 .... 58.2
Slade v Fooks (1838) 9 Sim 386, 8 LJ Ch 41, 2 Jur 961 .... 71.4
Slade's (Lady) Goods, Re (1869) 33 JP 311, 20 LT 330 .... 18.19, 18.22
Slaney v Slaney (1864) 33 Beav 631 .... 97.5
Slaney v Watney (1866) LR 2 Eq 418, 35 LJ Ch 783, 14 WR 818, 14 LT 657 .... 27.6, 30.15
Slanning v Style. See Stanway v Styles
Slark v Dakyns (1874) 10 Ch App 35, 44 LJ Ch 205, 23 WR 118, 31 LT 712 .... 94.44, 94.47, 94.48
Slater, Re (1964) 46 DLR (2d) 359, [1964] 2 OR 692 .... 90.1
Slater, Re, Slater v Jonas (1915) 85 LJ Ch 432, 113 LT 691 .... 38.19, 38.23
Slater, Re, Slater v Slater [1906] 2 Ch 480, 75 LJ Ch 660, 54 WR 602, 50 Sol Jo 594, 95 LT 350; affd [1907] 1 Ch 665, 76 LJ Ch 472, 51 Sol Jo 426, 97 LT 74, CA 41.1, 41.2, 41.4, 41.13, 41.14, 58.12, 59.2
Slater v Dangerfield (1846) 16 LJ Ex 51, 15 M & W 263, 7 LTOS 113 ... 76.1, 76.2, 85.4
Slatter's Will Trusts, Re, Turner v Turner [1964] Ch 512, [1964] 2 All ER 469, [1964] 3 WLR 18, 108 Sol Jo 378 .... 103.3
Slaughter, Re, Trustees Corpn Ltd v Slaughter [1945] Ch 355, [1945] 2 All ER 214, 115 LJ Ch 1, 89 Sol Jo 350, 173 LT 81, 61 TLR 453 .... 80.3, 216.30
Slavinsky's Estate, Re (1989) 53 SASR 221 .... 10.14
Slee, Re, Midland Bank Executor and Trustee Co Ltd v Slee [1962] 1 All ER 542, [1962] 1 WLR 496, 106 Sol Jo 352 .... 44.6, 100.5
Sleech v Thorington (1754) 2 Ves Sen 560 .... 30.8, 30.24, 69.2
Slevin, Re, Slevin v Hepburn [1891] 2 Ch 236, 60 LJ Ch 439, 39 WR 578, [1891–4] All ER Rep 200, 64 LT 311, 7 TLR 394, CA 102.20, 103.3, 103.18
Slingsby v Grainger (1859) 7 HL Cas 273, 28 LJ Ch 616, 5 Jur NS 1111 .... 50.21, 57.3, 58.6, 64.23
Slinn's Goods, Re (1890) 15 PD 156, 59 LJP 82, 39 WR 175, 63 LT 229 .... 1.2, 10.4
Sloan, Re, Stevens v Sloan (1943) ALR 132, [1943] VLR 63 .... 31.1
Slobodiniak v Podlasiewicz (2003) 228 DLR (4th) 610 .... 5.4
Smaling, Re, Johnson v Smaling (1877) 26 WR 231, 37 LT 392 .... 97.6

Smallbone v Brace (1677) Cas temp Finch 303 .... 30.3
Smalley, Re, Smalley v Scotton [1929] 2 Ch 112, 98 LJ Ch 300, 73 Sol Jo 234, 141 LT 158, 45 TLR 396, CA 80.2
Smalley, Re, Smalley v Smalley (1883) 49 LT 662 .... 64.45
Smallman v Goolden (1787) 1 Cox Eq Cas 329 .... 30.3
Smallwood, Re, Smallwood v Martins Bank Ltd [1951] Ch 369, [1951] 1 All ER 372, 95 Sol Jo 108, [1951] 1 TLR 331 .... 105.25
Smart v Clark (1827) 3 Russ 365, 5 LJOS Ch 111 .... 97.2
Smart v Prujean (1801) 6 Ves 560 .... 15.1, 81.5
Smart v Tranter (1890) 43 Ch D 587, 59 LJ Ch 363, 38 WR 530, 62 LT 356, CA 49.7
Smart's Goods, Re [1902] P 238, 71 LJP 123, 46 Sol Jo 587, 87 LT 142, 18 TLR 663 .... 15.2, 15.4
Smee v Baines (1861) 29 Beav 661, 31 LJ Ch 63, 7 Jur NS 902, 9 WR 802, 4 LT 573 .... 30.12
Smee v Smee (1879) 5 PD 84, 44 JP 220, 49 LJP 8, 28 WR 703 .... 4.11, 4.13, 4.15
Smeed, Re, Archer v Prall (1886) 54 LT 929, 2 TLR 535 .... 218.66
Smell v Dee (1707) 2 Salk 415 .... 93.26
Smeltzer, Re (1976) 72 DLR (3d) 280 .... 52.1
Smethurst v Tomlin and Bankes (1861) 25 JP 777, 30 LJPM & A 269, 7 Jur NS 763, 2 Sw & Tr 143, 4 LT 712 .... 25.4
Smidmore v Smidmore (1905) 3 CLR 344 .... 52.1, 52.6
Smiley, Re (1908) 28 NZLR 1 .... 69.1, 74.1, 81.3
Smilter, Re, Bedford v Hughes [1903] 1 Ch 198, 72 LJ Ch 102, 51 WR 231, 47 Sol Jo 146, 87 LT 644 .... 72.3
Smith, Re (1862) 2 John & H 594 .... 20.3, 52.11, 66.9, 91.6
Smith, Re (1889) 58 LJ Ch 661 .... 86.5
Smith, Re [1955] SASR 227 .... 11.8, 11.14
Smith, Re (1956) 20 WWR 254 .... 82.2
Smith, Re [1956] NZLR 593 .... 5.7
Smith, Re [1957] VLR 683 .... 91.2
Smith, Re, Arnold v Smith [1896] 1 Ch 171, [1895–9] All ER Rep 1175, 65 LJ Ch 269, 74 LT 14 .... 205.25
Smith, Re, Bilke v Roper (1890) 45 Ch D 632, [1886–90] All ER Rep 503, 60 LJ Ch 57, 39 WR 93, 63 LT 448, 6 TLR 484 .... 20.3, 22.2
Smith, Re, Bull v Smith [1933] Ch 847, [1933] All ER Rep 981, 102 LJ Ch 359, 149 LT 382 .... 78.1
Smith, Re, Dowzer v Dowzer (1914) 48 ILT 236 .... 30.31
Smith, Re, Eastick v Smith [1904] 1 Ch 139, 73 LJ Ch 74, 52 WR 104, 89 LT 604, 20 TLR 66 .... 212.5
Smith, Re, Henderson-Roe v Hitchins (1889) 42 Ch D 302, 58 LJ Ch 860, 37 WR 705, 61 LT 363 .... 29.14, 32.26
Smith, Re, Hillgrove v Smith [1956] NZLR 841 .... 63.1, 64.27
Smith, Re, Johnson v Bright-Smith [1914] 1 Ch 937, 83 LJ Ch 687, 58 Sol Jo 494, 110 LT 898, 30 TLR 411 .... 9.35, 9.36, 66.19, 102.26
Smith, Re, Keeling v Smith (1890) 44 Ch D 654, 59 LJ Ch 284, 38 WR 380, 62 LT 181, 6 TLR 183 .... 34.21, 35.16
Smith, Re, Lord v Hayward (1887) 35 Ch D 558, 56 LJ Ch 771, 35 WR 663, 56 LT 878 .... 74.1
Smith, Re, Phillips v Smith [1915] WN 12 .... 210.61

Smith, Re, Prada v Vandroy [1916] 2 Ch 368, 85 LJ Ch 657, 60 Sol Jo 603, 115 LT 161, CA 1.1, 20.3, 47.1
Smith, Re, Public Trustee v Aspinall [1928] Ch 915, 97 LJ Ch 441, 140 LT 369 .... 210.56
Smith, Re, Public Trustee v Smith [1932] 1 Ch 153, 100 LJ Ch 409, [1931] All ER Rep 617, 75 Sol Jo 780, 146 LT 145, 48 TLR 44, CA 102.10
Smith, Re, Royal Exchange Assurance Co v Lee (1923) 130 LT 185, [1923] All ER Rep 694, 67 Sol Jo 457 .... 33.5, 211.17
Smith, Re, Smith v Smith [1913] 2 Ch 216, 83 LJ Ch 13, 108 LT 952 .... 206.21
Smith, Re, Smith v Smith [1916] 1 Ch 369, 85 LJ Ch 473, [1916] HBR 66, 60 Sol Jo 368, 114 LT 680 .... 99.3
Smith, Re, Smith v Smith [2001] 3 All ER 552, [2001] 1 WLR 1937, [2001] 28 LS Gaz R 43, [2001] NLJR 784 .... 1.8, 46.1
Smith, Re, Veasey v Smith [1948] Ch 49, [1947] 2 All ER 708, [1949] LJR 765, 91 Sol Jo 664, 63 TLR 608 .... 50.2, 52.3, 101.2
Smith v Butcher (1878) 10 Ch D 113, 48 LJ Ch 136, 27 WR 281 .... 50.6, 78.4
Smith v Butler (1846) 3 Jo & Lat 565 .... 64.40
Smith v Campbell (1815) Coop G 275, 19 Ves 400 .... 79.5
Smith v Chishome (1888) 15 AR 738 .... 40.5
Smith v Claremont Haynes & Co (1991) Times, 3 September 1.14
Smith v Coffin (1795) 2 Hy Bl 444 .... 50.21
Smith v Conder (1878) 9 Ch D 170, 47 LJ Ch 878, 27 WR 149 .... 100.7
Smith v Coney (1801) 6 Ves 42 .... 58.10
Smith v Cowdery (1825) 2 Sim & St 358, 3 LJOS Ch 205 .... 34.19, 35.6
Smith v Crabtree (1877) 6 Ch D 591, 25 WR 824 .... 52.6, 100.4
Smith v Cuninghame (1884) 13 LR Ir 480 .... 94.7, 94.38, 95.8
Smith v Cunningham (1823) 1 Add 448 .... 18.5, 22.3
Smith v Davis (1866) 35 LJ Ch 874, 14 WR 942, CA 38.10
Smith v Farr (1839) 3 Y & C Ex 328, 8 LJ Ex Eq 46 .... 94.4
Smith v Fitzgerald (1814) 3 Ves & B 2 .... 52.11
Smith v Harris (1845) 1 Rob Eccl 262, 9 Jur 406, 4 Notes of Cases 48 .... 11.21
Smith v Houblon (1859) 26 Beav 482 .... 40.10
Smith v Jackson (1823) 1 LJOS Ch 231 .... 66.13
Smith v Jobson [1886–90] All ER Rep 1024, 59 LT 397 .... 72.2
Smith v Kerr [1902] 1 Ch 774, 71 LJ Ch 369, 86 LT 477, 18 TLR 456, CA 102.8
Smith v Layh (1953) 90 CLR 102 .... 1.8
Smith v Lidiard (1857) 3 K & J 252 .... 71.1
Smith v Lucas (1881) 18 Ch D 531, 30 WR 451, 45 LT 460 .... 42.6
Smith v Martin (1672) 2 Wms Saund 394 .... 64.26
Smith v Meriam (1878) 25 Gr 383 .... 14.6
Smith v Milles (1786) 1 Term Rep 475 .... 25.14
Smith v Oliver (1848) 11 Beav 494 .... 47.24
Smith v Osborne (1857) 6 HL Cas 375, 3 Jur NS 1181, 6 WR 21, 30 LTOS 57 .... 57.3, 67.4
Smith v Palmer (1848) 7 Hare 225 .... 68.11, 79.7
Smith v Pepper (1859) 27 Beav 86 .... 74.8
Smith v Perpetual Trustee Co Ltd and Delohery (1910) 11 CLR 148 .... 99.8
Smith v Plummer (1848) 9 JP 376, 17 LJ Ch 145, 9 Jur 352, 10 LTOS 38 .... 40.10
Smith v Pybus (1804) 9 Ves 566 .... 52.6

Smith v Ridgway (1866) LR 1 Exch 331, 35 LJ Ex 198, 12 Jur NS 742, 14 WR 868, 14 LT 632 .... 58.6, 63.4, 64.2, 64.26
Smith v Ruger (1859) 23 JP 581, 5 Jur NS 905, 33 LTOS 282 .... 103.7
Smith v Smith (1688) 2 Vern 92 .... 93.44
Smith v Smith (1837) 8 Sim 353, 6 LJ Ch 175 .... 47.32, 68.9
Smith v Smith (1861) 3 Giff 263, 31 LJ Ch 91, 7 Jur NS 1140, 5 LT 302 .... 30.10, 44.15
Smith v Smith (1866) LR 1 P & D 143, 35 LJP & M 65, 12 Jur NS 674, 14 WR 648, 14 LT 417 .... 12.3
Smith v Smith (1870) 5 Ch App 342, 18 WR 742 .... 94.21
Smith v Smith (Smith intervening) [1992] Fam 69, [1991] 2 All ER 306, [1991] 3 WLR 646, [1991] FCR 791, [1991] 2 FLR 432, [1991] Fam Law 412, CA 105.6, 105.39
Smith v Spencer (1856) 6 De GM & G 631, 3 Jur NS 193, 5 WR 136, 29 LTOS 59 .... 97.5
Smith v Stewart (1851) 4 De G & Sm 253, 20 LJ Ch 205, 15 Jur 834, 17 LTOS 195 .... 97.4, 97.5
Smith v Tebbitt (1867) LR 1 P & D 398, 36 LJP & M 97, 16 WR 18, 16 LT 841 .... 4.15, 4.16, 4.20
Smith v Thompson (1931) 75 Sol Jo 555, 146 LT 14, 47 TLR 603 .... 18.8
Smith and McKay, Re (1994) 116 DLR (4th) 308 (Man CA) 47.6
Smith's Estate, Re [1945] 3 WWR 216 .... 4.17
Smith's Estate, Re [1948] 2 WWR 55 .... 11.20
Smith's Estate, Re (1985) 38 SASR 30 .... 10.1
Smith's Goods, Re (1864) 29 JP 199, 34 LJPM & A 19, 10 Jur NS 1243, 3 Sw & Tr 589, 11 LT 684 .... 38.10
Smith's Goods, Re (1869) LR 1 P & D 717, 33 JP 712, 38 LJP & M 85, 17 WR 1110, 21 LT 340 .... 1.5, 1.6
Smith's Goods, Re (1889) 15 PD 2, 59 LJP 5, 54 JP 183, 38 WR 384, 62 LT 183 .... 9.8
Smith's Goods, Re [1904] P 114, 73 LJP 28, 90 LT 169, 20 TLR 119 .... 201.11
Smith's Trusts, Re (1865) LR 1 Eq 79 .... 93.15, 93.19, 101.4
Smith's Trusts, Re (1875) 5 Ch D 497n, 46 LJ Ch 388n 9.2
Smith's Trusts, Re (1878) 9 Ch D 117, 27 WR 132, 38 LT 905 .... 47.32
Smith's Will, Re (1855) 20 Beav 197, 24 LJ Ch 466, 1 Jur NS 220, 3 WR 277, 24 LTOS 322 .... 93.30
Smith's Will, Re [1965] Qd R 177 .... 11.4
Smith's Will, Re, Watson v Smith [1916] VLR 540 .... 64.8
Smith's Will Trusts, Re, Barclays Bank Ltd v Mercantile Bank Ltd [1962] 2 All ER 563, [1962] 1 WLR 763, 106 Sol Jo 389, CA 102.10, 103.10
Smithers, Re, Watts v Smithers [1939] Ch 1015, [1939] 3 All ER 689, 108 LJ Ch 369, 83 Sol Jo 689, 161 LT 193 .... 10.14, 64.35, 64.53
Smithson v Smithson (1915) 33 WLR 230, 22 BCR 326, 9 WWR 501 .... 25.4
Smithwick v Hayden (1887) 19 LR Ir 490 .... 94.13
Smyth v Power (1876) IR 10 Eq 192 .... 98.3
Smyth v Smyth (1878) 8 Ch D 561, 26 WR 736, 38 LT 633 .... 38.3, 38.4, 38.5, 64.16
Smyth's Goods, Re (1898). See Piazzi-Smyth's Goods, Re
Smythe, Re, Guinness v Smythe [1932] IR 136 .... 87.2
Smythies, Re, Weyman v Smythies [1903] 1 Ch 259, 71 LJ Ch 216, 51 WR 284, 87 LT 742 .... 44.2, 44.8
Snadden's Will, Re [1962] VR 571 .... 35.2

Snaith, Re, Snaith v Snaith (1894) 8 R 561, 42 WR 568, 38 Sol Jo 564, 71 LT 318 .... 32.15, 32.21
Snook v Watts (1848) 11 Beav 105, 12 Jur 444, 12 LTOS 1 .... 4.20
Snow v Poulden (1836) 1 Keen 186 .... 93.4, 93.14
Snow v Teed (1870) LR 9 Eq 622, 39 LJ Ch 420, 18 WR 623, sub nom Sum v Teed 23 LT 303 .... 77.1, 79.2
Snowden, Re, Smith v Spowage [1979] Ch 528, [1979] 2 All ER 172, [1979] 2 WLR 654, 123 Sol Jo 323 .... 36.7
Snowden's Goods, Re (1896) 75 LT 279 .... 21.7
Soames, Re, Church Schools Co Ltd v Soames (1897) 13 TLR 439 .... 3.2
Soames v Martin (1839) 10 Sim 287, sub nom Somes v Martin 8 LJ Ch 367, 3 Jur 1144 .... 33.18
Soar v Dolman, Re Rippin's Goods (1842) 3 Curt 121, 6 Jur 512, 1 Notes of Cases 513 .... 14.1
Society for the Propagation of the Gospel v A-G (1826) 3 Russ 142 .... 103.11
Solicitor, a, Re [1975] QB 475, [1974] 3 All ER 853, [1975] 2 WLR 105, 118 Sol Jo 737 .... 5.5, 200.4
Solly v Solly (1858) 5 Jur NS 36, 32 LTOS 293 .... 56.5, 68.1
Solomon, Re, Solomon v Solomon [1946] ALR 195, [1946] VLR 115 .... 35.31
Solomon v Solomon (1864) 33 LJ Ch 473, 10 Jur NS 331, 12 WR 540, 10 LT 54 .... 38.23
Solomons Estate, Re [1957] SASR 240 .... 96.1
Somech, Re, Westminster Bank Ltd v Phillips [1957] Ch 165, [1956] 3 All ER 523, [1956] 3 WLR 763, 100 Sol Jo 801 .... 9.39, 210.36, 232.67
Somers, Re [1941] 1 DLR 674, 15 MPR 335 .... 10.1
Somerville and Turner's Contract, Re [1903] 2 Ch 583, 72 LJ Ch 727, 52 WR 101, 47 Sol Jo 727, 89 LT 405 .... 64.52
Somes, Re, Smith v Somes [1896] 1 Ch 250, 65 LJ Ch 262, 44 WR 236, 40 Sol Jo 210, 74 LT 49, 12 TLR 152 .... 40.10, 40.15
Somes v Martin. See Soames v Martin
Songest, Re, Mayger v Forces Help Society and Lord Roberts Workshops [1956] 2 All ER 765, [1956] 1 WLR 897, 100 Sol Jo 528, CA 103.3
Sony KK v Saray Electronics (London) [1983] FSR 302, CA 21.25
Soper, Re, Naylor v Kettle [1912] 2 Ch 467, 81 LJ Ch 826, 107 LT 525 .... 77.1
Sotheran v Dening (1881) 20 Ch D 99, CA 18.8
Souch, Re [1938] 1 DLR 563, [1938] OR 48 .... 4.17, 5.2
South v Williams (1842) 12 Sim 566, 11 LJ Ch 410, 6 Jur 332 .... 47.22
South Place Ethical Society, Re, Barralet v A-G. See Barralet v A-G
Southampton (Lord) v Marquis of Hertford (1813) 2 Ves & B 54 .... 95.2, 95.8
Southcot v Watson (1745) 3 Atk 226 .... 64.53
Southerden's Estate, Re, Adams v Southerden [1925] P 177, 95 LJP 1, 69 Sol Jo 723, 133 LT 505, 41 TLR 539, CA 18.5, 19.1, 19.3, 19.5
Southern v Wollaston (1852) 16 Beav 166, 1 WR 86 .... 93.39
Southmolton Corpn v A-G (1854) 5 HL Cas 1, 23 LJ Ch 567, 18 Jur 435, 23 LTOS 117 .... 38.1, 103.14, 103.15, 103.16
Southouse v Bate (1851) 16 Beav 132, 18 LTOS 218 .... 83.13
Soutter's Executry v IRC [2002] STC (SCD) 385, [2002] WTLR 1207 .... 241.14
Sowerby's Trusts, Re (1856) 2 K & J 630 .... 47.21
Spackman v Timbrell (1837) 8 Sim 253, Donnelly 171, 209, 6 LJ Ch 147 .... 31.18
Spain, Re (1915) 31 TLR 435 .... 18.12

Spark v Purnell (1615) Hob 75, Moore KB 864 .... 84.2
Spark's Estate, Re [1941] P 115, [1941] 2 All ER 782, 110 LJP 71, 85 Sol Jo 370, 165 LT 234, 57 TLR 643 .... 16.2
Sparkes, Re, Kemp-Welch v Kemp-Welch (1911) 56 Sol Jo 90 .... 100.4
Sparks v Restal (1857) 24 Beav 218 .... 68.1
Sparrow, Re [1967] VR 739 .... 44.2
Sparrow, Re [1984] 1 NZLR 750 .... 38.3, 50.3
Sparrow v Royal Trust Co (1932) 40 Man LR 211, [1932] 1 WWR 379 .... 44.15
Speak, Re, Speak v Speak (1912) 56 Sol Jo 273 .... 67.6, 74.1
Speaker's Executor v Spicker 1969 SLT (Notes) 7 .... 64.10
Speakman, Re, Unsworth v Speakman (1876) 4 Ch D 620, 46 LJ Ch 608, 25 WR 225, 35 LT 731 .... 47.25, 50.2
Speakman v Speakman (1850) 8 Hare 180 .... 51.4, 56.5, 68.1, 94.5
Spearing v Hawkes (1857) 6 I Ch R 297 .... 38.3
Speedy, Re, Guardian Trust and Executors Co of New Zealand Ltd v Speedy [1964] NZLR 961 .... 48.8
Speir, Re, Holt v Speir [1924] 1 Ch 359, 93 LJ Ch 225, [1923] All ER Rep 640, 68 Sol Jo 251, 130 LT 564, CA 64.54
Spence, Re [1990] Ch 197, [1989] 3 WLR 834, [1990] 1 FLR 286, [1990] Fam Law 140, 133 Sol Jo 1513, sub nom Re Spence, Spence v Dennis [1989] 2 All ER 679, [1989] FCR 651; affd [1990] Ch 652, [1990] 2 All ER 827, [1990] 2 WLR 1430, [1990] FCR 983, [1990] 2 FLR 278, [1990] Fam Law 475, CA 72.15
Spence, Re, Barclays Bank Ltd v Stockton-on-Tees Corpn [1938] Ch 96, [1937] 3 All ER 684, 107 LJ Ch 1, 81 Sol Jo 650, 53 TLR 961 .... 102.10
Spence, Re, Ogden v Shackleton [1979] Ch 483, [1978] 3 WLR 483, 122 Sol Jo 574, sub nom Re Spence's Will Trusts, Ogden v Shackleton [1978] 3 All ER 92 .... 103.2, 103.3
Spence, Re, Spence v Dennis. See Spence, Re
Spence, Re, Wilkinson v Arlow [1939] NI 83 .... 64.7
Spencer, Re (1973) 42 DLR (3d) 127 .... 76.3
Spencer, Re, Hart v Manston (1886) 34 WR 527, 54 LT 597 .... 10.17, 52.9
Spencer (Lord) v Duke of Marlborough. See Marlborough (Duke) v Earl Godolphin
Spencer v Harrison (1879) 5 CPD 97, 44 JP 235, Colt 61, 49 LJQB 188, 41 LT 676 .... 38.25
Spencer v Metropolitan Board of Works (1882) 22 Ch D 142, 52 LJ Ch 249, 31 WR 347, 47 LT 459, CA 50.6
Spencer v Spencer (1856) 21 Beav 548 .... 63.1
Spencer v Ward (1870) LR 9 Eq 507, 18 WR 858, 22 LT 702 .... 69.2
Spencer v Wilson (1873) LR 16 Eq 501, 42 LJ Ch 754, 21 WR 838, 29 LT 19 .... 47.32, 93.31
Spencer Cooper, Re, Poë v Spencer Cooper [1908] 1 Ch 130, 77 LJ Ch 64, 98 LT 344 .... 55.7, 210.3, 210.7, 214.17, 214.64
Spencer's Case (1622) Win 51 .... 61.1
Spencer's Will, Re (1887) 57 LT 519, 3 TLR 822, CA 36.13
Spens v IRC [1970] 3 All ER 295, [1970] 1 WLR 1173, 46 TC 276, 49 ATC 89, [1970] TR 85, 114 Sol Jo 668 .... 218.95

Spensley's Will Trusts, Re, Barclays Bank Ltd v Staughton [1952] Ch 886, [1952] 2 All ER 49, 96 Sol Jo 412, [1952] 1 TLR 1435; on appeal [1954] Ch 233, [1954] 1 All ER 178, [1954] 2 WLR 145, 98 Sol Jo 77, CA 18.10, 18.15, 102.10, 102.17, 102.26, 103.17
Sperling's Goods, Re (1863) 27 JP 777, 33 LJPM & A 25, 9 Jur NS 1205, 3 Sw & Tr 272, 12 WR 354, 9 LT 348 .... 12.12
Spicer, Re, Spicer v Richardson [1949] P 441, [1949] 2 All ER 659, [1949] LJR 1588, 93 Sol Jo 679, 65 TLR 590 .... 16.4, 16.5
Spiller, Re, Spiller v Madge (1881) 18 Ch D 614, 50 LJ Ch 750, 29 WR 782, 45 LT 41 .... 47.32
Spiller v Maude (1881) 32 Ch D 158n 102.16
Spink v Lewis (1791) 3 Bro CC 355 .... 77.3
Spire v Smith (1839) 1 Beav 419 .... 33.10
Spitzel's Will Trusts, Re, Spitzel v Spitzel [1939] 2 All ER 266, 83 Sol Jo 378 .... 35.52
Spong v Spong (1829) 3 Bli NS 84, 1 Dow & Cl 365, HL 82.1
Spooner's Trust, Re, ex p Mouritz (1851) 2 Sim NS 129, 21 LJ Ch 151, 18 LTOS 269 .... 39.12, 39.14, 47.39
Spracklan's Estate, Re [1938] 2 All ER 345, 82 Sol Jo 373, CA 18.16
Sprackling v Ranier (1761) 1 Dick 344 .... 66.20
Sprague, Re, Miley v Cape (1880) 43 LT 236 .... 101.9
Spratt's Goods, Re [1897] P 28, 66 LJP 25, 45 WR 159, 75 LT 518 .... 1.5
Spread v Morgan (1865) 11 HL Cas 588, 6 New Rep 269, 13 LT 164 .... 42.12
Sprigge v Sprigge (1868) LR 1 P & D 608, 33 JP 104, 38 LJP & M 4, 17 WR 80, 19 LT 462 .... 18.5, 18.7, 18.31
Springett v Jenings (1871) 6 Ch App 333, 40 LJ Ch 348, 19 WR 575, 24 LT 643 .... 36.2, 36.4, 47.7
Spurway v Glynn (1804) 9 Ves 483 .... 32.8
Squire, Re (1962) 34 DLR (2d) 481, [1962] OR 863 .... 34.5
Squire's Trusts, Re, Chester and Flower v Oxford and Cambridge Universities and A-G (1901) 17 TLR 724 .... 103.17
Stable, Re, Dalrymple v Campbell [1919] P 7, 88 LJP 32, [1918–19] All ER Rep 299, 120 LT 160 .... 16.4
Stacey v Elph (1833) 1 My & K 195, 2 LJ Ch 50, 36 RR 306 .... 27.6, 45.1
Stackpole v Beaumont (1796) 3 Ves 89 .... 35.3
Stackpoole v Howell (1807) 13 Ves 417 .... 30.14, 30.15
Stackpoole v Stackpoole (1843) 6 I Eq R 18, 2 Con & Law 489, 4 Dr & War 320 .... 40.21
Stadder v Canadian Bank of Commerce [1929] 3 DLR 651, 64 OLR 69 .... 83.12
Staffordshire County Council v B [1999] 2 FCR 333, [1998] 1 FLR 261, [1998] Fam Law 8 .... 75.3, 245.96
Staines v Maddock. See Maddox v Staines
Stalker's Executors, Petitioners, Re 1977 SLT (Notes) 4 .... 50.6
Stalman, Re, Stalman v Jones [1931] WN 143, [1931] All ER Rep 193, 145 LT 339, CA 11.2, 11.9
Stamford (Earl), Re, Hall v Lambert (1906) 22 TLR 632, CA 63.1, 204.41
Stamford (Earl), Re, Payne v Stamford [1896] 1 Ch 288, 65 LJ Ch 134, 44 WR 249, 40 Sol Jo 114, 73 LT 559, 12 TLR 78 .... 30.42
Stamford v White [1901] P 46, 70 LJP 9, 84 LT 269 .... 18.22, 19.5

Stamford and Warrington (Earl), Re, Payne v Grey [1912] 1 Ch 343, 81 LJ Ch 302, 56 Sol Jo 204, 105 LT 913, 28 TLR 159, CA 51.4, 94.7, 94.14, 95.2
Stammers v Elliott (1868) 3 Ch App 195, 37 LJ Ch 353, 16 WR 489, 18 LT 1 .... 30.11, 30.13
Stammvoll v Hales, Re Johnstone. See Stummvoli v Hales
Stamp Duties Comr v Bone [1977] AC 511, [1976] 2 All ER 354, [1976] 2 WLR 968, [1976] STC 145, [1976] TR 117, 120 Sol Jo 421, PC 30.4, 30.12, 31.4, 47.22
Stamp Duties Comr (Queensland) v Livingston [1965] AC 694, [1964] 3 All ER 692, [1964] 3 WLR 963, 43 ATC 325, [1964] TR 351, 108 Sol Jo 820, PC 1.8, 7.14, 25.18, 205.12, 241.8
Stamper v Pickering (1838) 9 Sim 176 .... 33.24
Stanford, Re, Cambridge University v A-G [1924] 1 Ch 73, 93 LJ Ch 109, [1923] All ER Rep 589, 68 Sol Jo 59, 130 LT 309, 40 TLR 3 .... 102.20, 103.6, 103.13
Stanford v Stanford (1886) 34 Ch D 362, 35 WR 191, sub nom Re Stanford, Stanford v Stanford 56 LJ Ch 273, 55 LT 765 .... 66.10, 93.20
Stanhope's Trusts, Re (1859) 27 Beav 201 .... 47.29, 47.32, 85.5
Stanier v Hodgkinson (1903) 73 LJ Ch 179, 52 WR 260, 48 Sol Jo 143 .... 38.23, 93.20
Stanley, Re, Tennant v Stanley [1906] 1 Ch 131, 75 LJ Ch 56, 54 WR 103, 93 LT 661 .... 38.10
Stanley v Bond [1913] 1 IR 170 .... 67.6
Stanley v IRC [1944] KB 255, [1944] 1 All ER 230, 113 LJKB 292, 26 TC 12, 170 LT 140, 60 TLR 209, CA 218.56
Stanley v Lennard (1758) Amb 355, 1 Eden 87 .... 98.4
Stanley v Potter (1789) 2 Cox Eq Cas 180 .... 41.19
Stanley v Stanley (1809) 16 Ves 491 .... 93.16
Stanley v Stanley (1862) 2 John & H 491, 10 WR 857, 7 LT 136 .... 50.2, 58.6
Stanley v Wise (1788) 1 Cox Eq Cas 432 .... 66.6
Stanley's Estate, Re [1916] P 192, 85 LJP 222, [1916–17] All ER Rep 352, 60 Sol Jo 604, 114 LT 1182, 32 TLR 643 .... 16.2, 16.3
Stanley's Settlement, Re, Maddocks v Andrews [1916] 2 Ch 50, 85 LJ Ch 809, 60 Sol Jo 478, 114 LT 933 .... 86.6, 101.6
Stansfield, Re, Stansfield v Stansfield (1880) 15 Ch D 84, 49 LJ Ch 750, 29 WR 72, 43 LT 310 .... 47.12, 47.32
Stanway v Styles (1734) 2 Eq Cas Abr 156n, sub nom Slanning v Style 3 P Wms 334, 24 ER 1089 .... 64.28
Staple, Re [1954] QWN 54 .... 238.3
Staples, Re, Fitzherbert v Midland Bank Executor and Trustee Co Ltd [1933] IR 126 .... 40.21
Stapleton, Re [1938] 3 DLR 752 .... 39.14
Stapleton, Re, Stapleton v Stapleton [1946] 1 All ER 323, 90 Sol Jo 139, 174 LT 188 .... 32.21, 218.47
Stapleton v Cheales (1711) 1 Eq Cas Abr 295, Gilb Ch 76, Prec Ch 317, 2 Vern 673 .... 93.26, 93.27
Stapleton v Conway (1750) 3 Atk 727, 1 Ves Sen 427 .... 30.43, 32.33, 64.28
Stapleton v Stapleton (1852) 2 Sim NS 212, 21 LJ Ch 434 .... 56.8
Stares v Penton (1867) LR 4 Eq 40 .... 100.4
Stark, Re (1969) 7 DLR (3d) 313, [1969] 2 OR 881 .... 71.1, 71.5
Stark's Trustees v Stark 1948 SC 41 .... 63.8, 64.8

Starr v Newberry (1857) 23 Beav 436 .... 77.2
Staveley, Re, Dyke v Staveley (1920) 90 LJ Ch 111, 65 Sol Jo 154, 124 LT 466 .... 35.52, 40.21, 94.46, 94.48
Stavers v Barnard (1843) 2 Y & C Ch Cas 539, 7 Jur 1080, 2 LTOS 95 .... 74.1
Stead, Re, Witham v Andrew [1900] 1 Ch 237, 69 LJ Ch 49, 48 WR 221, 44 Sol Jo 146, 81 LT 751 .... 36.4, 36.7, 36.8, 36.13
Stead v Newdigate (1817) 2 Mer 521 .... 37.5, 39.12
Stead v Platt (1853) 18 Beav 50 .... 67.4
Stead v Stead [1985] FLR 16, [1985] Fam Law 154, CA 105.9
Stedham's Goods, Re, Re Dyke's Goods (1881) 6 PD 205, 46 JP 40, 45 JP 784, 50 LJP 75, 29 WR 743, [1881–5] All ER Rep 410, 45 LT 192 .... 21.6, 21.7, 21.8, 22.5
Steed v Calley (1836) 1 Keen 620 .... 4.14
Steel, Re, Public Trustee v Christian Aid Society [1979] Ch 218, [1978] 2 All ER 1026, [1978] 2 WLR 950, 122 Sol Jo 148 .... 38.3, 50.15, 57.5, 64.50, 90.6
Steel, Re, Wappett v Robinson [1903] 1 Ch 135, 72 LJ Ch 42, 51 WR 252, 47 Sol Jo 31, 87 LT 548 .... 50.12
Steele, Re (1915) 15 SRNSW 247, 32 WNNSW 66 .... 30.14
Steele, Re, Steele v Steele [1913] 1 IR 292 .... 20.4
Steele's (or Steel) Goods, Re, Re May's Goods, Re Wilson's Goods (1868) LR 1 P & D 575, 32 JP 791, 37 LJP & M 68, 72, 17 WR 15, [1861–73] All ER Rep 209, 19 LT 91 .... 20.4, 21.5, 21.6
Steer, Re (1858) 3 H & N 594, 28 LJ Ex 22, 32 LTOS 130 .... 236.10
Stein v Ritherdon (1868) 37 LJ Ch 369, 16 WR 477, 19 LT 184 .... 38.5, 60.2, 64.19, 64.40
Steinberg's Will, Re (1968) 63 WWR 649 .... 33.12, 62.1
Stelfox v Sugden (1859) John 234 .... 33.23, 33.26
Stemson's Will Trusts, Re, Carpenter v Treasury Solicitor [1970] Ch 16, [1969] 2 All ER 517, [1969] 3 WLR 21, 113 Sol Jo 465 .... 58.11, 103.3
Stenhouse v Mitchell (1805) 11 Ves 352 .... 64.39
Stent v Robinson (1806) 12 Ves 461 .... 32.5
Stephanides v Cohen [2002] EWHC 1869 (Fam), [2002] WTLR 1373 .... 105.9, 105.21
Stephen, Re, Stephen v Stephen [1913] WN 210 .... 38.12
Stephens, Re, Giles v Stephens (1892) 36 Sol Jo 713, 8 TLR 792 .... 102.10
Stephens, Re, Kilby v Betts [1904] 1 Ch 322, 73 LJ Ch 3, 52 WR 89, 48 Sol Jo 15, 91 LT 167 .... 66.13, 66.21, 95.9, 95.11
Stephens, Re, Tomalin v Tomalin's Trustee [1927] 1 Ch 1, 95 LJ Ch 493, 135 LT 503, CA 66.6, 96.1
Stephens v Gadsden (1855) 20 Beav 463 .... 82.4
Stephens v Powys (1857) 1 De G & J 24 .... 53.1
Stephens v Stephens (1857) 1 De G & J 62, 3 Drew 697, 3 Jur NS 525, 5 WR 540, 29 LTOS 271 .... 42.5
Stephens v Taprell (1840) 2 Curt 458 .... 18.17, 18.25
Stephens v Tolley [1954] SASR 97 .... 82.4
Stephenson, Re, Donaldson v Bamber [1897] 1 Ch 75, 66 LJ Ch 93, 45 WR 162, 41 Sol Jo 96, 75 LT 495, 13 TLR 67, CA 53.1, 53.5, 57.9, 57.19, 69.2
Stephenson, Re, Stephenson v Stephenson (1885) 54 LJ Ch 928; affd sub nom Stephenson v Stephenson (1887) 56 LT 75, CA 48.9

Stephenson (Inspector of Taxes) v Barclays Bank Trust Co Ltd [1975] 1 All ER 625, [1975] 1 WLR 882, [1975] STC 151, 50 TC 374, 53 ATC 357, [1974] TR 343, 119 Sol Jo 169 .... 200.57, 220.73
Stephenson v Dowson (1840) 3 Beav 342, 10 LJ Ch 93, 4 Jur 1152 .... 30.5, 30.8, 64.39
Stephenson's Trusts, Re (1870) 18 WR 1066 .... 35.16
Sterling v Bruce [1973] NI 255 .... 11.4, 19.4
Stevens, Re [1918] NZLR 940 .... 14.5
Stevens, Re [1946] 4 DLR 322 .... 41.7
Stevens, Re, Clark v Stevens (1896) 40 Sol Jo 296 .... 66.16
Stevens, Re, Cooke v Stevens [1897] 1 Ch 422, 66 LJ Ch 155, 45 WR 284, 76 LT 18; affd [1898] 1 Ch 162, 67 LJ Ch 118, 46 WR 177, 42 Sol Jo 113, 77 LT 508, 14 TLR 111, CA 25.12
Stevens, Re, Pateman v James [1952] Ch 323, [1952] 1 All ER 674, 96 Sol Jo 182, [1952] 1 TLR 590 .... 51.2, 53.4
Stevens, Re, Stevens v Keily [1888] WN 110 .... 64.7, 64.37, 64.39
Stevens, Re, Stevens v Stevens [1915] 1 Ch 429, 84 LJ Ch 432, 59 Sol Jo 441, 112 LT 982 .... 32.28
Stevens, Re, Trustees, Executors and Agency Co Ltd v Teague [1912] VLR 194 .... 66.5, 66.13
Stevens v King [1904] 2 Ch 30, 73 LJ Ch 535, 52 WR 443, [1904–7] All ER Rep 951, 90 LT 665 .... 47.21, 47.38, 47.39
Stevens v Mossisroe (2001) 202 DLR (4th) 577 .... 5.4
Stevens v Pyle (1860) 28 Beav 388 .... 101.14
Stevens v Pyle (1861) 30 Beav 284 .... 81.3
Stevens' Trusts, Re (1872) LR 15 Eq 110, 21 WR 119, 27 LT 480 .... 78.4
Stevenson, Re [1944] 1 DLR 267, 51 Man R 221, [1943] 3 WWR 519 .... 38.3
Stevenson v Abington (1862) 31 Beav 305, 8 Jur NS 811, 10 WR 591, 6 LT 345 .... 71.4
Stevenson v Abington (1863) 9 Jur NS 1063, 11 WR 935, 9 LT 74 .... 35.38
Stevenson v Gullan (1854) 18 Beav 590 .... 87.2
Stevenson v Liverpool Corpn (1874) LR 10 QB 81, 44 LJQB 34, 23 WR 346, 31 LT 673 .... 8.5
Stevenson v Masson (1873) LR 17 Eq 78, 43 LJ Ch 134, 22 WR 150, 29 LT 666 .... 44.12
Stevenson (Inspector of Taxes) v Wishart [1987] 2 All ER 428, [1987] 1 WLR 1204, [1987] STC 266, 59 TC 740, 131 Sol Jo 744, [1987] LS Gaz R 1574, CA 218.39
Steward v Cotton (1777) 5 Russ 17n 8.4
Steward's Will, Re [1964] VR 179 .... 18.13
Stewart, Re [1976] 1 NZLR 661 .... 92.3, 92.4, 92.5
Stewart, Re, Stewart v Bosanquet (1913) 57 Sol Jo 646 .... 32.20
Stewart, Re, Stewart v Hislop (1905) 23 NZLR 797 .... 35.19, 83.6
Stewart, Re, Stewart v McLaughlin [1908] 2 Ch 251, 77 LJ Ch 525, [1908–10] All ER Rep 133, 99 LT 106, 24 TLR 679 .... 30.18, 57.32
Stewart v Garnett (1830) 3 Sim 398 .... 62.1
Stewart v Green (1870) IR 5 Eq 470 .... 9.35
Stewart v Jones (1859) 3 De G & J 532, 5 Jur NS 229, 7 WR 184, 33 LTOS 114 .... 47.25
Stewart v MacLaren (1920) 57 SLR 531, 1920 SC (HL) 148, 1920 SLT 134 .... 21.7
Stewart v Murdoch [1969] NI 78 .... 35.8

Stewart v Stewart (1880) 15 Ch D 539, 49 LJ Ch 763, 29 WR 275, 43 LT 370 .... 100.4
Stibbe, Re, Cleverley v Stibbe (1946) 175 LT 198 .... 44.12, 44.15
Stickland v Aldridge (1804) 9 Ves 516, [1803–13] All ER Rep 554 .... 36.2, 36.4
Stilborn Estate, Re (1966) 58 DLR (2d) 575, 57 WWR 446 .... 30.43
Stiles v Guy (1832) 4 Y & C Ex 571 .... 25.12, 64.53
Stiles's Goods, Re [1898] P 12, 67 LJP 23, 46 WR 444, 78 LT 82, 14 TLR 61 .... 25.13
Still v Hoste (1821) 6 Madd 192 .... 57.22
Stillman, Re (1966) 52 DLR (2d) 601, [1966] 1 OR 113 .... 67.2
Stillman v Weedon (1848) 16 Sim 26, 18 LJ Ch 46, 12 Jur 992 .... 39.20
Stilwell v Mellersh (1851) 20 LJ Ch 356 .... 20.4, 22.3
Stimpson's Trusts, Re, Stimpson v Stimpson [1931] 2 Ch 77, [1931] All ER Rep 809, 100 LJ Ch 312, 145 LT 249 .... 218.90, 218.93
Stinson, Re (1973) 30 DLR (3d) 519 .... 38.3, 64.38
Stirling, Re, Union Bank of Scotland Ltd v Stirling [1954] 2 All ER 113, [1954] 1 WLR 763, 98 Sol Jo 337 .... 36.6
Stobie Estate, Re [1942] 3 WWR 414 .... 10.8
Stock v Brown [1994] 2 FCR 1125, [1994] 1 FLR 840, [1994] Fam Law 254 .... 105.5
Stockdale v Bushby (1815) Coop G 229, 19 Ves 381 .... 58.10
Stocken v Stocken (1831) 4 Sim 152; on appeal (1833) 2 My & K 489; on appeal (1838) 4 My & Cr 95, 7 LJ Ch 305, 2 Jur 693, 41 ER 38 .... 3.11, 44.15
Stocks v Barre (1859) John 54, 33 LJOS 8, 5 Jur NS 537, 7 WR 247 .... 64.35
Stocks v Dodsley (1836) 1 Keen 325 .... 83.3
Stockwell v Ritherdon (1848) 1 Rob Eccl 661, 12 Jur 779, 12 LTOS 107, 6 Notes of Cases 409 .... 18.3
Stoddart, Re, Bird v Grainger [1916] 2 Ch 444, 86 LJ Ch 29, 60 Sol Jo 586, 115 LT 540 .... 214.66, 235.22
Stoddart v Grant (1852) 19 LTOS 305, 1 Macq 163, HL 1.1, 18.31
Stoddart v Nelson (1855) 6 De GM & G 68, 25 LJ Ch 116, 2 Jur NS 27, 4 WR 109, 26 LTOS 210 .... 71.4
Stodworthy v Sancroft. See Stolworthy v Sancroft
Stokes, Re, Bowen v Davidson [1928] Ch 716, 97 LJ Ch 273, [1928] All ER Rep 406, 72 Sol Jo 384, 139 LT 331 .... 32.5, 32.22
Stokes, Re, Public Trustees v Brooks [1922] 2 Ch 406, 91 LJ Ch 774, 66 Sol Jo 523, 127 LT 92 .... 39.14
Stokes, Re, Stokes v Ducroz (1890) 38 WR 535, 62 LT 176, 6 TLR 154 .... 23.4
Stokes v Cheek (1860) 28 Beav 620, 29 LJ Ch 922 .... 33.5, 33.7
Stokes v Heron. See Heron v Stokes
Stolworthy v Sancroft (1864) 33 LJ Ch 708, 10 Jur NS 762, 12 WR 635, sub nom Stodworthy v Sancroft 10 LT 223 .... 101.9
Stone, Re [1954] NZLR 1170 .... 64.45
Stone, Re [1958] SASR 246 .... 67.2
Stone, Re [1959] QWN 2 .... 17.5
Stone, Re, Baker v Stone [1895] 2 Ch 196, 64 LJ Ch 637, 12 R 415, 44 WR 235, 72 LT 815, CA 50.21, 87.1, 87.2
Stone v Greening (1843) 13 Sim 390 .... 58.6, 64.22
Stone v Hoskins [1905] P 194, 74 LJP 110, 54 WR 64, 93 LT 441, 21 TLR 528 .... 2.3, 2.5, 2.6, 2.7, 2.8, 3.13

Stone v Maule (1829) 2 Sim 490 .... 98.13
Stone v Parker (1860) 1 Drew & Sm 212, 29 LJ Ch 874, 8 WR 722, 3 LT 79 .... 35.19, 38.10, 83.6
Stone's Trusts, Re (1866) 12 Jur NS 447, 14 LT 542 .... 34.21, 35.48
Stoneham, Re, Stoneham v Stoneham [1919] 1 Ch 149, 88 LJ Ch 77, [1918–19] All ER Rep 1051, 63 Sol Jo 192, 120 LT 341 .... 30.18, 57.32
Stonham, Re, Lloyds Bank Ltd v Maynard [1963] 1 All ER 377, [1963] 1 WLR 238, 107 Sol Jo 74 .... 64.38
Stoodley, Re, Hooson v Locock [1916] 1 Ch 242, [1916–17] All ER Rep 761, 114 LT 445, sub nom Re Stoodley, Hooson v Stoodley 85 LJ Ch 226, 60 Sol Jo 221, CA 18.33, 52.9
Stooke v Stooke (1866) 35 Beav 396, 14 WR 564 .... 64.35, 64.36
Stopford v Chaworth (1845) 8 Beav 331, 9 Jur 363, 5 LTOS 142 .... 74.1
Stopford v Stopford (1903) 19 TLR 185 .... 16.2
Storer v Prestage (1818) 3 Madd 167 .... 33.11
Storrs v Benbow (1833) 2 My & K 46, 2 LJ Ch 201; revsd (1853) 3 De GM & G 390, 22 LJ Ch 823, 17 Jur 821, 1 WR 420, 21 LTOS 189 .... 65.3, 66.20, 73.1
Storrs v Benbow (1853) 3 De GM & G 390, 22 LJ Ch 823, 17 Jur 821, 1 WR 420, 21 LTOS 189 .... 73.1, 94.11, 94.21
Stott, Re, Klouda v Lloyds Bank Ltd [1980] 1 All ER 259, [1980] 1 WLR 246, 123 Sol Jo 422 .... 5.2, 5.3, 5.4, 5.9
Stracey's Goods, Re (1855) Dea & Sw 6, 1 Jur NS 1177, 4 WR 164, 26 LTOS 127 .... 2.2
Strakosch, Re, Temperley v A-G [1949] Ch 529, [1949] 2 All ER 6, [1949] LJR 1477, 93 Sol Jo 372, 65 TLR 383, CA 102.10
Strange, Re, Lamb v Bossi Leu (1916) 60 Sol Jo 640 .... 33.8
Strange (Lord) v Smith (1755) Amb 263 .... 35.16
Stratford v Powell (1807) 1 Ball & B 1 .... 42.8, 84.2, 89.1
Stratheden and Campbell (Lord), Re, Alt v Lord Stratheden and Campbell [1894] 3 Ch 265, 63 LJ Ch 872, 8 R 515, 42 WR 647, 38 Sol Jo 602, 71 LT 225, 10 TLR 574 .... 94.13, 102.10, 102.26
Stratton, Re, Knapman v A-G [1931] 1 Ch 197, 100 LJ Ch 62, [1930] All ER Rep 255, 74 Sol Jo 787, 144 LT 169, 47 TLR 32, CA 102.17
Stratton v Grymes (1698) 2 Vern 357 .... 34.14
Stratton's Disclaimer, Re, Stratton v IRC [1958] Ch 42, [1957] 2 All ER 594, [1957] 3 WLR 199, 36 ATC 145, [1957] TR 161, 101 Sol Jo 533, CA 46.5
Strauss v Schmidt (1820) 3 Phillim 209 .... 1.5
Streatfeild v Cooper (1859) 27 Beav 338 .... 60.2
Streatfield v Streatfield (1735) Cas temp Talb 176, 1 Swan 436n, 1 White & Tud LC 400 .... 42.11
Streatley's Goods, Re [1891] P 172, 60 LJP 56, 39 WR 432 .... 12.11, 12.14, 12.15
Street, Re, Vevers v Holman [1922] WN 291 .... 33.27
Street v Street (1863) 2 New Rep 56, 8 LT 306 .... 33.34
Stretch v Watkins (1816) 1 Madd 253 .... 32.21, 62.1, 93.27
Stretton v Fitzgerald (1889) 23 LR Ir 466 .... 56.1
Stride v Sandford (1853) 17 Jur 263, 21 LTOS 24 .... 21.8
Stringer v Gardiner (1859) 27 Beav 35, 4 De G & J 468, 7 WR 602, 33 LTOS 295 .... 57.15, 58.10, 71.5
Stringer's Estate, Re, Shaw v Jones-Ford (1877) 6 Ch D 1, 46 LJ Ch 633, 25 WR 815, 37 LT 233, CA 43.3, 83.9, 83.11, 83.12, 99.1

Strode (Sir Litton) v Lady Russel and Lady Falkland (1707) 3 Rep Ch 169, 2 Vern 621; on appeal sub nom Viscountess Falkland v Lytton (1708) 3 Bro Parl Cas 24, HL 53.5, 57.22
Strombeck Estate, Re, Royal Trust Co v Children's Hospital (1956) 2 DLR (2d) 109, 17 WWR 588 .... 30.23, 54.2
Strong, Re, Strong v Meissner (1925) 95 LJ Ch 22, 69 Sol Jo 693 .... 24.12, 24.16
Strong v Bird (1874) LR 18 Eq 315, 43 LJ Ch 814, 22 R 788, [1874–80] All ER Rep 230, 30 LT 745 .... 30.18, 57.32
Strong's Estate, Re, Strong v Hadden [1915] P 211, 84 LJP 188, 112 LT 997, 31 TLR 256 .... 13.2
Strother v Dutton (1857) 1 De G & J 675 .... 68.15, 93.29
Stroud v Gwyer (1860) 28 Beav 130, 6 Jur NS 719, 126 RR 57, 2 LT 400 .... 38.23
Struthers, Re (1980) 114 DLR (3d) 492 .... 33.23
Struthers v Struthers (1857) 5 WR 809 .... 41.4, 58.12, 207.3
Stuart v Babington (1891) 27 LR Ir 551 .... 94.48
Stuart v Bruce (1798) 3 Ves 632 .... 86.2
Stuart v Clemons [1951] Tas LR 23 .... 15.1
Stuart v Cockerell (1870) 5 Ch App 713, 39 LJ Ch 729, 18 WR 1057, 23 LT 442, CA 66.1, 94.8
Stuart v Marquis of Bute (1806) 11 Ves 657; on appeal (1813) 1 Dow 73, HL 38.10, 63.1, 64.25
Stuart v Norton (1860) 14 Moo PCC 17, 9 WR 320, 3 LT 602 .... 40.5
Stuart Estate, Re (1964) 47 WWR 500 .... 47.32
Stubbings v Clunies-Ross (1911) 27 TLR 361 .... 201.11
Stubbs v Sargon (1837) 2 Keen 255, 6 LJ Ch 254; on appeal (1838) 3 My & Cr 507, 7 LJ Ch 95, 2 Jur 150, 44 RR 241 .... 56.9
Stuckey, Re, Executor Trustee and Agency Co of South Australia Ltd v Stuckey [1915] SALR 190 .... 97.5
Studd v Cook (1883) 8 App Cas 577, 10 R 53, 20 SLR 566, HL 24.6, 50.19
Studholme v Hodgson (1734) 3 P Wms 300 .... 98.13
Stulz's Trusts, Re, ex p Kingsford and Stulz (1853) 4 De GM & G 404, 22 LJ Ch 917, 1 Eq Rep 334, 17 Jur 749, 1 WR 499, 22 LTOS 9 .... 99.9
Stummvoli v Hales (1864) 34 Beav 124, 10 Jur NS 716, 4 New Rep 473, 12 WR 1137, sub nom Stammvoll v Hales, Re Johnstone 10 LT 807 .... 74.2
Stump v Gaby (1852) 2 De GM & G 623, 22 LJ Ch 352, 17 Jur 5, 1 WR 85, 20 LTOS 213 .... 7.8
Sturge and Great Western Rly Co (1881) 19 Ch D 444, 51 LJ Ch 185, 30 WR 456, sub nom Sturge v Sturge, Sturge to Great Western Rly Co, Re Vendor and Purchaser Act 1874 45 LT 787 .... 77.4
Sturgess v Pearson (1819) 4 Madd 411, 20 RR 316 .... 67.7
Sturgis, Re, Webling v Van Epery (1889) 17 OR 342 .... 9.8
Sturt, Re, De Bunsen v Hardinge [1922] 1 Ch 416, 91 LJ Ch 289, 66 Sol Jo 236, 126 LT 460 .... 37.8
Sturton v Whetlock (1883) 47 JP 232, 52 LJP 29, 31 WR 382, 48 LT 237 .... 14.1, 19.4
Sudbrook Trading Estate Ltd v Eggleton [1983] 1 AC 444, [1982] 3 All ER 1, [1982] 3 WLR 315, 44 P & CR 153, 126 Sol Jo 512, 265 Estates Gazette 215, HL 92.3
Sudbury v Brown (1856) 4 WR 736, 27 LTOS 260 .... 64.31
Sudeley (Lord) v A-G [1897] AC 11, 61 JP 420, 66 LJQB 21, 45 WR 305, 75 LT 398, 13 TLR 38, [1895–9] All ER Rep Ext 1904, HL 1.8, 38.16

Sudlow, Re, Smith v Sudlow [1914] WN 424, 59 Sol Jo 162 .... 64.30
Suenson-Taylor's Settlement, Re, Moores v Moores [1974] 3 All ER 397, [1974] 1 WLR 1280, 118 Sol Jo 757 .... 220.69
Sugden v Lord St Leonards (1876) 1 PD 154, 45 LJP 49, 2 Char Pr Cas 160, 24 WR 479, 860, [1874–80] All ER Rep 21, 34 LT 369, 372, CA 15.5, 18.12, 18.29
Suisse v Lord Lowther (1843) 2 Hare 424, 12 LJ Ch 315, 7 Jur 252, 367 .... 44.4, 44.8, 88.3, 88.4
Sullivan, Re, Dunkley v Sullivan [1930] 1 Ch 84, 99 LJ Ch 42, [1929] All ER Rep 564, 142 LT 187, 45 TLR 590 .... 38.24, 38.25, 46.3, 104.14
Sullivan, Re, Sullivan v Sullivan [1917] 1 IR 38 .... 42.5
Sullivan v Sullivan (1870) IR 4 Eq 457 .... 57.19
Sullivan v Sullivan (1879) 3 LR Ir 299 .... 12.7
Sullivan v Sullivan [1903] 1 IR 193 .... 9.4, 36.13
Sum v Teed. See Snow v Teed
Summers's Goods, Re (1850) 2 Rob Eccl 295, 14 Jur 791, 15 LTOS 478, 7 Notes of Cases 562 .... 11.24
Summers's Goods, Re (1901) 45 Sol Jo 327, 84 LT 271, 17 TLR 325 .... 18.10
Sumner's Will Trusts, Re, Midland Bank Executor and Trustee Co Ltd v Sumner [1969] 1 All ER 779, [1969] 1 WLR 373, 113 Sol Jo 209 .... 55.5
Sumpton v Downing [1947] ALR 513 .... 87.2
Sunderland's Goods, Re (1866) LR 1 P & D 198, 35 LJP & M 82, 14 WR 971, 14 LT 741 .... 15.1
Supple v Lowson (1773) Amb 729 .... 79.4
Supple v Pender [2007] EWHC 829 (Ch), [2007] All ER (D) 195 (Feb) 5.9
Surridge, Re, Sparks v Kingdom (1970) 114 Sol Jo 208, CA 19.1
Surridge v Clarkson (1866) 14 WR 979 .... 66.19
Surtees v Surtees (1871) LR 12 Eq 400, 19 WR 1043, 25 LT 288 .... 89.1
Susanni's Trusts, Re (1877) 47 LJ Ch 65, 26 WR 93 .... 47.38, 101.9
Sutcliffe, Re, Alison v Alison [1934] Ch 219, 103 LJ Ch 154, [1933] All ER Rep 773, 150 LT 391 .... 66.2, 76.1
Sutcliffe, Re, Sutcliffe v Robertshaw [1929] 1 Ch 123, 98 LJ Ch 33, 72 Sol Jo 384, 140 LT 135 .... 77.2
Sutcliffe v Cole (1855) 3 Drew 135, 24 LJ Ch 486, 3 WR 265 .... 47.8, 47.9
Sutcliffe v Richardson (1872) LR 13 Eq 606, 41 LJ Ch 552, 20 WR 505, 26 LT 495 .... 33.13, 35.20, 83.7
Sutherland v Cooke (1844) 14 LJ Ch 71, 1 Coll 498, 8 Jur 1088, 4 LTOS 192 .... 38.23
Sutherland v Public Trustee [1980] 2 NZLR 536 .... 1.14
Sutherland's Trustee v Verschoyle 1968 SLT 43 .... 34.12
Sutton, Re [1952] NZLR 93 .... 74.2
Sutton, Re, Boscawen v Wyndham [1921] 1 Ch 257, 90 LJ Ch 71, 65 Sol Jo 155, 124 LT 526 .... 39.28
Sutton, Re, Evans v Oliver [1934] Ch 209, 103 LJ Ch 127, [1933] All ER Rep 671, 150 LT 453, 50 TLR 189 .... 77.2
Sutton, Re, Stone v A-G (1885) 28 Ch D 464, 54 LJ Ch 613, 33 WR 519 .... 64.35, 102.23
Sutton v Sadler (1857) 3 CBNS 87, 26 LJCP 284, 3 Jur NS 1150, 5 WR 880, 30 LTOS 65 .... 4.11, 4.13
Sutton v Sharp (1826) 1 Russ 146 .... 38.10

Sutton v Sutton (1892) 30 LR Ir 251, CA 90.2, 101.13
Sutton v Torre (1842) 11 LJ Ch 255, 6 Jur 234 .... 85.3
Swabey v Goldie (1875) 1 Ch D 380, 34 LT 306, CA 87.1, 87.2
Swain, Re, Brett v Ward [1918] 1 Ch 399, 87 LJ Ch 305, 62 Sol Jo 308, 118 LT 439; on appeal [1918] 1 Ch 574, CA 76.1, 76.3, 93.22
Swain, Re, Monckton v Hands [1905] 1 Ch 669, 74 LJ Ch 354, 92 LT 715, CA 94.7, 95.7, 95.12, 102.26, 102.28, 103.11
Swain, Re, Phillips v Poole (1908) 99 LT 604, 24 TLR 882 .... 9.35, 102.26
Swain, Re, Swain v Bringeman [1891] 3 Ch 233, 61 LJ Ch 20, 65 LT 296 .... 30.38
Swaine v Kennerley (1813) 1 Ves & B 469 .... 72.2
Swan, Re, Witham v Swan [1915] 1 Ch 829, 84 LJ Ch 590, 113 LT 42, 31 TLR 266 .... 8.3, 204.45
Swan v Holmes (1854) 19 Beav 471 .... 42.3, 86.5, 101.4, 101.14
Swannell, Re, Morice v Swannell (1909) 101 LT 76 .... 99.8
Swanson Estate, Re [1941] 1 WWR 641 .... 51.2
Swayzie, Re [1912] 3 DLR 631, 3 OWN 621, 21 OWR 95 .... 52.7
Sweetapple v Bindon (1705) 2 Vern 536 .... 85.2
Sweetapple v Horlock (1879) 11 Ch D 745, 48 LJ Ch 660, 27 WR 865, 41 LT 272 .... 39.5
Sweeting, Re, Sweeting v Sweeting [1988] 1 All ER 1016 .... 41.20
Sweeting v Prideaux (1876) 2 Ch D 413, 45 LJ Ch 378, 24 WR 776, 34 LT 240 .... 101.1
Sweetland v Sweetland (1865) 29 JP 168, 34 LJPM & A 42, 11 Jur NS 182, 4 Sw & Tr 6, 13 WR 504, 11 LT 749 .... 11.3
Sweetman v Sweetman (1868) IR 2 Eq 141 .... 42.12
Swick, Re [1944] 4 DLR 55, [1944] OR 420, [1944] OWN 484 .... 41.9
Swift v Swift (1859) 1 De GF & J 160, 29 LJ Ch 121, 8 WR 100, 1 LT 150 .... 64.32
Swift v Swift (1863) 32 LJ Ch 479, 1 New Rep 353, 11 WR 334 .... 51.11, 91.5
Swift d Neale v Roberts (1764) Amb 617, 3 Burr 1488, 1 Wm Bl 476 .... 7.3
Swift's Goods, Re (1900) 17 TLR 16 .... 11.24, 12.3
Swifte v A-G for Ireland (No 2) [1912] 1 IR 133 .... 9.31, 50.9
Swinburne, Re, Swinburne v Pitt (1884) 27 Ch D 696, 54 LJ Ch 229, 33 WR 394 .... 39.22, 39.25, 39.26, 40.21
Swindlehurst, Re [1952] 3 DLR 561, [1952] OR 392, [1952] OWN 278 .... 64.37
Swinfen v Swinfen (No 4) (1860) 29 Beav 207, 7 Jur NS 89, 9 WR 175, 4 LT 194 .... 38.10, 63.1, 64.27
Swinford's Goods, Re (1869) LR 1 P & D 630, 33 JP 231, 38 LJP & M 38, 17 WR 536, 20 LT 87 .... 11.26, 13.2
Swires (Inspector of Taxes) v Renton [1991] STC 490, 64 TC 315 .... 218.102, 242.19
Swords' Goods, Re [1952] P 368, [1952] 2 All ER 281 .... 5.7
Sydall v Castings Ltd [1967] 1 QB 302, [1966] 3 All ER 770, [1966] 3 WLR 1126, 110 Sol Jo 790, CA 74.8
Sydney Homeopathic Hospital v Turner [1959] ALR 782 .... 103.3
Syer v Gladstone (1885) 30 Ch D 614, 34 WR 565 .... 46.3
Sykes, Re, Drake v Sykes (1907) 23 TLR 747, CA 18.26, 18.28, 18.29, 18.31
Sykes, Re, Skelton and Dyson v Sykes [1940] 4 All ER 10 .... 58.2, 64.7, 204.70, 204.80
Sykes, Re, Sykes v Sykes [1909] 2 Ch 241, 78 LJ Ch 609, 101 LT 1, CA 57.15, 205.75
Sykes v Carroll [1903] 1 IR 17, 36 ILT 125 .... 39.25
Sykes v Land [1984] 2 EGLR 8, 271 Estates Gazette 1264, CA 234.15

Sykes v Sykes (1867) LR 4 Eq 200 .... 47.27, 47.32
Sykes v Sykes (1868) 3 Ch App 301, 37 LJ Ch 367, 16 WR 545 .... 18.15, 20.5, 38.13, 47.6, 47.28
Sykes' Goods, Re (1873) LR 3 P & D 26, 37 JP 183, 42 LJP & M 17, 21 WR 416, 28 LT 142 .... 14.8, 14.11
Syme, Re [1980] VR 109 .... 48.6, 66.15
Syme, Re, Union Trustee Co of Australia Ltd v Syme [1933] VLR 282 .... 3.6, 3.12
Symers v Jobson (1848) 16 Sim 267 .... 78.4, 84.4
Symes v Appelbe (1887) 51 JP 632, 57 LT 599 .... 15.4
Symes v Green (1859) 28 LJP & M 83, 5 Jur NS 742, 1 Sw & Tr 401, 33 LTOS 168 .... 4.13, 4.15
Symes v Symes [1896] 1 Ch 272, 65 LJ Ch 265, 44 WR 521, 73 LT 684 .... 94.33
Symm's Will Trusts, Re, Public Trustee v Shaw [1936] 3 All ER 236, 80 Sol Jo 994 .... 94.12
Symmers Trustees v Symmers 1918 SC 337 .... 102.23
Symons, Re [1949] SASR 289 .... 93.16
Sympson v Hornsby. See Sympson v Hutton
Sympson v Hutton (1716) 2 Eq Cas Abr 439, sub nom Simpson v Hornby Gilb Ch 120, sub nom Sympson v Hornsby Prec Ch 452, sub nom Hutton v Simpson 2 Vern 722 .... 40.6, 47.23, 68.2
Symson v Kirton (1606) Cro Jac 115 .... 18.5
Synge v Synge (1874) 9 Ch App 128, 22 WR 227, 29 LT 855 .... 42.2
Synge v Synge [1894] 1 QB 466, 58 JP 396, 63 LJQB 202, 9 R 265, 42 WR 309, [1891–4] All ER Rep 1164, 70 LT 221, 10 TLR 194, CA 3.2, 3.3, 3.6
Synge's Trusts, Re (1854) 3 I Ch R 379 .... 74.1, 98.7, 98.13
Szabo v Boros (1967) 60 DLR (2d) 186, 58 WWR 247; on appeal (1967) 64 DLR (2d) 48, 60 WWR 754 .... 2.2
Szczutkowski Estate, Re (1955) 14 WWR 396; affd (1956) 15 WWR 480 .... 64.32

T

TWGS v G. See TWGS v JMG
TWGS v JMG [2000] 2 All ER 83; affd sub nom TWGS v G [2001] Ch 568, sub nom TWGS v JMG [2001] 1 All ER 97, [2000] 3 WLR 1910, [2001] 1 FCR 339, [2000] NLJR 1788, CA 1.6, 9.13, 9.17, 46.1, 46.5, 48.8, 104.9
Taaffe v Conmee (1862) 10 HL Cas 64, 8 Jur NS 919, 6 LT 666 .... 50.2, 67.1, 86.7
Taber, Re, Arnold v Kayess (1882) 51 LJ Ch 721, 30 WR 883, 46 LT 805 .... 33.12
Tabuteau v Nixon (1899) 15 TLR 485 .... 76.6
Talbot, Re [1925] SASR 100 .... 18.23
Talbot, Re [1932] IR 714 .... 35.40, 35.43
Talbot, Re, Jubb v Sheard [1933] Ch 895, [1933] All ER Rep 126, 102 LJ Ch 362, 77 Sol Jo 388, 149 LT 401, 49 TLR 462 .... 94.13, 94.34, 202.28
Talbot v Earl Radnor (1834) 3 My & K 252, 41 RR 64 .... 27.6, 46.3
Talbot v Talbot [1967] 1 All ER 601; affd [1968] Ch 1, [1967] 2 All ER 920, [1967] 3 WLR 438, 111 Sol Jo 278, CA 53.4, 92.1, 92.3
Talbot-Ponsonby's Estate, Re, Talbot-Ponsonby v Talbot-Ponsonby [1937] 4 All ER 309, 81 Sol Jo 883, 54 TLR 33 .... 34.11
Talbott v Duke of Shrewsbury (1714) 2 Eq Cas Abr 352, Gilb Ch 89, Prec Ch 394 .... 44.1, 44.15

Tallent v Scott (1868) 18 LT 900 .... 64.40
Tancred's Settlement, Re, Somerville v Tancred [1903] 1 Ch 715, 72 LJ Ch 324, 51 WR 510, [1900–3] All ER Rep 251, 47 Sol Jo 319, 88 LT 164 .... 99.4
Tankard, Re, Tankard v Midland Bank Executor and Trustee Co Ltd [1942] Ch 69, [1941] 3 All ER 458, 111 LJ Ch 70, 85 Sol Jo 475, 166 LT 65, 58 TLR 56 .... 30.30, 38.15
Tann v Tann (1863) 2 New Rep 412 .... 58.10, 63.4
Tanner, Re (1884) 53 LJ Ch 1108, 51 LT 507 .... 218.66
Tanner v New Zealand Guardian Trustee Co [1992] 3 NZLR 74 .... 93.28
Tanner v Tebbutt (1843) 2 Y & C Ch Cas 225, 12 LJ Ch 216, 7 Jur 339 .... 34.21, 35.48
Tapley v Eagleton (1879) 12 Ch D 683, 28 WR 239 .... 8.7
Tapley v Kent (1846) 1 Rob Eccl 400, 9 Jur 1041, 4 Notes of Cases 292 .... 10.9
Tapscott v Newcombe (1842) 6 Jur 755 .... 93.24
Tarbottom v Earle (1863) 11 WR 680 .... 33.23, 33.27
Tarbuck v Tarbuck (1835) 4 LJ Ch 129 .... 93.9, 96.1
Tarbutt v Nicholson (1920) 89 LJPC 127, 123 LT 638 .... 50.6
Tarca, Re (1981) 29 SASR 152 .... 41.4, 41.5
Targa, Re (1986) 43 SASR 234 .... 93.16
Target v Gaunt (1718) 1 Eq Cas Abr 193, Gilb Ch 149, 10 Mod Rep 402, 1 P Wms 432 .... 98.4
Tarnpolsk, Re, Barclays Bank Ltd v Hyer [1958] 3 All ER 479, [1958] 1 WLR 1157, 102 Sol Jo 857 .... 35.29, 35.31
Tarrant's Trust, Re (1889) 58 LJ Ch 780 .... 39.13
Tate, Re, Williamson v Gilpin [1914] 2 Ch 182, 83 LJ Ch 593, 58 Sol Jo 119, 109 LT 621 .... 86.6, 101.6
Tate v Clarke (1838) 1 Beav 100, 8 LJ Ch 60 .... 84.4, 85.4
Tatham, Re (1949) 51 WALR 39 .... 30.43
Tatham, Re, Huxtable v Princess Margaret Children's Hospital (1951) 81 CLR 639, [1951] ALR 1, 24 ALJ 416 (Aust HC) 5.7, 53.5
Tatham v Drummond (1864) 4 De GJ & Sm 484, 34 LJ Ch 1, 10 Jur NS 1087, 5 New Rep 24, 13 WR 61, 11 LT 324 .... 51.4, 57.3, 88.4
Tatham v Vernon (1861) 29 Beav 604, 7 Jur NS 814, 9 WR 822, 4 LT 531 .... 93.35
Tatham v Wright (1832) 2 Russ & M 1, sub nom Wright v Tatham 9 LJOS Ch 265 .... 4.14
Tattersall v Howell (1816) 2 Mer 26 .... 34.11, 35.45
Tavernor v Grindley (1875) 32 LT 424 .... 81.3
Tawney v Ward (1839) 1 Beav 563, 8 LJ Ch 319 .... 62.1, 93.34, 93.35
Taws v Knowles [1891] 2 QB 564, 56 JP 68, 60 LJQB 641, 39 WR 675, 65 LT 124, CA 61.1
Taylor, Re (1914) 28 WLR 630 .... 83.7
Taylor, Re [1924] NZLR 1109 .... 19.4
Taylor, Re [1949] ALR 863, [1949] VLR 201 .... 17.4
Taylor, Re (1972) 28 DLR (3d) 257, [1972] 3 OR 349 .... 68.2, 93.2
Taylor, Re, Cloak v Hammond (1886) 34 Ch D 255, 56 LJ Ch 171, 35 WR 186, 55 LT 649, 3 TLR 178, CA 57.15, 57.22, 58.9, 58.10, 71.1
Taylor, Re, Dale v Dale [1909] WN 59 .... 20.4
Taylor, Re, Hockley v O'Neal [1925] Ch 739, 95 LJ Ch 43, [1925] All ER Rep 662, 133 LT 602 .... 72.3
Taylor, Re, Illsley v Randall (1884) 53 LJ Ch 1161, 33 WR 13, 50 LT 717 .... 33.24

Taylor, Re, Lloyds Bank Ltd v Jones [1957] 3 All ER 56, [1957] 1 WLR 1043, 101 Sol Jo 816 .... 48.5, 48.6, 48.8
Taylor, Re, Martin v Freeman (1888) 58 LT 538, 4 TLR 302 .... 102.22, 103.11
Taylor, Re, Midland Bank Executor and Trustee Co Ltd v Smith [1940] Ch 481, [1940] 2 All ER 637, 109 LJ Ch 188, 84 Sol Jo 289, 163 LT 51, 56 TLR 588; affd [1940] Ch 834, CA 9.35
Taylor, Re, Pullan v Taylor [1931] 2 Ch 242, 100 LJ Ch 374, [1931] All ER Rep 387, 145 LT 417 .... 9.39
Taylor, Re, Read v Carr [1957] NZLR 647 .... 50.7, 54.2, 68.9
Taylor, Re, Smart v Taylor [1901] 2 Ch 134, 70 LJ Ch 535, 49 WR 615, 84 LT 758 .... 32.16
Taylor, Re, Taylor v Baker [1931] NZLR 352 .... 57.22
Taylor, Re, Taylor v Ley (1885) 52 LT 839, CA 77.6, 87.1
Taylor, Re, Taylor v Taylor [1931] 2 Ch 237, 100 LJ Ch 309, 75 Sol Jo 393, 145 LT 443 .... 47.25, 47.28
Taylor, Re, Taylor v Taylor [1961] 1 All ER 55, [1961] 1 WLR 9, 105 Sol Jo 37, CA 17.2
Taylor, Re, Taylor v Tweedie [1923] 1 Ch 99, 91 LJ Ch 801, 66 Sol Jo 693, 127 LT 684, 38 TLR 850, CA 50.2, 50.7, 64.35
Taylor, Re, Taylor v Wade [1894] 1 Ch 671, 63 LJ Ch 424, 8 R 186, 42 WR 373, 38 Sol Jo 288, 70 LT 556 .... 30.10
Taylor, Re, Whitby v Highton (1888) 57 LJ Ch 430, 36 WR 683, 58 LT 842 ... 20.4, 22.2
Taylor v Allhusen [1905] 1 Ch 529, 74 LJ Ch 350, 53 WR 523, 92 LT 382 .... 40.14
Taylor v Beverley (1844) 13 LJ Ch 240, 1 Coll 108, 8 Jur 265, 2 LTOS 516 .... 50.17
Taylor v Cartwright (1872) LR 14 Eq 167, 41 LJ Ch 529, 20 WR 603, 26 LT 571 .... 44.4
Taylor v Cooper (1846) 10 Jur 1078, 8 LTOS 134 .... 92.1
Taylor v Creagh (1858) 8 I Ch R 281 .... 5.8
Taylor v Dening. See Baker v Dening
Taylor v Dickens [1998] 3 FCR 455, [1998] 1 FLR 806, [1998] Fam Law 191 .... 43.1
Taylor v Earl Harewood (1844) 3 Hare 372, 13 LJ Ch 345, 8 Jur 419, 3 LTOS 73 .... 35.39
Taylor v Frobisher (1852) 5 De G & Sm 191, 21 LJ Ch 605, 16 Jur 283, 19 LTOS 242 .... 51.2, 93.1, 93.42
Taylor v Gerst (1728) Mos 98, sub nom Taylor v Johnson 2 P Wms 504, 2 Eq Cas Abr 566 pl 16 .... 32.23
Taylor v Graham (1878) 3 App Cas 1287, HL 57.3, 93.2
Taylor v Johnson. See Taylor v Gerst
Taylor v Lambert (1876) 2 Ch D 177, 45 LJ Ch 418, 24 WR 691, 34 LT 567 .... 93.44
Taylor v Martindale (1841) 12 Sim 158, 10 LJ Ch 339, 5 Jur 648 .... 33.12
Taylor v Popham (1782) 1 Bro CC 168 .... 34.25, 35.51
Taylor v Richardson (1853) 2 Drew 16, 23 LJ Ch 9, 2 Eq Rep 332, 2 WR 29, 22 LTOS 95 .... 57.10
Taylor v Shaw, Re Jones (1920) 89 LJPC 124, 123 LT 643 .... 50.2
Taylor v Stainton (1856) 2 Jur NS 634, 4 WR 588 .... 97.1, 97.2
Taylor v Sturrock [1900] AC 225, 69 LJPC 29, 82 LT 97, PC 50.5
Taylor v Taylor (1833) 6 Sim 246 .... 38.3
Taylor v Taylor (1837) 1 Jur 401 .... 64.40

Taylor v Taylor (1875) LR 20 Eq 155, 44 LJ Ch 718, 23 WR 719 .... 44.4
Taylor v Taylor (1910) 10 CLR 218 .... 102.10
Taylor v Taylor, Re Taylor's Estate Act (1874) LR 17 Eq 324, 43 LJ Ch 314, 22 WR 349, 30 LT 49 .... 33.23
Taylor v Web (or Webb) (1651) Sty 301 .... 84.2
Taylor d Smith v Biddall (1677) 2 Eq Cas Abr 335, Freem KB 243, 2 Mod Rep 289 .... 94.3
Taylor's Estate, Re [1929] P 260, 98 LJP 145, 73 Sol Jo 385, 141 LT 200, 45 TLR 481 .... 26.3
Taylor's Estate, Re (1950) 51 SRNSW 16 .... 92.1
Taylor's Estate, Re, Goldie v Adam. See Goldie v Adam
Taylor's Estate, Re, National and Provincial and Union Bank of England v Taylor (1919) 64 Sol Jo 148 .... 18.31
Taylor's Estate, Re, Tomlin v Underhay (1881) 22 Ch D 495, 48 LT 552, CA 43.6, 100.7
Taylor's Estate and Will Trusts, Re, Taylor v Taylor [1969] 2 Ch 245, [1969] 1 All ER 113, [1969] 2 WLR 1371, 113 Sol Jo 208 .... 55.7, 214.9
Taylor's Goods, Re (1890) 63 LT 230, 6 TLR 375 .... 18.22
Taylor's Trusts, Re, Taylor v Blake [1912] 1 IR 1 .... 76.1, 76.4, 85.5, 94.12
Tchilingirian v Ouzounian [2003] EWHC 1220 (Ch), [2003] All ER (D) 76 (Mar) 4.17, 5.2
Teague's Settlement, Re (1870) LR 10 Eq 564, 18 WR 752, 22 LT 742 .... 94.44
Teale, Re, Teale v Teale (1885) 34 WR 248, 53 LT 936 .... 96.1, 97.7
Teape's Trusts, Re (1873) LR 16 Eq 442, 43 LJ Ch 87, 21 WR 780, 28 LT 799 .... 39.22, 39.26
Teatt v Strong (1760) 3 Bro Parl Cas 219, HL 60.1
Tee v Ferris (1856) 20 JP 563, 2 K & J 357, 25 LJ Ch 437, 2 Jur NS 807, 110 RR 262, 4 WR 352 .... 36.2, 36.3, 36.4, 36.8
Teele v Federal Commission of Taxation (1940) 63 CLR 201, 46 ALR 74, 13 ALJ 507 .... 102.23
Tegg, Re, Public Trustee v Bryant [1936] 2 All ER 878, 80 Sol Jo 552 .... 35.30, 35.32, 35.36
Tegg's Goods, Re (1846) 4 Notes of Cases 531 .... 22.3
Tegler Estate, Re [1929] 1 DLR 445, 1 WWR 181 .... 93.6
Telfair, Re, Garrioch v Barclay [1900–3] All ER Rep 95, 86 LT 496 .... 33.14, 101.6
Telfer, Re [1964] 1 OR 373 .... 47.31
Tempest v Lord Camoys (1888) 52 JP 532, 58 LT 221 .... 27.3
Tempest v Tempest (1856) 2 K & J 635; on appeal (1857) 7 De GM & G 470 .... 9.5, 64.27
Temple, Re, ex p Thistlewood (1812) 1 Rose 290, sub nom Ex p Thistlewood 19 Ves 236 .... 33.37
Temple v Thring (1887) 56 LJ Ch 767, 56 LT 283 .... 8.3
Templeman v Warrington (1842) 13 Sim 267 .... 96.1
Templemore's Estate, Re (1925) 69 Sol Jo 382 .... 18.5, 18.26
Templeton Estate, Re, Templeton v Royal Trust Co [1936] 3 DLR 782, 44 Man R 154, [1936] 2 WWR 347 .... 83.16
Tench v Cheese (1854) 19 Beav 3, 3 WR 42; on appeal (1855) 6 De GM & G 453, 24 LJ Ch 716, 3 Eq Rep 971, 1 Jur NS 689, 3 WR 500, 582, 25 LTOS 189, 261 .... 95.7, 210.7
Tennent v Tennent (1844) 1 Jo & Lat 379 .... 60.1

Tennent's Estate, Re [1913] 1 IR 280 .... 43.3
Tenney's Goods, Re (1881) 45 LT 78 .... 40.3
Tepper's Will Trusts, Re, Kramer v Ruda [1987] Ch 358, [1987] 1 All ER 970, [1987] 2 WLR 729, [1987] 2 FLR 439, [1987] Fam Law 379, 131 Sol Jo 327, [1987] LS Gaz R 1057 .... 34.2, 34.9, 34.10, 34.11, 35.29, 35.31, 53.1, 53.2, 57.15, 217.40
Terrible's Goods, Re (1858) 1 Sw & Tr 140, 6 WR 816, 31 LTOS 318 .... 21.2, 21.6
Terry v Terry (1863) 33 Beav 232, 12 WR 66, 9 LT 469 .... 83.6
Tetley, Re, A-G v National Provincial and Union Bank of England. See A-G v National Provincial and Union Bank of England
Tetsall, Re, Foyster v Tetsall [1961] 2 All ER 801, [1961] 1 WLR 938, 105 Sol Jo 444 .... 57.14, 58.2, 61.1, 64.54
Tewart v Lawson (1874) LR 18 Eq 490, 43 LJ Ch 673, 22 WR 822 ..... 38.26, 38.28, 93.4
Thackeray v Dorrien. See Thackeray v Hampson
Thackeray v Hampson (1825) 2 Sim & St 214, sub nom Thackeray v Dorrien 3 LJOS Ch 89 .... 56.3
Thamer v Jundt (1912) 4 DLR 753, 3 OWN 1307, 22 OWR 206 .... 4.15
Tharp, Re, Longrigg v People's Dispensary for Sick Animals of the Poor Inc [1942] 2 All ER 358; revsd [1943] 1 All ER 257, 87 Sol Jo 102, CA 103.3
Tharp v Tharp [1916] 1 Ch 142, 85 LJ Ch 162, 60 Sol Jo 176, 114 LT 495; on appeal [1916] 2 Ch 205, CA 36.2, 36.13, 40.13, 40.14
Tharp's Estate, Re (1863) 1 De GJ & Sm 453, 33 LJ Ch 59, 2 New Rep 253, 11 WR 763, 8 LT 559 .... 67.4
Thatcher's Trusts, Re (1859) 26 Beav 365 .... 93.1, 93.39, 94.30
Theakston v Marson (1832) 4 Hag Ecc 290 .... 10.1
Thellusson v Lord Rendlesham (1859) 7 HL Cas 429, 28 LJ Ch 948, 5 Jur NS 1031, 7 WR 563, 33 LTOS 379 .... 50.2, 50.9, 51.8, 51.12, 81.3
Thellusson v Woodford (1799) 4 Ves 227; on appeal (1805) 1 Bos & PNR 357, 8 RR 104, 11 Ves 112, 32 ER 1030, [1803–13] All ER Rep 30, HL 9.13, 49.4, 50.2, 50.6, 53.2, 57.5, 94.2, 94.12, 94.13, 94.33, 95.2, 102.10
Thellusson v Woodford (1806) 13 Ves 209; affd sub nom Rendlesham v Woodford (1813) 1 Dow 249, HL 42.3
Thellusson v Woodford (1829) 5 Russ 100 .... 74.1
Thicknesse v Liege (1775) 3 Bro Parl Cas 365, HL 98.13
Thirlwell's Will Trusts, Re, Evans v Thirlwell [1958] Ch 146, [1957] 3 All ER 465, 101 Sol Jo 886 .... 39.14
Thistlethwayte's Trust, Re (1855) 24 LJ Ch 712, 1 Jur NS 881, 3 WR 629, 25 LTOS 293 .... 55.6
Thistlewood, ex p. See Temple, Re, ex p Thistlewood
Thomas, Re, Public Trustee v Falconer [1946] Ch 36, [1945] 2 All ER 586, 115 LJ Ch 145, 89 Sol Jo 565, 173 LT 365, 62 TLR 23 .... 33.3, 33.6, 33.7, 33.35, 33.45
Thomas, Re, Smith v Thomas (1915) 34 NZLR 1110 .... 57.15
Thomas, Re, Thomas v Thomas [1921] 1 Ch 306, 90 LJ Ch 113, 125 LT 606 .... 98.1, 98.7
Thomas, Re, Thomas v Thompson [1930] 1 Ch 194, [1929] All ER Rep 129, 99 LJ Ch 140, 142 LT 310 .... 220.80
Thomas, Re, Trustees Executors and Agency Co Ltd v Thomas [1925] VLR 488, 47 ALT 42 .... 50.9

Thomas, Re, Vivian v Vivian [1920] 1 Ch 515, 89 LJ Ch 251, 64 Sol Jo 359, 123 LT 40 .... 98.13
Thomas, Re, Wood v Thomas [1891] 3 Ch 482, 60 LJ Ch 781, 40 WR 75, 65 LT 142 .... 38.19, 38.23
Thomas v A-G (1837) 2 Y & C Ex 525 .... 32.10, 32.12
Thomas v Bennet (1725) 2 P Wms 341 .... 44.15
Thomas v Hole (1728) 2 Eq Cas Abr 368, Cas temp Talb 251, 1 Dick 50 .... 79.6
Thomas v Howell (1692) 2 Eq Cas Abr 360, 4 Mod Rep 66, 1 Salk 170, Holt KB 225, Skin 301 .... 19.1
Thomas v Howell (1874) LR 18 Eq 198, 43 LJ Ch 511 .... 19.5, 102.8, 102.22
Thomas v IRC [1981] STC 382, [1981] TR 83 .... 200.104
Thomas v Jones (1862) 2 John & H 475, 31 LJ Ch 732, 8 Jur NS 1124, 10 WR 853, 7 LT 154; affd (1862) 1 De GJ & Sm 63, 34 LJ Ch 139, 9 Jur NS 161, 11 WR 242, 7 LT 610 .... 39.14, 40.7
Thomas v Jones [1928] P 162, [1928] All ER Rep 704, 72 Sol Jo 255, 139 LT 214, 44 TLR 467, sub nom Re Jones' Estate, Thomas v Jones 97 LJP 81 .... 4.10, 4.17, 5.1
Thomas v Kent [2006] EWCA Civ 1485, [2006] All ER (D) 57 (May) 65.3
Thomas v Kent [2007] WTLR 177 .... 50.1
Thomas v Lane (1680) 2 Cas in Ch 26 .... 64.26
Thomas v Phelps (1828) 4 Russ 348, 6 LJOS Ch 110 .... 38.6, 64.51, 83.6
Thomas v Thomas (1864) 2 Drew & Sm 298, 13 WR 225, 11 LT 471 .... 9.2
Thomas v Thomas [1948] 2 KB 294, [1948] 2 All ER 98, 46 LGR 396, 112 JP 345, [1948] LJR 1943, 92 Sol Jo 393, 64 TLR 377 .... 105.14
Thomas v Wilberforce (1862) 31 Beav 299 .... 93.6, 93.35
Thomas and Agnes Carvel Foundation v Carvel [2007] EWHC 1314 (Ch), [2007] 4 All ER 81, [2007] WTLR 1297, [2007] All ER (D) 76 (Jun) 25.17
Thomas d Jones v Evans (1802) 2 East 488 .... 1.1, 18.6
Thomas d Evans v Thomas (1796) 3 RR 306, 6 Term Rep 671 .... 53.1, 57.9, 58.3
Thomas's Estate, Re, Public Trustee v Davies [1939] 2 All ER 567 .... 49.6
Thomas's Goods, Re (1859) 23 JP 72, 28 LJP & M 33, 5 Jur NS 104, 1 Sw & Tr 255, 7 WR 270, 32 LTOS 261 .... 13.3
Thomas's Will Trust, Re [1969] 3 All ER 1492. See Chitty's Will Trust, Re, Re Thomas's Will Trusts, Ransford (or Ransferd) v Lloyds Bank Ltd
Thomas's Will Trusts, Re, Powell v Thomas [1930] 2 Ch 67, 99 LJ Ch 286, 74 Sol Jo 201, 144 LT 64 .... 34.8
Thomason v Moses (1842) 5 Beav 77, 6 Jur 403, 59 RR 421 .... 51.12
Thomond (Earl) v Earl of Suffolk (1718) 2 Eq Cas Abr 567, 1 P Wms 461 .... 41.4
Thompson, Re (1943) 44 WALR 75 .... 25.2
Thompson, Re [1955] OWN 521 .... 31.1
Thompson, Re (1973) 41 DLR (3d) 305 .... 93.28
Thompson, Re, ex p Thompson (1864) 16 I Ch R 228, CA 84.2
Thompson, Re, Griffith v Thompson (1896) 44 WR 582, 40 Sol Jo 544 .... 34.6, 35.30, 93.27
Thompson, Re, Lloyds Bank Ltd v George [1939] 1 All ER 681, 83 Sol Jo 317 .... 35.35
Thompson, Re, Machell v Newman (1886) 55 LT 85 .... 79.7
Thompson, Re, Public Trustee v Husband [1936] Ch 676, [1936] 2 All ER 141, 105 LJ Ch 289, 80 Sol Jo 466, 155 LT 474 .... 33.1, 210.5, 210.6, 210.7

Thompson, Re, Public Trustee v Lloyd [1934] Ch 342, 103 LJ Ch 162, [1933] All ER Rep 805, 150 LT 451 .... 9.31
Thompson, Re, Thompson v Thompson [1906] 2 Ch 199, 75 LJ Ch 599, 54 WR 613, 95 LT 97 .... 1.2, 93.7, 94.11, 94.48
Thompson v Ahern [1958] Qd R 504 .... 93.22
Thompson v Beasley (1854) 3 Drew 7, 24 LJ Ch 327, 3 Eq Rep 59, 18 Jur 973 .... 76.6
Thompson v Clive (1857) 23 Beav 282 .... 68.11
Thompson v Lady Lawley (1800) 2 Bos & P 303 .... 64.33
Thompson v Leach (1690) Comb 468, 1 Com 45, 3 Lev 284, 1 Ld Raym 313, 12 Mod Rep 173, 3 Mod Rep 301, 3 Salk 300, 2 Salk 427, 576, 618, 675, Holt KB 357, 2 Vent 198, [1558–1774] All ER Rep 39, Carth 435, sub nom Leech's Case Freem KB 502, sub nom Leach v Thompson 1 Show 296; on appeal sub nom Leach v Thompson (1698) Show Parl Cas 150, sub nom Thompson v Leach 2 Vent 208, HL 46.1
Thompson v Robinson (1859) 27 Beav 486, 29 LJ Ch 280, 5 Jur NS 1196, 8 WR 34, 1 LT 121 .... 71.1
Thompson v Simpson (1841) 58 RR 298, 1 Dr & War 459 .... 40.15, 76.3
Thompson v Simpson (1881) 50 LJ Ch 461, 44 LT 710 .... 18.16
Thompson v Teulon (1852) 22 LJ Ch 243, 1 WR 97 .... 56.3, 88.2
Thompson v Thompson (1844) 13 LJ Ch 455, 1 Coll 381, 8 Jur 839, 3 LTOS 452 .... 53.4, 65.2, 102.7, 102.22
Thompson v Whitelock (1859) 4 De G & J 490, 28 LJ Ch 793, 5 Jur NS 991, 7 WR 625, 33 LTOS 339 .... 5.8, 57.5, 68.2
Thompson v Wylie (1938) 38 SRNSW 328, 55 WNNSW 107 .... 30.43
Thompson's Settlement, Re, Thompson v Thompson [1986] Ch 99, [1985] 2 All ER 720, [1985] 3 WLR 486, 129 Sol Jo 575 .... 221.4
Thompson's Trust, Re, ex p Oliver (1852) 5 De G & Sm 667, 22 LJ Ch 273, 17 Jur 16, 20 LTOS 289 .... 96.2
Thompson's Trusts, Re (1878) 9 Ch D 607, 48 LJ Ch 135, 27 WR 378 .... 56.5, 68.1
Thompson's Will, Re, Brahe v Mason [1910] VLR 251 .... 49.8, 65.3, 66.5
Thomson, Re [1956] SASR 188 .... 103.7
Thomson, Re, Thomson v Allen [1930] 1 Ch 203, 99 LJ Ch 156, 142 LT 253 .... 205.73
Thomson v Eastwood (1877) 2 App Cas 215, HL 58.10, 221.4
Thomson v Shakespear (1860) 24 JP 309, 1 De GF & J 399, 29 LJ Ch 276, 6 Jur NS 281, 8 WR 265, 2 LT 479 .... 9.35, 94.38, 103.11
Thomson and Baxter v Hempenstall (1849) 1 Rob Eccl 783, 13 Jur 814, 13 LTOS 449, 7 Notes of Cases 141 .... 57.3, 57.15
Thomson Settlement Trusts, Re, Robertson v Makepeace [1953] Ch 414, [1953] 1 All ER 1139, 97 Sol Jo 334 .... 100.2
Thomson's Estate, Re, Herring v Barrow (1880) 14 Ch D 263, 49 LJ Ch 622, 28 WR 802, 43 LT 35, CA 83.11, 83.12, 99.1
Thomson's Goods, Re (1844) 3 Notes of Cases 441 .... 14.9
Thomson's Trusts, Re (1870) LR 11 Eq 146, 19 WR 196, 23 LT 693 .... 93.41, 101.7
Thorleifson Estate, Re (1954) 13 WWRNS 515 .... 2.4
Thorley, Re, Thorley v Massam [1891] 2 Ch 613, [1891–4] All ER Rep Ext 2074, 60 LJ Ch 537, 39 WR 565, 64 LT 515, 7 TLR 479 .... 30.16
Thorn v IRC [1976] 2 All ER 622, [1976] 1 WLR 915, [1976] STC 208, [1976] TR 63, 120 Sol Jo 216 .... 241.18

Thornber, Re, Crabtree v Thornber [1937] Ch 29, [1936] 2 All ER 1594, 106 LJ Ch 7, 80 Sol Jo 689, 155 LT 223, CA 38.24, 61.1, 104.14
Thorncroft and Clarke v Lashmar (1862) 26 JP 567, 31 LJPM & A 150, 8 Jur NS 595, 2 Sw & Tr 479, 10 WR 783, 6 LT 476 .... 10.9
Thorne v Rooke (1841) 2 Curt 799, sub nom Langdon v Rooke 1 Notes of Cases 254 .... 18.14
Thorne v Thorne (1903) 33 SCR 309 .... 63.1
Thorne's Goods, Re (1865) 34 LJPM & A 131, 11 Jur NS 569, 4 Sw & Tr 36, 121 LT 639 .... 1.5, 16.8
Thornhill v Thornhill (1819) 4 Madd 377 .... 47.32, 68.8
Thornton v Curling (1824) 8 Sim 310 .... 24.1, 24.2, 49.7, 57.4
Thornton v Hawley (1804) 10 Ves 129 .... 37.4
Thornton v Thornton (1861) 11 I Ch R 474 .... 42.5
Thornton v Thornton (1875) LR 20 Eq 599 .... 39.22
Thornton's Goods, Re (1889) 14 PD 82, 53 JP 407, 58 LJP 82, 61 LT 200 ... 18.5, 18.17, 19.5
Thorp v Owen (1843) 2 Hare 607, 12 LJ Ch 417, 7 Jur 894, 1 LTOS 286 .... 82.5
Thorpe v Bestwick (1881) 6 QBD 311, 45 JP 440, 50 LJQB 320, 29 WR 631, 44 LT 180 .... 9.7
Thorpe v Thorpe (1862) 1 H & C 326, 32 LJ Ex 79, 8 Jur NS 871, 10 WR 778 .... 50.21, 78.3
Throckmorton, Re, ex p Eyston (1877) 7 Ch D 145, 47 LJ Bcy 62, 26 WR 181, 37 LT 447, CA 99.7
Thrupp v Collett (No 2) (1858) 26 Beav 147, 5 Jur NS 111 .... 30.24
Thruston's Will Trusts, Re (1849) 17 Sim 21, 18 LJ Ch 437 .... 93.31
Thurlow, Re, Riddick v Kennard [1972] Ch 379, [1972] 1 All ER 10, [1971] 3 WLR 881, 115 Sol Jo 813 .... 52.2, 52.3, 74.8
Thursby's Settlement, Re, Grant v Littledale [1910] 2 Ch 181, 79 LJ Ch 538, [1908–10] All ER Rep 505, 54 Sol Jo 581, 102 LT 838, CA 39.27
Thurston, Re, Thurston v Evans (1886) 32 Ch D 508, 55 LJ Ch 564, 34 WR 528, 54 LT 833 .... 39.7
Thwaites v Forman (1844) 1 Coll 409, 10 Jur 483; on appeal (1846) 15 LJ Ch 397 .... 33.33
Thynne (Lady) v Earl of Glengall (1848) 2 HL Cas 131, 12 Jur 805 ...... 44.1, 44.5, 44.7, 44.10, 44.12, 44.13, 44.15
Tibbits v Tibbits (1816) 2 Mer 96n, 19 Ves 656 .... 42.11
Tibbs v Elliott (1865) 34 Beav 424 .... 91.6
Ticehurst, Re, Midland Bank Executor and Trustee Co v Hankinson (1973) Times, 6 March 5.1, 5.4
Tidd v North. See Kidd v North
Tidwell v Ariel (1818) 3 Madd 403 .... 47.24
Tidy, Re [1949] 2 OLR 302, [1949] OWN 193 .... 39.14
Tiernan's Goods, Re [1942] IR 572, 76 ILTR 203 .... 11.4
Tiffin v Longman (1852) 15 Beav 275, 20 LTOS 13 .... 79.6
Tiger v Barclays Bank Ltd [1951] 2 KB 556, [1951] 2 All ER 262, 95 Sol Jo 400, [1951] 2 TLR 102; affd [1952] 1 All ER 85, CA 25.13, 30.42
Tighe v Featherstonehaugh (1883) 13 LR Ir 401 .... 38.10
Tilburgh v Barbut (1748) 1 Ves Sen 89 .... 84.2
Tilden, Re, Coubrough v Royal Society of London (1938) 82 Sol Jo 334 .... 47.9

Tilley v Berg and Berg (No 2) (1945) 4 DLR 179, 53 Man R 331, [1945] 3 WWR 81 .... 5.9
Tilly v Tilly (1743) 18 Ves 43 .... 101.3
Tilson v Jones (1830) 1 Russ & M 553 .... 97.2
Timberlake, Re, Archer v Timberlake (1919) 63 Sol Jo 286 .... 82.1, 205.58, 233.40
Timewell v Perkins (1740) 2 Atk 102 .... 38.11
Timins v Stackhouse (1858) 27 Beav 434 .... 87.2
Timlick Estate, Re, Timlick v Crawford (1965) 53 WWR 87 .... 5.4
Timmis, Re, Nixon v Smith [1902] 1 Ch 176, 71 LJ Ch 118, 50 WR 164, 46 Sol Jo 122, 85 LT 672 .... 30.38, 243.3
Timson, Re, Harper v Timson [1953] 2 All ER 1252, [1953] 1 WLR 1361, 97 Sol Jo 780 .... 20.3, 210.5, 210.7, 214.5, 214.6
Timson, Re, Smiles v Timson [1916] 2 Ch 362, 85 LJ Ch 561, 60 Sol Jo 526, 115 LT 55, CA 76.3
Tissen v Tissen (1718) 1 P Wms 500 .... 8.3
Titchfield (Marquis) v Horncastle (1838) 7 LJ Ch 279, 2 Jur 610 .... 38.7, 64.15
Tito v Waddell (No 2) [1977] Ch 106, [1977] 3 All ER 129, [1977] 2 WLR 496, 121 Sol Jo 10 .... 29.20
Tiverton Market Act, Re, ex p Tanner (1855) 20 Beav 374, 24 LJ Ch 657, 1 Jur NS 487, 25 LT 76 .... 86.3
Toates v Toates [1926] 2 KB 30, 90 JP 103, 95 LJKB 526, 135 LT 25 .... 27.15
Tod, Re, Bradshaw v Turner [1916] 1 Ch 567, 85 LJ Ch 668, [1916–17] All ER Rep 1054, 60 Sol Jo 403, 114 LT 839, 32 TLR 344 .... 100.5
Tod v Earl of Winchelsea (1826) 2 C & P 488, Mood & M 12 .... 12.6
Todd v Bielby (1859) 27 Beav 353 .... 33.36, 33.38
Tollemache, Re, Forbes v Public Trustee [1930] WN 138, 169 LT Jo 519, 69 L Jo 423 .... 44.6, 100.5
Tollemache v Earl of Coventry. See Deerhurst (Lord) v Duke of St Albans
Tollemache's Estate, Re [1917] P 246, 86 LJP 154, 61 Sol Jo 696, 116 LT 762, 33 TLR 505 .... 16.1
Tollner v Marriott (1830) 4 Sim 19, sub nom Tolner v Marriott 9 LJOS Ch 14 .... 34.21, 35.48
Tolner v Marriott. See Tollner v Marriott
Tolson v Collins (1799) 4 Ves 483 .... 44.15
Tom's Settlement, Re, Rose v Evans [1987] 1 All ER 1081, [1987] 1 WLR 1021, 131 Sol Jo 916, [1987] LS Gaz R 2045 .... 66.13, 66.20
Tomkins v Tomkins (1743) 2 Hov Supp 456, 19 Ves 126n, cited in 1 Burr 234 .... 101.7
Tomkinson, Re, M'Crea and Bell v A-G of Duchy of Lancaster (1929) 74 Sol Jo 77 .... 102.23
Tomkyns v Blane (1860) 28 Beav 422 .... 40.21
Tomlin v Hatfeild (1841) 12 Sim 167 .... 87.1
Tomline's Will Trusts, Re, Pretyman v Pretyman [1931] 1 Ch 521, 100 LJ Ch 156, [1931] All ER Rep 713, 144 LT 592, 47 TLR 274 .... 64.3
Tomlinson v Glyns Executor and Trustee Co [1970] Ch 112, [1969] 1 All ER 700, [1969] 2 WLR 283, 45 TC 600, 47 ATC 447, [1968] TR 425, 112 Sol Jo 986; on appeal [1970] Ch 112, [1970] 1 All ER 381, [1969] 3 WLR 310, 45 TC 600, 48 ATC 212, [1969] TR 211, 113 Sol Jo 367, CA 200.39
Tompson v Browne (1835) 3 My & K 32, 5 LJ Ch 64 .... 1.3, 10.6

Tong, Re, Hilton v Bradbury [1931] 1 Ch 202, [1930] All ER Rep 262, 100 LJ Ch 132, 144 LT 260, CA 214.7
Tonge's Goods, Re (1891) 66 LT 60 .... 10.14, 14.10, 14.11
Tonks v Crockett (1907) 25 NZLR 572 .... 52.1
Toole v Hamilton [1901] 1 IR 383 .... 41.16
Toomer v Sobinska [1907] P 106, 76 LJP 19, 96 LT 475 .... 18.6, 18.16
Tootal's Estate, Re, Hankin v Kilburn (1876) 2 Ch D 628, 24 WR 1031, CA 33.24
Toovey v Bassett (1809) 10 East 460 .... 98.11
Topham v Duke of Portland (1863) 1 De GJ & Sm 517, 32 LJ Ch 257, 1 New Rep 496, 11 WR 507, 8 LT 180; on appeal sub nom Portland (Duke of) v Lady Topham (1864) 11 HL Cas 32, 34 LJ Ch 113, 10 Jur NS 501, 12 WR 697, [1861–73] All ER Rep 980, 10 LT 355 .... 40.14, 40.15, 40.20
Topham v Duke of Portland (1869) 5 Ch App 40, 32 LJ Ch 257, 11 WR 507, 8 LT 180, CA 40.15
Topham and Tombs v Norris (1857) 29 LTOS 346 .... 18.7
Toplis v Baker (1787) 2 Cox Eq Cas 118 .... 47.22
Toplis v Vonder Heyde (1840) 4 Y & C Ex 173, 9 LJ Ex Eq 27 .... 64.7
Tormey, Re, Tormey v Tormey [1935] VLR 300, 41 Argus LR 420 .... 64.27
Torney v Lawrence (1967) 61 WWR 510 .... 33.12, 62.1
Toronto General Trusts Corpn v Fodey (1953) 9 WWRNS 660 .... 33.34
Torre v Browne (1855) 5 HL Cas 555, 24 LJ Ch 757, 26 LTOS 129 .... 33.31
Torre v Castle (1836) 1 Curt 303; affd sub nom Castle v Torre (1837) 2 Moo PCC 133, PC 10.7
Torre's Goods, Re (1862) 8 Jur NS 494 .... 11.6
Torrington (Lord) v Bowman (1852) 22 LJ Ch 236, 20 LTOS 153 .... 64.16
Toscani's Estate, Re [1912] P 1, 81 LJP 15, 56 Sol Jo 93, 105 LT 911, 28 TLR 84 .... 25.10
Tothill v Pitt (1766) 1 Madd 488; revsd (1770) 2 Dick 431; restored sub nom Chatham (Earl) v Tothill (1771) 7 Bro Parl Cas 453, cited in 5 De GM & G at 206, HL 49.4
Tottenham, Re, Public Trustee v Tottenham (1946) 115 LJ Ch 170, 90 Sol Jo 152, 174 LT 367, 62 TLR 245 .... 83.1
Tottrup v Patterson [1970] SCR 318, 71 WWR 388, sub nom Re Ottewell 9 DLR (3d) 314 .... 78.5, 83.1
Touchet and Touchet v Blais (1963) 40 DLR (2d) 961, 45 WWR 246 .... 102.9, 102.17
Tourton v Flower (1735) 3 P Wms 369 .... 25.15
Townend, Re, Knowles v Jessop [1914] WN 145 .... 30.34
Townley, Re, Townley v Townley (1884) 53 LJ Ch 516, 32 WR 549, 50 LT 394 .... 20.3, 64.35, 64.36
Townley v Bolton (1832) 1 My & K 148, 2 LJ Ch 25 .... 101.4, 101.6
Townley v Watson (1844) 3 Curt 761, 8 Jur 111, 2 LTOS 376, 3 Notes of Cases 17 .... 14.2
Towns v Wentworth (1858) 11 Moo PCC 526, 6 WR 397, 31 LTOS 274 .... 50.3, 98.3, 101.1
Townsend, Re (1970) 7 DLR (3d) 270, 69 WWR 630 .... 93.11
Townsend v Ascroft [1917] 2 Ch 14, 86 LJ Ch 517, 61 Sol Jo 507, 116 LT 680 .... 33.12, 83.13
Townsend v Early (1860) 3 De GF & J 1 .... 65.3
Townsend v Moore [1905] P 66, 74 LJP 17, 53 WR 338, 49 Sol Jo 146, 92 LT 335, CA 18.10, 18.11, 18.14, 52.7

Townsend's Estate, Re, Townsend v Townsend (1886) 34 Ch D 357, 56 LJ Ch 227, 35 WR 153, 55 LT 674, 3 TLR 204 .... 9.9, 48.5, 48.6, 48.7
Townshend, Re [1938] 3 DLR 767, 8 FLJ (Can) 68, 13 MPR 160 .... 33.1
Townshend, Re [1941] 3 DLR 609, 16 MPR 69 .... 34.5
Townshend v Mostyn (1858) 26 Beav 72 .... 88.3
Townshend v Windham and Robinson (1706) 2 Vern 546 .... 30.24
Townson v Tickell (1819) 3 B & Ald 31, 22 RR 291, [1814–23] All ER Rep 164 .... 27.6, 45.1, 46.1, 46.5
Towry's Settled Estate, Re, Dallas v Towry (1889) 41 Ch D 64, 58 LJ Ch 593, sub nom Re Towry, Dallas v Law 37 WR 417, 60 LT 715, CA 20.3, 29.14
Trafford v Ashton (1710) 2 Vern 660, 1 Eq Cas Abr 213 pl 8 .... 81.3
Trafford v Berrige (1729) 1 Eq Cas Abr 201 .... 38.10
Trafford v Boehm (1746) 3 Atk 440 .... 98.10
Trafford's Settlement, Re, Moore v IRC [1985] Ch 32, [1984] 1 All ER 1108, [1984] 3 WLR 341, 128 Sol Jo 333, [1984] LS Gaz R 900, sub nom Moore and Osborne v IRC [1984] STC 236 .... 200.94
Travers, Re, Hurmson v Carr (1916) 86 LJ Ch 123, [1916–17] All ER Rep 904, 61 Sol Jo 56, 115 LT 604, 33 TLR 17 .... 30.24
Travers v Blundell (1877) 6 Ch D 436, 36 LT 341, CA 58.3, 58.8
Travis, Re, Frost v Greatorex [1900] 2 Ch 541, 69 LJ Ch 663, 49 WR 38, 44 Sol Jo 625, 83 LT 241, CA 102.28
Treadwell v Hitchings [1925] NZLR 519 .... 59.1
Treasury Solicitor v Lewis [1900] 2 Ch 812, 69 LJ Ch 833, 48 WR 694, 83 LT 139, 16 TLR 559 .... 1.15
Treble, Re (1966) 56 DLR (2d) 402, [1966] 2 OR 153 .... 77.3
Tredennick v Tredennick [1900] 1 IR 354 .... 62.1, 94.44, 94.48
Tredgold, Re, Midland Bank Executor and Trustee Co Ltd v Tredgold [1943] Ch 69, [1943] 1 All ER 120, 112 LJ Ch 68, 87 Sol Jo 30, 168 LT 135, 59 TLR 99 .... 22.3
Tredwell, Re, Jaffray v Tredwell (No 2) (1891) 65 LT 742 .... 29.2
Tredwell, Re, Jeffray v Tredwell [1891] 2 Ch 640, 65 LT 399, sub nom Tredwell, Re, Jaffray v Tredwell 60 LJ Ch 657, CA 33.20, 50.21, 50.21, 93.18, 93.21
Tree, Re, Idle v Tree [1945] Ch 325, sub nom Re Tree, Idle v Hastings Corpn [1945] 2 All ER 65, 114 LJ Ch 247, 89 Sol Jo 293, 173 LT 42, 61 TLR 383 .... 102.7, 102.10
Treeby's Goods, Re (1875) LR 3 P & D 242, 44 LJP & M 44 .... 14.7
Tregonwell v Sydenham (1815) 3 Dow 194, 15 RR 40 .... 47.8, 94.15, 94.37
Treharne v Layton (1875) LR 10 QB 459, 44 LJQB 202, 23 WR 799, 33 LT 327, Ex Ch 96.2
Trelawney v Molesworth (1701) Colles 163, HL 66.5
Trelease, Re (1911) 30 NZLR 226 .... 18.13
Treloar, Re (1984) 36 SASR 41 .... 10.7
Treloar v Lean (1889) 14 PD 49, 58 LJP 39, 37 WR 560, 60 LT 512 .... 18.18, 18.23, 18.27
Tremayne v Rashleigh [1908] 1 Ch 681, 77 LJ Ch 292, 52 Sol Jo 263, 98 LT 615 .... 83.2
Tremblay, Re (1920) 56 DLR 281, 48 OLR 321 .... 45.2
Trenchard, Re, Trenchard v Trenchard [1902] 1 Ch 378, 71 LJ Ch 178, 50 WR 266, [1900–3] All ER Rep 289, 46 Sol Jo 231, 86 LT 196 .... 35.28, 83.6

Trenchard, Re, Trenchard v Trenchard [1905] 1 Ch 82, 74 LJ Ch 135, 53 WR 235, 92 LT 265 .... 33.1
Trethewy v Helyar (1876) 4 Ch D 53, 46 LJ Ch 125 .... 38.1, 47.24, 83.3
Trevelyan v Trevelyan (1810) 1 Phillim 149 .... 10.1
Trevor v Trevor (1847) 1 HL Cas 239, 73 RR 58 .... 76.5, 85.2, 85.4
Tribe, Re, Tribe v Dean and Chapter of Truro Cathedral (1915) 85 LJ Ch 79, 59 Sol Jo 509, 113 LT 313 .... 64.35
Tribe v Tribe (1849) 1 Rob Eccl 775, 13 Jur 793, 13 LTOS 449, 7 Notes of Cases 132 .... 12.6
Trickey v Trickey (1832) 3 My & K 560 .... 90.2
Trider, Re (1978) 84 DLR (3d) 336 .... 44.15
Trimmer, Re, Crundwell v Trimmer (1904) 91 LT 26 .... 57.3, 57.20
Trimmer v Bayne (1802) 7 Ves 508 .... 44.1, 44.9, 44.12, 44.14
Trimnell's Goods, Re (1865) 11 Jur NS 248 .... 12.6
Trinder v Trinder (1866) LR 1 Eq 695, 14 WR 557 .... 59.2
Trinder's Goods, Re (1844) 3 Notes of Cases 275 .... 12.3
Trollope's Will Trusts, Re, Public Trustee v Trollope [1927] 1 Ch 596, [1927] All ER Rep 365, 96 LJ Ch 340, 71 Sol Jo 310, 137 LT 375 ..... 27.15, 30.31, 38.25, 38.26, 220.23
Trotter, Re, Trotter v Trotter [1899] 1 Ch 764, 68 LJ Ch 363, 47 WR 477, 80 LT 647, 15 TLR 287 .... 9.5, 9.11
Trower v Butts (1823) 1 Sim & St 181, 1 LJOS Ch 115 .... 73.1
Trufort, Re, Trafford v Blanc (1887) 36 Ch D 600, 57 LJ Ch 135, 36 WR 163, 57 LT 674, 3 TLR 798 .... 23.7, 23.8
Trundle, Re, Emanuel v Trundle [1961] 1 All ER 103, [1960] 1 WLR 1388, 104 Sol Jo 1094 .... 64.37
Truro's (Lady) Goods, Re (1866) LR 1 P & D 201, 35 LJP & M 89, 14 WR 976, 14 LT 893 .... 15.2
Trustees, Executors and Agency Co Ltd v Bush (1908) 28 NZLR 117 .... 94.38
Trustees, Executors and Agency Co Ltd v Dimock (1892) 18 VLR 729 .... 33.27
Trustees, Executors and Agency Co Ltd v Engelbert (1951) 51 SRNSW 244 .... 77.3
Trustees, Executors and Agency Co Ltd v Jenner (1897) 22 VLR 584 .... 94.45
Trustees, Executors and Agency Co Ltd v Ramsay (1920) 27 CLR 279 .... 38.10
Trustees, Executors and Agency Co Ltd v Scott (1898) 24 VLR 522 .... 41.1
Trustees, Executors and Agency Co Ltd v Sleeman (1899) 25 VLR 187 .... 66.12, 73.1
Trusts of Arthur McDougall Fund, Re, Thompson v Fitzgerald [1956] 3 All ER 867, [1957] 1 WLR 81, 101 Sol Jo 63 .... 102.10
Tuck's Settlement Trusts, Re, Public Trustee v Tuck [1976] Ch 99, [1976] 1 All ER 545, [1976] 2 WLR 345, 119 Sol Jo 868; affd [1978] Ch 49, [1978] 1 All ER 1047, [1978] 2 WLR 411, 121 Sol Jo 796, CA 34.2, 34.9, 34.10, 34.11, 35.5, 35.29, 35.31, 49.8, 53.2, 217.40
Tucker, Re, Bowchier v Gordon (1887) 56 LJ Ch 449, 35 WR 344, 56 LT 118 .... 66.10
Tucker v Billing (1856) 2 Jur NS 483, 27 LTOS 132 .... 74.8
Tucker v Boswell (1843) 5 Beav 607 .... 38.25
Tucker v Ellick (1883) 49 LT 674 .... 77.1
Tucker v Harris (1832) 5 Sim 538, 2 LJ Ch 18 .... 51.9, 51.10
Tucker v Inman (1842) Car & M 82, 4 Man & G 1049, 5 Scott NR 843 .... 49.7
Tucker v Kayess (1858) 4 K & J 339 .... 47.8, 47.9
Tucker Estate, Re, Wilde v Lepper (1954) 13 WWRNS 351 .... 53.5

Tuckett's Will Trusts, Re, Williams v National Provincial Bank Ltd (1967) 111 Sol Jo 811 .... 77.3
Tuckey v Henderson (1863) 33 Beav 174, 9 Jur NS 1306, 11 WR 1013 .... 88.4
Tuckwell v Cornick (1844) 2 LTOS 336 .... 5.9
Tugman v Hopkins (1842) 11 LJCP 309, 4 Man & G 389, 5 Scott NR 464 .... 61.1
Tugwell v Scott (1857) 24 Beav 141, 3 Jur NS 633 .... 72.2
Tuite v Bermingham (1875) LR 7 HL 634, 24 WR 540 .... 81.3
Tulk v Houlditch (1813) 1 Ves & B 248 .... 34.21, 35.48
Tunaley v Roch (1857) 3 Drew 720, 5 WR 515, 29 LTOS 192 .... 50.4, 101.3
Tunno, Re, Raikes v Raikes (1890) 45 Ch D 66, 59 LJ Ch 573, 38 WR 636, 63 LT 23 .... 31.4
Tupper v Tupper (1855) 1 K & J 665, 1 Jur NS 917, 3 WR 616, 26 LTOS 47 .... 19.2
Turkington, Re, Owen v Benson [1937] 4 All ER 501, 81 Sol Jo 1041 .... 9.35
Turland, Re, Permanent Trustee Co v Macready [1964] NSWR 414 .... 30.8
Turnbull, Re, Skipper v Wade [1905] 1 Ch 726, 74 LJ Ch 438, 53 WR 440, 49 Sol Jo 417 .... 31.1, 51.5, 54.4
Turner, Re (1860) 2 De GF & J 527, 30 LJ Ch 144, 7 Jur NS 114, 9 WR 174, 3 LT 573 .... 237.11
Turner, Re (1865) 2 Drew & Sm 501, 34 LJ Ch 660, 13 WR 770, 12 LT 695 .... 68.2, 68.11
Turner, Re, Armstrong v Gamble (1908) 1 IR 274, 41 ILT 237 .... 31.3
Turner, Re, Arnold v Blades (1891) 36 Sol Jo 28 .... 38.10
Turner, Re, Carpenter v Staveley [1949] 2 All ER 935, 94 Sol Jo 114 .... 51.1, 51.2, 51.3, 53.4, 57.5
Turner, Re, Hudson v Turner [1932] 1 Ch 31, 101 LJ Ch 49, 146 LT 209 .... 47.37, 47.38
Turner, Re, Tennant v Turner [1938] Ch 593, [1938] 2 All ER 560, 107 LJ Ch 326, 82 Sol Jo 295, 159 LT 246, 54 TLR 697 .... 204.77, 204.78
Turner v A-G (1876) 10 IR Eq 386 .... 7.3
Turner v Brittain (1863) 3 New Rep 21 .... 80.1, 80.6
Turner v Buck (1874) LR 18 Eq 301, 43 LJ Ch 583, 22 WR 748 .... 32.9
Turner v Frampton (1846) 2 Coll 331, 10 Jur 24, 6 LTOS 314 .... 98.10
Turner v Gosset (1865) 34 Beav 593 .... 97.9
Turner v Hudson (1847) 10 Beav 222, 16 LJ Ch 180, 9 LTOS 215 .... 66.1
Turner v Martin (1857) 7 De GM & G 429, 26 LJ Ch 216, 3 Jur NS 397, 5 WR 277, 28 LTOS 349 .... 47.21
Turner v Mullineux (1861) 1 John & H 334 .... 33.47
Turner v Penny (1843) 1 LTOS 412 .... 4.13
Turner v Turner (1852) 21 LJ Ch 843, 20 LTOS 30 .... 39.12, 64.32, 64.35, 64.53
Turner v Turner (1880) 14 Ch D 829, 44 JP 734, 28 WR 859, 42 LT 495, [1874–80] All ER Rep Ext 1448 .... 30.42, 63.6
Turner v Turner [1911] 1 Ch 716, 80 LJ Ch 473, [1911–13] All ER Rep 962, 104 LT 901, CA 30.10, 30.12
Turner v Turner [1984] Ch 100, [1983] 2 All ER 745, [1983] 3 WLR 896, 127 Sol Jo 842 .... 53.6
Turner v Turner [2007] All ER (D) 238 (May) 4.11
Turner's Goods, Re (1872) LR 2 P & D 403, 36 JP 808, 21 WR 38, 27 LT 322 .... 18.15, 18.28
Turner's Estate, Re [2003] BCSC 1226, [2004] WTLR 1467, BC SC 22.1
Turner's Goods, Re (1891) 64 LT 805 .... 21.7

Turner's Trustees v Turner (1897) 24 R 619, 34 SLR 468, 4 SLT 332 .... 76.1
Turner's Will Trusts, Re, District Bank Ltd v Turner [1937] Ch 15, [1936] 2 All ER 1435, 106 LJ Ch 58, 80 Sol Jo 791, 155 LT 266, 52 TLR 713, CA 218.48, 218.52, 218.53, 218.71, 218.78, 221.35
Turner's Will Trusts, Re, Westminster Bank Ltd v Turner [1968] 1 All ER 321, [1968] 1 WLR 227, 111 Sol Jo 913 .... 44.6, 100.5
Turney, Re, Turney v Turney [1899] 2 Ch 739, 69 LJ Ch 1, 48 WR 97, 81 LT 548, CA 56.5, 68.1, 93.22, 93.38, 93.39, 93.42, 94.14
Turnour's Goods, Re (1886) 50 JP 344, 56 LT 671 .... 18.10
Turton, Re, Whittington v Turton [1926] Ch 96, 95 LJ Ch 136, [1925] All ER Rep 340, 134 LT 439 .... 34.2
Turvin v Newcome (1856) 3 K & J 16, 3 Jur NS 203, 5 WR 35 .... 95.8
Tussaud's Estate, Re, Tussaud v Tussaud (1878) 9 Ch D 363, 47 LJ Ch 849, 26 WR 874, 39 LT 113, CA 44.9, 44.12, 44.13, 44.14, 57.31
Tuttesham v Roberts (1603) Cro Jac 22 .... 63.3
Tweed, Re, Buckmaster v Moss (1902) 46 Sol Jo 634 .... 64.27
Tweedale v Tweedale (1878) 7 Ch D 633, 47 LJ Ch 530, 26 WR 457, 38 LT 137 .... 35.12, 35.13
Tweedale's Goods, Re (1874) LR 3 P & D 204, 39 JP 152, 44 LJP & M 35, 31 LT 799 .... 16.8
Twining v Powell (1845) 2 Coll 262, 5 LTOS 474 .... 38.11, 44.8, 44.13, 102.21
Twisden v Twisden (1804) 9 Ves 413 .... 44.1, 100.6
Twiss, Re, Barclays Bank Ltd v Pratt [1941] Ch 141, [1941] 1 All ER 93, 84 Sol Jo 719, 57 TLR 16 .... 33.36, 33.39, 33.40
Twohill's Goods, Re (1879) 3 LR Ir 21 .... 25.1, 57.15
Twopeny's Settlement, Re, Monro v Twopeny [1924] 1 Ch 522, 93 LJ Ch 323, 68 Sol Jo 402, 130 LT 816, CA 37.2
Twycross v Grant (1878) 4 CPD 40, 48 LJQB 1, 27 WR 87, 39 LT 618, CA 7.29
Twyford v Trail (1834) 7 Sim 92 .... 25.10
Tyler, Re, Tyler v Tyler (1891) 65 LT 367, 7 TLR 310; affd [1891] 3 Ch 252, 60 LJ Ch 686, 40 WR 7, 65 LT 367, 7 TLR 654, CA 9.29, 41.11, 102.26, 202.28, 212.13
Tyler v Merchant Taylors' Co (1890) 15 PD 216, 60 LJP 86, 63 LT 779 .... 14.8
Tyler's Fund Trusts, Re, Graves v King [1967] 3 All ER 389, [1967] 1 WLR 1269, 111 Sol Jo 794 .... 36.10, 103.17
Tylor, Re, Barclays Bank Ltd v Norris (1968) 112 Sol Jo 486 .... 71.1, 71.5
Tyndale v Wilkinson (1856) 23 Beav 74, 2 Jur NS 963, 4 WR 695 .... 87.1
Tyrone (Earl) v Marquis of Waterford (1860) 1 De GF & J 613, 29 LJ Ch 486, 6 Jur NS 567, 8 WR 454, 2 LT 397 .... 63.1, 84.4, 85.2, 89.1
Tyrrell, Re [1959] OR 248, [1959] OWN 138 .... 97.1
Tyrrell v Naylor (1892) 11 NZLR 118 .... 94.13
Tyrrell v Painton [1894] P 151, 6 R 540, 42 WR 343, [1891–4] All ER Rep 1120, 70 LT 453, CA 4.17, 5.1, 5.9
Tyrrell's Estate, Re [1907] 1 IR 292, CA 94.30
Tyssen, Re, Knight-Bruce v Butterworth [1894] 1 Ch 56, 63 LJ Ch 114, 8 R 22, 42 WR 172, 38 Sol Jo 58, 69 LT 689 .... 40.8, 213.12
Tytherleigh v Harbin (1835) 6 Sim 329, 5 LJ Ch 15 .... 68.10
Tzedeck v Royal Trust Co [1953] 1 SCR 31 .... 202.7

U

Ullersperger's Goods, Re (1841) 6 Jur 156 .... 11.21
Ullswater, Re, Barclays Bank Ltd v Lowther [1952] Ch 105, [1951] 2 All ER 989, [1951] 2 TLR 1024 .... 38.26, 214.19, 214.39
Ulverston and District New Hospital Building Trusts, Re, Birkett v Barrow and Furness Hospital Management Committee [1956] Ch 622, [1956] 3 All ER 164, [1956] 3 WLR 559, 100 Sol Jo 603, CA 103.6
Umbers v Jaggard (1870) LR 9 Eq 200, 18 WR 283 .... 35.39, 55.3
Umpherson, Re [1918] SALR 147 .... 68.6
Underhill v Roden (1876) 2 Ch D 494, 45 LJ Ch 266, 24 WR 574, 34 LT 227 .... 85.4, 93.20
Underwood v Morris (1741) 2 Atk 184 .... 34.15, 35.11
Underwood v Swain (1649) 1 Rep Ch 161 .... 34.25
Underwood v Wing (1855) 4 De GM & G 633, 24 LJ Ch 293, 3 Eq Rep 794, 1 Jur NS 169, 3 WR 228, 24 LTOS 304; on appeal sub nom Wing v Angrave (1860) 8 HL Cas 183, 30 LJ Ch 65 .... 47.23, 70.1, 93.9, 93.18, 93.19
Underwood Estate, Re (1959) 19 DLR (2d) 65, 28 WWR 602 .... 96.2
Ungly v Peale (1712) 2 Eq Cas Abr 358, sub nom Ongley v Peale 2 Ld Raym 1312, 10 Mod Rep 103 .... 89.1
Uniacke, Re (1844) 68 RR 220, 1 Jo & Lat 1 .... 27.5
Union Trustee Co of Australia Ltd v Pettit (1958) 76 WNNSW 110 .... 68.3
United Grand Lodge of Ancient Free and Accepted Masons of England v Holborn Borough Council [1957] 3 All ER 281, [1957] 1 WLR 1080, 56 LGR 68, 50 R & IT 709, 2 RRC 190, 121 JP 595, 101 Sol Jo 851, 170 Estates Gazette 507 .... 102.9
University College of North Wales v Taylor [1908] P 140, 77 LJP 20, 52 Sol Jo 44, 98 LT 472, 24 TLR 29, CA 15.1, 57.5, 102.8
University of London Medical Sciences Institute Fund, Re, Fowler v A-G [1909] 2 Ch 1, 78 LJ Ch 562, 53 Sol Jo 302, 100 LT 423, 25 TLR 358, CA 103.6
Unwin v Unwin (1914) 20 BCR 77, 6 WWR 1186, SC 18.29
Upton, Re, Barclays Bank Ltd v Upton (1965) 109 Sol Jo 236, CA 87.4
Upton v Hardman (1874) IR 9 Eq 157 .... 98.1
Upton v Prince (1735) Cas temp Talb 71 .... 44.4
Upton v Vanner (1861) 1 Drew & Sm 594, 8 Jur NS 405, 10 WR 99, 5 LT 480 .... 33.24
Upton's Estate, Re, Upton v National Westminster Bank [2004] EWHC 1962 (Ch), [2004] WTLR 1339 .... 72.10, 75.4
Urch v Walker (1838) 3 My & Cr 702, 7 LJ Ch 292, 2 Jur 487, 45 RR 360 .... 27.6
Urquhart v Butterfield (1887) 37 Ch D 357, 57 LJ Ch 521, 36 WR 376, 385n, 57 LT 780, 4 TLR 161, CA 7.9
Usborne's Goods, Re (1909) 25 TLR 519 .... 10.14
Ussher, Re, Foster and Ussher [1922] 2 Ch 321, 91 LJ Ch 521, 127 LT 453 .... 93.18, 93.37, 93.38, 210.49
Usticke, Re (1866) 35 Beav 338, 14 WR 447 .... 67.1, 67.4
Usticke v Peters (1858) 4 K & J 437, 4 Jur NS 1271, 32 LTOS 60 .... 42.5
Uttermare, Re, Leeson v Foulis [1893] WN 158 .... 64.32

V

Vachel v Vachel (1669) 1 Cas in Ch 129, sub nom Vachell v Leman 1 Eq Cas Abr 361 pl 7 .... 8.3
Vachell v Breton (1706) 2 Eq Cas Abr 437, 5 Bro Parl Cas 51, HL 101.2
Vachell v Leman. See Vachel v Vachel
Vaisey v Reynolds (1828) 5 Russ 12, 6 LJOS Ch 172 .... 64.20, 64.37, 64.53
Valdez's Trusts, Re (1888) 40 Ch D 159, 58 LJ Ch 861, 37 WR 162, 60 LT 42 .... 83.3, 97.1
Valentine, Re, Kennedy v Birchall [1940] Ch 424, [1940] 1 All ER 545, 109 LJ Ch 129, 162 LT 261, TLR 408, CA 68.9
Vallance, Re (1876) Seton's Judgments & Orders 7th ed 1304 .... 9.31
Vallance v Vallance (1863) 2 New Rep 229 .... 60.1, 61.1, 64.32
Van v Clarke (1739) 1 Atk 510, West temp Hard 699 .... 93.45
Van Cutsem's Goods, Re (1890) 63 LT 252 .... 21.6
Vandeleur v Sloane [1919] 1 IR 116 .... 35.39, 35.43, 45.2
Van Den Bergh's Will Trusts, Re, Van Den Bergh v Simpson [1948] 1 All ER 935, 92 Sol Jo 324 .... 44.1
Vander Byl, Re, Fladgate v Gore [1931] 1 Ch 216, 100 LJ Ch 108, 74 Sol Jo 770, 144 LT 401 .... 39.15
Vanderplank v King (1843) 3 Hare 1, 12 LJ Ch 497, 7 Jur 548 .... 94.10, 94.49
Vanderzee v Aclom (1799) 4 Ves 771 .... 101.9
Vandyke v Adams [1942] Ch 155, [1942] 1 All ER 139, 111 LJ Ch 110, 86 Sol Jo 56, 116 LT 117, 58 TLR 129 .... 99.8
Van Grutten v Foxwell [1897] AC 658, 66 LJQB 745, 46 WR 426, 77 LT 170, HL 18.6, 50.7, 50.9, 50.11, 51.7, 78.1, 87.2
Van Hagan, Re, Sperling v Rochfort (1880) 16 Ch D 18, 50 LJ Ch 1, 29 WR 84, 44 LT 161, CA 39.7
Van Lessen, Re, National Provincial Bank Ltd v Beamont [1955] 3 All ER 691, [1955] 1 WLR 1326, 99 Sol Jo 912 .... 64.56
Vanneck v Benham [1917] 1 Ch 60, [1916–17] All ER Rep 741, 86 LJ Ch 7, 115 LT 588 .... 29.17, 38.16, 204.21
Van Tassel v Frederick (1896) 27 OR 646 .... 98.7
Vardon, Re, Brown v Vardon [1938] 4 All ER 306, 82 Sol Jo 697, 159 LT 455 .... 33.3
Vardon's Trusts, Re (1884) 28 Ch D 124, 54 LJ Ch 244, 33 WR 297, 51 LT 884; revsd (1885) 31 Ch D 275, 55 LJ Ch 259, 34 WR 185, 53 LT 895, 2 TLR 204, CA 42.6, 42.16
Varley, Re, Thornton v Varley (1893) 62 LJ Ch 652, 68 LT 665 .... 35.39, 83.6
Varley v Winn (1856) 2 K & J 700, 25 LJ Ch 831, 2 Jur NS 661, 4 WR 792, 28 LTOS 80 .... 32.12, 51.7, 93.9, 97.4
Vatcher v Paull [1915] AC 372, 84 LJPC 86, [1914–15] All ER Rep 609, 112 LT 737, PC 40.14, 40.15
Vaudrey v Howard (1853) 2 WR 32 .... 20.5, 38.13, 47.28
Vaughan, Re, Scott v British and Foreign School Society (1901) 17 TLR 278 .... 57.15
Vaughan, Re, Vaughan v MacIver [1926] IR 67 .... 99.8
Vaughan, Re, Vaughan v Thomas (1886) 33 Ch D 187, 51 JP 70, 35 WR 104, 55 LT 547, 2 TLR 725 .... 102.9, 102.22
Vaughan v Booth (1852) 16 Jur 808 .... 30.24

Vaughan v Buck (1841) 1 Ph 75, 6 Jur 23 .... 38.23
Vaughan v Clerk (1902) 87 LT 144, 18 TLR 704 .... 5.7
Vaughan v Foakes (1836) 1 Keen 58 .... 52.11
Vaughan v Marquis of Headfort (1840) 10 Sim 639, 9 LJ Ch 271, 4 Jur 649 .... 85.3
Vaughan v Vanderstegen (1854) 2 Drew 165, 363, 23 LJ Ch 793, 2 Eq Rep 1229, 2 WR 599, 61 ER 759, 23 LTOS 309 .... 17.5
Vautier's Estate, Re (2000–01) 3 ITELR 566, Royal Ct Jersey 5.5, 6.2
Vaux, Re, Nicholson v Vaux [1939] Ch 465, [1938] 4 All ER 297, 703, 108 LJ Ch 60, 211, 82 Sol Jo 949, 1048, 160 LT 65, 74, 55 TLR 92, 230, CA 44.1, 44.11, 94.15, 94.47, 94.48
Vavasseur v Vavasseur (1909) 25 TLR 250 .... 30.18
Vawdry v Geddes (1830) 1 Russ & M 203, Taml 361, 8 LJOS Ch 63 .... 93.31, 93.38
Veal v Veal (1859) 27 Beav 303, 6 Jur NS 527, 8 WR 2, sub nom Re Veal, Veal v Veal 29 LJ Ch 321, 2 LT 228 .... 1.15
Veale's Trusts, Re (1876) 4 Ch D 61; on appeal (1877) 5 Ch D 622, 46 LJ Ch 799, 36 LT 346, CA 50.21
Vear, Re, Vear v Vear (1917) 62 Sol Jo 159 .... 57.13, 57.18, 57.20, 64.35, 64.37
Velasco v Coney [1934] P 143, 103 LJP 76, [1934] All ER Rep 630, 78 Sol Jo 431, 151 LT 307, 50 TLR 444 .... 23.13, 23.14, 24.11, 24.14
Vencatanarayana Pillay v Subammal (1915) 32 TLR 118, PC 18.10
Venn, Re, Lindon v Ingram [1904] 2 Ch 52, 73 LJ Ch 507, 52 WR 603, 90 LT 502 .... 20.3, 47.32, 52.11
Verdonk, Re (1979) 106 DLR (3d) 450 .... 64.20, 77.3, 87.1
Vere-Wardale, Re, Vere-Wardale v Johnson [1949] P 395, [1949] 2 All ER 250, [1949] LJR 1494, 93 Sol Jo 553, 65 TLR 493 .... 13.3
Veres, Re, Pirot v Veres [1942] 3 DLR 770, 2 WWR 529 .... 5.7, 35.20
Verge v Somerville [1924] AC 496, 93 LJPC 173, 68 Sol Jo 419, 131 LT 107, 40 TLR 279 .... 102.4
Vergers Will, Re [1956] VLR 94 .... 11.4
Verner v General and Commercial Investment Trust [1894] 2 Ch 239, 63 LJ Ch 456, 38 Sol Jo 308, 10 TLR 341; on appeal [1894] 2 Ch 239, 260, 63 LJ Ch 456, 1 Mans 136, 7 R 170, 38 Sol Jo 308, 384, 70 LT 516, 10 TLR 341, 393, [1891–4] All ER Rep Ext 409, CA 38.21
Vernon, Re, Garland v Shaw (1906) 95 LT 48 .... 3.2, 44.9, 44.12, 44.13, 48.5, 48.12
Vernon (Trustees of Employees Fund of William Vernon & Sons Ltd) v IRC [1956] 3 All ER 14, [1956] 1 WLR 1169, 36 TC 484, 35 ATC 176, 49 R & IT 396, [1956] TR 119, 100 Sol Jo 632 .... 102.24
Vernon Estate, Re, Boyle v Battye [1948] 2 WWR 46 .... 102.10
Vernon's Estate, Re (1916) 33 TLR 11 .... 16.4
Vernon's Will Trusts, Re, Lloyds Bank Ltd v Group 20, Hospital Management Committee (Coventry) [1972] Ch 300n, [1971] 3 All ER 1061n, [1971] 3 WLR 796n 58.11, 103.4, 103.5, 103.10
Verschoyle's Trusts, Re (1879) 3 LR Ir 43 .... 40.7
Vertannes v Robinson (1927) LR 54 Ind App 276, PC 64.15
Vestey's (Baron) Settlement, Re, Lloyds Bank Ltd v O'Meara [1951] Ch 209, [1950] 2 All ER 891, CA 218.51
Vezey v Jamson (1822) 1 Sim & St 69 .... 102.23
Vickers, Re (2001–02) 4 ITELR 584 .... 18.8, 201.11
Vickers, Re, Vickers v Mellor (1899) 44 Sol Jo 90, 81 LT 719 .... 41.22

Vickers, Re, Vickers v Vickers (1888) 37 Ch D 525, 57 LJ Ch 738, 36 WR 545, 58 LT 920 .... 44.11
Vickers (Estate of), Re [2001] 4 ITELR 584 .... 18.8
Vickers v Bell (1864) 4 De GJ & Sm 274, 10 Jur NS 376, 3 New Rep 624, 12 WR 589, 10 LT 77 .... 25.12
Vickers v Pound (1858) 6 HL Cas 885, 28 LJ Ch 16, 4 Jur NS 543, 6 WR 580, 31 LTOS 372 .... 50.21, 51.8
Vickers Will, Re [1912] VLR 385 .... 101.7
Viertel, Re [2003] WTLR 1075, SC Qd 41.1
Villar, Re, Public Trustee v Villar [1929] 1 Ch 243, [1928] All ER Rep 535, 98 LJ Ch 223, 72 Sol Jo 761, 140 LT 90, 45 TLR 13, CA 53.3, 53.7, 94.2
Villar v Gilbey [1907] AC 139, [1904–7] All ER Rep 779, 76 LJ Ch 339, 51 Sol Jo 341, 96 LT 511, 23 TLR 392, HL 50.6, 50.11, 73.1, 200.35, 235.25
Vincent v Newcombe (1832) You 599, 2 LJ Ex Eq 15 .... 30.8
Vincent v Vincent (1887) 56 LT 243, CA 3.3
Vine, Re, Perpetual Executors and Trustees Association of Australia Ltd v Vine [1955] ALR 499, [1955] VLR 200 .... 80.3
Viner, Re, Kreeger v Cooper [1978] CLY 3091 .... 105.19
Viner v Francis (1789) 2 Cox Eq Cas 190, 2 Bro CC 658 .... 66.5, 66.19
Vines' Estate, Re, Vines v Vines [1910] P 147, 79 LJP 25, 54 Sol Jo 272, 102 LT 141, 26 TLR 257 .... 1.5
Vinnicombe v Butler (1864) 29 JP 56, 34 LJPM & A 18, 10 Jur NS 1109, 3 Sw & Tr 580, 13 WR 392 .... 13.2
Violett v Brookman (1857) 26 LJ Ch 308, 5 WR 342, 29 LTOS 104 .... 20.4, 34.19
Vivian, Re, Vivian v Swansea (1920) 36 TLR 657, CA 35.19
Vivian v Mills (1839) 1 Beav 315, 8 LJ Ch 239 .... 93.22, 93.27
Vize v Stoney (1841) 1 Dr & War 337 .... 93.27, 93.33
Voges v Monaghan (1954) 94 CLR 232 .... 36.3
Voice Estate, Re, Voice v Voice (1964) 48 DLR (2d) 558, 50 WWR 499 .... 78.6
Von Brentano's Estate, Re [1911] P 172, 105 LT 78, 27 TLR 395, sub nom Re Brentano's Goods 80 LJP 80 .... 23.11
Von Brockdorff v Malcolm (1885) 30 Ch D 172, 55 LJ Ch 121, 33 WR 934, [1881–5] All ER Rep 1068, 53 LT 263 .... 39.18, 40.8, 51.4, 53.2, 94.48
Vorley v Richardson (1856) 8 De GM & G 126, 25 LJ Ch 335, 2 Jur NS 362, 4 WR 397, 27 LTOS 22 .... 67.2
Vout v Hay (1995) 125 DLR (4th) 431, Can SC 4.13, 5.4, 5.9
Vulliamy v Huskisson (1838) 3 Y & C Ex 80, 2 Jur 656 .... 96.7
Vynior's Case (1609) 8 Co Rep 81b 1.4

W

W (a minor) (claim from deceased's estate), Re [1995] 2 FCR 689, sub nom Re C (leave to apply for provision) [1995] 2 FLR 24, [1995] Fam Law 479 .... 105.5, 105.16
W v B (1849) 11 Beav 621 .... 35.6
WJGL, Re. See L (WJG), Re
Wachtel v Wachtel [1973] Fam 72, [1973] 1 All ER 113, [1973] 2 WLR 84, 116 Sol Jo 762; varied [1973] Fam 72, [1973] 1 All ER 829, [1973] 2 WLR 366, 117 Sol Jo 124, CA 105.9, 105.28

Walford v Gray (1865) 11 Jur NS 106, 5 New Rep 235, 13 WR 335, 11 LT 620; affd (1865) 11 Jur NS 473, 6 New Rep 76, 13 WR 761, 12 LT 437 .... 40.13
Walford v Walford [1912] AC 658, 81 LJ Ch 828, [1911–13] All ER Rep 950, 56 Sol Jo 631, 107 LT 657, HL 30.6, 30.32, 32.4, 32.11, 50.4, 50.21
Walker, Re (1871) 7 Ch App 120, 41 LJ Ch 219, 20 WR 171, 25 LT 775 .... 9.2
Walker, Re [1905] 1 Ch 160, 74 LJ Ch 86, 91 LT 713, CA 4.14
Walker, Re [1924] 1 DLR 719, 53 OLR 480 .... 57.15
Walker, Re, Clarke v Walker [1973] 1 NZLR 449 .... 5.7, 47.29, 57.8
Walker, Re, Dunkerly v Hewerdine [1917] 1 Ch 38, 86 LJ Ch 196, 115 LT 708 .... 66.2, 66.5
Walker, Re, MacColl v Bruce [1908] 1 Ch 560, 77 LJ Ch 370, 52 Sol Jo 280, 98 LT 524 .... 49.7
Walker, Re, Macintosh-Walker v Walker [1908] 2 Ch 705, 77 LJ Ch 755, 99 LT 469 .... 37.2
Walker, Re, Public Trustee v Walker [1939] Ch 974, [1939] 3 All ER 902, 109 LJ Ch 1, 83 Sol Jo 731, 161 LT 223, 55 TLR 1092 .... 33.41, 99.4, 99.10, 211.24
Walker, Re, Romilly v Robinson [1905] St R Qd 74 .... 101.7
Walker, Re, Walker v Duncombe [1901] 1 Ch 879, 70 LJ Ch 417, 49 WR 394, 84 LT 193 .... 218.66
Walker, Re, Walker v Lutyens [1897] 2 Ch 238, 66 LJ Ch 622, 45 WR 647, 41 Sol Jo 622, 77 LT 94, 13 TLR 499 .... 72.3
Walker, Re, Walker v Walker (1886) 54 LT 792 .... 95.7, 95.9
Walker, Re, Walker v Walker (1890) 59 LJ Ch 386, 62 LT 449 .... 29.10
Walker, Re, Walker v Walker [1930] 1 Ch 469, 90 LJ Ch 225, [1930] All ER Rep 392, 74 Sol Jo 106, 142 LT 472, CA 54.2, 66.12, 68.6
Walker v Boughner (1889) 18 OR 448 .... 3.2
Walker v Claridge (1968) 207 Estates Gazette 341 .... 3.3
Walker v Cusin [1917] 1 IR 63 .... 77.2, 78.4
Walker v Denne (1793) 2 Ves 170 .... 37.2
Walker v Geo H Medlicott & Son [1999] 1 All ER 685, [1999] 1 WLR 727, [1999] 1 FLR 1095, [1999] Fam Law 214, [1999] 01 LS Gaz R 24, CA ... 1.14, 6.1, 6.3, 6.4, 57.29
Walker v Irish Law Clerks Benefit Society [1946] IR 222 .... 47.1
Walker v Mackie (1827) 4 Russ 76 .... 39.19
Walker v Main (1819) 1 Jac & W 1 .... 93.29, 97.4, 97.8
Walker v Mower (1852) 16 Beav 365 .... 91.3, 93.6, 93.22, 93.43
Walker v Petchell (1845) 1 CB 652, 14 LJCP 211, 5 LTOS 126 .... 98.3
Walker v Shore (1808) 15 Ves 122 .... 66.11
Walker v Shore (1815) 19 Ves 387 .... 62.4, 64.2
Walker v Simpson (1855) 1 K & J 713, 1 Jur NS 637 .... 93.22
Walker v Smith (1861) 20 Beav 394 .... 5.9
Walker v Stones [2001] QB 902, [2000] 4 All ER 412, [2001] 2 WLR 623, [2000] 35 LS Gaz R 36, CA 221.13, 221.16, 221.21
Walker v Tillott (1835) 4 LJ Ch 232 .... 38.23
Walker v Tipping (1852) 9 Hare 800, 16 Jur 442, 19 LTOS 177 .... 50.6, 50.15
Walker v Walker (1860) 2 De GF & J 255, 29 LJ Ch 856 .... 34.2, 34.19
Walker and Elgee's Contract, Re (1918) 53 ILT 22 .... 40.15
Walker's Estate, Re, Watson v Treasury Solicitor (1912) 28 TLR 466 .... 4.14, 4.15

Walker's Goods, Re (1862) 26 JP 168, 31 LJPM & A 62, 8 Jur NS 314, 2 Sw & Tr 354, 5 LT 766 .... 11.6, 11.9
Walker's Settlement Trusts, Re, Watson v Walker [1936] Ch 280, 105 LJ Ch 49, [1934–1935] B & CR 279, 154 LT 564, 52 TLR 118 .... 38.28
Wall, Re, Pomeroy v Willway (1889) 42 Ch D 510, 59 LJ Ch 172, 37 WR 779, 61 LT 357 .... 102.5, 102.7
Wall v Tomlinson (1810) 16 Ves 413 .... 98.13
Wall v Wall (1847) 15 Sim 513, 16 LJ Ch 305, 11 Jur 403 .... 32.5
Wallace, Re, Champion v Wallace [1920] 2 Ch 274, 89 LJ Ch 450, 64 Sol Jo 478, 123 LT 343, 36 TLR 481, CA 8.1, 34.12, 35.47
Wallace v Bayldon (1825) 4 LJOS Ch 74 .... 64.6
Wallace v Pomfret (1805) 11 Ves 542 .... 44.16
Wallace v Seymour (1872) 20 WR 634, IR 6 CL 219 .... 18.14, 20.3
Wallace v Wallace (1898) 24 VLR 859 .... 35.38
Wallace's Estate, Re, Solicitor of Duchy of Cornwall v Batten [1952] 2 TLR 925 .... 4.17, 5.1
Wallace's Settlements, Re [1968] 2 All ER 209, [1968] 1 WLR 711, 112 Sol Jo 381 .... 40.16, 200.104, 216.8, 216.9
Waller, Re, White v Scoles (1899) 68 LJ Ch 526, 47 WR 563, 43 Sol Jo 569, 80 LT 701, CA 58.4
Waller v Stevenson (1912) 56 Sol Jo 666, HL 51.10
Walley, Re, National Westminster Bank Ltd v Williams [1972] 1 All ER 222, [1972] 1 WLR 257, 51 ATC 247, [1972] TR 213, 116 Sol Jo 146 .... 210.70, 214.70
Wallgrave v Tebbs (1855) 20 JP 84, 2 K & J 313, 25 LJ Ch 241, 2 Jur NS 83, 4 WR 194, 26 LTOS 147 .... 36.2
Wallinger's Estate, Re [1898] 1 IR 139 .... 39.3, 39.14
Wallis v Brightwell (1722) 2 P Wms 88, 2 Eq Cas Abr 62 pl 4 .... 30.43, 32.33
Wallis v Crimes (1667) 1 Cas in Ch 89 .... 34.25
Wallis v Solicitor-General for New Zealand [1903] AC 173, 72 LJPC 37, 88 LT 65, 19 TLR 230 .... 102.8, 102.26, 103.11
Wallis v Taylor (1836) 8 Sim 241, Donnelly 162, 6 LJ Ch 68 .... 83.3
Wallop v Darby (1612) Yelv 209 .... 84.2
Walmsley v Foxhall (1863) 1 De GJ & Sm 605 .... 68.1
Walmsley v Vaughan (1857) 1 De G & J 114, 26 LJ Ch 503, 3 Jur NS 497, 5 WR 549, 29 LTOS 204 .... 100.2
Walmsley's Settled Estates, Re (1911) 55 Sol Jo 600, 105 LT 332 .... 32.28
Walne v Hill [1883] WN 171 .... 30.15
Walpole, Re, Public Trustee v Canterbury [1933] Ch 431, 102 LJ Ch 209, [1933] All ER Rep 988, 148 LT 526 .... 37.7
Walpole v Apthorp (1867) LR 4 Eq 37, 15 WR 632 .... 30.3
Walpole (Lord) v Earl of Cholmondeley (1797) 7 Term Rep 138 .... 1.1
Walpole v Laslett (1862) 1 New Rep 180, 7 LT 526 .... 93.20, 93.21
Walpole (Lord) v Lord Orford (1797) 3 Ves 402 .... 2.4, 2.6, 2.10
Walpole's Marriage Settlement, Re, Thomson v Walpole [1903] 1 Ch 928, 72 LJ Ch 522, 51 WR 587, 88 LT 419 .... 39.5, 40.7
Walsh, Re, Keenan v Brown (1911) 30 NZLR 1166 .... 57.11
Walsh, Re, Public Trustee v Walsh [1936] 1 All ER 327, 80 Sol Jo 264, CA 77.2
Walsh, Re, Walsh v Walsh [1953] Ch 473, [1953] 1 All ER 982, [1953] 2 WLR 686, 97 Sol Jo 228 .... 64.42
Walsh v Gladstone (1843) 1 Ph 290, 8 Jur 25 .... 102.8

Walsh v Johnston [1899] 1 IR 501 .... 76.1
Walsh v Wallinger (1830) 2 Russ & M 78, Taml 425, 9 LJOS Ch 7 .... 83.17
Walsh v Walsh (1852) 1 Drew 64 .... 9.40
Walsh's Trusts, Re (1878) 1 LR Ir 320 .... 39.18
Walter, Re, Turner v Walter (No 2) (1912) 56 Sol Jo 632, CA 47.25
Walter v Drew (1723) 1 Com 373 .... 98.7
Walter v Makin (1833) 6 Sim 148, 2 LJ Ch 173 .... 79.7
Walter's Will's Trusts, Re, Stuart v Pitman [1949] Ch 91, [1948] 2 All ER 955, [1949] LJR 225, 92 Sol Jo 674 .... 90.3, 90.4
Waltham Forest London Borough Council v Thomas [1992] 2 AC 198, [1992] 3 All ER 244, [1992] 3 WLR 131, 90 LGR 385, [1993] Fam Law 67, 24 HLR 622, [1992] 2 EGLR 40, [1992] 28 LS Gaz R 32, [1992] NLJR 1005, [1992] 30 EG 87, 136 Sol Jo LB 200, HL 7.4
Walton's Estate, Re (1856) 8 De GM & G 173, 25 LJ Ch 569, 2 Jur NS 363, 4 WR 416, 27 LTOS 22 .... 49.8, 50.17
Wand, Re, Escritt v Wand [1907] 1 Ch 391, 76 LJ Ch 253, 96 LT 424 ... 20.5, 38.13, 47.1
Wandesforde v Carrick (1871) IR 5 Eq 486 .... 40.7
Wankford v Wankford (1699) 11 Mod Rep 38, 1 Salk 299, Holt KB 311 ...... 25.2, 25.10
Want v Stallibrass (1873) LR 8 Exch 175, 42 LJ Ex 108, 21 WR 685, 19 LT 293 .... 40.7
Warbrick v Varley (No 2) (1861) 30 Beav 347 .... 35.38
Ward, Re, Partridge v Hoare-Ward [1920] 1 Ch 334, 89 LJ Ch 181, 64 Sol Jo 115, 122 LT 336 .... 86.2
Ward, Re, Public Trustee v Ward [1941] Ch 308, 165 LT 115, sub nom Re Ward, Public Trustee v Berry [1941] 2 All ER 125, 110 LJ Ch 171, 85 Sol Jo 255, 57 TLR 473, CA 212.5
Ward, Re, Ward v Ward [1965] Ch 856, [1964] 3 WLR 957, 108 Sol Jo 801, sub nom Ward's Will Trusts, Re, Ward v Ward [1964] 3 All ER 442 .... 66.21
Ward, Re, Ward v Warwick [1946] 2 All ER 206, 90 Sol Jo 405, 175 LT 284 .... 1.15
Ward v Arch (1846) 15 Sim 389, 16 LJ Ch 66, 10 Jur 977, 8 LTOS 337 .... 37.6
Ward v Brown [1916] 2 AC 121, 85 LJPC 183, 113 LT 929, 31 TLR 545, PC 67.7, 93.2
Ward v Butler (1824) 2 Mol 533 .... 25.12
Ward v Crook (1896) 17 NSWLR (B) 64 .... 21.5
Ward v Grey (1859) 26 Beav 485, 29 LJ Ch 74, 5 Jur NS 948, 7 WR 569, 34 LTOS 50 .... 30.1, 30.3, 55.4, 85.3
Ward v Laverty [1925] AC 101, [1924] All ER Rep 319, 94 LJPC 17, 68 Sol Jo 629, 131 LT 614, 40 TLR 600, HL 203.62
Ward v Turner (1752) 1 Dick 170, 2 Ves Sen 431 .... 1.15
Ward v Van der Loeff [1924] AC 653, [1924] All ER Rep 542, 93 LJ Ch 397, 69 Sol Jo 517, 131 LT 292, 40 TLR 493, HL 18.10, 19.4, 20.4, 66.3, 71.1, 94.11, 237.11
Ward v Ward [1903] 1 IR 211 .... 33.12
Ward v Ward [1921] 1 IR 117 .... 85.2
Ward's Estate, Re [1957] SASR 125 .... 64.35, 83.15, 102.7
Ward's Trusts, Re (1872) 7 Ch App 727, 42 LJ Ch 4, 20 WR 1024, 27 LT 668 .... 82.7, 82.8
Ward's Will Trusts, Re, Ward v Ward. See Ward, Re, Ward v Ward
Warde, Re, Warde v Ridgway (1914) 58 Sol Jo 472, 111 LT 35 .... 100.4

Wardrop's Estate, Re [1917] P 54, 86 LJP 37, 61 Sol Jo 171, 115 LT 720, 33 TLR 133 .... 16.4, 16.10, 17.2
Wardroper v Cutfield (1864) 33 LJ Ch 605, 10 Jur NS 194, 12 WR 458, 10 LT 19 .... 93.20
Ware, Re, Re Rouse, Ware v Rouse [1926] WN 163, 70 Sol Jo 691 .... 44.8
Ware, Re, Cumberlege v Cumberlege-Ware (1890) 45 Ch D 269, 59 LJ Ch 717, 38 WR 767, 63 LT 52, 6 TLR 388 .... 47.37, 79.7
Ware v Watson (1855) 7 De GM & G 248, 3 WR 496 .... 68.1, 90.2
Wareham, Re, Wareham v Brewin [1912] 2 Ch 312, 81 LJ Ch 578, 56 Sol Jo 613, 107 LT 80, CA 38.23
Warin, Re [1919] NZLR 555 .... 10.1
Waring, Re, Hayward v A-G [1907] 1 Ch 166, 76 LJ Ch 49, 51 Sol Jo 101, 95 LT 859 .... 103.3
Waring, Re, Westminster Bank Ltd v Awdry [1942] Ch 309, [1942] 1 All ER 556, 111 LJ Ch 170, 86 Sol Jo 139, 166 LT 297, 58 TLR 281; revsd [1942] Ch 426, [1942] 2 All ER 250, 111 LJ Ch 284, 86 Sol Jo 310, 167 LT 145, 58 TLR 367, CA 22.3
Waring v Currey (1873) 22 WR 150 .... 49.2
Waring v Waring (1848) 6 Moo PCC 341, 12 Jur 947, 6 Notes of Cases 388 .... 4.11
Warn v Swift (1832) 1 LJ Ch 203 .... 4.10
Warner, Re, Watts v Silvey [1918] 1 Ch 368, 87 LJ Ch 234, 62 Sol Jo 159, 118 LT 353, 34 TLR 130 .... 66.10, 93.20
Warner v Latouche (1855) 8 Ir Jur 34 .... 44.1
Warner v Warner (1850) 20 LJ Ch 273, 15 Jur 141, 16 LTOS 320 .... 72.3, 72.4
Warner v White. See White d White v Warner
Warre's Will Trusts, Re, Wort v Salisbury Diocesan Board of Finance [1953] 2 All ER 99, [1953] 1 WLR 725, 97 Sol Jo 387 .... 102.25
Warren, Re (1922) 52 OLR 127 .... 59.2
Warren, Re, Warren v Warren [1932] 1 Ch 42, [1931] All ER Rep 702, 101 LJ Ch 85, 146 LT 224 .... 20.4, 22.4, 41.3, 41.18, 204.69
Warren v Kelson (1859) 28 LJP & M 122, 5 Jur NS 415, 1 Sw & Tr 290, 7 WR 348, 33 LTOS 12 .... 25.16
Warren v Rudall, ex p Godfrey (1860) 1 John & H 1, 29 LJ Ch 543, 6 Jur NS 395, 8 WR 331, 2 LT 693 .... 27.6, 46.3
Warren v Warren (1783) 1 Cox Eq Cas 41, 1 Bro CC 305 .... 44.5
Warren v Warren (1829) 3 Ir L Rec 1st ser 85 .... 31.19
Warren v Wright (1861) 12 I Ch R 401 .... 33.12
Warren's Trusts, Re (1884) 26 Ch D 208, 53 LJ Ch 787, 32 WR 641, 50 LT 454 .... 76.2, 94.47
Warter v Warter (1890) 15 PD 152, 54 JP 631, 59 LJP 87, 63 LT 250, 6 TLR 391, [1886–90] All ER Rep Ext 1223 .... 17.2
Warwick v Hawkins (1852) 5 De G & Sm 481, 21 LJ Ch 796, 16 Jur 902, 19 LTOS 243 .... 91.6
Warwick v Warwick (1918) 34 TLR 475, CA 10.9
Wass, Re, Re Clarke (1906) 95 LT 758 .... 38.7, 64.16, 64.18, 64.45
Wasserberg, Re, Union of London and Smiths Bank Ltd v Wasserberg [1915] 1 Ch 195, 84 LJ Ch 214, [1914–15] All ER Rep 217, 59 Sol Jo 176, 112 LT 242 .... 1.15
Waterhouse, Re, Waterhouse v Ryley (1907) 77 LJ Ch 30, 98 LT 30, CA 39.10, 39.13
Waterhouse v Stansfield (1851) 9 Hare 234, 21 LJ Ch 881 .... 23.4

Waterman's Will Trusts, Re, Lloyds Bank Ltd v Sutton [1952] 2 All ER 1054, 96 Sol Jo 850, [1952] 2 TLR 877 .... 203.31
Waters, Re, Preston v Waters [1889] WN 39 .... 29.2, 29.6, 29.9, 29.10
Waters, Re, Waters v Boxer (1889) 42 Ch D 517, 58 LJ Ch 750, 38 WR 57, 61 LT 431 .... 32.9
Waters v Thorn (1856) 22 Beav 547 .... 7.8
Waters v Waters (1857) 26 LJ Ch 624, 3 Jur NS 654, 112 RR 434, 29 LTOS 310 .... 97.3
Waters v Wood (1852) 5 De G & Sm 717, 22 LJ Ch 206, 17 Jur 33, 20 LTOS 76 .... 58.2, 64.29
Wathen v Smith (1819) 4 Madd 325 .... 44.15
Watkins, Re, James v Cordey (1889) 37 WR 609, CA 94.21
Watkins, Re, Maybery v Lightfoot [1912] 2 Ch 430, 81 LJ Ch 822, 107 LT 450; affd [1913] 1 Ch 376, 82 LJ Ch 240, 108 LT 237, CA; revsd sub nom Lightfoot v Maybery [1914] AC 782, 83 LJ Ch 627, 58 Sol Jo 609, 111 LT 300, HL 50.3, 78.2, 78.3, 93.2
Watkins v Cheek (1825) 2 Sim & St 199 .... 93.44
Watkins v Frederick (1865) 11 HL Cas 358 .... 101.1
Watkins v Weston (1863) 3 De GJ & Sm 434, 32 LJ Ch 609, 11 WR 408, 8 LT 406 .... 62.1, 62.4, 82.3
Watkins v Williams (1851) 21 LJ Ch 601, 16 Jur 181, 3 Mac & G 622, 87 RR 228, 19 LTOS 13 .... 34.6, 83.8, 99.1
Watkins' Goods, Re (1865) LR 1 P & D 19, 35 LJP & M 14, 12 Jur NS 12, 13 LT 445 .... 15.1
Watkins' Settlement, Re, Wills v Spence [1911] 1 Ch 1, 80 LJ Ch 102, 55 Sol Jo 63, 103 LT 749, CA 33.24
Watney, Re, Watney v Gold (1911) 56 Sol Jo 109 .... 44.4, 100.6
Watson, Re (1887) 13 VLR 599 .... 21.4
Watson, Re [1927] 4 DLR 626, 61 OLR 173 .... 47.6, 48.4
Watson, Re [1957] NZLR 544 .... 19.2
Watson, Re [1999] 3 FCR 595, [1999] 1 FLR 878, [1999] Fam Law 211, [1999] 02 LS Gaz R 28, 143 Sol Jo LB 51 .... 105.14, 105.16, 105.18
Watson, Re, Carlton v Carlton (1887) 35 WR 711 .... 23.7, 23.8
Watson, Re, Cox v Watson [1892] WN 192, 27 LJNC 174 .... 94.38
Watson, Re, Culme-Seymour v Brand [1930] 2 Ch 344, 99 LJ Ch 452, 143 LT 764 .... 73.1, 82.3, 217.41
Watson, Re, Turner v Watson [1896] 1 Ch 925, 65 LJ Ch 553, 44 WR 571, 74 LT 453 .... 30.11, 30.12, 30.13
Watson v Arundel (1876) IR 10 Eq 299 .... 64.27
Watson v Arundell (1876) IR 11 Eq 53, Ir CA 15.3, 57.20
Watson v Conant [1964] SCR 312, 44 DLR (2d) 346 .... 33.25
Watson v Donaldson [1915] 1 IR 63, Ir CA 47.28, 47.31, 47.32, 66.5
Watson v Hayes (1839) 5 My & Cr 125, 9 LJ Ch 49, 4 Jur 186, 48 RR 249 .... 93.32, 93.34
Watson v National Children's Home [1995] 37 LS Gaz R 24 .... 34.7, 35.12, 35.13, 57.23
Watson v Watson (1840) 11 Sim 73 .... 66.5, 66.8
Watson v Watson (1864) 33 Beav 574 .... 44.4, 44.5, 44.8
Watson v Young (1885) 28 Ch D 436, 54 LJ Ch 502, 33 WR 637 .... 66.13
Watson's Estate, Re (1986) 43 SASR 15 .... 1.3

Watson's Settlement Trusts, Re, Dawson v Reid [1959] 2 All ER 676, [1959] 1 WLR 732, 103 Sol Jo 528 .... 94.44
Watson's Trusts, Re (1870) LR 10 Eq 36, 39 LJ Ch 770, 18 WR 642 .... 66.2, 96.2
Watt, Re, Hicks v Hill [1932] 2 Ch 243n, 101 LJ Ch 417n, 147 LT 528n, CA 103.3
Watt v Wood (1862) 2 Drew & Sm 56, 31 LJ Ch 338, 10 WR 335 .... 38.3, 95.9
Watt's Will Trusts, Re, Watt v Watt [1936] 2 All ER 1555 .... 66.13, 95.3, 95.8, 218.72
Watts v Public Trustee for Western Australia [1980] WAR 97 .... 1.14
Watts, Re, Coffey v Watts [1931] 2 Ch 302, 100 LJ Ch 353, 145 LT 520 .... 39.2
Watts v Watts (1873) LR 17 Eq 217, 43 LJ Ch 77, 22 WR 105, 29 LT 671 .... 41.4, 41.5
Watts' Estate, Re (1889) 8 NZLR 72 .... 10.1
Watts's Goods, Re (1837) 1 Curt 594 .... 4.13, 4.14, 4.20
Waugh, Re [1955] NZLR 1129 .... 83.6
Waugh, Re, Waugh v Cripps [1903] 1 Ch 744, 72 LJ Ch 586, 51 WR 461, 88 LT 54, 19 TLR 283 .... 84.2
Wavertree of Delamere (Baron), Re, Rutherford v Hall-Walker [1933] Ch 837, [1933] All ER Rep 837, 102 LJ Ch 367, 77 Sol Jo 468, 149 LT 418, 49 TLR 515 .... 8.7, 64.27, 204.20, 204.21
Way, Re (1903) 6 OLR 614, 2 OWR 1072, 24 CLT 20 .... 64.45
Way's Goods, Re [1901] P 345, 71 LJP 13, 85 LT 643, 17 TLR 758 .... 25.2
Wayland's Estate, Re [1951] 2 All ER 1041, 95 Sol Jo 804 .... 18.8
Wayling v Jones (1993) 69 P & CR 170, [1996] 2 FCR 41, [1995] 2 FLR 1029, [1996] Fam Law 88, [1995] Conv 409, CA 43.1, 105.18
Waynford v Heyl. See Wainford v Heyl
Weakley d Knight v Rugg (1797) 7 Term Rep 322 .... 98.13
Weale v Ollive (No 2) (1863) 32 Beav 421 .... 50.2, 83.2, 83.8, 83.13
Weall v Rice (1831) 2 Russ & M 251, 9 LJOS Ch 116 .... 44.1, 44.2, 44.10, 44.14
Weatherhill v Pearce [1995] 2 All ER 492, [1995] 1 WLR 592 .... 11.6, 11.10, 11.11, 11.24, 11.26
Weaver, Re [1963] VR 257 .... 102.13
Webb, Re, Leedham v Patchett (1890) 63 LT 545 .... 33.24
Webb, Re, Smith v Johnston [1964] 2 All ER 91, [1964] 1 WLR 509, 108 Sol Jo 139 .... 18.12
Webb v Byng (1855) 1 K & J 580, 1 Jur NS 696 .... 57.18, 57.19, 58.12, 63.5
Webb v Byng (1856) 2 K & J 669, 4 WR 657, 6 LTOS 133; on appeal (1856) 8 De GM & G 633; affd sub nom Byng v Byng (1862) 10 HL Cas 171, 31 LJ Ch 470, 8 Jur NS 1135, 10 WR 633, 7 LT 1 .... 85.2
Webb v Grace (1848) 2 Ph 701, sub nom Grace v Webb 18 LJ Ch 13, 12 Jur 987 .... 33.20, 34.3, 35.2
Webb v Hearing (1617) 3 Bulst 192, Cro Jac 415, 1 Roll Rep 436, J Bridg 84, sub nom Anon Moore KB 852 .... 93.15
Webb v Hodge [1925] NZLR 22 .... 86.5
Webb v Honnor (1820) 1 Jac & W 352 .... 39.19
Webb v Kelly (1839) 9 Sim 469 .... 33.18
Webb v Sadler (1873) 8 Ch App 419, 42 LJ Ch 498, 21 WR 394, 28 LT 388 .... 40.5, 94.30, 94.44, 94.48
Webb v Webb (1840) 2 Beav 493 .... 95.7, 95.9
Webb v Webb (1900) 17 WN 188, 21 NSW Eq 245 .... 44.15
Webb v Webb Estate [1995] 6 WWR 52 .... 4.10
Webb's Case (1607) 1 Roll Abr 609 .... 53.5

Webb's Goods, Re (1855) Dea & Sw 1, 1 Jur NS 1096, 4 WR 92, 26 LTOS 111 .... 12.7
Webb's Goods, Re (1864) 28 JP 696, 33 LJPM & A 182, 10 Jur NS 709, 4 New Rep 486, 3 Sw & Tr 482, 11 LT 277 .... 10.1
Webber, Re, Barclays Bank Ltd v Webber [1954] 3 All ER 712, [1954] 1 WLR 1500, 98 Sol Jo 871 .... 102.8
Webber v Corbett (1873) LR 16 Eq 515, 43 LJ Ch 164, 29 LT 365 ..... 53.3, 57.20, 57.22
Webber v Stanley (1864) 16 CBNS 698, 33 LJCP 217, 10 Jur NS 657, 4 New Rep 192, 12 WR 833, 10 LT 417 .... 49.3, 58.1, 58.6, 63.2
Webber v Webber (1823) 1 Sim & St 311, 1 LJOS Ch 219 .... 29.4, 30.33
Webster, Re, Goss v Webster [1937] 1 All ER 602, 156 LT 128, CA 30.6
Webster, Re, Pearson v Webster [1912] 1 Ch 106, 81 LJ Ch 79, 56 Sol Jo 90, 105 LT 815 .... 103.3
Webster v Boddington (1858) 26 Beav 128 .... 94.24
Webster v Hale (1803) 8 Ves 410 .... 32.4, 32.5
Webster's Estate, Re, Widgen v Mello (1883) 23 Ch D 737, 52 LJ Ch 767, 49 LT 585 .... 68.6
Wecke's Will, Re, Montreal Trust Co v Sinclair and Wecke (1958) 15 DLR (2d) 655, 26 WWR 164 .... 34.10
Weddell v Mundy (1801) 6 Ves 341 .... 56.1
Wedge, Re (1968) 67 DLR (2d) 433, 63 WWR 396 .... 102.7
Wedge's Goods, Re (1842) 2 Notes of Cases 14 .... 10.8
Wedgwood, Re, Allen v Public Trustee [1921] 1 Ch 601, 90 LJ Ch 322, 125 LT 146, CA 29.14
Wedgwood, Re, Allen v Wedgwood [1915] 1 Ch 113, 84 LJ Ch 107, 59 Sol Jo 73, 112 LT 66, 31 TLR 43, CA 9.31, 102.13
Wedgwood, Re, Sweet v Cotton [1914] 2 Ch 245, 83 LJ Ch 731, 58 Sol Jo 595, 111 LT 436, 30 TLR 527 .... 58.11, 103.8
Wedgwood v Denton (1871) LR 12 Eq 290, 40 LJ Ch 526, 25 LT 379 .... 20.4, 34.19, 35.26, 207.4
Wedmore, Re, Wedmore v Wedmore [1907] 2 Ch 277, 76 LJ Ch 486, 97 LT 26, 23 TLR 547 .... 30.3, 30.4, 31.2, 31.4, 44.15, 47.22, 204.64, 210.27
Weeding, Re, Armstrong v Wilkin [1896] 2 Ch 364, 65 LJ Ch 743, 44 WR 556, 40 Sol Jo 565, 74 LT 651 .... 58.4, 64.11, 64.54, 64.57
Weeding v Weeding (1861) 1 John & H 424, 30 LJ Ch 680, 7 Jur NS 908, 9 WR 431, 4 LT 616 .... 41.20
Weeds v Bristow (1866) LR 2 Eq 333, 35 LJ Ch 839, 12 Jur NS 446, 14 WR 726, 14 LT 587 .... 71.5
Weekes' Settlement, Re [1897] 1 Ch 289, 66 LJ Ch 179, 45 WR 265, 41 Sol Jo 225, 76 LT 112 .... 1.6, 83.18, 101.9
Weeks, Re (1972) 28 DLR (3d) 452 .... 18.27
Weiner's Will Trusts, Re, Wyner v Braithwaite [1956] 2 All ER 482, [1956] 1 WLR 579, 100 Sol Jo 400 .... 30.9, 30.36, 200.57
Weir v Chamley (1850) 1 I Ch R 295 .... 40.15
Weir v Crum-Brown [1908] AC 162, 77 LJPC 41, 52 Sol Jo 261, 98 LT 325, 24 TLR 308, HL 102.7
Weir Hospital, Re [1910] 2 Ch 124, 79 LJ Ch 723, 54 Sol Jo 600, 102 LT 882, 26 TLR 519, CA 103.18

Weir's Settlement Trusts, Re, MacPherson and Viscount Weir v IRC [1971] Ch 145, [1970] 1 All ER 297, [1969] 3 WLR 860, 48 ATC 392, [1969] TR 369, 113 Sol Jo 627, CA 214.50
Welbrock, Re [1920] NZLR 1 .... 18.28
Welby v Rockcliffe (1830) 1 Russ & M 571, 8 LJOS Ch 142 .... 45.2
Welby v Welby (1813) 2 Ves & B 187 .... 63.8
Welch v Phillips (1836) 1 Moo PCC 299 .... 18.31
Welch and Freeman v Gardner (1887) 51 JP 760 .... 19.4
Weld v Bradbury (1715) 2 Vern 705, 1 Eq Cas Abr 203 pl 25 .... 66.5, 87.1
Weldon v Hoyland (1862) 4 De GF & J 564, 6 LT 96 .... 76.4, 87.1
Weldon v Weldon [1911] 1 IR 177 .... 98.2
Welford's Will Trusts, Re, Davidson v Davidson [1946] 1 All ER 23, 90 Sol Jo 54 .... 39.22, 39.25, 39.26
Welland v Townsend [1910] 1 IR 177 .... 51.6
Wellesley (Lady) v Earl Mornington (1855) 2 K & J 143, 1 Jur NS 1202 .... 40.15, 100.3
Wellesley v Vere (1841) 2 Curt 917, 1 Notes of Cases 240 .... 4.18
Wellesley (Lord) v Withers (1855) 4 E & B 750, 24 LJQB 134, 1 Jur NS 706, 99 RR 727, 3 CLR 1187, 25 LTOS 79 .... 27.6
Wellington (Duke), Re, Glentanar v Wellington [1948] Ch 118, [1947] 2 All ER 854, [1949] LJR 612, 92 Sol Jo 11, 64 TLR 54, CA 201.12
Wellington v Shepherd (1872) 27 LT 832 .... 63.7
Wellington v Wellington (1768) 4 Burr 2165, 1 Wm Bl 645 .... 98.8
Wells, Re, Public Trustee v Wells [1940] Ch 411, [1940] 2 All ER 68, 109 LJ Ch 261, 84 Sol Jo 272, 162 LT 422, 56 TLR 443 .... 33.47
Wells, Re, Wells v Wells (1889) 43 Ch D 281, 59 LJ Ch 113, 38 WR 327, 61 LT 806 .... 32.23, 218.66
Wells v Horton (1826) 4 Bing 40, 5 LJOSCP 41, 12 Moore CP 177 .... 3.2
Wells v Wells (1874) LR 18 Eq 504, 43 LJ Ch 681, 22 WR 893, 31 LT 16 ... 57.22, 71.1
Wells v Wood (1861) 9 WR 780, 4 LT 768 .... 34.5
Wells' Estate, Re (1868) LR 6 Eq 599, 37 LJ Ch 553, 16 WR 784, 18 LT 462 .... 72.2, 72.3
Wells' Trusts, Re, Hardisty v Wells (1889) 42 Ch D 646, 58 LJ Ch 835, 38 WR 229, 61 LT 588 .... 39.20, 39.28, 59.1
Welply v Cormick (1864) 16 I Ch R 74 .... 35.4
Welsh, Re (1980) 111 DLR (3d) 390 .... 50.2
Welsh Hospital (Netley) Fund, Re, Thomas v A-G [1921] 1 Ch 655, 90 LJ Ch 276, [1921] All ER Rep 170, 65 Sol Jo 417, 124 LT 787 .... 102.7
Wenborn, Re [1923] NZLR 27 .... 19.4
Wenmoth's Estate, Re, Wenmoth v Wenmoth (1887) 37 Ch D 266, [1886–90] All ER Rep 591, 57 LJ Ch 649, 36 WR 409, 57 LT 709, 4 TLR 74 .... 51.2, 66.21
Wentworth v Cox (1882) 6 Madd 363 .... 60.1
Were's Will, Re (1886) 12 VLR 271 .... 25.1
Wernher, Re, Wernher v Beit [1918] 2 Ch 82, 87 LJ Ch 372, 62 Sol Jo 503, 118 LT 388, 34 TLR 391, CA 16.1, 16.6
Wernher's Settlement Trusts, Re, Lloyds Bank Ltd v Mountbatten [1961] 1 All ER 184, [1961] 1 WLR 136, 105 Sol Jo 88 .... 66.13, 66.20
Wescombe, Re (1944) Tas LR 35 .... 78.1
Wesley v Wesley (1998) 71 SASR 1 .... 73.1
Wesslbenyi v Jamieson [1907] AC 440, HL 78.1

West, Re [1942] SCR 120, [1942] 1 DLR 754 .... 31.4
West, Re, Denton v West [1921] 1 Ch 533, 90 LJ Ch 342, 65 Sol Jo 379, 125 LT 117, 37 TLR 433 .... 100.2
West, Re, George v Grose [1900] 1 Ch 84, 69 LJ Ch 71, 48 WR 138, 44 Sol Jo 89, 81 LT 720 .... 82.5
West, Re, West v Roberts [1909] 2 Ch 180, 78 LJ Ch 559, 101 LT 375 .... 25.16, 31.20
West, Re, Westhead v Aspland [1913] 2 Ch 345, [1911–13] All ER Rep 692, 82 LJ Ch 488, 109 LT 39 .... 32.20, 218.59
West v Kerr (1853) 23 LTOS 24 .... 33.20
West v Lawday (1865) 11 HL Cas 375, 13 LT 171 .... 58.3, 58.6, 58.8
West v Moore (1807) 8 East 339 .... 64.20
West v Ray (1854) Kay 385, 23 LJ Ch 447, 2 Eq Rep 431, 2 WR 319, 23 LTOS 9 .... 213.1
West v West (1863) 4 Giff 198, 32 LJ Ch 240, 9 Jur NS 400, 1 New Rep 258, 7 LT 779 .... 93.2
West v West [1921] 2 IR 34 .... 19.4
West Australian Trustee Executor and Agency Co Ltd v O'Connor (1955) 57 WALR 25 .... 18.13, 18.17
West Sussex Constabulary's Widows, Children and Benevolent (1930) Fund Trusts, Re, Barnett v Ketteringham [1971] Ch 1, [1970] 1 All ER 544, [1970] 2 WLR 848, 114 Sol Jo 92, 134 JP Jo 119, 120 NLJ 225 .... 103.6
West's Goods, Re (1863) 28 JP 9, 32 LJPM & A 182, 9 Jur NS 1158, 12 WR 89 .... 11.4, 12.11
Westby's Settlement, Re, Westby v Ashley [1950] Ch 296, [1950] 1 All ER 479, 66 (pt 1) TLR 515, CA 99.4
Westerman's Executor v Schwab (1905) 43 SLR 161, 8 F 132, 13 SLT 594 .... 23.15
Western Australian Trustee, Executor and Agency Co Ltd v Young (1958) 59 WALR 42 .... 52.3
Westendorp v Warwick [2006] EWHC 915 (Ch), [2006] All ER (D) 248 (Apr) 4.11, 4.21
Westfaling v Westfaling (1746) 3 Atk 460 .... 64.32
Westhaver v Flett (1917) 36 DLR 251, 51 NSR 235 .... 35.21
Westminster Bank Ltd's Declaration of Trust, Re [1963] 2 All ER 400n, [1963] 1 WLR 820, sub nom Abbott v Service 107 Sol Jo 681 .... 66.3, 216.31
Westminster City Council v Peart (1991) 24 HLR 389, CA 105.14
Westminster's (Duke) Settled Estates, Re, Westminster (Duke) v Earl of Shaftesbury [1921] 1 Ch 585, [1921] All ER Rep 702, 90 LJ Ch 305, 125 LT 82, 37 TLR 529 .... 207.7
Weston (Weston's Executors) v IRC [2000] STC 1064, [2001] 02 LS Gaz R 41 .... 205.8
Weston's Goods, Re (1844) 8 JP 362, 3 LTOS 140 .... 11.20
Weston's Goods, Re (1869) LR 1 P & D 633, 33 JP 312, 38 LJP & M 53, [1861–73] All ER Rep 364, 20 LT 330 .... 19.3
Weston's Settlement, Re, Neeves v Weston [1906] 2 Ch 620, 76 LJ Ch 54, 95 LT 581 .... 39.17, 39.25
Westropp, Re (1903) 37 ILT Rep 183 .... 100.2
Westwick v Wyer (1591) 4 Co Rep 28a 25.18
Westwood v Southey (1852) 2 Sim NS 192, 21 LJ Ch 473, 16 Jur 400, 20 LTOS 7 .... 98.3, 98.10

Wetherell v Wetherell (1862) 4 Giff 51, 8 Jur NS 814, 10 WR 818, 7 LT 89; on appeal (1863) 1 De GJ & Sm 134, 32 LJ Ch 476, 9 Jur NS 368, 11 WR 274, 8 LT 39 .... 101.10
Wetherell v Wetherell (1863) 1 De GJ & Sm 134, 32 LJ Ch 476, 9 Jur NS 368, 11 WR 274, 8 LT 39 .... 66.19, 93.22
Wetherell v Wilson (1836) 1 Keen 80, Donnelly 4, 5 LJ Ch 235 .... 82.5
Whale, Re [1977] 2 NZLR 1 .... 17.4
Whale v Booth (1784) 4 Term Rep 625n, 4 Doug KB 36 .... 25.18
Whaley, Re, Whaley v Roehrich [1908] 1 Ch 615, 77 LJ Ch 367, 98 LT 556 .... 64.26
Whaley v Cox (1736) 2 Eq Cas Abr 549, West temp Hard 700 .... 30.31
Whalley v Tompson (1799) 1 Bos & P 371 .... 7.26
Wharton v Barker (1858) 4 K & J 483, 4 Jur NS 553, 6 WR 534 .... 51.7, 77.3, 77.4
Wharton v Earl of Durham. See Durham (Earl) v Wharton
Wharton v Gresham (1776) 2 Wm Bl 1083 .... 85.2
Wharton v Masterman. See Harbin v Masterman [1894] 2 Ch 184
Whateley v Spooner (1857) 3 K & J 542 .... 100.7
Whateley v Whateley (1867) 14 Gr 430 .... 60.1
Wheable v Withers (1849) 16 Sim 505, 18 LJ Ch 156 .... 97.6
Wheatley (Wheatley's Executors) v IRC [1998] STC (SCD) 60 .... 234.4
Wheeler, Re, Hankinson v Hayter [1904] 2 Ch 66, 73 LJ Ch 576, 52 WR 586, 48 Sol Jo 493, 91 LT 227 .... 30.11, 30.12, 64.40
Wheeler, Re, Jameson v Cotter [1929] 2 KB 81n, [1928] WN 225, [1928] All ER Rep 510, 141 LT 322 .... 41.18
Wheeler v Bingham (1746) 3 Atk 364, 1 Wils 135 .... 34.14
Wheeler v Humphreys [1898] AC 506, 67 LJ Ch 499, 47 WR 17, [1895–9] All ER Rep 362, 78 LT 799, HL 100.4
Wheeler v Sheer (1730) Mos 288, 301 .... 102.22
Wheeler v Warner (1823) 1 Sim & St 304, 24 RR 176 .... 35.13
Wheeler and Batsford v Alderson (1831) 3 Hag Ecc 574 .... 4.19, 4.20, 5.9
Wheeler's Goods, Re (1879) 49 LJP 29, 44 JP 285, 28 WR 476, 42 LT 60 .... 18.22
Wheelwright's Goods, Re (1878) 3 PD 71, 47 LJP 87, 42 JP 680, 27 WR 139, 39 LT 127 .... 25.10
Whelan, Re [1961] VR 706 .... 52.3
Whichelow, Re, Bradshaw v Orpen [1953] 2 All ER 1558, [1954] 1 WLR 5, 98 Sol Jo 12 .... 66.3, 216.31
Whicker v Hume (1851) 14 Beav 509; affd (1858) 7 HL Cas 124, [1843–60] All ER Rep 450, 28 LJ Ch 396, 22 JP 591, 4 Jur NS 933, 6 WR 813, 31 LTOS 319 .... 23.2, 24.1, 24.2, 25.15, 30.1, 49.7, 55.4, 103.1
Whieldon v McCarogher. See McCarogher v Whieldon
Whishaw v Stephens. See Gulbenkian's Settlements, Re, Hacobian v Maun
Whistler v Webster (1794) 2 Ves 367 .... 42.3, 42.4, 42.7, 42.9
Whiston, Re, Whiston v Woolley [1924] 1 Ch 122, 93 LJ Ch 113, 68 Sol Jo 116, 130 LT 437, CA 47.32, 69.2, 93.1
Whitaker v Forbes (1875) LR 10 CP 583; affd (1875) 1 CPD 51, 40 JP 436, 45 LJQB 140, 24 WR 241, 33 LT 582, CA 23.4
Whitbread v Lord St John (1804) 10 Ves 152 .... 66.18, 66.20
Whitby, Re, Public Trustee v Whitby [1944] Ch 210, [1944] 1 All ER 299, 113 LJ Ch 170, 88 Sol Jo 111, 170 LT 176, 60 TLR 224, CA 59.3, 64.25, 64.31, 104.4

Whitby v Mitchell (1889) 42 Ch D 494, 59 LJ Ch 8, 38 WR 5, 61 LT 353; affd (1890) 44 Ch D 85, 59 LJ Ch 485, 38 WR 337, 62 LT 771, CA ... 94.44, 94.47, 94.48
Whitby v Von Luedecke [1906] 1 Ch 783, 75 LJ Ch 359, 54 WR 415, 94 LT 432 ... 93.5, 94.8, 94.12, 94.48
Whitcher, Re [1982] 2 NZLR 416 ... 68.2
Whitcher v Penley (1846) 9 Beav 477, 7 LTOS 488 ... 68.1
White, Re [1948] 1 DLR 572, 21 MPR 331 ... 11.13
White, Re [1957] OWN 465 ... 35.8
White, Re (1962) 33 DLR (2d) 185, [1962] OR 590 ... 83.9
White, Re [1965] VR 250 ... 48.15
White, Re (1987) 38 DLR (4th) 631 ... 1.3
White, Re, Barker v Gribble [1991] Ch 1, [1990] 3 All ER 1, [1990] 3 WLR 187, [1991] 1 FLR 112, [1991] Fam Law 60 ... 9.5, 11.10, 11.11, 11.24, 12.4, 14.1
White, Re, Knight v Briggs [1925] Ch 179, 94 LJ Ch 211, [1924] All ER Rep 630, 69 Sol Jo 213, 132 LT 481 ... 20.2, 36.6, 57.5, 57.11
White, Re, McCann v Hull [1958] Ch 762, [1958] 1 All ER 379, [1958] 2 WLR 464, 102 Sol Jo 195 ... 64.7
White, Re, Mastaka v Midland Bank Executor and Trustee Co Ltd. See Mastaka v Midland Bank Executor and Trustee Co Ltd
White, Re, Perpetual Trustees Estate and Agency Co Ltd v Milligan [1963] NZLR 788 ... 53.5, 102.17
White, Re, Theobald v White [1913] 1 Ch 231, 82 LJ Ch 149, 57 Sol Jo 212, 108 LT 319 ... 204.61
White, Re, White v Shenton (1909) 101 LT 780 ... 32.9, 32.10, 210.23
White, Re, White v White [1893] 2 Ch 41, [1891–4] All ER Rep 242, 62 LJ Ch 342, 2 R 380, 41 WR 683, 37 Sol Jo 249, 68 LT 187, CA ... 102.22, 103.1
White, Re, White v White [1916] 1 Ch 172, 85 LJ Ch 368, 60 Sol Jo 210, 114 LT 353 ... 64.8, 64.27, 104.4
White v Baker (1860) 2 De GF & J 55, 29 LJ Ch 577, 6 Jur NS 591, 8 WR 533, 2 LT 583 ... 67.2, 67.3, 67.7
White v Barber (1771) Amb 701, 5 Burr 2703 ... 101.2
White v Barton (1854) 18 Beav 192 ... 27.5
White v Birch (1867) 36 LJ Ch 174, 15 WR 305, 15 LT 605 ... 63.7
White v Briggs (1848) 2 Ph 583, 15 Sim 300, 17 LJ Ch 196, 78 RR 203 ... 79.1
White v Chitty (1866) LR 1 Eq 372, 35 LJ Ch 343, 12 Jur NS 181, 14 WR 366, 13 LT 750 ... 99.10
White v Grier (1841) Milw 602 ... 14.6
White v Hight (1879) 12 Ch D 751, 41 LT 17 ... 96.4
White v Hill (1867) LR 4 Eq 265, 16 LT 826 ... 51.10, 96.2
White v Jones [1995] 2 AC 207, [1993] 3 All ER 481, [1993] 3 WLR 730, [1993] 23 LS Gaz R 43, [1993] NLJR 473, CA; affd [1995] 2 AC 207, [1995] 1 All ER 691, [1995] 2 WLR 187, [1995] 3 FCR 51, [1995] NLJR 251, 139 Sol Jo LB 83, HL ... 1.14, 200.25, 200.46, 223.1
White v M'Dermott (1872) IR 7 CL 1 ... 27.6, 35.13, 35.16
White v Paine. See Paine v Countess of Warwick
White v Parker (1835) 1 Bing NC 573, 4 LJCP 178, 1 Hodg 112, 1 Scott 542 ... 52.8
White v Repton (1844) 3 Curt 818, 8 Jur 562, 3 LTOS 322, sub nom Whyte v Repton 3 Notes of Cases 97 ... 16.2

White v Springett (1869) 4 Ch App 300, 38 LJ Ch 388, 17 WR 336, 20 LT 502 ..... 77.6
White v Stamps Comr (1908) 25 WN 104, 8 SRNSW 287 ..... 94.48
White v Summers [1908] 2 Ch 256, 77 LJ Ch 506, 98 LT 845, 24 TLR 552 ..... 50.21, 93.13
White v Supple (1842) 2 Dr & War 471 ..... 56.6, 56.9
White v Tunnicliffe (1897) 13 TLR 469 ..... 11.26
White v Turner (1858) 25 Beav 505 ..... 100.4
White v Vitty (1826) 2 Russ 484 ..... 58.6
White v White (1778) 1 Bro CC 12 ..... 103.17
White v White (1908) 28 NZLR 129 ..... 10.7, 53.4
White v White [2001] 1 AC 596, [2001] 1 All ER 1, [2000] 3 WLR 1571, [2000] 3 FCR 555, [2000] 2 FLR 981, [2001] Fam Law 12, [2000] 43 LS Gaz R 38, [2000] NLJR 1716, 144 Sol Jo LB 266, HL 105.9
White v Wilson (1852) 1 Drew 298, 22 LJ Ch 62, 17 Jur 15, 1 WR 47 ..... 40.5
White Trust, Re [1952] 4 DLR 711, [1952] OWN 748 ..... 39.14
White d White v Warner (1728) 11 East 552n, 3 Doug KB 4, sub nom Warner v White 3 Bro Parl Cas 435, 1 Bro CC 219n, HL 68.2
White's Goods, Re (1843) 7 Jur 1045, 2 Notes of Cases 461 ..... 12.12
White's Goods, Re (1860) 24 JP 792, 30 LJPM & A 55, 6 Jur NS 808 ..... 14.12
White's Goods, Re (1879) 3 LR Ir 413 ..... 18.22, 18.33
White's Goods, Re (1882) 7 PD 65, 46 JP 424, 51 LJP 40, 30 WR 660, 46 LT 695 ..... 64.35
White's Goods, Re [1896] 1 IR 269 ..... 14.12
White's Trusts, Re (1860) John 656 ..... 56.5, 68.1, 101.9
White's Trusts, Re (1886) 33 Ch D 449, 50 JP 695, 55 LJ Ch 701, 34 WR 771, 55 LT 162, 2 TLR 830 ..... 102.7, 102.26
White's Will Trusts, Re, Barrow v Gillard [1955] Ch 188, [1954] 2 All ER 620, [1954] 3 WLR 314, 98 Sol Jo 541 ..... 102.20
White's Will Trusts, Re, Tindall v Board of Governors of United Sheffield Hospitals [1951] 1 All ER 528, 95 Sol Jo 205 ..... 103.10
Whiteford, Re, Inglis v Whiteford [1903] 1 Ch 889, 72 LJ Ch 540, 51 WR 491, 47 Sol Jo 336 ..... 66.8, 100.5, 100.6
Whiteford, Re, Whiteford v Whiteford [1915] 1 Ch 347, 84 LJ Ch 584, 59 Sol Jo 272, 112 LT 577 ..... 94.13
Whitehead, Re, Peacock v Lucas [1894] 1 Ch 678, 63 LJ Ch 229, 8 R 142, 42 WR 491, [1891–4] All ER Rep 636, 38 Sol Jo 183, 70 LT 122 ..... 38.28
Whitehead, Re, Whitehead v Hemsley [1920] 1 Ch 298, 89 LJ Ch 155, [1918–19] All ER Rep 1170, 122 LT 767, 36 TLR 129 ..... 78.5, 86.5
Whitehead, Re, Whitehead v Street [1913] 2 Ch 56, 82 LJ Ch 302, 57 Sol Jo 323, 108 LT 368 ..... 31.1, 31.2, 44.15
Whitehead v Bennett (1853) 22 LJ Ch 1020, 1 Eq Rep 560, 18 Jur 140, 1 WR 406, 21 LTOS 178 ..... 94.24
Whitehead's Will Trusts, Re, Burke v Burke [1971] 2 All ER 1334, [1971] 1 WLR 833, 115 Sol Jo 389 ..... 27.3
Whitehead's Will Trusts, Re, Public Trustee v White [1959] Ch 579, [1959] 2 All ER 497, 103 Sol Jo 491 ..... 38.28
Whitehorne, Re, Whitehorne v Best [1906] 2 Ch 121, 75 LJ Ch 537, 54 WR 580, 94 LT 698 ..... 48.9

Whitehouse, Re, Whitehouse v Edwards (1887) 37 Ch D 683, 57 LJ Ch 161, 36 WR 181, 57 LT 761 .... 30.12, 100.6
Whitelaw v Wilson (1934) 3 DLR 554, [1934] OR 415, 62 CCC 172 .... 9.18
Whiteley, Re, London (Bishop) v Whiteley [1910] 1 Ch 600, 79 LJ Ch 405, 55 Sol Jo 291, 102 LT 313, 26 TLR 309 .... 50.4, 102.7, 221.29
Whiteley, Re, Whiteley v Bishop of London (1909) 101 LT 508, 26 TLR 16, CA 32.4
Whiteley v King (1864) 17 CBNS 756, 10 Jur NS 1079, 5 New Rep 12, 13 WR 83, 11 LT 342 .... 18.29
Whitelock v Heddon (1798) 1 Bos & P 243 .... 73.1
Whiter, Re, Windsor v Jones (1911) 105 LT 749 .... 55.3, 97.9
Whiteside v Whiteside [1950] Ch 65, [1949] 2 All ER 913, 66 (pt 1) TLR 126, CA 6.1
Whiteway v Fisher (1861) 9 WR 433 .... 41.5
Whitfield v Langdale (1875) 1 Ch D 61, 45 LJ Ch 177, 24 WR 313, 33 LT 592 .... 58.1, 58.6, 63.3, 63.5
Whiting, Re [1957] VLR 400 .... 35.30
Whiting, Re, Ormond v De Launay [1913] 2 Ch 1, 82 LJ Ch 309, 57 Sol Jo 461, 108 LT 629 .... 18.33, 20.5, 38.13, 47.28
Whiting v Force (1840) 2 Beav 571, 9 LJ Ch 345 .... 97.7
Whiting v Turner (1903) 47 Sol Jo 470, 89 LT 71 .... 11.24, 13.2
Whiting v Whiting [1988] 2 All ER 275, [1988] 1 WLR 565, [1988] FCR 569, [1988] 2 FLR 189, [1988] Fam Law 429, 132 Sol Jo 658, [1988] NLJR 39, CA 105.12
Whiting's Settlement, Re, Whiting v De Rutzen [1905] 1 Ch 96, 74 LJ Ch 207, 53 WR 293, 49 Sol Jo 83, 91 LT 821, 21 TLR 83, CA 34.13, 34.14, 35.9
Whitley v Whitley (1862) 31 Beav 173 .... 42.12
Whitman v Aitken (1866) LR 2 Eq 414, 12 Jur NS 350, 14 LT 248 .... 97.7, 97.8
Whitmore, Re, Walters v Harrison [1902] 2 Ch 66, 71 LJ Ch 673, 87 LT 210, CA 47.25, 51.7, 219.26
Whitmore v Regina Branch of Canadian Legion of British Empire Service League [1940] 3 WWR 359 .... 102.10
Whitrick, Re, Sutcliffe v Sutcliffe [1957] 2 All ER 467, [1957] 1 WLR 884, 101 Sol Jo 574, CA 52.2, 52.3
Whitrod, Re, Burrows v Base [1926] Ch 118, 95 LJ Ch 205, 70 Sol Jo 209, 134 LT 627 .... 38.1, 38.13, 47.7, 47.28
Whittaker, Re, Whittaker v Whittaker (1882) 21 Ch D 657, 51 LJ Ch 737, 30 WR 787, 46 LT 802 .... 32.5, 34.1
Whittaker v Kershaw (1890) 45 Ch D 320, sub nom Re Kershaw, Whittaker v Kershaw 60 LJ Ch 9, 39 WR 22, 63 LT 203, CA 31.7
Whitter v Bremridge (1866) LR 2 Eq 736, 35 LJ Ch 807, 14 WR 912 .... 93.16, 93.22
Whittet's Trustees v Whittet (1892) 19 R 975, 29 SLR 834 .... 74.1
Whitting v Whitting (1908) 53 Sol Jo 100 .... 94.48
Whittingham v Crease & Co (1978) 88 DLR (3d) 353, [1978] 5 WWR 45, BC SC 1.14, 4.21
Whittingham's Case (1603) 8 Co Rep 42b 34.24, 35.39
Whitty, Re, Evans v Evans (1881) 43 LT 692 .... 82.5
Whorwood, Re, Ogle v Lord Sherborne (1887) 34 Ch D 446, 56 LJ Ch 340, 35 WR 342, 56 LT 71, 3 TLR 307, CA 57.15, 57.19, 65.2

Whyte v Pollok (1882) 7 App Cas 400, 47 JP 340, 47 LT 356, HL 1.2, 10.1, 10.7, 10.18
Whyte v Repton. See White v Repton
Whyte v Rose (1842) 3 QB 493, 11 LJ Ex 457, 2 Gal & Dav 312, 4 Jur 986, 4 Per & Dav 199, Ex Ch 25.15
Whyte v Whyte (1873) LR 17 Eq 50, 43 LJ Ch 104, 22 WR 180 .... 44.1, 88.4
Whytte (or Whyte) v Ticehurst [1986] Fam 64, [1986] 2 All ER 158, [1986] 2 WLR 700, [1986] 2 FLR 83, [1986] Fam Law 192, 130 Sol Jo 185, [1986] LS Gaz R 875 .... 105.6, 105.16
Widdicombe v Muller (1853) 1 Drew 443, 22 LJ Ch 614, 1 WR 223 .... 66.1
Widdison v Hodgkin (1823) 2 LJOS Ch 9 .... 84.4
Widrig v Strazer and Konish and BC Yukon Air Service Ltd [1964] SCR 376, 47 WWR 268 .... 30.8
Wienholt v Logan. See Logan v Wienholt
Wigan v Rowland (1853) 11 Hare 157, 23 LJ Ch 69, 1 Eq Rep 213, 17 Jur 910, 1 WR 383, 21 LTOS 150 .... 9.8
Wigg v Wigg (1739) 1 Atk 382, West temp Hard 677 .... 8.2
Wiggins v Horlock (1888) 39 Ch D 142, 58 LJ Ch 46, [1886–90] All ER Rep 1125, 59 LT 710, CA 44.15
Wiggins v Wiggins (1852) 2 Sim NS 226, 21 LJ Ch 742 .... 51.2
Wight v Olswang (1999) Times, 18 May, CA 221.13
Wightman's Estate, Re (1945) 4 DLR 754, [1945] 3 WWR 14 .... 38.12
Wightwick v Lord (1857) 6 HL Cas 217, 28 LJ Ch 825, 3 Jur NS 699, 5 WR 713, 29 LTOS 303 .... 38.15
Wightwick's Will Trusts, Re, Official Trustees of Charitable Funds v Fielding-Ould [1950] Ch 260, [1950] 1 All ER 689, 94 Sol Jo 239, 66 (pt 1) TLR 592 .... 94.38
Wilce v Wilce (1831) 7 Bing 664, 9 LJOSCP 197, 5 Moo & P 682 .... 38.3, 51.3
Wilcock, Re, Kay v Dewhirst [1898] 1 Ch 95, 67 LJ Ch 154, 46 WR 153, 42 Sol Jo 115, 77 LT 679 .... 18.6, 20.3, 82.4
Wilcocks v Wilcocks (1706) 2 Vern 558 .... 3.11
Wilcocks' Settlement, Re (1875) 1 Ch D 229, 45 LJ Ch 163, 24 WR 290, 33 LT 719 .... 34.6
Wilcox, Re, Wilcox v Wilcox [1978] Tas SR 82 .... 34.5
Wild's Case (1599) 6 Co Rep 16b, sub nom Anon Gouldsb 139, sub nom Richardson v Yardley Moore KB 397 .... 50.18, 73.1, 76.1, 85.1, 85.2, 85.4
Wilday v Barnett (1868) LR 6 Eq 193, 16 WR 961 .... 39.12
Wildbore v Gregory (1871) LR 12 Eq 482, 41 LJ Ch 129, 19 WR 967 .... 39.19
Wilder's Trusts, Re (1859) 27 Beav 418 .... 47.24, 91.5
Wildes v Davies (1853) 22 LJ Ch 495, 1 Sm & G 475, 1 WR 253, 21 LTOS 206 .... 30.14, 88.2, 95.9
Wiley v Chanteperdrix [1894] 1 IR 209 .... 62.1, 67.2, 67.7, 86.7
Wilford's Estate, Re, Taylor v Taylor (1879) 11 Ch D 267, 48 LJ Ch 243, 27 WR 455 .... 2.1, 2.4, 225.27
Wilkes, Re, Wilkes v Wilkes (2000) [2006] WTLR 1097 .... 4.10, 4.11, 4.17, 4.20, 5.1, 5.2, 5.4, 5.9
Wilkes v Allington [1931] 2 Ch 104, 100 LJ Ch 262, 75 Sol Jo 221, 144 LT 745, 47 TLR 307 .... 1.15
Wilkes v Collin (1869) LR 8 Eq 338, 17 WR 878 .... 64.53
Wilkes' Estate, Re (1880) 16 Ch D 597, 50 LJ Ch 199 .... 38.28

Wilkie v Wilkie (1915) 17 WALR 156 .... 4.10
Wilkins, Re, Spencer v Duckworth (1881) 18 Ch D 634, 50 LJ Ch 774, 29 WR 911, 45 LT 224 .... 97.7
Wilkins, Re, Wilkins v Rotherham (1884) 27 Ch D 703, 54 LJ Ch 188, 33 WR 42 .... 33.38
Wilkins, Re, Wilkins v Wilkins [1920] 2 Ch 63, 89 LJ Ch 507, 64 Sol Jo 530, 123 LT 571 .... 18.33, 20.5, 38.13, 237.11
Wilkins v Jodrell (1863) 11 WR 588 .... 63.1
Wilkins v Jodrell (1879) 13 Ch D 564, 49 LJ Ch 26, 28 WR 224, 41 LT 649 .... 33.18
Wilkinson, Re (1869) 4 Ch App 587, 17 WR 839 .... 39.14
Wilkinson, Re, Neale v Newell [1978] Fam 22, [1978] 1 All ER 221, [1977] 3 WLR 514, 7 Fam Law 176, 121 Sol Jo 375 .... 105.18, 105.19
Wilkinson, Re, Page v Public Trustee [1926] Ch 842, 95 LJ Ch 528, [1926] All ER Rep 357, 135 LT 736 .... 33.19, 34.10, 34.11, 35.19, 35.20, 35.22, 35.23, 35.25
Wilkinson, Re, Thomas v Wilkinson [1910] 2 Ch 216, 79 LJ Ch 600, 54 Sol Jo 563, 102 LT 854 .... 39.3, 39.13
Wilkinson v Adam (1813) 1 Ves & B 422; affd (1823) 12 Price 470, [1814–23] All ER Rep 688, HL 20.4, 72.2, 72.4, 101.1
Wilkinson v Bewicke (1853) 3 De GM & G 937, 22 LJ Ch 781, 1 Eq Rep 12 .... 58.6, 63.8
Wilkinson v Dent (1871) 6 Ch App 339, 40 LJ Ch 253, 19 WR 611, 25 LT 142, CA 42.3
Wilkinson v Duncan (1861) 30 Beav 111, 30 LJ Ch 938, 7 Jur NS 1182, 9 WR 915, 5 LT 171 .... 94.21
Wilkinson v Joughin (1866) LR 2 Eq 319, 30 JP 452, 35 LJ Ch 684, 12 Jur NS 330, 14 LT 394 .... 58.10, 80.6
Wilkinson v Lindgren (1870) 5 Ch App 570, 30 LJ Ch 722, 18 WR 961, [1861–73] All ER Rep 279, 23 LT 375 .... 102.25
Wilkinson v O'Sullivan (1953) 27 ALJ 541 .... 38.3
Wilkinson v Thornhill (1889) 61 LT 362 .... 40.7
Wilkinson v Wilkinson (1819) 2 Wils Ch 47, 3 Swan 515 .... 99.8
Wilkinson v Wilkinson (1825) 2 Sim & St 237 .... 35.49
Wilkinson v Wilkinson (1871) LR 12 Eq 604, 40 LJ Ch 242, 19 WR 558, 24 LT 314 .... 34.24, 35.23, 35.35
Wilkinson's Goods, Re (1881) 6 PD 100, 45 JP 716, 29 WR 896 .... 11.3
Wilkinson's Goods, Re [1892] P 227, 61 LJP 134, 67 LT 328 .... 25.2
Wilkinson's Settlement, Re, Butler v Wilkinson [1917] 1 Ch 620, 86 LJ Ch 511, [1916–17] All ER Rep 326, 61 Sol Jo 414, 117 LT 81, 33 TLR 267 .... 24.12, 24.16
Wilkinson's Settlement Trusts, Re (1869) LR 8 Eq 487; affd (1869) 4 Ch App 587 .... 39.12
Wilkinson's Trusts, Re (1887) 19 LR Ir 531 .... 9.35, 9.36
Wilks v Bannister (1885) 30 Ch D 512, 54 LJ Ch 1139, 33 WR 922, 53 LT 247, 1 TLR 680 .... 71.4, 97.7
Wilks v Williams (1861) 2 John & H 125, 10 WR 55, 5 LT 445 .... 101.7, 101.8
Willatts, Re, Willatts v Artley [1905] 1 Ch 378, 74 LJ Ch 269, 92 LT 195, 21 TLR 194; on appeal [1905] 2 Ch 135, 74 LJ Ch 564, 93 LT 256, 21 TLR 571, CA 101.4
Willcocks, Re [1959] Qd R 349 .... 62.1

Willcocks, Re, Warwick v Willcocks [1921] 2 Ch 327, 91 LJ Ch 27, [1921] All ER Rep 161, 65 Sol Jo 793, 126 LT 86 ... 30.8
Willes v Greenhill (1860) 29 Beav 376; affd (1861) 4 De GF & J 147, 31 LJ Ch 1, 7 Jur NS 1134, 10 WR 33, 5 LT 336 ... 30.11, 30.12
Willetts v Willetts (1848) 7 Hare 38, 17 LJ Ch 457, 12 Jur 670 ... 67.4
Willey, Re, Goulding v Shirtcliffe (1929) 45 TLR 327 ... 64.27
Williames, Re, Andrew v Williames (1885) 54 LT 105, CA ... 45.2, 208.27
Williams, ex p (1819) 1 Jac & W 89 ... 47.38
Williams, Re (1849) 12 Beav 317, 19 LJ Ch 46, 13 Jur 1110, 14 LTOS 393 ... 97.8
Williams, Re (1877) 5 Ch D 735, 47 LJ Ch 92, 25 WR 689, 36 LT 939 ... 9.29, 102.22
Williams, Re, Bendigo and Northern District Base Hospital of Bendigo v A-G [1955] VLR 65 ... 62.1
Williams, Re, Cunliffe v Williams [1915] 1 Ch 450, 84 LJ Ch 578, 110 LT 569 ... 42.1, 42.5
Williams, Re, Foulkes v Williams (1889) 42 Ch D 93, 53 LJ Ch 451, 61 LT 58, CA ... 39.11, 39.16, 39.18, 39.20
Williams, Re, James v Williams (1910) 26 TLR 307 ... 59.1, 102.9
Williams, Re, Metcalf v Williams [1914] 1 Ch 219, 83 LJ Ch 255, 58 Sol Jo 198, 110 LT 60; affd [1914] 2 Ch 61, 83 LJ Ch 570, 58 Sol Jo 470, 110 LT 923, CA ... 50.21, 68.9
Williams, Re, Public Trustee v Williams [1927] 2 Ch 283, 96 LJ Ch 449, 71 Sol Jo 605, 137 LT 477 ... 102.9, 102.22
Williams, Re, Spencer v Brighouse (1886) 54 LT 831 ... 93.6, 93.13, 93.17
Williams, Re, Taylor v University of Wales (1908) 24 TLR 716 ... 34.7, 102.8
Williams, Re, Wiles v Madgin [1985] 1 All ER 964, [1985] 1 WLR 905, 129 Sol Jo 469, [1985] LS Gaz R 2996 ... 6.2, 53.4, 57.25, 57.27
Williams, Re, Williams v All Souls, Hastings (Parochial Church Council) [1933] Ch 244, 102 LJ Ch 58, [1932] All ER Rep 724, 148 LT 310 ... 36.13, 82.5
Williams, Re, Williams v Ball [1917] 1 Ch 1, 86 LJ Ch 36, [1916–17] All ER Rep 354, 61 Sol Jo 42, 115 LT 689, CA ... 10.5, 12.3
Williams, Re, Williams v Templeton [1936] Ch 509, [1936] 1 All ER 175, 105 LJ Ch 362, 80 Sol Jo 223, 154 LT 640, CA ... 33.47
Williams, Re, Williams v Williams (1895) 64 LJ Ch 349, 13 R 316, 43 WR 375, 39 Sol Jo 285, 72 LT 324 ... 33.11
Williams, Re, Williams v Williams [1897] 2 Ch 12, 66 LJ Ch 485, 45 WR 519, 41 Sol Jo 452, 76 LT 600, CA ... 91.1, 200.22
Williams, Re, Williams v Williams [1907] 1 Ch 180, 76 LJ Ch 41, 51 Sol Jo 68, 95 LT 759 ... 93.35, 93.37, 210.47
Williams, Re, Williams and Glyn's Trust Co Ltd v Williams [1974] 1 All ER 787, [1974] 1 WLR 754, [1974] STC 123, 118 Sol Jo 390, sub nom Williams' Executor v Williams 52 ATC 409, [1973] TR 339 ... 55.7
Williams v Arkle (1875) LR 7 HL 606, 45 LJ Ch 590, 33 LT 187 ... 83.3
Williams v Ashton (1860) 1 John & H 115, 3 LT 148 ... 14.4, 77.1
Williams v Clark (1851) 4 De G & Sm 472 ... 93.27
Williams v Davies, Re Williams (1864) 33 LJPM & A 127, 28 JP 664, 4 New Rep 301, 3 Sw & Tr 437, 10 LT 583 ... 210.17
Williams v Goude (1828) 1 Hag Ecc 577 ... 4.20, 5.9
Williams v Haythorne (1871) 6 Ch App 782 ... 51.10, 65.1, 93.1
Williams v Jekyl (1755) 2 Ves Sen 681 ... 54.5
Williams v Johns [1988] 2 FLR 475, [1988] Fam Law 257 ... 105.16, 105.25

Williams v Jones (1826) 1 Russ 517 .... 47.26
Williams v Jones (1849) 7 Notes of Cases 106 .... 18.18, 18.26
Williams v Knipe (1842) 5 Beav 273 .... 35.51
Williams v Lewis (1859) 6 HL Cas 1013, 28 LJ Ch 505, 5 Jur NS 323, 7 WR 349, 33 LTOS 23 .... 84.4
Williams v Owen (1863) 2 New Rep 585, 9 LT 200 .... 59.3
Williams v Owens (1794) 2 Ves 595 .... 41.22
Williams v Papworth [1900] AC 563, 69 LJPC 129, 83 LT 184 .... 33.18, 94.38
Williams v Roberts [1986] 1 FLR 349, [1984] Fam Law 210 .... 105.18
Williams v Russell (1863) 10 Jur NS 168 .... 65.1, 93.1
Williams v Teale (1847) 6 Hare 239, 77 RR 100 .... 54.5, 94.8, 94.10, 94.15
Williams v Williams (1835) 5 Cl & Fin 111n, 1 Keen 274n, 5 LJ Ch 84 .... 102.23
Williams v Williams (1851) 1 Sim NS 358, 20 LJ Ch 280, 15 Jur 715 .... 79.2
Williams v Williams (1878) 8 Ch D 789, 47 LJ Ch 857, 27 WR 100, 39 LT 180, CA 64.35, 64.36
Williams v Williams (1882) 20 Ch D 659, [1881–5] All ER Rep 840, 51 LJ Ch 385, 46 JP 726, 15 Cox CC 39, 30 WR 438, 46 LT 275 .... 7.33, 202.3
Williams v Wilson (1865) 5 New Rep 267 .... 33.11
Williams' Estate, Re (1985) 36 SASR 423 .... 10.1
Williams' Executor v Williams. See Williams, Re, Williams and Glyn's Trust Co Ltd v Williams
Williams' Goods, Re (1865) LR 1 P & D 4, 35 LJP & M 2, 11 Jur NS 982, 14 WR 111, 13 LT 304 .... 11.12
Williams' Settlement, Re, Greenwell v Humphries [1929] 2 Ch 361, [1929] All ER Rep 632, 98 LJ Ch 358, 73 Sol Jo 384, 141 LT 579, 45 TLR 541, CA 80.3, 80.4, 83.7, 216.30
Williams' Trustees v IRC [1947] AC 447, [1947] 1 All ER 513, 27 TC 409, [1948] LJR 644, 176 LT 462, 63 TLR 352, HL 102.10
Williams' Will Trusts, Re, Rees v Williams [1949] 2 All ER 11, [1949] LJR 1234, 93 Sol Jo 319, 65 TLR 322 .... 97.5
Williamson, Re, Murray v Williamson (1906) 94 LT 813 .... 83.6
Williamson v Farwell (1887) 35 Ch D 128, 56 LJ Ch 645, 36 WR 37, 56 LT 824 .... 40.5, 40.21
Williamson v Jeffreys (1854) 18 Jur 1071 .... 100.2
Williamson v Moore (1862) 8 Jur NS 875, 10 WR 536 .... 71.5, 74.8
Williamson v Naylor (1838) 3 Y & C Ex 208 .... 47.21
Williamson v Ough (Inspector of Taxes) [1936] AC 384, 105 LJKB 193, 20 TC 194, 80 Sol Jo 244, 154 LT 524, HL 216.27
Williamson v Williamson [1974] NI 92 .... 66.13
Williamson's Goods, Re (1902) 46 Sol Jo 552 .... 15.1
Willing v Baine (1731) Kel W 12, 3 P Wms 113 .... 38.13, 97.4, 97.8
Willis, Re, Crossman v Kirkaldy [1917] 1 Ch 365, 86 LJ Ch 336, 61 Sol Jo 233, 115 LT 916 .... 48.8
Willis, Re, Shaw v Willis [1921] 1 Ch 44, 90 LJ Ch 94, 65 Sol Jo 43, 124 LT 290, 37 TLR 43, CA 102.22, 103.1, 103.17
Willis, Re, Spencer v Willis [1911] 2 Ch 563, 81 LJ Ch 8, 55 Sol Jo 598, 105 LT 295 .... 58.12, 59.3, 64.26, 64.57
Willis v Black (1828) 4 Russ 170, 7 LJOS Ch 3 .... 3.2
Willis v Curtois (1838) 1 Beav 189, 8 LJ Ch 105 .... 64.6
Willis v Plaskett (1841) 4 Beav 208, 5 Jur 572 .... 64.35, 64.36, 67.7, 93.29

Willmott v Jenkins (1838) 1 Beav 401 .... 29.14, 29.15
Willmott's Goods, Re (1858) 1 Sw & Tr 36, 6 WR 409, 30 LTOS 370 .... 10.9
Willock v Noble (1875) LR 7 HL 580 .... 4.4
Willoughby, Re, Willoughby v Decies [1911] 2 Ch 581, 80 LJ Ch 562, 104 LT 907, CA 66.7, 100.5
Willoughby v Storer (1870) 18 WR 658, 22 LT 896 .... 15.5
Wills, Re, Dulverton v Macleod [1939] Ch 705, [1939] 2 All ER 775, 108 LJ Ch 286, 83 Sol Jo 438, 160 LT 635, 55 TLR 822 .... 100.5, 237.14
Wills, Re, Wills v Hamilton [1915] 1 Ch 769, 84 LJ Ch 580, [1914–15] All ER Rep 289, 59 Sol Jo 477, 113 LT 138 .... 38.26
Wills, Re, Wills v Wills [1909] 1 IR 268 .... 57.15
Wills v Palmer (1904) 53 WR 169, 49 Sol Jo 165 .... 9.2
Wills v Wills (1875) LR 20 Eq 342, 44 LJ Ch 582, 23 WR 784 .... 52.3, 87.2
Wills' Trust Deeds, Re, Wills v Godfrey [1964] Ch 219, [1963] 1 All ER 390, [1963] 2 WLR 1318, 107 Sol Jo 475 .... 40.10, 101.9
Wills' Will Trusts, Re, Wills v Wills [1959] Ch 1, [1958] 2 All ER 472, [1958] 3 WLR 101, 102 Sol Jo 490 .... 218.94, 218.95, 218.99
Willson v Cobley [1870] WN 46 .... 94.30
Wilmer's Trusts, Re, Moore v Wingfield [1903] 1 Ch 874, 72 LJ Ch 378, 51 WR 395, 47 Sol Jo 336, 88 LT 379; affd [1903] 2 Ch 411, 72 LJ Ch 670, 51 WR 609, 47 Sol Jo 602, 89 LT 148, CA 73.1, 94.4
Wilmot, Re (1861) 29 Beav 644 .... 39.18
Wilmot, Re, Wilmot v Betterton (1897) 45 WR 492, 76 LT 415 .... 85.3, 85.4, 85.5
Wilmot v Flewitt (1865) 11 Jur NS 820, 13 WR 856, 13 LT 90 .... 90.1
Wilmot v Wilmot (1802) 8 Ves 10 .... 67.4
Wilmot's Trusts, Re (1864) 10 LT 563 .... 35.13
Wilson, Re (1891) 14 PR 261 .... 32.21
Wilson, Re (1900) 19 NZLR 406 .... 67.1
Wilson, Re [1954] NZLR 880 .... 32.28, 93.29
Wilson, Re [1958] Qd R 559 .... 41.2
Wilson, Re, Hartley v Marie Curie Hospital [1940] Ch 966, sub nom Re Wilson, Hurtley v Marie Curie Hospital [1940] 4 All ER 57, 109 LJ Ch 413, 84 Sol Jo 537, 164 LT 245, 57 TLR 8 .... 33.45
Wilson, Re, Lothian v Wilson (1920) 89 LJ Ch 216, 64 Sol Jo 389, 123 LT 165 .... 47.12, 47.18
Wilson, Re, Moore v Wilson [1907] 1 Ch 394, 76 LJ Ch 210, 96 LT 453 .... 38.18, 38.23
Wilson, Re, Parker v Winder (1883) 24 Ch D 664, 53 LJ Ch 130 .... 47.31, 87.4
Wilson, Re, Twentyman v Simpson [1913] 1 Ch 314, 82 LJ Ch 161, [1911–13] All ER Rep 1101, 57 Sol Jo 245, 108 LT 321 .... 103.1, 103.6, 103.18
Wilson, Re, Wilson v Batchelor [1907] 1 Ch 450, 76 LJ Ch 228, 96 LT 392; affd [1907] 2 Ch 572, 77 LJ Ch 13, 52 Sol Jo 11, 97 LT 656, CA 77.4
Wilson, Re, Wilson v Mackay [1967] Ch 53, [1966] 2 All ER 867, [1966] 3 WLR 365, 110 Sol Jo 605 .... 30.3, 38.3, 210.7
Wilson, Re, Wilson v Wilson [1908] 1 Ch 839, 77 LJ Ch 564, 98 LT 828 .... 92.2
Wilson v Barnes (1886) 38 Ch D 507, CA 102.10
Wilson v Bayly (1760) 3 Bro Parl Cas 195, HL 56.8
Wilson v Beddard (1841) 12 Sim 28, 10 LJ Ch 305, 5 Jur 624 .... 11.13
Wilson v Duguid (1883) 24 Ch D 244, 53 LJ Ch 52, 31 WR 945, 49 LT 124 .... 101.9
Wilson v Eden (1848) 11 Beav 237, 17 LJ Ch 459, 12 Jur 488; on appeal sub nom Eden v Wilson (1852) 4 HL Cas 257 .... 50.2, 52.2, 64.32, 64.33

Wilson v Eden (1852) 16 Beav 153, 20 LTOS 13 .... 64.32
Wilson v Knox (1884) 13 LR Ir 349 .... 93.26, 93.34, 93.39
Wilson v Maddison (1843) 2 Y & C Ch Cas 372, 12 LJ Ch 420, 7 Jur 572, 1 LTOS 336 .... 32.5, 82.5
Wilson v Mount (1854) 19 Beav 292, 2 WR 448 .... 66.2
Wilson v O'Leary (1872) 7 Ch App 448, 41 LJ Ch 342, 20 WR 501, 26 LT 463, CA 88.4
Wilson v Piggott (1794) 2 Ves 351 .... 40.3, 100.2
Wilson v Spencer, Wilson v Smith (1732) Cooke Pr Cas 72, sub nom Wilson v Spencer 3 P Wms 172 .... 30.31
Wilson v Squire (1842) 1 Y & C Ch Cas 654 .... 57.20, 103.7
Wilson v Squire (1842) 13 Sim 212, 12 LJ Ch 139 .... 29.14
Wilson v Toronto General Trust Corpn and Saskatchewan University Board of Governors [1954] 3 DLR 136, 12 WWRNS 302 .... 102.8
Wilson v Wilson (1847) 1 De G & Sm 152, 11 Jur 793, 9 LTOS 291 .... 8.7, 46.1, 64.57
Wilson v Wilson (1851) 1 Sim NS 288, 20 LJ Ch 365, 15 Jur 349 .... 95.2
Wilson v Wilson (1858) 28 LJ Ch 95, 4 Jur NS 1076, 7 WR 26, 32 LTOS 122 .... 94.25
Wilson's Estate, Re, Wilson v Coleclough [1952] P 92, [1952] 1 All ER 852, [1952] 1 Lloyd's Rep 292, 96 Sol Jo 231, [1952] 1 TLR 911 .... 16.3
Wilson's Goods, Re (1866) LR 1 P & D 269, 36 LJP & M 1, 15 WR 229, 15 LT 191 .... 12.11, 12.14
Wilson's Will, Re [1935] 2 WWR 111 .... 38.3
Wilson's Will, Re [1954] 3 DLR 161, [1954] 11 WWRNS 497 .... 33.23
Wilton, Re [1958] Qd R 559 .... 58.2
Wiltshire, Re, Eldred v Comport (1916) 142 LT Jo 57 .... 83.7
Wiltshire v Rabbits (1844) 14 Sim 76, 13 LJ Ch 284, 8 Jur 769 .... 33.1
Wimperis, Re, Wicken v Wilson [1914] 1 Ch 502, 83 LJ Ch 511, 58 Sol Jo 304, 110 LT 477 .... 46.2, 46.3, 241.16
Winans v A-G [1904] AC 287, [1904–7] All ER Rep 410, 73 LJKB 613, 90 LT 721, 20 TLR 510, HL 236.10
Winchester's (Marquess) Case (1598) 6 Co Rep 23a 4.10
Winchilsea v Wauchope (1827) 3 Russ 441, 5 LJOS Ch 167 .... 12.6
Windham, Re (1862) 4 De GF & J 53, 31 LJ Ch 720, 8 Jur NS 448, 10 WR 499, 6 LT 479 .... 4.20
Windsor, Re, Public Trustee v Windsor (1913) 57 Sol Jo 555, 108 LT 947, 29 TLR 562 .... 64.35, 64.38
Windus v Windus (1856) 6 De GM & G 549, 26 LJ Ch 185, 2 Jur NS 1101, 28 LTOS 31 .... 30.1, 38.12
Wing v Angrave. See Underwood v Wing
Wing v Wing (1876) 24 WR 878, 34 LT 941 .... 68.2
Wingfield v Newton (1739) 2 Coll 520n, 9 Mod Rep 428 .... 41.13
Wingfield v Wingfield (1878) 9 Ch D 658, 47 LJ Ch 768, 26 WR 711, 39 LT 227 .... 56.5, 68.12
Wingham, Re, Andrews v Wingham [1949] P 187, [1948] 2 All ER 908, [1949] LJR 695, 92 Sol Jo 660, 64 TLR 594, CA 16.2
Wingrove v Wingrove (1885) 11 PD 81, 50 JP 56, 55 LJP 7, 34 WR 260 .... 5.9
Wingrove's Goods, Re (1850) 15 Jur 91, 16 LTOS 347 .... 14.6
Wink's Executors v Tallent 1947 SC 470 .... 102.23

Winn, Re, Brook v Whitton [1910] 1 Ch 278, 79 LJ Ch 165, [1908–10] All ER Rep 593, 101 LT 737 .... 66.5, 77.3, 77.4
Winn, Re, Burgess v Winn (1916) 86 LJ Ch 124, [1916–17] All ER Rep 758, 61 Sol Jo 99, 115 LT 698 .... 71.1
Winn v Fenwick (1849) 11 Beav 438, 18 LJ Ch 337, 13 Jur 996, 13 LTOS 155 .... 101.9
Winn's Goods, Re (1861) 7 Jur NS 764, 2 Sw & Tr 147, 9 WR 852, 4 LT 655 .... 1.5
Winslow, Re, Frere v Winslow (1890) 45 Ch D 249, 60 LJ Ch 20, 39 WR 120, 63 LT 485 .... 29.11, 29.14, 31.10
Winter, Re [1926] VLR 300, 48 ALT 23, [1926] Argus LR 288 .... 12.5
Winter v Crichton (1991) 23 NSWLR 116 .... 5.9
Winter v Winter (1846) 5 Hare 306, 16 LJ Ch 111, 11 Jur 10, 8 LTOS 252, 5 Notes of Cases 2n 7.22, 20.4
Winterstoke's Will Trusts, Re, Gunn v Richardson [1938] Ch 158, [1937] 4 All ER 63, 107 LJ Ch 122, 81 Sol Jo 882, 158 LT 404, 54 TLR 20 .... 216.37
Winterton v Crawfurd (1830) 1 Russ & M 407, 8 LJOS Ch 134 .... 67.4
Wintle, Re, Tucker v Wintle [1896] 2 Ch 711, 65 LJ Ch 863, 45 WR 91, 75 LT 207 .... 93.39
Wintle v Nye [1959] 1 All ER 552, [1959] 1 WLR 284, 103 Sol Jo 220, HL 5.1, 5.2, 5.3, 5.4, 5.9
Wintour v Clifton (1856) 8 De GM & G 641, 26 LJ Ch 218, 3 Jur NS 74, 5 WR 129, 28 LTOS 194 .... 42.5
Winzar, Re, Public Trustee v Winzar (1953) 55 WALR 35 .... 35.33, 79.4, 81.3, 81.4
Wipperman, Re, Wissler v Wipperman [1955] P 59, [1953] 1 All ER 764, [1953] 2 WLR 706, 97 Sol Jo 231 .... 18.12
Wisden v Wisden (1854) 18 Jur 1090, 2 Sm & G 396, 2 WR 616, 24 LTOS 250 .... 47.12, 83.1, 86.7
Wise, Re, Jackson v Parrott [1896] 1 Ch 281, 65 LJ Ch 281, 44 WR 310, 73 LT 743 .... 94.38
Witham, Re [1938] 3 DLR 142 .... 18.18, 18.29
Witham v Witham (1861) 3 De GF & J 758, 30 LJ Ch 888, 9 WR 854, 5 LT 133 .... 96.7
Wither v King. See King v Withers
Withy v Mangles (1841) 4 Beav 358; affd (1843) 10 Cl & Fin 215, 8 Jur 69, HL 77.1
Witkowska v Kaminski [2006] EWHC 1940 (Ch), [2006] 3 FCR 250, [2007] 1 FLR 1547, [2006] All ER (D) 357 (Jul) 105.14, 105.18
Witts v Boddington (1789) cited in 5 Ves 503 .... 101.9
Witty, Re, Wright v Robinson [1913] 2 Ch 666, 83 LJ Ch 73, 58 Sol Jo 30, 109 LT 590, CA 40.21, 94.49
Wohlgemuth, Re, Public Trustee v Wohlgemuth [1949] Ch 12, [1948] 2 All ER 882, [1949] LJR 231, 92 Sol Jo 660, 64 TLR 587 .... 72.2
Wokingham Fire Brigade Trusts, Re, Martin v Hawkins [1951] Ch 373, [1951] 1 All ER 454, 49 LGR 335, 115 JP 159, 95 Sol Jo 137, [1951] 1 TLR 446 .... 102.10
Wolfe v Wolfe [1902] 2 IR 246 .... 1.3, 10.1
Wolfe's Goods, Re [1919] 2 IR 491 .... 38.3, 64.17, 64.18
Wolff's Estate, Re (1960) 32 WWR 550 .... 30.14

Wolffe's Will Trusts, Re, Shapley v Wolffe [1953] 2 All ER 697, [1953] 1 WLR 1211, 97 Sol Jo 539 .... 34.3, 34.18, 34.19
Wollaston v King (1869) LR 8 Eq 165, 38 LJ Ch 61, 392, 17 WR 641, 20 LT 1003 .... 40.5, 42.2, 42.3, 94.30, 94.44, 94.48
Wollaston's Goods, Re (1845) 3 Notes of Cases 599 .... 22.3
Wolson, Re, Wolson v Jackson [1939] Ch 780, [1939] 3 All ER 852, 108 LJ Ch 399, 83 Sol Jo 605, 161 LT 168, 55 TLR 923 .... 47.12, 47.18
Wolstenholme, Re, Marshall v Aizlewood (1881) 39 WR 414, 43 LT 752 .... 99.1, 99.5
Wolverhampton and Staffordshire Banking Co v George (1883) 24 Ch D 707 .... 46.3
Wolverton Mortgaged Estates, Re (1877) 7 Ch D 197, sub nom Re Woolverton Mortgaged Estates 47 LJ Ch 127, 26 WR 138, 37 LT 573 .... 57.22
Wombwell v Hanrott (1851) 14 Beav 143, 20 LJ Ch 581, 18 LTOS 60 .... 100.2
Wong v Wong [2003] WTLR 1161 .... 6.2
Wong Kee Kit, Re (1956) 7 DLR 124 .... 53.5
Wong Oi King v Lai Lok Yee Catherine [2003] 4 HKC 438 .... 10.4
Wood, Re [1943] 3 DLR 84, [1943] OR 278 .... 33.12
Wood, Re [1952] VLR 450 .... 38.3
Wood, Re, Hardy v Hull (1923) 68 Sol Jo 186, 130 LT 408 .... 67.2, 67.3, 67.7
Wood, Re, Moore v Bailey (1880) 29 WR 171, 43 LT 730 .... 66.5, 96.1
Wood, Re, Tullett v Colville [1894] 3 Ch 381, 63 LJ Ch 790, 7 R 495, 71 LT 413, CA 94.11, 94.13, 94.37
Wood, Re, Ward v Wood (1886) 32 Ch D 517, 55 LJ Ch 720, 34 WR 788, sub nom Re Wood's Estate, Wood v Ward 54 LT 932 .... 43.6, 100.7
Wood, Re, Wodehouse v Wood [1913] 1 Ch 303, 82 LJ Ch 203, 57 Sol Jo 265, 108 LT 31; affd [1913] 2 Ch 574, 83 LJ Ch 59, 57 Sol Jo 835, 109 LT 347, CA 100.3
Wood, Re, Wood v Wood [1902] 2 Ch 542, 71 LJ Ch 723, 50 WR 695, 46 Sol Jo 632, 87 LT 316, 18 TLR 710, CA 50.3, 72.3
Wood v Baron (1801) 1 East 259 .... 85.2
Wood v Briant (1742) 2 Atk 521 .... 44.17
Wood v Drew (1864) 33 Beav 610 .... 53.4, 93.7
Wood v Gaynon (1761) Amb 395, sub nom Gaynon v Wood 1 Dick 331, 1 P Wms 410n 44.15, 61.1
Wood v Penoyre (1807) 13 Ves 325 .... 30.31, 32.4, 32.5
Wood v Richardson (1840) 4 Beav 174, 5 Jur 623 .... 82.5
Wood v Smith [1993] Ch 90, [1991] 2 All ER 939, [1991] 3 WLR 514; affd [1993] Ch 90, [1992] 3 All ER 556, [1992] 3 WLR 583, [1992] 17 LS Gaz R 43, 136 Sol Jo LB 99, CA 4.11, 11.10, 11.11
Wood v Wood (1811) 1 Phillim 357 .... 4.11
Wood v Wood (1861) 23 D 338 .... 66.5
Wood v Wood (1866) 35 Beav 587 .... 97.5
Wood v Wood (1867) LR 1 P & D 309, 31 JP 567, 36 LJP & M 34, 15 LT 593 .... 18.13
Wood's Estate, Re, Wood v Ward (1886). See Wood. Re, Ward v Wood
Wood's Will, Re (1861) 29 Beav 236 .... 18.33, 20.5, 38.13
Wood's Will, Re (1862) 31 Beav 323 .... 47.32, 68.6
Wood's Will Trusts, Re, Wood v Donnelly [1952] Ch 406, [1952] 1 All ER 740, 96 Sol Jo 261, [1952] 1 TLR 670 .... 35.40, 206.27, 235.27

Woodard v Woodard [1995] 3 All ER 980, [1992] RTR 35, [1997] 1 FCR 533, [1996] 1 FLR 399, [1991] Fam Law 470, CA 1.15
Woodburne v Woodburne (1850) 3 De G & Sm 643, 19 LJ Ch 88, 14 Jur 565, 15 LTOS 21 .... 96.7
Woodburne v Woodburne (1853) 23 LJ Ch 336, 18 Jur 184, 2 WR 131, 22 LTOS 314 .... 97.6
Woodcock v Renneck (1841) 4 Beav 190; affd (1842) 1 Ph 72, 11 LJ Ch 110, 6 Jur 138 .... 40.2, 47.37
Woodgate v Atkins. See Woodgate v Unwin
Woodgate v Unwin (1831) 4 Sim 129, sub nom Woodgate v Atkins 9 LJOS Ch 166 .... 86.4
Woodhall (Woodhall's Personal Representative) v IRC [2000] STC (SCD) 558 .... 208.34, 208.40
Woodhams, Re, Lloyds Bank Ltd v London College of Music [1981] 1 All ER 202, [1981] 1 WLR 493, 125 Sol Jo 275 .... 102.8, 103.1, 103.11, 103.18
Woodhead v Perpetual Trustee Co Ltd (1987) 11 NSWLR 267 .... 4.15
Woodhouse, Re, Public Trustee v Woodhouse [1941] Ch 332, [1941] 2 All ER 265, 110 LJ Ch 214, 85 Sol Jo 367, 165 LT 368, 57 TLR 598 ... 38.17, 38.22, 38.23, 38.25
Woodhouse v Balfour (1887) 13 PD 2, 52 JP 7, 57 LJP 22, 36 WR 368, 58 LT 59 .... 13.2
Woodhouse v Herrick (1855) 1 K & J 352, 24 LJ Ch 649, 3 Eq Rep 817, 3 WR 303 .... 34.2, 35.39, 66.23, 93.3
Woodhouse v Meredith (1816) 1 Mer 450 .... 64.32
Woodhouselee (Lord) v Dalrymple (1817) 2 Mer 419 .... 72.2
Woodin, Re, Woodin v Glass [1895] 2 Ch 309, 64 LJ Ch 501, 12 R 302, 43 WR 615, 39 Sol Jo 558, 72 LT 740, CA 32.3, 32.15, 32.21, 210.46
Woodington's Goods, Re (1839) 2 Curt 324 .... 11.6
Woodisse, Re (1943) 3 DLR 385, [1943] OR 365 .... 35.21
Woodman v Blake (1691) 2 Vern 222 .... 34.25
Woodright v Wright (1717) 10 Mod Rep 370, sub nom Goodright v Wright 1 P Wms 397, 1 Stra 25 .... 47.23
Woodroofe v Woodroofe [1894] 1 IR 299, 28 ILT 304 .... 97.2, 97.5, 97.6
Woods, Re [1947] 4 DLR 386, [1947] OR 753, [1947] OWN 738 .... 37.2
Woods, Re, Gabellini v Woods [1904] 2 Ch 4, 73 LJ Ch 204, 48 Sol Jo 207, 90 LT 8 .... 38.19
Woods, Re, Woods v Creagh [1931] 2 Ch 138, 100 LJ Ch 385, [1931] All ER Rep 696, 145 LT 206 .... 38.13, 47.28, 47.29
Woods v Townley (1853) 11 Hare 314, 23 LJ Ch 281, 1 WR 504, 22 LTOS 75 .... 34.24, 35.19
Woods v Woods (1836) 1 My & Cr 401, Donnelly 61, 43 RR 214 .... 79.1, 82.5
Woods' Goods, Re (1868) LR 1 P & D 556, 32 JP 168, 37 LJP & M 23, 16 WR 407, 17 LT 583 .... 25.1
Woodward v Glasbrook (1700) 2 Vern 388 .... 56.2, 90.1
Woodward's Goods, Re (1871) LR 2 P & D 206, 35 JP 216, 40 LJP & M 17, 19 WR 448, 24 LT 40 .... 18.23
Woolcomb v Woolcomb (1731) 2 Eq Cas Abr 326, 3 P Wms 112 .... 38.10, 64.25
Woolf, Re, Public Trustee v Lazarus [1920] 1 Ch 184, 89 LJ Ch 11, 122 LT 457 .... 61.1, 93.18

Woolley v Clark (1822) 5 B & Ald 744, 1 Dow & Ry KB 409, [1814–23] All ER Rep 584 .... 25.14
Woolley, Re, Cathcart v Eyskens [1918] 1 Ch 33, 87 LJ Ch 169, 117 LT 511 .... 60.1, 64.35
Woolley, Re, Wormald v Woolley [1903] 2 Ch 206, 72 LJ Ch 602, 89 LT 16 .... 68.2, 68.11, 86.2, 86.5
Woolmore v Burrows (1827) 1 Sim 512 .... 94.15
Woolrich, Re, Harris v Harris (1879) 11 Ch D 663, 48 LJ Ch 321, 27 WR 429, 41 LT 309 .... 68.9
Woolridge v Woolridge (1859) John 63, 28 LJ Ch 689, 5 Jur NS 566, 33 LTOS 254 .... 42.4
Woolverton Mortgaged Estates, Re. See Wolverton Mortgaged Estates, Re
Wootton's Will Trusts, Re, Trotter v Duffin [1968] 2 All ER 618, [1968] 1 WLR 681, 112 Sol Jo 174 .... 50.4, 53.6, 102.23
Wordingham v Royal Exchange Trust Co Ltd [1992] Ch 412, [1992] 3 All ER 204, [1992] 2 WLR 496, [1992] 17 LS Gaz R 44 .... 6.2
Wordsworth v Wood (1847) 1 HL Cas 129, 11 Jur 593, 9 LTOS 489 .... 57.5, 67.2, 97.9
Wormald, Re, Frank v Muzeen (1890) 43 Ch D 630, 59 LJ Ch 404, 38 WR 425, 62 LT 423 .... 99.4, 99.5
Wormald v Muzeen (1881) 50 LJ Ch 776, 29 WR 795, 45 LT 115, CA 33.23
Worrell, Re (1970) 8 DLR (3d) 36, [1970] 1 OR 184 .... 4.21
Worsley v Wood (1796) 6 Term Rep 710, [1775–1802] All ER Rep 59 .... 34.21
Worth v Clasohm (1952) 86 CLR 439 .... 4.13
Worthing Corpn v Heather [1906] 2 Ch 532, [1904–7] All ER Rep 530, 75 LJ Ch 761, 4 LGR 1179, 50 Sol Jo 668, 95 LT 718, 22 TLR 750 .... 202.28
Worthington, Re, Nichols v Hart [1933] Ch 771, [1933] All ER Rep 189, 102 LJ Ch 273, 77 Sol Jo 371, 149 LT 296, 49 TLR 444, CA 214.7, 214.9
Worthington v Evans (1823) 1 Sim & St 165, 1 LJOS Ch 126 .... 35.13, 35.16
Worthington v Wiginton (1855) 20 Beav 67, 24 LJ Ch 773, 1 Jur NS 1005, 26 LTOS 34 .... 42.12
Worthington & Co Ltd v Abbott [1910] 1 Ch 588, 79 LJ Ch 252, 54 Sol Jo 83, 101 LT 895 .... 31.15
Worthington's Goods, Re (1871) 36 JP 168, 20 WR 260, 25 LT 853 .... 17.5
Worts v Cubitt (1854) 19 Beav 421, 2 WR 633 .... 72.3
Wotton's Goods, Re (1874) LR 3 P & D 159, 38 JP 328, 43 LJP & M 14, 22 WR 352, [1874–80] All ER Rep 240, 30 LT 75 .... 11.2
Wozciechowiecz Estate, Re (1931) 4 DLR 585, 26 Alta LR 1, [1931] 3 WWR 283 .... 12.6
Wragg, Re, Hollingsworth v Wragg [1959] 2 All ER 717, [1959] 1 WLR 922, 103 Sol Jo 716, CA 32.17, 51.1, 51.2, 93.15
Wragg, Re, Wragg v Palmer [1919] 2 Ch 58, [1918–19] All ER Rep 233, 88 LJ Ch 269, 63 Sol Jo 535, 121 LT 78 .... 29.6, 29.9, 220.29, 220.71, 220.80
Wrangham's Trust, Re (1860) 1 Drew & Sm 358, 30 LJ Ch 258, 7 Jur NS 15, 9 WR 156, 3 LT 722 .... 93.26, 93.43
Wray, Re, Wray v Wray [1951] Ch 425, [1951] 1 All ER 375, 95 Sol Jo 107, CA 18.10, 18.15, 237.11
Wray v Field (1822) 6 Madd 300; affd (1826) 2 Russ 257 .... 88.4
Wren v Bradley (1848) 2 De G & Sm 49, 17 LJ Ch 172, 12 Jur 168, 10 LTOS 438 .... 35.35
Wrench v Jutting (1841) 3 Beav 521, 5 Jur 145 .... 38.3, 38.10

Wrench v Murray (1843) 3 Curt 623, 7 Jur 705, 1 LTOS 412 .... 4.20
Wrenn's Goods, Re [1908] 2 IR 370 .... 5.7
Wrey, Re, Stuart v Wrey (1885) 30 Ch D 507, 24 LJ Ch 1098, 53 LT 334 .... 93.27, 93.31, 93.32, 93.33
Wright, Re [1955] 1 DLR 213, [1954] OR 755, [1954] OWN 685 .... 218.66
Wright (bankrupt), Re, ex p Landau v Trustee [1949] Ch 729, [1949] 2 All ER 605, 93 Sol Jo 679, 65 TLR 564 .... 7.23
Wright, Re, Barclays Bank Ltd v Wright [1952] 2 All ER 698, 31 ATC 433, 45 R & IT 709, [1952] TR 429, [1952] 2 TLR 649 .... 33.47
Wright, Re, Blizard v Lockhart [1954] Ch 347, [1954] 2 All ER 98, [1954] 2 WLR 972, 98 Sol Jo 336, CA 102.20, 103.3, 103.11, 103.18
Wright, Re, Burrows v Honeysette [1937] 3 WWR 452 .... 1.5
Wright, Re, Hegan v Bloor [1920] 1 Ch 108, 88 LJ Ch 452, [1918–19] All ER Rep 825, 64 Sol Jo 21, 121 LT 549 .... 36.13, 40.15
Wright, Re, Mott v Issott [1907] 1 Ch 231, 76 LJ Ch 89, [1904–7] All ER Rep 169, 51 Sol Jo 47, 95 LT 697 .... 35.2, 35.19, 35.23, 50.3
Wright, Re, Public Trustee v Wright (1937) 81 Sol Jo 1022, 158 LT 368, 54 TLR 153 .... 35.30
Wright, Re, Whitworth v Wright [1906] 2 Ch 288, 75 LJ Ch 500, 54 WR 515, 94 LT 696 .... 42.4
Wright v Callender (1852) 2 De GM & G 652, [1843–60] All ER Rep 508, 21 LJ Ch 787, 16 Jur 647, 19 LTOS 308 .... 33.3, 33.35
Wright v Doe d Tatham (1834) 1 Ad & El 3, 3 LJ Ex 366, 3 Nev & MKB 268 .... 4.20
Wright v Goff (1856) 22 Beav 207, 25 LJ Ch 803, 2 Jur NS 481, 4 WR 522, 27 LTOS 179 .... 40.15
Wright v Marsom [1895] WN 148, 40 Sol Jo 67 .... 56.1
Wright v Morgan [1926] AC 788, 95 LJPC 171, [1926] All ER Rep 201, 135 LT 713 .... 92.1
Wright v Netherwood. See Wright v Sarmuda
Wright v Rogers (1869) LR 1 P & D 678, 33 JP 711, 38 LJP & M 67, 17 WR 833, 27 LT 156 .... 13.2, 13.3
Wright v Sanderson (1884) 9 PD 149, 48 JP 180, 32 WR 560, 50 LT 769, sub nom Re Sanderson, Wright v Sanderson 53 LJP 49, CA 11.26, 13.2
Wright v Sarmuda (1793) 2 Phillim 266n, sub nom Wright v Netherwood 2 Salk 593n 70.1
Wright v Shelton (1853) 18 Jur 445 .... 64.25
Wright v Tatham. See Tatham v Wright
Wright v Wilkin (1860) 2 B & S 232, 31 LJQB 7, 7 Jur NS 441, 10 WR 403, 6 LT 220; affd (1862) 2 B & S 259, 31 LJQB 196, 9 Jur NS 715, 11 WR 101, 6 LT 221 .... 34.4, 91.1, 91.2
Wright v Wright (1750) 1 Ves Sen 409, [1558–1774] All ER Rep 528 .... 56.5, 78.5
Wright v Wright (1852) 21 LJ Ch 775, 19 LTOS 311 .... 93.27
Wright d Burrill v Kemp (1789) 3 Term Rep 470 .... 56.1, 56.6
Wright's Goods, Re (1908) 25 TLR 15 .... 25.2
Wright's Trusts, Re (1857) 3 K & J 419, 112 RR 212 .... 30.42
Wright's Will, Re [1917] VLR 127 .... 62.1
Wrightson, Re, Battie-Wrightson v Thomas [1904] 2 Ch 95, 73 LJ Ch 742, 90 LT 748, CA 35.52, 93.1, 93.2, 94.14
Wrightson v Calvert (1860) 1 John & H 250 .... 58.6, 69.2

Wrightson v Macaulay (1845) 15 LJ Ex 121, 14 M & W 214, 5 LTOS 218 .... 78.3

Wrigley v Lowndes [1908] P 348, 77 LJP 148, 99 LT 879 .... 39.20, 39.22

Wrigley v Sykes (1856) 21 Beav 337, 25 LJ Ch 458, 2 Jur NS 78, 4 WR 228, 26 LTOS 252 .... 49.9

Wroe, Re, Frith v Wilson (1896) 74 LT 302 .... 52.3

Wroughton v Colquhoun (1847) 1 De G & Sm 357, 11 Jur 940 .... 33.2, 33.44

Wu Koon Tai v Wu Yau Loi [1995] 2 HKC 732, HK CA; revsd [1997] AC 179, [1996] 3 WLR 778, [1996] NPC 139, 140 Sol Jo LB 221, [1996] 3 HKC 559, PC 1.8

Wu Man Shan v Registrar of Probate [2006] 2 HKC 106 .... 6.2

Wyatt, Re [1952] 1 All ER 1030, 96 Sol Jo 362, [1952] 1 TLR 1294 .... 18.9

Wyatt, Re, Furniss v Phear (1888) 36 WR 521, 4 TLR 245 .... 57.5, 57.15

Wyatt v Berry [1893] P 5, 62 LJP 28, 1 R 462, 68 LT 416, 9 TLR 36 .... 12.3, 13.3

Wyatt v Ingram (1832) 3 Hag Ecc 466, sub nom Ingram v Wyatt 1 LJ Ch 135 .... 5.9

Wykes, Re, Riddington v Spencer [1961] Ch 229, [1961] 2 WLR 115, 105 Sol Jo 109, sub nom Re Wykes' Will Trusts, Riddington v Spencer [1961] 1 All ER 470 .... 102.24

Wylde's Estate, Re (1852) 2 De GM & G 724, 22 LJ Ch 87, 16 Jur 1029, 1 WR 9, 20 LTOS 162 .... 86.5

Wyles, Re, Foster v Wyles [1938] Ch 313, [1938] 1 All ER 347, 107 LJ Ch 164, 82 Sol Jo 95, 54 TLR 336, sub nom Re Wyles, Porter v Wyles 158 LT 147 .... 32.29, 32.32

Wylie v Wylie (1860) 1 De GF & J 410, 29 LJ Ch 341, 6 Jur NS 259, 8 WR 316, 1 LT 533; affd sub nom Enohin v Wylie (1862) 10 HL Cas 1, 31 LJ Ch 402, 8 Jur NS 897, 10 WR 467, 6 LT 263, [1861–73] All ER Rep Ext 2305 .... 51.3, 52.11, 64.40

Wylie's Trustees v Bruce (1919) 56 SLR 156, 1919 SC 211, 1919 1 SLT 41 ... 66.1, 78.2

Wynch v Wynch (1788) 1 Cox Eq Cas 433 .... 32.20

Wynch's Trusts, Re, ex p Wynch (1854) 5 De GM & G 188, 23 LJ Ch 930, 2 Eq Rep 1025, 18 Jur 659, 2 WR 570, 23 LTOS 259 .... 49.4, 51.4, 84.4

Wyndham v Wyndham (1789) 3 Bro CC 58 .... 32.15

Wyndham's Trusts, Re (1865) LR 1 Eq 290 .... 83.16, 98.3

Wynn, Re, Landolt v Wynn [1983] 3 All ER 310, [1984] 1 WLR 237, 128 Sol Jo 34 .... 93.23, 101.2

Wynn v Skegness UDC [1966] 3 All ER 336, [1967] 1 WLR 52, 12 RRC 220, 130 JP 404 .... 102.2, 102.12

Wynn's Will Trusts, Re, Public Trustee v Newborough [1952] Ch 271, [1952] 1 All ER 341, 96 Sol Jo 120, [1952] 1 TLR 278 .... 35.38, 49.8, 202.7, 221.18

Wynne v Fletcher (1857) 24 Beav 430 .... 34.11, 34.23, 35.19, 35.22

Wynne v Wynne (1837) 2 Keen 778, 7 LJ Ch 45 .... 62.1

Wynne v Wynne (1840) 10 LJCP 23, Drinkwater 52, 4 Jur 1114, 2 Man & G 8, 2 Scott NR 278, 133 ER 642 .... 34.11, 35.45

Wytcherley v Andrews (1871) LR 2 P & D 327, 35 JP 552, 40 LJP & M 57, 19 WR 1015, 25 LT 134 .... 43.4

X

X v A [2005] EWHC 2706 (Ch), [2006] 1 All ER 952, [2006] 1 WLR 741, [2006] 2 P & CR D7, [2006] 3 FCR 148, (2006) Times, 10 January, [2005] All ER (D) 379 (Nov) 218.98
X v Woolcombe Yonge [2001] WTLR 301 .... 223.1

Y

Yalden, Re (1851) 1 De GM & G 53 .... 34.6, 83.8
Yardley v Yardley (1858) 26 Beav 38 .... 91.5
Yarmie v Panchyshyn [1952] 3 DLR 693, 6 WWR 173 .... 82.2
Yates, ex p (1869) 17 WR 872, 20 LT 940 .... 64.45
Yates, Re, Bostock v D'Eyncourt [1891] 3 Ch 53, 39 WR 573, 64 LT 819 .... 68.13, 86.5
Yates, Re, Singleton v Povah (1922) 128 LT 619, 66 Sol Jo 523 .... 20.4, 52.11, 237.11
Yates, Re, Throckmorton v Pike (1907) 96 LT 758, CA 32.4
Yates, Re, Yates v Wyatt [1901] 2 Ch 438, 70 LJ Ch 725, 49 WR 646, 45 Sol Jo 652, 85 LT 398 .... 33.18
Yates v Compton (1725) 2 Eq Cas Abr 457, 2 P Wms 308, Cas temp King 54 .... 33.5
Yates v Maddan (1851) 21 LJ Ch 24, 16 Jur 45, 3 Mac & G 532 .... 33.12
Yates v Thomson (1835) 3 Cl & Fin 544, sub nom Yeats v Thomson 1 Sh & Macl 795, HL 49.7, 57.3
Yates v University College, London (1873) 8 Ch App 454; on appeal (1875) LR 7 HL 438, 45 LJ Ch 137, 23 WR 408, 32 LT 43 .... 34.2, 34.7, 102.8
Yates v Yates (1860) 28 Beav 637, 29 LJ Ch 872, 6 Jur NS 1023, 3 LT 9 .... 38.25, 38.27
Yates v Yates (1905) 25 NZLR 263 .... 85.3, 99.1
Yates's Estate, Re [1919] P 93, 88 LJP 92, 63 Sol Jo 355, 120 LT 671, 35 TLR 301 .... 16.1, 51.5, 54.4
Yates's Trust, Re (1851) 21 LJ Ch 281, 16 Jur 78, 18 LTOS 298 .... 97.9
Yaxley v Gotts [2000] Ch 162, [2000] 1 All ER 711, [1999] 3 WLR 1217, 79 P & CR 91, [1999] 2 FLR 941, [1999] Fam Law 700, 32 HLR 547, [1999] EGCS 92, 78 P & CR D33, CA 2.8, 3.4
Yeap Cheah Neo v Ong Cheng Neo (1875) LR 6 PC 381 .... 8.7, 79.2, 94.1
Yearwood, Re (1982) 30 SASR 169 .... 25.4
Yearwood v Yearwood (1846) 9 Beav 276, 10 Jur 151 .... 53.5, 57.9
Yeats v Thomson. See Yates v Thomson
Yelland, Re, Broadbent v Francis (1975) 119 Sol Jo 562 .... 18.12
Yerburgh, Re, Yerburgh v Yerburgh [1928] WN 208 .... 9.40, 27.15
Yockney v Hansard (1844) 3 Hare 620, 8 Jur 822 .... 33.10, 44.1, 88.2
Yonge v Furse. See Younge v Furse
Young, Re (1915) 34 NZLR 950 .... 11.12
Young, Re [1928] 2 DLR 966, 62 OLR 275 .... 77.1
Young, Re [1969] NZLR 454 .... 12.5, 13.1
Young, Re, Brown v Hodgson [1912] 2 Ch 479, 81 LJ Ch 817, 107 LT 380 .... 33.24, 33.26, 62.2
Young, Re, Fraser v Young [1913] 1 Ch 272, 82 LJ Ch 171, 57 Sol Jo 265, 108 LT 292, 29 TLR 224 .... 46.4

Young, Re, Public Trustee v Walker [1920] 2 Ch 427, 89 LJ Ch 614, 64 Sol Jo 615, 124 LT 59 .... 38.2, 39.4
Young, Re, Trustees, Executors and Agency Co Ltd v Wilson [1925] VLR 672, 47 ALT 82, 31 Argus LR 485 .... 87.2
Young, Re, Young v Young [1914] 1 Ch 581; affd [1914] 1 Ch 976, 83 LJ Ch 453, 111 LT 265, CA 100.4
Young, Re, Young v Young [1951] Ch 185, 94 Sol Jo 762, sub nom Re Young's Will Trusts, Young v Young [1950] 2 All ER 1040 .... 104.14
Young, Re, Young v Young [1951] Ch 344, [1950] 2 All ER 1245, 94 Sol Jo 839, [1951] 1 TLR 262 .... 9.4, 34.4, 36.9, 38.3, 64.25, 102.7
Young v Bain, Re Young (1902) 21 NZLR 503 .... 63.1
Young v Burdett (1724) 5 Bro Parl Cas 54, HL 52.8
Young v Davies (1863) 2 Drew & Sm 167, 32 LJ Ch 372, 9 Jur NS 399, 1 New Rep 419, 11 WR 452, 8 LT 80 .... 9.9, 76.6, 84.4
Young v Elworthy (1833) 1 My & K 215 .... 49.7
Young v Hassard (1841) 1 Dr & War 638 .... 18.14
Young v Holloway [1895] P 87, [1891–4] All ER Rep Ext 1478, 64 LJP 55, 11 R 596, 43 WR 429, 72 LT 118, 11 TLR 128 .... 25.16, 43.4
Young v Lord Waterpark (1842) 13 Sim 199, 11 LJ Ch 367, 6 Jur 656; affd (1845) 15 LJ Ch 63, 10 Jur 1, 6 LTOS 517 .... 32.33
Young v Midland Rly Co (1892) 16 OR 738 .... 61.1
Young v Richards (1839) 2 Curt 371 .... 4.20
Young v Robertson (1862) 8 Jur NS 825, 4 Macq 314, HL 50.21, 67.2, 97.10
Young v Sealey [1949] Ch 278, [1949] 1 All ER 92, [1949] LJR 529, 93 Sol Jo 58 .... 1.3, 1.9, 10.1
Young v Sheppard (1847) 10 Beav 207, 16 LJ Ch 247, 9 LTOS 331 .... 89.1
Young v Young (1918) 52 ILT 40 .... 83.12, 85.3
Young's Estate, Re (1934) 103 LJP 75, 78 Sol Jo 431, 151 LT 221, 50 TLR 424 .... 203.30
Young's Settlement Trusts, Re, Royal Exchange Assurance v Taylor-Young [1959] 2 All ER 74, [1959] 1 WLR 457, 103 Sol Jo 328 .... 48.5, 48.8
Young's Trustees v M'Nab etc (1883) 10 R 1165, 20 SLR 789 .... 76.1
Young's Trustees v Shelton's Executors 1937 SC 28 .... 33.13
Young's Will Trusts, Re, Westminster Bank Ltd v Sterling [1955] 3 All ER 689, [1955] 1 WLR 1269, 99 Sol Jo 873 .... 102.15
Young's Will Trusts, Re, Young v Young [1950] 2 All ER 1040. See Young, Re, Young v Young [1951] Ch 185 Younge v Furse (1857) 8 De GM & G 756, sub nom Yonge v Furse 26 LJ Ch 352, 3 Jur NS 603, 5 WR 394, 29 LTOS 34 .... 35.2, 35.3, 91.5
Younghusband v Gisborne (1844) 1 Coll 400; affd (1846) 15 LJ Ch 355, 10 Jur 419, 66 RR 120, 7 LTOS 221 .... 33.18
Yule's Trustees v Deans 1919 SC 570 .... 93.2, 93.15

Z

Zamet v Hyman [1961] 3 All ER 933, [1961] 1 WLR 1442, 105 Sol Jo 911, CA 3.5
Zehr, Re [1944] 2 DLR 670, [1944] OWN 334 .... 74.1
Zeis's Will, Re (1877) 3 VLR 110 .... 25.2

Zerny's Will Trusts, Re, Symons v Zerny [1968] Ch 415, [1968] 1 All ER 686, [1968] 2 WLR 1066, 111 Sol Jo 927, CA 92.1
Zimmer's Estate, Re (1924) 40 TLR 502 .... 14.13, 19.1
Zouche (Baroness), Re, Dugdale v Baroness Zouche [1919] 2 Ch 178, 88 LJ Ch 274, 63 Sol Jo 554, 121 LT 82 .... 63.1, 64.27, 204.41
Zurowski, Re [1928] 1 DLR 357, [1927] 3 WWR 745, 22 Sask LR 249 .... 5.7

VOLUME 2

Precedents and statutes

PART A

Introductory note

Introductory note

I. General .... [200.1]
- (a) Capacity and freedom from influence .... [200.2]
- (b) Form of will .... [200.9]
- (c) Other points .... [200.27]
- (d) The Trusts of Land and Appointment of Trustees Act 1996 and the Trustee Act 2000 .... [200.48]

II. Inheritance tax ('IHT') .... [200.68]
- (a) Main characteristics .... [200.69]
- (b) Exemptions and reliefs relevant to testamentary dispositions .... [200.84]
- (c) Will trusts .... [200.92]
- (d) Incidence of IHT .... [200.111]
- (e) Partially exempt estates .... [200.112]
- (f) The consequences of IHT for dispositions by will (other than will trusts) .... [200.119]
- (g) Trusts in dispositions by will—usefulness, the alternatives, and tax consequences .... [200.125]
- (h) Review of existing wills after FA 2006 and the Pre-Budget Report of 9 October 2007 .... [200.134]

I. GENERAL

[200.1]
The purpose of this first section of Part A is to mention some of the practical matters that ought to be borne in mind when taking instructions for, preparing and executing wills and codicils. Most of these matters are fully considered in the text as well as in notes to precedents or groups of precedents and it is not proposed to touch on any of them more than briefly here. Nor is it claimed that the matters mentioned below constitute an exhaustive list but only that they are some of the matters more commonly encountered.

(*a*) *Capacity and freedom from influence*

[200.2]
A person's capacity to dispose of his property by will is affected by a number of factors. Most obviously the would-be testator will need to be of full age (now 18 except in the case of privileged wills) and of a sound disposing mind. If instructions for a will are taken in circumstances where an attack on the testator's mental capacity is anticipated, it is a wise precaution for the will to be witnessed if at all possible by the testator's medical attendant and his solicitor and for these witnesses to make statements as to the testator's capacity: see Templeman J's remarks in *Kenward v Adams* [1975] CLY 3591; *Re Simpson* (1977) 121 Sol Jo 224; and see *Buckenham v Dickinson* [1997] CLY 4733. A solicitor may now witness a will appointing him an executor without forfeiting his right to the benefit of a charging clause: Trustee Act 2000 (TrA 2000), ss 28(4)(a) and 35(1) (Part G, paras **[246.160]** and **[246.167]**; see also the commentary at para **[221.42]** ff).

[200.3]
Even if the testator's mental capacity is not in doubt, it is important to make sure that the testator fully and freely intends the dispositions proposed. The testator should be seen on his or her own or, if that is not possible, in the absence of interested parties, and the instructions and attendance notes should be retained, especially where the testator is elderly or infirm, and even more so where the solicitor preparing the will has never acted for the testator before and has been instructed through someone who is a potential beneficiary under the will.

[200.4]
In any subsequent dispute the testator's solicitor may be called upon to give a statement to any interested party: see (1959) 56 Law Society's Gazette 619, and *Re Moss, Larke v Nugus* [2000] WTLR 1033 (also reported sub nom *Larke v Nugus* in (1979) 123 Sol Jo 337), CA. If a solicitor, or indeed any other person, preparing a will takes any substantial interest under it he must see that the testator obtains independent advice (see *Re a Solicitor* [1975] QB 475, [1974] 3 All ER 853; *Tristram and Coote's Probate Practice* (30th edn) LexisNexis Butterworths, para 34.50; and the Solicitors Regulation Authority's 'Solicitors' Code of Conduct 2007', para 3.04).

[200.5]
The Law Society's 'The Guide to the Professional Conduct of Solicitors' (8th edn), para 24.02, has some further guidance in the commentary which should be noted. It states that if the client declines to take independent advice, the solicitor must refuse to act in drawing the will, that it is not sufficient just to have the will witnessed by an independent solicitor, and that the same rules apply to gifts to an employee of a solicitor. It also states that, where the client wishes to leave all or a substantial part of his or her estate to a solicitor to be dealt with in accordance with the testator's wishes as communicated to the solicitor either orally or in a document, or as a secret trust, independent advice is not needed if the solicitor will not benefit personally or financially, but that the solicitor should preserve the instructions (which is a sensible thing to do in relation to any will) and should make sure that the testator signs or initials a statement in writing of 'such secret trust'. It is not entirely clear from this statement whether independent advice is thought by the Law Society to be unnecessary where the solicitor will as a matter of strict law be entitled beneficially to property of the testator but intends in fact to distribute that property to others in accordance with a non-binding request of the testator, and we therefore recommend that independent advice is insisted on where it is proposed that this will be the case. An alternative, which would clearly not require independent advice, would be for the will to create a discretionary trust (under which the solicitor is not a beneficiary), combined with a non-binding memorandum of wishes. For secret trusts see Vol 1, paras **[36.1]**–**[36.13]** and for provision by will for discretionary distribution of chattels see the Preliminary Note on personal chattels in B4 at para **[204.7]**.

[200.6]
It often happens that a solicitor receives instructions to draft wills for husband and wife, which include an instruction that the wife's will is to

contain a gift of all or nearly all her property to the husband if he survives her, but the instructions are communicated wholly by the husband. There is nothing especially suspect or unusual about this, but we do feel that a solicitor should in these circumstances make sure from direct contact with the wife that these really are her instructions.

[200.7]
A foreign domicile (or foreign matrimonial domicile) may affect a would-be testator's power to dispose by will of movables or even of English immovable property: *Re De Nicols, De Nicols v Curlier* [1900] 2 Ch 410. A wife's domicile will almost always be the same as her husband's, but as a result of the enactment of the Domicile and Matrimonial Proceedings Act 1973 this can no longer be taken for granted.

[200.8]
Other restrictions may be dictated by the nature of the testator's assets or of his interest in them (see generally Vol 1, paras **[7.1]**–**[7.32]**). The testator may own foreign property which is not freely alienable under the *lex situs*. He may be entitled to an interest in realty as a beneficial joint tenant in which case he will be unable to dispose of it by will unless he has first severed the joint tenancy (eg by notice) during his lifetime. He may be entitled to a capital sum under a pension scheme over which he has a power of nomination which must be exercised in accordance with the rules of the scheme or in respect of which his power of disposition may be restricted. He may have a limited interest in settled property or have a power of appointment limited to a particular class. In all cases the extent of the testator's property and his power of disposition over it must be carefully considered if possible by reference to the relevant documents.

(*b*) *Form of will*

[200.9]
The will is a flexible instrument capable of accommodating the universal beneficiary at the one extreme and the large discretionary class at the other. Many considerations (some of which have been referred to above) will dictate the form of the will. The extent and nature of the testator's property (and liabilities) and the circumstances and needs of the members of his family or dependants will loom large. Unless a testator has a substantial estate he should be discouraged from making elaborate provision in his will which may make the administration of the estate difficult and expensive. A number of the more common forms of testamentary provision are briefly considered below together with some of the difficulties that may arise in connection with them.

[200.10]
Pecuniary legacies. These are frequently given as a token of friendship or for some charitable purpose which the testator has supported in his lifetime. There is a danger, however, that a testator's generosity in giving legacies may seriously prejudice the interests of the persons interested in residue who will ordinarily either be relatives or dependants. This danger may be aggravated

by the fact that the testator's circumstances may deteriorate between the date of his will and the date of his death and by the fact that he may not fully appreciate either the extent of his existing liabilities or the effect or the incidence of IHT. Where the estate is relatively small or the aggregate amount of the legacies relatively large, provision ought to be made for ensuring that residue does not fall below a certain value. See eg Form B10.54 at para **[210.75]**.

[200.11]
Life interests. Life interests in residue or a settled fund are frequently employed as a means of giving income security to a surviving spouse or other relative, where the capital is intended to go ultimately to another or others. One of the difficulties that life interests pose is that it is not easy to predict what the amount of income is likely to be especially in the case of a life interest in residue. Further the amount of income may fluctuate with changing economic circumstances. One way of protecting the life tenant from a reduction in income is to empower the trustees to resort to capital for the benefit of the life tenant. It should be remembered, however, that such a power may be framed or exercised in such a way as to render capital paid over to the life tenant income in his or her hands and taxable accordingly. For suitable precedents see Forms B18.7 and B18.8 at paras **[218.39]** and **[218.40]** and the notes thereto, and Form C2.3 at paras **[224.58]**–**[224.72]**. For life interest forms in complete wills see, for example, Forms C2.3 at paras **[224.58]** ff or C3.2 at paras **[225.23]** ff. The rules for IHT on settled property subject to a life interest or other interest in possession have been radically altered by FA 2006. Property settled by the testator's will which is subject to a life interest commencing from the testator's death will be subject to IHT as if the settled property is the life tenant's property, but otherwise property settled by will (other than certain trusts for minors or disabled persons) is subject to the IHT 'discretionary trust' or 'relevant property' regime, for which see paras **[200.92]** ff and **[200.126]** ff below. A positive aspect of the change is that there is a wider choice as to tax treatment. In particular, it is possible to have a life interest which is treated as such for income tax purposes while the underlying settled property is for IHT purposes 'relevant property' (for the advantages of relevant property treatment in some circumstances see para **[200.131]**).

[200.12]
Annuities. Testamentary annuities, giving a fixed sum of money each year, were common in the 19th century to make income provision for relatives or other dependants at a time when monetary values were stable. In subsequent times of high inflation annuities naturally ceased to be used very much. Although inflation has declined in recent years, there have been few signs of revival of use of annuities. A section on annuities is retained in Part B11 at para **[211.1]** ff. The grant of an annuity to be charged on property cany create IHT problems which are avoidable if the annuity is provided for in some other way. Income tax considerations also arise. Is the annuity to be paid 'free of tax' and, if so, free of tax at the basic rate or at some higher rate? And what is to become of any tax repayments to which the annuitant may become entitled? These matters are best dealt with by express provision, as in the alternatives in Form B11.3 (at para **[211.10]**).

[200.13]
Specific gifts. Specific gifts of property, though frequently resorted to, are liable to ademption by a subsequent sale or other disposition during the testator's lifetime. This may not matter much where the gift is of some small personal item but where, for example, a specific gift of the testator's residence is adeemed, the testator's calculations (as well as the beneficiary's expectations) may be seriously upset. The testator may wish to include an express provision against such an event and Form B6.16 (at para **[206.25]**) may be used or adapted for this purpose. A testator should be informed that where property is specifically given the donee is liable to discharge any incumbrances, unless express provision is made to the contrary (AEA 1925, s 35: Part G, **[246.62]**). This is a particularly important point where a specific gift of a house which is subject to a mortgage is contemplated. The testator should also be informed that all foreign property prima facie bears its own IHT, though this is now no longer true of UK real property, and has never been true of UK personalty (see the notes on incidence at paras **[214.55]**–**[214.75]**). He may wish to vary the incidence of IHT on specific gifts: see eg Forms B6.30 and B6.31 (at paras **[206.39]** and **[206.40]**) and B14.33 and B.14.34 (at paras **[214.76]** and **[214.77]**).

[200.14]
Personal chattels. Because of the difficulties of keeping track of chattels and keeping them in repair, and because the expense of trust administration is usually out of proportion with the capital value, these should not be settled except in special cases such as high value or strong historical associations. A frequent device is to make an outright gift of such chattels coupled with a non-binding expression of desire as to their distribution. See the Note in B4 (at paras **[204.7]** and **[204.8]**) and Forms B4.6 to B4.11 (at paras **[204.20]**–**[204.25]**).

[200.15]
Business and partnership interests. These call for special care. If it is intended that the business should continue to be run by the beneficiary or the trustees suitable powers must be conferred and sufficient working capital made available. The incidence of IHT and the interaction of business property relief and the spouse exemption, must also be considered. See the Preliminary Note to B5 at paras **[205.1]**–**[205.57]** and the Forms in B5 at paras **[205.58]**–**[205.79]**. See also C11 at para **[233.1]** ff.

[200.16]
Rights of residence. Testators are often as much concerned to provide their dependants with a roof over their heads as to provide income. The use of a strict settlement coupled with a supporting rentcharge is no longer an option: see para **[200.52]**. But it can be effected in a number of other ways, and the Trusts of Land and Appointment of Trustees Act 1996 (TLATA 1996) has simplified the task. For alternative forms for the various options now available and a discussion of their respective merits, see the forms in B8 and the Preliminary Note to it at para **[208.1]** ff. See also the notes on the TLATA 1996 at para **[200.48]** ff.

[200.17]
'Commorientes' provisions. It is a standard professional practice in wills for spouses, civil partners, or any couple living together, to make any gift between them conditional on the donee surviving the donor by a specified period. This is often referred to as a commorientes provision, though survivorship condition is a more accurate description. Where two persons die in a common accident, and are not spouses or civil partners, a survivorship condition in any gift by one to the other avoids the same property being charged to IHT twice (subject to quick succession relief). Where they are spouses or civil partners, on the other hand, because of the IHT exemption for gifts between them (see paras **[200.84]** ff), and the introduction of nil-rate band carry-forward (see para **[200.75]**), it is only in very special circumstances that a survivorship condition can have any IHT advantage, and in some circumstances it could be a disadvantage. We no longer in general recommend their use as between spouses or civil partners: for the details of the reasoning see B19 at para **[219.1]** ff and C2 at paras **[224.6]–[224.10]**. In cases where there are no issue or dependants, imposing a survivorship condition can also avoid the joint estate going entirely to the kin of the survivor, a consequence which neither testator may have envisaged. Even where there is a survivorship condition, this can happen if the second to die survives the relevant period, and it is much better for the dispositions in both wills to be so structured that this does not happen irrespective of the period by which one survives the other: see paras **[219.2]**, **[219.3]** and **[231.2]**.

[200.18]
Discretionary trusts. What is primarily meant by the term 'discretionary trust' is a trust where the income is distributed among a defined class of beneficiaries (or, in some cases, accumulated) at the discretion of the trustees. Such trusts give maximum flexibility, but at the cost of adverse income tax treatment, especially in relation to dividend income (see paras **[218.29]–[218.32]**). Such trusts are normally combined with wide discretionary powers to appoint or apply capital for the benefit of some or all of the beneficiaries, though such powers over capital can also be included in trusts where there are life interests or other fixed interests in income. Once very popular on account of its inherent estate duty advantages, the discretionary trust lost most of its former appeal with the introduction of capital transfer tax (now IHT) by the Finance Act 1975. This Act introduced a system of charging discretionary trusts to tax which was widely considered to be very unfavourable. However, the IHT regime for such trusts was modified considerably in 1982, and was extended to most other categories of trust by FA 2006 (see para **[200.92]** ff). It is now contained in IHTA 1984, Part III, Ch III. Because of the FA 2006 changes, it is more accurate to refer to this IHT regime as the 'relevant property' charging regime rather than the discretionary trust charging regime: see **[200.92]**. The current relevant property regime has caused discretionary trusts to regain some of their popularity, and in many situations it has advantages over other IHT regimes. See further paras **[200.125]** ff and the Note on discretionary trusts in B18 at para **[218.1]** ff, where the circumstances in which a discretionary trust can be advantageous are considered. Some possible uses of discretionary trusts are also mentioned in B4 (at paras **[204.7]** and **[204.8]**) and in the note to Form

C3.6 (at para **[225.83]** ff). Where the reason for wanting a discretionary trust is the IHT treatment it will receive, there is now the alternative of an interest in possession trust which gets 'relevant property' IHT treatment: see **[200.126]**.

[200.19]
Trusts for minors. The former IHT-privileged category of accumulation and maintenance trusts within IHTA 1984, s 71 for minors and young persons has been abolished by FA 2006 for trusts created after 21 March 2006, and in particular for trusts created by the wills of persons dying after that date. FA 2006 created two much more limited categories of IHT-privileged trust for minors, namely trusts for bereaved minors for persons under 18 falling within IHTA 1984 s 71A, and 18-to-25 trusts for persons under 25 falling within IHTA 1984, s 71D: see paras **[200.108]** and **[200.109]** for the details of the qualifying conditions and the advantages. Such trusts can only be created by testamentary provision by the will of a parent or step-parent of the beneficiary or beneficiaries, or by a person with parental responsibility for the beneficiary or beneficiaries. Where any beneficiary under a will may still be a minor when the testator dies, and is a child or stepchild of the testator (or someone he has parental responsibility for), consideration should be given as to whether the trusts for the beneficiary should be so structured as to satisfy s 71A or 71D. See further, paras **[200.108]**, **[200.109]**. For examples see eg Forms C2.1, cl 7, at para **[224.35]** and C2.3, cl 6, at para **[224.65]**. Where these are not available, or, if available, are not wanted, the choice of provision for minor children lies among: immediate post-death interests in possession (see para **[200.98]**), relevant property trusts (see paras **[218.8]** ff), or bare trusts (see para **[200.110]**). For further discussion of the alternatives see paras **[200.131]**, **[200.132]**.

[200.20]
Protective trusts. If a testator is making a will for the benefit of anyone who might become insolvent, it will be a good idea to provide either a protective trust, where the beneficiary has a life interest until he goes bankrupt (or tries to dispose of the interest) to be followed after any such forfeiture by a discretionary trust for him and his family, or a fully discretionary trust from the outset. For appropriate clauses see Forms B16.1 and B16.2 at paras **[216.6]** and **[216.7]** (protective trusts), Form B18.1 at para **[218.31]** (discretionary trusts); and for relevant complete forms, see Forms C3.5 at para **[225.68]** ff and C6.2 at para **[228.19]** ff. For the statutory protective trusts, see the Trustee Act 1925 (TA 1925), s 33 (Part G, para **[246.31]**). For the IHT treatment of protective trusts, see para **[200.104]**.

[200.21]
Additions to existing settlements and referential trusts. It is not uncommon for a testator to wish to transfer property by will to the trustees of an existing settlement rather than settle it on trusts declared by the will itself. It should be noted, however, that the addition of funds to a discretionary settlement made by the testator may be disadvantageous for IHT purposes, particularly if the settlement was made before 27 March 1974; for the rather complex IHT provisions relating to the addition of property to an existing

discretionary settlement see *Foster's Inheritance Tax*, E4.15, E4.33. However, there can be circumstances where it is advantageous to do this, in order to avoid aggregation of the property with other property settled by the will when calculating the IHT rate on subsequent taxable events: see *Foster's Inheritance Tax*, M7.05 If the testator wishes to transfer property by his will to an existing settlement, the draftsman will need to take care to use appropriate language, eg 'I give my residuary estate to the trustees at my death of the settlement made by me on the – to hold on the trusts thereof and as an accretion to the trust fund therein defined for all purposes'. By contrast a gift of property 'on the like trusts as' or 'on similar trusts to' those contained in an existing settlement will not amount to a gift of property to the trustees of that settlement but a declaration of trusts of that property by reference to it, a rather inconvenient result as the trustees of the will will end up holding property on trusts contained not in the will but in another instrument. For examples of gifts of these kinds see Forms B6.22 (at para **[206.31]**), B6.23 (at para **[206.32]**) and B10.31 (at para **[210.45]**) respectively and the notes to those forms.

[200.22]
Precatory words. Testators often wish to make an absolute gift subject to a request, which is not intended to be legally binding, that the donee will use the gift to benefit others. It is important where this is being done to make the intention clear, because words of recommendation, confidence, request or desire have been construed as creating a legally-enforceable trust: see, eg *Comiskey v Bowring-Hanbury* [1905] AC 84, HL (and contrast *Re Williams, Williams v Williams* [1897] 2 Ch 12, CA). The only safe course is to negate any obligation by clear words such as 'I request, without imposing any trust or obligation'. The most common use of precatory words is in gifts of chattels: see, eg Form B4.9 at para **[204.23]**. For the law on whether words of request etc create a trust, see Vol 1, paras **[82.5]–[82.6]**, and Underhill & Hayton, *Law Relating to Trusts and Trustees* (17th edn), paras 8.214 ff. Expressions of wishes may also influence how various provisions of the TLATA 1996 are to operate: see paras **[200.56]**, **[200.62]**, **[208.18]**, sub-para (6) and **[220.57]**.

[200.23]
Ademption, lapse and incidence of IHT and other liabilities. Any one of these may defeat either wholly or partly a testator's intentions. Ademption, mentioned at para **[200.13]**, is fully considered in Vol 1 at para **[41.1]** ff and for a precedent for its exclusion see Form B6.16 at para **[206.25]**. The effect of the incidence of IHT and other liabilities has also been referred to at paras **[200.13]**, **[200.15]** and **[200.16]** and is further considered in the Preliminary Note to Form B14 at paras **[214.55]–[214.71]**. Lapse, which has not so far been mentioned, like ademption, often presents a trap for the unwary testator, for if the donee predeceases him then unless the donee is also a child or issue of the testator and leaves issue surviving the testator, the gift fails and there is no substitution of the donee's issue. If the donee is the testator's spouse or civil partner the gift may fail as a result of a subsequent divorce or dissolution (see para **[200.24]**; see also Vol 1, paras **[47.2]–[47.3]** and the Preliminary Note to Form C2 at para **[224.16]** ff). If the testator's attention

is drawn to these possibilities he may wish to make alternative or substitutional gifts so as to avoid them. These matters are more fully discussed in Vol 1 at para **[68.1]** ff, and for relevant precedents see Forms B6.27 (at para **[206.36]**), B19.5 and B19.6 (at paras **[219.18]** and **[219.19]**) and B19.9 to B19.15 (at paras **[219.22]–[219.28]**).

[200.24]

Wills in favour of spouses or civil partners—whether mutual. Where, as is commonly the case, a husband and wife or civil partners have made at the same time wills in favour of each other and in the same terms mutatis mutandis, the question whether they intended the wills to be mutual wills (see Vol 1, paras **[2.1]–[2.10]**) sometimes arises, often years later after one or both of them have died. Where instructions are being taken for wills to be made at the same time by spouses or civil partners we recommend that they are asked whether they intend the wills to be mutual wills, and, whether they intend mutual wills or intend otherwise, that a declaration as to whichever is intended be included in both wills. It is particularly important to do this where there is any indication that there are circumstances of a sort which can give rise to succession disputes, eg, in the case of spouses, the children being treated unequally, or the marriage being a second marriage for one or both parties and there being issue by a previous marriage. For mutual wills see Form B1.8 at para **[201.13]** and for a declaration making it clear that wills are not mutual, see Form B1.9 at para **[201.14]**.

[200.25]

Wills in favour of spouses or civil partners–effect of divorce. By virtue of the Wills Act 1837, s 18A, added by the Administration of Justice Act 1982, s 18(2) (see Part G, para **[244.18]** for the text of s 18A as currently in force; see also Vol 1, paras **[47.2]–[47.3]** and C2 at para **[224.16]** ff for a commentary on it) a gift by will to the testator's spouse will lapse if the marriage has ended in divorce after the will was made (unless the will shows a contrary intention). For deaths on or after 1 January 1996, the amendments made to s 18A by the Law Reform (Succession) Act 1995, s 3 achieve this by deeming the spouse to have died on the date of the decree of divorce for the purposes of the devolution of property which the spouse was given (or was given an interest in). This means that an alternative gift to the spouse's gift which is expressed to take effect in the event of the spouse predeceasing the testator will take effect if there has been a divorce and the spouse survives the testator (in relation to deaths before 1 January 1996 such an alternative gift did not take effect in these circumstances, see Vol 1, para **[47.2]**). It is not necessary to make express provision for the possibility of divorce in such gifts (or in an alternative appointment of an executor to one in favour of the testator's spouse): for a more detailed discussion see the Preliminary Note to C2 at para **[224.16]** ff. Parallel provision is made for gifts by will to a civil partner of the testator where the civil partnership is dissolved or annulled after the date of the will. The will takes effect as if the civil partner had died on the date of the dissolution or annulment: Wills Act 1837, s 18C, inserted by Civil Partnership Act 2004 ss 71, 263(2), Sch 4 paras 1 and 2 (see Part G, para **[244.20]**).

[200.26]
Wills in favour of spouses or civil partners – IHT. A special factor affecting the provision which a testator should make by will for his spouse or civil partner is the exemption from IHT for gifts to spouses or civil partners, for which see further paras **[200.84]–[200.86].** The former problems of trying to make use of the IHT nil rate band of the testator if he predeceases his spouse or civil partner are being largely eliminated, in cases where the surviving spouse or civil partner dies after 8 October 2007, by the legislation allowing nil-rate band carry-forward which was announced in the Pre-Budget Report of 9 October 2007: see para **[200.75]**.

(*c*) *Other points*

[200.27]
The age of majority. As from 1 January 1970, this was reduced from 21 to 18 by the Family Law Reform Act 1969 (FLRA 1969), s 1 (Part G, para **[246.89]**; see also Vol 1, para **[4.7]**). Testators had in the past very frequently adopted 21 as the age contingency which a beneficiary has to satisfy in order to attain a vested interest. No doubt some testators have begun to adopt 18 instead, but many feel that is too soon for vesting of capital and prefer 21 or 25. However, the FA 2006 changes to IHT and the FA 2004 income tax and capital gains tax provisions for 'trusts for the vulnerable' (see paras **[200.108]** and **[217.4]**) confer, in relation to will trusts for the testator's own minor children, tax advantages where the capital vests absolutely at the age of 18. A will trust for the testator's minor children where the capital vests over the age of 18 but not later than the age of 25 can also have some IHT advantage: see para **[200.109]**. If a testator wishes to enable a minor to be able to give a good receipt then Form B10.19 (at para **[210.32]**), Form B21.18 (at para **[221.22]**) or Form C2.1, cl 8(3) (at para **[224.36]**) may be employed. It should be noted that the ChA 1989, s 3(3) (Part G, para **[244.114]**) provides that a parent or guardian of a minor with 'parental responsibility' for him or her (see Vol 1, para **[28.2]** for the meaning of this term) has the right to receive or recover for the benefit of the minor any property which the minor is entitled to receive or recover. This seems to mean that a trustee or personal representative can always accept a receipt from a parent or guardian with parental responsibility for a minor in respect of income or capital to which that minor is entitled. See also Vol 1, para **[9.42]**.

[200.28]
Children, issue and other words descriptive of relationship. The rules of construction relating to references in wills and other instruments to children and issue and to any other terms used to denote a blood relationship have undergone major reform in recent years. For the development of the new statutory rules and the application of the former rules to existing instruments, reference should be made to Vol 1 (at paras **[72.1]**, **[74.1]** and **[75.1]** ff) and the statutes printed in Part G2 (at para **[245.1]** ff) and the notes thereto. The current position as regards the devolution of property on death, under a will made now, may be summarised as follows:

(a) ***Adoption.*** The governing statute is the Adoption and Children

Act 2002 (ACA 2002), replacing with effect from 30 December 2005 the similar provisions of the Adoption Act 1976 (the relevant provisions of ACA 2002 are printed at paras **[245.92]–[245.101]** and discussed in Vol 1 at paras **[75.1]–[75.7]**). ACA 2002 provides that a child adopted under the Adoption Act 1976 or ACA 2002 or by any adoption recognised as valid by English law is to be treated for the purposes of the devolution of property, whether under a will or on an intestacy, as the legitimate child of his adoptive parent or parents (who can be same-sex couples). Effectively therefore any disability previously attaching to adopted status is removed. The one exception relates to property settled to devolve with a dignity or title of honour.

(b) ***Legitimation.*** The rights of persons who are legitimated by the subsequent marriage of their parents are governed by the Legitimacy Act 1976 (Part G, paras **[245.44]–[245.54]** and considered in Vol 1 at paras **[72.15]–[72.17]**) which provides that for succession purposes legitimated persons are to be treated as if born legitimate. There is a similar saving for property settled to devolve with a dignity or title of honour.

(c) ***Illegitimacy.*** The position is now governed by the Family Law Reform Act 1987 (FLRA 1987) (Part G, paras **[245.70]–[245.81]** and considered in Vol 1 at para **[72.14]**) which again effectively removes any disability to which persons who were either illegitimate or were claiming through illegitimate persons have in the past been subject, and in particular they are treated in the same way as legitimate children of the same parent when it comes to determining who is to benefit under a gift to, eg 'my children' or 'my nephews and nieces', unless a contrary intention is expressed. Again there is a saving for property settled to devolve with a dignity or title of honour. The FLRA 1987 replaces the FLRA 1969 and is wider in some respects than it (see para **[245.69]** for a summary of the main differences), although in the majority of cases where the meaning of a gift in a will is in issue the FLRA 1987 will have no different effect from that which the FLRA 1969 would have had.

(d) ***Artificial insemination and in vitro fertilisation.*** Recent medical developments have resulted in the enactment of special rules concerning the rights of succession of persons born in consequence of artificial insemination or other techniques designed to overcome infertility. These are now to be found in the Human Fertilisation and Embryology Act 1990 (Part G, paras **[245.83]–[245.91]** and considered in Vol 1 at paras **[74.5]–[74.7]**). Where a woman carries a child as a result of the use of any of these techniques, the child is treated as her child in law and no other woman's; her husband (or in certain cases her partner) will be treated as the father unless it is shown that he did not consent to the use of artificial insemination or other technique. If the man and woman are married, the child will seemingly be treated as their legitimate offspring. For the purposes of succession to property it is provided that any enactment, deed, instrument or other document (whenever made) is to be construed in accordance with the rules summarised above with the consequence that a child born as a result of one of the techniques in question will be eligible under a will or on an intestacy as if he were the legitimate or (as the case may be) the illegitimate child of his 'parent' or 'parents'. Again there is a saving for property settled to devolve with a dignity or title of honour.

(e) ***Gender change.*** Under GRA 2004 (Part G, paras **[245.102]** ff and considered in Vol 1 at para **[81.1]**) a change of gender in accordance with that Act has effect for all legal purposes (except under a will or other instrument made before 4 April 2005). This is capable of changing the effect of any gift by will where the designation of the donee or donees is gender specific.

[200.29]

The present position is thus that for all practical purposes children who are adopted, legitimated or illegitimate, and children who are born to 'parents' as a consequence of the medical techniques just mentioned, are treated for succession purposes on an equal footing with legitimate children. In the case of testamentary succession this is subject to any contrary intention being expressed in the particular will. The earlier law on the rights of adopted, legitimated or illegitimate children (Part G, para **[245.1]** ff) remains relevant to the administration of estates or will trusts where the testator died or, in cases involving succession by illegitimate persons, made his will before the law on one or more of the above topics was changed, and to making an appointment under a special power of appointment where the power was created by a will or other instrument to which the earlier law applied (see B13 at para **[213.1]** ff). Where illegitimate persons are involved, the earlier law remains relevant (irrespective of the date of death of the testator) to wills made before the FLRA 1987 came into force on 4 April 1988 (see FLRA 1987, s 19(7): Part G, para **[245.72]**), and, more importantly, to wills made before its predecessor the FLRA 1969 came into force on 1 January 1970 (see FLRA 1969, s 15(8): Part G, para **[245.39]**). It should be noted that a codicil which confirms a will made before one or both of these Family Law Reform Acts came into force does not by the fact of doing so cause the will to be treated as made after that or those Acts came into force (see the Preliminary Note to Part D at para **[237.8]**). By contrast, the rules in the Human Fertilisation and Embryology Act 1990 referred to at para **[200.28]**, sub-para (d) apply to any instrument, whenever made, and this includes all wills irrespective of their date or the date of death of the testator.

[200.30]

Drafting wills using words descriptive of relationship. The statutory rules just mentioned, so far as they relate to adopted or legitimated children, or ones born as a result of the use of the medical techniques referred to above, will normally reflect what the testator would have wished anyway. This will not always be the case for the statutory rules relating to illegitimate children. The draftsman will need to bear in mind the new statutory rules, particularly those relating to the rights of illegitimate children, when taking instructions for a will. A married man with legitimate children may possibly have one or more illegitimate children as well, and not intend them to benefit to the same extent as his legitimate children, or at all. However, a gift to 'my children' without more will include the illegitimate children. Since it is now conclusively established that a solicitor taking instructions for a will owes a duty of care to take all usual steps to ensure that persons intended to benefit do in fact benefit and can be liable in damages to a disappointed beneficiary if he fails to discharge that duty (see *White v Jones* [1995] 2 AC 207, [1995] 1 All ER 691, HL; see also para **[200.46]**), the draftsman cannot leave the matter to chance. One way of dealing with the problem is to identify the children in the will by name, but this may not be convenient if the client is capable of having further children. Another possible course is to limit the gift to the children of the marriage. But the safest course (though not a very appealing one) is to enquire specifically of the client whether he has any illegitimate children and if he has (or may have) whether he wishes to exclude them, and, if he has and does, to exclude them expressly or exclude the Family Law Reform Acts from applying. For the latter purpose, we recommend the use of words such as 'Words descriptive of relationship shall be construed in all respects as if the Family Law Reform Act 1969, s 15 and the Family Law Reform Act 1987 had not been enacted'. A reference to the FLRA 1969 should be retained; since the FLRA 1987 repeals the FLRA 1969, s 15, such a provision which referred to the FLRA 1987 alone could be construed as a direction that the gift should be read as subject to the FLRA 1969.

[200.31]
Another point to remember is that where a testator leaves his estate to 'my children' without more, his executors will no longer be protected if they distribute to his legitimate children if unknown to them he happens to leave an illegitimate child: see the FLRA 1987, s 20 (Part G, para **[245.75]**) repealing the FLRA 1969, s 17 (Part G, para **[245.41]**). In such a case the executors are protected if they have advertised for claims pursuant to the TA 1925, s 27 (Part G, para **[246.25]**) and distributed the estate before becoming aware of the existence of the illegitimate child (*Re Aldhous* [1955] 2 All ER 80, [1955] 1 WLR 459).

[200.32]
Non-beneficial provisions and illegitimacy. As noted in Part G (at para **[245.69]**), there are few practical differences relevant to will drafting between the effect of the FLRA 1987, ss 1 and 19 (Part G, paras **[245.70]** and **[245.72]**) and the effect of its predecessor the FLRA 1969, s 15 (Part G, para **[245.39]**). However, one is that the FLRA 1969 only applied to provisions that were for the benefit of a person who was illegitimate or claimed through someone who was illegitimate (FLRA 1969, s 15(2)) while the FLRA 1987 is not so restricted. This means that the FLRA 1987 should be excluded in relation to a reference to the descendants of a named monarch when defining a royal lives perpetuity period, and that if there is a condition imposed on a gift such as 'if X shall predecease me leaving issue' where no benefit is conferred on the issue of X, the reference to issue will now include illegitimate issue where it would not have done under the FLRA 1969.

[200.33]
Nephews, nieces and cousins. As mentioned at paras **[200.28]** and **[200.29]**, references to nephews, nieces and cousins and other classes of relative are now also construed in accordance with the statutory rules referred to above.

References to relatives such as nephews, nieces or cousins may give rise to particular difficulty where relatives of the half-blood or spouses of relatives are or may be involved. (See generally Vol 1, para **[71.1]** ff). It is advisable to take detailed instructions about such relatives, especially where a gift to a class rather than an individual is contemplated. Where possible, it is safer to refer to such relatives by name. However, this has its own hazards where an elderly testator has an inaccurate recollection of the names of young relations.

[200.34]

Family provision. Testators who anticipate that unwelcome claims may be made on their deaths under the Inheritance (Provision for Family and Dependants) Act 1975 (I(PFD)A 1975) (Part G, para **[247.2]** ff; see also Vol 1, para **[105.1]** ff) may seek to guard against the risk by inserting in their wills some form of declaration setting out the reasons for not making any or only limited provision for the potential claimant; for examples of such declarations see Form B2.15 at para **[202.40]**. The utility of such declarations is fairly limited, though they may be useful as a record of any special factors militating against the making of an award which might otherwise be overlooked, e g substantial lifetime gifts to the potential claimant which the executors and beneficiaries under the will might not otherwise know about. Perhaps a more effective way of deterring a possible claimant is for the testator to face up to the likelihood of a claim and make some provision for the potential claimant—potential claimants whom testators do not wish to provide for are usually former or current spouses, or in some cases children—but at the lower end of the scale in the hope that he or she will take what is offered rather than running the risk of making a claim and failing to establish that the will does not make reasonable provision for him or her. If the provision exceeds the capital limits for public funding for the claimant's claim that can also help to avert a claim. Special considerations apply in the case of a potential claimant under the I(PFD)A 1975, s 1(1)(e) (Part G, para **[247.2]**) as such claimant must show that he or she was being maintained by the deceased immediately before his death. If the testator wishes to ensure that such a person will be unable to claim he could do so, at least in theory, by ceasing to maintain such person.

[200.35]

Gifts to 'surviving' relatives. The words 'survive' and 'surviving' should be used with great care and deliberation as they, perhaps more than any other, frequently give rise to difficulty by arguably limiting a gift in a way which is unexpected and which the testator would not have intended. The words 'survive' and 'surviving' in their natural meaning require that the person who is to survive must be living at the time of the event which he is to survive. Thus a gift to 'such of my grandchildren as survive me and attain 25' is prima facie confined to grandchildren living at the testator's death. There is a benevolent rule of construction which will let in a grandchild who is *en ventre sa mère* at the date of the testator's death (see *Villar v Gilbey* [1907] AC 139, HL, as explained in *Elliot v Joicey* [1935] AC 209, HL), but otherwise after-born grandchildren may not be admitted to the class even though none of the grandchildren has attained 25 at the date of the testator's death. This may of course be what the testator intends, but frequently it is either contrary to his wishes or would be if his attention were drawn to the point. In *Blech v Blech* [2002] WTLR 483, and *Marshall v Hill* [2003] All ER (D) 304 (Mar), Chancery Division 20 March 2003, (see Vol 1, para **[67.1]**) the courts have recently shown a greater willingness to depart from the strict meaning of 'survive' in this type of context. However, it was necessary in those cases to go to court to achieve this result, and when it comes to drafting wills there is no substitute for a clear expression of the testator's intention. The word 'surviving' when used in a gift over in favour of a class may also give rise to constructional problems if the time at which the surviving members of the class are to be ascertained is not clearly stated in the will. For a more detailed review of the relevant rules of construction see Vol 1, paras **[67.1]–[67.8]** and **[73.1]–[73.2]**.

[200.36]
Rules of apportionment. The rules of apportionment laid down by the Apportionment Act 1870, and the rules of apportionment between capital and income known as the rules in *Howe v Earl of Dartmouth* (1802) 7 Ves 137, *Re Earl of Chesterfield's Trust* (1883) 24 Ch D 643 and *Allhusen v Whittell* (1867) LR 4 Eq 295 are widely regarded as an administrative inconvenience, especially in the case of smaller estates, and are frequently excluded. For a more detailed discussion of these rules see B14 at paras **[214.35]–[214.38]**, **[214.43]** and **[214.44]** and for suitable precedents, see Forms B14.1 to B14.3 at paras **[214.10]–[214.12]**, B14.10 at para **[214.19]**, B14.24 to B14.27 at paras **[214.39]–[214.42]** and **B14.28** to **B14.30** at paras **[214.45]–[214.47]**.

[200.37]
'Free of tax'. 'Free of tax' in relation to annuities refers to income tax. It must not be confused with 'free of inheritance tax', which is a direction concerning the incidence of the IHT on the testator's death (see further para **[214.55]** ff). 'Free of duty' and 'free of capital transfer tax' are phrases which can still be used (IHTA 1984, Sch 6, para 1 and Finance Act 1986 (FA 1986), s 100(1)(b)), but 'free of inheritance tax' is preferable.

[200.38]
Meanings given by statute. The Law of Property Act 1925 (LPA 1925), s 61 (Part G, para **[246.54]**) applies to wills, so that, in the absence of the context otherwise requiring, 'month' means calendar month, 'person' includes a corporation, the singular includes the plural and vice versa, and the masculine includes the feminine *and vice versa* (emphasis supplied). Thus a will need make no express provision for any of these matters. The statutory definitions in the Interpretation Act 1978 (IA 1978) do not apply to wills or other written instruments, but there is one provision of that Act which does apply to them, this is the IA 1978, s 23(3) (Part G, para **[246.97]**). The drafting of this provision by reference to the IA 1978, s 17(2)(a) (Part G, para **[246.96]**) is somewhat opaque, but the effect seems to be that if a will or other written instrument refers to a legislative provision, and that legislative provision is repealed and re-enacted (with or without modification), the reference in the will or other instrument to the original provision will operate as a reference to its re-enactment.

[200.39]

Capital gains tax. The death of a person is not an occasion of capital gains tax charge on his assets, but it is an occasion on which the acquisition value of his assets is uprated to the value of them as at his death in relation to future occasions of capital gains charge: see the Taxation of Chargeable Gains Act 1992 (TCGA 1992), s 62(1). No special provision need therefore be made for the incidence of such tax on the death of the person whose will is being prepared. The death of someone who has a beneficiary-taxed interest in possession (see para **[200.92]** for this term) in settled property for IHT purposes is also an occasion of uprating of the value of the assets subject to the interest for capital gains tax purposes without a tax charge (TCGA 1992, ss 72, 73) except where hold-over relief was obtained on making the settlement (TCGA 1992, s 74). This uprating does not apply to settled property deemed to be subject to a beneficiary-taxed interest in possession by virtue of IHTA 1984, ss 88 (protective trusts after a forfeiture—see para **[200.104]**) or 89 (trusts for the disabled—see para **[200.99]**, **[200.105]**). However, where settled property vests absolutely in anyone, other than on the death of someone entitled to a beneficiary-taxed interest in possession (see para **[200.92]** for this term), it is an occasion of capital gains tax charge on that property under TCGA 1992, s 71, on the ground that he then becomes absolutely entitled to the property as against the trustees: *Tomlinson (Inspector of Taxes) v Glyns Executor and Trustee Co* [1970] Ch 112, [1969] 1 All ER 700. If the settled property is subject to a beneficiary-taxed interest in possession (see **[200.92]**) for this term) immediately before such absolute vesting, and the absolute vesting occurs during the lifetime of the person entitled to that interest in possession, hold-over relief will be available only if business or agricultural assets are involved (TCGA 1992, s 165). For other kinds of asset there is hold-over relief available on the absolute vesting of settled property where it is an IHT chargeable transfer which is not potentially exempt (TCGA 1992, s 260(1) and (2)(a)), or where it is the absolute vesting of property in a beneficiary on the coming to an end of a trust for a bereaved minor within IHTA 1984, s 71A (see para **[200.108]**) or an age 18-to-25 trust within IHTA 1984, s 71D (see para **[200.109]**):TCGA 1992, s 260(1) and (2)(a), (da), (db). In the case of an age 18-to-25 trust, hold-over relief will be available by virtue of it being a chargeable transfer within TCGA 1992, s 260(2)(a), where the property vests in the beneficiary after attaining the age of 18. In particular, it will be a chargeable transfer entitled to hold-over relief where there is an occasion of charge under the IHTA 1984, s 65 on property leaving a relevant property trust (see para **[200.92]**, **[200.126]** (2) and (3), and the Preliminary Note to B18 at paras **[218.8]**–**[218.10]** and **[218.27]**), even where no IHT is payable because the tax threshold is not exceeded. This will apply to interest in possession trusts where the interest or interests in possession are not beneficiary-taxed for IHT purposes as well as fully discretionary trusts (see para **[200.92]**). The only types of beneficiary-taxed interest in possession for IHT purposes which can now be created by will out of free estate are immediate post-death interests (see para **[200.98]**) and disabled persons' interests (see para **[200.99]**). The non-availability of hold-over relief where a beneficiary becomes absolutely entitled to settled property in which there is a beneficiary-taxed interest means that it is good capital gains tax planning, where such an interest is being created, to make it an interest for life with flexible powers to distribute capital, rather than provide for absolute vesting at a specified age, so that there is maximum flexibility as to when, if at all, the beneficiary becomes absolutely entitled and a capital gains tax charge arises. For examples of wills making this type of provision see Forms C2.2 (at paras **[224.42]** ff) and C3.2 (at para **[225.23]**).

[200.40]
Capital gains tax rates. Until 5 April 2008, capital gains realised by individuals are charged to capital gains tax as if they are income, and capital gains realised by settlements and estates of deceased persons in the course of administration are charged to capital gains tax at the income tax trust rate, currently (in 2007–08) 40 per cent: TCGA 1992, s 4, ITA 2007, s 9. However, the changes to capital gains tax announced in the Pre-Budget Report on 9 October 2007 include a flat rate of capital gains tax of 18 per cent for individuals, estates of deceased persons, and trusts alike, with effect from 6 April 2008, and if that passes into law this difference between individual and trust rates of capital gains tax will then disappear. These tax rates are applied to the gains after deduction of annual exemption, which is more generous for individuals, and for estates in administration (until the end of the first two complete tax years after the deceased's death), than for settlements. Trust capital gains can obtain the more generous capital gains tax annual exemption attributable to a beneficiary where that beneficiary is a bereaved minor or disabled person and the trust is such that it qualifies for special treatment under FA 2005, ss 23–43 (see paras **[217.4]**, **[226.9]** ff).

[200.41]
Income tax. Different forms of disposition have different income tax consequences. Where a beneficiary is entitled to the income of an asset or a fund of assets, or to a fixed proportion or amount of such income (whether by virtue of an absolute or limited interest), that income will be taxed as his income (see *Simon's Direct Tax Service* C4.221), although income of a deceased person's residuary estate in the course of administration is only taxed as the beneficiary's when it is distributed to him, and what remains undistributed is taxed as his when the administration is completed (see *Simon's Direct Tax Service,* C4.107–111). Income which is accumulated or which is to be distributed under the exercise of a discretion is charged to income tax at the trust rate, currently (in 2007–08) 40 per cent, but can come to be treated for income tax purposes as the income of a beneficiary after it has been distributed to him: see B18 at paras **[218.29]** and **[218.30]** and *Simon's Direct Tax Service* C4.226. However, discretionary trusts have the income tax disadvantage as compared with interest in possession trusts that if there is dividend income which is then distributed to a beneficiary the tax credit on the dividend does not carry through to the beneficiary: see para **[218.31]**. Undistributed trust income may be taxed at the personal income tax rate or rates of a beneficiary where that beneficiary is a bereaved minor or disabled person and the trust is such that it qualifies for special treatment under FA 2005, ss 23–43 (see paras **[217.4]**, **[226.9]** ff).

[200.42]
Income tax advantages of generation skipping dispositions. A reason in favour of 'generation skipping' dispositions in wills (see para **[200.125]**) is that they may avoid the income tax disadvantage of which the following is an illustration. If a testator, T, makes a gift by will of property to an adult, A, and after T's death A makes a lifetime gift or settlement of that property in favour of A's minor children, A will be the 'settlor' for income tax purposes of that gift or settlement and the income of the property will be treated as that of A so far as it is applied for the benefit of A's children (ITTOIA 2005, s 629: see *Simon's Direct Tax Service* at C4.315 ff). This would be so even if A made the gift or settlement by deed of variation within two years of T's death; there is no relieving provision for income tax purposes corresponding with the IHTA 1984, s 142, (see F3 at para **[241.19]**). The above income tax disadvantage would be avoided if T made a gift by will directly in favour of A's children.

[200.43]
Codicils. Codicils can be useful where a small variation of a testamentary provision is to be effected, e g the increase or reduction of a legacy. Where the changes are more substantial it is advisable where time permits for a fresh will to be prepared and executed, since the combined operation of will and codicil may produce unintended effects which a fresh will would have avoided. For the law relating to codicils, see Vol 1, paras **[20.1]–[20.9]** and for suitable precedents see the forms in Part D at para **[237.1]** ff.

[200.44]
Execution. The formal requirements for the due execution of an English will are set out in Vol 1 at paras **[10.1]–[12.17]**. A testator who executes a will without a solicitor being present should be informed of these requirements in detail. He should also be warned that neither a witness to a will nor the spouse of such witness can in general take a benefit under the will. Such gifts will only be saved by the Wills Act 1968 (Part G, para **[244.84]** ff) if such attestation is superfluous. To be valid, a will does not in general have to be dated (*Corbett v Newey* [1998] Ch 57, [1996] 2 All ER 914, CA), but it is preferable and usual for a will to be dated by the testator when it is executed, and if wills are undated it may be difficult to determine which is the last will and accordingly entitled to probate. However, there is one circumstance where dating is a legal requirement, namely where there is an appointment by will of a guardian—to be valid it must be dated: see Vol 1, para **[28.5]** and the ChA 1989, s 5(5), (Part G, para **[244.116]**).

[200.45]
Revocation. Testators should be discouraged from retaining custody of the executed will. If a testator insists on so doing he should be warned that if the will is not forthcoming on his death it will be presumed to have been revoked. Testators should also be advised that their subsequent marriage or formation of a civil partnership will automatically revoke their wills unless expressed to be made in expectation of the particular marriage or civil partnership. See generally as to revocation Vol 1, Chapters 17, 18 and 19 and for wills made in expectation of marriage or civil partnership see Forms B1.2

and B1.3 at paras **[201.6]** and **[201.7]** and Form C6.1 at para **[228.5]**. It should also be noted that where a will contains an appointment of a guardian, that appointment can be revoked by a subsequent non-testamentary instrument: see Vol 1, para **[28.6]** and the ChA 1989, ss 5(3)–(5) and 6(1) and (2) (Part G, paras **[244.121]** and **[244.122]**).

[200.46]

Mistake. The court of probate has always possessed jurisdiction to rectify wills by omitting words if it can be shown that the testator either did not know or did not approve them: see, eg *Re Morris* [1971] P 62. But until the AJA 1982, s 20 (Part G, para **[244.98]**) came into force in relation to the wills of persons dying on or after 1 January 1983, there was no jurisdiction to add words. It should be noted, however, that the statutory jurisdiction is narrower than the equitable jurisdiction to rectify deeds and other instruments in that it is available only where the will fails to carry out the testator's intentions by reason of (a) a clerical error, or (b) a failure on the part of the draftsman to understand his instructions. There is no remedy where the draftsman understands his instructions but fails to employ language in the will which is appropriate to give effect to them, although there would be a remedy if the document was a deed (as in *Re Butlin's Settlement Trusts* [1976] Ch 251, [1976] 2 All ER 483). For a more detailed discussion of the jurisdiction to rectify wills see Vol 1, paras **[6.1]**–**[6.5]**. Mistakes can have other consequences. It is now conclusively established by the House of Lords that mistakes on the part of the draftsman can give rise to liability for damages in negligence at the suit of a disappointed beneficiary: *White v Jones* [1995] 2 AC 207, [1995] 1 All ER 691 (a case of delay on the part of the solicitor and the consequent failure of the client to execute the will for which he had given instructions thereby depriving the plaintiffs of their intended legacies) and see *Gartside v Sheffield Young and Ellis* [1983] NZLR 37, NZCA (referred to in *White v Jones*) and *Hooper v Fynmores (*2001) 145 Sol Jo LB 156 (also delay cases). For other instances of negligence see *Carr-Glynn v Frearsons (a firm)* [1999] Ch 326, [1999] 4 All ER 225, CA, and *Kecskemeti v Rubens Rabin & Co* (1992) Times, 31 December, (in both of which a solicitor instructed to draft a will who failed to advise the client to sever the beneficial joint tenancy of the matrimonial home was held liable in damages to the residuary beneficiary who was thereby deprived of an undivided half-share of the proceeds of sale). See also Vol 1, para **[1.13]**.

[200.47]

Custody of wills. In view of the presumption that a will which is traced to the custody of the testator but is not forthcoming on his death is revoked clients should be discouraged from retaining possession of their own wills. It is better to leave original wills where possible with the solicitors who drew them, though it is essential to ensure that the executors and other members of the family are fully informed of their whereabouts. Alternatively there is a system, not much used, for the deposit of wills at any probate registry and this facility will be extended under provisions contained in the Administration of Justice Act 1982 when (and if) these are brought into force. See generally Vol 1, para **[10.20]**.

(*d*) *The Trusts of Land and Appointment of Trustees Act 1996 and the Trustee Act 2000*

[200.48]

The Trusts of Land and Appointment of Trustees Act 1996. The TLATA 1996 (Part G, para **[246.103]** ff) has made fundamental changes to the law relating to land held on trust, and has also effected limited, though significant, changes to the law relating to the appointment and retirement of trustees whether of realty or personalty. These changes have important consequences for dispositions of land by will, and for the drafting of wills. Attention is drawn to such changes, where appropriate, in the notes to the forms, but, to avoid excessive repetition of the same basic points, an outline is given below. With one minor exception (s 27(3)), the TLATA 1996 extends to England and Wales only. It came into force on 1 January 1997: The Trusts of Land and Appointment of Trustees Act 1996 (Commencement) Order 1996 (SI 1996/2974).

[200.49]

If a will draftsman goes on using pre-TLATA 1996 forms it is unlikely to have serious adverse consequences in most cases (except in the rare case of trying to create an entail—see para **[200.53]**). He will, however, be wasting the opportunities provided by the TLATA 1996 to make drafting simpler, more comprehensible, and more concise, by, eg not using trusts for sale, or omitting administrative powers or provisions as to occupation by beneficiaries, which are adequately covered by the statutory provisions.

[200.50]

One of the main ideas behind the TLATA 1996 is that a trust for sale is an inappropriate conveyancing fiction to use as a basis for co-ownership of houses for the co-owners to live in. As a result, the trust of land has features, particularly the statutory right of occupation and the power to postpone sale implied in a trust for sale, which reflect a bias in favour of land which is being retained for occupation, but which create difficulties for trusts of land to be held as an investment, or for trusts for sale of land where the trust to sell is a reality rather than a fiction, such as a testamentary trust for several beneficiaries in undivided shares (where it is necessary to sell in order to be able to distribute to the beneficiaries).

[200.51]

Trusts of land. The major change made by the TLATA 1996 is a single system of trusts of land replacing the former trusts for sale and the Settled Land Act 1925 (SLA 1925) systems, with features of both but resembling the former trusts for sale system more than the settled land one. The SLA 1925 ceases to apply to new trusts, but continues to apply to ones to which it already applied (see para **[200.52]**), while all other trusts involving land fall within the TLATA 1996's provisions, whether or not there is a trust for sale. The TLATA 1996, s 1 defines 'trust of land' and 'trustees of land', and most of the operative parts of the Act legislate for trusts of land or trustees of land, and so the definitions in s 1 are what determine which trusts the Act applies to. 'Trust of land' is defined by TLATA 1996, s 1(1)(a) as 'any trust of property which consists of or includes land', and 'trustees of land' are defined as 'trustees of a trust of land': TLATA 1996, s 1(1)(b). For this purpose a 'trust' is defined as 'any description of trust (whether express, implied, resulting or constructive), including a trust for sale and a bare trust': TLATA 1996, s 1(2)(a). It includes a trust created before the commencement of the TLATA 1996 (s 1(2)(b)), but there is an exception for land which continues to be settled land under the SLA 1925 (TLATA 1996, s 1(3)) on or after that date. The TLATA 1996 thus applies to all trusts for sale of land created before 1 January 1997, and indeed to any other trust before that date apart from one which continues to be within the SLA 1925, and all trusts involving land of any kind created on or after that date. 'Land' here has the same meaning as in the LPA 1925: see TLATA 1996, s 23(2) (Part G, para **[246.126]**) and the LPA 1925, s 205(1)(ix) for the relevant definition. It apparently includes undivided shares of land.

[200.52]
Settled land. Strict settlements have not been abolished, but no new settlements can be created under the SLA 1925 on or after 1 January 1997, the commencement date of the TLATA 1996: TLATA 1996, s 2(1) (Part G, para **[246.104]**). There is a saving for SLA 1925 settlements in existence at the commencement of the TLATA 1996, and for any settlement which derives from such a settlement in existence at that date: TLATA 1996, s 2(2). (It is not clear when a settlement 'derives' from another as this term is not defined by the TLATA 1996, but it would seem to include settlements created in exercise of powers to resettle capital.) These settlements will continue to be governed by the SLA 1925 and to that extent the assimilation of SLA 1925 settlements and trusts for sale effected by the TLATA 1996 will not be completely achieved for many years to come. A settlement to which TLATA 1996, s 2(2) applies will cease to be a settlement governed by the SLA 1925 as soon as there is no 'relevant property' subject to the settlement after the commencement of the TLATA 1996, 'relevant property' being land and heirlooms to which the SLA 1925, s 67(1) applies: TLATA 1996, s 2(4) (not to be confused with 'relevant property' for IHT purposes, for which see para **[218.8]**). The trustees of such a settlement, after all 'relevant property' has been disposed of, will have a statutory power to buy more land by virtue of the Trustee Act 2000, s 8 if they do not have an express power to do so. Any land acquired by the trustees of such a settlement after the SLA 1925 has ceased to apply will be held on a trust of land within the TLATA 1996. Section 2(4) seems to have the following consequences—

(1) If trustees of a settlement subject to the SLA 1925 held no relevant property immediately after midnight of 31 December 1996, the SLA 1925 ceases to apply to it at that point and the TLATA 1996 applies to any land subsequently acquired.
(2) If trustees of a settlement subject to the SLA 1925 held relevant property immediately after midnight of 31 December 1996, but subsequently sell all relevant property either at once or in stages, the SLA 1925 ceases to apply when the last piece of relevant property is sold.
(3) If trustees of a settlement subject to the SLA 1925 held relevant property immediately after midnight of 31 December 1996, but subsequently sell the relevant property in stages, but as they sell some

relevant property they buy other such property, in such a way that at all times they hold *some* relevant property, the SLA 1925 will continue to apply, and this seems to be so even if all the relevant property held when the TLATA 1996 came into force has been disposed of.

For a more detailed examination of the machinery of the strict settlement, reference should be made to *Cheshire & Burn's Modern Law of Real Property* (16th edn, 2000), pp 188–215.

[200.53]
Entailed interests. Entailed interests have suffered the same fate as strict settlements. Entails created prior to the commencement of the TLATA 1996 are not affected, but new entails cannot be created after the commencement of the Act and any entailed interest purportedly granted thereafter will take effect as an absolute interest: TLATA 1996, s 2(6) and Sch 1, para 5 (Part G, paras **[246.104]** and **[246.131]**).

[200.54]
Trusts for sale. Trusts for sale of land, whether created before or after the commencement of the TLATA 1996, have now become trusts of land. Statutory trusts for co-owners under the LPA 1925, ss 34 (tenants in common) and 36 (joint tenants), and of intestates' estates under the Administration of Estates Act 1925, s 33, have ceased to be trusts for sale and have become trusts of land without any duty to sell (but with a power of sale) by virtue of the amendments to those sections made by the TLATA 1996, Sch 2 (the sections are printed as amended in Part G at paras **[246.51]**, **[246.53]** and **[244.60]**). Trusts for sale are not abolished, but the TLATA 1996 tries to (and perhaps does) create a set of rules under which it makes no practical difference whether or not there is a trust for sale. The main way in which it does this is to provide a common set of powers and provisions which apply to all 'trusts of land' whether or not there is a trust for sale, but there are also two specific provisions which affect the operation and legal consequences of trusts for sale of land—

(1) In all trusts for sale of land created by a disposition a power to postpone sale is implied *despite any provision to the contrary made by the disposition* (emphasis supplied): TLATA 1996, s 4(1). This provision is worded in the same way as the LPA 1925, s 25(1) (which is repealed by the TLATA 1996 and replaced by the TLATA 1996, s 4(1)), but it differs from the SLA 1925, s 25(1) in that the latter only implied a power to postpone sale where no contrary intention appeared. The reasoning behind s 4(1) seems to be that a trust for sale of land should have the same consequences in practice as a trust of land with a power of sale, and that there should not be the presumption in favour of sale which there appeared to be under the pre-1 January 1997 law. The consequences of this power to postpone are discussed further at paras **[200.57]–[200.59]**.
(2) The other specific change made by the TLATA 1996 to trusts for sale is that the doctrine of conversion is abolished by TLATA 1996, s 3 in relation to express trusts for sale, whether made before or after the commencement of the Act, with the consequence that land held on

trust for sale is no longer to be regarded as personalty. (There is an exception for trusts for sale created by the wills of testators dying before the commencement of the Act.) For consequences of this see Vol 1, para **[41.18]** and the notes to Forms B4.45 (at para **[204.67]**), B14.15 and B14.16 (at paras **[214.24]** and **[214.25]**).

[200.55]
Trusts for sale no longer necessary. In general, therefore, it is no longer necessary for gifts of land by will (or by inter vivos instrument) to be effected by way of disposition on trust for sale. Before 1 January 1997, if land was directed to be held on successive, contingent, discretionary or other trusts, but there was no direction to hold it on trust for sale, the SLA 1925 would apply. This reason for imposing a trust for sale has now been removed, and as explained above at para **[200.54]**, trusts for sale are made virtually if not totally indistinguishable in their practical consequences from trusts of land where there is no trust for sale. The objection to continuing to use the trust for sale is that it is an artificial and technical concept that is not readily comprehensible to the client, and is also counter-intuitive. Trustees do not in practice sit around considering whether to postpone sale all the time; they hold the property unsold without thinking about it at all until they have some reason for considering a sale. We therefore recommend that in general trusts for sale should not be included in trusts of land (and in particular not in administration trusts of residue). For administration trusts of residue after the TLATA 1996, see para **[214.1]** ff.

[200.56]
A trust for sale might still be appropriate as follows—

(i) where the settlor or testator particularly wants there to be an early sale, an express trust for sale would emphasise his intention, but would not impose any greater legal obligation to sell (because the TLATA 1996, s 4 confers a non-excludable power to postpone sale);
(ii) where land is intended to be held as an investment, and not for the occupation of beneficiaries, again the traditional trust for sale wording might be a way of emphasising this (see the Preliminary Note to B8 at para **[208.1]** ff concerning rights of occupation), although the strict legal position would probably be little or not at all different from one where there was no trust for sale; or
(iii) where there is a gift of or including land, eg a gift of a residuary estate, which includes land, to two or more persons as tenants in common (or joint tenants) absolutely and beneficially, the minority in terms of the aggregate value of their interests may have a stronger right to an immediate sale against the wishes of the majority if there is a trust for sale. If that is what is intended, the TLATA 1996, s 11 should be excluded (for which, see para **[220.58]**). See also paras **[200.58]** and **[200.59]** and Form B15.8 at para **[215.8]**.

In all the above cases an expression of intention should be included as well as a trust for sale (because a trust for sale may always have been included continuing to use old forms rather than because of a specific intent), and it may well be that the expressions of intention will be more decisive than the presence of a trust for sale. But the inclusion of a trust for sale can do no harm and may, at any rate in a case such as that described in sub-para (iii), turn out to make a real difference as to whether the court will order a sale on an application to it under the TLATA 1996, s 14: see paras **[200.59]** and **[200.62]**.

[200.57]
Distribution of land held in undivided shares—the need for a sale. Where property is held on trust for beneficiaries in absolute undivided shares and it is of a kind which is readily divisible, such as cash or stock exchange investments, and the trustees do not have a subsisting power to appropriate, each beneficiary is entitled to have transferred to him or her his or her proportionate share of each asset, but this is not so in the case of land, private company shares in special circumstances, and mortgage debts, where a sale or other conversion into cash is usually necessary before a beneficiary is entitled to a distribution (*Re Marshall* [1914] 1 Ch 192; *Re Weiner's Will Trusts* [1956] 2 All ER 482, [1956] 1 WLR 579; *Stephenson v Barclays Bank Trust Co Ltd* [1975] 1 All ER 625 at 637; *Lloyds Bank plc v Duker* [1987] 3 All ER 193, [1987] 1 WLR 1324). Thus where property given by will is or includes land, and it is given to a number of beneficiaries in equal or unequal undivided shares, a sale of that land is a necessary part of the working out of the trust, because usually the land cannot be finally distributed among the beneficiaries without a sale and distribution of the proceeds. There is also the possibility of partition (TLATA 1996, s 7: Part G, para **[246.109]**), or exercise of any available power of appropriation (see para **[220.70]** ff), but this is often impracticable. If the trustees are different persons from the beneficiaries they can insist on conveying the land to the beneficiaries as co-owners under the power in the TLATA 1996, s 6(2), but this just transfers the problem of distribution to the beneficiaries to sort out among themselves.

[200.58]
Sale of land held in undivided shares. Before the TLATA 1996 came into force, the law in relation to a gift by will of land on trust to sell it and hold the proceeds of sale on trust for beneficiaries in undivided shares seems to have been that the trustees' power to postpone sale came to an end when the beneficiaries' interests were absolutely vested and any prior life or other limited interest had come to an end (and the administration of the estate was complete): *Re Ball, Jones v Jones* [1930] WN 111. Although the LPA 1925, s 25 implied a power to postpone sale in any trust for sale of land, it yielded to a contrary intention, and it seems from *Re Ball, Jones v Jones* that a trust to sell with an express power to postpone sale excluded the statutorily implied power to postpone sale, at any rate once the moment for sale and division of the fund had arrived. Also, even where there was a continuing power to postpone sale, where the trustees were not unanimous in agreeing to do so, the trust to sell had to be executed, and the court would not interfere with that (*Re Mayo, Mayo v Mayo* [1943] Ch 302, [1943] 2 All ER 440), unless there was a continuing purpose of the trust, which is not usually the case with tenancies in common arising under a will. With effect from 1 January 1997 the position is altered significantly by the TLATA 1996 in a

number of respects. The TLATA 1996, s 4 (Part G, para **[246.106]**; see also para **[200.54]**), by implying a power to postpone sale in any trust for sale of land *despite any provision to the contrary* made by the disposition creating the trust for sale, means that *Re Ball, Jones v Jones* [1930] WN 111 can no longer be good law according to its precise ratio decidendi. This is because whatever the express trusts under a trust for sale, and however imperative is the direction to sell, the trustees always have the statutorily implied power to postpone sale. Accordingly, when land becomes vested in beneficiaries absolutely in undivided shares under, eg a will trust, and there is no continuing trust purpose which justifies the continued retention of the land, the remedy of a beneficiary who wants a sale (if the trustees are refusing to sell) is to apply to the court for an order for sale under the TLATA 1996, s 14 (Part G, para **[246.117]**; see also para **[200.62]**). The power of the court to order a sale is discretionary and there is not the same certainty of outcome which an application for a sale based on *Re Ball, Jones v Jones* would have had before the Act came into force: see further paras **[200.59]** and **[200.62]**.

[200.59]
Whether someone with an undivided share can obtain an order for sale. It should be noted that the TLATA 1996, ss 14 and 15 (Part G, paras **[246.117]** and **[246.118]**; see also para **[200.62]**) give the court a wider discretion than the former LPA 1925, s 30, and would seem to override the former rule (see para **[200.58]**) that a sale must be ordered where the trustees cannot agree to postpone sale. It should also be noted that the TLATA 1996, s 15, which sets out the matters to which the court is to have regard on a s 14 application, also includes in sub-s (3) the wishes of any beneficiaries of full age and entitled to an interest in possession, or (in case of dispute) of the majority according to value. If the applicant for a sale under the TLATA 1996, s 14 is in a minority by value, the majority will argue that the TLATA 1996, s 15(3) means that the court should not order a sale. However, the court is only directed by s 15(3) to 'have regard' to the wishes of the majority, and that the weight to be given to those wishes will depend on the circumstances. It is tentatively suggested that if the time for distribution has arrived, and there is no continuing trust purpose which justifies further postponement of sale, and the TLATA 1996, s 11 (Part G, para **[246.114]**; see also para **[220.58]**) does not apply to the trust, then a sale should be ordered and the wishes of the majority should have little weight. If this were not the case, the liberty given by TLATA 1996, s 11(2)(a) to exclude s 11 from applying would be of little consequence. On the other hand, if TLATA 1996, s 11 applies, it is arguable that the court should not order a sale if the majority of the beneficiaries by value do not want a sale. Section 11 can be excluded by the will or other disposition creating the trust (TLATA 1996, s 11(2)(a)), and this is something to consider doing in any will trust of land of this type where a sale and division of the proceeds is intended.

[200.60]
Repeal of trust for sale provisions of the Law of Property Act 1925. The TLATA 1996, Sch 4 repealed (without replacing) the following provisions of the LPA 1925 which were formerly relevant to will and other trust drafting—

(a) **Section 25(4)** – used to provide that a trust to retain or sell land took effect as a trust for sale with power to postpone sale. A trust to retain or sell land now has effect according to its terms.

(b) **Section 28(1)** – conferred various statutory powers set out in the SLA 1925 on trustees for sale, and is naturally repealed by the TLATA 1996 in view of the different and wider administrative powers conferred on trustees of land by the TLATA 1996, s 6. However, the SLA 1925, s 28(1) used also to provide that land acquired by trustees for sale should be conveyed to them on trust for sale, and that the statutory powers of leasing, improvement, etc of trustees for sale should be exercised with the consents (if any) required for a sale. The repeal of the SLA 1925, s 28(1) means that now trustees of land (including trustees for sale) whose power or trust to sell the land is subject to a requirement of obtaining the consent of someone do not need that person's consent to the exercise of their other powers over the land unless the will or settlement expressly says so.

(c) **Section 28(2)** – used to provide that subject to express provision to the contrary, the net rents and profits of land held on trust for sale, after payment for repairs insurance and other outgoings, should be paid or applied, except so far as liable to be set aside as capital money under the SLA 1925, in the like manner as the income of investments representing the purchase money would be payable or applicable if a sale had been made and the proceeds duly invested. This probably enacted what was broadly the position under the general law, but to be on the safe side any new will or settlement creating a trust for sale should now include an express trust of the net rents and profits of the land before sale. Further, the repeal of this provision for setting aside rents as capital money under the SLA 1925 means that there is now uncertainty as to whether any, and, if so, how much, of mining royalties and the proceeds of timber should be capitalised, and express provision should be made in this respect in any trust of land where there may be exploitation of minerals or sales of timber: see Form B20.12 at para **[220.61]** and the notes thereto.

(d) **Section 32** – used to provide that land acquired by a personalty settlement under an express power to do so was to be held on trust for sale (subject to an express contrary intention). This is repealed, although many personalty settlements contain express provision that any land acquired by the trustees shall be held on trust for sale.

[200.61]

Purchasers. The TLATA 1996, s 16 (Part G, para **[246.119]**) provides protection for purchasers dealing with trustees of unregistered land. A purchaser of land that is or has been subject to a trust of land need not be concerned to see that any requirement imposed on the trustees by the TLATA 1996, ss 6(5), 7(3) or 11(1) (all of which require the trustees to consult the beneficiaries or have regard to their rights) has been complied with: TLATA 1996, s 16(1). Further, a conveyance of land in contravention of any order, enactment or rule of law or equity to a purchaser who has no notice of the contravention is not invalidated by the contravention: TLATA 1996, s 16(2). In the case of registered land purchasers dealing with trustees need only have regard to restrictions registered on the title, there being a new restriction (Land Registry restriction no. 11A) to deal with cases where the statutory administrative powers are restricted by the will or settlement (the vendor trustees or their lawyers have to declare or certify that the restrictions have been complied with). The purchase money still has to be paid to or applied by the direction of two persons as trustees or a trust corporation (LPA 1925, s 27, as amended).

[200.62]

Powers of the court. The TLATA 1996, ss 14 and 15 (Part G, paras **[246.117]** and **[246.118]**) replace the LPA 1925, s 30, giving the court a wider jurisdiction than that under the LPA 1925, s 30 to make orders with respect to the exercise by trustees of land of any of their functions (whereas the LPA 1925, s 30 only applied where trustees were refusing to sell or exercise statutory powers over the land, or a beneficiary was refusing his consent to sale or such an exercise). The TLATA 1996, s 15 sets out the matters to which the court is to have regard, and they include the intentions of the testator (or settlor), and the purposes for which the land is held. The latter is an enactment of the case law principle under the LPA 1925, s 30 that sale would not be ordered where the land had been acquired for a purpose which had not come to an end, eg a house bought as a residence for a husband and wife (*Jones v Challenger* [1961] 1 QB 176, [1960] 1 All ER 785, CA), and will not usually be relevant in the case of property given in trust by will. The testator's expressions of intention, on the other hand, as to matters such as occupation by beneficiaries or sale, could be an important factor in such cases. The circumstances and wishes of beneficiaries will also be taken into account (see also para **[200.59]**).

[200.63]

Personal representatives. The provisions of the TLATA 1996 are declared to apply with exceptions and appropriate modifications to personal representatives: TLATA 1996, s 18(1), (2) (Part G, para **[246.121]**). The duty to consult beneficiaries under the TLATA 1996, s 11 and the right to apply to the court under s 14 are omitted from the list. The abolition of the doctrine of conversion does not apply to personal representatives if the death occurred before the commencement of the Act: TLATA 1996, s 18(3). The TLATA 1996 also amends the Administration of Estates Act 1925, s 39 (Part G, para **[246.63]**) so as to give personal representatives all the powers of trustees under the TLATA 1996 in relation to land.

[200.64]

Other provisions of the Trusts of Land and Appointment of Trustees Act 1996. Rights of occupation of trust land under the TLATA 1996 are discussed at para **[208.5]** ff, powers of management of land under the Act at paras **[220.49]**–**[220.52]**, powers to delegate the powers of management of land to beneficiaries at paras **[220.54]**–**[220.56]**, consultation with beneficiaries at para **[220.58]** and the appointment of trustees under the Act in the notes at para **[221.39]**.

[200.65]

The Trustee Act 2000. The TrA 2000 is set out in Part G (at para **[246.132]** ff). It confers on trustees and personal representatives newer and wider powers of investment, powers to delegate investment and investment-holding powers, and powers to charge, while imposing an excludable statutory duty of care. See paras **[220.12]–[220.18]** (powers of investment), **[220.36]–[220.38]** (delegation of investment powers), **[221.42]–[221.48]** (powers of charging) and **[221.15]** (statutory duty of care). One consequence of the Act is that it makes all kinds of investment (apart from equitable interests in land) authorised investments (see paras **[220.12]–[220.18]**). This may turn out to have consequences for other rules: for example, it may have the effect of abolishing or marginalising the rule in *Howe v Dartmouth* (1802) 7 Ves 137 (see para **[214.35]** ff), or causing all trustees to have powers of appropriation (see para **[220.71]**).

[200.66]

Review of existing wills in relation to TLATA 1996 and TrA 2000. (For review of wills for recent IHT changes see **[200.134]** ff). In what circumstances (if any) should someone who made a will before the TLATA 1996 or the TrA 2000 came into force consider making a new will or a codicil by reason of the changes to the law made by these Acts? It seems that it is only in unusual circumstances that either or both of these Acts are likely to provide a compelling reason for reviewing an existing will. We suggest the following circumstances might justify revision in the light of the TLATA 1996 without other reasons for doing so–

(1) Where SLA 1925 forms have been used, particularly if a will has used a form such as 'I give Blackacre to my wife for her life … I appoint X and Y to be the trustees for the purposes of the Settled Land Act 1925'. In such a case there could be doubt as to who are the trustees of the land in whom Blackacre should be vested by the executors. It would be a good idea to prepare a codicil substituting 'I give Blackacre to X and Y to hold it on trust for my wife for life' (or to my wife and X, or otherwise as appropriate – it may be that X and Y were willing to be SLA 1925 trustees but would not want the greater burden of being trustees of land under the TLATA 1996).
(2) Where an entail is purportedly created. The prohibition of new entails, and conversion of purported entails into absolute interests (see para **[200.53]**) applies to trusts arising on a death on or after 1 January 1997 even though the will was made before that date. See Form C13.2 at para **[235.18]** ff for a substitute for the traditional strict settlement.
(3) It was intended that the trustees' powers over land should be more restricted than the powers of an absolute owner under the TLATA 1996, s 6(1) (Part G, para **[246.108]**; see also paras **[220.49]–[220.52]**). Express restriction of the TLATA 1996, s 6 should be made.
(4) Where in a trust for sale a beneficiary's (or other person's) consent is required to a sale, and it was intended that other administrative powers of the trustees over the land should require the same consent by virtue of the LPA 1925, s 28(1) (now repealed). See Form B20.13 at para **[220.62]**. Revision of the will is probably not required simply to maintain as effective an express requirement of a beneficiary's consent to exercise of one of the trustees' administrative powers.

(5) To exclude the TLATA 1996, ss 19 or 20 in a trust created to protect the beneficiaries from their own improvidence: see Form B21.34 at para **[221.39]**.
(6) The rare case of a will which relies on the doctrine of conversion under a trust for sale for a particular disposition to be effective according to the testator's intention, eg which contains a gift of personalty which is intended to include an undivided share of land. See further, Vol 1, para **[41.18]**; and paras **[200.59]** and **[214.24]**.
(7) There is a specific gift of an undivided share in land which might possibly be at risk of ademption by reverse application of *Re Newman* [1930] 2 Ch 409, ie because the gift is phrased as a bequest of personalty and the interest has been changed to an interest in realty by the TLATA 1996 (see Vol 1, paras **[41.18]** and **[200.54]**). 'I give all my interest in Blackacre to X' should in our opinion remain effective; what is perhaps more at risk of ademption (but it is hard to believe that a court would now hold that there is ademption) is a gift of 'my interest in the proceeds of sale of Blackacre to X', and the undivided share of Blackacre is not under an express trust for sale but is governed by the LPA 1925, s 34 (which is now amended by the TLATA 1996 so as no longer to impose a trust for sale, even in relation to pre-1 January 1997 dispositions: see para **[200.54]**). A simple affirmatory codicil would deal with the point.

It is not necessary to make a new will or codicil simply in order to exclude the TLATA 1996, s 11 (consultation of beneficiaries) (see para **[220.58]**), as s 11 does not apply to wills made before 1 January 1997 even if the testator dies on or after that date (TLATA 1996, s 11(2)(b): Part G, para **[246.114]**). There does not seem to be anything in the TrA 2000 which might make a testator want to change his will, but a potential executor or trustee of a will of a testator who is still alive might want him to make a new will or codicil which excludes or restricts the statutory duty of care (see para **[221.15]**).

[200.67]
If a new will or a codicil is being made, consider eliminating trusts for sale and unnecessary duplication of the statutory powers over land, omitting powers of insurance (see para **[220.51]** for the statutory power of insurance introduced by the TrA 2000), remember that the TLATA 1996, s 11 (and ss 19 and 20) will apply unless excluded, make any restrictions on administrative powers relate expressly to the TLATA 1996, ss 6 and 7, and if you are creating a trust for sale, provide expressly that the net rents and profits pending sale are to be held on the same trusts as the income of the proceeds of sale (because of the repeal of the LPA 1925, s 28(2): see para **[200.60]**). If it is intended that the liability for negligence of all or any of the executors or trustees is to be limited or excluded, consider introducing wording to this effect which refers to the statutory duty of care under the TrA 2000. For the requirements of professional practice when including such limitation or exclusion see **[221.13]** ff. There should also be review of the will for recent IHT changes: see **[200.134]** ff.

II. INHERITANCE TAX

[200.68]
These notes in this second section of Part A are concerned with more general IHT topics. There are also notes to particular precedents or groups of precedents on IHT points which affect them. In taking account of the changes made to IHT by FA 2006, the IHT notes concentrate on the implications of those changes for will drafting after 21 March 2006. They discuss the current, post-21 March 2006, rules for deaths and dispositions after that date, and so do not in general discuss the transitional provisions for pre-22 March 2006 settlements. These notes also take into account nil-rate band carry-forward (see para **[200.75]**), as announced in the Pre-Budget Report of 9 October 2007. The following terms, used in Part A and elsewhere, are explained in the following paras: 'beneficiary-taxed interest', a term which does not appear in the legislation: para **[200.92]**; 'immediate post-death interest' (abbreviated as 'IPDI'): para **[200.98]**; 'transitional serial interest': para **[200.100]**; 'bereaved minor's trust' or 's 71A trust': para **[200.108]**; '18-to-25 trust' or 's 71D trust': para **[200.109]**; 'disabled person's interest': para **[200.99]**.

(*a*) *Main characteristics*

[200.69]
Introductory. IHT is a tax which is imposed principally on the property owned by a person at his death, or on gifts made by him within the seven years preceding his death. It applies to deaths and lifetime gifts occurring on or after 18 March 1986, and was introduced mostly by way of amendment of the pre-existing capital transfer tax legislation, with the 1984 consolidation of the capital transfer tax legislation being renamed the IHTA 1984. There are exemptions from the tax, principally for gifts to the spouse or civil partner of the giver and to charity (see paras **[200.84]** ff below), and reliefs for agricultural and business property (see paras **[205.1]**–**[205.57]**, **[233.1]** ff and **[234.1]**–**[234.10]**). Settled property falls into the following three main categories: settled property in which an individual has an interest in possession (such as a right to the income or a right of occupation), or is deemed to do so, and where the property is subject to IHT as if that individual owned it (a 'beneficiary-taxed' interest in possession – see paras **[200.92]** ff); settled property which is taxed under the 'relevant property' rules, which originally related to discretionary and other trusts with no interest in possession but which from 22 March 2006 can also apply to many kinds of interest in possession trust (see paras **[218.8]**–**[218.15]**); or property held on trusts for bereaved minors or young persons within IHTA 1984, ss 71A or 71D (see paras **[200.108]** and **[200.109]**).

[200.70]
Lifetime gifts. These can be:

(i) wholly exempt transfers which are not charged to IHT at all, such as gifts to the donor's spouse or civil partner or to charity (see paras

[200.84] ff) – there are also certain categories of exemption specific to lifetime transfers, such as annual exemption (see the IHTA 1984, ss 19–22);
(ii) potentially exempt transfers which are only chargeable to tax if the donor of the gift dies within seven years of it (IHTA 1984, s 3A); or
(iii) immediately chargeable transfers, which are immediately chargeable to IHT at half the tax rate for transfers on death (but there may be more tax to pay if the donor dies within seven years of the gift).

[200.71]
Potential exemption applies to gifts (other than wholly exempt ones) made by one individual to another individual, or into a trust for a disabled person, and potential exemption also applies to the termination of an interest in possession in settled property where the interest in possession is such that the settled property is treated for IHT purposes as if it were the property of the person entitled to the interest (a 'beneficiary-taxed interest'), and it is succeeded by an absolute interest or another beneficiary-taxed interest (see paras **[200.98]–[200.100]** below for the categories of beneficiary-taxed interest). There is one specific category of potentially exempt transfer relevant to drafting wills, where an 'immediate post-death interest' ends in favour of property going into a 'bereaved minor's trust': see para **[200.128]** below.

The main category of immediately chargeable lifetime transfers is transfers of property into a trust other than a trust for a disabled person, or the termination of a beneficiary-taxed interest in possession in settled property where it is followed by continuing trusts which do not include a beneficiary-taxed interest (for a full list of immediately chargeable transfers see *Foster's IHT*, C3.19). In the case of trusts arising under a will of someone dying after 21 March 2006, there can only be potential exemption where a beneficiary-taxed interest in possession comes to an end, and another interest in possession succeeds it, if the successor interest is a disabled person's interest (see para **[200.99]** below) or falls within IHTA 1984, s 71A (see **[200.108]** below).

[200.72]
The IHT charge on death. When someone dies, there is an IHT charge imposed on the aggregate of the property to which he was beneficially entitled immediately before his death (IHTA 1984, ss 4(1), 5(1)), including settled property in which he had a beneficiary-taxed interest in possession (IHTA 1984, s 49 – and see para **[200.92]**) and certain property subject to a gift with reservation (see para **[200.76]**). The tax rate is calculated taking into account transfers made in the seven years preceding the death (see paras **[200.73]** and **[200.74]** below), and where there is more than one fund, e g free estate and settled property subject to an interest in possession, the tax is apportioned rateably between them. The main exceptions or reliefs from this charge are as follows:

(i) the deduction of debts and funeral expenses in determining the value of the estate (see para **[200.77]** below);
(ii) where the deceased was domiciled and resident outside the UK, property with a foreign situs, exempt UK government stock, and

foreign currency bank accounts in the UK owned by him may be left out of account (IHTA 1984, ss 6 and 157);

(iii) exemptions for gifts to spouses and civil partners, charities, political parties, housing associations, etc (see paras **[200.84]** ff below);

(iv) the exception from charge for the estate of someone who dies as a result of active service in the armed forces (IHTA 1984, s 154);

(v) certain exceptions relating to settled property: reversionary interests owned by the deceased (IHTA 1984, s 48(1)), property in which the deceased had an interest in possession which on his death reverted to the settlor or the settlor's spouse (IHTA 1984, s 54), and property in which the deceased had an interest in possession which was entitled to the estate duty surviving spouse exemption (IHTA 1984, Sch 6, para 2);

(vi) conditional exemption for works of art, land etc of historical artistic etc interest (IHTA 1984, ss 30–34; see also the Note in B4 at para **[204.11]**);

(vii) relief for business or agricultural property, which can be 100 per cent, i e amount to a complete exemption (see the Preliminary Notes to B5 at paras **[205.1]**–**[205.57]**; C11 at paras **[233.1]** ff and C12 at paras **[234.1]** ff);

(viii) relief for woodlands (IHTA 1984, ss 125–130);

(ix) relief in the form of a reduction of the taxable value where quoted shares which were owned by the deceased are sold within a year of death or land owned by him is sold within four years of death (IHTA 1984, ss 178–198);

(x) where the deceased died within five years of inheriting property on the death of someone else, there may be relief in respect of the IHT paid on the earlier death (IHTA 1984, s 141);

(xi) where the deceased and another person died in circumstances that the order of deaths cannot be known they are treated as dying simultaneously, so that neither's taxable estate on death will be treated as including property inherited from the other (IHTA 1984, s 4(2); see also B19 at para **[219.5]**);

(xii) double tax relief where property in the estate is subject to foreign death duties (IHTA 1984, s 158, 159);

(xiii) nil-rate band carry-forward relief where the deceased dies after 8 October 2007 and is a surviving spouse or civil partner of someone who did not make full use of his or her nil-rate band: see para **[200.75]**.

There are complicated rules for establishing the taxable value of the estate where there is partial exemption: see paras **[200.112]** ff and the Preliminary Note to C11 at paras **[233.1]** ff.

[200.73]

Tax rates. There is a single tax-rate scale which applies in full to the estate on death and to lifetime transfers made within three years before death. It currently (in the tax year 2007–08) consists of a nil rate for the first £300,000 and a single rate of 40 per cent once the nil-rate band is exceeded. The nil-rate band will be £312,000 for 2008–09 and £325,000 for 2009–10 unless there is further legislation on the subject. This is also subject to the nil-rate band carry-forward for spouses and civil partners announced in the Pre-Budget Report on 9 October 2007: see para **[200.75]**. The rate of IHT on lifetime transfers is a percentage of a full charge where the period between the transfer and the transferor's death is more than three years but fewer than seven years, the percentage being reduced for every year beyond three years that the transferor has survived (IHTA 1984, s 7). Transfers which are immediately chargeable (eg gifts into a settlement) are charged to tax at half full rates initially, but if the transferor dies within seven years the tax charge is recalculated, taking into account among other things the date of the transferor's death, any loss of business or agricultural relief by virtue of the disposal of business or agricultural property before the transferor's death (see the IHTA 1984, ss 113A, 113B, 124A, and 124B), and the tax rates prevailing at the transferor's death. If the tax so recalculated exceeds the tax already paid, the excess then becomes payable: IHTA 1984, s 7(2), (4), and (5). See para **[200.74]**.

[200.74]
Aggregation. A potentially exempt transfer which becomes a chargeable transfer as a result of the transferor's death within seven years is not treated as forming part of the estate charged to IHT on the transferor's death, although the tax on such a transfer becomes payable six months after the end of the month in which the death occurred (IHTA 1984, s 226(3A)) and the rate-scale on which the tax is charged is that prevailing at the time of the death (IHTA 1984, Sch 2, para 1A). A potentially exempt transfer which becomes chargeable is a lifetime chargeable transfer belonging, for the purposes of aggregation, to the time when it was made; it is one of the chargeable transfers which enters into the cumulative total of chargeable transfers of the previous seven years which is taken into account in calculating the IHT charge on the transferor's estate on death (IHTA 1984, s 7(1)). The tax charge on a potentially exempt transfer which has become chargeable is calculated taking into account the chargeable transfers made by the transferor in the seven years preceding it. These would include immediately chargeable transfers made in that period even though made more than seven years before the transferor's death and thus not taken into account when calculating the tax charge on the estate on death. It should be noted that the value transferred by a potentially exempt transfer is aggregated in full when calculating the IHT charge on death unless the transferor survives a full seven years after the transfer. Therefore, where a lifetime transfer of value is made and the value transferred does not exceed the nil-rate band (there being no previous transfers aggregable), there would be no advantage in that transfer being a potentially exempt transfer as opposed to an immediately chargeable transfer unless there were subsequent lifetime immediately chargeable transfers of value. The chargeable estate on death is aggregated with the lifetime chargeable transfers, if any, including any potentially exempt transfers, which were made by the deceased in the seven years preceding his death. Any of the nil-rate band not used up by those lifetime transfers will be available in relation to the taxable estate on death, and the excess of the estate on death over the available nil-rate band (if any) will be charged to IHT at the 40 per cent rate (tax year 2001–02). Obviously if the nil-rate band is entirely used up by lifetime chargeable transfers in the seven

years preceding the death, the chargeable estate on death will all be taxed at 40 per cent. Under the proposed nil-rate band carry-forward rules announced in the Pre-Budget Report on 9 October 2007 (see para **[200.75]**), the additional nil-rate band will only be available in relation to the IHT charge on the death of the second to die of a married couple or civil partnership. If the lifetime chargeable transfers made by the second to die within the seven years preceding his or her death have exhausted the unaugmented nil-rate band, however, the additional nil-rate band will still be available in relation to the estate on death.

[200.75]

Nil-rate band carry-forward. This was announced by the Chancellor of the Exchequer in the Pre-Budget Report of 9 October 2007, to apply with effect from that date as described further below. This paragraph is based on the draft legislation published on 9 October 2007, which will insert new IHTA 1984, ss 8A–8C. The draft legislation could change in material respects before becoming law, which is likely to take until July 2008, but is unlikely to be altered so as to become less generous to the taxpayer. The draft legislation, if enacted, will allow the estate of anyone who dies after 8 October 2007 who was the survivor of a marriage or civil partnership to make use of nil rate band which was not used on the death of the predeceasing spouse or civil partner, irrespective of when the predeceasing spouse or civil partner died. It will be unused where more of the first to die's estate is exempt than the value of the excess of that estate over the nil-rate band (for the exemptions see paras **[200.84]** ff). The carry-forward is calculated as follows, where A is the first to die of a married couple or civil partnership, and B is the second to die:

(1) Work out the maximum which could have been transferred on the death of A at a nil tax rate. It is stated in the guidance note published with the draft clauses that this maximum is not intended to be reduced where the value of the assets owned by A at death was less than the then nil-rate band, though the relevant wording of the draft legislation (in the proposed IHTA 1984, s 8A(2), definition of 'M') seems ambiguous on the point. This maximum will thus apparently be the amount of the nil-rate band under the rate table in force at the date of A's death, minus the aggregate of any lifetime chargeable transfers made or deemed to have been made by A in the seven years preceding his or her death, but increased by the previous application of these provisions if A died after 8 October 2007 and had had a previous spouse or civil partner who died without making full use of the nil-rate band.

(2) Then calculate the value actually transferred by the chargeable transfer taking effect on A's death, ie the value of the part of A's estate which has not on A's death gone to B, or a charity or other exempt recipient, or on IPDI trusts for B (for the exemptions see paras **[200.84]** ff). Where relevant this could include, for example, settled property in which A had an interest in possession or property subject to reservation in relation to A at death.

(3) Then deduct the amount arrived at under (2) above from the amount arrived at under (1) above. If the difference is a positive figure, there is

available carry-forward. If the difference is zero or a negative quantity, there is no carry-forward and the calculation stops here (see the proposed IHTA 1984, s 8A(2)).

(4) If stage (3) above shows that there is carry-forward, arrive at the percentage of the nil-rate band not used. The amount arrived at under (3) above is divided by the nil-rate band in the rate table in force at the death of A, and the result is multiplied by a hundred (see the proposed IHTA 1984, s 8A(4)).

(5) Subject to (6)–(9) below, the nil-rate band in the rate table in force at the death of B is then increased by the percentage arrived at under (4) above when it comes to calculating the IHT on B's estate (see the proposed IHTA 1984, s 8A(3)).

(6) If the above calculations result in an increase in the nil-rate band in relation to B's estate on death of more than 100 per cent, the increase is limited to 100 per cent. This could occur where B had had one or more predeceased spouses or civil partners other than A who failed to make full use of their nil-rate band, or where A died after 8 October 2007 and had an enhanced nil-rate band as a result of a previous application of these rules (see the proposed IHTA 1984, s 8A(5), (6)).

(7) A claim for carry-forward will have to be made (see the draft s 8A(3) and s 8B). It may be made by B's personal representatives within two years from the end of the month in which B died, or, if it ends later, within three months of them first acting as B's personal representatives. HMRC will have power to specify a longer period. If the personal representatives do not make a claim, anyone else liable for the IHT on B's death may do so within a period to be specified by HMRC. The burden will be on the taxpayer to show that the dispositions on A's death did not make full use of the available nil-rate band. It will be important to retain relevant records, particularly where A died intestate, or was a joint tenant of property, or left a will which did not leave all A's estate to B, or had an interest in possession in settled property. Estate accounts, any IHT assessments, and any deeds of variation, disclaimers, or appointments within two years of A's death made out of discretionary trusts created by A's will, particularly need to be retained so as to be available to B's personal representatives.

(8) If in relation to A's death there were deferred tax charges, under the rules for heritage property, non-agricultural woodlands, or alternatively secured pensions, there are draft rules in the proposed IHTA 1984, s 8C, and in proposed amendments to IHTA 1984, 151BA, to make sure that either the deferred tax charge is taken into account in determining carry-forward relief, or that any carry-forward relief is taken into account in determining the amount of the deferred tax charge.

(9) If A has died not only before 9 October 2007 but also before 18 March 1986, ie the date when IHT replaced capital transfer tax, the rules will be subject to modification by statutory instrument.

Assuming these rules pass into law, they will eliminate the need for nil-rate band discretionary trusts in the majority of cases. For discussion of circumstances where such trusts might still be useful see para **[200.130]**.

[200.76]
Gifts with reservation. Property which has been the subject-matter of a gift, made on or after 18 March 1986, from the enjoyment of which or benefit from which the donor has not been entirely excluded after the gift was made ('property subject to a reservation') is taxed as if it had remained part of the donor's estate if the reserved enjoyment or benefit continues until his death, and if the reserved benefit or enjoyment ceased within seven years of his death the property is taxed as if he had made a potentially exempt transfer of it when the enjoyment or benefit ceased. The fact that the latter type of event is treated as a potentially exempt transfer means among other things that the IHT on it becomes payable only after the donor's death and at the rates then prevailing, and the liability for the tax is the same as for potentially exempt transfers (see below). The essential legislative wording (FA 1986, s 102) and rules for tracing the property comprised in a gift (FA 1986, Sch 20) for the purposes of gifts with reservation are derived with very little modification, from the former estate duty rules on the subject. Most types of exempt gift, including ones within the spouse exemption, are excluded from being gifts with reservation (FA 1986, s 102(5)). There has been major legislation to counter avoidance schemes. FA 1999 inserted in the FA 1986 new ss 102A, 102B, and 102C, to counter the type of avoidance scheme where someone retains a lease of a house or other real property at a nominal rent but gives away the freehold, as was held to be effective to avoid the gift with reservation rules by the House of Lords in *Ingram v IRC* [2000] 1 AC 293, [1999] 1 All ER 297. FA 2003 inserted new sub-ss (5A)–(5C) in FA 1986, s 102 to counter schemes where the donor's spouse is given a short-term initial life interest to exploit the exclusion of spouse exempt gifts from the gift with reservation rules. FA 2004 introduced the pre-owned assets income tax charge to impose tax on various schemes or arrangements for giving away property and continuing to enjoy it which had slipped through the holes in the gift with reservation net. An anti-avoidance provision of particular relevance to advising on and drafting wills is the new s 102ZA, introduced into FA 1986 by FA 2006, which treats, for gift with reservation purposes, any termination after 21 March 2006 of a beneficiary-taxed interest in possession (see paras **[200.98]–[200.100]** below for these), during the life of the person entitled to the interest, as if it were a gift of the settled property subject to the interest made by the person who had been entitled to the interest. Consequently, if such an interest in possession comes to an end during the life of the person entitled to it, and that person continues to benefit or retain the possibility of benefit from the settled property, that property will be taxed as property subject to a reservation in relation to him.

[200.77]
Deduction of liabilities on death. Liabilities of the deceased are deductible in determining his taxable estate on death for IHT purposes, so far as they were incurred for consideration in money or money's worth or imposed by law (IHTA 1984, s 5(5)), unless there is a right of reimbursement reasonably likely to be obtained (IHTA 1984, s 162(1)) or the consideration was given by a person with property deriving from the deceased (see below). Liabilities which are incumbrances on property are deducted first from that property (IHTA 1984, s 162(4)), and liabilities to persons outside the UK which do

not fall to be discharged in the UK and are not charged on property in the UK are deducted so far as possible from property outside the UK: IHTA 1984, s 162(5). If the deceased was entitled to a beneficiary-taxed interest in possession in settled property, but his free estate is insolvent, the excess of his liabilities over the assets of his free estate cannot then be deducted from the settled property in diminution of the IHT chargeable on the settled property on the deceased's death: *St Barbe Green v IRC* [2005] EWHC 14 (Ch), [2005] STC 288. Reasonable funeral expenses are deductible (IHTA 1984, s 172) including a reasonable amount for mourning apparel (Inland Revenue Concession F1) and the cost of a tombstone or gravestone (Inland Revenue Statement of Practice SP 7/87). The administration expenses are not deductible, save that the expenses of administering or realising foreign property may be deductible if attributable to the location of the property and subject to a limit of five per cent of the value of the property (IHTA 1984, s 173), and the part of the estate spent on administration expenses apparently escapes being charged to IHT so far as the expenses are paid out of exempt residue (see para **[200.116]** below).

[200.78]
A liability incurred for no consideration, such as a deed of covenant, is not deductible for IHT purposes. A liability incurred on or after 18 March 1986 for full consideration where the lender had previously been given property by the deceased is also not deductible, as a result of the reintroduction of some estate duty rules on this subject by the FA 1986: FA 1986, s 103(1)–(6). Also non-deductible is any liability connected with insurance made on or after 1 July 1986, unless the sums assured are part of the estate: FA 1986, s 103(7).

[200.79]
Liability for IHT. IHT on potentially exempt transfers, and additional IHT on chargeable transfers (never potentially exempt), made within seven years of the transferor's death, and IHT on property subject to a reservation, is a liability of both the transferor's personal representatives (IHTA 1984, ss 199(2) and 200(1)(a)), and of any person whose estate was increased by the transfer or in whom the property which was the subject-matter of the transfer or reservation is vested (IHTA 1984, ss 199(1) and 200(1)). The liability of the transferor's personal representatives is, however, one which will in most cases only arise if such tax is unpaid twelve months after the end of the month in which the transferor or donor died (IHTA 1984, s 204(8) and (9)). The possibility of a liability for IHT on lifetime gifts is a problem for personal representatives, who may not know about them: see, further, para **[200.123]**. If nothing is agreed as to who will pay the IHT arising from the transferor's death within seven years, and the transferee fails to pay it and the transferor's personal representatives have to do so, it is most unclear whether the personal representatives have any right of recovery of the tax against the transferee. Agreement as to the burden of this tax should always be made at the time of the gift.

[200.80]
Liability for the IHT on a person's death is that of his personal representatives in relation to the deceased's free estate and any settled land in the UK

which was comprised in a settlement before the death and which vests in them (IHTA 1984, s 200(1)(a)), but not other settled property in which the deceased had an interest in possession. There is a concurrent liability of anyone who becomes interested in the property, and the trustees of a settlement in which the deceased had a beneficiary-taxed interest in possession are primarily liable for the IHT on the property in that settlement (IHTA 1984, s 200(1)(b)–(d)). The personal representatives' liability is limited to the assets of the estate they have received or should have received (IHTA 1984, s 204(1)), and where the primary liability for the IHT on any property subject to the IHT charge on death is not that of the residuary estate, the personal representatives may recover the tax from the person primarily liable (IHTA 1984, s 211(3)). As already mentioned in para **[200.79]**, the personal representatives have no express right of recovery in relation to any IHT paid by them on a lifetime potentially exempt or other transfer made by the deceased in the seven years before his death, in the absence of an express agreement having been made by the transferee with the deceased to pay it. For the incidence of IHT on death see the Preliminary Note to B14 at paras **[214.55]** ff.

[200.81]
Valuation of the estate on death. The valuation is on the basis of a hypothetical sale on the open market immediately before the deceased's death (IHTA 1984, ss 4(1) and 160), taking into account additions to the deceased's property and increases or decreases in the value of his property which have occurred by reason of his death, other than decreases arising from alterations in unquoted shares and any changes by way of accrual of property by survivorship or the termination of any interest: IHTA 1984, s 171. Property subject to a restriction on alienation is valued on the assumption that it could be sold freely but that the purchaser will be subject to the same restriction when he has acquired it (*IRC v Crossman* [1937] AC 26, [1936] 1 All ER 762; *Alexander v IRC* [1991] STC 112), and it is assumed for the purposes of valuation that the hypothetical seller took the course of action which would get the largest price, such as, for example, dividing property up into lots, or selling separate items together, provided that this would not have entailed undue expenditure of time and effort (*IRC v Gray* [1994] STC 360).

[200.82]
The deceased's free estate and settled property in which he had a beneficiary-taxed interest in possession (see paras **[200.98]** ff below) will be valued together if that produces a higher value (IHTA 1984, ss 4(1), 5(1) and 49(1)), and any property in the deceased's estate (including property in which he had an interest in possession) which has a higher value if it is valued as a proportionate part of the aggregate of it and related property will be so valued (IHTA 1984, s 161(2)). Related property is property owned (absolutely or for a beneficiary-taxed interest in possession) by the deceased's spouse or civil partner, or which was owned at his death, or had during the preceding five years been owned, by a charity or similar body as a result of a post-15 April 1976 exempt transfer by the deceased or his spouse or civil partner (IHTA 1984, s 161(2)). Another category of property which may be

valued in aggregation with the rest of the deceased's taxable estate is property subject to a reservation (see para **[200.76]** above) at the deceased's death of which the deceased was the donor (FA 1986, s 102(3)). There is relief for falls in the value of property after death, in relation to quoted investments sold within one year of death (IHTA 1984, ss 178–189) and land sold within four years of death: IHTA 1984, ss 190–198.

[200.83]
Post-death rearrangement. It is often desired by the beneficiaries to alter the dispositions taking effect on the testator's death, sometimes to increase or alter the benefit taken by a particular beneficiary, sometimes to make better use of exemptions or reliefs, sometimes so as to pass assets on to the next generation. It is often possible to rearrange the devolution of the estate within two years of the testator's death so that the rearrangement is treated for IHT purposes as if done by the deceased, so that, for example, a rearrangement which gives more property to the deceased's surviving spouse obtains a corresponding increase in the amount of the estate which is exempt (see paras **[200.84]** ff below for the spouse exemption), and, if post 8 October 2007 nil-rate band carry-forward passes into law (see para **[200.75]**), increases the amount of such carry-forward. The main methods of making such rearrangements are disclaimers or instruments of variation under the IHTA 1984, s 142 (see F3 at paras **[241.1]** ff) and distributions out of discretionary trusts created by will in accordance with the IHTA 1984, s 144 (see C3 at paras **[225.83]** ff). There are also distribution in accordance with the deceased's wishes of personal property in accordance with the IHTA 1984, s 143 (see B4 at paras **[204.9]** and **[204.10]**) and court orders (including certain kinds of agreed order) under the I(PFD)A 1975 (see the I(PFD)A 1975, s 19: Part G, para **[247.25]**; and the IHTA 1984, s 146; see also Vol 1, para **[105.51]**).

(*b*) *Exemptions and reliefs relevant to testamentary dispositions*

[200.84]
The exemption for gifts to spouses or civil partners. A transfer of value between spouses or civil partners is ordinarily exempt, to the extent of the value of property which thereby becomes comprised in the spouse's or civil partner's estate, or, where no property becomes so comprised, to the extent that the spouse's or civil partner's estate is thereby increased: IHTA 1984, s 18(1) (as amended by SI 2005/3229, regs 3 and 7 for civil partnership with effect from 5 December 2005). The exemption can apply to a transfer whereby the transferor's spouse or civil partner acquires a beneficiary-taxed interest in possession in settled property (see paras **[200.92]** and **[200.98]** ff for beneficiary-taxed interests), as well as to an outright gift to the transferor's spouse or civil partner. In the case of lifetime dispositions, it is only if the spouse or civil partner of the settlor is a disabled person within IHTA 1984, s 89(4)–(6) (see para **[200.99]**) that it is possible for a settlor to provide a beneficiary-taxed interest in possession for the benefit of such spouse or civil partner and thus qualify for the spouse or civil partnership exemption. On the other hand, in the case of testamentary dispositions, if an immediate interest in possession in settled property is given to the testator's spouse or

civil partner out of the testator's fere estate it will be a beneficiary-taxed interest in possession (an 'IPDI': for IPDIs see para **[200.98]**), and the property can thus qualify for the spouse or civil partnership exemption whether or not the spouse or civil partner is a disabled person.

[200.85]

The extent of the IHT spouse or civil partnership exemption is restricted if the transferor but not the transferor's spouse or civil partner is domiciled in the UK, for which see the IHTA 1984, s 18(2). The overall limit for transfers in these circumstances is currently £55,000, although in some cases there is a greater amount of exemption under a relevant double tax treaty.

[200.86]

The Pre-Budget Report of 9 October 2007, in which was announced the introduction of nil-rate band carry forward between spouses and civil partners (see para **[200.75]**), has the effect of reversing much standard tax-planning advice. Previously, spouses and civil partners were advised to try to make sure that the first to die would at death own sufficient assets to make use of all of his or her nil-rate band, and that the first to die should create a nil-rate band discretionary trust in his or her will (see para **[218.16]** ff for nil-rate band discretionary trusts). The proposed carry-forward rules will make the first of these completely unnecessary (see para **[200.75]** sub-para (1)), and in most cases the sensible advice will be to rely on nil-rate band carry forward and not create a nil-rate band discretionary trust by the will of the first to die. For the circumstances in which a nil-rate band discretionary trust might still be appropriate see para **[200.130]**.

[200.87]

Gifts to charities, political parties, housing associations, or for national purposes, and gifts to maintenance funds for historic buildings. There is exemption for all of these: IHTA 1984, ss 23–25 and 27. A political party has to have attained a specified level of success in the most recent general election for a gift to it to qualify for exemption: IHTA 1984, s 24(2). 'Gifts for national purposes' for the purposes of the exemption means gifts to any of the institutions (such as national museums and galleries, universities, local authorities and government departments) specified in the IHTA 1984, Sch 3: IHTA 1984, s 25(1). For charitable gifts, see B12, and for a gift by will to provide a maintenance fund, see Form C13.2 at para **[235.18]**.

[200.88]

IHTA 1984, ss 23(2) to (5), 24(3) and 25(2) contain restrictions which ensure that these exemptions (subject to very limited exceptions) only apply to absolute gifts of the donor's entire interest in the property given.

For forms of charitable gifts and notes thereon, see B12 at paras **[212.1]** ff.

[200.89]

Gifts made by persons with a foreign domicile. Property situated outside the UK and beneficially owned absolutely by someone with a foreign domicile (the rules are quite different for settled property, for which see the IHTA 1984, s 48(3)) is 'excluded property' (IHTA 1984, s 6(1)), which does not form part of that person's estate for the purposes of the charge to IHT on death: IHTA 1984, s 5(1). It must always be remembered that under the IHTA 1984, s 267 certain persons with a foreign domicile are treated as having a UK domicile for IHT purposes; in particular, anyone now giving up his UK domicile has to have a foreign domicile and be a foreign resident for three years before he loses UK domicile for these purposes.

[200.90]
Persons with a foreign domicile but deemed to have a UK domicile under the IHTA 1984, s 267 are, however, helped by the IHTA 1984, ss 6(2) and 48(4)–(7). By virtue of those provisions, exempt government securities are 'excluded property' while beneficially owned by someone not domiciled or ordinarily resident in the UK and IHTA 1984, s 267 does not apply for the purposes of that paragraph: IHTA 1984, s 267(2). There is an additional exception for persons domiciled in the Channel Islands or the Isle of Man who are entitled to certain types of government bonds or rights under certificated contractual savings schemes: IHTA 1984, s 6(3). The deemed domicile provisions are excluded in this case also: IHTA 1984, s 267(2).

For the advantages of creating will trusts where the testator is domiciled outside the UK see C14 at paras **[236.1]** ff.

[200.91]
Exemptions and reliefs for particular kinds of asset. There are elaborate provisions for conditional exemption for works of art, historic buildings, etc (see the IHTA 1984, ss 30 ff and B4 at paras **[204.11]** ff), and for relief for business property (IHTA 1984, s 103), agricultural property (IHTA 1984, s 115) and woodlands (IHTA 1984, s 125) which are discussed in B5 at paras **[205.1]** ff, C11 at paras **[233.1]** ff and C12 at paras **[234.1]** ff.

(*c*) *Will trusts*

[200.92]
Beneficiary-taxed interest in possession or relevant property. The rules for charging IHT on settled property are set out in the IHTA 1984, Part III. This Part provides two contrasting principal methods of charging tax, and some subsidiary special treatments for specific types of trust. Taking account of the changes made by FA 2006, the two principal methods of charging IHT will be referred to here as 'beneficiary-taxed' and 'relevant property'. 'Relevant property' is a term found in the legislation (see IHTA 1984, ss 58 ff), but 'beneficiary-taxed' is not. The term 'beneficiary-taxed' refers to cases where there is an interest in possession in settled property, and the interest is in one of the specific categories of interest in possession where the owner of the interest is treated for IHT purposes as if he were the owner of the settled property in which the interest subsists (by virtue of IHTA 1984, s 49(1), and 49(1A) inserted by FA 2006, Sch 20, para 4). Before 22 March 2006 this is the IHT treatment which applied to all settled property which was subject to an interest in possession to which an individual was beneficially entitled. With effect from 22 March 2006, FA 2006 has confined this treatment to interests in possession in the categories of beneficiary-taxed interest in possession which are summarised in paras

[200.98]–[200.100] below. There are two categories of beneficiary-taxed interest which can be created by a will of a person dying after 21 March 2006: immediate post-death interests or IPDIs (see para **[200.98]**), and disabled person's interests (see para **[200.99]**). Relevant property is settled property not subject to a beneficiary-taxed interest in possession. Typically it is settled property subject to discretionary trusts, but it can now also be property subject to an interest in possession which is not a beneficiary-taxed interest. IHT is charged periodically on relevant property so long as it remains relevant property, and there is also an 'exit' charge whenever property in the settlement ceases to be relevant property. The relevant property charging provisions are considered in B18 at paras **[218.16]** ff. The charging rules for relevant property have not been changed significantly by FA 2006 except so as to make them apply to settled property which is subject to an interest in possession where the interest is not a beneficiary-taxed interest. Relevant property is thus the default charging regime, which applies unless it can be established that there is a beneficiary-taxed interest in possession, or that there is a trust in one of the categories which obtain special treatment, such as trusts for bereaved minors (see para **[200.108]** for these). In deciding whether there is a beneficiary-taxed interest in possession, there is a two-stage process: first, it must be determined whether there is an interest in possession, and, secondly, it must be determined whether it is an interest in possession which is in one of the beneficiary-taxed categories. FA 2006, which extended the relevant property rules to most new interest in possession trusts, was a complex piece of legislation which gives rise to a number of interpretative questions. There have so far been three published statements about some of these, agreed between STEP and HMRC, the texts of which can be found in Foster's IHT. They are referred to here as '*STEP/CIOT/HMRC April 2007*' (the set of 43 questions with HMRC's answers as revised in April 2007 and printed at *Foster's Inheritance Tax* X6.78), '*Transitional regime guidance May 2006*' (see *Foster's Inheritance Tax X6.80*), and '*S 71A etc guidance June 2007*' (see *Foster's Inheritance Tax X6.81*).

[200.93]

Interest in possession. This term is not defined in the IHT legislation, but in their press notice dated 12 February 1976 the Inland Revenue expressed the view that:

> '… an interest in possession in settled property exists where the person having the interest has the immediate entitlement (subject to any prior claim by the trustees for expenses or other outgoings properly payable out of income) to any income produced by that property as the income arises; but that a discretion or power, in whatever form, which can be exercised after income arises so as to withhold it from that person negatives the existence of an interest in possession. For this purpose a power to accumulate income is regarded as a power to withhold it, unless any accumulations must be held solely for the person having the interest or his personal representatives.
>
> On the other hand the existence of a mere power of revocation or appointment, the exercise of which would determine the interest wholly or in part (but which, so long as it remains unexercised, does not affect the

beneficiary's immediate entitlement to income) does not in the Board's view prevent the interest from being an interest in possession.'

[200.94]
After the notice quoted at para **[200.93]** above was issued, the meaning of 'interest in possession' for capital transfer tax (IHT) purposes was authoritatively determined by a bare majority of the House of Lords (reversing the High Court and the Court of Appeal) in *Pearson v IRC* [1981] AC 753, [1980] 2 All ER 479. The House of Lords held that the Inland Revenue view is largely correct, and that where trustees have power, eg, to accumulate the income of any settled property, or to distribute such income among a class of beneficiaries, and subject to such power that income is held on trust for a specific person, the last-mentioned person does not have an interest in possession in the settled property for the purposes of the tax. The rationale of the decision is that a beneficiary has an interest in possession only if he is entitled to call for the income as it arises. Income which can be distributed to others or accumulated does not satisfy this test: see also *Re Trafford's Settlements, Moore v IRC* [1985] Ch 32, [1984] 1 All ER 1108. On the other hand an overriding power of appointment exercisable prospectively only is not inconsistent with the existence of an interest in possession. The House of Lords decision is also important in drawing a distinction between 'dispositive' powers, eg a power to distribute or accumulate income, and 'administrative' powers, eg a power to pay expenses, expressing the view that only powers of the former sort were capable of negativing interests in possession. For discussion of administrative powers and interests in possession, see B20 at paras **[220.4]** ff and for more detailed discussion of interests in possession generally, see *Foster's Inheritance Tax*, E1.41–E1.49. Someone who has an annuity arising under a will and charged on the testator's estate, is treated as having an interest in possession in part of that estate for IHT purposes. This may give rise to problems: see further B11 at paras **[211.1]** ff.

[200.95]
Interest in possession through enjoyment of assets in kind. If a residence is given on trust to permit a beneficiary to occupy it for life, or is given a life interest in a fund which includes a residence which the beneficiary is permitted to occupy, that is an interest in possession, and if it commences at the death of the testator it will be an IPDI (see para **[200.98]**). In HMRC's opinion interest in possession can also be created where none would otherwise subsist if trustees allow a discretionary beneficiary to have the free use of a house or chattels. This opinion is based on the capital gains tax case of *Sansom v Peay* [1976] 3 All ER 375, [1976] 1 WLR 1073. In that case beneficiaries were permitted by the trustees of a discretionary settlement to occupy a house under a power contained in the settlement. It was held that such beneficiaries were 'entitled to occupy it under the terms of the settlement' within the Finance Act 1965, s 29(9) (now the TCGA 1992, s 225) with the consequence that the house was exempt from capital gains tax on its disposal by the trustees. The wording of that subsection is not identical with any provision in the capital transfer tax (IHT) legislation but the similarities, especially with what is now the IHTA 1984, s 50(5) are striking, and the Inland Revenue therefore announced that it would in future regard someone

having the use of a house held on trust by permission of the trustee as having an interest in possession in many cases, particularly where the power is exercised to provide a permanent home for a beneficiary: see IR Statement of Practice SP10/79, 15 August 1979. Before 22 March 2006 this had the consequence that an exercise by trustees of a discretionary settlement of a power to permit a beneficiary to occupy a residence often meant that the beneficiary thereby became entitled to an interest in possession falling within the beneficiary-taxed settled property rules. In relation to events after 21 March 2006 the problem is reduced, because the creation of an interest in possession for a beneficiary in property subject to a discretionary trust will only cause the settled property to move from the relevant property rules into the beneficiary-taxed rules in the limited circumstances discussed at para **[200.133]** below or if the beneficiary is a disabled person within IHTA 1984, s 89(4)–(6) (see para **[200.99]** below). For a discussion of the meaning of 'interest in possession' in TLATA 1996, for the purposes of the right of occupation under that Act, see paras **[208.12]** ff.

[200.96]
Interests in possession and overriding powers. In spite of the rather narrower meaning put on the term 'interest in possession' by the House of Lords in *Pearson v IRC,* it is possible to retain some flexibility in a settlement by giving a life interest which is a beneficiary-taxed interest in possession but which is subject to overriding powers of appointment or application under which capital can be distributed to, or appointed on trust for, the life tenant or other specified persons. If such overriding powers are not capable of exercise in any manner which might affect the life tenant's right to income arising before such exercise, their existence will not prejudice the existence of an interest in possession (see the Inland Revenue statement quoted at para **[200.93]** above). If such powers are exercised so that the life tenant becomes beneficially entitled to property which was subject to his life interest, there is no IHT charge: IHTA 1984, s 53(2). If such powers are exercised in favour of a person or persons other than the life tenant, the IHT consequences are as if the life tenant had made a transfer of value of the capital over which the powers are exercised: IHTA 1984, s 52(1). If the power is exercised so as to terminate a beneficiary-taxed interest in possession, but the settled property remains settled (whether or not subject to an interest in possession) it is likely to be an occasion of immediate IHT charge: see, further, para **[200.71]** above.

[200.97]
Deemed interests in possession during the administration of the estate and survivorship periods. A person who has been given by will an interest in possession in a residuary estate is not entitled to an equitable interest in the estate, or to be paid the income as it arises, until the administration of the estate is completed: see Vol 1, paras **[1.12]**, **[38.16]**. However, such a person is still treated for IHT purposes as becoming entitled to the interest in possession as from the deceased's death: IHTA 1984, s 91. This means that if he dies, or assigns or surrenders the interest, before the administration of the estate has been completed, the same IHT consequences follow as if the administration had been completed. Thus if someone entitled as from the

testator's death under his will to a life interest in the testator's residuary estate dies while the estate is still being administered, the residuary estate will be taxed on his death as if he had had an interest in possession in it, even though the trust fund had not been constituted by the time of his death. However, someone entitled to an interest in possession in an estate may be able to assign or surrender the interest by instrument of variation or disclaimer under the IHTA 1984, s 142 within two years of the testator's death without adverse IHT consequences (see paras **241.1]** ff). IHTA 1984, s 91 also means that an interest in possession in residue can qualify as an 'immediate post-death interest' or 'IPDI' (for which see para **[200.98]** below). Where there is a specific gift by will of property to be held on an immediate interest in possession trust, IHTA 1984 s 91 does not apply, but it seems from cases such as *IRC v Hawley* [1928] 1 KB 578 (see also Vol 1 paras **[1.12]**, **[32.2]**) that the interest in possession runs from the death under the general law. Where under the terms of a will (or otherwise) property is held for any person on condition that he survive another for a specified period of not more than six months, IHTA 1984 applies as if the disposition taking effect at the end of the period or the earlier death of the person in question had had effect from the beginning of the period: IHTA 1984 s 92. This means that if someone is given by will an interest in possession contingently on surviving the testator by a period not exceeding six months, the interest in possession will be treated as starting from the testator's death if the person entitled to the interest does survive the period in question. In relation to events after 21 March 2006, s 92 has the additional effect that the interest will be an IPDI (for which see para **[200.98]** below).

[200.98]

Beneficiary-taxed interests in possession – immediate post-death interests ('IPDIs'). This is the most important category of beneficiary-taxed interest for the will draftsman (IHTA 1984, s 49A inserted by FA 2006, Sch 20, para 5). To be an IPDI an interest in possession must have arisen under a settlement effected by the testator's will or under the law relating to intestacy, and a person must have become beneficially entitled to it on the death of the testator or intestate. The following should be noted:

(1) An immediate interest in possession given by will can be an IPDI despite the technicalities of the period of administration of the estate, and even where the interest is conditional on surviving the testator by a specified period (provided it is a period not exceeding six months): see IHTA 1984, ss 91 and 92 and para **[200.97]** above.

(2) It will not be an IPDI if IHTA 1984, s 71A (trusts for bereaved minors – see para **[200.108]** below) applies, nor if it is a disabled person's interest (see para **[200.99]** below).

(3) An IPDI will continue to be an IPDI so long as the person who became entitled to the interest at the testator's or intestate's death continues to be beneficially entitled to it. If he assigns the interest to someone else it will be treated as coming to an end (IHTA 1984, s 51(1)), and so it will not revert to being an IPDI if it is then assigned back to him.

(4) Overriding powers can be combined with an IPDI, provided that they do not prevent the person entitled to the IPDI from being entitled to

the income as it arises (see para **[200.96]**). It is important to make sure when providing such a power that it should be exercisable so as to vary or replace the trusts in remainder which follow the IPDI while leaving the IPDI to continue. There is a risk with some conventional forms of power of appointment or application that they can only be exercised by creating completely new trusts of the property subject to an appointment with effect from the date of the appointment or application. If, while an IPDI is continuing, a power of appointment or application of capital is exercised so as to terminate the IPDI and create new trusts of the property previously subject to the IPDI, this will be an occasion of deemed immediately chargeable transfer of the settled property by the person entitled to the IPDI for IHT purposes, even if under the appointment or application of capital the person who was previously entitled to the terminated IPDI continues to be entitled to an interest in possession in the same property (IHTA 1984, ss 49A (3), 52(1) and 53(1), (2) and (2A)).

(5) HMRC recognise that an interest in possession starting from the testator's death created in exercise of a *general* power of appointment can be an IPDI (*STEP/CIOT/HMRC April 2007*, question 15), but fairly plainly one created by exercise of a special power cannot. In some circumstances it may be possible for a testator in exercise of a special power by will to create a transitional serial interest in favour of his or her spouse or civil partner: see para **[200.100]** below.

(6) In *Transitional regime guidance May 2006* there is consideration of a number of examples of changes in beneficial interests over time, with HMRC's views as to which do or do not count as continuation of the same interest in possession. This is for the purposes of the transitional provisions, but it seems to us that the same should apply for the purposes of determining whether an IPDI continues or terminates. The main points of interest for drafting wills are that HMRC accept that where the trusts declared by the trust instrument take the form of an initial trust for a class of persons contingently upon attaining a specified age, followed by a provision directing the vested shares to the retained by the trustees and held on life interest trusts, each beneficiary has a single interest in possession before and after attaining a contingency rather than two different interests in possession in succession. On the other hand, where the initial trust is declared by the trust instrument but the subsequent superimposed life interest is declared in exercise of a power of appointment or application at a later date, the superimposed interest is a new one and not a continuation of the old one.

(7) An interest in possession which is not expressed to commence at the death of the testator but commences, whether by express provision in the will or in exercise of a power, during the period of two years immediately following the testator's death, is likely to become an IPDI as a result of the operation of IHTA 1984, s 144 (see para **[200.133]**). This is a point to watch out for particularly where it is intended to create interest in possession trusts which are desired to fall within the relevant property regime.

(8) Careful thought needs to be given to the remainder trusts after an

IPDI. If it terminates during the life of the person entitled to it, the deemed transfer of value caused thereby will only be potentially exempt (see para **[200.71]**) if the settled property vests absolutely in somebody, or is succeeded by trusts for a bereaved minor (see para **[200.108]**) or a disabled person's interest (see para **[200.99]**), and will only be totally exempt if it vests absolutely in the person entitled to the IPDI or his spouse or civil partner. Otherwise, and in particular if the property continues to be settled property, there will be an immediate IHT charge. There will be no capital gains tax hold-over relief on any such absolute vesting unless the underlying assets qualify for business assets hold-over (see para **[200.39]**). If the IPDI terminates on the death of the person entitled to it, the IHT consequences are the same whether or not the property subject to the IPDI continues to be settled property after the death of that person, except that there will be spouse or civil partnership exemption if the property vests absolutely in the spouse or civil partner of the person who was entitled to the IPDI. There are particular problems about what happens after the termination of an IPDI where the testator is or may be domiciled outside the UK: see para **[236.6]**.

(9) If the person beneficially entitled to an IPDI dies still so entitled to it, there is capital gains tax acquisition-value uprating on his death: see para **[200.39]**.

[200.99]

Beneficiary-taxed interests in possession – disabled persons' interests. Disabled persons for this purpose are persons mentally incapable of managing their affairs, or in receipt of, or qualified to receive, attendance allowance (persons of 65 or over), or in receipt of, or qualified to receive, disability living allowance with the care component at the highest or middle rate (persons under 65) (IHTA 1984, s 89(4)–(6)). The term 'disabled person's interest' is defined in IHTA 1984, s 89B. It includes an interest in possession in settled property to which a disabled person is beneficially entitled, and a non-interest in possession trust falling within IHTA 1984, s 89 which is treated as being an interest in possession trust. Both these types of trust are beneficiary-taxed. See IHTA 1984, ss 49(1A), 89, 89B. See, further, C4 at paras **[226.1]** ff. Some trusts for disabled persons can also obtain a measure of income tax and capital gains tax relief under FA 2005, ss 23–45, but the qualifying requirements which the trusts have to satisfy to obtain the relief are narrower than those relating to the IHT special treatment: see Part C4, paras **[226.3]** ff below. There is uprating of acquisition value on the death of the disabled person for capital gains tax purposes (see **[200.39]**) where he has an actual interest in possession which is beneficiary-taxed, but not if he is deemed to have a beneficiary-taxed interest in possession under IHTA 1984, s 89.

[200.100]

Beneficiary-taxed interests in possession – transitional provisions. In addition to the general categories of beneficiary-taxed interest in possession described above, there are two transitional categories of interest in possession which remain beneficiary-taxed. These are interests in possession which commenced before 22 March 2006, and 'transitional serial interests'. The latter term comprises three sub-categories: interests in possession which follow on from a pre-22 March 2006 interest in possession in the same property and commence after 21 March 2006 but before 6 April 2008 (IHTA 1984, s 49C); a person's interest in possession under a pre-22 March 2006 settlement which commences on the death after 5 April 2008 of the spouse or civil partner of that person, where the deceased spouse or civil partner had been entitled to an interest in possession which had commenced before 22 March 2006 and had been in the same property (IHTA 1984, s 49D); certain successive interests in life insurance policies which were settled before 22 March 2006 (IHTA 1984, s 49E). These are not interests which can be created by a will disposing of free estate, but the rules concerning them can be relevant to the preparation of a will. Where a testator has an interest in possession in settled property it is necessary for estimating the likely IHT position on his death to know whether his interest is a beneficiary-taxed one. If it is, there is then the question of whether it will be fully taxable as part of the testator's estate on death and thus affect the rate of tax on the testator's free estate, and, if it potentially will be so taxable, whether anything can be done about it. For example, if the testator has a special power of appointment over the settled property it may be possible for him to make an appointment in favour of his spouse or civil partner. If the testator has an interest in possession which commenced before 22 March 2006 the appointment of an interest in possession to the surviving spouse or civil partner could cause the settled property to be exempt on the testator's death (by virtue of IHTA 1984, s 49D), whereas if the testator has a transitional serial interest it will be necessary to appoint an absolute interest to the surviving spouse or civil partner in order to obtain the exemption.

[200.101]
Will precedents and IHT status. Plainly some of the most important questions which now have to be answered in respect of any precedent for the creation of settled interests is whether it creates an interest in possession or not, and, if it does, whether the interest is beneficiary-taxed. A life or similar interest in income is on any view of the meaning of the term an interest in possession, and so also is a right of residence arising under a trust. If the interest arises under a settlement created by the testator's will and commences from his or her death, it will be an IPDI and therefore beneficiary-taxed. A minor child or young adult who has a right to the income as it arises of a fund pending attaining an absolute interest in the capital at a specified age will have an interest in possession, but it will not be an IPDI if it falls within IHTA 1984, s 71A (for which see para **[200.108]**). In the notes to the precedents we indicate where relevant or important whether we believe a beneficiary-taxed interest is created. For discussion of the possible types of trust to include in wills see paras **[200.125]** ff below. For a discussion of the meaning of 'interest in possession' in TLATA 1996, see paras **[208.12]** ff.

[200.102]
IHT and capital gains tax consequences of settled property being subject to a beneficiary-taxed interest in possession. If an individual is beneficially entitled to a beneficiary-taxed interest in possession in settled property, he is treated for IHT purposes as if he were beneficially entitled to the property:

IHTA 1984, s 49(1). If the interest comes to an end during his life without him becoming absolutely entitled to the property itself, a set of IHT charging provisions apply which parallel, but are not quite the same in some respects as, the provisions for charging IHT on lifetime transfers of absolutely owned property (see the IHTA 1984, ss 51–53 and *Foster's Inheritance Tax*, E2.21–30). The individual who was entitled to the interest is treated as having made a transfer of value of the settled property in which the interest in possession subsisted (IHTA 1984, s 52(1)), and this is capable of being a potentially exempt transfer where someone else becomes absolutely entitled to the property, or becomes entitled to another beneficiary-taxed interest in possession, or where a s 71A trust (see para **[200.108]** below) follows an IPDI in certain circumstances: IHTA 1984, ss 3(4), 3A(1), (1A), (3B) and (7) and see paras **[200.70]** and **[200.71]** above and **[200.128]** below. Where someone dies while beneficially entitled to a beneficiary-taxed interest in possession in settled property, the settled property subject to the interest is charged to IHT as part of his estate immediately before his death (IHTA 1984, ss 4(1), 5(1) and 49(1)), and so on death settled property subject to such an interest in possession is taxed under the rules for absolutely-owned property: see para **[200.72]** above. However, the general personal representatives are not liable for the IHT on such settled property unless it was settled land (see para **[200.80]** above). The incidence of capital gains tax on settled property is for the most part the same whether or not there is a beneficiary-taxed interest in possession, subject to two important exceptions. One is that on the death of a person who is beneficially entitled to a beneficiary-taxed interest in possession there is in most cases acquisition-value uprating for capital gains tax purposes: see **[200.39]**. The other is that there is no capital gains tax hold-over relief when settled property subject to a beneficiary-taxed interest in possession vests absolutely in the person entitled to that interest, or anyone else, during the life of the person entitled to the beneficiary-taxed interest (unless business or agricultural assets are involved): again see para **[200.39]**.

[200.103]
Will trusts of foreign domiciled testators. If a testator has a foreign domicile for IHT purposes (see paras **[200.89]** and **[200.90]** above), and some or all of the beneficiaries intended to benefit under his will are UK resident, he should consider making a will settling the property intended for UK beneficiaries so as to take advantage of the excluded property rules: see C14 at para **[236.3]**.

[200.104]
Protective trusts. These (see para **[200.20]** above) receive special treatment under the IHTA 1984, s 88, which eliminates the charge which would otherwise arise under the IHTA 1984, s 52(1) on a forfeiture of a beneficiary-taxed interest in possession occurring, and provides for the 'principal beneficiary' to be treated as continuing to have the interest in possession after forfeiture. Where an IPDI is a protective life interest, and a forfeiture occurs, the deemed interest in possession after the forfeiture is deemed to be a continuation of the IPDI (IHTA 1984, s 88(4) and (5)). However, if the beneficiary has already become bankrupt before the testator's death with the result that the interest is forfeited before it commences, it

seems that s 88(4) and (5) cannot apply, with the result that the IHT relevant property regime will apply to the property subject to the interest. A testator who feels that imposing protective trusts would be appropriate for a particular beneficiary in favour of whom an IPDI is intended need not be discouraged from doing so by the IHT consequences. HMRC have indicated that they do not accept as falling within IHTA 1984, s 88 a protective trust which by comparison with the statutory form has a larger class of objects of the discretionary trust of income arising after a forfeiture, but do accept a power to pay capital to the principal beneficiary ([1976] BTR 421). We infer they would probably accept a trustee's power to lift the protection. HMRC's opinion on this point cannot easily be reconciled with *Re Wallace's Settlements* [1968] 2 All ER 209, [1968] 1 WLR 711 (in which Megarry J said of the rather similar words of the Variation of Trusts Act 1958, s 1(2) that the word 'like' required not identity but similarity) or *Thomas v IRC* [1981] STC 382, but it is wiser not to depart from the TA 1925, s 33 (Part G, para **[246.31]**) unless absolutely necessary. See B16 at paras **[216.6]** and **[216.7]** and Form C3.5 at para **[225.68]** for protective trust precedents.

[200.105]
Trusts for persons mentally disabled or in receipt of attendance allowance. The testator's main concern is usually that the beneficiary's means-tested social security benefits should be affected as little as possible, and that the beneficiary should not be entitled to any income or capital but it should be applicable at the trustees' discretion. If a testator wishes to make provision for a disabled person, a discretionary trust of income is usually the most appropriate method. If the beneficiary is a disabled person within IHTA 1984, s 89(4)–(6) (see **[200.99]**), for IHT purposes there is a choice between such a trust being beneficiary-taxed under IHTA 1984, s 89 (see para **[200.99]** above and pars **[226.4]** ff) or relevant property (see paras **[218.36]** ff). For a fuller discussion, see C4 at para **[226.3]** ff, and for precedents see Forms B18.4 at para **[218.34]**, C4.1 and C4.2 at paras **[226.13]** and **[226.40]**. It is also possible for a trust for a disabled person to obtain special income tax and capital gains tax treatment under FA 2005, ss 23–45, for which also see the notes below to C4, paras **[226.6]** ff.

[200.106]
Discretionary trusts. See B18 at paras **[218.8]**–**[218.15]** for discussion of these. The rules there discussed also apply to a post 21 March 2006 interest in possession trust where the interest is not beneficiary-taxed.

[200.107]
Abolition of accumulation and maintenance trusts within IHTA 1984, s 71. The former provision for accumulation and maintenance trusts for children contained in IHTA 1984, s 71 cannot apply to trusts created after 21 March 2006. For an account of them see *Foster's Inheritance Tax*, E5. Where someone dies after 21 March 2006 leaving a will which contains a trust intended to fall within s 71 (and which does not come within s 71A or 71D – for which see paras **[200.108]**, **[200.109]**), and where the interests are not vested absolutely by the time of his death, the IHT treatment of the trusts will vary according to the ages reached by the beneficiaries: see paras

[200.136] and **[217.2]** below. In relation to trusts coming into effect after 21 March 2006, including wills of persons dying after that date, there are two much more limited categories of trust for minor children which receive advantageous treatment for IHT purposes: under IHTA 1984, s 71A ('trusts for bereaved minors') and 71D ('age 18-to-25 trusts'). For either section to apply at least one of the beneficiary's parents must have died, and a trust in a will can only fall within either section if it is established under *the will of a parent of the child*. Parents for this purpose, however, extend to step-parents and anyone who at his or her death has parental responsibility for the child: see s 71H. A s 71D trust is essentially a variant on a s 71A trust which permits a higher vesting age, at the cost of possibly incurring an IHT charge of probably modest proportions.

[200.108]

Trusts for bereaved minors. As mentioned in para **[200.107]**, a trust can only fall within IHTA 1984, s 71A trust if one of the beneficiary's parents has died, and if the trust (if created by will) is created by the will of a parent of the child. The main requirement as to the form taken by such a trust, for IHTA 1984, s 71A to apply, is that the beneficiary will become absolutely entitled to the income and capital on or before attaining the age of 18. The trusts must also be such that the income arising before the beneficiary attains 18 is either income to which the beneficiary is entitled as it arises, i e it is held on an interest in possession trust for the beneficiary, or it is subject to a power to apply the income for the benefit of the beneficiary (and there is no power to apply it for anyone else) and the rest of the income is accumulated and held on trust for the beneficiary absolutely on attaining 18. Note the following:

(1) If the beneficiary has an interest in possession as from the testator's death, the trust will nevertheless fall within s 71A rather than be an IPDI trust (IHTA 1984, s 49A(4)(a)). However, a bare trust for a minor does not fall within s 71A, not being settled property (see para **[200.110]**), and a disabled person's interest (see para **[200.99]**) does not fall within s 71A either (s 71A(1)).

(2) Powers over capital must be limited to a power to apply capital for the benefit of the beneficiary. However, it is expressly provided that the possession by the trustees of the power of advancement under Trustee Act 1925, s 32, or a similar express power, even if expanded to be exercisable over more than half of the beneficiary's prospective entitlement, does not prevent the section from applying: s 71A(7). This, together with the provision that an application of capital for the benefit of a beneficiary is not an occasion of IHT charge (s 71B(2)(c)), means that it is possible in an appropriate case to defer vesting beyond 18 by an exercise of a power of advancement before the beneficiary attains that age, provided that the exercise is genuinely for the benefit of the beneficiary, at an acceptable cost in terms of IHT – there is no IHT charge on the exercise of power, but the relevant property or 18-to-25 trust regimes will apply there after: see, further, para **[224.24]**.

(3) The compatibility with s 71A trusts of a Trustee Act 1925, s 32 power applying to the whole of a presumptive share, as just described, is thus made clear, while its compatibility with trusts for the vulnerable within

FA 2005, ss 23–45 for income-tax and capital gains tax purposes remains uncertain (see para **[217.2]**). It is possible that if a power of advancement applies which is exercisable over the whole of a presumptive share the trust may be prevented from falling within FA 2005, s 35 even though it falls within IHTA 1984, s 71A.

(4) HMRC accept that IHTA 1984, s 71A can apply to a class gift where each beneficiary has a presumptive undivided share of an entire fund, and that it can apply to some undivided shares but not to others: *STEP/CIOT/HMRC April 2007,* questions 26 and 27.

(5) It might be thought that where there is, for example, a class gift to the children of the testator, the individual presumptive shares have to be looked at separately to see if IHTA 1984, s 71A applies. This would mean that for the trusts to fall within s 71A, the prospective share to which each beneficiary will become entitled if he attains the age of 18 must be fixed from the outset, and that a trust will not fall within s 71A if there is power to vary the shares to be taken by each beneficiary before they attain the age of 18. However, HMRC have stated, without explaining how they derive this from the wording of s 71A, that they accept that it is compatible with s 71A to have a class gift where the shares ultimately taken by the beneficiaries may be varied as between or among beneficiaries who are for the time being living and under the age of 18, provided that all the beneficiaries retain continuously some presumptive share, however small (*S 71A etc guidance June 2007,* para 1). Thus it is HMRC's opinion, first that for s 71A to apply, the trusts must be such that a beneficiary's share of capital will be irrevocably determined no later than attaining the age of 18, and secondly that s 71A will cease to apply if a power to vary shares is exercised revocably so as to reduce the presumptive share of one of several beneficiaries to nil in circumstances where that beneficiary could have a presumptive share restored to him on a revocation of that exercise of the power. On the other hand, HMRC say that the mere existence of an unexercised power that can be exercised in this way does not prevent s 71A from applying.

(6) As regards the income of each share, the choice is between TA 1925, s 31 applying unamended, or interest in possession treatment of the income during the minority. The latter has the advantage that the income will be subject to income tax as the income of the minor beneficiary rather than under the discretionary trust income regime (see B18 at paras **[218.29]** and **[218.32]** for the latter).

(7) HMRC accept that a trust within s 71A can be created by the exercise of a special power of appointment created by the testator's will, but not by exercise of a general power (*STEP/CIOT/HMRC April 2007,* question 19). An example would be where a testator's will gives his surviving spouse a life interest and confers on the trustees a special power of appointment exercisable for the benefit of the testator's issue, and that power is exercised by the trustees to create a trust which satisfies the s 71A preconditions.

(8) If s 71A applies, there is no IHT on the fund during the child's minority or on the child attaining his or her majority and becoming entitled to the capital, in the same way as formerly under IHTA 1984

s 71. If a 'vulnerable person election' can be made (see (3) above) and is made (FA 2005, ss 24, 37 – see para **[217.2]** below), the trustees' capital gains and undistributed income will be taxed as the beneficiary's (FA 2005, ss 25–33): see para **[217.2]**.

(9) If an IPDI comes to an end during the life of the person entitled to it (typically an IPDI given to the testator's surviving spouse), to be followed by a s 71A trust under the same settlement, the resulting deemed transfer of value on the termination of the IPDI is potentially exempt: see IHTA 1984, s 3A(1A)(c)(iii), (3B), and para **[200.128]**.

(10) One advantage of a s 71A trust is that capital gains tax hold-over relief is available on the property vesting in the beneficiary at or before attaining the age of 18: TCGA 1992, s 260(2)(da) as inserted by FA 2006. However, if the underlying property is land and the s 71A trust is a class gift for, for example, three children of the testator of different ages, none of the beneficiaries will become absolutely entitled to any of the trust property for capital gains tax purposes until the youngest attains the age of 18 (assuming all the land is retained until then and none of it is appropriated to an individual share). In such a situation there would only be holdover relief on the share of the youngest (unless business assets holdover relief is available under TCGA 1992, s 165). If this is a cause for concern a relevant property trust or even a bare trust may be more appropriate.

[200.109]

Age 18-to-25 trusts for a bereaved minor. These are trusts within IHTA 1984, s 71D. Apart from two important differences, the conditions for a trust to be within s 71D are the same as for trusts within s 71A, including the requirements that a parent of the beneficiary must have died, that (in the case of a trust created by a will) the trust must be established under the will of a deceased parent of the beneficiary or beneficiaries, and that it is not a trust for a disabled person within the rules referred to in para **[200.99]**. The main difference in the requirements for s 71D from those for s 71A is that the trusts should provide for absolute vesting of the capital and unapplied income no later than the age of 25, as opposed to the age of 18 in the case of s 71A trusts. The points made about IHTA 1984, s 71A trusts in sub-paras (2), (4), (5), and (7) of para **[200.108]** apply equally, mutatis mutandis, to s 71D trusts. The corresponding provision ensuring compatibility of s 71D applying with a Trustee Act 1925, s 32 power being exercisable, including being exercisable over the whole of a presumptive share, is in IHTA 1984, s 71D(7). The HMRC view of acceptable variability of the shares referred to in para **[200.108],** sub-para (5), where a trust is intended to be within s 71D, is of course that a beneficiary's share must become fixed irrevocably no later than attaining the age of 25. The second, more technical difference, between the preconditions for s 71D to apply and those for s 71A, is that if an under-25 beneficiary has an interest in possession commencing at the testator's death (and the trusts would otherwise fall within s 71D) it is an IPDI trust not a s 71D trust (s 71D(5)(c)). There are three main differences of s 71D from s 71A in its tax consequences, as follows:

(1) A s 71D trust does not fall within FA 2005, ss 23–45, ie the special

income tax and capital gains tax treatment for trusts for bereaved minors, for which see para **[217.2]**).

(2) The property in a s 71D trust will be subject to an IHT charge on the property vesting in the s 71D beneficiary, but only if absolute vesting occurs after the beneficiary has attained the age of 18. Where this happens, the property is subject to a 'relevant property' IHT exit charge, is not subject to the periodic charge, and the exit charge is calculated on the basis of the property having been relevant property only since the later to occur of the death of the testator or beneficiary attaining the age of 18 (s 71F).

(3) If an IPDI comes to an end during the life of the person entitled to it to be succeeded by a s 71D trust, the deemed transfer of value on the coming to an end of the IPDI is not potentially exempt.

As regards the income, the choice is between TA, 1925 s 31 applying unamended so that the beneficiary gets an interest in possession at 18, or extending the TA 1925, s 31 treatment of the income beyond the age of 18 if there is an available accumulation period in relation to it. It is strongly recommended that in all s 71D trusts the accumulation and maintenance trusts of income of TA 1925, s 31 are expressly extended to continue until the earlier to occur of the beneficiary attaining the age of 25 or the end of the 21-year accumulation period from the death of the testator. This is to avoid the possibility of it accidentally turning out to be an IPDI trust as a result of the testator dying when the beneficiary is between the ages of 18 and 25 in circumstances where s 31 applies without amendment. For extended accumulation and maintenance trusts see B18 at paras **[218.74]** ff, and Form C2.1, cl 8 at para **[224.36]**. Capital gains tax holdover relief is available on the property vesting in the beneficiary if it does so on or before he or she attains the age of 18 (TCGA 1992, s 260(2)(db) as inserted by FA 2006) or over 18 (TCGA 1992, s 260(2)(a)). The problem for the availability of holdover relief where the underlying property is land and the beneficial shares vest at different times, referred to in para **[200.108]** sub-para (10), is equally relevant to s 71D trusts.

[200.110]
Bare trusts. A bare trust created by will, i e where a trustee holds property on trust for someone absolutely, is of little practical difference from an outright gift where the recipient is an adult who does not suffer from a mental disability. The possibility of creating by testamentary gift a bare trust for someone who is still a minor, however, is a possibility of increased interest after the FA 2006 changes to IHT. HMRC accept that the trust property is not 'settled property' for IHT purposes, and that this is so whether or not Trustee Act 1925, s 31 has been excluded (*STEP/CIOT/HMRC April 2007*, question 33). The practical effect of a bare trust for a minor is not very different from an IHTA 1984, s 71A trust for a bereaved minor (see para **[200.108]** for the latter). The main difference is that on the death of the minor beneficiary of a bare trust under the age of 18 the trust property will pass under the intestacy rules, and be subject to IHT on his or her death, while under a s 71A trust the trust property can devolve under the trusts of the will and will not be subject to IHT on the beneficiary's death. Also, where there is a class of minor beneficiaries, there can be no flexibility as to

the shares taken by each in the case of a bare trust, while some limited flexibility is permitted, according to HMRC, in the case of a s 71A trust (see para **[200.108]**, sub-para (5)). The fact that the property passes under the intestacy rules has the disadvantage that if there is a surviving parent or parents the property is likely to devolve on him, her or them, but this disadvantage could perhaps be avoided where there is a class of beneficiaries, by making them entitled to the trust property as joint tenants (provided a least one survives the age of 18). The IHT charge on death will not be a disadvantage if the property is worth less than the nil-rate band at the beneficiary's death. A bare trust for a minor is the nearest to a s 71A trust which can be created in a will of a person who is not a parent of the intended beneficiary. If a will gives someone an IPDI (see para **[200.108]**), and that comes to an end during that person's life in favour of a bare trust for a minor, the deemed transfer of value on the coming to an end of the IPDI can be a potentially exempt transfer. For income tax and capital gains tax purposes the property subject to a bare trust arising under a will is the beneficiary's. The problem relating to s 71A trusts for the availability of holdover relief where the underlying property is land and the beneficial shares vest at different times, referred to in para **[200.108]**, sub-para (10), would not apply to a bare trust. A bare trust for a minor could and should include power for the trustees to apply income and capital for the benefit of the beneficiary, typically by Trustee Act 1925, ss 31 and 32 applying, preferably with s 32 applying to the whole of the beneficiary's entitlement.

(*d*) *Incidence of IHT*

[200.111]
The decision of the Court of Session in *Re Dougal* [1981] STC 514 to the effect that capital transfer tax (now IHT) on heritable property is prima facie a testamentary expense payable out of residue gave rise to the enactment of what is now the IHTA 1984, s 211 (Part G, para **[246.100]**) giving legislative effect to that decision throughout the UK in relation to deaths occurring on or after 26 July 1983. Incidence is more fully discussed in B14 at paras **[214.55]**–**[214.75]** and there are also notes on provisions concerning incidence as follows: in relation to specific bequests in B4 at para **[204.1]**; in relation to specific gifts of land in B6 at para **[206.3]**; and in relation to pecuniary legacies in B10 at para **[210.3]**. We would particularly draw attention to the absurd rule that in the absence of contrary provision, pecuniary legacies charged on a mixed fund of UK and foreign property bear their own tax to the extent that they are payable out of the foreign property, and to possible methods of excluding the rule, for which see B14 at paras **[214.64]** and **[214.71]**.

(*e*) *Partially exempt estates*

[200.112]
The IHTA 1984, Part II, Ch III contains rules to be applied when an estate is partially exempt to determine the extent of the exempt part or parts and the incidence of IHT. As regards incidence, IHTA 1984, s 41 has the effect, put broadly, overriding the terms of any will, that the recipients of the exempt

parts of the estate cannot be made to bear any of the IHT on the non-exempt parts. The only advantage gained by the beneficiaries interested in the non-exempt parts is thus the reduction in the overall tax rate as a consequence of there being parts of the estate which are exempt. That is the position where the estate is being administered in England. In the New Zealand case of *McGowan v Hamblett* (2005–06) 8 ITELR 943 it was held that IHTA 1984, s 41 had no application in an estate being administered in New Zealand, where there was UK property bearing IHT comprised in a residuary estate of which a quarter was exempt as going to the deceased's widow. The benefit of the exemption was in effect ordered to be shared rateably among the residuary beneficiaries, exempt and non-exempt alike.

[200.113]
Another matter dealt with in the IHTA 1984, Part II, Ch III is the allocation of exemption where the total value of gifts of some exempt type exceeds the limit for that exemption. The only types of testamentary gift to which this could now be relevant (most of the former limits on exemptions having been removed) are gifts by a person domiciled in the UK to a foreign domiciled spouse or civil partner (limited to an aggregate of £55,000: see the IHTA 1984, s 18(2)). By the IHTA 1984, s 38(2) the excess over the exemption in these cases is attributed to gifts not bearing their own tax before gifts bearing their own tax and otherwise attributed to the relevant gifts in proportion to their values. This rule appears to be incapable of variation by the terms of a will (though obviously it is the terms of the will which determine which gifts bear their own tax and which do not).

[200.114]
The remainder of the IHTA 1984, Part II, Ch III is mostly concerned with fixing the extent of the exempt portion of any partially exempt estate. A full account of these provisions is beyond the scope of this note, and we refer the reader to *Foster's Inheritance Tax*, D2.31–43 for this. We can only mention a few practical points for the draftsman.

[200.115]
Technical differences in drafting a will in ways relevant to the partial exemption rules can make only marginal differences to the amount of IHT paid. The main point to bear in mind is that some fairly elaborate calculations are required if the will involves either of the following:

(i) a wholly exempt residue combined with a mixture of specific gifts and/or legacies, some of which are free of and some subject to IHT;
(ii) a partially exempt residue combined with specific gifts and/or legacies of which some or all are free of IHT.

The deterrent effect of the rules applicable here lies not in the advanced mathematics involved (the worst you have to do is gross up tax-free gifts) but the complexity of the rules which have to be mastered. In circumstances where these complex rules have to be mastered and applied there may be, it seems to us, a very small IHT saving, which may pay for the extra administration costs involved.

[200.116]
Where residue is wholly or partially given to exempt beneficiaries, the partial exemption rules have some interesting consequences. One is that the amount of the estate which is chargeable to IHT on the death can be affected, sometimes very much affected, where there are non-exempt specific gifts, by whether those specific gifts bear their own IHT or not: see B14 at para **[214.74]**. Another is that where administration expenses such as legal fees are payable out of residue, it seems that the exempt residue used to pay them is still treated as exempt, so that in effect IHT is not charged on the part of the estate used to pay such administration expenses so far as they are met out of exempt residue. This is because the partial exemption rules operate by determining the value for IHT purposes of specific gifts (IHTA 1984, s 38), and then providing that what is left of the value of the estate is attributed to residue (IHTA 1984, s 39); the size of residue for the purposes of these rules is not affected by the payment of administration expenses out of it. By contrast, a liability of the estate which is not deductible (see para **[200.78]** for non-deductible debts) is treated as a specific gift under the partial exemption rules (IHTA 1984, s 38(6)), so that the value of such a liability does not fall out of charge when it is paid out of exempt residue. Another consequence of having a partially exempt residue used to be uncertainty as to how the residuary estate should be divided between exempt and non-exempt beneficiaries. The position has now become clearer but express provision is still advisable: see para **[200.118]** and B14 at para **[214.72]**.

[200.117]
The IHTA 1984, s 39A makes express provision for allocation of an estate between exempt and non-exempt gifts where there is business or agricultural relief. The relief is allocated rateably between the exempt and non-exempt parts of the estate, save that where there is a specific gift (whether or not to an exempt beneficiary) of business or agricultural property, the business or agricultural relief attributable to that property is allocated to that gift (see *Foster's IHT* D2.40 and C11 at paras **[233.1]** ff). Thus, where a testator has any property which may qualify for business or agricultural relief on his death, and the estate will be partially exempt, it will save IHT to make a specific gift of that property to a non-exempt beneficiary, or, if that is not practical, to avoid making a specific gift of that property to an exempt beneficiary. This has been an even more important topic ever since the higher rate of business and agricultural relief was increased to 100 per cent (see B5 at para **[205.5]** and C12 at para **[234.7]**), and it is discussed at some length in the Preliminary Note to C11 at paras **[233.1]** ff.

[200.118]
Where residue is divided into two or more proportionate shares, where at least one is exempt and at least one non-exempt, there is a question whether the shares should be on the basis of gross (of IHT) proportions or net ones. In *Re Benham's Will Trusts* [1995] STC 210, High Court, where there was no express provision on the point, net division was favoured. However, in *Re Ratcliffe* [1999] STC 262, also High Court, *Re Benham's Will Trusts* was not followed and gross division was held to be the correct method in the absence of express provision. The issue has not been considered at appellate level,

and uncertainty can arise on the wording of a will as to which basis of division was intended. Accordingly, despite *Re Ratcliffe*, it is strongly recommended that express provision is made even where gross division is intended, and it is clearly needed where net division is intended. See also B14 at paras **[214.72]** ff, and see Forms B14.35– B14.37 at paras **[214.78]–[214.80]** for examples of declarations to deal with this point.

(f) The consequences of IHT for dispositions by will (other than the creation of will trusts)
For IHT and will trusts see **[200.125]** ff.

[200.119]
Choice between lifetime and testamentary dispositions. Where the extent and nature of a person's assets enable him to make, and contemplate with equanimity making, potentially exempt transfers without any reservation of enjoyment or benefit, and that person has a reasonable chance of living for the next seven years, he has a strong incentive to make immediate lifetime gifts rather than retain property to devolve on his death. The changes made to IHT on settled property by FA 2006 mean that with rare exceptions potential exemption can only be obtained by making absolute lifetime gifts. Any new settlement made by way of lifetime gift is now subject to IHT under the 'relevant property' regime (ie that which previously applied to discretionary trusts), except so far as the settled property is immediately subject to a disabled person's interest within the new IHTA 1984, s 89B (see paras **[200.99]** and **[200.105]** and the notes in C4 at para **[226.1]** ff). This means that there will be an immediate charge to IHT if the value transferred by a lifetime transfer into a settlement (other than one creating a disabled person's interest), together with the value of other immediately chargeable transfers made during the preceding seven years, exceeds the nil-rate band. The provisions concerning gifts with reservation and non-deduction of debts discourage lifetime gifts by persons with modest assets, who do not feel that they can afford to divest themselves completely of a significant part of what they have. Another problem for making lifetime dispositions can be capital gains tax, if the assets most suitable for giving away are ones which have gone up in value a lot since they were acquired. There will be a chargeable capital gains tax disposal on giving them away, unless they are put into a settlement such that the gift is an immediately chargeable transfer for IHT purposes and hold-over relief can be claimed under the TCGA 1992, s 260; however, in such case there will be IHT immediately payable if the nil-rate band is exceeded. The change to a single capital gains tax rate of 18 per cent which was announced in the Pre-Budget Report of 9 October 2007 will mean, if it passes into law, that there will be a twofold choice. On the one hand, it could be a potentially exempt transfer giving rise to no immediate IHT charge but on which capital gains tax of 18 per cent of the excess of the value over acquisition cost (minus available annual exemption) is payable. On the other hand, it could be an immediately chargeable transfer where the capital gain can be held over, but IHT of 20 per cent is payable on the excess of the value over the available nil rate band. Lifetime gifts should always contain express provision as to who is to pay the IHT or additional IHT payable in the event of the donor dying within seven years: see para **[200.79]**.

There are special considerations where a person has business or agricultural property: see the Preliminary Note to B5 at paras **[205.1]** ff.

[200.120]
Business and agricultural relief and partial exemption. See C11 at paras **[233.1]** ff.

[200.121]
IHT payable out of residue. The IHT rules have the effect that the possible tax liabilities which may arise on death include the tax on potentially exempt transfers made within seven years of the transferor's death, additional tax on chargeable (not potentially exempt) transfers made within seven years before the transferor's death, and tax on property subject to a reservation within seven years of, or at, the donor's death. These tax liabilities are primarily payable by the transferees or donees or out of the property to which they relate (see paras **[200.79]** and **[200.80]** above), and will not be borne by the transferor's or donor's residuary estate in the absence of express provision to that effect (see B14 at para **[214.60]**), except where the persons primarily liable fail to pay the tax and the personal representatives pay it and cannot recover it from them. The law is unclear on whether the personal representatives have a right to reclaim any such tax which they have paid in the absence of express agreement between the deceased and the transferee or donee that the latter should pay it. However, any express direction in a will as to the incidence of IHT needs to be considered carefully to see if it might unintentionally include within its scope any tax in these categories (see B14 at para **[214.70]**). The liability rules also include the special category of non-deductible debt where the creditor held property derived from the debtor (see para **[200.78]** above), and the IHT payable by reason of the debtor's death and attributable to such debts will be payable out of his residuary estate in the absence of provision to the contrary.

[200.122]
The IHT rules may also make it more difficult to decide when making a will what IHT on the estate should be borne by residue, in that the extent of the ultimate IHT liability of a testator's estate, and therefore the consequences of the various possible provisions he might make in his will for the incidence of IHT, will be very uncertain at the time when his will is made if he has just made or is about to make substantial potentially exempt transfers. If he does not survive those transfers by seven years, not only will the rate of the IHT charge on his death be much higher, but there will be the possibility that the estate may have to bear the IHT on the lifetime transfers if the persons primarily liable do not or cannot pay, or there is no right of recovery (see paras **[200.79]** and **[200.80]** above).

On these topics see, further, the Notes in B10 at paras **[210.64]**–**[210.67]** and B14 at paras **[214.55]** ff.

[200.123]
Administration of estates. Administration of estates may be seriously delayed by executors who are concerned about their liability for IHT on lifetime gifts made by the deceased. Personal representatives can apply under the IHTA

1984, s 239 for certificates of discharge in respect of such of these as they know about, and if the tax has been paid HMRC has a duty to issue such a certificate if the transferor has died (IHTA 1984, s 239(2)). Note that in the case of potentially exempt transfers which become chargeable, an application for a certificate of discharge can only be made after two years have elapsed from the transferor's death, unless HMRC think fit to entertain an earlier application made after the transferor's death (IHTA 1984, s 239(2A)). However, neither s 239 nor any other provision of the IHTA 1984 seems to make available any protection for personal representatives against IHT liabilities in respect of lifetime transfers or property subject to a reservation of which they are wholly ignorant. Because a personal representative's liability for IHT is an original liability and not a representative one (*IRC v Stannard* [1984] 2 All ER 105, [1984] 1 WLR 1039), it is submitted that personal representatives will not be protected against unforeseeable claims for IHT by statutory advertisements under the TA 1925, s 27. However, HMRC have said that they will not usually pursue further IHT personal representatives who have done their best to discover lifetime transfers and disclose them to HMRC, and have obtained a certificate of discharge and distributed the estate before a chargeable lifetime transfer comes to light (letter to the Law Society published in *Law Society's Gazette* 13 March 1991, reproduced in *Foster's Inheritance Tax*, X6.44).

[200.124]
Personal representatives who delay applying for a grant of representation for more than a year after the end of the month in which the deceased died may find that it is a condition of obtaining a grant of representation that they pay IHT which is still unpaid in respect of lifetime gifts or property subject to a reservation of which the deceased was the donor. This is because it is a statutory precondition of obtaining a grant that they must pay all IHT for which they are liable (Supreme Court Act 1981, s 109(1) and IHTA 1984, s 226(2)), and they become liable for IHT on lifetime gifts and property subject to a reservation if it remains unpaid after 12 months have elapsed from the end of the month in which the deceased died: IHTA 1984, s 204(8) and (9).

(*g*) *Trusts in dispositions by will – usefulness, the alternatives, and tax consequences*

[200.125]
Settlements by will – possible purposes of trusts

(1) To protect principal beneficiar(y)(ies) from their own improvidence, or from losing it all on divorce, or having it all spent on care home fees.
(2) To determine the ultimate destination of property after the death of the immediate beneficiar(y)(ies). The testator may want it to go in the end to the younger generation, to the testator's own relatives rather than the beneficiary's, or to a favourite charity.
(3) Save tax, in particular IHT, or at any rate minimise it so far as compatible with other objectives.

A particular use of a will trust is to provide generation-skipping dispositions. Suppose a testator, T, is making his will. He has an adult child, B, who has two children, M and N. If he gives the property to B, B can make potentially exempt transfers in favour of M and N, but under IHT there remain several good reasons why a 'generation skipping' disposition by T's will directly in favour of M and N could be an advantage. If M and N are minors, it will be an advantage if B is not the 'settlor' for income tax purposes of property given to M and N (see para **[200.42]**). B can only (post 21 March 2006) make potentially exempt transfers in favour of M and N by way of absolute gifts. A gift by T's will directly to M and N will ensure that some property reaches M and N instead of being squandered on riotous living by B. If T owns property which in aggregate has a value higher than the sum of the values of its parts, such as a majority holding of the ordinary shares of a property company, there may be advantages in the future if it has been split by T's will among separate gifts to B, M and N, each gift being of a minority holding. A direct gift by T's will to M and N will also avoid the disadvantage of potentially exempt transfers by B to M and N that perhaps substantial amounts of IHT may be payable if B does not survive the transfer by seven years, and the disadvantage of lifetime transfers by B to M and N that the gifts with reservation rules could apply. Where it is uncertain when T is making his will whether B will need the property which might be given directly to M and N, T's choice will lie between making a gift to B, creating an IPDI trust for B, and creating a discretionary trust under which B, M and N are beneficiaries. If T makes an absolute gift to B, or creates an IPDI in his favour, B will still be able to make potentially exempt transfers in favour of M and N, and can make gifts to M and N by deed of variation within two years of T's death which will be treated for IHT purposes as dispositions by T's will (see F3 at paras **[241.1]**–**[241.21]**). There will be the disadvantage, if M and N are minors, that B will be the 'settlor' for income tax purposes (see para **[200.42]**), and in the case of potentially exempt transfers the other disadvantages mentioned above. If T creates a discretionary trust by his will, distributions of capital in favour of B or M or N will give rise to an IHT charge but this may be quite low or even nil, and in the case of distribution to M and N the IHT position could in many circumstances be better than it would have been on a transfer by B from absolute property or settled property in which B had an interest in possession (see para **[200.131]**, **[200.132]** and B18 at para **[218.6]** ff).

[200.126]
Possible types of trust which can be created by post-21 March 2006 wills, classified by their IHT treatment:

(1) *Immediate post-death interests* ('IPDIs'), i e interest in possession trusts which are treated for IHT in the same way as interests in possession trusts were treated before 22 March 2006. The property subject to the IPDI is beneficiary-taxed for IHT purposes, i e treated as if it were the property of the person entitled to the IPDI: see paras **[200.98]** and **[200.102]**. Overriding powers can be combined with an IPDI, but such powers should be ones under which the interests in remainder can be altered without the IPDI being terminated: see paras **[200.96]** and **[200.98]**. The settled property is not subject to periodic charges while the IPDI continues, but is subject to what could be a substantial IHT charge on the death of the person entitled to the IPDI, aggregated with

that person's free estate. The most important use of IPDIs is for surviving spouses or civil partners, to obtain the spouse or civil partnership exemption while determining the destination of the settled property after the death of the spouse or civil partner. For the capital gains tax position see para **[200.127]**.

(2) *Interest in possession trusts which are subject to IHT as relevant property*, ie any interest in possession trust where there is not an IPDI, disabled person's interest, or s 71A trust, but where a beneficiary or beneficiaries have an interest or interests in possession (and which will be subject to income tax as interest in possession trusts). For IHT on relevant property see para **[218.8]** ff. Creation of this type of interest by will is not straightforward – if done by means of an initial discretionary trust of income followed by an interest in possession, it needs to be done in such a way that IHTA 1984, s 144 does not convert the interest in possession into an IPDI: see para **[200.133]** below. Relevant property interest in possession trusts can and normally should be combined with wide overriding powers. There is a periodic charge, but the property is not taxed as part of the estate of a beneficiary, and in appropriate cases this can result in less IHT being paid than would be paid if there was an IPDI. The capital gains tax position is that there can be hold-over relief on someone becoming absolutely entitled to trust property, but there is no acquisition-value uprating on the death of someone entitled to an interest in possession: see para **[200.39]**.

(3) *Fully discretionary trusts*, ie where the income is subject to a discretionary trust or power to distribute the income among a class of beneficiaries at the discretion of the trustees from time to time, usually combined with power to accumulate income. These should always be combined with overriding powers of appointment and/or application of capital. The IHT and capital gains tax treatment is now the same as for trusts falling under (2) above, but the income tax treatment is in accordance with ITA 2007, ss 479–483: see paras **[218.29]** ff.

(4) *Protective trusts*. If the initial interest in possession is an IPDI the beneficiary will continue to be treated as having an IPDI after forfeiture, provided that forfeiture has not occurred before the testator's death: see para **[200.104]** above. Otherwise, settled property subject to a protective trust will be subject to IHT as relevant property.

(5) *Beneficiary-taxed trusts for disabled persons*. A disabled person within the definition in IHTA 1984, s 89(4)–(6) may be given a disabled person's interest within IHTA 1984, s 89B, which could be *either* an actual interest in possession, *or* a discretionary trust of income for the life of the disabled person with restrictions on the power to apply capital so that IHTA 1984, s 89 applies. In either case the settled property subject to the disabled person's interest will be beneficiary-taxed, ie treated for IHT purposes as if it were part of the disabled person's estate. The capital gains tax position is more complicated. A further alternative for the benefit of a disabled person is a discretionary relevant property trust as under (3) above. See, further paras **[200.99]** and **[200.105]** and C4, paras **[226.13]** ff.

(6) *Trusts for bereaved minors* within IHTA 1984, s 71A and possibly also

FA 2005, ss 35 and 39: see para **[200.108]** above and para **[217.4]** below. These can only be created for the testator's own minor children.

(7) *Age 18-to-25 trusts* within IHTA 1984, s 71D: see para **[200.109]** above. These can also only be created for the testator's own children.

(8) *Bare trusts for minors*: see para **[200.110]** above. The trust property is the absolute property of the beneficiary for all tax purposes, and is not settled property for IHT or capital gains tax purposes.

[200.127]

Absolute interests as against trust interests – capital gains tax aspects. The capital gains tax rules, like the IHT rules, are mostly neutral between making an absolute gift to a person and making a settlement under which that person has an IPDI (for IPDIs see paras **[200.98]** and **[200.102]**). In particular, the capital gains tax exemption for private residences under TCGA 1992, ss 222–225 can apply where a beneficiary has an interest in possession in a property comprised in a settlement which is his principal private residence, and in most cases there is capital gains tax acquisition-value uprating on the death of the beneficiary: see para **[200.39]**. The main exceptions to capital gains tax neutrality between an absolute interest and an IPDI are that the amount of annual exemption available to trustees is less than would be available to the beneficiary if he were absolutely entitled, and that if a beneficiary entitled to an IPDI becomes absolutely entitled to the settled property it is a capital gains tax disposal, and one in relation to which there is no hold-over relief unless the settled property is business or agricultural assets within TCGA 1992, s 165. In a relevant property trust (see para **[218.8]** ff for IHT on relevant property), on the other hand, the capital gains tax position is that there can be hold-over relief on someone becoming absolutely entitled to trust property, but there is no acquisition-value uprating on the death of someone entitled to a beneficial interest: see para **[200.39]**. Particularly after the Finance Act 2006 changes, it is possible for the capital gains tax private residence exemption under TCGA 1992, ss 222–225 to apply to relevant property. A disadvantage of settled property, as opposed to absolutely owned property, has been that the capital gains tax rate on disposals of settled property has been the trust rate, in 2007–08 40 per cent, the same as the higher rate of income tax paid by individuals, whereas an individual's disposal of an absolutely-owned asset could be wholly or partly taxed at the basic rate so far as his income and capital gains in any particular tax year did not reach the threshold of the higher rate. However, the changes to capital gains tax announced in the Pre-Budget Report on 9 October 2007 include a flat rate of capital gains tax of 18 per cent for individuals and trusts alike, with effect from 6 April 2008, and so this disadvantage of a trust interest as against an absolute interest will disappear as from that date if this passes into law. In the same Pre-Budget Report it was also announced that taper relief would cease with effect from 6 April 2008. Accordingly, the former advantage of settling property on trusts so that property remained in the same ownership for capital gains tax purposes through successive beneficial interests, so as to maximise taper relief, no longer exists.

[200.128]
Trusts in the wills of spouses or civil partners – younger couples. Trusts are not usually appropriate to wills for young couples, especially ones with young children and/or modest assets, where the purpose of the will is to make provision against the possibility of early death of one of them. Here the importance of the survivor having maximum financial support is what is usually most important, and an absolute gift of all the first to die's property to the other spouse or civil partner will usually be preferred (see C2 at paras **[224.1]** ff). If it is decided to provide an IPDI for the surviving spouse or civil partner where there are minor children or stepchildren of the testator, a possibility is either to provide a s 71A trust for the minor children to follow the IPDI, or, better but more complicated, provide flexible powers of appointment which would enable the appointment of such trusts. This is because, if the IPDI of the surviving spouse or civil partner is brought to an end during his or her lifetime, to be followed by trusts for the testator's children, the deemed transfer of value for IHT purposes will be a potentially exempt transfer where it is followed by a s 71A trust under the same settlement (IHTA 1984, s 3A(1A)(c)(iii), (3B)). Such an event is only a potentially exempt transfer if the settled property 'continues to be held on the trusts of the settlement' when s 71A starts to apply (s 3A(3B)(e)(i)). HMRC accept that this would be satisfied if the s 71A trust arises under the exercise of a special power of appointment created by the will rather than under the words of the will itself (*STEP/CIOT/HMRC April 2007,* question 19). For IPDIs see para **[200.98]**, and for s 71A see para **[200.108]**. On the death of the surviving spouse or civil partner a s 71D trust (see para **[200.109]**) is a possible choice, but may not be wanted where the assets are substantial and there is concern about vesting of capital at too early an age. In the latter case a relevant property trust might be preferable. Beneficiary-taxed treatment will not be available for any continuing trust after the termination of an IPDI (except for a disabled person's interest—see paras **[200.99]**, **[200.105]** for these). See, further, C2 at para **[224.1]** ff.

[200.129]
Trusts in the wills of spouses or civil partners – older couples. Assuming that nil-rate band carry-forward, as announced in the Pre-Budget Report of 9 October 2007 (see para **[200.75]**), passes into law, nil-rate band discretionary trusts are no longer needed to make sure of making use of the first to die's nil-rate band, except in special circumstances. See para **[200.130]** for the circumstances in which nil-rate band discretionary trusts may still be worth using. The usual arrangement, and one which will take maximum advantage of nil-rate band carry forward, will be an exempt testamentary gift by the first to die of substantially the whole of his or her estate for the benefit of the survivor. This can be an absolute gift or an interest in possession which is an IPDI. The advantages and disadvantages of an IPDI as opposed to an absolute interest are:

(1) The ultimate destination of the property can be determined by the testator – of particular importance for childless couples or persons in second or subsequent marriages or civil partnerships.
(2) *IHT.* Property subject to an IPDI in favour of the surviving spouse or

civil partner gets the spouse or civil partnership exemption in the same way as an absolute gift, and is otherwise subject to IHT in the same way as absolute property.

(3) *Capital Gains Tax*. There are the advantages and disadvantages mentioned in para **[200.127]**.

(4) *Income Tax*. There is no significant income tax advantage or disadvantage in interest in possession trusts as opposed to absolute ownership.

If an IPDI is decided on, the matrimonial home, or the first to die's interest in it, will normally be part of residue. The trustees should be given power to purchase an undivided share of a property in the event of purchase of a replacement property, and combine with other proprietors of a property to sell or purchase the home or any other such property which may wholly or partly form part of residue: see, for example, Form B8.1 at para **[208.38]**, sub-clause (6). On the death of the survivor the choice of remainder interests in relation to the estate of the first to die is among: absolute interests, typically for issue or other relations who are adult, a relevant property trust, typically for infant or young grandchildren or other class of younger relations, or exempt gifts to charity or a political party etc. As regards the dispositions to take effect on the death of the survivor in relation to his or her own estate there is the additional possibility of an IPDI trust. See, further, paras **[200.131]**, **[200.132]**.

[200.130]

Continuing uses for nil-rate band discretionary trusts. In wills for married couples or civil partners, the whole elaborate structure of nil-rate band discretionary trusts is no longer needed or advisable in the majority of cases, if, as seems likely, nil-rate band carry-forward passes into law as announced in the Pre-Budget Report of 9 October 2007 (see para **[200.75]**). The important point about the carry-forward rules is that if none of the first to die's nil-rate band is used, the nil-rate band *at its level at the time of the survivor's death* is doubled. A nil-rate band discretionary trust fund would have to grow in value by a greater percentage than the percentage increase in the nil-rate band between the first and second deaths for it to produce a better result than the carry-forward rules. It is difficult to predict at the time of making a will either the future growth of the nil-rate band or of the value of particular assets. There are all kinds of difficulties about nil-rate band discretionary trusts, and setting them up and keeping them on the go is trouble and expense. In general, nil-rate band carry-forward seems a much better option than a nil-rate band discretionary trust. There remain the following situations in which a nil-rate band discretionary trust is still worth considering:

(1) Where either or both testators have an asset which, or a part of which, could be appropriated to the nil rate band discretionary trust fund, and which they are confident will grow in value between the two deaths at a rate which would be likely to exceed the expected rate of increase of the nil-rate band.

(2) Where the testator wishes to target the benefit of his nil-rate band if he predeceases his or her spouse or civil partner. For example, a childless married couple might decide to make wills where the first to die gives

the survivor an IPDI life interest in his or her estate followed by the fund going to that testator's relatives, and the survivor leaves her or his estate to her or his relatives. If their estates are or might turn out to be unequal, they might prefer that the ultimate beneficiaries under the first to die's will should have the benefit of all of the first to die's nil rate band. If the matter was left to the carry-forward rules, the combined nil-rate bands on the death of the survivor would be shared rateably between the life interest fund and the survivor's free estate. A possible option would be a nil-rate band discretionary trust in the first to die's will which devolves on the death of the survivor on that testator's beneficiaries. There would then be the problem that if the first to die also leaves his or her residuary estate on an IPDI trust for the survivor, on the death of the survivor the survivor's nil rate band will be shared rateably between the IPDI trust and the survivor's free estate. If the nil-rate band trust fund is wanted for the reason just given, it is likely that it would also be desired that the survivor's relatives get the full benefit of the survivor's nil rate band. The first to die's IPDI trust could contain provision for some of the fund to go to the survivor's relatives, according to a formula based on the amount of the survivor's nil-rate band going to the IPDI trust.

(3) Where one or both testators have been married or in a civil partnership previously, where that previous marriage or civil partnership ended with the death of the other party and that other party did not make full use of his or her nil-rate band. In this situation, some nil-rate band will be wasted unless the first to die's will creates a nil-rate band discretionary trust of the usual kind or otherwise makes non-exempt gifts equal to the available nil-rate band at the first to die's death. This is because nil-rate band carry-forward is to be limited to the maximum of a doubling of the nil-rate band on the death of the survivor: see the proposed IHTA 1984, s 8A(5) and (6). See further, para **[200.75]**. If that limit is relaxed, either in the legislation as it eventually passes into law, or subsequently, this reason for using a nil-rate band discretionary trust may become less strong or disappear.

(4) Where one or both testators have assets which potentially qualify for 100 per cent business or agricultural relief. It could be worthwhile to put such assets into a discretionary trust in the event of the spouse or civil partner who owns them being the first to die. The main point of doing this would be in case the assets cease to qualify for the relevant relief before the death of the survivor. A specific gift of the relevant assets would probably be more appropriate than a nil-rate band pecuniary legacy. See paras **[233.8]** ff.

(5) Where it is desired to maximise the protection of the first to die's assets, during the survivor's period of survivorship, from the depredations of creditors, care home fees, subsequent spouses or civil partners, etc, of the survivor, while avoiding any IHT being paid on the first death. A nil-rate band trust where the income is held on discretionary trusts, combined with an IPDI for the survivor in the rest of the estate, will be the best that can be done in this regard, and will be particularly effective where the nil-rate band trust fund contains the first to die's income-yielding assets and residue wholly or mainly consists of non

income-yielding assets such as a dwelling house occupied by the survivor. For an example see Form C3.5 at paras **[225.68]** ff.

If it is possible but uncertain that a nil-rate band discretionary trust would be beneficial, the best course of action could be to include nil-rate band discretionary trusts, which include the surviving spouse or civil partner as a beneficiary, on the footing that if after the death of the first to die it does not appear to be the best arrangement, an absolute interest or an IPDI can be appointed to the surviving spouse or civil partner within two years of the death in reliance on IHTA 1984, s 144 (see paras **[200.133]** and **[225.83]** ff for s 144).

[200.131]

Trusts for non-exempt beneficiaries other than minor children. The choice for IHT purposes, if absolute gifts are decided against, is between an IPDI or a relevant property trust (see paras **[200.98]** and **[218.8]** ff for these respectively). In this kind of case a relevant property trust will usually save IHT, unless the aggregate of the personal assets of the intended primary beneficiary and the fund being used to benefit him or her will be plainly below the IHT threshold, or the property will go to charity on the primary beneficiary's death, or the beneficiary is young and in good health and might survive for many years. The advantages of a relevant property trust are particularly strong where a testator wants to leave some money to boost the income of a not very well-off sibling or friend of mature years, or wants to provide for a partner who is not a spouse or civil partner, but wants the property to go ultimately to other persons, or where the testator wishes to benefit some or all of the members of a class such as the testator's descendants of more than one generation and wishes to maintain flexibility as to the relative amounts ultimately taken by each beneficiary. There is also the advantage of a relevant property trust that capital gains tax hold-over relief is available if assets vest absolutely. Some more detailed points to bear in mind are:

(1) The initial IHT cost of setting up such a trust by will, ie the IHT charge on the death of the testator or of the testator's spouse or civil partner (where he or she has an IPDI under the testator's will), is exactly the same for creating a relevant property trust as it is for creating an IPDI trust for a non-exempt beneficiary, or making an absolute gift to the non-exempt beneficiary (in contrast to setting up trusts by lifetime disposition).
(2) Once a relevant property trust is up and running, it will have to run for really quite a long time before it runs up aggregate IHT charges greater than would be paid on the death of someone with an interest in possession whose combined free estate and deemed estate subject to an interest in possession significantly exceeds the nil-rate band and is chargeable on his or her death. Your client will often not know what the personal assets of the person or persons whom he or she wants to benefit will be. However, where the intended beneficiary or beneficiaries are likely to be young at the testator's death, an IPDI can be a sensible choice.
(3) Relevant property has the advantage where the underlying property is business or agricultural assets which qualify for IHT business or

agricultural relief, because the ownership remains wholly vested in the trustees at all material times, instead of it shifting between the person entitled to the IPDI and the trustees.

(4) In a situation of uncertainty as to what will be the most beneficial arrangement after the death of a testator, a discretionary trust is probably the best option. This is because it is in general easier, after the testator's death, to convert a discretionary trust into an IPDI one with retrospective effect, by an appointment under IHTA 1984, s 144 as amended (see paras **[200.133]** and **[225.83]** ff), than it is to turn an IPDI trust into a discretionary one under s 142 by a deed of variation made by the person entitled to the IPDI, and which will not be possible if he or she dies before doing so.

(5) As mentioned in para **[200.76]** above, the new FA 1986, s 102ZA (inserted by FA 2006, Sch 20, para 33) treats the termination of an IPDI (or other beneficiary-taxed interest in possession) during the life of the person entitled to the interest as a gift of the underlying settled property, for gift with reservation purposes. Also as a result of FA 2006, if an IPDI (or other beneficiary-taxed interest in possession) terminates during the life of the person entitled to it in favour of anything other than absolute interests (or disabled person's interests) there will be an immediate IHT charge, and if it terminates in favour of absolute interests there is a capital gains tax disposal without hold-over relief (unless the settled property is business or agricultural assets within TCGA 1992, s 165). Under a relevant property settlement, different beneficiaries can receive income or similar benefits from the settled property at different times without there being adverse IHT consequences when benefit to one beneficiary ceases and benefit to another commences, or when there remains a possibility of later benefit to a beneficiary who has for the time being ceased to receive benefit.

(6) *Capital Gains Tax.* There are the advantages and disadvantages of settled as opposed to absolutely-owned property mentioned in para **[200.127]**. There is no advantage or disadvantage in terms of tax rate between a relevant property and an IPDI trust. Relevant property, as opposed to property subject to an IPDI, has the disadvantage of no acquisition value uprating on the death of a beneficiary, but in the case of an IPDI this will often only be obtainable at the cost of an IHT charge on that beneficiary's death. In favour of a relevant property settlement is the fact that hold-over relief can be obtained on property leaving the settlement. It is also possible now, post-FA 2006, for a beneficiary under a discretionary trust to be permitted to occupy trust property as a principal residence, for the private residence relief from capital gains tax to apply, but for it to continue to be relevant property for IHT purposes.

(7) *Income Tax.* There is an income tax disadvantage of a discretionary trust in the need for trustees to account for tax at the trust rate (ITA 2007, ss 479–483), and in relation to dividend income there is a disadvantage in lack of carry-across of tax credit to the beneficiaries to whom the income is distributed. See paras **[218.29]** ff. However, this

can now be avoided by having an interest in possession relevant property trust: see para **[200.126]** (2) above.

[200.132]

Trusts for minor children, grandchildren, nieces, nephews etc. Where what is wanted is a trust for the testator's own minor children or stepchildren there are, in addition to the possibilities discussed in para **[200.131]**, the options of a s 71A or a s 71D trust: see paras **[200.108]** and **[200.109]** above for the requirements and advantages, and para **[200.128]** for the possibility of potential exemption where a s 71A trust succeeds an IPDI. If the testator is a parent or step-parent of the prospective beneficiaries but does not want vesting of capital in the beneficiaries by the age of 25, or he is not a parent or step-parent of the prospective beneficiaries, there are the possibilities of IPDIs (see para **[200.98]**), or a relevant property trust (see para **[218.8]** ff). For the comparative merits of IPDI and relevant property trusts see para **[200.131]**. Another option in the opposite direction is a bare trust: see para **[200.110]**. Where an IPDI is provided for a person under 18, or a s 71A trust is created with an interest in possession in the income while a beneficiary is under the age of 18, the beneficiary will become entitled to call for the current income from the age of 18, and on attaining that age to call for any income which has arisen during the minority which has not been applied for his or her benefit. If an IPDI is being provided for someone who may be a minor at the testator's death, remember to modify TA 1925, s 31 so that he or she will be absolutely entitled to the income as it arises while he or she is a minor: see Form C2.1, cl 8 at para **[224.36]**, for an example. TA 1925, s 31 unmodified makes contingent on attaining 18 the right to the income arising during the minority which is not applied for the beneficiary's benefit, and so prevents there being an interest in possession. Bare trusts, on the other hand (see para **[200.110]**), do not require express modification of s 31 in this manner because s 31 provides that unapplied income during the minority is added to capital if the beneficiary dies under the age or 18, and the beneficiary is entitled to the capital in any event. Where a trust of capital vesting contingently on attaining a specified age greater than 18 is being created for a minor or minors which will not fall within IHTA 1984, ss 71A or 71D, and where it is intended that the relevant property rather than the IPDI regime should apply, it is recommended that the accumulation and maintenance trusts of income of TA 1925, s 31 are expressly extended to continue until the earlier to occur of the beneficiary attaining the age of vesting or the end of the 21-year accumulation period from the death of the testator. This is to avoid the possibility of it accidentally turning out to be an IPDI trust as a result of the testator dying when the beneficiary is between the ages of 18 and the vesting age in circumstances where s 31 applies without amendment. For extended accumulation and maintenance trusts see B18 at paras **[218.74]** ff, and Form C2.1, cl 8 at para **[224.36]**.

[200.133]

The revised IHTA 1984, s 144, and creating non-IPDI interests in possession. (For IHTA 1984, s 144, see also paras **[225.83]** ff.) FA 2006 amended IHTA 1984, s 144 in relation to the estate of any testator dying after 21 March 2006 who has settled some or all of his or her estate by his or her will. It now contains two independent provisions, as follows:

(a) Section 144(1)–(2) deal with cases where, before there is an IPDI for a disabled person's interest in the settled property, there is an event giving rise to a relevant property exit charge within two years after the death of the testator, treating the state of affairs after the event as if it were contained in the will in the same way as before 22 March 2006. Typically this will be where an absolute interest or a disabled person's interest is created or arises. The trap for the unwary that these provisions do not apply if the event in question occurs within three months of the testator's death will continue. These subsections can apply where an absolute interest or disabled person's interest is created or arises out of an IHTA 1984, s 71D trust in relation to which the beneficiary is over the age of 18, as well as where it is created or arises out of a relevant property trust.

(b) Section 144(3) and (4) apply where an IPDI or a s 71A or s 71D trust is created or arises, before there is an IPDI for a disabled person's interest, during the two-year period following the death of the testator. This separate provision is required because these are interests the creation of which out of relevant property are not inherently occasions of relevant property exit charge: an IPDI has to start from the testator's death, and a s 71A or s 71D trust has to be established by the will of a deceased parent of a beneficiary. The IPDI or s 71A or s 71D trust will be treated as if they had been contained the testator's will. Note that s 144(3) and (4) do apply where the event in question is within three months of the testator's death. This provision could be used to turn a s 71A or s 71D trust into an IPDI trust.

As already mentioned, one of the main new possibilities opened up by the new rules is the possibility of having an interest in possession trust which is taxed as relevant property. If this is what is wanted, it is necessary to avoid an IPDI arising. This has a technical problem arising from IHTA 1984, s 144 as amended by FA 2006 (for the amended text of which see paras **[225.83]**–**[225.91]**), as follows:

(1) There is an interpretative problem as to what is required for IHTA 1984, s 144(3)(c) to apply to an IPDI attemptedly created or arising after the testator's death but within two years of it, perhaps best explained by an example. Suppose a testator T has by his will left his residuary estate on discretionary trusts of income and subject to a trustees' power of appointment. One year after T's death the trustees appoint a life interest in the residuary estate to Mrs T. Will the interest so appointed qualify as an IPDI for the purposes of IHTA 1984, s 144(3)(c) if it commences from the date of the appointment, or will it only do so if the appointment in favour of Mrs T includes the income of the residuary estate which has arisen between T's death and the date of the appointment? The critical question is whether the appointment, if it does not include the arrears of income between T's death and the date of the appointment, causes the residuary estate to be held on trusts that would, if they had in fact been established by T's will, have resulted in an IPDI subsisting in the residuary estate.

(2) Until there is clarification of the problem referred to in (1) above by legislative amendment or HMRC statement of practice, the cautious

view must be that an appointment of an IPDI should carry the arrears of income from death, and that where an IPDI is not wanted the interest in possession should commence more than two years after the testator's death. Early indications are that HMRC regard s 144(3) as applying to any interest in possession which commences during the two years after the testator's death (see *STEP/CIOT/HMRC April 2007*, question 14).

(3) Section 144 does not just apply where the trustees make an appointment or application of capital, but also where under the provisions of the will a period of discretionary trust is followed by an event within two years of the death which falls within s 144(1) or (3). This, together with the point discussed in paras (3) and (4) above, has implications for the kind of case where what is wanted is an interest in possession but with the settled property being subject to the IHT relevant property regime. The safe course will be for the initial discretionary trust to last for more than two years from the death before the intended interest in possession commences.

(4) An alternative method of obtaining relevant property treatment for an interest in possession created by will would be, for example, a short interest in possession (of less than a year) for X followed by an interest in possession for Y, in order that Y's interest should not be an IPDI. This would mean that the termination of X's interest would be treated as an immediately chargeable lifetime transfer by X, but this could be acceptable in some circumstances, e g where the value of the fund is less than the nil-rate band, or there will be quick succession relief, or X is the testator's spouse or civil partner and Y is not. If this method is adopted, make sure that X is wholly excluded from benefiting from the trust fund after the termination of X's interest: see para **[200.76]**.

(5) In the present state of interpretative uncertainty, and where, as is usually the case, there is uncertainty as to what will be the best arrangement in the period following the testator's death, a wide discretionary trust with wide trustees' powers of appointment and application of capital, exercisable before grant of probate, combined with a statement of wishes, will often be the best arrangement.

On IHTA 1984, s 144 see also paras **[225.83]–[225.91]** below.

(*h*) *Review of existing wills after FA 2006 and the Pre-Budget Report of 9 October 2007*

[200.134]

Wills of married couples or civil partners—provision for the survivor on the death of the first to die. Wills for married couples or civil partners have been typically structured so that under the will of the first to die there will be a nil-rate band discretionary trust, with an absolute interest or an interest in possession in the remainder of the estate given to the survivor. The requirements for creating an IPDI (see para **[200.98]**) are such that an interest in possession such as a life interest for the surviving spouse or civil partner in the testator's free estate, starting at the death of the testator, will be an IPDI and therefore beneficiary-taxed, and the spouse exemption will apply to the property subject to it on the first to die's death (see para **[200.84]**). The FA

2006 rules therefore do not have the effect of taking away the spouse exemption from wills which give the survivor of a marriage or civil partnership an interest in possession in the first to die's free estate, and review of wills made before 22 March 2006 is not needed on that account. The same is true where a testator has an interest in possession under a pre 22 March 2006 settlement, has a power of appointment exercisable by will under that settlement, and has exercised the power by his will to appoint an interest in possession to his or her spouse or civil partner to commence at the testator's own death. The successor's interest in possession will be a transitional serial interest (IHTA 1984, s 49C or s 49D) and therefore beneficiary-taxed.

[200.135]
Wills of married couples or civil partners—nil-rate band discretionary trusts. For the reasons given in **[200.75]** and **[200.130]**, nil-rate band discretionary trusts in the wills of the first to die of a married couple or civil partnership are no longer necessary or desirable in most cases. It will usually be better to rely on the nil-rate band carry-forward announced in the Pre-Budget Report on 9 October 2007. To do this to the maximum it is necessary for the will of the first to die to leave everything to the survivor. Accordingly, most nil-rate band discretionary trusts contained in wills made before 22 March 2006 will not be wanted. However, it will not be essential for persons who have made wills in this form to make a new will or codicil to eliminate the nil-rate band discretionary trust, provided that the surviving spouse or civil partner is a beneficiary under it. If after the death of the first to die the trustees of the nil-rate band discretionary trust make an appointment of an absolute interest or an interest in possession to the surviving spouse or civil partner within two years of the death, IHTA 1984, s 144 will have the effect (see paras **[200.133]** and **[225.83]–[225.91]**) that the first to die is treated as having made an exempt gift in favour of the survivor of the nil-rate band discretionary trust fund. There will be cases where the first to die's nil-rate band is used up by a non-exempt gift which is either not a discretionary trust or is a discretionary trust which does not include the surviving spouse or civil partner among the beneficiaries. In such cases a review of existing dispositions will be appropriate.

[200.136]
Trusts for minor children and young persons. This is the category of testamentary provision which is most affected by FA 2006. Wills which were made before 22 March 2006 which contain trusts for minor children drafted with the former IHTA 1984, s 71 (accumulation and maintenance trusts) in mind will in many cases have different tax consequences from those originally contemplated when the will was made. How different will depend on the terms of the trust and what has happened by the time of the death of the testator. The main possibilities are as follows:

(1) The existing will contains a simple accumulation and maintenance trust where the beneficiaries are the children of the testator, capital vests in equal or other fixed shares at the age of 18, and Trustee Act 1925, s 31 applies to the income. It will fall within IHTA 1984, s 71A (see para **[200.108]**) and the tax consequences are much as originally contemplated. A codicil or new will is not needed.

(2) The existing will contains a simple accumulation and maintenance trust where the beneficiaries are the children of the testator, capital vests in equal or other fixed shares at the age of 25, and Trustee Act 1925, s 31 applies to the income. It falls within IHTA 1984, s 71D (see para **[200.109]**). The tax consequences are not as originally contemplated in that, in relation to the share of any beneficiary who has not attained the age of 25 before the testator's death, there will be an IHT charge on capital vesting at an age greater than 18 (see para **[200.109]**). Such IHT charge will in most cases be modest, and a price worth paying for postponement of vesting where such postponement is found to be appropriate. Further, if, as will often be the case, there is a full power of advancement, or similar power (typically the Trustee Act 1925, s 32 power expanded expressly apply to the whole of a presumptive share), the potential IHT charge can be avoided or substantially mitigated by the exercise of the power within two years of the testator's death to make the beneficiary absolutely entitled. Such a power may also be exercisable so as to create a short-term IPDI trust (IHTA 1984, s 144 would enable this – see para **[200.133]**). Review of such a will is not a pressing matter, but the testator could consider the alternative of IPDI trusts if the will was reviewed for other reasons.

(3) The existing will contains simple accumulation and maintenance trusts of the kinds described in (1) or (2) above of this paragraph, but the testator is not a parent of the beneficiaries, or he or she is but there is some element in the trust which prevents IHTA 1984, s 71A or 71D from applying. In this case the settled property will fall within the relevant property rules to the extent that the beneficiary or beneficiaries interested in it are under the age of vesting of capital at the testator's death, subject to one point. If the trusts are such that a beneficiary attains an interest in possession in his presumptive share before attaining the age of vesting of capital, and by the time of the testator's death a beneficiary has attained the age at which an interest in possession is attained but not attained the age of vesting of capital, the position is as described under (4) below of this paragraph. As regards the whole or part of the fund which is relevant property at the death of the testator, if there is a sufficient power of advancement or similar power of the kind referred to under (2) above, the property can be converted into being subject to a bare trust or an IPDI trust by exercise of the power within two years of the testator's death. Review of the will would be appropriate if the trusts lack such a power and the potential beneficiaries are in their infancy, particularly if the fund could turn out to be substantial, or if there is a serious risk of part or all the fund being subject to interest in possession trusts at death. See (4) below for this last point.

(4) The existing will contains accumulation and maintenance trusts of the more complex kind, where there are initial accumulation and maintenance trusts, followed by interests in possession. Where the trust is of the testator's free estate (i e not created in exercise of a special power of appointment exercisable by will over a fund subject to an existing settlement) the FA 2006 rules can have a capricious effect. So far as the

fund subject to this trust is held on trust for a beneficiary or beneficiaries who have by the time of the death of the testator attained the age at which an interest in possession commences, it will be subject to IPDIs and so beneficiary-taxed. So far as the fund is held for a beneficiary or beneficiaries who have not attained that age, it will be relevant property. It will continue to be relevant property after that beneficiary or those beneficiaries attain interests in possession, unless they become entitled to interests in possession within the period of two years following the testator's death, in which case they will become entitled to IPDIs by virtue of IHTA 1984, s 144. Thus different members of a class of beneficiaries may find that their funds are subject to quite different IHT treatment, depending on how old they are at the testator's death. For a comparison of relevant property and IPDI trusts see para **[200.131]**. However, it will be possible (if there are wide enough powers conferred on the trustees) to convert the relevant property to IPDIs within two years of the testator's death. IPDIs will have the tax treatment which was contemplated by the testator when he made the will, except where powers were conferred with the specific purpose of enabling the shares taken by different beneficiaries to be varied after interests in possession are attained (see **[200.131]**)(5) for the disadvantages of varying beneficiary-taxed shares post FA 2006). Review of such a will is called for, therefore, if the powers are not adequate for conversion of relevant property to IPDI property, or variability of shares after interests in possession are obtained is particularly important to the testator. In the latter case the substitution of a fully discretionary trust should be considered.

(5) The existing will contains accumulation and maintenance trusts of any of the kinds mentioned above, in exercise of a power of appointment under an existing settlement. If the power is a general power (ie, broadly, one which can be exercised in favour of anybody, including the testator's own estate), the position will be as set out above, since for this purpose a general power over property is equivalent to ownership. Where it is the exercise of a special power of appointment under an existing settlement, IPDIs cannot be created and the trust property will be wholly relevant property from the testator's death, irrespective of the ages of beneficiaries and whether they have interests in possession (unless there is a disabled person entitled to an interest in possession). Although this is not the tax treatment intended by the testator, IPDIs are not available, and IHTA 1984, ss 71A, 71D, 142 and 144 cannot apply. If the appointment were reviewed, the only alternative with a different IHT outcome would be to appoint absolute interests. Review of the will could be carried out, but is not a high priority so long as the trustees of the settlement will have power to distribute the trust property absolutely soon after the testator's death. This is because the relevant property exit charge would be small or nil if such a distribution were done promptly (where the settled property is beneficiary-taxed property before the death), or very little increased (where the settled property is relevant property before the death), as compared with an absolute appointment taking effect on the death.

PART B

Clauses in wills

B1 Commencement of will

Preliminary Note .... [201.1]

FORMS

B1.1 Ordinary commencement .... [201.6]

B1.2 Commencement of will made in expectation of marriage........ [201.7]

B1.3 Commencement of will made in expectation of forming a civil partnership .... [201.8]

B1.4 Commencement of will made in expectation of marriage—conditional form .... [201.9]

B1.5 Commencement of will made in expectation of civil partnership—conditional form .... [201.10]

B1.6 Commencement of will of testator with UK and foreign property confining the will to UK property........ [201.11]

B1.7 Commencement of concurrent will of testator with UK and foreign property confining the will to UK property........ [201.12]

B1.8 Commencement of mutual will made in pursuance of an agreement that it shall not be revoked .... [201.13]

B1.9 Commencement of mirror but not mutual wills........ [201.14]

B1.10 Commencement of will made on behalf of a mentally disordered person pursuant to an order of the Court of Protection .... [201.15]

PRELIMINARY NOTE

[201.1]

General words of commencement. A will should commence with the name of the testator, a declaration that all former testamentary dispositions made by him are revoked and a declaration that it is his last will. It is important that a will should be dated, although this is not a legal requirement except where a guardian is being appointed (see Vol 1, para **[28.5]**). Some practitioners place the date of the will at the commencement, but the usual practice is to insert it in the testimonium and that is the style adopted in these forms. For examples of testimonium clauses see B22 at **[222.1]** ff. In preparing the commencement of a will, care should be taken to ascertain the correct full name of the testator as any inaccuracy will lead to the probate having to be taken in both the correct full name of the testator and his name as it appears in the will. If possible, it should be ascertained that the testator's name and its spelling in the will agree with the name and spelling in the testator's birth certificate. If the testator is commonly known by a name which is not in his birth certificate, it is a good idea to put this in as well.

[201.2]

Revocation of previous wills. Every will should contain an express revocation of all former testamentary dispositions if that is intended. Wills limited to England and Wales should contain a more limited revocation if extra-jurisdictional testamentary dispositions are to survive. See Forms B1.6 and B1.7 at **[201.11]** and **[201.12]**. The declaration that a will is the testator's 'last will' does not generally work a revocation and usually means no more than that the document is intended to be the testator's will (see Vol 1, paras **[1.6]**, n 7 and **[18.9]**). Although in a particular case it may be certain that there are no former testamentary dispositions to revoke, it is usually safer to include an express revocation. The term 'testamentary dispositions' is generally used in this context in preference or in addition to the term 'wills', although the only reason why it might be preferable or necessary is in the comparatively rare case these days where a testator has made an informal testamentary disposition while a serviceman on active service (see Vol 1, para **[16.1]** ff).

[201.3]
Revocation of appointments of guardians. It is only necessary to include in a revocation clause an express revocation of a former appointment of a guardian of minor children (which appointment may have been included in a former will or in another written instrument which is not a will) where it is desired to revoke the appointment without making a new one. If a new appointment of a guardian is made in a will, a previous appointment contained in a former will or other instrument is thereby revoked without any express revocation: ChA 1989, s 6(1) (Part G, para **[244.117]**). For the revocation of appointments of guardians see Vol 1, para **[28.6]** and B3 at para **[203.47]** ff. If an express revocation is required it could run as follows: 'I hereby revoke all former testamentary dispositions and appointments of guardians made by me.'

[201.4]
Wills made in expectation of marriage. As a general rule a will is revoked by the subsequent marriage of the testator. However, a will made on or after 1 January 1983 from which it appears that at the time it was made the testator was expecting to be married to a particular person and that he intended that the will should not be revoked by the marriage is not revoked by his marriage to that person: Wills Act 1837 (WA 1837), s 18 (as substituted by the Administration of Justice Act 1982 (AJA 1982), s 18), Part G, para **[244.16]**, replacing the Law of Property Act 1925 (LPA 1925), s 177 (Part G, para **[244.56]**) in respect of wills made on or after 1 January 1983. Therefore, if a will is not to be revoked by a subsequent marriage, it must appear from the will itself that the testator was expecting to marry a particular person and he intended that the will should not be revoked in that event. For wills made in expectation of marriage, see generally Vol 1 at para **[17.6]** ff, and for the commencement of such a will see Forms B1.2 at para **[201.6]** and B1.4 at para **[201.9]**.

[201.5]
Wills made in expectation of civil partnership. Since the commencement of CPA 2004 on 5 December 2005 (see Part G, paras **[244.130]**–**[244.134]**), the rule is extended so that a will is also revoked by the formation of a civil partnership between the testator and another person: WA 1837, s 18B(1) (as added by CPA 2004, s 71, Sch 4, para 2. See Part G, para **[244.19]**). However, a will from which it appears that at the time it was made the testator was expecting to form a civil partnership with a particular person and that he intended that the will should not be revoked by the formation of the civil partnership is not revoked by its formation: see the WA 1837, s 18B(3) (as added by CPA 2004, s 71, Sch 4, para 2. See Part G, para **[244.19]**). Therefore, if a will is not to be revoked by the subsequent formation of a civil partnership, it must appear from the will itself that the testator was

expecting to form a civil partnership with the person with whom it has been formed, and that he intended that the will should not be revoked in that event. See Forms B1.3 at para **[201.8]** and B1.5 at para **[201.10]**. The formation of a civil partnership could not happen before 5 December 2005, but it seems to us that a will made before that date, but after CPA 2004 passed into law, showing the relevant expectation, would probably not be revoked by the subsequent formation of a civil partnership.

[201.6]

Form B1.1: Ordinary commencement[1]

I [*testator*] of [*address*] hereby revoke all former testamentary dispositions made by me and declare this to be my last will.

1 See the Preliminary Note at para **[201.1]**.

[201.7]

Form B1.2: Commencement of will made in expectation of marriage[1]

I [*testator*] of [*address*] hereby revoke all former testamentary dispositions made by me. I declare that I make this will in expectation of my intended marriage with [*name of intended wife or husband*] and that it shall not be revoked by reason of the said marriage. I further declare that it shall be effective even if the said marriage is not solemnised.

1 See the Preliminary Note at para **[201.1]** ff. In this form the word 'expectation' is used in conformity with the WA 1837, s 18, as amended by the AJA 1982, s 18 (Part G, para **[244.16]**) but the word 'contemplation', as in the previous statutory provision (LPA 1925, s 177: Part G, para **[244.56]**) is probably still effective.

[201.8]

Form B1.3: Commencement of will made in expectation of forming a civil partnership[1]

I [*testator*] of [*address*] hereby revoke all former testamentary dispositions made by me. I declare that I make this will in expectation of my intended civil partnership with [*name of intended civil partner*] and that it shall not be revoked by reason of the said civil partnership. I further declare that it shall be effective even if the said civil partnership is not registered.

1 See para **[201.5]** above. In this form the word 'expectation' is used in conformity with the WA 1837, s 18B as added by CPA 2004, s 71, Sch 4, para 2.

[201.9]

Form B1.4: Commencement of will made in expectation of marriage—conditional form[1]

I [*testator*] of [*address*] hereby make this will in expectation of my intended marriage with [*name of intended wife or husband*]. I declare that this will shall not be effective unless the said marriage is solemnised within —— months from the date hereof [or I die within —— months from the date hereof while still engaged to be married to [*name of intended wife or husband*]]. Upon this will so becoming effective, I declare that all former testamentary dispositions made by me shall be revoked and this will shall then be my last will.

1 See paras **[201.4]** and **[201.7]**, n 1. For conditional wills see Vol 1, para **[1.10]**.

[201.10]

Form B1.5: Commencement of will made in expectation of civil partnership – conditional form[1]

I [*testator*] of [*address*] hereby make this will in expectation of my intended civil partnership with [*name of intended civil partner*]. I declare that this will shall not be effective unless the said civil partnership is registered within —— months from the date hereof [or I die within —— months from the date hereof without having revoked my intention to form a civil partnership with [*name of intended civil partner*]]. Upon this will so becoming effective, I declare that all former testamentary dispositions made by me shall be revoked and this will shall then be my last will.

1 See para **[201.5]**, above and para **[201.8]**, n 1, above.

[201.11]

Form B1.6: Commencement of will of testator with UK and foreign property confining the will to UK property[1]

I [*testator*] of [*address*] hereby make this my will which shall affect only my property of every kind in the United Kingdom of Great Britain and Northern Ireland and no other part of my property of any kind. I hereby revoke all former testamentary dispositions made by me to the extent that and so far only as they affect my property of every kind in the United Kingdom of Great Britain and Northern Ireland. I declare that I am domiciled in England[2] and that the proper law of this my will shall be the law of England and Wales.

1 Where a testator is possessed of property outside the United Kingdom and is able to dispose of such property and the greater part thereof to persons residing outside that area, there are obvious advantages in arranging for the distribution of such estate in the country outside the United Kingdom so far as possible in order to avoid the difficulties and expense of transferring such sums from one country to another. This is also true in the case of property situated in a dominion or colony, and it can often be appropriate to make separate and entirely independent wills with respect to the property in the United Kingdom and that situated outside the United Kingdom. Probate of a will granted in England does not extend to such property (*Re Murray's Goods* [1896] P 65), unless some of it is brought to England (*Stubbings v Clunies-Ross* (1911) 27 TLR 361). For the converse case of probate granted in a British possession, or by a British court in a foreign country, see the Colonial Probates Act 1892; and as to a limited colonial grant, see *Re Smith's Goods* [1904] P 114. (See generally as to probate *Tristram and Coote's Probate Practice* (30th edn).) See also *In the Estate of Vickers* (2001–02) 4 ITELR 584, discussed in the note to para **[18.8]**. See also C14 at para **[236.1]** ff.

2 Such a declaration as to domicile will not be conclusive as to domicile at the date of death, nor indeed to domicile at the date of the declaration (see para **[236.10]**, n 1).

[201.12]

Form B1.7: Commencement of concurrent will of testator with UK and foreign property confining the will to UK property[1]

I [*testator*] of [*address*] hereby revoke all testamentary dispositions made by me prior to the date hereof and hereby declare that this will and another will of even date herewith together constitute my last will. This will shall affect only my property of every kind in the United Kingdom of Great Britain and Northern Ireland and no other part of my property of any kind. [*or* This will shall not affect my property of any kind in the United States of America [*or as the case may be*] which I have disposed of by the said will of even date herewith.]

1 Care must be taken that the will dealing with the foreign property should be properly executed to pass all kinds of property according to the law of the foreign country, and for this purpose a lawyer of the foreign country should be consulted. In some cases, eg the United States, it is necessary to consider the law of the particular State in which the property is situated. Though an English will may by its words imply that foreign property is excluded, yet those words may be inserted because the testator believes he has otherwise effectively disposed of such property. If that other disposition has failed, the foreign property will pass under the English will: *Re Duke of Wellington, Glentanar v Wellington* [1948] Ch 118, [1947] 2 All ER 854.

[201.13]

Form B1.8: Commencement of mutual will made in pursuance of an agreement that it shall not be revoked[1]

I [*testator*] of [*address*] hereby revoke all former testamentary dispositions made by me and declare this to be my last will. I declare that my wife[2] [*name*] [*or as the case may be*] and I have agreed with one another to execute wills of even date and in similar terms and in consideration of such promise we have agreed that such respective wills shall not hereafter be revoked or altered either during our joint lives (so long as we shall remain married[2]) or by the survivor of us (if surviving as the lawful spouse[2] of the other).

1 As to mutual wills generally, see Vol 1, paras **[2.3]**–**[2.10]**. For the doctrine of mutual wills to apply it is not necessary for the second testator to die to have obtained a personal financial benefit under the will of the first testator to die: *Re Dale* [1994] Ch 31, [1993] 4 All ER 129. Careful thought should be given to the making of mutual wills because, for example, in the case of husband and wife, a remarriage by the survivor leads to obvious complications: see *Re Green, Lindner v Green* [1951] Ch 148, [1950] 2 All ER 913. If mutual wills are made by a husband and wife with their children as ultimate beneficiaries, the latter should be expressed to be the children of the marriage rather than eg 'my children'.

2 In order to adapt the form to take account of civil partnerships formed pursuant to CPA 2004, 'civil partner' may be substituted for 'wife', 'civil partners' may be substituted for 'married' and 'civil partner' may be substituted for 'spouse'.

[201.14]

Form B1.9: Commencement of mirror but not mutual wills[1]

I [*name*] of [*address*] revoke all former testamentary dispositions made by me and declare this to be my last will And I further declare that notwithstanding that my wife[2] [*name*] [*or as the case may be*] is making a will in similar terms we have agreed that our wills are not mutual wills and accordingly that each of us shall be free to revoke his or her will at any time whether before or after the death of the other and shall be free to dispose of his or her property or any property derived from the other as he or she thinks fit.

1 The purpose of this form is to prevent argument or even litigation arising at a later date. Such an argument may not be limited to a claim that the wills were intended to be mutually binding but could extend to litigation under the Inheritance (Provision for Family and Dependants) Act 1975: see *Re Goodchild, Goodchild v Goodchild* [1996] 1 All ER 670; affd [1997] 3 All ER 63, CA. See also the Introductory Note on wills in favour of spouses in Part A at para **[200.24]** ff. There should be a similar declaration in the other will.

2 In order to adapt the form to take account of civil partnerships formed pursuant to CPA 2004, 'civil partner' may be substituted for 'wife'.

[201.15]

Form B1.10: Commencement of will made on behalf of a mentally disordered person pursuant to an order of the Court of Protection[1]

This is the last will of me [*Name of Patient*] of [*address*] acting by [*name of authorised person*] of [*address of authorised person*] the person authorised in that behalf by an Order dated the [*date*] made by the Court of Protection pursuant to s 18(1)(i) of the Mental Capacity Act 2005. I hereby revoke all former Wills and Codicils made by me and declare this to be my last Will.

1 MCA 2005 (in force from 1 October 2007) confers wide powers on the Court of Protection in relation to the property and affairs of any person who is found to be 'unable to make a decision for himself in relation to the matter because of an impairment of, or a disturbance in the functioning of, the mind or brain', such a person lacks mental capacity and is referred to by the MCA as 'P'. (under the previous legislation (MeHA 1983, s 94(2)) the test was whether a person was 'incapable, by reason of mental disorder, of managing his property and affairs' and such person was defined as a 'patient'.

By the MCA 2005, ss. 16, 18(1)(i) and Sch 2 the court may authorise the execution on behalf of a person who lacks mental capacity ('P') of a will (or codicil: see s 64(1)) containing any provision (whether by way of disposing of property or exercising a power or otherwise) which could be made by a will executed by P if he had capacity to make it. These powers are not to be exercised while P is under the age of 18 years (MCA 2005, s. 18(2)) and the court considers that he is incapable of making a valid will for himself. The mode in which a will made on behalf of a patient is to be executed is laid down in the MCA 2005, Sch 2, para 3: see Form B22.14 at para **[222.16]** for a form of testimonium and attestation clause and see the note to that form for details of the requirements for due execution of P's will.

The wording set out in this form and in Form B22.14 at para **[222.16]** for the testimonium and attestation is based upon the statutory requirements and is intended to provide precedents for those parts of a will made under this jurisdiction which must necessarily differ from the corresponding parts of an ordinary will. Apart from them, it is thought, a will made under this jurisdiction need not differ in any way from a will made by a testator who is sui juris. These precedents are not in any sense official. In particular, it is a function of the Court of Protection to consider and criticise draft wills when they are submitted, and this function cannot be fettered in advance; but it is thought that objection would not normally be made to formal parts of a will couched in the terms set out in this form and Form B22.14.

The provisions relevant to the jurisdiction are to be found in the MCA 2005, ss. 16, 18 and Sch 2 (Part G, paras **[244.140]**–**[244.141]**, **[244.142]**). A Code of Practice exists in draft form, as to which see Vol 1 at para **[4.9]**.

B2 Miscellaneous declarations and desires sometimes included in wills

General note .... [202.1]
DISPOSAL OF BODY .... **[202.2]**
FORMS
B2.1 Direction as to place of burial and tombstone .... [202.3]
B2.2 Expressions of desire as to cremation .... [202.4]
B2.3 Direction that only necessary expense shall be incurred .... [202.5]
B2.4 Directions as to the ascertainment of the testator's death in order to prevent his being buried alive .... [202.6]
B2.5 Power for executor to incur expense in respect of directions .... [202.7]
ANATOMICAL RESEARCH AND ORGAN TRANSPLANTATION .... **[202.8]**
FORMS
B2.6 Direction for anatomical examination and corneal grafting .... [202.16]
B2.7 Clause providing for the use of the testator's body for therapeutic purposes, but not for medical education or research .... [202.17]
MAINTENANCE OF GRAVES .... **[202.18]**
FORMS
B2.8 Gift for the upkeep of a particular grave during a perpetuity period .... [202.31]
B2.9 Perpetual gift for the upkeep of a churchyard with a request to maintain a particular grave .... [202.32]
B2.10 Gift for the upkeep of a particular grave in a churchyard during a perpetuity period followed by a perpetual gift for the upkeep of the churchyard with a request to maintain the particular grave .... [202.33]
B2.11 Direction to executors to enter into an agreement for the maintenance of a grave in a local authority cemetery .... [202.34]
B2.12 Gift to a charity conditional upon the maintenance of a particular grave with a gift over on breach of the condition to another charity .... [202.35]
MAINTENANCE OF ANIMALS .... **[202.36]**
FORMS
B2.13 Gift for the maintenance and upkeep of an animal .... [202.37]
B2.14 Combined gift of legacy and pet animal coupled with a non-binding expression of hope that the legatee will look after the animal .... [202.38]
DECLARATIONS UNDER THE INHERITANCE (PROVISION FOR FAMILY AND DEPENDANTS) ACT 1975 .... **[202.39]**
FORM
B2.15 Declarations under the Inheritance (Provision for Family and Dependants) Act 1975—Alternative forms .... [202.40]
CLAUSE HEADINGS OR MARGINAL NOTES .... **[202.41]**
FORM
B2.16 Direction regarding clause headings or marginal notes .... [202.42]

GENERAL NOTE

[202.1]

This Section brings together a number of provisions which have little in common with each other save that they are difficult to classify under any of the more conventional headings but are often found towards the beginning of a will.

Disposal of body

[202.2]

Note. The following declarations and expressions of desire should ideally be communicated to two or three near relatives or friends and confirmed by letter during the testator's lifetime. But it is not uncommon to confirm them also by will and to give the executors an express power to determine what is reasonable and proper and to incur any necessary expense in carrying out the testator's wishes. For the law relating to these matters see Vol 1, para **[7.33]**.

[202.3]

Form B2.1: Direction as to place of burial and tombstone

I desire that my body may be buried in my family grave in the —— Cemetery which is in the part of that cemetery for burials of deceased members of the [Church of England[1]] in Section —— Grave No ——[2] I further direct that my executors shall expend a sum of money [not exceeding £——] upon the erection of a suitable inscription upon a tombstone upon the said grave.[3]

1 Or such other part of the cemetery as may be desired.

2 A direction of this nature cannot be enforced: *Williams v Williams* (1882) 20 Ch D 659. The executors have a right to possession of the body and their duty is to bury it (*Williams v Williams; Dobson v North Tyneside Health Authority* [1996] 4 All ER 474): see also Vol 1, para **[7.33]**. As to upkeep of graves, see paras **[202.18]** ff.

3 For a direction that only necessary expense be incurred see Form B2.3 at para **[202.5]**; and for power to incur reasonable expense, see Form B2.5 at para **[202.7]**. Note that reasonable funeral expenses are allowed in valuing a deceased person's estate for inheritance tax purposes: ITA 1984, s 172. By Revenue concession such funeral expenses are taken to include the cost of a tombstone: SP7/87 (15 July 1987).

[202.4]

Form B2.2: Expressions of desire as to cremation

A. I desire that my body may be cremated [in the crematorium at ——] and my ashes deposited at —— [or scattered on consecrated ground at ——][1] *or*

B. [*If the testator desires a more elaborate form of words, the following may be suggested:*] I desire that my trustees shall dispose of my remains by the cleansing fires of cremation and that my ashes shall be spread upon the garden of remembrance at ——[2] *or*

C. I direct that my body shall not be cremated.[3]

1 As to the law relating to cremation, see Vol 1, para **[7.33]**. Cremation must take place in a recognised crematorium. Written directions for cremation are not essential, see also n 3 infra. The Cremation Society of Great Britain, Second Floor Brecon House, 16/16A Albion Place, Maidstone, Kent, ME14 5DZ; tel: (01622) 688 292, issue a printed form of this direction, which, when completed, they undertake to register in their records; and they endeavour to give effect to the expressed desire. The printed form is in duplicate, one part

for registration with the society and the other to be handed to the executor or selected relative. The Cremation Society has a website at www.cremation.org.uk.

As to disposal of the ashes, disputes sometimes arise as to where ashes should be scattered, as in *Fessi v Whitmore* [1999] 1 FLR 767.

2 This wording is based upon an actual will.

3 It is no longer unlawful to cremate a body where such a direction has been given, and whether cremation takes place is solely in the discretion of the deceased's executors or nearest relative, who are apparently free to disregard the deceased's wishes: see Vol 1, para **[7.33]**, n 4.

[202.5]

Form B2.3: Direction that only necessary expense shall be incurred[1]

I desire that at my death there shall be [no ostentation or show of any kind, that there shall be] no flowers and that mourning shall not be worn by my relatives and generally that no expense beyond what is necessary shall be incurred.

1 This direction is merely indicative of what some testators desire to be inserted and is, in fact based upon actual wills. Executors may incur all reasonable expenses in connection with the funeral and burial of the deceased without any direction or power in the will, though the amount they are allowed to spend is less where the estate is insolvent than where it is solvent: *Hancock v Podmore* (1830) 1 B & Ad 260; *Edwards v Edwards* (1834) 2 Cr & M 612. In the latter case it is said that even in the case of an insolvent estate reasonable (as contrasted with necessary) expenses are allowed. Insolvency Act 1986, s 421 and Administration of Insolvent Estates of Deceased persons Order 1986, SI 1986/1999, Art 4(2) confirm that reasonable funeral and testamentary expenses take priority over preferential debts. Express directions, such as contained in this form, may limit the amount and, on the other hand, specific directions to spend large sums on tombs and monuments can be followed, certainly to any reasonable extent: *Paice v Archbishop of Canterbury* (1807) 14 Ves 364 at 372. At common law the husband was liable for the funeral expenses on the wife's death, but the Married Woman's Property legislation has removed the foundation of this rule and the wife's executors are now responsible for any expense so incurred: *Rees v Hughes* [1946] KB 517, [1946] 2 All ER 47.

[202.6]

Form B2.4: Direction as to the ascertainment of the testator's death in order to prevent his being buried alive[1]

I direct my executors to take all necessary steps and for this purpose to employ and pay such doctors or other skilled persons as they in their sole discretion may think proper for the purpose of ascertaining that I am in fact dead and not in any state having only the semblance of death in order so far as possible to avoid all risk of my being buried alive.

1 Although all necessary and proper expenses for this purpose are payable by the executor without express authority, it is wiser in this case to include in the will an express power as in Form B2.5 at para **[202.7]**.

[202.7]

Form B2.5: Power for executor to incur expense in respect of directions[1]

[*Set out the directions in the will in addition to leaving such directions addressed to the executor and continue as follows*] and I hereby authorise my executor to spend such sums in carrying out the above directions as may appear to him to be reasonable and his decision as to what is reasonable in the circumstances shall be final and binding upon all beneficiaries under this my will.

1 In order to avoid questions about incorporation of documents in the will and as to what documents should be admitted to probate, the directions should be set out in the will as well as in a letter to the executor or nearest relative. The executor under such a clause must act reasonably having regard to the directions given by the testator. The clause does not, of course, oust the jurisdiction of the court to determine what expenses it is proper to allow in all the circumstances, but it does show that the testator intended his bounty to the beneficiaries to be subject to these directions: see *Re Wynn's Will Trusts* [1952] Ch 271, [1952] 1 All ER 341; *Re Bromson* [1958] OR 367. Where it is alleged that there are customs relating to burial, such customs must be proved to be legal customs, and, if such is not shown, then only a reasonable sum can be claimed against the estate: *Tzedeck v Royal Trust Co* [1953] 1 SCR 31. For the case of insolvent estates see the note to Form B2.3 at **[202.5]**.

Anatomical research and organ transplantation

[202.8]
Donor cards. For obvious reasons it is essential that any directions concerning these matters should be given immediate effect. Such directions should therefore be communicated by the testator during his lifetime as well as incorporated in his will. Where appropriate, donor cards should be carried.

1. Anatomical research and examination

[202.9]
Arrangements for anatomical examination. Anatomical examination and research is quite distinct from organ transplantation in that it is limited in scope to the macroscopic examination by dissection for the purposes of teaching or studying or researching into the gross structure of the human body[1] and does not involve the transfer or transplantation of tissue from one (deceased) body to a living person. Arrangements for the donation of a body for anatomical examination should be made before death. Since the commencement of the Human Tissue Act 2004[2] on 1 September 2006 the Human Tissue Authority is the regulatory body for all matters concerning the removal, storage, use and disposal of human tissue. Information and help for those who wish to donate their body for medical education, training or research, and for bereaved relatives of a deceased person who has expressed such a wish during their lifetime can be obtained from the Human Tissue Authority of Finlaison House, 15–17 Furnival Street, London EC4A 1AB; Tel: 020 7211 3400. Further information can be found on the Human Tissue Authority website at www.hta.gov.uk.

Those in Northern Ireland should contact: The Department of Anatomy at Queen's University, Belfast, Medical Biology Centre, 97 Lisburn Road, Belfast BT9 7BL; Tel: 028 9097 2131.

Those in Scotland should contact their nearest medical school at: Aberdeen – Department of Anatomy (Tel: 01224 274 320/01224 272 000); Dundee – Faculty of Life Sciences, University of Dundee (Tel: 01382 344 206); Edinburgh – Department of Biomedical Sciences, University of Edinburgh (Tel: 0131 650 2997/0131 650 8318); Glasgow – The Anatomy Department,

University of Glasgow (Tel: 0141 330 4296/0141 339 8855); St Andrews – Department of Anatomy, University of St Andrews (Tel: 01334 463 601).

1 Anatomical examination is defined at HTA 2004, s 54(1).
2 HTA 2004 repeals both AA 1984 and HTA 1961 and, as a result, the position of HM Inspector of Anatomy has ceased to exist.

[202.10]
Despite the overriding brief of the Human Tissue Authority, a person in England and Wales who wishes to donate their body in this way should complete a consent form obtained from local medical schools. A comprehensive list of medical schools (see **[202.12]** below) setting out which postcode falls within the ambit of each together with the contact details of the Bequethal Secretaries at each can be found on the Human Tissue Authority website. Those without internet access should contact the Human Tissue Authority directly. The completed and witnessed consent form should then be kept with the will and a copy lodged with the local medical school.

The Human Tissue Authority states that in certain circumstances a body cannot be accepted for donation unless appropriate consent has been given. Where a body is to be stored for use or used for public display or for anatomical examination other than examination of excepted material), appropriate consent means that the deceased's agreement must have been written down and witnessed and the consent document produced on death. HTA 2004 does not, however, require the use of a specific form of consent and written consent is not required in all cases although it is necessary for most purposes. Where written consent is necessary, the consent of an adult must be in writing signed by the person concerned in the presence of at least one witness who attests the signature; or at the direction of the person concerned, in his presence and in the presence of at least one witness who attests the signature; or by will made in accordance with WA 1837, s 9.[1] Only the donor is capable of giving this consent but, provided the consent does not concern excepted material,[2] an adult may appoint one or more persons to represent him after his death in relation to consent for the purposes of the Act and such an appointment may be made orally (in the presence of two witnesses) or in writing signed by the donor in the presence of one attesting witness, at the direction of the donor in his presence and in the presence of at least one witness or in a will.[3] .

Practitioners asked to draw up a will with a direction permitting anatomical examination would be well advised to obtain the necessary forms and follow Human Tissue Authority Guidance.

1 HTA 2004, s 3(3),(5).
2 Excepted material is material that has come from a living person or has come from the body of a deceased person otherwise than in the course of anatomical examination: HTA 2004, s 12.
3 HTA 2004, s 4.

[202.11]
As to procedure on death it is recommended that the executors should immediately contact the Local Medical School using the details provided with the consent form. Arrangements will then be made to have the body removed.

[202.12]
The following list of the principal University Medical Schools (with telephone numbers) may be of assistance in this connection:

Birmingham (Tel: 0121 414 6811); Bristol (Tel: 0117 928 8137); Cambridge (Tel: 01223 336 776); Cardiff (Tel: 02920 874 370); Leeds (Tel: 0113 343 4297); Leicester (Tel: 0116 252 3021); Liverpool (Tel: 0151 794 5442); Manchester (Tel: 0161 275 5241); Newcastle-upon-Tyne (Tel: 0191 222 6616); Nottingham (Tel: 0115 823 0143); Oxford (Tel: 01865 272 181); Sheffield (Tel: 0114 222 4642); and Southampton (Tel: 02380 594465).

2. Organ transplantation

[202.13]
Use of organs for therapeutic purposes. Human Tissue Act 2004 authorises the use of the deceased's organs for therapeutic purposes subject to the following conditions. The deceased may authorise such use at any time in writing (witnessed as described at **[202.10]** above) or orally in the presence of two witnesses during his last illness. The party lawfully in possession of the deceased's body may authorise such removal unless he has reason to believe that the deceased had expressed an objection and not withdrawn it or the surviving spouse or any surviving relative objects. The removal must be by a registered medical practitioner who has satisfied himself that life is extinct. No authority can be given where an inquest is likely to be held nor by a person entrusted by another with the burial or cremation of the body. Where the body is in hospital, the person having control and management of the hospital can authorise such removal or that person may delegate power to authorise such removal to any officer or persons designated by him. The use of organs for therapeutic purposes requires that the removal shall be effected on death or, in the case of eyes, within a few hours of death and therefore in most cases the deceased should give some oral indication of his wishes to his doctors during his last illness in addition to this direction if it is to serve any practical purpose.

[202.14]
Eye hospitals. A list of Eye Hospitals which would probably be interested in receiving eyes for corneal grafting is set out below. It is not suggested that the list is complete but it is hoped that it may assist practitioners who may be asked to advise on this matter.

[202.15]
Birmingham and Midland Eye Hospital; Sussex Eye Hospital, Brighton; Bristol Eye Hospital; Royal Victoria Eye and Ear Hospital, Dublin; Glasgow Eye Infirmary; St Paul's Eye Hospital, Liverpool; Moorfields Eye Hospital, London EC1; Western Ophthalmic Hospital, London NW1; Kent County Ophthalmic and Aural Hospital, Maidstone, Kent; Manchester Royal Eye Hospital; North Riding Infirmary, Middlesbrough; Newcastle-upon-Tyne Ophthalmic Out-patients Department, Walkergate Hospital, Newcastle-upon-Tyne; Nottingham and Midland Eye Infirmary; Oxford Eye Hospital; Royal Eye Infirmary, Plymouth, Devon; Wolverhampton and Midland County Eye Infirmary, Wolverhampton; Eye, Ear and Throat Hospital, Shrewsbury.

[202.16]

Form B2.6: Direction for anatomical examination and corneal grafting[1]

1. I desire that after my death my body may be made available [to ——] for such anatomical examinations as may be thought desirable but in accordance with the provisions of the Human Tissue Act 2004 (HTA 2004)[2] [and in due course the institution receiving it shall have it cremated[3]]. Such use may be made of all or any part thereof as may be lawful.

2. I hereby request that my body or any part thereof [*or if the testator so desires specify a particular part of the body*] may be used for therapeutic purposes or for the purposes of medical education or research.[4]

1 See Vol 1, para **[7.34]**. It must be remembered that the surviving spouse or nearest known relative can require interment without such examination. Here again it will be wiser to include an express power to pay expenses. See Form B2.5 at para **[202.7]**.

As a deceased person has no power of disposition over his body it might perhaps be more suitable if this direction accompanied the will rather than being embodied in it although it is not suggested that it is of any great moment where the direction appears so long as it is kept in a place where it will be brought to the attention of the executors as soon as possible. It is, however, important to comply with the requirements of the HTA 2004 (see para **[202.10]**.

2 The HTA 2004, which replaced the Anatomy Act 1984, came into force on 1 September 2006.

3 The institution receiving the body is responsible for seeing that it is decently interred in consecrated ground or in a public burial ground in use for persons of the religious persuasion to which the person whose body has been removed for examination belonged. Only a very simple funeral can be provided however and if any special arrangements (e g such as cremation) are required it is expected that the executors or next of kin will meet the additional cost so incurred.

4 For the law and other information concerning organ transplantation, see paras **[202.8]–[202.15]**.

[202.17]

Form B2.7: Clause providing for the use of the testator's body for therapeutic purposes, but not for medical education or research[1]

(a) I desire that after my death any part or parts of my body which may be of use for therapeutic purposes (including corneal grafting in the case of my eyes and transplantation in the case of any other part of my body) shall be removed with a view to their use for those purposes.

(b) For the avoidance of doubt I declare that the foregoing provisions shall not authorise the use of my body or any part of it for medical education or research.

(c) I desire that my body after the removal of such parts of it as may be removed with a view to their use for therapeutic purposes shall be cremated and I declare that arrangements for its cremation may be made either by my executors or (if my executors think fit) by any hospital or other institution which has custody of my body after such removal has been completed.

(d) I authorise my executors to spend as much money from my estate as they may in their absolute discretion think fit in implementing the wishes which I have expressed in the foregoing provisions of this clause.

1 With the development of transplantation surgery, some testators wish to include in their wills a provision permitting their bodies to be used for the purposes of such surgery, but not for medical education or research. This clause is designed to fulfil these requirements. It is

thus a variant of Form B2.6 at para **[202.16]**. It can of course be readily adapted to meet the needs of testators who wish to permit educational and research use as well as transplantation.

Maintenance of graves

[202.18]

Note. There are several methods of providing for the upkeep of a tomb or grave, none of them wholly satisfactory (See also Vol 1, para **[9.29]**).

[202.19]

Gifts for maintenance of graves are not charitable. A gift for the maintenance of a grave or family tomb (not being part of the fabric of a church) is not charitable, but such gift may be valid as a private trust if it does not infringe the rule against perpetuities: see *Pirbright v Salwey* [1896] WN 86, followed in *Re Hooper, Parker v Ward* [1932] 1 Ch 38. It is therefore possible to leave a legacy on trust to apply the income for the maintenance of a grave during a perpetuity period, as in Form B2.8 at para **[202.31]**. The disadvantage of a gift in this form is that it is of limited duration and that while it is lawful for the trustees to give effect to the trust, there is no beneficiary to enforce it and its efficacy therefore depends upon the goodwill and conscientiousness of the trustees. Doubts have been expressed as to whether it is possible to provide for such a gift to take effect for one of the perpetuity periods permitted by the Perpetuities and Accumulations Act 1964 (PAA 1964) because of the terms of s 15(4) of the PAA 1964. The authors take the view that s 15(4) does not prevent the 80-year perpetuity period from being employed in trusts such as these in Form B2.8 at para **[202.31]**.

[202.20]

Gifts for the upkeep of churchyards etc are charitable. Although a gift for the maintenance of a particular grave is not charitable, a gift for the upkeep of the churchyard of a parish church or church of any other religious denomination is a valid charitable gift: *Re Manser, A-G v Lucas*[1]. Further, such a gift will not be vitiated by the addition of words such as 'and in particular the grave of' a designated person[2] or some other merely precatory request for the maintenance of a particular tomb or grave. A gift in this form is contained in Form B2.9 at para **[202.32]**. It has the advantage over the gift in Form B2.8 at para **[202.31]** of not being of limited duration, but the extent to which effect is given to the wish of the testator to have a particular grave maintained again depends entirely on the trustees.

1 [1905] 1 Ch 68.
2 [1905] 1 Ch 68, at 75.

[202.21]

Combined gifts are permitted. Where the grave is in a churchyard, a combination of the two forms of gift contained in Forms B2.8 and B2.9 at paras **[202.31]** and **[202.32]** can be employed: see Form B2.10 at para **[202.33]**.

[202.22]

Local Authority Cemeteries. Where the grave is in a cemetery maintained by a local authority, a charitable gift in the form sanctioned in *Re Manser*[1] is not available, but the local authority has power by statute to enter into arrangements for the maintenance of particular graves. The position is now governed by the Parish Councils and Burial Authorities (Miscellaneous Provisions) Act 1970 and the Local Authorities' Cemeteries Order 1977 (SI 1977/204), made under powers conferred by the Local Government Act 1972 and replacing earlier legislation. Article 10 of the 1977 Order provides that a burial authority may grant (inter alia) exclusive burial rights in any grave space or grave or the right to construct a walled grave or vault together with exclusive burial rights therein together with the right to place and maintain a tombstone or other memorial thereon. The authority may also enter into maintenance agreements for a period not exceeding 100 years, though there is power to extend this period.

1 [1905] 1 Ch 68.

[202.23]
The method of providing for the maintenance of a grave which the Order affords is clearly more simple, and probably more satisfactory, than the provisions to this end which have usually been employed in wills in the past. On the face of it, the testator need only direct his executors to enter into an agreement under the Order. But the following points should be noted.

[202.24]
(1) No agreement made under the Order may impose an obligation to maintain for longer than 100 years. It is conceivable that the authority might be prepared to indicate its willingness to continue maintenance beyond that period if circumstances permitted, particularly as there is now power to extend the period of maintenance, though it may not wish to impose upon itself a binding obligation. This would be a matter for discussion with the individual authority and might require the payment of an increased charge.

[202.25]
(2) The Order is permissive only and does not impose any obligation upon the authority to enter into such agreements. Even if the authority is willing to do so, it seems that it may limit its obligations to some period less than 100 years if it wishes to do this. Therefore a testator can do no more than direct that his executors shall enter into an agreement if the authority is willing, and that the agreement shall provide for maintenance for as long as the authority is prepared to undertake it. With many Metropolitan authorities contemplating the future re-use of existing graves in order to alleviate overcrowding, lengthy maintenance agreements may become less common.

[202.26]
(3) Although the Local Government Act 1972, s 214(3) confers a ministerial power to amend other Acts which are inconsistent with, or unnecessary in consequence of, the new provisions, it is possible that local Acts are still in operation in certain areas. It seems advisable, therefore, to permit the agreement also to be made under any local Act.

[202.27]
Form B2.11 at para **[202.34]** confers power on a deceased person's executors to enter into a maintenance agreement with a local authority under any statutory power.

[202.28]

Perpetual gifts from charity to charity are permissible. An alternative method of providing for the maintenance of a particular grave, which is embodied in Form B2.12 at para **[202.35]**, is also based on the law of charity but, unlike the provision contained in Form B2.9 at para **[202.32]**, is available wherever the grave is situated. The particular formula derives from the decision in *Re Tyler, Tyler v Tyler* [1891] 3 Ch 252, CA and involves: (i) an initial gift of property to a charity to be held on trust to apply the income in perpetuity either for its general purposes or for a particular charitable purpose administered by the selected charity; (ii) a condition requiring the charity to maintain the particular grave; and (iii) a gift over to a second charity on breach of that condition. The perpetuity rule does not apply to a gift from one charity to another, though it does apply where the gift over is from a charity to an individual (*Re Davies, Lloyd v Cardigan County Council* [1915] 1 Ch 543; *Re Talbot, Jubb v Sheard* [1933] Ch 895), or where the gift over is from an individual to a charity (*Worthing Corpn v Heather* [1906] 2 Ch 532). It must be noticed that the first gift must not be for the maintenance of the grave, as an indefinite gift for such a purpose will be invalid even though the first donee is a charity: see *Re Elliott, Lloyds Bank Ltd v Burton-on-Trent Hospital Management Committee* [1952] Ch 217, [1952] 1 All ER 145. Where the gift over is not to a charity it must be limited to take effect only within the perpetuity period, and, if the trust fails after the perpetuity period, the gift will automatically fall into residue. The efficacy of a gift in this form depends on the willingness of the second donee to enforce the condition. It is therefore advisable that the second donee should be a body having a permanent existence which is likely to be interested in ensuring that the grave is maintained. However, it should be noted that the decision of *Tyler v Tyler* was not followed by the High Court of Australia in *RSPCA of NSW v Benevolent Society of New South Wales* (1960) 102 CLR 629 where the non-charitable conditions imposed upon a charity to which property was left were considered to be part of the trust and the dominant purpose of the gift.

[202.29]

Reverter gifts no longer effective. A further device, based on the decision in *Re Chardon, Johnston v Davies* [1928] Ch 464, but now no longer available, was to give a fund to trustees to pay the income thereof to a cemetery company or the persons responsible for the maintenance of the cemetery or burial ground so long as they should keep a particular grave or graves in repair. The efficacy of this method depended inter alia upon the rule that while a gift over on condition broken (other than a gift over as between charities) had to comply with the rule against perpetuities, a possibility of reverter did not. The PAA 1964, s 12(1) (Part G, para **[246.85]**) has now subjected possibilities of reverter to the perpetuity rule with the consequence that this method no longer works. The form based on *Re Chardon, Johnston v Davies* is accordingly omitted.

[202.30]

Value of gift for maintenance of grave. In the case of a gift from charity to charity the capital value of the gift to the charity should be substantially in excess of the cost of maintaining the grave so that the device works, because if the gift is small there is no incentive for the charity to enforce it and it may be invalid. However, in all cases where gifts are made for the maintenance of graves, care should be taken in calculating an appropriate capital value of the gift. There are two problems which may arise where the capital value of the gift is substantial. First, if excessive, it could be viewed as capricious thus rendering the whole of the gift void.[1] Secondly, if the capital value of the gift is such that it yields a greater income than that necessary for the maintenance of the grave the gift should specify what is to become of the excess income in the interim and, in particular, after the expiry of any accumulation period included in the terms of the gift.

1 There is no English authority on this point, but various US decisions have held gifts capricious. See, for example, *Clark v Portland Burying Ground Association* 151 Conn 527 (1964); *In Filoon Estate* 71 D & C 506 (1950); and *In Shepp Estate* 29 D & C 2d 385 (1962).

[202.31]

Form B2.8: Gift for the upkeep of a particular grave during a perpetuity period[1]

I give to my trustees the sum of £—— upon trust to invest the same and during the period of eighty years[2] from my death (which period shall be the perpetuity period applicable to the disposition hereby effected)[3] to apply the income thereof in keeping the grave and gravestone of my late wife and of myself (if I shall be buried there) in good order and repair and in keeping the lettering thereon legible and causing the same to be re-cut from time to time when necessary for that purpose.

1 See para **[202.19]**.
2 For concerns about the permissible perpetuity period see para **[202.19]**.
3 See the PAA 1964, s 1(1): Part G, para **[246.74]**.

[202.32]

Form B2.9: Perpetual gift for the upkeep of a churchyard with a request to maintain a particular grave[1]

I give to the vicar and churchwarden of the parish church of —— and their successors the sum of £—— upon trust to invest the same and to apply the income thereof in keeping the graveyard of the said church in good order and repair and I request but without imposing any legal obligation on them that they will keep in good order and repair the grave and gravestones of my late wife and of myself (if I shall be buried there) and will keep the lettering thereon legible and will cause the same to be re-cut from time to time when necessary for that purpose.

1 For the general law relating to gifts in this form see para **[202.20]**.

[202.33]

Form B2.10: Gift for the upkeep of a particular grave in a churchyard during a perpetuity period followed by a perpetual gift for the upkeep of the churchyard with a request to maintain the particular grave[1]

(1) I give to the vicar and churchwardens of the parish church of —— and their successors the sum of £—— upon trust to invest the same and during

the period of eighty years[2] from my death (which period shall be the perpetuity period applicable to the disposition hereby effected[3] to apply the income thereof in keeping the grave and gravestone of my late wife —— and of myself (if I shall be buried there) in good order and repair and in keeping the lettering thereon legible and causing the same to be re-cut from time to time when necessary for that purpose and to apply any balance of the said income not required for such purpose in keeping the said graveyard in good order and repair.

(2) After the expiration of the said period of eighty years the said vicar and churchwardens and their successors shall hold the said sum and the investments representing the same upon trust to apply the income thereof in keeping the said graveyard in good order and repair. And I request but without imposing any legal obligation on them that they will maintain the grave and gravestone of my said wife and of myself (if I shall be buried there) in the manner mentioned in subclause (1) hereof.

1 This form in effect combines the gifts contained in the two preceding forms: see paras **[202.19]–[202.21]**.
2 For concerns about the permissible perpetuity period, see **[202.19]**.
3 See para **[202.31]**, n 2.

[202.34]

Form B2.11: Direction to executors to enter into an agreement for the maintenance of a grave in a local authority cemetery[1]

If the burial authority or local authority which provides or maintains the burial ground where my body is buried [in accordance with the direction given in clause —— of this will] is willing to make an agreement (whether under the provisions of the Parish Councils and Burial Authorities (Miscellaneous Provisions) Act 1970 or any statutory modification or re-enactment thereof or under those of any local Act or other enabling power) with my executors [trustees] for the maintenance of my grave and of the tombstone or other memorial placed upon it then I direct my executors [trustees] to make an agreement with that authority providing for such maintenance to be carried out for the longest period for which the authority is prepared to undertake it and to pay from my estate the sum required by the authority as consideration therefor and any other costs which may reasonably be incurred in implementing the provisions of this clause.

1 For the general law on agreements for the maintenance of graves in local authority cemeteries, see para **[202.22]**. This Form provides for the care of a grave with a tombstone but can be readily adapted to meet the particular circumstances.

[202.35]

Form B2.12: Gift to a charity conditional upon the maintenance of a particular grave with a gift over on breach of the condition to another charity[1]

I give to [*charity*] the sum of £—— upon trust to apply the income thereof to its general purposes [*or name of particular purpose*] so long as the said [*charity*] shall maintain [*description of grave*] as the same has been maintained during my lifetime and upon the said [*charity*] failing so to maintain the said grave I give the said sum of £—— to [*second charity*] [*or* if before the expiration of twenty-one years from the death of the last survivor of all the descendants living and actually born at the date of my death of his late Majesty King George V the said [*charity*] shall fail so to maintain the said grave then I give the said sum of £—— to [*name of individual*] absolutely].

I declare that neglect to tend and replant the said grave for a period of [two] years shall constitute a failure to maintain the said grave and that allowing more than one third of the lettering of the tombstone on the said grave to be illegible for the same period shall also constitute such a failure.

The receipt of the proper officer of either the said [*charities*] or any person purporting to be such shall be a sufficient discharge to my trustees in respect of the said legacy.

1 For the law relating to gifts in this form see para **[202.28]**.

Maintenance of animals

[202.36]

Note. A gift, such as that contained in Form B2.13 at para **[202.37]**, for the upkeep of a particular animal is not charitable, but is valid if confined within perpetuity limits: see *Re Dean, Cooper-Dean v Stevens* (1889) 41 Ch D 552. In so far as this case decides that a dog's life is a life for the purposes of the perpetuity rule, it is generally considered to be wrong: see *Re Kelly, Cleary v James* [1932] IR 255 and Vol 1, para **[9.31]**. Since there is no beneficiary to enforce the trust, the efficacy of the gift depends entirely on the trustees' willingness to perform the trust. It may be preferable to give the pet animal together with a legacy to some person whom the testator can rely upon to look after it. It is possible to adapt Form B2.14 (at para **[202.38]**) for this purpose.

[202.37]

Form B2.13: Gift for the maintenance and upkeep of an animal

I give to my trustees the sum of £—— upon trust to invest the same and to apply the income therefrom for the upkeep and maintenance of my [dog *or other animal, describing it*] for the period of [twenty-one years[1]] from the date of my death if my said [dog] shall so long live and after the death of my said [dog] or after the expiration of the said period of twenty-one years whichever shall first happen the said sum shall fall into and form part of my residuary estate.

1 The period need not be confined to 21 years, provided that it does not exceed perpetuity limits.

[202.38]

Form B2.14: Combined gift of legacy and pet animal coupled with a non-binding expression of hope that the legatee will look after the animal[1]

I give to [*name*] a legacy of the sum of £—— together with my dog [or other animal, describing it] (if living at my death) and I express the hope (but without imposing any binding obligation on him) that the said [*name*] will look after the said dog [or other animal].

1 The legacy will take effect even if the dog or other animal is dead at the testator's death.

Declarations under the Inheritance (Provision for Family and Dependants) Act 1975

[202.39]

Note. The provisions of the Inheritance (Provision for Family and Dependants Act 1975 (I(PFD)A 1975))[1] are considered in more detail in Vol 1 at para **[105.1]** ff. The court may receive in evidence oral and documentary statements by the deceased: Civil Evidence Act 1995, s 1. A testator may wish to take advantage of this provision by incorporating a statement in his will or by leaving a signed statement with his will. The court is not of course bound to accept the deceased's reasons as conclusive: see eg, *Re Preston, Preston v Hogarth* [1969] 2 All ER 961, [1969] 1 WLR 317. However, the court cannot entertain any application under the I(PFD)A 1975 made by the surviving party to a marriage or a former marriage, in contravention of an order made on the grant of a divorce, a decree of nullity of marriage or a decree of judicial separation that that party should not be entitled to apply for an order under the I(PFD)A 1975. Either party to a marriage may apply to the court for such an order excluding an application: I(PFD)A 1975, s 15[2]. A similar provision applies to civil partners: I(PFD)A 1975, s 15ZA.

1 See Part G, paras **[247.1]**–**[247.33]**.
2 See Part G, para **[247.17]**.

[202.40]

Form B2.15: Declarations under the Inheritance (Provision for Family and Dependants) Act 1975—Alternative forms

(1) I hereby declare that no provision is hereby made for my wife [*name*] for the reason that by a deed of separation dated —— and made between [*parties*] I covenanted to pay her a clear annuity of £—— during her life and such annuity will after my death be a charge upon my estate.[1]

(2) I hereby declare that no provision is hereby made for my civil partner [*name*] for the reason that by a deed of separation dated —— and made between [*parties*] I covenanted to pay [him]/[her] a clear annuity of £—— during [his]/[her] life and such annuity will after my death be a charge upon my estate.

(3) No provision is hereby made for my wife [*name*] for the reasons set out in a statement signed by me and deposited with ——.[2]

(4) No provision is hereby made for my civil partner [*name*] for the reasons set out in a statement signed by me and deposited with ——.[2]

(5) I hereby declare that my reason for making no provision for my present husband [*name*] or the infant children of my present marriage is that the whole of my real and personal estate was left to me by my first husband [*name*] and I consider that the whole of the beneficial interest therein should go to the children of my first marriage [more especially as my present husband is possessed of adequate means].

(6) I hereby declare that the reason for making no provision in this my will for my unmarried daughter [*name*][3] is that she left home many years ago and I consider that my married daughter [*name*][3] with whom I have made my home for many years has a much greater claim on me.

(7) I declare that my reason for making no provision in this my will for my infant son [*name*] is that he is already well provided for under the will of his godfather the late [*name*] while my other children have no means of their own.

(8) I hereby declare that my reason for making no greater provision in this my will for [*name*] with whom I have lived for many years is that she has her own financial resources and has never been maintained by me during my lifetime.

1 Unless a contrary intention is expressed, an agreement for maintenance will bind the husband's estate: *Kirk v Eustace* [1937] AC 491, [1937] 2 All ER 715.

2 Where the testator's reasons for making no provision for any dependant are such that, if published, they would give rise to scandal, they should be stated in a separate document, for such matter is excluded from the probate: *Re Hall's Estate* [1943] 2 All ER 159.

3 Note that in alternative (6) it is important to name the persons concerned for reasons including the introduction of GRA 2004.

Clause headings or marginal notes

[202.41]

Note. If clause headings or marginal notes are used in a will for more convenient reference it may be wise to include a declaration that they are not to be used in construing the will.

[202.42]

Form B2.16: Direction regarding clause headings or marginal notes

I declare that the [clause headings] *or* [marginal notes] added hereto are added for the sole purpose of more convenient reference and not for the purpose of the construction of the clauses herein.

B3 Appointment of executors, trustees and guardians

Preliminary Note on executors and trustees .... [203.1]

INDIVIDUALS

FORMS

B3.1 Appointment of wife as sole executrix and trustee with alternative appointment .... [203.7]

B3.2 Appointment of civil partner as sole executor and trustee with alternative appointment .... [203.8]

B3.3 Appointment of executors .... [203.9]

B3.4 Appointment of same persons as executors and trustees .... [203.10]

B3.5 Appointment of executors and of different persons as trustees .... [203.11]

B3.6 Appointment of wife during widowhood adult son and infant son when he attains majority to be executors and trustees .... [203.12]

B3.7 Appointment of three persons, one of whom is abroad, to be executors and trustees, and also trustees for the purposes of the Settled Land Act 1925 .... [203.13]

B3.8 Appointment of executors and trustees with provisions for substitution in case of vacancy .... [203.14]

SOLICITORS

Note .... [203.15]

FORMS

B3.9 Appointment of future partners in a solicitors' firm as executors and trustees .... [203.24]

B3.10 Appointment of members of solicitors' incorporated practice including a limited liability partnership .... [203.25]

B3.11 Appointment of members and employees held out as partners of solicitors' incorporated practice including a limited liability partnership .... [203.26]

B3.12 Appointment of future partners in a solicitors' firm or future members of the body of limited liability partnership in the event of incorporation .... [203.27]

CORPORATIONS

Note .... [203.28]

FORMS

B3.13 Appointment of a bank together with individuals as executors and trustees .... [203.32]

B3.14 Appointment of bank as sole executor and trustee .... [203.33]

B3.15 Appointment of insurance company as executor and trustee .... [203.34]

B3.16 Remuneration clause for bank appointed as executor and trustee ... [203.35]

THE PUBLIC TRUSTEE

FORMS

B3.17 Application by an intending testator to the Public Trustee to act as executor and trustee under a will .... [203.36]

B3.18 Clause in will appointing the Public Trustee as sole executor and trustee or jointly with others .... [203.37]

B3.19 Clauses in will appointing executors and trustees, the Public Trustee being only a trustee or custodian trustee .... [203.38]

B3.20 Clauses in will of a person domiciled elsewhere than in England and Wales appointing an individual executor and providing for transfer of the residuary estate or of a legacy to the Public Trustee to be held upon English trusts .... [203.39]

B3.21 Codicil revoking appointment of executors and trustees and

appointing the Public Trustee sole executor and trustee in their place .... **[203.40]**
B3.22 Codicil appointing the Public Trustee as executor and trustee jointly with executors and trustees previously appointed or in place of one who has died .... **[203.41]**
B3.23 Clause in will prohibiting appointment of the Public Trustee as a trustee .... **[203.42]**

SEPARATE EXECUTORS FOR PARTICULAR ASSETS

FORMS

B3.24 Appointment of literary executors .... **[203.43]**
B3.25 Appointment of separate executors for testator's business .... **[203.44]**
B3.26 Appointment of separate executors for UK property and foreign property .... **[203.45]**
B3.27 Appointment of special executors of settled land .... **[203.46]**

GUARDIANS

Note .... **[203.47]**

FORMS

B3.28 Appointment of guardian to take effect only if the other parent predeceases the appointor, with optional wording making it also take effect if the other parent does not make an effective appointment .... **[203.60]**
B3.29 Appointment of guardian which takes effect if the other parent predeceases the appointor or if there is a residence order in favour of the testator at his or her death, with optional wording making it also take effect if the other parent does not make an effective appointment .... **[203.61]**
B3.30 Appointment of two guardians with expression of wishes about religious education .... **[203.62]**
B3.31 Appointment of a guardian with an alternative appointment if the first choice predeceases the testator or disclaims .... **[203.63]**
B3.32 Appointment by the mother of illegitimate children, appointing the father as guardian with alternative appointment in the event of him predeceasing her .... **[203.64]**
B3.33 Appointment of wife to be the guardian of children by a former marriage with general revocation of previous appointments .... **[203.65]**
B3.34 Appointment of a guardian by a guardian .... **[203.66]**

PRELIMINARY NOTE ON EXECUTORS AND TRUSTEES

[203.1]

Number of executors. In his will, a testator should appoint an executor or executors to administer his property and carry into effect the provisions of the will. The number of executors to be appointed needs to be considered. Probate and letters of administration cannot be granted to more than four persons in regard to the same part of a deceased's person's estate: Supreme Court Act 1981 (SCA 1981), s 114. A single executor can always take a grant of probate to a will, although where a grant of administration has to be taken (for example, where the executors named in the will have predeceased the testator) and a minority or a life interest arises under a will, administration can only be granted either to a trust corporation (with or without an individual) or to not fewer than two individuals: SCA 1981, s 114(2). In many cases it may be wise to appoint at least two executors. Two executors may exercise, by virtue of the Trustee Act 1925 (TA 1925), s 18(2), any trust or power which was vested in the testator as a sole or last surviving trustee. If the will creates a trust for sale of land, although one executor can sell as personal representative, there must be at least two trustees if the sale is by trustees. In the case of settlements and dispositions on trust for sale of land, the number of trustees is not to exceed four: TA 1925, s 34(2) (Part G, para **[246.32]**). There are circumstances in which separate executors ought to be appointed for particular assets as in the case of literary executors (see form B3.24 at **[203.43]** below) and in some cases particular consideration ought to be given to the identity of executors. For example, in the case of a farmer who has Single Payment Scheme entitlements, it may help in the preservation during administration of the estate of the entitlements for the future, and also in being able to claim the payments during the administration, if a farmer is among the executors.

[203.2]
Trust Corporations. A trust corporation may be an executor either alone or jointly with another person: SCA 1981, s 115. For the meaning of 'trust corporation' and other aspects of the appointment of corporations as executors or trustees see para **[203.28]** ff. See also Forms B3.13 to B3.16 at paras **[203.32]**–**[203.35]** for examples of appointments of corporations.

[203.3]
Trustees. It is usually more convenient if the same persons are appointed both executors and trustees. However, they need not necessarily be the same persons. For a form appointing different persons as trustees see Form B3.4 at para **[203.10]** and for an example of a complete will appointing trustees who are not also the personal representatives see Form C5.4 at paras **[227.50]** ff.

[203.4]
Executors and the Settled Land Act 1925. The Settled Land Act 1925 (SLA 1925) cannot apply to new settlements or trusts of land created on or after 1 January 1997, but existing Settled Land Act settlements continue to be subject to the SLA 1925 unless and until sale of all the land (and heirlooms, if any). If a testator is the tenant for life of land under an existing strict settlement for the purposes of the SLA 1925, the settled land will normally be vested in him in fee simple. The Administration of Estates Act 1925 (AEA 1925), s 22 provides that a testator may appoint, and in default of appointment shall be deemed to have appointed, as his special executors in regard to settled land the persons who are trustees of the settlement at his death. These special executors will have the prior right to a grant of administration limited to the settled land: Non-Contentious Probate Rules 1987, r 29 (SI 1987/2024) (as amended with effect from 14 October 1991 by SI 1991/1876; before this amendment was made, *probate* limited to the settled land was granted to such special executors). For a form of appointment of special executors see Form B3.27 at para **[203.46]**. If there are no special executors, or there are but they do not take out a grant, the trustees of the settlement at the date of the grant are next in order of priority to take out a grant of administration, and failing them the testator's

general personal representatives may take a grant: Non-Contentious Probate Rules 1987, r 29 (as amended by SI 1991/1876). In the case of the testator's personal representatives taking a grant, the Court has power to appoint a special or additional personal representative in respect of the settled land: AEA 1925, s 23. See further Vol 1, para **[26.1]** ff.

[203.5]
Settled land to vest in tenant for life. The personal representatives in respect of the settled land (whoever they may happen to be) will hold the settled land on trust, if and when required to do so, to vest it in the person who under the trust instrument or by virtue of the SLA 1925, becomes the tenant for life or statutory owner. This right is subject to and without prejudice to the rights and powers of the personal representatives for the purposes of administration: SLA 1925, s 8(3). They may be liable for inheritance tax on the settled land (IHTA 1984, s 200(1)(a), and may transfer or create legal estates pro tanto overriding the settlement for raising money or indemnifying themselves: SLA 1925, s 8(5) and (6).

[203.6]
Acceptance and renunciation. As to acceptance and renunciation or disclaimer of the office of executor or trustee, see Vol 1, paras **[25.12]–[25.13]**. For forms of renunciation of executorship and trusteeship see Forms F1.1 to F1.4 at paras **[239.2]–[239.5]**.

For executors generally, see Vol 1, para **[25.1]** ff.

Individuals

[203.7]

Form B3.1: Appointment of wife as sole executrix and trustee with alternative appointment[1]

I appoint my wife [*name*] sole executrix and trustee of this my will but if my wife shall die in my lifetime or shall refuse or be unable to act as such executrix and trustee[2] then I appoint [*name*] of [*address*] and [*name*] of [*address*] to be the executors and trustees of this my will and I declare that in this will the expression 'my trustee' shall where the context so admits include my personal representatives or personal representative for the time being and the trustees or trustee for the time being of this will.

1 The appointment of a sole executor and trustee of a will is inadvisable except where there is a sole beneficiary of full age or the executor is a trust corporation. This Form assumes that the main gift in the will is to the testator's wife, with an alternative gift to take effect if the gift to her fails.

2 The appointment of a spouse as executor or as executor and trustee will fail, and the spouse will be deemed to predecease the testator for the purposes of the alternative appointment (testators dying on or after 1 January 1996), if the marriage is after the date of the will dissolved, annulled or declared void, unless a contrary intention appears by the will: WA 1837, s 18A (Part G, para **[244.18]**), see also Vol 1, para **[47.2]** and C2 at paras **[224.12]–[224.19]**.

[203.8]

Form B3.2: Appointment of civil partner as sole executor and trustee with alternative appointment[1]

I appoint my civil partner [*name*] sole executor and trustee of this my will but if my civil partner shall die in my lifetime or shall refuse or be unable to act as such executor and trustee[2] then I appoint [*name*] of [*address*] and [*name*] of [*address*] to be the executors and trustees of this my will and I declare that in this will the expression 'my trustee' shall where the context so admits include my personal representatives or personal representative for the time being and the trustees or trustee for the time being of this will.

1 The appointment of a sole executor and trustee of a will is inadvisable except where there is a sole beneficiary of full age or the executor is a trust corporation. This Form assumes that the main gift in the will is to the testator's civil partner, with an alternative gift to take effect if the gift to him fails.

2 The appointment of a civil partner as executor or as executor and trustee will fail, and the civil partner will be deemed to predecease the testator for the purposes of the alternative appointment, if the civil partnership is after the date of the will dissolved or annulled, unless a contrary intention appears by the will: the WA 1837, s 18C (as added by CPA 2004, s 71, Sch 4, para 2 – see Part G, Statutes, para **[244.20]**, below), see also Vol 1, para **[47.3]** and C2 at paras **[224.16]–[224.23]**.

[203.9]

Form B3.3: Appointment of executors[1]

I appoint [*name*] of [*address*] and [*name*] of [*address*] to be the executors of this my will.

1 While a mere appointment of executors in this form may be sufficient where there is a universal beneficiary or all the gifts in the will are immediate and final distribution can be made as soon as the estate is cleared, it is always preferable that trustees of the will should be appointed as in the next following precedent. As to when executors, though not appointed trustees, become trustees, see *Re Ponder, Ponder v Ponder* [1921] 2 Ch 59 and Vol 1, para **[27.1]**. A grant will not be made to more than four persons in respect of the same part of a deceased person's estate but there is no longer any overall limit to the number of personal representations where separate grants are taken to different parts of the same estate: see s 114 (1) of the SCA 1981 reversing *Re Holland's Estate* [1936] 3 All ER 13.

[203.10]

Form B3.4: Appointment of same persons as executors and trustees[1]

I appoint [*name*] of [*address*] and [*name*] of [*address*] (hereinafter called 'my trustees' which expression shall include the trustees[2] for the time being hereof) to be the executors and trustees of this my will [and also to be the trustees hereof for the purposes of the Settled Land Act 1925][3] [If real or leasehold estate in Northern Ireland also is settled add: and of the Settled Land Acts 1882–1890, and s 42 of the Conveyancing Act 1881].[4]

1 It is usually convenient to appoint the same persons both executors and trustees though it is sometimes desired to appoint different persons, usually because the executors desire to be released from their duties as soon as possible. The following form is suitable where different persons are appointed, but such procedure will also entail some differences in the later part of the will, see paras **[227.46]–[227.48]**. As to the desirability of appointing at least two persons, see para **[203.1]**.

2 Since the plural now includes the singular and vice versa (LPA 1925, s 61: Part G, para **[246.54]**) it is not strictly necessary to say 'the trustees or trustee' as in the common form

before 1926, although it is still customary to do so. *Re Hayes' Will Trusts, Pattison v Hayes* [1971] 2 All ER 341, [1971] 1 WLR 758 establishes that where, as here, a will appoints the same persons as executors and trustees and defines them as 'my trustees', powers conferred on 'my trustees' elsewhere in the will may be exercisable by those persons in either capacity. It is doubtful whether it is sufficient for the will to appoint the persons concerned as executors and trustees and then to contain a definition clause which merely makes it clear that 'my trustees' includes additional or substituted *trustees*. But each case must depend upon the intention of the testator to be deduced from the will as a whole.

3 These words will only be necessary where the provisions of the will are such that land becomes settled land within the SLA 1925. Their insertion is not essential as the SLA 1925, s 30(3), makes the personal representatives such trustees where none are appointed by the will and there are none by virtue of the provisions of the earlier part of that section. However, it is better practice to make an appointment in the will than to rely on the SLA 1925, s 30(3).

4 The changes made to the law of settled land by the English 1925 legislation have not been made to the law of settled land in any part of Ireland.

[203.11]

Form B3.5: Appointment of executors and of different persons as trustees[1]

I appoint [*name*] of [*address*] and [*name*] of [*address*] to be the executors of this my will and [*name*] of [*address*] and [*name*] of [*address*] (hereinafter called 'my trustees' which expression shall include the trustees for the time being hereof) to be the trustees of this my will [and I appoint my trustees to be the trustees hereof for the purposes of the Settled Land Act 1925].

1 See notes to last precedent. For a form of will where there are trustees who are different persons from the executors see Form C5.4 at para **[227.50]**.

[203.12]

Form B3.6: Appointment of wife / civil partner during widowhood/until formation of a civil partnership adult son and infant son when he attains majority to be executors and trustees

I appoint to be the executors and trustees of this my will my wife[1] [*name*] [so long as she shall not remarry or form a civil partnership][2] my son [*name*][3] and also my son [*name*] if and when such last-named son shall attain the age of eighteen years[4] who are hereinafter called 'my trustees' which expression where used throughout this my will shall (where the context permits) include the trustees for the time being of this my will whether original or substituted [and if there shall for the time being be no such trustees or trustee shall (where the context permits) include the persons or person empowered by statute to exercise or perform any power or trust hereby or by statute conferred upon my trustees willing or bound to exercise or perform the same][5] [and I appoint my trustees to be trustees hereof for the purposes of the Settled Land 1925].[6]

1 In order to adapt the form to take account of civil partnerships formed pursuant to CPA 2004 replace the opening references to wife and widowhood with the following words: 'I appoint to be the executors and trustees of this my will my civil partner [*name*] [so long as [he]/[she] shall not marry or form another civil partnership]...'

2 It is inadvisable to direct a person to cease to be an executor on the happening of a certain event or to become an executor on the happening of a certain event. If this clause is used at all, the wife and son should be trustees only, and even with this limitation, the clause is likely to cause difficulty and should be used only on the express instructions of the testator.

Note that a widowhood interest can end either by remarriage or by the formation by the widow of a civil partnership (which need not involve any sexual relations) and it is no longer satisfactory to refer only to an interest ceasing on a person ceasing to be a widow.

3 Following the commencement of GRA 2004 on 4 April 2005 it is important to name the son referred to. See para **[81.1]** above.

4 As to the effect of appointing an infant as a sole or joint executor, see s 118 of the SCA 1981.

5 See s 18(2) of the TA 1925 (Part G, para **[246.16]**) and s 30(3) of the SLA 1925. It is submitted that this addition is in law unnecessary because under these statutes the personal representative may either assume the position of trustee or appoint others to be trustees. If he assumes the position of trustee he becomes a trustee for the time being of the will. However, the words may be included if it is desired to make the position quite clear. As to executors generally, see Vol 1, para **[25.1]** ff. As to the validity of appointment of a wife as executor during her widowhood see Wentworth, Off Ex 14th ed 29; Goldolphin, Part II, c 2, s 3. Probate or letters of administration will not be granted to more than four persons in respect of the same part of the estate of a deceased person, but there is no longer any limit to the total number of executors or administrators where separate grants are made to different parts of the estate: see para **[203.8]**, n 1. As to the position where an executor renounces, but is subsequently permitted to withdraw his renunciation and to prove, see s 6(1) of the AEA 1925.

6 See para **[203.9]**, n 4.

[203.13]

Form B3.7: Appointment of three persons, one of whom is abroad, to be executors and trustees, and also trustees for the purposes of the Settled Land Act 1925

I appoint [*name*] of [*address*] and [*name*] of [*address*] and also [*name*] of [*address*] [if and when such last-named person returns to England with the intention of permanently residing there][1] (hereinafter called 'my trustees'[2] which expression shall include the trustees or trustee for the time being hereof whether original or substituted) to be the executors and trustees of this my will and I appoint my trustees to be trustees hereof for all the purposes of the Settled Land 1925.[3] [If real or leasehold estate in Northern Ireland also is settled add: and of the Settled Land Acts 1882 to 1890 and section 42 of the Conveyancing Act 1881].[4]

1 An appointment of this kind is very inadvisable. For the difficulties that may arise under it, see *Re Arbib and Class's Contract* [1891] 1 Ch 601. If any named executor does not prove, those who do prove can validly execute a conveyance of real estate (AEA 1925, s 2(2), and note that 'real estate' in s 2(2) includes leaseholds: AEA 1925, s 3(1)).

2 See para **[203.9]**, n 3.

3 See para **[203.9]**, n 4. Settled Land Act trustees are also trustees for management of land during the minority of a person entitled in possession, unless their appointment provides to the contrary: SLA 1925, s 102.

4 The English 1925 legislation does not apply to any part of Ireland.

[203.14]

Form B3.8: Appointment of executors and trustees with provisions for substitution in case of vacancy[1]

I appoint [*name*] of [*address*] [*name*] of [*address*] and [*name*] of [*address*] to be executors and trustees of this my will and in case any one or more of them shall die in my lifetime or shall refuse or be unable to act in the office of executor and trustee then I appoint [*name*] of [*address*] [*name*] of [*address*] and [*name*] of [*address*] in the order named to fill any vacancy in the office of executor and trustee hereof that may occur by reason of such death refusal or inability as aforesaid. [And I declare that the expression 'my trustees' used throughout this my will shall include (where the context permits) my personal representatives for the time being and the trustees for the time being of this my will whether original or substituted. And if there shall for the time being be no such trustee the said expression shall (where the context permits) include the person empowered by statute to exercise or perform any power or trust hereby or by statute conferred upon my trustees and willing or bound to exercise or perform the same.] [I appoint my trustees to be the trustees hereof for the purposes of the Settled Land Act 1925.][2]

1 Where executors renounced, a grant was made to substituted executors: *Re Freeman's Estate* (1831) 146 LT 143. See also para **[203.9]**, n 3 as to the effect of the definition of 'my trustees'. For a form of appointment of a spouse as executor with an alternative appointment in case of a vacancy, see Form B3.1 at para **[203.7]**. The formula used in this form can now be used where a spouse is initially appointed executor despite the possibility of the appointment failing by reason of the marriage ending in divorce, being annulled or being declared void: see para **[203.7]**, n 2. For the equivalent form where there is a civil partnership, see para **[203.8]**.

2 See para **[203.10]**, n 4.

Solicitors

[203.15]

Partners in firms of solicitors. The two forms of B3.9 (at para **[203.24]**) are designed to cater for the wish of a client to appoint as executors and trustees of his will persons who will be partners in a firm of solicitors at the date of his death. Form A is based on a precedent which in the case of *Re Horgan* [1971] P 50, [1969] 3 All ER 1570 was considered by Latey J to be 'probably the best which could be devised'. It provides that all the partners at the date of death are appointed as both executors and trustees, but the intention is (if the precatory words in square brackets are included) that only two shall accept the appointment and that the remainder (if any) shall act neither as the executors nor as the initial trustees. It is important to phrase the appointment in this way to avoid uncertainty as to who has been appointed—a purported appointment of 'two of the partners in X firm' will be void: *Re Baylis' Goods* (1862) 2 Sw & Tr 613; *Re Blackwell's Goods* (1877) 2 PD 72.

[203.16]

Two partners as executors and trustees. Where Form A in B3.9 at para **[203.24]** is used, so far as the executorship is concerned, the two who decide to act can prove the will and the others can renounce probate or simply refrain from proving. But renunciation of probate or failure to prove the will does not necessarily amount to disclaimer of the trusteeship, so that when the administration is complete and the trusts begin to operate it is arguable that the trustees, prima facie, are all the partners and not merely the two who have proved the will. On the other hand, this difficulty may be more apparent than real. However many people may be appointed trustees, the only people who actually become trustees are those who expressly or impliedly accept office, and if the other partners do not accept the trusteeship they will not become trustees. So far as conveyancing is concerned they will be hidden behind the curtain mechanism; the legal estate in the land will not leave the hands of the two proving executors unless and until they make an assent, and when they do make an assent the assent is, in favour of a purchaser, to be taken as sufficient evidence that the persons to whom it is made are those to whom it should have been made: AEA 1925, s 36(7). Nor is there any risk of the beneficiaries making the other partners liable as trustees unless they have actually intermeddled in the trusts (though having regard to the fact that they are partners in the same firm of solicitors as the 'real' trustees and might on occasion take on some of their work, there might be a slight risk that intermeddling could be inferred).

[203.17]
A drafting problem which can arise where Form A in B3.9 at para **[203.24]** is used in the more complicated type of will, where powers of appointment or application of capital are conferred on the executors and trustees, is avoiding the possibility that the powers can only be exercised by all the partners in the firm including those who do not take out a grant.

[203.18]
These difficulties with Form A appointment can be avoided by an appointment made along the lines of Form B of B3.9 at para **[203.24]**. This provides that the only partners to be trustees are those who actually prove the will. It also provides a definition of 'my trustees', for use when conferring powers and creating trusts, which excludes from the definition persons appointed executors who do not take out a grant of probate.

[203.19]
Even where a definition of 'my trustees' is included on the lines of the one in Form B, this type of appointment is not a good one to choose if the will creates discretionary trusts with a view to taking advantage of the ITA 1984, s 144 (see C3 at paras **[225.83]–[225.91]**), at any rate where it may be desired to make an appointment under a power in the will before the grant of probate has been obtained, because the agreement to and execution of the appointment by all the partners in the firm at the testator's death will be needed for an appointment to be made before the grant of probate, even where Form B is used.

For forms of executors' oaths which may be applicable where partners of a firm of solicitors are appointed executors, see Form F2.3 at para **[240.3]**.

[203.20]
Solicitors' incorporated practices. By virtue of the Administration of Justice Act 1985, s 9 and the Solicitors' Incorporated Practice Rules 1988 solicitors may now act through bodies corporate rather than a partnership firm provided the body is recognised by the Law Society. The corporate body itself cannot take out a grant of probate or letters of administration to a person's estate because it is not a trust corporation, but its directors, members and the owners of its shares may. There are hardly any incorporated practices at present, but it is possible that the number will increase. Where Form B3.9 (at para **[203.24]**) has been used and the firm has become incorporated before the testator's death, there would be a question whether

the appointment of executors was still effective. Unlike Limited Liability Partnerships (see below), not much use has been made of the Solicitors' Incorporated Practice Rules.

[203.21]
Forms B3.9 and B3.10 (at paras **[203.24]** and **[203.25]**) are designed to cater respectively for a solicitors' practice which has already been incorporated, and for the possibility that what is at present a firm may become incorporated before the testator's death, where the testator wishes to appoint the members of the incorporated practice or firm as executors.

[203.22]
Solicitors' limited liability partnerships. By virtue of Limited Liability Partnerships Act 2000, s 1 and the Limited Liability Partnerships Regulations 2001 (SI 2001/1090) solicitors may now act through limited liability partnerships. A limited liability partnership falls within the broader category of an incorporated practice and so is within the scope of the Solicitors' Incorporated Practices Order 1991 (SI 1991/2684) (as amended by SI 2001/645). The effect is that the limited liability partnership, like the corporate body of an incorporated practice, cannot itself take out a grant of probate or letters of administration to a person's estate because it is not a trust corporation, but its members (sometimes described as partners) may. Many limited liability partnerships act in concert with trust corporations incorporated for the purpose of obtaining probate etc on behalf of the incorporated firm (see para **[203.28]** onwards). In such cases the trust corporation ought to be appointed executor and trustee.

As with incorporated practices, where a precursor to Form B3.9, para **[203.24]** (see form B3.8 in the previous edition at **[203.21]**), has been used and the firm has become a limited liability partnership before the testator's death, there may be a question whether the appointment of executors is still effective. This is resolved in the case of statutes and statutory instruments by the Solicitors' Incorporated Practices Order 1991, art 4 but there is no equivalent in the case of wills and other private instruments.

[203.23]
An appointment of the partners in a firm may not be effective if the firm subsequently converts into an incorporated practice or a limited liability partnership. At their annual conference in 2003 the Probate Registrars decided that on a firm becoming a limited liability partnership, an appointment of 'the partners in the firm' would cease to be effective because the members of a successor limited liability partnership could not be described as 'partners' in a 'firm'. This caused obvious problems for a number of firms. As a result of pressure from the Probate Section of the Law Society, a test case, *Re Rogers (deceased)*[1] was brought.

Re Rogers (deceased) was a case in which the will adopted the wording suggested by Latey J in *In re Horgan*[2] and provided:

> 'I appoint the partners at the date of my death in the firm … or in the firm which at that date has succeeded to and carried on its practice to be the Executors and Trustees of this my Will (and I express the wish that two and only two of them shall prove my Will and act initially in its trusts).'

The firm in question had merged with another firm and subsequently formed a limited liability partnership ('the LLP'). Lightman J held that upon the true construction of the will probate could be granted to the profit-sharing members of the LLP but not to non-profit sharing employees of the LLP. In reaching that conclusion, Lightman J also held that even the term 'partner in the partnership' means in the case of a partnership (as opposed to an LLP) a profit sharing partner and not merely a salaried partner or a person merely held out as (but not in fact) a partner. The judge added that testators ought to make express provision whether on the conversion of any appointed firm of solicitors or successor firm, for the appointment of employee and profit sharing members. Forms 3.9 to 3.12 below have been redrawn to take account of that decision.

1 *Re Rogers (deceased)* [2006] EWHC 753 (Ch), [2006] 2 All ER 792.
2 *Re Horgan* [1971] P 50 at 61.

[203.24]

Form B3.9: Appointment of future partners in a solicitors' firm as executors and trustees

FORM A. ORIGINAL FORM (adapted for LLPs):

I appoint the partners (which term includes [employees described or held out as partners] directors members or beneficial owners[1]) at the date of my death in the firm of [*name of firm*] of [*address*] or the firm which at that date has succeeded to and carries on its practice including a firm which has been incorporated or has formed a limited liability partnership to be the executors and trustees of this my will [and I express the wish that no more than two of them shall prove my will and act initially in its trusts and that [*name*] if then a partner [or an employee of the firm or any successor thereto][2] should be one of them].

FORM B. ALTERNATIVE (PREFERRED) FORM (adapted for LLPs):

(a) As executors of this will I appoint the partners at the date of my death in the firm of [*name of firm*] of [*address*] or the firm which at that date has succeeded to and carries on its practice including a firm which has been incorporated or has formed a limited liability partnership [and I express the wish that no more than two of them shall prove the will and that [*name*] if then a partner [or an employee of the firm or any successor thereto][3] should be one of them].

(b) In this clause the expression 'partners' includes any [employees described or held out as partners] directors members or beneficial owners of the firm or any successor thereto[4].

(c) As trustees of this will I appoint the persons who take out a grant of probate [not being a grant limited to settled land][5] by virtue of the foregoing appointment of executors[6].

(d) The expression 'my trustees' in this my will means my personal representatives and the trustees of this will from time to time (whether original or substituted) but after there has been a grant of probate or letters of administration in respect of my estate [(other than a grant limited to settled land)][7] it shall not include, by virtue of the foregoing appointment of executors[8], any person appointed an executor who for the time being has not proved this will.

1 See the note at **[203.22]**. If it is only intended that profit-sharing partners, members, directors and beneficial owners of the firm or any successor firm should be appointed then the reference to employees ought to be deleted and the form might be amended (in either version) by adding the somewhat inelegant subclause: 'In this clause the words firm and partner are to be construed as if Solicitors' Incorporated Practices Order 1991, art 4 applied to this will.'

Except where there is a desire to appoint a particular member of the firm (who might be the [*name*] referred to) with whom the testator has had a long-standing relationship it is likely that both testator and firm will be wary of permitting the appointment of employees, including salaried partners.

2 If the particular solicitor who the testator would like to appoint is not a partner or is likely to retire from the partnership but remain on the payroll as a consultant, these words ought to be included.

3 If the particular solicitor who the testator would like to appoint is not a partner or is likely to retire from the partnership but remain on the payroll as a consultant, these words ought to be included.

4 See the note at **[203.22]**. If it is only intended that profit-sharing partners, members, directors and beneficial owners of the firm or any successor firm should be appointed then the reference to employees ought to be deleted. Except where there is a desire to appoint a particular consultant with whom the testator has had a long-standing relationship it is likely that both testator and firm will be wary of permitting the appointment of employees, including salaried partners.

5 These words could be included if the testator is a tenant for life under a SLA 1925 settlement which will continue after his death, because the first persons to take out a grant might be the trustees of the strict settlement. However, these words are now not strictly necessary in this context: as a result of the changes made to Non-Contentious Probate Rules 1987, r 29 by SI 1991/1876 (with effect from 14 October 1991) all grants in respect of settled land of which the deceased was the life tenant are now grants of *administration* not probate. See **[203.4]–[203.6]**.

6 This subclause is intended to include in the appointment of trustees anyone who takes out a grant including a grant subsequent to the first, e g where the partners in the firm who take out the initial grant and die while the estate is still in the course of administration, and another partner or partners take out a grant under the power reserved.

7 These words should be included if the testator is a tenant for life under a SLA 1925 settlement which will continue after his death, because the first persons to take out a grant of probate or letters of administration might be the trustees of the settled land. In contrast to these words in the preceding subclause these words are needed in this subclause despite the changes to Non-Contentious Probate Rules 1987, r 29 noted in n 1 above because here there is a reference to grants of administration as well as probate.

8 The reason for including these words is to make it clear that someone who is initially appointed an executor, who does not take a grant of probate, but is later appointed a trustee by, eg, an appointment under TA 1925, s 36, is not excluded from the definition.

[203.25]

Form B3.10: Appointment of members of solicitors' incorporated practice including a limited liability partnership

(a) As executors of this will I appoint the persons who at the date of my death are the directors, members and beneficial owners of any share of the incorporated practice or limited liability partnership of [*name of incorporated practice or limited liability partnership*] of [*address of registered office*] and I express the wish that no more than two of them [including [*name*] if he/she should be a[n employee][1] director, member or beneficial owner of any share at the time of my death] shall prove my will.

(b) As trustees of this will I appoint the persons who take out a grant of probate [not being a grant limited to settled land][2] by virtue of the foregoing appointment of executors.

(c) The expression 'my trustees' in this my will means my personal representatives and the trustees of this will from time to time (whether original or substituted) but after there has been a grant of probate or letters of administration in respect of my estate [(other than a grant limited to settled land)][3] it shall not include, by virtue of the foregoing appointment of executors,[4] any person appointed an executor who for the time being has not proved this will.

1 If the particular solicitor whom the testator would like to appoint is not a member, director or beneficial owner or is likely to retire from that position but remain on the payroll as a consultant, these words ought to be included.
2 See para **[203.24]**, n 5.
3 See para **[203.24]**, n 6.
4 See para **[203.24]**, n 7.

[203.26]

Form B3.11: Appointment of members and employees held out as partners of solicitors' incorporated practice including a limited liability partnership[1]

(a) As executors of this will I appoint the persons who at the date of my death are the [employees held out as partners], directors, members or beneficial owners of any share of the incorporated practice or limited liability partnership of [*name of incorporated practice or limited liability partnership*] of [*address of registered office*] and I express the wish that no more than two of them [including [*name*] if he/she should be a[n employee][2] director, member or beneficial owner of any share at the time of my death] shall prove my will.

(b) As trustees of this will I appoint the persons who take out a grant of probate [not being a grant limited to settled land][3] by virtue of the foregoing appointment of executors.

(c) The expression 'my trustees' in this my will means my personal representatives and the trustees of this will from time to time (whether original or substituted) but after there has been a grant of probate or letters of administration in respect of my estate [(other than a grant limited to settled land)][4] it shall not include, by virtue of the foregoing appointment of executors,[5] any person appointed an executor who for the time being has not proved this will.

1 Sometimes the testator wants to appoint a solicitor with whom he has had dealings for many years but that solicitor is actually a salaried consultant, or at least not a profit-sharing member, director or beneficial owner of the limited liability partnership. In such a case the testator ought to appoint employees of the 'firm' as well.
2 If the particular solicitor whom the testator would like to appoint is not a member, director or beneficial owner or is likely to retire from that position but remain on the payroll as a consultant, these words ought to be included.
3 See para **[203.24]**, n 5.
4 See para **[203.24]**, n 6.
5 See para **[203.24]**, n 7.

[203.27]

Form B3.12: Appointment of future partners in a solicitors' firm or future members of the body or limited liability partnership in the event of incorporation

(a) As executors of this will I appoint the partners[1] at the date of my death in the firm of [*name of firm*] of [*address*] or the firm which has succeeded to and carries on its practice but in the event of such firm being incorporated whether by the formation of a limited liability partnership or otherwise at the date of my death I appoint the directors, members and beneficial owners of any share of the incorporated practice or limited liability partnership at the date of my death.

(b) I express the wish that no more than two persons shall prove my will [including [*name*] if he/she should be partner, director, member or beneficial owner (as the case may be) at the time of my death][2].

(c) As trustees of this will I appoint the persons who take out a grant of probate [not being a grant limited to settled land][3] by virtue of the foregoing appointment of executors.

(d) The expression 'my trustees' in this my will means my personal representatives and the trustees of this will from time to time (whether original or substituted) but after there has been a grant of probate or letters of administration in respect of my estate [(other than a grant limited to settled land)][4] it shall not include, by virtue of the foregoing appointment of executors,[5] any person appointed an executor who for the time being has not proved this will.

1 Following *Re Rogers (deceased) (see* **[203.22]***)*, this form does not appoint salaried partners or persons held out as partners in a limited liability partnership but who are, in reality, employees. It is thought that, except where there is a desire to appoint a particular consultant with whom the testator has had a long-standing relationship it is likely that both testator and firm will be wary of permitting the appointment of employees, including salaried partners. If that is desired, Form B3.9 should be adapted.

2 If the particular solicitor whom the testator would like to appoint is not a member, director or beneficial owner or is likely to retire from that position but remain on the payroll as a consultant, the previous form should be adapted.

3 See para **[203.24]**, n 5.

4 See para **[203.24]**, n 6.

5 See para **[203.24]**, n 7.

Corporations

[203.28]

Trust corporations. A trust corporation may be an executor either alone or jointly with another person: SCA 1981, s 115. A trust corporation is the Public Trustee or a corporation appointed by the court as a trustee or entitled under the Public Trustee Rules to act as custodian trustee: TA 1925, s 68(18) (Part G, para **[246.38]**) and the LPA 1925, s 205(1)(xxviii) (Part G, para **[246.59]**). For the last mentioned category, see r 30 of the Public Trustee Rules 1912 (SR & O 1912/348), as substituted by the Public Trustee (Custodian Trustee) Rules 1975 (SI 1975/1189) and subsequently amended (Part G, para **[246.73]**). Certain EC corporations can qualify as trust corporations. Any authorised officer of a trust corporation may on its behalf swear affidavits, give security, and do any other act or thing which the court may require with a view to taking a grant, and the acts of such officer will be binding on the corporation.

[203.29]

Appointment of trust corporation. Most banks and insurance companies are trust corporations or have subsidiaries which are trust corporations. If it is proposed to appoint a bank or insurance company as executor or trustee, it must be ascertained whether the trustee department is a separate company, and if so, it must be referred to by its proper name. The institution's common form clauses should be obtained and agreed, with or without modification, together with the scale of fees. The will should be submitted to the institution in draft, so that it may inform the testator or those advising him whether it will accept office. Generally speaking all ordinary wills are accepted, but wills requiring the trustees to carry on a business are usually refused.

[203.30]

Charging clause. Where a will appoints a trust corporation as executor and/or trustee, a clause authorising it to charge for acting on its standard terms should be included. There is now a statutory power for a trust corporation to charge reasonable remuneration under the Trustee Act 2000, s 29 (Part G, para **[246.161]**), but it is not clear that it would include power to charge scale fees: see para **[221.48]**. Where a corporation is appointed administrator of an estate, the court can authorise remuneration both under the TA 1925, s 42 and its inherent jurisdiction: *Re Young's Estate* (1934) 103 LJP 75 and *Re Masters, Coutts & Co v Masters* [1953] 1 All ER 19.

[203.31]

Fees charged by banks. Where a bank was by codicil appointed executor and trustee of a will in place of a solicitor who was given the benefit of a charging clause, the bank was entitled to its ordinary scale of fees at the date of the codicil although nothing was said in the codicil as to charging: *Re Campbell's Estate* [1954] 1 All ER 448. Where a clause appointing a bank as executor and trustee included the following: 'and may without accounting for any resultant profit act as banker and perform any service on behalf of my estate on the same terms as would be made with a customer', it was held that where considerable funds of the estate remained uninvested for some four years while on deposit with the bank, the bank was under no duty to account for the profit gained by its employment of the money deposited with it, such procedure being justified by the charging clause: *Re Waterman's Will Trusts, Lloyds Bank Ltd v Sutton* [1952] 2 All ER 1054. The statutory power of a trust corporation to charge includes a power for one which is a bank to charge reasonable charges for its banking services: TrA 2000, s 29(3) (Part G, para **[246.161]**); see also para **[221.48]**.

[203.32]

Form B3.13: Appointment of a bank together with individuals as executors and trustees

I appoint [*names*] of [*address*] and the —— Bank plc to be executors and trustees of this my will.

[203.33]

Form B3.14: Appointment of bank as sole executor and trustee

I appoint —— Bank plc to be the executor and trustee [or the custodian trustee] of this my will. [*Add the clauses required by the bank.*] [I hereby also appoint the said bank to be the trustees hereof for the purposes of the Settled Land Act 1925.][1]

1 See para **[203.9]**, n 4.

[203.34]

Form B3.15: Appointment of insurance company as executor and trustee

I appoint —— Insurance Co plc to be the executor and trustee [*or* the custodian trustee] of this my will. If in relation to my will or the trusts thereof it shall become necessary to effect any policy of insurance such insurance may be effected with the said —— Insurance Co plc at their usual rates for such insurance and the said —— Insurance Co plc shall not be accountable to my estate in respect of any profit it may make in respect thereof. [*Add any special clauses required by the insurance company.*] [I hereby also appoint the said —— Insurance Co plc to be the trustee hereof for the purposes of the Settled Land Act 1925.][1]

1 See para **[203.9]**, n 4.

[203.35]

Form B3.16: Remuneration clause for bank appointed as executor and trustee

(a) The bank shall have power to act by its proper officers and shall be entitled to remuneration for acting as executor and trustee [in accordance with the bank's published scale of fees contained in a letter dated —— written to me by the bank] *or* [in accordance with the bank's published scale of fees from time to time] *or* [in accordance with such scale of fees as may be agreed upon after my death between the bank and the other persons nominated herein as my executors and trustees or such of them as shall be living at my death].

(b) The bank may act as bankers to and make advances or loans to my trustees or my estate upon the usual terms as to interest and charges in the ordinary course of the bank's business and share stockbrokers' commissions and generally act as a banker may in relation to his customer and without accounting for any profit so made.

[(c) The bank shall hold all moneys deeds and documents relating to the trusts of this my will subject to proper facilities for my other trustees to inspect and verify the same and the name of the bank shall be placed first in the register of all registered securities or property.][1]

1 This subclause is not needed if the bank is sole executor.

The Public Trustee

[203.36]

Form B3.17: Application by an intending testator to the Public Trustee to act as executor and trustee under a will[1]

(*All information placed before the Public Trustee will be treated as confidential.*)

To the Public Trustee,
81 Chancery Lane, London, WC2A 1DD / DX 0012 London / Chancery Lane.

Dear sir.

I shall be glad to learn if you will be prepared to act as

1. Executor [co-executor] *or*	}	
2. Trustee [co-trustee] *or*		under my will.
3. Executor and trustee [co-executor and co-trustee]		

I CONTEMPLATE disposing of my property in the following manner ——.

The original will (*with other testamentary documents, if any*) is [*will be*] deposited at ——.

My bankers are ——.

The stockbrokers I usually employ are Messrs —— of ——.

The solicitors whom I desire the Public Trustee to employ for any necessary professional work incidental to the administration of my estate are Messrs —— of ——.

Name of testator (in full) ——.

Signature ——.

Residence ——.

Occupation (if any) ——.

Date ——.

The property which will pass under the will will probably consist of the following:[2]

	Approximate value or amount.
Stocks and shares fully paid	£——
Stocks and shares partly paid	£——
Life insurances	£——
Real property in the United Kingdom	£——
Real property abroad	£——
Leasehold property in ——	£——
Mortgages on property in ——	£——
Other property ——	£——
Approximate total	£——

1 It is not essential to supply detailed information, but it is desirable that the form should be filled in and returned to the Public Trustee, who is then in the position to say, from the details submitted to him, whether he can act or not. On receipt of the form duly filled in, the Public Trustee's formal consent to act is forwarded to the applicant, and in this way a suitable record is established on either side. The submission of this form is in no way binding upon the applicant. The Public Trustee will not act where the carrying on of a business for an indefinite period is involved nor will he undertake a trust where the whole of the trust property is devoted to religious or charitable purposes, but this latter restriction does not apply to executorships. A testator may appoint the Public Trustee without first obtaining his consent, but the appointment does not have effect unless the Public Trustee consents to act: r 8 of the Public Trustee Rules 1912 (SR & O 1912/348).

2 It is not essential to fill in this portion of the form, but it is convenient to the Public Trustee to see the general character of the estate with which it is proposed he shall deal.

[203.37]

Form B3.18: Clause in will appointing the Public Trustee as sole executor and trustee or jointly with others[1]

I appoint the Public Trustee [and [*first executor*] and [*second executor*] who and the survivors and survivor of them are hereinafter referred to as 'my trustees'] to be [sole] executor[s] and trustee[s] of this my will [and to be trustee[s] thereof for the purposes of the Settled Land Act 1925].[2]

1 For power to appoint the Public Trustee either solely or jointly with others: Public Trustee Act 1906 (PTA 1906), s 2(2).

2 It is desirable that the Public Trustee's name should appear first in order to secure that all communications, etc from companies should be addressed to him as the first-named holder.

[203.38]

Form B3.19: Clauses in will appointing executors and trustees, the Public Trustee being only a trustee or custodian trustee

I appoint [*first executor*] and [*second executor*] (hereinafter called 'my executors') to be the executors of this my will and my executors and the Public Trustee (who and the survivors and survivor of whom are hereinafter referred to as 'my trustees') to be the trustees of this my will [and to be trustees thereof for the purposes of the Settled Land Act 1925][1]

OR

I appoint [*first executor*] and [*second executor*] (who and the survivors and survivor of whom and other the managing trustees for the time being hereof are hereinafter referred to as 'my trustees') to be executors and the managing trustees of this my will and the Public Trustee to be the custodian trustee thereof [and I further appoint [*trustees, including Public Trustee if so desired*] to be the trustees hereof for the purposes of the Settled Land Act 1925].[2]

On the death of the said [*first executor*] or [*second executor*] I appoint the survivor and the Public Trustee to be the trustees of my will and the expression 'my trustees' shall thereafter mean and include such survivor and the Public Trustee and other the trustees or trustee for the time being thereof provided always that the trust funds and property from time to time subject to the trusts of this my will shall be held in the sole name of the Public Trustee.[3]

1 See para **[203.10]**, n 4.

2 The Public Trustee may act as sole trustee including Settled Land Act trustee (PTA 1906, s 5(1); LPA 1925, s 27(2), as amended by the Law of Property (Amendment) Act 1926: Part G, para **[246.46]**). See also para **[203.10]**, n 4.

3 The appointment of the Public Trustee as both managing trustee and custodian trustee might be ineffective: see *Forster v Williams Deacon's Bank Ltd* [1935] Ch 359, [1935] All ER Rep 374, and *Arning v James* [1936] Ch 158.

[203.39]

Form B3.20: Clauses in will of a person domiciled elsewhere than in England and Wales appointing an individual executor and providing for transfer of the residuary estate or of a legacy to the Public Trustee to be held upon English trusts[1]

I appoint [*executor*] to be executor of this my will and direct that my executor shall pay a legacy of £—— free from inheritance tax [*or* that after payment of my funeral and testamentary expenses and debts and the inheritance tax payable in respect of my death and all legacies given by this my will or any codicil thereto my executor shall pay or transfer the whole of my residuary estate] to the Public Trustee constituted by the Public Trustee Act 1906 to be held by him upon the trusts and with and subject to the powers and provisions hereinafter declared and contained concerning the same.

I declare that the trust to be created in respect of my residuary estate [or the said legacy of £——] shall be considered to be an English trust and that the Public Trustee in his character of trustee thereof shall be exempted from being subject to the process or decision of any tribunal other than the High Court of Justice in England.

[*Set out trusts upon which the legacy or share of residue is to be held.*]

1 The validity of the direction in favour of the Public Trustee may depend upon the law of the country of domicile of the testator.

[203.40]

Form B3.21: Codicil revoking appointment of executors and trustees and appointing the Public Trustee sole executor and trustee in their place

I [*Testator*] of [*address*] declare this to be a codicil (*or* the —— codicil) to my will dated ——.

I revoke the appointment contained in my said will [or in the —— codicil thereto] of [*names*] as executors and trustees [and also as trustees for the purposes of the Settled Land Act 1925] and in lieu thereof:

I appoint the Public Trustee to be sole executor and trustee of my said will [and the —— codicil[s] thereto] [and to be trustee thereof for the purposes of the Settled Land Act 1925].[1]

And in all other respects I confirm my said will [and —— codicils].

IN WITNESS ETC.[2]

1 See para **[203.38]**, n 2 and para **[203.10]**, n 4.
2 For a form of execution and attestation, see Form B22.9 at para **[222.11]**.

[203.41]

Form B3.22: Codicil appointing the Public Trustee as executor and trustee jointly with executors and trustees previously appointed or in place of one who has died

I [*Testator*] of [*address*] declare this to be a codicil [or the —— codicil] to my will dated ——.

[*Recite, if appropriate, the death of any executor and trustee previously appointed.*]

I appoint the Public Trustee to be an executor and trustee of my said will [and the —— codicil[s] thereto] [in place of [*name*] who has died and] jointly with [*names of surviving executors and trustees*] [and also as trustee of my said will jointly with [*names of surviving executors and trustees*] for the purposes of the Settled Land Act 1925].[1]

And I declare that my said will [and the —— codicil[s] thereto] shall be read and construed in all respects as if the official name of the Public Trustee had been inserted throughout as an executor and trustee [but so that the Public Trustee shall not be entitled to receive any legacy [*or* annuity] given to the said [*name of the deceased executor and trustee*] for acting as executor and trustee of my will].

And in all other respects I confirm my said will [and the —— codicil[s] thereto].

In witness etc.[2]

1 See para **[203.10]**, n 4.
2 For form of execution and attestation, see Form B22.9 at para **[222.11]**.

[203.42]

Form B3.23: Clause in will prohibiting appointment of the Public Trustee as a trustee[1]

PROVIDED ALWAYS and I hereby direct and declare that the Public Trustee [or a trust corporation] shall in no event be appointed a new or additional trustee or custodian trustee of this my will or any codicil hereto or of any trust or duty by such will or codicil declared.

1 PTA 1906, s 5(3). A direction such as the above is not binding on the court (s 5(3)). Presumably the direction can be made in respect of trust corporations in general, though the subsection is confined to the Public Trustee.

Separate executors for particular assets

[203.43]

Form B3.24: Appointment of literary executors[1]

I hereby appoint [*name*] of [*address*] and [*name*] of [*address*] (hereinafter called 'my trustees') to be the executors and trustees of this my will except as to the part of my estate hereby given to my literary executors as hereinafter mentioned. I appoint [*name*] of [*address*] and [*name*] of [*address*] (hereinafter called 'my literary executors') to be the executors of this my will to administer only the part of my estate hereinafter given to them [and I direct that the inheritance tax attributable to the said part of my estate and the expenses paid and incurred by them in taking out a limited grant of probate shall be borne by and payable out of the said part of my estate so given to them and as a first charge thereon].[2]

1 It is sometimes desired that special literary executors should be appointed. If so they should be persons having a special knowledge of the administration of literary assets or the interests in them under the will. The difficulties associated with a special grant make this a course which should not be adopted unless there are unpublished works likely from the reputation of the testator to be of considerable value and the publication of which require the supervision of a person experienced in such matters or where there are manuscripts of importance which are to be given to one person and it is desired to keep them separate from the general estate, see *Re Holland's Estate* [1936] 3 All ER 13. Where all the works have been published and it is merely a question of collecting royalties, the matter can in general be safely left to the general executors who can obtain such advice as they may require from qualified persons. A gift of an unpublished manuscript to literary executors carries with it the copyright unless a contrary intention is expressed: CDPA 1988, s 93. In the case where the literary assets are given to the executor for his absolute use and benefit, there is much more reason for adopting this course. As to the number of such executors to be appointed the following considerations may be relevant. If the literary assets are to be given to one person it seems best to appoint him the sole literary executor. If they are given upon special trusts or to be handed over to the general trustees to form part of the residue, then it seems better that there should be two such executors for the simple reason that one such may well predecease the testator and still more likely may die before the completion of his task and the whole object of the special appointment would be frustrated. There is no reason in law for the appointment of only one literary executor especially now that there is no limit to the overall total number of executors in cases where separate grants are made to different parts of the estate: see para **[203.8]**, n 1. See Forms B4.50 and B4.51 at paras **[204.72]** and **[204.73]**, for forms of gifts to and specific powers for literary executors.

2 In the absence of a direction such as this throwing the burden of inheritance tax attributable to the separate property upon the separate property, it would be borne by the testator's residuary estate, see the Preliminary Note to B14 at para **[214.55]** ff.

[203.44]

Form B3.25: Appointment of separate executors for testator's business[1]

I hereby appoint [*name*] of [*address*] and [*name*] of [*address*] (hereinafter called my trustees) to be executors and trustees of this my will for all purposes other than the purpose of dealing with my business assets given by Clause [number] below and I appoint [*name*] of [*address*] and [*name*] of [*address*] (hereinafter called 'my business trustees') to be executors and trustees to administer and hold on trust my said business assets.

1 See Form B5.1 at para **[205.58]** for a gift of a business, and Form B5.6 at para **[205.63]** and Form C11.3 at paras **[233.36]**–**[233.51]** for other forms dealing with business property and appointing separate executors of it.

[203.45]

Form B3.26: Appointment of separate executors for UK property and foreign property

(a) I hereby appoint [*name*] of [*address*] and [*name*] of [*address*] to be executors and trustees of this my will for the purpose of dealing with all real or personal property belonging to me and situate in the United Kingdom at my death [and for the purpose of receiving from my foreign trustees hereinafter appointed and dealing with the income and proceeds of sale and property vesting in my foreign trustees which my foreign trustees may hand over to them pursuant to the directions in that behalf hereinafter contained].

(b) I hereby appoint [*names of individuals or of trust corporation*] [of] *or* [whose registered office is situate at] [*address*] to be executors and trustees of this my will in regard to and for the purpose of dealing with all property (movable or immovable) belonging to me and situate in [*name of country*] at my death.

[203.46]

Form B3.27: Appointment of special executors of settled land[1]

I appoint as my special executors in regard to settled land of which at my death I shall be the tenant for life or the person having the powers of a tenant for life the respective persons who shall be at the time of my death the trustees for the purposes of the Settled Land Act 1925 of such settlements provided the land settled thereby continues to be settled land after my death.

1 This form is included for completeness, but in the absence of an express appointment such an appointment is implied by statute: AEA 1925, s 22. See paras **[203.4]**–**[203.6]** generally on special executors.

Guardians

[203.47]

Note. The law of guardians has been much revised and completely restated by the Children Act 1989 (ChA 1989), and when it comes to drafting appointments of guardians the provisions of that Act are all that need to be considered. Its provisions are considered in detail in Vol 1, para **[28.1]** ff and printed in Part G at para **[244.112]** ff. For the power of a guardian to receive or recover the property of a minor see the ChA 1989, s 3(3) (Part G, para **[244.114]**) and Vol 1, paras **[9.38]**–**[9.42]**. Although the law has been made more complicated, its practical effect on the making of appointments of guardians is probably to simplify matters. Anyone making a will who has 'parental responsibility' (see Vol 1, para **[28.2]** for the meaning of this) for minor children should consider including in his will an appointment of a guardian to look after them in the event of his or her death. Anyone with parental responsibility for minor children who does not want to make a will should at least consider making an appointment of a guardian, which can be done by a signed and dated written instrument without observing the formal requirements for making a will, and which can like a will be revoked or changed subsequently (see Vol 1, para **[28.5]**). If a will is being made, we recommend putting any appointment of a guardian in it, since the appointment is more likely to be found and acted on after the appointor's death if it is in a will.

We have the following points and recommendations to make about the appointment of guardians.

[203.48]

(a) **Children with two parents with parental responsibility.** This category comprises children of a marriage, children whom the law deems to be the children of both the parties to a marriage, and children whose parents are not and have not been married to each other but whose fathers have acquired parental responsibility (for which see Vol 1, para **[28.2]**). Children deemed to be children of both parties to a marriage include children legitimated by the subsequent marriage of their parents, adopted by a married couple, or conceived by artificial insemination or in vitro fertilisation in circumstances that they are treated as the child of both parties to a marriage (ChA 1989, s 2(1) and (3): Part G, para **[244.113]**; and HFEA 1990, ss 27 to 29: Part G, paras **[245.85]**–**[245.87]**).

[203.49]
An appointment of a guardian by the father of a child born out of wedlock will only be valid if it is made after he has acquired parental responsibility for the child, which he can do by agreement with the mother or a court order (see Vol 1, paras **[28.2]** and **[28.4]**), or by marrying the mother, which will have the effect that the child will be deemed to be the child of the marriage with both parents having parental responsibility (ChA 1989, s 2(1) and (3): Part G, para **[244.113]**; and FLRA 1987, s 1(2) and (3): Part G, para **[245.70]**). An appointment made by him before he has acquired parental responsibility will be of no effect even if he subsequently acquires it. It should be remembered that if he and the mother do decide to make a parental responsibility agreement the father will not acquire parental responsibility unless and until the agreement has been made in the prescribed form and has been registered with the Principal Registry of the Family Division of the High Court (see Vol 1, para **[28.2]**).

[203.50]
In addition to agreement (a 'parental responsibility agreement') or the court (on his application) ordering that he shall have parental responsibility for a child, the unmarried father of a child may acquire parental responsibility for a child if he becomes registered as the child's father. See ChA 1989, s 4, as amended by the Adoption and Children Act 2002 with effect from 30 December 2005 (see Vol 1, para **[28.1]**). Under the ChA 1989, as amended by the Adoption and Children Act 2002, a person married to, or in a civil partnership with, a child's parent may acquire parental responsibility for a stepchild by agreement or by order declaring that he shall have parental responsibility for the child. See ChA 1989, s 4A, as inserted by the Adoption and Children Act 2002 with effect from 30 December 2005. However, ChA 1989 and Adoption and Children Act 2002 draw a distinction between a parent and a step-parent. The latter is not a parent and so cannot appoint a guardian under ChA 1989.

[203.51]
The main thing to bear in mind, and this is an innovation of the Children Act 1989, is that if one of two parents with parental responsibility for minor children dies leaving the other surviving, an appointment of a guardian made by the first to die will not take effect until the death of the other parent (unless the first to die had a residence order in his or her favour, to the exclusion of the other parent, at his or her death): see Vol 1, para **[28.4]** and ChA 1989, s 5(8) (Part G, para **[244.116]**). We recommend, at any rate where the parents' marriage or relationship is reasonably harmonious, for each parent's appointment of a guardian to be such that it will take effect only if the other has predeceased him or her, so that in the event of the death of both while any of the children are still under 18 it is only the appointment made by the second to die which will take effect. This will leave the survivor, after the death of the first to die, with a free hand as to the choice of a guardian to look after the children in the event of the survivor also dying while some of them are still minors, whereas if the first to die has left an effective appointment it will take effect on the death of the second to die and nothing (short of obtaining a court order) can be done to revoke or prevent

it after the first to die's death. See Form B3.2 at para **[203.60]** for an example of an appointment which only takes effect if the other parent has predeceased the testator.

[203.52]
If an appointment of the kind just recommended has been made, it could have an effect which is not what the testator would have wanted if by the time of his or her death (predeceasing the other parent) there is a residence order made by the court in his or her favour (and which is not in favour of the other parent); an appointment of a guardian expressed to take effect only if the other parent predeceases the testator would not take effect in these circumstances, even though it could have taken effect immediately on the death of the first to die if it had been unconditional (see Vol 1, para **[28.4]** and ChA 1989, s 5(7) to (9): Part G, para **[244.116]**). See Form B3.29 at para **[203.61]** for an appointment which will take effect where there is a residence order at the testator's death, while still leaving the choice of guardian to the surviving parent if there is not a residence order.

[203.53]
A further point about leaving the surviving parent with a free hand as to the appointment of guardians is that he or she might not make any appointment, though appointing a guardian is perhaps unlikely to be neglected by someone who has had the experience of the death of the other parent. See Forms B3.28 and B3.29 at paras **[203.60]** and **[203.61]** for optional wording which will enable an appointment to take effect on the death of the survivor of the two parents if the survivor does not make an effective appointment. It seems unnecessary to include wording of this type where at the same time both parents are making wills containing appointments of guardians.

[203.54]
(b) **Children with only one parent with parental responsibility.** This category includes children of a marriage where one parent has died, and children whose parents have never been married to each other and whose fathers have not acquired parental responsibility.

[203.55]
It is particularly important for a sole parent with parental responsibility of a child to make an appointment of a guardian. Where an unmarried couple are living together, and the father has not acquired parental responsibility, the mother should consider making an appointment of the father as guardian. She could also consider making a parental responsibility agreement giving the father parental responsibility; an important difference is that an appointment of a guardian is revocable by the appointor, while a parental responsibility agreement can only be terminated by a court order (see Vol 1, para **[28.2]**). On the other hand parental responsibility is a permanent acceptance of responsibility by the father, whereas he can always disclaim an appointment as guardian after the death of the mother (see Vol 1, paras **[28.6]** and **[28.7]**).

For forms for appointment of a guardian by a sole parent see Forms B3.31 and B3.32 at paras **[203.63]** and **[203.64]**.

Similarly, where a widow or widower has minor children by her or his first marriage, and marries again, she or he should consider making an appointment of her or his second spouse as guardian of the children: see Form B3.33 at para **[203.65]**.

[203.56]
(c) **Children in the care of guardians.** A guardian of a minor child has power to appoint a successor to act as guardian in the event of his own death (see Vol 1, para **[28.4]**). Such an appointment will take effect on his death even if the child has another guardian who is still living after the death, provided that there is no surviving parent with parental responsibility. For a form for an appointment by a guardian of a successor to himself see Form B3.34 at para **[203.66]**.

[203.57]
(d) **Number and identity of guardians.** There is no limit to the number of guardians of the same child who may be appointed, and the ChA 1989 expressly contemplates that more than one may be appointed (ChA 1989, s 6(1): Part G, para **[244.117]**). As a practical matter the sensible course is to appoint one guardian, or at the most two who are eg a married couple. Only individuals may be appointed, and as the duties are looking after the child rather than looking after the child's property the chosen guardian will often be a different person from any of the executors, and it will normally be appropriate to appoint named persons, and not for instance 'my Executors' or 'my Trustees', especially when the latter are widely defined to include any personal representatives or trustees.

[203.58]
(e) **Alternative appointments; successive or delegated appointments.** It will often be appropriate, eg when someone elderly is the first choice as the guardian of a child, to appoint a second guardian to act if the first one dies or disclaims before becoming a guardian. There is nothing in the ChA 1989 to prevent appointments of this kind being made. See Forms B3.31 and B3.32 at paras **[203.63]** and **[203.64]** for examples.

The ChA 1989 does not enable a parent or guardian to appoint a guardian to act after the death of another guardian after the latter guardian has acted as guardian, nor does it enable a parent or guardian to authorise someone else to exercise his or her power of appointing a guardian. As mentioned above, a guardian has his own directly-conferred statutory power to appoint his own successor as guardian.

[203.59]
(f) **Revocation of previous appointments.** The standard words of general revocation (see B1 at para **[201.2]** ff) of previous wills or testamentary dispositions would probably not be effective by themselves to revoke any earlier appointments of guardians which were in a written instrument which was not a will. However, s 6(1) of the ChA 1989 provides that an appointment of a guardian under that Act revokes an earlier appointment by the same person in respect of the same child unless it is clear from the appointment that its purpose was to appoint an additional guardian. It

should also be noted that if a previous will or codicil is revoked, as it will be by a general revocation clause revoking 'all former testamentary dispositions', any appointment of a guardian in that will or codicil is revoked (ChA 1989, s 6(4): Part G, para **[244.117]**). It is therefore not really necessary to provide expressly that earlier appointments of guardians are revoked when making an appointment of a guardian (unless there is something in the will which might suggest that the appointment was of an additional guardian). Cautious draftsmen may wish to include such a provision, and an example is given in Form B3.33 at para **[203.65]**. Note also that an appointment of the spouse of the appointor as guardian is revoked by divorce or annulment of the marriage: see n 2 to Form B3.33 at para **[203.65]**.

For power to lend trust money to guardians, see Forms B18.30 and B18.31 at paras **[218.116]** and **[218.117]**. For examples of complete forms including the appointment of guardians see C2 at para **[224.27]** ff, C6 at para **[228.5]** ff and C7 at para **[229.2]** ff.

[203.60]

Form B3.28: Appointment of guardian to take effect only if the other parent predeceases the appointor, with optional wording making it also take effect if the other parent does not make an effective appointment

If my [wife]/[husband] [*name*] dies before me [or survives me but does not make any effective appointment of a guardian of our minor children which is not disclaimed by the person appointed][1] then I appoint [*name*] of [*address*] to be the guardian of our minor children in the event of my death.[2]

1 The inclusion of these words in square brackets will allow the appointment to take effect if the other (surviving) parent fails to make an appointment. In order to adapt the form to take account of civil partnerships formed pursuant to CPA 2004, replace the references to wife and husband with civil partner.

2 For reasons given in the note at para **[203.51]** above, this is the recommended form for the appointment of a guardian where there are two parents with parental responsibility. The point is that after the death of one parent the survivor has a free hand as to the choice of guardian in the event of him or her also dying while the children are still minors.

[203.61]

Form B3.29: Appointment of guardian which takes effect if the other parent predeceases the appointor or if there is a residence order in favour of the testator at his or her death, with optional wording making it also take effect if the other parent does not make an effective appointment

I appoint [*name*] of [*address*] to be the guardian of the minor children of myself and [my husband [*name*]] in the event of my death Provided that if [my said husband] survives me and the foregoing appointment does not take effect on my death [and there is at least one effective appointment by [my said husband] of a guardian of our minor children which is not disclaimed by the person appointed][1] then the foregoing appointment of a guardian by me shall be void and of no effect.[2]

1 The inclusion of these words in square brackets will allow the appointment to take effect if the other (surviving) parent fails to make an appointment. In order to adapt the form to take account of civil partnerships formed pursuant to CPA 2004, replace the references to wife and husband with civil partner.

2 This is an alternative to the preceding form for cases where there is another parent with parental responsibility, and is appropriate where the testator is concerned about the possibility of the marriage or relationship breaking up. Again the other parent if surviving the testator has a free hand as to the choice of guardian in the event of he or she also dying while the children are still minors, but under this form this is subject to the testator's appointment taking effect if he or she is the first to die in circumstances that at his or her death there is a residence order relating to the children in his/her favour (which is not also in favour of the other parent). See the note to these forms at paras **[203.52]** and **[203.53]**.

[203.62]

Form B3.30: Appointment of two guardians with expression of wishes about religious education[1]

I appoint [my sister [*name*] and her husband [*name*] both of [*address*]] to be the guardians of my minor children in the event of my death and it is my particular wish that my children shall be brought up [[in the Protestant religion] *or* [as members of the Church of England] *or* [as Roman Catholics] *or as may be*].[2]

1 The wishes of a parent as to the faith in which his or her child should be brought up after his or her death will be taken into account by the court if there are proceedings in which the court has to make a decision on the upbringing of the child, but such wishes will be considered along with the other relevant factors, including the child's own wishes, and it is the welfare of the child that is the paramount consideration: *Ward v Laverty* [1925] AC 101; *Re Collins* [1950] Ch 498, [1950] 1 All ER 1057. Given that this is the legal position, it will not make provisions of this kind any more effective to word them more strongly as, for example, directions as to the children's religious education, although this might give them a more persuasive effect.

2 In order to adapt the form to take account of civil partnerships formed pursuant to CPA 2004, replace the references to wife and husband with civil partner. Following the commencement of GRA 2004 on 4 April 2005 it is important to name the sister referred to. See Vol 1 at para **[81.1]** above.

[203.63]

Form B3.31: Appointment of a guardian with an alternative appointment if the first choice predeceases the testator or disclaims

I appoint [my mother [*name*] of [*address*]] to be the guardian of my minor children in the event of my death but if [she] shall die before me or disclaim the appointment then I appoint [*name*] of [*address*] to be such guardian.

[203.64]

Form B3.32: Appointment by the mother of illegitimate children, appointing the father as guardian with alternative appointment in the event of him predeceasing her

I appoint [*name*] of [*address*] to be the guardian of my minor children in the event of my death but if he shall die before me then I appoint [*name*] of [*address*] to be such guardian.[1]

1 This is for a case where the father has not acquired parental responsibility, which he can only do under a court order, or a parental responsibility agreement with the mother made in the prescribed form and registered with the Family Division of the High Court, by becoming registered as the father, or by marrying the mother: see Vol 1, para **[28.2]** and the notes at paras **[203.54]** and **[203.55]**. The conditions introducing the alternative appointment could also include the possibility of the father disclaiming (see the last preceding

form), but the testator might not wish to contemplate, or wish to encourage the father to think, that he might disclaim. The alternative person chosen would very likely be appointed guardian by the court if the father did disclaim.

[203.65]

Form B3.33: Appointment of wife to be the guardian of children by a former marriage with general revocation of previous appointments

I appoint my wife [*name*] to be the guardian in the event of my death of such of my children [*names*] being children of my late wife [*name*] as may be minors at my death[1] and I revoke all previous appointments of guardians of my said children which I may have made.[2]

1 In the absence of agreement or order (see **[203.50]**), a step-parent would not become responsible for the children on the parent's death unless appointed a guardian, unless he or she had become a parent of them by legal adoption. In order to adapt the form to take account of civil partnerships formed pursuant to CPA 2004, replace the references to wife and husband with civil partner.

2 A general revocation clause is not really necessary: see the note at para **[203.59]**. Note that an appointment of this sort is revoked if the testator and his spouse are divorced (or the marriage is annulled), unless a contrary intention appears by the appointment: ChA 1989, s 6(3A) (Part G, para **[244.117]**) inserted by Law Reform (Succession) Act 1995, s 4 in relation to deaths on or after 1 January 1996 (see also Vol 1, para **[28.6]**).

[203.66]

Form B3.34: Appointment of a guardian by a guardian

I appoint [*name*] of [*address*] to take my place in the event of my death as the guardian of such of [*names*] as may be minors at my death, of whom I am the guardian appointed by the will of their [mother [*name*]] (who died on [*date*]).[1]

1 The details of the guardian's own appointment are not strictly necessary for the appointment to be valid. However, if any question arises after his death as to whether he had power to appoint a guardian, the provision of these details will make it easier for his own appointment to be checked. For the power conferred by the ChA 1989, s 5(4) (Part G, para **[244.116]**) for a guardian to appoint his own successor, see Vol 1, para **[28.2]** and the note at para **[203.58]**.

B4 Specific gifts

Note on the incidence of inheritance tax .... **[204.1]**
PERSONAL CHATTELS
Preliminary Note .... **[204.2]**
FORMS
B4.1 Gift of personal chattels by incorporation of Statutory Will Forms 1925, Form 2 .... **[204.15]**
B4.2 Gift of personal chattels by incorporation of definition in the Administration of Estates Act 1925 .... **[204.16]**
B4.3 Gift of personal chattels to wife .... **[204.17]**
B4.4 Gift of personal chattels to wife—alternative form .... **[204.18]**
B4.5 Gift of personal chattels—short form .... **[204.19]**
B4.6 Gift to wife of such articles as she may select .... **[204.20]**
B4.7 Gift to wife of such articles as she may select up to a stated amount and of the residue to testator's daughters .... **[204.21]**
B4.8 Gift of articles of personal adornment to daughters as trustees shall determine .... **[204.22]**
B4.9 Gift of articles with request to distribute them in accordance with testator's wishes .... **[204.23]**
B4.10 Gift of chattels selected by trustees on life interest trusts .... **[204.24]**
B4.11 Gift to trustees of chattels upon a short-term discretionary trust.... **[204.25]**
B4.12 Gift of chattels in specific dwellinghouse .... **[204.26]**
B4.13 Gift of chattel with residuary estate paying costs of preservation, transport, packing and insurance .... **[204.27]**
B4.14 Gift of item which might be conditionally exempt from inheritance tax .... **[204.28]**
B4.15 Gift to a public collection or the nation of a work of art .... **[204.29]**
B4.16 Gift of a library .... **[204.30]**
B4.17 Gift of sporting implements .... **[204.31]**
B4.18 Gift of wearing apparel to servants .... **[204.32]**
B4.19 Gift of letters and papers .... **[204.33]**
B4.20 Gift by reference to a document already in existence .... **[204.34]**
CONSUMABLE STORES
Note .... **[204.35]**
FORM
B4.21 Gift of consumable stores .... **[204.36]**
FURNITURE
Note .... **[204.37]**
FORMS
B4.22 Gift of furniture to wife .... **[204.40]**
B4.23 Gift of furniture in a certain house .... **[204.41]**
B4.24 Gift of furniture to such of testator's children as survive him .... **[204.42]**
B4.25 Gift to a daughter of furniture and effects in her bedroom .... **[204.43]**
B4.26 Gifts of furniture and effects to daughters contingently on their attaining eighteen or twenty-one or marrying .... **[204.44]**
B4.27 Gift of furniture and effects to wife for life or during widowhood; no inventory .... **[204.45]**
B4.28 Gift of furniture and effects to civil partner for life or until marriage or formation of civil partnership; no inventory .... **[204.46]**
B4.29 Gift of furniture to wife during widowhood; repairs and insurance to be provided for by her, and an inventory made .... **[204.47]**

B4.30 Gift of furniture to civil partner until marriage or formation of civil partnership; repairs and insurance to be provided for by him, and an inventory made .... **[204.48]**
B4.31 Gift of furniture to wife or civil partner during life and thereafter for children: directions for inventory, and for repairs and insurance out of income during life .... **[204.49]**
B4.32 Gift of furniture to widow for life and then to son, incorporation of Statutory Will Form as to inventory .... **[204.50]**

STOCKS AND SHARES

Note .... **[204.51]**

FORMS

B4.33 Gift of stock as a general legacy .... **[204.55]**
B4.34 Specific gift of stock .... **[204.56]**
B4.35 Gift of shares held by testator at death and of shares to which he will be entitled at death .... **[204.57]**
B4.36 Gift of shares in public company .... **[204.58]**
B4.37 Gift of shares in public or private company—provision for only a lesser number of shares being available .... **[204.59]**
B4.38 Gift of shares with provision for amalgamation, reconstruction, reorganisation or demerger .... **[204.60]**
B4.39 Specific legacy of shares with added words negativing apportionment .... **[204.61]**

DEBTS

FORMS

B4.40 Gift of a debt .... **[204.62]**
B4.41 Gift of principal of a debt but not of arrears of interest .... **[204.63]**
B4.42 Release to a debtor of debts present or future .... **[204.64]**
B4.43 Release of children's debts with optional provision for hotchpot .... **[204.65]**
B4.44 Gift of debt to a legatee of a share of residue with provision for hotchpot .... **[204.66]**
B4.45 Gift of mortgage debt to the mortgagor .... **[204.67]**
B4.46 Declaration that sums advanced were by way of gifts .... **[204.68]**

UNDIVIDED SHARES AND CLAUSE DEALING WITH JOINT PROPERTY

FORMS

B4.47 Gift of undivided share in equity of real property .... **[204.69]**
B4.48 Gift of undivided share in personal property .... **[204.70]**
B4.49 Clause dealing with property held in joint tenancy .... **[204.71]**

INTELLECTUAL PROPERTY

FORMS

B4.50 Absolute gift of copyrights and unpublished works to literary executor .... **[204.72]**
B4.51 Same—proceeds to be transferred to general executors .... **[204.73]**
B4.52 Gift of patents .... **[204.74]**

MISCELLANEOUS GIFTS

FORMS

B4.53 Gift of entailed personalty .... **[204.75]**
B4.54 Gift of a reversionary interest .... **[204.76]**
B4.55 Gift of money secured by an insurance policy on testator's life .... **[204.77]**
B4.56 Clause exonerating specific gifts from charges .... **[204.78]**
B4.57 Gift of live and dead stock .... **[204.79]**
B4.58 Gift of farming stock .... **[204.80]**
B4.59 Gift of ready money .... **[204.81]**

B4.60 Gift of proceeds of premium savings bonds and prizes received or awarded since the testator's death .... [204.82]

NOTE ON THE INCIDENCE OF INHERITANCE TAX

[204.1]
The incidence of inheritance tax payable on death on chattels and things in action is the same as in the case of estate duty: if they are situated in the United Kingdom the inheritance tax on them will be borne by residue as a testamentary expense, and if situated elsewhere they bear their own inheritance tax (see para **[214.55]** ff), subject, of course, to any direction to the contrary. However, a possible consequence of the Scottish case of *Re Dougal* [1981] STC 514 is that personal or movable property outside the United Kingdom does *not* bear its own tax (as to which see para **[214.58]**). It is also possible for a valuable chattel to be accidentally located outside the United Kingdom at the testator's death. It is therefore preferable to make express provision for the inheritance tax on property which will or might be outside the United Kingdom at the testator's death (see further paras **[214.63]** and **[214.71]**).

For circumstances in which it may be preferable to make chattels in the UK bear their own inheritance tax, see para **[204.28]**, n 1. Property located abroad will bear any foreign death duties payable in respect of it in the absence of a direction to the contrary: see Vol 1, para **[30.34]**.

Personal chattels

[204.2]
General considerations. Where a testator is giving all or nearly all his estate to his spouse, civil partner or to his children absolutely, it will usually be unnecessary for his will to contain a separate disposition of his personal chattels, which will form part of his residuary estate. A separate gift is obviously needed where the testator wants to give his chattels to different persons from those who take residue, or to the same persons but for different interests from those they are given in residue. Where the testator's spouse or civil partner, or any other person, is given a life or other limited interest in residue, it is better to make a separate absolute gift of the testator's personal chattels, because chattels, with the possible exception of things such as paintings and antique furniture, are most unsuitable for holding on trust. The expense, difficulty, and potential for dispute, when they are administered as part of a trust fund, is out of all proportion to their value. Trusts are sometimes created of, eg, furniture, or more valuable chattels: for examples see Form B4.10 at para **[204.24]** and Forms B4.26 to B4.30 at paras **[204.44]**–**[204.48]**. See also the Note on gifts of furniture at paras **[204.37]**–**[204.39]** concerning life interest trusts of chattels.

[204.3]
Choice of words. A mere gift of 'personal chattels' without more may involve a difficult question of what passes under those words, but the older practice

of setting out a long list of such chattels can now be avoided either by incorporating the definition of such chattels in the Administration of Estates Act 1925 (AEA 1925), s 55(1)(x) (Part G, para **[246.67]**) or Form 2 of the Statutory Will Forms 1925 (reproduced at para **[238.8]**). The two forms are in practically the same terms save for the reference to 'wearing apparel' in the statutory will form. The will may, of course, come into the hands of persons who have no ready access to these definitions and it may be thought to be more convenient to set out one of the forms at length, though where wills have to be prepared hurriedly incorporation by reference may be unavoidable. There is some advantage in using forms rather than a specially prepared list of articles because they include many words which have already been judicially considered and which are likely from time to time to be construed by the court. Any such general gift must be made subject to specific dispositions of such or similar articles. These precedents may be adapted where the gift is to some person other than the testator's spouse or civil partner, but in that case more attention should be paid to the inheritance tax position (see para **[204.1]**). For gifts of individual chattels the draftsman must try to find a description which sufficiently identifies the item in question, making sure, where the testator has more than one item of the same kind, that there is no ambiguity as to which is meant. As to particular descriptions of property, see Vol 1, para **[64.1]** ff.

[204.4]

Expenses of transport and preservation, and money charged on chattels specifically given. After the executor has assented to a specific gift of chattels, the cost of packing, transportation etc of them is normally borne by the legatee, including where they have to be transported from abroad: see Vol 1, para **[30.34]**. The cost of storing and preserving chattels specifically given is also probably something which should be borne by the legatee as from the testator's death (in the absence of contrary provision in the will), unless the legatee takes under a right of selection in which case such costs are borne by the estate until the selection takes place: see Vol 1, para **[30.34]**. For an example of a gift including the costs of transport see Form B4.13 at para **[204.27]**. A gift of a chattel, like a testamentary gift of any other property, is subject to any mortgage or charge on it which is outstanding at the testator's death, in the absence of an expression of a contrary intention: AEA 1925, s 35 (Part G, para **[246.62]**). However, a gift of a car (and this apparently applies to any other chattel) which has not been paid for or delivered is not a gift subject to a charge for the purchase price: *Re Coxen* [1948] Ch 747 [1948] 2 All ER 492.

[204.5]

Collections. Where a testator owns a valuable collection, for example, of stamps or coins, it is probably wise to make it the subject of a specific gift and not leave it to be decided following death whether it passes by a gift of personal chattels or not: see *Re Crispin's Will Trusts, Arkwright v Thurley* [1975] Ch 245, [1974] 3 All ER 772, CA and *Re Reynolds' Will Trusts, Dove v Reynolds* [1965] 3 All ER 686, [1966] 1 WLR 19, in which a valuable clock and watch collection and a valuable stamp collection respectively were held to pass under gifts of personal chattels.

[204.6]
Right of selection of chattels. A testator who is not living alone will normally want to leave all or most of his chattels to the person or persons he is living with. If he does not want to make a list of specific bequests of chattels, whether because he is uncertain as to who would like which of his chattels or for whatever reason, the testator can grant a right of selection. This can be in the form of a simple right of selection with a provision that those chattels not selected should fall into residue, as in Form B4.6 at para **[204.20]** or one with a gift over to other beneficiaries after selection is complete, as in Form B4.7 at para **[204.21]**. To avoid complications over rights of selection testators should provide, so far as they are able, that a selection exercised in a particular manner or before the expiration of a particular period is to be treated as irrevocable and executors should abide by such directions. For the sake of certainty testators and executors should make it quite clear that once a selection has been made and the executors notified that selection is irrevocable both as to the items selected and as to those over which no right has been exercised.

[204.7]
Discretionary distribution of chattels. The chattels of a testator who is living alone will be dispersed after his death. If he is concerned that these should be distributed among his friends or relations, and would prefer not just to leave his chattels to fall into residue to be sold, thrown away, or distributed among the residuary beneficiaries by the executors, then there are two main possibilities. One is to give the chattels to a particular legatee, with a precatory request that the legatee distribute the chattels in accordance with any written expression of wishes left by the testator, as in Form B4.9 at para **[204.23]**, the other is to give the chattels to the executors (or separate trustees) subject to a discretionary trust to distribute the chattels, with or without precatory expressions of wishes as to distribution (whether in the will or elsewhere), as in Form B4.11 at para **[204.25]** (for the inheritance tax implications see the notes on inheritance tax on discretionary distributions at paras **[204.9]** and **[204.10]**). A discretionary trust has the disadvantage that the discretion is limited to benefiting the beneficiaries specified in the will, but it is possible to define the objects widely, and to confer power to add to the class of objects (for an example of a very wide power see *Re Beatty's Will Trusts, Hinves v Brooke* [1990] 3 All ER 844, [1990] 1 WLR 1503).

[204.8]
In our opinion, where there is no relative or friend of the testator to whom it would be appropriate to bequeath the chattels beneficially in the hope that he or she will carry out a distribution in accordance with the testator's wishes, there should be a discretionary trust. It is not appropriate for professional executors who have no connection with the testator, except that of professional adviser, to take the chattels beneficially subject to precatory wishes as to distribution, at any rate where the chattels are of any significant value. There will be a serious question as to whether they, being persons appointed to act in a wholly fiduciary capacity, really are intended to take the chattels beneficially, and if in truth they are not intended to do so, then Inheritance Tax Act 1984 (IHTA 1984), s 143 (see below) will not apply. If

they really are intended to take the chattels beneficially, and they have also prepared the will, and the chattels are of significant value, they may be in breach of professional etiquette, or the gift may be overturned if the testator did not have independent advice on it (see Part A, para **[200.5]**).

[204.9]

Inheritance tax—discretionary distribution of chattels. Where a testator bequeaths property by his will, and leaves a memorandum or otherwise expresses a wish (not necessarily in writing) that any of the property should be transferred by the legatee to other persons, and the legatee transfers it in accordance with the testator's wishes within two years of the testator's death, there will be no inheritance tax charge on the transfers, and they are treated as having being made under the terms of the testator's will: see IHTA 1984, s 143 (and s 17). For HMRC's treatment see *Inheritance Tax Manual* IHTM35171–IHTM35173, and see IHTM35121.The main purpose of s 143 is to provide for gifts of chattels, but it can apply to any gift by will of personal property; the use of the word 'bequeath' in s 143 implies that it would not apply to a gift of freehold land. It should be noted that a disadvantage of s 143 applying to any property given to the testator's spouse or civil partner is that the spouse exemption from inheritance tax on the testator's death (see Part A, para **[200.84]** ff) is lost in relation to that property. Where the property is sufficiently valuable for there to be a significant amount of inheritance tax at stake, s 143 can be avoided by waiting for two years from the testator's death before making the transfer. It should, however, be borne in mind that this will mean that the distribution is a lifetime transfer by the spouse or civil partner, chargeable to inheritance tax if the spouse dies within seven years of the distribution.

[204.10]

Section 143 of the IHTA 1984 only applies where the legatee is given the property absolutely: *Harding (executors of Loveday) v IRC* [1997] STC (SCD) 321. Where property is given to trustees on trust to make a discretionary distribution, a similar result to the effect of s 143 can be achieved by ensuring that there is no interest in possession pending the distribution of the chattels, so that the IHTA 1984, s 144 will apply so as to treat the distributions as if they were gifts in the testator's will: for s 144 see the *note* in C3 at para **[225.83]** ff and for a discretionary trust of chattels of this type see Form B4.11 at para **[204.25]**. For HMRC's treatment of IHTA 1984, s 144 see *Inheritance Tax Manual* IHTM35181–IHTM35184. ITA, s 144 is amended by FA 2006 with effect from 22 March 2006. For the effect of the amendment see paras **[225.83]** ff below.

[204.11]

Inheritance tax—chattels of artistic or historic interest given to individuals. Some personal chattels may qualify for conditional exemption from inheritance tax if they are works of art or otherwise of sufficient public interest to qualify to form part of the national heritage. In the case of chattels (unlike land) it is not possible to obtain from the Capital Taxes Office in advance an opinion as to whether any articles will qualify for conditional exemption. The relief is allowed on a conditional basis in return for undertakings from the legatee relating to the preservation of the property and for securing reasonable public access to it. Upon the sale of the property or upon any breach of an undertaking, the conditional exemption is withdrawn and a charge to tax arises. A claim for conditional exemption must be made to the Capital Taxes Office following the testator's death with full particulars being provided and, ideally, an opinion from an appropriate expert, together with the address at which the property can be inspected and details of any previous exemptions. The Capital Taxes Office refers the papers to an appropriate specialist, who inspects the items, gives his opinion, and the Capital Taxes Office informs the taxpayer if conditional exemption is to be granted and submits the appropriate undertakings for signature. The undertaking for reasonable public access may be that the object is lent to a public collection for display on a long-term basis, or perhaps, that details of the object and its location be listed on a register which is open for public inspection giving details of how the objects may be inspected. See cl 10 of Form C13.2 at para **[235.18]** for a gift of heirlooms, and *Foster's Inheritance Tax*, G5, for a more detailed treatment of the topic of conditional exemption for heritage property and for HMRC's treatment, see *Inheritance Tax Manual,* Annex: *Guidance Notes on Public Access*.

[204.12]
Where a will is being prepared containing a general direction to pay inheritance tax out of residue, and the testator has chattels which may qualify for conditional exemption, care should be taken to make sure that the tax payable in the event of a sale of the chattels after conditional exemption has been obtained is not within the scope of that general direction, since that could hold up the administration of the estate indefinitely and would anyway not be appropriate.

[204.13]
It is strongly recommended that any specific gift of a chattel (or any other property) which might qualify for conditional exemption should be made to bear its own inheritance tax: see para **[204.28]**, n 1 and para **[214.55]** ff.

[204.14]
Inheritance tax—chattels of artistic or historic interest given to museums etc.
If any property is given by will to a museum or other institution which is a charity or a public body listed in the IHTA 1984, Sch 3 the gift is exempt from inheritance tax (see Part A, paras **[200.87]** and **[200.88]**), and so a gift of a chattel of historic or artistic interest to such an institution will be exempt. However, where the testator has chattels of historic or artistic etc interest which would be likely to qualify for conditional exemption, and they are of significant value, another option, which confers more benefit on the non-exempt beneficiaries of the estate, is for such chattels to fall into residue with a view to their being accepted by the Revenue in satisfaction of inheritance tax on the other parts of the estate under the IHTA 1984, s 230. The disadvantage of doing this is that the testator has no control over where the chattels will end up, and if the Revenue decide that they are not of sufficient interest for acceptance under s 230 they will probably not end up in a public collection at all. Where s 230 is to be relied on and residue will be

settled on trusts, it is probably not necessary to provide express powers for the trustees to transfer assets in satisfaction of inheritance tax, as they are conferred by the IHTA 1984, s 231.

[204.15]

Form B4.1: Gift of personal chattels by incorporation of Statutory Will Forms 1925, Form 2

I give to my wife [*name*] absolutely all my personal chattels and for the purposes of this gift Form 2 of the Statutory Will Forms 1925 is incorporated in this my will.[1]

1 The terms of this form are set out in Part E at para **[238.8]**. In order to adapt this form for use where the testator is in a civil partnership, 'civil partner' may be substituted for 'wife'.

[204.16]

Form B4.2: Gift of personal chattels by incorporation of definition in the Administration of Estates Act 1925

I give to my wife[1] [*name*] absolutely all my personal chattels as defined in section 55(l)(x) of the Administration of Estates Act 1925,[2] but this gift shall take effect subject to any specific gift herein contained or made by any codicil hereto.

1 In order to adapt this form for use where the testator is in a civil partnership, 'civil partner' may be substituted for 'wife'.

2 See Part G, para **[246.67]**. Where the will is being prepared in an emergency, the reference to the section can be omitted and a mere reference to the Act is sufficient. Included in this definition are a motor yacht used for pleasure purposes: *Re Chaplin* [1950] Ch 507, [1950] 2 All ER 155; racehorses: *Re Hutchinson Holt v Huchinson* [1955] Ch 255, [1955] 1 All ER 689; a stamp and coin collection and a motor car: *Re Collin's Settlement Trusts, Donne v Hewetson* [1971] 1 All ER 283, [1971] 1 WLR 37; and a collection of clocks: *Re Crispin's Will Trusts, Arkwright v Thurley* [1975] Ch 245, [1974] 3 All ER 772, CA.

[204.17]

Form B4.3: Gift of personal chattels to wife[1]

I give to my wife [*name*] absolutely all my horses, stable furniture and effects, motor cars and accessories, garden effects, domestic animals, plate,[2] plated articles, linen, china, glass, books,[3] pictures,[4] prints, furniture,[5] jewellery,[6] articles of household or personal use or ornament (including wearing apparel),[7] also musical and scientific instruments and apparatus, wines, liquors and consumable stores, but there is not included herein any chattels used at my death for business purposes, nor money[8] or securities for money,[9] and this gift shall take effect subject to any specific disposition.

1 This clause is in the terms of the Statutory Will Form, No 2, which follows the definition in the AEA 1925, s 55(l)(x) (Part G, para **[246.67]**), except for the addition of the words 'including wearing apparel.' In order to adapt this form for use where the testator is in a civil partnership 'civil partner' may be substituted for 'wife'.

2 See Vol 1, para **[64.47]**.

3 See Vol 1, para **[64.6]**.

4 See Vol 1, para **[64.46]**.

5 See Vol 1, para **[64.27]**.

6 See Vol 1, para **[64.31]**.

7 See Vol 1, para **[64.45]**.
8 See Vol 1, paras **[64.35]**–**[64.40]**.
9 See Vol 1, para **[64.53]**.

[204.18]

Form B4.4: Gift of personal chattels to wife—alternative form[1]

I give all my household furniture plate plated articles linen wearing apparel china books stamp collections manuscripts pictures drawings prints photographs engravings etchings lithographs printed music musical instruments (including equipment for the reproduction of sound with all rolls tapes records or discs for the same) wireless and television sets works of art clocks watches jewellery articles of virtue clothing cycles motor cars motorcycles and garage furniture and other articles of household domestic garden or personal use or ornament to my wife [*name*] absolutely but this gift shall not include any article or thing used for business purposes or forming part of the stock in trade of any business in which I am interested nor shall it include any article fixed to the premises wherein it is situated even though the same would not be a fixture in law[2] and shall take effect subject to any specific disposition contained herein or in any codicil hereto.

1 For what has been held to fall within the various descriptions included in this gift, see Vol 1, para **[64.1]** ff. In order to adapt this form for use where the testator is in a civil partnership 'civil partner' may be substituted for 'wife'.
2 This seems a necessary addition in these days of built-in furniture and accessories: see *Gray v Fidler* [1943] KB 694, [1943] 2 All ER 289; *Property Holding Co Ltd v Mischeff* [1946] KB 645, [1946] 2 All ER 294.

[204.19]

Form B4.5: Gift of personal chattels—short form

I give to my wife[1] [*name*] absolutely all articles of personal domestic household or garden use or ornament not hereby or by any codicil hereto specifically disposed of.

1 In order to adapt this form for use where the testator is in a civil partnership 'civil partner' may be substituted for 'wife'.

[204.20]

Form B4.6: Gift to wife of such articles as she may select[1]

I give to my wife[2] [*name*] absolutely such of my furniture plate household linen and articles of personal domestic household or garden[3] use[2] as she may[4] select[3] within six months after my decease and any such articles not selected by her within the said time shall fall into and form part of my residuary estate provided always that this gift is subject to any specific disposition contained herein or in any codicil hereto

[Provided further that during the said period of six months from my decease my trustees shall pay or apply any income arising from the articles referred to above during such period to or for the benefit of all or any one or more of my wife and my issue as my trustees may in their absolute discretion think fit and no person shall be entitled to the enjoyment in specie of any such articles] *or*

[Provided further that during the said period of six months from my decease my wife shall be entitled to the enjoyment in specie of all articles to which this clause applies (whether or not for the time being selected by her) and she shall be entitled to be paid any income arising therefrom during such period].[5]

1 Since no limit except as to time is placed upon the right of selection, the wife is entitled to select the whole of such articles not specifically given: *Arthur v Mackinnon* (1879) 11 Ch D 385; *Re Sharland, Kemp v Rozey (No 2)* (1896) 74 LT 664; *Re Baron Wavertree of Delamere, Rutherford v Hall-Walker* [1933] Ch 837, [1933] All ER Rep 837. Should the wife die within the six months her right of selection ceases and cannot be exercised by her personal representatives: *Re Madge, Pridie v Bellamy* (1928) 44 TLR 372; *Skelton v Younghouse* [1942] AC 571, [1942] 1 All ER 650. See Vol 1, para **[8.7]**.

2 In order to adapt this form for use where the testator is in a civil partnership 'civil partner' may be substituted for 'wife'. Care should also be taken with the use of 'she' if inappropriate.

3 The list of articles may be expanded if desired as in Forms B4.1 to B4.4 at paras **[204.15]–[204.18]**.

4 For the need to ensure finality where rights of selection are exercised see para **[204.6]**. The executors should ensure that such a right is exercised with certainty by, for example, providing the widow with a comprehensive list of available items and requiring a written exercise of the right.

5 The two possible provisos have different inheritance tax consequences. The first proviso creates a discretionary trust of income during the selection period of six months so that the IHTA 1984, s 144 should apply on the expiry of the period of six months, with the consequence that the resulting distribution will be treated as having taken effect on the testator's death, see paras **[204.10]** and **[225.83]** ff. The second alternative proviso will give the surviving spouse an interest in possession for inheritance tax purposes from the testator's death until she makes a selection or the time runs out for doing so. This will mean that the spouse exemption will apply to all the chattels whether she selects them or not, but she will be deemed to make a transfer of value in respect of those which she does not select. This may not be too disadvantageous if the residue is given absolutely, or on interest in possession or accumulation and maintenance trusts, and the spouse survives the transfer by seven years, see Part A, paras **[200.70]** and **[200.71]**. Also the values involved may not be very great.

[204.21]

Form B4.7: Gift to wife of such articles as she may select up to a stated amount and of the residue to testator's daughters

I give to my[1] wife [*name*] such of my furniture plate and household[2] linen[1] as she may within six months after my decease[3] select[2] to the value of £——[4] the value of the selected articles to be determined by my personal representatives and the whole of such property if my wife should not make any selection or the residue thereof not selected by her as the case may[5] be[4] I give and bequeath to my daughters in equal shares [and in case any dispute shall arise with regard to the allotment of any of the above articles among my said daughters I direct that my personal representatives shall sell the same and divide the net proceeds after payment of the costs of such sale among my said daughters equally].[6]

1 In order to adapt this form for use where the testator is in a civil partnership 'civil partner' may be substituted for 'wife'. Care should also be taken with the use of 'she' and 'her' if inappropriate.

2 See para **[204.20]**, n 2, above.

3 For the need to ensure finality where rights of selection are exercised see para **[204.6]**, above. The executors should ensure that such a right is exercised with certainty by, for example, providing the widow with a comprehensive list of available items and requiring a written exercise of the right.

4 See Vol 1, para **[8.7]**. In *Re Baron Wavertree of Delamere, Rutherford v Hall-Walker* above, a right of selection 'of such effects as may be in either of my houses H or S' gave power to take all in both houses. If no provision had been made in case of disagreement, presumably the daughters would have had to draw lots as to who should have the first right of selection: see *Re Knapton, Knapton v Hindle* [1941] Ch 428, [1941] 2 All ER 573, though it may be that this being a gift to tenants in common, the division in default of agreement must be by sale and division of the net proceeds; see *Vanneck v Benham* [1917] 1 Ch 60. Daughters entitled to half or more of the furniture can apply to the court under the LPA 1925, s 188, for an order for division and the court can make such order and give such consequential directions as it thinks fit.

5 If the mother should predecease the testator so that she could not make a selection and only the residue after the mother's selection was given to the daughters, the gift to the daughters would fail: *Boyce v Boyce* (1849) 16 Sim 476.

6 See para **[204.20]**, n 2 and add one of the provisos at the end of Form B4.6 at para **[204.20]** if appropriate.

[204.22]

Form B4.8: Gift of articles of personal adornment to daughters as trustees shall determine[1]

I give all my jewellery lace furs and all other articles of personal adornment to such of my daughters [*naming them*][2] as shall survive me to be divided among them as they shall agree and in default of agreement the same to be divided equally among my said daughters by my trustees as near as may be according to the value of the several articles the value thereof to be determined by my trustees and the division by my trustees shall be final and binding upon all my said daughters.

1 This form of gift is sometimes desired but it places an invidious duty upon trustees and the testatrix should if possible make specific gifts of the various articles, at least so far as they are of any substantial value.

2 Following the commencement of GRA 2004 on 4 April 2005 it is important to name the daughters referred to. See Vol 1 at para **[81.1]**.

[204.23]

Form B4.9: Gift of articles with request to distribute them in accordance with testator's wishes[1]

I give to [*name*] absolutely my furniture plate and articles of household domestic or personal use or ornament and without imposing any trust or binding obligation upon [him]/[her] or conferring any interest upon any other person I request [him]/[her] to distribute the same in accordance with any existing or future memorandum of my wishes left by me and that in default of any such memorandum [he]/[she] will divide the said articles between [himself]/[herself] and [*names or descriptions*] as [he]/[she] thinks fit.

1 As any memorandum referred to may come into existence after the will is made it will not be incorporated in the will or included in probate (see Vol 1, para **[15.1]** ff). This is in its legal effect an absolute gift and there is nothing to prevent the recipient from keeping the articles given, but if the recipient is someone the testator can trust to carry out his wishes this type of disposition enables him to retain a latitude as to the disposition of personal effects without the necessity for making a new will or codicil whenever he changes his mind. It should be emphasised to the testator that the persons whom he wishes to benefit are

entirely at the mercy of the person to whom the assets are given. Since the transfer will be gratuitous, it may well constitute a disposal for capital gains tax purposes. But the articles will have been revalued on the death and if they are promptly distributed, no chargeable gain should in practice accrue on the disposal. In any event small gifts exemption under the Taxation of Chargeable Gains Act 1992 (TCGA 1992), s 262 may be available. A gain will not be chargeable if it arises from a disposal of any one chattel or set of chattels where the consideration or deemed consideration (ie. the market value where it is gratuitous) for the disposal is £6,000 or less. For inheritance tax purposes the distribution made by the legatee will be treated as made by the testator if the distribution is made within two years of the testator's death: see the IHTA 1984, s 143. Section 143 apparently applies to any personal property given to a legatee where that legatee transfers it to another person or persons in accordance with wishes left by the testators. Other possibilities are a discretionary trust of chattels (see paras **[204.7]** and **[204.8]**, above and Form B4.11 at para **[204.25]**) and a disposition in accordance with a pre-existing memorandum (see Form B4.20 at para **[204.34]**).

[204.24]

Form B4.10: Gift of chattels selected by trustees on life interest trusts[1]

I give to my trustees such of my jewels jewellery plate plated articles furniture pictures books prints china and glass as in the uncontrolled opinion of my trustees are suitable to be held upon the trusts set out below, and the following trusts powers and provisions shall apply:

(1) My trustees shall hold the said articles and the assets from time to time representing the same on trust for the use and enjoyment of my daughter [*name*][2] during her lifetime or upon trust to pay the income thereof to my said daughter during her lifetime (according to the nature of the property) and subject thereto on trust for the children of my son [*name*][2] living at the death of my daughter in equal shares absolutely.

(2) So soon as conveniently may be after my death my trustees shall cause an inventory to be made of the said articles and such inventory shall be retained by my trustees and a copy thereof signed by my trustees shall be delivered to my daughter who shall on the delivery to her of the said articles sign and deliver to my trustees a receipt therefor.

(3) The said articles shall at all times during the lifetime of my daughter be kept insured to the full insurable value thereof against loss or damage by fire (so far as the same are capable of being insured) and properly preserved at the expense of my daughter.

(4) After such receipt shall have been signed as aforesaid my trustees shall not be bound to see to the insurance or preservation of the said articles or any of them during the lifetime of my daughter and shall not be responsible for any omission or neglect on the part of my daughter with respect to the insurance or preservation thereof nor for any loss or damage occasioned by any other act or omission but nevertheless my trustees shall not be precluded from interfering for the protection of the said articles or any of them when and as they shall think fit.

(5) The said articles or any of them may from time to time be exchanged for any other articles of a like nature or the form thereof altered at the expense of my daughter but so that the intrinsic value thereof shall not be diminished.

(6) My trustees may at their absolute discretion sell any of the articles held by them under this clause and shall in relation to the proceeds of sale have the same powers of investment and changing investments at their absolute discretion as a sole beneficial owner and shall also shall have power at their absolute discretion to apply the money arising from the sale of any articles held by my trustees under this clause or any investments made as aforesaid in the purchase of chattels to be held on the foregoing trusts.

(7) My trustees shall hold any investments made as aforesaid and the assets from time to time representing the same on trust to pay the income thereof to my daughter during her lifetime and subject thereto upon trust for the said children of my son [*name*][2] living at the death of my daughter in equal shares absolutely.

(8) My trustees may exercise the powers of appropriation conferred upon personal representatives by statute without the necessity of obtaining any consents.

1 For deaths on or after 22 March 2006, this life interest should be an immediate post-death interest if it takes effect immediately on the testator's death (or is subject only to a survivorship condition permitted by IHTA 1984, s 92: see paras **[219.6]**–**[219.7]**), and is not, for example, postponed to another interest (see the note to para **[216.1]**). The gift over to the son's children is not an immediate post-death interest but takes effect absolutely on the daughter's death.

2 Following the commencement of GRA 2004 on 4 April 2005 it is important to name the daughter and son referred to. See Vol 1, para **[81.1]**.

[204.25]

Form B4.11: Gift to trustees of chattels upon a short-term discretionary trust[1]

(1) I give to my trustees my personal chattels as defined in section 55(1)(x) of the Administration of Estates Act 1925 to hold the same upon the following trusts and subject to the following powers.

(2) My trustees shall during the period of two years less one day from my death ('the relevant period') have power to distribute the said articles among the beneficiaries as hereinafter defined or any one or more of them in such manner as my trustees shall think fit.

(3) I request my trustees in exercising the said power to give effect to any memorandum of wishes left by me but no such memorandum shall have any testamentary character or create any trust right or obligation whatsoever.

(4) [Subject to subclause (5) below][2] the beneficiaries for the purposes of this clause are [my wife[3] my children and remoter issue my parents my uncles and aunts my friends [*names*] and the children and remoter issue and spouses[3] of all the foregoing] [and the public bodies specified in Schedule 3 to the Inheritance Tax Act 1984 as amended][4] and shall include all persons satisfying the foregoing descriptions at the date hereof or at any time hereafter not later than the date of my death.

[(5) My trustees shall have power [with the written consent of [*name*]] by written instrument to add any body of persons having wholly charitable purposes or any person other than one of my trustees to the beneficiaries for the purposes of this clause].[5]

(6) During the relevant period my trustees shall pay or apply any income arising from any of the said articles for the time being undistributed to or for the benefit of all or any one or more of the beneficiaries as my trustees may in their absolute discretion think fit and no person shall be entitled to enjoy in kind any of the said articles which are for the time being undistributed.

[(7) My trustees shall in relation to all or any of the said articles have power to delegate in writing their said power of distribution of the same to any one or more of the beneficiaries.][6]

(8) My trustees shall during the relevant period have power at their absolute discretion to sell any of the said [7]articles[6] and to dispose of any of the said articles which are of little value to whomsoever or in whatever manner (including for no consideration) as they think fit.[8]

[(9) My trustees shall have power to insure the said articles against any risk and to any value and pay the premiums out of my residuary estate and to pay for the storage of the said articles out of my residuary estate.]

(10) Subject as aforesaid the said articles or their proceeds of sale shall form part of my residuary estate.

1 This involves a discretionary distribution of chattels in relation to which there is or may be a memorandum of wishes of no legally binding effect. The persons who are to make the distribution are in a fiduciary position and will not benefit personally if the discretionary distribution does not occur. The IHTA 1984, s 144 (see para **[204.10]**) will apply so that for inheritance tax the distribution (providing it is made more than three months after the testator's death) or the taking effect of the remainder trusts will be treated as occurring on the testator's death. Capital gains tax is unlikely to be a problem. The ultimate donees may be deemed to take as 'legatees' within the TCGA 1992, ss 62 and 64 if the distribution takes place during the course of administration, with the consequence that they will be deemed to acquire the chattels at the value at which the executors are treated as having acquired them, ie their market value at the date of the testator's death. If the administration is complete and the distribution constitutes a deemed disposal by the trustees under the TCGA 1992, s 71(1), the chattel exemption under s 262 of that Act (annually £6,000) will apply in most cases. The trustees would also be entitled to relief from tax on gains up to a fixed limit (£4,600 in the year 2007–08): TCGA 1992, s 3 and Sch 1, para 2. For a discussion of the effect of FA 2006 on short-term discretionary trusts, see paras **[225.83]** ff.

2 To be omitted if sub-cl (5) is not included.

3 In order to adapt this form for use where the testator is in a civil partnership 'civil partner' may be substituted for 'wife' and 'spouses' might be amended to 'spouses or civil partners'.

4 The IHTA 1984, Sch 3 is a convenient list of public bodies, including museums, universities, conservation and heritage bodies, which might be appropriate to include where the testator has chattels of historic or artistic etc interest which he wishes to go to public collections. For the alternative possibility of taking advantage of the IHTA 1984, s 230 (transfer of property of artistic etc interest in satisfaction of inheritance tax): see para **[204.14]**, above.

5 This is thought to be valid despite the wide discretion involved: see para **[225.92]**, n 2. Its purpose is to enable items to be distributed to persons who turn out to be deserving but not beneficiaries within the definition in the preceding subclause. However, for some testators it may be felt to give the trustees too wide a discretion.

6 This is a power which could be useful where there are professional executors and there may be a friend or relative of the testator who could, for example, distribute the testator's house contents, saving the considerable cost of the executors doing it and also having more idea of what would be an appropriate distribution.

7 There will often be items which for one reason or another should be sold immediately, eg because no beneficiary wants them and they are difficult to store or insure. This provision as it stands enables the trustees to sell everything without offering them to the beneficiaries first, but it is difficult to devise a restriction to make sure that the articles are first offered to the beneficiaries without imposing excessive restrictions on the trustees.

8 There will often be items which no beneficiary wants and which have no sale value. Further, since 1 March 1993, it has been illegal, other than for a private individual, to sell upholstered furniture which does not meet the Furniture and Furnishings (Fire) (Safety) Regulations 1988, SI 1988/1324. Therefore a professional trustee may be unable to sell such furniture.

[204.26]

Form B4.12: Gift of chattels in specific dwellinghouse

I give to [*name*] absolutely the whole of the chattels (including motor cars animals and consumable stores) in or about or used in connection with my dwellinghouse at —— or the garage outbuildings gardens or curtilage thereof with the exception of (a) money securities for money deeds contracts or other legal instruments[1] and (b) any chattels hereby or by any codicil hereto specifically given to any other person.

1 Such items would not normally pass under a gift of contents of a residence: see Vol 1, para **[63.1]**.

[204.27]

Form B4.13: Gift of chattel with residuary estate paying costs of preservation, transport, packing and insurance

I give to my son [*name*][1] absolutely [my grand piano] and I direct that all costs of storage preservation and insurance of it while it remains in the control of my trustees and of transport packing and insurance in transit of it when it is transferred into the possession of my son shall be paid out of and borne by my residuary estate.[2]

1 Following the commencement of GRA 2004 on 4 April 2005 it is important to name the son referred to: see Vol 1 at **[81.1]**.

2 Without these express provisions the legatee would bear the cost of transport etc: see Vol 1, para **[30.34]**. It is also important to ensure that an item as large as a grand piano or a billiard table is capable of being removed from the property. If not, difficulty may result.

[204.28]

Form B4.14: Gift of item which might be conditionally exempt from inheritance tax

I give to my niece [*name*][1] [my picture by Rowlandson known as 'Landscape with Foxhounds Chasing an Attorney'] and I declare that the inheritance tax payable on my death which is attributable thereto (if any) shall be borne by my niece in exoneration of my residuary estate.[2]

1 Following the commencement of GRA 2004 on 4 April 2005 it is important to name the niece referred to: see Vol 1 at para **[81.1]**.

2 See paras **[204.11]–[204.13]**, above generally for conditional exemption. A gift of property for which conditional exemption is claimed will, without express direction, be subject to any inheritance tax charge which arises from a subsequent sale or breach of undertaking. It would be better to make such a gift expressly subject to any inheritance tax which would arise on the testator's death if conditional exemption was not claimed, because otherwise the legatee might prefer that the exemption is not claimed (to which end he could refuse to give the appropriate undertakings) so that he takes the property free of a potential tax liability, at the expense of residue.

[204.29]

Form B4.15: Gift to a public collection or the nation of a work of art[1]

I give my [collection of antique snuff boxes] to the [British Museum].

1 A gift of an article pre-eminent for its national, scientific, historic or artistic interest to an institution named in or approved by the Treasury for the purposes of the IHTA 1984, Sch 3 will be exempt from inheritance tax under s 25 of that Act. If a testator wishes such an article to pass into a public collection, but not any particular one, it will be advantageous if it passes into non-exempt residue and offered in satisfaction of tax under s 230 of the IHTA 1984; if accepted it would find its way into an appropriate collection. See further para **[204.14]**.

[204.30]

Form B4.16: Gift of a library

I give to [*name*] my bookcases and library books except such books as my wife may select for her own use within the period of six months from my decease [to a value not exceeding £——] which I give to her absolutely [and I direct that in case of disagreement such value shall be ascertained in such manner as my personal representatives shall determine] [and I direct that the value to be taken shall be the value agreed with the Capital Taxes Office for probate purposes].[1] [Provided that during the said period of six months from my decease no beneficiary under this will or any codicil hereto shall be entitled to the enjoyment in specie of any such articles and all income (if any) thereof shall be paid or applied at the absolute discretion of my trustees to or for the benefit of all or any one or more of [*names or descriptions of beneficiaries*]].[2]

1 The phrase 'taken at probate valuation' has been held to mean taken at the valuation put upon the gift in the Inland Revenue affidavit leading to probate: *Re Eumorfopoulos, Ralli v Eumorfopoulos* [1944] Ch 133, [1943] 2 All ER 719. But the phrase 'at the valuation agreed for probate' has been held to mean 'at the valuation ultimately agreed with the Estate Duty Office': *Re De Lisle's Will Trusts, White v De Lisle* [1968] 1 All ER 492, [1968] 1 WLR 322. It is better for the will to make the position absolutely clear as in this precedent. The first alternative appearing in this precedent is recommended on the grounds that a valuation inserted in an Inland Revenue account may be unrealistically low and may be rather arbitrary and the valuation ultimately agreed with the Capital Taxes Office may be on the low side.

2 See para **[204.20]**, n 2.

[204.31]

Form B4.17: Gift of sporting implements

I give to [*name*] absolutely all my fishing tackle guns and sporting implements.

[204.32]

Form B4.18: Gift of wearing apparel to servants[1]

I give my wearing apparel to my indoor female servants in my service at my death to be distributed amongst them in such manner and in such shares as my trustees think fit.

1 As to gifts to servants see Vol 1, para **[30.23]** and see legacies to employees at paras **[210.58]–[210.63]**.

[204.33]

Form B4.19: Gift of letters and papers[1]

I give to my wife [*name*][2] absolutely all my letters copies of letters papers personal manuscripts memoranda diaries and writings but not legal documents [paper money] securities for money or books of account.[3]

1 A gift of letters, papers and manuscripts does not include the copyright in any of them unless it is expressly given: *Re Dickens* [1935] Ch 267.

2 In order to adapt this form for use where the testator is in a civil partnership 'civil partner' may be substituted for 'wife'.

3 It is the duty of the executors to examine all letters and papers belonging to their testator. As to the meaning of 'books' see Vol 1, para **[64.6]**. If a testator possesses any documents which his executors are not to examine, he should bequeath them to the person whom he desires to have them, and appoint such a person a special executor as to them. This may sometimes be the case where the testator releases a debt, though he desires until his death to keep all the relevant documents. See para **[203.12]**, n 3 as to the limitation of the number of executors who can prove. The appointment of a special executor should be avoided wherever possible. See also Form B3.24 at para **[203.43]**.

[204.34]

Form B4.20: Gift by reference to a document already in existence

I give my watches jewellery trinkets and other articles of personal use and ornament unto [*name*] upon trust to distribute the same to the persons if living and in the manner set out in a list dated —— which I have already prepared and signed and which will be found with this my will at my death and in so far as the said articles are not subject to any directions contained in the said list I give the same to the said [*name*] absolutely.[1]

1 For the incorporation of documents see Vol 1, para **[15.1]** ff. It is important to remember that future documents cannot be incorporated: *Re Jones, Jones v Jones* [1942] Ch 328, [1942] 1 All ER 642. The list will be admitted to probate as part of the will. This creates a binding obligation but the testator cannot change his mind without changing his will. Other forms offer greater flexibility but no binding obligation, as in Form B4.9 at para **[204.23]**, or create a discretionary trust as in Form B4.11 at para **[204.25]**.

Consumable stores

[204.35]

Note. In general a gift of successive interests in such things will fail and in a will where chattels, such as furniture or valuable ornamental articles, are given for successive interests, it may be advisable to make a separate absolute gift of consumable stores. The matter is dealt with in Vol 1 at para **[8.3]**.

[204.36]

Form B4.21: Gift of consumable stores

I bequeath to my wife [name][1] absolutely all my wines liquors and consumable stores [add if such is the intention other articles such as a motor car, a particular picture or other article which it is desired that the wife should take absolutely].

1 In order to adapt this form for use where the testator is in a civil partnership 'civil partner' may be substituted for 'wife'.

Furniture

[204.37]

Note. Where the gift of furniture is absolute there is not a great deal that requires consideration, and it is usual and preferable for gifts of furniture to be made absolutely. Under a gift of furniture generally only ordinary household and movable furniture will pass, and if there are books, fixtures, china, pictures or similar articles of any value, it will be of some importance to say whether these are included in or excluded from the gift (see Vol 1, para **[64.27]**). Where the donee or donees are to have a power of selection, the gifts will follow the forms already given for gifts of personal chattels (see paras **[204.20]** and **[204.21]**), care being taken to provide for any necessary valuation and for cases of disagreement. Where the gift is of furniture in a house regard must be had to the possibility of removal and to the fact that the furniture may at the time of death be in storage though, perhaps, the latter can be effectively dealt with only by a codicil executed when the facts are known. Gifts of specific articles of furniture are necessarily liable to ademption by the testator parting with that article in his lifetime or the article ceasing to exist by wearing out or some form of destruction.

[204.38]

Furniture settled on trust. Where the gift is not absolute but gives successive interests in the furniture, there is the question whether there shall be an inventory of the furniture. Where the gift is to the wife for life or widowhood and the furniture on the cesser of that interest is to fall into residue, an inventory is often dispensed with and, in ordinary cases, this is the more reasonable course as the wife has treated the furniture as her own during the husband's life and it would be irksome to place restrictions upon her in the continued use of the furniture. In other cases it is probably desirable to provide for an inventory as in the following forms. In these cases of successive gifts, care should be taken not to include in the gift consumable goods, for these would vest in the first taker absolutely (see Vol 1, para **[8.4]**). It is also a good idea to provide an express power of sale and investment of the proceeds, in case some or all of the furniture becomes surplus to the life tenant's requirements. Prior to the commencement of the Trustee Act 2000 (TrA 2000) on 1 February 2001, where powers of sale and investment were not provided for expressly there was sometimes doubt as to whether any power of sale existed at all, and even if there was an implied or statutory power of sale the powers of investment were limited to those in Trustee Investments Act 1961. Trustees may now make any kind of investment that they could make if they were absolutely entitled to the assets of the trust ('the general power of investment'): TrA 2000, s 3 (see the Preliminary Note on Investment Powers in B20 at para **[220.11]** ff). It is, however, sensible to provide an express power of sale. Insurance of the furniture should also normally be provided for and this is probably better left to the trustees until such time as the furniture vests absolutely in later donees. Apart from any direction by the testator, the trustees have a statutory power to insure: TA 1925, s 19 (as substituted by the TrA 2000, s 34(1): Part G, para **[246.166]**). However, it is advisable to provide for such insurance by a specific direction for there will be no income from the subject-matter of these gifts. A duty to repair is sometimes placed upon the limited owner, but with the greatly increased cost of such repairs this may now often become an impossible burden, having regard to the resources of the limited owner.

[204.39]

The subject-matter of the gift. In all cases it must be ascertained that the business of the testator in no way concerns the sale or use of furniture for where that is the case the furniture held or used for business purposes must usually be excepted from the gift though it may be assumed that a gift of 'household' furniture does not include furniture used for business purposes unless the latter is expressly mentioned: *Re Seton-Smith, Burnand v Waite* [1902] 1 Ch 717. There may thus be an automatic exception where the gift is of 'household furniture' or 'furniture for domestic use,' but even in the case of such gifts words of exception may be necessary and are certainly advisable where the testator is concerned with such occupations as boarding-house proprietor, private hotel proprietor or the letting of furnished accommodation. Again, it must be ascertained that the furniture is the testator's absolute property and not subject to a hire-purchase agreement. If a house and the furniture in it are given to different persons, it may well be the case that certain items now classed as furniture will be fixtures and pass with the house and not under a gift of furniture. Further it is possible that many such articles may be easily removable (eg by taking out a few screws), but such removal might reduce considerably the value of the house and it may be preferable for such articles of furniture to be excepted from the clause giving the furniture and made to pass with the house.

See the text on Personal Chattels at paras **[204.2]–[204.14]** for other aspects.

[204.40]

Form B4.22: Gift of furniture to wife

I give to my wife [*name*][1] absolutely all my furniture except such as shall be used for business purposes and such as is fixed to the premises [whether or not the same is in law a fixture].[2]

1 In order to adapt this form for use where the testator is in a civil partnership 'civil partner' may be substituted for 'wife'.

2 See para **[204.18]**, n 2.

[204.41]

Form B4.23: Gift of furniture in a certain house

I give to [*name*] absolutely all articles of household or domestic furniture which shall be in or about my house —— [or such other house as I may reside in] at my death.[1]

1 For a discussion as to what passes under such a gift, see *Re Baroness Zouche, Dugdale v Baroness Zouche* [1919] 2 Ch 178; see also Vol 1, para **[64.27]**. If instead of the words 'at my death,' the words 'now' or 'at present' are used, the will may still speak from death: *Re Ashburnham, Gaby v Ashburnham* (1912) 107 LT 601; see also Vol 1, paras **[59.1]–[59.3]**. Where the testator has two houses, furniture, etc, may be moved from one house to another. For a consideration of these circumstances, see *Re Earl of Stamford, Hall v Lambert* (1906) 22 TLR 632; see also Vol 1, para **[63.1]**.

[204.42]

Form B4.24: Gift of furniture to such of testator's children as survive him

I give all my household furniture and effects to such of my children as shall survive me if more than one to be divided among them as nearly as may be in equal shares in such manner as my trustees in their absolute discretion think fit.[1]

1 It may be that the absolute discretion of the trustees would not in every case prevent children entitled to half or more of the furniture applying to the court under the LPA 1925, s 188, but they would have to make out a strong case against the trustees before any relief could be obtained.

[204.43]

Form B4.25: Gift to a daughter of furniture and effects in her bedroom

I give to my daughter [*name*][1] all household furniture pictures and other effects whatsoever ordinarily used by her in her bedroom in my house known as —— [or such other house as I may reside in at my death].

1 Following the commencement of GRA 2004 on 4 April 2005 it is important to name the daughter referred to: see Vol 1 at **[81.1]**.

[204.44]

Form B4.26: Gifts of furniture and effects to daughters contingently on their attaining eighteen or twenty-one or marrying[1]

I give all my household furniture [but excluding such furniture as is fixed to the premises whether or not the same is in law a fixture] to such one or more of my daughters [name] and [name][2] as shall survive me and attain the age of [eighteen] [twenty-one] years or marry under that age if more than one to be divided between them in equal shares or as nearly thereto as my trustees in their absolute discretion think[3] fit[2] and I declare that my trustees may at their sole discretion permit any of my daughters to have the use and enjoyment of any of such furniture to which she is for the time being presumptively entitled under the foregoing trust or may deposit the same for safe custody in such place or places as they think fit and also may make such provisions for the insurance repair and preservation thereof [out of the income or capital of my residuary estate] as they think fit but without being liable for any omission or neglect so to do or for any loss or damage that may happen to any of the said furniture in any manner[4] whatsoever[3] and all insurance moneys received shall be held on the same trusts and subject to the same powers as proceeds of sale of the said furniture.

I declare that my trustees may with the consent of my daughters who have attained the age of [eighteen] [twenty-one] years or married under that age but otherwise at their discretion sell any part or parts of the said furniture and my trustees shall in relation to the proceeds of sale have all the powers of investment, changing investments, and purchase of further chattels of a sole beneficial owner and shall hold the net proceeds of sale and the assets from time to time representing the same upon the trusts applicable to the furniture given by this clause (which shall be deemed to carry the intermediate income).

[I direct that an inventory of the furniture subject to this gift shall be made by my trustees and copies thereof delivered to all my daughters benefiting thereby who are of full age or married under age. Where any daughter is permitted to have the use and enjoyment of any such furniture she shall sign a list of the articles she is permitted so to use and enjoy and deliver the same to my trustees and, if she so desires, she shall be entitled to a copy of such list signed by my trustees. On any change of the right to use and enjoy a new list or lists shall be signed and delivered as aforesaid. My trustees may exclude from any such list any articles of such trifling value or wearing out nature as they may consider should be so excluded. After delivery of such articles my trustees shall not be liable for any unauthorised dealing with such articles but shall keep up the policy of insurance (if any) which they have effected in respect of such articles.]

1 For deaths on and after 22 March 2006, however, it is no longer possible to create trusts which have the inheritance tax benefits of IHTA 1984, s 71 (see para **[200.119]** above). In respect of deaths after that date, the trusts which a testator might declare for his young children which will fall outside the inheritance tax relevant property charging regime are trusts for bereaved minors, age 18-to-25 trusts, or trusts under which the children take immediate post-death interests (see para **[200.126]** above for these different kinds of trusts). Thus, if the selected specified age in the first clause is 18, the trust should be a trust for bereaved minors (see para **[200.108]** above), and if the specified age is 21 (or any other age between 18 and 25), the trust should be an age 18-to-25 trust (see para **[200.109]** above).

2 Following the commencement of GRA 2004 on 4 April 2005 it is important to consider whether the daughters ought to be named: see Vol 1 at **[81.1]**.

3 See para **[204.42]** n 1, above. It should be remembered, however, that actual use and enjoyment of any articles of furniture by a beneficiary presumptively entitled to it will probably give rise to an interest in possession. While the creation of an interest in possession will have no inheritance tax consequences in the present case, the termination of such interest before the beneficiary attains an absolute interest may have adverse consequences, at any rate in theory.

4 As to the application of the insurance money, see the TA 1925, s 20 (as amended by the TrA 2000, s 34(2): Part G, para **[246.18]**); as to the statutory power of insurance, see s 19 of the same Act (substituted by the TrA 2000, s 34(1): Part G, para **[246.17]**).

[204.45]

Form B4.27: Gift of furniture and effects to wife for life or during widowhood; no inventory[1]

I give all my household furniture to my wife[2] during her life [so long as she shall not marry or form a civil partnership][2] she keeping the same in good repair and insured so far as practicable against fire to the full value thereof at her own cost in the names of my trustees and after her decease [or remarriage or formation of a civil partnership whichever shall first happen[2]] I direct that the same shall fall into and form part of my residuary estate and I declare that my wife[2] shall not be bound to sign an inventory of such furniture and that it shall not be obligatory on my trustees to make an[3] inventory[2] or to see to the repair or insurance of the said furniture and that they shall not be personally liable by reason of the neglect or omission of my wife[2] to repair or insure such furniture or by reason of any loss resulting therefrom but that nevertheless my trustees may take such steps as they think fit for the protection and preservation of the said [4] furniture[3] [but all moneys received in respect of any insurance of the said furniture shall be applied in the replacement and reinstatement thereof].

1 In this form it will be noticed that the furniture is not (as it is in the next form) given in the first place to the trustees. It is permissible to give chattels in this way to a tenant for life with a remainder to another person or as here to residue, though the first taker appears in strictness not to be a tenant for life but a trustee for himself and the remainderman. See *Re Swan, Withan v Swan* [1915] 1 Ch 829; see also Vol 1, para **[8.1]**. This form is generally only suitable for use in simple wills. Articles which are consumed in their use cannot be given in this way. It would be unwise to include a direction to keep up the value of the property given, for if the value increased during the lifetime of the widow, her estate would be entitled to the increase in value: *Re Powell, Dodd v Williams* [1921] 1 Ch 178. It should be noted that no power of sale is conferred, and it is not clear whether one is implied by statute or the general law. This form creates an immediate post-death interest within IHTA 1984, s 49A, so the spouse exemption from inheritance tax should be available (see para **[200.128]** above). One point to note, however, is that the termination of an immediate post-death interest on or after 22 March 2006 will be deemed to be a gift of the underlying settled property for the purposes of FA 1986, s 102, so that unless the beneficiary of the immediate post-death interest is excluded altogether from benefit after the termination, the gift with reservation rules could apply: see FA 1986, s 102ZA and the note to para **[200.76]** above. Where the immediate post-death interest terminates on death that problem will not arise but if the interest terminates on remarriage and the spouse has an interest in residue, there could be a difficulty.

2 The following form is to be used for civil partners. In this form it should also be noted that a widowhood interest can be brought to an end by remarriage or the formation of a civil partnership (and vice versa).

3 Apart from a special direction of this nature, a tenant for life is bound to sign an inventory: *Foley v Burnell* (1783) 1 Bro CC 274; *Conduitt v Soane* (1844) 1 Coll 285.

4 As to insurance moneys, see the TA 1925, s 20 (as amended by the TrA 2000, s 34(2): Part G, para **[246.18]**).

[204.46]

Form B4.28: Gift of furniture and effects to civil partner for life or until marriage or formation of civil partnership; no inventory[1]

I give all my household furniture to my [*civil partner*][2] [*name*] [*during his life*]/[*so long as he shall not form another civil partnership or marry*] he keeping the same in good repair and insured so far as practicable against fire to the full value thereof at his own cost in the names of my trustees and after his [*decease*]/[*or marriage or formation of another civil partnership whichever shall first happen*][2] I direct that the same shall fall into and form part of my residuary estate and I declare that my civil partner[2] shall not be bound to sign an inventory of such furniture and that it shall not be obligatory on my trustees to make an inventory[3] or to see to the repair or insurance of the said furniture and that they shall not be personally liable by reason of the neglect or omission of my civil partner[2] to repair or insure such furniture or by reason of any loss resulting therefrom but that nevertheless my trustees may take such steps as they think fit for the protection and preservation of the said furniture[4] [but all moneys received in respect of any insurance of the said furniture shall be applied in the replacement and reinstatement thereof].

1 See para **[204.45]**, n 1.
2 See para **[204.45]**, n 2.
2 See para **[204.45]**, n 3.
4 See para **[204.45]**, n 4.

[204.47]

Form B4.29: Gift of furniture to wife during widowhood; repairs and insurance to be provided for by her, and an inventory made[1]

(1) I give my furniture to my trustees upon trust to permit my wife to have the use and enjoyment thereof so long as she shall not marry or form a civil partnership[2] she keeping the same in good repair and condition (reasonable wear and tear excepted)[3] and insured at her own cost but in the names of my trustees so far as is practicable against loss or damage by fire [and theft] in such an amount as my trustees may think proper and from and after the death or remarriage or formation of a civil partnership[2] of my wife the said furniture shall fall into and form part of my residuary estate.

(2) I direct that as soon as conveniently may be after my death my trustees shall cause an inventory to be made of the said furniture and that the same shall be signed by my wife and retained by my trustees and that a copy of such inventory signed by my trustees shall be delivered to my wife and that when an inventory has been duly signed and a copy thereof delivered as aforesaid my trustees shall not be bound to see to the repair or insurance of the said furniture and shall not be subject to any liability whatsoever by reason of the neglect of my wife to do such repairs or effect such[4] insurance[3] and all insurance money received shall be held on the same trusts and subject to the same powers as proceeds of sale of the said furniture.

(3) My trustees may with the consent of my wife during her life and thereafter at their absolute discretion sell any of the said furniture and my trustees shall in relation to the proceeds of sale have the same powers of investment and changing investments and purchase of further chattels as a sole beneficial owner and shall hold the net proceeds of sale and the assets from time to time representing the same upon the same trusts as the furniture given by this clause.

1 See para **[204.45]**, n 1, above.
2 The following form is to be used for civil partners. In this form it should also be noted that a widowhood interest can be brought to an end by remarriage or the formation of a civil partnership (and vice versa).
3 As to the liability to repair under this exception, see *Brown v Davies* [1958] 1 QB 117, [1957] 3 All ER 401; *Regis Property Co Ltd v Dudley* [1959] AC 370, [1958] 3 All ER 491.
4 As to insurance moneys, see the TA 1925, s 20 (as amended by the TrA 2000, s 34(2): Part G, para **[246.18]**).

[204.48]

Form B4.30: Gift of furniture to civil partner until marriage or formation of civil partnership; repairs and insurance to be provided for by him, and an inventory made[1]

(1) I give my furniture to my trustees upon trust to permit my civil partner to have the use and enjoyment thereof so long as he shall not form another civil partnership or marry[2] he keeping the same in good repair and condition (reasonable wear and tear excepted)[3] and insured at her own cost but in the names of my trustees so far as is practicable against loss or damage by fire [and theft] in such an amount as my trustees may think proper and from and

after the death or formation of a new civil partnership or marriage[2] of my civil partner the said furniture shall fall into and form part of my residuary estate.

(2) I direct that as soon as conveniently may be after my death my trustees shall cause an inventory to be made of the said furniture and that the same shall be signed by my civil partner and retained by my trustees and that a copy of such inventory signed by my trustees shall be delivered to my civil partner and that when an inventory has been duly signed and a copy thereof delivered as aforesaid my trustees shall not be bound to see to the repair or insurance of the said furniture and shall not be subject to any liability whatsoever by reason of the neglect of my civil partner to do such repairs or effect such insurance[4] and all insurance money received shall be held on the same trusts and subject to the same powers as proceeds of sale of the said furniture.

(3) My trustees may with the consent of my civil partner during his life and thereafter at their absolute discretion sell any of the said furniture and my trustees shall in relation to the proceeds of sale have the same powers of investment and changing investments and purchase of further chattels as a sole beneficial owner and shall hold the net proceeds of sale and the assets from time to time representing the same upon the same trusts as the furniture given by this clause.

1 See para **[204.45]**, n 1.
2 See para **[204.47]**, n 2.
2 See para **[204.47]**,n 3.
4 See para **[204.47]**, n 4.

[204.49]

Form B4.31: Gift of furniture to wife or civil partner during life and thereafter for children: directions for inventory, and for repairs and insurance out of income during life[1]

I bequeath all my household furniture to my trustees upon trust that they shall permit my [*wife*]/[*civil partner*] to have the use and enjoyment thereof during [*her*]/[*his*] life and after [*her*]/[*his*] decease shall divide the same equally between such of [*my children*]/[*the persons entitled to my residuary estate*][2] as survive [*her*]/[*him*] in such manner as my trustees in their uncontrolled discretion shall think proper. And I direct as follows:

(1) So soon after my death as may be convenient my trustees shall cause an inventory to be made of the said furniture and the same shall be signed by my said [*wife*]/[*civil partner*] and retained by my trustees and a copy thereof signed by my trustees shall be delivered to my [*wife*]/[*civil partner*] [and to any child of mine surviving me who shall require a copy thereof such child paying the reasonable costs of making a copy].

(2) My trustees shall during the life of my [*wife*]/[*civil partner*] out of the income payable to [*her*]/[*him*] under the trusts hereinafter declared repair the said furniture so far as may in their opinion be necessary and insure the same against any risks they think fit in their names to the full value thereof such value to be determined by them in any manner they think proper. All

moneys received in respect of any insurance of the said furniture shall be held on the same trusts and subject to the same powers as proceeds of sale of the said furniture.

(3) [*Power of sale with consent of wife as in paragraph (3) of* Form B4.29, para **[204.47]**.]

(4) My trustees may with the consent of my [*wife*]/[*civil partner*] during [*her*]/[*his*] life and thereafter at their absolute discretion sell any of the said furniture and my trustees shall in relation to the proceeds of sale have the same powers of investment and changing investments and purchase of further chattels as a sole beneficial owner and shall hold the net proceeds of sale and the assets from time to time representing the same upon the same trusts as the furniture given by this clause.

1 It is thought that this form will be the most satisfactory arrangement where the wife or civil partner is given the income of the whole residuary estate during her/his life and such income is amply sufficient for her needs. However, it is really only if the residue is to be subject to different remainder interests from those intended for the furniture that this separate provision is necessary (instead of the furniture being included in residue). It is thought that this clause also confers an interest in possession on the widow/surviving civil partner (since the exemption from inheritance tax is available in the same way as between civil partners as it is between married couples (see the Note to para **[200.84]** above)). As to the effect of FA 2006, see para **[204.25]** above.

2 For the construction of this word see Vol 1, paras **[72.1]**–**[72.18]** and **[74.1]**–**[75.9]**.

[204.50]

Form B4.32: Gift of furniture to widow for life and then to son, incorporation of Statutory Will Form as to inventory[1]

I bequeath all my furniture to my trustees upon trust that they shall permit my wife [*name*] to have the use and enjoyment thereof during her life and after her decease to hold the same for my son [*name*] absolutely and Form No. 3 of the Statutory Will Forms 1925 is hereby incorporated in this my will. My trustees may [*continue as in third paragraph of* Form B4.29 *at para* **[204.47]**, *giving the trustees a power of sale with the consent of the wife*].

1 For the terms of the statutory form, see Part E at para **[238.9]**. In order to adapt this form for use where the testator is in a civil partnership 'civil partner' may be substituted for 'wife'. Following the commencement of the GRA 2004 on 4 April 2005 it may be important to name the son referred to: see Vol 1 at para **[81.1]**.

Stocks and shares

[204.51]

Note. In the case of these gifts, the great difficulty is to decide whether they are specific or general gifts. The matter is discussed with the authorities in Vol 1 at para **[30.8]**. If it is desired that the gift shall be specific the following appear to be the most suitable expressions to use: (a) 'all my stock' or 'shares' of a stated description; (b) the use of 'my' or any possessive word; (c) the use of the words 'standing in my name.' If the gift is intended to be a general gift then apparently it may be made so by adding the words 'as a general and not as a specific gift.' But whether the gift is specific or general ultimately depends on the wording of the particular will, for, any rule there may be necessarily yields to any indications in the will construed with reference to such surrounding circumstances as may be legitimately taken into account: *Re Hawkins, Public Trustee v Shaw* [1922] 2 Ch 569. As to what passes under such words as 'investments,' 'securities,' 'shares,' stock,' etc, see Vol 1, paras **[64.30]**, **[64.53]** and **[64.54]**.

[204.52]

Inheritance tax relief. Shares in a company of which the business is something other than dealing in or holding property or investments can be the subject of business relief if owned for two years: relief is given by means of a reduction in value of 100 per cent where the testator held securities forming part of a controlling holding of unquoted shares and securities or held unquoted shares, and 50 per cent for quoted controlling holdings of shares or securities. For fuller details of this relief see *Foster's Inheritance Tax*, G1, and for more detailed discussion of the drafting of wills when the testator has shares qualifying for business relief see the notes to B5 at paras **[205.5]–[205.16]** and **[205.29]–[205.33]** and C11 at paras **[233.1]–[233.13]**. See Forms B5.9 and B5.10 at paras **[205.66]** and **[205.67]**, for gifts of shares with a business relief element.

[204.53]

Shares in a farming company of which the testator had control and in which agricultural land is vested can qualify for agricultural relief to the extent that the value of the shares is attributable to the land: see *Foster's Inheritance Tax*, G3 for a full account of the relief and paras **[234.1]–[234.10]** for will drafting points in relation to assets qualifying for agricultural relief.

[204.54]

Situs of shares and inheritance tax. By virtue of the IHTA 1984, s 211, personalty situated within the United Kingdom does not bear its own inheritance tax but personalty situated outside the United Kingdom does so (see B14 at paras **[214.55]–[214.72]**), though slight doubt remains as to the incidence of tax on foreign movable property in consequence of the decision in *Re Dougal* [1981] STC 514 (see B14 at para **[214.63]**). It should be noted that in general the situs of registered shares and securities is determined by the location of the register (see *Foster's Inheritance Tax*, J4.11), but that this rule is often displaced for the purposes of double taxation relief by Double Taxation Conventions so as to be determined by the place of incorporation (see *Foster's*, J5.32).

[204.55]

Form B4.33: Gift of stock as a general legacy

I give to [name] £—— 21/2 per cent consolidated stock as a general and not as a specific legacy.[1]

1 As to the last words, see *Re Compton, Vaughan v Smith* [1914] 2 Ch 119, where such words converted an otherwise specific legacy into a general legacy. The legatee under such a gift in the case of abatement has to bring the legacy in at the value of the stock at one year after the testator's death and without any of the income from the stock in the interval (*Re Compton, Vaughan v Smith*). See generally Vol 1, paras **[30.1]–[30.9]**. See Forms B5.9 and B5.10 at paras **[205.66]** and **[205.67]**, for gifts of stocks and shares with business or agricultural property relief.

[204.56]

Form B4.34: Specific gift of stock

I bequeath to [*name*] all my £—— 4 per cent consolidated stock now standing in my name.[1]

1 Whether a legacy is specific or general is in every case a question of construction, but the above wording combined with the fact that it is all the stock of the designated kind the testator has will generally make the legacy specific: see generally Vol 1, paras **[30.1]**–**[30.9]**.

[204.57]

Form B4.35: Gift of shares held by testator at death and of shares to which he will be entitled at death

I give to [*name*] all of the shares in [*name of company*] which I shall hold at the date of my death and all of the shares in such company which I shall not hold but to which I shall be entitled at the date of my death.

[204.58]

Form B4.36: Gift of shares in public company[1]

I give to [*name*] absolutely [20] of my shares in —— plc [and if I do not at my death hold sufficient shares in the said company to satisfy this gift I give to the said [*name*] in lieu of said gift the sum of £——]. I declare that any charge on the said shares existing at my death shall be paid out of my residuary estate.[2]

1 This will normally be a general legacy of the shares (see Vol 1, paras **[30.8]** and **[30.9]**). Any difficulty arising from the fact that the testator does not hold such shares at his death is provided for by the substitutionary money gift which here replaces the whole gift of the shares. For a form replacing a partial failure, see the next following form.

2 Charges on personalty are on the same footing as those on realty and the gift is subject to them unless a contrary intention is shown: AEA 1925, s 35 (Part G, para **[246.62]**); the declaration here included is a clear expression of a contrary intention. See para **[204.75]**, n 1 and para **[206.22]**, n 1.

[204.59]

Form B4.37: Gift of shares in public or private company—provision for only a lesser number of shares being available[1]

I give to my son [*name*] absolutely [50] of my shares in —— [plc] [Limited] and if and in so far as I do not at my death hold sufficient shares to answer the above gift in lieu of each share by which my holding in the said company falls short of the said number of shares I give to my said son a sum equivalent to the mean market value of such share on the day of my death [*if the shares are not officially quoted* equivalent to the value of such share at my death such value to be certified by the secretary of the said company or if he refuses to certify to be fixed by my trustees]. I declare that any charge which at my death may be existing upon the shares hereby given shall to the extent to which it affects the said shares be paid out of my residuary estate.

1 See para **[204.56]**, nn 1 and 2. Following the commencement of the GRA 2004 on 4 April 2005 it may be important to name the son referred to: see Vol 1 at para **[81.1]**.

[204.60]

Form B4.38: Gift of shares with provision for amalgamation, reconstruction, reorganisation or demerger

I bequeath all my [*number*] ordinary shares in —— [plc] [Limited] now standing in my name to [*name*] and declare that if at my death the said shares shall by virtue of any amalgamation reconstruction or reorganisation of the capital of the said company or sale of the said company's business or demerger of the said company (whether direct or indirect) be represented by a different capital holding or holdings whether in the said company or in any other company or in government local authority or other public stock to which I am entitled or which I possess at my death then the said gift shall take effect as if it had been a gift of the capital holding or capital holdings which as the result of such amalgamation reconstruction or rearrangement of capital or sale or demerger took the place of such shares.[1]

1 The purpose is to prevent ademption, but the gift will still be adeemed if the testator in his lifetime disposes of the substituted capital. As to ademption in such cases see Vol 1, para **[41.11]**.

[204.61]

Form B4.39: Specific legacy of shares with added words negativing apportionment

I give to [*name*] all my [ordinary shares] *or* [[——] 5 per cent preference shares] in —— [plc] [Limited] now standing in my name together with all dividends thereon received after my death (which shall not be apportioned to any period before my death).[1]

1 In the ordinary way accruing dividends must be apportioned upon the death of the testator, the specific legatee taking only such dividend as accrues subsequent to the death (Apportionment Act 1870: Part G, para **[246.2]** ff; see also B14 at paras **[214.48]**–**[214.52]**). The above addition excludes such apportionment: *Re Lysaght, Lysaght v Lysaght* [1898] 1 Ch 115. The necessity for apportionment is not restricted to preference shares, but applies generally to securities of both public and private companies: *Re White, Theobald v White* [1913] 1 Ch 231. In the case of loan securities, such as debentures, it will be necessary to change the word 'dividends' to 'interest'. Arrears of dividends on cumulative preference shares are not apportioned, see *Re Wakley, Wakley v Vachell* [1920] 2 Ch 205; followed in *Re Buck* [1964] VR 284; *Re Marjoribanks, Marjoribanks v Dansey* [1923] 2 Ch 307. As to a gift of shares with 'current' dividends: see *Re Raven, Spencer v Raven* (1914) 111 LT 938, and compare *Re Joel, Johnson v Joel* [1936] 2 All ER 962, and *Re McCutcheon's Will* [1960] VLR 289. In the case of a general legacy of shares the legatee is not entitled to any dividends until the shares are transferred to him. If this is not done before the expiration of a year from the testator's death, the legatee gets neither dividends nor interest on the value of his legacy, but after the expiration of one year, he is entitled to interest on the value of the legacy until such time as the shares are transferred to him: *Re Hall* [1951] 1 All ER 1073. See Vol 1, para **[32.4]**, n 1 for the rate of interest.

Debts

[204.62]

Form B4.40: Gift of a debt[1]

I give to [*name*] all sums of money owing to me at the date of my death from [*name of debtor*] and all interest due and unpaid at the date of my death and to become due thereafter in respect thereof and all mortgages or other securities for the same [and I appoint him executor of this my will so far as regard the said sums of money interest mortgages and securities[2]].

1 For what passes under such a gift, see Vol 1, para **[7.28]** (choses in action). It is important to make clear whether arrears of interest are included or not in a gift of a debt, because the law on whether they are (in the absence of express provision) is most unclear: see Vol 1, para **[64.39]**.

2 The legatee, being appointed executor as regards the particular debt, can sue for it in his own name, if he proves the will; as to arrears of interest, see *Re Ford* [1911] 1 Ch 455.

[204.63]

Form B4.41: Gift of principal of a debt but not of arrears of interest

I give to [*name*] all principal sums of money owing to me at the date of my death from [*name of debtor*] but not any arrears of interest thereon which shall be outstanding at the date of my death.

[204.64]

Form B4.42: Release to a debtor of debts present or future

I forgive and release unto [*name*] [free of inheritance tax] all sums whether for principal or interest which at my death may be owing by him to me on the security of any mortgages bills bonds or other security or otherwise and I direct that all such mortgages bills bonds or other securities shall as soon as may be after my death be delivered by my executors to the said [*name*] or cancelled and that for the purposes aforesaid my personal representatives shall at the cost of my estate execute and deliver to the said [*name*] all necessary receipts reconveyances or reassignments and I declare that if the said same [*name*] shall predecease me his legal personal representatives shall be entitled to the benefit of this gift as if he had died immediately after my death.[1]

1 A general forgiveness of debts should never be inserted in a will. Such a clause raises questions of difficulty about debentures owned by a testator and his balances at a bank, etc (*Re Neville, Neville v First Garden City Ltd* [1925] Ch 44, [1924] All ER Rep 377; *Midland Bank Executor and Trustee Co Ltd v Yarners Coffee Ltd* [1937] 2 All ER 54). There may also be a doubt as to whether both secured and unsecured debts are included: *Re Coghill* [1948] 1 All ER 254; *Re Leach* [1948] Ch 232, [1948] 1 All ER 383 (direction to pay son's debts). As to business debts where there are running accounts, see *Crane v Maritime Trust Co* (1954) 33 UPR 15. Since the release of a debt is a specific gift, it abates as such (*Re Wedmore* [1907] 2 Ch 277 at 283) and lapses if the debtor predeceases the testator unless, as here, there is express provision against lapse.

[204.65]

Form B4.43: Release of children's debts with optional provision for hotchpot

I release each of my children [and their spouses [or civil partners]] from any legal liability to pay any debt which may be due from him or her to me at the date of my death together with any arrears of interest thereon [but each of my children shall bring into hotchpot against the capital of his or her share of my residuary estate such total sum from which such child and/or such child's spouse [or civil partner] shall have been released as aforesaid].

[204.66]

Form B4.44: Gift of debt to a legatee of a share of residue with provision for hotchpot[1]

I forgive and release unto [*name*] all sums whether for principal or interest which at my death may be owing by him to me whether secured by mortgage bills bonds covenants or otherwise or unsecured and I direct that all such securities shall as soon as may be after my death be cancelled and delivered up by my trustees to the said [*name*] and that at the cost of my estate my trustees shall execute and deliver to the said [*name*] all necessary receipts reconveyances or reassignments Provided always that all sums of money hereby released (whether or not the same constitute legal debts) with interest thereon at the rate of —— per cent per annum from the date of my death but not in any case for any period prior to my death shall be brought into hotchpot as against the said [*name*] in the share of my residuary estate hereby given to him [*or if the named person takes a life interest in a settled share of residue:* as against the share of my residuary estate in which the said [*name*] takes a life interest hereunder].

1 Release of debts of 'pecuniary beneficiaries' includes the release of debts of beneficiaries entitled to residue. Such forgiveness could not be defeated by distribution of the estate in specie: *Re Epstein* [1963] 2 OR 276.

[204.67]

Form B4.45: Gift of mortgage debt to the mortgagor

I bequeath to [*mortgagor*] absolutely all sums both for principal and interest which shall be due or accruing due at the date of my death and secured on property situate at —— by a mortgage dated —— and made between [*parties*] [and the further charges endorsed thereon dated —— and ——] [and I direct my trustees at the cost of my residuary estate to execute in favour of the said [*mortgagors*] a full discharge of the said mortgage and of all claims thereunder and to deliver up to him all title deeds and other documents held by me in respect thereof] *or* [and subject to the said [*mortgagor*] paying or providing for the costs thereof I direct my trustees to execute in his favour a full discharge of the said mortgage and of all claims thereunder and to deliver up to him all title deeds and other documents held by me in respect thereof].[1]

1 The usual form of indorsed receipt would, it is thought, be effective for the discharge of the mortgage, the trustees stating that they had received all moneys due under the mortgage, but it is obviously more proper to execute a surrender since there will in fact be no payment. There will be no stamp duty in either case.

[204.68]

Form B4.46: Declaration that sums advanced were by way of gifts

I declare that the various sums of money that have from time to time or at any time been given by me to or on account of [*name*] were gifts and nothing is now due to me in respect thereof and no claim can be made and no such claim shall be made against the said [*name*] or his personal representatives nor shall the said [*name*] be liable to bring into account any such sum or sums.

Undivided shares and clause dealing with joint property

[204.69]

Form B4.47: Gift of undivided share in equity of real property[1]

I hereby give unto [*name*] all that my share and interest in equity of and in [parcels] *or* [all that my one equal third share and interest of and in [*parcels*]] absolutely [subject to and charged with the recoupment to my residuary estate of the proper proportion of the inheritance tax leviable on my death attributable to such share and interest and with interest on such proportion].

1 A devise in a will executed before 1926 of 'all my freehold property' or of 'all my moiety or equal half part and all other my share in' freehold property was not effective to pass an undivided share in the property owing to the conversion of the 1925 legislation of such interests into interests in the proceeds of sale: *Re Kempthorne, Charles v Kempthorne* [1930] 1 Ch 268, [1929] All ER Rep 495; and *Re Newman, Slater v Newman* [1930] 2 Ch 409, [1930] All ER Rep 617. Where, however, a codicil was executed after 1925, not dealing with the particular devise but confirming the will, it was held that the devise was not adeemed and the devise of the undivided share was effective to pass the corresponding interest in the proceeds of sale: *Re Warren, Warren v Warren* [1932] 1 Ch 42, [1931] All ER Rep 702. By virtue of the Trusts of Land and Appointment of Trustees Act 1996 (TLATA 1996) an undivided share is now an equitable interest in land whether under a trust for sale or not. It follows that: (a) a gift of an undivided share in land ought to be expressed as a gift and not a bequest; and (b) following the abolition of the doctrine of conversion, no reference should be made to an interest in the 'proceeds of sale' of land. There has thus been a partial reversion to the position as it was before 1 January 1926.

Inheritance tax on undivided shares of the proceeds of sale of land in the UK held on trust for sale is borne by residue in the absence of a direction to the contrary: See B14 at para **[214.55]** ff.

Note that this form and the next one will not operate as intended if the testator is in fact a joint tenant of the relevant property, and that making a will does not effect a severance. The testator's title should always be examined carefully when a will is being prepared containing a disposition of this kind, and a notice of severance served where appropriate. If it is not, and the beneficiary named in the will is disappointed at the expense of the surviving joint tenant, the legal adviser may be held liable in negligence to the disappointed beneficiary, see *Kecskemeti v Rubens Rabin & Co* (1992) Times, 31 December and *Carr-Glynn v Frearsons (a firm)* [1998] 4 All ER 225, [1999] Ch 326, CA.

For another form of gift of an undivided share in land see Form B8.11 at para **[208.48]**.

[204.70]

Form B4.48: Gift of undivided share in personal property[1]

I hereby bequeath unto [*name*] all my share and interest in any [*description of personal property*] owned by me as tenant in common with [*co-owner*] or with any other person.

1 An undivided share in racehorses will not pass under a gift of horses (*Re Sykes, Skelton and Dyson v Sykes* [1940] 4 All ER 10). See *Re Lewis's Will Trusts, Lewis v Williams* [1984] 3 All ER 930, [1985] 1 WLR 102. Note that for the reasons given in the note to para **[204.67]** an undivided share in land is no longer personal property and this form should not be used to dispose of such an interest.

[204.71]

Form B4.49: Clause dealing with property held in joint tenancy[1]

As to [*Whiteacre*] of which I and A are beneficial joint tenants in fee simple in possession I make the following provisions:

(a) If there is in my lifetime a severance of the said joint tenancy then I give all my interest in the said property to my nephew X.

(b) If there is no such severance and I survive the said A then I give the said property to my nephew X.

1 The provision here made is unusual, but it seems necessary as a precautionary measure in case on the severance it should be forgotten to make the necessary provision. A testator cannot sever an equitable joint tenancy by will and it would be left until the happening of

one of the events mentioned in the clause before any such provision would be made. It has, however, been rightly pointed out that circumstances may arise in which there would be no opportunity of making these later provisions by codicil and it is as well to provide contingently for such events. In the ordinary case it would be simpler to sever by notice (as provided by the LPA 1925, s 36(2), proviso) and to dispose of the severed share by will.

Intellectual property

[204.72]

Form B4.50: Absolute gift of copyrights and unpublished works to literary executor[1]

I bequeath unto my literary executor absolutely all my published and unpublished works together with all manuscripts letters notes and other writings including those in electronic form [together also with including sound recordings films and other visual recordings howsoever recorded and stored][2] and the copyrights and all other rights and privileges therein for his own absolute use and benefit and declare that all administration expenses other than those arising out of the special grant of probate and the payment of inheritance tax necessary to secure such grant shall be borne by my general estate in exoneration of the gift hereby made and further that all debts and inheritance tax (except as already provided) shall also be borne by my general estate.

1 In this form the donee of the copyrights of unpublished works is the person appointed sole literary executor. For a form appointing the literary executor, see Form B3.24 at para **[203.43]**. It is not necessary to expressly provide that the copyright in unpublished works is to pass with the gift since a gift of an unpublished manuscript will carry with it the copyright unless a contrary intention is expressed: Copyright, Designs and Patents Act 1988, s 93. See also Vol 1, para **[61.2]**.

2 Similar provisions as to copyright apply to sound recordings and films: Copyright, Designs and Patents Act 1988, s 93. See also Vol 1, para **[61.2]**.

[204.73]

Form B4.51: Same—proceeds to be transferred to general executors[1]

(1) I bequeath unto my literary executors all my published and unpublished works together with all manuscripts letters notes and other writings including those in electronic form[2] [together also with including sound recordings films and other visual recordings howsoever recorded and stored][3] (except those necessary to the administration of my general estate) and the copyright and all other rights and privileges therein with full right to publish any such unpublished works and to complete or have completed any unfinished work and to publish the same in such manner and subject to such terms and conditions as my literary executors may in their uncontrolled discretion determine.

(2) Any loss sustained in the exercise of the foregoing discretion shall be borne by the literary assets hereby given to my literary executors or in case of deficiency of such assets by my general estate to the exoneration of my literary executors who shall not be accountable for any loss so incurred.

(3) My literary executors shall be entitled to receive all payments of

every kind made in respect of my published or unpublished works and after defraying thereout all expenses incurred in the carrying out of this gift shall transfer the net proceeds to my trustees to hold upon the same trusts as are herein declared in respect of the settled legacy hereinafter called the —— Fund *or* [upon the trusts herein declared in respect of my residuary estate].

[(4) I declare that for the proper execution of any trust or duty hereby vested in my literary executors my trustees in their discretion may but shall not be bound to lend to my literary executors any sum or sums of money not exceeding in the whole the sum £—— (that being the total amount to be advanced irrespective of the fact that some sums may have already been repaid)].

1 In this case it may be advisable to appoint more than one literary executor but the total number of literary executors should not exceed four. The former restriction on the *total* number of executors to prove where separate grants are made to different parts of the same estate has now been abolished: see para **[203.8]**, n 1. See para **[203.43]**, n 1 for the appointment of literary executors. See also para **[204.70]**, n 1, above and Vol 1, para **[61.2]**.

2 Letters pertaining to the general estate and necessary to its administration must be available to the general executors. The literary executors on the other hand may need private correspondence for the preparation of a biography.

3 See para **[204.70]**, n 2, above.

[204.74]

Form B4.52: Gift of patents

(1) I bequeath all patents and interest in patents to which I am entitled to my trustees. I direct that my trustees shall have the fullest powers to sell and deal with the same including power to grant licences or rights (whether exclusive or not) of manufacturing selling using or working the subject-matter of any such patents and that any such sale or dealing may be made wholly or partly in consideration of royalties to be paid to my trustees: and I declare that my trustees may join with other persons interested in any such patent in any such sale or dealing as aforesaid.

(2) My trustees shall hold the said patents upon the same trusts as are herein declared in respect of the settled legacy hereinafter called the —— Fund [*or* upon the trusts herein declared in respect of my residuary estate] *or* [upon the following trusts and subject to the following powers and provisions:][1]

1 For a wasting asset like a patent there could be an inheritance tax advantage in a discretionary trust of income, particularly where the patent would expire before the first ten-yearly periodic charge occurred. In the latter case the income can be distributed according to maximum income tax advantage, and there need be no inheritance tax charge unless income is accumulated. For further points on the advantages and disadvantages of discretionary trusts, see para **[218.6]** ff.

Miscellaneous gifts

[204.75]

Form B4.53: Gift of entailed personalty[1]

I give all my personal property of which I am tenant in tail in possession under [*particulars of will or settlement*] to [*name*] absolutely.

1 The express reference to entails is not superseded by the TLATA 1996, although the creation of new entails on or after 1 January 1997 is prevented by the TLATA 1996, Sch 1, para 5 and any attempt to create one gives rise to an absolute interest. It is, however, still possible for a testator to be a tenant in tail under a pre-1997 disposition by which a tenant in tail in possession has power to dispose by will of entailed property referring specifically either to the property or the instrument under which it was acquired or to entailed property generally: LPA 1925, s 176 (Part G, para **[244.55]**). The gift takes effect as if the entail had been duly barred. There must be a reference either to the property or the document under which the interest arises. A reference to the property sufficiently refers to an entailed interest in an undivided share: *Acheson v Russell* [1951] Ch 67, sub nom *Re Manor Farm, Kytes Hardwick, Acheson v Russell* [1950] 2 All ER 572. It should be remembered, however, that this power of disentailing is available only if the testator is tenant in tail in possession at the date of his death.

[204.76]

Form B4.54: Gift of a reversionary interest[1]

I give unto [*name*] of [*address*] all that the one equal [fifth] part or share and all other the share (if any) to which under the trusts of the will date —— of —— deceased I am at my death or thereafter entitled in reversion expectant on the death [or remarriage or the formation of a civil partnership] of —— of and in the investments and property representing the residuary estate of the said —— deceased and all other the reversionary interest or interests under the said will to which whether at the time of my death or thereafter I may be or become entitled under the trusts of the said will.

1 Where the reversionary interest may be affected by advances or the operation of accruer clauses, it is necessary in order to avoid disputes to include words in this clause which will make it certain that the beneficiary is to take the whole benefit of the reversionary interest subject to advances received by the present testator in his lifetime. This gift is confined to reversionary interests and will not include eg interests vested in possession under the will which have not been distributed at the time of the present testator's death. A reversionary interest under a trust is 'excluded property' for inheritance tax purposes (unless purchased for a consideration at any time or vested at present or previously in the settlor or his wife) and is left out of account in charging inheritance tax on death: IHTA 1984, ss 5(1) and 48(1).

[204.77]

Form B4.55: Gift of money secured by an insurance policy on testator's life

I give to [*name*] absolutely the policy of assurance on my life for the sum of £—— effected with the —— Life Assurance Society dated —— and numbered —— and the said sum of £—— and all bonuses and other sums payable in respect thereof. [Any charge upon the said policy including any charge made in connection with any charge upon any freehold or leasehold property shall be discharged out of my residuary estate[1]].

1 See the AEA 1925, s 35 (Part G, para **[246.62]**). In the absence of such a clause as above, any property or interest in property charged with the payment of money has to bear the charge. A letter saying how the charge is to be met will be insufficient to show a contrary intention unless it shows how that charge is to be met between the specific donee and the residuary estate: *Re Wakefield* [1943] 2 All ER 29; *Re Birmingham, Savage v Stannard* [1959] Ch 523, [1958] 2 All ER 397. Particular care should be exercised in the case of specific gifts of shares, etc, and policy moneys which are in practice frequently used to secure a temporary loan, see *Re Turner* [1938] Ch 593, [1938] 2 All ER 560. Where a testator has made a gift of land contracted to be purchased and dies before completion, the unpaid purchase money becomes a charge on the property: *Re Birmingham, Savage v Stannard*; see also n 1 to Form B6.13 at para **[206.22]**.

[204.78]

Form B4.56: Clause exonerating specific gifts from charges

I direct that if at the date of my death any property comprised in any specific gift made by this my will or any codicil thereto is charged with the payment of money such charge shall be discharged primarily out of my residuary estate in exoneration of the property so charged.[1]

1 See the AEA 1925, s 35 (Part G, para **[246.62]**). In the absence of such a clause as above, any property or interest in property charged with the payment of money has to bear the charge. A letter saying how the charge is to be met will be insufficient to show a contrary intention unless it shows how that charge is to be met between the specific donee and the residuary estate: *Re Wakefield* [1943] 2 All ER 29; *Re Birmingham, Savage v Stannard* [1959] Ch 523, [1958] 2 All ER 397. Particular care should be exercised in the case of specific gifts of shares, etc, and policy moneys which are in practice frequently used to secure a temporary loan, see *Re Turner* [1938] Ch 593, [1938] 2 All ER 560. Where a testator has made a gift of land contracted to be purchased and dies before completion, the unpaid purchase money becomes a charge on the property: *Re Birmingham, Savage v Stannard*; see also n 1 to Form B6.13 at para **[206.22]**.

[204.79]

Form B4.57: Gift of live and dead stock

I give to my wife[1] all my cows pigs and poultry and all my plants garden stock gardening implements and all other my live and dead stock [in or about my house —— or the grounds and other buildings occupied therewith].

1 In order to adapt this form for use where the testator is in a civil partnership 'civil partner' may be substituted for 'wife'.

[204.80]

Form B4.58: Gift of farming stock[1]

I give to my son [*name*][2] absolutely all my stock of cattle corn hay and grain horses cows calves sheep lambs swine live stock and animals of all kinds and also my farming utensils and implements of husbandry tools haymaking harvesting and other agricultural machines whether self-propelled or not tractors lorries wagons carts trailers harness saddles and other accoutrements [and the motor car which I use in connection with my farming business] and all other my live and dead stock whatsoever which shall at my decease be used on my farm at —— [or any other farm belonging to me at the date of my death].

1 A gift of 'all my horses' will not pass an interest in horses owned as tenant in common. There is quite commonly a partnership in racehorses and sometimes in other pedigree stock. See *Re Sykes, Skelton and Dyson v Sykes* [1940] 4 All ER 10. See also *Cochrane v Moore* (1890) 25 QBD 57 at 73 and *Re Lewis's Will Trusts, Lewis v Williams* [1984] 3 All ER 930, [1985] 1 WLR 102.

In *Re Sykes* it was held that extrinsic evidence that the testator owned no horses but owned half shares of three horses was not admissible in evidence to assist in the interpretation of 'all my horses,' in contrast to the position where the testator is referring to some specific item of property but what he owned did not exactly fit the description. It is thought that the new rules for the admission of extrinsic evidence contained in the AJA 1982, s 21 (see the commentary on it in Vol 1, paras **[57.22]–[57.26]**, and the text of it in Part G at para **[244.99]**) do not alter this rule.

2 Following the commencement of the GRA 2004 on 4 April 2005 it may be important to name the son referred to: see Vol 1 at **[81.1]**.

[204.81]

Form B4.59: Gift of ready money

I give to my wife[1] absolutely all ready money[1] which at my death may be in or about my place of residence and also all money standing to my credit on current account at the —— Bank [or at my banker's *or* at any bank].

1 In order to adapt this form for use where the testator is in a civil partnership 'civil partner' may be substituted for 'wife'.

2 A gift of 'money' is a form of gift likely to cause difficulty owing to the numerous decisions construing such a gift. For a consideration of the cases, see Vol 1, paras **[64.35]–[64.40]**. As to gifts for immediate necessities, see the note to B10 at paras **[210.15]–[210.18]**.

[204.82]

Form B4.60: Gift of proceeds of premium savings bonds and prizes received or awarded since the testator's death[1]

I direct my trustees to encash all premium savings bonds which I may own at my death and to give the net proceeds thereof and any prize money in respect of them received after my death (whether awarded before or after my death) to [*name of beneficiary*].

1 Premium bonds are not transferable: see reg 3(4) of the Premium Savings Bonds Regulations 1972 (SI 1972/765). It is not therefore possible to give them away, but it is possible to direct that they be encashed and the proceeds given away.

B5 Gifts and other provisions relating to business property

B5.22 Powers to give warranties etc on the sale of a business or private company shares .... [205.79]

PRELIMINARY NOTE

[205.1]
There is (for deaths, transfers and other events after 9 March 1992) 100 per cent business relief (in effect complete exemption) for many types of business asset: Inheritance Tax Act 1984 (IHTA 1984), s 104(1). This means that the incentive to dispose of them by lifetime gift is less than it was previously (see para **[205.46]**) and that testamentary gifts of such property assume a greater importance.

[205.2]
B5 is concerned with testamentary dispositions of business assets, and powers and other ancillary provisions which may be relevant to such dispositions, and mentions some of the inheritance tax aspects which should be borne in mind. For testamentary options relating to business property see B9 at para **[209.1]** ff and for a right of a beneficiary to have particular property appropriated to his share see Form B17.22 at para **[217.30]**. For further trustees' powers relevant to business property see Forms B20.17 to B20.19 (at paras **[220.66]**–**[220.68]**) and for complete wills involving business and agricultural assets, and the attendant problems of providing appropriately for the whole of the testator's family and avoiding waste of business and agricultural relief, see C11 (business) and C12 (agricultural) at paras **[233.1]** and **[234.1]** ff and the Preliminary Notes thereto. For inheritance tax agricultural relief, see the Preliminary Note to C12 at para **[234.1]** ff.

[205.3]
The main kinds of business asset which can qualify for business relief and which may be disposed of by will are sole traders' businesses, partnership shares, company shares (typically shares in a private family company), and assets owned personally by the testator which are used in a business carried on by a partnership or company in which he is interested.

Business assets and inheritance tax—general points

[205.4]
For a complete account of inheritance tax on business assets we refer the reader to *Foster's Inheritance Tax*, in particular Divisions G1 (business relief), G3 (agricultural relief), H2 (principles of valuation), H3 (valuation of particular types of property) and L5 (payment by instalments). The notes in this work concentrate on inheritance tax aspects of business assets which are relevant to drafting wills and advising persons who are making wills. For a further account of inheritance tax on business assets see Inheritance Tax Manual IHTM25000 and subsequent paragraphs.

[205.5]
Assets qualifying for relief and the rates of relief. There is at the moment (in relation to transfers after 5 April 1996) 100 per cent relief, subject to satisfying the preconditions mentioned further below, for the following types of business property:

(a) businesses of sole traders;
(b) partnership shares;
(c) holdings of unquoted voting securities of a company controlled by the transferor;
(d) holdings of unquoted shares.

[205.6]
There is at the moment (in relation to transfers after 9 March 1992) 50 per cent relief, subject to satisfying the preconditions mentioned further below, for the following types of business property:

(a) holdings of quoted shares or securities giving control of the company;
(b) land, buildings, machinery or plant owned personally and used in the business of a company which the owner of the asset controls or a partnership in which he is a partner, provided that the testator's interest or shares in the business in which it is used also qualify for business relief: IHTA 1984, s 105(6);
(c) land, buildings, machinery or plant comprised in a settlement and used in a business carried on by someone who has an interest in possession in such land, buildings, machinery or plant. On the death of someone with an interest in possession in settled property used in a business carried on by him there will normally be 100 per cent business relief on the business itself and the settled property used in it taken together as 'a business' (*Finch v IRC* [1985] Ch 1, sub nom *Fetherstonaugh v IRC* [1984] STC 261), and this separate 50 per cent relief category is only relevant where the settled property is comprised in a transfer of value which does not also include the business itself. Accordingly, this business relief category will not often be relevant to the inheritance tax charge on a person's death.

[205.7]
See the IHTA 1984, ss 104(1) and 105(1). 100 per cent relief means that the value transferred is reduced by 100 per cent of the value of the asset qualifying for relief, and 50 per cent relief means that the value transferred is reduced by 50 per cent of that value: IHTA 1984, s 104(1). For the allocation of the reduction where parts of an estate or transfer are exempt and parts not exempt, under the IHTA 1984, s 39A see the Preliminary Note to C11 at para **[233.2]** ff.

[205.8]
Types of business qualifying for business relief. Subject to the exceptions mentioned below, any trade or profession can qualify for inheritance tax business relief, either where it (or a partnership share of it) is directly owned by the testator, or where it is carried on by an unquoted company in which he has shares or a quoted company which he controls. The exceptions to this

are for businesses of dealing in securities, stocks or shares, or land or buildings, or making or holding investments (IHTA 1984, s 105(3)), but that itself is subject to exceptions for UK discount houses, and market makers on the stock exchange or the London International Financial Futures and Options Exchange: IHTA 1984, s 105(4), (7) and SI 1992/3181. The Special Commissioners have held that ownership and management of land let to tenants is making or holding investments within the above exception and does not qualify for business relief, and this approach has been approved by the High Court in *Weston v IRC* [2000] STC 1064 (see for the now numerous cases in this area *Foster's Inheritance Tax*, G1.12). There is no territorial limit on the location of the business, and it can be anywhere in the world (whereas agricultural relief can apply only to land in the UK, Channel Islands, or Isle of Man). The assets of a farming business other than the agricultural land itself can only qualify for business relief not agricultural relief, as the latter relief is confined to land and buildings etc attached to land. See para **[205.15]** below and C12 at para **[234.8]** for what happens when both reliefs might apply to agricultural land.

[205.9]
Excepted assets. The value of individual assets is excepted from the relief if they have not been used in the business for two years and are not required for use in it at the time of the transfer or death (IHTA 1984, s 112), and land, buildings, plant or machinery personally owned and used in a business by a company which the testator controls or a partnership in which he is a partner is excepted unless it has been used in the business for two years or it and an asset it replaced have together been used in it for two out of the previous five years: IHTA 1984, s 112(3).

[205.10]
Liabilities. Section 162(4) of the IHTA 1984 provides that a liability which is an incumbrance on any property shall, so far as possible, be taken to reduce the value of that property. Liabilities incurred for the purposes of a business will be taken into account in valuing it (or the company or partnership shares which it underlies) whether or not charged on the business assets, but s 162(4) could reduce relief further where borrowing for some other purpose is charged on business property. Where there is a choice between charging a liability on business or non-business property it may thus be better to choose the latter.

[205.11]
Required period of ownership, and succession. To qualify for business relief on a testator's death, business property must have been owned by the testator throughout the two years preceding his death: IHTA 1984, s 106. If he inherited it he can count in the whole period from the death of the person from whom he inherited it, and if that person was his spouse he can count in the spouse's period of ownership as well as his own: IHTA 1984, s 108. If he was given the business property by lifetime gift or inherited it, and business relief applied to the transfer by which he acquired it, the relief will also apply on his death if the only obstacle to it applying under the main rules is that he has not owned the property for two years by that time: IHTA 1984, s 109.

[205.12]
The Inland Revenue regard these provisions as applying where the succession is by virtue of a gift by will of residue, notwithstanding that for a period after the death the business property will have been comprised in an estate in the course of administration and not strictly speaking held on trust for the person entitled to residue (*Stamp Duties Comr (Queensland) v Livingston* [1965] AC 694: see Vol 1, para **[1.12]**). This is because the IHTA 1984, s 91 applies to treat the situation as the same as it would have been if the residue had been ascertained as from the relevant death.

[205.13]
For possible provision in a will where business property has not been owned for two years by the time of making a will, see paras **[205.31]** and **[205.50]**.

[205.14]
Contracts of sale and company liquidations. If business property is under contract of sale at the time of the death of its owner or any other occasion of inheritance tax charge, business relief does not apply to that property on that death or other occasion unless the contract provides for the transfer of the business to a company in return for shares in it, or for the reconstruction or amalgamation of a company: IHTA 1984, s 113. This is a point of particular concern in relation to partnership shares which are subject to rights of acquisition vested in the other partners: see para **[205.28]**. Similarly, business relief does not apply to company shares on a death or other occasion of inheritance tax charge if at that time the company has gone into liquidation, unless it has done so as part of a reconstruction or amalgamation after which its business will continue: IHTA 1984, s 105(5).

[205.15]
Relationship with agricultural relief. Where both reliefs are capable of applying, it is agricultural relief alone which applies: IHTA 1984, s 114. There are notes on agricultural relief in the Preliminary Note to C12 at para **[234.1]** ff.

[205.16]
Testamentary options. For the inheritance tax aspects of these, see the Preliminary Note to B9 at para **[209.1]** ff.

Payment of inheritance tax by instalments

[205.17]
Under ss 227 and 228 of the IHTA 1984 there is provision for payment by instalments over ten years, at the option of the person paying it, of the inheritance tax on death on the types of asset listed below. In addition, for certain categories, which almost but not quite coincide with the types of property which may qualify for business or agricultural relief, there is a right to pay by instalments which are *interest-free* under the IHTA 1984, s 234, i e interest is only payable if an instalment is paid after it has become due (as opposed to interest being payable on an instalment from what would have been the due date for payment of the tax if there was no instalment option). Property with an interest-free instalment option for the payment of the inheritance tax on death is as follows:

(a) sole traders' businesses: IHTA 1984, ss 227(2)(c) and 234(1)(a);
(b) partnership shares: IHTA 1984, ss 227(2)(c) and 234(1)(a);
(c) land subject to agricultural relief: IHTA 1984, ss 227(2)(a) and 234(1)(a);
(d) controlling shareholdings, quoted or unquoted (IHTA 1984, ss 227(2)(b), 228(1)(a) and 234(1)(a)), provided that the company's business is not one of the kinds excluded from business relief by reason of being a land or investment dealing or holding company (IHTA 1984, s 234(3); see also para **[205.8]**), and in judging whether the deceased had control, related property and settled property in which he had an interest in possession will be taken into account (IHTA 1984, s 269(2), (3));
(e) unquoted shareholdings, which do not give control, again provided that the company's business is not one of the kinds excluded from business relief by reason of being a land or investment dealing or holding company (IHTA 1984, s 234(3); see also para **[205.8]**) in any of the following three categories:
  (i) if the tax on them, together with the tax on any other property to which the instalment payment option applies, represents at least 20 per cent of the tax on the deceased's death for which the person paying the tax on the shares is liable in the same capacity: IHTA 1984, s 228(1)(b), (2);
  (ii) if they have a taxable value on the death of more than £20,000, *and* either were in their nominal value at least ten per cent of the nominal value of the capital of the company at the time of the deceased's death, *or* are ordinary shares which in their nominal value were at least ten per cent of the nominal value of the ordinary share capital of the company at that time: IHTA 1984, s 228(1)(d), (3);
  (iii) if the Inland Revenue are satisfied that the tax on them cannot be paid in one sum without due hardship: IHTA 1984, s 228(1)(c).

Shares which would fall within the above-listed categories qualifying for interest-free instalment payment if it were not for the fact that the company's business is land or investment dealing or holding, will qualify for *interest-bearing* instalment payment. Land or buildings not falling within categories (a), (b) or (c) above also qualify for *interest-bearing* instalment payment. For HMRC's treatment of payments by instalments see IHTM30191 and subsequent paragraphs.

[205.18]

Payment by instalments and 100 per cent relief property. It will be apparent from the above that business or agricultural property of a kind which can qualify for 100 per cent relief will all qualify also for interest-free instalment payment, save for certain shareholdings (see further para **[205.34]** ff). Property subject to 100 per cent business relief is of course property on which there should be no inheritance tax at all, but the right to pay inheritance tax by instalments can be relevant to it, for the reasons given at para **[205.51]**.

[205.19]
Payment by instalments and 50 per cent relief property. The only category of business property qualifying for 50 per cent relief which coincides more or less with a category of property qualifying for interest-free instalment payments is controlling shareholdings of *quoted* shares. The categories of unquoted shares which qualify for interest-free instalment payment are quite differently defined from those which qualify for 50 per cent business relief, and some 50 per cent relief unquoted holdings will qualify for interest-free instalment payment and some will not: see further para **[205.34]** ff. Land, buildings, machinery or plant owned personally by the deceased or subject to an interest in possession of his, and qualifying for 50 per cent business relief (in the circumstances summarised at paras **[205.6]** and **[205.41]** ff) does not qualify for interest-free instalment payment, but land and buildings can qualify for *interest-bearing* instalment payment: IHTA 1984, s 227(2)(a) and IA 1978, Sch 1 (definition of 'land').

[205.20]
Subsequent sale. The unpaid instalments or an appropriate part of them become due immediately on a sale of all or a part of the property: IHTA 1984, s 227(4) and (6). This can have implications for testamentary options: see the Preliminary Note to B9 at para **[209.1]** ff.

Sole traders

[205.21]
In modern conditions limited companies tend to be preferred for any but the smallest businesses, and farms and shops are probably now the most common examples of businesses carried on by sole traders.

[205.22]
Business relief for a sole trader. A business of a sole trader qualifies for business relief at the 100 per cent rate, but it must be emphasised that to qualify for the relief the testator must at his death own a business which is *his* business—this does not mean that he is necessarily working very hard in it (he could employ a manager), but the risk of loss and the hope of profit must be his, and a bundle of assets which adds up to being a business must be his property, although property he uses in the business and is deemed to own by virtue of it being settled property in which he has an interest in possession may be treated as part of the business assets for relief purposes (*Finch v IRC* [1985] Ch 1, sub nom *Fetherstonaugh v IRC* [1984] STC 261). An individual business asset which is not part of the assets of a business owned by the testator, eg because it is used by somebody else in that other person's business, will not qualify for the relief. Where someone wishes to hand over his business to someone else while retaining a stake in it which will qualify for business relief he should consider forming a partnership or a company.

[205.23]
As has been established in a number of cases on capital gains tax retirement relief, an asset used in a business is not 'a business': see, eg *McGregor v*

Adcock [1977] STC 206, *Pepper v Daffurn* [1993] STC 466, and *Jarmin v Rawlings* [1994] STC 1005. Thus a lifetime gift by a sole trader of a single asset used in his business will not qualify for business relief. This is a less significant point in relation to inheritance tax on death, because if a person is in business as a sole trader at his death the entire business will be included in his deemed transfer of value on death. However, it is significant in relation to inheritance tax on death where the estate is partially exempt, because it affects the application of the IHTA 1984, s 39A (business or agricultural relief and partial exemption), and specific gifts by will of individual assets of the business should be avoided where there are exempt gifts: see the Preliminary Note to C11 at para **[233.6]**.

[205.24]
The value for relief purposes. The business relief is on the net value of the business, ie the value of the assets owned by the testator and used in the business (including goodwill) less the liabilities incurred for the purposes of the business: IHTA 1984, s 110. This deduction of liabilities occurs whether or not they are charged on the business assets; if there are any liabilities incurred other than for the purposes of the business which are charged on the business assets, then those liabilities will also go to reduce the amount of relief by virtue of the IHTA 1984, s 162(4), which provides that an incumbrance on any property is (so far as possible) taken to reduce the value of that property. For HMRC's treatment of valuation of a business see IHTM25081 and IHTM25082.

[205.25]
Dispositions of businesses: executors' and trustees' powers. For specific dispositions of businesses see Forms B5.1 to B5.4 at paras **[205.58]–[205.61]**.

The addition of specific powers for running the testator's business should be considered where there is any possibility that it might be necessary or convenient for the executors or trustees to carry it on. Executors or trustees do not have power to carry on the testator's business in the absence of authority, express or implied, to do so (*Kirkman v Booth* (1848) 11 Beav 273), except that they may carry on a business for a reasonable time with a view to a beneficial sale (*Garrett v Noble* (1834) 6 Sim 504). A power to postpone sale and conversion of the testator's estate may authorise the carrying on of a business not only with a view to sale but so long as the power to postpone continues (*Re Crowther, Midgley v Crowther* [1895] 2 Ch 56), but not where there is a direction to sell the business as well as a power to postpone sale (*Re Smith, Arnold v Smith* [1896] 1 Ch 171). A direction in a will to carry on the testator's business does not of itself authorise the employment therein of more of the testator's assets than were employed in it at his death (*M'Neillie v Acton* (1853) 4 De GM & G 744). In the absence of express authority to write off losses against capital, a loss in one year must ordinarily be made good out of the profits of future years and not out of capital and a provision enabling the trustees to make reserves for depreciation reinforces this view: *Rutherford v IRC* [1965] NZLR 444. For power to carry on a business and employ capital of the estate in doing so see Form B5.13 at para **[205.70]**.

Partnership interests

[205.26]
Partnership, like sole trading, is not very often used for trading or manufacturing, the private company usually being preferred. Partnership has always been the rule for many professions which perform services rather than trade, for example, solicitors, doctors, accountants, architects, and surveyors, although incorporation is becoming an option for many professions, including solicitors. However, in many cases farming is still carried on in family or other partnerships. When preparing a will for someone who is a partner in a firm it is important to look at the terms of the partnership agreement and the partnership accounts to see whether the testator's partnership share is likely to have any significant value on his death, because if it will not there is no need to make any special provision. Further, partnership agreements usually contain terms as to what happens in the event of the death of a partner, and these need to be considered both for their inheritance tax implications (see para **[205.28]**), and for what (if anything) may be disposed of by the testator's will.

[205.27]
Business relief. Business relief, if it applies, is at the rate of 100 per cent on a partnership share. The value on which it is calculated will be based on the net value of the partnership share, ie the testator's appropriate part or portion of the net value of the partnership assets (after deduction of partnership liabilities). If the testator owns personally assets which are used in the partnership business, those assets and the partnership share may be valued as if sold together and the combined value apportioned between them: *IRC v Gray* [1994] STC 360.

[205.28]
Buy and sell agreements. Provision in a partnership agreement for the death of a partner often provides for the purchase by the surviving partner or partners of the testator's interest. This can take the form of automatic accruer of his share to the other partners with an obligation on them to make a payment to his personal representatives, an obligation by the surviving partners to buy and the testator's personal representatives to sell his share, or an option for the surviving partners to buy his share. Clearly the obligation to buy and sell will prevent business relief from applying if it causes the share to be under contract of sale at death: IHTA 1984, s 113. There has been some uncertainty as to whether the Revenue regarded in the same way automatic accruer provisions, but it now seems clear the Revenue's view is that s 113 does not apply to them. An option provided in the partnership agreement for the surviving partners to acquire the share will not affect the availability of business relief. The right to payment by instalments of the inheritance tax on the partnership share will be terminated by the exercise of an option, but of course this is inevitable in any arrangement whereby the surviving partners buy the testator's share.

Private company shares

[205.29]
Any unquoted shares, and this includes shares dealt in on the Alternative Investment Market (IHTA 1984, s 105(1ZA)), can qualify for business relief, although the exclusions of land or investment dealing or holding businesses, value attributable to excepted assets, assets held for fewer than two years, etc should not be overlooked.

[205.30]
100 per cent relief shareholdings. There are two categories of holding which get 100 per cent relief, both unquoted: securities forming part of a controlling holdings of unquoted shares and securities (IHTA 1984, s 104(1)(b)) and unquoted shares: IHTA 1984, s 104(1)(bb). It is thought that 'securities' includes things like debenture stock, but it is not common for these to carry any votes.

[205.31]
Ownership requirement. Unquoted shares, in common with the other categories, have to have been owned for two years to qualify for the relief (see para **[205.11]**). Form B5.9 at para **[205.66]** is a gift of such of a particular class of share as the testator has owned for two years, which could be used in a case where he is continuing to buy more shares but wishes to make a non-exempt specific gift of only those which qualify for relief. There could, however, be difficulties of identification of the shares which have been held for two years if the testator has at his death shares of the same kind which have been owned for fewer than two years, and the shares of the class in question are not numbered by the company which issued them. It will anyway be important for him to keep careful records of his purchases if he is making a disposition of this type.

[205.32]
50 per cent relief shareholdings. The holdings of shares or securities which qualify for 50 per cent relief are quoted controlling holdings of shares or securities, subject to the qualifying conditions noted at para **[205.8]** ff as to type of business, length of ownership, etc.

[205.33]
Quoted controlling holdings, as is the case with unquoted controlling holdings, can qualify for relief where they have been owned for two years and are part of a controlling holding at the testator's death, even if he has not had control for as long as two years, and related property and settled property in which the testator has an interest in possession is taken into account.

[205.34]
Payment by instalments and shareholdings qualifying for business relief. The types of shareholdings in relation to which the option to pay the inheritance tax on death by interest-free instalments is available are listed at para **[205.17]**. Where shares qualify for business relief and instalment payment,

the instalments are interest-free: IHTA 1984, s 234. However, not all shareholdings which qualify for business relief do qualify for payment by instalments. Where the relief will be 100 per cent, there may not be any tax to pay and, if so, the availability of the instalment option will not matter, but this is not always the case: see para **[205.51]**.

[205.35]
A controlling quoted or unquoted holding of shares or securities qualifies for instalment payment: IHTA 1984, s 228(1)(a).

[205.36]
As regards unquoted non-controlling holdings there are three possible ways of qualifying for payment by instalments, one of which, the discretion of the Revenue to allow it in a case of hardship (IHTA 1984, s 228(1)(c)), cannot be relied on in advance as being something which will apply. When a will is being made, attention should be focused on whether the case will fall within one of the two categories where payment by instalments is available as of right.

[205.37]
The first question is whether the testator's shareholding is likely at the testator's death to be worth more than £20,000, and to represent in its nominal value either ten or more per cent of the nominal value of the company's share capital, or (being ordinary shares) ten or more per cent of the nominal value of the company's ordinary shares: IHTA 1984, s 228(1)(d) and (3). Ordinary shares are defined here as ones which are entitled to dividends other than ones restricted to a fixed rate (IHTA 1984, s 228(4)), and so voting powers are not relevant. It should also be noted that related property will not be taken into account in assessing the size of the testator's shareholding for this purpose, although it is possible that shares in which he has an interest in possession and ones in his free estate would be aggregated for this purpose when it comes to the inheritance tax charge on death under the general rule that the tax charge is on the value of the estate, which is defined as the aggregate of all property to which he is beneficially entitled (IHTA 1984, ss 4(1) and 5(1)) and includes property in which he has an interest in possession to which he is beneficially entitled: IHTA 1984, s 49(1).

[205.38]
However, it is also possible (from the wording of the IHTA 1984, s 227(1)), and the Inland Revenue's attitude to this point is not known, that where different people are liable for the tax on different parts of a holding, the part of the holding which each person is liable to pay the tax on has to be considered separately to see if it passes the ten per cent test, and, if that is so, interest in possession property would not be likely to be aggregated in this way (as the persons liable will not usually be the same). Thus making a number of different gifts of part of a holding, some or all of which bear their own inheritance tax, may reduce the chances of the shareholding or parts of it qualifying for instalment payment under this head (though it may increase the chances of it doing so under the other head discussed below). Even if a holding is prima facie likely to qualify for payment by instalments

under the ten per cent of nominal capital rule, it is possible that it will cease to do so by the time of the testator's death, e g by the company increasing the amount of other classes of ordinary share capital, and where a will is made on the basis that shares will fall into this category the testator needs to be warned that he may need to review his will if there is an alteration in the company's capital.

[205.39]
If there is or might be difficulty about an unquoted holding qualifying for instalment payment on the testator's death under the ten per cent of capital qualification described above, the other possibility is that it could qualify on the basis (which is only available in relation to the charge on death) that 20 per cent or more of the tax on the testator's death for which the person paying the tax is liable (in the same capacity) is the tax on the holding in question and on any other property on which payment by instalments is available: IHTA 1984, s 228(1)(b) and (2). This appears to mean that if the holding is given free of tax (expressly or by reason of the IHTA 1984, s 211 for which see para **[214.55]** ff), whether the tax on it amounts to the necessary 20 per cent will be assessed with reference to the tax being paid by the personal representatives, but that if the holding or a part of the holding is given subject to tax this will be assessed with reference to the tax being paid by the person it is given to. If this is correct, a reason for making a subject to tax gift of unquoted shares (see para **[205.52]** ff for other reasons) can be, in an appropriate case, to increase the chances of the right to pay by instalments being available. Note that the calculation is by reference to relative amounts of tax, not property values, so that the tax on shares on which there will be business relief will be a smaller proportion of the entire tax on the estate than the proportion which the actual value of the underlying property is of the entire value of the estate. If there are exempt gifts and the unquoted shares are the subject of a non-exempt gift, the greater the proportion of the estate which is exempt the greater will be the proportion of the tax payable on death which is represented by the shares.

[205.40]
What dispositions to make of shares qualifying for business relief. This topic is discussed at para **[205.46]** ff.

Land, buildings, plant and machinery

[205.41]
Land, buildings, plant and machinery which is owned by the testator but used by a partnership in which he is a partner or a company which he controls can qualify for business relief on his death, but, if it does, only 50 per cent relief will be available (unless it is farmland, in which case it might get 100 per cent agricultural relief—see the Preliminary Note to C12 at para **[234.1]** ff). For such assets to qualify for the relief under this head the testator's relevant company shares or partnership interest must themselves be property which qualifies for business relief (IHTA 1984, s 105(6)), and the land, buildings, machinery or plant must have been used in the business for the two years preceding the testator's death, or it and property it replaced

must have been used in the business for two years or more in the five years preceding the testator's death: IHTA 1984, s 112(3). In determining whether the testator has control of a company for this purpose, related property and interest in possession property are taken into account: IHTA 1984, s 269. It should be noted that if land, buildings, machinery or plant are used by a company in which the testator has shares but not control, then the land, buildings, machinery or plant will get no business relief, even though the shares themselves may get business relief at the rate of 100 per cent.

[205.42]
One tax planning move to consider making with this type of asset is therefore a lifetime transfer of it to the partnership or company which uses it for business purposes, so as to get the higher rate of relief for it on the testator's death; as just mentioned, there are particularly strong reasons for doing so where it is used by a company in relation to which the testator does not have control. However, the capital gains tax consequences, and inheritance tax consequences (if it is to be done by gift), of doing so need to be analysed carefully, particularly where it is a transfer to a company which is contemplated.

[205.43]
Instalment payment of the inheritance tax on this type of asset is available for land and buildings, but not plant and machinery unless it counts as land. If the inheritance tax on land or buildings is paid in instalments, and the land or buildings do not qualify for agricultural relief (see para **[234.1]** ff), the instalments are not interest-free, ie they all carry interest from what would be the due date for payment if there were no instalment option (see paras **[205.17]** and **[205.19]**).

[205.44]
Valuation and aggregation. It has now been held in *IRC v Gray* [1994] STC 360, by the Court of Appeal reversing the Lands Tribunal, that land owned by a deceased person and used by a partnership in which he was a partner can be valued as part of the aggregate of it and the partnership share, so that, for example, if the testator is in partnership with his spouse in a business which uses land owned by him alone there would be a vacant possession valuation of the land valued in aggregation with the partnership shares, and the total value apportioned between the testator's interest in the land, his partnership share, and his spouse's partnership share. This is another reason, in a case of this kind, to make the land a partnership asset so that it qualifies for 100 per cent relief, if it can be done without undue capital gains tax cost and the testator is prepared to allow his spouse or other partners to acquire an interest in it. It should be remembered, however, that if the land owned by the testator and used by a partnership is agricultural land it can qualify for 100 per cent agricultural relief without being a partnership asset: see the Preliminary Note to C12 at para **[234.1]** ff.

[205.45]
Options. Where the partnership or company has other partners or shareholders who are outside the testator's family, it may be desired to give the

other partners or the company the option to purchase the land etc being used in the business. For options see B9 at para **[209.1]** ff and note that the exercise of an option may terminate any right to pay the inheritance tax by instalments.

Implications of inheritance tax business relief and instalment payment for what dispositions to make

[205.46]

Whether to make lifetime gifts of business property. Where someone has property which qualifies for 100 per cent relief, ie in effect a complete exemption from inheritance tax, the obvious strategy, other things being equal, is for him to retain the property, in a state which continues to attract the relief at this rate, until his death, and, where there is a choice between exempt and non-exempt gifts, to make a specific gift of it by his will to a non-exempt beneficiary (ie his children or relatives, but not his spouse or charity). The main reasons are that although a lifetime gift of the property would also qualify for 100 per cent relief, the inheritance tax position is just as good on death, the capital gains tax position is often better if the property is retained until death (a complete rebasing instead of hold-over relief and the testator may come to need the money before he dies. When it comes to making a will, business relief is wasted if it is made the subject of a gift which would be exempt anyway. For the rules governing the allocation of business relief between exempt and non-exempt parts of an estate see the Preliminary Note to C11 at para **[233.2]** ff.

[205.47]

Considerations which weigh against retaining 100 per cent relief property until death are the possibility that the 100 per cent rate of relief might be replaced with a lesser relief (or none at all) before the testator's death (whereas a lifetime gift made by him now is more likely to retain the right to 100 per cent relief), and the possibility that the testator may want to retire and hand over ownership and running of the business to others.

[205.48]

Whether shareholdings of private company shares which attract 100 per cent relief should be kept together is considered at para **[205.56]**.

[205.49]

Where property qualifies for only 50 per cent relief there is more incentive to give it away by lifetime gift in the hope of surviving the gift by seven years so that it becomes wholly free of inheritance tax. There are also special reasons for making a lifetime disposition of land, buildings, machinery or plant used by a company or partnership in which the testator has a stake: see paras **[205.41]** and **[205.42]**. If 50 per cent relief property is to be retained, and given by will, it is worth considering whether to make the gift bear its own inheritance tax, and, where there may be exempt gifts (to the testator's spouse or charity), whether to make it a non-exempt specific gift: see para **[205.52]** ff and for business relief and exempt gifts see the Preliminary Note to C11 at para **[233.2]** ff.

[205.50]
Property not owned for long enough. Where a testator acquires business property to which business relief will apply when it has been owned long enough, but makes a will before he has owned the business property for two years (and none of the succession provisions apply), he might be advised to do either or both of two things. One is to leave the business property to a non-exempt beneficiary contingently on the testator having survived the acquisition of the business property by two years (see Form B5.9 at para **[205.66]** for a disposition of this type, but note the possible problem of identification mentioned at para **[205.31]**), and the other is to leave the business property to his spouse, if he has one, in the event of his dying within two years of acquiring the property. The point of the latter is not only to make an exempt gift, but also to take advantage of the rule (see para **[205.11]**) that one spouse who inherits the other spouse's business property also inherits the other spouse's period of ownership for business relief purposes: IHTA 1984, s 108.

[205.51]
When there may be inheritance tax on relieved property. When a will is being made by a party to a marriage who has substantial property prima facie attracting 100 per cent relief, and he or she is inclined to make a specific gift of that property to a non-exempt beneficiary, leaving most or all the remainder of the estate as an exempt gift to his or her spouse, some thought should be given to the possibility that there may in the event be inheritance tax on the non-exempt gift on his or her death. Possible circumstances in which this might occur are as follows:

(a) such property may not have been owned long enough for business or agricultural relief to apply (see para **[205.11]**), or may fail to qualify for relief by being under contract of sale or by the company being in liquidation: the property not having been owned for long enough will not exclude the right to pay by interest-free instalments except in the case of agricultural land, where it will mean that there will be an instalment option, but not interest-free;
(b) there may be 'excepted assets' (IHTA 1984, s 112; see also para **[205.9]**) in relation to the value of which there is no relief;
(c) even if the asset in question wholly qualifies for 100 per cent relief at the time of making the will, the position could change before the testator's death, particularly in the case of private company shares: the company's business might be sold and the proceeds invested, substantial profits might come to be invested in 'excepted assets', or the company's share capital may be diluted or the rights attached to it altered;
(d) the 100 per cent rate of business relief might have been replaced by a lesser rate for the type of asset in question by the time of the testator's death;
(e) in the case of property to which 100 per cent agricultural relief applies, the relief only relates to the agricultural value of it, and if it has hope value arising from a possibility of planning permission for another use that will not qualify for agricultural relief. Other possibilities are that the farmhouse may have a value in excess of agricultural value or not

be occupied for agricultural purposes for the relevant period (see para **[234.3]**), or that the land or some of it may be used for a non-agricultural purpose (see para **[234.4]**).

One possibility to consider is to make such a gift subject to tax, if any (see para **[205.52]** ff), and another is to make the gift conditional on there being substantial or total relief from inheritance tax. See Forms B5.9 and B5.10 at paras **[205.66]** and **[205.67]**. See also the Preliminary Note to C11 at para **[233.10]**.

[205.52]

Subject to tax gifts. A specific gift by will of any property situated in the UK is prima facie free of tax, so that any inheritance tax on it is paid out of residue, unless the will directs to the contrary or the property was comprised in settled property immediately before the testator's death; property situated outside the UK bears its own inheritance tax unless the will directs to the contrary: IHTA 1984, s 211 and see B14 at para **[214.55]**. Assets outside the UK can qualify for business relief, but cannot qualify for agricultural relief unless they are in the Isle of Man or Channel Islands.

[205.53]

There are often good reasons for a specific gift of business property to be made to bear its own inheritance tax. These include the following:

(1) Where substantial property prima facie entitled to 100 per cent business relief is being given by specific gift to a non-exempt beneficiary, or property prima facie entitled to 50 per cent relief is being given by such a gift having a prospective taxable value falling within the inheritance tax nil-rate band, with in either case most or all of the remainder of the estate being given to the testator's spouse, with the intention that the estate will not be charged to inheritance tax, it would be a sensible precaution to make the gift subject to tax, if any, in case there is tax on it. See para **[205.51]** for the circumstances in which there might be tax on apparently 100 per cent relief property, and in the case of 50 per cent relief property it could turn out to have a taxable value in excess of the nil-rate band or the nil-rate band might come to be wholly or partly used up in making lifetime gifts. Making such a gift subject to tax means that the taxable estate will be smaller than it would be if the specific gift were tax-free and grossed up (see B14 at para **[214.74]**). Further, if there does turn out to be substantial tax on the gift the beneficiary can disclaim or assign the property to the surviving spouse under a Deed of Variation (see F3 at para **[241.1]** ff). If the gift to him is made tax-free (or the property is in the UK and there is no direction as to incidence) the benefit and the burden will be separated and he can elect to take the gift and leave residue to pay the tax, even though the tax is more than the testator had contemplated.

(2) Where the testator is contemplating a specific gift of business assets to a non-exempt beneficiary, and there is likely to be, or might be, inheritance tax on it, but which could be paid by instalments, one possible way in which the tax might be funded is for the donee to retain the property and pay the inheritance tax himself by instalments. This is

of course most likely to be a viable option if the instalments will be interest-free instalments (see paras **[205.17]** ff and **[205.34]** for what is meant by this and the types of property where it is available). If this is likely or appropriate, the gift should be made expressly subject to its own inheritance tax. Whether to do so depends on many factors, such as the value of the property, whether any of the estate will be exempt and the intended size of the non-exempt part, and what exactly the testator is trying to achieve. See further the Preliminary Note to C11 at paras **[233.7]**–**[233.11]** for relevant factors where the estate is partially exempt.

(3) In the case of some unquoted shareholdings it seems that the chances of there being a right to pay the inheritance tax by instalments can be increased by making a gift of them subject to tax: see para **[205.39]**.

(4) Where there is a right to pay inheritance tax on a specific gift by instalments, and the tax is to be paid out of residue, the final distribution of the residuary estate could be held up for years—the instalments are ten annual ones—while the executors retain enough from the residuary estate to pay the instalments and any interest on them.

For subject to tax gifts of business property, see Forms B5.1 (at para **[205.58]**), B5.4 (at para **[205.61]**), B5.9 (at para **[205.66]**) and B5.10 (at para **[205.67]**).

[205.54]
Where a specific gift of business property is directed to bear its own inheritance tax, the tax it bears ought on equitable principles to be the inheritance tax at the estate rate attributable to the taxable value of the business after the deduction of business relief, and in the event of a dispute we would expect a court so to hold, in the absence of clear contrary directions. However, it can save argument to deal with such a point expressly, and there are examples of clauses which do so in Forms B5.9 and B5.10 (at paras **[205.66]** and **[205.67]**) and Forms C11.1, cl 2(1)(a) (at para **[233.17]**) and C11.3, cl 2 (at para **[233.40]**).

[205.55]
Nil-rate band gifts and property qualifying for business relief. See the Preliminary Note to C11 at paras **[233.8]**–**[233.10]**.

[205.56]
Dividing up or keeping together shareholdings. On death a large shareholding can be divided among a number of different legatees or kept together and given to a single legatee, and whichever is done will usually make no difference to the amount of the inheritance tax charge on the testator's death (except so far as an exempt legatee or exempt legatees are involved in either alternative). Where the testator owns a majority or large minority holding which does not qualify for business relief (eg a holding in a property company), dividing up ownership will have the advantage that each legatee will have a holding which will on a future occasion of inheritance tax charge be valued at a lower, sometimes a very much lower, amount per share than

that of the single holding held by the testator. Now that 100 per cent business relief applies to unquoted holdings irrespective of the amount of votes (if any) controlled by the transferor, there is no longer any compelling inheritance tax reason for keeping a holding which qualifies for the relief together in order to maintain qualification for the relief. Capital gains tax business assets taper relief also no longer requires unquoted holdings to be of a minimum size to qualify for the relief.

[205.57]

Shareholdings where the relief depends on control. Agricultural relief for shares in a company owning agricultural property (see para **[234.6]**), business relief for land, building, plant or machinery owned by the testator and used but not owned by a company in which he is a shareholder (see para **[205.41]**), and the rare cases of business relief on securities forming part of an unquoted controlling holding or quoted shares forming part of a controlling holding (see paras **[205.5]** and **[205.6]**), depend on the testator having control of the company (taking into account related property and settled property in which he has an interest in possession). Where a testator has a controlling holding which qualifies for the relief of any of these kinds it will often be desirable to keep the holding together after his or her death so as to maintain the qualification for the relief on future occasions of inheritance tax charge. If it is desired to keep the holding together but enable many people to benefit, a possible solution is a discretionary trust as in Form C11.1 at para **[233.13]** ff. Where spouses between them have control, a gift by the first to die to the survivor so as to enable the survivor to have control after the death of the first to die, with the balance going into a non-exempt gift, is a possible option, based on Form C11.2 at para **[233.26]** ff.

[205.58]

Form B5.1: Bequest of a sole trader's business[1]

I give to [*name*] the goodwill of my business[2] of a *description of business*] carried on by me at *location*] and all the [equipment plant stock-in-trade][3] vehicles and all other assets of any kind employed or used in carrying on the same at my death and all book debts then owing to me in respect of such business together with the then balances (if any) to the credit of the current [and business reserve] accounts of the said business at the [*name*] Bank Plc[4] and the benefit of all contracts relating thereto but subject to taking over all my liabilities in connection with the said business existing at my death and indemnifying my estate against the same but subject as follows:

(1) [the foregoing gift shall include the freehold or such other estate or interest I may have at my death in the premises in which the said business is carried on but subject to any mortgage charge or other liability on or of such premises subsisting at my death][5] *or where the premises are leasehold* [the foregoing gift shall include the lease or tenancy of the premises on which the said business is carried on but subject to accepting the covenants liabilities and obligations thereunder and keeping my estate indemnified against all liability under the said lease or tenancy whether or not such liability has arisen in my lifetime or arises from acts or omissions done or occurring during

my lifetime] *or where the donee is not to be given the testator's interest in the premises* [the foregoing gift shall not include my interest in the premises in which the said business is carried on but the said [*name*] shall be entitled to a non-assignable [monthly] tenancy thereof [without any obligations in respect of external or structural repair] on such terms and at such market rent as shall be determined by my Trustees (and the said [*name*] may disclaim the foregoing gift at any time up to four weeks after being notified by the trustees of the rent and other terms which they have determined upon for such tenancy)];[6]

(2) if there is any inheritance tax payable on my estate by reason of my death which is attributable to the foregoing gift (after allowing for any reduction in value for inheritance tax purposes which is attributed thereto) then the foregoing gift shall be subject to such inheritance tax and it shall be borne by the said [*name*] in exoneration of the rest of my estate.[7]

1 The rate of business relief should be 100 per cent if the business has been owned for two years: see the Note at para **[205.22]** ff. For complete wills where there is business relief: see C11 at para **[233.1]** ff. This Form is not intended for use as a gift of a farming business (for wills disposing of farms, see C12 at para **[234.1]** ff) nor for a partnership share (for a gift of which see B5.6 at para **[205.63]**). In order to avoid disputes, it is better to give a business to one person who takes the benefit and assumes the liabilities. For an appointment of a separate executor of the testator's business, see Form B3.25 at para **[203.44]**.

2 The word 'business' has no definite legal meaning. In its narrowest sense it may pass the mere right to carry on the business as the testator's successor and to use his trade name; in its widest sense it may include everything enumerated in this Form: see generally Vol 1, para **[64.7]**. The draftsman should consider in each case which of the things enumerated in this Form are intended to pass and specify them. It is important to state whether the gift of the business is subject to trade liabilities (see *Re Timberlake, Archer v Timberlake* (1919) 63 Sol Jo 286).

3 The list may need amendment depending on the kind of business.

4 Banking arrangements vary, and the conscientious will-draftsmen should enquire into those of his client's business and get instructions on what bank balances to include in the gift.

5 A bequest of a business prima facie passes all the testator's interest in all the assets of the business, including the business premises: *Re Rhagg, Easton v Boyd* [1938] Ch 828, [1938] 3 All ER 314, and under the AEA 1925, s 35 (Part G, para **[246.62]**) a gift is subject to any mortgages or charges on the property in the absence of the expression of a contrary intent. However, to avoid doubt and possible dispute, we recommend that express provision is made about the business premises, and charges on it where relevant. There may need to be amendment where the business is carried on on part only of premises owned or leased by the testator, and the donee of the business is not intended to receive the whole of the premises.

6 The third option given here is an example and many other possible arrangements can be made. Excluding the testator's interest in the business premises from the gift may mean that business relief is not fully utilised, particularly where the gift of the business is not exempt and the premises themselves fall into an exempt residue. It should be remembered that a tenancy will have security of tenure under the LTA 1954, Pt II and that the trustees may need special powers or directions as to, e g how often to seek a rent increase if the premises which they will hold subject to the tenancy are to be held on trust.

7 There should be no inheritance tax on the gift because of 100 per cent business relief (see the Note at para **[205.22]**), but for the circumstances in which tax may be paid on such property see para **[205.51]**. Adding this subclause is a precaution, for use particularly where much or all of the remainder of the estate may be exempt.

[205.59]

Form B5.2: Bequest to trustees of a business carried on on leasehold premises upon trust to carry on for a limited period

I bequeath my leasehold premises at *address of business premises*] for all my estate term and interest therein and the goodwill of my business[1] of a —— now carried on there by me and all the machinery plant stock-in-trade and effects employed or used in carrying on the same and all book debts owing to me in respect of my said business together with the balance (if any) to the credit of my said business at the —— Bank [*or if the business account is not kept separately* together with the sum of £—— for carrying on the business[2]] and the benefit of all contracts relating thereto but subject to all my liabilities in connection with the said business unto my trustees[3] upon the trusts hereinafter declared concerning the same (that is to say):

(1) upon trust that my trustees shall continue to carry on the said business on the said premises or any other suitable premises during such period as they in their sole discretion may think fit and subject thereto—

(2) upon trust to sell the said premises on which the said business may be carried on and the said business as a going concern with the goodwill thereof and all the then existing assets thereof or such of them as my trustees think fit but subject to the liabilities thereof or such of them as my trustees think fit upon such terms as they may in their sole discretion think proper [*add such of* Forms B5.14 *at para* **[205.71]**, B5.15 *at para* **[205.72]**, B5.17 *at para* **[205.74]**, B5.18 *at para* **[205.75]**, B5.20 *at para* **[205.77]** *and* B5.21 *at para* **[205.78]** *as may be necessary*].

1 The bequest of a business prima facie passes all the testator's interest in all the assets of the business, including the business premises (*Re Rhagg, Easten v Boyd* [1938] Ch 828).

2 See para **[205.58]** n 4.

3 Care should be taken to choose trustees who will be prepared to carry on the business even if only with a view to its sale. It may be appropriate for the gift to be subject to its own inheritance tax: see the Preliminary Note to B5 at paras **[205.52]–[205.54]** and the final subclause of Form B5.1 at para **[205.58]** for a form of words.

[205.60]

Form B5.3: Trusts of net profits and proceeds of sale of a business[1]

I declare that my trustees shall stand possessed of the said business and the annual profits thereof after payment of all the expenses of carrying on the same until the said business shall be sold and of the net proceeds of sale thereof after the same shall be sold and of any other moneys arising therefrom or in connection therewith and of the income of such proceeds of sale and other moneys upon trust to pay such annual profits or income as the case may be to my daughter [*name*][2] during her life and after her death as to the said business and the said annual profits or (as the case may be) the said proceeds of sale and other moneys and the income thereof respectively upon trust etc.

1 This could be combined with Form B5.2 at para **[205.59]**. For deaths on or after 22 March 2006, this life interest should be an immediate post-death interest if it takes effect immediately on the testator's death (or is subject only to a survivorship condition permitted

by IHTA 1984, s 92: see paras **[219.6]–[219.7]**), and is not, for example, postponed to another interest (see the Note to para **[216.1]**). The gift over is not an immediate post-death interest and the assets, if they remain settled, would then fall within the inheritance tax charging regime for relevant property (see para **[200.92]**). The termination of an immediate post-death interest on or after 22 March 2006 will be deemed to be a gift of the underlying settled property for the purposes of FA 1986, s 102.

2 Following the commencement of GRA 2004 on 4 April 2005 it is important to name the daughters referred to. See Vol 1 at **[81.1]**.

[205.61]

Form B5.4: Gift of Lloyd's underwriting business[1]

I give to [*name*] of [*address*] the assets of my business as an underwriting member at Lloyd's subject to payment thereout of the liabilities of such business Provided that:

(1) [subject as set out below][2] the assets given hereby shall include the following (as at or ascertained after my death):

(a) my syndicate capacity, all my investments and cash deposited at Lloyd's, all investments and cash comprised in my special reserve, personal reserve, and premiums trust funds, and any balances on my personal account with my underwriting agent;

[(b) any property charged as security for a guarantee or letter of credit provided by a bank or other financial institution to support my membership at Lloyd's in respect of my Lloyd's deposit or personal or other reserve;][3]

(c) all profits of the said business received after my death whatever the year to which they relate and any tax repayments received after my death attributable to my said business;[4] and

(d) the benefit of any stop loss insurance or estate protection plan.

(2) [Subject as set out below][5] the liabilities to which the foregoing gift is subject shall include liabilities for income tax and capital gains tax on the foregoing assets and any losses paid after my death of the said business.

[(3) The assets given hereby and liabilities to which they are subject shall exclude:

[(a) any property charged as security for a guarantee or letter of credit provided by a bank or other financial institution to support my membership at Lloyd's in respect of my Lloyd's deposit or personal or other reserve;][6]

[(b) any profits received on an underwriting year of account which shall have been closed before my death;]

[(c) any losses of the said business for any underwriting year of account which shall have been closed before my death].]

(4) If the assets comprised in the foregoing gift are exceeded by the liabilities to which it is subject then this Clause shall be of no effect.

[(5) If any of the assets comprised in the foregoing gift do not wholly qualify for business property relief under Chapter I of Part V of the Inheritance Tax Act 1984 or if any of the foregoing liabilities to which the foregoing gift is made subject are not wholly taken into account as a deduction from the assets qualifying for such relief in determining the amount of such relief then the foregoing gift shall comprise only such assets and/or parts of assets as qualify for such relief and shall be subject only to such liabilities and/or parts of liabilities as are a deduction in determining the amount of such relief.][7]

(6) If there is any inheritance tax payable on my estate by reason of my death which is attributable to the foregoing gift (after allowing for any business property relief reducing its value for inheritance tax purposes which is attributed thereto) then the foregoing gift shall be subject to such inheritance tax and it shall be borne by the said [*name*] in exoneration of the rest of my estate.[8]

1 A Lloyd's underwriting interest will at least as to part enjoy 100 per cent relief as a 'business', and is thus something particularly worth making a specific gift of to a non-exempt beneficiary, especially because if it is given to the testator's spouse he or she may not become an underwriting member of Lloyd's (and so the business relief will not be carried forward to the spouse's death), and if he or she does become one he or she will have a new business and will not succeed to the testator's period of ownership for business relief purposes. However, not all the value of the Lloyd's deposit or the various reserves will necessarily be accepted by the Revenue as qualifying for the relief, on the grounds that they are in excess of what is really required for the business. It is important to investigate what the testator's underwriting assets consist of, and whether there is an estate protection plan, and consider to what extent these should be included in the gift. See further the footnotes on specific points below.

2 These words should be omitted if the exclusionary sub-cl (3) is omitted.

3 Before including this item consideration should be given to what it consists of and its value. The Revenue are unlikely to concede business property relief on it beyond the amount of the guarantee, and possibly not on any of it if it is in personal use, e g where it is the testator's residence, and this has now been confirmed by the decision in *IRC v Mallender* [2001] STC 514, High Court. This subclause should be omitted if sub-cl (3)(a) excluding such property is included.

4 There will be at least two, possibly more, underwriting years of account for which the profits will not have been received (or losses notified) by the time of the testator's death. It has been held by a Special Commissioner in *Hardcastle v IRC* [2000] STC (SCD) 532 that underwriting losses not notified at an underwriter's death were not liabilities deducted in valuing the business for relief purposes, but this may imply that profits not so notified would not qualify for the relief.

5 These words should be omitted if the exclusionary sub-cl (3) is omitted.

6 See n 3 above. This subclause should be omitted if sub-cl (1)(b) including such property is included.

7 Such a provision may well be desirable for inheritance tax purposes, but there could be difficulty, where the Revenue only agree to relief on part of an asset or fund, as to whether it is possible to make a gift of only that part which gets the business relief: see the Preliminary Note to C11 at para **[233.10]**. Profits and losses of open years which have not been notified at the testator's death will apparently be excluded by this provision: see n 4 above. There is thus a risk in this type of provision of throwing large liabilities on to the residuary estate, and, for example, reducing by too much the provision made for the testator's surviving spouse.

8 Where sub-cl (5) is not included it will often be appropriate to make the gift subject to inheritance tax, particularly where the residue is exempt and it is hoped to avoid inheritance tax on the estate (see the Note at paras **[205.52]**–**[205.54]**). Even where sub-cl (5) is included, it would be a sensible precaution to include this, in case the whole of the business relief on the underwriting assets cannot be marshalled against the gift.

[205.62]

Form B5.5: Clause providing that inheritance tax on business premises be paid by trustees and repaid to them by son[1]

I direct my trustees to pay out of my residuary estate all inheritance tax payable in respect of the said property in which the business of the said [company] is carried on and which is devised to my said son [*name*][2] as provided above.

Upon such payment in respect of inheritance tax being made by my trustees I direct that my son shall at the expiration of [six] months from the date of such payment repay the same to my trustees to be held by them as part of my residuary estate. PROVIDED always that such payment may at the election of my son be made by [ten] equal annual payments the first of such payments to be made at the expiration of the period of [six] months aforesaid. The said sum paid for inheritance tax by my trustees shall carry interest at the rate of [three] per cent until repayment and when paid by instalments such interest shall be charged only on the amount from time to time outstanding. If my trustees so require my son shall charge the said property with the repayment of the said sum or so much thereof as is for the time being outstanding and with the interest thereon. All instalments shall be held by my trustees as part of the capital of my residuary estate and the interest thereon shall be applicable as income of my residuary estate.

1 Where the inheritance tax will be payable by instalments (see paras **[205.17]**–**[205.20]**) the gift could simply be made subject to inheritance tax as in Form B5.1 at para **[205.58]**. The instalments would be interest-bearing ones (see para **[205.19]**), but would be ten annual instalments. This express provision could be used to give the son a lower rate of interest than that charged on inheritance tax, but the instalment number and period should be at least as generous as those under IHTA 1984, s 227 because the son will have a statutory right to repay in not less than the statutory instalments by virtue of the IHTA 1984, s 213. If the testator controls the company which uses the property, the property could qualify for 50 per cent business relief: see para **[205.41]**.

2 Following the commencement of GRA 2004 on 4 April 2005 it is important to name the daughters referred to. See Vol 1 at para **[81.1]**.

[205.63]

Form B5.6: Nomination of a son to succeed testator in partnership and gift to him of partnership share if he becomes a partner

In exercise of the power contained in the Articles of Partnership[1] dated —— and executed by the partners in the firm of —— carrying on business as —— in which firm I am a partner and of every other power enabling me at my death in this behalf I hereby nominate my son [*name*][2] to succeed me as a partner in the said firm on the terms contained in the said articles of partnership or on the terms contained in any articles of partnership in force with regard to the said firm at the date of my death.

I bequeath unto my said son [*name*] in the event of his becoming a partner in the said firm under this clause all my share and interest of and in the capital goodwill stock-in-trade plant machinery and assets of the said firm but my said son [*name*] shall indemnify and keep indemnified my estate to the satisfaction of my trustees from all debts and liabilities of the said firm and shall account for any sum due or owing to me from the said firm by way of profit at my death.

[I appoint my said son [*name*] my special executor as to the said partnership share and the expenses of obtaining a grant limited to such property shall be paid by him][3].

[Take in sub-cl (2) of Form B5.1 at para **[205.58]**].

In the event of my said son [*name*] refusing or failing [within —— months from the date of my death] to become a partner in the said firm I direct that all my share and interest in the said business shall fall into my residuary estate and be held by my trustees upon the trusts and subject to the powers and provisions hereinafter declared concerning the same and in the like event I bequeath to my said son [*name*] a [further] legacy of £——.

1 This clause can be used only in the rare case where the partnership articles contain a special provision allowing such nomination and where the testator is at his death a partner in the firm.

2 The articles may allow the nomination of some relative other than a son. A nomination is not restricted to sons or even relatives but only persons who are mentioned in the articles can be nominated. The person to be nominated and his rights on nomination are fixed by the articles. Following the commencement of GRA 2004 on 4 April 2005 it is important to name the son referred to. See Vol 1 at para **[81.1]**.

3 This is unnecessary if the partnership is a family one and the general executors are not likely to be adverse to the partnership. It is of importance only where the partners might object to the general executors seeing the private papers of the partnership.

[205.64]

Form B5.7: Clause giving effect to provision in partnership deed and granting widow a share of the profits during the joint lives of the widow and the surviving partner[1]

In exercise of the power in that behalf conferred on me by a partnership agreement dated —— and made between myself of the one part and AB of the other part I hereby direct that if I shall die during the continuance of the partnership thereby constituted and the said AB shall exercise the option given to him by the said agreement of purchasing my share in the capital and assets of the partnership business then there shall be paid to my wife [*name*][2] in accordance with the terms of the said agreement out of the net profits of the partnership business an annuity equal to —— parts of such net profits from time to time during the joint lives of my said wife[2] and the said AB such annuity to commence from the date of my death and that my executors shall require the said AB to enter into a proper deed of covenant for payment of the said annuity to my said wife[2] in a form to be approved by my executors.

1 This clause assumes that the partnership deed provides that, on the death of the partner, the other partner (usually the original owner of the partnership business) shall instead of paying a capital sum for the deceased's share in the partnership provide an annuity out of the partnership profits for the deceased's widow. Notice that the annuity is for the joint lives of the surviving partner and the widow and is, therefore, liable to cease during the widow's lifetime on the death of the surviving partner. Apparently the annuity is not part of the testator's estate and is free from the claims of his creditors: see *Re Flavell, Murray v Flavell* (1883) 25 Ch D 89, nor does the annuity render the widow liable as a partner: Partnership Act 1890, s 2(3)(c).

2 In order to adapt this form for use where the testator is in a civil partnership 'civil partner' may be substituted for 'wife'.

[205.65]

Form B5.8: Clauses giving assistance to son in acquiring partnership share, with alternative provision for realisation of the share[1]

POWER TO TRUSTEES TO LEAVE CAPITAL IN BUSINESS IF SON BECOMES A PARTNER

(1) In the event of my dying while I am a member of the firm of [*firm name*] I direct my trustees to allow any capital of mine which at my death is invested in the business carried on by the said firm to remain in such business as a loan at [£5] per cent per annum until the expiration of three months from the date of my death or from the date of my son [*name*][2] attaining the age of [18]/[21] years whichever is later. If on or before the expiration of the period applicable in the event which happens the then members of the said firm enter into articles of partnership with my said son upon the terms (inter alia) that my said son shall have not less than a [one-fourth] share of the profits of the said partnership then and in that event I direct my trustees to authorise the members of the said firm to retain a sum of £[10,000] out of my capital employed in the said business such sum of £[10,000] to belong to my said son as his share in the capital of the said business. And I further authorise and empower my trustees to allow the residue of my capital to remain in the said business upon the terms of the same being paid out to my trustees by the said firm by equal annual payments extending over a period of not more than [six] years from the admission of my said son into partnership with interest on the capital for the time being unpaid at [£5] per cent per annum.[3]

SON TO BRING AMOUNT OF CAPITAL INTO ACCOUNT IN DISTRIBUTION OF RESIDUE

(2) In the event of my said son being admitted as a partner in the said firm as aforesaid and receiving the said sum of £[10,000] as his share in the capital of the said business I direct that neither he nor his children shall take anything under the residuary gift hereinbefore contained without bringing such sum of £[10,000] into hotchpot and accounting therefor and further that in the event of the said sum of £[10,000] exceeding the respective shares of my other children in my residuary estate my said son or his personal representatives shall repay to my trustees a capital sum equal to the difference between the said sum of £[10,000] and the sum which on an equal division of my residuary estate (including for the purpose of computation the said sum of £[10,000]) my said son would receive [or would (if he had survived me and my said wife) have received][4] as his share thereof such capital sum to be paid by equal yearly instalments extending over a period of not more than —— years with interest at the rate of [five] per cent per annum on such part of the said capital sum as for the time being remains unpaid and I direct that my son shall secure such payment as aforesaid by his personal covenant. And I direct that such capital sum when paid and the interest thereon or on such part thereof as for the time being remains unpaid shall be paid and divided by my trustees to and among the persons other than my said son who are entitled under the residuary gift hereinbefore contained in favour of my children and issue in the proportions in which they respectively benefit under such residuary gift.

POWERS TO TRUSTEES IF SON DOES NOT BECOME PARTNER

(3) As and when it appears that such partnership as aforesaid has become impossible of effectuation (either through the refusal of the then partners or of my said son to entertain the proposition or by reason of the death of my said son or otherwise) I authorise my trustees:

(a) To ascertain my share in the said business and either to procure immediate payment to them of the value of the same or in their discretion to allow the whole or any part of my share to remain in the said business as a loan bearing interest at [five] per cent per annum for any period not exceeding —— years from the date of my death and to arrange for the payment of my said share by instalments either with or without taking security for payment thereof and without being responsible for any loss occasioned thereby.

(b) To sell or concur with other partners or partner in selling the said business to any company or individual or in winding up the affairs thereof and on any sale to agree that the purchase money therefor shall remain on loan for any period not exceeding —— years from such sale or shall be payable by instalments and on every sale to a company to accept in payment [of an amount not exceeding one-half] of the purchase-money for my share in the said business fully paid preference or ordinary shares or debentures or debenture stock of such company and to retain the same as authorised investments under this my will.

(c) In winding up such business to pay compound or submit to arbitration all accounts debts or other sums due to or owing from such business upon such evidence whether strictly legal or not as to them may seem satisfactory and to sell upon such credit and give time for payment of any sums due to my estate from any person or persons upon such terms as my trustees may think fit and generally to enter into execute and do all such agreements releases and acts as may be necessary to wind up the same in the manner most beneficial to my estate.

DEFINITION OF FIRM, ETC

(4) Any reference in this my will to the said firm of [*name*] or the business thereof or partnership therein shall be deemed to extend to and include the firm howsoever varied or constituted as to the members or member thereof for the time being and from time to time carrying on the business howsoever varied extended or limited now at the date of execution of this my will carried on by the said firm [*name*] and the business thereof and partnership therein.

1 This form assumes that residue has been given to the testator's children in equal shares, and that that gift might be subject to a life interest given to his widow.

2 Following the commencement of GRA 2004 on 4 April 2005 it is important to name the son referred to. See Vol 1 at para **[81.1]**.

3 The terms of the partnership articles, particularly in relation to repayment of capital and to interest on capital, should be ascertained, and considered. When this provision takes effect in favour of the son while the widow has a life interest it could cause a partial termination of the widow's interest in possession, which could be unsatisfactory in its inheritance tax consequences: see Part A, para **[200.102]**.

4 These words should be included if the son's interest in the residuary estate is contingent on surviving the widow.

[205.66]

Form B5.9: Gift of such of unquoted shares as shall have been owned for two years by the time of testator's death, subject to inheritance tax

I give to [*name*] such [25p ordinary shares in ABC Ltd] as I shall have owned throughout the period of two years immediately preceding my death[1] (if any) subject to the said [*name*] paying any inheritance tax which is payable in respect of such shares by reason of my death (taking into account any business property relief reducing the value of such shares for inheritance tax purposes which is attributed thereto).[2]

1 The gift is thus contingent on the shares having been owned long enough to qualify for business relief: see the Preliminary Note at para **[205.11]**. There may be difficulties of identification of the shares in some circumstances: see the Note at para **[205.31]**, in which case it may be better not to use this form. It is not necessary to provide an express alternative gift if falling into residue is what is wanted in the event of this gift not taking effect, and the wording of the residuary gift is wide enough. The main point of a gift of this type is to make an inheritance tax-free gift to a non-exempt beneficiary, where the residue of the estate is given to the testator's spouse. This form does not allow for subsequent company or capital reconstruction: see Form B5.10 at para **[205.67]** for a form which does this.

2 There are various ways in which property apparently attracting 100 per cent business relief may give rise to an inheritance tax charge. For reasons for making the gift subject to inheritance tax, see the Note at paras **[205.52]–[205.54]**. Where this is the only (or only significant) non-exempt gift, the legatee can choose between taking a larger gift subject to paying some tax or assigning shares in excess of the nil-rate band to the widow by Deed of Variation within two years of the testator's death so as to eliminate the inheritance tax liability. To make this even easier, power to disclaim part of the gift could be included as in Form B5.10, sub-cl (3) at para **[205.67]**.

[205.67]

Form B5.10: Gift of unquoted shares or any substitute shares on condition that they qualify for business relief, subject to inheritance tax, and with power to disclaim part of the gift[1]

(1) If at my death I own any [ordinary shares in ABC Ltd] or any substitute shares (as defined below) which at my death qualify for any business property relief under Chapter I of Part V of the Inheritance Tax Act 1984 then I give such shares to [*name*] subject to [his] bearing any inheritance tax which is payable (after making allowance for such business property relief as is attributed thereto) in respect of such shares by reason of my death.[2]

(2) For the foregoing purposes substitute shares are any ordinary shares which at my death would under any of the provisions of sections 126 to 136 of the Taxation of Chargeable Gains Act 1992 be identified with [ordinary shares in ABC Ltd] previously owned by me.[3]

(3) The said [*name*] may by written instrument made within two years of my death disclaim irrevocably the foregoing gift of any one or more of the foregoing shares without disclaiming the entire gift, and any of the said shares which are so disclaimed shall devolve as if the said [*name*] had predeceased me.[4]

1 See Form B5.9, nn 1 and 2 at para **[205.66]** and the Preliminary Note at para **[205.11]**. This form is similar in its effect to B5.9, but it will fail if any factor, not just period of ownership, prevents any business relief from being available. It also makes provision for alterations in the company's capital, takeovers, etc and provides power to disclaim part of the gift.

2 For reasons for making the gift subject to inheritance tax, see the Note at paras **[205.52]–[205.54]**.
3 These are the provisions which, for capital gains tax purposes, identify one shareholding with an earlier one where there has been a reorganisation of share capital, conversion of securities, or company reconstruction or amalgamation.
4 If the total of the value of this gift, and the value of any other parts of the estate which are chargeable to inheritance tax, exceeds the available nil-rate band, the legatee may wish to reduce this gift to a size which does not give rise to an inheritance tax charge, making use of the IHTA 1984, s 142 (see F3 at paras **[241.1]–[241.15]**). This provision makes a tax-effective reduction in the size of the gift easier for the legatee to accomplish, assuming that residue is given to the testator's spouse. Even if this provision were not included in the testator's will the legatee could still effect such a reduction of the size of the gift by an instrument of variation, but a disclaimer is simpler and involves fewer parties than an instrument of variation, and no election is needed for the IHTA 1984, s 142 to apply. However, a disclaimer of part of a gift is thought not to be possible, in the absence of a provision of this kind: see the Preliminary Note to F3 at para **[241.16]**.

[205.68]

Form B5.11: Bequest of an annuity to widow of principal director from shares in a family company, the shares being given to sons on the widow's death[1]

I bequeath my —— shares in —— Company Limited to my trustees upon trust during the lifetime of my wife [*name*][2] to pay from the income accruing therefrom an annuity[3] to my said [2]wife of £—— per annum [free of all deductions whatsoever and free of income tax at the basic rate] and subject thereto during the lifetime of my said wife[2] to divide the said income equally between my sons —— and —— and after the death of my said wife the said shares shall be held in trust for my said two sons[4] equally, provided always that in the event of the income therefrom in any year providing insufficient to satisfy the said annuity to my said wife[2] the deficiency shall be raised by charges upon or sale of the said shares or some part thereof.

I direct that any rebate allowance or repayment of income tax which may be made or allowed to my said wife shall enure for her own benefit.

1 This clause is designed to provide for the widow of a principal director of a small company. Though not in strictness a bequest of the business, it will in many cases amount to much the same thing in practice. The wife's income may be raised from capital, but any capital so raised will be subject to income tax: *Cunard's Trustees v IRC* [1946] 1 All ER 159.
2 In order to adapt this form for use where the testator is in a civil partnership 'civil partner' may be substituted for 'wife'.
3 The gift of an annuity has certain fiscal disadvantages which are discussed in B11 at para **[211.1]** ff. Also, changing an annuity in favour of the testator's widow on property entitled to business relief is wasteful of the relief and better avoided if possible: see C11 at para **[233.1]** ff.
4 Following the commencement of GRA 2004 on 4 April 2005 it is important to consider whether it is necessary to name the sons referred to. See Vol 1 at para **[81.1]**.

[205.69]

Form B5.12: Appointment by will of permanent director of private company[1]

In pursuance of article—of the articles of association of the —— Company Limited I hereby appoint [*widow or one of the trustees or as otherwise authorised by the article*] to be a permanent director of the said company subject always to the provisions of the said articles of association.[2]

1 For an article giving power to make such an appointment, see 9 Encyclopaedia of Forms and Precedents (5th edn, 2000 Reissue), Form 219 at para [1362].
2 Such an article may limit such an appointment to the duration of the life of the surviving original permanent director, and any director so appointed is liable to removal by simple resolution of the company in general meeting under the Companies Act 1985, s 303 though it is possible to provide by the articles for the weighting of votes on a resolution for the removal of a director so as in effect to entrench a director's position: *Bushell v Faith* [1970] AC 1099, [1970] 1 All ER 53.

Trustees' powers[1]

[205.70]

Form B5.13: Power to carry on business[2]

My trustees may carry on any business either alone or in partnership and may employ in it any capital of my residuary estate [*an indemnity as in* Form B5.15 *at para* **[205.72]** *could be added*].

1 See also Forms B20.17 to B20.19 at paras **[220.66]–[220.68]**, Forms B21.9 to B21.11 at paras **[221.10]–[221.12]**, B21.17 at para **[221.21]** and Form C11.1, cl 6(f)–(i) at para **[233.21]**.
2 See the Note at para **[205.25]** for trustees' powers to carry on a business.

[205.71]

Form B5.14: Power to turn business into limited or unlimited company

I declare that my trustees may form or join in forming a limited or unlimited company to take over or purchase such business or may sell the said business to a limited or unlimited company and I direct—

(a) that all or any part of the expenses in connection with such formation and sale may be paid out of my residuary estate;
(b) that my trustees or any of them may become directors or servants of the company and may receive the remuneration attaching to such office without being liable to account for the same and that any trustee may become qualified as a director (if the articles so allow) by the holding in his own name of shares belonging to my estate provided that he executes a declaration of trust thereof in favour of my trustees generally accompanied by the certificates of such shares and that he accounts to my estate for all dividends and bonuses payable in respect thereof;
(c) that the consideration for any such sale may comprise either cash debentures or debenture stock, preference or ordinary or deferred shares [fully paid] [whether fully or partly paid] or may comprise all or any of the aforesaid in such proportions as my trustees may think fit;
(d) that the sale may comprise the whole or some part only of the assets and liabilities of the said business;
(e) that the price shall be fixed in such manner as my trustees may determine;
[(f) that any debentures, debenture stock or shares of any kind in such company shall be an authorised investment under this my will][1].

1 This subclause will only be needed if there is a restricted power of investment which would not include such debentures, stock, or shares. For powers of investment see B20 at para **[220.1]** ff.

[205.72]

Form B5.15: Indemnity to trustees carrying on business[1]

I declare that every trustee hereof shall be fully and effectually indemnified out of my estate and every part thereof in respect of any personal liability which he may incur in connection with the said business and I further declare that no trustee hereof shall be liable to my estate or to any person claiming any interest under this my will for any loss which may be incurred in carrying on the said business.

1 For a more general form of indemnity see Form B21.12 at para **[221.16]**.

[205.73]

Form B5.16: Power to trustees to carry on business where the will contains a general trust for conversion[1]

I declare that notwithstanding the trust for sale hereinbefore contained[2] it shall be lawful for my trustees to carry on [with a view to selling the same as a going concern] the business of a —— carried on by me at ——[3] and that in carrying on the said business they shall be free from the control or interference of any person or persons beneficially entitled under this my will and may employ in it any capital of my residuary estate.

1 See the Note at para **[205.25]**. Trustees carrying on a business under such a power are in a fiduciary relationship to the beneficiaries and cannot set up a competing business on their own account without severing all connection with the trust (*Re Thomson, Thomson v Allen* [1930] 1 Ch 203).

2 If a power to postpone sale is conferred the trustees would have an implied power to continue the business in the meantime: *Re Crowther, Midgley v Crowther* [1895] 2 Ch 56. But it is preferable to make express provision.

3 Under a direction to carry on the testator's business, the trustees or executors are entitled to the free use of the business premises and the fixed plant and machinery therein so long as they are entitled under the will to carry on the business (*Re Cameron, Nixon v Cameron* (1884) 26 Ch D 19). The trustees will be entitled to set aside sums for depreciation of assets and a reserve fund: *Re Crabtree, Thomas v Crabtree* (1911) 106 LT 49; *Re Robertson* [1953] 2 SCR 1. Such a setting aside is not an accumulation and is not subject to the LPA 1925, s 164 (Part G, para **[246.66]**).

[205.74]

Form B5.17: Power for some of the trustees only to carry on testator's business

I declare that in case any one or more of my trustees shall be unwilling to carry on such business then it shall be lawful for the others or other of such trustees to carry on such business and to exercise alone all powers authorities and discretions hereby conferred on my trustees in relation to carrying on the said business or winding up the affairs thereof or otherwise howsoever in respect thereof[1] and I declare that any one or more of my trustees may act as manager or managers of the said business at such salary[2] as may be agreed upon by the other or others of my trustees for the time being without being liable to account to my estate in respect thereof.

1 See *Re Mellor, ex p Butcher* (1880) 13 Ch D 465.

2 The salary would technically be legacy: *Re Salmen, Salmen v Bernstein* (1912) 107 LT 108.

[205.75]

Form B5.18: Provision for exercise of powers though trustees interested in business[1]

All or any of the above powers granted to my trustees in relation to the said business and premises may be exercised [by my executors and][2] by any of my trustees and may be exercised although he or she may be interested as a partner in the said business or as a beneficiary under this my will.

1 For a clause practically in these terms, see *Re Sykes, Sykes v Sykes* [1909] 2 Ch 241.

2 Where the will appoints the same persons both executors and trustees and defines them as 'my trustees,' these words are not necessary, but they might be of importance where different persons were so appointed in a case where the powers had to be exercised during the ordinary administration of the estate by executors as such.

[205.76]

Form B5.19: Power to lend money to legatee of business

My trustees may at any time lend trust moneys to my said son[1] to whom my business is bequeathed to an amount not exceeding £—— at any one time and not exceeding £—— in all such loan or loans to be for such period or periods and at such commercial rate or rates of interest [not being less than—per cent per annum] and upon such other terms as my trustees may think fit and my trustees shall not in any event be under any liability in respect of money so advanced or the interest thereon.

1 Following the commencement of GRA 2004 on 4 April 2005 it is important to consider whether it is necessary to name the sons referred to. See Vol 1 at **[81.1]**.

[205.77]

Form B5.20: Power to employ a manager

My trustees may appoint any person (including any one or more of themselves) manager servant or agent to act in [the said business] at a salary or otherwise.

[205.78]

Form B5.21: Powers relating to sale of a business

My trustees shall have the following additional powers in any sale of [the said business]:

(1) to allow the purchase money to remain on loan for any period not exceeding [five] years payable by instalments at such rate of interest as they may think proper and to pay compound or submit to arbitration all accounts debts or other sums due or owing from such business upon such evidence whether strictly admissible in a court of law or not as to them may seem proper and to sell upon credit and give time for payment of any sums due to [the said business] from any person or persons upon such terms as they may think fit;

(2) in the event of [the said business] being sold to any company to accept, in satisfaction of the whole or any part of the purchase money payable in respect of such sale, shares in such company

(whether wholly or partly paid up or preference or ordinary shares) or debentures or debenture stock in such company.

[205.79]

Form B5.22: Powers to give warranties etc on the sale of a business or private company shares

My trustees may in connexion with the sale of any assets of my estate (in particular the sale of any business or any private company shares) give any warranty indemnity or other agreement or covenant whatever and shall be fully indemnified out of [my residuary estate] against any liability they may incur thereunder.

B6 Gifts of freehold land

Preliminary Note .... [206.1]

FORMS

B6.1 Absolute general gift of freeholds or lands generally .... [206.10]

B6.2 General gift of lands in a particular place .... [206.11]

B6.3 Gift of freehold lands purchased in a certain year .... [206.12]

B6.4 Specific gift of freeholds .... [206.13]

B6.5 Specific gift of property with provision against apportionment .... [206.14]

B6.6 Specific gift of registered land .... [206.15]

B6.7 Gift to joint tenants or tenants in common .... [206.16]

B6.8 Gift to minor .... [206.17]

B6.9 Gift of land of which the testator is tenant in tail .... [206.18]

B6.10 Gift of entailed property generally .... [206.19]

B6.11 Gift of freeholds subject to the payment of a legacy .... [206.20]

B6.12 Gift subject to the payment of debts, funeral, and testamentary expenses .... [206.21]

B6.13 Gift subject to a mortgage .... [206.22]

B6.14 Gift freed from a mortgage debt .... [206.23]

B6.15 Gift of lands, and in the event of such lands being sold during testator's lifetime, bequest of the proceeds of sale of such lands .... [206.24]

B6.16 Gift of lands which the testator has contracted to purchase .... [206.25]

B6.17 Gift of certain freehold lands to a charity .... [206.26]

B6.18 Gift subject to a condition as to taking a name .... [206.27]

B6.19 Gift to a person with a gift over on death without issue .... [206.28]

B6.20 Gift in exercise of a special power of appointment .... [206.29]

B6.21 Expression of testator's intention not to exercise a general power of appointment over land .... [206.30]

B6.22 Gift of lands upon the trusts of a settlement .... [206.31]

B6.23 Gift by reference to a settlement on trust for sale .... [206.32]

B6.24 Gift of lands to testator's sons, with successive gifts over if sons predecease or without issue [male] .... [206.33]

B6.25 Gift for the benefit of testator's children and the issue of deceased children at eighteen or marriage .... [206.34]

B6.26 Gift with provision against lapse .... [206.35]

B6.27 Clause creating an easement over land given to one person in favour of devisee of other land .... [206.36]

B6.28 Gift of part of land to one person and the other part to another by reference to a plan, with cross easements .... [206.37]

B6.29 Declaration as to payment of inheritance tax on specific gifts .... [206.38]

B6.30 Specific gift subject to inheritance tax .... [206.39]

B6.31 Specific gift of land which may qualify for agricultural property relief subject to inheritance tax .... [206.40]

Cross References

For rights of residence see B8 at para **[208.1]** ff. For testamentary options see B9 at para **[209.1]** ff. For gifts of land into trust see Forms B17.34 to B17.35 at paras **[217.42]**–**[217.43]**. For trustees' powers to permit enjoyment in kind see Forms B18.24 to B18.26 at paras **[218.109]**–**[218.112]**. For trustees' powers in the management of land see Forms B20.10 to B20.13 at paras **[220.49]**–**[220.62]**. For discussion of trusts of land under the Trusts of Land and Appointment of Trustees Act 1996 see Part A, para **[200.48]** ff.

PRELIMINARY NOTE

[206.1]
Strictly, the correct term for a gift of real property as opposed to personal property is a 'devise', and so apt to describe a gift of freehold land but not of leasehold land (which is, properly speaking, 'a bequest'). However, in this edition the words 'bequeath' and 'devise' have both been replaced with 'give' which is now in common usage.

[206.2]
In the case of an absolute gift there is probably little that need be considered save that testators are often misinformed as to the description of their interest in property and are apt to describe properties in terms which are difficult to reconcile with the title deeds. Where time permits, therefore, these matters should be checked with the deeds in order to prevent later dispute.

[206.3]
Inheritance tax. Whether the gift is to be free of, or subject to, inheritance tax, should also be given careful consideration. In the absence of contrary provision inheritance tax on a specific gift of land in the United Kingdom is now a testamentary expense payable out of residue: Inheritance Tax Act 1984 (IHTA 1984), s 211 (Part G, para **[246.100]**). This is subject to the point that s 211 does not treat as a testamentary expense the inheritance tax attributable to property comprised in a settlement immediately before the testator's death. The relevant definition of settlement (IHTA 1984, s 43(2)) would include entailed property. Therefore, property disposed of by will by virtue of a special or general power of appointment of settled property, or by virtue of the power conferred by the Law of Property Act 1925 (LPA 1925), s 176 (Part G, para **[244.55]**) to dispose of entailed property by will, bears its own inheritance tax in the absence of an expression of a contrary intention in the will. See C11 at para **[233.1]** ff for business relief and C12 at para **[234.1]** ff for agricultural and woodlands relief.

[206.4]
Gifts to minors. A minor cannot have a legal estate vested in him. A gift of land to a minor under a will of a person dying on or after 1 January 1997 will have effect as a trust for the minor and the Settled Land Act 1925 (SLA 1925) will no longer apply: TLATA 1996, Sch 1, para 2 (Part G, para **[246.131]**). The personal representatives will hold the land on trust for the minor as a trust of land (TLATA 1996, s 2) and will transfer it to him when he attains 18 (the age of majority pursuant to Family Law Reform Act 1969 (FLRA 1969), s 1). The conveyancing is now much simplified and it makes no practical difference whether or not a trust for sale is included in the gift. While the donee is a minor the personal representatives no longer need to set up a settlement subject to the SLA 1925 by execution of a vesting assent, but will be able to assent to the vesting of the land in themselves as trustees and to appoint new trustees of land under the TA 1925, s 36 (Part G, para **[246.34]**).

[206.5]
If a minor dies on or after 1 January 1997 without having been married and without issue, any fee simple estate or absolute interest in freehold land to

which he would otherwise have been entitled under a trust or settlement (including a will) he will be deemed to have had a life interest in and the trust or settlement is to be construed accordingly. Any freehold land so given to such a minor will accordingly revert to the testator's estate on the minor's death (see the AEA 1925, s 51(3), as amended by the TLATA 1996, s 25(1), Sch 3, paras 6(1), (4)(a): Part G, para **[244.81]**). In this respect an absolute gift of land to a minor without the interposition of a trust for sale is less 'absolute' than a gift of the proceeds of sale of land subject to a trust for sale.

[206.6]
Successive interests. Following the commencement of the TLATA 1996 on 1 January 1997, where a gift of freehold land is not absolute but creates successive interests it takes effect as a trust of land under that Act. It was at one time thought desirable that successive interests should be effected by creating a trust for sale in order to avoid the necessity for a special grant but because the SLA 1925 cannot apply it now makes little or no difference whether or not there is a trust for sale.

[206.7]
Administrative powers. Subject to the application of the duty of care under the Trustee Act 2000, s 1 (if not excluded by the will), for the purpose of exercising their functions as trustees, the trustees of land have in relation to the land subject to the trust all the powers of an absolute owner (TLATA 1996, s 6: Part G, para **[246.108]**) and if the land is sold the trustees have a general power of investment (TrA 2000, s 3: Part G, para **[246.135]**). Thus, the need to confer express administrative powers is much reduced and in many cases it will not be necessary to include any express powers at all. For examples of express powers see paras **[220.49]**–**[220.58]** and Forms B20.10 to B20.13 at paras **[220.59]**–**[220.62]**.

[206.8]
Existing liability for repairs. When a testator is the owner in fee simple of property and gives it subject to a lease in which he has covenanted to keep the exterior in repair, the cost of such repairs necessary at the date of death, if executed after the death of the testator, must (in the absence of any direction to the contrary) be met out of the residue of the estate and not paid for by the donee. In one case the repairs had been discussed by the testator with builders but no definite order for their execution was given: *Re Day's Will Trusts, Lloyds Bank Ltd v Shafe* [1962] 3 All ER 699, [1962] 1 WLR 1419.

[206.9]
Ademption. It must be remembered that a sale of the property given after the execution of the will will result in ademption. For a codicil for use where there has been such a sale, see Form D7 at para **[237.14]**.

[206.10]

Form B6.1: Absolute general gift of freeholds or lands generally

I give all my freehold property[1] [including all my undivided shares therein][2] whatsoever and wheresoever whether in possession reversion remainder or expectancy or over which I may have any general power of disposition [including all freehold land of which I am tenant in tail in possession under [*describe the will or settlement*]] to [*name*] absolutely.[3]

1 Since the change in the law of intestacy and the abolition of descent to the heir, rendering the word 'heir' obsolete, the word 'hereditaments' has become rather meaningless. The word 'property' is here substituted but some may think that that word is insufficient in the case of incorporeal hereditaments and for the sake of completeness there may be added after the word property 'including incorporeal hereditaments'.

2 By virtue of the TLATA 1996 an undivided share is now an equitable interest in land. This does not mean that a phrase such as 'freehold property' will now include an undivided share of a freehold, because it is an interest in a freehold rather than being itself a freehold. However, it could save argument to make it clear whether or not undivided shares are included in the gift by including the words in parenthesis.

3 The express reference to entails is not superseded by the TLATA 1996, although the creation of new entails on or after 1 January 1997 is prevented by Sch 1, para 5 of that Act, and any attempt to create one gives rise to an absolute interest. It is, however, still possible for a testator to be a tenant in tail under a pre-1997 disposition. As to a gift of property of which the testator is tenant in tail in possession, see the LPA 1925, s 176 (Part G, para **[244.55]**). Such a gift operates as if the tenants in tail in possession had barred the entail and become owner of the fee simple. A reference to entailed property generally would be sufficient.

A gift of the land of the testator or of the land of the testator described in a general manner is to be construed to include leasehold estates of the testator unless a contrary intention appears (WA 1837, s 26: Part G, para **[244.28]**), see Vol 1, paras **[64.32]–[64.34]**. If the words were 'all my lands', they would pass a testator's freeholds and leaseholds, and also, by virtue of the WA 1837, s 27 (Part G, para **[244.29]**), pass all similar property over which he has a general power of appointment, but this clause is restricted to freeholds.

[206.11]

Form B6.2: General gift of lands in a particular place[1]

I give all my freehold property in the parish of —— *or* in the county of ——] including all my undivided shares therein[2] to [*name*] absolutely [in fee simple for his own absolute use and benefit].

1 The properties should be specified if possible but such general gifts may be used in cases where no better description is possible. They have in the past, however, often led to difficulty and contention: see Vol 1, para **[63.1]** ff. See notes to the immediately preceding precedent.

2 See para **[206.10]**, n 2.

[206.12]

Form B6.3: Gift of freehold lands purchased in a certain year[1]

I give my freehold lands[2] at —— which I purchased from —— in the year —— to my daughter [*name*] absolutely.

1 See the notes to the immediately preceding precedents.

2 See para **[206.10]**, n 2.

[206.13]

Form B6.4: Specific gift of freeholds[1]

I give to [*name*] in fee simple my freehold property[2] situate at —— in the county of —— and known as —— [together with all easements appurtenances and other rights thereto belonging or appertaining or reputed to appertain thereto or to any part thereof or enjoyed or reputed or known as part or parcel thereof[3]].

1 While it will often not be possible to describe the property in the terms of the description in the title deeds, it is most desirable that whatever short description is adopted is part of the fuller description in those deeds so that the property is identified with the property there described.
2 See para **[206.10]**, n 2.
3 The words in brackets are required only where the testator owns adjoining property.

[206.14]

Form B6.5: Specific gift of property with provision against apportionment

I give to [*name*] in fee simple my freehold property[1] at —— in the county of —— and known as —— together with the rents and profits due or accruing due[2] in respect thereof at the date of my death but subject to the payment by him of all outgoings and expenses usually chargeable against the income of such property.[3]

1 See para **[206.10]**, n 2.
2 Where rent is paid in arrear, these words will exclude the Apportionment Act 1870, s 2 (Part G, para **[246.3]**) which would otherwise require the rent to be considered as accruing from day to day and apportioned between the part of the rent period preceding the testator's death (that portion of rent passing with residue if not otherwise specifically given) and the part of the rent period following the testator's death (which portion of rent would pass with the specific gift). The Act does not apply where rent is paid in advance (*Ellis v Rowbotham* [1900] 1 QB 740) and so the words 'or accruing due' should perhaps not be included where the gift is of land subject to a lease under which the rent is payable in advance because their inclusion might lead to a question over whether the gift is intended to carry rent for the part of the rent period following the testator's death.
3 As to outgoings usually chargeable against income, see *Eccles v Mills* [1898] AC 360; *Re Hughes, Ellis v Hughes* [1913] 2 Ch 491. In the case of land subject to leases, only expenses incident to the relationship of landlord and tenant are properly chargeable against income. This excludes expenses preparatory to the relationship of landlord and tenant such as expending money to put the property in a certain state of repair or condition required by the tenant as a condition of accepting a lease.

[206.15]

Form B6.6: Specific gift of registered land

I give to [*name*] [in fee simple] my freehold lands registered in HM Land Registry as County [*or* County Borough] —— Title No —— Property —— [and declare that all cost of the registration of the said [*donee*] with an absolute title thereto in the Land Register shall be payable out of my residuary estate].[1]

1 In the case of a specific gift the cost of vesting it in the beneficiary is to be borne by him in the absence of a direction to the contrary: *Re Grosvenor, Grosvenor v Grosvenor* [1916] 2 Ch 375.

[206.16]

Form B6.7: Gift to joint tenants or tenants in common

I give my freehold[1] house and premises known as —— and now in the occupation of [*tenant*] to my daughters [*name*] and [*name*][2] as joint tenants [*or* as tenants in common in equal shares[3]].

1 See para **[206.10]**, n 2.
2 Following the commencement of GRA 2004 on 4 April 2005 it is important to name the daughters referred to. See Vol 1 at para **[81.1]**.
3 See the LPA 1925, s 36, as to joint tenancy; and s 34, as to tenancy in common. A joint tenancy may be severed either expressly by service of a notice under LPA 1925, s 36, or by operation of law, e g by the beneficiary charging his interest in favour of a third party, and after severance the party severing will be a tenant in common with the other or others: that is, if there are two joint tenants, they become tenants in common; but if there are more than two, then the severer is a tenant in common with the others who remain joint tenants among themselves. The personal representatives will hold the land on trust for the beneficial tenants in common or joint tenants (LPA 1925, ss 34(2), (3) and 36(1)), but they can require the beneficiaries to accept a transfer of the land (TLATA 1996, s 6(2)). For a gift of the beneficial interest of a tenant in common, see Form B4.47 at para **[204.69]** and for a clause dealing with property held in joint tenancy, see Form B4.49 at para **[204.71]**.

[206.17]

Form B6.8: Gift to minor[1]

I give my freehold land[2] at —— in the county of —— known as —— to [*minor*] absolutely provided that if the said [*minor*] shall predecease me without leaving issue[2] living at my death or then en ventre but born thereafter or if he shall survive me and die under the age of [eighteen] [twenty-one] years without leaving children[2] living at his death then I give the said land unto —— and provided further that if the said [*minor*] shall predecease me leaving issue[3] living at my death or then en ventre but born thereafter then I give the said land to such issue and if more than one as tenants in common in equal shares per stirpes but so that no issue shall take whose parent is living at my death and so capable of taking.[4]

1 As to effect of such a gift, see the General Note to gifts at paras **[206.4]** and **[206.5]**. For trusts for minors generally see paras **[217.1]** ff and for taxation of these gifts see Part A, paras **[200.107]** ff.
2 See para **[206.10]**, n 2.
3 Any reference to issue or children will, in the absence of a contrary intention, be construed as including illegitimate and adopted issue and children. For wills made after 3 April 1988 the inclusion of illegitimate issue and children will be by virtue of the FLRA 1987, ss 1 and 19 (Part G, paras **[245.70]** and **[245.72]**). (For wills made prior to that and after 1 January 1970, see FLRA 1969, s 15(1): Part G, para **[245.39]**). The inclusion of adopted children and issue is by virtue of Adoption Act 1976, ss 39 and 42, replacing (by way of consolidation) the Children Act 1975, Sch 1, paras 3 and 5 as from 1 January 1976, and brought into force on 1 January 1988. The Human Fertilisation and Embryology Act 1990, as from 1 August 1991, also affects the meaning of 'children' and 'issue' in some circumstances (see Part G, para **[245.83]** ff). See generally Vol 1, paras **[71.1]**–**[76.6]**, for the meaning of the terms 'children' and 'issue'.
4 It seems that these words are necessary to avoid any question arising in the rare case where there is a child and grandchildren or other issue of differing generations.

[206.18]

Form B6.9: Gift of land of which the testator is tenant in tail[1]

I give all the land of which I am tenant in tail in possession under [*particulars of will or settlement*] to [*name*] in fee simple.

1 The express reference to entails is not superseded by the TLATA 1996, although the creation of new entails on or after 1 January 1997 is prevented by Sch 1, para 5 of that Act, and any attempt to create one gives rise to an absolute interest. It is, however, still possible for a testator to be a tenant in tail under a pre-1997 disposition by which a tenant in tail in possession has power to dispose by will of entailed property referring specifically either to the property or the instrument under which it was acquired or to entailed property generally: see the LPA 1925, s 176(1) (Part G, para **[244.55]**). A tenant in tail in this section includes the owner of a base fee in possession (sub-s (3)). This gift will bear its own inheritance tax unless there is some provision to the contrary in the will: see para **[206.3]** and paras **[214.4]–[214.7]**.

[206.19]

Form B6.10: Gift of entailed property generally[1]

I give all entailed property whatsoever and wheresoever of which, by virtue of section 176 of the Law of Property Act 1925, I have power to dispose by will to [*name*] absolutely [*or* in fee simple *or* for all the residue of the several terms of which the same are held *or* absolutely *according to the nature of the property*].

1 See para **[206.18]**, n 1. The LPA 1925, s 176 (Part G, para **[244.55]**), gives power not only to dispose by will of property of which the testator is tenant in tail in possession, but also of money (including the proceeds of property directed to be sold) subject to be invested in the purchase of property, of which, if it had been so invested, he would have been the tenant in tail in possession at his death. This gift will bear its own inheritance tax unless there is some provision to the contrary in the will: see paras **[206.3]** and **[214.4]–[214.7]**.

[206.20]

Form B6.11: Gift of freeholds subject to the payment of a legacy[1]

I give my lands situate at —— to [*donee*] subject to and charged with the payment of [the clear sum of] £—— to [*legatee*] and the [*donee*] accepting this gift shall [not] be personally liable for such payment.

[*OR*

I charge my lands situate at —— with payment of [the clear sum of] £—— to etc and subject to such charge give the same to etc.[2]]

1 A gift of land upon the condition that certain payments are made is usually construed as constituting those payments a charge upon the land. If, therefore, the words 'and charged with' were omitted from the above clause, the payment would probably still be a charge upon the land, but whether it was so or not would be a question of construction of the will taken as a whole. The inclusion of these words, therefore, will remove any difficulty of this nature which might arise. See *Re Lester, Lester v Lester* [1942] Ch 324, [1942] 1 All ER 646, and the cases there reviewed. As to such a gift creating a trust, see Vol 1, para **[91.2]**. A legacy charged on realty will not, as was formerly the case, bear a due proportion of the inheritance tax attributable to such realty, as tax on realty is now prima facie a testamentary expense: see the IHTA 1984, s 211 (Part G, para **[246.100]**; see also paras **[214.4]–[214.7]** and **[214.55]–[214.74]**).

2 This form removes any doubt as to the land being charged with the legacy and is preferable to that first given.

[206.21]

Form B6.12: Gift subject to the payment of debts, funeral, and testamentary expenses

I give my freehold lands situate at —— but subject to and charged [in exoneration of my personal estate[1]] with the payment of my debts funeral and testamentary expenses and the legacies and annuities given by this my will or any codicil hereto and the inheritance tax on any legacy or annuity given free of inheritance tax to [*donee*] absolutely [and I declare that all inheritance tax payable in respect of any such legacy or annuity shall be born or paid by the said [*donee*] or the said lands in exoneration of the legatees or annuitants[2]].

1 These words must be inserted if such is the testator's intention (*Bootle v Blundell* (1815) 1 Mer 193 at 219), even if the land is outside the jurisdiction (*Re Smith, Smith v Smith* [1913] 2 Ch 216). The general practice now is to make the residuary realty and personalty subject to a trust for sale and to pay all these sums out of the proceeds in priority to all other sums.

2 A legatee whose legacy is charged on land is no longer liable to bear a proportion of the inheritance tax (see para **[206.20]**, n 1) and this express exoneration is therefore not strictly necessary.

[206.22]

Form B6.13: Gift subject to a mortgage

I give my freehold land situate at —— subject to and charged with the payment of all principal sums and interest secured thereon by way of mortgage or otherwise at my death to [*name*] absolutely.[1]

1 Every kind of property which a person dies possessed of or entitled to, or which he disposes of by his will under a general power of appointment (including entailed property under the statutory power) is now, in the absence of a contrary intention as between the different persons claiming through the deceased, primarily liable for the payment of any money charged on that property at the time of the deceased's death. See the AEA 1925, s 35 and the definition of 'property' in s 55(1)(xvii) (Part G, paras **[246.62]** and **[246.67]**). The results would, therefore, be the same if the land were given without reference to the mortgage, but it may be convenient to refer to it. The gift of an option to purchase at a price below the portion of a mortgage debt attributable to the specifically given property does not show a contrary intention within this section: *Re Biss, Heasman v Biss*, below.

Where the property here specifically given has been mortgaged or charged with other property which is included in the residue, then the specifically given property must bear a proportionate part of the mortgage debt or charge: *Re Neeld, Carpenter v Inigo-Jones* [1962] Ch 643, [1962] 2 All ER 335, overruling *Re Biss, Heasman v Biss* [1956] Ch 243, [1956] 1 All ER 89, and *Re Cohen, National Provincial Bank Ltd v Katz* [1960] Ch 179, [1959] 3 All ER 740 on this point.

[206.23]

Form B6.14: Gift freed from a mortgage debt

I give my freehold lands situate at —— to [*name*] absolutely freed and discharged from all sums secured thereon by way of mortgage or otherwise at my death and I direct that such sums and all interest in respect thereof and costs and expenses relating to the discharge thereof shall be paid out of my residuary estate.[1]

1 See para **[206.22]**, n 1. There must be express words making this gift free of the mortgage or charge on the property.

[206.24]

Form B6.15: Gift of lands, and in the event of such lands being sold during testator's lifetime, bequest of the proceeds of sale of such lands

I give my freehold land at —— in the county of —— and known as —— to [*name*] absolutely and in case the said land [or any part thereof] shall be sold or contracted to be sold[1] by me in my lifetime then in lieu thereof [or of such part thereof] I give to the said [*name*] free of inheritance tax[2] the sum of £—— [*or* a sum equal in amount to the sum received as purchase-money in respect of such sale after the deduction of all expenses of such sale] [and I direct that in the event of there being an insufficiency of assets in my estate the legacy hereby given shall be treated as if it were property specifically given for the purposes of abatement[3]].

1 A binding contract for sale will effect an ademption: *Farrar v Lord Winterton* (1842) 5 Beav 1 and see Vol 1, paras **[41.1]–[41.8]**.
2 Inheritance tax on land is now prima facie payable out of residue, but a legacy may have to contribute to the payment of inheritance tax if residue includes foreign property: see para **[214.62]**.
3 But for these words the legacy would abate rateably other general legacies, whereas the specific gift of the property, had it not been adeemed, would have abated only with property specifically given.

[206.25]

Form B6.16: Gift of lands which the testator has contracted to purchase

I give the freehold lands at —— which I have lately agreed to purchase from [*vendor*] of etc to [*donee*] absolutely and I direct that the purchase-money payable in respect thereof and the costs of and incidental to such purchase or so much thereof respectively as shall remain unpaid at my death shall be paid out of my residuary personal estate.[1] [And in case the said contract shall be determined either in my lifetime or after my death I give to the said *donee*] in lieu of such lands a sum equal in amount to the agreed purchase money in respect of such purchase.]

1 The devisee takes subject to the vendor's lien for the purchase money: *Re Cockcroft, Broadbent v Groves* (1883) 24 Ch D 94, and *Re Birmingham, Savage v Standard* [1959] Ch 523, [1958] 2 All ER 397, unless there is an express direction for it to be paid out of the personal estate. See *Re Rix, Steward v Lonsdale* (1921) 90 LJ Ch 474, as to the position if the contract goes off before testator's death. See also *Re Riddell, Public Trustee v Riddell* [1936] Ch 747, [1936] 2 All ER 1600, where the balance of the purchase money on completion was paid by the testator's solicitors shortly before his death.

[206.26]

Form B6.17: Gift of certain freehold lands to a charity

I give my freehold lands at —— in the county of ——[1] and known as —— to the [*charity*] absolutely[2] [and I accordingly direct my personal representatives to vest the same in or cause the same to be vested in the trustees of the said [*charity*].[3]

1 If the gift is to be limited to such lands as the testator owns at the date of his will, the lands must be accurately described, as in a conveyance.
2 Such a gift was subject to the Mortmain and Charitable Uses Act 1891, s 5 but that provision has been repealed by the Charities Act 1960, s 38 and this gift now takes effect

according to its terms. The gift will be free of inheritance tax under the IHTA 1984, s 23(1): see further Part A, paras **[200.87]** and **[200.88]** and **[212.2]**.

3 Land held for charitable purposes is land subject to a trust of land within the meaning of the TLATA 1996, ss 1 and 2(5) (Part G, paras **[246.103]** and **[246.104]**). Accordingly the charity trustees will have all the powers of an absolute owner (s 6(1)) and these cannot be restricted or excluded by the instrument creating the trust (s 8(3)). The gift should not name the Official Custodian for Charities. If the charity so desires then it is for the charity to have the land vested in the Official Custodian for Charities as custodian trustee.

[206.27]

Form B6.18: Gift subject to a condition as to taking a name

I give my freehold lands at —— to [*donee*] in fee simple on condition that he shall within —— months after my death unless already using the surname of —— take and use upon all occasions the surname of —— in addition to [*or* in substitution for] his own surname but if the said [*donee*] shall neglect or refuse within such period as aforesaid to take and use the said surname or if the said [*donee*] using such surname shall discontinue such use then and in every such case immediately after the expiration of the said period of —— months or immediately after such discontinuance as aforesaid the estate of the said [*donee*] shall immediately cease and determine and I give the said lands unto my trustees in fee simple upon the trusts and with and subject to the powers and provisions hereinafter declared and contained of and concerning my residuary estate or such of the same as may for the time being be subsisting and capable of taking effect.[1]

1 See generally Vol 1, paras **[35.39]–[35.44]**. See also Form C13.2, cl 9 at para **[235.27]** and the notes thereto. Where this clause included the provision against discontinuance of the use of the name it had been held to be void for uncertainty: *Re Lewis' Will Trust, Whitelaw v Beaumont* [1951] WN 591; *Re Bouverie, Bouverie v Marshall* [1952] Ch 400, [1952] 1 All ER 408; *Re Wood's Will Trusts, Wood v Donnelly* [1952] Ch 406, [1952] 1 All ER 740, but these cases have been overruled by the decision in *Re Neeld, Carpenter v Inigo-Jones* [1962] Ch 643, [1962] 2 All ER 335.In the case of the will of a person dying on or after 1 January 1997 the land will be held on a trust of land within the meaning of the TLATA 1996. The land would otherwise have been settled land.

[206.28]

Form B6.19: Gift to a person with a gift over on death without issue

I give my freehold lands at —— to [*name*] absolutely but if he predeceases me without leaving [male] issue[1] living at my death or then en ventre but born thereafter or if he shall survive me and die under the age of [eighteen] [twenty-one] years without leaving [male] issue[1] living at his death then I give the said lands to [*name*] in fee simple[2] and if he predeceases me leaving [male] issue[1] living at my death or then en ventre but born thereafter then I give the said lands to such issue in equal shares per stirpes and that no such issue shall take whose parent is living at my death and so capable of taking.

1 For wills made after 3 April 1988 the inclusion of illegitimate issue and children will be by virtue of the FLRA 1987, ss 1 and 19 (Part G, paras **[245.70]** and **[245.72]**). (For wills made prior to that and after 1 January 1970, see the FLRA 1969, s 15(1): Part G, para **[245.39]**). The inclusion of adopted children and issue is by virtue of the AA 1976, ss 39 and 42, replacing (by way of consolidation) the Children Act 1975, Sch 1, paras 3 and 5 as from 1 January 1976, and brought into force on 1 January 1988. The HFEA 1990, as from

1 August 1991, also affects the meaning of 'children' and 'issue' in some circumstances (see Part G, paras **[245.83]** ff). See generally Vol 1, paras **[72.1]–[76.6]**, for the meaning of the terms 'children' and 'issue'

2 Land given by a gift as in Form B6.19 is settled land in the case of a person dying before 1997 but in the case of a will of a person dying on or after 1 January 1997 the land will be subject to a trust of land within the meaning of the TLATA 1996.

[206.29]

Form B6.20: Gift in exercise of a special power of appointment[1]

In exercise of the power for this purpose given to me by the will dated —— of my deceased father [*name*] who died on —— and whose said will was proved in the [Principal] [—— District] [Registry of the Family Division] on —— [*or* by deed dated —— and made between [*parties*]] and of every or any other power enabling me in this behalf I give and appoint [all the freehold lands [capital moneys and investments][2] which may at my death be subject to such power of appointment to my sons [*name*] and [*name*][3] in equal shares as tenants in common absolutely[4]] [the freehold lands known as [*description*] to my son [*name*] and the freehold lands known as [*description*] to my son [*name*][3] and all the remainder of the freehold lands which may at my death be subject to such power of appointment to my said two sons in equal shares as tenants in common absolutely[5]].

1 If, as would normally be the case, the property subject to the power is settled property for inheritance tax purposes in which the testator has an interest in possession immediately before his death, it will bear its own inheritance tax unless there is express provision in the will to the contrary: see the Preliminary Note at para **[206.3]** and para **[208.41]**, n 1.

2 *Mills v Fox* (1887) 37 Ch D 153 at 162, shows the advantage of including these words for the property may be sold or compulsorily acquired before the death of the testator.

3 Following the commencement of GRA 2004 on 4 April 2005 it is important to name the sons referred to. See Vol 1 at **[81.1]**.

4 LPA 1925 undivided shares in land remain equitable interests but, as of 1 January 1997, if they do not arise under an express trust for sale they no longer take effect under a statutory trust for sale (LPA 1925, s 34, as amended by the TLATA 1996). The personal representatives will hold the land on trust for the beneficial tenants in common, but they can require the beneficiaries to accept a transfer of the land (TLATA 1996, s 6(2): Part G, para **[246.108]**).

5 A sale of any of the specific lands before the testator's death will vitiate the intention. If thought fit, express provision may be made for the death of one of the sons before the testator.

[206.30]

Form B6.21: Expression of testator's intention not to exercise a general power of appointment over land

Whereas under and by virtue of the will dated —— and duly proved in the [Principal] [—— District] [Registry of the Family Division] on —— of [*testator*] who died on ——I have a general power of appointment over certain freehold lands in the parish of —— in the county of —— now I hereby declare that it is not my intention to exercise the said power and that no clause of this my will shall operate as an exercise thereof.[1]

1 See the WA 1837, s 27 (Part G, para **[244.29]**) and Vol 1, paras **[39.8]–[39.15]**. This declaration is a clear expression of a contrary intention within the section so that the general power is not exercised by a general gift of real estate.

[206.31]

Form B6.22: Gift of lands upon the trusts of a settlement[1]

I give [*description of land*] to my trustees upon the same trusts and subject to the same powers and provisions [(including the trust for sale)] [2] as are declared in the settlement [dated etc] of and concerning the property thereby settled so far as the same shall at my death be still subsisting and capable of taking effect.

1 This form should be used where the trustees of the settlement are the same as those of the will or where, for any reason, such as urgency, although there are different trustees it is desired to use this short form. It is, of course, highly inconvenient where trustees do not hold the document setting out the trusts which they are to administer. Adding property to existing settlements should be avoided if possible: see Part A, para **[200.23]** generally, and see paras **[218.11]–[218.14]** for the addition of property to settlements where the settled property is held on discretionary trusts.

2 The trust created by this clause will now (from 1 January 1997) be a trust of land within the TLATA 1996, whether or not it creates a trust for sale, and even if the settlement by reference to the trusts of which property is settled is a pre-1997 one to which the SLA 1925 applies.

[206.32]

Form B6.23: Gift by reference to a settlement on trust for sale[1]

I give all my real estate unto my trustees upon trust that they shall convey the same to or otherwise vest the same in the trustees for the time being of a conveyance dated —— and made between [*parties*] upon trust for sale and to hold the rents profits and other income thereof until sale and the net proceeds of sale and the income thereof upon the trusts declared by the trust instrument in the said conveyance referred to or such of the same as are for the time being subsisting and capable of taking effect in like manner in all respects as though the property hereby given had formed part of the property assured by the said conveyance.

1 See Part A, para **[200.23]** generally for the addition of property to existing settlements and paras **[218.11]–[218.14]** for the addition of property to settlements where the settled property is held on discretionary trusts.

[206.33]

Form B6.24: Gift of lands to testator's sons, with successive gifts over if sons predecease testator without issue [male]

I give my freehold lands at —— in the county of —— known as the —— Estate to my eldest son [*name*][1] in fee simple but if my said son dies in my lifetime leaving [male] issue living at my death or then en ventre but born thereafter[2] then to his personal representatives as part of his estate and in default of my said son[1] or his personal representatives becoming entitled thereto hereunder I give the same to my second son [*name*][1] in fee simple but if my said son dies in my lifetime leaving [male] issue living at my death or then en ventre but born thereafter then to his personal representatives as part of his estate and in default of my said son or his personal representatives becoming entitled thereto hereunder [I give the same [*similarly for third son if required*][1]] and subject as aforesaid I declare that the said lands shall fall into and form part of my residuary estate.

1 Following the commencement of GRA 2004 on 4 April 2005 it is important to name the son referred to. See Vol 1 at **[81.1]**.
2 As this is a gift to the testator's child, the WA 1837, s 33, as substituted by the AJA 1982, s 19 (see the commentary in Vol 1 at paras **[47.11]–[47.16]** and the text in Part G at para **[244.36]**) would apply so as to confer an interest on the issue by substitution in the event of the son predeceasing the testator, if it were not for the provisions of this clause vesting the gift in this event in the son's estate. This clause is similar in effect to the former s 33 of the WA 1837 (see Vol 1, paras **[47.11]–[47.16]** and Part G, para **[244.35]**) but with the difference that, unlike the former s 33, the gift to the testator's son's estate takes effect if the son predeceases the testator leaving only issue en ventre at the testator's death. It is thought that no inheritance tax will be payable on the estate of the son if predeceasing the testator: see para **[219.21]**, n 1. For substitution of children, see Form B17.1 at para **[217.6]** and the note thereto. For alternative forms of declaration against lapse, see Forms B19.10 to B19.16 at paras **[219.23]–[219.29]**.

[206.34]

Form B6.25: Gift for the benefit of testator's children and the issue of deceased children at eighteen or marriage

I give all my real estate whatsoever and wheresoever [*or* my freehold houses known as etc] unto my trustees upon the same trusts for my own issue as if I had died possessed thereof intestate leaving no wife surviving me.[1]

1 The above clause carries the subdivision of the property through all the generations living at the testator's death in the proper shares. The intestacy rules now in force give vested interests to all issue, whether male or female, legitimate or illegitimate, attaining eighteen or marrying under that age: AEA 1925, s 46(1)(i) and s 47(1)(i), as amended (Part G, paras **[244.62]** and **[244.63]**). In order to adapt this form for use where the testator is in a civil partnership 'civil partner' may be substituted for 'wife'.

[206.35]

Form B6.26: Gift with provision against lapse

I give my freehold lands at —— and known as —— to my nephew [*name*][1] absolutely and if my said nephew shall die in my lifetime [leaving issue living at my death or then en ventre but born afterwards[2]] then to his personal representatives as part of his estate as if his death had happened immediately after mine.[3]

1 Following the commencement of GRA 2004 on 4 April 2005 it is important to name the nephew referred to. See Vol 1 at **[81.1]**.
2 See para **[206.33]**, n 1.
3 For substitution of children, see Form B17.34 at para **[217.39]** and the note thereto. See also as to such provisions against lapse as this Vol 1, para **[47.23]** and the various alternative forms of declaration against lapse in Forms B19.7 to B19.16 at paras **[219.20]–[219.29]**.

[206.36]

Form B6.27: Clause creating an easement over land given to one person in favour of devisee of other land

I direct that the said [devisee of Blackacre] and his successors in title and all persons authorised by him or them shall have the right in fee simple in common with the said [devisee of Whiteacre] and his successors in title and all persons authorised by him or them at all times and either with or without animals or vehicles of any kind to pass and repass over and along the private road constructed by me and leading from —— to —— for the purpose of access thereby to [Blackacre] subject to the payment of a fair proportion of the expense of maintaining and keeping the said private road and the gates and fences thereof in repair and my personal representatives shall if so required by the said [devisee of Blackacre] give effect to this direction in their assents to the said gifts or otherwise as may be necessary subject to the payment of the costs incurred therein by the said [devisee of Blackacre].

[206.37]

Form B6.28: Gift of part of land to one person and the other part to another by reference to a plan, with cross easements

(1) I give to my son [*name*][1] that part of my freehold land at —— and known as —— which part is more particularly described in the plan[2] entitled [Freehold land at —— and known as ——'] dated —— and signed by me and which part is delineated by being hatched black in such plan.

(2) I give to my daughter [*name*][1] all the rest and residue of my said freehold land.

(3) I direct that my son and his successors in title and all persons authorised by him or them shall have the right in fee simple in common with my daughter and her successors in title and all persons authorised by her or them at all times to run electricity mains water soil and surface water and other services through any sewers drains water courses pipes cables wires or other channels or conductors which are now in under or over the land hereby given to my daughter for all purposes in connection with any user of the land hereby given to my son.

(4) I direct that my daughter and her successors in title and all persons authorised by her or them shall have the right in fee simple in common with my son and his successors in title and all persons authorised by him or them at all times to run electricity mains water soil and surface water and other services through any sewers drains water courses pipes cables wires or other channels or conductors which are now in under or over the land hereby given to my son for all purposes in connection with any user of the land hereby given to my daughter.

1 Following the commencement of GRA 2004 on 4 April 2005 it is important to name the son and daughter referred to. See Vol 1 at para **[81.1]**.

2 A plan may be admitted to probate with the testator's will if it is referred to in the will, the reference being sufficient to identify it, and if it is already in existence at the date of the will (for incorporation of documents generally, see Vol 1, para **[15.1]** ff). It may save trouble in obtaining probate if colour is not used on the plan.

[206.38]

Form B6.29: Declaration as to payment of inheritance tax on specific gifts

I declare that the inheritance tax payable on my death in respect of the lands and hereditaments hereinbefore given to —— and —— respectively [and the inheritance tax payable on my death in respect of the lands and hereditaments hereinbefore given to my trustees in trust for my daughter[1] and —— her issue] shall be a charge on such specifically given lands and hereditaments in exoneration of my residuary [personal] estate.[2]

1 Following the commencement of GRA 2004 on 4 April 2005 it is important to name the daughter referred to. See Vol 1 at para **[81.1]**.

2 For the incidence of inheritance tax see para **[214.55]** ff. As mentioned there, inheritance tax on land in the UK is, in the absence of any expressed intention to the contrary, now prima facie payable out of residue, unless the land is comprised in a settlement immediately before the testator's death (see paras **[206.3]** and **[214.58]** and **[214.59]**). See also para **[206.39]**, n 1.

[206.39]

Form B6.30: Specific gift subject to inheritance tax

I give to [*name*] in fee simple my freehold property at —— in the county of —— and known as —— subject to all inheritance tax (of any) attributable thereto and payable by reason of my death.[1]

Land which may be conditionally exempt under IHTA 1984, s 30 (ie because of some scenic, artistic, historic, etc interest) should normally be given subject to payment of the inheritance tax attributable to it.

1 This form can be used to exclude the IHTA 1984, s 211 (inheritance tax on UK free estate payable out of residue: see para **[214.55]** ff and Part G, para **[246.100]**) in relation to a particular gift, and may also be used to qualify a general direction as to inheritance tax such as that in Form B14.33 at para **[214.76]**.

[206.40]

Form B6.31: Specific gift of land which may qualify for agricultural property relief subject to inheritance tax[1]

I give to [*name*] my freehold farm land situate at —— and known as —— and I declare that the proportion of the inheritance tax payable on my estate by reason of my death which is attributable to the value of the said land (allowing for any reduction in value for inheritance tax purposes) shall be charged upon the said land and shall be borne by [*name of devisee*] in exoneration of my residuary estate.

1 The 'subject to tax' formula used in this form may also be used where business property relief may be granted. For agricultural and business property relief generally, see para **[233.1]** ff. If the testator's estate may be partially exempt and include agricultural or business property other than the property specifically given, consider using the 'subject to tax' formula in Form B14.34 at para **[214.79]**; see also para **[214.73]**.

B7 Gifts of leasehold land

Preliminary Note .... [207.1]

FORMS

B7.1 Gift of leaseholds .... [207.15]

B7.2 Gift of leasehold flat and devise of any interest in freehold of premises in which flat is contained .... [207.16]

B7.3 Gift of leasehold house free from mortgage .... [207.17]

B7.4 Gift of leaseholds with a direction that the legatee is to pay all arrears of rent and cost of dilapidations .... [207.18]

B7.5 Gift of leaseholds to trustees upon trust to pay rents and profits to a person for life, and after his death to assign to another .... [207.19]

B7.6 Declaration that gift of lease includes the freehold reversion or any renewal if subsequently acquired .... [207.20]

B7.7 Contingent gift of leaseholds .... [207.21]

B7.8 Gift of undivided share in leaseholds .... [207.22]

B7.9 Gift of sinking fund policies in respect of leasehold properties .... [207.23]

B7.10 Declaration as to inheritance tax on settled leaseholds .... [207.24]

B7.11 Gift of leaseholds upon trust out of the rents and profits to form sinking fund .... [207.25]

B7.12 Alternative provision for sinking fund to replace leasehold value .... [207.26]

Cross References

For rights of residence see B8 at para **[208.1]** ff, especially Forms B8.5 at para **[208.41]**. For trustees' powers to permit enjoyment in kind see Note and Forms B18.24 to B18.26 at paras **[218.108]–[218.111]**. For trustee's powers in the management of land see Note and Forms B20.10 to B20.13 at paras **[220.49]–[220.62]**.

PRELIMINARY NOTE

[207.1]

Leaseholds are personalty. Since leaseholds are personalty, it is common practice to 'bequeath' leaseholds rather than 'devise' them, though it is generally unimportant which term is used but see para **[207.3]**. However, in this edition the words 'bequeath' and 'devise' have been replaced with 'give' which is now in common usage. Care should of course be taken in distinguishing gifts of a freehold and a leasehold interest in the same property. There is no harm in continuing to use the term 'bequeath' in the context of leaseholds except where there is a possibility that the freehold reversion will be acquired before death under, for example, the Leasehold Reform Act 1967 (LRA 1967) (see para **[207.9]** ff). Leaseholds, though not real property, are commonly included in the term 'land' (see Vol 1, para **[64.33]**) and for that reason the word 'land' should not in general be used without some qualification restricting it to freehold land or to leasehold land depending on the testator's intention. The form of a gift of leaseholds has varied from time to time but at the present time such a gift seldom contains more than the following: 'I give to —— my leasehold premises at ——.' It necessarily follows that the donee takes them subject to the rent, the lessee's covenants and the conditions in the lease and these are now seldom referred to. There may be special cases where the lease requires to be specifically referred to, but having regard to the fact that every properly drawn assignment of leaseholds commences with a recital of the lease, this can seldom be of any practical value. A gift of leaseholds has since 1877 borne its own charges and there can be no question of a mortgage being paid off out of the personal estate unless the will contains a direction to that effect. Inheritance tax in respect of leaseholds in the UK is prima facie a testamentary expense (see para **[214.55]** ff) and it will not normally be necessary to include a direction expressly freeing a gift of leasehold property from inheritance tax.

[207.2]

Liability for repair. In the case of an absolute donee of leaseholds, he will be bound to perform the tenant's continuing obligations under the lease, including repair, which arise after the testator's death: *Re Betty, Betty v A-G* [1899] 1 Ch 821. He usually takes the property as he finds it though it has been suggested that he has a remedy against the residuary estate of the testator in respect of dilapidations in the testator's lifetime: see *Harris v Poyner* (1852) 1 Drew 174 doubting *Hickling v Boyer* (1851) 3 Mac & G 635 on this point to the contrary. He can disclaim the gift and thus free himself from liability, but he may not be able to disclaim onerous leaseholds if the gift of them is only part of the bounty of the testator towards himself and it appears that other property has been given to him because the gift of the leaseholds carried heavy burdens without disclaiming all such other property also: see *Re Baron Kensington, Earl of Longford v Baron Kensington* [1902] 1 Ch 203, and see generally Vol 1 at para **[46.3]**, but see *Re Lysons, Beck v Lysons* (1912) 107 LT 146, where a donee was allowed to disclaim the leaseholds but to take the chattels given with it. Where, however, the gift is to a tenant for life and then to a remainderman the position is different. A trust for persons in succession of any leasehold property will (after 1 January 1997) be a trust of land under the TLATA 1996. Whereas the leasehold would formerly have vested in the tenant for life under a Settled Land Act settlement it now vests in the trustees who are thus liable to the landlord on the covenants for repair and the like. The trustees will have power to effect repairs, and a discretion as to how the repairs are paid for (under s 6(1) of the TLATA 1996: Part G, para **[246.108]**). If the life tenant has a right of occupation under s 12 of the 1996 Act, and exercises it, the trustees will be able to require him to accept the obligation to repair if it is reasonable to require this (s 13(3) and (5) of the TLATA 1996: Part G, para **[246.116]**). The extent to which the life tenant and/or the trustees under a trust of land will be liable to the remaindermen for non-repair depends on what exoneration from or imposition of liability (if any) there is in the will or settlement, and, subject to that, in the case of trustees will depend on whether they have acted prudently and carefully and in the case of the life tenant it will depend on whether any obligation has been imposed as a condition of occupation. In general trustees cannot be expected to effect repairs at their own personal expense, and their liability to beneficiaries for non-repair will depend on (inter alia) the extent to which there is available income or capital of the trust fund to pay for the repairs. See further paras **[208.26]**–**[208.28]**.

[207.3]

Changes in the asset after the will is made. It is usually the sale during the testator's lifetime of property specifically given by his will which gives rise to questions of ademption. In the case of leaseholds additional problems may arise as a leasehold interest in property may cease to exist by merger on the purchase of the reversion expectant on the determination of the lease. However, merger has generally been construed as not amounting to an ademption. In some cases it has been considered as falling within the WA 1837, s 23 (Part G, para **[244.25]**), which provides that no alteration of the testator's interest shall operate to revoke a devise or bequest, be it greater or smaller at the time of his death than at the date of his will, and by the WA 1837, s 24 (Part G, para **[244.26]**) the will as to the property included within any devise or bequest speaks as from the testator's death. Again what passes under a gift is a question of construction of the words used by the testator and if he merely 'devises' his interest in certain lands, clearly this may pass the fee and this has been held to be so even where the testator has included the word 'term' in his description: see *Saxton v Saxton* (1879) 13 Ch D 359 ('all his term and interest') and an even stronger case: *Struthers v Struthers* (1857) 5 WR 809 (where the devise was for all the residue of the terms). Other cases in this line of cases are *Miles v Miles* (1866) LR 1 Eq 462; *Cox v Bennett* (1868) LR 6 Eq 422 and most recently of all *Re Fleming's Will Trusts, Ennion v Hampstead Old People's Housing Trust Ltd* [1974] 3 All ER 323, [1974] 1 WLR 1552 ('my leasehold house, 54 Narcissus Road'). A case contrary to the foregoing is *Emuss v Smith* (1848) 2 De G & Sm 722, which is generally explained as being a devise of specific property. In that case a testator by his will as varied by a codicil gave all his freehold property at B which he had purchased from C. A small part of the land purchased was leasehold of which he purchased the freehold after the date of the codicil, but this was held not to pass under the devise. In *Ross v Perrin-Hughes* [2004] EWHC 2559 (Ch), [2004] All ER (D) 159 (Nov) a testator who had purchased the lease of a first floor maisonette and the freehold reversion to the building in which the maisonette was situated at the same time was held to have given both in a gift of '... my apartment and contents'.

[207.4]

Renewed leases. In the case of a specific gift of 'my present lease' where the lease has expired but been renewed the donee may take the renewed lease: *Re Reeves, Reeves v Pawson* [1928] Ch 351, [1928] All ER Rep 342 (the will was confirmed by a codicil executed after the renewal); but where the old lease was surrendered, the donee took only so much of the new term as corresponded with the unexpired part of the old on surrender: *Wedgwood v Denton* (1871) LR 12 Eq 290.

[207.5]

For a form of declaration which makes it clear that the freehold or a successor lease is carried by the gift, see Form B7.6 at para **[207.20]**. For a form of a gift of a leasehold flat which will carry with it any new lease with an extended term and any interest in the freehold obtained under the provisions of the LRA 1967 or the Leasehold Reform, Housing and Urban Development Act 1993 (LRHUDA 1993), see Form B7.2 at para **[207.16]**.

[207.6]
Settled leaseholds. The Settled Land Act 1925 (SLA 1925) can no longer apply to new trusts of land created on or after 1 January 1997 all of which are trusts of land within the meaning of the TLATA 1996 (see para **[207.2]**).

[207.7]
Old settled leaseholds. In relation to Settled Land Act settlements which existed and held land on 31 December 1996 and which have continued to do so the old learning still applies. In such cases under the SLA 1925, s 79, if the tenant for life of such leaseholds exercises his power of sale, the trustees may, notwithstanding anything in the SLA 1925, require the purchase money to be laid out, invested, accumulated or paid in such manner as in their judgment will give to the parties interested in that money the like benefit as they might lawfully have had from the lease. Parties interested may apply for an order of the court in these terms. In general the operation of the section is to give the tenant for life not only the income from the purchase money or the investments representing it but also in each year a part of the capital so that the fund will be exhausted at the time when the lease would have expired (see *Re Simpson, Clarke v Simpson* [1913] 1 Ch 277). This power is wholly discretionary in the trustees or in the court (*Re Duke of Westminster Settled Estates, Duke of Westminster v Earl of Shaftesbury* [1921] 1 Ch 585 at 599, [1921] All ER Rep 702 at 707), and a declaration to the contrary in the will would seem a sufficient safeguard against the exercise of such a power. Where the lease is short, the exclusion of the power may result in harsh treatment of the life tenant, for, having regard to allowance for dilapidations, the lease will not realise a great sum and the interest on the purchase money will be much less than the rent. A rather similar provision in principle provides for the capitalisation of the rent of a mining lease: SLA 1925, s 47. Under the new regime applicable to trusts of land there is no equivalent to the SLA 1925, s 79 which was a provision which went with the tenant for life having a power of sale.

[207.8]
A testator wishing to leave a leasehold upon trust for successive interests may wish to establish a sinking fund to secure the replacement of the wasting value of the leasehold. If the sinking fund is to be funded from the rents and profits of the leasehold before payment of the net rents and profits to the person entitled to the same for the time being, unless the direction for the establishment of the sinking fund is regarded as an administrative provision rather than a dispositive provision the settled leasehold will be treated for inheritance tax purposes as if there was no interest in possession in at least a part, and possibly the whole, of it. However, it seems that such a direction can be regarded as an administrative provision rather than a dispositive provision so that the person entitled to the net rents and profits should be regarded as having an interest in possession in the whole, see *Miller v IRC* [1987] STC 108. For a discussion of the difference between dispositive provisions and administrative provisions, see *Foster's Inheritance Tax*, E1.42 and E1.43, and for the charge to inheritance tax where there is no interest in possession, see paras **[208.30]–[208.35]** and **[218.6]** ff. For two forms establishing sinking funds, see Forms B7.11 and B7.12 at paras **[207.25]** and **[207.26]**.

[207.9]
The Leasehold Reform Act 1967. The LRA 1967 (whose scope has been extended by the LRHUDA 1993 and the Housing Act 1996 (HA 1996) to cover high value houses and those which fail the low rent test of the LRA 1967), the terms of which have been held by the European Court of Human Rights not to infringe the European Convention on Human Rights, allows certain tenants, occupying under long leases at low rents, either to purchase the freehold of their premises or to extend their leases for a further period of 50 years.

Where a flat forming part of a house is let to a person who is a qualifying tenant, one of the conditions to be fulfilled is that the tenant must, when he gives notice under the LRA 1967, have been occupying the premises as his only or main residence (s 1(1ZB)(a)) for the last two years or for periods amounting to two out of the last ten years (s 1(1ZB)(b) as amended by the Commonhold and Leasehold Reform Act 2002). Section 6 is relevant to cases involving the occupation of premises by beneficiaries under trusts, created by will or otherwise. The primary relevance of s 6 is to strict settlements under the SLA 1925 (which cannot be created after 1 January 1997). Briefly it provides:

(a) That a tenant who currently occupies premises as a direct tenant and who formerly occupied them either as a sole tenant for life under a strict settlement or as a beneficiary under a trust of land, who was entitled or permitted to occupy the premises by reason of his beneficial interest (including an interest as beneficial joint tenant or tenant in common), may treat periods of occupation in the earlier capacity as qualifying periods under the Act. It is not clear whether this includes an interest in an estate in the course of administration; where the person entitled under the will to a lease of a house is already in occupation, the executors should consider making an early assent in his favour. Where a tenant of a house dies and, immediately before his death, he had the right to acquire the freehold or the right to an extended lease, the right is exercisable by his personal representatives while the lease is vested in them.
(b) That an individual who is currently a sole tenant for life under a strict settlement shall have the same rights in respect of his occupation as if the tenancy belonged to him beneficially.
(c) That where premises are vested in trustees and a beneficiary under the trust is entitled or permitted to occupy them by reason of his beneficial interest, the *trustees* shall have the same rights as the occupant himself would have had if he were occupying in right of the tenancy.
(d) That without prejudice to any powers exercisable under the SLA 1925 by tenants for life or statutory owners, where the tenancy of premises is vested in trustees, then unless the instrument regulating the trusts (made after the passing of the Act) provides to the contrary the trustees shall have power to acquire and retain the freehold or an extended lease under the Act.
(e) That the purposes authorised for the application of capital money under a strict settlement or a trust for sale, and the purposes for which money may be raised by mortgage, shall include the payment of any

expenses incurred in or in connection with proceedings taken in virtue of the provisions summarised in sub-paras (b) and (c) above.

[207.10]

Testator's period of residence may count in favour of successor. If the testator had a lease of a house such that enfranchisement under the LRA 1967 would have been possible if the residence condition had been fulfilled, anyone who inherits the lease from the testator under his will or intestacy, and is a member of the testator's family (within the definition in the LRA 1967, s 7(7)) who has been living with him in the property, may be able to count his or her period of residence with the testator in the house as part of his or her three-year period of residence as tenant, for the purposes of qualifying for enfranchisement: see the LRA 1967, s 7, which applies even where the lease is inherited as a part of a residuary gift (s 7(2)(b)). It is therefore advisable, where practical, for a testator to leave a lease which could qualify for enfranchisement to a member of the testator's family who has been living with him, especially if it is a lease with only a few years to run which might run out before someone who inherited it had himself lived there for two years.

[207.11]

The Leasehold Reform, Housing and Urban Development Act 1993. Sections 1 to 38 give to long leaseholders of flats paying a low rent in a predominantly residential building ('qualifying tenants') the right to purchase collectively at market value the freehold of the building. Where trustees are a qualifying tenant of a flat their powers include the participation in a claim to collective enfranchisement or to apply for a new lease unless the trust instrument was made on or after 1 October 1996 and contains an explicit direction to the contrary: LRHUDA 1993, s 93A, as inserted by the HA 1996.

[207.12]

Death of participating tenant. Where an initial notice has been given for collective enfranchisement and one of the participating tenants dies his personal representatives must within 56 days of his death notify the nominee purchaser who is conducting the sale on behalf of the participating tenants of his death and whether or not they are electing to withdraw from participation in the proposed transaction, and unless they elect to withdraw they will be regarded as a participating tenant as from the death of the tenant and so long as the lease is vested in them: LRHUDA 1993, s 14(5) and (6). Where personal representatives then assent to the vesting of the lease in any person, that person must within 14 days notify the nominee purchaser of the assignment and whether or not he is electing to participate in the proposed transaction: LRHUDA 1993, s 14(2).

[207.13]

Acquisition of new lease. Sections 39 to 62 of the LRHUDA 1993 give to a person who has been a qualifying tenant for the last two years the right to acquire a new lease of his flat: LRHUDA 1993, s 39(2). On the death of a person who has been a qualifying tenant for two years before his death, the right to enfranchise under LRHUDA 1993 extends to his personal representatives (s. 39(3A)). Where the lease by virtue of which the qualifying tenant is a qualifying tenant is vested in trustees (other than a sole tenant for life within the meaning of the SLA 1925), the right arises if an individual having an interest under the trust satisfies the occupation conditions: LRHUDA 1993, s 39(2A), as inserted by the HA 1996. If a tenant who has given notice of his claim to acquire a new lease dies, his personal representatives and their assigns stand in his place: LRHUDA 1993, s 43.

[207.14]

Inheritance tax relief. As already mentioned, inheritance tax payable on a specific gift of a leasehold property is prima facie a testamentary expense payable out of residue. For notes on business relief see C11 at para **[233.1]** ff and for notes on agricultural and woodlands relief see C12 at para **[234.1]** ff.

[207.15]

Form B7.1: Gift of leaseholds

I give to [*name*] my leasehold property [together with the outbuildings and garage thereto] situate at —— in the county of —— and known as No —— Street[1] [for all the residue which shall at my death be unexpired of the term for which the same are held [*or* of the term created by the lease dated —— and made between *parties*] subject to the rent lessees' covenants and conditions therein reserved and contained]].

1 The bequest will normally end here for the donee could not take the benefit of the gift without assuming its burdens. The donee will be at liberty to disclaim the gift provided it is not associated with some other benefit given in consideration of his accepting the burden of this gift, eg where the term is short and the liability for dilapidations may be heavy (see *Re Lysons, Beck v Lysons* (1912) 107 LT 146).

[207.16]

Form B7.2: Gift of leasehold flat and devise of any interest in freehold of premises in which flat is contained[1]

I give to [*name*] my leasehold flat known as —— and situate at —— for all the residue which shall at my death be unexpired of the term for which the same is held subject to the rent lessees' covenants and conditions therein reserved and contained and I also give all that my interest if any in the freehold of the premises in which the said flat is contained.

1 This gift would carry the residue of any lease which the testator has at his death in the named premises. So if, for example, he is granted before his death a new lease under the LRHUDA 1993, Pt I, Ch III extending his original term by 90 years this lease will pass under this gift. Also this gift will carry with it any interest in the freehold which the testator may have acquired by virtue of the exercise of the rights for collective enfranchisement under the LRHUDA 1993.

One of the conditions which must be met for a tenant to acquire a 90-year extension of the lease of his flat under the LRHUDA 1993 is that he must have been a qualifying tenant for two years. It is no longer necessary for the tenant to have occupied the flat as his only or principal home.

[207.17]

Form B7.3: Gift of leasehold house free from mortgage

I give my leasehold residence and premises known as —— to my wife absolutely freed and discharged from any mortgage debt or other charge affecting the same which I direct shall be paid out of my residuary [personal] estate.[1]

1 See s 35 of the AEA 1925 (Part G, para **[246.62]**) under which section the property would bear its own charges if this contrary intention had not been shown. See also paras **[204.76]**, n 1 and **[206.23]**, n 1.

[207.18]

Form B7.4: Gift of leaseholds with a direction that the legatee is to pay all arrears of rent and cost of dilapidations

I give my leasehold residence and premises at —— to [*name*] absolutely he paying the rent payable in respect thereof and performing and observing the covenants in the lease thereof contained and on the lessee's part to be performed and observed and I declare that the rent in respect thereof owing or accruing at my death and the costs and expenses of putting the said premises into repair in compliance with the provisions of the said lease shall be borne and paid by the said [*name*] in exoneration of my residuary estate.[1]

1 As to disclaimer of onerous gifts, see *Guthrie v Walrond* (1883) 22 Ch D 573; *Re Loom, Fulford v Reversionary Interest Society Ltd* [1910] 2 Ch 230; *Re Lysons, Beck v Lysons* (1912) 107 LT 146 and Vol 1, para **[46.3]**. For forms of disclaimer see Forms F3.1 to F3.3 at paras **[241.22]–[241.24]**.

[207.19]

Form B7.5: Gift of leaseholds to trustees upon trust to pay rents and profits to a person for life, and after his death to assign to another

I give my leasehold property situate at —— in the county of —— known as —— and now in the occupation of —— [or all my leasehold property lands and hereditaments] to my trustees for all the residue unexpired of any term [or terms] for which I may hold the same [respectively] at my death. Upon trust that my trustees shall out of the rents and profits thereof pay the rent and all other expenses charges and outgoings payable from time to time in respect thereof and perform and observe the covenants on the part of the lessee to be performed or observed and shall pay the residue of such rents and profits to [*name*] during his life and after his death shall stand possessed of the said leasehold premises and the rents and profits thereof in trust for and shall assign the same to [*name*] absolutely.[1]

1 See para **[207.6]**.

[207.20]

Form B7.6: Declaration that gift of lease includes the freehold reversion or any renewal if subsequently acquired

I declare that if in my lifetime I shall by purchase or otherwise become and be at my death the owner of the freehold reversion expectant on the determination of any leasehold term hereby given the same shall notwithstanding any gift in this my will or any codicil hereto contained enure for the benefit of the person or persons for the time being and from time to time beneficially entitled to such leasehold term and the property comprised therein and shall pass to or be held in trust for him or them as if included in the gift of such property hereinbefore contained and similarly if any such lease shall expire in my lifetime and shall be renewed by the lessor or if I shall surrender any such lease in consideration of the grant of a new lease, then such renewed or new lease shall pass to or be held in trust for him or them as if included in the gift of such property hereinbefore contained.[1]

1 See the Preliminary Note at paras **[207.9]–[207.13]**. The insertion of this clause prevents any question arising as to the testator's intention.

[207.21]

Form B7.7: Contingent gift of leaseholds

I give my leasehold house known as —— unto my trustees upon trust for my niece [A] if and when she attains the age of twenty-five years.[1]

1 A contingent or future specific devise or bequest carries the intermediate income (subject to the provisions as to accumulations contained in the Act) from the death of the testator, except so far as the income is otherwise *expressly* disposed of (LPA 1925, s 175: Part G, para **[244.54]**). During the minority of the beneficiary, the income will be available for maintenance; if the beneficiary on attaining eighteen has not yet obtained a vested interest, the whole income will be payable to the beneficiary until he attains a vested interest, or dies, or his interest is otherwise defeated (TA 1925, s 31, as amended by the FLRA 1969, s 1(3) and Sch 1, Pt 1: Part G, para **[246.28]**). By virtue of the LPA 1925, s 165 (Part G, para **[246.57]**) any period of minority during which accumulations are made under statutory power (e g the above section of the TA 1925) is not to be taken into account in determining whether a direction for accumulation goes beyond the period permitted by the LPA 1925, ss 164 or 166 (Part G, paras **[246.56]** and **[246.58]**) and the PAA 1964, s 13 (Part G, para **[246.86]**). See generally Vol 1, at para **[95.1]** ff and the note in B18 at para **[218.41]** ff. There will thus be accumulation and maintenance trusts within the IHTA 1984, s 71, for which see Part A, para **[200.107]** ff.

[207.22]

Form B7.8: Gift of undivided share in leaseholds

I give all my undivided share[s] in the leasehold premises situate at —— in the county of —— known as ——to [*name*] absolutely [*or* to my trustees upon trust to etc].[1]

1 See para **[204.67]**, n 1.

[207.23]

Form B7.9: Gift of sinking fund policies in respect of leasehold properties

I give to my trustees my sinking fund policies upon trust to hold the moneys received in respect of such policies and the proceeds of the sale or surrender of such policies under the power hereinafter contained on the trusts hereinafter declared concerning my residuary [personal] estate.

My trustees shall pay all premiums and other sums payable in respect of the said policies out of the income of my residuary [personal] estate.

If my trustees shall sell any leasehold property covered by any such policy they may at their absolute discretion sell or surrender any policy maintained in respect of the property so sold.

[207.24]

Form B7.10: Declaration as to inheritance tax on settled leaseholds[1]

I declare that the inheritance tax upon and by reason of my death attributable to the settled gift of leaseholds contained in clause —— hereof shall be borne by and paid out of the leasehold property thereby settled in exoneration of my personal estate and shall be raised by my trustees by mortgage or charge thereof or by a sale of a competent part thereof and be paid accordingly.

1 Inheritance tax on leaseholders will in the absence of a direction such as this be payable out of residue: see the note to B14 at para **[214.59]** ff.

[207.25]

Form B7.11: Gift of leaseholds upon trust out of the rents and profits to form sinking fund[1]

I give all my leasehold lands to my trustees upon the trusts and with the directions following:

(1) In the first place to pay out of the rents and profits thereof the rents payable in respect of the leases under which the same are held and perform and observe the lessees' covenants therein contained.

(2) In the next place to raise out of the said rents and profits any such annual sum (either for the premium or premiums in respect of a policy or policies of insurance to be effected by my trustees or by way of investment in their names and accumulation during any period allowed by law[2]) as shall be sufficient in their opinion to provide at the expiration of the respective leases for which I hold the said leasehold lands a capital sum of £—— and to apply the annual sum so raised in paying the premiums for keeping on foot such policy or policies of insurance or by way of investment in the names of my trustees and accumulation accordingly.

(3) Subject thereto to stand possessed of my said leasehold lands and the rents and profits thereof upon trust etc [*set out the trusts of the surplus rents and profits*]

(4) My trustees shall invest the said sum of £—— as and when received or provided as aforesaid in manner herein mentioned and shall stand possessed thereof and of the investments for the time being representing the same and the income thereof upon the like trusts and subject to the like provisions in all respects as are hereinbefore declared and contained concerning my said leasehold lands and the rents and profits thereof so far as the same trusts and provisions may then be subsisting and capable of taking effect.

1 See para **[207.6]**. A clause of this kind could have adverse inheritance tax consequences in that it could be said that as part of the income of the trust property is to be accumulated there will be no interest in possession in at least a part of it, and possibly the whole, since the amount of income is decided by the trustees in their discretion. However, if the capital

sum for which the trustees are to make provision at the expiry of the leases is no greater than the value of the leases as at the testator's death, so that the provision is merely one which directs the trustees to meet depreciation and not to increase the capital value of the trust assets, it may be that this can properly be regarded as an administrative provision rather than a dispositive provision, so that there will be an interest in possession in the whole: see *Miller v IRC* [1987] STC 108.

2 Accumulations are now governed by the LPA 1925, s 164 ff (Part G, para **[246.66]** ff) and the PAA 1964, s 13 (Part G, para **[246.86]**) but this clause seems to be valid for any accumulation and certainly in so far as it provides for keeping up a policy however long its provisions continue: *Re Gardiner, Gardiner v Smith* [1901] 1 Ch 697.

[207.26]

Form B7.12: Alternative provision for sinking fund to replace leasehold value[1]

I give all my leasehold lands unto my trustees upon the trusts and with the directions following:

(1) Upon trust in the first place to pay out of the rents and profits thereof the rents payable in respect of the leases under which the same are held and to perform and observe the lessees' covenants therein contained and subject thereto to set aside out of the rents and profits of each such leasehold in each year such a sum and for such period as hereinafter directed.

(2) Subject as aforesaid my trustees shall stand possessed of the said leasehold lands and the rents and profits thereof upon trust [*set out the trusts of the leaseholds and the rents and profits*].

(3) The sum so to be set aside (as a sinking fund to secure the replacement of the wasting value of each leasehold) out of the net rents and profits of each leasehold in each year shall be calculated by dividing the net rents and profits of the year by one more than the number of complete years which at the date of my death the lease of that property has to run.

[(4) But such setting aside shall not be made for a longer period than twenty-one years from my death.]

(5) In respect of each such leasehold the said annual sums deducted or set aside as aforesaid shall be invested as one fund and shall be accumulated by investing the income thereof as an accretion to that fund.

(6) Such accumulations shall cease [at the expiration of twenty-one years from my death *or*] upon the expiration of such lease while still held by my trustees or upon the sale of the leasehold in respect of which the said fund is being set aside and accumulated whichever period shall be the shortest.

(7) Thereafter the fund so formed and the future income thereof shall be held by my trustees upon the same trusts (save for the setting aside of a sum out of income) as the leasehold itself is being held by my trustees or would be held if it had not expired or been sold, as the case may be, so far as the same trusts and provisions may then be subsisting and capable of taking effect.

(8) And I specially declare that the fund so set aside and accumulated in respect of a leasehold shall be primarily liable for all claims for

dilapidations and breaches of covenant if such leasehold shall be still held by my trustees at the date of expiration of the lease thereof.[2]

1 See para **[207.25]**, n 1. This form is preferable in that the sum to be set aside is expressly to form a sinking fund to meet depreciation, and so is arguably an administrative provision rather than a dispositive provision. But if it should be thought to be a dispositive provision rather than an administrative provision, since the amount to be accumulated is determined by a formula, there is less risk of the clause causing there to be no interest in possession in the entire property.

2 A direction to set aside annual sums out of rents to secure replacement is not within the Thellusson Act, whether the sums be expended in keeping up a policy or in actual investment; neither is the direction to accumulate the income of the sums invested, see *Re Gardiner, Gardiner v Smith* [1901] 1 Ch 697, and *Re Hurlbatt, Hurlbatt v Hurlbatt* [1910] 2 Ch 553, at any rate as long as it is made bona fide for replacement, and not for the purpose of evading the Act. The same principle applies to a reserve fund where the executors are empowered to carry on a business: *Re Crabtree* (1911) 106 LT 49; *Re Robertson* [1953] 2 SCR 1. Sections 164 ff of the LPA 1925 (Part G, para **[246.66]** ff) (which replace the Thellusson Act), do not appear to alter the position. For the taxation of accumulated income see the note to B18 at para **[218.30]**.

B8 Rights of residence

Preliminary Note .... **[208.1]**
THE STATUTORY RIGHT OF OCCUPATION UNDER A TRUST OF LAND .... **[208.5]**
GIVING RIGHTS OF RESIDENCE BY WILL .... **[208.19]**
OTHER ASPECTS .... **[208.29]**
TRUSTS OF LAND
FORMS
B8.1 Interest of beneficiary limited to a right of residence with provision for changing residences .... **[208.38]**
B8.2 Interest of beneficiary limited to right of residence, with the beneficiary's consent to a sale being required generally, with provision for changing residences .... **[208.39]**
B8.3 Trust to permit residence and use of furniture etc by the testator's wife and children .... **[208.40]**
B8.4 Trust for wife for life or until she remarries and then for son, with power to permit residence .... **[208.41]**
B8.5 Trust for civil partner for life or until marriage or the formation of another civil partnership and then for son, with power to permit residence .... **[208.42]**
B8.6 Gift of residence for wife for life with the intention that she reside there—fuller form, providing for the possibility of a change of house by the testator before his death or by the trustees after his death .... **[208.43]**
B8.7 Clause in will of widow or widower providing residence and furniture for children .... **[208.44]**
MISCELLANEOUS
FORMS
B8.8 Gift with the object of ensuring personal residence, giving the right to a series of short leases .... **[208.45]**
B8.9 The like—in the form of a lease determinable on death with rentcharge to support residence .... **[208.46]**
B8.10 Gift with the object of ensuring personal residence by the devisee—alternative form using a periodic tenancy .... **[208.47]**
B8.11 Gift of the testator's interest as tenant in common in a house, the gift being postponed to allow the other tenants in common to continue to reside in the house .... **[208.48]**

PRELIMINARY NOTE

[208.1]
Cases often arise in which the testator wishes to provide a house for a beneficiary or beneficiaries to live in. Where the beneficiary or beneficiaries are also interested in residue a separate gift of a residence may be unnecessary; instead the trustees of residue can be given power to purchase, retain etc a residence for a beneficiary as in, eg Form C2.1, cl 9(3)(h) at para **[224.37]** or Forms B18.24 to B18.26 at paras **[218.110]–[218.112]**. However, a specific gift of the kind considered here can still be appropriate even if the beneficiary or beneficiaries are interested in residue, for example where it is

desired to give provision of a residence priority over legacies and residuary gifts, or to make sure the property concerned is resorted to last to pay liabilities of the estate.

[208.2]
Two methods of providing a residence by specific gift are to be found in the forms in B8 as explained at paras **[208.3]** and **[208.4]**.

[208.3]
The first method—a trust of land under the Trusts of Land and Appointment of Trustees Act 1996. The Trusts of Land and Appointment of Trustees Act 1996 (TLATA 1996) (Part G, para **[246.103]** ff) has, in relation to the creation of new trusts (whether by will or lifetime disposition), replaced the former alternative regimes of trusts for sale and settled land with a single trust of land, which can still be a trust for sale but it makes little or no difference whether there is a trust for sale or not. The basic scheme of the TLATA 1996 and its consequences are described in Part A at para **[200.48]** ff. The notes below first discuss the rights of occupation given to beneficiaries by the TLATA 1996 (see paras **[208.5]**–**[208.18]**) and then more specific points to consider when getting instructions for and drafting trusts to provide a residence (see paras **[208.19]**–**[208.37]**). The TLATA 1996 is particularly orientated towards trusts of land for occupation by beneficiaries, and it does enable some simplification of the drafting of trusts of this type. For reasons given at paras **[200.55]** and **[200.56]** it is recommended that trusts for sale should not in general be used in trusts of land, and it is particularly inappropriate to provide a trust for sale where the purpose of the trust is or includes providing a property for residential or other occupation by a beneficiary.

[208.4]
The second method—grant of a lease by the trustees to the beneficiary. This may be a suitable method in some cases, but may in others be unsatisfactory. In particular, it should be noted that the gift of a lease terminable on or by reference to a death is now treated as the equivalent of a life interest in settled property for inheritance tax purposes (see the Inheritance Tax Act 1984 (IHTA 1984), s 43(3)) and on disadvantageous terms compared with a true settlement since the reversion is not excluded property: IHTA 1984, s 48(1)(c). It is thus better in general to create a life interest under a settlement, but we have retained the lease precedents for the sake of completeness and because some may fall outside the ambit of the IHTA 1984, s 43(3). See Forms B8.8 to B8.10 at paras **[208.45]**–**[208.47]**. For HMRC's treatment of leases for life for inheritance tax purposes, see their Inheritance Tax Manual at IHTM16191.

The statutory right of occupation under a trust of land

[208.5]
The statutory right of occupation. The statutory rights of occupation described below are not confined in their application to residential property held on trust, but can be relevant to any kind of land in England and Wales

held on trust which is capable of being occupied by a beneficiary, eg a farm or business premises. These rights are discussed in this part of this work because trusts to provide residences are probably the most common type of trust of land for occupation by a beneficiary created by will. Section 12(1) of the TLATA 1996 (Part G, para **[246.115]**) provides a right of occupation for a beneficiary 'who is beneficially entitled to an interest in possession' in land subject to a trust of land (see para **[200.51]** for the meaning of 'trust of land' and para **[208.12]** ff for the meaning of 'interest in possession') at any time if at that time *either* (a) the purposes of the trust include making the land available for his occupation (or for the occupation of a class of which he is a member or of beneficiaries in general) *or* (b) the land is held by the trustees so as to be so available. This is subject to the right not being available if the land is either unavailable or unsuitable for occupation by him: TLATA 1996, s 12(2). The trustees may impose reasonable conditions on a beneficiary in relation to his occupation of land including payment of outgoings and assuming any other obligation in relation to the land or any activity conducted there (eg a farming business): TLATA 1996, s 13(3), (5) (Part G, para **[246.116]**). Where two or more beneficiaries are entitled to occupy land the trustees may exclude or restrict the entitlement to occupy of one or more but not all of them, but may not do so unreasonably (TLATA 1996, s 13(1), (2)), and the trustees can require compensatory provision to be made for anyone excluded: TLATA 1996, s 13(6). Section 13(6) contemplates two possibilities, that a beneficiary who occupies the land may be required to pay a 'rent' to an excluded beneficiary or beneficiaries, or that he forgoes benefit from another part of the trust fund so that a compensating additional benefit from that other part is received by the excluded beneficiary or beneficiaries.

[208.6]
Comparison with previous law. This right of occupation is completely new as compared with the previous statutory provisions concerning trusts for sale, under which there were no statutory rights of occupation for beneficiaries. The courts had held that beneficial joint tenants and tenants in common had rights of occupation (*Bull v Bull* [1955] 1 QB 234; *City of London Building Society v Flegg* [1988] AC 54), but it was not clear whether the same was true of someone with a life interest under a trust for sale of land, and it was common to provide expressly in trusts for sale for persons in succession that the trustees either should permit, or had a power to permit, occupation by a beneficiary or beneficiaries. The new statutory right of occupation puts someone with a life interest under a trust of land in a position similar (as regards the right to occupy trust property) to that of a tenant for life under a Settled Land Act 1925 settlement (because a tenant for life of settled land under that Act has a right of occupation of the land by virtue of having the legal estate vested in him).

[208.7]
Land available for occupation. There are two main requirements of the TLATA 1996, s 12 (Part G, para **[246.115]**) for a beneficiary to have the right to occupy trust land. First, he must be beneficially entitled to an interest in possession in it, a separate topic discussed at paras **[208.12]** and **[208.13]**.

Secondly, either the purposes of the trust must include making the land available for occupation by the beneficiary (or beneficiaries of a class of which he is a member or of beneficiaries in general) (TLATA 1996, s 12(1)(a)), or the land must be held by the trustees so as to be so available: TLATA 1996, s 12(1)(b). Could s 12(1)(a) apply solely by virtue of the will or settlement conferring a standard-form administrative power to permit occupation by beneficiaries? The words in brackets in s 12(1)(a) suggest that this may be so, but it seems peculiar that the existence of express powers of this kind in the will or settlement could confer such a right when those powers duplicate powers which are conferred on all trustees of land by statute. Does s 12(1)(b) confer a right of occupation of any land held by the trustees which is for the time being vacant (subject to suitability, etc under the TLATA 1996, s 12(2)), or must the trustees make some decision or take some action to make it available first? We feel that the latter view would produce a more sensible result, but the position is unclear, and it is certainly possible that any beneficiary with an interest in possession can claim the right to occupy land which is for the time being vacant (again subject to suitability, etc within s 12(2)). This can be illustrated by the example of a residuary estate consisting of residential properties let to tenants, with the testator's widow having a life interest, and the purposes of the trust within s 12(1)(a) not including making land available for her occupation. A tenant of a residential property departs, leaving it vacant. Does the life tenant then have a right of occupation of that property, ie is it one which is held by the trustees so as to be available for occupation by her within s 12(1)(b), or does it only become so held if the trustees decide eg not to re-let and to repair it and offer it to the widow as a residence?

[208.8]
Suitability for occupation. Even where the requirements of the TLATA 1996, s 12(1) are met (see para **[208.7]**), s 12(2) qualifies the right by excluding it where the land is unavailable or unsuitable for occupation by him. The duplication of the availability test, i.e. that it appears in both s 12(1)(b) and in s 12(2), is slightly puzzling, but the explanation may be that 'unavailable' in terms of s 12(2) is intended for s 12(1)(a) cases, i.e. where the purposes of the trust are to make the land available. The exclusion by s 12(2) of a beneficiary's right of occupation where the land is unsuitable for that beneficiary's occupation is perhaps aimed at the kind of case where say the land is 6,000 acres of prime agricultural land and the beneficiary is bankrupt and has a drink problem. However, this would be better characterised as the beneficiary being unsuitable for occupation of the land rather than the land being unsuitable for the beneficiary's occupation. If the land is a light industrial unit and the beneficiary is looking for a residence, it seems clear that the right of occupation is excluded by s 12(2), although whether this is a case of unsuitability or unavailability it is probably not necessary to decide. A large country house would presumably be 'unsuitable' within s 12(2) for say an elderly widow who only needs a bed-sitting room. In general, s 12(2) is conceptually fuzzy and in many circumstances will create uncertainty as to whether the right to occupy has arisen or not, and it has potential for dispute between trustee and beneficiary.

[208.9]

Two or more beneficiaries. A more complicated difficulty arises where there are beneficiaries with similar concurrent interests but only some of whom for the time being have interests in possession. This is best illustrated by an example. Suppose that there is a trust of a farm for a class of four minor beneficiaries, who get vested interests in capital and income in equal shares at the age of 25 and attain interests in possession in their respective presumptive shares at the age of 18 under the Trustee Act 1925, s 31 by virtue of becoming entitled to be paid the current income of those shares (see para **[208.12]** as to whether this is an interest in possession in the land). The trustees farm the land themselves, employing a manager. The eldest of the beneficiaries then attains 18. Suppose that the TLATA 1996, s 12(1)(a) or (b) applies, either because a purpose of the trust is occupation by beneficiaries, or because (contrary to the tentative view expressed at para **[208.7]**) s 12(1)(b) is satisfied by the mere fact of there being vacant land in the trust. He then becomes a beneficiary entitled to occupy the land under the TLATA 1996, s 12 and cannot be prevented from doing so, subject only to the possible arguments that the land is not 'available' or not 'suitable' for occupation by him (TLATA 1996, s 12(2)) and to the right of the trustees to impose reasonable conditions on him in relation to his occupation: TLATA 1996, s 13(3) and (5). The trustees cannot exclude a beneficiary under the power in s 13(1) unless there are at least two beneficiaries with interests in possession, and then they cannot exclude all of them. It seems likely that 'reasonable conditions' would include requiring him to take over the farming business, including its liabilities, in particular the trustees' existing contractual liabilities to the farm manager and any borrowing secured on the land: TLATA 1996, s 13(5)(b). This may be impossible for the beneficiary to satisfy but if he is able to do so the difficult question then arises as to whether he can be required to pay compensation for the benefit of the beneficiaries who are still under 18. Section 13(6) of the TLATA 1996 (under which the trustees can require a beneficiary who is in occupation to make compensation arrangements in favour of beneficiaries who are not) only applies where there are two or more beneficiaries with interests in possession, and it has no application to this example of one of a class of beneficiaries having an interest in possession while the others do not. There is thus a lack of specific express provision for such a case. However, the question then arises whether the trustees can impose compensatory provisions on the occupying beneficiary for the benefit of the other three beneficiaries under the general power to impose reasonable conditions in the TLATA 1996, s 13(3). The appropriate condition would be that an appropriate rent for three-quarters of the value of the land be paid to the trustees to be treated as income of the three-quarters of the fund still subject to accumulation and maintenance trusts. The occupying beneficiary could, however, put up a strong case for saying that a condition as to compensation of this kind can only be imposed to compensate other beneficiaries *who have a right of occupation under the Act which they are not able to exercise* (and this idea is supported by the TLATA 1996, s 15(2)). The trustees could reply that it is only fair to require compensation in circumstances where other beneficiaries have an interest in the property which would, in the absence of such compensation, bring them no benefit, but which would bring them an income benefit if the property was yielding income.

[208.10]
Sub-trusts. Another somewhat unexpected result arises where there is a sub-trust of a beneficial interest, again best illustrated by an example. Suppose that a husband H and his wife W own a house as tenants in common. H dies, leaving his half share to his executors and trustees to hold it on trust for their daughter D for life. It seems from the TLATA 1996, ss 12(1) and 22(1), (2) (Part G, paras **[246.115]** and **[246.125]** respectively) that W has a right of occupation of the house under s 12 and D and H's will trustees do not have such a right: see '*Trustees with a Part Interest in Land: The impact of the Trusts of Land and Appointment of Trustees Act 1996*', Chris Jarman, [2007] PCB 263. This is because s 22(1) provides that 'beneficiary' in relation to a trust means any person who *under the trust* (emphasis supplied) has an interest in property subject to the trust, which seems to exclude D from being a beneficiary under the trust of the house for the purposes of the TLATA 1996, s 12(1), and because, while s 22(1) provides that 'beneficiary' includes trustees of a sub-trust, s 22(2) provides that beneficiaries who are beneficially entitled do not include such trustees, with the consequence that the trustees of H's will do not have a right of occupation which they can allow D to use. As in the example at para **[208.9]**, there is a question as to whether the trustees of the house could require W to pay compensation to the trustees of H's will for D's benefit, as a reasonable condition within the TLATA 1996, s 13(3) in relation to W's continued occupation of the house (subject to the possibility that s 13(7), discussed at para **[208.11]**, prevents its imposition). The arguments for and against are the same as in the example given at para **[208.9]**.

[208.11]
Termination of occupation. A further point to note is that the termination of a beneficiary's occupation is made more difficult under the TLATA 1996 than it was under trusts for sale with a power to permit residence before 1 January 1997. Under the latter, the trustee could revoke the permission to reside and bring a possession action, whereas now the trustee will have to apply under the TLATA 1996, ss 13(7) or 14 (Part G, paras **[246.116]** and **[246.117]**) if there is some strong reason for the occupation to cease (e g the beneficiary is disabled or the house is falling into disrepair) and the beneficiary will not co-operate or is failing to fulfil obligations reasonably imposed by the trustee as a condition of occupation. Section 13(7) prohibits the powers of the trustees under s 13 being exercised so as to terminate the occupation of a beneficiary who is in occupation, or in a way likely to cause that beneficiary's occupation to cease, without that beneficiary's consent or the court's approval. Further, the right to occupy is not made conditional on observing the conditions reasonably imposed by the trustees under s 13(3), and the trustees cannot keep a beneficiary out of occupation while they decide on what conditions to impose. The trustees may well find that they have a more limited power to impose conditions if a beneficiary is in occupation than if he is not.

[208.12]

Meaning of 'interest in possession'. For a beneficiary to have a right to occupy trust land under the TLATA 1996, s 12(1) (Part G, para **[246.115]**) he must be 'beneficially entitled to an interest in possession' in it. This is perhaps the most important context in the TLATA 1996 where the expression 'interest in possession' appears, but it is also relevant to the power to delegate management of trust land in the TLATA 1996, s 9 (Part G, para **[246.111]**; see also para **[220.54]** ff) and the duty to consult beneficiaries in the TLATA 1996, s 11 (Part G, para **[246.112]**; see also para **[220.58]**). As in the inheritance tax legislation, there is no definition of 'interest in possession'. The only express provision in the TLATA 1996 is the exclusion of annuitants from having interests in possession in land subject to a trust: see the TLATA 1996, s 22(3) (Part G, para **[246.125]**) for inheritance tax purposes an annuitant does have an interest in possession in a share of the trust property. The use of the term 'interest in possession' in the TLATA 1996 is probably influenced by the IHTA 1984, but it does not follow that what is an interest in possession for the purposes of the IHTA 1984 is also one within the TLATA 1996, as the statutory purposes of the use of the term are different. However, as a working hypothesis, anything which is an interest in possession in land for inheritance tax purposes is likely to be one for the purposes of the TLATA 1996, subject to the differences noted at para **[208.13]**. For the meaning of 'interest in possession' for inheritance tax purposes see paras **[200.125]–[200.130]** and *Foster's Inheritance Tax*, E1.41–E1.49. For HMRC's treatment of interests in possession, see their Inheritance Tax Manual IHTM16061 and subsequent paragraphs.

[208.13]

The main differences between 'interest in possession' in the Trusts of Land and Appointment of Trustees Act 1996 and in the Inheritance Tax Act 1984—

(1) A trust of a property for X and Y as beneficial joint tenants, or as beneficial tenants in common in equal (or unequal) shares, fairly clearly gives both X and Y interests in possession in that property for the purposes of the TLATA 1996. They may also have interests in possession within the meaning of the IHTA 1984, but it is an academic question (except in relation to the IHTA 1984, s 91) because they are not interests in possession *in settled property* for the purposes of the IHTA 1984. Settled property in the IHTA 1984 (see IHTA 1984, s 43(2)) is trust property subject to interests other than absolute ones.

(2) In *Pearson v IRC* [1981] AC 753 it was held that a right to the income of a fund, but subject to a trustees' power to accumulate that income, is not an interest in possession for inheritance tax purposes. It is, however, likely that this is an interest in possession for the purposes of the TLATA 1996, and in relation to the TLATA 1996, s 12 there is the further point that s 12 will only apply where the land is available for occupation and so unlet and not yielding income, so that for the time being there is no question of the trustees being able to exercise the power of accumulation (for possible inheritance tax consequences of this see para **[208.17]**).

(3) Occupation of a trust property by a beneficiary under a discretionary trust as his permanent residence under an exercise of the trustees'

powers to permit it is regarded by HMRC as giving the beneficiary an interest in possession in that property for inheritance tax purposes (for the consequences post-Finance Act 2006 see Part A, para **[200.127]**). It may be that it is also an interest in possession for the purposes of the TLATA 1996, and in particular s 12, but this has no practical consequences, since if there is an interest in possession within the meaning of s 12 it is co-terminous with the occupation, i.e. there is no interest in possession, distinct from the permission to occupy, which gives rise to a right of occupation independently of the permission given by the trustees.

(4) As already mentioned, an annuity is an interest in possession under inheritance tax, and is not for the purposes of the TLATA 1996: TLATA 1996, s 22(3).

(5) In the sub-trust example discussed at paras **[208.10]** and **[208.16]**, the daughter D who has a life interest under a sub-trust of a half undivided share of a property is not a beneficiary in relation to the underlying co-ownership trust of the property. The normal inheritance tax rule is that she is treated as entitled to half the property for inheritance tax purposes; she has an interest in possession in the sub-trust's share of the property, and so by the IHTA 1984, s 49 she is treated as beneficially entitled to it if her interest in possession is one of those which, post Finance Act 2006, is not subject to the relevant property regime for inheritance tax purposes (see Part A, para **[200.127]**)). There is the possibility, discussed at paras **[208.10]** and **[208.16]**, that the operation of the TLATA 1996, ss 12, 13 and 22 might deprive her of any benefit from the property while W is living in it, but it may well be that this would not prevent her from being entitled to an interest in possession in half the property for inheritance tax purposes if she is otherwise so interested: see *Foster's Inheritance Tax*, E1.46.

(6) The view has been expressed (see Kenny and Kenny, *The Trusts of Land and Appointment of Trustees Act 1996* (1997), pp 47–15 and 47–16) that where property is held on trust for sale to hold the proceeds of sale and the net rents and profits until sale on trust for X, X does not have an interest in possession in the land for the purposes of the TLATA 1996. If this were correct, this type of case would be one where there could be an interest in possession for inheritance tax purposes but not under the TLATA 1996. However, it seems doubtful whether this is correct. It seems to us that to be entitled under a trust of land to be paid the current income of the land subject to the trust (other than by way of annuity) is to have an interest in possession in that land for the purposes of the TLATA 1996, irrespective of whether there is a trust for sale. If that were not the case, it would probably be unnecessary for the TLATA 1996, s 22(3) to exclude annuitants from the category of persons with interests in possession in land, and it would be the case that beneficial tenants in common or joint tenants under an express trust for sale would not have interests in possession in that land, and thus no right of occupation.

(7) Someone entitled to an interest in residue does not have a beneficial interest in the strict sense in the assets of the estate while it is in the course of administration: see Vol 1, para **[1.12]**. It therefore seems

likely that a residuary beneficiary does not have an interest in possession giving him a right of occupation under the TLATA 1996, s 12 while the estate is in the course of administration, particularly as the TLATA 1996, s 18 provides that the TLATA 1996 applies to personal representatives without prejudice to their functions for the purposes of administration. On the other hand, the IHTA 1984 has (in s 91) a provision that someone who would have an interest in possession in residue during the administration of the estate is treated as having it for inheritance tax purposes. It is thought that someone with an interest in possession in a specific gift by will has it from the testator's death both under the TLATA 1996 and the IHTA 1984.

[208.14]
Tax aspects of the right of occupation. The types of interest in possession which post-21 March 2006 result in their holders being treated as beneficially entitled to the underlying settled property under IHTA 1984, s 49(1) are: an interest in possession to which a person became beneficially entitled before 22 March 2006 (unless it is an interest in possession under a trust for a bereaved minor within IHTA 1984, s 71A (see Part A, para **[200.108]**)), or an interest in possession to which a person became beneficially entitled on or after 22 March 2006 and which is an immediate post-death interest within IHTA 1984, s 49A (see Part A, para **[200.98]**); a disabled person's interest within IHTA 1984, s 89B (see Part A, para **[200.99]**); or a transitional serial interest within IHTA 1984, s 49B (see Part A, para **[200.100]**). An interest in possession arising by virtue of a right of occupation will usually qualify for this treatment because it starts at the testator's death and so be an immediate post-death interest (or 'IPDI').

Where the person being given a right of residence is the spouse or civil partner of the testator, it will normally be desirable that they should have an IPDI in order that the spouse or civil partnership exemption should apply (see Part A, paras **[200.84]** and **[200.98]**). In other cases, particularly where the person intended to have the right of residence is elderly, it will often be preferable for the relevant property rules to apply (see Part A, para **[200.131]**) so that there is not a further inheritance tax charge on the death of the occupant. One important consequence of the changes made by FA 2006 is that it makes it possible for there to be an interest in possession trust which is not taxed as such but is subject to the relevant property taxation regime. Achieving this in the case of a right of residence is not straightforward and is discussed further in para **[208.32]** below.

If the trustees exercise their powers under the TLATA 1996, s 13 to exclude or restrict the rights of someone with an interest in possession, it might have the effect of terminating the excluded beneficiary's interest in possession. HMRC has expressed the tentative view that an administrative adjustment which does not affect the value of the respective interests (i.e. the excluded beneficiary receives full compensation from the occupying beneficiaries for his non-occupation) is not likely to be the termination of an interest in possession, and that the existence of the s 13 powers before they are exercised does not prejudice the existence of an interest in possession: see HMRC's answers to questions put by Chris Jarman published in the *Tax Journal*, 30 January 1997, p 19 and 6 February 1997, p 19 (reprinted in

Foster's Inheritance Tax, X6.69). If, on the other hand, a beneficiary with a right of occupation but out of occupation is not fully compensated, in their view he might have given up his interest in possession; but each case will depend on its own facts. These articles also discuss income tax aspects of beneficiary exclusion subject to compensatory rental payments under the TLATA 1996, s 13 and make the point that there would be no tax deduction for the compensation payments unless they were a business expense, and that they would be likely to be taxable income of the excluded beneficiary who received them. What is not discussed directly is the situation where a number of beneficiaries are entitled to occupy a property (typically this happens where a testator confers a right of residence on some or all of his children), and some live there and some do not, the ones out of occupation not being formally excluded and retaining the right of occupation. This situation was considered by a Special Commissioner in *Woodhall v IRC* [2000] STC (SCD) 558, in a case where under their father's will two brothers had rights of residence in a house (held on trust for sale), but only one had lived there. The one who lived there had died in April 1997. It was held that he had had an interest in possession in the house for inheritance tax purposes, but because his brother had an equal right (albeit unexercised) to occupy the house it was held (applying the IHTA 1984, s 50(5)) that the deceased brother's interest in possession was in half the house, not the whole of it. This could offer a method of saving inheritance tax in some situations—see Form B8.3 at para **[208.40]**.

An important point to note, however, is that the termination of an IPDI during the life of the person entitled to it on or after 22 March 2006 will be deemed to be a gift of the underlying settled property for the purposes of FA 1986, s 102, so that unless the person entitled to the immediate post-death interest is excluded altogether from benefit after the termination, the gift with reservation rules could apply: see FA 1986, s 102ZA and Part A, para **[200.76]**. Thus, if a beneficiary is given a right of occupation (which gives rise to an immediate post-death interest) and is also interested or partially interested in the property (or the proceeds of sale of the property) on the termination of that right of occupation, the end of that beneficiary's occupation will give rise to a gift by him or her which will be treated as a gift with reservation.

[208.15]

Tax aspects—trusts for children and the right of occupation. The questions discussed in the *Tax Journal* articles mentioned at para **[208.14]** do not include whether the existence of the rights and powers under the TLATA 1996, ss 12 and 13 could prejudice the application of the IHTA 1984, s 71 to accumulation and maintenance trusts. For deaths on and after 22 March 2006, it is no longer possible to create trusts which fall within IHTA 1984, s 71 and such trusts as were previously in existence will cease to attract special treatment under s 71 from 6 April 2008 (see Part A, para **[200.107]**) and further discussion of this issue is no longer necessary.

Reverting to the children's trust example discussed at para **[208.9]**, above, there is unlikely to be difficulty in relation to the more limited types of interest for young children which replace s 71. If the testator declares a trust of land for his young children which falls within IHTA 1984, s 71A (trusts for bereaved minors) or 71D (age 18-to-25 trusts), the situation discussed in para **[208.9]** would not cause those sections to cease to apply (see Part A, paras **[200.108]** and **[200.109]** for these kinds of trust). Where there are trusts under which the children take IPDIs, the problem discussed in para **[208.9]** does not arise because the beneficiaries would all simultaneously have interests in possession at all relevant times.

Where the situation discussed in para **[208.9]** could cause trouble is where there is a trust for a class of children of the kind that used to fall within IHTA 1984, s 71 but which does not fall within ss 71A or 71D because, typically, the children attain interests in possession on or before attaining the age of 25, but the trusts are such that they become entitled to capital either at a greater age, or not necessarily at all because they get life interests with remainders over (possibly combined with a power to pay capital to them). This type of trust has the problem (see para **[217.2]** below) that it will be a matter of chance whether at the testator's death it is an IPDI trust or a relevant property trust, or partly one and partly the other, depending on whether any or all of the beneficiaries have attained the age at which they become entitled to interests in possession by the time of the testator's death. There is the further complication that if one or more of the beneficiaries attain interests in possession in the period of two years after the testator's death, IHTA 1984, s 144 may have the effect of turning the interests in possession retrospectively into IPDIs (see Part A, para **[200.133]**). The situation discussed in para **[208.9]** could have the disastrous effect that the eldest of several beneficiaries has an interest in possession in the entire property which is an IPDI, and is then in stages divested of the interest in appropriate parts of the property as the other beneficiaries attain the age at which interests in possession commence. Each time his interest is divested in relation to part of the fund it will be an occasion of immediate inheritance tax charge as a deemed lifetime (non-potentially exempt) transfer by him (see Part A, para **[200.71]**).

[208.16]

Tax aspects—sub-trusts. The sub-trust example discussed at para **[208.10]**, i.e. the house owned as to half by W and as to half by H's will trustees holding it on trust for D for life, is discussed in the *Tax Journal* articles mentioned at para **[208.14]**, on the assumption that W cannot be required to make compensation payments for the benefit of D. HMRC accepts (see the *Tax Journal*, 30 January 1997, p 19 and 6 February 1997, p 19) that no taxable benefit flows from D to W in that example. There is a further question whether in these circumstances W has an interest in possession for inheritance tax purposes in H's former half of it with the result that it is subject to inheritance tax as part of W's estate on her death as well as her own absolute share. HMRC's answer that W is entitled to occupy the property pursuant to her statutory right as tenant in common and beneficiary of the trust of land, and is not, therefore, in receipt of a benefit from either the trustees of H's will or D, would seem to imply that W's taxable interest continues to be limited to half the property only. If so, this arrangement is a way of using H's nil rate band up, while giving W security of exclusive possession of the house. If the trustees could require W to pay compensation for use of H's will trustees' half of the property but did not do so, the position might be different.

[208.17]

Interests in possession for inheritance tax purposes. The property subject to an interest in possession arising under a will of someone dying after 21 March 2006 will be taxed as relevant property unless the interest in possession is an IPDI (or the beneficiaries are disabled persons): see Part A, paras **[200.92]**, **[200.98]** and **[200.99]**. As mentioned at paras **[208.12]** and **[208.13]**, the meaning of 'interest in possession' is not necessarily the same in the TLATA 1996 as it is in the IHTA 1984. It is thus possible that a beneficiary might have a right of occupation under the TLATA 1996 by virtue of an interest which is an interest in possession for the purposes of the TLATA 1996, but which is not an interest in possession for inheritance tax purposes, whether taxed as such or not. For example, it is possible that an interest such as that which was the subject matter of *Pearson v IRC* [1981] AC 753, [1980] 2 All ER 479, [1980] STC 318, which was there held not to be an interest in possession for inheritance tax purposes (i.e. a right to the income of settled property subject to a trustees' power to accumulate the income), constitutes an interest in possession for the purposes of the TLATA 1996, s 12 where land is held on trusts of that kind. It is then possible that if a beneficiary takes up occupation by virtue of an interest of this type he becomes entitled to an interest in possession for inheritance tax purposes. However, it is no longer necessarily the case that an interest in possession in property arising under TLATA 1996 in the ways discussed in the main work will cause the property to be taxed as part of the estate of the person entitled to the interest on his or her death. A beneficiary under a discretionary trust who is permitted to occupy the land in exercise of a trustees' power might then have an interest in possession for inheritance tax purposes – although this is unlikely – (see para **[200.95]**), but would not have an interest in possession such as to give him a right of occupation under the TLATA 1996.

[208.18]

Drafting points concerning the right of occupation—

(1) The right of occupation cannot be excluded, and once it arises it will continue (while the conditions as to availability and suitability of land etc are fulfilled) so long as the beneficiary has an interest in possession. However, the TLATA 1996 places no constraints on when an interest in possession comes into existence or ceases, and, for example a trust will not give rise to rights of occupation under the Act if it is wholly discretionary and does not confer an interest in possession.

(2) In addition, the trustees' power to impose reasonable conditions on an occupying beneficiary under the TLATA 1996, s 13(3) is a discretionary power to be exercised from time to time taking into account the matters set out in s 13(4), which include the beneficiaries' circumstances and wishes as well as the intentions of the testator (or settlor) and the purposes for which the land is held, and which is subject to

s 13(7) (protection of existing beneficiary occupation). It seems that the will (or settlement) cannot determine in advance what conditions it will be reasonable to impose. It is more realistic therefore to express an intention that occupation should be subject to repair, payment of outgoings, etc than to direct that it shall be. It would be possible to provide that the occupying beneficiary's interest in possession comes to an end in the event of, eg failure to repair or pay outgoings, but this could be excessively draconian in its practical operation, at any rate unless there was a relief from forfeiture provision, and if provision of the latter kind was included there could be inheritance tax problems, with an interest in possession terminating as a result of the failure with the possibility of there being a gift with reservation if the beneficiary had an IPDI and then has an interest in residue.

(3) If problems under the TLATA 1996, ss 12 and 13 might arise, it will often not be an available option to provide eg a discretionary trust or some other non-interest in possession trust. Usually a beneficiary taxed interest in possession is wanted because of its tax consequences. It is important to note that for deaths on and after 22 March 2006 it is no longer possible to create trusts which fall within IHTA 1984, s 71 (see Part A, para **[200.107]**), and it is possible to have an interest in possession trust which is taxed as relevant property. The important thing is to decide whether a trust should be an IPDI trust, a relevant property trust, or an IHTA 1984, s 71A or s 71D trust, and draft the will accordingly. The problem discussed here will only arise where an IPDI trust is decided on. If overriding powers combined with an IPDI are included the power should be one which enables the remainder trusts to be changed without disturbing the IPDI for the reasons given in Part A, para **[200.98]**.

(4) Where an interest in possession is wanted, for tax or other reasons, it would still be possible to include an overriding power of appointment which enabled the interest in possession to be terminated if the exercise by a beneficiary of the right of occupation was causing problems for the administration of the trust. Such a power could, if so exercised, apparently be effective to give the trustee a right to possession, but of course there might be tax or other reasons for not wanting to exercise the power in this way, and if the trustee and beneficiary were already in dispute the trustee would be open to accusations of improper use of the power. However, the possible existence of rights under the TLATA 1996, ss 12 and 13 could be a reason for including a wide overriding power of appointment in an interest in possession trust of land.

(5) Whether the TLATA 1996, s 12(1)(a) applies to a will or settlement will be a matter of how it is worded, and this is a point where the drafting can affect the operation of ss 12 and 13, but however strongly the wording prevents s 12(1)(a) from applying it cannot be sure of preventing s 12(1)(b) from ever doing so.

(6) The TLATA 1996, s 13(4) declares that the matters to which trustees are to have regard when exercising their powers to impose conditions on occupying beneficiaries or to exclude beneficiaries from occupation include the intentions of the person creating the trust, the purposes for which the land is held, and the circumstances and wishes of each

beneficiary entitled to occupy. These are also relevant under the TLATA 1996, s 15 to the court's decision in the event of a dispute. There is thus some scope for influencing the position in a will by including statements with regard to the testator's intention.

(7) On the positive side, the TLATA 1996, especially the trustees' powers in s 6 and the rights of occupation, makes it possible to have more concise forms of trust when the purpose of the trust is that a beneficiary or beneficiaries should occupy the trust property. See para **[208.19]** and Forms B8.1 and B8.5 at paras **[208.38]** and **[208.43]**, below.

Giving rights of residence by will

[208.19]

Main features of a trust to provide a residence. These should, we suggest, be the following—

(1) An interest in possession in the property, either a life or similar interest or one ending when ceasing to reside in the property—see para **[208.21]**. Although the TLATA 1996 confers the right of residence on any beneficiary with an interest in possession, it does not impose any restrictions on the circumstances in which an interest in possession may come to an end.

(2) No trust for sale (see Part A, paras **[200.55]** and **[200.56]**). Also unnecessary and probably redundant in an interest in possession trust are a power to permit occupation, because the beneficiary will have a statutory right of occupation (see para **[208.5]** ff), or power to impose conditions as to repair, insurance, etc by the beneficiary (because that is provided for by the TLATA 1996, s 13(3), (5): Part G, para **[246.116]**). A power to permit occupation by a beneficiary and impose conditions on the beneficiary as to repair, insurance, etc should be included in a discretionary trust.

(3) An expression of intention that the trust is to provide a residence for the beneficiary, where the main trust does not make that clear, so as to make plain that the statutory right of occupation applies: TLATA 1996, s 12(1)(a) (Part G, para **[246.115]**; see also para **[208.7]**).

(4) No exclusion of the duty of trustees to consult beneficiaries who have an interest in possession in trust land about the exercise of powers or duties in relation to the land under the TLATA 1996, s 11 (Part G, para **[246.114]**; see also para **[220.58]**).

(5) The rights of the beneficiary can be further enhanced by providing that the trustees' powers of sale, and possibly other powers or discretions as well, may only be exercised with the consent of the beneficiary: the TLATA 1996, s 8(2) (Part G, para **[246.110]**) expressly contemplates that the statutory powers of management may be subject to consents. Where the interest in possession ceases on giving up residence in the property, consideration should be given to whether the requirement of consent should cease at the same time: see para **[208.21]**. If it becomes necessary for the trustees to sell the property against the wishes of the beneficiary, e g because of serious disrepair or, where the property is leasehold, failure to observe the lessee's covenants, then the trustees

may apply to the court for an order under the TLATA 1996, s 14, in particular s 14(2)(a) (Part G, para **[246.117]**; see also Part A, para **[200.62]**). It is no longer the case that making sale of land subject to a beneficiary's consent causes the same consent to be required for the exercise of other powers over the land (see para **[220.62]**) and express provision must be made in relation to all powers or discretions which it is intended to make subject to a requirement of consent.

(6) The testator can also express a wish that the trustees should delegate all their powers of management of the land to the beneficiary under the TLATA 1996, s 9 (Part G, para **[246.111]**; see also para **[220.54]** ff). An expression of wishes rather than a direction is appropriate because it appears that trustees cannot be obliged to exercise the power.

(7) Where the beneficiary's rights cease on giving up residence, it is preferable if the trusts provide for sale of one residence and purchase another with the proceeds.

[208.20]

Whether to provide a life interest or only a right to reside. When a testator wants to provide a right of residence, he usually intends that it should be no more than that, so that on the giving up of occupation by the beneficiary, or the sale of the property, the beneficiary's interest will terminate and the persons interested in remainder under the trusts of the property (often the persons interested in residue) will become entitled in possession to the property or its proceeds of sale. If such a testator could be persuaded to confer a full life interest not dependent on continued residence it would be much kinder to the beneficiary, because it could be extremely hard on a beneficiary who wanted to live somewhere else but did not want to forfeit permanently a valuable right. The beneficiary's position is even worse where there is no provision for changing residences, so that the beneficiary might have to carry on living in a house which is in the wrong area or too large because leaving that particular house means forfeiture of all benefit. There could also be dilemmas for the trustees, who might for example find that there are grounds for thinking that the beneficiary has given up residence, but they are not sure, they are under pressure from the remaindermen to sell the property and hand the capital over to them, and do not have any funds (apart from the house) for legal proceedings (see further para **[208.21]**). Providing a full life interest, as in Forms B8.4 to B8.6 at paras **[208.41]** to **[208.43]**, avoids these problems. It also means that the arrangements for residence do not need to be so tightly drafted, more can be left to the discretion of the trustees and to be taken care of by the TLATA 1996, and a much more concise clause is possible than in the case of trust to provide a right of residence only.

[208.21]

Interests ceasing on sale or on giving up residence. Where the testator particularly wants to create a trust for the beneficiary which terminates when the beneficiary gives up residence or the property is sold, the condition of obtaining the beneficiary's consent to a sale can either be general, i.e. a prerequisite for a sale whether or not the beneficiary is living in the property, or only a prerequisite for a sale so long as the beneficiary is in residence. If the beneficiary's consent is a general requirement, the beneficiary has more protection from precipitate action by the trustees, but there is more uncertainty about the position where the beneficiary leaves the property but will not consent to a sale. In these circumstances the trustees could have the dilemma that the property is a sterilised asset, perhaps a deteriorating one, particularly if the power to lease the property requires the beneficiary's consent and it is being withheld, and if they cannot be sure that they would be successful if they applied to the court under the TLATA 1996, s 14 to dispense with the beneficiary's consent to a sale. There might also be doubt as to whether the beneficiary's rights are really at an end or not.

[208.22]
Such possible difficulties could be reduced by not providing that *leasing* the property requires the beneficiary's consent after the beneficiary has given up residence (or at all), and/or by providing that any rents and profits of the property before it is sold should go to the beneficiary and not to the remainderman. Providing that the rents and profits before sale should go to the beneficiary rather than the remainderman in this situation would have a possible inheritance tax advantage (see paras **[208.31]** to **[208.33]**) and if the beneficiary's consent was needed for letting the property, it would of course encourage the beneficiary to consent to it. If the beneficiary's consent was not needed for letting the property when he or she was out of possession it would enable the trustees to obtain an income from which repairs, insurance, etc could be funded. These two provisions would also reduce ambiguity and make it fairly clear that the beneficiary, when out of residence, was entitled to block a sale with a view to resuming occupation, but of course his or her rights would in effect be very similar to having a full life interest.

[208.23]
The potential difficulties just described are avoided if the requirement of the beneficiary's consent to a sale ceases on him or her ceasing to reside. The problem which could then arise for the trustees is whether the beneficiary has in fact ceased to reside, but if they can establish that he or she has ceased to do so they can at least be sure that the beneficiary's rights are at an end and the property should be sold. The authorities on construction of conditions as to residence, considered in Vol 1 at paras **[35.18]**–**[35.28]**, may provide some guidance as to when residence by the beneficiary should be regarded as having ceased. There is also the question whether involuntary cesser of residence should be declared not to amount to ceasing to reside. Without express provision involuntary cesser of residence would probably terminate the beneficiary's veto on sale. If words to this effect are included, it could be difficult for the trustees if the beneficiary is say taken to prison or hospital, or just disappears so that the trustees do not know what his or her circumstances are, and the house is in disrepair or perhaps at risk of vandalism or of being taken over by squatters and needs to be sold. In these circumstances the trustees would have to apply to the court for an order dispensing with the beneficiary's consent to a sale—either an application under the TLATA 1996, s 14 (Part G, para **[246.117]**) or if the beneficiary was mentally incapacitated, an application under the Mental Capacity Act 2005, ss 16 and 18 (Part G, para **[244.139]**). On the other hand, there

could be unfairness in omitting this provision. The beneficiary might be taken to hospital and then recover, or be remanded in custody and then acquitted of the crime of which he or she was accused, and find that his or her residence had been sold. Deciding whether to include this provision is a matter of balancing the protection of the beneficiary's position against administrative convenience. A possible compromise is the provision in Form B8.1, sub-cl (8)(a) at para **[208.38]**, under which involuntary ceasing to reside does not terminate the beneficiary's interest, but does do so if he or she does not notify the trustees within a specified period that he or she intends to return.

[208.24]

Remainder trusts and avoiding gaps in the beneficial interests. Where the beneficiary has a life interest in the proceeds of sale the chances of failure to dispose fully of income or capital are small. Where the interest ceases on the remarriage of the beneficiary, however, the draftsman should make sure that the remainder trusts will take effect on his or her remarriage as well as his or her death. Similar principles apply to civil partners and it should be noted that a widowhood can come to an end because of remarriage or the formation of a civil partnership and a surviving civil partner might form a new civil partnership or marry. The chances of error are further reduced by using remainder trusts of the kind which begin 'subject to the foregoing trusts', as opposed to those which begin 'on the death of the said ——'.

[208.25]

The chances of an accidental failure to dispose fully of the beneficial interest are increased where the beneficiary is only given a right of residence; it can sometimes happen that a will gives a beneficiary an interest in a house which ends when the beneficiary ceases to reside there, but then creates a remainder trust of the house which apparently only takes effect on the beneficiary's death. Even where it is made clear that the remainderman becomes entitled when the property is sold, there can still be a question (which will not very often arise in practice, though it could) as to who is entitled to the rent if the property is let before it is sold. It is better to make express provision for this if there would otherwise be any ambiguity about it.

[208.26]

Repairs, payment of outgoings, etc. Where a residential property is held on trust for a beneficiary under a specific gift it is very often without any additional endowment of capital held on the same trusts which could be used to pay for repairs, insurance, etc. Where a beneficiary has an interest in possession in a residential property (or land of any other kind) which gives rise to a right of occupation of that land under the TLATA 1996, s 12 (Part G, para **[246.115]**) that right is subject to a power of the trustees to impose reasonable conditions on the beneficiary in relation to his occupation of that land under s 12: TLATA 1996, s 13(3) (Part G, para **[246.116]**; see also para **[208.5]**). It seems from the structure of the TLATA 1996, ss 12 and 13 and the lack of any provision permitting the exclusion of ss 12 and 13, that the right of occupation is subject only to the conditions which are reasonably imposed by the trustees under s 13(3) after taking into account not only the intentions of the testator and the purposes for which the land is held but also the circumstances and wishes of the beneficiaries: TLATA 1996, s 13(4). Accordingly, it seems that the will cannot predetermine what would be reasonable conditions for the trustees to impose, but that an expression of the testator's intentions as to the burdens to be assumed by an occupying beneficiary will carry weight under s 13(4) and, in the event of a dispute about the discharge of such burdens going to court, under the TLATA 1996, s 15(1) (Part G, para **[246.118]**).

[208.27]

Remedies for failure by a beneficiary to repair, pay outgoings, etc. It should be noted that the conditions imposed under the TLATA 1996, s 13(3) are not conditions for the right of occupation continuing to be exercisable; in other words the right of occupation does not come to an end if those conditions are broken. However, the practical position is likely to be that if an occupying beneficiary is in serious breach of reasonably imposed conditions relating to his or her occupation, one option will be for the trustees to apply to the court under the TLATA 1996, s 14 (Part G, para **[246.117]**) for an order for sale with vacant possession (and dispensing with the beneficiary's consent if the will makes that a requirement for a sale) on the grounds, for example, that the beneficiary cannot be relied on to observe the obligations which go with his or her occupation, the property is deteriorating, and the only hope of saving something for the remaindermen is a sale as soon as possible before the property deteriorates further. The trustees can also ask the court for directions as to what they should do if sale is not ordered. An alternative course of action would be proceedings against the beneficiary for compensation for failure to carry out the obligations imposed. It seems that by taking up occupation (or continuing in it after the testator's death) under a right given by the will (or an exercise of a power under the will) which is subject to repairing, insuring, etc the beneficiary cannot take the benefit without accepting the burden, so that for example, the trustees could sue the beneficiary for reimbursement of insurance premiums, or they (or possibly the persons interested in remainder) could sue the beneficiary's estate for compensation after his or her death if he or she had failed to keep the property in repair. See *Re Williames* (1885) 54 LT 105; *Jay v Jay* [1924] 1 KB 826; *Re Field* [1925] Ch 636; and *Haskell v Marlow* [1928] 2 KB 45; these are all cases concerning obligations to repair of tenants for life of settled land (where the trusts expressly imposed a repairing obligation), but we can see no reason why the benefit and burden principle set out in those cases should not equally apply to someone with a life or lesser interest occupying property held on a trust of land subject to obligations to repair, etc reasonably imposed by the trustees under the TLATA 1996, s 13(3). The TLATA 1996 makes no express provision as to how conditions imposed on occupying beneficiaries are to be enforced, but the terms of the TLATA 1996, s 13(3) and (5) seem to imply that if a beneficiary breaks a condition reasonably imposed upon him he will be personally liable.

[208.28]

In practice, the lack of any additional endowment will make it extremely difficult for the trustees to take any steps to enforce the beneficiary's obligations, as there may be no funds even to pay for a simple application to the court for directions, without first selling the property. It is advisable to make it clear, where the trustees might be in this position, that they are not to be liable for any failure to enforce the beneficiary's obligations, although this would probably be implicit in trusts of this type. Other possibilities which could be considered are to restrict the liability to repair to keeping the property in the state it is in at the testator's death (where it is likely to be in a poor state of repair), and providing an endowment fund to pay for repairs, insurance, etc. Simply providing for expenses to be paid out of residue could hold up the distribution of residue for a long time. Where the beneficiary's own estate is likely to go on his or her death to the persons who are the remaindermen under the trusts of the residential property, precise definition of the beneficiary's obligations as to repair and outgoings is less important.

Other aspects

[208.29]

Freedom from liabilities. The intention of providing a residence could be frustrated if a gift for that purpose is burdened with a charge which is not directed to be paid out of residue (see the AEA 1925, s 35: Part G, para **[246.62]**). Inheritance tax in respect of land in the UK is now prima facie payable out of residue as a testamentary expense (IHTA 1984, s 211: Part G, para **[246.100]**) and the incidence of inheritance tax no longer poses a problem in this respect. Where the beneficiary is the testator's widow, widower or surviving civil partner, and she or he becomes entitled to an immediate post-death interest in possession (within IHTA 1984, s 49A) or a disabled person's interest (within the meaning of IHTA 1984, s 89B) in the residence under the trusts of the will, the gift will normally be exempt from inheritance tax and the question of incidence will not arise: see Part A, para **[200.84]**.

[208.30]

Taxation. A beneficiary with a life interest in a property or its proceeds of sale will clearly have an interest in possession but if that arises under the will of someone dying after 21 March 2006, it does not necessarily have to be a beneficiary-taxed (see Part A, para **[200.92]** for this term) interest in possession for inheritance tax purposes. If the interest commences at the testator's death (occurring after 21 March 2006) it will be an IPDI within IHTA 1984, s 49A (see Part A, para **[200.98]**), and therefore a beneficiary-taxed interest. If it starts at a later date, unless it does so in circumstances that IHTA 1984, s 144 turns it into an IPDI (see Part A, para **[200.133]**), or the beneficiary is disabled within the meaning of IHTA 1984, s 89(4)–(6) (see Part A, para **[200.99]**), it will be subject to inheritance tax under the 'relevant property' rules which formerly applied only to non-interest in possession property. The same will almost certainly be true where the beneficiary is entitled to reside in the property but has no larger beneficial interest. Where the trusts are discretionary, or are fixed trusts in favour of persons other than the beneficiary, and the beneficiary occupies the property by virtue of the trustees' exercise of a power to permit him or her to reside there, it is likely that this will also give the beneficiary an interest in possession in the property which may be a beneficiary taxed interest in possession for inheritance tax purposes, and HMRC are likely to so regard it: see *Foster's Inheritance Tax*, E1.47 and Part A, para **[200.95]**.

[208.31]
The consequence of a beneficiary having a beneficiary-taxed interest in possession is that the death of the beneficiary while the interest in possession continues will give rise to an inheritance tax charge on the property as part of the beneficiary's estate (IHTA 1984, ss 4(1), 5(1) and 49(1)), and that the termination of the interest in possession during his or her life will be an inheritance tax transfer of value, which may be a potentially exempt transfer if the termination of the interest is followed by an absolute interest, a disabled person's interest (see Part A, para **[200.99]**), or (if the terminating interest is an IPDI) a trust for a bereaved minor within IHTA 1984, s 71A (see Part A, para **[200.108]**): IHTA 1984, s 3A. If it is a potentially exempt transfer, inheritance tax will only be payable in respect of the termination of the interest if the beneficiary dies within seven years of the termination. The termination of a beneficiary-taxed interest on or after 22 March 2006 will be deemed to be a gift of the underlying settled property for the purposes of FA 1986, s 102, so that unless the beneficiary entitled to the beneficiary-taxed interest is excluded altogether from benefit after the termination, the gift with reservation rules could apply: see FA 1986, s 102ZA and Part A, para **[200.76]**.

[208.32]
It is therefore a bad idea for a will to create trusts of a residence which may give rise to a series of beneficiary taxed interests in possession for different people, with successive lifetime terminations of interests in possession, each with a potential for giving rise to an inheritance tax charge. This unsatisfactory result formerly arose where the beneficiary's interest in a property exclusively arises from a power to permit him or her to occupy, as the power will only come to be first exercised after some time has elapsed from the testator's death, and may not be exercised continuously thereafter, or from the beneficiary having a right of occupation which is interrupted by a period during which the property is let to a tenant and the rents are payable to the remainderman (who would thus have an interest in possession while entitled to the rents). However, a series of interests in possession in a property for different people can, post-21 March 2006, be provided by a will without these adverse inheritance tax consequences. This will be so if none of the interests in possession are beneficiary-taxed ones, with the consequence that the 'relevant property' inheritance tax rules will apply throughout. Provided that none of the beneficiaries turns out to be disabled, this can be achieved so long as the first interest or interests in possession provided by the will are not IPDIs. See para **[208.33]** below for a discussion of the methods by which creating an IPDI might be avoided in relation to a right of residence which would (apart from the tax disincentive) commence from the testator's death. Before 22 March 2006, giving concurrent rights of residence to a number of persons could effect an inheritance tax saving by dividing the value of the property among different estates (see para **[208.14]**), even though some of those persons will not exercise the right of residence. See Form B8.3 at para

[208.40] and the notes thereto. A right of residence arising under the exercise of a power in a discretionary trust to permit a beneficiary to occupy property does not now (in respect of deaths after 21 March 2006) present the same problem, provided that the interest commences more than two years after the death of the testator (see Part A, para **[200.133]** for the latter point). The idea of giving concurrent rights of residence to a number of persons remains a valid idea for diluting the inheritance tax effect of one or more IPDIs. However, it is not a good idea to provide for several people to be entitled to parallel IPDIs in the same property, with the trusts being such that the IPDI of each beneficiary will terminate when he or she ceases to reside or dies, and his or her share will accrue to the remaining occupants' shares. This is likely to result in inheritance tax charges arising on death, and immediate lifetime inheritance tax charges arising when a beneficiary ceases to reside, which would all be avoided if the property was subject to the relevant property regime throughout. Where the beneficiary is the testator's spouse or civil partner, it is important that the beneficiary's interest in possession should commence from the testator's death, if it is desired that the spouse exemption (under the IHTA 1984, s 18: see Part A, para **[200.84]**) should apply to the property on the testator's death; again this means that the will should provide a trust entitling him or her to occupation of the property, or a life (or until remarriage or the formation of a (new) civil partnership) interest.

[208.33]

Where a right of residence is being provided for the testator's surviving spouse or civil partner an IPDI will usually be wanted for the sake of the inheritance tax exemption. Where such a right is being given to someone other than the testator's surviving spouse or civil partner it will often be preferable, particularly where the beneficiary is elderly, to avoid creating an IPDI and have the property taxed under the relevant property rules (for further discussion of the merits of these alternatives see Part A, para **[200.131]**). In principle what is needed is a period of discretionary trust immediately following the testator's death followed by the commencement of the intended interest in possession. If the interest in possession commences during the period of two years following the testator's death HMRC's view is that IHTA 1984, s 144 will have the effect of turning it into an IPDI (see Part A, para **[200.133]**). It should therefore be an initial discretionary trust of just over two years followed by the intended right of residence, or else just a conventional discretionary trust with wide powers which would enable the trustees to allow the particular beneficiary to occupy the property in question. In the absence of any clear indications from HMRC as to what in their view will or will not give rise to an IPDI in this context, a full discretionary trust seems the better option. It is very often the case that the intended beneficiary will be living in the property in question at the testator's death. There is a question, where there is a discretionary trust commencing at the testator's death, whether the executors or trustees leaving the beneficiary in the property for two years without making any decision will or will not give rise to an interest in possession commencing within the two-year period. The decision of the Special Commissioner in *Judge v Revenue and Customs Comrs* [2005] STC (SCD) 863 gives some encouragement to the idea that it need not give rise to an interest in possession. This was a case where a beneficiary was permitted to continue residing in a property because the trustee believed that the will gave the beneficiary a right of residence, but it was in fact a discretionary trust and the beneficiary was only entitled to occupy the property if the trustees made a discretionary decision to permit the beneficiary to do so. They made no such decision and so it was held that there was no interest in possession. It will be more credible that no interest in possession has arisen during the two-year period after the testator's death if the trusts are conventional discretionary trusts continuing for a lengthy trust period after death without a supervening trust to provide the beneficiary with a residence. If the beneficiary can only obtain a right of occupation if the trustees exercise their discretion in his or her favour, and they only get around to exercising their discretion in that way after the two years have elapsed, it will be a clearer case of there being no interest in possession during the two years after the testator's death than if a right of occupation is conferred by the will commencing just over two years after the testator's death. In the latter case the discretionary trust for the initial two-year period will lack credibility because the will is so structured that no sensible executor would do other than leave the beneficiary in occupation during that period. Where it is desired to avoid a discretionary trust, an alternative possibility which might work satisfactorily and could be considered is for the will to commence by giving the beneficiary a right to be granted a lease of the property in question for two years and one month from the death of the testator (and which does not terminate on the beneficiary's earlier death), adapting Form B8.8 at para **[208.45]**. The lease would be at a modest rent, and the rent or other income would be held on discretionary trusts for the period of the lease. From the date of expiry of the lease the beneficiary would then be given a conventional right of residence under a trust. This could have an adverse effect on capital gains tax private residence relief if the property were sold subsequently.

[208.34]
Another inheritance tax problem for residences is the effectiveness of the nil rate band-using strategy of husband and wife owning the matrimonial home as tenants in common, and the first to die leaving his or her share of the home to a non-exempt beneficiary or beneficiaries such as their children, on the basis or with the intention that the surviving spouse will go on living there. An outright gift to the children is probably effective to keep the first to die's share out of the taxable estate of the survivor, but at the cost of the survivor being at risk of the children seeking an order for sale. However, writing protection from this risk for the survivor into the trusts is likely to cause the survivor to have an interest in possession in the first to die's share. For example, the arrangement of this kind in Form B8.10 (at para **[208.48]**) was held to have this effect in *IRC v Lloyd's Private Banking* [1998] STC 559, High Court (see n 1 to para **[208.48]**). Another arrangement which might work is to give the child or children a life interest or interests in the share of the first to die, because the TLATA 1996, ss 12 and 13 seem to have the effect that the surviving spouse has security of exclusive possession of the property while having, it is hoped, a taxable interest in only half the property: see paras **[208.10]** and **[208.16]**. The latter scheme is untested and the Inland

Revenue have not expressed views on it. The most popular method of late, and one which has the considerable advantage of having been accepted as effective, at least in some form, by the Inland Revenue, is a nil rate band discretionary trust fund under the first to die's will where the trust fund is constituted by a personal obligation of the surviving spouse or by a charge on the first to die's share of the matrimonial home: see para **[218.19]** ff. Following the introduction, on 9 October 2007, of new rules providing for a carry forward of an unused nil-rate band, these schemes will largely be unnecessary.

The new inheritance tax rules under FA 2006 make inclusion of parts or shares of a private residence in a nil-rate band discretionary trust easier. This is because it is now possible to have an interest in possession in property and have the property within the relevant property charging regime: see paras **[208.31]** ff above. A possible strategy will be to appropriate an undivided share of the first to die's share of the property to the nil-rate band discretionary trust fund after two years have elapsed from the death: see paras **[218.19]**–**[218.22]** below.

There have been several recent Special Commissioner cases on whether occupation rights gave an interest in possession and, if so, to what extent: see *Woodhall v IRC* [2000] STC (SCD) 558, *Faulkner v IRC* [2001] STC (SCD) 112, *Cook v IRC* [2002] STC (SCD) 318, *Oakley v IRC* [2005] STC (SCD) 343, and *Judge v Revenue and Customs Comrs* [2005] STC (SCD) 863 (see para **[208.33]** above).

The nil-rate inheritance tax band for 2007–8 is £300,000: see FA 2005, s 98. For 2008–9 it will be £312,000, for 2009–10 it will be £325,000: see FA 2006, s 155. For 2010–11 it will be £350,000: see FA 2007, s 4.

[208.35]

The capital gains tax private residence exemption should apply, as long as the property is the beneficiary's main residence: TCGA 1992, ss 222 and 225. This is likely to be so even where the beneficiary occupies by virtue of the exercise of a discretionary power: see *Sansom v Peay* [1976] 3 All ER 375, [1976] 1 WLR 1073, the decision on the basis of which the Inland Revenue regard occupation under the exercise of a power as giving rise to an interest in possession for inheritance tax purposes. Under TCGA 1992, s 225A, (replacing Extra-Statutory Concession ESC D5) principal private residence relief is allowed to personal representatives on the disposal, during the administration period, of a house which both before and after a deceased person's death was the only or main residence of individuals who, under the will or intestacy, are entitled to the whole or to at least 75 per cent of the proceeds of sale of the house, either absolutely or for life. Where such relief is due it is computed in the same manner as relief under TCGA 1992, s 225.

[208.36]

Administrative powers. Where a residence may be held on trust for some time there are various administrative powers and provisions which it might be appropriate to include in the will, such as: power to borrow (see Form B20.20 at para **[220.69]**), power to lend to the life tenant (see Form B18.27 at para **[218.113]**), power for a trustee to contract with the trust fund (see Form B21.7 at para **[221.8]**), power to appoint foreign trustees (see Form B21.36 at para **[221.41]**), and a professional trustee charging clause (see Forms B21.37 and B21.38 at paras **[221.49]** and **[221.50]**). An express power of investment is only needed if it is desired to confer on the trustees power to acquire land outside the UK or undivided shares of land (or other equitable interests in land), or unsecured loans—the statutory powers of investment enable purchase of most kinds of asset apart from these categories: see the Trustee Act 2000 (TrA 2000), ss 3 and 8 (Part G, paras **[246.135]** and **[246.140]**) and para **[220.12]** ff. Express powers of management of land are needed if land outside England and Wales might be held, but for most purposes in relation to a trust to provide a residence the statutory powers over land in England and Wales are likely to be adequate: see the TLATA 1996, s 6(1) (Part G, para **[246.108]**) and para **[220.64]** ff. Where any such provisions are being included in the will in relation to a residuary trust fund, it may be possible to make them applicable also to a specific gift of a residence, but care should be taken for inheritance tax reasons to make sure that powers over one fund or asset cannot be used to benefit beneficiaries interested in another fund or asset (see the Note in B18 at para **[218.109]** and the General Preliminary Note to B20 at paras **[220.1]**–**[220.10]**).

[208.37]

Furniture. Sometimes it is desired to provide a life or other limited right to the use of some or all of the house contents along with the house. Except possibly in the case of really valuable furniture and fittings, it is better to make an absolute gift of chattels because the expense, difficulty, and potential for dispute of administering chattels as part of a trust fund is usually out of all proportion to their value. For forms for use in cases where the testator cannot be dissuaded from settling furniture and/or other chattels, see Forms B4.10 (at para **[204.24]**), B4.26 to B4.30 (at paras **[204.44]**–**[204.48]**), B8.3 (at para **[208.40]**) and B8.7 (at para **[208.44]**). For notes on settling chattels see the Note on furniture in B4 at para **[204.38]** ff.

Trusts of land

[208.38]

Form B8.1: Interest of beneficiary limited to a right of residence with provision for changing residences[1]

(1) I give my freehold dwellinghouse known as ————, or (if the same shall be sold or otherwise disposed of before my death) the dwellinghouse which I shall own at the date of my death, to my trustees free of all sums charged or otherwise secured thereon at my death (which sums shall be paid out of my residuary estate) to hold the same and any dwellinghouse acquired in substitution therefor (as provided below) upon trust to provide a residence for [my wife] so long as she wishes to reside there subject as provided below.

(2) If at my death I own more than one dwellinghouse the foregoing gift shall be of my principal place of residence at my death and if none of them is my principal place of residence then the foregoing gift shall be of the dwellinghouse which has the highest capital value (as determined by my trustees) at my death but [my wife] shall have the right to select by notice in

writing to my trustees another dwellinghouse of mine to be the subject-matter of the foregoing gift in place that which would otherwise be the subject-matter of it provided that—

(a) the foregoing right of selection shall cease if such notice of selection has not been received by my trustees within one year of my death or within two months of the grant of probate or letters of administration to my estate if later;

(b) my trustees may extend the time for service of such notice of election for any period they think fit and if they do not inform [my wife] of her foregoing right of selection within six months of my death they shall extend the time for service thereof at least until the expiry of six months from her being so informed;

(c) if [my wife] is one of my trustees the references to my trustees in this subclause are to my trustees other than [my wife] and if [she] alone constitutes my trustees for the time being proviso (b) above to this subclause shall not apply and [my wife] shall give notice of selection by endorsing notice of it on the probate or letters of administration;

(d) if more than one dwellinghouse of mine has the same capital value or if for any other reason there is a question as to which of my dwellinghouses is the subject-matter of the foregoing gift it shall be determined by notice of selection by my wife as set out above and if she shall not give valid notice of selection within the time for doing so it shall be determined by my trustees by notice in writing to [my wife].[2]

(3) My trustees shall not exercise their power to sell the said or any substitute dwellinghouse or their power to purchase any substitute dwellinghouse or exercise any of their other powers (conferred hereby or by law)[3] over any such dwellinghouse without the consent in writing of [my wife] so long as her interest continues and (if for the time being a dwellinghouse is held subject to the provisions of this clause) so long as she shall perform and observe any conditions reasonably imposed by my trustees in relation to her residence in any such dwellinghouse.[4]

(4) I wish my trustees to impose as a condition in relation to [my wife]'s residence in any such dwellinghouse that she should keep the same fully insured in the name of my trustees, keep the same in good repair, observe and perform the lessee's covenants (if the dwellinghouse is leasehold), and pay all taxes and other outgoings in respect thereof[5] and my trustees shall not be liable for lack of insurance repair or payment of outgoings or for not taking steps to enforce any reasonable conditions imposed in relation to [my wife]'s residence in any such dwellinghouse.[6]

(5) I also wish my trustees to delegate to [my wife] their powers of sale of any such dwellinghouse.[7]

(6) If [my wife] gives up residence in one dwellinghouse subject to this clause so as to enable it to be sold and some other dwellinghouse to be acquired for her to reside in then her interest shall not cease and she shall be entitled to be paid the income of the proceeds of sale of one dwellinghouse pending purchase of another,[8] and—

(a) my trustees may apply such proceeds of sale in the purchase of a dwellinghouse in any location they think fit (whether in England and

Wales or elsewhere) to provide a residence for [my wife] and may apply some of the proceeds of sale of one dwellinghouse in the purchase of another dwellinghouse and some in the improvement and/or repair of that other dwellinghouse;[9]

(b) without prejudice to the generality of the foregoing, my trustees shall have power to purchase the substitute dwellinghouse together with [my wife] as tenants in common in such shares as my trustees may deem appropriate according to the respective contributions of my trustees and [my wife] and notwithstanding that [my wife] may be one of my trustees;[10]

(c) if my trustees decide to acquire an undivided share of a replacement dwellinghouse my trustees may join with [my wife] and/or the other co-owner or co-owners in charging the property to assist [my wife] or any other co-owner in borrowing money to finance the purchase of her or his share thereof on such times as my trustees think fit;

(d) my trustees shall have power to pay out of the proceeds of sale of the dwellinghouse sold any reasonable costs of temporary accommodation and/or storage of chattels for [my wife] between her moving out of the dwellinghouse sold and moving into the replacement dwellinghouse;

(e) any of the proceeds of sale of the dwellinghouse sold which are not applied in the purchase or purchase and improvement and/or repair of another dwellinghouse or in assisting [my wife] as aforesaid shall fall into my residuary estate;

(f) if the period of twelve months elapses after the sale of one dwellinghouse without the acquisition of another dwellinghouse then [my wife]'s interest shall cease and all the proceeds of sale of the dwellinghouse sold shall fall into my residuary estate (but my trustees may by writing extend the period of continuance of [my wife]'s interest pending purchase of another dwellinghouse at any time or times when such period including any previous extension of it under this power has not expired).[11]

(7) On the death of [my wife] or (subject to subclause (6) above) in the event of her giving up residence, such dwellinghouse and any property representing it shall fall into my residuary estate.

(8) For the purposes of this clause—

(a) no involuntary ceasing by [my wife] to reside in a dwellinghouse subject to this clause shall be treated as ceasing to reside therein unless [my wife] shall have been out of residence continuously for six months and shall not have expressed in writing to my trustees her intention to take up residence again;[12]

(b) references to a dwellinghouse include a flat and an interest in, or undivided share of, a dwellinghouse.

(9) All the powers of my trustees may be exercised by them in favour of or for the benefit of [my wife] even though she may be one of my trustees but not if she is sole trustee.

[(10) My trustees shall have the same powers and [my wife] shall have the same rights in relation to any dwellinghouse subject to this clause which is situated outside England and Wales as they would have if it were situated in England and Wales.][13]

[*Take in administrative powers and provisions as appropriate* (*see para* **[208.36]**), *such as Form B20.20* (*borrowing*) *at para* **[220.69]**, *Form B21.12* (*trustee indemnity*) *at para* **[221.16]** *and Form B21.37* (*trustee power to charge*) *at para* **[221.49]**.]

1 This form is more complicated than the full life interest Form B8.6 (at para **[208.43]**), because it is essential in this type of trust to make provision for sale of one residence and purchase of another. If the client can be persuaded to give a full life interest, or at any rate an interest not ceasing on giving up residence, the drafting can be much simplified, and in some ways it is fairer on the beneficiary, since he or she will not be constrained to linger on in a property which he or she should move out of only because the benefit of it is lost if he or she does so. If the interest given is one which ceases on residence being given up by the beneficiary, where the beneficiary is someone with a claim on the testator, he or she may be able to apply under the I(PFD)A 1975 for the interest to be enlarged to a full life interest or even an absolute interest. Because the Form gives the widow a right of occupation over property comprised in a specific gift from the testator's death, an immediate post-death interest in possession in the property is almost certainly conferred on the beneficiary from the testator's death (see Part A, paras **[200.98]** and **[208.14]**). Accordingly, where the beneficiary is the testator's spouse the gift should be exempt from inheritance tax on the testator's death as a gift to a spouse, unless at the testator's death the testator is domiciled in the UK, his spouse is not, and the £55,000 limit for exempt gifts in such circumstances is exceeded (see Part A, para **[200.85]**). Where the property is or may be outside the UK, it may be appropriate to make the gift free of inheritance tax or foreign death duties: see Form B8.6, n 1 at para **[208.43]**. In order to adapt the form to take account of civil partnerships formed pursuant to CPA 2004, substitute 'civil partner' for 'wife' and amend 'she' to 'he' as appropriate.

2 Sub-clause (2) can be omitted if it is likely that the testator will have only one dwellinghouse at his death. If it is omitted, the words 'or the principal dwellinghouse (if I have more than one)' could be inserted in sub-cl (1) between '... before my death) the dwellinghouse' and 'which I shall own at the date of my death ... '. It is not clear whether exercise of the right of selection will terminate the beneficiary's interest in possession in the whole of the property given under sub-cl (1), or whether the IHTA 1984, s 52(3) will apply to relieve it from being an occasion of charge save in respect of the difference in value (if any) between the original property and the selected one. Any occasion of charge will be potentially exempt or immediately chargeable (see paras **[200.71]** and **[200.102]**) according to what the trusts of residue are.

3 This is no longer statutorily implied from the requirement of consent to a sale as a result of the repeal of the LPA 1925, s 28(1): see para **[200.60]**. The TLATA 1996, s 8(2) (Part G, para **[246.110]**) provides that exercise of the trustees' powers may be subject to consents (see para **[200.66]**).

4 Subclause (3) could be omitted, since so long as the beneficiary is in residence the trustees cannot sell the property without first applying to the court under the TLATA 1996, s 14 (Part G, para **[246.117]**) and making the requirement of her consent end if she does not fulfil the conditions of her occupation does not help the trustees much if she is still in occupation.

5 See para **[208.18]**, sub-para (2) for the reasons for making this an expression of wishes rather than a direction that the beneficiary's occupation shall be subject to these burdens.

6 Although it is thought that the will cannot predetermine what obligations an occupying beneficiary will be subject to (see para **[208.18]**, sub-para (2)) there is nothing to prevent the trustees being absolved from liability for want of repair, etc which it is contemplated will be the beneficiary's responsibility.

7 For the power of delegation, and the reasons for thinking that the most that can be provided in relation to it is an expression of wishes, see para **[220.57]** and the TLATA 1996, s 9 (Part G, para **[246.111]**).

8 The main reason for this provision is so that the beneficiary has an interest in possession in the proceeds of sale for inheritance tax purposes. It could have adverse inheritance tax consequences if the residuary beneficiaries had interests in possession in the proceeds of sale for a short period between the sale of one property and the purchase of another. See the note on taxation at para **[208.30]**.

9 It is not clear that the proceeds of sale of one property could be spent on improving another property under the powers conferred by the TLATA 1996 or the TrA 2000 in the absence of express authorisation by the will. It is arguably not a power of an absolute owner in relation to the land within the TLATA 1996, s 6(1) since it is something done in relation to the cash received from a sale of the land, and it is not the purchase of a legal estate in land within the TrA 2000, s 8(1) (Part G, para **[246.140]**; see also para **[220.52]**).

10 The purchase of an undivided share in land is not authorised by the TrA 2000, s 8 (Part G, para **[246.140]**) and express power is needed to be able to do so. If an undivided share is subject to these trusts (either under the original gift or as a matter of subsequent acquisition) the beneficiary will apparently not have a right of occupation of the property under the TLATA 1996 in respect of that share: see para **[208.10]**. Usually the beneficiary will be the absolute owner of the other share, and have a right of occupation by virtue of owning it. If on a purchase of a substitute property the beneficiary is not one of the other co-owners the trustees should obtain the agreement of the other co-owners to the beneficiary's occupation before entering into the purchase.

11 Subclause (f) is a long stop provision to prevent the beneficiary refusing consent to purchase of a new property in order to go on enjoying the income. Some or all of sub-cls (a) to (d) of this proviso may in particular cases be unnecessary elaboration and if so can be omitted. If (a) and/or (d) are omitted there will be consequential amendment to make to (e).

12 The idea here is to protect the beneficiary against precipitate sale if she is hospitalised after an accident or illness, but if she is hospitalised and is mentally incapacitated she will not be able to express an intention to return and the trustees will be free to sell the property after six months. See also para **[208.23]**. This paragraph may be omitted if preferred.

13 The statutory rights and powers under the TLATA 1996, s 6(1) (Part G, para **[246.108]**; see also para **[220.52]**) only apply to land in England and Wales: TLATA 1996, s 27(3) (Part G, para **[246.130]**). If land in Scotland or Northern Ireland is acquired under the statutory power to do so in the TrA 2000, s 8(1) (Part G, para **[246.140]**), they have the same statutory powers of management in relation to that land (TrA 2000, s 8(3)), but this will not apply to land in Scotland or Northern Ireland acquired under an express power or comprised in the testator's estate at his death. This subclause may be omitted if there is no likelihood of the beneficiary wanting to live outside England and Wales.

[208.39]

Form B8.2: Interest of beneficiary limited to right of residence, with the beneficiary's consent to a sale being required generally, with provision for changing residences

[(1) *As sub-cl (1) of* Form B8.1 *at para* **[208.38]**.]

[(2) *As sub-cl (2) of* Form B8.1 *at para* **[208.38]**.]

(3) My trustees shall not during the lifetime of [my wife] sell the said or any substitute dwellinghouse or exercise their power to purchase any substitute dwellinghouse or exercise any of their other powers (conferred hereby or by law) over any such dwellinghouse without the consent in writing of [my wife] [Provided that while [my wife] is not in residence in any such dwellinghouse my trustees may grant leases or tenancies of it or of any part or parts of it without her consent].[1]

[(4) *As sub-cl (4) of* Form B8.1 *at para* **[208.38]**.]

[(5) *As sub-cl (5) of* Form B8.1 *at para* **[208.38]**.]

[(6) *As sub-cl (6) of* Form B8.1 *at para* **[208.38]**.]

(7) My trustees shall pay the net rents and profits of any such dwellinghouse arising before the sale thereof (if any) to [my wife].[2]

[(8) *As sub-cl (7) of* Form B8.1 *at para* **[208.38]**.]

[(9) *As sub-cl (8) of* Form B8.1 *at para* **[208.38]**.]

[(10) *As sub-cl (9) of* Form B8.1 *at para* **[208.38]**.]

[(11) *As sub-cl (10) of* Form B8.1 *at para* **[208.38]**.]

[Take in administrative powers and provisions as appropriate (see para **[208.36]**), such as Form B20.20 (borrowing) at para **[220.69]**, Form B21.12 (trustee indemnity) at para **[221.16]** and Form B21.37 (trustee power to charge) at para **[221.49]**.]

1 On this subclause, see paras **[208.21]** and **[208.22]**. In order to adapt the form to take account of civil partnerships formed pursuant to CPA, substitute 'civil partner' for 'wife' and amend 'she' to 'he' as appropriate.

2 See paras **[208.21]** and **[208.22]**. This subclause will prevent interests in possession stopping and starting where the beneficiary goes out of occupation, the property is let, and later the beneficiary returns to live there. It also will encourage the beneficiary to consent to a letting while she is out of residence, where her consent to such letting is not dispensed with.

[208.40]

Form B8.3: Trust to permit residence and use of furniture etc by the testator's wife and children[1]

(1) I devise my freehold residence known as —— to my trustees upon trust for my wife and my children to reside therein so long as they so desire and so long as they or any of them shall so desire and so reside the said property shall not be sold without the consent of such one or more of them so desiring to reside.[2] I declare that no involuntary ceasing to reside in the said property shall be construed as a ceasing to reside therein[3] and I wish my trustees to impose as a condition in relation to such residence that it shall be subject to the payment by those or the one so residing as the case may be of the council tax, cost of keeping the said property in reasonable repair and other outgoings. My trustees shall not be responsible for any neglect of the obligations of those or the one so residing. Subject as aforesaid my trustees shall hold the said property and any assets representing the same and the income thereof as part of my residuary estate as hereinafter defined.

(2) If those so residing in —— aforesaid under the provisions of the last preceding subclause shall desire to reside in some other house then I hereby further authorise my trustees to sell the said house and out of the proceeds of sale thereof to purchase such other house as those so residing shall choose, provided always that no more than the proceeds of such sale shall be required to cover all the costs of sale and purchase and conveyance or transfer of the properties. In case immediate possession cannot be secured of such alternative residence I authorise my trustees at their absolute discretion to raise a sum not exceeding £—— out of my residuary estate and apply the same to the reasonable expenses incurred by those so residing in securing accommodation pending taking possession of the alternative residence. Such alternative residence [shall be situated in the United Kingdom and] may be freehold or leasehold the term of which has not fewer than 60 years unexpired and shall be vested in my trustees upon trust subject to the requirement of consent or consents to a sale as aforesaid such alternative residence to be held upon the trusts of this my will concerning —— aforesaid.

(3) I bequeath to my trustees all my furniture and household and domestic effects upon trust with power to sell the same at their discretion

and declare that no sale thereof shall be had without the consent of my wife and my children or such of them as shall for the time being be residing in —— aforesaid or the house substituted thereof under the provisions of the last preceding subclause. My trustees shall allow my wife and my children for the time being residing in the property specified in subclause (1) or subclause (2) of this clause the use of such furniture and they or such of them as shall for the time being be residing in the said property shall be responsible for the repair upkeep and insurance of such furniture. My trustees shall not be responsible for the neglect of the above obligations in respect of such furniture but nevertheless my trustees may take such steps as they think fit for the protection and preservation thereof. All moneys received in respect of any insurance of such furniture shall be applied in replacement or reinstatement thereof. Subject as aforesaid the said furniture or the proceeds of sale thereof shall fall into my residuary estate as hereinafter defined.[4]

1 The inheritance tax implications of this form need to be considered carefully if its use is contemplated—it could have advantages or disadvantages depending on the facts. The widow and children will have interests in possession in equal shares of the property and because these arise immediately upon the testator's death they will be IPDI's: see paras **[200.98]** and **[208.31]**). This is likely to be disadvantageous for inheritance tax purposes for reasons given in para **[208.32]** above. It would be better to interpose initial discretionary trusts so that they are not IPDIs: see para **[208.33]** above for discussion of possible methods of IPDI avoidance in relation to rights of residence. It is not entirely clear whether one of them leaving to live elsewhere will cause a lifetime termination of his or her interest in possession. It seems from the Special Commissioner's decision in *Woodhall v IRC* [2000] STC (SCD) 558 that the interest in possession of one of them who is not living there may continue so long as at least one of them is still living in the house and the one not living there retains the right to return (see para **[208.14]**). This could have considerable advantages on the death of the widow as it would reduce the proportion of the house treated as part of her taxable estate on death if some or all of the children had interests in possession in the property even if not actually living there. There will clearly be a lifetime termination if occupation ceases and the house is sold, or where one of them irrevocably renounces the right. This will not matter if the termination is a potentially exempt transfer (see Part A, para **[200.70]**) and he or she survives the occasion by seven years or does not do so but does not turn out to have had taxable assets (including his or her estate on death and the capital value of his or her former deemed share of the property) in excess of the inheritance tax nil-rate band. It should be remembered, however, that the spouse exemption (see Part A, paras **[200.71]** and **[200.84]**) will only apply on the testator's death as respects the part or share subject to the widow's immediate post-death interest in possession. This could give rise to unnecessary tax charges on the testator's death, but will not do so if the children's shares and any other non-exempt parts of the estate do not exceed the inheritance tax nil-rate band. If the *Woodhall* decision stands this could be a tax efficient form of disposition to provide a residence for someone who is not the testator's spouse, eg by adding that person's children to the beneficiaries and so reducing the inheritance tax charge on that person's death.

For administrative powers which could suitably be added, see para **[208.36]**.

In order to adapt the form to take account of civil partnerships formed pursuant to CPA 2004, substitute 'civil partner' for 'wife' and amend 'she' to 'he' as appropriate.

2 This sentence makes a distinction between the requirement as to when consent is needed, and the requirement as to whose consent is needed when it is needed. If at least one of the beneficiaries is residing in the property and the trustees wish to sell the house the trustees must get the consent of all those who wish to reside there, including those who wish to reside there but are not actually doing so. If none of the wife or the children is in residence the trustees are free to sell the property without the consent of any of them *whether or not any of them wants to reside there*. If the words 'and so reside' are omitted from this sentence the consent of all those who wish to reside is needed even when none of them is in residence, but the trustees' task is made more difficult in the event of them all ceasing to live

in the property. If those words are omitted, the words in the next sentence from 'that no involuntary ceasing' to 'reside therein and' (inclusive) should also be omitted.

3 See para **[208.23]**.

4 For settlements of chattels, see also the Note on furniture in B4 at para **[204.37]** ff and Forms B4.10 (at para **[204.24]**) and B4.26 to B4.30 (at paras **[204.44]–[204.48]**).

[208.41]

Form B8.4: Trust for wife for life or until she remarries and then for son, with power to permit residence[1]

I devise my freehold house and land known as No —— —— Street —— in the county of —— [free of all sums charged or otherwise secured thereon at my death (which sums shall be paid out of my residuary estate)] to my trustees to hold the same and the assets from time to time representing the same upon trust for my wife during her life [until she remarries or forms a civil partnership] [2] and after her death [or remarriage or the formation of a civil partnership][2] my trustees shall hold the said property if unsold or the assets representing the same for my son CB[3] absolutely. I intend the said property to be available for occupation by my wife and that my trustees should during the period of such occupation require her to pay all council tax and other outgoings payable in respect of the same and keep the said property in good repair and condition and refund to my trustees the cost of keeping the same insured. My trustees shall not be liable to see to such repair or the effecting or keeping up of such insurance or for any breach of the obligations hereby imposed on my wife.[4]

1 Unless the testator is domiciled in the UK and the wife has a foreign domicile, this gift will be exempt from inheritance tax on the testator's death (see Part A, paras **[200.84]** and **[200.85]**), but the property will be charged to inheritance tax on her death as part of her estate unless the interest ends on remarriage and she has remarried (see Part A, para **[200.86]**). If the interest is made to terminate on remarriage, and she remarries, the remarriage will cause a lifetime termination of an interest in possession, which will be treated as a lifetime transfer by her of the property, and which may be potentially exempt (see Part A, para **[200.70]**). The right of residence will be an IPDI (see paras **[200.98]** and **[208.31]** above), and the exemption for gifts to spouses still applies, and will also apply where the beneficiary is the surviving spouse of the testator. If the alternative of termination of the wife's interest on marriage is included, as the property will vest absolutely in the son if the wife remarries, this should be a potentially exempt transfer: see para **[200.71]** above.

2 Both alternatives should be included; it is not inconceivable that a widowhood will end by the formation of a civil partnership rather than by remarriage.

3 Following the commencement of GRA 2004 on 4 April 2005, it is important to name the son referred to. See Vol 1 at **[81.1]**.

4 For administrative powers which could suitably be added, see para **[208.36]**.

[208.42]

Form B8.5: Trust for civil partner for life or until marriage or the formation of another civil partnership and then for son, with power to permit residence[1]

I devise my freehold house and land known as No —— —— Street —— in the county of —— [free of all sums charged or otherwise secured thereon at my death (which sums shall be paid out of my residuary estate)] to my trustees to hold the same and the assets from time to time representing the same upon trust for my [*civil partner*] [*name*] [*during his life*] / [*so long as he shall not form another civil partnership or marry*] and after his [*decease*] / [*or marriage or formation of another civil partnership whichever shall first happen*][2] my trustees shall hold the said property if unsold or the assets representing the same for my son CB[3] absolutely. I intend the said property to be available for occupation by my civil partner and that my trustees should during the period of such occupation require her to pay all council tax and other outgoings payable in respect of the same and keep the said property in good repair and condition and refund to my trustees the cost of keeping the same insured. My trustees shall not be liable to see to such repair or the effecting or keeping up of such insurance or for any breach of the obligations hereby imposed on my civil partnership.[4]

1 See Form 8.4, n 1 above. The right of residence will be an IPDI (see paras **[200.98]** and **[208.31]** above), and the exemption for gifts to spouses still applies, and will also apply where the beneficiary is the surviving civil partner of the testator. If the alternative of termination of the civil partner's interest on the formation of another civil partnership or on marriage is included, as the property will vest absolutely in the son if the civil partner marries or forms a new civil partnership, this should be a potentially exempt transfer: see para **[200.71]** above.

2 Both alternatives should be included; it is not inconceivable that the situation will change by the formation of a civil partnership or a marriage.

3 Following the commencement of GRA 2004 on 4 April 2005, it is important to name the son referred to. See Vol 1 at **[81.1]**.

4 For administrative powers which could suitably be added, see para **[208.36]**.

[208.43]

Form B8.6: Gift of residence for wife for life with the intention that she reside there—fuller form, providing for the possibility of a change of house by the testator before his death or by the trustees after his death[1]

(1) I give my [interest in the] freehold dwellinghouse known as ——, or (if the same shall be sold or otherwise disposed of before my death) the estate or interest owned by me at my death in my then dwellinghouse or my then principal dwellinghouse (if I have more than one),[2] to my trustees free of all sums charged or otherwise secured thereon at my death (which sums shall be paid out of my residuary estate) to hold the same and the assets from time to time representing the same on trust for [my wife] during her life and subject to [my wife's] said interest on trust as part of my residuary estate.

(2) It is a purpose of the foregoing trust to provide a home for [my wife] so long as she so desires[3] and I declare that my trustees shall not be liable for lack of insurance repair or payment of outgoings of any home occupied by her under the foregoing trust or for not taking steps to enforce any reasonable conditions imposed by my trustees on [my wife] in relation to her occupation of any such home.[4]

(3) In addition to their statutory powers of investment and acquisition of assets my trustees may acquire [land or buildings outside the United Kingdom or] any undivided share (whether in co-ownership with [my wife] or any other person) in land or buildings [in the United Kingdom or elsewhere] for any purpose including provision of a home for [my wife], and may apply capital in the improvement or repair of any land or buildings for the time being subject to the foregoing trust.[5]

[(4) My trustees shall have the same powers and [my wife] shall have the same rights in relation to any property subject to this clause which is situated outside England and Wales as they would have if it were situated in England and Wales.][6]

(5) All the powers of my trustees may be exercised by them in favour of or for the benefit of [my wife] even though she is one of my trustees, and at any time when she is not one of my trustees her consent shall still be required to any exercise of the trustees' powers of sale purchase or leasing in relation to any land or buildings or interest therein subject to this clause.[7]

[Other provisions of Form B8.1 at para **[208.38]** which could be added here are: sub-cl (4), (5)(c), (d), (7)(b) and (9). Take in administrative powers and provisions as appropriate (see para **[208.36]**), such as Form B20.20 (borrowing) at para **[220.69]**, Form B21.12 (trustee indemnity) at para **[221.16]** and Form B21.37 (trustee power to charge) at para **[221.49]**.]

1 This Form shows the TLATA 1996 at its best. The removal of the need for a trust for sale (see para **[200.55]**), the statutory right of occupation (see para **[208.5]** ff) and the wide administrative powers given to trustees of land (see para **[220.49]** ff), reduce the amount of express provision needed and enable clauses of this kind to be more concise and comprehensible. The right of residence can also be made to terminate on, eg remarriage or the formation of a civil partnership although this is not recommended because the wife will have limited security and may bring a claim under the Inheritance (Provision for Family and Dependants) Act 1975 (see Vol 1 at **[105.1]** ff). Under this clause, if the house is sold and the beneficiary goes to live with a relative or in rented accommodation, she will be entitled to the income of the proceeds of sale as invested. Because this Form gives the widow an interest in possession (the right of residence will be an IPDI, see paras **[200.98]** and **[200.31]**) in the property from the testator's death, the gift should be exempt from inheritance tax on the testator's death as a gift to a spouse, unless at the testator's death the testator is domiciled in the UK, his wife is not, and the £55,000 limit for exempt gifts in such circumstances is exceeded: see Part A, para **[200.85]**. If the house is outside the UK (or might be replaced by a property outside the UK), the inclusion of a provision freeing the gift from foreign death duties should be considered. If the form is being adapted for use for someone other than the testator's spouse, or the testator is domiciled in the UK but his spouse is not (so that the gift will not necessarily be wholly exempt from inheritance tax—see Part A, para **[200.85]**), and the inheritance tax on the gift might not be borne by residue in the absence of express provision to that effect (eg the property is or might be outside the UK or the gift is an exercise of a general power of appointment over settled property: see the Preliminary Note to B14 at para **[214.60]**) a provision freeing the gift from inheritance tax should also be considered. In order to adapt the form to take account of civil partnerships formed pursuant to CPA 2004, substitute 'civil partner' for 'wife' and amend 'she' to 'he' as appropriate.

2 If the testator might have more than one property at his death, Form B8.1, sub-cl (2) (at para **[208.38]**) would provide more comprehensively for this eventuality. The words 'interest in the' in the first line, in square brackets, are to be left in or omitted depending on whether the testator owns an undivided share of the property or the whole of it at the time of making the will.

3 This should be sufficient to confer the statutory right of occupation on the beneficiary under the TLATA 1996, s 12(1)(a) (Part G, para **[246.144]**): see para **[208.7]**.

4 In the interests of economy there is no expression of wishes as to the conditions to be imposed on the beneficiary, but such could be included as in Form B8.1, sub-cl (4) at para **[208.38]**. See also nn 5 and 6 to that subclause.

5 These are all thought to be applications of capital money which are not authorised by the TLATA 1996 or the TrA 2000 (see para **[220.52]** ff and Form B8.1, nn 9 and 10 at para **[208.38]**. This subclause can be omitted in whole or in part if there are provisions elsewhere in the will to the same effect which apply to this clause. See note 6 concerning the words in square brackets other than 'my wife'. The statutory powers of acquisition of assets are now in the TrA 2000, ss 3 and 8 (Part G, paras **[246.135]** and **[246.140]**; see also para **[220.11]** ff).

6 The statutory rights and powers under the TLATA 1996, s 6(1) (Part G, para **[246.108]** and see para **[220.49]**) only apply to land in England and Wales: TLATA 1996, s 27(3) (Part G, para **[246.130]**). If land in Scotland or Northern Ireland is acquired under the statutory power to do so in the TrA 2000, s 8(1) (Part G, para **[246.140]**), they have the same statutory powers of management in relation to that land (TrA 2000, s 8(3)), but this will not apply to land in Scotland or Northern Ireland acquired under an express power or comprised in the testator's estate at his death. This subclause may be omitted if there is no likelihood of the beneficiary wanting to live outside England and Wales, and if it is omitted the words in square brackets other than 'my wife' in the preceding subclause should also be omitted.

7 The TLATA 1996, s 8(2) enables exercise of the trustees' powers over land to be made subject to consents. The repeal of the LPA 1925, s 28(1) (see para **[200.60]**) means that a requirement of consent to a sale is no longer applied by statute to other powers.

[208.44]

Form B8.7: Clause in will of widow or widower providing residence and furniture for children [1]

If any of my children are under [18]/[21] when I die then I give to my trustees free of [inheritance tax foreign death duties and][2] all sums of money charged or otherwise secured thereon at my death (which sums shall be paid out of my residuary estate) my freehold house known as [description] or other the house which I may own as my [principal] residence at the date of my death together with all my household furniture and household effects therein to hold such house furniture and effects and the assets from time to time representing the same ('the Fund') upon the following trusts and in accordance with the following provisions—

(a) my trustees shall hold the Fund in trust for such of my children as [are under the age [18]/[21] at my death and][3] shall attain the age of 25 years if more than one in equal shares;

(b) all of my children who have a vested or presumptive share under the foregoing trust shall be entitled to reside in the said house or any house representing the same free of charge and to use the said furniture and effects;[4]

(c) my trustees may allow such other persons as they think fit to reside in the house free of charge with any of my children who are for the time being residing there;

(d) my trustees shall keep the said house and the furniture and effects in good repair and insured comprehensively and to their full value and ensure that the rates and other outgoings are paid and the money required to discharge these obligations shall be found out of the income (or if that is insufficient then out of the capital) of the share or shares of my residuary estate in which the children who are residing in the house have for the time being a vested or contingent interest.

1 This clause contemplates a situation in which the testator's spouse is dead and in which he wishes to make express provision for his house to be used by his children while they are under 18 or 21. If the spouse is still alive the clause can be worded so as to take effect only if the spouse predeceases the testator, but it is not suitable for use in the event of the spouse surviving the testator. If the selected specified age is 18, the trust should be a trust for bereaved minors (see para **[200.108]**), and if the specified age is 21 (or another age between 18 and 25), the trust should be an age 18-to-25 trust (see para **[200.109]**).

The express right of occupation and the right of occupation under the TLATA 1996, s 12 (see para **[208.5]** ff) mean that the beneficiaries will have interests in possession for inheritance tax purposes (see para **[200.93]** ff). If the house is sold and the fund becomes one of investments, interests in possession in the more usual sense of being entitled to a share of the income (if any) will be attained at 18 (see the Note on maintenance in B18 at para **[218.50]**), this being a trust which carries the intermediate income: LPA 1925, s 175 (Part G, para **[244.54]**).

If full powers over residue are given to the trustees (e g as in Form C2.1 at para **[224.20]**), the trustees could allow the children to reside in the house. The main use of this clause will be where the trusts of residue are unsuitable for this purpose, the testator wishes to give priority to provision of a house, or there is a wide disparity in the ages of his children and it is desired to make this provision for younger children only (see n 3 infra).

The clause must, of course, be made consistent with the rest of the will. In particular, sub-cl (e) should be varied if necessary.

2 The words 'free of inheritance tax' will be unnecessary if the house is in the UK (see B14 at para **[214.55]** ff).

3 Clearly if the ages of the testator's children are widely separated the eldest will attain an absolute interest well before the younger ones cease to need the house to live in. These parts in square brackets can be used to cut down the membership of the class of children interested under this clause, and so postpone absolute vesting, but of course they also have the effect of excluding the older children from participating in the capital.

4 The reason for this subclause is that without it interests in possession would probably only arise at 18 (see note 1), with the consequence that the children over 18 would apparently have a statutory right of occupation under the TLATA 1996, s 12 (see para **[208.5]** ff) while those under 18 would not. This also means that those who are over 18 should not be able to argue that their statutory rights give them a right to occupy to the exclusion of those who are under 18 and do not have the statutory right to occupy. There might be difficulties about the interaction of the express and statutory rights of occupation, but it is submitted that this provision will give those under 18 interests in possession within the meaning of TLATA 1996, s 12.

Miscellaneous

[208.45]

Form B8.8: Gift with the object of ensuring personal residence, giving the right to a series of short leases[1]

I give my freehold residence situate at —— and known as —— to my trustees in fee simple upon trust that my trustees shall grant a lease thereof to my wife[2] for a period not exceeding [three] years at a yearly rent of £[5] if she shall within one month from my death in writing request them so to do such lease to commence from my death and to contain an absolute covenant against assignment or underletting or parting with the possession thereof or any part thereof binding only on my said wife[2] personally[3] and such other provisions as to my trustees shall seem reasonable including a proviso for re-entry on non-payment of rent or breach of any covenant or provision therein contained and to be renewable from time to time for like periods upon request in writing made by her to my trustees not less than one month before the expiration of each period unless any lease shall have been determined under such power of re-entry but without any fine being paid for such renewal and after the death of my wife[2] or on her failing or becoming disentitled to request in manner aforesaid a grant or renewal of the said lease whichever shall first happen [and in the meantime subject to such lease and any renewal thereof under the aforesaid provisions] my trustees shall hold the said residence upon trust for [*name*] absolutely.

1 See the Preliminary Note at para **[208.4]**. This form makes the testator's wife a mere lessee for years at a rent. Now that new settled land. See also Form B8.10 at para **[208.47]** and note thereto. The inheritance tax consequences of this form are obscure. HMRC would no

doubt want to argue that the widow had an interest in possession in the property, but there are difficulties in such a view. If it does it will be one commencing from the testator's death and therefore an IPDI. The uncertainty makes this an inadvisable form to use in the present state of the law. It should be noted that if it does not create an interest in possession (so that there is no inheritance tax charge as a result of the death of the devisee) it will not be all fiscal gain, for the extent of the spouse's exemption on the testator's death will be much less. See also Part A, para **[200.84]**. It should also be noted that once the aggregate of the terms of the successive leases comes to exceed 21 years, the widow would be likely to become entitled to acquire the freehold under the LRA 1967 if the property is a house: see the LRA 1967, s 3(4). If the property is a flat she might similarly become entitled to a lease under the LRHUDA 1993, Pt I, Ch II: LRHUDA 1993, s 7(4).

2 In order to adapt the form to take account of civil partnerships formed pursuant to CPA 2004, substitute 'civil partner' for 'wife' and amend 'she' to 'he' as appropriate.

3 *Seers v Hind* (1791) 1 Ves 294. Notwithstanding the covenant against assignment, the executors will be entitled to assign any part.

[208.46]

Form B8.9: The like—in the form of a lease determinable on death with rentcharge to support residence[1]

If within three months from my death my wife shall request my personal representatives so to do they shall grant to my wife a lease of my freehold residence [*description*] for the term of 90 years determinable after the death of my wife by one month's notice in writing at an annual rent of £1 [without impeachment of waste]. Such lease shall contain her absolute covenant against assignment underletting or parting with the possession of all or any part of the property so leased and such other covenants (if any) by her as lessee as my personal representatives shall in their uncontrolled discretion think fit and a proviso for re-entry on breach of any covenant and shall be made determinable at any time by my wife on three months' notice.

If my wife shall accept such lease she will be entitled to an annual rentcharge of £—— issuing out of and charged upon [*description of the property to be charged omitting therefrom the property comprised in the lease*] commencing as from the date of such lease and continuing so long only during her life as such lease shall remain subsisting and to be payable quarterly the first quarter's payment to be made at expiration of three months from the date of the commencement of said lease.[2]

[The said lease and rentcharge are given free of inheritance tax or contribution thereto [and as regards such rentcharge free of income tax at the basic rate but not at any higher rate] and the inheritance tax attributable to the said lease and rentcharge [and the said income tax] shall be exclusively charged on the property subject to such rentcharge [but as to income tax my wife[2] shall account to my trustees for all tax repaid or otherwise allowed in account to her in respect of the tax on the said rentcharge]].[3]

1 This form undoubtedly creates a lease terminable on death within the IHTA 1984, s 43(3) so that it is treated for inheritance tax purposes as a settlement. For the effect of this as compared with a true settlement see the Preliminary Note at para **[208.4]**, above. In order to adapt the form to take account of civil partnerships formed pursuant to CPA 2004, substitute 'civil partner' for 'wife' and amend 'she' to 'he' as appropriate. After the amendments made to IHTA 1984 by FA 2006 a lease for a life or lives continues to be treated as an interest in possession under a settlement, with the consequence that this Form creates an IPDI.

2 See further the Preliminary Note to B11 at para **[211.1]** ff and Form B11.6 at para **[211.13]**.

3 This paragraph shifts the inheritance tax liability from residue to the property subject to the rentcharge.

[208.47]

Form B8.10: Gift with the object of ensuring personal residence by the devisee—alternative form using a periodic tenancy

I give my freehold residence and land at —— and known as —— to my trustees in fee simple upon trust that my trustees shall if my wife so desire let the same to her on a yearly tenancy at a rent of £[1] per annum without power for her to assign sublet or part with the possession of the same premises or any part thereof except as a furnished house for a period or periods not exceeding —— months in any one year and upon the terms of my wife[1] keeping the said premises in good and tenantable repair and insured against all damage by fire. Provided that so long as my wife [*so long as she shall not marry or form a civil partnership* and] [1] shall duly observe and perform the conditions aforesaid a notice to determine such tenancy shall not be effectual unless signed by all my trustees for the time being but after the remarriage of my wife or any default on her part in observing and performing the conditions aforesaid such notice shall be effectual if signed by my trustees other than my wife.[2]

1 In order to adapt the form to take account of civil partnerships formed pursuant to CPA 2004, account must be taken of the possibility that a widowhood will end by the formation of a civil partnership rather than by remarriage. Accordingly, for '*shall remain my widow*' in line eight, substitute '*so long as she shall not marry or form a civil partnership*'. In order to adapt the form for use by one of two civil partners, substitute 'civil partner' for 'wife' and amend 'she' to 'he' as appropriate. For '*shall remain my widow*' substitute '*shall not form another civil partnership or marry*'.

2 As with Form B8.8 (at para **[208.45]**) it is not clear whether this form creates a lease for a life for inheritance tax purposes; though we feel that the case for saying so is stronger here than in relation to Form B8.8. The remarks concerning inheritance tax in Form B8.8, n 1 at para **[208.45]** apply here also. If it does create an interest in possession it will be one commencing from the testator's death and therefore an IPDI.

In this case the wife could herself be made one of the trustees. By this means she cannot be given notice to quit against her will, whilst entitled to the tenancy.

[208.48]

Form B8.11: Gift of the testator's interest as tenant in common in a house, the gift being postponed to allow the other tenants in common to continue to reside in the house[1]

I give free of inheritance tax all my share as beneficial tenant in common in the freehold property known as [*description of property*] and all other (if any) my interest therein to my trustees to hold the same upon and subject to the following trusts and provisions—

(a) while any one or more of the following persons namely [*names of the other tenants in common*] remain alive and desire to reside in the property (and provided that the property is kept in good repair and insured comprehensively and to its full value with insurers approved by my trustees (their interest being noted on the policy) at no cost to my trustees and that my trustees are kept indemnified against all rates taxes and other outgoings in respect of the property) my trustees shall not make any objection to such residence and shall not disturb or restrict it in any way and shall not take any steps to enforce the trust for sale on which the property is held or to realise my share therein or to obtain any rents or profits from the property.

(b) subject as aforesaid my trustees shall hold the same as to both capital and income upon trust absolutely for [*name*].

1 Several people sometimes contribute to the purchase of a house as tenants in common, with the intention that all of them shall be allowed to live there for as long as they wish. Their rights in this respect may of course be defined in an agreement made between them at the time of purchase or at some later date. Failing this, however, it is necessary to include some suitable provision in their wills, and the clause which follows may be found appropriate for this purpose. From an inheritance tax point of view a provision of this kind is a 'settlement' (see the IHTA 1984, s 43(2)(a)) under which the testator's co-tenants in common may attain immediate post-death interests in possession: see *IRC v Lloyd's Private Banking Ltd* [1998] STC 559, High Court. This may not matter if their estates will be too small to attract inheritance tax charges on their deaths. Alternatively, if the co-owners are of commensurate age and hold in equal shares, an inter-vivos mutual agreement that there shall be no sale until they all die or cease to reside ought for each co-owner to be a restriction on dealing with his share incurred for full consideration, and which would minimise the incidence of inheritance tax. For trustees' powers in relation to undivided shares, see the TA 1925, s 24 (Part G, para **[246.22]**).

B9 Testamentary options

Preliminary Note .... [209.1]
FORMS
B9.1 Clause giving option to purchase land .... [209.6]
B9.2 Direction to trustees to offer farm and farming assets to the testator's sons successively at a valuation before selling under a trust .... [209.7]
B9.3 Devise of freehold property conditional upon the donee conferring a right of pre-emption on another person .... [209.8]
B9.4 Clause giving option to testator's wife to purchase retail business... [209.9]
B9.5 Clause giving option to son to take lease or purchase freehold of business premises .... [209.10]
B9.6 Clause giving option to purchase shares in family company........... [209.11]
B9.7 Clause giving option to purchase shares in private company (longer form) .... [209.12]

PRELIMINARY NOTE

[209.1]

Testamentary options generally. For an account of the general law relating to testamentary options, see Vol 1, para **[92.1]** ff. Testamentary options are a peculiarity. The gift of an option to acquire property at its market value is not really a gift at all and might be described as beneficial only in the sense that the donee is given the opportunity of acquiring the property which he would not otherwise have. An option might also be beneficial (and often is) in the sense that it gives the donee the opportunity to acquire the property at an undervalue. But the nature of a testamentary option itself is quite uncertain. The person entitled to the option may not get the asset because the personal representatives might have to sell it to pay debts or testamentary expenses (*Re Eve* [1956] Ch 479 where Roxburgh J held (at 483) that: 'in so far as the property subject to the option is required for the payment of debts, the option over that property cannot be exercised at all, and the benefit of it is totally destroyed by operation of law.'

[209.2]

Validity of testamentary options to purchase land. To be enforceable, an option to purchase land must comply with the Law of Property (Miscellaneous Provisions) Act 1989 (LP(MP)A 1989), s 2, which requires contracts for the sale or other disposition of an interest in land to be made in writing signed by or on behalf of each party to the contract. A testamentary option to purchase land will not, by its very nature, comply with that requirement. The donee could attest the will but if he is a necessary witness the gift will be void: WA 1837, s 15 (Part G, para **[244.12]**). However, a testamentary option takes effect under the will and not by way of contract, so the fact that it does not comply with the LP(MP)A 1989, s 2, would not seem to be fatal. Testamentary options are not really options in the strict sense at all but fall somewhere between options and pre-emption rights: see *Re Avard Deceased,*

Hook v Parker [1948] Ch 43 and *Brooke v Garrod* (1857) 3 K & J 608. It is advisable to ensure that a binding procedure for exercising the option is put in place by the will (see para **[209.5]**, below). Because of the decision in *Re Eve* [1956] Ch 479 it is also important to provide a relatively long period within which the personal representatives are required to set the option procedure in motion, so that they do not find that the will obliges them to sell property at a favourable price before ascertaining the debts and liabilities of the estate as this may lead to uncertainty and, possibly, the insolvency of the estate.

[209.3]
Inheritance tax and testamentary options. In estate duty days the grant of an option to purchase realty at an undervalue was treated as a gift of part of the interest in the property. Thus in the absence of a direction to the contrary in the will, the donee of the option was liable for the duty attributable to the excess value: *Re Lander, Lander v Lander* [1951] Ch 546. This was thought to have been the position for capital transfer tax until the Court of Session undermined that assumption with its decision in *Re Dougal* [1981] STC 514. The present position is that the inheritance tax attributable to *all* property in the UK (including realty) which on the death of a person vests in his personal representatives is prima facie a testamentary expense payable out of residue: see now the Inheritance Tax Act 1984 (IHTA 1984), s 211 (Part G, para **[246.100]**); see also the Note at para **[214.55]** ff for a general discussion of this topic. The tax attributable to any excess value conferred on the donee of the option is thus prima facie a testamentary expense whatever the nature of the property, provided that it is located in the UK. Foreign property, whether real or personal, prima facie bears its own tax (see para **[214.63]**) and where an option to buy foreign property at an undervalue is given but is not exonerated from inheritance tax the rule in *Re Lander* will apply.

[209.4]
Capital gains tax and testamentary options. On the transfer of an asset to a legatee, the personal representatives make neither gain nor loss for capital gains tax purposes and the legatee acquires the asset at the personal representatives' base value together with the expenses of effecting the transfer: TCGA 1992, ss 62(4) and 64(1). If the option permits the donee to acquire the asset at a favourable price he may well be regarded as a person taking under a testamentary disposition and would therefore be taken to have acquired the property at the value placed on it at the testator's death and the personal representatives will not make a gain. Some support for this view may be derived from *Re Lander, Lander v Lander* [1951] Ch 546 in which Roxburgh J held that the right to acquire property at a favourable value was a beneficial interest created by the will.

On the other hand, where the donee merely has the right to acquire the asset at market value the acquisition does not arise under the will but as a result of an independent transaction. The donee acquires the asset at its market value at the time the option is exercised, and the personal representatives dispose of it at that time and at that value. Any gain since the death ought to be subject to capital gains tax: see Whiteman, *Capital Gains Tax*

(4th edn), paras 28–45 and 28–46 and *Supplement*. This situation is not dissimilar to the case of a residuary beneficiary who makes a payment to the personal representatives in order to preserve a specific asset for his own use although he otherwise has no title to it: *Passant v Jackson* [1985] STC 133.

[209.5]
Drafting testamentary options. In drafting options the draftsman should bear the following points in mind:

(1) Although an option which does not specify a particular time for its exercise is valid, it is clearly desirable in the interests of a speedy and efficient administration for a time limit to be imposed. The Perpetuities and Accumulations Act 1964, s 9(2) (Part G, para **[246.82]**) imposes a maximum time limit of 21 years for options relating to land but a period of a month or so is all that will ordinarily be required. At the same time an option can be exercised only if the donee is aware of its existence. A time limit computed by reference to the death or the grant of probate may work unfairly if the donee is left in ignorance of his rights until too late. Older authority is to the effect that, in the context of testamentary options, time limits are enforced strictly: the rule being that equity will not enlarge the time specified in the will (see *Master v Willoughby* (1705) 2 Bro Parl Cas 244). With the exception of cases of fraud and, perhaps, laches, the older cases tend to hold that this is so even if blame for the failure to exercise the option within time can be laid at the door of the personal representatives: *Dawson v Dawson* (1837) 8 Sim 346. Thus, in *Re Avard Deceased, Hook v Parker* [1948] Ch 43, a decision of Roxburgh J, an option had to be exercised within three months of the death of a life tenant. An attempt to exercise the option out of time failed. One method of reconciling the objectives of efficiency and fairness is to impose a primary duty on the trustees to give notice of the option to the donee and to compute the time for its exercise from the service of the notice. Forms B9.1 and B9.2 at paras **[209.6]** and **[209.7]** contain options in this form.

Recently, however, two first instance decisions have sought to bypass the strict rule as to time as described above by construing the will in such a way as to conclude that time is not of the essence in the exercise of testamentary options. These are *Allardyce v Roebuck* [2004] EWHC 1538 (Ch), [2004] 3 All ER 754 and *Re Bowles Deceased* [2003] EWHC 253 (Ch), [2003] Ch 422, both of which are discussed in Vol 1 at **[92.4]**. The problem may, therefore, be less acute if tackled by a more flexible court.

(2) Where options are granted to purchase property at a valuation rather than at a fixed price, it is essential to ensure that the gift contains adequate machinery for having the price determined. Thus, an option to purchase property at the value agreed with the district valuer for probate purposes will not be capable of operating in accordance with its terms if the district valuer declines to agree the value of the property, eg because the estate is exempt from inheritance tax: *Re Malpass, Lloyds Bank plc v Malpass* [1985] Ch 42 (where, however, Megarry V-C gave effect to the option by directing an inquiry as to the value of the property to which the district valuer could have been expected to agree for probate purposes). It is also important to ensure

that the time limit imposed for exercise of the option is not inconsistent with the mechanism devised for valuation: there is little point in requiring that an option be exercised within three months of death at the value agreed with the District Valuer if that value is unlikely to be fixed until much later. Care should also be taken to ensure that the testator owns the whole of the property concerned and, if not, that there is a proper mechanism for determining the value of his interest: *Dutton v Dutton* [2001] WTLR 553.

(3) Where an option is given to purchase property at a valuation, the testator may wish also to give the donee the right to resile from the option should the price be higher than expected by him. Sub-clause (e)(v) of Form B9.3 at para **[209.8]** can be used or adapted for this purpose.

(4) It is inadvisable to confer options to purchase foreign property, particularly immovable property and possibly also shares in a foreign company, without first taking the advice of a local lawyer. It may be preferable for the testator to execute a will in accordance with the local law disposing of such property: see generally the Preliminary Note to C14 at paras **[236.1]** ff.

(5) Where an option is given to purchase business property and the property attracts an inheritance tax liability, eg because it qualifies only for 50 per cent relief or because there are 'excepted assets' which reduce the value to which the relief applies (as to which, see the Preliminary Note to B5 at para **[205.9]**) and the right to pay by instalments is available (see under 'Payment of inheritance tax by instalments' at paras **[205.17]**–**[205.20]**) the right to pay by instalments will cease when a sale of the property pursuant to an exercise of the option takes place. This could cause particular difficulty where the option is to purchase at below market value as it is not clear that the option to pay by instalments will continue to be available in relation to that proportion of the market value which is effectively given to the option-holder.

(6) Where an estate is partially exempt from inheritance tax, eg because part of it is given to the testator's spouse, it is not clear whether the gift by will of an option to purchase business or agricultural property qualifying for relief will constitute a specific gift of that property for the purposes of the IHTA 1984, s 39A so as to attract all the relief attributable to the property. If it does not, the relief will be apportioned with a resultant reduction in the size of the exempt estate: see generally the Preliminary Note to C11 at para **[233.1]** ff.

[209.6]

Form B9.1: Clause giving option to purchase land

I direct my trustees to offer my freehold property known as —— situate at —— in the county of —— to my son [*name*][1] for the purchase of the same by him at the price of £——[2] such offer to be made in writing within thirty-six[3] months of the date of my death or within twelve[3] months of the date of the grant of probate or administration to my estate (whichever shall be the longer period) and to be accepted in writing by my son within three months from the date on which such offer made by my trustees is received by my said son [but notwithstanding anything herein contained the option hereby conferred on my said son shall lapse and shall cease to be exercisable by him at the expiration of the period of thirty-nine months immediately following my death[4]].

And I declare that:

(i) such option is personal to my son to be exercised by him during his lifetime and not by any person (not even his personal representative) after his death;

(ii) the inheritance tax payable in respect of the said property on or by reason of my death or in the administration of my estate including any of the same payable by reason of the above price not being the full value of the said property shall be paid out of my residuary estate;[5]

(iii) if in their absolute and uncontrolled discretion they see fit to do so my trustees may accept from my said son a mortgage upon the said property for an amount not exceeding one-half of the above-stated option price upon such terms as to interest repayment and therein as my trustees think fit;

(iv) upon my said son exercising the said option he shall be entitled to a conveyance of the fee simple of the said property free from incumbrances other than a mortgage to secure a part of the option price in accordance with the last foregoing provision my said son paying such costs as are paid by a purchaser for value. My said son shall not be entitled to any abstract of title but shall accept without investigation such title as my trustees have at the time of the exercise of the said option save that the property shall be vested in him free from incumbrances other than as aforesaid. The incumbrances other than as aforesaid (if any) upon the said property shall be discharged out of my residuary estate and all costs of such discharge shall also be borne by my residuary estate;[6]

(v) upon any sale or other transaction by my trustees in respect of or relating to the said property any recital or statement in writing by my trustees that no offer as hereinbefore provided has been accepted by my said son shall in favour of a purchaser or other person dealing with my trustees for money or money's worth be conclusive evidence of the fact thus stated; and

(vi) my trustees shall accumulate the income of the said property until the earlier to occur of the exercise of the said option or the expiry of the time for its exercise and hold such accumulations as part of my residuary estate.[7]

1 Following the commencement of GRA 2004 on 4 April 2005, it may be important to name the son referred to. See Vol 1 **at para [81.1]**.

2 If the price is below the portion of a mortgage debt attributable to the property here in question, that fact does not show a contrary intention within the AEA 1925, s 35 (Part G, para **[246.62]**), i e an intention that the property shall be taken free from the charge: *Re Biss, Heasman v Biss* [1956] Ch 243, [1956] 1 All ER 89. The sale is expressly provided to be free from incumbrances in sub-cl (iv) of this form.

3 Long option periods are provided for because the personal representatives will not want to be compelled to sell before they know whether or not they need to sell the property on the

open market in order to discharge liabilities so it is well to provide long periods within which the option should be exercised. On the other hand, too long an option period can hamper the proper distribution of an estate.

4 The words in square brackets if included, will enable the administration to be completed even though it proves impossible to trace the beneficiary.

5 If the stated price is not the full value of the property, there is a gift of the excess to the donee. Under estate duty law the donee would have been liable for the duty in respect of such excess: see *Re Lander, Lander v Lander* [1951] Ch 546. As mentioned in the Preliminary Note to this section (at para **[209.3]**) the inheritance tax position is now different as tax in respect of land in the UK is prima facie a testamentary expense payable out of residue: IHTA 1984, s 211 (Part G, para **[246.100]**; see also para **[214.55]** ff).

6 The donee would be entitled in any event to the property free from incumbrances created after the death of the testator: *Re Fison's Will Trusts, Fison v Fison* [1950] Ch 394. This clause entitles the donee to the property free from incumbrances created at any time other than a mortgage to secure part of the option price.

7 This provision is intended to prevent there being any immediate post-death interest in possession in the shares pending exercise of the option. It is thought that without such a provision it is possible to argue (though probably incorrectly) that before the option is exercised the shares are settled property and subject to an immediate post-death interest in possession if residue is subject to such an interest. If so, the immediate post-death interest in possession would terminate, with the usual inheritance tax consequences, when the option was exercised. The termination of an immediate post-death interest on or after 22 March 2006 will be deemed to be a gift of the underlying settled property for the purposes of FA 1986, s 102, so that unless the beneficiary of the immediate post-death interest is excluded altogether from benefit after the termination, the gift with reservation rules could apply: see FA 1986, s 102ZA and para **[200.76]**.The argument has more force where the option price is below the market value. If this subclause is included the IHTA 1984, s 144 (see the Note in C3 at para **[225.83]** ff) will apply when the option is exercised.

[209.7]

Form B9.2: Direction to trustees to offer farm and farming assets to the testator's sons successively at a valuation before selling under a trust[1]

I direct my trustees as soon as conveniently may be after my death to give in writing to my adult sons [*names*][2] living at my death successively accordingly to seniority the option of purchasing my [freehold] farm and lands known as —— Farm and the live and dead stock farming machines implements and utensils therein or belonging thereto at a price to be determined by a valuer appointed by my trustees and I declare that each of my said adult sons shall have one month from the date of the giving of such respective options within which to give notice in writing to my trustees accepting the same and that my trustees shall not sell my said farm and effects unless and until all my said adult sons shall have neglected or refused to accept in writing such right of pre-emption within the time aforesaid but that no purchaser from my trustees shall be affected by the said right of pre-emption. [I declare that the right of pre-emption hereby granted is personal to my said sons and shall not be exercisable by their respective personal representatives.[3]]

1 For the inheritance tax implications of the grant of options over business or agricultural property see the Preliminary Note at para **[209.5]** and the Preliminary Note to C11 at para **[233.7]**.

2 Following the commencement of GRA 2004 on 4 April 2005, it may be important to consider whether the gift is to sons born male or to sons whether born male or female. Naming the donees also avoids the trustees being caught out by the existence of illegitimate sons who are otherwise included in the gift. See Vol 1 at **para [81.1]**.

3 The addition would avoid any suggestion that this option was exercisable after the decease of any such son, a contention which has often given rise to difficulty. See on this point *Skelton v Younghouse* [1942] AC 571, [1942] 1 All ER 650.

[209.8]

Form B9.3: Devise of freehold property conditional upon the donee conferring a right of pre-emption on another person[1]

(a) Subject to the condition imposed by subclause (b) of this clause (if it arises under the provisions of that subclause) I give my freehold property known as, etc [and registered, etc] (in this clause called the property) absolutely to [*name*] of, etc [(hereinafter called the donee)] *or* if he predeceases me then to [*name*] of, etc (and such one of these two persons as becomes entitled (subject as aforesaid) to the property on my death is in this clause called the donee)].

(b) If [*name*] of, etc (in this clause called the option holder) survives me then the gift made by subclause (a) of this clause shall be conditional upon the donee entering into an agreement with the option holder by deed signed by him or on behalf of each of them and embodying the terms set out in subclause (e) of this clause (the cost of its preparation and stamping to be paid out of my residuary estate) and if the donee refuses to accept this condition then the gift of the property to the donee shall not take effect and I give the same instead absolutely to the option holder [*or*, [*name*] of, etc] [*or*, it shall fall instead into my residuary estate].

(c) My trustees shall within six months of my death give written notice to the donee of the contents of this clause and (unless in the meantime the donee has indicated his refusal to accept the condition imposed by subclause (b)) shall as soon as possible thereafter prepare an assent to vest the property in the donee and given written notice of its preparation to the donee informing him that they will deliver the assent or authorise its delivery duly executed to the donee or to the donee's agent if at the same time the donee will deliver to the option holder or to the option holder's agent the agreement referred to in subclause (b) of this clause duly executed by the donee and if the donee does not comply with the terms of such latter notice within two months of its receipt (he being given a reasonable opportunity to do so) then he shall be deemed to have refused to accept the condition imposed by subclause (b) of this clause.

(d) My trustees shall accumulate the income of the said property until the earliest to occur of the donee's acceptance of the property on the foregoing terms the donee's rejection of the same (including any deemed refusal under the foregoing subclause) or the expiry of the period of two years less one day from my death and shall hold such accumulations on trust for the donee if he accepts the property as aforesaid and otherwise [upon trust for [the option holder] [*name of alternative donee*] [as an accretion to my residuary estate].[2]

(e) The agreement referred to in subclause (b) of this clause shall embody the following terms:

- (i) That it shall remain binding and effective until the end of the period of 21 years from my death or until the death of the option holder (whichever shall happen first).
- (ii) That if the donee dies and the option holder within two months of the death gives written notice (in this clause called the option notice) to the donee's personal representatives of the option holder's desire

to purchase the property then the terms set out in paragraphs (iv) and (v) of this subclause shall take effect.

(iii) That if the donee desires to dispose (whether by sale letting gift or otherwise) in his lifetime of the property or any part of it he shall give written notice of such desire to the option holder and if the option holder within two months of the receipt of such notice gives written notice (in this clause called the option notice) to the donee of the option holder's desire to purchase the property then the terms set out in paragraphs (iv) and (v) of this subclause shall take effect.

(iv) That if the option holder serves the option notice within the time prescribed by paragraphs (ii) or (iii) (as the case may be) of this clause then the option holder and the donee (or the donee's personal representatives) shall attempt to reach agreement on the value of the property in the open market and with vacant possession at the time of the service of the option notice and if such agreement has not been reached within one month from the service of the option notice then an independent surveyor shall be appointed to make a valuation binding on both parties and at their joint expense such appointment to be made by agreement between the parties or in default of agreement by the President for the time being of the Royal Institution of Chartered Surveyors to whom application may be made by either party.

(v) That once such valuation has been agreed or made in the manner stated and communicated to both parties the option holder shall have one month in which to decide whether he wants to proceed with his intended purchase of the property at that valuation and if within that month he serves written notice on the donee (or his personal representatives) of his desire to proceed then he shall be entitled on paying the amount of the valuation to the donee (or his personal representatives) to a conveyance of the property free from all incumbrances (except for any exceptions reservations and restrictive or other covenants and conditions to which it is already subject at the date of my death) and the option holder shall not be entitled to any abstract of title but shall accept such title as the donee has (or his personal representatives have) to the property save that it shall be vested in him free from incumbrances (except as stated) that the title deeds shall be handed to him and that the donee (or his personal representatives) shall supply him with such other evidence required to perfect the title (if any) as he (or they) may be able to provide.

(vi) That if the option holder does not serve the option notice within the time prescribed by paragraphs (ii) or (iii) of this subclause or if having done so he does not serve written notice within the time prescribed by and under the provisions of paragraph (v) of his desire to proceed with the purchase then the donee (or his personal representatives) may deal with or dispose of the property free in all respects from the rights of the option holder and the option holder shall forthwith effect the cancellation of any entry which he may have made under the provisions of the Land Charges Act 1972 the Land Registration Act 2002 (or any enactments amending or replacing them) in respect of his rights under the agreement.

(vii) That whilst the option holder has rights under the agreement the donee (or his personal representatives) shall keep the property in repair and insured comprehensively and to its full value (and with the option holder's interest noted on the policy) in some insurance office of repute and shall produce to the option holder on demand the insurance policy and the receipt for the last premium.

(viii) That the rights of the option holder under the agreement are personal to him and are not exercisable by his personal representatives.

(ix) That for the purposes of all the foregoing provisions time shall be of the essence of the contract.

1 Testators sometimes desire to make a gift of property to one donee but to ensure that if he wants to dispose of it he shall offer it first to some specified third party. The form which follows provides one method of carrying out such a desire. An advantage of requiring the donee to enter into an agreement with the third party lies in the fact that the third party can then register a class C (iv) land charge against the donee (or make an entry on the Register in the case of registered land) and thus safeguard his rights. The PAA 1964, s 9 (Part G, para **[246.82]**) provides that in the case of a disposition which consists in the conferring of an option to acquire for valuable consideration any interest in land, the perpetuity period shall be 21 years. It is assumed that the property will not be mortgaged on the testator's death: if it may be, special provision should be made (e g that any mortgage shall be discharged out of residue).

2 See para **[209.6]**, n 6 and the Note in C3 at para **[225.83]** ff. As to length of option period, see para (1) of the Preliminary Note at para **[209.5]**.

[209.9]

Form B9.4: Clause giving option to testator's wife to purchase retail business[1]

I grant to my wife[2] the option of purchasing my retail business of —— carried on by me at [*address*] upon the following terms namely: my trustees shall either by themselves (and in such case in such manner as they shall in their absolute discretion think fit) or by an agent engaged by them for that purpose (and in such case at the cost of my residuary estate) fix the value of the said business as a going concern. If my wife[2] shall desire to purchase the same she shall give to my trustees written notice of said intention within three months after they have been granted probate of this will and shall give such security for the payment of the sum so fixed as my trustees shall demand the sum so secured to be payable by weekly instalments of [£——] or such other instalments as my trustees may think fit without interest and either with or without a proviso that the unpaid amount for the time being shall become payable on default in the payment of any instalment or shall become payable if my wife[2] shall sell the business or die before the price is fully paid provided that my trustees shall not be bound to enforce the payment of any instalment of purchase money if having regard to the circumstances my wife is in their opinion not in a position to pay the same. And I declare that for the purpose of this clause my business shall include all assets [including my interest in the premises on which the business is carried on] stock in trade book debts and goodwill [and moneys in the —— Bank standing to the credit of my [business] account] on the one hand and all liabilities in connection therewith on the other hand [but shall not include moneys at the bank] [nor shall it include the premises on which my said business is carried on].

1 The disposition of small businesses such as are carried on in retail shops requires very careful consideration in each individual case. The testator's wife may have taken a considerable part in the business and may frequently be capable of carrying it on. Indeed she may have become entitled to a beneficial interest in the business. In such circumstances the simplest course would be to give her the business outright. The testator may, however, wish to make provision for his children in which case a sale of the business to the wife provides a solution. Trustees cannot usually be advised to carry on the business themselves, even through the managership of the wife, as they may become personally liable for debts in the event of the failure of the business. The course suggested in this precedent is a sale to the wife on very easy terms, such as weekly payments made to a National Savings Bank account. If all goes well, the value of the business will gradually be restored for the benefit of the children, and there will be some salvage, even if the business ultimately comes to grief. Before the purchase price has been fully paid, the wife is entitled to the weekly profits which remain after the instalments have been paid to the trustees without any liability to account, and she therefore has every inducement to try and make a success of it. This clause is expressed in the simplest terms since it will obviously concern a small estate.

2 This form can be adapted for use by civil partners (pursuant to CPA 2004), by substituting 'civil partner' for 'wife' and amending 'she' to 'he' as appropriate.

[209.10]

Form B9.5: Clause giving option to son to take lease or purchase freehold of business premises[1]

I direct my trustees if requested in writing so to do by my son [*name*][2] within six months after my death or within three months of the grant of probate or administration being taken to my estate (whichever shall be the longer period)[3] to grant to him a lease of the freehold premises on which my —— business is carried on at my death. And I further direct that such lease shall be for any term not exceeding [30] years from my death as my said son shall require and shall be at a yearly rent of £—— and shall contain all such covenants and conditions as my trustees shall think fit and such lease if and when granted shall be held by my said son as part of the assets of the said business. [And I authorise my said trustees if my said son shall be desirous of purchasing the said premises instead of taking a lease thereof and upon such a request in writing as aforesaid to sell the said freehold premises to my said son at the price of £—— or at such less price as some competent valuer to be nominated by my trustees other than my son shall determine to be the fair value thereof such determination to be conclusive and the basis or method of valuation not to be questioned and in the event of such sale being made I authorise my trustees to allow such part of the purchase money as my trustees other than my said son may think fit to remain on mortgage of the said freehold premises such mortgage to be upon such terms and to contain such provisions including a provision that the mortgage money shall not be called in for any fixed term as my trustees other than my said son may think fit.]

1 This clause is intended for use in conjunction with a gift of the business itself. For a precedent for a gift of such a business see Form B5.1 at para **[205.58]**.

2 Following the commencement of GRA 2004 on 4 April 2005, it may be important to consider whether to name the son. See Vol 1 at para **[81.1]**.

3 The grant of an option exercisable within a period measured by reference to the death only can cause difficulties if no grant is taken out within that time.

[209.11]

Form B9.6: Clause giving option to purchase shares in family company[1]

I direct my trustees as soon as conveniently may be after my death to give in writing to my son ——[2] living at my death the option to purchase —— shares in the —— Company Limited at a price to be determined by an accountant to be agreed upon by my son and my trustees and in default of such agreement to be nominated by my trustees [*or other person*]. I declare that my son shall have one month from the date of the receipt of such notice[3] in which to exercise the same but no purchaser of the said shares shall be in any way affected by the terms of this clause.

1 For the inheritance implications of the grant of options to purchase business property, see the Preliminary Note to this section at para **[209.3]**. The company will be a private company and there will be some restriction on the transfer of shares which might interfere with the registration of transfers of shares to the sons. Restrictions which restrict the disposition by will are sometimes directed to the prevention of a substantial interest in the company becoming vested in a stranger.

2 Following the commencement of GRA 2004 on 4 April 2005, it may be important to consider whether to name the son. See Vol 1 at **para [81.1]**.

3 It is assumed that the whereabouts of all the sons are known to the trustees. If not, the posting of such a notice addressed to his last known address should be made sufficient service of such a notice, and the period of one month should be made to run from the time of such posting. In such a case the period of one month may have to be lengthened if it is thought any son is in a part of the world difficult to reach by post. However, the only practical course in such a case is to make the period run from the date of posting.

[209.12]

Form B9.7: Clause giving option to purchase shares in private company (longer form)[1]

I direct my trustees to offer my shares in —— Limited (*if necessary limit the number and description of the shares*) to my son [*name*][2] for the purchase of the same by him at the price of £—— per share [*or* at the current market value determined as provided below] such offer to be made within twelve months of the date of my death or within six months of the grant of probate or administration to my estate (whichever shall be the longer period)[3] and to be accepted by my son within six months from the date on which such offer made by my trustees is received by my said son [but notwithstanding anything herein contained the option hereby conferred on my said son shall lapse and shall cease to be exercisable by him at the expiration of the period of two years immediately following my death[4]].

And I declare that:

(i) such option is personal to my son to be exercised by him during his lifetime and not by any person (not even his personal representatives) after his death;

[(ii) the inheritance tax payable in respect of the said shares on or by reason of my death including any payable by reason of the above price not being the full value of the said shares shall be paid out of my residuary estate;[5]]

(iii) if in their absolute and uncontrolled discretion they see fit to do so my trustees may accept from my said son a charge upon the said shares for an amount not exceeding one-half of the above-stated option price.

(iv) upon my said son exercising the said option he shall be entitled to a transfer of the said shares free from all liens and charges other than a charge to secure a part of the option price in accordance with the last foregoing provision my said son paying such costs and stamp duty as are paid by a purchaser for value. Any lien or charge other than as aforesaid (if any) upon the said shares shall be discharged out of my residuary estate and all costs of such discharge shall also be borne by my residuary estate;[6]

(v) upon any sale or other transaction by my trustees in respect of or relating to the said shares after the expiration of the above-mentioned period of two years a statement in writing by my trustees that no offer as hereinbefore provided has been accepted by my said son shall in favour of a purchaser or other person dealing with my trustees for money or money's worth be conclusive evidence of the fact thus stated;

[(iv) the current market value aforesaid shall be determined in accordance with subsection (3) of section 272 of the Taxation of Chargeable Gains Act 1992 (taking the day before the service of the notice exercising the said option as the 'relevant date' therein referred to) unless the said subsection does not apply in which case the said market value shall be determined as at the date of service of such notice by an accountant acting as expert and not as arbitrator to be agreed upon by my said son and my trustees or in default of agreement to be nominated upon the application of my said son or my trustees by the President of the Institute of Chartered Accountants in England and Wales the costs of such valuation to be borne equally by my said son and my estate;]

(vii) my trustees shall accumulate the income of the said shares until the earlier to occur of the exercise of the said option or the expiry of time for its exercise and hold such accumulations as part of my residuary estate.[7]

1 See para **[209.11]**, n 2.

2 Following the commencement of GRA 2004 on 4 April 2005, it may be important to consider whether to name the son. See Vol 1 at para **[81.1]**.

3 See sub-para (1) of the Preliminary Note at para **[209.5]**.

4 See para **[209.6]**, n 3.

5 Where the option price is less than the full value of the shares there is a gift of the excess value to the donee, the inheritance tax in respect of which will prima facie come out of residue. In estate duty days where there was a beneficial option to purchase property which bore its own duty, the duty attributable to the excess value was payable by the donee: *Re Lander, Lander v Lander* [1951] Ch 546, [1951] 1 All ER 622.

Since real estate now bears its own tax, this principle will no longer apply save possibly in relation to foreign property: see Preliminary Note at para **[209.3]** and see generally the Note to B14 at para **[214.55]** ff. The benefit of the option being exercisable at a price below the full value of the shares is not a specific gift. If the residue is insufficient to pay debts, etc, then the shares are the last property available for debts and as long as the other assets together with the purchase price of the shares are sufficient to meet the liabilities of the estate, then the purchase price and not the shares constitute part of the fund available for payment of debts, etc: *Re Eve, National Provincial Bank Ltd v Eve* [1956] Ch 479, [1956] 2 All ER 321.

6 The donee would be entitled in any event to the shares free from incumbrances created after the death of the testator: *Re Fison's Will Trusts, Fison v Fison* [1950] Ch 394, [1950] 1 All ER 501. This clause entitles the donee to the property free from incumbrances created at any time other than a charge to secure part of the option price.

7 See para **[209.6]**, n 6.

B10 Pecuniary legacies

Preliminary Note ..... [210.1]

ABSOLUTE GIFTS

FORMS

B10.1 Legacy to one individual ..... [210.9]
B10.2 Gift of a number of legacies ..... [210.10]
B10.3 Legacies given by reference to a schedule..... [210.11]
B10.4 Legacy to husband and wife or survivor ..... [210.12]
B10.5 Direction as to payment of interest at a variable rate ..... [210.13]
B10.6 Legacy uprated by reference to Index of Retail Prices..... [210.14]

PROVISION FOR IMMEDIATE NEEDS

Note..... [210.15]

FORM

B10.7 Immediate legacy to wife or civil partner or other person in charge of testator's household ..... [210.19]

DEFERRED AND PRIOR LEGACIES

FORMS

B10.8 Legacy payable six months after the death of the survivor of testator and his wife ..... [210.20]
B10.9 Legacy with priority..... [210.21]
B10.10 Declaration as to time of payment and priority of legacies..... [210.22]
B10.11 Legacy payable on death of life tenant ..... [210.23]
B10.12 Power to trustees to postpone payment of legacies..... [210.24]

LEGACIES WITH SUBSTITUTIONAL PROVISIONS

FORMS

B10.13 Legacy with a clause of substitution in the case of an individual legate ..... [210.25]
B10.14 Legacy to nieces, and the children of deceased nieces..... [210.26]

LEGACIES TO DEBTORS AND CREDITORS

Note..... [210.27]

FORMS

B10.15 Legacy to a creditor ..... [210.28]
B10.16 Declaration as to legacies to creditors..... [210.29]
B10.17 Legacy to debtor without forgiveness of debt ..... [210.30]
B10.18 Legacy to debtor with forgiveness of debt ..... [210.31]
B10.19 Legacy to a son subject to deduction of sums owing..... [210.32]

MINORS AND CHILDREN

FORMS

B10.20 Legacy to minor ..... [210.34]
B10.21 Small legacy to minor with provision for opening National Savings Bank account..... [210.35]
B10.22 Legacy to a minor who is married ..... [210.36]
B10.23 Legacy to minor to be applied in maintenance ..... [210.37]
B10.24 Legacy to minor to provide an allowance for him ..... [210.38]
B10.25 Legacy of a capital sum for the education of children..... [210.39]
B10.26 Legacy to grandchildren..... [210.40]
B10.27 Legacy to an adopted child ..... [210.41]
B10.28 Legacy to children and an illegitimate child..... [210.42]
B10.29 Legacy to illegitimate children of the testator, including one en ventre sa mère ..... [210.43]
B10.30 Legacy to legitimate and illegitimate children of a brother of the testator ..... [210.44]

B10.31 Legacy to married daughters to become subject to the trusts of their respective marriage settlements, the amount of the legacies varying in order to equalise the provisions made by the testator for all his daughters .... **[210.45]**

CONTINGENT AND CONDITIONAL LEGACIES

FORMS

B10.32 Legacy contingent on attaining eighteen or twenty-one .... **[210.46]**

B10.33 Legacy contingent on attaining eighteen or twenty-one carrying interest .... **[210.47]**

B10.34 Legacies to two persons contingently on their attaining eighteen or twenty-one years of age with survivorship .... **[210.48]**

B10.35 Legacy contingent on attaining twenty-five or marrying, relying on the statutory powers of maintenance .... **[210.49]**

B10.36 Legacy subject to discharge of guarantee .... **[210.50]**

LEGACIES TO EXECUTORS AND TRUSTEES

Note .... **[210.51]**

FORMS

B10.37 Legacies to executors .... **[210.52]**

B10.38 Legacies to executors and annuities to trustees .... **[210.53]**

LEGACIES FOR IMPROVIDENT PERSONS

FORMS

B10.39 Legacy with provision for forfeiture on alienation .... **[210.55]**

B10.40 Legacy to improvident person payable by instalments .... **[210.56]**

LEGACIES TO EMPLOYEES

FORMS

B10.41 Legacy to a servant, if not under notice to leave at testator's death .... **[210.58]**

B10.42 Legacy to chauffeur with alternative gift if he shall have left the testator's service .... **[210.59]**

B10.43 Legacies to indoor servants .... **[210.60]**

B10.44 Legacies to servants—longer form .... **[210.61]**

B10.45 Legacy to clerks .... **[210.62]**

B10.46 Adjustment of legacies to servants or employees occasioned by redundancy payments under the Employment Rights Act 1996 .... **[210.63]**

INHERITANCE TAX AND FOREIGN DEATH DUTIES

Note .... **[210.64]**

FORMS

B10.47 Legacies free of inheritance tax and duties payable outside Great Britain .... **[210.68]**

B10.48 Clause dealing with inheritance tax on lifetime gifts made by the testator .... **[210.69]**

B10.49 Clause providing for payment out of residue of inheritance tax on property not passing under the will .... **[210.70]**

B10.50 Clause providing for payment by the donee of the inheritance tax on a testamentary gift which would otherwise be free of inheritance tax .... **[210.71]**

NIL-RATE BAND LEGACIES

FORMS

B10.51 Nil-rate band legacy .... **[210.72]**

MISCELLANEOUS

FORMS

B10.52 Legacies with provision for some of the legatees not being able to be found .... **[210.73]**

B10.53 Demonstrative legacy .... **[210.74]**

B10.54 Bequest of legacies payable exclusively out of a particular property with provision for abatement and interest .... **[210.75]**
B10.55 Clause providing for reduction of legacies where the testator's estate proves to have decreased in value .... **[210.76]**
B10.56 Declaration as to currency in which legacies payable .... **[210.77]**
B10.57 Direction as to rate of exchange for payment of legacies in a foreign currency .... **[210.78]**
B10.58 Legacy for purchase of customary mourning .... **[210.79]**

PRELIMINARY NOTE

[210.1]
Legacies as gifts to relatives including minors. Legacies are generally a method of remembering the relatives and friends who are not included among the main beneficiaries of the estate, but they may in some cases be used for the purpose of increasing the benefit given to one of the principal beneficiaries. Particular types of legacy may require the insertion of special provisions. See, for example para **[210.33]**.

[210.2]
Legacies to debtors or creditors. A testator must be carefully questioned as to whether the intended beneficiaries either owe money to him, or, on the other hand, he owes money to them. The debts may have to be brought into account and the position in such cases should be made clear in the will.

[210.3]
Inheritance tax a testamentary expense payable out of residue. As stated in the note at para **[214.55]** ff it is thought that the incidence of inheritance tax in respect of legacies is much the same as that of estate duty. But in one important aspect the law has changed. Under estate duty law it was settled that to the extent that a pecuniary legacy was payable out of realty (for which see below) it had to be considered as realty and bore the estate duty attributable to it: *Re Spencer Cooper, Poe v Spencer Cooper* [1908] 1 Ch 130; and *Re Owers* [1941] Ch 17. It was thought that inheritance tax payable in respect of real property was likewise prima facie payable out of the realty. But this assumption was not accepted in the context of Scottish Law by the Court of Session in *Re Dougal* [1981] STC 514. In the light of the uncertainties caused by that decision Parliament has intervened and the current position, now embodied in the Inheritance Tax Act 1984 (IHTA 1984), s 211 (Part G, para **[246.100]**) is that tax on realty is prima facie a testamentary expense payable out of residue. The problems which used to arise in cases where legacies were changed on a mixed fund of realty and personalty are now largely a thing of the past. However, a rather similar problem remains where the fund includes foreign property. It is thought that in the absence of a direction to the contrary legacies charged on such a fund, unless they are given to charity, will be liable to contribute a rateable proportion of the tax attributable to the foreign property: see *Re Sebba, Lloyds Bank Ltd v Hutson* [1959] Ch 166 at 178 (declaration (3); not reported

on this point in [1958] 3 All ER 393). A mixed fund of UK and foreign property is by no means an unlikely eventuality. It is therefore advisable to continue to include words expressly exonerating pecuniary legacies from inheritance tax, or to include a general declaration exonerating legacies from inheritance tax as in Forms B10.47 (at para **[210.68]**) and B14.33 (at para **[214.76]**).

[210.4]

Inheritance tax on legacies payable out of settled property. It is thought that legacies might also bear their own inheritance tax (in the absence of a direction to the contrary) to the extent that they are payable out of property which was settled property immediately before the testator's death, because the IHTA 1984, s 211 does not treat the inheritance tax on such property as a testamentary expense (see s 211(1)(b): Part G, para **[246.100]**). This is a point which will not arise very often in modern conditions, but it could do so where legacies are payable out of residue, and residue includes formerly settled property over which the testator had a general power of appointment or the statutory power (under the Law of Property Act 1925 (LPA 1925), s 176: Part G, para **[244.55]**) to dispose of entailed property.

[210.5]

The funds from which legacies are payable. There is a considerable body of case law on this subject, much of which is superseded or has become of small practical importance, through changes in the customary patterns of disposition and changes in the law. The principal questions which have arisen are the following (references to realty and personalty below refer to realty and personalty which is not the subject of a specific gift):

(1) Whether the legacies are payable out of realty, or only out of personalty with the consequence that they abate if personalty is insufficient.
(2) Where the legacies are payable out of both realty and personalty, whether they are payable rateably out of both or only out of realty to the extent to which personalty is insufficient.
(3) Where there is an undisposed of share of residue, whether the legacies are payable out of it in priority over other shares of residue, or whether all shares of residue, disposed of or undisposed of, bear the legacies rateably.

Of these three questions, the third is the one which is most likely to arise in modern conditions, and the one which is affected by the 1925 property legislation, and it is discussed together with the similar problems which arise in relation to debts and administration expenses at para **[214.7]**. The law relevant to the first two questions was not altered by the 1925 property legislation (see *Re Thompson, Public Trustee v Husband* [1936] Ch 676, [1936] 2 All ER 141; *Re Rowe, Bennetts v Eddy* [1941] Ch 343; *Re Ridley, Nicholson v Nicholson* [1950] Ch 415, [1950] 2 All ER 1; and *Re Timson, Harper v Timson* [1953] 2 All ER 1252). The factors which have rendered the first two of the above questions less important than formerly are—

(a) it is now usual for a single combined residuary gift to be made of realty and personalty;

(b) it is very unusual to make separate gifts of residuary realty and residuary personalty; realty and personalty are, and have been since 1925, subject to a common set of intestacy rules; and
(c) the former rule that personalty was free of estate duty but realty bore its own duty (in the absence of express provision) has been altered in favour of both realty and personalty (situated in the UK) being free of inheritance tax in the absence of express provision (see para **[214.55]** ff).

These are all factors which do not abolish the previous law on these topics, but which have the consequence either that the issues do not arise, or that where they could arise on the wording of the will, the determination of the issue does not matter because the outcome either way produces the same result for who gets what. On the other hand, in consequence of some of the changes to the law made by the TLATA 1996, it has become possible to abandon the former almost universal practice of imposing a trust for sale and conversion of the assets comprised in residue (see paras **[214.5]** and **[214.6]**). A check on the law concerning the burden of legacies is therefore called for, so as to make sure that this change in practice would not have unexpected consequences.

[210.6]
Liability of realty for legacies. Where the estate is wholly disposed of by will (for the effect of partial intestacy see paras **[214.4]** and **[214.5]**), in the absence of provision to the contrary, legacies are payable only out of personalty not specifically bequeathed: *Robertson v Broadbent* (1883) 8 App Cas 812; *Re Rowe, Bennetts v Eddy* [1941] Ch 343, [1941] 2 All ER 330; *Re Ridley, Nicholson v Nicholson* [1950] Ch 415. One very common form of contrary provision is where there is a gift of legacies followed by a residuary gift of real and personal estate, in which case either the real estate is liable for the payment of the legacies if personalty is insufficient (*Greville v Browne* (1859) 7 HL Cas 689; *Re Thompson, Public Trustee v Husband* [1936] Ch 676, [1936] 2 All ER 141), or, where the testator created by his will a mixed fund for such payment, realty and personalty are liable rateably to provide the legacies: *Roberts v Walker* (1830) 1 Russ & M 752; *Re Boards, Knight v Knight* [1895] 1 Ch 499. Where realty is liable for payment of legacies, and there is no difference in the destination of residuary realty and personalty, it will not usually matter whether realty is liable for them rateably with personalty or only after personalty is exhausted, but there could be exceptional circumstances where it would matter. One possible example is where there is a life interest in residue, the rule in *Howe v Earl of Dartmouth* (see para **[214.35]**) is not excluded, and there are wasting assets to which the rule applies which are comprised in the residuary personalty, with the consequence that the amount of income which is treated as capital is different according to whether the legacies are payable primarily out of personalty or rateably out of realty and personalty. Another possibility is where personalty includes assets situated outside the UK, the legacies are not expressed to be free of inheritance tax, and the circumstances are such that the legacies are liable to bear some inheritance tax so far as payable out of the foreign assets

(see para **[214.57]**): in such a case the amount of inheritance tax borne by the legacies would be different according to whether the tax was borne rateably or by personalty before realty.

[210.7]
Liability of realty for legacies—what provision produces what result.

(1) Gifts of legacies followed by a gift of all the testator's real estate and the residue of his personal estate (and without a trust for sale or any other relevant provisions) will usually mean that the legacies are payable only out of the personalty, and therefore abate if the personalty is insufficient to pay them all in full: *Re Rowe, Bennetts v Eddy* [1941] Ch 343, [1941] 2 All ER 330; *Re Wilson, Wilson v McKay* [1967] Ch 53; and *Re Ridley, Nicholson v Nicholson* [1950] Ch 415).

(2) Gifts of pecuniary legacies followed by a gift of the residue of both the testator's real and personal estate (and without a trust for sale or any other relevant provisions) will normally mean that the realty is available to pay legacies, but that the legacies will be payable primarily out of residuary personalty, and out of residuary realty only if the personalty is exhausted: *Re Thompson, Public Trustee v Husband* [1936] Ch 676, [1936] 2 All ER 141; *Re Anstead* [1943] Ch 161.

(3) However, a gift of residuary realty and personalty without a trust for sale can have the effect that legacies are payable rateably out of realty and personalty if an intention to create a mixed fund is shown: *Allan v Gott* (1872) 7 Ch App 439 (a number of factors showed this, including a power to sell realty and personalty as and when they thought fit), *Re Timson, Harper v Timson* [1953] 2 All ER 1252, [1953] 1 WLR 1361 (where the will gave the real estate and the residuary personal estate upon trust after payment thereout of debts, funeral and testamentary expenses, death and legacy duties to the daughter of the testatrix; by a codicil, the same property was given to trustees upon trust for sale; the codicil was in the events which happened ineffective, but it was held to show an intention to create a mixed fund and that the testatrix regarded her estate as a single indivisible entity and the pecuniary legacies were payable rateably out of the real and personal estate).

(4) A trust for sale and conversion of residuary realty and personalty together normally creates a mixed fund where the realty and personalty bear any legacies rateably: *Roberts v Walker* (1830) 1 Russ & M 752; *Tench v Cheese* (1855) 6 De GM & G 453; *Re Spencer Cooper, Poë v Spencer Cooper* [1908] 1 Ch 130.

(5) The above points are of course subject to any express direction as to how the legacies are to be paid. A direction to pay legacies out of particular property will often have the effect that they are not payable out of other assets of the estate if the particular property is insufficient: see *Halsbury's Laws of England*, vol 17(2) Reissue, paras 411 and 530. Where a testator gave three legacies and stated expressly that they were to be first second and third charges on his real estate, the legacies were payable in the first instance out of the proceeds of sale of his real estate and only so far as that proved insufficient out of personalty: *Re Pollock* [1964] VR 554.

(6) Where there is nothing in the will which varies the statutory rules in the

AEA 1925, ss 33 and 34 and Sch 1, Pt II, and there is part of the estate which is not disposed by the will, the legacies are payable out of that part, including any realty comprised in it: see paras **[214.4]** and **[214.5]**.

[210.8]
Interest on legacies. The traditional fixed rates of interest on legacies (see Vol 1, para **[32.1]** ff) may not be appropriate in times of very low or very high interest rates. Therefore, a testator may wish to direct that interest will be payable on legacies given by his will at a variable rate based on bank base rates (see Form B10.5 at para **[210.13]**). Where a legacy carries interest, that interest is payable out of the income of the estate after payment of income tax. But the payment of interest to the legatee is gross, and the legatee will be liable to tax on that interest.

Absolute gifts

[210.9]

Form B10.1: Legacy to one individual

I. GENERAL FORM

I give to [*name*] of etc the sum of £—— free of inheritance tax.[1]

II. LEGACY PAYABLE AT FIXED TIME

I give to [*name*] of etc the sum of £—— free of inheritance tax[1] to be paid—months[2] after my death.[3]

III. LEGACY MAKING GIFTS TO CHARITY UP TO A NAMED AMOUNT

I give to the [*name of charity or similar body*] such a sum as will with the moneys I have already given to the said [*charity*] amount to £——.[4]

1 The inclusion of these words is still desirable; see the Preliminary Note at paras **[210.3]** and **[210.4]**.
Where several legacies are given, all free of inheritance tax, it is a prudent course to give the legacies simply, and add immediately after the gift of them a direction that all the legacies are to be paid free of inheritance tax. This may save mistakes, as the words 'free of inheritance tax' might easily be omitted in reference to one among a number of legacies, and this might influence the construction of the will as to the incidence of inheritance tax: see *Re King, Barclays Bank v King* [1942] Ch 413, [1942] 2 All ER 182.

2 'Months' means 'calendar months' and it is unnecessary to insert the word 'calendar': LPA 1925, s 61 (Part G, **[246.54]**). See as to this section *Re Figgis, Roberts v Maclaren* [1969] 1 Ch 123, [1968] 1 All ER 999.

3 This will not make the legacy payable at the stated time if that time is within the executor's year: see Vol 1, para **[30.31]**, but interest on the legacy will run from the stated date. There is, however, nothing to prevent the executor paying the legacy at the stated time if he is satisfied that he has assets.

4 There is no cash limit on gifts for charitable purposes made on or within 12 months before death. A rule to this effect has been abolished and it is no longer important for inheritance tax purposes to impose a monetary limit or to provide that the legacy is to be free of inheritance tax. For the former law see *Re Dawson's Will Trusts, National Provincial Bank Ltd v National Council of the YMCA Inc* [1957] 1 All ER 177, [1957] 1 WLR 391, in which a clause in similar terms expressly free of tax was held to mean that the charity was to receive the clear sum without any deduction in respect of duty payable on the lifetime gift.

[210.10]

Form B10.2: Gift of a number of legacies[1]

I give to [*name*] the sum of £——.

I give to [*name*] the sum of £——.

I give to each of my trustees who shall prove my will and act in the trusts thereof the sum of £——.[2]

All the above legacies are given free of inheritance tax.[3]

1 Where a number of legacies are given they are better set out in separate lines or paragraphs rather than in a schedule. For those who prefer a schedule, Form B10.3 (at para **[210.11]**) is included.
2 As to legacies to executors and trustees, see Form B10.35 at para **[210.49]**.
3 It is a wise precaution where all the legacies are to be free of inheritance tax to say so in an added sentence as here, for if the words are accidentally omitted in the case of one legacy then that legacy may not be free of tax; see *Re King, Barclays Bank Ltd v King* [1942] Ch 413, [1942] 2 All ER 182. See also paras **[210.3]** and **[210.9]**, n 1.

[210.11]

Form B10.3: Legacies given by reference to a schedule[1]

I give to the several persons and institutions whose names are set forth in the first column of the schedule to this clause of my will the respective legacies set opposite to such names in the second column of the said schedule and I declare that all such legacies shall be paid free of inheritance tax and that the receipt of the treasurer or other proper officer for the time being of any institution named in the said schedule shall be a sufficient discharge for the legacy given to such institution.

THE SCHEDULE ABOVE REFERRED TO.

Name of Legatee.	Amount of Legacy.

1 See para **[210.9]**, nn 1 to 4. Notice that the schedule follows the clause giving the legacies and is not placed at the end of the will as is usual in the case of deeds. Care should be taken to see that the space in the schedule is either completely occupied by the names and amounts or else it is carefully ruled through so that there can be no question of further addition after the execution of the will.

[210.12]

Form B10.4: Legacy to husband and wife or survivor

I give to [*name*] and his wife [*name*][1] the sum of £—— in equal shares absolutely provided that if either of them shall predecease me I give to the survivor the whole of such legacy absolutely.

1 This form can be adapted for use by civil partners (pursuant to CPA 2004) by substituting 'civil partner' for 'wife'.

[210.13]

Form B10.5: Direction as to payment of interest at a variable rate

I hereby declare that interest shall be payable upon legacies given by this my will during the period between the first anniversary of the date of my death and the date of payment of such legacies and such interest shall be paid at the rate of —— per cent per annum above —— Bank's base rate from time to time during such period.

[210.14]

Form B10.6: Legacy uprated by reference to Index of Retail Prices[1]

I give to [*name*] free of inheritance tax a sum determined by dividing the sum of £—— by the index figure in the Index of Retail Prices for the month in which this my will is executed and (having made allowance for any re-basing of the Index which may have happened in the meantime) multiplying it by the index figure in that Index for the month in which my death occurs. For the purposes hereof the Index of Retail Prices shall mean the Index of Retail Prices published by HM Stationery Office or any official publication substituted therefor and in the event of any change after the date hereof in the reference base used to compile the said Index the figure taken to be that at which the said Index stands after such change shall be the figure at which the said Index would have stood if the reference base current at the date hereof had been retained.

1 The Index of Retail Prices is published monthly in the Department of Employment Gazette. The current index was introduced in 1956 and replaced earlier indexes to which it can be linked back (see Industrial Relations Handbook and a publication of the Stationery Office 'Method of Construction and Calculation of the Index of Retail Prices').

Provision for immediate needs

[210.15]

Date on which legacies payable. Where on the death of a spouse, more usually the husband, the income of the wife will practically cease for the reason that during marriage she was wholly dependent on him financially, it is advisable to provide for her immediate necessities until such time as the will can be proved and there are assets which can be made available to her, though now it must be remembered that a surviving spouse or civil partner may be entitled to a pension or allowance under the Social Security Acts or under the pension scheme of the deceased spouse's or civil partner's employers and most insurance companies have policies designed to meet this need. A pecuniary legacy given to a widow 'for her immediate necessities,' though a very usual provision, hardly fulfils this requirement, for such a legacy is not in strictness immediately payable. Payment could not even in the case of clearly solvent estates be required before the end of the executor's year and this is the case even where the will expressly provides for payment at some time within the year. Where, however, the legacy is to be paid immediately after the testator's death, it has been said that the legatee is entitled to immediate payment (see *Re Riddell, Public Trustee v Riddell* (1936), as reported in 155 LT 247; *Re Pollock, Pugsley v Pollock* [1943] Ch 338, [1943]

2 All ER 443), but the decision in these cases concerns the date from which interest is payable, so that it is clear that payment of the legacy was not in fact made until some time later. There appears to be a clear distinction between legacies 'immediately payable' and those payable 'as soon as possible' after the testator's death. If it should happen that the assets are insufficient to pay all the legacies in full, such a legacy will (apart from some further provision) abate with other legacies (see Vol 1, paras **[31.1]**–**[31.5]**). This last difficulty may be overcome by giving the legacy express priority over all other legacies. The increase in the classes of possible claimants for family provision and the expansion of the court's jurisdiction made by the Inheritance (Provision for Family and Dependants) Act 1975 (Part G, paras **[247.2]** ff), for which see Vol 1, para **[105.1]** ff, make it more risky for personal representatives to make early distributions. They are only with certainty free from liability if they distribute at least six months after the date on which representation is first taken out, and without notice of any family provision claims (see s 20 of the I(PFD)A 1975). They would be wise to make a search for any proceedings which may have been issued within the time limit of six months after the date on which representation is first taken out, but which may not have been served (the period for service being four months after the date of issue).

[210.16]
Need for priority. These considerations make it essential that, if immediate necessities are to be met out of a legacy, the legacy must be made payable within a short time after the testator's death (this provision being inserted for what it is worth) but more particularly, it must be given priority over all other legacies, so that (in an ordinary case where no question of insolvency arises) it can be paid in full without any fear of questions of abatement arising. It is also important to make sure that the legacy does not bear any inheritance tax (see the note at para **[214.55]** ff).

[210.17]
Alternative provision. The desire in general being to provide for the period immediately following the testator's death may be met in a much more practical way by the husband during his life opening a current account at a bank in the joint names of himself and his wife, and the mandate to the bank stating that cheques shall require the signature of only one of the persons in whose names the account stands. There will be no inheritance tax problem in view of the spouse exemption, and it will ensure that the wife will have funds available for her immediate day-to-day requirements which might not otherwise be available, for the property in such money passes to the wife by survivorship as a joint owner thereof and the will and the personal representative are not concerned in the matter at all: *Williams v Davies* (1864) 3 Sw & Tr 437; *Re Harrison, Day v Harrison* (1920) 90 LJ Ch 186; and see *Hirschhorn v Evans* [1938] 2 KB 801, [1938] 3 All ER 491. The same principle applies for civil partners.

[210.18]
Provision of funds for immediate payment of inheritance tax. Another immediate necessity is the obtaining of sufficient funds for the payment of the

inheritance tax in order to obtain a grant of probate. Such funds are often supplied by a bank and the form of undertaking usually required is given below.

[210.19]

Form B10.7: Immediate legacy to wife or civil partner or other person in charge of testator's household

I give to [my wife] *or* [my civil partner] *or* [my friend [*name*] *or as the case may be*] the sum of £—— [free of inheritance tax] to be paid to her immediately after my death in priority to all other bequests hereby or by any codicil hereto made such legacy to be a first charge upon my estate and to carry interest from the date of my death at the rate of [—— per cent per annum] *or* [—— per cent per annum above —— Bank's base rate from time to time between the date of my death and payment].[1]

1 The payment of interest from the testator's death is the law whenever the legacy is payable on death: *Re Pollock, Pugsley v Pollock* [1943] Ch 338, [1943] 2 All ER 443, but it is better stated in the will so that no question can arise, and the opportunity can be taken to fix a realistic rate of interest. A legacy for immediate needs has no priority over other legacies: *Re Schweder's Estate* [1891] 3 Ch 44, unless expressly provided, as here.

Deferred and prior legacies

[210.20]

Form B10.8: Legacy payable six months after the death of the survivor of testator and his wife

I give to each of my nephews and nieces [*names*] the sum of £—— free of all inheritance tax[1] to be paid within six months from the death of the survivor of myself and my said wife[2] [and I direct that such legacies shall carry interest after but not before the expiration of the said period of six months].

1 It is a wise precaution where all the legacies are to be free of inheritance tax to say so in an added sentence as here, for if the words are accidentally omitted in the case of one legacy then that legacy may not be free of tax; see *Re King, Barclays Bank Ltd v King* [1942] Ch 413, [1942] 2 All ER 182. See also paras **[210.3]** and **[210.9]**, n 1.
2 This form can be adapted for use by civil partners (pursuant to CPA 2004) by substituting 'civil partner' for 'wife'.

[210.21]

Form B10.9: Legacy with priority

I give to [*name*] of etc the sum of £—— free of inheritance tax[1] to be paid in priority to all other legacies hereby or by any codicil hereto given.[2]

1 See paras **[210.3]** and **[210.9]**, n 1.
2 The effect of this provision is that the legacy will not abate with other legacies in the case of a deficiency of assets. Such a provision is not generally necessary except in the case of a legacy for immediate needs given to a wife: see paras **[210.16]** and **[210.17]**. A legacy does not take priority unless it is expressly given priority by the will: see *Re Schweder's Estate, Oppenheim v Schweder* [1891] 3 Ch 44, unless it was given in lieu of dower. A legacy to whomsoever given may be given such priority and the expression is not confined to gifts for immediate needs, though it would add to the difficulties of administration if such priority were given to a legacy payment of which was postponed for a long period.

[210.22]

Form B10.10: Declaration as to time of payment and priority of legacies

I give the following legacies which I declare shall be paid within [three] months of my death and in priority to all other legacies hereby or by any codicil hereto given [and shall be free of inheritance tax[1]] and shall carry interest from the day of my death at the rate of £—— per cent per annum that is to say [*specify the legacies intended to have priority*].

1 See paras **[210.3]** and **[210.9]**, n 1.

[210.23]

Form B10.11: Legacy payable on death of life tenant

I give to [*name*] of etc the sum of £—— and to [*name*] of etc the sum of £—— to be paid on the death of [*life tenant*] or if [*life tenant*] predeceases me to be paid on my death. And I direct that such legacies are to be paid free of all inheritance tax payable on my death or the death of the said [*life tenant*] and shall carry interest from the death of the said [*life tenant*] or if he predeceases me from the first anniversary of my death.[1]

1 Legacies of this nature are more commonly included at a later stage in the will. After a gift of immediate legacies and specific bequests, a trust for payment of debts immediate legacies and inheritance tax the income is given to the life tenant. Then follows a direction to hold the capital upon trust to pay these postponed legacies and further gifts of capital. There is, however, no objection to all the legacies being dealt with together. The postponed legacies will not be payable until the event happens upon which they are stated to be payable and they will carry interest only from the happening of that event. If the event happens in the lifetime of the testator, the legacies become immediate legacies and the better view seems to be that they then carry interest only from one year after the testator's death (as provided here): see *Re Palfreeman, Public Trustee v Palfreeman* [1914] 1 Ch 877, where certain earlier decisions were not followed. If the event happens after the death of the testator but within the executor's year, apparently interest runs from the happening of the event: *Re White, White v Shenton* (1909) 101 LT 780 (where the tenant for life died one month after the testator). It is desirable to exonerate the legacy expressly from inheritance tax on both deaths; see paras **[210.3]** and **[210.4]** and *Foster's Inheritance Tax*, K2.03.

[210.24]

Form B10.12: Power to trustees to postpone payment of legacies

I declare that the payment of the legacies hereinbefore given to [*names*] and to the trustees of the marriage settlement of my daughter [*name*][1] may if my trustees think fit be postponed for a period not exceeding [five] years from my death and shall until the same be paid carry interest at the rate of —— per cent per annum above —— Bank's base rate from time to time from the date of my death payable half-yearly [and in aid of my residuary personal estate I charge all my real estate with the payment of the said legacies and the interest thereon].[2]

1 Following the commencement of GRA 2004 on 4 April 2005, it is important to name the daughter referred to. See Vol 1, at para **[81.1]**.

2 Without such a power as this the trustees cannot ordinarily refuse to pay a legacy, if payment is demanded by a legatee of full age and there are assets available. See also paras **[210.34]**, n 1 and **[210.36]**, n 3. If any of the assets on which the legacies are charged or out of which they are payable are ones which ordinarily bear their own inheritance tax (see the Preliminary Note at paras **[210.3]** and **[210.4]**), there should be included an express direction freeing the legacies from inheritance tax.

Legacies with substitutional provisions

[210.25]

Form B10.13: Legacy with a clause of substitution in the case of an individual legatee[1]

I give £—— free of inheritance tax[2] to AB but if the said AB be dead at the time of payment I give the said legacy to CD.

1 See Vol 1, paras **[30.30]** and **[30.31]** for the time of payment. A legacy of this nature does not lapse if AB, the original legatee, dies in the lifetime of the testator but it is payable to CD in order to prevent a lapse; *Ive v King* (1852) 16 Beav 46, 54, and this is so whether AB the original legatee dies before the date of the will or after the date of the will and before the death of the testator or after the death of the testator and before the date of payment. In short it is immaterial when AB died so long as it is before the date of payment: *Ive v King* above; *Ashling v Knowles* (1856) 3 Drew 593. See also Vol 1, para **[68.2]**.

2 See paras **[210.3]** and **[210.4]** and **[210.9]**, n 1.

[210.26]

Form B10.14: Legacy to nieces, and the children of deceased nieces

I give to each of the daughters [*names*][1] living at my death [or born afterwards] of my brother [*name*] [except his daughter [*name*]] the sum of £—— free of inheritance tax[2] and if any daughter of my said brother [except the said [*name*]] shall have died in my lifetime leaving a child or children living at my death I give to such child or children the said sum of £—— free of inheritance tax[1] to be divided amongst them if more than one in equal shares.[3]

1 Following the commencement of GRA 2004 on 4 April 2005, it is important to consider whether to name the daughters. If they cannot be named, an alternative formulation such as 'children born female' might be employed, if desired. See Vol 1, at **[81.1]**.

2 See paras **[210.3]**, **[210.4]** and **[210.9]**, n 1.

3 The benefit of the WA 1837, s 33, as substituted by the AJA 1982, s 19, is confined to children or issue of the testator: for the text of s 33, as substituted, see Part G, para **[244.36]**. For a discussion of the operation of the new s 33 see Vol 1, para **[47.14]**.

Legacies to debtors and creditors

[210.27]

Presumed satisfaction of debt. In the absence of a direction to pay debts, a legacy to a creditor of a sum equal to or greater than the debt is prima facie presumed to be in satisfaction of the debt: see *Re Rattenberr, Ray v Grant* [1906] 1 Ch 667. But the presumption may be rebutted on various grounds: see Vol 1, para **[44.14]**. The testator should, in order to avoid any question being raised, expressly direct whether the legacy is in satisfaction of the debt or not. A legacy to a creditor in satisfaction of his debt has no priority over other general legacies: see *Re Wedmore, Wedmore v Wedmore* [1907] 2 Ch 277, but it carries interest from the testator's death: see *Clark v Sewell* (1744) 3 Atk 96.

For forms relating to bequests and releases of debts, see Forms B4.38 to B4.44 at paras **[204.60]–[204.66]**.

[210.28]

Form B10.15: Legacy to a creditor[1]

I give to [*creditor*] free of inheritance tax[2] the sum of £—— and I declare that this legacy is not to be taken in satisfaction of the debt due by me to him but is additional thereto.

1 For the law relating to satisfaction of debts by legacies see Vol 1, para **[44.14]**.
2 The inclusion of these words is still desirable; see Preliminary Note at paras **[210.3]** and **[210.4]**. Where several legacies are given, all free of inheritance tax, it is a prudent course to give the legacies simply, and add immediately after the gift of them a direction that all the legacies are to be paid free of inheritance tax. This may save mistakes, as the words 'free of inheritance tax' might easily be omitted in reference to one among a number of legacies, and this might influence the construction of the will as to the incidence of inheritance tax: see *Re King, Barclays Bank v King* [1942] Ch 413, [1942] 2 All ER 182.

[210.29]

Form B10.16: Declaration as to legacies to creditors[1]

In so far as any of the legacies hereby given are given to persons to whom I am indebted, I declare that such legacies are given in addition to the payment of the debts owing to them and are not to be in satisfaction of such debts.

1 See para **[210.28]**, n 2.

[210.30]

Form B10.17: Legacy to debtor without forgiveness of debt[1]

I give to [*name*] free of inheritance tax[2] the sum of £—— and I declare (but without hereby releasing or forgoing the debt hereinafter mentioned) that this legacy shall be paid to him without requiring him to bring into account the debt of £—— now owing by him to me if the same shall remain undischarged at the time when this legacy is paid.

1 Where a legacy is given to a debtor of the testator, the personal representative has a right to set off the debt against the legacy and to pay to the legatee only such balance as may then remain (if any): see Vol 1, paras **[30.10]**–**[30.13]**. If this is not intended, the declaration above may be added. The result would be to leave the debt still recoverable provided it was not statute-barred. The above right of set-off extends to statute-barred debts. The alternative in brackets releases the debt and it will not then be recoverable at all. As to release of debts see Vol 1, para **[30.4]**.
2 See paras **[210.3]**, **[210.4]** and **[210.9]**, n 1.

[210.31]

Form B10.18: Legacy to debtor with forgiveness of debt

I give to [*name*] free of inheritance tax[1] the sum of £—— and I hereby forgive and release unto him free of inheritance tax[1] all principal sums owing by him to me at the date of my death on the security of any mortgages bills bonds or other securities or otherwise together with any arrears of interest thereon which shall be outstanding at the date of my death and I direct that all such mortgages bills bonds or other securities shall as soon as may be after my death be delivered by my trustees to the said [*name*] or cancelled and that for the purposes aforesaid my trustees shall at the cost of my estate execute and deliver to the said [*name*] all necessary receipts reconveyances or reassignments and if the said [*name*] shall predecease me his legal personal representatives shall be entitled to the benefit of this release and forgiveness as if the said [*name*] had died immediately after my death.

1 See paras **[210.3]**, **[210.4]** and **[210.9]**, n 1.

[210.32]

Form B10.19: Legacy to a son subject to deduction of sums owing[1]

I give to my son [*name*][2] the sum of £—— free of inheritance tax[3] subject to the deduction therefrom of any sums of principal and interest owing by him to me at my death [and in so far as the said sums may be secured but deducted as aforesaid I direct my personal representatives to hand over to my said son all documents and securities for the same and to execute [but only at the sole cost and expense of my said son] *or* [at the expense of my residuary estate] all proper releases surrenders or other necessary documents for the discharge of such security] and I declare that in the event of the sums owing exceeding the said sum of £—— that sum of £—— shall be deducted in full and the amount of the excess shall remain due and owing.

1 See para **[210.30]**, n 1. This form, though arranged for the case of a son which is the case most commonly occurring, may be used with proper adaptation in the case of any other person.
2 Following the commencement of GRA 2004 on 4 April 2005, it is important to consider whether to name the son. See Vol 1, at **[81.1]**.
3 See paras **[210.3]**, **[210.4]** and **[210.9]**, n 1.

Minors and children

[210.33]
In the case of an absolute legacy to a minor, if the legacy is small and the minor nearing his or her majority, a testator may consider making provision in his will for the trustees to be fully discharged by a receipt given by the minor. However, it now seems that in contrast to the position in the past when trustees (in the absence of an express provision to the contrary) in order to get a sufficient discharge had to retain a minor's legacy until the minor was of full age (ie 18: FLRA 1969, s 1 (Part G, para **[246.89]**)) and able to give a good receipt, a person with parental responsibility for a minor can receive a legacy on the minor's behalf: see the ChA 1989, s 3(3) (Part G, para **[244.114]**), which came into force on 14 October 1991. The provisions of ss 2 to 4 of ChA 1989 are supplemented by ss 111 and 112 of ACA 2002 with effect from 1 December 2003 (s 111): and 30 December 2005 (s 112). ACA 2002 inserts a new s 4A providing for the acquisition of parental responsibility by a step-parent and the provisions are extended to civil partners by CPA 2004, s 75(1)(2) and Civil Partnership Act 2004 (Commencement No 2) Order 2005, SI 2005/3175. A legacy which is contingent on the minor attaining full age must be retained until the attainment of that age or previous death. Where a legacy is contingent, express provision should be made as to intermediate income as a contingent legacy is not deemed to carry income under the LPA 1925, s 176 (Part G, para **[244.55]**).

[210.34]

Form B10.20: Legacy to minor[1]

I give to [*minor*] of etc the sum of £—— free of inheritance tax[2] and if at the time when such legacy would be paid the said [*minor*] shall not have attained the age of eighteen years then I declare as follows:

(i) If the said [*minor*] shall at the time when the above legacy is paid have attained the age of sixteen years then the receipt of the said [*minor*] shall be a full and proper discharge to my trustees for the payment of the same.

(ii) If the said [*minor*] shall at the time when the above legacy is paid not have attained the age of sixteen years then the receipt of his parent or guardian shall be a full and proper discharge to my trustees for the payment of the same.

1 This form enables the personal representatives to get a good receipt on payment to the minor after he or she has attained the age of sixteen. Otherwise it now seems that the person with parental responsibility for the minor can receive the legacy on the minor's behalf: See the ChA 1989, s 3(3) (Part G, para **[244.114]**) and para **[210.33]**. If, however, the person with parental responsibility will not accept the legacy (and the trustees do not pay it to the minor under an express power) then one of three courses is available to the trustees of the will: (i) they can retain the sum until the minor attains full age (now 18: FLRA 1969, s 1: Part G, para **[246.89]**); (ii) they can pay it into court under the TA 1925, s 63; (iii) the personal representatives can appoint trustees of the legacy under the AEA 1925, s 42 (Part G, para **[246.66]**). Trustees retaining such sums may invest them in some government stock redeemable at about the time the minor attains eighteen years. This would almost certainly ensure that the capital is intact.

2 See paras **[210.3]**, **[210.4]** and **[210.9]**, n 1.

[210.35]

Form B10.21: Small legacy to minor with provision for opening National Savings Bank account[1]

I give to [*minor*] of [*address*] the son of —— the sum of £—— free of inheritance tax[2] and I direct that my trustees may if in their absolute discretion they so decide open an account in the National Savings Bank in the name of the said [*minor*] and pay the said legacy and such interest (if any) as may be due thereon into such account. Thereupon my trustees may hand the National Savings Bank book relating to such account to the said [*minor*] and his acknowledgement of the receipt of the same shall be a full and proper discharge to my trustees in respect of the said legacy. If at the time when the said legacy falls to be paid there is an account in the said Bank in the name of the said [*minor*] it shall be sufficient if my trustees pay the legacy and interest into such account and such payment shall be a full discharge to my trustees in respect of the said legacy.

1 Where a minor is given a small legacy of the order of £50 or £100 it is a matter of inconvenience to the trustees to keep this sum until the minor attains eighteen years of age and the convenience of all parties is met by providing for the legacy to be paid into the National Savings Bank, see *Elliott v Elliott* (1885) 54 LJ Ch 1142. An alternative is by a similar clause to authorise the purchase of National Savings Certificates.

2 See paras **[210.3]**, **[210.4]** and **[210.9]**, n 1.

[210.36]

Form B10.22: Legacy to a minor who is married

I give to [*name*] the sum of £—— free of inheritance tax[1] and I declare that notwithstanding that the said [*name*] shall be under the age of eighteen years the same shall be paid to her or as she shall direct as soon as may be after my death and that her receipt shall be a sufficient discharge to my trustees for the same[2] [and this gift is additional to and not in [part] satisfaction of a sum I have covenanted to pay to the trustees of her marriage settlement dated ——].[3]

1 See paras **[210.3]**, **[210.4]** and **[210.9]**, n 1.

2 A minor who is married can give a receipt for income (LPA 1925, s 21: Part G, para **[246.42]**) but not for a capital sum. The form is drafted for a female minor but is equally applicable for a male minor. Payment may be made to the minor where the will so authorises: *Re Denekin, Peters v Tanchereau* (1895) 72 LT 220, but the trustee or personal representative has a discretion despite the direction to pay or to withhold payment until the infant attains the age of eighteen years. The same law applied to a legacy to a minor to be paid on marriage: *Re Somech, Westminster Bank Ltd v Phillips* [1957] Ch 165, [1956] 3 All ER 523. The will ought to add that the receipt of the minor shall be a sufficient discharge (*Re Somech*); and see *Re Robertson* (1908) 17 OLR 568.
See also paras **[210.33]** and **[210.34]**, n 1. For a general receipt clause see Form B21.20 at para **[221.24]**.

3 It should be ascertained whether there is any sum of which the legacy could be in satisfaction (see Vol 1, para **[44.1]** ff) and then if there is any such sum, it must be expressly stated whether the legacy is to be in satisfaction of that obligation or additional to it. If desired, this form could be adapted to cope with a settlement made on the formation of a civil partnership (in place of the marriage referred to) pursuant to CPA 2004.

[210.37]

Form B10.23: Legacy to minor to be applied in maintenance[1]

I give to [*name*] the sum of £—— free of inheritance tax[2] and I declare that if the said [*name*] shall be under the age of eighteen years at my death my trustees may apply the same or any part thereof for the maintenance education advancement or benefit of the said [*name*] in such manner as they think proper or pay the same or any part thereof to the guardian for the time being of the said [*name*] without being responsible to see to the application thereof.

I direct that the said legacy shall carry interest at the rate of —— per cent per annum from the date of my death until the said sum shall be paid or invested and that section 31 of the Trustee Act 1925 shall apply to such interest and to the income of the said legacy when invested.

1 The statutory powers of maintenance and advancement (the TA 1925, s 31 being the statutory power of maintenance out of income, and trust to accumulate the surplus, relating to property held for a minor) are set out in Part G at para **[246.29]**. The power herein contained is wider than the statutory power of advancement. As to when a legacy to a minor carries interest from the death of the testator, see Vol 1, paras **[32.18]**–**[32.27]**, but, if it is intended that it should, it is better to avoid all question by saying so in express terms. A legacy to provide education carries interest from the testator's death: *Re Selby-Walker, Public Trustee v Selby-Walker* [1949] 2 All ER 178. We recommend, at any rate when such a legacy is of any size, that it carry income from the death of the testator, so that there is no argument that there is an occasion of inheritance tax charge at the point when the legacy begins to carry income with it. See also para **[210.46]**, n 1. It now means that a person with parental responsibility for the minor could call for the legacy on the minor's behalf, see para

[210.33]. If a testator does not want this to happen, the form below, which does not give the minor an absolute and indefeasible entitlement to the legacy prior to the age of eighteen, is to be preferred.

2 See paras **[210.3]**, **[210.4]** and **[210.9]**, n 1.

[210.38]

Form B10.24: Legacy to minor to provide an allowance for him[1]

I give to my trustees the sum of £—— free of inheritance tax[2] to be invested in any manner they think fit with power to vary the investment of the same and to be held in trust for my son [*name*][3] and to be paid to him by way of allowance during his minority in such sums at such times or to be otherwise applied for his education or benefit in such manner as my trustees shall in the exercise of their absolute discretion determine and if all or any part of the said sum shall not be applied in the above manner during the minority of my said son [*name*] the said sum or so much thereof as shall not have been so applied shall be paid to my said son [*name*] on his attaining the age of eighteen years. If my said son [*name*] shall predecease me or having survived me die under the age of eighteen years the said sum or the unapplied part thereof shall fall into and form part of my residuary estate. I direct that the said legacy shall carry interest at the rate of —— per cent per annum from the date of my death until the said sum shall be paid or invested and that section 31 of the Trustee Act 1925 shall apply to such interest and the income of the said legacy when invested.

1 This form is in a sense alternative to the immediately preceding form but it is submitted that it meets the requirements of the testator more fully and is in a form more readily understood by him. The intended effect of this clause is that the son shall receive an annual allowance much in the same way as he would if the testator were alive. The son will not have any right to call for the capital until he is eighteen. If it is desired that he shall not receive the capital until he is of some greater age than eighteen, the gift over to residue must be adapted so that it operates on his death before attaining that later age, otherwise he would have a right to call for the capital at eighteen. The gift is not peculiar to the case of a son but is generally applicable to any minor either male or female.

See para **[210.37]**, n 1 concerning inheritance tax, and the Note in B18 at paras **[218.43]**–**[218.78]** for the TA 1925, s 31 (set out in Part G at para **[246.29]**). For deaths on and after 22 March 2006 it is no longer possible to create trusts which have the inheritance tax benefits of IHTA 1984, s 71 (see the Note to para **[200.107]** above). The trusts which a testator might now declare for *his* young children which will fall outside the inheritance tax relevant property charging regime are trusts for bereaved minors, age 18-to-25 trusts, or trusts under which the children take immediate post-death interests (see para **[200.109]** for these different kinds of trusts). If the minor is the testator's child then this form creates a trust for bereaved minors within IHTA 1984, s 71A (see para **[200.108]**).

2 See paras **[210.3]**, **[210.4]** and **[210.9]**, n 1.

3 Following the commencement of GRA 2004 on 4 April 2005, it is important to consider whether to name the son. See Vol 1, at **[81.1]**.

[210.39]

Form B10.25: Legacy of a capital sum for the education of children[1]

I give to my trustees the sum of £—— free of inheritance tax[2] upon trust to invest the same on any investments hereby authorised with power to vary and transpose the same and to hold such investments and the income thereof upon the following trusts:

(a) Upon trust to apply the income thereof at the sole discretion of my trustees for the education of my children who shall be under the age of [thirty] years or any one or more of them to the exclusion of the other or others in such shares as my trustees shall in their absolute discretion deem proper.

(b) Upon trust in the event of the income of the said fund not proving sufficient for the purposes of the education of my said children to raise so much as in the absolute discretion of my trustees they shall deem necessary of the capital of the said fund and apply the same as aforesaid for the education of my said children.[3]

(c) Until the expiration of twenty-one years from my death my trustees shall invest any surplus income from the fund in investments hereby authorised to be held as augmentations of the said fund and after the expiration of the said twenty-one years all surplus income shall be distributed as part of my residuary estate.

(d) Without prejudice to their absolute discretion in the matter it is my desire that my trustees shall provide for the education of my said children at the following schools colleges or institutions ——.

(e) In addition to providing for the education in schools colleges or institutions my trustees may provide out of the said fund for my said children such books of reference or of an educational nature and all such instruments and other things as may be reasonably required for purposes of such education and as my trustees in their absolute discretion think fit and in so far as my trustees in the exercise of such discretion think advisable and may apply the fund for securing any of the said children to become articled for the purpose of any profession or to be received as a pupil of any professional practitioner.

(f) When all my children then surviving shall have attained the age of [thirty] years or all have died under that age the said fund or so much thereof as has not been expended in the execution of the foregoing trusts shall fall into and form part of my residuary estate.

1 IHTA 1984. For deaths on and after 22 March 2006 it is no longer possible to create trusts which have the inheritance tax benefits of IHTA 1984, s 71, for which this Form was designed (see para **[200.107]**). The settled property subject to the trusts of this form falls within the inheritance tax charging regime for relevant property (see para **[200.92]**) and so if the legacy is sizable it would be worthwhile considering a fully discretionary trust.

2 See paras **[210.3]**, **[210.4]** and **[210.9]**, n 1.

3 Any capital so applied would be deemed to be income of the beneficiary concerned: see *Cunard's Trustees v IRC* [1946] 1 All ER 159.

[210.40]

Form B10.26: Legacy to grandchildren

I give the sum of £—— free of inheritance tax[1] to my trustees to invest the same in any manner they think fit with power to vary the investment of the same and to hold the same upon trust for such of my grandchildren as shall attain the age of [eighteen] [twenty-one] years or marry [or form a civil partnership]' under that age if more than one in equal shares. For the avoidance of doubt I hereby declare that the class of my grandchildren shall not close on the attainment by any grandchild of the age of [eighteen] [twenty-one] years or marrying [or forming a civil partnership] thereunder whether in my lifetime or after my death but shall include all my grandchildren whenever born.[2] The said sum shall carry interest at —— per cent per annum from the date of my death until the same shall be paid or invested and section 31 of the Trustee Act 1925 shall apply to such interest and the income of the said legacy when invested.

1 See paras **[210.3]**, **[210.4]** and **[210.9]**, n 1.
2 As to closing of classes under the rules of convenience, see Vol 1, paras **[65.1]–[66.23]**. Prima facie illegitimate grandchildren will be eligible: see generally Vol 1, para **[72.6]**. For the TA 1925, s 31 (Part G, para **[246.29]**) see B18 at paras **[218.43]–[218.78]** and Part A at paras **[200.107]** ff for inheritance tax and trusts of this type. The trusts which a testator might now declare for *his* young children which will fall outside the inheritance tax relevant property charging regime are trusts for bereaved minors, age 18-to-25 trusts, or trusts under which the children take immediate post-death interests. Trusts for grandchildren of this sort will fall within the inheritance tax charging regime for relevant property whatever age contingency is employed. Thus, the choice of eighteen or twenty-one will have more to do with the testator's belief about the maturity of the grandchildren than inheritance tax.

[210.41]

Form B10.27: Legacy to an adopted child[1]

I give to my adopted daughter [*or* son] [*name*][2] the sum of £—— free of inheritance tax[3] [*if the adopted child is still under age add provision for discharge of trustees as in* Form B10.20 *at para* **[210.34]**].

1 As to adopted children see Vol 1, para **[75.1]** ff.
2 Following the commencement of GRA 2004 on 4 April 2005, it is important to consider whether to name the daughter or son referred to. See Vol 1, at para **[81.1]**.
3 See paras **[210.3]**, **[210.4]** and **[210.9]**, n 1.

[210.42]

Form B10.28: Legacy to children and an illegitimate child[1]

I give to each of my children (including my child [*name*]) the sum of £—— free of inheritance tax.[2]

1 The expressions 'child', 'son', 'issue' and the like now prima facie include illegitimate children, sons or issue: FLRA 1987, ss 1 and 19(1) (Part G, paras **[245.70]** and **[245.72]**) and see generally Vol 1, para **[72.14]**. But it is wiser to be explicit, especially in the case of a father if there could be any doubt as to paternity, as this will avoid uncertainty and delay.
2 See paras **[210.3]**, **[210.4]** and **[210.9]**, n 1.

[210.43]

Form B10.29: Legacy to illegitimate children of the testator, including one en ventre sa mère[1]

I give to each of the children whom I have or am reputed to have by [*name of mother*] (including the child of which she is now enceinte) the sum of £—— free of inheritance tax.[2]

1 See para **[210.42]**, n 1.
2 See paras **[210.3]**, **[210.4]** and **[210.9]**, n 1.

[210.44]

Form B10.30: Legacy to legitimate and illegitimate children of a brother of the testator

I give [to each of the children of my brother [*name*] and to each of his reputed children [*name*] and [*name*] now of the respective ages of —— and —— years] *or* [to each of the children of my brother [*name*] namely [*insert names*][1]] the sum of £—— free of inheritance tax.[2]

1 See para **[210.42]**, n 1.
2 See paras **[210.3]**, **[210.4]** and **[210.9]**, n 1.

[210.45]

Form B10.31: Legacy to married daughters to become subject to the trusts of their respective marriage settlements, the amount of the legacies varying in order to equalise the provisions made by the testator for all his daughters

I give to or for the benefit of each of my married[1] daughters[2] free of inheritance tax[3] [such a sum as with any sum paid by me to them or for their benefit in my lifetime or covenanted to be so paid on their respective marriages will make up] the clear sum of £—— and I declare that such respective legacies shall not be paid to my said respective daughters personally but shall (whether or not all or any of such daughters shall die in my lifetime) be paid clear of all deductions to the trustees or trustee for the time being of the respective marriage settlements of my said daughters and shall be held by them or him respectively upon the trusts and with and subject to the powers and provisions therein respectively declared and contained of and concerning the trust funds and property thereby settled by or for the benefit of my said daughters respectively and as an accretion to such respective trust funds.[4]

1 In order to adapt the form to take account of civil partnerships formed pursuant to CPA 2004, substitute 'daughters [*names*] who is married or in a registered civil partnership' for 'married daughters' and 'marriages or civil partnerships' for 'marriages'. A further adaptation will be necessary where the form refers to a marriage settlement. See para **[210.36]**, n. 3.
2 Following the commencement of GRA 2004 on 4 April 2005, it is important to consider whether to name the daughters. See Vol 1, at para **[81.1]**.
3 See paras **[210.3]**, **[210.4]** and **[210.9]**, n 1.
4 It should be ascertained whether the marriage settlements contain an ultimate trust for the testator or for the daughter, and generally what the provisions may be and what exercises of powers there have been. Questions may arise as to whether this bequest may not in the circumstances give the testator (i e his residuary estate) an interest on default of issue of the daughters (*Re Powell, Bodvel-Roberts v Poole* [1918] 1 Ch 407; or the principle of *Lassence v Tierney* (1849) 1 Mac & G 551, may apply; *Re Currie's Settlement, Re Rooper, Rooper v Williams* [1910] 1 Ch 329; *Re Burtons Settlement Trusts, Public Trustee v Montefiore* [1955] Ch 348, [1955] 1 All ER 433; compare also *Re Beaumont, Bradshaw v Parker* [1913] 1 Ch 325); see also Vol 1, para **[82.1]**; and the cases there cited. It is often better not to add property to existing settlements: see Part A, para **[200.21]** and the Preliminary Note at paras **[218.11]**–**[218.14]**.

Contingent and conditional legacies

[210.46]

Form B10.32: Legacy contingent on attaining eighteen or twenty-one[1]

I give the sum of £—— free of inheritance tax[1] to [*name*] if he shall attain the age of [eighteen] [twenty-one] years [or marry under that age and in the latter event his or her receipt shall be a sufficient discharge to my trustees[2]] [and I direct that such sum shall carry interest at the rate of —— per cent per annum from my death until the said [*name*] attains the said age of [eighteen] [twenty-one] years [or marries under that age]].

1 Normally a contingent pecuniary legacy does not carry interest and the LPA 1925, s 175 (Part G, para **[244.54]**) which enacts that certain contingent testamentary gifts shall carry the intermediate income, does not apply to pecuniary legacies (*Re Raine, Tyerman v Stansfield* [1929] 1 Ch 716). A contingent legacy given by the parent of, or a person *in loco parentis* to, the legatee carries interest for the purpose of maintenance (see the TA 1925, s 31(3): Part G, para **[246.29]**). The rate of interest is fixed in s 31(3) at five per cent per annum, but this is 'subject to any rules of court to the contrary'. Practice Direction – Accounts, Inquiries etc para 15 provides that: 'Where an account of legacies is directed by any judgment, then, subject to – (a) any directions contained in the will or codicil in question; and (b) any order made by the court, interest shall be allowed on each legacy at the basic rate payable for the time being on funds in court or at such other rate as the court shall direct, beginning one year after the testator's death.' The rate has been 4% per annum since 1 February 2002.

This provision is limited to accounts taken under judgment, and although it is widely thought that this is the rate governing interest on legacies generally (see Vol 1, para **[32.4]**, n 1), it is submitted that this is not a rule of court to the contrary in the context of s 31(3), except where an account is directed by judgment, in which case the particular legacy will carry interest at the rate of four per cent. A direction to set a legacy apart will usually cause it to carry interest or income (*Re Woodin, Woodin v Glass* [1895] 2 Ch 309); see also para **[218.57]**. This result can be effected by making the legacy a trust legacy as in the next precedent. See generally Vol 1, para **[32.1]** ff. In the case of legacies of any size, we feel that there may be inheritance tax disadvantages if they do not convey the intermediate income from death. The fund out of which they are to be paid will be settled property for inheritance tax purposes (see the IHTA 1984, s 43(2)), at any rate in the case of contingent legacies (the position as regards vested ones is less clear). If they do not carry the intermediate income there will apparently be no interest in possession in favour of the legatees. In respect of deaths on and after 22 March 2006 it is no longer possible to create trusts which have the inheritance tax benefits of IHTA 1984, s 71 (see para **[200.107]**). The trusts which a testator might now declare for *his* young children which will fall outside the inheritance tax relevant property charging regime are trusts for bereaved minors, age 18-to-25 trusts, or trusts under which the children take immediate post-death interests (see para **[200.126]** for these different kinds of trusts). In other cases the trusts will fall within the relevant property regime.

2 The provision for vesting on marriage under the specified age contingency is often restricted to female legatees, but in this form male and female beneficiaries are treated on an equal basis in this respect as is done in the AEA 1925, s 47 (Part G, para **[244.61]**). An adaptation for civil partnerships is straightforward.

[210.47]

Form B10.33: Legacy contingent on attaining eighteen or twenty-one carrying interest[1]

I give to my trustees the sum of £—— free of inheritance tax[2] upon trust to invest the same in any investments authorised by law for the investment of trust moneys with power from time to time to vary such investments and to hold the said sum and the investments representing the same and the income therefrom in trust for [*minor*] if he shall attain the age of [eighteen] [twenty-one] years but if the said [minor] shall die under that age [*gift over or direction that the sum and the investments and any accumulations of income shall fall into residue*].

1 The direction to set apart the sum given will cause the legacy to carry interest and the provisions of the TA 1925, s 31 (Part G, para **[246.29]**), will apply to it: see *Re Raine, Tyerman v Stansfield* [1929] 1 Ch 716. When a legacy is payable at a certain age, but is, in terms, contingent, the legacy becomes vested when there is a direction to pay the interest in the meantime to the person to whom the legacy is given; and not less so when there is superadded a direction that the trustees shall pay the whole or such part of the interest as they shall think fit: *Re Parker, Barker v Barker* (1880) 16 Ch D 44, at 45, 46, approved in *Re Williams, Williams v Williams* [1907] 1 Ch 180 at 183. The effect, therefore, of an express gift of the income would be to make the legacy vest at the testator's death, with a result very different from that intended by the above clause.

See generally Vol 1, para **[32.1]** ff.

2 See paras **[210.3]**, **[210.4]** and **[210.9]**, n 1.

[210.48]

Form B10.34: Legacies to two persons contingently on their attaining eighteen or twenty-one years of age with survivorship

I give to each of [*name*] and [*name*] the sum of £—— free of inheritance tax[1] contingently on his attaining the age of [eighteen] [twenty-one] years and direct that interest thereon at the rate of —— per cent per annum shall be paid from my death until the said [*name*] and [*name*] respectively attain the said age and in the event of either of them dying under the said age the legacy hereby given to him with all interest thereon shall be paid to the survivor of them on his attaining the said age and in the event of both of them dying under the said age both the above legacies and all interest thereon shall fall into and form part of my residuary estate. Section 31 of the Trustee Act 1925 shall apply to the said interest.

1 See paras **[210.3]**, **[210.4]** and **[210.9]**, n 1.

[210.49]

Form B10.35: Legacy contingent on attaining twenty-five or marrying, relying on the statutory powers of maintenance

I give to [*name*] if he [she] shall attain the age of twenty-five years [or marry under that age] the sum of £—— free of inheritance tax[1] with interest thereon from my death at the rate of £—— per cent per annum until the same be set apart or invested. And I declare that if the said [*name*] shall die under the age of twenty-five years [and a spinster] the said legacy and all unapplied accumulations of the income thereof and the investments then representing the said legacy and the said accumulations shall fall into and form part of my residuary estate.[2]

1 See paras **[210.3]**, **[210.4]** and **[210.9]**, n 1.

2 The statutory power of maintenance will apply. After the age of eighteen the legatee will be entitled to payment of the full income both of the legacy and of the past accumulations of income (the TA 1925, s 31, as amended: Part G, para **[246.29]**; see also B18 at paras **[218.43]**–**[218.79]**).

Where there is no gift over, a gift at 25 with a trust or direction to apply income for maintenance is a vested and not a contingent gift (*Re Gossling, Gossling v Elcock* [1903]

1 Ch 448), even if the direction is to apply such part only of the income as the trustees think fit (*Fox v Fox* (1875) LR 19 Eq 286; *Re Parker, Barker v Barker* (1880) 16 Ch D 44; *Re Ussher, Foster v Ussher* [1922] 2 Ch 321).

In a gift to A when he shall attain the age (or at the age) of twenty-five, the attainment of that age may be a part of the description of the legatee, so that the gift is contingent on his attaining the age: *Re Francis, Francis v Francis* [1905] 2 Ch 295; *Re Astor, Astor v Astor* [1922] 1 Ch 364; see also Vol 1, para **[93.6]**. If the gift is a pecuniary legacy it only carries interest if directed to be set apart as in this precedent.

[210.50]

Form B10.36: Legacy subject to discharge of guarantee[1]

If the guarantee dated —— and entered into by me to secure the banking account of —— Co, Ltd at —— Bank (—— Branch) shall when the legacy hereby given becomes payable have been fully discharged otherwise than by payment by me in my lifetime or by my trustees [personal representatives] after my death then I give my husband[2] a legacy of £—— free of inheritance tax. If the said guarantee shall not have been so fully discharged then I give my husband[2] free of inheritance tax such sum (if any) as shall remain after deduction from the said sum of £—— of the amount or amounts paid by me or by my trustees [personal representatives] in discharge of the said guarantee.

1 The position here intended to be provided for is that the wife has guaranteed the banking account of a one-man company, of which the husband is the principal director. She wishes to give her husband a legacy provided she or her estate is not called upon to meet the liability under the guarantee. It is assumed that the guarantee is a limited one and that the legacy is of about the same amount as the total liability thereunder. Provision is made for a corresponding part of the legacy to be received if the wife or her estate have only to meet part of the total sum guaranteed.

2 In order to adapt the form to take account of civil partnerships formed pursuant to CPA 2004, substitute 'civil partner' for 'husband' on each occasion.

Legacies to executors and trustees

[210.51]

Remuneration by way of lump sum and annuity. The duties of executors become more exacting with the increase of the number of statutory enactments affecting the proper administration of a testator's estate and in the case of a lay executor some recompense for the time and trouble spent in such matters should be given. At the same time it must be remembered that the duties of a trustee, though not inconsiderable, are much less arduous and generally capable of being spread over a much greater space of time and, therefore, not as likely to interfere with the personal affairs of the person appointed. It follows, therefore, that the executorship should attract higher remuneration than that of the trustee. The common practice is to grant a lump sum to a person who proves the will and accepts the trusts thereof. A more equitable practice is to give a lump sum to persons acting as executors and a small annuity to persons acting in the trusts thereof. It would not seem equitable to restrict such annuity to the first trustees, but, if later trustees are to receive payment, that should be expressly stated in the will, for a lay trustee can not receive any payment not provided for in the will; although a corporate trustee or a trustee acting in a professional capacity now can: TrA

2000, s 29 (Part G, para **[246.161]**). Note, however, that a trust corporation or a trustee who acts in a professional capacity will be entitled to receive 'reasonable remuneration' (TrA 2000, s 29(1) and (2)) but the provision of an annuity by the will denies that entitlement (TrA 2000, s 29(5)) and so may result in professional trustees refusing to take up the trusteeship. Remuneration to trustees in this way can only be given where the estate is a substantial one, and the annuity should bear a reasonable relation to the amount of the estate. A legacy given to an executor or trustee is presumed to be annexed to the office, and is forfeited if he does not prove or act in the trusts (*Re Appleton, Barber v Tebbit* (1885) 29 Ch D 893). The presumption may, however, be rebutted; the will should, therefore, contain an express statement whether the legacy is given conditionally on the legatee proving or acting in the execution of the trusts of the will, or otherwise. A legacy to an executor 'for his trouble' had, under the old law (prior to 1 February 2001 and the commencement of the TrA 2000), no priority over other legacies (*Duncan v Watt* (1852) 16 Beav 204) but the situation in respect of remuneration of professional and corporate trustees is now different: TrA 2000, s 28(4)(b) (Part G, para **[246.160]**).

[210.52]

Form B10.37: Legacies to executors

I give to each of my trustees[1] [*names*] free of inheritance tax[2] the sum of £—— if he shall prove my will and act in the administration thereof.[3]

1 It is assumed that the same persons are appointed executors and trustees and are stated to be referred to as 'my trustees'.
2 See paras **[210.3]**, **[210.4]** and **[210.9]**, n 1.
3 As to what amounts to acting in the administration of a will, see *Re Sharman's Will Trusts, Public Trustee v Sharman* [1942] Ch 311, [1942] 2 All ER 74 (where the legacy was £1,000 and the trustee, though he apparently continued to act for some years, did little in the trusts) and see also *Re Parry, Dalton v Corke* [1969] 2 All ER 512, [1969] 1 WLR 614; see generally Vol 1, paras **[30.14]**–**[30.18]**.

[210.53]

Form B10.38: Legacies to executors and annuities to trustees

I give to each of my trustees[1] [*names*] free of inheritance tax[2] the sum of £—— if he shall prove my will and act as executor thereof.[3]

I give to each of the trustees for the time being of this my will[4] an annuity of £—— per annum to be paid in equal quarterly payments and to be clear of all deductions including income tax deductible at the source.

Such annuities shall in the case of the first trustees commence from the expiration of one year from the date of my death and in other cases from the date of the appointment of the trustee and continue as long as the trustee acts in the trusts of my will.

The first payment to each trustee shall be made three months after the commencement of the annuity and the payments shall accrue from day to day and be apportionable in respect of any broken period.

Provided always that a trustee who acts in a professional capacity or is a trust corporation shall be entitled to reasonable remuneration as defined by section 29(3) of the Trustee Act 2000 in place of the annuity hereinbefore provided for.[5]

1 See para **[210.52]**, n 1.
2 See paras **[210.3]**, **[210.4]** and **[210.9]**, n 1.
3 This sum is intended to be earned by merely proving the will, clearing the estate and executing any necessary assents.
4 Though this seems a very reasonable provision, a provision in these terms is seldom made. To the extent that the annuity represents reasonable remuneration its termination by the death of the trustee or otherwise is not an occasion of an inheritance tax charge: IHTA 1984, s 90.
5 The purpose of this proviso is to ensure that corporate and professional trustees are entitled to their statutory reasonable remuneration without being limited to the annuity (which may be inadequate): TrA 2000, s 29 (Part G, para **[246.161]**).

Legacies for improvident persons

[210.54]

Settled legacies for children. The method of providing for children by means of a settled legacy is not now as common as in the past but it is still an appropriate course where the beneficiary is improvident or easily influenced, though, of course, a share of residue can be settled in similar terms. Form 7 of the Statutory Will Forms 1925 (at para **[238.13]**) provides a means of greatly shortening the lengthy clause formerly necessary, but there is always the difficulty that trustees may not have a ready access to the form or know where to find it. For settled legacies see Forms B16.25 and B16.26 (at paras **[216.30]** and **[216.31]**) and C3.4 (at para **[225.57]** ff).

[210.55]

Form B10.39: Legacy with provision for forfeiture on alienation[1]

I give to [*name*] a legacy of £—— free of inheritance tax[2] but if (whether before or after my death) any act or event shall have happened whereby the whole or any part of such legacy would but for this provision have before such legacy becomes payable at the expiration of one year from the date of my death become payable to or charged in favour of some person[3] other than the said [*name*] then the right of the said [*name*] to receive such legacy shall absolutely cease and determine and the same shall be held by my trustees as part of my residuary estate and subject to the trusts thereof.

1 The main object of this clause is to prevent a legacy becoming payable to the legatee's trustee in bankruptcy. It can be adapted to all legacies by commencing: 'Provided that in the case of every legacy hereby or by any codicil hereto given if whether before or after——.'
2 See paras **[210.3]**, **[210.4]** and **[210.9]**, n 1.
3 'Person' will include the plural 'persons' and also a corporation: LPA 1925, s 61 (Part G, para **[246.54]**).

[210.56]

Form B10.40: Legacy to improvident person payable by instalments[1]

I give to my trustees the sum of £—— free of inheritance tax payable on my death[2] as to the income thereof upon protective trusts for the benefit of [*A*] the wife[3] of [*B*] during her life and my trustees shall until the failure or determination of the trust of income in favour of the said [*A*] have the further power at their absolute discretion and without being liable in any way for the exercise of such discretion to raise and pay to the said [*A*] for her absolute use and benefit at any time or times as my trustees shall determine any sum or sums not exceeding on any one occasion £—— clear of expenses out of the capital of the said sum of £—— and my trustees shall hold any part of the said sum of £—— not so transferred to the said [*A*] during her life as the said [*A*] shall by will or codicil appoint and in default of and subject to any such appointment [*gift over in default*] and I direct that my trustees shall on no account be liable or responsible for making any such payment whether of income or capital to the said [*A*] after the failure or determination of her said determinable life interest unless or until they shall have received express notice of the act or event causing such failure or determination.

1 The provisions of this clause make it possible for the capital of the legacy to be received by the legatee in instalments as required by her needs and are a safeguard against influence by her husband or others and generally against her own discretion. The clause can be used for any legatee who it is feared may squander the legacy. Obviously it will be required only where the income is insufficient for the support of the legatee. It must be remembered that the legatee can combine with the person or persons entitled to the gift over and call upon the trustees to pay over the whole capital sum to them as the persons absolutely entitled, see *Re Smith, Public Trustee v Aspinall* [1928] Ch 915, [1928] All ER Rep 520. For the inheritance tax implications of protective trusts and in relation to powers to pay capital to a life tenant, see Part A, para **[200.104]**.

2 See paras **[210.3]**, **[210.4]** and **[210.9]**, n 1.

3 In order to adapt the form to take account of civil partnerships formed pursuant to CPA 2004, substitute 'civil partner' for 'wife'.

Legacies to employees

[210.57]

Legacies to employees. Many of the difficulties of legacies to servants or employees will now be non-existent because there are now few establishments with a large staff of indoor and outdoor servants; and as far as servants are concerned they can now in practically every case be made as a legacy to a named person. They should be made additional to wages or other payment due to the servant or accruing due at the time of the testator's death but can be drafted so as to take into hotchpot any statutory redundancy payment.

[210.58]

Form B10.41: Legacy to a servant, if not under notice to leave at testator's death

I give to my butler [*name*] if he shall be in my service at my death and shall not then be under notice given by him or by me to quit my service the sum of £—— free of inheritance tax[1] in addition to any sums then owing to him for wages or otherwise.[2]

1 See paras **[210.3]**, **[210.4]** and **[210.9]**, n 1.

2 The bequest of a stated sum is preferable to 'a year's wages' since the latter has been held to restrict servants to those hired by the year: *Re Ravensworth, Ravensworth v Tindale* [1905] 2 Ch 1, but this rule does not apply to a gift of the amount of one year's wages: *Re Earl of Sheffield, Ryde v Bristow* [1911] 2 Ch 267. For a legacy intended to vary in accordance with size of redundancy payment, see Form B10.46 at para **[210.63]**.

[210.59]

Form B10.42: Legacy to chauffeur with alternative gift if he shall have left the testator's service

I give to my chauffeur [*name*] if in my service at the time of my death[1] the sum of £—— free of inheritance tax[2] in addition to any sums then owing to him for wages or otherwise and if he shall have left my service I give him the sum of £—— free of inheritance tax.[2,3]

1 Without the words 'at my death' a servant who has left the service can claim the legacy: *Re Sharland, Kempt v Rozey* [1896] 1 Ch 517. For provisions concerning redundancy payments see Form B10.46 at para **[210.63]** and as to redundancy payments generally, see **[210.63]**, n 1.

2 See paras **[210.3]**, **[210.4]** and **[210.9]**, n 1.

3 The bequest of a stated sum is preferable to 'a year's wages' since the latter has been held to restrict servants to those hired by the year: *Re Ravensworth, Ravensworth v Tindale* [1905] 2 Ch 1, but this rule does not apply to a gift of the amount of one year's wages: *Re Earl of Sheffield, Ryde v Bristow* [1911] 2 Ch 267. For a legacy intended to vary in accordance with size of redundancy payment, see Form B10.46 at para **[210.63]**.

[210.60]

Form B10.43: Legacies to indoor servants

I give to my maid [*name*] [in recognition of her long and faithful service] the sum of £—— free of inheritance tax[1] and if she shall still be in my service at my death the said legacy shall be in addition to any wages or other sums then owing to her.

I give to each of my indoor servants (other than my said maid) in my service at my death[2] the sum of £—— free of inheritance tax[1] such legacies to be in addition to any sums owing to them respectively for wages or otherwise.

1 See paras **[210.3]**, **[210.4]** and **[210.9]**, n 1.

2 Without the words 'at my death' a servant who has left the service can claim the legacy: *Re Sharland, Kempt v Rozey* [1896] 1 Ch 517. For provisions concerning redundancy payments see Form B10.46 at para **[210.63]** and as to redundancy payments generally, see para **[210.63]**, n 1.

[210.61]

Form B10.44: Legacies to servants—longer form

To each of my servants who shall be in my service at my death[1] and shall then have been in my service for one year or more continuously and shall not then be under notice to leave such service (whether given by him or her or me) and whether he or she be at yearly monthly weekly or other wages[2] a sum equal to the wages [net of income tax and national insurance contributions][3] earned by such servant for the last year preceding my death and to each of my servants who shall be in my service at my death and shall have been in my service for less than a year a sum equal to the wages [also net of income tax and national insurance contributions] earned by such servant up to the date of my death and I declare that such legacies shall be free of inheritance tax[4] and in addition to any sums then owing to them respectively for wages or otherwise.

1 See para **[210.60]**, n 2.

2 The form of this gift avoids the question whether only servants hired by the year can take: see *Re Ravensworth, Ravensworth v Tindale* [1905] 2 Ch 1; and *Re Earl of Sheffield, Ryde v Bristow* [1911] 2 Ch 267. This form is specially drawn to avoid the difficulties which have arisen in the construction of such gifts: see Vol 1, paras **[30.23]–[30.29]**.

3 'Wages' does not include extra allowances, perquisites and similar benefits: *Re Peacock* (1929) 45 TLR 301; *Re Smith, Phillips v Smith* [1915] WN 12 (commission). See Form B10.46 at para **[210.63]** as to redundancy payments.

4 See paras **[210.3]**, **[210.4]** and **[210.9]**, n 1.

[210.62]

Form B10.45: Legacy to clerks

To each of the clerks employed by me at my death in my business of —— if I shall then be carrying on such business who shall have been in my service for upwards of —— years the sum of £—— free of inheritance tax[1] and I declare that such legacies shall be in addition to any salaries or other sums owing to them at my death. [In computing such periods of service any temporary absence shall not be considered an interruption of service but the period of such absence shall be excluded when determining the length of such service.][2]

1 See paras **[210.3]**, **[210.4]** and **[210.9]**, n 1.

2 Where the testator from a certain time carried on his business under a declaration of trust so that certain persons were entitled to certain shares in the profits but to all appearances and as far as his employees knew was carrying on the same for his own benefit it was held that the whole period could be included in such a computation: *Re Howell's Trusts, Barclays Bank Ltd v Simmons* [1937] 3 All ER 647. See Form B10.46 at para **[210.63]** as to redundancy payments.

[210.63]

Form B10.46: Adjustment of legacies to servants or employees occasioned by redundancy payments under the Employment Rights Act 1996[1]

I

Such sum shall be in addition to any redundancy payment payable to the said [*employee or servant*] under the Employment Rights Act 1996 or any succeeding or supplementary Act.

II

Provided always as follows:

(i) If the said *employee or servant*] shall be paid any redundancy payment under the Employment Rights Act 1996 or any succeeding or supplementary Act and such payment is equal to or more than the said sum of £—— then the above legacy shall not be payable.

(ii) If the said payment under the said Act (which term includes any succeeding or supplementary Act) shall be less than the said legacy then I give the said [*employee or servant*] such sum free of inheritance tax as is equal to the difference between the said legacy and the redundancy payment and in addition to any sum then owing to him [her] for wages or otherwise.

[(iii) If the said [*employee or servant*] shall within the terms of Chapter II of the said Act unreasonably refuse an offer to renew his employment or a re-engagement by my personal representatives then the above legacy and any addition thereto hereby authorised shall not be payable].

1 It has long been the custom to leave legacies to servants or employees of long-standing but it may well be that with the enactment of the Redundancy Payments Act 1965, re-enacted in the Employment Rights Act 1996 that this custom may cease or testators may wish to leave only such sum as with the redundancy payment will amount to a stated sum. No payment is made where the contract of employment is renewed by the personal representative of the testator or the employee is re-engaged by the personal representative as long as such renewal or re-engagement takes effect within eight weeks of the death of the testator. Nor is any payment to be made where the personal representative has made the employee an offer in writing to renew the contract or to re-engage the employee where the renewal of re-engagement will take effect not less than eight weeks after the testator's death as long as the terms of the renewal or re-engagement are not different from those prevailing before the testator's death or the offer constitutes an offer of suitable employment of the employee and in either case the employee has unreasonably refused the offer. The substitution of the personal representatives for the deceased is not to be taken as making any material difference in the contract of employment nor whether the refusal was unreasonable. The proviso in respect of this renewal or re-engagement has been placed in brackets. It is a matter for the testator to decide whether he wishes payment to be withdrawn in these circumstances. It would seem that as the period of eight weeks is to be reckoned from the death of the testator, it is a very short period for any action to be taken as it may well be that eight weeks will have elapsed before a grant of probate can be obtained.

Inheritance tax and foreign death duties

[210.64]
Legacies free of or subject to inheritance tax. In the absence of express provision, pecuniary legacies bear inheritance tax or are free of it according to whether the assets out of which they are payable are of a kind which are tax-free or subject to tax. This means that pecuniary legacies will be free of inheritance tax to the extent that they are payable out of UK free estate (whether realty or personalty), and will be subject to tax to the extent that they are payable out of property which bears its own inheritance tax, such as foreign property or property which was comprised in a settlement immediately before the testator's death. See paras **[210.3]** and **[210.4]** and the note to B14 at para **[214.55]** ff.

[210.65]
Freeing legacies from inheritance tax. Form B10.47 at para **[210.68]** (see also Form B14.33 at para **[214.76]**) is a direction freeing all legacies from inheritance tax and foreign death duties, for use in a case where the fund out of which legacies are payable (typically the testator's residuary estate) might be or include property which normally bears its own inheritance tax and Form B10.50 at para **[210.71]** is a form of direction that a legacy shall bear its own inheritance tax for use in the unusual case where that is desired. For incidence of inheritance tax and directions as to incidence see further the note at para **[214.55]** ff and Forms B14.33 and B14.34 at paras **[214.76]** and **[214.77]**.

[210.66]
Gifts of the inheritance tax on lifetime transfers. As described in Part A at paras **[200.70]**–**[200.76]**, the Finance Act 1986 (FA 1986) has increased very

significantly the potential for the death of a person to cause inheritance tax to become payable in respect of lifetime gifts which he has made. The possible categories of inheritance tax liability which may arise on a testator's death in respect of his lifetime gifts are as follows:

(i) Until March 1989 there could arise additional inheritance tax on a lifetime transfer of value made before 18 March 1986 and three years or less before the testator's death. Where a testator died on or after 18 March 1986, the pre-18 March 1986 capital transfer tax rules were preserved in relation to any pre-18 March 1986 lifetime transfers he had made (FA 1986, Sch 19, para 40). Under these rules, if the testator died three years or less after a transfer, inheritance tax on the transfer was calculated on the rate scale applicable to the inheritance tax charge on death. The amount of tax then payable in respect of the transfer as a result of his death was the difference between that amount of tax and the tax already paid at the lifetime rates applicable to the transfer (IHTA 1984, s 7(2) before it was amended by the FA 1986). There was no additional tax payable if he died more than three years after the transfer. This was subject to the tax rate table used for calculating the additional inheritance tax being that which was in force at the time of the testator's death, not that in force at the date of the transfer (IHTA 1984, Sch 2, para 2 before it was amended by the FA 1986), and to the possibility of relief under the IHTA 1984, Pt V, Ch IV where property subject to the transfer had gone down in value since the transfer was made. Since the death rates were reduced as from 18 March 1986, and the lifetime rates had been half the death rates, the amount of additional tax on a pre-18 March 1986 lifetime transfer where the transferor died within three years but after that date would thus be less, but not usually very much less, than the amount of tax already paid in respect of the transfer.

(ii) Inheritance tax on potentially exempt transfers (for which see Part A, para **[200.71]**) made by the testator on or after 18 March 1986 but which have become chargeable transfers as a result of the testator dying within seven years of the transfer (IHTA 1984, s 3A(4)). Prior to 22 March 2006 such transfers included the making of an interest in possession settlement, the making of an accumulation and maintenance settlement, the termination of an interest in possession in favour of an absolute interest, or another or other interests in possession, or an accumulation and maintenance trust. Substantial liabilities could be involved here, since no tax will have been paid in respect of such a transfer. The tax rates are the full rates appropriate to the inheritance tax charge on death where the testator has survived the transfer by three years or less, but are a percentage of a full charge if the transferor has survived more than three years after the transfer, the percentage being reduced further for every year beyond three that he has survived the transfer (IHTA 1984, s 7(1) and (4), as amended by the FA 1986, Sch 19, para 2). Again the rate table is that in force at the testator's death (IHTA 1984, Sch 2, para 1A). From and after 22 March 2006 it is no longer possible to create trusts which have the inheritance tax benefits of IHTA 1984, s 71 (see para **[200.107]** above). The types of interest in possession which post-21 March 2006 result in their holders being treated as beneficially entitled to the underlying settled property under IHTA 1984, s 49(1) are an interest in possession to which a person became beneficially entitled before 22 March 2006 (unless it is an interest in possession under a trust for a bereaved minor), or an interest in possession to which a person became beneficially entitled on or after 22 March 2006 and which is an immediate post-death interest, a disabled person's interest, or a transitional serial interest (see para **[200.93]**). As to the termination of a pre-existing interest in possession, from 22 March 2006, potential exemption will only be available if the determination results in another person acquiring an absolute interest, or an interest in possession which has the result that its holder is treated as beneficially entitled to the underlying settled property under IHTA 1984, s 49(1) (such as a disabled person's interest), or causes the settled property to become subject to a trust for a bereaved minor (see para **[200.71]**).

A transfer of value made by an individual on or after 22 March 2006 is a potentially exempt transfer (para **[200.71]**) if it would be a chargeable transfer and constitutes:

(1) a gift to another individual,
(2) a gift into a disabled trust, or
(3) a gift into a bereaved minor's trust on the coming to an end of an immediate post-death interest. A transfer of value falls within this category to the extent that the value transferred is attributable to settled property (whenever settled) that becomes property to which IHTA 1984, s 71A below applies in the following circumstances:
    (a) under the settlement, a person ('L') is beneficially entitled to an interest in possession in the settled property,
    (b) the interest in possession is an immediate post-death interest,
    (c) on or after 22 March 2006, but during L's life, the interest in possession comes to an end,
    (d) L is beneficially entitled to the interest in possession immediately before it comes to an end, and
    (e) on the interest in possession coming to an end, the property (i) continues to be held on the trusts of the settlement, and (ii) becomes property to which IHTA 1984, s 71A applies.

(See IHTA 1984, s 3A(1A), (3A) as inserted by FA 2006, s 156, Sch 20, para 7).

(iii) Additional inheritance tax payable in respect of chargeable (not potentially exempt) transfers made by the testator on or after 18 March 1986 and within seven years of his death. Such transfers will usually be the making of discretionary settlements, the termination of an interest in possession in favour of a discretionary trust or a transfer of value by a close company in which the testator was a participator, all of which are transfers or deemed transfers which are incapable of being potentially exempt transfers (IHTA 1984, s 3A(1), (2), (3), and (6)). A chargeable (not potentially exempt) transfer is taxed at half rates initially (IHTA 1984, s 7(2), as substituted by the FA 1986, Sch 19, para 2), but if the transferor dies within seven years of it, and the inheritance tax on it, recalculated on the same basis as the tax on a potentially exempt transfer (including the reducing percentages and the use of the rate table in force at the transferor's death) exceeds the inheritance tax already paid on it, the excess becomes payable (IHTA 1984, s 7 and Sch 2, para 2, as amended by the FA 1986, Sch 19). It might be thought that, like the additional tax referred to under (i) above, this type of liability could never exceed the amount of tax already paid, but this is not so. First, the death of the transferor may cause potentially exempt transfers made before the chargeable transfer, but (as it turns out) within seven years before his death, to become aggregable with the chargeable transfer, and thus cause the chargeable transfer to be subject to a higher marginal rate when the amount of the inheritance tax charge on it comes to be recalculated as a result of the transferor's death. Such previous potentially exempt transfers would not have been aggregated with the chargeable transfer when the lifetime charge on it was calculated (see the IHTA 1984, s 3A(5)). Secondly, there could have been business or agricultural relief on the chargeable transfer which is not available when the tax is recalculated on the transferor's death, because the transferee has disposed of the business or agricultural property in question before the transferor's death (see the IHTA 1984, ss 113A and 124A).

(iv) Inheritance tax on property comprised in a gift with reservation made by the testator on or after 18 March 1986 (see the FA 1986, s 102), where the reservation continued until his death or ceased within seven years of it. If the reservation ceased during his life but within seven years of his death, he is treated as having made a potentially exempt transfer of the property at the time when the reservation ceased, and if the reservation continues until his death the property is taxed as if it was part of his estate on death (FA 1986, s 102(3) and (4)). The termination of an immediate post-death interest on or after 22 March 2006 will be deemed to be a gift of the underlying settled property for the purposes of FA 1986, s 102, so that unless the beneficiary of the immediate post-death interest is excluded altogether from benefit after the termination, the gift with reservation rules could apply: see FA 1986, s 102ZA and para **[200.76]**. This category includes property brought within the gift with reservation regime by virtue of an election made pursuant to the pre-owned assets legislation introduced by FA 2004, s 84, Sch. 15, para 21.

In all the above cases the inheritance tax or additional inheritance tax liability is prima facie borne by the donee (including within that expression the settlement trustees if the gift was by way of settlement), although the FA 1986 (in the amendments to the IHTA 1984, ss 199 and 204) introduced a secondary liability on the part of the transferor's personal representatives. There is no reason why the donor should not direct that such liabilities should be paid out of his estate, such direction being in effect the gift of a pecuniary legacy of the amount of tax payable (see Form B10.48 at para **[210.69]**). Before directions are included in a will for the payment out of the testator's estate of any of these liabilities, careful consideration should be given to the sums possibly involved, which could be substantial, and the consequences of such a direction for the other dispositions intended to be made by the will, particularly in the case of transfers made on or after 18 March 1986 (see sub-paras (ii) to (iv)).

[210.67]

Gifts of the inheritance tax on property passing on death but not under the testator's will. There are various categories of property, notably settled property in which a testator had an interest in possession and a testator's severable share of property of which he was a joint tenant, which does not form part of his free estate disposed of by his will, but which devolves in some way on his death, and is charged to inheritance tax as if it was part of his estate on death. Property subject to a reservation of which the testator was the donor, and which remains subject to a reservation at his death, is also charged to inheritance tax as part of his estate on death (FA 1986, s 102). In the absence of express provision to the contrary, property in all these categories bears its own inheritance tax (see the note at para **[214.70]** ff). Again, there is no reason why a testator should not make gifts of the inheritance tax arising on his death in respect of such property if he wants to, but again careful consideration should be given to the possibly substantial amounts involved. See Form B10.49 at para **[210.70]** which gives further examples of such property.

[210.68]

Form B10.47: Legacies free of inheritance tax and duties payable outside Great Britain[1]

All legacies and annuities hereby or by any codicil hereto given shall be paid free of inheritance tax and all duties or taxes upon or by reason of my death in whatsoever country or place the same may be payable.

1 'Death duties' will not prima facie include foreign duties (i e duties other than those leviable under UK legislation): *Re Goetze, National Provincial Bank Ltd v Mond* [1953] Ch 96, [1953] 1 All ER 76; see also *Re Cunliffe-Owen, Mountain v Comber* [1951] Ch 964, [1951] 2 All ER 220, and *Re Sebba, Lloyds Bank Ltd v Hutson* [1959] Ch 166, [1958] 3 All ER 393 (which latter decisions also considered the treatment of tax credits, whether concessionary or available under double taxation conventions). In Scotland the rule is different: *Maclean's Trustees v M'Nair* 1969 SC 65, expressly not following *Re Goetze*. A fortiori 'free of inheritance tax' will not include foreign death duties.

[210.69]

Form B10.48: Clause dealing with inheritance tax on lifetime gifts made by the testator[1]

(1) I declare that if any additional taxes (as defined in subclause (2)) shall be payable by reason of my death then my trustees shall provide for the payment of such taxes (and any interest on them) [free of all taxes payable on my death][2] out of my residuary estate [except to the extent that the liability has been provided for by insurance effected for that purpose].[3]

(2) 'Additional taxes' shall mean the following liabilities to inheritance tax or additional inheritance tax payable by reason of my death:

- tax on any lifetime absolute gift made by me [except tax charged in respect of any settled property in which an interest in possession of mine shall have terminated during my lifetime][4];

- tax on any lifetime transfer by me of property into a settlement [except tax charged in respect of any settled property in which an interest in possession of mine shall have terminated during my lifetime][5];
- tax charged in respect of any settled property in which interest in possession of mine shall have terminated during my lifetime;
- tax charged under Part IV of the Inheritance Tax Act 1984 (close companies);
- in the case of property subject to a reservation in relation to me (within the meaning of sections 102 to 102C of the Finance Act 1986) at or within seven years of my death [any tax chargeable thereon by virtue of section 102(3) or (4) of the Finance Act 1986][6] *or* [an amount limited to the amount of inheritance tax (if any) which would have been chargeable if sections 102 to 102C of the Finance Act 1986 had not applied to such property].[7]

1 This clause can be modified to suit the testator's requirements, omitting those taxes which the testator does not wish to be paid from his residuary estate.

2 Since this is a pecuniary legacy, these words should be included where residue might include property which bears its own inheritance tax, e g foreign property, see the Preliminary Note at paras **[210.3]** and **[210.4]**.

3 A donee of a lifetime gift will often insure against the risk of inheritance tax or additional inheritance tax becoming payable by him on the donor's death. Therefore, the testator may wish to exclude from this provision for the payment of tax out of his residuary estate that tax which has been insured against.

4 If the testator does not wish tax charged in respect of the termination of an interest in possession to be paid from his estate, these words should be included to make this absolutely clear. Following the changes to the inheritance tax treatment of trusts wrought by FA 2006, on and from 22 March 2006 only certain life interests or other interests in possession have the result which formerly all interests in possession had of causing their holder to be treated as being beneficially entitled to the property in which the interest subsists under IHTA 1984, s 49(1). The types of interest in possession which post-21 March 2006 result in their holders being treated as beneficially entitled to the underlying settled property under IHTA 1984, s 49(1) are an interest in possession to which a person became beneficially entitled before 22 March 2006 (unless it is an interest in possession under a trust for a bereaved minor), or an interest in possession to which a person became beneficially entitled on or after 22 March 2006 and which is an immediate post-death interest, a disabled person's interest, or a transitional serial interest (see para **[200.93]**). While settled property is subject to this type of interest in possession, it is not subject to the inheritance tax charging regime for relevant property (see para **[200.92]**).

5 If the testator does not wish tax charged in respect of the termination of an interest in possession to be paid from his estate, the words 'tax charged in respect of any settled property in which an interest in possession of mine shall have terminated during my lifetime' should be included to make this absolutely clear: Under IHTA 1984, s 52(1), where at any time during the life of a person beneficially entitled to an interest in possession in settled property his interest comes to an end, inheritance tax is charged as if at that time he had made a transfer of value and the value transferred had been equal to the value of the property in which his interest subsisted unless tax is not charged by virtue of IHTA 1984, s 53. However, where the interest concerned is one to which the person became beneficially entitled on or after 22 March 2006, this provision applies in relation to the coming to an end of the interest only if the interest is an immediate post-death interest within IHTA 1984, s 49A (see para **[200.98]**), a disabled person's interest within IHTA 1984, s 89B (see para **[200.99]**), or a transitional serial interest within IHTA 1984, s 49B (see para **[200.100]**).

6 Where a person has made a gift of property and reserved a benefit to himself, which benefit continues until his death, inheritance tax is charged as if he was beneficially entitled to the

property at his death (FA 1986, s 106(3)). The termination of an immediate post-death interest on or after 22 March 2006 will be deemed to be a gift of the underlying settled property for the purposes of FA 1986, s 102, so that unless the beneficiary of the immediate post-death interest is excluded altogether from benefit after the termination, the gift with reservation rules could apply: see FA 1986, s 102ZA and para **[200.76]**. If the benefit ceases within seven years of his death, he is treated as having made a potentially exempt transfer of the property at the time when the benefit ceases (FA 1986, s 106(4)). By virtue of the Inheritance Tax (Double Charges Relief) Regulations 1987, where there are two possible charges to inheritance tax in respect of property subject to a reservation of benefit, i e an inheritance tax charge as a result of the original lifetime gift (which may either have been a potentially exempt transfer or a chargeable transfer) and as a result of the FA 1986, s 106(3) or (4), only the higher amount of tax is charged. It is more likely that the tax charged as a result of the FA 1986, s 106(3) or (4) will be higher than that on the original gift, and so these words cover this tax.

7 See previous note. These words will only cover an amount up to the amount of tax which would be payable upon the original lifetime gift. So if under the Inheritance Tax (Double Charges Relief) Regulations 1987 such amount is the lesser amount of tax, the amount chargeable under the FA 1986, s 106(3) or (4) being higher and so the amount payable, the lesser amount will be payable out of the testator's residuary estate, and the balance due will be the primary liability of the donee of the gift.

[210.70]

Form B10.49: Clause providing for payment out of residue of inheritance tax on property not passing under the will[1]

Even though they do not pass under this will inheritance tax payable upon and by reason of my death on the following types of property shall be paid free of inheritance tax[2] out of my residuary estate:

(a) Any interest which I may have at my death in any property of whatever kind [or, if the provision is to apply only to land, in the proceeds of sale of any freehold [or leasehold] property] as a beneficial joint tenant.

(b) If and to the extent that it does not fall within the provisions of subclause (b) of this clause any money standing to the credit of any current [or deposit] bank account in the joint names of [name] and myself.

(c) Any donationes mortis causa made by me or the property comprised in them.

(d) Any lump sum payment annuity or other benefit arising under any life insurance or other policy effected by me to which any person becomes entitled on my death otherwise than by virtue of this will.

(e) Any property of any of the following kinds to which a person becomes entitled on my death by virtue of a nomination made by me in my lifetime in favour of that person:

  (i) Money standing to the credit of any Trustee Savings Bank account of mine.

  (ii) Money standing to the credit of any National Savings Bank account of mine.

  (iii) Savings certificates of mine.

  (iv) Stock or securities of mine on the National Savings Stock Register.

  (v) Money payable on my death by any Friendly Society of which I am or may become a member.

(f) Any property subject to an interest in possession (within the meaning of Part III of the Inheritance Tax Act 1984) to which I am beneficially entitled immediately before my death.[3]

(g) Any property which immediately before my death is property subject to a reservation in relation to which I am the donor within the meaning of section 102 of and the Twentieth Schedule to the Finance Act 1986 where the inheritance tax is payable by virtue of section 102(3) or (4) of the Finance Act 1986.

1 This form is designed to cast onto residue the burden of certain inheritance tax which would not otherwise fall on it. It is assumed that the inheritance tax on any gifts actually made by the will has been dealt with elsewhere in the will. It is not suggested that the form should be adopted in its entirety: only those parts of it which are (or may be) relevant to the testator's circumstances should be used. For the incidence of inheritance tax see the Note at para **[214.55]** ff.

Subclause (a) deals with the inheritance tax attributable to any interest of the testator in property as a joint tenant. Such an interest accrues automatically to the other joint tenant(s) who thus become(s) (unless provision is made to the contrary) liable for the tax.

Subclause (b) is designed to counter the result of *Re Figgis, Roberts v MacLaren* [1969] 1 Ch 123, [1968] 1 All ER 999, in which it was held that a gift of the duty on gifts inter vivos did not apply to money placed by the testator in a bank account in the joint names of himself and his wife. Such a provision is not always needed, of course: thus, if the other joint tenant receives the residuary estate in any case, there would be no point in including it. The spouse exemption will normally make it unnecessary in relation to the joint accounts of spouses.

Subclause (c) relates to donationes mortis causa for which see Vol 1, para **[1.14]**.

Subclause (d) relates to life insurance money, etc, which does not pass under the will: see further Vol 1, para **[7.11]**.

Subclause (e) deals with property which passes, by virtue of a nomination made by the testator in his lifetime, to the person nominated. A number of enactments permit or used to permit such nominations to be made in respect of certain types of property all of which, it is thought, are mentioned in this subclause; see further Vol 1, para **[7.9]**. Although it is no longer possible to make nominations in relation to any of the categories in sub-cl (e) apart from money in Friendly Societies (Vol 1, para **[7.10]**), nominations made before the right was withdrawn are still capable of taking effect. The fact that inheritance tax on nominated property should be expressly dealt with is demonstrated by *Re Walley, National Westminster Bank Ltd v Williams* [1972] 1 All ER 222, [1972] 1 WLR 257. Although on the particular facts of that case the estate duty on nominated property was held to be covered by the particular wording used, in relation to a general direction to pay estate duty or inheritance tax out of residue this would not normally be so.

Subclause (f) deals with settled property in which the testator had an interest in possession and sub-cl (g) deals with property subject to a reservation at the testator's death of which he was the donor. See the Note at para **[210.67]**.

2 See para **[210.69]**, n 2.

3 It is possible for settled property to be disposed of by will by virtue of a power of appointment or the statutory power to dispose of entailed property (LPA 1925, s 176: Part G, para **[244.55]**) and where this may happen care should be taken to see that a provision of this kind is consistent with the parts of the will which dispose of settled property. A person beneficially entitled to an interest in possession in settled property is treated for the purposes of inheritance tax as beneficially entitled to the property in which the interest subsists (IHTA 1984, s 49(1)). However, s 49(1) only applies to an interest in possession to which the person becomes beneficially entitled on or after 22 March 2006, if, and for so long as, it is an immediate post-death interest within IHTA 1984, s 49A (see para **[200.98]**), a transitional serial interest within IHTA 1984, s 49B (see para **[200.100]**) or a disabled person's interest within IHTA 1984, s 89B (see para **[200.99]**). Furthermore, the provision does not apply where the interest in possession is one to which the person became beneficially entitled before 22 March at any time when there is a trust for bereaved minors within IHTA 1984, s 71A (see para **[200.108]**).

[210.71]

Form B10.50: Clause providing for payment by the donee of the inheritance tax on a testamentary gift which would otherwise be free of inheritance tax[1]

I give [*subject matter of gift*] to [*donee*] absolutely but declare that the property [sum] comprised in this gift shall bear its own inheritance tax.

1 Most types of property now devolve free of inheritance tax unless a contrary intention is shown: see generally the Note at para **[214.55]** ff. But testators may wish to direct that a particular gift should bear its rateable proportion of tax. This form is for use in such a case. If the estate will or may be partially exempt, and includes business or agricultural property, consider the use of Form B14.36 at para **[214.79]** and see the Note at para **[214.73]**. See also Forms B5.1 at para **[205.58]** and B6.29 to B6.31 at paras **[206.38]–[206.40]**.

Nil-rate band legacies

[210.72]

Form B10.51: Nil-rate band legacy[1]

If the gift of my residuary estate to [my wife, civil partner *or other exempt person, eg a charity*] shall take effect[2] I give to such of my children [*name*] [*name*] and [*name*] who shall survive me if more than one in equal shares absolutely a legacy of the maximum sum of money which can in the circumstances subsisting at my death be given by this clause without any liability being incurred for the payment of inheritance tax on or by reason of my death. And in particular but without prejudice to the generality of the foregoing the circumstances to be taken into account for the foregoing purpose shall include any chargeable transfers made by me during my lifetime (or events treated as such for inheritance tax purposes) the dispositions taking effect under this my will (apart from this present clause) or under any codicil hereto and any property treated as if it were part of my estate immediately before my death for inheritance tax purposes [provided that if such maximum sum exceeds [one-third] of the probate value of my estate (disregarding for this purpose any business [or agricultural] relief applicable thereto) then the amount of the foregoing legacy shall be equal to [one-third] of the said probate value] *or* [provided that if such maximum sum shall exceed [£300,000] I give instead of such maximum sum the said sum of [£300,000]].[3]

1 Where a testator's estate is likely to exceed the inheritance tax threshold, and his residuary estate will be exempt from inheritance tax because he is leaving it to an exempt person, for example, his spouse or civil partner, he may wish to leave to non-exempt persons, such as his children, the maximum amount which he can leave without incurring any inheritance tax liability. This clause makes provision for this. See Part A, paras **[200.84]–[200.91]** on this topic generally, the Note to B18 at para **[218.16]** ff and Form B18.2 at para **[218.32]** for nil-rate band discretionary trusts.

2 The gift should be made conditional upon the testator's residuary estate being exempt from inheritance tax because in the event of the testator's taxable estate exceeding the available nil-rate inheritance tax band, nothing will be payable according to the formula.

3 For 2007–8 the nil-rate sum is £300,000: see FA 2005, s 98. For 2008–9 it will be £312,000, for 2009–10 it will be £325,000: see FA 2006, s 155; and for 20010–11 it will be £350,000: see FA 2007, s 4. Where the testator's residuary estate may include property with the benefit of business or agricultural property relief, in particular property qualifying for such relief at the rate of 100 per cent, the maximum sum of money which could pass under this clause could exceed by a very considerable amount the sum which is the inheritance tax

threshold, and leave the surviving spouse with less, perhaps much less, than the testator intends (see para **[233.9]**). The testator would be well advised to place a limit on the amount of the legacy in these circumstances, as provided here. For business relief see the Preliminary Notes to B5 at para **[205.1]** ff, C11 at paras **[233.1]–[233.13]** and for agricultural relief, see the Preliminary Note to C12 at paras **[234.1]** ff.

Miscellaneous

[210.73]

Form B10.52: Legacies with provision for some of the legatees not being able to be found

I give the sum of £—— free of inheritance tax to each of my nephews [*names*][1] provided that if the address of any such nephew is not known to my trustees and such nephew does not claim the said legacy within two years of my decease then the sum or sums given to that nephew or those nephews shall fall into or form part of my residuary estate.[2]

1 Following the commencement of GRA 2004 on 4 April 2005, it is important to name the nephews referred to. See Vol 1 at para **[81.1]**.

2 See *Hawkes v Baldwin* (1838) 9 Sim 355. The condition in this clause is binding on the legatee whether or not he is aware of it. He cannot claim the legacy after the expiration of the two years on the ground that he was ignorant of it, nor is the executor bound to inform any such legatee of the terms of the legacy. See Vol 1, paras **[30.32]–[35.48]**.

[210.74]

Form B10.53: Demonstrative legacy[1]

I give to [*name*] the sum of £—— free of inheritance tax to be raised primarily out of my [4 *per cent Consolidated Stock*] but if I shall not have sufficient of such stock at my death then out of my residuary estate.

1 Such a legacy will not abate with the general legacies until after the particular fund out of which it is to be paid is exhausted: see Vol 1, para **[30.6]**.

[210.75]

Form B10.54: Bequest of legacies payable exclusively out of a particular property with provision for abatement and interest

I give to my trustees free of inheritance tax [my freehold property known as ——] upon trust to sell the same and from the net proceeds of sale (after payment of all of the costs of the sale including legal fees and estate agents' commission) I direct them to pay the following legacies to the following persons: [*set out the names of the legatees and the amounts of the legacies*] and I declare that if the net proceeds of sale of the property shall be less than the total of the said legacies (other than those that shall have failed or lapsed) such legacies shall abate between themselves rateably according to value and further I declare that such legacies shall carry interest from the first anniversary of my death until payment at the rate of —— per cent per annum such interest to be payable upon such payment and to be payable in the first place from the net rents and profits of the said property in the second place from the amount (if any) by which the net proceeds of sale exceed the total of such legacies and in the third place from my residuary estate.

[210.76]

Form B10.55: Clause providing for reduction of legacies where the testator's estate proves to have decreased in value[1]

In deciding on the amount of the above legacies I have estimated the net value of my estate after payment of my debts and the inheritance tax thereon on my death at about £100,000 at the time of making this my will and accordingly I declare that the said legacies to the said [*legatees*] given by me in this clause shall be subject to abatement and reduction as follows: if the value of my estate at the date of my death after payment of my funeral and testamentary expenses and debts and the inheritance tax in respect thereof shall amount to less than £100,000 then the said pecuniary legacies given by this clause of this my will shall abate and be diminished so that the proportion of such legacies to be paid by my trustees to such legatees in satisfaction of their said legacies respectively shall be the same proportion as the net value of my estate (ascertained as aforesaid) shall bear to £100,000.

1 It is by no means impossible that the testator's estate will prove to be much less in value than could have been reasonably expected. The common practice is to give a number of legacies of stated amount and to divide the residue amongst the family. If the estate is greatly reduced, the legacies may exhaust the whole estate, and the family will in consequence be left unprovided for. This precedent provides for the reduction of the legacies, so that such a result may be avoided.

[210.77]

Form B10.56: Declaration as to currency in which legacies payable[1]

I declare that all legacies annuities and all other sums of money payable under this my will shall be paid in pounds sterling.

1 Prima facie the currency a legacy is to be paid in is that of the domicile of the testator, but where a different currency is expressly indicated in the will, the legacy is to be paid in that currency, see Vol 1, para **[30.43]**. This clause will generally be required where there may be a doubt or there are legatees or annuitants resident in different countries or there are legacies charged on different properties in different countries.

[210.78]

Form B10.57: Direction as to rate of exchange for payment of legacies in a foreign currency[1]

I declare that all legacies payable under my will in a currency other than in pounds sterling although the same are expressed in pounds sterling shall be computed according to the applicable rate of exchange of the —— Bank prevailing [on such date prior to payment as my trustees shall in their absolute discretion (without being liable for loss) select] *or* [on the first anniversary of my death].

1 This direction should be used where a testator has expressly directed that certain legacies should be paid in a currency other than pounds sterling. In the absence of an express direction, the applicable rate of exchange is that prevailing on the first anniversary of the testator's death: see Vol 1, para **[30.43]**.

[210.79]

Form B10.58: Legacy for purchase of customary mourning

I give to my wife[1] and to each of my sons[2] such sums as shall in the absolute discretion of my trustees be sufficient to provide them with suitable mourning apparel.

1 In order to adapt the form to take account of civil partnerships formed pursuant to CPA 2004, substitute 'civil partner' for 'wife'.

2 Following the commencement of GRA 2004 on 4 April 2005, it is important to name the sons referred to. See Vol 1 at **[81.1]**.

B11 Annuities

Preliminary Note .... [211.1]
FORMS
B11.1 Gift of simple annuity .... [211.8]
B11.2 Gift of annuity tax-free .... [211.9]
B11.3 Gift of annuity with reference to liability of annuitant to account for reliefs and repayments—alternative forms .... [211.10]
B11.4 Gifts of annuity of such sum as after deduction of income tax at the basic rate for the time being will amount to a stated sum to be varied with reference to the Index of Retail Prices .... [211.11]
B11.5 Gift of several annuities .... [211.12]
B11.6 Gift of annuities charged on land .... [211.13]
B11.7 Power to purchase annuities, the capital cost being recouped out of income .... [211.14]
B11.8 Power to trustees to appropriate investments to answer annuities1—separate fund for each annuity .... 211.15]
B11.9 Power to trustees to appropriate investments to answer annuities—aggregate fund for all annuities .... [211.16]
B11.10 Gift of annuity with direction to purchase .... [211.17]
B11.11 Annuity provisions designed to mitigate inheritance tax and income tax .... [211.18]
B11.12 Gift of annuity and direction to trustees to purchase; the annuity to cease on alienation, and the annuitant not to be entitled to purchase-money in lieu of the annuity .... [211.19]
B11.13 Proviso for cesser of annuities on alienation .... [211.20]
B11.14 Declaration that annuities are to be paid clear of all deductions .... [211.21]
B11.15 Gift of several annuities to same person, being annuities to widow with reduction on remarriage and provision for minor children residing with widow .... [211.22]
B11.16 Gift of an annuity to a trustee in trust for a mentally disabled daughter .... [211.23]
B11.17 Gift of an annuity upon trust for a spendthrift son and his wife and children .... [211.24]
B11.18 Direction as to payment of an annuity not created by the will for insertion where the residue is settled .... [211.25]

PRELIMINARY NOTE

[211.1]
Annuities are unsatisfactory. Annuities used to be a convenient method of providing maintenance for persons to whom the testator felt an obligation but who were not primary objects of the testator's bounty. They are no longer very satisfactory, for two main reasons.

[211.2]
Inflationary devaluation of annuities. In a period of high inflation the real value of an annuity will decline rapidly, both between the making of the will and the testator's death, and during the period in which the annuity is payable. This can be compensated for by 'index-linking' the annuity (as in

Form B11.4 at para **[211.17]**), but that could have the effect, if the value of the fund out of which the annuity is paid fails to keep pace with inflation, that the annuity grows to consume all the income, and possibly capital as well, of the fund.

[211.3]
Taxation problems of annuities. Inheritance tax on funds out of the income of which annuities are payable is charged in a manner which can operate unfairly, though it is also possible for it to be turned to advantage. An annuitant is treated as having an interest in possession in the same proportion of the capital fund as the proportion the annuity bears to the income of the fund (Inheritance Tax Act 1984 (IHTA 1984), s 50(2)) but subject to prescribed maximum and minimum rates for the income of the fund (s 50(3)) which only apply when they favour the Inland Revenue. Thus, if the income of the fund is above the prescribed maximum or below the prescribed minimum there could be inheritance tax charges on more than the overall value of a fund if the annuitant and the person entitled to the rest of the income of the fund died within a short period of each other. Also the charge to inheritance tax on the death of the annuitant could be on a larger share of the settled property than was exempt on the testator's death, where the annuitant is his spouse or civil partner. On the other hand, within the limits of these prescribed rates advantage can sometimes be obtained by deliberate reinvestment to obtain a different income return for the fund or by appropriating an annuity to a small fund with a high income yield. The prescribed maximum and minimum rates for the purposes of s 50(3) after 15 August 1980 and before 18 February 2000 are contained in the Capital Transfer Tax (Settled Property Income Yield) Order 1980 (SI 1980/1000). The rates applicable after 17 February 2000 are contained in the Inheritance Tax (Settled Property Income Yield) Order (SI 2000/174). The latter Order designates the following rates of yield in the FT Actuaries Share Indices for the higher and lower rates: for the higher rate – the Irredeemables' yield shown in the indicies of FTSE Actuaries Government Securities UK Indices; for the lower rate – the rate of the All-Share actual dividend yield shown in the FTSE Actuaries Share Indices. In each case the applicable rate is determined using the indices produced for the date on which the value in question is to be determined or, if those indices are not produced for that date, for the latest date preceding that date for which those indices are produced. There are also obscurities about these inheritance tax provisions: it is not clear what period is to be taken for the purposes of s 50(2), and although it seems most unlikely that a change in the income rate of the fund or an appropriation of an annuity fund could be an occasion of an inheritance tax charge, the possibility cannot be finally ruled out. These inheritance tax problems of course relate only to annuities charged (wholly or partly) on the income of property, and do not apply to purchased life or covenanted annuities. See further *Foster's Inheritance Tax*, E 2.11–E2.14. For HMRC's treatment of interests in possession, see IHTM16061 and subsequent paragraphs. An interest to which a person becomes beneficially entitled after 22 March 2006 can only be an interest in possession if it is an immediate post-death interest (IPDI), a disabled person's interest or a

transitional serial interest (see Part A at paras **[200.92]**) ff. The gift of an annuity by will after 22 March 2006 will, in most cases, give rise to an IPDI.

[211.4]
Alternatives. Other methods of providing maintenance are to give a life interest in a proportionate share of a fund (or a proportionate share of the income of a fund, ie so that there can be no appropriation of capital to the share of income—see *Re Freeston's Charity* [1979] 1 All ER 51, [1978] 1 WLR 741), or a life interest in a settled legacy, or a legacy of a capital sum with which the legatee may purchase an annuity: see further method (4) at para **[211.6]**.

[211.5]
General considerations. The various methods of providing annuities are discussed in detail at para **[211.6]**. The following general considerations should be mentioned:

(i) An annuity is a form of pecuniary legacy, and it abates and bears inheritance tax in the same manner. It is important therefore to ensure that it is expressed to be free of inheritance tax, for, if it is not, administrative complications may ensue. This situation is less likely to arise now that tax on realty is prima facie treated as a testamentary expense. But although an annuity which is charged on a mixed fund of realty and personalty will no longer be required to contribute to the payment of inheritance tax, it will be otherwise if the fund includes foreign property: see the Preliminary Note to B10 at paras **[210.3]** and **[210.4]** and the Note to B14 at para **[214.63]**.
(ii) Where an annuity is charged on a fund, the extent to which the fund is liable to inheritance tax on the death of the annuitant can be a complex and difficult matter to determine: see *Foster's Inheritance Tax*, E2.12 and K2.03. From a fiscal and administrative point of view there is much to be said for giving annuities (if at all) only to individuals whose personal circumstances are such that no charge to inheritance tax on his death is likely to arise.
(iii) Annuities are payable subject to deduction of income tax at the basic rate. It is possible in wills, unlike other kinds of instrument, to provide income tax free annuities, and where the rule in *Re Pettit, Le Fevre v Pettit* [1922] 2 Ch 765 applies to such an annuity an annuitant whose personal circumstances entitle him to a refund of tax is required to account to the trustees for the proportionate part of such refund which is attributable to the annuity (see *Simon's Taxes*, E2.1119–E2.1128). While a testator who wants to ensure that the annuitant receives a net sum and no more may regard this as a fair arrangement, it will be an unwelcome administrative chore for all parties. Forms are given below which provide for the rule in *Re Pettit* to apply, but their use is not recommended.
(iv) Administrative difficulties may also arise if an annuity is given of a net amount computed by reference to tax rates which are higher than the basic rate. Effect can be given to such a direction only after the end of

the relevant year of assessment when the annuitant's personal tax liability has been settled. Gifts of annuities on this basis are similarly not recommended.

[211.6]

Means of providing annuities. There are several methods of providing for the payment of an annuity given by will and these will be discussed in turn:

(1) The 'appropriated fund' method whereby the trustees have power to set aside part of the capital of the estate as an appropriated fund to answer the annuity by its income and, if necessary, by its capital. Where this gives the annuitant a beneficiary taxed interest in possession under IHTA 1984, s 49(1) such as an interest in possession to which the annuitant became beneficially entitled before 22 March 2006 (other than an interest in possession under a trust for a bereaved minor); an immediate post-death interest; a disabled person's interest; or a transitional serial interest (see Part A, para **[200.92]**).If the annuity is a beneficiary taxed interest in possession then this has the disadvantages of inheritance tax on the annuitant's death and delay in the distribution of the estate. Furthermore, if the trustees are given power to resort to the capital of the appropriated fund in order to pay the annuity, and they exercise this power, the capital paid to the annuitant will be taxable in his hands as income.

(2) A *direction* to the trustees to purchase an annuity for the annuitant. This does avoid inheritance tax on the annuitant's death (since the annuity is not then supported by any slice of capital) – but see para (3) below – and it also avoids the delay in the distribution of the estate. But:

   (a) the annuitant can at once demand the capital which the trustees are directed to spend on the purchase of the annuity and can spend it as he likes, though this result can be avoided by a carefully-drafted provision in the will: see eg Form B11.12 at para **[211.25]**; and

   (b) the advantage of the normal rule applicable to a purchased annuity whereby the 'capital element' in the periodical annuity payments is exempt from income tax (Income and Corporation Taxes Act 1988 (ICTA 1988), ss 656 and 657) will be lost because this rule does not apply 'to any annuity purchased in pursuance of any direction in a will, or to provide for an annuity payable by virtue of a will or settlement out of income of property disposed of by the will or settlement (whether with or without resort to capital)' (ICTA 1984, s 657(2)(c)). It follows that the purchase of an annuity by the trustees is much less advantageous than the purchase of such an annuity by the annuitant himself.

(3) A gift of an annuity coupled with a *power* for the trustees to satisfy it by purchasing an annuity for the annuitant. The only difference here is that the right of the annuitant to demand the capital sum arises only when the trustees have decided to exercise their power to purchase the annuity. Otherwise, the position is the same as in (2) above. The purchased annuity to which the annuitant becomes entitled will normally be worth less than the share of capital in which the annuitant

was treated as having an interest in possession for inheritance tax purposes (see above), so that arguably the purchase of the annuity could be an occasion of charge under the IHTA 1984, s 52(4)(b). Although if there is an occasion of charge under s 52, and the property released from the annuity vests absolutely in an individual, or becomes subject to an interest in possession to which an individual is beneficially entitled, or subject to accumulation and maintenance trusts, the deemed transfer of value may be potentially exempt and thus exempt if the annuitant survives it by seven years. As annuitants are usually elderly, this is perhaps of limited assistance. However, the Inland Revenue do not regard the substitution of a purchased annuity for an annuity paid out of the income of the testator's estate in exercise of a power given by the will, or in pursuance of a direction made by the will, as an occasion of charge under the IHTA 1984, s 52 (see *Dymond's Capital Taxes*, para 16.509), although they do regard such a substitution as an occasion of tax charge where it is done by agreement with the annuitant (see *Dymond's Capital Taxes*, paras 16.510–16.512). A cautious draftsman could put the matter beyond doubt by creating an annuity fund in which there was no interest in possession until the trustees had decided how the annuities were to be met; if they did so within two years of the death their actions would be treated as those of the deceased for inheritance tax purposes under the IHTA 1984, s 144 (see the note in C3 at para **[225.83]** ff).

(4) A simple gift to the annuitant of a lump sum, either without any further provision or with some purely precatory suggestion that he might use the money to buy an annuity; or else a gift to the annuitant of such a sum as in the opinion of the trustees, or of insurance brokers designated by trustees or in some other way, is sufficient to allow the annuitant to buy an annuity of specified amount. There is of course no way here of avoiding the risk that the annuitant may spend the money otherwise than in buying an annuity, but apart from that this method has the great advantage over methods (2) and (3) that the capital element of the annuity payments is not taxable in the hands of the annuitant, so that less capital needs to be spent to provide the annuitant with the same net income.

(5) A gift of an annuity coupled with a power for the trustees to *commute* the annuity by paying a lump sum to the annuitant. The idea behind this method is that the annuitant will, with the lump sum, purchase an annuity for himself and thus gain the income tax advantages which he would have lost if the trustees had purchased it for him. The results of this method, once the trustees exercise their power to commute, are the same as the results of method (4) but it may be preferred to method (4) because it gives the trustees a discretion as to whether, and if so when, to exercise the power, and they can make this decision in the light of all the circumstances which for the time being exist. This also has the tax disadvantage (although also the possibility of potential exemption) mentioned at (3) above.

(6) A method whereby the annuity is neither purchased nor secured upon capital but payable by some third person as a personal obligation. This third person is usually a residuary beneficiary, because he is the person

who stands to gain by accepting this obligation, and one difficulty in employing this method lies in the fact that there may be no residuary beneficiary who is adult, able and willing to undertake it. Assuming that there is, however, there are several ways in which the method may be employed. The testator may, for instance, make the residuary gift conditional upon the residuary beneficiary (or beneficiaries) entering into a deed of covenant to pay the annuity. Alternatively, he may give the annuity and couple it with a power for the trustees to release the capital fund out of which it would otherwise be payable upon the residuary beneficiary (or beneficiaries) entering into such a deed of covenant or otherwise undertaking to pay it. This latter method is probably to be preferred because, again, it allows the trustees to make their decision in the light of current circumstances, but the inheritance tax disadvantage mentioned in (3) above (although subject again to the availability of potential exemption) would be more serious in this case, as it could involve a charge on the whole of the share of the estate in which the annuity was treated as subsisting. For the purposes of this inheritance tax charge, the value of the covenant would apparently only be deductible from the value of the capital deemed to have been subject to the terminated annuity under the IHTA 1984, s 52(2) if the *annuitant* agreed to the surrender of the annuity in return for the covenant. It should be emphasised that the use of this method provides less security for the annuitant than any of the others, because the continued payment of his annuity depends upon the residuary beneficiary's (and perhaps his personal representatives') continued goodwill and solvency. If these can be relied upon, however, it can be an advantageous method to adopt. It solves the two problems of inheritance tax on the annuitant's death and delay in distribution, but it enables the residuary beneficiary to obtain the whole of the residuary estate unencumbered and unreduced. The income tax rules for non-charitable covenants were altered by the Finance Act 1988 (adding new ss 347A and 347B to the ICTA 1984 which have now been rewritten into ITA 2007, Part VII, Chapter 4 (principally at ss 453 and 454)) so that they are not income tax deductible by the payer, but are not charged to income tax in the hands of the recipient. Since the covenantor would more likely be a higher rate taxpayer, and the convenantee not, this could be a disadvantage.

[211.7]
The draftsman will have to decide, in conjunction with the testator and in the light of the considerations outlined above, how best to provide for the annuity in question. Often it will be best to give the trustees several alternative powers, leaving them to decide between them when the time comes. They will then have an opportunity of assessing all the relevant points, including the age, health, wealth and character of the annuitant and of any person from whom a personal covenant may be taken, the size and nature of the estate as a whole, and any changes which may have been made in the law. Form B11.11 at para **[211.18]** is designed to give the trustees a fair range of alternative powers.

[211.8]

Form B11.1: Gift of simple annuity[1]

I give to [*name*] for [his]/[her] life[2] to be paid free of all deductions[3] by equal quarterly payments the first payment to be made at the end of three months after my death an annuity of £—— per annum.

1 See notes to Form B11.2 at para **[211.9]**. In this form the annuity is not tax-free and must be paid subject to deduction in respect of income tax. The word deduction does not include income tax, see note 3 below. For a tax-free annuity, see Form B11.2 at para **[211.9]**.

2 A gift of an annuity to a person without more is a gift of the annuity during the life of such person only (*Blight v Hartnoll* (1881) 19 Ch D 294), and see *Re Jackson, Day v Atkin* [1946] 1 All ER 327, where an annuity was coupled with a direction that it should be applied to the donee's maintenance and education until twenty-one, and it was held to be an annuity for life. But in order that no question may be raised, the duration of an annuity should always be expressed. As to duration of annuities, see Vol 1, paras **[33.11]–[33.22]** and as to annuities during widowhood or spinsterhood, see Vol 1, para **[33.20]**.

3 Words such as 'free of all deductions' or 'a clear annuity' were held in *Re Skinner, Milbourne v Skinner* [1942] Ch 82, [1942] 2 All ER 32 to exonerate an annuity from estate duty but not income tax. It is thought that such words will likewise exonerate annuities from inheritance tax. See also Vol 1, paras **[33.46]–[33.47]**. As to the importance of freeing annuities from inheritance tax, see the Preliminary Note to this section, sub-para (i) at para **[211.5]**.

[211.9]

Form B11.2: Gift of annuity tax-free[1]

I give to [*name*] for [his]/[her] life to be paid free of all deductions[2] whatsoever and free of income tax at the basic rate for the time being [*or if desired* free of income tax up to —— p in the £] by equal quarterly payments [the first payment to be made at the end of three months from my death an annuity of £—— per annum] *or* [the first payment to be made on the first usual quarter day occurring after the end of three months from my death such payment to include a proportionate payment in so far as the period for which it is paid exceeds the quarter ending on such day of payment].

[*Add one of the following as the intention may be*] I declare and direct that any rebate allowance or repayment of income tax which may be allowed or made to the said [*name*] shall enure for his [her] benefit [*or* shall be accounted for the said [*name*] to my trustees].[3]

1 A gift in this form provided the estate is sufficient will not allow the annuitant to claim the value of the annuity in a lump sum. Where, however, the estate is sufficient he can claim the lump sum, but the amount of it will, if necessary, have to abate in proportion to the abatement of other general legacies. See Vol 1, paras **[33.35]–[33.45]**.

2 See para **[211.8]**, n 3.

3 There are many decisions upon particular wording of the gifts as to whether there is liability to account for income tax repayments: see *Simon's Taxes*, E2.1122. The position can no doubt be made clear by adopting one of the special forms of words construed in the cases, but it seems preferable to put the question beyond doubt by expressly stating that the annuitant can retain the repayment or stating that it must be accounted for to the trustees. The annuitant must make the claim for the repayment where she is bound to hand it over to the trustees: *Re Kingcome, Hickley v Kingcome* [1936] Ch 566, [1936] 1 All ER 173.

[211.10]

Form B11.3: Gift of annuity with reference to liability of annuitant to account for reliefs and repayments—alternative forms[1]

I. PROVISION FOR PAYMENT OF ANNUITY FREE OF INCOME TAX (THE RULE IN *RE PETTIT* BEING APPLICABLE) BUT NOT AT ANY RATE HIGHER THAN THE BASIC RATE

I give to A for [his]/[her] life an annuity of such sum as after deduction of income tax at the basic rate for the time being (but not at any higher rate) amounts to clear[2] sum of £—— and I direct that any relief rebate allowance or repayment of income tax which may be allowed to A shall be accounted for by [him]/[her] to my trustees.

II. PROVISION FOR PAYMENT OF ANNUITY FREE OF INCOME TAX AT THE BASIC RATE (THE RULE IN *RE PETTIT* NOT BEING APPLICABLE) BUT NOT AT ANY HIGHER RATE

I give to A for [his]/[her] life an annuity of such sum as after deduction of income tax at the basic rate for the time being amounts to the clear[2] sum of £—— and I direct that A shall be entitled to retain for [his]/[her] own benefit all reliefs rebates allowances and repayments of income tax made or allowed to [him]/[her].

III. PROVISION FOR PAYMENT OF ANNUITY FREE OF INCOME TAX (THE RULE IN *RE PETTIT* BEING APPLICABLE) WHETHER AT THE BASIC OR AT ANY HIGHER RATE

My trustees shall pay to A for [his]/[her] life an annuity of such sum as after deduction of all income tax payable in respect thereof (whether at the basic or at any higher rate) amounts to the clear[2] sum of £—— and I direct that any relief rebate allowance or repayment of income tax which may be allowed to A shall be accounted for by [him]/[her] to my trustees.

IV. PROVISION FOR PAYMENT OF ANNUITY FREE OF INCOME TAX AT THE BASIC RATE (THE RULE IN *RE PETTIT* NOT BEING APPLICABLE) AND OF INCOME TAX AT ANY HIGHER RATE

I give to A for [his]/[her] life an annuity of such sum as after deduction of income tax at the basic rate and of all income tax payable in respect thereof at any higher rate amounts to the clear[2] sum of £—— and I direct that A shall be entitled to retain for [his]/[her] own benefit all reliefs rebates allowances and repayments made or allowed to [him]/[her].

1 There are many decisions upon particular wording of the gifts as to whether there is liability to account for income tax repayments: see *Simon's Taxes*, E2.1122. The position can no doubt be made clear by adopting one of the special forms of words construed in the cases, but it seems preferable to put the question beyond doubt by expressly stating that the annuitant can retain the repayment or stating that it must be accounted for to the trustees. The annuitant must make the claim for the repayment where she is bound to hand it over to the trustees: *Re Kingcome, Hickley v Kingcome* [1936] Ch 566, [1936] 1 All ER 173.

2 For the effect of this word see para **[211.8]**, n 3.

[211.11]

Form B11.4: Gifts of annuity of such sum as after deduction of income tax at the basic rate for the time being will amount to a stated sum to be varied with reference to the Index of Retail Prices[1]

I give to my wife [*name*][2] for her life an annuity of such sum as after deduction of income tax at the basic rate for the time being in force will amount to the clear[3] sum of £—— or such other clear[2] sum as may be substituted therefor as hereinafter provided such annuity to be paid in monthly instalments and the first payment to be made one month after my death.

As to such annuity I hereby declare and direct as follows:

(i) The amount thereof shall be increased or decreased by dividing the sum of £—— by the index figure in the Index of Retail Prices for the month in which my will is executed and (having made allowance for any rebasing of the Index which may have happened in the meantime) multiplying it by the index figure in that Index for the month in which my death occurs.

(ii) Any rebate allowance or repayment of income tax which may be allowed or made to my said wife [shall enure for her benefit] or [shall be accounted for by my said wife to my trustees].

(iii) My trustees [shall]/[may] provide for the payment thereof by setting apart and appropriating in respect thereof such part of my residuary estate as shall in their opinion be sufficient by the income thereof to pay such annuity (hereinafter called the annuity fund). My trustees shall have absolute discretion in assessing the amount so to be set apart having regard to any possible increase in the said Index and shall not be liable for any loss incurred by the annuitant by reason of the annuity fund subsequently proving insufficient.[4]

(iv) When such appropriation has been made the annuity shall be wholly charged on the annuity fund in exoneration of the rest of my estate but the capital of such fund may be resorted to in case at any time the income thereof is insufficient to pay the annuity.

(v) In so far as the income from the annuity fund shall in any year exceed the sum required to pay the annuity my trustees shall accumulate the same during the lifetime of my said wife or for 21 years from the date of my death whichever period shall be the shorter by investing the same in any investments hereby authorised as my trustees shall think fit. Such accumulations and the interest or income thereof shall be held by my trustees to make up any deficiency of the annuity in any subsequent year and in so far as they are not so required they shall form an accretion to the annuity fund and on the determination of the said annuity shall with the annuity fund fall into and form part of my residuary estate.[5]

For the purposes hereof the Index of Retail Prices shall mean the Index of Retail Prices published by HM Stationery Office or any official publication substituted therefor and in the event of any change after the date hereof in the reference base used to compile the said Index the figure taken to be that at which the said Index stands after such change shall be the figure at which the said Index would have stood if the reference base current at the date hereof had been retained.

1 The Index of Retail Prices is published monthly in the Department of Employment Gazette. The current index was introduced in 1956 and replaced earlier indexes to which it can be linked back (see Industrial Relations Handbook and a publication of the Stationery Office 'Method of Construction and Calculation of the Index of Retail Prices').
2 In order to adapt the form to take account of civil partnerships formed pursuant to CPA 2004, substitute 'civil partner' for 'wife' and substitute 'his' for 'her' where appropriate.
3 See para **[211.8]**, n 3.
4 In economic conditions of high inflation and a tendency of most investments to fail to maintain their value in real terms, the use of this form is likely to present the trustees with considerable difficulty in deciding what size fund is appropriate, and a discretion not to do so may be preferred. In such economic conditions there is a serious risk of a large proportion of the estate being used up to meet an annuity in this form, with much capital being paid out, and charged to income tax, as income.
5 As to the right to 'hold up' income to meet future annuity instalments, see *Re Berkeley, Inglis v Countess Berkeley* [1968] Ch 744, [1968] 3 All ER 364, CA and see generally Vol 1, para **[33.25]**. This subclause will mean that there is no interest in possession in the part of the annuity fund not treated as subject to the annuitant's interest in possession for inheritance tax purposes (see para **[211.3]**), and that that part will be subject to the 'discretionary trust' inheritance charging regime described in the Note to B18 at para **[218.1]** ff.

[211.12]

Form B11.5: Gift of several annuities

I give free of all deductions[1] the following annuities to the following persons for their respective lives to be paid free of all deductions by equal half-yearly payments the first whereof respectively shall be made at the end of six months after my death. [*Add particulars of annuities and annuitants in separate paragraphs.*]

And I direct my trustees to appropriate in respect of each such annuity[2] [out of my personal estate] in their names investments of any nature hereinafter authorised of an amount sufficient at the date of such appropriation in the opinion of my trustees to answer out of the income thereof the annuity in respect of which such appropriation is made [and an increased margin of income not exceeding 10 per cent of that annuity] and I declare that such income shall be the primary fund for answering the said annuity and the capital of the said investments shall form the secondary fund for answering the same in the event of the income proving insufficient and further that after any such appropriation shall have been made my residuary estate or the income thereof shall no longer be liable to provide for the annuity in respect of which such appropriation shall have been made.

[*If annuities are to be charged on income only omit declaration as to primary and secondary fund and substitute*: And I declare that after such appropriation as aforesaid such income shall be the primary and only fund for answering the said annuity and that any deficiency of such income in any year shall be borne by the annuitant and shall not be made good to the annuitant.]

And I declare that the balance (if any) of the income of [the] [each] appropriated fund not required in any year for answering the annuity [in respect of which the fund was appropriated] shall form part of the income of my residuary estate and shall be distributed accordingly.

[*If an annuity is given free of income tax, add the following*: I direct that all rebates, allowances or repayments which may be made to or recovered by the said [*names*] in respect of income tax shall enure for the benefit of the said [*names*] [respectively] and that the said [*names*] shall not account to my trustees for the same or any part thereof *or* I direct that the said [*names*] shall respectively account to my trustees for all rebates allowances or repayments which may be made or allowed to them in respect of income tax.]

1 See para **[211.8]**, n 3.

2 It is probably convenient to have a separate fund for each annuity, so as to ensure that definite investments shall fall into residue automatically on the cesser of the annuity in question and be divisible as residue without question.

[211.13]

Form B11.6: Gift of annuities charged on land

I give the following annuities (that is to say) to [*names of annuitants and amounts and periods of duration of annuities*] and I hereby charge my lands and premises at —— in the county of —— with the payment of the said annuities [in exoneration of the rest of my estate[1]] and I direct that the said annuities shall be paid clear of all deductions[2] by equal quarterly payments the first whereof shall respectively be made three months after my death [and I further direct that no part of the inheritance tax payable by reason of my death in respect of such lands and premises shall be borne or paid by the said annuities or the said annuitants or any of them but all such tax shall be borne and paid by the person or persons entitled (subject to the said annuities) to the said lands and premises].

1 If the land is to be charged with the payment of the annuities in exoneration of the testator's personal estate, this must be expressly stated. Such a charge will result in the land being held on trust to give effect to the charge and there will be a trust of land within the TLATA 1996, s 2 and Sch 1, para 3 (Part G, paras **[246.104]** and **[246.131]**). Such an annuitant will not be regarded as having an interest in possession in the land within the meaning of the TLATA 1996 and so no question of a right to occupy the land or a right to be consulted or to have trustees' powers delegated to him can arise: TLATA 1996, ss 9, 11, 12 and 22 (Part G, paras **[246.111]**, **[246.114]**, **[246.115]** and **[246.125]**).

An annuity charged only on land in the absence of any contrary intention was liable to bear a proportionate part of the interest on the sum required for estate duty upon the land (see Finance Act 1894, s 14; and *Re Parker-Jervis, Salt v Locker* [1898] 2 Ch 643), and the same used to be thought to be the case in relation to capital transfer (now inheritance) tax. However, as a result of legislative clarification following the Scottish decision in *Re Dougal* [1981] STC 514, it is now settled that tax on realty is prima facie a testamentary expense payable out of residue: see now the IHTA 1984, s 211 (Part G, para **[246.100]**). Accordingly, an annuity charged on land will not now be burdened with payment of inheritance tax arising from the testator's death (unless there is some direction to that effect by the testator).

The description of the land charged should be as specific as possible.

If the land is eg agricultural land with a very low income yield there could be a serious inheritance tax disadvantage in the annuities being charged on it: see the Preliminary Note at para **[211.3]**.

2 See para **[211.8]**, n 3.

[211.14]

Form B11.7: Power to purchase annuities, the capital cost being recouped out of income[1]

1. I give free of all deductions[2] the following annuities [*particulars of names of annuitants and amounts and periods of duration of annuities*].

2. I empower my trustees if in their discretion they think such a course in the best interests of my estate to purchase out of my residuary [personal] estate the above annuities from an insurance office of repute.

3. In each of the twenty-one years from my death my trustees shall out of the income of my residuary estate add to the capital thereof a sum equal [either] to one twenty-first part of the sum required to purchase the annuities hereby bequeathed [or a sum equal to the balance of income remaining after paying to the person entitled from time to time to the income of my residuary estate the sum of £—— whichever shall be the less].[3]

1 For various reasons it is more convenient for purposes of administration to direct the purchase of an annuity than to charge it on the estate. In this form the trustees are given a discretionary power to purchase. For a direction to purchase, see Form B11.10 at para **[211.17]**. From the time when the trustees finally determine to exercise the power, the annuitant can claim to have the value of the annuity paid over to him. It may be desired to recoup the capital loss out of income. It is important to make sure that the income will be sufficient to stand this burden and provision is here made to ensure that the life tenant will receive a minimum sum. See however, sub-para (2)(b) of the Preliminary Note at para **[211.6]** and n 3 below.

2 See para **[211.8]**, n 3.

3 Clause 3 apparently has the effect that a portion of the capital of the residuary estate will be treated as not being subject to a beneficiary taxed interest in possession for inheritance tax purposes, and thus subject to the 'discretionary trust' charging règime outlined in the Preliminary Note to B18 at para **[218.1]** ff. For this reason it may in many cases be preferable to omit this clause when this form is used.

[211.15]

Form B11.8: Power to trustees to appropriate investments to answer annuities[1]—separate fund for each annuity

I authorise my trustees to provide for the payment of any annuity hereby or by any codicil hereto bequeathed by setting apart and appropriating in respect of each such annuity such part or parts of my residuary [personal] estate as shall in their opinion be sufficient by the income thereof to pay such annuity.

I declare that when such appropriation shall have been made the annuity in respect of which the appropriation shall be made shall be wholly charged on the investments so appropriated (hereinafter referred to as 'the annuity fund') in exoneration of the rest of my estate but that the capital of the annuity fund may be resorted to in case at any time the income thereof is insufficient to pay such annuity.

I further declare that on the cesser of any annuity the annuity fund appropriated to such annuity shall revert to and form part of my residuary estate and that any surplus income arising from any annuity fund shall be applied as income of my residuary estate.

1 As stated in the Preliminary Note to these forms on annuities (see paras **[211.1]**–**[211.7]**), if this procedure is adopted the annuitant cannot claim to have the capital value of the

annuity paid over to him unless the estate proves insufficient to set aside a sufficient sum to answer the annuities: see Vol 1, para **[33.3]**. In this form a separate fund is to be set aside to answer each separate annuity and then on the cesser of such annuity, that fund falls into residue. It is perhaps more economical to set aside an aggregate fund to answer all the annuities, but in that case, particularly where economy has been exercised, there may be a question as to how much of the aggregate fund can be released on the cesser of any particular annuity and this may lead to disputes between the trustees and those entitled to the residue in cases where the residuary legatees are entitled to immediate payment of the amount of the fund released.

[211.16]

Form B11.9: Power to trustees to appropriate investments to answer annuities—aggregate fund for all annuities[1]

[I authorise] *or* [I direct] my trustees to provide for the payment of the annuities hereby or by any codicil hereto bequeathed by setting apart and appropriating in respect of those annuities such part or parts of my residuary personal estate as shall in their opinion be sufficient by the income thereof to pay such annuities.

I declare that:

(i) when such appropriation shall have been made the annuities shall be wholly charged on the investments so appropriated (hereinafter called 'the annuity fund') in exoneration of the rest of my estate but that the capital of the annuity fund may be resorted to if at any time the income thereof is insufficient to pay such annuities;

(ii) on the cesser of any annuity such part of the annuity fund as my trustees in their absolute and uncontrolled discretion shall determine shall be released to and thereafter be treated as part of my residuary estate my trustees retaining such part of the annuity fund as they may consider sufficient to produce by the income thereof an annual sum equal to the amount of any subsisting annuities;

(iii) any surplus income at any time arising from the annuity fund shall be applied as income of my residuary estate;

(iv) my trustees may from time to time vary any of the investments from time to time constituting the annuity fund in exercise of the general power of investment.[2]

OR

[Form 5 of the Statutory Will Forms 1925 is hereby incorporated in this my will.[3]]

1 See notes to Form B11.8 at para **[211.15]**. For the statutory will form, see Form E5 at para **[238.11]**. Since surplus income is applied as income of the residuary estate, this form is preferable to, e g Form B11.4 at para **[211.11]**, in its inheritance tax consequences: see para **[211.11]**, n 4.

2 For the general power of investment, see the TrA 2000, s 3 (Part G, para **[246.135]**).

3 For the text of this form, see Form E5 at para **[238.11]**. This form includes the usual provisions where one fund is made answerable for several annuities and by incorporating this Form it may well be that a number of annuities can be provided for more economically than by appropriating a separate fund to each annuity.

[211.17]

Form B11.10: Gift of annuity with direction to purchase[1]

I give free of all deductions[2] to A an annuity of £—— for the period of [his]/[her] life to commence from my decease and payable every three months the first payment to be made three months after my decease and I direct my executors to provide for the payment of the said annuity by purchasing the same from any public company.

1 Where there is a *direction* to purchase an annuity (as distinct from a *power* to purchase) the annuitant becomes immediately entitled if he or she so elects to be paid the sum necessary for such purchase and, even if he or she dies before any payment of the annuity becomes payable (but after the death of the testator), his or her personal representatives are entitled to the sum necessary for such purchase: *Re Robbins, Robbins v Legge* [1907] 2 Ch 8; *Re Brunning, Gammon v Dale* [1909] 1 Ch 276. In the case of a *power* to purchase the personal representatives of the annuitant have no such right.

This form may be both a grant of the annuity and a direction to purchase or merely a direction to purchase when the form will be: 'I direct my executors to purchase an annuity for A payable during her life of £—— per annum from any public company.'

If the will states that the purchase may be from any public company, the testator's executors have a discretion from whom they will purchase the annuity and, if a capital sum is claimed, it is only the sum required to purchase the annuity from the source chosen by the executors: *Re Smith, Royal Exchange Co v Lee* (1923) 130 LT 185. If for any reason the executors do not exercise that discretion or option, it is thought that the annuitant or his or her personal representatives could demand the cost of the annuity as determined in accordance with the Government annuity tables which remain in force despite the discontinuance of the sale of Government annuities in 1962. The tables now in force are those laid down by the following Government Annuity Table Orders: SI 1963/1178, SI 1968/1731, SI 1973/1407, SI 1974/1935, SI 1975/692, and SI 1977/1536.

The position where there is a power to purchase is rather different. It is not until the trustees have decided to exercise the power, that the annuitant can demand the sum required to purchase the annuity and in such a case the annuitant's personal representatives have no claim whatsoever in any event. See also Form B11.12 at para **[211.19]** and Vol 1, paras **[33.4]–[33.10]**.

2 See para **[211.8]**, n 3.

[211.18]

Form B11.11: Annuity provisions designed to mitigate inheritance tax and income tax[1]

(a) I give free of inheritance tax[2] to [*name*] of [*address*] (in this clause called 'the annuitant') for his life and payable by equal quarterly instalments (the first payment to be made three months after my death) [an annuity of £——] *or* [an annuity of such sum as after deduction of income tax at the basic rate in force for the time being (the annuitant being entitled to retain any repayment of tax made to him) amounts to £——[3]].

(b) My trustees may provide for or in relation to the said annuity at their discretion at any time in any one or more of the following ways:

(i) By appropriating such part of my residuary estate as will in their opinion yield sufficient income to pay the annuity and the cost of paying it and if they exercise this power then the annuity shall be charged wholly on the appropriated fund (to which the powers of investment hereafter given shall apply) in exoneration of the rest of my estate but the capital of the appropriated fund may be resorted to if it is at any time insufficient to pay the annuity and when the annuity ceases the appropriated fund shall form part of my residuary estate and any surplus income which may arise from it in the mean time shall be applied as income of my residuary estate.[4]

(ii) By purchasing in their names an annuity from any public company and paying it to the annuitant but if my trustees exercise this power and the annuitant then does or permits any act or event or process by which the annuity thus provided would or might (but for this provision) become vested in or payable to any other person then his annuity shall immediately cease and the payments received during the remainder of his life under the purchased annuity shall be applied as income of my residuary estate and I declare that if my trustees decide to exercise this power the annuitant shall not be entitled to receive the capital value of the annuity given to him.[5]

(iii) By commuting the annuity with the annuitant's consent and paying to him such capital sum as they may in their discretion consider reasonable in all the circumstances (having regard in particular to the fact that any inheritance tax otherwise payable on the death of the annuitant may be avoided and that the administration of my estate may be simplified and to the position in relation to income tax) and if my trustees exercise this power the annuitant shall have no further claim against my estate in respect of this annuity.[6]

(iv) [By accepting from [name of residuary legatee]] or [By accepting from any one or more of the following persons namely [names of residuary legatees or others who might be willing to provide the annuity]] a Deed of Covenant in a form approved by my trustees and providing for the payment of the annuity by such person [or jointly and severally by such persons] and [his]/[her]/[their] personal representatives (and with any personal guarantees or sureties which my trustees may require) for the remainder of the annuitant's lifetime and if such a Deed is made and accepted by my trustees then the gift of the annuity made by subclause (a) of this clause shall not take effect or shall cease to have effect (as the case may be).[7]

1 See para **[211.6]** for a possible disadvantage of the powers to commute the annuity.

2 For the importance of this direction see para **[211.3]**.

3 For alternative forms of 'tax-free' annuity provisions see Form B11.3 at para **[211.10]**.

4 See para **[211.16]**, n 1.

5 This power is for the trustees to purchase an annuity and is worded in such a way that the annuitant cannot call for the capital even when they have decided to exercise it. Its use is virtually confined to circumstances in which the trustees feel that if the annuitant received a lump sum he might, to his own detriment, spend it otherwise than on an annuity. If they do not feel this, they would do better to act under the power to commute, which immediately follows. There would, it seems, be an inheritance tax charge on the forfeiture of a purchased annuity under this subclause under the IHTA 1984, s 52(1), (2A) if the annuity is a beneficiary taxed interest in possession of the type specified in IHTA 1984, s 52(2A) or subsisted before 22 March 2006: The types of interest in possession which post-21 March 2006 result in their holders being treated as beneficially entitled to the underlying settled property under IHTA 1984, s 49(1) are an interest in possession to which a person became beneficially entitled before 22 March 2006 (unless it is an interest in possession under a trust for a bereaved minor), or an interest in possession to which a person became beneficially entitled on or after 22 March 2006 and which is an immediate post-death interest, a disabled person's interest, or a transitional serial interest (see para **[200.93]**). Under IHTA 1984, s 52(2A) (inserted by FA 2006, s 156, Sch 20, para 7) where the interest in possession concerned is one to which the person became beneficially entitled on or after 22 March

2006, this provision applies in relation to the coming to an end of the interest only if the interest is an immediate post-death interest within IHTA 1984, s 49A (see para **[200.99]**), a disabled person's interest within IHTA 1984, s 89B (see para **[200.98]**), or a transitional serial interest within IHTA 1984, s 49B (see para **[200.100]**). As to the termination of a pre-exisiting interest in possession, from 22 March 2006, potential exemption will only be available if the determination results in another person acquiring an absolute interest, or an interest in possession which has the result that its holder is treated as beneficially entitled to the underlying settled property under IHTA 1984, s 49(1) (such as a disabled person's interest), or causes the settled property to become subject to a trust for a bereaved minor (see para **[200.71]**).

For those transfers of value made by an individual which, on or after 22 March 2006, will be potentially exempt transfers see Part A, para **[200.71]**.

6 A power of this kind has been suggested by Messrs E F and J H George in *Brighouse's Short Forms of Wills*, where it is pointed out that since the use of the power will benefit the estate financially (by saving inheritance tax on the annuitant's death), and will benefit the annuitant as well (for the capital element in the annuity which he buys will be exempt from income tax), it may be possible for the trustees to grant a lump sum which will enable the annuitant to buy an annuity which gives him a higher net income than he would have had under the will and still leave the estate better off. For the inheritance implications of the exercise of such a power, see para **[211.6]**.

7 For an inheritance tax disadvantage of the exercise of such a power see para **[211.6]**.

[211.19]

Form B11.12: Gift of annuity and direction to trustees to purchase; the annuity to cease on alienation, and the annuitant not to be entitled to purchase-money in lieu of the annuity

I give to [*name of annuitant*] during [his]/[her] life an annuity of £—— [free of inheritance tax] to be paid by equal quarterly payments the first whereof shall be made three calendar months after my death and I direct my trustees [unless they see special reason to the contrary[1]] to purchase in their names and at the expense of my estate from some insurance office of repute an annuity for the life of the said [*annuitant*] of the above amount and I declare that my trustees shall stand possessed of such annuity when purchased upon trust to pay the same to the said [*annuitant*] in manner above directed and that until such purchase the said annuity shall be paid out of the income of my residuary estate. Provided always that if the said [*annuitant*] shall commit permit or suffer any act default or process whereby the said annuity or any part thereof would or might but for this present provision become vested in or payable to any other person or persons then such annuity shall immediately thereupon absolutely cease and determine as if the said [*annuitant*] were dead and any purchased annuity shall thenceforth during the life of the said [*annuitant*] be paid to [*name of person entitled on gift over*] and I declare that the said [*annuitant*] shall not be entitled to receive the capital value of the said annuity in lieu thereof.

1 If these words are omitted and the clause were ended at the words 'of the above amount' in the third line below these words, the annuitant would have the right to claim the cash value of the annuity. If the trustees had not, as here, been given the right to purchase from an insurance company, the cash value would have to be calculated by reference to the Government Tables: see para **[211.17]**, n 1 and Vol 1, paras **[33.4]**–**[33.10]**. The latter part of this clause makes the receipt of the capital sum altogether contrary to the intention of the testator and the right is in the last words of the clause expressly negatived; but these are insufficient to prevent the claim being sustained. The right to receive the capital sum can be prevented only by a gift over; see Vol 1, para **[33.7]**. As to valuation of annuities see Vol 1, paras **[33.35]**–**[33.43]**. For a possible inheritance tax disadvantage of this form see para

[211.6]. Further, this would not seem to be a protective trust within the IHTA 1984, s 88 (see Part A, para **[200.104]**) and there would be an inheritance tax charge under the IHTA 1984, s 52(1) on a forfeiture occurring unless potential exemption was available. For commentary on protective trusts see para **[200.104]**. As to the termination of an interest in possession and potential exemption, see Form B11.1, n 5.

[211.20]

Form B11.13: Proviso for cesser of annuities on alienation

Provided always that if any of the said annuitants [*or* any [*or* either] of them the said [*names of particular annuitants*]] shall commit permit or suffer any act default or process whereby but for this present provision the said annuity hereinbefore bequeathed to [him] *or* [her] or any part thereof would or might become vested in or payable to any other person or persons then such annuity shall immediately thereupon absolutely cease and determine as if such annuitant were dead.

[211.21]

Form B11.14: Declaration that annuities are to be paid clear of all deductions[1]

I declare that all the annuities bequeathed hereby or by any codicil hereto shall be paid clear of all deductions whatsoever [including income tax at the basic rate deductible at source] and that the expenses of and incidental to the purchase of any annuity under the provisions of this my will shall be borne by my residuary estate. I further declare that any rebate, allowance or repayment of income tax which may be allowed or made to any annuitant under this my will shall enure for the benefit of such annuitant[2].

1 See para **[211.5]**, sub-paras (iii) and (iv) and para **[211.8]**, n 2.
2 See para **[211.10]**, n 1.

[211.22]

Form B11.15: Gift of several annuities to same person, being annuities to widow with reduction on remarriage and provision for minor children residing with widow[1]

I give to my wife the following annuities [free of inheritance tax[2]] [and to have priority over all other pecuniary legacies and annuities hereby or by any codicil hereto bequeathed]:

(1) as from my death so long as she does not remarry or form a civil partnership[3] an annuity of £—— [4]

(2) as from her remarriage or formation of a civil partnership[3] an annuity of £—— during the residue of her life and

(3) as from my death so long as any child of mine[5] being a minor and unmarried resides with her[2] an annuity of £—— in respect of each such child. As to such annuities I declare as follows:

  (a) Such annuities if and when respectively payable shall be paid clear of all deductions[6] by equal quarterly payments on the usual quarter days with all necessary apportionments thereof respectively and my trustees shall not be bound to see to the application of any annuity payable under the trusts hereof to my said wife in respect of any child of mine.

(b) My trustees shall as soon as conveniently may be provide for the payment of the said annuities by setting apart and appropriating a sufficient part of my residuary personal estate to produce by the income thereof such annuities and when that has been done such annuities shall be wholly charged on the investments so appropriated (hereinafter referred to as 'the annuity fund') in exoneration of the rest of my estate but the capital of the annuity fund may be resorted to if at any time the income thereof is insufficient to pay such annuities.

(c) Till such appropriation the said annuities shall be paid out of [the income of] my residuary estate.

(d) On the cesser of any of the said annuities the annuity fund or such part thereof as shall not in the opinion of my trustees be required for payment of the annuity or annuities for the time being remaining payable shall revert to and form part of my residuary estate and any surplus income arising from the annuity fund in each year shall be applied as income of my residuary estate.

1 These annuities are not given free of income tax. If the widow has little other income they will no doubt become virtually free of tax by reason that the widow's total income is not taxable. If the widow has an income of her own, a provision making them tax-free may lead to involved calculations if the widow is to account for reliefs, etc. In order to adapt the form to take account of civil partnerships formed pursuant to CPA 2004, substitute 'civil partner' for 'wife', substitute 'his' for 'her' where appropriate; replace 'does not remarry or form a civil partnership' in sub-clause (1) with 'does not form a new civil partnership or remarry' and replace 'remarriage or formation of a civil partnership' in sub-clause (2) with 'formation of a new civil partnership or marriage'.

2 See para **[211.5]**, sub-para (i). These words should be omitted unless there are grounds for thinking that the gift might not be wholly exempt from inheritance tax, such as the testator being domiciled in the UK and his wife not.

3 Account should be taken of the possibility of a widow forming a civil partnership and so ending her widowhood interest that way.

4 The remarriage of the widow and the leaving home or coming of age of each child will be occasions of inheritance tax charge under the IHTA 1984, s 52(1) unless potential exemption applies. See para **[211.6]** ff. As to the termination of an interest in possession and potential exemption, see Form B11.1, note 5.

5 Illegitimate and adopted children will be included: see Vol 1, paras **[72.1]** ff and **[75.1]** ff.

6 See para **[211.8]**, n 2.

[211.23]

Form B11.16: Gift of an annuity to a trustee in trust for a mentally disabled daughter[1]

I give to [*trustee*] during the life of my daughter [*name*][2] an annuity of £—— free of all inheritance tax[3] to be paid by equal quarterly payments the first whereof shall be made three months after my death and I authorise my trustees either to purchase from some insurance society of good repute an annuity of the above amount[4] or set apart and appropriate so much of my residuary estate (hereinafter called 'the annuity fund') as shall in their opinion be sufficient by means of the income thereof to pay such annuity and I direct as follows:

(1) When the annuity shall have been provided for in either of the ways aforesaid the rest of my estate shall be exonerated from payment thereof and my trustees shall have recourse only to the annuity or the annuity fund to pay such annuity.

(2) The capital of the annuity fund (if any) may be resorted to in case at any time the income thereof is insufficient to pay the said annuity.

(3) On the cesser of the said annuity the annuity fund (if any) shall revert to my residuary estate and any surplus income arising in any year from the annuity fund shall be applied as income of my residuary estate.

(4)

(a) The said [*trustee*] shall stand possessed of the said annuity of £—— upon trust to pay or apply the same for the maintenance or benefit of my said daughter [*name*] including the payment of all expenses of and incidental to the provision of a home for and the care and maintenance of my said daughter [*name*] and the said [*trustee*] shall have full and uncontrolled discretion with respect to the application of the said annuity and if and so long as my said daughter shall reside with the said [*trustee*] [he] *or* [she] shall be entitled to retain for [his] *or* [her] own benefit out of the said annuity the sum of £—— by way of rent in respect thereof.[5]

(b) If at the date of the death of my said daughter there shall be any moneys resulting from any unapplied part of such annuity the same shall [fall as capital into my residuary estate]/[be paid by the said [*trustee*] to the treasurer for the time being of the —— Home for Incurables [*address*] whose receipt shall be a good discharge].

1 It is thought that this gives the annuitant an interest in possession for inheritance tax purposes which, because arising immediately on the death of the testator, will be an IPDI (see Part A at para **[200.98]**). If it does not do so, the annuitant, if incapable of administering her property or managing her affairs within the meaning of the Mental Health Act 1983 (see Vol1 para **[4.12]**) at the date of the testator's death (or in receipt of an attendance allowance at that time), will be deemed to have an interest in possession under the IHTA 1984, s 89. For a commentary on trusts for the vulnerable for disabled persons see C4 at para **[226.8]**, below. See para **[226.3]** ff. and Part A, para **[200.99]**.

2 It may be important to name the daughter referred to in order to take account of GRA 2004 although in this context the point is unlikely. See Vol 1 at para **[81.1]**.

3 See para **[211.5]**, sub-para (i).

4 For a possible inheritance tax disadvantage of the exercise of this power see para **[211.6]**.

5 Compare Form B18.4 at para **[218.34]**.

[211.24]

Form B11.17: Gift of an annuity upon trust for a spendthrift son and his wife and children

[*Gift of annuity, as in last form, down to the words* income of my residuary estate, *substituting* son *for* daughter *throughout.*]

(4) [The said [*trustee*] shall stand possessed of the said annuity of £—— upon trust to pay or apply the same to or for the benefit of my said son during his life or until he shall alienate or charge the same or become bankrupt or do or suffer any act or thing whereby the same

or any part thereof would or might but for this present provision become vested in or payable to any other person or persons.]

(5) [*If the annuity is to cease on alienation*: After the happening of any of the events hereinbefore mentioned the said annuity (if purchased) shall be applied as income of my residuary estate].[1]

[*If the 'protected' interest is to continue during the life of the son substitute the following for (4) and (5):* The said [*trustee*] shall hold the said annuity on protective trusts for the benefit of my said son for the period of his life].[2]

1 Under this alternative there may be an occasion of inheritance tax charge when forfeiture occurs under the IHTA 1984, s 52(1) (termination of an interest in possession) unless potential exemption is available. See para **[211.6]** ff. As to the termination of an interest in possession and potential exemption, see Form B11.1, note 5.

2 See the TA 1925, s 33 (Part G, para **[246.31]**), Part A, para **[200.104]** and Form B16.2 at para **[216.7]**. Where the annuitant was bankrupt at the death of the testator, but obtained his discharge before the first instalment of the annuity became payable, there was a forfeiture of the annuity (*Re Walker, Public Trustee v Walker* [1939] Ch 974, [1939] 3 All ER 902). A forfeiture of a protected life interest will not give rise to a charge to inheritance tax despite the termination of the life tenant's interest in possession: see the IHTA 1984, s 88.

[211.25]

Form B11.18: Direction as to payment of an annuity not created by the will for insertion where the residue is settled[1]

I direct that the payment of the annuity to [*name*] payable under a deed dated —— and made between —— shall be payable out of the capital of my residuary estate.

1 Where an annuity not created by the will is payable out of settled residue the strict rule is to apply either of two complicated methods of calculation: see Vol 1, para **[38.26]**. This form will not make a great deal of difference unless the amount of the annuity is considerable but it is a far simpler method of dealing with the matter. The annuity could of course be made payable out of income only, but unless the annual income of the estate is considerable, this may place an unfair burden on the tenant for life.

B12 Charitable gifts

Preliminary Note .... [212.1]

FORMS

B12.1 Gifts to several charitable institutions .... [212.3]

B12.2 Gifts of shares of residue to individual and charitable institutions . [212.4]

B12.3 Gift of a share of residue upon trust for charitable objects to be selected by trustees .... [212.5]

B12.4 Gift of residue upon a charitable trust .... [212.6]

B12.5 Gift to a Church of England Board of Finance .... [212.7]

B12.6 Gift to vicar for poor of a parish .... [212.8]

B12.7 Bequest coupled with a request to effectuate a purpose which the law will not enforce .... [212.9]

B12.8 Bequest for religious purposes in a particular parish .... [212.10]

B12.9 Bequest of legacy to provide Sunday school prizes .... [212.11]

B12.10 Legacy to a religious community .... [212.12]

B12.11 Bequests for masses .... [212.13]

B12.12 Gift to the representative body of the Church in Wales .... [212.14]

B12.13 Gift to the Salvation Army .... [212.15]

B12.14 Bequest to the Trustees for Methodist Church Purposes on the model trusts of the Methodist Church Act 1976 .... [212.16]

B12.15 Bequest to the Baptist Union .... [212.17]

B12.16 Gift to the United Reformed Church .... [212.18]

B12.17 Bequest to the Congregational Federation .... [212.19]

B12.18 Bequest to the Presbyterian Church of Wales (Calvinistic Methodists)1 .... [212.20]

B12.19 Devise for the Presbyterian Church of Wales (Calvinistic Methodists) .... [212.21]

B12.20 Bequest to the Unitarian and Free Christian Churches .... [212.22]

B12.21 Gift of land or houses to the Unitarian and Free Christian Churches .... [212.23]

B12.22 Gift to the United Synagogue .... [212.24]

B12.23 Gift to a hospital supported by public funds .... [212.25]

B12.24 Bequest to school for provision of playing fields .... [212.26]

B12.25 Bequest to school to be applied for the encouragement of sport ..... [212.27]

B12.26 Gift of residue to found college fellowships .... [212.28]

B12.27 Legacies in favour of the Scout Association .... [212.29]

B12.28 Legacies in favour of the Guide Association .... [212.30]

B12.29 General provision against lapse of charitable gifts .... [212.31]

PRELIMINARY NOTE

[212.1]

For a statement of the general law relating to charities see Vol 1, paras **[102.1]–[103.21]**. And see the Note in B2 at para **[202.28]** ff for charitable gifts for the maintenance of graves. The Charities Act 2006 received Royal Assent on 8 November 2006 but at the time of writing not all of the Act is in force. Although the charitable status of some entities which are presently charities will be affected, Charities Act 2006 is unlikely to affect the making of testamentary gifts to charities described in this Chapter.

[212.2]

Charitable gifts are wholly exempt from inheritance tax: Inheritance Tax Act 1984 (IHTA 1984), s 23. It is thought that, like the exemption for charities from income tax, the inheritance tax exemption is confined to charities established in the UK (see the income tax case of *Camille and Henry Dreyfus Foundation v IRC* [1956] AC 39, [1955] 3 All ER 97). Gifts to certain institutions, eg the British Museum, the National Gallery and the National Trust are wholly exempt: IHTA 1984, s 25 and Sch 3. Gifts to political parties may in certain circumstances enjoy a similar exemption: IHTA 1984, s 24. Gifts to housing associations may also be exempt: IHTA 1984, s 24A. For HMRC's treatment of charitable gifts for inheritance tax purposes, see the Inheritance Tax Manual at IHTM11101.

Many charitable gifts are concerned with quite small charities in which the testator has taken an active interest. It is with such charities that practical difficulties may occur: that is, that they have very little organisation and it may be difficult to find someone who can give a proper receipt for the legacy. It is wise in such cases to provide not only that the receipt of the treasurer or other proper officer shall be a full discharge, but to go further and say that the receipt of the person who professes to be the proper officer shall be such a discharge. In all cases it is important for those drawing the will to ascertain the precise name of the charity which the testator intends to benefit, for, on the one hand, there are many with very similar names and, on the other hand, testators commonly speak of a charity by a name which is quite different from its proper name. Failure to give the charity's correct name may result in the gift going to the wrong charity or even failing altogether. At the very least a misdescription of a charity can lead to delay and expense in the administration of the estate, and often greater expense than the value of the gift itself. Now that most charities can be registered the name should be checked with the Charity Commission and there is no excuse for failing to do so. The Charity Commission's Register of Charities can be consulted online at www.charity-commission.gov.uk (England and Wales) and www.o-scr.org.uk (Scotland) to find the correct name and address of any registered charity which a testator wishes to benefit (but some charities are of course exempt from registration).

[212.3]

Form B12.1: Gifts to several charitable institutions[1]

I give[2] to the following institutions the sums set opposite their names and declare that the receipt of [the person who professes to be][3] the treasurer or other proper officer for the time being of the institution shall in each case be a sufficient discharge to my trustees

To [*name of first institution*] the sums of £——

To [*name of second institution*] the sum of £—— [*and similarly for all other institutions*].

1 The trustees should be discharged upon obtaining a receipt from an officer of the institution. Some small charities may not be constituted in any regular way and the trustees may have to accept the best receipt they can obtain for the legacy. The legacy, however, does not fail because there is no one who can give a receipt: *Re Meyers* [1951] Ch 534, [1951] 1 All ER 538; *Re Hutchinson's Will Trusts, Gibbons v Nottingham, Area No 1 Hospital Management Committee* [1953] Ch 387, [1953] 1 All ER 996. Another provision which can

help in cases where there is a problem in identifying someone to whom a charitable gift can properly be paid is an anti-lapse clause as in Form B12.29 at para **[212.31]**.

2 The words 'free of inheritance tax' are not necessary now that the £100,000 limit on the exemption for gifts on or within one year of death has been removed: see para **[212.2]**. The words should be inserted at this point if the form is used for any gift to an institution which is not charitable, and the fund out of which the legacies will be paid includes assets which bear their own inheritance tax (see paras **[210.3]** and **[210.4]**).

3 To avoid practical difficulties in obtaining a receipt it is wise to include these words.

[212.4]

Form B12.2: Gifts of shares of residue to individual and charitable institutions

My trustees shall hold my residuary estate and the income thereof upon trust as to:

(a) a one third share for my son [*name*][1] for his own use and benefit absolutely;

(b) a one third share for the charity known as [*name and address of charity*] for its general purposes (the receipt of the person who professes to be the treasurer or other proper officer for the time being of the charity to be sufficient discharge to my trustees); and

(c) a one third share for such charitable institution or institutions in England [which have amongst their objects the relief of aged and infirm persons][2] as my trustees may in their absolute discretion within the period of one year from my death select and if more than one in such proportions as my trustees may think proper (the receipt of the person who professes to be the treasurer or other proper officer for the time being of any selected charitable institution to be sufficient discharge to my trustees) and in default of or subject to any such selection for the aforesaid charity [*name of charity*] for its general purposes.

And I hereby declare that in determining the said one third shares of my residuary estate my trustees shall divide my residuary estate into three shares without making any allowance for the inheritance tax payable by reason of my death and attributable to my residuary estate and then reducing such shares as are not exempt from inheritance tax by the inheritance tax attributable thereto.[3]

1 Following the commencement of GRA 2004 on 4 April 2005, it may be important to name the son referred to. See Vol 1 at para **[81.1]**.

2 A charity for 'the relief of aged and infirm persons' is currently a recognised head of charity but under Charities Act 2006 a new head of charity is recognised for 'the relief of those in need by reason of youth, age, ill-health, disability, financial hardship or other disadvantage' provided that the purpose is also for the public benefit.

3 Where other shares of residue will not be exempt from inheritance tax, a declaration such as this should be included to avoid complicated calculations, see para **[214.72]**.

[212.5]

Form B12.3: Gift of a share of residue upon trust for charitable objects to be selected by trustees[1]

(1) My trustees shall hold one equal [fourth] part of my residuary estate and the income thereof upon trust to apply the same for such charitable

institutions or such other charitable objects in England as my trustees may in their absolute discretion select and to pay such share and income to or for such institutions or objects if more than one in such proportions as my trustees may think proper and I declare that the receipt of the [person who professes to be the][2] treasurer or other proper officer for the time being of any such charity shall be an effectual discharge to my trustees in respect of any sum (whether of capital or income) allocated under this gift.

(2) I express the wish without imposing any binding trust or obligation that my trustees should distribute the whole of the said equal [fourth] part of my residuary estate and the income thereof within the period of two years from my death [and until such distribution is complete my trustees shall have power to invest all moneys liable to be invested in any property of whatever description or location as if they were a sole beneficial owner of such moneys].[3]

(3) The fractional shares of my residuary estate shall be determined by dividing my residuary estate into the fractional shares set out above without making any allowance for the inheritance tax payable by reason of my death and attributable to my residuary estate and then reducing such shares as are not exempt from inheritance tax by the inheritance tax attributable thereto.[4]

1 This form will be suitable where it is envisaged that the distribution will take place shortly after the testator's death. For a long-term discretionary trust, see Form C13.1 at para **[235.2]**. Care must be taken as to the description of the objects to be benefited in a gift such as this. It is clear that a gift for 'charitable objects' is good. A gift for 'charitable and benevolent objects' has also been held to be good (*Re Best, Jarvis v Birmingham Corpn* [1904] 2 Ch 354). On the other hand, a gift for 'charitable or benevolent objects' will be void for uncertainty (*Hunter v A-G* [1899] AC 309; *Re Horrocks, Taylor v Kershaw* [1939] P 198, [1939] 1 All ER 579; *Chichester Diocesan Fund and Board of Finance Inc v Simpson* [1944] AC 341, [1944] 2 All ER 60); but 'a gift for charitable or religious purposes' is good (*Re Ward, Public Trustee v Ward* [1941] Ch 308, [1941] 2 All ER 125, CA); the Charitable Trusts (Validation) Act 1954 validated certain existing charitable trusts that would otherwise have been void but did not have an effect on trusts created thereafter. See generally Vol 1, para **[102.23]**.

There is a prima facie presumption that every power given to a trustee, even one involving the exercise of a very wide discretion such as the above is vested in them virtue officii and accordingly passes with the office to the holders for the time being thereof (*Re Smith, Eastick v Smith* [1904] 1 Ch 139). If, therefore, the testator desires that the power of selection is only to be exercised by the individuals named as trustees special provision must be made. A testator may leave the selection of charity beneficiaries to trustees: see *A-G v National Provincial Bank* [1924] AC 262, [1923] All ER Rep 123 at 264 and 126 respectively.

2 To avoid practical difficulties in obtaining a receipt it is wise to include these words.

3 These words could be left out, because they are no broader than the general power of investment by which personal representatives can now make any kind of investment which they could make if they were absolutely entitled to the assets of the estate: TrA 2000, ss 3 and 35 (Part G, paras **[246.135]** and **[246.167]**).

4 If other shares of residue will not be exempt from inheritance tax, a declaration such as this should be included to avoid complicated calculations, see para **[214.72]**.

[212.6]

Form B12.4: Gift of residue upon a charitable trust[1]

I give my residuary estate (hereinafter called 'the trust fund') to my trustees to hold the same upon the following trusts with and subject to the following powers and provisions:

[(1) In this clause 'charity' means any purpose which is exclusively charitable according to the law of England and Wales and any institution whether corporate or not (including any trust or undertaking) which is established for purposes which are exclusively charitable according to the law of England and Wales and 'charities' has a corresponding meaning.][2]

OR

[(1) In this clause 'charity' shall have the same meaning as under the Charities Act 2006.][3]

(2) My trustees shall pay the income of the trust fund to such charity or charities if more than one in such shares and in such manner generally as my trustees shall in their absolute discretion think fit provided that until the expiration of the period of 21 years from my death my trustees shall have power to accumulate the whole or any part of such income by investing the same and the resulting income thereof in any manner hereby authorised so that any accumulations so made shall form an accretion to the capital from which such income arose for all purposes.

(3) Notwithstanding the foregoing trust of income my trustees shall have power at any time or times to pay transfer or apply the whole or any part or parts of the capital of the trust fund to or for the benefit of such charity or charities in such shares if more than one and in such manner generally as my trustees shall in their absolute discretion think fit.

(4) I express the wish without imposing any trust or legal obligation that my trustees should consider the purpose of the relief of poor persons resident in the county of —— and charities which have amongst their objects the relief of such persons as the principal beneficiaries of the trust fund and the income thereof.

(5) The receipt of the person who professes to be the treasurer or other proper officer for the time being of any charity shall be sufficient discharge to my trustees.[4]

1 See also Form C13.1 at para **[235.2]**. The will should include suitable investment powers for the trustees as this trust may continue for some time.

2 This definition of charity is derived from the CA 1993, ss 96 and 97. This reflects the definition still in force at the time of writing.

3 Under Charities Act 2006 Charity is defined as an institution which is established for charitable purposes only, and falls to be subject to the control of the High Court in the exercise of its jurisdiction with respect to charities and the term 'Charitable purpose' is defined for the first time. See Vol 1, at para **[102.3]**. Use the second alternative if the Charities Act 2006 is wholly in force.

4 To avoid practical difficulties in obtaining a receipt it is wise to include these words.

[212.7]

Form B12.5: Gift to a Church of England Board of Finance[1]

I give the sum of £ —— to [the Central Board of Finance of the Church of England of Church House, Great Smith Street, London SW1[2]] [the Board of Finance of the Diocese of —— of [*address*][3]] for such ecclesiastical charitable purposes as the Board shall in its absolute discretion decide [*or* in aid of the fund for ——] [*or* for the following charitable purpose namely —— [*eg* the training of ordination candidates both male and female in the Church of England]] and I declare that the receipt of the secretary for the time being of the Board shall be a full and sufficient discharge to my trustees.

1 This form is based on forms recommended by the Central Board of Finance of the Church of England.
2 In *Re Barnes, Simpson v Barnes* [1930] 2 Ch 80n, it was held that a gift to 'the Church of England' was a good charitable gift, but the question whether the Central Board of Finance (a body incorporated in 1914 which administers the Central Church Fund which was established the year following) was entitled to call for the property given as of right was left undecided. If, therefore a gift for Church of England purposes is intended, it is advisable for the gift to be made in favour of the Central Board of Finance or one of the diocesan boards of finance (as to which see n 3 below).
3 In every diocese there is a diocesan board of finance incorporated under the Companies Acts. A diocesan board of finance is empowered by its constitution to hold property for purposes connected with the Church of England.

[212.8]

Form B12.6: Gift to vicar for poor of a parish[1]

I give to the vicar [parish priest] for the time being of the parish of —— near —— in the County of —— the sum of £—— to be used by him for the assistance in such manner in all respects as he shall determine of the poor of the said parish and the receipt of the said vicar [parish priest] shall be a full discharge to my trustees for the said sum and my trustees shall in no way be responsible for the application thereof.

1 It seems proper for such a gift to be made to the priest in charge, but it may, if the testator desires, be made to the parochial church council. As to gifts for parish purposes, see Form B12.8 at para **[212.10]** and Vol 1, para **[102.16]**.

[212.9]

Form B12.7: Bequest coupled with a request to effectuate a purpose which the law will not enforce[1]

I give £—— [free of inheritance tax] to [*name of person or the holder of an office* at the date of my death or if the said office is then vacant to the first holder thereof within five years after the date of my death] absolutely. Without any intention of creating a trust or legal obligation I request the said —— to devote the said sum of £—— to [*the purpose desired*].

1 This is the form of bequest formerly in common use when it was desired to devote money to what were known as superstitious uses, such as the saying of masses for the dead. That purpose has now been held to be legal (see Form B12.11 at para **[212.13]**), but the form may still be wanted for some purposes. It can also be used for cases where the testator does not desire that the purpose shall be known except to some confidential agent who will apply the money according to his direction, though the purpose is one which the law allows. As this is not a charitable gift it will not be exempt from inheritance tax and the words 'free of inheritance tax' will be appropriate for inclusion where the legacy might be payable out of assets which bear their own inheritance tax. See paras **[210.3]**, **[214.59]** and **[214.60]**.

[212.10]

Form B12.8: Bequest for religious purposes in a particular parish[1]

I bequeath the sum of £—— to [the vicar and churchwardens for the time being] *or* [parochial church council] of the parish of —— on trust for such religious purposes in the said parish as [the said vicar and churchwardens] *or* [parochial church council] shall in their absolute discretion think fit and I declare that the receipt of [the said vicar and churchwardens] *or* [the treasurer of the said parochial church council] shall be a sufficient discharge to my trustees for the said sum and that my trustees shall not be bound to see to or inquire into the application thereof and I further declare that [the said vicar and churchwardens or their respective successors] *or* [the said parochial church council] shall be entitled at any time to expend the whole capital of the said sum in the manner aforesaid.

1 As to gifts for religious purposes, see Vol 1, paras **[102.9]** and **[102.17]**.

[212.11]

Form B12.9: Bequest of legacy to provide Sunday school prizes[1]

1. I give to my trustees the sum of £——.

2. My trustees shall pay or transfer the said sum (which and the investments for the time being representing the same are hereinafter called the trust fund) to or into the name of [the Parochial Church Council of ——] *or* [the vicar and churchwardens of the parish of ——[2]] *or* [the minister and deacons of the —— Congregational Church at ——] *or* [*as the case may be*] and [the Parochial Church Council] *or* [the vicar and churchwardens for the time being of the said parish] *or* [the minister and deacons for the time being of the said church] *or* [*as the case may be*] (hereinafter called the special trustees) shall hold the trust fund upon the trusts following:

(a) Out of the yearly dividends of the trust fund the special trustees shall as they in their discretion think fit [grant prizes or awards] *or* [shall purchase prizes or awards of books] for deserving scholars attending a Sunday school in connection with [the church of St —— in the said parish] *or* [the said church] [for proficiency in religious knowledge] *or* [for good conduct regularity in attendance and progress in religious knowledge] provided that no one scholar shall receive any prizes or awards in respect of any one year exceeding in total [amount] *or* [value] the sum of ——.

(b) If the whole of the dividends produced by the trust fund in any year shall not be applied in the [grant] *or* [purchase] of prizes or awards under the provision hereinbefore contained the special trustees shall at any time before the expiration of 21 years from my death invest and accumulate so much of the said dividends as is not so applied in their names [in any investments of whatever description or location as they may in their absolute discretion think fit][3] with power for the special trustees at their discretion to vary any investment for others of any nature hereby authorised and stand possessed of the said accumulations upon the same trusts as are hereby declared concerning the trust fund but so that the whole or any part of such accumulations may at any time be applied for the purposes aforesaid as if the same had been dividends arising in the year in which the same shall be so applied[4] and after the expiration of 21 years from my death my special trustees shall pay or apply so much of the said dividends as is not applied as aforesaid for such religious purposes [in the said parish] *or* [of the said church] as they shall in their absolute discretion think fit.

1 The promotion of education in Christian knowledge is a charitable purpose: *A-G v Stepney* (1804) 10 Ves 22. See Vol 1, para **[102.8]**.
2 It would seem the proper course to vest the legacy in the parochial church council, but, as the Parochial Church Councils (Powers) Measure 1956, s 5, is permissive in character, it may be that the legacy may still be vested in the vicar and churchwardens, as was the universal practice before 1921.
3 See para **[212.5]**, n 3.
4 As to this clause, see *Wharton v Masterman* [1895] AC 186 at 200.

[212.12]

Form B12.10: Legacy to a religious community[1]

I give the sum of £—— to the person who at the time my trustees shall be ready to pay this legacy shall be or shall act as the [abbess] of the Convent of —— at —— in the county of —— [*or* as the case may be] upon trust to apply the income thereof for the general purposes of the said convent and the receipt of the said abbess or the person acting as such shall be a full discharge to my trustees for this gift.

1 The capital of the legacy is not disposed of, but a perpetual trust of income for charitable purposes is valid: *Re Levy, Barclays Bank Ltd v Board of Guardians and Trustees for the Relief of the Jewish Poor* [1960] Ch 346, [1960] 1 All ER 42. Those advising the testator must take particular care to obtain the correct name of the convent or community and the description of the person in charge. In many cases the person in charge will hold office for only a short period, a new head being elected or appointed from time to time. The descriptions of such persons vary considerably according to the religious order concerned. For a case where the will was witnessed by two nuns, one of whom had become abbess of the convent at the death of the testator, see *Re Ray's Will Trusts, Re Ray's Estate, Public Trustee v Barry* [1936] Ch 520, [1936] 2 All ER 93 (being a gift for the purposes of the convent and not a beneficial gift to either of the attesting witnesses, it was not rendered void by such attestation). If there is any doubt about the charitable status of the body in question, it would seem preferable to use a receipt clause in the terms of Form B12.1 at para **[212.3]** and to provide for the legacy to be free of inheritance tax where it may be payable wholly or partly out of assets which bear their own inheritance tax (see paras **[210.3]**, **[214.59]** and **[214.60]**).

[212.13]

Form B12.11: Bequests for masses[1]

I. Gift to Parish Priest

I give the sum of £—— to the priest in charge of the Roman Catholic Church at —— to be applied to the offering of masses in public for the repose of the soul[s] of —— and I declare that the receipt of the priest in charge of the said church at the time of the payment of the said sum of £—— shall be a full discharge to my executors in respect of the same.

II. Gift for a Foundation Mass

[I give to the treasurer for the time being of the Roman Catholic diocese of —— the sum of £——] *or* [I direct my trustees to give to the treasurer for the time being of the Roman Catholic diocese of —— such sum as may be necessary] for the foundation of a [mass] *or* [masses] to be offered in public at the Roman Catholic church at —— for the repose of soul[s] of —— and I declare that the receipt of the treasurer for the time being of the said diocese shall be a full discharge to my executors in respect of the same.

III. Gift of a Sum of Money the Income Thereof to be Applied for the Offering of Masses for the Dead

I give to the trustees of this my will the sum of £—— upon trust to apply the income thereof [for a period of —— years from the date of my death] in payment of the stipends [offerings][2] to the priest for the saying of masses in public for the repose of the soul[s] of —— such masses to be said as far as reasonably possible at the Roman Catholic church at —— the whole income in any one year being so expended as nearly as may be in the course of the year in which it is received and the receipt of the priest or priests saying such masses shall be a full discharge to my trustees in respect of the sums so paid [*add gift over if a limited period is provided for*].

1 At one time it was thought that a gift for masses was void as being for a superstitious use, but this view was held to be ill founded by the decision of the House of Lords in *Bourne v Keane* [1919] AC 815. It still remained to be decided whether such a gift was in law a charitable bequest, and it was decided to be so in *Re Caus, Lindeboom v Camille* [1934] Ch 162, [1933] All ER Rep 818. (This case was before the House of Lords in *Gilmour v Coats* [1949] AC 426, [1949] 1 All ER 848, and though it may be said that the House did not seem to regard the decision with any favour, their lordships refrained from expressing any definite view as to its correctness, and, indeed, the point of the decision did not arise in the case then decided.) The effect of the former decision was to confirm the validity of the bequest given in the first clause of this form. The latter decision made possible gifts, such as those in the remaining clauses, for the application of the income of an invested fund to defray the expenses of such masses. The more recent decision of *Re Hetherington* [1990] Ch 1, [1989] 2 All ER 129, has confirmed that a gift for the saying of masses in public, as opposed to in private, contains a sufficient element of public benefit to make the gift charitable. Where the gift is made by the payment of a lump sum to the parish priest, it will be presumably expended in defraying the mass stipends of the priest in saying masses within a short period of the date of the death of the person for whom they are to be said. A lump sum should be of a moderate amount. When a sum of £1,000 was given, it was decided by the diocesan authorities that such a gift was impossible of performance and the gift had to be refused. A foundation mass is a mass said once a year in perpetuity and is usually said upon the anniversary of the date of the death of the deceased, or possibly upon the Sunday nearest thereto. In such a case, a sum is paid to, and invested by, the diocesan treasurer, and out of the income thereof the treasurer for the time being pays the stipend of the priest saying the mass. The mass itself is usually said at the church which the deceased attended during his or her lifetime, which, of course, will be within the diocese. Where it is intended that the masses shall be paid for out of income, the arrangements for foundation masses will probably meet the desires of the testator and be the most convenient course to adopt. The third clause can be adopted where the arrangements for a foundation mass or foundation masses are thought to be insufficient, or where, for any other reason, they do not meet with the testator's approval. The third clause is also appropriate where the income is to be applied for the provision of masses for a limited time, after which the capital or the income of the fund is to be given over. Such a gift over must vest within the period limited by the rule against perpetuities, unless it is also in itself a charitable gift (*Re Tyler, Tyler v Tyler* [1891] 3 Ch 252).

2 Payment made to the priest for the saying of a mass is variously called a stipend or an offering. The amount of such stipend or offering is not invariable, and is often varied according to the means of the person desiring the mass to be said.

[212.14]

Form B12.12: Gift to the representative body of the Church in Wales[1]

I give [*description of property*] [the sum of £——] unto the representative body of the Church in Wales whose office is at 39 Cathedral Close, Cardiff, South Glamorgan CS1 9XF to be held and dealt with by them under and in accordance with the regulations and provisions contained in their charter of incorporation or otherwise for the time being in force respecting property held by them so far as the same are applicable Nevertheless upon trust that the said representative body shall from time to time apply at their discretion the income [and also if and when they see fit the capital] of the said [property] [sum] and of all or any property from time to time representing the same for the benefit of the bishop for the time being of [*or* for charitable Church purposes in] the diocese of —— [*or* the incumbent for the time being of [*or* for charitable Church purposes in] the parish of —— in the County of —— or any parish with or into which such parish may for the time being be united or merged] [*or* for charitable Church purposes in Wales] and the receipt of the treasurer or the other proper officer for the time being of the said representative body shall be an effectual discharge to my trustees in respect of this gift.

1 This form is based on precedents originally supplied by the Representative Body of the Church in Wales.

[212.15]

Form B12.13: Gift to the Salvation Army[1]

I give [the sum of £——] [*description of property*] to the Salvation Army for its general purposes[2] and direct that the receipt of the treasurer or finance secretary for the time being of the Salvation Army at its UK and International Headquarters, 101 Queen Victoria Street, London EC4P 4EP, shall be a good discharge to my trustees.

1 This form is based on a precedent supplied by the Salvation Army. Further information and advice regarding clauses making gifts for specific Salvation Army purposes is available from the Finance Secretary, The Salvation Army, 101 Queen Victoria Street, London EC4P 4EP.

2 Substitute here 'for its social work' if it is desired that the gift be used for Salvation Army social work.

[212.16]

Form B12.14: Bequest to the Trustees for Methodist Church Purposes on the model trusts of the Methodist Church Act 1976[1]

I give to the Trustees for Methodist Church Purposes of Central Buildings, Oldham Street, Manchester M1 1JQ (hereinafter called 'the Board') the sum of £—— to be held by the board as custodian trustees upon the model trusts for the time being contained in the Methodist Church Act 1976 and I desire the said sum to be applied for the ——[2] purposes (as defined in the said Act) of ——.[3]

1 This is based on a precedent provided by the Trustees for Methodist Church Purposes at the address given in the form (telephone no: 0161 236 5194). The model trusts referred to in this form are set out in Pt III of Sch 2 to the Methodist Church Act 1976, and are trusts generally for the purposes of the Methodist Church. However, declarations of preferences for particular churches or purposes may be included. Indeed where there is a gift of property in a will to any local Methodist church without any express declaration of trust effecting the property, then the Methodist Church Act 1976, s 15(2) provides that the gift will have effect as if the gift had been made to the Trustees for Methodist Church Purposes upon the model trusts containing a declaration of preference for the application of the property for the purposes of the local church referred to in the gift. Advice can be obtained on the wording of gifts for specific Methodist Church Purposes from the Trustees and from the Methodist Church Property Division (of the same address and telephone no). This form

enables the testator to specify by precatory words some particular object which he or she wants the gift devoted to, but to avoid the danger of the gift failing by reason of the particular object ceasing before his or her death.

2 Insert 'local', 'circuit', 'district', 'connexional', or 'divisional' as required.

3 Insert name of church, circuit, district, division or fund.

[212.17]

Form B12.15: Bequest to the Baptist Union[1]

I give and bequeath to the Baptist Union of Great Britain and Ireland, the sum of £—— and I declare that the receipt of the treasurer for the time being of the said Baptist Union shall be sufficient discharge for the same. [I wish the said sum to be earmarked for the following purpose ——.[2]]

1 This form is based on a precedent supplied by the Bapist Union Corporation, Ltd. Any further information may be obtained from the Corporation at Baptist House, PO Box 44, 129 Broadway, Didcot, Oxon OX11 8RT.

2 A number of separate funds are mentioned as particular purposes and it may be important to make proper inquiries as to the proper name of the fund to which the legacy is to be applied. If no special fund is mentioned, the gift will be used for any of the purposes of the Union.

[212.18]

Form B12.16: Gift to the United Reformed Church[1]

I give to the United Reformed Church of 86 Tavistock Place, London WC1H 9RT for its general purposes (being charitable) [the sum of ——] [*description of property*] and I direct that the receipt of the treasurer for the time being of such church shall be a sufficient discharge for the same.

1 This form is based on a precedent supplied by the United Reformed Church of the address given in the form, from whom advice should be sought if it is desired to make a gift for some specific United Reformed Church purpose.

[212.19]

Form B12.17: Bequest to the Congregational Federation

I bequeath the sum of £—— to the Congregational Federation of 4 Castle Gate, Nottingham NG1 7AS and I declare that the receipt of the treasurer for the time being of the Federation shall be a sufficient discharge for the legacy.

[212.20]

Form B12.18: Bequest to the Presbyterian Church of Wales (Calvinistic Methodists)[1]

I give and bequeath to the treasurer for the time being of ——[2] in connection with the General Assembly of the Presbyterian Church of Wales (Calvinistic Methodists) the sum of £—— and the receipt of such treasurer to be sufficient discharge to my executors.

1 This form is based on a precedent supplied by the General Assembly of the Presbyterian Church of Wales, 53 Richmond Road, Cardiff CF2 3UP. The property of the Calvinistic Methodist or Presbyterian Church of Wales is by the Calvinistic Methodist or Presbyterian Church of Wales Act 1933 to be vested so far as it consists of land in the Properties Board

of the Church but it is optional whether personal property is so vested unless the will expressly directs that the property be vested in the Properties Board. The above precedent is therefore applicable to personalty only.

2 Fill in here: 'for the general purposes of the connexion' or for a named church or for any of the particular funds administered by the connexion. In the last case it may be of importance to inquire as to the particular description of the fund.

[212.21]

Form B12.19: Devise for the Presbyterian Church of Wales (Calvinistic Methodists)[1]

I give to the Properties Board of the Calvinistic Methodist Church of Wales, or the Presbyterian Church of Wales as a custodian trustee [*describe property*] in trust for [*state specific connexional object or objects which it is desired to benefit*].

1 By the Calvinistic Methodist or Presbyterian Church of Wales Act 1933, s 7(2) (as to which see para **[212.18]**, n 1), the transfer of property to the board by trustees or personal representatives is a good discharge to them for the property so transferred.

[212.22]

Form B12.20: Bequest to the Unitarian and Free Christian Churches[1]

I give to the society now known as the General Assembly of Unitarian and Free Christian Churches the sum of £—— and the receipt of the Treasurer or secretary of such society for the time being shall be a sufficient discharge to my executors.

1 This form and the following form are based on precedents supplied by the General Assembly of Unitarian and Free Christian Churches, Essex Hall, 1–6 Essex Street, London WC2R 3HY.

[212.23]

Form B12.21: Gift of land or houses to the Unitarian and Free Christian Churches

I devise to the society now known as the General Assembly of Unitarian and Free Christian Churches my house [*describe the premises*] upon trust for the general purposes of the said society.

[212.24]

Form B12.22: Gift to the United Synagogue[1]

I give to the United Synagogue [to be applied for the benefit of the synagogue at ——] the sum of £—— and I declare that the receipt of one of the treasurers for the time being of the United Synagogue shall be a sufficient discharge to my trustees.

1 This form is adapted from a form recommended by the United Synagogue, Woburn House, Upper Woburn Place, London, WC1H 0EZ. Many, though by no means all, Orthodox Jewish Synagogues in the United Kingdom are constituents of the United Synagogue, which is a corporate body. Gifts may be made to the United Synagogue either for its general purposes, or for the benefit of a constituent synagogue.

[212.25]

Form B12.23: Gift to a hospital supported by public funds[1]

I give the sum of £—— to the appropriate hospital authority for —— Hospital to be invested by the said authority in any investments [permitted by law for the investment of trust funds or by this my will] *or* [of whatever description or location as it may in its absolute discretion think fit] with power from time to time to transfer any such investments into others of a like nature upon trust to apply the income from such investments for any one or more of the following purposes [*insert such of the following purposes as may be desired*]:

(i) For the provision of prizes for student nurses undergoing training at the said —— Hospital.

(ii) For the provision of prizes or otherwise for the benefit of the —— Nurses' School attached to the said —— Hospital.

(iii) For the provision of extra comforts for the patients of the said —— Hospital including gifts of clothing or additional medical or surgical appliances on leaving the said —— Hospital.

(iv) For the provision of extra comforts for or the general welfare of the staff of the said —— Hospital.

(v) For the provision of accommodation for the use of the relatives who come from a distance of patients who are critically ill.[2]

(vi) For the purposes of any research [or name a particular branch of research] carried on at the said —— Hospital.

(vii) Generally for purposes relating to the said —— Hospital or any research carried out therein.

The above legacy is conditional upon the said authority undertaking [*or* It is my desire that in consideration of the said legacy the said authority shall undertake] to name and maintain in perpetuity a bed [cot] in the said hospital to be known as the —— Bed [Cot].[3]

I desire that the said gift shall always be known as the —— Fund [in memory of [my wife]/[my civil partner] who was for many years on the staff of the said hospital].

I declare that the receipt purporting to be signed by the treasurer or other proper officer of the said authority shall be sufficient discharge to my trustees in respect of the above legacy.

1 By the NHSA 2006, ss 90 and 91, a gift may be made to a health authority upon trust for purposes relating to the health service or to an NHS trust for purposes relating to the hospital aimed and managed by the NHS trust. This Form refers to 'the appropriate health authority'. This will be the appropriate NHS trust or area health authority save where there are special trustees for the hospital. This form is so worded that if the hospital to be benefited should become an NHS trust between the date of the will and the date of the death, the gift will be to the appropriate NHS trust.

2 See *Re Dean's Will Trusts* [1950] 1 All ER 882.

3 See *Re Ginger* [1951] Ch 458, [1951] 1 All ER 422; *Re Mills, Midland Bank Executor and Trustees Co Ltd v United Birmingham Hospitals Board of Governors* [1953] 1 All ER 835, [1953] 1 WLR 554. Where the gift was for providing beds for paying patients as to one-half at one hospital where there were none and as to the other half at another hospital where there were such beds it was held that both gifts were charitable: *Re Adams, Gee v Barnet Group Hospital Management Committee* [1968] Ch 80, [1967] 3 All ER 285.

[212.26]

Form B12.24: Bequest to school for provision of playing fields

I give the sum of £ —— free of inheritance tax to the governors of —— School to be applied by them in the purchase of a field or fields to be used for the school games and the school sports and similar purposes. [I also give to my trustees the sum of £—— free of inheritance tax [to invest in securities and investments of whatever description or location as my trustees shall in their absolute discretion think fit][1] and to pay the income therefrom to the said governors to be applied by them for the upkeep of the said playing fields and any buildings thereon. I empower my trustees as soon as the said playing fields have been purchased to transfer the said investments to trustees appointed by the said governors or to such persons as my trustees shall in their discretion think fit.][2]

1 See para **[212.5]**, n 3.

2 The first gift of a capital sum is good in any event, but the second gift is probably only charitable if the school is itself a charity, see *Re Mariette, Mariette v Aldenham School Governing Body* [1915] 2 Ch 284; *Re Gray, Todd v Taylor* [1925] Ch 362, [1925] All ER Rep 250; for a case against such a gift being charitable where the school is not a charity, see *Re Nottage, Jones v Palmer* [1895] 2 Ch 649. See also *IRC v McMullen* [1981] AC 1, [1980] 1 All ER 884 (trust for the promotion of the physical education and development of pupils at schools and universities upheld as a valid charitable trust) and see generally Vol 1 at para **[102.10]**, and cases cited at para **[102.12]**, n 9. Under Charities Act 2006 some schools which are presently considered charitable may struggle to satisfy the public benefit test and so lose their charitable status.

In case the gift is non-charitable (and thus not exempt from inheritance tax) and is payable wholly or partly out of assets which bear their own inheritance tax, a direction freeing the gift from inheritance tax may be appropriate (see paras **[210.3]** and **[210.4]** and **[214.59]** and **[214.60]**).

[212.27]

Form B12.25: Bequest to school to be applied for the encouragement of sport[1]

I bequeath the sum of £—— free of inheritance tax to the governing body of —— School at —— for the purpose of acquiring land and preparing and equipping the same for the playing of [lawn tennis or *such other game for which amount of the bequest may be sufficient*]. I also bequeath to the said governing body the sum of £—— for providing by the income therefrom a prize or trophy for the winner of [the 1,500 metres race] at the school's annual sports.

1 See para **[212.26]**, n 2.

[212.28]

Form B12.26: Gift of residue to found college fellowships

(1) As to the net residue of the proceeds of my residuary real and personal estate I give and bequeath the same unto my trustees upon trust subject to the conditions hereinafter mentioned to pay the same to the treasurer or person or persons for the time being authorised and acting as treasurer of —— College in the University of —— for the purpose of founding fellowships in the said college of not less than £—— per annum according to the following conditions or provisions[1] namely:

(a) that the said fellowships shall [from time to time be given to such candidates as shall from time to time be adjudged to be the most fit and proper to receive the same upon the result of an examination in the higher branches of classics or of mathematics or of both combined all such candidates to] be confined to such persons as shall have been former students of the said college and shall have obtained certificates in the [tripos or final public] examination held in the said university for [classical or mathematical or medical or chemical or scientific or other honours] [provided also that the examiners for such fellowships shall be of opinion that such candidates possess sufficient merit and distinction].

(b) [That persons shall be selected for or elected to such fellowships from time to time in such manner as is usual in respect of other fellowships of the said college or in such special manner as the governing body of the college shall from time to time decide.]

(c) That such fellowships shall be tenable for [seven] years and not longer unless the governing body of the said college shall for special reasons consider that in any particular case the term [seven] years ought to be extended and in such case such term may be extended from time to time at the sole discretion of such governing body.

(d) [That such fellowships may be given to any such person as aforesaid who is undertaking or desires to undertake any branch of research or experimental work.]

(e) That the holders of such fellowships shall be styled Fellows of the said college and shall have a reasonable share in the government and management of the college pursuant to the constitution and regulations thereof as established [but need not be resident Fellows].

(f) [That the governing body of the college shall be at liberty to expend not only the income but also the capital of the said moneys in providing such fellowships as aforesaid since I consider it more beneficial to provide for the near than for the distant future, and I suggest to the said governing body that the whole of the said moneys both principal and interest might well be expended within the period of [twenty-one] years from the date of the receipt of the said moneys.]

(2) The offer and payment to the said treasurer or other persons acting as such shall be made subject to the acceptance by the said college and the governing body thereof of all and singular the above-mentioned conditions (with such modifications as may be approved by my trustees pursuant to clause (4) hereof) and in case of non-acceptance thereof within the period of three months from the date of such offer or within such extended period not exceeding twelve months as my trustees shall deem expedient my trustees shall make the same offer or payment to or in favour of [*name*] college upon the same conditions in all respects as if the name of the college lastly hereinbefore named were substituted for the college firstly hereinbefore named.

(3) In case neither of the said colleges shall accept the said conditions my trustees shall stand possessed of the said net residue of the proceeds of my real and personal estate upon trust for ——.

(4) I declare that my trustees shall have full power to vary or modify the said conditions of acceptance by [*name*] College and [*name*] College respectively provided that the paramount general intention of such conditions is effectuated.

1 Some of the following paragraphs are inserted as instances which have in fact proved useful, though in most cases the conditions will generally be left to the discretion of the governing body of the college. It may be mentioned that fellowships conferred after a qualifying examination are not usual at the universities.

[212.29]

Form B12.27: Legacies in favour of the Scout Association[1]

I. LEGACY FOR THE GENERAL PURPOSES OF THE SCOUT ASSOCIATION

I hereby give to the Scout Association (incorporated by Royal Charter) the sum of £—— for the general purposes of such association and I declare that receipt of the treasurer for the time being of such association shall be a good discharge to my executors.

II. LEGACY FOR THE BENEFIT OF A SCOUT GROUP OR DISTRICT OR COUNTY SCOUT COUNCIL[2]

I hereby give to the Scout Association (incorporated by Royal Charter) the sum of £—— for the general purposes of such association and I express the desire but without imposing any trust that the said sum shall be used for the —— [Group] [District/County Scout Council] of the Scout Association and I declare that the receipt of the treasurer for the time being of such association shall be a good discharge to my executors.

1 These forms are based on precedents supplied by the Scout Association.
2 In the event of the named group or district or council having ceased to exist at the date of the testator's death, it would be the normal practice of the association to apply the legacy for the benefit of scouting in the same locality.

[212.30]

Form B12.28: Legacies in favour of the Guide Association[1]

I. LEGACY FOR THE GENERAL PURPOSES OF THE GUIDE ASSOCIATION

I hereby give to the Guide Association (incorporated by Royal Charter) the sum of £—— for the general purposes of such association and I declare that the receipt of the treasurer for the time being of such association shall be a good discharge to my executors.

II. LEGACY FOR THE BENEFIT OF A UNIT OR AREA OF THE GUIDE ASSOCIATION[2]

I GIVE [the sum of £—— free of all tax] [a—— share of my Residuary Estate] to The Guide Association Trust Corporation of 17–19 Buckingham Palace Road London SW1W 0PT to hold the same upon the trusts of the Guide Association Trust Deed of 1938 as trustee for [—— County] of the Guide Association a registered charity number [——] or if the said Guide [County] has ceased to exist following amalgamation reorganisation disbandment or otherwise then for the Guide Association County [or Counties] which in the discretion of the Trust Corporation most nearly represents the present [—— County] as it exists at the date of this my will and I express the wish (but without imposing any binding trust or obligation) that the legacy shall be applied in or towards the [purchase and any subsequent improvement repairs and maintenance of a Pack Holiday House to belong to the Guide County but to be used particularly to enable inner city children to experience the fun of Pack Holidays].

1 These forms are based on precedents supplied by the Guide Association.
2 See para **[212.29]**, n 2.

[212.31]

Form B12.29: General provision against lapse of charitable gifts

If any institution society trust or body of persons (incorporated or unincorporated) which is intended to be the recipient of any gift made by me herein or in any codicil hereto [and which is referred to hereby or by such codicil as a charity or charitable[1]] shall be found never to have existed or to have ceased to exist or to have been amalgamated with another institution society or body of persons or changed its name or constitution before my death the benefit intended to be given under such gift shall be paid transferred or applied to such charitable institutions societies or bodies of persons established in the United Kingdom of Great Britain and Northern Ireland or for such charitable purposes in the said United Kingdom and if more than one in such shares as my trustees in their absolute discretion think fit and I express the wish without imposing any trust or obligation that in carrying out the foregoing trust my trustees should seek to benefit a charity or charities as close as possible in purpose to those of the institution society or body of persons intended to be benefited by my said original gift.

1 Some draftsmen may prefer to add these words, as otherwise a gift to any institution, even though not intended as a charitable gift, will be caught. But if such words are included, care must be taken to describe expressly all intended charitable objects as charities.

B13 Exercises of special powers of appointment

Preliminary Note .... **[213.1]**

FORMS

B13.1 Appointment by widow of her husband's residuary estate among children and issue .... **[213.12]**

B13.2 Appointment by woman of fund in which she has a life interest in unequal shares, one child's share appointed direct to his own children, another's settled on him for life, the others appointed absolutely .... **[213.13]**

B13.3 Exercise by married woman of powers of appointment contained in her marriage settlement in favour of her husband for life and if she has no children in favour of her husband absolutely .... **[213.14]**

PRELIMINARY NOTE

[213.1]

Special powers of appointment may often be exercised by will. Where a settlement, will or other instrument confers on any person a special power of appointment, it is often the case that the donee is expressly authorised to execute the power by will or codicil. In the absence of such express authorisation it is a matter of construction of the instrument as a whole whether the donee may exercise such a power validly by will or codicil. A power to be executed by 'an instrument in writing' may be executed by will: *West v Ray* (1854) Kay 385. When a testator desires to exercise a power of appointment, the terms of the power must be carefully considered and followed.

[213.2]

For a full treatment of the exercise of special powers of appointment, see Vol 1, **[39.1]** ff. Some general observations on some points which often arise in practice appear below.

[213.3]

Objects of Power

Generally, a power may only be exercised for the benefit of the objects of the power. A common special power of appointment is a power to appoint among a person's 'children'. In this case, 'children' will have the same meaning as in the instrument creating the power, so that even if before the date of exercise of the power the law has changed the meaning of 'children' from the meaning it has in the instrument creating the power, 'children' must still be identified according to the meaning in the instrument creating the power. Where an appointment is made to a person who is not a proper object according to the terms of the power, it will be void, see *Re Hoff* [1942] Ch 298, [1942] 1 All ER 547 and *Re Brinkley* [1968] Ch 407, [1967] 3 All ER 805. For the meanings of 'children' and 'issue' see Vol 1, paras **[74.1]–[74.9]** and **[76.1]–[76.6]**.

[213.4]
Death of appointee in testator's lifetime. Where a testator exercises a special power of appointment in his will and before his death the appointee dies, the appointment lapses, and the property which the appointee would have taken passes in default of appointment. Special powers are not within the WA 1837, s 33 (Part G, para **[244.36]**), so that appointments are not saved when made in favour of a child of the testator who predeceases him: *Holyland v Lewin* (1884) 26 Ch D 266. Neither is an appointment saved on the death of an appointee if the appointment is made to the appointee or his personal representatives, unless the personal representatives are objects of the power. To save against lapse, an appointment could contain a substitutional gift to other objects to take effect in the event of the death of a primary appointee during the testator's lifetime.

[213.5]
A special power of appointment often has as its objects the appointor's issue of all degrees, with a trust in default of appointment for the appointor's children. Such a special power can be usefully exercised to make an appointment in favour of the children of any child who has predeceased the appointor.

[213.6]

Delegation
A special power of appointment cannot be delegated and so on the exercise of such a power, trusts, powers and discretions should not be delegated to anyone unless the terms of the power authorise such a delegation. So, for example, an appointment should not (unless the power expressly or impliedly authorises it) appoint the settled funds upon discretionary trusts, or appoint the income upon protective trusts because of the discretionary trust arising on a forfeiture: *Re Boulton's Settlement Trust, Stewart v Boulton* [1928] Ch 703. However, some fairly standard special powers will authorise some delegation such as the inclusion of the statutory power of advancement (*Re Hunter's Will Trusts, Gilks v Harris* [1963] Ch 372, [1962] 3 All ER 1050) and new administrative provisions (*Re Rank's Settlement Trusts, Newton v Rollo* [1979] 1 WLR 1242). See also Vol 1, paras **[40.4]–[40.5]**.

[213.7]

Perpetuities
The perpetuity period applicable to the interests created under a special power of appointment is the perpetuity period applicable to the instrument creating the special power. So when exercising a special power of appointment, care must be taken to ensure that the interests which it creates vest in interest within the perpetuity period applicable to the instrument creating the power. This is particularly important where the instrument creating the special power of appointment took effect before 16 July 1964 because in this case there is no 'wait and see' rule which might save an otherwise perpetuitous appointment by enabling it to be treated as valid until it is apparent that the interests must vest, if at all, outside the perpetuity period. The 'wait and

see' rule would only apply in relation to instruments creating a power which took effect on or after 16 July 1964, see the Perpetuities and Accumulations Act 1964 (PAA 1964), ss 3 and 15(5) (Part G, paras **[246.76]** and **[246.88]**). In some cases, instruments creating a special power of appointment will expressly define the applicable perpetuity period, for example, in the case of instruments taking effect on or after 16 July 1964 a period of 80 years or less may have been selected as provided by the PAA 1964, s 1(1), (Part G, para **[246.74]**). If there is no express perpetuity period in the instrument creating the power the period of a life or lives in being plus 21 years should be used. For perpetuities generally see Vol 1, para **[94.1]** ff and for perpetuities in relation to powers of appointment see para **[94.41]** ff.

[213.8]

Accumulations
If a power expressly or impliedly authorises the appointment of a trust or power of accumulation, excessive accumulations should not be directed, ie accumulation for a longer period than that authorised by law and by the instrument creating the power. The periods of accumulation permitted by law are contained in the Law of Property Act 1925 (LPA 1925), s 164 (Part G, para **[246.56]**) and (for instruments taking effect on or after 16 July 1964) the PAA 1964, s 13 (Part G, para **[246.86]**). The instrument creating the power will sometimes expressly incorporate one of these periods of accumulation, otherwise it is a matter of construction of the instrument as a whole whether a period has been selected and which period it is. These periods, only one of which may apply in respect of any disposition, are in addition to any accumulations pursuant to the TA 1925, s 31 (Part G, para **[246.29]**), see the LPA 1925, s 165 (Part G, para **[246.57]**). For accumulations generally see Vol 1, para **[95.1]** ff.

[213.9]

Some Tax Considerations
Very often a person with a special power of appointment will have a beneficiary taxed interest in possession in the property over which the power is exercisable (see Part A, paras **[200.92]** ff), and so on his death the value of the property will be treated as forming part of his estate for inheritance tax purposes. Therefore, if an appointor's spouse or (sometimes) civil partner is an object of the power, it may be advantageous if an immediate post-death interest in possession (a life or lesser interest) is appointed to the spouse so that the spouse exemption will be available on the appointor's death. The partial exemption rules of the Inheritance Tax Act 1984 (IHTA 1984), ss 36 to 42, for charging tax on death where the deemed transfer of value on death is partly exempt and partly chargeable will apply separately to such property from the appointor's free estate: IHTA 1984, s 40.

[213.10]
Under the terms of a settlement, the settlor or the settlor's spouse may have an interest in possession (see Part A, para **[200.93]**) in the settled property and a special power of appointment in respect of the settled property. If he

exercises his special power to create discretionary trusts (assuming they are authorised by the power) to take effect immediately after his interest in possession, he will be regarded, for the purposes of the charging rules for relevant property (ie settled property in which there is no interest in possession), as the settlor of a new discretionary settlement at the time when his interest in possession ceases, see the IHTA 1984, s 80 (but see also the IHTA 1984, s 61(2)) which provides that for the purposes of calculating the ten year anniversary for the periodic charge to inheritance tax, the settlement should be regarded as having commenced when the property first became settled). In circumstances where s 80 applies, for the relevant property to qualify after the cessation of the interest in possession as excluded property under the IHTA 1984, s 48(3)(a), or for the exemption in s 65(8) from an inheritance tax exit charge when relevant property becomes invested in exempt government securities, the condition as to the domicile of the settlor outside the UK at the time of his settlement must be satisfied both by the original settlor and his spouse or civil partner at the times when their respective settlements were made or deemed to be made, see the IHTA 1984, s 82. (See *Foster's Inheritance Tax*, E4.52, for a more detailed treatment of the IHTA 1984, s 80, and its consequences.)

[213.11]
If an appointor has a life interest in the settled property over which he exercises, by will or codicil, his special power of appointment, his death will not usually be the occasion of a capital gains tax charge, whether he appoints the settled property on further trusts or absolutely, see the TCGA 1992, ss 72 and 73. There will usually be an uplift in the value of the assets on his death for capital gains tax purposes (the exception for reverter to the original settlor in the TCGA 1992, s 73(1)(b) not being relevant to a will trust where the settlor is ex hypothesi deceased).

[213.12]

Form B13.1: Appointment by widow of her husband's residuary estate among children and issue

In exercise of the power of appointment conferred on me by [the will of my late husband[1] who died on —— which was proved *etc*] to appoint the capital and income of my late husband's[1] residuary estate [to or for the benefit of our children and issue in such shares and with such trusts powers and provisions for their respective benefit exercisable at the discretion of any person or persons as I shall appoint[2]] I hereby direct that the trustees of the will of my said husband[1,3] shall after my death stand possessed of my late husband's[1] residuary estate upon trust to divide the same into three equal parts and hold the same upon the trusts and with and subject to the powers and provisions following:

(1) As to one equal third part and the income thereof upon trust for such of the children of my late son [*name*][4] as shall survive me and attain the age of twenty-one if more than one in equal shares absolutely provided that if any of such children shall predecease me or survive me but die without having attained the age of twenty-one leaving a child or children living at my death or born thereafter such

child or children shall take if more than one equally between them the share which his her or their parent would have taken if he or she had survived me and attained the age of twenty-one[5];

(2) As to one equal third part and the income thereof upon trust for my daughter [*name*][4] absolutely;

(3) As to the remaining one equal third part upon trust to pay the income thereof to my son [*name*][4] for his life[6] and subject thereto as to both capital and income for such of his children living at my death or born thereafter who shall attain the age of twenty-one if more than one in equal shares absolutely;

(4) If the foregoing trusts herein declared of any equal third part of my late husband's residuary estate shall fail then each such part (together with any part or parts which may accrue thereto under this present provision) shall accrue to the other part or parts hereby appointed the trusts whereof shall not at the date of such accrual have failed;

(5) The powers of section 32 of the Trustee Act 1925 shall apply to the foregoing trusts [as if the words 'one half of' were omitted from proviso (a) to subsection (1) thereof[7]].

1 In order to adapt the form to take account of civil partnerships formed pursuant to CPA 2004, substitute 'civil partner' for 'husband' throughout. The references to children and issue might still be relevant but the form will otherwise require significant amendment to suit the requirements of civil partners.

2 The terms of this power are based on the power considered in *Re Hunter's Will Trusts, Gilk v Harris* [1963] Ch 372, [1962] 3 All ER 1050. They were held not to authorise the creation of an immediate discretionary trust for a class of appointees.

3 In exercising a special power of appointment the appointor should not (unless the power expressly or impliedly authorises it, see *Re Redgate, Marsh v Redgate* [1903] 1 Ch 356) appoint the settled funds to the trustees of the appointor's will. Under such an appointment the trustees of the settled property in respect of which the power is exercised are not bound to transfer the settled funds to the trustees of the will, but ought to carry out and execute the appointor's directions themselves (see *Busk v Aldam* (1874) LR 19 Eq 16; *Scotney v Lomer* (1886) 31 Ch D 380; *Re Tyssen, Knight-Bruce v Butterworth* [1894] 1 Ch 56; *Re Mackenzie, Bain v Mackenzie* [1916] 1 Ch 125).

4 Following the commencement of GRA 2004 on 4 April 2005, it is important to name the sons and daughter referred to. See Vol 1 at para **[81.1]**.

5 Assuming that no perpetuity period has been defined in the husband's will, the common law perpetuity period will apply. Since the power is conferred by the husband's will which would only have come into force on his death his widow and the children of the marriage will be lives in being for the purposes of the common law rule against perpetuities. Therefore appointments to the children which vest in interest during their lifetimes will be valid, as will be appointments to their children which vest on the death of the widow or at or before they attain 21, and to the children of such a child who predeceases the widow or dies under 21 so long as there is no contingency such as the attainment of a specified age.

6 The terms of the power as recited would not permit an appointment of the income on protective trusts because the discretionary trust of income arising after any forfeiture would be an improper delegation of the power. It is not clear whether a power to pay or apply capital to a life tenant would be permitted.

7 The incorporation of the statutory power of advancement of the TA 1925, s 32 (Part G, para **[246.30]**) to pay one half of a beneficiary's presumptive share for his advancement or benefit, will not be an improper delegation, and it is thought that in the case of the terms of the recited power it will not be an improper delegation to extend the power to be exercisable in respect of the whole of a beneficiary's presumptive share.

[213.13]

Form B13.2: Appointment by woman of fund in which she has a life interest in unequal shares, one child's share appointed direct to his own children, another's settled on him for life, the others appointed absolutely[1]

In exercise of the power of appointment conferred on me by [the will of my late father who died on —— which was proved etc] to appoint the capital and income of his residuary estate in which I have a life interest [to all or any one or more exclusively of the others or other of my issue at such times and if more than one in such shares with such provisions for maintenance education and advancement and otherwise at the discretion of any person and with such gifts over and generally in such manner for the benefit of my issue or some or one of them as I shall appoint[2]] I hereby direct that the trustees of the will of my late father[3] shall after my death stand possessed of my late father's residuary estate upon trust to divide the same into five equal parts and hold the same upon the trusts and with and subject to the powers and provisions following:

(1) As to two equal fifth parts upon trust to pay the income thereof to my daughter [*name*][4] for her life and subject thereto as to both capital and income for such of her children living at my death or born thereafter before the vesting day (as defined in my late father's will)[5] who shall attain the age of twenty-one or shall be living on the vesting day if earlier if more than one in equal shares absolutely.

(2) As to one equal fifth part and the income thereof upon trust for such of the children of my daughter [*name*][4] living at my death or born thereafter before the vesting day who shall attain the age of twenty-one or shall be living on the vesting day (as defined in my late father's will)[6] if earlier if more than one in equal shares absolutely.

(3) As to one equal fifth part and the income thereof upon trust for my son [*name*][4] absolutely.

(4) As to the remaining one equal fifth part and the income thereof upon trust for my son [*name*][4] absolutely.

(5) The powers and provisions of section 32 of the Trustee Act 1925 shall apply to the foregoing trusts as if the words 'one half of' were omitted from proviso (a) to subsection (1) thereof.

(6) I declare that in the foregoing subclauses of this present clause the terms 'child' and 'children' shall have the same meanings as they have in my late father's will.[7]

(7) The administrative powers and provisions of clauses —— of my late father's will shall continue to apply to my late father's residuary estate so far as consistent with the beneficial interests hereby appointed and the trustees of my late father's will shall have the following additional powers:[8]

   (i) power to invest trust moneys in any property of whatever description or location as if they were a sole beneficial owner of such moneys;

   (ii) power to borrow money with or without giving security and on such terms as to interest repayment and otherwise for any purpose connected with the trusts hereby appointed and no lender from whom the trustees borrow money in purported exercise of this power shall be concerned to enquire as to the propriety amount or purpose of any such borrowing.

1 For the purposes of this form it is assumed that the appointor's father died before 16 July 1964 and before the birth of any of the appointor's children. Therefore, the interests created must be certain to vest within the perpetuity period because there will be no 'wait and see' rule to save an otherwise perpetuitous appointment, see para **[213.7]**.

2 The terms of this power are based on the power considered in *Re Rank's Settlement Trusts, Newton v Rollo* [1979] 1 WLR 1242.

3 See para **[213.12]**, n 2.

4 Following the commencement of GRA 2004 on 4 April 2005, it is important to name the sons and daughters referred to. See Vol 1 at para **[81.1]**.

5 It is assumed that the appointor's father's will contains an express perpetuity restriction, with a defined vesting day 21 years from the death of the last survivor of the appointor and Royal lives. If it is not defined the common law period of a life or lives in being plus 21 years will apply, so that if the appointor's grandchildren's interests were expressed to vest at the latest on the expiry of the period of 21 years from the death of the appointor there would be no perpetuity problem.

6 See n 5, above.

7 See para **[213.7]**.

8 In *Re Rank's Settlement Trusts, Newton v Rollo,* above, the terms of the power were held to authorise the creation of additional administrative powers.

[213.14]

Form B13.3: Exercise by married woman of powers of appointment contained in her marriage settlement in favour of her husband for life and if she has no children in favour of her husband absolutely

Whereas under a settlement dated —— and made between [*parties*] and executed in contemplation of my marriage with my husband [*name*] I have:

(a) power to appoint to my said husband a life or less interest in the funds subject to the trusts thereof in the event of my husband surviving me; and

(b) a general power of appointment by will in respect of the said funds in the event of no child of my said marriage attaining the age of twenty-one years or being female marrying subject to the interest so appointed to my said husband as aforesaid and also subject to any exercise of the special powers of appointment in favour of issue of our marriage conferred by such settlement on my husband and myself jointly and on the survivor of us.

Now in exercise of the said respective powers of appointment and of all other powers (if any) enabling me in this behalf I hereby direct and appoint that:

(1) in the event of my said husband surviving me the trustees for the time being of the said settlement[2] shall from and after my death stand possessed of the said funds upon trust to pay the income thereof to my said husband during the residue of his life; and

(2) in the event of my said husband surviving me and no child of our marriage attaining the age of twenty-one or being female marrying and subject to any exercise of such special powers conferred on my husband and myself jointly as aforesaid the trustees for the time being of the said settlement shall stand possessed of the capital and income of the said funds in trust for my said husband absolutely.

1 A settlement on civil partners akin to a marriage settlement is not impossible although the beneficial class is likely to be different from that contemplated by this form. In order to adapt the form to take account of civil partnerships formed pursuant to CPA 2004, substitute 'civil partner' for 'husband' throughout and replace 'marriage' with 'civil partnership' where appropriate. As to other beneficiaries, the form will require significant amendment to suit the situation of the civil partners.

2 See para **[213.12]**, n 2.

B14 Residue

ADMINISTRATION TRUSTS

Note .... **[214.1]**

FORMS

B14.1 Administration trust without a trust for sale .... **[214.10]**

B14.2 Administration trust without a trust for sale, concise form .... **[214.11]**

B14.3 Residuary disposition to trustees on trust for sale, with administration trusts, directions as to inheritance tax, and exclusion of equitable and statutory apportionment .... **[214.12]**

B14.4 Residuary disposition with power of sale with respect to personalty so as to prevent the rules in Howe v Dartmouth and Re Chesterfield's Trusts from applying, with administration trusts and exclusion of statutory apportionment and the rule in Allhusen v Whittell .... **[214.13]**

B14.5 Residuary gift with no trust for sale and a power of sale which is to be used only if appropriation in specie not practicable .... **[214.14]**

B14.6 General residuary gift to trustees—direction to pay inheritance tax on specific gifts, pecuniary legacies, and lifetime gifts .... **[214.15]**

B14.7 Trust for conversion .... **[214.16]**

B14.8 Trust to pay debts and invest residue—directions as to inheritance tax .... **[214.17]**

B14.9 Gift of residue to trustees who are different persons from the executors .... **[214.18]**

B14.10 Gift of residue on trust for sale—exclusion of equitable apportionment rules .... **[214.19]**

B14.11 The same by incorporation of Statutory Will Forms 1925, Form 8. **[214.20]**

B14.12 Definition of residuary estate .... **[214.21]**

B14.13 Declaration negativing the exercise of the statutory power to dispose of entailed property or the exercise of a general power of appointment .... **[214.22]**

B14.14 Devise and bequest of residue charged with payment of debts........ **[214.23]**

B14.15 Bequest of residuary personal estate only .... **[214.24]**

B14.16 Devise of residuary real estate only .... **[214.25]**

B14.17 Trusts of proceeds of sale of residue with general direction to pay inheritance tax on free estate out of residue .... **[214.26]**

POWERS AND DIRECTIONS FOR THE ADMINISTRATION OF AN ESTATE

Note .... **[214.27]**

FORMS

B14.18 Power to trustees to sell or mortgage for payment of incumbrances .... **[214.29]**

B14.19 Power to trustees to postpone conversion except as to certain property .... **[214.30]**

B14.20 Power to trustees to defer the calling in of certain debts .... **[214.31]**

B14.21 Direction to determine tenancy of a house .... **[214.32]**

B14.22 Direction to trustees to convert foreign property, with powers of management .... **[214.33]**

B14.23 Direction to foreign trustees to remit proceeds of sale to English trustees .... **[214.34]**

EXCLUSION OF APPORTIONMENT BETWEEN CAPITAL AND INCOME (RULES IN *HOWE V EARL OF DARTMOUTH* AND *RE CHESTERFIELD'S TRUSTS*)
Note .... **[214.35]**
FORMS
B14.24 Exclusion of rule in Howe v Earl of Dartmouth .... **[214.39]**
B14.25 Exclusion of rule in Re Chesterfield's Trusts .... **[214.40]**
B14.26 Exclusion of rules in Howe v Earl of Dartmouth and Re Chesterfield's Trusts—short form naming case .... **[214.41]**
B14.27 Exclusion of rules in Howe v Earl of Dartmouth and Re Chesterfield's Trusts—alternative form .... **[214.42]**
EXCLUSION OF RULE FOR APPORTIONMENT OF LIABILITIES BETWEEN CAPITAL AND INCOME (RULE IN *ALLHUSEN V WHITTELL*)
Note .... **[214.43]**
FORMS
B14.28 Trustees given a discretion as to allocation .... **[214.45]**
B14.29 Liabilities to be paid out of capital .... **[214.46]**
B14.30 Liabilities to be paid out of capital, but interest on them payable for periods after the testator's death to be paid out of income as far as possible .... **[214.47]**
EXCLUSION OF TIME APPORTIONMENT
Note .... **[214.48]**
FORMS
B14.31 Exclusion of Apportionment Acts as between before and after testator's death .... **[214.53]**
B14.32 Exclusion of Apportionment Acts generally .... **[214.54]**
INCIDENCE OF INHERITANCE TAX
Note .... **[214.55]**
FORMS
B14.33 General declaration making all inheritance tax and foreign death duties on free estate payable out of residue .... **[214.76]**
B14.34 Declaration that inheritance tax and foreign death duties on pecuniary legacies and personal chattels shall be paid out of residue .... **[214.77]**
B14.35 Declaration concerning partially exempt residue – Re Ratcliffe direction .... **[214.78]**
B14.36 Alternative declaration concerning fractional shares of partially exempt residue – Re Benham direction .... **[214.79]**
B14.37 Alternative declaration concerning equal shares of partially exempt residue – Re Benham direction .... **[214.80]**
B14.38 Specific gift subject to inheritance tax where the estate may turn out to be partially exempt and include business or agricultural property .... **[214.81]**
B14.39 Declaration that free of inheritance tax provisions relate only to tax on the testator's death .... **[214.82]**

ADMINISTRATION TRUSTS

[214.1]

Note

Administration trusts and trusts of land. Residuary gifts are fully considered in Vol 1, Ch 38. The coming into force of the Trusts of Land and Appointment of Trustees Act 1996 (TLATA 1996) on 1 January 1997 has important implications for the drafting of administration trusts. The Act prohibits the creation of new settlements under the Settled Land Act 1925, although there is a saving for existing strict settlements. The Act introduces the 'trust of land' as the vehicle for all other settlements of land. The trust for sale of land is not abolished but is largely assimilated. A particularly significant change in the context of administration trusts is the abolition of the doctrine of conversion in relation to trusts for sale of land. (For a fuller discussion of the changes effected by the TLATA 1996, see Part A, para **[200.48]** ff.) Under the former law it was usual to include in an administration trust an express trust for sale and conversion of all the property not otherwise disposed of, and to provide expressly for the payment of debts, funeral and testamentary expenses, inheritance tax and legacies out of it. This practice may well continue and in any event, many pre-TLATA 1996 wills will remain unaltered. But a trust for sale is no longer necessary and although forms of administration trust incorporating a trust for sale are included in B14, we recommend administration trusts which include a power of sale, rather than a trust for sale, unless there are special reasons for including the latter: see paras **[200.55]**, **[200.56]** and **[214.2]**. This is the formula which is adopted in the complete will forms in Part C.

[214.2]

Trust for sale and conversion or power of sale. It is now (ie from the commencement of the TLATA 1996 on 1 January 1997) no longer necessary or important to provide a trust for sale and conversion in administration trusts of residue, because it is no longer the case that the Settled Land Act 1925 will apply to land comprised in residue in the event of residue being subject to trusts for persons in succession, subject to a contingency, etc: see paras **[200.51]** and **[200.52]**). If there is land in residue held on trust it will be a 'trust of land' within the TLATA 1996, and it makes little or no difference whether or not there is a trust for sale: see para **[200.54]**). We recommend that, in general, trusts for sale are not provided (see paras **[200.55]** and **[200.56]**). We do, however, recommend the express provision of a power of sale if there is no provision of a trust for sale, even though there are wide powers of sale conferred by the Administration of Estates Act 1925 (AEA 1925), ss 39 and 40 (Part G, paras **[246.63]** and **[246.64]**) and the TLATA 1996, s 6(1) (Part G, para **[246.108]**) for the purposes of the administration. This is because once the administration is over the trustees of the will are not given by the general law any general power of sale over residuary personalty (see para **[220.23]**), and it is an unusual residuary estate which does not contain some personalty, and because it is not clear to what extent s 39 of the AEA 1925 confers power to sell assets situated outside England and Wales, particularly land. For examples of administration trusts without a trust for sale, see Form B14.1 at para **[214.10]**, and the statutory administration trust for intestates' estates in the AEA 1925, s 33(1), as substituted by the TLATA 1996, Sch 2, para 5(2) which provides that the estate shall be held in trust by the personal representatives with the power to sell it (Part G, para **[244.60]**). For circumstances in which a trust for sale may still be appropriate see Part A, para **[200.56]** and Form B15.8 at para **[215.8]** for an example of use of a trust for sale to maximise the chances of an early sale. It seems that if all residuary realty and personalty are together disposed of, made subject to a power of sale and charged with payment of debts and testamentary expenses, this will still create a mixed fund from which the debts and testamentary expenses are payable generally rather than from an undisposed of share (ie the statutory order of application of assets under the AEA 1925, Sch I, Pt II is still varied to that extent): see *Allan v Gott* (1872) 7 Ch App 439 and para **[214.6]**. The provision of a power of sale rather than a trust for sale, together with an indication of intention that the time of sale should be within the trustees' discretion, may have the effect that the rule in *Howe v Dartmouth* does not apply: see para **[214.38]**. It is the provision of a power rather than a trust for sale which provides a concise method of excluding the rule in *Howe v Dartmouth*: see para **[214.38]**.

The Law of Property Act 1925 (LPA 1925), s 25(3) used to provide that a power to retain or sell land was to be treated as a trust for sale with power to postpone sale. This is now repealed with effect from 1 January 1997 by the TLATA 1996, Sch 4.

[214.3]

Power to sell or postpone sale. If the personal representatives and trustees are given a power of sale, as opposed to holding on trust for sale, they of course have a complete discretion as to whether and when to sell. Such a power is conferred on trustees in relation to land by the TLATA 1996, s 6(1) (Part G, para **[246.108]** and see generally para **[220.23]** ff) unless excluded or restricted by the will, but because there is likely to be, or there could turn out to be, personalty in any residuary estate we recommend the provision of an express power of sale where no trust for sale is provided (see para **[214.2]**).

Where a trust for sale and conversion is provided in relation to land (in England and Wales) it is still the case, indeed it is even more the case, that statute implies a power to postpone the sale of that land, and provides that the trustees are not liable for postponing sale (in the exercise of their discretion) for an unlimited period. This is by virtue of the TLATA 1996, s 4(1) (Part G, para **[246.106]**; see also para **[200.54]**) which replaces the LPA 1925, s 25 in materially identical terms, with one crucial difference: the TLATA 1996, s 4(1) applies *despite any provision to the contrary made by the disposition*, while the LPA 1925, s 25(1) and (2) only applied so far as a contrary intention did not appear. The TLATA 1996, s 4(1) applies to personal representatives: TLATA 1996, s 18(1) (Part G, para **[246.121]**).

The TLATA 1996, s 4 means that a will cannot impose on the personal representatives a binding obligation to sell land at any particular point. Cases such as *Bate v Hooper* (1855) 5 De GM & G 338 (in which it was held that where a will contained a direction to sell and convert without conferring a power to postpone sale the conversion ought to take place within a year of the testator's death), *Re Rooke's Will Trust, Taylor v Rooke* [1953] Ch 716,

[1953] 2 All ER 110 (in which a direction to sell land as soon as possible after the testator's death was held to negative the implied power to postpone sale) and *Re Ball, Jones v Jones* [1930] WN 111 (in which it was held that the power to postpone sale ceased as soon as all the beneficial interests vested absolutely) are superseded in relation to land. The *Bate v Hooper* point that there should be sale within a year of death if there is no power to postpone sale cannot arise in relation to land because there is now always power to postpone sale; and *Re Rooke* and *Re Ball* are decisions that the express provisions of the will in each case showed a contrary intention which excluded the LPA 1925, s 25(1). The grounds for those decisions are no longer available now that the power to postpone sale under the TLATA 1996, s 4(1) cannot be excluded or cut down. If a beneficiary is aggrieved that trustees are postponing sale of land for too long he should apply to the court for an order for sale under the TLATA 1996, s 14 (Part G, para **[246.117]**; see also paras **[200.57]** and **[200.59]**) if the administration is complete and the personal representatives have become trustees, or under the court's inherent jurisdiction over the administration of estates if the administration of the estate is still continuing (as s 14 of the TLATA 1996 does not apply to personal representatives: TLATA 1996, s 18(1) (Part G, para **[246.121]**)). For a form for a case where early sale is contemplated, see Form B15.8 at para **[215.8]** and the Note thereto.

It is still the case that no power to postpone sale is conferred on trustees holding personalty on trust to sell and convert, and so we still recommend the provision of an express power to postpone sale in relation to any mixed fund of realty and personalty held on trust for sale.

The TLATA 1996, s 4(1) provides (as had the LPA 1925) that where there is a power to postpone the sale of land, the trustees are not liable for postponing such sale for an indefinite period. The exercise of the power to postpone, as with the exercise of other fiduciary powers, requires the concurrence of all the trustees. Under the former law, in the absence of agreement to postpone a sale of property the sale generally had to take place: *Re Roth, Goldberger v Roth* (1896) 74 LT 50 and *Re Mayo, Mayo v Mayo* [1943] Ch 302 (decisions on the LPA 1925, s 25(2)). Neither of these decisions is a safe guide to the manner in which the court's jurisdiction will be exercised under the TLATA 1996, s 14: see Part A, paras **[200.59]** and **[200.62]**. Generally the power of postponement can be exercised only as a power of management for the general benefit of the estate and not so as to alter the rights of the parties: *Rowlls v Bebb* [1900] 2 Ch 107 at 116, but it seems it is no objection to the legitimate exercise of such discretion that it will benefit one beneficiary at the expense of another: *Re Sewell's Estate* (1870) LR 11 Eq 80; *Re Schneider, Kirby v Schneider* (1906) 22 TLR 223, and the court will not interfere with the bona fide exercise of the discretion: *Gisborne v Gisborne* (1877) 2 App Cas 300; *Re Burrage, Burningham v Burrage* (1890) 62 LT 752; *Re Charteris, Charteris v Kenyon* [1917] 2 Ch 257, and will presume that the discretion has been properly exercised: *Re Oddy, Connell v Oddy* (1911) 104 LT 128.

[214.4]
Order of application of assets to pay testamentary expenses, debts, etc. Whether undisposed of residue is primarily liable for debts, administration

expenses and legacies remains one question which sometimes still arises in modern conditions, where there is an undisposed of share of residue and the persons who take on intestacy are not the same as the persons who take the disposed of residuary estate, or if they are, do not take in the same proportions. The abolition of hotchpot in the partial intestacy rules (see Vol 1, paras **[104.13]** and **[104.14]**) means that where the testator leaves issue and an undisposed share of residue the chances of this question arising have slightly increased. The order of application of assets where the estate is solvent is laid down by the AEA 1925, Sch 1, Pt II (Part G, para **[246.69]**). By the AEA 1925, s 32 all liabilities of the testator have to be satisfied out of his estate, but by s 34(3) (Part G, para **[246.61]**) where the estate is solvent the real and personal property is subject to rules of court and the provisions as to charges on property in s 35 (Part G, para **[246.62]**) *and to the provisions, if any, contained in the will* applicable to the discharge of funeral testamentary and administration expenses debts and liabilities in the order mentioned in the AEA 1925, Sch 1, Pt II.

[214.5]
One of the main provisions of a will which may vary the statutory order of application is the creation of a mixed fund. Where a testator combines his real and personal estate into one general fund and states that the whole of that fund is to be applied for the payment of the liabilities of his estate including legacies the statutory order is excluded (*Re Petty, Holliday v Petty* [1929] 1 Ch 726, [1929] All ER Rep 493) so that debts, etc are not payable out of a lapsed share of residue (*Re Petty* above, *Re Kempthorne, Charles v Kempthorne* [1930] 1 Ch 268, [1929] All ER Rep 495). The usual clause giving all property, subject to the exception of that specifically disposed of, to trustees upon trust for sale and conversion and for the payment of debts, etc, out of the proceeds, created a mixed fund for this purpose under the former law (*Bedford v Bedford* (1865) 35 Beav 584). It is not thought that the abolition of the doctrine of conversion in relation to trusts for sale of land will affect matters. A direction for real estate to be deemed to be personalty had a similar result (*Simmons v Rose* (1856) 6 De GM & G 411) The testator was also able to create a mixed fund by codicil (*Re Timson, Harper v Timson* [1953] 2 All ER 1252, [1953] 1 WLR 1361). But the mere gift of real and personal estate together coupled with a direction to pay debts, etc did not constitute a mixed fund (*Boughton v Boughton* (1848) 1 HL Cas 406); there had to be a direction to pay the debts, etc out of the mixed fund.

[214.6]
As mentioned in para **[214.2]** in relation to trusts for sale and conversion, it seems that if all residuary realty and personalty are together disposed of, made subject to a power of sale, and charged with payment of debts and testamentary expenses, this still creates a mixed fund from which the debts and testamentary expenses are payable generally, rather than from an undisposed of share, the statutory order of application of assets under the AEA 1925, Sch I, Pt II being varied to that extent (*Allan v Gott* (1872) 7 Ch App 439). The question is whether the real and personal estate are intended to be combined into a general fund for the payment of liabilities: *Boughton v Boughton* (1848) 1 HL Cas 406 at 437; *Allan v Gott* (1872) 7 Ch App 439; *Re Timson, Harper v Timson* [1953] 2 All ER 1252, [1953] 1 WLR 1361.

[214.7]
Other matters by which the statutory order may be displaced are a direction for the payment of such expenses out of the proceeds of the conversion of the personal estate (*Re Atkinson, Webster v Walter* [1930] 1 Ch 47, [1929] All ER Rep 491; *Re Martin, Midland Bank Executor and Trustee Co Ltd v Marfleet* [1955] Ch 698, [1955] 1 All ER 865) or a gift of residue subject to such expenses (*Re Kempthorne, Charles v Kempthorne,* [1930] 1 Ch 268, [1929] All ER Rep 495; *Re Harland Peck, Hercy v Mayglothing* [1941] Ch 182, [1940] 4 All ER 347; *Re Berrey's Will Trusts, Greening v Warner* [1959] 1 All ER 15, [1959] 1 WLR 30). These provisions exclude the statutory order so far as it provides primarily for payment out of property undisposed of by the will. (In the case of a gift of residue subject to such expenses the presence or absence of a trust for sale is irrelevant.) On the other hand, a mere direction to pay such expenses followed by a residuary gift (*Re Lamb, Vipond v Lamb* [1929] 1 Ch 722, [1929] All ER Rep 82; *Re Kempthorne; Re Tong, Hilton v Bradbury* [1931] 1 Ch 202, [1930] All ER Rep 262; *Re Worthington, Nichols v Harl* [1933] Ch 771, [1933] All ER Rep 189) or a gift of residue followed by a direction to pay duty (*Re Sanger, Taylor v North* [1939] Ch 238, [1938] 4 All ER 417) does not exclude the statutory order. An express charge of such expenses on specific gifts followed by a residuary gift to persons other than the specific legatees excludes the statutory order (*Re Littlewood, Clark v Littlewood* [1931] 1 Ch 443, [1930] All ER Rep 151; *Re James, Lloyds Bank Ltd v Atkins* [1947] Ch 256, [1947] 1 All ER 402; *Re Meldrum, Swinson v Meldrum* [1952] Ch 208, [1952] 1 All ER 274; *Re Ridley, Nicholson v Nicholson* [1950] Ch 415, [1950] 2 All ER 1) but a charge of such expenses on a legacy, the residue being undisposed of, does not exclude it (*Re Gordon, Watts v Rationalist Press Association Ltd* [1940] Ch 769, [1940] 3 All ER 205). (It is thought that these estate duty cases will apply equally under inheritance tax.)

[214.8]
It should be noted that where under the former law the residuary assets were directed by the will to be held on trust to sell or convert, and the debts, testamentary expenses, legacies, etc were directed to be paid out of the proceeds of such sale or conversion, the statutory order of application of assets to pay these would ordinarily be varied with the result that they would be paid out of residue generally, rather than an undisposed of share of residue: see paras **[214.4]** and **[214.5]**. It is not thought that an administration trust which confers a power of sale will have different consequences, provided that there is a clear intention to create a general fund out of which the liabilities are to be paid.

[214.9]
Order of application of the estate to pay legacies. There are two main issues which can arise: first, the extent to which real estate is available for payment of legacies, and, secondly, where there is a partial intestacy, whether legacies are payable out of the undisposed of residue or out of residue generally. The first of these is discussed in B10 at paras **[210.5]–[210.7]**. The second is a question of the extent to which the AEA 1925, ss 33(2), 34(3) and Sch 2, Pt II, para 1 (Part G, paras **[244.60]**, **[246.61]** and **[246.69]**) operate to direct

payment of legacies primarily out of undisposed of estate, and what express provisions of a will are effective to displace those provisions. It should be noted that legacies for this purpose will include inheritance tax on specific gifts or general legacies which the will directs to be paid out of residue, and which would be borne by the gift itself in the absence of such direction, but not inheritance tax which is treated as a testamentary expense by the IHTA 1984, s 211 (see para **[214.65]**). Subject to the provisions of the will, pecuniary legacies are first payable out of a lapsed share of residue or other property undisposed of by the will: *Re Worthington, Nichols v Hart,* [1933] Ch 771, [1933] All ER Rep 189; *Re Sanger, Taylor v North,* [1939] Ch 238, [1938] 4 All ER 417; *Re Gillett's Will Trusts, Barclays Bank Ltd v Gillett* [1950] Ch 102, [1949] 2 All ER 893; *Re Beaumont's Will Trusts, Walker v Lawson* [1950] Ch 462, [1950] 1 All ER 802; *Re Martin, Midland Bank Executor and Trustee Co Ltd v Marfleet,* [1955] Ch 698, [1955] 1 All ER 865; *Re Midgley, Barclays Bank Ltd v Midgley* [1955] Ch 576, [1955] 2 All ER 625; *Re Berrey's Will Trusts, Greening v Warner* [1959] 1 All ER 15, [1959] 1 WLR 30; and *Re Taylor's Estate and Will Trusts, Taylor v Taylor* [1969] 2 Ch 245, [1969] 1 All ER 113. The important question is what provisions of the will displace the statutory order. An express direction for payment of pecuniary legacies out of residue before it is divided into shares will naturally displace the statutory order, as in the case of liabilities (see para **[214.4]** ff). The difficult point has been whether the presence of an express trust for sale in the will, without any express direction as to payment of legacies, excludes the statutory order so that the rule is that which prevailed before 1925, namely that the legacies are payable generally out of residue rather than out of the undisposed share. The most recent decision, *Re Taylor's Estate and Will Trusts* above, following *Re Beaumont* above, and not following *Re Midgley* above, held that the presence of an express trust for sale was sufficient by itself to displace the statutory order. There are two main parts to the reasoning: first that the AEA 1925, s 33(2), which applied to undisposed of estate where s 33(1) imposing a statutory trust for sale applied, and which has the effect that the pecuniary legacies are primarily paid out of undisposed of property if it applies (see *Re Worthington* above and *Re Berrey* above), did not apply where there was an express trust for sale which displaced s 33(1), and secondly that AEA 1925, Sch 1, Pt II does not require the pecuniary legacies to be provided first out of undisposed of residue. This decision has been the subject of convincing criticism (see MJ Albery QC at (1969) 85 LQR 464), but even if it is not overruled the position may now be different after the coming into force of the TLATA 1996. This is because the AEA 1925, s 33 has been amended by the TLATA 1996, s 5 and Sch 2, para 5 (see Part G, para **[244.60]**) so that the AEA 1925, s 33(1) does not contain a trust for sale and s 33(2) arguably is not dependent on s 33(1) applying, and because the former reason for providing an express trust for sale in administration trusts of residue no longer holds good as a result of the TLATA 1996 (see paras **[200.55]** and **[214.2]**). It is therefore possible that s 33(2) would now apply to an undisposed of share of residue even where there is a trust for sale of residue provided by the will, and even more likely that it would do so where, as in the form of administration trust recommended in para **[214.2]**, the will provides a power of sale not a trust for sale.

[214.10]

Form B14.1: Administration trust without a trust for sale

Note. For reasons mentioned at paras **[214.1]** and **[214.2]** it is no longer necessary for the administration trusts of residue to contain a trust for sale and conversion, and we recommend that they do not do so unless there is some specific reason for including a trust for sale. It is particularly appropriate not to provide one where there are life interest or other trusts which may continue for some time after the testator's death, and even more so where occupation of land by beneficiaries is contemplated. Where the gift of residue is into immediate and absolute fractional shares a trust for sale is arguably still appropriate: see Form B15.8 at para **[215.8]**.

If there is no trust for sale it is still appropriate to include an express power of sale, because the general law confers no general power to sell personalty (there is a power to sell it for purposes of administration under the AEA 1925, s 39 and a power to sell it in order to invest in investments authorised by the Trustee Act 2000 (TrA 2000)). The administration trust of an intestate's estate under the AEA 1925, s 33(1) has been amended by the TLATA 1996, Sch 2, para 5(2) so as to provide a power, not a trust, to sell: it is printed as so amended in Part G at para **[244.60]**.

The form below excludes the rules in *Howe v Dartmouth* and *Re Chesterfield's Trusts*, and statutory apportionment, but contains no directions as to the incidence of inheritance tax (except in so far as inheritance tax is a testamentary expense). It also provides a discretion as to the burden of liabilities as between capital and income instead of the total exclusion of the rule in *Allhusen v Whittell*. For a direction as to inheritance tax see eg Form C3.1, cl 5 at para **[225.15]**.

FORM

(1) I give all my property not hereby or by any codicil hereto otherwise effectively disposed of [(including any entailed or other property over which I shall have at my death a general power of disposition by will)][1] to my trustees upon trust with power at their discretion to sell all or any of it when they think fit.[2]

(2) My trustees shall pay my funeral and testamentary expenses my debts and any legacies given by this will or any codicil hereto out of such property or its proceeds of sale and shall have a discretion as to how such payments shall be borne as between capital and income.[3]

(3) None of the equitable rules of apportionment between capital and income shall apply in any circumstances whatever.

(4) Subject as aforesaid my trustees shall invest all money comprised in such property or arising from its sale in any of the investments hereby authorised with power to change such investments into any others hereby authorised and the said property and the assets from time to time representing the same (hereinafter called 'my residuary estate') shall be held on the trusts hereinafter declared.

(5) All income of my residuary estate shall be treated as accruing on the date on which it becomes payable and there shall be no statutory apportionment of it to any other time or period.[4]

1 Subject to any express contrary intention property subject to a general power will be carried by a residuary gift under the WA 1837, s 27 (Part G, para **[244.29]**), but in the case of entailed property the will must refer to the property, or the instrument under which it was acquired, or entailed property generally for the statutory power of disposition to be exercised: LPA 1925, s 176(1) (Part G, para **[244.55]**). Although no new entails can be created on or after 1 January 1997 (see para **[200.55]**), entails created before that date can continue to exist and, if they do, the statutory power of disposition of them by will continues to be available.

2 This wording could be made even more concise, such as 'My trustees shall have power to sell all or any of such property'. One reason for using the slightly more elaborate wording in this Form is that it follows the wording which was held in *Re Pitcairn* [1896] 2 Ch 199 to prevent the rule in *Howe v Dartmouth* from applying, but out of caution sub-cl (3) is also included. See further, para **[214.38]**.

3 The words from 'and shall have' are intended to exclude the rule in *Allhusen v Whittell* and give the trustees a complete discretion over the burden of debts and testamentary expenses as between capital and income. See paras **[214.43]** and **[214.44]** for exclusion of this rule.

4 For exclusion of statutory apportionment see paras **[214.51]** and **[214.52]**.

[214.11]

Form B14.2: Administration trust without a trust for sale, concise form[1]

(1) My trustees shall hold all my property not hereby or by any codicil hereto otherwise effectively disposed of [(including any entailed or other property over which I shall have at my death a general power of disposition by will)][2] and the assets from time to time representing the same ('my residuary estate') with power to sell the same as and when they think fit upon the trusts set out below.

(2) In the administration of my estate and the execution of the trusts hereof or of any codicil hereto:

(a) none of the equitable rules of apportionment between capital and income shall apply in any circumstances whatever and my trustees shall have a discretion as to how expenses debts and legacies shall be borne as between capital and income;

(b) my trustees shall treat all income as accruing on the date on which it becomes payable regardless of the period in respect of which it shall have accrued and shall not make any statutory apportionment of the same.[3]

1 This form omits any direction as to incidence of debts, administration expenses and legacies and leaves the incidence of them to statute. For the statutory order see paras **[214.4]–[214.9]**.

2 See para **[214.10]**, n 1.

3 See para **[214.10]**, nn 3 and 4.

[214.12]

Form B14.3: Residuary disposition to trustees on trust for sale, with administration trusts, directions as to inheritance tax, and exclusion of equitable and statutory apportionment

I give all my property not hereby or by any codicil hereto otherwise effectively disposed of (including any entailed or other property over which I shall have at my death a general power of disposition by will)[1] to my trustees to hold on trust as follows:

(1) My trustees shall hold such property upon trust to sell the same[2] or such part thereof as shall not consist of money with full power to postpone the sale of all or any part thereof[3] without being responsible for loss;

(2) Out of the net moneys to arise from such sale and any ready moneys comprised in my estate my trustees shall pay my funeral and testamentary expenses, my debts, any taxes or duties referred to in the next following subclause, and any legacies given by this will or any codicil hereto;

(3) There shall be paid out of the said moneys (in addition to any inheritance tax on my death which is a testamentary expense) any inheritance tax or other tax or duty payable on or by reason of my death which is attributable to any gift in this will or any codicil hereto which is made free of such tax or duty;[4]

(4) In the administration of my estate and the execution of the trusts hereof:

(a) all income from my estate or any part thereof shall be treated as accruing on the date on which it becomes payable regardless of the period in respect of which it shall have accrued and it shall not be the subject of any statutory apportionment;[5]

(b) the equitable rules of apportionment between capital and income shall not apply in any circumstances whatever and furthermore shall not apply to any assets in respect of which my trustees have not made any deliberate decision to postpone the sale thereof;[6] and

(c) debts, testamentary expenses, inheritance tax or similar taxes, and legacies shall be paid out of capital but any interest on any such debts, expenses, taxes or legacies which may become payable in respect of any period falling after my death shall so far as possible be paid out of income;[7]

(5) My trustees shall invest the residue of the said moneys in any of the investments hereby authorised with power to change the investment thereof into any other investment hereby authorised;

(6) My trustees shall hold the residue of such moneys and the assets from time to time representing the same and all parts of my estate for the time being unsold (all of which property is hereinafter collectively referred to as 'my residuary estate') upon the trusts and with and subject to the powers and provisions hereinafter contained.

1 As to power to dispose by will of entailed property, see the LPA 1925, s 176 (Part G, para **[244.55]**) and Vol 1, para **[7.2]**; a general reference to entailed property is sufficient. Although entailed interests can no longer be created, existing interests can continue to exist, in which case this section will apply: see para **[200.53]**. For the exercise of general powers of appointment by will, see Vol 1, paras **[39.10]–[39.15]**.

2 Although we recommend the inclusion in administration trusts of a power of sale rather than a trust for sale (see para **[214.1]**), a trust for sale remains a perfectly acceptable alternative.

3 The power to postpone sale implied by the TLATA 1996, s 4(1) (Part G, para **[246.89]**) only applies in relation to *land* held on trust for sale.

4 See para **[214.71]**, sub-para (1).

The inheritance tax on the testator's free estate in the UK will be paid out of residue as a testamentary expense, in the absence of the expression of a contrary intention: see para **[214.59]** ff. Any inheritance tax which is not a testamentary expense (e g the tax on foreign property: see para **[214.63]**) and is attributable to a pecuniary legacy or specific gift which is made elsewhere in the will, or in a codicil to it, and which is expressed to be free of inheritance tax, will be payable out of residue by virtue of this subclause. The reason for the somewhat long-winded treatment of inheritance tax is so that what is a standard form is not construed so as to have an unintended effect where there are no gifts in the will to which it applies: see para **[214.70]**.

It should therefore be noted that where this form is used, individual specific gifts or pecuniary legacies which prima facie bear some or all of their own inheritance tax (or foreign death duties) must be stated to be free of inheritance tax (and foreign death duties where appropriate) if the testator wants them to be free of such tax or duties. Pecuniary legacies should be expressed to be free of inheritance tax unless it is absolutely certain that there will be no property with a foreign location in the residuary estate: see para **[214.64]**.

5 For statutory apportionment, between different periods of time, see paras **[214.48]–[214.52]**.

6 For exclusion of the rules in *Howe v Dartmouth* and *Re Chesterfield's Trusts* see paras **[214.35]–[214.38]**. The words from 'and in particular' are intended to exclude what we refer to as the rule in *Re Rowlls* [1900] 2 Ch 107: see also para **[214.38]**.

7 For the reasoning behind this see para **[214.44]**.

[214.13]

Form B14.4: Residuary disposition with power of sale with respect to personalty so as to prevent the rules in *Howe v Dartmouth* and *Re Chesterfield's Trusts* from applying, with administration trusts and exclusion of statutory apportionment and the rule in *Allhusen v Whittell*

I give all my property not hereby or by any codicil hereto otherwise effectively disposed of (including any entailed or other property over which I shall have at my death a general power of disposition by will[1]) to my trustees upon trust as follows:

(1) My trustees shall have power to sell any of such property whenever they think fit but shall hold any freehold or leasehold land on trust for sale with full power to postpone the sale of all or any part thereof without being responsible for loss;[2]

(2) Out of the net moneys to arise from sale of such property and any ready moneys comprised in my estate my trustees shall pay my funeral and testamentary expenses, my debts, and any legacies given by this will or any codicil hereto;[3]

(3) In the administration of my estate and the execution of the trusts hereof:

(a) all income from my estate or any part thereof shall be treated as accruing on the date on which it becomes payable regardless of the period in respect of which it shall have accrued and it shall not be the subject of any statutory apportionment;[4] and

(b) the rule of equity as to the apportionment between capital and income of payments made in the course of administration shall not apply to my estate, and debts, testamentary expenses, inheritance tax or similar taxes, and legacies shall be paid out of capital while any interest on any such debts, expenses, taxes or legacies which may become payable in respect of any period falling after my death shall as far as possible be paid out of income;[5]

(4) [As sub-clause (5) in Form B14.3 at para **[214.12]**].

(5) [As sub-clause (6) in Form B14.3 at para **[214.12]**].

1 See Form B14.1, n 1 at para **[214.10]**.

2 Where there is a power to sell personalty when the trustees think fit, it seems that the rules in *Howe v Dartmouth* and *Re Chesterfield's Trusts* cannot apply: see Vol 1, para **[38.23]**, n 11. For these rules and their exclusion see paras **[214.35]–[214.38]**. A disadvantage of using this method of excluding these rules is that it will not be as readily apparent that these apportionment rules do not apply as it would be if there were words of express exclusion of them. See further para **[214.38]**.

3 This form makes no provision for inheritance tax or foreign death duties from which specific gifts or pecuniary legacies are freed. See Form B14.3 at para **[214.12]** for an example of such provision.

4 For statutory apportionment, between different periods of time, see paras **[214.48]–[214.52]**.
5 For the reasoning behind this see para **[214.44]**.

[214.14]

Form B14.5: Residuary gift with no trust for sale and a power of sale which is to be used only if appropriation in specie not practicable[1]

(1) I give all the rest of my property both real and personal whatsoever and wheresoever situate to [all my children] in equal shares if more than one.

(2) My trustees may in extension of the power of appropriation conferred on personal representatives by section 41 of the Administration of Estates Act 1925 at any time or times without any of the consents required by that section appropriate any part of my residuary estate in its then actual condition or state of investment in or towards the satisfaction of the share of any infant beneficiary interested in my residuary estate.[2]

(3) If at the expiration of three months after the submission of any proposal for appropriation by my trustees or such further period as my trustees in their absolute discretion shall allow the persons entitled thereto or whose consent is required as aforesaid have not consented in writing to such appropriation of any asset of my residuary estate under the preceding subclauses hereof such asset shall be sold by my trustees (with power at their absolute discretion to postpone such sale for so long as they shall think fit without being liable for loss) and the net proceeds of sale and the net income until sale shall be divided amongst [my said children].[3]

1 Although formerly less popular, the inclusion of a power of sale rather than a trust for sale in administration trusts is the authors' preferred option in the light of the changes in the law relating to settlements of land introduced by the TLATA 1996: see para **[214.2]**. This form leaves the incidence of debts, administration expenses etc to the general law, and if there is a lapsed share of residue these will be primarily payable out of the lapsed share of residue rather than residue generally: see para **[214.5]**.
2 This provision only slightly extends the common law duty of executors. If an estate is given to a number of persons without any trust for sale, the duty of the executors is to appropriate the estate to the beneficiaries, and, if division of certain property is or becomes impossible, they must sell the property and divide the proceeds. See *Re Beverly* [1901] 1 Ch 681 at 685, and compare *Cooper v Cooper* (1874) LR 7 HL 53 at 65. If it was instead provided that exercise of the power of appropriation did not need any consents at all, not even those of the adult beneficiaries, it would make the administration of the estate easier, and might give a stamp duty advantage where there was land comprised in the residuary estate: see the Note and Forms concerning powers of appropriation in B20 at para **[220.70]** ff.
3 See n 2 above. This is a statement of what the executors would have to do anyway, in the absence of express provision, if they could not appropriate the entire estate, but its presence may reduce the scope for dispute.

[214.15]

Form B14.6: General residuary gift to trustees—direction to pay inheritance tax on specific gifts, pecuniary legacies, and lifetime gifts

I give my trustees all my real and personal estate whatsoever and wheresoever including both entailed[1] and all other property over which I have any power of disposition by will[2] excepting only the property hereby or by any codicil hereto specifically devised or bequeathed [*if the property is not to be made subject to a trust for sale, add* subject to the payment in due course of administration of my debts funeral and testamentary expenses inheritance tax and any death duties payable outside the United Kingdom in respect of any specific gift or pecuniary legacy hereby made[3] [and in respect of any gift or other transaction given or effected in my lifetime and giving rise to a claim for any inheritance tax or additional inheritance tax on my death[4]] and the legacies and annuities hereby or by any codicil hereto bequeathed].

1 As to power to dispose by will of entailed property, see the LPA 1925, s 176 (Part G, para **[244.55]**) and Vol 1, para **[7.2]**. A general reference to entailed property is sufficient. Although entailed interests can no longer be created, existing interests can continue to exist, in which case this section will apply: see para **[200.53]**.
2 This may include property subject to a general power of appointment: see Vol 1, paras **[39.10]**–**[39.15]**.
3 See the Note on the incidence of inheritance tax at paras **[214.55]** ff and Forms B14.3 (at para **[214.12]**), B14.17 (at para **[214.26]**), B14.33 (at para **[214.76]**) and B14.34 (at para **[214.77]**) for alternative forms of direction concerning inheritance tax and foreign death duties.
4 The reference to inter vivos gifts should not be included without careful thought for the likely sums involved. It will refer to the inheritance tax or additional inheritance tax payable on any inter vivos chargeable or potentially exempt transfer made within seven years before the testator's death. See further the note in B10 at para **[210.66]**. A provision concerning the payment of inheritance tax on lifetime transfers such as this will in effect be one or more pecuniary legacies (e g for the purposes of abatement: see para **[214.65]**).

[214.16]

Form B14.7: Trust for conversion

I direct my trustees to sell call in and convert into money all such parts of my said real and personal estate as shall not consist of money [or investments of the kinds hereinafter authorised] / [*or* investments authorised by law for the investment of trust funds][1] with power to postpone such sale calling in and conversion for such time as my trustees in their absolute discretion and without being liable to account shall think fit.[2]

1 The first alternative words in brackets will be used where the will contains an express investment clause. Where there is no such clause, the second alternative words in brackets should be used.
2 See Note on power to postpone sale at para **[214.3]**. This form could be followed by Form B14.17 at para **[214.26]**.

[214.17]

Form B14.8: Trust to pay debts and invest residue—directions as to inheritance tax[1]

Out of my ready money and the clear moneys to arise from such sale calling and conversion as aforesaid my trustees shall pay or provide for my debts funeral and testamentary expenses (including inheritance tax treated as such by statute)[2] and the inheritance tax [and foreign death duties] payable on any gift caused to be free of inheritance tax [and foreign death duties] by any declaration in this will or any codicil hereto and the pecuniary legacies and annuities hereby or by any codicil hereto given (which shall not bear any inheritance tax [or foreign death duties] even if they are wholly or partly paid out of foreign assets and whether or not they are herein elsewhere expressed to be free of inheritance tax [or foreign death duties])[3] and subject thereto my trustees shall invest in manner hereinafter authorised with power to vary any such investments for others of a like nature the residue of the said moneys and stand possessed of such investments and of the residue of such investments as aforesaid which formed part of my estate at the time of my death and of all parts of my estate for the time being unsold and any ready money (hereinafter called 'my residuary estate') upon the trusts hereinafter declared concerning the same.

1 This form provides for all legacies and annuities to be free of inheritance tax, for specific gifts of property in the UK also to be free of it, but for specific gifts of foreign property to be free of inheritance tax only if specifically declared to be.
2 As to the meaning of 'testamentary expenses' see Vol 1, para **[55.7]**, and for the inheritance tax treated as such (ie that on UK property), see the IHTA 1984, s 211 (Part G, para **[246.100]**) and paras **[214.55]** ff.
3 The residue constitutes a mixed or blended fund and without these words, if the estate includes foreign assets, the legacies and annuities not expressed to be free of inheritance tax would be payable rateably out of UK and foreign assets and the part paid out of foreign assets would be liable to bear inheritance tax and foreign death duties paid in respect of it: *Re Spencer Cooper, Poë v Spencer Cooper* [1908] 1 Ch 130; *Re Owers* [1941] Ch 17, [1940] 4 All ER 225; *Re Sebba, Lloyds Bank Ltd v Hutson* [1959] Ch 166 at 178 (see the declaration on question (3)—the report at [1958] 3 All ER 393 does not report this point). See further para **[214.64]**. These words are not necessary if the legacies and annuities are all expressed to be free of inheritance tax, but the chances of error are less if a general provision of this type is used than if directions relating to individual gifts are used.

[214.18]

Form B14.9: Gift of residue to trustees who are different persons from the executors[1]

The executors after paying or satisfying my debts funeral and testamentary expenses inheritance tax and the aforesaid pecuniary and specific legacies shall transfer all the residue of my estate (including all property over which I have a power of appointment or disposition by will and all entailed property of which by virtue of section 176 of the Law of Property Act 1925 or any other statutory provision I can dispose by will[2]) to —— and —— (hereinafter called my trustees) to hold the same upon the following trusts: [*administration trusts*].

1 Will forms generally assume that the same persons are appointed both executors and trustees of the will. Where different persons are appointed trustees, a variation of the residuary gift is necessary. If desired the following form may used: Subject to my debts funeral and testamentary expenses inheritance tax and the aforesaid pecuniary and specific legacies, I give all my real and personal property wheresoever situate and of whatsoever kind (including, etc) to —— and —— (hereinafter called my trustees) to hold, etc, as above.
2 See para **[214.10]**, n 1.

[214.19]

Form B14.10: Gift of residue on trust for sale—exclusion of equitable apportionment rules[1]

I give all my real and personal movable and immovable property of whatever nature and wheresoever situate not hereby or by any codicil hereto otherwise disposed of unto my trustees upon trust to sell call in and convert the same into money with power to postpone such sale calling in and conversion as long as they shall in their absolute discretion think fit without being liable for loss and so that the income of all parts of my estate however constituted or invested (including the income of property required for the payments of debts and other payments made in due course of administration in payment whereof the proceeds of such sale calling in and conversion are hereinafter directed to be applied) shall as from my death be treated and applied as income and so that no reversionary or future interest shall be sold prior to the falling into possession thereof unless my trustees shall see special reason for an earlier sale and no such interest shall before falling into possession be treated as producing income and that the net rents and profits of my real and leasehold estate for the time being unsold after payment thereout of all outgoings which my trustees shall consider payable out of income shall go and be applied as if the same were income of authorised investments made of the proceeds of an actual sale thereof.

1 This form includes in a comprehensive paragraph several of the foregoing clauses, including a trust for sale (as to the implications of which see para **[214.2]**). It will then be followed by the trusts upon which the residue is to be held, for example, a trust to pay debts and expenses, a trust for investment where a short form of that trust is used, followed by the beneficial trusts of income and capital. Under this form the rule in *Howe v Earl of Dartmouth* (as to which, see paras **[214.35]–[214.38]**) is excluded in all its branches and the rule in *Allhusen v Whittell* (as to which, see paras **[214.43]** and **[214.44]**): see *Re Ullswater* [1952] Ch 105, [1951] 2 All ER 989 (the relevant words are the ones in brackets), but not apportionment under the Apportionment Act 1870 (Part G, para **[246.2]** ff); see also paras **[214.48]–[214.52]**.

[214.20]

Form B14.11: The same by incorporation of Statutory Will Forms 1925, Form 8

I devise and bequeath all my real and personal estate not hereby or by any codicil hereto specifically devised or bequeathed unto my trustees and the Statutory Will Forms 1925, Form 8 (Administration Trusts) shall be incorporated herein and apply to this residuary gift.[1]

1 For Statutory Will Forms 1925, Form 8, see para **[238.14]**. If desired the Statutory Form can be incorporated with the exception or variation of certain parts. For example after the word 'incorporated' above may be inserted: 'with the exception of paragraph 7(b) of the said Form (Leasehold Sinking Fund).' For forms providing such a sinking fund, see Forms B7.11 and B7.12 at paras **[207.25]** and **[207.26]**.

[214.21]

Form B14.12: Definition of residuary estate

My trustees shall stand possessed of such investments and of the residue of such investments as aforesaid which form part of my estate at the time of my death and all parts of my estate for the time being unsold and any ready money and the assets from time to time representing the same all of which are together hereinafter referred to as 'my residuary estate' [and of the income thereof] upon the following trusts.[1]

1 Some of the more usual forms of these trusts are set out in B15 to B19 (at paras **[215.1]** ff and **[219.1]** ff) and see Statutory Wills Forms 1925, Forms 9 and 10 (Part E, paras **[238.15]** and **[238.16]**).

[214.22]

Form B14.13: Declaration negativing the exercise of the statutory power to dispose of entailed property or the exercise of a general power of appointment[1]

I hereby declare that nothing herein contained is intended to or shall operate as an exercise of any general power of appointment vested in me nor as the exercise of the statutory power to dispose of entailed property.

1 A general declaration in these terms is probably the most convenient way. For the power to dispose of entailed property by will see Vol 1, para **[7.2]** and for the exercise of general powers of appointment by will see Vol 1, paras **[39.10]**–**[39.15]**.

[214.23]

Form B14.14: Devise and bequest of residue charged with payment of debts

I devise and bequeath all my real and personal estate whatsoever and wheresoever not hereby or by any codicil hereto otherwise specifically disposed of (including any real or personal property over which I may have any general power of appointment [and including also any entailed property of which I have power to dispose by will]) unto [*donee*] absolutely but subject to and charged with the payment of my debts [including debts charged upon any property specifically devised or bequeathed] funeral and testamentary expenses and legacies and annuities bequeathed hereby or by any codicil hereto [and the inheritance tax on any such legacies or annuities].

[214.24]

Form B14.15: Bequest of residuary personal estate only

I bequeath all other personal estate (including [*or* except] leasehold property [and including also such part of any entailed property of which I have power to dispose by will as is in fact represented by personal estate]) not hereby or by any codicil hereto otherwise specifically disposed of to which I may be entitled at my death or over which I may have at my death any general power of appointment unto [*legatee*] absolutely.[1]

1 The effect of this Form and Form B14.16 at para **[214.25]** is probably altered by the TLATA 1996 in relation to undivided shares of land. Before the TLATA 1996 came into force an undivided share of land was an interest in the proceeds of sale of land held on trust for sale and was treated as an interest in personalty by virtue of the doctrine of conversion (*Re Kempthorne, Charles v Kempthorne* [1930] 1 Ch 268, CA). From the coming into force of the TLATA 1996 (1 January 1997) an undivided share of land is either an equitable interest in land directly (ie without the interposition of a trust for sale), or it is an interest under a trust for sale but with the doctrine of conversion abolished: see Vol 1, paras **[41.18]**, **[64.52]** and **[200.54]**. The only exception is an undivided share of land under an express trust for sale created by the will of a person who died before 1 January 1997 (in relation to which the doctrine of conversion still applies). Accordingly, it would seem that contrary to the position between 1 January 1926 and 31 December 1996 (inclusive), a gift as in Form B14.15 will not now include an undivided share of freehold land, and a gift as in Form B14.16 will do so. It is thought that an equitable interest in freehold land counts as real property, as such an interest devolved on the heir before 1926 (see, eg *Re Somerville and Turner's Contract* [1903] 2 Ch 583).

[214.25]

Form B14.16: Devise of residuary real estate only

I devise all the residue of the real estate other than [*or* including] leaseholds[1] not hereby or by any codicil hereto otherwise specifically disposed of to which I may be entitled at my death or over which I may have any general power of appointment [and all real estate other than [*or* including] leaseholds of which I am tenant in tail in possession under a settlement dated etc *or* under the will of etc] unto [*devisee*] absolutely.

1 See the WA 1837, s 26 (Part G, para **[244.28]**). Where there are freeholds, a devise of 'real estate,' without more, will not include leaseholds (*Butler v Butler* (1884) 28 Ch D 66), but if words of description are added to 'real estate', leaseholds may be included (*Moase v White* (1876) 3 Ch D 763).
If there are no freeholds, a devise of 'real estate' will pass leaseholds (*Re Holt, Holt v Holt* [1921] 2 Ch 17). Undivided shares of real estate would probably now pass under this clause (see para **[214.24]**, n 1).
As to whether this devise of residuary realty is a specific gift: see Vol 1, para **[30.3]**, nn 12 and 13.

[214.26]

Form B14.17: Trusts of proceeds of sale of residue with general direction to pay inheritance tax on free estate out of residue

I declare that my trustees shall stand possessed of the net moneys arising from the sale of my said residuary real and personal estate and of my ready money upon trust as follows:

(1) To pay and discharge my funeral and testamentary expenses[1] and debts other than mortgage debts or charges on property specifically devised or bequeathed[2] which shall be paid out of the property charged therewith.

(2) Except so far as is otherwise provided by this will or any codicil hereto to pay all inheritance tax [and foreign death duties (if any)] payable by reason of my death in respect of all property wherever situated disposed of by me by this will or any codicil hereto (other than property appointed under a special or general power of appointment or entailed property).[3]

(3) To pay the legacies bequeathed hereby or by any codicil hereto and to provide for the annuities bequeathed hereby or by any codicil hereto

(4) My trustees shall invest the residue of such moneys in their names in any of the modes of investment hereby authorised with power from time to time [with the consent of —— if living] to vary such investments for others of the nature aforesaid.[4]

1 As to the expression 'testamentary expenses', see Vol 1, para **[55.7]**.
2 Specifically bequeathed personalty bears its own money charges: AEA 1925, s 35 (Part G, para **[246.62]**). If thought fit, property specifically given can be exonerated by a special direction. See Form B4.56, n 1 at para **[204.78]**.
3 See the Note on the incidence of inheritance tax at para **[214.55]** ff and Forms B14.3 (at para **[214.12]**) and B14.33 and B14.34 (at paras **[214.76]** and **[214.77]**) for alternative forms.
4 These are the administration trusts. For beneficial trusts, see precedents in B15 to B19 (at paras **[215.1]**–**[219.1]** ff). A devise of realty on trust to pay debts extended the period of limitation to twelve years as against the realty (*Re Balls, Trewby v Balls* [1909] 1 Ch 791).

POWERS AND DIRECTIONS FOR THE ADMINISTRATION OF AN ESTATE

[214.27]

Note

Dispositions of residue. The beneficial interests commonly given in a residuary gift necessarily vary according to the circumstances of the testator. The common form in the case of a married person has changed as a result of the introduction of capital transfer tax (now inheritance tax). In the estate duty era the usual disposition was for the surviving spouse for life or until remarriage and then for the children of the marriage. Under inheritance tax there is no advantage in giving the testator's spouse or civil partner a life interest (see para **[200.84]**), and it is now becoming more common to make an absolute gift to the surviving spouse or civil partner with an alternative gift to the testator's children in case the spouse does not survive the testator. This is particularly the case with younger testators who are making wills principally to dispose of their property in the event of an unexpectedly early death. Older testators, in the interests of using up their inheritance tax nil-rate band (see para **[200.86]**), may wish to leave part of the residue to their spouses and part to their children or on discretionary trusts under which the surviving spouse can benefit without the discretionary fund forming part of his or her taxable estate. They may also be more likely to want a traditional form of will which leaves only a life interest to their spouses, particularly if they have married a second time and wish to ensure that their property will go to their children by an earlier marriage after their spouses have died. Further, if they have grandchildren, there can be an inheritance tax advantage in leaving property on trust for their grandchildren so that it passes to them directly, missing out the intervening generation and an intermediate tax charge. For examples of such wills see C2 and C3 at paras **[224.1]** ff and **[225.1]** ff.

[214.28]

Prior to 22 March 2006 the types of trust most likely to be required were trusts for minors or young persons drafted so as to satisfy the requirements of the IHTA 1984, s 71 (accumulation and maintenance trusts). For deaths on and after 22 March 2006, however, it is no longer possible to create trusts which have the inheritance tax benefits of IHTA 1984, s 71. After 22 March 2006, the trusts which a testator might declare for his young children which will fall outside the inheritance tax relevant property charging regime are trusts for bereaved minors within IHTA 1984, s 71A (see para **[200.108]**), age 18-to-25 trusts within IHTA 1984, s 71D (see para **[200.109]**), or trusts under which the children take immediate post-death interests within IHTA 1984, s 49A (see para **[200.98]**). See para **[200.126]** above for these different kinds of trusts generally. There will be some demand for such things as life interests and protective trusts, for non-fiscal reasons.

There has been a significant revival of interest in discretionary trusts as a result of the changes in the system of charging now inheritance tax on them introduced in 1982 and the subsequent reductions in inheritance tax rates: see the Note in B18 at para **[218.1]** ff. This interest is likely to be increased by the changes wrought by Finance Act 2006 with effect from 22 March 2006 which have brought many trusts formerly charged as interest in possession trusts within the relevant property charging regime.

In the case of unmarried persons, the residue, unless given to strangers must go to collaterals and then care should be taken to include or exclude, as the intention may be, those who are only collateral through marriage. For example, a nephew's wife may be commonly spoken of by a testator as his niece and, though she is not properly speaking his niece, it may be intended to include her. In such cases there may be much to be said for making the gifts to named persons rather than to classes, though this may involve more complication in making provision for those dying in the testator's lifetime or in infancy. For the simpler method of dealing with this difficulty, see Form B19.11 at para **[219.24]**. The statutory rules of construction including illegitimate children and issue, discussed in Vol 1 at para **[72.1]** ff, should not be overlooked, nor should the rules including adopted children which are considered in Vol 1 at para **[75.1]** ff.

Many examples of different dispositions of residue will be found in Part C, classified according to the family or other circumstances of the testator.

[214.29]

Form B14.18: Power to trustees to sell or mortgage for payment of incumbrances

I authorise my trustees at any time or times and from time to time in their discretion to sell or mortgage at such price and upon such terms and conditions as they may think fit all or any part of the real or leasehold property forming part of my residuary estate for the purpose of paying or of securing to the respective mortgagers or mortgagee for the time being any mortgage debt or debts owing by me at my death or to effect and keep on foot out of the income or if necessary out of the capital of my residuary estate any policy or policies of assurance for the purpose of discharging such mortgage debt or debts and I declare that no purchaser or mortgagee shall be concerned to inquire as to the propriety of any sale or mortgage under this power or as to the application of any money raised thereby.[1]

1 Under the TLATA 1996, s 6(1) (Part G, para **[246.108]**) trustees of land have all the powers of an absolute owner in relation to the land they hold.

[214.30]

Form B14.19: Power to trustees to postpone conversion except as to certain property[1]

I declare that it shall be lawful for my trustees to postpone the sale calling in and conversion of my said residuary real and personal estate or any part thereof (except shares in companies with unlimited liability which I direct shall be sold as soon as conveniently may be after my death[2]) so long as my trustees shall in their uncontrolled discretion think proper.

1 A power to postpone sale is, in the case of every trust of land, implied despite any provision to the contrary made by the disposition: TLATA 1996, s 4(1) (Part G, para **[246.106]**). As to the effect of a power to postpone upon the application of the rule in *Howe v Earl of*

Dartmouth: see *Re Berry, Lloyds Bank Ltd v Berry* [1962] Ch 97, [1961] 1 All ER 529 and Vol 1, para **[38.19]**. See also notes on the power to postpone sale at paras **[214.3]** and **[214.37]**.

2 As to the adequacy of these words, see *Re Rooke's Will Trusts, Taylor v Rooke* [1953] Ch 716, [1953] 2 All ER 110. (The decision in this case, which concerned land, has been superseded by the TLATA 1996, s 4(1) (Part G, para **[246.106]**), but remains good law as to other forms of property.)

[214.31]

Form B14.20: Power to trustees to defer the calling in of certain debts

I authorise my trustees to defer the calling in of any debt or debts carrying interest which may be owing to me from [*name*] at my decease for any period not exceeding [five] years and I declare that my trustees shall not be bound to require any security or further security for such debt or debts provided such interest be regularly paid and that they shall not be responsible for any loss that may occur by reason of deferring such calling in or of any omission to require such security.

[214.32]

Form B14.21: Direction to determine tenancy of a house

I direct that my trustees shall as soon as conveniently may be after my death use their best endeavours to sell or by surrender including a release from liability[1] thereunder determine the tenancy of my leasehold premises known as ——. They may for the purposes aforesaid pay out of the capital of my residuary estate to the purchaser or a reversioner as the case may be such sum as they in their uncontrolled opinion think reasonable not exceeding the clear sum of £——.

1 See *Richmond v Savill* [1926] 2 KB 530, [1926] All ER Rep 362.

[214.33]

Form B14.22: Direction to trustees to convert foreign property, with powers of management[1]

With regard to property whether real or personal movable or immovable belonging to me or to which I may be entitled at the time of my decease in [Canada] I direct as follows:

(1) My trustees shall sell convert into money and get in all such property at such time or times and in such manner and upon such terms and conditions as in their uncontrolled discretion they shall think fit with full power to buy in rescind or vary any contract of sale and to resell any property intended to be included in any such sale without being answerable for any loss and with power in the like discretion to postpone any such sale conversion or realisation for such periods as they may think fit.

(2) Pending such sale conversion and realisation my trustees may let on lease for any term not exceeding [twenty-one] years manage and superintend the whole or any part of the said property and receive the rents and profits thereof and out of any moneys coming into their hands from my property in [Canada] execute and pay for all

such cultivation improvements repairs insurances and other matters as my trustees may think expedient.

(3) As regards any undivided share or interest to which I may be entitled at my decease in any property situate receivable or recoverable in [Canada] my trustees may concur with any person or persons entitled to or having power in that behalf over the other shares or interests in any such property in exercising any powers of sale leasing or managing hereinbefore conferred. And also if deemed expedient they may partition or concur in partitioning the same or any part thereof and for that purpose may agree to any apportionment of purchase-money rent expenses of sale or other matters and pay or receive money for equality of exchange or partition.[2]

1 See also Form C14.1 at para **[236.9]**.

2 The TrA 2000, Pt IV (Part G, paras **[246.143]–[246.159]**) gives to trustees and personal representatives very wide powers to delegate their functions which would include power to delegate their functions in relation to foreign property. Special power is therefore not required; it may, however, sometimes be advisable to insert full powers in order that persons in the foreign country may see upon the face of the will that the trustees have certain powers.

If a will is being made in England of a person domiciled abroad, the section could easily be adapted so as to give the trustees of the will an express power of delegation in respect of land in England, if it were considered desirable for the powers to appear on the face of the will.

A foreign country, as the words are used above, includes all countries except England and Wales, although they may be in the UK or the Commonwealth. The point is that such countries are not necessarily subject to precisely the same law, even though they may be common law jurisdictions. This form and adaptations of it may be useful where restrictions on foreign exchange make it difficult to send money from one jurisdiction to another. As far as possible all payments which can be made in the foreign jurisdiction should be made there and as little as possible remitted.

[214.34]

Form B14.23: Direction to foreign trustees to remit proceeds of sale to English trustees[1]

(1) I declare that subject to the retention of such sums or sums as they may consider necessary for all or any of the purposes aforesaid in connection with any unrealised portion of my said real or personal estate in [*foreign country*] my foreign trustees shall from time to time hand over and remit to my English trustees through such bank as my English trustees may direct the net proceeds of all real and personal estate sold converted got in or realised by my foreign trustees in [*foreign country*] after paying all expenses of and incident to any such sale conversion and realisation and after deducting thereout the commission payable to my foreign trustees for their services and all taxes and duties of whatsoever description which may be payable in [*foreign country*] in respect of my estate and also after paying thereout all pecuniary legacies bequeathed by this my will to any person or persons for the time being resident in [*foreign country*].

(2) I direct that as regards any income which may be received by my foreign trustees from any property of mine in [*foreign country*] pending the sale and conversion thereof and the handing of the proceeds of such sale and conversion over to my English trustees the same shall after payment thereout of all taxes and duties which may be payable in respect thereof in

[*foreign country*] and subject to deduction therefrom of the commission payable in respect of such income to my foreign trustees be paid over to my English trustees and shall be applicable as income in their hands.

(3) The receipt of my English trustees [or other the trustees in England of this my will for the time being] shall be a good and complete discharge for all moneys paid over to them by my foreign trustees.

1 Compare Form C14.1, cl 5 at para **[236.15]**; see also Form B1.6, n 1 at para **[201.11]**.

EXCLUSION OF APPORTIONMENT BETWEEN CAPITAL AND INCOME (RULES IN *HOWE V EARL OF DARTMOUTH* AND *RE CHESTERFIELD'S TRUSTS*)

[214.35]

Note

The rules in *Howe v Earl of Dartmouth* and *Re Chesterfield's Trusts*. The rules in *Howe v Earl of Dartmouth* (income of assets of a wasting or hazardous nature or other unauthorised assets apportioned partly to capital) and the rule in *Re Chesterfield's Trusts* (reversions or other non-income yielding property apportioned retrospectively partly to income when they fall in or are sold) are commonly excluded. The rules, which are described in Vol 1 at paras **[38.17]–[38.27]**, only apply to personal property comprised in residue which is held on trust for persons in succession. There is copious case law on when the rules apply, and the rules concerning their exclusion are by now a nightmare of complexity and technicality. Indeed the precise basis of the rules is uncertain. The conventional view, adopted in the notes which follow, is that the rules apply in relation to investments which are unauthorised. On this view the introduction of a very wide statutory power of investment by the TrA 2000, s 3 (Part G, para **[246.135]**) will have excluded the rules in all but very exceptional cases. An alternative view is that the rules apply to assets which are of a wasting or hazardous nature, whether authorised or not: see Robert Mitchell 'Trusts for Sale in Wills – Excess Baggage' (1999) 63 Conv 84 at 98–103. This view, if correct, affords a further reason for excluding the rules. Note the following points:

(1) 'Personal property' here originally included leasehold land (but not of course freehold land), and a classic example of the type of wasting asset to which *Howe v Earl of Dartmouth* applied was a leasehold with only a few years to run. However, prior to 1 January 1997 the LPA 1925, s 28(2) effectively excluded the rule in relation to leaseholds held on trust for sale, and it was arguable that because the *Howe v Earl of Dartmouth* rule applied to assets not expressly held on trust for sale by implying a trust for sale, s 28(2) had the curious effect of also excluding the rule in relation to leaseholds not held on trust for sale (see Wolstenholme & Cherry's *Conveyancing Statutes* (13th edn), vol 1, pp 85–6), but the point was uncertain. The repeal of the LPA 1925, s 28(2) therefore may mean that leaseholds fall back into the rule in *Howe v Earl of Dartmouth*, unless it is the case that the rule does not apply to authorised investments (see above), in which case the wide power to

invest in leaseholds in TrA 2000, s 8(1) (Part G, para **[246.140]**; see also para **[220.17]**) has the effect (in relation to a will where this TrA 2000 power of investment is not excluded) that the rule in *Howe v Earl of Dartmouth* again does not apply to them.

(2) If it is the case that the rule in *Howe v Earl of Dartmouth* does not apply to authorised investments (see above), 'authorised investments' here includes investments authorised by the will (see *Brown v Gellatly* (1867) 2 Ch App 751 at 758–9) so that if the investment clause is wide enough to authorise investment in all the types of asset which are comprised in residue, as is now the case under the TrA 2000, ss 3 and 8 the rules will not apply. The main types of personalty which might be comprised in residue but still fall outside the new statutory power and some of the modern forms of wide investment powers are businesses (see eg *Re Berry, Lloyds Bank Ltd v Berry* [1962] Ch 97 at 111) and reversionary interests: see the Preliminary Note on Investment Powers in B20 at paras **[220.33]** and **[220.34]**.

(3) 'Trusts for persons in succession' here obviously includes a life interest with remainders and does not include an absolute interest. But what of eg a gift of capital contingent on obtaining the age of 30 and carrying the intermediate income? If the beneficiary dies at, say, 29 he will have been entitled to the current income since he attained 18 but the capital will go to somebody else. It may be that the equitable apportionment rules could apply to such a case; the only relevant authority seems to be *Re Bland, Miller v Bland* [1899] 2 Ch 336, where it was held that the rules did not apply on the particular facts of the case to a defeasible gift, but the judgment did not rule out the possibility that the rules could apply to such a gift. We recommend exclusion of the rules wherever the interests in residue are not immediate and absolute.

[214.36]
Why exclude the *Howe v Dartmouth* and *Re Chesterfield's Trusts* rules? The main reason for doing this is to avoid the administrative expense and difficulty in operating them. In addition they are out of date in various ways — the four per cent rate of assumed income yield is only occasionally in line with current interest rates, there is an assumption behind the rule in *Howe v Earl of Dartmouth* that rates of yield of unauthorised investments will be higher than those of authorised investments, and also an assumption that reversionary interests are readily saleable assets, which is no longer the case. It is also arguable in theory that the *Howe v Earl of Dartmouth* rule would prevent someone with a life interest from having an interest in possession for inheritance tax purposes in the whole of the property to which the rule applied (since some of the income would be added to capital rather than paid to the life tenant) though we think it unlikely that such a point would be taken by the Inland Revenue in practice, and the Scottish decision of *Miller v IRC* [1987] STC 108, in which it was decided that a power to set aside income in a sinking fund to meet depreciation of capital value was compatible with there being an interest in possession for inheritance tax purposes, weighs heavily against this argument.

[214.37]
How to exclude the *Howe v Earl of Dartmouth* and *Re Chesterfield's Trusts* rules. The main traditional exclusionary formula is to direct that the actual income of the estate is from the testator's death to be treated as income: see Forms B14.10 (at para **[214.19]**) and B14.24 (at para **[214.39]**) and the AEA 1925, s 33(5) (Part G, para **[244.60]**) for the use of this formula for the estates of intestates. This formula excludes the rule in *Re Chesterfield's Trusts* as well as the rule in *Howe v Earl of Dartmouth* (see *Re Rowlls* [1900] 2 Ch 107), as does a declaration that the rule in *Howe v Earl of Dartmouth* in all its branches shall not apply (see *Re Hey's Settlement Trusts, Hey v Nickell-Lean* [1945] Ch 294). However, neither of these formulae excludes what might be called the rule in *Re Rowlls* [1900] 2 Ch 107, namely that where there is a trust for sale with power to postpone sale, and either of these exclusionary formulas is used, the rules in *Howe v Earl of Dartmouth* and *Re Chesterfield's Trusts* are only excluded in relation to any particular property which is an unauthorised investment, reversionary interest, etc if the trustees make a conscious discretionary decision to postpone its sale: see *Re Hey's Settlement Trusts, Hey v Nickell-Lean* [1945] Ch 294. If they did not know the property formed part of the estate (something which can easily happen in the case of a reversionary interest) or failed to address their minds to the point, equitable apportionment will still occur. We refer the reader whose reaction to this is disbelief to Vol 1, para **[38.23]**, n 15 for other decisions to the same effect.

[214.38]
It should be possible to exclude the rule in *Re Rowlls*, ie provide that even if the trustees fail to make an exercise of their discretion to postpone sale the equitable apportionment rules will still not apply. It would appear that the formula 'a reversionary interest shall not be sold unless the trustees see special reason for sale' which formerly appeared in the statutory trust for sale of the estates of intestates (AEA 1925, s 33(1) before its amendment by the TLATA 1996 and appears in Form B14.25 at para **[214.40]**) may well be effective to exclude the rule in *Re Rowlls* in relation to reversionary interests, but it should be remembered that 'reversionary interest' does not include every kind of interest to which the rule in *Re Chesterfield's Trusts* can apply (see eg *Re Fisher, Harris v Fisher* [1943] Ch 377—annuity paid under a life assurance policy). We put forward a suggestion for the exclusion of apportionment where residue is held on trust for sale, even if the trustees do not exercise their discretion to postpone sale, in Form B14.27 at para **[214.42]**. An alternative is to provide administration trusts of residue which do not include a trust to sell or convert, and which confer a power to sell the assets at the discretion of the trustees when they think fit (an administration trust which provides a power of sale rather than a trust to sell is in general what we recommend on other grounds: see para **[214.2]**). The rule in *Howe v Dartmouth* apparently does not apply where there is a clear intention that the time of sale should be within the trustees' discretion: see Vol 1, para **[38.23]**, n 11 and the cases there cited, especially *Re Pitcairn, Brandreth v Colvin* [1896] 2 Ch 199. These decisions could still be overruled or held inapplicable, however, and it is not readily apparent to those who have not made a detailed study of this area of the law that the effect of such wording is to

exclude the rule in *Howe v Dartmouth*. Accordingly, the cautious draftsman will prefer to use express exclusionary words (and see Robert Mitchell, 'Trusts for Sale in Wills – Excess Baggage' (1999) 63 Conv 84 at 99). See Forms B14.1 at para **[214.10]** and B14.4 at para **[214.13]** for examples of the *Re Pitcairn* formula.

[214.39]

Form B14.24: Exclusion of rule in *Howe v Earl of Dartmouth*[1]

The income of all parts of my estate for the time being unsold however constituted or invested shall as from my death be treated and applied as the income of investments authorised hereby or by the general law.

1 For a form incorporating much the same formula in a gift of residue on trust for sale see Form B14.10 at para **[214.19]**. Note also that this form is probably also effective to exclude the rule in *Re Chesterfield's Trusts*, but will exclude neither rule if there is a trust for sale with power to postpone sale and the trustees do not make a deliberate exercise of the latter power: see *Re Rowlls* [1900] 2 Ch 107; and para **[214.37]**. This form does not exclude the rule in *Allhusen v Whittell* (1867) LR 4 Eq 295 (*Re Ullswater, Barclays Bank Ltd v Lowther* [1952] Ch 105).

[214.40]

Form B14.25: Exclusion of rule in *Re Chesterfield's Trusts*[1]

No reversionary or future interest shall be sold prior to falling into possession unless my trustees see special reason for sale and no reversionary future or other property not producing income shall be treated as producing income.

1 For the rule itself see Vol 1, paras **[38.22]–[38.23]**: for notes on excluding it see para **[214.37]** and for much the same formula incorporated into a gift of residue on trust for sale, see Form B14.10 at para **[214.19]**. It may be that the direction not to sell in this form means that the rule in *Re Chesterfield* is excluded even if the trustees make no deliberate decision to postpone sale: see para **[214.37]**.

[214.41]

Form B14.26: Exclusion of rules in *Howe v Earl of Dartmouth* and *Re Chesterfield's Trusts*—short form naming case[1]

The rule in *Howe v Earl of Dartmouth* in all its branches shall not apply.

1 The authority that this excludes both rules is *Re Hey's Settlement Trusts, Hey v Nickell-Lean* [1945] Ch 294; it is also authority that if residue is held on trust for sale with power to postpone, the rules are only excluded by these words if the trustees make a deliberate decision to postpone sale: see para **[214.37]**.

[214.42]

Form B14.27: Exclusion of rules in *Howe v Earl of Dartmouth* and *Re Chesterfield's Trusts*—alternative form[1]

The rules of equity concerning the apportionment (between income and capital) of income from assets which are unauthorised investments or of capital arising from non-income yielding assets are hereby excluded from applying to any asset subject to the trusts of this will or of any codicil hereto in any circumstances whatever and notwithstanding that my trustees may not have made any deliberate decision to postpone the sale of such asset.[2]

1 This has the advantage over Form B14.24 (at para **[214.39]**) of being more direct and making its purpose clear, and has the advantage over Form B14.26 (at para **[214.40]**) of not using the case name and making some attempt to describe the rules it refers to. (Form B14.24 will convey nothing to non-lawyers, and little to many lawyers, and would be difficult to persuade some testators to accept.) This form also tries to exclude what we refer to as the rule in *Re Rowlls* (see para **[214.37]**). It has the disadvantage of not having been considered by the courts.

2 The words from 'notwithstanding' are our attempt to exclude what we refer to as the rule in *Re Rowlls* (see para **[214.37]**). A trust for sale with power to postpone sale affecting the whole of residue is assumed.

EXCLUSION OF RULE FOR APPORTIONMENT OF LIABILITIES BETWEEN CAPITAL AND INCOME (RULE IN *ALLHUSEN V WHITTELL*)

[214.43]

Note

Exclusion of the rule in *Allhusen v Whittell*. This rule (apportionment of estate liabilities between income and capital) applies to the administration expenses, inheritance tax payable out of residue and legacies as well as debts and is described in Vol 1 at para **[38.25]**. It is again a rule which only has any relevance where residue is settled (so that income and capital will or may go to different beneficiaries), but it can apply to realty as well as personalty and is of course a rule which will apply to authorised and unauthorised investments alike. It is thus of potentially wider application than the rules in *Howe v Earl of Dartmouth* and *Re Chesterfield's Trusts*.

[214.44]

It is usual to exclude the rule to avoid intricate calculations, and it seems to us that in addition to just excluding it an express indication as to how liabilities etc are to be borne should be given. There are two main possibilities: the executors can be given a discretion as to the apportioning of liabilities etc between capital and income (see Form B14.28 at para **[214.45]**), or the liabilities can be directed to be paid out of capital (see Form B14.29 at para **[214.46]**). It should be noted that a likely consequence of a direction to pay debts and testamentary expenses out of capital is that interest on inheritance tax and on income tax arrears will be payable out of capital: *Re Hogg* (11 July 1983, unreported) Ch D (see McCutcheon 'Going the Whole Hogg?' [1986] *Capital Taxes* 27). This would seem to mean also that where a direction to pay liabilities etc out of capital applies to legacies, the interest on the legacies should also be paid out of capital. It does seem inappropriate for interest on debts, administration expenses (in particular interest on overdue inheritance tax) and legacies, where the interest arises in respect of a period after the death of the testator, to be paid out of capital. A possible solution is to provide that the principal amounts are to be paid out of capital but that interest arising after the testator's death should as far as possible be paid out of income: see Forms B14.3 (at para **[214.12]**), B14.4 (at para **[214.13]**) and B14.30 (at para **[214.47]**).

[214.45]

Form B14.28: Trustees given a discretion as to allocation[1]

My trustees may at their absolute discretion allocate the burden of payments made in the due course of administration to or between income or capital of my estate and shall have no obligation to apply the rule [of equity as to such allocation[2]].

1 For the rule in *Allhusen v Whittell* see Vol 1, para **[38.25]** and the notes on excluding the rule at paras **[214.43]** and **[214.44]**. Form B14.10 at para **[214.19]** contains another formula for excluding the rule of a rather oblique kind – see n 1 thereto.
2 For the words in square brackets substitute 'in *Allhusen v Whittell*' if preferred.

[214.46]

Form B14.29: Liabilities to be paid out of capital[1]

My trustees shall pay all payments made in due course of administration of my estate out of capital and the rule [of equity as to the apportionment of the same between capital and income[2]] shall not apply.

1 For the rule in *Allhusen v Whittell* see Vol 1, para **[38.25]** and the notes on excluding the rule at paras **[214.43]** and **[214.44]**. Form 14.10 at para **[214.19]** contains another exclusionary formula – see n 1 thereto. Note that this form may cause interest on, e g inheritance tax, to be payable out of capital: see para **[214.44]**.
2 For the words in square brackets substitute 'in *Allhusen v Whittell*' if preferred.

[214.47]

Form B14.30: Liabilities to be paid out of capital, but interest on them payable for periods after the testator's death to be paid out of income as far as possible

The rule of equity as to the apportionment between capital and income of payments made in the course of administration shall not apply to my estate, and debts, testamentary expenses, inheritance tax or similar taxes, and legacies shall be paid out of capital while any interest on any such debts, expenses, taxes or legacies which may become payable in respect of any period falling after my death shall as far as possible be paid out of income.[1]

1 For the reasoning behind this see para **[214.44]**.

EXCLUSION OF TIME APPORTIONMENT

[214.48]

Note

The Apportionment Acts. The Apportionment Act 1870 (AA 1870) (Part G, para **[246.2]** ff) provides that rents annuities dividends and other periodical payments in the nature of income are treated as accruing from day to day and apportionable in respect of time accordingly (AA 1870, s 1). This means that where an instalment of income is received after some change has occurred in the ownership of the right to receive the income, and the instalment is in respect of a period partly preceding the change, it is to be apportioned between the period before and the period after the change occurred.

[214.49]
The effect of the AA 1870 on dividends on ordinary shares is particularly notable, because the apportionment is to be to the period for which the dividend is declared (AA 1870, s 5 definition of 'dividends': Part G, para **[246.6]**), which is typically a period ending six months or so before the dividend becomes payable. The Act does not apply to the profits of a business, and does not apply to instalments of rent paid in advance (*Ellis v Rowbotham* [1900] 1 QB 740); since rent is almost invariably payable in advance under modern leases the Act has ceased to have much relevance to rent.

[214.50]
The AA 1870 is applicable on the death of the testator (see below), the death of a life tenant, and when there is a gift to a class of minor beneficiaries to which the Trustee Act 1925, s 31 (Part G, para **[246.29]**) applies and the class increases or decreases by birth or death (*Re Joel's Will Trusts, Rogerson v Brudenell-Bruce* [1967] Ch 14, [1966] 2 All ER 482). It does not apply in relation to the forfeiture of a protective life interest (*Re Jenkins, Williams v Jenkins* [1915] 1 Ch 46) or on the commencement or determination of any discretionary trust of income (*Weir's Settlement Trusts* [1971] Ch 145 at 167).

The Apportionment Act 1834 (AA 1834) is superseded, but not repealed, by the AA 1870.

[214.51]
Exclusion of the Apportionment Acts. The Acts apply subject to a contrary stipulation: AA 1870, s 7 (Part G, para **[246.8]**) and AA 1834, s 3. The reason for excluding them is essentially the same as for excluding the other apportionment rules, namely to avoid troublesome calculations for no very advantageous result. In relation to the testator's own death the significance of the Acts applying to the income of residuary assets is that part of the income received shortly after death will be apportioned to capital, and the significance of it applying to assets comprised in a specific gift is that part of the income received shortly after death is likely to be apportioned to residue (as capital) instead of going to the person entitled to the specific gift. It is usual to exclude the Apportionment Acts in relation to the testator's death by a clause such as that in Form B14.31 at para **[214.53]**. For specific gifts including anti-apportionment provision (so that the income payable after the testator's death goes to the specific legatee or devisee) see Forms B4.39 (at para **[204.61]**) and B6.5 (at para **[206.14]**). There could be some advantage in not excluding the Acts if the person who will be entitled to the income of residue will have a high personal income tax rate, since if some of the income is apportioned to capital it will not form part of that person's income for the purposes of higher rate income tax, although this may still be so where that person is entitled absolutely to the capital as well as the income.

[214.52]
If the will settles any property, Form B14.31 (at para **[214.53]**) will not exclude the Apportionment Acts in relation to any event subsequent to the testator's death, such as the death of a life tenant. We recommend excluding the Apportionment Acts in relation to such subsequent events, especially if there are accumulation and maintenance trusts (see *Re Joel's Will Trusts, Rogerson v Brudenell-Bruce* [1967] Ch 14, [1966] 2 All ER 482 mentioned at para **[214.50]**), by use of a general exclusion clause such as Form B14.32 at para **[214.54]**. If the AA 1870 is excluded by express reference to that Act, the AA 1834 might nevertheless still apply if not also expressly excluded. See also the exclusionary formula in Form B14.3 at para **[214.12]**.

[214.53]

Form B14.31: Exclusion of Apportionment Acts as between before and after testator's death[1]

All income of my estate (whether the same be received in respect of a period wholly or only partly prior to my death) which shall be actually received after my death shall be treated as accruing wholly after my death and shall not be apportioned to or treated as capital.

1 See para **[214.44]**. Exclusion of the Apportionment Acts will probably not prevent any of the income element of National Savings Certificates which has been capitalised before the testator's death from being treated as capital of his estate: *Re Holder, National Provincial Bank Ltd v Holder* [1953] Ch 468, [1953] 2 All ER 1.

[214.54]

Form B14.32: Exclusion of Apportionment Acts generally[1]

All income of my estate or of any property held from time to time on any of the trusts of this will or of any codicil hereto shall be treated as accruing at the time when it is payable and shall not be apportioned to any other time or period under the Apportionment Acts of 1834 or 1870.[2]

1 A general exclusion of this type is recommended where there is any interest in possession or accumulation and maintenance trusts: see para **[214.52]**. For an alternative form, see Form B14.3, sub-cl 4(a) at para **[214.12]**.
2 Specific reference to the Acts is preferable. The AA 1834 has never been repealed, although its provisions are duplicated by the more general provisions of the AA 1870. If the AA 1870 only is excluded there is a possibility that the AA 1834 might still apply. For the text of the AA 1870 see Part G, para **[246.2]** ff.

INCIDENCE OF INHERITANCE TAX

[214.55]

Note
The Inheritance Tax Act 1984, s 211. The provisions now contained in the IHTA 1984, s 211 (Part G, para **[246.100]**) apply in relation to deaths on or after 26 July 1983. They were previously contained in the Finance Act 1975, s 28, as amended by the Finance (No 2) Act 1983, s 13. We are here

concerned with drafting wills for persons living after publication of this edition of this work, so we do not consider the previous law of incidence.

[214.56]

Section 211 of the IHTA 1984 (Part G, para **[246.100]**) is a provision which was introduced to resolve the difficulties caused by the decision of the Court of Session in *Re Dougal* [1981] STC 514, a decision which contradicted the commonly held opinion that under Scottish law land comprised in a deceased person's free estate bore its own capital transfer tax (now inheritance tax) in the absence of express provision in the will, and instead held that the tax on it was to be paid out of residue. It had also been thought that land comprised in free estate bore its own capital transfer tax (now inheritance tax) in English law; it was possible that English law on the point might turn out to be different from the Scottish law, but there were sufficient resemblances between the two systems in material respects for there to be a real question as to whether *Re Dougal* might not be followed in England. The point has not been, and probably never will be, litigated, and the conclusion reached in *Re Dougal* has now been given statutory effect for the future by s 211 so that realty and personalty are now treated alike as regards incidence.

[214.57]

A slight doubt about s 211. The crucial part of the IHTA 1984, s 211 is in sub-s (1); tax is treated as part of testamentary expenses *but only* so far as attributable to the UK free estate (real or personal). It thus expressly provides that the inheritance tax on assets other than UK free estate is not a testamentary expense. Subsection (3) provides for repayment of tax paid by personal representatives which is not a testamentary expense 'where occasion requires', but does not in any way determine what occasions do and do not so require, and it is really only sub-s (1) which has any effect on who should bear the inheritance tax on different parts of an estate.

[214.58]

However, the decision in *Re Dougal* [1981] STC 514 did not say anything about capital transfer tax (now inheritance tax) being a testamentary expense, but said that the tax is calculated by reference to the entire estate regardless of the nature of the chargeable property and that it is a debt for which the estate as a whole is liable and which the personal representatives are obliged to pay on all the estate, irrespective of the type of property; therefore there were no grounds for distinguishing land and other assets as regards incidence. There thus remains the possibility that it follows from *Re Dougal* that any inheritance tax for which the personal representatives are liable is to be borne by residue, though not as an administration expense under the IHTA 1984, s 211 and that this includes the inheritance tax on foreign property, or perhaps even the tax on property which does not vest in the personal representatives at all, such as the severable share of jointly tenanted property. The incidence of inheritance tax on any deceased person's estate could be put beyond all doubt by his will providing expressly for the incidence of all inheritance tax for which the personal representatives may be liable (see eg Form B14.33 at para **[214.76]**). However, in our view it is most unlikely that the courts of England and Wales would hold that the IHTA 1984, s 211 does not exhaustively define the categories of property in respect of which the inheritance tax is borne by residue, as opposed to being borne by the property itself (in the absence of a contrary direction).

[214.59]
Inheritance tax which is a testamentary expense. Close examination shows that for inheritance tax to be a testamentary expense of a testator's estate by virtue of the IHTA 1984, s 211(1) (Part G, para **[246.100]**):

(a) his personal representatives must be liable for the tax;
(b) the tax must relate to the inheritance tax charge on the testator's 'estate' immediately before his death for inheritance tax purposes (ie the charge under the IHTA 1984, s 4);
(c) the property to which it relates must be in the UK (at the testator's death, it would seem);
(d) it must relate to property which vests in the testator's personal representatives; and
(e) it must relate to property which was not comprised in a settlement immediately before the testator's death.

[214.60]
Property which bears its own inheritance tax. The collection of often overlapping conditions (set out at para **[214.59]**) excludes from being a testamentary expense by virtue of the IHTA 1984, s 211 any inheritance tax arising from a testator's death which falls into any of the following categories (with the result that such tax is borne by the property to which it relates in the absence of express provision):

(1) The inheritance tax on property of the testator situated outside the UK at his death.
(2) The inheritance tax on the testator's severable share of jointly tenanted property (see Vol 1, para **[7.3]**), property which devolves under a nomination (see Vol 1, paras **[7.9]**–**[7.11]**), or property comprised in a donatio mortis causa (see Vol 1, para **[1.14]**). Section 211(1) of the IHTA 1984 does not apply to property devolving in any of these ways because such property does not vest in the testator's personal representatives, although such property is part of his estate on death for inheritance tax purposes and the personal representatives are liable for the inheritance tax on it.
(3) The inheritance tax on property which was comprised in a settlement immediately before the testator's death. The IHTA 1984, s 211(1) therefore does not apply to the inheritance tax which is charged by reason of the testator's death on settled property in which the testator had a beneficiary taxed interest in possession (see Part A, para **[200.92]**) immediately before his death (IHTA 1984, ss 4(1), 5(1) and 49(1)), and this is so even if such property vests in the testator's personal representatives or is disposed of by the testator's will. In particular, inheritance tax arising from the testator's death in respect of property which was settled immediately before the testator's death, but which is disposed of by his will in exercise of a general or special power

of appointment, or in exercise of the statutory power to dispose of entailed property which is conferred by the LPA 1925, s 176 (Part G, para **[244.55]**; see also Vol 1, para **[7.2]**), will fall outside s 211(1). It will be recalled that property subject to a general power of appointment exercisable by a testator's will can very easily fall into his residuary estate by virtue of a general residuary gift which expresses no intention that the power should not be exercised: WA 1837, s 27 (Part G, para **[244.29]**; see also Vol 1, para **[39.2]** ff).

(4) Inheritance tax or additional inheritance tax payable as a result of the testator's death in respect of potentially exempt transfers or chargeable transfers he has made during his life, but within seven years of his death (see paras **[200.70]** and **[200.71]** and B10 at para **[210.66]**). IHTA 1984, s 211(1) will also not apply to the inheritance tax on events which are charged to inheritance tax as if they were lifetime potentially exempt transfers, such as property of which the testator was the donor ceasing to be subject to a reservation within seven years of his death (Finance Act 1986, s 102 (4): see para **[200.76]**), or the repayment by the testator within seven years of his death of a debt which would not have been a deductible liability on his death because the consideration for it derived from him (see the Finance Act 1986, s 103(1) to (6) and para **[200.77]**). This inheritance tax or additional inheritance tax arising on death in respect of lifetime transfers, or events treated as lifetime potentially exempt transfers, falls outside s 211(1) because it is not tax on the chargeable transfer on death, and the property concerned does not vest in the personal representatives.

(5) Inheritance tax on property comprised in a lifetime gift made by the testator which is property subject to a reservation (see para **[200.76]**) at the testator's death. Such property is comprised in the chargeable transfer made on death (see the Finance Act 1986, s 102(3)) and the personal representatives are liable for the tax on it, though as a secondary liability (see the IHTA 1984, s 204(9) and para **[200.78]**). However, the property does not vest in the personal representatives and so IHTA 1984, s 211(1) does not apply. The position is quite the opposite in relation to debts not deductible by virtue of the Finance Act 1986, s 103 (see para **[214.61]**).

(6) Inheritance tax on works of art, etc or woodlands where exemption or relief from the inheritance tax charge on death is obtained, but an inheritance tax charge arises from a subsequent sale or breach of undertakings. The IHTA 1984, s 211(1) does not apply to the inheritance tax arising on such a subsequent event because it is not tax on the chargeable transfer on death and because the personal representatives are not liable for it: IHTA 1984, ss 207 and 208.

[214.61]

Non-deductible liabilities. Debts or other liabilities of a testator's estate may not be deductible for inheritance tax purposes because they were not incurred or not wholly incurred for a consideration in money or money's worth (IHTA 1984, s 5(5)), or because the consideration for the debt or other liability derived from the testator or came from a person who had property derived from the testator: Finance Act 1986, s 103(1)–(6). Whatever the inheritance tax treatment of such a liability, it remains a liability of the estate which is payable out of it in priority to all beneficial interests in the estate and it will not be subject to any deduction for the inheritance tax arising from the testator's death and attributable to such liability (*Re Gray* [1896] 1 Ch 620) unless the terms on which the liability was incurred provided for its payment or repayment to be subject to payment of such tax. If the liability was not incurred on such terms it is difficult to see how any provision of the testator's will could impose the burden of the inheritance tax attributable to such liability on the liability itself, although the burden could be thrown on to some other gift made by the will to the person to whom the liability is owed (unless that gift is exempt: see the IHTA 1984, s 41).

[214.62]
What has just been said is subject to the possibility that where a non-deductible liability is payable out of property which bears its own inheritance tax, eg because the testator leaves no free estate in the UK or charges foreign property with the payment of his debts, the liability itself may bear its own inheritance tax, although the estate duty cases which suggest that this might be the case (*Re Hacket, Hacket v Gardiner* [1907] 1 Ch 385; *Re Hartland, Banks v Hartland* [1911] 1 Ch 459) depend on a provision of the estate duty legislation (Finance Act 1894, s 14(1)) which has no equivalent in the inheritance tax legislation and are concerned with non-deductible liabilities charged on real estate by a lifetime disposition. Where the total of non-deductible and other liabilities of an estate and the inheritance tax on the estate exceeds the value of the estate it seems that the estate is insolvent and that the inheritance tax which is a testamentary expense will have priority over the debts (under the Administration of Insolvent Estates of Deceased Persons Order 1986, SI 1986/1999, art 4 — in force from 29 December 1986). If in such a case there is inheritance tax which does not fall within the IHTA 1984, s 211(1) and therefore is not a testamentary expense, such inheritance tax would presumably have priority over payment of non-deductible debts, perhaps by virtue of the Inland Revenue charge (under the IHTA 1984, s 237) or on the basis that non-deductible liabilities bear their own inheritance tax where they are payable out of assets which bear their own inheritance tax.

[214.63]
Foreign property. At the time when the anomalous difference in the incidence of capital transfer tax (now inheritance tax) between realty and personalty was abolished by what is now the IHTA 1984, s 211(1), an increase in ownership of foreign assets had been taking place as a result of the abolition of exchange control. Section 211(1) leaves foreign assets bearing their own tax, in the absence of an expressed contrary intention, just as under estate duty law, and it seems likely that many of the estate duty rules of incidence and cases on construction of free of duty provisions remain relevant. For many testators, whether they want to make specific gifts free from or subject to inheritance tax will have little to do with the location of the assets. Further, it is most unusual for a testator to want pecuniary legacies to bear any inheritance tax or foreign death duties, which they might do in the

absence of express provision to the contrary if they are payable wholly or partly out of foreign property (see para **[214.64]**). There is the further problem which could arise in relation to specific gifts of chattels that it is possible for chattels to be unexpectedly outside the UK at the testator's death, although it would be in an unusual case (yachts, aircraft, jewellery) that items of significant value would be involved. For possible methods of dealing with these problems see para **[214.71]**.

[214.64]
General and pecuniary legacies. Despite the IHTA 1984, s 211 it remains probable that pecuniary or general legacies, in the absence of express provision to the contrary, are subject to inheritance tax as far as they are payable out of a fund which consists of or includes assets which bear their own inheritance tax, such as foreign property or property which was comprised in a settlement immediately before the testator's death. It was held in *Re Spencer Cooper, Poë v Spencer Cooper* [1908] 1 Ch 130 and *Re Owers, Public Trustee v Death* [1941] Ch 17, [1940] 4 All ER 225, CA that general or pecuniary legacies charged on a mixed fund of realty and personalty bore a proportion of the estate duty on the fund corresponding to the proportion of the fund that the realty represented, and in particular that this was so in the case of such legacies payable out of a mixed residuary fund directed to be held on trust for sale. The same principle applied to legacies charged on a mixed fund of British and foreign personalty: see *Re Sebba* [1959] Ch 166 at 178 (the declaration on question (3) — the reasoning is not reported, and the report at [1958] 3 All ER 393 does not report the decision on this point). Inheritance tax seems sufficiently similar to estate duty for it to be likely that this rule would apply to the incidence of inheritance tax on legacies paid out of a mixed fund of UK and foreign assets. It also seems likely that this rule would apply where residue (or some other fund out of which pecuniary or general legacies are to be paid) includes property which was comprised in a settlement immediately before the testator's death and was, eg subject to a general power of appointment which he exercised by his will (see para **[214.59]**, sub-para (c)).

[214.65]
Abatement. Inheritance tax on UK free estate will be a testamentary expense which will be satisfied out of the assets of the estate in the order prescribed by the AEA 1925, Sch 1, Pt II (Part G, para **[246.69]**) for debts and administration expenses. Inheritance tax on other assets, such as foreign assets, which the will directs to be paid out of residue, will constitute legacies (see the definition of 'pecuniary legacy' in the AEA 1925, s 55(1)(ix): Part G, para **[246.67]**) and will abate rateably with ordinary pecuniary legacies in the absence of a direction to the contrary. An example of a direction which would give priority over ordinary precuniary legacies to the inheritance tax on a specific gift of foreign property is contained in a proviso to Form B14.33 at para **[214.76]**.

[214.66]
Inheritance tax on events subsequent to the testator's death. There are some rather unreliable decisions from the 1914–18 War period (eg *Re Stoddart,*

Bird v Grainger [1916] 2 Ch 444) which suggest that a general direction that duty be paid out of residue might easily include duty arising on the death of a tenant for life under the will trusts, but more recent cases (such as *Re Howell* [1952] Ch 264 and *Re Embleton's Will Trusts, Sodeau v Nelson* [1965] 1 All ER 771, [1965] 1 WLR 840) show the courts leaning heavily against such a conclusion. However, the possibility that a direction as to incidence might in some circumstances be interpreted as referring to tax on events subsequent to the testator's death should be borne in mind when drafting such directions.

[214.67]
Works of art, etc woodlands, and property on which the inheritance tax may be payable by instalments. Any testator who is thinking of making a specific gift of a work of art or other property which might qualify for conditional exemption under the IHTA 1984, Pt II, Ch II ('heritage property'), or woodlands in the UK, could be well advised to make the gift bear its own inheritance tax. It will be apparent from what is said above that where there are no express directions about incidence, the effect of claiming exemption or relief from the inheritance tax charge on death in relation to either type of property is not only to defer the tax charge but to shift its incidence from residue to the property itself. If the specific legatee or devisee has not been given any share or interest in residue, he may prefer that the exemption or relief should not be claimed so that he takes the property free of the potential tax liability at the expense of residue. In the case of woodlands the decision whether to claim the relief would be the personal representatives' (IHTA 1984, s 125(2)), and this could put them in an invidious position; in the case of heritage property the specific legatee could prevent conditional exemption being obtained by refusing to give the undertakings that he would almost certainly be asked to give as a condition of the exemption: IHTA 1984, ss 30(1)(b) and 31(2)–(4). On the subject of heritage property, see also the Preliminary Note on chattels in B4 at para **[204.2]** ff.

[214.68]
A testator might also consider whether it would be more appropriate to make subject to inheritance tax a specific gift of property in respect of which the inheritance tax might be paid by instalments, such as land, businesses, or majority shareholdings (see the IHTA 1984, ss 227–229). This would enable the estate to be administered more rapidly, as the executors would be less likely to have to retain assets of the residuary estate with which to pay the instalments of tax for ten years after the testator's death. For further points favouring subject to tax gifts of business or agricultural property see the Note to B5 at paras **[205.52]**–**[205.54]** and the Preliminary Note to C11 at para **[233.10]**.

[214.69]
Partially exempt estates and incidence of inheritance tax. For points on incidence of inheritance tax specific to partially exempt estates, see paras **[214.72]**–**[214.75]**.

[214.70]
Drafting hazards. We suggest that the following are points to watch when formulating directions as to incidence of inheritance tax and foreign duties:

(1) There are many categories of property which are chargeable to inheritance tax or additional inheritance tax as a result of a testator's death which do not form part of his free estate disposed of by his will: see paras **[214.59]** and **[214.60]**. Formulae such as 'all the inheritance tax payable by reason of my death' without some words restricting the liability to the tax on the free estate, could be construed as including the inheritance tax on some or all of those categories of property, contrary to the likely intentions of the testator. References to 'my estate' could in some contexts be construed as having the extended meaning which the term 'estate' is given by the IHTA 1984.

(2) A direction of the type often found in administration trusts to pay testamentary expenses and inheritance tax out of residue prima facie throws on to residue the burden of all the inheritance tax arising on the testator's death on his free estate, including the tax on property (such as foreign property) which normally bears its own inheritance tax (*Re Pimm, Sharpe v Hodgson* [1904] 2 Ch 345). However, such a direction may be construed as having a wider meaning and as including inheritance tax on death on property which is not part of the testator's free estate where all the inheritance tax on the free estate is a testamentary expense and the reference to inheritance tax would be redundant if not given the wider meaning: see *Re Walley, National Westminster Bank Ltd v Williams* [1972] 1 All ER 222, [1972] 1 WLR 257, where a direction to pay 'testamentary expenses … and all death duties' out of residue was treated as including the estate duty on a Post Office Savings Bank account which devolved by nomination (see para **[214.60]**, sub-para (2)). The main ground for the decision was that the free estate consisted entirely of UK personalty, the duty on which was a testamentary expense anyway. Now that the IHTA 1984, s 211(1) provides that inheritance tax on realty as well as personalty in the UK is a testamentary expense the possibility of a general reference of this kind to inheritance tax being redundant if not construed as referring to something other than the tax on free estate is much greater, and it is advisable to make clear what inheritance tax a general direction as to inheritance tax is intended to refer to.

(3) On the other hand, a general direction of the kind referred to under (2) above could be narrowed in its scope if the will also contains gifts of a kind which might otherwise be subject to tax which are specifically made free of tax and there are other gifts of the same kind which are not specifically made free of tax. In such cases the courts have tended to construe the general direction as referring only to the inheritance tax on those gifts which are specifically declared to be free of tax: see *Re Phuler's Will Trusts, Midland Bank Executor and Trustee Co Ltd v Logan* [1964] 2 All ER 948, [1965] 1 WLR 68 and *Re Neeld, Carpenter v Inigo-Jones* [1964] 2 All ER 952n, [1965] 1 WLR 73n. Therefore, any specific provisions as to inheritance tax made in relation to particular gifts need to be harmonised with any general directions as to incidence.

[214.71]

Recommendations for provisions as to incidence. Where there is no real possibility of the testator dying possessed of foreign property, or exercising by will any power of disposition over settled property, one course of action would be to rely entirely on the IHTA 1984, s 211, refrain from including in the will any general direction as to the payment or incidence of inheritance tax, and include a specific direction only where a particular gift is to bear its own inheritance tax. If there is a possibility of there being any property comprised in the estate disposed of by will of a kind which bears its own inheritance tax (see para **[214.60]**, sub-paras (1) and (3)) the possibilities are to:

(1) Use 'free of inheritance tax and foreign death duties' or some such words in relation to individual gifts, such as pecuniary legacies and specific gifts of foreign property, which might otherwise bear inheritance tax, as far as it is desired that they should be free of tax and duties, and confine any general direction to referring to the tax on gifts made free of tax (see eg Forms B14.3 and B14.8 at paras **[214.12]** and **[214.17]**). This is the strategy adopted in the forms of complete wills in Part C.

(2) Include a general direction that all pecuniary and general legacies and gifts of personal chattels are free of inheritance tax and foreign death duties (see Form B14.34 at para **[214.77]**), with the result that specific gifts of foreign property (other than chattels) or settled property are subject to inheritance tax and foreign death duties unless specifically declared to be free of them.

(3) Include a general direction that the inheritance tax on the entire free estate is payable out of residue save in so far as it is declared to be subject to tax (see Forms B14.17 at para **[214.26]** and B14.33 at para **[214.76]**). If such a general direction is used, no individual gifts should be expressed to be free of inheritance tax. For specific gifts subject to inheritance tax, see Forms B5.1 (at para **[205.58]**), B5.4 (at para **[205.61]**), B6.31 (at para **[206.40]**), B10.50 (at para **[210.71]**) and B14.36 (at para **[214.79]**).

For directions for payment out of residue of inheritance tax on lifetime gifts and property not comprised in free estate, see Forms B10.48 and B10.49 at paras **[210.69]** and **[210.70]**. Most of the forms of complete will in Part C have directions as to incidence: see eg C3.1 at para **[225.9]** ff and C11.1 at para **[233.13]** ff.

[214.72]

Partially exempt residue. The special rules for partially exempt estates are described in outline in Part A at para **[200.112]** ff. They give rise to a drafting problem where residue is given in fractional shares to different people, at least one of whom is an exempt beneficiary (most commonly the testator's spouse or a charity) and at least one of whom is not. Are the fractional shares to be calculated before deducting the tax attributable to the non-exempt shares so that the net benefit will not be in the proportions that the fractions prescribed in the will would suggest? Or are they fractional shares of the net benefit, and, if so, how is the inheritance tax charge to be calculated without throwing the burden of any of the tax on to exempt gifts (which is prohibited by the IHTA 1984, s 41 notwithstanding the terms of any disposition)? In *Re Benham's Will Trusts* [1995] STC 210 the shares prescribed by the will were held to relate to the net benefit, with grossing up of the non-exempt shares to achieve this result. In *Re Ratcliffe* [1999] STC 262, however, it was held that the shares were to be ascertained first and tax imposed on the non-exempt shares so ascertained; *Re Benham* was regarded as a decision on its own special facts and can in practice now be disregarded. To eliminate any possible doubt on the point a declaration such as Form B14.35 at para **[214.78]** may be used. This makes it clear that the solution adopted in *Re Ratcliffe* is to prevail – it may not produce quite the result the testator wants, but it is probably the most practical and workable solution.

[214.73]
Gifts subject to inheritance tax where there is business or agricultural relief. The rules effective for occasions of tax charge on or after 18 March 1986 for partially exempt estates where there is business or agricultural relief (see the IHTA 1984, s 39A, added by the Finance Act 1986, s 105; and the Preliminary Note to C11 at para **[233.1]** ff) present a drafting problem for gifts subject to inheritance tax which is best explained by an example. Suppose a testator makes by his will a specific gift of his house to his son, and leaves residue to be divided equally between a charity and his daughter. Suppose also that the gift of the house is made subject to the inheritance tax attributable to it, and that the residuary estate turns out to include property on which there is business relief. Under the IHTA 1984, s 39A the business relief will be apportioned rateably between the exempt and non-exempt parts of the estate in the process of determining the extent of the non-exempt part, and the house will be treated as having a value reduced by a rateable share of the business relief for this purpose. It seems to us that in these circumstances there could be doubt as to whether the tax attributable to the house which is to be borne by the son is the tax attributable to the value of the house as reduced by business relief under s 39A, or the tax attributable to its actual value. Form B14.36 (at para **[214.79]**) is an example of a declaration intended to deal with this point.

[214.74]
Subject to inheritance tax/free of inheritance tax specific gifts. Where some or all of residue is exempt, and there are any non-exempt specific gifts, the size of the non-exempt estate and thus the amount of tax payable on the testator's death will be much less if the non-exempt specific gifts bear their own inheritance tax. Inheritance tax free specific gifts are grossed up in the process of establishing the size of the chargeable estate: IHTA 1984, s 38(3). There is nothing unfair about this, because the net amount after inheritance tax received by the persons entitled to the non-exempt specific gifts is correspondingly greater where the inheritance tax on those gifts is paid out of residue rather than out of their gifts, and the amount of net residue received by the exempt beneficiary or beneficiaries is correspondingly less. However, the fact that specific gifts of UK free estate are, in the absence of express provisions to the contrary, inheritance tax free and grossed up under the partial exemption rules can get overlooked when the inheritance tax consequences of proposals for a will which includes specific gifts to non-exempt beneficiaries and residuary gifts to exempt beneficiaries (ie the testator's spouse/civil partner and/or charity) are being considered, or when

proposals for a deed of variation on these lines is being considered: see F3 at para **[241.12]**. For example, if the dispositions are calculated to use up the testator's nil rate band, and it is not intended that the non-exempt beneficiaries should receive more than they may receive without any inheritance tax being paid on the testator's death, the inheritance tax consequences of the gift to the non-exempt beneficiaries turning out to be over the inheritance tax threshold will be much less serious if the non-exempt gift is subject to inheritance tax.

[214.75]

Testamentary expenses. Where residue is wholly or partly exempt, and administration expenses such as legal fees are payable out of residue, it seems that the exempt residue used to pay them is still treated as exempt, so that in effect inheritance tax is not charged on the part of the estate used to pay such administration expenses as far as they are met out of exempt residue: see Part A, para **[200.116]**.

[214.76]

Form B14.33: General declaration making all inheritance tax and foreign death duties on free estate payable out of residue[1]

Except to the extent that provision to the contrary is made elsewhere in this will or any codicil hereto all inheritance tax [and foreign death duties] payable by reason of my death in respect of all property wherever situated which is disposed of by this will or any codicil hereto[2] (other than property which is disposed of in exercise of a special or general power of appointment or the statutory power to dispose of entailed property without becoming thereby comprised in my residuary estate[3]) shall be paid out of my residuary estate in exoneration of all specific gifts or general or pecuniary legacies (if any) and no inheritance tax on other property for which my personal representatives are liable shall be paid out of my residuary estate[4] [and the inheritance tax [and foreign death duties] payable out of my residuary estate shall be treated for all purposes (including abatement) as a testamentary expense[5]].

1 See paras **[214.55]–[214.71]**, in particular para **[214.71]**, sub-para (3). The main purpose of this form is to exonerate specific gifts of foreign property, and pecuniary legacies payable out of a residuary fund which contains foreign property or property which was comprised in a settlement immediately before the testator's death, from bearing any inheritance tax (or foreign death duties), except for specific gifts or pecuniary legacies expressly declared to be subject to tax or duties. See Forms B5.1 (at para **[205.58]**), B5.4 (at para **[205.61]**), B6.31 (at para **[206.40]**), B10.50 (at para **[210.71]**) and B14.36 (at para **[214.79]**) for specific gifts made subject to inheritance tax.

If this form is used any woodlands, works of art etc which are specifically given by the will should be given subject to the tax attributable thereto and payable by reason of the testator's death. This is a sound idea anyway (see para **[214.67]**) and also there is a slight risk that unless such property bears its own inheritance tax it could be argued that under this form inheritance tax 'payable by reason of my death' includes the tax payable after the death of the testator on a sale of the property or (in the case of works of art etc) a breach of undertakings where exemption or relief from the charge on death has been obtained under the IHTA 1984, s 30 (works of art etc) or s 125 (woodlands).

See also Forms B14.6 (at para **[214.15]**), B14.8 (at para **[214.17]**) and B14.17 (at para **[214.26]**). For an alternative approach see Form B14.3 (at para **[214.12]**).

2 This slightly elaborate formula is used instead of 'comprised in my estate' because of the special meaning 'estate' has in the context of inheritance tax, including as it does settled

property in which the testator had a beneficiary taxed interest in possession, any severable share of jointly tenanted property, and any property subject to a reservation at the testator's death of which he was the donor (see para **[214.60]**). This formula may make this clause unsuitable for a testator with a foreign domicile whose estate may be subject to compulsory portions.

3 These words are intended to exclude any property which was comprised in a settlement immediately before the testator's death which might be disposed of by the will, except for any such property which falls into residue. The latter exception is for the sake of drafting consistency with making pecuniary and general legacies free of inheritance tax. Property which was settled property immediately before the testator's death prima facie bears its own inheritance tax (see para **[214.60]**, sub-para (3)), and legacies prima facie bear their own tax to the extent that they are payable out of property which bears its own tax (see para **[214.64]**). Therefore, if tax-free legacies are payable out of a residuary estate which includes settled property it seems inconsistent for that property to be directed to bear its own inheritence tax.

For the statutory power to make a testamentary disposition of entailed property see the LPA 1925, s 176 (Part G, para **[244.55]**; see also Vol 1, para **[7.2]**).

4 The words 'And no inheritance tax ... residuary estate' are in our view unnecessary, but inclusion of them would eliminate the slight doubt about the effect of the IHTA 1984, s 211(1) which arises from the decision in *Re Dougal* [1981] STC 514: see para **[214.58]**. It would not be appropriate to include these words if there were provision in the will for payment out of residue of the inheritance tax on lifetime gifts or on property charged to inheritance tax on death but not disposed of by the will, such as in Forms B10.48 at para **[210.69]** and B10.49 at para **[210.70]**.

5 Any inheritance tax on property which is freed from bearing it by express direction in a will is a pecuniary legacy for the purposes of abatement (see **[214.65]**), while inheritance tax which falls within the IHTA 1984, s 211(1) (Part G, para **[246.100]**; see also paras **[214.55]**–**[214.65]**) is a testamentary expense which has priority over pecuniary legacies in the event of abatement. This proviso has the effect that the inheritance tax which is directed to be paid out of residue but which would otherwise not be so paid, and foreign death duties if that is desired, will have priority over ordinary pecuniary legacies if residue is insufficient to pay all debts administration expenses taxes and legacies, and the legacies have to abate. Whether to include this proviso is a matter for the testator's choice—whether he is more concerned about the donees of specific gifts of foreign or settled property receiving their gifts of tax or about the pecuniary legatees receiving maximum benefit.

[214.77]

Form B14.34: Declaration that inheritance tax and foreign death duties on pecuniary legacies and personal chattels shall be paid out of residue[1]

Any dispositions of any personal chattels (as defined in section 55(1)(x) of the Administration of Estates Act 1925[2]) or pecuniary or general legacies made or given by this will or any codicil hereto shall be free of any inheritance tax or foreign death duties payable by reason of my death and attributable thereto (which shall accordingly be payable out of my residuary estate) save in so far as any such dispositions or legacies are declared elsewhere in this will or any codicil hereto to be subject to inheritance tax or foreign death duties.

1 The purpose of this form is to prevent the pecuniary legacies being subject to any inheritance tax or foreign death duties in the event of their being paid out of a fund which includes property which bears its own inheritance tax and foreign death duties (see para **[214.60]**, sub-para (2), and to prevent specific gifts of personal chattels which are fortuitously outside the UK at the testator's death (see paras **[214.63]** and **[214.70]**, sub-para (2)) being subject to inheritance tax or foreign duties. If this form is used any specific gifts or dispositions made by the will of foreign property (other than chattels) or settled property will be subject to inheritance tax unless specifically directed to be free of it.

Any chattels which are works of art etc which are eligible for conditional exemption under the IHTA 1984, s 30 and are specifically given (including ones comprised in a gift of 'my personal chattels') should be given subject to inheritance tax for the reasons given at para **[214.67]** and in Form B14.33, n 1 at para **[214.76]**.

2 See Vol 1, para **[64.44]** and Part G, para **[246.67]**.

[214.78]

Form B14.35: Declaration concerning partially exempt residue – *Re Ratcliffe* direction[1]

The entitlement of the [charities and][2] persons interested in [my residuary estate[3]] shall be determined by dividing [my residuary estate[3]] into the fractional shares set out above without making any deduction or allowance for the inheritance tax payable by reason of my death and attributable to [my residuary estate[4]] and then reducing such shares as are not exempt from inheritance tax by the inheritance tax attributable thereto.

1 See para **[214.69]** for the purpose of this form.

2 These words should be included if, as is likely in a case where this clause is relevant, charities are among the exempt beneficiaries interested in the residuary estate. If there is a residuary gift in favour of the testator's spouse it is usually a gift of the whole of residue, and cases where residuary estate is divided between exempt and non-exempt beneficiaries are usually ones where the exempt beneficiaries are charities.

Further words may be needed if the residuary beneficiaries include a political party (a gift to which can also be exempt — see Part A, para **[200.87]**) or a non-charitable club or institution. In such circumstances a formula such as 'persons trusts and bodies of persons (corporate or unincorporated)' or 'societies trusts associations institutions and persons' could be used instead of 'charities and persons'.

3 It is assumed that the expression used here refers to the net residue after payment of debts, administration expenses, inheritance tax and legacies.

4 See the Preliminary Note to C11 at para **[233.1]** ff for the IHTA 1984, s 39A. See Form B5.1 at para **[205.58]** for a gift of business property bearing its own inheritance tax.

[214.79]

Form B14.36: Alternative declaration concerning fractional shares of partially exempt residue – *Re Benham* direction[1]

The entitlement of the persons societies trusts associations institutions and bodies of persons (corporate or unincorporated) ('the residuary beneficiaries') interested in [my residuary estate[2]] shall be determined by grossing up the shares of those who are not exempt from inheritance tax so that after making any deduction or allowance for the inheritance tax payable by reason of my death and attributable to [my residuary estate[2]] the residuary beneficiaries shall receive the fractional shares set out above so that net of inheritance tax the shares actually received by the residuary beneficiaries shall bear to one another the same proportions as the fractional shares set out above whether or not any of them is exempt from inheritance tax.

1 The purpose of this form is to allow a testator to provide for a *Benham (Re Benham's Will Trusts* [1995] STC 210) type of division of residue in preference to the *Re Ratcliffe* [1999] STC 262 type of division provided for in the previous form. The *Benham* division results in exempt and non-exempt residuary beneficiaries receiving residue net of inheritance tax in the same proportions as actually contemplated by the testator in any fractional division set out in the will. This is generally known as net division or net equality and results in the payment of more inheritance tax than the gross division contemplated by the previous form because, in order to achieve net equality the non-exempt beneficiaries' shares are artificially grossed up. See para **[214.69]**.

2 It is assumed that the expression used here refers to the net residue after payment of debts, administration expenses, inheritance tax and legacies. See also the Preliminary Note to C11

at para **[233.1]** ff for the IHTA 1984, s 39A. See Form B5.1 at para **[205.58]** for a gift of business property bearing its own inheritance tax.

[214.80]

Form B14.37: Alternative declaration concerning equal shares of partially exempt residue – *Re Benham* direction[1]

A – Widow or civil partner and child

My residuary estate[2] shall be held on trust to pay my debts and funeral and testamentary expenses thereout (other than the inheritance tax attributable to [*name of child*]'s share of my residuary estate) and subject thereto on trust for [*name of child*] and [my wife]/[civil partner] in such proportions that, after payment of the inheritance tax attributable to [*name of child*]'s share out of that share, [*name of child*] and [my wife]/[civil partner] are entitled to equal shares.

B – Charity and non-exempt individual

My residuary estate[2] shall be held on trust to pay my debts and funeral and testamentary expenses thereout (other than the inheritance tax attributable to [*Name of non-exempt beneficiary*]'s share of my residuary estate) and subject thereto on trust for [*Name of non-exempt beneficiary*] and [*Name of Charity*] in such proportions that, after payment of the inheritance tax attributable to [*Name of non-exempt beneficiary*]'s share out of that share, [*Name of non-exempt beneficiary*] and [*Name of Charity*] are entitled to equal shares.

1 See previous form n 1 and para **[214.69]**. For the origin of this form see *Foster's Inheritance Tax* at D2.39. The two versions of the form used here illustrate that the same difficulty is encountered between a spouse and a child as between a charity and an individual (other than the spouse).

2 It is assumed that the expression used here refers to the net residue after payment of debts, administration expenses, inheritance tax and legacies but the following words are intended to clarify the meaning. See also the Preliminary Note to C11 at para **[233.1]** ff for the IHTA 1984, s 39A. See Form B5.1 at para **[205.58]** for a gift of business property bearing its own inheritance tax.

[214.81]

Form B14.38: Specific gift subject to inheritance tax where the estate may turn out to be partially exempt and include business or agricultural property[1]

I give to [*name*] my [house known as 'Laburnums', Acacia Avenue, Tuliptree Park, Sevenoaks, Kent] subject to payment of the inheritance tax attributable thereto and payable by reason of my death and I declare that if part of my estate is exempt from inheritance tax and the value of the foregoing gift is treated as reduced by virtue of section 39A of the Inheritance Tax Act 1984 the tax attributable to the foregoing gift for the foregoing purposes shall be the tax attributable to the value of the said gift as so reduced.[2]

1 See para **[214.73]** for the purpose of this form, and the Preliminary Note to C11 at para **[233.1]** ff for the IHTA 1984, s 39A. See Form B5.1 at para **[205.58]** for a gift of business property bearing its own inheritance tax.

2 It would be possible to provide that the donee pays the tax attributable to the full value of the gift, but it seems to us that this could cause uncertainty as to whether, when it comes to calculating the extent of the chargeable part of the estate under the IHTA 1984, Pt II,

Ch III (ss 36–42), the value of the gift should in some way be treated as reduced by the tax it bears in excess of the tax attributable to the value the property is treated as having by s 39A.

[214.82]

Form B14.39: Declaration that free of inheritance tax provisions relate only to tax on the testator's death

I declare that where any gift is hereby given free of inheritance tax, such gift shall be free only of inheritance tax payable on or by reason of my death.[1]

1 This expressly excludes any possibility that words freeing gifts of inheritance tax might be construed as including inheritance tax on events subsequent to the testator's death, although it is unlikely that words such as 'free of inheritance tax' would be so construed. See para **[214.66]**.

B15 Absolute and simple contingent gifts

FORMS

B15.1 Residuary bequest to one person .... **[215.1]**
B15.2 Trusts of residue, as two persons jointly or the survivor of them shall appoint .... **[215.2]**
B15.3 Gift of residuary estate to three named persons .... **[215.3]**
B15.4 Gift of residue to named children making provision for death in testator's lifetime or after his death in the latter case without leaving issue .... **[215.4]**
B15.5 Clause disposing of residue in unequal shares, the interest of one of the beneficiaries being contingent, and with substitutional gifts to spouses and children and accruer provisions .... **[215.5]**
B15.6 Clause disposing of residue in percentage shares .... **[215.6]**
B15.7 Residuary gift without administration trusts .... **[215.7]**
B15.8 Absolute residuary gift to three children of the testator: land to be sold .... **[215.8]**

Cross Reference

See also Form B19.16 at para **[219.29]**

[215.1]

Form B15.1: Residuary bequest to one person[1]

Subject to the payment of my debts funeral and testamentary expenses, inheritance tax legacies and annuities I devise and bequeath all my real and personal estate whatsoever and wheresoever of which I have any power of disposition by will whatsoever not hereby or by any codicil hereto specifically disposed of unto [*name*] absolutely.

1 Where there is an absolute gift to one person there is little point in interposing elaborate administration trusts. If the personal representatives need to realise assets for the payment of debt, they have power to do so under the AEA 1925, s 39 (Part G, para **[246.63]**) and the general law.

[215.2]

Form B15.2: Trusts of residue, as two persons jointly or the survivor of them shall appoint

I direct my trustees to stand possessed of the investments from time to time representing my residuary estate (hereinafter called the trust fund) and of the income thereof upon the following trusts. In trust for such persons and purposes and generally in such manner as —— and —— shall at any time or times by deed revocable or irrevocable jointly appoint and in default of and subject to any such appointment as the survivor of them shall [in manner aforesaid or] by will or codicil appoint.[1]

1 This form of disposition common in the case of a resettlement may be useful where the property is to go to an only son and his wife/civil partner or only daughter and her husband/civil partner who can then either take absolutely or settle it upon their children according to their own desires or the altered circumstances which may exist some years after the testator's death.

[215.3]

Form B15.3: Gift of residuary estate to three named persons[1]

My trustees shall hold my residuary estate in trust for A B and C as tenants in common in equal shares. In the event of the death of the said A B or C in my lifetime leaving issue[2] him or her surviving his or her share shall be held in trust for such issue living at my death and attaining the age of [eighteen] [twenty-one] years or marrying[3] under that age in equal shares per stirpes but so that no issue shall take whose parent is alive at my death and so capable of taking. In the event of any of the said A B or C dying in my lifetime leaving no issue living at my death [or then en ventre and born afterwards] or leaving such issue all of whom die under the age of [eighteen] [twenty-one] and unmarried[3] the share of anyone so dying shall be held for the other persons entitled to my residuary estate as if the one or more so dying had been originally excluded from taking a share therein.

1 This form can be adapted for any number of named persons.

2 Illegitimate issue will prima facie be included and so should be subject to express exclusion if they are not to form part of the class. See Part A, para **[200.28]**.

3 In order to adapt the form to take account of civil partnerships formed pursuant to CPA 2004, substitute 'marrying or forming a civil partnership' for 'marrying' and 'unmarried or not in a civil partnership' for 'unmarried'.

[215.4]

Form B15.4: Gift of residue to named children making provision for death in testator's lifetime or after his death in the latter case without leaving issue[1]

My trustees shall hold my residuary estate in trust for my three children [*names*] as tenants in common in equal shares. In the event of any of my said children dying in my lifetime leaving issue[2] him or her surviving his or her share shall be held in trust for such issue living or en ventre at my death and attaining the age of [eighteen] [twenty-one] years or marrying[3] under that age as tenants in common in equal shares per stirpes. In the event of any of my said children dying in my lifetime without leaving any such issue as aforesaid the share of such child of mine so dying shall be held for the other persons entitled to my residuary estate as if the one or more so dying had for all the purposes of this clause been originally excluded from taking a share therein. In the event of [any of my said children dying after my death leaving no issue him or her surviving *or*[4]] none of the issue living or en ventre at my death of a child of mine who has predeceased me attaining a vested interest under the foregoing trust the share of such child of mine and any share which may accrue thereto by virtue of the provisions of this clause shall be held by my trustees as an accretion to the other shares (and equally if more than one) the trusts whereof shall not at the date of such accruer have failed or determined and upon the trusts powers and provisions applicable thereto herein contained or such of them as at the date of such accruer shall be capable of taking effect.

1 This clause makes a rather complicated provision and the complication can be avoided by the testator making a new will or codicil on the death of any child in his lifetime. Clauses of this nature are, however, often preferable because they are some protection against a testator neglecting to make new provisions on an alteration in the circumstances of his family.

2 Prima facie, illegitimate issue will be included: see Part A, para **[200.28]**.
3 In order to adapt the form to take account of civil partnerships formed pursuant to CPA 2004, substitute 'marrying or forming a civil partnership' for 'marrying'.
4 If the part in square brackets is included, each child of the testator will have a vested interest subject to divestment on dying without issue, and distribution could be long postponed. We do not recommend its inclusion unless a power of advancement exerciseable over the whole of a presumptive share (see e g Form B18.20 at para **[218.104]**) is included as well.

[215.5]

Form B15.5: Clause disposing of residue in unequal shares, the interest of one of the beneficiaries being contingent, and with substitutional gifts to spouses and children and accruer provisions[1]

My trustees shall hold my residuary estate[2] upon trust to divide it or to treat it as being divided into fifteen shares of equal value and shall hold them upon the following trusts and subject to the following provisions:

(a) My trustees shall hold such shares upon trust absolutely:
(i) As to three of them for [*donee*].
(ii) As to four of them for [*donee*].
(iii) As to one of them for such of my friends [*donees*] as survive me and if more than one in equal shares.
(iv) As to one of them for [*donee*] but if he predeceases me then for his wife [*donee*][3].
(v) As to two of them for [*donee*].
(vi) As to four of them for [*donee*] contingently upon his reaching the age of [twenty-one] [eighteen] or marrying[3] under that age.

(b) Provided that if any of the persons named in paragraphs (i) (ii) and (v) or if both of those named in paragraph (iv) of subclause (a) of this clause predecease me leaving a child or children living at my death who reach the age of [eighteen] [twenty-one] or marry[3] under that age then such child or children shall take absolutely and if more than one equally between them the share or shares of my residuary estate which his her or their parent would have taken if such parent had survived me.[4]

(c) Provided also that if at any time the trusts declared by subclause (a) read in conjunction with subclause (b) of this clause in respect of any share or shares of my residuary estate lapse or fail then from the date of such lapse or failure such share or shares (and any further share or shares or part thereof which may have accrued thereto by virtue of this provision) shall accrue to the other share or shares (and equally if more than one [or and if more than one in the proportions which they bear to each other][5]) the trusts of which have not at that date lapsed or failed and be held upon the trusts and with and subject to the powers and provisions from time to time affecting such other share or shares.

1 Testators often wish their estates to be divided into unequal shares, each affected by a different set of trusts. This form is designed to illustrate some of the many possible variations and the way in which they may be fitted together. To avoid disappointment or partial intestacy care should be taken to ensure that the sum of the fractional shares is

singular. For problems, which can arise where residue is divided into fractional shares and some of the beneficiaries are exempt from inheritance tax see Part A, paras **[200.112]**–**[200.119]** and Form B14.35 at para **[214.78]**.

2 Or substitute 'the trust fund' or some similar expression if this has already been defined and use the same expression throughout the clause.

3 In order to adapt the form to take account of civil partnerships formed pursuant to CPA 2004, substitute 'wife or civil partner' for 'wife' in sub-clause (a)(iv), 'marrying or forming a civil partnership' for 'marrying' in sub-clause (a)(vi) and 'marry or form a civil partnership' for 'marry' in sub-clause (b).

4 The settled property subject to the gift over falls within the inheritance tax charging regime for relevant property (see para **[200.92]**).

5 If the words 'and equally if more than one' are used then, although the property was originally divided into unequal shares, any share of which the trusts fail will be divided *equally* amongst the remaining shares. This is the simplest method to adopt. But if the testator wishes to perpetuate the original inequality, so that a share of which the trusts fail is divided amongst the remaining shares in the original *unequal* proportions, the words in square brackets should be substituted.

[215.6]

Form B15.6: Clause disposing of residue in percentage shares[1]

My trustees shall hold my residuary estate[2] upon trust to hold the same upon the following trusts and subject to the following provisions:

(a)

(i) As to forty per cent (40%) thereof for [*donee*].
(ii) As to fifteen per cent (15%) thereof for [*donee*].
(iii) As to fifteen per cent (15%) thereof for [*donee*].
(iv) As to ten per cent (10%) thereof for [*donee*].
(v) etc.

[(b) Provided that if any of the persons named in paragraphs (i) (ii) and (iv) or if both of those named in paragraph (iii) of subclause (a) of this clause predecease me leaving a child or children living at my death who reach the age of [eighteen] [twenty-one] or marry[3] under that age then such child or children shall take absolutely and if more than one equally between them the share or shares of my residuary estate which his her or their parent would have taken if such parent had survived me.] [4]

(c) Provided also that if at any time the trusts declared by subclause (a) read in conjunction with subclause (b) of this clause in respect of any share or shares of my residuary estate lapse or fail then from the date of such lapse or failure such share or shares (and any further share or shares or part thereof which may have accrued thereto by virtue of this provision) shall accrue to the other share or shares (and equally if more than one [*or* and if more than one in the proportions which they bear to each other][5]) the trusts of which have not at that date lapsed or failed and be held upon the trusts and with and subject to the powers and provisions from time to time affecting such other share or shares.] [4]

1 To avoid disappointment or partial intestacy, care should be taken to ensure that the percentage shares add up to 100%. For problems which can arise where residue is divided into shares and some of the beneficiaries are exempt from inheritance tax see Part A, paras **[200.112]**–**[200.119]** and Form B14.35 at para **[214.78]**.

2 Or substitute 'the trust fund' or some similar expression if this has already been defined and use the same expression throughout the clause.

3 In order to adapt the form to take account of civil partnerships formed pursuant to CPA 2004, substitute 'marry or form a civil partnership' for 'marry' in sub-clause (b).

4 These provisions are similar to those included at para **[215.5]** but others could easily be devised in their place. The settled property subject to the gift over falls within the inheritance tax charging regime for relevant property (see para **[200.92]**).

5 If the words 'and equally if more than one' are used, then although the property was originally divided into unequal shares, any share of which the trusts fail will be divided *equally* amongst the remaining shares. This is the simplest method to adopt. But if the testator wishes to perpetuate the original inequality, so that a share of which the trusts fail is divided amongst the remaining shares in the original *unequal* proportions, the words in square brackets should be substituted. See para **[215.5]**, n 3.

[215.7]

Form B15.7: Residuary gift without administration trusts[1]

(1) I give all the rest of my property both real and personal whatsoever and wheresoever situate to all my children[2] in equal shares if more than one.

(2) My executors may in extension of the power of appropriation conferred on personal representatives by section 41 of the Administration of Estates Act 1925, at any time or times with the consent in writing only of all other persons for the time being entitled to share in my estate who are of full age and capacity appropriate any part of my residuary estate in its then actual condition or state of investment in or towards satisfaction of the share of any infant beneficiary in my residuary estate.[3]

[(3) If at the expiration of three months after the submission of any proposal for appropriation by my executor or such further period as my executor in his absolute discretion shall allow the persons entitled thereto or whose consent is required as aforesaid have not consented in writing to such appropriation of any article or other part of my estate under the preceding clauses hereof such article or part of my estate shall be sold by my executor (with power in his absolute discretion to postpone such sale for as long as he shall think fit) and the net proceeds of sale and the net income until sale shall be divided amongst my said children.][4]

[(4) Provided that if any child of mine shall die in my lifetime leaving issue[2] living at my death such issue if and when they attain the age of [eighteen] [twenty-one] years or marry[5] under that age shall take by substitution and if more than one in equal shares per stirpes the share of my estate which such deceased child of mine would have taken if he or she had survived me but so that no issue shall take whose parent is alive at my death and so capable of taking.] [6]

1 This form of will avoids the conventional administration trusts, which are no longer as necessary as formerly because of the provisions of the TLATA 1996. See n 3 below. This form is most suitable where all the gifts are immediate and of the simple nature here shown. See further para **[215.1]**, n 1.

2 References to children and issue in this clause will prima facie include illegitimate and legitimated children and issue: see Part A, para **[200.28]**.

3 This provision is designed for use where all the gifts under the will are immediate and the desire is to distribute the estate as far as possible at the earliest date. As soon as the estate is cleared the trustees (which by the usual express definition will include the executors, so that there is no question of the power of appropriation being given both to the executors and to the trustees and it is not necessary to show that the executors have become trustees before they are entitled to exercise this power) can proceed to distribution, except in the case of the shares of minors which must be held pending the attainment of full age. See Part G, para **[246.65]** for s 41 of the AEA 1925.

4 See n 3 above. This in fact optional provision is only a statement of the duties of the executors but expressly stated in terms which may no doubt help to avoid disputes among the beneficiaries.

5 In order to adapt the form to take account of civil partnerships formed pursuant to CPA 2004, substitute 'marry or form a civil partnership' for 'marry' in sub-clause (4).

6 This provision is included for clarity and because of the option of providing that issue of children who predecease the testator are to take other than at the age of 18 years, but the statutory exception from lapse contained in s 33 of the WA 1837 renders the provision otherwise unnecessary. See Part G, para **[244.36]** for s 33 of the WA 1837 (as substituted by the AJA 1982, ss 19 and 73(6).

[215.8]

Form B15.8: Absolute residuary gift to three children of the testator: land to be sold

Note. This form is an attempt to make as effective as possible within the constraints of the Trusts of Land and Appointment of Trustees Act 1996 (TLATA 1996) a residuary trust under which the trustees are to sell any land comprised in residue and divide the proceeds: see Part A, paras **[200.57]**–**[200.59]** for the problems which arise under the TLATA 1996 for making sure that a sale takes place. As mentioned there, the key question is what happens should the majority by value want to retain the property, but a minority want a sale so that they can have their share in cash. The main matters in this form designed to maximise the chances that there will be a sale are that there is a trust for sale; the provision for having regard to majority wishes in the TLATA 1996, s 11 is excluded; and provisions which might be thought to show that a long-term trust administration is contemplated are tied specifically to the substitution clause. There is also an express exclusion of occupation by beneficiaries as a purpose of the trust to minimise the risk that a beneficiary who was in occupation of any property comprised in residue could claim that he had a right of occupation (compare *Barclay v Barclay* [1970] 2 QB 677 and see now the statutory right of occupation discussed at para **[208.5]** ff). It is not clear to what extent it makes any difference to have a trust for sale in this context. It may well be that the court, on an application for an order for sale under the TLATA 1996, s 14 would make the same decision on the basis of the same factors (such as the beneficial trusts and the lack of a continuing trust purpose) whether there was a trust for sale or a power of sale. However, the presence of a trust for sale may make sale more imperative, and also may help to exclude any right of occupation (see *Barclay v Barclay* [1970] 2 QB 677 at 684C–E).

FORM

I give all my property not hereby or by any codicil hereto otherwise effectively disposed of [(including any entailed or other property over which I shall have at my death a general power of disposition by will)][1] to my trustees upon trust as follows—

(a) my trustees shall hold the same upon trust to sell the same or such part thereof as shall not consist of money with power to postpone such sale;

(b) my trustees shall pay my funeral and testamentary expenses my debts and any legacies given by this will or any codicil hereto out of the proceeds of any such sale and any ready money comprised in such property;

(c) subject as aforesaid my trustees shall hold such moneys and any of my said property for the time being unsold and any other assets for the time being representing the foregoing (hereinafter called 'my residuary estate') upon trust for such of my three children AB CD and EF as shall survive me if more than one in equal shares absolutely;

(d) all income of my residuary estate shall be treated as accruing on the date on which it becomes payable and there shall be no statutory apportionment of it to any other time or period;[2]

(e) if any of my said children has already died or shall die before me leaving issue living at or after my death who shall satisfy the Vesting Condition (as hereinafter defined) then such issue shall take if more than one equally between them per stirpes the share of my residuary estate which such child of mine would have taken if he or she had survived me but so that no issue shall take whose parent is living at or after my death and satisfies the Vesting Condition;

(f) for the purposes of the last foregoing subclause the Vesting Condition is attaining the age of [25] years before my death or before or at the expiry of the period of 80 years from the date of my death or being living but under the age of [25] years at the expiry of such period of 80 years from the date of my death which shall be the perpetuity period applicable to the foregoing disposition of my residuary estate;

(g) if any substitutional trusts shall have effect under the foregoing subclauses in relation to any part or parts of my residuary estate:

  (i) none of the equitable rules of apportionment between capital and income shall apply to such part or parts of residuary estate;

  (ii) section 31 of the Trustee Act 1925 (accumulation and maintenance trusts of income) shall apply to the income of such part or parts;

  (iii) section 32 of the Trustee Act 1925 (payment or application of capital) shall apply to such part or parts as if the words 'one-half of' were omitted from proviso (a) to subsection (1) of the said s 32;

  (iv) my trustees shall have power to appropriate assets in their current state of investment to any share or shares of my residuary estate (whether the share or shares of any substituted beneficiaries or of any of my said children) without any consents being required to such appropriation;

(h) section 11(1)(b) of the Trusts of Land and Appointment of Trustees Act 1996 (giving effect to beneficiaries' wishes) shall not apply to the exercise by my trustees of any of their functions relating to any land comprised in my residuary estate unless all my children or remoter issue who are for the time being interested under the foregoing trust and are of full age are unanimous as to their wishes and in particular I intend that after the expiry of one year from my death my trustees shall sell any land so comprised if requested to do so in writing by any one or more of my said children or remoter issue who are interested as aforesaid and of full age;[3]

(i) it is not my intention that any land comprised in my estate at any time should be made available for the occupation of any beneficiaries under the foregoing trusts;[4]

(j) my trustees shall have all the powers of a sole beneficial owner to invest trust moneys and change investments comprised in my residuary estate.

1 Subject to any express contrary intention, property subject to a general power will be carried by a residuary gift under the WA 1837, s 27 (Part G, para **[244.29]**), but in the case of entailed property the will must refer to the property, or the instrument under which it was acquired, or entailed property generally for the statutory power of disposition to be exercised: LPA 1925, s 176(1) (Part G, para **[244.55]**). Although no new entails can be created on or after 1 January 1997 (see Part A, para **[200.53]**), entails created before that date can continue to exist and, if they do, the statutory power of disposition of them by will continues to be available.

2 For exclusion of statutory apportionment of income over time see paras **[214.48]**–**[214.52]**. This clause has a function even if the substitution clause does not take effect in preventing apportionment as between before and after the testator's death.

3 For the TLATA 1996, s 11 see Part G, para **[246.114]** and B20 at para **[220.58]**. It does not apply insofar as provision that it does not apply is made by the disposition (s 11(2)(a)), and so it is thought that partial exclusion of it in this way is permitted.

4 For the statutory right of occupation see para **[208.5]** ff and for drafting aspects see para **[208.18]**.

B16 Life interests

Preliminary Note .... **[216.1]**

FORMS

B16.1 Statutory protective trusts, varied by allowing accumulation for a period of years after a forfeiture has occurred .... **[216.8]**

B16.2 Protective income trusts for woman for life .... **[216.9]**

B16.3 Determinable life interest .... **[216.10]**

B16.4 Life or widowhood interest to wife .... **[216.11]**

B16.5 Life interest to wife reducible on remarriage .... **[216.12]**

B16.6 Trust for wife during widowhood subject to an obligation to maintain children .... **[216.13]**

B16.7 Same where no legal obligation imposed .... **[216.14]**

B16.8 Gift of income of residuary estate to a reputed wife as long as she is unmarried .... **[216.15]**

B16.9 Trust of income for several persons for life giving a general testamentary power of disposition to the survivor .... **[216.16]**

B16.10 Trust for wife for life and then to children in equal shares1 .... **[216.17]**

B16.11 Trust for wife for life and then to children in equal shares by incorporation of Statutory Will Forms 1925, Form 10 .... **[216.18]**

B16.12 Trust for wife for life and then to unmarried daughters for life .... **[216.19]**

B16.13 Trust for wife for life and then to children as she shall appoint, with hotchpot provision .... **[216.20]**

B16.14 Trust for wife for life and then to issue upon such trusts as she shall appoint .... **[216.21]**

B16.15 Trust for wife during widowhood, then to son for life with remainder to his children .... **[216.22]**

B16.16 Trust for wife for life and then to children for life with substitution of their issue .... **[216.23]**

B16.17 Trust for wife for life and then to children as she shall appoint incorporating Statutory Will Forms 1925, Form 9 .... **[216.24]**

B16.18 Clause directing trustees to resort to the capital of residue in order to make up income to a minimum amount .... **[216.25]**

B16.19 Clause empowering trustees to resort to capital .... **[216.26]**

B16.20 Clause empowering trustees to lend capital money to make up income of a share of residue to a stated amount .... **[216.27]**

B16.21 Gift of residue to children incorporating Statutory Will Forms 1925, Form 7, with modification .... **[216.28]**

B16.22 Gift of residue incorporating intestacy provisions .... **[216.29]**

B16.23 Settlement of child's share of residuary estate .... **[216.30]**

B16.24 Provision directing payment of capital to a female life tenant having no likelihood of children, where she has herself a general power of appointment in default of children .... **[216.31]**

SETTLED LEGACIES

FORMS

B16.25 Settled legacy—concise form .... **[216.32]**

B16.26 Settled legacy—full form .... **[216.33]**

ANCILLARY PROVISIONS

FORMS

B16.27 Trust for accumulation of income .... **[216.34]**

B16.28 Payment of income to banker .... **[216.35]**

B16.29 Clause as to annual sums payable under an insurance policy .... **[216.36]**
B16.30 No apportionment on death of life tenant .... **[216.37]**

PRELIMINARY NOTE

[216.1]

Using life interests. Although a testator's priority may be to ensure that following his death his spouse or civil partner has adequate financial resources, he may also wish to ensure that so much of his property as is not needed by his spouse or civil partner passes to his children and grandchildren, or perhaps other persons. This desire can often be best met by the conferral of a life interest in residue upon a spouse or civil partner, with remainder trusts for children, more remote issue or other persons. The conferral of a life interest on a spouse or civil partner may also have considerable IHT advantages. The benefit of the spouse or civil partner exemption can be claimed on the testator's death in respect of the property in which his spouse or civil partner has a life interest if that life interest is an immediate post-death interest, see para **[216.2]**, and Part A, paras **[200.99]**–**[200.101]**. On the death of the surviving spouse or civil partner, to the extent that the testator had not fully utilised his nil-rate band allowance, a nil-rate band carry forward allowance will be available on and from 9 October 2007 (assuming the same becomes law) in addition to the surviving spouse's or civil partner's own nil-rate band allowance, (see para **[200.75]** above), so particularly if there is not much else which falls into the charge to IHT other than the property in which her life interest subsists, the property may devolve with little or even no tax being payable (depending on its value). Alternatively, if the surviving spouse or civil partner surrenders her life interest in part or parts of the property during her lifetime in favour of the remainder trusts she will be deemed to make transfers of value which may be potentially exempt from IHT if the remainder gift is to persons absolutely, so that if she survives by seven years no tax is payable. Thus, it is possible that a testator's property may pass to his issue with no IHT being payable.

[216.2]

Immediate post-death interests. An interest in possession is an immediate post-death interest if four conditions are met:

(a) Condition 1 is that the interest in possession arises under a settlement effected by will or under the law relating to intestacy;
(b) Condition 2 is that the person became beneficially entitled to the interest on the death of the testator or intestate;
(c) Condition 3 is that IHTA 1984, s 71A (trust for bereaved minors, see para **[200.108]** above) does not apply to the property in which the interest subsists, and the interest is not a disabled person's interest (see para **[200.99]**); and
(d) Condition 4 is that Condition 3 has been satisfied at all times since the person became beneficially entitled to the interest in possession.

Therefore, where a testator leaves property by his will upon trust immediately for another person for their life, or for a shorter period, that person's interest in possession should be an immediate post-death interest (unless it is a disabled person's interest or arises under a trust for a bereaved minor). If the gift is subject to a survivorship condition, provided the condition is within IHTA 1982, s 92, see paras **[219.6]–[219.7]**), then on satisfaction of that condition the gift should be treated for IHT purposes as having had effect from the date of death so that Condition 2 should be satisfied. Further, where the interest in possession is in residue, IHTA 1984, s 91 has the effect that the interest in possession will be treated as arising on death even if residue is not then ascertained, so again Condition 2 should be satisfied.

An important consequence of the beneficiary of an immediate post-death interest being treated as beneficially entitled to the property in which the immediate post-death interest subsists under IHTA 1984, s 49(1) is that exemption from IHT should be available under IHTA 1984, s 18 on the testator's death to the extent of the property in his estate which becomes subject to an immediate post-death interest for his or her surviving spouse or civil partner. So the conferral of an immediate post-death interest on or after 22 March 2006 has the same consequences as the conferral of any interest in possession before 22 March 2006, although on and after 22 March 2006 the consequences of the termination of an immediate post-death interest may be very different. In the first place, the termination of an immediate post-death interest will generally be a chargeable transfer, unless it results in another person acquiring an absolute interest, or an interest in possession which has the result that its holder is treated as beneficially entitled to the underlying settled property under IHTA 1984, s 49(1) (such as a disabled person's interest), or causes the settled property to become subject to a trust for a bereaved minor (see para **[200.108]** above). In these cases, the termination may be a potentially exempt transfer. In the second place, the termination of an immediate post-death interest on or after 22 March 2006 will be deemed to be a gift of the underlying settled property for the purposes of FA 1986, s 102, so that unless the beneficiary of the immediate post-death interest is excluded altogether from benefit, the gift with reservation rules could apply: see FA 1986, s 102ZA and para **[200.76]** above.

To the extent that by taking advantage of the spouse or civil partner exemption by conferring a life interest on his spouse or civil partner, a testator does not fully utilise his nil-rate band allowance, a nil-rate band carry forward allowance will be available on and from 9 October 2007 (assuming the same becomes law) to the spouse or civil partner in addition to their own nil-rate band allowance. See para **[200.75]** above. So a testator will not waste his nil-rate allowance by conferring a life interest on his spouse or civil partner since the nil-rate allowance allowable on the death of the spouse or civil partner will be correspondingly increased. Indeed, if the spouse or civil partner's life interest terminates wholly or partly by way of potentially exempt transfer in favour, say, of the testator's children, and she survives seven years, no tax will be payable on the lifetime transfer of the testator's property to the next generation, and the nil-rate band carry forward allowance will still be available on the death of the spouse or civil partner.

It may still be good tax-planning therefore in an appropriate case (eg where the testator is satisfied that his surviving spouse or civil partner will be well provided for), to give trustees overriding powers to terminate a spouse's (or civil partner's) interest in possession without her participation or consent, and to appoint new trusts. Although any such termination may be a chargeable transfer, and a gift for the purposes of the IHT gift with reservation rules, it is thought that the beneficiary of the terminated interest in possession cannot be treated as a settlor for income tax purposes (as is the case following a surrender, see *IRC v Buchannan* [1957] 2 All ER 400) so that the income tax settlement provisions taxing income on a settlor who is not wholly excluded from that income (ITTOIA 2005, s 624), or which is paid to or for the benefit of her infant, unmarried children (ITTOIA, s 629) cannot apply.

An important tax-planning role for immediate post-death interests in relation to deaths on or after 22 March 2006 will not just be to secure the spouse or civil partner exemption from IHT where the beneficiary is the spouse or civil partner of the testator, but also to settle property upon trust but outside of the IHT charging regime for relevant property (see para **[218.8]** ff above). In particular, where a testator wishes to provide for children who are either not his own, or who are but he is unhappy about their taking absolute interests at 18 or 25 (as under a trust for bereaved minors within IHTA 1984, s 71A (see para **[200.108]** above), or an age 18-to-25 trust within IHTA 1984, s 71D (see para **[200.109]** above)), he might give them immediate post-death interests. The trustees could have powers to pay or apply capital to them or for their benefit and provision could be made for capital to vest absolutely at whatever age the testator considered appropriate, eg 40. The property subject to the immediate post-death interest would not be relevant property, so there would be no exit or periodic charges, nor any IHT implications when the beneficiary of the immediate post-death interest became absolutely entitled to capital. While the immediate post-death interest beneficiary was an infant, income could be applied for his maintenance or other benefit and any not so applied could be accumulated, but when he attained 18 he would be entitled to those accumulations as of right (or if he died under 18, his estate would be entitled to those accumulations) and henceforth would be entitled to the income as it arose. The underlying trust property would be treated throughout as comprised in the child's estate for IHT purposes, so would be taxable as such on his or her death, but this may be considered an acceptable risk.

[216.3]

Life interests which are not immediate post-death interests. A life interest or other interest in possession which arises under a will after an immediate post-death interest, or otherwise than on the death of the testator cannot be an immediate post-death interest. So unless it is a disabled person's interest (see para **[200.99]** above), or arose before 22 March 2006 or in succession to a pre-22 March 2006 interest in possession so that it is a transitional serial interest (see para **[200.100]**), it will not be the type of interest in possession which results in the life tenant being treated as beneficially entitled to the underlying settled property under IHTA 1984, s 49(1). Instead the underlying settled property will fall within the IHT charging regime for relevant property (see para **[218.8]** ff).

[216.4]
Perpetuities. When drafting the trusts which are to take effect following a life interest, care must be taken that they do not infringe the rule against perpetuities. The rule, simply stated, is that every future interest in property must vest in interest (not necessarily in possession) within a perpetuity period allowed by law. The statutory perpetuity period is 80 years, and if this period (or a lesser period) is chosen by a will draftsman, it must be expressly stated to be the perpetuity period in the will: see the Perpetuities and Accumulations Act 1964 (PAA 1964), s 1 (Part G, para **[246.74]**). The common law perpetuity period is for a life or lives in being plus 21 years. The measuring life or lives may be, or may include, lives which have no connection with the trusts created, for example, those descendants of George V living at the testator's death, but then they must be expressly specified in the will as measuring lives. However, the more common and often more appropriate measuring lives are of those persons connected with the trusts. In this case it is not always necessary to specify expressly that those persons are the measuring lives. For example, a gift to such of the testator's grandchildren who attain the age of 21 and survive the testator's widow does not infringe the rule against perpetuities because the grandchildren's interests must necessarily vest within 21 years of the death of the last survivor of the testator's widow and children.

[216.5]
Wait and see rule. Although it is better if all interests created by will are certain to, or are expressly stated to, vest within the chosen perpetuity period (whether it be the statutory or common law period), since 1964 the 'wait and see' rule has meant that if it is not certain when a disposition takes effect that all of the interests will vest within a perpetuity period (before 1964 this lack of certainty was fatal to the interests which might not necessarily vest) then one can wait and see if the interest does in fact vest within an available perpetuity period (taking into account, if relevant, the lives specified in the PAA 1964, s 3(5) (Part G, para **[246.76]**). In none of the forms which follow has it been necessary to specify a perpetuity period because all of the interests must vest within the common law perpetuity period of a life or lives in being (of persons connected with the trusts), plus 21 years.

For a fuller account of perpetuities, see Vol 1, para **[94.1]** ff.

[216.6]
Vesting. Where, as is commonly the case, a testator wishes to give a life interest to his spouse, with remainder to his children, the question arises as to whether the remainder gift should be contingent only on the children's surviving the testator so that the gift vests in interest absolutely on the testator's death and is not liable to divestment, or whether it should also be contingent on surviving the spouse (or liable to be divested on not surviving the spouse). In favour of the extra contingency (or the divestment) is the fact that by use of substitutional gifts or gifts over in the event of the contingency not being fulfilled (or the divestment), the destination of the testator's property can be determined by the testator's will instead of passing under the child's will or intestacy to persons whom the testator might not wish to benefit. The most common substitutional gift is for the children or issue of a

child who does not satisfy all the conditions of the gift. They usually take the share which that child would have taken if he had satisfied all of the conditions. This is often a preferable course to the trust property being divided between those children who do satisfy the conditions. If a substitution clause or gift over is incorporated in a will, care should be taken to ensure that it will take effect in whatever circumstances the primary gift fails.

[216.7]

However, the more contingencies or possibilities of divestment are introduced, the more difficult it is for the beneficiaries to terminate or rearrange the trusts by agreement, which may often be desirable in changing personal circumstances and a changing fiscal climate, and if children's interests remain contingent, it is more difficult for them to sell or raise a loan on their interests before they fall into possession. These disadvantages can to some extent be overcome if the trustees are given overriding powers to pay or advance capital or even alter the trusts.

[216.8]

Form B16.1: Statutory protective trusts, varied by allowing accumulation for a period of years after a forfeiture has occurred[1]

Note. It is possible for a life interest subject to the statutory protective trusts to be an immediate post-death interest (see IHTA 1984, s 88(4)(b)(i) and para **[200.104]** above), although it is unlikely that HMRC would accept that where the protective trusts are varied as in this Form, the relief of IHTA 1984, s 88 will apply. Nevertheless, for deaths on or after 22 March 2006 and pending any forfeiture, the life interest in this Form should be an immediate post-death interest if it takes effect immediately on the testator's death (or is subject only to a survivorship condition permitted by IHTA 1984, s 92: see paras **[219.6]**–**[219.7]**), and is not, for example, postponed to another interest (see para **[216.2]** above). If it is not afforded relief under IHTA 1984, s 88 its termination may occasion an IHT charge under IHTA 1984, s 52(1) which would be immediately chargeable, and since the termination of an immediate post-death interest on or after 22 March 2006 will be deemed to be a gift of the underlying settled property for the purposes of FA 1986, s 102, and since the life tenant may continue to benefit under the protective trusts, the gift with reservation rules could apply: see FA 1986, s 102ZA and para **[200.76]** above. Accordingly, a testator wishing to establish a protective life interest which is an immediate post-death interest is probably best advised to rely on statutory protective trusts without any amendment so that relief under IHTA 1984, s 88 will apply. However, where the protected life interest would not qualify as an immediate post-death interest (eg. because it takes effect on the termination of an immediate post-death interest) and the underlying settled property would be within the IHT charging regime anyway, this Form would not have these disadvantageous IHT consequences.

Form

I declare that the income hereinbefore directed to be held upon trust for or to be paid to the said [*name*] for life shall not vest absolutely in the said [*name*] but shall be held by my trustees [*or* I declare that the annuity hereinbefore bequeathed to the said [*name*] shall not vest in the said [*name*] absolutely but shall be received and held by my trustees] upon the statutory protective trusts (subject to the variations hereinafter mentioned) for the benefit of the said [*name*] for the period of his [*her*] life.

Provided however that in each year prior to the expiration of twenty-one years from my death during which my trustees under the said statutory trusts have a discretion as to the application of the said income [annuity] my trustees shall from time to time determine in their uncontrolled discretion how much (if any part at all) of the income of the current year they will apply under the statutory trusts and the said trusts shall apply to the amount so determined and my trustees shall accumulate the balance of the said income [annuity] in the way of compound interest by investing the same and the resulting income thereof[2] but with power for my trustees in their uncontrolled discretion to determine from time to time during the said period of twenty-one years that any part of the past accumulations shall be income of the current year and be applicable accordingly at the discretion of my trustees, and I declare that after the death of the said [*name*] the said accumulations or the balance thereof shall be an accretion to the capital of the property from which such accumulations arose and be one fund with such capital for all purposes and shall be held by my trustees upon trust accordingly [*in the case of an annuity*, fall into the capital of my residuary estate and be distributed accordingly].[3]

1 See the TA 1925, s 33 (Part G, para **[246.31]**), which provides a statutory method of effecting a 'protected life interest'. The section contemplates that the whole of the yearly income (or annuity) must be applied every year, and does not provide for any accumulations (*Re Gourju's Will Trusts* [1943] Ch 24, [1942] 2 All ER 605; compare *Re Mellor, Alvarez v Dodgson* [1922] 1 Ch 312, [1922] All ER Rep 735; *Re Peel, Tattersall v Peel* [1936] Ch 161).

2 A period of 21 years from the testator's death is a permitted period of accumulation: see the LPA 1925, s 164(1)(b) (Part G, para **[246.56]**).

3 Although these variations of the trusts set out in the TA 1925, s 33 (Part G, para **[246.31]**) preserve its basic scheme, it seems that HMRC will not be prepared to accept these forms as 'to the like effect' for the purposes of IHT relief under the IHTA 1984, s 88 which disregards a forfeiture of an immediate post-death interest for IHT purposes (for which see Part A, para **[200.104]**). Therefore, the occasion of the forfeiture of the life interest (if it is an immediate post-death interest) when such discretionary trusts take effect will be a chargeable transfer for IHT purposes under the IHTA 1984, ss 2(1) and 52(1), and a gift of the underlying settled property for the purposes of FA 1986, s 102. For some guidance on what trusts might be like to those of the TA 1925, s 33 (Part G, para **[246.31]**), see *Re Wallace's Settlements, Fane v Wallace* [1968] 2 All ER 209, [1968] 1 WLR 711. See also Form C3.2, cl 4(4) at para **[225.32]** and *Foster's Inheritance Tax*, E6.21.

[216.9]

Form B16.2: Protective income trusts for woman for life[1]

Note. It is possible for a life interest subject to the statutory protective trusts to be an immediate post-death interest (see IHTA 1984, s 88(4)(b)(i) and para **[200.104]** above), although it is unlikely that HMRC would accept that where the protective trusts are varied as in either of the alternative Forms below, the relief of IHTA 1984, s 88 will apply. Nevertheless, for deaths on or after 22 March 2006 and pending any forfeiture, the life interest in either of the alternative Forms should be an immediate post-death interest if it takes effect immediately on the testator's death (or is subject only to a survivorship condition permitted by IHTA 1984, s 92: see paras **[219.6]–[219.7]**), and is not, for example, postponed to another interest (see para **[216.2]** above). If it is not afforded relief under IHTA 1984, s 88 its termination may occasion an IHT charge under IHTA 1984, s 52(1) which would be immediately chargeable, and since the termination of an immediate post-death interest on or after 22 March 2006 will be deemed to be a gift of the underlying settled property for the purposes of FA 1986, s 102, and since the life tenant may continue to benefit under the protective trusts, the gift with reservation rules could apply: see FA 1986, s 102ZA and para **[200.76]** above. Accordingly, a testator wishing to establish a protective life interest which is an immediate post-death interest is probably best advised to rely on statutory protective trusts without any amendment so that relief under IHTA 1984, s 88 will apply. However, where the protected life interest would not qualify as an immediate post-death interest (eg. because it takes effect on the termination of an immediate post-death interest) and the underlying settled property would be within the IHT charging regime anyway, neither of these Forms would have these disadvantageous IHT consequences.

(A)USING THE STATUTORY PROTECTIVE TRUSTS

My trustees shall hold the income of [my residuary estate] upon protective trusts for the benefit of [*name*] during her life provided that the discretionary trusts by statute implied to arise after the failure or determination during the life of the said [*name*] of the trust to pay such income to her shall be varied as follows:

(i) My trustees may in their discretion apply any income accrued but unapplied in any previous year for the purposes of such discretionary trusts in any subsequent year but at a time not exceeding twenty-one years after the date of my death.

(ii) After the death of any object of such discretionary trusts my trustees may in their discretion while [*name*] is still living within three years of the date of such death apply any income which accrued in his or her lifetime in or towards the discharge of any liability incurred by or on behalf of any such object which my trustees may think fit to satisfy.

(iii) Notwithstanding the protective trusts hereinbefore declared and without determining her life interest thereunder the said [*name*] may by deed or deeds but with the consent of my trustees therein expressed (which consent my trustees shall have absolute power to give or withhold) assign any part or parts not exceeding in the whole one half of the income of [my residuary estate] to any her child children or issue[2] who shall at the date of such assignment have attained the age of [eighteen] [twenty-one] years or have married or shall marry within one month after such assignment.[3]

(iv) Further and notwithstanding the protective trusts hereinbefore declared and without determining the life interest thereunder of the said [*name*] my trustees shall have power at any time or times during the lifetime of the said [*name*] either before or after her life interest shall have failed or determined to pay or apply the whole or any part or parts of the capital of [my residuary estate] to or for the benefit of the said [*name*].

(v) My trustees shall have power at any time or times before the life interest of the said [*name*] shall have failed or determined by deed or deeds to declare that they shall henceforth hold the income of [my residuary estate] or any part or share thereof upon trust to pay the same to the said [*name*] during her life and not upon protective trusts for her benefit.

(B)ALTERNATIVE FORM—WITHOUT USING REFERENCE TO THE STATUTORY PROTECTIVE TRUSTS[4]

My trustees shall pay the income of [my residuary estate] to the said [*name*] during her life unless or until some act or event shall have happened or shall happen whereby the said income or any part thereof if belonging absolutely to her would become vested in or charged in favour of some other person.[5] And in the event of the failure or determination during her life of the trust last above declared in her favour my trustees shall during the remainder of her life pay or apply such income unto or for or towards the personal support maintenance and education of the said [*name*] [her husband] and her issue[6] for the time being and the person who if she were dead would for the time being be interested in [my residuary estate] or such one or more to the exclusion of the others or other of such objects of this discretionary trust in such manner and if more than one in such shares as my trustees shall think proper with power while [*name*] is still living within three years after the death of any object of such discretionary trust to apply any income which accrued in his or her lifetime in or towards the discharge of any liability incurred by or on behalf of any such object which my trustees shall think fit to satisfy.

[*Add sub-cls* (*iii*), (*iv*) *and* (*v*) *of alternative* Form (A) *above*.]

1 Although these variations of the trusts set out in the TA 1925, s 33 (Part G, para **[246.31]**) preserve its basic scheme, it seems that HMRC will not be prepared to accept these forms as 'to the like effect' for the purposes of IHT relief under IHTA 1984, s 88 which disregards a forfeiture of an immediate post-death interest for IHT purposes (for which see Part A, para **[200.104]**). Therefore, the occasion of the forfeiture of the life interest (if it is an immediate post-death interest) when such discretionary trusts take effect will be a chargeable transfer for IHT purposes under IHTA 1984, ss 2(1) and 52(1). Further, since the termination of an immediate post-death interest on or after 22 March 2006 will be deemed to be a gift of the underlying settled property for the purposes of FA 1986, s 102. For some guidance on what trusts might be like to those of the TA 1925, s 33 (Part G, para **[246.31]**); see *Re Wallace's Settlements, Fane v Wallace* [1968] 2 All ER 209, [1968] 1 WLR 711. See also Form C3.2, cl 4(4) at para **[225.32]** and *Foster's Inheritance Tax*, E6.21.

2 These words prima facie include illegitimate children or issue: see Part A, paras **[200.28]** and **[200.29]**.

3 This provision will enable a settlement to be made on the marriage of a child of the protected life tenant.

4 See n 2 to Form B16.1 at para **[216.8]**. The differences between the trusts of this clause and those of the TA 1925, s 33 (Part G, para **[246.31]**) are the same as the differences between those of the preceding Form (A) and s 33 with the additional variation that the remainder-man is an object of the discretionary trust of income even if the principal beneficiary has a spouse or civil partner or issue living (compare s 33(1)(ii)(b)).

5 Singular includes plural and vice versa, and person a corporation (LPA 1925, s 61: Part G, para **[246.54]**). See on this clause, *Re Pilkington's Will Trusts, Pilkington v Harrison* [1937] Ch 574, [1937] 3 All ER 213.

6 See n 2, above.

[216.10]

Form B16.3: Determinable life interest[1]

Until the death of my son [*name or as the case may be*] my trustees shall, if no act or thing shall have been done permitted or suffered by my said son or shall have been attempted to have been done and if no event shall have happened (other than a consent to any advancement under any statutory or express power) whereby the income of [my residuary estate *or as the case may be*] or some part thereof would or might if belonging absolutely to my said son become vested in or charged in favour of some other persons or a corporation or my said son would or might be deprived of the right to receive the same or any part thereof, pay the said income to my said son during his life until some such act or thing as aforesaid shall be done permitted or suffered or be attempted to be done by my said son or some such event as aforesaid shall happen.

And after the death or earlier failure or determination in the lifetime of my said son of the trust in his favour hereinbefore contained my trustees shall stand possessed of [my residuary estate *or* his share of my residuary estate *or as the case may be*] and the income thereof in trust etc.[2]

1 For deaths on or after 22 March 2006, and pending any determination, the life interest in this Form should be an immediate post-death interest if it takes effect immediately on the testator's death (or is subject only to a survivorship condition permitted by IHTA 1984, s 92: see paras **[219.6]**–**[219.7]**), and is not, for example, postponed to another interest (see para **[216.2]** above). On and after 22 March 2006, its termination may occasion an IHT charge under IHTA 1984, s 52(1) and potential exemption will only be available if the determination results in another person acquiring an absolute interest, or an interest in possession which has the result that its holder is treated as beneficially entitled to the underlying settled property under IHTA 1984, s 49(1) (such as a disabled person's interest, see para **[200.99]**), or causes the settled property to become subject to a trust for a bereaved minor (see para **[200.108]** above). Further, the termination of an immediate post-death interest on or after 22 March 2006 will be deemed to be a gift of the underlying settled property for the purposes of FA 1986, s 102, so that unless the beneficiary of the immediate post-death interest is excluded altogether from benefit after the termination, the gift with reservation rules could apply: see FA 1986, s 102ZA and para **[200.76]** above.

2 TA 1925, s 33 (Part G, para **[246.31]**) cannot readily be adapted to the case considered in this form. This form may be adapted to a legacy (see Form B10.39 at para **[210.55]**) to prevent the legacy becoming payable, e g to a trustee on bankruptcy. This is not a protective trust for IHT purposes.

[216.11]

Form B16.4: Life or widowhood interest to wife[1]

My trustees shall pay the income of my residuary estate to my wife for her life [*or* as long as she shall remain my widow[2]].

1 For deaths on or after 22 March 2006, this life or widowhood interest should be an immediate post-death interest if it takes effect immediately on the testator's death (or is subject only to a survivorship condition permitted by IHTA 1984, s 92: see paras **[219.6]**–**[219.7]**), and is not, for example, postponed to another interest (see para **[216.2]** above).

2 As to the meaning of this term, see Vol 1, paras **[80.1]** and **[80.2]**. If the wife's interest is limited to her widowhood, her remarriage will determine her interest and may occasion an IHT charge under IHTA 1984, s 52(1) unless potential exemption is available, see Part A, para **[200.71]**. On and after 22 March 2006, potential exemption will only be available if the determination results in another person acquiring an absolute interest, or an interest in possession which has the result that its holder is treated as beneficially entitled to the underlying settled property under IHTA 1984, s 49(1) (such as a disabled person's interest, see para **[200.99]**), or causes the settled property to become subject to a trust for a bereaved minor (see para **[200.108]** above). Further, the termination of an immediate post-death interest on or after 22 March 2006 will be deemed to be a gift of the underlying settled property for the purposes of FA 1986, s 102, so that unless the wife is excluded altogether from benefit after the termination, the gift with reservation rules could apply: see FA 1986, s 102ZA and para **[200.76]** above.

[216.12]

Form B16.5: Life interest to wife reducible on remarriage[1]

My trustees shall pay the income of my residuary estate to my wife during her life Provided that in the event of her remarriage they shall cease to pay her the income from [one half of] my residuary estate.[2]

1 For deaths on or after 22 March 2006, the wife's interest should be an immediate post-death interest if it takes effect immediately on the testator's death (or is subject only to a survivorship condition permitted by IHTA 1984, s 92: see paras **[219.6]**–**[219.7]**), and is not, for example, postponed to another interest (see para **[216.2]** above).

2 It is advisable following the widow's remarriage to give the widow the income of half the estate rather than half the income of the estate since this will allow one half of the estate to be distributed on remarriage. For this distinction see *Re Freeston's Charity, Sylvester v*

University College Oxford [1979] 1 All ER 51, [1978] 1 WLR 741. There will of course be a partial termination of an interest in possession on remarriage which may attract a charge to IHT under the IHTA 1984, s 52(1) unless potential exemption is available, see Part A, para **[200.71]**. On and after 22 March 2006, potential exemption will only be available if the determination results in another person acquiring an absolute interest, or an interest in possession which has the result that its holder is treated as beneficially entitled to the underlying settled property under IHTA 1984, s 49(1) (such as a disabled person's interest, see para **[200.99]**), or causes the settled property to become subject to a trust for a bereaved minor (see para **[200.108]** above). Further, the termination of an immediate post-death interest on or after 22 March 2006 will be deemed to be a gift of the underlying settled property for the purposes of FA 1986, s 102, so that unless the widow is excluded altogether from benefit after the termination, the gift with reservation rules could apply: see FA 1986, s 102ZA and para **[200.76]** above.

[216.13]

Form B16.6: Trust for wife during widowhood subject to an obligation to maintain children

In trust to pay the income thereof to my wife during her widowhood she thereout maintaining and educating my sons while under the age of twenty-five years and my unmarried daughters but my wife so long as she maintains and educates my children to the satisfaction of my trustees shall not be liable to account for the said income.[1]

1 *Re Booth, Booth v Booth* [1894] 2 Ch 282; *Re G (Infants)* [1899] 1 Ch 719; *Comiskey v Bowring-Hanbury* [1905] AC 84; *Re Ramsay, Thorpe v Ramsay* [1917] 2 Ch 64. This form imposes an obligation, and is not merely a precatory direction. If no obligation is to be imposed, this should be expressly stated as in the next following form. If the income in question is the income of a legacy, the legacy will carry interest from the testator's death where the primary object is maintenance (*Re Ramsay, Thorpe v Ramsay*), but not otherwise (*Re Crane, Adams v Crane* [1908] 1 Ch 379). For the purposes of IHT the wife will not have an interest in possession and so if the trust takes effect immediately on the testator's death it will not create an immediate post-death interest and the underlying settled property will be relevant property for IHT purposes (see para **[218.8]** ff).If this is not desired it will be safer to use the next following form instead.

[216.14]

Form B16.7: Same where no legal obligation imposed[1]

In trust to pay the income thereof to my wife during her widowhood[2] and I request her, but so as not to impose any legal obligation upon her, thereout to educate and maintain my sons while under the age of twenty-five years and my daughters while under that age and unmarried.

1 For deaths on or after 22 March 2006, this interest should be an immediate post-death interest if it takes effect immediately on the testator's death (or is subject only to a survivorship condition permitted by IHTA 1984, s 92: see paras **[219.6]–[219.7]**), and is not, for example, postponed to another interest (see para **[216.2]** above).

2 Since the wife's interest is limited to her widowhood, her remarriage will determine it and may occasion an IHT charge under IHTA 1984, s 52(1) unless potential exemption is available. On and after 22 March 2006, potential exemption will only be available if the determination results in another person acquiring an absolute interest, or an interest in possession which has the result that its holder is treated as beneficially entitled to the underlying settled property under IHTA 1984, s 49(1) (such as a disabled person's interest, see para **[200.99]**), or causes the settled property to become subject to a trust for a bereaved minor (see para **[200.108]** above). Further, the termination of an immediate post-death interest on or after 22 March 2006 will be deemed to be a gift of the underlying settled

property for the purposes of FA 1986, s 102, so that unless the wife is excluded altogether from benefit after the termination, the gift with reservation rules could apply: see FA 1986, s 102ZA and para **[200.76]** above.

[216.15]

Form B16.8: Gift of income of residuary estate to a reputed wife as long as she is unmarried[1]

My trustees shall pay the income of my residuary estate[2] to my wife [*name of reputed wife*] during her life or until after my death she shall marry and from and after the death or such marriage[3] of my said wife my trustees shall hold my residuary estate and the income thereof [*add gift over*].

1 This form will, it is thought, be found useful where the testator desires to conceal the true status of a reputed wife to whom he has never been legally married, but nevertheless wishes her interest to cease on her marriage after his death to any other person. See generally Vol 1, para **[80.1]** ff. For deaths on or after 22 March 2006, this life interest should be an immediate post-death interest if it takes effect immediately on the testator's death (or is subject only to a survivorship condition permitted by IHTA 1984, s 92: see paras **[219.6]**–**[219.7]**), and is not, for example, postponed to another interest (see para **[216.2]** above).

2 It is assumed that the 'residuary estate' has been defined. In the event of the reputed wife marrying the testator, he will have to make a fresh will since marriage generally revokes a will, see Vol 1, para **[17.1]** ff.

3 Her marriage will determine her interest and may occasion an IHT charge under the IHTA 1984, s 52(1) unless potential exemption is available, see Part A, para **[200.71]**. On and after 22 March 2006, potential exemption will only be available if the determination results in another person acquiring an absolute interest, or an interest in possession which has the result that its holder is treated as beneficially entitled to the underlying settled property under IHTA 1984, s 49(1) (such as a disabled person's interest, see para **[200.99]**), or causes the settled property to become subject to a trust for a bereaved minor (see para **[200.108]** above). Further, the termination of an immediate post-death interest on or after 22 March 2006 will be deemed to be a gift of the underlying settled property for the purposes of FA 1986, s 102, so that unless the reputed wife is excluded altogether from benefit after the termination, the gift with reservation rules could apply: see FA 1986, s 102ZA and para **[200.76]** above.

[216.16]

Form B16.9: Trust of income for several persons for life giving a general testamentary power of disposition to the survivor[1]

In trust to pay the income thereof to my three daughters [*names*] and the survivors and survivor of them during their or her respective lives or life and after the death of such survivor in trust as to both the capital and income of the trust fund for such persons and in such manner as such survivor shall by will or codicil appoint [*add gift over in default of appointment as desired*].[2]

1 For deaths on or after 22 March 2006, the initial life interest each daughter takes should be an immediate post-death interest if it takes effect immediately on the testator's death (or is subject only to a survivorship condition permitted by IHTA 1984, s 92: see paras **[219.6]**–**[219.7]**), and is not, for example, postponed to another interest (see para **[216.2]** above). However, the further life interest a survivor acquires on the death of any of them, will not be an immediate post-death interest so that the settled property subject to it may then fall within the IHT charging regime for relevant property (see para **[218.8]** ff above).

2 It is not unusual to make the ultimate gift to the last survivor absolutely but the result of giving him a general testamentary power of appointment is much the same as he can dispose of it as his property. If this form is used for the exercise of a special power of appointment care should be taken to keep within the common law perpetuity rule for the

gift to the survivor is contingent: see *Re Legh's Settlement Trusts, Public Trustee v Legh* [1938] Ch 39, [1937] 3 All ER 823. An exercise of the power which is invalid at common law might nevertheless be saved under the 'wait and see' provision of the PAA 1964, s 3 (Part G, para **[246.76]**).

[216.17]

Form B16.10: Trust for wife for life and then to children in equal shares[1]

(i) Upon trust to pay the income from my residuary estate to my wife for life [during her widowhood] [and I direct that if in any year the income of my residuary estate does not amount to £—— then my trustees shall resort to the capital of my residuary estate to make good the deficiency].

(ii) After the death [*or if wife's interest is restricted to widowhood*, After the death or remarriage] of my wife my trustees shall hold my residuary estate in trust in equal shares if more than one for all my children who attain the age of eighteen years[2] provided that if any child shall have died in my lifetime whether before or after the date hereof leaving issue living at my death such issue shall take by substitution and if more than one in equal shares per stirpes the share of my residuary estate that such deceased child of mine would have taken had he or she survived me and attained a vested interest but so that no issue shall take whose parent is alive at my death and so capable of taking.

1 This is the common form of gift to wife for life and then for children in equal shares. For deaths on or after 22 March 2006, the life or widowhood interest for the wife should be an immediate post-death interest if it takes effect immediately on the testator's death (or is subject only to a survivorship condition permitted by IHTA 1984, s 92: see paras **[219.6]–[219.7]**), and is not, for example, postponed to another interest (see para **[216.2]** above). Variations are shown for the case where the gift is for widowhood and where, as may be necessary in a small estate, there is a discretion to make the income up out of capital to a stated amount. Although these payments are made from capital, they attract income tax: *Cunard's Trustees v IRC* [1946] 1 All ER 159. HMRC will treat payments out of capital as the income of the beneficiary where, by the terms of the trust instrument, payments out of capital are required to be made, or may be made, in order to supplement income to a fixed amount or a certain defined level, see the Trusts, Settlements and Estates Manual, TSEM 3757. There is no IHT disadvantage in paying capital to someone who has an immediate post-death interest in it: see Part A, para **[200.96]**. If such a clause as this is worded as a trust for the wife for life and then to children and the *issue* of any then dead, the issue must survive the wife: *Mousley v Rigby* [1955] Ch 139, [1954] 3 All ER 553, following *Re Embury* (1913) 109 LT 511; see also Vol 1, para **[68.11]**. Illegitimate children and issue will be eligible under this clause; see Part A, paras **[200.28]** and **[200.29]**.

2 This trust for the testator's children should be a trust for bereaved minors if it comes into possession while the children are under 18 (see para **[200.108]** above). If the widow's life interest determines on her remarriage this may occasion an IHT charge under IHTA 1984, s 52(1), but potential exemption should be available since if the children are under 18 (and unmarried) the termination will be in favour of a trust for bereaved minors, see para **[200.108]**, and if they are over 18 or married, they will be absolutely entitled (see para **[200.71]** above).

[216.18]

Form B16.11: Trust for wife for life and then to children in equal shares by incorporation of Statutory Will Forms 1925, Form 10[1]

Statutory Will Forms 1925, Form 10, is hereby incorporated in this my will and shall apply to my residuary estate.[2]

1 This form settles any property directed to be subject to it upon trust for the surviving spouse for life, and after her death for the testator's children at 21 or earlier marriage. If the spouse's life interest takes effect immediately on death (or subject only to a survivorship condition permitted by IHTA 1984, s 92: see paras **[219.6]**–**[219.7]**) it will be an immediate post-death interest within IHTA 1984, s 49A, so spouse exemption from IHT should be available, see para **[216.2]** above. The remainder trust for the children should be an age 18-to-25 trust within IHTA 1984, s 71D to the extent that any of the children are under 21 on the date it takes effect (see para **[200.109]** above) (unless it has taken effect immediately on the testator's death, and any child was over the age of 18 but under the age of 21, and immediately entitled to an interest possession by virtue of TA 1925, s 31(1)(ii) (see Part G, para **[246.29]**), so that he or she would have an immediate post-death interest).

2 This assumes that the term 'residuary estate' has already been defined. For Form 10 of the Statutory Will Forms 1925 see Part E, para **[238.16]**.

[216.19]

Form B16.12: Trust for wife for life and then to unmarried daughters for life[1]

My trustees shall hold my [residuary estate] upon the following trusts:

(i) Upon trust to pay the income thereof to my wife [*name*] during her life.

(ii) If both my daughters [*name*] and [*name*] shall be living and unmarried at the death of my said wife[2] to pay the income thereof to my said daughters in equal shares either for the period of their joint lives or until the marriage of either of them whichever period shall be the shorter and on the death or marriage of one of my said daughters to pay the income of the appropriated fund hereinafter defined to my surviving or unmarried daughter (as the case may be) until her death or marriage.

(iii) If only one of my said daughters shall survive my said wife and shall at the death of my said wife be unmarried then to pay the income of the appropriated fund to such unmarried daughter until her death or marriage.

(iv) The appropriated fund hereinbefore mentioned shall be a fund set aside either at the death of my wife or at the death or on the marriage of the first of my said daughters to die or marry as the case may be and shall consist of investments sufficient at the time when such fund shall be set aside to produce the gross yearly sum before deduction of income tax of £——.[3]

(v) Subject to the above provisions and subject as hereinafter provided to hold [my residuary estate] in trust both as to capital and income in trust for all my children [who shall attain the age of eighteen] in equal shares.[4] Provided that if any child of mine has died or shall die in my lifetime leaving issue living at my death such issue shall stand in the place of such deceased child and take per stirpes and equally between them if more than one the share of [my residuary estate] which such deceased child of mine would have taken if he or she had survived me and had attained a vested interest but so that no issue shall take whose parent is alive and capable of taking under this provision of my will.

(vi) So long as either of my said daughters remain unmarried such unmarried daughters shall not take any share or interest in the income of [my residuary estate] without bringing her share of the income of the appropriated fund into hotchpot and accounting for the same.

1 For deaths on or after 22 March 2006, the life interest for the wife should be an immediate post-death interest if it takes effect immediately on the testator's death (or is subject only to a survivorship condition permitted by IHTA 1984, s 92: see paras **[219.6]**–**[219.7]**), and is not, for example, postponed to another interest (see para **[216.2]** above). However, the subsequent life interests for the daughters, will not be immediate post-death interests (unless the wife has predeceased the testator so her life interest has not taken effect) so that unless they, or any of them are disabled person's interests (see para **[200.99]** above), the settled property subject to it may then fall within the IHT charging regime for relevant property (see para **[218.8]** ff above).

2 This clause assumes that the wife survives the husband, but if at this point and at corresponding points later in the clause, the words 'at the death of my said wife' are replaced by the words 'at the death of the survivor of myself and my said wife,' the clause will be applicable to the case where the wife predeceases the testator. There seems little reason to doubt that, as the clause stands, if the wife's interest fails, the later interests will be accelerated.

3 The unmarried daughter may not be entitled to much in the way of rebates or allowances, and it seems that a gross sum will be as convenient as any.

4 This trust for the testator's children should be a trust for bereaved minors if it comes into possession while the children are under 18 (see para **[200.108]** above).

[216.20]

Form B16.13: Trust for wife for life and then to children as she shall appoint, with hotchpot provision[1]

(i) Upon trust to pay the income thereof [of my residuary estate] to my wife for her life[2] and subject thereto.

(ii) Upon trust as to both capital and income for all or any one or more of my children and remoter issue in such shares and subject to such powers provisions and generally in such manner as my said wife shall by deed or will appoint[3] and subject to any such appointment upon trust for all my children living at my death if more than one in equal shares as tenants in common.

(iii) Any child who or whose issue takes any interest under the foregoing provision in default of appointment shall not take such interest in default of appointment without bringing into hotchpot any share or shares appointed to him or her or his or her issue and accounting for the same unless the appointment shall direct to the contrary.

1 This is a very short form and makes no provision under the trusts in default of appointment for children who die in the testator's lifetime leaving issue although the power of appointment can be exercised in favour of such issue. For a longer form, see Form B17.4 at para **[217.12]** and for a form with a wider power of appointment, see Forms B16.14 at para **[216.21]**. Illegitimate children will be eligible: see Part A, paras **[200.28]** and **[200.29]**.

2 For deaths on or after 22 March 2006, the life interest for the wife should be an immediate post-death interest if it takes effect immediately on the testator's death (or is subject only to a survivorship condition permitted by IHTA 1984, s 92: see paras **[219.6]**–**[219.7]**), and is not, for example, postponed to another interest (see para **[216.2]** above).

3 The wife could use this special power to appoint trusts for the testator's children which could qualify as trusts for bereaved minors or age 18–25 trusts (see para **[200.108]** ff above).

[216.21]

Form B16.14: Trust for wife for life and then to issue upon such trusts as she shall appoint[1]

(i) Upon trust to pay the income thereof of [my residuary estate] to my wife for her life[2] and subject thereto.

(ii) Upon trust as to both capital and income for all or any one or more of my children and remoter issue for such interests at such ages or times in such shares and with and subject to such powers and discretions exercisable over capital or income by any person or persons as my wife shall by deed or will (without transgressing the rules against perpetuities) appoint.[3]

(iii) In default of and subject to any such appointment in trust for all my children living at my death if more than one in equal shares as tenants in common provided that if any child of mine shall have died in my lifetime whether before or after the date hereof leaving issue living at my death such issue shall take by substitution and if more than one in equal shares per stirpes the share of my residuary estate that such deceased child of mine would have taken in default or subject to any appointment as aforesaid had he or she survived me but so that no issue shall take whose parent is alive at my death and so capable of taking.

1 This form authorises the testator's widow to appoint new trusts, including discretionary trusts, for the benefit of the testator's issue.

2 For deaths on or after 22 March 2006, the life interest for the wife should be an immediate post-death interest if it takes effect immediately on the testator's death (or is subject only to a survivorship condition permitted by IHTA 1984, s 92: see paras **[219.6]**–**[219.7]**), and is not, for example, postponed to another interest (see para **[216.2]** above).

3 The wife could use this special power to appoint trusts for the testator's children which could qualify as trusts for bereaved minors or age 18-to-25 trusts (see para **[200.108]** ff above).

[216.22]

Form B16.15: Trust for wife during widowhood, then to son for life with remainder to his children[1]

(i) Upon trust to pay the income of [my residuary estate] to my wife during her widowhood.

(ii) After the death or remarriage of my wife my trustees shall hold my residuary estate upon trust to pay the income thereof to my son [*name*] during his life and subject thereto upon trust in equal shares for all the children of my said son who shall attain the age of [eighteen] [twenty-one] years or marry thereunder.

1 For deaths on or after 22 March 2006, the life interest for the wife should be an immediate post-death interest if it takes effect immediately on the testator's death (or is subject only to a survivorship condition permitted by IHTA 1984, s 92: see paras **[219.6]**–**[219.7]**), and is not, for example, postponed to another interest (see para **[216.2]** above). The son's successive life interest will not be an immediate post-death interest (unless the wife has predeceased the testator so her life interest has not taken effect), and unless it is a disabled person's interest (see para **[200.99]** above), the settled property then subject to it will fall within the IHT charging regime for relevant property and remain there during the subsistence of any trusts for the son's children. If the widow's life interest determines on her remarriage this may occasion an IHT charge under IHTA 1984, s 52(1), and this will be immediately chargeable unless the son's successive life interest is a disabled person's interest.

[216.23]

Form B16.16: Trust for wife for life and then to children for life with substitution of their issue[1]

My trustees shall hold my residuary estate and the income thereof upon the following trusts:

(a) Upon trust to pay the income thereof to my wife if she shall survive me during her life and subject thereto

(b) Upon trust to divide my residuary estate into equal shares the number of such shares being equal to the number of my children living at the death of the survivor of myself and my said wife together with the number of my children who have died (whether before or after the date hereof) prior to such date as aforesaid leaving issue living at such date. Such shares to be held upon the trusts and subject to the powers and provisions hereinafter contained.

(c) In the case of each such living child of mine one share shall be held upon the following trusts:

(i) upon trust to pay the income thereof to such child during his or her life [*or* upon protective trusts for such child's benefit during his or her life] and after the death of such child.

(ii) upon trust to pay the said income to any wife or husband of such child of mine who shall survive him or her during the residue of such wife's or husband's life.

(iii) upon trust as to both capital and income of such share for all or such one or more exclusively of the others or other of the children or remoter issue of such child of mine born within twenty-one years of the death of the survivor of myself and my said wife [and my children] at such times and if more than one in such shares and with such provisions for maintenance advancement and otherwise for the benefit of such children or remoter issue or some or one of them at the discretion of my trustees or any other persons and generally in such manner in all respects as such children of mine shall by deed revocable or irrevocable or by will or codicil appoint.[2] And subject to any such appointment.

(iv) upon trust for the child or children of such child of mine who attain the age of [eighteen] [twenty-one] years or being female attain that age or marry under that age and if more than one in equal shares.

(v) provided always that no child of such child of mine who or whose issue shall take any part of such share by virtue of any appointment by such child of mine under the power aforesaid shall unless such child of mine so direct share in the unappointed part of such share without bringing the part so appointed into hotchpot and accounting therefor.

(d) In the case of the issue of each such deceased child of mine one share shall be held upon the following trusts: upon trust in equal shares (if more than one) for all or any of the children or child of such deceased child of mine living at the date of the death of the survivor of myself and my said wife who attain the age of [eighteen] [twenty-one] years or marry under that age and for all or any of the issue living at the date aforesaid who attain the age of [eighteen] [twenty-one] years or marry under that age of any child (who dies before the aforesaid date leaving issue living at the aforesaid date) of such child of mine such issue to take through all degrees according to their stocks in equal shares (if more than one) the share which their parent would have taken if living at the aforesaid date and so that no issue shall take whose parent is living at the aforesaid date and so capable of taking.[3]

(e) If the trusts of any such share as aforesaid shall fail by reason of no person attaining a vested interest therein then I direct that subject to the trusts powers and provisions herein contained or which may be applicable thereto by statute the said share and any share or shares which may accrue thereto by virtue of this present proviso shall be held by my trustees as an accretion to the other share or shares (and equally if more than one) the trusts whereof shall not at the date of such accruer have failed as aforesaid and upon the trusts powers and provisions applicable thereto herein contained or such of them as at the date of such accruer shall be capable of taking effect.

1 For deaths on or after 22 March 2006, the life interest for the wife should be an immediate post-death interest if it takes effect immediately on the testator's death (or is subject only to a survivorship condition permitted by IHTA 1984, s 92: see paras **[219.6]**–**[219.7]**), and is not, for example, postponed to another interest (see para **[216.2]** above). The children's successive life interests will not be immediate post-death interests (unless the wife has predeceased the testator so her life interest has not taken effect), and unless they are disabled person's interests (see para **[200.99]** above), the settled property then subject to it will fall within the IHT charging regime for relevant property and remain there during the subsistence of the subsequent trusts.

2 A joint power of appointment can be given to a daughter and her husband. At common law a power of appointment could not be given to the husband alone if he survived (*Re Abbott, Peacock v Frigout* [1893] 1 Ch 54), because such husband might be a person not born in the testator's lifetime, but would now be saved, at least partially, by the 'wait and see' provisions introduced by the PAA 1964, s 3 (Part G, para **[246.76]**).

3 Compare the AEA 1925, s 47(1) (Part G, para **[244.63]**).

[216.24]

Form B16.17: Trust for wife for life and then to children as she shall appoint incorporating Statutory Will Forms 1925, Form 9[1]

Statutory Will Forms 1925, Form 9, is hereby incorporated in this my will and shall apply to my residuary estate.

1 This statutory form makes provisions for children dying in the lifetime of the testator, for hotchpot and other matters. For the terms of this statutory will form, see Part E, para **[238.15]**.

[216.25]

Form B16.18: Clause directing trustees to resort to the capital of residue in order to make up income to a minimum amount[1]

I direct that if in any year the net income from [my residuary estate] in the hands of my widow she retaining all rebates allowances and repayments for her own benefit which shall be included in the computation of the said net income does not amount to £—— then my trustees shall [at the written request of my widow] resort to the capital of my residuary estate to make good the deficiency.

1 This clause directs trustees to make up income to a specified amount. It is thought that the total sum paid to the beneficiary is liable to income tax, see *Cunard's Trustees v IRC* [1946] 1 All ER 159, and HMRC have said they will treat payments out of capital as the income of the beneficiary where, by the terms of the trust instrument, payments out of capital are required to be made, or may be made, in order to supplement income to a fixed amount or a certain defined level, see the Trusts, Settlements and Estates Manual, TSEM 3757. See n 1 to Form B16.20 at para **[216.27]**.

[216.26]

Form B16.19: Clause empowering trustees to resort to capital[1]

My trustees may at the written request of my widow at any time or times raise any sum or sums [(not exceeding £—— in any one year and not exceeding £—— in all)] out of the capital of my residuary estate and pay such sum or sums to or for the absolute benefit of my widow in addition to the income of my residuary estate hereinbefore given to her but in any such case my trustees shall have an absolute discretion whether or not they will raise such sums notwithstanding the written request of my said widow.

1 This form gives trustees power to resort to capital to make up income, rather than, as in the immediately preceding form, directing them to do so to make up income to a specified sum. The trustees must be satisfied that the raising of such sums is for the benefit of the wife or for that of the children whom the wife is supporting: *Re Powles, Little v Powles* [1954] 1 All ER 516, [1954] 1 WLR 336. It is not clear whether sums paid to the beneficiary will be liable to income tax, see n 1 to Form B16.20 at para **[216.27]**.

[216.27]

Form B16.20: Clause empowering trustees to lend capital money to make up income of a share of residue to a stated amount[1]

I direct that if in any year during the lifetime of the said [*beneficiary*] the income of the share of residue hereinbefore bequeathed to the said [*beneficiary*] [*or* for the benefit of the said [*beneficiary*] and [her]/[his] children [and issue]] shall after deduction therefrom of income tax at the basic rate for the time being in force but without taking into account rebates allowances or repayments of tax be less than £—— my trustees may in their absolute discretion out of the capital of the said residue lend to the said [*beneficiary*] upon her [his] written undertaking that such moneys shall be recoverable and that interest shall be paid thereon as hereinafter stated the difference between the net income of the said share of residue and the sum of £—— provided that the said [*beneficiary*] shall not be called upon by my trustees to repay any such moneys during [her]/[his] lifetime but that they shall be recoverable only after [her]/[his] death from [her]/[his] estate and provided that in arriving at the sum to be borrowed the interest on any previous loan shall not be taken into consideration.

[*Add rate and terms of payment of interest.*]

1 Form B16.18 at para **[216.25]** directs trustees to make up income to a stated amount by resorting to capital, and B16.19 at para **[216.26]** gives a power to trustees to make up

income by resorting to capital. If an arrangement such as that of Form 16.18 is adopted (that is, directing a resort to the capital of the residuary estate) it is thought that the total sum paid to the beneficiary is liable to income tax, see *Cunard's Trustees v IRC* [1946] 1 All ER 159, and HMRC have said they will treat payments out of capital as the income of the beneficiary where, by the terms of the trust instrument, payments out of capital are required to be made, or may be made, in order to supplement income to a fixed amount or a certain defined level, see the Trusts, Settlements and Estates Manual, TSEM 3757. It is less clear that this result follows if Form 16.19 is adopted, but it is possible that it does. It would seem that this result may be avoided by giving the trustees a right to recover the sums advanced from the beneficiary so advanced: see *Williamson v Ough* [1936] AC 384, HL.

[216.28]

Form B16.21: Gift of residue to children incorporating Statutory Will Forms 1925, Form 7, with modification[1]

I give the residue of my real and personal estate to my trustees to hold the same upon trust for such of my children who shall be living at my death and if more than one in equal shares and I direct that Form 7 of the Statutory Will Forms 1925 (except clause (5) thereof) is hereby incorporated in my will and shall apply to the share in my residuary estate of each child of mine and to the investments representing the same as if such share were a legacy and instead of clause (5) of the said Form 7 I direct that if any such child of mine shall not have any child who under the incorporated trusts in default of appointment attains a vested interest in such child's share then subject to the incorporated trusts and powers in favour of such child and his or her issue the said share and the income thereof and all statutory accumulations (if any) of income and any share which shall accrue thereto under this present provision shall accrue to the other shares (and if more than one equally between them and whether such other shares are settled or not settled) in my residuary estate the trusts whereof shall not at the date of such accruer have failed or determined otherwise than by absolute vesting.

1 This statutory form makes provision for the payment of income to a life tenant, with remainder for the issue of the life tenant as he or she should appoint, with default provisions. For Form 7 see Part E, para **[238.13]**.

[216.29]

Form B16.22: Gift of residue incorporating intestacy provisions[1]

I devise and bequeath all the residue of my property to my trustees upon the same trusts and powers both as to the sale investment and administration thereof and as to the beneficial interests therein as if I had died intestate in respect thereof.

1 Subject to appointing executors and making some specific legacies, a person may wish his estate to pass as on an intestacy, or be prepared for this to happen if a will has to be made urgently. For the provisions which apply on an intestacy see the AEA 1925, ss 33 and 47 (Part G, paras **[244.60]** and **[244.63]**). If a testator leaves a spouse or civil partner and issue, the spouse or civil partner takes the personal chattels, a net sum currently of £125,000 with interest currently at 6% from the date of death, and a life interest in half the residue. Subject to the interest of the widow or civil partner, the issue take the residue with stirpital substitution throughout. For deaths on or after 22 March 2006, the life interest for a widow or civil partner under the intestacy provisions should be an immediate post-death interest, and the statutory trusts for the minor children of the testator should be a trust for bereaved minors within IHTA 1984, s 71A (see para **[200.108]** above).

[216.30]

Form B16.23: Settlement of child's share of residuary estate[1]

My trustees shall hold my residuary estate upon trust for such of my children who shall survive me if more than one in equal shares. Provided that the share of my residuary estate of all such children who shall survive me shall not vest absolutely in such child but shall be retained by my trustees and held upon the following trusts:

(1) To pay the income from such share to such child for life and such child shall have power by will or codicil to appoint to any spouse or civil partner who shall survive him or her a life or less interest in such income[2] [And so that if and so long as such child is under the age of 18 years my trustees may pay or otherwise apply for or towards the maintenance education or benefit of such child the whole or such part or parts of the income of such share as my trustees in their absolute discretion think fit and shall retain the balance of such income upon trust for such child absolutely but my trustees may at any time or times while such child is under the age of 18 years pay or apply such retained income as if it were income arising in the then current year and section 31 of the Trustee Act 1925 shall not apply to such share][3]

(2) From and after the death of such child [and subject to any such appointment as aforesaid to a surviving spouse or civil partner] such share and the income thereof shall be held upon such trusts for such one or more of his or her children and remoter issue as he or she may by deed with or without power of revocation and new appointment or by will or codicil appoint.

(3) In default of any such appointment and so far as any such appointment shall not extend such share shall be held upon trust for all the children or any child of such child of mine who [being male] — shall attain the age of [eighteen] [twenty-one] years or [being female shall attain that age or] previously marry or form a civil partnership and if more than one equally as tenants in common. Provided that no child of any such child of mine shall take any part of my child's share in default of appointment under this present trust without bringing into hotchpot any part of the share of my child which he or she may have appointed in favour of such child or of any of such child's issue under the power in that behalf hereinbefore contained unless my child making the appointment shall direct to the contrary.

(4) If the share of my child or any part thereof shall not vest absolutely in some person or persons under the foregoing trusts then after the death of my child his or her share or the part thereof which shall not so vest shall (subject to the trusts powers and provisions hereby or by statute vested in my trustees in respect of the income or the capital thereof and to every exercise of the same by my trustees) be held in trust for such persons or person as he or she shall by will or codicil appoint and in default of any such appointment in trust for the statutory beneficiaries entitled as if he or she had died intestate

without ever having married or formed a civil partnership and without leaving a parent and such share had formed part of his or her estate.

(5) If at the date when such child of mine attains the age of [fifty] years he or she shall never have had a child or if at the said date all the children he or she shall then have had shall have died without attaining a vested interest in his or her share or if subsequently to the said date all the children he or she shall have had shall die without any of them attaining such a vested interest as aforesaid then my trustees may at any time or times after the date when such child of mine attains the age of fifty years or the subsequent date when his or her last surviving child shall die without attaining such a vested interest as aforesaid as the case may be and during the life of such child of mine transfer the whole or any part or parts of his or her share in its then actual state of investment to such child of mine absolutely freed and discharged from the trusts powers and provisions hereof.[3]

1 If this clause is used it will be advisable to add a clause expressly authorising the executors or trustees to appropriate; see Form B20.24 at para **[220.77]**. As to the construction of the words children and issue, see Part A, paras **[200.28]** and **[200.29]**. For deaths on or after 22 March 2006, the initial life interest each child takes should be an immediate post-death interest if it takes effect immediately on the testator's death (or is subject only to a survivorship condition permitted by IHTA 1984, s 92: see paras **[219.6]**–**[219.7]**), and is not, for example, postponed to another interest. However, a further life interest appointed to a spouse (or civil partner) under the power of sub-clause (1) of the Form will not be an immediate post-death interest, and unless it is a disabled person's interest within IHTA 1984, s 89B (see para **[200.99]** above), the settled property subject to it will then fall within the IHT charging regime for relevant property and remain there during the subsistence of any further trusts which are not disabled person's interests (see para **[200.107]** above).

2 Such an appointment would fail if a divorce (or dissolution of a civil partnership) takes place, since a divorced spouse cannot be a spouse (and a former civil partner cannot be a civil partner) who survives a named person: *Re Kettlewell, Jones v Kettlewell* (1907) 98 LT 23; *Re Williams' Settlement, Greenwell v Humphries* [1929] 2 Ch 361, [1929] All ER Rep 632; *Re Slaughter, Trustees Corpn Ltd v Slaughter* [1945] Ch 355, [1945] 2 All ER 214; *Re Allan, Allan v Midland Bank Executor and Trustee Co Ltd* [1954] Ch 295, [1954] 1 All ER 646.

3 This provision should be included where the testator may have a minor child living at his death, and he wishes such child to have a life interest which will be an immediate post-death interest within IHTA 1984, s 49A (see para **[216.2]** above). TA 1925, s 31 needs to be excluded because the trust of accumulations under the TA 1925, s 31 (Part G, para **[246.29]**) which applies where a minor beneficiary has a life interest is such as to give the minor beneficiary a contingent interest in such accumulations. The purpose of this substitution for s 31 is to cause the income which is not applied for the child's benefit during his minority to be held on trust absolutely for the child, so as to confer an interest in possession for IHT purposes. An infant cannot be paid income to which he is entitled (see Vol 1, para **[9.39]**) but it is thought that he or she has an interest in possession in income if it would form part of his estate if he or she died under the age of 18 (and unmarried and without a civil partner).

3 See n 2 to Form B16.24 at para **[216.31]**.

[216.31]

Form B16.24: Provision directing payment of capital to a female life tenant having no likelihood of children, where she has herself a general power of appointment in default of children

If at the date when [*name*] [any daughter of mine] attains the age of [50] years she shall never have had a child[1] or if at the said date all the children[1] she shall then have had shall have died without attaining a vested interest in the [*property*] [*share of my residuary estate*] of which [she] [such daughter] is life tenant hereunder or if subsequently to the said date all the children [she] [such daughter] shall have had shall die without any of them attaining such a vested interest as aforesaid then my trustees shall at the date when the said [*name*] [such daughter] attains the age of [50] years or upon the subsequent date when the last surviving child of the said [*name*] [such daughter] shall die without attaining such a vested interest as aforesaid as the case may be transfer such [*property*] [*share*] as aforesaid in its then actual state of investment to the said [*name*] [such daughter] freed and discharged [from any life interest in the whole or a part thereof to which any husband of the said [*name*] [such daughter] who might survive her would or might have become entitled after her death whether under any appointment actually then made or otherwise and] from every [other] trust or power to take effect after her death under the trusts hereinbefore contained.[2]

1 Including an illegitimate child unless a contrary intention is shown: see Part A, paras **[200.28]** and **[200.29]**.

2 This precedent is for use when a female life tenant is entitled, in default of children attaining a vested interest, to a general power of appointment, or where in similar circumstances the property would otherwise go direct to her next of kin on her death. Any appointment to a surviving husband made under a power is overridden. It has been suggested that, where there is no longer any prospect of children, it is better that the life tenant should be able to break the trust even to the disadvantage of a husband who may survive her rather than that the money should go to (possibly) distant relatives. As to when the court used to presume a woman to be past childbearing, see *Re Whichelow, Bradshaw v Orpen* [1953] 2 All ER 1558, [1954] 1 WLR 5; *Allen v Crane* [1953] ALR 959, St R Qd 95; *Re Pettifor's Will Trusts* [1966] Ch 257, [1966] 1 All ER 913; and *Re Westminster Bank Ltd's Declaration of Trust* [1963] 2 All ER 400n, [1963] 1 WLR 820; see also the PAA 1964, s 2(1)(a) (Part G, para **[246.75]**) for the presumption in the context of the rule against perpetuities. These authorities can no longer be relied on: see para **[221.34]**, n 1. For this form in the context of a set of beneficial trusts see Form B 16.23 at para **[216.30]**.

Settled Legacies

[216.32]

Form B16.25: Settled legacy—concise form[1]

(i) I give to my trustees the sum of £—— [free of IHT and foreign death duties[1]] upon trust to invest the same in any investments hereby authorised or authorised by law for the investment of trust funds with power to vary the same and to hold the same in trust to pay the income therefrom to A. during his life.

(ii) Subject thereto as to both capital and income for all or any the children or child[2] of A. who attain the age of [eighteen] [twenty-one] years or marry under that age and if more than one in equal shares.[3]

[(iii) I hereby declare that the administrative provisions of this my will relating to residue shall apply to this legacy].

[*If it is desired to impose protective trusts, substitute the following in clause* (*i*) *above*: and to hold the income of the same upon protective trusts for the benefit of A. during his life.[4]]

1 For deaths on or after 22 March 2006, the initial life interest of A should be an immediate post-death interest if it takes effect immediately on the testator's death (or is subject only to a survivorship condition permitted by IHTA 1984, s 92: see paras **[219.6]**–**[219.7]**), and is not, for example, postponed to another interest (see para **[216.2]** above). If the property remains on trust after A's death, the settled property will then fall within the IHT charging regime for relevant property (see para **[218.8]** ff above), unless A's children are also the testator's children in which case if the selected age of contingency for the children's remainder trust is 18, it should be a trust for bereaved minors (see para **[200.108]** above), and if the specified age is 21 (or another age between 18 and 25), the trust should be an age 18-to-25 trust (see para **[200.109]** above).

2 See paras **[210.3]**, **[210.4]** and **[214.64]** for IHT and pecuniary legacies. These words are unnecessary if there is a general direction covering inheritance such as Forms B14.33 at para **[214.76]** or B14.34 at para **[214.77]** or the legacy will be payable wholly out of UK free estate.

3 Illegitimate and legitimated children will now be included; see Part A, paras **[200.28]** and **[200.29]**.

4 Where the income was given until marriage and upon marriage settled on the beneficiary and her children and in fact the beneficiary never married, the capital on the death of the beneficiary fell into residue: *Re Henry Will Trust, Mussett v Smith* [1953] 1 All ER 531, [1953] 1 WLR 376.

5 For the IHT treatment of protective trusts, see Part A, para **[200.104]**. For TA 1925, s 33, which defines protective trusts, see Part G, para **[246.31]**.

[216.33]

Form B16.26: Settled legacy—full form

I.FORM INCORPORATING STATUTORY WILL FORM[1]

I give to [*legatee*] the sum of £—— [free of IHT and foreign death duties[2]] and I declare that Form 7 of the Statutory Will Forms 1925 is incorporated in this my will and shall apply to this legacy [subject to the following modification, *add any necessary modification*].

II.FORM SETTING OUT THE TRUSTS[3]

I give to my trustees the sum of £—— [free of IHT and foreign death duties] upon trust to invest the same in any investments hereby authorised [*or* authorised by law for the investment of trust funds] with power to vary and transpose the same and to hold such investments and the income thereof:

(a) Upon trust to pay the income of the said investments to A. during his life and after his death;

[*or, if the life interest is to be protected:*

(a) Upon trust to hold the income of the said investments on protective trusts for A. during his life[4]];

(b) Upon trust if the said A. shall so direct by will to pay the income of the said investments or such part thereof as the said A. shall so direct to any wife [or civil partner] of the said A. who shall survive him during the residue of her life or for such less period as the said A. shall so direct and subject thereto;

(c) Upon trust as to both capital and income of the said investments for all or such one or more exclusively of the others or other of the children or remoter issue[5] of the said A. at such time and if more than one in such shares and with such provisions for maintenance advancement and otherwise for the benefit of such children or issues[5] or some or one of them at the discretion of my trustees or any other persons and generally in such manner in all respects as the said. A. shall by deed revocable or irrevocable or by will or codicil appoint And in default of and subject to any such appointment;

(d) Upon trust for all or any the children or child[5] of the said A. who shall attain the age of [eighteen] [twenty-one] years or marry under that age if more than one in equal shares as tenants in common;

(e) Provided always that no child of the said A. who or whose issue shall take by virtue of any appointment under the aforesaid power any share of the said investments shall unless the said A. so direct share in the unappointed part of the said investments without bringing the share so appointed into hotchpot and accounting therefor;

(f) If there shall be no child of the said A. who under the trust in default of appointment hereinbefore contained shall attain a vested interest in the said investments then the said investments and the income thereof and all accumulations of income shall be held upon trust for such persons and purposes and generally in such manner as the said A. shall by deed revocable or irrevocable by will or codicil appoint and subject to any such appointment;

(g) Upon trust for the next of kin of the said A. ascertained according to and in the shares provided by the law relating to intestacy as if the said A. had died intestate and a bachelor;

[(h) I hereby declare that the administrative provisions of this my will relating to residue shall apply to this legacy.]

1 For Form 7 see Part E, para **[238.13]**.

2 See n 1 to Form B16.25 at para **[216.32]**.

3 For deaths on or after 22 March 2006, the initial life interest of A should be an immediate post-death interest if it takes effect immediately on the testator's death (or is subject only to a survivorship condition permitted by IHTA 1984, s 92: see paras **[219.6]**–**[219.7]**), and is not, for example, postponed to another interest (see para **[216.1]** above). This is the case even if the protective trust option is chosen (see IHTA 1984, s 88(4)(b)(i) and para **[200.104]** above). A further life interest appointed to a spouse (or civil partner) under the power of sub-clause (b) of the Form will not be an immediate post-death interest, and unless it is a disabled person's interest within IHTA 1984, s 89B (see para **[200.99]** above), spouse or civil partner exemption will not be available on A's death, and the settled property subject to it will then fall within the IHT charging regime for relevant property (see para **[218.8]** ff above).

4 See n 4 to Form B16.25 at para **[216.32]**.

5 Including an illegitimate child unless a contrary intention is shown: see Part A, paras **[200.28]** and **[200.29]**.

Ancillary provisions

[216.34]

Form B16.27: Trust for accumulation of income[1]

[Subject to the payment of the said annuity to my wife [*name*]] my trustees shall accumulate for the period of twenty-one years from the date of my death [if my wife shall so long live] the [surplus] income of my residuary estate by investing the same and the income therefrom in any investments hereby authorised with power to vary such investments as my trustees shall think fit until the termination of the said period of twenty-one years [or until the death of my wife whichever shall first happen] and shall then hold the accumulated fund as capital of my residuary estate but so that no part of such fund shall be invested in the purchase of land.

1 The periods allowed for accumulation are stated in the LPA 1925, s 164 (Part G, para **[246.56]**) and the PAA 1964, s 13 (Part G, para **[246.86]**). This clause assumes that the income of the residuary estate is more than sufficient to maintain the widow and children and provides for the accumulation of the surplus income in order to provide more capital for the children.

For the taxation of accumulated income see paras **[218.29]**–**[218.36]**.

This clause could be unsatisfactory for IHT reasons. Part of the residuary estate will be treated as subject to the annuitant's interest in possession which could be an immediate post-death interest if it takes immediate effect on the testator's death (see the Preliminary Note to B11 at para **[211.1]** ff) and the remainder will be taxed as relevant property (see para **[218.8]** ff).

[216.35]

Form B16.28: Payment of income to banker[1]

My trustees may and if any beneficiary entitled hereunder to receive any income so requests them in writing shall pay such income to any banker to be chosen from time to time by such beneficiary to be held by such banker for the account of such beneficiary and my trustees shall not be liable for any loss arising from payment so made but my trustees may from time to time if they think fit disregard in whole or in part any such request by such a beneficiary with respect to any income subject to a provision for forfeiture on alienation or to a discretionary trust or if at any time my trustees should not be satisfied as to the continued existence of such beneficiary.

1 This clause may be helpful on occasion, but in general this will be a matter for arrangement between the beneficiary and the trustees where the beneficiary is absolutely entitled to the income.

[216.36]

Form B16.29: Clause as to annual sums payable under an insurance policy[1]

I declare that the annual sums payable to my estate under a policy of insurance issued by —— and numbered —— shall [during the widowhood of my wife] be treated when received as income of my estate [and paid to my widow accordingly].

1 An insurance policy may provide for the payment of a lump sum on death followed by an annual payment for a number of years and then, on the cesser of such payments, a final lump sum. These annual payments have been held to be capital of the testator's estate: *Re Fisher, Harris v Fisher* [1943] Ch 377, [1943] 2 All ER 615, and it therefore becomes necessary to include a clause such as this if such payments are to be treated as income. The same rule was applied where a testator was entitled to receive a percentage of the net profits of a business for some years after his death: see *Re Payne, Westminster Bank Ltd v Payne* [1943] 2 All ER 675. This clause is only necessary where the will gives a life interest. The wording here assumes that the will gives the income of the residuary estate to the widow during her widowhood. The wording must be adapted where the wife's interest is not restricted to widowhood and can be used where some person other than the wife takes a life interest in residue. It should be noted, however, that such sums may be taxable as income in the hands of the widow.

[216.37]

Form B16.30: No apportionment on death of life tenant[1]

I declare that the personal representatives of any person who under the trusts thereof is life tenant of any property shall not be entitled to receive any part of any dividends rents interest royalties or moneys of the nature of income which shall be actually received in respect of such property after the death of such life tenant, notwithstanding that the same be paid in respect of a period wholly or partly prior to the death of such life tenant; but the same when received shall belong to the person or persons who under the said trusts would have been entitled thereto if the same had been paid in respect of a period immediately subsequent to the death of such life tenant.

1 It seems that the general rule is that apart from express provision no apportionment is proper where shares are sold cum dividend on the death of the life tenant: see *Re Firth, Sykes v Ball* [1938] Ch 517, [1938] 2 All ER 217; distinguishing *Re Winterstoke's Will Trusts, Gunn v Richardson* [1938] Ch 158, [1937] 4 All ER 63. When, however, the shares are appropriated to beneficiaries in satisfaction of their interests on the death of the life tenant, an apportionment under the Apportionment Act 1870 is proper: *Re Henderson, Public Trustee v Reddie* [1940] Ch 368, [1940] 1 All ER 623, where the position is discussed and all the authorities considered. See Form B14.32 at para **[214.54]** for a shorter and more general form. See also the Note to B14 at paras **[214.48]–[214.52]** concerning the Apportionment Acts and their exclusion.

B17 Trusts for children

B17.26 Trust for wife and children equally .... [217.34]
B17.27 Trust after life interest to a wife for nephews and nieces as wife shall appoint, and in default of appointment equally .... [217.35]
B17.28 Trust for brothers and sisters and children of deceased brothers and sisters .... [217.36]
B17.29 Trust of child's share by reference .... [217.37]
B17.30 Trust of child's share by reference—another form .... [217.38]
B17.31 Declaration excluding s 33 of the Wills Act 1837 .... [217.39]
B17.32 Clause providing for forfeiture of gift on marriage to person not professing a certain religion .... [217.40]
B17.33 Child en ventre—general clause .... [217.41]
GIFTS OF LAND
FORMS
B17.34 Gift of land for the benefit of testator's children and issue of deceased children, sons taking at eighteen or twenty-one, and in either case with the alternative of taking on previous marriage—variation for children of a person other than testator .... [217.42]
B17.35 Gift of land to minor with provision for his death under eighteen or twenty-one leaving issue .... [217.43]
DECLARATIONS CONCERNING HOTCHPOT
FORMS
B17.36 Declaration that provisions made by will for testator's wife and children are in addition to and not in substitution for provisions made for them in his lifetime .... [217.44]
B17.37 Declaration that provisions made by will for children are not to be in addition to provisions made for them by the testator's marriage settlement .... [217.45]
B17.38 Declaration that certain children are to bring specified sums into hotchpot .... [217.46]
B17.39 Declaration negativing ademption of a gift by will by subsequent gift .... [217.47]
B17.40 Declaration that certain future gifts are to be brought into hotchpot .... [217.48]
B17.41 Express provision against satisfaction and ademption .... [217.49]

PRELIMINARY NOTE

[217.1]

Trusts for bereaved minors and age 18-to-25 trusts within IHTA 1984, ss 71A and 71D. The former provision for accumulation and maintenance trusts for children contained in IHTA 1984, s 71 cannot apply to trusts created or coming into possession after 21 March 2006. In relation to trusts coming into effect after 21 March 2006, including wills of persons dying after that date, there are two much more limited categories of trust for minor children which receive advantageous treatment for IHT purposes: under IHTA 1984, ss 71A ('trusts for bereaved minors') and 71D ('age 18-to-25 trusts). For either section to apply, at least one of the beneficiary's parents must have died, and a trust in a will can only fall within either section if it is established under *the will of a parent of the child.* Parents for this purpose extend to step-parents and anyone who at his or her death has parental responsibility for the child: see s 71H. The s 71D trust is essentially a variant on the s 71A trust which permits a higher vesting age, at the cost of possibly incurring an IHT charge of probably modest proportions.

For a fuller account of these two forms of testamentary trust see the Notes to paras **[200.108]**–**[200.109]** above. For a summary of the available types of testamentary trusts for minors see para **[224.24]**, and for examples of immediate post-death interest and relevant property trusts for minors in Forms C2.2 at **[224.42]** ff and C2.6 at **[224.102]** ff.

[217.2]

Tax consequences of accumulation and maintenance trusts outside ss 71A and 71D. Suppose someone dies on or after 22 March 2006 having made a will containing an accumulation and maintenance trust of the type which used to fall within IHTA 1984, s 71, under which the beneficiaries attain interests in possession on or before attaining the age of 25, but the capital either vests in them at a greater age than 25 or they are given life interests (so that neither s 71A nor s 71D will apply). The effect of the FA 2006 IHT rules on such a trust will depend on the ages which the beneficiaries have reached by the time of the testator's death. The shares of beneficiaries who at the time of the testator's death are below the age at which interests in possession are attained will be within the relevant property regime, whereas the shares of those who have by the time of the testator's death attained that age will have immediate post-death interests which are beneficiary-taxed. Where a beneficiary is at the testator's death below the age of attaining an interest in possession, his or her share will continue to be subject to the relevant property rules when he or she attains an interest in possession, unless it happens within two years of the testator's death and IHTA 1984, s 144 has the effect of converting the interest to an immediate-post death interest (see para **[200.136]** for this possibility).

[217.3]

Income tax and capital gains tax. The income tax rate applicable to trusts is 40 per cent, (32.5% for dividends) and has been since the tax year 2004–05 (Income Tax Act 2007, s 9, formerly ICTA 1988, s 686(1A)). Until 6 April 2008, the rate of capital gains tax on trusts is 40 per cent, subject to indexation relief and taper relief, (TCGA 1992, s 4(1AA) as amended). The Government has announced that on and from 6 April 2008 there will be a flat rate of capital gains tax applicable across the board, including trusts, of 18 per cent, without indexation relief or taper relief. In the case of a 'trust for the vulnerable' within FA 2005, ss 23–45, gains are taxed as if they were the principal beneficiary's: see the Notes to para **[217.4]** and Part C4 below. Whereas this could produce a significant capital gains tax advantage before 6 April 2008, on and after that date when the rate of capital gains tax should be a uniform 18 per cent (if the Government proposal becomes law), the only advantage would seem to be that the trust would have the benefit of the beneficiary's annual exempt amount rather than the trust's (which is only one-half of an individual's). The 40 per cent rate applies until 6 April 2008 to capital gains realised by estates in the course of administration: TCGA 1992, s 4(1AA) as amended. On and after 6 April 2008, the 18 per cent rate should apply.

[217.4]

Trusts for the vulnerable. A type of trust for minor children with special tax treatment is created by FA 2005, ss 23–45. This is a 'trust for the vulnerable' for a 'relevant minor', which broadly corresponds with the trust for a bereaved minor discussed in the Note to para **[217.1]** above. This type of trust enables the trustees and beneficiary to elect for the income and capital gains to be taxed as if the trust assets and income were the property of the relevant minor instead of being taxed at the trust rates. Whereas this could produce a significant capital gains tax advantage before 6 April 2008 since trust rates have increased considerably in recent years, on and after that date when the Government has announced a uniform rate of capital gains tax of 18 per cent, the only capital gains tax advantage of a trust for the vulnerable would seem to be that the trust would have the benefit of the beneficiary's annual exempt amount rather than the trust's (which is only one-half of an individual's) (see the Notes to para **[200.40]** above). This note and the form set out below concentrate on the aspects of the new rules which fall within the scope of *Williams on Wills*, namely the drafting problems of creating, by testamentary disposition, trusts which qualify for this special treatment. The details of what the special treatment is and how it is obtained will be found in HMRC's 'An introduction to the new special tax treatment for certain trusts with vulnerable beneficiaries', and *Tolley's Income Tax 2007–08*, paras 75.18–75.20.

For the purposes of FA 2005, ss 23–45, a relevant minor is a child under the age of 18 who has at least one deceased parent (s 39). Creating a qualifying 'trust for the vulnerable' is thus a possibility for a testator who has minor children to consider when deciding what provisions to include in his will to take effect in the event of him dying while one or more of them are still minors. It is important to note that where it is a question of creating by will a 'trust for the vulnerable' for a 'relevant minor' within FA 2005, ss 23–45, it can only be done by the will of a parent of the relevant minor, and other relatives are not able to do so (see s 35(2)(a)).

For a trust fund held for a minor child to be able to qualify for this special treatment it has to be one under which he will become absolutely entitled to the trust property and its income at the age of 18, and also to any income of the property which has been accumulated before that time (s 35(3)(a)). As regards the trusts while the relevant minor is under 18 there is one condition as to the trusts of capital and one as to the trusts of income. The capital condition is that while the relevant minor is living and under 18 there must be no power to apply capital other than for the benefit of the relevant minor (s 35(3)(b)). The income condition is that while the relevant minor is living and under 18 either he must be entitled to the income (if any) as it arises or the income may not be applied for anyone else's benefit (s 35(3)(c)). In other words a trust of capital and income for a relevant minor contingently on attaining the age of 18, to which TA 1925, ss 31 and 32 apply, would qualify.

It is expressly provided that the application of the statutory power of advancement (the Trustee Act 1925, s 32 or the Northern Irish equivalent) or an express power of advancement which subject to the same restrictions as the statutory power does not prevent the trusts from being qualifying trusts (FA 2005, s 35(4) as amended by FA 2006, s 88, Sch 12, para 48(3),(5)). This provision, coupled with the (in our view correct) published opinion of

HMRC that if the statutory power is modified to apply to the whole of a presumptive share, or if there is an express power extending to the whole of a presumptive share, this provision does not apply, may cause confusion as to what is permissible in relation to the relevant minor himself. FA 2005, s 35(3)(b) says that a qualifying trust must be such that while the relevant minor is living and under the age of 18, if any property is applied for the benefit of a beneficiary it must be applied only for the benefit of the relevant minor. This expressly contemplates that capital may be applied for the benefit of the relevant minor, without any limit on the amount or proportion, and seems therefore to imply that an express power of application of capital, or TA 1925, s 32 power extended to apply to the whole of a presumptive share, *which is limited to enabling the capital of the relevant minor's share to be applied for the benefit of the relevant minor*, is compatible with the trusts being qualifying trusts for the purposes of the special treatment for trusts for the vulnerable. On the other hand, the provision in FA 2005, s 35(4) that the application of TA 1925, s 32 does not prevent a trust from being a qualifying trust might be thought to mean that without such a provision the application of s 32 in relation to the interest in capital of the relevant minor would prevent the trust being a qualifying trust, and therefore that any power of application in favour of the relevant minor beyond that provided by s 32 will prevent a trust from being a qualifying trust. (In this regard trusts for vulnerable minors differ from trusts for bereaved minors in respect of which an unrestricted power of advancement is expressly permitted: s 71A(4).) The possibilities for a trust for a vulnerable minor are as follows:

(1) Despite FA 2005, s 35(3)(b), an express power of application or s 32 applied to the whole of a presumptive share in relation to the interest of a relevant minor is not compatible with the trust being a qualifying trust;

(2) FA 2005, s 35(4) has the sole purpose of enabling a trust to be a qualifying trust where TA 1925, s 32 power applies in relation to the beneficial interest of someone other than the relevant minor, such as a person who would take the trust fund in the event of the relevant minor dying under the age of 18. The trouble with this theory is that it is difficult to imagine circumstances where the application of TA 1925, s 32 power in favour of beneficiaries other than the relevant minor could, apart from FA 2005, s 35(4), prevent the conditions in FA 2005, s 35(3) from applying. This is because the Trustee Act 1925, s 32(1)(c) provides that the power cannot be exercised so as to prejudice any person entitled to a prior interest unless such person is in existence, of full age, and consents in writing to the exercise. The nature of the requirements for a trust for a relevant minor which appear in FA 2005, s 35(3) are such that TA 1925, s 32(1)(c) would seem to prevent any exercise of the s 32 power in favour of any person with an interest over which the relevant minor's interest has priority while the relevant minor is living and under the age of 18. Where another beneficiary has priority over the relevant minor's interest, it is difficult to see how the trust for the relevant minor could be a qualifying trust quite apart from any question of the application of TA 1925, s 32; and

(3) FA 2005, s 35(4) has been included in imitation of the similar provision in IHTA 1984, s 89(3) without a full analysis of the need for it, and it is in fact redundant.

HMRC's guidance in their publication 'An introduction to the new special tax treatment for certain trusts with vulnerable beneficiaries' is equivocal on whether it is compatible with a trust being a qualifying trust for there to be a power of application in favour of the relevant minor which is wider than the unamended TA 1925, s 32. Therefore, the cautious advice is to avoid including an express power of application, or an expansion of the s 32 power to apply more than half of a presumptive share, in relation to the interest of a relevant minor unless and until it becomes clear that HMRC accept that this is compatible with a trust being a qualifying trust.

FA 2005, s 36 makes clear that trusts can qualify for the special treatment if they relate to part rather than the whole of an asset, provided that the part of the asset and its income are sufficiently identifiable to be able to determine whether it is held on qualifying trusts. It seems likely that a trust of an undivided fractional or percentage share of an asset or fund of assets and of the income of that share would have sufficiently definite subject-matter for it to be possible for the qualifying conditions to apply. HMRC's guidance notes on this topic are not very clear on whether they regard a trust of a fractional undivided share of a fund as being capable of qualifying for this special treatment. The main practical point here is to make sure that there is a power of appropriation without any consents being required, so that if there turns out to be a difficulty about obtaining the special tax treatment for an undivided share of a fund, specific assets can be appropriated to the trust for the relevant minor in order to obtain the special treatment.

The requirements for a trust to qualify for the special capital gains tax and income tax treatment for trusts for the vulnerable under FA 2005, ss 23–45 are narrower than the requirements for IHTA 1984, s 71A (trusts for bereaved minors). IHTA 1984, s 71A can apply collectively to a class of minors without individual members of the class being certain of becoming entitled to any specific part or share of the fund, and an express power of application of capital, or an expanded TA 1925 s 32 power can apply to more than half of a presumptive share.

Although the intestacy trusts are expressly declared to qualify as trusts for the vulnerable for a relevant minor (FA 2005, s 35(1)(a)), when drafting will trusts intended to fall within FA 2005, ss 23–45, it will not be sufficient to copy out the statutory trusts in the AEA 1925. This is because marriage under the age of 18 is an alternative contingency under the intestacy trusts but is not a permitted alternative contingency in the case of express trusts appearing in a will: compare IHTA 1984, s 71A(3)(a) with FA 2005, s 35(3)(a). In this respect also trusts for vulnerable minors appear to differ from a trust for bereaved minors. For a precedent for a trust for vulnerable minors see Form B17.1 below under para **[217.9]**.

[217.5]

Substitution. When trusts for the testator's children or remoter issue are being drafted it should be remembered that the new s 33 of the Wills Act 1837 (WA 1837) (substituted by the AJA 1982, s 19: Part G, para

[244.36]) provides a statutory substitution clause in some circumstances, even in relation to class gifts: see Vol 1, para **[47.14]** ff. The substitutional provisions for class gifts are of such uncertain application to the more common kinds of class gift that we recommend that express provision is made for substitution, or that s 33 is expressly excluded. Also, they can only apply where a child or remoter descendant of the testator predeceases him, and will not operate to substitute issue of someone who survives the testator but dies before attaining some age upon the attaining of which the gift is contingent. Express substitutional clauses can and should be made to apply in whatever circumstances a primary gift fails.

One feature of the provisions relating to trusts for bereaved minors within IHTA 1984, s 71A, or age 18-to-25 trusts within IHTA 1984, s 71D, contained in a will which should be noted is that they only apply to *children* of the deceased parent. If, therefore, the trusts include a substitutional proviso in favour of the children of a child dying under the age of 18 and the proviso takes effect, the property or share of property which then devolves on the deceased parent's grandchildren will become 'relevant property' for IHT purposes, though without any charge to tax on the death of the child where that occurs after the testator's death: IHTA 1984, s 71B(2)(b). The same is true in relation to age 18-to-25 trusts for children of the testator where a child dies under 18: s 71E(2)(b). If the child attains the age of 18, the property will become liable to tax under ss 71E and 71F in the same manner as if it were relevant property (with no possibility of a periodic charge, however). If the child thereafter dies before attaining 25, there will be in addition an exit charge in respect of such property under s 71F, save where the death occurs within two years of the testator's death: s 144(1)(a).

[217.6]

Perpetuities. When drafting trusts for children and issue care must be taken that they do not infringe the rule against perpetuities, see the Preliminary Note to B16 at paras **[216.2]** and **[216.3]** and for a fuller account of perpetuities, see Vol 1, para **[94.1]** ff.

[217.7]

Vesting. If a gift to a minor is absolutely vested as from the testator's death, it now seems that in contrast to the position in the past when trustees (in the absence of an express provision to the contrary) in order to get a sufficient discharge had to retain the gift until the minor was of full age and able to give a good receipt, a person with parental responsibility for a minor can receive the gift on the minor's behalf: ChA 1989, s 3(3) (Part G, para **[244.114]**), which came into force on 14 October 1991 and Vol 1, para **[9.41]**.

For some considerations as to whether a gift to children should be made contingent upon their attaining a certain age or being living at a specified time, see the Preliminary Note to B16 at paras **[216.4]** and **[216.5]**.

[217.8]

Meaning of children and issue. When drafting a trust for a class of children, whether the testator's or someone else's, the testator should be asked to confirm that he wishes illegitimate, legitimated and adopted children and issue to be included because references to children and issue in wills will be construed as including such persons unless a contrary intention is expressed. For wills made after 3 April 1988 the inclusion of illegitimate issue and children will be by virtue of the Family Law Reform Act 1987 (FLRA 1987), ss 1 and 19 (Part G, paras **[245.70]** and **[245.72]**). (For wills made prior to that and after 1 January 1970, see the Family Law Reform Act 1969 (FLRA 1969), s 15(1): Part G, para **[245.39]**.) The inclusion of adopted children and issue is by virtue of the Adoption and Children Act 2002, ss 66–73 in relation to adoptions occurring on or after 30 December 2005 (and prior thereto the Adoption Act 1976 (AA 1976), ss 39 and 42, replacing (by way of consolidation) Children Act 1975, Sch 1, paras 3 and 5 as from 1 January 1976, and brought into force on 1 January 1988). The Human Fertilisation and Embryology Act 1990 (HFEA 1990), as from 1 August 1991, also affects the meaning of 'children' and 'issue' in some circumstances (see Part G, para **[245.82]** ff). See generally Vol 1, Chs 71 to 76 for the meaning of the terms 'children' and 'issue'.

[217.9]

Form B17.1: Trust for the minor children of the testator at age 18 falling within Inheritance Tax Act 1984, s 71A (trusts for bereaved minors) and Finance Act 2005, ss 23–45 (special income tax and capital gains tax treatment for trusts for the vulnerable)[1]

(1) My trustees shall hold [my residuary estate][2] upon trust for such of my children as are living at my death and attain the age of 18 years if more than one in equal shares absolutely.

(2) If for any reason any child of mine does not attain a vested interest under the foregoing trust and there are descendants of his or hers who are living at my death (or the death of such child of mine if later) and who attain the age of 18 years such descendants shall take in equal shares per stirpes the share such child of mine would have taken if he had attained a vested interest and so that no descendant shall take whose parent attains a vested interest under the foregoing trust.

(3) The foregoing trusts shall carry the intermediate income and section 31 of the Trustee Act 1925 shall apply thereto.[3]

(4) My trustees shall have power at their absolute discretion to appropriate specific assets to or towards the vested or presumptive share under the foregoing trusts of any child or remoter descendant of mine and on the basis of such evidence of values or advice as to values as they think fit.

1 See the notes to paras **[217.1]–[217.4]** above.

2 An earlier definition of the trust fund is assumed, which could be a pecuniary legacy or a specific gift or residue or a share of residue, and which should be defined as including the assets from time to time representing whatever is initially given.

3 If it becomes clear that HMRC will accept that a power of application of the whole of a presumptive share in favour of a relevant minor is compatible with the trusts falling within the Finance Act 2005, ss 23–45, add as a separate sub-clause 'Section 32 of the Trustee Act 1925 (relating to payment or application of capital) shall apply to the foregoing trust for my children (but not the foregoing trust for my remoter descendants) as if the words 'one-half of' were omitted from sub-section (1)(a) thereof.' See the note under para **[217.4]** above.

[217.10]

Form B17.2: Trust for children of the testator at twenty-five falling within Inheritance Tax Act 1984, s 71D (age 18 to 25 trusts) with substitutional trusts for those who die in testator's lifetime or after testator's death

In trust for such of my children as attain the age of twenty-five years and if more than one in equal shares absolutely[1] provided always that if any child of mine shall die or has already died in my lifetime or shall die after my death under the age of twenty-five years leaving a child or children living at my death or born thereafter who attains or attain the age of twenty-one years then the share which such child of mine would have taken had such child survived me and obtained a vested interest in such share shall be held in trust for such child or children as aforesaid of such child of mine and if more than one in equal shares.[2]

1 These trusts should be capable of qualifying as age 18-to-25 trusts within IHTA 1984, s 71D (see para **[200.108]** above). But if they come into possession immediately following the testator's death, and any child is over the age of 18 but under the age of 25, and entitled to an interest possession by virtue of TA 1925, s 31(1)(ii), he or she would have an immediate post-death interest in a share of the trust fund rather than his or her share being subject to age 18-to-25 trusts (see IHTA 1984, s 71D(5)(c)). Further, if a child attained an interest in possession within two years of the testator's death, IHTA 1984, s 144 might have the effect of converting the interest to an immediate post-death interest (see para **[200.136]** for this possibility). An immediate post-death interest could have a capital gains tax disadvantage over age 18-to-25 trusts because although a beneficiary's absolute entitlement at age 25 would not trigger an IHT charge if he or she had an immediate post-death interest (by virtue of IHTA 1984, s 53(2)), no capital gains tax hold-over relief would be available to relieve any gain accruing under TCGA 1992, s 71 on that absolute entitlement. However, although there could be an IHT charge on a beneficiary's absolute entitlement at age 25 under age 18-to-25 trusts (under IHTA 1984 s. 71E(1)), hold-over relief would be available under TCGA 1992, s 260(2)(d). Immediate post-death interests could be avoided if TA 1925, s 31 was modified to allow accumulation of income for the testator's children beyond their 18th birthdays, such as in Form B18.13, para **[218.81]**.

2 If these substitutional trusts take effect the property or share of property which devolves on the deceased child's children will be relevant property for IHT purposes, though without any charge to tax on the death of the child where that occurs after the testator's death: s 71E(2)(b). If they take effect immediately on the testator's death however, and any grandchild is over the age of 18 but under the age of 21, and entitled to an interest possession by virtue of TA 1925, s 31(1)(ii), he or she would have an immediate post-death interest in a share of the trust fund rather than his or her share being relevant property. Further, if a grandchild attained an interest in possession within two years of the testator's death, IHTA 1984, s 144 might have the effect of converting the interest to an immediate post-death interest (see para **[200.153]** for this possibility). As mentioned in the above footnote, immediate post-death interests would be avoided if TA 1925, s 31 was modified to allow accumulation of income for the testator's grandchildren beyond their 18th birthdays, such as in Form B18.13, para **[218.81]**.

[217.11]

Form B17.3: Trust for the children of the testator falling within Inheritance Tax Act 1984, s 71A (trusts for bereaved minors) or s 71D (age 18-to-25 trusts), in variable shares

My trustees shall hold my residuary estate upon trust for such of my children as shall survive me and attain the age of [18/25][1] years and if more than one in such shares as my trustees shall from time to time by deed or deeds revocable or irrevocable appoint in accordance with the provisions below[2] and in default of such appointment in equal shares Provided that if any child of mine shall die in my lifetime or having survived me shall die before attaining a vested interest leaving a child or children living at or born after my death who shall attain the age of [18/21] years such last-mentioned child or children shall take if more than one equally between them the share of my residuary estate to which their deceased parent would have become entitled had he or she lived to attain a vested interest and provided further that no appointment under the power aforesaid shall be made and no appointment shall be revoked so as to

(i) diminish or increase the share (or the accumulations of income forming part of the share) of a child who at the date of such appointment or revocation has reached the age of [18/25] years;

(ii) diminish or increase the share (or the accumulations of income forming part of the share) devolving on his or her child or children of a child who has died under the age of [18/25] years; or

(iii) give a share (or accumulations of income forming part of the share) to a child who at the date of such appointment has been excluded from benefit as a result of an exercise of the power.

1 If the age contingency of 18 is adopted, a trust in this form will, in relation to the testator's living children, comply with the requirements for trusts for bereaved minors, and if the age contingency of 25 is adopted, it should comply with the requirements for age 18-to-25 trusts. But if the age contingency of 25 is adopted and the trusts come into possession immediately following the testator's death, and any child is over the age of 18 but under the age of 25, and entitled to an interest possession by virtue of TA 1925, s 31(1)(ii), he or she would have an immediate post-death interest in a share of the trust fund rather than his or her share being subject to age 18-to-25 trusts (see IHTA 1984, s 71D(5)(c)). Further, if a child attained an interest in possession within two years of the testator's death, IHTA 1984, s 144 might have the effect of converting the interest to an immediate post-death interest (see para **[200.136]** for this possibility). An immediate post-death interest could have a capital gains tax disadvantage over age 18-to-25 trusts because although a beneficiary's absolute entitlement at age 25 would not trigger an IHT charge if he or she had an immediate post-death interest (by virtue of IHTA 1984, s 53(2)), no capital gains tax hold-over relief would be available to relieve any gain accruing under TCGA 1992, s 71 on that absolute entitlement. However, although there could be an IHT charge on a beneficiary's absolute entitlement at age 25 under age 18-to-25 trusts (under IHTA 1984, s. 71E(1)), hold-over relief would be available under TCGA 1992, s 260(2)(d). Immediate post-death interests could be avoided if TA 1925, s 31 was modified to allow accumulation of income for the testator's children beyond their 18th birthdays, such as in Form B18.13, para **[218.81]**.

2 HMRC have confirmed that they consider that a power to vary shares may be compatible with trusts for bereaved minors and age 18-to-25 trusts, so long as the share of a child who has attained 18 or 25 (as the case may be), or who has died leaving children on whom his share devolves cannot be varied, and also so long as a child who has been excluded from benefit on an exercise of the power cannot be reinstated as a beneficiary.

[217.12]

Form B17.4: Trust for children or issue as life tenant shall appoint: variation where there is a joint power of appointment[1]

In trust for all or such one or more exclusively of the others or other of the children or remoter issue[2] of the said —— [and ——] at such time and if more than one in such shares and with such provisions for maintenance advancement and otherwise for the benefit of such children or issue or some or one of them at the discretion of my trustees or any other persons and with such gifts over and generally in such manner as the said —— [and —— shall by deed revocable or irrevocable jointly appoint and in default of and subject to any such appointment as the survivor of them] shall by deed revocable or irrevocable or by will or codicil appoint and subject to any such appointment in trust for the child or children of the said —— [and ——] who shall attain the age of [eighteen] [twenty-one] years or [being female] previously marry and if more than one in equal shares as tenants in common provided that if any child of the said —— [and ——] dies in the lifetime of —— [*or* before the death of the survivor of —— and ——] leaving issue living at the death of [the survivor of —— and] —— then such issue if and when they attain the age of [eighteen] [twenty-one] years or marry thereunder shall take by substitution and if more than one in equal shares per stirpes the share of my residuary estate which such child would have taken had he or she survived [the survivor of —— and] —— but so that no issue shall take whose parent is alive and so capable of taking.

Any child who or whose issue take any interest under the foregoing provision in default of appointment shall not take such interest in default of appointment without bringing into hotchpot any share or shares appointed to him or her or his or her issue and accounting for the same unless the appointment shall direct to the contrary.

1 Though it may be more common to give the capital of the residue to children equally, it is certainly a wise precaution, where there is a life interest given to a wife, that she should be given a power of appointment, for this enables the division of the estate to be considered at the last possible moment. By this means those who have prospered or married well may be given less than those who have suffered misfortune and all inequalities of fortune may be compensated for to a great extent. Class gifts – The 'rules of convenience' are fully stated in Vol 1 at para [66.1] ff.

2 Illegitimate children and issue will be objects of the power: see Vol 1, para **[72.14]**.

[217.13]

Form B17.5: Trust for children at eighteen, with alternative contingency of previous marriage with consent of guardians[1]

In trust for my children[2] who [being male] attain the age of eighteen years or [being female either attain that age or[3]] marry under that age with the consent (if marrying after my death) of their [his] or her guardians or guardian[4] and if more than one in equal shares as tenants in common[5] provided always that if any child of mine shall die or has already died in my lifetime or shall die after my death without obtaining a vested interest leaving a child or children living at my death or born thereafter who attains or attain the age of eighteen years then the share which such child of mine would have taken had such child survived me and obtained a vested interest in such share shall be held in trust for such child or children as aforesaid of such child of mine and if more than one in equal shares.

1 While this Form satisfies the requirements in relation to the testator's children for trusts for bereaved minors for IHT purposes within IHTA 1984, s 71A, it is doubtful whether it also satisfies the requirements for trusts for a vulnerable minor for income and capital gains tax purposes within FA 2005, ss 23–45 in view of the inclusion of entitlement on the alternative contingency of marriage with consent: see the Notes to paras **[217.1]**–**[217.4]** above. If there is any substitution of a child's children the substitutional trust cannot fall within s 71A: see para **[217.1]** above.

2 Illegitimate children may share: see para **[217.12]**, n 2.

3 A child or daughter (as the case may be) who marries without the necessary consent will nevertheless attain a vested interest on attaining her majority. If the guardians die before the marriage, the law dispenses with their consent (*Dawson v Oliver-Massey* (1876) 2 Ch D 753).

4 A person under 18 who is not a widow or widower cannot marry without the consent of parents or guardians, though, if such consent is refused, it may be given by the court: see the Marriage Act 1949, ss 3 and 78(1) (27 Halsbury's Statutes (4th edn) (2000 Reissue) 622), as amended by the FLRA 1969, s 2(1). In the case of marriage after banns the marriage may be celebrated provided such persons do not dissent. To satisfy the clause consent is required though it may be presumed from conduct, see Vol 1, paras **[35.9]**–**[35.17]**.

5 If it is desired to substitute a higher age as the age contingency then the words 'under the age of eighteen years' should be added to the words in brackets 'if marrying after my death', since it is only in such a case that consent to a marriage will be required. If the sons and daughters are to be put on a level as regards marriage under eighteen, omit the first two parts in square brackets and include the third. This used not to be the usual practice, but was adopted in the statutory trusts for issue of an intestate (AEA 1925, s 47(1): Part G, para **[244.63]**) and now the desire to make no distinction between the sexes is almost invariable.

[217.14]

Form B17.6: Trust for children; sons at twenty-five or on marriage after twenty-one, and daughters at twenty-one or on previous marriage[1]

In trust for my children[2] living at my death who being male attain the age of twenty-five years or marry under that age but over the age of twenty-one years or being female attain the age of twenty-one years or marry under that age if more than one in equal shares as tenants in common.[3]

1 For IHT purposes a trust in the form of this precedent complies with requirements for age 18-to-25 trusts. But if it comes into possession immediately following the testator's death, and any child is over the age of 18 but under the vesting age, and entitled to an interest possession by virtue of TA 1925, s 31(1)(ii), he or she would have an immediate post-death interest in a share of the trust fund rather than his or her share being subject to age 18-to-25 trusts (see IHTA 1984, s 71D(5)(c)). Further, if a child attained an interest in possession within two years of the testator's death, IHTA 1984, s 144 might have the effect of converting the interest to an immediate post-death interest (see para **[200.136]** for this possibility). An immediate post-death interest could have a capital gains tax disadvantage over age 18-to-25 trusts because although a beneficiary's absolute entitlement at age 25 would not trigger an IHT charge if he or she had an immediate post-death interest (by virtue of IHTA 1984, s 53(2)), no capital gains tax hold-over relief would be available to relieve any gain accruing under TCGA 1992, s 71 on that absolute entitlement. However, although there could be an IHT charge on a beneficiary's absolute entitlement at age 25 under age 18-to-25 trusts (under IHTA 1984, s. 71E(1)), hold-over relief would be available under TCGA 1992, s 260(2)(d). Immediate post-death interests could be avoided if TA 1925, s 31 was modified to allow accumulation of income for the testator's children beyond their 18th birthdays, such as in Form B18.13, para **[218.81]**. It is doubtful whether this trust also satisfies the requirements for trusts for a vulnerable minor in view of the inclusion of entitlement on the alternative contingency of marriage: see the Notes to paras **[217.1]** and **[217.2]** above.

2 Illegitimate and legitimated children will be eligible: see Part A, para **[200.28]** ff.

3 It should be borne in mind that although the WA 1837, s 33 (as substituted by the AJA 1982, s 19: Part G, para **[24.36]**) can apply to a class gift, its application to contingent class gifts where a member of the class predeceases the testator is unclear, and it cannot apply where a member of the class survives the testator but dies without having attained a vested interest (see Vol 1, para **[47.14]** ff). An express substitution clause should be included, such as in Forms B17.7 or B17.9 at paras **[217.15]**, **[217.17]**. Gifts to the testator's own children can of course be made to vest at any age, for the children are all 'lives in being.' For a clause where the children of a person other than the testator are to take, see Form B17.8 at para **[217.16]**. Testators should be warned that it is possible to defeat this clause so far as it postpones vesting until 25, for a son could raise money on his interest by mortgaging it with the usual insurance policy. It may be preferable to settle the share and give trustees a power to determine the settlement on the son attaining 25.

[217.15]

Form B17.7: Trust for children at twenty-one by settling each child's share and giving trustees power to pay or apply capital in favour of life tenant[1]

In trust for my children[2] living at my death who attain the age of twenty-one years or marry thereunder if more than one in equal shares.

Provided that the share of my residuary trust fund so given to every child of mine who shall survive me and attain twenty-one years or marry shall not vest absolutely in such child but shall be retained by my trustees upon the following trusts:

(i) The income of such share shall be paid to such child during his or her life.

(ii) Provided that my trustees shall have power in their absolute discretion from time to time during the life of such child after such child shall have attained the age of twenty-one years to pay transfer or apply to or for the benefit of such child the whole or any part or parts of the capital of such share freed and discharged from the trusts and powers hereof.

(iii) Subject as aforesaid such share and the income thereof shall be held upon trust for such one or more of his or her issue[3] immediate or remote as he or she may by deed with or without power of revocation and new appointment or by will or codicil appoint.

(iv) In default of such appointment and in so far as any such appointment shall not extend and subject to the foregoing trusts and powers such share shall be held for all the children or the child of such child of mine who attain the age of twenty-one years or marry thereunder if more than one as tenants in common in equal shares provided that no such child shall take in default of appointment without bringing into hotchpot any part of such share my child may have appointed in his or her favour or in favour of his or her issue under the power in that behalf hereinbefore contained unless my child making such appointment shall direct to the contrary.

1 This may seem an involved provision but its purpose is to protect a child from becoming entitled to capital at too young an age. The settled property subject a trust in this form will be relevant property for IHT purposes and thus liable to periodic and exit charges, or else beneficiary-taxed, if the trusts come into possession on the testator's death and the children have attained interests in possession at the time of the testator's death or within two years of it: see para **[217.2]** above.

2 Illegitimate and legitimated children will be eligible: see Part A, para **[200.28]**.

3 Illegitimate issue may take: see Part A, para **[200.28]**.

[217.16]

Form B17.8: Trust for children of a person who takes no life interest

In trust for all the children[1] of [*name*] [whenever born during the lifetime of [*name of parent*][2]] who attain the age of [eighteen] [twenty-one] years [or being female marry under that age] if more than one in equal shares as tenants in common.

1 It is not envisaged that the trust in this form will be for the testator's children, so the settled property subject to it will be relevant property for IHT purposes and thus liable to periodic and exit charges, or else beneficiary-taxed if the trusts come into possession on the testator's

death and the children have attained interests in possession at the time of the testator's death or within two years of it: see para **[217.2]** above. See n 2 to Form B17.4 at para **[217.12]**. Illegitimate issue may take: see Part A, para **[200.29]**.

2 See Vol 1, para **[66.1]** ff, on gifts to a class. If the gift is to children of a person who is not life tenant and the class is definitely extended to *all* his children, distribution will be delayed until his death, for until then the number cannot be ascertained. Where there is a life interest, words such as 'born or to be born' are referred to birth before the death of the life tenant and do not further extend the class (*Mogg v Mogg* (1815) 1 Mer 654), and so with 'all and every the children' (*Andrews v Partington* (1791) 3 Bro CC 401). If the class is to remain open indefinitely there should be a power of advancement exercisable over the whole of a presumptive share (see Form B18.20 at para **[218.105]**), so that the trusts can be terminated when it becomes reasonably certain that no more members of the class will be born.

[217.17]

Form B17.9: Trust for children of testator, including children dying in testator's lifetime leaving issue[1]

In trust for my children living at my death who attain the age of [eighteen] [twenty-five] years or die under that age leaving issue and for any children of mine who may have died in my lifetime whether before or after the date hereof leaving issue living at my death or then en ventre but born afterwards if more than one in equal shares as tenants in common but so that the share of any child of mine dying in my lifetime shall pass to his or her personal representatives as part of such child's estate as if such child had survived me.[2]

1 For IHT purposes a trust in this form will, in relation to the testator's living children, comply with the requirements for trusts for bereaved minors if the age contingency of 18 is adopted and with the requirements for age 18-to-25 trusts if the age contingency of 25 is adopted. But if the age contingency of 25 is adopted and the trusts come into possession immediately following the testator's death, and any child is over the age of 18 but under the vesting age, and entitled to an interest possession by virtue of TA 1925, s 31(1)(ii), he or she would have an immediate post-death interest in a share of the trust fund rather than his or her share being subject to age 18-to-25 trusts (see IHTA 1984, s 71D(5)(c)). An immediate post-death interest could have a capital gains tax disadvantage over age 18-to-25 trusts because although a beneficiary's absolute entitlement at age 25 would not trigger an IHT charge if he or she had an immediate post-death interest (by virtue of IHTA 1984, s 53(2)), no capital gains tax hold-over relief would be available to relieve any gain accruing under TCGA 1992, s 71 on that absolute entitlement. However, although there could be an IHT charge on a beneficiary's absolute entitlement at age 25 under age 18-to-25 trusts (under IHTA 1984, s. 71E(1)), hold-over relief would be available under TCGA 1992, s 260(2)(d). Further, if a child attained an interest in possession within two years of the testator's death, IHTA 1984, s 144 might have the effect of converting the interest to an immediate post-death interest (see para **[200.136]** for this possibility). Immediate post-death interests could be avoided if TA 1925, s 31 was modified to allow accumulation of income for the testator's children beyond their 18th birthdays, such as in Form B18.13, para **[218.81]**. See n 2 to Form B17.4 at para **[217.12]**. Illegitimate issue may take: see Part A, para **[200.28]**.

2 It must be remembered that a share thus passing to the representatives of a deceased child becomes liable to the payment of the debts of that child. A direct gift to the child's issue may therefore in certain cases be more expedient. Forms B17.9 and B17.12 at paras **[217.17]** and **[217.20]** or Form B19.11 at para **[219.24]** may be used to prevent the share becoming available to satisfy the debts of a deceased child. Children of a deceased parent taking in substitution do not bring into account a debt owing by the deceased parent to the testator (*Re Binns, Public Trustee v Ingle* [1929] 1 Ch 677, [1929] All ER Rep 542). See also n 1 to Form B17.8 at para **[217.16]**.

[217.18]

Form B17.10: Trust for children of another, including children dying in testator's lifetime leaving issue[1]

In trust for the children of [*name*] living at my death or born afterwards who attain the age of [eighteen] [twenty-one] years or die under that age leaving issue and any children of the said [*name*] who may have died in my lifetime whether before or after the date hereof leaving issue living at my death or then en ventre but born afterwards if more than one in equal shares as tenants in common but so that the share of any child of the said [*name*] dying in my lifetime shall pass to his or her personal representatives as part of such child's estate and as if such child had survived me.[2]

1 The settled property subject a trust in this form will be relevant property for IHT purposes and thus liable to periodic and exit charges, or else beneficiary-taxed if the trusts come into possession on the testator's death and the children have attained interests in possession at the time of the testator's death or within two years of it: see para **[217.2]** above. Illegitimate issue may take: see Part A, para **[200.28]**.

2 See n 2 to Form B17.7 at para **[217.15]**.

[217.19]

Form B17.11: Trust for children of testator living at his decease and issue of deceased children then living at eighteen or twenty-one or on previous marriage[1]

In trust in equal shares (if more than one) for all my children living at my death and for all or any of the issue living at my death who attain the age of [eighteen] [twenty-five] years or marry under that age of any child of mine who predeceases me or has already predeceased me leaving issue living at my death, such issue to take through all degrees according to their stocks in equal shares (if more than one) the share which their parent would have taken if living at my death and so that no issue shall take whose parent is living at my death and so capable of taking.

1 For IHT purposes a trust in this form will, in relation to the testator's living children, comply with the requirements for trusts for bereaved minors if the age contingency of 18 is adopted and with the requirements for age 18-to-25 trusts if the age contingency of 25 is adopted. But if the age contingency of 25 is adopted and the trusts come into possession immediately following the testator's death, and any child is over the age of 18 but under the vesting age, and entitled to an interest possession by virtue of TA 1925, s 31(1)(ii), he or she would have an immediate post-death interest in a share of the trust fund rather than his or her share being subject to age 18-to-25 trusts (see IHTA 1984, s 71D(5)(c)). Further, if a child attained an interest in possession within two years of the testator's death, IHTA 1984, s 144 might have the effect of converting the interest to an immediate post-death interest (see para **[200.136]** for this possibility). An immediate post-death interest could have a capital gains tax disadvantage over age 18-to-25 trusts because although a beneficiary's absolute entitlement at age 25 would not trigger an IHT charge if he or she had an immediate post-death interest (by virtue of IHTA 1984, s 53(2)), no capital gains tax hold-over relief would be available to relieve any gain accruing under TCGA 1992, s 71 on that absolute entitlement. However, although there could be an IHT charge on a beneficiary's absolute entitlement at age 25 under age 18-to-25 trusts (under IHTA 1984, s 71E(1)), hold-over relief would be available under TCGA 1992, s 260(2)(d). Immediate post-death interests could be avoided if TA 1925, s 31 was modified to allow accumulation of income for the testator's children beyond their 18th birthdays, such as in Form B18.13, para **[218.81]**. Illegitimate children and issue may take: see Part A, para **[200.28]**.

[217.20]

Form B17.12: The same by reference to the statutory trusts for issue[1]

Upon the same statutory trusts for my issue as if I had died possessed thereof domiciled in England and intestate and without leaving a wife me surviving.[2]

1 Illegitimate children and issue may take: see Part A, para **[200.28]**.

2 See the statutory trusts of the AA 1976, s 47. The trusts give a vested interest not only to a female marrying under eighteen but also to a male marrying under that age. For deaths on or after 1 January 1996 the trusts no longer provide for the bringing into hotchpot of money or property, etc, paid or settled or advanced or covenanted to be paid or settled to or on a child (see Vol 1, para **[104.7]**). If this is not desired, the following words excluding hotchpot should be added: 'Provided that the said statutory trusts shall apply as if the former s 47(1)(iii) of the AA 1976 (advances, gifts on marriage etc to be taken into hotchpot) had not been repealed'. If the testator leaves infant children, these trusts should qualify as trusts for bereaved minors within IHTA 1984, s 71A (see the note to para **[200.108]** above), but may not be 'qualifying trusts' for the benefit of 'vulnerable beneficiaries' such as would allow a claim for special tax treatment bringing the trustees' income and capital gains tax liability into line with what the vulnerable beneficiaries' liability would have been had they received the income directly or had realised the trust gains (see FA 2005, ss 23–45). Although the intestacy trusts are expressly declared to qualify as trusts for the vulnerable for a relevant minor (FA 2005, s 35(1)(a)), if they do not arise by operation of statute, but rather by disposition of a testator, they may not fall within FA 2005, s 35(1)(a), and neither will they qualify under FA 2005, s 35(1)(b) since marriage under the age of 18 is an alternative contingency under the intestacy trusts but is not a permitted alternative contingency in the case of trusts appearing in a will. See para **[217.4]** above.

[217.21]

Form B17.13: Trust for children at discretion of trustees until the youngest attains eighteen or twenty-one years of age[1]

Until my youngest surviving child shall attain the age of [eighteen] [twenty-one] years my trustees may at their absolute discretion apply the income of my residuary trust fund [*or as the case may be*] to or for the maintenance education and support or otherwise for the benefit of all or any to the exclusion of the others or other of my children for the time being living in such shares and manner as the trustee shall think fit with power to pay such income to and to accept the receipt of the guardian or guardians of my said children and shall accumulate as an accretion to the capital of the said fund for all purposes the balance of such income and upon the youngest surviving child attaining the age of [eighteen] [twenty-one] years my trustees shall hold the said fund and the income thereof in trust for my said children in equal shares absolutely.[2]

1 Illegitimate children and issue as well as children and issue adopted at any time will prima facie be eligible; see Part A, para **[200.28]**.

2 This form will not comply with the requirements either for trusts for bereaved minors or for age 18-to-25 trusts; the property subject to a trust in this form will therefore be relevant property for IHT purposes and thus liable to periodic and exit charges if the youngest child is under the age of 18 or 21 (as the case may be) at the testator's death: see para **[217.1]** above.

[217.22]

Form B17.14: Remainder trust for children and issue of deceased children of life tenant at eighteen or twenty-one or on previous marriage[1]

In trust in equal shares (if more than one) for all or any the children or child of [*life tenant*] living at the date of the death of the survivor of myself and the said [*life tenant*] who attain the age of [eighteen] [twenty-one] years or marry under that age and for all or any of the issue living at the said date who attain the age of [eighteen] [twenty-one] years or marry under that age of any child of the said [*life tenant*] who dies before the said date or is already dead leaving issue living at the said date such issue to take through all degrees according to their stocks in equal shares (if more than one) the share which their parent would have taken if living at the said date and so that no issue shall take whose parent is living at the said date and so capable of taking.

1 Illegitimate children and issue as well as children and issue adopted at any time will prima facie be eligible; see Part A, para **[200.28]**. If the life tenant dies or surrenders his or her interest before the interests of any of the children or issue have attained absolute interests this trust will only qualify for favoured IHT treatment under IHTA 1984, s 71A or 71D in relation to any beneficiaries who are children or stepchildren of the testator. See para **[217.1]** above.

[217.23]

Form B17.15: The same by reference to the statutory trusts for issue[1]

Upon the same statutory trusts for the issue of [*life tenant*] as if he had died at the date of the death of the survivor of himself and myself possessed thereof domiciled in England and intestate and without leaving a wife him surviving.[2]

1 If the life tenant dies or surrenders his or her interest before the interests of any of the children or issue have attained absolute interests this trust will only qualify for favoured IHT treatment under IHTA 1984, s 71A or 71D in relation to any beneficiaries who are children or stepchildren of the testator. See para **[217.1]** above.

2 Illegitimate children and issue may take: see Part A, para **[200.28]**. See n 2 to Form B17.10 at para **[217.18]** and n 1 to Form B17.12 at para **[217.20]**. As to the ascertainment of a class of next of kin at an artificial point in time, not being the date of the testator's death, see *Hutchinson v National Refugee for Homeless and Destitute Children* [1920] AC 795, [1920] All ER Rep 701 and Vol 1, paras **[77.2]** and **[77.3]**. In the absence of a contrary intention in a will the class will be ascertained at the testator's death, see *Gundry v Pinniger* (1852) 1 De GM & G 502.

[217.24]

Form B17.16: Trust for children of another person who attain twenty-five within the limits of the rule against perpetuities[1]

In trust for the children of [*name*] born in my lifetime or after my death[2] who before the expiration of the period of twenty-one years from the death of the survivor of myself and the said [*name*] attain the age of twenty-five years or marry under that age or are living but under the said age and unmarried at the expiration of such period if more than one in equal shares as tenants in common.[3]

1 As to the construction of children and issue see Part A, para **[200.28]**.

2 The words 'after my death' extend the trust to children whenever born.
3 The settled property subject to a trust in this form will be relevant property for IHT purposes and thus liable to periodic and exit charges, or else beneficiary-taxed if the trusts come into possession on the testator's death and the children have attained interests in possession at the time of the testator's death or within two years of it: see para **[217.2]** above.

[217.25]

Form B17.17: Trust for children with entitlement to income during minority[1]

In trust for my children who attain the age of [eighteen] [twenty-one years] if more than one in equal shares absolutely and I declare that section 31 of the Trustee Act 1925 shall apply hereto as if in subsection (2) thereof the words 'as follows:– ' and paragraphs (i) and (ii) were replaced by the words 'upon trust for that person absolutely'.

1 If this form is used, the modification to the Trustee Act 1925 (TA 1925), s 31 (see paras **[218.53]–[218.56]** and Part G, para **[246.29]**) that any accumulations of income made by the trustees during a minority should belong to the minor absolutely, will mean that a child will be regarded by HMRC as having an interest in possession during his or her minority. For IHT purposes a trust in this form will comply with the requirements for trusts for bereaved minors within IHTA 1984, s 71A if the age contingency of 18 is adopted. If a greater age is adopted the beneficiaries will have immediate post-death interests: IHTA 1984 ff. There is a possible advantage over accumulation and maintenance trusts in that income will not be taxed at the trust rates (see paras **[218.28]–[218.30]**) but at the beneficiary's own rate of tax (which rate may well only be the lower or basic rate of tax depending upon the size of the fund) with his or her exemptions. There will be hold-over relief in respect of any capital gains tax charge which arises when a beneficiary becomes absolutely entitled to his share of the settled property if the age contingency is 18, see TCGA 1992, s 260(2)(da), (see para **[200.135]**), but not if the age contingency is a higher age. There may be an IHT disadvantage in that there may be an IHT charge if a beneficiary dies while entitled to an immediate post-death interest, although this will depend upon the size of the fund and whether or not it comes within the nil-rate IHT threshold according to the beneficiary's circumstances.

[217.26]

Form B17.18: Gift to children absolutely[1]

In trust for my children living at my death if more than one in equal shares absolutely.

1 This form will mean that a child will be regarded by HMRC as being absolutely entitled to capital and income during his or her minority. The same income tax considerations as noted in note 1 to Form B17.17 above will apply, but capital gains will be taxed at the beneficiary's own rate with his or her own personal exemption. A person with parental responsibility for a minor can now receive an absolute gift to a minor on the minor's behalf: ChA 1989, s 3(3) (Part G, para **[244.114]**), which came into force on 14 October 1991.

[217.27]

Form B17.19: Trusts for children, sons taking double shares[1]

In trust for my children who attain the age of [eighteen] [twenty-five] years or marry under that age if more than one as tenants in common in equal shares except that each son of mine entitled under this bequest shall take a share double the amount of the share of each daughter of mine [*or* except that my son [*name*] if he survives me and attains the age of [eighteen] [twenty-five] years shall take a share double the amount of the share of each of his brothers and sisters].[2]

1 As to the construction of children and issue see Part A, para **[200.28]**.

2 For IHT purposes a trust in this form will comply with the requirements for trusts for bereaved minors if the age contingency of 18 is adopted and with the requirements for age 18-to-25 trusts if the age contingency of 25 is adopted. But if the age contingency of 25 is adopted and the trusts come into possession immediately following the testator's death, and any child is over the age of 18 but under the age of 25, and entitled to an interest possession by virtue of TA 1925, s 31(1)(ii), he or she would have an immediate post-death interest in a share of the trust fund rather than his or her share being subject to age 18-to-25 trusts (see IHTA 1984, s 71D(5)(c)). Further, if a child attained an interest in possession within two years of the testator's death, IHTA 1984, s 144 might have the effect of converting the interest to an immediate post-death interest (see para **[200.136]** for this possibility). An immediate post-death interest could have a capital gains tax disadvantage over age 18-to-25 trusts because although a beneficiary's absolute entitlement at age 25 would not trigger an IHT charge if he or she had an immediate post-death interest (by virtue of IHTA 1984, s 53(2)), no capital gains tax hold-over relief would be available to relieve any gain accruing under TCGA 1992, s 71 on that absolute entitlement. However, although there could be an IHT charge on a beneficiary's absolute entitlement at age 25 under age 18-to-25 trusts (under IHTA 1984, s 71E(1)), hold-over relief would be available under TCGA 1992, s 260(2)(d). Immediate post-death interests could be avoided if TA 1925, s 31 was modified to allow accumulation of income for the testator's children beyond their 18th birthdays, such as in Form B18.13, para **[218.81]**.

[217.28]

Form B17.20: Trusts for various persons unequally[1]

In trust to divide the [trust] [said] fund into —— equal shares (and the words share or shares in this clause shall be always read as referring to such equal shares) and to hold —— shares in trust for [*name*] and if he shall die in my lifetime then in trust for such of his children who shall be living at my death who being male attain the age of [eighteen] [twenty-one] years or attain that age or marry and if there be more than one such child equally between them. And to hold —— shares in trust for [*name*] etc [*as above and continuing until all the shares are allotted*] Provided that if any of the trusts declared by this clause shall lapse or fail then the share or shares as to which the said trusts shall so lapse or fail (including any share or shares accruing by virtue of this provision) shall accrue to and be added equally to the other shares hereby given and be held in trust accordingly.[2]

1 See also Form B15.5 at para **[215.5]**. As to the construction of children and issue see Part A, para **[200.28]**. The effect of this clause may be shown by a simple example. In the case of three nephews who are to take the fund thus: A taking 1/2, B 1/3, and C 1/6, it is clear that there must be 12 shares, of which A will take six, B will take four, and C will take two. As the word 'share' throughout refers to such equal twelfth part, if A's interest fails, then his six shares are added equally to the remaining six shares, so that B will still receive twice as much as C. For problems which can arise where residue is divided into fractional shares and some of the beneficiaries are exempt from IHT see the Note to B14 at para **[214.72]** and Form B14.35 at para **[214.78]**.

2 The shares of any substituted beneficiaries who have not attained the age of vesting at the testator's death will be subject to IHT as relevant property unless they have interests in possession in their shares at the testator's death in which case they will have immediate post-death interests. They may also have immediate post-death interests if they become entitled to interests in possession within two years of the testator's death, see IHTA 1984, s 144(3)–(6).

[217.29]

Form B17.21: Trust for children in unequal shares[1]

In trust as to two equal sixth parts for my son [*name*] absolutely as to one other equal sixth part for my son [*name*] if and when he attains the age of [eighteen] [twenty-five] years and as to the remaining three equal sixth parts in trust in equal shares for my grandchildren —— and —— if and when they shall respectively attain the age of [eighteen] [twenty-one] years or marry under that age[2] [*add gift over of shares which fail to vest*].

1 For IHT purposes the trust in this form in relation to the share of the second son, if he is under the age of vesting at the testator's death, will comply with the requirements for trusts for bereaved minors if the age contingency of 18 is adopted and with the requirements for age 18-to-25 trusts if the age contingency of 25 is adopted. But if the age contingency of 25 is adopted and the trusts come into possession immediately following the testator's death, and the second son is over the age of 18 but under the age of 25, and entitled to an interest possession by virtue of TA 1925, s 31(1)(ii), he would have an immediate post-death interest in his share rather than his share being subject to age 18-to-25 trusts (see IHTA 1984, s 71D(5)(c)). Further, if the second son attains an interest in possession within two years of the testator's death, IHTA 1984, s 144 might have the effect of converting his interest in possession to an immediate post-death interest (see para **[200.136]** for this possibility). An immediate post-death interest could have a capital gains tax disadvantage over age 18-to-25 trusts because although a beneficiary's absolute entitlement at age 25 would not trigger an IHT charge if he or she had an immediate post-death interest (by virtue of IHTA 1984, s 53(2)), no capital gains tax hold-over relief would be available to relieve any gain accruing under TCGA 1992, s 71 on that absolute entitlement. However, although there could be an IHT charge on a beneficiary's absolute entitlement at age 25 under age 18-to-25 trusts (under IHTA 1984, s 71E(1)), hold-over relief would be available under TCGA 1992, s 260(2)(d). An immediate post-death interest could be avoided if TA 1925, s 31 was modified to allow accumulation of income for the second son beyond his 18th birthday, such as in Form B18.13, para **[218.81]**.The shares for the grandchildren will be taxed as relevant property unless they have attained absolute interests, or interests in possession by the time of the testator's death (or within two years of it).

2 A contingent gift of residuary personal estate has long since been held to carry the intermediate income. As to other gifts which now carry the intermediate income, see the LPA 1925, s 175 (Part G, para **[244.52]**). As to the statutory power of maintenance, see the TA 1925, s 31 (Part G, para **[246.26]**) and notes to B18 at para **[218.41]** ff.

[217.30]

Form B17.22: Gift to class of children with one child having the option to have assets appropriated in satisfaction of his share

(i) My trustees shall hold my residuary estate in trust for my children living at my death if more than one in equal shares absolutely.

(ii) Provided that my trustees shall as soon as conveniently may be after my death give to my son [*name*] notice in writing of the option to have shares in the —— Company Limited which form part of my estate ('the Company Shares') to the value of his share of my residuary estate appropriated to him in satisfaction of his share of my residuary estate and [also the option to purchase such of the Company Shares not so appropriated at a price equivalent to their value] *or* [if the value of the Company Shares should exceed the value of my son's share of my residuary estate I give so many of the Company Shares as exceed that value to my son absolutely and the shares of my other children in my residuary estate shall abate equally amongst themselves by that excess value].

(iii) The value of the Company Shares for the purposes of this clause shall be determined by an accountant nominated by my trustees as on the day of my death.

(iv) I declare that my said son shall have one month from the date of receipt of such notice in which to exercise the option but no purchaser of the said shares shall be in any way affected by the terms of this clause.

[217.31]

Form B17.23: Trust for children, in definite sums

In trust as to £[20000] or investments of that value for my daughter [*name*] if and when she attains the age of [eighteen] [twenty-five] years or marries under that age and as to £[20000] or investments of that value for my daughter [*name*] if and when she attains the age of [eighteen] [twenty-five] years or marries under that age and as to the residue (if any) for my son [*name*] absolutely.[1]

1 See n 1 to Form B17.19 at para **[217.27]**. The gift will carry the intermediate income, the beneficiaries being children of the testator. Such income will be available for maintenance purposes until the beneficiary attains majority, unless TA 1925 is varied to allow accumulation until the daughters attain the vesting age. See the Note in B18 at paras **[218.55]–[218.59]** generally for what interests carry intermediate income. For IHT purposes the trust in this form for a daughter, if she is under the age of vesting at the testator's death, will comply with the requirements for trusts for bereaved minors if the age contingency of 18 is adopted and with the requirements for age 18-to-25 trusts if the age contingency of 25 is adopted. But if the age contingency of 25 is adopted and the trusts come into possession immediately following the testator's death, and the daughter is over the age of 18 but under the age of 25, and entitled to an interest possession by virtue of TA 1925, s 31(1)(ii), she would have an immediate post-death interest in her share rather than her share being subject to age 18-to-25 trusts (see IHTA 1984, s 71D(5)(c)). Further, the daughter attains an interest in possession within two years of the testator's death, IHTA 1984, s 144 might have the effect of converting her interest in possession to an immediate post-death interest (see para **[200.136]** for this possibility). An immediate post-death interest could have a capital gains tax disadvantage over age 18-to-25 trusts because although a beneficiary's absolute entitlement at age 25 would not trigger an IHT charge if he or she had an immediate post-death interest (by virtue of IHTA 1984, s 53(2)), no capital gains tax hold-over relief would be available to relieve any gain accruing under TCGA 1992, s 71 on that absolute entitlement. However, although there could be an IHT charge on a beneficiary's absolute entitlement at age 25 under age 18-to-25 trusts (under IHTA 1984, s 71E(1)), hold-over relief would be available under TCGA 1992, s 260(2)(d). An immediate post-death interest could be avoided if TA 1925, s 31 was modified to allow accumulation of income for the daughter beyond her 18th birthday, such as in Form B18.13, para **[218.81]**.

[217.32]

Form B17.24: Trust for children other than a child who becomes entitled to settled estates[1]

In trust for the children of [*name*] who attain the age of [eighteen] [twenty-one] years or being female marry under that age if more than one in equal shares as tenants in common (other than and except any son or sons of the said [*name*] who on or before attaining the age of [eighteen] [twenty-one] years or any daughter or daughters of the said [*name*] who on or before attaining that age or marrying shall become entitled as tenant in tail [*or* in tail male] in possession or in remainder immediately expectant upon the determination of a life interest in possession to the —— Estates settled by etc *or* devised by etc)[2] and if there shall be no child (other than and except as aforesaid) who shall attain the age of [eighteen] [twenty-one] years or being female shall marry under that age then in trust for such of the excepted children as attain the age of [eighteen] [twenty-one] years or being female marry under that age if more than one in equal shares.

1 If this form is used, and the age of vesting is greater than 18 years, accumulation and maintenance trusts of income should continue until the age of vesting (but not longer than a period of accumulation permitted by law), otherwise there could be the termination of an immediate post-death interest which would be treated as a chargeable transfer for IHT purposes (under the IHTA 1984, ss 2 and 52(1)) where one of the beneficiaries comes to be within the exception after becoming entitled to an immediate post-death interest in his presumptive share. See Forms B18.11 to B18.13 at paras **[218.77]–[218.79]** for extended accumulation and maintenance provisions. See also B18 at paras **[218.72]–[218.76]** on the advantages of extended accumulation and maintenance provisions. As the beneficiaries are not children of the testator, IHTA 1984, ss 71A or 71D cannot apply to the trusts, and the funds will either be relevant property, absolute property, or immediate post-death interest property depending on the ages of the beneficiaries at the testator's death and whether TA 1925, s 31(1) (see para **[246.29]**) applies modified or unmodified.

2 Although no new entails can be created after 1 January 1997 (see paras **[200.52]** and **[200.53]**, entails created before that date can continue to exist.

[217.33]

Form B17.25: Trust for two persons as tenants in common on attaining twenty-five, with a gift over on the death of either to the other of them

In trust for [*name*] and [*name*] if and when they shall respectively attain the age of twenty-five years in equal shares as tenants in common and in case either of them is already dead or shall die in my lifetime or before attaining the age of twenty-five years I bequeath the share [of residue] hereinbefore bequeathed to the one so dying to the other of them if and when [he] shall attain the age of twenty-five years.[1]

1 This trust will not fall within IHTA 1984, s 71D unless the beneficiaries are children of the testator. Even then, if the trust comes into possession immediately following the testator's death, and either child is over the age of 18 but under the age of 25, and entitled to an interest possession by virtue of TA 1925, s 31(1)(ii), he or she would have an immediate post-death interest in his or her share rather than the share being subject to age 18-to-25 trusts (see IHTA 1984, s 71D(5)(c)). Further, if either attains an interest in possession within two years of the testator's death, IHTA 1984, s 144 might have the effect of converting it to an immediate post-death interest (see para **[200.136]** for this possibility). An immediate post-death interest could have a capital gains tax disadvantage over age 18-to-25 trusts because although a beneficiary's absolute entitlement at age 25 would not trigger an IHT charge if he or she had an immediate post-death interest (by virtue of IHTA 1984, s 53(2)), no capital gains tax hold-over relief would be available to relieve any gain accruing under TCGA 1992, s 71 on that absolute entitlement. However, although there could be an IHT charge on a beneficiary's absolute entitlement at age 25 under age 18-to-25 trusts (under IHTA 1984, s 71E(1)), hold-over relief would be available under TCGA 1992, s 260(2)(d). An immediate post-death interest could be avoided if TA 1925, s 31 was modified to allow accumulation of income for the children beyond their 18th birthdays, such as in Form B18.13, para **[218.81]**. If the beneficiaries are not children of the testator, the property will be relevant property while they are under the age of twenty-five, unless they have immediate post-death interests.

[217.34]

Form B17.26: Trust for wife and children equally[1]

In trust for such of my wife [*name*] and my children as survive me in equal shares as tenants in common.

1 All children alive at the testator's death will take. As to the construction of the word 'children', see Part A, para **[200.28]**. The gift to the wife is exempt from IHT, the gifts to the children are not. For the problems this could cause see the note to B14 at para **[214.72]** ff and for a declaration to deal with the problem see Form B14.35 at para **[214.78]**.

[217.35]

Form B17.27: Trust after life interest to a wife for nephews and nieces as wife shall appoint, and in default of appointment equally[1]

In trust for all or any one or more exclusively of the others or other of my nephews and nieces children of my [deceased] brothers or sisters in such shares and generally in such manner as my wife shall by deed revocable or irrevocable or by will or codicil appoint and subject to any such appointment in trust for all my said nephews or nieces living at my death [*or* the death of my wife] if more than one in equal shares as tenants in common.

1 Nephews and nieces should always be carefully defined otherwise relations by marriage or even great-nephews and great-nieces may make a claim. As to the meaning of nephews and nieces, see Vol 1, para **[71.5]**.

[217.36]

Form B17.28: Trust for brothers and sisters and children of deceased brothers and sisters[1]

In trust for my brothers and sisters living at my death and the children then living of any then deceased brother or sister of mine [who attain the age of [eighteen] [twenty-one] years or being female marry under that age][2] if more than one in equal shares as tenants in common but so that the children of any such deceased brother or sister shall take equally between them as tenants in common only the share their parent would have taken had he or she survived me.

1 As to the construction of words describing a blood relationship, see Part A, para **[200.28]** ff.

2 If an age contingency is included, and the trust for children of a deceased sibling takes effect, the property subject to it will be relevant property while the children are under the specified age, unless they have immediate post-death interests.

[217.37]

Form B17.29: Trust of child's share by reference

Upon the like trusts for the benefit of my daughter [*or* son] [*name*] and her [*or* his] children or issue and with the like gift over in favour of her [*or* his] [brothers and] sisters and their children and issue respectively as are hereinbefore expressed concerning the share of residue hereinbefore bequeathed for the benefit of my daughter [*or* son] [*name*] and her [*or* his] children or issue.[1]

1 This form is for use where children's shares are settled separately.

[217.38]

Form B17.30: Trust of child's share by reference—another form

Upon and subject to the same trusts powers and provisions as if clause —— of my will were herein repeated verbatim but with the substitution of the name of my daughter B. for that of my said son A. and of the word 'husband' for that of 'wife' and with the requisite change of genders.[1]

1 This form is for use where children's shares are settled separately.

[217.39]

Form B17.31: Declaration excluding s 33 of the Wills Act 1837[1]

Section 33 of the Wills Act 1837 (as substituted by section 19 of the Administration of Justice Act 1982) shall not apply to any of the foregoing trusts.

1 See the WA 1837, s 33, as substituted by the AJA 1982, s 19 (Part G, para **[244.36]**); see also Vol 1, para **[47.14]** ff. The main use of this form would be where there is a gift to a class contingent on their attaining some specified age, and it is desired to eliminate the uncertainty as to whether and how s 33 would apply. (See Vol 1, para **[47.14]** ff for the difficulties of applying s 33 to such a gift.)

[217.40]

Form B17.32: Clause providing for forfeiture of gift on marriage to person not professing a certain religion[1]

I hereby direct that if either[2] during my lifetime whether before or after the date of execution of this my will or after my decease any one or more of my children has or shall have married or shall marry a person who did not at the time of such marriage openly profess the —— religion then in every such case and in the case of marriage after my death as from the occurrence of such event such child or children shall absolutely forfeit and lose all interest in and right to the capital or income of any share in my residuary estate [gift hereby made] to such my child or children and the gift so forfeited shall [*add gift over*].

[But this clause shall have no operation in relation to any marriage that may have already occurred or shall hereafter in my lifetime occur and which in the uncontrolled opinion of my trustees I shall have approved at the time of marriage or shall have subsequently forgiven.]

For the purpose of deciding whether a person openly professes the —— religion my trustees shall accept a statement in writing by a priest or minister or any officer of a church of that religion and I declare that any such statement shall be final and binding upon all beneficiaries claiming under this my will.[3]

1 Such a forfeiture clause was held good in *Hodgson v Halford* (1879) 11 Ch D 959, and the decision of the House of Lords in *Clayton v Ramsden* [1943] AC 320, [1943] 1 All ER 16, which suggested that expressions referring to a particular religion are too uncertain, has been distinguished by the House of Lords in *Blathwayt v Baron Cawley* [1976] AC 397, [1975] 3 All ER 625, where a clause causing forfeiture on becoming a Roman Catholic was upheld as valid. A defining condition such as 'of the Jewish faith' without further definition of what is meant and without providing a procedure for determining whether it is broken, is at risk of being void, particularly if it is a condition subsequent, see *Re Tepper's Will Trusts*

[1987] Ch 358, [1987], 1 All ER 970. If in themselves such conditions are too uncertain, it does not seem to be possible to make them certain by making the opinion of the trustees the criterion in such a case: see *Re Coxen, McCallum v Coxen* [1948] Ch 747 at 761, [1948] 2 All ER 492 at 502. The risk of the clause being void is best minimised by providing, as in the final paragraph of this form, for some kind of certification by an officer of the faith in question. Such a provision has recently been upheld as valid in *Re Tuck's Settlement Trusts, Public Trustees v Tuck* [1978] Ch 49, [1978] 1 All ER 1047, CA. The clause must be so drafted as not to interfere with the right of a parent or guardian in the exercise of his parental duty as regards the religious instruction of a child, see *Re Borwick, Borwick v Borwick* [1933] Ch 657, [1933] All ER Rep 737. See Vol 1, paras **[35.5]** and **[35.29]**.

2 There might have been a secret marriage before or after the date of the will, or the testator might have forgiven or approved a marriage. A clause of this nature may be so drawn that unintentionally the words apply only to marriage after the death of the testator, contrast *Re Evans, Hewitt v Edwards* [1940] Ch 629, with *Hodgson v Halford.*

3 It may be that in the case of some religions the proof can be much more precise, e g the person might shortly before marriage become a convert to the particular religion and have been baptised in that faith and these facts could be proved from the records of the church. See Vol 1, para **[35.29]** ff.

[217.41]

Form B17.33: Child en ventre—general clause[1]

For the purposes of this my will any child en ventre at the date of my or any other death or other event referred to in my will but born alive[2] in due time[3] thereafter shall be deemed to be living at that date.

1 See generally Vol 1, paras **[73.1]** and **[73.2]** for the law relating to children en ventre.

2 A still-born child is not issue at all.

3 As to this expression, see *Re Watson, Culme-Seymour v Brand* [1930] 2 Ch 344. (It refers to the period of gestation and not to the period allowed by the perpetuity rule.)

Gifts of land

[217.42]

Form B17.34: Gift of land for the benefit of testator's children and issue of deceased children, sons taking at eighteen or twenty-one, and in either case with the alternative of taking on previous marriage—variation for children of a person other than testator[1]

I give my freehold lands and property at —— and known as —— to my trustees upon trust [to sell the same and to hold the net proceeds of sale both as to capital and income and the net rents and profits until sale on trust][2] for all and every my children or child (if only one) [*or* the children or child (if only one) of —— deceased] who attain the age of [eighteen] [twenty-one] years or previously marry and if more than one in equal shares as tenants in common. Provided nevertheless that if any child of mine [*or* of the said ——] has died or shall die in my lifetime leaving issue living at my death who attain the age of [eighteen] [twenty-one] or previously marry such issue shall stand in the place of such deceased child and take per stirpes and equally between them if more than one the share of the proceeds of sale which such deceased child would have taken if he or she had survived me and attained a vested interest but so that no issue shall take whose parent is alive at my death and so capable of taking. [And provided further that the gift in this clause contained shall be construed as if section 15 (1) of the Family Law Reform Act 1969 and the Family Law Reform Act 1987 had not been enacted].[3]

1 For IHT purposes a trust in this form will, in relation to the testator's children, comply with the requirements for trusts for bereaved minors if the age contingency of 18 is adopted and with the requirements for age 18-to-25 trusts if the age contingency of 21 is adopted. But if the age contingency of 21 is adopted, and any child is at the testator's death over the age of 18 but under 21, and entitled to an interest possession by virtue of TA 1925, s 31(1)(ii), he or she would have an immediate post-death interest in a share of the trust fund rather than his or her share being subject to age 18-to-25 trusts (see IHTA 1984, s 71D(5)(c)). Further, if a child attained an interest in possession within two years of the testator's death, IHTA 1984, s 144 might have the effect of converting the interest to an immediate post-death interest (see para **[200.136]** for this possibility). An immediate post-death interest could have a capital gains tax disadvantage over age 18-to-25 trusts because although a beneficiary's absolute entitlement at age 25 would not trigger an IHT charge if he or she had an immediate post-death interest (by virtue of IHTA 1984, s 53(2)), no capital gains tax hold-over relief would be available to relieve any gain accruing under TCGA 1992, s 71 on that absolute entitlement. However, although there could be an IHT charge on a beneficiary's absolute entitlement at age 25 under age 18-to-25 trusts (under IHTA 1984, s 71E(1)), hold-over relief would be available under TCGA 1992, s 260(2)(d). Immediate post-death interests could be avoided if TA 1925, s 31 was modified to allow accumulation of income for the testator's children beyond their 18th birthdays, such as in Form B18.13, para **[218.81]**. If the trust takes effect for children other than the testator's children, the property subject to it will be relevant property while the children are under the specified age, unless they have immediate post-death interests.

2 A trust for sale is not strictly necessary in the light of the TLATA 1996, but may be desirable in any particular case where it is wished to emphasise that any beneficiary is entitled to a sale and the division of the proceeds of sale.

3 But for these words the references to children and issue would be deemed to include references to illegitimate children and issue: see generally Part A, para **[200.28]**. References to both statutes should be included because the FLRA 1987 repeals FLRA 1969, s 15 and so a provision which referred to the FLRA 1987 alone could be construed as a direction that the gift should be read as subject to the FLRA 1969, s 15 (Part G, para **[245.39]**). Adopted children and issue will be included by virtue of the AA 1976, ss 39 and 42. The HFEA 1990 also affects the meaning of issue in some circumstances: see Part G, para **[245.82]** ff.

[217.43]

Form B17.35: Gift of land to minor with provision for his death under eighteen or twenty-one leaving issue[1]

I give my lands at —— in the county of —— to my trustees in fee simple upon the following trusts.

(i) If [*minor*] shall predecease me without leaving issue living at my death [or then en ventre but born afterwards] upon trust for [*gift over*].

(ii) If the said [*minor*] shall predecease me leaving issue living at my death [or then en ventre but born afterwards] upon trust for such issue and if more than one in equal shares per stirpes as tenants in common but so that no issue shall take whose parent is living at my death and so capable of taking.

(iii) If the said [*minor*] shall be living at my death and have attained the age of [eighteen] [twenty-five] years upon trust for the said [*minor*] absolutely.

(iv) If the said [*minor*] shall survive me but shall not at my death have attained the age of [eighteen] [twenty-one] years upon trust to apply such part or the whole of the income as my trustees shall in their uncontrolled discretion think proper for the maintenance education or benefit of the said [*minor*] and to accumulate any surplus income by way of compound interest by investing the same and the resulting income thereof from time to time in authorised investments but with power to apply any such surplus income or such accumulations or any part thereof as if they were income in the then current year until the happening of one of the following events.

(a) If the said [*minor*] shall die under the age of [eighteen] [twenty-one] years leaving no children then surviving [or then en ventre but born afterwards] then all capital income and accumulations shall be held upon trust for [*gift over*].

(b) If the said [*minor*] shall die under the age of [eighteen] [twenty-one] years leaving children then surviving [*or* then en ventre but born afterwards] then all capital and accumulations and the income thereof (to which income section 31 of the Trustee Act 1925 as amended shall apply) shall be held upon trust for such children and if more than one in equal shares as tenants in common.

(c) If the said [*minor*] being under [eighteen] [twenty-one] at the date of my death shall thereafter attain the age of [eighteen] [twenty-one] years then all capital income and accumulations shall be held upon trust for the said [*minor*] absolutely.[2]

[The foregoing gift shall be construed in all respects as if section 15(1) of the Family Law Reform Act 1969 and the Family Law Reform Act 1987 had not been enacted.[3]]

1 The expressions 'issue' and 'children' in this form include illegitimate and adopted issue and children: FLRA 1987, ss 1 and 19 and AA 1976, ss 39 and 42. They will also be affected by the HFEA 1990 (Part G, para **[245.82]**). See para **[206.4]** for gifts to minors of land.

2 If the minor is a child of the testator, this trust should be a trust for a bereaved minor if the age contingency of 18 is adopted and an age 18-to-25 trust if the age contingency of 21 is adopted.

3 The references to issue and children in this form will now be construed as including references to illegitimate issue and children unless the final words are added: see generally Part A, para **[200.28]**. References to both statutes should be included because the FLRA 1987 repeals the FLRA 1969, s 15 and so a provision which referred to the FLRA 1987 alone could be construed as a direction that the gift should be read as subject to the FLRA 1969, s 15. These references will also include children or issue by adoption, whenever the adoption occurs: see the AA 1976, ss 39 and 42. The HFEA 1990 also affects the meaning of issue in some circumstances (Part G, para **[245.82]**).

Declarations concerning hotchpot

[217.44]

Form B17.36: Declaration that provisions made by will for testator's wife and children are in addition to and not in substitution for provisions made for them in his lifetime

I declare that the provisions hereby made for my wife and children [and their issue] are in addition to and not in substitution for the provisions in their favour respectively contained in my marriage settlement dated —— [and in the settlement made by me upon the marriages of my daughters A and B] [*or as the case may be*].[1]

1 In the absence of special provision a 'portion' given by will to a child will be presumed to be given in satisfaction or part satisfaction of the liability incurred by a testator in some former instrument to pay or provide a 'portion' for the same child.

Having regard to the fact that the presumption against 'double portions' has the effect of depriving a child of one of the 'portions' without any word being said by the testator to that effect and to the fact that the presumption may be rebutted (in some cases by verbal evidence), it is advisable to inquire whether the testator has made any provision by covenant or gift for any of his children and to provide that the gift by will shall be in addition to the former provision or on the contrary shall be in substitution or part substitution therefor as the testator may desire.

As to the presumption against 'double portions' see Vol 1, para **[44.1]** ff. Form 1 of the Statutory Will Forms 1925, (Part E, para **[238.7]**), could be incorporated instead of this clause. The presumption only arises when the testator is the parent of or in loco parentis to the beneficiary.

[217.45]

Form B17.37: Declaration that provisions made by will for children are not to be in addition to provisions made for them by the testator's marriage settlement

(1) Any child of mine [and any issue of a child of mine] who becomes entitled hereunder to a share in my residuary estate and who also becomes entitled under my marriage settlement dated … (either by appointment or in default of appointment) to a share in the property thereby settled shall upon the division of my residuary estate bring into hotchpot and account for the actual net value of such last-mentioned share such value to be ascertained as at the date when it becomes actually payable to him or her.

(2) [If my residuary estate shall in the events which happen become divisible before the property settled by the said marriage settlement becomes divisible then the division of my said residuary estate shall not be deferred but any child [person] who under the aforesaid provisions is liable to bring into hotchpot a share in the property settled by the said settlement shall assign such last-mentioned share to my trustees and also if my trustees think fit execute to my trustees a bond in such form and for the payment of such sum as my trustees may think fit before being entitled to receive his or her share in my residuary estate, and upon the said share in the property settled by the said settlement becoming payable my trustees shall receive and distribute the same among the persons entitled to my residuary estate under the provisions of this my will in such manner as to give effect as nearly as possible to the aforesaid provisions.[1]]

(3) [Where any such child of mine is entitled hereunder to a life interest only in a share in my residuary estate and also where under the provisions hereof some other person or persons shall take by substitution the share in my residuary estate primarily given hereby to any such child the share in the property settled by the settlement directed to be brought into account by such child shall be brought into account as against such child and also as against all other persons interested in such share in my residuary estate.[2]]

1 If the division of the marriage settlement property may occur later than the division of the testator's residuary estate the administration of the latter will be rendered difficult. This clause may be adapted so as to enable the testator's estate to be distributed at once.
2 Where there are settled shares or a substitution in the case of the death before the testator of one of the primary residuary legatees provision should be made that the sums are still to be brought into account as against persons interested in the shares.

[217.46]

Form B17.38: Declaration that certain children are to bring specified sums into hotchpot

Having already transferred money or property to several of my children absolutely I direct that my children hereafter named shall bring into hotchpot upon the division of my residuary estate the respective sums following, namely, my son [A] the sum of £[X] my daughter [B] the sum of £[Y] etc. [And I direct that where any such child is entitled hereunder to a life interest only in a share of my residuary estate and where under the provisions hereof some other person or persons shall take by substitution the share in my residuary estate primarily given hereby to any such child the sum directed to be brought into account by such child shall be brought into account as against such child and also as against all persons interested in such share.[1]]

1 Gifts completely made over before the date of the will are not, in the absence of special directions, liable to be brought into account under the doctrine against double portions. As this clause is drafted the various persons will not be in a position to dispute the amount to be brought into account; see Vol 1, para **[44.2]**. If they are to have that privilege, as they might where the specified sums are stated to be loans and not gifts as in this case, add 'or so much of the said sums as remains unpaid'.

[217.47]

Form B17.39: Declaration negativing ademption of a gift by will by subsequent gift

I declare that no gift of money or property made by me after the date hereof to any child of mine and no covenant or obligation entered into by me after the date hereof for the benefit of any child of mine shall adeem in whole or in part any gift or provision made by this my will for such child or shall be brought into hotchpot by such child unless at the time of or within six months from the time of making such gift or entering into such covenant or obligation I shall in writing signed or initialled by me declare to the contrary.[1]

1 Under the doctrine of 'double portions' a cash payment of a 'portion' to, and an obligation entered into to provide a 'portion' for, a child of the testator is presumed to adeem, in whole or in part, a 'portion' provided for that child by a will already in existence.

[217.48]

Form B17.40: Declaration that certain future gifts are to be brought into hotchpot

I declare that every gift at any one time of money or property of a greater amount or value at the time of such gift than £[—] made by me after the date of this my will to any child of mine and every sum of money or any property settled or agreed to be settled by me for the benefit of any child of mine after the date hereof shall be brought into hotchpot by such child upon the division of my residuary estate at the value thereof at the time of such gift or settlement and be accounted for accordingly, unless at the time of or within six months from the time of making such gift or settlement or agreement I shall in writing signed or initialled by me declare to the contrary[1] but save as aforesaid no future gift and no sum of money or property which I may hereafter give settle or agree to settle shall be brought into hotchpot by any such child.

1 See note to Form B17.39 at para **[217.47]**. The incorporation of a future declaration may be questioned: see *Re Deprez, Henriques v Deprez* [1917] 1 Ch 24, and *Re Jones' Will Trusts, Jones v Jones* [1942] Ch 328, [1942] 1 All ER 642. As to the calculation of shares on bringing money into hotchpot see Vol 1, paras **[100.1]–[100.7]**.

[217.49]

Form B17.41: Express provision against satisfaction and ademption[1]

I expressly direct that no child or issue of mine taking any share or interest under the trusts aforesaid shall be liable to bring into account any sum of money or the value of any property or interest which I may have already paid or transferred to or settled upon such child or issue or for his her or their benefit or covenanted so to do or which I may hereafter pay or transfer to or settle upon such child or issue or for his, her or their benefit or covenant so to do [unless at the time of or within six months from the time of making such payment transfer settlement or covenant I shall in writing signed or initialled by me declare to the contrary].

1 As to bringing advances and settled shares into account see Vol 1, paras **[100.1]–[100.7]**.

B18 Discretionary trusts and powers

DISCRETIONARY TRUSTS
Note .... **[218.1]**
FORMS
B18.1 Discretionary trust for the testator's family .... **[218.33]**
B18.2 Legacy equal to inheritance tax threshold to be held on discretionary trusts .... **[218.34]**
B18.3 Devise to beneficiary on discretionary trusts .... **[218.35]**
B18.4 Trusts for a disabled person .... **[218.36]**
POWERS
FORMS
B18.5 Power to daughter to appoint life interest in a settled share to her husband .... **[218.37]**
B18.6 Power to trustees to settle child's share .... **[218.38]**
B18.7 Protective life interest with a power to raise and pay capital .... **[218.39]**
B18.8 Life interest subject to trustees' power to pay or apply capital to or for the benefit of the life tenant, with remainders to the life tenant's children subject to powers of the life tenant to appoint a life interest to his spouse and to appoint capital among his issue .... **[218.40]**
B18.9 Power to pay, to children who have life interests, increasing proportions of capital as they grow older .... **[218.41]**
B18.10 Power to trustees to vary trusts of child's settled share .... **[218.42]**
MAINTENANCE
Note .... **[218.43]**
FORMS
B18.11 Variation of the statutory provision for maintenance and accumulation to maximise the trustees' discretion .... **[218.79]**
B18.12 Statutory maintenance and accumulation to continue to the age of twenty-one .... **[218.80]**
B18.13 Statutory maintenance and accumulation to continue to maximum possible age .... **[218.81]**
B18.14 Variation of the statutory provision for maintenance and accumulation—on the birth of a new member of the class existing accumulations are shared with the new member .... **[218.82]**
B18.15 Variation of the statutory provision for maintenance and accumulation—accumulations vesting absolutely .... **[218.83]**
B18.16 Maintenance of a class; applicable to shares in income as well as in capital **[218.84]**
B18.17 Another clause providing for maintenance out of a common fund . **[218.85]**
B18.18 Maintenance clause; simple express trusts .... **[218.86]**
ADVANCEMENT
Note .... **[218.87]**
FORMS
B18.19 Statutory advancement clause restricted .... **[218.104]**
B18.20 Statutory advancement clause varied to apply to the whole of a presumptive share .... **[218.105]**
B18.21 Express Advancement clause; ordinary form .... **[218.106]**
B18.22 Variation for advancement to life tenant .... **[218.107]**
B18.23 Expressions of desire for the guidance of trustees in exercising powers of advancement and of lending capital to the testator's spouse .... **[218.108]**
ENJOYMENT IN KIND
Note .... **[218.109]**

FORMS
B18.24 Powers to permit enjoyment in kind—restricted to prevent prejudice to inheritance tax status of beneficial trusts .... **[218.110]**
B18.25 Clause where trustees are to have power to purchase property for use of beneficiary .... **[218.111]**
B18.26 Power where wife is given residence for life or house is bought for beneficiary to invest trust money in purchase of furniture .... **[218.112]**
LOANS TO BENEFICIARIES
FORMS
B18.27 Loans to a life tenant .... **[218.113]**
B18.28 Loans to individuals without security .... **[218.114]**
B18.29 Loans to beneficiary to whom a business is bequeathed .... **[218.115]**
B18.30 Power for trustees to make loans to guardians .... **[218.116]**
EXERCISE AND RELEASE OF POWERS
FORMS
B18.31 Testator's wishes as to the exercise of powers of maintenance and advancement [and power to make loans to guardians] during period of guardianship .... **[218.117]**
B18.32 Powers and discretions exercisable in favour of a beneficiary trustee .... **[218.118]**
B18.33 Power to release powers .... **[218.119]**

DISCRETIONARY TRUSTS

[218.1]

Note. Many kinds of trusts confer discretions on the trustees (and sometimes on beneficiaries) by means of which, to a greater or lesser extent, they may alter or determine what the beneficiaries will receive and when. What distinguishes a discretionary trust, as the term is commonly understood, is that the income is subject to the trustees' discretion to determine who receives it and in what shares, and none of the beneficiaries has an entitlement to any of the income as it arises (so that there is no interest in possession for tax purposes—see Part A, para **[200.93]**). Such a discretion as to income is of course usually combined with wide discretionary powers over capital and future income, so that the trustees can, in exercise of those powers, distribute capital to any of the beneficiaries, apply it for the benefit of any of them, or appoint other trusts.

[218.2]

There are both fiscal and non-fiscal reasons for providing discretionary trusts in wills. Some of their fiscal aspects are noted briefly below in this Note. The main non-fiscal reasons are to protect beneficiaries from their own improvidence, to prevent them (where they are children or young persons) from having too much money at too early an age, to prevent the creditors of a beneficiary who goes bankrupt from being able to get at the trust capital or income, and to maintain flexibility of responses to the different needs of the different beneficiaries from time to time. Another reason with the advent of the Trusts of Land and Appointment of Trustees Act 1996 (TLATA 1996) is to give trustees maximum discretion over the occupation and use of land comprised in the trust fund. If interests in possession are given, the beneficiaries could have statutory rights of occupation of the land under the TLATA 1996, s 12 (see para **[208.5]** ff), but this may not be desirable where the property is essentially an investment property. A discretionary trust may be the solution since the beneficiaries will not automatically have rights of occupation. A discretionary trust may also be a good way of providing for someone who is disabled in some way and not able to manage his own property (see C4 at para **[226.1]** ff). Form B18.1 at para **[218.33]** is an example of a straightforward discretionary trust of the usual type, and there are various examples of wills containing discretionary trusts in Part C, eg Forms C6.2 at para **[228.19]** and C10.2 at para **[232.15]**.

[218.3]

Discretionary trusts and the rule that a testator cannot delegate his power of testamentary disposition. In *Re Beatty's Will Trusts* [1990] 3 All ER 844, [1990] 1 WLR 1503 the creation by will of an extremely wide trustees' fiduciary power to distribute assets, which included power to distribute to themselves, was held to be valid and effective, and not an invalid attempt to delegate the testator's powers of testamentary disposition. It was held that a power which would be valid if it was contained in a settlement is equally valid if it is contained in a will. The test as to whether the objects of a power are sufficiently certain for the power to be valid is a test which applies equally to powers created by will and those created by settlement. See further Vol 1, para **[9.45]**. At the end of his judgment in *Re Beatty's Will Trusts* Hoffmann J remarked that to hold otherwise would be an injustice to beneficiaries of testators who in reliance on earlier decisions to the same effect had conferred wide powers on their trustees. He gave as an example the wide power of appointment in the precedent in the sixth edition of this work ((6th edn), Vol 2, Form C10.2) which appears in this edition as Form C3.6 at para **[225.101]**, remarking that no warning was there given that such a power might be invalid, and that in his judgment there was no reason why there should have been.

[218.4]

Trustees as objects of powers. In framing discretionary trusts and powers the draftsman should bear in mind one particular application of the doctrine that a trustee may not profit from his trust, namely that the donee of a fiduciary power (ie a power given to trustees in their capacity as trustees, as opposed to one given to a beneficiary) may not exercise such a power for his own benefit unless authorised to do so by the settlement or will creating the power: see *Re Edward's Will Trusts, Dalgleish v Leighton* [1947] 2 All ER 521 at 524; and *Re Beatty's Will Trusts* [1990] 3 All ER 844, [1990] 1 WLR 1503 at 844–847 and 1506 respectively. It may be that when a power of appointment is conferred on trustees, a person who is named by the will or settlement as one of the original trustees and who is also a member of the class of objects of the power would be held to be impliedly authorised to join in an exercise of the power in his own favour, (see *Sargeant v National Westminster Bank plc* (1990) 61 P&CR 518 and *Edge v Pensions Ombudsman* [1998] Ch 512; [1998] 2 All ER 547), but a trustee who is not so named would not, it seems, be so authorised in the absence of an express provision to that effect. The same would probably apply to the exercise of a discretion over income under a discretionary trust of income, and to the exercise of the statutory power of advancement (ie the Trustee Act 1925 (TA 1925), s 32: considered at paras **[218.87]–[218.103]**).

[218.5]
This point, though frequently overlooked, is of particular relevance to discretionary trusts created by will, where it is often convenient and desirable that members of the testator's family should act as trustees. It is therefore advisable to remove any doubt by providing expressly that objects of a discretionary power or trust who agree to act as trustees are authorised to benefit under the exercise of any of the powers and discretions, subject to suitable safeguards, eg that the power can only be exercised if the trustees are not fewer than two in number or that the trustees exercising the power should include at least one person who is not interested in the exercise or not a beneficiary. See Form B18.32 at para **[218.118]** for a provision of this kind.

[218.6]
Inheritance tax advantages of discretionary trusts. Throughout most of the history of estate duty, discretionary trusts were an attractive option because they were not subject to estate duty until the Finance Act 1969 introduced a not wholly successful attempt to subject them to it. Perhaps because of the difficulties which had been encountered in trying to subject discretionary trusts to estate duty, capital transfer tax (introduced by the Finance Act 1975) taxed them with particular severity, and their popularity was much reduced. A less severe set of rules for imposing capital transfer tax on discretionary trusts was introduced by the Finance Act 1982. The introduction of inheritance tax in 1986 made only minor differences to the position of discretionary trusts, but the subsequent reduction in inheritance tax rates and simplification of the rate bands to a single 40 per cent rate over and above a high tax threshold (from March 1988) on which the rates of tax on discretionary trusts are based (see paras **[218.11]–[218.15]**), have made discretionary trusts much more attractive.

[218.7]
The short point about a discretionary trust is that the property subject to it is not treated for inheritance tax purposes as if it were owned by one or more of the beneficiaries. On and after 22 March 2006 it shares this feature with certain trusts with interests in possession, namely interests in possession arising on or after 22 March 2006 which do not fall into the categories of immediate post-death interest, disabled person's interest, or transitional serial interest (see the Notes to paras **[200.98]–[200.100]** above). This treatment contrasts with the treatment afforded to trusts where there is a pre-22 March 2006 interest in possession or an immediate post-death interest, disabled person's interest, or transitional serial interest, where the settled property is treated as belonging to the beneficiaries. (see Part A, para **[200.92]** ff). A discretionary trust forms an 'estate' by itself, though in some ways taxed as an emanation of the settlor or testator, and pays inheritance tax in fairly easy instalments which can be very small or nothing at all where the fund is of modest size. Particular uses of a discretionary trust are to provide a fund equal to the testator's nil-rate band from which the testator's spouse can benefit without it being treated as part of her estate (see paras **[218.16]–[218.18]** and Forms B18.2 at para **[218.34]** and C11.1 at para **[233.13]**) and to empower the executors to make the most tax-efficient distribution of the estate in reliance on Inheritance Tax Act 1984 (IHTA 1984), s 144 (see Form C3.6 at para **[225.92]**).

[218.8]
Inheritance tax charges on discretionary trusts. The rules for charging inheritance tax on discretionary trusts are those which apply to what is called "relevant property" in the inheritance tax legislation. Some forms of trust where there is no interest in possession receive privileged treatment, such as trusts for bereaved minors (see para **[200.108]** above), age 18-to-25 trusts (see para **[200.109]** above), protective trusts (see Part A, para **[200.104]**), trusts for disabled persons (see Part A, para **[200.117]** and C4 at para **[226.1]** ff), discretionary will trusts lasting not more than two years (see C3 at para **[225.1]** ff), charitable trusts, superannuation schemes, trusts for employees and trusts of shares in newspaper publishing companies: see *Foster's Inheritance Tax*, E5 and E6.

[218.9]
The rules for charging inheritance tax on relevant property are described in detail in *Foster's Inheritance Tax*, E3 and E4. We can only give an outline of some of the main features of these rules here. There are two types of inheritance tax charge on relevant property. These are a periodic charge and an 'exit charge'. The periodic charge is imposed (s 64) at every tenth anniversary of the day on which property first became comprised in the settlement, on all property which immediately before the anniversary is comprised in the settlement and 'relevant property'. There is also an inheritance tax 'exit charge' on property ceasing to be 'relevant property' or dispositions which depreciate the value of relevant property (s 65), subject to certain exemptions, such as where relevant property goes to charity or a public body or authority specified in the IHTA 1984, Sch 3 (s 76).

[218.10]
The rules for calculating the rate of periodic and exit charges are essentially similar. The periodic charge is the basic charge, and the exit charge can be looked upon as a means of collecting the periodic charge for which a potential liability has arisen since the last occasion of inheritance tax charge to affect the property, a potential liability which has arisen by virtue of the length of time for which that property has been relevant property.

[218.11]
Calculation of the rate of inheritance tax charge. There are two main stages to the calculation of the tax charge. First, the overall rate of inheritance tax on a hypothetical lifetime chargeable transfer is determined, the hypothetical value transferred and the hypothetical amount of previous chargeable transfers for this purpose being determined by reference to the history of the settlor and the settlement (see below). Secondly, the rate of tax so determined is reduced so that in the case of a periodic charge where the property has been relevant property comprised in the settlement for the previous ten years, the charge is 30 per cent of the overall rate at which inheritance tax would be charged on the hypothetical lifetime transfer (s 66(1)); in the case of a periodic charge where the property has not been relevant property comprised in the settlement for the previous ten years and in the case of any exit charge, the charge is that proportion of 30 per cent of the rate of

inheritance tax on the hypothetical lifetime chargeable transfer which corresponds to the proportion of ten years represented by the period since the most recent occasion of periodic charge (if any) during which the property has been relevant property comprised in the settlement (ss 66(2), 68(1)–(3), 69(1) and (4)). The rate of inheritance tax on a lifetime chargeable transfer is half the death rates (IHTA 1984, s 7(2)), and so relevant property bears tax at 15 per cent of a charge at death rates for every ten years that it is relevant property. This is 1.5 per cent of such a charge per year of property being relevant property, and would mean that a complete charge at death rates would be incurred in instalments if property remained relevant property for 67 years. As the highest marginal rate of inheritance tax at the rates charged on death is now 40 per cent, the highest marginal rate of a periodic charge on property which has been relevant property for a full ten years is now six per cent.

[218.12]

The hypothetical transfer used to calculate the tax rate in the case of a periodic charge at a ten-year anniversary is a transfer of the aggregate of the value of the relevant property on which tax is being charged, the value of any property comprised in the same settlement which has never been 'relevant property' comprised in the settlement (taken at its value when it first became comprised in the settlement), and any property comprised in a 'related settlement' (s 66(4)). The related settlement rules are of particular relevance to dispositions by will, and we mention them further below. The hypothetical previous transfers for calculating the rate of a periodic charge are the aggregate of the chargeable transfers made by the settlor in the seven years before he made the settlement, disregarding transfers made on the day he made the settlement (although a different period of aggregation of his transfers may be taken for this purpose where he has subsequently added property to the settlement—see s 67), and the values on which 'exit charges' have been charged on the settlement in the ten years preceding the anniversary (s 66(5) and (6)).

[218.13]

In the case of exit charges occurring after the first ten-year anniversary the calculations are based on the same hypothetical lifetime chargeable transfer as the most recent periodic charge was based, subject to adjustments for any property which may have been added to the settlement or become relevant property on or after the most recent occasion of periodic charge (s 69). In the case of an exit charge occurring before the first ten-year anniversary the tax rate is calculated on a hypothetical transfer of the value of the property comprised in the settlement immediately after it was made (whether relevant property or not), any property subsequently added to the settlement at its value when added, and the value of any related settlement (s 68(5)—see below for related settlements). The assumed previous chargeable transfers are those of the settlor in the seven years preceding the making of the settlement, not including the day on which the settlement was made (s 68(4)(b)).

[218.14]
Two settlements are 'related' to one another if neither is wholly and permanently charitable, they have the same settlor, and property first became comprised in both of them on the same day (ss 60 and 62). This is subject to the point that if the property first comprised in a settlement is subject to a pre-22 March 2006 interest in possession, an immediate post-death interest or a disabled person's interest to which the settlor or his or her spouse (including his or her widow or civil partner or widower or surviving civil partner) is beneficially entitled, that property will be treated for the purposes of the discretionary trust charging rules as not becoming comprised in that settlement at that time (s 80). Accordingly a settlement commencing with such an interest in possession in favour of the settlor or his or her spouse or civil partner will not be 'related' to a settlement in which property becomes first comprised at the same time. Where property comprised in a related settlement is taken into account for inheritance tax rate calculation purposes under the above rules it is taken at its value immediately after it first became comprised in the related settlement.

[218.15]
Inheritance tax on discretionary trusts created by will. Where property is settled by will it is treated as becoming comprised in the settlement when the testator dies (IHTA 1984, s 83) and of course references to the settlor for the above purposes are to the testator (s 44). Some points to note about including discretionary trusts in wills are as follows:

(i) As mentioned above, the rate of tax charged on an occasion of exit charge during the first ten years of a settlement is calculated by reference to a hypothetical chargeable transfer equal to the value of the settled property at the time when it first became comprised in the settlement (assuming that there is no related settlement and no subsequently added property). The relevant tax rate table is that which is in force at the time when the occasion of exit charge occurs (ss 66(3)(b), 68(4)(b) and Sch 2, para 3). Thus if the nil-rate band in the rate table in force at the time of an occasion of exit charge exceeds the value of the settled property when it first became comprised in the settlement, and there are no aggregable lifetime transfers made by the testator (see sub-para (iii) below) and no related settlement, no tax will be payable on such occasion of exit charge.

(ii) The tax rate calculations for any exit or periodic charge will not take into account any of the property passing under the testator's will except for property which goes into a related settlement. Thus where the testator by his will makes absolute gifts or settles property on trust for his or her surviving spouse or civil partner for life for an immediate post-death interest so that s 80 applies (see para **[218.14]**), the property so given or settled will not come into the calculations of periodic charges or exit charges on property settled on discretionary trusts by the same will.

(iii) Lifetime chargeable transfers (including of course potentially exempt transfers) made or treated as made by the testator during the seven years preceding his death will always be taken into account in calculating exit or periodic charges, but ones made seven years or more before his death will not be taken into account (unless property is added by the will to an existing discretionary settlement—s 66(5)).

[218.16]

Nil-rate band discretionary trusts. The inheritance tax nil-rate band is now (in tax year 2007–08) £300,000. (For 2008–09 it is proposed that it will be £312,000; for 2009–10, £325,000: see FA 2006, s 155; and for 2010–11, £350,000).If a testator leaves his entire estate to his spouse or civil partner in the event of the spouse or civil partner surviving him, and at the time of his death has not made any lifetime gifts in the previous seven years, he will not have used any of his nil-rate band in the event of his spouse or civil partner surviving him. Prior to new rules introduced on 9 October 2007, this would have wasted his nil-rate band. He could have left up to his available nil-rate band to non-exempt recipients, eg his children, without any inheritance tax being payable. However, he may not have wanted to leave up to £300,000 direct to the children in the event of his dying survived by his spouse or civil partner if such survivor would or might need access to the income or even the capital of the whole of the testator's estate after his death. So, a testator who wished to enable his spouse or civil partner to be able to benefit from his entire estate and its income if need be, but who nevertheless wished to provide for a nil-rate band's worth of his estate to devolve on eg his children, without it being charged to inheritance tax as part of the spouse's or civil partner's estate, often did so by means of a discretionary trust. On and from 9 October 2007 new rules provide (assuming they become law) that to the extent that a testator does not fully utilise his nil-rate band allowance, a nil-rate band carry forward allowance will be available to his spouse or civil partner in addition to her own nil-rate band allowance: see para **[200.75]** above. Therefore, the device of the nil-rate band discretionary trust will no longer figure as such an essential tool of inheritance tax planning. Nevertheless, there will be instances where it may still be appropriate to incorporate a nil-rate band discretionary trust in a will. For example, if a testator has assets which are predicted to increase more in value than the nil-rate band, it may be advantageous for inheritance tax purposes if a nil-rate band trust is incorporated in his will with power for the executors to appropriate those assets to the value of the nil-rate band to the trust. Or, a nil-rate band discretionary trust may be desirable for non-fiscal reasons, eg. to make income and capital immediately available to beneficiaries other than the testator's spouse or civil partner, or to keep assets out of the surviving spouse's or civil partner's estate if, for example, it is possible that she may be declared bankrupt, or perhaps require long-term care when her own assets would be taken into account in determining her entitlement to local authority funding, but assets in a discretionary trust may not.

[218.17]

The usual method for incorporating a nil-rate band discretionary trust in a will before the introduction of the nil-rate band carry forward allowance was for a legacy equal to the amount of the nil-rate band to be given by the will to trustees to hold it on discretionary trusts for his spouse or civil partner and children with residue to his spouse or civil partner. This will continue to be the appropriate method where it is desired to incorporate a nil-rate band discretionary trust in a will. If the testator has by the time of his death made no lifetime transfers within the seven years before his death (apart from permanently exempt ones such as to his spouse or civil partner or charity), and leaves no other non-exempt gifts by his will, his estate will not incur a liability for inheritance tax on his death. The income of the legacy can be paid to the spouse or civil partner and, should the need arise, the capital also. But unless the capital of it is paid to the spouse or civil partner, the legacy will not form part of the spouse's or civil partner's taxable estate and will escape being charged to inheritance tax in aggregation with the rest of the spouse's or civil partner's estate on death. The legacy will of course be liable to periodic charges to inheritance tax and to a charge when distributed. Such charges should amount to nothing or very little during the first ten years after the testator's death, and are unlikely to be very much even after that. See paras **[218.11]–[218.14]**.

[218.18]
The following further points should be noted:

- The tax effectiveness of a testamentary discretionary trust is normally increased if the testator does not by his will create any trusts of the balance of his estate, the reason being that the value of any such 'related settlement' will be taken into account in computing the rate of tax on the discretionary legacy: IHTA 1984, s 68(5)(b); see also para **[218.13]**. However, trusts under which the surviving spouse or civil partner takes an immediate interest in possession which is an immediate post-death interest do not have this consequence, because of the provisions of the IHTA 1984, s 80 (see para **[218.14]**). The testator's will could therefore give the spouse or civil partner a life interest in residue instead of an absolute interest without increasing the rate of exit or periodic charges affecting the nil-rate band discretionary trust.
- The nil-rate band discretionary trust can only be relied on to work where the fund consists of income-yielding assets. If it were to consist of eg the matrimonial home, and the surviving spouse or civil partner was permitted to occupy it as a residence under the terms of the trust, the surviving spouse or civil partner would almost certainly be regarded by HMRC as having an interest in possession for inheritance tax purposes. Whereas an interest in possession arising post-21 March 2006 will not necessarily be the type of interest in possession which would cause the property to be treated as part of his or her estate for inheritance tax purposes, in the context of discretionary trusts established by will, if it arises within two years of the testator's death, it may be back-dated to the testator's death under IHTA 1984, s 144, so that it would be an immediate post-death interest and result in the property being treated as part of the surviving spouse's 'estate' for inheritance tax purposes and chargeable to inheritance tax as such on the surviving spouse's or civil partner's death: see Part A, para **[200.98]** ff and Sansom v Peay [1976] 3 All ER 375, [1976] 1 WLR 1073. This would have the result that the inheritance tax exemption of IHTA 1984, s 18 would be available in relation to the trust property on the testator's death. Therefore, following the introduction on and from 9 October 2007 of new rules providing that to the extent that a testator does not

fully utilise his nil-rate band allowance, a nil-rate band carry forward allowance will be available to his spouse or civil partner in addition to her own nil-rate band allowance (see para **[200.75]** above), it may not matter particularly if the survivor is treated as having an immediate post-death interest in the trust property, and it may even be preferable for inheritance tax purposes if the value of the property in the trust does not increase as much in value as the inheritance tax nil-rate band. But prior to these new rules, it was essential that the trust property should not form part of the surviving spouse's or civil partner's estate. So the strategy which became popular for cases where there were insufficient assets apart from the matrimonial home to provide a nil-rate band trust fund was a debt or charge scheme, where the fund was constituted wholly or partly by a personal debt of the surviving spouse or civil partner or a charge on the house or the testator's interest in the house (see para **[218.19]**).

- The device of the discretionary legacy may be inconvenient and disproportionately expensive to administer. Testators may prefer the greater flexibility of the fully discretionary will or the will creating a two-year discretionary trust of residue: see Forms B18.1 (at para **[218.33]**) and C3.6 (at para **[225.92]**) and for the rules for charging inheritance tax on discretionary trusts see paras **[218.11]**–**[218.14]**.

Form B18.2 at para **[218.34]** is an example of a nil-rate band legacy subject to discretionary trusts. Forms C3.4 at para **[225.57]** and C3.5 at para **[225.68]** are examples of complete wills incorporating such a legacy.

[218.19]
Nil-rate band discretionary trust funds constituted by a debt or charge. Where it may not be possible to constitute the nil-rate band trust out of assets of the estate without using some or all of the matrimonial home, there is the problem that if the matrimonial home (or a share of it) is in the discretionary trust fund, and the surviving spouse or civil partner is permitted to occupy the home, the latter may have an interest in possession in the discretionary trust fund. Whereas an interest in possession arising post-21 March 2006 will not necessarily be the type of interest in possession which would cause the property to be treated as part of her estate for inheritance tax purposes, in the context of discretionary trusts established by will, if it arises within two years of the testator's death, it may be back-dated to the testator's death under IHTA 1984, s 144, so that it would be an immediate post-death interest with the consequence that the underlying property would be taxed as part of the survivor's estate on her death (see para **[200.98]**). This would also have the result that the inheritance tax exemption of IHTA 1984, s 18 would be available in relation to the trust property on the testator's death. Following the introduction on and from 9 October 2007 of new rules providing that to the extent that a testator does not fully utilise his nil-rate band allowance, a nil-rate band carry forward allowance will be available to his spouse or civil partner in addition to her own nil-rate band allowance (see para **[200.75]** above), it may not matter particularly if the survivor is treated as having an immediate post-death interest in the trust property, and it may even be preferable for inheritance tax purposes if the value of the property in the trust does not increase as

much in value as the inheritance tax nil-rate band. But prior to these new rules, it was essential that the trust property should not form part of the surviving spouse's or civil partner's estate. A possible solution to this problem which became popular was a debt or charge scheme, whereby the discretionary trust fund is constituted either by a personal obligation on the part of the surviving spouse or civil partner to pay a sum of money to the trustees of the discretionary trust fund, or by a sum of money charged on the matrimonial home or a share of it. If the discretionary trust fund is a personal debt it is repayable on demand but interest free, and if it is a charge it is enforceable on demand or notice and interest free. The charge scheme is generally to be preferred since it avoids an SDLT liability and may avoid a problem under the Finance Act 1986, s 103 (see para **[218.21]**). Both schemes have the advantage that the house is owned by or held beneficially for the surviving spouse or civil partner, so that the capital gains tax private residence exemption can (if the appropriate conditions are fulfilled) apply to the whole of it in the event of a decision to sell the existing one and buy another. However, following the introduction of the nil-rate band carry forward allowance (see para **[200.75]** above), constituting a nil-rate band discretionary trust by a debt or charge may not be particularly advantageous from an inheritance tax point of view, especially where, as is usually the case, the value of the debt or charge (and so the value of the deduction from the survivor's estate) will not increase more than in line with the Index of Retail Prices. Assuming the nil-rate band allowance increases at a greater rate, it could be better for inheritance purposes if the nil-rate band discretionary trust had not been established on the testator's death, and instead his whole estate had passed to his spouse or civil partner with his nil-rate band carried forward. Nevertheless, there may be non-fiscal reasons to constitute a nil-rate band discretionary trust by a debt or charge, for example to keep assets out of the surviving spouse's or civil partner's estate if it is possible that she may be declared bankrupt, or perhaps require long-term care when the value of her own assets would be taken into account in determining her entitlement to local authority funding. For a will clause enabling such an arrangement to be entered into, see Form B18.2 at para **[218.34]** and for documentation putting such schemes into effect, see Forms F5.3 and F5.4 at paras **[243.4]** and **[243.5]**.

[218.20]

Debt or charge schemes appear, at least in some forms, to be accepted as effective for inheritance tax purposes by IR Capital Taxes. The theory behind them is that the debt or charge which constitutes the discretionary fund is a deduction from the surviving spouse's or civil partner's estate on the latter's death, but the surviving spouse or civil partner does not have an interest in possession in the discretionary trust fund. In the case of a debt scheme, the surviving spouse or civil partner has entered into the obligation in return for being distributed the residuary estate, and it is therefore incurred for full consideration, and deductible, if the estate distributed to her exceeds the amount of the debt. In the case of a charge scheme, the property in the residuary estate on which the charge is imposed is distributed to or held on trust for the surviving spouse or civil partner subject to the charge (without the surviving spouse or civil partner having a personal obligation), and should therefore be a deduction from the value of the property, but of course only to the extent that the amount of the charge does not exceed the unencumbered value of the property. Although allowing a beneficiary to occupy trust property may create an interest in possession, the better view is probably that lending to a beneficiary all or part of a trust fund interest-free and repayable on demand does not give that beneficiary an interest in possession in the whole or part of the trust fund which is lent. Where a nil-rate band trust fund is constituted by a debt or charge of this type, it is thought that the inheritance tax status of the fund (as between being or not being subject to an interest in possession) is determined by reference to the trusts which would apply to the income which would be yielded by the debt or charge if interest were payable (see also *Foster's Inheritance Tax*, E1.45 and E1.46).

[218.21]

The reason for using the charge scheme—Finance Act 1986, s 103. Where a nil-rate band discretionary trust is to be constituted by a debt or charge, if a simple personal obligation is entered into by the surviving spouse or civil partner to pay the amount of the trust legacy to the trustees of it, there could be a question whether the debt is deductible on the death of the surviving spouse or civil partner if the testator had during his life been given property by the survivor. This is because the Finance Act 1986, s 103 may apply in these circumstances so as to abate the liability of the survivor to the discretionary trust fund when it comes to determining the amount of the survivor's taxable estate on the latter's death. This is what happened in *Phizackerley v Revenue and Customs Comrs* [2007] WTLR 745. In that case a husband and wife purchased a house as joint tenants. The funds, including repayments on a small mortgage, were provided by the husband. Later, the husband and wife severed the joint tenancy. On the wife's death, she left her estate by will as to the nil rate band on discretionary trusts for the husband, her children and remoter issue, and the residue for the husband absolutely. Her half-share of the house, valued at £150,000, was assented to the husband on his promising to pay £150,000 (subject to indexation) to the trustees of the ni-rate band discretionary trust. Following the husband's death, HMRC issued a notice of determination that the liability of £150,000 (with indexation) incurred by the husband was not deductible in computing the value of his estate for inheritance tax by virtue of FA 1986, s 103. The argument before the Special Commissioner was that the deceased's contribution to the house purchase (and so his wife's half share) was not a transfer of value (so could be ignored under FA 1986, s 103(4)) but a disposition for the maintenance of his wife within IHTA 1984 s 11. The Special Commissioner considered, however, that the disposition was not for 'maintenance' on the facts of the case. The ordinary meaning of maintenance had 'a flavour of meeting recurring expenses', in which case inheritance tax was unlikely to be relevant, but it was wide enough to cover the transfer of a house or part interest in a house if, and only if, it relieved the recipient from income expenditure, for example on rent. When a husband put a house in the joint names of himself and his wife during their marriage that did not fall within the ordinary meaning of 'maintenance'. In the present case the only evidence of their purpose was the daughter's evidence that the deceased thought it appropriate that the house be owned by them jointly so that the wife would enjoy the security of joint ownership. That was not 'for the maintenance' of the other party; it was to give the other party security. Therefore the Special Commissioner confirmed the notice of determination.

The charge schemes are an attempt to get round the problem highlighted by *Phizackerley v Revenue and Customs Comrs* by creating a charge on one or more assets in the residuary estate, typically the first to die's share of the matrimonial home, which is not 'an incumbrance created by a disposition made by' the surviving spouse (see FA 1986, s 103(1) for the significance of this wording). It would be a charge on the property, but without the surviving spouse being personally liable. Where it is possible that the surviving spouse might want to change homes, at least within the first two years after the testator's death, it is advisable for the first to die's will to give the surviving spouse a life interest in residue (qualifying as an immediate post-death interest) rather than an absolute interest. This is because if the surviving spouse owns absolutely the house which is subject to the charge, a replacement charge on a new house (replacing that which passed on the death) will have to be imposed by the surviving spouse, and so the arrangement may then become caught by s 103 even though it was not so caught in relation to the original house (because the original charge was made by the executors of the first to die before distributing the original house to the surviving spouse). Where there is a life interest trust of residue for the surviving spouse, the trustees of the residuary estate are the appropriate persons to create the charge and they could also enter into a liability to pay the amount (and if they do, it should be limited to the amount of the available trust assets in their hands); alternatively they could enter into a personal liability (limited as just described) without charging the assets.

So long as the acquisition of the new home does not take place within two years of the testator's death however, it may not be necessary for a replacement charge or debt to be entered into. Following a sale of the original property, the discretionary trust could invest the monies paid to it in discharge of the debt or charge in the purchase of a new property for the surviving spouse to live in, and even though this might mean the surviving spouse acquires an interest in possession in the new property (or a share of it) for inheritance tax purposes, this should not matter if this interest in possession arises only after the second anniversary of the testator's death since then ITA 1944, s 144 cannot apply to backdate it to the testator's death to become an immediate post-death interest. The only circumstance where such an interest in possession arising more than two years after the testator's death should be avoided would be where the surviving spouse is disabled at the date of the testator's death within the meaning of IHTA 1984, s 89(4) (amended by FA 2006, Sch 20, para 6(2), (4)). If the surviving spouse was disabled at the date of the testator's death, their interest in possession would be a disabled person's interest and so would be the type of interest in possession which would cause the property to be treated as part of his or her estate for inheritance tax purposes: see para **[200.99]** above).

Following the introduction on and from 9 October 2007 of new rules providing that to the extent that a testator does not fully utilise his nil-rate band allowance, a nil-rate band carry forward allowance will be available to his spouse or civil partner in addition to her own nil-rate band allowance (see para **[200.75]** above), the inheritance tax complications described above may be avoided by the simple expedient of the testator not including a nil-rate band discretionary trust in his will, and allowing his unused nil-rate band to be carried forward to the survivor's death. If a will already incorporates a nil-rate band discretionary trust the same result can be achieved if within 2 years of the testator's death (but not within the first three months), an appointment of the nil-rate legacy is made to the surviving spouse or civil partner relying on IHTA 1984, s 144 to backdate the appointment to the testator's death for inheritance tax purposes (see para **[218.26]** below).

[218.22]

Another reason for using the charge scheme—SDLT. Where, nevertheless, a nil-rate band discretionary trust is to be constituted by a debt or charge, the charge scheme is to be preferred to the debt scheme, because if properly implemented HMRC's view is that it will not give rise to stamp duty land tax, whereas a debt scheme will (at least if the value charged against the residential property exceeds the nil-rate threshold for residential property which is £150,000 on and from 23 March 2006). HMRC's views appeared in *Modernising Stamp Duty on land and buildings in the UK*: Practitioners' Newsletter, Issue 4 (7 December 2004). They cite the commonest examples of such transactions and their stamp duty land tax consequences as follows:

- The legacy trustees accept the surviving spouse's promise to pay in satisfaction of the pecuniary legacy and in consideration of that promise land is transferred to the surviving spouse. The promise to pay is chargeable consideration for stamp duty land tax purposes.
- The legacy trustees accept the personal representatives' promise to pay in satisfaction of the pecuniary legacy and land is transferred to the surviving spouse in consideration of the spouse accepting liability for the promise. The acceptance of liability for the promise is chargeable consideration for stamp duty land tax purposes. The amount of chargeable consideration is the amount promised (not exceeding the market value of the land transferred).
- Land is transferred to the surviving spouse and the spouse charges the property with payment of the amount of the pecuniary legacy. The legacy trustees accept this charge in satisfaction of the pecuniary legacy. The charge is money' s worth and so is chargeable consideration for stamp duty land tax purposes.

- The personal representatives charge land with the payment of the pecuniary legacy. The personal representatives and legacy trustees also agree that the trustees have no right to enforce payment of the amount of the legacy personally against the owner of the land for the time being. The legacy trustees accept this charge in satisfaction of the legacy. The property is transferred to the surviving spouse subject to the charge. There is no chargeable consideration for stamp duty land tax purposes provided that there is no change in the rights or liabilities of any person in relation to the debt secured by the charge.

[218.23]
Debt and charge schemes—practical points.

Some practical points are noted below as to the constitution of a debt or charge scheme. In the light of some of them, a testator may reasonably take the view that such a scheme post-8 October 2007 is more trouble than it is worth and rely instead on the nil-rate band carry forward allowance for effective inheritance tax planning (see para **[200.75]** above).

(1) Specific powers to constitute the discretionary trust fund as a debt or charge are needed, since it is a form of investment of the discretionary trust fund which is disadvantageous to the beneficiaries of it compared with more conventional kinds of investment (see Form B18.2 at para **[218.34]** for an example).

(2) Similarly, it is important that all relevant trustees should be exonerated from liability for the fund being worth less than it would have been if conventionally invested, and from liability for a failure of the surviving spouse's resources (in the case of a debt) or the value of the property (in the case of a charge) to be sufficient to meet the amount of the debt or charge in full.

(3) For a debt scheme where the surviving spouse is to be the debtor, the legacy trustees should include at least one person who is not the surviving spouse, because a person cannot make a contract with himself. However, the legacy trustees and the general trustees could be the same persons. The surviving spouse can enter into a contract with himself and others: Law of Property Act 1925 (LPA 1925), s 82.

(4) Where the charge scheme might be used, the surviving spouse should not be one of the personal representatives or trustees who create the charge (but he could be a legacy trustee). This is so as to avoid any argument that the Finance Act 1986, s 103 applies to a charge created by trustees who include the surviving spouse among their number (see para **[218.21]**). As the charge would be created in exercise of a fiduciary power by trustees or personal representatives acting in that capacity, this seems unlikely to be correct, but the non-participation of the surviving spouse will reduce the number of contentious points to argue about.

(5) Where the charge scheme might be used, or there is a life interest trust of residue for the surviving spouse (so that the legacy fund will be a debt or charge, or both, incurred or made by the trustees of the residuary estate), the legacy trustees and the general trustees should not be exactly the same persons, again because of the problem of someone creating an interest in favour of himself. The LPA 1925, s 72(3) authorises a conveyance of land by a person to himself, but it is doubtful whether 'land' as defined for this purpose in the LPA 1925, s 205(1)(ix) (Part G, para **[246.59]**), includes mortgages and charges (because they did not devolve on the heir before 1926 and are thus probably not 'hereditaments' within the definition). The LPA 1925, s 72(1), (2), and (4) makes it clear that if the two sets of trustees are not exactly the same persons, a charge will be valid even though one or more persons are members of both sets of trustees.

(6) Where the testator and spouse own the matrimonial home together, if

they are joint tenants they need to sever the joint tenancy by agreement or notice before either has died (although it may be possible to remedy failure to do this by a deed of variation). The share of the first to die will form part of his residuary estate in which the surviving spouse will have an absolute or life interest. If a charge rather than debt scheme is used, the charge will be an equitable charge on the first to die's undivided share, not a charge on the house itself. This will mean that there will be a continuing trusteeship of the house itself, since one undivided share is subject to a charge and the other not.

(7) A personal debt will only be deductible to the extent that the surviving spouse has received property from the first to die's estate equal to the amount of the debt. A charge (without any personal liability) will only be deductible so far as it does not exceed the value of the property it is charged upon.

[218.24]

Discretionary trusts where there is no spouse or civil partner exemption. There can be advantages in having a discretionary trust in a will to which the spouse or civil partner exemption is not relevant, particularly where the testator is elderly and making a will leaving all or most of his property in favour of a friend or relative who is also elderly. With a discretionary trust the income of the property of the testator can be enjoyed by the beneficiary without being charged to inheritance tax as part of the beneficiary's estate on his or her death, and is likely to be taxed much more lightly, if at all, when the discretionary trust terminates. This is particularly beneficial where the testator leaves an estate which is wholly or mostly free of inheritance tax, being within or mostly within the nil-rate band, and where the beneficiary already has property which will mostly or wholly use up the nil-rate band on his death, so that the testator's property, if it were added to the beneficiary's property and taxed as the latter's property on his death, would on the beneficiary's death give rise to an inheritance tax charge equivalent to 40 per cent of the testator's property. In this situation there would be no or hardly any successive charges relief under the IHTA 1984, s 141 where the beneficiary died within five years, because little or no tax would have been paid on the testator's death. Even where there will be inheritance tax payable on the testator's death, creating a discretionary trust will often be likely to have an inheritance tax advantage over giving an absolute interest or interest in possession where the beneficiary is elderly and has property of his own exceeding or not much less than the nil-rate band.

[218.25]

Further, where a gift of an absolute interest or an immediate post-death interest to a beneficiary would not be exempt from inheritance tax, so that the inheritance tax charge on the testator's death is the same irrespective of the type of trust created for the benefit of the beneficiary, it is much less important to confine any discretionary trust to assets of the testator's estate equal to the nil-rate band. Doing so should ensure (where there are no aggregable lifetime chargeable transfers and no other property is settled by the will—see para **[218.15]**) that there is no inheritance tax charge on the termination of the discretionary trusts in the first ten years after the testator's death. However, avoiding an inheritance charge on the discretionary fund might be achieved at the cost of a much higher charge on absolute or immediate post-death interest property on the death of the beneficiary. Where the fund intended to benefit the beneficiary will or may exceed the nil-rate band, it will often be the case that putting the whole of that fund into a discretionary trust will be likely to save inheritance tax on the beneficiary's death, as compared with a discretionary trust of part of the fund equal to the nil-rate band and the beneficiary being given an absolute interest or immediate post-death in the remainder of the fund. See paras **[218.11]–[218.15]**. For a deed of variation which converts a life interest under a will to a discretionary trust see Form F3.9 at para **[241.30]**.

[218.26]
Two-year discretionary trusts to take advantage of IHTA 1984, s 144. A distribution or appointment within two years after a testator's death out of a discretionary trust created by his will may be treated as a disposition by the will for inheritance tax purposes, and a will can thus be made which subjects all or most of the testator's estate to a discretionary trust, with a view to the executors making the most tax-efficient disposition in the light of the circumstances at or shortly after the testator's death. An appointment in favour of the testator's spouse or civil partner would, for example, enable advantage to be taken of the new rules for the nil-rate band carry forward allowance (see para **[200.75]** above). This topic is discussed in more detail in the text in C3 at paras **[225.83]** ff, an example of such a will is Form C3.6 at para **[225.92]**. See also paras **[225.83]** ff.

[218.27]
Capital gains tax and discretionary trusts. Prior to 6 April 2008, the rates of capital gains tax for an individual are arrived at by adding the capital gains made in a tax year to his or her income and charging them in effect to income tax. By contrast, capital gains tax on the gains of a settlement prior to 6 April 2008 is charged at the income tax trust rate under the Income Tax Act 2007, s 9(1) (formerly known as the rate applicable to trusts under Income and Corporation Taxes Act 1988 (ICTA 1988), s 686), currently 40 per cent in the tax year 2007–08 (see the Taxation of Chargeable Gains Act 1992 (TCGA 1992), s 4(1AA)(a)). The realisation of a chargeable gain on the sale of assets held in a discretionary trust before 6 April 2008 will thus involve paying more capital gains tax than would be paid if the assets were owned absolutely by an individual who, after taking into the account the chargeable gain, was not a higher rate tax payer. The Government has announced though that on and from 6 April 2008 there will be a flat rate of capital gains tax applicable across the board, including individuals and trusts, of 18 per cent (without indexation relief or taper relief). Therefore, on and after 6 April 2008 (assuming the proposal becomes law) a discretionary trust will not pay significantly more capital gains tax than an individual would, although it will pay a little more since a trust only has the benefit of up to one-half (maximum) of an individual's annual exempt amount.

[218.28]
General capital gains tax hold-over relief for gifts and transfers in and out of settlements was abolished by the Finance Act 1989, leaving more limited

hold-over reliefs for gifts of business and agricultural property (TCGA 1992, s 165 and Sch 7) and gifts on which inheritance tax is chargeable (TCGA 1992, s 260). The latter type of hold-over relief is available when property is distributed out of a discretionary trust and it is an occasion of inheritance tax 'exit charge' under IHTA 1984, s 65, even if the hypothetical transfer on the basis of which the tax rate is calculated (see paras **[218.12]** and **[218.13]**) is such that no tax is in fact payable on the distribution. This is an advantage of a discretionary trust over a trust with, for example, an immediate post-death interest.

[218.29]
Income tax and discretionary trusts. Discretionary trusts still have some income tax advantages where the income received is not UK company dividends, in that the trustees are enabled to distribute income to those beneficiaries who pay the least tax. However, the provisions for the taxation of the income of certain discretionary trusts contained in the Income Tax Act 2007, ss 479–483 (formerly ICTA 1988, ss 686 and 687), should be borne in mind, and there are now distinct disadvantages where the trust receives UK company dividends subject to the dividend trust rate (formerly known as the Schedule F trust rate of tax).

[218.30]
The Income Tax Act 2007, s 479(4) (formerly ICTA 1988, s 686(1)) provides that non-UK company dividend income is to be taxed on the trustees at 'the trust rate' (currently 40 per cent) The income caught by the section includes inter alia income which falls to be accumulated and income which is payable to a beneficiary under a discretion (whether or not there is power to accumulate) (see the Income Tax Act 2007, s 480(1), (2)). Income applicable under the TA 1925, s 31 (Part G, para **[246.29]**) during the minority of a beneficiary would fall within this definition. Various categories of income are excluded from the operation of s 479(4), of which it is sufficient to mention income applied in defraying trust expenses which are properly chargeable to income (or would be so chargeable but for some express provision of the trust): a restrictive interpretation of these words was adopted by the House of Lords in *Carver v Duncan* [1985] 2 All ER 645. The Income Tax Act 2007, ss 493–4 (formerly ICTA 1988, s 687) provide that income paid to a beneficiary as income is to be treated as income net of the trust rate. The trustees are responsible for the payment of the amount of such tax subject to set off of the 'tax pool' which will include the income tax already paid to HMRC. A beneficiary who receives income under a discretion and who pays tax at a rate below 40 per cent or who has unused personal reliefs available to him may be able to recover some part of the tax paid by the trustees in respect of such income. The ultimate burden of tax on income to which these sections apply is thus unaffected as long as such income is distributed as income, but if, for example, income is accumulated and subsequently distributed in the form of capital there can be no recovery of any part of the tax paid in respect of such accumulations. Now that investment income surcharge is abolished for individuals and the higher income tax rates for individuals are comparatively low accumulation of trust income (excluding UK company dividends) is fiscally unattractive in most cases.

[218.31]

If the trust includes UK company dividend income, however, new rules which came into force in 1999–2000 mean that accumulation of such income will generally be preferable to distribution. A dividend from a UK company comes with a tax credit (currently 1/9 of the amount distributed), and under the Income Tax Act 2007, ss 9(2), 479(3) (formerly ICTA 1988, s 686), tax on such income is charged on the trustees at the dividend trust rate (formerly the Schedule F trust rate) (currently 37.5 per cent). If the trustees distribute the dividend income, they are deemed to make a payment grossed up at the normal trust rate (currently 40 per cent), and are liable under Income Tax Act 2007, ss 493–4 (formerly ICTA 1988, s 687) to tax on this grossed up amount. The tax credit on the dividends does not, however, go into the 'tax pool' to reduce this liability, so the trustees are only able to set off the tax actually paid by them under Income Tax Act 2007, s 479. The beneficiary who receives the dividend income is liable for tax on that payment at his own income tax rate, but with the benefit of a credit for the amount paid by the trustees, so he is entitled to a tax repayment or liable for further tax, as appropriate. The overall effect of the rules is that if a discretionary trust is to invest in UK company shares it will probably be better for the income produced thereby to be accumulated, rather than distributed, and for capital payments or loans to be made to the beneficiaries rather than income distributions.

[218.32]

For 2005–6 and onwards there is a new special trust tax rate which applies to the first £1000 (£500 for 2005–6) which would otherwise be chargeable to tax at the trust rate or the dividend trust rate: see the Income Tax Act 2007, s 491 (formerly TA 1988, s 686D). Such income is instead chargeable to income tax at the basic rate, the lower rate or the dividend ordinary rate, depending on the nature of the income (Income Tax Act 2007, s 491(3), formerly TA 1988, s 686(3)).

[218.33]

Form B18.1: Discretionary trust for the testator's family

(1) In this clause:

  (i) 'the trust period' means the period starting with the date of my death and ending 80 years afterwards (and that period shall be the perpetuity period applicable hereto);[1]

  (ii) 'the beneficiaries' means [*here set out the persons comprising the class of beneficiaries. An example would be*: my wife my sister [*name*] and all the children and remoter issue of myself or of my said sister who may be born before the end of the trust period together with any spouse civil partner widow widower or surviving civil partner of any such children or remoter issue (and so that the expressions 'widow', 'widower' and 'surviving civil partner' shall include a widow widower or surviving civil partner who has married or formed a civil partnership)].

(2) My trustees shall hold the capital and income of the trust fund upon trust for all or such one or more of the beneficiaries at such ages or

times in such shares and upon such trusts for the benefit of all or any one or more of the beneficiaries as my trustees (being at least two in number or a [trust] corporation)[2] may by deed or deeds[3] revocable or irrevocable at any time or times during the trust period appoint and in making any such appointment my trustees shall have powers as full as those which they could possess if they were the absolute beneficial owner of the trust fund and in particular (but without prejudice to the generality of the foregoing words) may:

(i) appoint new trustees of the whole or any part or parts of the trust fund and provide for the remuneration of any who may be professional or corporate trustees;

(ii) create or delegate powers and discretions over capital or income (including powers of further delegation) whether of a dispositive or administrative nature;

Provided that:

(a) no appointment shall be capable of being made and no revocable appointment shall be capable of being revoked after the expiration of the trust period;

(b) no appointment shall prejudice or affect any prior payment transfer or application of income or capital hereunder;

(c) any appointment under the foregoing power may be made subject and without prejudice to any existing interests trusts or powers;

(d) any such appointment may be made of income without any appointment of capital; and

(e) my trustees (being at least two in number or a [trust][4] corporation) may at any time or times by deed or deeds extinguish, or release or restrict the foregoing power in any manner and to any extent.[5]

(3) In default of and subject to and until any appointment made under the provisions of the preceding subclause:

(i) during the trust period my trustees shall pay or apply the income of the trust fund to or for the maintenance or support or otherwise for the benefit of all or any one or more of the beneficiaries as my trustees may in their absolute discretion think fit; provided that during the 21 years immediately following my death[6] my trustees may if they in their absolute discretion think fit accumulate such income or any part of it by way of compound interest by investing the same and its resulting income in any way authorised by this will and if they do so they shall hold such accumulations as part of the capital of the trust fund but may nonetheless in any future year during the trust period apply them or any part of them as if they were arising in that year;

(ii) upon the expiry of the trust period my trustees shall hold the trust fund as to both capital and income absolutely for [*here insert the dispositions to take effect at the end of the trust period in default of previous appointment. For example*: such of the beneficiaries as are then living and if more than one in equal shares.

or such of my children and remoter issue as are then living and if more than one in equal shares according to their stocks and so that no issue shall take whose parent is still alive and so capable of taking].

(4) [As Form B18.32 at para **[218.118]**.][7]

1 The disadvantage of adopting the 80-year (or lesser fixed term) perpetuity period for a discretionary trust is that it then becomes the *only* available perpetuity period when drafting an appointment in exercise of the power: see the PAA 1964, s 1 (Part G, para **[246.74]**). Accordingly, an appointment under the power of, say, a life interest to someone living at the testator's death, with remainder to someone born before the life tenant's death vesting at or before the age of 21, needs to be expressly limited so that all interests vest (in interest if not in possession) and all powers are exercised within the 80-year period, whereas no express perpetuity restrictions would be needed in such an appointment if the 80-year period (or a lesser fixed term) had not been adopted by the testator's will as the perpetuity period. We should add that if this is not done in an appointment where there is a relevant fixed-term perpetuity period, there will still be 'wait and see' under the PAA 1964, s 3 (Part G, para **[246.76]**), but it is better practice to draft trusts of which it is clear from the outset that they will vest within the relevant perpetuity period.

2 For the meaning of trust corporation see the Preliminary Note to B3 at para **[203.28]**. If a foreign corporate trustee might be appointed, the word 'trust' should be omitted.

3 For precedents, see Forms F4.1 to F4.4 at paras **[242.7]–[242.11]**.

4 See n 2, above.

5 A power conferred on trustees in that capacity cannot be released by them unless they have express power to do so: see Vol 1, para **[40.10]**.

6 A period of 21 years from the testator's death is a permitted period of accumulation: see the LPA 1925, s 164(1)(b) (Part G, para **[246.42]**).

7 This will enable the trustees to exercise their powers and discretions in favour of one of their number.

[218.34]

Form B18.2: Legacy equal to inheritance tax threshold to be held on discretionary trusts[1]

(1) In this clause the following expressions have the following meanings—

(a) 'the trust legacy' means the legacy by this clause bequeathed to my legacy trustees and the assets for the time being representing the same;

(b) 'the beneficiaries' means and includes [my wife [*name*]] and my children and remoter issue;[2]

(c) 'the trust period' means the period commencing on my death and expiring on the twenty-first anniversary of the death of [my wife];[3]

(d) 'the accumulation period' means the period commencing with my death and expiring on the twenty-first anniversary thereof;[4] and

(e) 'my legacy trustees' means [*name*] of [*address*] and [*name*] of [*address*] or other the trustee or trustees for the time being of the trust legacy].[5]

(2) If [my wife] shall survive me[6] then I bequeath to my legacy trustees free of inheritance tax and foreign death duties[7] a legacy of [£300,000][8] *or* [the maximum sum of money (if any) which can in the circumstances subsisting at my death be given by this clause without any liability being incurred for the payment of inheritance tax on or by reason of my death. And in particular but without prejudice to the generality of the foregoing the circumstances to be taken into account for the foregoing purpose shall include any chargeable transfers made by me during my lifetime (or events treated as such for inheritance tax purposes) the dispositions taking effect

under this Will (apart from this present clause) or under any codicil hereto and any property treated as if it were part of my estate immediately before my death for inheritance tax purposes].[9]

(3) My legacy trustees shall hold the trust legacy and the income thereof upon such trusts for the benefit of all or any one or more exclusively of the others or other of the beneficiaries and if more than one in such shares and with such trusts and powers [(including trusts and powers conferring a discretion as to the distribution of capital or income exercisable by my legacy trustees or by any other person or persons)][10] and with such provisions generally as my legacy trustees (not being fewer than two in number or being a corporation) shall by any deed or deeds revocable or irrevocable appoint provided that no appointment shall be made and no revocable appointment shall be revoked after the expiration of the trust period.

[(4) At any time or times during the trust period my legacy trustees (not being fewer than two in number or being a corporation) may raise the whole or any part or parts of the trust legacy and pay or apply the same to or for the advancement or benefit of any of the beneficiaries for the time being living in such manner as they think fit.][11]

(5) Subject to any exercise of the foregoing power[s] my legacy trustees shall during the trust period hold the trust legacy upon trust to pay or apply the income thereof to or for the maintenance education or benefit of all or any one or more of the beneficiaries for the time being living in such shares if more than one and generally in such manner as they think fit provided that my legacy trustees may during the accumulation period accumulate the whole or any part of the income of the trust legacy by investing the same and the resulting income thereof in any of the investments hereby authorised and any accumulations of income so made shall form part of the capital of the trust legacy for all purposes.

(6) Subject to any exercise of the foregoing powers the trust legacy and the income thereof shall be held at the expiration of the trust period in trust absolutely for such of my children and remoter issue as shall then be living in equal shares per stirpes.

(7) Any capital or income of the trust legacy not otherwise disposed of by this clause shall be held in trust for such of my children as survive me if more than one in equal shares absolutely.

(8) Any of my trustees or my legacy trustees may exercise any power or discretion hereby or by law conferred notwithstanding that he or she has a direct or indirect personal interest in the mode or result of such exercise.[12]

(9) Instead of the trust legacy being satisfied by the payment of cash or by the appropriation of property—[13]

(a) my trustees may charge (with or without there being any personal liability of any person or persons) any property which is (or but for this clause would be) comprised in [my residuary estate] with payment of a sum of money equal to or less than the amount of the trust legacy to my legacy trustees and my legacy trustees shall accept such charge for such sum as the whole or a part (as the case may be) of the trust legacy; and

(b) my trustees may require my legacy trustees to accept in satisfaction of all or part of the trust legacy a binding promise of payment (secured or unsecured) made personally by [my wife] or by my trustees as trustees of [my residuary estate] which debt shall be payable on demand and my legacy trustees shall accept such debt as the whole or a part (as the case may be) of the trust legacy.

(10) The following shall apply in relation to the powers in the last preceding subclause—

(a) my trustees may require to be included such terms if any as they think fit in relation to a charge under subclause (9)(a) above or a debt under subclause (9)(b) above including terms as to interest (if any) and terms linking the debt or sum charged to the Retail Prices Index or otherwise providing for its amount to vary with the passage of time according to a formula provided that the debt or sum charged shall be payable to my legacy trustees on demand and the charge shall be enforceable by my legacy trustees at any time;

(b) my legacy trustees may leave the charge or debt outstanding for as long as they think fit and refrain from exercising their rights in relation to it and waive the payment of all or any part of any interest due in respect of it and may accept any substitute debt or charge undertaken or created by any person;

(c) my trustees may assent to the vesting of [my residuary estate] subject to an outstanding obligation to pay or satisfy the trust legacy and my legacy trustees may appoint new trustees in exercise of the statutory power to do so before the trust legacy has been paid or satisfied;[14]

(d) my legacy trustees and my trustees shall not be liable if [my wife] is or becomes unable to pay the debt or any security is or becomes inadequate or for any other loss or disadvantage which may occur as a result of their exercising or choosing not to exercise any of the foregoing powers; and

(e) the foregoing powers are in addition to any other powers given by this will or any codicil or by the general law and the foregoing powers may be exercised even though my trustees and my legacy trustees are the same persons or [my wife] is among either or both sets of trustees provided that such powers shall not be exercisable by a sole trustee who is [my wife].

(11) My trustees may constitute the trust legacy wholly or partly by appropriating to it at their discretion any property or proportionate share of any property and for this purpose may take such advice as to the value of the said property or proportionate share as they think fit.[15]

(12) Where the trust legacy is for the time being wholly or partly constituted by a proportionate share of a dwellinghouse or other property my legacy trustees shall have all the powers of an absolute owner in relation to such share and property and in particular may at their discretion join with the other proprietor or proprietors of such property:

(i) to permit a beneficiary under the trusts of the trust legacy to have the use or enjoyment of the property in kind on such terms as my legacy trustees think fit; or

(ii) to effect or enable a sale of the property and the purchase of another property in the same or similar co-ownership with the trust legacy constituted by a proportionate share thereof.

1 See paras **[218.16]–[218.19]** for the purpose of this form, and whether or not it is still advisable following the introduction on 9 October 2007 of rules to carry forward an unused nil-rate band allowance. It may be adapted for use where the testator may leave a husband or civil partner. It is to go with a gift of the rest of the testator's estate to his spouse or civil partner, either absolutely or for life (or another interest in possession, but in either case such that the spouse or civil partner has an immediate post-death interest or a disabled person' s interest: see paras **[200.98]–[200.99]** above). See Forms C3.4 at para **[225.57]** and C3.5 at para **[225.68]** for forms of complete wills incorporating a disposition of this type.

2 The definition of the discretionary class may need to be enlarged or adapted in individual cases. See also n 2 to Form C3.6 at para **[225.100]**.

3 The trust period is longer than may be desired in most cases, but gives considerable flexibility.

4 A period of 21 years from the testator's death is a permitted period of accumulation: see the LPA 1925, s 164(1)(b) (Part G, para **[246.42]**).

5 The main circumstances in which there should be separate trustees of the legacy are where a charge scheme might be entered into, in which case the testator's spouse or civil partner should not be one of the executors and trustees but could be a trustee of the legacy, or where the testator's spouse or civil partner is or might be sole executor and a debt scheme might be entered into, or where there is a life interest trust of residue for the surviving spouse or civil partner. See para **[218.22]**.

6 This form assumes an exempt gift of residue to the testator's spouse or civil partner, or a gift of it on an interest in possession trust for the spouse or civil partner (e g a life interest) such that the spouse or civil partner has an immediate post-death interest or a disabled person's interest: see paras **[200.98]–[200.99]** above, so that the estate is wholly or mostly exempt apart from this gift. This gift of a nil-rate band fund on discretionary trusts should not be subject to a condition that the spouse or civil partner survives the testator by a certain period (and note that an omnibus commorientes clause such as Form B19.2 at para **[219.15]** could have this effect). This is because the IHTA 1984, s 92 may not apply to such a survivorship condition, since the condition would not be as to the survival of the beneficiary under the nil-rate fund, as the section appears to require; see para **[219.8]**.

7 See the Preliminary Note to B14 at para **[214.35]** ff for the reasons for having these words if the testator has any foreign assets. It can be better to make this gift *subject* to tax. Making the gift subject to inheritance tax will, in the event of this gift taking the non-exempt estate over the inheritance tax threshold (e g because of changes in the law or the testator having made lifetime gifts during the seven years preceding his death), cause the size of the chargeable estate to be less than it would be if the gift was free of inheritance tax: see B14 at para **[214.74]**.

8 The current threshold is £300,000 (tax year 2007–08). (For 2008–9 it will be £312,000, and for 2009–10 it will be £325,000, see FA 2006, s 155. For 2010–11 it will be £350,000, see FA 2007, s 4.) If a legacy of £300,000 is settled on discretionary trusts and if, as in this form, all other benefits devolve on the spouse, no inheritance tax will be payable on the testator's death unless lifetime transfers fall to be taken into account or there is property treated as part of the testator's estate for inheritance tax purposes such as property subject to a reservation (see Part A, para **[200.76]**), or settled property in which he had an interest in possession within IHTA 1984, s 49(1).

9 The formula in square brackets is designed to ensure that the amount of the discretionary legacy does not exceed the inheritance tax threshold where other non-exempt gifts are made or where lifetime chargeable transfers fall to be taken into account on the death. Where a legacy subject to a discretionary trust is included in a will where the residuary gift will not be exempt from inheritance tax (see paras **[218.24]** and **[218.25]**), the second alternative formula for defining the amount of the settled legacy should not be used. This is because the amount of inheritance tax payable on the estate will be the same whatever the size of the legacy. The probable result of using the second alternative formula where none of the residue was exempt would be that if the taxable estate were within the nil-rate band and no inheritance tax was payable, the legacy would use up the entire residue, and that if any inheritance tax were payable on the estate the legacy would be nil. We suggest that where there is no exempt residue either a specified cash sum should be settled on discretionary trusts, or residue should be left on discretionary trusts with the idea that an appointment

falling within the IHTA 1984, s 144 (for which see the Note in C3 at para **[225.83]** ff) can be made if the discretionary trust fund turns out after the testator's death to be larger than is appropriate.

10 The words in square brackets authorise the creation of discretionary powers, eg powers to advance capital to a life tenant, which may not otherwise be valid: see Vol 1, para **[40.5]**.

11 A power to pay or apply capital, being exercisable in a less formal manner than a power of appointment, may be a useful power to confer. It is essential that its exercise is adequately evidenced.

12 This will enable the trustees to exercise their powers and discretions in favour of one of their number.

13 These powers and the provisions of the next subclause are included so as to enable a debt or charge scheme to be used as a means of avoiding the surviving spouse or civil partner having an interest in possession in the trust fund subject to the trusts of this clause, where there are insufficient assets other than the matrimonial home with which to constitute that trust fund. See paras **[218.19]–[218.22]**.

14 The purpose of this is so that new trustees of the residuary estate can be appointed before a charge is entered into, in a case where the surviving spouse is one of the personal representatives or the personal representatives and the trustees of the discretionary legacy are the same persons, and to make clear that new or additional trustees of the discretionary trust legacy can be appointed before the legacy is constituted as a debt from the surviving spouse or civil partner where the surviving spouse or civil partner is the sole trustee of it: see para **[218.22]** for the reasons for avoiding these states of affairs.

15 If post-21 March 2006 a beneficiary is permitted to occupy a property owned by a discretionary trust, whereas this may give that beneficiary an interest in possession, it will not necessarily be the type of interest in possession which will cause the property to be treated as part of his or her estate for inheritance tax purposes. Only an interest in possession which is an immediate post-death interest, a disabled person's interest, or a transitional serial interest (see paras **[200.98]–[200.100]** above) will have this result. In the context of a discretionary trust established by will, if a permission to occupy is given within two years of the testator's death, and this gives rise to an interest in possession this may be back-dated to the testator's death under IHTA 1984, s 144, so that it would be an immediate post-death interest and result in the property being treated as part of the beneficiary's estate for inheritance tax purposes: see para **[225.83]** ff. But if the permission is not granted until after the second anniversary of the testator's death, and the beneficiary to whom it is granted is not a disabled person within the meaning of IHTA 1984, s 89(4) at the testator's death so that her interest is not a disabled person's interest within IHTA 1984, s 89B (see the para **[200.99]** above), it should not result in the property being treated as part of the beneficiary's estate for inheritance tax purposes. Therefore, an express power to appropriate property or a share of property may be given to trustees to exercise in appropriate circumstances, and sub-clauses (11) and (12) contain such a power and associated provisions.

[218.35]

Form B18.3: Devise to beneficiary on discretionary trusts[1]

I devise my freehold land at —— in the county of —— known as —— to my trustees upon trust to sell the same and to hold the rents and profits until sale after payment thereout of all outgoings usually chargeable against income and the net income from the proceeds of sale in trust for [*name*] during [his]/[her] life provided always that at any time or times instead of paying any such rents and profits or income accruing during the life of the said [*name*] to [him]/[her] my trustees may apply any such rents and profits or income for or towards the personal support maintenance and education of the said [*name*] or [his]/[her] issue for the time being or such one or more to the exclusion of the others or other of such objects of this discretionary power in such manner and if more than one in such shares as my trustees shall think proper with power within three years after the death of any object of such discretionary power to apply any income which accrued in his or her lifetime in or towards the discharge of any liability incurred by or on behalf of any such object which my trustees shall think fit to satisfy, and after the death of the said [*name*] [*gift over to remainderman or as the beneficiary shall appoint*].

1 This form may be appropriate as an alternative to a protected life interest, (see eg Forms B16.1 to B16.3 at paras **[216.6]–[216.8]** and Form B18.7 at para **[218.39]**) where a testator feels that the object of his bounty may be at risk of bankruptcy, divorce or some other calamity when it would be advantageous for the trustees to be able to divert income from the beneficiary to, eg persons dependent upon him. The trust for sale is not strictly necessary in the light of the TLATA 1996 (see para **[200.48]** ff), but since the purpose of the form is to provide the beneficiary with an income rather than a place to live, it may be appropriate The trusts of this clause, which give the beneficiary a life interest subject to power for the trustees to divert the income elsewhere, are of a type which does not confer an interest in possession on the main beneficiary for inheritance tax purposes; see *Pearson v IRC* [1981] AC 753; see generally Part A, paras **[200.93]–[200.97]**. However, it is possible that she would have an interest in possession for the purposes of the TLATA 1996, so that unless the land devised was unavailable (eg let) or unsuitable (eg business premises) for her occupation, she might have a right to occupy the land under the TLATA 1996, s 12 (Part G, para **[246.115]**; see also para **[208.5]** ff). Therefore, if the testator wishes to avoid this, a full discretionary trust form should be used, eg Form B18.1 at para **[218.33]**.

For the taxation of the income and capital gains of discretionary trusts, see paras **[218.27]–[218.32]**.

[218.36]

Form B18.4: Trusts for a disabled person[1]

If my said son A (hereinafter called 'A') shall be living and be a disabled person within the meaning of the Inheritance Tax Act 1984, s 89[2] at the time of my death the said [share of my residuary estate] directed to be held upon trust for him as aforesaid (hereinafter called 'the share') shall not vest absolutely in A but shall be retained by my trustees and held upon the following trusts and with and subject to the following powers:

(1) My trustees shall have power at their absolute discretion to pay or apply the whole or any part or proportion of the income of the share to or for the benefit of A during his life.

(2) My trustees shall during the period of 21 years commencing with my death while A is living accumulate the income of the share which shall not be paid or applied for the benefit of A as aforesaid as an accretion to the capital of the share but shall have power to pay or apply such accumulations during the life of A as if the same were income of the then current year.

(3) If A is still living at the expiration of the said period of 21 years my trustees shall from the expiration of such period during the remainder of the life of A pay or apply all income of the share arising after the expiration of the said period of 21 years which shall not be paid or applied to or for the benefit of A under the foregoing power to or for the benefit of all or any one or more of [my children and remoter issue for the time being living other than A] in such shares and proportions as my trustees think fit.

(4) Notwithstanding the foregoing trusts and power my trustees shall have power during the life of A to pay or apply the whole or any part or parts of the capital of the share to or for the benefit of all or such one or more of [my children and remoter issue] and in such

proportions as my trustees think fit provided that the foregoing power shall not be exercisable so as to cause the aggregate amount or value of the capital of the share which shall for the time being have been paid or applied to or for the benefit of persons other than A at any time to exceed the aggregate amount or value of such capital which shall for the time being have been paid or applied to or for the benefit of A.

(5) Subject to the foregoing trusts and to any or every exercise of the foregoing powers my trustees shall hold the share or such part thereof as shall not have been paid or applied as aforesaid and the income thereof [upon trust for all or any my grandchildren or grandchild whenever born during the lifetime of the last of my children to die who shall attain the age of 18 years if more than one in equal shares].

(6) Section 32 of the Trustee Act 1925 (relating to the payment or application of capital) shall apply to the last foregoing trust without modification during the life of A but after the death of A the said section 32 shall apply to the said trust in all respects as if the words 'one-half of' had been omitted from proviso (a) of subsection (1) thereof.

1 This form is intended to satisfy the conditions laid down in the IHTA 1984, s 89 (see the Preliminary Note to C4 at paras **[226.1]** ff). It assumes that the testator has made a gift in an earlier clause of the will to his disabled son, and that it is an absolute gift conditional only on surviving the testator. The trusts of the clause only come into operation if the disabled son 'A' is still disabled within the meaning of s 84(4) at the testator's death because it seems that the section will only apply if he is disabled at the time of the testator's death. During A's life current income is only paid for his benefit at the discretion of the trustees and is otherwise accumulated or distributed to other beneficiaries, but he will be deemed for inheritance tax purposes to have an interest in possession. Subclause (4) confers a wide power to apply capital with a proviso that is intended to 'secure that not less than half of the settled property which is applied during [A's] life is applied for his benefit' within the meaning of s 89(1)(b).

Subclause (6) provides for the statutory power of advancement to apply without modification during A's life, so that the existence of the power does not prejudice the application of s 89: see sub-s (3). After A's death the power is made applicable to the whole of a presumptive share.

This form will not qualify as a trust for the benefit of a 'vulnerable beneficiary'. A trust so qualifying allows a claim – for tax years 2004–5 onwards – for special tax treatment bringing the trustees' income and capital gains tax liability into line with what the vulnerable beneficiary's liability would have been if he or she had received the income directly or had realised the trust gains (see FA 2005, ss 23–45 and para **[226.7A]**). For a form of trust which would qualify, see para **[226.34A]**, below.

2 A disabled person may be someone: (i) incapable by reason of mental disorder within the meaning of the Mental Health Act 1983 of administering his property or managing his affairs; (ii) in receipt of an attendance allowance under the Social Security Contributions and Benefits Act 1992, s 64 or the Social Security Contributions and Benefits (Northern Ireland) Act 1992, s 64; (iii) in receipt of a disability living allowance under the Social Security Contributions and Benefits Act 1992, s 71 or the Social Security Contributions and Benefits (Northern Ireland) Act 1992, s 71, by virtue of entitlement to the care component at the highest or middle rate (IHTA 1984, s 89(4)); or (iv) not in receipt of attendance allowance or disability living allowance at either of the appropriate rates, but who would be in such receipt were he not undergoing treatment for renal failure in hospital or provided with certain accommodation or non-UK resident: see IHTA 1984, s 89 (4), (5), (6) added by FA 2006, Sch 20, para 6.

POWERS

[218.37]

Form B18.5: Power to daughter to appoint life interest in a settled share to her husband[1]

Provided always and I hereby declare that notwithstanding the trusts hereinbefore contained my said daughter [*name*] shall have power[2] by deed revocable or irrevocable or by will or codicil to appoint to any husband who may survive her for the residue of his life or for any less period [the whole or] any part [not exceeding one-half] of the income of my said daughter's share[3] or the income of any asset or assets comprised in such share or of any part or share of such share [not exceeding one-half of the value at the date of such deed will or codicil of such share (all values for this purpose to be determined conclusively by my trustees)] and she may if she thinks fit appoint protective trusts of such income for his benefit during his life or any less period.

1 Such a power may be less desirable than previously, at least from an inheritance tax perspective, on and after 22 March 2006. Where the daughter is entitled to a life interest which arises after 22 March 2006 and is an immediate post-death interest, any interest in possession appointed to her husband will not attract the spouse exemption from inheritance tax unless her husband was disabled at the date of the testator's death since then his interest would be a disabled person's interest (see para **[200.112B]** above). This would be the only relevant type of interest in possession which would have the result of treating her husband as beneficially entitled to the underlying trust property for inheritance tax purposes under IHTA 1984, s 49(1), (1A)(b) thus enabling the spouse exemption to be claimed. Unless the husband has a disabled person's interest, the underlying trust property will then fall into the relevant property regime. A testator may still, however, wish to confer such a power for the benefit of the daughter's husband. For an alternative form see Form 18.8 at para **[218.40]**.

2 If this power is only to be effectually exercised in default of children or issue attaining a vested interest, insert here: 'in case no child or other issue of such daughter shall attain a vested interest in such daughter's share.'

3 It is assumed that the fund is divided into shares, each of which is settled on a child of the testator with remainder to his or her own children. For examples see Forms C2.6 at para **[224.95]** and C7.4 at para **[229.37]**.

[218.38]

Form B18.6: Power to trustees to settle child's share[1]

Provided always and I hereby declare that in case any child of mine shall marry before attaining the age of [eighteen] [twenty-five] [*the age mentioned in the primary gift*] years my trustees shall have power in their absolute discretion until such child shall attain the said age to appoint by deed or deeds executed either before and contingent upon any such marriage or after such marriage to settle the whole or any part of the share of residue hereinbefore bequeathed to such child or the whole or any part of any specific property appropriated to the said share upon such trusts for the benefit of such child and his or her spouse or intended spouse and their children or issue or any of them in such manner and form and with such provisions stipulations and agreements as my trustees may think proper including discretionary trusts and powers and administrative powers and provisions as my trustees think fit.

1 This clause contemplates a compulsory settlement by the trustees before the child attains a vested interest, here supposed to be at eighteen or twenty-five years or another age. It may be appropriate where the testator wishes the child to be protected in the event of an early and improvident marriage. If this power is included, and the initial trust for the testator's child or children provided for vesting at 18 or 25, it would be neither a trust for bereaved minors within IHTA 1984, s 71A (see para **[200.108]** above), or an age 18-to-25 trust within IHTA 1984, s 71D (see para **[200.109]** above). Rather, the settled property subject to it would be within the IHT charging regime for relevant property (see para **[200.92]** above).

[218.39]

Form B18.7: Protective life interest with a power to raise and pay capital[1]

I give to my trustees the sum of £—— free of inheritance tax payable on my death [*or* the residue of my property both real and personal wherever situate being or arising] as to the income thereof upon protective trusts for the benefit of A during his life and my trustees shall until the failure or determination of the trust of income in favour of the said A have the further power at their absolute discretion and without being liable in any way to account for the exercise of such discretion to raise and pay to the said A for his own absolute use and benefit at any time or times as my trustees shall determine [the whole or any part or parts of] [any sum or sums not exceeding on any one occasion £—— clear of expenses out of] the capital of the said fund [*or* residue] and my trustees shall hold any part of the said fund [residue] not so transferred to the said A during his lifetime as the said A shall by will or codicil appoint and in default of and subject to any such appointment [*set out trusts in remainder*] and I direct that my trustees shall on no account be liable or responsible for making any such payment whether of income or capital to the said A after the failure or determination of his said determinable life interest unless or until they shall have received express notice of the act or event causing such failure or determination.

1 The effect of this clause is that trustees can pay sums out of capital to the beneficiary and this may prove a very useful provision where the beneficiary has only a life interest whether protected or not. Care should be taken not to exercise the power in such manner as to encourage HMRC to claim that the capital advanced is liable to tax as income in the beneficiary's hands, eg by making advances of regular amounts at regular intervals to pay everyday living expenses. In *Stevenson v Wishart* [1987] STC 266 recurring payments of large sums out of trust capital for a discretionary beneficiary's nursing-home expenses were held not to be income, but the decision leaves open the question whether it is possible that recurring payments of capital made by trustees under a power of the kind in this Form could be taxed as income if they were intended to defray ordinary living expenses. HMRC will treat payments out of capital as the income of the beneficiary where, by the terms of the trust instrument, payments out of capital are required to be made, or may be made, in order to supplement income to a fixed amount or a certain defined level. See the *Trusts, Settlements and Estates Manual*, TSEM 3757. It is possible for a life interest subject to the statutory protective trusts to be an immediate post-death interest (see IHTA 1984, s 88(4)(b)(i) and para **[200.104]** above), and the exercise of a power to pay capital to a life tenant with an immediate post-death interest does not involve a charge to inheritance tax: see Part A, para **[200.96]** and the IHTA 1984, s 53(2), (2A). For a shorter form of power to pay or apply capital for the benefit of a life tenant see Form B18.8 at para **[218.40]** and for a form by reference to the statutory power of advancement see Form B18.22 at para **[218.107]**.

[218.40]

Form B18.8: Life interest subject to trustees' power to pay or apply capital to or for the benefit of the life tenant, with remainders to the life tenant's children subject to powers of the life tenant to appoint a life interest to his spouse and to appoint capital among his issue

(1) My trustees shall hold [the trust fund] on trust to pay the income thereof to [my son] during his life;[1]

(2) provided that my trustees shall have power in their absolute discretion from time to time during the life of [my son] to pay transfer or apply the whole or any part or parts of the capital of [the trust fund] in which [my son] has for the time being an interest in possession (within the meaning of Part III of the Inheritance Tax Act 1984)[2] to or for the benefit of [my son] in such manner as they shall in their absolute discretion think fit;[3]

(3) subject to the foregoing trust and any or every exercise of the foregoing power my trustees shall hold [the trust fund] and the income thereof upon such trusts in such shares or proportions and with and subject to such powers and provisions (which may include discretionary trusts or powers or administrative powers or provisions) for the benefit of all or such one or more of [my son's] children and remoter issue as [he] may by deed (revocable or irrevocable) or by will or codicil appoint;

(4) in default of and subject to any such appointment and subject to the foregoing trusts and any or every exercise of the foregoing powers my trustees shall hold [the trust fund] and the income thereof upon trust for the child or children of [my son] who shall attain the age of 21 years if more than one in equal shares;

(5) notwithstanding the foregoing trusts and powers for the benefit of the issue of [my son] he shall have power by deed (revocable or irrevocable) or by will or codicil to appoint to any wife of his who may survive him as his widow a life or lesser interest (or a life or lesser interest on protective trusts) in the whole or any part or parts of [the trust fund] and the foregoing trusts for [my son's] children and any or every exercise of the foregoing power for the benefit of his issue shall take effect subject to such life or lesser interest;[4]

(6) [*As* Form B18.32 *at para* **[218.118]**].[5]

1 For deaths on or after 22 March 2006, the son's life interest should be an immediate post-death interest if it takes effect immediately on the testator's death (or is subject only to a survivorship condition permitted by IHTA 1984, s 92, see para **[219.6]**-**[219.7]**), and is not, for example, postponed to another interest (see para **[216.1]** above). If after his death the property remains in trust, it will fall within the inheritance tax charging regime for relevant property (see the Note to para **[200.92]** above).

2 The point of restricting the power to property in which the life tenant has an interest in possession is that if his life interest is terminated by him, e g surrendering or assigning it in favour of the remaindermen, the power will automatically cease to be exercisable.

3 See n 1 to Form B18.7 at para **[218.39]**. This power would authorise lending capital to or for the benefit of the life tenant in an appropriate case (*Re Kershaw's Trusts* (1868) LR 6 Eq 322), although an express power to lend such as Form B18.27 at para **[218.113]** could usefully be incorporated. The case law on the scope of the statutory power of advancement, discussed at paras **[218.87]**–**[218.103]** is also relevant to an express power of this kind.

4 Where the son becomes entitled to his interest in possession on or after 22 March 2006, any interest in possession appointed to his spouse will only attract the spouse exemption from inheritance tax if it is also a disabled person's interest, which will require his spouse or civil partner to have been disabled at the date of the testator's death (see para **[200.99]** above). This would be the only relevant type of interest in possession which would have the result of

treating his spouse or civil partner as beneficially entitled to the underlying for inheritance tax purposes under IHTA 1984, s 49(1), (1A)(b) thus enabling the spouse exemption to be claimed.

5 This will enable the trustees to exercise their power to pay or apply capital to the life tenant and the statutory power of advancement (for which see paras **[218.87]**–**[218.103]**) in favour of one of their number.

[218.41]

Form B18.9: Power to pay, to children who have life interests, increasing proportions of capital as they grow older[1]

Notwithstanding the trust hereinbefore declared my trustees may in the exercise of their absolute discretion as they think fit on or after the attainment of the age of [25] years by any child of mine pay transfer or apply to or for the benefit of such child one third or any less part of the share of such child and on or after the attainment of the age of [30] years by any child of mine pay transfer or apply to or for the benefit of such child a further third or any less part of the share of such child and on or after the attainment of the age of [35] years by any child of mine pay transfer or apply to or for the benefit of such child the whole or any part or parts of the share (or such of the same as has not previously been so paid transferred or applied) of such child [and I express the wish but without restricting my trustees' discretion in any way that each of my children shall receive all the capital of his share by the time he attains the age of 35 years].

1 This form presupposes a trust for the testator's children in shares which are settled on them for life with remainders to their own children. For a form of complete will containing a clause of this kind see Form C8.6 at para **[230.81]**.

[218.42]

Form B18.10: Power to trustees to vary trusts of child's settled share

Provided always and I hereby declare that my trustees shall have power during the lifetime of any child of mine by any deed or deeds to vary all or any of the trusts in this my will contained concerning the share of residue whether original or accruing hereby bequeathed to such child and to settle the whole or any part of such share upon such trusts for the benefit of such child and his or her spouse and his children or issue or any of them in such manner and form and with such provisions stipulations and agreements as my trustees may think proper including discretionary trusts and powers and administrative powers and provisions as my trustees think fit.

MAINTENANCE

[218.43]

Note. The TA 1925, s 31 (Part G, para **[246.29]**) which contains the statutory power of maintenance was amended by the Family Law Reform Act 1969, s 1(3) and Sch 1, Part 1 which substituted for references therein to twenty-one years references to eighteen years. This amendment did not affect interests arising under instruments made *before* the commencement of the 1969 Act (i e before 1 January 1970), s 1(4) and Sch 3, para 5(1)(a) in which case the relevant age remained twenty-one years. For this purpose an interest created by an appointment made after 31 December 1969, under a special power is *not* an interest under an instrument made before the commencement of the Act, even if the power was created by an instrument made before then: see *Re Dickinson's Settlements, Bickersteth v Dickinson* [1939] Ch 27 (this is a decision on the TA 1925, s 31(5), but the relevant wording of the Family Law Reform Act 1969, Sch 3, para 5(1)(a) is virtually the same), and *Begg-McBrearty v Stilwell* [1996] 4 All ER 205 where it was held that where a settlement was made before the coming into force of FLRA 1969 creating a special power of appointment which was exercised after the 1969 Act came into force, and the trusts under the appointment incorporated the provisions of TA 1925, s 31, the appointment was the relevant instrument under which the beneficiary's interest existed, so the trusts under the appointment were affected by the statutory reduction of the age of majority, with the result that the beneficiary obtained a vested interest in income on the attainment of her majority at 18.

[218.44]
The TA 1925, s 31 applies where a trust carries the intermediate income and so should be read in conjunction with the LPA 1925, s 175 (Part G, para **[244.54]**), which extends the categories of interest which will now carry the intermediate income, unless that income is otherwise *expressly* disposed of. Our comments on the TA 1925, s 31 (the full text of which is set out in Part G at para **[246.29]**) are as follows:

[218.45]
(a) **Type of beneficiary.** The section does not authorise maintenance when apart from the section the beneficiary on attaining a vested interest in capital would not be entitled to the income (*Re Raine, Tyerman v Stansfield* [1929] 1 Ch 716).

[218.46]
(b) **Commencement.** The powers of maintenance contained in the TA 1925, s 31 do not apply where the will or instrument under which the interest arises came into operation before 1 January 1926. For this purpose a document exercising a special power of appointment is the instrument (*Re Dickinson's Settlements, Bickersteth v Dickinson* [1939] Ch 27 and *Begg-McBrearty v Stilwell* [1996] 4 All ER 205). It is conceived that despite the repeal of the LPA 1925, Sch 7 (20 *Halsbury's Statutes* (2nd edn) 895) by the Statute Law Revision Act 1950 (41 *Halsbury's Statutes* (4th edn) 743), the Conveyancing Act 1881, s 43 (37 *Halsbury's Statutes* (4th edn) 59) still applies to instruments which came into operation before 1925.

[218.47]
(c) **Relationship to the terms of the will.** The powers of maintenance are in addition to any powers conferred by the will. They apply without any incorporation in the will, but so far only as a contrary intention is not expressed in the will, and have effect subject to the terms of the will (TA 1925, s 69(2): Part G, para **[246.40]**). Where there is a specific direction to accumulate the whole income there is no power to apply it in maintenance: *Re Reade-Revell, Crellin v Melling* [1930] 1 Ch 52, [1929] All ER Rep 506; even where the direction to accumulate is void: *Re Erskine's Settlement Trusts, Hollis v Pigott* [1971] 1 All ER 572, [1971] 1 WLR 162. Where there is no direction to accumulate during a minority, the section allows maintenance even though there is a direction to accumulate after the attainment of the age of eighteen (or twenty-one): *Re Leng, Dodsworth v Leng* [1938] Ch 821, [1938] 3 All ER 181. The decision in *Re Reade-Revell, Crellin v*

Melling was followed in *Re Stapleton, Stapleton v Stapleton* [1946] 1 All ER 323, where it was explained that in *Re Reade-Revell, Crellin v Melling* there was a specific direction to accumulate, but in *Re Leng, Dodsworth v Leng* there was only an implied direction. A positive direction to apply the entire income in maintenance precludes accumulation of surplus (*Re Peel, Tattersall v Peel* [1936] Ch 161).

[218.48]
(d) Prior interests. The provisions of the TA 1925, s 31 are subject to any prior interests or charges which affect the property: *Re Turner's Will Trusts, District Bank Ltd v Turner* [1937] Ch 15 at 28, [1936] 2 All ER 1435 at 1448.

[218.49]
(e) Interests to which s 31 of the TA 1925 applies. The provisions apply to any property held by trustees for any person for any interest, whether vested or contingent, but, in the case of contingent interests, only if the limitation or trust carries the intermediate income. As to what interests carry the intermediate income, see Vol 1, paras **[32.3]**, **[32.15]**–**[32.17]** and **[218.57]**–**[218.61]**. As to the effect of s 31 on vested interests, see para **[218.54]**.

[218.50]
(f) Where income of another fund is also available. The statutory scheme is, in some respects, rather elaborate. Under its provisions, trustees, who have notice of any other income available for the maintenance of a minor, should attempt to agree with the trustees of the fund producing such other income upon a proper figure for the maintenance of the minor (a matter upon which there may be a divergence of opinion); the figure having been agreed each set of trustees is to apply, out of the income in their hands, a proportionate part only of the amount so agreed, the proportion being based on the incomes of the two funds. Where the two funds will, upon the failure of the minor's contingent interest, pass to different persons, the provision is eminently fair; but it may lead to difficulty and delay (eg where one set of trustees is in another country) in cases where it is essential that maintenance should be given promptly; however it only applies 'so far as practicable', and if difficulties arise it can be disregarded. The proviso to s 31(1) which provides for this is commonly excluded: see eg, Form B18.11 at para **[218.79]**.

[218.51]
(g) The trustees' discretion. Trustees must exercise a conscious discretion. They *are* to have regard to the age of the minor and his requirements and generally to the circumstances of the case. The trustees should take the income of a parent into account, for though they *may* apply income whether or not there is any person bound by law to provide, etc, yet it is only such part as may, in all the circumstances, be reasonable which may be applied. Where there is a discretionary trust to pay or apply income to or for the benefit of minors, who have only a contingent reversionary interest in the corpus which does not carry the intermediate income, any payment or application of income in pursuance of such discretionary trust is not made in pursuance of this section, for sub-s (3) excludes the case where there is no

right to the intermediate income: *Re Vestey's Settlement, Lloyds Bank Ltd v O'Meara* [1951] Ch 209, [1950] 2 All ER 891.

[218.52]
(h) Income interests of contingent beneficiaries of full age. If a person on attaining eighteen has not a vested interest in the income (eg is still only entitled contingently as tenant for life or as owner of the corpus), he will be entitled personally to receive the income both of the property and of past accumulations until he attains a vested interest (eg until he becomes a tenant for life or owner of the corpus), or until he dies, or until failure of his interest. This will be an interest in possession for tax purposes (see Part A, para **[200.108]** ff). But an express direction for maintenance etc to continue to a later age will usually amount to a contrary intention within the TA 1925, s 69(2) (Part G, para **[246.40]**) so as to exclude the statutory entitlement to income: *Re Turner's Will Trusts, District Bank Ltd v Turner,* [1937] Ch 15 at 28, [1936] 2 All ER 1435 at 1448. The court has power, where the testator was a parent or in loco parentis, to allow maintenance in the case of a legacy contingent on the minor attaining an age other than full age (*Re Jones, Meacock v Jones* [1932] 1 Ch 642, [1932] All ER Rep 804).

[218.53]
(i) Destination of accumulation of surplus income. Under the TA 1925, s 31(2) (Part G, para **[246.29]**) accumulations will cease in any event on the attainment of eighteen, unless there be an overriding direction in the will to the contrary (*Re Turner's Will Trusts, District Bank Ltd v Turner,* [1937] Ch 15 at 28, [1936] 2 All ER 1435 at 1448).

In three cases the accumulations will belong to the person who has been the object of the maintenance:

(i) If the income during the minority or until marriage or formation of a civil partnership has been nominally vested in the minor (eg if he were—although still a minor—tenant for life or tenant in tail), and he attains eighteen or marries or forms a civil partnership under that age.

(ii) If the minor on attaining eighteen or on marriage or formation of a civil partnership under that age becomes entitled to the property itself either in fee simple, absolute or determinable, or absolutely, or for an entailed interest.

(iii) He or his estate will be entitled to the accumulations even if he dies under eighteen if he had a vested annuity (TA 1925, s 31(4)), or an absolutely vested interest in capital (because the accumulations are added to capital but he is entitled to the capital), or there is some express provision of the trust instrument which has this effect (as in *Re Delamere's Settlement Trust, Kenny v Cunningham-Reid* [1984] 1 All ER 584, [1984] 1 WLR 813). It is thought that in any of these circumstances he will have an interest in possession for tax purposes during his minority. See Form B18.15 at para **[218.83]** for a variation of TA 1925, s 31 which provides for the accumulations to vest absolutely.

[218.54]
Where a minor child is absolutely and indefeasibly entitled to any of the income of a fund during his minority, he cannot insist on it being handed

over to him while he is a minor, although the trustees will have power to pay it to him and accept his receipt if he marries while still a minor (LPA 1925, s 21) or there is specific power to accept his receipt in the will (such as Form B21.20 at para **[221.24]**). However, a parent or guardian with 'parental responsibility' (see Vol 1, para **[28.2]** for this term) for such a child could require such income to be handed over to the parent or guardian, and could give a good receipt where the trustees wish to hand it over, in reliance on the ChA 1989, s 3(3) (Part G, para **[244.114]**; see also Vol 1, para **[9.42]**).

[218.55]
If the person who has had income applied for his maintenance is not, and does not become, entitled to the accumulations in any of the ways described above, the accumulations are held as an accretion to 'the capital of the property from which such accumulations arose' and as one fund with it for all purposes, although the trustees have power to apply them as income of the current year while the beneficiary remains a minor and his interest continues (TA 1925, s 31(2)(ii): Part G, para **[246.29]**). What is 'the property from which such accumulations arose' presents difficulty in some circumstances. If there is eg a testamentary gift of a fund on trust for the children of A who attain the age of twenty-five in equal shares, with the TA 1925, s 31 applying, and A has two children X and Y of whom X is alive at the testator's death and Y is born five years after the testator's death, both of whom then attain the age of twenty-five, are the accumulations of the income of the fund which arose after the testator's death and before the birth of Y an accretion to the entire fund to which X and Y are both entitled, or are they an accretion to X's half share of the fund only? According to *Re Joel's Will Trusts* [1967] Ch 14 at 36–37, following *Re King* [1928] Ch 330 at 337–338, such accumulations would in this example be an accretion to X's half share of the fund only. See Form B18.14 at para **[218.82]** for a form which varies s 31 so that the accumulations go with the capital, with the result in this example that Y would get a half share of them.

[218.56]
It should be noted that a minor who is entitled to a defeasible interest in personalty does not have an 'absolute' interest so as to be entitled to the accumulation of income thereon on attaining full age or marriage, even though an equivalent interest in realty would so entitle him: *Re Sharp's Settlement Trusts, Ibbotson v Bliss* [1973] Ch 331, [1972] 3 All ER 151. The effect of s 31(2) is, however, to give a minor who would otherwise be entitled to a vested interest in income but not in capital only a contingent interest in the surplus income during his minority and he is not assessable to higher rate income tax in respect thereof: *Stanley v IRC* [1944] KB 255, [1944] 1 All ER 230. For the taxation of income in such a case see para **[218.67]**.

[218.57]
(j) What interests carry intermediate income. The section must be read in conjunction with the LPA 1925, s 175 (Part G, para **[244.54]**). That section enacts that, except so far as the income or any part of it is otherwise *expressly* disposed of, the following interests *shall* (subject to statutory

provisions as to accumulations: LPA 1925, ss 164–166: Part G, paras **[246.56]–[246.58]**; and the PAA 1964, s 13: Part G, para **[246.86]**) carry the intermediate income:

(a) A contingent or future specific devise or bequest of any property: 'specific' applies to 'bequest' as well as to 'devise' (*Re Raine, Tyerman v Stansfield* [1929] 1 Ch 716), and consequently a contingent pecuniary legacy is not within these words.
(b) A contingent residuary devise of freehold land.
(c) A specific or residuary devise of freehold land to trustees upon trust for persons whose interests are contingent or executory.

[218.58]
Having regard to the rules under the general law (eg that a contingent residuary bequest and also a contingent residuary devise and bequest of mixed realty and personalty carry the intermediate income), it would appear that all contingent specific and residuary devises and bequests will now carry the intermediate income, unless that income is otherwise expressly disposed of.

[218.59]
The question of contingent or future pecuniary legacies to minors still remains to be considered under the general law. The testator may, or may not, be the parent of or in loco parentis to the legatee:

(a) If he is a parent or in loco parentis (a grandfather is not usually in loco parentis as regards grandchildren; *Re Dawson, Swainson v Dawson* [1919] 1 Ch 102, and see generally, as to who is in loco parentis, Vol 1, para **[44.7]**), the general rule is that a contingent legacy to a minor carries interest:
    (i) if the contingency is the attaining of full age or marriage. It appears that such a contingent legacy carries interest for the benefit of the legatee, even if there is another fund the income of which is available for his maintenance (*Re Moody, Woodroffe v Moody* [1895] 1 Ch 101; *Re Raine, Tyerman v Stansfield* [1929] 1 Ch 716 at 721). But if the contingency is the attaining of a greater age than full age, the legacy does not carry interest (*Re Abrahams, Abrahams v Bendon* [1911] 1 Ch 108).
    (ii) in any case in which a contingent legacy to a minor, where the testator is not the parent of or in loco parentis to the legatee, would carry interest (see below).

In all cases where the testator is the parent or in loco parentis to the minor legatee, and where the legacy carries interest under the general law, the rate of interest is 5 per cent per annum if the income is sufficient and subject to any rules of court to the contrary (TA 1925, s 31(3): Part G, para **[246.29]**), and the statutory rules of maintenance apply. It may be that the rate of interest on legacies provided by CPR 40, PD 15 (currently 4 per cent—see Vol 1, para **[32.4]**) for cases where the court orders an account of legacies, is a rate contained in a rule of court to the contrary for this purpose.

(b) If the testator is not the parent or in loco parentis, still, under the general law, a contingent legacy to an infant carries interest if—
   (i) the legacy is directed to be set apart; but in this case the court would not as a rule order maintenance if the father is living: *Re Boulter, Capital and Counties Bank v Boulter* [1918] 2 Ch 40 at 45; in cases of setting apart the general rule is that the income is added to and awaits the vesting of the capital; or
   (ii) an intention is manifested in the will that the minor should be maintained; but if the income of any other fund under the will (residue for instance) is available for maintenance, the contingent legacy will not carry interest (*Re West, Westhead v Aspland* [1913] 2 Ch 345; *Re Raine, Tyerman v Stansfield* [1929] 1 Ch 716 at 720).

[218.60]
A future defeasible gift does not carry the intermediate income: *Re Gillett's Will Trusts, Barclays Bank Ltd v Gillett* [1950] Ch 102, [1949] 2 All ER 893 (gift of capital in default of appointment); *Re Geering, Gulliver v Geering* [1964] Ch 136, [1962] 3 All ER 1043 (where there was an express provision which carried the intermediate income), see also Vol 1, paras **[32.15]**–**[32.17]**.

[218.61]
Where income is available in such cases as these, the statutory rules as to maintenance will no doubt apply and carry interest. It should be noted that the general law does not give interest on a contingent legacy to a minor when there is a trust for accumulating the income which precedes the contingent gift (*Re George* (1877) 5 Ch D 837). On these subjects, see Vol 1, para **[32.1]** ff.

[218.62]
(k) Annuities. By s 31(4) of the TA 1925 (Part G, para **[246.29]**) a *vested* annuity is to be treated for the purpose of maintenance as if it were income of property, save that any accumulations during infancy belong in any case to the infant or his personal representatives.

[218.63]
(l) Adaptations of the TA 1925, s 31. A number of testators will no doubt be content to rely on the statutory powers. Others may prefer to give their own trustees what may be a wider discretion by omitting the reference to other available income. Section 31(1)(i) (standing alone at any rate) gives the impression that the amount of income to be applied depends upon a standard of reasonableness, and that it cramps the discretion of the trustees (but see para **[218.51]**). Form B18.11 at para **[218.79]** meets this point by expressly giving an absolute discretion.

[218.64]
It will be appreciated that where the TA 1925, s 31 applies to property held on trust for a class of minors, several of whom are in existence, it applies severally to each presumptive share; that is, in each year all the income has to be divided up among the beneficiaries in accordance with their interests in

capital, and then the share of income allocated to each beneficiary has to be applied for his benefit or accumulated for him in accordance with s 31.

[218.65]
Special provision will still have to be made if it is desired to use the income for the common maintenance of a class of individuals, and such provision may have inheritance tax disadvantages. See para **[218.69]** and Forms B18.16 at para **[218.84]** and B18.17 at para **[218.85]**. For extended accumulation and maintenance provisions continuing after the age of eighteen see para **[218.74]**. For provision in relation to an open class of beneficiaries of which new members are born after the trust for that class commenced, so that such new members participate in accumulations of income made before they are born, see para **[218.55]** and Form B18.14 at para **[218.82]**. For provision entitling a beneficiary absolutely to the accumulations of income of his share, and therefore it seems conferring an interest in possession on him for tax purposes, see para **[218.53]** and Form B18.15 at para **[218.83]**.

[218.66]
(m) The powers of the court. The court can order maintenance and, where there is already a provision for maintenance, increased maintenance. The court has jurisdiction with respect to the income of property belonging to or held in trust for a minor, to take care of it and apply it for his maintenance or otherwise for his benefit and accumulate any surplus not required to be so applied (*Havelock v Havelock, Re Allan* (1881) 17 Ch D 807; *Re Smeed, Archer v Prall* (1886) 2 TLR 535). Where, however, property is vested in trustees upon whom a power has been expressly conferred (which includes the statutory power) of applying at their discretion all or any part of the income for maintenance, education or benefit, the court will not override or interfere with that discretion, if the trustees actually exercise it (*Re Wells, Wells v Wells* (1889) 43 Ch D 281 at 286, 287) and are not doing so in a manner prejudicial to the infant's interests (*Re Lofthouse* (1885) 29 Ch D 921; *Re Bryant, Bryant v Hickley* [1894] 1 Ch 324). If there are two funds available for maintenance, the court orders maintenance from the fund from which it is most beneficial to the minor that it should be taken (*Re Wells*). Maintenance will be ordered out of income directed to be accumulated where there is a paramount intention that the beneficiary should be maintained (*Havelock v Havelock, Re Allan*; *Re Collins, Collins v Collins* (1886) 32 Ch D 229; *Walker v Duncombe* [1901] 1 Ch 879; *Re Wright* [1954] OR 755). Where necessary, maintenance will be ordered out of capital or income in which the minor has only a reversionary or contingent interest subject to the rights of creditors (*Revel v Watkinson* (1748) 1 Ves Sen 93 at 95) and recoupment of such expenditure may be secured by a policy of assurance (*Re Bruce* (1882) 30 WR 992; *Re Tanner* (1884) 53 LJ Ch 1108 at 1110) or by a charge on the property (*Re Colgan* (1881) 19 Ch D 305; *Re Tanner*; but see *Re Hambrough's Estate, Hambrough v Hambrough* [1909] 2 Ch 620, as explained in *Re Gower's Settlement* [1934] Ch 365 at 371, [1934] All ER Rep 796 at 798, but this difficulty has been removed by the enactment of the TA 1925, s 53). The jurisdiction under the TA 1925, s 53 is only applicable where money is required for the maintenance, education or benefit of a minor and cannot be used merely to put an end to a settlement (*Re Heyworth's*

Settlements [1956] Ch 364, [1956] 2 All ER 21), but where the proceeds of a sale under that section are to be settled, it seems they are to be 'applied' for maintenance, education or benefit of a minor (*Re Meux, Gilmour v Gilmour* [1958] Ch 154, [1957] 2 All ER 630).

[218.67]

(n) Income tax. It should be remembered that income which is to be accumulated or which is payable at the discretion of the trustees or any other person in so far as it is not used to defray trust expenses is taxable in the hands of the trustees at the trust rate applicable to trusts (currently 40 per cent), (unless it is UK company dividend income when it is taxable at the dividend trust rate, currently 37.5 per cent): Income Tax Act 2007, s 479 (formerly ICTA 1988, s 686). This provision will apply to express discretionary and accumulation trusts, but it will also apply in cases where the maintenance and accumulation provisions of the TA 1925, s 31 apply, ie until the beneficiary has attained full age. Income applied for the benefit of a beneficiary under a power will be treated as such beneficiary's income for tax purposes and he or she may be able to recover some part of the tax already paid by the trustees: Income Tax Act 2007, ss 493–4 (formerly ICTA 1988, s 687). See also paras **[218.29]**–**[218.32]**.

[218.68]

(o) Time apportionment of income. Where the TA 1925, s 31 applies to property held on trust for an open class of minors contingently upon their attaining a particular age, the birth of an additional member of the class or the death of an existing one could cause elaborate apportionment calculations under the Apportionment Act 1870 if it is not excluded: see *Re Joel's Will Trusts; Rogerson v Brudenell-Bruce* [1967] Ch 14, [1966] 2 All ER 482. It is better to exclude the Act using eg Form B14.32 at para **[214.54]**.

[218.69]

(p) Inheritance tax. ff The new categories of trust for children and young persons, namely trusts for bereaved minors within IHTA 1984, s 71A (see the Note to para **[200.108]** above) and age 18-to-25 trusts within IHTA 1984, s 71D (see the Note to para **[200.109]** above), have two conditions in common, which are met by the application of TA 1925, s 31. One of these conditions is that pending a beneficiary's attainment of an absolute interest, the beneficiary must be entitled to all the income (if there is any) arising from the settled property, or no income may be applied for the benefit of any other person: see IHTA 1984, ss 71A(3)(c), 71D(6)(c). The other condition is that the beneficiary must become entitled to any accumulations of income on or before the age of 18 (in the case of a trust for bereaved minors), or the age of 25 (in the case of age 18-to-25 trusts). Both of these will be satisfied where TA 1925, s 31 applies to the income.

[218.70]

It seems that the application of each of IHTA 1984, s 71A and s 71D is viewed collectively in relation to a class of 'beneficiaries' interested in settled property, so that a provision for maintenance and accumulation for a class of 'beneficiaries' out of a common fund of income may be within IHTA 1984, ss 71A(3)(c), 71D(6)(c), but care has to be taken to see that such a provision does not prejudice the application of s 71A or s 71D by postponing the time when some of the 'beneficiaries' attain absolute interests until after they attain the age of 18 or 25 (as the case may be) or by allowing those who have attained 18 or 25 to benefit from income held for those who are under that age. We do not recommend the use of such provisions, even though they may be slightly more convenient administratively, because they increase the chances of something going wrong. See further, *Foster's Inheritance Tax*, E5.

[218.71]
(q) **Section 31 and the permitted periods of accumulation.** It seems that accumulation under the TA 1925, s 31 during a minority is always valid, irrespective of whether a permitted accumulation period is available under the LPA 1925, s 164 (Part G, para **[246.56]**) or the PAA 1964, s 13 (Part G, para **[246.86]**) because it is directed by statute. Section 165 of the LPA 1925 (Part G, para **[246.57]**) provides that where accumulations of surplus income are made during a minority under any statutory power (or under the general law), the period for which such accumulations are permitted to be made is not to be taken into account in determining the periods for which accumulations are permitted to be made by the LPA 1925, s 164 (which is treated by the PAA 1964, s 13 as including those added by that section), and accordingly an express trust for accumulation for any other permitted period will not be invalidated by reason of accumulations also having been made during a minority under a statutory power (or the general law). It is not easy to work out exactly what the LPA 1925, s 165 is providing, and there is very little authority on it. The reference to a statutory power is a reference to the provisions for accumulation under the TA 1925, s 31; although the latter are strictly speaking a *trust* to accumulate, they are ancillary to the statutory power of maintenance (see *Re Turner's Will Trusts, District Bank Ltd v Turner* [1937] Ch 15).

[218.72]
Only one of the permitted periods of accumulation under the LPA 1925, s 164 is available in relation to any particular disposition, and it is a matter of construction of the instrument making the disposition to determine which period has seemingly been chosen: see eg *Jagger v Jagger* (1883) 25 Ch D 729; *Re Watt's Will Trusts, Watt v Watt* [1936] 2 All ER 1555, 1562, and *Re Ransome* [1957] Ch 348, 361. A possible interpretation is therefore that the LPA 1925, s 165 means no more than that a will or other disposition is not deprived of choice of accumulation period by providing trusts to which accumulation under the TA 1925, s 31 applies; for example, providing trusts to which s 31 applies does not amount to a selection of the duration of minorities of persons who would be entitled to the income if of full age (the period permitted by the LPA 1925, s 164(1)(d): Part G, para **[246.42]**), and the 21-year accumulation period can still be used.

[218.73]
There is a more radical interpretation of the LPA 1925, s 165, which is that it permits accumulation under the TA 1925, s 31 cumulatively with accumulation under the relevant period under s 164. This argument is really only of

interest in relation to the 21-year period under s 165(1)(b) (or the PAA 1964, s 13(1)(a)); it would mean that the accumulation period was suspended during a period of accumulation under the TA 1925, s 31, but started again where it left off once the accumulation under s 31 had finished. If this was correct it would be possible for accumulation for a beneficiary to continue until he reached the age of 25 outside the period of 21 years from the testator's death, unless and until there had been accumulation other than under the TA 1925, s 31 for a total of 21 years, and this was the interpretation apparently accepted by Astbury J in *Re Maber* [1928] Ch 88 at 93, although it was not necessary for his decision in that case. This seems too good to be true, and it would have the inconvenient consequence that the 21-year period would apply differently to different parts of the same trust fund where there was a trust for eg the children of a named person. It is, however, an interpretation which cannot be completely ruled out on the wording of the LPA 1925, ss 164 and 165. From the point of view of drafting will (or any other) trusts it is not an argument which can safely be relied on unless and until there is a decision of the court more directly in point, particularly bearing in mind the often adverse consequences of provisions which go beyond the permitted accumulation periods (see Vol 1, paras **[95.8]** and **[95.13]**). For the practical purposes of will drafting, unless and until there is clear authority to the contrary, it should be assumed that the 21-year accumulation period under the LPA 1925, s 164(1)(b) (Part G, para **[246.56]**) runs out 21 years from the testator's death, irrespective of whether there has been accumulation under TA 1925, s 31 during that period.

[218.74]

(r) **Extended accumulation and maintenance provisions.** The accumulation and maintenance provisions of the TA 1925, s 31, as amended by the FLRA 1969 (Part G, para **[246.29]**), only apply during the minority of a beneficiary, that is, until the age of 18. Thus if there is a gift of capital to members of a class contingently on attaining 25 (for example as in an age 18-to-25 trust, see para **[200.109]** above), and s 31 applies, each member of the class will be entitled to be paid the income of his presumptive share on attaining the age of 18, and will have an interest in possession in his presumptive share from that time. Where an age 18-to-25 trust is proposed, it may be desired to extend accumulation and maintenance provisions so as to continue beyond 18, to 25 if possible. This may be desirable for personal considerations (it is often felt that 18 is too early an age to start receiving a sometimes substantial income), but it may also be desirable to avoid the children having immediate post-death interests (see para **[200.98]** above) from the testator's death, which they would do if they were over 18 at his death (and under 25) and TA 1925, s 31 applied to give them interests in possession from his death. This is because although the income condition of IHTA 1984, s 71D(6)(c) (ie. that pending a beneficiary's attainment of an absolute interest, the beneficiary must be entitled to all the income arising from the settled property, or no income may be applied for the benefit of any other person) may be satisfied where the beneficiary has an interest in possession, if the beneficiary has an interest in possession immediately from the testator's death (or it arises within two years of death, see para **[200.136]**) it will be an immediate post-death interest, which will prevent the underlying trust property being subject to an age 18-to-25 trust, see IHTA 1984, s 71D(5)(c)(ii). Whereas an immediate post-death interest would have the advantage that no inheritance tax would be payable when the beneficiary attained an absolute vested interest at (or under) 25 (see IHTA 1984, s 53(2)), it would have the disadvantage that capital gains tax hold-over relief would not be available in respect of any gain on the trustees' deemed disposal under TCGA 1992, s 71. Conversely, if the property was subject to an age 18-to-25 trust, then there would be an occasion of inheritance tax exit charge when the beneficiary attained an absolute vested interest at (or under) 25 (see IHTA 1984, s 71E(1)(a), but capital gains tax holdover relief would be available under TCGA 1992, s 260(2)(a). Since any inheritance tax exit charge may be nil or small, an age 18-to-25 trust could therefore have an advantage over an immediate post-death interest.

[218.75]
If extended accumulation and maintenance provisions are to be included in a will, one of the accumulation periods permitted by the LPA 1925, s 164 will have to be used. The period of 21 years from the death of the testator will normally be the most appropriate: see paras **[218.71]–[218.73]** for its relationship with accumulation under TA 1925, s 31. If it is certain that all the beneficiaries will be over the age of 4 at the testator's death, the 21-year accumulation period will continue until all have attained 25 and accumulation and maintenance provisions can continue to that age. If the class is to consist only of persons living at the testator's death, accumulation and maintenance provisions can be made to continue until the age of 21. See Form B18.12 at para **[218.80]**.

[218.76]
Where the class of beneficiaries is to remain open after the testator's death (eg. where there is a trust for grandchildren, which necessarily cannot be an age 18-to-25 trust), none of the above methods can be used for the presumptive shares of beneficiaries born after his death. Express accumulation and maintenance provisions could be drafted in respect of the income of the shares of such afterborn beneficiaries which continue to the end of the 21-year accumulation period.

[218.77]
It should be emphasised that extended accumulation and maintenance trusts will be of no effect if the capital vests indefeasibly in the beneficiary on or before he attains the age of eighteen. In these circumstances he will be able to call for the capital at that age, and since any accumulations would be added to that capital (see para **[218.53]**) he can call for the capital and the future income of it despite the fact that the future income has been directed to be accumulated. This is the rule in *Saunders v Vautier* (1841) Cr & Ph 240; affg 4 Beav 115.

[218.78]
The directory provisions of the TA 1925, s 31 (Part G, para **[246.29]**), eg the trust to accumulate, are capable of being varied by the provisions of a will or

settlement creating the trusts to which s 31 applies, even though the TA 1925, s 69(2) only states that the *powers* conferred by the Act are subject to the terms of the trust instrument: see *Re Turner's Will Trusts, District Bank Ltd v Turner* [1937] Ch 15.

[218.79]

Form B18.11: Variation of the statutory provision for maintenance and accumulation to maximise the trustees' discretion[1]

I declare that in the application to the trusts hereof of the statutory power of maintenance given to trustees by section 31 of the Trustee Act 1925 as amended[2] the proviso to subsection (1) of that section shall not apply and shall be deemed to be omitted[3] and that paragraph (i) of subsection (1) of the said section shall be read as if the words 'as the trustees think fit' were substituted for the words 'as may, in all the circumstances, be reasonable'.[4]

1 This Form should be compatible with trusts for bereaved minors within IHTA 1984, s 71A (see para **[200.108]** above) and age 18-to-25 trusts within IHTA 1984, s 71D (see para **[200.109]** above).
2 The section is set out as amended in Part G at para **[246.29]**. It should be remembered that the statutory power of maintenance will cease when the child attains 18, after which he or she will be entitled to the income: see para **[218.43]**.
3 This part of the clause excludes the reference in the section to the available income from another fund and the special statutory scheme where other available income exists; but it does not, of course, mean that the trustees are not to consider other available income as part of the 'circumstances'. See sub-para (f) of para **[218.50]**.
4 This part of the clause enlarges the discretion of the trustees. See para **[218.51]**.

[218.80]

Form B18.12: Statutory maintenance and accumulation to continue to the age of twenty-one[1]

Section 31 of the Trustee Act 1925 [as amended by the Family Law Reform Act 1969[2]] shall apply to the foregoing trust [provided that in relation to the presumptive share of any of [*beneficiaries*] who is actually in existence at the time of my death the said section 31 shall have effect[2]] as if section 1 of the Family Law Reform Act 1969 had not been enacted.

1 See paras **[218.74]–[218.78]**. The idea behind this clause is to allow maintenance and accumulation to continue for a period of 21 years from the testator's death, 21 years being a permitted period of accumulation: see LPA 1925, s 164(1)(b) (Part G, para **[246.56]**). The FLRA 1969, s 1 substituted in the TA 1925, s 31 references to 18 years for references to 21 years, so that if it is deemed not to have been enacted, the TA 1925, s 31 will apply as if the age up to which maintenance and accumulation is possible is 21. Any beneficiary actually in existence (and not merely en ventre sa mere) at the testator's death will necessarily attain 21 within the permitted accumulation period of 21 years from the testator's death, so that accumulation will be permissible until he attains the age of 21. This Form should be compatible with age 18-to-25 trusts within IHTA 1984, s 71D (see para **[200.109]** above).
2 If it is certain that all the beneficiaries will be in existence at the testator's death, the parts in square brackets may be omitted.

[218.81]

Form B18.13: Statutory maintenance and accumulation to continue to maximum possible age[1]

(1) Section 31 of the Trustee Act 1925 (as amended by the Family Law Reform Act 1969) shall apply to the foregoing trusts Provided that in

relation to the presumptive share of any of the [*beneficiaries*] in relation to whom the specified age (as hereinafter defined) exceeds 18 years the said section 31 (as amended as aforesaid) shall have effect as if the age of majority were the specified age (the expressions 'infant' 'infancy' and 'minority' therein being construed accordingly) and as if there were substituted the specified age for the words 'eighteen years' wherever the same occur in the said section 31 (as amended as aforesaid).

(2) In the last preceding subclause 'the specified age' in relation to any of the [*beneficiaries*] means whichever is the less of (i) the age which he or she will attain (if he or she so long lives) on his or her last birthday occurring not later than the expiration of 21 years from my death or (ii) the age of [25] years.[2]

1 See paras **[218.74]**–**[218.78]**.

2 This definition has the function of preventing accumulation continuing beyond the permitted maximum of 21 years from the testator's death (see s 164(1)(b) of the LPA 1925: Part G, paras **[246.56]** and **[218.71]**–**[218.73]**), and also that of preventing accumulation beyond the specified age. The latter should not exceed 25 years if the trusts are to satisfy the IHTA 1984, s 71D (see Part A, para **[200.109]**) and should not exceed the age of absolute vesting of capital if that is earlier than 25.

[218.82]

Form B18.14: Variation of the statutory provision for maintenance and accumulation—on the birth of a new member of the class existing accumulations are shared with the new member[1]

Section 31 of the Trustee Act 1925 shall apply to the foregoing trust[2] Provided that if after my death the class of [beneficiaries][3] interested or presumptively interested under the foregoing trust is increased by the birth of a further member of that class any accumulations of income which are held immediately before such birth on the trusts set out in subsection (2) of the said section 31 for any existing member of the class shall from such birth be held on those trusts for the respective benefit of such existing member and such new-born member in the same respective proportions as the proportions in which the share of capital in which such existing member is interested immediately before such birth comes to be held for such existing and newborn members respectively immediately after such birth.

1 Where there is an open class of beneficiaries, if there is no provision of this kind any accumulations of income held in relation to a beneficiary will continue to be held for him contingently on attaining 18 (or marrying or forming a civil partnership) or as an accretion to his share after the birth of a further member of the class. The purpose of this provision is that accumulations made before the birth of a new member of the class are shared with that member in the same way as the underlying capital. See para **[218.55]** for further explanation of the effect of the TA 1925, s 31 (Part G, para **[246.29]**) which this form is intended to counteract. See n 2 below for the type of trust to which this form is relevant.

2 This form assumes that the trust to which it applies is one for an open class of beneficiaries, e g a trust for the testator's grandchildren who attain the age of 25, so that it is possible for there to be members of it who are born after the testator's death. It also assumes that the trusts upon which any accumulations of income are to be held are those in the TA 1925, s 31(2) without any other variation. A provision of this kind is not relevant to a closed class, such as the testator's children, and it would be completely inconsistent with, and must not be combined with, a provision such as Form B18.15 at para **[218.83]** under which accumulations of income are vested absolutely in the beneficiaries from the outset. This

provision could be combined with one that continued the accumulation and maintenance trusts of s 31 to an age greater than 18, such as B18.12 at para **[218.80]** and B18.13 at para **[218.81]**.

3 It will usually be appropriate to substitute a description of the class in question for 'beneficiaries', e g where the trust is for the testator's grandchildren who attain the age of 25 substitute 'my grandchildren' at this point.

[218.83]

Form B18.15: Variation of the statutory provision for maintenance and accumulation—accumulations vesting absolutely[1]

Section 31 of the Trustee Act 1925 shall apply to the foregoing trusts[2] as if in subsection (2) therereof there were substituted for the words from 'as follows' to the end of the subsection the words 'upon trust for such infant or his personal representatives absolutely'.

1 See para **[218.53]** for the trusts of accumulations of income under the TA 1925, s 31 (Part G, para **[246.29]**), which unless varied are such as usually to give minor beneficiaries a contingent interest in such accumulations, even if they have a vested interest in the income (unless they have an annuity). The purpose of this variation of s 31 is to cause the accumulations to be held on trust absolutely for the beneficiary in relation to whose interest the income arose, so as to confer an interest in possession for inheritance tax purposes. A minor cannot be paid income to which he is entitled (see Vol 1, para **[9.39]**) but it is thought that he has an interest in possession in income if it would form part of his estate if he died under the age of 18 (and unmarried and without having formed a civil partnership).

2 This provision can be combined with any trust of capital but is not appropriate where the accumulations will vest absolutely without such a provision (see para **[218.53]**). If it is used in conjunction with a trust for the testator's child or children contingently on attaining the age of 18, that trust should be a trust for bereaved minors within IHTA 1984, s 71A (see para **[200.108]** above). It could also be used to give a minor an immediate post-death interest within IHTA 1984, s 49A (see the Note to para **[200.98]** above). If its effect is to give a minor an immediate post-death interest it will prevent the trust for that minor being an age 18-to-25 trust within IHTA 1984, s 71D, even if capital is to vest at age 25 (see IHTA 1984, s 71D(5)(c)(ii) and para **[200.109]** above). It is inconsistent with, and should not be combined with, any provision extending the accumulation and maintenance trusts of TA 1925, s 31 to an age greater than 18, such as Forms B18.12 at para **[218.80]** and B18.13 at para **[218.81]**, nor with any provision altering the trusts of the accumulations such as Form B18.14 at para **[218.82]**.

[218.84]

Form B18.16: Maintenance of a class; applicable to shares in income as well as in capital[1]

With regard to maintenance I direct as follows:

(1) Subject to any prior interests in the income hereinafter mentioned my trustees shall receive such part of the income arising from [my residuary estate] as is for the time being attributable to the shares or presumptive or prospective shares in my residuary estate or in the income thereof of such of [my children] [the children of the said [*name*]] as for the time being are under the age of [eighteen] [twenty-one] years and they may pay or apply the whole or so much thereof as they in their discretion think fit for or towards the maintenance education or benefit of such children for the time being under the said age of [eighteen] [twenty-one] years as a class and if my trustees think fit unequally as between such children and shall not be bound to consider whether or not there is any other income

applicable for the same purposes or whether or not there is any person bound by law to provide for the maintenance or education of such children or any of them.

(2) My trustees may pay the whole or any part of the said income to the parent or guardian or guardians of any of such children or to any such children if of the age of sixteen years or more without seeing to the application thereof and shall accumulate the surplus (if any) of the said income in each year by investing the same and the resulting income thereof in manner hereby authorised and subject to sub-clause (3) below my trustees may at any time apply such accumulations as if the same were income of the current year.

(3) When and so often as any child of [mine] [the said [*name*]] attains the age of [eighteen] [twenty-one] years a share in the then existing accumulations corresponding to the share of my residuary estate to which or to the income of which such child shall then be entitled shall be transferred to the capital of such last-mentioned share and be dealt with accordingly and so that if any share in which or in the income of which any of the said children shall for the time being have a vested interest shall be increased by any event which may happen a share in the accumulations which exist at the date of such event proportionate to the increase in such share shall be transferred to the capital of such share and be dealt with accordingly.[2]

1 For consideration of this type of provision which can be used where a testator has left property to a class of beneficiaries in specified shares and whether it is compatible with IHTA 1984, s 71A or s 71D see paras **[218.69]** and **[218.70]**. Twenty-one should only be chosen as the relevant age if all the children in question will be in existence by the time of the testator's death: see further n 2 to Form B18.17 at para **[218.85]**.

2 Paragraph (3) contemplates a division and transfer of the accumulations from time to time as and when any child becomes absolutely entitled.

Under the usual form of maintenance clause (including the statutory clause: TA 1925, s 31 (Part G, para **[246.29]**)) trustees ought to keep the accumulated income of each child's share distinct, though they frequently do not do so.

[218.85]

Form B18.17: Another clause providing for maintenance out of a common fund[1]

With regard to maintenance I direct as follows:

(1) Subject to any prior interests in the income hereinafter mentioned my trustees shall receive the income arising from my residuary estate or from so much thereof as shall not for the time being have become subject to an absolute interest or an interest in possession of any child[2] [of mine] [of the said [*name*]] under the trusts hereinbefore contained and may pay or apply such income or so much thereof as my trustees shall think fit for the maintenance education or benefit of such [of my children] [children of the said [*name*]] as shall for the time being be under the age of [eighteen] [twenty-one] years or any one or more exclusively of the others or other of such children in such proportions at such time and in such manner in all respects as my trustees shall in their sole discretion think proper with liberty to my trustees to pay the whole or any part of the said income to the

guardian or guardians of any of the said children for the purposes aforesaid without seeing to the application thereof; and

(2) My trustees shall invest the surplus (if any) of the said income in investments of the nature hereby authorised and shall accumulate the same at compound interest by investing the resulting income thereof as an accretion thereto and shall hold such accumulations as accretions to the capital of the whole part or parts of my residuary estate from which they arose and as one fund therewith for all purposes.[3]

1 For consideration of this type of clause in relation to IHTA 1984, s 71A and 71D, see paras **[218.69]** and **[218.70]**.

2 If the class has not closed at the death, e g because the gift is to the children of a person who may still be living at the testator's death, the age contingency specified throughout the clause should be 18 not 21. Otherwise the accumulation provision in sub-cl (2) may be invalid: see the LPA 1925, s 164(1)(d) (Part G, para **[246.56]**) restricting the power to accumulate to the minority (which now ends at 18) of any beneficiary otherwise entitled to income.

3 For fear of possible inheritance tax difficulties as regards the application of IHTA 1984, s 71A and 71Dff, there is no power to apply accumulations as income of the current year. We recommend that a power of advancement over the whole of a presumptive share is added to make up for this.

[218.86]

Form B18.18: Maintenance clause; simple express trusts[1]

(1) Subject and without prejudice to any prior interest or charge affecting the income hereinafter mentioned, I empower my trustees during the minority [or minority and spinsterhood as the case may be] of any child [of mine] [*or* grandchild of mine] [*or* of the said [*name*]] to apply the whole or such part as my trustees shall think fit of the income of the expectant or presumptive share[2] of such child [*or* grandchild] for or towards his or her maintenance education or benefit with power to pay the same to the parent or to the guardian or guardians of such child [*or* grandchild] for the purposes aforesaid without seeing to the application thereof.[3]

(2) My trustees may exercise the power aforesaid whether or not there is any other fund or income available for any of the aforesaid purposes and whether or not there is any person bound by law to provide for such maintenance or education.

(3) The surplus income shall be accumulated by investing the same and the resulting income thereof in any investments of the kind hereby authorised and such accumulations shall be added to the property or to the share therein from which the same was derived and shall devolve therewith so as to follow the destination of such property or share but my trustees shall be entitled at any time to apply any part of such accumulations for any of the purposes aforesaid as if the same were income arising in the then current year.

1 This form may be useful where the will may have to be acted on abroad, or where it is desired to express an ordinary maintenance clause in a will rather than to let the statutory clause apply. Further, it is a form which can be readily adapted to provide express accumulation and maintenance trusts to a higher age than 18. If, for example, it is desired to have these to the age of 21 for the testator's children, substitute for the words 'during the minority ... of any child of mine' the words 'while any child of mine has not attained the

age of 21 years'. There must of course be an available accumulation period for this to be valid: see paras **[218.74]–[218.78]**. This Form would be compatible with trusts for bereaved minors within IHTA 1984, s 71A (see para **[200.108]** above) or age 18-to-25 trusts within IHTA 1984, s 71D (see para **[200.109]** above).

It excludes the necessity of applying only a portion of the income where the trustees have notice of other available income (TA 1925, s 31: Part G, para **[246.29]**). In the Canadian case of *Re Larsen's Will* (1968) 66 WWR 358 a clause in similar terms was held wide enough to authorise the purchase by the trustees of an annuity for a beneficiary in need.

2 Where a woman was entitled to a share on birth of issue and, being over 50 years of age, had no children, the court refused to hold that she was past childbearing, and she was, therefore, entitled to an expectant or presumptive share and to maintenance under an express maintenance clause: *Re Allen* [1953] ALR 959, St R Qd 95.

3 Giving a person power to maintain the minor out of income will not make the gift to the minor vested, if it is otherwise contingent: *Re Rogers, Lloyds Bank Ltd v Lory* [1944] Ch 297, [1944] 2 All ER 1.

ADVANCEMENT

[218.87]

Note. TA 1925, s 32 (statutory power of advancement), as amended by the TLATA 1996, s 25(1), Sch 3, para 3(1), (8) subject to savings contained in s 25(4) thereof, is set out in Part G at para **[246.27]**. We have the following points concerning it:

[218.88]

(a) Age. A 'specified age' in TA 1925, s 32(1) includes a double event, eg surviving another and attaining eighteen (or twenty-one): *Re Garrett, Croft v Ruck* [1934] Ch 477.

[218.89]

(b) Extent of power. The amount which may be raised and applied is not to exceed one-half of the presumptive or vested share or interest of the person to be advanced; the amount advanced is to be brought into account if the person is or becomes absolutely entitled to a share in the property; but the advancement may be made notwithstanding that his interest is liable to be defeated by the exercise of a power of appointment, or to be diminished by an increase of the class to which he belongs. It will not therefore be necessary to make an absolute appointment to a person in order that he may be advanced; and again, if the class be merely the children of A, and A's wife dies, the whole class can be advanced up to the limit, notwithstanding that A might marry again and have a second family. We recommend that the power is always made exercisable over the whole of a presumptive share (see eg Form B18.20 at para **[218.105]**). An extended power of advancement exercisable over the whole of a beneficiary's presumptive share, is compatible with trusts for bereaved minors within IHTA 1984, s 71A (see para **[200.108]** above) and age 18-to-25 trusts within IHTA 1984, s 71D (see para **[200.109]** above). It may, however, prevent a vulnerable person election being made for the trustees' capital gains and undistributed income will be taxed as the beneficiary's (see FA 2005, ss 25–33 and para **[217.4]**).

[218.90]

(c) Effect of advancements on prior interests, including interests under protective trusts. The advancement cannot be made so as to prejudice any person entitled to a prior life or other interest, vested or contingent: *Re Bainbridge* [1948] Ch 717, [1948] 2 All ER 657 (and see *IRC v Bernstein* [1960] Ch 444, [1960] 1 All ER 697, as to what is a prior interest), but any such person who is of full age may consent in writing. Objects of a discretionary trust do not have a vested or contingent interest within TA 1925, s 32(1)(c), though all together if of age they can put an end to the trust (*Re Beckett's Settlement, Re Beckett, Eden v Von Stutterheim* [1940] Ch 279). A married woman validly restrained from anticipation could give such consent (*Re Garrett, Croft v Ruck* [1934] Ch 477). It is clear that the consent of a life tenant whose interest is determinable on alienation, etc under protective trusts will not occasion a forfeiture in the following cases:

(i) Where the provision for forfeiture in the protective trusts is expressly stated not to affect any steps taken by the life tenant to enable advances to be made by the trustees in accordance with the advancement clause contained in the settlement. This goes without saying, but the point is discussed in *Re Shaw's Settlement Trusts, Shaw v Shaw* [1951] 1 All ER 656 at 658.

(ii) Where the statutory protective trusts (TA 1925, s 33: Part G, para **[246.31]**) are incorporated because these trusts include a provision to that effect.

(iii) Where though the protective trusts do not include such a provision, there is an express protective trust and an express advancement clause in the settlement, because the whole document must be construed together and it is not to be supposed that it was intended that, if the advancement was to be made, the life tenant would forfeit his interest: *Re Hodgson, Weston v Hodgson* [1913] 1 Ch 34; *Re Shaw's Settlement Trusts, Shaw v Shaw* [1951] 1 All ER 656 at 659.

(iv) Where the settlement is made after 1925, and there is no express advancement clause and the provisions of the TA 1925, s 32 are implied, a consent to an advancement does not cause a forfeiture of the life interest because the draftsman must be deemed to have had in mind the statutory power and could not have intended that consent to its exercise should work a forfeiture: *Re Rees' Will Trusts, Lloyds Bank Ltd v Rees* [1954] Ch 202, [1954] 1 All ER 7. There remains the reported decision in *Re Stimpson's Trusts, Stimpson v Stimpson* [1931] 2 Ch 77, [1931] All ER Rep 809. This would not seem to be good law though it has not been expressly overruled. In this case the will was made in 1906 and the testatrix died in 1929. There was no express advancement clause, but, in the circumstances, the implied advancement clause under the TA 1925, s 32 applied, and it was held that a consent to an advancement would forfeit the life interest. No reasons for this are given and, it seems, that the only distinction which can be made is that the draftsman of the will in 1906 could not have had in mind and relied upon a clause in the 1925 Act.

[218.91]

(d) The circumstances in which s 32 of the TA 1925 applies. Where the protective trusts were set out in the will and the trust after the cesser of the life interest was 'to apply any sums not exceeding in any one year the amount of the annuity or life interest' for certain beneficiaries, this reference to 'the amount' is not an expression of a contrary intention within the TA 1925, s 69(2) (Part G, para **[246.40]**), which would exclude the application of s 32: *Re Rees' Will Trusts* [1954] Ch 202, [1954] 1 All ER 7.

[218.92]
The power given by s 32 of the TA 1925 is not applicable as long as a trust for accumulation is effective, since such a trust is inconsistent with an advance being made and a contrary intention within the TA 1925, s 69(2) is shown: *IRC v Bernstein* [1961] Ch 399, [1961] 1 All ER 320. The inclusion of an express power of advancement may also be evidence of a contrary intention within the meaning of the subsection: *Re Evans' Settlement, Watkins v Whitworth Jones* [1967] 3 All ER 343, [1967] 1 WLR 1294.

[218.93]
TA 1925, s 32 applies to all kinds of trust property other than capital money arising under the Settled Land Act 1925 (unless expressly declared to apply) (TA 1925, 32(2), as substituted by the TLATA 1996, s 25(1), Sch 3, para 3(1), (8) subject to savings contained in s 25(4) thereof). Since no new settlements can be created under the Settled Land Act 1925 on or after 1 January 1997, this exclusion will be of diminishing importance. Prior to 1 January 1997, when land was either held on trust for sale or was settled land, the section only applied where the trust consisted of money or securities, or property held upon trust for sale, calling in, and conversion where the money or securities, or proceeds of sale, were not by statute or in equity considered as land, or applicable as capital money under the Settled Land Act 1925, eg where there was no direction to reconvert into land (*Re Stimpson's Trusts, Stimpson v Stimpson* [1931] 2 Ch 77, [1931] All ER Rep 809, and Vol 1, para **[37.1]**).

The section does not apply to trusts constituted or created before 1 January 1926, and, contrary to the position under s 31, where the will comes into operation before 1926 does not apply where a special power of appointment arising under such a will is exercised after 1925 (*Re Batty* [1952] 1 All ER 425; see also *Re Leigh's Marriage Settlement* [1952] 2 All ER 57). The case is otherwise in the case of a general power of appointment: *Re Bransbury's Will Trusts, Grece v Bransbury* [1954] 1 All ER 605.

Under the TA 1925, s 69(2) (Part G, para **[246.40]**), the testator can negative or vary the statutory power; if he does not wish *any* power of advancement to apply, he should expressly negative the statutory power.

Section 32 is, speaking generally, a statutory enactment of the power of advancement which was usually inserted in settlements of personalty.

[218.94]
(e) **Meaning of 'benefit' in s 32.** The power of advancement under the Act is a power the exercise of which must have some reference to the actual circumstances of the object of the power requiring to be benefited at the time of the exercise of the power. An advancement in its strict sense is something given by the parent to establish the child in life or to make what is called a provision for him; but where, as in the TA 1925, s 32 the power of application of capital may be exercised for advancement or benefit in such manner as the trustees may in their absolute discretion think fit, the power is

not confined to the making of advancements in the strict sense and is a very wide power indeed. The cited cases usually start with *Roper-Curzon v Roper-Curzon* (1871) LR 11 Eq 452, but that case merely decided that, while the advancement would not be authorised if the money were handed over to the son, it would be authorised if the money were settled upon himself, his wife and children upon the ordinary trusts of such a settlement. *Re Halsted's Will Trusts, Halsted v Halsted* [1937] 2 All ER 570, was a somewhat similar case on its facts but it was clearly held that, where the son had no other resources, such a settlement was for the 'benefit' of the son. In the first case the advancement was required for the pursuit by the son of the legal profession, but in the second there was no such requirement, the money being advanced merely for the purpose of the son making provision for his family. In *Re Ropner's Settlement Trusts, Ropner v Ropner* [1956] 3 All ER 332, the benefit was the possible avoidance of death duties in an otherwise similar case. The avoidance of death duties was the benefit in *Re Meux, Gilmour v Gilmour* [1958] Ch 154, [1957] 2 All ER 630 (a decision under the TA 1925, s 53 which does not deal with advancement) and in *Re Wills' Will Trusts, Wills v Wills* [1959] Ch 1, [1958] 2 All ER 472. Thus we have two points decided:

(i) the avoidance of taxation may be a benefit within the meaning of that word in a power of advancement; and
(ii) a settlement of the sum advanced is permissible under the power.

[218.95]
There has since been further authority on the scope of the power to settle capital in exercise of the power under the TA 1925, s 32. In *Re Wills' Will Trusts, Wills v Wills* [1959] Ch 1, [1958] 2 All ER 472, there was an express power of advancement which allowed application for the benefit of any child, children or wife of the person advanced and it was held that a provision for recently born twins of a beneficiary, whose interest might be defeated by his death under twenty-five, such beneficiary being engaged in war service, was a good exercise of the power. It was stated that such advancement though on contingent trusts was *in the circumstances* for the benefit of the twins. In *Pilkington v IRC* [1964] AC 612, [1962] 3 All ER 622, the statutory power was applicable. The beneficiary proposed to be advanced was a child of two years, the daughter of a wealthy parent well able to provide for her maintenance and education. The proposed trusts of the sum advanced were for the infant absolutely if she attained the age of thirty years and in the event of her death under that age leaving children then for such children on attaining twenty-one years of age and subject thereto for all the other children of the infant's father on attaining full age or marrying. It was held by the House of Lords that it was not possible to introduce into the statutory power a qualification which would exclude its exercise in such circumstances since the propriety of requiring a settlement of the money advanced had been recognised as lawful ever since *Roper-Curzon v Roper-Curzon* (1871) LR 11 Eq 452 was decided in 1871. It was also held that the statutory power of advancement must be treated as a provision written into the will and, therefore, so far as the rule of perpetuities is concerned, the trusts of the new settlement had to be read back into the will and their validity under the perpetuity rule decided as if they were contained in the

will just as is done in the case of special powers. This is a matter of considerable importance, as the whole advance may fail if the trusts of the new settlement are substantially invalid: see *Re Hastings-Bass, Hastings-Bass v IRC* [1975] Ch 25, [1974] 2 All ER 193, and *Re Abrahams' Will Trusts, Caplan v Abrahams* [1969] 1 Ch 463, [1967] 2 All ER 1175. Such invalidity may have serious fiscal consequences: *Spens v IRC* [1970] 3 All ER 295, [1970] 1 WLR 1170.

[218.96]
Another point that has been discussed is whether the trustees of the settled advanced sum can be given a discretion and more particularly whether that sub-settlement can include discretionary trusts. In view of the extremely wide scope of the powers under the TA 1925, s 32, as shown by *Pilkington v IRC* [1964] AC 612, [1962] 3 All ER 622, *Re Clore's Settlement Trusts, Sainer v Clore* [1966] 2 All ER 272, [1966] 1 WLR 955, and most recently by *Re Hampden Settlement Trusts*, [1977] TR 177, we take the view that discretionary trusts could be created in a proper case in exercise of the powers conferred by s 32. This has certain IHT consequences, for which see para **[218.101]**.

[218.97]
Other illustrations of applications of capital under a power to apply it for someone's benefit are as follows. In *Re Kershaw's Trusts* (1868) LR 6 Eq 322 the court authorised trustees with such a power to make a loan of trust money to the beneficiary's husband to provide him with capital to continue in business, and in *Lowther v Bentinck* (1874) LR 19 Eq 166 payment of the beneficiary's debts was held to be within such a power.

[218.98]
There are three important modern decisions on applications for a beneficiary's benefit which take the form of the satisfaction of a moral or legal obligation of his to others. In *Re Clore's Settlement Trusts, Sainer v Clore* [1966] 2 All ER 272, [1966] 1 WLR 955 the trustees were authorised to apply a proportion of a beneficiary's presumptive share in donations to charity, the beneficiary being a wealthy man who regarded himself as under a moral obligation to make substantial charitable donations. In *Re Hampden Settlement Trusts* [1977] TR 177 the court held that the trustees had validly exercised an express power to apply capital (in similar terms to the power under the TA 1925, s 32: Part G, para **[246.30]**) for the benefit of an object of the power by settling the trust property on immediate trusts for the benefit of his minor child and any future children of his, again satisfying a moral (and legal) obligation of the beneficiary, in this case to maintain and educate his own minor children. It should be noted that in the *Clore* and *Hampden* cases the beneficiary was comfortably off independently of the funds which were being applied to or on trust for others in satisfaction of his obligations; the court would be unlikely to approve or uphold an application of this type which stripped a beneficiary of all means of support. In such a case, it might not be presumed that there was a moral obligation to be satisfied, and indeed in *X v A* [2005] EWHC 2706 (Ch), [2006] 1 All ER 952, Hart J did not authorise the payment of £2.46m from a £3.21m fund to charity as for the

benefit of the life tenant in respect of whose benefit the trustees had a power to apply capital, and who distrusted inherited wealth and gave most of her property to charity. The judge held that such a payment could not be said to improve her material situation since it was not relieving her of an obligation she would otherwise have to meet out of her own resources which were not as great as the trust resources. Her sense of moral obligation was not sufficient to justify such a payment, there had to be a moral obligation capable of being recognised by the court.

For the capital gains tax significance of the possibility of creating new trusts in exercise of the power conferred by TA 1925, s 32, see paras **[218.102]–[218.104]**.

[218.99]
(f) **Transfers of property in specie under s 32.** The trustees are empowered by the section to pay or apply any capital money subject to the trust. The point has arisen whether this provision allows the conveyance of land so subject. The trustees could, of course, pay the purchase price to the beneficiary and with that money he could purchase the property. The court, however, has decided that such circuity of action would not be insisted on and the trustees might execute the conveyance forthwith under the terms of the power: see *Re Collard's Will Trusts, Lloyds Bank Ltd v Rees* [1961] Ch 293, [1961] 1 All ER 821 and *Pilkington v IRC* [1964] AC 612, [1962] 3 All ER 622, HL. In *Re Wills' Will Trusts, Wills v Wills* [1959] Ch 1, [1958] 2 All ER 472, the trustees were empowered to raise any part of his or her presumptive share and to pay or apply the same for the benefit of the beneficiary. Certain investments which had been appropriated to the beneficiary's share were directed to be held on certain new trusts and this was held to be a 'raising' within this special power of advancement.

[218.100]
(g) **Exercise of s 32 powers in breach of trust.** Where trustees have a power of advancement with the consent of the tenant for life or other beneficiary, such exercise may be a breach of trust on the part of the trustees despite the consent of the tenant for life. The court has to consider all the circumstances in order to see whether it is fair and equitable that the person injured by such exercise should sue the trustees. It is not necessary that he should know that he is concurring in a breach of trust provided he fully understands in what he is concurring, nor is it necessary that he himself should have benefited by the breach of trust: *Re Pauling's Settlement Trusts, Younghusband v Coutts & Co* [1964] Ch 303, [1963] 3 All ER 1. In this case advances were made in respect of a child's share and applied for the benefit of the parents.

[218.101]
(h) **Inheritance tax.** The statutory power of advancement, whether extended so that it is exercisable over the whole of a beneficiary's presumptive share or not, or a like power, would be compatible with trusts for bereaved minors within IHTA 1984, s 71A (see IHTA 1984, s 71A(5) and para **[200.108]** above) and age 18-to-25 trusts within IHTA 1984, s 71D (see IHTA 1984, s 71D(7) and para **[200.109]** above). The power could be exercised so as to prevent capital vesting absolutely in a beneficiary at 18 or

25 (as the case may be), eg. by deferring vesting to a later age or giving the beneficiary a life interest rather than an absolute contingent interest. In either of these cases, from the exercise of the power, the advanced property would cease to be within IHTA 1984, s 71A or s 71D (as the case may be), although the possibility that the power might be so exercised would not prevent the property being within either section prior to such exercise. It seems that it would only be in the event of property being advanced from an age 18-to-25 trust when the advanced beneficiary is over 18, that there would be an inheritance tax charge (see IHTA 1984, s 71E(1)(a)). Otherwise, ie. where property is advanced from a trust for bereaved minors, or from an age 18-to-25 trust for the benefit of a beneficiary under 18, there would not, see IHTA 1984 ss. 71B(2)(c), 71E(2)(d).

[218.102]

(i) **Capital gains tax.** Where a power of application of capital, such as that conferred under the TA 1925, s 32, is exercised so as to create new trusts, this can be, for capital gains tax purposes, the creation of a new settlement (as opposed to being a continuation of the one under which the power arose). In such a case there is a deemed disposal for capital gains tax purposes of all the assets put into the new settlement under the TCGA 1992, s 71: see *Hoare Trustees v Gardner* [1979] Ch 10, [1978] 1 All ER 791. (New trusts created in exercise of a special power of appointment, on the other hand, are in a normal case regarded as a continuation of the existing settlement, and no such deemed disposal arises on their creation—see *Bond (Inspector of Taxes) v Pickford* [1983] STC 517.) It has sometimes been thought that new trusts created under an exercise of the power of payment or application of capital conferred by the TA 1925, s 32 must always give rise to a new settlement, and thus to a deemed disposal, for capital gains tax purposes. However, it was held in *Swires v Renton* [1991] STC 490 that the question whether or not a new settlement was created, where new trusts were created in exercise of an express power which in material respects resembled the wording of s 32, was a question of intention to be gathered from the language of the instrument exercising the power. Accordingly, with careful drafting it is possible to create new trusts in exercise of a power to pay or apply, such as s 32, without giving rise to a deemed disposal for capital gains tax purposes.

[218.103]

This possibility of creating new trusts under the TA 1925, s 32 without creating a new settlement is important now that general hold-over relief from capital gains tax has been abolished, because it means that where a beneficiary is about to reach an age of absolute vesting of capital which will be a capital gains tax deemed disposal under the TCGA 1992, s 71, and hold-over is not available, it may be possible to defer the impending capital gains tax charge by a timely imposition of further trusts on the capital in exercise of the s 32 power (particularly where the power applies to the whole of a presumptive share), without this exercise of the power itself being a deemed disposal for capital gains tax. However, capital gains tax hold-over relief will be available under TCGA 1990, s 260(2)(d), (da), (db) when capital vests from relevant property trusts, trusts for bereaved minors and age

18-to-25 trusts, and the main circumstance when hold-over will not be available (in the context of wills) is where a beneficiary with an immediate post-death interest becomes absolutely entitled to capital.

[218.104]

Form B18.19: Statutory advancement clause restricted

I declare that the statutory power of advancement given to trustees by section 32 of the Trustee Act 1925,[1] shall apply to the trusts hereof as if incorporated herein save that the limit of advancement shall instead of being one-half of the value of the property or share be [one-third thereof] [the sum of £—— to be raised out of the property or share]

1 See Part G, para **[246.30]**.

[218.105]

Form B18.20: Statutory advancement clause varied to apply to the whole of a presumptive share

Section 32 of the Trustee Act 1925 shall apply to the trusts hereof as if the words 'one-half of' were omitted from proviso (a) to subsection (1) thereof.[1]

1 In our view this is a better formula than declaring that proviso (a) to s 32(1) is to be treated as omitted, because a provision of the latter kind might permit the payment or application of *more than* a beneficiary's presumptive share for his advancement or benefit. This Form would be compatible with trusts for bereaved minors within IHTA 1984, s 71A (see IHTA 1984, s 71A(5) and para **[200.108]** above) and age 18-to-25 trusts within IHTA 1984, s 71D (see IHTA 1984, s 71D(7) and para **[200.109]**).

[218.106]

Form B18.21: Express Advancement clause; ordinary form

I declare that my trustees may raise any part or parts not exceeding altogether [one-half] [*or* any sum or sums not exceeding £—— in the whole] out of the then presumptive contingent expectant or vested [legacy or] share of any child [*or* grandchild] of mine [of the said [*name*]] under the trusts hereinbefore declared and may pay or apply the same as my trustees shall think fit for the advancement or benefit[1] of such child [*or* grandchild]. Provided that no such payment or application shall be made so as to prejudice any person entitled to any prior life or other interest whether vested or contingent in the money so to be paid or applied without the consent of such person.[2]

1 The essential wording of this power is the same as that of the statutory power under the TA 1925, s 32 (Part G, para **[246.30]**). For the scope of the power see paras **[218.94]**–**[218.98]** and for the capital gains tax aspects see paras **[218.102]**–**[218.104]**. This Form would be compatible with trusts for bereaved minors within IHTA 1984, s 71A (see IHTA 1984, s 71A(5) and para **[200.108]** above) and age 18-to-25 trusts within IHTA 1984, s 71D (see IHTA 1984, s 71D(7) and para **[200.109]**).

2 This may be usefully inserted in a will which may have to be acted upon abroad. The statutory power may be relied on in a simple case.

[218.107]

Form B18.22: Variation for advancement to life tenant

I declare that the statutory power of advancement given to trustees by section 32 of the Trustee Act 1925 shall apply to the trusts hereof and I declare that my trustees shall have a similar power of advancement out of the trust property or a share thereof in favour of a person who is entitled to a life interest only in the property or share or is contingently entitled to a life interest therein. Such power shall extend to [one-half of] the capital value of such property or share.[1]

1 See *Lowther v Bentinck* (1874) LR 19 Eq 166; *Re Brittlebank, Coates v Brittlebank* (1881) 30 WR 99 and paras **[218.94]**–**[218.97]**.

[218.108]

Form B18.23: Expressions of desire for the guidance of trustees in exercising powers of advancement and of lending capital to the testator's spouse[1]

In the hope that an indication of my own feelings in regard to the power conferred on my trustees by clause ... of this will to raise capital for my wife [husband] may be of some help to them in exercising that power but without imposing any trust or obligation binding upon them at law or in equity or seeking to fetter their absolute discretion to exercise the power in such a way as may seem to them right in the light of current circumstances I would state that in conferring the power I contemplate that:

(a) my trustees will be less ready to pay capital to my wife [husband] outright than to lend it to her [him]; and

(b) subject to that they will not hesitate to exercise the power liberally for my wife's [husband's] benefit;

[OR

(b) they will in any case regard the power as one to be exercised only in emergency].

1 Although it is not customary to include in a will provisions which are of no legal effect, there may sometimes be a case for doing so. One example arises in connection with the exercise of powers of maintenance and advancement during a period of guardianship: as to this, see Form B18.31 at para **[218.117]**. The point may also be illustrated in connection with the power commonly conferred on trustees to raise capital for a surviving spouse to whom a life interest is given. This power (partly for income tax reasons) normally contains no binding stipulation as to the exact extent to which it is to be exercised, and it is thought that trustees might welcome some indication of what the testator had in mind in this regard when he conferred it. The provision set out above may prove helpful in this connection. There is of course no need to include it in the will itself: it could (with any necessary variations) be the subject of a separate note addressed to the trustees. This form assumes that the will gives the trustees power either to give capital to the spouse outright or to lend it and will need amendment to fit it for other circumstances.

ENJOYMENT IN KIND

[218.109]

Note. Trustees' powers of investment are generally not sufficient to enable to acquire property for enjoyment in kind by a beneficiary (see the Preliminary Note to B20 at para **[220.30]**). However, trustees (whether of land or not) do now have statutory powers to acquire UK freehold or leasehold land for occupation by a beneficiary—under the Trustee Act 2000 (TrA 2000), s 8(1)(b) (Part G, para **[246.140]**). Freehold or leasehold land in this context is defined to mean a legal estate in land or the equivalent in Scotland: TrA 2000, s 8(2) (Part G, para **[246.140]**). A beneficiary with an interest in possession in the land will be entitled to a right of occupation if the purposes of the trust include making the land available for his occupation, or it is held by the trustees so as to be so available (TLATA 1996, s 12: Part G, para **[246.144]**; see also the Preliminary Note to B8 at paras **[208.5]**–**[208.8]**). However, the trustees will require a specific power to enable a beneficiary of a discretionary trust, without an interest in possession, to occupy a property, and the statutory powers do not enable trustees to acquire an undivided share in a property to be occupied by a beneficiary (eg to purchase a property jointly with a beneficiary) or to purchase land outside the UK for such occupation, nor are there statutory powers to enable trustees to acquire chattels for use by a beneficiary. Therefore, express provision should still be made for these circumstances. When drafting powers to permit enjoyment in kind it is important to keep in mind the beneficial interests and their intended inheritance tax status. The exercise of a power to provide a beneficiary with a residence or other assets to enjoy in kind is likely to be regarded by HMRC as creating an interest in possession for inheritance tax purposes in favour of that beneficiary if he does not already have one (Inland Revenue Statement of Practice SP 10/79 dated 15 August 1979). See further Part A, paras **[200.95]** ff. Accordingly:

(1) Where settled property is subject to an interest in possession, a power to permit the beneficiary entitled to that interest in possession to enjoy in kind assets comprised in that settled property (or the statutory right of occupation if it is land) should not cause any prejudice to the existence or continuance of that beneficiary's interest in possession. If the express power extended to permitting enjoyment in kind of assets comprised in the settled property by a person who did not already have the interest in possession in the settled property, the existence of the power would probably not prejudice the existence of that interest in possession, but its exercise would. If it is desired to provide power to benefit persons other than the life tenant in this way it would be better practice to provide an overriding power of appointment.

(2) The existence of an express power to enjoy assets in kind should not prejudice an IHTA 1984, s 71A or s 71D trust (see Part A, paras **[200.108]**–**[200.109]** ff) provided that the power cannot be exercised in favour of anyone who is not for the time being one of the beneficiaries of the s 71A or 71D trust.

(3) The exercise of such a power in favour of a beneficiary under a s 71A or 71D trust may create an interest in possession in his favour; that should not matter since an interest in possession may be compatible with trusts within IHTA 1984, s 71A or 71D (see Part A, paras **[200.108]**–**[200.109]**).

(4) Although it could be argued that the same considerations apply to trustees making a loan on beneficial terms to a beneficiary, the better view is probably that doing this does not confer an interest in possession on the beneficiary, at any rate where the loan is repayable on demand (see para **[218.20]**). However, it may in many cases be preferable, in the interests of certainty, or in order to make sure that only a particular beneficiary or beneficiaries can benefit from a particular fund, to restrict the exercise of a power to make beneficial loans so that it can only be done in favour of persons with beneficial interests in the fund from which money is lent. There may be a stronger case for saying that an interest in possession is conferred where the right to repayment of the loan is restricted or deferred, but it seems more likely that in such a case no interest in possession is conferred, but that it is a transaction which diminishes the value of the settled property and gives rise to an inheritance tax charge under s 52(3) of the IHTA 1984 (where, for example, there is an immediate post-death interest), s 65(1)(b) (relevant property), s 71B(1)(b) (bereaved minors trust property), or s 71D(1)(b) (age 18-to-25 trust property).

See Form B18.24 at para **[218.110]** for restrictions which it is thought would prevent a power to permit enjoyment in kind from prejudicing the existence of an interest in possession. See the Preliminary Note to B8 at para **[208.1]** ff for specific gifts to provide a residence.

[218.110]

Form B18.24: Powers to permit enjoyment in kind—restricted to prevent prejudice to inheritance tax status of beneficial trusts[1]

My trustees may permit any beneficiary hereunder who for the time being is entitled to be paid the income of the whole or some part of [my residuary estate] (or would be so entitled if it yielded income) or to whom or for whose benefit for the time being the income of the whole or some part of [my residuary estate] may be paid or applied in exercise of a discretion (or might be so paid or applied if it yielded income) to have the use or enjoyment in kind of any land building chattel or other property which or the proceeds of sale of which or a share of which is comprised in such whole or part of [my residuary estate] upon such conditions as to payment by such beneficiary for outgoings insurance and repair as my trustees think fit (and my trustees shall not be liable for any failure to pay outgoings or insure or repair such property if a beneficiary is responsible for the same under the terms of such use or enjoyment).[2]

1 This express power is not necessary to enable a beneficiary with an interest in possession in land suitable and available for his occupation to occupy that land, since he has a right of occupation under the TLATA 1996, s 12 (Part G, para **[246.144]**; see also para **[208.5]** ff). However, it will be necessary to enable a beneficiary without an interest in possession to occupy or enjoy land, and to enable any beneficiary (ie with or without an interest in possession) to use any chattel. For a corresponding power to purchase property for enjoyment in kind see Form B20.5 at para **[220.44]**. For the reasons behind the restrictions in this form, see para **[218.109]**.

2 See the Preliminary Note to B8 at para **[208.1]** ff for a discussion of the effect of imposing these obligations on beneficiaries occupying trust property.

[218.111]

Form B18.25: Clause where trustees are to have power to purchase property for use of beneficiary[1]

The trustees shall have power to purchase land (or a share in land) situate in any part of the world for the purpose of providing a place of residence for one or more of the beneficiaries and to purchase chattels for the use and enjoyment of one or more of the beneficiaries with power from time to time to sell any property so purchased and to invest the proceeds of sale in the purchase of further property for the same purpose.

1 This clause is goes beyond the statutory powers to acquire land in that it permits the purchase of an undivided share in land, and also land in any part of the world.

[218.112]

Form B18.26: Power where wife is given residence for life or house is bought for beneficiary to invest trust money in purchase of furniture[1]

If my wife shall elect to reside in the said property [*or* If my trustees shall purchase property for providing a residence for the said [*beneficiary*]] my trustees may in their uncontrolled discretion purchase with any trust money in their hands for the time being such furniture as they think fit but not exceeding in value the sum of £—— to be used and enjoyed by my wife [*or* the said [*beneficiary*]] during her life she keeping the same fully insured against fire and such other risks as my trustees may require and also keeping the same in good repair. Such furniture shall on the death of my wife [*or* the said [*beneficiary*]] fall into and form part of my residuary estate.

I direct that upon any such purchase my trustees shall cause an inventory to be made of the furniture so purchased and that the same shall be signed by my wife [*or* the said [*beneficiary*]] and retained by my trustees and that a copy of such inventory signed by my trustees shall be delivered to my wife [*or* the said [*beneficiary*]] and when such inventory and a copy thereof shall be signed and delivered as aforesaid my trustees shall not be bound to see to the repair and insurance of the said furniture and shall not be liable in any respect if my wife [*or* the said [*beneficiary*]] shall neglect to do such repairs or effect to keep up such insurance.

1 There is no statutory power for trustees to purchase chattels for a beneficiary's use, so an express power such as this should be conferred on trustees if they are to be able to make such purchases.

LOANS TO BENEFICIARIES

[218.113]

Form B18.27: Loans to a life tenant

I declare that my trustees may lend money comprised in the whole or any part of my residuary estate to any person entitled for the time being to be paid the income of such whole or part of my residuary estate upon such terms as to the payment or non-payment of interest and otherwise as my trustees think fit.[1]

1 For the reasons for restricting the power to being exercisable in favour of someone who is already entitled to the income, see the Note on Enjoyment in Kind at para **[218.109]**. For a wider power, which also permits loans to discretionary beneficiaries, see Form C2.1, cl 9(3)(e) at para **[224.30]**, but note that such a power should be made subject to the inheritance tax restriction in cl 9(2) of Form C2.1.

[218.114]

Form B18.28: Loans to individuals without security

I declare that my trustees may make loans out of any moneys subject to the trusts hereof to [each of my sons A and B] to an amount not exceeding [£——] in respect of [each such son] upon [their] personal security only.

[218.115]

Form B18.29: Loans to beneficiary to whom a business is bequeathed

I declare that my trustees may lend out of any moneys subject to the trusts of this my will to the said *donee of business*] any sum or sums not exceeding in the whole the sum of £—— my trustees being satisfied that such sum or sums is or are required for and intended to be for the purposes of the said business. The rate of interest upon such sums shall not be less than the current base rate of the —— Bank subject however to a minimum rate of [5] per cent per annum and such sums shall be subject to such terms as to repayment and otherwise as my trustees shall think fit without being liable for loss *where the beneficiary is also a trustee add*: provided that my trustees other than the said *donee of business*] may call in and compel payment of such loan or loans as and when payment shall become due [but shall not be liable for loss for neglecting so to do]].

[218.116]

Form B18.30: Power for trustees to make loans to guardians[1]

My trustees shall have power at any time and from time to time if they consider it to be for the benefit of any minor child of mine to raise capital of the presumptive share of the trust fund[2] of such child and lend it to any person who is a guardian of such child of mine [(even though that person may also be a trustee)] with or without charging interest or taking security and on such terms as to repayment and otherwise as my trustees may in their discretion (without being liable for loss) think fit.

1 If an appointment of guardians is made, the testator should consider the practical problems with which the guardians may be presented in looking after the children and ensure that the other provisions of the will are calculated to minimise rather than to exacerbate these problems. The direct financial needs of the children themselves should be covered by the normal powers of maintenance and advancement, which apply automatically. But other problems may arise. To take one example, the guardians may find themselves compelled to have a larger house than they would otherwise need in order to provide adequate accommodation for the children, and they may have difficulty in finding the money to purchase and maintain it. Various detailed provisions could be designed to guard against possibilities such as this, but it is suggested that a simple but wide power for the trustees to lend capital money to the guardians is not only desirable but also, in most cases, adequate. It is not thought that a power in this form would be inconsistent with the conditions for trusts for bereaved minors within IHTA 1984, s 71A (see para **[200.108]** above) or age 18-to-25 trusts within IHTA 1984, s 71D (see para **[200.109]** above). Attention is drawn also to Form B18.31 at para **[218.117]**. For the appointment of guardians see B3 at paras **[203.43]** ff.

2 It is assumed that 'the trust fund' has already been defined, (but if this is not so a suitable alternative, eg 'my residuary estate', should be used), and that the fund is given to the children in specific shares contingently upon attaining 18 or some greater age.

EXERCISE AND RELEASE OF POWERS

[218.117]

Form B18.31: Testator's wishes as to the exercise of powers of maintenance and advancement [and power to make loans to guardians] during period of guardianship[1]

I should like my trustees to ensure (so far as seems to them reasonable having regard to the funds at their disposal and other relevant matters) that no guardian of any minor child of mine suffers any financial burden or loss by reason of anything he may do in the course of his guardianship (whether or not the act in question falls strictly within the ambit of his duties as guardian) and I therefore express the hope (but without imposing any trust or obligation binding at law or in equity) that my trustees will exercise any powers of maintenance and advancement or any similar powers which they may have in regard to that child by statute or under this will [and the power to lend money to the guardian which is given them by clause [*insert clause number*] of this will] in such a way as to ensure (so far as mentioned above) that no such burden or loss is suffered and I trust that the guardian himself will accept it as my wish that these powers should be exercised in that way.

1 If an appointment of guardians is made, doubt may arise during the period of guardianship as to how far the guardians should shoulder the financial burdens of caring for the children. They themselves may sometimes feel reluctant to accept money for this purpose from the trust set up by the will for the children's benefit. If the testator does not want the guardians to incur financial burdens in the performance of their functions (as normally, it is thought, he would not) it may therefore be useful to make this clear by including in the will some such provision as the following. The provision contains a variation designed to fit it for use in cases where the will gives the trustees power to make loans to guardians (see the preceding form). Of course the provision has no legal effect and so it could (with any necessary variations) be the subject of a separate note addressed to the trustees. It is not thought that a provision in this form, being merely precatory, would be inconsistent with the conditions for trusts for bereaved minors within IHTA 1984, s 71A (see the Note to para **[200.108]** above) or age 18-to-25 trusts within IHTA 1984, s 71D (see the Note to para **[200.109]** above): see also n 1 to Form B 18.30 at para **[218.116]**.

[218.118]

Form B18.32: Powers and discretions exercisable in favour of a beneficiary trustee

Any power or discretion hereby or by law vested in my trustees may be exercised in favour of a person who is an object of such power or discretion notwithstanding that he or she is one of my trustees provided that any such exercise of such a power or discretion is made by at least one of my trustees who does not have a personal interest in the mode or result of exercising the same.[1]

1 It is important to include a provision of this kind in wills under which significant discretions are conferred: see paras **[218.4]** and **[218.5]**.

[218.119]

Form B18.33: Power to release powers[1]

My trustees (being at least two in number or a [trust] corporation[2]) may at any time or times by deed release or restrict in any manner whatever and in whole or in part the future exercise of any powers or discretions hereby or by law conferred on them in such manner as to bind their successors as trustees hereof notwithstanding that the same shall be vested in them in a fiduciary capacity but no such release or restriction shall prejudice or affect any exercise of any of such powers made before any such release or restriction is made.

1 Trustees who have a power conferred on them *virtute officii* cannot release it unless they have express power to do so: see Vol 1, para **[40.10]**.

2 For the meaning of trust corporation see the Preliminary Note to B3 at para **[203.24]**. If there is a possibility of a foreign corporate trustee being appointed, the word 'trust' should be omitted.

B19 Provisions for failure of primary trusts

COMMORIENTES PROVISIONS
Note .... **[219.1]**
FORMS
B19.1 Contingent gift of property which does carry intermediate income during the commorientes period .... **[219.14]**
B19.2 'Omnibus' commorientes provision extending to all gifts in the will .... **[219.15]**
B19.3 Spouse or civil partner survivorship clause for will of older spouse or civil partner only .... **[219.16]**
B19.4 Proviso for will of older spouse or civil partner only to be added at the end of a general survivorship clause .... **[219.17]**
SUBSTITUTION CLAUSES
FORMS
B19.5 Substitution clause limited to children of deceased children .... **[219.18]**
B19.6 Trust for testator's children at twenty-five with substitution of issue of a child who predeceases the testator and further substitution of children on death after the testator's death without attaining a vested interest .... **[219.19]**
ACCRUER CLAUSES
FORMS
B19.7 Accruer of share .... **[219.20]**
B19.8 Accruer of settled share .... **[219.21]**
B19.9 Accruer where shares given to named children .... **[219.22]**
PROVISIONS CONCERNING LAPSE
FORMS
B19.10 Declaration against lapse in the case of a gift to a named person .... **[219.23]**
B19.11 Clause providing against lapse in the case of a gift to a named person and that the clause shall operate as a direct gift to the substituted persons .... **[219.24]**
B19.12 Declaration against lapse in the case of a class gift of residue .... **[219.25]**
B19.13 Declaration against lapse of settled share .... **[219.26]**
B19.14 Clause as to application of lapsed share of residue .... **[219.27]**
B19.15 General form of gift over on failure of the trusts of residue .... **[219.28]**
B19.16 Gift to testator's wife with alternative gift to take on the failure for any reason of the primary gift .... **[219.29]**
PROVISION CONCERNING DISCLAIMER
FORM
B19.17 Clause allowing for a partial disclaimer, the property disclaimed devolving as if the person disclaiming had predeceased the testator .... **[219.30]**
PROVISION CONCERNING FORFEITURE
FORM
B19.18 Forfeiture on contesting the will or attempting to intermeddle .... **[219.31]**

Cross References

For other discussion of survivorship or *commorientes* clauses see C2 at para **[224.1]** ff. For other substitution clauses see Forms B6.19 at para **[206.28]**, B6.24 at para **[206.33]**, B6.25 at para **[206.34]**, B10.13 at para **[210.25]**, B10.14 at para **[210.26]**, B17.7 to B17.13 at paras **[217.12]**–**[217.18]**, B17.33 at para **[217.38]** and B17.34 at para **[217.39]**. For other declarations against lapse see Forms B6.27 at para **[206.36]** and (for charitable gifts) B12.29 at para **[212.31]**. For declarations against ademption see Forms B4.36 at para **[204.58]**, B6.15 at para **[206.24]** and B7.6 at para **[207.20]**. For provision for forfeiture see Form B17.31 at para **[217.36]**.

COMMORIENTES PROVISIONS

[219.1]

Note. Survivorship clauses—or *commorientes* clauses as they are commonly, if less accurately known—i e provisions whereby a gift by will is made to take effect only if the donee survives the testator by a given period, usually a month—are very commonly included in wills. The principal purpose of *commorientes* provisions is the practical one of enabling the testator to control the devolution of his estate in circumstances in which the beneficiary dies either at the same time as him or shortly thereafter. The justification on practical grounds for such clauses is considered more fully below. Such clauses also have fiscal implications and these are also considered. However, survivorship conditions are no longer recommended as between spouses and civil partners, for reasons given in paras **[224.7]**, **[224.8]**.

[219.2]

(a) **Practical considerations.** The LPA 1925, s 184 (Part G, para **[244.58]**) provides that if two or more persons die in circumstances rendering it uncertain which of them survived the other or others, their deaths are, for all purposes affecting their title to property, presumed to have occurred in order of seniority. Thus, if the donee is younger than the testator and the order of their deaths is uncertain, the testator will be deemed to have died first. The statutory presumption may have anomalous consequences as is demonstrated by the classic case of *Re Rowland, Smith v Russell* [1963] Ch 1, [1962] 2 All ER 837. In that case a husband and wife made wills leaving their estates to one another. The husband's will went on to provide that 'in the event of the decease of [his wife] preceding or coinciding with [his] own decease' his estate was to go to his brother and his wife's nephew. The wife's will correspondingly went on to provide that in a similar event her estate was to go to her niece. The parties died in circumstances rendering the order of their deaths uncertain but since there was no evidence that the deaths 'coincided', the wife, being the younger, was deemed to have survived the husband under s 184. Their combined estates accordingly passed to the wife's niece and the husband's beneficiaries took nothing. If the husband had died *intestate*, this unfortunate result would not have occurred as the statutory presumption as between the parties to a marriage where one of them dies intestate in circumstances rendering it uncertain which of them survived is that the other is *not* deemed to survive the intestate: AEA 1925, s 46(3): Part G, para **[244.62]**. The result would also have been avoided by a *commorientes* clause making the gift to the wife dependent upon her survival for a month (or some such period) because then she would never have become entitled under the husband's will: the husband's estate would have passed to his beneficiaries and hers to hers. Hence, the argument runs, *commorientes* clauses are desirable.

[219.3]

Useful though *commorientes* clauses may often be, it must be observed that they will not necessarily provide a complete answer. The fault in *Re Rowland* lay as much in the substantive provisions of the two wills as in the absence of *commorientes* provisions. It is never wise for a husband to leave his estate to his wife or, if she predeceases him, to the persons *he* wants to benefit and for the wife to leave her estate to him or, failing him, to the different persons *she* wants to benefit. In the nature of things one of them is bound to die first and the combined estates are (unless the surviving spouse has the opportunity to change his or her will in the meantime and does so) bound to devolve—later if not sooner—on the beneficiaries of the surviving spouse alone. This problem is further discussed, and forms providing solutions are printed in C9 at para **[231.1]** ff. It follows that the unhappy results in *Re Rowland* could have been avoided by the draftsman without recourse to a *commorientes* clause—and they would have been better avoided without such recourse because even if a *commorientes* clause had been used it would not have helped if the wife had happened to die just outside the *commorientes* period.

[219.4]
Furthermore, although the trouble inherent in the ill-advised provisions of the two wills in *Re Rowland* would *in the circumstances which happened* have been avoided by a *commorientes* clause, cases can be imagined in which the trouble inherent in other ill-advised provisions would in certain circumstances be precipitated rather than avoided by such a clause. Suppose a widower left his estate equally between such of his children as survived him by one month, that one of his children survived him (or was presumed under s 184 to have survived him) but died within the month and that this child left a wife and young children of his own. The testator would (let us suppose) have wanted the bereaved family to take the share which his son would have had, but because he used a *commorientes* clause they cannot do so. If the testator had omitted the *commorientes* clause the bereaved family would (assuming they were beneficiaries of the son's estate) have benefited as the testator would have wished. Here again, however, the trouble arises basically, not from the presence or absence of a *commorientes* clause, but from the substantive provisions of the will: a substitutional gift should have been included for the benefit of the family of any child who failed to take under the will; for a child might equally well have died just before the testator as just after him, and the former possibility needs to be guarded against just as much as the latter. But while *commorientes* provisions may not provide a complete answer, they can serve a useful function. A testator will usually want the beneficiaries named in his will themselves to enjoy the gifts thereby made and not the persons who may be entitled under their wills or intestacies. If the original donees cannot enjoy the gifts in this way, the testator would probably like them to pass instead to whoever would have had them if the donees had predeceased him. The inclusion of a *commorientes* clause may therefore be desirable because it goes some way towards ensuring that the only people who take the estate are those who are alive when it is actually distributed.

See also the Preliminary Note to C2 at para **[224.1]** ff, and forms providing solutions at C9 at para **[231.1]** ff.

[219.5]
(b) Fiscal implications. The Inheritance Tax Act 1984 (IHTA 1984), s 4(2) provides that where it cannot be known which of two or more persons who

have died survived the other or others they shall be assumed for the purposes of the charge to inheritance tax on death to have died at the same instant (IHTA 1984, s 54(4)). Multiple charges to tax on simultaneous deaths are thus excluded. But this relieving provision does not extend to cases where the order of deaths is known however close in point of time they may be. In such cases relief may be available under the quick succession relief provisions contained in the IHTA 1984, s 141, but such relief is at best only partial. Where the testator and beneficiary are married or are civil partners the assets devolving on the survivor are ordinarily exempt from IHT on the first death. In such cases the property will prima facie fall to be aggregated with the estate of the surviving spouse (or civil partner) for tax purposes. However, with the advent of nil-rate band carry-forward (see para **[200.75]**) this will not be an IHT disadvantage except where one or other has a potential entitlement to carry-forward from a previous marriage or civil partnership which ended with the death of the other party: see paras **[200.75]** and **[224.7]**.

[219.6]
The effect of *commorientes* provisions in cases where deaths are close but not simultaneous is governed by the IHTA 1984, s 92. Provided that the period for survival does not exceed six months from the testator's death, the dispositions taking effect at the end of that period or on the death of the beneficiary if earlier are to be treated as having had effect from the date of the death. IHTA 1984, s 144 (see para **[225.83]** ff and **[242.4]**) will have the same effect if there is no beneficiary-taxed interest in possession (see para **[200.92]** for this term) in the period between the testator's death and the end of the survivorship period or the earlier death of the beneficiary, provided that that is more than three months after the death where what then takes effect is an absolute gift or a disabled person's interest. The main point about s 92 is that it will apply even if a beneficiary is entitled to the income during the survivorship period and it is a beneficiary-taxed interest (typically an IPDI, for which see para **[200.98]**), and even where the period ends within three months of the death.

[219.7]
Where the beneficiary is the testator's spouse (or civil partner), special considerations apply. This is because of the exemption under IHTA 1984, s 18 (see para **[200.84]**) for property passing from one to the other. The announcement of nil-rate band carry-forward (see para **[200.75]**) means that survivorship conditions as between husband and wife or civil partners are not needed and should not be included for purely IHT reasons: see para **[224.7]**. The only useful function a survivorship clause might have as between husband and wife or civil partners is where their wills contain absolute gifts to each other but the alternative gifts taking effect in the event of the other predeceasing are not the same (this is not recommended, see para **[219.3]**, but sometimes clients cannot be persuaded otherwise), or a will containing an absolute gift to the other is being made for one of them only and it is not known what the other's dispositions will be.

[219.8]
A further circumstance where a survivorship condition is not needed is where the testator has left his estate to his spouse (or civil partner), subject to

a legacy to non-exempt persons or a discretionary trust of the maximum sum he can leave without incurring inheritance tax (a 'nil-rate band legacy'). See Form B18.2 at para **[218.32]** and Form C3.1 at para **[225.13]** for nil-rate band legacies, and note that after the announcement of nil-rate band carry-forward (see para **[200.75]**) there are only certain special circumstances where these are still advisable, discussed in para **[200.130]**. The nil-rate band legacy will be subject to the condition that the gift to the spouse (or civil partner) takes effect, so if the gift to the spouse (or civil partner) is subject to a survivorship condition, then the gift of the nil-rate legacy is impliedly subject to the same condition. However, the IHTA 1984, s 92 may not apply to this implied survivorship condition since the condition is not as to the survival of the beneficiary of the nil-rate gift, as the section appears to require. Where the spouse dies within a short period of the testator, there is no inheritance tax disadvantage in not having included a survivorship condition, since the testator will have fully utilised his nil-rate band by the nil-rate band legacy.

[219.9]
A further point should be noted about inheritance tax where spouses (or civil partners) die in circumstances where it cannot be known which of them survived the other. Where this happens, s 4(2) of the IHTA 1984 applies, but it only applies for the purposes of s 4(1). It does not apply for the purposes of s 18 (the spouse or civil partner exemption). Accordingly, if a husband and wife (or civil partners) die in these circumstances, and they have each made a will leaving the other his or her entire estate (with no *commorientes* or survivorship provision) with, say, an alternative gift to their children, the estate of the older will devolve on the younger by virtue of Law of Property Act 1925, s 184; it will not be charged to inheritance tax on the death of the younger because of the IHTA 1984, s 4(2); and it will not be charged to inheritance tax as part of the estate on death of the older because of the spouse or civil partner exemption. If there had been a survivorship condition in the older spouse's (or civil partner's) will this advantage would be lost because the older spouse's (or civil partner's) estate would not devolve on the younger.

[219.10]
Therefore if a survivorship clause, general or specific, is being included in a will so as to apply to gifts by the testator to his spouse (or civil partner), and the testator is older than the spouse (or civil partner), there could be an IHT advantage in excluding the survivorship condition in the event of their dying in circumstances where it is uncertain which has survived the other. HMRC accept this point: see HMRC Inheritance Tax Manual, para 12197. It may not be appropriate to do this, despite the IHT advantages, where the alternative gift in the other spouse's or civil partner's will, taking effect if the testator predeceases the other, is different from the testator's. We suggest as suitable wording (to go in the will of the older spouse only), where the will incorporates a survivorship condition, Form B19.3 at para **[219.15]**. A proviso to be added at the end of a general survivorship clause can be found in Form B19.4 at para **[219.16]**. However, for reasons given in paras **[224.7]**

and **[224.8]** below, we do not recommend the inclusion for purely fiscal reasons of survivorship conditions as between husband and wife or civil partners.

[219.11]
There is no capital gains tax provision corresponding with IHTA 1984, s 92. However, capital gains tax is unlikely to be a significant factor. If the property given subject to a survival contingency is a pecuniary legacy a charge to capital gains tax cannot in any event arise. Even if the gift is of a specific asset a charge to tax is unlikely to accrue during the contingency period which cannot exceed six months and is frequently no more than a month. The satisfaction of the contingency or the prior death of the beneficiary could be a deemed disposal under the settled property provisions. Since, however, the administration would very probably continue until after that time the settled property provisions would, it is thought, be excluded. Thus a beneficiary who became absolutely entitled to property one month after the death of the testator would ultimately take as 'legatee' under the Taxation of Chargeable Gains Act 1992, ss 62(4) and 64, ie he would be treated as having acquired it at its value at the testator's death, and there would be no deemed disposal under the TCGA 1992, s 71.

[219.12]
(c) **Conclusions.** *Commorientes* or survivorship provisions can have a useful role to play but the substantive dispositions affected by the will are more important. Wills of husbands and wives or civil partners should have the same ultimate destination for their combined assets, or else should give each other life interests only. Where that is so, survivorship conditions imposed on gifts to each other are superfluous and could have an IHT disadvantage. Substantial gifts to issue or near relations should provide substitution of the issue of the donee or donees in case the latter predecease the testator. In the case of the latter type of gift a survivorship condition can usefully be added. Although deeds of variation and disclaimers (as to which see F3 at para **[241.1]** ff) may be capable of rearranging beneficial dispositions in a more convenient or economic manner, this is not always the case. For an alternative approach to the problems which *commorientes* provisions are intended to solve the two-year discretionary trust might be considered: see C3 at para **[225.1]** ff. Another alternative is the nil-rate band legacy, as in Form C3.4 at para **[225.57]**.

[219.13]
Of the first two forms which follow, Form B19.1 is specific, and Form B19.2 is general. In both cases it is provided that intermediate income should not be carried. In view of the short period involved this seems the more convenient course administratively.

[219.14]

Form B19.1: Contingent gift of property which does carry intermediate income during the *commorientes* period

I give [*property*] to [*donee*] absolutely but contingently upon his surviving me for [one] calendar month and if he dies within the calendar month [*or as the case may be*] following my death he shall be treated as having predeceased me and the intermediate income from the said [*property*] shall not belong to him [*add alternative disposition, which should mention the intermediate income, thus*: and in that event I give the said [*property*] including the intermediate income thereof to [*alternative donee*] [*or* the said [*property*] including the intermediate income thereof shall form part of my residuary estate]].

[219.15]

Form B19.2: 'Omnibus' *commorientes* provision extending to all gifts in the will

Every person who would otherwise benefit under this will but who fails to survive me for [three calendar months[1]] shall be treated for all purposes connected with the devolution of my estate[2] [[including] [but not including] s 33 of the Wills Act 1837[3]] as having predeceased me and my estate and the intermediate income thereof shall devolve accordingly to the intent that no such person shall be entitled to any intermediate income from my estate or any part of it if he dies within that period or acquire therein or in any part thereof a vested interest (or a vested interest subject to defeasance) before the end of it.

1 This period must not exceed six months.
2 These words cover the possibility of a partial intestacy.
3 For the operation of the new s 33 of the WA 1837 (as substituted by the AJA 1982, s 19 (Part G, para **[244.36]**)) see Vol 1, paras **[47.14]**–**[47.19]**. Since the new section creates what is in effect a substitutional gift in favour of the issue of a predeceasing child or remoter descendant of the testator, there may be advantages in preserving its effect. It is advisable to make the position absolutely clear by expressly including or excluding the section.

[219.16]

Form B19.3: Spouse or civil partner survivorship clause for will of older spouse or civil partner only[1]

I give [*property*] to my wife [*name*] if she shall survive me by the period of six months provided that if she and I shall die in circumstances where it cannot be known which of us survived the other then the foregoing survival condition shall not apply and the foregoing gift shall take effect.

1 For the possible inheritance tax advantage of including such a clause as this in the will of the older of two spouses or civil partners, and what other gifts should be included in the will if this clause is used, see paras **[219.7]**–**[219.10]**.

[219.17]

Form B19.4: Proviso for will of older spouse or civil partner only to be added at the end of a general survivorship clause[1]

Provided that if my [wife][husband][civil partner] [*name*] and I shall die in circumstances where it cannot be known which of us survived the other then the foregoing survival condition shall not apply and all gifts in her favour herein [other than ——] shall take effect.

1 For the possible inheritance tax advantage of including such a clause as this in the will of the older of two spouses or civil partners, and what other gifts should be included in the will if this clause is used, see paras **[219.7]**–**[219.10]**.

SUBSTITUTION CLAUSES

[219.18]

Form B19.5: Substitution clause limited to children of deceased children[1]

Provided that if any of my said children is already dead or shall predecease me or shall die after my death without attaining the age of [eighteen] [twenty-one] [thirty] years leaving a child or children who shall attain the age of [eighteen] [twenty-one] years or marry thereunder such child or children shall take by substitution and if more than one in equal shares the share of my residuary estate [the trust fund] which his her or their parent would have taken if he or she had survived me and attained a vested interest.

1 As to the construction of children and issue see Vol 1, Chs 71 to 76.

[219.19]

Form B19.6: Trust for testator's children at twenty-five with substitution of issue of a child who predeceases the testator and further substitution of children on death after the testator's death without attaining a vested interest[1, 2]

(1) My trustees shall hold [my residuary estate] in trust for such of my children as shall be living at my death and attain the age of [25] years if more than one in equal shares.

(2) Provided that if any of my children is already dead or predeceases me the share of [my residuary estate] to which such child would be entitled if he or she survived me and attained a vested interest shall be held in trust for such of his or her children and remoter issue (if any) as shall be living at my death and attain the age of [21] years in equal shares per stirpes and so that no issue shall take whose parent is living at my death and capable of taking.

(3) Provided further that if any child of mine or any remoter issue of mine presumptively entitled under the foregoing proviso is living at or after my death but dies without attaining a vested interest under the foregoing trusts the share of [my residuary estate] to which such child or issue of mine would be entitled if he or she lived to attain such a vested interest shall be held in trust for such of his children (if any) as attain the age of 21 years or marry under that age if more than one in equal shares.

1 As to the construction of children and issue see Vol 1, Chs 71 to 76.

2 The initial trusts of Clause (1) for the testator's children should qualify as age 18-to-25 trusts within IHTA 1984, s 71D if the age of vesting is 25 (see para **[200.109]** above), although if the children's trust came into possession immediately following the testator's death, and is not postponed to any other interest, and any child is over the age of 18 but under the specified age, and entitled to an interest possession by virtue of TA 1925, s 31(1)(ii) (see para **[246.29]**), he or she would have an immediate post-death interest. If and when the trusts of Clauses (2) or (3) come into effect, the property subject to them would fall within the inheritance tax charging regime for relevant property (see the Note to para **[200.92]** above).

ACCRUER CLAUSES[1]

[219.20]

Form B19.7: Accruer of share[2]

If the gift of any such share as aforesaid shall fail by reason of no person attaining a vested interest therein then I direct that the said share and any share or shares which may accrue thereto by virtue of this present provision shall be held by my trustees as an accretion to the other share or shares [(and equally if more than one)] / [(if more than one in the proportion which such other shares bear to one another)][3] the gift or gifts whereof shall not at the date of such accruer have failed as aforesaid.

1 As to these clauses, see Vol 1, paras **[90.1]–[90.6]**.
2 This simple form is for use where the testator has left shares of residue or of a legacy to beneficiaries without any contingencies which might not be satisfied until after the testator's death (other than a survivorship condition). For a form for use where there are contingencies or the shares are settled, see Form B19.8 at para **[219.21]** below.
3 Where shares are equal, the testator may wish any shares, the gifts of which have failed, to accrue equally to the others; but where the shares are initially unequal, he may wish the accrual to be in proportion to the relative sizes of the remaining shares.

[219.21]

Form B19.8: Accruer of settled share[1]

If the trusts of any such share as aforesaid shall fail or determine (other than by absolute vesting) then I direct that subject to the trusts powers and provisions herein contained or which may be applicable thereto by statute the said share and any share or shares which may previously have accrued thereto by virtue of this present provision shall be held by my trustees as an accretion to the other share or shares [(and equally if more than one)] / [(if more than one in the proportion which such other shares bear to one another)][2] the trusts whereof shall not at the date of such accruer have failed or determined (other than by absolute vesting) as aforesaid and as one fund therewith for all purposes.

1 This form is for use where the testator has left a share or shares of residue or of a legacy subject to contingencies which might not be satisfied until after the testator's death, or has otherwise settled some or all of the shares. (For a simple form for use where there are no contingencies or settlements, see Form B19.7 at para **[219.20]**). Where beneficiaries are given an absolute interest and trusts are engrafted thereon and all die without issue, the absolute interests remain and, although the shares may have accrued as to income, the capital passes under the absolute interest of each beneficiary: *Re Atkinson's Will Trusts, Prescott v Child* [1957] Ch 117, [1956] 3 All ER 738.
2 Where shares are equal, the testator may wish any shares, whose trusts have failed, to accrue equally to the others; but where the shares are initially unequal, he may wish the accrual to be in proportion to the relative sizes of the shares.

[219.22]

Form B19.9: Accruer where shares given to named children

[*Where residue divided into four shares, two for a named son and one each for each of two daughters.*]

If my son [*name*] shall predecease me or shall survive me and fail to attain a vested interest in such two shares then I direct that my trustees shall stand possessed of one half of my said son's shares as an accretion to the share hereby given to and hereinafter settled on my said daughter [*name*] and her issue and of the other half of my said son's shares as an accretion to the share hereby given to and hereinafter settled on my said daughter [*name*] and her issue.

PROVISIONS CONCERNING LAPSE

[219.23]

Form B19.10: Declaration against lapse in the case of a gift to a named person[1]

I declare that the [legacy of £——] [share of residue] hereinbefore bequeathed to [*name*] shall not lapse by reason of the death in my lifetime of the said [*name*] but shall in that event pass to his [*or* her] personal representatives as part of his estate.[2]

1 The words 'to the effect that my will shall take effect whether I survive or predecease my husband' are not sufficient to prevent lapse in the case of the husband predeceasing the testatrix (*Re Ladd, Henderson v Porter* [1932] 2 Ch 219). Where a person to whom a lapsed gift would pass also predeceased the testator, the gift lapses in the testator's estate (*Re Cousen's Will Trusts, Wright v Killick* [1937] Ch 381, [1937] 2 All ER 276). It is thought that if the primary beneficiary dies before the testator there will not be a charge to inheritance tax on the gift as part of the primary beneficiary's estate as well as the charge as part of the testator's estate because the primary beneficiary will not at his death be beneficially entitled to anything under the testator's will.

2 This provision will not of course be inserted if issue are substituted, or if the WA 1837, s 33 (substituted by the AJA 1982, s 19: Part G, para **[244.36]**) can be relied on to effect the substitution which is desired: for the scope and effect of this provision see Vol 1, para **[47.14]**.

[219.24]

Form B19.11: Clause providing against lapse in the case of a gift to a named person and that the clause shall operate as a direct gift to the substituted persons[1]

I declare that if my said nephew or my said niece shall die in my lifetime [leaving issue[2] living at my death or then *en ventre* but born afterwards] the [devises and] bequests herein contained to him or her so dying shall not lapse but shall go and devolve in the same manner as if he or she had survived me and died immediately after my death provided that this direction shall take effect by way of direct gift to the persons (if any) beneficially interested under the will or on the intestacy (as the case may be) of my said nephew or niece and shall not make the said [devises or] bequests part of his or her estate so as to be liable for his or her debts or inheritance tax on his or her estate.

1 See para **[219.23]**, n 1.

2 Illegitimate issue are prima facie included: FLRA 1987; ss 1 and 19 (Part G, paras **[245.70]** and **[245.72]**). The HFEA 1990, as from 1 August 1991, also affects the meaning of issue in some circumstances: Part G, para **[245.82]** ff.

[219.25]

Form B19.12: Declaration against lapse in the case of a class gift of residue

I declare that if any person who at or before the date of his or her death would have taken a vested interest in my residuary estate if the provisions of my will had at that date been operative shall die before me then the share which such person would have taken in my residuary estate if such person had survived me shall at my death pass to the personal representatives of such person as part of his or her estate as if such person had died immediately after me.[1]

1 See para **[219.23]**, n 1.

[219.26]

Form B19.13: Declaration against lapse of settled share

I declare that in case any daughter [*or* child] of mine shall die or has already died in my lifetime leaving issue living at my death or then en ventre but born afterwards [the legacy of £—— and] the share of residue hereinbefore bequeathed to her [*or* such child] whether original or accruing shall be retained by my trustees upon the like trusts in all respects as if such daughter [*or* child] had died immediately after me.[1]

1 For a case of lapse, see *Re Roberts, Tarleton v Bruton* (1885) 30 Ch D 234; for the more ordinary cases where there was held not to be a lapse, see *Re Pinhorne, Moreton v Hughes* [1894] 2 Ch 276; *Re Powell, Campbell v Campbell* [1900] 2 Ch 525; *Re Whitmore, Walters v Harrison* [1902] 2 Ch 66; *Re Harward, Newton v Bankes* [1938] Ch 632, [1938] 2 All ER 804.

[219.27]

Form B19.14: Clause as to application of lapsed share of residue[1]

I direct that any lapsed share of residue causing an intestacy as to that share shall be primarily applied in or towards the payment of debts funeral and testamentary expenses and pecuniary legacies hereby or by any codicil hereto bequeathed before recourse is had to any other property hereby or by any codicil hereto devised or bequeathed.

1 The order of application of assets where the estate is solvent is stated in the AEA 1925, Sch 1, Pt II (Part G, para **[246.59]**). Although the AEA 1925 provides for testamentary expenses, debts etc to be paid primarily out of a lapsed share, this can easily be displaced by the creation of a mixed residuary fund. Accordingly, this form could be used to prevent the creation of such a fund from having such an effect. See further the Preliminary Note to B14 at para **[214.4]** ff.

[219.28]

Form B19.15: General form of gift over on failure of the trusts of residue[1]

If [any share or shares of] my residuary estate shall not vest absolutely in some person or persons under the preceding trusts, then [such undisposed of share or shares of] my residuary estate shall (subject to the trusts powers and provisions hereby or by statute vested in my trustees in respect of the income or capital thereof and to every exercise of the same by my trustees) be held by my trustees [for such person or persons as *some previous beneficiary*] shall by will or codicil appoint and in default of such appointment] in trust for my brothers and sisters living at my death and the children of any then deceased brother or sister of mine who attain the age of [eighteen] [twenty-one] years or marry thereunder if more than one in equal shares as tenants in common but so that the children of any such deceased brother or sister shall take between them as tenants in common only the share their parent would have taken had he or she survived me.

1 This form assumes that the residue is given to the testator's immediate family. It may readily be adapted to cases where the testator has no brothers or sisters and wishes to benefit more remote relatives or strangers.

As to the construction of words denoting a blood relationship see Vol 1, paras **[71.1]–[71.5]**.

[219.29]

Form B19.16: Gift to testator's wife with alternative gift to take on the failure for any reason of the primary gift[1]

I give [my residuary estate] to my wife [*name*] absolutely [if she shall survive me by the period of [one month][2]] and if she shall predecease me [or fail to survive me by the said period of [one month]s] or if the foregoing gift in her favour shall lapse or fail for any other reason then [I give [my residuary estate] to [*name*] absolutely] [my trustees shall hold [my residuary estate] upon the following trusts namely [*specify desired trusts*]].

1 This form incorporates a primary absolute gift in favour of the testator's wife with a gift over on the failure for any reason of the primary gift. The wording of this form was designed to overcome the difficulties which could be encountered in relation to deaths before 1 January 1996 if the parties were divorced after the date of the will. The primary gift lapsed under the WA 1837, s 18A (as introduced by the AJA 1982, s 18(2): Part G, para **[244.17]**), but if the ex-wife survived the testator and satisfied any survival contingency which might attach to the primary gift, the gift over would not take effect even though the primary gift had failed: see *Re Sinclair, Lloyds Bank plc v Imperial Cancer Research Fund* [1985] Ch 446, [1985] 1 All ER 1066 and Vol 1, paras **[47.2]** and **[47.3]**. In relation to deaths on or after 1 January 1996 a divorced spouse is treated as having predeceased the testator for the purposes of a gift of this kind, and reference to failure of the gift to the spouse 'for any other reason', as here, is not necessary: see Preliminary Note to C2 at paras **[224.12]–[224.19]**.

2 A survival contingency may also be incorporated, if desired. The survival period should on no account exceed six months. There may be an inheritance advantage in excluding a survivorship provision in the will of the older of two spouses in the event that the spouses die in circumstances where it cannot be known who died first. For clauses providing for this exclusion, see Forms B19.3 and B19.4. See generally the notes on *commorientes* provisions at paras **[219.7]–[219.10]**.

PROVISION CONCERNING DISCLAIMER

[219.30]

Form B19.17: Clause allowing for a partial disclaimer, the property disclaimed devolving as if the person disclaiming had predeceased the testator[1]

I declare that any person may disclaim in whole or in part any gift in his or her favour contained in this my will or any codicil hereto and in the event of such disclaimer either in whole or part the gift or part thereof disclaimed shall devolve as if the person disclaiming had predeceased me.

1 A disclaimer of a whole gift is possible in law and its effect is usually to accelerate gifts taking effect in remainder. So, for example, a disclaimed legacy falls into residue, and a disclaimed residuary gift passes as on an intestacy. This clause may vary the destination of a disclaimed gift. It is not possible as a matter of general law to disclaim a part of a gift (the position is otherwise in Scotland), so this clause expressly provides for it to be possible. For disclaimer generally, see Vol 1, paras **[46.1]–[46.6]**.

PROVISION CONCERNING FORFEITURE

[219.31]

Form B19.18: Forfeiture on contesting the will or attempting to intermeddle

Provided that if any of [*names or description of beneficiaries*] shall either (i) dispute the validity of this will or any of the dispositions of my estate effected by it or (ii) at any time without reasonable cause interfere in or intermeddle with or attempt to interfere in or intermeddle with the administration or management of my estate then notwithstanding anything herein elsewhere provided that person shall forfeit his interest in [my residuary estate] and be deemed to have predeceased me for the purposes of the devolution of my estate.

B20 Administrative powers and provisions

General preliminary note .... [220.1]
Preliminary note on investment powers .... [220.11]

INVESTMENT POWERS

FORMS

B20.1 Power of investment confined to fixed interest investments quoted shares and legal estates in land .... [220.40]
B20.2 Full discretion—long form .... [220.41]
B20.3 Full discretion—short form .... [220.42]
B20.4 Statutory power subject to an ethical investment policy .... [220.43]
B20.5 Retention of shares in family company .... [220.44]
B20.6 Powers of sale and transposing assets .... [220.45]
B20.7 Power to give warranties on the sale of private company shares .... [220.46]
B20.8 Power to delegate investment powers and vest assets in nominees .... [220.47]
B20.9 Clause as to bonus shares .... 220.48]

MANAGEMENT OF LAND

Note .... [220.49]

FORMS

B20.10 Power of management in relation to land in any location .... [220.59]
B20.11 Power to apply other capital in improving land .... [220.60]
B20.12 Treatment of mining rent and royalties and proceeds of timber .... [220.61]
B20.13 Exercise of powers to be subject to beneficiary's consent .... [220.62]

POWERS RELATING TO FOREIGN PROPERTY

FORMS

B20.14 Powers of management of foreign land .... [220.63]
B20.15 Declaration that statutory provisions shall apply to foreign property .... [220.64]
B20.16 Power to pay foreign tax .... [220.65]

BUSINESSES

FORMS

B20.17 Power to carry on business .... [220.66]
B20.18 Power to carry on farming business .... [220.67]
B20.19 Power to incorporate business .... [220.68]

BORROWING

FORM

POWERS OF APPROPRIATION

Note .... [220.70]

FORMS

B20.21 Power for trustees to appropriate .... [220.74]
B20.22 Another power for trustees to appropriate .... [220.75]
B20.23 Short form of power of appropriation, by reference to the statutory power .... [220.76]
B20.24 Clause allowing appropriation without the beneficiary's consent and where trustees are beneficially interested—alternative form .... [220.77]
B20.25 Clause as to appropriation incorporating Statutory Will Forms 1925, Form 6 .... [220.78]
B20.26 Power of appropriation with consent of beneficiaries of full age .... [220.79]
B20.27 Power for trustees to partition and appropriate land [220.80]

INHERITANCE **TAX**

FORM

B20.28 General restriction to prevent administrative powers prejudicing inheritance tax status of beneficial trusts .... [220.81]

MISCELLANEOUS
FORM
B20.29 Power to give guarantees for loans to companies wholly or substantially owned by trustees .... **[220.82]**

Cross references

For powers relating to business property see B5 at para **[205.1]** ff. For administration trusts, declarations concerning apportionment and incidence of IHT see B14 at para **[214.1]** ff. For maintenance and advancement powers, powers to permit enjoyment in kind and general declarations concerning the exercise of powers see B18 at para **[218.41]** ff. For trustees and executors—self-dealing, retention of benefits, indemnities, appointment of new trustees and charging see B21 at para **[221.4]**. For complete sets of administrative provisions see Form C2.1, cl 9 at para **[224.37]** and C11.1, cl 6 at para **[233.21]**. For disclaimer and renunciation of probate or trusteeship see F1 at para **[239.1]** ff.

GENERAL PRELIMINARY NOTE

[220.1]
The extent of the administrative powers and provisions which need to be included in a will depends on the nature of the beneficial interests given; none (or none except perhaps a professional trustee charging clause) may be needed if the only gifts are absolute gifts to adults or to charity, while a variety of administrative provisions might be included where all or part of the estate is settled on trust. However, with the enactment of the Trusts of Land and Appointment of Trustees Act 1996 (TLATA 1996) and the Trustee Act 2000 (TrA 2000), the need to include express powers in the general run of cases is less pressing than was formerly the case. By virtue of the TLATA 1996, wide powers in relation to land are conferred on trustees of land, ie trustees of any trust of property which consists of or includes land (or the proceeds of sale of land): TLATA 1996, ss 1 and 3 (Part G, paras **[246.103]** and **[246.105]**). Subject to certain exceptions, these powers will also apply to personal representatives where the estate they administer includes land: TLATA 1996, s 18 (Part G, para **[246.121]**). The TrA 2000 is of wider application, and, with certain exceptions, applies to trustees (including personal representatives: TrA 2000, s 35, Part G, para **[246.167]**) whether they hold land or not. It provides a new wider statutory power of investment to replace the limited powers under the Trustee Investments Act 1961 (TIA 1961), and new powers to appoint agents (including investment managers), nominees and custodians, to insure trust property, and to pay professional trustees. These new powers generally apply to trusts whenever created. However, as under the present law, they will generally be in addition to any express powers and only apply to the extent that the will permits. Even after these two major enactments, however, there are still administrative powers and provisions which it might be considered advisable to include in any particular will. The preliminary notes to the subdivisions of B20 indicate what may be lacking under the general law, even after the TLATA 1996 and the TrA 2000, in response to which the various categories of express provision might be considered useful.

[220.2]
B20 is concerned with powers and provisions relating to the administration of trust assets; powers and provisions concerning executors and trustees are in B21, and administration trusts of residue and directions concerning apportionment are in B14. The complete forms of will in Part C give examples of appropriate administrative provisions to combine with particular beneficial interests.

[220.3]
Where there are settled specific gifts or general legacies it is important to check that the administrative powers contained in the will apply to them and not just to the residuary trust fund. It is also important where there are any settled funds to make sure that provisions such as powers of appropriation, directions concerning the Apportionment Acts, and professional charging clauses will continue to apply after the administration of the estate is complete and the personal representatives give way to trustees.

[220.4]
Inheritance tax. A headache of which will draftsmen will be aware, is the danger that wide administrative provisions may prejudice the intended IHT status trusts. Prior to 22 March 2006, the concern was that certain wide powers might prejudice the status of interest in possession trusts or of trusts intended to fall within IHTA 1984, s 71 (accumulation and maintenance trusts). Post 21-March 2006, the concern will be that wide powers might prejudice the status of immediate post-death interest trusts (see para **[200.98]** above), or trusts intended to fall within IHTA 1984, s 71A or 71D, ie trusts for bereaved minors and age 18-to-25 trusts (see paras **[200.108]–[200.109]** above).

[220.5]
In the case of immediate post-death trusts which are a species of interest in possession trusts (see Part A, para **[200.98]**) the main concern is to avoid powers which, by their very existence, prevent the person prima facie entitled to the immediate post-death interest from being entitled to the income of the relevant settled property as it arises. It is a natural incident of an interest in possession that it is subject to certain expenses being payable out of income: for example, rates, repairs and fire insurance premiums relating to land held on trust for sale, and income tax and interest on charges and incumbrances (see *Carver v Duncan (Inspector of Taxes)* [1985] AC 1082 at 1120, [1985] 2 All ER 645 at 652). It seems clear from *Pearson v IRC* [1981] AC 753, [1980] 2 All ER 479, HL, at 774–5 and 784–5 and 486 and 494 respectively that administrative powers to pay such expenses out of income do not prevent anyone from having an interest in possession for inheritance tax purposes. The passages in *Pearson v IRC* just cited, particularly the remarks of Lord Dilhorne, seem to be saying that a power to pay capital taxes out of income would not prejudice the existence of an interest in possession, but it is the authors' opinion that so liberal a view should not in the present state of authority (and bearing in mind *Carver v Duncan (Inspector of Taxes)*) be relied on.

[220.6]
What should be avoided is conferring express powers to pay capital expenses, such as life assurance premiums, capital taxes, or permanent improvements to land, or expenses attributable to some other share or fund, out of income. We should add that powers of this kind will not always prejudice the existence of an interest in possession, first, because a general discretion as to the burden of particular types of expense will not necessarily displace the trustees' normal duty to allocate the burden of expenditure equitably according to the various beneficial interests in the trust fund and its income; and second, because many such powers may not be exercisable until some other event happens, for example, life assurance premiums cannot be paid out of income until the trustees acquire or effect a life assurance policy.

[220.7]
There is a subsidiary category of administrative powers whose existence (unexercised) does not prevent some intended interest in possession from subsisting, but whose exercise might cause an interest in possession to terminate. The exercise of some powers to effect life policies might have this consequence, as might exercise of a power to allow a beneficiary other than the person entitled to an interest in possession to occupy a house comprised in the trust fund or have other enjoyment in kind of trust assets. (HMRC take the view that enjoyment in kind of trust assets by virtue of an exercise of a power of the trustees to permit it can give rise to an interest in possession, and there are convincing reasons for their view—see Part A, para **[200.95]** and *Foster's Inheritance Tax*, E1.47.)

[220.8]
In the case of trusts intended to fall within the Inheritance Tax Act 1984 (IHTA 1984), s 71A or 71D, ie. trusts for bereaved minors and age 18-to-25 trusts (see paras **[200.108]–[200.109]** above) the requirements are more stringent and even more care must be taken to see that there are no administrative powers which prevent the conditions for such trusts from applying. It will be appreciated that a power to pay expenses not properly attributable to capital (or not properly attributable to the settled property in question), whether or not it is actually exercised, could prevent the beneficiaries becoming entitled to that capital on or before attaining either 18 or 25 (as the case may be)—ie it could prevent the trusts from satisfying s 71A(3)(a) or s 71D(6)(a). Further, the same would be the consequence of the existence of a power to permit enjoyment in kind of trust assets which was capable of being exercised in favour of persons other than the beneficiaries. Similarly, a power that permitted the income to be applied in some way other than to or for the benefit of the beneficiaries or accumulation would prejudice the application of s 71A(3)(c) or 71D(6)(c).

[220.9]
On the other hand, the references to settled property and to the income from it in s 71A(3) and 71D(6) must be references respectively to the property net of the expenses properly attributable to it and to the income net of the expenses properly attributable to it.

[220.10]
We have tried in the forms in B20 to indicate what restrictions (if any) we regard as appropriate where there are immediate post-death interest or s 71A or 71D trusts. We have also included a form of general restriction intended to prevent any administrative powers from prejudicing the intended IHT status of the beneficial trusts (see Form B20.28 at para **[220.81]** and Form C2.1, cl 9 at para **[224.37]**). For further discussion of these points, see *Foster's Inheritance Tax*, E1.43 and E5.14.

PRELIMINARY NOTE ON INVESTMENT POWERS

[220.11]
The main points to consider when drafting investment clauses seem to us to be as follows:

[220.12]
Statutory investment power. The TrA 2000 came into force on 1 February 2001 (Trustee Act 2000 (Commencement) Order 2001, SI 2001/49), and has replaced the provisions of the TIA 1961 as to trustees' powers of investment. The provisions of the TIA 1961 were widely considered to be too elaborate and troublesome to follow correctly, unduly restrictive, and particularly in relation to their policy of only permitting up to a specific proportion of a fund to be invested in ordinary shares, out-of-date. The power conferred on trustees (and personal representatives) by the TrA 2000 is referred to as 'the general power of investment'. It is a power to make (subject to the further provisions of the TrA 2000, described below) any kind of investment, including loans secured on land but otherwise excluding land (power to invest in which is dealt with separately–see para **[220.17]**), that they could make if they were absolutely entitled to the assets of the trust: TrA 2000, s 3(1)–(3) (Part G, para **[246.1135]**). By an irony of fate, the TrA 2000 conferred a full power to invest an entire fund in ordinary shares just in time to catch the substantial falls in the value of quoted shares in the summer and autumn of 2001. The new statutory power of investment is in addition to any other powers conferred on the trustees (eg by the will), but subject to any restriction or exclusion imposed by, eg the will: TrA 2000, s 6(1) (Part G, para **[246.138]**). It applies in relation to trusts whether created before or after the commencement of the Act on 1 February 2001, and in the case of a trust created by will, whenever the will was made or the testator died: TrA 2000, s 7(1) (Part G, para **[246.129]**). It applies to personal representatives as well as trustees: TrA 2000, s 35 (Part G, para **[246.167]**).

[220.13]
Duty to have regard to standard investment criteria. In exercising the general power of investment (or indeed any investment power, whether conferred expressly by the will or by some other statutory provision such as the TrA 2000, s 8(1)(a); for which see para **[220.17]**), trustees (or personal representatives) must have regard to 'the standard investment criteria'. These criteria are first, the suitability to the trust of investments of the same kind as any particular investment proposed to be made or retained and of that particular

investment as an investment of that kind; and second, the need for diversification of investments of the trust, insofar as is appropriate to the circumstances of the trust. The trustees must also, from time to time, review the investments of the trust and consider whether, having regard to the standard investment criteria, they should be varied: TrA 2000, s 4 (Part G, para **[246.136]**). No indication is given as to how often trustees must review the investment, but once a year must surely be the minimum, and in the case of a large trust fund or one invested on the stock market at times of particular volatility, more reviews might be required. This in substance re-enacts the provisions of the TIA 1961, s 6(1), which also applied to express as well as statutory powers of investment. The only difference is that the wording of the TrA 2000, s 4 makes it even plainer than the TIA 1961, s 6(1) did that the requirement of having regard to the standard investment criteria applies to all powers of investment, and that it is not capable of being excluded. Although it cannot be excluded, trustees' liability for negligence, and therefore for negligent failure to have regard to the standard investment criteria, can be excluded or limited (see para **[221.15]**). Where it is intended that trustees should retain a particular asset, eg land or private company shares, thought should be given to adding an expression of wishes to that effect, by way of guidance on the question of whether diversification is 'appropriate to the circumstances of the trust'. More important than expressions of wishes, however, is the purpose of the trust. For example, if the purpose of a trust of family company shares is to retain it in the family while various members of the family work in it, or if the purpose of a trust of land is to provide a residence for a beneficiary or preserve a farm or landed estate for family business use or pleasure, those will be strong reasons why diversification is not appropriate. For private company shares, see Form B20.5 at para **[220.44]**. For land, see Forms B8.1 to B8.6 at paras **[208.37]** to **[208.42]** and Form C13.2 at para **[235.18]** ff.

[220.14]

Duty to take advice. Before exercising their statutory investment power (or indeed any investment power, whether conferred expressly by the will or by some other statutory provision such as the TrA 2000, s 8(1)(a); for which see para **[220.17]**) and when reviewing their investments, trustees must obtain and consider proper advice about the way in which, having regard to the standard investment criteria, their powers to invest or vary investments should be exercised. However, they do not need to obtain such advice if they reasonably conclude that in all the circumstances it is unnecessary or inappropriate to do so. Proper advice is the advice of a person who is reasonably believed by the trustees to be qualified to give it by his ability in and practical experience of financial and other matters relating to the proposed investment. (TrA 2000, s 5: Part G, para **[246.137]**). Circumstances where trustees might reasonably conclude that they do not need to obtain advice might be where one of their number is an investment specialist, or where the proposed investment is small in comparison to the size of the trust fund. This provision derives from the TIA 1961, s 6(2)–(4), but under that Act the duty to take advice applied only to making certain categories of investment, and when exercising the statutory powers of investment only. The change made by the TrA 2000, s 5 is that the duty applies to all types of investment and to the exercise of all powers of investment, not just the statutory one. As with the duty to have regard to the standard investment criteria (see para **[220.13]**), the duty to take advice cannot be excluded, but again the exclusion or limitation of liability for negligence (see para **[221.13]** ff) will limit the practical effect of this duty.

[220.15]

Statutory duty of care. A concern that trustees might abuse the greater ambit of discretion given to them by 'the general power of investment', even with the requirement to take proper advice, has been met by the imposition on them when exercising those statutory powers, of a statutory duty of care. It is very important to note, however, that this statutory duty applies not only to trustees exercising the new powers conferred by the TrA 2000, but also to trustees exercising similar powers conferred on them expressly (e g by will) or by other Acts, whether before or after the passing of the TrA 2000. On the other hand, the TrA 2000 expressly permits the exclusion or limitation of the duty by express provision in the will. See para **[221.15]** ff.

[220.16]

Mortgages. It is clear from the TrA 2000, s 3(3) that as part of their general power of investment, trustees may invest in loans secured on land, such loans being defined in the TrA 2000, s 3(4) and (5), as where one person provides another with credit, be it a cash or other money loan, or other financial accommodation, and the obligation of the borrower to repay is secured on land. 'Land' here includes buildings and other structures, land covered with water, and any estate, interest, easement, servitude or right in or over land: Interpretation Act 1978 (IA 1978), Sch 1 (Part G, para **[246.98]**). This power is subject to the trustees having regard to the standard investment criteria, the requirement to obtain proper advice and the statutory duty of care: see paras **[220.12]** and **[221.15]**. The former detailed rules relating to investment in mortgages in the Trustee Act 1925 (TA 1925), ss 8 and 10 are, along with the rest of Part I of that Act, repealed by the TrA 2000, Sch 2, para 18. Additionally, trustees of land have power to purchase a legal estate in any land in England and Wales (see para **[220.17]**) and the corresponding interests in land in Scotland or Northern Ireland: TrA 2000, s 8(1) (Part G, para **[246.140]**), which would include acquiring a legal mortgage or a charge by way of legal mortgage (taking into account the relevant definition of 'land' referred to above). This power is more limited than the power in the TrA 2000, s 3 in that it only permits trustees to lend on the security of land situated in the UK, but wider in that it permits trustees to lend on the security of land for purposes other than investment: e g trustees could make an interest-free loan to a beneficiary to enable him to purchase a property for his occupation, taking the property as security for the loan. In exercising the power for non-investment purposes, the trustees will not be under duties to have regard to the standard investment criteria or to obtain proper advice (but will be under such duties when doing so for investment): see paras **[220.13]** and **[220.14]**. They will be subject to the statutory duty of care (see the TrA 2000, Sch 1, para 2: Part G, para **[246.173]** and B21 at para **[221.15]**) unless it is expressly excluded.

[220.17]

Power to acquire land. Trustees may acquire freehold or leasehold land in the UK as an investment, for occupation by a beneficiary, or for any other reason: TrA 2000, s 8(1) and (2) (Part G, para **[246.140]**). 'Land' here includes buildings and other structures, land covered with water, and any estate, interest, easement, servitude or right in or over land (IA 1978, Sch 1: Part G, para **[246.98]**), but 'freehold or leasehold land' for this purpose is specifically defined to mean, in relation to England, Wales and Northern Ireland, a legal estate (including in relation to Northern Ireland land held under a fee farm grant), and in relation to Scotland, the estate or interest of the proprietor if the dominium utile, or in the case of land not held on feudal tenure, the estate or interest of the owner, or a tenancy: TrA 2000, s 8(2). Therefore, it is clear that trustees are not permitted to acquire any undivided share in land in England and Wales under this power, since an undivided share exists only in equity and cannot subsist as a legal estate. If trustees are acquiring the land as an investment, they will be under duties to have regard to the standard investment criteria and to obtain and consider proper advice (see paras **[220.13]** and **[220.14]**), and also the statutory duty of care, if it has not been limited or excluded by the will or trust instrument. However, if they are acquiring it for a non-investment purpose, eg for occupation by a beneficiary, it seems that they will only be subject to the statutory duty of care (again, if it has not been limited or excluded by the will or other trust instrument): TrA 2000, Sch 1, para 2 (Part G, para **[246.173]**; see also para **[221.15]**). Prior to the enactment of the TrA 2000, there was no power to invest trust moneys in land (apart from mortgages) unless such power was expressly conferred, or the assets originally settled were land.

[220.18]

Express provision and the statutory powers. The general power of investment and the power to acquire land in the TrA 2000, ss 3 and 8 respectively (see paras **[220.12]** and **[220.17]**) are in addition to powers conferred on the trustees by the will or other trust instrument, and are subject to any restriction or exclusion imposed by the will or other trust instrument: TrA 2000, ss 6(1) and 9 (Part G, paras **[246.138]** and **[246.141]**). It is therefore possible to provide wider powers than the statutory powers, and to restrict the statutory powers. The main reasons for providing a wider express power are to enable the trustees to acquire land outside the UK, to acquire equitable interests in land such as undivided shares of land, and to acquire any other interests in or rights over land which are not legal estates (see para **[220.17]** for the limits of the statutory power to acquire land). There is also the possibility that the general power of investment does not include power to make unsecured personal loans or invest in non-income producing assets: see paras **[220.31]–[220.33]**. The TrA 2000, ss 6(1) and 9 also make it possible to impose a narrower choice of investments than that permitted by the statutory powers, eg to ensure a cautious, low-risk, investment policy, or to ensure an ethical investment policy. It is probably better to express wishes about investment policy than to deprive trustees completely of power to purchase particular types of investment, since doing the latter could put the trustees in a difficult position where, for example, a company whose shares were an authorised investment was taken over by one which was not. Where express powers are provided it is recommended that they are expressed to be in addition to those conferred by the general law, so as to avoid the possibility that a power which overlaps with the statutory power is intended to exclude it, just in case a situation arises where the statutory power enables something to be done which the express power does not.

[220.19]
It is no longer the case that land purchased in exercise of a power conferred by a settlement of personal property is, by the Law of Property Act 1925 (LPA 1925), s 32(1), directed to be held on trust for sale in the absence of contrary provision in the settlement. Nor is it any longer the case that land purchased by trustees for sale in exercise of their statutory powers is directed to be held on trust for sale by the LPA 1925, s 28(1) (both were repealed as from 1 January 1997 by the TLATA 1996). It is no longer necessary or desirable in clauses which confer power to invest in land to provide that any land in England and Wales acquired under the power shall be held on trust for sale. All land held on trust under a trust created on or after 1 January 1997 is subject to the trust of land provisions of the TLATA 1996, irrespective of whether there is a trust for sale: see Part A, para **[200.51]**.

[220.20]
Company shareholdings. The former provisions of the TA 1925, s 10(3) and (4) which gave extensive powers to trustees holding shares or other securities in a company to concur in schemes or arrangements for company reconstruction, etc have been repealed, along with the remainder of the TA 1925, Part I by the TrA 2000, Sch 2, para 18. This is because the point of the powers conferred by the TA 1925, s 10(3) and (4) was to permit acceptance and retention of new holdings which were not authorised investments but which replaced or arose from old holdings which were authorised investments, and the powers are not needed now that the general power of investment conferred by the TrA 2000, s 3 (see para **[220.12]**) permits a complete discretion as to type of investment at any rate in relation to company shareholdings.

[220.21]
Bearer securities. The general power of investment in the TrA 2000, s 3 (Part G, para **[246.135]**; see also **[220.12]**) is clearly in wide enough terms to authorise investment in bearer securities. Where trustees hold bearer securities they are (unless express provision is made to the contrary in the will or other trust instrument) required to deposit them with a custodian: TrA 2000, s 18 (Part G, para **[246.150]**). Where this statutory requirement applies, the custodian must be someone who carries on business acting as a custodian, a body corporate controlled by the trustees, or an incorporated solicitors practice: TrA 2000, s 19(2) (Part G, para **[246.151]**), and there are statutory restrictions on the terms on which the custodian is appointed and requirements as to review of the appointment: TrA 2000, ss 20 and 22 (Part G, paras **[246.152]** and **[246.154]**).

[220.22]
Foreign investment. The investments authorised by the TrA 2000, s 3(1) (the general power of investment: see para **[220.12]** and Part G, para **[246.135]**)

are not subject to any territorial limit. The power to acquire land conferred by the TrA 2000, s 8(1) (see para **[220.17]** and Part G, para **[246.140]**) is confined to the acquisition of land in the UK. Trustees can therefore under the statutory powers of investment acquire investments anywhere in the world, except for land and interests in land outside the UK, but with the latter exception being subject to an exception for loans secured on land (ie with the consequence that such loans outside the UK can be invested in), and with the power to acquire land in the UK being confined to the acquisition of legal estates.

[220.23]
Powers of sale. The TrA 2000, s 3(1) (the general power of investment—see para **[220.12]** and Part G, para **[246.135]**) by implication authorises the sale of the assets currently held so as to invest in other investments authorised under that power: compare *Re Pratt's Will Trusts, Barrow v McCarthy* [1943] Ch 326, [1943] 2 All ER 375 where the power of investment in the TA 1925, s 1 was held to authorise sale of assets in order to exercise that power of investment. The Administration of Estates Act 1925, s 39 (Part G, para **[246.53]**) confers power to sell personal estate for the purposes of the administration, but these powers cease when the administration is complete (see *Re Trollope's Will Trusts* [1927] 1 Ch 596). The TA 1925, s 16 (Part G, para **[246.14]**) authorises the sale of trust assets to raise money to pay or apply for any purpose or in any manner which the payment or application of capital money is authorised by the trust instrument or by law. Apart from these powers, there is no general power of trustees to sell property other than land.

[220.24]
Trustees of land which is located in England and Wales have in relation to the land all the powers of an absolute owner (TLATA 1996, s 6(1): Part G, para **[246.108]**), and trustees who have acquired land in the UK under the power in the TrA 2000, s 8(1) (see para **[220.17]**) have in relation to it all the powers of an absolute owner: TrA 2000, s 8(3) (Part G, para **[246.140]**). Both powers clearly include a power of sale. The relevant definition of 'land' for the TLATA 1996 is that in the LPA 1925, s 205(1)(ix) (Part G, para **[246.59]**) (incorporated by reference by the TLATA 1996, s 23(2): Part G, para **[246.128]**) and includes rights privileges or benefits in over or derived from land. The relevant definition of 'land' for the TrA 2000 is that in the IA 1978, Sch 1 and includes buildings and other structures, land covered with water, and any estate, interest, easement, servitude or right in or over land: IA 1978, Sch 1 (but it should be remembered that the power in the TrA 2000, s 8(3) is confined to being exercisable over land acquired under s 8(1) and the latter only confers power to purchase legal estates in land). These powers apply also to personal representatives: TLATA 1996, s 18 (Part G, para **[246.121]**, TrA 2000, s 35 (Part G, para **[246.167]**); and the AEA 1925, s 39 (Part G, para **[246.53]**) has been amended by the TLATA 1996, Sch 3, para 6 so that a personal representative's powers of sale, etc in relation to real estate for the purposes of administration are those of the TLATA 1996, s 6(1). The ancillary powers and provisions in relation to sale of property in the TA 1925, ss 12 and 13 (Part G, paras **[246.10]** and **[246.11]**) continue to apply.

[220.25]
The powers conferred by the TLATA 1996, s 6(1) can be restricted or excluded by the will or other trust instrument, and can be made subject to a requirement of consent to their exercise by some specified person (usually a beneficiary): TLATA 1996, s 8(1), (2), and the powers conferred by the TrA 2000, s 8(3) can be restricted or excluded: TrA 2000, s 9. It is therefore possible, though not advisable, to exclude the power to sell land, and render the land inalienable for a full perpetuity period. This would be subject to the possibility that the trustees could apply to the court to be given power to do so under the TA 1925, s 57 and also it is unlikely that an exclusion of power to sell land would be effective to prevent personal representatives from selling it to pay debts or administration expenses. As regards alienability of land, the previous law is therefore reversed. Before the TLATA 1996 came into force it was not possible to tie up land in trust and exclude the power to sell it, but it was possible to impose a binding obligation to sell. Now exclusion of all powers to sell land is permitted, but (because of the non-excludable power to postpone sale under the TLATA 1996, s 4, for which see paras **[220.28]** and **[200.54]**) it is no longer possible to impose an obligation to sell land without a power to retain it. For a discussion of ways of causing an early sale to take place, see paras **[200.56]**–**[200.59]**. The above described statutory powers in relation to land do not apply to land situated outside the UK, and only apply to land outside England and Wales where it has been acquired in exercise of the power in the TrA 2000, s 8(1).

[220.26]
Accordingly, where there are will trusts which include powers of investment that are wider than those conferred by statute, it is important to provide an express power or trust to sell the assets. For the usual trust for sale or powers of sale with respect to residue, see B14 at paras **[214.1]** ff and **[214.10]** ff and for powers of sale and changing investments, see Form B20.6 at para **[220.45]**.

[220.27]
There is normally implied in a power to invest trust moneys in investments of a particular kind a power to vary those investments (*Re Pope's Contract* [1911] 2 Ch 442), and so it is not so important to provide express power to vary investments, but it is better practice to do so.

[220.28]
Power to postpone sale. A trust to sell land is subject to a non-excludable power to postpone sale: TLATA 1996, s 4(1) (Part G, para **[246.106]**; see further Part A, para **[200.54]**).This is implied in a trust for sale of land in England and Wales, but not in a trust for sale of personalty. Express power to postpone sale is thus needed in relation to a trust for sale of personalty or a mixed fund of realty and personalty (see further B14 at para **[214.1]** ff).

[220.29]
Construction of express powers. Despite the standard textbook proposition that powers of investment going beyond those conferred on trustees by the general law will be construed restrictively, in practice wide words will be

given a wide meaning: see eg *Re Wragg, Wragg v Palmer* [1919] 2 Ch 58 ('… stocks funds shares securities or other investments of whatsoever nature and wheresoever … to the intent that the trustees should have the same full and unrestricted powers … as if … absolutely entitled …'—held to authorise purchase of land as an investment); *Re Harari's Settlement Trust, Wordsworth v Fanshawe* [1949] 1 All ER 430 ('shall invest … the moneys in or upon such investments as to them [the trustees] may seem fit'—not restricted to trust investments under the ordinary law); *Re Peczenik's Settlement Trusts, Cole v Ingram* [1964] 2 All ER 339, [1964] 1 WLR 720 ('in any stocks shares property' and an express declaration that trustees not restricted to 'trustee stocks'—held they could invest in any type of property which can properly be regarded as an investment). However wide and general the wording, specific provision may be needed as regards the matters mentioned in the succeeding paragraphs of this Note (see Form B20.2 at para **[220.41]** for an investment clause which makes provision for all these except for businesses).

[220.30]
Enjoyment in kind by beneficiaries. When exercising an *investment* power, however widely worded, the trustees must choose assets capable of being treated as investments ('not property which is acquired merely for use and enjoyment'—*Re Peczenik's Settlement Trusts, Cole v Ingram* [1964] 1 WLR 720 at 723), and choose and retain assets according to proper investment criteria, and may not, eg use investment powers to benefit particular beneficiaries, or, a fortiori, themselves. Hence, eg there must be express power for trustees to be able to purchase a residence for a beneficiary to live in (*Re Power, Public Trustee v Hastings* [1947] Ch 572), and the same must be so of the purchase of other types of asset for enjoyment in kind by a beneficiary; however, there is now an express statutory power to purchase a legal estate in land in the UK for occupation by a beneficiary: TrA 2000, s 8(1)(b) (Part G, para **[246.140]**). Express power is still needed for the purchase of land outside the UK for occupation by a beneficiary, purchase of an undivided share of land in the UK for this purpose, and for purchase of chattels for enjoyment in kind by a beneficiary. See further the Note and Forms concerning enjoyment of assets in kind in B18 at para **[218.108]** ff and Form B20.2 at para **[220.41]**.

[220.31]
Loans. For the same sort of reason as that given above in relation to purchase of assets for enjoyment in kind, express power is needed to leave a loan outstanding to accommodate the borrower (Underhill and Hayton, *Law of Trusts and Trustees* (18th edn, 2007), paras **[53.47]** ff) and, it is submitted, to make loans to beneficiaries on other than commercial terms. See, further, the Note and Forms concerning enjoyment of assets in kind and loans to beneficiaries in B18 at para **[218.108]** ff and Form B20.2 at para **[220.41]**.

[220.32]
Unsecured personal loans. Powers to invest are normally regarded as limited to the acquisition of some sort of property. Accordingly, unsecured personal loans are normally only permitted if the investment clause expressly says so

(Underhill and Hayton, *Law of Trusts and Trustees* (18th edn 2007), para **[53.47]** ff, and see *Re Peczenik's Settlement Trusts, Cole v Ingram* [1964] 1 WLR 720 at 723). It is possible, though not certain, that making unsecured personal loans is outside the statutory general power of investment in the TrA 2000, s 3(1) (Part G, para **[246.135]**; see also para **[220.12]**).

[220.33]
Non-income-yielding assets. The trustees must consider the interests of the beneficiaries as a whole, and in particular must hold the balance between the income and capital beneficiaries (Underhill and Hayton, *Law of Trusts and Trustees* (18th edn, 2007), para **[48.1]** ff). Prima facie they should be investing in income producing assets, and if it is intended that they should be able to acquire and retain non-income producing assets, or eg retain shares in a private company and permit the company to continue not to pay dividends, the will or settlement should say so. In practice the acquiescence of the life tenant may often be sufficient in the absence of such powers. If there is a good investment reason for acquiring a non-income-yielding asset, and it is not unfair on any category of beneficiary to do so, it seems likely that doing so would be within the general power of investment, but it is better to confer express authority to acquire non-income-yielding assets.

[220.34]
Businesses. Express power is always needed for trustees to be able to trade with trust assets: see eg *Re Berry* [1962] Ch 97 at 111, B5 at para **[205.25]**, Forms B5.13 to B5.22 at paras **[205.70]–[205.79]** and Forms B20.17 and B20.18 at paras **[220.82]** and **[220.83]**.

[220.35]
Delegation. It is becoming increasingly common for stock exchange investments comprised in trust funds to be managed by a professional fund manager, with the investments vested in nominees who are or are controlled by the fund manager. The fund manager makes the decisions as to purchase or sale without reference to the trustees, but in accordance with an investment policy chosen by the trustees and periodically reconsidered by them. The conventional power of investment, however wide it may be as to the type of investment, confers the power to select investments and decide when to sell them on the trustees only, and it is not a power which the trustees can delegate in the absence of express authority to do so. However, the TrA 2000, Pt IV, ss 11–27, (Part G, paras **[246.143]–[246.159]**) now confers power on trustees and personal representatives to delegate investment functions to investment managers and to vest trust assets in nominees. The question from a draftsman's point of view is now whether to rely on the statutory powers or whether express provision should still be made.

[220.36]
The statutory power to delegate. The statutory power to delegate is contained in the TrA 2000, s 11(1) (Part G, para **[246.143]**), and in the case of non charitable trusts it enables trustees to authorise an agent to exercise any of their delegable functions—those are all functions other than those specified in s 11(2). The most important non-delegable functions specified in s 11(2)

are those relating to asset distribution (eg powers of appointment), and the appointment of new trustees. The power to appoint nominees and vest assets in them is in TrA 2000, s 16 (Part G, para **[246.148]**). The power to remunerate agents and nominees, provided the terms of engagement include agreement to remunerate them, and the amount of the remuneration does not exceed what is reasonable in the circumstances, is in TrA 2000, s 32 (Part G, para **[246.164]**). The aspects of the statutory powers which might make express provision seem appropriate are—

(a) Although trustees may delegate to an agent who is one or more of themselves, and to a person who is also acting as a nominee, they may not do so in favour of a beneficiary: TrA 2000, s 12 (Part G, para **[246.144]**).

(b) The terms on which a delegation of powers to an agent is carried out may not include, *unless it is reasonably necessary for the trustees to agree to such terms* (emphasis supplied), a term permitting the agent to appoint a substitute, a term restricting the liability of the agent, or a term permitting the agent to act in circumstances capable of giving rise to a conflict of interest. See the TrA 2000, s 14 (Part G, para **[246.146]**). These last two are terms commonly sought to be imposed by professional investment managers. If all known fund managers seek to impose such terms, there will not be much difficulty in deciding that it is reasonably necessary to accept them. However, what is the position if trustees have a choice between investment manager A and investment manager B, where A insists on limitation of liability and self-dealing being permitted, and B does not, but A is thought to be a better investment manager who will achieve more capital growth? It might be thought desirable to give trustees an untrammelled discretion as to whether to accept terms such as these, but it is not at all clear that the requirements of s 14 can be excluded or by-passed by express provision in the will or other trust instrument: see para **[220.37]**.

(c) Section 15 of the TrA 2000 (Part G, para **[246.147]**) imposes detailed requirements on agreements to delegate asset management functions to an agent, ie functions of acquiring and disposing of assets, and managing assets while they are held. The agreement must be or be evidenced in writing, the trustees must prepare a prior written policy statement, formulated with a view to ensuring that the asset management functions will be exercised by the agent in the best interest of the trust, and the agreement delegating these functions must include terms which secure compliance by the agent with the policy statement. It should be noted that these requirements can apply to, eg an estate agent to whom functions of management of commercially let land or buildings are delegated, as well as someone to whom investment of a stock exchange portfolio of shares is delegated. These are of course all things which it would be sensible for trustees to do in many or most cases, but it might be unduly constricting and expensive for the trust funds if the trustees are required to produce a policy statement whenever they delegate any of these matters. However, as with s 14, it is not at all clear that these requirements can be excluded or by-passed by express provision in the will or other trust instrument: see para **[220.37]**.

(d) The persons who may be appointed nominees under the statutory power are confined to persons carrying on a business which consists of or includes acting as a nominee, a body corporate controlled by the trustees, or a body corporate which is an incorporated solicitors' practice: see TrA 2000, s 19(1), (2) (Part G, para **[246.151]**).

(e) The terms on which a person may be appointed to act as nominee may not include, *unless it is reasonably necessary for the trustees to agree to such terms* (emphasis supplied), a term permitting the nominee to appoint a substitute, a term restricting the liability of the nominee, or a term permitting the nominee to act in circumstances capable of giving rise to a conflict of interest. See TrA 2000, s 20 (Part G, para **[246.152]**).

(f) While an agent or nominee continues to act, the trustees must keep the arrangements under review, and must consider whether there is a need to intervene if circumstances make it appropriate to do so. If they do consider that there is a need to intervene, they must do so. Where the agent is managing trust assets, this duty includes considering whether to revise or replace the policy statement and doing so where this is considered by them to be needed, and assessing whether the policy statement is being complied with. See TrA 2000, s 22 (Part G, para **[246.154]**). These again are things which it will often be sensible for trustees to do, but which it may be unduly constricting and expensive for the trust funds if they are required to do these things in all cases all the time.

[220.37]

How far the statutory requirements can be excluded or restricted. It is clear that the provisions relating to the statutory powers of delegation and appointment of nominees listed at para **[220.36]** can all be excluded or restricted, or by-passed by an express power not subject to the same restrictions, apart from the TrA 2000, ss 14 and 15, referred to at para **[220.36]**, sub-paras (b) and (c). The excludability of the provisions other than ss 14 and 15 is clear either from the relevant provisions stating that they only apply to the statutory powers (see TrA 2000, ss 12(1), 19(1) and 20(1)), or from express provision that may be excluded (see TrA 2000, s 21(3), which makes such provision in relation to s 22). Sections 14 and 15 are not expressly confined to imposing restrictions on the exercise of the statutory powers of delegation, but their context and wording suggest that they may have been intended to apply only to the statutory powers in s 11, and that any more general application may be an accident arising from the use of an economical drafting style. It is worth noting that in ss 4 and 5 (standard investment criteria and advice on investment: see paras **[220.13]** and **[220.14]**) the intention that those sections should apply to express powers of investment is made much more explicit by the wording of TrA 2000, ss 4(1) and 5(1) respectively (Part G, paras **[246.136]** and **[246.137]**). The TrA 2000, s 26 (Part G, para **[246.158]**) states that the statutory powers of delegation and appointing nominees are in addition to any express powers, and that they are subject to any restriction or exclusion by the trust instrument. This enables greater restrictions than the statutory restrictions to be imposed on the statutory powers, but does not permit exclusion of statutory restrictions imposed on express powers. Our conclusion is therefore that it is not clear whether ss 14 and 15 are excludable. If a will or other trust instrument purports to exclude them, or an express power is conferred which is so worded as to purport not to be subject to them, we recommend that the trustees act as if ss 14 and 15 apply unless and until it becomes clear from a court decision (or legislation) that they are not subject to them. See Form B20.8 at para **[220.47]** for a clause purporting to exclude the statutory restrictions on delegation and nomineeship.

[220.38]

Delegation, nomineeship, and liability. The statutory duty of care (see para **[220.15]**) applies to trustees when exercising powers of delegation or of appointing nominees, whether the powers exercised are those under the TrA 2000, ss 11 or 16, or are conferred by the will or other trust instrument, or otherwise: TrA 2000, Sch 1, para 3(1)(a), (b), (d), and para 3(2) (Part G, para **[246.173]**). It also applies when exercising the powers of review of delegation or nomineeship under the TrA 2000, s 22: Sch 1, para 3(1)(e). The duty of care can be excluded by the will or other trust instrument: TrA 2000, Sch 1, para 7 (Part G, para **[246.173]**). Trustees are not liable for any act or default of a person to whom powers have been delegated, or of a nominee appointed, under the powers in the TrA 2000 unless they have failed to comply with the duty of care when entering into the arrangements for the delegation or nomineeship, or when carrying out their duties of review etc under s 22: TrA 2000, s 23(1) (Part G, para **[246.155]**) and see s 21(1) for the confinement of s 23 to applying to the statutory powers (Part G, para **[246.153]**). This might appear to mean that trustees are not liable for the acts or defaults of a delegate or nominee where the trustees fail completely to carry out their duties of reviewing the delegation or nomineeship under s 22, as opposed to carrying out those duties without sufficient care, but this is probably illusory. Section 22 imposes a duty to review, and if trustees fail to do it, and the consequence is that, eg inadequately supervised investment managers cause a loss to the trust fund, the trustees will have an original (as opposed to vicarious) liability for a loss consequent on their own failure. What s 23(1) does is to make clear that there is no vicarious liability where trustees are not themselves at fault.

[220.39]

Other powers of delegation. The general power of delegation by trustees acting together as a body under the TrA 2000, s 11 should be distinguished from the power under the TA 1925, s 25 (as substituted by the Trustee Delegation Act 1999), which is a power of an individual trustee to delegate all his trusts powers and discretions by power of attorney for up to a year at a time, and is outside the scope of this work. There is also a power under the TLATA 1996, s 9 to delegate functions as trustees of land to a beneficiary entitled to an interest in possession in the land: see para **[220.54]** ff.

Investment powers

[220.40]

Form B20.1: Power of investment confined to fixed interest investments quoted shares and legal estates in land[1]

Trust moneys may be invested in any of the following (and the statutory general power of investment and power to acquire land shall not apply)—

(a) the public stocks funds or government securities of the United Kingdom of Great Britain and Northern Ireland or any member state of the British Commonwealth or any member state of the European Union or any province or state having a separate local legislature and forming part of any of the foregoing;

(b) bonds stocks debentures or other securities of any municipal or local body or authority in the British Commonwealth or the European Union;

(c) the units of any authorised unit trust scheme for the time being authorised under the Financial Services Act 1986 or the Financial Services and Markets Act 2000;

(d) the shares or deposits of any building society within the meaning of the Building Societies Act 1986 registered in the United Kingdom;

(e) in any investments of whatsoever nature which at the date of purchase are or on allotment will be listed on the Stock Exchange or on any of the stock exchanges of New York, Montreal, Paris, Frankfurt, Amsterdam, Milan, Madrid, Zurich, Tokyo, Hong Kong or Johannesburg;

(f) in the acquisition of freehold and leasehold legal estates (including legal mortgages or charges) in land situate in the United Kingdom including land for occupation by a beneficiary [pursuant to the power hereinafter contained][2] provided that—

  (i) leasehold estates in land shall be purchased only if at the date of the purchase the unexpired term exceeds fifty years,

  (ii) in relation to land in Scotland what may be acquired under the foregoing power is the estate or interest of the proprietor of the dominum utile or, in the case of land not held on feudal tenure, the estate or interest of the owner, or (subject to proviso (a) above) a tenancy, and

  (iii) 'land' includes buildings and rights over land.[3]

1 This is narrower than the statutory powers of investment (for which see paras **[220.12]** and **[220.17]**), for the cautious testator. It is intended to cover the main types of fixed interest investment, quoted shares, and legal estates in land other than leases of 50 years or less unexpired. In practice these are probably all that prudent trustees with a fund of cash to invest, maintaining a balance of income and capital growth, would want to invest in, but it could turn out to be unduly restrictive. Where a testator is inclined towards something of this sort, it might be better to put it as an expression of wishes rather than a restriction on the trustees' powers. For the power to restrict or exclude the statutory powers of investment see the TrA 2000, ss 6(1) and 9 (Part G, paras **[246.138]** and **[246.141]**). For the non-excludable requirements of the TrA 2000, ss 4 and 5 as to having regard to the standard investment criteria and obtaining advice see paras **[220.13]** and **[220.14]**. The power permits investment in mortgages secured on UK land, whereas the statutory powers under the TrA 2000, s 3 (see para **[220.16]**) permit investment in mortgages secured on land anywhere.

2 The cautious draftsman will include this restriction for IHT reasons: see para **[220.4]** ff and the Note in B18 at paras **[218.67]** and **[218.68]**. For a power to permit beneficiaries to occupy or enjoy in kind trust assets, see Form B18.17 at para **[218.83]**.

3 This is based on the TrA 2000, s 8 (see para **[220.17]** and Part G, para **[246.140]**), but subject to the restriction (deriving from the more traditional investment clauses) that leasehold land with 50 or less years to run should not be acquired.

[220.41]

Form B20.2: Full discretion—long form[1]

Trust moneys may be invested in such stocks funds shares securities assurance policies land interests in land or other assets of any nature and wheresoever situate whether involving liability or not and whether yielding income or not including secured or unsecured loans [the purchase or improvement of dwellinghouses or other assets for occupation or enjoyment in kind by beneficiaries hereunder and secured or unsecured loans to beneficiaries hereunder[2]] as my trustees in their absolute discretion shall think fit and my trustees may grant indulgence to or release any debtor give and take guarantees enter into profit-sharing agreements or give and take options and accept substitution of any security for other security or of one debtor for another debtor to the intent that my trustees shall have the same unrestricted powers of investing and using trust moneys and managing investments as if they were absolutely entitled provided that:

(i) no loan shall be made to a beneficiary hereunder unless it is either made for full consideration in money or money's worth or made in exercise of the power to make free or advantageous loans to beneficiaries hereinafter contained;[3]

(ii) no beneficiary hereunder shall be permitted to have the occupation or enjoyment in kind of any asset except in exercise of the powers to permit such occupation or enjoyment hereinafter contained;[4] and

(iii) in the professed exercise of the foregoing powers my trustees [and any person to whom such powers are delegated in pursuance of the power of delegation hereinafter contained[5]] shall not be liable for any loss arising from any purchase investment or other dealing made in good faith.[6]

1 This form is wider than the statutory powers in that it permits the acquisition of land outside the UK and equitable interests in land, and makes it clear that non income-yielding assets and unsecured loans may be acquired or made. See para **[220.18]**. For the non excludable requirements of the TrA 2000, ss 4 and 5 as to having regard to the standard investment criteria and obtaining advice, see paras **[220.13]** and **[220.14]**.

2 These words in square brackets are restricted by provisos (i) and (ii) and no amendment of these words should be considered without also considering those provisos and vice versa. See also the notes to the provisos.

3 This proviso is probably not needed for IHT reasons, but together with an appropriately restricted power will ensure that the power is only exercised in accordance with the beneficial interests. See the Notes at para **[220.4]** ff and the Note in B18 at paras **[218.67]** and **[218.68]**. For a power to make beneficial loans to a beneficiary entitled to an interest in possession see Form B18.26 at para **[218.107]**, and for a power to do so where a beneficiary has an interest in possession or has an interest in income as the object of a discretion see Form C2.1, cl 9 at para **[224.37]**.

4 This proviso is included for IHT reasons. See the Notes at para **[220.4]** ff and the Note in B18 at paras **[218.67]** and **[218.68]**. For a power to permit beneficiaries to occupy or enjoy in kind trust assets see Form B18.24 at para **[218.109]**.

5 Omit the words in square brackets if there is no power to delegate investment powers; see Form B20.8 at para **[220.47]** for such a power.
6 For a more general clause exonerating trustees from liability, see Form B21.12 at para **[221.16]**.

[220.42]

Form B20.3: Full discretion—short form[1]

My trustees may invest trust moneys in any property of whatever description or location including land buildings and interests in land or buildings, unsecured personal loans, non-income yielding property, and land or buildings or interests in land or buildings for occupation or use by beneficiaries pursuant to the power for that purpose set out below[2] as if they were a sole beneficial owner of such moneys.

1 This form is wider than the statutory powers in that it permits the acquisition of land outside the UK and equitable interests in land, and makes it clear that non-income-yielding assets and unsecured loans may be acquired or made. See para **[220.18]**. See also Form C2.1, cl 9 at para **[224.30]**. For the non excludable requirements of the TrA 2000, ss 4 and 5 as to having regard to the standard investment criteria and obtaining advice, see paras **[220.13]** and **[220.14]**.
2 This assumes a separate power to permit the use of land and chattels by beneficiaries: see Form B18.24 at para **[218.109]**.

[220.43]

Form B20.4: Statutory power subject to an ethical investment policy[1]

(1) Subject as set out below, my trustees shall have the general power of investment and the power to acquire land respectively conferred by sections 3 and 8 of the Trustee Act 2000.

(2) [I request that my trustees do not] *or* [My trustees shall not][2] acquire or retain any shares securities bonds debentures land or other assets which are or include, or underlying which directly or indirectly are assets which include, any business which to a significant extent deals in, makes, promotes, provides services in respect of, or is otherwise commercially involved with, any of the following products—

(a) cigarettes cigars pipe tobacco snuff or other tobacco products;
(b) arms explosives mines bombs missiles or other weapons, or military or naval vehicles ships aircraft or other equipment, for use in or ancillary to the conduct of warfare, rebellion, suppression of rebellion or dissent, or other violent action against persons or property;
(c) timber or timber products from non-renewable sources;
(d) products which have been tested on live animals;
(e) products produced by the labour of children under the age of [15] years;
(f) alcoholic liquor of any kind;
(g) oil and petroleum products;
(h) chemical fertilisers or chemical pesticides or herbicides;
(i) plants or animals genetically modified by the manipulation of DNA.

(3) [I request that my trustees do not] *or* [My trustees shall not][3] acquire or retain any shares securities bonds debentures land or other assets which are or include, or underlying which directly or indirectly are assets which

include, assets which are located in [*name*(*s*) *of country*(*ies*)] *or, eg* [any country state or territory where there is for the time being believed by my trustees to be abuse of human rights (as defined in the European Convention for the Protection of Human Rights and Fundamental Freedoms agreed by the Council of Europe in 1950 and the protocols thereto) or where there is capital punishment].

(4) I declare that my trustees shall not be liable for any loss which may arise from compliance or purported compliance with the foregoing, or from taking steps or refraining from taking steps in the belief that they are acting or refraining from acting in accordance with the foregoing, and that they shall be fully indemnified out of [my residuary estate] against the cost of obtaining information relevant to compliance with the foregoing.

1 This form in sub-cl (2) sets out a number of types of business which a testator might desire to exclude, either as the subject of precatory words of exclusion, or by express exclusion from the scope of the statutory powers of investment (on the relative merits of these alternatives see n 2 below). From these, the provisions desired in any particular case can be selected, or others added or substituted. Subclause (3) excluding investments connected with particular countries or countries of a particular description, can be used either together with or separately from sub-cl (2). For the statutory powers of investment and purchase of land, and power to restrict them, see paras **[220.12]**, **[220.17]** and **[220.18]**.

2 One of these alternatives should be deleted. The use of precatory words is preferable because it is difficult to draft the descriptions of the excluded categories in a sufficiently definite and comprehensive manner to be workable as a matter of legal obligation, and because putting trustees under an obligation to avoid the specified types of investment puts a heavy burden on them, not only of interpreting the wording of the exclusion, but of obtaining sufficient information to establish whether particular investments fall within a prohibited category. The practical difference between imposing an obligation and using precatory words is not great, because if an obligation is imposed, the prohibited investments are not in a prohibited category because they carry a high risk of loss or poor prospects of income or capital profits, but because of moral disapproval. If trustees breach the obligation by investing in a company whose business is on the prohibited list, but the investment performs well as an investment, it is difficult to see how the trustees could be liable to the beneficiaries for the breach. The main things a testator should concentrate on if he wants an ethical investment policy is to absolve the trustees from liability for following it, and to choose trustees who share his outlook.

3 One of these alternatives should be deleted, and where sub-cl (2) is also included, it should be the same alternative. See n 2 above for discussion of the relative merits of these alternatives.

[220.44]

Form B20.5: Retention of shares in family company

If I hold at my death any shares or securities in the [*name*] Company Limited (whether or not it has undergone any change of name) or in any company which as a result of any reconstruction amalgamation demerger or sale shall be a successor to any business of the said company or of any subsidiary of it, it is my wish that my trustees shall retain such shares or securities or any shares or securities they may come to hold in any successor company as aforesaid [if and so long as any of my children or remoter issue are employed in any of such businesses, and if and when none of them are so employed] unless and until it is in their opinion necessary in the interests of the beneficiaries to sell or otherwise dispose of such shares or securities or any of them and I declare that my trustees shall not be liable for any loss arising from investment in or retention of any shares or securities of the foregoing kinds.[1]

1 This form is for a testator who wants the trustees to continue to hold private company shares which he owns. The expression of a wish as to retention of the shares is intended as a counterweight to the duty to consider the need for diversification imposed by the TrA 2000, s 4 (see para **[220.13]**). This duty cannot be excluded, but diversification out of a holding of this kind may not be 'appropriate to the circumstances of the trust' (see the TrA 2000, s 4(3)(b): Part G, para **[246.136]**) where there is some special reason for retention, such as one or more beneficiaries working in the business. Although s 4 cannot be excluded, exclusion of liability for failure to diversify is possible, and the exclusion of liability for retaining the shares is perhaps the most effective step which can be taken towards bringing about retention of them. The specific exclusion of liability is not needed if there is a general exclusion of such liability elsewhere in the will.

[220.45]

Form B20.6: Powers of sale and transposing assets[1]

My trustees may at their discretion retain as invested or sell or otherwise convert into money [the property [other than money[2]] settled under clause —— of this will] and invest the moneys arising thereby [and such of the said property as may be money[2]] in any investments hereby or by law authorised with power from time to time to change such investments for others hereby authorised and in exercising the foregoing powers shall have all the powers of disposition and acquisition of an absolute owner.

1 A provision such as this is not necessary where the trust fund is net residue subject to administration trusts for conversion into money with power to postpone conversion, or subject to a power of sale, but such a provision is needed where specific property is settled on trust. Accordingly, this Form is assumed to refer to a clause of the will containing a specific gift. Powers of sale and changing investments are often integrated into the main trusts; see eg Form B16.26 at para **[216.31]**.

2 Omit 'other than money' and 'and such of the said assets as may be money' if the property settled does not include money.

[220.46]

Form B20.7: Power to give warranties on the sale of private company shares

My trustees shall have power on the sale or transfer of any private company shares to give any warranty indemnity guarantee or undertaking in relation to the shares and the company and any other matter in connection with such sale or transfer as they shall in their absolute discretion think fit and they shall be fully indemnified out of [my residuary estate] against any liability they may incur thereunder.

[220.47]

Form B20.8: Power to delegate investment powers and vest assets in nominees[1]

(1) My trustees may delegate with respect to the whole or any part of [my residuary estate] their powers hereunder of investing trust moneys and changing trust investments and any other of my trustees' powers hereby or by law conferred relating to the management or administration of trust moneys or other trust assets to any person carrying on the business of

management of investments to any extent for any period on any terms (which may include authorising self-dealing or limiting the liability of the person to whom such powers are delegated) and in any manner and may remunerate such person and s 22 of the Trustee Act 2000 shall not apply.

(2) My trustees shall have power to vest or register any property in any person or persons whether individual or corporate and whether or not an investment manager to whom powers have been delegated under the foregoing power (and who may be or include one or more of my trustees or the beneficiaries hereunder) as nominee or nominees for my trustees upon such terms as to remuneration or otherwise (including terms authorising self-dealing or providing for the limitation of the liability of the nominee) as my trustees think fit and s 22 of the Trustee Act 2000 shall not apply.[2]

1 Express provision for delegation of investment management powers is not as important as it formerly was because there is now the statutory power to appoint investment managers in the TrA 2000, Pt IV, ss 11–15 (Part G, paras **[246.143]–[246.147]**; see also para **[220.36]**). This clause differs from the statutory power in that the detailed procedural requirements of the TrA 2000, s 15 do not apply; the trustees have a wider discretion as to restricting an investment manager's liability or permitting self-dealing by him (compare the TrA 2000, s 14(2): Part G, para **[246.146]**, under which these can only be done if it is reasonably necessary); beneficiaries can be appointed (this is forbidden in exercise of the statutory power by the TrA 2000, s 12(3)); and the duty to review the arrangement from time to time under the TrA 2000, s 22 (Part G, para **[246.143]**) does not apply. The by-passing of the TrA 2000, ss 14 and 15 is only effective if those statutory provisions apply solely to the statutory powers of delegation, and do not apply to express powers to delegate investment management functions, something which is not at all clear (see para **[220.37]**). Even though trustees have an express power of this kind, unless and until there is either a definitive decision of the courts or amending legislation which makes it certain that ss 14 and 15 are excluded by such a power, trustees should regard themselves as bound by ss 14 and 15.

2 This is wider than the statutory power to appoint nominees in the TrA 2000, Pt IV, ss 16–20 (Part G, paras **[246.148]–[246.152]**; see also para **[220.35]** ff), in that the trustees have a wider discretion as to restricting a nominee's liability or permitting self-dealing by him (compare the TrA 2000, s 20(2): Part G, para **[246.152]** under which these can only be done if it is reasonably necessary); the persons who may be appointed nominees are not confined to persons carrying on a business as nominees, a company controlled by the trustees, or a solicitors' incorporated practice (compare TA 2000, s 19(2): Part G, para **[246.151]**); and the duty to review the arrangement from time to time under the TrA 2000, s 22 (Part G, para **[246.154]**) does not apply.

[220.48]

Form B20.9: Clause as to bonus shares[1]

If my trustees shall by virtue of any shareholding in any company for the time being held by my trustees upon the trusts hereof and listed on a stock exchange become entitled to any shares or stocks or securities distributed as dividend such that in the opinion of my trustees the capital value of the shares in respect of which the dividend is distributed is diminished by more than 10 per cent (comparing with their listed value immediately before and immediately after they became listed ex dividend but leaving out of account so far as possible any other factors influencing value other than the holdings becoming ex dividend) my trustees may apportion such whole or part of the said bonus shares stocks or securities to capital as in their opinion shall be just and reasonable.

1 For clauses negativing rules of apportionment generally, see Forms B14.24 to B14.29 at paras **[214.39]–[214.46]**. This clause is intended to deal with a case where a substantial

dividend based on accumulated profits or capital profits of the company over a long period is declared in the form of distribution of shares in a subsidiary in order to achieve a demerger or a reduction in capital. The law seems to be that if it is a direct demerger the shares distributed will be income, but if it is an indirect one they are capital: see *Sinclair v Lee* [1993] Ch 497, sub nom *Re Lee, Sinclair v Lee* [1993] 3 All ER 926. Thus what is in substance a capital split or repayment is treated under the general law in some situations as a distribution which constitutes income, and where this involves a substantial diminution of the capital value of the original holding this is unfair on the capital beneficiaries and a windfall to the income beneficiaries. There are objections to using this clause, however. First, its effects for IHT purposes in relation to fixed interest trusts or bereaved minor or age 18-to-25 trusts are unclear and such effects may be adverse–treating what would otherwise be income as capital might affect the intended IHT status of the trusts (but *Miller v IRC* [1987] STC 108, for which see n 1 to para **[220.61]** gives some support to the view that the intended IHT status would not be prejudiced). Secondly, a clause in this form may involve an unlawful direction to accumulate after the expiration of the relevant accumulation period.

Management of land

[220.49]

The statutory powers. Trustees holding on trust land situated in England and Wales are given a wide power to manage that land by the TLATA 1996, s 6(1) (Part G, para **[246.108]**), and trustees holding on trust land in the UK which they have acquired in exercise of their powers to acquire land under the TrA 2000, s 8(1) are given the same power of management of such land by the TrA 2000, s 8(3) (Part G, para **[246.140]**). In both cases, they have in relation to the land all the powers of an absolute owner, for the purposes of exercising their functions as trustees. These powers apply also to personal representatives: TLATA 1996, s 18 (Part G, para **[246.104]**) and TrA 2000, s 35 (Part G, para **[246.167]**). For newly created trusts of land (see Part A, para **[200.51]** for this term) these powers replace the extensive and detailed powers of management of land which are conferred on tenants for life of settled land by the Settled Land Act 1925 (SLA 1925), and which also, before 1 January 1997 (the commencement of the TLATA 1996), applied to trustees for sale of land by virtue of the LPA 1925, s 28(1) (repealed by the TLATA 1996). The new statutory powers give the widest discretion in respect of such matters as sale, insurance, repair, improvement, mortgaging and leasing, and apply to all trusts of any kind involving land created on or after 1 January 1997, and all created before that date apart from ones to which the SLA 1925 continues to apply (see Part A, para **[200.48]** ff).

[220.50]

Restrictions on the statutory powers. The powers may be restricted or excluded (TLATA 1996, s 8(1) and TrA 2000, s 9) or made subject to consents: TLATA 1996, s 8(2) (Part G, para **[246.110]**). It is thought that in relation to trusts created before the Act came into force the trustees will have the full s 6 powers, notwithstanding any express restriction on the trustees' powers in the disposition creating the trust, but that any requirement of consent will continue to be binding, because s 8(1) seems only to relate to specific exclusion of the powers conferred by the Act, whereas s 8(2) seems to refer to requirements of consent in relation to powers of a kind conferred by the Act. However, the LPA 1925, s 28(1) used to provide that land acquired by trustees for sale should be conveyed to them on trust for sale, and that the statutory powers of leasing, improvement, etc of trustees for sale should be exercised with the consents (if any) required for a sale. The repeal of the LPA 1925, s 28 from 1January 1997 by the TLATA 1996 means that now trustees of land (including trustees for sale) whose power or trust to sell the land is subject to a requirement of obtaining the consent of someone do not need that person's consent to the exercise of others of their powers over the land unless the will or settlement expressly says so.

[220.51]

Insurance. A new TA 1925, s 19 (power of insurance: see Part G, para **[246.17]**) is substituted by the TrA 2000, s 34 with effect from 1 February 2001, but in relation to trusts created before, on, or after that date. It provides that a trustee may insure any property subject to the trust against risks of loss or damage due to any event, and pay the premium out of any income or capital funds of the trust. This remedies the deficiencies of the previous statutory trustees' powers of insurance, and it is no longer necessary to make express provision. The power is also exercisable by personal representatives: TA 1925, s 69(1) and TrA 2000, s 35 (Part G, paras **[246.40]** and **[246.167]**). The TA 1925, s 20 makes full provision for the application of moneys received under a policy of insurance against loss, whatever the risk and whether the insurance was under an express or a statutory power.

[220.52]

The limitations of the statutory administrative powers. The limitations of the powers conferred by the TLATA 1996, s 6(1) and the TrA 2000, s 8(3) in relation to land which should in our opinion be borne in mind and which should be compensated for by express provision, either generally or in particular cases, are as follows—

(1) They only apply to land in England and Wales, and to land in Scotland and Northern Ireland acquired under the power in the TrA 2000, s 8(1) (see para **[220.17]** for this). Express powers are needed for management of any other land. Further, the meaning of 'land' in England and Wales for the purposes of the TLATA 1996, s 6(1) is that given by the LPA 1925, s 205(1)(ix) (see TLATA 1996, s 23(2)) and this is a definition which is difficult to construe and which possibly does not include mortgages or charges or all kinds of equitable interest in land (although it may include undivided shares of land). For an extended power of management see Form B20.10 at para **[220.59]**.

(2) The TLATA 1996, s 6(1) and the TrA 2000, s 8(3) only apply 'in relation to the land'. It is not clear whether this would include power to use the capital or income of other trust assets, eg stock exchange investments, to pay for, eg repairs or improvements of the land. In the case of the construction of new buildings, it seems likely that the power of acquisition of land in the TrA 2000, s 8(1), which is of course a power to use any trust money to acquire land, would include power to pay for a new building on land already owned (provided the trustees own a legal estate in the land). This is because the verb is 'acquire' rather than 'purchase', and because the relevant definition of 'land' (IA 1978, Sch 1) includes buildings. The SLA 1925, s 73(1)(iii) did

authorise capital money to be spent on improvements to land, and like other powers under that Act also applied to trusts for sale, and it is unlikely that the new powers are narrower than those which they replace. We recommend an express power in order to avoid uncertainty: see Form B20.11 at para **[220.60]**.

(3) Similarly, it is not absolutely clear that the statutory powers in TrA 2000, s 6(1) would authorise borrowing on the security of the land held in trust to purchase, eg company shares as an investment, although again we think it likely that this is authorised. See Form B20.20 at para **[220.69]** for a power to borrow and note 1 thereto for the statutory powers to borrow.

(4) It seems to us that the TLATA 1996, s 6(1) and TrA 2000, s 8(3) do not confer on the trustees of land sufficient powers to carry on a business such as farming on the land. They clearly authorise the use of the land in the business, but do not authorise the use of trust assets other than the land as capital for the business, or the incurring of business liabilities to be met out of the trust fund. A life tenant in occupation of land held on trust can of course carry on his own business there without special powers.

(5) For the limitations of the statutory powers to purchase land see paras **[220.17]** and **[220.18]**.

[220.53]

Express provision. For the reasons given at para **[220.52]**, express powers of management should be conferred in relation to land outside England and Wales to which the statutory powers would not extend, and the recommended method is to follow the wording of the statutory powers: see Form B20.10 at para **[220.59]**. An express power to apply capital held on the same trusts as trust land in making improvements to the land is also recommended. Such a power is unlikely to cause IHT difficulties of the kind considered at paras **[220.4]–[220.10]** since expenditure which increases the capital value of the trust fund is prima facie properly payable out of capital. On the other hand, it would be better not to confer express powers to pay for improvements out of income where there are intended to be immediate post-death interest trusts or trusts for bereaved minors or age 18-to-25 trusts for IHT purposes (see paras **[200.112A]**, **[200.120]–[200.121]** above). See Form B20.11 at para **[220.60]**. It would give greater flexibility for the trustees to be given a power to pay for repairs out of capital, but this is something better avoided in the case of trusts for bereaved minors or age 18-to-25 trusts; repair is something which is prima facie something to be paid for out of income and power to pay for it out of capital might prejudice the application of the ITA 1984, s 71 (see para **[220.4]** ff).

[220.54]

Power to delegate powers of sale and management of land to a beneficiary. By the TLATA 1996, s 9 (Part G, para **[246.111]**), trustees of land acting together jointly as trustees are given power to delegate by power of attorney to any beneficiary or beneficiaries of full age and beneficially entitled to an interest in possession in land any of their functions which relate to the land, for any period or indefinitely (but apparently not irrevocably—see para

[220.55]). The corresponding power formerly vested in trustees for sale by the LPA 1925, s 29 was narrower in that it was only exercisable in respect of the trustees' powers of leasing and management, while the powers now delegable to a beneficiary include sale. The reason for this wider power of delegation is to make up for the non-availability of the SLA 1925 for trusts of land created after 1996 (for which see Part A, para **[200.52]**). After a full delegation of powers under the TLATA 1996, s 9 the beneficiary will be in a similar position to that of a tenant for life under the SLA 1925, but with the difference that he only gets in that position if the trustees make a discretionary decision to put him there, while a tenant for life under the SLA 1925 had the land vested in him and the powers of sale, leasing, etc as of right. Where the power of sale is delegated, the power to receive the purchase money cannot be delegated and remains in the hands of the trustees: TLATA 1996, s 9(7).

[220.55]
Delegation to beneficiaries—revocability. It seems from the TLATA 1996, s 9(3) and (4) (Part G, para **[246.111]**) that where the trustees decide to delegate to a beneficiary or beneficiaries, even if they express the delegation to be irrevocable, unless the power of attorney is given by way of security and is expressed to be irrevocable it can be revoked at any time by any one of the trustees, and is automatically revoked on appointment of a new trustee, or by the beneficiary's interest in possession coming to an end, or the beneficiary ceasing to be beneficially entitled to it. This underlines another essential difference between being a beneficiary with delegated powers under the TLATA 1996, s 9 and a tenant for life under the SLA 1925, because in the latter case the trustees have no power to terminate the tenant for life's powers. The TLATA 1996, s 9A(3) (inserted by the TrA 2000, s 40, Sch 2, para 47: Part G, para **[246.112]**) imposes duties on trustees to keep any delegation under review and intervene where it is needed, if the delegation is not irrevocable: TLATA 1996, s 9A(2)(b). Since no delegation under s 9 seems to be irrevocable unless done by way of security (which, it is suggested, would be a very unusual use of this power), these duties are more general than the wording of s 9A might suggest.

[220.56]
Delegation to beneficiaries—liability. A beneficiary in whose favour there is delegation under the TLATA 1996, s 9 (see para **[220.54]**) is liable as a trustee for his conduct in carrying out the delegated functions: TLATA 1996, s 9(7). The trustees are by the TLATA 1996, s 9A (inserted by the TrA 2000, s 40, Sch 2, para 47: Part G, para **[246.95]**) subject to the TrA 2000, s 1 duty of care (for which see para **[220.15]**) when deciding whether to exercise the power of delegation: TLATA 1996, s 9A(1). Where the delegation is not irrevocable (see para **[220.55]** for what this seems to mean), trustees are under a continuing duty to review the delegation and intervene where needed, with the duty of care applying to carrying out the latter duties: TLATA 1996, s 9A(2)–(5). The trustees are not liable for the conduct of a beneficiary to whom they have delegated unless they have failed to comply with the duty of care in deciding to delegate or reviewing the delegation: TLATA 1996, s 9A(6). There is a question as to how far the statutory duty of

care can be excluded or cut down by express provision in relation to the substituted TLATA 1996, s 9A. The duty of care is defined in the TrA 2000, s 1, and s 2 states that Sch 1 makes provision about when the duty applies to a trustee. Schedule 1 lists a number of situations where the duty of care applies, which do not in terms include the TLATA 1996, s 9A (but arguably it is one of the powers in relation to land referred to by Sch 1, para 2(c)), and Sch 1, para 7 (Part G, para **[246.131]**) states that the duty of care does not apply if or insofar as it appears from the trust instrument that the duty is not meant to apply. The application of the duty of care to the power of delegation in the TLATA 1996, s 9 is by virtue of the TLATA 1996, s 9A, not by virtue of the TrA 2000, Sch 1. The difficulty is whether TrA 2000, Sch 1, para 7 applies generally, or only in relation to the matters listed in Sch 1, and if the latter, whether the TLATA 1996, s 9A is among the powers referred to by Sch 1, para 2(c). It would be anomalous if the duty of care could not be excluded in relation to the power of delegation to a beneficiary, but could be excluded in relation to many equally important matters (and it would almost certainly arise from an accident of drafting), but it is possible.

[220.57]
Delegation to beneficiaries—express provision. It would seem that the power under the TLATA 1996, s 9 cannot be excluded or varied or its exercise made mandatory by express provisions of the will or other disposition, and there is the difficulty of construction as to whether the TrA 2000, s 1 duty of care can be excluded in relation to it (see para **[220.56]**). The most that can be done is to request the trustees to exercise the power (or not exercise it) in particular ways or in general, and if it is desired to encourage them to exercise it, to make the exercise of any of their powers over the land subject to obtaining the consent of the life tenant(s) in possession for the time being, and not to exclude the TLATA 1996, s 11 (see para **[220.58]**). Non-binding requests will not be legally binding on the trustees, but will be a factor to which the court is to have regard under ss 14 and 15 of the TLATA 1996 in the event of a dispute about the exercise or non-exercise of the power of delegation getting to court. For an example, see Form C13.2 at para **[235.18]** ff, in particular cl 8 at para **[235.26]**.

[220.58]
Duty to consult beneficiaries. The TLATA 1996, s 11 (Part G, para **[246.114]**) imposes a duty on trustees of land in the exercise of any function relating to the land subject to the trust 'so far as practicable' to consult the beneficiaries of full age and beneficially entitled to an interest in possession, and so far as consistent with the general interest of the trust to give effect to the wishes of those beneficiaries, or (in the event of a dispute) the majority by value. This is in the same terms as the former LPA 1925, s 26(3) (which was repealed by the TLATA 1996). The difference between the TLATA 1996, s 11 and the former LPA 1925, s 26(3) is that the latter only applied to an express trust for sale created by deed or will if it was expressly declared to apply, whereas the former will apply to any trust created on or after 1 January 1997, unless expressly excluded: TLATA 1996, s 11(2)(a). As it could add appreciably to the burdens and difficulties of the trustees, in general we recommend its routine exclusion unless there are special reasons for not doing so. Circumstances where it might be appropriate not to exclude it are a co-ownership

trust of a house in which the co-owners are going to live, in a trust to provide a residence for, e g the testator's widow, or any other land where it is intended that a beneficiary will occupy it. It is particularly something to exclude in relation to a gift by will where it is intended that any land shall be sold and the proceeds divided (see further Part A, paras **[200.56]–[200.59]**). For a clause excluding s 11, see Form B21.23 at para **[221.27]**. It should be noted that s 11 does not apply to a will made before 1 January 1997 of a person who dies on or after that date: TLATA 1996, s 11(2)(b).

[220.59]

Form B20.10: Power of management in relation to land in any location[1]

My trustees shall have all the powers of an absolute owner in relation to any land held by them (wherever situated) and for this purpose 'land' includes buildings and estates interests or rights of any kind in or over land.

1 See para **[220.52]**, sub-para (1) for the reasons for this type of provision.

[220.60]

Form B20.11: Power to apply other capital in improving land[1]

My trustees whether acting as trustees or personal representatives shall have power to apply capital held on the same trusts as any land or interest in land (or which would be so held if the administration of my estate had been completed) in the improvement of such land and to apply such capital or the income of such capital on the repair or maintenance of such land.[2]

1 See para **[220.52]**, sub-para (2) for the reasons for this type of provision.

2 The restriction to capital held on the same trusts helps to ensure fairness as between beneficiaries, and is also intended to avoid the prejudice to the IHT status of settled property which might arise from the possibility that it might bear expenses attributable to other settled property in the same settlement but held on different trusts. The restriction to spending capital on improvements avoids expenditure normally properly payable out of capital being paid out of income (see paras **[220.4]–[220.10]**).

[220.61]

Form B20.12: Treatment of mining rent and royalties and proceeds of timber[1]

(1) All the rent or royalties from any mining lease or licence of land held by my trustees shall be treated as income and none shall be apportioned to capital.[2]

(2) The net proceeds of sale of any timber which is cut and sold from any land held by my trustees shall be treated wholly as income.[3]

1 This form makes clear that mineral rents and royalties and the proceeds of sale of timber are to be treated wholly as income. Before 1 January 1997, the SLA 1925, ss 47 (mineral rents) and 66 (timber), which apportion these between capital and income, applied to land held on trust for sale by virtue of the LPA 1925, s 28(2) (subject to express provision in the trust instrument). The LPA 1925, s 28(2) was repealed by the TLATA 1996, and these provisions of the SLA 1925 do not apply to trusts of land within the meaning of the TLATA 1996 (see Part A, para **[200.51]** for this term). It is uncertain whether the non-application of these provisions means that the former rule of the general law that the whole of mineral rents and proceeds of timber are capital (see nn 2 and 3) are revived, or whether the wide power of management of land in the TLATA 1996, s 6(1) (see para

[220.49]) has the effect that mineral rents and royalties and the sale proceeds of timber are income, or at any rate that it is within the trustees' powers to treat them as such. In this state of uncertainty, where trust property may include mining leases or saleable timber it will save argument to include provision of this kind. The other possible ways of dealing with the problem are to give the trustees a discretion to apportion some to capital, or to provide that a fixed proportion is apportioned to capital. Both these options risk treating what is really income as capital, and prejudicing the existence of an interest in possession (and in particular an immediate post-death interest, see para **[200.198]** above) for IHT purposes or the application of the IHTA 1984, s 71A (trusts for bereaved minors, see para **[200.120]** above) or s 71D (age 18-to-25 trusts, see para **[200.121]** above), but a discretionary power would probably not have this effect, although it would have the problem that the trustees would have very little guidance as to how to exercise it. In *Miller v IRC* [1987] STC 108 it was held by the Court of Session that a power of the trustees to set aside income for meeting depreciation of the capital value of trust assets, or for any other reason the trustees thought advisable or necessary, was an administrative power which did not prevent the liferentrix from having an interest in possession for IHT purposes. There is an express exception from the rules against excessive accumulations for the accumulation of the proceeds of timber or wood (LPA 1925, s 164(2)(iii): Part G, para **[246.44]**), but no similar provision for mineral rents, so treating the latter as capital when they were really income might be a breach of the rules against accumulations.

2 Under the general law, before statutory intervention originally by the Settled Land Act 1882, mineral rents counted as capital if the tenant for life was impeachable for waste: *Re Ridge, Hellard v Moody* (1885) 31 Ch D 504 at 508. Under the SLA 1925, s 47 if the tenant for life is impeachable for waste, three-quarters of the rents are capitalised and he is entitled to a quarter, and if he if he is not so impeachable, one-quarter is capital. This could be varied by express provision, and it has been common to exclude this provision in settled land settlements and provide that the entire rents are income. Without express provision, someone with a life interest in the proceeds of sale under a trust for sale had the same rights to income as a tenant for life impeachable for waste (*Re Ridge, Hellard v Moody*), so that the capitalisation was of three-quarters of the mineral rents.

3 Under the general law, before statutory intervention originally by the Settled Land Act 1882, the proceeds of sale of timber counted as capital if the tenant for life was impeachable for waste: *Honeywood v Honeywood* (1874) LR 18 Eq 306. Under the SLA 1925, s 66 if the tenant for life is impeachable for waste three-quarters of the net proceeds of timber are capitalised. 'Timber' in this context is oak, ash and elm of the age of 20 years or more but not so old as not to have useable timber (*Honeywood v Honeywood*), but this can be varied by local custom. As mentioned in n 1, the SLA 1925, s 66 does not apply to trusts of land within the meaning of the TLATA 1996, and there is uncertainty as to whether or not proceeds of timber should be capitalised in the absence of express provision.

[220.62]

Form B20.13: Exercise of powers to be subject to beneficiary's consent[1]

My trustees shall not exercise their powers (whether conferred by statute or otherwise) of sale lease licence mortgage or charge, or of effecting improvements or development, of any land comprised in [my residuary estate] without the consent of [my wife]/[any person for the time being beneficially entitled to an interest in possession in such land].

1 TLATA 1996, s 8(2) (Part G, para **[246.110]**) expressly contemplates that exercise of the statutory powers of management of land can be made subject to consents, as the powers of trustees for sale often were before the TLATA 1996. The kind of trust where this is most appropriate is one to provide a residence, or any other trust where the beneficiary is likely to occupy the land. It may in many circumstances be felt to be sufficient to protect the interests of the beneficiaries, however, to do no more than refrain from excluding the operation of the TLATA 1996, s 11 (duty to consult beneficiaries, see para **[220.58]**). It should be noted that the LPA 1925, s 28(1) was repealed by the TLATA 1996, so it is no longer the case that making sale of the land subject to consent has the effect that exercise of the trustees' powers of management is also subject to requiring that consent. It is unnecessarily burdensome for

the trustees to make all exercises of their powers to be subject to consent, and this clause is confined to making the more major types of disposition or action subject to it.

Powers relating to foreign property

[220.63]

Form B20.14: Powers of management of foreign land

In relation to any land or immovable property outside England and Wales my trustees shall in addition to the powers conferred hereby have all the powers of an absolute owner and a sole trustee for the time being of this my will may exercise all or any of such powers.

[220.64]

Form B20.15: Declaration that statutory provisions shall apply to foreign property

I declare that my trustees shall in addition to any powers authorities or discretions hereby expressly conferred on them have with respect to any property belonging to me in [*foreign country*] or elsewhere all such powers authorities and discretions as are conferred on trustees of property and personal representatives in England by statute or the general law.

[220.65]

Form B20.16: Power to pay foreign tax

My trustees shall have power in their absolute discretion to pay any tax in any part of the world for which they may be liable even though such tax may not be enforceable against them.

Businesses[1]

[220.66]

Form B20.17: Power to carry on business

My trustees shall have power to carry on any business either alone or in partnership and employ therein any capital of [my residuary estate] and they shall be fully indemnified thereout in respect of any liabilities they may incur in connection with any such business and none of my trustees shall be liable to any of the beneficiaries hereunder for any losses sustained in the course of my trustees' conduct of any such business in the absence of deliberate fraud or wrongdoing on the part of such trustee personally.

1 See also B5 at para **[205.1]** ff, especially Forms B5.13 to B5.22 at paras **[205.70]**–**[205.79]**. Express power is always needed to carry on a business, and essential ancillary powers are powers to invest capital in the purchase of business assets, and power to incur trading liabilities and satisfy them out of the trust fund. See the Preliminary Note to B5 at para **[205.25]**.

[220.67]

Form B20.18: Power to carry on farming business

My trustees may manage stock farm and cultivate alone or in partnership any farm or agricultural land or woodlands anywhere in the world which are comprised in [my residuary estate] and may employ any capital of [my residuary estate] held on the same trusts as such farm agricultural land or woodland is held for such purpose or for the purpose of paying or compensating outgoing tenants and shall have all the powers of a sole absolute owner in relation to such farm agricultural land or woodlands and shall be fully indemnified out of [my residuary estate] in respect of any loss arising from the exercise of these powers.

[220.68]

Form B20.19: Power to incorporate business

My trustees may at the expense of [my residuary estate] form or join in forming a limited or unlimited company to carry on any business or to acquire any business already carried on (alone or in partnership) by my trustees or an interest therein and may sell lease or otherwise dispose of any such business to any limited or unlimited company in consideration (partly or wholly) of shares stock or debentures of such company or for any other consideration.

Borrowing

[220.69]

Form B20.20: Power to borrow[1]

My trustees may borrow money with or without giving security and on such terms as to interest repayment and otherwise as my trustees may think fit for any purpose connected with the trusts affecting [my residuary estate] (including the purchase of or subscription for assets to be held as part of [my residuary estate] or any part or share thereof) and no lender from whom my trustees borrow money in purported exercise of this power shall be concerned to enquire as to the propriety amount or purpose of any such borrowing.[2]

1 In the absence of express power the only powers of trustees to borrow are the power under the TA 1925, s 16 (Part G, para **[246.14]**) to borrow on mortgage to raise money for payment or application in some way which is authorised in relation to capital money, and the powers of an absolute owner in relation to land under the TLATA 1996, s 6(1) and the TrA 2000, s 8(3) (all of which powers also apply to personal representatives). Personal representatives also have power to borrow on the security of personal estate for the purposes of administration of the estate: AEA 1925, s 39 (Part G, para **[246.53]**). TheTA 1925, s 16 does not permit borrowing to finance the purchase of further investments (*Re Suenson-Taylor's Settlement, Moores v Moores* [1974] 3 All ER 397 [1974] 1 WLR 1280), does not permit unsecured borrowing, and does not apply to settled land unless the trustees are statutory owners: TA 1925, s 16(2). It is possible, but not certain, that the powers of an an absolute owner in relation to land under the TLATA 1996, s 6(1) and the TrA 2000, s 8(3) would enable borrowing on the security of the land to finance the purchase of some other investment, but it does not authorise unsecured borrowing. Express powers of this kind are therefore desirable.

2 The TA 1925, s 17 (Part G, para **[246.15]**) gives protection of this kind to mortgagees, but not to lenders of unsecured loans.

Powers of appropriation

[220.70]

Note. The AEA 1925, s 41 (Part G, para **[246.65]**) confers extensive powers of appropriation on personal representatives, but mostly subject to obtaining the consent of the beneficiary or trustees in favour of whom the appropriation is made. There are three main reasons for making express provision for appropriation. The first is to dispense with the requirement of consent: see para **[220.74]**, n 3. The second, in a case where property is to be held on trust, is to confer powers of appropriation on the trustees of the will which will be exercisable when administering the will trusts after the administration of the estate is complete (when the statutory power will have ceased to apply)—although trustees have power of appropriation under the general law, there are uncertainties about the scope of it (see para **[220.71]**), and it is better to make express provision. The third reason is to authorise exercise of the power by a personal representative or trustee in his own favour. In *Re Radley-Kane, Kane v Radley-Kane* [1999] Ch 274, [1998] 3 All ER 753 it was held that a personal representative cannot as a matter of general law exercise the statutory power of appropriation in his own favour unless the assets appropriated are cash or the equivalent of cash such as stock exchange investments. Forms B20.21 at para **[220.74]**, B20.22 at para **[220.75]**, B20.23 at para **[220.76]** and B20.24 at para **[220.77]** confer power of appropriation on the will trustees when acting as trustees, but Form B20.26 at para **[220.79]** does not, and it is not entirely clear whether Statutory Will Form No 6 (see Form B20.25 at para **[220.78]**) does so, but it probably does.

[220.71]

Trustees' powers under the general law. The wide powers of investment in land and other assets now conferred by the TrA 2000, ss 3 and 8 possibly mean that trustees (as opposed to personal representatives) have power under the general law to appropriate any asset to any interest, provided that it is an interest of a kind which can be satisfied by appropriation (see *Re Freeston's Charity, Sylvester v University College Oxford* [1979] 1 All ER 51, [1978] 1 WLR 741 for an example of an interest not so susceptible, namely a right to receive half the income of a fund, as contrasted with a right to the income of half a fund, which could be the subject of an appropriation). This is because it seems there is always power to appropriate an asset which is an authorised investment, and without the consent of the beneficiaries to whose interests it is appropriated: *Re Wragg, Wragg v Palmer* [1919] 2 Ch 58 (a case concerning the power of trustees to appropriate land and private company shares to settled shares of a trust fund). The TrA 2000 renders legal estates in land and all assets other than land authorised investments (see paras **[220.12]** and **[220.17]**). Therefore, trustees have a general power to appropriate trust assets. However, it is not an entirely certain conclusion, and there are the other reasons for conferring express power to appropriate mentioned in this paragraph, see paras **[220.70]**, **[220.72]** and **[220.73]**. We therefore still recommend that express powers of appropriation are conferred in wills. Where land is held on trust in undivided shares for absolutely entitled beneficiaries of full age, the trustees of the land are given power by the TLATA 1996, s 7 (Part G, para **[246.109]** corresponding with the power formerly vested in trustees for sale by the LPA 1925, s 28(3)) to partition land with the beneficiaries' consent. This power may now be redundant, at any rate in respect of land held for a legal estate, if the view expressed here that trustees have power of appropriation under the general law anyway is correct. On appropriation, see further Vol 1, paras **[29.1]** ff.

[220.72]
Tax aspects. An appropriation by personal representatives does not generally give rise to any capital gains tax charge (Taxation of Chargeable Gains Act 1992, s 62(4), together with ss 64(2) and 62(3)). However, if an asset with a value in excess of a beneficiary's entitlement under the will is transferred to the beneficiary upon the beneficiary paying the excess, a capital gains tax charge may arise because this will be treated as a sale of the asset, see *Passant v Jackson* [1986] STC 164.

Generally, an appropriation of an interest in land by personal representatives is exempt from stamp duty land tax, even if made with consents. This is achieved by FA 2003, Sch 3, para 3A(1) which provides that the acquisition of property by a person in or towards satisfaction of his entitlement under or in relation to the will of a deceased person, or on the intestacy of a deceased person, is exempt from charge. This exemption does not apply, however, if the person acquiring the property gives any consideration for it, other than the assumption of secured debt (FA 2003, Sch 3, para 3A(2)). Here a secured debt means an obligation, whether certain or contingent, to pay a sum of money either immediately or at a future date, and which immediately after the death of the deceased person is secured on the property (FA 2003, Sch 3, para 3A(4)). So, for example, the appropriation of a house subject to a mortgage at the deceased's death, in satisfaction of a legacy of an amount equivalent to the value of the equity of redemption will not be liable to stamp duty land tax. Conversely, if a house is appropriated in full satisfaction of a legacy for a lesser amount than the value of the house, with the legatee paying the difference to the personal representatives, this difference will be liable to stamp duty land tax.

Further, even after the administration of an estate is complete, an appropriation of land by trustees, even with consents, may be exempt from stamp duty land tax. FA 2003, Sch 16, para 8 (added by FA 2006, s 165 with effect in relation to any acquisition of which the effective date is on or after 19 July 2006) provides that where trustees of a settlement reallocate trust property in such a way that a beneficiary acquires an interest in certain trust property and ceases to have an interest in other trust property, and the beneficiary consents to ceasing to have an interest in that other property, the fact that he gives consent does not mean that there is chargeable consideration for the acquisition such as to give rise to an SDLT liability.

Stamp duty still applies to stock or marketable securities, and the requirement of a beneficiary's consent will not make an appropriation by personal representatives of stock or marketable securities in satisfaction of a general legacy of money subject to stamp duty (Finance Act 1985, s 84(4), and the Stamp Duty (Exempt Instruments) Regulations 1987). However, an appropriation by trustees rather than by personal representatives with the consent of a beneficiary would probably be liable to ad valorem stamp duty because there is no specific exemption for such an appropriation, and there is authority for saying that the requirement of consent makes an appropriation subject to stamp duty, see *Jopling v IRC* [1940] 2 KB 282, [1940] 3 All ER 279, and Vol 1, para **[29.16]**.

[220.73]

Tax aspects—capital gains tax deemed disposal deferment. The presence or absence of an express power of appropriation can also be important as to whether and when there is a capital gains tax charge on beneficiaries becoming absolutely entitled. This is best illustrated by an example. Suppose that a trust fund is held on trust for such of three siblings A, B, and C as attain the age of 25, if more than one in equal shares. A is three years older than B, and B is three years older than C. When A attains 25, he becomes absolutely entitled to one third of the fund and thus there is a deemed disposal at market value of that one third by virtue of the Taxation of Chargeable Gains Act 1992, s 71 if neither of the exceptions referred to below applies. The first exception is that if and insofar as the trust fund consists of land, when A attains 25 he will not become absolutely entitled to any of that land or assets representing it until the land is sold or there is an appropriation or partition, or C attains twenty-five (A and B already having attained that age) so that all three then become together absolutely entitled to the land. This follows from *Stephenson v Barclays Bank Trust Co* [1975] 1 All ER 625, [1975] 1 WLR 882, *Pexton v Bell* [1975] 1 All ER 498, [1975] 1 WLR 707 and *Crowe v Appleby* [1975] 3 All ER 529, [1975] 1 WLR 1539 (High Court—the CA decision is on a different point). The second exception is that where the assets are not land but there is an express power of appropriation, HMRC take the view that the effect is the same as if the assets were land, the point presumably being that (continuing the above example) when A attains 25 he cannot claim any specific assets of the trust fund because the trustees could still exercise their power of appropriation to decide which specific assets he receives in satisfaction of his share (see HMRC's *Capital Gains Manual*, para 37530). If the argument set out at para **[220.71]** that the TrA 2000 has had the effect of conferring a general power of appropriation on all trustees is correct, HMRC practice should now be extended to all trusts including ones without an express power of appropriation. This HMRC view may be beneficial to the taxpayer because it enables the capital gains tax charge under the TCGA 1992, s 71 to be deferred, although there are situations where or it can be a disadvantage, for example where absolute entitlement when A attains eighteen, for example, would be an occasion when holdover relief could be obtained (for example where A is a beneficiary under a trust for bereaved minors or age 18-to-25 trusts, see paras **[200.108]–[200.109]** above), but the subsequent event (which is when A becomes absolutely entitled as a result of the presence of the power of appropriation) is one where hold-over relief is not obtainable.

[220.74]

Form B20.21: Power for trustees to appropriate

I declare that [notwithstanding the trust for sale hereinbefore contained][1] my trustees (whether acting as personal representatives or as trustees) may appropriate any real or personal property forming part of [my residuary estate] to or towards the share or interest whether settled or not of any person or persons in the proceeds of sale thereof under the trusts hereinbefore contained and may set apart any investments to answer any annuity hereby bequeathed and for the purposes aforesaid shall have and may at any time exercise all such powers of appropriation and other powers conferred upon personal representatives by section 41 of the Administration of Estates Act 1925[2] and with the same effect as set out in such section provided always that the power hereby conferred shall be additional to any power of appropriation or partition conferred upon my trustees by statute,[3] any such appropriation shall be valid and binding without the consent of the beneficiary or of any other person,[4] and any such appropriation shall be valid and binding notwithstanding that one or more of my trustees may be beneficially interested in the exercise of the said power.[5]

1 Trusts for sale are no longer necessary or desirable (see Part A, para **[200.55]**. Omit these words if there is no trust for sale.
2 As to the desirability of an express clause, see paras **[220.70]**–**[220.72]** and n 3 below.
3 Trustees have a statutory power of partition of land (TLATA 1996, s 7) but only where the beneficiaries are of full age, absolutely entitled in undivided shares, and consent.
4 Dispensing with consents to appropriations may make the administration easier: see para **[220.70]**.
5 See para **[220.70]** for the importance of including this provision.

[220.75]

Form B20.22: Another power for trustees to appropriate

I declare that my trustees (whether acting as personal representatives or as trustees) may at any time appropriate any part of the real or personal property (including things in action) forming part of [my residuary estate] in the actual condition or state of investment thereof at the time of appropriation in or towards satisfaction of any share or subdivided share in [my residuary estate] or the proceeds of sale of [my residuary estate] whether such share be settled or not and may for that purpose ascertain or fix the value of the property so to be appropriated [in accordance with the powers conferred on trustees by section 22(3) of the Trustee Act 1925] [as they shall think fit] [provided however that no such appropriation shall be made hereunder in respect of any share or subdivided share to which some person of full age and capacity is absolutely and beneficially entitled in possession without the consent of such person and no appropriation shall be made hereunder in respect of a settled share to the income whereof some person of full age and capacity is beneficially entitled in possession without the consent of such person but save as aforesaid no consent of any person shall be required].[1]

Every appropriation made thereunder [with such consent (if any) as aforesaid] shall bind all persons interested under this my will whether in the said share or subdivided share to which the appropriation is made or in any other share or otherwise under this my will, and every such appropriation shall be valid and binding notwithstanding that one of more of my trustees may be beneficially interested in the exercise of the said power.[2]

1 See para **[220.74]**, n 4.
2 See para **[220.70]** for the importance of this type of provision.

[220.76]

Form B20.23: Short form of power of appropriation, by reference to the statutory power

My trustees shall have all the powers of appropriation and other incidental powers conferred on personal representatives by statute whether they are acting as trustees or as personal representatives and although one or more of such trustees may be beneficially interested in the exercise of such powers[1] and without requiring any of the consents required by statute.

1 See Vol 1, para **[29.13]**.

[220.77]

Form B20.24: Clause allowing appropriation without the beneficiary's consent and where trustees are beneficially interested—alternative form[1]

I declare that my trustees may exercise the power of appropriation conferred upon them by section 41 of the Administration of Estates Act 1925[2] without obtaining any of the consents required by that section.

My trustees may so exercise such power of appropriation whether they are acting as personal representatives or as trustees, and even though they (or one or more of them) may be beneficially interested in such exercise.

My trustees shall wherever possible give to the persons whose consent would but for this provision be required by the said Act one month's notice of any intended appropriation but no purchaser shall be concerned to see or inquire whether such notices have been given.

1 See paras **[220.70]** and **[220.72]**.
2 See Part G, para **[246.65]**.

[220.78]

Form B20.25: Clause as to appropriation incorporating Statutory Will Forms 1925, Form 6

Statutory Will Forms 1925, Form No 6 is incorporated herein.[1]

1 For this form, see Part E, Form E6 at para **[238.12]**.

[220.79]

Form B20.26: Power of appropriation with consent of beneficiaries of full age[1]

My trustees may in extension of the power conferred on them by section 41 of the Administration of Estates Act 1925, at any time or times with the consent in writing only of all other persons for the time being entitled to share in my estate who are of full age and capacity appropriate any part of my residuary estate in its then actual condition of state of investment in or towards satisfaction of the share of any infant beneficiary in my estate. [For the purposes of this clause no consent shall be required in the case of any beneficiary or possible beneficiary whose address is not at the time of such intended appropriation known to my trustees. In all other cases my trustees shall give notice of such appropriation to all such beneficiaries of full age and capacity by sending notice thereof to the last known address of such beneficiary and if all such addresses are in Great Britain and Ireland then if no objection to the intended appropriation is received within one month of the date of posting of such notice my trustees shall assume that such consent has been given and be entitled to proceed with such appropriation without such consent in writing. If all such addresses are not in Great Britain and Ireland the last provision of this clause shall apply with the substitution of 'three months' for 'one month'.]

1 This clause is designed for use where all the gifts under the will are immediate and the desire is to distribute the estate as far as possible at the earliest date. As soon as the estate is cleared the trustees (which by the usual express definition will include the executors, so that there is no question of the power of appropriation being given both to the executors and to the trustees and it is not necessary to show that the executors have become trustees before they are entitled to exercise this power) can proceed to distribution, except in the case of the shares of minors which must be held pending the attainment of full age.

[220.80]

Form B20.27: Power for trustees to partition and appropriate land[1]

(a) My trustees may at any time partition any land for the time being unsold which forms part of my residuary estate among all or some of the aforesaid shares in my residuary estate and may also appropriate land to one only of such shares without partitioning or appropriating land to any other of such shares.

Provided that:

(i) An appropriation of land to any such share as aforesaid may be made without the consent or consents of any person or persons including that of the person (if any) of full age and capacity for the time being entitled as tenant for life under the trusts aforesaid to the income of such share.

(ii) An appropriation of land to any such share as aforesaid which has become absolutely vested in possession in a person of full age and capacity or in several persons in undivided shares may be made without the consent or consents of any person or persons.

(b) An appropriation of land made as aforesaid shall be binding upon all persons interested in the share to which the appropriation is made and upon all persons interested in every other share in my residuary estate notwithstanding that such persons may not be in existence or may be under disability or cannot be found or ascertained at the time of such appropriation or that one or more of the trustees making the appropriation are beneficially interested in my residuary estate.

In making any such partition or appropriation my trustees may arrange that land appropriated to any share in my residuary estate shall stand charged with any sum of money whether or not by way of equality money or partition in favour of my trustees as part of my undivided or undistributed residuary estate or in favour of some other share or shares.

(c) My trustees shall give effect to any such partition or appropriation hereunder by proper conveyance or other deeds and (if required) by executing or obtaining the execution of proper mortgages or charges and my trustees may appoint persons other than themselves to be trustees of any share in my residuary estate in the place of my trustees.

(d) For the purpose of any such partition or appropriation my trustees may (by duly qualified agents) ascertain and fix the value of any land proposed to be or about to be partitioned or appropriated in such manner as they think proper and any valuation so made shall be binding upon all persons interested under this my will.

1 The TLATA 1996, s 7 gives to trustees of land a power to partition unsold land, but only where the land has become absolutely vested in undivided shares. Where at the time of partition the trustees for sale themselves hold any individual share directly in trust for any immediate beneficiary for his life or other interest less than an absolute interest, such share is not absolutely vested for this purpose: *Re Thomas, Thomas v Thompson* [1930] 1 Ch 194, [1929] All ER Rep 129 (a case on the LPA 1925, s 28(3), but the provisions of it material to the decision on this point were essentially the same). Where at such time the trustees hold any individual share in trust for other trustees that share is absolutely vested in the other trustees within the meaning of the subsection: *Re Gorringe and Braybons Ltd's Contract* [1934] Ch 614n, *Re Brooker, Public Trustee v Young* [1934] Ch 610. Where trustees have at any time held a share for a person absolutely that share is held absolutely within the subsection although the owner may have subsequently settled it.

Apart from statute, or special provisions, trustees having a power to invest in land can, but trustees holding land on trust for sale cannot, appropriate land to a settled share (*Re Wragg, Wragg v Palmer* [1919] 2 Ch 58). Since all trustees now have power to invest in land (see para **[220.17]**) and trusts for sale are not necessary and no longer implied by law where there is co-ownership (see Part A, para **[200.54]**), trustees of land probably can all appropriate land to a settled share in the absence of express provision to this effect in the trust instrument, except, perhaps, where there is a trust for sale.

Inheritance tax

[220.81]

Form B20.28: General restriction to prevent administrative powers prejudicing inheritance tax status of beneficial trusts[1]

No power or provision herein contained shall be capable of being exercised or operating in any manner such that (if the same were capable of being so exercised or operating) the existence of such power or provision would either:

(a) prevent any person who would (in the absence of such power or provision) have had an interest in possession falling within section 49(1A) of IHTA 1984 in any fund or part or share of a fund from having such an interest in possession as aforesaid; or

(b) prevent section 71A or 71D of IHTA 1984 from applying to any trust to which (in the absence of such power or provision) either section would have applied.

1 For the reason for this form, see the Note on IHT at paras **[220.4]–[220.9]**. It has the disadvantage that when the trustees want to make some particular exercise of their powers this restriction might in some circumstances cause doubt as to whether they have power to do what they want.

Miscellaneous

[220.82]

Form B20.29: Power to give guarantees for loans to companies wholly or substantially owned by trustees

My trustees shall have power in their absolute discretion to give guarantees for the repayment of any loans made to companies wholly or substantially owned by them and shall be entitled to charge the whole or any part or parts of [the trust fund] in connection with such guarantees and be fully indemnified out of [the trust fund] against any personal liability to which they may become subject by reason of giving any such guarantees.

B21 Trustees and executors

MEANING OF 'MY TRUSTEES'
FORMS
B21.1 Definition of 'my trustees' .... **[221.1]**
B21.2 Short definition 'my trustees' .... **[221.2]**
B21.3 Powers conferred on trustees and executors .... **[221.3]**
SELF-DEALING
Note **[221.4]**
FORMS
B21.4 Clause giving named trustee power to purchase part of testator's estate with safeguard against improper purchase .... **[221.5]**
B21.5 Power to trustees to purchase the trust property—no safeguards .... **[221.6]**
B21.6 Power to trustees to purchase with safeguard against improper purchase .... **[221.7]**
B21.7 Power to a trustee to enter into any transaction provided there is at least one other trustee .... **[221.8]**
B21.8 Power to trustees to enter into transactions in two capacities .... **221.9]**
RETENTION OF DIRECTORS' REMUNERATION ETC
FORMS
B21.9 Power for trustees to become directors and to retain remuneration—short form .... **[221.10]**
B21.10 Power for trustees to become directors, retain remuneration and to hold shares as qualifying shares .... **[221.11]**
B21.11 Retention of benefits—fuller form including benefits from subsidiary companies .... **[221.12]**
INDEMNITIES, RELEASES AND RECEIPTS
Note .... **[221.13]**
FORMS
B21.12 General indemnity clause—proviso excluding professional and corporate trustees .... **[221.16]**
B21.13 Clause excluding the statutory duty of care .... **[221.17]**
B21.14 Indemnity to trustees acting on counsel's opinion .... **[221.18]**
B21.15 Liability for acts of an agent, nominee or custodian appointed under the Trustee Act 2000 .... **[221.19]**
B21.16 Liability for attorney's acts .... **[221.20]**
B21.17 No duty to intervene in the affairs of a private company .... **[221.21]**
B21.18 Power to life tenants of settled shares to give releases to trustees .... **[221.22]**
B21.19 Power to insure against liability for inheritance tax on lifetime dispositions .... **[221.23]**
B21.20 Receipts by or on behalf of minors .... **[221.24]**
B21.21 Receipts on behalf of charities and unincorporated associations .... **[221.25]**
B21.22 Missing beneficiaries .... **[221.26]**
CONDUCT OF TRUSTEESHIP
FORMS
B21.23 Clause excluding trustees' duty to consult with beneficiaries as to land .... **[221.27]**
B21.24 Direction as to order of names of trustees in the registers of companies to secure voting rights .... **[221.28]**
B21.25 Direction that opinion of majority of trustees is to prevail .... **[221.29]**
B21.26 Power authorising an audit .... **[221.30]**
B21.27 Direction to employ a named solicitor .... **[221.31]**
B21.28 Nomination of trust corporation to receive notices .... **[221.32]**

B21.29 Power to vest assets in nominees .... [221.33]
B21.30 Power to distribute on assumption that no further children .... [221.34]
APPOINTMENT AND RETIREMENT OF TRUSTEES
Note .... [221.35]
FORMS
B21.31 Power to appoint new trustees conferred by the Trustee Act 1925... [221.36]
B21.32 Power to appoint separate trustees of parts of trust property .... [221.37]
B21.33 Power to remove trustees .... [221.38]
B21.34 Clause excluding beneficiaries' statutory right to direct retirement and appointment of trustees .... [221.39]
B21.35 Direction as to keeping up the number of trustees .... [221.40]
B21.36 Variation of statutory power to facilitate appointment of foreign trustees, and a sole trustee .... [221.41]
POWER TO CHARGE
Note—Powers of charging after Trustee Act 2000 .... [221.42]
FORMS
B21.37 Power to professional trustee to charge—concise form .... [221.49]
B21.38 Power to professional trustee to charge—full form .... 221.50]
B21.39 Proviso enabling professional trustee to elect not to charge .... [221.51]
B21.40 Provision for appointment of trust corporation .... [221.52]

Cross References

For administration trusts, declarations concerning apportionment, incidence of IHT, see B14 at para **[214.1]** ff. For maintenance and advancement powers, powers to permit enjoyment in kind, general declarations concerning the exercise of powers, see B18 at para **[218.1]** ff. For administrative powers and provisions, see B20 at para **[220.1]** ff. For disclaimer and renunciation of probate or trusteeship, see F1 at para **[239.1]** ff.

MEANING OF 'MY TRUSTEES'

[221.1]

Form B21.1: Definition of 'my trustees'

I declare that in the interpretation of this my will the expression 'my trustees' shall (where the context permits) mean and include my personal representatives and the trustees hereof whether original or substituted and if there shall be no such trustees shall (where the context permits) include the persons empowered by statute to exercise or perform any power or trust hereby or by statute conferred upon my trustees and willing or bound to exercise or perform the same.[1]

1 It will be remembered that in all instruments the plural includes the singular and vice versa and the word person includes a corporation (LPA 1925, s 61: Part G, para **[246.54]**). As to persons, other than actual trustees, who are empowered to act, see the AEA 1925, s 1(2); the TA 1925, s 18(2) (Part G, para **[246.16]**) and the SLA 1925, s 30(3). For a definition of 'my trustees' where the partners of a solicitors' firm or members of an LLP are appointed, see Form B3.8 at para **[203.21]**.

[221.2]

Form B21.2: Short definition 'my trustees'

The expression 'my trustees' herein includes my personal representatives and the trustees of this Will for the time being.

[221.3]

Form B21.3: Powers conferred on trustees and executors

For the avoidance of doubt it is hereby declared that every power hereby or by any codicil hereto conferred on my trustees including any power of appointment or application of capital or income (but excluding any power relating to the payment or satisfaction or incidence as between persons interested in my estate of debts administration expenses taxes and general legacies) shall be exercisable both during and after the completion of the administration of my estate and whether my trustees are for the time being holding as personal representatives or as trustees the property comprised in or derived from my estate in relation to which they exercise such power.[1]

1 Where, as is usually the case, the definition of 'my trustees' includes both personal representatives and trustees, and a power is conferred on 'my trustees', it seems obvious that the power can be exercised whether 'my trustees' are for the time being personal representatives or trustees. However, HMRC have in the past tried in some cases to argue that powers of appointment conferred on 'my trustees' cannot be exercised until the administration is complete (so as to argue that advantage cannot be taken of the ITA 1984, s 144 before the administration is complete—for s 144 see C3 at para **[225.83]** ff). This provision is intended to make the position clear. Where a testator granted remuneration to 'my trustees' for services as executors and trustees, and further defined trustees as the trustees whether original substituted or otherwise, the right to remuneration was not confined to trustees who also acted as executors: *Re Chirnside, Lewis v Forrest* [1956] VLR 295. For exercise of a power before grant of probate, see Form C3.6, cl 3(2)(ii) and (iii) at para **[225.101]**.

SELF-DEALING

[221.4]

Note. As to the fiduciary position of trustees which prevents them in ordinary circumstances purchasing the trust property or any part of it, see *Mackreth v Fox* (1791) 4 Bro Parl Cas 258; *Thomson v Eastwood* (1877) 2 App Cas 215. For a case in which the self-dealing rule was held in the special circumstances of the case not to apply to a purchasing executor who had renounced probate see *Holder v Holder* [1968] Ch 353, [1968] 1 All ER 665. The rule extends to any transaction where a trustee's duty as trustee and his personal interest conflict, including one with a company in which the trustee has a substantial interest: see *Re Thompson's Settlement, Thompson v Thompson* [1986] Ch 99, [1985] 2 All ER 720. The rule also applies to personal representatives or trustees exercising powers relating to beneficial interests in their own favour. See para **[218.4]** for the rule as it applies to the exercise of powers of appointment and similar powers or discretions. The rule against self-dealing has also been held to apply to the widow and sole administratrix of the estate of an intestate purporting to make an appropriation of private company shares in satisfaction of her statutory legacy—the purported appropriation was held to be invalid on this ground: see *Kane v Radley-Kane* [1999] Ch 274, [1998] 3 All ER 753. Self-dealing can be authorised by the will, and authorising it should be considered where executors are being appointed who might have the greatest interest in purchasing property in the estate, such as farming partners of the deceased or co-directors or co-shareholders of a private company, or where the trustees or personal representatives are or might be persons who are also beneficially interested. Forms B21.4 to B21.8 at paras **[221.5]–[221.9]** are powers for the trustees to enter into purchases, sales or similar dealings with the trust funds. For a power for trustees to exercise beneficial powers in their own favour, see Form B18.32 at para **[218.117]**. For powers for trustees to appropriate in their own favour, see Forms B20.21 ff at para **[220.74]** ff.

[221.5]

Form B21.4: Clause giving named trustee power to purchase part of testator's estate with safeguard against improper purchase

I declare that the said A B one of the trustees of this my will shall have the power to buy any portion of my estate real or personal either by private treaty or public auction including the right to bid at any public auction notwithstanding he is a trustee of this my will and in the event of a sale by private treaty the price shall be such as may be agreed upon between the said A B and my other trustees provided that in the case of quoted securities the purchase price shall not be less than the current market price thereof at the time of the execution of the transfer and in the case of other property my trustees other than the said A B shall obtain a valuation of and a report on the property by an independent surveyor or valuer (to be paid for by the said A B) and the purchase price shall not be less than the amount of such valuation and no sale shall be made if the report shall advise against a sale for any reason whatsoever.

[221.6]

Form B21.5: Power to trustees to purchase the trust property—no safeguards

I authorise my son [*name*] notwithstanding that he shall be a trustee of this my will [*or* my trustees or any of them] at any time or times to purchase whether at any public auction or by private contract all or any part of the property forming my residuary estate.

[221.7]

Form B21.6: Power to trustees to purchase with safeguard against improper purchase

Any of my trustees may notwithstanding that he is a trustee purchase from or sell to my estate or any trust fund deriving therefrom any property provided that in the case of quoted securities the purchase price shall not be less than the current market price thereof at the time of the execution of the transfer or in the case of property of any other character my trustees shall previously have obtained a valuation and report on the proposed sale by an independent surveyor or professional valuer appointed by the trustees for the time being other than the proposed purchaser (such valuation and report to be paid for by the proposed purchaser) and that the purchase price shall not be less than the amount of such valuation and the said surveyor or valuer shall not have advised against such sale for any reason.

[221.8]

Form B21.7: Power to a trustee to enter into any transaction provided there is at least one other trustee

Any of my trustees may contract or otherwise deal with my trustees as vendor or purchaser or otherwise provided that there is at least one other of my trustees agreeing in writing to the contract or dealing who has no interest in such contract or dealing save as one of my trustees.

[221.9]

Form B21.8: Power to trustees to enter into transactions in two capacities

My trustees may in their absolute discretion enter into any agreement or effect any transaction (hereby or by law authorised) with the trustee or trustees of any settlement or will notwithstanding that my trustees or one or more of them may also be trustees or a trustee or the sole trustee of such settlement or such will and may enter into any agreement or effect any transaction (hereby or by law authorised) involving a company notwithstanding that they or any one or more of them may be in any capacity directors or a director shareholders or a shareholder of such company.

RETENTION OF DIRECTORS' REMUNERATION ETC

[221.10]

Form B21.9: Power for trustees to become directors and to retain remuneration[1]—short form

I declare that any one or more of my trustees may act as a director officer or other employee of [the said —— Company Limited] [any company] and may receive remuneration or any other benefit for so acting without being liable to account for the same to my estate or the persons beneficially interested therein.

1 A trustee cannot make any profit out of his trust and would in the ordinary course be liable to account for all director's fees received by him: *Re Macadam, Dallow v Codd* [1946] Ch 73, [1945] 2 All ER 664; *Re Llewellin's Will Trusts, Griffiths v Wilcox* [1949] Ch 225, [1949] 1 All ER 487. The ordinary charging clause would not give a trustee-director power to retain such remuneration: *Re Gee* [1948] Ch 284, [1948] 1 All ER 498. However, a trustee is not liable to account where his position as director, officer or employee is owed entirely to votes other than those attached to the trust assets (*Re Gee* above).

[221.11]

Form B21.10: Power for trustees to become directors, retain remuneration and to hold shares as qualifying shares

My trustees or any of them may become directors officers or employees of [—— Company Limited] [any company] and may receive the remuneration or other benefits attaching to such office or employment without being liable to account for the same and any trustee may become qualified as a director (if the articles of the said company so allow) by holding in his own name shares belonging to my estate provided that he executes a declaration of trust thereof in favour of my trustees generally accompanied by the certificates of such shares and that he accounts to my estate for all dividends and bonuses payable in respect therof.[1]

1 If the company is governed by Table A of the Companies Act 1948, a holding as trustee is sufficient qualification unless in the articles or the qualification as fixed in general meeting (see Table A, Part I, art 77 as contained in the Companies Act 1948, Sch 1) it is stated to the contrary: *Pulbrook v Richmond Consolidated Mining Co* (1878) 9 Ch D 610. The new Table A in the Companies (Tables A to F) Regulations 1985, SI 1985/805, does not contain the old art 77 as share qualifications for directors are now less common.

[221.12]

Form B21.11: Retention of benefits—fuller form including benefits from subsidiary companies

Any of my trustees may act as a director officer or employee of any company in which [my residuary estate] or any part or share thereof may be invested or as a director officer or employee of any subsidiary of any such company and any such trustee may retain any remuneration or benefit deriving from such office or employment for his own use and benefit absolutely notwithstanding that any votes or other rights incident to assets of [my residuary estate] may have been instrumental in procuring for him or continuing him in such office or employment or that his qualification for such office or employment may be constituted in whole or in part by assets comprised in [my residuary estate].

INDEMNITIES, RELEASES AND RECEIPTS

[221.13]

Note. What are usually referred to as trustee indemnity clauses are in reality clauses which absolve trustees or executors from liability for their own negligence or from vicarious liability for the negligence or fraud of co-trustees or agents. The ills of twenty-first century civilisation, and in particular monetary and other instabilities, volatility in investment markets, and the increased popularity of professional negligence litigation, make it understandable that anyone accepting office as an executor or trustee should want protection of this kind. Indeed, anyone accepting such an office as a personal favour, and who will not be covered by professional negligence insurance when acting as trustee or personal representative, should in our opinion have the benefit of such a clause. Absolution from negligence liability seems less appropriate in the case of a professional trustee who charges for his services and is covered by insurance, and especially inappropriate in the case of a trust corporation: see, for example, the view of Millett LJ as expressed in *Armitage v Nurse* [1998] Ch 241, [1997] 2 All ER 705. It was, however, confirmed in the latter case that the liability of trustees, including professional trustees, for negligence, can be excluded. In *Wight v Olswang* (1999) Times, 18 May, CA it was held that where a settlement had two trustee exemption clauses, one protecting all trustees from liability for breach of trust and one which expressly did not apply to paid trustees, the paid trustees could not rely on the general exemption. There is also a prudential reason for a professional trustee not to exclude negligence liability. This is that if it is excluded, and there are beneficiaries who become so indignant about something the trustees have done (or not done) as to be determined to sue, those beneficiaries will be driven back onto alleging fraud or deliberate wrongdoing, which will not normally be covered by the trustee's professional negligence insurance, and depending on the facts, the negligence insurers may have no obligation to pay for the defence of the trustee against the allegations or any interest in doing so. *Walker v Stones* [2001] QB 902, [2000] 4 All ER 412 is an example of beneficiaries making this sort of allegation where the trustees had the benefit of a clause in the settlement excluding liability for negligence—the trust fund sustained a substantial loss as a result of the trustees guaranteeing a loan as part of providing finance for a company run by the settlor (the settlor being excluded from benefit under the settlement); the trustees said that they believed it to be for the benefit of the beneficiaries; the Court of Appeal held that there was a triable issue as to whether this was a dishonest breach of trust, on the basis that it might have been so unreasonable a belief that, by any objective standard, no reasonable solicitor trustee could have thought that what he did was for the benefit of the beneficiaries.

It has been judicially observed that a solicitor should always draw the testator's attention to any indemnity clause which it is proposed be included in the will, and should advise him upon it. In that way there cannot be any argument that the testator did not know of it and approve it, so that the solicitor, if he is appointed executor and trustee, is entitled to the benefit of it. He does not though have to advise the testator to take separate legal advice upon it: see *Bogg v*

Raper (1998) Times, 22 April, CA. Now this area is the subject of a Law Commission Report on 'Trustee Exemption Clauses' (Law Com 301, July 2006) which has concluded that trustees should be required to ensure that settlors are aware of any trustee exemption clauses in their trust deeds. The idea of introducing a statutory requirement to this effect was rejected by the Law Commission on the grounds that it could be likely to give rise to delay and additional cost when setting up a trust and to uncertainty as to the validity of the clause. The Report therefore recommends a rule of practice that:

> 'Any paid trustee who causes a settlor to include a clause in a trust instrument which has the effect of excluding or limiting liability for negligence must before the creation of the trust take such steps as are reasonable to ensure that the settlor is aware of the meaning and effect of the clause.'

The Law Commission encourages relevant regulatory and professional bodies to adopt a version of the rule appropriate to the particular circumstances of their membership, and to enforce such regulation in accordance with their existing codes of conduct. Although breach of this rule would not give rise in itself to liability in damages, it could give rise to disciplinary measures by the relevant governing body.

Guidance notes 66 and 67 to Rule 2 of the Solicitors Code of Conduct, which came into force on 1 July 2007, provide as follows:

'66. Where you are preparing a trust instrument for a client and that instrument includes a term or terms which has or have the effect of excluding or limiting liability in negligence for a prospective trustee, you should take reasonable steps before the trust is created to ensure that your client is aware of the meaning and effect of the clause. Extra care will be needed if you are, or anyone in or associated with your firm is, or is likely later to become, a paid trustee of the trust.

67. Where you or another person in, or associated with, your firm is considering acting as a paid trustee you should not cause to be included a clause in a trust instrument which has the effect of excluding or limiting liability for negligence without taking reasonable steps before the trust is created to ensure that the settlor is aware of the meaning and effect of the clause.'

It would be prudent to ensure both that:

(a) there is evidence that you have taken the appropriate steps; and
(b) that evidence is retained for as long as the trust exists and for a suitable period afterwards.'

The Society of Trust and Estate Practitioners (England and Wales), STEP, have issued the following practice rule for its members to apply in relation to wills executed on or after 19 July 2006:

'STEP Practice Rule in relation to Trustee Exemption Clauses

1. Where a member prepares, or causes to be prepared, a will or other testamentary document or a trust instrument (each an 'Instrument'), or is aware of being named as an original trustee or executor in an Instrument:
   a)
      i) in which he, or any trustee or executor, is entitled to remuneration under the terms of the Instrument; or
      ii) where he has, or may expect to have, a Financial Interest in the trusteeship or executorship of the trust or will or the preparation of the Instrument; and
   b) any one or more of the circumstances described in paragraph 2 below applies (together 'the Disclosable Circumstances'), such member shall use his reasonable endeavours to ensure:
      (i) that he or another shall have notified the Settlor of the provisions in the Instrument or the original trustee or executor's terms and conditions relating to the Disclosable Circumstances; and
      (ii) that he has reasonable grounds for believing that the Settlor has given his full and informed acceptance of such provisions prior to his execution or approval of the Instrument.
2. The Disclosable Circumstances referred to in paragraph 1 above are the existence of

provisions in the Instrument or the original trustee or executor's terms and conditions the effect of which limit or exclude the liability of a trustee or executor for negligence.

3. In this rule

a) 'Financial Interest' means circumstances where the member benefits or reasonably expects to benefit (whether directly or indirectly) from providing a service as trust advisor or as trustee.

b) 'Settlor' means any person who would be a principal initial settlor in relation to a settlement, or at whose directions the Instrument is created.

4 This rule shall be subordinate to any legislation or other binding provision of law in any jurisdiction where the member shall practise and shall only apply to Instruments governed by the law of England and Wales.'

STEP has produced guidance notes on the application of this rule which amongst other things give a suggested form of disclosure as follows:

A STEP Member writing to the settlor/testator could state:

> 'I should also draw your attention to clause [X]. This clause provides that no [executor of your will/trustee] will be personally liable for any act by them in that capacity unless they are guilty of fraud. [If an [executor/trustee] is paid for their services then they will also be liable if they are negligent]. If you have any queries in relation to this, then please let me know.'

If the STEP Member is preparing the document for someone else to send to the settlor/testator then he might include the following:

> 'I should also draw your attention to the trustee exoneration clause in clause [X]. I recommend that you highlight this provision to the [settlor/testator] and explain that it provides that no [executor of the will/trustee] will be personally liable for any act by them in that capacity unless they are guilty of fraud. [If an [executor/trustee] is paid for their services then they will also be liable if they are negligent.]'

[221.14]

Where under the power in the Trusts of Land and Appointment of Trustees Act 1996 (TLATA 1996), s 9(1) (Part G, para **[246.111]**; see also para **[220.54]** ff), trustees of land delegate any of their functions relating to the land to a beneficiary, the TLATA 1996, s 9A (inserted by the Trustee Act 2000 (TrA 2000): Part G, para **[246.112]**), imposes a statutory duty of care on trustees when deciding to delegate the function to him, and when reviewing the delegation. It is not clear whether this liability is capable of being excluded by trustee indemnity clauses in the will or settlement: see para **[220.56]**. Trustees' liability for the acts and defaults of an agent, nominee or custodian appointed under the TrA 2000, ss 11, 16, 17 or 18, (Part G, paras **[246.144]** and **[246.158]**–**[246.160]**) is limited by the TLATA 1996, s 23 (Part G, para **[246.109]**) to cases where the trustees have failed to comply with their statutory duty of care when entering into or reviewing the arrangement (see para **[221.15]** for the statutory duty of care). The TrA 2000, s 21(3) provides that if the application of s 23 is inconsistent with the terms of the will, it does not apply. But whether this applies to the case where the trustees exercise the statutory powers, in addition to cases where they exercise express powers, is not clear. Whereas the TrA 2000, s 21(2), which provides for s 23 to apply to a case where trustees exercise express powers to appoint an agent, nominee or custodian, is expressly made subject to s 21(3), s 21(1)—which provides for s 23 to apply to a case where trustees exercise the statutory powers—is not. However, it may be possible to exclude liability for all acts or defaults of an agent, nominee or substitute appointed under the statutory powers by expressly excluding the statutory duty of care in the will: TrA 2000, Sch 1 para 7, (Part G, para **[246.173]**). If it is excluded, then it is difficult to see how the trustees can be made liable for failing to comply with it. For a form excluding the statutory duty of care in this regard, see Form B21.15 at para **[221.19]**. Where a personal representative or trustee takes advantage of the Trustee Act 1925, s 25 (on or after 1 March 2000, as substituted by the Trustee Delegation Act 1999: see Part G, para **[246.22]**) to delegate the execution or exercise of all or any of his trusts, powers and discretions, his liability for the acts or defaults of the donee imposed by subs (7) probably can be excluded, since the powers of the TA 1925 apply if and so far only as a contrary intention is not expressed, and subject to the terms of the will: see the TA 1925, s 69(2), the Note at para **[221.35]** and Form B21.16 at para **[221.20]**.

[221.15]

Statutory duty of care. The TrA 2000 imposes a statutory duty of care which applies (unless expressly excluded) not only to trustees or personal representatives exercising the new powers of investment conferred by the TrA 2000, but also to trustees exercising similar powers conferred on them expressly (eg by will) or by other Acts, whether before or after the passing of the TrA 2000, and to the exercise of various other powers, set out below. This statutory duty has both subjective and objective elements, and is a duty for the trustee to exercise such care and skill as is reasonable in the circumstances, having regard in particular to any special knowledge or experience that he has or holds himself out as having (the subjective element), and if he acts in the course of a business or profession, to any special knowledge or experience that it is reasonable to expect of a person acting in the course of that kind of business or profession (the objective element): see the TrA 2000, s 1 (Part G, para **[246.133]**). In the absence of this statutory duty, a trustee always has, of course, when exercising his powers, been subject to fiduciary duties of care arising under the general law, eg a duty to invest the trust fund as an ordinary prudent man of business, or according to a higher standard if he is a professional trustee: see *Bartlett v Barclay's Bank Trust Co Ltd* [1980] Ch 515, [1980] 1 All ER 139. However, it was thought by the Law Commission that by enshrining such a duty in statute, certainty and consistency would be brought to the standard of competence and behaviour expected of trustees.

The majority of the occasions when the statutory duty of care applies are set out in the TrA 2000, Sch 1 (Part G, para **[246.173]**) and are when trustees are exercising or carrying out—

(a) any power of investment, however conferred (eg by the TrA 2000, s 3 or by the will or other trust instrument), and the duties of having regard to the 'standard investment criteria' and obtaining advice, and of reviewing investments, as set out in TrA 2000, ss 4 and 5 (see Part G, paras **[246.136]** and **[246.137]**; see also **[220.12]** ff);

(b) the power to acquire land conferred by TrA 2000, s 8 (see para **[220.17]**) or any other such power (eg one conferred by the will or other trust instrument), or any power in relation to land acquired under such a power (see para **[220.49]** ff)—the latter category probably includes exercise of powers in relation to land acquired before 1 February 2001 under a power to do so, but clearly does not include exercise of powers in relation to land which is comprised in the testator's estate at his death and devolves on the trustees of his will;

(c) any power to appoint an agent, nominee or custodian, (however conferred, eg by the TrA 2000, ss 11, 16, 17 or 18 or by the will—see para **[220.35]** ff and Part G, paras **[246.143]** and **[246.148]–[246.150]**), and the duties to review such appointment (as set out in the TrA 2000, s 22: Part G, para **[246.154]**);
(d) any power to compound liabilities, compromise claims or any other powers contained in the TA 1925, s 15 (Part G, para **[246.13]**) or corresponding powers otherwise conferred;
(e) any power to insure property (however conferred, eg by the TA 1925, s 19: Part G, para **[246.17]** or by the will); and
(f) any power in relation to the valuation of reversionary property and other trust property (however conferred, eg by the TA 1925, s 22(1) or (3): Part G, para **[246.20]** or by the will).

The statutory duty of care may, however, be excluded or restricted by the will or other trust instrument (see the TrA 2000, Sch 1, para 7) and a testator may wish to exclude it, particularly if he is appointing family or friends to be his executors and trustees. See, eg Form B21.23 at para **[221.27]**. The statutory duty of care also applies in relation to delegation of land management powers to a beneficiary with an interest in possession, where it is not clear whether it may be excluded: see para **[220.56]**.

[221.16]

Form B21.12: General indemnity clause—proviso excluding professional and corporate trustees[1]

In the professed[2] administration of my estate[3] and the professed[4] execution of the trusts powers or provisions of this will or any codicil hereto none of my trustees shall be liable (whether for breach of the duty of care under the Trustee Act 2000 or otherwise) for any act or omission of his or for any act or omission of any co-personal representative or co-trustee of his or of any agent, nominee or custodian[5] employed in the administration of my estate or the execution of the said trusts powers and provisions save for any act or omission involving wilful fraud or dishonesty[6] committed by the personal representative or trustee sought to be made liable. And in particular but without prejudice to the generality of the foregoing provision none of my trustees shall be bound to take any proceedings against a co-trustee or past trustee or his personal representatives for any breach or alleged breach of trust committed or suffered by such co-trustee. [Provided that this clause shall not apply to a corporation and shall not apply to an individual authorised hereby or by law[7] to charge for acting as a personal representative or trustee [unless he has elected in writing not to charge for so acting at or before the time of his obtaining a grant of representation or (not having obtained such a grant) his being first appointed as trustee]].[8]

1 If a paid trustee is to rely on this indemnity clause which excludes liability in negligence, the testator should specifically be made aware of its meaning and effect (see para **[221.13]** above).

2 By applying to acts or defaults in the 'professed' administration of the estate and execution of the trusts, the trustees will be exonerated, save to the extent excluded by the clause, ie wilful fraud or dishonesty, for anything done by them in the 'purported' administration

and execution of the trusts of the will, i e even though in fact not done in the administration or execution: see *Walker v Stones* [2000] 4 All ER 412, [2001] 2 WLR 623, CA at 440E–F and 654A–B respectively.

3 It is doubtful whether a provision of this kind can limit the rights of the creditors to make claims for e g negligence against the personal representatives. It is unclear whether such a provision can absolve trustees of land from liability under the TLATA 1996, s 9A in respect of the delegation of their functions under the TLATA 1996, s 9(1): see para **[220.56]**.

4 See n 1 above.

5 If trustees are to be absolved from all liability for the acts or defaults of any agent, nominee or custodian appointed under the TrA 2000, the clause in Form B21.15 at para **[221.19]** should be used in addition to this clause. See para **[221.14]**.

6 In *Walker v Stones* [2000] 4 All ER 412, [2001] 2 WLR 623, CA Sir Christopher Slade considered that a clause exonerating trustees save for 'wilful fraud or dishonesty', as here, was not materially different from a clause exonerating trustees save for 'actual fraud', as was considered by the Court of Appeal in *Armitage v Nurse* [1998] Ch 241; [1997] 2 All ER 705. Millett LJ said in *Armitage v Nurse* that the words 'actual fraud' excluded constructive fraud and equitable fraud and simply connoted dishonesty. Accordingly, such a clause would exempt a trustee from liability for loss unless caused by his own dishonesty, however, indolent, imprudent, lacking in diligence, negligent or wilful he might have been, and was not void for repugnancy or on the grounds of public policy. A trustee would, however, be treated as acting dishonestly if he acted in a way which he did not honestly believe was in the interests of the beneficiaries, whether or not he stood to gain personally from his actions. Sir Christopher Slade in *Walker v Stones* at 660C qualified this, at least in the case of a solicitor-trustee, with the observation that a clause such as this would not exempt trustees from liability for breaches of trust, even if committed in the genuine belief that the course taken by them was in the interests of the beneficiaries, if such belief was so unreasonable that no reasonable solicitor trustee could have held that belief.

7 Under the TrA 2000, s 29(2) an individual who acts as trustee in a professional capacity is entitled to reasonable remuneration for his services provided on or after 1 February 2001, (whenever the will was made or the testator died: see s 33(1)) with the written agreement of his co-trustee or co-trustees if the will does not include a remuneration clause

8 It may be thought undesirable for a paid trustee to have the benefit of this indemnity, in which case provision can be made to that effect: see para **[221.13]**. Sometimes, however, a relative or friend of the testator may accept office as executor or trustee as a personal favour, but also be among the categories of person able to charge. He might prefer not to charge and have the benefit of this clause—indeed, he might be a non-practising solicitor and have no negligence insurance. For a complementary proviso to a charging clause, see Form B21.39 at para **[221.51]**.

[221.17]

Form B21.13: Clause excluding the statutory duty of care[1]

The duty of care contained in section 1 of the Trustee Act 2000 shall not apply in relation in relation to [any of] my trustees [who does not act as trustee in the course of a business or profession].[2]

1 For the statutory duty of care under the TrA 2000, s 1 and Sch 1, and its exclusion by express provision, see para **[221.15]** (Part G, paras **[246.133]** and **[246.173]**). Even though the statutory duty of care is excluded, a trustee is still, of course, subject to duties arising under the general law, e g a duty to invest the trust fund as an ordinary prudent man of business, unless he is a professional trustee when the standard of care will be higher: see *Bartlett v Barclay's Bank Trust Co Ltd* [1980] Ch 515, [1980] 1 All ER 139. Liability under the general law can also be excluded: see para **[221.13]** and Form B21.12 at para **[221.16]**.

2 See para **[221.16]**, n 7.

[221.18]

Form B21.14: Indemnity to trustees acting on counsel's opinion[1]

No trustee hereof shall be personally liable for any act or omission done or made in accordance with the written opinion of counsel [of at least [10]

years call] practising at the Chancery Bar upon any question whatsoever of interpretation including questions in connection with the administration of the trusts hereof.[2]

1 Sometimes clauses have been inserted in wills purporting to empower counsel employed by the trustees conclusively to determine the construction of a will. Such clauses try to oust the jurisdiction of the court and for this reason they are objectionable: see *Re Wynn* [1952] Ch 271, [1952] 1 All ER 341; *Re Bromson* [1958] OR 367. The insertion of a clause providing for the forfeiture of the interest of any beneficiary who disputes the decision of the trustees or of counsel advising the trustees is sometimes asked for but such a clause is not recommended. The court will always entertain bona fide proceedings in spite of any such clause and will not allow a forfeiture: *Adams v Adams* [1892] 1 Ch 369; *Re Raven, Spencer v National Association for the Prevention of Consumption and Other Forms of Tuberculosis* [1915] 1 Ch 673. It is quite a different matter to absolve the trustees from all personal liability if they act upon counsel's written opinion and this form of the clause, which has much the same result, is free from objection, though whether a trustee would be able to distribute on the strength of such an opinion if he knew of an adverse claim is open to doubt. For the High Court's power to authorise personal representatives and trustees to act on the opinion of counsel of ten years standing (or the opinion of any other person who has a ten year High Court qualification, within the meaning of the Courts and Legal Services Act 1990, s 71) without hearing argument, see the Administration of Justice Act 1985, s 48.

2 If a paid trustee is to rely on this indemnity clause which may limit his liability in negligence in that it may absolve him from negligent failure to question counsel's advice, the testator should specifically be made aware of its meaning and effect (see para **[221.13]** above).

[221.19]

Form B21.15: Liability for acts of an agent, nominee or custodian appointed under the Trustee Act 2000[1]

The duty of care of the Trustee Act 2000 shall not apply to any of my trustees when entering into any arrangements under the Trustee Act 2000 under which any person acts as agent nominee or custodian or when agreeing a term under which the agent nominee or custodian is permitted to appoint a substitute or when carrying out any duties under Section 22 of the Trustee Act 2000 and none of my trustees shall be liable for any act or default of any agent nominee or custodian appointed under the Trustee Act 2000 or of any substitute appointed by any such agent nominee or custodian[2] [Provided that this clause shall not apply to a corporation and shall not apply to an individual authorised hereby or by law to charge for acting as a personal representative or trustee [unless he has elected in writing not to charge for so acting at or before the time of his obtaining a grant of representation or (not having obtained such a grant) his being first appointed as trustee]].[3]

1 If a paid trustee is to rely on this indemnity clause which may limit his liability in negligence in that it may absolve him from negligent failure to intervene to prevent loss, the testator should specifically be made aware of its meaning and effect (see para **[221.13]** above).

2 It is thought that this clause should have the effect of excluding a trustee's liability for the acts or defaults of an agent, nominee or custodian (or their substitute) appointed under the TrA 2000. See para **[221.14]**.

3 See Form B21.12, nn 6 and 7 at para **[221.16]**.

[221.20]

Form B21.16: Liability for attorney's acts[1]

Notwithstanding subsection (7) of section 25 of the Trustee Act 1925 (as substituted by the Trustee Delegation Act 1999)[2] the donor of a power of attorney made pursuant to that section (as so substituted) shall not be liable for the acts or defaults of the donee.

1 If a paid trustee is to rely on this indemnity clause which may limit his liability in negligence in that it may absolve him from negligent failure to intervene to prevent loss, the testator should specifically be made aware of its meaning and effect (see para **[221.13]** above).

2 The TA 1925, s 25 has been substituted by the TDA 1999, s 5(1), (2) in relation to powers of attorney created on or after 1 March 2000, and is printed as so substituted in Part G, para **[246.21]**. For the ability to exclude a trustee's liability for the acts and defaults of an attorney appointed under this section, see para **[221.14]**.

[221.21]

Form B21.17: No duty to intervene in the affairs of a private company[1]

My trustees shall not be under any duty to require or compel the payment of any dividend by, or interfere in or inquire into the management or conduct of the business of, any company in which [my residuary estate] may wholly or partly be invested (however extensive may be the control of such company conferred by shares or securities comprised in [my residuary estate]) or may otherwise be interested directly or indirectly[2] and in the absence of actual notice of dishonesty on the part of the directors of such company may leave the conduct of such company's affairs and the payment or non-payment of dividends wholly to its directors.[3]

1 This form has two rather different functions. First, it gives the trustees a discretion as to whether to leave the profits of a private company in which the trustees have shares to be accumulated and reinvested inside the company instead of being distributed as dividends; without this clause they would be prima facie under a duty to obtain an income from the shares (see para **[220.33]**), but retention of profits by the company may have fiscal and investment advantages (albeit to the disadvantage of the income beneficiaries). Second, the clause absolves the trustees from negligent failure to intervene to prevent loss. For examples of the latter type of liability see *Re Lucking's Will Trusts, Renwick v Lucking* [1967] 3 All ER 726, [1968] 1 WLR 866 and *Bartlett v Barclays Bank Trust Co* [1980] Ch 515, [1980] 1 All ER 139. For a recent case where it was alleged that trustees had not merely failed to intervene in a company's improper affairs, but had co-operated in the improprieties, see *Walker v Stones* [2001] 2 WLR 623, CA.

2 A company in which the residuary estate may have some other direct or indirect interest would include a subsidiary or sub-subsidiary of a company in which the trustees directly hold shares. It was held in *Walker v Stones* [2001] 2 WLR 623, CA at 631A, that as a matter of construction of the trustee exoneration clause under consideration, the phrase 'any body corporate *in respect of which* the trustees shall hold shares' was wide enough to include subsidiaries or sub-subsidiaries of the company in which the trustees actually held shares.

3 If a paid trustee is to rely on this indemnity clause which limits a trustee's liability in negligence, the testator should specifically be made aware of its meaning and effect (see para **[221.13]** above).

[221.22]

Form B21.18: Power to life tenants of settled shares to give releases to trustees

I declare that the adoption or acceptance by any individual of any account which shall be submitted to him or her by my trustees in relation to any trust funds or property in which or in any part or share of which such individual has a life interest under this my will (of which adoption or acceptance the signature of any such individual to any such account shall be conclusive evidence) shall as against such individual and any spouse and issue of such individual operate as an absolute release and discharge to my trustees in respect of all dealings with such trust funds or property appearing in any such account.[1]

1 This form will be of use where the will contains a settlement of any legacy or a share of residue.

[221.23]

Form B21.19: Power to insure against liability for inheritance tax on lifetime dispositions[1]

My trustees may effect any policy or policies of insurance against any inheritance tax for which they may be or become liable for as my personal representatives whether or not there shall be any other person or persons liable for such tax and the cost of such insurance shall be paid out of my estate as a testamentary expense.

1 It is possible that there could be some lifetime dispositions of the testator which are not known to the personal representatives at the time of distribution of the estate, or that there were some dispositions to the testator which may become chargeable to IHT. See Part A, paras **[200.79]** and **[200.80]** and **[200.95]**–**[200.98]**.

[221.24]

Form B21.20: Receipts by or on behalf of minors[1]

Whenever they have an obligation or discretion under the provisions of this will or under the general law to pay or apply income or capital to a minor or for his benefit my trustees may discharge that obligation or exercise that discretion if they so desire by paying the same to any parent or guardian of the minor or to the minor himself if of the age of 16 and their respective receipts shall be a good discharge to my trustees who shall not be obliged to see how it is used.

1 This express provision may no longer be strictly necessary for a parent of a minor to give a good receipt. In contrast to the position in the past when trustees (in the absence of an express provision to the contrary) in order to get a sufficient discharge had to retain a minor's legacy until the minor was of full age (ie 18: FLRA 1969, s 1; 6 *Halsbury's Statutes* (4th edn) (1999 Reissue) 121) and able to give a good receipt, a person with parental responsibility for a minor can now receive a legacy on the minor's behalf, and can apparently require the trustees to hand over to him or her any income or capital to which the minor is absolutely and indefeasibly entitled: see the ChA 1989, s 3(3) (Part G, para **[244.114]**; see also Vol 1, para **[9.41]**) which came into force on 14 October 1991. Trustees also have power of this kind over income—power to pay income to a parent or guardian where the TA 1925, s 31 applied (see subs (1)(i): Part G, para **[246.29]**), and power to obtain a good receipt for income and statutory accumulations of income from a married minor under the LPA 1925, s 21 (Part G, para **[246.42]**).

[221.25]

Form B21.21: Receipts on behalf of charities and unincorporated associations

I declare that if the donee of any gift under this my will or any codicil hereto shall be a charitable institution or an unincorporated association the receipt of the person who professes to be the treasurer or other proper officer for the time being of such institution or association shall be a full and sufficient discharge to my trustees.

[221.26]

Form B21.22: Missing beneficiaries

I declare that if any donee hereunder cannot be found within the space of three years from the date when the gift to him or her becomes payable my trustees may distribute my estate upon the footing that such donee predeceased me.

CONDUCT OF TRUSTEESHIP

[221.27]

Form B21.23: Clause excluding trustees' duty to consult with beneficiaries as to land[1]

Section 11(1) of the Trusts of Land and Appointment of Trustees Act 1996 (consultation with beneficiaries) shall not apply to the exercise by my trustees of their functions in relation to any land held by them.

1 For the TLATA 1996, s 11 see para **[220.58]** and Part G, para **[246.114]**.

[221.28]

Form B21.24: Direction as to order of names of trustees in the registers of companies to secure voting rights[1]

I direct that the name of my son [*name*] shall be placed first in the register of all registered stocks shares securities or property.

1 This clause, which is a common form where a bank or insurance company is one of several trustees, may be useful where it is desired that one of the trustees shall exercise the votes in respect of shares in a company, usually a private company. Table A, art 55 of the Companies (Tables A-F) Regulations 1985 (SI 1985/805) (replacing in identical terms, art 63 of Table A, Sch 1 to the Companies Act 1948) provides that in the case of joint holders the vote of the senior who tenders a vote, whether in person or by proxy, shall be accepted to the exclusion of the other joint holders; and for this purpose seniority shall be determined by the order in which the names stand in the register of members. The voting trustee must, however, exercise his votes in accordance with the directions of the trustees as a body, but being the first-named holder gives such trustee an added degree of control.

[221.29]

Form B21.25: Direction that opinion of majority of trustees is to prevail[1]

I declare that should any difference of opinion at any time exist between the trustees for the time being of this my will in relation to the commission or omission of any act or otherwise howsoever in the execution of the trusts of this my will or any codicil hereto the opinion of the majority of such trustees shall prevail and shall do so even if any one or more of such trustees may be personally interested or concerned in the matter in dispute or question provided that at least one trustee in the majority has no such personal interest.

1 Trustees other than trustees of a charity cannot without this special provision act by a majority: *Blacket v Blizard* (1829) 9 B & C 851; *Luke v South Kensington Hotel Co* (1879) 11 Ch D 121; *Re Roth, Goldberger v Roth* (1896) 74 LT 50; *Astbury v Astbury* [1898] 2 Ch 111. As to charity trustees, see *Re Whiteley, Bishop of London v Whiteley* [1910] 1 Ch 600; and the Charities Act 1993, s 82; 5 *Halsbury's Statutes* (4th edn) (1998 Reissue) 1043.

[221.30]

Form B21.26: Power authorising an audit

I declare that the provisions of section 22(4) of the Trustee Act 1925[1] (relating to the audit of the accounts of the trust property) shall apply hereto with the variation that two years shall be substituted for three years in such provisions[2] [and with the addition that any apportionment between capital and income of the costs of examination and audit made by the auditor at the request of the trustees shall be binding upon the persons entitled respectively to the capital and to the income of the trust property].

1 See Part G, para **[246.20]**.
2 The trustees may allocate the cost to capital or income partly to each; in default of any direction by them, costs attributable to capital will be borne by capital, and costs attributable to income by income. It would seem advisable to ask the auditor to apportion the costs himself.

[221.31]

Form B21.27: Direction to employ a named solicitor[1]

It is my wish that [*name of solicitor*] shall be employed in proving this my will and in transacting any legal business in the administration of the trusts hereof.

1 This form may be included where a family member or friend is appointed executor and trustee.

[221.32]

Form B21.28: Nomination of trust corporation to receive notices[1]

I nominate [*trust corporation*] as the trust corporation to which notices of dealings affecting real or personal property which is subject to any trust hereunder may be given.

1 LPA 1925, s 138. This nomination is not usually required unless property is settled under the will and is then only really essential where there are numerous beneficiaries who may charge their interests and it becomes of advantage to have an effective register of such dealings.

[221.33]

Form B21.29: Power to vest assets in nominees[1]

My trustees may vest or register any property which or the proceeds of sale of which form part of [my residuary estate] in the name or names of any person or persons (including any one or more of my trustees) or body or bodies corporate resident in the UK or elsewhere as nominee or nominees for my trustees and remunerate such nominee or nominees[2] and agree with such nominee or nominees such terms as in their absolute discretion they think fit including (without prejudice to the generality of the foregoing) terms permitting the nominee or nominees to appoint a substitute restricting the liability of the nominee or nominees (or substitute) to my trustees or to any beneficiary hereunder and permitting the nominee or nominees (or substitute) to act in circumstances capable of giving rise to a conflict of interest [Provided always that:

[(i) Section 22 of the Trustee Act 2000 (review of agents, nominees and custodians etc) shall not apply][3]

[(ii) Section 23 of the Trustee Act 2000 (liability for nominees) shall not apply but none of my trustees shall be liable for any act or default of any nominee appointed hereunder or substitute of such nominee][4]

[(iii) the duty of care of the Trustee Act 2000 shall not apply hereto].[5]

1 Personal representatives and trustees now have statutory powers to vest assets in nominees or custodians by virtue of the TrA 2000, ss 16–20 (Part G, paras **[246.148]**–**[246.152]**). However, this express power is wider than the statutory powers in that it authorises trustees to appoint one individual only of their number to be a nominee. Under TrA 2000, s 19(5)(a) trustees may only vest assets in one of their number if that one is a trust corporation, or otherwise in two or more of their number. Further, the terms expressly mentioned in this Form as terms which the trustees can agree 'in their absolute discretion' can only be agreed by trustees when making the appointment under their statutory powers if they consider it 'reasonably necessary for them to do so': TrA 2000, s 20(3). For a power to delegate investment powers, see Form B20.8 at para **[220.56]**.

2 Under the TrA 2000, s 32(2), (3) (Part G, para **[246.164]**) trustees may pay reasonable remuneration to a nominee, and reimburse him for any proper expenses.

3 Under the TrA 2000, s 22 (Part G, para **[246.154]**) trustees appointing a nominee under an express power (as well as under the statutory power) have duties to review and vary the arrangements of the appointment: TrA 2000, s 21(2) (Part G, para **[246.153]**). These duties may, however, be expressly excluded: TrA 2000, s 21(3) (Part G, para **[246.153]**). It is submitted, however, that in most cases it will be wise to retain these duties.

4 Under the TrA 2000, s 23 (Part G, para **[246.155]**) trustees appointing a nominee under an express power (as well as under the statutory power), are not liable for the acts and defaults of the nominee unless they have failed to comply with their statutory duty of care when entering into or reviewing the arrangement. This section can, however, be excluded (see TrA 2000, s 21(3): Part G, para **[246.153]**) and a wider indemnity can then be included so that trustees are exonerated from liability for all acts or defaults of the nominee even if they have not complied with the statutory duty of care. For the statutory duty of care, see note 5. If this sub-clause is included and a paid trustee is to rely on the indemnity contained in it which may limit his liability in negligence in that it may absolve him from negligent failure to intervene to prevent loss, the testator should specifically be made aware of its meaning and effect (see para **[221.13]** above).

5 Under the TrA 2000, s 2 and Sch 1, para 3(1)(d), (e) (Part G, paras **[246.134]** and **[246.173]**) the statutory duty of care applies where trustees appoint a nominee under an express power. The statutory duty is to exercise such care and skill as is reasonable in the circumstances, having regard in particular to any special knowledge or experience that they have or hold themselves out as having, and if they act as trustees in the course of a business or profession, to any special knowledge or experience that it is reasonable to expect them to have: TrA 2000, s 1(1) and Sch 1, para 3(1)(d), (e) (Part G, paras **[246.172]** and **[246.173]**). It can, however, be excluded: TrA 2000, Sch 1, para 7 (Part G, para **[246.173]**).

[221.34]

Form B21.30: Power to distribute on assumption that no further children

My trustees shall have power at their absolute discretion to distribute income or capital of my estate or of any fund deriving from it on the assumption that a woman who has attained the age of 55 years will have no further children and if they exercise this power my trustees shall not be liable for the assumption turning out to be incorrect (without prejudice to any beneficiary's right to trace trust assets against any other beneficiary).[1]

1 Existing authority that trustees can distribute on the assumption that a woman of 55 is past the age of childbearing (see Vol 1, paras **[66.3]** and **[216.29]**) can no longer be relied on, because advances in medical science mean that a woman who has passed the menopause could still have a child by means of in vitro fertilisation using donated eggs, and because if this were to happen she would be treated as the mother of the child for all purposes, including gifts by will, by virtue of the HFEA 1990, ss 27 and 29 (Part G, paras **[245.85]** and **[245.87]**). It is still possible to apply to the court for liberty to distribute on the basis of evidence that a particular person having another child is impossible or very unlikely (see *Re Levy Estate Trust* [2000] CLY, para 5263 and *Re Cassidy* [1979] VR 369). There is a statutory presumption that a woman over 55 will not adopt a child: see the AA 1976, s 42(5) (Part G, para **[245.60]**). Provision as in this clause is not usually needed if the beneficial trusts, powers and provisions themselves confer powers, such as a wide power of appointment or powers of advancement over the whole of a presumptive share, which would enable a trust fund to be appointed absolutely or distributed absolutely without waiting to see if more members of a class are born.

APPOINTMENT AND RETIREMENT OF TRUSTEES

[221.35]

Note. Some of the forms below vary the statutory powers and provisions for the appointment of new trustees contained in the TA 1925, ss 36 and 37. A variation of the powers conferred by the TA 1925 is generally permissible since the TA 1925, s 69(2) provides that the powers conferred by the Act are in addition to powers conferred by a trust instrument and have effect subject to the terms of the instrument. However, it is also thought that a variation of provisions which are ancillary to and part of the powers, though themselves not powers since they are imperative in nature, is also permissible, see *Re Turner's Will Trusts, District Bank Ltd v Turner* [1937] Ch 15 and *London Regional Transport Pension Fund Trustee Co Ltd v Hatt* [1993] PLR 227.

[221.36]

Form B21.31: Power to appoint new trustees conferred by the Trustee Act 1925

I declare that the statutory power of appointing new trustees hereof shall be vested in my said wife during her life [*or* widowhood] and after her death [*or* remarriage] in such one or more of my children [*names*] as shall for the time being have attained the age of eighteen years [*or* in such person during his or her life if of full age as shall for the time being have an interest in possession in the trust property in respect whereof a new trustee is to be appointed].[1]

1 The words in these brackets will be applicable where the testator has created several separate and distinct trusts.

A full power of appointing new trustees is in practice no longer necessary, and is omitted. The TA 1925, s 36 (Part G, para **[246.34]**), confers full powers of appointing new trustees, and (in certain circumstances) power to appoint additional trustees where no trustee is being replaced.

[221.37]

Form B21.32: Power to appoint separate trustees of parts of trust property[1]

My trustees shall have power to appoint a separate set of trustees for the part of the trust fund held on trusts for [the children and issue of my son] and a separate set of trustees for the part of the trust fund held on trusts for [the children and issue of my daughter] and any one or more of my trustees making such an appointment may appoint himself or herself to be one of such trustees.

1 The TA 1925, s 37(1)(b), (Part G, para **[246.35]**) authorises the appointment of separate sets of trustees for parts of trust property held on distinct trusts. This express provision would serve as a reminder. Such an appointment might be desirable where a testator has left property upon trusts for his grandchildren, where the trusts for the children of each child of his are distinct.

[221.38]

Form B21.33: Power to remove trustees

Any of my trustees may be removed by deed executed by [my widow] during her lifetime.

[221.39]

Form B21.34: Clause excluding beneficiaries' statutory right to direct retirement and appointment of trustees

Section[s]19[1] [and 20][2] of the Trusts of Land and Appointment of Trustees Act 1996 shall not apply to the trusts of this my will so that the beneficiaries shall not be entitled to direct any trustee to retire or to direct the appointment of any new trustee.

1 The TLATA 1996, s 19 provides that where no person is nominated for the purpose of appointing new trustees and the beneficiaries under the trust are of full age and capacity and between them absolutely entitled to the settled property, the beneficiaries may give a written direction to a trustee to retire from the trust or give a written direction to the trustees to appoint as a trustee or trustees the person or persons specified in the direction (Part G, para **[246.122]**). This reverses by statute the decision in *Re Brockbank, Ward v Bates* [1948] Ch 206, [1948] 1 All ER 287. The beneficiaries must act unanimously. TLATA 1996, s 19 may, however, be excluded in relation to new settlements and wills: TLATA 1996, s 21(5) (Part G, para **[246.124]**). The requirement of unanimity of the beneficiaries means that theoretically the beneficiaries have protection from each other, but exclusion could well be appropriate where trusts have been or are being created to protect beneficiaries from their own improvidence, or where one beneficiary has too much influence over another. As a practical matter settlements set up with this sort of purpose in mind are unlikely to be ones which will reach a stage where the beneficiaries become collectively entitled (because there are likely to be protective trusts or wide powers of appointment).

2 The TLATA 1996, s 20 gives power, again, to beneficiaries who are of full age and collectively entitled to the beneficial interest, where a trustee is mentally incapacitated and there is nobody with power to appoint a new trustee under the TA 1925, s 36 to direct the trustee's receiver or attorney under an enduring power to appoint a new trustee or trustees specified by the beneficiaries (Part G, para **[246.123]**). It may be excluded in relation to new wills: TLATA 1996, s 21(5) (Part G, para **[246.124]**). In the absence of such a power, an application would have to be made to the Court of Protection for the appointment of a replacement trustee under the Mental Capacity Act 2005, ss 16, 18(1)(j) (replacing the Mental Health Act 1983, s 96(1)(k) on and from 1 October 2007) (Part G, para **[244.129]**). However, even if the TLATA 1996, s 20 does apply, and the beneficiaries direct the appointment of a new trustee, there is no express provision for the trustee's receiver or attorney to vest any trust property which is not subject to automatic vesting under the TA 1925, s 40 (e g stocks and shares) in the new trustee. Therefore, an application to the Court of Protection may still be required.

[221.40]

Form B21.35: Direction as to keeping up the number of trustees[1]

I direct that the trustees of this my will shall be never less than [three] in number and that any vacancy in the trusteeship hereof shall be filled up as soon as conveniently may be but nevertheless that the trustees hereof for the time being shall during any vacancy have the same powers authorities and discretions and may act in all respects as if there were [three] or more trustees hereof.

1 It must be remembered that not more than four executors will be allowed to take a grant, but where separate grants are taken to different parts of the estate, the number of executors is limited to four in respect of each grant and is no longer limited to four in all: see the SCA 1981, s 114(1), reversing *Re Holland's Estate* [1936] 3 All ER 13 on this point. In the case of a private trust the trustees should be not more than four. A single trustee can act for most purposes, but a single trustee cannot give a valid receipt for capital moneys on a disposition of land unless a trust corporation.

[221.41]

Form B21.36: Variation of statutory power to facilitate appointment of foreign trustees, and a sole trustee

The statutory power to appoint new trustees shall apply subject to the following—

(i) Any person or persons who may be resident outside the United Kingdom may be appointed as a trustee or trustees hereof and the administration of the trusts hereof may be transferred to a place outside the United Kingdom and from and after any such transfer of the administration of the trusts hereof to a place outside the United Kingdom references in section 36 of the Trustee Act 1925 to the United Kingdom[1] shall in relation to each trustee hereof be treated as references to the territory or jurisdiction in which such trustee was resident at the time when he first became a trustee hereof.

(ii) Any company corporation or similar incorporated body which undertakes the management and administration of trusts (whether or not a trust corporation) shall be capable of being appointed a trustee hereof and shall be entitled to payment of its normal fees and charges as are from time to time applicable.

(iii) A corporation or body satisfying the requirements of the last preceding sub-clause or an individual may be appointed as sole trustee hereof.

(iv) When more than one person wishes to retire as trustees hereof at the same time and by the same instrument one person or fewer persons than the number retiring may be appointed in their place in exercise of the powers in the said section 36.[2]

(v) Any appointment of new trustees or deed of retirement of a trustee made with the consent of the co-trustees of the retiring trustee shall be effective to discharge from all the trusts hereof the persons or person expressed therein to be ceasing to be trustees or a trustee hereof provided that after such discharge there shall be at least one individual or a corporation or body satisfying the requirements of sub-clause (ii) above acting as the trustees hereof and sections 37(1)(c) and 39(1) of the Trustee Act 1925 so far as they would prevent any such appointment of new trustees or deed of retirement from being an effective discharge as aforesaid shall be of no effect.[3]

(vi) In this clause the expressions 'United Kingdom' and 'trust corporation' have the same meanings as in the Trustee Act 1925.[4]

1 TA 1925, s 36(1) (Part G, para **[246.34]**) provides that absence from the UK for more than twelve months is grounds for replacing a trustee.

2 This counters the effect of the decision in *Adam & Co International Trustees v Theodore Goddard* [2000] WTLR 349 that where more than one trustee wishes to retire by means of an appointment of new trustees in their place under the TA 1925, s 36 they cannot do so by the appointment of fewer trustees in their place. For a cogent criticism of this decision see The Appointment of Trustees: A disappointing decision by Francis Barlow, Conv 2003, Jan/Feb, 15–27.

3 TA 1925, ss 37(1)(c) and s 39(1) (as amended by the TLATA 1996 with effect from 1 January 1997: Part G, paras **[246.35]** and **[246.37]**) normally render an appointment of new trustees or a deed of retirement of a trustee ineffective to discharge any retiring trustees or trustee if there will not be two persons or a trust corporation as the trustees immediately afterwards. Trust corporation has a specific meaning that excludes most foreign trust corporations. Therefore, this form enables a single individual or a single non-trust corporation company to be appointed as sole trustee. For a case concerned with the situation where the statutory provisions for the discharge of trustees were not observed, see *Jasmine Trustees Ltd v Wells & Hind (a firm)* [2007] EWHC 38 (Ch), [2007] 1 All ER 1142.

4 TA 1925, s 68(18), (20) (Part G, para **[246.39]**). For the meaning of 'trust corporation' see para **[221.46]**. It includes certain EC corporations with a place of business in the UK but does not otherwise include non-UK corporations.

POWER TO CHARGE

[221.42]

Note.– Powers of charging after the trustee act 2000.

Statutory and express powers for trustees to charge for their services. It was formerly the case that generally, a solicitor or other professional person could not charge for acting as executor or trustee unless the will authorised him to charge for his services. However, the position has been changed by the TrA 2000 in relation to services provided on and after 1 February 2001, whatever the date of creation of the trusts: TrA 2000, s 33(1) (Part G, para **[246.165]**). Now TrA 2000, s 29(2) provides that in the absence of an express remuneration clause, a trustee or personal representative acting in a professional capacity and who is not a sole trustee is entitled to receive reasonable remuneration for any services he provides (including services capable of being provided by a lay trustee: s 29(4)) if each other trustee has agreed in writing that he may be remunerated (Part G, para **[246.161]**; see also the TrA 2000, s 35: Part G, para **[246.167]** for the application of these provisions to personal representatives). 'Reasonable remuneration' means in relation to the provision of services by a trustee (or personal representative), such remuneration as is reasonable in the circumstances for the provision of those services to or on behalf of that trust (or estate) by him (TrA 2000, s 29(3): Part G, para **[246.161]**). Furthermore, a trust corporation (see para **[221.47]** for the meaning of this term), including where it is a sole trustee, is also entitled to receive reasonable remuneration (TrA 2000, s 29(1)) and special provision is made for trustees of charitable trusts: TrA 2000, s 30 (Part G, para **[246.162]**). It is still advisable to include an express remuneration clause in a will if it is possible that a professional person will act as executor or trustee, because the statutory provisions will not enable a sole executor or trustee to charge, and where there are two or more trustees or executors, a professional person among them will need the written agreement of his co-trustee(s) or executor(s) to do so. Further, a trustee acting in a professional capacity for the purposes of s 29 is in some respects quite a narrow concept: see further para **[221.46]**. Therefore, an express remuneration clause entitling any professional or business person to charge is also advisable in case such a person falls outside this definition—eg a testator may appoint a business partner to be executor and trustee and wish him to have the benefit of a charging clause in respect of carrying on or winding up the business, or wish a professional or business person whose practice or business is not concerned with trusts or estates, but who can lend wisdom and experience to the trustees' deliberations, to be able to charge (and see further para **[221.46]**).

[221.43]

Professional trustees' charges for services capable of being provided by a lay trustee. In addition to the statutory power of charging described above, the TrA 2000 makes two important changes to the law regarding trustee or personal representative remuneration under express powers of charging in wills or other trust instruments. The first is that a trustee or personal representative acting in a professional capacity (see TrA 2000, s 28(5): see Part G, para **[246.160]** and para **[221.46]** for this term) or a trust corporation (see para **[221.47]** for this term), in relation to whom there is provision in the will or other trust instrument entitling him to receive payment for services provided to or on behalf of the trust or estate, is entitled to receive payment in respect of services even if they are services which are capable of being provided by someone who is not a trust corporation or someone acting in a professional capacity: TrA 2000, s 28(1)–(3), (6) (Part G, para **[246.160]**). This is subject to any inconsistent provision made by the will or other trust instrument (TrA 2000, s 28(1)) but it applies to any services performed on or after 1 February 2001 even if the trust is created before that date: TrA 2000, s 33(1) (Part G, para **[246.165]**). Before the TrA 2000 came into force, a charging clause which conferred power to charge for professional services did not authorise charging for services which a non-professional trustee could have done unless there was express provision to that effect (*Re Chapple* (1884) 27 Ch D 584, *Clarkson v Robinson* [1900] 2 Ch 722). This change in the law means that if the only trustees or executors who might wish to charge are persons, such as solicitors or accountants, who will act in a professional capacity within the meaning of TrA 2000, s 28, or a trust corporation, the charging clause could be made more concise by leaving out provision that the persons enabled to charge by the clause may charge for things which a lay trustee could do personally (see Form B21.32 at para **[221.49]**). However, express authority to charge for what a lay trustee could do is still relevant where the persons authorised to charge include, or might turn out to include, persons who are not trust corporations and are or may be outside the definition of a trustee acting in a professional capacity in the

TrA 2000, s 28(5) (see Part G, paras **[246.160]** and **[221.46]** for the meaning of this), or where a new long-term charitable trust is created. The reason for the latter exception is that the statutory extension of an express power to charge for services to matters which a non-professional trustee could do only applies to a trustee of a charitable trust (who is not a trust corporation) if he is not a sole trustee and the other trustees, or a majority of them, agree to him doing so: TrA 2000, s 28(3). The more general point to bear in mind, however, is that as discussed further at para **[221.46]**, 'acting in a professional capacity' is in some respects quite a narrow concept. Accordingly, we recommend that express provision continues to be made that a trustee in a profession or business can charge for services which a non-professional non-business trustee might have performed.

[221.44]

Trustees' remuneration no longer a legacy (in some respects). The second change made by the TrA 2000 to express powers for professional trustees to charge is that it provides that a trustee's (and a personal representative's) remuneration is no longer, for certain purposes, to be regarded as a species of gift, but only in relation to the wills of testators dying on or after the commencement date of the Act, ie 1 February 2001: see TrA 2000, ss 33(2) and 35(4) (Part G, paras **[246.165]** and **[246.167]**) for this restriction on the commencement of this change in the law and the Trustee Act 2000 (Commencement) Order 2001, SI 2001/49 for the commencement date of the Act. It should also be noted that these provisions only relate to the remuneration of a trust corporation: TrA 2000, s 28(1) (for which term see para **[221.47]**), or a trustee acting in a professional capacity within the meaning of TrA 2000, s 28(5) (for which see para **[221.46]**). Thus—

(1) It is to be regarded as remuneration, and not as a gift, for the purposes of the Wills Act 1837, s 15 (Part G, para **[244.12]**; see also Vol 1, para **[9.3]** ff): TrA 2000, s 28(4)(a) (Part G, para **[246.160]**). Therefore, where a testator has died on or after 1 February 2001, and a solicitor or other professional person who witnessed his will (whether before, on or after that date) becomes executor or trustee of it, such executor or trustee is not deprived of the benefit of a charging clause by the operation of the Wills Act 1837, s 15 which renders void gifts to any attesting witness. Under common law, remuneration is a gift, and hence an individual who witnessed the will of a testator who died before 1 February 2001 cannot make charges for acting as executor or trustee under an express remuneration clause: see Vol 1, para **[9.11]**. It is not clear, however, whether such an individual is now entitled to remuneration under the statutory entitlement to charge in the TrA 2000, s 29(2) for services provided on or after 1 February 2001 (see para **[221.42]** for this entitlement). This entitlement depends upon there being no provision about his entitlement to remuneration in the will or in any enactment: TrA 2000, s 29(5). Since the effect of the Wills Act 1837, s 15 is to render 'utterly null and void' a remuneration clause in the will so far as regards that individual, it could be said that the will has not made any provision about his entitlement. But then should it be said that the Wills Act 1837, s 15 (ie an enactment) has made provision about his

entitlement to remuneration, by denying him an entitlement so that s 29(2) cannot apply? The position is unclear.

(2) It is to be regarded as remuneration and an administrative expense for the purposes of the AEA 1925, s 34(3) (order in which estate to be paid out: Part G, para **[246.51]**; TrA 2000, ss 28(4)(b) and 35(3)(a): Part G, paras **[246.160]** and **[246.167]**). Formerly, ie in relation to deaths before 1 February 2001, remuneration was regarded as a species of legacy which would abate along with other pecuniary or general legacies if residue was insufficient (see the AEA 1925, Sch 1, Pt II: Part G, para **[246.59]** for the order of application of the assets of a solvent estate in the absence of contrary directions). However, in relation to deaths on or after 1 February 2001, remuneration is now regarded as an administrative expense and so payable as such in priority to legacies.

(3) It is to be regarded as an administrative expense for the purposes of any provision giving reasonable administrative expenses priority over the preferential debts listed in the Insolvency Act 1986, Sch 6: TrA 2000, s 35(3)(b). The rules regulating the administration of insolvent estates are contained in the Administration of Insolvent Estates of Deceased Persons Order 1986, SI 1986/1999, as amended by the Administration of Insolvent Estates of Deceased Persons (Amendment) Order 2002, SI 2002/1309) and Art 4(2) of that Order provides that reasonable funeral, testamentary and administration expenses have priority over the preferential debts listed in the Insolvency Act 1986, Sch 6 as amended by the Enterprise Act 2002, s 251(1), Sch 26 (ie contributions to occupational pension schemes and state scheme premiums; remuneration of employees; and levies on coal and steel production. The Crown's preference for debts due to the Inland Revenue, to customs and excise and for social security contributions was lost on 15 September 2003 when Enterprise Act 2002, s 251(1), Sch 26 came into force). Therefore, in relation to deaths occurring on or after 1 February 2001, an executor's reasonable remuneration will be payable in priority to preferential debts, other debts and legacies. This means that where an estate is insolvent, a professional need not be deterred from taking a grant of probate, as he may have been in relation to a death prior to 1 February 2001, when he would not have been able to rely upon a remuneration clause in the will to charge for his services since it would have been regarded as a legacy.

[221.45]

Limits of the statutory treatment of trustees' charges as remuneration rather than gift. It should be noted that the change from treating payment to trustees for their services as a legacy, to treating it as remuneration is for the above purposes only; the rule that such payment is a legacy continues to be relevant in at least two contexts and there may be others. The first is that of a professional executor who pays himself fees, after which the grant of probate is revoked. He does not have the protection afforded to purchasers dealing in good faith: see *Gray v Richards Butler* (1996) [2001] WTLR 625 where part of the reasoning behind the decision was that the remuneration counted as a legacy. The second context is where a trustee or personal representative is entitled to charge under the express provisions of the will (or other trust instrument) but is not a trust corporation (see para **[221.47]**) or does not fall within the definition of a trustee acting in a professional capacity in the TrA 2000, s 28(5) (Part G, para **[246.160]**; see also para **[221.46]**).

[221.46]

Trustee acting in a professional capacity. All the provisions of the TrA 2000, ss 28, 29, and 35 concerning trustee and personal representative remuneration discussed at paras **[221.42]–[221.44]** only apply to a trustee acting in a professional capacity, or to a trust corporation (for the latter see para **[221.47]**). The definition of what it is to be a trustee acting in a professional capacity is in TrA 2000, s 28(5) (Part G, para **[246.160]**). To come within this definition it seems that a trustee or personal representative has to satisfy two main requirements. First, he has to be in a profession or business which consists of or includes the provision of services in connection with the management or administration of trusts generally or a particular kind of trust, or which consists of or includes the provision of services in connection with any particular aspect of the management or administration of trusts generally or a particular kind of trust (this is referred to below as 'the qualifying profession or business'). Second, he must act in the course of that profession or business to provide services to or on behalf of the trust which are services in connection with the management or administration of trusts generally or a particular kind of trust, or which are services in connection with any particular aspect of the management or administration of trusts generally or a particular kind of trust (these are referred to below as 'the qualifying services'). It seems that 'trust' here includes 'estate', by virtue of TrA 2000, s 35 (Part G, para **[246.167]**). With respect to these requirements for being a trustee acting in a professional capacity—

(1) It is not clear whether, in order to be engaged in a qualifying profession or business, it is sufficient to be a member of a profession (such as solicitor) which includes trusts work among the possible kinds of work done by that profession, or whether the trustee must practise, or be a member of a firm which practises, in the management or administration of trusts (or one of the other categories in TrA 2000, s 28(5)). We are inclined to think the latter, but the position is not crystal clear.
(2) It seems that the qualifying services do not have to be ones which are normally or generally provided in the course of the qualifying profession or business.
(3) It is clear, however, that the qualifying services have to be provided in the course of the qualifying profession or business. Accordingly, some of the tasks which might be carried out by a trustee who is engaged in a qualifying profession or business might fall outside the clause. Managing the testator's business is a possible example: see *Clarkson v Robinson* [1900] 2 Ch 722 where it was held that a solicitor, an architect, and an accountant could not charge for the time they spent managing the testator's silk-mercer's business where the charging clause confined the right to charge to charging for things done in the course of the trustees' own respective businesses.
(4) Further to the last point, it seems reasonably clear that the entitlement to charge for services capable of being provided by a lay trustee (TrA

2000, ss 28(2) and 29(4): Part G, paras **[246.160]** and **[246.161]**) is limited to things done in the course of the qualifying profession or business. Thus (for example) a stockbroker who is appointed an executor, and who is in a qualifying profession because he regularly gives investment advice to trustees, would not be able to charge under s 28(2) for attending an executors' meeting to decide on the appropriation of assets to beneficiaries, but could charge for giving investment advice to the executors. An express power of charging such as B21.38 at para **[221.50]** would enable him to charge for attending the trustees' meeting, irrespective of whether he provided services as a stockbroker to the executors.

(5) The requirement of being in a qualifying profession or business means that a retired member of one would not fall within the statutory provisions, but it should be added that the standard charging clauses do not enable retired members of professions to be able to charge. The requirement also means that persons in professions or businesses unconnected with trusts (e g a doctor) cannot charge under the statutory power, although they could charge for time spent on the affairs of the estate or trust under the usual form of professional trustee charging clause.

(6) The definition is not confined to individuals, and a company or other corporate body which is not a trust corporation (see para **[221.47]** for what is a trust corporation) can qualify as a trustee acting in a professional capacity, but it would have to be carrying on a qualifying business of providing trust and estate services, and a company incorporated just for the purpose of being trustee of one particular trust (for example) would not qualify.

[221.47]

Meaning of trust corporation. 'Trust corporation' has the same meaning in the TrA 2000 as in the TA 1925: TrA 2000, s 39(1) (Part G, para **[246.168]**). By virtue of the TA 1925, s 68(18) (Part G, para **[246.39]**) 'trust corporation' is confined to the Public Trustee and the corporations specified in the Public Trustee Rules 1912, r 30, as amended (Part G, para **[246.63]**), and corporations appointed by the court to be trustees. See also the Law of Property (Amendment) Act 1926 (Part G, para **[246.61]**) for certain further categories of trust corporation of small relevance to will drafting. The corporations specified in the Public Trustee Rules 1912, r 30 include certain EC corporations with a place of business in the UK but do not otherwise include non-UK corporations. Those included have to satisfy certain requirements, including requirements as to minimum capital, or be incorporated by statute or royal charter, or fall within one of the more specialised categories of, e g public authority, there set out. A corporate trustee outside the UK will thus not usually qualify as a trust corporation for the purposes of the TA 1925 or the TrA 2000, although it may qualify as a trustee acting in a professional capacity for the purposes of the TrA 2000, ss 28 and 29 if it carries on a business of administering trusts (see para **[221.46]**). For the appointment of a trust corporation as executor, see the Notes and Forms in B3 at para **[203.24]** ff.

[221.48]
Charging by trust corporations. Prior to the coming into force of the TrA 2000, where a power of charging was inserted because a solicitor was appointed trustee it operated to allow a bank to charge its usual fees upon the bank being substituted by codicil for the solicitor: *Re Campbell's Estate* [1954] 1 All ER 448, [1954] 1 WLR 516. On the other hand, in *Re Cooper, Le-Neve Foster v National Provincial Bank* (1939) 160 LTR 453 (not reported on this point in the report at [1939] Ch 580) it was held that a standard professional trustee charging clause did not enable a trust corporation to charge, but no reasons were given and no attention was paid to the LPA 1925, s 61(b) ('person' in a document includes a corporation—see Part G, para **[246.54]**). A standard professional trustee charging clause would only enable a trust corporation to charge on a time basis for work done, however, and would probably not permit charging scale fees based on a percentage of the value of the funds irrespective of the amount of work done. If, in the circumstances of a particular case, the will and codicil cannot be so construed as to confer an entitlement to remuneration upon a trust corporation, then in relation to services performed on or after 1 February 2001, a trust corporation is entitled to reasonable remuneration under the TrA 2000, s 29: see Part G, paras **[246.161]**; see also para **[221.42]**. It is entitled to this remuneration by virtue of being a trust corporation, and does not have to satisfy any of the rules as to co-trustees' agreement (see para **[221.42]**), or as to being in a qualifying profession or business or providing qualifying services (see para **[221.46]**) which an individual (or a corporation which is not a trust corporation) has to satisfy to be entitled to charge under the TrA 2000, s 29. Reasonable remuneration means, in relation to the provision of services by a trustee, such remuneration as is reasonable in the circumstances for the provision of those services to or on behalf of that trust by that trustee and, if the trustee is a trust corporation (and not trustee of a charitable trust) and an authorised institution under the Banking Act 1987 (ie a bank), it includes in relation to the provision of banking services by that trustee, its reasonable charges for doing so: TrA 2000, s 29(3) (Part G, para **[246.161]**; see also para **[203.27]**). It seems quite possible that s 29 of the TrA 2000 would not entitle a trust corporation to charge scale fees. Trust corporations will still want express powers to charge scale fees, and will not wish to rely on the statutory power to charge. Where the court appoints a trust corporation as a trustee, it can authorise remuneration under the TA 1925, s 42 and the inherent jurisdiction of the court (see para **[203.26]**). There is no need to provide for the appointment or payment of the Public Trustee as the statute provides for his appointment and gives him power to charge: Public Trustee Act 1906, s 5. The Public Trustee cannot be appointed where the will expressly forbids such appointment: Public Trustee Act 1906, s 5(3), unless the court orders such appointment. For a declaration that the Public Trustee or a trust corporation shall not be appointed, see Form B3.21 at para **[203.38]**.

[221.49]

Form B21.37: Power to professional trustee to charge—concise form[1]

Any of my trustees being a professional or business person may be paid reasonable remuneration for services provided by him in connection with the administration of my estate or any trust of this will or of any codicil hereto.

1 Where the only trustees or executors who might wish to charge will be trustees or personal representatives acting in a professional capacity within the meaning of the TrA 2000, s 28 (Part G, para **[246.160]**; see also para **[221.46]**), it is not necessary to provide expressly that such persons can charge for services which a non-professional trustee could provide, as this is permitted by the TrA 2000, s 28(2): see para **[221.43]**. This form could be used in wills for use in emergencies and simple wills giving immediate and absolute interests, but otherwise we recommend the traditional form of charging clause: see paras **[221.36]**, n 1, **[221.43]** and **[221.46]**.

[221.50]

Form B21.38: Power to professional trustee to charge—full form

Any of my trustees being in a profession or business may charge and be paid all usual professional and other proper charges for business transacted acts done advice given and time spent by him or his firm in connection with the administration of my estate or in connection with the trusts hereof including acts which a personal representative or trustee not being in any profession or business could have done personally.[1]

1 The express provision for a trustee to charge for acts which a lay trustee or personal representative could have done is no longer strictly necessary where the trustee will be acting in a professional capacity within the meaning of the TrA 2000, s 28(5) (Part G, para **[246.160]**; see also paras **[221.43]** and **[221.46]**), because the TrA 2000, s 28(2) provides that where there is an express remuneration clause, such a trustee or personal representative is entitled to receive payment for services which are capable of being provided by a lay trustee. As noted at para **[221.46]** the definition of a trustee acting in a professional capacity is quite narrow in scope. We therefore recommend that the traditional form of charging clause, as in this Form, continues to be used (except in the situations mentioned at para **[221.49]**, n 1.

[221.51]

Form B21.39: Proviso enabling professional trustee to elect not to charge[1]

... provided that any of my trustees being engaged in a profession or business who elects in writing not to charge for acting as my personal representative or as a trustee of this will at or before the time of his obtaining a grant of representation or (not having obtained such a grant) his being first appointed as a trustee hereof shall not be entitled as provided in the foregoing clause or by statute[2] (but shall be entitled to be relieved from liability under Clause —— above).[3]

1 This is a proviso which can be added to a professional charging clause such as Form B21.37 at para **[221.49]** or B21.38 at para **[221.50]**, where there is an indemnity clause such as Form B21.12 at para **[221.16]**, inclusive of the parts in square brackets.

2 Ie the TrA 2000, s 29(1) (see para **[221.42]**).

3 See Form B21.12 at para **[221.16]** and n 2 thereto.

[221.52]

Form B21.40: Provision for appointment of trust corporation[1]

My trustees in exercising the power of appointment vested in them by statute may if they so desire appoint a trust corporation to be either the sole trustee hereof or to be a trustee along with another or other trustees and in the event of a trust corporation being so appointed I hereby authorise such trust corporation to charge and my trustees to pay out of my estate such fees and remuneration[2] as is agreed upon between my trustees and the said trust corporation at the time of such appointment [*or* according to the scale of fees charged by such trust corporation from time to time].[3]

1 Most trust corporations have their own form of clause and it is wiser to ask for their consent to act in advance and to incorporate their form of clause. For the meaning of trust corporation, see para **[221.47]**. As mentioned in that paragraph, certain foreign corporations of EC countries now fall within the meaning of the term. See also Form B21.36 at para **[231.41]** and for forms appointing corporations as executors see Forms B3.11 to B3.13 at paras **[203.28]**–**[203.31]**. Trust corporations now have a statutory power to charge under the TrA 2000, s 29 (see para **[221.42]**) but will still want an express clause so as to be certain of being able to charge scale fees (see para **[221.48]**).

2 The trust corporation will be entitled to receive payment in respect of services even if they are services which are capable of being provided by a lay trustee: TrA 2000, s 28(2): Part G, para **[246.160]**; see also para **[221.43]**.

3 For the entitlement of a trust corporation to remuneration under the TrA 2000, s 29 (Part G, para **[246.161]**) in the absence of express provision, and which is not thought to include charging scale fees, see para **[221.48]**.

B22 Testimonium and attestation clauses

Preliminary note .... [222.1]
FORMS
B22.1 Usual form of testimonium and attestation .... [222.3]
B22.2 Short form of testimonium and attestation .... [222.4]
B22.3 Alternative form of attestation clause .... [222.5]
B22.4 Further alternative form of attestation clause .... [222.6]
B22.5 Form where testator signs with his mark .... [222.7]
B22.6 Form where another signs on behalf of the testator .... [222.8]
B22.7 Form where the testator is blind .... [222.9]
B22.8 Form of attestation where the testator is deaf and dumb but is able to read .... [222.10]
B22.9 Form of testimonium and attestation clause to a codicil .... [222.11]
B22.10 Form of attestation where the testator acknowledges a signature which he or another has made previously .... [222.12]
B22.11 Form of attestation where the testator acknowledges a signature which he has made previously—short form .... [222.13]
B22.12 Form of attestation where the will has been altered .... [222.14]
B22.13 Attestation clause where the testator has an imperfect knowledge of English .... [222.15]
B22.14 Forms of testimonium and attestation clause for will made on behalf of a mentally disordered person pursuant to an order of the Court of Protection .... [222.16]

PRELIMINARY NOTE

[222.1]
Care must be taken to use a recognised form of attestation clause, since if such a clause is used, a grant in common form will be obtained almost as a matter of course and no further proof of due attestation according to law will be required. The ordinary procedure for attestation is: (i) signature by the testator; (ii) the testator's signature must be written or acknowledged in the presence of two witnesses; (iii) the two witnesses then sign in the presence of the testator and of each other. That at any rate is the ordinary practice but it is not essential in law that the witnesses should sign in the presence of each other, and a witness may now sign before, and acknowledge his signature after, the testator has signed or acknowledged (See Vol 1, para **[12.1]**). The witnesses must sign or acknowledge in the presence of the testator, which means that he should be able to see the act of signing of the signature if he cares to do so. A blind person cannot witness a will. See the WA 1837, s 9, substituted by the AJA 1982, s 17 (Part G, para **[244.7]**; see also Vol 1, para **[12.15]**). In accordance with the wording of the substituted s 9, the attestation clauses which follow now state that the witnesses 'have signed our names below as witnesses' instead of the former 'have here unto subscribed our names as witnesses'.

[222.2]
To prevent disputes arising afterwards, it is usual to make certain variations in the attestation clause in certain circumstances. If there are alterations or

interlineations or erasures in the will, it is an advantage though not essential to note these in the attestation clause in order to provide evidence that they were made before execution of the will. It is in law quite sufficient if the alterations etc are initialled by the testator and the witnesses at or near the place where they occur without being mentioned in the attestation clause. Where the testator is suffering from any infirmity it is usual for the attestation clause to add that the testator had the will read over to him and appeared fully to understand it. If despite the infirmity the testator can read though it might be thought that he would not be able to do so, then the fact that he read and understood the will should be noted in the clause. Where the infirmity is such that his testamentary capacity might be impugned then care must be taken to choose witnesses of such standing that there can be no doubt that their opinion as to his mental capacity is to be trusted. In any case where the will is likely to be contested on this ground, the witnesses should preferably be persons who can readily be traced if difficulties arise. A common precaution in such cases is to arrange for one witness to be a medical practitioner and the other a solicitor and to take statements as to the question of the testator's capacity from them both. It must be remembered that neither witness nor the spouse or civil partner of a witness can take any benefit under the will. Where a testator died before 1 February 2001, a solicitor's charging clause creates such a benefit so that a solicitor will be unable to take advantage of it if he is a witness. The only exception is where such attestation is superfluous within the Wills Act 1968 (Part G, para **[244.84]**). However, in respect of deaths on or after 1 February 2001, a professional charging clause will not be regarded as such a benefit, so that a solicitor who witnessed the will of a testator dying on or after 1 February 2001, will be able to take advantage of it: TrA 2000, ss 28(4)(a) and 33(2)(a) (Part G, paras **[246.160]** and **[246.165]**; see also Vol 1, para **[9.11]**). For the particular requirements for the execution of a will on behalf of a patient see Vol 1, paras **[4.21]**–**[4.24]**, Form B22.14 at para **[222.16]** and the note thereto and the Mental Capacity Act 2005, Sch 2, para 3 (replacing the Mental Health Act 1983, s 97 on and from 1 October 2007) (Part G, para **[244.145]**).

[222.3]

Form B22.1: Usual form of testimonium and attestation[1]

IN WITNESS whereof I have hereunto set my hand this —— day of —— 20—[2].

SIGNED by the above-named [*testator*] as his last will in the presence of us present at the same time who at his request and in his presence and in the presence of each other have signed our names below as witnesses:	}	[*Signature of testator.*]

[*Signatures, addresses and descriptions of two witnesses*]

1 This is the full form of attestation clause. The shorter forms given in the three following forms are also accepted.

As to the formalities required for execution and attestation, see Vol 1, Chs 11 and 12. It is not necessary that the witnesses should sign in the presence of each other, but it has long been the practice for them to do so. The addresses and descriptions of the witnesses should be added to their signatures. No one who or whose spouse or civil partner takes a benefit under the will can be a witness without that benefit being lost, but the fact that a person is executor or trustee does not per se prevent such person or his or her spouse or civil partner from being a witness, though any legacy to which he or she would otherwise have been entitled will be forfeited. Whether remuneration under a professional charging clause is lost depends on the date of death of the testator: if he died before 1 February 2001, it is lost; if he died on or after 1 February 2001 the witness may take advantage of it, see para **[222.2]** above and Vol 1, paras **[9.3]–[9.12]**.

2 Wills are usually dated in the testimonium clause, but there is no objection to the date appearing at the commencement of the will when this clause may be adapted by use of the words 'the day and year first above written.' Though the words 'In witness' are commonly associated with execution as a deed, they are almost invariably used in the testimonium of a will although that document is now executed under hand. Execution as a deed might possibly be required if some foreign element is involved, but not otherwise.

[222.4]

Form B22.2: Short form of testimonium and attestation[1]

AS WITNESS my hand this —— day of —— 20 —.

SIGNED by the testator in our presence and then by us in his: } [*Signature of testator.*]

[*Signatures, addresses and descriptions of two witnesses*]

1 This is thought to be the shortest acceptable form of attestation clause. It makes it clear that all the statutory requirements have been complied with. It was learned from the Principal Probate Registry (now the Principal Registry of the Family Division) that this form is accepted in that Registry and all District Registries, and is indeed welcomed because it enables Registrars to see at a glance that the requirements are all satisfied.

[222.5]

Form B22.3: Alternative form of attestation clause[1]

SIGNED by the above-named [*testator*] as his last will in the joint presence of himself and us who at his request and in such joint presence have signed our names below as witnesses } [*Signature of testator.*]

[*Signatures, addresses and descriptions of two witnesses*]

1 See notes to Form B22.1 at para **[222.3]**. One point of a shortened form is that, where wills are prepared in an emergency, it is often necessary to write down an attestation clause from memory and the shorter the clause the easier it is to memorise. There is, however, so little difference between this clause and Form B22.1 at para **[222.3]**, that it is almost as easy to memorise the full clause as this version. Form B22.2 supra is the shortest and easiest to memorise of these attestation clauses.

[222.6]

Form B22.4: Further alternative form of attestation clause[1]

SIGNED by the above-named [*testator*] in our presence and attested by us in the presence of him and each other }	[*Signature of testator*.]

[*Signatures, addresses and descriptions of two witnesses*]

1 This form was approved in *Re Selby-Bigge* [1950] 1 All ER 1009.

[222.7]

Form B22.5: Form where testator signs with his mark

IN WITNESS whereof I have hereunto set my hand this —— day of —— 20 —.

SIGNED by the said [*testator*] with his mark as his last will (the same having been previously read over to him by [*name*] [me the undersigned [*name*]] when he seemed thoroughly to understand the same) in the presence of us present at the same time who at his request in his presence and in the presence of each other have signed our names below as witnesses }	[*Testator's mark*.]

[*Signatures, addresses and descriptions of two witnesses*]

[222.8]

Form B22.6: Form where another signs on behalf of the testator

IN WITNESS whereof I have hereunto set my hand this —— day of —— 20—.

SIGNED by [*person signing*] with the name of the said [*testator*] as his last will (the same having been previously read over to him by [*name*] [me the undersigned [*name*]] when he seemed thoroughly to understand the same) in his presence and by his direction and in the presence of us present at the same time who at the request and in the presence of the said [*testator*] and in the presence of each other have signed our names below as witnesses }	[*Testator's name*.]

[*Signatures, addresses and descriptions of two witnesses*]

[222.9]

Form B22.7: Form where the testator is blind[1]

IN WITNESS whereof I have hereunto set my hand this —— day of —— 20—.

THIS will having been first read over to the said [*testator*] (who is blind) [by me the undersigned [*name*] in the presence also of me the undersigned [*name*]] [in our presence] when the said [*testator*] appeared thoroughly to understand the same and to approve the contents thereof was signed by the said [*testator*][2] as his last will in the presence of us present at the same time who at his request in his presence and in the presence of each other have signed our names below as witnesses	}	[*Testator's signature or name if another signs for him.*]

[*Signatures, addresses and descriptions of two witnesses*]

1 In this and the following form the clause must be so worded that so far as possible the testator's infirmity has been provided for. The essentials are to show that (i) the testator despite his infirmity understood the document, (ii) that he intended it for his will, (iii) that he signed it either with a signature or mark or authorised someone to sign it on his behalf. Appropriate words from these clauses should be inserted in any particular case with respect to the particular matters which may be in doubt. As to attestation clauses in cases of blind persons, see Non-Contentious Probate Rules 1987, r 13.

2 It is not impossible for a blind testator to sign. If, however, he is unable to sign he may make his mark, when after the word 'signed' there should be added 'by his mark'. Alternatively another may sign for him, when the clause should run as follows: 'was signed by [*name of person signing*] by his direction as his last will in the presence,' etc.

[222.10]

Form B22.8: Form of attestation where the testator is deaf and dumb but is able to read

SIGNED as and for his last will by the above-named [*testator*] who is deaf and dumb but is able to read he having first read over the contents hereof and signified his understanding and approval thereof in the presence of us present at the same time who at his request in his presence and in the presence of each other have signed our names below as witnesses	}	[*Signature of testator.*]

[*Signatures, addresses and descriptions of two witnesses*]

[222.11]

Form B22.9: Form of testimonium and attestation clause to a codicil

IN WITNESS whereof I have hereunto set my hand this —— day of —— 20—.

SIGNED by the said [*testator*] as a codicil to his will which bears date the—day of—in the presence of us present at the same time who at his request in his presence and in the presence of each other have signed our names below as witnesses } [*Signature of testator.*]

[*Signatures, addresses and descriptions of two witnesses*]

[222.12]

Form B22.10: Form of attestation where the testator acknowledges a signature which he or another has made previously

SIGNED by the said [*testator*] [*or* by *person signing*] with the name of the said [*testator*] in his presence and by his direction] and acknowledged by him as his last will in the presence of us present at the same time who at his request in his presence and in the presence of each other have signed our names below as witnesses } [*Signature of testator.*]

[*Signatures, addresses and descriptions of two witnesses*]

[222.13]

Form B22.11: Form of attestation where the testator acknowledges a signature which he has made previously—short form[1]

SIGNED by the testator and his signature acknowledged by him in our presence and our names then signed by us in his presence } [*Signature of testator.*]

[*Signatures, addresses and descriptions of two witnesses*]

1 The WA 1837, s 9 (Part G, para **[244.7]**) allows the witnesses to witness the acknowledgment rather than the signing by the testator of his signature, provided that the signature was previously put there by the testator or by some other person in the testator's presence and by his direction. It is also possible for a witness to acknowledge his signature in some circumstances (see s 9(d)(ii)).

[222.14]

Form B22.12: Form of attestation where the will has been altered[1]

SIGNED by the above-named [*testator*] as his last will in the presence of us present at the same time who at his request and in his presence and in the presence of each other have signed our names below as witnesses the alteration [*or* erasure *or* interlineation] in line—on page—hereof having been made previously thereto }	[*Signature of testator.*]

[*Signatures, addresses and descriptions of two witnesses*]

1 The alterations, erasures or interlineations will be initialled in the margin by the testator and the witnesses where they occur. As to this, see Vol 1, Ch 14. Although only one alteration is noted in the precedent, the clause should refer to all alterations made in the will if more than one.

[222.15]

Form B22.13: Attestation clause where the testator has an imperfect knowledge of English[1]

THIS will having first been read over to the said [*testator*] (who understands the [Italian] language but has an imperfect knowledge of and cannot read the English language) by me the undersigned [*first witness*] in English and having been truly interpreted to the said [*testator*] by me the undersigned [*second witness*] who understands both the English and [Italian] languages [*or* both of whom the said [*witnesses*] understand both the English and [Italian] languages] which reading and interpretation were both done in our presence when the said [*testator*] appeared thoroughly to understand this will and to approve the contents thereof was signed by the said [*testator*] with his mark as his last will in the presence of us both present at the same time who at his request in his presence and in the presence of each other have signed our names below as witnesses }	[*Signature of testator.*]

[*Signatures, addresses and descriptions of two witnesses*]

1 As to attestation clauses in cases of illiterate persons, see Non-Contentious Probate Rules 1987, r 13.

[222.16]

Form B22.14: Forms of testimonium and attestation clause for will made on behalf of a mentally disordered person pursuant to an order of the Court of Protection[1]

A. TESTIMONIUM CLAUSE

IN WITNESS of which this will is signed by me [*testator*] acting by [*authorised person*] under the Order mentioned above[2] on [*date*].

B. ATTESTATION CLAUSE

SIGNED by the said [*testator*] by the said [*authorised person*] and by the said [*authorised person*] with his own name pursuant to the said Order in our both signatures being made in our presence and attested by us in the presence of the said [*authorised person*]. [Names and addresses of witnesses] Sealed with the official seal of the Court of Protection this day of 20	}	[*Testator*] by [*Authorised person*]

[*Signatures, addresses and descriptions of witnesses.*]

1 For the powers of the Court of Protection to order a will to be made on behalf of a patient, see note to Form B1.8 at para **[201.12]**. The requirements for the execution of a will on behalf of a patient are set out in the Mental Capacity Act 2005, Sch 2, para 3 (replacing the Mental Health Act 1983, s 97 on and from 1 October 2007) and are reflected in the terms of this Form. It should be noted that Sch 2, para 3 also requires that the will should be sealed with the official seal of the Court of Protection, (Part G, para **[244.145]**). See generally Vol 1, paras **[4.21]**–**[4.24]**.

2 The order will be mentioned in the commencement of the will.

PART C

Complete wills

C1 Wills for use in emergency

Note .... [223.1]

FORMS

C1.1 Gift of entire estate to one person .... [223.2]
C1.2 Gift of entire estate to children .... [223.3]
C1.3 Will incorporating gift of residue on discretionary charitable trusts .... [223.4]
C1.4 Will incorporating instructions for will .... [223.5]
C1.5 Settled gift of residue on trusts for spouse and children by reference to Statutory Will Forms .... [223.6]
C1.6 Will expressly incorporating intestacy rules .... [223.7]
C1.7 Adoption of intestacy rules by revocation of former wills .... [223.8]
C1.8 Settled gift of residue on express trusts for spouse and children .... [223.9]
C1.9 Gift of estate on discretionary trusts for family .... [223.10]
C1.10 Codicil reviving a former will and codicils which have been revoked .... [223.11]
C1.11 Codicil reviving a will which has been revoked by marriage or civil partnership .... [223.12]
C1.12 Codicil adding legacy and increasing the share of residue of one of the testator's children .... [223.13]

[223.1]

Note. This section contains a selection of short forms which may be used or adapted for use in emergency. The advent of word processors and data banks has made it much easier than formerly to produce at speed a full form of will. But situations may still arise when this is not possible and a short will may be necessary. A short will may not be ideal but can be replaced by a fuller form of will if time allows and will undoubtedly be preferable to no will at all. For the professional adviser there is the added consideration that the failure to prepare a will for execution in a death-bed situation may expose him to a liability in negligence to the intended beneficiary for the loss caused by such failure: see *White v Jones* [1995] 2 AC 207, [1995] 1 All ER 691, HL; *Gartside v Sheffield Young and Ellis* [1983] NZLR 37, NZCA; and *Hooper v Fynmores* (2001) 5 Sol Jo LB 156, in each of which a relatively short delay in the preparation of a will by a professional draftsman was held to give rise to liability in negligence (by contrast in *X v Woolcombe Yonge* [2001] WTLR 301 a very short delay was held on the facts not to give rise to liability).

As wide powers of investment are now conferred by Parts II and III of the Trustee Act 2000 (TrA 2000) (Part G, paras **[246.135]**–**[246.142]**; see also paras **[220.11]**–**[220.39]**), none need be included. Professional executors and trustees now have power to charge under TrA 2000, ss 29 and 35 (Part G, paras **[246.161]** and **[246.167]**; see also paras **[221.42]**–**[221.48]**), but this power is not available to a sole executor or trustee and is not otherwise available unless all the co-executors or co-trustees agree in writing. Forms C1.8 at para **[223.9]** and C1.9 at para **[223.10]** accordingly contain a short-form charging power which will not be subject to these restrictions.

[223.2]

Form C1.1: Gift of entire estate to one person[1]

I [*name*] of [*address*] revoke all former testamentary dispositions and declare this to be my last will.

I give all property real and personal over which I have power to dispose by will to my [wife/husband/civil partner] [*name*] absolutely and appoint [her/him] to be the sole [executrix/executor] hereof.

AS WITNESS my hand this —— day of —— 20——

SIGNED by the [testator/testatrix] in our presence and then by us in [his/hers][2] [*Signature of testator/testatrix*]

[*Signatures, addresses and descriptions of two witnesses*]

1 This form will usually be used by one spouse or civil partner in favour of the other. But it can be used in any situation where one person wishes to give his or her entire estate to another person, e g a common law spouse or unmarried partner. In the latter case a will, however rudimentary in form, will be essential as the intended beneficiary will almost certainly have no rights on intestacy.

2 In the forms in this section this short form of attestation clause has been used, which is thought to be the shortest acceptable form of attestation clause. It makes it clear that all the statutory requirements have been complied with. It was learned from the Principal Probate Registry (now the Principal Registry of the Family Division) that this form is accepted in that Registry and all District Registries, and is indeed welcomed because it enables Registrars to see at a glance that the requirements are all satisfied.

[223.3]

Form C1.2: Gift of entire estate to children[1]

I [*name*] of [*address*] revoke all former testamentary dispositions and declare this to be my last will.

I appoint [*name*] of [*address*] and [*name*] of [*address*] to be the executors and trustees of this my will.

Subject to the payment thereout of my funeral and testamentary expenses and debts I give all my real and personal property to my trustees upon trust for such of my children as survive me and if more than one in equal shares.

AS WITNESS my hand this —— day of —— 20——

SIGNED by the [testator/testatrix] in our presence and then by us in [his/hers][2] } [*Signature of testator/testatrix*]

[*Signatures, addresses and descriptions of two witnesses*]

1 This form does not contain a substitutional provision in favour of the children of a child who predeceases the testator. Such a provision is unnecessary as it is supplied by the WA 1837, s 33, as substituted by the AJA 1982 (Part G, para **[244.36]** and discussed in Vol 1, paras **[47.10]**–**[47.19]**).

[223.4]

Form C1.3: Will incorporating gift of residue on discretionary charitable trusts[1]

I [*name*] of [*address*] revoke all former testamentary dispositions and declare this to be my last will.

I appoint [*name*] of [*address*] and [*name*] of [*address*] to be the executors and trustees of this my will.

[I give the following pecuniary legacies free of inheritance tax:
(a) to [*name*] the sum of £——
(b) to [*name*] the sum of £——
(c) to [*name*] the sum of £——].

Subject to the payment thereout of my funeral and testamentary expenses and debts [and the legacies hereby given] I give all property over which I have power to dispose by will to my trustees upon trust for such charitable purposes or charitable bodies as my trustees may determine and I request my trustees (but without imposing any binding trust or obligation on them) to distribute my residuary estate [amongst charities established for charitable purposes connected with——][2] [equally between the following charities namely:
(a) [*name*]
(b) [*name*]
(c) [*name*].]

AS WITNESS my hand this —— day of —— 20——

SIGNED by the [testator/testatrix] in our presence } [*Signature of*
and then by us in [his/hers][2] *testator/testatrix*]

[*Signatures, addresses and descriptions of two witnesses*]

1 This will is intended for a childless and unmarried person who wishes to give some legacies to friends and the residue of his estate to charities of his choice but in circumstances where there is no time to confirm the existence or ascertain the correct description of such charities.

2 The first alternative enables the testator to indicate what type of charity he would like to benefit, e g charities connected with animal welfare or the relief of child poverty, rather than having to specify the charity or charities by name.

[223.5]

Form C1.4: Will incorporating instructions for will[1]

I [*name*] of [*address*] hereby revoke all former testamentary dispositions and declare this to be my last will.

I appoint [*name*] of [*address*] and [*name*] of [*address*] to be the executors and trustees of this my will.

I give all my real and personal property over which I have any power to dispose by will to my trustees upon trust to carry out the instructions attached hereto.

I declare that in giving effect to the said instructions my trustees shall have all the powers of management administration and investment of a sole beneficial owner of my estate.

AS WITNESS my hand this —— day of —— 20——

SIGNED by the [testator/testatrix] in our presence } [*Signature of*
and then by us in [his/hers][2] *testator/testatrix*]

[*Signatures, addresses and descriptions of two witnesses*]
[*Annex instructions*]

1 This form is intended for use only where the state of health of the testator is such that the will must be executed without delay. Where a will in this form is executed and the testator recovers sufficiently to execute a longer form of will, it would be advisable for him to do so. The efficacy of this form obviously depends on whether the instructions as taken down by the solicitor are sufficiently clear and certain in their legal consequences to be taken as the testator's dispositions.

[223.6]

Form C1.5: Settled gift of residue on trusts for spouse and children by reference to Statutory Will Forms[1]

I [*name*] of [*address*] hereby revoke all former testamentary dispositions and declare this to be my last will.

1. I appoint [*name*] of [*address*] and [*name*] of [*address*] to be the executors and trustees hereof.

2.
(a) I bequeath to [*name*] [my gold watch and chain] [my emerald necklace] free of inheritance tax.
(b) I bequeath the residue of my personal chattels to my [wife/husband] [*name*].

3. I bequeath the following pecuniary legacies free of inheritance tax:
(a) To [*name*] the sum of £——.
(b) To [*name*] the sum of £——.

4. I devise and bequeath all my estate both real and personal whatsoever and wheresoever to my trustees.

5. Form 8 of the Statutory Will Forms 1925[2] is incorporated in this my will and shall apply to all my estate [save that any income of my estate which has accrued in respect of a period wholly or partly before my death but is actually received after my death shall be deemed to have accrued after my death and shall not be apportioned] [and] [save that no sale shall be made of the dwellinghouse in which I now reside known as [*name*] during the lifetime of my [wife/husband] without [her/his] consent in writing and that until the sale thereof my trustees shall permit my [wife/husband] to occupy the same so long as [she/he] shall so desire].[3]

6. Form 10 of the Statutory Will Forms 1925[4] is incorporated in this my will and subject as provided in clause 5 hereof shall apply to all my property.

7. Any of my trustees being a solicitor or other person engaged in any profession or business shall be entitled to charge and be paid all usual professional or other proper charges for all business transacted or acts done by him or his firm in the administration of my estate or in connection with the trusts hereof including acts which a personal representative or trustee could have done personally.

AS WITNESS my hand this —— day of —— 20——

SIGNED by the [testator/testatrix] in our presence and then by us in [his/hers][2] } [*Signature of testator/testatrix*]

[*Signatures, addresses and descriptions of two witnesses*]

1 The Statutory Will Forms (which are printed in full at paras **[238.7]–[238.16]**) provide a useful shorthand method of incorporating fairly elaborate beneficial and administrative provisions. The disadvantage is that the testator cannot immediately see the nature and effect of his will.

2 Form 8 of the Statutory Will Forms, the text of which is set out at para **[238.14]**, contains an elaborate administration trust which includes (in para (5)) a power to invest in 'authorised investments'. This paragraph now incorporates by implication the wide powers of investment conferred by Pts II and III of the TrA 2000 (Part G, paras **[246.115]–[246.142]**). No express power of investment is therefore required and none is included. (As to investment powers generally see the Preliminary Note to B20 (para **[220.11]** ff) and Forms B20.1 to B20.9 at paras **[220.40]–[220.48]**. Form 8 of the Statutory Will Forms excludes the rule in *Howe v Dartmouth,* but not apportionment of income at the testator's death. If it is desired to exclude such apportionment, the first proviso should be added. The provisions of Form 8, cl (7)(c) leave the trustees free to apply or to exclude the rule in *Allhusen v Whittell.* For the rules of equitable apportionment see Vol 1, para **[38.17]** ff, and for a discussion of methods of excluding them see the Note to B14 at para **[214.35]** ff.

3 As to conferring rights of residence, see the Preliminary Note to B8 (para **[208.19]** ff). The right of occupation conferred on the wife by this clause does not create a strict settlement as it has not been possible to create strict settlements after 1996: TLATA 1996, s 2 (Part G, para **[246.87]**.

4 Form 10 of the Statutory Will Forms, the text of which is set out at para **[238.16]**, confers a life interest on the testator's spouse with remainder on stirpital trusts for his issue at 21 (Form 10 of the Statutory Will Forms has not been amended so as to reduce the vesting age to 18 despite the reduction of the age of majority to 18 by the FLRA 1969, s 1). The Statutory Will Forms have not been amended to provide for civil partners, so should not be used where a testator has a civil partner for whom he wishes to provide. See n 1, para **[238.16]**, for the IHT implications of incorporating Form 10 of the Statutory Will Forms 1925.

[223.7]

Form C1.6: Will expressly incorporating intestacy rules[1]

I [*name*] of [*address*] hereby revoke all former testamentary dispositions and declare this to be my last will.

1. I appoint [*name*] of [*address*] and [*name*] of [*address*] to be the executors and trustees of this my will.

2. I give the following pecuniary legacies free of inheritance tax:

(a) to [*name*] the sum of £——

(b) to [*name*] the sum of £——

(c) to [*name*] the sum of £——.

3. Subject as aforesaid I give all my real and personal property to my trustees upon the same trusts as to the sale and administration thereof and as to the beneficial interests therein as if I had died intestate in respect thereof.[2]

4. Any of my trustees being a solicitor or other person engaged in any profession or business shall be entitled to charge and be paid all professional or other proper charges for all business transacted or acts done by him or his firm in the administration of my estate or in connection with the trusts hereof including acts which a personal representative or trustee could have done personally.

AS WITNESS my hand this —— day of —— 20——

SIGNED by the [testator/testatrix] in our presence } [*Signature of*
and then by us in [his/hers][2] *testator/testatrix*]

[*Signatures, addresses and descriptions of two witnesses*]

1 This form engrafts the appointment of executors and the bequest of legacies on to a disposition of residue by reference to the intestacy rules. If the testator recovers he would be well advised to execute a new will declaring express trusts of residue.

2 See the AEA 1925, ss 33, 46 and 47 (Part G, paras **[244.60]**, **[244.62]** and **[244.63]**). The spouse or civil partner takes the 'personal chattels' (as to these, see Vol 1, para **[64.44]** and the definition in the AEA 1925, s 55(1)(x): Part G, para **[246.57]**), a net sum (currently of £125,000 where there are surviving issue, although the Government has published a consultation paper, Administration of Estates – Review of the Statutory Legacy (CP 11/05), proposing an increase) with interest (at the current rate of 6 per cent per annum) from the date of death until payment or appropriation and a life interest in half the residue. Subject to the interests of the spouse or civil partner the issue take the residue with stirpital substitution throughout. By expressly incorporating the intestacy rules, if the testator dies leaving a spouse or civil partner, his or her interest in possession in half of the residue should be an immediate post-death interest within IHTA 1984, s 49A (see para **[200.98]**). If the testator leaves infant children for whose benefit part of his estate will be held on the like trusts as the statutory trusts for issue, these trusts should qualify as trusts for bereaved minors within IHTA 1984, s 71A (see para **[200.120]** above), but may not be 'qualifying trusts' for the benefit of 'vulnerable beneficiaries' such as would allow a claim for special tax treatment bringing the trustees' income and capital gains tax liability into line with what the vulnerable beneficiaries' liability would have been had they received the income directly or had realised the trust gains (see FA 2005, ss 23–45). Although the intestacy trusts are expressly declared to qualify as trusts for the vulnerable for a relevant minor (FA 2005, s 35(1)(a)), if they do not arise by operation of statute, but rather by disposition of a testator, they may not fall within FA 2005, s 35(1)(a), and neither will they qualify under FA 2005, s 35(1)(b) since marriage under the age of 18 is an alternative contingency under the intestacy trusts but is not a permitted alternative contingency in the case of trusts appearing in a will. See para **[217.4]** above.

[223.8]

Form C1.7: Adoption of intestacy rules by revocation of former wills[1]

I [*name*] of [*address*] hereby revoke all former testamentary dispositions and declare that it is my intention to die intestate.

AS WITNESS my hand this —— day of —— 20——

SIGNED by the [testator/testatrix] in our presence } [*Signature of*
and then by us in [his/hers][2] *testator/testatrix*]

[*Signatures, addresses and descriptions of two witnesses*]

1 It is generally more convenient to prove a will than to obtain a grant of administration. A will in the form of the previous precedent is therefore preferable. But a revocation is a very short form which may be convenient to use in an emergency. A revocation must be executed in the same way as a will: see the WA 1837, s 20 (Part G, para **[244.22]**. See also Vol 1, para **[18.1]** ff. If the testator dies leaving a spouse or civil partner, his or her interest in possession in half of residue arising under the intestacy rules should be an immediate post-death interest within IHTA 1984, s 49A (see para **[200.98]** above and para **[216.1]** above). If the testator leaves infant children for whose benefit part of his estate will be held on the statutory trusts for issue, these trusts should qualify as trusts for bereaved minors within IHTA 1984, s 71A (see para **[200.108]** above), Further, in this case, unlike the former case (i e Form C1.6, para **[223.7]**), the intestacy trusts will arise by statute rather than disposition of the testator, so that if the testator dies leaving infant children for whose benefit part of

his estate will be held on the statutory trusts for issue, these trusts should be 'qualifying trusts' for the benefit of 'vulnerable beneficiaries' such as would allow a claim for special tax treatment bringing the trustees' income and capital gains tax liability into line with what the vulnerable beneficiaries' liability would have been had they received the income directly or had realised the trust gains (see FA 2005, ss 23–45). See para **[217.4]**, above and para **[223.7]**, above.

[223.9]

Form C1.8: Settled gift of residue on express trusts for spouse and children

I [*testator*] of [*address*] hereby revoke all former testamentary dispositions and declare this to be my last will.

1. I appoint [*name*] of [*address*] and [*name*] of [*address*] (hereinafter called 'my trustees' which expression shall include the trustees for the time being of this will) to be the executors and trustees hereof.

2. (1) I bequeath the following items free of inheritance tax:

(a) to my son [*name*] my father's cuff-links

(b) to my daughter [*name*] my mother's engagement ring.

(2) Subject as aforesaid I bequeath all my personal chattels within the meaning of section 55(1)(x) of the Administration of Estates Act 1925[1] to my [wife/ husband] absolutely.

3. I bequeath:

(a) £—— to my [wife/husband] absolutely to be paid as soon as possible and in priority to all other legacies.

(b) £—— free of inheritance tax to each of my executors who shall prove my will.

4. Subject to the payment thereout of my debts and funeral and testamentary expenses and the legacies hereby given my trustees shall hold the residue of my estate both real and personal:

(a) Upon trust to pay the income thereof to my [wife/husband] during [her/his] life [or until [she/he] shall remarry][2] [with power for my trustees (not being fewer than two in number) during such period to pay or apply the whole or any part of the capital thereof to [her/him] or for [her/his] benefit in such manner as they think fit[3]] and subject thereto.

(b) Upon trust as to capital and income for such of my children as shall survive me [and attain the age of [18/25] years][4] and if more than one in equal shares [provided that if any of my children shall predecease me or survive me but fail to attain a vested interest leaving a child or children surviving me or born after my death who shall attain the age of [18/21] years such last-mentioned child or children shall take and if more than equally between them the share which their parent would have taken had he or she lived to attain a vested interest].[5]

5. In relation to my estate my trustees shall have all the powers of management and investment of a sole beneficial owner.

6. The power of appointing trustees of my will shall be vested in my [wife/husband] during [her/his] life.

7. Any of my trustees being a professional or business person may be paid reasonable remuneration for services provided by him as personal representative or trustee.[6]

[8. My [wife/husband] may join in exercising the power to pay or apply capital for [her/his] benefit hereby conferred notwithstanding that [she/he] is a trustee hereof.][7]

AS WITNESS my hand this —— day of —— 20——

SIGNED by the [testator/testatrix] in our presence and then by us in [his/hers][2]	}	[*Signature of testator/testatrix*]

[*Signatures, addresses and descriptions of two witnesses*]

1 See para **[246.67]** below for the wording of this definition, and for further discussion of the meaning of 'personal chattels' see Vol 1, para **[64.44]**.

2 For deaths on or after 22 March 2006, the life interest for the surviving spouse or civil partner should be an immediate post-death interest within IHTA 1984, s 49A, so spouse or civil partner exemption from IHT should be available (see para **[216.1]**).

3 If the power to apply capital is included, it would be advisable to include a provision in the terms of cl 8 in case there is subsequently appointed a trustee. But such provision will not be necessary if the spouse is named as a trustee by the will itself: *Sargeant v National Westminster Bank plc* (1990) 61 P & CR 518, CA, 523; and *Edge v Pensions Ombudsman* [1998] Ch 512, 540–542.

4 If the age contingency of attaining 18 is included, and the trusts for children come into possession while they are still infants, these trusts should be trusts for bereaved minors within IHTA 1984, s 71A and so exempt from the IHT relevant property regime (see para **[200.108]**). They should also be 'qualifying trusts' for the benefit of 'vulnerable beneficiaries'. Such trusts will allow a claim for special tax treatment bringing the trustees' income and capital gains tax liability into line with what the vulnerable beneficiaries' liability would have been had they received the income directly or had realised the trust gains (see FA 2005, ss 23–45). See para **[217.4]**. If the age contingency selected is 25 and the trusts for children come into possession while they are under 25, these trusts should be age 18–25 trusts within IHTA 1984, s 71D and so exempt from the IHT relevant property regime although an IHT charge will arise on a beneficiary becoming absolutely entitled to capital when over the age of 18 (see para **[200.109]** above). However, if the children's trust comes into possession immediately following the testator's death, e g because he is not survived by his widow, and any child is over the age of 18 but under 21, and entitled to an interest possession by virtue of TA 1925, s 31(1)(ii) (see para **[246.29]**), he or she would have an immediate post-death interest.

5 If an age contingency is included in the primary gift for the children, the substitutional proviso should be added. This is because it is not clear whether the WA 1837, s 33 (Part G, para **[244.36]**) will apply where there is a class gift subject to a contingency of attaining a particular age, and anyway s 33 will not apply to the share of a child who survives the testator but fails to attain the specified age: see Vol 1, para **[47.17]**.

6 A professional executor or trustee is only entitled to charge under the powers conferred by the TrA 2000, ss 29 and 35 (Part G, paras **[246.161]** and **[246.167]**) if his co-executors or co-trustees agree in writing. A sole executor or trustee is not entitled to charge under the statutory power. An express charging provision as in cl 7 enables a professional executor or trustee to charge without obtaining the consent of his co-trustees and to charge if he is a sole executor or trustee. Under the TrA 2000, s 28(2) (Part G, para **[246.160]**) a professional trustee (and executor: see s 35) who has the benefit of an express power to charge is entitled to charge for services which are capable of being provided by a lay trustee and so a short form such as this will be adequate for the purpose.

7 See n 2 above.

[223.10]

Form C1.9: Gift of estate on discretionary trusts for family[1]

I [*name*] of [*address*] revoke all former testamentary dispositions and declare this to be my last will.

1. I appoint [*name*] of [*address*] and [*name*] of [*address*] (hereinafter called 'my trustees' which expression shall include the trustees for the time being of this will) to be the executors and trustees of this will.

2. Subject to the payment thereout of my debts and my funeral and testamentary expenses my trustees shall hold all my estate both real and personal upon the trusts and with and subject to the powers and provisions hereinafter declared and contained.

3. (1) In this clause—

(a) 'the beneficiaries' means and includes
  (i) my [wife/husband/civil partner] [*name*]
  (ii) my children and remoter issue
  (iii) the spouse civil partner widow widower or surviving civil partner of any of my children and remoter issue;[2]

(b) 'the trust period' means the period of 80 years immediately following my death[3] which shall be the perpetuity period applicable to the disposition effected by this will.

(2) My trustees shall have the following powers exercisable at any time and from time to time during the trust period:

(a) Power by deed or deeds to appoint that they shall hold the whole or any part or parts of my estate upon trust for all or such one or more of the discretionary beneficiaries and if more than one in such shares and with such trusts and powers (including trusts and powers conferring a discretion as to the disposition of capital or income) and provisions (including provisions for the accumulation of income during any period or periods permitted by law) as my trustees think fit,[4]

(b) Power to pay or apply the whole or any part or parts of my estate to or for the advancement support or benefit of all or any one or more of the discretionary beneficiaries in such manner as my trustees think fit.[5]

(3) Subject to any exercise of the foregoing powers my trustees shall hold my estate during the trust period upon trust to pay or apply the income thereof to or for the maintenance education support or benefit of all or any one or more of the discretionary beneficiaries for the time being living and if more than one in such shares and generally in such manner as my trustees shall think fit and shall hold the capital of my estate at the expiration of the trust period upon trust for such of my children and remoter issue then living and if more than one in equal shares per stirpes each child of mine being treated as a head of stock.

(4) The power to appoint capital conferred by subclause (2) hereof shall be exercisable whether or not a grant of administration has been obtained and whether or not the administration of my estate is complete.[6]

(5) The powers to appoint and apply capital and the discretion as to the distribution of income conferred by subclauses (2) and (3) hereof shall be

exercisable notwithstanding that any of my trustees has a personal interest in such exercise provided that there are not fewer than two trustees and that at least one of them has no such personal interest.[7]

4. In relation to my estate my trustees shall have all the powers of management and investment of a sole beneficial owner.[8]

5. The power of appointing trustees of this will shall be vested in my [wife/husband/civil partner] during [her/his] life.

6. Any of my trustees being a professional or business person may be paid reasonable remuneration for services provided by him as personal representative or trustee.[9]

AS WITNESS my hand this —— day of —— 20——

SIGNED by the [testator/testatrix] in our presence and then by us in [his/hers][2]	}	[*Signature of testator/testatrix*]

[*Signatures, addresses and descriptions of two witnesses*]

1 This form is intended for use by a testator who is uncertain as to the ultimate disposition of his estate and is content to leave the decision to his trustees.
2 The composition of the discretionary class will vary according to the circumstances of the individual testator.
3 This is the longest period which can be specified under the PAA 1964, s 1, the text of which appears in Part G, para **[246.74]**.
4 This is a wide power of appointment which expressly authorises the creation of discretions as to the disposition of capital and income.
5 A power to apply capital is a useful adjunct which can be exercised without any formality.
6 Although not strictly necessary, this provision may be useful in cases where a speedy appointment is required, e g an appointment within two years of the death complying with the IHTA 1984, s 144 (see para **[225.83]** ff), in view of arguments which HMRC has been known to advance to the effect that no appointment can be made before the completion of the administration. It should be remembered that for the technical reason discussed in the note to C3.6 (para **[225.85]**) an appointment or application of capital within three months of the testator's death will not attract the operation of s 144.
7 Since family trustees may well be appointed, a provision in this form is desirable.
8 This clause confers wide powers of investment and management. For administrative powers generally see B20 at para **[220.11]**.
9 See n 4 to Form C1.8 at para **[223.9]**.

[223.11]

Form C1.10: Codicil reviving a former will and codicils which have been revoked[1]

I [*testator*] of [*address*] declare this to be a [[second][third]] codicil to my will dated the [*date 1*].[2]

Whereas I made my most recent will on [*date 2*] and thereby revoked my said will dated [*date 1*] [and [two] codicil—[s] [respectively] dated [*date*] [and [*date*]]].

Now I hereby revive and confirm the said will dated [*date 1*] [and the said codicil[s] thereto] and hereby revoke [the said will dated [*date 2*] and] all testamentary dispositions made by me other than the said will dated [*date 1*] [and the said codicil[s] thereto].

AS WITNESS my hand this —— day of —— 20——

SIGNED by the [testator/testatrix] in our presence } [*Signature of testator/testatrix*]
and then by us in [his/hers][2]

[*Signatures, addresses and descriptions of two witnesses*]

1 It is advisable to execute a new will in the same terms as the revoked will, but in cases of emergency and where a copy of the former will exists, it may be necessary to use this form. If the previous will was revoked by destruction animo revocandi and no copy thereof is in existence, it will not be possible to adopt this course. A new will must in such a case be executed. On revival of wills see Vol 1, para **[21.1]** ff.

2 In the interests of clarity, in this form the date of the revoked will which is being revived is referred to as '*date 1*', and the date of the most recent will which is being revoked is referred to as '*date 2*'.

[223.12]

Form C1.11: Codicil reviving a will which has been revoked by marriage or civil partnership[1]

I [*name*] of [*address*] declare this to be a codicil to my will dated [*date*].

whereas;

(1) By my said will I left my residuary estate to [*name*].

(2) On [*date*] I [married]/[formed a civil partnership with] the said [*name*] and my said will was accordingly revoked.

Now I hereby revive and confirm my said will.

AS WITNESS my hand this —— day of —— 20——

SIGNED by the [testator/testatrix] in our presence } [*Signature of testator/testatrix*]
and then by us in [his/hers][2]

[*Signatures, addresses and descriptions of two witnesses*]

1 This will is designed for use in cases where a couple who have been living together and have made wills in favour of each other subsequently marry or form a civil partnership. The wills will be revoked by the marriage or civil parteneship by WA 1837, s 18 or 18B as inserted by CPA 2004, Sch 4, para 2 (Part G, paras **[244.16]**, **[244.19]**; see also Vol 1, paras **[17.5]**–**[17.8]**). Although it is preferable to execute a new will embodying the terms of the revoked will, this form may be used in an emergency.

[223.13]

Form C1.12: Codicil adding legacy and increasing the share of residue of one of the testator's children[1]

I [*testator*] of [*address*] declare this to be a codicil to my will dated the [*date*].

1. I give a pecuniary legacy of £—— to [*name*].

2. Whereas by my said will my residuary estate (as therein defined) is directed to be held on trust for such of my children as survive me and if more than one in equal shares NOW I hereby declare that on the division of my residuary estate my son [*name*] if surviving me shall be entitled to double the share of any other surviving child or children of mine.

3. In all other respects I confirm my said will.

AS WITNESS my hand this —— day of —— 20——

SIGNED by the [testator/testatrix] in our presence and then by us in [his/hers][2] } [*Signature of testator/testatrix*]

[*Signatures, addresses and descriptions of two witnesses*]

1 For further examples of codicils varying the terms of existing wills see Part D, para **[237.1]** ff.

C2 Wills for married couples (or civil partners) with young children

Preliminary note .... [224.1]

FORMS

C2.1 Reciprocal wills giving entire estate to spouse absolutely, with alternative gift to issue .... [224.27]

C2.2 Reciprocal wills giving entire estate to spouse absolutely with alternative gift of IPDIs to issue .... [224.42]

C2.3 Reciprocal wills leaving entire estate to spouse for life with power to resort to capital and with remainder to children .... [224.58]

C2.4 Reciprocal wills giving spouse life interest with power of appointment amongst issue, incorporating Statutory Will Forms.... [224.73]

C2.5 Will of husband who owns matrimonial home giving wife income of residue and right of residence for life or until remarriage .... [224.86]

C2.6 Will of husband settling residue on wife for life with remainder on discretionary trusts .... [224.102]

PRELIMINARY NOTE

[224.1]

General strategy and IHT. This section contains a selection of forms for use by married couples or civil partners with young children. Such couples are likely to be young or middle-aged, and the main purpose of wills for such couples is to provide for the possibility of one or other spouse or civil partner meeting an early death. If this happens it is likely on average that the other will survive for a long period. Providing for the survivor will be more important than IHT saving, and anyway nil-rate band carry-forward, announced on 9 October 2007 (see para **[200.75]**), means (assuming it becomes law) that the first to die making an exempt gift to the survivor of all his or her estate is a sound IHT-minimising strategy in most cases. Accordingly, all the forms in this section provide for the entire estate or virtually the entire estate of the first to die to devolve on the surviving spouse or civil partner either absolutely or for a life or widowhood or other limited interest. Such a limited interest will be an immediate post-death interest ('IPDI') within IHTA 1984, s 49A, and thus 'beneficiary-taxed' (see para **[200.98]**). Whether the gift to the survivor is absolute or for an interest in possession, the transfer on the death of the first to die will be exempt from IHT by virtue of the exemption for gifts to spouses or civil partners (see para **[200.84]**). The property of the first to die which goes to the survivor will be subject to IHT on the latter's death, so far as it has not been given away by the latter by lifetime potentially exempt transfers made seven years or more before his or her death. However, the IHT charge on the second death will be mitigated by nil-rate band carry-forward: see para **[200.75]**. For the circumstances where a nil-rate band discretionary trust could still be worth including in the will of the first to die of a married couple or civil partnership see para **[200.130]**ff.

[224.2]
It should be noted that on and after 22 March 2006, the opportunity for the survivor of a married couple or civil partners to make potentially exempt transfers remains, but is more limited than it formerly was. Potential exemption will only be available if the survivor's gift (or deemed transfer of value on the termination of his or her IPDI) results in another person acquiring the property absolutely, or an interest in possession which has the result that its holder is treated as beneficially entitled to the underlying settled property under IHTA 1984, s 49(1), the only available category where an IPDI commenced after 21 March 2006 being a disabled person's interest: see para **[200.71]** above. Additionally, in relation to the survivor's deemed transfer of value on the termination of his or her IPDI, potential exemption will be available if it results in the settled property becoming subject to trusts for bereaved minors within IHTA 1984, s 71A (see para **[200.128]** above). Also, it must be borne in mind that the termination of an IPDI on or after 22 March 2006 will be deemed to be a gift of the underlying settled property for the purposes of FA 1986, s 102, so that unless the beneficiary of the IPDI is excluded altogether from benefit after the termination, the gift with reservation rules could apply, see FA 1986, s 102ZA, (see para **[200.76]** above). Therefore, the former IHT advantage of a life interest for the survivor subject to overriding powers of appointment so that the life interest could be terminated in favour of new trusts under which the survivor might possibly benefit without inheritance reservation of benefit concerns, no longer exists.

[224.3]
Further changes to IHT which took effect on 22 March 2006 have a significant impact on dispositions in favour of children. For deaths on and after 22 March 2006, it is no longer possible to create trusts which have the IHT benefits of IHTA 1984, s 71 (see para **[200.107]** above), but two new categories of trust are specifically introduced for a testator's children, namely a trust for bereaved minors within IHTA 1984, s 71A (see para **[200.108]** above) and an age 18-to-25 trust within IHTA 1984, s 71D (see para **[200.109]** above). These trusts have the IHT advantage that, unlike most other trusts created after 21 March 2006, they will not be subject to the IHT relevant property regime, although in the case of an age 18-to-25 trust there is an occasion of IHT charge when a beneficiary becomes entitled to capital between ages 18 and 25. As alternatives to trusts for bereaved minors and age 18-to-25 trusts, children might be given IPDIs, or property may be settled on full discretionary trusts or other trusts which would be within the IHT relevant property regime, or they may be given assets absolutely in a bare trust. All of these options are considered in more detail at para **[224.24]** below, and also paras **[200.125]** ff.

[224.4]
Civil partners. The forms of C2 are drafted principally for married couples with children, but Forms C2.1, C2.2 and C2.3 can be easily adapted for use by civil partners with children. Forms C2.5 and C2.6 can be easily adapted for use by a civil partner with children. The Notes to the beginning of these Forms and the footnotes indicate what amendments may be required.

[224.5]
Uncertain order of deaths. Where two persons die in circumstances rendering it uncertain which of them survived the other, the younger is generally presumed for succession purposes to have survived the older: Law of Property Act 1925 (LPA 1925), s 184 (Part G, para **[244.58]**; see also Vol 1, paras **[70.1]**–**[70.4]**). The rule is excluded where the older person dies intestate and the younger person is his or her spouse or civil partner; in such a case the younger spouse or civil partner is treated as not having survived: Administration of Estates Act 1925 (AEA 1925), s 46(3) (Part G, para **[244.62]**). In the legislation relating to IHT the latter rule has been adopted and extended to all cases, so that where any two persons, whether married or civil partners or not, and whether testate or intestate, die in circumstances rendering it uncertain which of them survived they are treated as having died simultaneously for the purposes of the charge to IHT on death (IHTA 1984, s 4(2)). This means that where spouses or civil partners die in circumstances rendering it uncertain which survived, neither will be treated as having survived the other for IHT purposes, even if the estate of the older devolves on the younger under the older's will by virtue of the LPA 1925, s 184 (Part G, para **[244.58]**; see also para **[224.9]** and Vol 1, paras **[70.1]**–**[70.4]**). In these circumstances the older's estate will devolve on the younger and then under the will of the younger (or the intestacy rules as they apply to the younger), but it will not be added to the younger's estate for the purposes of the IHT charge on the younger's death. The nil-rate band of each will be fully utilised, provided that each has assets of a value equal to or more than the upper limit of the nil-rate band, or there will be the even more favourable result, mentioned at para **[224.9]** of this Preliminary Note, of the spouse or civil partner exemption applying to the estate of the first to die without that estate being charged to IHT on the survivor's death. It should be noted that in the event of husband and wife or civil partners dying in circumstances rendering it uncertain which of them survived the other, it seems that there will be no nil-rate band carry-forward (see para **[200.75]** for this), because it will not be possible to show that either survived the other. This will only be an IHT disadvantage where one of them owned assets with a total value less than the upper limit of the nil-rate band, and the other had assets with a total value which exceeds it.

[224.6]
Survivorship conditions. See also the Note on survivorship provisions in B19 at paras **[219.1]**–**[219.13]** and for further forms see Forms B19.1 to B19.4 at paras **[219.14]**–**[219.17]**. It has become a common practice to include in wills survivorship conditions whereby gifts by will are made conditional on the donee surviving the testator by a specified period. Where the period so specified does not exceed six months and the donee dies during that period, the disposition of the testator's will taking effect as a result of the donee's death during the survivorship period is treated by the IHTA 1984, s 92 as having had effect on the testator's death. The testator's estate will thus be treated for IHT purposes as devolving directly on the beneficiaries to whom the estate is given if the gift to the donee does not take effect. This has been a particularly common practice as between husband and wife or civil partners for the good reason that before the advent of nil-rate band

carry-forward (see para **[200.75]** for this) it could save IHT where, apart from the effect of the survivorship clause, all the estate of the first to die was given to the survivor. It meant that two nil-rate bands were utilised instead of one in the event of the survivor dying within the survivorship period. However, nil-rate band carry-forward means that survivorship clauses are no longer advantageous for IHT purposes save in exceptional circumstances, though in most cases their inclusion will not be a disadvantage: see para **[224.7]**.

[224.7]

Survivorship conditions and nil-rate band carry-forward. Nil-rate band carry-forward (see para **[200.75]** for this), assuming it becomes law, has the implication that from an IHT point of view survivorship conditions as between husband and wife or civil partners are less important than formerly, and in some situations counterproductive. Suppose A and B are husband and wife, and B is known to have died six weeks after A's death. A's will leaves the whole of his estate to B, and contains a survivorship clause whereby B only takes if she survives A by two months. Both estates are given, in the event of the other not surviving by two months, to their children. The position can be summarised as follows:

(1) If B had at her death assets of a total value less than the nil-rate band, while A had assets of a value which exceeded it, less IHT would be paid on the combined estates if there were no survivorship clause. This is because if there were no survivorship clause, under nil-rate band carry-forward, in combination with the whole of A's estate being inherited by B, the combined assets of both would get the benefit of a doubled nil-rate band on B's death. The survivorship clause means that A's nil-rate band is used in full on his death, and that on B's death the excess of B's nil-rate band over the value of B's assets goes to waste; there is no proposal for nil-rate band carry-back.

(2) If A died shortly before 6 April, and B died on or after that date, and the nil-rate band in the IHT rate table was (as has happened with every new tax year since 1995–96) increased with effect from that 6 April, less IHT would be paid on the combined estates if there were no survivorship clause (assuming that both have assets in excess of any relevant nil-rate band). This is because with the survivorship clause operating A's nil-rate band, used in full on his death, is at the pre 6 April level. If all A's estate had gone to B, nil-rate band carry-forward would have given their combined estates a nil-rate band of double the nil-rate band at its level on or after 6 April.

(3) If either or both of A or B was entitled to an increased nil-rate band by reason of carry-forward from a previous marriage or civil partnership which ended in the death of the other party, the survivorship clause will have saved IHT as compared with there being no survivorship clause. This is because under nil-rate band carry-forward, the uplift of the nil-rate band on B's death is limited to 100 per cent.

Otherwise the presence of the survivorship clause in the above example appears to be IHT neutral, ie it makes no difference to the amount of IHT paid on the combined estates whether or not it was included in A's will.

[224.8]
Survivorship clauses are thus in most cases better left out of wills as between husband and wife or civil partners. Although a survivorship clause could have a beneficial effect where either or both has potential nil-rate band carry-forward from a previous marriage or civil partnership which ended in the death of the other party, a survivorship clause is not the best solution where this is the case. This is because the survivorship clause will only have any effect if the survivor dies within the survivorship period. What is needed in this situation is a nil-rate band discretionary trust provided by the will of the first to die, and where a nil-rate band discretionary trust is provided a survivorship clause is still not appropriate: see para **[219.8]**. The only circumstance where a survivorship clause between husband and wife or civil partners can have a significant function is where their wills do not provide the same ultimate destination for their assets in the event of the other predeceasing: see C9.4 at para **[231.42]**.

The forms in C2 are all ones where all or nearly all the estate of the first to die goes into the IHT 'estate' of the survivor (ie absolutely or for an interest in possession which would be an IPDI). For the reasons given in paras **[224.7]** and **[224.9]**, the forms in C2 do not contain survivorship provisions as between the spouses or civil partners. For further discussion of survivorship conditions see the Note on commorientes provisions in B19 at paras **[219.1]**–**[219.13]** and for further forms see Forms B19.1 to B19.4 at paras **[219.14]**–**[219.17]**. For gifts in reciprocal wills which are intended to take effect only once, and survivorship clauses, see paras **[231.7]**, **[231.8]**.

[224.9]
Advantages of no survivorship condition where order of deaths of spouses or civil partners is uncertain. Where spouses or civil partners who make wills leaving their estates to each other happen to die in a common accident and the order of their deaths is uncertain, there can be an advantage if no survivorship condition takes effect in relation to the inter-spouse or -civil partner gift in the will of the older of them. Although for the purposes of the IHT charges on their deaths the two spouses or civil partners will be treated as dying simultaneously by virtue of the IHTA 1984, s 4(2) (see para **[224.2]**), the estate of the older will still devolve on the younger under the LPA 1925, s 184 (see para **[224.2]**) and will therefore become 'comprised in the estate of the transferor's spouse or civil partner' so as to qualify for exemption under the IHTA 1984, s 18 (see para **[200.84]** ff). IHTA 1984, s 4(2) applies to s 4(1) but not s 18. On the other hand the younger will be treated for IHT purposes as not having survived the older so that his or her separate estate will alone be taxable. HMRC accept that the spouse or civil partnership exemption is available in these circumstances (HMRC Inheritance Tax Manual para 12197). For forms of survivorship clause for husband and wife or civil partners, for cases where a survivorship clause is still wanted, which exclude the survivorship condition in the will of the older in the event of the order of deaths being unknown, see Forms B19.3 and B19.4 at paras **[219.16]** and **[219.17]**. See also the Note on commorientes provisions in B19 at para **[219.1]** ff.

[224.10]
Survivorship conditions and gifts to persons other than the testator's spouse or civil partner. The use of survivorship provisions and the scope of the IHTA 1984, s 92 are not confined to inter-spouse or -civil partner gifts. The main purpose of putting a condition of surviving the testator for a specified period in a gift to someone other than the testator's spouse or civil partner is usually to control the ultimate devolution of the property in question in the event of the early death of the primary beneficiary. However, it will also mean that if the primary beneficiary dies within the survivorship period and the IHTA 1984, s 92 applies, there is only one occasion of charge to IHT on death in relation to the property subject to the gift instead of two, and some IHT may be saved. There will not always be an IHT saving as a result of the operation of the survivorship condition because one or other estate may be below the tax threshold, and where both are large enough for tax to be payable successive charges relief under the IHTA 1984, s 141 will be available if there is no survivorship condition. See also paras **[231.7]**, **[231.8]**.

[224.11]
Guardians. Since the forms in C2 are for testators with young children, provision for the appointment of guardians is included in all cases. Under the Children Act 1989 where both parents have 'parental responsibility' (which will ordinarily be the case with married couples with young children) an appointment of guardians by one parent will not take effect during the lifetime of the other. It seems more convenient in these circumstances for the effective appointment to be made by the survivor. The forms in this section therefore provide that the appointment will not take effect if the other spouse survives. Where the forms are being adapted for use by civil partners, alternative forms of appointment of guardians should be used, see Forms B3.28 and B3.29. For the law relating to guardianship see Vol 1, paras **[28.1]–[28.8]**, and for the appointment of guardians see the Note in B3 at paras **[203.43]–[203.54]**, and Forms B3.26 to B3.32 at paras **[203.55]–[203.61]**.

[224.12]
Reciprocal and mutual wills. It is contemplated that most of the forms in this section will be used by both husband and wife (or both civil partners) and can be readily adapted for use by either. In this sense they are 'reciprocal', but they are not intended to be 'mutual' in the strict sense, ie executed pursuant to an agreement not to revoke them. If the parties wish to execute mutual wills in this sense, the formula used in Form B1.6 at para **[201.10]** should be adopted, but this course is not recommended. For the general law relating to mutual wills see Vol 1, paras **[2.3]–[2.9]**. If a husband and wife or civil partners want to make sure in the will of the first of them to die that that person's property will go to eg the children, on the death of the survivor, then a life interest trust for the survivor, perhaps with a power to apply capital for his or her benefit, with remainder to the children, is a better arrangement than mutual wills. See eg Forms C2.3 to C2.6 at para **[224.51]** ff and C3.2 and C3.5 at paras **[225.23]–[225.41]** and **[225.92]–[225.109]** respectively. For a form containing a declaration against mutual wills, see Form C2.1 at para **[224.28]**.

[224.13]
Reciprocal wills and the ultimate destination of property. Forms C2.1 and C2.2 (at paras **[224.27]–[224.57]**), in which each spouse leaves his or her estate (or most of it) to the other absolutely, are only suitable for use where the alternative gift, which takes effect where the other has predeceased the testator or testatrix (or failed to survive the survivorship period), is to the same beneficiaries in the wills of both spouses, ie to the children of their marriage. Where one or other of them has children who are not (or not treated in law) as children of the marriage (ie he or she has illegitimate children or children of another marriage), it is not appropriate for both spouses simply to make wills which contain absolute gifts to each other with an alternative gift to 'my children', since this will mean that the children who have as a parent one of the spouses but not the other will only inherit anything if their parent survives the other spouse. If such children are intended to benefit under their parent's will, other forms (such as those in C5 at para **[227.1]** ff) should be used. If they are not intended to take any benefit, words need to be added to the alternative gift so as to exclude them from its scope.

[224.14]
One method of excluding *illegitimate* children of one or other party to the marriage from taking under a gift is to exclude the statutory rules of construction which include illegitimate persons in words descriptive of relationship (see Part A, paras **[200.28]–[200.33]** and Vol 1, para **[72.14]**). This will not be sufficient where there are children who are intended to be excluded from the gift who are children of another marriage of one of the spouses. In Forms C2.1 (at para **[224.27]**) and C2.2 (at para **[224.42]**) where the primary gift of residue is an absolute gift to the surviving spouse, optional words are included in the alternative gift which restrict the donees of the gift to the children of the marriage (see paras **[224.35]** and **[224.50]**). If such words are included, any illegitimate children of the testator or testatrix, or children by some other marriage, will be excluded, but the gift will include legitimated children of the marriage (see the Legitimacy Act 1976, s 5(3): Part G, para **[245.48]**), adopted children of the marriage (see the Adoption Act 1976, s 39(1), Part G, para **[245.58]**, and the Adoption and Children Act 2002, s 67, Part G, para **[245.93]**) and children of the marriage born as a result of in vitro fertilisation or artificial insemination with the husband's consent (see the Human Fertilisation and Embryology Act 1990, s 28(2) and 29(1), (3): Part G, paras **[245.86]** and **[245.87]**). On these topics see also Vol 1, paras **[72.15]–[72.18]**, **[74.5]–[74.7]**, and **[75.1]–[75.9]** respectively.

[224.15]
This is a less significant point where the will takes the form of a life interest with remainders, because each spouse's estate will ultimately go to his own children, instead of the estate of the first to die being added to that of the survivor and going to the survivor's children. Of the life interest with remainder forms in C2, Form C2.3 (at para **[224.58]**) has, like Forms C2.1 (at para **[224.27]**) and C2.2 (at para **[224.42]**), optional words confining the trust for the children to the children of the marriage (see para **[224.65]**), but in Forms C2.4 to C2.6 (at paras **[224.73]–[224.118]**) the remainder trusts are for all the testator's children without such a restriction.

[224.16]
The possibility of divorce or dissolution of civil partnership. In relation to deaths on or after 1 January 1996, the dissolution or annulment of a testator's marriage after he has made a will causes his or her spouse to be deemed to have died on the date of the decree of divorce or annulment, for the purposes of any provisions of that will:

(i) conferring a power of appointment, if it is conferred on the spouse;
(ii) appointing executors or trustees, if the spouse is so appointed;
(iii) which relate to the devolution of property which, or an interest in which, is given to the spouse.

See the Wills Act 1837 (WA 1837), s 18A(1), as amended by the Law Reform (Succession) Act 1995, s 3 (Part G, para **[244.18]** and discussed in Vol 1 (at paras **[25.7]** and **[47.2]**), in Part A (at para **[200.26]**) and below.

The dissolution of a testator's civil partnership will have a like effect on his or her will in relation to his or her former civil partner as divorce would have in relation to his or her former spouse, see the WA 1837, s 18C as inserted by CPA 2004, Sch 4, Pt 1, para 2 (see Part G, para **[244.20]** and Vol 1, para **[47.3]**).

[224.17]
This treatment of the spouse or civil partner as having died on the date the marriage or civil partnership is dissolved or annulled has the effect not only of causing a provision in favour of the testator's spouse or civil partner of any of the kinds just mentioned to fail, but also of causing any alternative provision contained in the will, which is expressed to take effect in the event of the spouse or civil partner predeceasing the testator, to take effect instead. It is thus not necessary to make any express provision in wills for the possibility of s 18A or 18C applying, save that there is some uncertainty as to its effect on discretionary trusts and powers of which the testator's spouse or civil partner is an object: see paras **[224.21]**–**[224.23]**. By contrast, the WA 1837, s 18A as originally enacted (by the AJA 1982, s 18: Part G, para **[244.17]**), which applies in relation to deaths before 1 January 1996, causes any appointment as executor, or gift by will, in favour of the testator's spouse to lapse if there has been a divorce, but does not always cause alternative gifts or other provisions which are contained in the will, and expressed to take effect in the event of the spouse predeceasing the testator, to be effective (see Vol 1, para **[47.2]**). In particular, it fails to bring into operation a gift which is expressed to take effect if the testator's spouse predeceases the testator in the alternative to an absolute gift to the spouse (*Re Sinclair* [1985] Ch 446, [1985] 1 All ER 1066).

[224.18]
In wills made before 1 January 1996, therefore, a cautious draftsman will have provided for the possibility of the testator and his spouse becoming divorced by introducing any alternative appointment of executors which is to take effect in the event of the failure of an appointment of the testator's spouse, or any alternative gift which is provided in the event of the failure of a gift to the testator's spouse, with words such as 'if my [wife/husband] shall predecease me or the foregoing [gift to/appointment of] [her/him] shall fail

for any other reason' (see cls 1 and 5 of Form C2.1 at paras **[224.29]** and **[224.33]**). This is not necessary after 31 December 1995. There is no harm in retaining such wording, and its presence will mean that in the event of a disclaimer of the primary gift the alternative gift will take effect (which it would probably not otherwise do in the event of such a disclaimer—see Vol 1, para **[48.8]**). However, most draftsmen will probably prefer not to include such wording now that it is not necessary to do so in order to deal with the difficulties created by the WA 1837, s 18A as originally enacted (Part G, para **[244.17]**). Where a testator is happily married it is not appropriate when taking instructions for a will, nor likely to improve the reputation of the legal profession, to discuss providing in it for the eventuality of a divorce.

[224.19]
For completeness we retain an example of the use of wording which refers to failure of an appointment or gift in favour of a spouse for reasons other than predeceasing the testator: see Form C2.1, cls 1 and 5 at paras **[224.29]** and **[224.33]**. We do not include such wording in the other forms in Part C which contain provisions in favour of the testator's spouse.

[224.20]
The reason why even the revised WA 1837, s 18A, and new s 18C, do not go so far as to say that a will shall have effect for *all* purposes as if the testator's spouse or civil partner had died on the date on which the marriage or civil partnership is dissolved or annulled is presumably that this could upset provisions for the benefit of persons other than the spouse or civil partner which are contingent on, eg, the testator's spouse or civil partner not surviving the testator. An example is Form C3.1, cl 2 at para **[225.12]** where both spouses make wills with the same set of pecuniary legacies which are intended to take effect only once, on the death of the survivor. If s 18A applied to the construction of this clause and there was a divorce, the legacies would have effect on both deaths.

[224.21]
The possibility of divorce or dissolution of civil partnership – Wills Act 1837, ss 18A, 18C and discretionary trusts or powers. What effect, if any, the WA 1837, s 18A, as amended by the Law Reform (Succession) Act 1995, s 3 in relation to deaths on or after 1 January 1996 (see Part G, para **[244.18]** for the text of it), or WA 1837, s 18C (as inserted by CPA 2004, Sch 4, Pt 1, para 2 – se Part G, para **[244.20]** for the text of it), has on discretionary trusts or powers under which the testator's spouse or civil partner is a beneficiary is not obvious and requires some careful thought. WA 1837, ss 18A(1)(a) and 18C(1)(a) are not relevant because they concern powers of appointment which are to be *exercised* by the spouse or civil partner, not ones under which the spouse or civil partner may benefit. WA 1837, ss 18A(1)(b) and 18C(1)(b) provide that any property which, or an interest in which, is devised or bequeathed to the former spouse or civil partner shall pass as if the former spouse or civil partner had died on the date the marriage or civil partnership is dissolved or annulled. It seems to us that if a will gives the testator's spouse or civil partner a life interest in property with

a power to pay or apply capital of that property to or for the benefit of the spouse or civil partner, there is a divorce or dissolution of the civil partnership before the testator's death, and the testator predeceases his or her former spouse or civil partner without changing the will, then that property will be property an interest in which (ie the life interest) is devised or bequeathed to the former spouse or civil partner, s 18A(1)(b) or 18C(1)(b) will apply so as to cause that property to pass as if the spouse or civil partner died on the date of the decree of divorce or dissolution, and that will probably mean that the power to pay or apply capital, as well as the life interest, will not have effect.

[224.22]
On the other hand, if the will created a discretionary trust or power over capital or income of a fund which could be exercised in favour of the testator's spouse or civil partner, without the spouse or civil partner having any other beneficial interest in that fund, it is not clear that s 18A(1)(b) or s 18C(1)(b) would have any effect where a former spouse or civil partner did not predecease the testator. This is because it is not clear that making someone a discretionary object of a trust or power relating to particular property (and conferring no other benefit arising from that property) is to devise or bequeath to him or her an interest in that property within the meaning of s 18A(1)(b) or s 18C(1)(b). In practice it is only in rare cases that this point will matter. If a former spouse or civil partner turns out to be one of a class of discretionary beneficiaries under a will made before the dissolution of the marriage or civil partnership, it will be open to the trustees to decide that it is not appropriate to exercise their discretion in his or her favour.

[224.23]
Despite the view expressed above about the position under WA 1837, ss 18A(1)(b) and 18C(1)(b) in relation to a life interest for a spouse or civil partner coupled with a power to pay or apply capital to or for him or her, we recommend that any such power is limited so as to be exercisable only over capital which is for the time being subject to the life interest, and in the forms in Part C where this type of provision is made we have mostly so provided. This eliminates any uncertainty as to the operation of s 18A(1)(b) or s 18C(1)(b) on this type of provision, by making sure that if the life interest is rendered ineffective by s 18A(1)(b) or s 18C(1)(b) the power will be rendered ineffective as well, and also ensures that (where there is no dissolution and the spouse or civil partner survives the testator) if the spouse or civil partner assigns or surrenders the life interest the power will automatically be extinguished. There are various possible adverse fiscal consequences where a power to pay or apply capital to or for the benefit of the life tenant continues to be exercisable over capital in relation to which the life interest has ceased. One is that the termination of an IPDI (see **[200.98]** for these) on or after 22 March 2006 will be deemed to be a gift of the underlying settled property for the purposes of FA 1986, s 102, so that unless the beneficiary entitled to the IPDI is excluded altogether from benefit after the termination, the gift with reservation rules could apply, see FA 1986, s 102ZA, (see para **[200.76]** above). If a power to pay or apply capital

continues to be exercisable in his or her favour, he or she will not be excluded. Another is that the result of an assignment or surrender of a life interest may be a settlement under which the former life tenant is a settlor (by virtue of settling the life interest) for income tax purposes, but is not wholly excluded from benefit (because the power to pay or apply capital continues to be exercisable) with the result that the settlement income continues to be charged to income tax as his or her income (as happened in *IRC v Cookson* [1977] 2 All ER 331, [1977] 1 WLR 962). Another is that the continued existence of the power could wreck the intended IHT status of the trusts as trusts for bereaved minors within IHTA 1984, s 71A, (see para **[200.108]** above) or age 18-to-25 trusts within IHTA 1984, s 71D, (see para **[200.109]** above). For a power in favour of a surviving spouse or civil partner which is limited to capital of which he or she has an interest in the income, see eg Form C2.3, cl 5 at para **[224.64]**.

[224.24]

Trusts for the testator's children and IHT. For deaths on and after 22 March 2006, there are five different IHT regimes which might apply to trusts for the testator's children established by will. These are (and see also para **[200.125]** ff)—

(a) Trusts for bereaved minors within IHTA 1984, s 71A. The main characteristics of such trusts are described in para **[200.108]** above, but they are essentially trusts under which the testator's children (or stepchildren, or children for whom the testator has parental responsibility) will be fully entitled to the assets in the trust at age 18. For parental responsibility see Vol 1, para **[28.2]**, and for the meaning of step-parent where there is a civil partnership see para **[224.35]**, n 1. The main IHT advantages of such trusts are threefold: firstly, property subject to such trusts will be exempt from the relevant property regime; secondly, the lifetime termination of an IPDI (eg. for the surviving spouse) in favour of such trusts will be a potentially exempt transfer (see IHTA 1984, s 3A(3B)); and thirdly, there will be no IHT charges when a beneficiary becomes absolutely entitled to the settled property or dies under the age of 18, or on its being paid or applied for the advancement or benefit of a beneficiary (see IHTA 1984, s 71B(2)). There is also a capital gains tax advantage in that when assets are paid out of the trusts and the trustees are deemed under TCGA 1992, s 71 to make a disposal of them at market value, hold-over relief may be available under TCGA 1992, s 260(2)(da). The obvious disadvantage of trusts for bereaved minors is the fact that the children must become absolutely entitled to capital at a young age (ie. 18), however since TA 1925, s 32, extended to enable the whole of a beneficiary's share to be applied for his or her benefit, is compatible with a trust for bereaved minors (see IHTA 1984, s 71A(4)), it may be possible if shortly before the 18th birthday of a particular beneficiary the trustees consider him or her to be too immature to handle large sums of money, for them to exercise this power to prolong the trusts, eg. by postponing the beneficiary's entitlement to a later age. Such an exercise would not trigger any IHT by reason of IHTA 1984, s 71B(2)(c), although the settled property would then fall within the IHT relevant property regime. Forms C2.1, C2.3 and C2.5 below provide options to include trusts for bereaved minors.

(b) Age 18-to-25 trusts within IHTA 1984, s 71D. The main characteristics of such trusts are described in para **[200.109]** above, but they are essentially trusts under which the testator's children (or stepchildren, or children for whom the testator has parental responsibility) will be fully entitled to the assets in the trust at age 25. For parental responsibility see Vol 1, para **[28.2]**, and for the meaning of step-parent where there is a civil partnership see para **[224.35]**, n 1. The main merit of these trusts over trusts for bereaved minors is that they permit postponement of absolute vesting of capital, albeit at a (usually modest) cost in IHT. Property subject to them will be exempt from the relevant property regime and there will be no IHT charges when a beneficiary becomes absolutely entitled to the settled property under the age of 18, or dies under the age of 18, or on the property being paid or applied for the advancement or benefit of a beneficiary under the age of 18 (see IHTA 1984, s 71E(2)), but if the property remains settled after a beneficiary reaches 18, an IHT charge would arise on his or her absolute entitlement after that date, on his or her death, and on any application of capital for his or her benefit, up to a maximum of 4.2% (on present rates of IHT): see IHTA 1984, s 71E(1), (2). There is a capital gains tax advantage in such trusts in that when assets are paid out and the trustees are deemed under TCGA 1992, s 71 to make a disposal of them at market value, hold-over relief should be available under TCGA 1992, s 260(2)(d) (if there is also an IHT charge) or s 260(2)(db) (if there is not). Forms C2.1, C2.3 and C2.5 below provide options to include age 18-to-25 trusts. It is appropriate to continue accumulation and maintenance trusts beyond the age of 18 and so far as possible (compatible with the rule against excessive accumulations) to ensure that the trusts do not take effect as IPDI trusts on the testator's death, see para **[224.25]**.

(c) IPDIs within IHTA 1984, s 49A. These are described at para **[200.98]** above, but are essentially interests in possession which take immediate effect on the testator's death (subject only to a permissible survivorship clause under IHTA 1984, s 92). They cannot therefore arise in succession to a life interest for the testator's spouse. Where the surviving spouse or civil partner is given a life interest in the estate of the first to die, and subject to that both wills give the children interests in possession in both estates, after the death of the survivor the same trusts will give rise to relevant property IHT treatment for the estate of the first to die, and IPDI treatment for the estate of the second to die. Where the surviving spouse is given a life interest, therefore, it is probably better to provide relevant property trusts for the children if s 71A or 71D trusts are not wanted or available. An IPDI can be coupled with a power for the trustees to pay or apply capital to or for the benefit of the beneficiary of the interest, and even a provision for absolute entitlement to capital at a specified age. While the beneficiary is a minor, TA 1925, s 31 must be excluded or amended so that the beneficiary is treated as having an interest in possession (see for example, clause 8.2 of Form C2.2 below where TA 1925, s 31 is excluded), but while the beneficiary is a minor income may still be applied for his maintenance or other benefit and any not so applied may be accumulated, When the beneficiary attains 18, he would be entitled to those accumulations as of right. The essential advantage of such trusts over trusts for bereaved minors and age 18-to-25 trusts is that the beneficiaries do not have to become absolutely entitled to capital at an early age, whilst at the same time the property is outside the relevant property regime. Whether it is a significant advantage to be outside the relevant property regime is debatable and may depend on the value of the property concerned, since although there will be no IHT charge when the beneficiary becomes entitled to capital (by reason of IHTA 1984, s 53(2)), no hold-over relief would be available to postpone a capital gains tax charge on such an event, and there could be an IHT charge on the beneficiary's death since the underlying trust property would be treated as comprised in the beneficiary's estate for IHT purposes (under IHTA 1984, s 49(1), (1A)(a)). See also paras **[200.131]** ff. Form C2.2 below includes IPDIs for the testator's children.

(d) The relevant property regime (see para **[200.92]** above). This regime will, broadly speaking, cover any trusts which do not fall within the above categories. So, for example, it would cover discretionary trusts where trustees have wide discretions over income and capital, and also more rigid trusts which do not fall within any of the above categories because, for example, the age of vesting is too high, or the trustees have overriding powers over capital. The flexibility which wide discretionary trusts provide may mean that it is worth being within the relevant property regime (even if the value of the property concerned is such that periodic and exit charges will give rise to actual tax charges). Form C2.6 below includes wide discretionary trusts for the testator's children and remoter issue.

(e) A bare trust. This produces a result similar to a IHTA 1984, s 71A trust, but not identical: see para **[200.110]**. Where the testator is a parent of the beneficiary or beneficiaries, a s 71A trust is an available option and will probably seem a better choice than a bare trust. A bare trust is an option of more interest to a testator who is not a parent of the beneficiary or beneficiaries, and therefore does not have the option of a s 71A trust.

[224.25]

Haphazard IHT status—relevant property trusts and age 18-to-25 trusts which may turn out to be IPDIs. Something to avoid is a trust which is haphazard as to whether it will be an IPDI or relevant property trust, for IHT purposes, depending on the ages of the beneficiaries at the death of the testator. An obvious example is a type of trust which used to be drafted to fall within IHTA 1984, s 71, which begins with an accumulation and maintenance trust and then gives the beneficiaries interests in possession for their lives commencing at a specified age or time. The share of a beneficiary who, by the time of the death of the testator or within two years after his death, attains the age at which his or her interest in possession starts, will get IPDI treatment, and the share of any beneficiary who is still under that age by at least two years after the death of the testator will get relevant property treatment. See also para **[200.136]**, (4). In the interests of fairness and certainty, trusts should either be wholly IPDI trusts, with the beneficiaries having interests in possession with effect from the testator's death even while they are under the age of 18 (see Form 18.15, para **[218.81]** for an example of a relevant modification of Trustee Act 1925, s 31), or wholly relevant property trusts, to achieve which any interest in possession should only commence after at least two years have elapsed from the testator's death: see para **[200.133]**. Where a trust of capital vesting contingently on attaining a specified age greater than 18 is being created for a minor or minors which will not fall within s 71D, and, where it is intended that the relevant property rather than the IDPI regime should apply, it is recommended that the accumulation and maintenance trusts of income of TA 1925, s 31 are expressly extended to continue until the earlier to occur of the beneficiary attaining the age of vesting or the end of the 21-year accumulation period from the death of the testator: see Form C2.1, cl 8 at para **[224.36]** for an example. This will make sure that the trust will have IHT relevant property status if the beneficiary is under the age of vesting at the testator's death, irrespective of what that age is. Without such extended accumulation and maintenance trusts, so that a beneficiary becomes entitled under TA 1925, s 31 to be paid the current income at the age of 18, he would have an IPDI if he is between the ages of 18 and the vesting age at the death of the testator. The same point arises, with the same solution, where an IHTA 1984, s 71D trust is being created: see para **[200.109]**. For extended accumulation and maintenance trusts see also B18 at paras **[218.74]** ff.

[224.26]
Trusts for the testator's children and income tax and capital gains tax. As well as there being special IHT regimes which may be applicable to trusts for the testator's children, there is also a special income tax and capital gains tax regime. For tax years 2004–5 onwards there is a special tax treatment available for 'qualifying trusts' for 'vulnerable beneficiaries', who include infants, at least one of whose parents has died. A trust so qualifying allows a claim for tax treatment bringing the trustees' income and capital gains tax liability into line with what the vulnerable beneficiary's liability would have been if he or she had received the income directly or had realised the trust gains (see FA 2005, ss 23–45 and para **[217.4]** above). None of the trusts for children in the forms in C2 may be qualifying trusts for these purposes, even if the age contingency of attaining 18 is included, because the statutory power of advancement is incorporated with the usual modification of enabling the whole of a beneficiary's presumptive share of capital, and not merely one half, to be paid or applied for his or her advancement or benefit (see, for example, Form C2.1, clause 8(2), para **[224.36]**). HMRC do not consider the incorporation of such a wide power as being compatible with the status of qualifying trusts, see HMRC's *An introduction to the new special tax treatment for certain trusts with vulnerable beneficiaries*, paras 17 and 22 and para **[217.4]** above. Without resorting to FA 2005, ss 23–45, it is possible to obtain treatment of the income for income tax purposes as the minor beneficiary's, as opposed to it being subject to the trust rate under ITA 2007,

ss 479–483, by giving the beneficiary an interest in possession while under the age of 18. This is compatible with the trust falling within IHTA 1984, s 71A: see IHTA 1984, ss 49A(4) and 71A(1)(c)(i). The special capital gains tax treatment under FA 2005, ss 23–45 will apparently cease to be of any benefit after 5 April 2008 because of the changes to capital gains tax announced in the Pre-Budget Report on 9 October 2007. These include a flat rate of capital gains tax of 18 per cent for individuals and trusts alike, with effect from 6 April 2008.

[224.27]

Form C2.1: Reciprocal wills giving entire estate to spouse absolutely, with alternative gift to issue

Note. This form is intended to cater for the situation where the husband and wife are relatively young and their estates are not large. In such a case it will usually be appropriate for the survivor to take the estate of the first to die absolutely and for the children to take an interest only on the death of the survivor. The trusts for the children should qualify as either trusts for bereaved minors within IHTA 1984, s 71A, or age 18-to-25 trusts within IHTA 1984, s 71D (see para **[224.24]** above), depending on the age of contingency selected and if they come into effect while the children are under the age of contingency. See also the Preliminary Note on general strategy and IHT at para **[224.1]** ff, and also paras **[200.125]** ff.
This form can be adapted for use by civil partners with children. The words 'my wife/husband' should be replaced with 'my civil partner' throughout. The definition of the children by reference to parentage in clause 7, para **[224.35]**, will require attention, as will the reference to 'child of mine' in the proviso to clause 8 (if it is included).

[224.28]

REVOCATION CLAUSE AND DECLARATION AGAINST MUTUAL WILLS

I [*name*] of [*address*] revoke all former testamentary dispositions made by me and declare this to be my last will [And I further declare that notwithstanding that my [wife/husband] is making a will in similar terms we have agreed that our wills are not mutual wills and accordingly that each of us shall be free to revoke his or her will at any time whether before or after the death of the other and shall be free to dispose of his or her property or any property derived from the other as he or she thinks fit].[1]

1 There is no presumption that two wills in similar form are mutual wills in the technical sense, but the inclusion of the words in square brackets will remove any doubt on the point. If mutual wills are intended, then an express clause to that effect, such as Form B1.6 at para **[201.10]**, should be used instead of this clause. For the law on mutual wills see Vol 1, paras **[2.3]**–**[2.9]**. We recommend life interest trusts rather than mutual wills where a testator wishes to determine the destination of his property after the death of his spouse in the event of his spouse surviving him.

[224.29]

APPOINTMENT OF SPOUSE AS SOLE EXECUTOR/EXECUTRIX, WITH ALTERNATIVE APPOINTMENT

1. I appoint my [wife/husband] [*name*] ('my [wife/husband]') the sole [executrix/executor] of this will but if [she/he] predeceases me or renounces probate or dies without having proved this will [or if the foregoing appointment shall fail for any other reason][1] then I appoint [*name*] of [*address*] and [*name*] of [*address*] to be the executors and trustees hereof.

1 These words allow for the possibility of the appointment ceasing to have effect as a result of a divorce, by virtue of the WA 1837, s 18A(1)(a) (Part G, para **[244.17]**) in the event of the testator's death before 1 January 1996. They are not necessary in relation to deaths on or after that date but have been included for completeness. See the Preliminary Note on the possibility of divorce at paras **[224.16]**–**[224.23]**.

[224.30]

DEFINITION OF 'MY TRUSTEES'

2. In this will the expression 'my trustees' shall where the context permits mean my personal representatives for the time being and the trustees for the time being hereof.

[224.31]

APPOINTMENT OF GUARDIANS[1]

3. If my [wife/husband] shall predecease me I appoint [*name*] of [*address*] [and [*name*] of [*address*]] to be the [guardian/guardians] of my children during their respective minorities.

1 For the reasons given in the Preliminary Note at para **[224.11]**, the appointment of guardians incorporated in the forms in this section will only take effect if the other spouse dies first.

[224.32]

PRIMARY GIFT OF ESTATE TO SPOUSE

4. If my [wife/husband] shall survive me[1] then subject to the payment thereout of my debts and funeral and testamentary expenses I give devise and bequeath all my estate both real and personal [including any entailed or other property over which I shall have a general power of disposition at my death][2] to [her/him] absolutely.

1 If a survivorship clause is wanted the words 'for the period of one month' can be added at this point. See the Preliminary Note on survivorship conditions at paras **[224.5]**–**[224.10]** for the reasons for not including a survivorship clause as between husband and wife or civil partners. If a survivorship period is included it could be any period up to six months and still take advantage of the IHTA 1984, s 92 (see para **[224.6]**); if a survivorship period longer than a month is being considered, it should be remembered that it will not usually be possible to pay income or capital to the spouse before he or she has survived the period.

2 Subject to any contrary intention expressed in the will property subject to a general testamentary power will be carried by a residuary gift under the WA 1837, s 27 (see Part G, para **[244.29]** and Vol 1, paras **[38.1]** and **[38.2]**) without express reference to the property or power. In the case of entailed property, however, the property or the instrument under which it was acquired, or entailed property generally, must be referred to: LPA 1925, s 176(1) (see Part G, para **[244.55]** and Vol 1, para **[7.1]**).

[224.33]

ALTERNATIVE PROVISIONS IF SPOUSE DOES NOT SURVIVE

5. If my [wife/husband] shall predecease me[1] [or if the foregoing gift shall fail for any other reason][2] then the following provisions shall have effect.

1 If a survivorship condition is included in the gift to the spouse in clause 4 (para **[224.31]**) add the words 'or shall not survive me for the period aforesaid' at this point. See para **[224.31]**, n 1.

2 These words catered for the possibility that the gift may lapse by reason of divorce under the WA 1837, s 18A(1)(b) (Part G, para **[244.17]**) in the event of the testator's death before 1 January 1996. They are not necessary in relation to deaths on or after that date and should be omitted in most cases. See the Preliminary Note on the possibility of divorce at paras **[224.21]**–**[224.23]**.

[224.34]

ADMINISTRATION TRUSTS OF RESIDUE

6. (1) I give all my property not hereby or by any codicil hereto otherwise effectively disposed of [(including any entailed or other property over which I shall have at my death a general power of disposition by will)][1] to my trustees to hold on the trusts set out below with power at their discretion to sell all or any of it as and when they think fit.[2]

(2) My trustees shall pay my funeral and testamentary expenses[3] and debts and any legacies given by this will or any codicil hereto out of such property or its proceeds and shall have a discretion as to how such payments shall be borne as between capital and income.[4]

(3) Subject as above my trustees shall hold such property and the assets from time to time representing the same (hereinafter called 'my residuary estate') on the trusts set out below and shall invest all money comprised in such property or arising from its sale in any of the investments hereby authorised with power to change such investments into any others hereby authorised.

(4) In the administration of my estate and the execution of the trusts of this will or of any codicil to it:

(a) my trustees shall treat all income as accruing on the date on which it becomes payable regardless of the period in respect of which it shall have accrued and shall not make any statutory apportionment of the same;[5] and

(b) none of the equitable rules of apportionment between capital and income shall apply in any circumstances whatever.[6]

1 Subject to any express contrary intention property subject to a general power will be carried by a residuary gift under the WA 1837, s 27 (Part G, para **[244.29]**), but in the case of entailed property the will must refer to the property, or the instrument under which it was acquired, or entailed property generally for the statutory power of disposition to be exercised: LPA 1925, s 176(1), (Part G, para **[244.55]**). Although no new entails can be created on or after 1 January 1997 (see paras **[200.52]** and **[200.53]**), entails created before that date can continue to exist and, if they do, the statutory power of disposition of them by will continues to be available.

2 For the reasons for providing a power of sale rather than a trust for sale, see para **[214.1]** ff. This wording could be made even more concise, such as: 'My trustees shall have power to sell all or any of such property' or as appears in the AEA 1925, s 33(1), as amended by the TLATA 1996, Sch 2, para 5. One reason for using the slightly more elaborate wording in this form is that it follows the wording which was held in *Re Pitcairn* [1896] 2 Ch 199 to prevent the rule in *Howe v Dartmouth* from applying, (see Note at paras **[214.35]**–**[214.37]** for exclusion of the rule), although to save possible argument about the effect of this wording the express exclusion of the apportionment rules is also retained in sub-cl (4) below. Another reason is that this wording should also serve to create a mixed fund of residuary realty and personalty (see para **[214.64]** for the significance of this).

3 Testamentary expenses will include IHT on UK free estate, including real property: IHTA 1984, s 211(1) (Part G, para **[246.100]** and see the Preliminary Note to B14 at paras **[214.55]**–**[214.63]**). Accordingly, even if specific gifts or pecuniary legacies are intended to be free of IHT, it will not be necessary to make express provision for the incidence of IHT, unless (in the case of a specific gift) the gift is of property of a kind which bears its own tax,

or (in the case of a pecuniary legacy) the legacy is payable out of property (usually residue) which includes property of a kind which bears its own tax. The main relevant categories of property bearing its own tax are foreign property and property which is settled property immediately before the testator's death: see the Preliminary Note to B14 at paras **[214.55]**–**[214.63]** (settled property can be disposed of under a will where it is subject to a general testamentary power of appointment or is entailed—see n 1 above).

4 A discretion as to the apportionment between capital and income of the burden of liabilities is a middle way between the strict rule in *Allhusen v Whittell* (1867) LR 4 Eq 295 (see Vol 1, para **[38.26]** and para **[214.43]**) with its complex calculations, and a direction to pay the liabilities out of capital which can have the unsatisfactory consequences referred to at para **[214.44]**.

5 See the Preliminary Note to B14 at paras **[214.48]**–**[214.52]** for statutory apportionment of income over time and its exclusion.

6 See Vol 1, paras **[38.17]**–**[38.27]** for the rules of equitable apportionment between capital and income, and the Preliminary Note to B14 at para **[214.35]** ff for the reasons and techniques for excluding those rules. It is hoped that these words will exclude the rule in *Howe v Earl of Dartmouth* (1802) 7 Ves 137 and *Re Earl Chesterfield's Trusts* (1883) 24 Ch D 643. The power of sale in sub-cl (1) of this clause may also serve to do so (see n 2 above). For alternative strategies, see further the Preliminary Note to B14 at para **[214.38]**, Forms B14.4 (at para **[214.13]**) and B14.27 (at para **[214.42]**).

[224.35]

BENEFICIAL TRUSTS FOR ISSUE

7. My trustees shall hold my residuary estate and the income thereof upon trust for such of my children [by my [wife/husband]][1] as shall survive me and attain the age of [18/25] years[2] and if more than one in equal shares Provided that if any such child shall die before attaining a vested interest under the foregoing trust leaving a child or children living at or born after my death who shall attain the age of [18/21] years[3] [or marry or form a civil partnership under that age] then such last-mentioned child or children shall take and if more than one equally between them the share of my residuary estate which their deceased parent would have taken had he or she lived to attain a vested interest.

1 These words ensure that the alternative gifts in the wills of both spouses are identical in terms of whom they benefit, in circumstances where one spouse has children who are not children of the other spouse, and it is desired to exclude them. See, further, the Preliminary Note on reciprocal wills and the ultimate destination of property at paras **[224.13]**–**[224.15]** and for forms for use where one spouse has children who are not children of the marriage and wishes to benefit them by his or her will see C5 at para **[227.1]** ff. If there are intended beneficiaries under this trust who are the children of one spouse but not of the other, or if this Form is being adapted for use by civil partners either or both of whom have children, the children could be identified as 'my children and the children of my [wife/husband/civil partner] as shall be living at my death'. In this case it needs to be made clear whether or not children of the other spouse or civil partner born after the testator's death are excluded, and it should be borne in mind that inclusion of the children of both would include illegitimate children who might be forgotten or not known about. A testator can create trusts within IHTA 1984, ss 71A or 71D for his or her stepchildren (IHTA 1984, s 71H), and in the case of a testator who is in a civil partnership this includes children of the other civil partner (IHTA 1984, s 272, definition of 'stepchild', and CPA 2004, s 246).

2 Since the children will all be lives in being for perpetuity purposes, the age contingency does not have to be restricted to 21. If the age contingency of attaining 18 is included, and the trusts for children come into possession while they are still infants, these trusts should be trusts for bereaved minors within IHTA 1984, s 71A and so exempt from the IHT relevant property regime (see para **[224.24]** above). They will not, however, be 'qualifying trusts' for the benefit of 'vulnerable beneficiaries' for income tax purposes under FA 2005, ss 23–45 because the statutory power of advancement is incorporated in clause 8 with the usual modification of enabling the whole of a beneficiary's presumptive share of capital, and not

merely one half, to be paid or applied for his or her advancement or benefit: see para **[217.4]** above. If the age contingency selected is 25 and the trusts for children come into possession while they are under 25 these trusts should be age 18-to-25 trusts within IHTA 1984, s 71D and so exempt from the IHT relevant property regime although an IHT charge will arise on a beneficiary becoming absolutely entitled to capital when over the age of 18 (see paras **[200.109]** and **[224.24]** above). If the age contingency selected is 25, the trusts would not also be 'qualifying trusts' for the benefit of 'vulnerable beneficiaries' within FA 2005, ss 23–45 (see para **[217.4]** above).

3 The grandchildren will not necessarily be alive at the testator's death and it is therefore important to restrict the age contingency to 21 so as not to infringe the rule against perpetuities. If this trust for grandchildren takes effect, the property subject to it would be within the IHT relevant property regime, except so far as they are entitled to interest in possession by the time of the death of the testator, in which case the property will be subject to an IPDI or IPDIs (see paras **[200.125]** ff, **[224.24]**).

[224.36]

MAINTENANCE, ACCUMULATION AND ADVANCEMENT

Either

[8. (1) Section 31 of the Trustee Act 1925 (relating to accumulation and maintenance) shall apply in relation to the trusts hereby or by any codicil hereto declared as if:

(a) in paragraph (i) of subsection (1) of the said section the words 'as the trustees think fit' were substituted for the words 'as may in all the circumstances be reasonable'; and

(b) the proviso to the said subsection (1) were omitted][1].

[Provided that in relation to any presumptive share of my residuary estate of any child of mine [by my [wife/husband]][2]] the said section 31 (amended as aforesaid) shall have effect as if the age of majority were the lesser of the age which he or she will attain (if he or she so long lives) on his or her last birthday occurring not later than the expiration of 21 years from my death and the age of 25 years (and so that the expressions 'infancy', 'minority' and 'infant' and all references to the age of eighteen years in the said Section 31 shall be construed accordingly).][3]

Or

[8. (1) The income of the presumptive share of my residuary estate of any beneficiary which arises while he or she is living and under the age of 18 years shall be held on trust for him or her absolutely and indefeasibly and section 31 of the Trustee Act 1925 shall not apply to such income Provided that my trustees may pay or apply all or any part or parts of such income for his or her benefit at any time or times during his or her minority.][4]

(2) Section 32 of the Trustee Act 1925 (relating to advancement) shall apply in relation to the said trusts as if the words 'one half of' were omitted from proviso (a) to subsection (1) thereof.[5]

(3) Whenever my trustees shall have an obligation or discretion under the provisions of this will or any codicil hereto or under the general law to apply income or capital for the benefit of a minor beneficiary they may either pay the same without liability to account to his or her parent guardian or any other adult person with whom such beneficiary may be residing or to such beneficiary himself or herself if of the age of 16 years or more and so

that the receipt of such parent guardian or other person or of such minor beneficiary shall be a full and sufficient discharge to my trustees for the income or capital so applied.[6]

1 Where the primary trust in clause 7, para **[224.35]**, has a vesting age of 18, either include this subclause (1), without the proviso, or include the alternative subclause below which confers an interest in possession (for which see further n 4 below). Where the primary trust in clause 7, para **[224.35]**, has a vesting age of 25, include this subclause together with the proviso (for which see further n 3 below).

2 This reference needs to be to the same persons as the beneficiaries under the primary trust in clause 7: see **[224.35]** and n 1 to it.

3 This proviso is for inclusion where the age contingency for the alternative gift for the testator's children in clause 7, para **[224.35]**, is the age of 25. It extends the period during which income may be accumulated for as long as the law currently allows (ie. 21 years from the testator's death). See para **[224.25]**.The Law Commission have recommended the abolition of the statutory restrictions on accumulation so that accumulation is permissible for a full perpetuity period. It is possible that this might have happened by the time of the testator's death. It is not practical to provide for this possibility without knowing the final form of the legislation, and this proviso does not attempt to do so.

4 A trust can fall within IHTA 1984, s 71A even if the beneficiary has an interest in possession while under 18 (see paras **[200.108]**, **[224.24]**). If the first alternative subclause (1) is included, the income of a beneficiary's share while he or she is under 18 will be subject to the trust rate under ITA 2007, ss 479–483 (see para **[224.26]**), whereas if this second alternative is included the income will be subject to income tax as the beneficiary's. The disadvantage of this is that if he or she dies under the age of 18 the income will devolve under the intestacy rules as they apply to him or her instead of devolving with the capital.

5 This should be included whichever sub-cl (1) is chosen. The extended power is compatible with trusts for bereaved minors within IHTA 1984, s 71A (see para **[200.108]** above) and age 18-to-25 trusts within IHTA 1984, s 71D (see para **[200.109]** above).

6 This should be included whichever subclause (1) is chosen. A parent (with parental responsibility) and a guardian of a minor are empowered by the ChA 1989, s 3(3) (Part G, para **[244.114]**) to give a good receipt for the minor's property: see Vol 1, para **[9.41]**. The power in this subclause is wider in that it authorises the payment of income or capital to a parent who does not have parental responsibility, any adult with whom the minor is residing, and the minor himself or herself if 16 or over.

[224.37]

ADMINISTRATIVE POWERS[1]

9. (1) In this clause where the context so admits—

(a) the expression 'land' includes buildings and estates interests or rights of any kind in or over land; and

(b) during the administration of my estate the expression 'beneficiary' includes any person who would be a beneficiary if such administration had been completed and the expression 'beneficially interested' and references to income of any asset being payable or capable of being paid to or for the benefit of a beneficiary shall be construed accordingly.

(2) None of the powers or provisions contained in subclause (3) below of this clause shall be capable of being exercised or operating in any manner such that if such power or provision were capable of being so exercised or so operating the existence of the same would either—

(i) prevent any person who would in the absence of such power or provision have been entitled to an interest in possession falling within section 49(1A) of the Inheritance Tax Act 1984 in any property from being entitled to such interest; or

(ii) prevent section 71A or 71D of the Inheritance Tax Act 1984 from applying to any property to which in the absence of such power or provision either section would have applied.[2]

(3) In the administration of my estate and the execution of the trusts hereof or of any codicil hereto my trustees shall have the following powers in addition to those conferred by law but subject to the last foregoing subclause—

(a) power to invest moneys sell assets and change investments with the unrestricted freedom of choice and powers of disposition and acquisition of a sole beneficial owner with in particular power to make unsecured loans, acquire non-income yielding assets, and purchase land anywhere in the world or chattels for any purpose including occupation or enjoyment in kind by a beneficiary under the power set out below;[3]

(b) power to delegate all or any of their investment powers to a professional investment manager or managers whether individual or corporate and whether or not also a nominee holder of assets for my trustees (and who may be or include one or more of my trustees or the beneficiaries hereunder) upon such terms as to remuneration and otherwise (including terms authorising self-dealing or providing for the limitation of the liability of the investment manager or managers) as my trustees think fit and section 22 of the Trustee Act 2000 shall not apply;[4]

(c) power to vest or register any property in any person or persons whether individual or corporate and whether or not an investment manager to whom powers have been delegated under the foregoing power (and who may be or include one or more of my trustees or the beneficiaries hereunder) as nominee or nominees for my trustees upon such terms as to remuneration or otherwise (including terms authorising self-dealing or providing for the limitation of the liability of the nominee) as my trustees think fit and section 22 of the Trustee Act 2000 shall not apply;[5]

(d) power to borrow money with or without giving security and on such terms as to interest and repayment and otherwise as my trustees may think fit for any purpose connected with the administration of my estate or the trusts declared herein or in any codicil hereto (including investment) And no lender from whom my trustees borrow money in purported exercise of this power shall be concerned to enquire as to the proprietary amount or purpose of any such borrowing;[6]

(e) power to lend money to a beneficiary to whom any of the income of such money is payable or to whom or for whose benefit any income of such money is capable of being paid or applied in exercise of a discretion (or who would be such a beneficiary if such money yielded income) and to do so at a full or concessionary rate of interest or interest free;[7]

(f) all the powers of an absolute owner in relation to any land (wherever situated) held by them;[8]

(g) power to apply capital held on the same trusts as any land (or which would be so held if the administration of my estate had been completed) in the improvement of such land and to apply such capital or the income of such capital on the repair or maintenance of such land;[9]

(h) power to permit any beneficiary to have the beneficial occupation use or enjoyment in kind of any land or chattel or other tangible property on such terms as to repair insurance or payment of outgoings by the beneficiary or otherwise howsoever as my trustees think fit Provided that the foregoing power shall only be exercisable and such permission to occupy or enjoy in kind may only continue in the following circumstances—

  (i) so long as any of the income of such land chattel or other tangible property is payable to such beneficiary or capable of being paid or applied to him or for his benefit in exercise of a discretion (or would be so payable or capable of being so paid or applied if such land chattel or other property yielded income);

  (ii) in the case of land, so long as for the time being the occupation thereof by such beneficiary is compatible with any statutory rights of occupation of any other beneficiary or beneficiaries;[10]

(i) power to exercise all the powers of appropriation (and other incidental powers) conferred by statute on a personal representative without the necessity of obtaining any consents and notwithstanding that one or more of my trustees may be beneficially interested in the exercise of such power.[11]

1 For notes on administrative powers and the powers conferred by the general law, and for other examples of administrative powers, see B20 at para **[220.1]** ff. For a set of administrative powers which include powers in respect of business assets see Form C11.1, cl 6 at para **[233.21]**. The TLATA 1996 and the Trustee Act 2000 (TrA 2000) have much increased the statutory powers of trustees, and many wills and will trusts could manage without any of the powers in this clause being conferred expressly, or just with the power to borrow and the power of appropriation without consent. The differences from the relevant statutory powers of the powers in this clause which overlap with statutory powers are noted in the notes below. The only power which, before 1997, was included in this clause which has been omitted because there are now statutory powers which render express provision unnecessary is the power to insure: TA 1925, s 19, as substituted by the TrA 2000, s 34 (Part G, para **[246.17]**), and para **[220.51]**.

2 This is a general restriction so as to prevent the administrative powers prejudicing the intended IHT status of the beneficial trusts, either as IPDI trusts or trusts within IHTA 1984, s 71A or s 71D. See, further, the General Preliminary Note to B20 at para **[220.5]**.

3 This power is wider than the statutory powers of investment in the TrA 2000, ss 3 and 8 (Part G, paras **[246.135]** and **[246.140]**) for these and the notes on them at paras **[220.12]**–**[220.19]**) in that it permits unsecured loans, the purchase of land outside the UK, and the purchase of interests in land (such as undivided shares) which are not legal estates. The attempt can be made to exclude the statutory obligations relating to diversification and suitability of investments, and the requirement of taking advice, but as now enacted in the TrA 2000 these cannot be excluded (although their effect can be cut down by clauses exonerating trustees from liability for negligence): TrA 2000, ss 4 and 5 (see Part G, paras **[246.136]**, **[246.137]** and **[220.37]**).

4 This is wider than the statutory power to appoint investment managers in the TrA 2000, Pt IV, ss 11–15 (see Part G, paras **[246.143]**–**[246.147]** and B20 at paras **[220.35]** and **[220.36]**) in that the detailed procedural requirements of the TrA 2000, s 15 do not apply, the trustees have a wider discretion as to restricting an investment manager's liability or permitting self-dealing by him (compare the TrA 2000, s 14(2): Part G, para **[246.146]**, under which these can only be done if it is reasonably necessary), beneficiaries can be

appointed (this is forbidden in exercise of the statutory power by the TrA 2000, s 12(3)), and the duty to review the arrangement from time to time under the TrA 2000, s 22 (Part G, para **[246.154]**) does not apply. The by-passing of the TrA 2000, ss 14 and 15 is only effective if those statutory provisions apply only to the statutory powers of delegation, and do not apply to express powers to delegate investment management functions, something which is not at all clear (see para **[220.37]**). Even though trustees have an express power of this kind, unless and until there is either a definitive decision of the courts, or amending legislation, which makes it certain that ss 14 and 15 are excluded by such a power, trustees should regard themselves as bound by ss 14 and 15.

5 This is wider than the statutory power to appoint nominees in the TrA 2000, Pt IV, ss 16–20 (see Part G, paras **[246.148]**–**[246.152]** and **[220.36]**) in that the trustees have a wider discretion as to restricting a nominee's liability or permitting self-dealing by him (compare the TrA 2000, s 20(2): Part G, para **[246.152]**, under which these can only be done if it is reasonably necessary), the persons who may be appointed nominees are not confined to persons carrying on a business as nominees, a company controlled by the trustees or a solicitors' incorporated practice (compare the TrA 2000, s 19(2): Part G para **[246.151]**), and the duty to review the arrangement from time to time under the TrA 2000, s 22 (Part G, para **[246.154]**) does not apply.

6 There is no power under the general law for trustees to borrow money for the purposes of investment: see para **[220.69]**, n 1.

7 The investment power in sub-cl (a) above permits unsecured lending on a commercial basis, but express authorisation as in this subclause is needed to lend or continue to lend for the purpose of benefiting the borrower: see para **[220.32]**. A power to apply capital for the benefit of a beneficiary could in appropriate circumstances enable capital to be lent to him on beneficial terms.

8 The statutory power of management of land in similar terms in the TLATA 1996, s 6(1) (Part G, para **[246.108]**) applies only to land in England and Wales, and that in the TrA 2000, s 8(3) (Part G, para **[246.140]**) applies only to land acquired under the power in that section. As the power to acquire land in this clause is wider than the statutory power (see n 3 above) it is appropriate to provide an express power rather than rely on the statute.

9 See para **[220.52]** for the reasons for this provision.

10 See the Note and forms concerning enjoyment in kind in B18 at para **[218.108]** and the Preliminary Note on investment powers in B20 at para **[220.30]**. For the statutory rights of occupation under the TLATA 1996, see paras **[208.5]**–**[208.18]** and the TLATA 1996, ss 12 and 13 (Part G, paras **[246.115]** and **[246.116]**). A power as in this subclause is primarily relevant to a wholly discretionary trust, and it is made subject to any statutory rights of occupation because interest in possession trusts might come to be created in exercise of a power of appointment or application. A power to permit occupation by a beneficiary of trust land is not needed in relation to land in an interest in possession trust, because the statutory rights of occupation will be sufficient provision for beneficiary occupation and anyway are likely to leave no room for permissive occupation by beneficiaries who have no rights of occupation. A clause of this kind can be included in relation to trusts intended to be within the IHTA 1984, s 71A or 71D, but should always be subject to an overriding restriction to prevent the power prejudicing the s 71A or 71D status of the trusts, such as the proviso at the beginning of this clause. For the effect of conditions as to repair etc imposed on a beneficiary occupying or enjoying in kind trust property see the Preliminary Note to B8 at paras **[208.26]**–**[208.28]**.

11 For the statutory power of partition of land see the TLATA 1996, s 7 (Part G, para **[246.109]**) and for the statutory power of appropriation referred to here see the AEA 1925, s 41 (Part G, para **[246.65]**; see also Vol 1 paras **[29.17]**–**[29.23]** and **[220.70]**). A power of appropriation as in this subclause will be exercisable in circumstances when the power in the TLATA 1996, s 7 cannot be exercised, e g where a share of the land is still settled, and without the consent of beneficiaries. Exercise of a power of this kind which does not require the consent of beneficiaries may have stamp duty or capital gains tax advantages over one which does: see para **[220.72]**.

[224.38]

TRUSTEE LIABILITY

10. (1) My trustees shall not be liable for any act or default of any investment manager or nominee employed in good faith to manage or hold assets of my estate nor for any act or default of any beneficiary having the occupation use or enjoyment of property in kind.[1]

(2) Section 11(1) of the Trusts of Land and Appointment of Trustees Act 1996 (consultation with beneficiaries) shall not apply to the exercise by my trustees of any of their powers in relation to land subject to the trusts hereof. [2]

1 This makes it clear that the trustees are not liable for the defaults of others who may have possession or control of trust property. If a paid trustee is to rely on this indemnity clause which may limit his liability in negligence in that it may absolve him from negligent failure to intervene to prevent loss, the testator should specifically be made aware of its meaning and effect (see para **[221.13]** above). For a wider form of indemnity, see Form B21.12 at para **[221.16]**.

2 The requirement that trustees of land, in exercise of any function relating to land subject to the trust, consult with beneficiaries of full age beneficially entitled to an interest in possession in the land can be excluded: see the TLATA 1996, s 11 (Part G, para **[246.97]**.

[224.39]

PROFESSIONAL TRUSTEE CHARGING CLAUSE

11. Any of my trustees being a professional or business man may charge and be paid all usual professional and other proper charges for business transacted acts done advice given and time spent by him or his firm in connection with the administration of my estate or in connection with the trusts hereof including acts which a personal representative or trustee not being in any profession or business could have done personally.

[224.40]

TESTIMONIUM

IN WITNESS whereof I have hereunto set my hand this —— day of —— 20——.

[224.41]

ATTESTATION CLAUSE

SIGNED by the above-named [testator/testatrix] as [his/her] last will in the presence of us both present at the same time who at [his/her] request and in [his/her] presence and in the presence of each other have signed our names below as witnesses:	}	[*Signature of testator/testatrix*]

[Signatures, addresses and descriptions of two witnesses]

[224.42]

Form C2.2: Reciprocal wills giving entire estate to spouse absolutely with alternative gift of IPDIs to issue

Note. Form C2.2 is an alternative to Form C2.1, and provides for the gift to the children, which takes effect where the testator's spouse predeceases the testator, to be a settled gift under which each child (or a grandchild by substitution) is given a life interest in his or her share with remainder to his or her children, but subject to a power to pay to each child (or grandchild) the capital of his or her share. The life interest of each child (or grandchild) will be an IPDI within IHTA 1984, s 49A, (see para **[200.98]** above), even while they are infants, (see para **[200.132]** above). The main reasons for using a form such as Form C2.2 in preference to Form C2.1 are to allow property to be retained on trust for children longer, delaying the time when the children obtain dominion over the capital of their shares until the trustees decide to exercise their powers to pay it to them. Form C2.2 is therefore for couples who between them have a reasonable amount of property which they would not wish their children to become entitled to at too early an age, and which they wish to keep out of the IHT relevant property regime. For a form with more flexibility in the trusts for children and remoter issue see Form C2.6 at para **[224.102]** ff.

This form can be adapted for use by civil partners with children, where either or both civil partners are parents. The words 'my wife/husband' should be replaced with 'my civil partner' throughout. The definition of the children by reference to parentage in clause 7 (in sub-clauses (1) and (2)), and the opening of clause 8 (in its references to 'child' and 'grandchild'), will require adaptation: see para **[224.35]**, n 1.

[224.43]

REVOCATION CLAUSE

I [*name*] of [*address*] hereby revoke all former testamentary dispositions made by me and declare this to be my last will.[1]

1 See the note to the revocation clause in Form C2.1 at para **[224.28]**.

[224.44]

APPOINTMENT OF SPOUSE AS SOLE EXECUTOR/EXECUTRIX WITH ALTERNATIVE APPOINTMENT

1. [*As in cl 1 of* Form C2.1 *at para* **[224.29]**.]

[224.45]

DEFINITION OF 'MY TRUSTEES'

2. [*As in cl 2 of* Form C2.1 *at para* **[224.30]**.]

[224.46]

APPOINTMENT OF GUARDIANS

3. [*As in cl 3 of* Form C2.1 *at para* **[224.31]**.]

[224.47]

PRIMARY GIFT OF ESTATE TO SPOUSE

4. [*As in cl 4 of* Form C2.1 *at para* **[224.32]**.]

[224.48]

ALTERNATIVE PROVISIONS IF SPOUSE DOES NOT SURVIVE

5. [*As in cl 5 of* Form C2.1 *at para* **[224.33]**.]

[224.49]

ADMINISTRATION TRUSTS OF ESTATE

6. [*As in cl 6 of* Form C2.1 *at para* **[224.34]**.]

[224.50]

BENEFICIAL TRUSTS FOR CHILDREN AND ISSUE

7. (1) Subject to the direction for retention and settlement hereinafter contained my trustees shall hold my residuary estate upon trust for such of my children [by my [wife/husband]][1] as shall survive me if more than one in equal shares.

(2) If any such child shall die before me leaving a child or children surviving me then subject to the direction for retention and settlement hereinafter contained such last-mentioned child or children shall take and if more than one equally between them the share of my residuary estate which their deceased parent would have taken had he or she survived me.

1 See Form C2.1, cl 7, n 1 at para **[224.35]**.

[224.51]

SETTLEMENT OF CHILD'S OR GRANDCHILD'S SHARE OF RESIDUE

8. The share of my residuary estate to which any child or grandchild of mine[1] shall become entitled under the last foregoing clause hereof shall not vest in such child or grandchild but shall be retained by my trustees and held upon the following trusts:

(1) my trustees shall hold such share (hereinafter called 'the settled share') upon trust to pay the income thereof to such child or grandchild (hereinafter called 'the primary beneficiary') for life;

(2) if and so long as the primary beneficiary is under the age of 18 years my trustees may pay or otherwise apply for or towards the maintenance education or benefit of the primary beneficiary the whole or such part or parts of the income of the settled share as my trustees in their absolute discretion think fit and shall retain the balance of such income upon trust for the primary beneficiary absolutely but my trustees may at any time or times while the primary beneficiary is living and under the age of 18 years pay or apply such retained income as if it were income arising in the then current year and section 31 of the Trustee Act 1925 shall not apply to the settled share;[2]

(3) I declare that the purpose and intent of sub-clauses (1) and (2) above of this clause is that the primary beneficiary shall from my death have an interest in possession (within the meaning of Part III of the Inheritance Tax Act 1984) in the settled share during his or her life and even if and while such primary beneficiary is a minor;

(4) subject as aforesaid my trustees shall hold the settled share upon trust for all or any of the children or child of the primary beneficiary and if more than one in equal shares;[3]

(5) the provisions of section 32 of the Trustee Act 1925 (as hereinafter modified) shall apply in relation to the settled share;

(6) notwithstanding the trusts aforesaid so long as the primary beneficiary is entitled to be paid the income of all or any part of the capital of the settled share (or would be so entitled if such capital yielded income)[4] my trustees shall have power in their absolute discretion from time to time to pay transfer or apply the whole or any part or parts of such capital to or for the benefit of the primary beneficiary in such manner as they shall in their absolute discretion think fit;

(7) subject as above the settled share (or so much as has not been applied under any of the above powers) shall accrue to the share or shares of the other primary beneficiaries (and if more than one in the proportion which such other shares bear to one another) the trusts of which have not at the date of accruer failed or determined (otherwise than by absolute vesting) and shall form one fund with such other share or shares for all purposes and if there is no such share at the date of such accruer it shall be held upon trust for the estate of the primary beneficiary absolutely.

1 This needs to be consistent with the identification of the beneficiaries in clause 7: see para **[224.35]** n 1 above. Add 'or my husband/wife/civil partner' after 'of mine' where the primary class includes the other spouse's or civil partner's children who are not children of the testator.

2 See para **[218.53]** ff for the trusts of accumulations under the TA 1925, s 31 (Part G, para **[246.29]**) which unless varied or excluded are such as usually to give minor beneficiaries a contingent interest in such accumulations, even if they have a vested interest in the income. The purpose of this substitution for s 31 is to cause the income which is not applied for the primary beneficiary's benefit during his minority to be held on trust absolutely for the primary beneficiary, so as to confer an interest in possession for IHT purposes. An infant cannot be paid income to which he is entitled (see Vol 1, para **[9.39]**) but it is thought that he or she has an interest in possession in income if it would form part of his estate if he or she died under the age of 18 (and unmarried and without a civil partner). Such interest in possession will be an IPDI within IHTA 1984, s 49A (see paras **[200.98]** and **[224.24]** ff above).

3 The remainder interests are absolute. This is essentially in the interests of keeping it simple, on the footing that the capital will probably be distributed to the primary beneficiaries during their lifetimes. For greater flexibility as to the trusts in remainder see Form 3.2, para **[225.23]**, cl 4(3), para **[225.32]**.

4 The reason for restricting the power in this way is to ensure that if the principal beneficiary releases his life interest in favour of the remainderman this power automatically ceases to apply.

[224.52]

MAINTENANCE, ACCUMULATION AND ADVANCEMENT

9. (1) Section 31 of the Trustee Act 1925 (relating to accumulation and maintenance) shall apply (subject as hereinbefore provided in clause 8(2)) in relation to the trusts hereby or by any codicil hereto declared as if:

(a) in paragraph (i) of subsection (1) of the said section the words 'as the trustees think fit' were substituted for the words 'as may in all the circumstances be reasonable'; and

(b) the proviso to the said subsection (1) were omitted.

(2) Section 32 of the Trustee Act 1925 (relating to advancement) shall apply in relation to the said trusts as if the words 'one half of' were omitted from proviso (a) to subsection (1) thereof.

(3) Whenever my trustees shall have an obligation or discretion under the provisions of this will or any codicil hereto or under the general law to apply income or capital for the benefit of a minor beneficiary they may either pay the same without liability to account to his or her parent guardian or any other adult person with whom such beneficiary may be residing or to such beneficiary himself or herself if of the age of 16 years or more and so that the receipt of such parent guardian or other person or of such minor beneficiary shall be a full and sufficient discharge to my trustees for the income or capital so applied.[1]

1 A parent (with parental responsibility) and a guardian of a minor are empowered by the ChA 1989, s 3(3) (Part G, para **[244.114]**) to give a good receipt for the minor's property: see Vol 1, para **[9.41]**. The power in this sub-clause is wider in that it authorises the payment of income or capital to a parent who does not have parental responsibility, any adult with whom the minor is residing, and the minor himself or herself if 16 or over.

[224.53]

ADMINISTRATIVE POWERS

10. [*As in cl 9 of* Form C2.1 *at para* **[224.37]**.]

[224.54]

TRUSTEE LIABILITY

11. [*As in cl 10 of* Form C2.1 *at para* **[224.38]**.]

[224.55]

EXERCISE OF POWERS[1]

12. Any power or discretion hereby or by law conferred on my trustees (including a power or discretion as to the disposition of capital or income) shall be exercisable notwithstanding that any of my trustees has a personal interest in such exercise provided that there are not fewer than two trustees and that at least one of them has no such personal interest.

1 This clause permits a member of the family to be a trustee without disqualifying him or her from benefit under any exercise of statutory or express powers of payment or application of capital, appointment, etc. See the Note in B18 at para **[218.4]**.

[224.56]

PROFESSIONAL TRUSTEE CHARGING CLAUSE

13. [*As in cl 11 of* Form C2.1 *at para* **[224.39]**.]

[224.57]

[*Testimonium and attestation clause as in* Form C2.1 *at paras* **[224.40]** and **[224.41]**.]

[224.58]

Form C2.3: Reciprocal wills leaving entire estate to spouse for life with power to resort to capital and with remainder to children

Note. This form confines the interest of the surviving spouse to a life interest only in the property of the first to die, which life interest will be an IPDI within IHTA 1984, s 49A, (see para **[200.98]**), but gives the trustees power to pay, transfer or apply capital of the estate of the first to die to or for the benefit of the survivor. Accordingly, the property of the first to die will ultimately go to the children of the marriage so far as not so paid transferred or applied by the trustees. This contrasts with an absolute gift of the property of the first to die to the survivor, where in the absence of mutual wills (see Form B1.6 at para **[201.10]**) the survivor will of course be free to dispose of the property he or she has inherited from the first to die.

The matrimonial home will often be the couple's main or only significant asset and the purpose of putting the property of the first to die in trust for the children will be frustrated if his or her interest in the house passes to the other absolutely under a joint tenancy. *It is essential when preparing wills of this type to examine the title to the matrimonial home carefully to see how it is held*; if it is owned as joint tenants beneficially the parties must be advised to effect a severance. If the position is obscure, then effect a severance anyway. It is assumed for the purposes of this form that the matrimonial home is owned by the testators as tenants in common; if one of the spouses is sole owner of the matrimonial home, Form C2.5 (at para **[224.86]** ff) would be more appropriate. Where the testators' property is small, the expense of administering trusts may be difficult to justify and Form C2.1 (at paras **[224.27]**–**[224.41]**) may be more appropriate.

This form can be adapted for use by civil partners with children. The words 'my wife/husband' should be replaced with 'my civil partner' throughout. The definition of the children by reference to parentage and further references to such children in either alternative clause 6, will require attention (see para **[224.35]**, n 1), as will the reference to 'child of mine' in the proviso to clause 7 (if it is included).

[224.59]

REVOCATION CLAUSE

I [*name*] of [*address*] hereby revoke all former testamentary dispositions made by me and declare this to be my last will.[1]

1 If the wills are not mutual wills in the technical sense, this clause could be extended as in the revocation clause in Form C2.1 at para **[224.28]** (see also the note thereto).

[224.60]

APPOINTMENT OF EXECUTORS AND TRUSTEES

1. I appoint my [wife/husband] [*name*] ('my [wife/husband]'), [*name*] of [*address*] and [*name*] of [*address*][1] (hereinafter called 'my trustees' which expression shall include my personal representatives for the time being and the trustees for the time being hereof) to be the executors and trustees of this will.

1 If there are two executors as well as the wife/husband, there will still be two effective appointments if there is a divorce and the appointment of the wife/husband is nullified by the WA 1837, s 18A (Part G, para **[244.18]**).

[224.61]

APPOINTMENT OF GUARDIANS

2. [*As in cl 3 of* Form C2.1 *at para* **[224.31]**.]

[224.62]

GIFT OF PERSONAL CHATTELS TO SPOUSE[1]

3. I give to my [wife/husband] absolutely all my personal chattels as defined by section 55(1)(x) of the Administration of Estates Act 1925[2] [And I request [her/him] (but without imposing any trust or binding obligation on

[her/him]) to give effect to any wishes as to the disposition of such chattels which may be contained in any memorandum that may be found amongst my papers at my death or which may have otherwise been communicated to [her/him] during my life].[3]

1 It is not a good idea to settle chattels, because the trouble and expense of administering them as part of a trust fund is usually out of all proportion to their value, though it may sometimes be appropriate in the case of valuable ones. Accordingly an absolute gift of these to the surviving spouse is included in this Form.

2 See Part G, para **[246.67]** for the wording of this definition, and for further discussion of the meaning of 'personal chattels' see Vol 1, para **[64.44]**.

3 If property bequeathed by a will to one person is distributed to another person in accordance with wishes expressed by the testator within two years of his death, it is treated for IHT purposes as having been bequeathed by the will to that other person: IHTA 1984, s 143; see also B4 at para **[204.8]**. Where it is the testator's spouse to whom the property is bequeathed in the first place, s 143 may operate disadvantageously as it will cause the property so distributed by the spouse to cease being part of an exempt gift and to become part of a chargeable one. Where this is a problem, e g where large values are involved, the spouse could wait until after two years from the testator's death to distribute in accordance with his wishes.

[224.63]

ADMINISTRATION TRUSTS OF RESIDUE

4. [*As in cl 6 of* Form C2.1 *at para* **[224.34]**.]

[224.64]

PRIMARY TRUST FOR SPOUSE

5. If my [wife/husband] shall survive me my trustees shall hold my residuary estate upon trust to pay the income thereof to my [wife/husband] for life[1] Provided that so long as my [wife/husband] is entitled to be paid the income of all or any part of the capital of my residuary estate (or would be so entitled if such capital yielded income)[2] my trustees shall have power in their absolute discretion from time to time to pay transfer or apply the whole or any part or parts of such capital to or for the benefit of my [wife/husband] in such manner as they shall in their absolute discretion think fit.

1 The life interest for the surviving spouse will be an IPDI within IHTA 1984, s 49A (see para **[200.98]**), so spouse exemption from IHT should be available. For the reasons for not including a survivorship condition see the Preliminary Note on survivorship conditions at paras **[224.5]** ff and Form C2.1, cl 4, n 1 at para **[224.31]**.

2 There are two reasons for restricting the power to capital in which the spouse has an interest in possession: first, to ensure that the power is not exercisable if there is a divorce and the primary trust lapses (see the Preliminary Note at paras **[224.16]**–**[224.23]**) and, secondly, to ensure that the power ceases to be exercisable if the spouse assigns or surrenders his or her life interest. It is important that this power should cease to be exercisable in such an event because the termination of an IPDI on or after 22 March 2006 will be deemed to be a gift of the underlying settled property for the purposes of FA 1986, s 102, so that unless the beneficiary of the IPDI is excluded altogether from benefit after the termination, the gift with reservation rules could apply, see FA 1986, s 102ZA, (see para **[200.76]** above).

[224.65]

REMAINDER TRUSTS FOR CHILDREN AND ISSUE[1]

Either

[6. Subject to the trust and to any exercise of the power aforesaid my trustees shall hold my residuary estate upon trust for such of my children [by my [wife/husband]][2] as shall survive me and attain the age of [18/25][3] years and if more than one [in such shares as my trustees shall from time to time by deed or deeds revocable or irrevocable appoint in accordance with the provisions below and in default of such appointment][4] in equal shares Provided that if any such child shall die in my lifetime or having survived me shall die before attaining a vested interest leaving a child or children living at or born after my death who shall attain the age of [18/21] years such last-mentioned child or children shall take if more than one equally between them the share of my residuary estate to which their deceased parent would have become entitled had he or she lived to attain a vested interest [and provided further that no appointment under the power aforesaid shall be made and no appointment shall be revoked so as to

(i) diminish or increase the share (or the accumulations of income forming part of the share) of a child who at the date of such appointment or revocation has reached the age of [18/25] years;

(ii) diminish or increase the share (or the accumulations of income forming part of the share) devolving on his or her child or children of a child who has died under the age of [18/25] years; or

(iii) give a share (or accumulations of income forming part of the share) to a child who at the date of such appointment has been excluded from benefit as a result of an exercise of the power][5].]

Or

[6. (1) Subject to the trust and to any exercise of the power aforesaid my trustees shall hold my residuary estate and the income thereof upon trust for such of my children and remoter issue and if more than one in such shares and with such trusts powers and provisions (including trusts and powers conferring on any person or persons a discretion as to the disposition of capital or income and including provisions for the accumulation of income during any period permitted by law) as my [wife/husband] shall by any deed or deeds revocable or irrevocable or by will or codicil appoint.

(2) Subject to and in default of any such appointment my trustees shall hold my residuary estate upon trust for such of my children [by my [wife/husband]][6] as survive me and attain the age of 18 years[7] and if more than one in equal shares provided that:

(a) if [any child of mine]/[any child of mine by my [wife/husband]][8] shall die in my lifetime or having survived me shall die before attaining a vested interest leaving a child or children surviving me or born after my death who shall attain the age of [18/21] years such last-mentioned child or children shall take if more than one equally between them the share of my residuary estate to which such deceased child of mine would have become entitled had he or she lived to attain a vested interest; and

(b) no person who or whose issue shall take an interest in any part or share of my residuary estate under any such appointment as aforesaid shall participate in the unappointed part without bringing into account the appointed part or share and accounting for the same accordingly.]

1 Alternative clauses are set out, the first giving the children fixed interests, the second conferring an overriding power of appointment amongst issue on the spouse. Under neither alternative are the interests of the children contingent on surviving the life tenant, so that the interest of a child who survives the testator and attains the vesting age (if any) but predeceases the life tenant will vest in his or her personal representatives as part of his or her estate on death.

2 These words will ensure that the ultimate remainders in the wills of both spouses are identical in terms of whom they benefit, in circumstances where one spouse has children who are not children of the other spouse and who are not intended to benefit. See, further, the Preliminary Note on reciprocal wills and the ultimate destination of property at paras **[224.13]–[224.15]** and for forms for use where one or both spouses have children who are not children of the marriage, and who are intended to benefit, see C5 at para **[227.1]** ff. If there are intended beneficiaries under this trust who are the children of one spouse but not of the other, or if this Form is being adapted for use by civil partners either or both of whom have children, see para **[224.35]**, n 1.

3 If the age contingency of attaining 18 is included, and the trusts for children come into possession while they are still infants, these trusts should be trusts for bereaved minors within IHTA 1984, s 71A and so exempt from the IHT relevant property regime (see para **[224.24]** above). (See the following footnote for a possible advantage in the trusts for the children being bereaved minor trusts in the event of the surviving spouse wishing to release her life interest during her life). They may not, however, be 'qualifying trusts' for the benefit of 'vulnerable beneficiaries', for income tax and capital gains tax purposes within FA 2005, ss 23–45, because the statutory power of advancement is incorporated in clause 8 with the usual modification of enabling the whole of a beneficiary's presumptive share of capital, and not merely one half, to be paid or applied for his or her advancement or benefit, see para **[217.4]** above. If the age contingency selected is 25 and the trusts for children come into possession while they are under 25 these trusts should be age 18-to-25 trusts within IHTA 1984, s 71D and so exempt from the IHT relevant property regime although an IHT charge will arise on a beneficiary becoming absolutely entitled to capital when over the age of 18 (see para **[224.24]** above). If the age contingency selected is 25, the trusts would not also be 'qualifying trusts' for the benefit of 'vulnerable beneficiaries' (see para **[217.4]** above).

4 HMRC have confirmed that they consider that a power to vary shares may be compatible with trusts for bereaved minors and age 18-to-25 trusts, so long as the share of a child who has attained 18 or 25 (as the case may be), or has died leaving children on whom his share devolves cannot be varied, and also so long as a child who has been excluded from benefit on an exercise of the power cannot be reinstated as a beneficiary: see paras **[200.108]** and **[200.109]**.

5 Include this proviso if the power for the trustees to vary the shares of the children is included. See n 4 above.

6 As the age of contingency is 18, if these trusts for children come into possession following the surviving spouse's death while they are still infants, they should be trusts for bereaved minors within IHTA 1984, s 71A and so exempt from the IHT relevant property regime (see para **[224.24]** above). If the surviving spouse were to surrender her life interest (wholly or partially) during her lifetime while the children were under the age of 18, and release her power of appointment, so that the trusts for the children were accelerated, potential exemption from IHT should be available under IHTA 1984, s 3A(3B) because the accelerated trusts will be trusts for bereaved minors (see para **[200.128]** above). So as to avoid the surviving spouse being deemed to make a gift with reservation for IHT purposes under FA 1986, s 102ZA, (see para **[200.76]** above), which would nullify the IHT effectiveness of the early surrender of her life interest, it will be important that she is not capable of benefiting in the future from the property in which she surrenders her life interest. So, for example, her surrender should be coupled with an assignment of any interest she may have in the settled property in which she surrenders her life interest in the event of none of the children attaining the age of 18 (eg. as on a partial intestacy of the testator).

7 See n 6 above. Even if this trust is restricted in this way it is not necessary to impose the same restriction on the objects of the power in the preceding clause.

8 The second of these alternatives is appropriate where the primary trust is confined to the children of the marriage.

[224.66]

MAINTENANCE, ACCUMULATION AND ADVANCEMENT

7. Section 31 of the Trustee Act 1925 (relating to accumulation and maintenance) shall apply in relation to the trusts hereby or by any codicil hereto declared as if:

(a) in paragraph (i) of subsection (1) of the said section the words 'as the trustees think fit' were substituted for the words 'as may in all the circumstances be reasonable'; and

(b) the proviso to the said subsection (1) were omitted[1]

[Provided that in relation to any presumptive share of my residuary estate of any child of mine the said section 31 (amended as aforesaid) shall have effect as if the age of majority were the lesser of the age which he or she will attain (if he or she so long lives) on his or her last birthday occurring not later than the expiration of 21 years from my death and the age of 25 years (and so that the expressions 'infancy', 'minority' and 'infant' and all references to the age of eighteen years in the said Section 31 shall be construed accordingly).][2]

(2) Section 32 of the Trustee Act 1925 (relating to advancement) shall apply in relation to the said trusts as if the words 'one half of' were omitted from proviso (a) to subsection (1) thereof.[3]

(3) Whenever my trustees shall have an obligation or discretion under the provisions of this will or any codicil hereto or under the general law to apply income or capital for the benefit of a minor beneficiary they may either pay the same without liability to account to his or her parent guardian or any other adult person with whom such beneficiary may be residing or to such beneficiary himself or herself if of the age of 16 years or more and so that the receipt of such parent guardian or other person or of such minor beneficiary shall be a full and sufficient discharge to my trustees for the income or capital so applied.[4]

1 Where the contingency for the testator's children is attaining the age of 18 there is the alternative possibility of the beneficiaries having interests in possession and during their minorities. See the second alternative clause 8(1) in para **[224.36]** and n 4 thereto. However, combining this with the shares being variable is not recommended, because it is capable of causing considerable confusion about who is entitled to what income if the shares are varied.

2 This proviso is for inclusion where the age contingency for the testator's children in the first alternative clause 6 is the age of 25. It extends the period during which income may be accumulated for as long as the law currently allows (ie. 21 years from the testator's death). See para **[224.25]** and para **[224.36]** n 3.

3 The extended power is compatible with trusts for bereaved minors within IHTA 1984, s 71A (see para **[200.108]** above) and age 18-to-25 trusts within IHTA 1984, s 71D (see para **[200.109]** above).

4 A parent (with parental responsibility) and a guardian of a minor are empowered by the ChA 1989, s 3(3) (Part G, para **[244.114]**) to give a good receipt for the minor's property: see Vol 1, para **[9.41]**. The power in this subclause is wider in that it authorises the payment of income or capital to a parent who does not have parental responsibility, any adult with whom the minor is residing, and the minor himself or herself if 16 or over.

[224.67]

ADMINISTRATIVE POWERS

8. [*As in cl 9 of* Form C2.1 *at para* **[224.37]**.]

[224.68]

TRUSTEE LIABILITY

9. [*As in cl 10 of* Form C2.1 *at para* **[224.38]**.]

[224.69]

EXERCISE OF POWERS

10. [*As in cl 12 of* Form C2.2 *at para* **[224.55]**.]

[224.70]

APPOINTMENT OF NEW TRUSTEES

[11. The power of appointing new trustees shall be vested in my [wife/husband] during [her/his] life].

[224.71]

PROFESSIONAL TRUSTEE CHARGING CLAUSE

12. [*As in cl 11 of* Form C2.1 *at para* **[224.39]**.]

[224.72]

[*Testimonium and attestation clause as in* Form C2.1 *at paras* **[224.40]** and **[224.41]**.]

[224.73]

Form C2.4: Reciprocal wills giving spouse life interest with power of appointment amongst issue, incorporating Statutory Will Forms

Note. The Statutory Will Forms, the text of which appear in Part E at para **[238.1]** ff provide a shorthand method of incorporating fairly elaborate beneficial and administrative provisions. The disadvantage is that the testator cannot immediately see the nature and effect of his will. This form is similar in effect to, but not identical with, Form C2.3 (see paras **[224.58]**–**[224.72]**), where the second alternative version of Form C2.3, cl 6 is used; attention is drawn to the Note at the beginning of Form C2.3 (see para **[224.58]**) and in particular the point that it is important to investigate the title to the matrimonial home and see that any joint tenancy is severed where wills of this kind are being made.

The main difference in the beneficial trusts between this form and Form C2.3 is that this form does not contain a power to pay or apply capital to or for the benefit of the surviving spouse, and a child's interest will vest on marriage if that takes place before he or she attains the vesting age. Also, in relation to the remainder trust for the children of the testator or testatrix there is no option of confining it to being a trust for the children of the marriage (see the Preliminary Note at para **[224.10]** for the significance of this point).

Although the will is shortened by the use of the Statutory Will Forms, it is necessary in order to produce a will which is reasonably in accordance with modern conditions and practice to include a fair number of express administrative and other provisions, still producing quite a long document, and it must be questioned whether use of the Statutory Will Forms is worthwhile.

This form is not suitable for a testator who wishes to make a gift of residue on trust for his civil partner and issue, as Form 9 of the Statutory Will Forms 1925 which it incorporates makes provision for a spouse and not a civil partner.

[224.74]

REVOCATION CLAUSE

I [*name*] of [*address*] hereby revoke all former testamentary dispositions made by me and declare this to be my last will.[1]

1 If the wills are not mutual wills in the technical sense, this clause could be extended as in the revocation clause in Form C2.1 at para **[224.27]** (see the note thereto).

[224.75]

APPOINTMENT OF EXECUTORS AND TRUSTEES

1. [*As in cl 1 of* Form C2.3 *at para* **[224.60]**.]

[224.76]

APPOINTMENT OF GUARDIANS[1]

2. [*As in cl 3 of* Form C2.1 *at para* **[224.31]**.]

1 For the reasons given in the Preliminary Note (see para **[224.11]**), the appointment of guardians incorporated in the forms in this section will take effect only if the other spouse dies first.

[224.77]

GIFT OF PERSONAL CHATTELS TO SPOUSE

3. I give to my [wife/husband] absolutely all my personal chattels as defined by Form 2 of the Statutory Will Forms 1925[1] which is hereby incorporated in this will.

1 The text of Form 2 of the Statutory Will Forms is set out at para **[238.8]**. It is almost exactly the same as the definition of 'personal chattels' in the AEA 1925, s 55(1)(x) (Part G, para **[246.67]**) (which is the definition used in Form C2.3, cl 3 at para **[224.62]**) and almost certainly the same in its effect. The only significant verbal difference is that the Statutory Will Forms makes an express reference to wearing apparel as included in articles of household or personal use or ornament.

[224.78]

ADMINISTRATION TRUSTS OF RESIDUE

4. I give all my property not hereby or by any codicil hereto otherwise effectively disposed of to my trustees and Form 8 of the Statutory Will Forms 1925[1] shall apply thereto [provided that all income of my estate received at any time after my death shall be deemed to accrue on the date on which it is payable and shall not be apportioned to any other time or period].

1 Form 8 of the Statutory Will Forms (at para **[238.14]**) contains an elaborate administration trust but includes only a narrow power of investment. A wide power of investment is included in cl 7 of this form (see Form C2.1, cl 9(a) at para **[224.37]**) which displaces the power contained in Form 8 of the Statutory Will Forms (see Form C1.5, n 5 at para **[223.6]**). Form 8 excludes the rule in *Howe v Dartmouth*, but not time apportionment either at the testator's death or at any subsequent time. If time apportionment is to be excluded,

the proviso to this clause in square brackets should be included. The provisions of Form 8, cl 7(c) leave the trustees free to apply or exclude the rule in *Allhusen v Whittell.* For a general discussion of the equitable rules of apportionment and the statutory rules of apportionment over time see Vol 1, paras **[38.17]–[38.25]** and B14 at paras **[214.35]–[214.37]**.

[224.79]

BENEFICIAL TRUSTS FOR SPOUSE AND ISSUE

5. Form 9 of the Statutory Will Forms 1925[1] is incorporated in this will and shall apply to so much of my estate as devolves on my trustees under clause 4 hereof as is not required for administration purposes.

1 Form 9 of the Statutory Will Forms (at para **[238.15]**) creates trusts under which the spouse takes a life interest (which would be an IPDI, so spouse exemption from IHT should be available) coupled with a power to appoint among issue exercisable by deed or will with a default trust equally between all surviving children of the testator who attain 21 or marry under that age subject to hotchpot. The default remainder trust for the children should be an age 18-to-25 trust within IHTA 1984, s 71D to the extent that any of the children are under 21 on the date it takes effect (see para **[200.109]** above) (unless it has taken effect immediately on the testator's death, and any child was over the age of 18 but under the age of 21, and immediately entitled to an interest possession by virtue of TA 1925, s 31(1)(ii), so that he or she would have an IPDI). The spouse could appoint trusts for the testator's children which would be within IHTA 1984, s 71A (see para **[200.108]** above) if they took effect while the children were under the age of 18.

[224.80]

MAINTENANCE, ACCUMULATION AND ADVANCEMENT

6. (1) Section 31 of the Trustee Act 1925 (relating to accumulation and maintenance) shall apply in relation to the trusts hereby or by any codicil hereto declared as if:

(a) in paragraph (i) of subsection (1) of the said section the words 'as the trustees think fit' were substituted for the words 'as may in all the circumstances be reasonable'; and

(b) the proviso to the said subsection (1) were omitted

Provided that in relation to the presumptive share of any property of any child of mine living at my death the said section 31 (amended as aforesaid) shall have effect as if the age of majority were the age of 21 years (and so that the expressions 'infancy', 'minority' and 'infant' and all references to the age of eighteen years in the said Section 31 shall be construed accordingly).[1]

(2) Section 32 of the Trustee Act 1925 (relating to advancement) shall apply in relation to the said trusts as if the words 'one half of' were omitted from proviso (a) to subsection (1) thereof.[2]

(3) Whenever my trustees shall have an obligation or discretion under the provisions of this will or any codicil hereto or under the general law to apply income or capital for the benefit of a minor beneficiary they may either pay the same without liability to account to his or her parent guardian or any other adult person with whom such beneficiary may be residing or to such beneficiary himself or herself if of the age of 16 years or more and so that the receipt of such parent guardian or other person or of such minor beneficiary shall be a full and sufficient discharge to my trustees for the income or capital so applied.[3]

1 This proviso allows the income of the presumptive share of any child of the testator living at his death to be accumulated until such child attains an absolute interest at age 21 since the law currently allows accumulation for up to 21 years from the testator's death).
2 The extended power is compatible with age 18-to-25 trusts within IHTA 1984, s 71D (see para **[200.109]** above).
3 A parent (with parental responsibility) and a guardian of a minor are empowered by the ChA 1989, s 3(3) (Part G, para **[244.114]**) to give a good receipt for the minor's property: see Vol 1, para **[9.41]**. The power in this subclause is wider in that it authorises the payment of income or capital to a parent who does not have parental responsibility, any adult with whom the minor is residing, and the minor himself or herself if 16 or over.

[224.81]

ADMINISTRATIVE POWERS

7. [*As in cl 9 of* Form C2.1 *at para* **[224.37]**.]

[224.82]

EXERCISE OF POWERS

8. [*As in cl 12 of* Form C2.2 *at para* **[224.55]**.]

[224.83]

APPOINTMENT OF NEW TRUSTEES

9. [*As in cl 11 of* Form C2.3 *at para* **[224.70]**.]

[224.84]

PROFESSIONAL TRUSTEE CHARGING CLAUSE

10. [*As in cl 11 of* Form C2.1 *at para* **[224.39]**.]

[224.85]

[*Testimonium and attestation clause as in* Form C2.1 *at paras* **[224.40]** and **[224.41]**.]

[224.86]

Form C2.5: Will of husband who owns matrimonial home giving wife income of residue and right of residence for life or until remarriage

Note. This form caters for the situation where the matrimonial home is owned by one spouse only and assumes, as is more often the case, that that spouse is the husband. The form can, however, be readily adapted for use by a wife. The form contains alternative provisions giving the wife a full interest or an interest during widowhood only. The latter alternative may not be very effective in view of the power to advance capital to the wife and in view of the more ready acceptance nowadays of couples living together without marrying. A gift during widowhood is restored on the annulment of a second or subsequent marriage being made absolute (*Re Dewhirst, Flower v Dewhirst* [1948] Ch 198, [1948] 1 All ER 147), though not where the subsequent marriage is voidable (as distinct from void): see the Matrimonial Causes Act 1973, s 16 and see Vol 1, para **[35.8]**. A transaction carried into execution before annulment cannot be set aside, *Re Eaves, Eaves v Eaves* [1940] Ch 109, [1939] 4 All ER 260, CA. If the widowhood option is adopted, it may be desired to make a reduced provision after remarriage: see, for example, Form B16.5 at para **[216.10]**.
This form can be adapted for use by a civil partner with children. The words 'my wife' should be replaced with 'my civil partner' throughout, and the reference to widowhood in clause 8(a) appropriately amended.

[224.87]

REVOCATION CLAUSE

I [*name*] of [*address*] hereby revoke all former testamentary dispositions made by me and declare this to be my last will.[1]

1 See n 1 to the revocation clause in Form C2.1 at para **[224.28]**.

[224.88]

APPOINTMENT OF EXECUTORS AND TRUSTEES

1. I appoint my wife [*name*] ('my wife'), [*name*] of [*address*] and [*name*] of [*address*][1] (hereinafter together called 'my trustees' which expression shall include my personal representatives for the time being and the trustees for the time being hereof) to be the executors and trustees of this will.

1 See the note to Form C2.3, cl 1 at para **[224.60]**.

[224.89]

APPOINTMENT OF GUARDIANS[1]

2. If my wife shall not survive me I appoint [*name*] of [*address*] [and [*name*] of [*address*]] to be the [guardian/guardians] of my children during their respective minorities.

1 On this form of appointment of guardians see the Preliminary Note at para **[224.7]** and the Note in B3 at paras **[203.43]–[203.54]**; for alternative forms see Forms B3.26 to B3.32 at paras **[203.55]–[203.61]**; for the relevant law see Vol 1, para **[28.1]** ff. If this will is being adapted for a civil partner with children, and his or her partner is not also a parent of or does not otherwise have parental responsibility for his children, he or she may wish to appoint the surviving civil partner as guardian, in which case the opening words 'If my wife shall not survive me' should be deleted.

[224.90]

GIFT OF PERSONAL CHATTELS TO WIFE[1]

3. I give to my wife all my personal chattels as defined by section 55(1)(x) of the Administration of Estates Act 1925.

1 See Form C2.3, cl 3, n 1 at para **[224.62]**.

[224.91]

GIFT OF PECUNIARY LEGACIES

4. I give the following pecuniary legacies free of tax:[1]
   (a) to my wife the sum of £—— to be paid to her immediately after my death and in priority to all other legacies hereby given[2];
   (b) to [name] the sum of £——;
   (c) to [name] the sum of £——.

1 There is a risk with pecuniary legacies, particularly when given by a better-off testator, that they may be payable out of a residuary estate which includes property situated outside the UK, with the consequence that the legacies may be liable to bear their own IHT so far as payable out of the foreign property: see the Note in B14 at para **[214.63]**. Accordingly, it is better to provide expressly for the incidence of the IHT (and foreign death duties) on

legacies. The expression 'free of tax' is employed here in conjunction with the definition and direction as to payment in cl 7 of this Form at para **[224.94]**.

2 In the absence of express provision a legacy will not take priority even though it is to be paid to a wife for her immediate needs: *Re Schweder's Estate, Oppenheim v Schweder* [1891] 3 Ch 44. The legacy should therefore be given priority so as to ensure that it does not abate with any other legacies which are given. The legacy should also be made payable on death so as to carry interest from that date: *Re Pollock, Pugsley v Pollock* [1943] Ch 338, [1943] 2 All ER 443.

[224.92]

RIGHT FOR WIFE TO OCCUPY MATRIMONIAL HOME[1]

5. (1) If my wife shall survive me[2] I give my freehold dwellinghouse[3] known as ———, or (if the same shall be sold or otherwise disposed of before my death) the dwellinghouse or the principal dwellinghouse (if I have more than one) which I shall own at the date of my death,[4] to my trustees free of all sums charged or otherwise secured thereon at my death (which sums shall be paid out of my residuary estate) to hold the same and the assets from time to time representing the same on trust for my wife during her life.

(2) It is a purpose of the foregoing trust to provide a home for my wife so long as she so desires[5] and I declare that my trustees shall not be liable for lack of insurance repair or payment of outgoings of any home occupied by her under the foregoing trust or for not taking steps to enforce any reasonable conditions imposed by my trustees on my wife in relation to her occupation of any such home.[6]

(3) My trustees may invest trust moneys and change investments with the same unrestricted freedom of choice as a sole beneficial owner, may apply the same in the purchase of any undivided share (whether in co-ownership with my wife or any other person) in a home to be occupied by my wife, and may apply the same in the improvement or repair of any land or buildings for the time being subject to the foregoing trusts.[7]

(4) All the powers of my trustees may be exercised by them in favour of or for the benefit of my wife even though she is one of my trustees, and at any time when she is not one of my trustees her consent shall still be required to any exercise of the trustees' powers of sale purchase or leasing in relation to any land or buildings subject to this Clause.[8]

(5) Subject as aforesaid the said dwellinghouse and the assets representing the same shall fall into my residuary estate.

1 The widow is given a life or widowhood interest in residue, into which the matrimonial home would fall if this clause were omitted. However, this separate provision makes it clearer that the statutory right of occupation of a beneficiary under the TLATA 1996, s 12(1)(a) (Part G, para **[246.115]**) is to apply, makes the matrimonial home further on in the order in which assets are applied to pay debts and testamentary expenses, and means that the widow's right of occupation will not cease on any remarriage. For rights of residence and alternative forms for providing such rights see the Preliminary Note and Forms in B8 at para **[208.1]** ff.

2 If a survivorship clause is wanted the words 'for the period of one month' (or other period up to six months) can be added at this point. See the Preliminary Note on survivorship conditions at paras **[224.5]–[224.10]** for the reasons for not including a survivorship clause as between husband and wife or civil partners. If there is no survivorship condition in this clause but there is one in the trusts of residue, and the wife dies after the testator but within the survivorship period, she will have a brief interest in possession in the house but not in residue. However, if the survivorship condition is included in this clause but not in the residuary trusts, the effect will be the same as having no survivorship condition in either

place, i e the wife will have a brief interest in possession in the entire estate apart from the pecuniary legacies, because the house will fall into residue if the survivorship condition is not fulfilled.

3 If the testator has more than one house there could be merit in tightening the definition of the house with the words 'in which my wife and I now reside' or similar.

4 These words will create a right of residence in any house purchased in place of the matrimonial home occupied at the date of the will. Without such words the sale of the original matrimonial home prior to the testator's death would cause the gift of the right of residence to fail (although the widow would still have a life or widowhood interest in residue which would include any subsequently acquired home).

5 This should be sufficient to confer the statutory right of occupation on the beneficiary under the TLATA 1996, s 12(1)(a) (Part G, para **[246.115]**), and see the preliminary note to B8 at para **[208.5]**.

6 In the interests of economy there is no expression of wishes as to the conditions to be imposed on the beneficiary, but such could be included. See B8 at para **[208.19]**.

7 These are all thought to be applications of capital money which are not authorised by the TLATA 1996 (see Part G, para **[246.108]** and B8 at para **[208.26]**). This subclause can be omitted in whole or in part if there are provisions elsewhere in the will to the same effect which apply to this clause. It is not clear that the proceeds of sale of one property could be spent on improving another property under the powers conferred by the TLATA 1996 in the absence of express authorisation by the will. It is arguably not a power of an absolute owner in relation to the land within TLATA 1996, s 6(1), since it is something done in relation to the cash received from a sale of the land, and it is not the purchase of a legal estate in land within s 6(3).

8 TLATA 1996, s 8(2) (Part G, para **[246.110]**) enables exercise of the trustees' powers over land to be made subject to consents. The repeal by the TLATA 1996 of the LPA 1925, s 28(1) means that a requirement of consent to a sale is no longer applied by statute to other powers.

[224.93]

ADMINISTRATION TRUSTS OF RESIDUE

6. [*As in cl 6 of* Form C2.1 *at para* **[224.34]**.]

[224.94]

GIFTS MADE FREE OF TAX

7. Any specific gift or pecuniary or general legacy made by this will or any codicil hereto which is expressed to be 'free of tax' shall be free from the payment of any inheritance tax or foreign tax or duty payable on or by reason of my death to which such gift or legacy would otherwise be subject and such inheritance tax or foreign tax or duty shall be paid out of my residuary estate.[1]

1 See cl 4, n 1 of this form at para **[224.91]**. Where specific gifts and pecuniary legacies are of, or wholly payable out of, free estate in the UK, the IHT on them will be a testamentary expense payable out of residue without any express provision, and it is only where there is foreign property or settled property being disposed of by the will that a gift which is intended to be free of tax needs to be expressly declared to be free of tax: see further the Preliminary Note to B14 at para **[214.55]** ff.

[224.95]

BENEFICIAL TRUSTS OF RESIDUE

8. My trustees shall hold my residuary estate upon the following trusts:

(a) if my wife shall survive me[1] my trustees shall pay the income of my residuary estate to my wife during her [life/widowhood];[2]

(b) provided that my trustees shall have power in their absolute discretion from time to time so long as my wife is entitled to be paid the income of all or any part of the capital of my residuary estate (or would be so entitled if such capital yielded income) to pay transfer or apply the whole or any part or parts of such capital[3] to her or for her benefit in such manner as they shall in their absolute discretion think fit;

(c) subject as aforesaid my trustees shall hold my residuary estate in trust as to both capital and income in equal shares if more than one for all my children[4] who attain the age of [18/25] years[5] [or marry under that age][6] provided that:

(i) if any such child of mine shall have died in my lifetime whether before or after the date of this my will leaving issue living at my death who attain the age of [18/21] years [or marry under that age] then such issue shall take if more than one in equal shares per stirpes the share of my residuary estate which their deceased parent would have taken had he or she survived me and attained a vested interest but so that no issue shall take whose parent is alive at my death and so capable of taking;

(ii) if any such child of mine shall survive me but shall die before attaining a vested interest under the foregoing trust leaving a child or children who attain the age of [18/21] years or marry under that age then such child or children shall take by substitution if more than one in equal shares the share of my residuary estate which such child of mine would have taken if he or she had attained a vested interest;[7]

(d) subject as aforesaid my trustees shall hold my residuary estate in trust as to both capital and income for [the children of my sister [*name*] in equal shares] absolutely.

1 If a survivorship clause is wanted the words 'for the period of one month' (or other period up to six months) can be added at this point. See the Preliminary Note on survivorship conditions at paras **[224.5]–[224.10]** for the reasons for not including a survivorship clause as between husband and wife or civil partners. If there is a survivorship condition in this subclause, one should also be included in cl 5 above: see cl 5, n 2 at para **[224.92]**.

2 The wife's interest in possession, whether it be for life or widowhood, will be an IPDI within IHTA 1984, s 49A, so spouse exemption from IHT should be available (see para **[200.84]** above). Post-21 March 2006, the provision for automatic termination of an IPDI on events such as remarriage is probably not advisable because potential exemption from IHT will only be available if the termination results in another person acquiring an absolute interest or a disabled person's interest, or causes the settled property to become subject to a trust for bereaved minors (see paras **[200.71]**, **[200.128]**). Therefore, if the testator wishes his spouse's interest to be only an interest during her widowhood it may be advisable if the age contingency in the trusts for children (in sub-cl (c)) is 18 so that the trusts for children will either be trusts for bereaved minors (if the children are under 18 at the time the spouse remarries), or absolute interests (if they are over 18), and either way potential exemption should be available. Further, so as to avoid the surviving spouse being deemed to make a gift with reservation for IHT purposes under FA 1986, s 102ZA, (see para **[200.76]** above), which would nullify the IHT effectiveness of the termination of her life interest being a potentially exempt transfer, it will be important that she is not capable of benefiting in the future from the residuary estate (for example on a partial intestacy of the testator in the event of the testator's issue not attaining vested interests), therefore an ultimate default trust should be included, as in sub-clause (d).

If this form is being adapted for use by a civil partner with children, and the testator wishes his civil partner's interest to terminate on his forming another civil partnership (or marrying), the interest should be expressed to last during the civil partner's life 'or only until he forms a civil partnership or marries'.

3 There are two reasons for restricting the power to being exercisable only over capital in which the wife has an interest in possession: first, to ensure that the power is not exercisable if there is a divorce and the primary trust fails; and second, to ensure that the power ceases to be exercisable if the wife assigns or surrenders her life interest. See the Preliminary Note at paras **[224.16]–[224.23]**.

4 This trust is not confined to being in favour of the children of the marriage. See the Preliminary Note on reciprocal wills and the ultimate destination of property at paras **[224.13]–[224.15]**.

5 If the age contingency of attaining 18 is included, and the trusts for children come into possession while they are still infants, these trusts should be trusts for bereaved minors within IHTA 1984, s 71A and so exempt from the IHT relevant property regime (see para **[224.24]** above).They would not, however, be 'qualifying trusts' for the benefit of 'vulnerable beneficiaries' within FA 2005, ss 23–45, because the statutory power of advancement is incorporated in clause 9 with the usual modification of enabling the whole of a beneficiary's presumptive share of capital, and not merely one half, to be paid or applied for his or her advancement or benefit, see para **[217.4]** above. If the age contingency selected is 25 and the trusts for children come into possession while they are under 25, these trusts should be age 18-to-25 trusts within IHTA 1984, s 71D and so exempt from the IHT relevant property regime although an IHT charge will arise on a beneficiary becoming absolutely entitled to capital when over the age of 18 (see para **[224.24]** above). If the age contingency selected is 25 the trusts would not also be 'qualifying trusts' for the benefit of 'vulnerable beneficiaries' (see para **[217.4]** above).

6 This form follows the rules of intestate succession and makes no difference between sons and daughters as regards marriage under the vesting age: AEA 1925, s 47(1)(i) (Part G, para **[244.63]**). Where it is desired to make a distinction between sons and daughters, the words 'or marry under that age' should be changed to 'or being daughters attain that age or marry under that age' on each occasion where it occurs.

7 Clause 8(c) combines two different sorts of substitution, the substitution of issue remoter than children being only relevant to cases where the testator's child has predeceased the testator, since a child could not leave issue remoter than his own children if he died under the vesting age. If either substitutional provision takes effect, the property subject to it would be within the IHT relevant property regime, and any termination of the spouse's life interest on her remarriage in relation to it would be an immediately chargeable transfer.For a slightly more comprehensive clause on the same lines, see Form B19.6 at para **[219.19]**.

[224.96]

MAINTENANCE, ACCUMULATION AND ADVANCEMENT

9. Section 31 of the Trustee Act 1925 (relating to accumulation and maintenance) shall apply in relation to the trusts hereby or by any codicil hereto declared as if:

(a) in paragraph (i) of subsection (1) of the said section the words 'as the trustees think fit' were substituted for the words 'as may in all the circumstances be reasonable'; and

(b) the proviso to the said subsection (1) were omitted

[Provided that in relation to any presumptive share of my residuary estate of any child of mine the said section 31 (amended as aforesaid) shall have effect as if the age of majority were the lesser of the age which he or she will attain (if he or she so long lives) on his or her last birthday occurring not later than the expiration of 21 years from my death and the age of 25 years (and so that the expressions 'infancy', 'minority' and 'infant' and all references to the age of eighteen years in the said Section 31 shall be construed accordingly).][1]

(2) Section 32 of the Trustee Act 1925 (relating to advancement) shall apply in relation to the said trusts as if the words 'one half of' were omitted from proviso (a) to subsection (1) thereof.[2]

(3) Whenever my trustees shall have an obligation or discretion under the provisions of this will or any codicil hereto or under the general law to apply income or capital for the benefit of a minor beneficiary they may either pay the same without liability to account to his or her parent guardian or any other adult person with whom such beneficiary may be residing or to such beneficiary himself or herself if of the age of 16 years or more and so that the receipt of such parent guardian or other person or of such minor beneficiary shall be a full and sufficient discharge to my trustees for the income or capital so applied.[3]

1 This proviso is for inclusion where the age contingency for the testator's children in clause 8(c) is the age of 25. It extends the period during which income may be accumulated for as long as the law currently allows (ie 21 years from the testator's death). See, further, para **[224.25]**and para **[224.36]** n 3.

2 The extended power is compatible with trusts for bereaved minors within IHTA 1984, s 71A (see para **[200.108]** above) and age 18-to-25 trusts within IHTA 1984, s 71D (see para **[200.109]** above).

3 A parent (with parental responsibility) and a guardian of a minor are empowered by the ChA 1989, s 3(3) (Part G, para **[244.114]**) to give a good receipt for the minor's property: see Vol 1, para **[9.41]**. The power in this subclause is wider in that it authorises the payment of income or capital to a parent who does not have parental responsibility, any adult with whom the minor is residing, and the minor himself or herself if 16 or over.

[224.97]

ADMINISTRATIVE POWERS

10. [*As in cl 9 of* Form C2.1 *at para* **[224.37]**.]

[224.98]

EXERCISE OF POWERS

11. [*As in cl 12 of* Form C2.2 *at para* **[224.55]**.]

[224.99]

APPOINTMENT OF NEW TRUSTEES

12. [*As in cl 11 of* Form C2.3 *at para* **[224.70]**.]

[224.100]

PROFESSIONAL TRUSTEE CHARGING CLAUSE

13. [*As in cl 11 of* Form C2.1 *at para* **[224.39]**.]

[224.101]

[*Testimonium and attestation clause as* Form C2.1 *at paras* **[224.40]** and **[224.41]**.]

[224.102]

Form C2.6: Will of husband settling residue on wife for life with remainder on discretionary trusts

Note. Like Form C2.5, this is for the wealthier spouse, again assumed to be the husband, but the form could be readily adapted for a wife. It is similar to Form C2.5 in its provision for the testator's wife if she survives him (she is given a full life interest in residue), save that her interest is subject to the wide overriding powers in favour of other beneficiaries (mentioned further below) as well as a power to pay her capital. The remainder trusts are, however, fully discretionary, and are subject to overriding powers to appoint or apply capital amongst the testator's issue and their spouses. A will of this type gives maximum flexibility. It enables potentially exempt transfers to be made of the residuary estate during the widow's life in favour of the testator's issue by exercise of the trustees' powers (if, for example, property is appointed absolutely or on trusts for bereaved minors), the remainder trusts can be varied from time to time, and the vesting of capital in any of the children can be deferred indefinitely if that seems beneficial taking into account the tax which will be charged after the death of the testator's spouse under the IHT relevant property regime (for which see **[218.8]** ff).

Providing interest in possession trusts for the children is something to avoid where the testator's spouse is given a life interest, because if the spouse does not survive the testator the fund when held for the children will be subject to IPDI treatment for IHT purposes, whereas if the spouse does survive the testator it will be subject to IHT relevant property treatment after the death of the surviving spouse. See para **[224.24]**. The relevant property regime will apply after the death of the surviving spouse as if the surviving spouse were the settlor: see IHTA 1984, s 80.

This form can be adapted for use by a civil partner with children. The words 'my wife' should be replaced with 'my civil partner' throughout.

[224.103]

REVOCATION CLAUSE

I [*name*] of [*address*] hereby revoke all former testamentary dispositions made by me and declare this to be my last will.[1]

1 See n 1 to the revocation clause in Form C2.1 at para **[224.28]**.

[224.104]

APPOINTMENT OF EXECUTORS AND TRUSTEES

1. [*As in cl 1 of* Form C2.5 *at para* **[224.88]**.]

[224.105]

APPOINTMENT OF GUARDIANS

2. [*As in cl 2 of* Form C2.5 *at para* **[224.89]**.]

[224.106]

GIFT OF PERSONAL CHATTELS TO WIFE

3. [*As in cl 3 of* Form C2.5 *at para* **[224.90]**.]

[224.107]

GIFT OF PECUNIARY LEGACIES

4. [*As in cl 4 of* Form C2.5 *at para* **[224.91]**.]

[224.108]

RIGHT FOR WIFE TO OCCUPY MATRIMONIAL HOME FOR LIFE[1]

5. [*As in cl 5 of* Form C2.5 *at para* **[224.92]**, *deleting 'widowhood' in both places where it appears.*]

1 The separate provision of this clause gives the widow security of occupation, and the trustees' powers of appointment or application in cl 11 will only arise in relation to the house if it is sold with the widow's consent. Accordingly, the widow will arguably be settlor for income tax purposes of any money or other property representing the house which is appointed or applied in favour of other beneficiaries, at any rate where she has consented to a sale in order to enable such appointment or application (although there are some indications that this may not be a point taken by HMRC). If it is preferred to avoid this risk, this clause could be omitted, and the house will be in residue subject to a trustees' power to permit the widow to reside. If the house is owned jointly or in common by the testator and his wife this clause is not appropriate and should be omitted. See Form C2.5, cl 5, n 2 at para **[224.92]** with respect to the inclusion or omission of a survivorship condition.

[224.109]

ADMINISTRATION TRUSTS OF RESIDUE

6. [*As in cl 6 of* Form C2.1 *at para* **[224.34]**.]

[224.110]

GIFTS MADE FREE OF TAX

7. [*As in cl 7 of* Form C2.5 *at para* **[224.94]**.]

[224.111]

BENEFICIAL TRUSTS OF RESIDUE FOR WIFE

8. My trustees shall hold my residuary estate upon the following trusts:

(1) if my wife shall survive me my trustees shall pay the income of my residuary estate to my wife during her life;[1]

(2) provided that my trustees (being at least two in number) shall have power in their absolute discretion from time to time so long as my wife is entitled to be paid the income (if any) of all or any part of the capital of my residuary estate

(a) to pay transfer or apply the whole or any part or parts of such capital[2] to her or for her benefit in such manner as they shall in their absolute discretion think fit; and

(b) to terminate by declaration contained in any deed or deeds her right to be paid the income (if any) of all or any part of the capital of my residuary estate from a date not earlier than the date of any such deed and so accelerate the trusts hereinafter contained or appointed under the powers hereinafter contained and in any such deed my trustees may also declare that my wife shall thenceforth [cease to be among the discretionary beneficiaries (defined below) and] be excluded from all benefit of any kind whatsoever in relation to the capital and income of such part of my residuary estate.[3]

(3) subject as aforesaid my trustees shall hold my residuary estate upon the trusts and with and subject to the powers and provisions of clause 9 below.

1 The surviving spouse's life interest will be an IPDI within IHTA 1984, s 49A, so that the spouse exemption from IHT should be available in respect of the testator's residuary estate (see para **[200.84]** above).

2 The power is exercisable only over capital in which the surviving spouse has an interest in possession to ensure that the power ceases to be exercisable if the interest in possession terminates during her lifetime.

3 This power will enable the trustees to terminate the surviving spouse's interest in possession in the whole or part of the residuary estate. If it is terminated in favour of absolute interests, a disabled person's interest or a trust for bereaved minors (which may all be appointed under the powers below in advance of the termination), the termination of the life interest will be potentially exempt from IHT (see paras **[200.71]** and **[200.128]**). Otherwise it will be a chargeable transfer. It is also provided in this subclause that if the trustees terminate the spouse's life interest in any part of the residuary estate they will have power to exclude her from being a discretionary beneficiary or otherwise benefiting from that part. This is important because such termination will be treated for IHT gift with reservation purposes as a gift of that part of the residuary estate by the surviving spouse (under FA 1986, s 102ZA, see para **[200.76]** above), so it is important that she is excluded from all possibility of benefit after such termination. To give some measure of protection to the spouse this power will only be exercisable by at least two trustees acting unanimously. Nevertheless it should perhaps only be included if the testator fully understands its implications, and the couple's circumstance make it appropriate, e g if they each have sufficient assets in their own name so that the survivor will not necessarily require all of the income or capital from the residuary estate of the first-to-die. The words in square brackets should be omitted if the testator's wife is not included in the class of discretionary beneficiaries (see para **[224.112]**, n 2).

[224.112]

Discretionary trusts

9.(1) In this clause the following expressions have the following meanings, namely:

- (a) 'the trust fund' means the property directed to be held on the trusts of this clause and the assets for the time being representing the same;
- (b) 'the discretionary beneficiaries' means my children and remoter issue and the spouses civil partners widows widowers and surviving civil partners of my children and remoter issue[1] [and (subject to clause 8(2)(b) above) my wife][2].
- (c) 'the trust period' means the period commencing on my death and expiring on the twenty first anniversary of the death of the survivor of my [wife and] children and remoter issue living at the date of my death;
- (e) 'the accumulation period' means the period commencing with my death and expiring on the twenty-first anniversary thereof.

(2) My trustees shall hold the trust fund and the income thereof upon trust for all or such one or more of the discretionary beneficiaries at such ages or times in such shares and upon such trusts for the benefit of the discretionary beneficiaries as my trustees (being at least two in number) may by deed or deeds revocable or irrevocable executed at any time or times during the trust period appoint and in making any such appointment my trustees shall have powers as full as those which they would possess if they were an absolute beneficial owner of the trust fund and in particular (but without prejudice to the generality of the foregoing words) my trustees may in any exercise of the foregoing power as they in their absolute discretion think fit:

- (a) delegate give or impose to or upon themselves or any other person or persons and in relation to any trust or disposition any discretionary powers or discretionary trusts conditions limitations restrictions or provisions including powers of further delegation or powers to create further discretionary trusts or powers;[3]
- (b) create trusts or powers for the accumulation of income for any period permitted by law[4];

(c) appoint or create administrative powers or provisions of whatever nature;

Provided that:

(i) no such appointment shall invalidate any payment transfer or application of capital or income previously made under any of the trusts or powers herein elsewhere contained;

(ii) every interest limited under any exercise of such power shall vest in interest (if at all) not later than the expiration of the trust period;

(iii) any appointment may if my trustees think fit be made subject and without prejudice to any existing interest or interests in possession or to any other existing interests trusts or powers;[5]

(iv) any such appointment may be made in respect of income alone without any appointment of capital; and

(v) any such revocable appointment shall (so far as then unrevoked) cease to be revocable on the expiration of the trust period.

(3) In default of and subject to any exercise of the foregoing power my trustees (being at least two in number) may at their discretion at any time or times during the trust period pay transfer or apply the whole or any part or parts of the trust fund to or for the benefit of all or any one or more of the discretionary beneficiaries for the time being living in such manner as my trustees think fit.[6]

(4) Subject to any or every exercise of the foregoing powers my trustees shall during the trust period hold the trust fund upon trust to pay or apply the income thereof to or for the maintenance education or benefit of all or any one or more of the discretionary beneficiaries for the time being living in such shares if more than one and generally in such manner as they think fit provided that my trustees may during the accumulation period or any other period in which accumulation by them is permitted by law[7] accumulate the whole or any part of the income of the trust fund by investing the same and the resulting income thereof in any of the investments hereby authorised and any accumulations of income so made shall form part of the capital of the trust fund for all purposes.

(5) Subject to the foregoing trust and any or every exercise of the foregoing powers my trustees shall hold the trust fund and the income thereof at the expiration of the trust period in trust absolutely for such of my children and remoter issue as shall then be living in equal shares per stirpes so that no child or remoter issue shall take as share whose parent is then living and capable of taking.

(6) Any capital or income of the trust fund not otherwise disposed of by this clause shall be held in trust for such of my children as shall survive me if more than one in equal shares.

1 The definition of the discretionary class may need to be enlarged or adapted in individual cases, for example if issue of the spouse who are not issue of the testator are intended to be capable of benefiting.

2 The surviving spouse is entitled to the income and can have capital paid to her or for her benefit under the power in clause 8 (2)(a), and so it is not essential for her to be a member of the class of discretionary beneficiaries from the point of view of providing her with access to income or capital. The reason for including her in this class is that it provides greater flexibility as to what can be achieved in exercise of the power of appointment. The danger of including her is that the need to remove her from the class may be overlooked if her life interest is terminated during her life: see para **[224.111]**, n 3.

3 These words authorise the creation of discretionary powers, e g powers to advance capital to a life tenant, which might not otherwise be valid: see Vol 1, para **[40.5]**.

4 The Law Commission have recommended the abolition of the statutory restrictions on accumulation so that accumulation is permissible for a full perpetuity period. It is possible that this might have happened by the time of the testator's death.

5 This confirms that the trustees could make an appointment in remainder expectant upon the surviving spouse's life interest, and so in effect vary the remainder capital trusts, without causing her IPDI to come to an end (see para **[200.98]**). Trusts for bereaved minors can arise by appointment under a will (see paras **[200.108]**, **[200.128]** above), so if circumstances were appropriate it would be possible for the trustees to appoint a trust for bereaved minors in relation to a part, say, of the residuary estate, and then terminate the surviving spouse's IPDI in that part by way of potentially exempt transfer (see para **[200.108]** above).

6 A power to apply capital, being exercisable in a less formal manner, may be useful. But it is essential that its exercise should be adequately evidenced.

7 See note 4 above.

[224.113]

ADMINISTRATIVE POWERS

10. [*As in cl 9 of* Form C2.1 *at para* **[224.37]**.]

[224.114]

TRUSTEE LIABILITY

11. [*As in cl 10 of* Form C2.1 *at para* **[224.38]**.]

[224.115]

EXERCISE OF POWERS

12. [*As in cl 12 of* Form C2.2 *at para* **[224.55]**.]

[224.116]

APPOINTMENT OF NEW TRUSTEES

13. [*As in cl 11 of* Form C2.3 *at para* **[224.70]**.]

[224.117]

PROFESSIONAL TRUSTEE CHARGING CLAUSE

14. [*As in cl 11 of* Form C2.1 *at para* **[224.39]**.]

[224.118]

[*Testimonium and attestation clause as in* Form C2.1 *at paras* **[224.40]** and **[224.41]**.]

C3 Wills for married couples (or civil partners) with adult children

Preliminary note .... **[225.1]**

FORMS

C3.1 Reciprocal wills giving nil-rate band legacy to children and residue to spouse with default gift to children in equal/unequal shares .... **[225.9]**

C3.2 Reciprocal wills with nil-rate band legacy on trust for the children, residue on trust for spouse for life and then on trust for the children, son taking a life interest and daughter a protected life interest .... **[225.23]**

C3.3 Will dividing residue between spouse and issue .... **[225.42]**

C3.4 Reciprocal wills containing nil-rate band legacy on discretionary trusts with gift of residue to spouse .... **[225.57]**

C3.5 Reciprocal wills giving nil-rate band legacy on discretionary trusts and settling residue on protective trusts for spouse for life, with overriding trustees' powers over capital, and discretionary trusts for issue after the surviving spouse's death .... **[225.68]**

NOTE ON TWO-YEAR DISCRETIONARY TRUSTS (IHTA 1984, S 144) .... **225.83]**

FORMS

C3.6 Will providing two-year discretionary trust .... **[225.92]**

C3.7 Reciprocal wills giving entire estate to spouse absolutely, with alternative gift to issue .... **[225.110]**

PRELIMINARY NOTE

[225.1]

This section contains a selection of forms for use by married couples with adult children. Accordingly, trusts for their children are mostly in favour of named children, and are not contingent on attaining a specified age. The announcement of nil-rate band carry-forward on 9 October 2007 (see para **[200.75]**) has simplified IHT planning by making it unnecessary in most cases to include nil-rate band discretionary trusts in the will of the first to die. There are only certain special situations where they are advisable on IHT-saving grounds: see para **[225.2]**. Although much of the commentary below relates to married couples, the same considerations will apply to civil partners. The forms may be adapted for cases where civil partners (or either of them) have adult children.

[225.2]

Nil-rate band discretionary and other trusts. As discussed in para **[200.130]**, in view of the announcement of nil-rate band carry-forward on 9 October 2007 (see para **[200.75]**), there are only certain situations where there is a potential IHT advantage in having a nil-rate band gift or discretionary trust in the will of the first to die of a married couple or civil partnership. The reasons for continuing to include nil-rate band gifts or trusts in the will of the first to die which are relevant to C3 are, first, where there is an asset which could be appropriated to the nil-rate band trust fund which can confidently be expected to grow in value at a rate more rapid than increases in the nil-rate band, and, secondly, where either spouse or civil partner has been married or in a civil partnership before, the marriage or civil partnership ended on the death of the other party, and the dispositions taking effect on the death of the other party did not make full use of his or her IHT nil-rate band. A nil-rate band discretionary trust can also be useful where it is desired to keep to a minimum the assets of the first to die to which the survivor is entitled, so far as that is compatible with not paying IHT on the death of the first to die. For nil-rate band discretionary trusts see the Notes on them in B18 at paras **[218.16]–[218.24]**.

[225.3]
General strategy. Accordingly, some of the forms in C2 will be appropriate for married couples or civil partners who do not wish to have any IHT non-exempt gifts taking effect on the death of a first to die. The forms in C3, apart from Forms C3.6 and C3.7, all contain a non-exempt gift taking effect on the death of the first to die with the remainder of the first to die's estate being an exempt gift in favour of the survivor. Forms C3.1 to C3.3 are for cases where for non-fiscal reasons it is desired that the testators' children or other issue should be directly benefited on the death of the first to die without having to wait for the death of the survivor. Form C3.3 divides residue equally between spouse and issue, and provides an element of generation-skipping by settling the son's share directly on his children. Forms C3.4 and C3.5 are appropriate for the special cases where a nil-rate band discretionary trust taking effect on the death of the first to die could be beneficial from an IHT point of view, and Form C3.5 is also a form for use where it is desired, for asset protection reasons, to keep to a minimum the assets of the first to die to which the survivor is entitled. Form C3.6 subjects residue to a two-year discretionary trust in effect leaving it to the trustees to decide what is the best arrangement from a personal and tax point of view. This type of disposition relies on IHTA 1984, s 144, and a Note on s 144 precedes Form C3.6 (see para **[225.83]** ff). Form C3.7 is a simple form for the case where there is insufficient IHT advantage, and/or insufficient assets to spare, to justify making a non-exempt gift on the death of the first to die. Special considerations arise when the estate includes business or agricultural property. These are discussed in the Preliminary Notes to C11 and C12 at paras **[233.1]** ff and **[234.1]** ff.

[225.4]
Survivorship conditions. See the Preliminary Note to C2 at paras **[224.6]–[224.10]** for a discussion of survivorship conditions (they are also discussed in B19 at paras **[219.1]–[219.13]**), and for a discussion of survivorship conditions and gifts only intended to take effect once in reciprocal wills see paras **[231.7]**, **[231.8]**. For the reasons there given, there is no IHT advantage in making the gift to the spouse or civil partner subject to a survivorship condition, and it could be an IHT disadvantage (see paras **[224.7]**, **[224.8]**). Accordingly survivorship conditions are not included in inter-spouse gifts in C3. Survivorship conditions in gifts to persons other than the testator's spouse or civil partner are discussed in the Preliminary Note to C2 at para **[224.10]**. They are also not included in the forms in C3.

[225.5]

Guardians. It is assumed for the purposes of the forms in C3 that the testators' children have grown up, and no appointment of guardians is included in any of them.

[225.6]

Reciprocal and mutual wills. The Preliminary Note to C2 on this topic (at para **[224.12]**) applies also to C3.

[225.7]

Reciprocal wills and the ultimate destination of property. See the Preliminary Note to C2 at paras **[224.13]–[224.15]**. Where a husband and wife will not have any more children, it is possible to ensure that the alternative gift or remainder trust to or for the children is in favour of the same persons, in the wills of both spouses, by naming the children. Most of the forms in C3 provide for this to be done, and where they do not there are optional words confining the gift or trust to the children of the marriage.

[225.8]

The possibility of divorce or dissolution of a civil partnership. The Preliminary Note to C2 on this topic (at paras **[224.16]–[224.23]**) applies also to C3.

[225.9]

Form C3.1: Reciprocal wills giving nil-rate band legacy to children and residue to spouse with default gift to children in equal/unequal shares

Note. This form is of wills for a couple who have between them sufficient assets for the first to die to be able to give at least a nil-rate band's worth to the children, but wish to postpone paying any IHT to the second death. It will not be suitable where the surviving spouse might need access to the whole estate. For cases where the testators want there to be a significant gift to the children in the will of the first to die, but are concerned that a gift to the children equal in value to the whole of the nil-rate band might not leave enough for the maintenance of the surviving spouse (bearing in mind that there could in the next few years be substantial increases in the nil-rate band), there are the following possibilities. One is that an upper limit could be imposed on the amount of the legacy to the children, as in this form. Another possibility is that instead of the nil-rate band legacy being given directly to the children there is a discretionary trust of the nil-rate band legacy under which the surviving spouse is a beneficiary, as in Form C3.4 at para **[225.57]**, with a letter of wishes expressing the wish that the trustees in consultation with the surviving spouse should decide how much can be spared to go to the children immediately and should appoint it out to them

This Form C3.1 may be adapted for use for civil partners, the words 'my wife/husband' being replaced with 'my civil partner' throughout. Care should be taken to identify correctly in each will the children who are to benefit.

[225.10]

REVOCATION CLAUSE[1]

I [*name*] of [*address*] hereby revoke all former testamentary dispositions made by me and declare this to be my last will.

1 There is no presumption that wills in similar form are mutual wills in the technical sense, but the matter can be put beyond doubt by incorporating an express provision to that effect: see Form B1.6 at para **[201.10]** and the revocation clause to Form C2.1 at para **[224.28]** and the note thereto.

[225.11]

APPOINTMENT OF EXECUTORS AND TRUSTEES

1. I appoint my [wife/husband] [*name*] ('my [wife/husband]') [*name*] of [*address*] and [*name*] of [*address*][1] (hereinafter together called 'my trustees' which expression shall include my personal representatives for the time being and the trustees for the time being hereof) to be the executors and trustees of this will.

1 If there are two executors as well as the wife/husband, there will still be two effective appointments if there is a divorce and the appointment of the wife/husband is nullified by the Wills Act 1837, s 18A (Part G, para **[243.18]**). If this will is being adapted for civil partners, the same will apply mutatis mutandis, see Wills Act 1837, s 18C (Part G, para **[243.20]**). See also the Preliminary Note to C2 at paras **[224.16]–[224.19]**.

[225.12]

PECUNIARY LEGACIES

2. [If I survive my [wife/husband]][1] I give the following pecuniary legacies free of tax:[2]

(a) to [*name*] the sum of £——;
(b) to [*name*] the sum of £——;
(c) to [*name*] the sum of £——.

1 The words in square brackets should be included where these are intended to be legacies which are given once only, on the death of the second of the spouses to die. For reciprocal wills containing legacies intended to take effect under only one of the wills where there is a survivorship condition in the main gift see Form C9.2 at para **[231.14]** ff.

It should be noted that if there is a divorce, these legacies will still take effect, and only take effect, on the death of the survivor of the former spouses, if they do not change their wills.

2 See Form C2.1, cl 6, n 3 at para **[224.34]** and n 1 to cl 5 of this form at para **[225.15]**. These pecuniary legacies are declared to be 'free of tax' to take account of the risk that they may be payable out of a residuary estate which includes property of a kind which bears its own IHT, such as property situated outside the UK, with the consequence that the legacies might without this declaration be liable to bear their own IHT so far as payable out of that property: see the Preliminary Note to B14 at paras **[214.59]** and **[214.60]**. The expression 'free of tax' is employed here in conjunction with the definition and direction as to payment in cl 5 of this form at para **[225.15]**.

[225.13]

GIFT OF NIL RATE BAND LEGACY TO CHILDREN1

3. (1) If my [wife/husband] shall survive me[2] then I give to my trustees a pecuniary legacy of the maximum sum (if any) [not exceeding £——][3] which can in the circumstances subsisting at my death be given by this clause without any liability being incurred for the payment of inheritance tax on or by reason of my death and in particular (without prejudice to the generality of the foregoing) for the purpose of determining the amount of such maximum sum the circumstances to be taken into account shall include all chargeable transfers made by me during my life (or events treated as such for inheritance tax purposes) so far as relevant for the computation of inheritance tax on my death the dispositions taking effect under this will (apart from this clause) or under any codicil hereto and any property treated as if it were part of my estate for inheritance tax purposes].

Either[4]

(2) My trustees shall hold the said legacy upon trust for such of my children [*name*] [*name*] and [*name*][5] as shall survive me and if more than one in equal shares Provided that if any of my said children shall predecease me leaving a child or children surviving me [who shall attain the age of [18/21/25] years[6]] such last-mentioned child or children shall take and if more than one equally between them the share of the said legacy which such deceased child of mine would have taken had he or she survived me.

Or

(2) My trustees shall hold the said legacy upon trust to divide the same into [10] equal parts and shall hold:

(a) [5] of such parts upon trust for [my son] [name];

(b) a further [3] of such parts upon trust for [my daughter] [*name*]; and

(c) the remaining [2] of such parts upon trust for [my daughter] [*name*][7]

Provided that:

(i) if any of my said children shall predecease me leaving a child or children living at my death [who shall attain the age of [18/21/25] years[8]] such last-mentioned child or children shall take and if more than one equally between them the share of the said legacy which such deceased child of mine would have taken had he or she survived me;

(ii) if the trusts of any share of the said legacy shall fail because a child of mine predeceases me without leaving a child who attains a vested interest under paragraph (i) of this proviso then such share (and any share which may have accrued thereto hereunder) shall accrue to the other shares or share of the said legacy the trusts of which have not failed and if more than one [in equal shares]/[in the proportions which such shares bear to each other].

(3) The said legacy shall carry interest at the yearly rate of 6 per cent from my death until the same shall be paid or satisfied or set apart and invested and section 31 of the Trustee Act 1925 (as hereinafter modified) shall apply thereto.[9]

1 Subclause (1) of this clause gives a legacy of a sum determined in accordance with a formula which represents the maximum sum which can be given without incurring a liability for IHT. The current IHT threshold (tax year 2007–2008) is £300,000. For 2008–9 it is due to be £312,000, and for 2009–10, £325,000, see FA 2006, s 155. For 2010–11 it is due to be £350,000, see FA 2007, s 4. The formula for ascertaining the amount of the legacy is intended to ensure that the amount of the discretionary legacy does not exceed the IHT threshold where other non-exempt gifts are made by the will, or where there are non-exempt lifetime chargeable transfers or property treated as part of the testator's estate to be taken into account on the death. It also adjusts the legacy to any future increases in the nil-rate band where the IHT threshold is increased after the will has been made.

2 This precondition is imposed to avoid unnecessary duplication of gifts (ie this one and the residuary gift) in the event of the spouse not surviving the testator.

3 In view of the possible large increases in the nil-rate band in the next few years it would be advisable to set a cash limit on the amount of this gift. See para **[225.9]**. Another reason for setting a cash limit on it is where the testator has business or agricultural property: see the Preliminary Note to C11 at paras **[233.8]**–**[233.10]**.

4 The alternative forms give the legacy to the children either in equal or unequal shares, with substitutional provisions for the children of a predeceasing child. Similar alternatives are provided in the gift of residue which takes effect if the spouse does not survive the testator.
5 See the Preliminary Note on reciprocal wills and the ultimate destination of property at para **[225.7]**.
6 The grandchildren will be lives in being at the testator's death for perpetuity purposes, so if the gift to them is to be subject to a contingency that they attain a certain age, there is no risk of infringing the rule against perpetuities in specifying an age exceeding 21. If the gift to them is subject to an age contingency, and any of them have not satisfied it at the testator's death, but the substitutional trust takes effect, the property subject to it will be within the IHT charging regime for relevant property, unless they are entitled to interests in possession by the time of the testator's death and thus have IPDIs (see paras **[200.92]**, **[224.25]** above).
7 See the Preliminary Note on reciprocal wills and the ultimate destination of property at para **[225.7]**.
8 The grandchildren will be lives in being at the testator's death for perpetuity purposes, so if the gift to them is to be subject to a contingency that they attain a certain age, there is no risk of infringing the rule against perpetuities in specifying an age exceeding 21. If the gift to them is subject to an age contingency, and any of them have not satisfied it at the testator's death, but the substitutional trust takes effect, the property subject to it will be within the IHT charging regime for relevant property, unless they are entitled to interests in possession by the time of the testator's death and thus have IPDIs (see paras **[200.92]** and **[224.25]** above).
9 There is a contingency in the substitutional provision in proviso (i) to sub-cl (2) of this clause. A contingent legacy does not ordinarily carry the intermediate income, but one of the exceptions to this is where the legacy is directed to be set apart, invested and held on trust (see Vol 1, para **[32.15]**). This clause directs the trustees to hold the legacy on trust, and that may be sufficient to carry the intermediate income, but sub-cl (3) makes the position clear.

[225.14]

ADMINISTRATION TRUSTS OF RESIDUE

4. (1) I give all my property not hereby or by any codicil hereto otherwise effectively disposed of [(including any entailed or other property over which I shall have at my death a general power of disposition by will)][1] to my trustees to hold on the trusts set out below with power at their discretion to sell all or any of it as and when they think fit.[2]

(2) My trustees shall pay my funeral and testamentary expenses[3] and debts and any legacies given by this will or any codicil hereto out of such property or its proceeds and shall have a discretion as to how such payments shall be borne as between capital and income.[4]

(3) Subject as above my trustees shall hold such property and the assets from time to time representing the same (hereinafter called 'my residuary estate') on the trusts set out below and shall invest all money comprised in such property or arising from its sale in any of the investments hereby authorised with power to change such investments into any others hereby authorised.

(4) In the administration of my estate and the execution of the trusts of this will or of any codicil to it:

(a) my trustees shall treat all income as accruing on the date on which it becomes payable regardless of the period in respect of which it shall have accrued and shall not make any statutory apportionment of the same;[5] and

(b) none of the equitable rules of apportionment between capital and income shall apply in any circumstances whatever[6].

1 See Form C2.1, cl 6, n 1 at para **[224.27]**.
2 See Form C2.1, cl 6, n 2 at para **[224.27]**.
3 See Form C2.1, cl 6, n 3 at para **[224.27]**.
4 See Form C2.1, cl 6, n 4 at para **[224.27]**.
5 See Form C2.1, cl 6, n 5 at para **[224.27]**.
6 See Form C2.1, cl 6, n 6 at para **[224.27]**.

[225.15]

GIFTS MADE FREE OF TAX

5. Any specific gift or pecuniary or general legacy made by this will or any codicil hereto which is expressed to be 'free of tax' shall be free from the payment of any inheritance tax or foreign tax or duty payable on or by reason of my death to which such gift or legacy would otherwise be subject and such inheritance tax or foreign tax or duty shall be paid out of my residuary estate.[1]

1 See Form C2.1, cl 6, n 3 at para **[224.27]**. Where specific gifts and pecuniary legacies are of, or wholly payable out of, free estate in the UK, the IHT on them will be a testamentary expense payable out of residue without any express provision, and it is only where there is foreign property or settled property being disposed of by the will that a gift which is intended to be free of tax needs to be expressly declared to be free of tax. See also the Preliminary Note to B14 at paras **[214.59]–[214.60]**.

[225.16]

BENEFICIAL TRUSTS OF RESIDUE[1]

6. (1) My trustees shall hold my residuary estate upon trust for my [wife/husband] if [she/he] shall survive me.

Either

[(2) If my [wife/husband] fails to survive me my trustees shall hold my residuary estate upon trust for such of my children [*name*] [*name*] and [*name*][2] as shall survive me and if more than one in equal shares Provided that if any of my said children shall predecease me leaving a child or children surviving me [who shall attain the age of [18/21/25] years[3]] such last-mentioned child or children shall take and if more than one equally between them the share of my residuary estate which such deceased child of mine would have taken had he or she survived me.]

Or

[(2) If my [wife/husband] fails to survive me my trustees shall hold my residuary estate upon trust to divide the same into [10] equal parts and shall hold:

(a) [5] of such parts upon trust for [my son] [*name*];
(b) a further [3] of such parts upon trust for [my daughter] [*name*]; and
(c) the remaining [2] of such parts upon trust for [my daughter] [*name*];[4]

provided that:

(i) if any of my said children predeceases me leaving a child or children living at my death [who shall attain the age of [18/21/25] years[5]] such last-mentioned child or children shall take and if more than one equally between them the share of my residuary estate which such deceased child of mine would have taken had he or she survived me;

(ii) if the trusts of any share of my residuary estate shall fail because a child of mine predeceases me without leaving a child who attains a vested interest under paragraph (i) of this proviso then such share (and any share which may have accrued thereto hereunder) shall accrue to the other shares or share of the said legacy the trusts of which have not failed and if more than one [in equal shares]/[in the proportions which such shares bear to each other].

1 Residue devolves on the other spouse, if surviving. If the other spouse does not survive the testator, residue is given to the children. Two alternatives are given for the trust for the children; the alternatives correspond with the alternatives in the legacy contained in cl 3(2) of this form at para **[225.13]**.

2 See the Preliminary Note on reciprocal wills and the ultimate destination of property at para **[225.7]**.

3 The grandchildren will be lives in being at the testator's death for perpetuity purposes, so if the gift to them is to be subject to a contingency that they attain a certain age, there is no risk of infringing the rule against perpetuities in specifying an age exceeding 21. If the gift to them is subject to an age contingency, and any of them have not satisfied it at the testator's death, but the substitutional trust takes effect, the property subject to it will be within the IHT charging regime for relevant property, unless they are entitled to interests in possession by the time of the testator's death and thus have IPDIs (see paras **[200.92]**, **[224.25]** above).

4 See the Preliminary Note on reciprocal wills and the ultimate destination of property at para **[225.7]**.

5 The grandchildren will be lives in being at the testator's death for perpetuity purposes, so if the gift to them is to be subject to a contingency that they attain a certain age, there is no risk of infringing the rule against perpetuities in specifying an age exceeding 21. If the gift to them is subject to an age contingency, and any of them have not satisfied it at the testator's death, but the substitutional trust takes effect, the property subject to it will be within the IHT charging regime for relevant property, unless they are entitled to interests in possession by the time of the testator's death and thus have IPDIs (see paras **[200.92]** and **[224.25]** above).

[225.17]

MAINTENANCE, ACCUMULATION AND ADVANCEMENT[1]

7. (1) Section 31 of the Trustee Act 1925 (relating to accumulation and maintenance) shall apply in relation to the trusts hereby or by any codicil hereto declared as if:

(a) in paragraph (i) of subsection (1) of the said section the words 'as the trustees think fit' were substituted for the words 'as may in all the circumstances be reasonable'; and

(b) the proviso to the said subsection (1) were omitted.

(2) Section 32 of the Trustee Act 1925 (relating to advancement) shall apply in relation to the said trusts as if the words 'one half of' were omitted from proviso (a) to subsection (1) thereof.

(3) Whenever my trustees shall have an obligation or discretion under the provisions of this will or any codicil hereto or under the general law to apply income or capital for the benefit of a minor beneficiary they may either pay the same without liability to account to his or her parent guardian or any other adult person with whom such beneficiary may be residing or to such beneficiary himself or herself if of the age of 16 years or more and so

that the receipt of such parent guardian or other person or of such minor beneficiary shall be a full and sufficient discharge to my trustees for the income or capital so applied.[2]

1 For alternative provisions relating to maintenance and advancement see Forms B18.11 to B18.23 and the text thereto at paras **[218.77]–[218.107]**.

2 A parent (with parental responsibility) and a guardian of a minor are empowered by the ChA 1989, s 3(3) (Part G, para **[244.114]**) to give a good receipt for the minor's property: see Vol 1, para **[9.41]**. The power in this subclause is wider in that it authorises the payment of income or capital to a parent who does not have parental responsibility, any adult with whom the minor is residing, and the minor himself or herself if 16 or over.

[225.18]

ADMINISTRATIVE POWERS[1]

8. (1) In this clause where the context so admits:
   (a) the expression 'land' includes buildings and estates interests or rights of any kind in or over land; and
   (b) during the administration of my estate the expression 'beneficiary' includes any person who would be a beneficiary if such administration had been completed and the expression 'beneficially interested' and references to income of any asset being payable or capable of being paid to or for the benefit of a beneficiary shall be construed accordingly.

(2) None of the powers or provisions contained in subclause (3) below of this clause shall be capable of being exercised or operating in any manner such that if such power or provision were capable of being so exercised or so operating the existence of the same would either:
   (i) prevent any person who would in the absence of such power or provision have been entitled to an interest in possession falling within section 49(1A) of the Inheritance Tax Act 1984 in any property from being entitled to such interest; or
   (ii) prevent section 71A or 71D of the Inheritance Tax Act 1984 from applying to any property to which in the absence of such power or provision either section would have applied.[2]

(3) In the administration of my estate and the execution of the trusts hereof or of any codicil hereto my trustees shall have the following powers in addition to those conferred by law but subject to the last foregoing subclause—
   (a) power to invest moneys sell assets and change investments with the unrestricted freedom of choice and powers of disposition and acquisition of a sole beneficial owner with in particular power to make unsecured loans, acquire non-income yielding assets, and purchase land anywhere in the world or chattels for any purpose including occupation or enjoyment in kind by a beneficiary under the power set out below;[3]
   (b) power to delegate all or any of their investment powers to a professional investment manager or managers whether individual or corporate and whether or not also a nominee holder of assets for my trustees (and who may be or include one or more of my trustees or the beneficiaries hereunder) upon such terms as to remuneration and

otherwise (including terms authorising self-dealing or providing for the limitation of the liability of the investment manager or managers) as my trustees think fit and section 22 of the Trustee Act 2000 shall not apply;[4]

(c) power to vest or register any property in any person or persons whether individual or corporate and whether or not an investment manager to whom powers have been delegated under the foregoing power (and who may be or include one or more of my trustees or the beneficiaries hereunder) as nominee or nominees for my trustees upon such terms as to remuneration or otherwise (including terms authorising self-dealing or providing for the limitation of the liability of the nominee) as my trustees think fit and section 22 of the Trustee Act 2000 shall not apply;[5]

(d) power to borrow money with or without giving security and on such terms as to interest and repayment and otherwise as my trustees may think fit for any purpose connected with the administration of my estate or the trusts declared herein or in any codicil hereto (including investment) And no lender from whom my trustees borrow money in purported exercise of this power shall be concerned to enquire as to the propriety amount or purpose of any such borrowing;[6]

(e) power to lend money to a beneficiary to whom any of the income of such money is payable or to whom or for whose benefit any income of such money is capable of being paid or applied in exercise of a discretion (or who would be such a beneficiary if such money yielded income) and to do so at a full or concessionary rate of interest or interest free;[7]

(f) all the powers of an absolute owner in relation to any land (wherever situated) held by them;[8]

(g) power to apply capital held on the same trusts as any land (or which would be so held if the administration of my estate had been completed) in the improvement of such land and to apply such capital or the income of such capital on the repair or maintenance of such land;[9]

(h) power to permit any beneficiary to have the beneficial occupation use or enjoyment in kind of any land or chattel or other tangible property on such terms as to repair insurance or payment of outgoings by the beneficiary or otherwise howsoever as my trustees think fit Provided that the foregoing power shall only be exercisable and such permission to occupy or enjoy in kind may only continue in the following circumstances—

(i) so long as any of the income of such land chattel or other tangible property is payable to such beneficiary or capable of being paid or applied to him or for his benefit in exercise of a discretion (or would be so payable or capable of being so paid or applied if such land chattel or other property yielded income);

(ii) in the case of land, so long as for the time being the occupation thereof by such beneficiary is compatible with any statutory rights of occupation of any other beneficiary or beneficiaries;[10]

(i) power to exercise all the powers of appropriation (and other incidental powers) conferred by statute on a personal representative without the necessity of obtaining any consents and notwithstanding that one or more of my trustees may be beneficially interested in the exercise of such power.[11]

1 See Form C2.1, cl 9, n 1 at para **[224.37]**.
2 See Form C2.1, cl 9, n 2 at para **[224.37]**.
3 See Form C2.1, cl 9, n 3 at para **[224.37]**.
4 See Form C2.1, cl 9, n 4 at para **[224.37]**.
5 See Form C2.1, cl 9, n 5 at para **[224.37]**.
6 See Form C2.1, cl 9, n 6 at para **[224.37]**.
7 See Form C2.1, cl 9, n 7 at para **[224.37]**.
8 See Form C2.1, cl 9, n 8 at para **[224.37]**.
9 See para **[220.52]** for the reasons for this provision.
10 See Form C2.1, cl 9, n 10 at para **[224.37]**.
11 See Form C2.1, cl 9, n 11 at para **[224.37]**.

[225.19]

TRUSTEE LIABILITY

9. [(1)] My trustees shall not be liable for any act or default of any investment manager or nominee employed in good faith to manage or hold assets of my estate nor for any act or default of any beneficiary having the occupation use or enjoyment of property in kind.[1]

[(2) Section 11(1) of the Trusts of Land and Appointment of Trustees Act 1996 (consultation with beneficiaries) shall not apply to the exercise by my trustees of their functions in relation to any land subject to the trusts of this my will.][2]

1 This makes it clear that the trustees are not liable for the defaults of others who may have possession or control of trust property. In respect of the defaults of an investment manager or nominee, this indemnity may be wider than that of the Trustee Act 2000 (TrA 2000), s 23 (1) (Part G, para **[246.155]**) which only exempts a trustee from liability for such defaults if he has complied with the statutory duty of care, a standard which may be higher than that of 'good faith'. Whereas it is clear that a wider indemnity such as this can apply where trustees have exercised an express power to appoint an investment manager or nominee, it is not clear that a wider indemnity can be conferred where trustees have exercised the statutory power (see n 4 to Form C2.1, cl 9 at para **[224.37]** and the Preliminary Note to B21 at para **[221.14]**). If a paid trustee is to rely on this indemnity clause which may limit his liability in negligence in that it may absolve him from negligent failure to intervene to prevent loss, the testator should specifically be made aware of its meaning and effect (see para **[221.13]** above). For a wider form of indemnity, see eg Form B21.12 at para **[221.16]**.
2 The testator may wish to exclude the duties of trustees of land to consult the beneficiaries of full age and beneficially entitled to an interest in possession, and so far as consistent with the general interest of the trust to give effect to the wishes of those beneficiaries or (in the event of a dispute) the majority by value, see the TLATA 1996, s 11 (Part G, para **[246.114]** and see Preliminary Note to B20 at para **[220.58]**).

[225.20]

PROFESSIONAL TRUSTEE CHARGING CLAUSE

10. Any of my trustees being a professional or business man may charge and be paid all usual professional and other proper charges for business transacted acts done advice given and time spent by him or his firm in connection with the administration of my estate or in connection with the

trusts hereof including acts which a personal representative or trustee not being in any profession or business could have done personally.[1]

1 In spite of the TrA 2000, s 29(2) (Part G, para **[246.161]**) giving certain professional trustees authority to charge for their services on or after 1 February 2001, an express remuneration clause entitling any professional or business person to charge may still be advisable: see **[221.42]**.

[225.21]

TESTIMONIUM

IN WITNESS whereof I have hereunto set my hand this —— day of —— 20——.

[225.22]

ATTESTATION CLAUSE

SIGNED by the above-named [testator/testatrix] as [his/her] last will in the presence of us both present at the same time who at [his/her] request and in [his/her] presence and in the presence of each other have signed our names below as witnesses: [*Signatures, addresses and descriptions of two witnesses*]	}	[*Signature of testator/testatrix*]

[225.23]

Form C3.2: Reciprocal wills with nil-rate band legacy on trust for the children, residue on trust for spouse for life and then on trust for the children, son taking a life interest and daughter a protected life interest

Note. This, like Form C3.1, is of wills for a couple who have between them sufficient assets for the first to die to be able to give at least a nil-rate band's worth to the children, but wish to postpone paying any IHT to the second death. The form assumes a husband and wife with two adult children, a son and a daughter. On the death of the first spouse to die his or her will provides for:

(i) a nil-rate band legacy for the children in equal shares, the son having a life interest in his share and the daughter a protected life interest in hers (but with powers to pay or apply capital of their shares to them) with remainders to their respective children;

(ii) the settlement of residue on the surviving spouse for life with a power to pay or apply capital in the surviving spouse's favour. The remainder interests for the children are the same as under the nil-rate band legacy.

This Form C3.2 may be adapted for use for civil partners, the words 'my wife/husband' being replaced with 'my civil partner' throughout. Care should be taken to identify correctly in each will the children who are to benefit.

[225.24]

The life interests for the surviving spouse, and for the children under the nil-rate band legacy (including the protected life interest for the daughter) will be IPDIs within IHTA 1984, s 49A (see paras **[200.98]** and **[216.1]**). The IHT spouse exemption will apply to the fund held for the surviving spouse. On the death of the surviving spouse the remainder trusts of residue under the will of the first to die, and the trusts of residue under the will of the second to die, become the same as the trusts of the nil-rate band legacy for the children under the will of the first to die, ie life interest or protective trusts for the children with powers to pay or apply capital, and remainders to their children.

[225.25]

However, and this is a disadvantage of this form, the funds in existence after the death of the survivor will have different IHT treatment. The nil-rate band trust under the will of the first to die and the residuary estate of the second to die will be beneficiary-taxed IPDI trusts, and the funds subject to these could be amalgamated. By contrast, the residuary estate of the first to die, in which the surviving spouse had a life interest, will be within the IHT charging regime for relevant property (except to the extent that the trusts qualify as disabled persons' trusts) even during the children's life interests since they will not be IPDIs: see paras **[200.92]**, **[200.98]**, **[200.99]** above. An alternative strategy is for all three trusts for the children to be relevant property trusts, as in Form C3.5. Even here, it will be necessary to keep funds separate for IHT relevant property charging purposes: see para **[225.75]**.

[225.26]

The main point of using this form in preference to, say, Form C3.1, is mainly non-fiscal; the fact that the surviving spouse is given only a life interest in the residuary estate of the first to die makes it more likely that that estate will ultimately go to the children, the settlement of the children's interests is a restraint on them squandering capital, and the protective life interest gives protection against creditors.

[225.27]

The matrimonial home will usually be a major item of property owned by the couple; the purpose of putting the residuary estate of the first to die in trust for the eventual benefit of the children may be frustrated if his or her interest in the house passes to the other absolutely under a joint tenancy. *It is essential when preparing wills of this type to examine the title to the matrimonial home carefully to see how it is held*; if it is owned as joint tenants beneficially the parties must be asked whether they wish the interest in the home of the first of them to die to be settled on trust under his or her will. If so, they must be advised to effect a severance, and, if not, it should be recorded that they intend the joint tenancy to continue. If similar wills are entered into by both spouses, each with the agreement of the other, then this fact may operate as a severance of the joint tenancy (see *Re Wilford's Estate* (1879) 11 Ch D 267 and *Re Hey's Estate* [1914] P 192), but if there is no clear expression of the intentions of the parties in this respect, there will be uncertainty and the possibility of litigation.

[225.28]

REVOCATION[1]

I [*name*] of [*address*] hereby revoke all former testamentary dispositions made by me and declare this to be my last will.

1 If the wills are not mutual wills in the technical sense, this clause could be extended as in the revocation clause in Form C2.1 at para **[224.28]**. See n 1 to that clause at para **[224.28]**, and the Preliminary Note to C2 on reciprocal and mutual wills at para **[224.12]**.

[225.29]

APPOINTMENT OF EXECUTORS AND TRUSTEES

1. [*As in cl 1 of* Form C3.1 *at para* **[225.11]**.]

[225.30]

PECUNIARY LEGACIES

2. [*As in cl 2 of* Form C3.1 *at para* **[225.12]**.]

[225.31]

GIFT OF PERSONAL CHATTELS TO SPOUSE[1]

3. I give my personal chattels as defined by section 55(1)(x) of the Administration of Estates Act 1925[2] to my wife if she shall survive me and if

she shall not survive me I give the same free of tax to such of my son [*name*] and my daughter [*name*] as shall survive me if both in equal shares.

1 Since residue is settled on the surviving spouse, and then on the children, a specific gift of chattels is provided. It is not a good idea to settle chattels, because the trouble and expense of administering them as part of a trust fund is usually out of all proportion to their value, though it may sometimes be appropriate in the case of valuable ones. For the reason for the inclusion of the words 'free of tax' is in case any of the chattels are outside the UK at the testator's death, and thus 'subject to tax' in the absence of a direction to the contrary. See paras **[214.59]** and **[214.60]**.

2 See Part G, para **[245.67]** for the wording of this definition, and for further discussion of the meaning of 'personal chattels' see Vol 1, para **[64.44]**.

[225.32]

GIFT OF NIL-RATE BAND LEGACY ON TRUST FOR CHILDREN[1]

4. (1) If my [wife/husband] shall survive me[2] then I give to my trustees a pecuniary legacy of the maximum sum (if any) [not exceeding £——][3] which can in the circumstances subsisting at my death be given by this clause without any liability being incurred for the payment of inheritance tax on or by reason of my death and in particular (without prejudice to the generality of the foregoing) for the purpose of determining the amount of such maximum sum the circumstances to be taken into account shall include all chargeable transfers made by me during my life (or events treated as such for inheritance tax purposes) so far as relevant for the computation of inheritance tax on my death the dispositions taking effect under this will (apart from this clause) or under any codicil hereto and any property treated as if it were part of my estate for inheritance tax purposes.

(2) My trustees shall hold the said legacy upon trust to invest the same in any investments hereby authorised with power to vary the same and shall hold the same and the assets from time to time representing the same (hereinafter called 'the trust legacy') upon trust to divide the same into two equal shares hereinafter respectively called 'my son's share' and 'my daughter's share'.

(3) My trustees shall hold my son's share upon the following trusts:

(a) my trustees shall pay the income of my son's share to my son [*name*] ('my son') during his life;[4]

(b) provided that my trustees shall have power in their absolute discretion from time to time during my son's life to pay transfer or apply the whole or any part or parts of my son's share to him or for his benefit in such manner as they shall in their absolute discretion think fit;

(c) subject as aforesaid my son shall have power at any time by deed or deeds revocable or irrevocable or by will or codicil to appoint to any wife who may survive him as his widow (including power to appoint to a named wife contingently on her surviving him as his widow) an interest in the income of the whole or any part or parts of my son's share for the residue of her life or for any lesser period;[5]

[(d) subject as aforesaid my trustees shall hold my son's share upon such trusts for the benefit of all or such one or more exclusive of the others or other of my son's children and remoter issue if more than one in such shares and with such trusts and powers for their respective benefit (including trusts and powers conferring a discretion as to the disposition of capital or income by whomsoever exercisable) and such provisions (including provisions for the accumulation of income during any period permitted by law and administrative provisions of whatever nature) as my son may by any deed revocable or irrevocable or by will or codicil appoint;]

[(d)/(e)] subject as aforesaid my trustees shall hold my son's share upon trust for such of the children of my son as shall attain the age of [18/21] years if more than one in equal shares;

[(e)/(f)] subject as aforesaid my trustees shall hold my son's share as an accretion to my daughter's share and as one fund therewith for all purposes.

(4) My trustees shall hold my daughter's share upon the following trusts:

(a) my trustees shall hold my daughter's share upon protective trusts[6] for the benefit of my daughter [*name*] ('my daughter') during her life provided that none of my trustees shall be liable for paying to my daughter the income of my daughter's share accruing after the forfeiture of her protected life interest unless such trustee shall have express notice of the act thing or event giving rise to the forfeiture[7]

(b) Provided further that my trustees shall have power in their absolute discretion from time to time during my daughter's life to pay transfer or apply the whole or any part or parts of my daughter's share to her or for her benefit in such manner as they shall in their absolute discretion think fit and whether or not any forfeiture of her foregoing protective life interest shall have occurred;

(c) subject as aforesaid my daughter shall have power at any time by deed or deeds revocable or irrevocable or by will or codicil to appoint to any husband who may survive her as her widower (including power to appoint to a named husband contingently on him surviving her as her widower) an interest in the income of the whole or any part or parts of my daughter's share for the residue of his life or for any lesser period;[8]

[(d) subject as aforesaid my trustees shall hold my daughter's share upon such trusts for the benefit of all or such one or more exclusive of the others or other of my daughter's children and remoter issue if more than one in such shares and with such trusts and powers for their respective benefit (including trusts and powers conferring a discretion as to the disposition of capital or income by whomsoever exercisable) and such provisions (including provisions for the accumulation of income during any period permitted by law and administrative provisions of whatever nature) as my daughter may by any deed revocable or irrevocable or by will or codicil appoint;]

[(d)/(e)] subject as aforesaid my trustees shall hold my daughter's share upon trust for such of the children of my daughter as shall attain the age of [18/21] years if more than one in equal shares;

[(e)/(f)] subject as aforesaid my trustees shall hold my daughter's share as an accretion to my son's share and as one fund therewith for all purposes.

(5) The trusts hereinbefore declared of the capital of my son's share and my daughter's share shall carry the intermediate income (so far as not disposed of under any trust having priority thereto) and section 31 of the Trustee Act 1925 (as hereinafter modified) shall apply thereto.

(6) Section 32 of the Trustee Act 1925 (as hereinafter modified) shall apply in relation to the said trusts.

1 See Form C3.1, cl 3, n 1 at para **[225.13]**.
2 See Form C3.1, cl 3, n 2 at para **[225.13]**.
3 See Form C3.1, cl 3, n 3 at para **[225.13]**.
4 The son's life interest should be an IPDI within IHTA 1984, s 49A (see paras **[200.98]** and **[216.1]** above), so the property subject to it should be outside of the relevant property regime for IHT purposes. But if he appoints an interest in possession to his spouse or civil partner under sub-clause (c) it will only attract the spouse or civil partner exemption from IHT if it is also a disabled person's interest, which will require his spouse or civil partner to have been disabled at the date of the testator's death (see para **[200.99]** above). This would be the only relevant type of interest in possession which would have the result of treating his spouse or civil partner as beneficially entitled to the underlying settled property for IHT purposes under IHTA 1984, s 49(1), (1A)(b) thus enabling the spouse or civil partner exemption to be claimed. During the subsistence of the spouse's or civil partner's interest in possession (unless it is a disabled person's interest) and any continuing trusts for his children whether appointed or taking effect in default, the property would fall within the IHT charging regime for relevant property (see para **[200.92]** above).
5 This power will have the practical advantage of enabling the son to make provision for his widow, but will have no IHT advantage unless the interest appointed is a disabled person's interest which will require the spouse to have been disabled at the testator's death (see n 4 above).
6 The statutory protective trusts are set out in the TA 1925, s 33 (Part G, para **[246.31]**). The daughter's protected life interest should be an IPDI within IHTA 1984, s 49A (see para **[200.98]** above), so the property subject to it should be outside the relevant property regime for IHT purposes. It would remain so even if she forfeited her life interest, see IHTA 1984, s 88 (amended by FA 2006, Sch 20, para 24), see para **[200.104]**. But if she appoints an interest in possession to her spouse or civil partner under sub-clause (c) it will only attract the spouse or civil partner exemption from IHT if it is also a disabled person's interest, which will require her spouse or civil partner to have been disabled at the date of the testator's death (see para **[200.99]** above). This would be the only relevant type of interest in possession which would have the result of treating his spouse or civil partner as beneficially entitled to the underlying for IHT purposes under IHTA 1984, s 49(1), (1A)(b) thus enabling the spouse or civil partner exemption to be claimed. During the subsistence of the spouse's or civil partner's interest in possession (unless it is a disabled person's interest) and any continuing trusts for her children whether appointed or taking effect in default, the property would fall within the IHT charging regime for relevant property (see para **[200.92]** above).
7 The proviso to this subclause will protect an innocent trustee who continues to pay income to the protected life tenant after the forfeiture of her interest unless he has express notice of the event giving rise to the forfeiture.
8 This power will have the practical advantage of enabling the daughter to make provision for her widower, but will have no IHT advantage unless the interest appointed is a disabled person's interest which will require the spouse to have been disabled at the testator's death (see n 6 above).

[225.33]

ADMINISTRATION TRUSTS OF RESIDUE

5. (1) I give all my property not hereby or by any codicil hereto otherwise effectively disposed of [(including any entailed or other property over which I shall have at my death a general power of disposition by will)][1] to my trustees to hold on the trusts set out below with power at their discretion to sell all or any of it as and when they think fit[2] [provided that my trustees

shall not seek to sell the freehold dwellinghouse situate at [*address*]] which is owned by my [wife/husband] and me as beneficial tenants in common in equal shares so long as my [wife/husband] shall continue to occupy the same as [her/his] only or main residence].[3]

(2) My trustees shall pay my funeral and testamentary expenses[4] and debts and any legacies given by this will or any codicil hereto out of such property or its proceeds and shall have a discretion as to how such payments shall be borne as between capital and income.[5]

(3) Subject as above my trustees shall hold such property and the assets from time to time representing the same (hereinafter called 'my residuary estate') on the trusts set out below and shall invest all money comprised in such property or arising from its sale in any of the investments hereby authorised with power to change such investments into any others hereby authorised.

(4) In the administration of my estate and the execution of the trusts of this will or of any codicil to it:

(a) my trustees shall treat all income as accruing on the date on which it becomes payable regardless of the period in respect of which it shall have accrued and shall not make any statutory apportionment of the same;[6] and

(b) none of the equitable rules of apportionment between capital and income shall apply in any circumstances whatever.[7]

1 Subject to any express contrary intention property subject to a general power will be carried by a residuary gift under the WA 1837, s 27 (Part G, para **[244.29]**), but in the case of entailed property the will must refer to the property, or the instrument under which it was acquired, or entailed property generally for the statutory power of disposition to be exercised: LPA 1925, s 176(1) (Part G, para **[244.55]**). Although no new entails can be created on or after 1 January 1997 (see para **[200.53]**), entails created before that date can continue to exist and, if they do, the statutory power of disposition of them by will continues to be available.

2 For the reasons for providing a power of sale rather than a trust for sale see para **[214.1]** ff. This wording could be made even more concise, such as 'My trustees shall have power to sell all or any of such property' or as appears in the AEA 1925, s 33(1), as amended by the TLATA 1996, Sch 2, para 5 (Part G, para **[244.60]**). One reason for using the slightly more elaborate wording in this form is that it follows the wording which was held in *Re Pitcairn* [1896] 2 Ch 199 to prevent the rule in *Howe v Dartmouth* from applying (see Note at paras **[214.35]**–**[214.38]** for exclusion of the rule), although to save possible argument about the effect of this wording the express exclusion of the apportionment rules is also retained in sub-cl (4) below. Another reason is that this wording should also serve to create a mixed fund of residuary realty and personalty (see paras **[210.6]** and **[214.5]** for the significance of this).

3 The proviso assumes that the matrimonial home is vested in the husband and wife as beneficial tenants in common in equal shares and, in conjunction with the TLATA 1996, s 12 (Part G, para **[246.115]**), ensures that the surviving spouse (who has a life interest in residue) has the right to continue to reside in it for so long as he or she wishes since it makes clear that the purposes of the trust include making it available for his or her occupation. See the Preliminary Note to B8 on rights of residence generally at para **[208.1]** ff. The proviso will not be appropriate if the house is owned, and is to continue to be owned, by the husband and wife as beneficial joint tenants. Where wills of this type are being made it is important to determine how the matrimonial home is held, and for the husband and wife to decide whether they wish the interest in it of the first to die to pass to the survivor absolutely under a joint tenancy or to become settled on the survivor under the will of the first to die, and to take appropriate steps. See para **[225.27]**.

4 Testamentary expenses will include IHT on UK free estate, including real property: IHTA 1984, s 211(1) (Part G, para **[246.100]**; see also B14 at paras **[214.55]**–**[214.63]**). Accordingly,

even if specific gifts or pecuniary legacies are intended to be free of IHT, it will not be necessary to make express provision for the incidence of IHT unless (in the case of a specific gift) the gift is of property of a kind which bears its own tax, or (in the case of a pecuniary legacy) the legacy is payable out of property (usually residue) which includes property of a kind which bears its own tax. The main relevant categories of property bearing its own tax are foreign property and property which is settled property immediately before the testator's death: see B14 at paras **[214.55]–[214.63]** (settled property can be disposed of under a will where it is subject to a general testamentary power of appointment or is entailed – see n 1 to this clause).

5 A discretion as to the apportionment between capital and income of the burden of liabilities is a middle way between the strict rule in *Allhusen v Whittell* (1867) LR 4 Eq 295 (see Vol 1, para **[38.26]** and paras **[214.43]** and **[214.44]**) with its complex calculations, and a direction to pay the liabilities out of capital which can have unsatisfactory consequences.

6 See B14 at paras **[214.48]–[214.52]** for statutory apportionment of income over time and its exclusion.

7 See Vol 1, paras **[38.17]–[38.27]** for the rules of equitable apportionment between capital and income, and the Preliminary Note to B14 at para **[214.35]** ff for the reasons and techniques for excluding those rules. It is hoped that these words will exclude the rule in *Howe v Earl of Dartmouth* (1802) 7 Ves 137 and *Re Earl Chesterfield's Trusts* (1883) 24 Ch D 643. The power of sale in sub-cl (1) of this clause may also serve to do so (see n 2 to this clause). For alternative strategies see further the Preliminary Note to B14 at para **[214.35]** ff and Forms B14.4 at para **[214.13]** and B14.27 at para **[214.42]**.

[225.34]

GIFTS MADE FREE OF TAX

6. [*As in cl 5 of* Form C3.1 *at para* **[225.15]**.]

[225.35]

BENEFICIAL TRUSTS OF RESIDUE

7. (1) My trustees shall hold my residuary estate upon trust to pay the income thereof to my [wife/husband] during [her/his] life.[1]

(2) Provided that my trustees shall have power in their absolute discretion from time to time so long as my [wife/husband] is entitled to be paid the income of all or any part of the capital of my residuary estate (or would be so entitled if such capital yielded income) to pay transfer or apply the whole or any part or parts of such capital[2] to [her/him] or for [her/his] benefit in such manner as they shall in their absolute discretion think fit.

(3) Subject as aforesaid my trustees shall divide my residuary estate into two equal shares (hereinafter respectively called 'my son's residuary share' and 'my daughter's residuary share') and shall hold my son's residuary share upon the trusts and with and subject to the powers and provisions hereinbefore declared in respect of my son's share of the trust legacy and shall hold my daughter's residuary share upon the trusts and with and subject to the powers and provisions hereinbefore declared in respect of my daughter's share of the trust legacy.[3]

(4) The powers to pay transfer or apply capital of my son's residuary share to or for the benefit of my son and of my daughter's residuary share to or for the benefit of my daughter hereinbefore (by reference) declared shall be exercisable during the life of my [wife/husband] [with [her/his] written consent][4] and for this purpose my trustees shall have power during the life of my [wife/husband] to appropriate my residuary estate to or between my son's residuary share and my daughter's residuary share wholly or partially and in any manner they think fit.

1 The surviving spouse's life interest will be an IPDI within IHTA 1984, s 49A, so spouse exemption from IHT should be available (see paras **[200.84]**, **[200.98]**, **[216.1]** above).

2 There are two reasons for restricting the power to capital in which the spouse has an interest in possession: first, to ensure that the power is not exercisable if there is a divorce and the primary trust fails and, secondly, to ensure that the power ceases to be exercisable if the spouse assigns or surrenders his or her life interest. It is important that this power should cease to be exercisable in such an event because the termination of an IPDI on or after 22 March 2006 will be deemed to be a gift of the underlying settled property for the purposes of FA 1986, s 102, so that unless the beneficiary of the IPDI is excluded altogether from benefit after the termination, the gift with reservation rules could apply, see FA 1986, s 102ZA, (see para **[200.76]** above). On the possibility of divorce see the Preliminary Note to C2 at para **[224.16]**–**[224.23]**.

3 If the testator is not survived by his spouse, and the remainder trusts for the children take effect immediately on his death, then the IHT consequences will be as in the notes to Clauses 4(3) and 4(4) above. But if the spouse survives, and they take effect in remainder to the spouse's life interest, the property subject to the remainder trusts will be within the IHT charging regime for relevant property even during the childrens' life interests since they will not be IPDIs (and unless either child was disabled at the testator's death, they will not be disabled persons' interests) (see para **[225.25]** above).

4 Including these words will give the surviving spouse protection against losing the benefit of any of the fund against his or her will. The disadvantage of including them is that the surviving spouse will be the settlor of the income for income tax purposes if the power is exercised. The latter is probably not a serious disadvantage, as this only has adverse consequences where a 'settlor' retains a possibility of benefit or where he or she settles property on his or her minor children. This form is for use where the children are adult.

[225.36]

MAINTENANCE, ACCUMULATION AND ADVANCEMENT

8. [*As in cl 7 of* Form C3.1 *at para* **[225.17]**.]

[225.37]

ADMINISTRATIVE POWERS

9. [*As in cl 8(1), (2) and (3) of* Form C3.1 *at para* **[225.18]**.]

[225.38]

TRUSTEE LIABILITY

10. [*As in cl 9(1) of* Form C3.1 *at para* **[225.19]**.]

[225.39]

EXERCISE OF POWERS[1]

11. Any power or discretion hereby or by law conferred on my trustees shall be exercisable in favour of any person who is an object of such power or discretion notwithstanding that he or she is one of my trustees and shall be exercisable notwithstanding that any of my trustees has any other direct or indirect personal interest in the mode or result of such exercise provided that there are not fewer than two trustees and that at least one of them has no personal interest in the mode or result of exercising the same.

1 This clause permits a member of the family to be a trustee without disqualifying him or her from benefit under any exercise of statutory or express powers of payment or application of capital, appointment, etc. See the Preliminary Note to B18 at paras **[218.4]** and **[218.5]**.

[225.40]

APPOINTMENT OF NEW TRUSTEES

[12. The power of appointing new trustees shall be vested in my [wife/husband] during [her/his] life.][1]

1 This provision will not be appropriate if the testators decide to appoint trustees who are independent of the beneficiaries. However, if it is excluded, the TLATA 1996, s 19 (Part G, para **[246.122]**) provides that where no person is nominated for the purpose of appointing new trustees and the beneficiaries under the trust are of full age and capacity and between them absolutely entitled to the settled property, the beneficiaries may give a written direction to a trustee to retire from the trust or give a written direction to the trustees to appoint as a trustee or trustees the person or persons specified in the direction. For a provision excluding the beneficiaries' statutory right to direct retirement and appointment of trustees, see Form B21.34 at para **[221.39]**.

[225.41]

PROFESSIONAL TRUSTEE CHARGING CLAUSE

13. [*As in cl 10 of* Form C3.1 *at para* **[225.20]**.]

[*Testimonium and attestation clause as in* Form C3.1 *at paras* **[225.21]** *and* **[225.22]**.]

[225.42]

Form C3.3: Will dividing residue between spouse and issue

Note. This is a form for one spouse only, and makes provision for the other spouse if surviving by giving him or her the personal chattels and half the residuary estate, the balance being divided into two shares, one being settled on 'generation-skipping' (see Part A, paras **[200.42]** and **[200.125]**) trusts for the son's children and the other being settled on trusts for the benefit of the daughter and her children. It is assumed that the matrimonial home is held by the spouses on a joint tenancy, or that the other spouse owns the matrimonial home or some other residential property, or that for some other reason he or she is not in need of the testator's interest in the matrimonial home.

This Form C3.3 may be adapted for use for civil partners, the words 'my wife/husband' being replaced with 'my civil partner' throughout. Care should be taken to identify correctly in each will the children who are to benefit.

[225.43]

The IHT position in relation to this form is that if the testator is survived by the other spouse there will be some IHT payable if the value of a half share of residue turns out to be more than the IHT nil-rate band. If it turns out to be less, the unused nil-rate band of the first to die can be carried forward under the nil-rate band carry-forward rules announced in the Pre-Budget Report on 9 October 2007. This is subject to the point that if either of the spouses potentially has enhan ced carried-forward nil-rate band from the death of a previous spouse or civil partner, some nil-rate band may be wasted if the half share going to the children does not use up all the testator's nil-rate band. If this is the case a formula nil-rate band gift such as that in Forms C3.4 or C3.5 would be a better choice.

[225.44]

For other forms creating trusts for grandchildren, see Forms C8.3 and C8.4 at paras **[230.30]** and **[230.45]** ff.

[225.45]

REVOCATION

I [*name*] of [*address*] hereby revoke all former testamentary dispositions made by me and declare this to be my last will.[1]

1 If the wills are not mutual wills in the technical sense, this clause could be extended as in the revocation clause in Form C2.1 at para **[224.21]**. See n 1 to that clause at para **[224.21]** and the Preliminary Note to C2 on reciprocal and mutual wills at para **[224.8]**.

[225.46]

APPOINTMENT OF EXECUTORS AND TRUSTEES

1. I appoint my [wife/husband] [*name*] ('my [wife/husband]'), my son [*name*] ('my son') and my daughter [*name*] ('my daughter')[1] (hereinafter together called 'my trustees' which expression shall include my personal representatives for the time being and the trustees for the time being hereof) to be the executors and trustees of this will.

1 If there are two executors as well as the wife/husband, there will still be two effective appointments if there is a divorce and the appointment of the wife/husband is nullified by the WA 1837, s 18A (added by the AJA 1982, s 18 (Part G, para **[244.17]**). For similar provisions on the dissolution of civil partnerships, see WA 1837, s 18C (Part G, para **[244.20]**). See also the Note on the possibility of divorce (or dissolution of civil partnership) to C2 at paras **[224.12]**–**[224.19]**. As the spouse and the daughter get absolute interests, and the only long-term trusts will probably be for the son's children, it may be appropriate for the spouse and children to be executors.

[225.47]

PECUNIARY LEGACIES

2. [*As in cl 2 of* Form C3.1 *at para* **[225.12]**.]

[225.48]

GIFT OF PERSONAL CHATTELS TO SPOUSE[1]

3. [*As in cl 3 of* Form C3.2 *at para* **[225.31]**.]

1 As the spouse only takes half of the residuary estate, and part of it is settled for the son's children, a specific gift of chattels is appropriate.

[225.49]

ADMINISTRATION TRUSTS OF RESIDUE

4. [*As in cl 4 of* Form C3.1 *at para* **[225.14]**.]

[225.50]

GIFTS MADE FREE OF TAX

5. [*As in cl 5 of* Form C3.1 *at para* **[225.15]**.]

[225.51]

Beneficial trusts of residue

6. (1) My trustees shall hold one equal half share of my residuary estate upon trust for my [wife/husband] absolutely.[1]

(2) Subject as aforesaid my trustees shall hold my residuary estate[2] upon trust to divide the same into two equal shares (hereinafter respectively called 'my son's children's share' and 'my daughter's share').

(3) My trustees shall hold my son's children's share upon trust for such of the children of my son [(whenever born)][3] as shall be living on the vesting

day (as hereinafter defined)[4] or shall earlier attain the age of [18/21/25] years[5] and if more than one in equal shares provided that:

(a) if any child of my son shall predecease me or having survived me shall die before attaining a vested interest under the foregoing trust leaving a child or children surviving me or born after my death who shall be living on the vesting day or shall earlier attain the age of [18/21/25] years such last-mentioned child or children shall take if more than one equally between them the share of my son's children's share which such deceased child of my son would have taken had he or she lived to attain a vested interest therein;

(b) if there shall be no child or grandchild of my son who shall live to attain a vested interest under the foregoing trusts my trustees shall hold my son's children's share upon trust for my son absolutely.[6]

(4) My trustees shall hold my daughter's share upon trust for my daughter absolutely provided that if my daughter shall predecease me my trustees shall hold my daughter's share upon trust for such of her children as shall survive me and attain the age of [18/21/25] years and if more than one in equal shares.[7]

(5) The foregoing trusts shall carry the intermediate income of my residuary estate and section 31 of the Trustee Act 1925 (as hereinafter modified) shall apply thereto.

(6) Section 32 of the Trustee Act 1925 (as hereinafter modified) shall apply in relation to my residuary estate.

(7) If the trusts of either of my son's children's share or my daughter's share shall fail or determine the same shall accrue to and be held upon the trusts affecting the other such share or such thereof as are still subsisting and capable of taking effect at the date of such accruer.

(8) In this clause the expression 'the vesting day' means the day on which shall expire the period of 21 years immediately following the death of the last survivor of all my issue (whether children or more remote) living at my death.

(9) I declare that if the foregoing trust for my [wife/husband] shall take effect then the half share of my residuary estate to be held in trust for [her/him] shall be ascertained by equal division of my residuary estate inclusive of any inheritance tax payable by reason of my death and attributable to my son's children's share and my daughter's children's share (which shall be borne exclusively by the latter two shares).[8]

1 For the reasons for not including survivorship conditions as between husband and wife or civil partners see **[224.6]–[224.9]**.

2 The gift of the residuary estate contained in this subclause will carry the wife's share if she fails to survive or the gift to her fails as a result of a divorce. See the Note on the possibility of divorce (or dissolution of civil partnership) to C2.1 at paras **[224.16]–[224.23]**.

3 If included, the words in brackets will exclude the rule in *Andrews v Partington* and the class of eligible children will not be closed when the first child attains the specified age: *Re Edmondson's Will Trusts* [1972] 1 All ER 444, [1972] 1 WLR 183, CA. However, the trustees will be able to advance the entire presumptive share of any child in exercise of the power of advancement under the TA 1925, s 32 as extended to the whole of a presumptive share under cl 7 at para **[225.52]**.

4 Since after-born children may be eligible, not all the children will necessarily be lives in being for perpetuity purposes and an ultimate vesting provision is required: see sub-cl (9) for the definition of 'the vesting day'.

5 Since an ultimate vesting provision is incorporated, any age may be specified.

6 If the trusts for the children (or grandchildren) of the testator's son come into possession while they are under the specified vesting age, the trusts will be subject to the IHT relevant property regime (see paras **[200.92]**, **[224.24]** above). This is subject to the point that if interests in possession commence before the vesting of capital, and any child of the testator's son attains the age at which interests in possession commence (without also attaining the age of vesting of capital) before the testator dies or within two years after his death, the share held for such child will be subject to an IPDI and beneficiary-taxed: see paras **[218.74]**, **[224.25]**. The same could apply to the share of a grandchild of the testator's son who takes an interest under the substitution clause by reason of his or her parent predeceasing the testator, but not to a grandchild of the testator's son who takes by substitution as a consequence of the death after the death of the testator of his or her parent before attaining the vesting age. To avoid so far as possible an accidental IPDI, extend accumulation and maintenance trusts to the maximum: see para **[225.52]**, n 1.

7 If the trusts for the daughter's children come into possession while they are under the specified vesting age, the trusts will be subject to the IHT relevant property regime (see paras **[200.92]**, **[224.24]**), subject to the same IPDI possibility as described in n 6 above.

8 See the Preliminary Note to B14 at para **[214.72]** for the reasons for making provision of this type in relation to residuary estates which are partially exempt from IHT.

[225.52]

MAINTENANCE, ACCUMULATION AND ADVANCEMENT

7. (1) Section 31 of the Trustee Act 1925 (relating to accumulation and maintenance) shall apply in relation to the trusts hereby or by any codicil hereto declared as if:

(a) in paragraph (i) of subsection (1) of the said section the words 'as the trustees think fit' were substituted for the words 'as may in all the circumstances be reasonable'; and

(b) the proviso to the said subsection (1) were omitted

[Provided that in relation to any presumptive share of my residuary estate of any person living at my death the said section 31 (amended as aforesaid) shall have effect as if the age of majority were the lesser of the age which he or she will attain (if he or she so long lives) on his or her last birthday occurring not later than the expiration of 21 years from my death and the age of [21/25] years (and so that the expressions 'infancy', 'minority' and 'infant' and all references to the age of eighteen years in the said Section 31 shall be construed accordingly).][1]

(2) Section 32 of the Trustee Act 1925 (relating to advancement) shall apply in relation to the said trusts as if the words 'one half of' were omitted from proviso (a) to subsection (1) thereof

(3) Whenever my trustees shall have an obligation or discretion under the provisions of this will or any codicil hereto or under the general law to apply income or capital for the benefit of a minor beneficiary they may either pay the same without liability to account to his or her parent guardian or any other adult person with whom such beneficiary may be residing or to such beneficiary himself or herself if of the age of 16 years or more and so that the receipt of such parent guardian or other person or of such minor beneficiary shall be a full and sufficient discharge to my trustees for the income or capital so applied.[2]

1 Where an age of vesting is included in the trusts in clause 6(3) and (5) and it is 21 or 25, this proviso should be included to enable income to be accumulated for as long as the law currently allows (ie 21 years from the testator's death). This will ensure so far as possible

that if the testator dies when a beneficiary is under the vesting age, the fund held for that beneficiary will be subject to the IHT relevant property regime rather than the IPDI regime (see para **[225.51]** n 6). Relevant property treatment will often be preferable to IPDI treatment (see paras **[200.131]**, **[200.132]**, **[224.24]**), and, where IPDI treatment seems to be preferable in the circumstances prevailing after the testator's death it will be possible to convert the trust retrospectively to an IPDI trust by exercise of the power of advancement within two years of the testator's death in reliance on IHTA 1984, s 144 (see para **[225.119]** ff). Conversion from an IPDI trust to a relevant property one would involve an IHT lifetime chargeable transfer by the beneficiary unless it can be achieved by a deed of variation within IHTA 1984, s 142. However, if it is desired to have IPDI treatment for these trusts, Trustee Act 1925, s 31 should be excluded, using a clause such as the second alternative clause 8(1) in Form C2.1, para **[224.36]**.

2 A parent (with parental responsibility) and a guardian of a minor are empowered by the ChA 1989, s 3(3) (Part G, para **[244.114]**) to give a good receipt for the minor's property: see Vol 1, para **[9.41]**. The power in this subclause is wider in that it authorises the payment of income or capital to a parent who does not have parental responsibility, any adult with whom the minor is residing, and the minor himself or herself if 16 or over.

[225.53]

ADMINISTRATIVE POWERS

8. [*As in cl 8 of* Form C3.1 *at para* **[225.18]**.]

[225.54]

TRUSTEE LIABILITY

9. [*As in cl 9 of* Form C3.1 *at para* **[225.19]**.]

[225.55]

EXERCISE OF POWERS

10. [*As in cl 11 of* Form C3.2 *at para* **[225.39]**.]

[225.56]

PROFESSIONAL TRUSTEE CHARGING CLAUSE

11. [*As in cl 10 of* Form C3.1 *at para* **[225.20]**.]

[*Testimonium and attestation clause as in Form* C3.1 *at paras* **[225.21]** *and* **[225.22]**.]

[225.57]

Form C3.4: Reciprocal wills containing nil-rate band legacy on discretionary trusts with gift of residue to spouse

Note. For a discussion of nil-rate band discretionary trusts, see the Note in B18 at paras **[218.16]**–**[218.22]**. This form is for use where it is thought that a nil-rate band discretionary trust taking effect on the death of the first to die might be advantageous, despite the availability of nil-rate band carry-forward (see paras **[200.75]**, **[200.130]**). Examples are where there is an asset which could be appropriated to the trust fund which might grow in value faster than the rate of increase in the nil-rate band, or where one of the spouses has accrued nil-rate band carry-forward from a previous marriage or civil partnership. If there is a possibility but not a certainty that such a trust will be advantageous, the best course will often be to include on the footing that the fund subject to it can be converted back to an IPDI or absolute gift to the surviving spouse within two years of the testator's death in reliance on IHTA 1984, s 144. This form can be used where the main asset of the testator's estate is likely to be the matrimonial home, or a share in it, which will be lived in by the surviving spouse. If the home (or share) is appropriated in satisfaction of the nil-rate band legacy, the spouse's continued occupation could confer an interest in possession (see para **[200.95]**). Now an interest in possession arising on or after 21 March 2006 will not necessarily be the type of interest in possession which would cause the underlying property to be treated as part of the spouse's estate for IHT purposes, but in the context of discretionary trusts established by will, if an interest in possession arises within two years of the testator's death, this may be backdated to the testator's death under IHTA 1984, s 144 (see para **[200.133]**), so that it would be an IPDI, thus defeating the object of keeping property out of the survivor's estate for IHT purposes. Accordingly this form contains provisions for establishing a debt or charge scheme, enabling the trustees to satisfy the nil-rate band legacy by a debt owed by the spouse or a charge on the matrimonial home or share (see Preliminary Note to B18 at paras **[218.19]–[218.22]**), and also power to appropriate the house or a share of it to the nil-rate band legacy with a view to the possibility of doing this after two years have elapsed from the testator's death. In this form, the gift of residue to the spouse is an absolute gift, but if it is possible that the surviving spouse might want to change homes (eg to move to a smaller property or to be nearer to children) particularly within two years of the testator's death, it may be advisable for the first to die's will to give the surviving spouse a life interest in residue rather than an absolute interest (see Preliminary Note to B18 at para **[218.21]**). Form C3.5 (at para **[225.68]** ff) is an example of such a will, with the further refinement that the spouse's life interest is a protective life interest.

This Form C3.4 may be adapted for use for civil partners, the words 'my wife/husband' being replaced with 'my civil partner' throughout. Care should be taken to identify correctly in each will the children who are to benefit.

[225.58]

REVOCATION CLAUSE

I [*name*] of [*address*] hereby revoke all former testamentary dispositions made by me and declare this to be my last will.[1]

1 There is no presumption that wills in similar form are mutual wills in the technical sense, but the matter can be put beyond doubt by incorporating an express provision to that effect: see Form B1.7 at para **[201.11]** and the revocation clause to Form C2.1 at para **[224.28]** and the note thereto.

[225.59]

APPOINTMENT OF EXECUTORS AND TRUSTEES

1. I appoint my [wife/husband] [*name*] ('my [wife/husband]') [*name*] of [*address*] and [*name*] of [*address*][1] (hereinafter together called 'my trustees' which expression shall include my personal representatives for the time being and the trustees for the time being of the trusts of this will save for those of the trust legacy (hereafter defined)) to be the executors of this will and trustees of the trusts of this will save for those of the said trust legacy.[2]

1 If there are two executors as well as the wife/husband, there will still be two effective appointments if there is a divorce and the appointment of the wife/husband is nullified by the WA 1837, s 18A (Part G, para **[244.18]**). If this will is being adapted for civil partners, the same will apply mutatis mutandis, see Wills Act 1837, s 18C (Part G, para **[244.20]**). See also the Preliminary Note to C2 at paras **[224.12]–[224.19]**.

2 If a debt or charge scheme may be entered into, a separate set of trustees of the discretionary trusts of the nil-rate band legacy contained in cl 2 needs to be appointed (see Preliminary Note to B18 at para **[218.22]** and cl 2(2)(a) and (b) at para **[225.60]**).

[225.60]

GIFT OF NIL-RATE BAND LEGACY ON DISCRETIONARY TRUSTS[1]

2. (1) If my [wife/husband] shall survive me[2] then I give to my legacy trustees (hereafter defined) a pecuniary legacy of the maximum sum (if any)[3]

which can in the circumstances subsisting at my death be given by this clause without any liability being incurred for the payment of inheritance tax on or by reason of my death and in particular (without prejudice to the generality of the foregoing) for the purpose of determining the amount of such maximum sum the circumstances to be taken into account shall include all chargeable transfers made by me during my life (or events treated as such for inheritance tax purposes) so far as relevant for the computation of inheritance tax on my death the dispositions taking effect under this will (apart from this clause) or under any codicil hereto and any property treated as if it were part of my estate for inheritance tax purposes.

(2) In this clause the following expressions have the following meanings, namely:

(a) 'the trust legacy' means the legacy by this clause bequeathed to my legacy trustees and the assets for the time being representing the same;

(b) 'my legacy trustees' means and includes [*name*] of [*address*] and [*name*] of [*address*] or other the trustee or trustees for the time being of the trust legacy[4];

(c) 'the beneficiaries' means and includes my [wife/husband] and my children and remoter issue;[5]

(d) 'the trust period' means the period commencing on my death and expiring on the twenty first anniversary of the death of my [wife/husband];[6]

(e) 'the accumulation period' means the period commencing with my death and expiring on the twenty-first anniversary thereof.

(3) My legacy trustees shall hold the trust legacy and the income thereof upon trust for all or such one or more of the beneficiaries at such ages or times in such shares and upon such trusts for the benefit of the beneficiaries as my legacy trustees (being at least two in number [or a trust corporation][7]) may by deed or deeds revocable or irrevocable executed at any time or times during the trust period appoint and in making any such appointment my legacy trustees shall have powers as full as those which they would possess if they were an absolute beneficial owner of the trust legacy and in particular (but without prejudice to the generality of the foregoing words) my legacy trustees may in any exercise of the foregoing power as they in their absolute discretion think fit:

(a) delegate give or impose to or upon themselves or any other person or persons and in relation to any trust or disposition any discretionary powers or discretionary trusts conditions limitations restrictions or provisions including powers of further delegation or powers to create further discretionary trusts or powers;[8]

(b) create trusts or powers for the accumulation of income during the accumulation period;

(c) appoint or create administrative powers or provisions of whatever nature;

Provided that:

(i) no such appointment shall invalidate any payment transfer or application of capital or income previously made under any of the trusts or powers herein elsewhere contained;

(ii) every interest limited under any exercise of such power shall vest in interest (if at all) not later than the expiration of the trust period;
(iii) any such appointment may be made in respect of income alone without any appointment of capital; and
(iv) any such revocable appointment shall (so far as then unrevoked) cease to be revocable on the expiration of the trust period.

(4) In default of and subject to any exercise of the foregoing power my legacy trustees (being at least two in number [or a trust corporation][9]) may at their discretion at any time or times during the trust period pay transfer or apply the whole or any part or parts of the trust legacy to or for the benefit of all or any one or more of the beneficiaries for the time being living in such manner as my legacy trustees think fit.[10]

(5) Subject to any or every exercise of the foregoing powers my legacy trustees shall during the trust period hold the trust legacy upon trust to pay or apply the income thereof to or for the maintenance education or benefit of all or any one or more of the beneficiaries for the time being living in such shares if more than one and generally in such manner as they think fit provided that my legacy trustees may during the accumulation period accumulate the whole or any part of the income of the trust legacy by investing the same and the resulting income thereof in any of the investments hereby authorised and any accumulations of income so made shall form part of the capital of the trust legacy for all purposes.

(6) Subject to the foregoing trust and any or every exercise of the foregoing powers my legacy trustees shall hold the trust legacy and the income thereof at the expiration of the trust period in trust absolutely for such of my children and remoter issue as shall then be living in equal shares per stirpes.

(7) Any capital or income of the trust legacy not otherwise disposed of by this clause shall be held in trust for such of my children as shall survive me if more than one in equal shares

(8) Instead of the trust legacy being satisfied by the payment of cash or by the appropriation of property[11]:

(a) my trustees may charge (with or without there being any personal liability of any person or persons) any property which is (or but for this clause would be) comprised in my residuary estate with payment of a sum of money equal to or less than the amount of the trust legacy to my legacy trustees and my legacy trustees shall accept such charge for such sum as the whole or a part (as the case may be) of the trust legacy; and
(b) my trustees may require my legacy trustees to accept in satisfaction of all or part of the trust legacy a binding promise of payment (secured or unsecured) made personally by my wife or by my trustees as trustees of my residuary estate which debt shall be payable on demand and my legacy trustees shall accept such debt as the whole or a part (as the case may be) of the trust legacy.

(9) The following shall apply in relation to the powers in the last preceding subclause:

(a) my trustees may require to be included such terms if any as they think fit in relation to a charge under subclause (8)(a) above or a debt under subclause (8)(b) above including terms as to interest (if any) and terms linking the debt or sum charged to the Retail Prices Index or otherwise providing for its amount to vary with the passage of time according to a formula provided that the debt or sum charged shall be payable to my legacy trustees on demand and the charge shall be enforceable by my legacy trustees at any time;

(b) my legacy trustees may leave the charge or debt outstanding for as long as they think fit and refrain from exercising their rights in relation to it and waive the payment of all or any part of any interest due in respect of it and may accept any substitute debt or charge undertaken or created by any person;

(c) my trustees may assent to the vesting of my residuary estate subject to an outstanding obligation to pay or satisfy the trust legacy and my legacy trustees may appoint new trustees in exercise of the statutory power to do so before the trust legacy has been paid or satisfied;[12]

(d) my legacy trustees and my trustees shall not be liable if my wife is or becomes unable to pay the debt or any security is or becomes inadequate or for any other loss or disadvantage which may occur as a result of their exercising or choosing not to exercise any of the foregoing powers; and

(e) the foregoing powers are in addition to any other powers given by this will or any codicil or by the general law and the foregoing powers may be exercised even though my trustees and my legacy trustees are the same persons or my wife is among either or both sets of trustees provided that such powers shall not be exercisable by a sole trustee who is my wife.

(10) My trustees may constitute the trust legacy wholly or partly by appropriating to it at their discretion any property or proportionate share of any property and for this purpose may take such advice as to the value of the said property or proportionate share as they think fit.[13]

(11) Where the trust legacy is for the time being wholly or partly constituted by a proportionate share of a dwellinghouse or other property my legacy trustees shall have all the powers of an absolute owner in relation to such share and property and in particular may at their discretion join with the other proprietor or proprietors of such property:

(i) to permit a beneficiary under the trusts of the trust legacy to have the use or enjoyment of the property in kind on such terms as my legacy trustees think fit; or

(ii) to effect or enable a sale of the property and the purchase of another property in the same or similar co-ownership with the trust legacy constituted by a proportionate share thereof.

1 See Form C3.1, cl 3, n 1 at para **[225.13]**. This trust will be subject to the IHT relevant property regime, for which see **[218.8]** ff. For nil-rate band discretionary trusts see para **[218.16]** ff.

2 See Form C3.1, cl 3, n 2 at para **[225.13]**.

3 At this point in this formula in Form C3.1, cl 3, at para **[225.13]** a maximum limit is imposed for the reasons given in n 3 at para **[225.13]**. It is not appropriate to do so here. In

Form C3.1 the nil-rate band legacy is given outright to the children, whereas here the surviving spouse is a beneficiary under the discretionary trust imposed on the nil-rate band legacy. Also, any excess over what turns out to be an acceptable size for the nil-rate band legacy could be appointed absolutely to the surviving spouse within two years of the testator's death and be treated as an exempt gift to the surviving spouse as a result of the application of IHTA 1984, s 144 (see paras **[225.83]**–**[225.91]**).

4 The main reasons for having separate trustees of the legacy are where a charge scheme might be entered into, in which case the testator's spouse should not be one of the executors and trustees but could be a trustee of the legacy, or where a debt scheme might be entered into and the testator's spouse might be sole executor: see para **[218.22]** above.

5 The definition of the discretionary class may need to be enlarged or adapted in individual cases.

6 The trust period is longer than may be needed in most cases, but gives considerable flexibility.

7 These words should be included if a trust corporation is to be an executor, or if there is a possibility that a trust corporation might subsequently be appointed a trustee. In either case express provision for the remuneration of a trust corporation so acting (not included in this form) may be added; see eg Forms B3.11 to B3.14 at paras **[203.28]**–**[203.31]** and Form B21.40 at para **[221.52]**. If express provision is not made, then the TrA 2000, s 29 authorises a trust corporation to receive reasonable remuneration (Part G, para **[246.161]**). Nonetheless, if a particular trust corporation is being appointed executor it should be ascertained whether it is content to receive only statutory remuneration or whether it requires express provision for its charges which may be in excess of those which might be authorised by statute. If it is desired to make it possible for a foreign corporation to be appointed as sole trustee, it will also be necessary to amend these words to '(being not fewer than two in number or a corporation)' and to vary the statutory power of appointment of new trustees as in Form B21.36 at para **[221.41]**.

8 These words authorise the creation of discretionary powers, eg powers to advance capital to a life tenant, which might not otherwise be valid: see Vol 1, para **[40.5]**.

9 See n 7 above.

10 A power to apply capital, being exercisable in a less formal manner, may be useful. But it is essential that its exercise should be adequately evidenced.

11 These powers and provisions are included so as to enable a debt or charge scheme to be used as a means of avoiding the surviving spouse having an interest in possession in the trust fund subject to the trusts of this clause, where there are insufficient assets other than the matrimonial home with which to constitute that trust fund. See para **[218.19]** ff.

12 The purpose of this is so that new trustees of the residuary estate can be appointed before a charge is entered into, in a case where the surviving spouse is one of the personal representatives or the personal representatives and the trustees of the discretionary legacy are the same persons, and to make clear that new or additional trustees of the discretionary trust legacy can be appointed before the legacy is constituted as a debt from the surviving spouse where the surviving spouse is the sole trustee: see para **[218.22]** for the reasons for avoiding these states of affairs.

13 If post-21 March 2006 a beneficiary is permitted to occupy a property owned by a discretionary trust, whereas this may give that beneficiary an interest in possession, it will not necessarily be the type of interest in possession which will cause the property to be treated as part of his or her estate for IHT purposes. Only an interest in possession which is an IPDI, a disabled person's interest, or a transitional serial interest (see paras **[200.98]**–**[200.100]** above) will have this result. In the context of a discretionary trust established by will, if a permission to occupy is given within two years of the testator's death, and this gives rise to an interest in possession this may be backdated to the testator's death under IHTA 1984, s 144, so that it would be an IPDI and result in the property being treated as part of the beneficiary's estate for IHT purposes: see para **[225.83]** ff. But if the permission is not granted until after the second anniversary of the testator's death, and the beneficiary to whom it is granted is not a disabled person within the meaning of IHTA 1984, s 89 (4) at the testator's death so that her interest is not a disabled person's interest within IHTA 1984, s 89B (see para **[200.99]** above), it should not result in the property being treated as part of the beneficiary's estate for IHT purposes. Therefore, an express power to appropriate property or a share of property may be given to trustees to exercise in appropriate circumstances, and sub-clauses (10) and (11) contain such a power and associated provisions.

[225.61]

ADMINISTRATION TRUSTS OF RESIDUE

3. (1) [*As in cl 4(1) of* Form C3.1 *at para* **[225.14]**.]
(2) [*As in cl 4(2) of* Form C3.1 *at para* **[225.14]**.]
(3) [*As in cl 4(3) of* Form C3.1 *at para* **[225.14]**.]
(4) In the administration of my estate and the execution of the trusts of this will or of any codicil to it:
(a) my trustees and my legacy trustees shall treat all income as accruing on the date on which it becomes payable regardless of the period in respect of which it shall have accrued and shall not make any statutory apportionment of the same;[1] and
(b) none of the equitable rules of apportionment between capital and income shall apply in any circumstances whatever.[2]

1 See Form C2.1, cl 6, n 5 at para **[224.27]**.
2 See Form C2.1, cl 6, n 6 at para **[224.27]**.

[225.62]

BENEFICIAL TRUSTS OF RESIDUE

4. (1) My trustees shall hold my residuary estate upon trust for my [wife/husband] [*name*] absolutely if [she/he] shall survive me.[1]
(2) If my [wife/husband] shall predecease me my trustees shall hold my residuary estate upon trust for such of my children [by my [wife/husband]][2] as shall survive me if more than one in equal shares, provided that if any of my [said][3] children shall predecease me leaving a child or children surviving me [who shall attain the age of [18/21/25] years][3] such last-mentioned child or children shall take if more than one equally between them the share of my residuary estate which such deceased child of mine would have taken had he or she survived me.
(3) The foregoing trusts shall carry the intermediate income of my residuary estate and section 31 of the Trustee Act 1925 (as hereinafter modified) shall apply thereto.
(4) Section 32 of the Trustee Act 1925 (as hereinafter modified) shall apply in relation to my residuary estate.

1 A survivorship condition is neither necessary nor advisable. See the Preliminary Note on survivorship conditions at para **[225.4]**.
2 These words ensure that the alternative gifts for the children in the wills of both spouses are identical in terms of whom they benefit, in circumstances where one spouse has children who are not children of the other spouse. See, further, the Preliminary Note to C2 on reciprocal wills and the ultimate destination of property at paras **[224.9]–[224.11]**. For forms for use where one spouse has children who are not children of the marriage and wishes to benefit them by his or her will see C5 at para **[227.2]** ff.
3 The grandchildren will be lives in being at the testator's death for perpetuity purposes, so if the gift to them is to be subject to a contingency that they attain a certain age, there is no risk of infringing the rule against perpetuities in specifying an age exceeding 21. If the gift to them is subject to an age contingency, and any of them have not satisfied it at the testator's death, but the substitutional trust takes effect, the property subject to it will be within the IHT charging regime for relevant property or the IPDI regime (see para **[225.51]** n 6 above).
3 To be included if the trust is confined to the children of the marriage.

[225.63]

MAINTENANCE, ACCUMULATION AND ADVANCEMENT

5. (1) Section 31 of the Trustee Act 1925 (relating to accumulation and maintenance) shall apply in relation to the trusts hereby or by any codicil hereto declared as if:

(a) in paragraph (i) of subsection (1) of the said section the words 'as the trustees think fit' were substituted for the words 'as may in all the circumstances be reasonable'; and

(b) the proviso to the said subsection (1) were omitted

[Provided that in relation to any presumptive share of my residuary estate of any grandchild of mine living at my death the said section 31 (amended as aforesaid) shall have effect as if the age of majority were the lesser of the age which he or she will attain (if he or she so long lives) on his or her last birthday occurring not later than the expiration of 21 years from my death and the age of [21/25] years (and so that the expressions 'infancy', 'minority' and 'infant' and all references to the age of eighteen years in the said Section 31 shall be construed accordingly).][1]

(2) Section 32 of the Trustee Act 1925 (relating to advancement) shall apply in relation to the said trusts as if the words 'one half of' were omitted from proviso (a) to subsection (1) thereof .

(3) Whenever my trustees or my legacy trustees shall have an obligation or discretion under the provisions of this will or any codicil hereto, or under the general law, to apply income or capital for the benefit of a minor beneficiary, they may either pay the same without liability to account to his or her parent, guardian or any other adult person with whom such beneficiary may be residing, or to such beneficiary himself or herself if of the age of 16 years or more and so that the receipt of such parent, guardian or other person or of such minor beneficiary shall be a full and sufficient discharge to my trustees or my legacy trustees (as the case may be) for the income or capital so applied.[2]

1 Where an age of vesting is included in the substitutional trust for grandchildren in clause 4(2), and it is 21 or 25, this proviso should be included to enable income to be accumulated for as long as the law currently allows (i e 21 years from the testator's death). See para **[225.52]** n 1.

2 A parent (with parental responsibility) and a guardian of a minor are empowered by the ChA 1989, s 3(3) (Part G, para **[244.114]**) to give a good receipt for the minor's property: see Vol 1, para **[9.41]**. The power in this subclause is wider, in that it authorises the payment of income or capital to a parent who does not have parental responsibility, any adult with whom the minor is residing, and the minor himself or herself if aged 16 or over.

[225.64]

ADMINISTRATIVE POWERS

6. (1) In this clause where the context so admits:

(a) the expression 'land' includes buildings and estates interests or rights of any kind in or over land;

(b) during the administration of my estate the expression 'beneficiary' includes any person who would be a beneficiary if such administration had been completed and the expression 'beneficially interested'

and references to income of any asset being payable or capable of being paid to or for the benefit of a beneficiary shall be construed accordingly; and

(c) the expression 'my trustees' includes 'my legacy trustees'.

(2) [*As in cl 8(2) of* Form C3.1 *at para* **[225.18]**.]

(3) [*As in cl 8(3) of* Form C3.1 *at para* **[225.18]**.]

[225.65]

TRUSTEE LIABILITY

7. Neither my trustees nor my legacy trustees shall be liable for any act or default of any investment manager or nominee employed in good faith to manage or hold assets of my estate nor for any act or default of any beneficiary having the occupation use or enjoyment of property in kind.[1]

1 See Form 3.1, cl 9, n 1 at para **[225.19]**.

[225.66]

EXERCISE OF POWERS

8. Any power or discretion hereby or by law conferred on my trustees or my legacy trustees shall be exercisable in favour of any person who is an object of such power or discretion notwithstanding that he or she is one of my trustees or my legacy trustees, and shall be exercisable notwithstanding that any of my trustees or my legacy trustees has any other direct or indirect personal interest in the mode or result of such exercise.[1]

1 This clause permits a member of the family to be a trustee without disqualifying him or her from benefit under any exercise of statutory or express powers of payment or application of capital, appointment, etc. See the Preliminary Note to B18 at paras **[218.4]** and **[218.5]**.

[225.67]

PROFESSIONAL TRUSTEE CHARGING CLAUSE

9. Any of my trustees or my legacy trustees being a professional or business man may charge and be paid all usual professional and other proper charges for business transacted acts done advice given and time spent by him or his firm in connection with the administration of my estate or in connection with the trusts hereof including acts which a personal representative or trustee not being in any profession or business could have done personally.[1]

[*Testimonium and attestation clause as in* Form C3.1 *at paras* **[225.21]** *and* **[225.22]**.]

1 In spite of the TrA 2000, s 29(2) (Part G, para **[246.161]**) giving certain professional trustees authority to charge for their services on or after 1 February 2001 in the absence of express provision, an express remuneration clause entitling any professional or business person to charge may still be advisable: see Note to B21 at para **[221.42]**.

[225.68]

Form C3.5: Reciprocal wills giving nil-rate band legacy on discretionary trusts and settling residue on protective trusts for spouse for life, with overriding trustees' powers over capital, and discretionary trusts for issue after the surviving spouse's death

Note. For a discussion of nil-rate band discretionary trusts, see the Note in B18 at paras **[218.16]–[218.22]**. This form, like Form C3.4, is for use where it is thought that a nil-rate band discretionary trust taking effect on the death of the first to die might be advantageous, despite the availability of nil-rate band carry-forward (see paras **[200.75]**, **[200.130]** and **[225.57]**). This form is a variant of the preceding form which is designed to give the maximum asset protection against, eg, bankruptcy or carelessness with money of the surviving spouse, and against the estate of the first to die getting used up in care-home fees for the surviving spouse. In addition it provides discretionary trusts for issue after the death of the surviving spouse. It is assumed that there are three grown-up children. If the husband and wife own the matrimonial home or any other property as joint tenants, a severance of the joint tenancy should be effected, since otherwise the first to die's severable share will accrue absolutely to the survivor and be wholly available to the latter's creditors. The form contains provisions (as in the previous Form C3.4) for establishing a charge scheme, enabling the trustees to satisfy the nil-rate band legacy by a charge on the matrimonial home or share (see B18 at paras **[218.19]–[218.22]**), and also power to appropriate a house or a share of it to the nil-rate band legacy with a view to the possibility of doing this after two years have elapsed from the testator's death (see para **[225.57]**). The wife is given a protective life interest rather than an absolute interest in residue, and so this trust will be appropriate (as would be a full life interest), if the charge scheme is used to constitute the nil-rate band trust fund, if it is possible that the surviving spouse might want to change homes (see B18 at para **[218.21]**).

This Form C3.5 may be adapted for use by a civil partner, the words 'my wife/husband' being replaced with 'my civil partner' throughout. Care should be taken to identify the children who are to benefit.

[225.69]

REVOCATION

I [*name*] of [*address*] hereby revoke all former testamentary dispositions and declare this to be my last will.

[225.70]

APPOINTMENT OF EXECUTORS AND TRUSTEES[1]

1. I appoint [*name*] of [*address*] and [*name*] of [*address*] (hereinafter together called 'my trustees' which expression shall include my personal representatives for the time being and the trustees for the time being of the trusts of this will save for those of the trust legacy (hereafter defined)) to be the executors of this will and trustees of the trusts of this will save for those of the trust legacy.[2]

1 It is assumed that the spouse will not be appointed an executor.
2 If a debt or charge scheme may be entered into, a separate set of trustees of the discretionary trusts of the nil-rate band legacy contained in cl 2 needs to be appointed (see B18 at para **[218.22]** and cl 2(2)(a) at para **[225.60]**).

[225.71]

GIFT OF CHATTELS TO SPOUSE[1]

2. [*As in cl 3 of* Form C3.2 *at para* **[225.31]**, *but with the gift taking effect if the spouse does not survive the testator being in favour of three children.*]

1 This clause is included because the spouse takes only a limited interest in residue. If, however, the chattels are valuable, it may not be appropriate and should be limited to household effects or omitted altogether. Reliance would have to be placed on the express power to permit a beneficiary to have the beneficial use and enjoyment of chattels contained in cl 8: see Form C3.1, cl 8(e) at para **[225.18]**.

[225.72]

GIFT OF NIL-RATE BAND LEGACY ON DISCRETIONARY TRUSTS[1]

3. [*As in cl 2 of* Form C3.4 *at para* **[225.60]**. *The beneficiaries as defined in this clause should include the surviving spouse and all the other persons included in the discretionary beneficiaries as defined in clause 7(1)(a) (para* **[225.76]**).]

1 See the notes to cl 2 of Form C3.4 at para **[225.60]**. Although the powers in sub-cl (8) ff of cl 2 of Form C3.4 empower the trustees to require the legacy trustees to accept an unsecured promise of payment from the spouse in satisfaction of the trust legacy, if the legacy trustees need to resort to a debt or charge scheme they should employ a charge scheme rather than a debt scheme. This is because this form provides for the spouse to have a (protective) life interest in residue, rather than an absolute interest, and this means that the trustees would not be in a position to provide full consideration for the spouse's promise to pay the debt if a debt scheme were attempted: see para **[218.20]**.

[225.73]

ADMINISTRATION TRUSTS OF RESIDUE

4. [*As in cl 3 of* Form C3.4 *at para* **[225.61]**.]

[225.74]

GIFTS MADE FREE OF TAX

5. [*As in cl 5 of* Form C3.1 *at para* **[225.15]**.]

[225.75]

BENEFICIAL TRUSTS OF RESIDUE

6. (1) My trustees shall hold my residuary estate upon protective trusts[1] for the benefit of my [wife/husband] during [her/his] life provided that none of my trustees shall be liable for continuing to pay the income of my residuary estate to my [wife/husband] after [she/he] has done or attempted to do or has suffered any act or thing or an event has occurred which has caused [her/his] interest to determine unless such trustee has had actual notice of such act thing or event.[2]

(2) Subject as aforesaid my trustees shall hold my residuary estate upon trust until the vesting day (defined below) to pay the income thereof to or for the maintenance education or benefit of all or any one or more of the discretionary beneficiaries (defined below) for the time being living in such shares if more than one and generally in such manner as they think fit provided that my trustees may during the period of 21 years from my death accumulate the whole or any part of the income of my residuary estate by investing the same and the resulting income thereof in any of the investments hereby authorised and any accumulations of income so made shall form part of the capital of my residuary estate for all purposes.[3]

(3) Subject to the foregoing my trustees shall hold my residuary estate and the income thereof in trust absolutely for such of my children and remoter issue as shall be living on the vesting day (defined below) in equal shares per stirpes so that no child or remoter issue shall take as share whose parent is then living and capable of taking.

(4) Any capital or income of my residuary estate not otherwise disposed of by this clause shall be held in trust for such of my children as shall survive me if more than one in equal shares.

1 The statutory protective trusts are set out in the TA 1925, s 33 (Part G, para **[246.31]**). Provided that no forfeiture has occurred before the testator's death, the spouse will be treated as having an IPDI for IHT purposes even if there is a forfeiture and the discretionary income trust arises: see the IHTA 1984, s 88 (amended by FA 2006, Sch 20 para 24), and Part A, paras **[200.20]**, **[200.104]**. No power to advance capital to the spouse is included in this clause in view of the wide overriding powers of appointment and application contained in cl 7. If the surviving spouse becomes bankrupt before the death of the testator, with the consequence that the interest in possession is forfeit with effect from the testator's death, it is arguable that IHTA 1984, s 88 would not have the effect of treating the surviving spouse as having an IPDI. This would mean that there would be no spouse exemption in relation to the residuary estate. If there is a risk that the surviving spouse might become bankrupt before the testator's death, and it is felt to be more important to obtain the spouse exemption from IHT than to keep all the income out of the clutches of the trustee in bankruptcy, add the following words at the end of the subclause "and provided further that section 33 of the Trustee Act 1925 shall have effect in relation to the foregoing trust as if in subsection (1)(i) thereof there were substituted the words 'after the commencement of the trust period' for the words 'whether before or after the termination of any prior interest'".

2 The proviso is included in order to protect the trustees who may well be ignorant of the events giving rise to a forfeiture.

3 Under these remainder trusts the residuary estate will fall within the IHT charging regime for relevant property after the death of the surviving spouse (see paras **[200.92]**, **[200.131]**, **[218.18]**). However similar the trusts of this fund and those of the nil-rate band legacy are, under the will of the first to die, the two funds are likely to have to remain separately identifiable for IHT charging purposes because this fund will be treated as a separate settlement made by the surviving spouse: see IHTA 1984, s 80.

[225.76]

OVERRIDING POWERS TO APPOINT AND APPLY CAPITAL

7. (1) In this clause and clause 6 above the following expressions have the following meanings:

(a) the expression 'the discretionary beneficiaries' means and includes:
   (i) my [wife/husband];
   (ii) my children and remoter issue whether living at my death or born thereafter;
   (iii) any spouse civil partner widow widower or surviving civil partner of any of my said children or remoter issue (and 'widow' 'widower' and 'surviving civil partner' shall include a widow widower or surviving civil partner who has married or formed a civil partnership);[1]

(b) 'the vesting day' means the day on which shall expire the period of 21 years immediately following the death of my [wife/husband].

(2) Notwithstanding and in derogation of the foregoing trusts my trustees (being not fewer than two in number [or a trust corporation][2]) may [with the

consent in writing of my [wife/husband] during [her/his] life and otherwise at their discretion][3] exercise any of the following powers:

(a) power at any time or times and from time to time before the vesting day by deed or deeds revocable or irrevocable to appoint the whole or any part or parts of my residuary estate and the income thereof upon such trusts and with and subject to such powers and provisions for the benefit of all or such one or more exclusive of the others or other of the discretionary beneficiaries as my trustees may in their absolute discretion think fit and my trustees may in exercise of the foregoing power:

(i) delegate or create powers or discretions over capital or income including powers of further delegation or powers to create further powers or discretions over capital or income;

(ii) create powers or trusts for the accumulation of income during any period permitted by law;

(iii) provide for the total or partial exclusion from benefit of any person or persons or class of persons;

(iv) create administrative powers or provisions of whatever nature;

(v) appoint income alone without any appointment of capital;

(vi) make any appointment having effect subject to and without prejudice to any pre-existing interest or interests in possession or to any other pre-existing interests trusts or powers;[4]

Provided that:

(1) no such appointment shall invalidate any payment transfer or application of capital or income previously made or any entitlement to income which has already accrued under any of the trusts or powers herein elsewhere contained;

(2) every interest limited under any exercise of such power shall vest in interest (if at all) not later than the vesting day; and

(3) any such revocable appointment shall (so far as then unrevoked) cease to be revocable on the vesting day;

(b) subject to any previous exercise of the foregoing power of appointment, power at any time or times and from time to time before the vesting day in their absolute discretion to pay transfer or apply the whole or any part or parts of my residuary estate to or for the benefit of all or any one or more exclusive of the others or other of the discretionary beneficiaries if more than one in such shares and generally in such manner as my trustees shall think fit;

(c) power at any time or times and from time to time before the vesting day by deed or deeds to release or restrict all or any of the powers contained in the present subclause (including this present power) either in whole or in part and in any manner they think fit.

1 The definition of the class will need to be framed so as to fit the particular circumstances of the testator.

2 See Form C3.4, cl 2, n 7 at para **[225.60]**.

3 These words are inserted for the spouse's protection, but have the disadvantage that any appointment or application of capital with his or her consent which cuts short his or her income interest may make him or her settlor of such income for tax purposes. As it is assumed that the children are grown up, being a settlor for income tax purposes will only be a disadvantage if an appointment or application of capital is being made under which the spouse will retain a possibility of benefit. If an appointment is made to terminate the

spouse's IPDI (other than in favour of the spouse absolutely) it is important that the spouse cannot benefit thereafter (whether under the appointed trusts, on a failure of the appointed trusts, on a revocation of the appointed trusts, or at all) since the termination of an IPDI on or after 22 March 2006 will be deemed to be a gift of the underlying settled property for the purposes of FA 1986, s 102, so that unless the spouse is excluded altogether from benefit after the termination, the gift with reservation rules could apply, see FA 1986, s 102ZA, (see para **[200.76]** above). A termination of the spouse's IPDI, other than in favour of absolute interests, a trust for bereaved minors or a disabled person's interest (when potential exemption should be available) will generally be a chargeable transfer.

4 This confirms that the trustees could make an appointment in remainder expectant upon the surviving spouse's life interest, and so in effect vary the remainder capital trusts, without causing the spouse's IPDI to come to an end (see para **[200.98]**).

[225.77]

ADMINISTRATIVE POWERS

8. [*As in cl 6 of* Form C3.4 *at para* **[225.64]**.]

[225.78]

TRUSTEE LIABILITY

9. [(1)] [*As in cl 7 of* Form C3.4 *at para* **[225.65]**.]

[(2) Section 11(1) of the Trusts of Land and Appointment of Trustees Act 1996 (consultation with beneficiaries) shall not apply to the exercise by my trustees or my legacy trustees of their functions in relation to any land subject to the trusts of this my will[1]]

1 See Form C3.1, cl 9, n 2 at para **[225.19]**. Section 11(1) does not apply to personal representatives (see the TLATA 1996, s 18(1): Part G, para **[246.104]**), so would not apply when the trustees are deciding in the administration of the estate how to satisfy the nil-rate band legacy. But if a charge scheme is entered into (charging the matrimonial home which will then form part of the residuary estate in which the spouse has an interest in possession) it will be relevant (unless excluded).

[225.79]

EXERCISE OF POWERS

10. [*As in cl 8 of* Form C3.4 *at para* **[225.66]**.]

[225.80]

APPOINTMENT OF NEW TRUSTEES

11. [*As in cl 12 of* Form C3.2 *at para* **[225.40]**.]

[225.81]

PROFESSIONAL TRUSTEE CHARGING CLAUSE

12. [*As in cl 9 of* Form C3.4 *at para* **[225.67]**.]

[225.82]

[*Testimonium and attestation clause as in* Form C3.1 *at paras* **[225.21]** and **[225.22]**.]

[225.83]

Note on two-year discretionary trusts (IHTA 1984, s 144)

NOTE

Section 144. On and after 22 March 2006, IHTA 1984, s 144 provides as follows:

(1) Subsection (2) below applies where property comprised in a person's estate immediately before his death is settled by his will and, within the period of two years after his death and before any interest in possession has subsisted in the property, there occurs—

(a) an event on which tax would (apart from subsection (2) below) be chargeable under any provision, other than section 64 or 79, of Chapter III of Part III of this Act, or

(b) an event on which tax would be so chargeable but for section 75 or 76 above or paragraph 16(1) of Schedule 4 to this Act.

(1A) Where the testator dies on or after 22nd March 2006, subsection (1) above shall have effect as if the reference to any interest in possession were a reference to any interest in possession that is—

(a) an immediate post-death interest, or

(b) a disabled person's interest.

(2) Where this subsection applies by virtue of an event within paragraph (a) of subsection (1) above, tax shall not be charged under the provision in question on that event; and in every case in which this subsection applies in relation to an event, this Act shall have effect as if the will had provided that on the testator's death the property should be held as it is held after the event.

(3) Subsection (4) below applies where—

(a) a person dies on or after 22nd March 2006,

(b) property comprised in the person's estate immediately before his death is settled by his will, and

(c) within the period of two years after his death, but before an immediate post-death interest or a disabled person's interest has subsisted in the property, there occurs an event that involves causing the property to be held on trusts that would, if they had in fact been established by the testator's will, have resulted in—

(i) an immediate post-death interest subsisting in the property, or

(ii) section 71A or 71D above applying to the property.

(4) Where this subsection applies by virtue of an event—

(a) this Act shall have effect as if the will had provided that on the testator's death the property should be held as it is held after the event, but

(b) tax shall not be charged on that event under any provision of Chapter 3 of Part 3 of this Act.

(5) Subsection (4) above also applies where—

(a) a person dies before 22nd March 2006,

(b) property comprised in the person's estate immediately before his death is settled by his will,

(c) an event occurs—

(i) on or after 22nd March 2006, and

(ii) within the period of two years after the testator's death,

that involves causing the property to be held on trusts within subsection (6) below,

(d) no immediate post-death interest, and no disabled person's interest, subsisted in the property at any time in the period beginning with the testator's death and ending immediately before the event, and

(e) no other interest in possession subsisted in the property at any time in the period beginning with the testator's death and ending immediately before 22nd March 2006.

(6) Trusts are within this subsection if they would, had they in fact been established by the testator's will and had the testator died at the time of the event mentioned in subsection (5)(c) above, have resulted in—

(a) an immediate post-death interest subsisting in the property, or

(b) section 71A or 71D above applying to the property.

Section 144 thus applies (inter alia) where discretionary trusts are created by will, and an appointment or distribution is made out of the property held on those trusts within two years of the testator's death (provided, in certain cases described below, that it is not made within three months after his death). Section 144 operates not only to relieve the appointment or distribution from any IHT charge which might otherwise arise, but also to treat the distribution or appointment as a disposition made by the testator's will. The second of these effects is very much more important than the first, because any IHT charge on property leaving a discretionary trust within two years of its commencement is unlikely to be very great (see the Note in B18 at paras **[218.8]**–**[218.18]**). The main importance of an appointment or distribution falling within s 144(1) is either that it makes an exemption from IHT on the testator's death applicable (e g spouse or civil partner exemption, charitable exemption), or that it changes the IHT status of settled property from being relevant property to being, eg, beneficiary-taxed (see para **[200.92]**) or a trust for a bereaved minor (see para **[200.108]**). See also para **[242.4]** for the operation of section 144.

[225.84]
Where s 144 applies – occasions of IHT charge. By virtue of the IHTA 1984, s 144(1)(a), s 144 applies to an appointment or distribution where there would apart from s 144 be a charge under any of the provisions of the IHTA 1984, Part III, apart from s 64 which imposes the ten-yearly periodic charge (see B18 at para **[218.8]**), and s 79 which imposes an IHT charge in some circumstances on works of art etc comprised in a settlement where exemption from the periodic charge has been obtained and a chargeable event occurs. The charging provisions in Part III of IHTA 1984 to which s 144(1) is relevant are the exit charges on relevant property trusts, in particular exit charges from ordinary discretionary trusts (see B18 at paras **[218.8]**–**[218.10]**), and the various charging provisions which apply to property leaving some of the categories of privileged trust, such as age 18-to-25 trusts within IHTA 1984, s 71D (see para **[200.109]** and B18 at para **[218.8]**). On and after 22 March 2006 the occasions when an appointment out of relevant property will give rise to an IHT exit charge are much reduced. But the appointment of an absolute interest will give rise to an exit charge (unless made within the first three months of death, as discussed in para **[225.85]** below), and so an appointment from discretionary trusts of property to the testator's spouse or civil partner absolutely, more than three months after death but within two years of it, should, by virtue of IHTA 1984, s 144(1), secure the spouse or civil partner exemption for that property.

[225.85]
Where s 144 applies – exempt distributions and the three-months-from-death trap. By virtue of the IHTA 1984, s 144(1)(b), s 144 applies to an appointment or distribution, made within two years of a testator's death under a discretionary trust created by his will, where IHTA 1984, ss 75 or 76, or Sch 4, para 16(1) apply so as to exempt the appointment or distribution from the exit charges imposed by Part III in cases where the property appointed or distributed vests in employee trusts, charities, qualifying political parties, exempt bodies, or maintenance funds for historic buildings etc. Thus, s 144(1)(b) enables the relevant exemption to be obtained from the IHT charge on the testator's estate on death where the appointment or distribution falls into one of these exempt categories, even though the appointment or distribution would not give rise to an IHT charge apart from the effects of s 144. Unfortunately, subsection (1)(b) does not include s 65(4) (distributions etc within three months of the commencement of a settlement) in its list of provisions which exempt an appointment or distribution from charge, and so any appointment or distribution within three months of the testator's death will not fall within s 144. This is something of a trap for the zealous executor: see *Frankland v IRC* [1996] STC 735, and the Special Commissioner's decision *Harding (executors of Loveday) v IRC* [1997] STC (SCD) 321 in

which it was held that the executors who had made an early distribution could not rely on IHTA 1984, s 143 (see paras **[204.9]** and **[204.10]**) as an alternative to s 144.

[225.86]

Where s 144 applies – IPDIs. As mentioned above, the occasions when an appointment from relevant property will give rise to an exit charge are much reduced as a result of the changes made by FA 2006 (see **[200.92]**). So, for example, an appointment of an interest in possession out of relevant property will not give rise to an exit charge unless the interest is a disabled person's interest (see para **[200.99]** above). Therefore, if s 144(1) were the only relieving provision in s 144, it would not be possible post-21 March 2006 to obtain the spouse or civil partner exemption by way of an appointment of an interest in possession to the testator's spouse or civil partner, unless the surviving spouse or civil partner was a disabled person at the testator's death with the consequence that his or her interest would then be a disabled person's interest (see para **[200.99]** above). Accordingly subsections (3)–(6) of s 144 (inserted by FA 2006) provide that where an appointment of trusts is made within two years of the testator's death, and it is such that if those trusts had been included in the testator's will they would have resulted in an IPDI (on the hypothesis, in the case of a testator dying before 22 March 2006, that he died at the date of the appointment), those trusts will be treated by virtue of subsection (4) of s 144 as having had effect from the testator's death. This means that, for example, if property is appointed within two years of the testator's death to the testator's spouse for life, out of a discretionary trust created by the testator's will, the spouse exemption will apply to that property as at the testator's death. It should be noted that s 144(3)–(6), in contrast to s 144(1) and (2) (see para **[225.85]**), can apply to an appointment made within three months of the testator's death. For further discussion of the interaction between the IPDI rules and IHTA 1984, s 144, and the problems of creating or avoiding creating an IPDI in the two years following a testator's death, see para **[200.133]**. See also para **[242.4]**.

[225.87]

Where s 144 applies – s 71A trusts and s 71D trusts. Subsections (3)–(6) of IHTA 1984, s 144 also cover appointments of trusts made within two years of the testator's death, which if they had been included in the testator's will would have resulted in trusts for bereaved minors (see para **[200.108]** above), or age 18-to-25 trusts (see para **[200.109]** above), (on the hypothesis in the case of a testator dying before 22 March 2006 that he died at the date of the appointment). Such trusts will be deemed to have arisen on the testator's death under the terms of his will by virtue of s 144(4). It may be noted that as in the case of the appointment of an IPDI (see **[225.86]**), an appointment of such trusts within three months of death can fall within this provision. See para **[242.4]**.

[225.88]

What property s 144 can apply to. Section 144 of the IHTA 1984 can apply to any property comprised in the testator's estate immediately before his death and settled by his will. It must therefore be property over which the testator had sufficient dominion to be able to settle it on trust by his will, but the reference in s 144 to property comprised in the testator's estate is not limited to his free estate as is the similar reference in s 142 (deeds of variation): see s 142(5) and the Preliminary Note to F3 at para **[242.5]**. Thus s 144 would apparently be capable of applying to settled property in which a testator had an interest in possession falling within IHTA 1984, s 49(1) (generally speaking a pre-22 March 2006 interest in possession, an IPDI, a transitional serial interest or a disabled person's interest), and over which he had a general testamentary power of appointment in exercise of which he settled the property by his will.

[225.89]

What trusts s 144 applies to. For deaths before 22 March 2006, IHTA 1984, s 144 only applies if there is no interest in possession between the testator's death and the time of the appointment or distribution (see s 144(1), (5)(d),(e)). For deaths on and after 22 March 2006, it applies if there is no IPDI or disabled person's interest (see s 144(2), (3)(c)) between the testator's death and the time of the appointment or distribution. It would not apply, for example, to will trusts arising on or after 22 March 2006 under which there was a life interest or absolute interest defeasible by exercise of a power arising immediately on death. (In this context the IHTA 1984, s 91 which deems an interest in possession in residue under a will or intestacy to commence at the testator's death for IHT purposes, disregarding the period of the administration of the estate, a provision which also applies to absolute interests.) But it would apply where the will creates discretionary trusts. It might even apply where the will creates age 18-to-25 trusts (e g on an advance when the beneficiary is over the age of 18, see para **[242.4]** for some more examples of how s 144 may operate in relation to age 18-to-25 trusts), or where the will creates trusts for bereaved minors (e g on an advance postponing the age of vesting from 18 to 25, when the trusts would become age 18-to-25 trusts under s 144(3)). In this part we are concerned, however, with s 144 in relation to ordinary discretionary trusts created by will.

[225.90]

Advantages of testamentary discretionary trusts invoking s 144. Wills taking advantage of the IHTA 1984, s 144 are popular, and Form C3.6 is a precedent for one. It provides a useful method of allowing for changes in circumstances which might occur between the testator's will and his death. Varying the dispositions of the deceased is easier if it can be done by a distribution or appointment falling under s 144 rather than by a variation or disclaimer under s 142 (for which see Note to F3 at paras **[241.1]**–**[241.21]**); it will usually require the agreement of fewer people, and there is no problem where minors or unborns are benefited by the will. Also, there is no question of anyone other than the deceased being the 'settlor' for income tax or capital gains tax purposes. (For the position where there is a variation by an instrument in writing within the IHTA 1984, s 142, see Note to F3 at paras **[241.11]**, **[241.17]** and **[241.19]**.) Ensuring that the testator is the settlor (and the only settlor) for capital gains tax purposes can be a particularly important point for a testator with a foreign domicile. This is because under an instrument of variation creating a settlement, the beneficiary of an absolute gift under the testator's will who makes the instrument will be the settlor for capital gains tax purposes (see TCGA 1992, s 68C(2) with effect in respect of variations made on or after 6 April 2006), and accordingly the settled property will be subject to the rules for offshore settlements with a UK domiciled settlor where it is administered abroad and the beneficiary settlor under the instrument of variation has a UK domicile, even if the testator had a foreign domicile (see F3 at para **[241.17]**). Where there is no foreign element, and a deed of variation is made by a beneficiary which puts an absolute interest into a settlement, the capital gains on the settled property will be taxed as the beneficiary's if he retains an interest under the trusts. However, it seems that after 5 April 2008 this is unlikely to matter very much because of the intention of the government, announced in the Pre-Budget Report of 9 October 2007, to introduce a uniform flat rate of capital gains tax of 18 per cent.

[225.91]
Disadvantages of testamentary discretionary trusts invoking s 144. The main disadvantages of this type of will are that the deceased's property can in practice only be distributed to the objects of the powers created by his will (whereas the IHTA 1984, s 142 applies to an instrument whereby the deceased's property is redirected to any person, whether a beneficiary under the will or intestacy or not), it may necessitate payment of a large sum in IHT before probate can be obtained (as compared with a will in favour of the testator's spouse or civil partner with a view to the spouse or civil partner executing a deed of variation), and strictly it may not amount to 'reasonable financial provision' within the meaning of the Inheritance (Provision for Family and Dependants) Act 1975, s 1 for the deceased's dependants (see Part G, paras **[247.1]–[247.29]** and Vol 1, para **[105.1]** ff). We comment on these as follows:

(1) As regards the first point, it will be appreciated that an appointment to a beneficiary to enable him to assign property to a non-object of the power would be a fraud on the power and void. However, it is possible to provide for a wide class of objects of the power by giving the trustees power to add persons to the class (see *Blausten v IRC* [1972] Ch 256, [1972] 1 All ER 41 and *Re Manisty's Settlement* [1974] Ch 17, [1973] 2 All ER 1203), and it seems from *Re Hay's Settlement Trusts* [1981] 3 All ER 786, [1982] 1 WLR 202 and *Re Beatty's Will Trusts* [1990] 3 All ER 844, [1990] 1 WLR 1503 that a fiduciary power conferred on trustees with no limits on the persons in whose favour it might be exercised can be valid. A form for a *Blausten* type of power is included in Form C3.6, cl 3(1)(b) at para **[225.100]**. In *Re Beatty's Will Trusts* [1990] 3 All ER 844, [1990] 1 WLR 1503 it was held that the provision of wide discretionary trusts or powers in a will is not invalid as a delegation of the testator's power of testamentary disposition, and Form C10.2 in the 6th edition of this work, on which Form C3.6 is based, was referred to by way of example.

(2) As regards the second point, attempts are sometimes made to appoint property in exercise of powers conferred by a will to the testator's widow or widower before a grant of probate is obtained. An executor's authority stems from the will, and if it is clear that the named

executors are, or are among, the persons on whom a power of appointment is conferred by the will, it is difficult to see why they should not make an appointment before the grant of probate. HMRC were at one time unwilling to accept this in relation to some forms of will, but more recently have seemed to be more ready to accept the validity of such appointments. Their view is that whether there is power to make an appointment before probate, or while the estate is in the course of administration, is a question of construction of the will in each case. It is a sensible precaution to provide expressly in the will that an appointment may be made before the grant of probate and before the administration of the estate is complete. In any event certain appointments should be avoided in the first three months after the death if s 144 is to be relied upon (see para **[225.85]**).

(3) As regards the third point, the court will presumably make no order on a family provision application if the executors make an appointment which makes reasonable provision for the applicant, but the two-year period in which they may make an appointment or distribution which satisfies s 144 may well expire long after the six-month time limit from a grant of representation for a family provision application prescribed by the I(PFD)A 1975, s 4 (see Part G, para **[247.5]** and Vol 1, para **[105.5]**). Dependants of the deceased may feel that it is necessary to protect themselves by issuing a claim form for family provision within the six-month time limit, if no distribution or appointment has been made by that time. Where a distribution or appointment which does not make reasonable financial provision is made after the six-month time limit has expired, the court may well permit a late application under the I(PFD)A 1975.

[225.92]

Form C3.6: Will providing two-year discretionary trust

Note. This form creates a two-year discretionary trust with wide powers to appoint new trusts and to pay or apply capital, with a discretionary trust of income pending exercise of the powers or the earlier expiry of two years from the testator's death. Just before the end of the two-year period fixed trusts come into operation if there has been no exercise of the powers, and the coming into operation of these trusts in these circumstances will fall within s 144 of the IHTA 1984. The fixed trusts are an absolute gift to the testator's spouse if surviving, and otherwise to the children. Different or more elaborate default trusts could be substituted, depending on what mixture of exempt and non-exempt gifts is desired, and whom the testator wishes to benefit in the event of no exercise of the powers being made. If the testator wants to have a long-term discretionary trust as the default arrangement then a form such as C6.2 (see para **[228.19]**) would be more appropriate. However, the powers in Form C3.6 would enable the trustees to create a long-term discretionary trust if they wished to do so. If the testator wants trusts in default of appointment under which the beneficiary or beneficiaries have IPDIs, those trusts should commence just before the end of two years from the testator's death, and if the testator wants interest in possession trusts which get IHT relevant property treatment the trusts should start after the end of two years from the testator's death: see paras **[200.131]**, **[200.133]**. As well as considering what is to happen if the powers are not exercised, the testator should also leave a clear written expression of his wishes (but without imposing any trust or obligation) as to how he would like the powers exercised.

This Form C3.6 may be adapted for use for civil partners, the words 'my wife/husband' being replaced with 'my civil partner' throughout. Care should be taken to identify correctly in each will the children who are to benefit.

[225.93]

Joint property. When a will of this type is being made, it should be considered whether the matrimonial home, or any other property, is owned jointly by the testator and his spouse. If the testator desires to include his interest in any jointly-owned property in the property which is settled by his will on discretionary trusts, so that the IHTA 1984, s 144 is capable of applying to it, or at any rate so that it is subject to the trustees' discretion before any fixed trusts come into operation, a severance of the joint tenancy should be carried out.

[225.94]

The matrimonial home. Where this, or the testator's interest in it, is included in the residuary estate subject to the discretionary trusts, and the surviving spouse is living in the home at the testator's death and continues to do so afterwards, there will be a question as to whether this gives rise to an interest in possession in the home (or the testator's interest in it) in favour of the surviving spouse from the death, which interest in possession if it does not arise immediately on death, but arises within two years, might be backdated to death under IHTA 1984, 144 so as to be an IPDI: see Part A, paras **[200.95]**, **[200.133]**. If the surviving spouse does have an IPDI, it would mean that an appointment falling within the IHTA 1984, s 144 could not be made of the home (or the testator's interest in it): see para **[225.89]** for the requirement that there must be no IPDI after the death and before a s 144 appointment or distribution is made. HMRC's statement (Statement of Practice SP 10/79) that they regard an interest in possession as arising where a discretionary beneficiary is allowed to occupy trust property refers principally to an exercise of the trustees' powers so as to provide a permanent home for the beneficiary. It would be consistent with that statement not to regard an interest in possession as arising where no steps are taken to terminate the surviving spouse's existing occupation of the matrimonial home, pending the administration of the estate and a decision of the trustees on how to exercise their powers. There would be a particularly strong case for saying that there is no interest in possession in these circumstances where the home had been owned by the spouses as tenants in common, with the result that the surviving spouse's continuing occupation of the home after the testator's death could be attributed to his or her own interest in the home. The case for saying that a spouse does not have an interest in possession pending a decision of the trustees on how to exercise their powers is supported by a recent decision of the Special Commissioners, *Judge v HMRC* [2005] STC (SCD) 874, [2005] WTLR 1311 that where trustees had failed to exercise a power to permit a spouse to continue to occupy the matrimonial home because they believed she had the right to occupy, no interest in possession arose.

[225.95]

There is nevertheless some risk that HMRC will regard an interest in possession in the home (or the testator's interest in it) on the part of the surviving spouse as having arisen before any appointment or distribution is made, and it is of course likely that if the home, or the testator's interest in it, is included in the property subject to the discretionary trust, the trustees will still appoint it to the surviving spouse for an absolute interest or an IPDI. Despite these factors, it could still be desirable for the home or the testator's interest in it to be included in the property made subject to the discretionary trusts: it could be useful for the trustees to have the option of appointing the home (or interest) away from the surviving spouse and arguing the interest in possession point with HMRC; the spouse might no longer be living in the home by the time of the testator's death, and it could be useful for the trustees to have power to decide whether the surviving spouse should have an absolute entitlement to the home (or to the testator's interest in it) or a more limited interest.

[225.96]

Chattels. A similar point to that just made concerning the matrimonial home can be made about the testator's chattels, where they are in the matrimonial home and likely to continue to be enjoyed in kind by the surviving spouse after the testator's death. However, it could save administrative difficulty, especially if the chattels are not very valuable, to include a specific gift of personal chattels to the spouse, as in Form C3.2, cl 3 at para **[225.31]**. This would also avoid questions as to which spouse owned what chattels.

[225.97]

REVOCATION OF FORMER WILLS

I [*name*] of [*address*] hereby revoke all former testamentary dispositions made by me and declare this to be my last will.

[225.98]

APPOINTMENT OF EXECUTORS[1]

1. I appoint [*name*] of [*address*] and [*name*] of [*address*] (hereinafter together called 'my trustees' which expression shall where the context so admits include my personal representatives for the time being[2] and the trustees or trustee hereof for the time being) to be the executors and trustees hereof.

1 Wide powers are conferred by this form and the choice of executors must be made with care. If members of the testator's family are included, the provisions of cl 7 (exercise by trustees of powers in their own favour) must be considered carefully. See cl 7, n 2 at para **[225.108]**.

2 This makes clear that administrators will, after obtaining a grant of letters of administration, be entitled to exercise the powers of appointment and distribution if the named executors do not take a grant of probate. For the power of the named executors to exercise the powers of appointment or distribution before a grant is obtained see the provisos (ii) and (iii) to cl 3(2)(d) at para **[225.101]**.

[225.99]

ADMINISTRATION TRUSTS OF ESTATE

2. [*As in cl 4 of* Form C3.1 *at para* **[225.14]**.]

[225.100]

DEFINITIONS

3. (1) In this clause the following expressions shall have the following meanings, namely:

(a) 'the discretionary period' shall mean the period beginning immediately after [the end of the period of three months from] the day of my death and ending with the day before the second anniversary of my death;[1]

(b) the expression 'the beneficiaries' shall mean [*here set out the class of beneficiaries. An example would be:* my [wife/husband] [*name*] the children and remoter issue of my parents [*names*] and the children and remoter issue of my [wife's/husband's] parents [*names*] the spouses and former spouses of any of the foregoing and any other person or persons who may during the discretionary period upon the nomination of my [wife/husband] or of any such children and remoter issue be appointed by my trustees at their absolute discretion by deed to be a member or members of the class of beneficiaries].[2]

1 The powers are only exercisable during this period. Under IHTA 1984, s 144, IPDIs, trusts for bereaved minors or age 18-to-25 trusts may be appointed at any time in the two-year period after the testator's death to have the benefits of s 144, but if absolute interests are to be appointed, it is not possible to make an appointment or distribution which fails to fall

within the IHTA 1984, s 144 within three months of the testator's death (see para **[225.85]** for the non-application of s 144 to such an appointment). The words in square brackets might be included therefore to prevent this point being overlooked in the case of an absolute appointment, although as seen it will not be necessary to so restrict the appointment period in relation to the appointment of IPDIs, trusts for bereaved minors or age 18-to-25 trusts. The period expires the day before the second anniversary of the testator's death, so that the default trust in cl 3(5) comes into operation on the second anniversary and thus commences within the two-year period from the testator's death and complies with the requirements of the IHTA 1984, s 144. It is important to note that the last day for exercising the powers will be the day *before* the second anniversary of the death.

2 A power of nomination in this form is thought to be valid (cf *Blausten v IRC* [1972] Ch 256, [1972] 1 All ER 41 and *Re Manisty's Settlement* [1974] Ch 17, [1973] 2 All ER 1203), and its inclusion gives maximum flexibility to the appointments which can be made: see para **[225.91]**. It would apparently be possible to have a very wide hybrid or intermediate fiduciary power with a class of objects of virtually everyone: see *Re Hay's Settlement Trusts, Greig v McGregor* [1981] 3 All ER 786, [1982] 1 WLR 202, *Re Beatty's Will Trusts* [1990] 3 All ER 844, [1990] 1 WLR 1503, and Vol 1, para **[39.31]**. Further, in *Re Beatty's Will Trusts*, this particular form, as it appeared in the 6th edition of this work (as Form C10.2 on pp 1473–1477 of that edition), was referred to by Hoffmann J as an example of a will containing wide discretionary powers and trusts which was not, in his judgment, invalid as a delegation of the testator's powers of testamentary disposition.

[225.101]

POWER OF APPOINTMENT

(2) My trustees shall hold the capital and income of my residuary estate upon trust for all or such one or more of the beneficiaries at such ages or times in such shares and upon such trusts for the benefit of the beneficiaries as my trustees[1] may by irrevocable[2] deed or deeds executed at any time or times during the discretionary period[3] appoint and in making any such appointment my trustees shall have powers as full as those which they would possess if they were an absolute beneficial owner of my residuary estate and in particular (but without prejudice to the generality of the foregoing words) my trustees may in any exercise of the foregoing power as they in their absolute discretion think fit:

- (a) delegate give or impose to or upon themselves or any other person or persons and in relation to any trust or disposition any discretionary powers or discretionary trusts conditions limitations restrictions or provisions including powers of further delegation or powers to create further powers or discretions;
- (b) create trusts or powers for the accumulation of income during the period of 21 years commencing on the date of my death;[4]
- (c) create administrative powers or provisions of whatever nature;
- (d) make provision for the burden of any testamentary expenses taxes or debts payable out of my estate as between different assets funds shares or interests in any manner and to any extent as my trustees think fit;

Provided that:

- (i) no such appointment shall invalidate any payment transfer or application of capital or income previously made under any of the trusts or powers herein elsewhere contained;
- (ii) the foregoing power shall be exercisable by my trustees at any time during the discretionary period[5] and any exercise thereof shall have immediate effect for all purposes notwithstanding

that at the date of exercise there shall have been no grant of probate or administration in respect of the property over which the said power shall be exercised or the administration of my estate shall not have been completed in respect of such property or any other property comprised in my estate;

(iii) the persons who may exercise the foregoing power before any such grant as aforesaid are the persons hereinbefore named as my executors other than any of them who shall have died [or whose appointment as my executor shall have ceased to have effect][6] or who shall have renounced probate of my will.[7]

1 There should be no restrictions on the character or number of the trustees for this purpose, as it is not entirely certain that the statutory power to appoint new trustees can be exercised while the estate is in the course of administration; an alternative, where such restrictions are thought necessary, would be to have express powers to appoint new trustees of the power during the administration of the estate.

2 There seems to be little point in the trustees being able to revoke an appointment since the exercise of any power of revocation would have to be limited to the two-year period, and if s 144 applied to a revocable appointment when made (eg one appointing an interest in possession to the surviving spouse), its application to that appointment would not be altered by subsequent revocation of the appointment.

3 See n 1 to sub-cl (1)(a) of this clause at para **[225.100]**.

4 See B18 at paras **[218.72]–[218.76]** for a discussion of extended accumulation provisions in relation to accumulation and maintenance trusts.

5 See n 1 to sub-cl (1)(a) of this clause at para **[225.100]**.

6 These words could be included if the testator's spouse is a named executor. If there is a subsequent divorce the provisions appointing executors and conferring powers of appointment will have effect as if the spouse had died: WA 1837, s 18A (Part G, para **[244.18]**) and see the Preliminary Note to C2 at paras **[224.12]–[224.19]**. Section 18A would probably apply to this proviso in the absence of these words but they make the position clear. Similar provisions apply on the dissolution of a civil partnership, see Part G, para **[244.20]**.

7 This proviso is included to make clear that an appointment may be made before probate is applied for, and by whom, so that where it is decided to appoint some or all of the estate to an exempt beneficiary, such as the testator's spouse or charity, the benefit of the relevant exemption can be claimed when it comes to paying the IHT due as a condition of obtaining a grant of probate.

[225.102]

POWER TO APPLY CAPITAL

(3) In default of and subject to any exercise of the foregoing power my trustees may at their discretion at any time or times during the discretionary period[1] pay transfer or apply to or for the benefit of all or any one or more of the beneficiaries the whole or any part or parts of my residuary estate absolutely freed and discharged from the trusts powers and provisions hereof.[2]

1 See n 1 to sub-cl (1)(a) of this clause at para **[225.100]**.

2 This power is not absolutely necessary but may be administratively convenient if the trustees wish to distribute a personal chattel or capital cash for emergency maintenance, as they will be able to do so without having to execute a deed first.

[225.103]

DISCRETIONARY TRUST OF INCOME AND POWER TO ACCUMULATE IT DURING THE TWO-YEAR PERIOD[1]

(4) In default of and subject to any exercise of the foregoing powers the income of my residuary estate which shall become due and payable[2] at any time during the period commencing with my death and ending at the expiration of the discretionary period[3] shall be held by my trustees on trust to pay or apply the same to or for the benefit of any one or more of the beneficiaries for the time being living as my trustees may in their discretion think fit provided that my trustees shall have power at their absolute discretion to accumulate the whole or any part or parts of such income as an accretion to my residuary estate for all purposes.

1 It is essential for the application of the IHTA 1984, s 144 that there should be no interest in possession before the powers in sub-cls (3) and (4) are exercised (see para **[225.89]**), and to this end a discretionary trust of income or a provision for accumulation, or both, is required.
2 These words exclude apportionment, so as to make it clear that the discretions relating to income do not affect income payable after the end of the two-year period.
3 The rather elaborate form of words is necessary in order to include the income arising in the three-month period immediately following the death, in case that period is excluded from the definition of the discretionary period in sub-cl (1)(a) of this clause (see n 1 at para **[225.100]**).

[225.104]

DEFAULT TRUSTS TO TAKE EFFECT AT THE END OF THE TWO-YEAR DISCRETIONARY PERIOD[1]

(5) Subject to the foregoing trusts and any or every exercise of the foregoing powers my trustees shall hold my residuary estate and the income thereof upon the following trusts and with and subject to the following powers and provisions:

(a) if my [wife/husband] shall survive me and be living at the expiration of the discretionary period my trustees shall hold my residuary estate and the income thereof in trust for [her/him] absolutely;[2]

(b) if my [wife/husband] shall predecease me or die before the expiration of the discretionary period my trustees shall hold my residuary estate and the income thereof upon trust for such of my children [*name*] [*name*] and [*name*] as shall be living at the expiration of the discretionary period if more than one in equal shares provided that if any of my said children is already dead or shall die before the expiration of the discretionary period leaving a child or children living at the expiration of the discretionary period such child or children shall take if more than one equally between them the share of my residuary estate which such deceased child of mine would have taken if he or she had lived until the end of the discretionary period.

1 Care should be taken to ensure that the default trusts reflect the testator's wishes in case there should be no appointment for any reason. Different residuary trusts could be provided, such as those in Form C3.3 at para **[225.51]** or Form C3.5 at para **[225.75]**.
2 It will be apparent that s 144 permits what amounts to an extended survivorship condition, provided that there is no interest in possession during the two-year period. Contrast the

IHTA 1984, s 92 which applies even if there is an interest in possession during the survivorship period but which limits that period to six months: see B19 at paras **[219.1]**–**[219.11]** and C2 at paras **[224.6]**–**[224.10]**.

[225.105]

MAINTENANCE, ACCUMULATION AND ADVANCEMENT

4. [*As in cl 7 of* Form C3.1 *at para* **[225.17]**.]

[225.106]

ADMINISTRATIVE POWERS

5. [*As in cl 8 of* Form C3.1 *at para* **[225.18]**.]

[225.107]

TRUSTEE LIABILITY

6. [*As in cl 9 of* Form C3.1 *at para* **[225.19]**.]

[225.108]

EXERCISE OF POWERS[1]

7. Any power or discretion hereby or by law conferred on my trustees shall be exercisable in favour of any person who is an object of such power or discretion notwithstanding that he or she is one of my trustees and shall be exercisable notwithstanding that any of my trustees has any other direct or indirect personal interest in the mode or result of such exercise [provided that there are not fewer than two trustees and that at least one of them has no personal interest in the mode or result of exercising the same].[2]

1 This clause permits a member of the family to be a trustee without disqualifying him or her from benefit under any exercise of the powers of appointment and payment or application of capital. See the Preliminary Note to B18 at paras **[218.4]** and **[218.5]**.

2 If all the executors are to be members of the testator's family and beneficiaries, it would be advisable to omit the words in square brackets. Even if there are some independent executors and some family members appointed as executors, it might still be better to omit these words in case the independent trustees never take office. If the proviso is omitted there is no requirement that there should be two trustees acting where a power is exercised in favour of a trustee, which might be advantageous because such a restriction could cause difficulty for exercise of the powers within two years after the testator's death (see cl 3(2), n 1 at para **[225.101]**).

If it is thought that family members cannot be relied on to act disinterestedly and without causing disputes, independent persons who are not beneficiaries should be appointed as executors, and perhaps excluded as potential objects of the power to add to the class of beneficiaries contained in cl 3(1)(b) at para **[225.100]**.

[225.109]

PROFESSIONAL TRUSTEE CHARGING CLAUSE

8. [*As in cl 10 of* Form C3.1 *at para* **[225.20]**.]

[*Testimonium and attestation clause as in* Form C3.1 *at paras* **[225.21]** and **[225.22]**.]

[225.110]

Form C3.7: Reciprocal wills giving entire estate to spouse absolutely, with alternative gift to issue

Note. This is a simple form for a husband and wife who do not wish to make non-exempt gifts on the death of the first to die, and have decided to rely on nil-rate band carry-forward to utilise the nil-rate band of the first to die.

This form can be adapted for use by civil partners with children. The words 'my wife/ husband' should be replaced with 'my civil partner' throughout.

[225.111]

REVOCATION CLAUSE AND DECLARATION AGAINST MUTUAL WILLS

I [*name*] of [*address*] revoke all former testamentary dispositions made by me and declare this to be my last will [And I further declare that notwithstanding that my [wife/husband] is making a will in similar terms we have agreed that our wills are not mutual wills and accordingly that each of us shall be free to revoke his or her will at any time whether before or after the death of the other and shall be free to dispose of his or her property or any property derived from the other as he or she thinks fit].[1]

1 There is no presumption that two wills in similar form are mutual wills in the technical sense, but the inclusion of the words in square brackets will remove any doubt on the point. If mutual wills are intended, then an express clause to that effect, such as Form B1.6 at para **[201.10]**, should be used instead of this clause. For the law on mutual wills see Vol 1, paras **[2.3]–[2.9]**. We recommend life interest trusts rather than mutual wills where a testator wishes to determine the destination of his property after the death of his spouse in the event of his spouse surviving him.

[225.112]

APPOINTMENT OF SPOUSE AS SOLE EXECUTOR/EXECUTRIX, WITH ALTERNATIVE APPOINTMENT

1. I appoint my [wife/husband] [*name*] ('my [wife/husband]') the sole [executrix/executor] of this will but if [she/he] predeceases me or renounces probate or dies without having proved this will then I appoint [*name*] of [*address*] and [*name*] of [*address*] to be the executors and trustees hereof.

[225.113]

DEFINITION OF 'MY TRUSTEES'

2. In this will the expression 'my trustees' shall where the context permits mean my personal representatives for the time being and the trustees for the time being hereof.

[225.114]

PECUNIARY LEGACIES

3. [*As in cl 2 of* Form C3.1 *at para* **[225.12]**.]

[225.115]

PRIMARY GIFT OF ESTATE TO SPOUSE

4. If my [wife/husband] shall survive me[1] then subject to the payment thereout of my debts and funeral and testamentary expenses I give devise

and bequeath all my estate both real and personal [including any entailed or other property over which I shall have a general power of disposition at my death][2] to [her/him] absolutely.

1 If a survivorship clause is wanted the words 'for the period of one month' can be added at this point. See the Preliminary Note on survivorship conditions at paras **[224.5]**–**[224.10]** for the reasons for not including a survivorship clause as between husband and wife or civil partners. If a survivorship period is included it could be any period up to six months and still take advantage of the IHTA 1984, s 92 (see para **[224.6]**); if a survivorship period longer than a month is being considered, it should be remembered that it will not usually be possible to pay income or capital to the spouse before he or she has survived the period.

2 Subject to any contrary intention expressed in the will property subject to a general testamentary power will be carried by a residuary gift under the WA 1837, s 27 (see Part G, para **[244.29]** and Vol 1, paras **[38.1]** and **[38.2]**) without express reference to the property or power. In the case of entailed property, however, the property or the instrument under which it was acquired, or entailed property generally, must be referred to: LPA 1925, s 176(1) (see Part G, para **[244.55]** and Vol 1, para **[7.1]**).

[225.116]

ALTERNATIVE PROVISIONS IF SPOUSE DOES NOT SURVIVE

5. If my [wife/husband] shall predecease me[1] then the following provisions shall have effect.

1 If a survivorship condition is included in the gift to the spouse in clause 4 (para **[225.115]**) add the words 'or shall not survive me for the period aforesaid' at this point. See para **[224.31]**, n 1.

[225.117]

ADMINISTRATION TRUSTS OF RESIDUE

6. [*As in cl 4 of* Form C3.1 *at para* **[225.14]**.]

[225.118]

GIFTS MADE FREE OF TAX

7. [*As in cl 5 of* Form C3.1 *at para* **[225.15]**.]

[225.119]

BENEFICIAL TRUSTS FOR ISSUE

8. My trustees shall hold my residuary estate and the income thereof upon trust for such of my children [and the children of my [wife/husband]] [*name*] [*name*] [*name*] and [*name*][1] as shall survive me and if more than one in equal shares Provided that if any of the said children shall predecease me leaving children or remoter iss ue who survive me then such children or remoter issue shall take through all degrees according to their stocks in equal shares if more than one the share which such deceased child of mine [or of my [wife/husband]][2] would have taken if such child had survived me and so that no issue shall take whose parent (being such issue as aforesaid) is living at my death and so capable of taking.[3]

1 See the Preliminary Note on reciprocal wills and the ultimate destination of property at para **[225.7]**. The reference to the children of the spouse is needed where some of the named beneficiaries are children of the other spouse who are not also children of the testator, and may only be appropriate in one of the two wills.

2 These words need to be included where children of the other spouse who are not children of the testator are among the named primary beneficiaries.

3 Where the children who are the primary beneficiaries are of mature years, a stirpital substitution clause for issue of this sort is appropriate in case any of their descendants predecease the testator leaving issue. Under this clause the interests of vest at the death of the testator irrespective of the age of the beneficiaries who take, and if any are under the age of 18 their shares will be held on a bare trust for them (see para **[200.110]** for the IHT treatment of bare trusts).

[225.120]

MAINTENANCE, ACCUMULATION AND ADVANCEMENT1

9. [*As in cl 7 of* Form C3.1 *at para* **[225.17]**.]

[225.121]

ADMINISTRATIVE POWERS1

10. [*As in cl 8 of* Form C3.1 *at para* **[225.18]**.]

[225.122]

TRUSTEE LIABILITY

11. [*As in cl 9 of* Form C3.1 *at para* **[225.19]**.].

[225.123]

PROFESSIONAL TRUSTEE CHARGING CLAUSE

12. [*As in cl 10 of* Form C3.1 *at para* **[225.20]**.]

[*Testimonium and attestation clause as in* Form C3.1 *at paras* **[225.21]** and **[225.22]**.]

C4 Wills providing for someone with a disability

Preliminary note .... [226.1]

FORMS

C4.1 Reciprocal wills for husband and wife with a disabled child and other children; gift by first to die of entire estate to survivor subject to a nil-rate band discretionary trust, and a discretionary trust of residue on the death of the survivor .... [226.13]

C4.2 Reciprocal wills for husband and wife with grown-up children of whom one is disabled; gift by first to die of entire estate to survivor subject to a nil-rate band discretionary trust; on the death of the survivor a trust of residue for the children in equal shares with the disabled child's share settled on a 'trust for the vulnerable' within the Finance Act 2005, ss 23–45........................... [226.40]

C4.3 Will providing for spouse suffering from mental disorder................ [226.57]

Cross References

See also Forms B11.16 (at para **[211.23]**) and B18.4 (at para **[218.34]**). For protective trusts see Forms C3.2 (at para **[225.23]** ff) and C3.5 (at para **[225.68]** ff).

PRELIMINARY NOTE

[226.1]

The main factors relevant to a will providing for someone suffering from a severe physical or mental disability will usually be the following:

(i) the needs of the disabled person;

(ii) where the disabled person is not capable of managing his or her own affairs, avoiding the necessity for the appointment of a deputy under MCA 2005 so far as possible (deputies under MCA 2005 replaced receivers under the Mental Health Act 1983 with effect from 1 October 2007);

(iii) minimising the adverse impact of IHT, income tax and capital gains tax, so far as compatible with other objectives;

(iv) trying to ensure that the benefit provided by the will does provide some genuine additional advantage to the disabled person, and does not simply cause a corresponding reduction in means-tested state benefits, thus leaving him or her no better off.

A discretionary trust will usually be the best solution, at any rate where the disabled person is incapable of managing his own affairs, although it may have income tax disadvantages (see paras **[226.6]** and **[226.7]**). In particular it will avoid the need for a deputy (at any rate as regards the trust property and its income), and is the best that can be done to provide for the disabled person but at the same time to avoid the trust property being taken into account for state benefit purposes (see para **[226.2]**). Further, the testator has a choice as to what IHT charging rules will apply, i e whether the trust fund is taxed as a fully discretionary trust under IHTA 1984, Part III or as a beneficiary-taxed interest in possession trust under the special provisions of

IHTA 1984, s 89 for discretionary trusts for a disabled person (see paras **[226.3]** ff). The other main possibilities are:

(i) an interest in possession trust, which may be better from the point of view of income tax (see para **[226.7]**) but disadvantageous in that the income will be taken into account in assessing means-tested benefit and a deputy might be needed to look after the income;
(ii) a gift to the disabled person himself, where he is physically disabled but capable of managing his affairs—the main question here is the effect on state benefits, where he is in receipt of them;
(iii) gifts of all the testator's property to other children or relatives of the testator in the hope or on the understanding that they will make provision for the disabled person when it is needed;
(iv) a gift to a charity for the disabled in the hope or on the understanding that it will provide assistance to the disabled person—some charities for the disabled have schemes along these lines and enquiries should be made of the charities relevant to the disabled person's disability;
(v) a discretionary charitable trust under which donations to charities which may help the disabled person can be made.

Any of (iii) to (v) will avoid the risk that the property given by the will of the testator will be taken into account as part of the disabled person's means when means-tested benefits are assessed, but of course run the risk that no benefit at all will reach the disabled person from the testator's gift. They also run the risk that proceedings under the I(PFD)A 1975 will be brought on behalf of the disabled person against the testator's estate.

[226.2]
State benefits. The benefits which may be available to a disabled person are many and complex, and frequently changing, and the details of them are outside the scope of this work. The main means-tested state benefit is income support, and the rules for assessing means for this purpose at the moment disregard income and capital available under a discretionary trust except so far as it is actually paid to or applied for the benefit of the disabled person. Where a disabled person has an interest in possession under a trust, the income to which he is entitled will be taken into account for these purposes. Increasingly the care of disabled persons is the responsibility of local authorities under the Community Care policy. Local authorities are entitled to take into account the resources of a person to whom they provide services in fixing the level of charge for them. There are no general rules as to whether, and, if so, how, discretionary trust income or capital will be taken into account by local authorities, but there would seem to be a better chance that the income and capital of a trust will not be taken into account, at any rate so long as not paid to or applied for the benefit of the disabled person, when it is only applicable under a discretion than when the disabled person has an entitlement under fixed trusts. However, there are many possibilities as to the type of discretionary trust. If there are wide and unrestricted powers over a substantial amount of capital exercisable in favour of the disabled person, the fund is more likely to be taken into account by the local authority (or under any future change of rules for state

benefits) than if the powers over capital are more restricted (or non-existent); similarly, a fund which is tailored to the disabled person's circumstances (eg the trusts come to an end when he dies, or the trustees are directed to have regard primarily to his interests when deciding whether to exercise their powers) is more likely to be taken into account than one which is not.

[226.3]

IHT treatment of trusts for the disabled. A choice of IHT regime is available in relation to a discretionary trust for a disabled person, ie between taxation as a beneficiary-taxed interest in possession trust or taxation as a 'relevant property' discretionary trust (the relative merits of these two options are considered at para **[226.5]**). This is because settled property subject to a discretionary trust which satisfies certain conditions in relation to a disabled person is treated for IHT purposes, by virtue of IHTA 1984, s 89, as if the disabled person has an interest in possession in it (s 89(2)), and because, post-21 March 2006, settled property subject to a disabled person's interest in possession or deemed interest in possession still gets beneficiary-taxed treatment (IHTA 1984, s 49(1A)(b)). Section 89 treats in this way any property which is held on trusts:

(a) under which, during the life of a disabled person, no interest in possession subsists (s 89(1)(a)), and
(b) which secure that not less than half the settled property which is applied during the disabled person's life is applied for his benefit (s 89(1)(b)).

There is now, post-21 March 2006, a definition of 'disabled person's interest' in IHTA 1984, s 89B. It embraces both a deemed interest in possession under s 89 and an actual interest in possession to which, when it commences, a disabled person within the definition in s 89 is beneficially entitled. Both continue to be beneficiary-taxed interests, that is, ones where the settled property is treated for IHT purposes as if it were the property of the beneficiary (see paras **[200.84]** and **[200.90]**. This means that a lifetime settlement for a disabled person can obtain potential exemption, but in the case of a settlement for a disabled person in a will the case is less overwhelming for creating a beneficiary-taxed interest, because the fund going into the settlement is nevertheless subject to IHT on the testator's death, and a relevant property settlement for disabled person can have the advantages discussed in para **[226.5]**. One change of substance made by FA 2006 is that in relation to property going into settlements after 21 March 2006 the definition of 'disabled person' is expanded: see para **[226.4]**.

[226.4]

Commentary on IHTA 1984, s 89. We have the following points concerning s 89:

(i) A disabled person for the purposes of s 89 is someone who is incapable of administering his property or managing his affairs by reason of mental disorder within the Mental Health Act 1983 (MeHA 1983) (see (ii) infra), or who is in receipt of attendance allowance under the Social

Security Contributions and Benefits Act 1992, s 64 (or the equivalent Northern Ireland legislation), or who is in receipt of a disability living allowance under the Social Security Contributions and Benefits Act 1992, s 71 (or the equivalent Northern Ireland legislation) by virtue of entitlement to the care component at the highest or middle rate (IHTA 1984, s 89(4)): see further (ii) infra. In relation to property transferred into a settlement after 21 March 2006 a person also qualifies as a disabled person by being eligible for attendance allowance or disability living allowance by virtue of entitlement to the care component of the highest or middle rate but not in fact receiving it for certain specified reasons, such as living in a care home or being in hospital for renal dialysis: see IHTA 1984, s 89(5) and (6), inserted by FA 2006. This brings the definition for the purposes of IHT in line with the definition for the purposes of trusts for the vulnerable in FA 2005, s 38, for which see para **[226.9]** ff below.

(ii) A mental disorder within the MeHA 1983 is defined as mental illness, arrested or incomplete development of mind, psychopathic disorder, and any other disorder or disability of mind (MeHA 1983, s 1(2)). Attendance allowance (which is for persons of 65 or more), and disability living allowance (which is for persons under 65) by virtue of entitlement to the care component at the highest or middle rate, are for persons who are so severely disabled physically or mentally that they require frequent attendance in connection with bodily functions, or continual supervision to avoid substantial danger to themselves or others either by day or by night (Social Security Contributions and Benefits Act 1992, ss 64 and 72, and see *Cockburn v Chief Adjudication Officer; Secretary of State for Social Security v Fairey* [1997] 3 All ER 844, [1997] 1 WLR 799, HL).

(iii) IHTA 1984, s 89 applies to property settled by will where the disabled person was disabled (within the meanings described in (i) and (ii) above) 'when the property was transferred into settlement' (see s 89(4)), i e at the time of the testator's death. Thus where a testator makes provision in the form required by s 89 for the benefit of a person who counts as disabled (see (i) and (ii) above) at the date of the will but who ceases to do so before the testator's death, s 89 will not apply. On the other hand where the beneficiary is a 'disabled person' within s 89 at the testator's death, and s 89 applies to funds given on trust for his benefit by the testator's will, if he subsequently ceases to count as disabled as defined in s 89, the section will nevertheless continue to apply to the funds.

(iv) IHTA 1984, s 89(3) provides that trusts shall not be treated as falling outside the section by reason only of the powers of advancement conferred by the TA 1925 (TA 1925), s 32 (or the Trustee Act (Northern Ireland) 1958, s 33). However, this is a reference to the statutory power as it stands, and not the statutory power as modified in any way. It would, it seems, not be compatible with IHTA 1984, s 89 for the statutory power of advancement to be made applicable to the whole of a presumptive or vested share (instead of one half as provided in the TA 1925, s 32(1), proviso (a)). Therefore, no modified statutory power of advancement which is exercisable during the disabled person's lifetime should be included. If the statutory power applies, and there are discretionary trusts of income, it is likely that the disabled person would not be someone having a 'prior life or other interest' within the TA 1925, s 32(1), proviso (c) so as to make his consent a prerequisite to any exercise of the power: see *Re Beckett's Settlement, Re Beckett, Eden v Von Stutterheim* [1940] Ch 279 and B18 at para **[218.90]**.

(v) IHTA 1984, s 89 only applies to property if the trusts are such that during the life of the disabled person no interest in possession subsists in that property (see s 89(1)). It follows that if there is a discretionary trust of income, the entire income could in theory be applied for the benefit of persons other than the disabled person without jeopardising the application of s 89. On the other hand it seems that s 89 will not apply to trusts under which it is possible that an interest in possession will arise subsequently during the life of the disabled person, even if currently there is no interest in possession. We therefore recommend that the trusts of income exclude any interest in possession during the disabled person's life. Unfortunately, if this is done, the trusts cannot also comply with the similar but not identical requirements of the Taxation of Chargeable Gains Act 1992 (TCGA 1992), Sch 1, para 1, for a trust for a disabled person to receive a full annual allowance for capital gains tax purposes (rather than the reduced one which normally applies to trustees): see para **[226.6]**.

(vi) A further point arises about the requirement of IHTA 1984, s 89(1) that there should be no interest in possession. If it really is a requirement that there must be no possibility of an interest in possession arising during the life of the disabled person, it could be argued that if s 89 is to apply there must be no powers which can be exercised so as to create an interest in possession. A power which can be of particular utility in trusts of this type is the power to permit the disabled person to occupy a residence comprised in the trust fund, or to have the use of furniture or equipment acquired by the trustees as part of the trust fund. The exercise of such powers so as, eg, to provide the disabled person with a permanent residence could have the effect of conferring an interest in possession (see Part A, para **[200.121]**). Therefore, it could be argued, if it is to be certain that a set of trusts comes within s 89, it is necessary to avoid conferring powers of this kind. However, this would be so inconvenient, and it would be such a bizarre consequence given that an actual interest in possession for a disabled person gets the same IHT treatment (see para **[200.84]**), that it is in our view better to include such powers (unless it is clear that the particular disabled person could not be benefited by the exercise of such powers), and hope that HMRC do not regard the existence of such powers as incompatible with s 89 applying (we know of no published views of HMRC concerning this point). There should be power to restrict such powers so that they can be appropriately cut down if it becomes apparent that HMRC do regard them as preventing s 89 from applying.

(vii) What is said in (vi) above applies equally to powers of appointment or powers to pay or apply capital, which are powers which clearly enable the creation of interests in possession unless specifically restricted so as not to be so exercisable. There is the practical difference that it would not usually be as inconvenient to prohibit the creation of an interest in possession during the life of the disabled person under an exercise of a power of appointment or a power to pay or apply capital than it would be to prohibit the creation of an interest in possession under an exercise of a power to permit occupation or enjoyment in kind of land or other trust assets. However, if HMRC accept that the existence of a power to create an interest in possession by allowing occupation or use of trust property is compatible with IHTA 1984, s 89, then they should also accept that the existence of a power of appointment or payment or application of capital which enables the creation of an interest in possession is also so compatible. We recommend the inclusion of a power to restrict any power of appointment or power to pay or apply capital, which can be used to bring the trusts within IHTA 1984, s 89 should it become apparent that HMRC regard the existence of a power to create an interest in possession as incompatible with the application of s 89.

[226.5]
Relative advantages of the different IHT regimes. The provision which became IHTA 1984, s 89 originated under capital transfer tax when discretionary trusts were subject to much more onerous tax charges than interest in possession ones. The general rules for capital transfer tax and its successor IHT on settled property have since then been transformed out of recognition, and it is not always an advantage for trusts to fall within IHTA 1984, s 89 where the trusts in question are being created by will. If a trust is being created by lifetime gift, a s 89 trust has the advantage that potential exemption will be available (see paras **[200.71]** and **[200.84]**), but where it is being created by will the IHT charge on the testator's estate will be the same whether the trust is a relevant property trust or a s 89 trust, unless the disabled person is the testator's spouse or civil partner. Probably the main situations, when making a will, where s 89 trusts have a clear advantage over relevant property trusts are where the disabled beneficiary is the testator's spouse or civil partner, because the spouse or civil partner exemption will apply on the testator's death, or where the fund will go to charity on the death of the disabled person, so that it will be exempt from IHT on the disabled person's death. Otherwise, the balance of advantage will vary from case to case, depending on factors such as the size of the fund, the expectation of life of the disabled beneficiary, and the likely availability of liquid assets with which to pay periodic charges if it is a relevant property trust. If IHTA 1984, s 89 applies to settled property, it treats the property as subject to an interest in possession to which the relevant disabled person is beneficially entitled (s 89(2)). This will mean that there should be no occasions of IHT charge during the disabled person's life, except where a payment or application of capital is made in favour of other beneficiaries and so gives rise to a deemed transfer of value by the disabled person (see Part A, para **[200.87]**). Payment of capital to the disabled person will be free of IHT charge (IHTA 1984, s 53(2)), and the application of capital for his

direct benefit will probably be treated in the same way (although s 53(2) does not expressly include this). The periodic and exit charges applicable to discretionary trusts (see IHTA 1984, Pt III, Ch III and B18 at paras **[218.8]** and **[218.9]**) will not apply. However, the deemed interest in possession also means that on the death of the disabled person the settled property will be charged to IHT as part of his 'estate'. This will not be disadvantageous if, as will often be the case, his 'estate' including the trust fund is unlikely to exceed the IHT threshold. For a fund substantially in excess of the IHT threshold a relevant property discretionary trust not falling within IHTA 1984, s 89 would probably be more lightly taxed under the IHT rules as they stand at the moment, unless the disabled person lives for a very long time after the testator's death; it will bear periodic charges and exit charges under IHTA 1984, Pt III, Ch III at a modest rate (see B18 at paras **[218.8]** and **[218.9]**) and will not be taxed as part of the disabled person's estate. Such a trust can also be available without restriction to benefit other members of the family. However, although the IHT legislation taxes relevant property trusts lightly at the moment, this could change, while the privileges of trusts specifically for the disabled are more likely to remain untouched. On the other hand, a relevant property trust can be converted free of IHT charge to a s 89 trust within two years after the testator's death in reliance on IHTA 1984, s 144 (see para **[225.83]** ff), but conversion in the opposite direction in that period is likely to be difficult or impossible, and if it can be done it could involve an IHT charge. For trusts falling within IHTA 1984, s 89 see Form B18.4 (at para **[218.34]**) and Forms C4.1 and C4.3 ff. Form C4.3 (at para **[226.57]**) creates a trust within s 89 for the testator's spouse, so as to obtain, on the testator's death, the IHT exemption for gifts to spouses.

[226.6]

Capital gains tax annual exemption. By the TCGA 1992, Sch 1, para 1, a trust for a person who satisfies the requirements for being a disabled person for the purposes of IHTA 1984, s 89 (there is no cross-reference but the relevant definitions in the TCGA 1992, Sch 1 are the same) has the advantage of the full amount of capital gains tax annual exemption of capital gains in any year of assessment (currently £9,200 for the tax year 2007–08), as opposed to the reduced amount usually available to trustees, where certain conditions are fulfilled. The first of these conditions, which is the same as the condition specified in IHTA 1984, s 89(1)(b), is that the trusts should secure that during the life of the disabled person not less than half the trust property which is applied is applied for his benefit. But the second condition, which provides that the trusts should also secure that during his life he is entitled to not less than half the income of the trust property, or that no such income may be applied for the benefit of any other person, is inconsistent with the condition specified in IHTA 1984, s 89(1)(a) (ie that no interest in possession subsists throughout the life of the disabled beneficiary: see para **[226.4]**, sub-para (v)). The second limb of the second condition could be met without creating an interest in possession by providing for income to be applied for the benefit of the disabled person at the discretion of the trustees, and any not so applied to be accumulated. But since accumulation of income is only possible during limited periods, eg 21 years from the death of the testator (see the LPA 1925, s 164(1)(b): Part G, para **[246.56]**), in order to wholly satisfy the second condition the trust would have to confer an actual interest in possession on the disabled person in at least half the fund once the accumulation period had expired, since income which cannot be accumulated must be distributed to or for the benefit of somebody.

[226.7]
Capital gains tax rates. It was announced in the Pre-Budget Report on 9 October 2007 that capital gains tax will be charged at a flat rate of 18 per cent on individuals and trusts alike, with effect from 6 April 2008. This removes as from that date the capital gains tax rate disadvantage of holding property in trust rather than absolutely. The pre-6 April 2008 position was that until 5 April 2008 the gains of a settlement (whether discretionary or subject to an interest in possession) were charged at the income tax rate applicable to trusts under ITA 2007, ss 9 and 479 ff (formerly the Income and Corporation Taxes Act 1988, ss 686, 687), latterly 40 per cent (TCGA 1992, s 4(1AA)(a)) (see Part A, paras **[200.40]** and **[200.41]**), subject to the possibility of a lower rate if the trusts fall within FA 2005 , ss 23–45 as a trust for the vulnerable, for which see para **[226.9]** ff below.

[226.8]
Income tax. Income tax will, generally, be charged at 'the rate applicable to trusts' (currently 40 per cent) unless there is an actual interest in possession (see Part A, para **[200.41]**). However, the tax on any of the income which is paid to or applied for the benefit of a beneficiary will be adjusted to that appropriate to the personal tax position of the beneficiary. For the rules specific to UK company dividend income arising to trustees of discretionary trusts, see Preliminary Note to B18 at para **[218.30]**. This is subject to the possibility of a trust for a disabled person qualifying as a trust for the vulnerable within FA 2005, ss 23–45, and receiving more favourable income tax treatment, for which see para **[226.9]** ff below.

[226.9]
Trusts for the vulnerable for disabled persons. A further possible type of trust for disabled persons conferring a tax advantage is created by FA 2005, ss 23–45. This is a 'trust for the vulnerable' for a 'disabled person', which has the advantage that the trustees and beneficiary can elect for the income to be taxed as if the income were the property of the disabled person instead of being taxed at the trust rates, which have been increased considerably in recent years (see para **[200.41]** above). This note and the form set out below concentrate on the aspects of the new rules which fall within the scope of *Williams on Wills*, namely the drafting problems of creating, by testamentary disposition, trusts which qualify for this special treatment. The details of what the special treatment is and how it is obtained will be found in HMRC's 'An introduction to the new special tax treatment for certain trusts with vulnerable beneficiaries', and *Tolley's Income Tax 2007–08,* para 73.18. The income tax advantage is essentially that undistributed income is taxed as if it were the beneficiary's income. This is not so very beneficial, because if income is distributed the trustees have to account for income tax at the trust

rate of 40 per cent, so far as not already paid on the income which is distributed, the beneficiary has to make a repayment claim if this is in excess of his liability, and there is still no carry-through to the beneficiary of the tax credit on dividends. FA 2005, ss 23–45 also provided advantageous treatment for capital gains tax purposes, but the introduction of a capital gains tax flat rate of 18 per cent for trusts and individuals alike as from 6 April 2008 (announced in the 9 October 2007 Pre-Budget Report) means that from that date there is no capital gains tax advantage in falling within these provisions. With the disappearance of the capital gains tax advantage, there is very little to be gained by causing a trust to fall within FA 2005, ss 23–45, in view of the very restrictive requirements as to the income trusts and the fact that there is no advantage where income is distributed to or applied for the benefit of the beneficiary. A form of trust which is thought to fall within FA 2005, s 34 is in cl 8(3) of Form C4.2, para **[226.49]**.

[226.10]
Trusts for the vulnerable—qualifying conditions. FA 2005, s 38 defines the disabled persons whose trusts can qualify for the special treatment under FA 2005, ss 23–45. They are now, as a result of the FA 2006 amending IHTA 1984, s 89, the same persons as those who qualify as disabled for the purposes of IHTA 1984, s 89: see para **[226.4]** (i) and (ii). FA 2005, s 34 defines the qualifying trusts for disabled persons. To be qualifying trusts the property subject to them must satisfy two conditions, one relating to capital (see para **[226.11**) and the other relating to income (see para **[226.12]**). Trusts are qualifying trusts for a disabled person if they satisfy the conditions set out in FA 2005, s 34 during his lifetime or until the termination of the trusts if that occurs before his death (s 34(1)). It is not clear what sort of trust with a possibility or certainty of termination before the death of the disabled person is capable of being a qualifying trust. For example, would trusts which for the time being satisfy the income and capital conditions, but which are subject to an overriding power of the trustees to appoint different trusts which would not qualify, be for the time being qualifying trusts? This seems unlikely. It may be that such an arrangement fails to satisfy the capital condition on the basis that the overriding power is or could create a power of application within the meaning of s 34(2)(a) which falls outside it, or that 'until the termination of the trusts' in s 34(1)(b) means 'until the entire settlement terminates' rather than 'until the qualifying trust for the benefit of the disabled beneficiary terminates'. Another possibility is that 'until the termination of the trusts' in s 34(1) refers to the termination of the trusts for the benefit of the disabled beneficiary by the passing of time where the date of termination is predetermined, rather than by the occurrence of a contingency or the exercise of a power. Section 34(4) is probably intended to enable protective trusts for a disabled person to fall within these provisions, until a forfeiture occurs, where they otherwise would not. If so, and if it is the case that a protective trust could not be a qualifying trust before a forfeiture occurred in the absence of a provision such as 34(4), 'until the termination of the trusts' in s 34(1)(b) has a very restricted meaning.

[226.11]
Trusts for the vulnerable—qualifying condition as to trusts of capital. The condition relating to capital is that the trusts must secure that the only

applications of capital which can be made are applications for the benefit of the disabled person (s 34(2)(a)). However, the fact that the statutory power of advancement (TA 1925, s 32 or the Trustee Act (N Ireland) 1958, s 33) applies to the trust will not prevent this condition from being satisfied (FA 2005, s 34(3)). For example, if the trust is that the income is to be paid to A for life, A being a disabled person, with the capital then going to B after A's death, the statutory power of advancement will apply to the trust for B, if it is not expressly excluded, and will enable capital to be applied in B's favour. This will not prevent the trusts from being qualifying trusts. This is not a big concession, because in this example the exercise of the statutory power in favour of B would require A's consent (TA 1925, s 32(1)(c)). Another restriction on the statutory power is that it can only be exercised over half of a presumptive share (TA 1925, s 32(1)(b)). If s 32 were varied by express provision in the instrument creating the trusts, for example so as to enable the whole of a presumptive share to be applied in favour of B, the trusts would be prevented from being qualifying trusts. This liberty to include a power of advancement has been slightly expanded by amendment by FA 2006 so as to allow an express power of advancement to be compatible with a trust being a qualifying trust for this purpose, provided that it is subject to the same restrictions as in provisos (a) and (c) to TA 1925, s 32(1), ie limited to advancement of half a presumptive share, and requiring the consent of a beneficiary with a prior interest: see FA 2005, s 34(3) as amended. This of course makes it clear that a power applicable to the whole of presumptive share would prevent a trust from being a qualifying trust.

[226.12]
Trusts for the vulnerable—qualifying condition as to trusts of income. The income condition is that the trusts secure that the disabled person is entitled to all the income arising from the property (if any) or that none of the income may be applied for the benefit of any other person (FA 2005, s 34(4)). Either the disabled person must have an interest in possession or, if not, there cannot be a discretion over income exercisable in favour of anyone other than the disabled person. If there is an available accumulation period, a trust which provided that the trustees should either apply the income for the beneficiary's benefit or accumulate it could satisfy the condition without being an interest in possession trust, but once such accumulation period had run out (usually after 21 years from the creation of the trust) the trust would have to be one which in effect gave the disabled person a right to the income, ie an interest in possession. This is unfortunate, because it is often desirable when creating trusts for disabled persons that they should not be interest in possession trusts, eg because they are not good at handling money, to avoid an IHT charge on death on the interest in possession basis, or to avoid the undistributed trust income being taken into account for social security purposes. This also means that IHTA 1984, s 89 will not apply to trusts to which FA 2005, s 34 applies because of the requirement of s 89 that there should be no interest in possession throughout the life of the disabled person. Legislation on the Law Commission's proposals for abolishing the restrictions on accumulation of income would make it possible to devise trusts for the disabled which fall within FA 2005, s 34 and which are not at risk of sooner or later giving rise to an interest in possession.

[226.13]

Form C4.1: Reciprocal wills for husband and wife with a disabled child and other children; gift by first to die of entire estate to survivor subject to a nil-rate band discretionary trust, and a discretionary trust of residue on the death of the survivor

Note. When wills are being made to provide for a disabled child, there will often be uncertainty as to the future condition of the child, and there will usually be uncertainty about the future availability of and rules surrounding state benefits and local authority care, and the future incidence of taxation. Where the child is currently in the care of his parents, there is also the considerable uncertainty as to what will happen to him on the death of the second to die of his parents. Accordingly, this form for the wills of both husband and wife, leaves the decision as to what provision to make for the disabled child on the death of the second parent to die, to the executors' discretion.

[226.14]

On the death of the first to die. Under the will of the first of the spouses to die there is a nil-rate band discretionary trust under which the surviving spouse and the children, including the disabled child, are beneficiaries, and subject to that the residuary estate goes to the surviving spouse absolutely. This nil-rate band trust falls within the ordinary discretionary trust IHT charging rules, and does not fall within IHTA 1984, s 89. Because of nil-rate carry-forward (see para **[200.74]**), the nil-rate band trust is not needed for IHT-saving reasons unless one of the special reasons discussed in para **[200.130]** applies, but it provides flexibility. The powers are wide enough to enable the trustees to turn it into a s 89 trust for the disabled child, if that turns out to be a good idea, or they can appoint it to the surviving spouse absolutely or for life if a discretionary trust is not wanted and nil-rate band carry-forward seems a better use of the first to die's nil-rate band. For notes on nil-rate band discretionary trusts see B18 at paras **[218.16]–[218.18]**.

[226.15]

On the death of the survivor. Under the will of the survivor there are some pecuniary legacies and a gift of the estate on wide discretionary trusts and powers for a class which includes the disabled child and charity among the beneficiaries, with the idea that the trustees can appoint whatever seems to be the best arrangement at the time, and rely on IHTA 1984, s 144 (see C3 at paras **[225.83]–[225.91]**) where the appointment has IHT implications, particularly where property is distributed to charity or a wholly charitable trust is set up in relation to part of the fund (see below). If no exercise of their powers is made by the trustees during the two years after the testator's death, the trusts of residue will continue as discretionary trusts after the end of that period. However, there are two alternatives as to the IHT status of the default discretionary trusts after the end of two years from the testator's death (ie the trusts taking effect in the absence of any exercise of the trustees' powers during those two years) according to whether sub-cls (4) and (5) of cl 10 (see para **[226.33]**) are included in the will or left out. If those subclauses are included, they will bring the trusts within IHTA 1984, s 89(1)(b) (see para **[226.3]**) by restricting the powers over capital after the end of the two-year period so that at least half the capital which is applied during the disabled child's life is applied for his benefit. If the existence of powers which authorise the trustees to create interests in possession during the disabled child's life does not prevent IHTA 1984, s 89 from applying (see para **[226.4]**, sub-paras (vi) and (vii)), the inclusion of sub-cls (4) and (5) of cl 10 will mean that in default of any exercise of the trustees' powers during the two years following the testator's death s 89 will apply and the disabled child will be treated for IHT purposes as entitled to an interest in possession in the whole of the residuary estate (see para **[226.5]**). If sub-cls (4) and (5) of cl 10 are not included in the will, the trusts in default of exercise of the trustees' powers within the two-year period will be subject to IHT under the ordinary relevant property discretionary trust charging rules (IHTA 1984, Pt III, Ch III: see B18 at paras **[218.6]–[218.15]**).

[226.16]

Scope of powers and IHTA 1984, s 89. We mention in sub-paras (vi) and (vii) of para **[226.4]** the possibility that the existence of powers which allow the trustees to create an interest or interests in possession is not compatible with IHTA 1984, s 89 applying. We also mention that this would be extremely inconvenient and that there is no indication that HMRC take this view. Accordingly the provisions in this form intended to cause s 89 to apply (i e sub-cls (4) and (5) of cl 10 at para [226.33]) do not in terms restrict the trustees' powers so as to prevent the creation of interests in possession during the life of the disabled beneficiary. There is a general restriction on the administrative powers in cl 9(2)(iii) to the effect that those powers are not to prevent s 89 from applying (see para [224.31]). Also, a power to release or restrict powers is included. If during the two years following the testator's death it is clear that HMRC do regard the existence of powers to create an interest or interests in possession during the disabled beneficiary's life as incompatible with s 89, and it is desired that s 89 should apply, an appropriate restriction could be imposed.

[226.17]

After the death of the disabled child. It should also be noted that in the absence of any exercise of the trustees' powers the discretionary trusts of the surviving spouse's residuary estate will continue well beyond the death of the disabled child (see the definition of 'the trust period' in cl 8(2)(b) and the discretionary trust of income in cl 8(4) at para **[226.30]**). This means that if sub-cls (4) and (5) of cl 10 are included in the will (see para **[226.16]**), and IHTA 1984, s 89 applies during the life of the disabled child so as to treat him as having an interest in possession in the residuary estate, the IHT status of the trusts from the death of the disabled child until the end of the trust period will be discretionary trusts falling within IHTA 1984, Pt III, Ch III (see B18 at paras **[218.6]**–**[218.15]**), and there will be an exit charge on property which is distributed out of the estate after the disabled child's death (in addition to the IHT charge on the residuary estate as part of the disabled child's estate on his death). Under the rules as they stand at the moment this exit charge will be very small if it occurs a short time after the disabled child's death (see B18 at para **[218.11]**). However, it can be avoided altogether if an appointment is made before the disabled child's death of fixed trusts which take effect on his death. If it is found desirable to restrict the trustees' powers, either in order to get the trusts within IHTA 1984, s 89 (see para **[226.4]**, sub-paras (vi) and (vii)), or to reduce the chances of the residuary estate being taken into account for state etc benefit purposes (see para **[226.2]**), it should be done so far as possible so as to leave the trustees with flexible powers to determine what the trusts will be on or after the disabled child's death.

[226.18]

Charities as objects of the discretions. The discretionary beneficiaries under both the nil-rate band legacy trusts and the residuary trusts include charities. This means that not only are the trustees able to distribute income or capital to charities at any time, but they are also able, by virtue of IHTA 1984, s 144 (see C3 at paras **[225.83]**–**[225.91]**), to obtain IHT charitable exemption on the death of the surviving spouse in relation to any of the residuary estate distributed to particular charities during the period of two years from the testator's death, or appointed during that period on permanent and irrevocable discretionary trusts which have charities as the only objects. This is also so in relation to the nil-rate band legacy under the will of the first to die, but there would be no IHT advantage in obtaining exemption for part of a fund which has not borne IHT in consequence of being below the tax threshold.

[226.19]

Power of advancement. Where trusts are being drafted so as to fall within IHTA 1984, s 89, or so as to be capable of doing so, it should be remembered that the statutory power of advancement, if it is declared or permitted to apply during the disabled child's life, should not be varied or modified in any way: see para **[226.4]**, sub-para (iv). There is no express provision in this form concerning the statutory power of advancement.

[226.20]

Letters of wishes. These should be left by the testators, setting out their wishes with regard to the discretionary trusts, and expressed not to create any legally binding trust or obligation. It is particularly important that they should indicate what proportion of the estate of the second of them to die they would like to go into a fund to help the disabled child and what proportion they would like to go to the other children immediately. Where the estate is likely to be fairly small it will usually be intended that the non-disabled children will only receive significant benefit after the death of the disabled child.

[226.21]

For another example of a trust falling within IHTA 1984, s 89 see Form B18.4 at para **[218.34]**.

This form may be adapted for use for civil partners, the words 'my wife/husband' being replaced with 'my civil partner' throughout. Care should be taken to identify correctly in each will the children who are to benefit.

[226.22]

REVOCATION CLAUSE

I [*name*] of [*address*] revoke all former testamentary dispositions made by me and declare this to be my last will.[1]

1 There is no presumption that wills in similar form are mutual wills in the technical sense, but in view of the close tailoring of the two wills to each other, it would be appropriate to add a declaration excluding mutual wills as in the revocation clause of Form C2.1 at para **[224.28]**.

[226.23]

APPOINTMENT OF EXECUTORS AND TRUSTEES AND DEFINITION OF 'MY TRUSTEES'

1. I appoint [*name*] of [*address*] and [*name*] of [*address*][1] (hereinafter together called 'my trustees' which expression shall where the context so admits include my personal representatives for the time being and the trustees for the time being hereof) to be the executors and trustees of this will.

1 For reasons given in para **[218.22]** (4) the surviving spouse should not be a general executor if the charge scheme method of constituting the nil-rate band trust is to be used.

[226.24]

APPOINTMENT OF GUARDIANS[1]

2. If my [wife/husband] shall predecease me I appoint [*name*] of [*address*] [and [*name*] of [*address*]] to be the [guardian/guardians] of my children during their respective minorities.

1 For reasons given in the Note on appointment of guardians in B3 (at paras **[203.47]**–**[203.59]**) it is better to provide appointments of guardians which take effect only on the death of the survivor. It should be noted that the legal status of guardians will cease in relation to a mentally disabled child when he or she attains the age of 18. This clause should be omitted if the children are all already over the age of 18.

[226.25]

LEGACIES TO TAKE EFFECT ON THE DEATH OF THE SECOND TO DIE

3. If I survive my [wife/husband][1] I give the following pecuniary legacies free of tax:[2]

[(a) To my son [*name*][3] the sum of £——;

(b) To my daughter [*name*][4] the sum of £——;

(c) To [*name*] of [*address*] the sum of £——.]

1 The words in square brackets should be included where these are intended to be legacies which are given once only, on the death of the second of the spouses to die. It should be noted that where the words in square brackets are not included, and the nil-rate band utilising legacy below is expressed as a specified sum of money, the latter needs to be reduced by the total amount or value of the legacies given by this clause which are not exempt legacies, such as ones to the surviving spouse or to charity. For reciprocal wills containing legacies intended to take effect under only one of the wills where there is a survivorship condition in the main gift see Form C9.2 at para **[231.14]** ff.

It should be noted that if there is a divorce, these legacies will still take effect, and only take effect, on the death of the survivor of the former spouses, if they do not change their wills.

2 These pecuniary legacies are declared to be 'free of tax' to take account of the risk that they may be payable out of a residuary estate which includes property of a kind which bears its own IHT, such as property situated outside the UK, with the consequence that the legacies might without this declaration be liable to bear their own IHT so far as payable out of that property: see the Preliminary Note to B14 at paras **[214.59]**–**[214.60]**. The expression 'free of tax' is employed here in conjunction with the definition and direction as to payment in cl 6 of this form at para **[226.28]**.

3 Ie one of the non-disabled children of the testator.

4 See n 3 above.

[226.26]

GIFT OF NIL-RATE BAND LEGACY ON DISCRETIONARY TRUSTS

4.(1) In this clause the following expressions have the following meanings:

(a) 'the trust legacy' means the legacy by this clause bequeathed to my legacy trustees and the assets for the time being representing the same;

(b) 'the beneficiaries' means:

(i) my [wife/husband];

(ii) my children and remoter issue;[1]

(iii) any spouse widow or widower of any of such children or remoter issue (and 'widow' and 'widower' shall include a widow or widower who has remarried);

(iv) any institution (whether corporate or not) which is established for purposes which are exclusively charitable under the law of England and Wales.[2]

(c) 'A' means my [son/daughter] A[3];

(d) 'the trust period' means the period commencing on my death and expiring on the twenty-first anniversary of the last survivor of the following persons, namely:

(i) my [wife/husband];

(ii) my children;[4]

(e) 'the accumulation period' means the period commencing with my death and expiring on the twenty-first anniversary thereof; and

(f) 'my legacy trustees' means [*name*] of [*address*] and [*name*] of [*address*][5] or other the trustee or trustees for the time being of the trust legacy.

(2) If my [wife/husband] shall survive me[6] then I bequeath to my legacy trustees free of tax a legacy of the maximum sum of money (if any) which can in the circumstances subsisting at my death be given by this clause without any liability being incurred for the payment of inheritance tax on or by

reason of my death. And in particular but without prejudice to the generality of the foregoing the circumstances to be taken into account for the foregoing purpose shall include any chargeable transfers made by me during my lifetime (or events treated as such for inheritance tax purposes) the dispositions taking effect under this Will (apart from this present clause) or under any codicil hereto and any property treated as if it were part of my estate immediately before my death for inheritance tax purposes.

(3) My legacy trustees shall hold the trust legacy and the income thereof upon such trusts for the benefit of all or any one or more exclusively of the others or other of the beneficiaries and if more than one in such shares and with such trusts and powers (which may include discretionary trusts or powers conferred on my legacy trustees or any other person or persons and may also include power to create further discretionary trusts or powers)[7] and with such provisions generally as my legacy trustees (not being fewer than two in number or being a corporation) shall by any deed or deeds revocable or irrevocable appoint provided that no appointment shall be made and no revocable appointment shall be revoked after the expiration of the trust period.

(4) At any time or times during the trust period my legacy trustees (not being fewer than two in number or being a corporation) may pay or apply the whole or any part or parts of the trust legacy to or for the advancement or benefit of any of the beneficiaries for the time being living in such manner as they think fit.[8]

(5) Subject to any exercise of the foregoing powers my legacy trustees shall during the trust period hold the trust legacy upon trust to pay or apply the income thereof to or for the maintenance education or benefit of all or any one or more of the beneficiaries for the time being living in such shares if more than one and generally in such manner as they think fit provided that my legacy trustees may during the accumulation period accumulate the whole or any part of the income of the trust legacy by investing the same and the resulting income thereof in any of the investments hereby authorised and any accumulations of income so made shall form part of the capital of the trust legacy for all purposes.

(6) Subject to any exercise of the foregoing powers the trust legacy and the income thereof shall be held at the expiration of the trust period in trust absolutely for such of my children and remoter issue by my [wife/husband][9] as shall then be living in equal shares per stirpes so that no issue shall take whose parent is living at the expiration of the trust period and capable of taking Provided that for the purposes of the foregoing trust A[10] shall (if then living) be deemed to have predeceased the expiration of the trust period and the share which apart from this proviso would be his share shall devolve on his issue (if any) or the other stirpes accordingly.

(7) After the death of my [wife/husband] my trustees shall have power during the trust period in their absolute discretion to transfer the trust legacy or any part or parts thereof to the trustees of any fund held on any discretionary or other trusts arising under the will of my [wife/husband] which are wholly or partly for the benefit of any one or more of the legacy beneficiaries (whether or not persons other than the legacy beneficiaries may also be benefited) to be held as an accretion to such fund and as one fund therewith for all purposes provided that the foregoing power shall not be

exercisable unless such transfer can be effected without infringing the rule against perpetuities as it affects the trust legacy.[11]

(8) Any capital or income of the trust legacy not otherwise disposed of by this clause shall be held in trust for such of my children other than A as survive me if more than one in equal shares absolutely.

(9) Instead of the trust legacy being satisfied by the payment of cash or by the appropriation of property:

(a) my trustees may charge (with or without there being any personal liability of any person or persons) any property which is (or but for this clause would be) comprised in my residuary estate with payment of a sum of money equal to or less than the amount of the trust legacy to my legacy trustees and my legacy trustees shall accept such charge for such sum as the whole or a part (as the case may be) of the trust legacy;

(b) my trustees may require my legacy trustees to accept in satisfaction of all or part of the trust legacy a binding promise of payment (secured or unsecured) made personally by my [wife/husband] or by my trustees as trustees of my residuary estate which debt shall be payable on demand and my legacy trustees shall accept such debt as the whole or a part (as the case may be) of the trust legacy; and

(c) without prejudice to the power of appropriation herein elsewhere contained my trustees may constitute the trust legacy wholly or partly by appropriating to it at their discretion any property or proportionate share of any property and for this purpose may take such advice as to the value of the said property or proportionate share as they think fit and where the trust legacy is for the time being wholly or partly constituted by a proportionate share of a dwelling-house or other property my legacy trustees shall have all the powers of an absolute owner in relation to such share and property and in particular may at their discretion join with the other proprietor or proprietors of such property:

  (i) to permit a beneficiary under the trusts of the trust legacy to have the use or enjoyment of the property in kind on such terms as my trustees think fit; or

  (ii) to effect or enable a sale of the property and the purchase of another property in the same or similar co-ownership with the trust legacy constituted by a proportionate share thereof.

(10) The following shall apply in relation to the powers in the last preceding sub-clause:

(a) my trustees may require to be included such terms if any as they think fit in relation to a charge under sub-clause (8)(a) above or a debt under sub-clause (8)(b) above including terms as to interest (if any) and linking the debt or sum charged to the Index of Retail Prices or otherwise providing for its amount to vary with the passage of time according to a formula provided that the debt or the sum of money secured by the charge shall be payable to my legacy trustees on demand and the charge shall be enforceable by my legacy trustees at any time;

(b) my legacy trustees may leave the charge or debt outstanding for as long as they think fit and refrain from exercising their rights in relation to it and waive the payment of all or any part of any interest due in respect of it and may accept any substitute debt or charge undertaken or created by any person;

(c) my trustees may assent to the vesting of my residuary estate subject to an outstanding obligation to pay or satisfy the trust legacy and my legacy trustees may appoint new trustees of the trust legacy in exercise of the statutory power to do so before the trust legacy has been paid or satisfied;

(d) my legacy trustees and my trustees shall not be liable if my [wife/husband] is or becomes unable to pay the debt or any security is or becomes inadequate or for any other loss or disadvantage which may occur as a result of their exercising or choosing not to exercise any of the foregoing powers; and

(e) the foregoing powers are in addition to any other powers given by this will or any codicil or by the general law and the foregoing powers may be exercised even though my trustees and my legacy trustees are the same persons or my [wife/husband] is among either or both sets of trustees provided that such powers shall not be exercisable by a sole trustee who is my [wife/husband].

(11) Clauses 9 to 14 inclusive below shall apply to the trusts of this clause as if references therein to my trustees were references to my legacy trustees.

1 Add 'by my wife/husband' if appropriate, here and in the definition of the trust period in cl 4(1)(d)(ii), and in the trusts of residue in clause 8(2)(a)(i) and (b) in para **[226.30]**. See the Preliminary Note to C2 at paras **[224.13]–[224.15]**. It is desirable that the nil-rate band legacy in the will of the first to die is held on trusts as similar as possible to those of the residuary estate of the survivor, so that the two funds can be amalgamated after the death of the latter if they are both trusts falling within IHTA 1984, s 89.

2 This definition is based on that contained in the Charities Act 1993, s 96(1). The latter definition will be replaced in the near future by Charities Act 2006, s 1(1), which has some verbal differences but is substantially the same: see Vol 1, para **[102.3]**. If the disabled child is being cared for by some charitable body, it may be useful to have express power to make appointments in favour of that charity.

3 This is the disabled child, in order to exclude him or her from the fixed trusts which take effect if the discretionary trusts come to an end without the trustees' powers being exhaustively exercised (see sub-clauses (6) and (7) of this clause).

4 For reasons given in para **[218.22]** (5) of Vol 2 the legacy trustees and general trustees should not be exactly the same persons, though there could be overlap, in case it turns out to be desired to use a charge scheme to constitute the trust fund.

5 The nil-rate band legacy in the one will and the residuary estate in the other should have the same perpetuity period. This is particularly important if the amalgamation of the funds is to be possible. See cl 4(7) of this form for the power to amalgamate them.

6 This precondition is imposed to avoid unnecessary duplication of gifts (ie this one and the residuary gift) in the event of the spouse not surviving the testator. Survivorship conditions are no longer recommended as between spouses or civil partners (see para **[224.6]** ff). Even if it is preferred in general to continue to include survivorship conditions, this gift should not be made conditional on the spouse surviving the testator by a survivorship period: see the Preliminary Note to C3 at para **[225.4]**.

7 These words authorise the creation of discretionary trusts or powers which might not otherwise be valid: see Vol 1, para **[40.5]**.

8 A power to apply capital, being exercisable in a less formal manner, may be useful, but it is essential that its exercise should be adequately evidenced. It is an important power to include where a disabled person is a beneficiary, because it will authorise, eg payments to be

made to persons or charities looking after or helping the disabled person, where such payments are beneficial to the disabled person. See the Note in B18 at para **[218.92]** ff for the wide scope of a power to apply property for a person's benefit. The reference to a trust corporation is for the reasons given in n 1 of para **[226.37]**.

9 See n 1 above.

10 Ie the name of the disabled child, whom it will probably be appropriate to exclude from this ultimate gift of capital.

11 In order to maximise the chances of this power being exercisable the trusts of the nil-rate band legacy and of the residue under the other spouse's will are made as similar as possible. It may be possible to amalgamate the funds if they are both subject to beneficiary-taxed deemed interests in possession of the same person, by virtue of IHTA 1984, s 89. If they are relevant property they will have to remain separately identifiable funds because they will have different settlors, different factors in their calculations of the tax rate on periodic charges and exit charges, and different dates of periodic charges.

[226.27]

ADMINISTRATION TRUSTS OF RESIDUE

5. (1) I give all my property not hereby or by any codicil hereto otherwise effectively disposed of [(including any entailed or other property over which I shall have at my death a general power of disposition by will)][1] to my trustees to hold on the trusts set out below with power at their discretion to sell all or any of it as and when they think fit.[2]

(2) My trustees shall pay my funeral and testamentary expenses[3] and debts and any legacies given by this will or any codicil hereto out of such property or its proceeds and shall have a discretion as to how such payments shall be borne as between capital and income[4].

(3) Subject as above my trustees shall hold such property and the assets from time to time representing the same (hereinafter called 'my residuary estate') on the trusts set out below and shall invest all money comprised in such property or arising from its sale in any of the investments hereby authorised with power to change such investments into any others hereby authorised.

(4) In the administration of my estate and the execution of the trusts of this will or of any codicil to it:

(a) my trustees shall treat all income as accruing on the date on which it becomes payable regardless of the period in respect of which it shall have accrued and shall not make any statutory apportionment of the same;[5] and

(b) none of the equitable rules of apportionment between capital and income shall apply in any circumstances whatever[6].

1 See Form C2.1, cl 6, n 1 at para **[224.34]**.
2 See Form C2.1, cl 6, n 2 at para **[224.34]**.
3 See Form C2.1, cl 6, n 3 at para **[224.34]**.
4 See Form C2.1, cl 6, n 4 at para **[224.34]**
5 See Form C2.1, cl 6, n 5 at para **[224.34]**.
6 See Form C2.1, cl 6, n 6 at para **[224.34]**.

[226.28]

GIFTS MADE FREE OF TAX

6. Any specific gift or pecuniary or general legacy made by this will or any codicil hereto which is expressed to be 'free of tax' shall be free from the

payment of any inheritance tax or foreign tax or duty payable on or by reason of my death to which such gift or legacy would otherwise be subject and such inheritance tax or foreign tax or duty shall be paid out of my residuary estate.[1]

1 Where specific gifts and pecuniary legacies are of, or wholly payable out of, free estate in the UK, the IHT on them will be a testamentary expense payable out of residue without any express provision, and it is only where there is foreign property or settled property being disposed of by the will that a gift which is intended to be free of tax needs to be expressly declared to be free of tax. See also the Note to B14 at paras **[214.59]**–**[214.60]**.

[226.29]

PRIMARY TRUST OF RESIDUE IN FAVOUR OF SPOUSE IF SURVIVING

7. If my [wife/husband] shall survive me[1] my trustees shall hold my residuary estate and the income thereof upon trust for [her/him] absolutely.

1 Residue devolves on the other spouse, if surviving. If the other spouse does not survive the testator, residue is given to the children, see cl 8 at para **[226.25]**. It is not appropriate to incorporate a survivorship condition in the gift to the spouse: see the Notes on survivorship conditions in C2 at **[224.6]** ff and C3 at para **[225.4]**. It may be preferable, if a charge scheme is to be entered into for the spouse (see the reasons given in para **[218.21]**), or if the testators are elderly, to have a life interest (and overriding powers) rather than absolute interest given to the surviving spouse. See, eg, Form C3.5, clauses 6(1) and 7, at paras **[225.75]** and **[225.76]**. If such provisions are substituted, Clause 8 below should be expressed to be subject to the surviving spouse's interest rather than having effect if he or she does not survive the testator, and clause 10(4) (para **[226.33]** – the IHTA 1984, s 89 restriction), if included, should be expressed to operate only if the spouse does not survive the testator (as well as being contingent on the disabled child surviving the relevant day).

[226.30]

ALTERNATIVE GIFT OF RESIDUE ON DISCRETIONARY TRUSTS FOR CHILDREN AND ISSUE

8. (1) If my [wife/husband] shall not survive me[1] my trustees shall hold my residuary estate and the income thereof upon the trusts and with and subject to the powers and provisions hereinafter in this clause declared and contained.

(2) In this clause the following expressions have the following meanings namely:

(a) 'the residuary beneficiaries' means and includes:[2]
  (i) my children and remoter issue;[3]
  (ii) any spouse widow or widower of any of such children or remoter issue (and 'widow' and 'widower' shall include a widow or widower who has remarried);[4]
  (iii) any institution (whether corporate or not) which is established for purposes which are exclusively charitable under the law of England and Wales;[5]

(b) 'the trust period' means the period commencing on the day of my death and expiring on the twenty-first anniversary of the death of the last survivor of my children;[6]

(c) 'the accumulation period' means the period commencing with my death and expiring on the twenty-first anniversary thereof;

(d) 'the relevant day' means the day falling two years less one day after my death.

(3) Subject as provided in clause 10 below[7] my trustees (being not less than two in number or a trust corporation except as hereinafter provided)[8] may at any time or times and from time to time during the trust period exercise either or both of the following powers namely:

(a) power at any time or times and from time to time by deed or deeds revocable or irrevocable to appoint the whole or any part or parts of my residuary estate upon trust for all or such one or more exclusive of the others or other of the residuary beneficiaries if more than one in such shares and either absolutely or at such age or time or respective ages or times and with such trusts and powers for their respective benefit and such provisions as my trustees may think fit and in making any such appointment my trustees shall have powers as full as those which they would possess if they were an absolute beneficial owner of my residuary estate and in particular (but without prejudice to the generality of the foregoing words) my trustees may in any exercise of the foregoing power as they in their absolute discretion think fit:
   (i) to delegate give or impose to or upon themselves or any other person or persons any discretionary powers or discretionary trusts conditions limitations restrictions or provisions including powers of further delegation or powers to create further discretionary trusts or powers;
   (ii) create powers or trusts for the accumulation of income during any period permitted by law;
   (iii) create administrative powers or provisions of whatever nature;

Provided that:
   (i) no such appointment shall invalidate any payment transfer or application of capital or income previously made under any of the trusts or powers herein elsewhere contained;
   (ii) every interest limited under any exercise of such power shall vest in interest (if at all) not later than the expiration of the trust period;
   (iii) any such appointment may be made in respect of income alone without any appointment of capital;
   (iv) any such revocable appointment shall (so far as then unrevoked) cease to be revocable on the expiration of the trust period;
   (v) in any appointment made before the relevant day (but not in any appointment made thereafter) my trustees may make provision for the burden of any testamentary expenses taxes or debts payable out of my estate as between different assets funds shares or interests in such manner and to such extent as my trustees think fit;
   (vi) the foregoing power of appointment may be exercised notwithstanding that there shall have been no grant of probate or administration in respect of the property over which the said power shall be exercised or that the administration of my estate shall not have been completed in respect of such property or any other property comprised in my estate and so long as no such grant as aforesaid has been obtained the persons

who may exercise the foregoing power are the persons hereinbefore named as my executors other than any of them who shall have died or whose appointment as my executor shall have ceased to have effect or who shall have renounced probate of my will;

(vii) the foregoing power of appointment may be exercised before the relevant day by a sole trustee who is not a trust corporation;[9]

(b) power (subject to any or every exercise of the foregoing power) at any time or times and from time to time in their absolute discretion to pay transfer or apply my residuary estate or any part or parts thereof to or for the benefit of all or any one or more exclusive of the others or other of the residuary beneficiaries for the time being in existence if more than one in such shares and generally in such manner as my trustees shall think fit provided that the foregoing power of payment transfer or application of capital may be exercised before the relevant day by a sole trustee who is not a trust corporation.[10]

(4) In default of and subject to any or every exercise of the foregoing powers my trustees shall hold my residuary estate during the trust period upon trust to pay or apply the income thereof to or for the maintenance education or benefit of all or any one or more of the residuary beneficiaries and if more than one in such shares and in such manner generally as my trustees think fit provided that during the accumulation period my trustees may accumulate all or any part or parts of such income by investing the same and the resulting income thereof in any investments hereby authorised and so that any accumulations so made shall form part of the capital of my residuary estate from which such income arose for all purposes.

(5) Subject as aforesaid my trustees shall hold my residuary estate and the income thereof at the expiration of the trust period upon trust for such of my grandchildren and remoter issue as shall be then living in equal shares per stirpes.

(6) Any capital or income of my residuary estate not otherwise disposed of by this clause shall be held in trust for such of my children other than [*name*][11] as shall survive me and if more than one in equal shares.

1 Residue devolves on the other spouse, if surviving. If the other spouse does not survive the testator, residue is given on discretionary trusts for the children etc. It will be taxed as relevant property (see para **[218.8]** ff) unless it is brought within IHTA 1984, s 89 by positive act of the trustees or by clause 10(4) (para **[226.33]**) operating. It is not appropriate to incorporate a survivorship condition in the gift to the spouse: see the Preliminary Notes on survivorship conditions in C2 at para **[224.6]** ff and C3 at para **[225.4]**.

2 For a wider class, including power to add to it, see Form C3.6, cl 3(1)(b) at para **[225.100]**.

3 See cl 4(2), n 1 at para **[226.26]**.

4 Instructions must be taken on the composition of the class. In settlements created after 21 March 2006, the IHT reasons for including spouses etc in a discretionary class are much diminished, because appointing successive interests in possession to spouses or civil partners no longer, in general, gets the spouse or civil partner exemption (see **[200.84]**, **[200.98]**, **[200.99]**).

5 See cl 4(2), n 2 at para **[226.26]**. See also the Note to this form at para **[226.18]**.

6 Since the trusts are principally for the benefit of the disabled child, a common law perpetuity period based on lives (including that of the disabled child) seems appropriate.

See cl 4, nn 1 and 5 at para **[226.26]** on the possibility of restriction of the class of beneficiaries and the relevant lives to those of the children of the marriage.

7 Clause 10 contains a power to release and restrict powers (cl 10(2) at para **[226.32]**) and an optional restriction intended to bring IHTA 1984, s 89 into operation (cl 10(4) and (5) at para **[226.32]**).

8 See proviso (viii) to sub-cl (3)(a) and sub-cl (3)(b) of this clause, for the modification of this provision during the two years following the testator's death. For the appointment of a trust corporation see cl 14 at para **[226.37]** and the note thereto.

9 If it were required that there should be two trustees during the two years after the testator's death, difficulty could arise if the number of trustees was reduced to one and the administration of the estate was not complete, as it is not clear that the statutory power to appoint new trustees could be exercised in such circumstances.

10 See cl 4(4), n 8 at para **[226.26]** and, for the reasons for the proviso, see n 9 above.

11 Ie the name of the disabled child, whom it will probably be appropriate to exclude from this ultimate gift of capital.

[226.31]

ADMINISTRATIVE POWERS[1]

9. (1) In this clause where the context so admits:

(a) the expression 'land' includes buildings and estates interests or rights of any kind in or over land; and

(b) during the administration of my estate the expression 'beneficiary' includes any person who would be a beneficiary if such administration had been completed and the expression 'beneficially interested' and references to income of any asset being payable or capable of being paid to or for the benefit of a beneficiary shall be construed accordingly.

(2) None of the powers or provisions contained in subclause (3) below of this clause shall be capable of being exercised or operating in any manner such that if such power or provision were capable of being so exercised or so operating the existence of the same would:

(i) prevent any person who would in the absence of such power or provision have been entitled to an interest in possession falling within section 49(1A) of the Inheritance Tax Act 1984 in any property from being entitled to such interest; or

(ii) prevent section 71A or 71D of the Inheritance Tax Act 1984 from applying to any property to which in the absence of such power or provision either section would have applied;[2] or

(iii) prevent any person who would in the absence of such power or provision have been treated as entitled to an interest in possession by virtue of section 89 of the Inheritance Tax Act 1984 in any property from being entitled to such interest.

(3) In the administration of my estate and the execution of the trusts hereof or of any codicil hereto my trustees shall (subject to clause 10 below) have the following powers in addition to those conferred by law but subject to the last foregoing subclause:

(a) power to invest moneys sell assets and change investments with the unrestricted freedom of choice and powers of disposition and acquisition of a sole beneficial owner with in particular power to make unsecured loans, acquire non-income yielding assets, and purchase land anywhere in the world ,or chattels for any purpose including occupation or enjoyment in kind by a beneficiary under the power set out below;[3]

(b) power to delegate all or any of their investment powers to a professional investment manager or managers whether individual or corporate and whether or not also a nominee holder of assets for my trustees (and who may be or include one or more of my trustees or the beneficiaries hereunder) upon such terms as to remuneration and otherwise (including terms authorising self-dealing or providing for the limitation of the liability of the investment manager or managers) as my trustees think fit and section 22 of the Trustee Act 2000 shall not apply;[4]

(c) power to vest or register any property in any person or persons whether individual or corporate and whether or not an investment manager to whom powers have been delegated under the foregoing power (and who may be or include one or more of my trustees or the beneficiaries hereunder) as nominee or nominees for my trustees upon such terms as to remuneration or otherwise (including terms authorising self-dealing or providing for the limitation of the liability of the nominee) as my trustees think fit and section 22 of the Trustee Act 2000 shall not apply;[5]

(d) power to borrow money with or without giving security and on such terms as to interest and repayment and otherwise as my trustees may think fit for any purpose connected with the administration of my estate or the trusts declared herein or in any codicil hereto (including investment) and no lender from whom my trustees borrow money in purported exercise of this power shall be concerned to enquire as to the propriety amount or purpose of any such borrowing;[6]

(e) power to lend money to a beneficiary to whom any of the income of such money is payable or to whom or for whose benefit any income of such money is capable of being paid or applied in exercise of a discretion (or who would be such a beneficiary if such money yielded income) and to do so at a full or concessionary rate of interest or interest free;[7]

(f) all the powers of an absolute owner in relation to any land (wherever situated) held by them;[8]

(g) power to apply capital held on the same trusts as any land (or which would be so held if the administration of my estate had been completed) in the improvement or adaptation of such land and to apply such capital or the income of such capital on the repair or maintenance of such land;[9]

(h) power to permit any beneficiary to have the beneficial occupation use or enjoyment in kind of any land or chattel or other tangible property on such terms as to repair insurance or payment of outgoings by the beneficiary or any other person or persons or otherwise howsoever as my trustees think fit including power for the benefit of a beneficiary to permit any other person or persons (whether beneficiaries or not) to occupy use or enjoy any of the types of asset aforesaid together with such beneficiary or otherwise.

Provided that the foregoing power shall only be exercisable and such permission to occupy or enjoy in kind may only continue in the following circumstances:

(i) so long as any of the income of such land chattel or other tangible property is payable to such beneficiary or capable of being paid or applied to him or for his benefit in exercise of a discretion (or would be so payable or capable of being so paid or applied if such land chattel or other property yielded income);

(ii) in the case of land, so long as for the time being the occupation thereof is compatible with any statutory rights of occupation of any other beneficiary or beneficiaries;[10]

(i) power to exercise all the powers of appropriation (and other incidental powers) conferred by statute on a personal representative without the necessity of obtaining any consents and notwithstanding that one or more of my trustees may be beneficially interested in the exercise of such power.[11]

1 See Form C2.1, cl 9, n 1 at para **[224.37]**.
2 See Form C2.1, cl 9, n 2 at para **[224.37]**. This restriction is not needed so long as the trusts are discretionary, but it is included in case trusts of any of these kinds are created by the trustees in exercise of any of their powers.
3 See Form C2.1, cl 9, n 3 at para **[224.37]**.
4 See Form C2.1, cl 9, n 4 at para **[224.37]**.
5 See Form C2.1, cl 9, n 5 at para **[224.37]**.
6 See Form C2.1, cl 9, n 6 at para **[224.37]**.
7 See Form C2.1, cl 9, n 7 at para **[224.37]**.
8 See Form C2.1, cl 9, n 8 at para **[224.37]**.
9 See para **[220.52]** for the reasons for this provision.
10 See Form C2.1, cl 9, n 10 at para **[224.37]**. Express provision for occupation etc by persons other than a beneficiary is added to this subclause to make it clear that the trustees may, eg provide a residence for a disabled beneficiary and someone who is looking after him.
11 See Form C2.1, cl 9, n 11 at para **[224.37]**.

[226.32]

EXERCISE AND RELEASE OF POWERS

10. (1) In this clause:

(a) the expression 'the relevant day' has the same meaning as in clause 8 above of this will;

(b) the expression 'the trust period' has in relation to the trust legacy the same meaning as in clause 4 above of this will and has in relation to my residuary estate the same meaning as in clause 8 above of this will.

(2) My trustees shall have power at any time or times and from time to time during the trust period by deed or deeds to release or restrict all or any of the powers hereinbefore contained (whether dispositive or administrative) or this present power either in whole or in part and in any manner they think fit Provided that except in the case of any exercise of the foregoing power in respect of my residuary estate before the relevant day the trustees shall be at least two in number or a trust corporation.[1]

(3) Any power or discretion hereby or by law conferred on my trustees (including a power or discretion as to the disposition of capital or income)

shall be exercisable notwithstanding that any of my trustees has a personal interest in such exercise [Provided that except in the case of any exercise of a power over my residuary estate before the relevant day[2] there are not fewer than two trustees and at least one of my trustees has no such personal interest].[3]

1 This power could be used to convert the trusts of the trust legacy into discretionary trusts falling within IHTA 1984, s 89 (see para **[226.4]**, sub-paras (vi) and (vii)), and also those of the residuary estate if sub-cls (4) and (5) of this clause are not included in the will. It could also be used to narrow the trustees' powers over capital if it is found that extensive powers over capital exercisable in favour of the disabled child are having an adverse effect on state benefits or local authority provision for him or her, or to restrict their powers so that they cannot create an interest or interests in possession during the disabled child's life if that turns out to be necessary for HMRC to accept that IHTA 1984, s 89 applies (see para **[226.4]**, sub-paras (vi) and (vii)), and it is desired that s 89 should apply.

2 This restriction is only imposed after the initial two-year period from the testator's death because it could cause difficulty for exercise of the powers during the initial period.

3 The words in square brackets should be omitted if the executors and trustees will or might all be members of the testator's family.

[226.33]

RESTRICTION FOR THE PURPOSES OF IHTA 1984, S 89

[(4) If my [son/daughter] [*name of disabled child*] shall be living after the relevant day none of the powers hereinbefore contained shall be exercisable after the relevant day during the life of my said [son/daughter] so as to cause the aggregate amount or value of the capital of my residuary estate which shall for the time being have been applied (within the meaning of section 89(1)(b) of the Inheritance Tax Act 1984) otherwise than for the benefit of my said [son/daughter] to exceed the aggregate amount or value of such capital which shall for the time being have been applied (within the meaning aforesaid) for the benefit of my said [son/daughter] to the intent that section 89 of the Inheritance Tax Act 1984 shall apply to my residuary estate after the relevant day during the life of my said [son/daughter].[1]

(5) Provided that my trustees may by any deed or deeds executed before the relevant day declare that the foregoing subclause (4) of this clause shall not apply to the whole or any part or share of my residuary estate which may be specified in such deed and the operation of the foregoing subclause (4) shall be excluded or restricted accordingly.[2]]

1 This and the next subclause, if included, will restrict the exercise of the trustees' powers after the expiry of two years from the surviving spouse's death in a way which will convert the trusts into 'disabled trusts' within IHTA 1984, s 89, provided that the disabled child is disabled within the meaning of s 89 at the testator's death (see para **[226.4]**, sub-paras (i) and (ii)), and provided that the existence of powers under which the trustees could create an interest in possession during the disabled child's life is compatible with s 89 (see para **[226.4]**, sub-paras (vi) and (vii) and cl 10(2), n 1 at para **[226.32]**). Since the restriction will come into effect no more than two years after the death, its doing so will not constitute a chargeable event and the disabled trusts will be deemed to have been a provision of the testator's will: IHTA 1984, s 144 (see C3 at paras **[225.83]**–**[225.91]**). The restriction applies to the powers in cl 9 as well as those in cl 8, as there are various powers in cl 9 which could be characterised as powers to apply capital, such as the power to permit enjoyment in kind in cl 9(h) and the power to lend in cl 9(e).

2 Subclause (5) enables the executors by deed executed within two years of the death to exclude the operation of sub-cl (4) in relation to the whole or any part of residue. If sub-cls (4) and (5) are omitted, or they are included but the power in sub-cl (5) is exercised, the residuary estate or the part to which the exercise of the power relates will continue to be

held on full discretionary trusts without any restriction on the powers of appointment or application and will be subject to IHT periodic and exit charges under the relevant property regime in IHTA 1984, Pt III, Ch III (see B18 at paras **[218.8]** and **[218.9]**).

[226.34]

RECEIPTS ON BEHALF OF CHARITABLE INSTITUTIONS

11. The receipt of any person who professes to be the treasurer or other proper officer for the time being of any institution (whether corporate or not) shall be a sufficient discharge to my trustees in respect of any money or other asset which becomes payable or transferable to such institution under any exercise of any power or discretion herein contained.

[226.35]

TRUSTEE INDEMNITY

12. (1) My trustees shall not be liable for any act or default of any investment manager or nominee employed in good faith to manage or hold assets of my estate nor for any act or default of any person having the occupation use or enjoyment of property in kind nor for any depreciation wear and tear or damage to any such property while in the possession of any such person.[1]

[(2) Section 11(1) of the Trusts of Land and Appointment of Trustees Act 1996 (consultation with beneficiaries) shall not apply to the exercise by my trustees of their functions in relation to any land subject to the trusts of this my will].[2]

1 This makes it clear that the trustees are not liable for the defaults of others who may have possession or control of trust property, nor for the depreciation of property (such as chattels made available to a disabled beneficiary) which remain trust assets but are being enjoyed in kind. In respect of the defaults of an investment manager or nominee, this indemnity may be wider than that of the TrA 2000, s 23(1) (Part G, para **[246.155]**) which only exempts a trustee from liability for such defaults if he has complied with the statutory duty of care, a standard which may be higher than that of 'good faith'. Whereas it is clear that a wider indemnity such as this can apply where trustees have exercised an express power to appoint an investment manager or nominee, it is not clear that a wider indemnity can be conferred where trustees have exercised the statutory power (see n 4 to cl 8 at para **[224.37]** and Preliminary Note to B21 at para **[221.14]**). For a wider form of indemnity, see e g Form B21.12 at para **[221.16]**. If a paid trustee is to rely on this indemnity clause which may limit his liability in negligence in that it may absolve him from negligent failure to intervene to prevent loss, the testator should specifically be made aware of its meaning and effect (see para **[221.13]** above).

2 The TLATA 1996, s 11(1) which obliges trustees of land to consult beneficiaries of full age and beneficially entitled to an interest in possession, and so far as consistent with the general interest of the trust to give effect to the wishes of those beneficiaries or (in the event of a dispute) the majority by value, will not be relevant so long as the trusts are discretionary, but it may become so in the event that interest in possession trusts are created by the trustees in exercise of any of their powers. In that case the testator may wish to exclude it (Part G, para **[246.114]** and see Preliminary Note to B20 at para **[220.58]**).

[226.36]

PROFESSIONAL TRUSTEE CHARGING CLAUSE

13. Any of my trustees being a professional or business man may charge and be paid all usual professional and other proper charges for business

transacted acts done advice given and time spent by him or his firm in connection with the administration of my estate or in connection with the trusts hereof including acts which a personal representative or trustee not being in any profession or business could have done personally[1].

1 In spite of the TrA 2000, s 29(2) (Part G, para **[246.161]**) giving certain professional trustees authority to charge for their services on or after 1 February 2001, an express remuneration clause entitling any professional or business person to charge may still be advisable: see B21 at para **[221.35]**.

[226.37]

APPOINTMENT OF A TRUST CORPORATION

14. A trust corporation (within the meaning of the Trustee Act 1925) may be appointed a trustee hereof (whether as a sole trustee or jointly with another trustee or trustees) and may charge for so acting in accordance with its published scale of charges at the time of its appointment or on such other basis as may be agreed between the trust corporation and the persons making the appointment.[1]

1 It may become necessary for a trust corporation to take on the trusteeship if suitable family members die or do not want to act. Further, it may be possible and appropriate to appoint a trust corporation which is connected with a charity for persons with the relevant disability. If express provision is not made for a corporate trustee's remuneration, then the TrA 2000, s 29 authorises it to receive reasonable remuneration (Part G, para **[246.161]**). Nonetheless, an express charging clause such as this may be desirable since a particular trust corporation might not be prepared to act in return for the statutory remuneration.

[226.38]

TESTIMONIUM

IN WITNESS whereof I have hereunto set my hand this —— day of ——20——.

[226.39]

ATTESTATION CLAUSE

SIGNED by the above-named [testator/testatrix] as [his/her] last will in the presence of us both present at the same time who at [his/her] request and in [his/her] presence and in the presence of each other have signed our names below as witnesses: [*Signatures, addresses and descriptions of two witnesses*]	}	[*Signature of testator/testatrix*]

[226.40]

Form C4.2: Reciprocal wills for husband and wife with grown-up children of whom one is disabled; gift by first to die of entire estate to survivor subject to a nil-rate band discretionary trust; on the death of the survivor a trust of residue for the children in equal shares with the disabled child's share settled on a 'trust for the vulnerable' within the Finance Act 2005, ss 23–45

Note. This is a variant of Form C4.1 where the trusts of residue on the death of the surviving spouse are completely different. The residuary estate of the second to die is given to the children in equal shares with substitution of remoter descendants in the case of a child predeceasing the testator, and the share of the disabled child is settled on trusts which it is thought will fall within FA 2005, s 34 (trusts for the vulnerable for disabled persons – see **[226.9]** ff above). The share of residue held for the disabled child should also fall within TCGA 1992, Sch 1, para 1, so as to qualify for a full capital gains tax annual exemption (see para **[226.6]** for this). It will apparently not fall within IHTA 1984, s 89 because of the requirement of the latter that there should be no interest in possession throughout the life of the disabled person (see para **[226.4]** (v)), and, if so, it will be subject to the relevant property IHT regime during the initial 21-year accumulation period, and thereafter will be a disabled person's interest in possession which will be beneficiary-taxed (see IHTA 1984, s 89B(1)(c) and para **[200.84]**).

This form may be adapted for use for civil partners, the words 'my wife/husband' being replaced with 'my civil partner' throughout. Care should be taken to identify correctly in each will the children who are to benefit.

[226.41]

REVOCATION CLAUSE

I [*name*] of [*address*] revoke all former testamentary dispositions made by me and declare this to be my last will.

[226.42]

APPOINTMENT OF EXECUTORS AND TRUSTEES AND DEFINITION OF 'MY TRUSTEES'

1. [*As in cl 1 of* Form C4.1 *at para* **[226.23]**.]

[226.43]

APPOINTMENT OF GUARDIANS

2. [*As in cl 2 of* Form C4.1 *at para* **[226.24]**.]

[226.44]

LEGACIES TO TAKE EFFECT ON DEATH OF SECOND TO DIE

3. [*As in cl 3 of* Form C4.1 *at para* **[226.25]**.]

[226.45]

GIFT OF NIL-RATE BAND LEGACY ON DISCRETIONARY TRUSTS

4. [*As in cl 4 of* Form C4.1 *at para* **[226.26]**.]

[226.46]

ADMINISTRATION TRUSTS OF RESIDUE

5. [*As in cl 5 of* Form C4.1 *at para* **[226.27]**.]

[226.47]

GIFTS MADE FREE OF TAX

6. [*As in cl 6 of* Form C4.1 *at para* **[226.28]**.]

[226.48]

PRIMARY TRUST OF RESIDUE IN FAVOUR OF SPOUSE IF SURVIVING

7. If my [wife/husband] shall survive me my trustees shall hold my residuary estate and the income thereof upon trust for [her/him] absolutely.[1]

1 See para **[226.29]** n 1.

[226.49]

TRUST OF RESIDUE FOR CHILDREN AND ISSUE IF SPOUSE NOT SURVIVING

8. (1) If my [wife/husband] shall not survive me my trustees shall hold my residuary estate and the income thereof upon trust for such of my children as shall survive me if more than one in equal shares absolutely subject as provided below.

(2) If for any reason any child of mine does not attain a vested interest under the foregoing trust and there are children or remoter issue of his or hers who survive me and attain the age of 18 years such children and remoter issue shall take in equal shares per stirpes the share such child of mine would have taken if he or she had attained a vested interest and so that no issue shall take whose parent attains a vested interest under the foregoing trust.

(3) If at the time of my death my said [son/daughter] A (hereinafter called 'A') shall be living as a disabled person within the meaning of section 38 of the Finance Act 2005, then the said share of my residuary estate directed to be held upon trust for [him/her] as aforesaid (hereinafter called 'the share') shall not vest absolutely in A but shall be retained by my trustees and held upon the following trusts and with and subject to the following powers:

(a) My trustees shall have power at their absolute discretion to pay transfer or apply the whole or any part or proportion of the income of the share to or for the benefit of A during [his/her] life.

(b) My trustees shall during the period of 21 years commencing with my death while A is living accumulate the income of the share which shall not be paid or applied for the benefit of A as aforesaid as an accretion to the capital of the share but shall have power to pay or apply such accumulations during the life of A as if the same were income of the then current year.

(c) If A is still living at the expiration of the said period of 21 years my trustees shall from the expiration of such period during the remainder of the life of A hold the income of the share arising after the expiration of the said period of 21 years and which shall not be paid or applied for the benefit of A as aforesaid on trust for A absolutely.

(d) Notwithstanding the foregoing trusts and power my trustees shall have power at their absolute discretion during the life of A to pay or apply the whole or any part or parts of the capital of the share to or for the benefit of A.

(e) Subject to the foregoing trusts and to any or every exercise of the foregoing powers my trustees shall hold the share or such part thereof as shall not have been paid or applied as aforesaid and the income thereof upon trust absolutely for such of my children other than A and remoter issue (including any issue of A) as shall be living at the death of A in equal shares per stirpes so that no issue shall take whose parent is living at the death of A and capable of taking.

(f) Section 32 of the Trustee Act 1925 (relating to the payment or application of capital) shall apply to the last foregoing trust without modification during the life of A but after the death of A the said section 32 shall apply to the said trust in all respects as if the words 'one-half of' had been omitted from proviso (a) of subsection (1) thereof.[1]

1 See para **[226.9]** ff for the thinking behind sub-clause (3).

[226.50]

ADMINISTRATIVE POWERS

9. [*As in cl 9 of* Form C4.1 *at para* **[226.31]**.]

[226.51]

EXERCISE AND RELEASE OF POWERS

10. [*As in cl 10(1)–(3) of* Form C4.1 *at para* **[226.32]**.]

[226.52]

RECEIPTS ON BEHALF OF CHARITABLE INSTITUTIONS

11.[As in cl 11 of Form C4.1 at para [226.34].]

[226.53]

TRUSTEE INDEMNITY

12. [*As in cl 12 of* Form C4.1 *at para* **[226.35]**.]

[226.54]

PROFESSIONAL TRUSTEE CHARGING CLAUSE

13. [*As in cl 13 of* Form C4.1 *at para* **[226.36]**.]

[226.55]

APPOINTMENT OF A TRUST CORPORATION

14. [*As in cl 14 of* Form C4.1 *at para* **[226.37]**.]

[226.56]

TESTIMONIUM AND ATTESTATION CLAUSES

[*As in* Form C4.1 *at paras* **[226.38]** *and* **[226.39]**.]

[226.57]

Form C4.3: Will providing for spouse suffering from mental disorder

Note. This form incorporates a nil-rate band legacy on discretionary trusts under which the mentally disabled spouse is a beneficiary, and then settles residue on trusts for the benefit of the spouse which by virtue of IHTA 1984, s 89 will be treated as conferring an interest in possession on the spouse. The estate is thus made fully available for the upkeep of the spouse while minimising the spouse's entitlement to assets, and making sure that no IHT is paid on the testator's death if the spouse survives the testator. It is no longer necessary to have a nil-rate band trust under the will of the first to die in order to avoid wasting the first to die's nil-rate band, except in the special circumstances discussed in para **[200.130]**. The main point of having such a trust in this case is that the nil-rate band trust fund is available for the benefit of the surviving spouse, but it is not subject to the restrictions required by IHTA 1984, s 89 and can thus be more freely used to benefit other beneficiaries if it is not needed for the support of the surviving spouse. If within the period of two years after the testator's death it is decided that the nil-rate band trust is not wanted, it can be appointed on appropriate trusts for the surviving spouse so that the estate is wholly exempt, in reliance on IHTA 1984, s 144 (see paras **[225.83]** ff).

This form may be adapted for use for civil partners, the words 'my wife/husband' being replaced with 'my civil partner' throughout. Care should be taken to identify correctly in each will the children who are to benefit.

[226.58]

REVOCATION CLAUSE

I [*name*] of [*address*] revoke all former testamentary dispositions made by me and declare this to be my last will.

[226.59]

APPOINTMENT OF EXECUTORS AND TRUSTEES AND DEFINITION OF 'MY TRUSTEES'

1. I appoint [*name*] of [*address*] and [*name*] of [*address*] (hereinafter together called 'my trustees' which expression shall where the context so admits include my personal representatives for the time being and the trustees for the time being hereof) to be the executors and trustees of this will.

[226.60]

BEQUEST OF PERSONAL CHATTELS[1]

2. (1) I give the following items free of tax:[2]
[(a) To my son [*name*] my father's signet ring;
(b) to my daughter [*name*] my mother's engagement ring;]

(2) If my [wife/husband] [*name*] ('my [wife/husband]') shall survive me then subject as aforesaid I give all my personal chattels as defined by section 55(1)(x) of the Administration of Estates Act 1925[3] to my trustees free of tax to hold the same upon trust as follows:
(a) my trustees shall have power during the life of my [wife/husband] to distribute the said chattels among the legacy beneficiaries (as defined in clause 3 below) or any one or more of them and in such manner as my trustees think fit;
(b) my trustees shall have power during the life of my [wife/husband] to sell any of the said chattels and to dispose of any thereof which are of little value to any person and in any manner (including power to dispose of the same for no consideration) as they think fit;
(c) subject to and in default of any distribution or disposal as aforesaid my trustees shall hold the said chattels and any proceeds of sale thereof on trust for my [wife/husband] during [her/his] life (and clauses 8 to 13 below shall apply to such chattels and proceeds of sale);
(d) subject as aforesaid my trustees shall hold the said chattels or their proceeds of sale as part of my residuary estate.[4]

1 If the testator's spouse survives the testator, it is not appropriate for the chattels to go to the spouse absolutely (because of the spouse's mental incapacity), nor is it appropriate for them

to fall into the residuary estate as there are no powers to distribute the capital of the latter to persons other than the spouse (contrast the extensive powers over residue in Form C4.1, cl 8, at para **[226.30]**).

2 See Form C3.1, cl 2, n 2 at para **[225.12]**. The words 'free of tax' would only be of significance if the items given were outside the UK at the testator's death.

3 See Part G, para **[246.67]** for the wording of this definition, and for further discussion of the meaning of 'personal chattels' see Vol 1, para **[64.44]**.

4 With a disposition in this form, if the testator's spouse survives the testator, the IHT spouse exemption will apply to the chattels on the testator's death, and that will not be affected by subsequent distribution to other persons: neither of IHTA 1984, s 143 (see B4 at paras **[204.9]** and **[204.10]**) or s 144 (see C3 at paras **[225.83]**–**[225.91]**) will apply. A wider class of objects of the discretion could be introduced as in sub-cls (4) and (5) of Form B4.11 at para **[204.25]**.

If it is preferred to have a non-exempt gift of chattels, at any rate so far as they do not fall into the residuary estate, a short-term discretionary trust such as that in Form B4.11 at para **[204.25]** could be used; if it is used, Form B4.11 should perhaps be varied so that the trustees can add chattels to the residuary estate before the period of two years from death has ended, so that the size of the non-exempt estate apart from cl 3, and thus the size of the nil-rate band legacy given by cl 3, can be ascertained at an early date.

[226.61]

GIFT OF NIL-RATE BAND LEGACY ON DISCRETIONARY TRUSTS

3. [*As in cl 4 of* Form C4.1 *at para* **[226.26]**.]

[226.62]

ADMINISTRATION TRUSTS OF RESIDUE

4. [*As in cl 5 of* Form C4.1 *at para* **[226.27]**.]

[226.63]

GIFTS MADE FREE OF TAX

5. [*As in cl 6 of* Form C4.1 *at para* **[226.28]**.]

[226.64]

BENEFICIAL TRUSTS OF RESIDUE FOR SPOUSE[1]

6. During the life of my [wife/husband] my trustees shall hold my residuary estate and the income thereof upon the trusts following:

[Either]

[(a) My trustees shall apply the income of my residuary estate for the maintenance or otherwise for the benefit of my [wife/husband] in such manner as they shall think fit]

[Or]

[(a) My trustees shall pay or apply the income of my residuary estate to or for the maintenance of any one or more of the following persons namely my [wife/husband] and children and remoter issue[2] and if more than one in such shares and generally in such manner as my trustees think fit [Provided that during the period commencing on my death and expiring on the twenty-first anniversary thereof or on the earlier death of my [wife/husband] my trustees may accumulate the whole or any part of such income by investing the same and the resulting income thereof in any of the investments hereby authorised and the accumulations so made shall form part of the capital of my residuary estate for all purposes;]]

(b) Notwithstanding the foregoing trust my trustees (being not fewer than two in number or a trust corporation) may at any time or times and from time to time during the life of my [wife/husband] apply the whole or any part or parts of my residuary estate for [her/his] maintenance support or benefit in such manner as they think fit.

1 This clause contains alternative forms of provision for the benefit of the mentally disabled spouse in sub-cl (a), the first requiring the trustees to apply all the trust income for her or his benefit, and the second creating a discretionary trust of income for the testator's spouse and the children and remoter issue (subject again to an optional power to accumulate income). Whichever is selected is followed by a power in sub-cl (b), which enables the trustees to resort to capital for the spouse's maintenance.

The first version of sub-cl (a) would give rise to an actual interest in possession for IHT purposes. If there is uncertainty as to whether the spouse will qualify as a disabled person within the definition in IHTA 1984, s 89(4)–(6), this will have the advantage that he or she will have an IPDI, qualifying for beneficiary-taxed treatment and thus spouse exemption, if the spouse does not qualify as a disabled person. It is thought that the second form of sub-cl (a) would (together with sub-cl (b)) be treated for IHT purposes as giving rise to a deemed interest in possession under IHTA 1984, s 89(1) and (2). It is thought that the first form of sub-cl (a) would qualify the trust for the full capital gains tax annual allowance: see in particular the TCGA 1992, Sch 1, para 1(1)(b) and para **[226.6]**. On the other hand, the first version of sub-cl (a) could result in the whole of the income being taken into account as the spouse's in any means test for benefit purposes. See for the social security and fiscal implications of disabled trusts the Preliminary Note at para **[226.2]** ff.

2 It may be advantageous to add spouses, widows and widowers of the children and remoter issue.

[226.65]

REMAINDER TRUSTS FOR CHILDREN AND ISSUE

7. (1) Subject as aforesaid my trustees shall hold my residuary estate and the income thereof upon trust for such of my children as shall survive me and if more than one in equal shares absolutely.

(2) Provided that if any of my children shall predecease me leaving a child or children surviving me such last-mentioned child or children shall take and if more than one equally between them the share of my residuary estate which such deceased child of mine would have taken had he or she survived me.

(3) Section 32 of the Trustee Act 1925 (relating to advancement) shall apply in relation to the foregoing trusts in this clause contained without modification during the life of my [wife/husband] but after the death of my [wife/husband] the said section 32 shall apply to the said trusts as if the words 'one half of' were omitted from proviso (a) to subsection (1) thereof.[1]

1 IHTA 1984, s 89 is not prevented from applying to settled property by reason of the statutory power of advancement applying to it during the disabled person's life, provided that it is not subject to modification: see IHTA 1984, s 89(3).

[226.66]

ADMINISTRATIVE POWERS

8. [*As in cl 9 of* Form C4.1 *at para* **[226.31]**, *amending '(subject to cl 10 below)' in the second line of cl 9(3) to '(subject to cl 9 below)'.*]

[226.67]

EXERCISE AND RELEASE OF POWERS

9. (1) My trustees (being not fewer than two in number or a trust corporation) shall have power at any time or times and from time to time during the life of my [wife/husband] by deed or deeds to release or restrict all or any of the powers hereinbefore contained (whether dispositive or administrative) or this present power either in whole or in part and in any manner they think fit.[1]

(2) Any power or discretion hereby or by law conferred on my trustees (including a power or discretion as to the disposition of capital or income) shall be exercisable notwithstanding that any of my trustees has a personal interest in such exercise [provided that at least one of my trustees has no such personal interest].[2]

(3) None of the powers hereinbefore contained shall be exercisable while my [wife/husband] is living so as to cause the aggregate amount or value of the capital of my residuary estate which shall for the time being have been applied (within the meaning of section 89(1)(b) of the Inheritance Tax Act 1984) other than for the benefit of my [wife/husband] to exceed the aggregate amount or value of such capital which shall for the time being have been applied (within the meaning aforesaid) for the benefit of my [wife/husband] to the intent that section 89 of the Inheritance Tax Act 1984 shall apply to my residuary estate during the life of my [wife/husband].][3]

1 The main reason for including such a power is in case any of the powers turn out to be regarded by HMRC as incompatible with IHTA 1984, s 89. For the main concern of this kind, see para **[226.4]**, sub-paras (vi) and (vii). It could also be useful where the first alternative cl 6(a) at para **[226.64]**, including the proviso permitting accumulation of income, has been included in the will, and it is found that HMRC will not accept that IHTA 1984, s 89 applies, but would accept that there would be an interest in possession if the power to accumulate were released; if the release were effected during the two years after the testator's death the spouse exemption might be obtained on the testator's death by virtue of IHTA 1984, s 144 (see C3 at paras **[225.83]**–**[225.91]**).

2 The words in square brackets should be omitted if the executors and trustees will or might all be members of the testator's family.

3 The purpose of this subclause is to make sure that the condition as to powers over capital in IHTA 1984, s 89(1)(b) is satisfied. Although the main dispositive power over capital in this form, ie cl 6(b) at para **[226.64]** can only be applied in favour of the spouse, it is possible that some of the administrative powers in cl 8 could be exercised so as to apply capital for other beneficiaries.

[226.68]

RECEIPTS ON BEHALF OF CHARITABLE INSTITUTIONS

10. [*As in cl 11 of* Form C4.1 *at para* **[226.34]**.]

[226.69]

TRUSTEE INDEMNITY

11. [*As in cl 12 of* Form C4.1 *at para* **[226.35]**.]

[226.70]

PROFESSIONAL TRUSTEE CHARGING CLAUSE

12. [*As in cl 13 of* Form C4.1 *at para* **[226.36]**.]

[226.71]

APPOINTMENT OF A TRUST CORPORATION

13. [*As in cl 14 of* Form C4.1 *at para* **[226.37]**.]

[*Testimonium and attestation clause as in* Form C4.1 *at paras* **[226.38]** and **[226.39]**.

C5 Wills where there is more than one family

Preliminary note .... [227.1]

FORMS

C5.1 Will of twice-married testator who has adult children from his first marriage and minor children from his second and who owns the matrimonial home; nil-rate band discretionary trust, and gift of residue on trust for second wife for life with remainder to all the testator's children .... [227.7]

C5.2 Reciprocal wills of spouses both having adult children by previous marriages (but none by their own), the first to die making a nil-rate band gift to his or her own children and giving the survivor a life interest in residue with remainder to his or her own children, and the survivor leaving his or her estate to his or her own children .... [227.25]

C5.3 Reciprocal wills of spouses both having adult children by previous marriages (but none by their own), the first to die giving the survivor his or her estate absolutely and the survivor dividing his or her estate between children and stepchildren .... [227.39]

C5.4 Will of married man with adult children making provision for an illegitimate child who is a minor by means of a settled legacy......... [227.50]

PRELIMINARY NOTE

[227.1]

This section contains forms for use by married couples where one or both of the spouses have children by someone other than his or her present spouse. They can be adapted for use by civil partners who have children. The forms in this section do not contain any provision for a former spouse or civil partner; it is assumed that either any former spouse or civil partner is either dead, or that there was a divorce or dissolution with a clean break financial settlement and with an order having been made by the court under the Inheritance (Provision for Family and Dependants) Act 1975 (I(PFD)A 1975), s 15 or 15ZA (as substituted by CPA 2004) that the former spouse or civil partner shall not be entitled on the death of the testator to make a claim under that Act (Part G, paras **[247.17]**, **[247.18]**).

For wills for unmarried couples see C6 at para **[228.1]** ff, for wills for childless couples see C9 at para **[231.1]**, and for a will of someone who is separated and may divorce see Form C6.3 at para **[228.33]** ff.

[227.2]

The destination of property after the second death. Wills for married couples where one or both has children by someone other than the other spouse frequently have in common with wills for childless couples (for which see C9 at para **[231.1]** ff) that each wants to benefit the other if he or she is the first to die, but wants to benefit different ultimate beneficiaries from those the other wants to benefit after the death of the survivor. Reciprocal wills and the ultimate destination of property is discussed in the Preliminary Note to

C2 at para **[224.9]** ff and in the Preliminary Note to C9 at para **[231.7]** ff. Forms C5.1 and C5.2 (at paras **[227.7]** and **[227.25]**) deal with this problem by providing a life interest in residue for the surviving spouse, with remainders to named children of the testator. Form C5.3 (at para **[227.39]**) adopts the strategy of the first to die leaving his or her estate to the other, and the survivor leaving his or her estate to the children and stepchildren in proportions intended to reflect the relative assets of each of the spouses (for an alternative approach see Form C9.6 at para **[231.62]**). Where both spouses have the same wishes as to the ultimate destination of their property, there may well be forms in C2 (at para **[224.1]** ff) and C3 (at para **[225.1]** ff) which will be readily capable of adaptation for their use.

[227.3]

Nil-rate band discretionary trusts. The announcement of nil-rate band carry-forward on 9 October 2007 (see para **[200.75]**) means that the inclusion of nil-rate band discretionary trusts (or other nil-rate band non-exempt gifts) in the will of the first to die of a married couple or civil partnership is in most cases no longer necessary or advisable in order to make use of the nil-rate band of the first to die. The circumstances in which a nil-rate band discretionary trust may still have a use are summarised in para **[200.130]**. One such use which can be of particular relevance to the forms in C5 is where either or both parties to a marriage or civil partnership have been in a previous marriage or civil partnership which ended with the death of the other party, and the . If that other party did not make full use of his or her available nil-rate band: see para **[227.8]** and Form C5.1, cl 5, at para **[227.14]**.

[227.4]

Survivorship conditions. On the utility of conditions as to surviving the testator by a particular period see the Preliminary Note to C2 at paras **[224.6]** ff. For the reasons there given survivorship conditions are no longer recommended as between spouses or civil partners. Accordingly the forms in C5 do not include them.

[227.5]

Trusts for children. The two categories of favoured trusts for minor children and young adults, 'trusts for bereaved minors' within IHTA 1984, s 71A (see para **[200.108]**) and 'age 18-to-25 trusts' within IHTA 1984, s 71D (see para **[200.109]**), can only be created by the will of a parent of the beneficiary or beneficiaries. Under general statutory provision this will include parents who have acquired that status through adoption (see Vol 1, paras **[75.1]**–**[75.4]**) or any of the processes falling within the Human Fertilisation and Embryology Act 1990 (see Vol 1, paras **[74.5]**–**[74.8]**). In addition, IHTA 1984, s 71H extends the meaning of 'parent', for the purposes of s 71A and 71D, to include a step-parent and someone who at the time of his death has parental responsibility for the beneficiary or beneficiaries. Further, step-parent includes the civil partner of a parent: CPA 2004, s 246, and see also the definition of 'stepchild' in IHTA 1984, s 272. It should be remembered, however, that parental responsibility ends when the child attains the age of 18, and that the status of step-parent is lost if there is a divorce or dissolution of the marriage or civil partnership.

Therefore, so far as a gift by will is to beneficiaries who are not children or stepchildren of the testator, nor ones for which he has parental responsibility, IHTA 1984, s 71A and 71D cannot apply. The property subject to trusts not so qualifying will be relevant property (see para **[218.8]** ff), except where a beneficiary has an interest in possession (while still under the age of vesting of capital, if any) commencing from the death of the testator or within two years after his or her death, in which case it will be subject to an IPDI.

For the possibilities for trusts for children see para **[200.132]**.

[227.6]

Guardianship. A guardian of a minor child can be appointed by anyone with parental responsibility for that child: see Vol 1, paras **[28.1]**, **[28.2]**. A way in which parental responsibility for a child may be acquired which is particularly relevant to C5 is that a person who is not a parent of that child, but is married to or in a civil partnership with a parent who has parental responsibility for that child, may acquire parental responsibility for that child by a parental responsibility agreement (to which both parents of the child must agree if they both have parental responsibility) or by a court order (ChA 1989, s 4A, inserted by the Adoption and Children Act 2002, Part G, para **[244.116]**). Where a step-parent does not have parental responsibility for a child, it may be appropriate for the parent's will to appoint the step-parent guardian of that child, particularly where the parent is the only person with parental responsibility for the child. A subsequent divorce or dissolution of the marriage or civil partnership of the parent and step-parent will revoke the appointment in the absence of a contrary intention expressed in the appointment (ChA 1989, s 6(3A) and (3B), Part G, para **[244.117]**).

[227.7]

Form C5.1: Will of twice-married testator who has adult children from his first marriage and minor children from his second and who owns the matrimonial home; nil-rate band discretionary trust, and gift of residue on trust for second wife for life with remainder to all the testator's children

Note. This is not one of a pair of wills. It is assumed that the husband is well-off, and wealthier than his wife, and that she will leave her estate exclusively to her children. This form can, however, be readily adapted for the converse situation. It is assumed that the testator wishes to provide support for his wife, and the children of the second marriage while minors, but wishes to ensure, so far as practical, that the capital goes ultimately to all his children including the children of the first marriage. It is also assumed that relations between his present wife and the children of his previous marriage are not especially warm, and that he feels that it is unlikely that any capital which he gives to his wife absolutely will be passed on by her to those children. This form can be adapted to cope with civil partners by substituting 'civil partner' for 'wife' where it occurs in clause 2 **[227.11]**, 5 **[227.14]**, 6 **[227.15]** and 9 **[227.18]**.

[227.8]

The will includes a nil-rate band discretionary legacy, for the following possible reasons. If the testator's previous marriage ended as a result of the death of his previous wife, and she did not make dispositions on her death which made full use of her nil-rate band, he will have a potential entitlement to additional nil-rate band. This will be wholly or partly wasted under the nil-rate carry-forward rules unless the first to die of the testator and his present wife makes a nil-rate band using-up non-exempt gift by his or her will, because of the overall limit on nil-rate band carry-forward of a 100 per cent uplift: see paras **[200.75]** and **[200.130]**, and the optional wording for this situation in cl 5(1) of this form at para **[227.14]**. Other purposes might be to provide a fund from which the children, in particular the children of the previous marriage, can benefit before the present wife's death, or to provide maximum asset protection from the wife's creditors or subsequent husbands or partners, or from being used up in care-home fees. Under this discretionary trust the income can be used to support the wife but the capital goes to the children, and residue is given to the wife for life with remainders to the children. There is an optional power to pay or apply part of the capital of residue to or for the benefit of the wife. It will be important for the testator to leave a letter of wishes. If there is a power to pay capital to or for the benefit of the wife it will be particularly important for him to indicate the circumstances in which he wants it to be exercised.

[227.9]

REVOCATION CLAUSE

I [*name*] of [*address*] hereby revoke all former testamentary dispositions made by me and declare this to be my last will.

[227.10]

APPOINTMENT OF EXECUTORS AND TRUSTEES

1. I appoint [*name*] of [*address*] and [*name*] of [*address*][1] (hereinafter together called 'my trustees' which expression shall include my personal representatives for the time being and the trustees for the time being hereof) to be the executors and trustees of this will.

1 It is assumed that the testator's wife is not appointed an executor or trustee. The choice of executors and trustees will have to be made carefully, as they may have to keep a balance between the widow and the children, especially the children of the first marriage.

[227.11]

APPOINTMENT OF GUARDIANS[1]

2. If my wife [*name*] ('my wife') shall predecease me I appoint [*name*] of [*address*] [and [*name*] of [*address*]] to be the [guardian/guardians] of the children of our marriage during their respective minorities.

1 This form assumes that the children of the second marriage are under 18. For the reasons given in the Preliminary Note to C2 at para **[224.1]**, the appointment will take effect only if the wife dies first. It is assumed that her will has a corresponding provision so that if she survives the testator but dies while the children are still minors the same persons will be appointed guardians.

[227.12]

GIFT OF CHATTELS[1]

3. (1) I give free of tax[2] the following items:
   (a) to my son [*name*] [my guns and fishing tackle];
   (b) to my daughter [*name*] [my mother's engagement ring];
   (c) to my son [*name*] [my gold watch].

(2) Subject as aforesaid I give all my personal chattels as defined by section 55(1)(x) of the Administration of Estates Act 1925[3] to my wife if she shall survive me [and I request her (but without imposing any trust or binding obligation on her) to give effect to any wishes as to the disposition of such chattels which may be contained in any memorandum that may be

found amongst my papers at my death or which may have otherwise been communicated to her during my life].[4]

1 It is not usually appropriate or practical to settle chattels, because the trouble and expense of administering them is usually out of all proportion to their value, unless they are exceptionally valuable ones. Accordingly, as the residuary estate is settled on trust for the testator's wife for life, this absolute gift of chattels is included. For alternative forms see B4, at paras **[204.15]–[204.34]**.

2 See Form C8.1, cl 3, n 2 at para **[230.6]**.

3 See Part G, para **[246.67]** for the wording of this definition, and for further discussion of the meaning of 'personal chattels' see Vol 1, para **[64.44]**.

4 If property bequeathed by a will to one person is distributed to another person in accordance with wishes expressed by the testator within two years of his death, it is treated for IHT purposes as having been bequeathed by the will to that other person: IHTA 1984, s 143, and see B4 at paras **[204.9]** and **[204.10]**. Where it is the testator's spouse to whom the property is bequeathed in the first place, s 143 will operate disadvantageously as it will cause the property so distributed by the spouse to cease being part of an exempt gift and to become part of a chargeable one. Where this is a problem, e g where large values are involved, the spouse could wait until after two years from the testator's death to distribute in accordance with his wishes.

[227.13]

GIFT OF LEGACIES

4. I give free of tax[1] the following legacies:
   (a) to [*name*] the sum of £——;
   (b) to [*name*] the sum of £——;
   (c) to [*name*] the sum of £——.

1 See Form C3.1, cl 2, n 2 at para **[225.12]**.

[227.14]

GIFT OF NIL-RATE BAND LEGACY ON DISCRETIONARY TRUSTS[1]

Either

5. (1) If my wife shall survive me[2] then I give to my legacy trustees (hereafter defined) a pecuniary legacy of the maximum sum (if any) which can in the circumstances subsisting at my death be given by this clause without any liability being incurred for the payment of inheritance tax on or by reason of my death and in particular (without prejudice to the generality of the foregoing) for the purpose of determining the amount of such maximum sum the circumstances to be taken into account shall include all chargeable transfers made by me during my life (or events treated as such for inheritance tax purposes) so far as relevant for the computation of inheritance tax on my death the dispositions taking effect under this will (apart from this clause) or under any codicil hereto and any property treated as if it were part of my estate for inheritance tax purposes [and furthermore in determining the foregoing maximum sum it shall be assumed that the nil-rate band maximum (within the meaning of Section 8A of the Inheritance Tax Act 1984) at the time of my death will be treated as increased for the purposes of the charge to inheritance tax on my death by any amount by which it would be treated as increased if a claim was made under that section and I direct my Trustees to make such a claim].[3]

Or

(1) If my wife shall survive me[4] then I give to my legacy trustees (hereafter defined) a pecuniary legacy of whichever is the less of:

(a) the amount by which the nil-rate band maximum (within the meaning of section 8A of the Inheritance Tax Act 1984) at the time of my death would be treated as increased for the purposes of the charge to inheritance tax on my death if a claim was made under that section; or

(b) the maximum sum (if any) which can in the circumstances subsisting at my death be given by this clause without any liability being incurred for the payment of inheritance tax on or by reason of my death and in particular (without prejudice to the generality of the foregoing) for the purpose of determining the amount of such maximum sum the circumstances to be taken into account shall include all chargeable transfers made by me during my life (or events treated as such for inheritance tax purposes) so far as relevant for the computation of inheritance tax on my death the dispositions taking effect under this will (apart from this clause) or under any codicil hereto and any property treated as if it were part of my estate for inheritance tax purposes and furthermore in determining such maximum sum it shall be assumed that the nil-rate band maximum (within the meaning of section 8A of the Inheritance Tax Act 1984) at the time of my death will be treated as increased for the purposes of the charge to inheritance tax on my death by any amount by which it would be treated as increased if a claim was made under that section and I direct my trustees to make such a claim.[5]

(2) In this clause the following expressions have the following meanings, namely:

(a) 'the income beneficiaries' means my wife and my children and remoter issue;

(b) 'the capital beneficiaries' means my children and remoter issue;

(c) 'my legacy trustees' means and includes [*name*] of [*address*] and [*name*] of [*address*] or other the trustee or trustees for the time being of the trust legacy[6];

(d) 'the trust period' means the period commencing on my death and expiring on the twenty-first anniversary of the death of my wife;[7]

(e) 'the accumulation period' means the period commencing with my death and expiring on the twenty-first anniversary thereof.

(3) My legacy trustees shall hold the said legacy upon trust to invest the same in any investments hereby authorised with power to vary the same and shall hold the said legacy and the assets from time to time representing the same (hereinafter called 'the trust legacy') and the income thereof upon trust for all or such one or more of the capital beneficiaries at such ages or times in such shares and upon such trusts for the benefit of the capital beneficiaries as my legacy trustees (being at least two in number [or a trust corporation][8]) may by deed or deeds revocable or irrevocable executed at any time or times during the trust period appoint and in making any such appointment my legacy trustees shall have powers as full as those which they would

possess if they were an absolute beneficial owner of the trust legacy and in particular (but without prejudice to the generality of the foregoing words) my legacy trustees may in any exercise of the foregoing power as they in their absolute discretion think fit:

(a) delegate give or impose to or upon themselves or any other person or persons and in relation to any trust or disposition any discretionary powers or discretionary trusts conditions limitations restrictions or provisions including powers of further delegation or powers to create further discretionary trusts or powers;[9]

(b) create trusts or powers for the accumulation of income during any period permitted by law;

(c) create administrative powers or provisions of whatever nature;

Provided that:

(i) no such appointment shall invalidate any payment transfer or application of capital or income previously made under any of the trusts or powers herein elsewhere contained;

(ii) every interest limited under any exercise of such power shall vest in interest (if at all) not later than the expiration of the trust period;

(iii) any such appointment may be made in respect of income alone without any appointment of capital; and

(iv) any such revocable appointment shall (so far as then unrevoked) cease to be revocable on the expiration of the trust period.

(4) In default of and subject to any exercise of the foregoing power my legacy trustees (being at least two in number [or a trust corporation][10]) may at their discretion at any time or times during the trust period pay transfer or apply to or for the benefit of all or any one or more of the capital beneficiaries for the time being living the whole or any part or parts of the trust legacy in any manner they in their absolute discretion think fit.[11]

(5) Subject to any or every exercise of the foregoing powers my legacy trustees shall during the trust period hold the trust legacy upon trust to pay or apply the income thereof to or for the maintenance education or benefit of all or any one or more of the income beneficiaries for the time being living in such shares if more than one and generally in such manner as they think fit provided that my legacy trustees may during the accumulation period accumulate the whole or any part of the income of the trust legacy by investing the same and the resulting income thereof in any of the investments hereby authorised and any accumulations of income so made shall form part of the capital of the trust legacy from which such income arose for all purposes [provided that my legacy trustees shall have power during the trust period to pay or apply such accumulations of income as if they were income of the current year].[12]

(6) Subject to the foregoing trust and any or every exercise of the foregoing powers my legacy trustees shall hold the trust legacy and the income thereof at the expiration of the trust period in trust absolutely for such of my children and remoter issue as shall then be living in equal shares per stirpes so that no child or issue of mine shall take a share if his or her parent is living at the expiration of the trust period and so capable of taking.

(7) Any capital or income of the trust legacy not otherwise disposed of by this clause shall be held in trust for such of my children as shall survive me if more than one in equal shares absolutely.

(8) Instead of the trust legacy being satisfied by the payment of cash or by the appropriation of property[13]:

(a) my trustees may charge (with or without there being any personal liability of any person or persons) any property which is (or but for this clause would be) comprised in my residuary estate with payment of a sum of money equal to or less than the amount of the trust legacy to my legacy trustees and my legacy trustees shall accept such charge for such sum as the whole or a part (as the case may be) of the trust legacy; and

(b) my trustees may require my legacy trustees to accept in satisfaction of all or part of the trust legacy a binding promise of payment (secured or unsecured) made personally by my wife or by my trustees as trustees of my residuary estate which debt shall be payable on demand and my legacy trustees shall accept such debt as the whole or a part (as the case may be) of the trust legacy.

(9) The following shall apply in relation to the powers in the last preceding subclause:

(a) my trustees may require to be included such terms if any as they think fit in relation to a charge under subclause (8)(a) above or a debt under subclause (8)(b) above including terms as to interest (if any) and terms linking the debt or sum charged to the Retail Prices Index or otherwise providing for its amount to vary with the passage of time according to a formula provided that the debt or sum charged shall be payable to my legacy trustees on demand and the charge shall be enforceable by my legacy trustees at any time;

(b) my legacy trustees may leave the charge or debt outstanding for as long as they think fit and refrain from exercising their rights in relation to it and waive the payment of all or any part of any interest due in respect of it and may accept any substitute debt or charge undertaken or created by any person;

(c) my trustees may assent to the vesting of my residuary estate subject to an outstanding obligation to pay or satisfy the trust legacy and my legacy trustees may appoint new trustees in exercise of the statutory power to do so before the trust legacy has been paid or satisfied;[14]

(d) my legacy trustees and my trustees shall not be liable if my wife is or becomes unable to pay the debt or any security is or becomes inadequate or for any other loss or disadvantage which may occur as a result of their exercising or choosing not to exercise any of the foregoing powers; and

(e) the foregoing powers are in addition to any other powers given by this will or any codicil or by the general law and the foregoing powers may be exercised even though my trustees and my legacy trustees are the same persons or my wife is among either or both sets of trustees provided that such powers shall not be exercisable by a sole trustee who is my wife.

(10) My trustees may constitute the trust legacy wholly or partly by appropriating to it at their discretion any property or proportionate share of any property and for this purpose may take such advice as to the value of the said property or proportionate share as they think fit.[15]

(11) Where the trust legacy is for the time being wholly or partly constituted by a proportionate share of a dwellinghouse or other property my legacy trustees shall have all the powers of an absolute owner in relation to such share and property and in particular may at their discretion join with the other proprietor or proprietors of such property:

(i) to permit an income beneficiary under the trusts of the trust legacy to have the use or enjoyment of the property in kind on such terms as my legacy trustees think fit; or

(ii) to effect or enable a sale of the property and the purchase of another property in the same or similar co-ownership with the trust legacy constituted by a proportionate share thereof.

(12) The powers and provisions of clauses 10 to 13 inclusive hereof shall apply to the trust legacy with references therein to 'my trustees' being treated as references to 'my legacy trustees'.

1 See Form C3.1, cl 3, n 1 at para **[225.13]**. For a discussion of nil-rate band discretionary trusts, see B18 at paras **[218.16]–[218.32]**. For the possible reasons for including a nil-rate band discretionary trust in a will of this type see para **[227.8]**. This trust will be subject to the IHT relevant property regime, for which see **[218.8]** ff.

The trusts of this legacy are such that the widow is an object of the discretionary trust of income, but capital can only be appointed, paid or applied for the benefit of the children and remoter issue. If the testator dies while the children of the second marriage are still minors the capital can be used to pay for their education or support, which will relieve the widow of expense she would otherwise incur.

If the testator prefers the trusts to include powers to appoint, pay or apply capital in favour of the widow, Form C3.4, cl 2 at para **[225.60]** could be substituted.

2 See Form C3.1, cl 3, n 2 at para **[225.13]**.

3 This sub-cl without the words at the end in square brackets is for use where the testator does not have a potential enhanced nil-rate band under the nil-rate band carry-forward rules (i e his previous marriage ended in divorce), but he has other reasons for including a nil-rate band discretionary trust (see paras **[200.130]** and **[227.8]**). The provision at the end in square brackets should be added if the testator does have a potential increased nil-rate band under the nil-rate band carry-forward rules (i e his previous marriage ended with the death of his previous wife, and she did not use all her nil-rate band), and he wishes the trust fund to be a legacy of the whole of his available nil-rate band. If the testator does have -a potential increased nil-rate band under the nil-rate band carry-forward rules his current wife should make a will containing a nil-rate band discretionary trust to take effect if she dies first, to avoid waste of the nil-rate band in the event of her doing so.

4 See Form C3.1, cl 3, n 2 at para **[225.13]**.

5 This second alternative sub-cl (1) is for the case where the testator does have a potential increased nil-rate band under the nil-rate band carry-forward rules (i e his previous marriage ended with the death of his previous wife, and she did not use all her nil-rate band), but he wishes the trust fund to be a legacy which is limited to the amount by which his available nil-rate band is potentially increased under the carry-forward rules. This would leave his basic nil-rate band to be carried forward and used on his current wife's death. If the testator does have a potential increased nil-rate band under the nil-rate band carry-forward rules his current wife should make a will containing a nil-rate band discretionary trust to take effect if she dies first, to avoid waste of nil-rate band in the event of her doing so.

6 The main reasons for having separate trustees of the legacy are where a charge scheme might be entered into, in which case the testator's spouse should not be one of the executors and trustees but could be a trustee of the legacy, or where a debt scheme might be entered into and the testator's spouse might be sole executor: see para **[218.22]** above.

7 The trust period is longer than may be needed in most cases, but gives considerable flexibility. In particular, if both parents were to die while the children of the second marriage were still minors, the whole of this fund would continue to be available for their support at the discretion of the trustees.

8 These words in square brackets should be included if a trust corporation is to be an executor, or there is a possibility that a trust corporation might subsequently be appointed a trustee. In either case express provision for the remuneration of a trust corporation so acting (not included in this form) should be added: see, eg Forms B3.13 to B3.16 at paras **[203.32]–[203.35]**, Form B21.40 **[221.52]** and Form C4.1, cl 1 at para **[226.18]**.

9 These words authorise the creation of discretionary powers which might not otherwise be valid: see Vol 1, para **[40.5]**.

10 See n 8 above.

11 Such a power to apply capital could be used to apply cash for the benefit of the children of the second marriage quickly and informally, eg paying fees for education or direct to the educational institution. However, it is essential that its exercise should be adequately evidenced.

12 The addition of these words will enable accumulated income to be paid or applied for the benefit of the wife; if they are omitted, any income which has been accumulated will form part of capital for all purposes and be unavailable for the wife.

13 These powers and provisions are included so as to enable a debt or charge scheme to be used as a means of avoiding the surviving spouse having an IPDI in the trust fund subject to the trusts of this clause, where there are insufficient assets other than the matrimonial home with which to constitute that trust fund. See para **[218.19]** ff and also n 15 below. As the wife is given a life interest, it is a charge scheme rather than a debt scheme which will be appropriate.

14 The purpose of this is so that new trustees of the residuary estate can be appointed before a charge is entered into, in a case where the surviving spouse is one of the personal representatives or the personal representatives and the trustees of the discretionary legacy are the same persons, and to make clear that new or additional trustees of the discretionary trust legacy can be appointed before the legacy is constituted as a debt from the surviving spouse where the surviving spouse is the sole trustee: see para **[218.22]** for the reasons for avoiding these states of affairs.

15 If post-21 March 2006 a beneficiary is permitted to occupy a property owned by a discretionary trust, whereas this may give that beneficiary an interest in possession, it will not necessarily be the type of interest in possession which will cause the property to be treated as part of his or her estate for IHT purposes. Only an interest in possession which is an IPDI, a disabled person's interest, or a transitional serial interest (see paras **[200.98]–[200.100]** above) will have this result. In the context of a discretionary trust established by will, if a permission to occupy is given within two years of the testator's death, and this gives rise to an interest in possession this may be backdated to the testator's death under IHTA 1984, s 144, so that it would be an IPDI and result in the property being treated as part of the beneficiary's estate for IHT purposes: see para **[225.83]** ff. But if the permission is not granted until after the second anniversary of the testator's death, and the beneficiary to whom it is granted is not a disabled person within the meaning of IHTA 1984, s 89 (4) at the testator's death so that her interest is not a disabled person's interest within IHTA 1984, s 89B (see para **[200.99]** above), it should not result in the property being treated as part of the beneficiary's estate for IHT purposes. Therefore, an express power to appropriate property or a share of property may be given to trustees to exercise in appropriate circumstances, and sub-cll (10) and (11) contain such a power and associated provisions.

[227.15]

ADMINISTRATION TRUSTS OF RESIDUE

6. (1) I give all my property not hereby or by any codicil hereto otherwise effectively disposed of [(including any entailed or other property over which I shall have at my death a general power of disposition by will)][1] to my trustees to hold on the trusts set out below with power at their discretion to sell all or any of it as and when they think fit.[2]

(2) My trustees shall pay my funeral and testamentary expenses[3] and debts and any legacies given by this will or any codicil hereto out of such property or its proceeds and shall have a discretion as to how such payments shall be borne as between capital and income.[4]

(3) Subject as above my trustees shall hold such property and the assets from time to time representing the same (hereinafter called 'my residuary estate') on the trusts set out below and shall invest all money comprised in such property or arising from its sale in any of the investments hereby authorised with power to change such investments into any others hereby authorised.

(4) In the administration of my estate and the execution of the trusts of this will or of any codicil to it:

(a) my trustees shall treat all income as accruing on the date on which it becomes payable regardless of the period in respect of which it shall have accrued and shall not make any statutory apportionment of the same;[5] and

(b) none of the equitable rules of apportionment between capital and income shall apply in any circumstances whatever.[6]

1 See Form C2.1, cl 6, n 1 at para **[224.34]**.
2 See Form C2.1, cl 6, n 2 at para **[224.34]**.
3 See Form C2.1, cl 6, n 3 at para **[224.34]**.
4 See Form C2.1, cl 6, n 4 at para **[224.34]**.
5 See Form C2.1, cl 6, n 5 at para **[224.34]**.
6 See Form C2.1, cl 6, n 6 at para **[224.34]**.

[227.16]

GIFTS MADE FREE OF TAX

7. Any specific gift or pecuniary or general legacy made by this will or any codicil hereto which is expressed to be 'free of tax' shall be free from the payment of any inheritance tax or foreign tax or duty payable on or by reason of my death to which such gift or legacy would otherwise be subject and such inheritance tax or foreign tax or duty shall be paid out of my residuary estate.[1]

1 See Form C3.1, cl 5, n 1 at para **[225.15]**.

[227.17]

BENEFICIAL TRUSTS OF RESIDUE

8. (1) My trustees shall hold my residuary estate upon trust to pay the income thereof to my wife during her life.[1]

[(2) Notwithstanding the foregoing trust my trustees (being not fewer than two in number [or a trust corporation][2] may at any time and from time to time during the life of my wife pay transfer or apply any part or parts not exceeding in the aggregate [one quarter]/[one half][3] of my residuary estate to or for the benefit of my wife in such manner as they think fit provided that the foregoing power shall only be exercisable over capital of which the income is for the time being payable to my wife (or would be payable if such capital yielded income).][4]

(3) Subject as aforesaid my trustees shall hold my residuary estate and the income thereof upon trust for such of my children as shall survive me

and in the case of those who are then under the age of [18/25] years as shall attain that age[5] and if more than one in equal shares provided that if any child of mine shall predecease me or having survived me shall fail to attain the age of [18/25] years leaving a child or children surviving me or born after my death who shall attain the age of [18/21] years such last-mentioned child or children shall take if more than one equally between them the share of my residuary estate which such deceased child of mine would have taken had he or she lived to attain a vested interest.[6]

1 The life interest for the surviving spouse will be an IPDI within IHTA 1984, s 49A (see para **[200.98]**), so spouse exemption from IHT should be available. For the reasons for not including survivorship condition see the Preliminary Note on survivorship conditions at paras **[224.5]** ff and Form C2.1, cl 4, n 1 at para **[224.31]**.

2 See n 8 to cl 5(3) of this form at para **[227.14]**.

3 One of these should be deleted, or both deleted and some other fraction substituted.

4 There are two reasons for restricting the exercise of the power to capital in which the widow has an interest in possession: first, to ensure that the power is not exercisable if there is a divorce and the life interest given by the previous subclause lapses (see the Preliminary Note to C2, at para **[224.16]** **]**–**[224.23]**ff); and secondly, to ensure that the power ceases to be exercisable if the wife assigns or surrenders her life interest. It is important that this power should cease to be exercisable in such an event because the termination of an IPDI on or after 22 March 2006 will be deemed to be a gift of the underlying settled property for the purposes of FA 1986, s 102, so that unless the beneficiary of the IPDI is excluded altogether from benefit after the termination, the gift with reservation rules could apply, see FA 1986, s 102ZA, (see para **[200.76]** above).

This entire clause can be omitted if the testator does not wish there to be any power to pay the widow capital. On the other hand, if he wants this power to apply to the whole of the residuary estate, a provision such as cl 7(2) of Form C3.2 at para **[225.35]** could be substituted.

5 Since the children will all be lives in being for perpetuity purposes the age contingency does not have to be restricted to 21. The choice here is between a vesting age of 18, which will mean that it is a trust for bereaved minors within IHTA 1984, s 71A (see para **[200.108]**), or a vesting age of 25, which will mean that it is an age 18-to-25 trust within IHTA 1984, s 71D (see para **[200.109]**). A s 71A trust would have the advantage that the termination of the widow's life interest during her life in favour of such a trust would be potentially exempt: see paras **[200.108]** and **[200.128]**. If a greater vesting age, or life interests, are desired, the choice is between IPDI trusts or relevant property trusts (see paras **[200.98]**, **[200.126]**, **[200.132]**). If trusts of this type but with an element of flexibility are desired cl 6 of C2.3 at para **[224.65]** could be adapted. If 25 is adopted as the vesting age, the accumulation and maintenance trusts of income under TA 1925, s 31 should be extended beyond the age of 18: see the proviso to cl 10(1) of this form at para **[227.18]**.

6 The grandchildren will not necessarily be alive at the testator's death, and it is therefore advisable to restrict the age contingency to not more than 21. Any settled property which becomes subject to this substitutional proviso will fall within the IHT charging regime for relevant property (see para **[218.8]** ff) if the relevant grandchildren are under the age of vesting at the death of the later to die of the testator and his wife, unless the testator dies after his wife, the age of vesting is 21, and a substituted grandchild has an IPDI as a result of being over 18 (and thus entitled to an interest in possession by virtue of TA 1925, s 31) but under 21 at or within two years after the testator's death (see para **[224.25]**). The possibility of a grandchild becoming entitled to an IPDI can be avoided by extending the accumulation and maintenance trusts of TA 1925, s 31 to the age of 21 for grandchildren.

[227.18]

MAINTENANCE, ACCUMULATION AND ADVANCEMENT[1]

9. (1) Section 31 of the Trustee Act 1925 (relating to accumulation and maintenance) shall apply in relation to the trusts hereby or by any codicil hereto declared as if:

(a) in paragraph (i) of subsection (1) of the said section the words 'as the trustees think fit' were substituted for the words 'as may in all the circumstances be reasonable'; and

(b) the proviso to the said subsection (1) were omitted;

[Provided that in relation to any presumptive share of my residuary estate of any child of mine the said section 31 (amended as aforesaid) shall have effect as if the age of majority were the lesser of the age which he or she will attain (if he or she so long lives) on his or her last birthday occurring not later than the expiration of 21 years from my death and the age of 25 years (and so that the expressions 'infancy', 'minority' and 'infant' and all references to the age of eighteen years in the said Section 31 shall be construed accordingly)][2].

(2) Section 32 of the Trustee Act 1925 (relating to advancement) shall apply in relation to the said trusts as if the words 'one half of' were omitted from proviso (a) to subsection (1) thereof.[3]

(3) Whenever my trustees shall have an obligation or discretion under the provisions of this will or any codicil hereto or under the general law to apply income or capital for the benefit of a minor beneficiary they may either pay the same without liability to account to his or her parent guardian or any other adult person with whom such beneficiary may be residing or to such beneficiary himself or herself if of the age of 16 years or more and so that the receipt of such parent guardian or other person or of such minor beneficiary shall be a full and sufficient discharge to my trustees for the income or capital so applied.[4]

1 For alternative provisions see the forms in B18 at paras **[218.79]–[218.108]**.

2 This proviso is for inclusion where the vesting age in the gift to children in cl 8(3) is the age of 25. It extends the period during which income may be accumulated for as long as the law currently allows (ie 21 years from the testator's death). See C2, para **[224.25]** and para **[224.36]** n 3.

3 The extended power is compatible with trusts for bereaved minors within IHTA 1984, s 71A (see para **[200.108]** above) and age 18-to-25 trusts within IHTA 1984, s 71D (see para **[200.109]** above).

4 A parent (with parental responsibility) and a guardian of a minor are empowered by the ChA 1989, s 3(3) (Part G, para **[244.114]**) to give a good receipt for the minor's property: see Vol 1, para **[9.41]**. The power in this subclause is wider in that it authorises the payment of income or capital to a parent who does not have parental responsibility, any adult with whom the minor is residing, and the minor himself or herself if 16 or over.

[227.19]

ADMINISTRATIVE POWERS[1]

10. (1) In this clause where the context so admits:

(a) the expression 'land' includes buildings and estates, interests or rights of any kind in or over land; and

(b) during the administration of my estate the expression 'beneficiary' includes any person who would be a beneficiary if such administration had been completed, and the expression 'beneficially interested' and references to income of any asset being payable or capable of being paid to or for the benefit of a beneficiary shall be construed accordingly.

(2) None of the powers or provisions contained in subclause (3) below of this clause shall be capable of being exercised or operating in any manner such that if such power or provision were capable of being so exercised or so operating the existence of the same would either:

(i) prevent any person who would in the absence of such power or provision have been entitled to an interest in possession falling within section 49(1A) of the Inheritance Tax Act 1984 in any property from being entitled to such interest; or

(ii) prevent section 71A or 71D of the Inheritance Tax Act 1984 from applying to any property to which in the absence of such power or provision either section would have applied.[2]

(3) In the administration of my estate and the execution of the trusts hereof or of any codicil hereto my trustees shall have the following powers in addition to those conferred by law but subject to the last foregoing subclause:

(a) power to invest moneys sell assets and change investments with the unrestricted freedom of choice and powers of disposition and acquisition of a sole beneficial owner with in particular power to make unsecured loans, acquire non-income yielding assets, and purchase land anywhere in the world or chattels for any purpose including occupation or enjoyment in kind by a beneficiary under the power set out below;[3]

(b) power to delegate all or any of their investment powers to a professional investment manager or managers whether individual or corporate and whether or not also a nominee holder of assets for my trustees (and who may be or include one or more of my trustees or the beneficiaries hereunder) upon such terms as to remuneration and otherwise (including terms authorising self-dealing or providing for the limitation of the liability of the investment manager or managers) as my trustees think fit and section 22 of the Trustee Act 2000 shall not apply;[4]

(c) power to vest or register any property in any person or persons whether individual or corporate and whether or not an investment manager to whom powers have been delegated under the foregoing power (and who may be or include one or more of my trustees or the beneficiaries hereunder) as nominee or nominees for my trustees upon such terms as to remuneration or otherwise (including terms authorising self-dealing or providing for the limitation of the liability of the nominee) as my trustees think fit and section 22 of the Trustee Act 2000 shall not apply;[5]

(d) power to borrow money with or without giving security and on such terms as to interest and repayment and otherwise as my trustees may think fit for any purpose connected with the administration of my estate or the trusts declared herein or in any codicil hereto (including investment) and no lender from whom my trustees borrow money in purported exercise of this power shall be concerned to enquire as to the propriety amount or purpose of any such borrowing;[6]

(e) power to lend money to a beneficiary to whom any of the income of such money is payable or to whom or for whose benefit any income of such money is capable of being paid or applied in exercise of a discretion (or who would be such a beneficiary if such money yielded income) and to do so at a full or concessionary rate of interest or interest free;[7]

(f) all the powers of an absolute owner in relation to any land (wherever situated) held by them;[8]

(g) power to apply capital held on the same trusts as any land (or which would be so held if the administration of my estate had been completed) in the improvement or adaptation of such land and to apply such capital or the income of such capital on the repair or maintenance of such land;[9]

(h) power to permit any beneficiary to have the beneficial occupation use or enjoyment in kind of any land or chattel or other tangible property on such terms as to repair insurance or payment of outgoings by the beneficiary or any other person or persons or otherwise howsoever as my trustees think fit including power for the benefit of a beneficiary to permit any other person or persons (whether beneficiaries or not) to occupy use or enjoy any of the types of asset aforesaid together with such beneficiary or otherwise. Provided that the foregoing power shall only be exercisable and such permission to occupy or enjoy in kind may only continue in the following circumstances:

   (i) so long as any of the income of such land chattel or other tangible property is payable to such beneficiary or capable of being paid or applied to him or for his benefit in exercise of a discretion (or would be so payable or capable of being so paid or applied if such land chattel or other property yielded income);

   (ii) in the case of land, so long as for the time being the occupation thereof is compatible with any statutory rights of occupation of any other beneficiary or beneficiaries;[10]

(i) power to exercise all the powers of appropriation (and other incidental powers) conferred by statute on a personal representative without the necessity of obtaining any consents and notwithstanding that one or more of my trustees may be beneficially interested in the exercise of such power.[11]

1 See Form C2.1, cl 9, n 1 at para **[224.37]**.

2 See Form C2.1, cl 9, n 2 at para **[224.37]**. This proviso is not needed so long as the trusts are discretionary, but it is included in case trusts of either of these kinds are created by the trustees in exercise of any of their powers.

3 See Form C2.1, cl 9, n 3 at para **[224.37]**.

4 See Form C2.1, cl 9, n 4 at para **[224.37]**.

5 See Form C2.1, cl 9, n 5 at para **[224.37]**.

6 See Form C2.1, cl 9, n 6 at para **[224.37]**.

7 See Form C2.1, cl 9, n 7 at para **[224.37]**. If a power to pay or apply capital is included in relation to a beneficiary, it will enable loans to be made to or for the benefit of that beneficiary (as an application of capital for his or her benefit), and a separate power to lend of this type is probably unnecessary. However, it is a useful power to include if, in relation to a particular beneficiary such as the testator's spouse, the testator does not wish there to be a power to pay or apply capital at all, or wants such power to be restricted to less than the entire fund.

8 See Form C2.1, cl 9, n 8 at para **[224.37]**.

9 See para **[220.52]** for the reasons for this provision.
10 See Form C2.1, cl 9, n 10 at para **[224.37]**. Express provision for occupation etc by persons other than a beneficiary are added to this subclause to make it clear that the trustees may eg, provide a residence for an orphaned minor beneficiary and someone who is looking after him. It is not entirely clear whether permitting such a person to reside with a beneficiary would give that person an interest in possession, but provided that the power is exercised more than two years after the testator's death the changes made to IHT by FA 2006 mean that it is not an important question (see paras **[200.126]** (2) and **[200.133]**).
11 See Form C2.1, cl 9, n 11 at para **[224.37]**.

[227.20]

TRUSTEE INDEMNITY

11. My trustees shall not be liable for any act or default of any investment manager or nominee employed in good faith to manage or hold assets of my estate nor for any act or default of any beneficiary having the occupation use or enjoyment of property in kind.[1]

1 This makes it clear that the trustees are not liable for the defaults of others who may have possession or control of trust property. In respect of the defaults of an investment manager or nominee, this indemnity may be wider than that of the TrA 2000, s 23(1) (see Part G, para **[246.155]**) which only exempts a trustee from liability for such defaults if he has complied with the statutory duty of care, a standard which may be higher than that of 'good faith'. Whereas it is clear that a wider indemnity such as this can apply where trustees have exercised an express power to appoint an investment manager or nominee, it is not clear that a wider indemnity can be conferred where trustees have exercised the statutory power (see Preliminary Note to B21 at para **[221.14]**). For a wider form of indemnity see eg Form B21.12 at para **[221.16]**. If a paid trustee is to rely on this indemnity clause, the testator should specifically be made aware of its meaning and effect (see para **[221.13]** above).

[227.21]

EXERCISE OF POWERS[1]

12. Any power or discretion hereby or by law conferred on my trustees shall be exercisable in favour of any person who is an object of such power or discretion notwithstanding that he or she is one of my trustees and shall be exercisable notwithstanding that any of my trustees has any other direct or indirect personal interest in the mode or result of such exercise provided that there are not fewer than two trustees and that at least one of them has no personal interest in the mode or result of exercising the same.

1 This clause permits a member of the family to be a trustee without disqualifying him or her from benefit under any exercise of statutory or express powers of payment or application of capital, appointment etc. See the Preliminary Note to B18 at paras **[218.4]** and **[218.5]**.

[227.22]

PROFESSIONAL TRUSTEE CHARGING CLAUSE

13. Any of my trustees being a professional or business man may charge and be paid all usual professional and other proper charges for business transacted acts done advice given and time spent by him or his firm in connection with the administration of my estate or in connection with the trusts hereof including acts which a personal representative or trustee not being in any profession or business could have done personally[1].

1 In spite of the TrA 2000, s 29(2) (Part G, para **[246.161]**) giving certain professional trustees authority to charge for their services on or after 1 February 2001, an express remuneration clause entitling any professional or business person to charge may still be advisable: see Preliminary Note to B21 at para **[221.42]** ff.

[227.23]

TESTIMONIUM

IN WITNESS whereof I have hereunto set my hand this —— day of —— 20——.

[227.24]

ATTESTATION CLAUSE

SIGNED by the above-named testator as his last will in the presence of us both present at the same time who at his request and in his presence and in the presence of each other have signed our names below as witnesses:	}	[*Signature of testator*]

[*Signatures, addresses and descriptions of two witnesses*]

[227.25]

Form C5.2: Reciprocal wills of spouses both having adult children by previous marriages (but none by their own), the first to die making a nil-rate band gift to his or her own children and giving the survivor a life interest in residue with remainder to his or her own children, and the survivor leaving his or her estate to his or her own children

Note. This form is for use by both spouses. It is assumed that they both have children of their own, but that there are no children of their marriage, and that none are likely to be born. It is also assumed that their previous marriages ended in divorce, so that neither has the possibility of an increased nil-rate band on death under the nil-rate band carry-forward rules as a result of the death of a previous spouse (see paras **[200.76]**, **[200.130]**, and also Form C5.1, the alternative clauses 5(1) and nn 3 and 5, at para **[227.14]**, for suggested wording of a nil-rate band gift to adopt if this is the case). In this form, on the death of the first to die a nil-rate band legacy goes direct to his or her children, and the surviving spouse is given a life interest only in residue with the capital passing to the testator's own children on the survivor's death. On the death of the survivor his or her own estate goes to his or her own children. *Where testators want an arrangement of this sort, the draftsman must find out whether they own the matrimonial home, or any other property of significant value, as joint tenants, and advise them to effect a severance if they do.* If the matrimonial home is owned, or an interest as tenant in common in it is owned, by the first of the spouses to die, the survivor will have a life interest in whatever interest in it was owned by the first to die, by virtue of that interest being comprised in the latter's residuary estate. This is on the assumption, of course, that it is not required to satisfy the nil-rate band legacy. If there is a possibility that it will be so required, the testators might wish to incorporate provisions in their wills for the establishment of a discretionary trust and a debt or charge scheme: see Preliminary Note to B18 at paras **[218.19]**–**[218.23]**, Form B18.2 at para **[218.34]**, and Form C3.4, cl 2, at para **[225.60]** ff. Alternatively, they could decide that the first to die's will should provide for the whole of the estate of the first to die to go into the residuary gift subject to the survivor's life interest, and rely on nil-rate carry-forward to use up the first to die's nil-rate band. Where neither has the possibility of an increased nil-rate band on death under the nil-rate band carry-forward rules as a result of the death of a previous spouse, the main purpose of a non-exempt gift of this type on the death of the first to die is to accelerate or preserve the interests of the ultimate beneficiaries rather than any IHT saving (see para **[200.130]**) ff. As in

Form C5.1, there is a power to pay or apply at least some of the capital of residue to or for the benefit of the surviving spouse, which can be omitted if that is preferred.

It will be important for the testators to leave letters of wishes. If there is a power to pay capital to or for the benefit of the survivor it will be particularly important for them to indicate the circumstances in which they want it to be exercised.

This form can be adapted to cope with civil partners by substituting 'civil partner' for 'wife/husband' where it occurs.

[227.26]

REVOCATION CLAUSE

I [*name*] of [*address*] hereby revoke all former testamentary dispositions made by me and declare this to be my last will.[1]

1 There is no presumption that wills in similar form are mutual wills in the technical sense, but it could save argument to add a declaration excluding mutual wills as in the revocation clause of Form C2.1 at para **[224.28]**.

[227.27]

APPOINTMENT OF EXECUTORS AND TRUSTEES[1]

1. I appoint [my [wife/husband] [*name*] ('my wife/husband')[2] my son [*name*] and my daughter [*name*]] (hereinafter together called 'my trustees' which expression shall where the context so admits include my personal representatives for the time being and the trustees for the time being hereof) to be the executors and trustees of this will.

1 The identity of the trustees will be of particular importance if a power to advance capital to the surviving spouse is included: see cl 5(2) of this form at para **[227.31]** and the notes thereto.

2 If the parties are divorced before the testator's death, the appointment of the other spouse as executor or executrix will fail (WA 1837, s 18A: see Vol 1, paras **[25.7]**, **[47.2]** and **[47.3]**, and Part G, para **[244.18]**). If two executors are appointed as well as the other spouse, there will still be two trustees in the event of a divorce, and of course the appointment will still be of two executors where the testator is predeceased by the other spouse. See also the Preliminary Note to C2 on the possibility of divorce at paras **[224.16]**–**[224.23]**.

[227.28]

GIFT OF CHATTELS TO SPOUSE[1]

2. I give to my [wife/husband] absolutely all my personal chattels as defined by section 55(1)(x) of the Administration of Estates Act 1925[2] if [she/he] shall survive me [and I request [her/him] (but without imposing any trust or binding obligation on her) to give effect to any wishes as to the disposition of such chattels which may be contained in any memorandum that may be found amongst my papers at my death or which may have otherwise been communicated to [her/him] during my life].[3]

1 See Form C5.1, cl 3, n 1 at para **[227.12]**.

2 See Part G, para **[246.67]** for the wording of this definition, and for further discussion of the meaning of 'personal chattels' see Vol 1, para **[64.44]**.

3 See Form C5.1, cl 3, n 4 at para **[227.12]**.

[227.29]

GIFT OF NIL RATE BAND LEGACY TO CHILDREN[1]

3. (1) If my [wife/husband] shall survive me[2] then I give a legacy of the sum hereinafter specified to such of my children [*name*] [*name*] and [*name*] as

survive me and if more than one in equal shares provided that if any of my said children shall predecease me leaving issue living at my death who shall attain the age of [18/21/25] years[3] such issue shall take and if more than one in equal shares per stirpes the share of the legacy hereby given which such deceased child of mine would have taken had he or she survived me but so that no issue shall take whose parent (being such issue as aforesaid) is living at my death.

[(2) The amount of the legacy hereby given shall be the maximum sum (if any)) [not exceeding £——][4] which can in the circumstances subsisting at my death be given by this clause without any liability being incurred for the payment of inheritance tax on or by reason of my death. And in particular (without prejudice to the generality of the foregoing) for the purpose of determining the amount of such maximum sum the circumstances to be taken into account shall include all chargeable transfers made by me during my life (or events treated as such for inheritance tax purposes) so far as relevant for the computation of inheritance tax on my death the dispositions taking effect under this will (apart from this clause) or under any codicil hereto and any property treated as if it were part of my estate for inheritance tax purposes.[5]

[(3)/(2)] The legacy hereby given shall carry interest at the yearly rate of [6 per cent] from my death until paid or satisfied and section 31 of the Trustee Act 1925 (as hereinafter modified) shall apply thereto.[6]

[[4)/(3)] Section 32 of the Trustee Act 1925 (as hereinafter modified) shall apply in relation to the foregoing trusts.

1 A legacy in favour of the children can be included if the estate is of sufficient value and the testators wish their own children not to have to wait to receive anything until both testators are dead. If the surviving spouse might need access to the income or capital of the legacy, a discretionary legacy such as that contained in Form C3.4, cl 2, (at para **[225.60]**), or Form C5.1, cl 5, (at para **[227.14]**) (which has more restricted powers to benefit the surviving spouse) could be substituted, or this clause can be omitted and nil-rate band carry-forward relied on to use the first to die's nil-rate band: see para **[227.25]**. For the continuing possible uses of nil-rate band gifts see paras **[200.130]**, **[227.8]** and for nil-rate band discretionary trusts see the Note in B18 at paras **[218.16]–[218.32]**.

As regards the formula used to determine the amount, see Form C3.1, cl 3, n 1 at para **[225.13]** and Form C3.4, cl 2, n 1 at para **[225.60]**.

2 This precondition is imposed to avoid unnecessary duplication of gifts (ie this one and the residuary gift), and to avoid difficulties as to the effect where the amount of the legacy is determined by a formula, in the event of the spouse not surviving the testator. This gift should not be made conditional on the spouse surviving the testator by a survivorship period: see the Preliminary Note to C3 at para **[225.4]**.

3 The grandchildren or remoter issue will be lives in being at the testator's death for perpetuity purposes, so if the gift to them is to be subject to a contingency that they attain a certain age, there is no risk of infringing the rule against perpetuities in specifying an age exceeding 21. On the other hand, the greater the vesting age, the greater is the risk that a descendant of the testator will die under the vesting age after the testator's death leaving issue—persons in the latter category will not take an interest. If the substitutional gift is subject to an age contingency, and any of the substituted beneficiaries have not satisfied it at the testator's death, but the substitutional trust takes effect, the property subject to it will be within the inheritance tax charging regime for relevant property (see para **[218.8]**). The possibility of substituted issue of the second of the testators to die becoming entitled to IPDIs (see paras **[200.92]**, **[224.25]** above) is avoided by the extended accumulation and maintenance trusts of income provided in cl 6(1) of this form at para **[227.32]**.

4 In view of the possible large increases in the nil-rate band in the next few years it would be advisable to set a cash limit on the amount of this gift. See para **[225.9]**. Another reason for

setting a cash limit on it is where the testator has business or agricultural property: see the Preliminary Note to C11 at paras **[233.8]–[233.10]**.

5 See Form C3.1, cl 3, n 1 at para **[225.13]**.

6 There is a contingency in the substitutional proviso to sub-cl (1) of this clause. A contingent legacy does not ordinarily carry the intermediate income, a factor which might have the unwelcome inheritance tax consequence that the surviving spouse has an interest in possession in the capital out of which the legacy is payable from the testator's death until the time when the legacy becomes payable. Subclause (3) is introduced to ensure that the legacy does carry the intermediate income.

[227.30]

ADMINISTRATION TRUSTS OF RESIDUE

4. [*As in cl 6 of* Form C5.1 *at para* **[227.15]**.]

[227.31]

BENEFICIAL TRUSTS OF RESIDUE

5. (1) My trustees shall stand possessed of my residuary estate upon trust to pay the income thereof to my [wife/husband] during [her/his] life.[1]

[(2) Notwithstanding the foregoing trust my trustees (being not fewer than two in number [or a trust corporation][2]) may at any time and from time to time during the life of my [wife/husband] pay transfer or apply [the whole or any part or parts of my residuary estate]/[any part or parts of my residuary estate not exceeding in the aggregate [one quarter]/[one half][3] thereof][4] to or for the benefit of my [wife/husband] in such manner as they think fit provided that the foregoing power shall only be exercisable over capital of which the income is for the time being payable to my [wife/husband] (or would be payable if such capital yielded income).][5]

[(3)/(2)] Subject as aforesaid my trustees shall stand possessed of my residuary estate upon trust for such of my children [*name*] [*name*] and [*name*] as shall survive me and if more than one in equal shares provided that if any of my said children shall predecease me leaving issue living at my death who shall attain the age of [18/21/25] years[6] such issue shall take and if more than one in equal shares per stirpes the share of my residuary estate which such deceased child of mine would have taken had he or she survived me but so that no issue shall take whose parent (being such issue as aforesaid) is living at my death.

[(4)/(3)] The trusts aforesaid shall carry the intermediate income of my residuary estate and section 31 of the Trustee Act 1925 (as hereinafter modified) shall apply thereto.

[(5)/(4)] Section 32 of the Trustee Act 1925 (as hereinafter modified) shall apply in relation to the foregoing trusts.

1 See Form C5.1, cl 8(1), n 1, at para **[227.17]**.

2 See Form C5.1, cl 5(3), n 5 at para **[227.14]**.

3 One of these should be deleted, or both deleted and some other fraction substituted.

4 The testators may wish to restrict the power to only a part of the residuary estate, in which case the second of these alternatives in square brackets should be used and the first alternative omitted. If they are content for the whole of residue to be subject to the power, the first alternative should be included and the second alternative should be omitted.

5 See Form C5.1, cl 8(2), n 4, at para **[227.17]**.ff

6 See cl 3 of this form, n 3, at para **[227.29]**.

[227.32]

MAINTENANCE, ACCUMULATION AND ADVANCEMENT

6. (1) Section 31 of the Trustee Act 1925 (relating to accumulation and maintenance) shall apply in relation to the trusts hereby or by any codicil hereto declared as if:

(a) in paragraph (i) of subsection (1) of the said section the words 'as the trustees think fit' were substituted for the words 'as may in all the circumstances be reasonable'; and

(b) the proviso to the said subsection (1) were omitted;

[Provided that in relation to any presumptive share of my residuary estate of any grandchild or remoter issue of mine the said section 31 (amended as aforesaid) shall have effect as if the age of majority were the lesser of the age which he or she will attain (if he or she so long lives) on his or her last birthday occurring not later than the expiration of 21 years from my death and the age of [21/25][1] years (and so that the expressions 'infancy', 'minority' and 'infant' and all references to the age of eighteen years in the said Section 31 shall be construed accordingly)][2].

(2) [*As in cl 9(2) of* Form C5.1 *at para* **[227.18]**.]

(3) [*As in cl 9(3) of* Form C5.1 *at para* **[227.18]**.]

1 The age here should be that which is the age of vesting in the substitution clauses in cll 3(1) and 5(3) of this form (paras **[227.29]** and **[227.31]**). If it is 18, this proviso is not needed.

2 This proviso is for inclusion where the vesting age in the substitutional gifts to grandchildren and remoter issue in cll 3(1) and 5(3) is greater than 18. It extends the period during which income may be accumulated until the age of vesting or, if sooner, the end of the permitted accumulation period of 21 years from the testator's death, so as to avoid any of these beneficiaries having accidental IPDIs. See C2, para **[224.25]** and para **[224.36]** n 3.

[227.33]

ADMINISTRATIVE POWERS

7. [*As in cl 10 of* Form C5.1 *at para* **[227.19]**.]

[227.34]

TRUSTEE INDEMNITY

8. [(1)] [*As in cl 11 of* Form C5.1 *at para* **[227.20]**.]

[(2) Section 11(1) of the Trusts of Land and Appointment of Trustees Act 1996 (consultation with beneficiaries) shall not apply to the exercise by my trustees of their functions in relation to any land subject to the trusts of this my will.[1]]

1 The testator may or may not wish to exclude the TLATA 1996, s 11(1) which obliges trustees of land to consult beneficiaries of full age and beneficially entitled to an interest in possession, and so far as consistent with the general interest of the trust, to give effect to the wishes of those beneficiaries, or (in the event of a dispute) the majority by value (see Part G, para **[246.114]** and the Note to B20 at para **[220.58]**).

[227.35]

EXERCISE OF POWERS

9. [*As in cl 12 of* Form C5.1 *at para* **[227.21]**.]

[227.36]

PROFESSIONAL TRUSTEE CHARGING CLAUSE

10. [*As in cl 13 of* Form C5.1 *at para* **[227.22]**.]

[227.37]

APPOINTMENT OF NEW TRUSTEES

[11. The power of appointing trustees hereof shall be vested in my [wife/husband] during [her/his] life.][1]

1 This provision will not be appropriate if the testators decide to appoint trustees who are independent of the beneficiaries, for example, where relations between the present spouse and the children of the previous marriage are not good, so that the presence of independent trustees might reduce the possibility of friction. However, if it is excluded, the TLATA 1996, s 19 (Part G, para **[246.122]**) provides that where no person is nominated for the purpose of appointing new trustees and the beneficiaries under the trust are of full age and capacity and between them absolutely entitled to the settled property, the beneficiaries may give a written direction to a trustee to retire from the trust, or give a written direction to the trustees to appoint as a trustee or trustees the person or persons specified in the direction. For a provision excluding the beneficiaries' statutory right to direct retirement and appointment of trustees, see Form B21.36 at para **[221.41]**.

[227.38]

ATTESTATION CLAUSE

SIGNED by the above-named [testator/testatrix] as [his/her] last will in the presence of us both present at the same time who at [his/her] request and in [his/her] presence and in the presence of each other have signed our names below as witnesses: [*Signatures, addresses and descriptions of two witnesses*]	}	[*Signature of testator/testatrix*]

[227.39]

Form C5.3: Reciprocal wills of spouses both having adult children by previous marriages (but none by their own), the first to die giving the survivor his or her estate absolutely and the survivor dividing his or her estate between children and stepchildren

Note. This is again a form for reciprocal wills, in which the entire estate of the first to die goes to the surviving spouse absolutely. On the death of the surviving spouse his or her estate is divided between the respective families of the two spouses in specified proportions, which may be equal or unequal. This form has the merit of administrative convenience, but should not be used unless the two spouses have complete confidence that the survivor will honour the arrangement and not cut out the children of the first to die. Even where this is not the case, it may be necessary to use this form where a couple have insufficient assets to justify the expense and complexity of life interest trusts such as those in Forms C5.1 or C5.2. It is also assumed that their previous marriages ended in divorce, so that neither has the possibility of an increased nil-rate band on death under the nil-rate band carry-forward rules as a result of the death of a previous spouse (see paras **[200.76]**, **[200.130]**, and also Form C5.1, the alternative cl 5(1) and nn 3 and 5, at para **[227.14]**, for suggested wording of a nil-rate band gift to adopt if this is the case).

This form can be adapted for civil partners by substituting 'civil partner' for 'wife/husband' where it occurs.

[227.40]

The proportions in which the estate of the survivor will be divided between the two families will require careful thought. What is envisaged is that the spouses should work out and agree the value of what each of them owns, and then agree to express what each of them owns as a percentage of their combined assets. The latter percentages would then be used to divide up the residuary estate of the survivor between the two families. It is assumed in this form that one spouse owns 63 per cent of the total of their assets and the other 37 per cent: see cl 3(2) and (3) of this form at para **[227.41]**. Other percentages can be substituted where indicated in cl 3(2). It may be appropriate to use this form even if it is decided that the spouses' combined assets should be shared equally between the two families, as it will ensure that each family gets half of the assets irrespective of what happens. If the trust was simply for the children of both spouses in equal shares, with substitution of issue, the ultimate division of the couple's assets between the two families would vary according to how many children each spouse had, or whether or not any of those children died without issue before the death of the survivor of the two spouses.

[227.41]

Where there is jointly-owned property, it is not absolutely essential for making the proposed testamentary dispositions that a severance of any joint tenancy should take place (compare, e g Form C5.2 at para **[227.21]** ff). Whether property passes from the first to die to the survivor under the will of the first to die, or under the right of accruer under a joint tenancy, the survivor will get an absolute interest, and the effect is the same.

[227.42]

REVOCATION CLAUSE

I [*name*] of [*address*] hereby revoke all former testamentary dispositions made by me and declare this to be my last will.[1]

1 If the spouses wish to ensure that the survivor has to abide by the arrangement, the wills could take effect as mutual wills in which case an express declaration to that effect would have to be included, though this course is not recommended: see the Preliminary Note to C2 at para **[224.8]**. For a declaration creating mutual wills see Form B1.8 at para **[201.13]**.

If there is no intention to create mutual wills, a declaration excluding mutual wills could be added as in the revocation clause of Form C2.1 at para **[224.21]**. There is no presumption that wills in similar form are mutual wills in the technical sense, but in the absence of an express declaration there is more scope for argument or even litigation on the point.

[227.43]

APPOINTMENT OF SPOUSE AS SOLE EXECUTOR/EXECUTRIX, WITH ALTERNATIVE APPOINTMENT

1. (1) I appoint my [wife/husband] [*name*] ('my [wife/husband]') the sole [executrix/executor] of this will but if [she/he] predeceases me or renounces probate or dies without having proved this will[1] then I appoint [*name*] of [*address*] and [*name*] of [*address*] to be the executors and trustees hereof.

(2) In this will the expression 'my trustees' shall where the context permits mean my personal representatives for the time being and the trustees for the time being hereof.

1 In the event of a divorce this alternative appointment will have effect as if the testator's husband or wife died on the date of the decree: WA 1837, s 18A (Part G, para **[244.18]** and the Preliminary Note to C2 at para **[224.12]** ff.

[227.44]

ADMINISTRATION TRUSTS OF RESIDUE

2. [*As in cl 6 of* Form C5.1 *at para* **[227.15]**.]

[227.45]

BENEFICIAL TRUSTS OF RESIDUE

3. (1) If my [wife/husband] shall survive me my trustees shall hold my residuary estate upon trust for my [wife/husband].

(2) If my [wife/husband] shall predecease me my trustees shall hold my residuary estate and the income thereof upon trust to divide the same into two shares as follows:

(a) a [63] per cent share of my residuary estate (hereinafter called 'the first share'); and

(b) a [37] per cent share of my residuary estate (hereinafter called 'the second share').

(3) My trustees shall hold the first share upon trust for such of my [children/stepchildren] [*name*] [*name*] and [*name*][1] as shall survive me if more than one in equal shares and shall hold the second share upon trust for such of my [stepchildren/children] [*name*] and [*name*][2] as shall survive me if more than one in equal shares Provided that:

(a) if any of my said children or stepchildren shall predecease me leaving issue living at my death who shall attain the age of [18/21/25] years[3] such issue shall take and if more than one in equal shares per stirpes the share of my residuary estate which such deceased child or stepchild of mine would have taken had he or she survived me but so that no issue shall take whose parent (being such issue as aforesaid) survives me;

(b) if the foregoing trusts for the benefit of my said stepchildren shall fail or determine then the share of my residuary estate hereinbefore directed to be held on trust for my said stepchildren shall devolve as if it formed part of my [wife's/husband's] estate and [she/he] had died intestate immediately after my death.[4]

1 The names at this point will be the same in both wills, but the description will be 'children' in one will and 'stepchildren' in the other. Care should be taken to get the names and descriptions the right way round, and the testators should be given drafts of their wills and asked specifically to confirm that the descriptions (ie 'children' or 'stepchildren') are correctly matched with the names in each will, and that the first share and second share are respectively given to the right families.

2 The names at this point will be the same in both wills, but the description will be 'stepchildren' in one will and 'children' in the other. See also the previous note.

3 See Form C5.2, cl 3, n 3, at para **[227.29]**.

4 Proviso (b) is designed to ensure that if the trusts of the stepchildren's share fail, the share will nevertheless go to their side of the family.

[227.46]

MAINTENANCE, ACCUMULATION AND ADVANCEMENT

4. (1) [*As in cl 6(1) of* Form C5.2 *at para* **[227.32]**.]

(2) [*As in cl 9(2) of* Form C5.1 *at para* **[227.18]**.]

(3) [*As in cl 9(3) of* Form C5.1 *at para* **[227.18]**.]

[227.47]

ADMINISTRATIVE POWERS

5. [*As in cl 10 of* Form C5.1 *at para* **[227.19]**.]

[227.48]

TRUSTEE INDEMNITY

6. [*As in cl 11 of* Form C5.1 *at para* **[227.20]**.]

[227.49]

PROFESSIONAL TRUSTEE CHARGING CLAUSE

7. [*As in cl 13 of* Form C5.1 *at para* **[227.22]**.]
[*Testimonium and attestation clause, as in* Form C5.2 *at para* **[227.38]**.]

[227.50]

Form C5.4: Will of married man with adult children making provision for an illegitimate child who is a minor by means of a settled legacy

Note. It is assumed in this form that the illegitimate child is living with his or her mother, and that the testator is not living with them

[227.51]

REVOCATION CLAUSE

I [*name*] of [*address*] hereby revoke all former testamentary dispositions made by me and declare this to be my last will.

[227.52]

APPOINTMENT OF EXECUTORS AND TRUSTEES

1. [*As in cl 1 of* Form C5.1 *at para* **[227.10]**.]

[227.53]

APPOINTMENT OF GUARDIANS[1]

2. [If [*name of mother of illegitimate child*] predeceases me I appoint [*name*] of [*address*] [and [*name*] of [*address*]] to be the [guardian/guardians] of my [son/daughter] [*name of illegitimate child*] during [his/her] minority.]

1 The testator will not have power to appoint a guardian of the child unless both parents have entered into an agreement in the prescribed form conferring parental responsibility on the testator (see Vol 1, para **[28.2]**), or the court has made an order conferring parental responsibility on him, or, if the birth was registered on or after 1 December 2003, his name appears on the birth certificate. If the testator does not have parental responsibility, it remains possible that the mother might appoint the testator to be the guardian of the child in the event of her death, and then predecease the testator (while the child is still under 18). If the testator becomes a guardian of the child in this way, he will then acquire parental responsibility and have power to appoint a successor to himself as guardian (see Vol 1, para **[28.2]**). It seems reasonably clear that the acquisition by the father of parental responsibility under a parental responsibility agreement will not retrospectively validate the appointment of a guardian by a will made by him at a time when he did not have parental responsibility (see Vol 1, para **[28.4]**), but it is not quite so clear that, if he becomes guardian of the child after the death of the child's mother, an appointment of a guardian to succeed him which was made before he became such guardian will not be valid, although it seems likely that this is the case. For the law relating to guardians generally, see Vol 1, para **[28.1]** ff and B3 at para **[203.47]** ff.

[227.54]

SETTLED LEGACY FOR ILLEGITIMATE CHILD[1]

3. (1) I give free of tax[2] a pecuniary legacy of £—— to [*name*] of [*address*] and [*name*] of [*address*].

(2) In this clause 'the legacy fund trustees' means and includes the said named persons or other the trustees or trustee for the time being of the legacy fund as hereinafter defined and pending the payment or transfer of the legacy fund as hereinafter defined shall also include my trustees.

(3) The said legacy shall carry interest from the date of my death at the rate of [4] per cent per annum until paid set aside or satisfied by appropriation.

(4) The legacy fund trustees shall hold the said legacy upon trust to invest the same in any investments hereby authorised with power to vary the same and shall hold the said legacy and the investments from time to time representing the same (in this clause together called 'the legacy fund') and the income thereof upon the trusts set out below.

(5) The legacy fund trustees shall hold the legacy fund and the income thereof upon trust for my [son/daughter] [*name of illegitimate child*] (hereinafter called 'the beneficiary') absolutely if [he/she] shall attain the age of 25[3] years provided that if [he/she] shall die before the said age of 25 years leaving a child or children [him/her] surviving who shall attain the age of 21 years such child or children shall take the legacy fund absolutely and if more than one equally between them.[4]

(6) The foregoing trusts shall carry the intermediate income of the legacy fund and section 31 of the Trustee Act 1925 (as hereinafter modified) shall apply thereto [provided that in relation to the beneficiary and his interest in the legacy fund the said section 31 (amended as aforesaid) shall have effect as if the age of majority were the lesser of the age which the beneficiary will attain (if [he/she] so long lives) on [his/her] last birthday occurring not later than the expiration of 21 years from my death and the age of 25 years (and so that the expressions 'infancy', 'minority' and 'infant' and all references to the age of eighteen years in the said Section 31 shall be construed accordingly)][5].

(7) Section 32 of the Trustee Act 1925 (as hereinafter modified shall apply to the foregoing trusts.

(8) Subject as aforesaid the legacy fund shall [fall into my residuary estate].

(9) The following provisions shall have effect with regard to the legacy fund trustees:

(a) if the said [*name of trustee appointed in subclause* (*1*)] shall die in my lifetime or shall refuse or be unable to act as a legacy fund trustee then I appoint [*name*] of [*address*] to be such a trustee in his place;

(b) if the said [*name of other trustee appointed in subclause* (*1*)] shall die in my lifetime or shall refuse or be unable to act as an original legacy fund trustee then I appoint [*name*] of [*address*] to be such a trustee in his place;

(c) if one of the persons appointed by name as an original trustee of the legacy fund in subclause (1) of this clause and the person appointed in his or her place under the foregoing provisions of this subclause shall both die in my lifetime or refuse or be unable to act as such a trustee then any other person appointed by name as an original trustee of the legacy fund by subclause (1) of this clause or the foregoing provisions of this subclause (as the case may be) may nominate additional trustees of the legacy fund;

(d) if all the persons hereinbefore appointed by name as original trustees shall die in my lifetime or shall refuse or be unable to act as such trustees then [*name*] of [*address*] [or failing [him/her] my trustees] may nominate additional trustees of the legacy fund;

(e) subject as aforesaid the power of appointing new trustees of the legacy fund [shall be vested in [the said] [*name*] of [*address*] during [his/her] life and otherwise] shall be the statutory power.[6]

1 In deciding what the amount of the legacy should be the testator needs to consider the level of support he is currently providing for the child, and what level of provision will be sufficient to avoid a claim being made under the Inheritance (Provision for Family and Dependants) Act 1975. He may need to make codicils from time to time to increase the legacy for inflation or to take account of changed circumstances. It could be tied to the inheritance tax threshold, as in Form C5.2, cl 3(2) at para **[227.29]**, but that could work capriciously and would not be a level of provision fixed by reference to the child's circumstances.

2 See Form C3.1, cl 2, n 2 at para **[225.17]**.

3 If the testator dies while the beneficiary is living and under the age of 25, the trust will be an age 18-to-25 trust within IHTA 1984, s 71D (see para **[200.109]** above). A possible alternative would be to substitute 18 as the age of vesting thus creating a trust for a bereaved minor within IHTA 1984, s 71A (see para **[200.108]** above).

4 A further alternative would be to provide a life interest with power to pay or apply capital to or for the benefit of the child; Form C2.2, cls 7 and 8 at paras **[224.50]** and **[224.51]** could be adapted for this purpose. It could either be a relevant property or an IPDI trust.

5 Advantage may be taken of the 21-year accumulation period following the testator's death which is sanctioned by the LPA 1925, s 164(1)(b) (Part G, para **[246.56]** to extend the provisions for maintenance and accumulation contained in the TA 1925, s 31 to the maximum age, up to the vesting age, which is possible within the 21-year accumulation period from death. For further discussion of the extension of accumulation and maintenance trusts in this way, and alternative forms for doing so, see B18 at paras **[218.74]**–**[218.78]**. It is a particularly good idea to extend accumulation and maintenance trusts of income in relation to a trust intended to be within IHTA 1984, s 71D (see para **[200.109]** above), as it ensures that IHTA 1984, s 71D will apply, if the beneficiary is under 25 at the testator's death, irrespective of the age of the beneficiary at the time of the testator's death: see para **[224.25]**.

6 The reason for these rather elaborate provisions is that the executors and the testator's immediate family may not be the most appropriate people to decide who should be trustees of this fund if the nominated persons do not take office. Further, the testator may not wish the child's mother to have too much influence on the trusteeship or administration of this fund. Accordingly, this subclause provides for alternative trustees to be nominated, and for someone to be nominated to decide who should be trustees in the absence of any of the named persons taking office. These provisions are mostly concerned with who will be the trustees in the first place; once the separate trustees are constituted they will appoint their own successors under the statutory power, unless someone is nominated to exercise it in sub-cl (9)(e).

[227.55]

ADMINISTRATION TRUSTS OF RESIDUE

4. [*As in cl 6 of* Form C5.1 *at para* **[227.15]**.]

[227.56]

GIFTS MADE FREE OF TAX

5. [*As in cl 7 of* Form C5.1 *at para* **[227.16]**.]

[227.57]

BENEFICIAL TRUSTS OF RESIDUE

6. (1) My trustees shall hold my residuary estate upon trust for my wife [*name*] absolutely if she shall survive me.[1]

(2) If my wife shall predecease me my trustees shall hold my residuary estate upon trust for such of my children [*name*] [*name*] and [*name*][2] as shall survive me if more than one in equal shares Provided that if any of my said children shall predecease me leaving a child or children surviving me who shall attain the age of [18/21/25] years such last-mentioned child or children shall take if more than one in equal shares the share of my residuary estate which such deceased child of mine would have taken had he or she survived me.

(3) The foregoing trusts shall carry the intermediate income of my residuary estate and section 31 of the Trustee Act 1925 (as hereinafter modified) shall apply thereto.

(4) Section 32 of the Trustee Act 1925 (as hereinafter modified) shall apply to the foregoing trusts.

1 Ie the children of the marriage.
2 See cl 3 of Form C5.2, n 3, at para **[227.29]**.

[227.58]

MAINTENANCE, ACCUMULATION AND ADVANCEMENT

7. (1) Section 31 of the Trustee Act 1925 (relating to accumulation and maintenance) shall apply in relation to the trusts hereby or by any codicil hereto declared as if:

(a) in paragraph (i) of subsection (1) of the said section the words 'as the trustees think fit' were substituted for the words 'as may in all the circumstances be reasonable'; and

(b) the proviso to the said subsection (1) were omitted.

(2) [*As in cl 9(2) of* Form C5.1 *at para* **[227.18]**.]

(3) [*As in cl 9(3) of* Form C5.1 *at para* **[227.18]**.]

[227.59]

ADMINISTRATIVE POWERS

8. [*As in cl 10 of* Form C5.1 *at para* **[227.19]**.]

[227.60]

TRUSTEE INDEMNITY

9. [*As in cl 11 of* Form C5.1 *at para* **[227.20]**.]

[227.61]

EXERCISE OF POWERS

10. [*As in cl 12 of* Form C5.1 *at para* **[227.21]**.]

[227.62]

PROFESSIONAL TRUSTEE CHARGING CLAUSE

11. [*As in cl 13 of* Form C5.1 *at para* **[227.22]**.]

[*Testimonium and attestation clause, as in* Form C5.1 *at paras* **[227.23]** and **[227.24]**.]

C6 Wills for unmarried couples with children

Preliminary note .... **[228.1]**

FORMS

C6.1 Reciprocal wills of couple living together who have young children and who are planning to marry .... **[228.5]**

C6.2 Reciprocal wills of couple living together who have children, leaving residue on discretionary trusts .... **[228.19]**

C6.3 Will of man separated (but not judicially separated) from wife and living with another woman, where divorce proceedings are contemplated .... **[228.33]**

PRELIMINARY NOTE

[228.1]

Special reasons for making wills. It is especially important for an unmarried heterosexual couple (whether or not they have children) to make wills providing for each other, because if one of them dies intestate the other will not inherit any of his or her estate. The same applies to a homosexual couple who have not formed a civil partnership. Making a will is not quite as important in the interests of any children, because illegitimate children inherit on the death of one of their parents intestate in the same way as legitimate ones (see Vol 1, para **[72.14]**), but it is still advisable, and of course it is necessary if the testator wishes to benefit children of a partner who are not the testator's. It is also important, so long as an unmarried couple have one or more minor children in respect of whom the father does not have parental responsibility, that the mother should appoint the father as guardian of the minor children in the event of her death: see B3 at para **[203.47]** ff and Vol 1, para **[28.2]**. Where a child's birth was registered before 1 December 2003 the father will only have parental responsibility if the mother has entered into a parental responsibility agreement with him or there has been a court order to that effect. If the registration of the birth was on or after 1 December 2003, the father will have parental responsibility if he is registered as the father on the birth certificate, but if he is not so registered it is still the case that he will only have it if there is a parental responsibility agreement with the mother or a court order to that effect. See ChA 1989, s 4, as amended by ACA 2002, s 111 (Part G, para **[244.115]**) and Vol 1, para **[28.2]**). Subsequent marriage of the parents will give the father parental responsibility: see ChA 1989, s 2(1), (3), FLRA 1987, s 1(2), (3), LA 1976, s 10 (Part G, paras **[244.113]**, **[245.70]**, **[245.51]**). Where an unmarried/non-civil partnership couple are looking after one or more children of which only one of them is a parent, the other will not be able to obtain parental responsibility for them unless he or she adopts them, or a court order is obtained conferring parental responsibility, but he or she can be appointed a guardian by the will of the one who is a parent in the event of the latter's death.

[228.2]
Special factors. When it comes to the preparation of wills for an unmarried heterosexual couple, or for a homosexual couple who have not formed a civil partnership, it should be remembered that the wills will be revoked by their subsequent marriage or formation of a civil partnership unless the wills are made in expectation of that marriage or civil partnership (see Vol 1, paras **[17.2]**, **[17.3]**, **[17.6]** and Form C6.1 at para **[228.5]** ff). Also, if the relationship breaks up without leading to marriage or civil partnership, any wills which they have made in favour of each other will continue in full force unless revoked (contrast the lapse by divorce of a gift to a spouse, and lapse by dissolution of a civil partnership of a gift to a civil partner, for which see the Preliminary Note to C2 at para **[224.16]** ff).

The principal IHT factor is that there is no exemption from IHT for gifts between persons who are neither married to each other nor in a civil partnership (see Part A, para **[200.84]** ff for this exemption for gifts between spouses or civil partners). This means that nil-rate band carry-forward and nil-rate band trusts (see paras **[200.75]** and **[200.130]**) are not relevant, and, more generally, that it makes no difference to the IHT charge on the death of the first to die how much or how little of the estate of the first to die is given to (or settled on interest in possession trusts for) the survivor. Thus a long-term discretionary trust of residue (see Form C6.2 at paras **[228.19]**–**[228.32]**), or a substantial proportion of residue going direct to the children (as in Form C3.3 at paras **[225.42]**–**[225.56]**, suitably adapted), are possibilities well worth considering for inclusion in the will of the first to die (see also paras **[200.131]**, **[200.132]**).

If fixed trusts of capital for children vesting at a specified age are wanted, trusts for them which fall within the favoured IHT categories in IHTA 1984, ss 71A or 71D (see paras **[200.108]**, **[200.109]**), are a possibility. This is subject to the point that someone who is not a biological or adoptive parent of a child, and not the spouse or civil partner of such a parent, can only create a trust falling within ss 71A or 71D by his or her will in favour of that child if he or she has parental responsibility for the child. In practice this will only be the case for such a person if he or she is a guardian of the child by virtue of the appointment of him or her as a guardian by an already deceased parent of the child, or if a court order conferring parental responsibility on him or her has been made. (The statutory power to confer parental responsibility for a child by a parental responsibility agreement can only be exercised to confer it on the child's father or step-parent – see Vol 1, para **[28.2]**).). If someone only qualifies as a parent of a child for the purposes of ss 71A or 71D by virtue of having parental responsibility for that child, and by his death he no longer has such parental responsibility, the trusts for that child will not qualify as trusts for bereaved minors or age 18-to-25 trusts, and in particular if the child is over the age of 18 (parental responsibility ceases when the child attains the age of 18) and the gift is contingent on attaining the age of 18, the trusts for them will not qualify as age 18-to-25 trusts. The property subject to trusts not so qualifying will be relevant property (see para **[218.8]**) except where a beneficiary attains an interest in possession (while still under the age of vesting of capital) at or within two years of the testator's death, in which case it will be subject to an IPDI.

[228.3]

Possible use of lifetime gifts. One possible IHT planning strategy for an unmarried heterosexual couple, or a homosexual couple who have not formed a civil partnership, where the poorer of them, in the event of him or her surviving the richer, will need to be provided for by the latter, is to try to make up for the lack of a general exemption for gifts between them by lifetime potentially exempt transfers from the richer of them to the poorer. These will be free of IHT if the transferor survives them by seven years (see Part A, para **[200.71]**), although as the couple are living together careful thought needs to be given to how to avoid making gifts with reservation of benefit (see Part A, para **[200.76]**), and it may not always be practical to do so. With effect from 22 March 2006 it is only absolute gifts which can obtain potential exemption (unless the recipient is disabled—see para **[200.99]**). Lifetime transfers have most to recommend them where the richer of the two is quite a lot older than the other, or there are other good reasons for thinking that the richer will die first, but, before such transfers are made, thought should always be given to the consequences if, contrary to expectations, the richer of the two outlives the other. It may be worth considering insurance against such an eventuality or against the IHT on the lifetime transfers. Another important factor is the likelihood of the couple marrying or forming a civil partnership; lifetime potentially exempt transfers could be very advantageous if the couple never marry or form a civil partnership, but if they do marry or form a civil partnership it could turn out that it would have been better to have left making transfers between them until after the marriage or formation of a civil partnership, when such transfers are wholly exempt. A couple's marriage or formation of a civil partnership will not cause the IHT exemption for transfers between spouses or civil partners to apply retrospectively to transfers previously made between them.

[228.4]

Forms of will for use by an unmarried/non-civil partnership couple with children. Despite the lack of the exemption for gifts to spouses, such couples will often make the same dispositions in their wills as they would make if they were married or in a civil partnership, and for many such couples with children there will be a form in C2 at para **[224.1]** ff, or C3 at para **[225.1]** ff (omitting, in the case of forms which contain them, the nil-rate band legacies) which will be suitable if adapted appropriately.

C6 contains some further forms with features specific to unmarried/non-civil partnership couples. As mentioned above, it is only a will made in expectation of marriage that is not revoked by marriage (see Vol 1, para **[17.6]**); accordingly, Form C6.1 at paras **[228.5]**–**[228.18]** provides an example of a will made in expectation of marriage which is intended to operate both before and after the marriage. However, if the parties do in fact marry, it would be wise for them to review their wills. Similarly, it is only a will made in expectation of forming a civil partnership which is not revoked by formation of a civil partnership (see Vol 1, para **[17.3]**) and alternative wording is provided in Form C6.1, cl 1, n 2, at para **[228.7]** for such a will.

There are special considerations surrounding the appointment of guardians in this type of will: see **[228.1]**, and Form C6.1, cl 2 at para **[228.8]** and

Form C6.2, cl 2 at para **[228.23]**. For the availability of trusts for children within IHTA 1984, ss 71A or 71D see para **[228.2]**.

As mentioned above, wills creating a discretionary trust, of all or most of the estate, are an option well worth considering by the better-off unmarried/non-civil partnership couple, because the absence of spouse exemption (see para **[228.2]**) means that a discretionary trust arising under the will of the first to die does not make any difference to the IHT charge on his or her death. For further aspects of this, see the Note to Form C6.2 at paras **[228.19]** and **[228.20]** and see Form C6.2 at paras **[228.21]**–**[228.32]** for an example of this type of will.

Finally, Form C6.3 at paras **[228.33]**–**[228.43]** is an example of a will for the situation where one of a heterosexual couple (assumed in this form to be the man) has a wife (by whom he has children) from whom he is separated, and whom he intends to divorce. It will be a sensible precaution for him to make a temporary will benefiting the new partner in case of death before a financial settlement is agreed and the divorce is finalised, to prevent the spouse becoming entitled to all his estate under the intestacy rules (or a previous will). He should also sever any beneficial joint tenancy of property he holds jointly with the wife.

[228.5]

Form C6.1: Reciprocal wills of couple living together who have young children and who are planning to marry

Note. This form is intended for an unmarried heterosexual couple with children, who are contemplating marriage. Wills in this form are intended to make continuing provision for the other partner and the children whether or not the marriage takes place. However, if the parties do in fact marry, they might do well to review their wills. The announcement of nil-rate band carry-forward (see para **[200.75]**) means that reviewing these wills after marriage is less important from an IHT point of view than formerly, except where one of the special reasons for having a nil-rate band discretionary trust applies: see para **[200.130]** for these. Marriage may also imply different arrangements as regards appointed guardians: see para **[228.1]** and cl 2 of this form, n 1, at para **[228.8]**.

This form may be adapted for homosexual couples contemplating civil partnership, and see cl 1, n 2, at para **[228.7]**, for the wording of a declaration of expectation of a civil partnership. References to children may have to be adjusted throughout according to circumstances.

[228.6]

REVOCATION

I [*name*] of [*address*] hereby revoke all former testamentary dispositions made by me and declare this to be my last will.[1]

1 There is no presumption that wills in similar form are mutual wills in the technical sense, but the matter can be put beyond doubt by incorporating an express provision to that effect: see Form B1.9 at para **[201.14]** for a precedent, and the revocation clause to Form C2.1 and the note thereto at para **[224.28]**.

[228.7]

EXPECTATION OF MARRIAGE

1. I declare that I make this will in the expectation of marrying [*name of intended spouse*] and that it shall not be revoked by reason of the said marriage[1] and I further declare that this will shall take effect whether or not the said marriage takes place.[2]

1 Marriage will revoke a will unless the will is made in expectation of marriage: see the WA 1837, s 18 (Part G, para **[244.16]**) and see generally Vol 1, para **[17.6]**). The expectation must be of marriage to a particular person not marriage in general. Similarly, the formation of a civil partnership will revoke a will unless the will is made in expectation of forming the particular civil partnership: see the WA 1837, s 18B (Part G, para **[244.21]**, and see generally Vol 1, para **[17.3]**).

2 This further declaration makes it plain that the will is to have immediate effect and is to govern the devolution of the estate whether or not the marriage takes place. For a homosexual couple substitute 'I declare that I make this will in the expectation of forming a civil partnership with [*name of intended civil partner*] and that it shall not be revoked by reason of the said civil partnership and I further declare that this will shall take effect whether or not the said civil partnership is formed.'

[228.8]

APPOINTMENT OF GUARDIANS[1]

[*In the will of the woman:*

2. (1) If I die without having been married to [*name of the man*] and he shall survive me then I appoint him to be the guardian of any child or children of ours who are minors at the date of my death.

(2) If the said [*name of the man*] shall predecease me then (whether or not he and I shall have been married) I appoint [*name*] of [*address*] [and [*name*] of [*address*]] to be the [guardian/guardians] of any child or children of ours who are minors at the date of my death.]

[*In the will of the man*:

2. If the said [*name of the woman*] shall predecease me I appoint [*name*] of [*address*] [and [*name*] of [*address*]] to be the [guardian/guardians] of any child or children of ours who are minors at the date of my death.]

1 These clauses are appropriate for an unmarried couple where the man does not have parental responsibility for their children. In these circumstances only the woman has such parental responsibility, and it is important that she should appoint the man to be the guardian of their children in the event of her death (see Vol 1, para **[28.2]**, B3 at para **[203.47]** ff and para **[228.1]**). It is arguable that an appointment of a guardian by the man which is made before he acquires parental responsibility will not be validated by him subsequently acquiring such responsibility, but, even if that is so, it is probably worthwhile for him to attempt to make such an appointment in case the argument is incorrect, and because, even if the argument is correct, the appointment will be an expression of wishes which the court can consider when appointing a guardian in the absence of a valid appointment by the mother.

If the man does have parental responsibility for the children at the time of making wills based on this Form then these clauses will not be appropriate, and the man and woman should each make an appointment of a guardian or guardians which takes effect only if the other does not survive him or her, such as Form B3.28 at para **[203.60]**, or Form C2.1, cl 3 at para **[224.31]**. They should also both make fresh appointments of the latter type if the man subsequently acquires parental responsibility for the children after they have made appointments of guardians as in these clauses of this form.

For the circumstances in which the father will have parental responsibility see para **[228.1]**.

[228.9]

GIFT OF ESTATE TO INTENDED SPOUSE

3. If the said [*name of intended spouse*] shall survive me then subject to the payment thereout of my funeral and testamentary expenses and my debts I give all my estate both real and personal (including all entailed or other

property over which I have a power of disposition by will at the time of my death)[1] to [her/him] absolutely and appoint [her/him] the sole [executrix/executor] hereof [provided that if the said intended marriage has not taken place by the time of my death the foregoing gift shall only have effect if the said [*name of intended spouse*] shall survive me by the period of [one month]][2].

1 Subject to any contrary intention expressed in the will property subject to a general testamentary power will be carried by a residuary gift under the WA 1837, s 27 (Part G, para **[244.31]**) without express reference to the property or power. In the case of entailed property, however, the property or the instrument under which the entailed interest arises or entailed property generally must be referred to: LPA 1925, s 176(1) (Part G, para **[244.57]**). Although no new entails can be created on or after 1 January 1997 (see para **[200.53]**), entails created before that date can continue to exist and, if they do, the statutory power of disposition of them by will continues to be available.

2 The words in square brackets will ensure that if the parties die in a common accident or within the period of one month of each other, before the marriage has taken place, the estates of both will devolve directly on the children. If the period does not exceed six months, the gifts to the children under both wills actually have taken effect, or will be treated (by IHTA 1984, s 92) for IHT purposes as having taken effect, on the testators' deaths. This survivorship condition is limited to operating if the parties have not married, because such a condition can have a useful function in relation to a non-exempt (from IHT) gift, but not in relation to a gift to a spouse or civil partner: see the Preliminary Note to C2 at paras **[224.6]–[224.10]**.

[228.10]

ALTERNATIVE APPOINTMENT OF EXECUTORS AND TRUSTEES AND DEFINITION OF 'MY TRUSTEES'

4. (1) If the foregoing appointment of [*name of intended spouse*] as executor and trustee fails for any reason or [she/he] dies before acting or refuses or is unable to act as executor and trustee hereof then I appoint [*name*] of [*address*] [and] [*name*] of [*address*] [and [*name*] of [*address*]] to be the executors and trustees hereof.

(2) In this will the expression 'my trustees' means and includes my personal representatives for the time being and the trustees for the time being hereof (including [*name of intended spouse*] if [she/he] becomes executor or trustee).

[228.11]

ALTERNATIVE PROVISIONS

5. If the foregoing gift to the said [*name of intended spouse*] does not take effect[1] then the following provisions of this will shall have effect.

1 If the couple marry and then divorce the gift to the other partner will fail and the alternative gift to the children will have effect: see the WA 1837, s 18A(1)(b) (Part G, para **[244.17]**). See the section in the Preliminary Note to C2 on the possibility of divorce at para **[224.12]** ff. Note that if the couple marry and then divorce the gift to the other will lapse; if they never marry and then separate the gift will remain effective.

[228.12]

ADMINISTRATION TRUSTS OF RESIDUE

6. (1) I give all my property not hereby or by any codicil hereto otherwise effectively disposed of [(including any entailed or other property over which

I shall have at my death a general power of disposition by will)][1] to my trustees to hold on the trusts set out below with power at their discretion to sell all or any of it as and when they think fit.[2]

(2) My trustees shall pay my funeral and testamentary expenses[3] and debts and any legacies given by this will or any codicil hereto out of such property or its proceeds and shall have a discretion as to how such payments shall be borne as between capital and income.[4]

(3) Subject as above my trustees shall hold such property and the assets from time to time representing the same (hereinafter called 'my residuary estate') on the trusts set out below and shall invest all money comprised in such property or arising from its sale in any of the investments hereby authorised with power to change such investments into any others hereby authorised.

(4) In the administration of my estate and the execution of the trusts of this will or of any codicil to it:

(a) my trustees shall treat all income as accruing on the date on which it becomes payable regardless of the period in respect of which it shall have accrued and shall not make any statutory apportionment of the same;[5] and

(b) none of the equitable rules of apportionment between capital and income shall apply in any circumstances whatever.[6]

1 See Form C2.1, cl 6, n 1 at para **[224.34]**.
2 See Form C2.1, cl 6, n 2 at para **[224.34]**.
3 See Form C2.1, cl 6, n 3 at para **[224.34]**.
4 See Form C2.1, cl 6, n 4 at para **[224.34]**.
5 See Form C2.1, cl 6, n 5 at para **[224.34]**.
6 See Form C2.1, cl 6, n 6 at para **[224.34]**.

[228.13]

BENEFICIAL TRUSTS OF RESIDUE

7. (1) My trustees shall hold my residuary estate upon trust for such of my children by the said [*name of intended spouse*] as survive me and attain the age of [18/25] years[1] and if more than one in equal shares provided that if any such child of mine shall predecease me or having survived me shall die before attaining the age aforesaid leaving a child or children living at or born after my death who shall attain the age of [18/21] years[2] such last-mentioned child or children shall take if more than one equally between them the share of my residuary estate to which such deceased child of mine would have become entitled had he or she lived to attain a vested interest.

(2) The foregoing trusts shall carry the intermediate income of my residuary estate and section 31 of the Trustee Act 1925 (as hereinafter modified) shall apply thereto accordingly [provided that in relation to any presumptive share of my residuary estate of any child of mine by the said [*name of intended spouse*][2] the said section 31 (as modified as aforesaid) shall have effect as if the age of majority were the lesser of the age which he or she will attain (if he or she so long lives) on his or her last birthday occurring not later than the expiration of 21 years from my death and the age of 25 years (and so

that the expressions 'infancy', 'minority' and 'infant' and all references to the age of eighteen years in the said Section 31 shall be construed accordingly)][3].

(3) Section 32 of the Trustee Act 1925 (as hereinafter modified) shall apply in relation to my residuary estate.

[(4) Subject as aforesaid my trustees shall hold my residuary estate and the income thereof [for [*name*] absolutely]/[for such charitable purposes as my trustees may declare]].

1 Since the children will all be lives in being for perpetuity purposes the age contingency does not have to be restricted to 21. The choice here is between a vesting age of 18, which will mean that it is a trust for bereaved minors within IHTA 1984, s 71A (see para **[200.108]**), or a vesting age of 25, which will mean that it is an age 18-to-25 trust within IHTA 1984, s 71D (see para **[200.109]**). If a greater vesting age, or life interests, are desired, the choice is between IPDI trusts or relevant property trusts (see paras **[200.98]**, **[200.126]**, **[200.132]**).

2 The grandchildren will not necessarily be alive at the testator's death, and it is therefore advisable to restrict the age contingency to not more than 21. Any settled property which becomes subject to this substitutional proviso will fall within the IHT charging regime for relevant property (see para **[218.8]** ff) unless the age of vesting is 21 and a substituted grandchild has an IPDI as a result of being over 18 (and thus entitled to an interest in possession by virtue of TA 1925, s 31) but under 21 at or within two years after the testator's death (see para **[224.25]**). The possibility of a grandchild becoming entitled to an IPDI can be avoided by having a second proviso to subclause (2) of this clause extending the accumulation and maintenance trusts of TA 1925, s 31 to the age of 21 for grandchildren.

3 This proviso should be included if the age of vesting is 25. It will ensure that the trusts for the children are within the age 18-to-25 trust regime of IHTA 1984, s 71D for beneficiaries under the age of 25 at the testator's death irrespective of the age they have attained by that time (see para **[224.25]**).

[228.14]

MAINTENANCE, ACCUMULATION AND ADVANCEMENT

8. (1) Section 31 of the Trustee Act 1925 (relating to accumulation and maintenance) shall apply in relation to the trusts hereby or by any codicil hereto declared as if:

(a) in paragraph (i) of subsection (1) of the said section the words 'as the trustees think fit' were substituted for the words 'as may in all the circumstances be reasonable'; and

(b) the proviso to the said subsection (1) were omitted.

(2) Section 32 of the Trustee Act 1925 (relating to advancement) shall apply in relation to the said trusts as if the words 'one half of' were omitted from proviso (a) to subsection (1) thereof.

(3) Whenever my trustees shall have an obligation or discretion under the provisions of this will or any codicil hereto or under the general law to apply income or capital for the benefit of a minor beneficiary they may either pay the same without liability to account to his or her parent guardian or any other adult person with whom such beneficiary may be residing or to such beneficiary himself or herself if of the age of 16 years or more and so that the receipt of such parent guardian or other person or of such minor beneficiary shall be a full and sufficient discharge to my trustees for the income or capital so applied.[1]

1 See Form C3.1, cl 7(3), n 3 at para **[225.17]**.

[228.15]

ADMINISTRATIVE POWERS[1]

9. (1) In this clause where the context so admits:

(a) the expression 'land' includes buildings and estates interests or rights of any kind in or over land; and

(b) during the administration of my estate the expression 'beneficiary' includes any person who would be a beneficiary if such administration had been completed and the expression 'beneficially interested' and references to income of any asset being payable or capable of being paid to or for the benefit of a beneficiary shall be construed accordingly.

(2) None of the powers or provisions contained in subclause (3) below of this clause shall be capable of being exercised or operating in any manner such that if such power or provision were capable of being so exercised or so operating the existence of the same would either:

(i) prevent any person who would in the absence of such power or provision have been entitled to an interest in possession falling within section 49(1A) of the Inheritance Tax Act 1984 in any property from being entitled to such interest; or

(ii) prevent section 71A or 71D of the Inheritance Tax Act 1984 from applying to any property to which in the absence of such power or provision either section would have applied.[2]

(3) In the administration of my estate and the execution of the trusts hereof or of any codicil hereto my trustees shall (subject to clause 10 below) have the following powers in addition to those conferred by law but subject to the last foregoing subclause:

(a) power to invest moneys sell assets and change investments with the unrestricted freedom of choice and powers of disposition and acquisition of a sole beneficial owner with in particular power to make unsecured loans, acquire non-income yielding assets, and purchase land anywhere in the world or chattels for any purpose including occupation or enjoyment in kind by a beneficiary under the power set out below;[3]

(b) power to delegate all or any of their investment powers to a professional investment manager or managers whether individual or corporate and whether or not also a nominee holder of assets for my trustees (and who may be or include one or more of my trustees or the beneficiaries hereunder) upon such terms as to remuneration and otherwise (including terms authorising self-dealing or providing for the limitation of the liability of the investment manager or managers) as my trustees think fit and section 22 of the Trustee Act 2000 shall not apply;[4]

(c) power to vest or register any property in any person or persons whether individual or corporate and whether or not an investment manager to whom powers have been delegated under the foregoing power (and who may be or include one or more of my trustees or the beneficiaries hereunder) as nominee or nominees for my trustees upon such terms as to remuneration or otherwise (including terms authorising self-dealing or providing for the limitation of the liability of the nominee) as my trustees think fit and section 22 of the Trustee Act 2000 shall not apply;[5]

(d) power to borrow money with or without giving security and on such terms as to interest and repayment and otherwise as my trustees may think fit for any purpose connected with the administration of my estate or the trusts declared herein or in any codicil hereto (including investment) and no lender from whom my trustees borrow money in purported exercise of this power shall be concerned to enquire as to the propriety amount or purpose of any such borrowing;[6]

(e) power to lend money to a beneficiary to whom any of the income of such money is payable or to whom or for whose benefit any income of such money is capable of being paid or applied in exercise of a discretion (or who would be such a beneficiary if such money yielded income) and to do so at a full or concessionary rate of interest or interest free;[7]

(f) all the powers of an absolute owner in relation to any land (wherever situated) held by them;[8]

(g) power to apply capital held on the same trusts as any land (or which would be so held if the administration of my estate had been completed) in the improvement or adaptation of such land and to apply such capital or the income of such capital on the repair or maintenance of such land;[9]

(h) power to permit any beneficiary to have the beneficial occupation use or enjoyment in kind of any land or chattel or other tangible property on such terms as to repair insurance or payment of outgoings by the beneficiary or any other person or persons or otherwise howsoever as my trustees think fit including power for the benefit of a beneficiary to permit any other person or persons (whether beneficiaries or not) to occupy use or enjoy any of the types of asset aforesaid together with such beneficiary or otherwise, provided that the foregoing power shall only be exercisable and such permission to occupy or enjoy in kind may only continue in the following circumstances:

   (i) so long as any of the income of such land chattel or other tangible property is payable to such beneficiary or capable of being paid or applied to him or for his benefit in exercise of a discretion (or would be so payable or capable of being so paid or applied if such land chattel or other property yielded income);

   (ii) in the case of land, so long as for the time being the occupation thereof is compatible with any statutory rights of occupation of any other beneficiary or beneficiaries;[10]

(i) power to exercise all the powers of appropriation (and other incidental powers) conferred by statute on a personal representative without the necessity of obtaining any consents and notwithstanding that one or more of my trustees may be beneficially interested in the exercise of such power.[11]

1 See Form C2.1, cl 9, n 1 at para **[224.37]**.

2 See Form C2.1, cl 9, n 2 at para **[224.37]**.
3 See Form C2.1, cl 9, n 3 at para **[224.37]**.
4 See Form C2.1, cl 9, n 4 at para **[224.37]**.
5 See Form C2.1, cl 9, n 5 at para **[224.37]**.
6 See Form C2.1, cl 9, n 6 at para **[224.37]**.
7 See Form C2.1, cl 9, n 7 at para **[224.37]**. If a power to pay or apply capital is included in relation to a beneficiary, it will enable loans to be made to or for the benefit of that beneficiary (as an application of capital for his or her benefit), and a separate power to lend of this type is probably unnecessary. However, it is a useful power to include if, in relation to a particular beneficiary such as the testator's spouse, the testator does not wish there to be a power to pay or apply capital at all, or wants such power to be restricted to less than the entire fund.
8 See Form C2.1, cl 9, n 8 at para **[224.37]**.
9 See para **[220.52]** for the reasons for this provision.
10 See Form C2.1, cl 9, n 10 at para **[224.37]**. Express provision for occupation etc by persons other than a beneficiary are added to this subclause to make it clear that the trustees may, e g provide a residence for an orphaned minor beneficiary and someone who is looking after him. It is not entirely clear whether permitting such a person to reside with a beneficiary would give that person an interest in possession, but provided that the power is exercised more than two years after the testator's death the changes made to IHT by FA 2006 mean that it is not an important question (see paras **[200.126]** (2) and **[200.133]**).
11 See Form C2.1, cl 9, n 11 at para **[224.37]**.

[228.16]

TRUSTEE INDEMNITY

10. [(1) My trustees shall not be liable for any act or default of any investment manager or nominee employed in good faith to manage or hold assets of my estate nor for any act or default of any beneficiary having the occupation use or enjoyment of property in kind.[1]

[[(2) Section 11(1) of the Trusts of Land and Appointment of Trustees Act 1996 (consultation with beneficiaries) shall not apply to the exercise by my trustees of their functions in relation to any land subject to the trusts of this my will].[2]

1 This makes it clear that the trustees are not liable for the defaults of others who may have possession or control of trust property. In respect of the defaults of an investment manager or nominee, this indemnity may be wider than that of the TrA 2000, s 23(1) (Part G, para **[246.155]**) which only exempts a trustee from liability for such defaults if he has complied with the statutory duty of care, a standard which may be higher than that of 'good faith'. Whereas it is clear that a wider indemnity such as this can apply where trustees have exercised an express power to appoint an investment manager or nominee, it is not clear that a wider indemnity can be conferred where trustees have exercised the statutory power (see Preliminary Note to B21 at paras **[221.13]** and **[221.14]**). For a wider form of indemnity see Form B21.12 at para **[221.16]**. If a paid trustee is to rely on this indemnity clause, the testator should specifically be made aware of its meaning and effect (see para **[221.13]**).
2 The Trusts of Land and Appointment of Trustees Act 1996 (TLATA 1996), s 11(1) which obliges trustees of land to consult beneficiaries of full age and beneficially entitled to an interest in possession, and so far as consistent with the general interest of the trust, to give effect to the wishes of those beneficiaries or (in the event of a dispute) the majority by value (Part G, para **[246.114]**; see also para **[220.58]**) will only be relevant in the circumstances contemplated by this form on the death of the survivor when children might become entitled to interests in possession in residue which might include land. It would probably be convenient for it to be excluded.

[228.17]

PROFESSIONAL TRUSTEE CHARGING CLAUSE

11. Any of my trustees being a professional or business man may charge and be paid all usual professional and other proper charges for business transacted acts done and advice given by him or his firm in connection with the administration of my estate or in connection with the trusts hereof including acts which a personal representative or trustee not being in any profession or business could have done personally[1].

1 In spite of the TrA 2000, s 29(2) (Part G, para **[246.161]**) giving certain professional trustees authority to charge for their services on or after 1 February 2001, an express remuneration clause entitling any professional or business person to charge may still be advisable: see Preliminary Note to B21 at para **[221.35]**.

[228.18]

TESTIMONIUM AND ATTESTATION CLAUSE

IN WITNESS whereof I have hereunto set my hand this —— day of —— 20——

SIGNED by the above-named [testator/testatrix] as [his/her] last will in the presence of us both present at the same time who at [his/her] request and in [his/her] presence and in the presence of each other have signed our names below as witnesses:	}	[*Signature of testator/testatrix*]

[*Signatures, addresses and descriptions of two witnesses*]

[228.19]

Form C6.2: Reciprocal wills of couple living together who have children, leaving residue on discretionary trusts

Note. Where a couple are unmarried there is no spouse exemption, and the IHT on the death of the first to die is the same whether his will creates a discretionary trust or gives an absolute interest or interest in possession to the survivor. A discretionary trust can thus be an appropriate option and this form provides an example of one. The main point of a discretionary trust would be to give greater flexibility and to avoid what in some circumstances might be a heavy IHT charge arising on the survivor's death in respect of property given to the survivor absolutely or for an interest in possession from the estate of the first to die. At the same time IHT on discretionary trusts is not too onerous a burden at the moment and for a fund of a size not exceeding the IHT threshold it can be nil (see B18 at paras **[218.8]**–**[218.20]**).

A discretionary trust would enable some or all of the income to be paid to the survivor without the latter having an interest in possession in the property subject to the trust, and thus without that property being treated as part of his or her estate for IHT purposes, and would enable income to be paid directly for the benefit of a child and treated as the child's for income tax purposes. Where the income is distributed in exercise of a discretion or accumulated the burdensome income tax provisions for such income under ITA 2007, ss 9, 479–483, 493–498, will apply, which bear particularly heavily on dividend income (see para **[218.29]**–**[218.32]**), but the post-21 March 2006 IHT rules mean that once two years have elapsed from the testator's death it will be possible to appoint interests in possession to beneficiaries to obtain the more favourable income tax treatment of this type of trust while retaining IHT 'relevant property' status (see para **[200.126]** (2)). The rate of capital gains tax on property subject to a trust is a flat rate of 40 per cent in 2007–08, but a new flat rate for individuals, estates and trusts alike, with effect from 6 April 2008, was announced on 9 October 2007: see para **[200.40]** and B18 at paras **[218.26]** and **[218.27]**.

A further consequence of the post-21 March 2006 IHT rules is that tangible property, such as a dwellinghouse used as a residence, or an interest in it, can be included in a discretionary trust even though the actual enjoyment of such items may constitute an interest in possession for IHT purposes: see Part A, paras **[200.92]**, **[200.95]**, **[200.126]** (2). If such property is to retain IHT relevant property status when included in the property settled by a will, it is important to avoid creating an interest in possession in it during the first two years after the death of the testator: see para **[200.133]**. If the testators own their principal residence, or any other property, as joint tenants, it will be essential to sever the joint tenancy if they desire the first to die's interest in such residence or other property to become subject to the discretionary trust under the will of the first to die. Chattels, however, unless they particularly valuable, are not suitable for inclusion in a trust, because the expense and difficulty of identifying and keeping track of them is usually out of all proportion to their value. Accordingly in this form these are given absolutely to the survivor.

[228.20]

In the case of an unmarried couple creating discretionary wills which might continue as discretionary trusts in the medium to long term, it is important that there should be no other settled gifts in the will without carefully weighing the consequences. Any other property which is settled will be taken into account as a 'related settlement' when it comes to calculating the IHT exit or periodic charges on the discretionary trust property (see B18 at para **[218.14]**), while property given absolutely by the will is not taken into account in this way. This difficulty can be avoided by the will adding property to a lifetime settlement made by the testator, but this is not always a practical course of action.

If it turns out after the death of the first to die that some other arrangement would be better, the trustees can, by virtue of the ITA 1984, s 144, make an appointment or distribution of some or all of the estate within two years of the death (but more than three months after in the case of certain appointments or distributions) which will be treated for IHT purposes as a disposition by the will (see C3 at paras **[225.83]**–**[225.91]**).

The provision of a discretionary trust is made with the will of the first to die principally in mind. However, the same discretionary trust arises on both deaths, with the difference that on the death of the survivor the chattels will go into the trust. It is of course possible that continuing discretionary trusts will not be wanted in relation to the estate of the survivor after his death, but a discretionary trust gives greater flexibility, and again a distribution of the estate can be made within two years of death (but more than three months after) which is treated for IHT as made by the will, in reliance on the ITA 1984, s 144 (see C3 at paras **[225.83]**–**[225.91]**).

[228.21]

REVOCATION CLAUSE[1]

I [*name*] of [*address*] hereby revoke all former testamentary dispositions made by me and declare this to be my last will.

1 There is no presumption that wills in similar form are mutual wills in the technical sense, but the matter can be put beyond doubt by incorporating an express provision to that effect: see Form B1.7 at para **[201.11]** for a precedent; see also the revocation clause to Form C2.1 at para **[224.21]**.

[228.22]

APPOINTMENT OF EXECUTORS AND TRUSTEES

1. I appoint [*name*] of [*address*] [and] [*name*] of [*address*] [and [*name*] of [*address*]] (hereinafter together called 'my trustees' which expression shall include my personal representatives for the time being and the trustees for the time being hereof) to be the executors and trustees hereof.

[228.23]

APPOINTMENT OF GUARDIANS[1]

[*In the will of the woman:*

2. (1) If [*name of the man*] shall survive me then I appoint him to be the guardian of any child or children of mine who are minors at the date of my death.

(2) If the said [*name of the man*] shall predecease me I appoint [*name*] of [*address*] [and [*name*] of [*address*]] to be the [guardian/guardians] of any child or children of mine who are minors at the date of my death.]

[*In the will of the man*:

2. If the said [*name of the woman*] shall predecease me I appoint [*name*] of [*address*] [and [*name*] of [*address*]] to be the [guardian/guardians] of any child or children of mine who are minors at the date of my death.]

1 See Form C6.1, cl 2, n 1 at para **[228.8]**. Like Form C6.1, cl 2 this clause is appropriate where the father does not have parental responsibility for the children. This clause differs from that in C6.1 in two respects: no provision is made for the possibility of marriage, and each partner makes an appointment in respect of his or her children whether or not they are also children of the other partner. For the circumstances in which the father will have parental responsibility see para **[228.1]**.

[228.24]

PECUNIARY LEGACIES

3. I give the following pecuniary legacies free of tax:[1]

(a) to [*name*] the sum of £——;

(b) to [*name*] the sum of £——;

(c) to [*name*] the sum of £——.

1 See Form C2.1, cl 6, n 3 at para **[224.34]** and n 1 to cl 6 of this form at para **[228.27]**. These pecuniary legacies are declared to be 'free of tax' to take account of the risk that they may be payable out of a residuary estate which includes property of a kind which bears its own inheritance tax, such as property situated outside the UK, with the consequence that the legacies might without this declaration be liable to bear their own inheritance tax so far as payable out of that property: see the Preliminary Note to B14 at paras **[214.59]** and **[214.60]**. The expression 'free of tax' is employed here in conjunction with the definition and direction as to payment in cl 6 of this form at para **[228.27]**.

[228.25]

GIFT OF CHATTELS TO PARTNER[1]

4. I give free of tax[2] all my personal chattels as defined by section 55(1)(x) of the Administration of Estates Act 1925[3] to [*name of partner*] absolutely.

1 It is not a good idea to settle personal chattels because the trouble and expense of administering them as part of a trust fund is usually out of all proportion to their value, though it may sometimes be appropriate in the case of valuable chattels. A couple living together will anyway normally want the chattels owned by the first to die to go to the survivor.

2 These words are only included in case any of the chattels might be outside the UK at the time of the testator's death. Property outside the UK bears its own IHT in the absence of express provision to the contrary: see the Note to B14 at para **[214.60]**. See also cl 6 of this form at para **[228.27]** for the definition of 'free of tax'.

3 See Part G, para **[246.67]** for the wording of this definition, and for further discussion of the meaning of 'personal chattels' see Vol 1, para **[64.44]**.

[228.26]

ADMINISTRATION TRUSTS OF RESIDUE

5. [*As in cl 6 of* Form C6.1 *at para* **[228.12]**.]

[228.27]

GIFTS MADE FREE OF TAX

6. Any specific gift or pecuniary or general legacy made by this will or any codicil hereto which is expressed to be 'free of tax' shall be free from the payment of any inheritance tax or foreign tax or duty payable on or by reason of my death to which such gift or legacy would otherwise be subject and such inheritance tax or foreign tax or duty shall be paid out of my residuary estate.[1]

1 See Form C2.1, cl 6, n 3 at para **[224.34]** and cll 3 and 4 of this form at paras **[228.24]** and **[228.25]**. Where specific gifts and pecuniary legacies are of, or wholly payable out of, free estate in the UK, the IHT on them will be a testamentary expense payable out of residue without any express provision, and it is only where there is foreign property or settled property being disposed of by the will that a gift which is intended to be free of tax needs to be expressly declared to be free of tax. See also the Note to B14 at para **[214.55]** ff.

[228.28]

DISCRETIONARY TRUSTS OF RESIDUE[1]

7. (1) In this clause the following expressions have the following meanings namely:

(a) 'the beneficiaries' means and includes:
- (i) the said [*name of partner*];
- (ii) my children and remoter issue whenever born;
- [(iii) the children and remoter issue whenever born of [*name of partner*]];[2]
- (iv) the spouses widows and widowers of any of the said children or remoter issue (and 'widow' and 'widower' shall include a widow or widower who has remarried);
- (v) any other person or persons or charitable institution or institutions (whether corporate or not) who may be added to the class of beneficiaries under the power for that purpose hereinafter contained; and
- (vi) any other persons who become beneficiaries under subclause (2) below of this clause;

(b) 'the trust period' means the period of 80 years immediately following my death (which period shall be the perpetuity period applicable hereto);[3]

(c) 'the accumulation period' means the period commencing with my death and expiring on the twenty-first anniversary thereof; and

(d) 'the relevant day' means the day falling two years less one day after my death.[4]

(2) If at any time during the trust period the said [*name of partner*] shall have died and there shall be no living child or remoter issue of mine then the beneficiaries shall also include:

(a) the children and remoter issue of each of my grandparents;
(b) the children and remoter issue of each of the grandparents of the said [*name of partner*]; and
(c) any institution (whether corporate or not) which is established for purposes which are exclusively charitable.[5]

(3) My trustees (being not less than two in number or a trust corporation except as hereinafter provided)[6] may at any time or times and from time to time during the trust period exercise any of the following powers, namely:

(a) power at any time or times and from time to time by deed or deeds[7] revocable or irrevocable to appoint the whole or any part or parts of my residuary estate upon trust for all or such one or more exclusive of the others or other of the beneficiaries if more than one in such shares and either absolutely or at such age or time or respective ages or times and with such trusts and powers for their respective benefit and such provisions as my trustees may think fit and in making any such appointment my trustees shall have powers as full as those which they would possess if they were an absolute beneficial owner of my residuary estate and in particular (but without prejudice to the generality of the foregoing words) my trustees may in any exercise of the foregoing power as they in their absolute discretion think fit:
   (i) delegate give or impose to or upon themselves or any other person or persons any discretionary powers or discretionary trusts conditions limitations restrictions or provisions including powers of further delegation or powers to create further discretionary trusts or powers;[8]
   (ii) create powers or trusts for the accumulation of income during any period permitted by law;
   (iii) create administrative powers or provisions of whatever nature;

Provided that:
   (i) no such appointment shall invalidate any payment transfer or application of capital or income previously made under any of the trusts or powers herein elsewhere contained;
   (ii) every interest limited under any exercise of such power shall vest in interest (if at all) not later than the expiration of the trust period;
   (iii) any such appointment may be made in respect of income alone without any appointment of capital;
   (iv) any such revocable appointment shall (so far as then unrevoked) cease to be revocable on the expiration of the trust period;
   (v) any such appointment may make provision for the burden of any testamentary expenses taxes or debts payable out of my estate as between different assets funds shares or interests in such manner and to such extent as my trustees think fit;
   (vi) the foregoing power of appointment may be exercised notwithstanding that there shall have been no grant of probate or administration in respect of the property over which the said power shall be exercised or that the administration of my

estate shall not have been completed in respect of such property or any other property comprised in my estate and so long as no such grant as aforesaid has been obtained the persons who may exercise the foregoing power are the persons hereinbefore named as my executors other than any of them who shall have died or whose appointment as my executor shall have ceased to have effect or who shall have renounced probate of my will;[9]

(vii) the foregoing power of appointment may be exercised before the relevant day by a sole trustee who is not a trust corporation;[10]

(b) power (subject to any or every exercise of the foregoing power) at any time or times and from time to time in their absolute discretion to pay transfer or apply my residuary estate or any part or parts thereof to or for the benefit of all or any one or more exclusive of the others or other of the beneficiaries for the time being in existence if more than one in such shares and generally in such manner as my trustees shall think fit provided that the foregoing power of payment transfer or application of capital may be exercised before the relevant day by a sole trustee who is not a trust corporation;[11]

(c) power at any time or times and from time to time to appoint at their absolute discretion by deed any person or persons or charitable institution or institutions (whether corporate or not) to be a member or members of the class of beneficiaries upon the nomination of the said [*name of partner*] or of any children or remoter issue of mine [or of [*name of partner*]][12] who are for the time being over the age of 16 years; provided that:

(i) the foregoing power may be exercised before the relevant day by a sole trustee who is not a trust corporation; and

(ii) proviso (vi) (exercise of power before probate or completion of the administration of my estate) to the power of appointment in subclause (3)(a) above shall apply to this power as if the references in it to the said power of appointment were references to this power and as if references to property comprised in my residuary estate were references to the whole of my residuary estate;[13]

(d) power at any time or times and from time to time by deed or deeds to release or restrict all or any of the foregoing powers or this present power either in whole or in part and in any manner they think fit provided that the foregoing power may be exercised before the relevant day by a sole trustee who is not a trust corporation.

(4) In default of and subject to any or every exercise of the foregoing powers my trustees shall hold my residuary estate during the trust period upon trust to pay or apply the income thereof to or for the maintenance education or benefit of all or any one or more of the beneficiaries and if more than one in such shares and in such manner generally as my trustees think fit; provided that during the accumulation period[14] my trustees may accumulate all or any part or parts of such income by investing the same and the resulting income thereof in any investments hereby authorised and so

that any accumulations so made shall form part of the capital of my residuary estate (or the part thereof from which such income arose) for all purposes.

(5) Subject as aforesaid my trustees shall hold my residuary estate and the income thereof at the expiration of the trust period upon trust for such of my grandchildren and remoter issue as shall be then living in equal shares per stirpes.

(6) Any capital or income of my residuary estate not otherwise disposed of by this clause shall be held in trust for such of my children as shall survive me and if more than one in equal shares.

1 Because it may be important to be able to make appointments or distributions within two years of death falling within the ITA 1984, s 144 (see C3 at paras **[225.83]–[225.91]**), various provisions are included to facilitate such appointments. However, in contrast with Form C3.6, cl 3 at paras **[225.100]–[225.104]** (which is formulated with s 144 in mind), in this form the discretionary trusts and powers continue for a full perpetuity period and do not cease at the end of two years from the testator's death.

2 This should be included where either partner has children by someone other than the current partner.

3 80 years is the maximum fixed period of years permissible under the PAA 1964, s 1 (Part G, para **[246.89]**). The disadvantage of adopting an 80-year period for these trusts is that when it comes to making an appointment of, eg a life interest with remainders, an old-style perpetuity period of a life in being plus 21 years cannot be used, and express perpetuity restrictions will often have to be imposed to make sure that the interests which are appointed vest within the perpetuity period. The discretionary trusts and powers continue throughout the perpetuity period: see n 1 to this clause below.

4 This definition relates to some short-term measures to make it easier for appointments within the ITA 1984, s 144 to be made.

5 If the primary beneficiaries die out, this will enables the trustees to distribute the estate to more distant relations or charity, and avoids an intestacy, or the class of beneficiaries being reduced to consisting only of the widows and widowers of issue.

6 See proviso (vii) to subclause (3)(a) and subclauses (3)(b), (c) and (d) of this clause for the modification of this provision during the two years following the testator's death, so as to make it easier for appointments within the ITA 1984, s 144 to be made.

7 For precedents of appointments see the forms in F4 at paras **[242.7]–[242.16]**.

8 These words authorise the creation of discretionary trusts or powers which might not otherwise be valid: see Vol 1, para **[40.5]**.

9 This is included so as to make it easier to make an appointment within the ITA 1984, s 144 at an early stage. The main reason for such a provision, ie to make exempt appointments before applying for a grant of probate (see C3 at paras **[225.83]–[225.91]**), is not likely to apply in relation to wills in this form, however, because of the lack of a spouse exemption.

10 This is included with the ITA 1984, s 144 (see C3 at paras **[225.83]–[225.91]**) in mind. If it were required that there should be two trustees during the two years after the testator's death, difficulty could arise if the number of trustees were reduced to one and the administration of the estate was not complete, as it is not clear that the statutory power to appoint new trustees could be exercised in such circumstances.

11 For the reasons for the proviso, see n 10 above. A power to apply capital is a useful alternative to a power of appointment, because fewer formalities are needed for its exercise, and because it permits a wide range of applications for a person's benefit such as lending him money, paying his debts, etc: see B18 at paras **[218.94]–[218.98]** for the scope of a power of this type. It is important that the exercise of such a power should be adequately evidenced.

12 To be included where either partner has children by someone other than the current partner.

13 See Form C3.6, cl 3(1)(b), n 2 at para **[225.100]**. In wills of this type for unmarried couples with children, it is a particularly good idea to include a power to add to the class of beneficiaries such as this subclause, as it will be a means of adding, eg unmarried partners of the testator's issue, or children of uncertain paternity, to the class of beneficiaries. The power to add charities would enable transfers to charity to be made so as to obtain IHT charitable gift exemption on the testator's death where the transfer fell within the ITA 1984,

s 144 (for which see C3 at paras **[225.83]**–**[225.91]**), and the second proviso enables charity to be added to the class of beneficiaries before probate is obtained. For the purpose of the first proviso see subclause 3(a)(vii), n 10 above.

14 Accumulation for the period of 21 years following the death of the testator is a permitted period under the LPA 1925, s 164(1)(b) (Part G, para **[246.71]**).

[228.29]

ADMINISTRATIVE POWERS

8. [*As in cl 9 of* Form C6.1 *at para* **[228.15]**.]

[228.30]

TRUSTEE INDEMNITY

9. [*As in cl 10(1) of* Form C6.1 *at para* **[228.16]**.]

[228.31]

EXERCISE OF POWERS[1]

10. Any power or discretion hereby or by law conferred on my trustees shall be exercisable in favour of any person who is an object of such power or discretion notwithstanding that he or she is one of my trustees and shall be exercisable notwithstanding that any of my trustees has any other direct or indirect personal interest in the mode or result of such exercise [provided that there are not fewer than two trustees and at least one of them has no personal interest in the mode or result of exercising the same].[2]

1 This clause permits a member of the family to be a trustee without disqualifying him or her from benefit under any exercise of statutory or express powers of payment or application of capital, appointment, etc. See the Preliminary Note to B18 at paras **[218.4]** and **[218.5]**.

2 If all the executors are to be members of the testator's family and beneficiaries, it would be advisable to omit these words in square brackets. Even if there are some independent executors and some family members as executors, it might still be better to omit these words in case the independent trustees never take office. It should also be noted that this clause does not impose a requirement that there should be two trustees acting where a power is exercised in favour of a trustee (compare Form C3.2, cl 11 at para **[225.39]**), because such a restriction could cause difficulty in exercising of the powers within two years after the testator's death (see cl 7, n 1 at para **[228.28]**).

If it is thought that family members cannot be relied on to act disinterestedly and without causing disputes, independent persons who are not beneficiaries should be appointed as executors, and perhaps excluded as potential objects of the power to add to the class of beneficiaries contained in cl 7(3)(c) at para **[228.28]**.

[228.32]

PROFESSIONAL TRUSTEE CHARGING CLAUSE

11. [*As in cl 11 of* Form C6.1 *at para* **[228.17]**.]

[*Testimonium and attestation clause as in* Form C6.1 *at para* **[228.18]**.]

[228.33]

Form C6.3: Will of man separated (but not judicially separated) from wife and living with another woman, where divorce proceedings are contemplated

Note. This will is intended as a temporary measure pending divorce proceedings. It is assumed that the testator is separated from his wife and children, and is living with another woman whom he wishes to benefit so far as practicable by his will. It is assumed that the wife and children are living in the former matrimonial home, and that the testator and his wife own that home as tenants in common, the testator having taken steps to sever any joint tenancy. This will should be reviewed as and when the divorce takes place and the financial arrangements are settled. The provision for the wife is confined to a right to occupy the former matrimonial home. Such provision will lapse on the dissolution of the marriage – the Wills Act 1837, s 18A (Part G, para **[244.17]**) – if it is not superseded by the financial settlement on divorce, which may well bring about some alteration of the ownership of the matrimonial home in the wife's or children's favour.

[228.34]

REVOCATION CLAUSE

I [*name*] of [*address*] hereby revoke all former testamentary dispositions made by me and declare this to be my last will.

[228.35]

APPOINTMENT OF EXECUTORS AND TRUSTEES

1. [*As in cl 1 of* Form C6.2 *at para* **[228.22]**.]

[228.36]

APPOINTMENT OF GUARDIANS[1]

2. If my wife [*name*] ('my wife') shall predecease me I appoint [*name*] of [*address*] [and [*name*] of [*address*]] to be the [guardian/guardians] of any child or children of ours who are minors at the date of my death.

1 For appointments of guardians where both parents are living and have parental responsibility, see the Note in B3 at para **[203.47]** ff and the Preliminary Note to C2 at para **[224.11]**.

[228.37]

GIFT OF INTEREST IN DWELLINGHOUSE ON TRUSTS PERMITTING WIFE TO OCCUPY DWELLINGHOUSE FOR LIFE OR DURING WIDOWHOOD[1]

3. (1) I give to my trustees all my interest in the dwellinghouse situate at [*address*] which is now occupied by my wife and which is vested in us both as beneficial tenants in common in equal shares to hold the same upon the trusts hereinafter declared.

(2) So long as my wife [shall not remarry and] shall desire to occupy the said dwellinghouse my trustees shall permit her to have the use and enjoyment thereof and shall not seek to bring about a sale of the same or take any step to prevent my wife from having the beneficial use and occupation thereof.

(3) Subject as aforesaid[2] my trustees shall hold the said interest and the assets for the time being representing the same (hereinafter called 'the trust fund') upon trust for such of my children as shall survive me and attain the age of 25 years[3] and if more than one in equal shares; provided that if any of my children shall not live to attain a vested interest under the foregoing trust leaving a child or children living at or born after my death who shall attain the age of 21 years[4] such last-mentioned child or children shall take and if more than one equally between them the share of the trust fund which his her or their parent would have taken had he or she lived to attain a vested interest.

(4) The foregoing trusts shall carry the intermediate income of the trust fund and section 31 of the Trustee Act 1925 (as hereinafter modified) shall apply thereto.

(5) Section 32 of the Trustee Act 1925 (as hereinafter modified) shall apply in relation to the said trusts.

[(6) I declare that I have made no further provision for my wife on the grounds that if she survives me as my widow she will become entitled to a widow's pension and that she is otherwise adequately provided for].[5]

1 This gift confers a residence right on the wife which will lapse on divorce. It will create a trust of an undivided share in land, which will be a trust of land within the TLATA 1996 (see the LPA 1925, s 205(1)(ix), as amended by the TLATA 1996, s 23(2) and Sch 4: Part G, para **[246.74]**). It is assumed that the testator has severed any joint tenancy to which the matrimonial home is subject. See the Note to this form at para **[228.33]**. It is thought that the wife will have an IPDI in the half share of the house and that the spouse exemption will apply (see paras **[200.84]**, **[200.95]** and **[200.98]**).

2 The gift in favour of the children will be accelerated on the dissolution of the marriage: see the WA 1837, s 18A (Part G, para **[244.18]**).

3 See Form C6.1, cl 7, n 1, at para **[228.13]**. See also the extended accumulation and maintenance provision in cl 6(1) of this form at para **[228.40]**, and Form C6.1, cl 7, n 3, at para **[228.13]**.

4 See Form C6.1, cl 7, n 2, at para **[228.13]**.

5 A declaration in this form may possibly be useful in the event that the husband dies before the marriage is dissolved and the wife makes a claim under the I(PFD)A 1975 (Part G, para **[247.1]** ff and discussed in Vol 1 at para **[105.1]** ff).

[228.38]

ADMINISTRATION TRUSTS OF RESIDUE

4. [*As in cl 6 of* Form C6.1 *at para* **[228.12]**.]

[228.39]

BENEFICIAL TRUSTS OF RESIDUE

5. (1) My trustees shall hold my residuary estate and the income thereof upon trust for [*name of partner*] if she survives me [by the period of one month][1] absolutely.

(2) If the said [*name of partner*] shall not survive me then my trustees shall hold my residuary estate upon trust for such of my children as shall survive me and attain the age of 25 years[2] and if more than one in equal shares provided that if any of my children shall not live to attain a vested interest under the foregoing trust leaving a child or children living at or born after my death who shall attain the age of [18/21] years[3] such last-mentioned child or children shall take and if more than one equally between then the share of my residuary estate which his her or their parent would have taken had he or she lived to attain a vested interest.

(3) The foregoing trust shall carry the intermediate income of my residuary estate and section 31 of the Trustee Act 1925 (as hereinafter modified) shall apply thereto.

(4) Section 32 of the Trustee Act 1925 (as hereinafter modified) shall apply in relation to the said trusts.

1 The words in square brackets will ensure that if the testator and partner die in a common accident or within the period of one month of each other, the residuary estate will devolve directly on the children. If the period does not exceed six months, the gift to the children

will be treated (by IHTA 1984, s 92) for IHT purposes as having taken effect, on the testator's death. Survivorship conditions can have a useful function in relation to a non-exempt (from IHT) gift, but not in relation to a gift to a spouse or civil partner: see the Preliminary Note to C2 at paras **[224.6]–[224.10]**.

2 See Form C6.1, cl 7, n 1, at para **[228.13]**. See also the extended accumulation and maintenance provision in cl 6(1) of this form at para **[228.40]**, and Form C6.1, cl 7, n 3, at para **[228.13]**.

3 See Form C6.1, cl 7, n 2, at para **[228.13]**.

[228.40]

MAINTENANCE, ACCUMULATION AND ADVANCEMENT

6. (1) Section 31 of the Trustee Act 1925 (relating to accumulation and maintenance) shall apply in relation to the trusts hereby or by any codicil hereto declared as if:

(a) in paragraph (i) of subsection (1) of the said section the words 'as the trustees think fit' were substituted for the words 'as may in all the circumstances be reasonable'; and

(b) the proviso to the said subsection (1) were omitted,

provided that in relation to any presumptive share or shares of any child of mine under any such trust or trusts the said section 31 (amended as aforesaid) shall have effect as if the age of majority were the lesser of the age which he or she will attain (if he or she so long lives) on his or her last birthday occurring not later than the expiration of 21 years from my death and the age of 25 years (and so that the expressions 'infancy', 'minority' and 'infant' and all references to the age of 18 years in the said Section 31 shall be construed accordingly).[1]

(2) [*As in cl 8(2) of* Form C6.1 *at para* **[228.14]**.]

(3) [*As in cl 8(3) of* Form C6.1 *at para* **[228.14]**.]

1 See Form C6.1, cl 7, n 3, at para **[228.13]**.

[228.41]

ADMINISTRATIVE POWERS

7. [*As in cl 9 of* Form C6.1 *at para* **[228.15]**.]

[228.42]

TRUSTEE INDEMNITY

8. [*As in cl 10(1) of* Form C6.1 *at para* **[228.16]**.]

[228.43]

PROFESSIONAL TRUSTEE CHARGING CLAUSE

9. [*As in cl 11 of* Form C6.1 *at para* **[228.17]**.]

[*Testimonium and attestation clause as in* Form C6.1 *at para* **[228.18]**.]

C7 Wills for sole parents with young children

Preliminary note .... **[229.1]**

FORMS

C7.1 Will of mother giving entire estate to her minor child .... **[229.2]**

C7.2 Will of mother appointing sister sole executrix and guardian of children and giving entire estate to her if accepting office, with alternative gift to children .... **[229.13]**

C7.3 Will of widow or widower in favour of children .... **[229.26]**

C7.4 Will of widow or widower settling residue on children equally for life with remainder to their children .... **[229.37]**

PRELIMINARY NOTE

[229.1]

This section is intended to cater for the needs of a sole parent with young children. The parent, usually the mother, may be single for one of a variety of reasons, but whatever the reason there will be no spouse or partner to provide for. Very often the sole parent will not have much to leave and making a will may not seem important. But a sole parent with young children would be wise to make a will, if only to appoint a guardian, and all the forms in the section contain provision for such an appointment. For a discussion of the law relating to guardianship see Vol 1, para **[28.1]** ff and the Note to Forms B3.28 to B3.34 at paras **[203.47]** ff.

The forms in this section contain a few alternative beneficial dispositions of the parent's estate. In Forms C7.1 (at paras **[229.2]**–**[229.12]**) and C7.3 (at paras **[229.26]**–**[229.36]**) the entire estate is left on contingent trusts for the child or children at 25 with substitutional trusts in favour of his, her or their children, whereas in Form C7.4 (at paras **[229.37]**–**[229.50]**) the entire estate is settled on the children for life with power to apply capital for their benefit and with remainder in favour of their children. Where the estate is small, the cost and trouble of administering trusts during a minority may be disproportionately great, and a possible solution would be to give the estate to the guardian if he or she accepts office as in Form C7.2 (at paras **[229.13]**–**[229.25]**). This might be a suitable course where the guardian is a close relative and the child would effectively become a member of the guardian's family. Where the estate is large or includes business or agricultural property or foreign property, the forms in this section may not be suitable and the forms in C11, C12 or C13 (at paras **[233.1]**–**[235.39]**) should be consulted.

Although Forms C7.3 and C7.4 are entitled wills for a widow or widower, they are suitable for other sole parents.

The forms in this section, which are intended to cater for the needs of a sole parent with young children, are not relevant to civil partners.

[229.2]

Form C7.1: Will of mother giving entire estate to her minor child

Note. This form is intended for a single mother with one child only.

[229.3]

REVOCATION CLAUSE

I [*name*] of [*address*] hereby revoke all former testamentary dispositions made by me and declare this to be my last will.

[229.4]

APPOINTMENT OF EXECUTORS AND TRUSTEES

1. I appoint [*name*] of [*address*] and [*name*] of [*address*] (hereinafter together called 'my trustees' which expression shall include my personal representatives for the time being and the trustees for the time being hereof) to be the executors and trustees of this will.

[229.5]

APPOINTMENT OF GUARDIANS[1]

2. I appoint [the said [*name*] and the said [*name*]]/[[*name*] of [*address*] [and [*name*] of [*address*]]] to be the [guardian/guardians] of my [son/daughter] [*name*] during [his/her] minority.

1 One of the main reasons for a sole parent with young children to make a will is to appoint a guardian or guardians. It may be possible or appropriate to appoint the same persons as executors and guardians. As to the appointment of guardians see the Note to Forms B3.28 to B3.34 at paras **[203.47]** ff and the more general discussion of the law in Vol 1 at para **[28.1]** ff.

[229.6]

ADMINISTRATION TRUSTS OF RESIDUE

3. (1) I give all my property not hereby or by any codicil hereto otherwise effectively disposed of [(including any entailed or other property over which I shall have at my death a general power of disposition by will)][1] to my trustees to hold on the trusts set out below with power at their discretion to sell all or any of it as and when they think fit.[2]

(2) My trustees shall pay my funeral and testamentary expenses[3] and debts and any legacies given by this will or any codicil hereto out of such property or its proceeds and shall have a discretion as to how such payments shall be borne as between capital and income[4].

(3) Subject as above my trustees shall hold such property and the assets from time to time representing the same (hereinafter called 'my residuary estate') on the trusts set out below and shall invest all money comprised in such property or arising from its sale in any of the investments hereby authorised with power to change such investments into any others hereby authorised.

(4) In the administration of my estate and the execution of the trusts of this will or of any codicil to it:

(a) my trustees shall treat all income as accruing on the date on which it becomes payable regardless of the period in respect of which it shall have accrued and shall not make any statutory apportionment of the same;[5] and

(b) none of the equitable rules of apportionment between capital and income shall apply in any circumstances whatever.[6]

1 See para **[224.34]**, n 1.
2 See para **[224.34]**, n 2.
3 See para **[224.34]**, n 3.
4 See para **[224.34]**, n 4.
5 See para **[224.34]**, n 5.
6 See para **[224.34]**, n 6.

[229.7]

BENEFICIAL TRUSTS OF ESTATE

4. (1) My trustees shall hold my residuary estate upon trust for my said [son/daughter] if [he/she] shall attain the age of 25 years[1] absolutely provided that if [he/she] shall predecease me or having survived me die before attaining the said age leaving a child or children [him/ her] surviving who attain the age of 21 years[2] such last mentioned child or children shall take my residuary estate and if more than one in equal shares.

(2) The foregoing trusts shall carry the intermediate income of my residuary estate and section 31 of the Trustee Act 1925 (as hereinafter modified) shall apply thereto provided that in relation to my said [son/daughter] the said section 31 (amended as aforesaid) shall take effect for all purposes as if the age of majority were the lesser of the age which my said [son/daughter] will attain (if [he/she] so long lives) on [his/her] last birthday occurring not later than the expiration of 21 years from my death and the age of 25 years[3] and so that all references in the said section 31 to 'infancy' 'minority' and 'infant' and all references therein to the age of eighteen years shall be construed accordingly.

(3) Section 32 of the Trustee Act 1925 (as hereinafter modified) shall apply in relation to my residuary estate.

(4) My trustees may exercise their powers to apply income or capital for the benefit of my said [son/daughter] by paying or transferring the same to [his/her] guardian for the time being.[4]

(5) Subject as aforesaid my trustees shall hold my residuary estate upon trust for such of my brothers and sisters [*name*] [*name*] [*name*] and [*name*] as survive me and if more than one in equal shares.

1 Since the child will be a life in being for perpetuity purposes, the age contingency does not have to be restricted to any particular age. If the vesting age is 25 or less the trust will fall within one of the favoured categories: the choice here is between a vesting age of 18, which will mean that it is a trust for a bereaved minor within IHTA 1984, s 71A (see para **[200.108]**), or a vesting age of 25, which will mean that it is an age 18-to-25 trust within IHTA 1984, s 71D (see para **[200.109]**). If a greater vesting age, or a life interest, is desired, the choice is between an IPDI trust or a relevant property trust (see paras **[200.98]**, **[200.126]** and **[200.132]**). If 25 is adopted as the vesting age, the accumulation and maintenance trusts of income under TA 1925, s 31 should be extended beyond the age of 18 as in sub-cl (2).

2 The grandchildren will not necessarily be lives in being and the age contingency is therefore restricted to 21. Any settled property which becomes subject to this substitutional proviso will fall within the IHT charging regime for relevant property (see para **[218.8]** ff) if the substituted grandchildren are under the age of vesting at the death of the testator, unless the age of vesting is 21 and a substituted grandchild has an IPDI as a result of being over 18 (and thus entitled to an interest in possession by virtue of TA 1925, s 31) but under 21 at or within two years after the testator's death (see para **[224.25]**). The possibility of a grandchild becoming entitled to an IPDI can be avoided by extending the accumulation and maintenance trusts of TA 1925, s 31 to the age of 21 for grandchildren. If the fund is likely to be below the IHT threshold, the IHT classification of this trust is not important.

3 It is possible to extend the statutory provisions for maintenance and accumulation to any age which will be attained during the period of 21 years following the testator's death (LPA 1925, s 164(1)(b): Part G, para **[246.56]**). See the note on extended accumulation and maintenance provisions in B18 at paras **[218.74]–[218.78]**. The age at which accumulation and maintenance trusts of income cease should not be greater than 25 where (as will usually be the case) it is desired that the IHTA 1984, s 71D should apply: see Part A, para **[200.109]**. On the other hand, it is strongly recommended, in relation to trusts of this type where capital vests contingently on attaining a specified age, that accumulation and maintenance trusts should be extended in this way to the maximum possible age (not more than the vesting age) to prevent the beneficiary having an IPDI in consequence of attaining the age at which the accumulation and maintenance trusts cease by the time of the testator's death or within two years after it (see para **[224.25]**).

4 It is not strictly necessary to include a power to pay income or capital to a guardian in view of the ChA 1989, s 3(3) (Part G, para **[244.114]**) which authorises any person with 'parental responsibility' in respect of a child to receive or recover property which the child is entitled to receive or recover, but it does no harm to include an express power.

[229.8]

MAINTENANCE, ACCUMULATION AND ADVANCEMENT[1]

5. (1) Section 31 of the Trustee Act 1925 (relating to accumulation and maintenance) shall apply in relation to the trusts hereby or by any codicil hereto declared as if:

(a) in paragraph (i) of subsection (1) of the said section the words 'as the trustees think fit' were substituted for the words 'as may in all the circumstances be reasonable'; and

(b) the proviso to the said subsection (1) were omitted.

(2) Section 32 of the Trustee Act 1925 (relating to advancement) shall apply in relation to the said trusts as if the words 'one half of' were omitted from proviso (a) to subsection (1) thereof.[2]

(3) Whenever my trustees shall have an obligation or discretion under the provisions of this will or any codicil hereto or under the general law to apply income or capital for the benefit of a minor beneficiary they may either pay the same without liability to account to his or her parent guardian or any other adult person with whom such beneficiary may be residing or to such beneficiary himself or herself if of the age of 16 years or more and so that the receipt of such parent guardian or other person or of such minor beneficiary shall be a full and sufficient discharge to my trustees for the income or capital so applied.[3]

1 For alternative provisions relating to maintenance and advancement see Forms B18.11 to B18.23 and the notes thereto at paras **[218.79]–[218.108]**.

2 An expanded TA 1925, s 32 power is expressly within the scope of IHTA 1984, ss 71A and 71D (see paras **[200.108]** and **[200.109]**).

3 A parent (with parental responsibility) and a guardian of a minor are empowered by the ChA 1989, s 3(3) (Part G, para **[244.114]**) to give a good receipt for the minor's property: see Vol 1, para **[9.42]**. The power in this subclause is wider in that it authorises the payment of income or capital to a parent who does not have parental responsibility, any adult with whom the minor is residing, and the minor himself or herself if 16 or over.

[229.9]

ADMINISTRATIVE POWERS[1]

6. (1) In this clause where the context so admits:

(a) the expression 'land' includes buildings and estates interests or rights of any kind in or over land; and

(b) during the administration of my estate the expression 'beneficiary' includes any person who would be a beneficiary if such administration had been completed and the expression 'beneficially interested' and references to income of any asset being payable or capable of being paid to or for the benefit of a beneficiary shall be construed accordingly.

(2) None of the powers or provisions contained in subclause (3) below of this clause shall be capable of being exercised or operating in any manner such that if such power or provision were capable of being so exercised or so operating the existence of the same would either:

(i) prevent any person who would in the absence of such power or provision have been entitled to an interest in possession falling within section 49(1A) of the Inheritance Tax Act 1984 in any property from being entitled to such interest; or

(ii) prevent section 71A or 71D of the Inheritance Tax Act 1984 from applying to any property to which in the absence of such power or provision either section would have applied.[2]

(3) In the administration of my estate and the execution of the trusts hereof or of any codicil hereto my trustees shall have the following powers in addition to those conferred by law but subject to the last foregoing subclause:

(a) power to invest moneys sell assets and change investments with the unrestricted freedom of choice and powers of disposition and acquisition of a sole beneficial owner with in particular power to make unsecured loans, acquire non-income yielding assets, and purchase land anywhere in the world or chattels for any purpose including occupation or enjoyment in kind by a beneficiary under the power set out below;[3]

(b) power to delegate all or any of their investment powers to a professional investment manager or managers whether individual or corporate and whether or not also a nominee holder of assets for my trustees (and who may be or include one or more of my trustees or the beneficiaries hereunder) upon such terms as to remuneration and otherwise (including terms authorising self-dealing or providing for the limitation of the liability of the investment manager or managers) as my trustees think fit and section 22 of the Trustee Act 2000 shall not apply;[4]

(c) power to vest or register any property in any person or persons whether individual or corporate and whether or not an investment manager to whom powers have been delegated under the foregoing power (and who may be or include one or more of my trustees or the beneficiaries hereunder) as nominee or nominees for my trustees upon such terms as to remuneration or otherwise (including terms authorising self-dealing or providing for the limitation of the liability of the nominee) as my trustees think fit and section 22 of the Trustee Act 2000 shall not apply;[5]

(d) power to borrow money with or without giving security and on such terms as to interest and repayment and otherwise as my trustees may think fit for any purpose connected with the administration of my estate or the trusts declared herein or in any codicil hereto (including investment) And no lender from whom my trustees borrow money in purported exercise of this power shall be concerned to enquire as to the propriety amount or purpose of any such borrowing;[6]

(e) power to lend money to a beneficiary to whom any of the income of such money is payable or to whom or for whose benefit any income of such money is capable of being paid or applied in exercise of a discretion (or who would be such a beneficiary if such money yielded income) and to do so at a full or concessionary rate of interest or interest free;[7]

(f) all the powers of an absolute owner in relation to any land (wherever situated) held by them;[8]

(g) power to apply capital held on the same trusts as any land (or which would be so held if the administration of my estate had been completed) in the improvement of such land and to apply such capital or the income of such capital on the repair or maintenance of such land;[9]

(h) power to permit any beneficiary to have the beneficial occupation use or enjoyment in kind of any land or chattel or other tangible property on such terms as to repair insurance or payment of outgoings by the beneficiary or otherwise howsoever as my trustees think fit Provided that the foregoing power shall only be exercisable and such permission to occupy or enjoy in kind may only continue in the following circumstances:

    (i) so long as any of the income of such land chattel or other tangible property is payable to such beneficiary or capable of being paid or applied to him or for his benefit in exercise of a discretion (or would be so payable or capable of being so paid or applied if such land chattel or other property yielded income);

    (ii) in the case of land, so long as for the time being the occupation thereof by such beneficiary is compatible with any statutory rights of occupation of any other beneficiary or beneficiaries;[10]

(i) power to exercise all the powers of appropriation (and other incidental powers) conferred by statute on a personal representative without the necessity of obtaining any consents and notwithstanding that one or more of my trustees may be beneficially interested in the exercise of such power.[11]

1 See para **[224.37]**, n 1.
2 See para **[224.37]**, n 2.
3 See para **[224.37]**, n 3.
4 See para **[224.37]**, n 4.
5 See para **[224.37]**, n 5.
6 See para **[224.37]**, n 6.
7 See para **[224.37]**, n 7.
8 See para **[224.37]**, n 8.
9 See para **[224.37]**, n 9.
10 See para **[224.37]**, n 10.
11 See para **[224.37]**, n 11.

[229.10]

TRUSTEE LIABILITY

7. (1) My trustees shall not be liable for any act or default of any investment manager or nominee employed in good faith to manage or hold assets of my estate nor for any act or default of any beneficiary having the occupation use or enjoyment of property in kind.[1]

(2) Section 11(1) of the Trusts of Land and Appointment of Trustees Act 1996 (consultation with beneficiaries) shall not apply to the exercise by my trustees of any of their powers in relation to land subject to the trusts hereof.[2]

1 This makes it clear that the trustees are not liable for the defaults of others who may have possession or control of trust property. For a wider form of indemnity, see e g Form B21.12 at para **[221.16]**. If a paid trustee is to rely on this indemnity clause, the testator should specifically be made aware of its meaning and effect (see para **[221.13]** above).

2 The requirement that trustees of land in exercise of any function relating to land subject to the trust consult with beneficiaries of full age beneficially entitled to an interest in possession in the land can be excluded: TLATA 1996, s 11 (Part G, para **[246.114]**).

[229.11]

PROFESSIONAL TRUSTEE CHARGING CLAUSE

8. Any of my trustees being a professional or business man may charge and be paid all usual professional and other proper charges for business transacted acts done advice given and time spent by him or his firm in connection with the administration of my estate or in connection with the trusts hereof including acts which a personal representative or trustee not being in any profession or business could have done personally.

[229.12]

TESTIMONIUM AND ATTESTATION CLAUSE

IN WITNESS whereof I have hereunto set my hand this —— day of —— 20——.

SIGNED by the above-named testatrix as her last will in the presence of us both present at the same time who at her request and in her presence and in the presence of each other have signed our names below as witnesses:	}	[*Signature of testatrix*]

[*Signatures, addresses and descriptions of two witnesses*]

[229.13]

Form C7.2: Will of mother appointing sister sole executrix and guardian of children and giving entire estate to her if accepting office, with alternative gift to children

Note. This form gives the entire estate to the guardian beneficially and is unlikely to be suitable unless the estate is relatively small: see the Preliminary Note to this section at para **[229.1]** ff. A will in this form will need to be kept under review especially as the children approach the age of majority.

[229.14]

REVOCATION CLAUSE

I [*name*] of [*address*] hereby revoke all former testamentary dispositions made by me and declare this to be my last will.

[229.15]

APPOINTMENT OF GUARDIAN[1]

1. If my children or any of them are minors at the time of my death I appoint my sister [*name*] of [*address*] to be the guardian of my children during their respective minorities.

1 See Form C7.1, cl 2, n 1 at para **[229.5]**.

[229.16]

GIFT OF ESTATE TO GUARDIAN AND APPOINTMENT OF GUARDIAN AS SOLE EXECUTRIX

2. If my children or any of them are minors at the time of my death and my said sister is willing to act as guardian then I appoint my said sister sole executrix of this will and subject to the payment thereout of any funeral and testamentary expenses and debts I give all of my estate both real and personal to my said sister absolutely [with the request (but not so as to impose on her any trust or obligation) that she apply the same and the income thereof for the benefit of my children].[1]

1 If included, the words in square brackets will impose on the sister only a moral obligation to apply the estate for the benefit of the deceased's children. To impose a legal obligation to do so would frustrate the purpose of the precedent which is to allow the guardian (in this form the sister of the testatrix) to treat the estate as her own and to avoid the need to administer a separate trust fund.

[229.17]

ALTERNATIVE PROVISIONS[1]

3. If my said sister shall predecease me or having survived me shall decline to accept office as guardian of such of my children as are minors at the time of my death or if at my death none of my children are minors then the following provisions shall have effect.

1 Alternative beneficial provisions similar to those contained in Form C7.1 are included in case the primary gift fails.

[229.18]

APPOINTMENT OF EXECUTORS AND TRUSTEES

4. [*As in cl 1 of* Form C7.1 *at para* **[229.4]**.]

[229.19]

APPOINTMENT OF GUARDIANS

5. I appoint [*name*] of [*address*] [and [*name*] of [*address*]] to be the [guardian/guardians] of my children during their respective minorities.

[229.20]

ADMINISTRATION TRUSTS OF ESTATE

6. [*As in cl 3 of* Form C7.1 *at para* **[229.6]**.]

[229.21]

BENEFICIAL TRUSTS OF ESTATE

7. (1) My trustees shall hold my residuary estate upon trust for such of my children as shall survive me and attain the age of 25 years[1] and if more than one in equal shares provided that if any of my children shall predecease me or survive me and die under the said age leaving a child or children living at or after my death who shall attain the age of 21 years[2] such last-mentioned child or children shall take and if more than one equally between them the share of my residuary estate which such deceased child of mine would have taken had he or she survived me.

(2) The foregoing trusts shall carry the intermediate income of my residuary estate and section 31 of the Trustee Act 1925 (as hereinafter modified) shall apply thereto provided that in relation to the presumptive share of my residuary estate of any child of mine the said section shall take effect for all purposes as if the age of majority were the lesser of the age which he or she will attain (if he or she so long lives) on his or her last birthday occurring not later than the expiration of 21 years from my death and the age of 25 years and so that all references in the said section 31 to 'infancy' 'minority' and 'infant' and all references therein to the age of eighteen years shall be construed accordingly.[3]

(3) Section 32 of the Trustee Act 1925 (as hereinafter modified) shall apply in relation to my residuary estate.

(4) My trustees may exercise their powers to apply income or capital for the benefit of any of my said children by paying or transferring the same to [his/her] guardian for the time being.[4]

(5) Subject as aforesaid my trustees shall hold my residuary estate upon trust for such of my brothers and sisters [*name*] [*name*] [*name*] and [*name*] as survive me if more than one in equal shares.

1 See Form C7.1, cl 4(1), n 1 at para **[229.7]**.
2 See Form C7.1, cl 4(1), n 2 at para **[229.7]**.
3 See Form C7.1, cl 4(2), n 3 at para **[229.7]**.
4 See Form C7.1, cl 4(4), n 4 at para **[229.7]**.

[229.22]

MAINTENANCE, ACCUMULATION AND ADVANCEMENT

8. [*As in cl 5 of* Form C7.1 *at para* **[229.8]**.]

[229.23]

ADMINISTRATIVE POWERS

9. [*As in cl 6 of* Form C7.1 *at para* **[229.9]**.]

[229.24]

TRUSTEE LIABILITY

10. [*As in cl 7 of* Form C7.1 *at para* **[229.10]**.]

[229.25]

PROFESSIONAL TRUSTEE CHARGING CLAUSE

11. [*As in cl 8 of* Form C7.1 *at para* **[229.11]**.]

[*Testimonium and attestation clause as in* Form C7.1 *at para* **[229.12]**.]

[229.26]

Form C7.3: Will of widow or widower in favour of children

Note. This form in effect reproduces the alternative provisions contained in cls 3 to 9 of Form C7.2 (at paras **[229.17]**–**[229.23]**).

[229.27]

REVOCATION CLAUSE

I [*name*] of [*address*] hereby revoke all former testamentary dispositions made by me and declare this to be my last will.

[229.28]

APPOINTMENT OF EXECUTORS AND TRUSTEES

1. [*As in cl 1 of* Form C7.1 *at para* **[229.4]**.]

[229.29]

APPOINTMENT OF GUARDIANS

2. [*As in cl 5 of* Form C7.2 *at para* **[229.19]**.]

[229.30]

ADMINISTRATION TRUSTS OF ESTATE

3. [*As in cl 3 of* Form C7.1 *at para* **[229.6]**.]

[229.31]

BENEFICIAL TRUSTS OF RESIDUE

4. [*As in cl 7 of* Form C7.2 *at para* **[229.21]**.]

[229.32]

MAINTENANCE, ACCUMULATION AND ADVANCEMENT

5. [*As in cl 5 of* Form C7.1 *at para* **[229.8]**.]

[229.33]

ADMINISTRATIVE POWERS

6. [*As in cl 6 of* Form C7.1 *at para* **[229.9]**.]

[229.34]

TRUSTEE LIABILITY

7. [*As in cl 7 of* Form C7.1 *at para* **[229.10]**.]

[229.35]

PROFESSIONAL TRUSTEE CHARGING CLAUSE

8. [*As in cl 8 of* Form C7.1 *at para* **[229.11]**.]

[229.36]

TESTIMONIUM AND ATTESTATION CLAUSE

IN WITNESS whereof I have hereunto set my hand this —— day of —— 20——.

SIGNED by the above-named [testator/testatrix] as [his/her] last will in the presence of us both present at the same time who at [his/her] request and in [his/her] presence and in the presence of each other have signed our names below as witnesses: } [*Signature of testator/testatrix*]

[*Signatures, addresses and descriptions of two witnesses*]

[229.37]

Form C7.4: Will of widow or widower settling residue on children equally for life with remainder to their children

Note. This form is an alternative to Form C7.3 in that the interest of each child instead of being a contingent interest in capital is settled on the child for life, with a power to pay capital to him or for his benefit. This is for a testator who does not want capital to vest as early as the age of 25, and so rejects the use of trusts falling within IHTA 1984, s 71 or 71A (see Part A, paras **[200.108]** **[200.109]**). The testator therefore has a choice between the trusts having beneficiary-taxed IHT status, by providing IPDIs (for which see para **[200.98]**), where the IHT periodic and exit charges on relevant property are avoided but capital gains tax hold-over relief is not available on distribution to a beneficiary, or being relevant property which is subject to the periodic charge and exit charges (for which see paras **[218.8]** ff) but where there can be capital gains tax hold-over relief on a distribution to a beneficiary (see para **[200.39]**). For further discussion of this choice see paras **[200.131]** and **[200.132]**. This form provides alternative wording for these possibilities in the alternative sub-cll (1) of cl 8 at para **[229.46]**.

[229.38]

REVOCATION CLAUSE

I [*name*] of [*address*] hereby revoke all former testamentary dispositions made by me and declare this to be my last will.

[229.39]

APPOINTMENT OF EXECUTORS AND TRUSTEES

1. [*As in cl 1 of* Form C7.1 *at para* **[229.4]**.]

[229.40]

APPOINTMENT OF GUARDIANS

2. [*As in cl 5 of* Form C7.2 *at para* **[229.19]**.]

[229.41]

PECUNIARY LEGACIES

3. I give free of tax[1] the following pecuniary legacies:

(a) to [*name*] of [*address*] the sum of ——;
(b) to [*name*] of [*address*] the sum of ——;
(c) to [*name*] of [*address*] the sum of ——.

1 See Form C3.1, cl 2, n 2 at para **[225.12]**. These words are included in case there is foreign or settled property comprised in residue. See cl 6 of this form for the definition of 'free of tax'.

[229.42]

SPECIFIC BEQUESTS

4. I make the following specific bequests free of tax:[1]
(a) to [my son] [*name*] [my/my late husband's] gold watch;
(b) to [my daughter] [*name*] [my/my late wife's] jewellery;
(c) to [my son] [*name*] [my/my late husband's] gold cuff-links.

1 These words are only included in case any of the chattels might be outside the UK at the time of the testator's death. Property outside the UK bears its own IHT in the absence of express provision to the contrary: see the Note to B14 at para **[214.63]**. See cl 6 of this form for the definition of 'free of tax'.

[229.43]

ADMINISTRATION TRUSTS OF RESIDUE

5. [*As in cl 3 of* Form C7.1 *at para* **[229.6]**.]

[229.44]

GIFTS MADE FREE OF TAX

6. Any specific gift or pecuniary or general legacy made by this will or any codicil hereto which is expressed to be 'free of tax' shall be free from the payment of any inheritance tax or foreign tax or duty payable on or by reason of my death to which such gift or legacy would otherwise be subject and such inheritance tax or foreign tax or duty shall be paid out of my residuary estate.[1]

1 See the note to Form C3.1, cl 5 at para **[225.15]**. Where specific gifts and pecuniary legacies are of, or wholly payable out of, free estate in the UK, the IHT on them will be a testamentary expense payable out of residue without any express provision, and it is only where foreign property or settled property is being disposed of by the will that a gift which is intended to be free of tax needs to be expressly declared to be free of tax. See also the Preliminary Note to B14 at para **[214.63]**.

[229.45]

BENEFICIAL TRUSTS OF RESIDUE FOR CHILDREN AND ISSUE

7. (1) My trustees shall hold my residuary estate upon trust for such of my children as shall survive me and if more than one in equal shares subject to clause 8 below provided that if any child of mine shall predecease me leaving a child or children living at my death who shall attain the age of [18/21] years[1] such last-mentioned child or children shall take absolutely and if more than one equally between them the share of my residuary estate which such deceased child of mine would (subject to clause 8 below) have taken had he or she survived me.

(2) The foregoing trust for children of any child of mine who predeceases me shall carry the intermediate income of my residuary estate and section 31 of the Trustee Act 1925 (as hereinafter modified) shall apply thereto.

(3) Section 32 of the Trustee Act 1925 (as hereinafter modified) shall apply in relation to the foregoing trust for children of any child of mine who predeceases me.

1 Any settled property which becomes subject to this substitutional proviso will fall within the IHT charging regime for relevant property (see para **[218.8]** ff) if the substituted grandchildren are under the age of vesting at the death of the testator, unless the age of vesting is 21 and a substituted grandchild has an IPDI as a result of being over 18 (and thus entitled to an interest in possession by virtue of TA 1925, s 31) but under 21 at or within two years after the testator's death (see para **[224.25]**). The possibility of a grandchild becoming entitled to an IPDI can be avoided by extending the accumulation and maintenance trusts of TA 1925, s 31 to the age of 21 for grandchildren. If the fund is likely to be below the IHT threshold, the IHT classification of this trust is not important.

[229.46]

SETTLEMENT OF CHILD'S SHARE OF RESIDUE[1]

8. The share of my residuary estate to which any child of mine shall become entitled under the last foregoing clause hereof shall not vest absolutely in such child ('the beneficiary') but shall be retained by my trustees and held upon the following trusts:

Either

(1) The income of such share ('the share') shall be held upon the following trusts during the beneficiary's life (and section 31 of the Trustee Act 1925 shall not apply to it):

(a) for the purposes of this subclause 'the discretionary period' means the period commencing at my death and ending on the third anniversary thereof or if earlier on the death of the beneficiary provided that if the beneficiary is living and under the age of 18 years at such third anniversary then 'the discretionary period' means the period commencing at my death and expiring on the beneficiary's 18th birthday or his or her earlier death;

(b) my trustees shall have power to pay to the beneficiary or to his or her parent or guardian or apply for the benefit of the beneficiary the whole or such part (if any) of the income of the share arising during the discretionary period as my trustees in their absolute discretion think fit and my trustees shall accumulate the income of the share arising during the discretionary period which is not so paid or applied as an accretion to the capital of the share but with power to apply such accumulations as income of the current year;

(c) subject as aforesaid my trustees shall hold the share upon trust to pay the income thereof to the beneficiary during his or her life;[2]

Or

(1) my trustees shall hold such share ('the share') upon trust to pay the income thereof to the beneficiary during his or her life provided that any income of the share which arises while the beneficiary is living and under the age of 18 years shall be held on trust for him or her

absolutely and indefeasibly and section 31 of the Trustee Act 1925 shall not apply to such income but provided further that my trustees may pay or apply all or any part or parts of such income for his or her benefit at any time or times during his or her minority.][3];

(2) subject as aforesaid my trustees shall hold the share upon trust for such of the children of the beneficiary as shall attain the age of [18/21] years and if more than one in equal shares absolutely;[4]

(3) the trust declared by subclause (2) above shall carry the intermediate income of such share and section 31 of the Trustee Act 1925 (as hereinafter modified) shall apply thereto;

(4) section 32 of the Trustee Act 1925 (as hereinafter modified) shall apply in relation to the trust declared by subclause (2) above;

(5) notwithstanding the trusts aforesaid so long as the beneficiary is entitled to be paid the income of all or any part of the capital of the share (or would be so entitled if such capital yielded income)[5] my trustees shall have power in their absolute discretion from time to time to pay transfer or apply the whole or any part or parts of such capital to or for the benefit of such child in such manner as they shall in their absolute discretion think fit;

(6) subject as aforesaid the share and any other share of my residuary estate which may have accrued thereto hereunder (or so much thereof as shall not have been paid or applied under any of the powers applicable thereto hereunder) shall go and accrue to the other shares or share of my residuary estate the trusts of which are at the date of such accruer subsisting and capable of taking effect;

(7) subject as aforesaid my trustees shall hold the share upon trust for [the beneficiary or his or her estate absolutely].

1 See the note at the beginning of this form at para **[229.37]**. The life interest trust is either subject to the relevant property regime or provides an IPDI within IHTA 1984, s 49A (see the Note to para **[200.98]** above) according to whichever version of sub-cl (1) is chosen: see nn 2 and 3 to this clause.

2 If this version of sub-cl (1) is used the trusts for the children will fall within the IHT relevant property regime (for which see para **[218.8]** ff). The initial non-interest in possession period needs to be more than two years for the reasons given in para **[200.133]**. Three years is adopted for drafting convenience but it could be a shorter period exceeding two years.

3 If this version of sub-cl (1) is used the children's interests will be IPDIs and therefore will fall within the IHT beneficiary-taxed regime (for which see paras **[200.92]**, **[200.98]**).

4 If any grandchild becomes entitled under this sub-clause while still under the vesting age his or her share will fall within the IHT charging regime for relevant property (see paras **[200.92]**, **[218.8]** ff) irrespective of whether during the testator's child's lifetime it was a relevant property or IPDI trust.

5 See Form C2.2, cl 8(6), n 4 at para **[224.51]**.

[229.47]

MAINTENANCE, ACCUMULATION AND ADVANCEMENT

9. (1) Section 31 of the Trustee Act 1925 (relating to accumulation and maintenance) shall subject to clause 8(1) above apply as if:

(a) in paragraph (i) of subsection (1) of the said section the words 'as the trustees think fit' were substituted for the words 'as may in all the circumstances be reasonable'; and

(b) the proviso to the said subsection (1) were omitted.

(2) Section 32 of the Trustee Act 1925 (relating to advancement) shall apply as if the words 'one half of' were omitted from proviso (a) to subsection (1) thereof.

(3) [*As in cl 5(3) of* Form C7.1 *at para* **[229.8]**.]

[229.48]

ADMINISTRATIVE POWERS

10. [*As in cl 6 of* Form C7.1 *at para* **[229.9]**.]

[229.49]

TRUSTEE LIABILITY

11. [*As in cl 7 of* Form C7.1 *at para* **[229.10]**.]

[229.50]

EXERCISE OF POWERS[1]

12. Any power or discretion hereby or by law conferred on my trustees (including a power or discretion as to the disposition of capital or income) shall be exercisable notwithstanding that any of my trustees has a personal interest in such exercise provided that at least one of them has no such personal interest.

1 This clause permits a member of the family to be a trustee without disqualifying him or her from benefit under any exercise of statutory or express powers of payment or application of capital. See the Preliminary Note to B18 at para **[218.4]**.

[229.51]

PROFESSIONAL TRUSTEE CHARGING CLAUSE

13. [*As in cl 8 of* Form C7.1 *at para* **[229.11]**.]

[*Testimonium and attestation clause as in* Form C7.3 *at para* **[229.36]**.]

C8 Wills for sole parents with adult children

Preliminary note .... **[230.1]**

FORMS

C8.1 Will of widow or widower leaving residue to children absolutely .... **[230.2]**

C8.2 Will of widow or widower dividing residue between son and daughter, son's share being settled on protective trusts for his benefit and daughter's share being either given to her absolutely or settled on trusts for her benefit .... **[230.16]**

C8.3 Will of widow or widower leaving one share of residue on trust for the children absolutely and the other share subjected to immediate post-death interests for the grandchildren........................ **[230.30]**

C8.4 Will of grandparent incorporating discretionary trusts of residue for grandchildren.. **[230.45]**

C8.5 Will of widow leaving her house to a daughter who is looking after her and residue to grandchildren on bare trusts .... **[230.62]**

C8.6 Will of widow or widower settling residue on trusts for children with progressive powers to pay them capital at different ages.......... **[230.73]**

PRELIMINARY NOTE

[230.1]

These forms are entitled forms for widows or widowers, but they are suitable for other sole parents. The forms in C7 for sole parents with young children concentrate on providing for the children, but where a sole parent's children are grown up there are wider possibilities as to the form which testamentary dispositions may take. In particular, there is the possibility of making 'generation skipping' provision for grandchildren, which has the advantages set out in Part A, para **[200.125]**. When making provision for infant grandchildren by way of trust, the choice lies among: immediate post-death interests in possession (see para **[200.98]**), relevant property trusts (see para **[200.108]**), or bare trusts (see para **[200.110]**). For further discussion of these options see paras **[200.131]** and **[200.132]**. The former IHT-privileged category of accumulation and maintenance trusts within IHTA 1984, s 71 for minors and young persons has been abolished by FA 2006 for trusts created after 21 March 2006, and in particular for trusts created by the wills of persons dying after that date. The FA 2006 created two much more limited categories of IHT-privileged trust for minors, namely trusts for bereaved minors falling within IHTA 1984, s 71A, and 18-to-25 trusts falling within IHTA 1984, s 71D, but such trusts can only be created by testamentary provision by the will of a parent or step-parent of the beneficiary or beneficiaries, or by a person with parental responsibility for the beneficiary or beneficiaries (see paras **[200.107]**) and **[200.108]**). Therefore, a grandparent cannot create such trusts for his or her grandchildren.

Where the testator is a widow, widower or surviving civil partner, she or he may have the benefit of nil-rate band carry-forward which (assuming it becomes law) will allow the estate of anyone who dies after 8 October 2007 who was the survivor of a marriage or civil partnership to make use of nil-rate band which was not used on the death of the predeceasing spouse or civil partner, irrespective of when the predeceasing spouse or civil partner died, see para **[200.75]**.

[230.2]

Form C8.1: Will of widow or widower leaving residue to children absolutely

Note. This form incorporates an absolute gift of residue to the testator's surviving children with a substitutional proviso in favour of the issue of any predeceasing child.

[230.3]

REVOCATION CLAUSE

I [*name*] of [*address*] hereby revoke all former testamentary dispositions made by me and declare this to be my last will.

[230.4]

APPOINTMENT OF EXECUTORS AND TRUSTEES

1. I appoint my son [*name*] my daughter [*name*] and my son [*name*] (hereinafter together called 'my trustees' which expression shall include my personal representatives for the time being and the trustees for the time being hereof) to be the executors and trustees of this will.

[230.5]

PECUNIARY LEGACIES

2. I give free of tax[1] the following pecuniary legacies:
   (a) to [*name*] of [*address*] the sum of £——;
   (b) to [*name*] of [*address*] the sum of £——;
   (c) to [*name*] of [*address*] the sum of £——.

1 Although the IHT on legacies or specific gifts of UK property is a testamentary expense, it is preferable to include an express direction that a pecuniary legacy is free of tax in case residue includes foreign property or settled property; if it does include such property, a proportion of the legacies, corresponding to the proportion of residue which is made up of foreign or settled property, would probably have to bear inheritance in the absence of a direction to the contrary. See, further, the Note to B14 at para **[214.63]**. For the definition of 'free of tax' see cl 5 of this form at para **[230.8]**.

[230.6]

GIFTS OF CHATTELS[1]

3. (1) I make the following specific bequests free of tax:[2]
   (a) to [my son] [*name*] [my/my late husband's] gold watch;
   (b) to [my daughter] [*name*] [my/my late wife's] jewellery;
   (c) to [my son] [*name*] [my/my late husband's] gold cuff-links.

(2) Subject as aforesaid I give all my personal chattels as defined by section 55(1)(x) of the Administration of Estates Act 1925[3] free of tax[4] to such of my said children [*name*] [*name*] and [*name*] as shall survive me if more than one in equal shares [And I request them (but without imposing any trust or binding obligation) to give effect to any wishes as to the

disposition of such chattels which may be contained in any memorandum that may be found amongst my papers at my death or which may have otherwise been communicated to her during my life].[5]

1 Gifts are made of specific items, and the remainder of the personal chattels are left to the children who survive the testator. Where all three children of the testator survive him or her, the latter gift will have the same effect as if the chattels had been left to fall into residue, but if a child predeceases the testator the chattels will go to the surviving children. This may introduce an element of unfairness as between families, but it avoids chattels being included in the deceased child's issue's share of residue, which may well have to be retained and managed by the trustees until the deceased child's issue attain the vesting age. It also means that the chattels are at the disposal of persons who are of full age who can (if they can agree among themselves) give away items to relatives and friends of the testator.

2 This is included in case any of the chattels are outside the UK at the testator's death, and thus 'subject to tax' in the absence of a direction to the contrary. See the Note to B14 at para **[214.71]** and the definition of 'free of tax' in cl 5 of this form at para **[230.8]**.

3 See Part G, para **[246.67]** for the wording of this definition, and for further discussion of the meaning of 'personal chattels' see Vol 1, para **[64.44]**.

4 See the note to the last preceding subclause at para **[230.5]**.

5 If property bequeathed by a will to one person is distributed to another person in accordance with wishes expressed by the testator within two years of his death, it is treated for IHT purposes as having been bequeathed by the will to that other person: Inheritance Tax Act 1984 (IHTA 1984), s 143; see also B4 at para **[204.6]**.

[230.7]

ADMINISTRATION TRUSTS OF RESIDUE

4. (1) I give all my property not hereby or by any codicil hereto otherwise effectively disposed of [(including any entailed or other property over which I shall have at my death a general power of disposition by will)][1] to my trustees to hold on the trusts set out below with power at their discretion to sell all or any of it as and when they think fit.[2]

(2) My trustees shall pay my funeral and testamentary expenses[3] and debts and any legacies given by this will or any codicil hereto out of such property or its proceeds and shall have a discretion as to how such payments shall be borne as between capital and income.[4]

(3) Subject as above my trustees shall hold such property and the assets from time to time representing the same (hereinafter called 'my residuary estate') on the trusts set out below and shall invest all money comprised in such property or arising from its sale in any of the investments hereby authorised with power to change such investments into any others hereby authorised.

(4) In the administration of my estate and the execution of the trusts of this will or of any codicil to it:

(a) my trustees shall treat all income as accruing on the date on which it becomes payable regardless of the period in respect of which it shall have accrued and shall not make any statutory apportionment of the same;[5] and

(b) none of the equitable rules of apportionment between capital and income shall apply in any circumstances whatever.[6]

1 Subject to any express contrary intention, property subject to a general power will be carried by a residuary gift under the WA 1837, s 27 (Part G, para **[244.29]**), but in the case of entailed property the will must refer to the property, or the instrument under which it was acquired, or entailed property generally for the statutory power of disposition to be

exercised: LPA 1925, s 176(1), (Part G, para **[244.55]**). Although no new entails can be created on or after 1 January 1997 (see para **[200.53]**), entails created before that date can continue to exist and, if they do, the statutory power of disposition of them by will continues to be available.

2 For the reasons for providing a power of sale rather than a trust for sale, see para **[214.1]** ff. This wording could be made even more concise, such as 'My trustees shall have power to sell all or any of such property' or as appears in the AEA 1925, s 33(1), as amended by the TLATA 1996, Sch 2, para 5 (Part G, para **[244.60]**). One reason for using the slightly more elaborate wording in this form is that it follows the wording which was held in *Re Pitcairn* [1896] 2 Ch 199 to prevent the rule in *Howe v Dartmouth* from applying, (see Note at paras **[214.35]**–**[214.37]** for exclusion of the rule), although to save possible argument about the effect of this wording the express exclusion of the apportionment rules is also retained in sub-cl (4). Another reason is that this wording should also serve to create a mixed fund of residuary realty and personalty (see para **[214.64]** for the significance of this).

3 Testamentary expenses will include IHT on UK free estate, including real property: IHTA 1984, s 211(1) (Part G, para **[246.100]**; see also the Note to B14 at paras **[214.55]**–**[214.63]**). Accordingly, even if specific gifts or pecuniary legacies are intended to be free of IHT, it will not be necessary to make express provision for the incidence of IHT unless (in the case of a specific gift) the gift is of property of a kind which bears its own tax, or (in the case of a pecuniary legacy) the legacy is payable out of property (usually residue) which includes property of a kind which bears its own tax. The main relevant categories of property bearing its own tax are foreign property and property which is settled property immediately before the testator's death: see the Note to B14 at paras **[214.55]**–**[214.63]** (settled property can be disposed of under a will where it is subject to a general testamentary power of appointment or is entailed—see n 1 above).

4 A discretion as to the apportionment between capital and income of the burden of liabilities is a middle way between the strict rule in *Allhusen v Whittell* (1867) LR 4 Eq 295 (see Vol 1, paras **[38.26]** and **[214.43]**) with its complex calculations, and a direction to pay the liabilities out of capital which can have the unsatisfactory consequences referred to at para **[214.44]**.

5 See the Note to B14 at paras **[214.48]**–**[214.52]** for statutory apportionment of income over time and its exclusion.

6 See Vol 1, paras **[38.17]**–**[38.27]**, for the rules of equitable apportionment between capital and income, and the Note to B14 at para **[214.35]** ff for the reasons and techniques for excluding those rules. It is hoped that these words will exclude the rule in *Howe v Earl of Dartmouth* (1802) 7 Ves 137 and *Re Earl Chesterfield's Trusts* (1883) 24 Ch D 643. The power of sale in sub-cl (1) of this clause may also serve to do so (see n 2 above). For alternative strategies see further the Note to B14 at para **[214.38]** and Forms B14.4 at para **[214.13]** and B14.27 at para **[214.42]**.

[230.8]

GIFTS MADE FREE OF TAX

5. Any specific gift or pecuniary or general legacy made by this will or any codicil hereto which is expressed to be 'free of tax' shall be free from the payment of any inheritance tax or foreign tax or duty payable on or by reason of my death to which such gift or legacy would otherwise be subject and such inheritance tax or foreign tax or duty shall be paid out of my residuary estate.[1]

1 See the note to Form C3.1, cl 5 at para **[224.15]** and the note to cl 2 of this form at para **[230.5]** and cl 3 of this form at para **[230.6]**. Where specific gifts and pecuniary legacies are of, or wholly payable out of, free estate in the UK, the IHT on them will be a testamentary expense payable out of residue without any express provision, and it is only where a specific gift or pecuniary legacy is of foreign or settled property, or wholly or partly payable out of such property, and intended to be free of tax, that it needs to be expressly declared to be free of tax. See also the Note to B14 at para **[214.55]**.

[230.9]

BENEFICIAL TRUSTS OF RESIDUE

6. (1) My trustees shall hold my residuary estate upon trust for such of my children [*name*] [*name*] and [*name*][1] as shall survive me and if more than one in equal shares.

(2) Provided that if any of my said children shall predecease me leaving issue me surviving who shall attain the age of 18 years[2] such issue shall take and if more than one in equal shares through all degrees according to their stocks the share of my residuary estate which such deceased child of mine would have taken had he or she survived me and so that no issue shall take whose parent (being such issue as aforesaid) survives me and attains the said age.[3]

(3) The trusts declared by the foregoing sub-clause shall carry the intermediate income of my residuary estate and section 31 of the Trustee Act 1925 (as hereinafter modified) shall apply thereto.

(4) Section 32 of the Trustee Act 1925 (as hereinafter modified) shall apply in relation to the said trusts.

(5) Subject as aforesaid my trustees shall hold my residuary estate and the income thereof upon trust for [such of my nephews and nieces [*name*] [*name*] [*name*] and [*name*]] as shall survive me if more than one in equal shares provided that if any of my said [nephews and nieces] shall predecease me leaving issue me surviving who shall attain the age of 18 years[4] such issue shall take and if more than one in equal shares through all degrees according to their stocks the share of my residuary estate which such deceased [nephew or niece] of mine would have taken had he or she survived me and so that no issue shall take whose parent (being such issue as aforesaid) survives me and attains the said age.[5]

(6) Subject as aforesaid my trustees shall hold my residuary estate and the income thereof upon trust for [such charitable purposes or institutions (whether corporate or not) having exclusively charitable purposes and in such proportions as they think fit].

1 Identifying the children who are intended to take by name will have the effect of excluding any other children, eg illegitimate children, who might otherwise be able to claim an interest.

2 Since the eligible issue are all ascertained at the testator's death, they will all be lives in being for perpetuity purposes and the vesting age for their interests need not therefore be limited to 18. However, the requirement in relation to all substituted issue that they be living at the testator's death means that where, for example, a child of the testator predeceases him, leaving a child who survives the testator but dies under the vesting age leaving a child of his who was born after the death of the testator, the latter will not take a share. The greater the age of vesting, the greater is the risk of this happening. An alternative which avoids this risk is for there to be no age contingency, so that the shares of the substituted beneficiaries vest absolutely at the testator's death even if they are under the age of 18: see cl 8 of Form C3.7 at para **[225.119]** for an example. If on the other hand it is preferred to take this risk and have an age of vesting greater than 18, then the accumulation and maintenance trusts of income in Trustee Act 1925 s 31 should be extended so far as possible to the vesting age: see cl 4(3) of Form C11.1 at para **[233.19]**.

The IHT consequences are that if there is an age contingency (and there are extended accumulation and maintenance trusts of income where that age is greater than 18), and the testator dies when the substitution clause has taken effect and any substituted beneficiary is under the age of vesting, the IHT relevant property rules (see para **[218.8]** ff) will apply until the age of vesting is reached. If there is no age contingency, the share of any substituted beneficiary who is under 18 at the time of the testator's death will be held on a bare trust for that beneficiary (see para **[200.110]**). The contingent gift to grandchildren cannot take effect as a trust for bereaved minors or an age 18-to-25 trust (see paras **[200.98]** and **[200.99]**).

3 The wording of the substitutional proviso is based on the wording of the statutory trusts contained in the AEA 1925, s 47(1)(i) (Part G, para **[244.63]**). A substitutional proviso which is limited to children may be more appropriate to the testator's family circumstances, in which case Form C4.2, cl 7(2) at para **[226.43]** may be adopted instead.

4 See n 2 above.

5 See n 3 above.

[230.10]

MAINTENANCE, ACCUMULATION AND ADVANCEMENT[1]

7. (1) Section 31 of the Trustee Act 1925 (relating to accumulation and maintenance) shall apply in relation to the trusts hereby or by any codicil hereto declared as if:

(a) in paragraph (i) of subsection (1) of the said section the words 'as the trustees think fit' were substituted for the words 'as may in all the circumstances be reasonable'; and

(b) the proviso to the said subsection (1) were omitted.

(2) Section 32 of the Trustee Act 1925 (relating to advancement) shall apply in relation to the said trusts as if the words 'one half of' were omitted from proviso (a) to subsection (1) thereof.

(3) Whenever my trustees shall have an obligation or discretion under the provisions of this will or any codicil hereto or under the general law to apply income or capital for the benefit of a minor beneficiary they may either pay the same without liability to account to his or her parent guardian or any other adult person with whom such beneficiary may be residing or to such beneficiary himself or herself if of the age of 16 years or more and so that the receipt of such parent guardian or other person or of such minor beneficiary shall be a full and sufficient discharge to my trustees for the income or capital so applied.[2]

1 For alternative provisions relating to maintenance and advancement see Forms B18.11 to B18.23 and the notes thereto at paras **[218.77]**–**[218.107]**.

2 A parent (with parental responsibility) and a guardian of a minor are empowered by the ChA 1989, s 3(3) (Part G, para **[244.114]**) to give a good receipt for the minor's property: see Vol 1, para **[9.42]**. The power in this subclause is wider in that it authorises the payment of income or capital to a parent who does not have parental responsibility, any adult with whom the minor is residing, and the minor himself or herself if 16 or over.

[230.11]

ADMINISTRATIVE POWERS[1]

8. (1) In this clause where the context so admits:

(a) the expression 'land' includes buildings and estates interests or rights of any kind in or over land; and

(b) during the administration of my estate the expression 'beneficiary' includes any person who would be a beneficiary if such administration had been completed and the expression 'beneficially interested' and references to income of any asset being payable or capable of being paid to or for the benefit of a beneficiary shall be construed accordingly.

(2) In the administration of my estate and the execution of the trusts hereof or of any codicil hereto my trustees shall have the following powers in addition to those conferred by law but subject to the last foregoing sub-clause:

(a) power to invest moneys sell assets and change investments with the unrestricted freedom of choice and powers of disposition and acquisition of a sole beneficial owner with in particular power to make unsecured loans, acquire non-income yielding assets, and purchase land anywhere in the world or chattels for any purpose including occupation or enjoyment in kind by a beneficiary under the power set out below;[2]

(b) power to delegate all or any of their investment powers to a professional investment manager or managers whether individual or corporate and whether or not also a nominee holder of assets for my trustees (and who may be or include one or more of my trustees or the beneficiaries hereunder) upon such terms as to remuneration and otherwise (including terms authorising self-dealing or providing for the limitation of the liability of the investment manager or managers) as my trustees think fit and section 22 of the Trustee Act 2000 shall not apply;[3]

(c) power to vest or register any property in any person or persons whether individual or corporate and whether or not an investment manager to whom powers have been delegated under the foregoing power (and who may be or include one or more of my trustees or the beneficiaries hereunder) as nominee or nominees for my trustees upon such terms as to remuneration or otherwise (including terms authorising self-dealing or providing for the limitation of the liability of the nominee) as my trustees think fit and section 22 of the Trustee Act 2000 shall not apply;[4]

(d) power to borrow money with or without giving security and on such terms as to interest and repayment and otherwise as my trustees may think fit for any purpose connected with the administration of my estate or the trusts declared herein or in any codicil hereto (including investment) and no lender from whom my trustees borrow money in purported exercise of this power shall be concerned to enquire as to the propriety amount or purpose of any such borrowing;[5]

(e) power to lend money to a beneficiary to whom any of the income of such money is payable or to whom or for whose benefit any income of such money is capable of being paid or applied in exercise of a discretion (or who would be such a beneficiary if such money yielded income) and to do so at a full or concessionary rate of interest or interest free;[6]

(f) all the powers of an absolute owner in relation to any land (wherever situated) held by them;[7]

(g) power to apply capital held on the same trusts as any land (or which would be so held if the administration of my estate had been completed) in the improvement of such land and to apply such capital or the income of such capital on the repair or maintenance of such land;[8]

(h) power to permit any beneficiary to have the beneficial occupation use or enjoyment in kind of any land or chattel or other tangible property on such terms as to repair insurance or payment of outgoings by the beneficiary or otherwise howsoever as my trustees think fit Provided that the foregoing power shall only be exercisable and such permission to occupy or enjoy in kind may only continue in the following circumstances:

(i) so long as any of the income of such land chattel or other tangible property is payable to such beneficiary or capable of being paid or applied to him or for his benefit in exercise of a discretion (or would be so payable or capable of being so paid or applied if such land chattel or other property yielded income);

(ii) in the case of land, so long as for the time being the occupation thereof by such beneficiary is compatible with any statutory rights of occupation of any other beneficiary or beneficiaries;[9]

(i) power to exercise all the powers of appropriation (and other incidental powers) conferred by statute on a personal representative without the necessity of obtaining any consents and notwithstanding that one or more of my trustees may be beneficially interested in the exercise of such power.[10]

1 For notes on administrative powers and the powers conferred by the general law, and for other examples of administrative powers, see B20 at para **[220.1]** ff. For a set of administrative powers which include powers in respect of business assets see Form C11.1, cl 6 at para **[233.21]**. The TLATA 1996 and the Trustee Act 2000 (TrA 2000) have much increased the statutory powers of trustees, and many wills and will trusts could manage without any of the powers in this clause being conferred expressly, or just with the power to borrow and the power of appropriation without consent. The differences to the relevant statutory powers of the powers in this clause that overlap with statutory powers are set out in the notes below. The only power which before 1997 was included in this clause that has been omitted because there are now statutory powers which render express provision unnecessary is the power to insure: see the Trustee Act 1925 (TA 1925), s 19, as substituted by the TrA 2000, s 34 (Part G, para **[246.17]**; see also B20 at para **[220.51]**).

2 This power is wider than the statutory powers of investment in the TrA 2000, ss 3 and 8 (Part G, paras **[246.135]** and **[246.140]** and the notes on them at paras **[220.12]**–**[220.19]**) in that it permits unsecured loans, the purchase of land outside the UK, and the purchase of interests in land (such as undivided shares) which are not legal estates. The attempt can be made to exclude the statutory obligations relating to diversification and suitability of investments, and the requirement of taking advice, but, as now enacted in the TrA 2000, these cannot be excluded (although their effect can be cut down by clauses exonerating trustees from liability for negligence): see the TrA 2000, ss 4 and 5 (Part G, paras **[246.136]** and **[246.137]**; see also para **[220.37]**.

3 This is wider than the statutory power to appoint investment managers in the TrA 2000, Pt IV, ss 11–15 (Part G, paras **[246.143]**–**[246.147]**; see also paras **[220.35]** and **[220.36]**), in that the detailed procedural requirements of the TrA 2000, s 15 do not apply; the trustees have a wider discretion as to restricting an investment manager's liability or permitting self-dealing by him (compare the TrA 2000, s 14(2): Part G, para **[246.146]**, under which these can only be done if it is reasonably necessary); beneficiaries can be appointed (this is forbidden in exercise of the statutory power by the TrA 2000, s 12(3)); and the duty to review the arrangement from time to time under the TrA 2000, s 22 (Part G, para **[246.154]**) does not apply. The by-passing of the TrA 2000, ss 14 and 15 is only effective if those statutory provisions apply only to the statutory powers of delegation, and do not apply to express powers to delegate investment management functions – something which is not at all clear (see para **[220.37]**). Even though trustees have an express power of this kind, unless and until there is either a definitive decision of the courts, or amending legislation, which makes it certain that ss 14 and 15 are excluded by such a power, trustees should regard themselves as bound by ss 14 and 15.

4 This is wider than the statutory power to appoint nominees in the TrA 2000, Pt IV, ss 16–20 (Part G, **[246.148]**– **[246.152]**; see also para **[220.36]**), in that the trustees have a wider discretion as to restricting a nominee's liability or permitting self-dealing by him (compare TrA 2000, s 20(2): Part G, para **[246.152]**, under which these can only be done if it is reasonably necessary); the persons who may be appointed nominees are not confined to persons carrying on a business as nominees, a company controlled by the trustees, or a solicitors' incorporated practice (compare the TrA, 2000, s 19(2): Part G, para **[246.151]**); and the duty to review the arrangement from time to time under the TrA 2000, s 22 (Part G, para **[246.154]**) does not apply.

5 There is no power under the general law for trustees to borrow money for the purposes of investment: see para **[220.69]**, n 1.

6 The investment power in sub-cl (a) above permits unsecured lending on a commercial basis, but express authorisation as in this subclause is needed to lend or continue to lend for the purpose of benefiting the borrower: see para **[220.32]**. A power to apply capital for the benefit of a beneficiary could in appropriate circumstances enable capital to be lent to him on beneficial terms.

7 The statutory power of management of land expressed in similar terms in the TLATA 1996, s 6(1) (Part G, para **[246.108]**) applies only to land in England and Wales, and that in the TrA 2000, s 8(3) applies only to land acquired under the power in that section. As the power to acquire land in this clause is wider than the statutory power (see n 3 above), it is appropriate to provide an express power rather than rely on the statute.

8 See para **[220.52]** for the reasons for this provision.

9 See the Note and forms concerning enjoyment in kind in B18 at para **[218.108]** and the Preliminary Note on investment powers in B20 at para **[220.30]**. For the statutory rights of occupation under the TLATA 1996, see paras **[208.5]**–**[208.18]** and ss 12 and 13: (Part G, paras **[246.115]** and **[246.116]**). A power as in this subclause is primarily relevant to a wholly discretionary trust, and it is made subject to any statutory rights of occupation because interest in possession trusts might come to be created in exercise of a power of appointment or application. A power to permit occupation by a beneficiary of trust land is not needed in relation to land in an interest in possession trust, because the statutory rights of occupation will be sufficient provision for beneficiary occupation and anyway are likely to leave no room for permissive occupation by beneficiaries who have no rights of occupation. A clause of this kind can be included in relation to an accumulation and maintenance trust intended to be within the IHTA 1984, s 71, but should always be subject to an overriding restriction to prevent the power prejudicing the s 71 status of the trusts, such as the proviso at the end of this clause. For the effect of conditions as to repair etc imposed on a beneficiary occupying or enjoying in kind trust property, see the Preliminary Note to B8 at paras **[208.26]**–**[208.28]**.

10 For the statutory power of partition of land, see the TLATA 1996, s 7 (Part G, para **[246.109]**) and for the statutory power of appropriation referred to here see the AEA 1925, s 41 (Part G, para **[246.65]**; see also Vol 1, paras **[29.17]**–**[29.23]** and B20 at para **[220.70]**. A power of appropriation as in this subclause will be exercisable in circumstances when the power in the TLATA 1996, s 7 cannot be exercised, eg where a share of the land is still settled, and without the consent of beneficiaries. Exercise of a power of this kind which does not require the consent of beneficiaries may have stamp duty or capital gains tax advantages over one which does: see para **[220.72]**.

[230.12]

TRUSTEE LIABILITY

9. (1) My trustees shall not be liable for any act or default of any investment manager or nominee employed in good faith to manage or hold assets of my estate nor for any act or default of any beneficiary having the occupation use or enjoyment of property in kind.[1]

(2) Section 11(1) of the Trusts of Land and Appointment of Trustees Act 1996 (consultation with beneficiaries) shall not apply to the exercise by my trustees of any of their powers in relation to land subject to the trusts hereof. [2]

1 This makes it clear that the trustees are not liable for the defaults of others who may have possession or control of trust property. For a wider form of indemnity, see e g Form B21.12 at para **[221.16]**. If a paid trustee is to rely on this indemnity clause, the testator should specifically be made aware of its meaning and effect (see para **[221.13]** above).

2 The requirement that trustees of land, in exercise of any function relating to land subject to the trust, consult with beneficiaries of full age beneficially entitled to an interest in possession in the land can be excluded: TLATA 1996, s 11 (Part G, para **[246.97]**).

[230.13]

RECEIPTS ON BEHALF OF CHARITABLE INSTITUTIONS

10. The receipt of the person who professes to be the treasurer or other proper officer for the time being of any institution (whether corporate or not) shall be a sufficient discharge to my trustees in respect of any money or other asset which becomes payable or transferable to such institution under any exercise of any power or discretion herein contained.

[230.14]

PROFESSIONAL TRUSTEE CHARGING CLAUSE

11. Any of my trustees being a professional or business man may charge and be paid all usual professional and other proper charges for business transacted acts done advice given and time spent by him or his firm in connection with the administration of my estate or in connection with the trusts hereof including acts which a personal representative or trustee not being in any profession or business could have done personally.

[230.15]

TESTIMONIUM AND ATTESTATION CLAUSE

IN WITNESS whereof I have hereunto set my hand this —— day of —— 20——

SIGNED by the above-named [testator/testatrix] as [his/her] last will in the presence of us both present at the same time who at [his/her] request and in [his/her] presence and in the presence of each other have signed our names below as witnesses: [*Signatures, addresses and descriptions of two witnesses*]	}	[*Signature of testator/testatrix*]

[230.16]

Form C8.2: Will of widow or widower dividing residue between son and daughter, son's share being settled on protective trusts for his benefit and daughter's share being either given to her absolutely or settled on trusts for her benefit

Note. In this form it is assumed that the son is in financial difficulty, e g because he is a Lloyd's name, or that he is otherwise in need of financial protection. His share of residue is settled on trusts for his benefit under which he takes a protected life interest which would qualify as an IPDI (see Part A, para **[200.104]**). Power is included for the trustees to apply capital for the son's benefit, something which HMRC have said they regard as not preventing a predecessor of the

IHTA 1984, s 88 from applying (see Part A, para **[200.116]**). There are also powers to appoint a life interest to a widow and a power to appoint capital among issue, exercisable by the trustees rather than the son, because of the possibility of the son becoming bankrupt.

[230.17]

As regards the daughter's share this form includes two options. Under the first she takes the share absolutely if surviving with a substitutional proviso for her children (or for her issue generally). Under the second her share is settled on conventional trusts giving her a life interest which would qualify as an IPDI (see Part A, para **[200.98]**), a power to appoint a life interest to a widower, a power of appointment amongst her issue and a default trust for her children (with substitution of issue). A power for the trustees to apply capital for her benefit is also included, and if she has no issue at or after attaining the age of 50 she has a general power to appoint her share by deed. If she dies at any time without issue she has a general testamentary power of appointment.

[230.18]

REVOCATION CLAUSE

I [*name*] of [*address*] hereby revoke all former testamentary dispositions made by me and declare this to be my last will.

[230.19]

APPOINTMENT OF EXECUTORS AND TRUSTEES

1. I appoint [my son [*name*]][1] [and] my daughter [*name*] [and [*name*] of [*address*]][2] (hereinafter together called 'my trustees' which expression shall include my personal representatives for the time being and the trustees for the time being hereof) to be the executors and trustees of this will.

1 Clause 9 of this form allows a trustee to exercise powers for his or her own benefit in certain circumstances. However, if there is a real risk that the son may become bankrupt, it would be better not to appoint him as an executor. It will in particular be an embarrassment if he has to join in any exercise of discretions or powers under which income or capital is diverted away from his trustee in bankruptcy.

2 If the son and daughter are appointed executors, it may be sensible to appoint a third, independent executor to act as a mediator should any disputes arise, and it will be useful to have a third appointee in case the son decides not to prove the will, eg because he has become bankrupt. There is also the point that exercise of powers in favour of the son and/or daughter will require an independent trustee also making the exercise: see cl 9 of this form at para **[230.27]**. If the son is not appointed an executor then another executor in addition to the daughter will of course be needed.

[230.20]

PECUNIARY LEGACIES

2. I give free of tax[1] the following pecuniary legacies:
   (a) to the Vicar and Churchwardens of [*name*] Church, [*location*], the sum of £—— [as an addition to the church restoration fund];
   (b) to the —— Golf Club the sum of £—— for the general purposes of the Club and the receipt of the person professing to be the treasurer or other proper officer of the Club shall be a full and sufficient discharge to my trustees;
   (c) to my friend [*name*] of [*address*] the sum of £——.

1 See the note to Form C8.1, cl 2 at para **[230.5]**.

[230.21]

GIFT OF CHATTELS[1]

3. I give free of tax[2] all my personal chattels as defined by section 55(1)(x) of the Administration of Estates Act 1925[3] to [such of my son and my daughter as shall survive me and if both in equal shares] [my daughter absolutely and I request her (but without imposing any trust or binding obligation upon her) to give effect to any wishes of mine as to the disposition of such chattels which may be contained in any memorandum which may be found amongst my papers at my death or which may have otherwise been communicated to her during my life].

1 A gift of chattels to the daughter with a request to distribute in accordance with the testator's known wishes is included as an alternative to a simple gift of chattels to the son and daughter equally in case there is a real danger of the son going bankrupt. A gift conferring power on the trustees to distribute the chattels amongst members of the family may be preferred in which case Form B4.11 at para **[204.25]** could be used.
2 See Form C8.1, cl 3, n 2 at para **[230.6]**.
3 See Form C8.1, cl 3, n 3 at para **[230.6]**.

[230.22]

ADMINISTRATION TRUSTS OF RESIDUE

4. [*As in cl 4 of* Form C8.1 *at para* **[230.7]**.]

[230.23]

GIFTS MADE FREE OF TAX

5. [*As in cl 5 of* Form C8.1 *at para* **[230.8]**.]

[230.24]

BENEFICIAL TRUSTS OF RESIDUE[1]

6. (1) My trustees shall hold my residuary estate upon trust to divide the same into two equal half shares (hereinafter respectively called 'my son's share' and 'my daughter's share').

(2) My trustees shall hold my son's share upon the following trusts:

(a) my trustees shall hold the income of my son's share upon protective trusts for my son's benefit during his life provided that none of my trustees shall be liable for paying to my son the income of my son's share accruing after the forfeiture of his protected life interest unless such trustee shall have express notice of the act thing or event giving rise to the forfeiture[2];

(b) subject as aforesaid my trustees shall have power at any time during the life of my son by deed or deeds revocable during his life or irrevocable to appoint to any wife [or civil partner] who may survive my son as his widow [or surviving civil partner] (including power to appoint to a named wife [or civil partner] contingently on her [or him] surviving him as his widow [or surviving civil partner]) an interest in the income of the whole or any part or parts of my son's share for the residue of her [or his] life or for any less period and in exercise of the foregoing power may appoint a protective trust of such income for the benefit of such widow [or surviving civil partner] for such period within the meaning of section 33 of the Trustee Act 1925;[3]

(c) subject as aforesaid my trustees shall hold my son's share upon trust for all or such one or more exclusive of the others or other of his children and remoter issue and if more than one in such shares and upon and with such trusts powers and provisions (including trusts and powers conferring a discretion on any person or persons as to the distribution of capital or income and including provisions relating to the accumulation of income during any period permitted by law and administrative provisions of whatever nature) as my trustees shall during the life of my son by deed or deeds revocable during the life of my son or irrevocable in their absolute discretion appoint;

(d) subject as aforesaid my trustees shall hold my son's share upon trust for such of his children as shall attain the age of 18 years and if more than one in equal shares;

(e) the foregoing trust shall carry the intermediate income of my son's share (so far as not disposed of under any trust or power having priority thereto) and section 31 of the Trustee Act 1925 (as hereinafter modified) shall apply thereto;

(f) section 32 of the Trustee Act 1925 (as hereinafter modified) shall apply in relation to the said trusts;

(g) notwithstanding the foregoing trusts powers and provisions my trustees may at any time or times and from time to time during my son's life pay transfer or apply the whole or any part or parts of the capital of my son's share to or for the benefit of my son in such manner as they think fit and whether or not any forfeiture of his foregoing protective life interest shall have occurred;

(h) if my son shall have no child who shall attain a vested interest under the foregoing trust of capital my son's share (or so much thereof as has not been paid transferred or applied under any of the powers aforesaid) shall accrue to and be held on the trusts applicable to my daughter's share and as one fund therewith for all purposes;

(i) my trustees shall have power at any time or times during the life of my son by deed to release or restrict the future exercise of any of their foregoing powers in any manner whatsoever.

Either

[(3) My trustees shall hold my daughter's share upon the following trusts:

(a) my trustees shall hold my daughter's share upon trust for my daughter if surviving me absolutely;

(b) if my daughter shall not survive me then my trustees shall hold my daughter's share upon trust absolutely for [such of the children of my daughter as shall survive me and attain the age of 18 years and if more than one in equal shares]/[such of the issue of my daughter who shall survive me and attain the age of 18 years and if more than one in equal shares through all degrees according to their stocks (each child of my daughter being for this purpose a head of stock) and so that no issue shall take whose parent survives me and attains the said age and is accordingly capable of taking];

(c) if my daughter shall predecease me without leaving any issue who shall attain a vested interest under the foregoing trust my daughter's share shall accrue to and be held on the trusts applicable to my son's share and as one fund therewith for all purposes.]

Or

[(3) My trustees shall hold my daughter's share upon the following trusts:

(a) my trustees shall hold my daughter's share upon trust to pay the income thereof to my daughter during her life;

(b) subject as aforesaid my daughter shall have power at any time by deed or deeds revocable or irrevocable or by will or codicil to appoint to any husband [or civil partner] who may survive her as her widower [or surviving civil partner] (including power to appoint to a named husband [or civil partner] contingently on him [or her] surviving her as her widower [or surviving civil partner]) an interest in the income of the whole or any part or parts of my daughter's share for the residue of his [or her] life or for any less period;[4]

(c) subject as aforesaid my trustees shall hold my daughter's share upon trust for all or such one or more exclusive of the others or other of her children and remoter issue and if more than one in such shares and upon and with such trusts powers and provisions (including trusts and powers conferring a discretion on any person or persons as to the distribution of capital or income and including provisions relating to the accumulation of income during any period permitted by law and administrative provisions of whatever nature) as my daughter shall by deed or deeds revocable or irrevocable or by will or codicil appoint;

(d) subject to and in default of any appointment under the foregoing power my trustees shall hold my daughter's share upon trust for such of my daughter's children as shall attain the age of 18 years and if more than one in equal shares provided that if any of my daughter's children shall predecease me or be living at or after my death but die under the said age of 18 years leaving issue who shall be living at or after my death such issue shall take and if more than one in equal shares through all degrees according to their stocks the share of my residuary estate which such deceased child of my daughter would have taken had he or she survived to attain a vested interest and so that no issue shall take whose parent (being such issue as aforesaid) attains a vested interest under the foregoing trusts;[5]

(e) the foregoing trusts shall carry the intermediate income of my daughter's share and section 31 of the Trustee Act 1925 (as hereinafter modified) shall apply thereto;

(f) section 32 of the Trustee Act 1925 (as hereinafter modified) shall apply in relation to the foregoing trusts;

(g) subject to the trusts and to any exercise of the powers aforesaid my trustees shall hold my daughter's share upon trust for such persons or purposes as she shall by will or codicil appoint;

(h) notwithstanding the foregoing trusts powers and provisions my trustees may at any time or times and from time to time during my daughter's life pay transfer or apply the whole or any part or parts of the capital of my daughter's share to or for the benefit of my daughter in such manner as they think fit;

(i) notwithstanding the foregoing trusts powers and provisions if at any time after my daughter shall have attained the age of 50 years there shall be no issue of hers living and no issue of hers shall have died after having attained a vested interest in my daughter's share under the foregoing trusts then my daughter shall have power to appoint by deed the whole or any part or parts of my daughter's share upon such trusts for such persons (including herself) or purposes as she shall think fit.][6]

1 This clause contains the beneficial trusts outlined in the Note to this form at paras **[230.16]** and **[230.17]**.

2 The proviso to this subclause will protect an innocent trustee who continues to pay income to the protected life tenant after the forfeiture of his interest unless he has express notice of the event giving rise to the forfeiture. In previous editions of this work, a further proviso was included which enabled the trustees to restore the beneficiary to a full protected life interest. It is not included in this edition since as well as it being not entirely clear whether HMRC accept that a protective trust with a power of reinstatement of this type falls within the IHTA 1984, s 88, it is unlikely that the reinstated life interest would qualify as an IPDI: see Note in **[230.16]**, Part A, para **[200.20]**.

3 A life interest for a spouse or civil partner appointed in exercise of this power will not (after 21 March 2006) enable IHT exemption for gifts to a spouse or civil partner to be claimed on the son's death, but it may still be desired that the son should have the ability to make this provision for a spouse or civil partner.

4 See n 3 above.

5 The substitutional proviso is not very likely to be relevant. The reason for including it is that without it the daughter would, in the event of her children dying under the vesting age leaving issue, be able to appoint the fund to persons other than her issue in exercise of the testamentary general power in sub-cl (g) below.

6 The main reason for providing that if the daughter attains 50 and has no issue, she becomes entitled to a general power over the fund, as in this subclause, rather than to an absolutely vested interest, is capital gains tax: she can choose the moment of becoming absolutely entitled to the fund, or put it off indefinitely if she does not need to have absolute ownership of it. Becoming absolutely entitled is an occasion of capital gains tax charge, with hold-over relief now available in only limited circumstances: see Part A, para **[200.39]**.
Ultimate trusts, as in Form C8.1, cl 6(5) and (6) at para **[230.9]**, could be added after this subclause.

[230.25]

MAINTENANCE, ACCUMULATION AND ADVANCEMENT

7. [*As in cl 7 of* Form C8.1 *at para* **[230.10]**.]

[230.26]

ADMINISTRATIVE POWERS[1]

8. (1) In this clause where the context so admits:

(a) the expression 'land' includes buildings and estates interests or rights of any kind in or over land; and

(b) during the administration of my estate the expression 'beneficiary' includes any person who would be a beneficiary if such administration had been completed and the expression 'beneficially interested'

and references to income of any asset being payable or capable of being paid to or for the benefit of a beneficiary shall be construed accordingly.

(2) None of the powers or provisions contained in subclause (3) below of this clause shall be capable of being exercised or operating in any manner such that if such power or provision were capable of being so exercised or so operating the existence of the same would prevent any person who would (in the absence of such power or provision) have had an interest in possession falling within section 49(1A) of the IHTA 1984 in any property from being entitled to such interest.[2]

(3) In the administration of my estate and the execution of the trusts hereof or of any codicil hereto my trustees shall have the following powers in addition to those conferred by law but subject to the last foregoing subclause—

(a) power to invest moneys sell assets and change investments with the unrestricted freedom of choice and powers of disposition and acquisition of a sole beneficial owner with in particular power to make unsecured loans, acquire non-income yielding assets, and purchase land anywhere in the world or chattels for any purpose including occupation or enjoyment in kind by a beneficiary under the power set out below;[3]

(b) power to delegate all or any of their investment powers to a professional investment manager or managers whether individual or corporate and whether or not also a nominee holder of assets for my trustees (and who may be or include one or more of my trustees or the beneficiaries hereunder) upon such terms as to remuneration and otherwise (including terms authorising self-dealing or providing for the limitation of the liability of the investment manager or managers) as my trustees think fit and section 22 of the Trustee Act 2000 shall not apply;[4]

(c) power to vest or register any property in any person or persons whether individual or corporate and whether or not an investment manager to whom powers have been delegated under the foregoing power (and who may be or include one or more of my trustees or the beneficiaries hereunder) as nominee or nominees for my trustees upon such terms as to remuneration or otherwise (including terms authorising self-dealing or providing for the limitation of the liability of the nominee) as my trustees think fit and section 22 of the Trustee Act 2000 shall not apply;[5]

(d) power to borrow money with or without giving security and on such terms as to interest and repayment and otherwise as my trustees may think fit for any purpose connected with the administration of my estate or the trusts declared herein or in any codicil hereto (including investment) And no lender from whom my trustees borrow money in purported exercise of this power shall be concerned to enquire as to the propriety amount or purpose of any such borrowing;[6]

(e) power to lend money to a beneficiary to whom any of the income of such money is payable or to whom or for whose benefit any income of such money is capable of being paid or applied in exercise of a discretion (or who would be such a beneficiary if such money yielded income) and to do so at a full or concessionary rate of interest or interest free;[7]

(f) all the powers of an absolute owner in relation to any land (wherever situated) held by them;[8]

(g) power to apply capital held on the same trusts as any land (or which would be so held if the administration of my estate had been completed) in the improvement of such land and to apply such capital or the income of such capital on the repair or maintenance of such land;[9]

(h) power to permit any beneficiary to have the beneficial occupation use or enjoyment in kind of any land or chattel or other tangible property on such terms as to repair insurance or payment of outgoings by the beneficiary or otherwise howsoever as my trustees think fit Provided that the foregoing power shall only be exercisable and such permission to occupy or enjoy in kind may only continue in the following circumstances:
   (i) so long as any of the income of such land chattel or other tangible property is payable to such beneficiary or capable of being paid or applied to him or for his benefit in exercise of a discretion (or would be so payable or capable of being so paid or applied if such land chattel or other property yielded income);
   (ii) in the case of land, so long as for the time being the occupation thereof by such beneficiary is compatible with any statutory rights of occupation of any other beneficiary or beneficiaries;[10]

(i) power to exercise all the powers of appropriation (and other incidental powers) conferred by statute on a personal representative without the necessity of obtaining any consents and notwithstanding that one or more of my trustees may be beneficially interested in the exercise of such power.[11]

1 See para **[230.11]**, n 1.
2 This is a general restriction so as to prevent the administrative powers prejudicing the intended IHT status of the IPDI trusts.
3 See para **[230.11]**, n 2.
4 See para **[230.11]**, n 3.
5 See para **[230.11]**, n 4.
6 See para **[230.11]**, n 5.
7 See para **[230.11]**, n 6.
8 See para **[230.11]**, n 7.
9 See para **[230.11]**, n 8.
10 See para **[230.11]**, n 9.
11 See para **[230.11]**, n 10.

[230.27]

EXERCISE OF POWERS[1]

9. Any power or discretion hereby or by law conferred on my trustees (including a power or discretion as to the disposition of capital or income) shall be exercisable notwithstanding that any of my trustees has a personal

interest in such exercise provided that there are not fewer than two trustees and that at least one of them has no such personal interest.

1 This clause permits a member of the family to be a trustee without disqualifying him or her from benefit under any exercise of statutory or express powers of payment or application of capital, appointment, etc. See the Note to B18 at para **[218.4]**.

[230.28]

TRUSTEE LIABILITY

10. [*As in cl 9 of* Form C8.1 *at para* **[230.12]**.]

[230.29]

PROFESSIONAL TRUSTEE CHARGING CLAUSE

11. [*As in cl 11 of* Form C8.1 *at para* **[230.14]**.]

[*Testimonium and attestation clause as in* Form C8.1 *at para* **[230.15]**.]

[230.30]

Form C8.3: Will of widow or widower leaving one share of residue on trust for the children absolutely and the other share subjected to immediate post-death interests for the grandchildren

Note. In this Form part of residue is given to the testator's children, but the Form also contains an element of 'generation skipping' by providing for the remainder of residue to be settled on the testator's grandchildren living at his or her death, giving each such grandchild an IPDI (for 'generation skipping' dispositions see Part A, para **[200.89]** and for IPDIs, see para **[200.98]**).

[230.31]

REVOCATION CLAUSE

I [*name*] of [*address*] hereby revoke all former testamentary dispositions made by me and declare this to be my last will.

[230.32]

APPOINTMENT OF EXECUTORS AND TRUSTEES

1. [*As cl 1 of* Form C8.1 *at para* **[230.4]**, *or cl 1 of* Form C8.2 *at para* **[230.19]**.][1]

1 The main long-term function of the trustees will be to administer the fund for the grandchildren. It will often be appropriate for the children to be these trustees, as in Form C8.1, cl 1, but if they are likely to disagree with each other it will be better to appoint an independent executor trustee as well, as in Form C8.2, cl 1, or to appoint wholly independent executors and trustees.

[230.33]

PECUNIARY LEGACIES

2. [*As in cl 2 of* Form C8.1 *at para* **[230.5]**.]

[230.34]

GIFTS OF CHATTELS

3. [*As in cl 3 of* Form C8.1 *at para* **[230.6]**.]

[230.35]

ADMINISTRATION TRUSTS OF RESIDUE

4. [*As in cl 4 of* Form C8.1 *at para* **[230.7]**.]

[230.36]

GIFTS MADE FREE OF TAX

5. [*As in cl 5 of* Form C8.1 *at para* **[230.8]**.]

[230.37]

BENEFICIAL TRUSTS OF RESIDUE

6. (1) My trustees shall hold [a two thirds share]/[one equal half share][1] of my residuary estate (hereinafter called 'my children's fund') upon trust for such of my children as shall survive me and if more than one in equal shares absolutely provided that if any of my children shall predecease me leaving a child or children surviving me such last-mentioned child or children shall take absolutely and if more than one equally between them the share of my children's fund which such deceased child of mine would have taken had he or she survived me.

(2) My trustees shall hold the balance[2] of my residuary estate (hereinafter called 'my grandchildren's fund') upon trust for such of my grandchildren living at my death and if more than one in equal shares [per stirpes each child of mine being for this purpose a head of stock].[3]

(3) The trusts declared by subclause (1) hereof shall carry the intermediate income of my residuary estate and section 31 of the Trustee Act 1925 (as hereinafter modified) shall apply thereto.

(4) Section 32 of the Trustee Act 1925 (as hereinafter modified) shall apply in relation to the said trusts of subclause (1).

1 One share of the residuary estate is given to the children equally with a substitutional proviso in favour of the children of any child of the testator who predeceases him.

2 The proportion of the residuary estate represented by the grandchildren's fund is not specified and will depend on the extent of the share given to the children by cl 6(1).

3 Without these words the grandchildren will share equally, so that a grandchild who is part of a family of three siblings will get the same share as a grandchild who is an only child; if these words are included each family will be treated equally, so that a family of three will together receive a share equal to that taken by an only child.

[230.38]

SETTLEMENT OF GRANDCHILDREN'S SHARES OF GRANDCHILDREN'S FUND[1]

8. The share of the grandchildren's fund to which any grandchild of mine shall become entitled under the last foregoing clause hereof shall not vest in such grandchild but shall be retained by my trustees and held upon the following trusts:

(1) my trustees shall hold such share (hereinafter called 'the settled share') upon trust to pay the income thereof to such grandchild (hereinafter called 'the primary beneficiary') for life;

(2) if and so long as the primary beneficiary is under the age of 18 years my trustees may pay or otherwise apply for or towards the maintenance education or benefit of the primary beneficiary the whole or

such part or parts of the income of the settled share as my trustees in their absolute discretion think fit and shall retain the balance of such income upon trust for the primary beneficiary absolutely but my trustees may at any time or times while the primary beneficiary is living and under the age of 18 years pay or apply such retained income as if it were income arising in the then current year and section 31 of the Trustee Act 1925 shall not apply to the settled share;[1]

(3) I declare that the purpose and intent of sub-clauses (1) and (2) above of this clause is that the primary beneficiary shall from my death have an interest in possession (within the meaning of Part III of the Inheritance Tax Act 1984) in the settled share during his or her life and even if and while such primary beneficiary is a minor;

(4) subject as aforesaid my trustees shall hold the settled share upon trust for all or any of the children or child of the primary beneficiary and if more than one in equal shares;[2]

(5) the provisions of section 32 of the Trustee Act 1925 (as hereinafter modified) shall apply in relation to the settled share;

(6) notwithstanding the trusts aforesaid so long as the primary beneficiary is entitled to be paid the income of all or any part of the capital of the settled share (or would be so entitled if such capital yielded income)[3] my trustees shall have power in their absolute discretion from time to time to pay transfer or apply the whole or any part or parts of such capital to or for the benefit of the primary beneficiary in such manner as they shall in their absolute discretion think fit;

(7) subject as above the settled share (or so much as has not been applied under any of the above powers) shall accrue to the share or shares of the other primary beneficiaries (and if more than one in the proportion which such other shares bear to one another) the trusts of which have not at the date of accruer failed or determined (otherwise than by absolute vesting) and shall form one fund with such other share or shares for all purposes and if there is no such share at the date of such accruer it shall be held upon trust for the estate of the primary beneficiary absolutely.

1 See para **[218.53]** ff for the trusts of accumulations under the TA 1925, s 31 (Part G, para **[246.29]**) which unless varied or excluded are such as usually to give minor beneficiaries a contingent interest in such accumulations, even if they have a vested interest in the income. The purpose of this substitution for s 31 is to cause the income which is not applied for the primary beneficiary's benefit during his minority to be held on trust absolutely for the primary beneficiary, so as to confer an interest in possession for IHT purposes. An infant cannot be paid income to which he is entitled (see Vol 1, para **[9.39]**) but it is thought that he or she has an interest in possession in income if it would form part of his estate if he or she died under the age of 18 (and unmarried and without a civil partner). Such interest in possession will be an IPDI within IHTA 1984, s 49A (see paras **[200.98]** and **[224.24]** ff above).

2 The remainder interests are absolute. This is essentially in the interests of keeping it simple, on the footing that the capital will probably be distributed to the primary beneficiaries during their lifetimes.

3 The reason for restricting the power in this way is to ensure that if the principal beneficiary releases his life interest in favour of the remainderman this power automatically ceases to apply.

[230.39]

MAINTENANCE, ACCUMULATION AND ADVANCEMENT

8. [*As in cl 7 of* Form C8.1 *at para* **[230.10]**.]

[230.40]

ADMINISTRATIVE POWERS

9. [*As in cl 8 of* Form C8.2 *at para* **[230.26]**.]

[230.41]

TRUSTEE LIABILITY

10. [*As in cl 9 of* Form C8.1 *at para* **[230.12]**.]

[230.42]

EXERCISE OF POWERS

11. [*As in cl 9 of* Form C8.2 *at para* **[230.27]**.]

[230.43]

PROFESSIONAL TRUSTEE CHARGING CLAUSE

12. [*As in cl 11 of* Form C8.1 *at para* **[230.14]**.]

[230.44]

[*Testimonium and attestation clause as in* Form C8.1 *at para* **[230.15]**.]

[230.45]

Form C8.4: Will of grandparent incorporating discretionary trusts of residue for grandchildren

Note. This form is primarily for a testator who wishes to benefit not just his grandchildren living at his death, but also grandchildren (and remoter issue) who might be born after his death. The form it takes is a discretionary trust which provides wide flexibility for residue to be utilised for the benefit of the grandchildren (and remoter issue). Discretionary trusts have the advantage that the individual beneficiaries do not automatically become entitled to capital at any age, and can be protected against any tendency they may develop to dissipate capital.

If considered appropriate at the time of the testator's death, appointments could be made from the discretionary trust within two years taking advantage of IHTA 1984, s 144, see paras **[225.83]**–**[225.91]**. For example, absolute interests might be appointed to grandchildren then living who were considered responsible and able to handle capital sums, or perhaps IPDIs might be appointed to living grandchildren to keep part of the residue out of the IHT relevant property regime. However, if it is expected that more grandchildren will be born, at least part of residue could be retained on full discretionary trusts for them.

Residue settled on discretionary trusts will be subject to the IHT relevant property rules (see para **[218.8]** ff). The capital gains tax rate for a discretionary trust is a flat rate (currently 40 per cent): TCGA 1992, s 4. But changes to capital gains tax announced in the Pre-Budget Report on 9 October 2007 include a flat rate of capital gains tax of 18 per cent with effect from 6 April 2008; see also Part A, paras **[200.39]** and **[200.40]**.

[230.46]

REVOCATION CLAUSE

I [*name*] of [*address*] hereby revoke all former testamentary provisions made by me and declare this to be my last will.

[230.47]

APPOINTMENT OF EXECUTORS AND TRUSTEES

1. [*As in cl 1 of* Form C8.1 *at para* **[230.4]**.]

[230.48]

PECUNIARY LEGACIES

2. [*As in cl 2 of* Form C8.1 *at para* **[230.5]**.]

[230.49]

GIFTS OF CHATTELS

3. [*As in cl 3 of* Form C8.1 *at para* **[230.6]**.]

[230.50]

ADMINISTRATION TRUSTS OF RESIDUE

4. [*As in cl 4 of* Form C8.1 *at para* **[230.7]**.]

[230.51]

GIFTS MADE FREE OF TAX

5. [*As in cl 5 of* Form C8.1 *at para* **[230.8]**.]

[230.52]

DEFINITIONS

6. (1) In this clause the following expressions shall have the following meanings, namely:

(a) 'the discretionary period' shall mean the period beginning immediately after the day of my death and ending with the day before the eightieth anniversary of my death and the period of eighty years from my death shall be the applicable perpetuity period;

(b) the expression 'the beneficiaries' shall mean my grandchildren and remoter issue Provided that if at any time no grandchild shall be living but a child or children of mine shall be living 'the beneficiaries' shall at that time include my children.[1]

1 Since it is assumed that the testator wishes principally to make provision for his grandchildren, they are the prime beneficiaries. But if at any time he should have no grandchildren living, this definition of 'beneficiaries' enables his children to benefit.

[230.53]

POWER OF APPOINTMENT

(2) My trustees shall hold the capital and income of my residuary estate upon trust for all or such one or more of the beneficiaries at such ages or times in such shares and upon such trusts for the benefit of the beneficiaries as my trustees may by deed or deeds (irrevocable or revocable during the discretionary period) executed at any time or times during the discretionary period appoint and in making any such appointment my trustees shall have

powers as full as those which they would possess if they were an absolute beneficial owner of my residuary estate and in particular (but without prejudice to the generality of the foregoing words) my trustees may in any exercise of the foregoing power as they in their absolute discretion think fit:

(a) delegate give or impose to or upon themselves or any other person or persons and in relation to any trust or disposition any discretionary powers or discretionary trusts conditions limitations restrictions or provisions including powers of further delegation or powers to create further powers or discretions;

(b) create trusts or powers for the accumulation of income during the period of 21 years commencing on the date of my death;

(c) create administrative powers or provisions of whatever nature;

(d) make provision for the burden of any testamentary expenses taxes or debts payable out of my estate as between different assets funds shares or interests in any manner and to any extent as my trustees think fit;

Provided that:

(i) no such appointment shall invalidate any payment transfer or application of capital or income previously made under any of the trusts or powers herein elsewhere contained;

(ii) the foregoing power shall be exercisable by my trustees at any time during the discretionary period and any exercise thereof shall have immediate effect for all purposes notwithstanding that at the date of exercise there shall have been no grant of probate or administration in respect of the property over which the said power shall be exercised or the administration of my estate shall not have been completed in respect of such property or any other property comprised in my estate

[230.54]

POWER TO APPLY CAPITAL

(3) In default of and subject to any exercise of the foregoing power my trustees may at their discretion at any time or times during the discretionary period pay transfer or apply to or for the benefit of all or any one or more of the beneficiaries the whole or any part or parts of my residuary estate absolutely freed and discharged from the trusts powers and provisions hereof.[1]

1 This power is not absolutely necessary but may be administratively convenient if the trustees wish to distribute a personal chattel or capital cash for emergency maintenance, as they will be able to do so without having to execute a deed first.

[230.55]

DISCRETIONARY TRUST OF INCOME AND POWER TO ACCUMULATE

(4) In default of and subject to any exercise of the foregoing powers the income of my residuary estate shall during the discretionary period be held by my trustees on trust to pay or apply the same to or for the benefit of any one or more of the beneficiaries for the time being living as my trustees may in their discretion think fit provided that my trustees shall have power during

the period of 21 years from my death at their absolute discretion to accumulate the whole or any part or parts of such income as an accretion to my residuary estate for all purposes

[230.56]

DEFAULT TRUSTS

(5) Subject to the foregoing trusts and any or every exercise of the foregoing powers my trustees shall hold my residuary estate and the income thereof upon trust for such of my grandchildren as shall be living at the expiration of the discretionary period if more than one in equal shares provided that if any of my said grandchildren shall die before the expiration of the discretionary period leaving a child or children living at the expiration of the discretionary period such child or children shall take if more than one equally between them the share of my residuary estate which such deceased grandchild of mine would have taken if he or she had lived until the end of the discretionary period.

[230.57]

ADMINISTRATIVE POWERS

7. [*As in cl 8 of* Form C8.1 *at para* **[230.11]**.]

[230.58]

EXERCISE OF POWERS

8. [*As in cl 9 of* Form C8.2 *at para* **[230.27]**.]

[230.59]

TRUSTEE LIABILITY

9. [*As in cl 9 of* Form C8.1 *at para* **[230.12]**.]

[230.60]

RECEIPTS ON BEHALF OF CHARITABLE INSTITUTIONS

10. [*As in cl 10 of* Form C8.1 *at para* **[230.13]**.]

[250.61]

PROFESSIONAL TRUSTEE CHARGING CLAUSE

11. [*As in cl 11 of* Form C8.1 *at para* **[230.14]**.]

[*Testimonium and attestation clause as in* Form C8.1 *at para* **[230.15]**.]

[230.62]

Form C8.5: Will of widow leaving her house to a daughter who is looking after her and residue to grandchildren on bare trusts

REVOCATION CLAUSE

I [*name*] of [*address*] hereby revoke all former testamentary dispositions made by me and declare this to be my last will.

[230.63]

APPOINTMENT OF EXECUTORS AND TRUSTEES

1. [*As in cl 1 of* Form C8.1 *at para* **[230.4]**.]

[230.64]

GIFT OF PERSONAL CHATTELS TO DAUGHTER

2. I give all my personal chattels (as defined by section 55(1)(x) of the Administration of Estates Act 1925)[1] to my daughter [*name*] free of tax[2] [and I request her (but without imposing any trust or binding obligation on her) to give effect to my wishes as to the disposition of such chattels which may be contained in any memorandum that may be found amongst my papers at my death or which may otherwise have been communicated to her during my life].[3]

1 See Form C8.1, cl 3, n 3 at para **[230.6]** and Part G, para **[230.67]**.
2 See Form C8.1, cl 3, n 2 at para **[230.6]**.
3 See Form C8.1, cl 3, n 5 at para **[230.6]**.

[230.65]

GIFT OF DWELLINGHOUSE OR ITS VALUE TO DAUGHTER[1]

3. (1) I give my freehold dwellinghouse known as [*address*] or (if it is sold during my lifetime) any other dwellinghouse which I may own at my death and which was purchased for use by me as my principal residence[2] to my said daughter [*name*] [free of all sums charged thereon or otherwise secured thereon at my death (which sums shall be paid out of my residuary estate)] [and] [free of tax].[3]

(2) If the foregoing gift shall fail by reason of the sale during my lifetime of the last dwellinghouse owned by me and used or intended to be used by me as my principal residence then I give to my said daughter free of tax[4] a pecuniary legacy equal in value to the net proceeds of such dwellinghouse.

1 This clause contains a gift not only of the dwellinghouse owned by the testatrix at the date of the will but of any dwellinghouse substituted for it and caters for the possibility of the testatrix having no home, e g because she has gone into a nursing home and has sold her house, by giving the daughter a legacy in lieu.
2 This form of words should ensure that the daughter takes any house purchased as a substitute residence even though it has ceased to be used as such by the testatrix, e g because she has gone into a home.
3 The IHT on land in the UK is a testamentary expense (see B14 at para **[214.55]**) and strictly speaking, these words are only needed if the residence is outside the UK or might be replaced by one which is. If the testator is already living outside the UK there are special factors to consider, such as foreign laws of succession: see further C14 at paras **[236.1]**–**[236.8]**. See Form C8.1, cl 5 at para **[230.8]** incorporated as cl 5 of this form, for the definition of 'free of tax'.

Where there are specific gifts or pecuniary legacies elsewhere in the will which are declared to be 'free of tax', it would be a good idea to include those words here as well, even if the residence is in the UK, to avoid any suggestion that, because of the absence of those words here when they are included elsewhere, this gift is intended to be subject to tax.

4 There are stronger reasons for including these words in relation to a pecuniary legacy than there are for land: see the note to Form C8.1, cl 2 at para **[230.5]**.

[230.66]

ADMINISTRATION TRUSTS OF RESIDUE

4. [*As in cl 4 of* Form C8.1 *at para* **[230.7]**.]

[230.67]

GIFTS MADE FREE OF TAX

5. [*As in cl 5 of* Form C8.1 *at para* **[230.8]**.]

[230.68]

BENEFICIAL TRUSTS OF RESIDUE[1]

6. (1) My trustees shall hold my residuary estate upon trust for such of my grandchildren as survive me and if more than one in equal shares absolutely.

(2) Section 31 of the Trustee Act 1925 (as hereinafter modified) shall apply to the share of my residuary estate of any of my grandchildren of mine while he or she is under the age of 18.

(3) Section 32 of the Trustee Act 1925 (as hereinafter modified) shall apply to the share of my residuary estate of any of my grandchildren of mine while he or she is under the age of 18.

1 The trusts of residue are for the grandchildren of the testatrix. If any of her grandchildren are under the age of 18 at her death, the share of such grandchild will be retained by the trustees on a bare trust for that grandchild. TA 1925, s 31 (Part G, para **[246.29]**) will apply to enable the trustees to apply income for the grandchild's maintenance, education or other benefit, and to accumulate any not so applied. This will not prevent the infant grandchild from being absolutely entitled to income since if the grandchild dies under the age of 18, the accumulations will belong to his or her estate (see TA 1925, s 31(2)(ii)). HMRC have confirmed that where property is held upon trust for a child absolutely, and TA 1925, s 31 applies, the property is not settled property (within IHTA 1984, s 43) but belongs to the child absolutely and will be taxed as such.

[230.69]

MAINTENANCE, ACCUMULATION AND ADVANCEMENT

7. [*As in cl 7 of* Form C8.1 *at para* **[230.10]**.]

[230.70]

ADMINISTRATIVE POWERS

8. [*As in cl 8 of* Form C8.1 *at para* **[230.11]**.]

[230.71]

TRUSTEE LIABILITY

9. [*As in cl 9 of* Form C8.1 *at para* **[230.12]**.]

[230.72]

PROFESSIONAL TRUSTEE CHARGING CLAUSE

10. [*As in cl 11 of* Form C8.1 *at para* **[230.14]**.]

[*Testimonium and attestation clause as in* Form C8.1 *at para* **[230.15]**.]

[230.73]

Form C8.6: Will of widow or widower settling residue on trusts for children with progressive powers to pay them capital at different ages

Note. In this form residue is settled in equal shares on the children for life with remainders over in favour of their children, the trustees being given power to apply each child's share for the benefit of such child which is initially fairly restricted but which increases in scope as the child gets older and which finally authorises the application of the entire share. If the testator or testatrix would prefer to include an unrestricted power, Form C2.2, cl 8(e) (at para **[224.44]**) could be substituted for cl 7(g) of this form. The children's life interests will be IPDIs, see para **[200.98]**.

[230.74]

REVOCATION CLAUSE

I [*name*] of [*address*] hereby revoke all former testamentary dispositions made by me and declare this to be my last will.

[230.75]

APPOINTMENT OF EXECUTORS AND TRUSTEES

1. [*As in cl 1 of* Form C8.1 *at para* **[230.4]**.]

[230.76]

PECUNIARY LEGACIES

2. [*As in cl 2 of* Form C8.1 *at para* **[230.5]**.]

[230.77]

SPECIFIC BEQUESTS

3. [*As in cl 3 of* Form C8.1 *at para* **[230.6]**.]

[230.78]

ADMINISTRATION TRUSTS OF RESIDUE

4. [*As in cl 4 of* Form C8.1 *at para* **[230.7]**.]

[230.79]

GIFTS MADE FREE OF TAX

5. [*As in cl 5 of* Form C8.1 *at para* **[230.8]**.]

[230.80]

BENEFICIAL TRUSTS OF RESIDUE FOR CHILDREN AND ISSUE

6. (1) Subject to the direction for retention and settlement hereinafter contained my trustees shall hold my residuary estate upon trust for such of my children as shall survive me and if more than one in equal shares provided that if any of my children shall predecease me leaving a child or children surviving me such last-mentioned child or children shall take and if more than one equally between them the share of my residuary estate which such deceased child of mine would have taken had he or she survived me.

(2) The trusts declared by the proviso to the foregoing subclause shall carry the intermediate income of any share of my residuary estate to which such proviso relates and section 31 of the Trustee Act 1925 (as hereinafter modified) shall apply thereto.

(3) Section 32 of the Trustee Act 1925 (as hereinafter modified) shall apply to the trusts declared by the proviso to the foregoing subclause.

[230.81]

SETTLEMENT OF CHILD'S SHARE OF RESIDUE

7. The share of my residuary estate to which any child of mine who survives me shall become entitled under the last foregoing clause hereof shall not vest in such child absolutely but shall be retained by my trustees and held upon the following trusts:

(a) my trustees shall hold such share upon trust to pay the income thereof to such child during his or her life;

(b) subject as aforesaid such child shall have power at any time by deed or deeds revocable or irrevocable or by will or codicil to appoint to any spouse [or surviving civil partner] who may survive him or her as his or her widow or widower [or surviving civil partner] (including power to appoint to a named spouse [or civil partner] contingently on such named spouse [or civil partner] surviving him or her as his or her widow or widower [or surviving civil partner]) an interest in the income of the whole or any part or parts of such share for the residue of such spouse's [or civil partner's] life or for any less period;[1]

(c) subject as aforesaid my trustees shall hold such share upon trust for the children of such child of mine and if more than one in equal shares;

(d) the trust declared by paragraph (c) above shall carry the intermediate income of such share and section 31 of the Trustee Act 1925 (as hereinafter modified) shall apply thereto;

(e) section 32 of the Trustee Act 1925 (as hereinafter modified) shall apply in relation to such share;

(f) if there shall be no child of such child of mine who shall attain a vested interest in such share then such share and any other share of my residuary estate as may have accrued thereunder (or so much thereof as shall not have been applied under any of the powers applicable thereto hereunder) shall accrue to the other shares or share of my residuary estate the trusts whereof are at the date of such accruer subsisting and capable of taking effect;

(g) notwithstanding the trusts aforesaid my trustees may from time to time pay transfer or apply to or for the benefit of such child of mine:

   (i) if such child shall have attained the age of [25] years any part or parts of the capital of such share not exceeding in the aggregate one quarter thereof;

   (ii) if such child shall have attained the age of [30] years any part or parts of the capital of such share not exceeding in the aggregate one half thereof;

   (iii) if such child shall have attained the age of [35] years any part or parts of the capital of such share not exceeding in the aggregate three quarters thereof; and

(iv) if such child shall have attained the age of [40] years the whole or any part or parts of the capital of such share.

1 A life interest for a spouse or civil partner appointed in exercise of this power will not (after 21 March 2006) enable IHT exemption for gifts to a spouse or civil partner to be claimed on the child's death, but it may still be desired that the child should have the ability to make this provision for a spouse or civil partner.

[230.82]

MAINTENANCE, ACCUMULATION AND ADVANCEMENT

8. [*As in cl 7 of* Form C8.1 *at para* **[230.10]**.]

[230.83]

ADMINISTRATIVE POWERS

9. [*As in cl 8 of* Form C8.2 *at para* **[230.26]**.]

[230.84]

EXERCISE OF POWERS

10. [*As in cl 9 of* Form C8.2 *at para* **[230.27]**.]

[230.85]

TRUSTEE LIABILITY

11. [*As in cl 9 of* Form C8.1 *at para* **[230.12]**.]

[230.86]

PROFESSIONAL TRUSTEE CHARGING CLAUSE

12. [*As in cl 11 of* Form C8.1 *at para* **[230.14]**.]

[*Testimonium and attestation clause as in* Form C8.1 *at para* **[230.15]**.]

C9 Wills for members of childless households

Preliminary note .... **[231.1]**

FORMS

C9.1 Reciprocal wills for a childless couple, each giving his or her entire estate to the other absolutely .... **[231.10]**

C9.2 Reciprocal wills for husband and wife or civil partners, each giving his or her entire estate to the other contingently on surviving him or her by a specified period, and providing in the alternative pecuniary legacies, a specific gift and a gift of residue in favour of the nephews and nieces of both testators in equal or other specified proportions .... **[231.14]**

C9.3 Reciprocal wills for a childless couple, the first to die giving entire estate to the survivor, and the survivor giving a legacy equal in value to the estate of the first to die to the latter's relatives and leaving residue to the survivor's own relatives .... **[231.30]**

C9.4 Reciprocal wills for couple each giving the other a life interest in residue with legacies payable on the death of the survivor and different ultimate trusts of their respective estates .... **[231.42]**

C9.5 Reciprocal wills for unmarried sisters leaving residue to survivor(s) with alternative gift to charity .... **[231.53]**

C9.6 Will of unmarried and childless testatrix giving her unmarried and childless sister a right of residence in her house and dividing residue between her nephews and nieces and charity .... **[231.62]**

PRELIMINARY NOTE

[231.1]

The wills in C9 are not only for childless married couples, but for any childless civil partners, or two or more childless persons living together where each wishes to provide for the other or others on his or her death. Except in the case of married couples or civil partners it is essential that such persons should make wills, because they will not (except possibly where they are siblings) benefit from each other's estates under the intestacy rules. The Forms in C9, apart from Form C9.5 (which is for three unmarried sisters), are for couples, but could be adapted for use by more than two persons.

When a couple are making wills, they may be only concerned with securing the position of the survivor after one of them has died, and thus may be content with a simple disposition of each to the other if surviving, leaving it entirely to the survivor to dispose of the joint estate. Such couples are catered for by Form C9.1 at para **[231.10]**. The obvious drawback to wills in this form is that the second of them to die, if he or she never gets round to making a further will, will die intestate, and where the testators are not blood relatives it will be only the relatives of the second to die who benefit from the combined estates, to the exclusion of the relatives of the first to die.

[231.2]

Gifts to take effect after the deaths of both. It is more common for each testator to want to make, in addition to a primary gift in favour of the other, an alternative disposition to take effect if the other predeceases him. This presents a problem where each of them has a different destination for his property in the event of the other not surviving him. If each testator makes a will leaving all his estate to the other if surviving, with an alternative gift to his own ultimate beneficiaries, one of the two sets of beneficiaries will inherit the combined estates of the two of them, with the other set of beneficiaries receiving nothing, and which set of beneficiaries inherits which will depend on which of the two testators dies first.

One solution, adopted in Form C9.2 (at para **[231.14]**), is for each spouse, civil partner or other partner to give his entire estate to the other if surviving and for the survivor to leave the combined estates on trust for the ultimate beneficiaries intended by both testators, either equally between the two sets of beneficiaries or, where the estates of the two testators differ significantly in value and they so wish, in unequal proportions. A variant of this solution, embodied in Form C9.3 (at para **[231.30]**), is for the survivor to leave a cash legacy equal in value to the estate of the first to die to the latter's chosen ultimate beneficiaries. Where the shares are proportional, as in Form C9.2, both sets of beneficiaries will share in any increase or decrease in the combined estates in the period between the death of the first to die and the death of the survivor, whereas if there is a legacy equal to the first to die's estate, as in Form C9.3, the ultimate beneficiaries chosen by the first to die will receive no increase for inflation in the period after the death of the first to die, but will have priority for what they are given over the ultimate beneficiaries chosen by the second to die if the combined estates come to be diminished by, eg, the second to die spending large amounts of capital. Either arrangement can cause unfairness if substantial lifetime gifts are made, although this is perhaps less likely to happen where the arrangement is a legacy to the beneficiaries of the first to die as in Form C9.3.

The solutions adopted in Forms C9.2 and C9.3 have the drawback that unless the wills are mutual wills in the technical sense (a course which is not recommended), the survivor will be free to change his or her will to the detriment of the chosen beneficiaries of the first to die. Many couples will have sufficient confidence in each other to take this risk, but if they are not content with such an arrangement the settlement of the first to die's estate on trust during the life of the survivor should be considered. A form of trust which could be used is Form C9.4 (at para **[231.42]**), where each spouse civil partner or other partner settles his estate on the other for life (with or without a power to apply capital) instead of giving it outright, and provides specifically in his will for the ultimate destination of his separate estate. Another possibility, which might be more efficient from an IHT point of view where the testators are not a married couple or civil partners, is a discretionary trust: see Form C6.2 and the Note thereto at para **[228.19]** ff.

[231.3]
The definition of the persons who take on the second death. The Forms in C9 all assume that the class of nephews and nieces or other persons who take on the death of the surviving testator are already a closed class. If it is desired to benefit a class which might include persons born after the death of the testator it is important that it is not defined as 'the children of X who survive

me' but, eg, 'the children of X who shall be living at or born after my death'. See, eg Form C10.1, cl 6(3) at para **[232.9]**.

[231.4]

Other provisions. Forms C9.5 and C9.6 (at paras **[231.53]** and **[231.62]**) are for households consisting of childless unmarried sisters. Form C9.5 contains a gift of residue by each sister to the survivors or survivor, and failing them to charity. Here it is assumed that they all wish to benefit the same charity when the last survivor of them dies, or else that they do not mind if it is the charity nominated by the last to die which scoops the pool. Where this is not the case Form C9.2 or Form C9.3 should be adopted. Form C9.6 contains a gift by one sister of a right of residence to the other, with the residue of her estate immediately, and the residence on the death of the other sister, being divided between charity and named nephews and nieces.

[231.5]

Inheritance tax. Members of childless households are less likely to be concerned about IHT saving than testators with children, and the forms in this section contain no devices designed to achieve any saving of IHT apart from some survivorship contingencies (for which see below). Nil-rate band carry-forward, announced on 9 October 2007 (see **[200.75]**), means (assuming it becomes law) that the first to die of a married couple or civil partners making an exempt gift to the survivor of all his or her estate is a sound IHT-minimising strategy in most cases. In cases where it might still be appropriate for a married person or civil partner to make a non-exempt gift so as to make use of their nil-rate band (for which see para **[200.130]**), reference should be made to the Preliminary Note to C3 at paras **[225.1]**–**[225.8]** and Form C5.1, cl 5 at para **[227.14]**. The main IHT-saving step which might be taken in cases of couples who are neither married or in a civil partnership is to provide a discretionary trust of the estate of the first to die. If it is desired to take such an IHT-saving step, see Form C6.2 and the Note thereto at para **[228.19]** ff.

[231.6]

Survivorship contingencies. In Forms C9.2, C9.3, and C9.5, which are all reciprocal wills, the primary gift made by each testator in favour of the other or others is contingent on the other or others surviving the testator by one month. This is principally in case they all die in a common accident. The purpose and effect of including such a provision are different according to whether the testators are a married or civil partnership couple, or not: see the Preliminary Note to C2 at para **[224.6]**–**[224.10]**. Where the testators are a married or civil partnership couple, nil-rate band carry-forward (see **[200.75]** for this), assuming it becomes law, has the implication that from an IHT point of view survivorship conditions as between husband and wife or civil partners are less important than formerly, and in some situations counterproductive (see para **[224.7]**). But where such testators have different plans for the ultimate devolution of their own separate assets, a survivorship condition may still be desired even where it may not be best from an IHT point of view.

[231.7]
Reciprocal wills, survivorship conditions, and gifts intended to take effect only once. Care needs to be taken where a couple make reciprocal wills under which each gives his entire estate to the other if surviving him by a specified period, with an alternative gift if the other does not survive by that period, and there is also any pecuniary legacy or specific gift which appears in both wills but which is intended to take effect only once. Care has to be taken to prevent any such legacy taking effect under both wills, and to see that any such pecuniary legacy or specific gift will be effective, in the event of the testators dying within the survivorship period of each other. The considerations relevant to pecuniary legacies are rather different from those relevant to specific gifts.

If such a pecuniary legacy is, like the alternative residuary gift, included in both wills and in both wills directed to take effect in the event of the failure of the other testator to survive the testator by the survivorship period, that legacy will take effect under both wills if they die within the survivorship period of each other. The simplest way of dealing with this problem is to provide in both wills that the legacy takes effect only in the event of the testator surviving the other testator (ie without reference to any survivorship period), and examples of pecuniary legacies of this type are included in Form C9.2, cl 2 at para **[231.17]**.

In relation to pecuniary legacies of this type, ie ones which are in both wills but intended to take effect once only, there is one circumstance where it could be appropriate to make special provision for the eventuality of the testators dying within the survivorship period of each other. This is where the estate of one of the testators by itself might, in the event of that testator dying within the survivorship period after the other's death (when that testator will not inherit the other's estate), be insufficient to pay all such legacies as well as make any other legacies or specific gifts which would take effect in the same event. In Form C9.2, cl 2 (at para **[231.17]**) an optional alternative is included under which these legacies take effect under the will of the wealthier testator, even if he dies first, where the testators die within the survivorship period of each other.

[231.8]
The position is rather different in the case of specific gifts. There is not a potential problem of duplication of a gift which is intended to have effect only once if it is a gift of specific property. If the testators die within the survivorship period of each other the property will either be owned in its entirety by one of them, in which case a gift of it in the other's will cannot have any effect, or it will be shared between the testators, in which case both shares will be intended to be given. It will usually be a workable arrangement if such a specific gift is worded so as to take effect in the same circumstances as the alternative gift of residue, ie in the event of the other testator predeceasing or failing to survive by the survivorship period. The main thing to avoid is any inappropriate duplication-avoiding formulae related to deaths within the survivorship period of the kinds sometimes found in precedents for pecuniary legacies.

If the specific gift is of property held by the testators as joint tenants, it is particularly important for the gift to take effect under the will of the second to die in all circumstances, including cases where the testators die within the survivorship period of each other; the first to die's interest in the property will accrue to the survivor even if the first to die's will does not take effect in favour of the survivor by reason of the latter surviving the first to die by less than the survivorship period.

Where the subject matter of the gift is or might be held by the testators as tenants in common, the gift should take effect under both wills in the event of the death of the testators within the survivorship period of each other, and should be of the entire property (in case one testator inherits the other's share) and of the testator's interest in it (in case neither inherits the other's share because they die within the survivorship period of each other): see Form C9.2, cl 6 at para **[231.21]** for an example. Where a property is held by them as joint tenants there is always a possibility that the joint tenancy might be severed before they die.

If the property is wholly owned by one testator it is also important that the gift should be worded so as to operate under that testator's will if he is the first to die and the other does not survive him by the survivorship period. The formula in Form C9.2, cl 6 at para **[231.21]** would be effective in this respect.

[231.9]

Gifts to nephews and nieces. Wills of childless persons often contain gifts in favour of collateral relatives such as nephews and nieces or cousins. These terms frequently give rise to difficulty. General descriptions by relationship will prima facie include persons related by the half blood as well as the whole blood but not those related by affinity only. The term nephews and nieces will not prima facie include great nephews or great nieces and the term cousins is prima facie confined to first cousins: see generally Vol 1, para **[71.5]**. The safest course is to describe the intended beneficiaries by name or as the children of named persons: see *Re Daoust, Dobell v Dobell* [1944] 1 All ER 443. Where they are named it is also a good idea to give their addresses, as it is quite possible for there to be more than one person with the same name in the same family. Naming the (legitimate) nephews and nieces is also a discreet way of excluding illegitimate ones if that is what the testator wishes; if they are referred to as the children of named persons, or as the nephews and nieces of either or both of the testators, illegitimate ones will be included (see Part A, para **[200.28]** and Vol 1, para **[72.1]** ff).

See also the note on the definition of the persons who take on the second death at para **[231.2]** of this Preliminary Note.

If trusts in favour of nephews and nieces are considered appropriate it should be noted that such trusts cannot be trusts for bereaved minors or age 18-to-25 trusts. See paras **[200.108]** and **[200.109]**.

[231.10]

Form C9.1: Reciprocal wills for a childless couple, each giving his or her entire estate to the other absolutely

Note. This form is only slightly more elaborate than the emergency will in favour of a single individual in Form C1.1 at para **[223.2]**. The obvious disadvantage of a will in this form is that a new will will be needed if the legatee predeceases the testator or if the parties are a married couple and get divorced, or civil partners and their civil partnership is dissolved, or neither married or in a civil partnership when they make their wills, but subsequently marry or form a civil partnership. A will containing an alternative gift (such as Form C9.2) is usually preferable particularly if the will is one of a pair of reciprocal wills and the joint estate will otherwise go in different directions depending on which one of them survives.

The form is very short but as executor and universal legatee the beneficiary has all the powers necessary to administer the estate and no express powers need be included. The form will not be suitable where the beneficiary is not of full age because a minor, though he may be appointed an executor, will not be granted probate: Supreme Court Act 1981, s 118. Furthermore a minor beneficiary, dying after the testator unmarried, not in a civil partnership and without issue, would not take any freehold property comprised in the estate absolutely but would be treated as having a life interest in it: AEA 1925, s 51(3) (as amended by TLATA 1996, s 25(1), (2), Sch 3, para 6(4), Sch 4) (Part G, para **[244.68]**).

[231.11]

REVOCATION CLAUSE

I [*name*] of [*address*] revoke all former dispositions made by me and declare this to be my last will.

[231.12]

GIFT OF ENTIRE ESTATE TO SPOUSE, CIVIL PARTNER OR OTHER PERSON AND APPOINTMENT OF THAT PERSON AS SOLE EXECUTOR

Subject to the payment thereout of my funeral and testamentary expenses[1] and debts I give all my estate both real and personal (including any entailed or other property over which I have a general power of disposition by will)[2] to [my [wife/husband/civil partner] [*name*]] [*name of partner or the other person*] absolutely and appoint [her/him] sole [executrix/executor] hereof.

1 This will include IHT payable in respect of the estate, though where the parties are married or civil partners the gift will be exempt.

2 Subject to any contrary intention expressed in the will property subject to a general testamentary power will be carried by a residuary gift under the Wills Act 1837 (WA 1837), s 27 (Part G, para **[244.31]**; see also Vol 1, paras **[38.1]** and **[38.2]**) without express reference to the property or power. In the case of entailed property, however, the property or the instrument under which it was acquired, or entailed property generally, must be referred to: LPA 1925, s 176(1) (Part G, para **[244.57]**; see also Vol 1, para **[7.1]**). Although no new entails can be created on or after 1 January 1997 (see paras **[200.52]** and **[200.53]**), entails created before that date can continue to exist and, if they do, the statutory power of disposition of them by will continues to be available.

[231.13]

AS WITNESS my hand this —— day of —— 20——

SIGNED by the [testator/testatrix] in our presence and then by us in [his/hers][1] } [*Signature of testator/testatrix*]

[*Signatures, addresses and descriptions of two witnesses*]

1 This is a short form of testimonium which is acceptable to the Probate Registry: see Form C1.1, n 2 at para **[223.2]**.

[231.14]

Form C9.2: Reciprocal wills for husband and wife or civil partners, each giving his or her entire estate to the other contingently on surviving him or her by a specified period, and providing in the alternative pecuniary legacies, a specific gift and a gift of residue in favour of the nephews and nieces of both testators in equal or other specified proportions

Note. This form is intended for use by a childless married couple or childless civil partners who wish the survivor to have the entire estate of both, but who each have their own relatives whom they ultimately wish to benefit after the death of both. Nil-rate band carry-forward, announced on 9 October 2007 (see **[200.75]**), means (assuming it becomes law) that the first to die of a married couple or civil partners making an exempt gift to the survivor of all his or her estate is a sound IHT-minimising strategy in most cases. In cases where it might still be appropriate for either to make a non-exempt gift so as to make use of their nil-rate band (for which see **[200.130]**), a legacy of an amount equal to the nil- rate band and settled on trusts under which the survivor is eligible to benefit could be used. Form C3.4 (at para **[225.60]**), cl 2 of which contains a legacy of this description, could readily be adapted for use in such a case.

This form divides up the survivor's residue between the two families, while Form C9.3 provides a legacy (on the survivor's death) equal to the value of the first to die's estate in favour of the latter's relatives. For discussion of the relative merits of the two forms see the Preliminary Note at para **[231.2]**. For further points on gifts as in this form, see the Note to Form C5.3 at paras **[227.35]**–**[227.45]**.

This form could also be used for a couple who are not married to each other or not in a civil partnership. The name of the other person should be substituted for 'my [wife/husband/civil partner]' throughout.

[231.15]

REVOCATION CLAUSE

I [*name*] of [*address*] revoke all former testamentary dispositions made by me and declare this to be my last will.

[231.16]

APPOINTMENT OF EXECUTORS AND TRUSTEES

1. (1) I appoint my [wife/husband/civil partner] [*name*] ('my [wife/husband/civil partner]') the sole [executrix/executor] of this will but if [she/he] predeceases me or renounces probate or dies without having proved this will[1] then I appoint [*name*] of [*address*] and [*name*] of [*address*] to be the executors and trustees hereof.

(2) In this will the expression 'my trustees' shall where the context permits mean my personal representatives for the time being and the trustees for the time being hereof.

1 If there is a divorce or civil partnership dissolution, the spouse or civil partner will be deemed to have died and the alternative appointment will take effect, by virtue of the WA 1837, ss 18A(1)(a), 18C (Part G, paras **[244.18]**, **[244.20]**). See the Preliminary Note to C2 on the possibility of divorce or civil partnership dissolution at paras **[224.16]**–**[224.23]**. Although the main gift to the spouse or civil partner is conditional on surviving the testator by the survivorship period which is provided in the primary gift in cl 3, it seems preferable not to make the appointment of the spouse or civil partner as executor similarly conditional since it would be inconvenient in some circumstances if he or she had to wait until the expiry of the survival period before being able to take steps as executor, and the alternative appointment takes effect if the spouse or civil partner dies without having proved the will.

[231.17]

PECUNIARY LEGACIES TO TAKE EFFECT ONLY ON ONE DEATH[1]

Either

[2. If my [wife/husband/civil partner] shall predecease me then I give the following pecuniary legacies free of tax:[2]
(a) to [*name*] the sum of ——;
(b) to [*name*] the sum of ——;
(c) to [*name*] the sum of ——].

Or

[2. [*In the will of the less well-off testator*: If I survive my [wife/husband/civil partner] by the period of one month]/[*In the will of the wealthier testator*: If my [wife/husband/civil partner] shall predecease me or fail to survive me for the period of [one month][3]] then I give the following pecuniary legacies free of tax:
(a) to [*name*] the sum of ——;
(b) to [*name*] the sum of ——;
(c) to [*name*] the sum of ——].

1 For the reasons behind these alternative provisions see the Preliminary Note at para **[231.7]**. Both alternatives are worded so that the legacies in this clause take effect under only one of the two wills. The only difference between them is that if the testators die within the specified survivorship period of each other (one month in this form), under the first alternative the legacies take effect under the will of the second to die, while under the second alternative the legacies take effect under the will of the wealthier of the two testators.

2 Although the IHT on legacies or specific gifts of UK property is a testamentary expense, it is preferable to include an express direction that a pecuniary legacy is free of tax in case residue includes foreign property or settled property; if it does include such property, a proportion of the legacies, corresponding to the proportion of residue which made up of foreign or settled property, would probably have to bear IHT in the absence of a direction to the contrary. See further the Note to B14 at para **[214.55]** ff. For the definition of 'free of tax', see cl 8 of this form at para **[231.23]**.

3 This period should be the same as the period by which the other spouse or civil partner has to survive the testator in order to become entitled to the testator's residuary estate under cl 3 of this form at para **[231.18]**.

[231.18]

GIFT OF RESIDUE TO SPOUSE OR CIVIL PARTNER AS UNIVERSAL LEGATEE

3. If my [wife/husband/civil partner] shall survive me for the period of [one month][1] then subject to the payment thereout of my funeral and testamentary expenses and debts and any legacies given hereby or by any codicil hereto I give all my estate both real and personal not otherwise disposed of hereby (including any entailed or other property over which I have a general power of disposition by will)[2] to [her/ him] absolutely and I declare that clauses 10 to 13 below hereof shall apply.[3]

1 For the IHT and other implications of such survivorship conditions see the Preliminary Note to C2 at para **[224.6]** ff and for the length of the survivorship period see Form C2.1, cl 4, n 1 at para **[224.32]**. Survivorship conditions are no longer recommended as between spouses or civil partners, for reasons given in paras **[224.7]**, **[224.8]**.

2 See Form C9.1, n 2 at para **[231.12]**.

3 An error which can easily creep into wills of this type is that all the ancillary administrative and other provisions have effect only in the event of the alternative gift taking effect. This declaration is one way round this problem.

[231.19]

ALTERNATIVE PROVISIONS

4. If [my [wife/husband/civil partner]] shall fail to survive me for the period aforesaid[1] then the following provisions shall have effect.

1 See cl 3, n 1 at para **[231.18]**.

[231.20]

DISCRETIONARY TRUST OF CHATTELS[1]

5. (1) I give all my personal chattels as defined by section 55(1)(x) of the Administration of Estates Act 1925[2] to my trustees free of tax.[3]

(2) My trustees may during the period of twelve months following the grant of probate to my will distribute the said chattels amongst any one or more of the children and remoter issue of my grandparents and the grandparents of my [wife/husband/civil partner] and the spouses [civil partners] and former spouses [or civil partners] of the foregoing[4] in such manner as they think fit And I request my trustees in making such distribution (but without imposing any binding trust or obligation on them) to have regard to any memorandum of wishes I may leave with my papers at my death or any wishes I may have communicated to any of them during my life.

(3) My trustees may delegate the exercise of their foregoing power as regards all or any of my personal chattels to such person or persons and to such extent and in such manner as they think fit.

(4) Subject as aforesaid my trustees shall hold my personal chattels upon trust to divide the same between such of my nephews and nieces and the nephews and nieces of [my wife/husband/civil partner] namely [*names of nephews and nieces of both spouses or civil partners*][5] as survive me as nearly as may be in equal shares according to value provided that my trustees shall not be obliged to obtain a valuation of the said chattels specifically for the foregoing purpose and may act on their own estimate of the value thereof or on any probate valuation obtained for the purposes of determining the inheritance tax arising on my death.

1 A large class of beneficiaries may be interested in residue, some of whom may be minors who take under the substitution clause. Dividing up chattels among residuary beneficiaries can cause difficulties, and there may be persons other than the residuary beneficiaries to whom it would be appropriate to distribute some of the chattels. A discretionary power to distribute the chattels as in this clause could therefore have much to recommend it. Where professional executors are appointed, or at any rate ones who are independent of the residuary beneficiaries, a trust in this form may serve to ensure that the distribution of chattels to persons other than the residuary beneficiaries is given serious consideration (it will also help to ensure that this is done if the testator also leaves a memorandum of wishes). The main alternative would be to make an absolute gift to some or all of the nephews and nieces, coupled with a precatory request, as in Form C8.1, cl 3(2) at para **[230.6]** or Form C8.2, cl 3 at para **[230.21]**.

The IHT consequence of the use of a simple trustees' discretionary power over chattels as in this clause is not entirely clear. It is thought that the nephews and nieces who survive the testator will have interests in possession (which would be immediate post-death interests) in all the chattels before any distribution to other beneficiaries takes place, and that neither s 143 (see B4 at para **[204.8]**) nor s 144 (see C3 at para **[225.83]** ff) of the IHTA 1984 will apply. This will mean that distributions under the power in cl 5(2) will be treated for IHT as gifts by the nephews and nieces rather than gifts by the testator, though they will usually be potentially exempt (see Part A, paras **[200.71]** and **[200.96]**). If substantial values could be involved, it would be preferable to provide a notional discretionary trust of income so that the IHTA 1984, s 144 could apply to distributions, as in Form B4.11 at para **[204.24]**.

2 See Part G, para **[246.67]** for the wording of this definition, and for further discussion of the meaning of 'personal chattels' see Vol 1, para **[64.44]**.

3 This is included in case any of the chattels are outside the UK at the testator's death, and thus 'subject to tax' in the absence of a direction to the contrary. See the Note to B14 at para **[214.63]** and the definition of 'free of tax' in cl 8 of this form at para **[231.23]**.

4 This class may need broadening further. An alternative would be a power to add beneficiaries as in Form C3.6, cl 3(1)(b) at para **[225.100]**.

5 It is advisable to give the names and addresses of the nephews and nieces or otherwise identify them: see the Preliminary Note to this section at para **[231.9]**.

[231.21]

SPECIFIC DEVISE OF HOUSE TO NEPHEW OF WIFE OR CIVIL PARTNER[1]

6. I give to my [wife's/civil partner's][2] nephew [*name*] of [*address*] free of tax[3] and free of all sums charged thereon or otherwise secured thereon at my death (which sums shall be paid out of my residuary estate) the freehold dwellinghouse and grounds situate at [*address*] if in my ownership at my death or all or any the estate or interest therein or in the proceeds of sale thereof to which I may be entitled at my death in fee simple or absolutely.

1 See the Preliminary Note at para **[231.2]**. This is a gift of the named property to the named nephew to take effect on the deaths of both testators, whether the property is owned by one of them or both and, if both, whether it is owned by them as tenants in common or joint tenants. It should be noted that this gift will be adeemed if the house is sold by one or both of the testators before the gift can take effect (see cl 3 of Form C8.5 at para **[230.73]** for a gift which makes provision for such an eventuality).

2 This word will be included in the husband's or one civil partner's will only. What is contemplated here is a gift in both wills to the same person.

3 If the property is in the UK the gift would be free of IHT under the general law (see the Note to B14 at para **[214.55]** ff). The main reason for putting these words here is to prevent it being argued, in the absence of these words, that because other gifts in the will are declared to be free of tax this gift is not intended to be.

[231.22]

ADMINISTRATION TRUSTS OF RESIDUE

7. (1) I give all my property not hereby or by any codicil hereto otherwise effectively disposed of [(including any entailed or other property over which I shall have at my death a general power of disposition by will)][1] to my trustees to hold on the trusts set out below with power at their discretion to sell all or any of it as and when they think fit.[2]

(2) My trustees shall pay my funeral and testamentary expenses[3] and debts and any legacies given by this will or any codicil hereto out of such property or its proceeds and shall have a discretion as to how such payments shall be borne as between capital and income[4].

(3) Subject as above my trustees shall hold such property and the assets from time to time representing the same (hereinafter called 'my residuary estate') on the trusts set out below and shall invest all money comprised in

such property or arising from its sale in any of the investments hereby authorised with power to change such investments into any others hereby authorised.

(4) In the administration of my estate and the execution of the trusts of this will or of any codicil to it:

(a) my trustees shall treat all income as accruing on the date on which it becomes payable regardless of the period in respect of which it shall have accrued and shall not make any statutory apportionment of the same;[5] and

(b) none of the equitable rules of apportionment between capital and income shall apply in any circumstances whatever.[6]

1 See para **[230.7]**, n 1.
2 See para **[230.7]**, n 2.
3 See para **[230.7]**, n 3.
4 See para **[230.7]**, n 4.
5 See para **[230.7]**, n 5.
6 See para **[230.7]**, n 6.

[231.23]

GIFTS MADE FREE OF TAX

8. Any specific gift or pecuniary or general legacy made by this will or any codicil hereto which is expressed to be 'free of tax' shall be free from the payment of any inheritance tax or foreign tax or duty payable on or by reason of my death to which such gift or legacy would otherwise be subject and such inheritance tax or foreign tax or duty shall be paid out of my residuary estate.[1]

1 Where specific gifts and pecuniary legacies are of, or wholly payable out of, free estate in the UK, the IHT on them will be a testamentary expense payable out of residue without any express provision, and it is only where foreign property or settled property is being disposed of by the will that a gift which is intended to be free of tax needs to be expressly declared to be free of tax. See also the Note to B14 at para **[214.55]** ff. See cls 2, 5, and 6 of this form for clauses which direct gifts to be free of tax.

[231.24]

BENEFICIAL TRUSTS OF RESIDUE

Either[1]

[9. (1) My trustees shall hold my residuary estate upon trust for such of my nephews and nieces and the nephews and nieces of [my wife/husband/civil partner] namely [*names of nephews and nieces of both spouse or civil partners*][2] as shall survive me and if more than one in equal shares provided that if any of the said nephews or nieces shall predecease me leaving a child or children living at my death such child or children shall take if more than one equally between them the share of my residuary estate which such deceased nephew or niece would have taken had he or she survived me[3].

(2) The foregoing trusts shall carry the intermediate income of my residuary estate and section 31 of the Trustee Act 1925 (as hereinafter modified) shall apply thereto.

(3) Section 32 of the Trustee Act 1925 (as hereinafter modified) shall apply in relation to my residuary estate.]

Or[4]

[9. (1) My trustees shall hold my residuary estate upon trust to divide the same into two shares as follows—

(a) a [70] per cent share (hereinafter called 'the first share'); and
(b) a [30] per cent share (hereinafter called 'the second share').

(2) My trustees shall hold the first share upon trust for such of [my nephews and nieces]/[the nephews and nieces of my [wife/husband/civil partner]] namely [*name*] [*name*] [*name*] and [*name*][5] as shall survive me and if more than one in equal shares and shall hold the second share upon trust for such of [the nephews and nieces of my [wife/husband/civil partner]]/[my nephews and nieces] namely [*name*] [*name*] and [*name*][6] as shall survive me and if more than one in equal shares provided that—

(a) if any of such nephews and nieces of myself or my [wife/husband/civil partner] shall predecease me leaving issue living at my death such issue shall take and if more than one in equal shares per stirpes the share of my residuary estate which such deceased nephew or niece would have taken had he or she survived me but so that no such issue shall take whose parent (being such issue as aforesaid) survives me [7];
(b) if the foregoing trusts for the benefit of the nephews and nieces of my [wife/husband/civil partner] shall fail or determine then the share of my residuary estate hereinbefore directed to be held on trust for them shall devolve as if it formed part of my [wife's/husband's/civil partner's] estate and [she/he] had died intestate immediately after my death.[8]

(3) The foregoing trusts shall carry the intermediate income of my residuary estate and section 31 of the Trustee Act 1925 (as hereinafter modified) shall apply thereto.

(4) Section 32 of the Trustee Act 1925 (as hereinafter modified) shall apply in relation to my residuary estate.]

1 The first alternative for cl 9 divides residue equally between the nephews and nieces of both parties. It should be noted that it produces equality between *beneficiaries*, not necessarily equality between *families*. If it is desired to have half or other specified proportion of the combined estates going to one spouse's or civil partner's relations and the balance to the other's, irrespective of the number of the relations of each who survive to attain an interest, then the second alternative cl 9 should be used with the 'first share' and 'second share' both set at the appropriate proportions.

2 It is advisable to give the names and addresses of the nephews and nieces or otherwise identify them: see the Preliminary Note to this section at para **[231.9]**.

3 Trusts in favour of children other than the testator's children, eg. children of nephews and nieces as here, cannot be trusts for bereaved minors or age 18-to-25 trusts. See the notes to paras **[200.108]** and **[200.109]**. Therefore to avoid property held for such children being within the relevant property regime, the substitutional trust for the children of nephews and nieces does not include any age contingency, and if the trust takes effect it will take effect in favour of minor children absolutely.

4 The second alternative cl 9 divides residue in specified proportions between the two sides of the family. It is phrased so as to require the minimum of alteration when adapting a draft prepared for one spouse or civil partner for use by the other spouse or civil partner. This alternative for cl 9 can be used where the two sides of the family are to receive unequal shares of the combined estates (e g where the parties' respective estates are of significantly different value), and where it is desired that each side of the family should receive half of the combined estates irrespective of the number of beneficiaries on each side of the family

(see also n 2, above). If there are substantial legacies taking effect in favour of any of the residuary beneficiaries, or a specific gift of a house to a nephew as in cl 6, these should not be forgotten in the calculations of the proportions which should go to each testator's relatives.

It should be noted that if the testators die within the survivorship period of each other, both estates are divided between the two families in the agreed proportions instead of the estate of each going to his or her own relatives exclusively. This is likely to be fairer, because the testators may make lifetime gifts to each other or share heavy expenditure unequally after the wills have been made, and it will clearly be fairer if there are any assets held by the testators as joint tenants, since these will end up wholly in the estate of the survivor even if he dies within the survivorship period following the other's death.

5 It is advisable to give the names and addresses of the nephews and nieces or otherwise identify them with precision: see the Preliminary Note at para **[231.9]**.

The names at this point will be the same in both wills, but the description will be 'my nephews and nieces' in the husband's or one civil partner's will and 'the nephews and nieces of my husband' in the wife's or other civil partner's. Care should be taken to get the names and descriptions the right way round, and the testators should be given drafts of their wills and asked specifically to confirm that the descriptions are correctly matched with the names in each will, and that the first share and second share are respectively given to the right families. There may be only nephews or only nieces in one or other category, in which case the description should be amended accordingly.

6 The names at this point will be the same in both wills, but the description will be 'the nephews and nieces of my wife' in the husband's will and 'my nephews and nieces' in the wife's will, or 'the nephews and nieces of my civil partner' in one civil partner's will and 'my nephews and nieces' in the other's will. See also the previous note.

7 See n 3, above.

8 Proviso (b) is designed to ensure that if the trusts of the share intended for the other spouse's or civil partner's nephews and nieces, that share will nevertheless go to their side of the family.

[231.25]

MAINTENANCE, ACCUMULATION AND ADVANCEMENT

10. (1) Section 31 of the Trustee Act 1925 (relating to accumulation and maintenance) shall apply in relation to the trusts hereby or by any codicil hereto declared as if:

(a) in paragraph (i) of subsection (1) of the said section the words 'as the trustees think fit' were substituted for the words 'as may in all the circumstances be reasonable'; and

(b) the proviso to the said subsection (1) were omitted.

(2) Section 32 of the Trustee Act 1925 (relating to advancement) shall apply in relation to the said trusts as if the words 'one half of' were omitted from proviso (a) to subsection (1) thereof.

(3) Whenever my trustees shall have an obligation or discretion under the provisions of this will or any codicil hereto or under the general law to apply income or capital for the benefit of a minor beneficiary they may either pay the same without liability to account to his or her parent guardian or any other adult person with whom such beneficiary may be residing or to such beneficiary himself or herself if of the age of 16 years or more and so that the receipt of such parent guardian or other person or of such minor beneficiary shall be a full and sufficient discharge to my trustees for the income or capital so applied.[1]

1 A parent (with parental responsibility) and a guardian of a minor are empowered by the ChA 1989, s 3(3) (Part G, para **[244.114]**) to give a good receipt for the minor's property: see Vol 1, para **[9.42]**. The power in this subclause is wider in that it authorises the payment of

income or capital to a parent who does not have parental responsibility, any adult with whom the minor is residing, and the minor himself or herself if 16 or over.

[231.26]

ADMINISTRATIVE POWERS[1]

11. (1) In this clause where the context so admits:
(a) the expression 'land' includes buildings and estates interests or rights of any kind in or over land; and
(b) during the administration of my estate the expression 'beneficiary' includes any person who would be a beneficiary if such administration had been completed and the expression 'beneficially interested' and references to income of any asset being payable or capable of being paid to or for the benefit of a beneficiary shall be construed accordingly.

(2) In the administration of my estate and the execution of the trusts hereof or of any codicil hereto my trustees shall have the following powers in addition to those conferred by law but subject to the last foregoing sub-clause:
(a) power to invest moneys sell assets and change investments with the unrestricted freedom of choice and powers of disposition and acquisition of a sole beneficial owner with in particular power to make unsecured loans, acquire non-income yielding assets, and purchase land anywhere in the world or chattels for any purpose including occupation or enjoyment in kind by a beneficiary under the power set out below;[2]
(b) power to delegate all or any of their investment powers to a professional investment manager or managers whether individual or corporate and whether or not also a nominee holder of assets for my trustees (and who may be or include one or more of my trustees or the beneficiaries hereunder) upon such terms as to remuneration and otherwise (including terms authorising self-dealing or providing for the limitation of the liability of the investment manager or managers) as my trustees think fit and section 22 of the Trustee Act 2000 shall not apply;[3]
(c) power to vest or register any property in any person or persons whether individual or corporate and whether or not an investment manager to whom powers have been delegated under the foregoing power (and who may be or include one or more of my trustees or the beneficiaries hereunder) as nominee or nominees for my trustees upon such terms as to remuneration or otherwise (including terms authorising self-dealing or providing for the limitation of the liability of the nominee) as my trustees think fit and section 22 of the Trustee Act 2000 shall not apply;[4]
(d) power to borrow money with or without giving security and on such terms as to interest and repayment and otherwise as my trustees may think fit for any purpose connected with the administration of my estate or the trusts declared herein or in any codicil hereto (including investment) and no lender from whom my trustees borrow money in

purported exercise of this power shall be concerned to enquire as to the propriety amount or purpose of any such borrowing;[5]

(e) power to lend money to a beneficiary to whom any of the income of such money is payable or to whom or for whose benefit any income of such money is capable of being paid or applied in exercise of a discretion (or who would be such a beneficiary if such money yielded income) and to do so at a full or concessionary rate of interest or interest free;[6]

(f) all the powers of an absolute owner in relation to any land (wherever situated) held by them;[7]

(g) power to apply capital held on the same trusts as any land (or which would be so held if the administration of my estate had been completed) in the improvement of such land and to apply such capital or the income of such capital on the repair or maintenance of such land;[8]

(h) power to permit any beneficiary to have the beneficial occupation use or enjoyment in kind of any land or chattel or other tangible property on such terms as to repair insurance or payment of outgoings by the beneficiary or otherwise howsoever as my trustees think fit Provided that the foregoing power shall only be exercisable and such permission to occupy or enjoy in kind may only continue in the following circumstances:

   (i) so long as any of the income of such land chattel or other tangible property is payable to such beneficiary or capable of being paid or applied to him or for his benefit in exercise of a discretion (or would be so payable or capable of being so paid or applied if such land chattel or other property yielded income);

   (ii) in the case of land, so long as for the time being the occupation thereof by such beneficiary is compatible with any statutory rights of occupation of any other beneficiary or beneficiaries;[9]

(i) power to exercise all the powers of appropriation (and other incidental powers) conferred by statute on a personal representative without the necessity of obtaining any consents and notwithstanding that one or more of my trustees may be beneficially interested in the exercise of such power.[10]

1 See para **[230.11]**, n 1.
2 See para **[230.11]**, n 3.
3 See para **[230.11]**, n 4.
4 See para **[230.11]**, n 5.
5 See para **[230.11]**, n 6.
6 See para **[230.11]**, n 7.
7 See para **[230.11]**, n 8.
8 See para **[230.11]**, n 9.
9 See para **[230.11]**, n 10.
10 See para **[230.11]**, n 11.

[231.27]

TRUSTEE LIABILITY

12. (1) My trustees shall not be liable for any act or default of any investment manager or nominee employed in good faith to manage or hold

assets of my estate nor for any act or default of any beneficiary having the occupation use or enjoyment of property in kind.[1]

(2) Section 11(1) of the Trusts of Land and Appointment of Trustees Act 1996 (consultation with beneficiaries) shall not apply to the exercise by my trustees of any of their powers in relation to land subject to the trusts hereof. [2]

1 This makes it clear that the trustees are not liable for the defaults of others who may have possession or control of trust property. For a wider form of indemnity, see e g Form B21.12 at para **[221.16]**. If a paid trustee is to rely on this indemnity clause, the testator should specifically be made aware of its meaning and effect (see para **[221.13]** above).

2 The requirement that trustees of land in exercise of any function relating to land subject to the trust consult with beneficiaries of full age beneficially entitled to an interest in possession in the land can be excluded: TLATA 1996, s 11 (Part G, para **[246.114]**).

[231.28]

PROFESSIONAL TRUSTEE CHARGING CLAUSE

13. Any of my trustees being a professional or business man may charge and be paid all usual professional and other proper charges for business transacted acts done advice given and time spent by him or his firm in connection with the administration of my estate or in connection with the trusts hereof including acts which a personal representative or trustee not being in any profession or business could have done personally.

[231.29]

TESTIMONIUM AND ATTESTATION CLAUSE

IN WITNESS whereof I have hereunto set my hand this —— day of —— 20——

SIGNED by the above-named testator as his last will in the presence of us both present at the same time who at his request and in his presence and in the presence of each other have signed our names below as witnesses: } [*Signature of testator*]

[*Signatures, addresses and descriptions of two witnesses*]

[231.30]

Form C9.3: Reciprocal wills for a childless couple, the first to die giving entire estate to the survivor, and the survivor giving a legacy equal in value to the estate of the first to die to the latter's relatives and leaving residue to the survivor's own relatives

Note. In this form the relatives of the first to die benefit from a legacy equal in value to his or her estate rather than participating in a share of residue as in the preceding form. This device has the disadvantage that inflation may erode the benefit received by this class especially if the survivor survives the first to die by a long period. By contrast Form C9.2 divides the survivor's residue between the two families. For discussion of the relative merits of the two forms see the Preliminary Note at para **[231.2]**.

This form could also be used for a couple who are not married to each other or in a civil partnership. The name of the other person should be substituted for 'my [wife/husband/civil partner]' throughout. There is also a modification which could be made to cl 4(1), noted in n 3 to that subclause at para **[231.35]**.

[231.31]

REVOCATION CLAUSE

I [*name*] of [*address*] hereby revoke all former testamentary dispositions made by me and declare this to be my last will.

[231.32]

GIFT OF ENTIRE ESTATE TO SPOUSE OR CIVIL PARTNER AND APPOINTMENT OF SPOUSE OR CIVIL PARTNER AS SOLE EXECUTOR

1. If my [wife/husband/civil partner] shall survive me for the period of one month[1] then subject to the payment thereout of my funeral and testamentary expenses[2] and debts I give all my estate both real and personal (including all entailed or other property over which I have at my death a general power of disposition by will)[3] to my [wife/husband/civil partner] and appoint [her/him] to be the sole [executrix/executor] hereof and I declare that clauses 6 to 9 below hereof shall apply.[4]

1 For the IHT and other implications of such survivorship conditions see the Preliminary Note to C2 at paras **[224.6]**–**[224.10]** and for the length of the survivorship period see Form C2.1, cl 4, n 1 at para **[224.32]**. It would not be appropriate to have a survivorship period longer than a month in this form because the appointment of the spouse or civil partner as executor is dependent on survival by the specified period as well as the primary gift to the spouse or civil partner. Survivorship conditions are no longer recommended as between spouses or civil partners, for reasons given in paras **[224.7]**, **[224.8]**.

2 See Form C9.1, n 1 at para **[231.12]**.

3 See Form C9.1, n 2 at para **[231.12]**.

4 See Form C9.2, cl 3, n 3 at para **[231.18]**.

[231.33]

ALTERNATIVE PROVISIONS

2. If my [wife/husband/civil partner] shall fail to survive me for the period aforesaid then the following provisions shall have effect.

[231.34]

APPOINTMENT OF EXECUTORS AND TRUSTEES

3. I appoint [*name*] of [*address*] and [*name*] of [*address*] (hereinafter together called 'my trustees' which expression shall include my personal representatives for the time being and the trustees for the time being hereof) to be the executors and trustees of this will.

[231.35]

GIFT TO OTHER SPOUSE'S OR CIVIL PARTNER'S BENEFICIARIES OF LEGACY EQUAL IN VALUE TO HIS OR HER ESTATE

4. (1) If any property shall have devolved upon me under my [wife's/husband's/civil partner's] will[1] or from my [wife/husband/civil partner] under any relevant joint tenancy (as defined below) I give to my trustees subject to and charged with a rateable proportion of any inheritance tax payable in respect of my death[2] a pecuniary legacy (hereinafter called 'the trust legacy') of such sum as shall be equal to the value (as at the date of the death of my

[wife/husband/civil partner]) of all such property as aforesaid[3] such legacy to carry interest at the rate of six per cent per annum from the date of my death until paid or satisfied by appropriation.

(2) For the foregoing purposes a relevant joint tenancy is one which has come to an end before my death and the value of property devolving upon me from my [wife/husband/civil partner] under a relevant joint tenancy shall be the value immediately before [her/his] death of [her/his] severable share of the property subject to such joint tenancy or (where there were other joint tenants in addition to the two of us) the proportion of such value as corresponds to the proportion of such severable share which shall have accrued to me on [her/his] death.

(3) In calculating the amount of the sum aforesaid my trustees may rely on such valuations (whether agreed for probate purposes or not) or other estimates of value as they may in their absolute discretion think fit and so that any calculation so made shall not be open to challenge to any person beneficially interested hereunder.

(4) My trustees shall hold the trust legacy upon trust for such of my [wife's/husband's/civil partner's] nephews and nieces [*name*] [*name*] [*name*] and [*name*][4] as shall survive me and if more than one in equal shares absolutely Provided that if any of my [wife's/husband's/civil partner's] said nephews and nieces shall predecease me leaving issue such issue shall take and if more than one in equal shares per stirpes the share of the trust legacy which such deceased would have taken had he or she survived me but so that no such issue shall take whose parent (being such issue as aforesaid) survives me[5].

(5) The foregoing trusts shall carry the intermediate income of the trust legacy and section 31 of the Trustee Act 1925 (as hereinafter modified) shall apply thereto.

(6) Section 32 of the Trustee Act 1925 (as hereinafter modified) shall apply in relation to the trust legacy.

1 If either spouse or civil partner will be exercising a testamentary power of appointment in favour of the other spouse or civil partner, words should be added to make clear whether or not the property appointed is to be included in this value.

2 Prima facie the IHT attributable to a legacy is a testamentary expense payable out of residue (IHTA 1984, s 211: Part G, para **[246.100]**; see also B14 at para **[214.55]** ff), but it will in most cases be fairer for this legacy to bear its due proportion of the tax payable in respect of the entire joint estate on the survivor's death. Although the beneficiaries of the legacy would have borne less IHT if the first to die's property had been left to them direct, it seems even more unfair that the testator's relations should have to bear all the IHT on this legacy.

3 If this Form is used for persons who are not married to each other, there should be express wording to make it clear that the value to be taken into account is after deduction of any IHT payable on the first to die's death, e g '(after deduction of any inheritance tax or foreign death duties arising from the death of [*name of other person*] and borne by me)'.

4 As to the desirability of identifying nephews and nieces (or other relatives) see the Preliminary Note to this section at para **[231.9]**.

5 See Form C9.2, cl 9, n 3 at para **[231.24]**.

[231.36]

ADMINISTRATION TRUSTS OF RESIDUE

5. [*As in cl 7 of* Form C9.2 *at para* **[231.22]**.]

[231.37]

BENEFICIAL TRUSTS OF RESIDUE

6. (1) My trustees shall hold my residuary estate upon trust for such of my nephews and nieces [*name*] [*name*] [*name*] and [*name*][1] as shall survive me and if more than one in equal shares absolutely provided that if any of my said nephews or nieces shall predecease me leaving issue who shall survive me such issue shall take and if more than one in equal shares per stirpes the share of my residuary estate which such deceased nephew or niece could have taken had he or she survived me but so that no such issue shall take whose parent (being such issue as aforesaid) survives me[2].

(2) The foregoing trusts shall carry the intermediate income of my residuary estate and section 31 of the Trustee Act 1925 (as hereinafter modified) shall apply thereto.

(3) Section 32 of the Trustee Act 1925 (as hereinafter modified) shall apply in relation to my residuary estate.

1 See para **[231.35]**, n 4.
2 See Form C9.2, cl 9, n 3 at para **[231.24]**.

[231.38]

MAINTENANCE, ACCUMULATION AND ADVANCEMENT

7. [*As in cl 10 of* Form C9.2 *at para* **[231.25]**.]

[231.39]

ADMINISTRATIVE POWERS

8. [*As in cl 11 of* Form C9.2 *at para* **[231.26]**.]

[231.40]

TRUSTEE LIABILITY

9. [*As in cl 12 of* Form C9.2 *at para* **[231.27]**.]

[231.41]

PROFESSIONAL TRUSTEE CHARGING CLAUSE

10. [*As in cl 13 of* Form C9.2 *at para* **[231.28]**.]

[*Testimonium and attestation clauses as in* Form C9.2 *at para* **[231.29]**.]

[231.42]

Form C9.4: Reciprocal wills for couple each giving the other a life interest in residue with legacies payable on the death of the survivor and different ultimate trusts of their respective estates

Note. This form deals with the problem outlined in the Preliminary Note of childless couples wishing to provide for each other while ensuring that their respective estates ultimately pass to their own relatives by settling residue on the survivor for life rather than making an outright gift of it. It is drafted for married couples or civil partners but may be adapted for others.

The home will usually be a major item of property owned by the couple; the purpose of putting the residuary estate of the first to die in trust for his or her relatives may be frustrated if his or her interest in the house passes to the other absolutely under a joint tenancy. *It is essential when preparing wills of this type to examine the title to the home carefully to see how it is held*; if it is owned by the testators as joint tenants beneficially the parties must be asked whether they wish the interest in the home of the first of them to die to be settled on trust under his or her will. If so, they must be advised to effect a severance, and, if not, a careful record should be made and retained of their intention that the joint tenancy should continue. Notwithstanding well reported authorities on the point, many cases of negligent will-drafting continue to arise as a result of a failure to take the elementary precaution of ensuring an unwanted joint tenancy is severed.

If a will of this type is being made for a married couple or civil partners who are concerned about the utilisation of the nil-rate band of the first to die, Form C3.2, cl 4 at para **[225.32]**, or Form C3.4, cl 2 at para **[225.60]** could be adapted for the purpose. With the introduction of nil-rate band carry-forward, announced on 9 October 2007 (see para **[200.75]**), (assuming it becomes law), this will be less of a concern than it was previously. For cases where it may still be a concern, see para **[200.130]**.

[231.43]

REVOCATION CLAUSE

I [*name*] of [*address*] hereby revoke all former testamentary dispositions made by me and declare this to be my last will.

[231.44]

APPOINTMENT OF EXECUTORS AND TRUSTEES[1]

1. I appoint my [wife/husband/civil partner] [*name*] [*name*] of [*address*] and [*name*] of [*address*][2] (hereinafter called 'my trustees' which expression shall include my personal representatives for the time being and the trustees for the time being hereof) to be the executors and trustees of this will.

1 The choice of executors and trustees will be especially important if a power to advance the capital of residue to the survivor is included.

2 If there are two executors as well as the wife/husband/civil partner, there will still be two effective appointments if there is a divorce or dissolution of civil partnership and the appointment of the wife/husband/civil partner is nullified by the WA 1837, s 18A or s 18C, s 3: Part G, paras **[244.18]**, **[244.20]**). See also the Preliminary Note on the possibility of divorce or civil partnership dissolution to C2 at paras **[224.12]**–**[224.19]**.

[231.45]

GIFT OF PERSONAL CHATTELS[1]

2. I give to my [wife/husband/civil partner] absolutely all my personal chattels as defined by section 55(1)(x) of the Administration of Estates Act 1925.[2]

1 As residue is settled on the survivor for life, and settling chattels is something to be avoided, an outright gift to the survivor of the personal chattels is included. However, one consequence is that all the combined chattels will fall into the residuary estate of the survivor, and go to the latter's relations, unless they are willing to give some of them to the first to die's relatives. It may be preferred to provide a discretionary trust or power arising under the will of the second to die with the relations of both testators made objects of the discretion. Forms which could be used are Form B4.11 at para **[204.25]** and Form C9.2, cl 5 at para **[231.20]**.

2 See Part G, para **[246.67]**. See also Vol 1, para **[64.44]** for discussion of the meaning of the term.

[231.46]

ADMINISTRATION TRUSTS OF RESIDUE

3. [*As in cl 7 of* Form C9.2 *at para* **[231.22]**.]

[231.47]

BENEFICIAL TRUSTS OF RESIDUE

4. (1) My trustees shall hold my residuary estate upon trust to pay the income thereof to my [wife/husband/civil partner] during [her/his] life[1] [provided that so long as my [wife/husband/civil partner] is entitled to be paid the income of all or any part of the capital of my residuary estate (or would be so entitled if it yielded income)[2] my trustees shall have power from time to time to pay transfer or apply the whole or any part or parts of such capital to or for the support or benefit of my [wife/husband/civil partner] as they shall in their absolute discretion think fit].[3]

(2) Subject to the trust [and to any exercise of the power] aforesaid my trustees shall hold my residuary estate upon trust on the later to occur of my death or the death of my [wife/husband/civil partner] to pay to the following persons [if then living][4] pecuniary legacies free of all inheritance tax and foreign death duties payable on or by reason of my death or the death of my [wife/husband/civil partner][5] (and with interest thereon at the yearly rate of 6 per cent from the later to occur of my death or the death of my [wife/husband/civil partner]) of the amounts hereinafter respectively mentioned namely:

(a) to [*name*] of [*address*] the sum of ——;
(b) to [*name*] of [address] the sum of ——;
(c) to [the Vicar and Churchwardens of the Parish of ——] the sum of £—— for such charitable purposes in the said Parish as they think fit.

(3) Subject as aforesaid my trustees shall hold my residuary estate and the income thereof upon trust for such of my nephews and nieces [*name*] [*name*] [*name*] and [*name*][6] as shall survive me and if more than one in equal shares absolutely provided that if any of my said nephews or nieces shall predecease me leaving a child or children surviving me such child or children shall take and if more than one equally between them the share of my residuary estate which such deceased nephew or niece would have taken had he or she lived to attain a vested interest.[7]

1 The life interest for the survivor will be an IPDI within IHTA 1984, s 49A (see para **[200.98]**), so where the survivor is a surviving spouse or civil partner, exemption from IHT should be available.

2 For the reasons for limiting the power in this way see the Preliminary Note to C2 at paras **[224.17]–[224.19]**.

3 For a provision of this type which limits the amount which can be paid or applied to or for the benefit of the beneficiary see Form C5.2, cl 5(2) at para **[227.27]**.

4 If the provisions of cl 4(1) fail by reason of divorce or dissolution of civil partnership, the remainder trusts will have effect as if the spouse or civil partner had died on the date of the decree: see the WA 1837, ss 18A, 18C (Part G, para **[244.18]**, **[244.20]**) and the Preliminary Note to C2 at paras **[224.17]–[224.19]**.

5 If the testator's spouse or civil partner survives the testator, the legacies are likely to be subject to a rateable share of the IHT arising on the spouse's or civil partner's death in the absence of an express direction to the contrary: see *Foster's Inheritance Tax*, K2.03.

6 As to the desirability of identifying nephews and nieces (or other relatives) see the Preliminary Note to this section at para **[231.9]**. The persons named at this point will be different persons in each will, and persons other than nephews and nieces can readily be substituted.

7 Trusts in favour of children other than the testator's own children, eg. children of nephews and nieces as here, cannot be trusts for bereaved minors or age 18-to-25 trusts. See the notes to paras **[200.151]** and **[200.152]**. Therefore to avoid property held for such children being within the relevant property regime, the substitutional trust for the children of nephews and nieces does not include any age contingency, and if the trust takes effect it will take effect in favour of minor children absolutely.

[231.48]

MAINTENANCE, ACCUMULATION AND ADVANCEMENT

5. [*As in cl 10 of* Form C9.2 *at para* **[231.25]**.]

[231.49]

ADMINISTRATIVE POWERS[1]

6. (1) In this clause where the context so admits:
   (a) the expression 'land' includes buildings and estates interests or rights of any kind in or over land; and
   (b) during the administration of my estate the expression 'beneficiary' includes any person who would be a beneficiary if such administration had been completed and the expression 'beneficially interested' and references to income of any asset being payable or capable of being paid to or for the benefit of a beneficiary shall be construed accordingly.

(2) None of the powers or provisions contained in subclause (3) below of this clause shall be capable of being exercised or operating in any manner such that if such power or provision were capable of being so exercised or so operating the existence of the same would prevent any person who would (in the absence of such power or provision) have had an interest in possession falling within section 49(1) of the IHTA 1984 in any property from having such interest.[2]

(3) In the administration of my estate and the execution of the trusts hereof or of any codicil hereto my trustees shall have the following powers in addition to those conferred by law but subject to the last foregoing subclause:
   (a) power to invest moneys sell assets and change investments with the unrestricted freedom of choice and powers of disposition and acquisition of a sole beneficial owner with in particular power to make unsecured loans, acquire non-income yielding assets, and purchase land anywhere in the world or chattels for any purpose including occupation or enjoyment in kind by a beneficiary under the power set out below;[3]
   (b) power to delegate all or any of their investment powers to a professional investment manager or managers whether individual or corporate and whether or not also a nominee holder of assets for my trustees (and who may be or include one or more of my trustees or the beneficiaries hereunder) upon such terms as to remuneration and otherwise (including terms authorising self-dealing or providing for the limitation of the liability of the investment manager or managers) as my trustees think fit and section 22 of the Trustee Act 2000 shall not apply;[4]

(c) power to vest or register any property in any person or persons whether individual or corporate and whether or not an investment manager to whom powers have been delegated under the foregoing power (and who may be or include one or more of my trustees or the beneficiaries hereunder) as nominee or nominees for my trustees upon such terms as to remuneration or otherwise (including terms authorising self-dealing or providing for the limitation of the liability of the nominee) as my trustees think fit and section 22 of the Trustee Act 2000 shall not apply;[5]

(d) power to borrow money with or without giving security and on such terms as to interest and repayment and otherwise as my trustees may think fit for any purpose connected with the administration of my estate or the trusts declared herein or in any codicil hereto (including investment) and no lender from whom my trustees borrow money in purported exercise of this power shall be concerned to enquire as to the propriety amount or purpose of any such borrowing;[6]

(e) power to lend money to a beneficiary to whom any of the income of such money is payable or to whom or for whose benefit any income of such money is capable of being paid or applied in exercise of a discretion (or who would be such a beneficiary if such money yielded income) and to do so at a full or concessionary rate of interest or interest free;[7]

(f) all the powers of an absolute owner in relation to any land (wherever situated) held by them;[8]

(g) power to apply capital held on the same trusts as any land (or which would be so held if the administration of my estate had been completed) in the improvement of such land and to apply such capital or the income of such capital on the repair or maintenance of such land;[9]

(h) power to permit any beneficiary to have the beneficial occupation use or enjoyment in kind of any land or chattel or other tangible property on such terms as to repair insurance or payment of outgoings by the beneficiary or otherwise howsoever as my trustees think fit Provided that the foregoing power shall only be exercisable and such permission to occupy or enjoy in kind may only continue in the following circumstances:

   (i) so long as any of the income of such land chattel or other tangible property is payable to such beneficiary or capable of being paid or applied to him or for his benefit in exercise of a discretion (or would be so payable or capable of being so paid or applied if such land chattel or other property yielded income);

   (ii) in the case of land, so long as for the time being the occupation thereof by such beneficiary is compatible with any statutory rights of occupation of any other beneficiary or beneficiaries;[10]

(i) power to exercise all the powers of appropriation (and other incidental powers) conferred by statute on a personal representative without the necessity of obtaining any consents and notwithstanding that one or more of my trustees may be beneficially interested in the exercise of such power. [11]

1 See para **[230.11]** n 1.
2 See para **[230.11]** n 2.
3 See para **[230.11]** n 3.
4 See para **[230.11]** n 4.
5 See para **[230.11]** n 5.
6 See para **[230.11]** n 6.
7 See para **[230.11]** n 7.
8 See para **[230.11]** n 8.
9 See para **[230.11]** n 9.
10 See para **[230.11]** n 10.
11 See para **[230.11]** n 11.

[231.50]

EXERCISE OF POWERS[1]

7. Any power or discretion hereby or by law conferred on my trustees (including a power or discretion as to the disposition of capital or income) shall be exercisable notwithstanding that any of my trustees has a personal interest in such exercise provided that there are not fewer than two trustees and that at least one of them has no such personal interest.

1 This clause will make it clear that the other spouse or civil partner, if he or she is a trustee, may join in exercising the power to pay or apply capital (see cl 4(1) at para **[231.46]**) in his or her favour. See the Preliminary Note to B18 at para **[218.4]** on this subject.

[231.51]

TRUSTEE LIABILITY

8. [*As in cl 12 of* Form C9.2 *at para* **[231.27]**.]

[231.52]

PROFESSIONAL TRUSTEE CHARGING CLAUSE

9. [*As in cl 13 of* Form C9.2 *at para* **[231.28]**.]

[*Testimonium and attestation clauses as in* Form C9.2 *at para* **[231.29]**.]

[231.53]

Form C9.5: Reciprocal wills for unmarried sisters leaving residue to survivor(s) with alternative gift to charity

Note. This form assumes a household of unmarried sisters but could be adopted for use by brothers or other relatives or friends living together. It also assumes that there are three members of such household who all make wills in similar form. Subject to the gift of legacies residue devolves on the surviving sisters or sister and the death of the last survivor goes to charity. As mentioned in the Preliminary Note, there is not much scope for tax-planning where the primary concern of the members of the household is to provide for each other, but an optional survival contingency is included in the residuary trusts.

[231.54]

REVOCATION CLAUSE AND DECLARATION AGAINST MUTUAL WILLS

I [*name*] of [*address*] revoke all former testamentary dispositions made by me and declare this to be my last will [and I further declare that notwithstanding that my sisters [*name*] and [*name*] are making wills in similar terms we have agreed that our wills are not mutual wills and accordingly that each of us shall be free to revoke her will at any time whether before or after the death of either of the others and shall be free to dispose of her property or any property derived from either of the others as she thinks fit].[1]

1 There is no presumption that two wills in similar form are mutual wills in the technical sense, but the inclusion of the words in square brackets will remove any doubt on the point. If mutual wills are intended, then an express clause to that effect, such as Form B1.6 at para **[201.10]** should be used instead of this clause. For the law on mutual wills see Vol 1, paras **[2.3]**–**[2.9]**. We recommend life interest trusts rather than mutual wills where a testator wishes to determine the destination of his property after the death of a primary beneficiary or beneficiaries.

[231.55]

DIRECTIONS AS TO BURIAL

1. I desire that my body may be buried in the family vault in the churchyard of the Church of —— in the Parish of ——.

[231.56]

APPOINTMENT OF EXECUTORS

2. I appoint [my sisters [*name*] and [*name*]] and [*name*] of [*address*] (hereinafter together called 'my trustees' which expression shall include my personal representatives for the time being and the trustees for the time being hereof) to be the executors and trustees of this will.

[231.57]

PECUNIARY LEGACIES

3. I give free of tax[1] the following pecuniary legacies—
   (a) to [my god-daughter [*name*]] the sum of £——;
   (b) to [my cousin [*name*]] the sum of £——;
   (c) to my friend [*name*] the sum of £——;
   (d) to [the Vicar and Churchwardens of the Parish of ——] the sum of £—— to be applied for such charitable purposes in the said Parish as they think fit.

1 See Form C9.2, cl 2, n 2 at para **[231.17]**.

[231.58]

ADMINISTRATION TRUSTS OF RESIDUE

4. [*As in cl 7 of* Form C9.2 *at para* **[231.22]**.]

[231.59]

GIFTS MADE FREE OF TAX

5. [*As in cl 8 of* Form C9.2 *at para* **[231.23]**.]

[231.60]

BENEFICIAL TRUSTS OF RESIDUE

6. My trustees shall stand possessed of my residuary estate—

(a) upon trust for such of my said sisters as shall survive me [for the period of one month][1] and if both in equal shares absolutely;

(b) in default of and subject to the foregoing trust upon trust for [*name of charity*] absolutely and I declare that the receipt of any person professing to be the treasurer or other proper officer of the said charity shall be a full and sufficient discharge to my trustees.

1 For the utility of survivorship conditions in gifts in favour of persons other than the testator's spouse or civil partner, see the Preliminary Note to C2 at para **[224.6]**.

[231.61]

PROFESSIONAL TRUSTEE CHARGING CLAUSE

7. [*As in cl 13 of* Form C9.2 *at para* **[231.28]**.]
[*Testimonium and attestation clause as in* Form C9.2 *at para* **[231.29]**.]

[231.62]

Form C9.6: Will of unmarried and childless testatrix giving her unmarried and childless sister a right of residence in her house and dividing residue between her nephews and nieces and charity

Note. The provision provided by this will for the unmarried sister is limited to a right of residence in the house. For alternative possibilities see Form C9.5 at paras **[231.53]–[231.61]** and Form C10.5 at paras **[232.52]–[232.63]**.

[231.63]

REVOCATION

I [*name*] of [*address*] hereby revoke all former testamentary dispositions made by me and declare this to be my last will.

[231.64]

APPOINTMENT OF EXECUTORS AND TRUSTEES

1. [*As in cl 3 of* Form C9.3 *at paras* **[231.34]**.]

[231.65]

GIFT OF CHATTELS TO SISTER

2. I give [free of tax][1] all my personal chattels as defined by section 55(1)(x) of the Administration of Estates Act 1925 to my sister [*name*] absolutely.

1 IHT on specifically given property is prima facie a testamentary expense payable out of residue unless the property is situate out of the United Kingdom: IHTA 1984, s 211(1) (Part G, para **[246.100]**; see also B14 at para **[214.55]** ff). However, the inclusion of the words 'free of tax' (ie free of inheritance tax: see the definition in cl 6) will do no harm and will exclude the tax charge in respect of any property which happens to be situate out of the jurisdiction at the death.

[231.66]

PECUNIARY LEGACIES

3. [*As in cl 3 of* Form C9.5 *at para* **[231.57]**.]

[231.67]

RIGHT OF RESIDENCE TO SISTER[1]

4. (1) I give my freehold dwellinghouse known as ———, or (if the same shall be sold or otherwise disposed of before my death) the dwellinghouse or the principal dwellinghouse (if I have more than one) which I shall own at the date of my death, to my trustees free of all sums charged or otherwise secured thereon at my death (which sums shall be paid out of my residuary estate) to hold the same and any dwellinghouse acquired in substitution therefor (as provided below) upon trust to provide a residence for my sister [*name*] so long as she wishes to reside there subject as provided below.

(2) My trustees shall not exercise their power to sell the said or any substitute dwellinghouse or their power to purchase any substitute dwellinghouse or exercise any of their other powers[2] over any such dwellinghouse without the consent in writing of my sister so long as her interest continues and (if for the time being a dwellinghouse is held subject to the provisions of this Clause) so long as she shall perform and observe any conditions reasonably imposed by my trustees in relation to her residence in any such dwellinghouse.[3]

(3) I wish my trustees to impose as a condition in relation to my sister's residence in any such dwellinghouse that she should keep the same fully insured in the name of my trustees, keep the same in good repair, observe and perform the lessee's covenants (if the dwellinghouse is leasehold), and pay all taxes and other outgoings in respect thereof[4] and my trustees shall not be liable for lack of insurance repair or payment of outgoings or for not taking steps to enforce any reasonable conditions imposed in relation to my sister's residence in any such dwellinghouse.[5]

(4) On the death of my sister or (subject to subclause (5) below) in the event of her giving up residence[6], such dwellinghouse and any property representing it shall fall into my residuary estate.

(5) For the purposes of this clause:

(a) no involuntary ceasing by my sister to reside in a dwellinghouse subject to this clause shall be treated as ceasing to reside therein unless my sister shall have been out of residence continuously for six months and shall not have expressed in writing to my trustees her intention to take up residence again; [7]

(b) references to a dwellinghouse include a flat and an interest in a dwellinghouse.

(6) All the powers of my trustees may be exercised by them in favour of or for the benefit of my sister even though she may be one of my trustees.

1 This is a simple form which permits the sister to reside only in the property held at the testator's death. For a more elaborate form which enables a replacement property to be purchased for her to live in, see Form B8.5 at para **[208.41]**. For a discussion of rights of residence see the Preliminary Note to B8 at para **[208.1]** ff. The sister's right to reside will give her an interest in possession in the house which will be an IPDI within IHTA 1984, s 49A (see para **[200.98]**).

2 This is no longer statutorily implied from the requirement of consent to a sale as a result of the repeal of the LPA 1925, s 28(1): see Part A, para **[200.60]**. The TLATA 1996, s 8(2) (Part G, para **[246.110]**) provides that exercise of the trustees' powers may be subject to consents (see Part A, paras **[200.60]** and **[208.19]**).

3 Subclause (2) could be omitted, since so long as the beneficiary is in residence the trustees cannot sell the property without first applying to the court under the TLATA 1996, s 14 (Part G, para **[246.117]**) and making the requirement of her consent end if she does not fulfil the conditions of her occupation does not help the trustees much if she is still in occupation.

4 See para **[208.26]** for the reasons for making this an expression of wishes rather than a direction that the beneficiary's occupation shall be subject to these burdens.

5 Although it is thought that the will cannot predetermine what obligations an occupying beneficiary will be subject to (see para **[208.26]**) there is nothing to prevent the trustees being absolved from liability for want of repair etc which it is contemplated will be the beneficiary's responsibility.

6 If the sister's IPDI comes to an end during her lifetime by her ceasing to reside, she will be deemed to make a transfer of value for IHT purposes, see IHTA 1984, s 52(1). However, to the extent that the property in which her IPDI terminates passes to charity (as part of it does under this Form), it should be an exempt transfer, and to the extent that it passes to individuals absolutely entitled (as the rest of it does under this Form), it should be potentially exempt.

7 The idea here is to protect the beneficiary against precipitate sale if she is hospitalised after an accident or illness, but if she is hospitalised and is mentally incapacitated she will not be able to express an intention to return and the trustees will be free to sell the property after six months. This paragraph may be omitted if preferred.

[231.68]

ADMINISTRATION TRUSTS OF RESIDUE

5. [*As in cl 7 of* Form C9.2 *at para* **[231.22]**.]

[231.69]

GIFTS MADE FREE OF TAX

6. [*As in cl 8 of* Form C9.2 *at para* **[231.23]**.]

[231.70]

DIVISION OF RESIDUE

7. (1) My trustees shall hold my residuary estate upon trust to divide the same into [two equal shares]/[two shares of one third and two thirds] (hereinafter respectively called 'the charity share' and 'the family share').

(2) The foregoing shares shall be determined by division of my residuary estate in the foregoing proportions before making any deduction for the inheritance tax payable by reason of my death and attributable to the family share and such inheritance tax shall then be borne by the family share as so determined.[1]

1 For the reasons for making provision of this sort, see paras **[200.138]** ff and **[214.69]**.

[231.71]

TRUSTS OF CHARITY SHARE

8. My trustees shall hold the charity share and the income thereof upon trust for such institution or institutions (whether corporate or not) having exclusively charitable purposes connected with the relief of poverty or for such exclusively charitable purposes connected with the relief of poverty as my trustees shall in their absolute discretion determine.

[231.72]

TRUSTS OF FAMILY SHARE

9. (1) My trustees shall hold the family share and the income thereof upon trust for such of my nephews and nieces [*name*] [*name*] [*name*] and [*name*][1] as shall survive me and if more than one in equal shares absolutely provided that if any of my said nephews or nieces shall predecease me leaving a child or children surviving me such child or children shall take and if more than one equally between them the share of my residuary estate which such deceased nephew or niece would have taken had he or she lived to attain a vested interest.[2]

1 It is advisable to give the names and addresses of them or otherwise identify them fully: see the Preliminary Note at para **[231.9]**.

2 Trusts in favour of children other than the testator's children, eg. children of nephews and nieces as here, cannot be trusts for bereaved minors or age 18-to-25 trusts. See the notes to paras **[200.108]** and **[200.109]**. Therefore to avoid property held for such children being within the relevant property regime, the substitutional trust for the children of nephews and nieces does not include any age contingency, and if the trust takes effect it will take effect in favour of minor children absolutely.

[231.73]

MAINTENANCE, ACCUMULATION AND ADVANCEMENT

10. [*As in cl 10 of* Form C9.2 *at para* **[231.25]**.]

[231.74]

ADMINISTRATIVE POWERS

11. [*As in cl 11 of* Form C9.2 *at para* **[231.26]**.]

[231.75]

TRUSTEE LIABILITY

12. [*As in cl 12 of* Form C9.2 *at para* **[231.27]**.]

[231.76]

PROFESSIONAL TRUSTEE CHARGING CLAUSE

13. [*As in cl 13 of* Form C9.2 *at para* **[231.28]**.]

[*Testimonium and attestation clause as in* Form C9.2 *at para* **[231.29]**.]

C10 Wills for childless individuals

Preliminary note .... **[232.1]**

FORMS

C10.1 Will of young person dividing his or her estate equally between his or her siblings but making a gift of the share of a sibling with living children direct to such children .... **[232.2]**

C10.2 Will of young person creating discretionary trust of residue for his or her parents and brothers and sisters and their issue .... **[232.15]**

C10.3 Will of older person in favour of brothers and sisters, with substitution of issue of those who predecease the testator .... **[232.27]**

C10.4 Will of older childless person settling residue in equal shares on brothers and sisters (or nephews and nieces) for life with remainders for their children .... **[232.39]**

C10.5 Will of unmarried childless person in favour of unmarried sister for life with remainders over to brothers and sisters or their issue... **[232.52]**

C10.6 Will of childless individual giving charitable and other legacies, with a specific gift of a house and residue given on trust for nephews and nieces for life with remainders for their children .... **[232.64]**

PRELIMINARY NOTE

[232.1]

The forms in this section provide a selection of alternative dispositions for childless individuals. These forms are in many respects similar to those in C7 and C8 for sole parents. One significant difference, however, is that in the case of wills of parents in favour of their own children, the class will necessarily close on the parent's death. In the case of an uncle or aunt, especially one who is relatively young, this is not necessarily so and, unless special provision is made, after-born nephews and nieces may be excluded from benefit. If the estate is substantial and includes landed estates, reference should be made to Form C13.2 at para **[235.18]** ff.

Another difference is that trusts in favour of children other than a testator's own children, cannot be trusts for bereaved minors or age 18-to-25 trusts. See the notes to paras **[200.151]** and **[200.152]**. Therefore if property is to be held on trust for children other than the testator's own, the children will have either IPDIs within IHTA 1984, s 49A (see para **[200.98]**), or the property will be within the IHT relevant property regime.

One tax planning possibility to bear in mind is generation skipping. Gifts direct to the youngest available generation could save significant amounts of IHT in the long run (see Part A, paras **[200.88]** and **[200.91]**). Form C10.1 is an example of a will which gives each sibling's share direct to his or her children if he or she has any at the testator's death.

Where it is desired to assist older generations, particularly where it is desired to benefit the elderly, a discretionary trust could save IHT. Form C10.2 at paras **[232.15]–[232.26]** is an example of this strategy.

[232.2]

Form C10.1: Will of young person dividing his or her estate equally between his or her siblings but making a gift of the share of a sibling with living children direct to such children

Note. The idea of this form is to include the maximum amount of generation skipping (for which see Part A, para **[200.91]**), according to the circumstances at the testator's death. The residuary estate is divided into shares according to the number of siblings then living, or then dead leaving issue. The share of any sibling of whom there are issue living at the testator's death goes direct to that issue, whether or not the sibling is still living.

[232.3]

REVOCATION CLAUSE

I [*name*] of [*address*] hereby revoke all former testamentary dispositions made by me and declare this to be my last will.

[232.4]

APPOINTMENT OF EXECUTORS AND TRUSTEES

1. I appoint [*name*] of [*address*] and [*name*] of [*address*] (hereinafter together called 'my trustees' which expression shall include my personal representatives for the time being and the trustees for the time being hereof) to be the executors and trustees of this will.

[232.5]

GIFT OF PERSONAL CHATTELS

2. I give free of tax[1] all my personal chattels as defined by section 55(1)(x) of the Administration of Estates Act 1925[2] to my [brother/sister] [*name*] absolutely and I request [him/her] (but without imposing any trust or binding obligation on [him/her]) to give effect to any wishes of mine as to the disposition of such chattels which may be contained in any memorandum which may be found amongst my papers at my death or which may have been otherwise communicated to [him/her] during my life.[3]

1 This is included in case any of the chattels are outside the UK at the testator's death, and thus subject to tax in the absence of a direction to the contrary. See the Note to B14 at para **[214.55]** and the definition of 'free of tax' in cl 5 of this form at para **[232.8]**.
2 See Part G, para **[246.67]** and Vol 1, para **[64.44]**.
3 A distribution in accordance with the testator's wishes within two years of the testator's death will be treated for IHT purposes as a direct gift by the testator's will (Inheritance Tax Act 1984 (IHTA 1984), s 143): see B4 at paras **[204.6]**–**[204.9]**.

[232.6]

PECUNIARY LEGACIES

3. (1) I give free of tax[1] pecuniary legacies of £—— to each of my godchildren [*name*] [*name*] and [*name*].[2]

(2) I give the following charitable legacies:[3]

(a) to [*name of charity*] the sum of £——;
(b) to [*name of charity*] the sum of £——;
(c) to [*name of charity*] the sum of £——;

And I declare that the receipt of the person professing to be the treasurer or other proper officer of any of the said charities shall be a full and sufficient discharge to my trustees for the legacy hereby given to such charity.[4]

1 Although the IHT on legacies or specific gifts of UK property is a testamentary expense, it is preferable to include an express direction that a pecuniary legacy is free of tax in case residue includes foreign property or settled property; if it does include such property, a proportion of the legacies, corresponding to the proportion of residue which made up of foreign or settled property, would probably have to bear inheritance in the absence of a direction to the contrary. See further the Note to B14 at para **[214.55]** ff. For the definition of 'free of tax' see cl 5 of this form at para **[232.8]**.

2 It is essential to identify godchildren by name.

3 Gifts for charitable purposes are exempt from IHT and it is not therefore necessary to incorporate the 'free of tax' formula.

4 If there is the slightest doubt as to whether any of these charitable donees are correctly described or still exist, a discretionary charitable trust to operate in case of difficulty, such as Form C10.6, cl 4 at para **[232.68]** could be added.

[232.7]

ADMINISTRATION TRUSTS OF RESIDUE

4. (1) I give all my property not hereby or by any codicil hereto otherwise effectively disposed of [(including any entailed or other property over which I shall have at my death a general power of disposition by will)][1] to my trustees to hold on the trusts set out below with power at their discretion to sell all or any of it as and when they think fit.[2]

(2) My trustees shall pay my funeral and testamentary expenses[3] and debts and any legacies given by this will or any codicil hereto out of such property or its proceeds and shall have a discretion as to how such payments shall be borne as between capital and income.[4]

(3) Subject as above my trustees shall hold such property and the assets from time to time representing the same (hereinafter called 'my residuary estate') on the trusts set out below and shall invest all money comprised in such property or arising from its sale in any of the investments hereby authorised with power to change such investments into any others hereby authorised.

(4) In the administration of my estate and the execution of the trusts of this will or of any codicil to it:

(a) my trustees shall treat all income as accruing on the date on which it becomes payable regardless of the period in respect of which it shall have accrued and shall not make any statutory apportionment of the same;[5] and

(b) none of the equitable rules of apportionment between capital and income shall apply in any circumstances whatever.[6]

1 See para **[230.7]**, n 1.

2 See para **[230.7]**, n 2.

3 See para **[230.7]**, n 3.

4 See para **[230.7]**, n 4.

5 See para **[230.7]**, n 5.

6 See para **[230.7]**, n 6.

[232.8]

GIFTS MADE FREE OF TAX

5. Any specific gift or pecuniary or general legacy made by this will or any codicil hereto which is expressed to be 'free of tax' shall be free from the payment of any inheritance tax or foreign tax or duty payable on or by reason of my death to which such gift or legacy would otherwise be subject and such inheritance tax or foreign tax or duty shall be paid out of my residuary estate.[1]

1 See Form C3.1, cl 5, n 1 at para **[225.15]**.

[232.9]

BENEFICIAL TRUSTS OF RESIDUE

6. (1) My trustees shall hold my residuary estate upon trust to divide the same into such number of equal shares as shall be equal to the number of such of my brothers and sisters as shall be living at the date of my death or shall have predeceased me (whether before or after the date of this will)[1] leaving children or grandchildren living at my death.

(2) In the case of any of my brothers or sisters who shall be living at the date of my death but who shall have no children or grandchildren then living my trustees shall hold one such equal share of my residuary estate upon trust for such brother or sister absolutely.

(3) In the case of any of my brothers and sisters who shall have children or grandchildren living at the date of my death (and whether or not such brother or sister shall himself or herself then be living) my trustees shall hold one such equal share of my residuary estate upon the following trusts:

(a) my trustees shall hold such share upon trust for such of the children of such brother or sister living at the date of my death[2] if more than one in equal shares;

(b) Provided that if any child of such brother or sister of mine shall predecease me leaving a child or children living at my death[3] such last-mentioned child or children shall take and if more than equally between them the share of such share of my residuary estate which his her or their parent would have taken had he or she lived to attain a vested interest;

(c) the foregoing trusts shall carry the intermediate income of such share and section 31 of the Trustee Act 1925 (as hereinafter modified) shall apply thereto;

(d) section 32 of the Trustee Act 1925 (as hereinafter modified) shall apply in relation to such share.

1 If any brother or sister is dead at the date of the will, it is likely that any issue of his or hers who may be living at the testator's death will be eligible under the trusts declared by sub-cl (3), but it is advisable to include the words in brackets so as to make this absolutely clear: cf *Re Earle's Settlement Trusts, Reiss v Norrie* [1971] 2 All ER 1188, [1971] 1 WLR 1118 and see generally Vol 1, paras **[68.3]–[68.9]**.

2 Trusts in favour of children other than the testator's own children, eg. children of brothers and sisters as here, cannot be trusts for bereaved minors or age 18-to-25 trusts. See the notes to paras **[200.107]** and **[200.108]**. Therefore to avoid property held for such children being within the IHT relevant property regime, the gift here is only to such children living at the testator's death, and with no age contingency.

3 See note 2 above.

[232.10]

MAINTENANCE, ACCUMULATION AND ADVANCEMENT[1]

7. (1) Section 31 of the Trustee Act 1925 (relating to accumulation and maintenance) shall apply in relation to the trusts hereby or by any codicil hereto declared as if:

(a) in paragraph (i) of subsection (1) of the said section the words 'as the trustees think fit' were substituted for the words 'as may in all the circumstances be reasonable'; and

(b) the proviso to the said subsection (1) were omitted.

(2) Section 32 of the Trustee Act 1925 (relating to advancement) shall apply in relation to the said trusts as if the words 'one half of' were omitted from proviso (a) to subsection (1) thereof.

(3) Whenever my trustees shall have an obligation or discretion under the provisions of this will or any codicil hereto or under the general law to apply income or capital for the benefit of a minor beneficiary they may either pay the same without liability to account to his or her parent guardian or any other adult person with whom such beneficiary may be residing or to such beneficiary himself or herself if of the age of 16 years or more and so that the receipt of such parent guardian or other person or of such minor beneficiary shall be a full and sufficient discharge to my trustees for the income or capital so applied.[2]

1 For alternative provisions see the forms in B18 at para **[218.77]** ff.

2 A parent (with parental responsibility) and a guardian of a minor are empowered by the ChA 1989, s 3(3) (Part G, para **[244.114]**) to give a good receipt for the minor's property: see Vol 1, para **[9.42]**. The power in this subclause is wider in that it authorises the payment of income or capital to a parent who does not have parental responsibility, any adult with whom the minor is residing, and the minor himself or herself if 16 or over.

[232.11]

ADMINISTRATIVE POWERS[1]

8. (1) In this clause where the context so admits:

(a) the expression 'land' includes buildings and estates interests or rights of any kind in or over land; and

(b) during the administration of my estate the expression 'beneficiary' includes any person who would be a beneficiary if such administration had been completed and the expression 'beneficially interested' and references to income of any asset being payable or capable of being paid to or for the benefit of a beneficiary shall be construed accordingly.

(2) In the administration of my estate and the execution of the trusts hereof or of any codicil hereto my trustees shall have the following powers in addition to those conferred by law but subject to the last foregoing subclause—

(a) power to invest moneys sell assets and change investments with the unrestricted freedom of choice and powers of disposition and acquisition of a sole beneficial owner with in particular power to make unsecured loans, acquire non-income yielding assets, and purchase land anywhere in the world or chattels for any purpose including occupation or enjoyment in kind by a beneficiary under the power set out below;[2]

(b) power to delegate all or any of their investment powers to a professional investment manager or managers whether individual or corporate and whether or not also a nominee holder of assets for my trustees (and who may be or include one or more of my trustees or the beneficiaries hereunder) upon such terms as to remuneration and otherwise (including terms authorising self-dealing or providing for the limitation of the liability of the investment manager or managers) as my trustees think fit and section 22 of the Trustee Act 2000 shall not apply;[3]

(c) power to vest or register any property in any person or persons whether individual or corporate and whether or not an investment manager to whom powers have been delegated under the foregoing power (and who may be or include one or more of my trustees or the beneficiaries hereunder) as nominee or nominees for my trustees upon such terms as to remuneration or otherwise (including terms authorising self-dealing or providing for the limitation of the liability of the nominee) as my trustees think fit and section 22 of the Trustee Act 2000 shall not apply;[4]

(d) power to borrow money with or without giving security and on such terms as to interest and repayment and otherwise as my trustees may think fit for any purpose connected with the administration of my estate or the trusts declared herein or in any codicil hereto (including investment) And no lender from whom my trustees borrow money in purported exercise of this power shall be concerned to enquire as to the propriety amount or purpose of any such borrowing;[5]

(e) power to lend money to a beneficiary to whom any of the income of such money is payable or to whom or for whose benefit any income of such money is capable of being paid or applied in exercise of a discretion (or who would be such a beneficiary if such money yielded income) and to do so at a full or concessionary rate of interest or interest free;[6]

(f) all the powers of an absolute owner in relation to any land (wherever situated) held by them;[7]

(g) power to apply capital held on the same trusts as any land (or which would be so held if the administration of my estate had been completed) in the improvement of such land and to apply such capital or the income of such capital on the repair or maintenance of such land;[8]

(h) power to permit any beneficiary to have the beneficial occupation use or enjoyment in kind of any land or chattel or other tangible property on such terms as to repair insurance or payment of outgoings by the beneficiary or otherwise howsoever as my trustees think fit Provided that the foregoing power shall only be exercisable and such permission to occupy or enjoy in kind may only continue in the following circumstances:

(i) so long as any of the income of such land chattel or other tangible property is payable to such beneficiary or capable of being paid or applied to him or for his benefit in exercise of a discretion (or would be so payable or capable of being so paid or applied if such land chattel or other property yielded income);

(ii) in the case of land, so long as for the time being the occupation thereof by such beneficiary is compatible with any statutory rights of occupation of any other beneficiary or beneficiaries;[9]

(i) power to exercise all the powers of appropriation (and other incidental powers) conferred by statute on a personal representative without the necessity of obtaining any consents and notwithstanding that one or more of my trustees may be beneficially interested in the exercise of such power.[10]

1 See para **[230.11]** n 1.
2 See para **[230.11]** n 3.
3 See para **[230.11]** n 4.
4 See para **[230.11]** n 5.
5 See para **[230.11]** n 6.
6 See para **[230.11]** n 7.
7 See para **[230.11]** n 8.
8 See para **[230.11]** n 9.
9 See para **[230.11]** n 10.
10 See para **[230.11]** n 11.

[232.12]

TRUSTEE LIABILITY

9. (1) My trustees shall not be liable for any act or default of any investment manager or nominee employed in good faith to manage or hold assets of my estate nor for any act or default of any beneficiary having the occupation use or enjoyment of property in kind.[1]

(2) Section 11(1) of the Trusts of Land and Appointment of Trustees Act 1996 (consultation with beneficiaries) shall not apply to the exercise by my trustees of any of their powers in relation to land subject to the trusts hereof.[2]

1 This makes it clear that the trustees are not liable for the defaults of others who may have possession or control of trust property. For a wider form of indemnity, see e g Form B21.12 at para **[221.16]**. If a paid trustee is to rely on this indemnity clause, the testator should specifically be made aware of its meaning and effect (see para **[221.13]** above).
2 The requirement that trustees of land in exercise of any function relating to land subject to the trust consult with beneficiaries of full age beneficially entitled to an interest in possession in the land can be excluded: TLATA 1996, s 11 (Part G, para **[246.114]**).

[232.13]

PROFESSIONAL TRUSTEE CHARGING CLAUSE

10. Any of my trustees being a professional or business man may charge and be paid all usual professional and other proper charges for business transacted acts done advice given and time spent by him or his firm in connection with the administration of my estate or in connection with the trusts hereof including acts which a personal representative or trustee not being in any profession or business could have done personally.

[232.14]

TESTIMONIUM AND ATTESTATION CLAUSE

IN WITNESS whereof I have hereunto set my hand this —— day of —— 20—

SIGNED by the above-named testator as his last will in the presence of us both present at the same time who at his request and in his presence and in the presence of each other have signed our names below as witnesses } [*Signature of testator*]

[*Signatures, addresses and descriptions of two witnesses*]

[232.15]

Form C10.2: Will of young person creating discretionary trust of residue for his or her parents and brothers and sisters and their issue

Note. For the taxation of property comprised in a discretionary trust see B18 at paras **[218.8]**ff. The reason for creating a discretionary trust of most of the estate as in this Form is that it enables income to be received by beneficiaries without the capital being treated as part of their 'estates' for IHT purposes. Accordingly, the death of any of the beneficiaries will not give rise to an IHT charge on the trust fund. It is particularly worth considering where those who are intended to receive benefit include the testator's parents, grandparents, or any other persons with a moderate or short expectation of life. For other points on the use of discretionary trusts in this way, see the Note to Form C6.2 at paras **[228.19]** and **[228.20]**.

If during the two years following the testator's death some other arrangement seems to the trustees to be better, they can make an appointment which is treated for IHT purposes as a disposition made by the testator's will by virtue of the IHTA 1984, s 144 (see the Note on s 144 in C3 at paras **[225.83]**–**[225.91]**). Section 144 applying is not likely to make a lot of difference unless the testator has a very substantial taxable estate, or the taxation of discretionary trusts becomes much heavier, or there might be substantial discretionary distributions to charity which would make the testator's estate exempt from IHT on his death if s 144 applied. The possibility of the testator getting married or forming a civil partnership, and thus the possibility of there being distributions to the testator's widow, widower or surviving civil partner which would be exempt if s 144 applied, is not relevant since a will made in this form will be revoked by the testator's marriage or civil partnership (WA 1837, ss 18(1), 18B: Part G, paras **[244.16]**, **[244.19]**). As matters stand at the moment, a distribution within a short period after the testator's death out of a discretionary trust created by his will is unlikely to be subject to very much IHT under the ordinary IHT charging rules for discretionary trusts (see B18 at para **[218.8]**), and the main advantage of s 144 applying is usually that spouse or civil partner or charitable exemption is obtained in relation to the testator's death.

If it might be important to be able to take advantage of the IHTA 1984, s 144 (eg because charity is an object of the power of appointment), it would be possible to add features to the provisos to the power of appointment making it easier for an appointment within s 144 to be made within the two years following the testator's death, such as appear in provisos (v) to (vii) of Form C6.2, cl 7(3)(a) at para **[228.28]** (and see also Form C3.6, cl 7 at para **[225.108]** and n 2 thereto). The only provision of this sort in the form as it stands is the provision in the opening words of cl 6(3) that the powers there referred to may be exercised before or after the grant of probate or the completion of the administration of the estate.

[232.16]

REVOCATION CLAUSE

I [*name*] of [*address*] hereby revoke all former testamentary dispositions made by me and declare this to be my last will.

[232.17]

APPOINTMENT OF EXECUTORS AND TRUSTEES

1. [*As in cl 1 of* Form C10.1 *at para* **[232.4]**.]

[232.18]

GIFT OF PERSONAL CHATTELS

2. [*As in cl 2 of* Form C10.1 *at para* **[232.5]**.]

[232.19]

PECUNIARY LEGACIES

3. [*As in cl 3 of* Form C10.1 *at para* **[232.6]**.]

[232.20]

ADMINISTRATION TRUSTS OF RESIDUE

4. [*As in cl 4 of* Form C10.1 *at para* **[232.7]**.]

[232.21]

GIFTS MADE FREE OF TAX

5. [*As in cl 5 of* Form C10.1 *at para* **[232.8]**.]

[232.22]

DISCRETIONARY TRUSTS OF RESIDUE

6. (1) My trustees shall hold my residuary estate and the income thereof upon the trusts and with and subject to the powers and provisions hereinafter declared and contained.

(2) In this clause the following expressions have the following meanings, namely:

(a) 'the residuary beneficiaries' means and includes:[1]

(i) my parents [*name*] and [*name*] [and my grandparents [*names of surviving grandparents*]];

(ii) my brothers and sisters [*name*] [*name*] [*name*] [*name*] and [*name*] and their respective children and remoter issue;

(iii) any spouse civil partner widow widower or surviving civil partner of any of my said brothers and sisters or their respective children or remoter issue (including any widow widower or surviving civil partner who has married or formed a civil partnership);

(b) 'the trust period' means the period commencing on the day of my death and expiring on [the twenty-first anniversary of the death of the last survivor of the residuary beneficiaries living at the date of my death]/[the eightieth anniversary thereof (and so that the perpetuity period applicable to the disposition hereby created shall be the period of 80 years from my death)];[2]

(c) 'the accumulation period' means the period commencing with my death and expiring on the twenty-first anniversary thereof.

(3) Subject as hereinafter provided my trustees (being not fewer than two in number or being a trust corporation)[3] may at any time or times and from time to time during the trust period (and whether before or after the grant of probate and regardless of whether the administration of my estate is complete) exercise either or both of the following powers namely:

(a) power at any time or times and from time to time by deed or deeds revocable or irrevocable to appoint the whole or any part or parts of my residuary estate upon trust for all or such one or more exclusive of the others or other of the residuary beneficiaries if more than one in such shares and either absolutely or at such age or time or respective ages or times and with such trusts and powers for their respective benefit and such provisions as my trustees think fit and in making any such appointment my trustees shall have powers as full as those which they would possess if they were an absolute beneficial owner of my residuary estate and in particular (but without prejudice to the generality of the foregoing words) my trustees may in any exercise of the foregoing power:
   (i) delegate give or impose to or upon themselves or any other person or persons any discretionary powers or discretionary trusts conditions limitations restrictions or provisions including powers of further delegation or powers of further creation of discretionary trusts or powers;
   (ii) create powers or trusts for the accumulation of income during any period permitted by law;
   (iii) create administrative powers or provisions of whatever nature;

Provided that:
   (i) no such appointment shall invalidate any payment transfer or application of capital or income previously made under any of the trusts or powers herein elsewhere contained;
   (ii) every interest limited under any exercise of such power shall vest in interest (if at all) not later than the expiration of the trust period;
   (iii) any such appointment may be made in respect of income alone without any appointment of capital; and
   (iv) any such revocable appointment shall (so far as then unrevoked) cease to be revocable on the expiration of the trust period;

(b) power (subject to any or every exercise of the foregoing power) at any time or times and from time to time in their absolute discretion to pay transfer or apply my residuary estate or any part or parts thereof to or for the benefit of all or any one or more exclusive of the others or other of the residuary beneficiaries for the time being in existence if more than one in such shares and generally in such manner as my trustees think fit.

(4) In default of and subject to any or every exercise of the foregoing powers my trustees shall hold my residuary estate during the trust period upon trust to pay or apply the income thereof to or for the maintenance education or benefit of all or any one or more of the residuary beneficiaries and if more than one in such shares and in such manner generally as my

trustees think fit provided that during the accumulation period my trustees may accumulate all or any part or parts of such income by investing the same and the resulting income thereof in any investments hereby authorised and so that any accumulations so made shall form part of the capital of my residuary estate (or the part thereof from which such income arose) for all purposes.

(5) Subject as aforesaid my trustees shall hold my residuary estate and the income thereof at the expiration of the trust period upon trust for such of the residuary beneficiaries as shall be then living in equal shares per capita.

(6) Any capital or income of my residuary estate not otherwise disposed of by this clause shall be held in trust for such of my brothers and sisters as shall survive me and if more than one in equal shares.

1 For an alternative definition, including power to add people to the class, see Form C3.6, cl 3(1)(b) at para **[225.100]** or Form C6.2, cl 7(1)(a) and (3)(c) at para **[228.28]**.

2 A common law perpetuity period and an 80-year period are included as alternatives. An 80-year period has the advantage that there is no difficulty in deciding when the period comes to an end, but the disadvantage that an appointment of, eg a life interest with remainders over, will need express perpetuity restrictions which it might not have needed if a common law period had been chosen.

3 For more elaborate provisions permitting the exercise of powers by a sole trustee during the two-year period following the death see Form C4.1, cl 8 at para **[226.25]**, see also the Note to this form at para **[232.15]**.

[232.23]

ADMINISTRATIVE POWERS

7. [*As in cl 8 of* Form C10.1 *at para* **[232.11]**.]

[232.24]

TRUSTEE LIABILITY

8. [*As in cl 9 of* Form C10.1 *at para* **[232.12]**.]

[232.25]

EXERCISE OF POWERS[1]

9. Any power or discretion hereby or by law conferred on my trustees (including a power or discretion as to the disposition of capital or income) shall be exercisable notwithstanding that any of my trustees has a personal interest in such exercise provided that there are not fewer than two trustees and that at least one of them has no such personal interest.

1 This clause enables a family member who may be an object of, eg a power of appointment or a power to apply capital, to be a trustee without being thereby disqualified from benefiting under an exercise of the power. See B18 at para **[218.4]**.

[232.26]

PROFESSIONAL TRUSTEE CHARGING CLAUSE

10. [*As in cl 10 of* Form C10.1 *at para* **[232.13]**.]

[*Testimonium and attestation clause as in* Form C10.1 *at para* **[232.14]**.]

[232.27]

Form C10.3: Will of older person in favour of brothers and sisters, with substitution of issue of those who predecease the testator

Note. This form contains a gift of residue to surviving brothers and sisters absolutely with a substitutional gift in favour of the issue of any deceased brother or sister. The form could readily be adapted so as to skip a generation by substituting references to nephews and nieces for references to brothers and sisters.

[232.28]

REVOCATION CLAUSE

I [*name*] of [*address*] hereby revoke all former testamentary dispositions made by me and declare this to be my last will.

[232.29]

APPOINTMENT OF EXECUTORS AND TRUSTEES

1. [*As in cl 1 of* Form C10.1 *at para* **[232.4]**.]

[232.30]

GIFT OF PERSONAL CHATTELS

2. [*As in cl 2 of* Form C10.1 *at para* **[232.5]**.]

[232.31]

PECUNIARY LEGACIES

3. [*As in cl 3 of* Form C10.1 *at para* **[232.6]**.]

[232.32]

ADMINISTRATION TRUSTS OF RESIDUE

4. [*As in cl 4 of* Form C10.1 *at para* **[232.7]**.]

[232.33]

GIFTS MADE FREE OF TAX

5. [*As in cl 5 of* Form C10.1 *at para* **[232.8]**.]

[232.34]

BENEFICIAL TRUSTS OF RESIDUE

6. My trustees shall hold my residuary estate and the income thereof upon trust for such of my brothers and sisters [*name*] [*name*] [*name*] and [*name*] as shall be living at my death and if more than in equal shares absolutely Provided that if any brother or sister of mine shall have predeceased me leaving issue surviving me such issue shall take and if more than one in equal shares per stirpes the share of my residuary estate which such deceased brother or sister of mine would have taken had he or she survived me and so that no issue shall take whose parent is living at my death and attains a vested interest.[1]

[1] Trusts in favour of children other than the testator's own children, eg. children of brothers and sisters as here, cannot be trusts for bereaved minors or age 18-to-25 trusts. See the notes to paras **[200.107]** and **[200.108]**. Therefore to avoid property held for such children being within the relevant property regime, the substitutional trust for the children of brothers and sisters does not include any age contingency, and if the trust takes effect it will take effect in favour of minor children absolutely.

[232.35]

MAINTENANCE, ACCUMULATION AND ADVANCEMENT

7. [*As in cl 7 of* Form C10.1 *at para* **[232.10]**.]

[232.36]

ADMINISTRATIVE POWERS

8. [*As in cl 8 of* Form C10.1 *at para* **[232.11]**.]

[232.37]

TRUSTEE LIABILITY

9. [*As in cl 9 of* Form C10.1 *at para* **[232.12]**.]

[232.38]

PROFESSIONAL TRUSTEE CHARGING CLAUSE

10. [*As in cl 10 of* Form C10.1 *at para* **[232.13]**.]

[*Testimonium and attestation clause as in* Form C10.1 *at para* **[232.14]**.]

[232.39]

Form C10.4: Will of older childless person settling residue in equal shares on brothers and sisters (or nephews and nieces) for life with remainders for their children

Note. This form is a variant of the preceding form and differs in that the interests of the brothers and sisters (or nephews and nieces) are settled on them for life with power (if desired) to advance the capital of each beneficiary's share to or for the benefit of such beneficiary. The life interest should qualify as IPDIs (see para **[200.98]** above). If any of the brothers and sisters (or nephews and nieces) have children an element of generation skipping might be considered appropriate, in which case Form C10.1 at paras **[232.4]**–**[232.14]** could be used or adapted.

[232.40]

REVOCATION CLAUSE

I [*name*] of [*address*] hereby revoke all former testamentary dispositions made by me and declare this to be my last will.

[232.41]

APPOINTMENT OF EXECUTORS AND TRUSTEES

1. [*As in cl 1 of* Form C10.1 *at para* **[232.4]**.]

[232.42]

GIFT OF PERSONAL CHATTELS

2. [*As in cl 2 of* Form C10.1 *at para* **[232.5]**.]

[232.43]

PECUNIARY LEGACIES

3. [*As in cl 3 of* Form C10.1 *at para* **[232.6]**.]

[232.44]

ADMINISTRATION TRUSTS OF RESIDUE

4. [*As in cl 4 of* Form C10.1 *at para* **[232.7]**.]

[232.45]

GIFTS MADE FREE OF TAX

5. [*As in cl 5 of* Form C10.1 *at para* **[232.8]**.]

[232.46]

BENEFICIAL TRUSTS OF RESIDUE

6. (1) Subject as hereinafter provided my trustees shall hold my residuary estate upon trust for such of my [brothers and sisters]/ [nephews and nieces] [*name*] [*name*] [*name*] [*name*] and [*name*][1] (hereinafter together called 'the beneficiaries') as shall survive me and if more than one in equal shares provided that if any of the beneficiaries shall predecease me leaving issue living at my death such issue shall take absolutely[2] and if more than one in equal shares per stirpes the share of my residuary estate to which such deceased beneficiary would have become entitled had he or she survived me and so that no such issue shall take whose parent is living at my death and attains a vested interest.

(2) The share of my residuary estate to which any of the beneficiaries shall become entitled under the foregoing subclause hereof on surviving me shall not vest in such beneficiary absolutely but shall be retained by my trustees and held on the following trusts:

(a) my trustees shall hold such share upon trust to pay the income thereof to such beneficiary during his or her life [provided that if and so long as such beneficiary is under the age of 18 years my trustees may pay or otherwise apply for or towards the maintenance education or benefit of such beneficiary the whole or such part or parts of the income of such share as my trustees in their absolute discretion think fit and shall retain the balance of such income upon trust for such beneficiary absolutely but my trustees may at any time or times while such beneficiary is living and under the age of 18 years pay or apply such retained income as if it were income arising in the then current year and section 31 of the Trustee Act 1925 shall not apply to the settled share[3]][[and] provided [further] that my trustees (being not fewer than two in number or being a trust corporation) may at any time or times and from time to time during the life of such beneficiary pay transfer or apply the whole or any part or parts of such share to or for the advancement support or benefit of such beneficiary in such manner as they think fit];

(b) subject as aforesaid my trustees shall hold such share upon trust for such one or more of the children and remoter issue of such beneficiary and if more than one in such shares and with such trusts powers and provisions (including trusts and powers conferring on my trustees or any other person or persons a discretion as to the disposition of capital or income or provisions for the accumulation of income during any period permitted by law or administrative powers) as such beneficiary shall by deed or deeds revocable or irrevocable or by will or codicil appoint;

(c) subject as aforesaid my trustees shall hold such share upon trust for such of the children of such beneficiary as shall survive him and if more than one in equal shares provided that no such child who or whose issue shall take any part of such share by virtue of any appointment under the foregoing power shall be entitled to participate in the unappointed part of such share without bringing the part so appointed into hotchpot and accounting for the same accordingly (except to the extent that there is a contrary direction in such appointment);

(d) the foregoing trusts shall carry the intermediate income of such share and section 31 of the Trustee Act 1925 (as hereinafter modified) shall apply thereto;

(e) section 32 of the Trustee Act 1925 (as hereinafter modified) shall apply in relation to such share;

(f) subject as aforesaid such share and the income thereof shall be held in trust for such beneficiary absolutely.

1 It is advisable to name the beneficiaries and give their addresses rather than describe them merely by relationship especially in the case of nephews and nieces or cousins: see the Preliminary Note to C9 at para **[231.9]** and Vol 1, para **[71.5]**.

2 It should be noted that the interests of substituted issue are not settled under cl 6(2).

3 This proviso must be included if any of the beneficiaries may be minors at the time of the testator's death, and if it is intended that their life interests should qualify as IPDIs. This is because unless TA 1925, s 31 (Part G, para **[246.29]**) is excluded, as here, or varied, it will give minor beneficiaries with a life interest only a contingent interest in accumulations made under TA 1925, s 31. The purpose of this substitution for s 31 is to cause the income which is not applied for the beneficiary's benefit during his minority to be held on trust absolutely for the beneficiary, so as to confer an interest in possession for IHT purposes. A minor cannot be paid income to which he is entitled (see Vol 1, para **[9.39]**) but it is thought that he or she has an interest in possession in income if it would form part of his estate if he or she died under the age of 18 (and unmarried and without a civil partner). Such interest in possession will be an IPDI within IHTA 1984, s 49A (see paras **[200.98]** and **[224.24]** ff above).

[232.47]

MAINTENANCE, ACCUMULATION AND ADVANCEMENT

7. [*As in cl 7 of* Form C10.1 *at para* **[232.10]**.]

[232.48]

ADMINISTRATIVE POWERS[1]

8. (1) In this clause where the context so admits:

(a) the expression 'land' includes buildings and estates interests or rights of any kind in or over land; and

(b) during the administration of my estate the expression 'beneficiary' includes any person who would be a beneficiary if such administration had been completed and the expression 'beneficially interested' and references to income of any asset being payable or capable of being paid to or for the benefit of a beneficiary shall be construed accordingly.

(2) None of the powers or provisions contained in subclause (3) below of this clause shall be capable of being exercised or operating in any manner such that if such power or provision were capable of being so exercised or so operating the existence of the same would prevent any person who would (in the absence of such power or provision) have had an interest in possession falling within section 49(1A) of the IHTA 1984 in any property from being entitled to such interest.[2]

(3) In the administration of my estate and the execution of the trusts hereof or of any codicil hereto my trustees shall have the following powers in addition to those conferred by law but subject to the last foregoing subclause—

(a) power to invest moneys sell assets and change investments with the unrestricted freedom of choice and powers of disposition and acquisition of a sole beneficial owner with in particular power to make unsecured loans, acquire non-income yielding assets, and purchase land anywhere in the world or chattels for any purpose including occupation or enjoyment in kind by a beneficiary under the power set out below;[3]

(b) power to delegate all or any of their investment powers to a professional investment manager or managers whether individual or corporate and whether or not also a nominee holder of assets for my trustees (and who may be or include one or more of my trustees or the beneficiaries hereunder) upon such terms as to remuneration and otherwise (including terms authorising self-dealing or providing for the limitation of the liability of the investment manager or managers) as my trustees think fit and section 22 of the Trustee Act 2000 shall not apply;[4]

(c) power to vest or register any property in any person or persons whether individual or corporate and whether or not an investment manager to whom powers have been delegated under the foregoing power (and who may be or include one or more of my trustees or the beneficiaries hereunder) as nominee or nominees for my trustees upon such terms as to remuneration or otherwise (including terms authorising self-dealing or providing for the limitation of the liability of the nominee) as my trustees think fit and section 22 of the Trustee Act 2000 shall not apply;[5]

(d) power to borrow money with or without giving security and on such terms as to interest and repayment and otherwise as my trustees may think fit for any purpose connected with the administration of my estate or the trusts declared herein or in any codicil hereto (including investment) And no lender from whom my trustees borrow money in purported exercise of this power shall be concerned to enquire as to the propriety amount or purpose of any such borrowing;[6]

(e) power to lend money to a beneficiary to whom any of the income of such money is payable or to whom or for whose benefit any income of such money is capable of being paid or applied in exercise of a discretion (or who would be such a beneficiary if such money yielded income) and to do so at a full or concessionary rate of interest or interest free;[7]

(f) all the powers of an absolute owner in relation to any land (wherever situated) held by them;[8]

(g) power to apply capital held on the same trusts as any land (or which would be so held if the administration of my estate had been completed) in the improvement of such land and to apply such capital or the income of such capital on the repair or maintenance of such land;[9]

(h) power to permit any beneficiary to have the beneficial occupation use or enjoyment in kind of any land or chattel or other tangible property on such terms as to repair insurance or payment of outgoings by the beneficiary or otherwise howsoever as my trustees think fit Provided that the foregoing power shall only be exercisable and such permission to occupy or enjoy in kind may only continue in the following circumstances:

   (i) so long as any of the income of such land chattel or other tangible property is payable to such beneficiary or capable of being paid or applied to him or for his benefit in exercise of a discretion (or would be so payable or capable of being so paid or applied if such land chattel or other property yielded income);

   (ii) in the case of land, so long as for the time being the occupation thereof by such beneficiary is compatible with any statutory rights of occupation of any other beneficiary or beneficiaries;[10]

(i) power to exercise all the powers of appropriation (and other incidental powers) conferred by statute on a personal representative without the necessity of obtaining any consents and notwithstanding that one or more of my trustees may be beneficially interested in the exercise of such power.[11]

1 See para **[230.11]**, n 1.
2 This is a general restriction so as to prevent the administrative powers prejudicing the intended IHT status of the IPDI trusts.
3 See para **[230.11]** n 3.
4 See para **[230.11]** n 4.
5 See para **[230.11]** n 5.
6 See para **[230.11]** n 6.
7 See para **[230.11]** n 7.
8 See para **[230.11]** n 8.
9 See para **[230.11]** n 9.
10 See para **[230.11]** n 10.
11 See para **[230.11]** n 11.

[232.49]

TRUSTEE LIABILITY

9. [*As in cl 9 of* Form C10.1 *at para* **[232.12]**.]

[232.50]

EXERCISE OF POWERS

10. [*As in cl 9 of* Form C10.2 *at para* **[232.25]**.]

[232.51]

PROFESSIONAL TRUSTEE CHARGING CLAUSE

11. [*As in cl 10 of* Form C10.1 *at para* **[232.13]**.]
[*Testimonium and attestation clause as in* Form C10.1 *at para* **[232.14]**.]

[232.52]

Form C10.5: Will of unmarried childless person in favour of unmarried sister for life with remainders over to brothers and sisters or their issue

REVOCATION CLAUSE

I [*name*] of [*address*] hereby revoke all former testamentary dispositions made by me and declare this to be my last will.

[232.53]

APPOINTMENT OF EXECUTORS AND TRUSTEES

1. [*As in cl 1 of* Form C10.1 *at para* **[232.4]**.]

[232.54]

GIFT OF PERSONAL CHATTELS

2. I give free of tax[1] all my personal chattels as defined by section 55(1)(x) of the Administration of Estates Act 1925[2] to my sister [*name of unmarried sister*] absolutely.

1 See Form C10.1, cl 2, n 1 at para **[232.5]**.
2 See Part G, para **[246.67]** and Vol 1, para **[64.44]**.

[232.55]

PECUNIARY LEGACIES

3. I give free of tax[1] to each of the children living at my death of my brothers and sisters [*name*] [*name*] and [*name*][2] a pecuniary legacy of £——.

1 See Form C10.1, cl 3, n 1 at para **[232.6]**.
2 The names here are intended of course to be those of the brothers and sisters, not those of their children. Illegitimate children are not excluded.

[232.56]

ADMINISTRATION TRUSTS OF RESIDUE

4. [*As in cl 4 of* Form C10.1 *at para* **[232.7]**.]

[232.57]

GIFTS MADE FREE OF TAX

5. [*As in cl 5 of* Form C10.1 *at para* **[232.8]**.]

[232.58]

BENEFICIAL TRUSTS OF RESIDUE

6. (1) My trustees shall hold my residuary estate upon trust to pay the income thereof to my said sister [*name of unmarried sister*] during her life[1] [provided that my trustees (being not fewer than two in number or being a trust corporation) may at any time or times and from time to time during the life of my said sister pay transfer or apply the capital of the whole or any part or parts of my residuary estate to or for the support or benefit of my said sister in such manner as they think fit].[2]

(2) Subject as aforesaid my trustees shall hold my residuary estate and the income thereof upon trust in equal shares for such of my brothers and sisters [*name*] [*name*] and [*name*][3] as shall be living at the later to occur of my death and the death of my said sister [*name of unmarried sister given the life interest under subclause* (*1*)] ('the vesting date') and the issue living at the vesting date of such of my said brothers and sisters as shall be dead at the vesting date such issue to take if more than one in equal shares per stirpes the share which such deceased brother or sister of mine would have taken had he or she lived to attain a vested interest and so that no issue shall take whose parent lives to attain a vested interest.[4]

(3) The foregoing trusts shall carry the intermediate income of such share and section 31 of the Trustee Act 1925 (as hereinafter modified) shall apply thereto.

(4) Section 32 of the Trustee Act 1925 (as hereinafter modified) shall apply in relation to the foregoing trusts.

1 This life interest will be an IPDI within IHTA 1984, s 49A (see para **[200.98]**).
2 For a power of this type which is limited to being exercisable only over part of the capital see Form C5.1, cl 9(2) at para **[227.13]**.
3 The names here will not include the unmarried sister who gets a life interest under the preceding subclause.
4 It is assumed that the unmarried sister who is given a life interest has no children. If she did have any children this clause would need modifying to enable them to be capable of benefiting under it. Trusts in favour of children other than the testator's own children cannot be trusts for bereaved minors or age 18-to-25 trusts. See the notes to paras **[200.107]** and **[200.108]**. Therefore to avoid property held for such children being within the IHT relevant property regime, the substitutional trust for issue does not include any age contingency, and if the trust takes effect it will take effect in favour of minor children absolutely.

[232.59]

MAINTENANCE, ACCUMULATION AND ADVANCEMENT

7. [*As in cl 7 of* Form C10.1 *at para* **[232.10]**.]

[232.60]

ADMINISTRATIVE POWERS

8. [*As in cl 8 of* Form C10.4 *at para* **[232.48]**.]

[232.61]

TRUSTEE LIABILITY

9. [*As in cl 9 of* Form C10.1 *at para* **[232.12]**.]

[232.62]

EXERCISE OF POWERS

10. [*As in cl 9 of* Form C10.2 *at para* **[232.25]**.]

[232.63]

PROFESSIONAL TRUSTEE CHARGING CLAUSE

11. [*As in cl 10 of* Form C10.1 *at para* **[232.13]**.]

[*Testimonium and attestation clause as in* Form C10.1 *at para* **[232.14]**.]

[232.64]

Form C10.6: Will of childless individual giving charitable and other legacies, with a specific gift of a house and residue given on trust for nephews and nieces for life with remainders for their children

REVOCATION CLAUSE

I [*name*] of [*address*] hereby revoke all former testamentary dispositions made by me and declare this to be my last will.

[232.65]

APPOINTMENT OF EXECUTORS AND TRUSTEES

1. [*As in cl 1 of* Form C10.1 *at para* **[232.4]**.]

[232.66]

GIFT OF PERSONAL CHATTELS TO BROTHER OR SISTER

2. [*As in cl 3 of* Form C10.1 *at para* **[232.6]**.]

[232.67]

PECUNIARY LEGACIES

3. I give the following pecuniary legacies free of tax:[1]
   (a) to each of my trustees [except [*name of professional trustee*]] who shall prove my will and act in the trusts thereof the sum of £——;[2]
   (b) to my brother [*name*] the sum of £—— and I direct that the same shall be paid to him as soon as possible after my death[3] and in priority to all other legacies hereby given;
   (c) to each of the children of my brother [*name*] who shall be living at the date of my death the sum of £—— with interest thereon from the date of my death at the rate of [6] per cent per annum;[4]
   (d) to my god-daughter [*name*] the sum of £—— and I declare that the receipt of the said [*name*] if of the age of 16 years or more shall be a full and sufficient discharge to my trustees for the same;[5]
   (e) to my chauffeur and handyman [*name*] if in service at my death[6] the sum of £—— in addition to any sums then owing to him for wages or otherwise [and if he shall then have left my service I give to him the sum of £——];
   (f) to my friend [*name*] the sum of £—— and without imposing any

trust or obligation upon him I desire that he may employ the same in the furtherance of the research project on which we have worked together for so many years;

(g) to the Management Committee of —— Hospital the sum of £—— to be applied in the provision of additional comforts for the inpatients of the said Hospital the receipt of the treasurer for the time being of the said hospital to be a sufficient discharge for such sum;[7]

(h) to the Vicar for the time being of the Parish of —— the sum of £—— to be applied by him in such manner as he may think best for the relief of the poor of the said Parish the receipt of the Vicar to be a sufficient discharge to my trustees for the said sum and so that my trustees are not to be bound to see to the application thereof;[8]

(i) to the Governing Body of —— School the sum of £—— for the purpose of [building] [enlarging] [equipping] [providing] [five courts] [a swimming bath] [a gymnasium] [playing fields] with power for the said governors to purchase thereout land for the purpose aforesaid and the receipt of the Chairman of the said Governing Body or other proper officer thereof for the said sum shall be a sufficient discharge to my trustees and so that my trustees shall not be bound to see to the application thereof.

1 See Form C10.1, cl 3, n 1 at para **[232.6]**.

2 As to this clause, see *Re Sharman's Will Trusts, Public Trustee v Sharman* [1942] Ch 311, [1942] 2 All ER 74, and *Re Parry, Dalton v Cooke* [1969] 2 All ER 512, [1969] 1 WLR 614, and see also Vol 1, paras **[30.14]–[30.18]** and B10 at paras **[210.51]–[210.53]**. This paragraph will provide legacies only for the executors who prove the will. A testator may wish to exclude a professional trustee from this clause if cl 14 is included.

3 The foregoing words providing for early payment would give the legacy no priority over other legacies without the words which follow (*Re Schweder's Estate, Oppenheim v Schweder* [1891] 3 Ch 44) and it would otherwise be liable to abate with other legacies. If executors have any doubt about the assets being sufficient, they must either withhold payment or obtain some security for repayment of any amount overpaid.

4 A contingent legacy does not ordinarily carry interest and in the absence of a specific direction will only carry interest from the end of the executor's year. See Vol 1, para **[32.1]** ff.

5 *Re Denekin, Peters v Tanchereau* (1895) 72 LT 220 shows that it is not sufficient to direct payment to a minor, and that the clause must go on to provide that the receipt of the minor shall be a sufficient discharge to the executors or trustees. Despite the specific provision for payment to the legatee while under 18 a trustee still has a discretion to withhold payment until the age of eighteen is attained: *Re Somech, Westminster Bank Ltd v Phillips* [1957] Ch 165, [1956] 3 All ER 523 (where the trustee surrendered his discretion to the court and an order for immediate payment was made). However, it seems that, while the legatee is a minor, a parent or guardian of the legatee with parental responsibility could insist on being paid the legacy: ChA 1989, s 3(3) (Part G, para **[244.114]**); see also Vol 1, para **[9.42]**.

6 As to the importance of these words, see *Re Sharland, Kemp v Rozey* [1896] 1 Ch 517. Testators should be reminded of the law relating to redundancy payments (now embodied in Pt VI of the Employment Protection (Consolidation) Act 1978). For a form which adjusts the servant's legacy by reference to the amount of any redundancy payment to which he may be entitled see Form B10.46 at para **[210.63]**.

7 Since the introduction of the National Health Service, gifts to the Hospital itself have in general been discontinued, but there are a number of ways in which a charitable testator can help patients, nurses and medical research. See Form B12.23 at para **[212.25]**.

8 This gift is obviously charitable. As to what gifts for parish work and such like are charitable, see Vol 1, para **[102.16]**.

[232.68]

PROVISION AGAINST LAPSE OF CHARITABLE GIFTS

4. If any institution society or body of persons (incorporated or unincorporated) or holder of an office which or who is intended to be the legatee under any legacy given by me herein or in any codicil hereto shall be found never to have existed or to have ceased to exist or to have been amalgamated with another institution society body of persons or office or changed its name or constitution before my death then such legacy shall be paid transferred or applied to such charitable institutions societies or bodies of persons established in the United Kingdom or for such charitable purposes in the said United Kingdom and if more than one in such shares as my trustees in their absolute discretion think fit and I express the wish without imposing any trust or obligation that in carrying out the foregoing trust my trustees should seek to benefit a charity or charities with objects as close as possible with those of the institution society body of persons or office-holder intended to receive the original legacy.

[232.69]

GIFT OF HOUSE AND CONTENTS

5. I give [free of tax][1] my property situate at [*address*] and my furniture and effects of household use or ornament therein or belonging thereto (save and except such of the same as may be otherwise specifically disposed of by this will or any codicil hereto) to my brother [*name*] absolutely.[2]

1 IHT on land in the UK which is specifically given is now a testamentary expense payable out of residue: IHTA 1984, s 211 (Part G, para **[246.100]**); see also B14 at para **[214.55]** ff. But if the 'free of tax' formula is being used elsewhere, it may be prudent to employ it here also, to avoid any suggestion that its absence here means that this gift was intended to be subject to IHT.

2 This gift will be subject to any sums charged on the property: AEA 1925, s 35 (Part G, para **[246.62]**).

[232.70]

ADMINISTRATION TRUSTS OF RESIDUE

6. [*As in cl 4 of* Form C10.1 *at para* **[232.7]**.]

[232.71]

GIFTS MADE FREE OF TAX

7. [*As in cl 5 of* Form C10.1 *at para* **[232.8]**.]

[232.72]

BENEFICIAL TRUSTS OF RESIDUE

8. (1) My trustees shall hold my residuary estate upon trust for such of my nephews and nieces (being children of my brothers [*name*] [*name*] and [*name*]) as shall be living at my death and if more than one in equal shares Provided that if any of my said nephews and nieces is now dead or shall predecease me leaving a child or children living at my death such child or

children shall take absolutely if more than one equally between them the share of my residuary estate which such deceased nephew or niece of mine would have become interested in had he or she lived to attain a vested interest.

(2) The foregoing trusts shall carry the intermediate income of my residuary estate and section 31 of the Trustee Act 1925 (as hereinafter modified) shall apply thereto.

(3) Section 32 of the Trustee Act 1925 (as hereinafter modified) shall apply in relation to the said trusts and shall apply in relation to the presumptive share of any such nephew or niece of mine notwithstanding the direction for retention and settlement hereinafter contained.

[232.73]

SETTLEMENT OF SHARES

9. The share of my residuary estate to which any nephew or niece of mine shall become entitled under the last foregoing clause hereof shall not vest in such nephew or niece absolutely but shall be retained by my trustees and held upon the trusts following namely (such nephew or niece hereinafter being referred to as 'the beneficiary'):

(a) my trustees shall hold such share upon trust to pay the income thereof to the beneficiary during his or her life [provided that if and so long as the beneficiary is under the age of 18 years my trustees may pay or otherwise apply for or towards the maintenance education or benefit of the beneficiary the whole or such part or parts of the income of such share as my trustees in their absolute discretion think fit and shall retain the balance of such income upon trust for the beneficiary absolutely but my trustees may at any time or times while the beneficiary is living and under the age of 18 years pay or apply such retained income as if it were income arising in the then current year and section 31 of the Trustee Act 1925 shall not apply to the settled share][1];

(b) provided that my trustees shall have power in their absolute discretion from time to time during the beneficiary's life and before the vesting day to pay transfer or apply the whole or any part or parts of such share to him or for his benefit in such manner as they shall in their absolute discretion think fit;

(c) subject as aforesaid the beneficiary shall have power at any time before the vesting day by deed or deeds revocable or irrevocable or by will or codicil to appoint to any spouse [or civil partner] who may survive him or her as his or her widow or widower [or surviving civil partner] in the event of his or her death before the vesting day (including power to appoint to a named spouse [or civil partner] contingently on such named spouse [or civil partner] surviving him or her as his or her widow or widower [or surviving civil partner] in such event) an interest in the income of the whole or any part or parts of such share for the residue of such spouse's [or civil partner's] life or for any less period;[2]

(d) subject as aforesaid if the beneficiary shall die before the vesting day my trustees shall hold such share upon trust as to both capital and income for all or such one or more exclusively of the others or other of the children and remoter issue of the beneficiary at such time or times and if more than one in such shares and with such trusts powers and provisions (including trusts and powers conferring on any person or persons a discretion as to the disposition of capital or income or provisions for the accumulation of income during any period permitted by law or administrative powers of whatever description) as the beneficiary shall before the vesting day by deed or deeds revocable or irrevocable or by will or codicil appoint;

(e) subject as aforesaid my trustees shall hold such share upon trust as to both capital and income for all or any the children or child of the beneficiary born before the vesting day and if more than one in equal shares [provided that no child of the beneficiary who or whose issue shall take any part of such share by virtue of any appointment under the foregoing power shall be entitled to participate in the unappointed part of such share without bringing the part so appointed into hotchpot and accounting for the same accordingly (except to the extent that there is a contrary direction in such appointment)];

(f) the trust declared by paragraph (e) above shall carry the intermediate income of such share and section 31 of the Trustee Act 1925 (as hereinafter modified) shall apply thereto;

(g) section 32 of the Trustee Act 1925 (as hereinafter modified) shall apply in relation to such share;

(h) subject as aforesaid if the beneficiary shall die before the vesting day my trustees shall hold such share upon trust as to both capital and income for such persons or purposes as the beneficiary shall by will or codicil appoint and subject to any such appointment;

(i) subject as aforesaid my trustees shall hold such share upon trust for the next of kin of the beneficiary living at his or her death or the earlier occurrence of the vesting day ascertained as if the beneficiary had died intestate without having married;

(j) in this clause 'the vesting day' means the day on which shall expire 21 years less three days after the death of the last survivor of such of my said nephews and nieces as shall be living at my death.

1 This proviso must be included if any of the beneficiaries may be minors at the time of the testator's death, and if it is intended that their life interests should qualify as IPDIs. This is because unless TA 1925, s 31 (Part G, para **[246.29]**) is excluded, as here, or varied, it will give minor beneficiaries with a life interest only a contingent interest in accumulations made under TA 1925, s 31. The purpose of this substitution for s 31 is to cause the income which is not applied for the beneficiary's benefit during his minority to be held on trust absolutely for the beneficiary, so as to confer an interest in possession for IHT purposes. A minor cannot be paid income to which he is entitled (see Vol 1, para **[9.39]**) but it is thought that he or she has an interest in possession in income if it would form part of his estate if he or she died under the age of 18 (and unmarried and without a civil partner). Such interest in possession will be an IPDI within IHTA 1984, s 49A (see paras **[200.98]** and **[224.24]** ff above).

2 A life interest for a spouse or civil partner appointed in exercise of this power will not (after 21 March 2006) enable IHT exemption for gifts to a spouse or civil partner to be claimed in relation to the share, but it may still be desired that a beneficiary should have the ability to make this provision for a spouse or civil partner.

[232.74]

MAINTENANCE, ACCUMULATION AND ADVANCEMENT

10. [*As in cl 7 of* Form C10.1 *at para* **[232.10]**.]

[232.75]

ADMINISTRATIVE POWERS

11. [*As in cl 8 of* Form C10.4 *at para* **[232.48]**.]

[232.76]

TRUSTEE LIABILITY

12. [*As in cl 9 of* Form C10.1 *at para* **[232.12]**.]

[232.77]

EXERCISE OF POWERS

13. [*As in cl 9 of* Form C10.2 *at para* **[232.25]**.]

[232.78]

PROFESSIONAL TRUSTEE CHARGING CLAUSE

14. [*As in cl 10 of* Form C10.1 *at para* **[232.13]**.]

[232.79]

[*Testimonium and attestation clause as in* Form C10.1 *at para* **[232.14]**.]

C11 Wills disposing of business property

Preliminary note .... **[233.1]**

ALLOCATION OF BUSINESS AND AGRICULTURAL RELIEF BETWEEN THE EXEMPT AND NON-EXEMPT PARTS OF AN ESTATE .... **[233.2]**

NON-EXEMPT GIFTS ON THE DEATH OF THE FIRST TO DIE (OF SPOUSES OR CIVIL PARTNERS) AND BUSINESS OR AGRICULTURAL PROPERTY .... **[233.8]**

OTHER FACTORS RELEVANT TO WILLS OF SPOUSES OR CIVIL PARTNERS .... **[233.11]**

WHERE ONLY ONE OR SOME OF THE TESTATOR'S CHILDREN WILL CARRY ON A BUSINESS .... **[233.13]**

FORMS

C11.1 Will settling private company shares entitled to business relief and optional 'top up' legacy on a nil-rate band discretionary trust, with residue given to wife with alternative gift to issue .... **[233.13]**

C11.2 Reciprocal wills for husband and wife who have recently acquired share capital of private trading company, the first to die making a direct gift of the shares to the children and otherwise leaving estate to the survivor .... **[233.26]**

C11.3 Will giving business carried on as sole trader or in partnership to sons, and legacies to daughters, with residue to wife for life with remainder to children with substitution clause and hotchpot of specific gifts .... **[233.36]**

PRELIMINARY NOTE

[233.1]

Notes on business property, IHT business relief, payment of IHT on business property by instalments, and the implications of these for testamentary dispositions, are to be found in the Preliminary Note to B5 at paras **[205.1]–[205.57]**, and clauses disposing of business property and ancillary provisions are to be found in B5 at paras **[205.58]–[205.79]**. For testamentary options see B9 at para **[209.1]** ff; for trustees' powers in relation to business property see B5 at paras **[205.70]–[205.79]**, B20 at paras **[220.66]–[220.68]** and B21 at para **[221.1]** ff; for agricultural property, including notes on IHT agricultural relief, see C12 at para **[234.1]** ff. For wills in favour of spouses and children see the Preliminary Notes to C2 and C3 at paras **[224.1]–[224.26]** and **[225.1]–[225.8]**.

This Preliminary Note is concerned with the IHT implications of the pattern of disposition in a will as a whole in cases where the testator has business property or agricultural property, and with certain other practical problems which can arise in wills where the testator has property of either kind (agricultural property is included because many of the points relating to business property are equally relevant to it).

Allocation of business and agricultural relief between the exempt and non-exempt parts of an estate

[233.2]
Where the testator has made exempt gifts by will to, eg his spouse or civil partner, or charity, and the remainder of the estate is not exempt, and the testator owns assets which qualify for business or agricultural relief, the amount of advantage gained from the relief depends on the form taken by his testamentary dispositions.

Business relief and agricultural relief operate to reduce the value transferred by a transfer of value, ie in the case of an estate on death, the value of the estate before any exempt parts are deducted to determine the extent of the chargeable transfer. Where an estate is partially exempt the transfer of value then has to be allocated between exempt and non-exempt gifts under the sometimes rather difficult rules in the Inheritance Tax Act 1984 (IHTA 1984), Part II, Ch III (ss 36–42: see Part A, paras **[200.112]–[200.118]** and *Foster's Inheritance Tax*, D2.31–43). As part of these rules, IHTA 1984, s 39A determines the allocation of any business or agricultural relief between exempt and non-exempt gifts for the purposes of determining the extent of the chargeable part of the transfer of value. Section 39A has at first sight an appearance of complexity (for a detailed account see *Foster's Inheritance Tax*, D2.40), but its effect can be summarised fairly simply in two propositions.

[233.3]
Summary of the effect of the Inheritance Tax Act 1984, s 39A.

(1) Any 'specific gifts of relevant business property or agricultural property' are treated as reduced by any business or agricultural relief relating to that property: IHTA 1984, s 39A(2). This is so whether the specific gift of the business or agricultural property is exempt or non-exempt; if it is non-exempt, all the business or agricultural relief relating to the property given by it will go to reduce the chargeable part of the estate, and if it is exempt the relief will reduce the exempt part of the estate and so will confer no tax saving.
(2) If available business or agricultural relief does not go to reduce the value of a specific gift of business or agricultural property as described under (1) above (in most cases this is where the business or agricultural property falls into the residuary estate), it is apportioned rateably between the exempt and non-exempt gifts, other than any specific gifts which have been reduced as described under (1) above: IHTA 1984, s 39A (3), (4).

Thus, when an estate is partially exempt, any available business or agricultural relief is likely to be most fully utilised by making non-exempt specific gifts of the business or agricultural property, and to be least or not at all utilised by making exempt specific gifts of it. In between lie cases where such property falls into residue. Where it is desirable or necessary for the surviving spouse or civil partner to have the benefit of property on which there will be business or agricultural relief, a discretionary trust could be considered, as in Form C11.1 at para **[233.13]** ff. Other possible ways of utilising the relief while arranging for the surviving spouse or civil partner to benefit from or obtain the business or agricultural property are considered at para **[233.7]**.

[233.4]

Gifts charged on business or agricultural property. A gift, typically a pecuniary legacy, which is payable out of business or agricultural property will not be treated as a specific gift of business or agricultural property, and will have allocated to it only a rateable part of any relief not attributed to specific gifts of business or agricultural property where the estate is partially exempt: IHTA 1984, s 39A(6). Charging pecuniary or general legacies on business or agricultural property which is the subject-matter of a non-exempt specific gift will therefore have the effect of reducing the benefit of the business or agricultural relief, and should be avoided so far as possible in a will where there are substantial exempt gifts.

[233.5]

Business or agricultural relief and specific gifts of other sorts of property. IHTA 1984, s 39A contains no provision treating a specific gift of property which is not business or agricultural property as having a value unreduced by business or agricultural relief. Accordingly, if there is any business or agricultural relief on property comprised in residue, for the purposes of the partial exemption rules an apportioned part of the relief will go to reduce the value of a specific gift of property (exempt or non-exempt) which does not itself attract either relief. This may cause uncertainty as to the tax payable by the donee where a subject to tax gift is made of such property in such circumstances: Form B14.36 at para **[214.79]** and Form C11.3, cl 4 at para **[233.42]** are examples of clauses which deal with this point.

[233.6]

What is a specific gift for the purposes of the Inheritance Tax Act 1984, s 39A. As stated above, a testator's estate will get maximum benefit from business relief or agricultural relief if there is a specific gift to a non-exempt beneficiary *of* 'relevant business property' (ie property qualifying for business relief) or *of* 'agricultural property' (see para **[234.2]** for the meaning of this expression). 'Specific gift' is defined in IHTA 1984, s 42(1) (which applies to s 39A, among other sections of the Act) to mean any gift other than a gift of residue or a share of residue, but this does not determine what is a specific gift *of* a particular kind of property. The only other provision with any relevance to its meaning is s 39A(6) mentioned at para **[233.4]**—gifts payable out of business or agricultural property are not for the purposes of s 39A specific gifts of that property.

It is our view that a specific gift will only qualify as a specific gift of relevant business property or agricultural property for the purposes of IHTA 1984, s 39A(2) if the property comprised in the gift and going to the beneficiary, considered in isolation from the rest of the estate, is relevant business property or agricultural property. If this is correct, the following points should be noted—

(1) When a business is carried on by the testator as sole proprietor and the business as a whole qualifies for business relief on his death as 'a

business' (see B5 at para **[205.22]**), a specific gift of an individual asset of that business by itself will on this view not be a specific gift of relevant business property (see B5 at para **[205.23]** for the distinction between a business and individual business assets). Whether business relief is available in respect of a business on a testator's death depends on the circumstances immediately before his death, not on the dispositions made by his will, and so it is thought that the business relief attributable to this individual asset comprised in a specific gift will not be lost completely in a case such as this, but will be divided rateably between the exempt and non-exempt parts of the estate instead of being concentrated on the specific gift.

(2) A similar point would arise in relation to a specific gift of a farm building or farm house, where the farm land itself was the subject of another gift. As stated in the Preliminary Note to C12 at paras **[234.2]** and **[234.3]**, buildings and farmhouses only qualify as agricultural property if they are combined with agricultural land and are of a character appropriate to it: IHTA 1984, s 115(2). Again, it is thought that a farm house or building given by a specific gift which did not also include the farm land would still qualify for agricultural relief on the testator's death, but that the relief attributable to the farmhouse would be apportioned rateably between the non-exempt and exempt parts of the estate because the house by itself is not 'agricultural property' for the purposes of IHTA 1984, s 39A(2).

(3) In the rare cases of controlling holdings of unquoted voting securities qualifying for 100 per cent business relief or controlling holdings of quoted shares or securities qualifying for 50 per cent business relief (IHTA 1984, ss 104(1) and 105(1)(b) and (cc)), the type of problem described above does not seem to arise where, for example, a testator makes a specific gift of part only of his holding. Shares or securities in either category qualify for the relief even if they do not by themselves give control, provided that they contribute to the testator's control of the company together with other shares or securities owned by him: see IHTA 1984, s 105(1)(b) and (cc).

(4) There is also a question as to whether a gift of relevant business property or agricultural property to one person, subject to a testamentary option for another to purchase it, is a specific gift of that property for the purposes of IHTA 1984, s 39A. It might be argued that it is not a gift of such property to the person to whom the primary gift is made, because he may end up with cash instead of the property, and that the option holder is not the recipient of a *gift* of such property (or not wholly—it depends on the price) and anyway might not exercise the option and receive the business (or agricultural) property. Such an arrangement is at its most provocative to HMRC where the property entitled to relief is given to a non-exempt beneficiary subject to an option given to the testator's spouse or civil partner to purchase it. However, whether or not it is an exempt beneficiary who is given the option is not strictly relevant to the legal merits of the argument. The attitude of HMRC to this point is not known, and in the absence of a clear indication that HMRC accept such arrangements as specific gifts

of the business or agricultural property within IHTA 1984, s 39A(2) they are better avoided if possible; see para **[233.7]** for alternatives.

[233.7]

Where the testator's spouse or civil partner is intended to benefit from or inherit the business (or agricultural) property. Where the testator wants his spouse or civil partner to be able to benefit from business or agricultural property after his death, but not necessarily to own it, a discretionary trust of the property such as in Form C11.1 at para **[233.13]** ff would be a way of taking advantage of the business or agricultural relief on the property on his death and keeping the property out of the taxable estate of the spouse or civil partner, while enabling the spouse or civil partner to benefit from the income. This is not an approach to adopt where the property is, e g agricultural land which it is intended that the trustees will permit the spouse or civil partner to occupy or use in carrying on the spouse's or civil partner's own business within two years of the testator's death, because that might have the effect of conferring an IPDI on the spouse or civil partner and thus including the property in the spouse's or civil partner's taxable estate (see *Foster's Inheritance Tax*, E1.47 and Part A, paras **[200.95]**, **[200.133]**).

Where it is necessary or desirable for the testator's spouse or civil partner to have after the testator's death an absolute interest or an interest in possession in business or agricultural property of the testator (being property entitled to business or agricultural relief), there may still be ways in which advantage could be taken of that relief in the event of the spouse or civil partner surviving the testator. For example, the property could be the subject-matter of a specific gift to the testator's son, with the idea that the son would sell it to, or exchange it for other assets with, the spouse or civil partner after the testator's death. However, a sale or exchange is likely to involve a stamp duty land tax and/or capital gains tax liability. Where there is doubt whether the potential non-exempt beneficiary will sell or exchange the property back to the spouse or civil partner, a testamentary option is not recommended, for the reasons given at para **[233.6]**, sub-para (4), but there are other possibilities.

One possibility is to create an interest in possession trust for the *non-exempt* beneficiary of the business or agricultural property, or a discretionary trust of it, so structured that the trustees can sell the business or agricultural assets back to the spouse or civil partner. See Form C11.1 at para **[233.13]** ff. Such arrangements have the disadvantage that the spouse or civil partner will not be able to have the testator's period of ownership taken into account for the purpose of business relief on his or her death under IHTA 1984, ss 108(b) or 109 (see B5 at para **[205.11]**), and any right to pay any IHT on the property by instalments will cease on its sale to the surviving spouse or civil partner (but the rate of relief may be 100 per cent with the result that there is no IHT). Again, there will or may be stamp duty land tax or capital gains tax payable.

A further possibility is the grant to the spouse or civil partner by inter vivos agreement of an option to purchase the business or agricultural property, combined with a non-exempt specific gift by will of that property. The existence at the testator's death of an (unexercised) option to purchase a property does not by itself affect the availability of business or agricultural relief in relation to that property: see B5 at para **[205.28]**. Consideration would need to be given to the tax consequences of the creation of the option, however. It should also be remembered that where the option is created after the date of the will its exercise after the testator's death could cause the gift to be adeemed under the rule in *Lawes v Bennett* (1785) 1 Cox Eq Cas 167: see Vol 1, para **[41.20]** and the second alternative cl 2(2) of Form C11.3 at para **[233.40]** for a form of words excluding ademption in these circumstances. Again there could be stamp duty land tax or capital gains tax to pay.

An arrangement which might avoid any stamp duty land tax or capital gains tax being payable on the exchange of assets is a single settlement created by will which contains all or most of the testator's assets, under which the business or agricultural property is subject to a relevant property trust or an IPDI trust for non-exempt beneficiaries, and his spouse or civil partner has an IPDI in the unrelieved property. This would be with a view to a cross-appropriation of assets between the two funds, so that the spouse or civil partner is interested in the business or agricultural property at death. The difficult part is achieving a single settlement with these characteristics, and a discretionary trust of the entire estate to be followed by the appointment of an IPDI to the spouse or civil partner would probably be the easiest way to do it.

Non-exempt gifts on the death of the first to die (of spouses or civil partners) and business or agricultural property

[233.8]

Nil-rate band gifts. These are gifts intended to use up some or all of the testator's nil-rate band on a non-exempt gift, in a will which is otherwise in favour of the testator's spouse or civil partner. Such gifts, of a value determined by a formula to the effect that it is the maximum which can be the subject of a non-exempt gift without any IHT being payable, and made into a discretionary trust from which the surviving spouse might benefit had, until the Pre-Budget Report of 9 October 2007, become a standard part of tax planning in wills for spouses or civil partners. This was so as to avoid wastage of the first to die's nil rate band. For discussion of nil-rate band discretionary trusts see the Note in B18 at para **[218.16]** ff. Examples of nil-rate band gifts without a business element are to be found in, eg Forms B10.51 at para **[210.72]**, B18.2 at para **[218.34]**, C3.1 at paras **[225.9]**–**[225.22]** and C3.4 at paras **[225.57]**–**[225.67]**. The announcement of nil-rate band carry-forward in the Pre-Budget Report of 9 October 2007 means that for the majority of testators nil-rate band discretionary trusts are no longer necessary or advisable. There remain some situations where they continue to be worth using: see para **[200.130]**. Where the circumstances are such that a nil-rate band discretionary trust on the death of the first to die is desirable, and there is business or agricultural property entitled to IHT business or agricultural relief, there are some additional factors to take into account. Also, even if there are no such circumstances, where a testator owns business or agricultural property, there are good reasons for making, in the event of the testator dying survived by his spouse or civil partner, a non-exempt gift of that business or agricultural property.

[233.9]

100 per cent relief property and 'formula' nil-rate band gifts. Where the testator has a significant amount of property entitled to 100 per cent business or agricultural relief, and it is decided for one or more of the reasons discussed in para **[200.130]** to include in his will a nil-rate band legacy given to non-exempt beneficiaries (or a discretionary trust) by reference to a formula such as 'the maximum sum I can give without any IHT being payable on my death', such a gift could operate to pass too much to the non-exempt beneficiaries. If after deduction of the relief the total transfer of value on death was less than the amount of the nil-rate band at death, the whole estate might pass under the nil-rate band gift leaving the surviving spouse or civil partner with nothing except a claim under the Inheritance (Provision for Family and Dependants) Act 1975 (see Vol 1, para **[105.9]**).

Consider this example: T dies in the tax year 2007–08 leaving business property, to which 100 per cent relief applies, and of which the market value is £500,000, and other assets worth £300,000. He had made no lifetime chargeable transfers. His will gives a legacy to the children of the maximum sum he can give without any IHT being payable on his death, with residue going to his spouse. The transfer of value on his death after business relief is £300,000. However, the legacy determined by the formula is £800,000, not £300,000. He can give a legacy of this amount without IHT being payable because if his will gave a legacy of £800,000 it would be treated as abated to £300,000 for the purposes of IHT on his death by virtue of IHTA 1984, s 37(2).

Where there is a risk of something like this happening, it may be advisable to set an upper limit of actual value on the amount to pass under the nil-rate band gift, as in Form C11.1, cl 2(1)(b) at para **[233.17]**. Where the nil-rate band legacy is to be held on a discretionary trust under which the spouse or civil partner will be a beneficiary, the consequences of the legacy being of the entire estate will not be as serious for the surviving spouse or civil partner as they would be if the legacy was given absolutely to, eg the children, but the testator may still want some of the estate to vest in his spouse or civil partner absolutely, in which case a limit on the size of the legacy will still be appropriate.

Where a testator has business or agricultural property, and intends to leave his residuary estate to his spouse or civil partner, it will be an excellent arrangement from a tax planning point of view to make a non-exempt specific gift of some or all of that property (see paras **[233.3]** and **[233.11]** for the advantages of such gifts), irrespective of whether it is also desired to provide a non-exempt top up legacy (defined by a formula) so as to use, or use the rest of, the nil-rate band (see Form C11.1, cl 2 at para **[233.17]**). The specific gift may have no taxable value because it gets 100 per cent relief (in which case any top up legacy will be the full amount of the available nil-rate band), or it may use up some or all of the nil-rate band because, for example it gets only 50 per cent relief or it is not wholly entitled to relief (see further B5 at para **[205.51]**). A consequence of a combination of specific gift and formula legacy, if the specific gift turns out to use up some of the nil-rate band, is that in order to determine the amount of the legacy it will be necessary to determine the value of the business or agricultural property comprised in the specific gift. This makes administrative difficulties for the executors where the specific gift is of assets which are very difficult to value, such as private company shares, particularly as it can take a long time for HMRC to express an opinion on the value of such property.

[233.10]

Non-exempt specific gifts of business or agricultural property. As described at para **[233.3]**, where there is an exempt gift of residue, the maximum use is made of business or agricultural relief by making a specific gift or gifts of the property qualifying for the relief(s) to non-exempt beneficiaries (which may be combined with a top up 'formula' pecuniary legacy, as in Form C11.1, cl 2 at para **[233.17]**, where one or more of the reasons discussed in para **[200.130]** for doing so apply. Where a non-exempt specific gift of business or agricultural property is made in this way, there may be a possibility that the taxable value of the specifically given property will exceed the available amount of nil-rate band, eg because the nil-rate available on death comes to be diminished by lifetime gifts, or because the business or agricultural property does not turn out to be entitled to as much relief or at as high a rate as expected. Possible ways of dealing with this or minimising its consequences are:

(1) Making the specific gift subject to IHT. This reduces considerably the adverse effect of the taxable value of the property turning out to exceed the nil-rate band, because it prevents grossing up of the non-exempt specific gift(s): see B5 at para **[205.52]** ff, and eg Form B5.1 at para **[205.58]**, Form C11.1, cl 2 at para **[233.17]** and Form C11.3, cl 2 at para **[233.40]**.
(2) Trying to limit the gift to such part of the business or agricultural assets as qualifies for business relief. It is questionable whether it is always possible to do this, and whether it is possible depends on the type of asset and the nature of the exclusionary provision involved. For example, where some of the testator's shares in a particular company have been owned for two years and some not, it should be possible to make a gift of only the shares which have been owned for two years (see Form B5.9 at para **[205.66]** and Form C11.2, cl 2 at para **[233.29]**). Where an asset is an 'excepted asset' (see B5 at para **[205.9]** for the meaning of this term) it should be possible to exclude it from a gift of a sole trader's business (see Form B5.4 at para **[205.61]**) or possibly from a gift of a partnership share in a business. On the other hand, if the assets owned by the testator are company shares, and the company owns 'excepted assets', it is difficult to see how the gift could be of that part of the company shares which is not attributable to the excepted assets, as the shares do not constitute a proprietary interest in particular assets of the company.
(3) Imposing an upper limit in monetary terms on the value of the specific gift, either by reference to its taxable value (ie as reduced by business or agricultural relief) or its actual value. A problem about this is that it makes difficulties for the executors, because they have to decide on the value to attribute to assets which may be very difficult to value, such as private company shares, and it can take a long time for HMRC to express an opinion on the value of the property in question.

(4) Making the specific gift of business or agricultural property subject to a discretionary trust under which the spouse or civil partner of the testator is a beneficiary. In principle it should be possible to avoid an IHT charge by making an appointment in favour of the spouse or civil partner of sufficient of the property to avoid an IHT charge, within two years of the testator's death in reliance on IHTA 1984, s 144 (see para **[225.83]** ff), if the combination of the value of the gift and the amount of relief available would otherwise cause IHT to be payable. This has the same problem as solution (3) above, namely that it may not be possible to get a definitive determination of the taxable value of the property before the expiry of two years from the death.

Other factors relevant to wills of spouses or civil partners

[233.11]
In some cases business or agricultural property owned by one party to a marriage or civil partnership is likely to qualify for agricultural or business relief on the death of the current owner of it, but will or might cease to qualify for the relief after his or her death, eg because it relates to a business which is personal to the current owner, or the executors may have to sell it, or it is a partnership share subject to an option for the surviving partners to buy it, or it is agricultural property where the farmhouse might cease to be occupied by anyone engaged in agriculture. It is obviously a good idea in such circumstances for the current owner to make a non-exempt gift of the property in the event of him or her predeceasing his or her spouse or civil partner. If the other spouse or civil partner might not have enough to live on without it, a discretionary trust with the spouse or civil partner as an object is a possible solution: see Form C11.1 at para **[233.15]**.

On the other hand, where the other spouse or civil partner would, if given the property, continue to hold it in such a way that it would continue to qualify for the relief (bearing in mind that the succession provisions—see B5 at para **[205.11]**—will probably apply) there is less disadvantage in leaving it to the other spouse. There is also the point that leaving the property to the other spouse or civil partner will enable there to be a tax-free uplift in the capital gains tax base value on the spouse's or civil partner's death, which will not occur if the property is settled by will on discretionary trusts. Private company shares are perhaps the type of property most likely to continue to qualify for business relief in the hands of the current owner's spouse or civil partner, but the possibility of a takeover or flotation should be borne in mind in appropriate cases. If there are no good reasons for creating a trust by will of business or agricultural property, an advantage of making an absolute gift, or creating a trust where all the beneficiaries are ascertained and of full age, is that it is easier for the beneficiaries to make a deed of variation to rearrange the assets into what is the most advantageous structure in the circumstances prevailing after the testator's death.

Where only one or some of the testator's children will carry on a business

[233.12]
Where there is a clear successor or successors, typically a child or children of the testator, who will carry on the testator's business after his death and to

whom the testator wishes to leave his business assets (whether directly owned or owned as a partnership interest or company shares), there are often other children or other relations with a claim on the testator who will not do so. There can then be a serious problem of what provision to make for the ones who will not carry on the business, if the testator does not have significant assets apart from his business assets. This problem is often at its most acute for farmers, particularly where there are no or hardly any assets apart from the farm and farming business, and where the child or children who want to carry on the farming will not be able to make a living if they have to pay a significant amount to acquire the farm and farming business. There is no easy solution to this, and to avoid over-burdening those who inherit the business it will often be necessary for the provision to be unequal. The rules for allocation of business relief where some of the estate is exempt (see paras **[233.2]**–**[233.7]**) can also render disadvantageous the making of cash provision for one set of beneficiaries out of a gift of business or agricultural property to another set of them (see para **[233.4]**). Ways in which provision for those who do not inherit the business assets may be made in appropriate cases are:

(1) Provision for the intended recipient(s) of the business or agricultural assets to buy them in easy or interest-free payments in instalments, the payments going into a trust fund for the other beneficiaries: see B9 at para **[209.1]** ff for options, and Form C12.1 at para **[234.17]** for a will on these lines. Dispositions in this form may affect the availability of the business or agricultural relief where the estate is partially exempt (see para **[233.6]**, sub-para (4)).

(2) Provision for the business or agricultural assets to go to the intended recipients subject to payment of legacies to the other beneficiaries. This can be by way of a charge of legacies on specific gifts, or a residuary gift of the business or agricultural assets subject to legacies (as in Form C12.2 at para **[234.31]** ff). Easy terms for payment of the legacies can be included, as in Form C12.2, cl 4(3) at para **[234.36]**. It should be remembered that charging a legacy on a specific gift of business or agricultural assets will affect the availability of the business or agricultural relief where the estate is partially exempt (see para **[233.4]**).

(3) A gift of residue in equal shares among all the beneficiaries, with those who will work in the business being given an option to purchase the business or agricultural property with the purchase money being set off so far as possible against their shares of residue (see Form C12.1 at para **[234.17]** ff).

(4) A specific gift of the business or agricultural property to the beneficiaries who will work in the business, with all the testator's other assets going to the other beneficiaries unless they exceed the value of the business assets, in which case there is an equal division. A possible way of doing this is through a hotchpot clause, as in Form C11.3 at para **[233.36]** ff (and for a similar provision see B5.8 at para **[205.65]**).

(5) Where what the testator owns is shares in a private company they can be divided up among the different beneficiaries if the beneficiary or beneficiaries who are going to run the business are safely installed as directors and managers. This is better from a business relief point of

view than charging legacies on the shares in favour of the beneficiaries who are not working in the business, but could lead to the beneficiaries running the business to lose control and be ousted, and could be of little benefit to the beneficiaries who do not work in the business if the shares never pay dividends. In the case of a company which owns agricultural property this course of action could prevent agricultural relief on subsequent deaths (see the Preliminary Note to C12 at para **[234.6]**).

(6) Another possibility for private company shares is a discretionary trust of the shares with those working in the business and those who are not as beneficiaries (see Form C11.1 at para **[233.15]** ff), thus keeping the holding together for relief purposes and preventing either faction from using their votes as shareholders against the interests of the other, but possibly creating a difficult task for the trustees of mediating between the conflicting interests.

[233.13]

Form C11.1: Will settling private company shares entitled to business relief and optional 'top up' legacy on a nil-rate band discretionary trust, with residue given to wife with alternative gift to issue

Note. The main point of this form is to make a specific gift of the testator's unquoted shareholding in a trading company on discretionary trusts. It is assumed that the shareholding is entitled to 100 per cent business relief (see the Preliminary Note to B5 at para **[205.5]** ff for the conditions for this). Even if there is thought to be 100 per cent relief, some IHT may turn out to be payable on the shares: see B5 at para **[205.51]** for circumstances in which this might occur.

This form can be adapted for use by civil partners if the words 'civil partner' are substituted for 'wife' throughout. As with other will forms adapted for use by civil partners, the references to the testator's children may have to be amended as appropriate.

There are a number of possible reasons for making a disposition in this form, as follows—

(1) If the testator's spouse survives the testator, it can be used to make a non-exempt gift of the shares, but one from which the surviving spouse can benefit, so as not to waste the business relief by making an exempt gift of the shares to the spouse (see para **[233.7]**). This is a particularly good idea where it is possible or likely that, if the shares were given to the spouse, business relief would not be available on the spouse's death for reasons such as those mentioned in para **[233.11]** or otherwise.

(2) If the testator's spouse survives the testator, to make a non-exempt gift of the shares where it is intended that the spouse will purchase some or all of the shares from the trustees. The business relief will thus be used to put funds in the hands of non-exempt beneficiaries, but the spouse can obtain the shares. This may be desirable because the spouse works in the business and/or has his or her own shares in it. It should be noted that it is not necessary for this purpose that the trust should be a discretionary trust; any trust, other than one which gives the surviving spouse an interest in possession or an absolute interest, will do. What is most important is that there should be no obstacles to the surviving spouse being able to buy the shares, such as him or her being a trustee without any specific authorisation to buy trust property (see cl 8(1) of this form at para **[233.23]** for such authorisation).

(3) Where some (or only one) of the testator's children work in the business, and the testator wants to enable the other children to benefit while keeping the holding together and to some extent under the control or influence those (or the one) who work in the business. The latter would be executors and trustees, but there could be a difficult problem as to whether the children who do not work in the business should also be represented among the executors or trustees.

[233.14]

One further point about creating a discretionary trust of this sort in cases where the testator's spouse survives the testator is that if the shares do turn out to be subject to more IHT than expected the liability can be reduced by making an appointment falling within IHTA 1984, s 144 (see C3 at para **[225.83]** ff) of some or all of the shares to the surviving spouse within two years of the testator's death, so as to increase the amount of the testator's estate to which the exemption for gifts to spouses applies.

A further feature of this form, (at para **[233.17]**, cl 2(1)(b)), is an optional 'top up' legacy, for use where the circumstances are such that it is appropriate to make use of the testator's nil-rate band as well as the business relief, if the testator's spouse survives the testator and the taxable value of the shares is less than the amount of nil-rate band available on the testator's death (see para **[233.9]** for the circumstances where this may be appropriate). For further discussion of this type of disposition see the Preliminary Note at para **[233.9]** and the Note on nil-rate band discretionary trusts in B18 at para **[218.16]** ff. The legacy is defined by a formula so as to be the maximum which can be given without an IHT charge arising on the testator's death. It is intended to ensure that the amount of the discretionary trust fund does not exceed the IHT threshold where other non-exempt gifts are made by the will, or where there are non-exempt lifetime chargeable transfers or other property treated as part of the testator's estate which have to be taken into account in determining the IHT charge on the testator's estate on death. However, in view of the presence of business relief it may be necessary or appropriate to impose an upper cash limit on the gift to prevent the entire estate going into the discretionary trust: see the Preliminary Note at para **[233.9]** and the words in square brackets in cl 2(1)(b) of this form at para **[233.17]** which are commented on in n 4 to that paragraph.

[233.15]

REVOCATION CLAUSE

I [*name*] of [*address*] hereby revoke all former testamentary dispositions made by me and declare this to be my last will.

[233.16]

APPOINTMENT OF EXECUTORS AND TRUSTEES

1. I appoint my wife [*name*] ('my wife') [*name*] of [*address*] and [*name*] of [*address*][1] (hereinafter together called 'my trustees' which expression shall include my personal representatives for the time being and the trustees for the time being hereof) to be the executors and trustees of this will.

1 If there are two executors as well as the wife, there will still be two effective appointments if there is a divorce and the appointment of the wife is nullified by the Wills Act 1837 (WA 1837), s 18A (added by the AJA 1982, s 18: Part G, para **[244.17]**). See also the Preliminary Note to C2 on the possibility of divorce at para **[224.16]** ff.

[233.17]

GIFT OF SHARES AND NIL-RATE BAND LEGACY ON DISCRETIONARY TRUSTS[1]

Either

2 (1) [If my wife shall survive me and the trust for her of my residuary estate hereinafter contained shall take effect][2] I give to my trustees all the [25p] ordinary shares in [Will Williams & Company Limited] (hereinafter called 'the company') which I shall own at my death subject to payment thereout of any IHT payable by reason of my death which is attributable thereto (after allowing for any reduction in value for inheritance tax purposes which is attributed thereto).[3]

Or

2 (1) [If my wife shall survive me and the trust for her of my residuary estate hereinafter contained shall take effect][4] I give to my trustees the following—

(a) all the [25p] ordinary shares in [Will Williams & Company Limited] (hereinafter called 'the company') which I shall own at my death subject to payment thereout of any IHT payable by reason of my death which is attributable thereto (after allowing for any reduction in value for inheritance tax purposes which is attributed thereto);[5] and

(b) the maximum sum (if any) [not exceeding £——][6] which can in the circumstances subsisting at my death be given by virtue of this subclause (b) without any liability being incurred for the payment of inheritance tax on or by reason of my death; and in particular (without prejudice to the generality of the foregoing) for the purpose of determining the amount of such maximum sum the circumstances to be taken into account shall include all chargeable transfers made by me during my life (or events treated as such for inheritance tax purposes) so far as relevant for the computation of inheritance tax on my death the dispositions taking effect under this will (apart from this subclause) or under any codicil hereto and any property treated as if it were part of my estate for inheritance tax purposes[7] [and furthermore in determining the foregoing maximum sum it shall be assumed that the nil-rate band maximum (within the meaning of Section 8A of the Inheritance Tax Act 1984) at the time of my death will be treated as increased for the purposes of the charge to inheritance tax on my death by any amount by which it would be treated as increased if a claim was made under that section and I direct my Trustees to make such a claim][8] [provided that the foregoing gift of a sum of money contained in this subclause (b) shall not have effect if my wife shall predecease me or the trust for her of my residuary estate hereinafter contained shall fail for any other reason].[9]

(2) In this clause the following expressions have the following meanings namely:

(a) 'the relevant beneficiaries' means and includes my wife my children and remoter issue (whether living at my death or born thereafter) and the spouses civil partners widows widowers and former civil partners (including those who have entered into a subsequent marriage or civil partnership) of my children and remoter issue;[10]

(b) 'the trust period' means the period commencing on my death and expiring on the twenty-first anniversary of the death of the last survivor of my wife and my children and remoter issue who shall be living at my death;

(c) 'the accumulation period' means the period commencing with my death and expiring on the twenty first anniversary thereof.

(3) My trustees may at their absolute discretion sell or retain the said shares for as long as they think fit and shall invest [the said legacy (if any)

and][11] the proceeds of sale of the said shares when and if sold in any investments hereby authorised with power to vary the same and shall hold the said shares [and the said legacy][12] and the assets from time to time representing the same (hereinafter called 'the trust fund') and the income thereof upon the trusts and with and subject to the powers and provisions hereinafter declared and contained.

(4) My trustees shall hold the trust fund and the income thereof upon trust for all or such one or more of the relevant beneficiaries at such ages or times in such shares and upon such trusts for the benefit of the relevant beneficiaries as my trustees (being at least two in number or a trust corporation) may by deed or deeds revocable or irrevocable executed at any time or times during the trust period appoint and in making any such appointment my trustees shall have powers as full as those which they would possess if they were an absolute beneficial owner of the trust fund and in particular (but without prejudice to the generality of the foregoing words) my trustees may in any exercise of the foregoing power as they in their absolute discretion think fit:

(a) delegate give or impose to or upon themselves or any other person or persons and in relation to any trust or disposition any discretionary powers or discretionary trusts including powers of further delegation or powers to create further discretionary trusts or powers;[13]

(b) create trusts or powers for the accumulation of income during any period permitted by law;

(c) create administrative powers or provisions of whatever nature;

Provided that:

(i) no such appointment shall invalidate any payment transfer or application of capital or income previously made under any of the trusts or powers herein elsewhere contained;

(ii) every interest limited under any exercise of such power shall vest in interest (if at all) not later than the expiration of the trust period;

(iii) any such appointment may be made in respect of income alone without any appointment of capital; and

(iv) any such revocable appointment shall (so far as then unrevoked) cease to be revocable at the expiration of the trust period.

(5) In default of and subject to any exercise of the foregoing power my trustees (being at least two in number or a trust corporation) may at their discretion at any time or times during the trust period pay transfer or apply the whole or any part or parts of the trust fund to or for the benefit of all or any one or more exclusive of the others or other of the relevant beneficiaries for the time being living if more than one in such shares and generally in such manner as my trustees shall think fit.[14]

(6) Subject to any or every exercise of the foregoing powers my trustees shall during the trust period hold the trust fund upon trust to pay or apply the income thereof to or for the maintenance education or benefit of all or any one or more of the relevant beneficiaries for the time being living in such shares if more than one and generally in such manner as they think fit

provided that my trustees may during the accumulation period accumulate the whole or any part of the income of the trust fund by investing the same and the resulting income thereof in any of the investments hereby authorised and any accumulations of income so made shall form part of the capital of the trust fund (or the part thereof from which such income arose) for all purposes.

(7) Subject to the foregoing trust and to any or every exercise of the foregoing powers my trustees shall hold the trust fund and the income thereof at the expiration of the trust period in trust absolutely for such of my children and remoter issue as shall then be living in equal shares per stirpes.

(8) Any capital or income of the trust fund not otherwise disposed of by this clause shall be held in trust for such of my children as shall survive me if more than one in equal shares absolutely.[15]

1 See the Note to this form at paras **[233.13]** and **[233.14]**.

2 Where the main or only objective of the discretionary trust is to make use of the business relief on the shares and the testator's nil-rate band if the testator's spouse survives the testator and becomes entitled to the residuary estate (see the Note to this form at para **[233.13]**), it is appropriate to impose this precondition. However, where an objective of the discretionary trust is to keep the holding together irrespective of whether the spouse becomes entitled to residue (see the Note to this form at para **[233.13]**), these words should be omitted.

3 Making the gift subject to IHT will, in the event of the testator's spouse surviving the testator and the gift of the shares giving rise to an IHT charge (see B5 at para **[205.51]** for possible reasons why this should happen), cause the size of the chargeable estate to be less than it would be if the gift was free of IHT: see B14 at para **[214.74]**. Without these words the gift of the shares will be free of IHT if they are located in the UK: see B14 at para **[214.55]** ff.

Where this gift is to take effect even if the testator's spouse does not survive the testator (see the last preceding note), it may be preferable for this gift to be free of IHT in those circumstances, which can be achieved by making the direction that the gift is subject to tax contingent on the spouse surviving the testator and becoming entitled to the residuary estate.

This first alternative version of sub-cl (1) is for use where the top up additional legacy is not wanted.

4 See n 2 above. If these words are omitted, the proviso to sub-cl (1)(b) should be included (see n 9 below).

5 See the first two paragraphs of n 3 above. This second alternative version of sub-cl (1) is for use where the top up additional legacy is wanted. See para **[200.130]** for the circumstances where such provision is still worth making despite nil-rate band carry-forward.

6 If the shares given by sub-cl (a) are entitled to 100 per cent business relief (see B5 at para **[205.29]** ff for 100 per cent relief on shares), and the testator has made no lifetime gifts within the seven years preceding his death, and there is no property outside his free estate which is taxable as part of his estate on his death, this legacy will be equal at least to the nil-rate band. Further, for reasons given in the Preliminary Note at para **[233.9]**, if there are other assets of the estate qualifying for business or agricultural relief then the cash legacy could exceed the nil-rate band or even, in an extreme case, use up the entire estate. In either case the testator might prefer to limit the amount of this legacy, as in these words in square brackets, so that his spouse gets some assets absolutely under the gift of residue.

However, the spouse is not excluded from benefit where the trusts of the legacy are, as in this form, discretionary trusts under which the spouse is a beneficiary. If the testator does not mind the possibility that the benefit to his spouse under the will might be solely that of being an object of a discretionary trust, he can take maximum advantage of the IHT reliefs if no upper limit is imposed on the legacy. It is much more important to impose an upper limit of this kind where the trusts of the legacy are such that the spouse is excluded from benefit, as in Form C11.2, cl 2 at para **[233.29]**.

7 See the Preliminary Note at para **[233.9]** and the Note to this form at para **[233.14]**.

8 These words should be included where the testator potentially has an increased nil-rate band on death under the nil-rate band carry-forward rules (see para **[200.75**) by reason of a previous marriage or civil partnership which ended in the death of the other party, and where the other party did not make full use of his or her nil-rate band in the dispositions taking effect on his or her death. Persons in this situation have a particularly strong IHT-planning reason for providing a nil-rate band discretionary trust in their wills to take effect in the event of their being survived by the current spouse or civil partner: see para **[200.130]**.

9 See n 4 above. This proviso should be included if the condition as to the wife's survival is omitted from the opening words of this alternative sub-cl (1) so that the discretionary trust of the shares takes effect even if the spouse predeceases the testator (for reasons given in the Note to this form at para **[233.13]**, sub-para (3)).

10 The definition of the discretionary class may need to be enlarged or adapted in individual cases. For wider classes, and power to add to the class of beneficiaries, see Form C3.6. cl 3(1)(b) at para **[225.100]**, Form C4.1, cl 8(2)(a) at para **[226.26]**, Form C6.2, cls 7(1)(a), (2) and (3)(c) at para **[228.28]**.

11 These words in square brackets should be omitted if the first alternative sub-cl (1) is adopted.

12 See n 11 above.

13 These words authorise the creation of discretionary trusts and powers which otherwise might not be within the scope of the power: see Vol 1, para **[40.5]**.

14 A power to apply capital, being exercisable in a less formal manner, may be useful. But it is essential that its exercise should be adequately evidenced.

15 If it may be necessary to resort to an appropriation of part of a principal private residence, or a debt or charge scheme, to satisfy the top up legacy then separate trustees of the legacy should be provided as in Form C5.1, cl 5, at para **[227.14]**, and the appropriate administrative powers added as in sub-cll (8)–(11) of that clause.

[233.18]

ADMINISTRATION TRUSTS OF RESIDUE

3. (1) I give all my property not hereby or by any codicil hereto otherwise effectively disposed of [(including any entailed or other property over which I shall have at my death a general power of disposition by will)][1] to my trustees to hold on the trusts set out below with power at their discretion to sell all or any of it as and when they think fit.[2]

(2) My trustees shall pay my funeral and testamentary expenses[3] and debts and any legacies given by this will or any codicil hereto out of such property or its proceeds and shall have a discretion as to how such payments shall be borne as between capital and income.[4]

(3) Subject as above my trustees shall hold such property and the assets from time to time representing the same (hereinafter called 'my residuary estate') on the trusts set out below and shall invest all money comprised in such property or arising from its sale in any of the investments hereby authorised with power to change such investments into any others hereby authorised.

(4) In the administration of my estate and the execution of the trusts of this will or of any codicil to it:

(a) my trustees shall treat all income as accruing on the date on which it becomes payable regardless of the period in respect of which it shall have accrued and shall not make any statutory apportionment of the same;[5] and

(b) none of the equitable rules of apportionment between capital and income shall apply in any circumstances whatever.[6]

1 See para **[230.7]**, n 1.

2 See para **[230.7]**, n 2.
3 See para **[230.7]**, n 3.
4 See para **[230.7]**, n 4.
5 See para **[230.7]**, n 5.
6 See para **[230.7]**, n 6.

[233.19]

BENEFICIAL TRUSTS OF RESIDUE

4. (1) My trustees shall hold my residuary estate upon trust for my wife absolutely if she shall survive me.

(2) If my wife shall predecease me my trustees shall hold my residuary estate upon trust for such of my children [by my wife][1] as shall survive me if more than one in equal shares[2] provided that if any of my children [by my wife][3] shall predecease me leaving a child or children surviving me who shall attain the age of [18/21/25] years such last-mentioned child or children shall take if more than one the share of my residuary estate which such deceased child of mine would have taken had he or she survived me.[4]

(3) The foregoing trusts for grandchildren of mine shall carry the intermediate income of my residuary estate and section 31 of the Trustee Act 1925 (as hereinafter modified) shall apply thereto [provided that in relation to any presumptive share of my residuary estate of any grandchild of mine the said section 31 (amended as aforesaid) shall have effect as if the age of majority were the lesser of the age which he or she will attain (if he or she so long lives) on his or her last birthday occurring not later than the expiration of 21 years from my death and the age of [21/25][5] years (and so that the expressions 'infancy', 'minority' and 'infant' and all references to the age of eighteen years in the said Section 31 shall be construed accordingly)][6].

(4) Section 32 of the Trustee Act 1925 (as hereinafter modified) shall apply in relation to my residuary estate.

1 These words are for inclusion where the testator has children other than children of the marriage who are not intended to benefit. An alternative, for where there will not be any more children of the marriage, is to make the gift to named children. See further the Preliminary Note to C2 on reciprocal wills and the ultimate destination of property at para **[224.13]** ff. For forms for use where one spouse has children who are not children of the marriage and wishes to benefit them by his or her will see C5 at para **[227.1]** ff.
2 It is assumed that the children are all adult and so there is no age contingency.
3 To be included if the trust is confined to the children of the marriage. See n 1 above.
4 The grandchildren will be lives in being at the testator's death for perpetuity purposes, so that there is no risk of infringing the rule against perpetuities in specifying an age exceeding 21. The substitutional gift to grandchildren, if it takes effect and a grandchild is under the age of vesting at the testator's death, will fall within the IHT relevant property regime (for which see para **[218.8]** ff). If the age of vesting is greater than 18, the extended accumulation and maintenance trusts of income in sub-cl (3) will make sure that the trust will fall within the relevant property rules whatever the age of a substituted grandchild if under the age of vesting at the testator's death, avoiding the possibility of the trust operating as an IPDI trust in the event of a substituted grandchild having attained the age of 18 but not the age of vesting of capital at the testator's death (see para **[224.25]**). The alternative possibility is to provide for substituted minor grandchildren to have interests in possession during their minorities so that the trust operates as an IPDI one: for such a provision see for example Form C2.1, second alternative cl 8(1), at para **[224.36]**.
5 This should be the same as the age of vesting in sub-cl (2).
6 This proviso is for inclusion if the age of vesting in sub-cl (2) is greater than 18. See n 4 above.

[233.20]

MAINTENANCE, ACCUMULATION AND ADVANCEMENT[1]

5. (1) Section 31 of the Trustee Act 1925 (relating to accumulation and maintenance) shall apply in relation to the trusts hereby or by any codicil hereto declared as if:

(a) in paragraph (i) of subsection (1) of the said section the words 'as the trustees think fit' were substituted for the words 'as may in all the circumstances be reasonable'; and

(b) the proviso to the said subsection (1) were omitted.

(2) Section 32 of the Trustee Act 1925 (relating to advancement) shall apply in relation to the said trusts as if the words 'one half of' were omitted from proviso (a) to subsection (1) thereof.

(3) Whenever my trustees shall have an obligation or discretion under the provisions of this will or any codicil hereto or under the general law to apply income or capital for the benefit of a minor beneficiary they may either pay the same without liability to account to his or her parent guardian or any other adult person with whom such beneficiary may be residing or to such beneficiary himself or herself if of the age of 16 years or more and so that the receipt of such parent guardian or other person or of such minor beneficiary shall be a full and sufficient discharge to my trustees for the income or capital so applied.[2]

1 For alternative provisions relating to maintenance and advancement see Forms B18.11 to B18.23 and the notes thereto at paras **[218.43]**–**[218.108]**.

2 A parent (with parental responsibility) and a guardian of a minor are empowered by the ChA 1989, s 3(3) (Part G, para **[244.114]**) to give a good receipt for the minor's property: see Vol 1, para **[9.42]**.The power in this subclause is wider in that it authorises the payment of income or capital to a parent who does not have parental responsibility, any adult with whom the minor is residing, and the minor himself or herself if 16 or over.

[233.21]

ADMINISTRATIVE POWERS[1]

6. (1) In this clause where the context so admits—

(a) the expression 'land' includes buildings and estates interests or rights of any kind in or over land; and

(b) during the administration of my estate the expression 'beneficiary' includes any person who would be a beneficiary if such administration had been completed and the expression 'beneficially interested' and references to income of any asset being payable or capable of being paid to or for the benefit of a beneficiary shall be construed accordingly.

(2) None of the powers or provisions contained in subclause (3) below of this clause shall be capable of being exercised or operating in any manner such that if such power or provision were capable of being so exercised or so operating the existence of the same would either—

(i) prevent any person who would in the absence of such power or provision have been entitled to an interest in possession within section 49(1A) of the Inheritance Tax Act 1984 in any property from being entitled to such interest; or

(ii) prevent section 71A or 71D of the Inheritance Tax Act 1984 from applying to any property to which in the absence of such power or provision either section would have applied.[2]

(3) In the administration of my estate and the execution of the trusts hereof or of any codicil hereto my trustees shall have the following powers in addition to those conferred by law but subject to the last foregoing subclause—

(a) power to invest moneys sell assets and change investments with the unrestricted freedom of choice and powers of disposition and acquisition of a sole beneficial owner with in particular power to make unsecured loans, acquire non-income yielding assets, and purchase land anywhere in the world or chattels for any purpose including occupation or enjoyment in kind by a beneficiary under the power set out below;[3]

(b) power to delegate all or any of their investment powers to a professional investment manager or managers whether individual or corporate and whether or not also a nominee holder of assets for my trustees (and who may be or include one or more of my trustees or the beneficiaries hereunder) upon such terms as to remuneration and otherwise (including terms authorising self-dealing or providing for the limitation of the liability of the investment manager or managers) as my trustees think fit and section 22 of the Trustee Act 2000 shall not apply;[4]

(c) power to vest or register any property in any person or persons whether individual or corporate and whether or not an investment manager to whom powers have been delegated under the foregoing power (and who may be or include one or more of my trustees or the beneficiaries hereunder) as nominee or nominees for my trustees upon such terms as to remuneration or otherwise (including terms authorising self-dealing or providing for the limitation of the liability of the nominee) as my trustees think fit and section 22 of the Trustee Act 2000 shall not apply;[5]

(d) power to borrow money with or without giving security and on such terms as to interest and repayment and otherwise as my trustees may think fit for any purpose connected with the administration of my estate or the trusts declared herein or in any codicil hereto (including investment) And no lender from whom my trustees borrow money in purported exercise of this power shall be concerned to enquire as to the propriety amount or purpose of any such borrowing;[6]

(e) power to lend money to a beneficiary to whom any of the income of such money is payable or to whom or for whose benefit any income of such money is capable of being paid or applied in exercise of a discretion (or who would be such a beneficiary if such money yielded income) and to do so at a full or concessionary rate of interest or interest free;[7]

(f) without prejudice to the generality of subclause (a) above power in connection with the sale of any assets (in particular the sale of any business or any private company shares) to give any warranty indemnity guarantee undertaking or other agreement or covenant whatever or to enter into any type of agreement they think fit;

(g) power to give guarantees or otherwise assist or finance any company or corporate body in which shares are held by my trustees or any beneficiary;

(h) power to carry on any business whether alone or in partnership or any other form of joint venture with others and to employ in it any capital held on the same trusts as the assets of the business or the partnership share (as the case may be) and to appoint any person (including any one or more of my trustees) manager servant or agent to act in any such business at a salary or otherwise;

(i) power to incorporate any company or other corporation in any part of the world with limited or unlimited liability for any purpose including the acquisition of any business or other assets subject to any of the trusts hereof (or of any codicil hereto) or the carrying on of any trade or business and any consideration for the acquisition of any such assets by any company incorporated under this subclause may consist wholly or partly of shares or securities (including unsecured loan stock) allotted to my trustees;[8]

(j) all the powers of an absolute owner in relation to any land (wherever situated) held by them;[9]

(k) power to apply capital held on the same trusts as any land (or which would be so held if the administration of my estate had been completed) in the improvement of such land and to apply such capital or the income of such capital on the repair or maintenance of such land;[10]

(l) power to permit any beneficiary to have the beneficial occupation use or enjoyment in kind of any land or chattel or other tangible property on such terms as to repair insurance or payment of outgoings by the beneficiary or otherwise howsoever as my trustees think fit Provided that the foregoing power shall only be exercisable and such permission to occupy or enjoy in kind may only continue in the following circumstances—

  (i) so long as any of the income of such land chattel or other tangible property is payable to such beneficiary or capable of being paid or applied to him or for his benefit in exercise of a discretion (or would be so payable or capable of being so paid or applied if such land chattel or other property yielded income),

  (ii) in the case of land, so long as for the time being the occupation thereof by such beneficiary is compatible with any statutory rights of occupation of any other beneficiary or beneficiaries;[11]

(m) power to exercise all the powers of appropriation (and other incidental powers) conferred by statute on a personal representative without the necessity of obtaining any consents and notwithstanding that one or more of my trustees may be beneficially interested in the exercise of such power.[12]

1 See para **[230.11]**, n 1.

2 See para **[230.11]**, n 2.
3 See para **[230.11]**, n 3.
4 See para **[230.11]**, n 4.
5 See para **[230.11]**, n 5.
6 See para **[230.11]**, n 6.
7 See para **[230.11]**, n 7.
8 The powers in sub-cls (f) to (i) are specific to business property of various kinds. Where the testator does not have a business owned personally and is not a partner in a business, and not likely to acquire a business or partnership interest before his death, his business interests all being held through companies, sub-cls (h) and (i) could be omitted.
9 See para **[230.11]**, n 8.
10 See para **[230.11]**, n 9.
11 See para **[230.11]**, n 10.
12 See para **[230.11]**, n 11.

[233.22]

EXERCISE OF POWERS[1]

7. Any power or discretion hereby or by law conferred on my trustees (including a power or discretion as to the disposition of capital or income) shall be exercisable notwithstanding that any of my trustees has a personal interest in such exercise provided that there are not fewer than two trustees and that at least one of them has no such personal interest.

1 This clause permits a member of the family to be a trustee without disqualifying him or her from benefit under any exercise of statutory or express powers of payment or application of capital, appointment, etc. See the Preliminary Note to B18 at para **[218.4]**.

[233.23]

TRUSTEE SELF-DEALING, INDEMNITY AND SIMILAR PROVISIONS

8. (1) Any of my trustees in his personal capacity or in a fiduciary capacity other than as one of my trustees may enter into any transaction (including a sale purchase lease loan or partnership) with my trustees provided that there is at least one other of my trustees agreeing in writing to the transaction who has no interest therein save as one of my trustees.[1]

(2) None of my trustees nor any officer or employee of any of my trustees shall be accountable for any remuneration or other benefit gained as an officer employee agent or adviser of any company body or firm notwithstanding that his situation or office may have been obtained or may be held or retained in right or by means or by reason of his position as one of my trustees or of any shares stock property rights or powers whatsoever held by my trustees.[2]

(3) In the professed administration of my estate and the professed execution of the trusts powers or provisions of this will or any codicil hereto none of my trustees (nor any officer or employee of any of my trustees) shall be liable (whether for breach of the duty of care under the Trustee Act 2000 or otherwise) for any act or omission of his or for any act or omission of any co-personal representative or co-trustee of his or of any agent adviser manager delegate nominee or other person employed in the administration of my estate or the execution of any of the said trusts powers and provisions save for any act or omission involving wilful fraud or dishonesty committed by the personal representative or trustee sought to be made liable.[3]

(4) Without prejudice to the generality of the foregoing none of my trustees shall be liable for leaving the conduct of the business and affairs

(including the payment and non-payment of dividends) of any company or corporation whose securities are subject to the trusts hereof or of any codicil hereto to the directors or other governing body thereof (whether or not such securities give control of the company or corporation) unless my trustees have express notice of some act of dishonesty or other misconduct on the part of such directors or governing body.

(5) My trustees shall be fully indemnified out of the assets they hold on the trusts hereof or of any codicil hereto against any liability they may incur in exercise of any of the powers hereby or by any codicil hereto or by law conferred.[4]

[(6) My trustees shall not be liable for any act or default of any investment manager or nominee employed in good faith to manage or hold assets of my estate nor for any act or default of any beneficiary having the occupation use or enjoyment of property in kind nor for any loss which may be incurred by reason of the carrying on a business in exercise of the foregoing power to do so.][5]

(7) Section 11(1) of the Trusts of Land and Appointment of Trustees Act 1996 (consultation with beneficiaries) shall not apply to the exercise by my trustees of any of their powers in relation to land subject to the trusts hereof. [6]

1 See para **[221.4]**. A power to purchase trust property or otherwise deal with the trustees is often a convenient power to have where business property or private company shares form part of the estate, because it is often necessary or appropriate to appoint executors and/or trustees who are involved in the business, and who are the most likely purchasers if the business assets or company shares have to be sold. It is particularly relevant if it is intended that the surviving spouse will purchase some or all of the shares. It could also be particularly relevant if the trustees wish to continue with a business which the deceased carried on in partnership where one of the trustees is also one of the partners.

2 Without a provision of this kind a trustee or employee of a trustee who owed his position in a company to the exercise or non-exercise of votes attached to shares held by the trustees would be accountable for his remuneration to the trust fund: see the note to Form B21.9 at para **[221.10]**. This is not so where his position is owed entirely to votes other than those attached to the trust assets (*Re Gee* [1948] Ch 284, [1948] 1 All ER 498). A provision of this kind should be included if the will disposes of private company shares, particularly where persons connected with the company are appointed executors or might subsequently become trustees.

3 This is a wide form of indemnity, and may not be appropriate where a professional executor and trustee, charging for his services, is being appointed. Further, if a paid trustee is to rely on this indemnity clause, the testator should specifically be made aware of its meaning and effect (see para **[221.13]**). Where the executors will include both professional and non-professional executors, it may be appropriate for this clause to be included but not to apply to a corporate or professional executor: see the proviso to Form B21.12 at para **[221.16]**. If this is omitted or restricted to non-professional executors, the more limited indemnity in sub-cl (6) could be included. For the duty of care under the TrA 2000 see para **[221.15]** and the TrA 2000, s 1 and Sch 1 at Part G, paras **[246.133]** and **[246.173]**.

4 This is implicit anyway in the powers concerned, which are principally the powers to give guarantees, and warranties on sale of shares or business assets, to carry on a business, and to borrow (cl 6(d), (f), (g), and (h)).

5 This makes it clear that the trustees are not liable for the defaults of others who may have possession or control of trust property or for carrying on a business in good faith. This clause should be omitted if sub-cl (3) is included and applies to all trustees: see n 3 supra.

6 The requirement that trustees of land in exercise of any function relating to land subject to the trust consult with beneficiaries of full age beneficially entitled to an interest in possession in the land can be excluded: see the TLATA 1996, s 11 (Part G, para **[246.114]**).

[233.24]

PROFESSIONAL TRUSTEE CHARGING CLAUSE

9. Any of my trustees being a professional or business man may charge and be paid all usual professional and other proper charges for business transacted acts done advice given and time spent by him or his firm in connection with the administration of my estate or in connection with the trusts hereof including acts which a personal representative or trustee not being in any profession or business could have done personally.

[233.25]

TESTIMONIUM AND ATTESTATION CLAUSE

IN WITNESS whereof I have hereunto set my hand this —— day of —— 20——.

SIGNED by the above-named testator as his last will in the presence of us both present at the same time who at his request and in his presence and in the presence of each other have signed our names below as witnesses:	}	[*Signature of testator*]

[*Signatures, addresses and descriptions of two witnesses*]

[233.26]

Form C11.2: Reciprocal wills for husband and wife who have recently acquired share capital of private trading company, the first to die making a direct gift of the shares to the children and otherwise leaving estate to the survivor

Note. It is assumed that the testators are husband and wife making wills shortly after acquiring part of the voting ordinary share capital of a private trading company. It is also assumed that the shares do not already qualify for business relief as replacement property within IHTA 1984, s 107 or under the succession provisions of IHTA 1984, ss 108 and 109 (see B5 at para **[205.11]**), but that the shares will qualify fully for IHT business relief after they have been owned by the testators for two years.

This form illustrates making a non-exempt gift of such shares which only takes effect in relation to those which qualify for business relief by the time of the testator's death, for the reasons discussed in paras **[233.9]** and **[233.11]** (see also B5 at para **[205.31]** and also Forms B5.9 and B5.10 at paras **[205.66]** and **[205.67]**).

It is possible that the company will change its name or be taken over, or shares with a different par value substituted, or more shares of the same type acquired by either testator (including by a bonus or rights issue), or some of the shares sold by either of them before the testator's death. It is not practicable to try to make provision for the numerous possibilities of this kind, and the testators will have to be warned (preferably in writing) that they must have their wills reviewed if there is a takeover, capital reconstruction, bonus or rights issue, change of name of the company, acquisition by either of them of more shares, or sale or other disposal by either of them of any of the shares, etc.

It is assumed that the testators' children are grown up. For notes on reciprocal wills for married couples with children, see the Preliminary Notes to C2 at paras **[224.12]**–**[224.15]** and C3 at para **[225.7]**.

[233.27]

REVOCATION CLAUSE

I [*name*] of [*address*] hereby revoke all former testamentary dispositions made by me and declare this to be my last will.

[233.28]

APPOINTMENT OF EXECUTORS AND TRUSTEES

1. I appoint my [wife/husband] [*name*] ('my [wife/husband]') [*name*] of [*address*] and [*name*] of [*address*][1] (hereinafter together called 'my trustees' which expression shall include my personal representatives for the time being and the trustees for the time being hereof) to be the executors and trustees of this will.

1 If there are two executors as well as the wife/husband, there will still be two effective appointments if there is a divorce and the appointment of the wife/husband is nullified by the WA 1837, s 18A (added by the AJA 1982, s 18): Part G, para **[244.17]**. See also the Preliminary Note to C2 on the possibility of divorce at paras **[224.16]–[224.23]**.

[233.29]

GIFT TO CHILDREN OF PRIVATE COMPANY SHARES[1]

2. (1) In this clause 'the relevant shares' means the [25p] ordinary shares in [Will Williams & Company Limited] owned by me at the date of this my will.

(2) If my [wife/husband] shall survive me[2] and if by the time of my death I shall have owned the relevant shares for a continuous period of two years[3] then I give [all]/[100][4] of the relevant shares subject to payment thereout of any inheritance tax payable by reason of my death which is attributable thereto (after allowing for any reduction in value for inheritance tax purposes which is attributed thereto)[5] to my trustees to hold the same on the trusts set out below.

(3) My trustees may at their absolute discretion sell or retain the said shares for as long as they think fit and shall invest the said legacy (if any) and the proceeds of sale of the said shares when and if sold in any investments hereby authorised with power to vary the same and shall hold the said shares and the said legacy and the assets from time to time representing the same (hereinafter called 'the trust fund') and the income thereof upon the trusts and with and subject to the powers and provisions hereinafter declared and contained.

(4) My trustees shall hold the trust fund and the income thereof upon trust for such of my children [*name*] [*name*] and [*name*][6] as shall survive me and if more than one in equal shares provided that if any of my said children shall predecease me leaving a child or children surviving me who shall attain the age of [18/21/25] years[7] such last-mentioned child or children shall take and if more than one equally between them the share of the trust fund which such deceased child of mine would have taken had he or she survived me.

(5) The foregoing trusts for grandchildren of mine shall carry the intermediate income of the trust fund and section 31 of the Trustee Act 1925 (as hereinafter modified) shall apply thereto [provided that in relation to any presumptive share of my residuary estate of any grandchild of mine the said section 31 (amended as aforesaid) shall have effect as if the age of majority

were the lesser of the age which he or she will attain (if he or she so long lives) on his or her last birthday occurring not later than the expiration of 21 years from my death and the age of [21/25][8] years (and so that the expressions 'infancy', 'minority' and 'infant' and all references to the age of eighteen years in the said Section 31 shall be construed accordingly)][9].

(6) Section 32 of the Trustee Act 1925 (as hereinafter modified) shall apply in relation to the trust fund.

1 See the Note above, for the importance of reviewing the terms of this gift if more of the same shares are acquired, or there is any relevant change in the company or its share capital. It may be preferred to have a discretionary trust of the property given by this clause, such as in Form C11.1, cl 2 at para **[233.17]**. It might also be desired to have a top up nil-rate band pecuniary legacy as in the second alternative sub-cl (1) of that clause.

2 The objective of this gift is to make use of the business relief on the shares if the testator's spouse survives the testator (see the Note to this form at para **[233.26]**), and this precondition is imposed to avoid unnecessary duplication of gifts (ie this one and the residuary gift) in the event of the spouse not surviving the testator. If the residuary gift to the spouse fails through divorce, there will be such duplication, but the trusts taking effect will be the same.

3 If the shares do not qualify for business relief by the time of the testator's death it is better for them to pass to the surviving spouse under the exempt residuary gift in the hope that the combined period of ownership of the testator and surviving spouse (taken into account together under IHTA 1984, s 108) will be sufficient for business relief to apply on the death of the spouse.

4 Delete one alternative, and if 'all' is deleted, amend the number of shares as appropriate. It is a matter for decision how much of the holding should be the subject of a non-exempt gift on the first death, and how much of it should go to the surviving spouse, depending on factors such as whether the shares may be entitled to business relief in the hands of the surviving spouse, what other resources the surviving spouse will have, and whether he or she will be working for the company (see also para **[233.11]**). If there is business or agricultural relief applicable which depends on control of the company (see paras **[205.5]**, **[205.6]** and **[234.6]** for the categories of relief depending on control) and the spouses between them have control of it, that will favour giving sufficient to the surviving spouse for him or her to maintain control.

5 Making the gift subject to IHT will, in the event of the gift of the shares giving rise to an IHT charge (see B5 at para **[205.51]** for possible reasons why this should happen), cause the size of the chargeable estate to be less than it would be if the gift was free of IHT: see B14 at para **[214.74]**. Without these words the gift of the shares will be free of IHT if they are located in the UK: see B14 at para **[214.59]**.

6 See the Preliminary Note to C2 on reciprocal wills and the ultimate destination of property at paras **[224.13]**–**[224.15]**.

7 See Form C11.1, cl 4(2), n 4 at para **[233.19]**.

8 This should be the same as the age of vesting in sub-cl (4).

9 See Form C11.1, cl 4(3), n 6 at para **[233.19]**.

[233.30]

ADMINISTRATION TRUSTS OF RESIDUE

3. [*As in cl 3 of* Form C11.1 *at para* **[233.18]**.]

[233.31]

BENEFICIAL TRUSTS OF RESIDUE

4. (1) My trustees shall hold my residuary estate upon trust for my [wife/husband] absolutely if [she/he] shall survive me.

(2) If my [wife/husband] shall predecease me my trustees shall hold my residuary estate upon trust for such of my children [*name*] [*name*] and

[*name*][1] as shall survive me if more than one in equal shares provided that if any of my said children shall predecease me leaving a child or children surviving me who shall attain the age of [18/21/25][2] years such last-mentioned child or children shall take if more than one the share of my residuary estate which such deceased child of mine would have taken had he or she survived me.

(3) The foregoing trusts for grandchildren of mine shall carry the intermediate income of my residuary estate and section 31 of the Trustee Act 1925 (as hereinafter modified) shall apply thereto [provided that in relation to any presumptive share of my residuary estate of any grandchild of mine the said section 31 (amended as aforesaid) shall have effect as if the age of majority were the lesser of the age which he or she will attain (if he or she so long lives) on his or her last birthday occurring not later than the expiration of 21 years from my death and the age of [21/25][3] years (and so that the expressions 'infancy', 'minority' and 'infant' and all references to the age of eighteen years in the said Section 31 shall be construed accordingly)][4].

(4) Section 32 of the Trustee Act 1925 (as hereinafter modified) shall apply in relation to my residuary estate.

1 See the Preliminary Note to C2 on reciprocal wills and the ultimate destination of property at paras **[224.13]–[224.15]**.
2 See Form C11.1, cl 4(2), n 4 at para **[233.19]**.
3 This should be the same as the age of vesting in sub-cl (5).
4 See Form C11.1, cl 4(3), n 6 at para **[233.19]**.

[233.32]

MAINTENANCE, ACCUMULATION AND ADVANCEMENT

5. [*As in cl 5 of* Form C11.1 *at para* **[233.20]**.]

[233.33]

ADMINISTRATIVE POWERS

6. [*As in cl 6 of* Form C11.1 *at para* **[233.21]**.]

[233.34]

TRUSTEE SELF-DEALING, INDEMNITY, AND SIMILAR PROVISIONS

7. [*As in cl 8 of* Form C11.1 *at para* **[233.23]**.]

[233.35]

PROFESSIONAL TRUSTEE CHARGING CLAUSE

8. [*As in cl 9 of* Form C11.1 *at para* **[233.24]**.]

[*Testimonium and attestation clause as in* Form C11.1 *at para* **[233.25]**.]

[233.36]

Form C11.3: Will giving business carried on as sole trader or in partnership to sons, and legacies to daughters, with residue to wife for life with remainder to children with substitution clause and hotchpot of specific gifts

Note. This form illustrates a possible solution to the problem which may arise where some of the testator's children are interested in carrying on the testator's business after his death and others are not (discussed in the Preliminary Note at para **[233.12]**): the business is specifically given to those who are interested in running it, but they have to bring it into hotchpot against their shares of residue. For other possibilities, see Form C11.1 at paras **[233.13]–[233.25]** and Forms C12.1 and C12.2 at paras **[234.17]–[234.44]**. This is a complicated form, not to be used without careful reflection on its consequences.

This form assumes that the testator has two sons who are interested in carrying on the business and a wife and two daughters who are not. The wife, if surviving, is given a life interest in residue, which will not include the business, which is the subject of an immediate gift to the sons (or the survivor of them if only one is living at the testator's death) whether or not the gift to the wife takes effect; there are alternative clauses, one for a sole proprietor's business, the other for a partnership share. To counterbalance the gift to the sons the daughters are given legacies in the event of the wife surviving and taking her life interest, so as to give them an immediate gift of whatever it is thought might be spared from what is needed for the wife's support.

When residue comes to be divided there is hotchpot of the specific gift to the sons and the legacies to the daughters (if any) at their value at the testator's death. The aim is that the estate other than the business goes to the daughters if its value is less than the value of the business, and if it is equal to or more than the value of the business the estate is ultimately divided in equal shares. It should be noted that, even where the widow's life interest takes effect, the interests of the children in residue vest on the testator's death, so that if one dies after the testator and before the testator's widow his or her share of residue will fall into his or her estate, and that the hotchpot is at the values at the testator's death. It would involve an unacceptable increase in the complexity of an already complicated form to provide otherwise on either of these points, but to compensate there is a power of appointment which enables alteration of the interests in residue during the widow's life if the trustees can agree on it (the suggested trustees are a son a daughter and the widow). This is a form for a united family, but there is an expression of wishes as to how the power of appointment should be exercised in cl 8 (at para **[233.46]**) in the hope that it will promote agreement.

[233.37]

The hope is that in the event of the wife's life interest taking effect the specific gifts will be within the IHT nil-rate band (assuming that the gift of the business property to the sons will obtain 100 per cent business relief), but they are made subject to IHT in case any IHT is payable, so as to avoid the adverse consequences of grossing up (see B5 at para **[205.52]** ff and B14 at para **[214.74]**).

Where, as in this form, a will gives a life interest to the testator's spouse, it is essential to find out whether the testator and his spouse own property (in particular a residence) jointly, and if so to obtain instructions as to whether the testator's interest in that property is to be included in the property passing under his will and becoming subject to the trusts of his residuary estate. If his interest in the property is to be included in the residuary estate it is then necessary to advise the testator to sever the joint tenancy (see further the Note to Form C3.2 at para **[225.27]**).

It is also essential to make sure exactly what the testator does own; for example, it is possible for him to talk of his business, when investigation might show that what he owned was shares in a private company which owned the business. A misdescription of this kind in the will could cause the gift to fail, as it did in *Re Lewis's Will Trusts* [1984] 3 All ER 930, [1985] 1 WLR 102, where a gift by will of a farm and farming business was ineffective because what the testator owned was shares in a company which owned the farm and business.

If the testator's business or the business in which he is a partner is transferred to a company after the will is made, with the testator receiving company shares in place of his interest in the business or partnership share, a new gift by will or codicil of the company shares will be needed in substitution for the gift of the business or partnership share, as the latter is most unlikely to have effect as a gift of the company shares.

[233.38]

REVOCATION CLAUSE

I [*name*] of [*address*] hereby revoke all former testamentary dispositions made by me and declare this to be my last will.

[233.39]

APPOINTMENT OF EXECUTORS AND TRUSTEES

1. (1) Subject to subclause (2) below I appoint my wife [*name*] ('my wife') my son [*name*] and my daughter [*name*][1] to be the executors and trustees of this will.

(2) If the gift in clause 2 below hereof takes effect I appoint my said son [*name*] and my son [*name*] to be the executors of the property comprised in such gift.[2]

(3) In this will the expression 'my trustees' shall where the context so admits mean and include my general personal representatives for the time being the trustees for the time being hereof and the executors of the said property comprised in the said gift in clause 2 hereof for the time being.

1 If there are two executors as well as the wife, there will still be two effective appointments if there is a divorce and the appointment of the wife is nullified by the WA 1837, s 18A (added by the AJA 1982, s 18): Part G, para **[244.17]**. See also the Preliminary Note to C2 on the possibility of divorce at paras **[224.16]–[224.23]**.

2 It may be inconvenient administratively to appoint the legatees of business property as special executors of it and this course should not be adopted where the legatees are not under the terms of the bequest entitled to the debts due to the business, or where the testator's estate may, apart from the business, be insufficient to pay his debts. On the other hand the legatees of a business who are also appointed executors for the purposes of the business are thereby enabled to sue in their own names for the debts due to the business, and the general executors of the will are relieved from trouble and responsibility with regard to the business. It may also be convenient to appoint special executors of a business where a testator's business is to be carried on after his death as part of the testator's residuary estate, and the business is extensive. Appointment of special executors is particularly appropriate where the persons appointed are already working in the business.

There may be up to four executors in respect of any part of a testator's estate: Supreme Court Act 1981, s 114(1), reversing the effect of the decision in *Re Holland's Estate* [1936] 3 All ER 13 that the limit of four executors imposed by the corresponding previous legislation related to the totality of a testator's estate.

It should be remembered that the Public Trustee may not carry on a business for more than a year, and he should never be appointed trustee of any estate which includes the carrying on of a business, and the same considerations in effect apply to the appointment of a bank or other trust corporation.

If the appointment in sub-cl (2) takes effect the general executors will not be entitled to probate of the property of which there are separate executors (*Re Wakeham's Goods* (1872) LR 2 P & D 395). The general executors alone can make a good title to the land not included in that property: *Re Cohen's Executors and LCC* [1902] 1 Ch 187.

[233.40]

GIFT OF BUSINESS PROPERTY TO SONS

Either[1]

[2. I give to such of my said sons [*name*] and [*name*] as shall be living at my death if both in equal shares absolutely the goodwill of my business[2] of a [description of business] carried on by me at [location] and all the [equipment plant stock-in-trade][3] vehicles and all other assets of any kind employed or used in carrying on the same at my death and all book debts then owing to me in respect of such business together with the then balances (if any) to the credit of the current [and business reserve] accounts of the said business at the [*name*] Branch of [*name*] Bank plc[4] and the benefit of all contracts relating thereto but subject to taking over all my liabilities in connection with the said business existing at my death and indemnifying the rest of my estate against the same and subject as follows:

(a) [the foregoing gift shall include the freehold or such other estate or interest I may have at my death in the premises in which the said business is carried on but subject to any mortgage charge or other liability on or of such premises subsisting at my death[5] *or where the premises are leasehold* [the foregoing gift shall include the lease or tenancy of the premises on which the said business is carried on but subject to accepting the covenants liabilities and obligations thereunder and keeping my estate indemnified against all liability under the said lease or tenancy whether or not such liability has arisen in my lifetime or arises from acts or omissions done or occurring during my lifetime];

(b) if there is any inheritance tax payable on my estate by reason of my death which is attributable to the foregoing gift (after allowing for any reduction in value for inheritance tax purposes which is attributed thereto) then the foregoing gift shall be subject to such inheritance tax and it shall be borne by my said sons or the survivor of them in exoneration of the rest of my estate.][6]

Or[7]

[2. (1) I give to such of my said sons [*name*] and [*name*] as shall be living at my death if both in equal shares all my share and interest of and in the capital goodwill stock-in-trade plant machinery and other assets of the firm of [*name*] carrying on business as [*description of business*] subject to:

(a) payment thereout of any IHT payable by reason of my death which is attributable thereto (after allowing for any reduction in value for inheritance tax purposes which is attributed thereto);[8] and

(b) my said sons or the survivor of them indemnifying my general estate from all debts and liabilities of the said firm and accounting to my general estate for any sum due or owing to me at my death from the said firm by way of profit.[9]

(2) If there shall be any exercise after my death of any option granted during my lifetime to which my said share and interest shall after my death be subject the foregoing gift shall take effect in relation to the consideration received for such share and interest and shall not be adeemed thereby.][10]

1 The first alternative is a gift of a sole trader's business, and the second a gift of a partnership share. See the Note at para **[233.37]** for the consequences of subsequent incorporation of the business.

2 The word 'business' has no definite legal meaning. In its narrowest sense it may pass the mere right to carry on the business as the testator's successor and to use his trade name; in its widest sense it may include everything enumerated in this clause: see generally Vol 1, para **[64.7]**. The draftsman should consider in each case which of the things enumerated in this clause are intended to pass and specify them. It is important to state whether the gift of the business is subject to trade liabilities (see *Re Timberlake, Archer v Timberlake* (1919) 63 Sol Jo 286).

3 The list may need amendment depending on the kind of business.

4 Banking arrangements vary, and the conscientious will-draftsmen should enquire into those of his client's business and get instructions on what bank balances to include in the gift.

5 A bequest of a business prima facie passes all the testator's interest in all the assets of the business, including the business premises: *Re Rhagg, Easten v Boyd* [1938] Ch 828, [1938] 3 All ER 314, and under the AEA 1925, s 35 (Part G, para **[246.62]**) a gift is subject to any

mortgages or charges on the property in the absence of the expression of a contrary intent. However, to avoid doubt and possible dispute, we recommend that express provision is made about the business premises, and charges on it where relevant. There may need to be amendment where the business is carried on on part only of premises owned or leased by the testator, and the donee of the business is not intended to receive the whole of the premises. There will be an avoidable loss of business relief where liabilities which are not incurred for the purposes of the business are charged on the business premises or other business assets: see the Preliminary Note to B5 at paras **[205.10]** and **[205.24]**.

6 There should be no IHT on the gift because of 100 per cent business relief (see B5 at para **[205.22]**), but see the Preliminary Note to B5 at para **[205.51]** for the circumstances in which IHT may be paid on such property. The advantage of including this subclause is that, if the residuary gift is exempt and there is any IHT payable on this gift, the amount of IHT payable on this gift will be much reduced if this gift is subject to tax rather than free of it: see B14 at para **[214.74]**.

If a possible reason for IHT being payable on this gift is the presence of excepted assets (see the Preliminary Note to B5 at para **[205.9]**) it would be possible to exclude these from the gift: see Form B5.4 at para **[205.61]** for an example.

7 This alternative is for a gift of a partnership share. See the Note to this form at para **[233.37]**, for the consequences of subsequent incorporation of the partnership business.

8 See n 6 to the first alternative cl 2 supra.

9 Alternatively undrawn profit could be included in the gift.

10 The gift could be adeemed under the rule in *Lawes v Bennett* (1785) 1 Cox Eq Cas 167 by exercise after the death of the testator of an option granted by lifetime disposition after the will was made (eg to the testator's partners), unless express provision is made to the contrary: see Vol 1, para **[41.20]**. An option granted but not exercised during the testator's life would not prevent there being business relief on the partnership share, although an automatic sale provision would probably exclude the relief: see the Preliminary Note to B5 at para **[205.28]** and also the Preliminary Note at para **[233.7]**. This clause is not intended to prevent ademption by exercise of an option before the testator's death, something which would of course prevent there being any business relief on the business property on his death even if the contract created by the exercise of the option had not been completed at the time of his death: IHTA 1984, s 113; see also B5 at para **[205.14]**.

[233.41]

GIFT OF PERSONAL CHATTELS TO SPOUSE OR CHILDREN[1]

3. I give my personal chattels as defined by section 55(1)(x) of the Administration of Estates Act 1925[2] to my wife if she shall survive me and if she shall not survive me I give the same to such of my children [*name*] [*name*] [*name*] and [*name*] as shall survive me if more than one in equal shares.[3]

1 Since residue is settled on the surviving spouse, and then on the children, a specific gift of chattels is provided. It is not a good idea to settle chattels, because the trouble and expense of administering them as part of a trust fund is usually out of all proportion to their value, though it may sometimes be appropriate in the case of valuable ones.

2 See Part G, para **[246.67]** for the wording of this definition, and for further discussion of the meaning of 'personal chattels' see Vol 1, para **[64.44]**.

3 The gift to the children will be free of IHT provided that all the chattels are in the UK: see B14 at paras **[214.59]**, **[214.60]** and **[214.63]**. If any might have a foreign location this gift to the children could be declared to be free of tax as in Form C3.2, cls 3 and 6 at paras **[225.31]** and **[225.34]**.

[233.42]

LEGACIES TO DAUGHTERS IF TRUST FOR WIDOW TAKES EFFECT

4. If the trust for my wife for life of my residuary estate hereinafter contained takes effect I give to each of my daughters [*name*] and [*name*] if she shall survive me the sum of [£25,000] subject to payment thereout of any

inheritance tax payable in respect thereof by reason of my death[1] [and I declare that if the value of the legacy or legacies given by this clause is treated as reduced by virtue of section 39A of the Inheritance Tax Act 1984 the inheritance tax attributable to the foregoing legacy or legacies and borne thereby shall be the inheritance tax attributable to such legacy or legacies as so reduced].[2]

1 These legacies are made subject to IHT to prevent grossing up of the gifts when the tax charge on death is calculated: see n 6 to the first alternative cl 2 at para **[233.40]**.

2 For a discussion of IHTA 1984, s 39A see the Preliminary Note at para **[233.2]** ff and for the reasons for a provision of this kind see B14 at para **[214.73]**. This is to be included if there is or might be property with business or agricultural relief comprised in residue; the business property subject to the gift in cl 2 is not relevant because the relief relating to it will be allocated wholly to that gift.

[233.43]

EXCLUSION OF WILLS ACT 1837, S 33 IN RELATION TO SPECIFIC GIFTS AND PECUNIARY LEGACIES

5. Section 33 of the Wills Act 1837 (as substituted by section 19 of the Administration of Justice Act 1982) shall not apply to the foregoing gifts and pecuniary legacies.[1]

1 For the WA 1837, s 33, as substituted by the AJA 1982, s 19: see Part G, para **[244.36]** and Vol 1, para **[47.15]** ff. Section 33 would provide substitution of issue for a child who predeceases the testator, and is excluded because the specific gifts are intended for surviving children only, with the trusts of residue having a substitution clause and hotchpot provisions, and in the case of the gift of chattels because it would be impractical to administer a trust for minors of a share of chattels. See n 1 to para **[233.41]**.

[233.44]

ADMINISTRATION TRUSTS OF RESIDUE

6. [*As in cl 3 of* Form C11.1 *at para* **[233.18]**.]

[233.45]

BENEFICIAL TRUSTS OF RESIDUE

7. (1) My trustees shall hold my residuary estate upon trust to pay the income thereof to my wife during her life[1].

(2) Provided that my trustees shall have power in their absolute discretion from time to time so long as my wife is entitled to be paid the income of all or any part of the capital of my residuary estate (or would be so entitled if such capital yielded income) to pay transfer or apply the whole or any part or parts of such capital[2] to her or for her benefit in such manner as they shall in their absolute discretion think fit.

(3) Subject as aforesaid my trustees shall hold my residuary estate upon such trusts for the benefit of all or such one or more exclusive of the others or other of my children and remoter issue if more than one in such shares and with such trusts and powers for their respective benefit (including trusts and powers conferring a discretion as to the disposition of capital and income by whomsoever exercisable) and such provisions (including provisions for the accumulation of income during any period permitted by law and administrative provisions of whatever nature) as my trustees may during

the life of my wife by any deed revocable during the life of my wife or irrevocable appoint provided that my trustees may at any time or times and from time to time during the life of my wife by deed or deeds release or restrict the foregoing power either in whole or in part and in any manner they think fit.[3]

(4) Subject as aforesaid my trustees shall hold my residuary estate upon trust for such of my children [*name*] [*name*] [*name*] and [*name*] as shall survive me if more than one in the shares set out below Provided that if any of my said children shall predecease me leaving a child or children surviving me who shall attain the age of [18/21/25] years[4] such last-mentioned child or children shall take and if more than one equally between them the share of my residuary estate which such deceased child of mine would have taken had he or she survived me.

(5) The shares referred to in the last foregoing subclause shall be equal shares provided that—

(a) any child of mine who is or has been entitled to a gift under clause 2 or 3 above shall bring the same into hotchpot as part of his or her share (net of inheritance tax) of my residuary estate and account for the same accordingly;[5]

(b) the value or amount of any gift brought into hotchpot as aforesaid shall be the net value or amount thereof (after deduction of any inheritance tax or other liabilities to which it is subject) at my death[6] and for this purpose my trustees may as soon as practical after my death (whether or not my wife's foregoing life interest takes effect) at the expense of my residuary estate obtain a professional valuation of whatever is taken by either of my said sons under clause 2 above and any such valuation shall be binding on all parties;[7] and

(c) for the avoidance of doubt I declare that if any gift to a child of mine directed to be brought into hotchpot as aforesaid exceeds the value of what would be that child's share if the property comprised in such gift formed part of my residuary estate then he or she shall not be under any obligation to make any repayment or transfer of any part of such gift to my residuary estate or to the other persons interested in my residuary estate and my residuary estate shall be divided among the other persons interested as if that child of mine was not entitled to a share thereof.[8]

(6) The foregoing trusts for grandchildren of mine shall carry the intermediate income of my residuary estate and section 31 of the Trustee Act 1925 (as hereinafter modified) shall apply thereto [provided that in relation to any presumptive share of my residuary estate of any grandchild of mine the said section 31 (amended as aforesaid) shall have effect as if the age of majority were the lesser of the age which he or she will attain (if he or she so long lives) on his or her last birthday occurring not later than the expiration of 21 years from my death and the age of [21/25][9] years (and so that the expressions 'infancy', 'minority' and 'infant' and all references to the age of eighteen years in the said Section 31 shall be construed accordingly)][10].

(7) Section 32 of the Trustee Act 1925 (as hereinafter modified) shall apply in relation to my residuary estate.

1 The gift of residue to the testator's spouse for life is an IPDI to which the spouse exemption can apply (see paras **[200.84]**, **[200.98]**).
2 There are two reasons for restricting the power to capital in which the wife has an interest in possession: first, to ensure that the power is not exercisable if there is a divorce and the primary trust lapses (see the Preliminary Note to C2 on the possibility of divorce at paras **[224.16]**–**[224.23]**); and, second, to ensure that the power ceases to be exercisable if the wife assigns or surrenders her life interest (for an example of the possible importance of the latter point see *IRC v Cookson* [1977] 2 All ER 331, [1977] 1 WLR 962).
3 This enables account to be taken of events occurring during the widow's life, such as the death of children of the testator, high inflation, or a major increase in the value of the business given to the sons. See cl 8 at para **[233.46]** for an expression of wishes as to how this power should be exercised, and the Note at para **[233.36]**.
4 See Form C11.1, cl 4(2), n 4 at para **[233.19]**.
5 It should be noted that the specific gifts do not have substitution clauses, and the testator's children's interests vest on the testator's death both under the specific gifts and the trusts of residue, so that these hotchpot provisions do not need to refer to the position of substituted beneficiaries. There is no hotchpot of interests appointed under the power of appointment.
6 This could clearly be very unfair, particularly if the testator's wife's life interest has taken effect and there has been significant inflation since the testator's death. However, it is not practical to make provision for all the things which might happen between the testator's and the wife's death; instead the arrangements can be varied by exercise of the power of appointment if the trustees can agree during the testator's widow's lifetime on how they should be varied.
7 It is not advisable to provide for the value to be that agreed with the Inland Revenue for probate purposes because if the business property given by cl 2 is subject to 100 per cent business relief, or it is not but the gifts in cls 2 and 3 are clearly within the testator's nil-rate band, the Inland Revenue will not wish to engage in negotiations over the value.
8 This is implicit in a direction for hotchpot, but this is not always readily appreciated and it can save disappointment and argument if it is spelt out expressly.
9 This should be the same as the age of vesting in sub-cl (4).
10 See Form C11.1, cl 4(3), n 6 at para **[233.19]** above.

[233.46]

EXPRESSION OF WISHES CONCERNING POWER OF APPOINTMENT

8. I express the wish without imposing any trust or obligation that my trustees shall exercise their foregoing power of appointment over the capital of my residuary estate as follows—

(a) in the event of the death of any child of mine after my death but before my wife's death so as to substitute the issue of that child if any and otherwise so as to extinguish that child's interest; and

(b) so as to maintain so far as possible equality of benefit among my children—

 (i) if there is any significant increase or decrease after my death in the value of the property given to my sons under clause 2 above not attributable to the efforts or defaults (respectively) of my sons or either of them;

 (ii) if there are high levels of inflation between my death and that of my wife;

 (iii) if a substantial proportion of my residuary estate is paid or applied to or for the benefit of my wife; or

 (iv) if there are any other events or circumstances which might produce an unfair distribution of my residuary estate between my sons and daughters in the absence of any exercise of the said power of appointment.

[233.47]

MAINTENANCE, ACCUMULATION AND ADVANCEMENT

9. [*As in cl 5 of* Form C11.1 *at para* **[233.20]**.]

[233.48]

ADMINISTRATIVE POWERS

10. [*As in cl 6 of* Form C11.1 *at para* **[233.21]**.]

[233.49]

EXERCISE OF POWERS

11. [*As in cl 7 of* Form C11.1 *at para* **[233.22]**.]

[233.50]

TRUSTEE SELF-DEALING, INDEMNITY, AND SIMILAR PROVISIONS

12. [*As in cl 8 of* Form C11.1 *at para* **[233.23]**.]

[233.51]

PROFESSIONAL TRUSTEE CHARGING CLAUSE

13. [*As in cl 9 of* Form C11.1 *at para* **[233.24]**.]

[*Testimonium and attestation clause as in* Form C11.1 *at para* **[233.25]**.]

C12 Wills disposing of farms and farming businesses

Preliminary note .... **[234.1]**
IHT AGRICULTURAL RELIEF .... **[234.1]**
OTHER ASPECTS .... **[234.11]**
FORMS
C12.1: Will of widower giving estate equally between his children, one son being given an option to purchase the farming assets .... **[234.17]**
C12.2: Will of farmer leaving legacies to his daughters, a right of residence in a farm cottage to his wife, and residue to his son if farming at his death, with residue given to the children in equal shares if he is not...... **[234.31]**
C12.3: Will of tenant farmer leaving his farming business either to his wife or his son with residue held on trust for wife for life with remainders to children with substitution of issue .... **[234.45]**

PRELIMINARY NOTE

IHT agricultural relief

[234.1]
Relief from IHT is available under IHTA 1984, Part V, Chapter II, in relation to agricultural property in certain circumstances. For a full discussion of the qualifying conditions the reader is referred to *Foster's Inheritance Tax*, Division G3. An outline of the relief and some notes of points particularly relevant to will-making are provided here. The rules for agricultural relief have many features in common with business relief, as a result of a revision of the agricultural relief rules by the Finance Act 1981 so as to bring them in line with the business relief rules so far as possible. Any agricultural property which is also an asset of a business is likely to satisfy the qualifying conditions for business relief as well, but where both reliefs would confer a reduction in taxable value it is agricultural relief which applies: IHTA 1984, s 114(1). A brief comparison of the scope of the two reliefs—when they overlap, when they do not—appears at para **[234.8]**.

For notes on business relief see the Preliminary Note to B5 at para **[205.1]** ff, and for notes on business and agricultural relief in relation to partially exempt estates, nil-rate band gifts, and gifts to spouses see the Preliminary Note to C11 at para **[233.1]** ff. For testamentary options see B9 at para **[209.1]** ff.

[234.2]
Meaning of agricultural property. This is defined by IHTA 1984, s 115(2) as agricultural land or pasture and as including woodland and any building used in connection with the intensive rearing of livestock or fish if such woodland or building is occupied with agricultural land or pasture and such occupation is ancillary to that of the land or pasture; the definition also includes such cottages, farm buildings and farmhouses and land occupied with them as are of a character appropriate to the property. Other assets which are included expressly or as a matter of Revenue practice are stud

farms (IHTA 1984, s 115(4)), milk quota when given or devolving on death with the land, ponds, land used for short-rotation coppice (IHTA 1984, as amended by Finance Act 1995, s 145), set aside land, and land in a wildlife habitat scheme (IHTA 1984, as amended by the Finance Act 1997, s 124C). In order to qualify for relief, agricultural property must be situated in the UK, the Channel Islands or the Isle of Man (IHTA 1984, s 115(5)).

[234.3]

The inclusion of houses and buildings. The Interpretation Act 1978 defines 'land' to include buildings so far as no contrary intention is expressed, and it applies to IHTA 1984. However, it has been held that the express reference in the IHTA 1984, s 115(2) to cottages, farm buildings and farmhouses of a character appropriate to the property excludes the general definition from applying, so that a house used for agricultural purposes but not owned together with agricultural land did not qualify for relief. The appropriate principles for determining whether a farmhouse is of a character appropriate to the agricultural property were summarised as follows:

'... first, one should consider whether the house is appropriate by reference to its size, content and layout, with the farm buildings and the particular area of farmland being farmed ...; secondly, one should consider whether the house is proportionate in size and nature to the requirements of the farming activities conducted on the agricultural land or pasture in question ...; thirdly that although one cannot describe a farmhouse which satisfies the "character appropriate" test one knows one when one sees it ...; fourthly, one should ask whether the educated rural layman would regard the property as a house with land or a farm ...; and, finally, one should consider the historical dimension and ask how long the house in question has been associated with the agricultural property and whether there was a history of agricultural production ...' (see *Lloyds TSB (personal representatives of Antrobus decd) v IRC* [2002] STC (SCD) 468 at para 48)

The inclusion of farmhouses is an important aspect of the relief; it enables a farmhouse which was occupied by the deceased (or by the transferor in the case of a lifetime transfer) as his residence to qualify for agricultural relief when it could never qualify for business relief, and such a house can represent a significant part of the value of agricultural property. Particularly in the case of substantial houses, it is important to consider the nature of the building in the context of the agricultural property generally. In *Arnander v Customs and Excise Comrs* [2006] STC (SCD) 800 the Special Commissioner held that a seven bedroom Grade 2* listed manor house, owned together with 110 acres of agricultural land failed to attract relief on three grounds: it was not a 'farmhouse', nor 'of a character appropriate to the farmland', nor was it 'occupied for the purposes of agriculture' because the owners had employed a contractor to farm for them because they were too ill to do so themselves.

The following points should be borne in mind:

(1) Severance of the agricultural land from the house, eg by making a lifetime gift of the farmland without the house, is to be avoided where possible because it will cause the relief to cease to be available in relation to the house.
(2) If the amount of agricultural land is perhaps on the low side in relation

to the house for the house to qualify for the relief, buying some extra adjacent land could be a worthwhile investment (it would still have to be occupied for two years or owned for seven years before it counted—see below).

(3) When it comes to making a will, a non-exempt gift of the farmhouse and an exempt gift of the farmland is not a good idea because the house by itself is not agricultural property—a non-exempt gift of the land and an exempt gift of the house would be better, and a non-exempt gift of both even better (from an IHT point of view). See the Preliminary Note to C11 at paras **[233.2]–[233.6]**.

(4) The farmhouse will not qualify for the relief unless it is occupied by someone engaged in agriculture for the required period (see para **[234.4]**). In *Harrold v IRC* [1996] STC (SCD) 195, the Special Commissioners held that the relief did not apply to a farmhouse which was unoccupied and awaiting renovation. A similar problem arises where the farmer has retired, as in *Arnander v HMRC* [2006] STC (SCD) 800.

(5) The relief is restricted to the agricultural value (see para **[234.7]**). Houses which are restricted to agricultural use (for planning purposes) often sell at a discount from the value they would have without the restriction. HMRC have taken to arguing that part of the value of any farmhouse which is not so restricted, typically a third of its value, is not entitled to the relief. They had a victory on this point in *Lloyds TSB Private Banking Plc v Peter Twiddy (Inland Revenue Capital Taxes)*, Lands Tribunal 10/10/2005, where the Lands Tribunal held that the agricultural value qualifying for agricultural relief of a farmhouse was 30 per cent below market value because it was an historic building in an attractive location which had the effect of uplifting its market value beyond what it would be if restricted to occupation for agriculture.

[234.4]

Conditions for relief. The principal condition for relief is that the property shall have been *either* (a) occupied by the deceased (or the transferor in the case of a lifetime transfer) for the purposes of agriculture throughout the period of two years ending with the date of the deceased's death (or the transfer)—it is immaterial whether the property is *owned* throughout the entirety of this period provided that it is owned on the death—*or* (b) owned by him throughout the period of seven years ending with that date *and* occupied throughout that period (whether by the transferor or another) for the purposes of agriculture (see IHTA 1984, s 117). If there has been replacement of one agricultural property by another the period of ownership or occupation of both can be taken into account (IHTA 1984, s 118). If a cottage on a farm is occupied by an employee working on a farm which was farmed (alone or in partnership) by the deceased (or the transferor under a lifetime transfer) that will be regarded as having been occupied by the deceased (or transferor), and by concession the same treatment is given to a cottage occupied by a retired agricultural employee or his or her widow or widower with statutory protection or a contractual equivalent (see *Foster's Inheritance Tax*, G3.11). It was held by the Special Commissioners in *Wheatley (Wheatley's Executors) v IRC* [1998] STC (SCD) 60 that use of a field for grazing by a horse kept for recreational riding was not occupation for an agricultural purpose (see also para **[234.3]** concerning the occupation requirement in relation to farmhouses).

[234.5]
Succession provisions. Section 120(1) of the IHTA 1984 provides (a) that in computing the period of two or seven years a transferor who succeeds to the property on the death of another person is deemed to have owned it and, if he subsequently occupies it, to have occupied it since the death of such other person and (b) that where that other person was his spouse he is deemed to have occupied it for the purpose of agriculture for any period for which it was so occupied by his spouse and to have owned it for any period for which his spouse owned it. Thus if the testator has not occupied or owned his agricultural property (including any it replaced) for long enough to qualify for relief on his death he should give it to his spouse by will, who will be able to carry on where he leaves off in building up a sufficient period of ownership or occupation, and be able to qualify for agricultural relief in relation to the property once the combined period of occupation or ownership by the testator and the testator's spouse is sufficient. Inheritance of the property by the spouse could be made to be contingent on the property not having been owned or occupied long enough to qualify for agricultural relief; compare Form B5.9 (at para **[205.66]**), which is a specific gift of shares contingent on them having been owned long enough to qualify for business relief—such a gift could be a non-exempt gift on failure of which the property subject to it falls into the residuary estate, and be combined with a gift of the residuary estate to the spouse.

HMRC regard the succession provisions in the IHTA 1984, s 120 as applying not only where agricultural property is specifically given, but also where it devolves under a residuary gift. They regard the IHTA 1984, s 91, which deems an interest in possession in a residuary estate to commence at the deceased's death (overriding the rule that strictly speaking no trust arises until the administration is complete), as applying to absolute gifts: see B5 at para **[205.12]**.

As already mentioned, a person's spouse, after succeeding to an agricultural property of that person, will only be able to count periods of occupation or ownership by him or her under the IHTA 1984, s 120(1)(b) where the spouse succeeded to the property on the *death* of the person and not where the spouse succeeded to the property on an inter vivos transfer. However, the IHTA 1984, s 121 provides an additional measure of relief in cases of successive transfers of agricultural property. Under this section where the property was eligible for relief on the earlier transfer (or would have been so eligible had the legislation been in force), relief will usually be available on the subsequent transfer, regardless of the length of the subsequent transferor's period of occupation or ownership, provided that either the earlier or the subsequent transfer was a transfer on death, and that at the time of the subsequent transfer the second transferor or the first transferor's personal representatives are in occupation of the property. The relief afforded by s 121 is general in its operation and is not confined to transfers as between spouses. It does mean, however, that where a person has acquired qualifying agricultural property from his spouse by way of inter vivos transfer and still owns and occupies such property at his death, agricultural relief will be available on his death, even though the requirements of ss 117 and 120 have not been satisfied, provided that at the time of the inter vivos transfer the transferor spouse had owned or occupied the property for long enough to qualify for the relief.

[234.6]

Farming companies. Shares in a farming company of which the testator had control and in which agricultural land is vested can also qualify for agricultural relief to the extent that the value of the shares is attributable to the land: see the IHTA 1984, s 122 and 123 and *Foster's Inheritance Tax*, G3.31–G3.35. If the testator's shareholding is not a controlling one it can qualify for business relief if the company is carrying on a farming business: see B5 at paras **[205.5]–[205.14]** and **[205.29]–[205.31]**.

[234.7]

The relief conferred. When it applies, agricultural relief (like business relief) operates by providing a percentage reduction of the taxable value of the property concerned, but the reduction relates only to the agricultural value, so that if and to the extent that the property has development or hope value it will not get agricultural relief (but might get business relief). HMRC have also taken to arguing that part of the value of many farmhouses is non-agricultural and does not qualify for the relief: see para **[234.3]**. There are two rates of agricultural relief, 100 per cent and 50 per cent. The 100 per cent relief is available under the IHTA 1984, s 116(2)(a) in cases where the interest of the transferor in the property carries the right to vacant possession or the right to obtain it within twelve months. The latter words cover the common situation of land being occupied for less than twelve months under a seasonal grazing licence, and by concession HMRC will treat them as applying to land where there is a right to vacant possession within 24 months, eg because the land is let for a term certain of more than one year and less than two, or a valid notice to quit has been served which takes more than twelve months to expire (see *Foster's Inheritance Tax*, G3.04).

An important extension to relief at the rate of 100 per cent took effect from 1 September 1995 (IHTA 1984, s 116(1)(c), added by Finance Act 1995, s 146): tenanted agricultural land, where the tenancy is granted on or after 1 September 1995, also qualifies for 100 per cent relief. This coincides with the date from which security of tenure under the Agricultural Holdings Act 1986 (AHA 1986) ceased to apply to most kinds of tenancy of agricultural land (Agricultural Tenancies Act 1995, s 4) granted on or after that date. It should be noted that it helps on the *rate* of relief but not on the qualifying conditions; anyone buying agricultural land with a view to letting it will still have to own it for seven years or occupy it for two years before qualifying for any agricultural relief. This 100 per cent relief has been extended to certain cases of tenanted land where, broadly, on or after 1 September 1995 a new tenancy was in the process of coming into existence when the taxpayer died (IHTA 1984, s 116(5A) to (5E), inserted by Finance Act 1996, s 185).

100 per cent agricultural relief is also available for tenanted land in cases where: (i) the transferor has been entitled to his interest since before

10 March 1981; (ii) the interest then qualified for agricultural relief under the now superseded provisions of Finance Act 1975, Sch 8 (as to which see *Foster's Inheritance Tax*, G2); and (iii) the transferor's interest has not at any time since then carried with it the right to vacant possession or to obtain it within twelve months and the transferor has not deliberately failed to obtain such a right: IHTA 1984, s 116(2)(b) and (3).

Section 116(2) of the IHTA 1984 provides that the 50 per cent relief is to apply in all other cases, ie land let on a tenancy granted before 1 September 1995 where the transitional relief just mentioned, for land entitled to relief under the superseded provisions of the Finance Act 1975, Sch 8, does not apply. It may be possible to cause land to become potentially entitled to 100 per cent relief where it is let on a pre-1 September 1995 tenancy by negotiating a surrender of the tenancy and a grant to the tenant of a new tenancy on or after that date: see *Foster's Inheritance Tax*, G3.04. Where land is tenanted but the value of the land for IHT purposes comes out at something close to a vacant possession value, eg where the tenancy is vested in a company wholly owned by the freeholder, or the tenancy is vested in a partnership consisting of the freeholder and his spouse (the spouse's interest being 'related property' within the IHTA 1984, s 161), HMRC will by concession allow 100 per cent relief: see *Foster's Inheritance Tax*, G3.04.

[234.8]

Comparison of agricultural relief and business relief. Where agricultural property is an asset of a business or a farming company, or is used by a partnership or company in which the owner of the land is a partner or shareholder, it will often satisfy the conditions for business relief as well as those for agricultural relief. Where there is such an overlap it is the agricultural relief which prevails; if agricultural relief gives a reduction in value, business relief is excluded from also reducing that value by the IHTA 1984, s 114(1).

Agricultural property in relation to which agricultural relief may apply where business relief would not apply includes: agricultural land which is not farmed by the owner of it, agricultural land owned by a company controlled by an individual where the company does not farm the land, farmhouses, and land farmed by but not owned by a company where the owner of the land does not control the company. Where someone owns agricultural land personally and it is farmed by a partnership in which he is a partner or a company which he controls, it can qualify for agricultural relief at the rate of 100 per cent, while it could only ever qualify for business relief at the rate of 50 per cent.

Agricultural property in relation to which business relief may apply where agricultural relief would not apply includes: a non-controlling shareholding in a farming company, development value in land forming part of the assets of a farming business or farming company, agricultural property which has not been owned or occupied long enough for agricultural relief where it was a replacement of a non-farming business property and the combined period of ownership of both properties is sufficient for business relief, and agricultural property outside the UK, the Channel Islands and the Isle of Man, which forms part of the assets of a farming business or farming company.

[234.9]
Agricultural relief and partially exempt estates. Like business relief, agricultural relief operates so as to reduce the value transferred by the transfer on death before exemptions are taken into account. Section 39A of the IHTA 1984, introduced by Finance Act 1986, s 105, applies where there is agricultural relief on assets comprised in a partially exempt estate (see the Preliminary Note to C11 at paras **[233.2]**–**[233.7]**). Accordingly, where a farmer owning qualifying agricultural property wishes to make provision for a wife and children, he would be well-advised to consider making a specific gift of agricultural property to the children and the balance of the estate to the spouse. This is likely to be considerably cheaper in fiscal terms than the other way round: see the Preliminary Note to C11 at paras **[233.6]**–**[233.10]**. On the other hand, as mentioned at para **[234.5]**, if agricultural property does not qualify for relief because it has not been owned or occupied by the transferor for either of the periods mentioned in the IHTA 1984, s 117, a gift of the property to the testator's spouse could enable the spouse to take advantage of the testator's period of ownership or occupation.

[234.10]
Debts charged on agricultural property. If agricultural property is subject to mortgages or other charges, they will reduce the 'agricultural value' of the property and therefore the amount of the relief: IHTA 1984, s 162(4). It would be of obvious advantage if loans for the purposes of the farming business or any other purposes could be charged or primarily charged on assets other than property qualifying for relief.

Other aspects

[234.11]
Business relief and farming businesses. Agricultural relief is available for land and buildings, and does not apply at all to the other assets of a farming business such as live and dead stock, farm machinery, etc. These may qualify for business relief: see B5 at para **[205.6]** ff for an outline of the conditions for this relief to apply.

[234.12]
Tenant farmers. Where a testator farms agricultural land under an AHA 1986 protected tenancy, he may have the right to designate a successor by will under the AHA 1986, Part IV unless he is a successor himself. These succession provisions, originally introduced in 1976, were abolished in relation to protected tenancies granted on or after 12 July 1984 subject to the limited exceptions referred to in the AHA 1986, s 34(1). But tenants farming under tenancies granted prior to that date continue to be able to designate successors and Form C12.3 contains a clause at para **[234.48]** exercising this right. There are advantages in designating a son or daughter rather than a spouse because only two successions are allowed, and business relief is likely to be wasted if the farming business is given to the spouse. However, the testator's spouse may in practice be the only person who could take over.

[234.13]
Farming partnerships with agricultural tenancies. Situations arise in which a testator who owns agricultural land farms the land in partnership with one

or more other persons under a tenancy granted to the partners. (The grant of an agricultural tenancy for full consideration is not a transfer of value: IHTA 1984, s 16.) The existence of the tenancy is likely to reduce the value of the freehold very considerably. But if the only other partner (and co-tenant) is his spouse, no reduction in value will be achieved for IHT purposes by virtue of the related property provisions contained in the IHTA 1984, s 161: see in particular s 161(2)(a). However, the Revenue will by concession allow 100 per cent agricultural relief on the property (if all the conditions for the relief are met) if the valuation comes out close to vacant possession value.

[234.14]

Woodlands. Woodlands which are not ancillary to agricultural land and which do not therefore qualify for agricultural relief may qualify for the separate relief which is available under the IHTA 1984, Part V, Chapter III for woodlands which have been beneficially owned for five years or acquired by gift: see generally *Foster's Inheritance Tax*, G4. The relief takes the form of a deferment of the charge to IHT on death until the woodlands are sold or given away by inter vivos transfer other than to the donor's spouse. This relief resembles the conditional exemption for works of art etc under the IHTA 1984, ss 30–34 but it is not strictly an exemption within the meaning of the Act, but a right to elect to have the woodlands left out of account in determining the chargeable transfer made on death: see ss 126(1)(a) and 130(1)(a). Since anyone who inherits woodlands which qualify for this relief will himself be qualified for the relief on his death however soon it may occur (see s 125(1)), there are less strong reasons than in the case of business assets or agricultural property for testators avoiding gifts of woodlands which qualify for relief to their spouses. It is advisable for specific gifts of woodlands to be made subject to IHT attributable thereto and payable on the testator's death for the reasons given in B14 at para **[214.67]**.

[234.15]

Where only one or some of the testator's children will carry on with farming. The problem of passing on business/farming assets to the child or children who want to carry on with the business or farming while making fair provision for the other children is discussed in the Preliminary Note to C11 at para **[233.12]**. Forms C12.1 and C12.2 at paras **[234.17]** ff and **[234.31]** ff illustrate two of the possibilities there mentioned.

One further possibility peculiar to farming is that either accidentally or deliberately the child or children who want to carry on with farming may already have an agricultural tenancy with security of tenure under the AHA 1986, or be partners in a partnership which does. Where the testator is the owner of the freehold and is a member of the partnership, the partners other than the testator may have security of tenure as against him or his successors in title: see *Sykes v Land* (1984) 271 Estates Gazette 1264, and *Featherstone v Staples* [1986] 2 All ER 461, [1986] 1 WLR 861. Where the child or children carrying on the farming have such security of tenure the testator can leave his estate in equal shares among his children without disturbing the child's or children's possession of the farm. It should be noted that tenancies granted on or after 1 September 1995 will not in general have security of tenure

(Agricultural Tenancies Act 1995, s 4). If someone who has already acquired an agricultural tenancy over the testator's land then becomes an executor of the testator, he will be under no obligation to the other beneficiaries to sell his tenancy along with the freehold to enable a better price to be obtained: *Sergeant v National Westminster Bank* (1988) 59 P & CR 182.

[234.16]

Checking the nature of the assets. In *Re Lewis's Will Trusts* [1984] 3 All ER 930, [1985] 1 WLR 102, the deceased had made a gift by will of a farm and farming business when what he owned was shares in a private company which owned the farm and business. The gift in the will was held to be ineffective. It is essential to check exactly what the form of the testator's ownership of the farm and farming business is. There are numerous possibilities, including companies and partnerships, and if there is a company or partnership the farmland may be owned by the company or partnership, or by the testator personally, or by him and others personally in a joint tenancy or tenancy in common.

[234.17]

Form C12.1: Will of widower giving estate equally between his children, one son being given an option to purchase the farming assets

Note. This form illustrates one possible solution to the problem of one or some of the testator's children wanting to carry on with the farming business and others not (see the Preliminary Note to C11 at para **[233.12]**). It is assumed that the testator is a widower with two sons ('AB' and 'EF') and a daughter ('CD'), of whom only the son AB has taken up farming and wishes to take over the testator's farmland and farming business. The residuary estate is given in equal shares, but AB is given an option to purchase the farming assets. There is some help given to him in the terms of the option, in particular the price could be directed to be less than market value, and the trustees are empowered to accept payment by instalments carrying low or no interest.

It has been mentioned in the Preliminary Note to C11 at para **[233.6]** that a testamentary option to purchase business or agricultural property might have adverse consequences for the allocation of any available business or agricultural relief where the estate is partially exempt. This problem does not arise where, as here, there are no exempt gifts.

For testamentary options see also B9 at para **[209.1]** ff.

[234.18]

REVOCATION CLAUSE

I [*name*] of [*address*] hereby revoke all former testamentary dispositions made by me and declare this to be my last will.

[234.19]

APPOINTMENT OF EXECUTORS AND TRUSTEES

1. I appoint my son AB ('AB') my daughter CD ('CD') and my son EF ('EF') (hereinafter together called 'my trustees' which expression shall include my personal representatives for the time being and the trustees for the time being hereof) to be the executors and trustees of this will.

[234.20]

GIFTS OF CHATTELS[1]

2. (1) I make the following specific bequests free of tax:[2]

(a) to AB my shot gun;
(b) to CD my late wife's jewellery;
(c) to EF the motor car I shall have at my death (and if I have more than one at my death he may select one of them).

(2) Subject as aforesaid I give all my personal chattels as defined by Section 55(1)(x) of the Administration of Estates Act 1925[3] free of tax[4] to such of AB CD and EF as shall survive me if more than one in equal shares [and I request them (but without imposing any trust or binding obligation) to give effect to any wishes as to the disposition of such chattels which may be contained in any memorandum that may be found amongst my papers at my death or which may have otherwise been communicated to them during my life][5] provided that section 33 of the Wills Act 1837 (as substituted by section 19 of the Administration of Justice Act 1982) shall not apply to the foregoing gift.[6]

1 Gifts are made of specific items, and the remainder of the personal chattels are left to the children who survive the testator. Where all three children of the testator survive him or her, the latter gift will have the same effect as if the chattels had been left to fall into residue, but if a child predeceases the testator the chattels will go to the surviving children. This may introduce an element of unfairness as between families, but it avoids chattels passing to the deceased child's issue', which may well have to be retained and managed by the trustees until such issue attain their majority. It also means that the chattels are at the disposal of persons who are of full age who can (if they can agree among themselves) give away items to relatives and friends of the testator.

2 This is included in case any of the chattels are outside the UK at the testator's death, and thus 'subject to tax' in the absence of a direction to the contrary. See the Preliminary Note to B14 at paras **[214.55]–[214.60]** and the definition of 'free of tax' in cl 5 of this form at para **[234.23]**. If there is no risk of this the words 'free of tax' can be omitted and so can cl 5.

3 See Part G, para **[246.67]** for the wording of this definition, and for further discussion of the meaning of 'personal chattels' see Vol 1, para **[64.44]**.

4 See n 2 to this clause, above.

5 If property bequeathed by a will to one person is distributed to another person within two years of the testator's death, in accordance with wishes expressed by the testator, it is treated for IHT purposes as having been bequeathed by the will to that other person: IHTA 1984, s 143, and see B4 at paras **[204.9]** and **[204.10]**.

6 See Part G, para **[244.36]** for this provision, and Vol 1, paras **[47.15]–[47.20]**. Section 33 would provide substitution of issue for a child who predeceases the testator, and is excluded because it would be impractical to administer a trust for minors of a share of chattels. See also n 1 to this clause.

[234.21]

OPTION FOR ONE OF THE SONS TO PURCHASE FARMING ASSETS[1]

3. (1) In this clause references to my trustees in relation to any time when AB is one of my trustees are references to my trustees other than AB and in relation to any time when there has been no grant of probate to this will are references to such of CD and EF as shall be living.

(2) In this clause 'my farming assets' means and includes such of the following as I may own at my death:

(a) any farm land farm buildings interests in farm land (or in the proceeds of sale thereof) equipment livestock milk quota growing or harvested crops and other assets of any farming business I may be carrying on at my death (other than any motor car hereinbefore specifically given and other than cash or bank accounts);[2]

(b) any assets of the foregoing types owned by me at my death which are of a kind which could be used in a farming business but which at my death are not in such use including any such assets which may be leased or licensed to AB or any other person;

(c) any shares in any company carrying on a farming business or any interest in any partnership carrying a farming business as may be owned by me at my death.[3]

(3) AB shall have an option to purchase my farming assets as set out below.

(4) As soon as practical after my death my trustees shall serve a written notice on AB notifying him of this option and specifying the assets to which it relates. My trustees shall have power to require AB to acquire my farming assets subject to such liabilities of any farming business which shall have been carried on by me or partnership in which I shall have been a partner or such incumbrances or charges to which my farming assets are subject as may be specified in such notice. My trustees shall make available to AB or his agents or advisers all documents of title books of account or other documents in their possession relevant to the decision whether to exercise the option.

(5) To exercise such option AB must serve a notice of exercise of it on my trustees within two months after service on AB of my trustees' said notice. If no notice as aforesaid by my trustees has been served on AB within 18 months of my death AB may serve a notice on my trustees exercising the option without the service of a notice by my trustees on him. AB's said option shall finally cease to be exercisable if no notice of exercise is served on my trustees by AB within two years of my death. A contract to sell and purchase binding on both parties shall arise on service of such notice by AB, subject to the right of rescission on the part of AB set out below and subject to the terms set out below. If land or an interest in land or in the proceeds of sale of land is included in the assets subject to the option the Standard Conditions of Sale in force at the date hereof shall apply so far as consistent with the terms set out herein.

(6) The option price shall be [[70] per cent of the net amount. The net amount shall be][4] the price which my farming assets might reasonably be expected to fetch if sold in the open market[5] [(with vacant possession in the case of any land)][6] at the date of AB's notice exercising the option less the value of such (if any) liabilities or incumbrances as AB's purchase may be subject to (as required by my trustees as provided above).

(7) After service of such notice by AB he and my trustees shall endeavour to agree the amount of the option price. My trustees shall have power to obtain such valuation or other relevant advice as they think fit at the expense of my residuary estate.

(8) If AB and my trustees are unable to agree the option price within two months of the service of such notice either AB or my trustees may at any time after expiry of that period of two months require (by notice served on the other) a reference to an expert (not acting as an arbitrator) to determine the price to be paid.

(9) Such expert shall in default of agreement be appointed by the President of the Royal Institution of Chartered Surveyors. The decision of such expert shall be final, and the costs of his determination and the

procedure adopted for his determination shall be at his discretion (but such costs shall be borne equally between AB and my trustees if no determination as to costs is made by such expert and there is no rescission by AB under the next following subclause).

(10) If the purchase price is determined by an expert as provided above then AB shall be entitled to rescind the agreement to purchase created by the option notice by a written notice served on my trustees within 21 days of AB first knowing the determination of such expert. In the event of such rescission by AB he shall pay or refund to the trustees any reasonable costs they shall have incurred in consequence of his service of the option notice including costs of advice in relation thereto and the costs of the said determination of the price by an expert.

(11) Completion of the said purchase by AB (if there shall be no rescission by AB as aforesaid) shall if the purchase price is fixed by agreement be 21 days after such agreement is reached and otherwise shall be 42 days after the price determined by such expert first becomes known to AB provided that the foregoing periods shall run from the date of first grant of probate or administration to my estate if that occurs after such agreement or determination.

(12) My farming assets shall be transferred or conveyed to AB free from incumbrances save in so far as the purchase is subject to such of the same as are specified in my trustees' said notice. The title to my farming assets deduced by my trustees shall not be open to objection by AB save in respect of matters which he did not know of and could not have known of from documents or information in his or his agents' possession before exercise of the option. On completion AB shall give my trustees a covenant of indemnity against all liabilities or sums charged on my farming assets to which the purchase is subject. AB and my trustees shall bear their own respective costs of such transfers or other assurances of property or covenants as may be required for completion as aforesaid.

(13) AB may require his share of my residuary estate (as defined below) to be offset against the purchase price. If the net value of my residuary estate has not been ascertained at the completion date and AB so requires completion shall be on the basis of my trustees' best estimate of AB's share of my residuary estate subject to further payment by my trustees or repayment by AB when AB's share of my residuary estate comes to be finally ascertained.

(14) My trustees shall have power to agree any terms they think fit for the purchase price to remain outstanding in whole or in part or to be paid in instalments after such completion provided that AB shall agree to complete payment of the purchase price within 10 years of my death and my trustees may renounce their vendor's lien to accept any security they think fit (or no security at all)[7] and shall not be obliged to charge interest at a full market rate or at all on outstanding purchase money or any money which may become repayable when AB's share of my residuary estate is ascertained and shall not be liable for any default of AB or any other adverse consequences of leaving purchase money outstanding.[8]

(15) I express the wish that unless a sale is necessary for carrying out their duties under the administration trusts in clause 4 below my trustees shall postpone the sale of my farming assets at least until the expiry of two

years from my death but no purchaser shall be concerned with the terms of this clause or whether the foregoing circumstances for a sale within two years of my death have arisen. Pending the exercise of AB's said option or the sale of my farming assets in the absence of such option being exercised my trustees may exercise their power hereinafter contained[9] to carry on any farming business comprised in my estate and/or may engage AB to carry on such business or join in carrying on such business on whatever terms they think fit.

(16) Time shall be of the essence of the time limits set out above for exercise of the option to purchase and right of rescission and either AB or my trustees may make time of the essence for completion of the purchase arising from any exercise of the foregoing option after the date for completion set out above has passed by service of at least 14 days' notice to that effect on the other party.

(17) The foregoing rights of AB shall be personal to him and shall not be exercisable by any personal representative or assign of AB or other successor in title of AB provided that if AB having during his lifetime served an effective notice of exercise of the foregoing option shall die before the same shall have been completed his personal representatives shall be obliged and entitled in relation thereto to the same extent as AB would have been if still living.

(18) Section 196 of the Law of Property Act 1925 shall apply to the service of all the foregoing notices.

[(19) Any inheritance tax attributable to the benefit of the foregoing option to AB (making due allowance for any reduction in value for inheritance tax purposes which is attributed thereto) shall be borne by AB in exoneration of my residuary estate.][10]

1 The basic division of the estate is in equal shares under the trusts of residue, but the son AB who wishes to carry on the farming business is given an option to acquire the farming assets under this clause, which can be on terms which have an element of bounty towards him. The option price could be a concessionary one, and provision is made for payment by instalments. His share of residue can be offset against the purchase price. For further discussion and examples of option clauses see B9 at para **[209.1]** ff.

2 There is not much point in the option holder paying cash to purchase cash.

3 Not all these categories will be appropriate and it may often be found that some of them can be omitted. However, it may be preferred to retain them all in case the testator changes his trading arrangements, or retires from active farming but retains ownership of some of the assets, before he dies.

4 This could be some other proportion or could be omitted completely so that he has to pay the full market price. The testator needs to consider how deserving AB is of a discount, how necessary a discount might be to enable him to acquire the assets, and how unfair to the other children such a discount will be. The reason for starting a new sentence in this way where the price is a reduced one is to make clear that the assets are valued and the liabilities are deducted before applying the percentage, as opposed to applying the percentage to the value and then deducting the liabilities in full.

5 It would be unsafe to provide that this should be the value agreed with the Revenue for IHT purposes because if there is 100 per cent agricultural relief and/or business relief the Revenue will not wish to agree a value for the farming assets.

6 If the person given the option is already farming the land, and there is any possibility that there might be an agricultural tenancy, it will be important (to save argument) that the basis of valuation is made clear. A tenanted valuation could alternatively be specified, but if this is done it will be important (if done by reference to a hypothetical tenancy) to specify what sort of tenancy should be assumed and when it should be assumed to have been granted.

Agricultural tenancies granted on or after 1 September 1995 will in general not have security of tenure under the AHA 1986: see the Agricultural Tenancies Act 1995, s 4.

7 If the purchase money is charged on the agricultural assets it will reduce the agricultural relief in the event of AB's death: see the Preliminary Note at para **[234.10]**. A vendor's lien for unpaid purchase money would constitute such a charge, and express waiver would be needed for there not to be such a lien while the purchase money remained outstanding.

8 This is needed in case there are minors interested in a share of residue by virtue of the substitution clause, or not all the persons beneficially interested in residue are executors (for without this subclause the other beneficiaries if of full age could always agree to such terms). If the value at the testator's death is less than the sale price there may be a capital gains tax charge, and if so the tax may be payable in full without any deferment even if the payment of the purchase price is in part deferred. However, if the option price is less than the market value it will be arguable that AB takes as 'legatee', with the result that there is no capital gains tax charge on the exercise of the option by virtue of the Taxation of Chargeable Gains Act 1992, s 62(4).

9 See cl 6(3)(h) of Form C11.1 at para **[233.21]**, incorporated in this form by reference in cl 8 at para **[234.26]**.

10 Assuming the farming assets are in the UK, any IHT attributable to the farming assets will be payable out of residue in the absence of a contrary direction (see B14 at paras **[214.55]**–**[214.60]**). There will be no IHT on the farming assets if they wholly qualify for 100 per cent agricultural relief, but if there is or might be some tax on these assets, and the option terms are beneficial to the option holder, the testator may want him to bear the tax attributable to that benefit. See the Preliminary Note to B9 at paras **[209.1]**–**[209.5]** for further discussion of testamentary options and their taxation and other aspects.

[234.22]

ADMINISTRATION TRUSTS OF RESIDUE

4. (1) I give all my property not hereby or by any codicil hereto otherwise effectively disposed of [(including any entailed or other property over which I shall have at my death a general power of disposition by will)][1] to my trustees to hold on the trusts set out below with power at their discretion to sell all or any of it as and when they think fit.[2]

(2) My trustees shall pay my funeral and testamentary expenses[3] and debts and any legacies given by this will or any codicil hereto out of such property or its proceeds and shall have a discretion as to how such payments shall be borne as between capital and income.[4]

(3) Subject as above my trustees shall hold such property and the assets from time to time representing the same (hereinafter called 'my residuary estate') on the trusts set out below and shall invest all money comprised in such property or arising from its sale in any of the investments hereby authorised with power to change such investments into any others hereby authorised.

(4) In the administration of my estate and the execution of the trusts of this will or of any codicil to it:

(a) my trustees shall treat all income as accruing on the date on which it becomes payable regardless of the period in respect of which it shall have accrued and shall not make any statutory apportionment of the same;[5] and

(b) none of the equitable rules of apportionment between capital and income shall apply in any circumstances whatever.[6]

1 See n 1 to cl 4 of Form C8.1 at para **[230.7]**.
2 See n 2 to cl 4 of Form C8.1 at para **[230.7]**.
3 See n 3 to cl 4 of Form C8.1 at para **[230.7]**.
4 See n 4 to cl 4 of Form C8.1 at para **[230.7]**.

5 See B14 at paras **[214.48]–[214.52]** for statutory apportionment of income over time and its exclusion.
6 See n 6 to cl 4 of Form C8.1 at para **[230.7]**.

[234.23]

GIFTS MADE FREE OF TAX

5. Any specific gift or pecuniary or general legacy made by this will or any codicil hereto which is expressed to be 'free of tax' shall be free from the payment of any inheritance tax or foreign tax or duty payable on or by reason of my death to which such gift or legacy would otherwise be subject and such inheritance tax or foreign tax or duty shall be paid out of my residuary estate.[1]

1 See n 3 to cl 4 of Form C8.1 at para **[230.7]** and n 2 to cl 2 of this form at para **[234.20]**. Where specific gifts and pecuniary legacies are of, or wholly payable out of, free estate in the UK, the IHT on them will be a testamentary expense payable out of residue without any express provision, and it is only where a specific gift or pecuniary legacy is foreign or settled property, or wholly or partly payable out of such property, and intended to be free of tax, that it needs to be expressly declared to be free of tax. See also B14 at paras **[214.55]–[214.60]**.

[234.24]

BENEFICIAL TRUSTS OF RESIDUE

6. (1) My trustees shall hold my residuary estate upon trust for such of my children AB CD and EF as shall survive me and if more than one in equal shares.

(2) Provided that if any of my said children shall predecease me leaving issue surviving me who shall attain the age of 18 years[1] such issue shall take through all degrees according to their stocks in equal shares if more than one the share of my residuary estate which such deceased child of mine would have taken had he or she survived me and so that no issue shall take whose parent (being such issue as aforesaid) survives me and attains the said age.[2]

(3) The trusts declared by the foregoing subclause shall carry the intermediate income of my residuary estate and section 31 of the Trustee Act 1925 (as hereinafter modified) shall apply thereto.

(4) Section 32 of the Trustee Act 1925 (as hereinafter modified) shall apply in relation to the said trusts.

1 Since the eligible issue are all ascertained at the testator's death, they will all be lives in being for perpetuity purposes and the vesting age for their interests need not therefore be limited to 18. However, the requirement in relation to all substituted issue that they be living at the testator's death means that where, for example, a child of the testator predeceases him, leaving a child who survives the testator but dies under the vesting age leaving a child of his who was born after the death of the testator, the latter will not take a share. The greater the age of vesting, the greater is the risk of this happening. An alternative which avoids this risk is for there to be no age contingency, so that the shares of the substituted beneficiaries vest absolutely at the testator's death even if they are under the age of 18: see cl 8 of Form C3.7, at para **[225.119]** for an example. If on the other hand it is preferred to take this risk and have an age of vesting greater than 18, then the accumulation and maintenance trusts of income in Trustee Act 1925 s 31 should be extended so far as possible to the vesting age: see cl 4(3) of Form C11.1 at para **[233.19]**.

The IHT consequences are that if there is an age contingency (and there are extended accumulation and maintenance trusts of income where that age is greater than 18), and the testator dies when the substitution clause has taken effect and any substituted beneficiary is under the age of vesting, the IHT relevant property rules (see para **[218.8]** ff) will apply until the age of vesting is reached. If there is no age contingency, the share of any substituted beneficiary who is under 18 at the time of the testator's death will be held on a bare trust for that beneficiary (see para **[200.110]**). The contingent gift to grandchildren cannot take effect as a trust for bereaved minors or an age 18-to-25 trust (see paras **[200.98]**, **[200.99]**).

2 The wording of the substitutional proviso is based on the wording of the statutory trusts contained in the AEA 1925, s 47(1)(i) (Part G, para **[244.63]**). A substitutional proviso which is limited to children may be more appropriate to the testator's family circumstances in which case cl 7(2) of Form C4.3 at para **[226.65]** may be adopted instead.

[234.25]

MAINTENANCE ADVANCEMENT AND ACCUMULATION

7. [*As in cl 5 of* Form C11.1 *at para* **[233.20]**.]

[234.26]

ADMINISTRATIVE POWERS[1]

8. [*As in cl 6 of* Form C11.1 *at para* **[233.21]**.]

1 The powers in cl 6 of Form C11.1 include power to carry on a business (see sub-cl (3)(h)), which would enable the executors to carry on the farming business.

[234.27]

EXERCISE OF POWERS

9. [*As in cl 7 of* Form C11.1 *at para* **[233.22]**.]

[234.28]

TRUSTEE SELF-DEALING, INDEMNITY, AND SIMILAR PROVISIONS

10. [*As in cl 8 of* Form C11.1 *at para* **[233.23]**.]

[234.29]

PROFESSIONAL TRUSTEE CHARGING CLAUSE

11. [*As in cl 9 of* Form C11.1 *at para* **[233.24]**.]

[234.30]

TESTIMONIUM AND ATTESTATION CLAUSE

SIGNED by the above-named testator as his last will in the presence of us both present at the same time who at his request and in his presence and in the presence of each other have signed our names below as witnesses: } [*Signature of testator*]

[*Signatures, addresses and descriptions of two witnesses*]

[234.31]

Form C12.2: Will of farmer leaving legacies to his daughters, a right of residence in a farm cottage to his wife, and residue to his son if farming at his death, with residue given to the children in equal shares if he is not

Note. This form illustrates another possible solution to the problem of one or some of the testator's children wanting to carry on with the farming business and others not (see the Preliminary Note to C11 at para **[233.12]**). It is assumed that the testator has a wife, a son, and two daughters, and that the son works on the farm (in partnership with the testator or otherwise) but the daughters do not. If the son is working on the farm at the testator's death he is given the residuary estate, which will include the farming assets owned by the testator apart from the cottage for the wife mentioned further below, and the daughters are given legacies, which will in practice be paid by the son and which he can be given time to pay. One of the farm cottages is given to the trustees to be held on trust as a residence for the testator's wife, which after her death or ceasing to reside falls into residue. Although this involves some waste of agricultural relief, it is thought that, because the cottage taken by itself is not agricultural property, the agricultural relief attributable to the cottage will be spread rateably between the exempt and non-exempt parts of the estate rather than concentrated entirely on the cottage: see the Preliminary Note to C11 at paras **[233.2]–[233.6]**. The hope is that the wife may have sufficient savings and pension entitlement for her support after the testator's death, and, if not, that the son will take her into partnership in the farming business and pay her some income from the farm profits. Although the cottage will form part of the wife's estate on death (if she has not by then given up residence) and will not qualify for agricultural relief on her death, her estate may be within the nil-rate band or may not much exceed it. The form can be adapted for use by civil partners if the words 'civil partner' are substituted for 'wife' throughout. As with other will forms adapted for use by civil partners, the references to the testator's children may have to be amended as appropriate. Care should be taken with the references to the various children throughout because of GRA 2004. See Vol 1 para **[81.1]**.

[234.32]

REVOCATION CLAUSE

I [*name*] of [*address*] hereby revoke all former testamentary dispositions made by me and declare this to be my last will.

[234.33]

APPOINTMENT OF EXECUTORS AND TRUSTEES

1. I appoint my wife [*name*] ('my wife') my son [*name*] and my daughters [*name*] and [*name*] (hereinafter together called 'my trustees' which expression shall include my personal representatives for the time being and the trustees for the time being hereof) to be the executors and trustees of this will.

[234.34]

GIFTS OF CHATTELS

2. (1) If my wife shall survive me I give her absolutely all my personal chattels as defined by section 55(1)(x) of the Administration of Estates Act 1925.[1]

(2) If my wife shall predecease me I give all my personal chattels as defined as aforesaid free of tax[2] to such of my said children as shall survive me if more than one in equal shares provided that section 33 of the Wills Act 1837 (as substituted by section 19 of the Administration of Justice Act 1982) shall not apply to the foregoing gift.[3]

(3) I request my wife or children who become entitled to my personal chattels under either of the foregoing gifts (but without imposing any trust or binding obligation) to give effect to any wishes as to the disposition of such chattels which may be contained in any memorandum that may be found amongst my papers at my death or which may have otherwise been communicated to her or them during my life.[4]

1 See Part G, para **[246.67]** for the wording of this definition, and for further discussion of the meaning of 'personal chattels' see Vol 1, para **[64.44]**.

2 This is included in case any of the chattels are outside the UK at the testator's death, and thus 'subject to tax' in the absence of a direction to the contrary. See B14 at paras **[214.55]–[214.60]** and the definition of 'free of tax' as incorporated by reference in cl 6 of this form at para **[234.38]**. If there is no risk of this the words 'free of tax' can be omitted and so can cl 6.

3 See Part G, para **[244.36]** for this provision, and Vol 1, paras **[47.15]–[47.20]**. Section 33 would provide substitution of issue for a child who predeceases the testator, and is excluded because it would be impractical to administer a trust for minors of a share of chattels.

4 If property bequeathed by a will to one person is distributed to another person within two years of the testator's death in accordance with wishes expressed by the testator, it is treated for IHT purposes as having been bequeathed by the will to that other person: IHTA 1984, s 143; see also B4 at paras **[204.9]–[204.10]**.

[234.35]

RIGHT OF RESIDENCE FOR WIFE[1]

3. (1) I give — Cottage [*address*] to my trustees free of all sums charged thereon or otherwise secured thereon at my death (which sums shall be paid out of my residuary estate)[2] to hold the same upon trust to provide a residence for my wife so long as she wishes to reside there.

(2) I declare that my trustees shall not be liable for lack of insurance repair or payment of outgoings or for not taking any steps to enforce any reasonable conditions[3] imposed by my trustees on my wife in relation to her occupation of my said cottage.

(3) On the death of my wife or in the event of her ceasing to reside in my said cottage my trustees shall hold the said cottage as part of my residuary estate as hereinafter defined.

(4) For the purposes of this clause no involuntary ceasing by my wife to reside in the said cottage shall be treated as ceasing to reside therein unless my wife shall have been out of residence continuously for six months and shall not have expressed in writing to my trustees her intention to take up residence again.

1 See the Note to this form at para **[234.31]**. This is a simple form of residence trust which permits the wife to reside only in the specified property held at the testator's death. In the event of her death or earlier ceasing to reside, it will fall into residue. For a more elaborate form which enables a replacement property to be purchased for her to live in, see Forms B8.1 and B8.2 at paras **[208.38]** and **[208.39]**. For a discussion of rights of residence see the Preliminary Note to B8 at paras **[208.1]–[208.37]**. The gift should be exempt from IHT on the basis that the widow has an IPDI (see para **[200.98]**) under these trusts. If her right to reside ceases during her lifetime so that the property falls into residue, and the substitution clause in cl 7(2) has not taken effect, her interest in possession in the same will terminate in favour of absolute interests of the son or son and daughter, with the result that she will be deemed to make a potentially exempt transfer of the property (see paras **[200.71]**, **[200.102]**). If the substitution clause has taken effect, and any of the substituted beneficiaries are under the age of vesting when her interest in possession terminates, there will be an immediately chargeable transfer (see para **[200.71]**, **[200.102]**). If her right continues until

her death, the property will be treated as part of her estate for IHT purposes transfer (see Part A, para **[200.102]** for the IHT consequences of a beneficiary-taxed interest in possession).

2 Where property specifically given is charged with the payment of money, then in the absence of a contrary intention expressed in the will, the property is primarily liable for the payment of the moneys so charged as between the persons claiming through the deceased: AEA 1925, s 35 (Part G, see para **[246.62]**).

3 By virtue of the TLATA 1996, s 13(3), (5) (Part G, para **[246.116]**), the trustees will be able to impose reasonable conditions on the wife's occupation, e g that she pay outgoings or assume other obligations such as insurance and repair.

[234.36]

PECUNIARY LEGACIES FOR DAUGHTERS

4. (1) If the gift of the whole of my residuary estate in favour of my son set out below shall take effect I give to each of my said daughters who shall survive me free of tax[1] the sum of [£50,000].

(2) Provided that if either of my said daughters shall predecease me leaving a child or children surviving me who shall attain the age of 18 years[2] such last-mentioned child or children shall take and if more than one equally between them the legacy which such deceased daughter of mine would have taken had she survived me.

(3) My trustees shall have power to assent to the vesting of the assets comprised in my residuary estate (as defined below) in my son before the foregoing legacies are paid or satisfied in full or at all and whether or not they have so assented my trustees may agree with my son any terms they think fit for deferment of the payment of the said legacies for up to [10] years from my death and my trustees may accept any security they think fit (or no security at all)[3] shall not be obliged to require interest to be paid at a full market rate or at all on any outstanding legacies and shall not be liable for any default of AB or any other adverse consequences of leaving payment of such legacies outstanding.[4]

1 The pecuniary legacies are declared to be 'free of tax' in case the residuary estate out of which they are payable includes property of a kind which bears its own tax, such as foreign property or settled property, with the consequence that without this express provision the legacies might, at least to some extent, have to bear their own tax. See B14 at paras **[214.55]–[214.60]**. The definition of 'free of tax' will be in cl 6 of this form. There is no IHT advantage in making the legacies subject to tax because residue is not exempt (contrast cl 4 of Form C11.3 at para **[233.42]**).

2 If the age of vesting is greater than 18 years, there is more risk of a grandchild dying after the death of the testator under the age of vesting and leaving children who do not benefit. If on the other hand it is preferred to take that risk and have an age of vesting greater than 18, then the accumulation and maintenance trusts of income in Trustee Act 1925, s 31 should be extended so far as possible to the vesting age: see cl 4(3) of Form C11.1 at para **[232.19]**. For the IHT consequences see Form C12.1, cl 6, n 1, at para **[234.24]**. The grandchildren will be lives in being at the testator's death for perpetuity purposes, so that there is no risk of infringing the rule against perpetuities in specifying a vesting age exceeding 21.

3 If the legacies are charged on the agricultural assets it will reduce the agricultural relief in the event of the son's death: see para **[234.10]**.

4 These powers are conferred expressly in case there are minors interested in one or both of the legacies or the daughters may not be willing to leave the legacies outstanding unless obliged to do so. If the farmland is subjected to a charge to secure the payment of the legacies in regular instalments over a fixed period there is a risk that this will cause the farmland to be settled property for IHT purposes (IHTA 1984, s 43(2)(c)) and that, if no interest is paid on the legacies, it might be argued that the son then has an interest in possession in the entire property which is partially terminated on the payment of any

instalment of the legacies (see Part A, para **[200.102]** for the IHT consequences of the termination of an interest in possession). It will be better either to have a personal covenant, or a charge for payment of a single sum on a particular date.

[234.37]

ADMINISTRATION TRUSTS OF RESIDUE

5. [*As in cl 4 of* Form C12.1 *at para* **[234.22]**.]

[234.38]

GIFTS MADE FREE OF TAX

6. [*As in cl 5 of* Form C12.1 *at para* **[234.23]**.]

[234.39]

BENEFICIAL TRUSTS OF RESIDUE

7. (1) If my son shall survive me and shall at my death be employed in agricultural work or engaged in a farming business on any land comprised in my residuary estate my trustees shall hold my residuary estate on trust for my son [*name*] absolutely if he shall survive me.

(2) Subject as aforesaid my trustees shall hold my residuary estate upon trust for such of my son and my said daughters as shall survive me if more than one in equal shares provided that if any of my said son or daughters shall predecease me leaving a child or children surviving me who shall attain the age of 18 years[1] such last-mentioned child or children shall take and if more than one equally between them the share of my residuary estate which such deceased son or daughter of mine would have taken had he or she survived me.

1 See Form 12.1, cl 6, n 1, at para **[234.24]** and cl 4 of this form, n 2, at para **[234.36]**.

[234.40]

MAINTENANCE ADVANCEMENT AND ACCUMULATION

8. [*As in cl 5 of* Form C11.1 *at para* **[233.20]**.]

[234.41]

ADMINISTRATIVE POWERS[1]

9. [*As in cl 6 of* Form C11.1 *at para* **[233.21]**.]

1 The powers in cl 6 of Form C11.1 include power to carry on a business (see sub-cl (3)(h)), which would enable the executors to carry on the farming business.

[234.42]

EXERCISE OF POWERS

10. [*As in cl 7 of* Form C11.1 *at para* **[233.22]**.]

[234.43]

TRUSTEE SELF-DEALING, INDEMNITY, AND SIMILAR PROVISIONS

11. [*As in cl 8 of* Form C11.1 *at para* **[233.23]**.]

[234.44]

PROFESSIONAL TRUSTEE CHARGING CLAUSE

12. [*As in cl 9 of* Form C11.1 *at para* **[233.24]**.]

[*Testimonium and attestation clause as in* Form C12.1 *at para* **[234.30]**.]

[234.45]

Form C12.3: Will of tenant farmer leaving his farming business either to his wife or his son with residue held on trust for wife for life with remainders to children with substitution of issue

REVOCATION CLAUSE

I [*name*] of [*address*] hereby revoke all former testamentary dispositions made by me and declare this to be my last will.

[234.46]

APPOINTMENT OF EXECUTORS AND TRUSTEES

1. [*As in cl 1 of* Form C12.2 *at para* **[234.33]**.]

[234.47]

GIFTS OF CHATTELS

2. [*As in cl 2 of* Form C12.2 *at para* **[234.34]**.]

[234.48]

BEQUEST OF FARMING BUSINESS AND NOMINATION OF SUCCESSOR TO TENANCY[1]

Either

[3. (1) I give to my wife my tenancy of —— Farm [*address*] and the assets of the farming business carried on by me thereat including live and dead stock agricultural equipment book debts growing crops milk quota and the money (if any) standing to the credit of my farm current [and business reserve] account[s] but [excluding any motor car and] subject to all debts and liabilities of my said business at my death [and for the purposes of Part IV of the Agricultural Holdings Act 1986 I designate my wife as the person whom I desire to succeed me as tenant of the said holding.[2]]

(2) If my wife shall predecease me then I give [and designate] as provided in the last preceding subclause in favour of my son [*name*] in place of my wife and as if the last foregoing subclause were written out again with references to my said son substituted for references to my wife.

(3) If the foregoing gift to my son [*name*] takes effect and there is any inheritance tax payable on my estate by reason of my death which is attributable to the foregoing gift (after allowing for any reduction in value for inheritance tax purposes which is attributed thereto) then such gift shall be subject to such inheritance tax and it shall be borne by my said son in exoneration of the rest of my estate.[3]]

Or

[3. (1) I give to my son [*name*] my tenancy of —— Farm [address] and the assets of the farming business carried on by me thereat including live and dead stock agricultural equipment book debts growing crops milk quota and the money (if any) standing to the credit of my farm current [and business reserve] account[s] but [excluding any motor car and] subject to all debts and liabilities of my said business at my death [and for the purposes of Part IV of the Agricultural Holdings Act 1986 I designate my said son as the person whom I desire to succeed me as tenant of the said holding.[4]]

(2) If there is any inheritance tax payable on my estate by reason of my death which is attributable to the foregoing gift to my said son (after allowing for any reduction in value for inheritance tax purposes which is attributed thereto) then the foregoing gift shall be subject to such inheritance tax and it shall be borne by my said son in exoneration of the rest of my estate.[5]]

1 This provides two alternatives: (i) a gift of the farming business to the testator's wife and designation of her as tenant (with alternative gift and nomination in favour of the son) or (ii) a gift of the business to and designation as successor of the son. There may be practical reasons why it is necessary for the farming business to go to the wife, but where it is practical there are two good reasons for the gift and designation being in favour of the son: (a) there can only be two successions to the agricultural tenancy; and (b) the business relief on the farming business (and agricultural relief on the tenancy if it has a value) will be wasted if the business is given to the wife (see the Preliminary Note to C11 at para **[233.3]**).

2 Where a testator farms agricultural land under an AHA 1986 protected tenancy granted before 12 July 1984 (or after that date in exceptional cases referred to in s 34(1)), he may have the right to designate a successor by will. To be effective a designation of a successor must specifically mention the holding, and must exclusively designate one person; different persons may be designated to be the successor in different circumstances, so long as the result is the designation of one person in the events which happen: AHA 1986, s 40(1) and (2). There will normally only be a right to succession to the tenancy if it was granted before 12 July 1984.

3 There should be no IHT on the gift because of 100 per cent business relief (see B5 at paras **[205.22]**–**[205.28]**), but for the circumstances in which tax may be paid on such property see B5 at para **[205.51]**. Making this gift subject to tax rather than free of it will have the effect, if the residuary gift is exempt and there is any IHT payable on this gift, that the amount of IHT payable will be much reduced: see B14 at para **[214.74]**. It would also be possible to exclude 'excepted assets' from the gift: see the Preliminary Note to B5 at para **[205.9]**, on excepted assets, and Form B5.4 at para **[205.61]**, for an example.

Another reason for making the gift subject to tax, even where the residuary gift is not exempt, is that it enables the administration of residue to be completed more quickly, since the IHT on the gift is likely to be payable by instalments (see the Preliminary Note to B5 at paras **[205.17]**–**[205.20]**) and part of residue might have to be retained for some time to pay the tax if it is payable out of residue.

4 See n 1 and 2, above.

5 See n 3, above.

[234.49]

ADMINISTRATION TRUSTS OF RESIDUE

4. [*As in cl 4 of* Form C12.1 *at para* **[234.22]**.]

[234.50]

GIFTS MADE FREE OF TAX

5. [*As in cl 5 of* Form C12.1 *at para* **[234.23]**.]

[234.51]

BENEFICIAL TRUSTS OF RESIDUE

6. (1) My trustees shall hold my residuary estate upon trust to pay the income thereof to my wife during her life.

(2) Provided that my trustees shall have power in their absolute discretion from time to time so long as my wife is entitled to be paid the income of all or any part of the capital of my residuary estate (or would be so entitled if such capital yielded income) to pay transfer or apply the whole or any part or parts of such capital[1] to her or for her benefit in such manner as they shall in their absolute discretion think fit.

(3) Subject as aforesaid my trustees shall hold my residuary estate upon trust for such of my children [*name*] [*name*] and [*name*] as shall be living at the death of the survivor of myself and my wife if more than one in equal shares Provided that if any of my said children shall die before the death of the survivor of myself and my wife leaving issue living at the death of the survivor of myself and wife who attain the age of 18[2] years such issue shall take and if more than one in equal shares per stirpes the share of my residuary estate which such deceased child of mine would have taken had he or she survived to attain a vested interest but so that no such issue shall take whose parent (being such issue as aforesaid) is living at the death of the survivor of myself and my wife and attains the said age.[3]

(4) The foregoing trusts of capital shall carry the intermediate income and section 31 of the Trustee Act 1925 (as hereinafter modified) shall apply thereto.

(5) Section 32 of the Trustee Act 1925 (as hereinafter modified) shall apply in relation to the foregoing trusts of capital.

1 There are two reasons for restricting the power to capital in which the spouse has an interest in possession: first, to ensure that the power is not exercisable if there is a divorce and the primary trust lapses and, secondly, to ensure that the power ceases to be exercisable if the spouse assigns or surrenders his or her life interest. See C2 on the possibility and effects of divorce at paras **[224.16]**–**[224.23]**. The gift of residue to the testator's spouse for life is an IPDI to which the spouse exemption applies.

2 See Form C12.1, cl 6, n 1, at para **[234.24]**.

3 In most remainder trusts of this type in the complete forms in Part C the interests of the primary class of beneficiaries vest on the death of the testator, and are not contingent on surviving the life tenant. This clause is an exception. Early vesting has the advantage that it makes it easier for the parties to rearrange or break the trusts, if they so desire, but the disadvantage that the estate of a child who predeceases the life tenant will take his or her share, which may thus pass to that child's widow or widower rather than to his or her issue. The inflexibility of the interests being contingent on surviving the life tenant is mitigated to some extent in this clause by the presence of a wide power of advancement.

[234.52]

MAINTENANCE, ACCUMULATION AND ADVANCEMENT

7. [*As in cl 5 of* Form C11.1 *at para* **[233.20]**.]

[234.53]

ADMINISTRATIVE POWERS

8. [*As in cl 6 of* Form C11.1 *at para* **[233.21]**.]

[234.54]

EXERCISE OF POWERS

9. [*As in cl 7 of* Form C11.1 *at para* **[233.22]**.]

[234.55]

TRUSTEE SELF-DEALING, INDEMNITY, AND SIMILAR PROVISIONS

10. [*As in cl 8 of* Form C11.1 *at para* **[233.23]**.]

[234.56]

PROFESSIONAL TRUSTEE CHARGING CLAUSE

11. [*As in cl 9 of* Form C11.1 *at para* **[233.24]**.]

[*Testimonium and attestation clause as in* Form C12.1 *at para* **[234.30]**.]

C13 Wills for owners of substantial property

Preliminary note .... [235.1]
FORMS
C13.1 Will of owner of substantial property with no immediate family containing specific gift of controlling shareholding in family company on trusts for the employees and leaving residue on charitable trusts .... [235.2]
C13.2 Will of a bachelor landowner settling the principal family estate together with a share of residue on one nephew and his issue, creating a maintenance fund for the upkeep of the mansion house and settled chattels and settling substantial legacies on two nieces and their issue .... [235.18]

PRELIMINARY NOTE

[235.1]
The two forms in this section are very different in character and both contain unusual features. The principal features of the first form are the gift of family company shares on trusts for the benefit of the employees and the settlement of residue on charitable trusts. The implications of these gifts are more fully explained in the Note preceding the form and in the footnotes to it. The principal feature of the second form is the inclusion of a settled gift of a landed estate with a maintenance fund for the restoration and upkeep of the mansion house and its contents. Formerly a strict settlement would have been an appropriate vehicle, but strict settlements can no longer be created: see Part A, para **[200.52]**; entailed interests have suffered the same fate: see Part A, para **[200.53]**. No form for a strict settlement is therefore included in this edition but Form C13.2, in particular cl 6 of it at para **[200.52]**, is intended to fulfil the same function by providing one or more life interests for persons in the line of succession who are living at the testator's death. However, the changes made by FA 2006 mean that after the initial life interest, which will be a beneficiary-taxed IPDI (see para **[200.98]**), any subsequent trusts which have effect before an absolute interest is attained will be subject to the relevant property regime (see para **[218.8]** ff). Unless the entire estate will be entitled to 100 per cent agricultural relief, or the nephew who is the first beneficiary in line of succession is likely to live on for a long time after the death of the testator, a discretionary trust commencing at the testator's death, together with a letter of wishes, is likely to pay less IHT than one which gives the first life tenant an IPDI to begin with (see also para **[200.131]**).

[235.2]

Form C13.1: Will of owner of substantial property with no immediate family containing specific gift of controlling shareholding in family company on trusts for the employees and leaving residue on charitable trusts

Note. The particular features of this form are (i) a specific gift of private company shares on trusts for the benefit of the company's employees and (ii) a gift of residue on charitable trusts. A detailed account of the law relating to employee trusts is beyond the scope of this work and reference should be made to *Foster's Inheritance Tax*, E6.31. The position briefly is that where settled property is held on discretionary trusts (whether indefinite or for a fixed period) for the benefit of all or most of the persons employed by or holding office with a body carrying on a trade or undertaking and their dependants (and whether or not those trusts also permit the settled property to be applied for charitable purposes), then such property is exempt from the periodic and exit charges applicable under the code for discretionary trusts contained in the Inheritance Tax Act 1984 (IHTA 1984), Part III, Ch III, and an interest in possession in any part not exceeding five per cent of the settled property will be disregarded: see the IHTA 1984, ss 58(1)(b) and 86(1), (2), (3)(a) and (4)(b). Following FA 2006, settled property to which IHTA 1984, s 86 applies will be relevant property if an interest in possession subsists in that property, and either:

(1) an individual became beneficially entitled to the interest in possession on or after 22 March 2006, and the interest is not an IPDI, a disabled person's interest, or a transitional serial interest (IHTA 1984, s 58(1B)); or
(2) a company, the business of which consists wholly or mainly in the acquisition of interests in settled property, is beneficially entitled to the interest in possession, having acquired the interest for full consideration in money or money's worth from an individual who became beneficially entitled to it on or after 22 March 2006, and immediately before the company acquired the interest, the interest in possession was neither an IPDI nor a transitional serial interest (IHTA 1984, s 58(1C)).

Additionally, if an individual settles shares in a company on employee trusts within s 86, then provided that the class of beneficiaries includes all or most of the persons employed by or holding office with the company and the shares comprised in the gift represent more than half the ordinary shares in the company and yield more than half the votes on all questions affecting the company as a whole, the initial gift will also be exempt: IHTA 1984, s 28. However, for this section to apply no part of the settled property should be capable of being applied for the benefit of any person who is at the date of the gift or has at any time thereafter or within the period of ten years immediately preceding the gift been a 'participator' in the company (or in any close company which settles property on the trusts by a disposition which is not a transfer of value by reason of s 13): s 28(4). (For this purpose a 'participator' is a person who is entitled to or entitled to acquire not less than five per cent of or of any class of the company's issued share capital or who is entitled on a winding up to not less than five per cent of its assets: s 28(5).) The specific gift of private company shares contained in this form is intended for use by a testator who not only wishes to make provision for the company employees but who has a controlling shareholding and is therefore in a position to do so by way of exempt transfer.

As the law stands, the gift of a controlling holding in a company (not being an investment company) would also attract 100 per cent business property relief under the IHTA 1984, ss 104(1)(a) and 105(1)(b) and (3). But it should be noted that by virtue of s 112 this relief (unlike the exemption under s 28) does not extend to the value of 'excepted assets' (as to which see the Preliminary Note to B5 at para **[205.9]**) and that the relief may quite possibly be reduced by a future government, whereas the exception for employee trusts is less likely to be affected.

The form also contains a charitable gift of residue which confers power on the trustees to form a new charitable company or trust and to transfer the assets comprised in residue to such new body.

[235.3]

REVOCATION CLAUSE

I [*name*] of [*address*] hereby revoke all former testamentary dispositions made by me and declare this to be my last will.

[235.4]

APPOINTMENT OF EXECUTORS AND TRUSTEES

1. I appoint [*name*] of [*address*] [*name*] of [*address*] and [*name*] of [*address*] (hereinafter together called 'my trustees' which expression shall include my

personal representatives for the time being and the trustees for the time being hereof) to be the executors and trustees of this will.

[235.5]

PECUNIARY LEGACIES

2. I give the following pecuniary legacies free of tax[1]—
   (a) to [*name*] the sum of £——;
   (b) to [*name*] the sum of £——;
   (c) to [*name*] the sum of £——.

1 IHT on assets situate in the UK, whether real or personal, is a testamentary expense and accordingly payable out of residue without express provision: IHTA 1984, s 211 (Part G, para **[246.100]** and see the Preliminary Note to B14 at paras **[214.55]**–**[214.58]**). The legacies are expressly declared to be 'free of tax' (a formula defined in cl 7 at para **[235.10]** in order to cater for the risk that residue includes property which bears its own tax, e g foreign property, in which event the legacies would be liable to contribute to the tax on such property unless expressly exonerated from it: see the notes to cls 6(1) and 7 at paras **[235.9]** and **[235.10]** and to Form C8.1, cl 4 at para **[230.7]**.

[235.6]

SPECIFIC GIFTS

3. I make the following specific gifts free of tax[1]—
   (a) to [*name*] all my vintage cars;
   (b) to [*name*] my guns and fishing tackle;
   (c) to [*name*] all my books and papers;
   (d) to [*name*] my sailing boat known as [*name of boat*].

1 See the preceding note. In the ordinary case a specific gift of personal chattels will devolve free of tax. The 'free of tax' formula is included in case any personal chattels, e g the sailing boat, happens to be situate out of the UK (e g the Channel Islands which are not part of the UK) at the testator's death and also to exclude any argument that the use of the 'free of tax' formula elsewhere in the will and its absence in the specific gift of the personal chattels implies that the chattels bear their own tax: cf *Re Phuler's Will Trusts* [1964] 2 All ER 948, [1965] 1 WLR 68.

[235.7]

GIFT OF COMPANY SHARES TO SEPARATE TRUSTEES ON EMPLOYEE TRUSTS

4. (1) I give free of tax[1] to [*name*] [and] [*name*] [and [*name*]][2] all my shares in my family company known as [*name of company*][3] to hold on the trusts and with and subject to the powers and provisions hereinafter declared and contained.

(2) In this clause the following expressions have the following meanings—
   (a) 'the company' means the said [*name of company*];
   (b) 'the company fund trustees' means the said [*name*] [and] the said [*name*] [and the said [*name*]] and the [survivors or] survivor of them or other the trustees or trustee for the time being of the company fund;[4]
   (c) 'the company fund' means the shares in the company hereby given to the company fund trustees and the assets from time to time representing the same;

(d) 'excluded person' means any person referred to in paragraphs (a) to (d) of subsection (4) of section 28 of the Inheritance Tax Act 1984 on the footing that—
  (i) the company referred to in paragraph (a) of the said subsection is the company as hereinbefore defined,
  (ii) the settlement referred to in paragraph (b) of the said subsection is the disposition on trust contained in this present clause,
  (iii) the transfer of value referred to in paragraph (c) of the said subsection is that which is deemed to occur immediately before my death for inheritance tax purposes, and
  (iv) the said paragraphs shall be construed and applied subject to and in accordance with all other statutory provisions to which they are subject or which contain definitions relevant to their interpretation.[5]

(e) 'the employees'[6] means and includes all persons who at any time after my death have either held office with or been employed (in whatever capacity) by the company (whether or not such person continues to hold office with or be employed by the company) and 'employee' means any one of the employees;

(f) 'dependants'[7] means in relation to any employee or deceased employee—
  (i) the spouse widow or widower of such employee,
  (ii) any child of such employee during his or her minority,
  (iii) any other person whom the company fund trustees may consider to be a dependant of such employee;

(g) 'the beneficiaries'[8] means and includes—
  (i) the employees,
  (ii) the dependants of any employee or deceased employee;

Provided that no excluded person shall be a beneficiary and any person who becomes an excluded person shall forthwith cease to be a beneficiary;

(h) 'the trust period' means the period of 80 years immediately following my death which shall be the perpetuity period applicable to the disposition made hereby;[9]

(i) 'the accumulation period' means the period of 21 years immediately following my death.[10]

(3) During the trust period the company fund trustees shall pay or apply the income of the company fund to or for the maintenance education support or benefit of all or such one or more exclusively of the others or other of the beneficiaries for the time being in existence and if more than one in such shares and generally in such manner [or for such charitable purposes generally][11] as the company fund trustees shall in their absolute discretion think fit Provided that during the accumulation period the company fund trustees may accumulate the whole or any part or parts of the income of the company fund by investing the same and the resulting income thereof in any of the investments hereby authorised and any accumulations so made shall form part of the capital of the company fund for all purposes.

(4) Notwithstanding the trust aforesaid the company fund trustees may at any time or times and from time to time during the trust period pay or apply the whole or any part or parts of the capital of the company fund to

or for the advancement or benefit of all or any one or more exclusively of the others or other of the beneficiaries for the time being in existence and if more than one in such shares and in such manner generally [or for such charitable purposes generally][12] as the company fund trustees may in their absolute discretion think fit.

(5) Subject to the trusts and to any exercise of the powers aforesaid the company fund trustees shall hold the company fund and the income thereof upon trust for such charitable purposes generally[13] as they may in their absolute discretion think fit.

(6) The administrative powers and provisions contained in clause 9 hereof shall apply in relation to the company fund and the income thereof as if references therein to 'my trustees' were references to 'the company fund trustees'.

1 See the notes to cls 2 and 3 at paras **[235.5]** and **[235.6]**. If the shares in the company confer control, the gift should be exempt from IHT: see the Note to this form at para **[235.2]**.
2 It may be convenient to appoint separate trustees of the company fund.
3 If the shares in the company confer control, the gift should be exempt from IHT: see the Note to this form at para **[235.2]**.
4 See n 2, above.
5 The excluded categories are essentially participators in the company entitled to five per cent or more of the share capital. It is not very satisfactory to use referential drafting of this kind, but the elaboration of the statutory provisions is such that it is not practical to attempt to reproduce them in full: see the IHTA 1984, ss 13(5), 28(4) to (7), and 102 and the Income and Corporation Taxes Act 1988, ss 414 to 417.
6 The definitions of 'the employees' and 'the beneficiaries' are based on the provisions of the IHTA 1984, ss 86(1) and (3)(a) and 28(1), (4) and (5).
7 The definition of 'dependants' is based on the IHTA 1984, s 86(1)(b).
8 See nn 6 and 7, above.
9 This is the maximum fixed period of years permitted by the PAA 1964, s 1 (Part G, para **[246.74]**).
10 The 21-year accumulation period is available under the LPA 1925, s 164(1)(b) (Part G, para **[246.56]**) and is the only suitable period.
11 It is permissible to include charitable objects without prejudicing the exempt status of the trusts: see the IHTA 1984, s 86(3) and the Note to this form at para **[235.2]**. If a power to benefit charity is not required the words in square brackets should be omitted.
12 See n 11, above.
13 See n 11, above. A trust for charitable purposes is a convenient ultimate trust.

[235.8]

GIFT OF FAMILY SEAT

5. I give free of tax[1] the mansion house and grounds known as [*name of house*] and situate in the Parish of [ ] in the County of [ ] and the contents thereof to my nephew [*name*] in fee simple and absolutely.

1 See n 3 to cls 2 and 3 of this form at paras **[235.5]** and **[235.6]**.

[235.9]

ADMINISTRATION TRUSTS OF RESIDUE[1]

6. (1) I give all my property not hereby or by any codicil hereto otherwise effectively disposed of [(including any entailed or other property over which I shall have at my death a general power of disposition by will)] to my trustees to hold on the trusts set out below with power at their discretion to sell all or any of it as and when they think fit.

(2) My trustees shall pay my funeral and testamentary expenses and debts and any legacies given by this will or any codicil hereto out of such property or its proceeds and shall have a discretion as to how such payments shall be borne as between capital and income.

(3) Subject as above my trustees shall hold such property and the assets from time to time representing the same (hereinafter called 'my residuary estate') on the trusts set out below and shall invest all money comprised in such property or arising from its sale in any of the investments hereby authorised with power to change such investments into any others hereby authorised.

(4) In the administration of my estate and the execution of the trusts of this will or of any codicil to it:

(a) my trustees shall treat all income as accruing on the date on which it becomes payable regardless of the period in respect of which it shall have accrued and shall not make any statutory apportionment of the same; and

(b) none of the equitable rules of apportionment between capital and income shall apply in any circumstances whatever.

1 See the notes to the administration trusts contained in Form C8.1, cl 4 at para **[230.7]**.

[235.10]

GIFTS MADE FREE OF TAX

7. Any specific gift or pecuniary or general legacy made by this will or any codicil hereto which is expressed to be 'free of tax' shall be free from the payment of any inheritance tax or foreign tax or duty payable on or by reason of my death to which such gift or legacy would otherwise be subject and such inheritance tax or foreign tax or duty shall be paid out of my residuary estate.[1]

1 See the notes to cls 2 and 3 of this form at paras **[235.5]** and **[235.6]**. Where specific gifts and pecuniary legacies consist of, or are wholly payable out of, free estate in the UK, the IHT on them will be a testamentary expense payable out of residue without any express provision, and it is only where foreign property or settled property is being disposed of by the will that a gift which is intended to be free of tax needs to be expressly declared to be free of tax. See also the Preliminary Note to B14 at para **[214.60]**.

[235.11]

CHARITABLE TRUSTS OF RESIDUE

8. (1) The charity hereby constituted shall be known as '[*name of charity*]'.

(2) In this clause the following expressions have the following meanings namely—

(a) 'charitable purposes' means purposes which are exclusively charitable under the law of England and Wales;

(b) 'charity' means any institution (whether corporate or unincorporated) established for charitable purposes only and 'charities' has a corresponding meaning. [1]

(3) My trustees shall hold my residuary estate upon trust to apply the income thereof[2] for such charitable purposes connected with [*here state nature of desired charitable purposes: eg* the relief of poverty *or* the promotion of research for the public benefit into the causes and treatment of

diabetes][3] [and for such charitable purposes generally][4] as my trustees may from time to time determine provided that my trustees may at any time or times during the accumulation period accumulate the whole or any part or parts of the income of my residuary estate by investing the same and the resulting income thereof in any of the investments hereby authorised and any accumulations so made shall form part of the capital of my residuary estate for all purposes.[5]

[(4) My trustees may at any time and from time to time resort to the whole or any part or parts of the capital of my residuary estate and apply the same as if it were income.][6]

(5) In the administration of the charity hereby constituted my trustees shall have the following powers (in addition to those conferred by clause 9 below)—

(a) power either themselves to apply the income [or capital][7] for the purposes hereby declared or for that purpose to pay the same to any other charity or charities having similar objects;

(b) power to do all such things as may in the opinion of my trustees be conducive to the promotion of the charitable objects hereby declared;

(c) power by deed to extend restrict vary or modify the trusts powers and provisions relating to my residuary estate in any manner whatever provided that the foregoing power shall not be exercisable so as to cause or permit any of my residuary estate or the income thereof to be payable or applicable otherwise than for charitable purposes;

(d) power to create a new charitable body (whether corporate or unincorporated) having exclusively charitable objects identical with or similar to the objects hereby declared and to confer on such body such administrative and other powers as my trustees think fit and as shall be consistent with charitable status and to transfer to such body the whole or any part of my residuary estate for the promotion of its objects.

1 Once Charities Act 2006 comes into force (probably at some time in 2008) these words will have the effect of referring to the definition of purposes in Charities Act 2006, s 2 (see Charities Act 2006, s 2(6), (7)). Charities Act 2006, s 1(1) has a definition of a charity which does not differ in substance from that in the previous legislation (ie Charities Act 1993, s 96(1)), but its definition of charitable purposes in s 2 differs from the preceding law in various respects, most notably by imposing a general requirement of public benefit (see Charities Act 2006, ss 2–5).

2 The primary (and only) trust is to apply the income of residue for charitable purposes, but power is conferred by cl 8(4) to resort to capital. A perpetual income trust for charitable purposes is valid: *Re Levy* [1960] Ch 346, [1960] 1 All ER 42. If the testator wishes to create such a trust, the power to resort to capital should be omitted.

3 Care should be taken to ensure that the charitable purposes are adequately described.

4 It is wise to include charitable purposes generally in case the specific purposes are defectively described or there is some development which makes it desirable to modify the original purposes.

5 The proviso confers a power to accumulate income for 21 years. The restrictions on accumulating income apply to charitable trusts as well as to private trusts.

The exemption from income tax for charity income is only available in relation to income of the appropriate kind which is 'applied' for charitable purposes: see the Income and Corporation Taxes Act 1988, s 505 for years prior to 2006/07, and Income Tax Act 2007, ss 507–564 for years 2007/08 onwards. It is therefore preferable, where trustees accumulate income of funds held on charitable trusts, that they should do so with some specific charitable objective in view. It is probable that income which is accumulated as a general accretion to the funds of a charity counts as 'applied' for charitable purposes and qualifies for this exemption, but it is not absolutely certain: see *IRC v Helen Slater Charitable Trust Ltd* [1982] Ch 49, [1981] 3 All ER 98.

6 See n 2, above.

7 If sub-cl (4) is not included, the words in square brackets should be omitted.

[235.12]

ADMINISTRATIVE POWERS[1]

9. (1) In this clause where the context so admits:

(a) the expression 'land' includes buildings and estates interests or rights of any kind in or over land; and

(b) during the administration of my estate the expression 'beneficiary' includes any person who would be a beneficiary if such administration had been completed and the expression 'beneficially interested' and references to income of any asset being payable or capable of being paid to or for the benefit of a beneficiary shall be construed accordingly.

(2) None of the powers or provisions contained in subclause (3) below of this clause shall be capable of being exercised or operating in any manner such that (if the same were capable of being so exercised or operating) the existence of such power or provision would either:

(i) prevent any person who would (in the absence of such power or provision) have had an interest in possession falling within section 49(1A) of the IHTA 1984 in any fund or part or share of a fund from having such an interest in possession as aforesaid; or

(ii) prevent section 71A or 71D of the IHTA 1984 from applying to any trust to which (in the absence of such power or provision) either section would have applied.

(3) In the administration of my estate and the execution of the trusts hereof or of any codicil hereto my trustees shall have the following powers in addition to those conferred by law but subject to the last foregoing subclause:

(a) power to invest moneys sell assets and change investments with the unrestricted freedom of choice and powers of disposition and acquisition of a sole beneficial owner with in particular power to make unsecured loans, acquire non-income yielding assets, and purchase land anywhere in the world or chattels for any purpose including occupation or enjoyment in kind by a beneficiary under the power set out below;

(b) power to delegate all or any of their investment powers to a professional investment manager or managers whether individual or corporate and whether or not also a nominee holder of assets for my trustees (and who may be or include one or more of my trustees or the beneficiaries hereunder) upon such terms as to remuneration and otherwise (including terms authorising self-dealing or providing for the limitation of the liability of the investment manager or managers) as my trustees think fit and section 22 of the Trustee Act 2000 shall not apply;

(c) power to vest or register any property in any person or persons whether individual or corporate and whether or not an investment manager to whom powers have been delegated under the foregoing power (and who may be or include one or more of my trustees or the beneficiaries hereunder) as nominee or nominees for my trustees upon such terms as to remuneration or otherwise (including terms authorising self-dealing or providing for the limitation of the liability of the nominee) as my trustees think fit and section 22 of the Trustee Act 2000 shall not apply;

(d) power to borrow money with or without giving security and on such terms as to interest and repayment and otherwise as my trustees may think fit for any purpose connected with the administration of my estate or the trusts declared herein or in any codicil hereto (including investment) and no lender from whom my trustees borrow money in purported exercise of this power shall be concerned to enquire as to the propriety amount or purpose of any such borrowing;

(e) power to lend money to a beneficiary to whom any of the income of such money is payable or to whom or for whose benefit any income of such money is capable of being paid or applied in exercise of a discretion (or who would be such a beneficiary if such money yielded income) and to do so at a full or concessionary rate of interest or interest free;

(f) all the powers of an absolute owner in relation to any land (wherever situated) held by them;

(g) power to apply capital held on the same trusts as any land (or which would be so held if the administration of my estate had been completed) in the improvement of such land and to apply such capital or the income of such capital on the repair or maintenance of such land;

(h) power to permit any beneficiary to have the beneficial occupation use or enjoyment in kind of any land or chattel or other tangible property on such terms as to repair insurance or payment of outgoings by the beneficiary or otherwise howsoever as my trustees think fit Provided that the foregoing power shall only be exercisable and such permission to occupy or enjoy in kind may only continue in the following circumstances:

   (i) so long as any of the income of such land chattel or other tangible property is payable to such beneficiary or capable of being paid or applied to him or for his benefit in exercise of a discretion (or would be so payable or capable of being so paid or applied if such land chattel or other property yielded income),

   (ii) in the case of land, so long as for the time being the occupation thereof by such beneficiary is compatible with any statutory rights of occupation of any other beneficiary or beneficiaries;

(i) power to exercise all the powers of appropriation (and other incidental powers) conferred by statute on a personal representative without the necessity of obtaining any consents and notwithstanding that one or more of my trustees may be beneficially interested in the exercise of such power.

1 See the notes to the administrative powers contained in Form C8.1, cl 8 at para **[230.11]**.

[235.13]

TRUSTEE LIABILITY

10. (1) My trustees shall not be liable for any act or default of any investment manager or nominee employed in good faith to manage or hold assets of my estate nor for any act or default of any beneficiary having the occupation use or enjoyment of property in kind.[1]

(2) Section 11(1) of the Trusts of Land and Appointment of Trustees Act 1996 (consultation with beneficiaries) shall not apply to the exercise by my trustees of any of their powers in relation to land subject to the trusts hereof.[2]

1 This makes it clear that the trustees are not liable for the defaults of others who may have possession or control of trust property. For a wider form of indemnity, see e g Form B21.12 at para **[221.16]**. If a paid trustee is to rely on this indemnity clause, the testator should specifically be made aware of its meaning and effect (see the Note *Indemnities, releases and receipts* to para **[221.13]** above).

2 The requirement that trustees of land in exercise of any function relating to land subject to the trust consult with beneficiaries of full age beneficially entitled to an interest in possession in the land can be excluded: see the Trusts of Land and Appointment of Trustees Act 1996 (TLATA 1996), s 11(2)(a) (Part G, para **[246.114]**).

[235.14]

RECEIPTS ON BEHALF OF CHARITABLE INSTITUTIONS

11. The receipt of the person who professes to be the treasurer or other proper officer of any institution shall be a sufficient discharge to my trustees in respect of any money or property payable or transferable thereto.

[235.15]

PROFESSIONAL TRUSTEE CHARGING CLAUSE

12. Any of my trustees being a professional or business man may charge and be paid all usual professional and other proper charges for business transacted acts done advice given and time spent by him or his firm in connection with the administration of my estate or in connection with the trusts hereof including acts which a personal representative or trustee not being in any profession or business could have done personally.

[235.16]

TESTIMONIUM

IN WITNESS whereof I have hereunto set my hand this —— day of —— 20——

[235.17]

ATTESTATION CLAUSE

SIGNED by the above-named [testator/testatrix] as [his/her] last will in the presence of us both present at the same time who at [his/her] request and in [his/her] presence and in the presence of each other have signed our names below as witnesses:	}	[*Signature of testator/testatrix*]

[*Signatures, addresses and descriptions of witnesses*]

[235.18]

Form C13.2: Will of a bachelor landowner settling the principal family estate together with a share of residue on one nephew and his issue, creating a maintenance fund for the upkeep of the mansion house and settled chattels and settling substantial legacies on two nieces and their issue

Note. This form replaces Form C13.2 of the seventh edition, which contained a precedent for a devise of land in strict settlement with remainders in tail. Strict settlements and entailed interests can no longer be created: see Part A, paras **[200.52]** and **[200.53]**. This form contains instead a settled devise of a landed estate on rather simpler trusts. The name and arms clause has been retained in modified form. There is also a gift of a substantial legacy on trusts for the maintenance, repair and preservation of the mansion house and contents. This gift will constitute an exempt transfer for IHT purposes but only if the mansion house and chattels qualify for conditional exemption and the appropriate undertakings are given. Substantial settled legacies for the benefit of the testator's nieces and their issue are also included.

REVOCATION CLAUSE

I [*name*] of [*address*] hereby revoke all former testamentary dispositions made by me and declare this to be my last will.

[235.19]

APPOINTMENT OF EXECUTORS AND TRUSTEES

I appoint [*name*] of [*address*] [*name*] of [*address*] and [*name*] of [*address*] to be executors and trustees of this will

[235.20]

INTERPRETATION CLAUSE

2. (1) I declare that in the interpretation of this will the following words and expressions have the following meanings, namely—

(a) 'my trustees' means and includes my personal representatives for the time being and the trustees or trustee for the time being hereof whether original or substituted and if there shall at any time be no such trustees shall (where the context permits) include the persons empowered by statute to exercise or perform any power or trust hereby or by statute conferred upon my trustees and willing or bound to exercise or perform the same;

(b) 'the mansion house' means the mansion house at present occupied by me known as ——— together with the outbuildings and appurtenances thereto belonging;

(c) 'the settled chattels' means the pictures items of furniture objets d'art and other chattels located at the mansion house which are listed in an inventory prepared by Messrs ——— and dated ———;

(d) 'the principal estate' means and includes:

  (i) the mansion house,

  (ii) the settled chattels,

  (iii) my agricultural estate known as the ——— estate situate at ——— in the County of ——— together with all other real and leasehold property and other interests in land in the said County to which I may be entitled at the time of my death,

  (iv) the share of my residuary estate hereinafter bequeathed to my trustees as part of the principal estate, and

  (v) the assets from time to time representing the premises respectively;[1]

(e) 'the maintenance fund' means the sum of [£2,000,000] hereinafter bequeathed for the maintenance repair and preservation of the heritage property and the investments for the time being representing the same;

(f) 'the [W] trust fund' shall mean the sum of [£500,000] hereinafter settled on my niece [MW] and her issue and the investments for the time being representing the same;

(g) 'the [L] trust fund' shall mean the like sum of [£500,000] hereinafter settled on my niece [VL] and her issue and the investments for the time being representing the same;

(h) 'younger children' or 'younger child' in relation to any person shall mean and include all daughters (including an eldest or elder daughter) of such person who shall live to attain the age [18/21] years or previously marry and also every son (except an eldest or only son) who shall live to attain the age of [18/21] years including any son who being originally a younger son shall after attaining the age of [18/21] years become an eldest son or only son by the death of an elder brother but (except for the purposes of any power of maintenance or advancement hereinafter contained or conferred upon my trustees by statute) shall not include any child who being male shall die under the age of [18/21] years or being female shall die under that age a spinster.

[(2) This will shall be read and construed as if section 15 of the Family Law Reform Act 1969 [the Children Act 1975/the Legitimacy Act 1976/the Adoption Act 1976], the Family Law Reform Act 1987 and the Human Fertilisation and Embryology Act 1990 had not been enacted.][2]

1 The clauses disposing of the principal estate are only appropriate to land in England and Wales.

2 References to children and issue will now, in the absence of a contrary intention, be read as including references to illegitimate, adopted and legitimated persons by virtue of the enactments mentioned in this paragraph: (Part G, paras **[245.39]**, **[245.48]**, **[245.60]**, **[245.72]** and **[245.77]** and Vol 1, paras **[72.10]–[72.18]** and **[74.3]–[74.7]**). If a testator also wishes to exclude the operation of GRA 2004 a reference to the Act should be included in this sub-clause. Although the Act, unlike the other statutes referred to in the sub-clause, does not expressly provide that for the purpose of construing a will or settlement or other disposition of property its provisions may be excluded, it is thought that a provision, such as sub-clause 2(2), which provides that a will is to be construed without reference to the

provisions of the Act is perfectly valid. In a will of this type the testator may desire to exclude the statutory rules of construction (or some of them) in which case this paragraph should be included and adapted as appropriate.

[235.21]

PECUNIARY LEGACIES

3. I give the following pecuniary legacies free of tax[1]—
   (a) to [*name*] the sum of £——;
   (b) to [*name*] the sum of £——;
   (c) to [*name*] the sum of £——.

1 See notes to cls 2 and 7 of Form C13.1 at paras **[235.5]** and **[235.10]**.

[235.22]

BEQUEST OF LEGACY ON TRUST

4. I bequeath to my trustees free of tax[1] the sum of [£500,000] with interest thereon from the date of my death until the appropriation thereof or of investments thereto at the basic rate payable for the time being on funds in court[2] upon trust to invest the said sum in or upon any of the investments hereinafter authorised and to hold such investments and the investments for the time being representing the same (hereinafter called 'the [W] trust fund') upon the following trusts, namely—
   (a) the income of the [W] trust fund and the said interest payable from the date of my death shall be held [upon trust to pay the same to]/[upon protective trusts[3] for the benefit of] my niece [MW] wife of [JW] during her life;
   (b) after the death of the said [MW] the [W] trust fund shall be held in trust for such one or more of the children and remoter issue of the said [MW] upon with and subject to such trusts powers and provisions (including trusts and powers conferring a discretion as to the disposition of capital and income or provisions for the accumulation of income during any period permitted by law) as the said [MW] may by deed or deeds with or without power of revocation and new appointment or by will or codicil appoint;
   (c) in default of any such appointment and subject to any partial appointment the [W] trust fund shall be held in trust for all the children or any the child of the said [MW] who have attained or shall attain the age of 18 years as tenants in common equally provided always that no child of the said [MW] shall take any part or share of and in the [W] trust fund in default of appointment without bringing into hotchpot any part or share therein which may have been appointed to him or her or to his or her issue;[4]
   (d) in default of any child or remoter issue of the said [MW] living to attain a vested interest in the whole of the [W] trust fund the same shall upon her decease be held in trust for such person or persons as she shall by will or codicil appoint and in default of any such appointment and subject to any partial appointment;[5]
   (e) in trust for her next of kin[6] living at her death [*alternatively* for the persons or person who would have been her statutory next-of-kin if

she had died intestate possessed thereof domiciled in England and a spinster [and without a parent] and (if more than one) in the same shares as those in which they would have been entitled to her estate];

(f) provided nevertheless that notwithstanding and in priority to the preceding trusts it shall be lawful for the said [MW] by will or codicil to appoint that the income of [any part not exceeding [two-thirds] of] the [W] trust fund shall be paid to any husband who may survive her during his life or for any less period or determinable upon the happening of any event;[7]

(g) the foregoing trusts shall carry the intermediate income of the [W] trust fund and the provisions of section 31 of the Trustee Act 1925 (as hereinafter modified) shall apply thereto;

(h) section 32 of the Trustee Act 1925 (as hereinafter modified) shall apply in relation to the [W] trust fund.

1 See notes to cls 2 and 7 of Form C13.1 at paras **[235.5]** and **[235.10]**. Where a legacy given free of IHT is settled, the freedom from the tax should extend only to tax payable upon or by reason of the death of the testator himself. Otherwise there is a danger that future taxes (eg IHT payable on the deaths of the tenants for life) may be thrown upon residue, a result which would render the administration of the residue impossibly difficult (see such cases as *Re Stoddart, Bird v Grainger* [1916] 2 Ch 444; *Re Eve, Hall v Eve* [1917] 1 Ch 562; *Re Kennedy, Corbould v Kennedy* [1917] 1 Ch 9).

2 See Civil Procedure Rules, Part 40, *Practice Direction – Accounts, Inquiries etc* para 15..

3 The protective life interest given to the niece will be a beneficiary-taxed IPDI unless she becomes bankrupt before the testator's death (see para **[225.75]**, n 1). She will continue to be treated as entitled to an IPDI if a forfeiture occurs after the testator's death (see para **[200.104]**).The trusts for her children will then fall within the IHT relevant property regime (see para **[218.8]** ff) until absolute vesting occurs if they have not attained the age of vesting by the time of the niece's death.

4 The trusts for her children will fall within the IHT relevant property regime (see para **[218.8]** ff) until absolute vesting occurs if they have not attained the age of vesting by the time of the later to occur of the testator's death or the niece's death.

5 For a clause allowing the fund to be paid to a female tenant for life who is past the age of childbearing, where the trusts are similar to these, see Form B16.24 at para **[216.31]** and for a form enabling her to take over the trust fund in these circumstances, see the second alternative cl 6(3) of Form C8.2 at para **[230.24]**.

6 See Vol 1, para **[77.1]** and see the AEA 1925, ss 46 to 50, (Part G, paras **[244.62]**–**[244.67]**).

7 The property subject to any interest appointed by the niece to her husband under this power will be subject to the IHT relevant property rules and so the exemption for transfers between spouses will not apply to this property on the death of the niece (see paras **[200.84]**, **[200.92]**).

[235.23]

BEQUEST OF LEGACY ON TRUSTS BY REFERENCE TO PRIOR LEGACY

5. I bequeath free of tax[1] to my trustees the further sum of [£500,000] with interest thereon at the rate of [six] per cent per annum[2] from the date of my death until the appropriation thereof or of investments thereto upon trust to invest the same upon any of the investments hereinafter authorised and to hold such investments and the investments for the time being representing the same (hereinafter called 'the [L] trust fund') and the said interest upon with and subject to similar trusts powers and provisions as are hereinbefore contained in relation to the [W] trust fund but substituting throughout the name of my niece [VL] for that of my said niece [MW] and the expression the [L] trust fund for the expression the [W] trust fund.

1 See Form C13.1, cl 2, n 1 at para **[235.5]**.
2 See n 2 to cl 4 of this form at para **[235.22]**.

[235.24]

SETTLED DEVISE OF PRINCIPAL ESTATE

6. I devise and bequeath the principal estate [free of tax]/[subject to payment thereout of any inheritance tax attributable thereto (making due allowance for any reduction in value for inheritance tax purposes which is attributed thereto)][1] unto my trustees upon the following trusts—

(a) upon trust for my nephew [JE the elder] the son of my late sister [SE] during his life with remainder;
(b) upon trust for [JE the younger] his only son living at the date of this my will during his life with remainder;
(c) upon trust for the first son of the said [JE the younger] to attain the age of 21 years absolutely with remainder;
(d) upon trust for the first daughter of the said [JE the younger] to attain the age of 21 years absolutely with remainder;
(e) upon trust for the first future-born son of the said [JE the elder] to attain the age of 21 years absolutely with remainder;
(f) upon trust for [ME] the only daughter living at the date of this my will of the said [JE the elder] during her life with remainder;
(g) upon trust for the first son of the said [ME] to attain the age of 21 years absolutely with remainder;
(h) upon trust for the first daughter of the said [ME] to attain the age of 21 years absolutely with remainder;
(i) upon trust for the first future-born daughter of the said [JE the elder] to attain the age of 21 years absolutely with remainder;
(j) upon trust for my own right heirs absolutely.[2]

1 This gift will be free of IHT unless the contrary is stated: see the Preliminary Note to B14 at paras **[214.55]–[214.58]**, although if it is intended to be free of tax it will be advisable to say so specifically at this point because other gifts are expressed to be free of tax, and the absence of any direction as to the burden of IHT in relation to this gift might give rise to doubt as to what was intended in this respect. If it is a substantial agricultural estate, in hand or let on tenancies commencing after 31 August 1995, it may be wholly entitled to 100 per cent agricultural relief: see the Preliminary Note to C12 at paras **[234.1]–[234.10]**.

However, there may be a likelihood or a risk that this gift will not be wholly free from IHT, and, if so, it may be appropriate to make it bear its own IHT. The IHT would be likely to be payable by instalments, and by interest-free instalments in relation to land on which there is an agricultural relief (see the Preliminary Note to B5 at paras **[205.17]–[205.20]**). It would enable the administration of the residuary estate to be speeded up if the executors did not have to retain any of it against the payment of the instalments of IHT on this estate. A share of the residuary estate is added to this gift which might be used to pay the tax.

2 It is assumed in the above clause that at the date of the will there are living only two children, i e one son and one daughter of the testator's nephew. For the effect of a gift to a person's right heirs, see Vol 1, para **[78.1]** ff. The IHT consequences of this clause are that the person who in the circumstances prevailing at the testator's death gets a life interest from his death will have a beneficiary-taxed IPDI (see para **[200.98]**). If his or her interest is succeeded by a further life interest or interests the property subject will fall into the IHT relevant property regime. A discretionary trust with a letter of wishes might save IHT (see para **[235.1]**), but the wishes might not be respected.

[235.25]

CLAUSE CUTTING DOWN ABSOLUTE INTERESTS TO LIFE INTERESTS

7. I declare that every child of the said [JE the elder] or of the said [JE the younger] or of the said [ME] who shall be hereafter born[1] in my lifetime shall instead of taking an absolute interest in the principal estate under the foregoing trusts take a life interest only therein with remainder to his or her first and other sons successively absolutely with remainder upon trust for his or her first and other daughters successively absolutely.

1 A child en ventre sa mère at the testator's death and born afterwards would not, it seems, come within this clause: see *Villar v Gilbey* [1907] AC 139, HL.

[235.26]

CONSULTATION AND CONSENTS OF, AND DELEGATION TO, BENEFICIARIES OF THE PRINCIPAL ESTATE[1]

8. If and so long as there is a person who is for the time being entitled to a life interest in possession in the principal estate under the foregoing trusts who has attained the age of 21 years—

(1) My trustees shall be under an obligation to consult such person as to their exercise of their functions in relation to any land comprised in the principal estate but subject as aforesaid section 11(1) of the Trusts of Land and Appointment of Trustees Act 1996[2] shall not apply in relation to such land or any other land comprised in my estate or any fund deriving therefrom and I request that so far as they may lawfully do so my trustees do delegate their functions in relation to the principal estate to such person;[3] and

(2) My trustees shall not exercise their powers (whether conferred by statute or otherwise) of sale lease licence mortgage or charge, or of effecting improvements or development, of any land comprised in the principal estate without the consent of such person.[4]

1 This provision is designed to put an adult life tenant in possession of the principal estate in a position as analogous to that of a tenant for life under a strict settlement as can be achieved under the TLATA 1996, see para **[220.54]**.

2 See the TLATA 1996, s 11 (Part G, para **[246.114]**); see also para **[220.55]**.

3 For the statutory power of delegation of management of land to a beneficiary with an interest in possession, under the TLATA 1996, s 9, see paras **[220.56]** and **[220.57]**. It is reasonably clear from the wording of the power that the trustees cannot be put under a duty to delegate, and an expression of wishes of this kind is the appropriate provision to make.

4 See note to Form B20.13 at para **[220.62]**.

[235.27]

NAME AND ARMS CLAUSE

9. Provided nevertheless that every person who under the trusts aforesaid (including the divesting limitations in this clause contained) shall become entitled in possession to the principal estate as tenant for life or contingently on attaining 21 years or absolutely and shall not then use[1] the name and arms of [*testator's family name*] shall within one year thereafter (or if a minor within one year after attaining majority) endeavour to procure the Royal Licence to take such name either alone or suffixed (but not prefixed)

to his or her previous surname and to use such arms either alone or quartered with his or her own arms and if such application be successful shall thenceforth use such name and arms for all purposes and in default of compliance with this condition[2] the trusts hereinbefore declared in favour of such person shall determine and become void as if such person (being a person entitled to a life interest or contingently on attaining 21 years) were then dead or (being a person otherwise entitled to an absolute interest) had died before attaining the age of 21 years provided always that if such person be under such trusts only tenant for life then during the rest of his of her life the principal estate shall be held by my trustees upon trust to receive the rents and profits thereof for the benefit of the person or persons who under the trusts following the said trust for such tenant for life hereinbefore contained would for the time being be entitled to the possession of the principal estate but for the trust for such tenant for life.

1 As to using a name, see *Re Drax, Dunsany v Sawbridge* (1906) 75 LJ Ch 317. See also as to disuse of a name, Vol 1, para **[35.43]** and the cases there cited. As to the effect of a 'name and arms' clause without a gift over, see *Re Evans's Contract* [1920] 2 Ch 469, and see generally, Vol 1, paras **[35.39]–[35.44]**. For an alternative precedent see Form B6.18 at para **[206.27]**.

2 If the clause goes on to prohibit disuse, it may be void for uncertainty: *Re Lewis' Will Trust, Whitelaw v Beaumont* [1951] 2 TLR 1032; *Re Bouverie, Bouverie v Marshall* [1952] Ch 400, [1952] 1 All ER 408; *Re Wood's Will Trusts, Wood v Donnelly* [1952] Ch 406, [1952] 1 All ER 740, but the present tendency is to hold such a clause certain; see *Re Howard's Will Trusts, Levin v Bradley* [1961] Ch 507, [1961] 2 All ER 413, and *Re Neeld, Carpenter v Inigo-Jones* [1962] Ch 643, [1962] 2 All ER 335, where all the authorities are considered, and see also *Re Neeld, Inigo-Jones v Inigo-Jones (No 3)* [1969] 2 All ER 1025, [1969] 1 WLR 988.

[235.28]

GIFT OF MAINTENANCE FUND

10. (1) In this clause the following expressions have the following meanings, namely—

(a) 'the heritage trustees' means such persons as my trustees may appoint and the Commissioners for Her Majesty's Revenue and Customs may approve pursuant to paragraph 2(1)(b) of Schedule 4;[1]

(b) 'the maintenance fund' means the fund so defined in subclause (2) hereof;

(c) 'the vesting day' means the day on which the principal estate shall vest in a beneficiary absolutely under the trusts declared by clause 6 hereof;

(d) 'the heritage period' means the period commencing on my death and expiring on the later to occur of the following two events:

 (i) the sixth anniversary of the day immediately following my death,[2] and

 (ii) the vesting day[3];

(e) 'the Act' means the Inheritance Tax Act 1984;

(f) 'Schedule 3' and 'Schedule 4' mean Schedule 3 and Schedule 4 respectively to the Act;

(g) 'the heritage property' means so much of the mansion house and the settled chattels as shall for the time being from time to time during the heritage period be qualifying property[4] within the meaning of paragraph 3(2) of Schedule 4;

(h) 'the heritage bodies' means and includes:
   (i) the bodies mentioned in Schedule 3,[5] and
   (ii) any body established for exclusively charitable purposes which is a qualifying charity within the meaning of paragraph 3(4) of Schedule 4.[6]

(2) For the purpose of maintaining repairing and preserving the heritage property I bequeath to the heritage trustees free of tax[7] the sum of [£2,000,000] with interest thereon from the date of my death until the appropriation thereof or of investments thereto at the basic rate payable for the time being on funds in court[8] upon trust to invest the said sum in or upon any of the investments hereinafter authorised and to hold such investments and the investments for the time being representing the same (hereinafter called 'the maintenance fund') upon the trusts hereinafter declared and contained And for the purpose aforesaid my trustees shall as soon as reasonably possible after my death and in any event within two years of my death[9] apply to the Commissioners for Her Majesty's Revenue and Customs[10] for a direction under paragraph 1 of Schedule 4 in relation to the bequest hereby made Provided that if no such direction shall be given the bequest made by this clause shall be null and void and the said sum of [£2,000,000] shall be deemed to have devolved on my death free of tax[11] as part of my principal estate.

(3) The heritage trustees shall stand possessed of the maintenance fund and the income thereof upon the trusts and with and subject to the powers and provisions following:

(a) the heritage trustees shall stand possessed of the maintenance fund upon trust during the heritage period to apply all or so much of the income thereof (including all income thereof accruing after my death) as may be required for the maintenance repair or preservation of or making provision for public access to the heritage property (by whomsoever the same may from time to time be owned and on whatever trusts the same may from time to time be held) or for defraying the expenses of the heritage trustees in relation to the maintenance fund;

(b) if at any time or times during the heritage period the income of the maintenance fund or some part thereof for any reason cannot be applied in accordance with paragraph (a) hereof the heritage trustees shall pay the same to all or any one or more of the heritage bodies and if more than one in such shares as the heritage trustees in their absolute discretion shall think fit;

(c) notwithstanding the foregoing trusts the heritage trustees shall have power during the accumulation period to accumulate the whole or any part or parts of the income of the maintenance fund by investing the same and the resulting income thereof in any of the investments hereby authorised and so that all such accumulations of income shall be held as a separate fund which shall be applied (as to both capital and income) at any time or times and from time to time during the heritage period and in any event not later than the expiration of the heritage period as if the same were income of the maintenance fund applicable under paragraphs (a) and (b) hereof;[12]

(d) notwithstanding the trusts and any exercise of the power aforesaid the trustees shall have power at any time or times and from time to time during the heritage period to raise any sum or sums [not exceeding in the aggregate the sum of £[500,000]] out of the capital of the maintenance fund (not for this purpose including any accumulations of income) and apply the same for any of the purposes for which income is applicable under paragraph (a) hereof;

Provided always that the heritage trustees shall have power by deed to modify the foregoing trusts to such extent as may be necessary to secure the approval of the Commissioners for Her Majesty's Revenue and Customs pursuant to paragraph 2(1)(a)(i) of Schedule 4.[13]

(4) For so long after the sixth anniversary of the day immediately following my death as the vesting day has not occurred the heritage trustees shall have power by deed or deeds to declare that as from the date of any such deed all or any part of the maintenance fund shall cease to be held on the trusts and with and subject to the powers set out in subclause (2) above and so that thereafter during the remainder of the heritage period the maintenance fund or such part thereof shall be held upon the trusts and with and subject to the powers and provisions applicable to the principal estate and as one fund therewith for all purposes.[14]

(5) Subject as aforesaid the heritage trustees shall hold the maintenance fund upon the trusts and with and subject to the powers and provisions as are hereinbefore declared of and concerning the principal estate and as one fund therewith for all purposes.

(6) The powers conferred on my trustees by this clause may be exercised before as well as after obtaining a grant of probate of this will and notwithstanding that the administration of my estate is not complete.[15]

1 The trustees must be approved by HMRC and must include a trust corporation, a solicitor, an accountant or a member of such professional body as they may allow in the case of the property concerned: IHTA 1984, Sch 4, para 2(1)(b).

The legislation refers to the Treasury but the Treasury's functions under Schedule 4 were transferred to the Revenue (now HMRC) by the Finance Act 1985, s 95.

2 The minimum duration required for the trusts a maintenance fund is six years: IHTA 1984, Sch 4, para 3(1)(a).

3 The heritage period is defined so as to last for six years or until the principal estate vests in a beneficiary absolutely under cl 6, whichever is the longer. During this period the maintenance fund will not form part of the taxable estate of a beneficiary unless the power conferred by sub-cl (3) is exercised.

4 Property is qualifying property if designated under the IHTA 1984, s 31 and if the requisite undertaking is given under s 30 (if conditional exemption is claimed) or under Sch 4, para 3(3) (if not).

5 The bodies mentioned in IHTA 1984, Sch 3 are national heritage bodies such as the National Gallery and the British Museum.

6 A charity is a qualifying charity if it exists wholly or mainly for maintaining, repairing or preserving heritage property: IHTA 1984, Sch 4, para 3(4).

7 This 'free of tax' formula is not strictly necessary as the gift will qualify as an exempt transfer under IHTA 1984, s 27 if the Revenue give a direction: IHTA 1984, Sch 4, para 1.

8 This is the rate of interest currently payable on legacies in an administration by the court: Civil Procedure Rules, Part 40, *Practice Direction – Accounts, Inquiries etc*, para 15.

9 The claim should ordinarily be made within two years: IHTA 1984, s 27(1A).

10 See n 1, above.

11 See Form C13.1, cl 2, n 1 at para **[235.5]**.

12 Although income accruing during the heritage period may be accumulated, it must be applied for heritage purposes: IHTA 1984, Sch 4, para 3(1)(c).

13 This power is inserted in case the Revenue insist on a modification of the trusts as a condition of giving a direction pursuant to the IHTA 1984, Sch 4, para 1.

14 This power enables the heritage trustees to determine the trusts after the minimum six-year period. The exercise of the power will trigger a tax charge under the IHTA 1984, Sch 4, Pt II.

15 The trustees are probably entitled to exercise their powers before the grant of probate and before the administration is complete, but this provision removes any doubt on the point.

[235.29]

CONTINGENT INTERESTS TO CARRY INTERMEDIATE INCOME

11. I declare that whenever any beneficiary is entitled under the trusts of this my will to an interest in any portion or any fund or share of a fund contingently on attaining the age of [18/21] years or (in the case of females) previous marriage such portion or fund or share therein as the case may be shall carry the intermediate income except so far as such income or any part thereof is under the provisions hereof expressly otherwise disposed of and section 31 of the Trustee Act 1925 (as hereinafter modified) shall apply.[1]

1 It is advisable to include an express provision to this effect as general legacies do not as a rule carry the intermediate income under the LPA 1925, s 175 (Part G, para **[244.54]**).

[235.30]

ADMINISTRATION TRUSTS OF RESIDUE

12. [*As in cl 6 of* Form C13.1 *at para* **[235.9]**.]

[235.31]

GIFTS MADE FREE OF TAX

13. [*As in cl 7 of* Form C13.1 *at para* **[235.10]**.]

[235.32]

BENEFICIAL TRUSTS OF RESIDUE

14. My trustees shall hold my residuary estate—

(a) as to a 40 per cent share thereof as part of the principal estate settled by this my will;

(b) as to a further 30 per cent share thereof upon trust to add the same to the [W] trust fund as an accretion thereto;

(c) as to the remaining 30 per cent share thereof upon trust to add the same to the [L] trust fund as an accretion thereto.

[235.33]

MAINTENANCE ACCUMULATION AND ADVANCEMENT

15. (1) Section 31 of the Trustee Act 1925 (relating to accumulation and maintenance) shall apply in relation to the trusts hereby or by any codicil hereto declared as if:

(a) in paragraph (i) of subsection (1) of the said section the words 'as the trustees think fit' were substituted for the words 'as may in all the circumstances be reasonable'; and

(b) the proviso to the said subsection (1) were omitted.

(2) Section 32 of the Trustee Act 1925 (relating to advancement) shall apply in relation to the said trusts as if the words 'one half of' were omitted from proviso (a) to subsection (1) thereof.

(3) Whenever my trustees shall have an obligation or discretion under the provisions of this will or any codicil hereto or under the general law to apply income or capital for the benefit of a minor beneficiary they may either pay the same without liability to account to his or her parent guardian or any other adult person with whom such beneficiary may be residing or to such beneficiary himself or herself if of the age of 16 years or more and so that the receipt of such parent guardian or other person or of such minor beneficiary shall be a full and sufficient discharge to my trustees for the income or capital so applied.[1]

1 A parent (with parental responsibility) and a guardian of a minor are empowered by the ChA 1989, s 3(3) (Part G, para **[244.114]**) to give a good receipt for the minor's property: see Vol 1, para **[9.42]**. The power in this subclause is wider in that it authorises the payment of income or capital to a parent who does not have parental responsibility, any adult with whom the minor is residing, and the minor himself or herself if 16 or over.

[235.34]

ADMINISTRATIVE POWERS

16. [*As in cl 9 of* Form C13.1 *at para* **[235.12]**.]

[235.35]

TIMBER AND MINERAL RENTS[1]

17. (1) All the rent or royalties from any mining lease or licence of land held by my trustees shall be treated as income and none shall be apportioned to capital.

(2) The net proceeds of sale of any timber which is cut and sold from any land held by my trustees shall be treated wholly as income.

1 See Form B20.12 at para **[220.61]** and the notes thereto.

[235.36]

TRUSTEE LIABILITY

17. [*As in cl 10(1) of* Form C13.1 *at para* **[235.13]**.]

[235.37]

PROFESSIONAL TRUSTEE CHARGING CLAUSE

18. [*As in cl 12 of* Form C13.1 *at para* **[235.15]**.]

[*Testimonium and attestation clause as in* Form C13.1 *at paras* **[235.16]** and **[235.17]**.]

C14 Wills with a foreign element

Preliminary note .... **[236.1]**
FORMS
C14.1 Will of English-domiciled testator/testatrix owning property in England and in foreign country, appointing separate executors to administer foreign property with direction to remit the proceeds of the foreign estate to the English executors .... **[236.9]**
C14.2 Reciprocal wills of English-domiciled couple who own foreign holiday home and who intend to execute foreign wills giving the home to their son on the death of the survivor, leaving their estates to each other with the survivor making a tax-free gift of holiday home to the son (with a tax-free legacy equal to the amount of the IHT on the home in the event that the foreign wills are executed), giving the daughter a compensating legacy and leaving residue to the son and daughter equally .... **[236.24]**
C14.3 Reciprocal wills of English-domiciled couple who own foreign holiday home and who have already executed foreign wills giving the home to their son on the death of the survivor, leaving their estates to each other with the survivor leaving a tax-free legacy to the son equal to the amount of the IHT on the holiday home, giving the daughter a compensating legacy and leaving residue to the son and daughter equally .... **[236.39]**

PRELIMINARY NOTE

[236.1]

Domicile. The forms in this work are for use by testators who have an English domicile. Catering for the needs of testators with a foreign domicile is a specialised topic and gives rise to fiscal and other considerations on which specialist advice, including the advice of foreign lawyers, will usually be required. However, some of the general considerations affecting testators with a foreign domicile are mentioned below, even though forms for wills with a foreign proper law, which are normally appropriate for testators with a foreign domicile, are outside the scope of this work. Domicile is itself a rather technical topic. For a discussion of the concept generally, see Vol 1, paras **[23.2]–[23.5]**, and for a more extended discussion reference should be made to *Cheshire and North's Private International Law* (13th edn), pp 134 ff and Dicey, Morris and Collins, *The Conflict of Laws* (14th edn), Vol 1, pp 130 ff.

[236.2]

Fiscal domicile. The basic territorial scope of IHT, subject to a number of qualifications and exceptions, is that it is imposed on the worldwide estate of someone who has a UK domicile, and on the UK property only of someone who has a non-UK domicile (see, further, *Foster's Inheritance Tax*, J1.01). Even if someone has an actual domicile outside the UK, he will be treated as having a UK domicile for IHT purposes if he has been domiciled in the UK within the preceding three years or has been resident in the UK for 17 out of the preceding 20 years of assessment ending with the year of assessment in which the relevant time falls: Inheritance Tax Act 1984 (IHTA 1984), s 267, and see *Foster's Inheritance Tax*, J2.06. The position as to fiscal domicile and charges to IHT (or foreign taxes of a similar sort) on the death or a transfer of value by someone with foreign domicile, nationality or residence, or who has property in a foreign country, can also be affected by one or more double taxation agreements which can, for example, define a 'treaty domicile'. See further *Foster's Inheritance Tax*, Division J5.

[236.3]

Persons with a foreign domicile. As mentioned above, forms which cater for testators who do not have a UK domicile are outside the scope of this work, but we would mention the following general points. Property situated outside the UK is 'excluded property' for IHT purposes if an individual domiciled outside the UK (and not deemed to be domiciled in the UK under IHTA 1984, s 267: see para **[236.2]**) is beneficially entitled to it: IHTA 1984, s 6(1). Settled property situated outside the UK which was settled by a settlor or testator who was not domiciled in the UK (or deemed to be so: see above) at the date of the settlement or death is also 'excluded property': s 48(3). Broadly speaking 'excluded property' escapes IHT altogether and settled property which is 'excluded property' will escape tax regardless of the domicile and residence of the beneficiaries. It would therefore be quite possible for an individual who is not domiciled in the UK (and not deemed to be so domiciled under IHTA 1984, s 267: see para **[236.2]**), even if he lives in the UK, to make a will leaving his foreign estate on discretionary trusts for beneficiaries who live in the UK which avoid future IHT charges. So long as the property remains situated outside the UK it will escape the periodic and exit charges which would otherwise apply (see B18 at paras **[218.8]–[218.15]** for these). The changes made to IHT by FA 2006 have introduced a new hazard for testators with a foreign domicile in that any continuing trust following an IPDI given to a testator's spouse or civil partner will be a relevant property trust, and will, by virtue of IHTA 1984, ss 80 and 82, be treated for the purposes of the relevant property rules, including the rules for determining whether the settled property is excluded property, as if the property were settled by the surviving spouse or civil partner on his or her death. This means that even if if the testator has a non-UK domicile at his or her death, the settled property will not be capable of being excluded property after the death of the surviving spouse or civil partner if the latter is domiciled (or deemed by IHTA 1984, s 267 to be domiciled) in the UK on his or her death. A testator with a non-UK actual and fiscal domicile, at any rate if he has substantial property outside the UK, will usually be advised to make appropriate arrangements, either by way of inter vivos settlement or by will, which are governed by foreign law rather than to incorporate such arrangements in his English will. (If he were to make a will in English form it might possibly prejudice his status as a non-UK domiciliary.) A non UK-domiciled testator may of course own property in the UK which will be liable to IHT in the normal way and may wish to make a will in English form disposing of such property. If so, he should use a commencement, such as that contained in Form B1.6 at para **[201.11]**, limiting the operation of his English will to his UK assets.

[236.4]

Spouses with different domiciles. Since the abolition of the wife's dependent domicile by the Domicile and Matrimonial Proceedings Act 1973, s 1 spouses have been able to have different domiciles from each other. If a case arises where one spouse or civil partner has a UK domicile and the other has a foreign domicile, the unlimited IHT exemption for inter-spouse or inter-civil partner transfers will apply only to transfers by the non-domiciled spouse or civil partner to the UK-domiciled spouse or civil partner. Transfers by the UK-domiciled spouse or civil partner to the non-domiciled spouse or civil partner will be exempt only up to a limit of £55,000: IHTA 1984, s 18(2). Lifetime transfers under which the non-domiciled spouse or civil partner takes an absolute interest or an interest in possession will qualify as potentially exempt transfers and will fall out of charge if the donor spouse or civil partner survives the transfer by seven years. The present amount of the limit on the spouse or civil partner exemption for a transfer by someone with a UK domicile to his foreign domiciled spouse or civil partner has been in force without increase with effect from 9 March 1982 (in the case of civil partners only from the introduction of civil partnership with effect from 5 December 2005). There is sometimes a relevant double taxation convention which provides for a more generous exemption in some circumstances: see eg the Convention with the USA of 19 October 1978 (SI 1979/1454), art 8(4).

[236.5]

Foreign property of UK domiciliaries. This section contains forms for use by individuals who are domiciled and resident in England but who own property situate abroad. In all such cases, especially where the foreign property is of substantial value or includes land, advice should be sought from local lawyers. One possible problem is that the local law may impose restrictions on an individual's freedom to dispose of his property which would be given effect to under English conflict of laws rules, at any rate in the case of immovable property, and there may also be local fiscal considerations to be taken into account. The forms in this section must be regarded as tentative solutions which may well have to be adapted to the local law and practice.

Form C14.1 may be appropriate for use in cases where the testator owns substantial assets in a foreign jurisdiction and where it may be convenient to have a separate administration of those assets. The form provides for the appointment of a separate set of local executors to administer the foreign assets and remit the proceeds to the English executors. In such cases it may be more convenient for the testator to execute a separate will governed by the local law dealing exclusively with such assets. If so, an English will confined to his property in the UK or a will dealing with all his property except that situate in one or more particular jurisdictions may be preferred, in which case a commencement provision such as Form B1.6 at para **[201.11]** may be appropriate. However, before this is done the possible IHT problem described at para **[236.8]** should be considered. The beneficial trusts of residue in Form C14.1 have no specific foreign element and others may be preferred: for alternatives see the forms in C2 and C3 at paras **[224.27]** ff and **[225.9]** ff.

Forms C14.2 and C14.3 are intended for use by couples who own a foreign holiday home which they wish to give to one of their children on the death of the survivor. As mentioned above, where foreign property is owned, especially land and other immovable property, it will be prudent to take the advice of local lawyers as to the manner and extent to which it may be disposed of on death. It is possible, for example, that the local law has forced heirship rules which may be recognised and enforced by English law in relation to immovables in that territory which a deceased person with an English domicile owns at his death. It may also turn out to be desirable to make wills in appropriate foreign form dealing with the foreign property. Form C14.2 contemplates a situation where it is intended to make such a will. It contains a specific free of tax gift of the foreign property by the survivor of the couple which is designed to take effect pending the execution of the intended foreign wills. (Unless the donee is to pay the IHT attributable to the property, the gift requires to be expressed to be free of tax: see para **[236.6]**.) The execution of the foreign wills will revoke the specific gift. In that event Form C14.2 provides for the donee to be given a tax-free legacy of a sum equal to the IHT and any foreign taxes attributable to the foreign property. Form C14.3 closely corresponds with Form C14.2, the difference being that in relation to C14.3 it is assumed that the foreign wills have already been executed. C14.3 therefore contains no specific free of tax gift of the foreign property, but simply a legacy equal to the IHT and local taxes on it.

[236.6]

Incidence of IHT on foreign property and of foreign taxes of a similar nature. Inheritance tax on foreign property in a deceased person's estate is not a testamentary expense but is (in the absence of express directions to the contrary) payable out of the property to which it relates: see the Preliminary Note to B14 at paras **[214.59]** and **[214.60]**. A specific gift of foreign property will also be subject to any foreign estate or inheritance taxes payable in respect of that property, in the absence of an express direction to the contrary: *Re Matthews's Will Trusts, Bristow v Matthews* [1961] 3 All ER 869, [1961] 1 WLR 1415. However, although it seems that a pecuniary legacy payable out of a residuary estate which includes foreign property will (in the absence of an express contrary direction) bear IHT so far as the legacy is to be regarded as paid out of the foreign property (see the Preliminary Note to B14 at para **[214.64]**), it also seems that such a legacy will not also (in the absence of an express contrary direction) bear any foreign estate taxes or duties which might be payable in respect of the foreign property (see *Peter v Stirling* (1878) 10 Ch D 279). It is important to make express 'free of tax' provision in relation to any specific gift of foreign property, or any pecuniary legacy payable out of a residuary estate which may include foreign property, if that is the testator's intention.

[236.7]

Inheritance tax and foreign liabilities and expenses. If a person has any liabilities to foreign resident persons, those liabilities will, for the purposes of IHT, be regarded as deducted so far as possible from property outside the UK, unless they are payable in the UK or charged on property in the UK: IHTA 1984, s 162(5). It is also HMRC practice to deduct debts in a particular country primarily from property in that country. These are points to remember when estimating the IHT on death likely to be attributable to particular foreign assets, or when advising on directions as to the incidence of IHT. They can also be important in the case of a foreign domiciled testator with some property in the UK and some outside it, as they could affect the extent to which liabilities can be deducted from the taxable estate in the UK.

The expense of administering or realising assets outside the UK which are comprised in the estate of a deceased person can be deducted from their value for the purposes of the IHT charge on them on that person's death, up to a limit of five per cent of their value, if the expense can be shown to be attributable to the situation of the property: IHTA 1984, s 173.

[236.8]

Testators with a UK domicile and substantial foreign assets. If a person is domiciled in the UK and owns assets which may be subject to IHT on his death and of which a high or significant proportion are foreign property, he should if possible make a single will disposing of all his property to the same beneficiaries and appoint either a single set of executors or foreign executors who will remit the net foreign assets to the UK executors (as in Form C14.1, cl 5 at para **[236.15]**). If there were separate wills and executors of the UK and foreign property, the UK executors might not be able to obtain probate without paying more IHT on his worldwide estate than the total value of his UK estate, and without any certainty that they could recover any of this tax out of his foreign estate. The same point applies to a foreign-domiciled testator living in the UK, because he might by the time of his death have resided in the UK long enough to have a deemed UK domicile for IHT purposes (see para **[236.2]**).

[236.9]

Form C14.1: Will of English-domiciled testator/testatrix owning property in England and in foreign country, appointing separate executors to administer foreign property with direction to remit the proceeds of the foreign estate to the English executors

Note. This form caters for the English-domiciled testator/testatrix whose dependants live in England but who owns property of significant value in a foreign jurisdiction as well as property in England (or elsewhere in the UK). It may well be difficult for English executors to exercise effective control and supervision over the administration of the foreign estate. This form caters for this difficulty by providing for the appointment of separate local executors to administer the foreign estate and remit the proceeds to the English executors. Such a device would normally be appropriate when the foreign estate is situate in a common law jurisdiction which recognises the office of executor, but it may not be suitable in other cases. The advice of lawyers practising in the particular jurisdiction should be taken. In the case of federal states, e g the United States, Canada and Australia, the relevant jurisdiction may be an individual state or province rather than the federal state itself.

In this form the gifts to the testator's children are in favour of all his children without being confined to children of the marriage or named children. See the Preliminary Note to C2 at para **[224.14]** for the significance of this point.

This form can be adapted for use by civil partners, substituting 'civil partner' for 'wife/husband'. References to children or other ultimate beneficiaries will have to be adapted according to circumstances.

[236.10]

REVOCATION CLAUSE AND DECLARATION OF DOMICILE

I [*name*] of [*address*] hereby revoke all former dispositions made by me and declare this to be my last will And I further declare that my domicile is English[1] and that my will is to be construed and to take effect according to English law[2] [and that all sums of money herein mentioned are stated and payable in sterling].[3]

1 A declaration by a testator to the above effect may be useful when, owing to the testator's birth or residence or the nature and location of his business interests, a reasonable doubt may arise as to his true domicile. Domicile is not, however, a mere question of intention, and such a declaration, if contradicted or unsupported by the actual facts, is inoperative: *Re Steer* (1858) 3 H & N 594; *Brunel v Brunel* (1871) LR 12 Eq 298; *Doucet v Geoghegan* (1878) 9 Ch D 441; *Bradford v Young* (1885) 29 Ch D 617; *Winans v A-G* [1904] AC 287; *Re Liddell-Grainger's Will Trusts, Dormer v Liddell-Grainger* [1936] 3 All ER 173. As to domicile generally see *Cheshire and North's Private International Law* (13th edn), pp 134 ff and Dicey, Morris and Collins, *The Conflict of Laws* (14th edn), Vol 1, pp 130 ff, especially at pp 142–143 with regard to the effect of declarations of this sort.

2 The general rule is that in the absence of any contrary indication the construction of a will of movables is governed by the law of the testator's domicile (*Re Cunnington, Healing v Webb* [1924] 1 Ch 68); it seems that the construction of a will of immovable property is also prima facie governed by the law of the domicile but subject to the constraints imposed by the local law: Dicey & Morris, *The Conflict of Laws* (14th edn), Vol 2, p 1255. This declaration resolves any possible doubt on this point in favour of English law. It should be noted, however, that the operation of such a declaration is confined to construction. The material or essential validity of any disposition of immovable property, e g the application of forced heirship rules, will depend on the local law: Dicey & Morris, op cit, Vol 2, pp 1251–1253.

3 References to currency in a will are prima facie to be construed in accordance with the law of the domicile: Dicey & Morris, *The Conflict of Laws* (14th edn), Vol 2, pp 1255–1257. Even so, difficulties can arise where a legacy expressed in 'pounds' is given to a beneficiary resident in a foreign jurisdiction that also denotes its money in 'pounds'. It is safer to make the position clear if legacies to non-residents are to be included.

[236.11]

APPOINTMENT OF ENGLISH EXECUTORS AND TRUSTEES

1. (1) I appoint my [wife/husband] [*name*] my solicitor [*name*] of [*address*] and my friend [*name*] of [*address*] to be the executors of this will for the purpose of administering and dealing with all my movable and immovable property[1] which is situate anywhere in the world at the time of my death except [*foreign country*][2] and for the purpose of receiving from my foreign trustees hereinafter appointed and administering the proceeds of property and any unsold property situate in [*foreign country*] which my foreign trustees are hereby directed to transfer to them and to be the trustees of this will for the purpose of executing the trusts hereby declared.[3]

(2) I declare that in this will the expression 'my trustees' shall mean and include my [wife/husband] and the said [*name*] and the said [*name*] and my

personal representatives for the time being for the purposes of administering all such property as aforesaid and the trustees for the time being of this will.

1 It is better to use the private international law terms, viz movable and immovable, to distinguish between the property to be administered by the English executors and the property to be administered by the foreign executors.
2 It is contemplated in this form that the foreign executors will be appointed to administer property situate in a particular foreign jurisdiction rather than foreign property generally.
3 It is contemplated that the English executors alone will become trustees of the trusts declared by the will.

[236.12]

APPOINTMENT OF FOREIGN EXECUTORS

2. (1) I appoint [*name*] of [*address*] and [*name*] of [*address*][1] to be the executors of this will for the purpose of administering all my movable and immovable property which is situate in [*foreign country*] at the time of my death.[2]

(2) I declare that in this will the expression 'my foreign trustees' shall mean and include the said [*name*] and the said [*name*] and my personal representatives for the time being for the purpose of administering all such foreign property as aforesaid.

1 It is contemplated that individuals will be appointed as executors to administer the foreign property. It may be possible to appoint a corporate trustee, eg a trust corporation or a locally incorporated trust company. This will depend on the local law. Although a trust corporation can take a grant of probate in England and Wales (see the Supreme Court Act 1981, s 115), this may not be the case in the foreign jurisdiction. For cases on the remuneration of foreign corporate trustees see *Re Sandys' Will Trusts, Sandys v Kirton* [1947] 2 All 302, CA, and *Re Northcote's Will Trusts, Northcote v Northcote* [1949] 1 All ER 442.
2 See n 2 to cl 1 of this form at para **[236.11]**.

[236.13]

GIFT OF PERSONAL CHATTELS TO SPOUSE

3. (1) I give to my [wife/husband] all my personal chattels as defined by section 55(1)(x) of the Administration of Estates Act 1925[1] not otherwise effectually disposed of hereby or by any codicil hereto.

(2) If my [wife/husband] does not survive me then I give the said chattels free of tax[2] to such of my children as shall survive me and if more than one in equal shares according to value and in the event of any dispute as to the value or distribution of such chattels the decision of my trustees shall be final and I declare that section 33 of the Wills Act 1837 shall not apply to the foregoing gift.[3]

1 See Part G, para **[246.67]** for the wording of this definition, and for further discussion of the meaning of 'personal chattels' see Vol 1, para **[64.44]**.
2 The words 'free of tax' are included in case any of the chattels are outside the UK at the testator's death, and thus subject to tax in the absence of a direction to the contrary. See the Preliminary Note to B14 at para **[214.63]** and the definition of 'free of tax' in cl 7 of this form at para **[236.17]**.
3 See Part G, para **[244.36]** for this provision, and Vol 1, paras **[47.15]**–**[47.19]**. Section 33 would provide substitution of issue for a child who predeceases the testator, and is excluded because it would be impractical to administer a trust for minors of a share of chattels.

[236.14]

GIFT OF LEGACIES

4. I give the following pecuniary legacies free of tax:[1]
   (a) to [*name*] the sum of £——;
   (b) to [*name*] the sum of £——;
   (c) to [*name*] the sum of £——.

1 These pecuniary legacies are declared to be 'free of tax' to take account of the real possibility that they may be payable out of a residuary estate which includes property situated outside the UK, with the consequence that the legacies might without this declaration be liable to bear their own IHT so far as payable out of that property: see the Preliminary Note to B14 at para **[214.64]**. The expression 'free of tax' is employed here in conjunction with the definition and direction as to payment in cl 7 of this form at para **[236.17]**.

[236.15]

GIFT OF FOREIGN PROPERTY TO FOREIGN TRUSTEES WITH DIRECTION TO CONVERT AND TRANSMIT PROCEEDS TO ENGLISH TRUSTEES

5. (1) I give to my foreign trustees all my movable and immovable property[1] which is situate in [*foreign country*] at the time of my death (hereinafter called my 'foreign estate') to administer the same in accordance with this clause.

(2) My foreign trustees shall hold so much of my foreign estate as shall not consist of money upon trust to sell the same with full power to postpone the sale thereof without being responsible for loss and to pay out of the moneys to arise from such sale and any ready moneys comprised in my foreign estate all taxes and duties due in respect of my foreign estate in [*foreign country*] all debts due to persons resident in [*foreign country*] and all expenses of the realisation and administration of my foreign estate.[2]

(3) I declare that in the administration of my foreign estate my foreign trustees shall have and may exercise all such powers of administration (including powers of charging) as are conferred on my trustees by this will or the general law and that all such other administrative provisions as are applicable hereunder or under the general law in relation to the residue of my estate shall apply in relation to my foreign estate.

(4) My foreign trustees shall hold the residue of all such moneys as aforesaid and all parts of my foreign estate for the time being unsold and the net income thereof (after deducting therefrom all liabilities properly payable thereout whether on account of taxes duties or otherwise) upon trust to transfer the same to my trustees to hold the same as hereinafter provided.

1 See n 1 to cl 1(1) of this form at para **[236.11]**.
2 For the limited right to deduct such expenses for IHT purposes, see the Preliminary Note at para **[236.7]**.

[236.16]

ADMINISTRATION TRUSTS OF RESIDUE[1]

6. (1) I give all my property not hereby or by any codicil hereto otherwise effectively disposed of [(including any entailed or other property over which I shall have at my death a general power of disposition by will)][1] to my

trustees to hold on the trusts set out below with power at their discretion to sell all or any of it as and when they think fit.[2]

(2) My trustees shall pay my funeral and testamentary expenses[3] and debts and any legacies given by this will or any codicil hereto out of such property or its proceeds and shall have a discretion as to how such payments shall be borne as between capital and income.[4]

(3) Subject as above my trustees shall hold such property and the assets from time to time representing the same (hereinafter called 'my residuary estate') on the trusts set out below and shall invest all money comprised in such property or arising from its sale in any of the investments hereby authorised with power to change such investments into any others hereby authorised.

(4) In the administration of my estate and the execution of the trusts of this will or of any codicil to it:

(a) my trustees shall treat all income as accruing on the date on which it becomes payable regardless of the period in respect of which it shall have accrued and shall not make any statutory apportionment of the same;[5] and

(b) none of the equitable rules of apportionment between capital and income shall apply in any circumstances whatever.[6]

1 See para **[230.7]**, n 1.
2 See para **[230.7]**, n 2.
3 See para **[230.7]**, n 3.
4 See para **[230.7]**, n 4.
5 See para **[230.7]**, n 5.
6 See para **[230.7]**, n 6.

[236.17]

GIFTS MADE FREE OF TAX

7. Any specific gift or pecuniary or general legacy made or given by this will or any codicil hereto which is expressed to be 'free of tax' shall be free from the payment of any inheritance tax or foreign tax or duty payable on or by reason of my death to which such gift or legacy would otherwise be subject and such inheritance tax or foreign tax or duty shall be paid out of my residuary estate.[1]

1 Testamentary expenses will include IHT on UK free estate, including real property, but not on foreign property of any description: IHTA 1984, s 211(1) (Part G, para **[246.100]** and see the Note to B14 at paras **[214.59]** and **[214.60]**). Accordingly, it is essential that any specific gift of foreign property and any pecuniary legacies should be expressly declared to be free of tax if that is the intention. In this form chattels are given 'free of tax' (the term is defined in cl 7) in case any of them are situated abroad, and pecuniary legacies are given 'free of tax' because residue is likely to include foreign property. See generally the Preliminary Note to B14 at para **[214.71]**. See the Preliminary Note at para **[236.6]** for the incidence of foreign estate tax or duty.

[236.18]

BENEFICIAL TRUSTS OF RESIDUE

8. My trustees shall hold my residuary estate:

(a) upon trust to pay the income thereof to my [wife/husband] during [her/his] life;[1]

(b) Provided that my trustees shall have power in their absolute discretion from time to time so long as my [wife/husband] is entitled to be paid the income of all or any part of the capital of my residuary estate (or would be so entitled if such capital yielded income) to pay transfer or apply the whole or any part or parts of such capital[2] to [her/him] or for [her/his] benefit in such manner as they shall in their absolute discretion think fit;

(c) subject as aforesaid upon trust as to both capital and income for all or such one or more exclusively of the others or other of my children or remoter issue at such times and if more than one in such shares and with such trusts and powers (including trusts and powers conferring a power or discretion on my trustees or any other person or persons as to the disposition of capital or income) and such provisions (including provisions for the accumulation of income during any period permitted by law and including administrative provisions of whatever nature) and generally in such manner as my [wife/husband] shall by deed revocable or irrevocable or by will or codicil appoint;[3]

(d) subject as aforesaid upon trust for such of my children[4] as survive me if more than one in equal shares;

(e) Provided always that if any child of mine dies (or has already died) in my lifetime leaving a child or children living at my death who attain the age of 18 years such child or children shall take if more than one equally between them the share which his her or their parent would have taken had such parent survived me;[5]

(f) Provided further that no child of mine who or whose children shall take by virtue of any such appointment as aforesaid shall unless my [wife/husband] so directs share in the unappointed part of my residuary estate without bringing the part appointed into hotchpot and accounting therefor;

(g) subject as aforesaid upon trust for the children of my deceased brother [*name*] living at my death and the children then living of any then deceased child of my said brother who whether children or children of children attain the age of 18 years in equal shares if more than one but so that the children of any then deceased child of my said brother shall take (if more than one equally between them) only the share which their parent would have taken had such parent lived to attain a vested interest;[6] and

(h) subject as aforesaid upon the trusts upon which the same would be held at my death if I had died possessed thereof intestate domiciled in England and Wales and without having married or had issue.[7]

1 The surviving spouse's interest will be a beneficiary-taxed IPDI which will qualify for the spouse exemption: see paras **[200.84]** and **[200.98]**.

2 There are two reasons for restricting the power to capital in which the spouse has an interest in possession: first, to ensure that the power is not exercisable if there is a divorce and the primary trust fails; and second, to ensure that the power ceases to be exercisable if the spouse assigns or surrenders his or her life interest. See the Note to C2 at paras **[224.16]**–**[224.23]**. It is particularly important for her to cease to be the object of this power if she assigns or surrenders her life interest because it will be a deemed gift of the settled property for gift with reservation purposes: see para **[200.76]**.

3 Any continuing trusts to follow the spouse's IPDI which are appointed under this power will be subject to the relevant property IHT regime unless there is a disabled person's interest: see paras **[200.92]** and **[218.8]** ff.
4 See the Note to this form at para **[236.9]**.
5 If this trust takes effect in possession, whether immediately on the death of the testator or after the death of the spouse, at a time when any of the grandchildren are under the age of 18, the shares of those grandchildren will be subject to the relevant property IHT regime unless there is a disabled person's interest: see paras **[200.92]** and **[218.8]** ff.
6 See n 5 above.
7 In some cases it may be appropriate to ascertain the class of next-of-kin at some other time, e g the death of the spouse if surviving, so as to confine the gift to the kin then living. There is no objection to so doing: see *Hutchinson v National Refuges for Homeless and Destitute Children* [1920] AC 795, [1920] All ER Rep 701.

[236.19]

MAINTENANCE, ACCUMULATION AND ADVANCEMENT[1]

9. (1) Section 31 of the Trustee Act 1925 (relating to accumulation and maintenance) shall apply in relation to the trusts hereby or by any codicil hereto declared as if:
(a) in paragraph (i) of subsection (1) of the said section the words 'as the trustees think fit' were substituted for the words 'as may in all the circumstances be reasonable'; and
(b) the proviso to the said subsection (1) were omitted.

(2) Section 32 of the Trustee Act 1925 (relating to advancement) shall apply in relation to the said trusts as if the words 'one half of' were omitted from proviso (a) to subsection (1) thereof.

(3) Whenever my trustees shall have an obligation or discretion under the provisions of this will or any codicil hereto or under the general law to apply income or capital for the benefit of a minor beneficiary they may either pay the same without liability to account to his or her parent guardian or any other adult person with whom such beneficiary may be residing or to such beneficiary himself or herself if of the age of 16 years or more and so that the receipt of such parent guardian or other person or of such minor beneficiary shall be a full and sufficient discharge to my trustees for the income or capital so applied.[2]

1 For alternative provisions relating to maintenance and advancement see Forms B18.11 to B18.23 and the notes thereto at paras **[218.43]–[218.108]**.
2 A parent (with parental responsibility) and a guardian of a minor are empowered by the ChA 1989, s 3(3) (Part G, **[244.114]**) to give a good receipt for the minor's property: see Vol 1, para **[9.42]**. The power in this subclause is wider in that it authorises the payment of income or capital to a parent who does not have parental responsibility, any adult with whom the minor is residing, and the minor himself or herself if 16 or over.

[236.20]

ADMINISTRATIVE POWERS[1]

10. (1) In this clause where the context so admits:
(a) the expression 'land' includes buildings and estates interests or rights of any kind in or over land; and
(b) during the administration of my estate the expression 'beneficiary' includes any person who would be a beneficiary if such administration had been completed and the expression 'beneficially interested'

and references to income of any asset being payable or capable of being paid to or for the benefit of a beneficiary shall be construed accordingly.

(2) None of the powers or provisions contained in subclause (3) below of this clause shall be capable of being exercised or operating in any manner such that if such power or provision were capable of being so exercised or so operating the existence of the same would either:

(i) prevent any person who would in the absence of such power or provision have been entitled to an interest in possession falling within section 49(1A) of the Inheritance Tax Act 1984 in any property from having such an interest in possession as aforesaid; or

(ii) prevent section 71A or 71D of the Inheritance Tax Act 1984 from applying to any property to which in the absence of such power or provision either section would have applied.[2]

(3) In the administration of my estate and the execution of the trusts hereof or of any codicil hereto my trustees shall have the following powers in addition to those conferred by law but subject to the last foregoing subclause:

(a) power to invest moneys sell assets and change investments with the unrestricted freedom of choice and powers of disposition and acquisition of a sole beneficial owner with in particular power to make unsecured loans, acquire non-income yielding assets, and purchase land anywhere in the world or chattels for any purpose including occupation or enjoyment in kind by a beneficiary under the power set out below;[3]

(b) power to delegate all or any of their investment powers to a professional investment manager or managers whether individual or corporate and whether or not also a nominee holder of assets for my trustees (and who may be or include one or more of my trustees or the beneficiaries hereunder) upon such terms as to remuneration and otherwise (including terms authorising self-dealing or providing for the limitation of the liability of the investment manager or managers) as my trustees think fit and section 22 of the Trustee Act 2000 shall not apply;[4]

(c) power to vest or register any property in any person or persons whether individual or corporate and whether or not an investment manager to whom powers have been delegated under the foregoing power (and who may be or include one or more of my trustees or the beneficiaries hereunder) as nominee or nominees for my trustees upon such terms as to remuneration or otherwise (including terms authorising self-dealing or providing for the limitation of the liability of the nominee) as my trustees think fit and section 22 of the Trustee Act 2000 shall not apply;[5]

(d) power to borrow money with or without giving security and on such terms as to interest and repayment and otherwise as my trustees may think fit for any purpose connected with the administration of my estate or the trusts declared herein or in any codicil hereto (including investment) and no lender from whom my trustees borrow money in purported exercise of this power shall be concerned to enquire as to the propriety amount or purpose of any such borrowing;[6]

(e) power to lend money to a beneficiary to whom any of the income of such money is payable or to whom or for whose benefit any income of such money is capable of being paid or applied in exercise of a discretion (or who would be such a beneficiary if such money yielded income) and to do so at a full or concessionary rate of interest or interest free;[7]

(f) all the powers of an absolute owner in relation to any land (wherever situated) held by them;[8]

(g) power to apply capital held on the same trusts as any land (or which would be so held if the administration of my estate had been completed) in the improvement of such land and to apply such capital or the income of such capital on the repair or maintenance of such land;[9]

(h) power to permit any beneficiary to have the beneficial occupation use or enjoyment in kind of any land or chattel or other tangible property on such terms as to repair insurance or payment of outgoings by the beneficiary or otherwise howsoever as my trustees think fit Provided that the foregoing power shall only be exercisable and such permission to occupy or enjoy in kind may only continue in the following circumstances:

  (i) so long as any of the income of such land chattel or other tangible property is payable to such beneficiary or capable of being paid or applied to him or for his benefit in exercise of a discretion (or would be so payable or capable of being so paid or applied if such land chattel or other property yielded income),

  (ii) in the case of land, so long as for the time being the occupation thereof by such beneficiary is compatible with any statutory rights of occupation of any other beneficiary or beneficiaries;[10]

(i) power to exercise all the powers of appropriation (and other incidental powers) conferred by statute on a personal representative without the necessity of obtaining any consents and notwithstanding that one or more of my trustees may be beneficially interested in the exercise of such power.[11]

1 See para **[230.11]**, n 1.
2 See para **[230.11]**, n 2.
3 See para **[230.11]**, n 3.
4 See para **[230.11]**, n 4.
5 See para **[230.11]**, n 5.
6 See para **[230.11]**, n 6.
7 See para **[230.11]**, n 7.
8 See para **[230.11]**, n 8.
9 See para **[230.11]**, n 9.
10 See para **[230.11]**, n 10.
11 See para **[230.11]**, n 11.

[236.21]

TRUSTEE LIABILITY

11. (1) My trustees shall not be liable for any act or default of any investment manager or nominee employed in good faith to manage or hold

assets of my estate nor for any act or default of any beneficiary having the occupation use or enjoyment of property in kind.[1]

(2) Section 11(1) of the Trusts of Land and Appointment of Trustees Act 1996 (consultation with beneficiaries) shall not apply to the exercise by my trustees of any of their powers in relation to land subject to the trusts hereof.[2]

1 This makes it clear that the trustees are not liable for the defaults of others who may have possession or control of trust property. For a wider form of indemnity, see e g Form B21.12 at para **[221.16]**. If a paid trustee is to rely on this indemnity clause, the testator should specifically be made aware of its meaning and effect (see para **[221.13]**).

2 The requirement that trustees of land in exercise of any function relating to land subject to the trust consult with beneficiaries of full age beneficially entitled to an interest in possession in the land can be excluded: see the TLATA 1996, s 11(2)(a) (Part G, para **[246.114]**.

[236.22]

PROFESSIONAL TRUSTEE CHARGING CLAUSE

12. Any of my trustees being a professional or business man may charge and be paid all usual professional and other proper charges for business transacted acts done advice given and time spent by him or his firm in connection with the administration of my estate or in connection with the trusts hereof including acts which a personal representative or trustee not being in any profession or business could have done personally.

[236.23]

TESTIMONIUM AND ATTESTATION CLAUSE

IN WITNESS whereof I have hereunto set my hand this —— day of —— 20——.

SIGNED by the above-named [testator/testatrix]as [his/her] last will in the presence of us both present at the same time who at [his/her] request and in [his/her] presence and in the presence of each other have signed our names below as witnesses:	}	[*Signature of testator/ testatrix*]

[*Signatures, addresses and descriptions of witnesses*]

[236.24]

Form C14.2: Reciprocal wills of English-domiciled couple who own foreign holiday home and who intend to execute foreign wills giving the home to their son on the death of the survivor, leaving their estates to each other with the survivor making a tax-free gift of holiday home to the son (with a tax-free legacy equal to the amount of the IHT on the home in the event that the foreign wills are executed), giving the daughter a compensating legacy and leaving residue to the son and daughter equally

Note. The ownership of foreign holiday homes is becoming increasingly common. This form is intended to cater for a couple who own such a home and intend that it should devolve on the death of the survivor on one of their children. Clients in the position of such a couple should be advised to take the advice of a local lawyer with a view to making wills in local form. (It is particularly important in the case of immovable property to establish whether there are any relevant forced heirship rules under the local law and whether English law would give effect to them where the property is owned by an English domiciliary.) This form contemplates that local wills will in due course be made revoking and replacing the specific gift of the house, but provides in the meantime for a specific free of tax gift of the holiday home to the son. (Foreign property prima facie bears its own IHT, and for most purposes also bears any foreign estate or inheritance taxes on it: see the Preliminary Note at para **[236.6]**.) The free of tax gift of the home will be revoked by the foreign wills when they are made and the form provides in that event for the gift to the son of a tax-free legacy of the amount of the IHT and any local taxes which would otherwise be payable by him.

This form can be adapted for use by civil partners, substituting 'civil partner' for 'wife/husband'. References to children or other ultimate beneficiaries will have to be adapted according to circumstances.

[236.25]

REVOCATION CLAUSE

I [*name*] of [*address*] hereby revoke all former testamentary dispositions made by me and declare this to be my last will.

[236.26]

GIFT OF ESTATE TO SPOUSE AND APPOINTMENT OF SPOUSE AS SOLE EXECUTRIX/EXECUTOR

1. If my [wife/husband] shall survive me then subject to the payment thereout of my funeral and testamentary expenses and debts I give all my estate of whatever nature and wherever situate to my [wife/husband] [*name*] and appoint [her/him] to be the sole [executrix/executor] hereof.

[236.27]

ALTERNATIVE PROVISIONS

2. If my [wife/husband] shall fail to survive me then the following provisions of this will shall have effect.

[236.28]

APPOINTMENT OF EXECUTORS AND TRUSTEES

3. I appoint my son [*name*] my daughter [*name*] and [*name*] of [*address*] (hereinafter together called 'my trustees' which expression shall include my personal representatives for the time being and the trustees for the time being hereof) to be the executors and trustees of this will.

[236.29]

GIFT OF CHATTELS TO SON AND DAUGHTER

4. I give free of tax[1] all my personal chattels (as defined by section 55(1)(x) of the Administration of Estates Act 1925)[2] not otherwise effectually disposed of hereby or by any codicil hereto or by any other will of mine to my said son and my said daughter in equal shares and I declare that section 33 of the Wills Act 1837 shall not apply to the foregoing gift.[3]

1 See Form C14.1, cl 3, n 2 at para **[236.13]**. The testator may have chattels outside the UK which do not form part of the contents of the holiday home and thus are not comprised in the specific gift of those contents to the son.

2 See Part G, para **[246.67]** for the wording of this definition, and for further discussion of the meaning of 'personal chattels', see Vol 1, para **[64.44]**.
3 See Form C14.1, cl 3, n 3 at para **[236.13]**.

[236.30]

GIFT OF LEGACY TO DAUGHTER

5. If a gift to my said son of the holiday home referred to below is effectually made by this will or by any further will of mine then I give to my said daughter a pecuniary legacy of £—— free of tax.[1]

1 See Form C14.1, cl 4, n 1 at para **[236.14]** as regards the 'free of tax' provision. As the legacy is intended to make up for the daughter not getting the holiday home, it is made contingent on the gift to the son taking effect.

[236.31]

SPECIFIC GIFT OF FOREIGN HOLIDAY HOME AND LEGACY OF THE IHT ON IT TO SON

6. (1) I give to my said son free of tax[1] all my interest in the family holiday home at [*address*] and the contents thereof[2] (hereinafter collectively called 'my foreign property').

(2) Whereas I intend to make a will in foreign form giving my foreign property to my said [wife/husband] if [she/he] survives me and if [she/he] fails to survive me to my said son Now I declare that if I make such a will and the same (or any will in foreign form subsequently executed by me and containing the like gift of my foreign property) is a valid and subsisting will at the date of my death (and if my said [wife/husband] fails to survive me) then I give to my said son free of tax[4] a pecuniary legacy of an amount equal to the inheritance tax and any local taxes or duties payable in respect of my foreign property on or by reason of my death.[5]

1 A specific gift of foreign property prima facie bears its own IHT and any foreign duties: see the Preliminary Note at para **[236.6]**. The 'free of tax' formula will exonerate the gift from all these liabilities: see Form C14.1, cl 7 at para **[236.17]** which is incorporated as cl 8 of this form.
2 For the effect of the gift of the contents of a property, see Vol 1, para **[63.1]**, n 1.
3 See n 1 to cl 1 of this form at para **[236.26]**.
4 See Form C14.1, cl 4, n 1 at para **[236.14]**.
5 If foreign wills are executed in the form contemplated, the son will receive the home under those wills and the IHT and any local duties to which the property will be subject are given to him in the form of a tax-free legacy. It is intended that whether cl 6(1) or cl 6(2) operates, the son will receive the home free of tax.

[236.32]

ADMINISTRATION TRUSTS OF RESIDUE

7. [*As in cl 6 of* Form C14.1 *at para* **[236.16]**.]

[236.33]

GIFTS MADE FREE OF TAX

8. [*As in cl 7 of* Form C14.1 *at para* **[236.17]**.]

[236.34]

BENEFICIAL TRUSTS OF RESIDUE

9. (1) My trustees shall hold my residuary estate upon trust for my said son and my said daughter in equal shares.

(2) Provided that if either of my said son or my said daughter shall predecease me leaving a child or children me surviving who shall attain the age of 18 years[1] such child or children shall take if more than one equally between them the share of my residuary estate which his her or their parent would have taken had he or she survived me.

(3) The trusts declared by the foregoing subclause hereof shall carry the intermediate income of my residuary estate and section 31 of the Trustee Act 1925 (as hereinafter modified) shall apply thereto.

(4) Section 32 of the Trustee Act 1925 (as hereinafter modified) shall apply in relation to the said trusts.

1 If this trust takes effect in possession on the death of the testator at a time when any of the grandchildren are under the age of 18, the shares of those grandchildren will be subject to the relevant property IHT regime unless there is a disabled person's interest: see paras **[200.92]** and **[218.8]** ff.

[236.35]

MAINTENANCE, ACCUMULATION AND ADVANCEMENT

10. [*As in cl 9 of* Form C14.1 *at para* **[236.19]**.]

[236.36]

ADMINISTRATIVE POWERS

11. [*As in cl 10 of* Form C14.1 *at para* **[236.20]**.]

[236.37]

TRUSTEE LIABILITY

12. [*As in cl 11 of* Form C14.1 *at para* **[236.21]**.]

[236.38]

PROFESSIONAL TRUSTEE CHARGING CLAUSE

13. [*As in cl 12 of* Form C14.1 *at para* **[236.22]**.]

[*Testimonium and attestation clause as in* Form C14.1 *at para* **[236.23]**.]

[236.39]

Form C14.3: Reciprocal wills of English-domiciled couple who own foreign holiday home and who have already executed foreign wills giving the home to their son on the death of the survivor, leaving their estates to each other with the survivor leaving a tax-free legacy to the son equal to the amount of the IHT on the holiday home, giving the daughter a compensating legacy and leaving residue to the son and daughter equally

Note. The form corresponds closely with Form C14.2, the difference being that this form is intended for use after foreign wills making gifts of the foreign holiday home (and its contents) have been executed. It is assumed that there is no relevant restriction on the power to dispose of the property under the local law, and that the wills made under the local law are ones whereby the husband and wife each gives his or her interest in the property (and contents) to the other, subject to the same survivorship condition (if any) as in this will, and in the alternative gives it to their son if the gift to the other does not take effect. This form is thus for wills which do not deal with the foreign holiday home and no specific gift of the holiday home is included, but the will of the survivor gives a tax-free legacy to the son of an amount equal to the IHT and any local taxes payable in respect of the holiday home if the gift of it in the foreign will to the son takes effect.

The holiday home is excluded from this will only to the extent that it is effectually disposed of under the foreign will, and so if the foreign will fails for some reason, this will will be effective to dispose of it.

This form can be adapted for use by civil partners, substituting 'civil partner' for 'wife/husband'. References to children or other ultimate beneficiaries will have to be adapted according to circumstances.

[236.40]

REVOCATION CLAUSE

I [*name*] of [*address*] hereby revoke all former testamentary dispositions made by me save for my will made according to the law of [*name of foreign country*] dated [*date*] (hereinafter called 'my foreign will') and declare this to be my last will in respect of all movable and immovable property of mine which is situate anywhere in the world at the time of my death except for the property disposed of by my foreign will.

[236.41]

GIFT OF ESTATE TO SPOUSE AND APPOINTMENT OF SPOUSE AS SOLE EXECUTRIX/EXECUTOR

1. If my [wife/husband] shall survive me then subject to the payment thereout of my funeral and testamentary expenses and debts I give all my estate of whatever nature and wherever situate other than property effectually disposed of by any other will of mine to my [wife/husband] [*name*] and appoint [her/him] to be the sole [executrix/executor] hereof.

[236.42]

ALTERNATIVE PROVISIONS

2. [*As in cl 2 of* Form C14.2 *at para* **[236.27]**.]

[236.43]

APPOINTMENT OF EXECUTORS AND TRUSTEES

3. I appoint my son [*name*] my daughter [*name*] and [*name*] of [*address*] (hereinafter together called 'my trustees' which expression shall include the executors or trustees for the time being of this will and any personal representatives of mine for the time being under letters of administration with this will annexed)[1] to be the executors and trustees of this will.

1 This definition is intended to exclude anyone who is a personal representative in respect of the foreign property. If the holiday home is in a civil law jurisdiction there may not be any personal representatives in respect of it.

[236.44]

SPECIFIC GIFT OF CHATTELS TO SON AND DAUGHTER

4. [*As in cl 4 of* Form C14.2 *at para* **[236.29]**.]

[236.45]

GIFT OF LEGACY TO DAUGHTER

5. If a gift to my said son of the holiday home referred to below is effectually made by my foreign will or by a further will of mine then I give to my said daughter a pecuniary legacy of £—— free of tax.[1]

1 See Form C14.1, cl 4, n 1 at para **[236.14]** on the significance of the 'free of tax' provision. As the legacy is supposed to make up for the daughter not getting the holiday home, it is made contingent on the gift of the holiday home to the son taking effect.

[236.46]

GIFT TO SON OF LEGACY EQUAL TO TAX ON FOREIGN PROPERTY[1]

6. Whereas by my foreign will I have given my interest in the family holiday home at [*address*] and the contents thereof (hereinafter together called 'my foreign property') to my said [wife/husband] if [she/he] survives me and if [she/he] fails to survive me to my said son Now I declare that if my foreign will (or any will in foreign form subsequently executed by me and containing the like gift of my foreign property) shall be a valid and subsisting will at the date of my death (and if my said [wife/husband] fails to survive me) then I give to my said son free of tax[2] a pecuniary legacy of an amount equal to the inheritance tax and any taxes or duties payable in [*name of foreign country*] in respect of my foreign property on or by reason of my death.

1 This clause in effect reproduces the alternative gift contained in Form C14.2, cl 6(2) at para **[236.31]**.

2 See Form C14.1, cl 4, n 1 at para **[236.14]**.

[236.47]

ADMINISTRATION TRUSTS OF RESIDUE

7. [*As in cl 6 of* Form C14.1 *at para* **[236.16]**.]

[236.48]

GIFTS MADE FREE OF TAX

8. [*As in cl 7 of* Form C14.1 *at para* **[236.17]**.]

[236.49]

BENEFICIAL TRUSTS OF RESIDUE

9. [*As in cl 8 of* Form C14.1 *at para* **[236.18]**.]

[236.50]

MAINTENANCE ACCUMULATION AND ADVANCEMENT

10. [*As in cl 9 of* Form C14.1 *at para* **[236.19]**.]

[236.51]

ADMINISTRATIVE POWERS

11. [*As in cl 10 of* Form C14.1 *at para* **[236.20]**.]

[236.52]

TRUSTEE LIABILITY

12. [*As in cl 11 of* Form C14.1 *at para* **[236.21]**.]

[236.53]

PROFESSIONAL TRUSTEE CHARGING CLAUSE

13. [*As in cl 12 of* Form C14.1 *at para* **[236.22]**.]

[*Testimonium and attestation clause as in* Form C14.1 *at para* **[236.23]**.]

PART D

Codicils

D Codicils

Preliminary Note .... **[237.1]**

CHANGES IN CIRCUMSTANCES OR WISHES

FORMS

D1 Codicil appointing an executor and trustee in substitution for an executor and trustee who has died; revocation of a gift of a one-fifth share of residue to a son by name, where such son has died without children, and gift of such share of residue to other children of testator .... **[237.11]**

D2 Codicil revoking settlement of a one-third share of testator's residuary estate on his sister, and giving such one-third share to a niece on the same trusts by reference .... **[237.12]**

D3 Codicil on a gift or advance being made to a child .... **[237.13]**

D4 Codicil directing sums given to daughters on marriage to be brought into hotchpot .... **[237.14]**

D5 Codicil altering the trusts of a settled share .... **[237.15]**

D6 Codicil on the occasion of testator's second marriage, reviving his will, substituting the name of his second wife for that of his first, and including any children by his second wife in the gift of residue contained in his will .... **[237.16]**

D7 Codicil where specifically devised realty has been sold after the execution of the will .... **[237.17]**

D8 Codicil after divorce .... **[237.18]**

D9 Codicil reducing benefits owing to reduction of estate .... **[237.19]**

D10 Codicil increasing an annuity .... **[237.20]**

D11 Codicil altering legacies .... **[237.21]**

D12 Codicil imposing protective trusts on share of a child who might become insolvent .... **[237.22]**

D13 Codicil appointing a guardian, the testator having acquired parental responsibility for his illegitimate children since making his will .... **[237.23]**

CHANGES IN THE LAW

FORMS

D14 Codicil revoking a nil-rate band legacy .... **[237.24]**

D15 Codicil ensuring that a trust for the testator's children is a trust for bereaved minors .... **[237.25]**

D16 Codicil substituting absolute gifts for a settled gift .... **[237.26]**

D17 Codicil making revisions consequent upon the Trusts of Land and Appointment of Trustees Act 1996 .... **[237.27]**

D18 Codicil excluding or restricting provisions of the Trustee Act 2000. **[237.28]**

D19 Codicil varying appointment of guardian .... **[237.29]**

D20 Codicil increasing the amount of a legacy to the current inheritance tax nil-rate band .... **[237.30]**

D21 Codicil imposing an actual value limit on a formula nil-rate band legacy to the testator's children .... **[237.31]**

CORRECTING ERRORS

FORMS

D22 Codicil correcting a clerical error in a will .... **[237.32]**

D23 Codicil to render valid alterations made in will .... **[237.33]**

REVIVAL AND REPUBLICATION

FORM

D24 Codicil reviving a former will and codicils thereto which have been revoked .... **[237.34]**

REVOCATION

FORM

PRELIMINARY NOTE

[237.1]

A codicil is a useful device for making changes to a will, such as a change of executors, or a change of the amount of a legacy. Great care should be taken, however, when drafting a codicil to ensure that it alters the will only to the required extent and that it does not affect other parts of the will. It should also be considered whether there are any consequential changes which need to be made to, eg the administration trusts of residue or the administrative provisions in the will, as a result of the main changes being made by the codicil. If a substantial amendment is to be made it may in most cases be preferable to execute a new will, and this will particularly be so if a significant reduction in the benefit given to a beneficiary is being made, as the beneficiary will be far less likely to find out what the testator's disposition in his favour was before the change was made if a completely new will is made.

[237.2]

Changes in the law since the date of a will may necessitate or make desirable changes to the provisions of the will. For instance, the changes made to the IHT treatment of trusts by the Finance Act 2006, Sch 20 may require wills to be reconsidered and amended. For example, for deaths on and after 22 March 2006, it is no longer possible to create trusts which have the IHT benefits of IHTA 1984, s 71, (see para **[200.119]** above), although it is still possible to create trusts for the testator's children which have certain IHT benefits, namely trusts for bereaved minors within IHTA 1984, s 71A, (see para **[200.108]** above), and age 18-to-25 trusts within IHTA 1984, s 71D, (see para **[200.109]** above). Further, although an interest in possession taking immediate effect on death on or after 22 March 2006 ('an immediate post-death interest' within IHTA 1984, s 49A, (see para **[200.98]** above)) will still have the result of treating the beneficiary of it as beneficially entitled to the underlying settled property, a subsequent interest in possession will not (unless it is a disabled person's interest within IHTA 1984, s 89B, (see para **[200.99]** above). Therefore, where a will contains trusts for children, or successive interests in possession they should be reviewed to ensure they achieve maximum IHT efficiency consistent with the testator's objectives. Although if changes to any trusts contained in the will are required as a result of this legislation, it may be preferable to make a new will rather than to try and incorporate them in a codicil.

[237.3]

The recent introduction on 9 October 2007 of rules to carry forward unused nil-rate band allowance (see para **[200.75]** above) may lead a testator to rethink the strategy of including a nil-rate discretionary trust in his will, and instead to leave the whole of his estate to his spouse or civil partner. If he prefers the simplicity of the carry forward rules, and there are no non-fiscal reasons for including a nil-rate discretionary trust in his will (eg. to make income and capital immediately available to beneficiaries other than his spouse or civil partner, or to keep assets out of the surviving spouse's or civil partner's estate if, for example, it is possible that she may be declared bankrupt, or perhaps require long-term care when her own assets would be taken into account in determining her entitlement to local authority funding), he may delete a legacy to a nil-rate band discretionary trust by codicil. See, for example, Form D14 at para **[237.24]**. However, given that it is possible to collapse a nil-rate band discretionary trust by an appointment out within two years of the testator's death (and in certain cases, not within the first three months), relying on IHTA 1984, s 144 to backdate the appointment to the testator's death for IHT purposes, it may not be essential for the testator to make this change to his will before his death, since his trustees may always achieve it after his death by an appropriate appointment in favour of the testator's surviving spouse or civil partner (see paras **[242.4]** ff).

[237.4]
Although less recent, the Trusts of Land and Appointment of Trustees Act 1996 (TLATA 1996) (see Part G, para **[246.102]** ff) and the Trustee Act 2000 (TrA 2000) (see Part G, para **[246.132]** ff) are two statutes making changes in the law which will have a bearing on a great many wills. It may be possible to incorporate such changes in a codicil, although again great care has to be taken to ensure that nothing is overlooked, and it may be preferable to make a new will. Also, some changes mean that there is an opportunity to simplify the provisions of many wills—eg as a result of the TLATA 1996 trusts for sale may not need to be created, (see paras **[200.55]** and **[214.1]** ff), or administrative powers or provisions as to occupation by beneficiaries could be excluded as they are adequately covered by the statutory provisions (see paras **[208.18]**, **[208.19]**, **[220.49]** ff). Therefore, a new, simpler, will may well be preferable to a codicil in such circumstances.

[237.5]
However, certain changes made by the TLATA 1996 could be dealt with by codicil, eg:

(a) No new Settled Land Act 1925 (SLA 1925) settlements can be created on or after 1 January 1997 (see para **[200.52]**), so SLA 1925 forms which may have been used in a pre-1997 will should be revised. See Form D14 at para **[237.24]**.
(b) Entailed interests cannot be created after the commencement of the TLATA 1996 and any entailed interest purportedly granted thereafter will take effect as an absolute interest (see para **[200.53]**). Therefore, where an entail is purportedly created, it should be replaced with new trust provisions. See Form D14 at para **[237.24]**.
(c) Trustees of land now have all the powers of an absolute owner under TLATA 1996, s 6(1). If it was intended that the trustees' powers over land should be more restricted, express restriction should be made (see TLATA 1996, s 8(1)). See Form D14 at para **[237.24]**.

(d) The Law of Property Act 1925, s 28(1) has been repealed by the TLATA 1996 (see para **[200.60]**) so that a requirement of consent to a sale is no longer applied by statute to other powers. Therefore, a testator may wish to provide expressly for the requirement of consent to the exercise of some or all of the trustees' powers in respect of land, (see the TLATA 1996, s 8(2), which enables the exercise of the trustees' powers over land to be made subject to consents). Revision of the will is probably not required simply to maintain as effective an express requirement of a beneficiary's consent to exercise of one of the trustees' administrative powers. See Form D14 at para **[237.24]**.

(e) Beneficiaries under a trust who are of full age and collectively entitled to the whole beneficial interest have powers under the TLATA 1996, ss 19 and 20, to direct the retirement of trustees and appoint new trustees (see para **[221.39]**). These powers may be excluded (see TLATA 1996, s 21(5)), and a testator may indeed wish to exclude them in a trust created to protect the beneficiaries from their own improvidence. See Form D14 at para **[237.24]**.

(f) The doctrine of conversion is abolished by the TLATA 1996, s 3, in relation to trusts for sale, whether made before or after the commencement of the Act, with the consequence that land held on trust for sale is no longer regarded as personalty. (There is an exception for trusts for sale created by the wills of testators dying before the commencement of the Act: see para **[200.54]**). Therefore, in the rare case of a will which relies on the doctrine of conversion under a trust for sale for a particular disposition to be effective according to the testator's intention (eg which contains a gift of all personalty which is intended to include an undivided share of land), a revision of the will should be made.

(g) Statutory trusts for co-owners under the Law of Property Act 1925, ss 34 (tenants in common) and 36 (joint tenants), and of intestates' estates under the Administration of Estates Act 1925, s 33, cease to be trusts for sale and become trusts of land without any duty to sell (but with a power of sale) by virtue of the amendments to those sections made by the TLATA 1996, Sch 2. Therefore, where there is a specific gift of an undivided share in land phrased as a bequest of personalty, eg: 'I bequeath my interest in the proceeds of sale of Blackacre to X', and Blackacre is no longer held upon trust for sale, a simple affirmatory codicil should be made.

[237.6]

The principal changes brought about by the TrA 2000 are the introduction of a standard duty of care which will apply to trustees in the exercise of many of their powers, the creation of a new wider statutory power of investment to replace the limited power under the Trustee Investments Act 1961, new powers to appoint agents, nominees and custodians; to insure trust property; and to pay professional trustees (see paras **[220.12]**, **[220.36]**, **[220.51]**, **[221.15]** and **[221.42]**). The new powers generally apply to trusts whenever created, however, as under the present law the new powers will only apply to the extent that the will permits. Therefore, a testator who has already made his will might conceivably wish to exclude or restrict some of the new powers. This could be achieved by codicil. See, for example Form D15 at para **[237.25]**.

[237.7]
Each codicil which follows contains a confirmation of the will which it is altering, so far as that will is not altered by it. The confirmation of a will may influence the construction of the will, as in *Re Clarke, Sheldon v Redrup* [1942] Ch 434, [1942] 2 All ER 294, and see also Vol 1, paras **[20.4]** (effect of confirmation of wills by codicils) and **[22.3]** (effect of republication of wills). Before adding into a codicil a confirmation of the will, it is as well to go through the will and make sure that there are no gifts of which the donees have died or otherwise become incapable of taking under the provisions of the will.

[237.8]
New statutory rules affecting wills or the interpretation of them sometimes apply according to the date of death of the testator, and sometimes according to the date of making the will. Two important statutory provisions which only apply to wills made after they came into force are the Family Law Reform Act 1969 (FLRA 1969), s 15 and the Family Law Reform Act 1987 (FLRA 1987), s 1, extending the rights of illegitimate persons so that, among other things, a gift to a person or persons defined by relationship to someone else is presumed to include illegitimate persons (see Vol 1, paras **[72.10]–[72.14]**, and Part A, paras **[200.28]–[200.32]**, and the statutes are set out in Part G, paras **[245.37]** ff and **[245.69]** ff). However, each of these statutory provisions also provides that the subsequent confirmation of a will which was made before the statute came into force, by a codicil made after it came into force, does not have the effect of treating the will as made after it came into force (FLRA 1969, s 15(8): Part G, para **[245.39]** and FLRA 1987, s 19(7): Part G, para **[245.72]**). As a result, the confirmation of a will made before the FLRA 1987 came into force (on 4 April 1988), by a codicil made on or after 4 April 1988, will not by itself cause the construction of the will to be governed by the 1987 Act; if the will was made after 1969 it will continue to be governed by the FLRA 1969 (see FLRA 1987, Sch 3, para 9: Part G, para **[245.80]**), although the practical consequences of this are quite likely to be the same as they would be if the will was governed by the FLRA 1987, and if it was made before 1970 it will continue to be governed by the common law rules whereby illegitimate persons were presumed to be excluded in the absence of words to the contrary. To avoid possible uncertainties of construction where a codicil is being made to a pre-4 April 1988 will, particularly where it is a pre-1 January 1970 will, it is recommended that express provision should be made either excluding the statutory rule or rules introduced since the will was made, or else making them applicable (see further Part A, para **[200.30]**): see cl 3 of Form D1 at para **[237.11]** for an example.

[237.9]
The TLATA 1996, s 11 imposes a duty on trustees of land in the exercise of any function relating to the land subject to the trust 'so far as practicable' to

consult the beneficiaries of full age and beneficially entitled to an interest in possession, and so far as consistent with the general interest of the trust, to give effect to the wishes of those beneficiaries or (in the event of a dispute) the majority by value: see para **[220.58]**. Section 11 will apply to any trust created on or after 1 January 1997 unless expressly excluded (see s 11(2)(a): Part G, para **[246.104]**), but it does not apply to a will made before 1 January 1997 of a person who dies on or after that date (s 11(2)(b)). However, confirmation of a pre-1997 will by a codicil made on or after 1 January 1997 could have the effect of causing s 11 to apply. Exclusion of s 11 should therefore be considered in such a codicil.

[237.10]
The statutory rules of construction relating to adopted persons which have had effect from 1 January 1976 (they were introduced by the Children Act 1975, consolidated into the Adoption Act 1976 as from 1 January 1988, and re-enacted in the Adoption of Children Act 2002, Pt 1, Ch 4, which came into force on 30 December 2005 (see Part H, Additional Statutes, para **[245.96]**, below), apply to the will of a person dying on or after 1 January 1976 regardless of the date of execution of the will, so that a confirmation of a codicil can make no difference (see Vol 1, para **[75.4]** and, see ACA 2002, s 73 (4), Sch 4, para 18, Part H, Additional Statutes, paras **[245.100]** and **[245.102]**, below. See also Chapter 75, above). The position is the same as regards the rules of construction relating to legitimated children contained in the Legitimacy Act 1976 (see Vol 1, para **[72.16]** and the Legitimacy Act 1976, s 10(3): Part G, para **[245.51]**). The Human Fertilisation and Embryology Act 1990 (HFEA 1990), ss 27 to 29, which came into force on 1 August 1991 and makes provision for who is to be treated as father and mother of a child produced by means (such as artificial insemination or in vitro fertilisation) regulated by the Act, seems to apply to dispositions made before or after the Act so that a post-Act confirmation of a pre-Act instrument will not bring these provisions into play; they will already apply (see Vol 1, para **[74.6]** and the HFEA 1990, s 29(3): Part G, para **[245.87]**). For the law relating to codicils generally, see Vol 1, para **[20.1]** ff.

Changes in circumstances or wishes

[237.11]

Form D1: Codicil appointing an executor and trustee in substitution for an executor and trustee who has died; revocation of a gift of a one-fifth share of residue to a son by name, where such son has died without children, and gift of such share of residue to other children of testator

I [*testator*] of [*address*] declare this to be a [first] codicil to my will which is dated the —— day of ——.

Whereas

RECITALS

(1) By my said will I have appointed my son [*name*] to be an executor and trustee thereof together with my brother [*name*].

(2) By my said will I have directed my trustees to stand possessed of one-fifth of my residuary estate in trust for my said son absolutely.

(3) My said son died on —— without leaving any issue him surviving.

REVOCATION OF APPOINTMENT OF SON AND APPOINTMENT OF A SUBSTITUTE

1. Now I hereby appoint my friend [*name*] of [*address*] to be executor and trustee thereof in place of my said son and I declare that my said will shall have effect as if the name of the said [*new trustee*] were substituted therein as an executor and trustee thereof for the name of my said son and I bequeath to the said [*new trustee*] a legacy of £—— if he accepts the office of [executor and] trustee.[1]

2. I hereby revoke the bequest to my said son of the said one-fifth share of my residuary estate and I direct my trustees to hold the same in trust for my children other than my said son as an accretion to their respective shares therein and upon the trusts in my said will declared of such shares and in the proportions which such respective shares bear to each other.[2]

CONFIRMATION OF WILL

3. In all other respects I hereby confirm my said will[3] [and I hereby declare that [for the purposes of construing my said will and this codicil Family Law Reform Act 1987 shall apply] [my said will and this codicil shall be construed as if section 15(1) of the Family Law Reform Act 1969 and the Family Law Reform Act 1987 had not been enacted][4] [and I further declare that section 11(1) of the Trusts of Land and Appointment of Trustees Act 1996 (consultation with beneficiaries) shall not apply to the exercise by my trustees of any of their functions in relation to any land subject to the trusts of my said will].[5]

TESTIMONIUM AND ATTESTATION CLAUSE

IN WITNESS whereof I have hereunto set my hand this —— day of —— 20——

SIGNED by the above-named [testator/testatrix] as a codicil to [his/her] will dated [date] in the presence of us both present at the same time who at [his/her] request and in [his/her] presence and in the presence of each other have signed our names below as witnesses:	}	[*Signature of testator/testatrix*]

[*Signatures, addresses and descriptions of two witnesses*]

1 What amounts to acceptance of the trusteeship is largely a question of fact, see *Re Sharman's Will Trusts, Public Trustee v Sharman* [1942] Ch 311, [1942] 2 All ER 74 and *Re Parry, Dalton v Cooke* [1969] 2 All ER 512, [1969] 1 WLR 614, and see generally Vol 1, para **[25.12]**. A distinction has been drawn between duties as an executor and those as a trustee and, as the duties as executor are commonly more arduous, it is usual to give a legacy conditionally on acceptance of the office of executor as well as that of trustee.

2 When an executor-beneficiary has died and a new executor is appointed by codicil, care should be taken that the substitution does not affect beneficial interests. It is dangerous merely to substitute the name of the new executor for that of the old (*Re Freeman, Hope v Freeman* [1910] 1 Ch 681; *Re Percival, Boote v Dutton* (1888) 59 LT 21; *Re Mellor, Dodgson v Ashworth* (1912) 28 TLR 473. See also *Re Wilkins, Wilkins v Wilkins* [1920] 2 Ch 63. See further as to revocation of gifts, *Re Yates, Singleton v Povah* (1922) 128 LT 619. *Re Joseph, Pain v Joseph* [1908] 2 Ch 507; *Re Backhouse, Salmon v Backhouse* [1916] 1 Ch 65; *Choa Eng*

Wan v Choa Giang Tee [1923] AC 469). The substitution of a new trustee by a codicil has been held to operate as a substitution of the new trustee as devisee in trust: *Re Turner* (1860) 2 De GF & J 527.

A gift of property by codicil which is itself void for perpetuity will not revoke a gift of the same property in the will unless there is an express revocation provision to that effect: *Ward v Van der Loeff, Burnyeat v Van der Loeff* [1924] AC 653. Where the gift in the will is revoked the revocation will stand despite the invalidity of the gift in the codicil unless there is a contrary intention: see *Quinn v Butler* (1868) LR 6 Eq 225 at 227. A clause in the codicil which is ambiguous will not operate to revoke a gift in the will: *Re Wray, Wray v Wray* [1951] Ch 425, [1951] 1 All ER 375.

3 For the effect of this confirmation, see Preliminary Note at para **[237.7]**.

4 See Preliminary Note at para **[237.8]** and Part A, para **[200.30]**. One of these alternatives must be omitted.

5 See Preliminary Note at para **[237.9]**.

[237.12]

Form D2: Codicil revoking settlement of a one-third share of testator's residuary estate on his sister, and giving such one-third share to a niece on the same trusts by reference

I [*testator*] of [*address*] declare this to be a [first] codicil to my will which is dated the —— day of ——.

Whereas by my said will I have bequeathed a one-third share of my residuary estate upon certain trusts therein declared for my sister [*name*] and her children issue general appointees and next-of-kin. Now I hereby revoke such bequest and declare that my trustees shall stand possessed of such one-third share of my residuary estate upon trusts and with and subject to powers and provisions in favour of my niece [*name*] her children issue general appointees and next-of-kin similar in all respects to the trusts powers and provisions by my said will declared in favour of my said sister as if the name of my said niece were throughout my said will substituted for the name of my said sister in respect of the said share of residue. In all other respects I confirm my said will.[1]

In witness etc.

[*Testimonium and attestation clause as in* Form D1 *at para* **[237.11]**.]

1 See Preliminary Note at paras **[237.7]**–**[237.10]** and cl 3 of Form D1 at para **[237.11]**.

[237.13]

Form D3: Codicil on a gift or advance being made to a child

I [*testator*] of [*address*] declare this to be a [first] codicil to my will which is dated the —— day of ——.

Whereas

RECITALS

(1) By my said will my residuary estate (as therein defined) is to be held for my children in equal shares.

(2) On —— last I gave to my son [*name*] a sum of £—— upon condition that it was an advance of part of his share of my said residuary estate.[1]

DUTY TO ACCOUNT

1. Now I hereby declare in distributing my residuary estate my trustees shall so distribute it that my said son [*name*] receives £—— [*the amount of the advance*] less than each of my other children sharing therein.

INTEREST

2. I direct that the said sum of £—— shall not carry interest.[2]

CONFIRMATION

3. In all other respects I hereby confirm my said will.[3]

[*Testimonium and attestation clause as in* Form D1 *at para* **[237.11]**.]

1 It is always wise, if possible, for a testator to declare by will or codicil whether a lifetime gift is to adeem a testamentary gift or not, so as to avoid disputes: see, for example, *Re Cameron* [1999] Ch 386, [1999] 2 All ER 924.
2 The advance would normally carry interest from the date of death. As to accounting for hotchpot generally, see Vol 1, paras **[100.1]**–**[100.5]**.
3 See Preliminary Note at paras **[237.7]**–**[237.10]** and cl 3 of Form D1 at para **[237.11]**.

[237.14]

Form D4: Codicil directing sums given to daughters on marriage to be brought into hotchpot[1]

I [*testator*] of [*address*] declare this to be a [second] codicil to my will which is dated the —— day of ——.

DIRECTION THAT SUMS GIVEN TO DAUGHTERS ON MARRIAGE TO BE BROUGHT INTO HOTCHPOT

1. Whereas by my said will I have given the proceeds of sale of my residuary estate to my trustees upon trust for the benefit of all my children who shall be living at my death in equal shares to hold the same upon the trusts declared therein and whereas on the marriage of each of my two daughters [*name*] and [*name*] I transferred to each of them on such marriage a sum of £10,000. Now I hereby declare that in ascertaining the amount of the settled shares of my children in my residuary estate, the said two sums of £10,000 so transferred as aforesaid shall be brought into hotchpot as part of the respective settled shares of my said two daughters in my residuary estate.

CONFIRMATION OF WILL AND EARLIER CODICIL

2. In all other respects I confirm my said will [and a first codicil thereto bearing date the —— day of ——].[2]

[*Testimonium and attestation clause as in* Form D1 *at para* **[237.11]**.]

1 It is always wise, if possible, for a testator to declare by will or codicil whether a lifetime gift is to adeem a testamentary gift or not, so as to avoid disputes: see, for example, *Re Cameron* [1999] Ch 386, [1999] 2 All ER 924. Interest on advances brought into hotchpot is charged at the rate of 4 per cent (*Re Wills, Dulverton v Macleod* [1939] Ch 705, [1939] 2 All ER 775).
2 See Preliminary Note at paras **[237.7]**–**[237.10]** and cl 3 of Form D1 at para **[237.11]**.

[237.15]

Form D5: Codicil altering the trusts of a settled share

I [*testator*] of [*address*] declare this to be a [first] codicil to my will which is dated the —— day of ——.

RECITAL OF ABSOLUTE LEGACY AND ONE-THIRD SHARE OF RESIDUARY ESTATE TO BROTHER

Whereas by my said will I have bequeathed to my brother [*name*] absolutely a legacy or sum of £—— and I have directed my trustees to stand possessed of a one-third share of my residuary estate upon certain trusts therein declared for (in effect) my said brother his wife and children issue and appointees.

REVOCATION OF LEGACY

1. I hereby revoke the said bequest of £—— to my said brother.

REVOCATION OF ONE-THIRD SHARE

2. I hereby revoke the said bequest of such one-third share of my residuary estate and all the trusts thereof declared in my said will.

RE-SETTLEMENT OF ONE-THIRD SHARE

3. I direct my trustees to stand possessed of such one-third share of my residuary estate upon trust [*here set out the new trusts.*]

CONFIRMATION

4. I confirm my said will as modified by this codicil.[1]

[*Testimonium and attestation clause as in* Form D1 *at para* **[237.11]**.]

1 See Preliminary Note at paras **[237.7]–[237.10]** and cl 3 of Form D1 at para **[237.11]**.

[237.16]

Form D6: Codicil on the occasion of testator's second marriage, reviving his will, substituting the name of his second wife for that of his first, and including any children by his second wife in the gift of residue contained in his will[1]

I [*testator*] of [*address*] declare this to be a [first] codicil to my will which is dated the —— day of ——.

Whereas

RECITALS

(1) Since the date of my said will my wife [*name*] died on the —— day of —— and on the —— day of —— I married [*name*].

(2) By my said will I have directed my trustees to stand possessed of my residuary estate in trust for my late wife [*name*] for life and after her death in trust for my children and issue as therein mentioned.

SUBSTITUTION OF SECOND WIFE FOR DECEASED WIFE AND DECLARATION THAT CHILDREN BY SECOND MARRIAGE SHALL TAKE

1. Now I hereby declare that the gift of my residuary estate in my said will contained shall have effect as if the name of my wife [*name*] had been substituted therein for the name of my late wife [*name*]. I further declare that the expression 'child children and issue' where used in my said will shall mean and include as well any child children and issue of mine by my present marriage as any child children and issue of mine by my said first marriage.

REVIVAL OF WILL

2. In all other respects I confirm and revive[2] my said will and declare that my said will as modified by this codicil shall operate and take effect as if it had been made since my marriage with my said wife [*name*].[3]

[*Testimonium and attestation clause as in* Form D1 *at para* **[237.11]**.]

1 This form is inserted as an example of a codicil reviving a revoked will. The better (and more tactful) course in the circumstances is for the testator to make a new will altogether; but cases may arise where the form is convenient as a temporary expedient.
2 Wills Act 1837 (WA 1837), s 22 (Part G, para **[244.24]**).
3 See Preliminary Note at paras **[237.7]**–**[237.10]** and cl 3 of Form D1 at para **[237.11]**.

[237.17]

Form D7: Codicil where specifically devised realty has been sold after the execution of the will[1]

I [*testator*] of [*address*] declare this to be a [first] [*or as the case may be*] codicil to my will which is dated the —— day of ——.

Whereas

DEVISE OF FREEHOLD

1. By my said will dated —— I have devised a freehold property known as —— and situated —— to my son —— in fee simple.

CONVEYANCE BY WAY OF SALE

2. The said property was on —— conveyed by way of sale to a purchaser for the sum of £——.

BEQUEST OF LEGACY

3. Now I hereby bequeath to my said son in place of the said devise which has been adeemed a legacy of the said sum of £—— [free of inheritance tax and foreign death duties].[2]

4. I confirm my said will as modified by this codicil.[3]

[*Testimonium and attestation clause as in* Form D1 *at para* **[237.11]**.]

1 As to ademption on sale of property specifically devised, see Vol 1, para **[41.5]**.
2 These words are appropriate where the testator's residuary estate will or may include property of a kind which bears its own tax: see the Preliminary Note to B14 at para **[214.71]**.
3 See Preliminary Note at paras **[237.7]**–**[237.10]** and cl 3 of Form D1 at para **[237.11]**.

[237.18]

Form D8: Codicil after divorce[1]

I [*testator*] of [*address*] declare this to be a [first] codicil to my will which is dated the —— day of ——.

Whereas

(1) By my said will dated the —— day of —— I made certain gifts to my then wife [*name*] and also gave my residuary estate upon trust for my said wife during her life and upon her death for my children as therein stated.

(2) By a decree absolute of divorce pronounced by the Family Division of the High Court of Justice on the —— day of —— the marriage between myself and my said wife was dissolved.

(3) By virtue of section 18A of the Wills Act 1837 my residuary estate and the other property given to my said former wife now devolve under my said will as if she died on the date of the said decree absolute.

Now I hereby direct that the gift in my said will to my said former wife of [my half share of the property known as [*address*]] shall continue to have effect [free of inheritance tax][2] despite the said dissolution of our marriage and I also bequeath the sum of £—— to [*name*] [free of inheritance tax].

I confirm my said will as modified by the said section 18A of the Wills Act 1837 and as further modified by this codicil.[3]

[*Testimonium and attestation clause as in* Form D1 *at para* **[237.11]**.]

1 For WA 1837, s 18A, as amended by Law Reform (Succession) Act 1995, s 3 in relation to deaths on or after 1 January 1996, see Part G, para **[244.18]**, and the discussion of it in Vol 1, para **[47.2]** and the Preliminary Note to C2 at paras **[224.12]–[224.19]**. Section 18A only applies to a will made before a divorce, and so a codicil made after a divorce to a will made before it could nullify the effect of s 18A by republishing the will (see Vol 1, paras **[20.4]** and **[22.3]**). Such a codicil should therefore make clear whether s 18A is to continue to apply or not. If the will contained an appointment of the wife as an executor a reference to that appointment and the effect of s 18A on it should be added to the recitals. (CPA 2004, which came into force on 5 December 2005, amends WA 1837 to provide that the dissolution of a testator's civil partnership will have a like effect on his will in relation to his or her former civil partner as divorce would have in relation to his or her former spouse, see WA 1837, s 18C as inserted by CPA 2004, Sch 4, para 2 (see para **[47.3A]**, above, and Part G, para **[244.20]**, below)).

2 The gift to the former spouse will not be exempt from IHT. It may be appropriate to make it subject to tax as in Form B6.30 at para **[206.39]**.

3 See Preliminary Note at paras **[237.7]–[237.10]**, n 1, above and cl 3 of Form D1 at para **[237.11]**.

[237.19]

Form D9: Codicil reducing benefits owing to reduction of estate

I [*testator*] of [*address*] declare this to be a [first] codicil to my will which is dated the —— day of ——.

RECITAL OF VALUE

1. Whereas I now know that the total value of my estate will be less than anticipated at the time when my said will was executed.

REVOCATION OF LEGACIES

2. Now I hereby revoke all pecuniary legacies given by my said will except that given to my wife for her immediate needs.

REDUCTION OF SETTLED LEGACY

3. I also revoke the settled legacy of £5000 settled on my daughter [and in its place I give my trustees a sum of £2000 to be subject to the same provisions in all respects as the said settled legacy of £5000 was by my said will].

4. I hereby confirm my said will in all other respects.[1]

[*Testimonium and attestation clause as in* Form D1 *at para* **[237.11]**.]

1 See Preliminary Note at paras **[237.7]–[237.10]** and cl 3 of Form D1 at para **[237.11]**.

[237.20]

Form D10: Codicil increasing an annuity[1]

I [*testator*] of [*address*] declare this to be a [first] codicil to my will dated the —— day of ——.

RECITAL

Whereas by my said will dated the —— day of —— I have directed my trustees to pay an annuity of the gross sum of £—— to [annuitant] on the days and out of the fund therein mentioned.

INCREASE

Now I hereby direct my trustees to increase the said annuity by the sum of £—— so that at the times and out of the fund mentioned in my said will my trustees shall pay to the said [*annuitant*] a total yearly gross sum of £—— being the said annuity mentioned in my will increased as above stated.

Except as modified by this codicil [and the codicils dated ——] I hereby confirm my said will.[2]

[*Testimonium and attestation clause as in* Form D1 *at para* **[237.11]**.]

1 As to annuities generally and their fiscal disadvantages, see para **[211.1]** ff.
2 See Preliminary Note at paras **[237.7]**–**[237.10]** and cl 3 of Form D1 at para **[237.11]**.

[237.21]

Form D11: Codicil altering legacies

I [*testator*] of [*address*] declare this to be a [first] codicil to my will which is dated the —— day of ——.

INCREASE IN AMOUNT OF LEGACY

1. Whereas by my said will I have bequeathed to [*name*] absolutely a legacy of £——. Now I hereby declare that the said legacy to the said [*name*] shall be increased to £——.

REVOCATION OF LEGACY

2. And whereas by my said will I have bequeathed to [*name*] absolutely a legacy of £——. Now I hereby revoke the said legacy of £—— to the said [*name*].

SUBSTITUTION OF ONE CHARITY FOR ANOTHER IN RESPECT OF A LEGACY

3. And whereas by my said will I have bequeathed to [*name of charity*] a legacy of £——. Now I hereby revoke the said legacy of £—— to the said [*name of charity*] and I give to [*name and address of substituted charity*] a legacy of £—— and I declare that the receipt of the person who professes to be the treasurer or other proper officer for the time being of the said [*name of substituted charity*] shall be a sufficient discharge to my trustees in respect of such legacy.

CONFIRMATION

4. In all other respects I hereby confirm my said will.[1]

[*Testimonium and attestation clause as in* Form D1 *at para* **[237.11]**.]

1 See Preliminary Note at paras **[237.7]**–**[237.10]** and cl 3 of Form D1 at para **[237.11]**.

[237.22]

Form D12: Codicil imposing protective trusts on share of a child who might become insolvent

I [*testator*] of [*address*] declare this to be a [first] codicil to my will which is dated the —— day of ——.

RECITAL OF LIFE INTEREST FOR SON

Whereas by my said will I have directed my trustees to stand possessed of a one-half share of my residuary estate to pay the income thereof to my son [*name*] for his life and subject thereto to hold the said one-half share of my residuary estate on the trusts declared in clauses —— to —— of my said will.

IMPOSITION OF PROTECTIVE TRUSTS ON SON'S LIFE INTEREST

1. Now I hereby revoke the said life interest for my said son in the said one-half share of my residuary estate and declare that my trustees shall stand possessed of the said one-half share of my residuary estate to hold the income thereof on protective trusts as defined by section 33 of the Trustee Act 1925 for the benefit of my said son for the period of his life[1] provided always that my trustees shall have power at any time or times while my said son shall be living to pay or apply all or any of the capital of the said one-half share of my residuary estate to or for the benefit of my said son.

2. Subject thereto my trustees shall hold the said one-half share of my residuary estate on the trusts declared in clauses —— to —— of my said will.

PROTECTION FOR TRUSTEES AGAINST LIABILITY FOR PAYMENT OF INCOME TO SON AFTER FORFEITURE WITHOUT NOTICE OF IT

3. My trustees shall not be liable for paying any income of the said one-half share of my residuary estate to my son or permitting him to receive such income after the failure or determination during his life of his right to receive such income if or whenever they shall do so without having had express notice of the act or event causing such failure or determination.

CONFIRMATION

4. In all other respects I hereby confirm my said will.[2]

[*Testimonium and attestation clause as in* Form D1 *at para* **[237.11]**.]

1 A life interest subject to protective trusts is capable of being an immediate post-death interest (see IHTA 1984, s 88(4)(b)(i) and para **[200.104]** above).

2 See Preliminary Note at paras **[237.7]**–**[237.10]** and cl 3 of Form D1 at para **[237.11]**.

[237.23]

Form D13: Codicil appointing a guardian, the testator having acquired parental responsibility for his illegitimate children since making his will

I [*testator*] of [*address*] declare this to be a [first] codicil to my will which is dated the —— day of ——.

1. Since my said will was made I and [*name of the mother of the children*] have made a parental responsibility agreement dated [*date*]

by which I have parental responsibility for our children [*name*] and [*name*] and the said agreement was registered with the Principal Registry of the Family Division of the High Court on [*date*].[1]

2. If the said [*name of the mother of the children*] dies before me I appoint [*name*] to be the guardian of such of our said children as shall be under the age of 18 years at my death.

CONFIRMATION

3. In all other respects I hereby confirm my said will.[2]

[*Testimonium and attestation clause as in* Form D1 *at para* **[237.11]**.]

1 For the appointment of guardians see B3 at paras **[203.43]–[203.54]** and Vol 1, para **[28.1]** ff. As stated there, it is thought that a parent can only make an appointment of a guardian of a child at a time when he or she has parental responsibility for the child, and the father of an illegitimate child only acquires parental responsibility for the child if there is a parental responsibility agreement between him and the mother (and in the prescribed form and duly registered with the Family Division), or he marries the mother, or the mother dies appointing him the guardian.

2 See Preliminary Note at paras **[237.7]–[237.10]** and cl 3 of Form D1 at para **[237.11]**.

Changes in the law

[237.24]

Form D14: Codicil revoking a nil-rate band legacy

I [*testator*] of [*address*] declare this to be a [first] codicil to my will which is dated the —— day of ——.

REVOCATION OF LEGACY

1. Whereas by Clause + of my said will I have bequeathed to my Trustees (in the event of my wife surviving me) a legacy of an amount calculated not to incur inheritance tax on my death. Now I hereby revoke the said legacy to my Trustees.

CONFIRMATION

2. In all other respects I hereby confirm my said will.[2]

[*Testimonium and attestation clause as in* Form D1 *at para* **[237.11]**.]

1 The recent introduction on 9 October 2007 of rules to carry forward unused nil-rate band allowance (see para **[200.75]** above) may lead a testator to rethink the strategy of including a nil-rate discretionary trust in his will, and instead to leave the whole of his estate to his spouse or civil partner (see para **[237.3]** above). This codicil assumes that the main dispositions of the testator's will are to leave a nil-rate band legacy to trustees to hold upon trust, with residue to his surviving spouse or civil partner. The effect of the codicil will therefore be to increase residue and so the amount of the testator's estate entitled to exemption under IHTA 1984, s 18 on the testator's death. To the extent that the testator's nil-rate band is unused, it can then be carried forward to the surviving spouse's or civil partner's estate.

2 See Preliminary Note at paras **[237.7]–[237.10]** and cl 3 of Form D1 at para **[237.11]**.

[237.25]

Form D15: Codicil ensuring that a trust for the testator's children is a trust for bereaved minors[1]

I [*testator*] of [*address*] declare this to be a [first] codicil to my will which is dated —— day of ——-.

1. Whereas by Clause [3] of my said will I have given a legacy of £200,000 to my trustees upon trust for such of my children as shall be living at my death and shall attain the age of 30 years and if more than one in equal shares absolutely.
2. Now I hereby declare that for the age of 30 years in Clause [3] there should be substituted the age of 18 years.
3. In all other respects I hereby confirm my said will.

[*Testimonium and attestation clause as in* Form D1 *at para* **[237.11]**.]

1 For deaths on or after 22 March 2006, the trusts which a testator might declare for his young children which will fall outside the IHT relevant property charging regime are trusts for bereaved minors, age 18-to-25 trusts, or trusts under which the children take immediate post-death interests (see the Notes to paras **[200.98]**, **[200.108]**–**[200.109]** above for these different kinds of trusts). This codicil contemplates that a testator with infant children has left a legacy to them in his will under which they will take at age 30, so unless at the date of his death they have attained ages at which they will have immediate interests in possession (eg age 18 if TA 1925, s 31 applies unmodified (see para **[246.29]**)) the legacy held on trust will be subject to the IHT relevant property charging regime (see para **[200.107]** above for this regime). To avoid this, this codicil reduces the age at which they will take to 18 so that the trust will be a trust for bereaved minors if it takes effect while they are infants, see para **[200.108]** above. In making this apparently simple amendment in this way, care must be taken to ensure that none of the other provisions in the will prevent the conditions for trusts for bereaved minors from being satisfied, eg overriding powers of appointment.

[237.26]

Form D16: Codicil substituting absolute gifts for a settled gift[1]

I [*testator*] of [*address*] declare this to be a [first] codicil to my will which is dated — day of ——.

1. Whereas by Clause [6] of my said will I have given my residuary estate to my trustees upon trust for such of my grandchildren as shall be living at my death and shall attain or have attained the age of 25 years if more than one in equal shares and have provided for the share of any such grandchild to be retained upon trust for the benefit of such grandchild during his or her life.
2. Now I hereby declare that in lieu of such gift and trusts of Clause [6] of my said will I give my residuary estate to my trustees upon trust for such of my grandchildren as shall be living at my death and if more than one in equal shares absolutely.
3. In all other respects I hereby confirm my said will.

[*Testimonium and attestation clause as* in Form D1 *at para* **[237.11]**.]

1 The trusts which this form of codicil varies will have been intended to be accumulation and maintenance trusts complying with IHTA 1984, s 71 (at least prior to the grandchildren attaining interests in possession). But for deaths on and after 22 March 2006, it is no longer possible to create trusts which have the IHT benefits of IHTA 1984, s 71 (see para **[200.107]** above). Therefore, if the gift was unvaried, the testator's residuary estate would fall into the IHT relevant property regime (see para **[200.92]** above), unless any of the grandchildren was immediately entitled to an interest possession from the testator's death when such grandchild would have an immediate post-death interest within IHTA 1984, s 49A (see para **[200.98]** above)) in his or her share so that that share would be outside of the relevant property regime. The testator may prefer to make absolute gifts to his grandchildren to avoid the possibility of the relevant property regime applying to his residuary estate. Since the testator here contemplated is making provision for his grandchildren, he cannot create a

trust for his grandchildren which is a trust for bereaved minors within IHTA 1984, s 71A (see para **[200.108]** above), or an age 18-to-25 trust within IHTA 1984, s 71D (see para **[200.109]** above).

[237.27]

Form D17: Codicil making revisions consequent upon the Trusts of Land and Appointment of Trustees Act 1996[1]

I [*testator*] of [*address*] declare this to be a [first] codicil to my will dated the —— day of ——.

WHERE A SETTLED LAND ACT 1925 SETTLEMENT WAS PURPORTEDLY CREATED BY THE WILL[2]

1. Whereas by clause [*clause*] of my said will dated the —— day of —— I have given my property known as Blackacre to my wife for her life and appointed X and Y to be the trustees for the purposes of the Settled Land Act 1925. Now I hereby revoke the said clause [*clause*] and declare that my said will shall be read and construed as if it contained the following clause:[2] 'I give Blackacre to [my wife and X][3]/[X and Y]/[*otherwise*][4] to hold it on trust for my wife for life'

WHERE AN ENTAILED INTEREST WAS PURPORTEDLY CREATED BY THE WILL[5]

1. Whereas by clause [*clause*] of my said will dated the —— day of —— I have purported to create an entailed interest of my property known as Blackacre. Now I hereby revoke the said clause [*clause*] and declare that my said will shall be read and construed as if it contained the following clause: 'I give Blackacre [set out the new gift and trusts of Blackacre]'

WHERE A TESTATOR WISHES TO RESTRICT THE POWERS OF TRUSTEES OF LAND[6]

1. Whereas under Section 6 of the Trusts of Land and Appointment of Trustees Act 1996 trustees of land have in relation to the land subject to the trust all the powers of an absolute owner including certain powers there expressly set out. Now I hereby declare that the trustees of this my will shall have only those powers in relation to land subject to the trusts of this my will as are set out [expressly in my will]/[below]:

WHERE A TESTATOR WISHES TO IMPOSE A REQUIREMENT OF CONSENT TO THE EXERCISE OF POWERS OVER LAND[7]

1. Whereas by clause [*clause*] of my said will dated the —— day of —— I have given my property known as Blackacre to my trustees upon to sell the same with the consent of my wife. Now I hereby declare that my wife's consent shall be required to any exercise of any of the trustees' powers over or in relation to Blackacre.

WHERE A TESTATOR WISHES TO RESTRICT BENEFICIARIES' POWERS IN RELATION TO THE RETIREMENT AND APPOINTMENT OF TRUSTEES OF LAND[8]

1. I hereby declare that Section[s] [19] [and] [20] of the Trusts of Land and Appointment of Trustees Act 1996 shall not apply to the trusts created by my said will.

2. Except as modified by this codicil [and the codicils dated ——] I hereby confirm my said will.[9]

[*Testimonium and attestation clause as in* Form D1 *at para* **[237.11]**.]

1 The TLATA 1996 came into force on 1 January 1997, and made fundamental changes to the law relating to land held upon trust. See Preliminary Note at paras **[237.4]** and **[237.5]**.

2 No new SLA 1925 settlements can be created on or after 1 January 1997, so SLA 1925 forms which may have been used in a pre-1997 will should be revised. See Preliminary Note at para **[237.5]**, sub-para (a).

3 A testator may have wished to create a settlement under the SLA 1925 because he wished the land to be vested in the tenant for life and to have the powers of disposition of a tenant for life. Therefore, he may now wish to make the tenant for life one of the trustees.

4 It may be that X and/or Y were willing to be SLA 1925 trustees but would not want the greater burden of being trustees of land under the 1996 Act.

5 Entailed interests cannot be created on or after 1 January 1997 and any entailed interest purportedly granted thereafter will take effect as an absolute interest. See Preliminary Note at para **[237.5]**, sub-para (b).

6 Trustees of land now have all the powers of an absolute owner under s 6(1) of the Act. A testator may wish to restrict these powers. See Preliminary Note at para **[237.5]**, sub-para (c).

7 See Preliminary Note at para **[237.5]**, sub-para (d).

8 Beneficiaries under a trust who are of full age and collectively entitled to the whole beneficial interest have powers under the TLATA 1996, ss 19 and 20, to direct the retirement and appointment of trustees. A testator may wish to exclude or restrict them. See Preliminary Note at para **[237.5]**, sub-para (e).

9 See Preliminary Note at paras **[237.7]–[237.10]** and cl 3 of Form D1 at para **[237.11]**.

[237.28]

Form D18: Codicil excluding or restricting provisions of the Trustee Act 2000[1]

I [*testator*] of [*address*] declare this to be a [first] codicil to my will dated the —— day of ——.

1. I hereby declare that the duty of care of the Trustee Act 2000 shall not apply to [any of] my trustees [who does not act as trustee in the course of a business or profession].[2]
2. I hereby declare that the general power of investment of the Trustee Act 2000 shall not apply to the trusts of this my will and trustees shall have only those powers of investment as are set out [expressly in my will]/[below].[3]
3. Except as modified by this codicil [and the codicils dated ——] I hereby confirm my said will.[4]

[*Testimonium and attestation clause as in* Form D1 *at para* **[237.11]**.]

1 The TrA 2000 came into force on 1 February 2000, and confers many new powers upon trustees. See Preliminary Note at para **[237.6]** ff.

2 TrA 2000, s 1, confers a duty of care on a trustee when exercising certain statutory or express powers, namely a duty to exercise such care and skill as is reasonable in the circumstances, having regard in particular to any special knowledge or experience that he has or holds himself out as having, and if he acts in the course of a business or profession, to any special knowledge or experience that it is reasonable to expect a person acting in the course of that kind of business or profession. The duty may, however, be excluded or restricted (see Sch 1, para 7) and a testator may wish to exclude it, particularly if he is appointing family or friends to be his executors and trustees. Even though the statutory duty of care is excluded, a trustee is still, of course, subject to duties arising under the general law, eg a duty to invest the trust fund as an ordinary prudent man of business, unless he is a professional trustee, when the standard of care will be higher; see *Bartlett v Barclay's Bank Trust Co Ltd* [1980] Ch 515, [1980] 1 All ER 139.

3 TrA 2000, ss 3 to 5, confer a general power of investment upon trustees namely, a power to make any kind of investment that they could make if they were absolutely entitled to the assets of the trust, having regard to the suitability of a particular investment to the trust,

and the need for appropriate diversification and upon taking advice, unless they reasonably conclude that in all the circumstances it is unnecessary or inappropriate to do so. The power may, however, be excluded or restricted; see s 6(1)(b).

4 See Preliminary Note at paras **[237.5]**–**[237.7]** and cl 3 of Form D1 at para **[237.8]**.

[237.29]

Form D19: Codicil varying appointment of guardian[1]

I [*testator*] of [*address*] declare this to be a [first] codicil to my will which is dated the —— day of ——.

RECITAL OF PREVIOUS APPOINTMENT

1. Whereas by my said will I have appointed my wife [*name*] and my brother [*name*] to be guardians of my minor children.

REVOCATION AND REAPPOINTMENT

2. I hereby revoke the said appointment of guardians and I hereby appoint my said brother [*name*] to be guardian of my minor children in the event of my said wife predeceasing me.

CONFIRMATION

3. In all other respects I hereby confirm my said will.[2]

[*Testimonium and attestation clause as in* Form D1 *at para* **[237.11]**.]

1 ChA 1988, s 5(8) provides that if one of two parents with parental responsibility for minor children dies leaving the other surviving, an appointment of a guardian made by the will of the first to die will not take effect until the death of the other parent, see Vol 1, para **[28.2]**. This codicil appoints a guardian only in the event of the testator being predeceased by his spouse, so if the spouse survives she will have a free hand to appoint a guardian in the event of her death leaving infant children. For various forms of appointments of guardians, see Forms B3.27 to B3.32 at paras **[203.56]**–**[203.61]** and see also the Note on appointment of guardians in B3 at paras **[203.43]**–**[203.54]**.

2 See Preliminary Note at paras **[237.7]**–**[237.10]** and cl 3 of Form D1 at para **[237.11]**.

[237.30]

Form D20: Codicil increasing the amount of a legacy to the current inheritance tax nil-rate band[1]

I [*testator*] of [*address*] declare this to be a [first] codicil to my will which is dated the —— day of ——.

RECITAL OF LEGACY

Whereas by my said will I have bequeathed to [*name*] a legacy of £—— which was the upper limit of the nil-rate inheritance tax band at the date of my said will and that upper limit has since increased to £——.

INCREASE OF LEGACY

1. Now I hereby increase the said legacy of £—— to the said [*name*] to the said sum of £——.

CONFIRMATION

2. In all other respects I hereby confirm my said will.[2]

[*Testimonium and attestation clause as in* Form D1 *at para* **[237.11]**.]

1 For nil-rate band legacies see Part A, para **[200.101]**, the Preliminary Note to B18 at para **[218.16]** ff and Form B10.51 at para **[210.72]**. The nil-rate IHT band for 2007–8 is £300,000:

see FA 2005, s 98. For 2008–9 it is proposed that it will be £312,000; for 2009–10, £325,000: see FA 2006, s 155; and for 2010–11, £350,000. The recent introduction on 9 October 2007 of rules to carry forward unused nil-rate band allowance (see para **[200.75]** above) may lead a testator to rethink altogether the strategy of including a nil-rate band gift in his will, (see para **[237.3]** above).

2 See Preliminary Note at paras **[237.7]–[237.10]** and cl 3 of Form D1 at para **[237.11]**.

[237.31]

Form D21: Codicil imposing an actual value limit on a formula nil-rate band legacy to the testator's children[1]

I [*testator*] of [*address*] declare this to be a [first] codicil to my will which is dated the —— day of ——.

RECITAL OF NIL-RATE BAND LEGACY

Whereas by clause —— of my said will I have bequeathed to my children in equal shares a legacy equivalent to the maximum sum of money which can in the circumstances subsisting at my death be given by the said clause without any liability being incurred for the payment of inheritance tax on or by reason of my death[2].

LIMIT ON LEGACY

1. Now I hereby declare that in the event that the said maximum sum of money exceeds the sum of £—— the said legacy to my children shall be the said sum of £——.

CONFIRMATION

2. In all other respects I hereby confirm my said will[3].

[*Testimonium and attestation clause as in* Form D1 *at para* **[237.11]**.]

1 A testator whose estate will include property with the benefit of business or agricultural property relief may wish to place a limit on a nil-rate legacy because the availability of such relief may cause the nil-rate legacy to exceed the upper limit of the nil-rate IHT band at the date of the testator's death. See the Preliminary Note to C11 at paras **[233.8]–[233.10]**. A limit may be particularly desirable where the bulk of the testator's estate comprises business property with the benefit of 100 per cent relief because then a nil-rate legacy without a limit might include most of the estate. Generally speaking, and particularly where part of the testator's estate may be exempt from IHT (eg. by reason of the spouse or civil partner exemption), it will be wise for IHT purposes if property with the benefit of business or agricultural property relief is the subject of a specific chargeable gift so that full advantage is taken of the business or agricultural property relief.

2 The nil-rate IHT band for 2007–8 is £300,000: see FA 2005, s 98. For 2008–9 it is proposed that it will be £312,000; for 2009–10, £325,000: see FA 2006, s 155; and for 2010–11, £350,000. The recent introduction on 9 October 2007 of rules to carry forward unused nil-rate band allowance (see para **[200.75]** above) may lead a testator to rethink altogether the strategy of including a nil-rate band gift in his will, (see para **[237.3]** above).

3 See Preliminary Note at paras **[237.7]–[237.10]** and cl 3 of Form D1 at para **[237.11]**.

Correcting errors

[237.32]

Form D22: Codicil correcting a clerical error in a will

I [*testator*] of [*address*] declare this to be a [first] codicil to my will dated the —— day of ——.

Whereas in my said will at line —— on page ——there are written the words [*set out wrong word or words in will with the remainder of the phrase or sentence in which they occur*] now I hereby declare that the words —— in that passage in my said will should be —— and that the passage should read [*set out quoted passage in its correct form*] and that my said will shall be read and construed as if the words —— had been written in the place of the words —— as aforesaid and in all other respects I confirm my said will.[1]

[*Testimonium and attestation clause as in* Form D1 *at para* **[237.11]**.]

1 See Preliminary Note at paras **[237.7]–[237.10]** and cl 3 of Form D1 at para **[237.11]**.

[237.33]

Form D23: Codicil to render valid alterations made in will[1]

I [*testator*] of [*address*] declare this to be [the second] codicil to my will dated the —— day of ——.

Whereas in my said will at
line —— on page ——;
line —— on page ——
certain words are crossed out and other words have been substituted by interlineations and such alterations were not initialled in the margin or elsewhere on the said will by myself and the attesting witnesses nor were such alterations noted in the attestation clause.

Now I hereby declare that the said alterations were made prior to the execution of my said will and that my said will shall at all times be read and construed subject to the said alterations and as if the said substituted words were the original words written in my said will and I hereby confirm my said will.[2]

[*Testimonium and attestation clause as in* Form D1 *at para* **[237.11]**.]

1 There is a presumption that alterations made in a will are made after execution and are invalid. The usual practice where alterations are necessary is for the testator and the witnesses to initial such alterations in the margin in which case the above presumption will be negatived and the will construed as altered: see Vol 1, paras **[14.3]–[14.14]**. This initialling must of course be done at the time of execution. If it has been omitted then the better plan is to execute a codicil in the above form. This form can be adapted to validate alterations made after execution by merely altering the recital of the facts. The general effect of a codicil upon alterations in a will is considered with the relevant cases in Vol 1, para **[14.9]**.

2 See Preliminary Note at paras **[237.7]–[237.10]** and cl 3 of Form D1 at para **[237.11]**.

Revival and republication

[237.34]

Form D24: Codicil reviving a former will and codicils thereto which have been revoked[1]

I [*testator*] of [*address*] declare this to be [a third] codicil to my will dated the ——.

Whereas I made my last will on the —— and thereby revoked my said will dated —— and [two] codicil[s] [respectively] dated the —— [and the ——].

Now I hereby revive and confirm the said will dated —— [and the said codicil[s] thereto] and hereby revoke [the said will dated —— and] all testamentary dispositions made by me other than the said will dated —— [and the said dated codicil[s] thereto].

[*Testimonium and attestation clause as in* Form D1 *at para* **[237.11]**.]

1 It is advisable to execute a new will in the same terms as the revoked will, but in cases of emergency and where a copy of the former will exists it may be necessary to use this form. If the previous will was revoked by destruction animo revocandi and no copy thereof is in existence, it will not be possible to adopt this course. A new will must in such a case be executed. See Vol 1, para **[21.3]**. See also Form D6 at para **[237.16]**.

Revocation

[237.35]

Form D25: Revocation of a will[1]

I [*testator*] of [*address*] hereby revoke my will dated —— and all other testamentary dispositions made by me and hereby declare that it is my intention to die intestate.

[*Testimonium and attestation clause as in* Form D1 *at para* **[237.11]**.]

1 This revocation will seldom be required as the testator will normally execute a new will. While the intestacy provisions may accord with the testator's testamentary wishes, it must be remembered that it is generally more convenient to prove a will than to obtain a grant of administration. A revocation must be executed in the same way as a will. See WA 1837, s 20 (Part G, para **[244.22]**) and see generally Vol 1, paras **[18.8]**–**[18.16]** ff.

PART E

Statutory Will Forms 1925

E Statutory Will Forms 1925

Preliminary Note .... **[238.1]**
The Statutory Will Forms Order 1925 (SR & O 1925 No 780) .... **[238.4]**
FORMS WHICH MAY BE APPLIED EITHER GENERALLY OR BY SPECIFIC REFERENCE
FORMS
E1 Statutory Will Forms 1925, Form 1: Confirmation of settlements .. **[238.7]**
E2 Statutory Will Forms 1925, Form 2: Meaning of 'personal chattels' .... **[238.8]**
E3 Statutory Will Forms 1925, Form 3: Inventories and provisions respecting chattels1 .... **[238.9]**
E4 Statutory Will Forms 1925, Form 4: Legacies to charities .... **[238.10]**
E5 Statutory Will Forms 1925, Form 5: Directions\respecting annuities1 .... **[238.11]**
E6 Statutory Will Forms 1925, Form 6: Power of appropriation .... **[238.12]**
FORMS WHICH MAY ONLY BE APPLIED BY SPECIFIC REFERENCE
FORMS
E8 Statutory Will Forms 1925, Form 8: Administration trusts .... **[238.14]**
E9 Statutory Will Forms 1925, Form 9: Trusts for spouse for life, with power to appoint to issue and gift over to them1 .... **[238.15]**
E10 Statutory Will Forms 1925, Form 10: Trusts for spouse and issue, without a power of appointment1 .... **[238.16]**

PRELIMINARY NOTE

[238.1]
Section 179 of the Law of Property Act 1925 (see Part G, para **[244.57]**) provides that the Lord Chancellor may from time to time prescribe and publish forms to which a testator may refer in his will, and give directions as to the manner in which they may be referred to, but, unless so referred to, such forms shall not be deemed to be incorporated in a will.

[238.2]
The Order printed below was made under the provisions of the section in 1925 and has not since been modified or replaced. It will be observed that the forms can be incorporated with or without modification.

[238.3]
Forms C1.5 (at para **[223.6]**) and C2.4 (at para **[224.73]**) incorporated a number of the forms. Certain of these forms were successfully incorporated in a will in Queensland: *Re Staple* [1954] QWN 54.

[238.4]

THE STATUTORY WILL FORMS ORDER 1925 (SR & O 1925 NO 780)

1. The forms hereinafter contained may be cited as the Statutory Will Forms 1925, and are divided into two groups called Part I and Part II respectively.

2. The forms in Part I may be incorporated in a will by a general reference to that part, and the forms in Part I and Part II or any of them may be incorporated in a will in manner indicated in the Schedule hereto in any other manner indicating an intention to incorporate them and in the case of forms in Part II also indicating what property or disposition is to be affected thereby.

3.—

(1) In any form when incorporated in a will—

(i) The provisions thereof shall have effect subject to the express provisions of the will;

(ii) 'Disposition' means a devise, bequest, and a testamentary appointment, whether in exercise of a general or special power includes a disposition under the statutory power to dispose of entailed interests by will; 'dispose of' has a corresponding meaning; and references to a testator's property include property which he disposes of in exercise of a power;

(iii) 'The trustees' mean the trustees appointed by the testator either generally or for a specific purpose, as the case may require, and the persons who by appointment by the court or otherwise become the trustees, and include his personal representatives, when acting as his trustees;

(iv) 'Authorised investments' mean investments authorised by the will creating the trust, for the investment of any money subject to the trusts of the will, or by the law.

(v) Other words and expressions have the same meanings as in the Law of Property Act 1925.

The Schedule is as follows:

Incorporation of all the Forms in Part I

All the forms contained in Part I of the Statutory Will Forms 1925, are incorporated in my will [subject to the following modifications, namely*].

* Here insert the modifications (if any).

Incorporation of specified Forms from Part I

The following forms contained in Part I of the Statutory Will Forms 1925, shall be incorporated in my will:

[*Specify those of the following forms which it is desired to incorporate.*]

Form 1 (*Confirmation of settlements*).
Form 2 (*Meaning of 'personal chattels'*).
Form 3 (*Inventories and provisions respecting chattels*).
Form 4 (*Legacies to charities*).
Form 5 (*Directions respecting annuities*).
Form 6 (*Power of appropriation*).

[subject to the following modifications, namely*].

* Here insert the modifications (if any).

Incorporation of specified Forms from Part II

Form 7: *Trusts of a Settled Legacy*

Form 7 of the Statutory Will Forms 1925, is incorporated in my will, and shall apply to the following legacies*
[subject to the following modifications].

* Here insert the legacies of money or investments to be settled.

Here insert the modifications (if any).
Form 8: *Administration Trusts*
Form 8 of the Statutory Will Forms 1925, is incorporated in my will, and shall apply to*
[subject to the following modifications].

* Here insert description of property to be held upon administration trusts.

Here insert the modifications (if any).
Form 9: *Trusts for Spouse for life with power to appoint to issue and gift over to them*
Form 9 of the Statutory Will Forms 1925, is incorporated in my will, and shall apply to*
[subject to the following modifications].

* Here insert description of property to be held on trusts for spouse for life with power to appoint to issue and gift over to them.

Here insert the modifications (if any).
Form 10: *Trusts for Spouse and issue without a power of appointment*
Form 10 of the Statutory Will Forms 1925, is incorporated in my will, and shall apply to*
[subject to the following modifications].

* Here insert description of property to be held on trusts for spouse and issue without power of appointment.

Here insert the modifications (if any).

[238.5]
The Statutory Forms are set out below. As appears from para 2 of the Order (at para **[238.4]**), all the forms in Part I may be incorporated in a will, eg by using the words 'All the forms contained in the Statutory Will Forms 1925 are incorporated in my will' or some only may be incorporated thus 'Form I of the Statutory Will Forms 1925 is incorporated in this my will'. It may be desired to refer in general terms to the nature of the form. The forms in Part II (at paras **[238.7]**–**[238.16]**) can be used only by specific reference and the property to which the form applies must be identified. For forms of will incorporating some of the statutory forms see Form C1.5 at para **[223.6]** and Form C2.4 at para **[224.73]**.

[238.6]
It should be noted that the statutory forms have not been amended to take account of the Family Law Reform Act 1969 (FLRA 1969), the Inheritance Tax Act 1984 (IHTA 1984), the Trusts of Land and Appointment of Trustees Act 1996 (TLATA 1996), or the Civil Partnership Act 2004 (CPA 2004). Accordingly while reference to persons of 'full age' in Form 3 are now to be construed as references to persons who have attained the age of 18 years, the express references to the age of 21 years contained in the beneficial

trusts set out in Forms 9 and 10 remain unchanged. The administration trusts set out in Form 8 continue to refer to 'duties' but this term is deemed to include a reference to IHT: see IHTA 1984, Sch 6, para 1 and Finance Act 1986, s 100(1)(b). Further, a trust for sale and conversion as appears in Form E8 at para **[238.14]** is in general no longer necessary in administration trusts as a result of the TLATA 1996: see para **[214.1]** ff.

Forms which may be applied either generally or by specific reference

[238.7]

Form E1: Statutory Will Forms 1925, Form 1: Confirmation of settlements

I confirm every settlement of property made by me which is subsisting at my death, and subject to any express provision to the contrary in my will, the provisions made by my will for the benefit of persons beneficially interested under such settlements, shall be in addition to, and not in satisfaction of, those made, or covenanted to be made by me in such settlement.

[238.8]

Form E2: Statutory Will Forms 1925, Form 2: Meaning of 'personal chattels'

(1) 'Personal chattels' shall mean 'carriages, horses, stable furniture and effects (not used for business purposes), motor cars and accessories (not used for business purposes), garden effects, domestic animals, plate, plate articles, linen, china, glass, books, pictures, prints, furniture, jewellery, articles of household or personal use or ornament (including wearing apparel), also musical and scientific instruments and apparatus, wines, liquors and consumable stores, but shall not include any chattels used at my death for business purposes, nor money or securities for money.'[1]

(2) But a general disposition of personal chattels shall take effect subject to any specific disposition.

1 This differs slightly from the definition of personal chattels in the AEA 1925, s 55(1)(x); (Part G, para **[246.67]**); see also B4 at paras **[204.2]** and **[204.3]** and Vol 1, para **[64.44]**.

[238.9]

Form E3: Statutory Will Forms 1925, Form 3: Inventories and provisions respecting chattels[1]

(1) An inventory of chattels given by my will, otherwise than by way of absolute gift, shall be made in duplicate, one part shall be retained by the trustees and the other part shall be delivered to the person of full age[2] for the time being entitled to the use or possession of the chattels, in this clause called the 'usufructuary'.

(2) A receipt shall be signed by the usufructuary, at the foot of the inventory retained by the trustees.

(3) The inventory delivered to the usufructuary shall, if he so requires, be signed at the foot thereof by the trustees.

(4) On any change of the right to the use or possession of the chattels a new receipt shall be signed by the usufructuary at the foot of the inventory retained by the trustees.

(5) Where, by reason of the exercise of any power to sell, exchange, purchase, alter the fashion of, or otherwise deal with the chattels, or of any destruction or loss of any chattel, the inventories become inaccurate, the inventories shall be altered and re-signed, or new inventories shall, if convenient, be made and signed.

(6) The trustees may, at their discretion, exclude from an inventory, any chattels which, by reason of their trifling value or wearing out nature, they may consider ought to be so excluded.

(7) Where the chattels have been delivered to the usufructuary and a receipt is given therefor, the trustees, so long as the usufructuary remains entitled to the use of the chattels, shall not be liable in any way—

(a) for any authorised disposition thereof or dealing therewith,

(b) to see the insurance (so far as the same are capable of being insured), repair, or safe custody of the chattels,

unless and until required, in writing, to insure the chattels or to take any proceedings in reference thereto, by some person beneficially interested in the chattels or by his guardian, committee or receiver, and unless also due provision be made, to the satisfaction of the trustees, for the payment of the costs of insurance or of any proceedings required to be taken.

(8) Where there is no person of full age[2] and capacity entitled to the use of the chattels, the trustees may, during the period of disability make such arrangements for the safe custody, repair, insurance and use of the chattels as, having regard to the circumstances of the case, they may in their absolute discretion, think expedient.

1 Compare Forms B4.1 and B4.2 at paras **[204.15]** and **[204.16]**.
2 The age of majority is 18 years: FLRA 1969, s 1 (Part G, para **[246.89]**).

[238.10]

Form E4: Statutory Will Forms 1925, Form 4: Legacies to charities

The receipt of the treasurer or other proper officer of a charitable benevolent or philanthropic institution, society or body of persons (corporate or incorporate), to which a legacy is given by my will shall be a complete discharge to my personal representatives.

[238.11]

Form E5: Statutory Will Forms 1925, Form 5: Directions\respecting annuities[1]

The following provisions shall have effect in regard to any annuities or annuity given by my will—

(1) The trustees may, and (if so requested by or on behalf of any person beneficially interested in the property affected), shall, as soon as may be after any annuity commences to accrue, set apart in their names or under their control authorised investments, to provide a fund, the income whereof will be sufficient, in the opinion of the trustees, to produce an annual sum equal to the amount of the annuities for the time being payable under my will.

(2) The income or, if necessary, the capital of the fund so appropriated, shall be applied in payment of every subsisting annuity.

(3) Until a fund shall be so appropriated, my residuary estate shall stand charged with the payment of every subsisting annuity, but, after appropriation, the said estate shall be thereby discharged therefrom.
(4) The appropriated fund, or, where more than one annuity is bequeathed, such parts thereof as, in the opinion of the trustees, may not be required to answer any subsisting annuity, shall, on the cesser of an annuity, fall into my residuary personal estate.
(5) Accordingly, as each annuity ceases, the trustees may treat as part of my residuary personal estate, the whole or a corresponding part of the appropriated fund, as the case may require, retaining only such part thereof (if any) as may, from time to time, in their opinion, be sufficient to produce, by the income thereof, an annual sum equal to the amount of any subsisting annuities.
(6) Any surplus income of the appropriated fund shall be applied in the same manner as the income of my residuary personal estate.
(7) The trustees may, at their discretion, vary any of the investments for the time being representing the appropriated fund for other authorised investments.
(8) In this clause 'annuity' includes any periodic payment (not being a rentcharge) for life or other terminable interest.

1 For the disadvantages of gifts of annuities, see the Preliminary Note to B11 at para **[211.1]** ff. For a direction to set apart separate funds for each annuity, see Form B11.8 at para **[211.15]**.

[238.12]

Form E6: Statutory Will Forms 1925, Form 6: Power of appropriation

(1) The power of appropriation conferred by the Administration of Estates Act 1925[1], shall be exercisable by the trustees, without any of the consents made requisite by that Act.[2]

(2) So far as practicable, the trustees shall give one month's notice, at least, of an intended appropriation, to the persons whose consent would, but for this clause, be required under that Act; but a purchaser shall not be concerned to see or inquire whether any such notices have been given.

(3) In this clause 'trustees' includes my personal representatives.

1 See TLATA 1996, s 41.
2 The main purpose of this qualification is to facilitate the administration. Generally, appropriations of interests in land by personal representatives are exempt from stamp duty land tax, even if made with consents. This is achieved by FA 2003, Sch 3, para 3A(1) which provides that the acquisition of property by a person in or towards satisfaction of his entitlement under or in relation to the will of a deceased person, or on the intestacy of a deceased person, is exempt from charge. Further, even where trustees appropriate property with the consents of beneficiaries after the completion of the administration of the estate, then (unless there is any extraneous consideration) there should be no stamp duty land tax liability for the beneficiaries since it is provided that where trustees reallocate trust property in such a way that a beneficiary acquires an interest in certain trust property and ceases to have an interest in other trust property, and the beneficiary consents to ceasing to have an interest in that other property, the fact that he gives consent does not mean that there is chargeable consideration for the acquisition, see FA 2003, Sch 16, para 8. Stamp duty still applies generally to instruments relating to stock or marketable securities, but not on appropriations, see FA 1985, s 84(4).

Forms which may only be applied by specific reference

[238.13]

Form E7: Statutory Will Forms 1925, Form 7: Trusts of a settled legacy[1]

Any legacy of money or investments to which this clause is applied shall be subject to the following provisions:

(1) The trustees shall stand possessed of the legacy upon trust to invest the same in their names or under their control in any authorised investments, with power, at the like discretion, to vary the investments thereof for others of a like nature.

(2) The trustees shall stand possessed of the legacy, and of the investments representing the same and all statutory accumulations, if any, of income thereof, hereinafter included in the description of such legacy upon trust to pay the income thereof to the legatee during the life of the legatee.

(3) After the death of the legatee, the capital and income of the legacy shall be held—

In trust for all or any one or more exclusively of the other or others, of the issue[2] of the legatee, whether children or remoter descendants, at such time, and if more than one in such shares, with such provisions for maintenance, education, advancement, and otherwise, at the discretion of any person or persons, and with such gifts over, and generally in such manner, for the benefit of such issue, or some or one of them, as the legatee shall, by deed, revocable or irrevocable, or by will appoint; but so that, under any appointment, a child shall not, otherwise than by way of advancement, take a vested interest, except upon attaining the age of twenty-one years or upon marriage.

And in default of and until and subject to any such appointment—

In trust for all or any the children or child[2] of the legatee, who attain the age of twenty-one years, or marry under that age, and if more than one in equal shares.

(4) Any child of the legatee, who, or whose issue, takes any part of the legacy under any appointment by the legatee, shall not, in the absence of any direction by the legatee to the contrary, take any share in the unappointed part without bringing the share or shares appointed to him or his issue into hotchpot and accounting for the same accordingly.

(5) If the legatee shall not have any child who, under the trusts in default of appointment hereinbefore contained, attains a vested interest in the legacy, then, subject to the trusts and powers hereinbefore expressed in favour of the legatee and his issue, the legacy and the income thereof and all statutory accumulations, if any, of income shall fall into and form part of my residuary personal estate.

(6) The legatee may, notwithstanding any of the trusts hereinbefore expressed concerning his legacy, from time to time or at any time by deed, revocable or irrevocable, or by will, appoint to or for the benefit of any spouse who may survive the legatee, during the residue of the life of such spouse or for any less period (and subject

or not to any conditions, and with such gifts over, and discretionary or other trusts for the benefit of the spouse and issue of the legatee, as the legatee may think fit), all or any part of the annual income of the legacy of the legatee, or of so much thereof as shall not before the death of the legatee, have been paid or applied under any power affecting the same.

And, upon any such appointment, the trusts and powers limited to take effect after the death of the legatee, shall take effect subject to the interest limited by any such appointment:

Provided that the power last aforesaid, to appoint by deed, shall not be exercisable by a woman while under coverture.

1 This form settles any legacy directed to be subject to it upon trust for the legatee for life, and after his death for his issue as he should appoint, and in default of appointment for his children at 21. If the legacy takes effect immediately on death (or subject only to a survivorship condition permitted by IHTA 1984, s 92: see paras **[219.6]**–**[219.7]**) and the legatee is not an infant it will be an immediate post-death interest within IHTA 1984, s 49A (see para **[200.98]** above and para **[216.1]** above). If the testator is the parent of the life tenant's children, the default remainder trust for the children will not be a trust for bereaved minors within IHTA 1984, s 71A (see para **[200.108]** above), but should be an age 18-to-25 trust within IHTA 1984, s 71D to the extent that any of the children are under 21 on the date it takes effect (see para **[200.109]** above) (unless it has taken effect immediately on the testator's death, and any child was over the age of 18 but under the age of 21, and immediately entitled to an interest possession by virtue of TA 1925, s 31(1)(ii), so that he or she would have an immediate post-death interest). Any life interest appointed to a spouse of the legatee under the power of Clause (6) will not be an immediate post-death interest within IHTA 1984, s 49A (see para **[200.98]** above and para **[216.1]** above).

2 Unless excluded, the statutory rules of construction, whereby references to children and issue include references to illegitimate, legitimated and adopted persons (Part G, Section 2, para **[245.1]**), will apply. For a form in which the statutory rules are excluded see Form C13.2, cl 2(f) at para **[235.18]**.

[238.14]

Form E8: Statutory Will Forms 1925, Form 8: Administration trusts

Any property disposed of by my will (otherwise than in exercise of a special power) to which this clause is applied shall be subject to the following provisions:

(1) The property shall be held—

(a) as to the real property, if any, including chattels real, upon trust to sell the same[1], and

(b) as to the personal property, if any, upon trust to call in, sell, and convert into money such part thereof as may not consist of money.

(2) The trustees shall have power to postpone such sale and conversion for such a period as they, without being liable to account, may think proper.

(3) A reversionary interest shall not be sold, until it falls into possession, unless the trustees see special reason for sale.

(4) The trustees shall out of the net money to arise from the sale and conversion of the property (after payment of costs) and out of any ready money of mine, included in the disposition, pay or provide for—

(a) my funeral and testamentary expenses;

(b) my debts, except charges on other property of mine so far as those charges are discharged out of the property primarily charged therewith under the Administration of Estates Act 1925;[2]

(c) the duties,[3] payable out of capital on my death, and not charged on or primarily payable out of other property;[4]

(d) any other liabilities properly payable out of the property, or the proceeds of sale thereof;

(e) the legacies (including money directed to be paid by my will), and annuities, bequeathed by me, but so that all legacies and annuities, and the duty[3] on all legacies and annuities bequeathed free of duty[3] shall be paid primarily out of personal property, if any, included in the disposition.

(5) The trustees may invest, in their names or under their control, the residue of the said money, or so much thereof as may not have been distributed, in any authorised investments, with power, at their discretion, to vary such investments for others of a like nature.

(6) The income (including net rents and profits of real property and chattels real, after payment of rates, taxes, rent, costs of insurance and of repairs and other outgoings properly attributable to income) of so much of the property as is not required for the administration purposes aforesaid shall, however the property is invested, as from my death, be treated and applied as income; and for that purpose any necessary apportionment may be made between capital and income.[5]

(7) Provided that

(a) statutory accumulations of income made during a minority[6], or pending a contingency, or accumulations made under an express trust for accumulation, may be added to capital;

(b) income may be applied in effecting and maintaining a leasehold sinking fund policy, or may be set aside and invested for providing a fund to answer any liabilities which in the opinion of the trustees ought to be borne by income;

(c) the trustees may in their discretion adjust, in such manner as they shall think fit, having regard to the circumstances of the case, the incidence, as between capital and income, of the payments made in due course of administration.[7]

1 A trust for sale and conversion is in general no longer necessary in administration trusts as a result of the TLATA 1996, see paras **[214.1]** ff. The inclusion of such a trust in this form might be a reason for not using it or expressly varying it.

2 See Administration of Estates Act 1925, s 35 (Part G, para **[246.62]**).

3 References in this clause to death duties are construed as including a reference to IHT: see the IHTA 1984, Sch 6, para 1 and FA 1986, s 100(1)(b).

4 It was held in *Re Previté, Sturges v Previté* [1931] 1 Ch 447 that cl (4)(c) of this form did not alter the incidence of estate duty. It is thought that the incidence of inheritance tax is similarly unaffected. Note the incidence of inheritance tax is not in some respects the same as the incidence of estate duty in that realty is not now prima facie subject to its own tax: see the Preliminary Note to B14 at paras **[214.55]** ff.

5 Clause (6) excludes the rule in *Howe v Earl of Dartmouth* as to which see Vol 1, para **[38.17]** ff and see also the Preliminary Note to B14 at paras **[214.37]** and **[214.38]**.

6 See Trustee Act 1925, s 31(2) (Part G, para **[246.29]**).

7 Clause (7)(c) does not expressly exclude the rule in *Allhusen v Whittell* (as to which see Vol 1, para **[38.25]** and the Preliminary Note to B14 at para **[214.43]**), but gives the trustees power to disregard it.

[238.15]

Form E9: Statutory Will Forms 1925, Form 9: Trusts for spouse for life, with power to appoint to issue and gift over to them[1]

Any property disposed of by my will (otherwise than in exercise of a special power) to which this clause is applied[2] shall be subject to the following provisions:

(1) The property (including the investments for the time being representing the same) shall be held upon trust to pay the income thereof to my spouse for life.

(2) After the death of my spouse, the capital and income of the property shall be held—

(i) In trust for all or any one or more, exclusively of the other or others, of my issue, whether children or remoter descendants,[3] at such time, and if more than one in such shares, with such provisions for maintenance, education, advancement and otherwise, at the discretion of any person or persons, and with such gifts over, and generally in such manner, for the benefit of such issue, or some or one of them, as my spouse shall, by deed, revocable or irrevocable, or by will, appoint; but so that, under any appointment, a child shall not, otherwise than by way of advancement, take a vested interest, except upon attaining the age of twenty-one years or upon marriage.

(ii) And in default of and until and subject to any such appointment in trust, in equal shares if more than one, for all or any of my children or child[3] who survive me and attain the age of twenty-one years[4] or marry under that age, and for all or any of the issue[3] living at my death who attain the age of twenty-one years[4] or marry under that age or any child of mine who predeceases me, such issue to take through all degrees, according to their stocks, in equal shares if more than one, the share or shares which his or their parent would have taken if living at my death and so that no issue shall take whose parent is living at my death and so capable of taking.

(3) Any person who, or whose issue, takes any part of the property, under any appointment by my spouse, shall not, in the absence of any direction by my spouse to the contrary, take any share in the unappointed part, without bringing the shares appointed to such person or his issue into hotchpot, and accounting for the same accordingly.

1 This form settles any property directed to be subject to it upon trust for the surviving spouse for life, and after her death for the testator's issue as the surviving spouse should appoint, and in default of appointment for the testator's children at 21 or earlier marriage. If the spouse's life interest takes effect immediately on death (or subject only to a survivorship condition permitted by IHTA 1984, s 92: see paras **[219.6]**–**[219.7]**) it will be an immediate post-death interest within IHTA 1984, s 49A so spouse exemption from inheritance tax should be available, see para **[216.1]** above. The default remainder trust for the children will not be a trust for bereaved minors within IHTA 1984, s 71A (see para

[200.108] above), but should be an age 18-to-25 trust within IHTA 1984, s 71D to the extent that any of the children are under 21 on the date it takes effect (see para **[200.109]** above) (unless it has taken effect immediately on the testator's death, and any child was over the age of 18 but under the age of 21, and immediately entitled to an interest possession by virtue of TA 1925, s 31(1)(ii) (see para **[246.29]**), so that he or she would have an immediate post-death interest). The spouse could appoint trusts for the testator's children which would be within IHTA 1984, s 71A (see para **[200.108]** above) if they took effect while the children were under the age of 18.

2 These provisions will commonly be applied to residue.

3 See para **[238.13]**, n 1, above.

4 The reference to 21 years in this and the following form are unaffected by the FLRA 1969.

[238.16]

Form E10: Statutory Will Forms 1925, Form 10: Trusts for spouse and issue, without a power of appointment[1]

Any property disposed of by my will (otherwise than in exercise of a special power) to which this clause is applied shall be subject to the following provisions:

(1) The property (including the investments for the time being representing the same) shall be held upon trust to pay the income thereof to my spouse for life.

(2) After the death of my spouse the capital and income of the property shall be held in trust, in equal shares if more than one, for all or any of my children or child,[2] who survive me and attain the age of twenty-one years[3] or marry under that age, and for all or any of the issue[2] living at my death, who attain the age of twenty-one years[1] or marry under that age, of any child of mine who predeceases me, such issue to take through all degrees, according to their stocks, in equal shares, if more than one, the share or shares which his or their parent would have taken if living at my death; and so that no issue shall take whose parent is living at my death and so capable of taking.

1 This form settles any property directed to be subject to it upon trust for the surviving spouse for life, and after her death for the testator's children at 21 or earlier marriage. If the spouse's life interest takes effect immediately on death (or subject only to a survivorship condition permitted by IHTA 1984, s 92: see paras **[219.6]**–**[219.7]**) it will be an immediate post-death interest within IHTA 1984, s 49A, so spouse exemption from inheritance tax should be available, see para **[216.1]** above. The remainder trust for the children will not be a trust for bereaved minors within IHTA 1984, s 71A (see para **[200.120]** above), but should be an age 18-to-25 trust within IHTA 1984, s 71D to the extent that any of the children are under 21 on the date it takes effect (see para **[200.121]** above) (unless it has taken effect immediately on the testator's death, and any child was over the age of 18 but under the age of 21, and immediately entitled to an interest possession by virtue of TA 1925, s 31(1)(ii), so that he or she would have an immediate post-death interest).

2 See para **[238.13]**, n 1.

3 See para **[238.15]**, n 3.

PART F

Non-testamentary instruments

F1 Renunciation of probate and disclaimer of trusteeships

Preliminary Note .... **[239.1]**
FORMS
F1.1 Renunciation of probate .... **[239.2]**
F1.2 Deed of disclaimer of the trusteeship of a will by an executor and trustee who has renounced probate .... **[239.3]**
F1.3 Deed of disclaimer of the trusteeship of a will—short form .... **[239.4]**
F1.4 Appointment of new trustees by disclaiming trustee who has proved testator's will .... **[239.5]**

PRELIMINARY NOTE

[239.1]
An executor appointed by the will of a deceased person who has not intermeddled with the estate may either reserve his position, in which case powers will be reserved to him to prove the will at a later stage if he so wishes, or he may renounce probate. The renunciation should be in writing and should be filed in court. A renunciation can be withdrawn but, if it has been filed, not without the leave of the court. See generally as to renunciation Vol 1, para **[25.13]**.

A renunciation of probate by an executor who is also appointed a trustee is not conclusive evidence that the trusteeship is renounced as well (see Vol 1, para **[27.4]**, n 8). He should therefore expressly disclaim the trusteeship, and a separate document is convenient because a renunciation of probate has to be filed with the court. A deed of disclaimer of the trusteeship will also be appropriate where someone appointed trustee but not executor wishes to disclaim. Where someone appointed a sole executor is willing to be executor but not trustee, he should take out probate and appoint new trustees in his place, when the administration is complete, under the statutory power in Trustee Act 1925 (TA 1925), s 36 (Part G, para **[246.34]**). See Form F1.4 at para **[239.5]**. If none of the named executors proves the will or accepts office as trustee of it the administrators will become trustees of the will on completion of the administration and among all the other usual powers of trustees will be able to appoint new trustees under the statutory power: see *Re Cockburn's Will Trusts, Cockburn v Lewis* [1957] Ch 438, [1957] 2 All ER 522.

Section 50 of the Administration of Justice Act 1985 confers jurisdiction on the High Court to appoint a new personal representative in substitution of some or all of the existing ones, or, if there are two or more of them, terminate the appointment of one or more, but not all, of the personal representatives. The Court is not empowered to increase the number of personal representatives. Application can be made by a personal representative or a beneficiary, and so an application under this section is a means whereby a personal representative can apply to be relieved of his office after he has obtained a grant. A personal representative who is substituted under this section is an executor (except for the purposes of any chain of representation) if he is appointed to act together with executors, and otherwise is an administrator.

[239.2]

Form F1.1: Renunciation of probate[1]

In the High Court of Justice.
Family Division.
The Principal [*or* The —— District] Probate Registry.
In the Estate of [*deceased's* [*name*], deceased.

WHEREAS [*deceased's* [*name*] late of [*deceased's last address*], deceased, died on the —— day of ——, 20—, at ——, having made and duly executed his last will and testament bearing date the —— day of ——, 20—, and thereof appointed the undersigned A B his sole executor; now I the said A B do hereby declare that I have not intermeddled in the estate of the said deceased and will not hereafter intermeddle therein with intent to defraud creditors, and I hereby renounce all my right and title to the probate and execution of the said will [and to letters of administration (with the said will annexed) of the estate of the said deceased[2]].

[*Signature of A B*]
Signed by the said A B this
—— day of ——, 20—, in
the presence of[3] ——,
Signature of Witness ——,
Address ——.

1 The renunciation is not effective until it is filed in the Registry: *Re Morant's Goods* (1874) LR 3 P & D 151. An executor cannot renounce until the testator is dead: *Re Fenton's Goods* (1825) 3 Add 35. Until that time the proper course is for the testator to execute a codicil revoking the appointment and, if necessary, making another appointment in its place. The executor need not renounce. He can if he wishes just stand aside and then if he is cited to come in and prove the will and simply refrains from doing so, his rights as executor wholly cease: AEA 1925, s 5(ii). The renunciation being filed in the appropriate Registry, it is sometimes executed in duplicate and the duplicate endorsed by the solicitor acting in the matter as follows: 'The instrument of renunciation of probate of which this is a duplicate was duly filed in the —— Registry of the Family Division on ——.' This, however, is not absolutely essential, since the grant will record the renunciation. If the disclaiming executor also intends to disclaim the office of trustee, Form F1.2 at para **[239.3]** or Form F1.3 at para **[239.4]**, should be used. As to probate generally see *Tristram and Coote's Probate Practice* (30th edn) LexisNexis Butterworths, and for renunciation of probate see Non-Contentious Probate Rules 1987, r 37 and Vol 1, para **[25.13]**.

2 This should be added if the executor might be entitled to a grant of administration in some other character under r 20 of the Non-Contentious Probate Rules 1987.

3 One disinterested witness is sufficient.

[239.3]

Form F1.2: Deed of disclaimer of the trusteeship of a will by an executor and trustee who has renounced probate[1]

THIS DEED OF DISCLAIMER is made the —— day of —— by [*disclaiming trustee*] of etc.

Whereas

(1) By his will dated —— [*testator*] late of etc (hereinafter called 'the testator') deceased devised and bequeathed all his real and personal property

unto [*disclaiming trustee*] and [*other trustees*] upon certain trusts therein mentioned and appointed the said [*disclaiming trustee*] and [*other trustees*] executors of his said will.

(2) The testator died on —— and his said will was on —— proved by the said [*other trustees*] alone in the [Principal] [—— District] [Registry of the Family Division] the said [*disclaiming trustee*] having renounced probate thereof [or having by an instrument dated —— duly renounced probate thereof which renunciation was duly filed in the said Registry].

(3) The said [*disclaiming trustee*] is desirous of disclaiming the trusts reposed in him by the said will.

NOW THIS DEED WITNESSES that the said [*disclaiming trustee*] hereby disclaims all the estate and interest in the real and personal estate of the testator devised and bequeathed to him by the said will as a trustee jointly with the said [*other trustees*] and the trusts and powers thereby reposed in him jointly with the said [*other trustees*].

[*If the disclaiming trustee is or may become entitled to a beneficial interest, add:* Provided that the disclaimer aforesaid shall not operate to disclaim or release any beneficial interest whether vested or contingent to which the said [*disclaiming trustee*] now is or may hereafter become entitled under the trusts or provisions of the said will [or any legacy thereby given to him for his own benefit] but any legacy or remuneration for acting in the trusts thereof is hereby disclaimed.[2]

In witness etc

[*Signature of and execution as a deed by disclaiming trustee.*][3]

1 As to disclaimer, see Vol 1, para **[27.4]**. Where a disclaimer is in writing it may be by deed: see LPA 1925, s 52(2)(b), and Vol 1, para **[27.4]**, n 2. Owing to the difficulty of proving a disclaimer by conduct, this deed should be executed in every case where the trustee does not intend to act in the trusts. In any ordinary case, the shorter form given in the next following precedent is quite sufficient.

2 The trustee would be disentitled to this benefit in any event if he did not act in the trusts. However, difficult questions sometimes arise as to whether a trustee has acted: see *Re Sharman's Will Trusts, Public Trustee v Sharman* [1942] Ch 311, [1942] 2 All ER 74.

3 For execution of an instrument as a deed, see the Law of Property (Miscellaneous Provisions) Act, 1989, s 1 and Form F3.3 at para **[241.24]**.

[239.4]

Form F1.3: Deed of disclaimer of the trusteeship of a will—short form[1]

BY THIS DEED made the —— day of —— I [*disclaiming trustee*] of etc hereby disclaim all the estate and interest in the real and personal estate of [*testator*] late of etc devolving upon me as [executor and] trustee of the will of the said [testator] deceased dated —— and the trusts and powers thereby reposed in me either solely or jointly with other persons [Provided that this disclaimer shall not operate to disclaim or release any beneficial interest to which I now am or may become entitled under the said will other than a benefit given to me for acting in the said trusts][2].

In witness etc

[*Signature of and execution as a deed by disclaiming trustee.*][3]

1 This short form is sufficient in practically every case. See notes to the immediately preceding precedent. It must be remembered that where a person is appointed executor and trustee, the taking out of probate is prima facie evidence of the acceptance of the trusts, and this is still more so where the trusts are engrafted on to the executorship without specifically

appointing the executor a trustee. In such cases, therefore, where a person has taken a grant (probably for the convenience of the estate) but does not intend to act in the trusts, he should either execute a disclaimer in this form or, better still, as soon as he has concluded the duties of the executorship secure the appointment of another trustee in his place. He cannot, of course, secure the appointment of anyone to perform the duties of executor without the concurrence of the court, but once those duties of clearing the estate are concluded, he is free to secure the appointment of a new trustee: see Vol 1, paras **[25.13]** and **[27.4]**. A trustee who has acted in the trusts cannot disclaim: *Re Sharman's Will Trusts, Public Trustee v Sharman* [1942] Ch 311, [1942] 2 All ER 74; he must secure the appointment of another trustee in his place.

2 See para **[239.3]**, n 2.

3 For execution of an instrument as a deed, see the Law of Property (Miscellaneous Provisions) Act 1989, s 1 and Form F3.3 at para **[241.24]**.

[239.5]

Form F1.4: Appointment of new trustees by disclaiming trustee who has proved testator's will[1]

THIS DEED OF APPOINTMENT OF NEW TRUSTEE is made the —— day of —— BETWEEN [*disclaiming trustee*] of etc (hereinafter called 'the appointor') of the one part and [*new trustees*] of etc (hereinafter called 'the new trustees') of the other part.

Whereas

(1) By his will dated —— [*testator*] late of —— (hereinafter called 'the testator') appointed the appointor to be the sole executor and trustee thereof and devised and bequeathed his property as therein mentioned and inter alia bequeathed an annuity of £—— per annum to the appointor in consideration of his acting as trustee of his will.

(2) The testator died on —— and the appointor on —— obtained a grant of probate thereof in the —— Probate Registry.

(3) The appointor though he has fulfilled the duties of executor of the said will desires to be discharged from the trusts thereof.

(4) The appointor has paid the funeral and testamentary expenses of the testator and discharged all taxes and duties for which he is accountable.[2]

(5) The new trustees are willing to act as the trustees of the said will in place of the appointor.

NOW THIS DEED WITNESSES as follows:

1. The appointor in exercise of the power given by the Trustee Act 1925 and every other power hereunto enabling him hereby appoints the new trustees to be the trustees of the said will in place of the appointor for all the purposes for which the appointor was appointed trustee thereof.

2. The appointor hereby disclaims all that the annuity of £—— per annum [*or* the legacy of £——] bequeathed to him as trustee of the said will.[3]

In witness etc

[*Signatures of and execution as a deed by all parties.*][4]

1 This is an appointment by a trustee refusing to act within the meaning of the TA 1925, s 36(1) (Part G, para **[246.34]**). The sole executor and trustee may be willing to take the grant to avoid delay in securing payment of policy moneys or to avoid the difficulty of securing an administrators' bond. He should in general appoint two new trustees.

2 It is thought that new trustees of a will can be appointed even though the administration is incomplete and no part of the estate has vested in the personal representative as trustee, though it would be unusual for an appointment to be made in such circumstances. In the

case of land a written assent is necessary to vest title in the trustees: *Re King's Will Trusts, Assheton v Boyne* [1964] Ch 542, [1964] 1 All ER 833.

3 It may be advisable to add a clause of this nature to make the position clear. If an annuity is given it will be reasonably clear that such gift was given to the disclaiming trustee as trustee and not as executor. In the case of a legacy it may well be if the amount is relatively small that the disclaiming party is entitled to it for acting in the executorship and it may not need to be disclaimed. These doubts may be resolved by the party disclaiming as in this second clause, but if he intends to claim a legacy as executor this clause should be omitted. At one time it was thought necessary to add a clause disclaiming the trusts and the trust property, but the appointment acts as a discharge of the trustee and the property either passes under the TA 1925, s 40 (Part G, para **[246.38]**), or under an assent by the personal representatives. It is not thought that this deed operates to divest a personal representative of property which he still holds as such and, despite the execution of this deed, all proving executors should also execute the usual assent.

4 For execution of an instrument as a deed, see the Law of Property (Miscellaneous Provisions) Act 1989, s 1 and Form F3.3 at para **[241.24]**.

F2 Executors and trustees

FORMS

F2.1	Notice to the Public Trustee of death of a testator who has appointed the Public Trustee as an executor of his will	**[240.1]**
F2.2	Notice to the Public Trustee of death of a testator who has appointed the Public Trustee as a trustee or as custodian trustee under his will	**[240.2]**
F2.3	Words to be included in executors' oath where partners in a solicitors' firm have been appointed executors	**[240.3]**
F2.4	Application for an advance from a bank by executors and undertaking to repay	**[240.4]**
F2.5	Declaration of trust of property devised or bequeathed by will on a secret trust	**[240.5]**

[240.1]

Form F2.1: Notice to the Public Trustee of death of a testator who has appointed the Public Trustee as an executor of his will[1]

[*Address and date.*]
[*Testator*] *deceased.*

To the Public Trustee,
81 Chancery Lane,
London, WC2A 1DD
DX 0012 London/Chancery Lane

Dear Sir,

I regret to inform you that the above-named formerly of etc died on ——. By his will dated —— (or by a codicil dated —— to his will dated ——) he appointed the Public Trustee and myself to be the executors and trustees thereof and I enclose a copy of the said will [and codicil[s]].
The solicitors who acted for the deceased in his lifetime are Messrs —— of [address] who have agreed, subject to your approval, to act in the administration and to look to the estate and not to the executors personally for their costs.
The funeral arrangements are being made by [name] in accordance with the wishes expressed by the deceased in his lifetime and I shall be glad to learn that this meets with your approval.
I enclose a short statement showing the assets and liabilities of the estate so far as they are known to me. So far as I can estimate the gross value of the estate is about £——.
I shall be glad to learn that the Public Trustee will join with me in proving the will.
[Signature of co-executor.]

1 It is the duty of any person appointed co-executor with the Public Trustee, and not renouncing, to give the Public Trustee notice in writing of such appointment as soon as

practicable after the same comes to his knowledge: Public Trustee Rules 1912, rr 8(3), 1, 6(c). See Forms B3.15 to B3.21 at paras **[203.32]–[203.38]**, for will clauses concerning the appointment of the Public Trustee.

[240.2]

Form F2.2: Notice to the Public Trustee of death of a testator who has appointed the Public Trustee as a trustee or as custodian trustee under his will[1]

[*Address and date.*]
[*Name of testator*] Will Trust..

To the Public Trustee,
81 Chancery Lane,
London, WC2A 1DD
DX 0012 London/Chancery Lane

Dear Sir,

I regret to inform you that the above
I enclose a copy of his will dated —— [and of the —— codicil[s] thereto [respectively] dated ——].
It will be observed that under the will [and codicils] —— and —— are appointed as executors and that the Public Trustee is appointed as sole [or custodian] trustee thereof [*or* as trustee thereof jointly with [*names*]] [*or* that by clause —— of the will [or by the —— codicil] a legacy of £—— is bequeathed to the Public Trustee upon the trusts thereby declared].
I enclose a short statement showing the assets and liabilities of the estate so far as they are known to me. So far as I can estimate the gross value of the estate is about £——.
I am acting for the executors of the will who are proposing to prove the same in due course and the estate is likely to comprise [*nature of assets*] to the value of about £—— [and the trust legacy is likely to be available in due course].
[*Where the Public Trustee is concerned with residue, add*: A copy of the Inland Revenue account will be supplied as soon as it has been agreed with the authorities and in due course a copy of the executors' accounts.]
I shall be glad to learn that the Public Trustee sees no difficulty in agreeing to act as [custodian] trustee [*or* trustee of the said legacy] in due course and to furnish any further information desired.
[*Signature of solicitor.*]

1 It is the duty of any person appointed co-trustee with the Public Trustee, and not disclaiming, to give the Public Trustee notice in writing of such appointment as soon as practicable after the same comes to his knowledge: Non-Contentious Probate Rules 1987, r 8(3). The notice may be given by the executors or one of them, but will commonly be given by their solicitor. No appointment is binding on the Public Trustee until he has sealed a formal consent to act: Public Trustee Rules 1912, rr 8(2), 10, and *Re Shaw, Public Trustee v Little* (1914) 110 LT 924. See Forms B3.15 to B3.21 at paras **[203.32]–[203.38]**, for will clauses concerning the appointment of the Public Trustee.

[240.3]

Form F2.3: Words to be included in executors' oath where partners in a solicitors' firm have been appointed executors[1]

I. Where There were Partners at the Date Other than Those Who are Applying.

That at the date of death of the said deceased there were [*state number*] partners in the firm of [*name*] of [*address*] [*add if it be the case*[2] the firm which had at that date succeeded to and at that date carried on the practice of [*name and address of firm stated in appointment clause in will*]] namely myself/ourselves and [*states names of other partners and if any has since died or renounced recite details*]. That I am/we are the surviving [*or* [*state number*] of the] executor[s] named in the said will.

II. Where There were No Partners at the Date Other than Those (or the One) Applying.

That at the date of death of the said deceased I was the sole principal of [*or* we were the only partners in] the firm of [*name*] of [*address*] [*add if it be the case*[2] the firm which had at that date succeeded to and at that date carried on the practice of [*name and address of firm stated in the appointment clause in will*]] and as such I am/we are the [sole] executor[s] named in the said will.

1 See B3 at paras **[203.14]–[203.20]** and Form B3.8 at para **[203.21]** generally for the appointment of partners in a solicitors' firm to be executors and trustees of a will. Where one or more partners apply for probate and power is to be reserved to other partners in the firm who have been appointed executors by reference to their being partners in that firm and not by their names, notice of the application need not be given to the partners to whom power is to be reserved; see the Non-Contentions Probate Rules 1987, r 27(1A), as amended by SI 1991/1876 as from 14 October 1991.

2 If the Oath states that the firm named in the appointment clause has been succeeded by another which carries on its practice, this must be established to the satisfaction of the district judge or registrar.

[240.4]

Form F2.4: Application for an advance from a bank by executors and undertaking to repay[1]

To —— Bank Plc.
[*Date*]
[*Branch*]

As executors of the will of [*testator*] deceased, which will we intend to prove at once, we have to request that you will advance to us the sum of £—— for payment of inheritance tax and expenses; and in consideration of your so doing we hereby undertake that the sum shall be so applied, and that we will duly obtain a grant of probate of the said will and forthwith produce the same to you for registration in your books and we hereby undertake to repay such advance out of the first moneys received on account of the estate of the deceased, and we hereby charge with such payment any cash and securities in your hands belonging to the deceased. The net value of the estate of the deceased is at present estimated to be £——.

1 An immediate necessity is the obtaining of sufficient funds for the payment of the inheritance tax in order to obtain a grant of probate. Such funds are often supplied by a

bank and this form of undertaking is usually required. An advance is usually given as soon as the bank are satisfied as to the solvency of the estate. Even if the estate proves insolvent, administration expenses have priority: Article 4(2) of the Administration of Insolvent Estates of Deceased Persons Order 1986 (SI 1986/1999), made under the Insolvency Act 1986, s 421. Executors can give a security of this nature before probate, though there would be a difficulty in suing upon it so as to bind the estate before probate was granted. It would be better from the purely legal aspect of this matter to make the personal representatives personally liable, but that is not always practicable and in any event is asking them to undertake a liability which they should not be asked to undertake.

[240.5]

Form F2.5: Declaration of trust of property devised or bequeathed by will on a secret trust[1]

THIS DECLARATION OF TRUST is made the —— day of —— BY [*declarants*] of etc (hereinafter called 'the declarants').

Whereas:

(1) [*Testator*] of etc has by his will intended to be executed shortly after the execution hereof devised [and bequeathed] certain property to the declarants for their own absolute use and benefit.

(2) The declarants as they hereby acknowledge are not to hold the said property for their own absolute use and benefit but upon the trusts hereinafter declared.

(3) The said property is specified in the schedule hereto.

NOW IT IS HEREBY DECLARED that if and when the said will shall become effective in law and the said property shall be vested in the declarants such property shall be held by the declarants upon the following trusts:

[Set out trusts.]

[Schedule.]

In Witness etc

[*Signatures and execution as a deed by declarants.*][2]

1 This declaration must be in existence at the time when the will is executed and the declaration cannot contain any provision for the alteration or revision of the trusts: see *Re Jones* [1942] Ch 328, [1942] 1 All ER 642. For secret trusts see, further, Vol 1,Ch 36.

2 For execution of an instrument as a deed, see the Law of Property (Miscellaneous Provisions) Act 1989, s 1 and Form F3.3 at para **[241.24]**.

F3 Disclaimers and variations of beneficial interests

Preliminary note .... [241.1]

FORMS

F3.1 Disclaimer by devisee of a gift under a will—short form.......... [241.22]

F3.2 Disclaimer—longer form.......... [241.23]

F3.3 Disclaimer of a life interest.......... [241.24]

F3.4 Deed of variation of dispositions effected by a will.......... [241.25]

F3.5 Deed of variation of disposition of property held by deceased and spouse on a joint tenancy.......... [241.26]

F3.6 Deed of variation creating a nil-rate band non-exempt legacy where entire estate given to the deceased's widow.......... [241.27]

F3.7 Deed of variation conferring a short-term interest in possession on a surviving spouse.......... [241.28]

F3.8 Deed of variation where spouses have died within two years of each other varying the disposition of the estate of the first to die... [241.29]

F3.9 Deed of variation of trusts of a will settling a life interest on discretionary trusts without disturbing remainders.......... [241.30]

F3.10 Deed of variation of trusts of a will settling a life interest on the same trusts as contingent remainders from time to time.......... [241.31]

PRELIMINARY NOTE

[241.1]

Disclaimers and variations have become important because the legislation relating to IHT allows the dispositions taking effect on a person's death to be rearranged by the beneficiaries within two years of the death, without tax being charged on the rearrangement but with the rearrangement being treated for IHT purposes as if effected by the deceased. There is a similar but more limited provision relating to capital gains tax. The relevant provisions are now embodied in the Inheritance Tax Act 1984 (IHTA 1984), s 142 and Taxation of Chargeable Gains Act 1992 (TCGA 1992), s 62(6)–(10). See also *Foster's Inheritance Tax*, D4.1123. Also, the IHTA 1984, s 17(*a*) provides that a variation or disclaimer to which s 142(1) applies is not a transfer of value for IHT purposes, ie the making of such a variation or disclaimer cannot be charged to IHT as the making of a lifetime disposition by the beneficiary or beneficiaries who make the variation or disclaimer.

[241.2]

Persons for whose benefit dispositions may be varied. It will be apparent that whether an instrument varying a deceased person's dispositions comes within the IHTA 1984, s 142 does not depend at all on who benefits from the variation. It can benefit absolutely anybody, and there is no requirement of any connection with the deceased.

[241.3]

Notice of intention for IHTA 1984, s 142 to apply. Since the effect of the IHTA 1984, s 142 is to treat a disposition made by a beneficiary as one made by the deceased, it can result in additional IHT becoming payable where an exempt beneficiary, such as the deceased's wife, assigns her interest. The personal representatives might not have enough assets left in their possession with which to pay the extra tax, and anyway s 142 not applying could be more advantageous in some circumstances (such as where the deceased has fully utilised his available nil-rate IHT band and the wife makes a substantial gift out of the deceased's assets). Section 142(2), (2A) therefore provides that for the section to apply to an instrument varying the deceased's dispositions, the instrument of variation must contain a statement, made by all the 'relevant persons', to the effect that they intend s 142(1) to apply to the variation. The 'relevant persons' are defined as the person or persons making the instrument, and where the variation results in additional tax being payable, the personal representatives. Personal representatives may, however, decline to join in such a statement if they have no or insufficient assets to discharge the additional tax. These requirements for a statement of intention were introduced for variations made after 31 July 2002 and replace the former requirement for an election to be made within six months of execution of the instrument of variation. If additional tax is payable as a result of the variation, there is an obligation on the relevant persons to deliver a copy of the instrument of variation to HMRC, and notify them of the amount of additional tax within six months: see IHTA 1984, s 218A, inserted by FA 2002, s 120(2), (4). Otherwise there is no obligation, as previously, to report the instrument.

If it is desired that some dispositions should be made to which s 142 applies, and some to which it does not, they could be made by separate instruments, with the one containing the appropriate statement, and the other not. It should also be noted that s 142(2) does not apply to *disclaimers* within s 142(1), and that the application of s 142 to disclaimers is thus automatic (unless they are made orally—in which case s 142 does not apply at all), so a statement within s 142(2) is not required, although it may be desirable for the sake of clarity. Where the deceased's surviving spouse makes an instrument of variation under which he or she assigns (to a non-exempt beneficiary) a specific gift or legacy which does not bear its own IHT, the persons interested in residue, out of which any extra tax will be paid, cannot, it seems, prevent a statement of intention under s 142(2) being made. A statement of intention under s 142(2), once made, cannot be revoked.

If it is intended that TCGA 1992, s 62(6) should apply to an instrument of variation (see para **[241.17]**), it must similarly contain a statement by the persons making the instrument that they intend s 62(6) to apply: see TCGA 1992, s 62(7) as substituted by FA 2002, s 52 with effect for instruments made after 31 July 2002. Note that there is no requirement for the personal representatives to join in this statement if they are not making the instrument.

For an example of a statement of intention within IHTA 1984, s 142(2) and TCGA 1992, s 62(7), see para **[241.25]**, below.

[241.4]

Receipt of benefit before the instrument is executed. The fact that a person has received a benefit under some interest in a deceased person's estate does not prevent him from transferring that interest to someone else by an instrument within the IHTA 1984, s 142. This is emphasised by the words in s 142(4) after the semicolon. It should be remembered, however, that as a matter of ordinary law a purported *disclaimer* will be ineffective if any benefit has been accepted under the gift purportedly disclaimed (see para **[241.16]**).

A separate but related problem is whether a person who is transferring by written instrument to another person some interest in a deceased person's estate must transfer also any benefit received by him or due to him, by virtue of that interest, during or in respect of the period between the death and the making of the instrument, for that instrument to fall within the IHTA 1984, s 142. In many cases this is strictly impossible (for example, where the benefit received was the occupation of a house) but there is no reason why the transferor should not assign income due but unpaid, or account for income already received, to the transferee (for the income tax consequences of doing so—see para **[241.19]**). It seems reasonably clear from the wording of s 142(1) that an instrument does not have to have retrospective effect in this manner to be within the section. There is specific provision in s 142(4) for variations which terminate an interest in possession (see para **[241.8]**).

[241.5]

Meaning of 'estate' for the purposes of section 142. Section 142(1) is expressly confined to variations or disclaimers relating to the property comprised in a deceased person's estate immediately before his death, which at first glance means the aggregate of all property to which that person was beneficially entitled other than excluded property (see IHTA 1984, s 5(1)). However, s 142(5) gives a special meaning to 'estate' for the purposes of s 142(1), by providing that it includes excluded property. It also provides that it does not include property in which the deceased had an interest in possession immediately before his death. This means that the only relieving provision where someone wishes not to receive an interest in settled property which falls into possession on the death of a life tenant is s 93 of the IHTA 1984, which applies only to a disclaimer made otherwise than for a consideration in money or money's worth.

It should also be noted that s 142 can apply to assets passing on a person's death, other than property which was settled property immediately before the death, which do not pass under that person's will, such as nominated savings bank accounts and interests in joint tenancies. For a form of variation of the disposition of a deceased's interest under a joint tenancy, see Form F3.5 at para **[241.26]**.

[241.6]

Form of instrument. Section 142 can only apply to a written instrument. Such instruments can take the form of disclaimers (provided that the requirements for a valid disclaimer are present, as to which see para **[241.16]**) or dispositions by assignment or conveyance. It is usual to call the latter 'deeds of variation'. Special provision will, however, be often needed where an assignment or conveyance is to operate as from the death of the deceased. Forms F3.4 to F3.10 at paras **[241.25]–[241.31]**, are intended to operate in this manner. HMRC take the view that an instrument of variation must identify the disposition of the deceased which is being varied, then vary the destination of that disposition as laid down by the terms of the will or the intestacy rules.

In practice instruments of variation are made by deed, to make sure that the variation is binding on the maker or makers of it, and are often expressed to vary the terms of the will or intestacy rules, as in the examples in Forms F3.4 to F3.10 at paras **[241.25]–[241.31]**.

As seen above, as from 31 July 2002, the instrument of variation must contain statements to the effect that IHTA 1984, s 142(1) and TCGA 1992, s 62(6) are to apply to the variation if such is the intention. See para **[241.3]**, above.

[241.7]

Consideration. Section 142(3) of the IHTA 1984 provides that s 142(1) does not apply to a variation or disclaimer made for any consideration in money or money's worth, other than consideration consisting of the making in respect of another of the deceased's dispositions of a variation or disclaimer to which s 142(1) applies. One particular point to watch in relation to this provision is that if the donee under an instrument of variation agrees to pay the costs of the instrument that could be consideration which takes the instrument outside s 142(1). For further points relating to this provision see paras **[241.13]** and **[241.14]**.

[241.8]

Interests in possession. Section 142(4) of the IHTA 1984 provides that where a variation within s 142(1) results in property being held in trust for a person which ends not more than two years after the deceased's death, the IHTA 1984 applies as if the disposition of the property that takes effect at the end of the period had had effect from the beginning of the period. It will be recalled that although a residuary estate will not strictly speaking be held on the trusts applicable to it under the testator's will until the administration of the estate is complete (*Stamp Duties Comr (Queensland) v Livingston* [1965] AC 694, [1964] 3 All ER 692), IHTA 1984, s 91 has the effect that, during the administration of the estate, any interest in possession which would subsist if the administration were complete is treated as subsisting for IHT purposes, and, consequently, that if there is an event which would be the coming to an end of an interest in possession in residue if the administration were complete it is treated as the termination of an interest in possession for IHT purposes. Section 142(4) can thus be relevant even where there is a variation relating to an interest in possession in unadministered residue.

An example of the operation of IHTA 1984, s 142(4) would be where the deceased's will gives his son a life interest in his residuary estate with effect from the deceased's death (so that if the deceased died on or after 22 March 2006 the life interest would be an immediate post-death interest within IHTA 1984, s 49A, (see para **[200.98]** above), and the son makes a deed of variation whereby his interest in possession terminates and the capital comes to be held on trust for the deceased's widow (either absolutely or for an interest in possession). Provided that the son's interest terminates by virtue of the deed of variation within two years from the deceased's death (and the other requirements of s 142 are satisfied), the variation will be treated as having effect from the deceased's death as well as not being itself a transfer of value by the son. This means that the property subject to the interest will be exempt from IHT on the deceased's death as going to the deceased's spouse (see Part A, para **[200.84]**), even if the son retains the income which accrued before the deed took effect. If the capital comes to be held on trust for the deceased's widow for an interest in possession, then since it will be treated as having effect from the deceased's death, it will be an immediate post-death interest within IHTA 1984, s 49A, (see para **[200.98]** above), therefore the spouse exemption from IHT should be available (see para **[216.1]** above).

However, s 142(4) contains a possible hazard for the unwary, and there is a limit on its scope—

(a) The possible hazard is that if a deed of variation creates a short-term interest in possession with the intention that the capital subject to that interest in possession will be treated by virtue of s 142 as if it were subject to the short-term interest in possession from the deceased's death, s 142(4) would have the effect of frustrating that intention if the short-term interest terminates within two years of the deceased's death because then the disposition taking effect on the termination of the interest in possession would be deemed to have had effect from the death of the deceased. A short-term interest created under an instrument of variation should thus be made to end more than two years after the deceased's death. For an example of this type of variation see Form F3.7 at para **[241.28]**. However, where a deed of variation creates an interest in possession, and the owner of it dies within two years of the deceased, it seems that HMRC do not regard s 142(4) as applying to treat the disposition taking effect on his death as having had effect from the death of the deceased: see *Foster's Inheritance Tax*, D4.14.

(b) The limit on the scope of s 142(4) is that it provides that it does not affect the application of the IHTA 1984 in relation to any distribution or application of property occurring before the termination of an interest in possession by virtue of a variation to which s 142(1) applies. This seems to mean, as regards property formerly subject to an interest in possession under the will and distributed in exercise of a power before the instrument of variation is made, that an instrument of variation cannot have a retrospective effect under s 142 (eg converting an exempt part of the deceased's estate on death to a non-exempt part or vice versa, or altering the IHT treatment of the distribution) in relation to that property: see further, *Foster's Inheritance Tax*, D4.14. The short point is that substantial discretionary distributions of capital subject to an interest in possession under a will should so far as possible be avoided until any proposals for an instrument of variation have been decided upon.

[241.9]

Consequences of s 142 applying. These have already been mentioned in general terms in the first paragraph of this Preliminary Note at para **[241.1]**. Further consequences of the provision in s 142(1) that IHTA 1984 applies as if a variation within s 142(1) was made by the deceased are worth noting. One is that if a variation within s 142 creates a settlement, the settlor of it for IHT purposes will be the deceased rather than the maker of the variation.

This could be significant for the application of the rules for charging IHT on discretionary trusts (see the Note on these in B18 at para **[218.6]** ff), or the application of the excluded property rules where the deceased had a non-UK domicile for IHT purposes (see the Preliminary Note to C14 at para **[236.1]** ff).

The second point is that it seems reasonably clear that the gift with reservation rules (see Part A, para **[200.76]**) apply as if the gift arising under an instrument of variation within s 142 is one made by the deceased and not by the maker of the instrument, ie in effect, the gift with reservation rules will not apply. Although the gift with reservation rules are contained in the Finance Act 1986, ss 102, 102A, 102B, 102ZA and Sch 20, those provisions are 'construed as one with' the IHTA 1984 (Finance Act 1986, s 114(5)). This means that an instrument of variation can eg create a discretionary trust under which the maker of the instrument is a beneficiary, and still be IHT effective: see Form F3.9 at para **[241.30]**.

A third point to note is that where the deceased died before 22 March 2006 (the date of the changes introduced by FA 2006, Sch 20), and a variation after that date (but within two years of his death), creates a new interest in possession which is deemed to have arisen on his death by virtue of IHTA 1984, s 142(1), that interest in possession will be deemed for IHT purposes to have arisen before 22 March 2006. One consequence of this is that it is possible that a subsequent interest in possession may be a transitional serial interest within IHTA 1984, s 49B (see para **[200.100]** above). Further, (and again where the deceased died before 22 March 2006) it may still be possible to create accumulation and maintenance trusts which have the IHT benefits of IHTA 1984, s 71 until 6 April 2008 (or beyond if capital will vest absolutely at age 18), since they will be deemed to have arisen pre-22 March 2006 (see para **[200.107]** above).

Where the deceased dies on or after 22 March 2006, and a variation after that date (but within two years of his death), creates a new interest in possession which is deemed to have arisen on his death by virtue of IHTA 1984, s 142(1), that interest in possession will be an immediate post-death interest within IHTA 1984, s 49A (see para **[200.98]** above and para **[216.1]** above). Therefore if the beneficiary of the interest in possession is the spouse or civil partner of the deceased, exemption from IHT should be available, see para **[216.1]** above.

Whether the deceased dies before, on or after 22 March 2006, leaving young children, it should be possible to establish for their benefit a trust for bereaved minors within IHTA 1984, s 71A (see para **[200.108]** above), or an age 18-to-25 trust within IHTA 1984, s 71D (see para **[200.109]** above).

A further consequence of s 142 applying (or more accurately, of IHTA 1984, s 17 applying, which provision prevents a variation or disclaimer within s 142(1) being a transfer of value) is that the pre-owned assets provisions of FA 2005, Sch 15 cannot apply. See para **[241.19]**, below.

[241.10]

Variations made before a grant of probate. If a variation of a deceased person's dispositions is decided on which will reduce or eliminate the IHT liability of his estate on his death, it will be an advantage if it can be put into effect before the grant of probate, so that the lesser amount consequent on the variation having been made is what is payable on account when applying for the grant. An instrument of variation may be made before there is a grant of representation and before the estate has been administered; although the right of a beneficiary who is interested in the unadministered estate of a deceased person does not amount to an equitable interest, he has a right to have the estate duly administered which he can make a disposition of: *Re Leigh's Will Trusts, Handyside v Durbridge* [1970] Ch 277, [1969] 3 All ER 432. HMRC accept that instruments of variation may validly be made before the grant of probate and their guidance note on Inland Revenue Accounts (January 1994—see *Foster's Inheritance Tax*, X3.53) says that such an instrument should state who are the proposed personal representatives and recite that they intend to apply for a grant at a (named) Probate Registry shortly. A copy of the deed containing the appropriate statement of intention must be submitted with the Account when applying for the grant if the IHT to be paid as a condition of probate is to be assessed on the basis that the variation has been made.

[241.11]
Necessary parties. Problems sometimes arise as to who are the necessary parties to an instrument of variation, typically where minors have beneficial interests in the estate, or there are beneficiaries who refuse to join in the variation, or are far away or difficult to contact. Section 142(1) requires that a variation of a disposition must be made by all those who benefit under the disposition. These might include not only persons with absolutely vested interests in the property whose disposition it is sought to vary, but also those with contingent interests, or those who are merely objects of a discretionary power over such property. On the other hand, where there is an absolute gift coupled with an expression of a wish which does not create a legal obligation that the donee should distribute the property in a particular way, only the donee would be a necessary party to a variation of the disposition.

Who are necessary parties to an instrument of variation is thus a matter of construction of the will in relation to the result which it is desired to achieve, and they are not necessarily everybody interested under the will. For example, if there are numerous pecuniary legacies in the will which it is not intended to cut down or alter in any way, the persons entitled to those legacies will not be needed as parties, or it may be possible to alter a life interest without altering remainder trusts under which minors are interested (for an example, see Form F3.9 at para **[241.30]**). The donees under a variation, or the trustees where the variation takes the form of creating or varying a trust, would usually be named as parties to the instrument, but the importance of their executing the instrument would usually be confined to showing that they accept the benefit conferred by it, unless they are also making some variation of dispositions in their favour under the same estate.

If there is the problem for a proposed deed of variation that the desired objectives cannot be attained without the variation of interests which are or might become vested in minors or unborn or unascertained persons, a possible solution is to apply for a variation of the trusts under the Variation of Trusts Act 1958. HMRC accept that an arrangement approved under that Act can be an instrument of variation within s 142. This is only a course to pursue where substantial amounts of tax are at stake, and if it is to be pursued proceedings need to be instituted promptly in order to get a court hearing date before two years have elapsed from the deceased's death.

As from 31 July 2002, the personal representatives will be necessary parties to an instrument of variation if it is intended that IHTA 1984, s 142(1) will apply, and if as a result additional tax will be payable, because of the requirement for an instrument of variation to contain a statement to the effect that IHTA 1984, s 142(1) is to apply, and that the personal representatives are to join in the statement if additional tax is payable as a result of the variation. See para **[241.3]**, above. In any event, it is important that the personal representatives should have notice of any instrument of variation, so that they know who to pay or distribute assets of the estate to.

For the appropriate parties to 'double death' variations see para **[241.14]**.

[241.12]

Subject to tax or free of tax. When framing a variation, careful consideration should be given to whether the dispositions which are to take effect as a result of the variation, and which will be deemed to have been made by the deceased, will be free of IHT or subject to IHT on the deceased's death. This is particularly important where the result of the variation is that part of the estate will be exempt from IHT and part will not, because if the non-exempt part of the estate exceeds the deceased's available nil-rate IHT band at the time of his death so that IHT will be payable, more IHT may be payable if non-residuary gifts to non-exempt persons are free of tax on the deceased's death than if they are subject to tax: see the Preliminary Note to B14 at para **[214.74]**. When drafting a variation by which a deceased person is deemed to have made non-residuary gifts to non-exempt persons these non-residuary gifts should be expressly made either free of tax or subject to tax on the testator's death (see, for example, cl 1 of Form F3.6 at para **[241.27]**). If no such direction is included, they will usually be free of tax: see the Preliminary Note to B14 at paras **[214.55]**–**[214.60]**.

[241.13]

Tax avoidance. A common type of variation has been one which results in an amount equal to the value of the testator's available nil-rate IHT band passing to non-exempt beneficiaries, and the rest of the estate passing to the surviving spouse (or civil partner) in order to obtain the spouse (or civil partner) exemption. Following the introduction on 9 October 2007 of rules to carry forward unused nil-rate band allowance (see para **[200.75]** above), variations to utilise the testator's available nil-rate IHT band may become less popular. But if the testator's estate includes property with the benefit of business or agricultural property relief, this can often be advantageously passed to non-exempt beneficiaries. In all cases where an estate containing such property is being varied, careful consideration should be given as to whether and how the dispositions of such property are to be varied. For the relevant considerations, see the Preliminary Notes to B5 at **[205.1]** ff and to C11 at **[233.1]** ff. There is also discussion of agricultural relief in the Preliminary Note to C12 at **[234.1]** ff.

When formulating and drafting a variation to take advantage of s 142(1), one must take care that HMRC will not be able to invoke s 142(3) (extraneous consideration—see para **[241.7]**) or the doctrine of *W T Ramsay Ltd v IRC* [1982] AC 300, [1981] 1 All ER 865, under which a step taken in a pre-ordained series of transactions and having no purpose other than tax avoidance can be disregarded. It is sometimes the case that on a testator's death a part, at least, of his estate passes to his children triggering an IHT charge. If his children entered into a deed of variation redirecting property they received under the will to the testator's widow so as to obtain the surviving spouse exemption on the testator's death, but upon the understanding that the widow later passed the property back to the children by a potentially exempt transfer, HMRC could contend either that extraneous consideration prohibited by s 142(3) had been provided for the variation, or else that the whole arrangement, ie the deed and the later transfer of property, is vitiated by an application of the *Ramsay* doctrine. It seems that HMRC does consider that *Ramsay* can apply in an IHT context, and in a case where property is redirected by instrument of variation to the testator's spouse they may enquire whether before the variation there was any discussion between the parties as to how the property redirected to the spouse should be dealt with and whether the spouse has made or is contemplating any transfers of the property redirected to her: see *Foster's Inheritance Tax*, D4.15.

However, the decision of the House of Lords in *Fitzwilliam v IRC* [1993] 3 All ER 184, [1993] 1 WLR 1189, that *Ramsay* did not apply in the particular circumstances of that case, may have paved the way for the contention that the *Ramsay* doctrine cannot apply where each step in a series of transactions has its own tax consequences. So where, for example, by virtue of a deed of variation a widow takes an interest in possession in property (which will be treated as a pre-22 March 2006 interest in possession or an immediate post-death interest, see para **[241.9]** above) which is to terminate some time after the date of the deed of variation (and after the expiry of the period of two years from the testator's death) when absolute remainder trusts for the children are to take effect, it is arguable that *Ramsay* cannot apply to prevent, first, the spouse exemption from being available in respect of the property on the testator's death, and secondly, to prevent the widow from being treated as making a potentially exempt transfer on the termination of her interest in possession, because while the widow is entitled to the interest in possession there are income tax and potential IHT consequences which make it impossible to ignore her brief entitlement and it is only if one can ignore such an entitlement that *Ramsay* can have any application. The effectiveness of this scheme and its immunity from a *Ramsay* attack can be further supported by reference to *MacNiven v Westmoreland Investments Ltd* [2001] UKHL 6, [2001] STC 237, which suggests that *Ramsay* cannot apply to recharacterise transactions involving 'purely legal concepts which have no broader commercial meaning'. Since IHT is essentially a tax on a 'transfer of value', which would seem to be a purely legal concept, it may be that a *Ramsay* challenge could not succeed in respect of this scheme.

Form F3.7 (at para **[241.28]**), is an example of a variation conferring a short-term interest in possession on a surviving spouse. The interest in possession should terminate under the terms of the deed after the expiry of two years after the testator's death for reasons given at para **[241.8]**. But it should be noted that HMRC are known not to approve of such variations: see *Foster's Inheritance Tax*, D4.15.

[241.14]

Double death variations. Prior to the introduction on 9 October 2007 of rules to carry forward unused nil-rate band allowance (see para **[200.75]** above), so-called 'double death variations' were a popular device where two spouses (or civil partners) died within two years of each other, and the estate, or part of the estate, of the first to die (a husband, say) had passed to the survivor (his wife) without his available nil-rate IHT band being fully utilised, but the wife's chargeable estate (enhanced by her husband's estate) exceeded her available IHT nil-rate band. The personal representatives and beneficiaries of the wife's estate may then have executed a deed of variation within two years of the husband's death, redirecting property up to the value of the husband's available unused IHT nil-rate band away from the wife's estate and into a non-exempt gift. In this way the husband's available nil-rate IHT band was fully utilised, and the wife's estate was reduced for IHT purposes, thereby reducing the amount of IHT payable. Even with the introduction of rules to carry forward unused nil-rate band allowance, such variations may still be advantageous in appropriate cases. For example, if the estate of the husband included property whose value was within his available nil-rate band at the time of his death, but which has risen substantially in value since then, eg. land which may have been granted planning permission, so that it is worth more than the nil-rate band carry forward allowance, a variation redirecting it by non-exempt gift so as to utilise the husband's nil-rate IHT band may produce a significant saving in IHT compared with allowing it to be taxed at a value in the wife's estate greater than the nil-rate band carry forward allowance.

HMRC accept that such a variation can fall within the IHTA 1984, s 142(1) if the appropriate statement of intention is made in the instrument of variation, even where no significant change of substance is made to the ultimate destination of the property subject to the instrument of variation. For it to be effective it must be made by the personal representatives of the second to die, but with the consent of the beneficiaries under the estate of the second to die (or at any rate those whose interests under the second estate are affected). HMRC will accept the written consent of such beneficiaries in a separate document (*Inland Revenue Tax Bulletin*, Issue 15 (February 1995); *Variation of inheritances following a death*—see *Foster's Inheritance Tax*, X6.63).

One important point to watch in relation to double death variations is the prohibition of extraneous consideration in s 142(3) (see para **[241.7]**). If a double death variation was to involve an exchange of beneficial interests under one estate for beneficial interests under the other, the arrangement would fall foul of s 142(3); the latter only permits exchanges of interests under the same estate to fall within s 142(1).

It seems that HMRC will regard the variation as ineffective if it purports to vary a life interest of the surviving spouse in the first to die's estate: see Inland Revenue Capital Taxes *IHT Newsletter* December 2001, p 5. It also seems, from the same source, that they will accept a disclaimer by the life tenant's personal representatives as effective where it is possible as a matter of general law for them to disclaim it. HMRC's non-acceptance of a variation of a life interest after the life tenant's death receives support from *Soutter's Executry v IRC* [2002] STC (SCD) 385, where a Scottish Special

Commissioner held that a variation of a liferent (a right to reside in a property for life) by the executors of the liferenter who died within two years of the testator from whom he derived his liferent, was ineffectual because following the liferenter's death there was nothing to vary.

Form F3.8 (at para **[241.29]**), is an example of a 'double death' variation.

[241.15]

Multiple variations. It was held in *Russell v IRC* [1988] 2 All ER 405, [1988] 1 WLR 834 that it is not possible in relation to an instrument of variation within s 142 to vary the dispositions of it in such a way as to have s 142 apply to such a variation of a variation. Thus if there is a mistake in an instrument of variation a further variation of it cannot be used as a remedy, although it may be possible (if there is appropriate evidence) to apply to the court for rectification of it (see *Foster's Inheritance Tax*, C1.34). On the other hand, it is possible to have more than one instrument of variation within s 142 relating to the same estate if each instrument affects different assets.

[241.16]

Disclaimers. If a disclaimer is contemplated the following points should be borne in mind:

(i) The law relating to disclaimers is technical and obscure. While some of its salient features are noted below, reference should be made to *Ing on Bona Vacantia* at pp 207 ff and *Halsbury's Laws of England*, 4th edn Reissue, Vol 50, paras **[390]**–**[392]** at pp 284–286, for a fuller treatment. See also Vol 1, para **[46.1]** ff.

(ii) The disclaimer does not strictly speaking operate as a disposition of property. As was said in an old case, a man 'cannot have an estate put into him in spite of his teeth'. Thus a disclaimer will not divest a gift in favour of the disclaiming beneficiary, but will prevent it from vesting in him. Acceptance of a gift or any part of it is inconsistent with an intention to renounce or disclaim it. The right to disclaim a gift is therefore extinguished as soon as any benefit has been received thereunder: see eg *Re Wimperis, Wicken v Wilson* [1914] 1 Ch 502. While it is usually possible to disclaim one testamentary gift without disclaiming another, this will not be permissible where such right is impliedly excluded. This will often be the case where gifts of onerous property and unencumbered property are made to the same person. Nor is it permissible to disclaim part only of a single gift. In *Re Joel, Rogerson v Joel* [1943] Ch 311, [1943] 2 All ER 263, CA, a gift of a leasehold house 'together with its contents' was in fact held to be a single gift and the legatee was accordingly held not to be entitled to disclaim the onerous leasehold whilst accepting the contents of the house.

(iii) Since, as we have already seen, disclaimers operate not to divest a gift but to prevent it from vesting, there is no requirement of form. A disclaimer even of an interest in land may thus be effected by informal writing, by conduct or even orally. But to be effective for the purposes of s 142 of the IHTA 1984 the disclaimer must be in writing. (IHTA 1984, s 142(1) applies automatically to a written disclaimer so long as it is made within two years of death and for no extraneous consideration, so a statement within s 142(2) is not required. See para **[241.3]**, above.) In general a disclaimer may also be retracted where nobody has altered his position on the faith of it. This right is not thought to be available where the disclaimer is by deed: see *Ing*, above at pp 209–210. In the interests of certainty it seems preferable for a disclaimer to be effected by deed.

(iv) It has sometimes been argued that it is not possible to disclaim an interest arising under an intestacy on the grounds that such interest is conferred by statute: see eg Sir William Goodhart QC's article 'Disclaimer of Interests on Intestacy?' in 40 *Conveyancer* at p 292. This would be an inconvenient restriction and, as Sir William himself points out, is inconsistent with the actual decision of Walton J in *Re Scott, Widdows v Friends of the Clergy Corpn* [1975] 2 All ER 1033, [1975] 1 WLR 1260, though the point was not in fact argued in that case.

(v) It is essential to give careful thought to what dispositions will take effect on a disclaimer being made. For example, sometimes a disclaimer of a life interest will accelerate the remainder interests, and sometimes it will give rise to a partial intestacy, depending on the nature of the remainder trusts; see Vol 1, para **[48.4]** ff. *Re Scott* discusses the effect of a disclaimer of certain interests arising under the intestacy rules, but the difficult problem as to the effect of a disclaimer by a child of a deceased intestate of his interest in that intestate's estate where that child himself has issue seems now to have been answered by the Court of Appeal in *Re DWS* [2001] Ch 568, [2001] 1 All ER 97, a case concerned with the effect on intestate succession of the forfeiture rule disqualifying a murderer from benefiting from his intestate victim's estate. Aldous LJ held that the Administration of Estates Act 1925, s 47(1)(I) was unambiguous and should be given its literal meaning that no issue could take if the parent was living at the death of the intestate; that if a surviving parent was prevented from taking by disclaimer or disqualification, the intestate's estate should pass not to the surviving parent's child, but to others. The Court was divided upon who should take, however, the majority holding in favour of the collateral relations within the Administration of Estates Act 1925, s 47(1)(v), but Sedley LJ preferring the estate to pass bona vacantia. See para **[9.13]**, above for Law Commission proposals that where a person who disclaims an inheritance, either under a will or under the law of intestacy, the inheritance should devolve as if the person disclaiming had died immediately before the deceased.

[241.17]

Capital gains tax. The TCGA 1992, s 62(6) to (10) contains provisions for capital gains tax which are for the most part identical with the IHTA 1984, s 142, though with some necessary differences arising from differences in the nature of the tax and one important difference of substance. These subsections apply to property of which the deceased was competent to dispose by will, other than under a power of appointment or the statutory power to dispose of entailed property, but with the express addition of any severable share under a joint tenancy (see sub-s (10)); it seems to us that this covers the same kinds of property as the differently worded provisions of IHTA 1984, s 142. Again a statement of intention is needed in the instrument of variation that the persons making the instrument intend s 62(6) to apply, (see

TCGA 1992, s 62(7) as substituted by FA 2002, s 52 with effect for instruments made after 31 July 2002). Though such a statement of intention is not required for a disclaimer, and in no circumstances do the personal representatives have to join in (unless they are parties to the instrument) (see s 62(7)).

The important difference between the TCGA 1992, s 62(6) and the IHTA 1984, s 142(1), however, is that whereas the result of the latter applying should apply is that the variation is treated as made by the deceased for all IHT purposes, the result of the corresponding capital gains tax provision applying is that the variation is treated as made by the deceased only for the purposes of the TCGA 1992, s 62, a section containing general provisions relevant to death (see *Marshall v Kerr* [1995] 1 AC 148, [1994] 3 All ER 106, HL), and for one other purpose mentioned below. So the consequences of a capital gains tax statement of intention are that the variation is not a disposal for capital gains tax purposes and the persons who have assets transferred to them pursuant to the variation will receive them 'as legatees' within the TCGA 1992, s 62(4), so that the acquisition value of the assets in their hands is that of the personal representatives.

Legislation has confirmed that the settlor for capital gains tax purposes of a settlement created by variation within TCGA 1992, s 62(6) is the person who made the variation, at least where that person would, in the absence of the variation, have been entitled to the varied property absolutely. TCGA 1992, s 68C(2), (3) (added by FA 2006, Sch 12, para 1(2) and coming into force on 6 April 2006 in relation to settlements whenever created), provides that where a disposition of property following a person's death is varied and becomes settled property in consequence of the variation (and would not, but for the variation, have become settled property), and TCGA 1992, s 62(6) applies in respect of the variation, the person who is to be treated as having made the settlement and provided the property for the purposes of the settlement is:

(a) a person who immediately before the variation was entitled to the property, or to property from which it derives, absolutely as legatee;
(b) a person who would have become entitled to the property, or to property from which it derives, absolutely as legatee but for the variation;
(c) a person who immediately before the variation would have been entitled to the property, or to property from which it derives, absolutely as legatee but for being an infant or other person under a disability; and
(d) a person who would, but for the variation, have become entitled to the property, or to property from which it derives, absolutely as legatee if he had not been an infant or other person under a disability.

The main implication of this is that where an instrument of variation settles property on trust it will be a settlement of which the maker of the instrument is the settlor for capital gains tax purposes. So for capital gains tax purposes such as identifying the settlor of a settlement for the purposes of charging capital gains tax on a settlor with an interest in a settlement under the TCGA 1992, s 77, or identifying the settlor of a settlement of foreign property, the person who made the variation will be the settlor and not the deceased.

However, if the varied property would have been settled property even apart from the variation (e g if property is settled by the deceased's will upon trust for his widow for life, remainder to his son, and the widow and son agree a variation to create new trusts for the son's children) the settlor for capital gains tax purposes is to be regarded as the deceased. More specifically, TCGA 1992, s 68C(4), (5) (added by FA 2006, Sch 12, para 1(2) and coming into force on 6 April 2006 in relation to settlements whenever created) provide that where property was or would have become comprised in a settlement which arose on the deceased person's death, but in consequence of the variation the property, or property derived from it, becomes comprised in another settlement, the deceased shall be treated as having made the other settlement.

Where a variation is entered into before the administration of an estate is complete, or before it is complete in respect of any property which is to be the subject of the variation, a statement of intention in accordance with the TCGA 1992, s 62(7) should always be made because the subject-matter of the variation is not strictly any specific asset of the estate but a chose in action, namely a right to have the estate duly administered, for which a beneficiary has no capital gains tax acquisition cost: *Re Leigh's Will Trusts, Handyside v Durbridge* [1970] Ch 277, [1969] 3 All ER 432 and *Marshall v Kerr* [1995] 1 AC 148, [1994] 3 All ER 106, HL. Therefore, a statement of intention would seem to be essential to prevent the variation from being a disposal for capital gains tax purposes.

[241.18]

Stamp duty and stamp duty land tax. An instrument within the IHTA 1984, s 142 other than a disclaimer used to attract ad valorem stamp duty as a voluntary disposition to the extent of the bounty passing thereunder: cf *Thorn v IRC* [1976] 2 All ER 622, [1976] 1 WLR 915. The charge to ad valorem stamp duty on voluntary dispositions was abolished as was the charge to ad valorem duty on instruments varying the dispositions of the estate of a deceased person where such instruments would formerly have attracted duty as conveyances on sale, provided that such instruments are executed within two years of the death: Finance Act 1985, ss 82(1) and 84(1). But the fixed £5 duty and the need for adjudication was avoided if the instrument was certified to be an instrument falling within category L or category M of the Schedule to the Stamp Duty (Exempt Instruments) Regulations 1987. But from 1 December 2003, stamp duty has been virtually abolished (save in respect of instruments relating to stock or marketable securities, see FA 2003, s 125) and replaced with stamp duty land tax. Accordingly, a certificate that an instrument falls within category L or category M of the Schedule to the Stamp Duty (Exempt Instruments) Regulations 1987 should no longer be necessary, apart from the case of an instrument varying the disposition of stock or marketable securities. However, in response to the introduction of stamp duty land tax, HMRC specifically amended its Inheritance Tax Manual IHTM 35060 on 10 April 2006, but to instruct its staff that where an instrument has not been duly stamped, or does not contain the appropriate exemption certificate within categories L or M in the schedule to the Regulations, they should apply the following procedure:

(a) any communication to the effect that IHTA 1984, s 142 applies must contain a caveat in such terms as 'provided the document is duly stamped and adjudicated, or the appropriate exemption certificate under the Stamp Duty/Exempt Instruments Regulations 1987 is attached';
(b) if the parties are relying on the instrument to reduce the liability to IHT, they must insist that the document is stamped, or the exemption certificate is attached, before giving effect to the terms of the instrument; but
(c) in other cases, having raised the caveat above, the matter need not be pursued further.

This guidance does not appear limited to variations effecting stock or marketable securities, although previously in their Customer Newsletters of April 2004 and August 2004, HMRC had indicated that an exemption certificate would only be required where both the deed effected a variation of stocks or shares, and unusually the deed acted as the transfer. In view of the more recent pronouncement of IHTM 35060, it may be wise to continue to include a stamp duty exemption certificate in all deeds of variation, if only to avoid unnecessary correspondence with HMRC.

Stamp duty land tax is essentially a tax on land transactions, charging ad valorem tax on the consideration given for the acquisition of an interest in land (see para **[220.72]**, above). Generally, s 142 variations in respect of land or interests in land will not give rise to a liability because they will not be made for consideration. But where they are so made (ie in consideration of the variation of other dispositions in the same estate) they will be exempt from stamp duty land tax by reason of FA 2003, Sch 3, para 4(1), (2), which provides that a transaction following a person's death that varies a disposition (whether effected by will, under the law relating to intestacy or otherwise) of property of which the deceased was competent to dispose is exempt from charge if:

(1) the transaction is carried out within the period of two years after a person's death; and
(2) no consideration in money or money's worth other than the making of a variation of another such disposition is given for it.

This exemption applies whether or not the administration of the estate is complete or the property has been distributed in accordance with the original dispositions (FA 2003, Sch 3, para 4(3)). It is not clear though, whether this exemption covers a variation involving a deceased's severable share of assets held on a joint tenancy since the same is not generally property *of which the deceased was competent to dispose*.

[241.19]
Income tax. There is no income tax provision exactly corresponding to the IHTA 1984, s 142, and an instrument within s 142 will not generally be treated as a disposition by the deceased for the purposes of income tax.

Rather, legislation has confirmed that the settlor for income tax purposes of a settlement created by variation is the person who made the variation, at least where that person would, in the absence of the variation, have been entitled to the varied property absolutely. ITA 2007, s 472 provides that where a disposition of property following a person's death is varied and becomes settled property in consequence of the variation (and would not, but for the variation, have become settled property), and TCGA 1992, s 62 (6) applies in respect of the variation, the person who is to be treated as having made the settlement and provided the property for the purposes of the settlement is:

(a) a person who immediately before the variation was entitled to the property, or to property from which it derives, absolutely as legatee;
(b) a person who would have become entitled to the property, or to property from which it derives, absolutely as legatee but for the variation;
(c) a person who immediately before the variation would have been entitled to the property, or to property from which it derives, absolutely as legatee but for being an infant or other person under a disability; and
(d) a person who would, but for the variation, have become entitled to the property, or to property from which it derives, absolutely as legatee if he had not been an infant or other person under a disability.

The main implication of this is that where an instrument of variation settles property on trust it will be a settlement of which the maker of the instrument is the settlor for income tax purposes. Accordingly, if the maker of the instrument retains a beneficial interest (eg he is a beneficiary under a discretionary trust), the income of the relevant property will be subject to income tax as his income under ITTOIA 2005, s 624 and, even if he is not a beneficiary, if his minor children are beneficiaries income which is applied for them will be taxed as his under ITTOIA 2005, s 629.

However, it is thought that the HMRC view is that a disclaimer does not constitute a 'settlement' for income tax purposes, and it is notable that ITA 2007, s 472 refers only to variations and not disclaimers. Thus if it is possible for a beneficiary under a deceased person's estate to achieve a desired result by a disclaimer rather than an instrument of variation, and that desired result would have adverse consequences under the provisions for charging income tax on settlors of settlements (for example, a parent wants to dispose of a life interest in favour of his minor children who are interested in remainder), a disclaimer would have the advantage that he would not be treated as the settlor.

However, if the varied property would have been settled property even apart from the variation (eg. if property is settled by the deceased's will upon trust for his widow for life, remainder to his son, and the widow and son agree a variation to create new trusts for the son's children) the settlor for income tax purposes is to be regarded as the deceased. More specifically, ITA 2007, s 473 provides that where property was or would have become comprised in a settlement which arose on the deceased person's death, but in consequence of the variation the property, or property derived from it, becomes comprised in another settlement, the deceased shall be treated as having made the other settlement.

An instrument of variation may have some further retrospective effect for income tax purposes, if the instrument relates to a residuary estate which is still in the course of administration when the instrument is made. Where this is the case, and there is any income of that residuary estate which has already accrued to the personal representatives before the date of the transfer, and which has not been distributed by them to any beneficiaries, then the Income and Corporation Taxes Act 1988, ss 695 to 701 (as amended by Finance Act 1995, Sch 18) have the effect that someone with an interest (absolute or limited) in a residuary estate still in the course of administration is able to transfer the right to such income so that the income is charged to income tax as the income of the person to whom the income is transferred. The essential scheme is, broadly, that any income of the estate which is distributed to a beneficiary while the estate is being administered is taxed as the income of that beneficiary, and any income which is still undistributed at the point when the administration is completed is taxed as the income of the person who is then entitled to it. These new rules can apply in relation to the estate of a person who died before 6 April 1995, if the administration of his estate had not been completed before that date. Accordingly, it can now be worthwhile from an income tax point of view to include in an instrument of variation, which disposes of the present or future right to income or capital of a residuary estate in the course of administration, a disposition of the right to undistributed income of the residuary estate which has accrued before the variation, if the personal income tax rates of the recipient of the income will be lower than those of the maker of the instrument.

FA 2004, Sch 15 introduced a new income tax charge for tax years 2005–6 onwards upon a taxpayer's occupation of land where he has previously disposed of an interest in that land, or for his use of chattels where he has previously disposed of an interest in them (FA 2004, Sch 15, paras 3, 6). It also deems intangible property in a settlor-interested settlement to produce an income at a prescribed rate, taxable on the settlor (FA 2004, Sch 15, para 8). However, any disposition made by a person ('the chargeable person') in relation to an interest in the estate of another person is to be disregarded for the purposes of Sch 15 if by virtue of IHTA 1984, s 17, the disposition is not treated for the purposes of IHT as a transfer of value by the chargeable person. IHTA 1984, s 17 prevents a variation or disclaimer within s 142(1) being a transfer of value. So, for example, where the devisee of a dwelling-house varies its disposition by a s 142 variation, perhaps transferring it to a discretionary trust, while continuing to occupy it as part of a debt or charge scheme (see para **[218.19]**), he will not be treated as making a transfer of value by virtue of IHTA 1984, s 17, so he will not have disposed of it for the purposes of FA 2004, Sch 15 and so no income tax charge tax charge can arise in respect of his continued occupation. Similarly, where the legatee of shares in a private company with a policy of not declaring dividends settles them on discretionary trusts of which he is a beneficiary by a s 142 variation, an income cannot be deemed under FA 2004, Sch 15, para 8 as for the purposes of Sch 15 he has not settled them as required by para 8(2).

[241.20]

Family provision claims. A provision with an effect similar to the IHTA 1984, s 142, is s 146 of the same Act, which treats an order made under the Inheritance (Provision for Family and Dependants) Act 1975, including the terms of a compromise scheduled to an order staying or dismissing proceedings under that Act, as dispositions made by the deceased. But s 29A of the IHTA 1984 reduces the exemption available on death where an exempt beneficiary settles a claim under the Inheritance (Provision for Family and Dependants) Act 1975 against the estate out of his or her own resources. Thus, if the deceased's widow takes the whole estate under his will but settles a claim by the deceased's mistress out of the widow's personal assets, the exempt part of the deceased's estate will be appropriately reduced.

Where a claim under the Inheritance (Provision for Family and Dependants) Act 1975 is settled without the issue of any proceedings and so without any court order, a question arises if the compromise is embodied in a deed of variation made within two years of the deceased's death as to whether IHTA 1984, s 142 can apply, since it cannot apply if a variation is made for any extraneous consideration (see IHTA 1984, s 142(3)), and the giving up of a right to bring a claim under the Act might be such extraneous consideration. Recently, HMRC have confirmed that IHTA 1984, s 142 can apply in these circumstances, saying 'The bar against consideration relates only to extraneous consideration and will not prevent a rearrangement of assets within the will', see Inheritance Tax Manual IHTM 35100.

For a more detailed treatment of the IHTA 1984, ss 146 and 29A, see *Foster's Inheritance Tax*, D4.41–D4.47.

[241.21]

Other events deemed to be dispositions by the deceased. For distributions of personalty in accordance with the deceased's wishes within two years of his death which are treated as dispositions by the deceased by virtue of the IHTA 1984, s 143, see B4 at paras **[204.9]** and **[204.10]**. For distributions out of discretionary trusts created by will within two years of the deceased's death which are treated as dispositions by the deceased see C3 at para **[225.83]** ff, the Preliminary Note to F4 at paras **[242.4]**–**[242.6]** and Form F4.1 at para **[242.7]**.

[241.22]

Form F3.1: Disclaimer by devisee of a gift under a will—short form[1]

BY THIS DEED I the undersigned [*name of devisee*] of etc hereby disclaim all benefit under the devise in my favour contained in the will of [*testator*] dated —— and proved in the —— Registry of the Family Division on —— by —— the executors named in the will and also disclaim all estate and interest in the property the subject of the said devise.

IN WITNESS WHEREOF I have executed these presents as my deed this —— day of ——

SIGNED and delivered as a deed by the said [*name*] in the presence of— } [*Signature of party*]
[*Signature, address and description of witness*]

[*Signature of and execution as a deed by the party disclaiming*][2]

1 Although a disclaimer may be effected informally, a deed is preferable: see para **[241.16]**, sub-para (iii). Devisees occasionally wish to disclaim property subject to onerous charges, covenants, or conditions. Forms F3.1 and F3.2 are alternatives. The shorter one is quite sufficient in the case of a specific devisee who is only once referred to in the will. The longer form may be required where it is necessary to set out the particular devise disclaimed in order to make the position clear. It must be remembered that there may be cases of related gifts where one cannot be disclaimed and the other accepted. See further Vol 1, paras **[46.1]** ff and **[241.16]**, sub-para (ii).

2 The requirements of the Law of Property (Miscellaneous Provisions) Act 1989, s 1, for the making of a deed are that it is clear on its face that it is intended by the parties to it to be a deed, that it is signed by each party in the presence of a witness who attests the signature (two witnesses if someone signs for a party), and that it is delivered as a deed by each party or someone authorised to do so on his behalf. Sealing is not necessary.

[241.23]

Form F3.2: Disclaimer—longer form[1]

THIS DEED OF DISCLAIMER is made the —— day of —— BY [*beneficiary*] of etc ('the beneficiary').

WHEREAS by his will ('the will') dated —— [testator] late of —— appointed —— ('the executors') to be executors and (inter alia) gave to the beneficiary [set out gift].

AND WHEREAS the said [testator] died on —— and the executors duly proved the will on —— in the —— Registry of the Family Division.

AND WHEREAS the beneficiary has duly notified the executors that he does not intend to accept the said gift and desires to disclaim all interest under the gift.

AND WHEREAS the executors have made no assent in respect of the said gift nor has the beneficiary in any way entered into possession of the property given or done any act or thing that might be or amount to an acceptance of the said gift.

NOW THIS DEED WITNESSES that the beneficiary hereby disclaims the said gift in his favour contained in the will and all benefit under the gift and further disclaims all estate and interest in the property given to him by the will [provided that nothing contained in this deed shall in any way affect his acceptance of and the right to receive all other gifts and benefits under the will nor his acceptance of his appointment as trustee made by the will].[2]

In witness etc[3]

1 Although a disclaimer may be effected informally, a deed is preferable: see para **[241.16]**, sub-para (iii). Devisees occasionally wish to disclaim property subject to onerous charges, covenants, or conditions. Forms F3.1 and F3.2 are alternatives. The shorter one is quite sufficient in the case of a specific devisee who is only once referred to in the will. The longer form may be required where it is necessary to set out the particular devise disclaimed in order to make the position clear. It must be remembered that there may be cases of related gifts where one cannot be disclaimed and the other accepted. See further Vol 1, paras **[46.1]** ff and **[241.16]**, sub-para (ii).

2 As to when one gift cannot be disclaimed if another is accepted, see Vol 1, para **[46.3]**.

3 For execution, see Form F3.1 at para **[241.22]**.

[241.24]

Form F3.3: Disclaimer of a life interest

THIS DEED OF DISCLAIMER[1] is made the [*date*] BETWEEN [*name*] of [*address*] ('the Widow') of the one part and [*name*] of [*address*] and [*name*] of [*address*] ('the Trustees') of the other part.

Whereas:

(A) By his last Will dated the [*date*] [*name*] late of [*address*] ('the Testator') appointed the Trustees to be executors and trustees and left his estate Upon Trust for the Widow for life with remainder Upon Trust for the Testator's children [*name*] and [*name*] in equal shares absolutely.[2]

(B) The Testator died on the [*date*][3] survived by the Widow and his said children [and on the [*date*] his said Will was duly proved by the Trustees].[4]

(C) The Widow has not received any benefit from the estate of the Testator[5] and desires to disclaim all her said life interest therein.

NOW THIS DEED made in pursuance of the said desire WITNESSES that the WIDOW HEREBY IRREVOCABLY DISCLAIMS AND RENOUNCES all right title or interest to or in the estate of the Testator and its income or any part of it respectively to which she is or may be entitled under the Testator's said Will or otherwise.[6]

IN WITNESS whereof the parties hereto have executed these presents as their deed the day and year first above written.[7]

SIGNED and delivered as a deed by the } [*Signature of party*]
said [*name*] in the presence of—
[*Signature, address and description of witness*]
[*The foregoing from 'SIGNED' to be repeated for each party to the deed*]

1 Although a disclaimer may be affected informally, a deed is preferable: see para **[241.16]**, sub-para (iii).

2 The consequence of the widow disclaiming her life interest will be that the children will take the testator's estate absolutely, and will be deemed to have so taken on the testator's death for all IHT purposes, see IHTA 1984, s 142(1), see para **[241.16]**, sub-para (iii). This may not trigger IHT so long as the value of the estate is within the testator's available nil-rate band, but to the extent that the testator's nil-rate band is utilised by the variation, the nil-rate band carry forward allowance will be reduced (see para **[200.75]** above).

3 The death must not be more than two years before the disclaimer if advantage is to be taken of the IHTA 1984, s 142(1).

4 It is not essential that the will of the testator should have been proved or that his estate should have been administered: see paras **[241.10]** and **[241.25]**, n 2.

5 It is essential if a disclaimer is to be effective that no benefit should have been received by the person disclaiming: see para **[241.16]**, sub-para (ii).

6 It is sometimes necessary (though not in this case) that the disclaimer should operate not only on the interest conferred by the will but also on any interest that the widow would take on an intestacy. See para **[241.16]**, sub-para (v).

7 The requirements of the Law of Property (Miscellaneous Provisions) Act 1989, s 1, for the making of a deed are that it is clear on its face that it is intended by the parties to it to be a deed, that it is signed by each party in the presence of a witness who attests the signature (two witnesses if someone signs for a party), and that it is delivered as a deed by each party or someone authorised to do so on his behalf. Sealing is not necessary.

[241.25]

Form F3.4: Deed of variation of dispositions effected by a will

THIS DEED OF VARIATION is made the [*date*] BETWEEN [*name*] of [*address*] ('the Widow') of the first part [*name*] of [*address*] ('the Son') of the second part and [*name*] of [*address*] and [*name*] of [*address*] ('the Trustees') of the third part.

Whereas:

(A) By his last Will ('the Will') dated [*date*] [*name*] late of [*address*] ('the Testator') appointed the Trustees to be executors and trustees and after bequeathing his personal chattels to the Widow absolutely left his residuary estate (subject to the payment of his funeral and testamentary expenses and debts) Upon Trust to pay its income to the Widow during her life and after her death Upon Trust as to both capital and income for the Son absolutely.

(B) The Testator died on the [*date*][1] [and on the [*date*] the Will was duly proved by the Trustees][2].

(C) The Son has two children only ('the Children') namely [*name*] and [*name*].

(D) The Widow and the Son desire to vary the trusts of the Will for the benefit of the Children in the manner appearing below.

NOW THIS DEED WITNESSES as follows:

1. IT IS HEREBY AGREED AND DECLARED by way of variation of the disposition of the Testator's residuary estate effected by the Will that the Will shall be construed and take effect and be deemed to have taken effect as from the death of the Testator[3] as if in lieu of the trusts there declared of the Testator's said residuary estate it had contained a direction that (subject to the payment of his funeral and testamentary expenses and debts) the said residuary estate and its income should be held IN TRUST for the Children in equal shares absolutely.[4]

2. The parties to this deed declare that they intend that the provisions of [Section 142(1) of the Inheritance Tax Act 1984] [and] [Section 62(6) of the Taxation of Chargeable Gains Act 1992] shall apply to the variations made by this deed, to the intent that such variations shall be treated as if they were made by the Deceased for the purposes of [inheritance tax] [and] [capital gains tax].[5]

3. The parties to this deed hereby certify that this instrument falls within category M in the Schedule to the Stamp Duty (Exempt Instruments) Regulations 1987.[6]

In witness etc[7]

1 The death must have occurred within the two years immediately preceding the deed to take advantage of the IHTA 1984, s 142(1): see para **[241.1]**.

2 It is not essential that the will should have been proved or the estate administered. Although the right of a beneficiary who is interested in the unadministered estate of a deceased person does not amount to an equitable interest, he has the right to have the estate duly administered and this right is transmissible: *Re Leigh's Will Trusts, Handyside v Durbridge* [1970] Ch 277, [1969] 3 All ER 432. Accordingly persons interested in unadministered estate can deal with their interests by way of deed of variation. However, in such a case a

statement of intention that the TCGA 1992, s 62(6) should apply should always be made, see Preliminary Note at para **[241.7]**. See the Preliminary Note at para **[241.10]** for HMRC practice on variations made before a grant of probate.

3 These words are designed to ensure that the variation is retrospective and that all intervening interests are eliminated. But it is probably not essential for intervening interests to be eliminated: see para **[241.4]**. However, it could be effective for income tax purposes: see para **[241.19]**.

4 The substituted trusts are of a very simple nature, but more elaborate trusts may be substituted.

5 If IHTA 1984, s 142(1) and TCGA 1992, s 62(6) are to apply, the instrument of variation must contain a statement to that effect. For further points on this statement see the Preliminary Note at para **[241.3]**. If IHTA 1984, s 142(1) is to apply, the children will be deemed to have taken testator's residuary estate absolutely on the testator's death for all IHT purposes. This may not trigger IHT so long as the value of the residuary estate is within the testator's available nil-rate band, but to the extent that the testator's nil-rate band is utilised by the variation, the nil-rate band carry forward allowance will be reduced (see para **[200.75]** above). If IHTA 1984, s 142 is not to apply, the widow will make a potentially exempt transfer, and the testator's unused nil-rate band will be carried forward.

6 This exemption certificate will be necessary to avoid a £5 fixed duty if the variation relates to stock or marketable securities, but may also be advisable where it does not in view of HMRC pronouncements. See the Preliminary Note at para **[241.18]**.

7 For execution, see Form F3.3 at para **[241.24]**.

[241.26]

Form F3.5: Deed of variation of disposition of property held by deceased and spouse on a joint tenancy

THIS DEED OF VARIATION is made the [*date*] BETWEEN [*name*] of [*address*] ('the Widow') of the one part and [*name*] of [*address*] ('the Daughter') of the other part.

Whereas:

(A) Immediately prior to the death on the [*date*][1] of [*name*] late of [*address*] ('the Deceased') the Deceased and the Widow held the property ('the Property') known as —— upon trust [to sell the same to hold the net proceeds of sale][2] for themselves as beneficial joint tenants.

(B) Following the death of the Deceased the Widow is absolutely entitled to the Property by right of survivorship.

(C) The Widow desires to vary the disposition of the Deceased's severable share in the Property [(or the net proceeds of sale)][3] effected by right of survivorship so as to benefit the Daughter in the manner appearing below.

NOW THIS DEED WITNESSES as follows:

1. The Widow and the Daughter hereby agree and declare by way of variation of the disposition of the Deceased's severable share in the Property [(or the net proceeds of sale)][4] which took effect on the Deceased's death by right of survivorship as follows—

   (1) That it shall be deemed that the beneficial joint tenancy of the Deceased and the Widow in the Property [(or the net proceeds of sale)][5] had been severed immediately prior to the death of the Deceased so that immediately prior to the death of the Deceased he and the Widow held the Property upon trust [to sell the same to hold the net proceeds of sale][6] for themselves as beneficial tenants in common in equal shares.

(2) That the Deceased's deemed one-half share of the Property [(or the net proceeds of sale)][7] as aforesaid shall be deemed to have been given to the Daughter absolutely by a will made by the Deceased (subject to the payment of any inheritance tax attributable thereto on or by reason of his death)[8] and the Widow shall henceforth hold the Property upon trust [to sell the same to hold the net proceeds of sale][9] for herself and the Daughter as beneficial tenants in common in equal shares.[10]

2. The parties to this deed hereby certify that this instrument falls within category M in the Schedule to the Stamp Duty (Exempt Instruments) Regulations 1987.[11]

3. The parties to this deed declare that they intend that the provisions of [Section 142(1) of the Inheritance Tax Act 1984] [and] [Section 62(6) of the Taxation of Chargeable Gains Act 1992] shall apply to the variations made by this deed, to the intent that such variations shall be treated as if they were made by the Deceased for the purposes of [inheritance tax] [and] [capital gains tax].[12]

In witness[13]

1 The deed must be made within two years of the death if IHTA 1984, s 142(1) is to apply: see the Preliminary Note at paras **[241.1]–[241.3]**.

2 These words will not be appropriate if the joint tenancy was not under a trust for sale at the Deceased's death, and should be omitted if it was not. The TLATA 1996 has the effect that it will not have been under a trust for sale if the Deceased died on or after 1 January 1997 and there was no express trust for sale in the disposition creating the joint tenancy.

3 See n 2 above.

4 See n 2 above.

5 See n 2 above.

6 See n 2 above.

7 See n 2 above.

8 A deceased's severable share of joint property bears its own tax on the deceased's death (see para **[214.60]**, sub-para (2)), but we would suggest that in the case of a variation of a deceased's severable share of joint property the variation should always be made expressly subject to its bearing any IHT payable on or by reason of the death of the deceased to avoid any doubt as to where the burden should fall. Although it would not seem necessary for a deceased's personal representatives to be a party to a variation of a severable share of joint property since it at no time vests in them, they are necessary parties to any statement of intention that the IHTA 1984, s 142(1) should apply to the variation where the variation results in additional tax being payable (IHTA 1984, s 142(2)(b)). They will be liable for this additional tax (IHTA 1984, s 200(1)), even if the ultimate burden of it will fall on the donee (see the Preliminary Note to B14 at para **[214.60]**, sub-para (2)).

9 If the parties wish that the Widow should hold the property upon trust for sale (whether it was so held at the time of the Deceased's death or not) these words should be included. Although held upon trust for sale, a power to postpone sale will be implied: see TLATA 1996, s 4(1) (Part G, para **[246.106]**). Otherwise, the words can be omitted and the Property will be held on a trust of land, with the Widow having wide powers to manage it, including power to sell it.

10 If the Deceased's estate apart from this severable share under the joint tenancy is or may be insolvent, it should be made clear that the deed is conferring an interest in the property on the Daughter or other donee under the deed, and not upon the Deceased's creditors. It was held in *Re Palmer (a debtor)* [1994] Ch 316, [1994] 3 All ER 835, CA that a deceased person's unsevered interest under a joint tenancy is not part of his estate available for creditors, where the estate goes into insolvent administration. This has now been reversed by the Insolvency Act 1986, s 421A, which enables an application to be made to the court for a surviving joint tenant to provide compensation to creditors of the deceased.

11 See the Preliminary Note at para **[241.18]**.

12 If IHTA 1984, s 142(1) and TCGA 1992, s 62(6) are to apply, the instrument of variation must contain a statement to that effect. For further points on this statement see the Preliminary Note at para **[241.3]**. If IHTA 1984, s 142(1) is to apply, the daughter will be deemed to have taken a half-share of the property on the testator's death for all IHT purposes. This may not trigger IHT so long as the value of the half-share is within the testator's available nil-rate band, but to the extent that the testator's nil-rate band is utilised by the variation, the nil-rate band carry forward allowance will be reduced (see para **[200.75]** above). If IHTA 1984, s 142 is not to apply, the widow will make a potentially exempt transfer, and the testator's unused nil-rate band will be carried forward, but there would be issues of reservation of benefit for IHT purposes if the widow continues to occupy the property alone (see FA 1986, s 102B), or pre-owned assets tax (see para **[241.19]** above). Therefore, it may usually be better for s 142 to apply.

13 For execution, see Form F3.3 at para **[241.24]**.

[241.27]

Form F3.6: Deed of variation creating a nil-rate band non-exempt legacy where entire estate given to the deceased's widow[1]

THIS DEED OF VARIATION is made the [*date*] BETWEEN [*name*] of [*address*] ('the Widow') of the first part [*name*] of [*address*] and [*name*] of [*address*] ('the Children') of the second part and [*name*] of [*address*] and [*name*] of [*address*] ('the Trustees') of the third part.

Whereas:

(A) By his last Will ('the Will') dated [*date*] [*name*] late of [*address*] ('the Testator') appointed the Trustees as executors and trustees.

(B) The Testator died on [*date*][2] [and on the [*date*] the Will was proved by the Trustees in the —— Probate Registry].[3]

(C) By Clause —— of the Will the Testator gave his residuary estate ('the Residuary Estate') to the Trustees to hold the same upon trust for the Widow absolutely.

(D) The Widow desires to vary the disposition of the Residuary Estate effected by the Will so as to benefit the Children in the manner appearing below.

NOW THIS DEED WITNESSES as follows:

1. By way of variation of the above-recited disposition of the Residuary Estate of the Testator effected by the Will the Widow the Children and the Trustees hereby agree and declare that the Will shall have effect and the estate of the Testator shall be administered as if the Testator had given by the Will a pecuniary legacy of [£300,000][4] to the Children in equal shares absolutely subject to payment of any inheritance tax payable in respect of the Testator's death and attributable thereto.[5]
2. Subject as aforesaid the provisions of the Will shall continue to have effect.
3. The parties to this deed hereby certify that this instrument falls within category M in the Schedule to the Stamp Duty (Exempt Instruments) Regulations 1987.[6]
4. The parties to this deed declare that they intend that the provisions of [Section 142(1) of the Inheritance Tax Act 1984] [and] [Section 62(6) of the Taxation of Chargeable Gains Act 1992] shall apply to the variations made by this deed, to the intent that such variations

shall be treated as if they were made by the Deceased for the purposes of [inheritance tax] [and] [capital gains tax].[7]

In witness etc[8]

1 This, at least prior to 9 October 2007, has perhaps been one of the commonest types of deed of variation. It makes use of the deceased's nil-rate band where it is wholly or largely unused as a result of all or most of the estate being given to his widow. Following the introduction on 9 October 2007 of rules to carry forward unused nil-rate band allowance it may no longer be so popular (see para **[200.75]** above). For nil-rate band gifts see Part A, para **[200.101]** and for nil-rate band discretionary trusts see the Note in B18 at para **[218.16]–[218.18]**.

2 The deed must be made within two years of the death if IHTA 1984, s 142(1) is to apply: see the Preliminary Note at paras **[241.1]** and **[241.3]**.

3 An instrument of variation can be made before probate is granted: see the Preliminary Note at para **[241.1]**.

4 This is the IHT threshold in relation to a death after 5 April 2007. For 2008–9 it is proposed that it will be £312,000; for 2009–10, £325,000: see FA 2006, s 155; and for 2010–11, £350,000. The legacy should be reduced from the amount of the nil-rate band at the deceased's death by any lifetime transfers of value made in the seven years before the deceased's death which are chargeable, by any non-exempt specific gifts or pecuniary legacies contained in the will, and by any other property which is chargeable to IHT as part of the deceased's estate on death. A formula can be used if there is uncertainty about the correct amount of the legacy: see cl 1 of Form F3.8 at para **[241.29]**.

5 These words are worth including if there is the slightest doubt as to whether there might be an IHT liability, and do no harm if there is not. See the Preliminary Note at para **[241.12]** and the Preliminary Note to B14 at para **[214.74]**.

6 This exemption certificate will be necessary to avoid a £5 fixed duty if the variation relates to stock or marketable securities, but may also be advisable where it does not in view of HMRC pronouncements. See the Preliminary Note at para **[241.18]**.

7 If IHTA 1984, s 142(1) and TCGA 1992, s 62(6) are to apply, the instrument of variation must contain a statement to that effect. See also the Preliminary Note at para **[241.3]**. If IHTA 1984, s 142(1) is to apply, the Children will be deemed to have taken the nil-rate band legacy on the testator's death for all IHT purposes, and there will be no nil-rate band carry forward allowance (see para **[200.75]** above). If IHTA 1984, s 142 is not to apply, the widow will make a potentially exempt transfer, and the testator's unused nil-rate band will be carried forward.

8 For execution, see Form F3.3 at para **[241.24]**.

[241.28]

Form F3.7: Deed of variation conferring a short-term interest in possession on a surviving spouse[1]

THIS DEED OF VARIATION is made the [*date*] BETWEEN [*name*] of [*address*] and [*name*] of [*address*] ('the Children') of the first part [*name*] of [*address*] ('the Widow') of the second part and [*name*] of [*address*] and [*name*] of [*address*] ('the Trustees') of the third part.

Whereas:

(A) By his last Will ('the Will') dated [*date*] [*name*] late of [*address*] ('the Testator') appointed the Trustees as executors and trustees.

(B) The Testator died on the [*date*][2] [and on the [*date*] the Will was duly proved by the Trustees].[3]

(C) By Clause —— of the Will the Testator gave his residuary estate ('the Residuary Estate') to the Trustees to hold the same upon trust for the Children in equal shares absolutely.

(D) The Children desire to vary the disposition of the Residuary Estate effected by Clause —— of the Will in the manner appearing below.

NOW THIS DEED made in pursuance of the said desire and by way of variation of the disposition of the Residuary Estate effected by Clause —— of the Will WITNESSES as follows:

1. The parties to this deed hereby agree and declare that the Will shall have effect and be deemed to have had effect as from the death of the Testator and the Testator's estate shall be administered as if in lieu of the above-recited direction to the Trustees to hold the Residuary Estate upon trust for the Children in equal shares absolutely the Will had contained[—
   (1) a legacy to the Children in equal shares absolutely of [£300,000][4] and a direction that any inheritance tax attributable to such legacy by reason of the death of the Testator should be borne by the Children in equal shares absolutely in exoneration of the Residuary Estate of the Testator;[5] and
   (2)][6] a direction to the Trustees to hold the Residuary Estate [(subject to the above-mentioned legacy)] upon trust to pay its income to the Widow for the period of her life or for a period expiring on the [*date*][7] (whichever shall be the shorter period) and subject thereto to hold the Residuary Estate (subject to the above-mentioned legacy) and its income upon trust for the Children in equal shares absolutely.
2. [*Stamp duty certificate as cl 3 of* Form F3.6 *at para* **[241.27]**.]
3. [*Statement of intention as cl 4 of* Form F3.6 *at para* **[241.27]**.]

In witness etc[8]

1 This form is designed to pass a testator's estate to non-exempt persons, but at least to the extent that it exceeds the testator's available nil-rate band, channelled through the estate of the surviving spouse by giving him or her a short-term interest in possession so that the spouse exemption may be claimed on the testator's death. (If the deceased died on or after 22 March 2006 the short-term interest in possession should be an immediate post-death interest within IHTA 1984, s 49A, (see para **[200.98]** above)). Upon the termination of the interest in possession, when the remainder gifts for non-exempt persons take effect, the surviving spouse should be treated as making a potentially exempt transfer which should escape a charge to IHT if the surviving spouse survives it for seven years. See Preliminary Note at para **[241.13]**. Since exemption from IHT is available in the same way between civil partners as it is between married couples (see para **[241.13]** above), this deed may be adapted to give a short-term interest in possession to a surviving civil partner.

2 The deed must be made within two years of the death if IHTA 1984, s 142(1) is to apply: see the Preliminary Note at paras **[241.1]** and **[241.3]**.

3 An instrument of variation can be made before probate is granted: see the Preliminary Note at para **[241.10]**.

4 See n 4 to cl 1 of Form F3.6 at para **[241.27]**.

5 See n 5 to cl 1 of Form F3.6 at para **[241.27]**.

6 Since the introduction on 9 October 2007 of rules to carry forward unused nil-rate band allowance (see para **[200.75]** above), it may be preferable from an IHT point of view for a nil-rate band legacy not to be carved out, and for the surviving spouse to take a short-term interest in possession in the whole of residue, thus preserving the nil-rate band carry forward allowance.

7 This date should be after the date of the deed of variation and after the expiry of the two-year period from the death of the testator, see Preliminary Note at para **[241.13]**.

8 For execution, see Form F3.3 at para **[241.24]**.

[241.29]

Form F3.8: Deed of variation where spouses have died within two years of each other varying the disposition of the estate of the first to die[1]

THIS DEED OF VARIATION is made the [*date*] BETWEEN [*name*] of [*address*] and [*name*] of [*address*] ('the Wife's Administrators') of the first part [*name*] of [*address*] [*name*] of [*address*] and [*name*] of [*address*] ('the Children') of the second part and [*name*] of [*address*] and [*name*] of [*address*] ('the Husband's Executors') of the third part.

Whereas:

(A) By his last Will ('the Husband's Will') dated [*date*] [*name*] late of [*address*] ('the Husband') appointed the Husband's Executors as executors and trustees and left his whole estate (subject to the payment of his funeral and testamentary expenses and debts) to his widow [*name*] ('the Wife').

(B) The Husband died on the [*date*][2] [and on the [*date*] the Husband's Will was duly proved by the Husband's Executors].[3]

(C) The Husband's estate includes a freehold property known as [*description*] ('the Property')

(D) The Wife died intestate on the [*date*] survived by her three children namely the Children who have all attained the age of 18 and on the [*date*] the Wife's Administrators were granted letters of administration to the Wife's estate.[4]

(E) Under the law relating to intestacy the Wife's residuary estate (as defined in section 33 of the Administration of Estates Act 1925) is held upon trust for the Children in equal shares absolutely.

(F) The parties hereto desire to vary the disposition of the Property effected by the Husband's Will in the manner appearing below.

NOW THIS DEED WITNESSES as follows:

1. The parties to this deed hereby agree and declare by way of variation of the disposition of the Property effected by the Husband's Will that the Husband's Will shall have effect and be deemed to have had effect as from the death of the Husband and the Husband's estate shall be administered as if the Husband's Will had contained a specific gift to the Children of the Property subject to payment of any inheritance tax payable in respect of the Husband's death and attributable thereto.[5]
2. Subject as aforesaid the Husband's Will shall continue to have effect.
3. [*Stamp duty certificate as cl 3 of* Form F3.6 *at para* **[241.27]**.]
4. The parties to this deed declare that they intend that the provisions of Section 142(1) of the Inheritance Tax Act 1984 and Section 62(6) of the Taxation of Chargeable Gains Act 1992 shall apply to the variations made by this deed, to the intent that such variations shall be treated as if they were made by the Deceased for the purposes of inheritance tax and capital gains tax.[6]

In witness etc[7]

1 This form is for use where two spouses (or civil partners) have died within two years of each other, the first spouse to die not having fully utilised his available nil rate IHT band: see Preliminary Note at para **[241.14]**. Following the introduction on 9 October 2007 of rules to

carry forward unused nil-rate band allowance, such variations may still be advantageous where, for example, the estate of the first-to-die includes property whose value was within his available nil-rate band at the time of his death, but which has risen substantially in value since then, eg. land which may have been granted planning permission, so that it is worth more than the nil-rate band carry forward allowance. A variation redirecting it to non-exempt beneficiaries so as to utilise the unused nil-rate IHT band may produce a significant saving in IHT compared with allowing it to be taxed at a value in the survivor's estate greater than the nil-rate band carry forward allowance. The variation must be made by the personal representatives of the second to die with the consent of the beneficiaries interested in the second to die's estate: see the Preliminary Note at para **[241.14]**. In this form the beneficiaries are actual parties to the deed, but HMRC will accept their consent being put in a separate instrument.

2 The deed must be made within two years of the husband's death if IHTA 1984, s 142(1) is to apply: see the Preliminary Note at paras **[241.1]** and **[241.3]**.

3 An instrument of variation can be made before probate is granted: see the Preliminary Note at para **[241.10]**.

4 The deed should be made after letters of administration to the wife's estate have been obtained, because the benefit of the disposition by the husband which is being varied is vested in the wife's estate, not the persons beneficially interested in it, and there are no personal representatives before a grant is obtained. If the wife had left a will which appointed executors, the named executors could arguably make the deed before obtaining a grant, but we recommend that a grant is obtained in respect of the second estate before making the deed, wherever possible, even where executors have been appointed.

5 If the value of this property at the date of the testator's death is within the testator's unused nil-rate IHT band, no IHT should be payable. If it is possible that the value might exceed the IHT threshold, a direction that the gift should be subject to tax should reduce the amount of tax payable.

6 For IHTA 1984, s 142(1) and TCGA 1992, s 62(6) to apply, the instrument of variation must contain a statement to that effect. See also the Preliminary Note at para **[241.3]**.

7 For execution, see Form F3.3 at para **[241.24]**.

[241.30]

Form F3.9 Deed of variation of trusts of a will settling a life interest on discretionary trusts without disturbing remainders[1]

THIS DEED OF VARIATION is made the [*date*] BETWEEN [*name*] of [*address*] ('the Life Tenant') of the one part and [*name*] of [*address*] and [*name*] of [*address*] ('the Trustees') of the other part.

Whereas:

(A) By his last Will ('the Will') dated [*date*] [*name*] late of [*address*] ('the Testator') appointed the Trustees as executors and trustees.

(B) The Testator died on the [*date*][2] [and on the [*date*] the Will was duly proved by the Trustees].[3]

(C) By Clause —— of the Will the Testator gave his residuary estate ('the Residuary Estate') to the Trustees to hold the same upon trust to pay its income to the Life Tenant for his life and subject thereto upon trust for such of the children of the Life Tenant who should attain the age of 21 and be living at his death in equal shares absolutely with a substitutional trust for the children of any such child who should die before attaining a vested interest.

(D) The Life Tenant desires to vary the disposition of the Residuary Estate effected by Clause —— of the Will for the benefit of his children and remoter issue (who together with the Life Tenant are 'the Beneficiaries')[4] in the manner appearing below.

NOW THIS DEED WITNESSES as follows:

1. By way of variation of the above-recited disposition of the Residuary Estate of the Testator made by Clause —— of the Will the Life Tenant HEREBY ASSIGNS his life interest in the Residuary Estate (which life interest shall include the net income of the Residuary Estate which shall have arisen between the Testator's death and the date of this Deed)[5] unto the Trustees to hold the same as follows—
   (1) The Trustees shall hold the income of the Residuary Estate arisen or arising during the life of the Life Tenant upon trust to pay or apply the same to or for the benefit of all or such one or more exclusively of the others or other of the Beneficiaries and if more than one in such shares and in such manner generally as the Trustees shall in their absolute discretion think fit Provided that until the expiration of the period of 21 years from the death of the Testator or until the death of the Life Tenant if sooner[6] the Trustees shall have power to accumulate the whole or any part of such income by investing the same and the resulting income in any manner authorised by the Will so that any accumulations shall be held as an accretion to the Residuary Estate but subject to a power exercisable by the Trustees at any time during the life of the Life Tenant to pay or apply any such accumulations or any part of them as if they were income of the Residuary Estate arising in the then current year.
   (2) Notwithstanding the foregoing the Trustees shall have power by any deed or deeds revocable or irrevocable from time to time during the life of the Life Tenant to appoint that all or any part or parts of the income of the Residuary Estate during the remainder of the life of Life Tenant or any less period shall be held upon with and subject to such trusts powers and provisions (including discretionary trusts or powers) in favour or for the benefit of all or such one or more exclusively of the others or other of the Beneficiaries if more than one in such shares and in such manner generally as the Trustees shall in their absolute discretion think fit Provided that no exercise of the said power shall invalidate any prior payment application or accumulation of income hereunder.[7]
2. Nothing contained in thus deed shall effect the devolution under the Will of the Residuary Estate on and following the death of the Life Tenant.
3. [*Stamp duty certificate as cl 3 of* Form F3.6 *at para* **[241.27]**.]
4. [*Statement of intention as cl 4 of* Form F3.6 *at para* **[241.27]**.]

In witness etc[8]

1 It can happen that a will leaves property upon trust for a life tenant for life, with remainder to individuals who are minors or whose identity cannot be finally ascertained until the death of the life tenant. This form allows a life tenant to remove property from his estate for IHT purposes by settling his life interest on discretionary trusts, with the remainder trusts taking effect on his death being unaffected. For the IHT charging regime for settlements without a qualifying interest in possession see B18 at para **[218.8]** ff. If the life tenant is elderly or infirm, check that he or she was not at the testator's death in receipt of attendance allowance or otherwise qualified under the IHTA 1984, s 89(4) as the principal beneficiary

under a disabled trust for IHT purposes (see para **[226.3]** ff). If so, the trusts might fall within the IHTA 1984, s 89 so that he or she is treated as retaining an interest in possession. This could be avoided by a variation which amends the powers over capital in such a way that s 89 does not apply, but if the remaindermen are minors or unborns this may only be achievable by applying to the court under the Variation of Trusts Act 1958.

Note also that HMRC will apparently not regard a variation varying or disposing of a life interest as effective for IHT purposes if the deed of variation is made after the life tenant's death: see *IHT Newsletter* December 2001, p 5 (but a disclaimer by the life tenant's personal representatives could in their view be effective). See Note at para **[241.14]**.

2 The deed must be made within two years of the death if IHTA 1984, s 142(1) is to apply: see the Preliminary Note at paras **[241.1]** and **[241.3]**.

3 An instrument of variation can be made before probate is granted: see the Preliminary Note at para **[241.10]**.

4 If the life tenant is to be an object of the discretionary trust, provided that a statement of intention is made that IHTA 1984, s 142(1) should apply to the variation, the life tenant's assignment should not be a gift subject to a reservation: see the Preliminary Note at para **[241.9]**.

It is not entirely clear what the effect of a statement of intention that the TCGA 1992, s 62(6) should apply would be for determining who the settlor is. Prior to the enactment of TCGA 1992, s 68C it was thought that whether or not TCGA 1992, s 62(6) applied, the deceased would be treated as the settlor of the capital of the residuary estate, and the life tenant as the settlor of the income arising during his lifetime, so that by being an object of the discretionary trust of income, any chargeable gains in respect of any accumulations of income would be taxed as the life tenant's as such accumulations would be property originating from him: see TCGA 1992, ss 77 and 79(2). However, TCGA 1992, s 68C now provides rules for who the settlor is in respect of variations made on or after 6 April 2006 (see Preliminary Note at para **[241.17]**). It is not entirely clear though how they operate in relation to variations such as the present where the will establishes a settlement, and the effect of the variation is to vary only the trust of income. It is submitted that the position is the same as it was thought to be before these rules were introduced. This is because either the rules do not apply in the precise circumstances of the case, so that one must determine who the settlor is under normal capital gains tax principles (as before), or because the rules apply separately to the income and the capital, and TCGA, 1992 s 68C(2) applies to treat the life tenant as the settlor of the income, and TCGA 1992, s 68C(5) or (6) applies to treat the deceased as settlor in relation to the capital. For income tax purposes the income would be treated as the life tenant's by reason of his being an object of the trust and the person who settled the income on the discretionary trusts: see Preliminary Note at para **[241.19]**.

5 If the deed is made before the administration is compete, this would be effective to transfer any undistributed income, for income tax purposes, from the life tenant to the discretionary trusts: see the Preliminary Note at para **[241.19]**.

6 Since the variation is to be deemed to have been made by the deceased for IHT purposes, it may be wise to limit accumulation to a period which the deceased could have chosen in his will, and which is also not longer than a period which the life tenant could have chosen for a lifetime disposition. A period of not longer than 21 years from the deceased's death could have been chosen by the deceased (see the LPA 1925, s 164(1)(b) (Part G, para **[246.42]**)), which allows accumulation for a period of 21 years from death, and is also within a period which the life tenant could have chosen for a lifetime disposition (see the PAA 1964, s 13(1)(a) (Part G, para **[246.71]**), which allows accumulation for a period of 21 years from the date of the disposition).

7 This power would permit the trustees to appoint an interest in possession to any of the beneficiaries. This might be desirable for income tax purposes.

8 For execution, see Form F3.3 at para **[241.24]**.

[241.31]

Form F3.10: Deed of variation of trusts of a will settling a life interest on the same trusts as contingent remainders from time to time[1]

THIS DEED OF VARIATION is made the [*date*] BETWEEN [*name*] of [*address*] ('the Life Tenant') of the one part and [*name*] of [*address*] and [*name*] of [*address*] ('the Trustees') of the other part.

Whereas:

(A) By his last Will ('the Will') dated [*date*] [*name*] late of [*address*] ('the Testator') appointed the Trustees as executors and trustees.

(B) The Testator died on the [*date*][2] [and on the [*date*] the Will was duly proved by the Trustees].[3]

(C) By Clause —— of the Will the Testator gave his residuary estate ('the Residuary Estate') to the Trustees to hold the same upon trust to pay its income to the Life Tenant for his life and subject thereto to hold the capital and income upon trust for such of the children of the Life Tenant who should attain the age of 21 and be living at the Life Tenant's death if more than one in equal shares provided that if any child of the Life Tenant should predecease the Life Tenant leaving issue who should attain the age of 21 such issue should take in equal shares per stirpes the share their parent would have become entitled to if surviving the Life Tenant.

(D) The Life Tenant desires to vary the disposition of the Residuary Estate effected by the Will in the manner appearing below.

NOW THIS DEED WITNESSES as follows:

1. By way of variation of the above-recited disposition of the Residuary Estate of the Testator made by Clause —— of the Will the Life Tenant HEREBY ASSIGNS his life interest in the Residuary Estate (which life interest shall include the net income of the Residuary Estate which shall have accrued between the Testator's death and the date of this Deed)[4] unto the Trustees to hold each instalment of the income of the Residuary Estate which shall arise or shall have arisen during the Life Tenant's life upon the trusts which would apply thereto under the Will if the Life Tenant had died immediately before such instalment arose.
2. Nothing contained in this deed shall affect the devolution under the Will of the Residuary Estate on and following the death of the Life Tenant.
3. [*Stamp duty certificate as cl 3 of* Form F3.6 *at para* **[241.27]**.]
4. [*Statement of intention as cl 4 of* Form F3.6 *at para* **[241.27]**.]

In witness etc[5]

1 Where the remainder trusts after a life interest are contingent on surviving the life tenant, particularly where the class of remainderman might include future born persons, it presents a problem for the termination of the life interest and acceleration of the remainders. This deed includes a formula for settling the life interest on the same trusts as the remainder from time to time. Once the deed is executed the trustees will have to retain the trust fund until the death of the life tenant, unless (i) they have a power of advancement exercisable over the whole of each presumptive share, or (ii) a scheme of distribution can be agreed with all the potential remaindermen who are in existence (and who are all of full age) and it is clear that no more persons entitled to an interest will be born, or (iii) an order of the court is obtained authorising distribution or varying the trusts under the Variation of Trusts Act 1958 in a way which allows a distribution to be made. Note that HMRC will apparently not regard a variation varying or disposing of a life interest as effective for IHT purposes if the deed of variation is made after the life tenant's death: see *IHT Newsletter* December 2001, p 5 (but a disclaimer by the life tenant's personal representatives could in their view be effective). See the Preliminary Note at para **[241.14]**.

The IHT treatment of the residuary estate after the variation will vary according to whether the remaindermen take interests in possession immediately after the variation or not, and according to whether the deceased died before 22 March 2006 or not. Say that the life tenant has 2 children at the date of the variation – one aged 19 and the other 17. If TA 1925, s 31 (see para **[246.19]**) applies, then following the variation, the elder child will be entitled to the income of a one-half share of the residuary estate by operation of TA 1925, s 31(1)(ii) and so will have an interest in possession in that half share, but the younger child will not have an interest in possession in the other half share as TA 1925, s 31(1)(i) will apply to its income pending his attainment of the age of 18. Now if the deceased died before 22 March 2006, then the effect of backdating the variation to the deceased's death should be that the elder son will have an interest in possession in a half share of the residuary estate which will be treated as having arisen before 22 March 2006 (hence the one-half share of the residuary estate in which his interest subsists will be treated as part of his estate for IHT purposes under IHTA 1984, s 49(1) and outside of the relevant property regime) and the trusts of the younger son's half share will be accumulation and maintenance trusts within IHTA 1984, s 71 until the younger son attains an interest in possession at age 18, or 6 April 2008 if sooner. On either of these events, his half share will then become subject to the relevant property regime. If the deceased died on or after 22 March 2006, the effect of IHTA 1984, s 142(1) applying to backdate the variation to the deceased's death, should be that the elder child's interest in possession should be an immediate post-death interest within IHTA 1984, s 49A, (see para **[200.98]** above), and hence the one-half share of the residuary estate in which his interest subsists will be treated as part of his estate for IHT purposes, and outside of the relevant property regime. Since no trusts created on or after 22 March 2006 can have the benefits of IHTA 1984, s 71, the younger son's half share will be relevant property (see para **[200.92]** above).

2 The deed must be made within two years of the death if IHTA 1984, s 142(1) is to apply: see the Preliminary Note at paras **[241.1]** and **[241.2]**.

3 An instrument of variation can be made before probate is granted: see the Preliminary Note at para **[241.10]**.

4 See the Preliminary Note at para **[241.19]** for the income tax consequences of disposing of the right to undistributed income of an unadministered estate.

5 For execution, see Form F3.3 at para **[241.24]**.

F4 Exercises of dispositive powers created by wills

Preliminary note ... **[242.1]**

FORMS

F4.1 Appointment from discretionary trust within two years of testator's death ... **[242.7]**

F4.2 Appointment to spouse from nil-rate band discretionary trust within two years of testator's death ... **[242.8]**

F4.3 Appointment from discretionary trust of money to beneficiaries who are sui juris ... **[242.9]**

F4.4 Appointment from discretionary trust of investments ... **[242.10]**

F4.5 Appointment of immediate post-death interests in residue for the testator's grandchildren ... **[242.12]**

F4.6 Appointment from discretionary trust of investments to a bereaved minor trust or age 18–25 trust ... **[242.13]**

F4.7 Appointment of a trust for bereaved minors terminating an immediate post-death interest ... **[242.15]**

F4.8 Exercise of power of advancement ... **[242.17]**

F4.9 Exercise of power of advancement for the benefit of someone by creating a trust for his minor children ... **[242.19]**

PRELIMINARY NOTE

[242.1]

When exercising a special power of appointment, care must be taken that the exercise is authorised by the terms of the power. For example, it can only be exercised for the benefit of the named objects of the power; trusts and powers should not be delegated (by eg the appointment of discretionary trusts and dispositive powers) unless the power authorises such delegation; the interests which it creates must vest within the perpetuity period applicable to the instrument creating the power; and excessive accumulations must not be directed. If the power requires, as powers of appointment usually do, an appointment by deed then a deed is necessary for the appointment to be valid. For some observations on these points in relation to exercises of special powers of appointment by will (which will apply with any necessary modifications to appointments made by an inter vivos instrument), see B13 at **[213.1]** ff (and for a fuller treatment of the exercise of special powers of appointment, see Vol 1, paras **[39.1]** and **[40.1]** ff).

One obvious, though important, difference between the exercise of a dispositive power by will or codicil, and the exercise of such a power by an inter vivos instrument such as a deed, is that an appointment by deed takes effect immediately following the execution of the deed whereas an appointment by will only takes effect upon the death of the appointor. Accordingly, an exercise by will can be revoked or altered at any time before the death of the appointor and before the appointment has taken effect. An appointment by deed, however, will have effect according to its terms unless and until it is made expressly revocable and is in fact revoked.

Some examples of the exercise of powers of advancement are also provided here (in Forms F4.8 and F4.9 at paras **[242.17]–[242.19]**). By powers of advancement we mean the statutory power of advancement (Trustee Act 1925, s 32: Part G, para **[246.30]**), or express powers in the same essential form, ie powers to pay or apply capital to or for the benefit of one or more persons, or the like. Such a power is, like a power of appointment, subject to the rule against perpetuities in such a way that interests created in exercise of the power need to vest within a perpetuity period calculated from the creation of the power (*Pilkington v IRC* [1964] AC 612, [1962] 3 All ER 622), but the rules as to what may be done in exercise of such a power may be more liberal and rather different from those surrounding a power of appointment: see B18 at para **[218.85]** ff. Also, it is usually the case that a power of advancement is not subject to the formal requirements for its exercise to which a power of appointment is commonly subject.

[242.2]

Inheritance tax consequences of an appointment or advance. On or after 22 March 2006, where an interest in possession in any property is brought to an end by an appointment or advance, different consequences will follow depending on whether the interest in possession is the type of interest in possession which post-21 March 2006 has the result that its holder is treated as beneficially entitled to the underlying settled property under IHTA 1984, s 49(1), or not. The types of interest in possession falling within the former category are an interest in possession to which a person became beneficially entitled before 22 March 2006 (unless it is an interest in possession under a trust for a bereaved minor), or an interest in possession to which a person became beneficially entitled on or after 22 March 2006 and which is an immediate post-death interest, a disabled person's interest, or a transitional serial interest (see para **[200.98]**–**[200.100]** above). The termination of such an interest in possession post-21 March 2006 will generally be a chargeable transfer, unless the appointment or advance causes another person to acquire an absolute interest, or an interest in possession which has the result that its holder is treated as beneficially entitled to the underlying settled property under IHTA 1984, s 49(1), or causes the settled property to become subject to a trust for a bereaved minor, see para **[200.108]** above). In these cases, the termination may be a potentially exempt transfer.

If the interest in possession which is terminated post-21 March 2006 is not the type of interest in possession which results in its holder being treated as beneficially entitled to the underlying settled property under IHTA 1984, s 49(1), or if the appointment or advance is made from property held on discretionary trusts, the settled property will generally have been relevant property and the consequence will be an exit charge as described in B18 at paras **[218.8]**–**[218.14]**, if the appointment or advance causes the settled property to cease to be relevant property, eg. if another person acquires an absolute interest, or a disabled person's interest within IHTA 1984, s 89B (see para **[200.99]** above).There remains, however, the special case of appointments or advances made within two years of a testator's death out of a discretionary trust created by his will, which do not give rise to an exit charge. Post-21 March 2006 this is extended to appointments or advances made within two years of a testator's death out of certain other trusts created by his will (see para **[242.4]** below).

[242.3]

Capital gains tax on appointments or advances. If an appointment or advance results in someone becoming absolutely entitled to any trust property that will be an occasion of deemed disposal for capital gains tax purposes: Taxation of Chargeable Gains Act 1992 (TCGA 1992), s 71(1). If property continues to be held on trust after the appointment or advance it will be an occasion of deemed disposal only if the property becomes comprised in a new or different settlement from that in which it was comprised before the appointment or advance: see further B18 at paras **[218.26]**, **[218.100]**–**[218.102]** and the notes to Form F4.3 at para **[242.9]** and Form F4.9 at para **[242.19]**. However, in either case, there may be no deemed disposal if the estate is still in the course of administration at the time of the appointment or advance, see para **[242.5]**.

Even where there is a deemed disposal for capital gains tax purposes, there may be hold-over relief where the property is business or agricultural property (TCGA 1992, s 165), or the appointment or advance is an occasion of immediate IHT charge (TCGA 1992, s 260(2)(a)), eg a chargeable transfer on the termination of an interest in possession which post-21 March 2006 has the result that its holder is treated as beneficially entitled to the underlying settled property under IHTA 1984, s 49(1) (see para **[242.2]** above), an exit charge under the relevant property regime (see paras **[218.8]** ff), or an exit charge under the age 18-to-25 trust regime (see para **[200.109]** above). Hold-over relief may also be available when the appointment or advance is from property subject to IHTA 1984, s 71 (so called accumulation and maintenance trusts, see para **[200.107]** above), IHTA 1984, 71A (trusts for bereaved minors, see para **[200.108]** above) or IHTA 1984, s 71D (age 18-to-25 trusts, see para **[200.109]** above) (TCGA 1992, s 260(2)(d), (da), (db)).

[242.4]

Inheritance Tax Act 1984, s 144. IHTA 1984, s 144 is a provision which, like IHTA 1984, s 142, enables changes made to the dispositions of a testator's estate within two years of his death to be backdated to the testator's death for IHT purposes.

Prior to 22 March 2006 and the changes to IHT introduced by FA 2006, Sch 20, it generally applied to cases where property was settled by will and within two years of the testator's death, but not sooner than three months after his death, and before an interest in possession had subsisted in the property, it was appointed or distributed to someone either absolutely or upon interest in possession trusts. The effect of IHTA 1984, s 144 applying was that there would be no IHT 'exit charge' on this event, and the will was treated for IHT purposes as if it had provided that on the testator's death the property should be held as it was held after the appointment. Accordingly, an appointment of property to a spouse would mean that the appointed property had the benefit of the spouse exemption upon the testator's death.

With the changes introduced by FA 2006, Sch 20, IHTA 1984, s 144 has been modified to enable a similar relief to continue to apply in the changed circumstances of the new IHT regime. The position for appointments made on or after 22 March 2006 is now broadly as follows:

(a) Where a testator died before 22 March 2006 settling property by his will, and within two years of his death, but not sooner than three months after his death, and before an interest in possession has subsisted in the property, it is appointed or distributed to someone either absolutely or for a disabled person's interest (see para **[200.99]** above) (or to charity, an employee trust or a maintenance fund), the appointment will not give rise to a charge to IHT, and will be treated as having had effect from the testator's death (IHTA 1984, s 144(1), (2)). So, for example, if property is appointed absolutely to the testator's spouse, the spouse exemption will apply to that property on the testator's death. The requirements that an appointment should not be made less than three months after the testator's death, and should be made absolutely or of a disabled person's interest (if not to charity, an employee trust or a maintenance fund), do not appear expressly in IHTA 1984, s 144(1). They follow from the fact that IHTA 1984, s 144(1) applies in the case of a death before 22 March 2006 where the property settled by the testator's will is relevant property (or would be relevant property if the administration of the estate had been completed, which amounts to the same thing for IHT purposes, see IHTA 1984, s 83), and where an event takes place within two years of death on which tax would be charged under IHTA 1984, Pt III Ch III (other than s 64 or 79), or an event on which tax would be charged but for IHTA 1984, s 75 (property becoming subject to employee trusts) or 76 (property becoming held for charitable purposes) or Sch 4 para 16(1) (property becoming comprised in maintenance funds). This essentially means that IHTA 1984, s 144(1) applies where, apart from it, there would be an exit charge under IHTA 1984, s 64, but there can be no such exit charge in the first three months of a settlement: IHTA 1984, ss 65(4), 83 and 144(1)(a). (This is confirmed by *Frankland v IRC* [1996] STC 735 and the Special Commissioner's decision in *Harding (executors of Loveday) v IRC* [1997] STC (SCD) 321.) Further, after 21 March 2006, occasions of exit charge are more restricted than was formerly the case, although absolute appointments and appointments of a disabled person's interest will give rise to an exit charge.

(b) Where a testator died before 22 March 2006 settling property by his will and an event occurs on or after 22 March 2006 and within two years of the testator's death before an immediate post-death interest (see para **[200.98]** above) or a disabled person's interest (see para **[200.99]** above) has subsisted in the property, (and when no other interest in possession has subsisted before 22 March 2006) that involves causing the property to be held on trusts such that had they been established by the testator's will (and he had died at the time of the event) they would have resulted in an immediate post-death interest, or a trust for bereaved minors (see para **[200.108]** above) or an age 18-to-25 trust (see para **[200.109]** above), they will be treated for IHT purposes as if they had been established by the testator's will, and tax shall not be charged (see IHTA 1984, s 144(4), (5), (6)). This separate provision is required (in addition to the provision set out in (a) above) because the appointment of a trust interest (other than a disabled person's interest) on or after 22 March 2006 out of relevant property is not an occasion of exit charge (as required by IHTA 1984, s 144(1)). It should be noted that an appointment within the first three months of the testator's death will be within these provisions. It should also be noted that although the appointment of an interest in possession will only be within these provisions if it would have qualified as an immediate post-death interest if it had been contained in the testator's will and he had died at the time of the appointment, the interest in possession will in fact be treated for IHT purposes as a result of these provisions as a pre-22 March 2006 interest in possession since it will be treated as having arisen before 22 March 2006 on the testator's death (IHTA 1984, s 144(4)(a)). Furthermore, while these provisions may be used to create trusts for bereaved minors or age 18-to-25 trusts, they may not be used to create accumulation and maintenance trusts with the benefits of IHTA 1984, s 71, even though the testator could have created such trusts by his will.

(c) Where a testator dies on or after 22 March 2006, settling property by his will, and within two years of his death, but not sooner than three months after his death, and before an immediate post-death interest (see para **[200.98]** above) or disabled person's interest (see para **[200.99]** above) has subsisted in the property, it is appointed or distributed to someone either absolutely or for a disabled person's interest (or to charity, an employee trust or a maintenance fund), the appointment will not give rise to a charge to IHT, and will be treated as having had effect from the testator's death (IHTA 1984, s 144(1), (1A), (2)). Again, the requirement that the appointment should be made absolutely or of a disabled person's interest (if not to charity, an employee trust or a maintenance fund) does not appear expressly in IHTA 1984, s 144(1), but follows from the fact that IHTA 1984, s 144(1) applies in the case of a death on or after 22 March 2006 where the property settled by the testator's will is relevant property, and occasions of exit charge are restricted to absolute appointments and appointments of a disabled person's interest. Similarly, the requirement that the appointment should not be made less than three months after the testator's death follows from the fact that an appointment in the first quarter after a testator's death will not give rise to an exit charge.

But for deaths on or after 22 March 2006, IHTA 1984, s 144 may also apply where the property settled by will is not relevant property, but property subject to an age 18-to-25 trust (see para **[200.109]** above). Say a testator dies in April 2006 leaving his residuary estate to his children at age 25. Assume he has two children, one who has attained the age of 25 at his death, and the other who is 23, and will be 25 in January 2008. The elder son will be entitled to a half share of the residuary estate immediately on the testator's death, but the younger son will not, and if TA 1925, s 31 applies, varied so that accumulation of income is possible until his 25th birthday so he does not have an immediate post-death interest (see para **[200.98]** above), his presumptive half share will be held on an age 18-to-25 trust. When he attains 25 in January 2008 and becomes absolutely entitled to his half share there will be an occasion of IHT charge under IHTA 1984, s 71E(1)(a) (which is contained in IHTA 1984, Pt III Ch III), and this situation would seem to come squarely within IHTA 1984, s 144(1), so that no

IHT will actually be charged on the younger son's 25th birthday, and for IHT purposes, he will be treated as having become absolutely entitled to his half share of the residuary estate on the testator's death. Even if the younger son attains 25 within three months of the testator's death, say in May 2006, IHTA 1984, s 144(1) would still seem to apply because although the IHT charge on such attainment will necessarily be nil (since there will be no complete quarter between the date when the property became subject to an age 18–25 trust, so the relevant fraction for calculating the IHT charge will also be nil, see IHTA 1984, s 71F(5)), it is still an occasion of charge.

IHTA 1984, s 144(1) might similarly apply upon an advance of capital to the beneficiary of an age 18-to-25 trust before his 25th birthday, (though after his 18th birthday, since there will be no IHT charge on an advance to a beneficiary before his 18th birthday, see IHTA 1984, s 71E(2)(a)) and within two years of the testator's death.

(d) Where a testator dies on or after 22 March 2006, settling property by his will, and within two years of his death, and before an immediate post-death interest (see para **[200.98]** above) or disabled person's interest (see para **[200.99]** above) has subsisted in the property, an event occurs that involves causing the property to be held on trusts such that had they been established by the testator's will they would have resulted in an immediate post-death interest, or a trust for bereaved minors (see para **[200.108]** above) or an age 18-to-25 trust (see para **[200.109]** above), they will be treated for IHT purposes as if they had been established by the testator's will, and tax shall not be charged (see IHTA 1984, s 144(3), (4)). Therefore it is possible to appoint an immediate post-death interest, a trust for bereaved minors or an age 18-to-25 trust within two years of the testator's death. It should be noted that such an event within the first three months of the testator's death will be within these provisions.

Again for deaths on or after 22 March 2006, IHTA 1984, s 144 may apply not only where property settled by will is relevant property, but also where property is subject to an age 18–25 trust. So if in the example given in (c) above, the younger son was 17 at the date of the testator's death, and say Trustee Act 1925, s 31 applies unvaried so that he attains an interest in possession on his 18th birthday within two years of the testator's death, it would seem that IHTA 1984, s 144(3), (4) will apply to treat him as having an immediate post-death interest from the testator's death. If this is right, then it would be possible if the will contained appropriate powers, to convert an age 18-to-25 trust to an immediate post-death interest within two years of a testator's death.

It is also possible that for deaths on or after 22 March 2006, IHTA 1984, s 144 can apply where property settled by will is subject to a bereaved minor's trust. For example, say that a testator leaves a nil-rate band legacy to his only child contingently on attaining the age of 18, with Trustee Act 1925, s 32 applying, but modified to enable the advance of the whole of the child's presumptive share before his 18th birthday. If within two years of the testator's death, and before the child has attained the age of 18, the trustees, being concerned about the child's ability to handle a large sum of money at the age of 18, exercise the power of advancement to declare an immediate life interest for the child in place of his contingent right to capital, it would seem that IHTA 1984, s 144(3), (4) will apply to treat him as having an immediate post-death interest from the testator's death.

Whether the above analysis is right, however, at least in relation to events happening automatically under the terms of the trust, is open to a small doubt. There is an interpretative problem as to what is required for IHTA 1984, s 144(3)(c) to apply to an interest in possession arising after the testator's death but within two years of it, and that is whether it will qualify as an immediate post-death interest for the purposes of IHTA 1984, s 144(3)(c) if it does not carry arrears of income arising since the testator's death. The critical question is whether if the interest in possession does not carry these arrears, an event has caused the property in which the interest in possession subsists to be held on trusts that would, if they had in fact been established by will, have resulted in an immediate post-death interest. So, for example, in the case where a beneficiary under an age 18-to-25 trust becomes entitled to an interest in possession when he attains 18 by operation of Trustee Act 1925, s 31(1)(ii), he will not also become entitled to income arising between the testator's death and his 18th birthday. However, if instead of becoming entitled to his interest in possession simply by operation of Trustee Act 1925, s 31(1)(ii) he became entitled by virtue of an exercise by the trustees of a power of advancement, by which exercise they also paid to him absolutely arrears of income arising since death, this would seem to fall squarely within IHTA 1984, s 144(3)(c), with the result that his interest in possession should be backdated to death to become an immediate post-death interest.

When making an appointment to come within s 144, and where part of the estate following the appointment will be exempt from IHT and part will not be exempt, and an appointment of specific property or a specified sum of cash is being made to a non-exempt beneficiary, it will often be advisable to make the appointment expressly subject to IHT payable in respect of the testator's death, particularly where the purpose of the exercise is to appoint property not exceeding the IHT nil-rate band to non-exempt beneficiaries with the rest of the estate going to the testator's surviving spouse. If in such a case the non-exempt part of the estate turns out to exceed the IHT threshold, less IHT will be payable on the estate if such appointments to non-exempt persons are subject to IHT in respect of the testator's death than if they are free of tax: see the Preliminary Note to B14 at para **[214.74]**. If no express direction as to IHT is included, a specific gift will usually be free of tax: see Preliminary Note to B14 at para **[214.55]** ff. On and from 9 October 2007, appointments within IHTA 1984, s 144 to utilise the deceased's nil-rate band by making appointments in favour of chargeable persons will become less common following the introduction of rules to carry forward unused nil-rate band allowance (see para **[200.75]**). Appointments in favour of a spouse (or civil partner), particularly from nil-rate band discretionary trusts, will become more popular. For such an appointment, see Form F4.2 at para **[242.8]**.

[242.5]

Capital gains tax and s 144 appointments. If an absolute appointment of trust property is made to which IHTA 1984, s 144 applies, there will be a deemed disposal by the trustees of the appointed assets at their market value under the TCGA 1992, s 71, and hold-over relief will not be available (because the appointment will not be a chargeable transfer for IHT purposes – see TCGA 1992, s 260) unless the assets are business or agricultural property which qualify for it under s 165 of the 1992 Act. Therefore a chargeable gain may accrue, the acquisition cost of the appointed assets being their market value as at the testator's death. Such gain will be chargeable to tax at the rate applicable to trusts under the TCGA 1992, s 5; see Part A, para **[200.39]**. However, if the appointment is made while the estate is still in the course of administration it is arguable that for capital gains tax purposes the appointees take the appointed assets as 'legatees' within the TCGA 1992, s 62(4), being persons who take under the will, with the consequence that no chargeable gain should accrue and the appointees will take the appointed assets with the personal representatives' acquisition cost for capital gains tax purposes, ie the market value of the assets at the date of death of the testator (TCGA 1992, ss 62 (4) and 64 (2)). This seems to be accepted by HMRC, see *Foster's Inheritance Tax*, D4.35. If an appointment within s 144 results in the property continuing to be held on trust and as property comprised in the same settlement, it is not an occasion of capital gains tax disposal.

[242.6]

Stamp duty and stamp duty land tax. Stamp duty remains applicable to instruments relating to stock or marketable securities, but is not payable on an instrument exercising a power of appointment or advancement. Stamp duty land tax is essentially a tax on land transactions, charging *ad valorem* tax on the consideration given for the acquisition of an interest in land (see para **[220.72]**, above), but usually no consideration will be given for the exercise of a power of appointment (unless perhaps property subject to a charge is appointed and the appointee assumes liability for the charge) so that stamp duty land tax will not usually be a concern. However, express provision is made in FA 2003 that where land or an interest in land is acquired by virtue of the exercise of a power of appointment there shall be treated as consideration for the acquisition of the interest any consideration given for the person in whose favour the appointment was made becoming an object of the power (FA 2003, Sch 16, para 7). The circumstances in which this might apply, particularly in relation to powers of appointment contained in wills, would be very rare indeed.

[242.7]

Form F4.1: Appointment from discretionary trust within two years of testator's death[1]

THIS DEED OF APPOINTMENT is made the [*date*] by [*name*] of [*address*] and [*name*] of [*address*] ('the Trustees').

Whereas:

(A) By his last Will ('the Will') dated [*date*] [*name*] late of [*address*] ('the Testator') appointed the Trustees to be the executors and trustees of the Will.

(B) The Testator died on the [*date*][2] and on the [*date*] the Will was duly proved by the Trustees.[3]

(C) By Clause —— of the Will the Testator directed the Trustees to hold the capital and income of his residuary estate ('the residuary estate') upon trust for all or such one or more of the beneficiaries ('the beneficiaries') at such ages or times in such shares and upon such trusts for the benefit of the beneficiaries as the Trustees should by irrevocable deed or deeds executed at any time or times during the discretionary period (as defined in the Will) appoint.

(D) The discretionary period was defined by Clause —— of the Will to mean the period beginning immediately after the end of the period of three months from the day of the Testator's death and ending with the day before the second anniversary of his death.

(E) The beneficiaries as defined in the Will include [*name*] who is the widow of the Testator and [*name*] and [*name*] who are the children of the Testator.

(F) The Trustees desire to exercise their above-mentioned power of appointment for the benefit of the said [*name*] [*name*] and [*name*] in the manner appearing below.

NOW THIS DEED WITNESSES that the Trustees in exercise of their above-mentioned power of appointment and each and every other power them enabling HEREBY IRREVOCABLY APPOINT that the residuary estate shall be held upon the following trusts:

(1) upon trust as to [£300,000] for the said children of the Testator [*name*] and [*name*] in equal shares absolutely [Provided that any inheritance tax attributable thereto and payable in respect of the death of the Testator should be borne by the said [*name*] and [*name*] in equal shares absolutely];[4] and

(2) subject as aforesaid upon trust for the said widow of the Testator [*name*] absolutely.

IN WITNESS whereof the Trustees have executed these presents as their deed the day and year first above written.[5]

SIGNED and delivered as a deed by the said [*name*] in the presence of— } [*Signature of trustee*]

[*Signature, address and description of witness*]

[*The foregoing from 'SIGNED' to be repeated for each trustee*]

1 This form is designed to take advantage of IHTA 1984, s 144. For a form of will which envisages such an appointment, see Form C3.6 at para **[225.92]** ff, and for notes on s 144 see C3 at para **[225.83]** ff and the Preliminary Note at para **[242.4]**, and the Preliminary Note at **[242.5]** on the capital gains tax consequences of an absolute appointment. The recitals of the terms of the will in this form are based on Form C3.6.

Provided that the appointment fulfils the conditions of s 144, there will be no exit charge under the IHTA 1984, s 65 on the appointment and the appointment will be treated as having effect from the deceased's death.

A type of appointment such as this, if the sum appointed to the testator's children is within the testator's available nil-rate band, has, at least prior to 9 October 2007, been one of the commonest types of appointment to take advantage of IHTA 1984, s 144, since if made within two years of death (and not within three months), it makes use of the deceased's nil-rate band. Following the introduction on 9 October 2007 of rules to carry forward unused nil-rate band allowance it may no longer be so popular, and it may be preferred to make an appointment to the testator's spouse because to the extent that the testator's nil-rate band is unused, it will be carried forward (see para **[200.75]** above).

2 To take advantage of the IHTA 1984, s 144, the appointment must be made not more than two years after the testator's death, but not within the first three months after his death: see the Preliminary Note at para **[242.4]**. Where the testator died before 22 March 2006, the relevant provisions, are IHTA 1984, s 144(1), (2), and where he dies on or after 22 March 2006 they are IHTA 1984, s 144(1), (1A), (2).

3 Whether or not the power of appointment may be exercised before the will has been proved, or before the executors have become trustees will depend upon the terms of the will. HMRC once took the view that executors could not exercise a power of appointment until the property which was to be appointed was vested in them as trustees, but they now seem to accept that a power may be exercised by executors if on the true construction of the will they have authority to exercise it in that capacity, for example, where a will expressly confers the power on them in their capacity as executors as well as trustees, or appoints the individuals who actually exercise the power as executors and trustees, referring to them in the will as 'my trustees' with the power being given to 'my trustees'.

4 So as to avoid IHT in respect of the death of the testator, the sum appointed should not be more than the maximum which non-exempt persons can take without any liability being incurred for IHT on or by reason of the testator's death, taking into account the testator's lifetime chargeable transfers, property treated as his for IHT purposes at the time of his death and the dispositions taking effect under his will and under the deed of appointment. In case this appointment should happen to push the testator's chargeable estate above the IHT threshold at the time of his death, for example, on its subsequently being discovered that the testator had made a lifetime chargeable transfer, a direction that any IHT should be borne by the appointees should result in less IHT being payable than if the legacy was free of tax: see the Preliminary Note at para **[242.4]**. £300,000 is the IHT threshold in relation to a death after 5 April 2007. For 2008–9 it is proposed that it will be £312,000; for 2009–10, £325,000: see FA 2006, s 155; and for 2010–11, £350,000.

5 The requirements of the Law of Property (Miscellaneous Provisions) Act 1989, s 1, for the making of a deed are that it is clear on its face that it is intended by the parties to it to be a deed, that it is signed by each party in the presence of a witness who attests the signature (two witnesses if someone signs for a party), and that it is delivered as a deed by each party or someone authorised to do so on his behalf. Sealing is not necessary.

[242.8]

Form F4.2: Appointment to spouse from nil-rate band discretionary trust within two years of testator's death[1]

THIS DEED OF APPOINTMENT is made the [*date*] BY [*name*] of [*address*] and [*name*] of [*address*] ('the Legacy Trustees').

SUPPLEMENTAL to the will ('the Will') dated [*date*] of [*name of testator*] ('the Testator') who died on [*date*][2] and which was proved by [*names*] on [*date*] in the [*name*] Registry

Whereas—

(A) By clause + of the Will the Testator gave to the Legacy Trustees a pecuniary legacy determined according to a formula ('the Trust Legacy') to hold the same upon trust for all or such one or more of the beneficiaries (as defined in the Will) at such ages or times in such shares and upon such trusts for the benefit of the beneficiaries as the

Legacy Trustees may be by deed or deeds revocable or irrevocable executed at any time or times during the trust period (as defined in the Will) appoint.

(B) The widow of the Testator [*name*] ('the Widow') is one of the beneficiaries.

(C) The Legacy Trustees desire to exercise their above-mentioned power of appointment for the benefit of the Widow in the manner appearing below.

NOW THIS DEED WITNESSETH that the Legacy Trustees in exercise of their above mentioned power of appointment and each and every other power them enabling HEREBY IRREVOCABLY APPOINT that the Trust Legacy[3] shall be held upon trust for the Widow absolutely

IN WITNESS whereof the Legacy Trustees have executed these presents as their deed the day and year first above written.[4]

SIGNED and delivered as a deed by the said [*name*] in the presence of— } [*Signature of trustee*]

[*Signature, address and description of witness*]

[*The foregoing from 'SIGNED' to be repeated for each trustee*]

1 This form assumes that the testator has settled a nil-rate band gift onto discretionary trusts in his will, with residue to his spouse, as in Form C3.4 at paras **[225.57]** ff. Generally, he will have done this to ensure that his nil-rate band was not wasted, although he will have wished his spouse to continue to be able to benefit from his estate. On and from 9 October 2007, however, new rules provide that to the extent that a testator does not fully utilise his nil-rate band allowance, a nil-rate band carry forward allowance will be available to his spouse or civil partner in addition to her own nil-rate band allowance, see para **[200.75]** above. Therefore, if the only or prime reason for the nil-rate band discretionary trust was IHT driven, it may now be considered appropriate to make an appointment within IHTA 1984, s 144 in favour of the testator's spouse, since the appointment will be backdated to the testator's death so that the spouse exemption from IHT will be available in relation to the nil-rate band legacy, and to the extent that the testator's nil-rate band is unused, a carry forward nil-rate band allowance will be available.

See the Preliminary Note at para **[242.5]** on the capital gains tax consequences of an absolute appointment.

2 To take advantage of the IHTA 1984, s 144, the appointment must be made not more than two years after the testator's death, but not within the first three months after his death: see the Preliminary Note at para **[242.4]**. Where the testator died before 22 March 2006, the relevant provisions are IHTA 1984, s 144(1), (2), and where he dies on or after 22 March 2006 they are IHTA 1984, s 144(1), (1A), (2).

3 Even if the estate of the Testator has not been fully administered by the time of the appointment and there has been no assent of the Trust Legacy in favour of the Legacy Trustees, in the view of the writers, the Legacy Trustees will be able to make a valid appointment of it provided that there is nothing in the will to limit the exercise of their power to a time when the Trust Legacy is actually vested in them.

4 The requirements of the Law of Property (Miscellaneous Provisions) Act 1989, s 1 for the making of a deed are that it is clear on its face that it is intended by the parties to it to be a deed, that it is signed by each party in the presence of a witness who attests the signature (two witnesses if someone signs for a party), and that it is delivered as a deed by each party or someone authorised to do so on his behalf. Sealing is not necessary.

[242.9]

Form F4.3: Appointment from discretionary trust of money to beneficiaries who are sui juris[1]

THIS DEED OF APPOINTMENT is made the —— day of —— BY [*names and addresses of trustees*] ('the Trustees') and is SUPPLEMENTAL to the Will ('the Will') dated —— of [*name of testator*] who died on —— and whose said will was on —— duly proved by [*names of executors*] the executors named in the Will

Whereas:

(1) The property now subject to the trusts of the will includes the sum of [*amount*] in cash

(2) The trustees desire by this deed to exercise the power of appointment given them by Clause [*insert number of relevant clause*] of the Will

NOW THIS DEED WITNESSES that the Trustees in exercise of their said power of appointment under the will hereby irrevocably appoint the said sum of [amount] upon the following trusts:

(a) As to [*amount*] upon trust as to both capital and income for [*beneficiary*] absolutely

(b) As to [*amount*] upon trust as to both capital and income for [*beneficiary*] absolutely

(c) Etc, etc.

In witness][2]

1 This form is for use in the simplest case – where the trust property has already been converted into cash and it is being appointed absolutely to beneficiaries who are all sui juris. There may be an exit charge for IHT purposes under IHTA 1984, s 65, see paras **[218.8]–[218.14]** (assuming the appointment does not come within IHTA 1984, s 144), but there will be no capital gains tax charge because the appointed property is cash.

2 For execution, see Form F4.1 at para **[242.7]**.

[242.10]

Form F4.4: Appointment from discretionary trust of investments Note

Note. This form presupposes that the trust property is still in the form of investments and that these are being appointed in specie amongst beneficiaries some of whom are not yet of age. The effect of the appointment is that they become absolutely entitled to the investments appointed to them so that there will be an exit charge under IHTA 1984, s 65 (see paras **[218.8]–[218.14]**), unless the appointment comes within IHTA 1984, s 144 (see para **[242.4]**), and a deemed disposal by the trustees for capital gains tax purposes under the TCGA 1992, unless, perhaps, the estate is still in the course of administration (see para **[242.3]**). The investments can be transferred to the appointees by the trustees in exchange for formal receipts, although if there is an election for capital gains tax hold-over relief under the TCGA 1992, s 260 (which allows hold-over relief in cases where the occasion of the disposal is also a chargeable transfer, and it seems that an exit charge is a chargeable transfer for these purposes) the trustees may need to retain some assets for six years in case a capital gains tax charge arises under the TCGA 1992, s 168, on the emigration of an appointee, for which the trustees are liable (see especially sub-ss (7) and (8)).

[242.11]

THIS DEED OF APPOINTMENT [*continue as in* Form F4.3 *at para* **[242.9]**.

Whereas:

(1) The property now subject to the trusts of the Will consists of the investments [and cash] set out in the schedule to this deed.

(2) The trustees desire by this deed to exercise the power of appointment given them by Clause [*insert number of relevant clause*] of the Will.

NOW THIS DEED WITNESSETH as follows:

1. The Trustees in exercise of their said power of appointment under the Will hereby irrevocably appoint the property set out in the said Schedule upon the following trusts:

   (a)

   (i) As to the property set out in the first part of the schedule upon trust as to both capital and income for [*adult beneficiary*] absolutely.

   (ii) As to the property set out in the second part of the schedule upon trust as to both capital and income for [*infant beneficiary*] absolutely.

   (iii) Section 32 of the Trustee Act 1925 (relating to advancement) shall apply in relation to the trust for [*infant beneficiary*] as if the words 'one half of' were omitted from proviso (a) to subsection (1).[1]

   (iv) Etc, etc.

2. All income of the said property shall be treated as accruing on the date on which it becomes payable regardless of the period in respect of which it shall have accrued and shall not be subject to statutory apportionment.[2]

In witness[3]

THE SCHEDULE

[*The schedule is to contain all the trust property and is to be divided into parts, the first part listing the property appointed to the first-named beneficiary, and so on*]

1 Where property is appointed to an infant beneficiary absolutely it will have to be retained upon a bare trust for that child and an extended power of advancement will be useful to enable the trustees to apply capital for his or her benefit.

2 For statutory apportionment over time and its exclusion see B14 at paras **[214.35]** ff.

3 For execution, see Form F4.1 at para **[242.7]**.

[242.12]

Form F4.5: Appointment of immediate post-death interests in residue for the testator's grandchildren

Note. This form presupposes that the testator has settled his residuary estate upon trusts for his grandchildren, which trusts bring residue within the IHT relevant property regime. For example, he may have settled residue upon usual form discretionary trusts, or (having died on or after 22 March 2006) upon trust for his grandchildren contingently upon attaining a specified age without any of them having attained that specified age at his death or being entitled to an interest in possession from his death (which interest in possession would be an immediate post-death interest, (see para **[200.98]** above)). The appointment will confer interests in possession on his grandchildren (even if any of them are minors), so that provided the appointment is made within two years of the testator's death, they will be treated as having immediate post-death interests by virtue of IHTA 1984, s 144(3)–(6), and there will be no IHT charge. If an appointment in this form was not made until after the expiry of two years from the testator's death, IHTA 1984, s 144 would not apply to backdate the appointed interests in possession to the testator's death, so they would not be immediate post-death interests and (unless any of the grandchildren was disabled at the time of the testator's death, in which case his interest in possession would be a disabled person's interest within IHTA 1984, s 89B (see para **[200.99]** above)) the residuary estate would remain within the relevant property regime for IHT purposes.

If the administration of the estate is complete at the time of the appointment, then whether or not there is a deemed disposal by the trustees of the property in question under the TCGA 1992, s 71 when new trusts are appointed depends upon whether the trust property moves to a new and separate settlement. If the power which is exercised does not authorise the trustees to remove the property from the original settlement, there will be no deemed disposal. If it does so authorise them, an Inland Revenue Statement of Practice, SP 7/84, 11 October 1984, states that there will be no deemed disposal where the appointed trusts are non-exhaustive or revocable, and that it is unlikely that a deemed disposal will occur when the duties with regard to the appointed assets fall to the trustees of the original settlement in their capacity as such. The trusts of this appointment are revocable, and also the trustees of the appointed assets are the trustees of the will, so that it is probable that no disposal can be deemed to have been made.

Form

THIS DEED OF APPOINTMENT is made the —— day of —— BY [*names and addresses of trustees*] ('the Trustees' which expression shall include the trustees for the time being of the Will defined below) and is SUPPLEMENTAL To the Will ('the Will') dated —— of [*name of testator*] ('the Testator') who died on —— and whose said will was on —— duly proved by the Trustees (being the executors named in the Will)

Whereas:

(1) By Clause [*insert number of relevant clause*] of the Will the Testator gave the Trustees power during the trust period (as defined in the Will) to appoint that his residuary estate be held upon such trusts for all or such one or more of his grandchildren and remoter issue at such ages or times in such shares and upon such trusts and with such powers for their benefit as the Trustees should think fit[1]

(2) The Testator left [six] grandchildren surviving him

(3) The Trustees desire by this deed to exercise the power of appointment given them by Clause [*insert number of relevant clause*] of the Will.

NOW THIS DEED WITNESSETH as follows:

1. The Trustees in exercise of their said power of appointment under the Will hereby appoint (subject to the power of revocation below) that the Testator's residuary estate shall be held upon trust for the Testator's grandchildren living at his death in equal shares but the share of the residuary estate to which a grandchild shall become entitled shall not vest in such grandchild but shall be retained by the Trustees and held upon the following trusts:

(a) the Trustees shall hold such share ('the settled share') upon trust to pay the income of the settled share [(including income which has arisen before the date of this deed and since the Testator's death)][2] to such grandchild ('the grandchild') for life;

(b) if and so long as the grandchild is under the age of 18 years the Trustees may pay or otherwise apply for or towards the maintenance education or benefit of the grandchild the whole or such part or parts of the income of the settled share as the Trustees in their absolute discretion think fit and shall retain the balance of such income upon trust for the grandchild absolutely but the Trustees may at any time or times while the grandchild is living and under the age of 18 years pay or apply such retained income as if it were income arising in the then current year and section 31 of the Trustee Act 1925 shall not apply to the settled share;[3]

(c) subject as above the Trustees shall hold the settled share upon trust for the children or child of the grandchild born during the trust period and if more than one in equal shares absolutely;[4]

(d) the provisions of section 32 of the Trustee Act 1925 shall apply in relation to the settled share as if the words 'one half of' were omitted from proviso (a) to subsection (1);

(e) notwithstanding the above trusts during the trust period and so long as the grandchild is entitled to be paid the income of all or any part of the capital of the settled share (or would be so entitled if such capital yielded income) the trustees shall have power in their absolute discretion from time to time to pay transfer or apply the whole or any part or parts of such capital to or for the benefit of the grandchild in such manner as they shall in their absolute discretion think fit; and

(f) subject as above the settled share (or so much as has not been applied under any of the above powers) shall accrue to the share or shares of the other grandchildren (and if more than one equally) the trusts of which have not at the date of accruer failed or determined (otherwise than by absolute vesting) to form one fund with such other share or shares for all purposes.

2. The administrative provisions of the will which are contained in Clauses [*set out here relevant clauses*] thereof shall apply to the trusts declared by this deed [save only for the following modifications [*set out any modifications which may be desired*].[5]

3. Provided always that the Trustees shall have power by deed or deeds executed during the trust period to revoke this deed in whole or in part Provided that no such revocation shall prejudice any person's entitlement to an interest in possession (within the meaning of Part III of the Inheritance Tax Act 1984) in any part of the Testator's residuary estate up to the time of such revocation nor invalidate any prior payment transfer or application of capital

In witness[6]

1 The precise terms of the power of appointment of the actual will must be considered carefully.

2 If the appointment is made within two years of the testator's death, and it is hoped to rely on the backdating effect of IHTA 1984, s 144, (and particularly where the testator died on or after 22 March 2006), the appointment should cover not only income arising in respect of residue following the date of the appointment, but also income arising since the testator's death, see the Preliminary Note at para **[242.4]**). Where residue is subject to usual form discretionary trusts under the terms of the testator's will, the trustees will have a discretion over income as well as capital so it should be possible for an appointment to cover income which has already arisen.

3 See para **[218.51]** for the trusts of accumulations under the TA 1925, s 31 (Part G, para **[246.29]**) which unless varied or excluded are such as usually to give minor beneficiaries a contingent interest in such accumulations, even if they have a vested interest in the income. The purpose of this substitution for s 31 is to cause the income which is not applied for the grandchild's benefit during his minority to be held on trust absolutely for the grandchild, so as to confer an interest in possession for IHT purposes. An infant cannot be paid income to which he is entitled (see Vol 1, para **[9.39]**) but it is thought that he or she has an interest in possession in income if it would form part of his estate if he or she died under the age of 18 (and unmarried and without a civil partner). Such an interest in possession will be an immediate post-death interest within IHTA 1984, s 49A (see para **[200.98]** above and para **[216.1]** above).

4 Although this gives the children of a grandchild absolute interests, these interests are in fact defeasible by exercise of the power of revocation contained below, so if and when they take effect on the termination of a grandchild's life interest, the settled share would become relevant property for IHT purposes (see para **[200.92]**).

5 Care should be taken to ensure that none of the administrative powers of the will is incompatible with an interest in possession.

6 For execution, see Form F4.1 at para **[242.7]**.

[242.13]

Form F4.6: Appointment from discretionary trust of investments to a bereaved minor trust or age 18–25 trust

Note. This form, like Form F4.4 above, presupposes that the trust property is still in the form of investments and that these are being appointed in specie amongst beneficiaries who are children of the testator. The appointment is not to those beneficiaries absolutely, but on continuing trusts. Since the appointees are children of the testator, a bereaved minor trust or age 18–25 trust may be appointed. If the selected age of contingency is 18, the trust appointed should be a trust for bereaved minors (see para **[200.108]** above), and if the specified age is 25, the trust should be an age 18–25 trust (see para **[200.109]** above). Although there is a question as to whether a trust for a bereaved minor or an age 18–25 trust can arise under the exercise of a special power of appointment rather than under the words of the will itself, it seems to the writers that such trusts can arise provided the appointment does not create a new and separate settlement (and HMRC seem to share this opinion) (see para **[200.107]** above). If the appointment is made within two years of the testator's death (whether the death occurred before or after 22 March 2006), there will be no IHT charge and the appointment will be backdated to the testator's death for IHT purposes (see IHTA 1984, s 144(3)–(6)). If the appointment is made more than two years after death, IHTA 1984, s 144 cannot apply, and there would be an exit charge under IHTA 1984, s 65 since trusts for bereaved minors and age 18-to-25 trusts are expressly excluded from the relevant property regime (see paras **[218.92]**).

If the same form were used for an appointment to children who were not children of the testator, the settled property appointed would remain subject to the IHT charging regime for relevant property, and even if the appointment is made within two years of the testator's death, IHTA 1984, s 144 has no backdating effect (see para **[200.107]** above). In any event there would be no exit charge under IHTA 1984, s 65 (see paras **[218.8]**–**[218.14]**) on the appointment. If it is the intention to avoid the relevant property regime, then an appointment to an infant (not being a child or stepchild of the testator) would have to be made to that infant absolutely.

As to whether or not there is a deemed disposal by the trustees of the property in question under the TCGA 1992, s 71 when new trusts are appointed, see the Note above. The trusts of this appointment are non-exhaustive, and the trustees of the appointed assets are the trustees of the will, so that it is probable that no disposal can be deemed to have been made.

[242.14]

THIS DEED OF APPOINTMENT is made the —— day of —— BY [*names and addresses of trustees*] ('the Trustees') and is SUPPLEMENTAL TO the Will ('the Will') dated —— of [*name of testator*] ('the Testator') who died on —— and whose said will was on —— duly proved by [*names of executors*] the executors named in the Will

Whereas:

(1) The Testator left [three] minor children surviving namely [*name*] who was born on [*date*] [*name*] who was born on [*date*] and [*name*] who was born on [*date*]

(2) The property now subject to the trusts of the Will consists of the investments [and cash] set out in the schedule to this deed ('the Appointed Property')

(3) The trustees desire by this deed to exercise the power of appointment given them by Clause [*insert number of relevant clause*] of the Will.

NOW THIS DEED WITNESSETH as follows:

1. The Trustees in exercise of their said power of appointment under the Will hereby irrevocably appoint the Appointed Property upon the following trusts:

(a)

(i) Upon trust as to both capital and income for such of the Testator's children as shall attain the age of [18]/[25][1] years and if more than one in equal shares absolutely.

(ii) The above trust shall carry the intermediate income [(including income which has arisen before the date of this deed and since the Testator's death)][2] and Section 31 of the Trustee Act 1925 (relating to accumulation and maintenance) shall apply [in relation to a child of the Testator in all respects as if the age of majority were the age of 25 years or such lesser age as that child will attain (if living) on his birthday immediately preceding the expiry of twenty one years from the date of the Testator's death (and so that the expressions 'infancy', 'minority' and 'infant' and all references to the age of eighteen years in the Section shall be construed accordingly)][3]

(iii) Section 32 of the Trustee Act 1925 (relating to advancement) shall apply in relation to the above trust as if the words 'one half of' were omitted from proviso (a) to subsection (1).[4]

(b) Provided that if any of the Testator's children dies before attaining a vested interest but leaving a child or children living at his death then such child or children shall take absolutely and if more than one in equal shares so much of the Appointed Property as that person would have taken had he attained a vested interest.[5]

2. The administrative provisions of the will which are contained in Clauses [*set out here relevant clauses*] thereof shall apply to the trusts declared by this deed [save only for the following modifications [*set out any modifications which may be desired*].[6]

In witness[7]

THE SCHEDULE

[*The schedule is to contain all the trust property which is being appointed*]

1 If the specified age is 18, the trust appointed should be a trust for bereaved minors (see para **[200.108]** above), and if the specified age is 25, the trust should be an age 18–25 trust (see para **[200.109]** above).

2 If the appointment is made within two years of the testator's death, and it is hoped to rely on the backdating effect of IHTA 1984, s 144, (and particularly where the testator died on or after 22 March 2006), the appointment should cover not only income arising in respect of the appointed property following the date of the appointment, but also income arising since the testator's death, see the Preliminary Note at para **[242.4]**). Where the appointed property is subject to usual form discretionary trusts under the terms of the testator's will, the trustees will have a discretion over income as well as capital so it should be possible for an appointment to cover income which has already arisen.

3 Inclusion of this modification to TA 1925, s 31 (see para **[246.29]**) should be considered if an age 18-to-25 trust is intended. Its effect will be to enable the income of each child's presumptive share to be accumulated for at least 21 years from the testator's death, or until the child attains 25 if sooner. So if all of the testator's children are aged at least 4 at the testator's death, accumulation of income will be possible until each attains 25. If the appointment is made within two years of the testator's death (so that IHTA 1984, s 144 would apply) and it is wished to create an age 18-to-25 trust rather than an immediate post-death interest, it will be important to include this clause if any of the testator's children have attained the age 18 at the testator's death. If Trustee Act 1925, s 31 applied unmodified, a child over 18 would be entitled to income absolutely (by virtue of TA 1925, s 31(1)(ii)) and the backdating effect of IHTA 1984, s 144(4) would be to treat that child as having an immediate post-death interest from the testator's death. It is not absolutely clear what the position would be if the child in question was under 18 at the date of the testator's death, but over the age of 18 at the date of the appointment, ie. whether the effect of the child having an interest in possession from the date of the appointment would be sufficient to treat him as having an interest in possession from the testator's death, so it is suggested that if an age 18-to-25 trust is intended in these circumstances, TA 1925, s 31 should apply as modified by this clause.

4 The extended statutory power of advancement is compatible with a trust for bereaved minors and an age 18-to-25 trust, see IHTA 1984, ss 71A(4)(b), 71D(7)(b).

5 Children of a child of the testator who does not reach the age of contingency will take their deceased parent's share of the appointed property absolutely. It is not possible to create a trust for bereaved minors or age 18-to-25 trust for persons other than the testator's children (or stepchildren or those for whom he has parental responsibility).

6 Care should be taken to ensure that none of the administrative powers of the will is incompatible with a trust for bereaved minors or an age 18-to-25 trust.

7 For execution, see Form F4.1 at para **[242.7]**.

[242.15]

Form F4.7: Appointment of a trust for bereaved minors terminating an immediate post-death interest

Note. This appointment partially terminates a surviving spouse's immediate post-death interest (see para **[200.98]** above) and appoints a trust for bereaved minors within IHTA 1984, s 71A for the testator's children (see para **[200.108]** above) so that the life tenant will be treated as having made a potentially exempt transfer: IHTA 1984, s 3A (1A)(a), (b), (c)(iii), (3B) and (7) and s 52. This is one of the few occasions when the termination of an immediate post-death interest in favour of continuing trusts will be a potentially exempt transfer. As well as the termination of a post-21 March 2006 immediate post-death interest in favour of a trust for bereaved minors being a potentially exempt transfer, it seems to be the case that the termination, in favour of a trust for bereaved minors, of an interest in possession which was subsisting before 22 March 2006 and which satisfies the conditions of an immediate post-death interest (see IHTA 1984, s 49A) will be a potentially exempt transfer. This is because the definition of immediate post-death interest is not confined to interests in possession arising on or after 22 March 2006, although generally the importance of an interest being an immediate post-death interest will be where it arises on or after 22 March 2006 (see IHTA 1984, s 49(1A)(a)).

Following the termination of an immediate post-death interest on or after 22 March 2006, it is vital for IHT purposes that the beneficiary of the immediate post-death interest is excluded from all possibility of future benefit from the property in which the interest subsisted. This is because the termination of an immediate post-death interest on and after 22 March 2006 will be treated as a gift of the underlying settled property by the beneficiary for the purposes of the gift with reservation rules of FA 1986, s 102 (see FA 1986, s 102ZA). The appointment below therefore appoints exhaustive trusts so as to remove the possibility of the life tenant's interest in possession being revived on a failure of the appointed trusts and is irrevocable so that again there is no possibility of a revival of her interest. It is also irrevocable since otherwise the appointed trusts would not qualify as trusts for bereaved minors. Although the appointed trusts are exhaustive and irrevocable, the trustees of the appointed trusts are expressed to be the trustees of the will, and the administrative powers and provisions of the will will continue to apply, so it is not thought that the appointment would be the occasion of a deemed disposal by the trustees under the TCGA 1992, s 71, (see Note to Form F4.4 at para **[242.10]**).

It is assumed that the will provides life interest trusts for the testator's widow subject to an overriding power of appointment.

[242.16]

THIS DEED OF APPOINTMENT is made the [*date*] BY [*name*] of [*address*] and [*name*] of [*address*] ('the Trustees' which expression shall where the context so admits include the trustee or trustees for the time being of the Will defined below).

Whereas:

(A) This deed is supplemental to the Will ('the Will') dated the [*date*] of [*name*] ('the Testator') who died on the [*date*] and which was duly proved by [*names of executors*] the executors named in the Will on the [*date*] in the [*name*] Probate Registry.

(B) By Clauses —— to —— of the Will the trustees of the Will were directed to hold the Testator's residuary estate ('the residuary estate') upon trust to pay its income to the Testator's widow [*name*] ('the Life Tenant') and subject to that upon certain trusts and subject to certain powers for the benefit of the Testator's children and remoter issue.

(C) By Clause —— of the Will notwithstanding and in derogation of the above-recited trusts and powers the Trustees (being not fewer than two in number or a trust corporation) have power at any time or times and from time to time before the vesting day (as defined in the Will) by any deed or deeds revocable or irrevocable to appoint any part or share of the residuary estate (up to the whole) upon trust for all or such one or more exclusive of the others or other of the discretionary beneficiaries (as defined in the Will and called 'the discretionary beneficiaries') if more than one in such shares and either absolutely or at such age or time or respective ages or times and with such trusts and powers for their respective benefit and such provisions as the Trustees think fit and the Trustees may in exercise of the foregoing power (inter alia) delegate or create powers or discretions over capital or income or appoint administrative powers or provisions but subject to a proviso that (inter alia) every interest limited under any exercise of the foregoing power shall vest in interest (if at all) not later than the vesting day.

(D) The Trustees are the present trustees of the Will and the residuary estate now consists of the assets specified in the Schedule hereto.

(E) The discretionary beneficiaries include the children and remoter issue of the Testator living at his death or born thereafter.

(F) There are now living [two] minor children of the Testator namely [*name*] who was born on the [*date*] and [*name*] who was born on the [*date*].[1]

(G) The Trustees desire to exercise their above-mentioned power of appointment for the benefit of the grandchildren and remoter issue of the Testator in the manner appearing below.

NOW THIS DEED WITNESSETH as follows:

1. The Trustees in exercise of their above-mentioned power of appointment and each and every other power them enabling HEREBY IRREVOCABLY APPOINT that the residuary estate and its income shall be held upon the following trusts (to the intent and so that the interest of the Life Tenant shall cease) and with and subject to the following powers:
   (1) The Trustees shall hold the residuary estate Upon Trust for such of the children of the Testator as shall attain the age of eighteen years if both in equal shares absolutely Provided always that if any of such children shall die without having attained the age of eighteen years leaving a child or children him or her surviving such child or children shall take if more than one equally between them the share of the residuary estate which their parent would have taken if he or she had lived to attain the age of eighteen years.[1]
   (2) Subject as above the Trustees shall hold the residuary estate upon trust for the Testator's children in equal shares absolutely.
   (3) The above trusts shall carry the intermediate income of the residuary estate and section 31 of the Trustee Act 1925 (relating to maintenance and accumulation) shall accordingly apply [as modified by the Will]/[as if the proviso to subsection (1) had been omitted].[2]
   (4) The powers in section 32 of the Trustee Act 1925 (relating to the payment or application of capital) shall apply to the above trusts [as modified by the Will]/[as if the words 'one-half of' were omitted from proviso (a) to subsection (1)].[3]
2. For the avoidance of doubt it is hereby declared that the powers and provisions of Clauses —— to —— of the Will shall continue to apply to the residuary estate.[4]
3. Without prejudice to and subject always to the Life Tenant's entitlement to income prior to this appointment all income of the residuary estate shall be treated as accruing on the date on which it

becomes payable regardless of the period in respect of which it shall have accrued and shall not be subject to statutory apportionment.[5]

In witness etc[6]

THE SCHEDULE

[*List of assets comprised in Trust Fund*]

1 It must be unlikely that this substitutional trust will take effect (ie. that an individual will die under 18 leaving a child or children), but if it does the children of a deceased child will take their deceased parent's share of the residuary estate absolutely. It is not possible to create a trust for bereaved minors or age 18-to-25 trust for persons other than the testator's children (or stepchildren or those for whom he has parental responsibility).

2 If the will has already modified TA 1925, s 31 in an appropriate way, use the first optional words.

3 If the will has already modified TA 1925, s 32 in an appropriate way, use the first optional words. The extended statutory power of advancement is compatible with a trust for bereaved minors, see IHTA 1984, s 71A(4)(b).

4 The administrative powers of the will will continue to apply. Care should be taken to ensure that none of them is incompatible with a trust for bereaved minors. The power of appointment recited is, however, wide enough for further administrative provisions to be included in the appointment.

5 If the will does not exclude statutory apportionment of income, it may be convenient to exclude it in the appointment. However, if apportionment is not excluded by the will, it will not be possible to exclude apportionment so as to deprive the Life Tenant of any income payable after the appointment, but apportionable to the period prior to the making of the appointment. For statutory apportionment of income over time and its exclusion see the Preliminary Note to B14 at para **[214.35]** ff.

6 For execution, see Form F4.1 at para **[242.7]**.

[242.17]

Form F4.8: Exercise of power of advancement

Note. This is a form of resolution (not executed as a deed) whereby trustees resolve to exercise the statutory power of advancement by transferring less than half of a beneficiary's presumptive share in a trust fund to that beneficiary. By transferring less than half of the beneficiary's presumptive share, in this case only a quarter of his share, the statutory power is not exhausted, and the trustees may later exercise their power with respect to the balance of a half share, see *Marquess of Abergavenny's Estate Act Trusts* [1981] 2 All ER 643, [1981] 1 WLR 843. In this form it is assumed that the advance is made from trusts under which the children of the testator take absolutely at age 25. Therefore the advance will be of property which is either subject to an age 18-to-25 trust (see para **[200.109]** above), or in which a child has an immediate post-death interest in the advanced assets at the time of the advance (for example under the Trustee Act 1925, s 31(1)(ii) where the child was over the age of 18 at the date of the testator's death) (see para **[200.98]** above). It is also assumed that the advance is made after the beneficiary has attained the age of 18. So if the advance is of property subject to an age 18-to-25 trust, the advance will trigger an IHT charge: see IHTA 1984, s 71E(1), and although the trustees will be deemed to have disposed of the advanced assets at their market value under the TCGA 1992, s 71, so that a capital gains tax charge may be triggered, hold-over relief will be available: see TCGA 1992, s 260(2)(a). (If, conversely, the advance is made before the beneficiary attains the age of 18, the advance would not trigger an IHT charge if made from age 18-to-25 trust property, but still hold-over would be available: see IHTA 1984, s 71E(2)(d), and TCGA 1992, s 260(2)(db).) If the advance is made from assets in which the beneficiary has an immediate post-death interest, it will not trigger an IHT charge: IHTA 1984, ss 53(2), and hold-over will not be available.

[242.18]

THIS RESOLUTION is made the [*date*] BY [*name*] of [*address*] and [*name*] of [*address*] ('the Trustees').

Whereas:

(A) This resolution is supplemental to the Will ('the Will') dated [*date*] of [*name*] ('the Testator') who died on the [*date*] and which was duly proved by [*names of executors*] the executors named therein.

(B) The Trustees are the present trustees of the Will.

(C) The Trust Fund which is defined in Clause —— of the Will is held by the Trustees upon trust for such of the children of the Testator as should attain the age of twenty-five years if more than one in equal shares absolutely.

(D) There are three children of the Testator who are now living none of whom has attained the age of twenty-five.

(E) The power conferred by section 32 of the Trustee Act 1925 (relating to the payment or application of capital) applies to the trusts of the Will.

(F) The Trustees desire to exercise the said statutory power for the benefit of the eldest child of the Testator [*name*] who has attained the age of eighteen in the manner appearing below.

NOW the Trustees in exercise of the power conferred on them by section 32 of the Trustee Act 1925 HEREBY RESOLVE to transfer[1] from the Trust Fund to the said [*name*] for his own use and benefit absolutely the assets listed in the Schedule to this Resolution which assets represent one-quarter of the presumptive share in the Trust Fund of the said [*name*].

[*Signatures of trustees*]

THE SCHEDULE

[*List of assets being transferred*]

1 Although the statutory power is to 'pay or apply any capital money subject to a trust' it seems that the power is properly exercised if trust property is transferred in specie: see B18 at para **[218.97]**.

If the resolution is in this form the advance may only become irrevocably effective at the point when the assets are transferred to the beneficiary. If it is important that the advance should take effect from the making of the resolution, it is recommended that the resolution is by deed and declares that the trustees hold the assets on trust for the beneficiary: see Form F4.9 at para **[242.19]**.

[242.19]

Form F4.9: Exercise of power of advancement for the benefit of someone by creating a trust for his minor children

Note. A power which may be exercised for the 'benefit' of a beneficiary, may be properly exercised in favour of, for example, his minor children to his own exclusion so long as the exercise can be said to be for his benefit, for example, where the beneficiary himself is well provided for and he has a moral and legal obligation to maintain the children: see *Re Hampden Settlement Trusts* [1977] TR 177 and B18 at paras **[218.92]**–**[218.96]**.

Assuming that prior to the advance the beneficiary has an immediate post-death interest (see para **[200.98]** above) in the fund which is being advanced, he will be treated as making a transfer of value on the advance: see para **[242.2]**. If the advanced fund is held for the children absolutely, the transfer will be potentially exempt, whereas if it is held on continuing trusts, as in the example below, it will be chargeable. Following the termination of an immediate post-death interest on or after 22 March 2006, it is vital for IHT purposes that the beneficiary of the immediate post-death interest is excluded from all possibility of future benefit from the property in which the interest subsisted. This is because the termination of an immediate post-death interest on and after 22 March 2006 will be treated as a gift of the underlying settled property by the beneficiary for the purposes of the gift with reservation rules of FA 1986, s 102 (see FA 1986, s 102ZA). The advance below therefore declares exhaustive trusts so there is no possibility of the beneficiary for whose benefit the advance is made benefiting again. Although the trusts of the advance are exhaustive, the trustees of the advanced fund are expressed to be the trustees of the will, and the administrative powers and provisions of the will will continue to apply, so it is not thought that the advance should be the occasion of a deemed disposal by the trustees under the TCGA 1992, s 71, (see Note to Form F4.4 at para **[242.10]**). Although in the past there has been some doubt as to whether an advance onto new trusts can ever be made without a new and separate settlement being created, the decision in *Swires v Renton* [1991] STC 490 which concerned a power to pay or apply capital similar to a power of advancement shows that this is not the case. See also B18 at paras **[218.100]–[218.102]**.

[242.20]

THIS DEED is made the [*date*] BY [*name*] of [*address*] and [*name*] of [*address*] ('the Trustees' which term shall where the context so admits include the trustee or trustees for the time being of the Will mentioned below).

Whereas:

(A) This Deed is supplemental to the Will ('the Will') dated the [*date*] of [*name*] who died on the [*date*] and which was duly proved by [*names of executors*] the executors named in the Will.

(B) The Trustees are the present trustees of the Will.

(C) The Trust Fund which is defined in Clause —— of the Will comprises the property set out in the Schedule hereto and in accordance with Clause —— of the Will is held by the Trustees upon trust for [*name*] contingently upon his attaining the age of ——.

(D) By Clause —— of the Will the power in section 32 of the Trustee Act 1925 (relating to the payment or application of capital) is modified so as to apply to the whole of the presumptive share of a beneficiary in the Trust Fund.

(E) The Trustees desire to exercise the above-mentioned power for the benefit of the said [*name*] in the manner appearing below.

NOW THIS DEED WITNESSETH as follows:

1. The Trustees in exercise of the above-mentioned power HEREBY DECLARE that they shall hold the Trust Fund and its income as follows—
   (1) upon trust for such of the children of the said [*name*] as shall attain the age of twenty-one if more than one in equal shares absolutely;
   (2) the above trust shall carry the intermediate income of the Trust Fund and section 31 of the Trustee Act 1925 (relating to maintenance and accumulation) shall accordingly apply as if the proviso to subsection (1) thereof had been omitted;
   (3) the powers in section 32 of the Trustee Act 1925 (relating to the payment or application of capital) shall apply to the above trusts as if the words 'one-half of' were omitted from proviso (a) to subsection (1);
   (4) subject as above upon trust for [*name*] absolutely[1]
2. For the avoidance of doubt it is declared that the powers and provisions of Clauses —— to —— of the Will shall continue to apply to the Trust Fund.

3. Without prejudice to and subject always to any entitlement to income prior to this advance all income of the Trust Fund shall be treated as accruing on the date on which it becomes payable regardless of the period in respect of which it shall have accrued and shall not be subject to statutory apportionment.[2]

In witness etc.[3]

THE SCHEDULE

[*List of assets in the Trust Fund*]

1 This default trust should be for someone other than the beneficiary whose immediate post-death interest is terminated. This is desirable so as to avoid the beneficiary being treated as making a gift with reservation of the Trust Fund (see the Note above). The default trust will have to be a trust which can be regarded as for the benefit of the beneficiary for whose benefit the advance is made.

2 If the will does not exclude statutory apportionment of income, it may be convenient to exclude it in the advance. However, if apportionment is not excluded by the will, it will not be possible to exclude apportionment so as to deprive of income anyone entitled to income immediately prior to the appointment. Therefore, any income payable after the advance, but apportionable to the period prior to the making of the advance, will still be apportioned. For statutory apportionment over time and its exclusion see the Preliminary Note to B14 at para **[214.35]** ff.

3 For execution, see Form F4.1 at para **[242.7]**.

F5 Miscellaneous documents giving effect to legacies

Preliminary note .... **[243.1]**

FORMS

F5.1 Resolution of appropriation .... **[243.2]**

F5.2 Assent .... **[243.3]**

F5.3 Deed of promise to give effect to a nil-rate band debt scheme .... **[243.4]**

F5.4 Deed of charge to give effect to a nil-rate band charge scheme .... **[243.5]**

PRELIMINARY NOTE

[243.1]

This section contains various forms for giving effect to the dispositions contained in a will. Form F5.1 can be used or adapted where executors exercise a power of appropriation (which could be that conferred by the Administration of Estates Act 1925 (AEA 1925), s 41 (Part G, para **[246.65]**) or by the will) and wish to have written evidence of it, particularly of the consents of the beneficiaries if their consents are required (as under the statutory power, or perhaps if the executor is also a beneficiary in whose favour an appropriation is to be made: see *Kane v Radley-Kane* [1999] Ch 274, [1998] 3 All ER 753). Form F5.2 is a general form of assent, and Forms F5.3 and F5.4 are forms to put into effect a nil-rate band debt or charge scheme, as described at paras **[218.19]**–**[218.22]** and to be used in conjunction with Form B18.2 at para **[218.32]**, Form C3.4 at paras **[225.57]** ff, or Form C3.5 at paras **[225.68]** ff. Even following the introduction of the nil-rate band carry forward allowance (see para **[200.75]** above), it may still be desirable in certain instances to keep in place a nil-rate band discretionary trust established by a testator's will and to constitute it by a debt or charge, rather than terminating the trust by an appointment to the surviving spouse or civil partner taking advantage of IHTA 1984, s 144 so that the carry-forward nil-rate band allowance will be available to the survivor's estate, (see paras **[218.19]** and **[242.4]** and Form F4.2 at para **[242.8]**). A debt or charge will keep value out of the survivor's estate which could be advantageous if she is declared bankrupt, or perhaps requires long-term care when the value of her own assets would be taken into account in determining her entitlement to local authority funding.

[243.2]

Form F5.1: Resolution of appropriation[1]

IN THE MATTER of the trusts of the Will ('the Will') dated [*date*] of [*name*] ('the Testator') who died on [*date*] which was proved on [*date*] by [*names of executors*] in the [*name*] Registry.

(1) We, the said [*names of executors*], have paid and discharged all of the Testator's debts, funeral and testamentary expenses and the specific and pecuniary legacies given by the Will.

(2) The property remaining in our hands which comprises the residuary estate of the Testator is described in the Schedule hereto.

(3) Under clause + of the Will the said residuary estate is to be divided into [equal one third shares to be paid as to one share to [*name of beneficiary*] one share to [*name of beneficiary*] and one share to [*names of trustees*] as trustees on the trusts set out in clause + of the Will].

(4) By virtue of [section 41 of the Administration of Estates Act 1925]/[clause + of the Will] we have power to appropriate any part or parts of the said residuary estate in or towards satisfaction of any share of the same given by the Will.

(5) [We have ascertained and fixed the values of the respective parts of the said residuary estate, for which purpose we have employed a duly qualified valuer namely [*name*] to value the freehold property known as and situate at [*address*], and] [t]/[T]he values of the property described in Part 1, Part 2 and Part 3 of the Schedule [are equal at the date hereof].[2]

[(6) The said [*name of beneficiary*] and [*names of trustees*] have consented to an appropriation of the property described in Part 1 of the Schedule hereto to [*name of beneficiary*], an appropriation of the property described in Part 2 of the Schedule hereto to [*name of beneficiary*], and an appropriation of the property described in Part 3 of the Schedule hereto to [*names of trustees*] in full and final satisfaction of their entitlements to the residuary estate].[3]

[(6)]/[(7)] We hereby resolve to appropriate the property described in Part 1 of the Schedule hereto to [*name of beneficiary*], the property described in Part 2 of the Schedule hereto to [*name of beneficiary*], and the property described in Part 3 of the Schedule hereto to [*names of trustees*] in full and final satisfaction of their entitlements to the residuary estate.

THE SCHEDULE

Part 1
Property appropriated to [name of beneficiary]

[*Description of property*]

Part 2
Property appropriated to [name of beneficiary]

[*Description of property*]

Part 3

Property appropriated to [*name of trustees*]
[*Description of property*]
[*Signatures of executors, and, if they are consenting, the beneficiaries and trustees*]
[*Date*]

1 Under the AEA 1925, s 41 (Part G, para **[246.67]**) personal representatives have power to appropriate any part of a testator's estate in or towards satisfaction of any legacy, subject to a number of provisos including the requirement of the consent of a beneficiary in whose favour the appropriation is made, and the requirement that a duly qualified valuer value property where necessary. However, an express power of appropriation is commonly conferred on executors removing the requirement of the beneficiaries' consents, (see for example sub-cl (3)(i) at para **[224.30]**). For appropriation generally, see Vol. 1, para **[29.1]** ff.

2 The value of property to be appropriated should be taken as at the date of appropriation, unless the will specifies some other date: see *Re Charteris, Charteris v Biddulph* [1917] 2 Ch 379 at 386.

3 If the consents of beneficiaries are required (as under the statutory power of appropriation, or perhaps if the executor is also a beneficiary in whose favour an appropriation is to be made: see *Kane v Radley-Kane* [1999] Ch 274, [1998] 3 All ER 753), this clause should be included. Under the statutory power the trustees of a settled legacy may consent to an appropriation in satisfaction of that legacy provided that they are not also the executors: see the AEA 1925, s 41(1)(ii)(b) (Part G, para **[246.65]**).

[243.3]

Form F5.2: Assent[1]

IN THE MATTER of the Will ('the Will') dated [*date*] of [*name*] ('the Testator') who died on [*date*] which was proved on [*date*] by [*names of executor*s] in the [*name*] Registry

We, [*names of executors*], as executors of the Will HEREBY ASSENT to the vesting in [*name of beneficiary*] of the property described in the Schedule hereto in [full and final]/[partial] satisfaction of the beneficial entitlement of the said [*name of beneficiary*] under the Will.

OR

We, [*names of executors*], as executors of the Will HEREBY ASSENT to the vesting in ourselves, as trustees of the trusts of the Will, of the property described in the Schedule hereto.[2]

THE SCHEDULE

[*Description of property*]
[*Signatures of executors*]
[*Date*]

1 It is only the assent of a legal estate in land which is required to be in writing (see the AEA 1925, s 36(4)); however, executors may wish to make a written assent in respect of other forms of property, particularly if it is not capable of physical delivery, e g an undivided share in land. If the assent is in respect of registered land, Land Registry Forms should be used: i e Form AS1 where the whole of the title is subject to the assent (prescribed under the Land Registration Rules 2003, SI 2003/1417, r 58, Sch 1), or Form AS3 where only part of a registered title is subject to the assent (prescribed under the Land Registration Rules 2003, SI 2003/1417, r 58, Sch 1). Form AS1 can also be used where the land to be assented is unregistered: an assent induces compulsory first registration, see the Land Registration Act 2002, s 4(1)(a)(ii).

2 This alternative form will be suitable where the executors have also been appointed trustees of trusts contained in the will, and upon the completion of the administration of the estate, or completion in respect only of a specific asset, wish to evidence the change in the capacity in which they hold the estate or asset from that of executors to that of trustees. This might be particularly desirable if there are powers they wish to exercise which are vested in them specifically as trustees rather than as executors. Even after such an assent, however, they are not discharged from any of their remaining duties as executors: see *Re Timmis, Nixon v Smith* [1902] 1 Ch 176 at 183. Where land is to be held subject to the trusts of the will, it appears that the executors must assent to its vesting in them as trustees in accordance with the AEA 1925, s 36(4): see *Re King's Will Trusts, Assheton v Boyne* [1964] Ch 542 (although the case of *Re Cockburn's Will Trusts, Cockburn v Lewis* [1957] Ch 438 which accepted that an assent was not necessary to pass the legal estate in such circumstances was not cited). In the case of registered land, the appropriate Land Registry forms should be used (see n 1 above).

[243.4]

Form F5.3: Deed of promise to give effect to a nil-rate band debt scheme[1]

Note: Even following the introduction of the nil-rate band carry forward allowance (see para **[200.75]** above), it may still be desirable in certain instances to keep in place a nil-rate band discretionary trust established by a testator's will and to constitute it by a debt or charge, see para **[243.1]** above. Where a promise is given to satisfy a pecuniary legacy, as in this Form, and as a result the promisor takes land (or an interest in land) which would otherwise have been used to satisfy the legacy, HMRC's view is that the promise is chargeable consideration for stamp duty land tax purposes so there could be a liability to stamp duty land tax. See paras **[218.19]**–**[218.22]** above, and para **[220.72]** above. Such a liability might be avoided if a charge was taken instead of a promise, as in Form F5.4.

THIS DEED is made the [*date*] BETWEEN (1) [*name of surviving spouse or civil partner*] of [*address*] ('the Promisor') (2) [*name of executor*] of [*address*] and [*name of executor*] of [*address*] ('the Executors') and (3) [*name of Legacy Trustee*] of [*address*] and [*name of Legacy Trustee*] of [*address*] ('the Legacy Trustees')[2]

SUPPLEMENTAL to the will ('the Will') dated [*date*] of [*name of testator*] ('the Testator') who died on [*date*] and which was proved by the Executors on [*date*] in the [*name*] Registry

Whereas—

(A) By clause + of the Will the Testator gave to the Legacy Trustees a pecuniary legacy determined according to a formula ('the Trust Legacy') to hold the same upon the trusts there set out.

(B) In the events which have happened the amount of the Trust Legacy is [£300,000].[3]

(C) By clause + of the Will the Executors were given power instead of satisfying the Trust Legacy by the payment of cash or the appropriation of property to require the Legacy Trustees to accept a binding promise of payment made personally by the Promisor which shall be repayable on demand.[4]

(D) The Executors have decided to satisfy the Trust Legacy by exercising such power to require the Legacy Trustees to accept a binding promise of payment of [£300,000] [linked to the Index of Retail Prices] made personally by the Promisor and the Promisor has agreed to make such promise.

NOW THIS DEED WITNESSETH:

1. The Promisor promises to pay on demand[5] to the Legacy Trustees the sum of [£300,000] [or (if greater) the sum determined under the following clause].

[2. The sum determined under this clause shall be the sum produced by dividing the sum of [£300,000] by the index figure in the Index of Retail Prices for the month in which this deed is executed and (having made allowance for any rebasing of the Index which may have happened in the meantime) multiplying it by the index figure in that Index for the month in which repayment is made. (For these purposes the Index of Retail Prices shall mean the Index of Retail Prices published by HM Stationery Office or any official publication substituted for it and in the event of any change after the date of this deed in the reference base used to compile the said Index the figure taken to be that at which the said Index stands after such change shall be the figure at which the said Index would have stood if the reference base current at the date of this deed had been retained.)]

[3. If a partial repayment is made, such repayment shall be treated as representing such part of the sum of [£300,000] as produces the amount of such partial repayment by the above method.]

[2.]/[4.] The Legacy Trustees declare that they hold the foregoing debt and all moneys payable thereunder upon the trusts declared by the Will in respect of the Trust Legacy.

IN WITNESS whereof the parties hereto have executed these presents as their deed the day and year first above written.[6]

SIGNED and delivered as a deed by the said [*name*] in the presence of— } [*Signature*]

[*Signature, address and description of witness*]
[*The foregoing from 'SIGNED' to be repeated for each party*]

1 This form is for use where a testator has given residue to his spouse or civil partner absolutely, made a nil-rate band gift onto discretionary trusts in his will, made provision for his executors to require the trustees of those trusts to accept a promise of payment from the surviving spouse or civil partner in satisfaction of the gift, as in Forms B18.2 or C3.4 at paras **[218.32]** and **[225.57]** ff, and the executors and surviving spouse or civil partner have agreed to satisfy the gift in this way. For an explanation of the scheme, see paras **[218.19]**–**[218.22]**.

2 The Legacy Trustees will have been appointed by the will and should include at least one person who is not the surviving spouse or civil partner: see para **[218.22]**, sub-para (3).

3 Insert the amount of the legacy ascertained in accordance with the terms of the will.

4 It is important that the loan is repayable on demand so as to assist the argument that an interest in possession is not created: see paras **[218.19]** and **[218.20]**.

5 See n 4 above.

6 The requirements of the Law of Property (Miscellaneous Provisions) Act 1989, s 1 for the making of a deed are that it is clear on its face that it is intended by the parties to it to be a deed, that it is signed by each party in the presence of a witness who attests the signature (two witnesses if someone signs for a party), and that it is delivered as a deed by each party or someone authorised to do so on his behalf. Sealing is not necessary.

[243.5]

Form F5.4: Deed of charge to give effect to a nil-rate band charge scheme[1]

Note. Even following the introduction of the nil-rate band carry forward allowance (see para **[200.75]** above), it may still be desirable in certain instances to keep in place a nil-rate band discretionary trust established by a testator's will and to constitute it by a debt or charge, see para **[243.1]** above.

THIS DEED is made the [*date*] BETWEEN (1) [*name of executor*] of [*address*] and [*name of executor*] of [*address*] ('the Executors')[2] and (2) [*name of Legacy Trustee*] of [*address*] and [*name of Legacy Trustee*] of [*address*] ('the Legacy Trustees')

SUPPLEMENTAL to the will ('the Will') dated [*date*] of [*name*] ('the Testator') who died on [*date*] and which was proved by the Executors on [*date*] in the [*name*] Registry

Whereas—

(A) By clause + of the Will the Testator gave to the Legacy Trustees a pecuniary legacy determined according to a formula ('the Trust Legacy') to hold the same upon the trusts there set out.

(B) In the events which have happened the amount of the Trust Legacy is [£300,000].[3]

(C) By clause + of the Will the Executors were given power instead of satisfying the Trust Legacy by the payment of cash or the appropriation of property to charge property comprised in the Testator's residuary estate (or but for clause + would be comprised) with payment of a sum of money equal to or less than the amount of the Trust Legacy.

(D) There is comprised in the Testator's residuary estate (or but for clause + would be comprised) [a one-half beneficial share in the property known as [*description*] ('the Beneficial Share')].

(E) The Executors have decided to satisfy the Trust Legacy by exercising such power to charge [the Beneficial Share] with payment to the Legacy Trustees on demand of the sum of [£300,000] [linked to the Index of Retail Prices] enforceable by the Legacy Trustees at any time (without there being any personal liability of any person).[4]

NOW THIS DEED WITNESSETH:

1. The Executors HEREBY CHARGE [the Beneficial Share] with payment to the Legacy Trustees on demand of the sum of [£300,000] [or (if greater) the sum calculated under the following clause] and such charge is to be enforceable by the Legacy Trustees at any time.[5]

[2. The sum determined under this clause shall be the sum produced by dividing the sum of [£300,000] by the index figure in the Index of Retail Prices for the month in which this deed is executed and (having made allowance for any re-basing of the Index which may have happened in the meantime) multiplying it by the index figure in that Index for the month in which repayment is made. (For these purposes the Index of Retail Prices shall mean the Index of Retail Prices published by HM Stationery Office or any official publication substituted for it and in the event of any change after the date of this deed in the reference base used to compile the said Index the figure taken to be that at which the said Index stands after such change shall be the figure at which the said Index would have stood if the reference base current at the date of this deed had been retained.)]

[3. If a partial repayment is made, such repayment shall be treated as representing such part of the sum of [£300,000] as produces the amount of such partial repayment by the above method.]

[2]/[4] The Legacy Trustees accept the above charge in [full]/[partial] satisfaction of the Trust Legacy and declare that they hold the foregoing charge and all moneys received thereunder upon the trusts declared by the Will in respect of the Trust Legacy and agree that the Legacy Trustees shall have no right to enforce payment of the amount charged personally against the owner or owners for the time being of the Beneficial Share.

IN WITNESS whereof the parties hereto have executed these presents as their deed the day and year first above written.[6]

SIGNED and delivered as a deed by the said [*name*] in the presence of— } [*Signature*]

[*Signature, address and description of witness*]
[*The foregoing from 'SIGNED' to be repeated for each party*]

1 This form is for use where a testator has made a nil-rate band gift onto discretionary trusts in his will, made provision for his executors to charge property comprised in his estate with payment of a sum of money in satisfaction of the gift, as in Forms B18.2, C3.4, or C3.5 at paras **[218.32]**, **[225.57]** ff and **[225.68]** ff, and the executors have decided to satisfy the gift in this way. For an explanation of the scheme, see paras **[218.19]**–**[218.22]** and for reasons for using the charge scheme rather than the debt scheme (as in Form F5.3 at para **[243.4]**), see also para **[218.21]**.
2 The surviving spouse or civil partner should preferably not be one of the executors in circumstances where FA 1986, s 103 might apply, and the executors and legacy trustees should not be exactly the same persons, see para **[218.22]**, sub-paras (4) and (5).
3 Insert the amount of the legacy ascertained in accordance with the terms of the will.
4 It is important that the charge is enforceable on demand so as to assist the argument that an interest in possession is not created, see paras **[218.19]**–**[218.20]**.
5 See n 4 above.
6 The requirements of the Law of Property (Miscellaneous Provisions) Act 1989, s 1 for the making of a deed are that it is clear on its face that it is intended by the parties to it to be a deed, that it is signed by each party in the presence of a witness who attests the signature (two witnesses if someone signs for a party), and that it is delivered as a deed by each party or someone authorised to do so on his behalf. Sealing is not necessary.

[243.6]

Form F5.5: Assent of property subject to a charge as part of a nil-rate band charge scheme

Note: To complete the implementation of a nil-rate charge scheme, the executors will need to assent the charged property to the beneficiary entitled to it. This will either be the surviving spouse or civil partner, or the trustees of residue where the surviving spouse or surviving civil partner has an interest in possession in residue. This Form is drafted in the light of HMRC's views of the type of charge scheme which will not give rise to a stamp duty land tax liability, i e where on the assent there is no change in the rights or liabilities of any person in relation to the debt secured by the charge (see paras **[218.19]**–**[218.22]**, above).

Form

IN THE MATTER of the Will ('the Will') dated [*date*] of [*name*] ('the Testator') who died on [*date*] which was proved on [*date*] by [*names of executors*] in the [*name*] Registry

We, [*names of executors*], as executors of the Will **HEREBY ASSENT** to the vesting in [*name of widow/widower/surviving civil partner or names of trustees of residue*] of the Testator's one-half beneficial share in the property known as [*description*] subject to the charge created by a Deed of Charge dated [*date*] and made between [*names of parties*] and so that [*name of widow/widower/surviving civil partner or names of trustees of residue*] shall not become personally liable for the amount secured by the said charge and neither shall any person's rights or liabilities in relation to the amount secured by the said charge be changed as a result of or in connection with this assent.

[*Signatures of executors*]
[*Date*]

PART G

Statutes

Contents

Section 1 – WILLS AND INTESTACY

Note .... **[244.1]**

WILLS ACT 1837

s 1 Meaning of certain words in this Act .... **[244.3]**
s 3 All property may be disposed of by will .... **[244.4]**
s 7 No will of a person under age valid .... **[244.5]**
s 9 (*Deaths before 1 January 1983*) Every will shall be in writing, and signed or acknowledged by the testator in the presence of two witnesses at one time, who shall attest the will .... **[244.6]**
s 9 (*Deaths on or after 1 January 1983*) Signing and attestation of wills .... **[244.7]**
s 10 Appointments by will to be executed like other wills, and to be valid, although other required solemnities are not observed .... **[244.8]**
s 11 Saving as to wills of soldiers and mariners .... **[244.9]**
s 13 Publication not to be requisite .... **[244.10]**
s 14 Will not to be void on account of incompetency of attesting witness .... **[244.11]**
s 15 Gifts to an attesting witness to be void .... **[244.12]**
s 16 Creditor attesting to be admitted a witness .... **[244.13]**
s 17 Executor to be admitted a witness .... **[244.14]**
s 18 (*Wills made before 1 January 1983*) Will to be revoked by marriage .... **[244.15]**
s 18 (*Wills made on or after 1 January 1983*) Wills to be revoked by marriage, except in certain cases .... **[244.16]**
s 18A (*Deaths on or after 1 January 1983 and before 1 January 1996*) Effect of dissolution or annulment of marriage on wills .... **[244.17]**
s 18A (*Deaths on or after 1 January 1996*) Effect of dissolution or annulment of marriage on wills .... **[244.18]**
s 18B Will to be revoked by civil partnership .... **[244.19]**
s 18C Effect of dissolution or annulment of civil partnership on wills .... **[244.20]**
s 19 No will to be revoked by presumption .... **[244.21]**
s 20 No will to be revoked otherwise than as aforesaid or by another will or codicil, or by destruction thereof .... **[244.22]**
s 21 No alteration in a will after execution except in certain cases, shall have any effect unless executed as a will .... **[244.23]**
s 22 No revoked will shall be revived otherwise than by re-execution or a codicil, etc .... **[244.24]**
s 23 A devise not to be rendered inoperative by any subsequent conveyance or act .... **[244.25]**
s 24 A will shall be construed to speak from the death of the testator .... **[244.26]**
s 25 A residuary devise shall include estates comprised in lapsed and void devises .... **[244.27]**
s 26 A general devise of the testator's lands shall include copyhold and leasehold as well as freehold lands .... **[244.28]**
s 27 A general gift shall include estates over which the testator has a general power of appointment .... **[244.29]**
s 28 A devise without any words of limitation shall be construed to pass the fee .... **[244.30]**
s 29 The words 'die without issue', or 'die without leaving issue', shall be construed to mean die without issue living at the death .... **[244.31]**
s 30 No devise to trustees or executors, except for a term or a presentation to a church, shall pass a chattel interest .... **[244.32]**
s 31 Trustees under an unlimited devise, where the trust may endure beyond the life of a person beneficially entitled for life, shall take the fee .... **[244.33]**

s 32 Devises of estates tail shall not lapse .... [244.34]
s 33 (*Deaths before 1 January 1983*) Gifts to children or other issue who leave issue living at the testator's death shall not lapse............ [244.35]
s 33 (*Deaths on or after 1 January 1983*) Gifts to children or other issue who leave issue living at the testator's death shall not lapse............ [244.36]
s 34 Act not to extend to wills made before 1838, nor to estates pur autre vie of persons who die before 1838.. [244.37]
s 35 Act not to extend to Scotland .... [244.38]

Wills Act Amendment Act 1852

s 1 Position of the testator's signature .... [244.40]
s 2 Act to extend to certain wills already made .... [244.41]
s 3 Interpretation of 'will' .... [244.42]

Wills Act 1861

s 1 Wills of personalty made by British subjects out of the United Kingdom to be admitted, if made according to the forms required by the law of the place where made, or the law of the domicile, or domicile of origin... [244.43]
s 2 Wills of personalty made in the United Kingdom to be admitted, if made according to the forms required by the law of the place where made .... [244.44]
s 3 Change of domicile not to invalidate will .... [244.45]
s 4 Nothing in this Act to invalidate wills of personalty otherwise valid.. [244.46]
s 5 Application of Act .... [244.47]

Wills (Soldiers and Sailors) Act 1918

s 1 Explanation of s 11 of Wills Act 1837... [244.48]
s 2 Extension of s 11 of Wills Act 1837 .... [244.49]
s 3 Validity of testamentary dispositions of real property made by soldiers and sailors .... [244.50]
s 4 Power to appoint testamentary guardians....................................... [244.51]
s 5 Short title and interpretation... [244.52]

Law of Property Act 1925

s 175 Contingent and future testamentary gifts to carry the intermediate income .... [244.54]
s 176 Power for tenant in tail in possession to dispose of property by specific devise or bequest .... [244.55]
s 177 (*Wills made before 1 January 1983*) Wills in contemplation of marriage .... [244.56]
s 179 Prescribed forms for reference in wills.. [244.57]
s 184 Presumption of survivorship in regard to claims to property .... [244.58]

Administration of Estates Act 1925

s 33 Trust for sale .... [244.60]
s 46 Succession to real and personal estate on intestacy .... [244.62]
s 47 Statutory trusts in favour of issue and other classes of relatives of intestate .... [244.63]
s 47A Right of surviving spouse to have his own life interest redeemed.... [244.64]
s 48 Powers of personal representative in respect of interests of surviving spouse .... [244.65]
s 49 Application to cases of partial intestacy .... [244.66]
s 50 Construction of documents... [244.67]
s 51 Savings.. [244.68]
s 52 Interpretation of Part IV.. [244.69]
s 54 Application of Act .... [244.70]

Intestates' Estates Act 1952

s 1 Succession to estate of intestate leaving a surviving spouse .... [244.72]

s 5 Rights of surviving spouse as respects the matrimonial home .... [244.73]
s 6 Interpretation and construction .... [244.74]
s 9 Short title and commencement .... [244.75]
Sch 2 Rights of surviving Spouse as respects the Matrimonial Home .... [244.76]

WILLS ACT 1963

s 1 General rule as to formal validity .... [244.77]
s 2 Additional rules .... [244.78]
s 3 Certain requirements to be treated as formal .... [244.79]
s 4 Construction of wills .... [244.80]
s 5 .... [244.81]
s 6 Interpretation .... [244.82]
s 7 Short title, commencement, repeal and extent .... [244.83]

WILLS ACT 1968

s 1 Restriction of operation of Wills Act 1837, s 15 .... [244.84]
s 2 Short title and extent .... [244.85]

FAMILY LAW REFORM ACT 1969

s 3 Provisions relating to wills and intestacy .... [244.87]

MATRIMONIAL CAUSES ACT 1973

s 18 Effects of judicial separation .... [244.89]

INTESTATE SUCCESSION (INTEREST AND CAPITALISATION) ORDER 1977, SI 1977/1491

art 1 Citation and Interpretation .... [244.91]
art 2 Interest on Statutory Legacy .... [244.92]
art 3 Capitalisation of Life Interests .... [244.93]

ADMINISTRATION OF JUSTICE ACT 1982

s 17 Relaxation of formal requirements for making wills .... [244.95]
s 18 Effect of marriage or its termination on wills .... [244.96]
s 19 Gifts to children etc who predecease testator .... [244.97]
s 20 Rectification .... [244.98]
s 21 Interpretation of wills—general rules as to evidence .... [244.99]
s 22 Presumption as to effect of gifts to spouses .... [244.100]
s 23 Deposit and registration of wills of living persons .... [244.101]
s 24 Designation of Principal Registry as national body under Registration Convention .... [244.102]
s 25 Regulations as to deposit and registration of wills etc .... [244.103]
s 26 .... [244.104]
s 27 The form of an international will .... [244.105]
s 28 International wills—procedure .... [244.106]
s 73 Transitional provisions and savings .... [244.107]
s 76 Commencement .... [244.108]
s 77 Extent .... [244.109]
s 78 Citation .... [244.110]
Sch 2 The Annex to the Convention on International Wills .... [244.111]

CHILDREN ACT 1989

s 2 Parental responsibility for children .... [244.113]
s 3 Meaning of 'parental responsibility' .... [244.114]
s 4 Acquisition of parental responsibility by father .... [244.115]
s 4A Acquisition of parental responsibility by step-parent .... [244.116]
s 5 Appointment of guardians .... [244.116A]
s 6 Guardians: revocation and disclaimer .... [244.117]
s 8 Residence, contact and other orders with respect to children .... [244.118]
s 105 Interpretation .... [244.119]
s 108 Short title, commencement, extent etc .... [244.120]
Sch 14 Transitional and Savings .... [244.121]
Sch 15 Repeals .... [244.123]

Law Reform (Succession) Act 1995
s 1 Intestacy and partial intestacy .... **[244.124]**
s 3 Effect of dissolution or annulment of marriage on will .... **[244.135]**
s 4 Effect of dissolution or annulment of marriage on appointment of guardian .... **[244.136]**
s 5 Repeals .... **[244.127]**
s 6 Citation and extent .... **[244.128]**
Sch Repeals .... **[244.129]**
Civil Partnership Act 2004
s 1 Civil partnership .... **[244.131]**
s 71 Wills, administration of estates and family provision .... **[244.132]**
Sch 4 Wills, Administration of Estates and Family Provision .... **[244.133]**
Mental Capacity Act 2005
s 1 The principles .... **[244.136]**
s 2 People who lack capacity .... **[244.137]**
s 3 Inability to make decisions .... **[244.138]**
s 4 Best interests .... **[244.139]**
s 16 Powers to make decisions and appoint deputies: general .... **[244.140]**
s 18 Section 16 powers: property and affairs .... **[244.141]**
s 42 Codes of practice .... **[244.142]**
s 64 Interpretation .... **[244.143]**
s 69 Short title .... **[244.144]**
Sch 2 Property and Affairs: Supplementary Provisions .... **[244.145]**
Code of Practice .... **[244.146]**
Section 2 – SUCCESSION RIGHTS AND ADOPTION, LEGITIMATION, ILLEGITIMACY AND CHANGE OF GENDER
Note .... **[245.1]**
Adoption of Children Act 1926
s 1 Power to make adoption orders .... **[245.3]**
s 5 Effect of adoption order .... **[245.4]**
s 12 Short title, commencement and extent .... **[245.5]**
Legitimacy Act 1926
s 1 Legitimation by subsequent marriage of parents .... **[245.7]**
s 3 Rights of legitimated persons, etc to take interests in property .... **[245.8]**
s 4 Succession on intestacy of legitimated persons and their issue .... **[245.9]**
s 5 Application to illegitimate person dying before marriage of parents .... **[245.10]**
s 8 Provisions as to persons legitimated by extraneous law .... **[245.11]**
s 9 Right of illegitimate child and mother of illegitimate child to succeed on intestacy of the other .... **[245.12]**
s 10 Savings .... **[245.13]**
s 11 Interpretation .... **[245.14]**
s 12 Short title and commencement .... **[245.15]**
Adoption Act 1950
s 1 Power to make adoption orders .... **[245.17]**
s 13 English intestacies, wills and settlements .... **[245.18]**
s 14 Provisions supplementary to s 13 .... **[245.19]**
s 45 Interpretation .... **[245.20]**
s 46 Transitional provisions .... **[245.21]**
s 47 Short title and commencement .... **[245.22]**
Sch 5 Transitional Provisions .... **[245.23]**
Adoption Act 1958
s 1 Power to make adoption orders .... **[245.25]**
s 16 English intestacies, wills and settlements .... **[245.26]**
s 17 Provisions supplementary to s 16 .... **[245.27]**
s 59 Transitional provisions .... **[245.28]**

s 60 Short title, extent and commencement .... [245.29]
Sch 5 Transitional Provisions .... [245.30]

Legitimacy Act 1959

s 1 Amendment of Legitimacy Act 1926 .... [245.32]
s 2 Legitimacy of children of certain void marriages .... [245.33]
s 6 Extent, short title, commencement, and saving .... [245.34]

Adoption Act 1960

s 1 Further provision for revocation of adoption orders in cases of legitimation .... [245.36]

Family Law Reform Act 1969

s 14 Right of illegitimate child to succeed on intestacy of parents, and of parents to succeed on intestacy of illegitimate child .... [245.38]
s 15 Presumption that in dispositions of property references to children and other relatives include references to, and to persons related through, illegitimate children .... [245.39]
s 16 Meaning of 'child' and 'issue' in s 33 of Wills Act 1837 .... [245.40]
s 17 Protection of trustees and personal representatives .... [245.41]
s 28 Short title, interpretation, commencement and extent .... [245.42]

Legitimacy Act 1976

s 1 Legitimacy of children of certain void marriages .... [245.44]
s 2 Legitimation by subsequent marriage of parents .... [245.45]
s 3 Legitimation by extraneous law .... [245.46]
s 4 Legitimation of adopted child .... [245.47]
s 5 Rights of legitimated persons and others to take interests in property .... [245.48]
s 6 Dispositions depending on date of birth .... [245.49]
s 7 Protection of trustees and personal representatives .... [245.50]
s 1 Interpretation .... [245.51]
s 11 Savings, amendments and repeals .... [245.52]
s 12 Short title, commencement and extent .... [245.53]
Sch 1 Savings .... [245.54]

Adoption Act 1976

s 12 Adoption orders .... [245.56]
s 38 Meaning of 'adoption' in Part IV .... [245.57]
s 39 Status conferred by adoption .... [245.58]
s 41 Adoptive relatives .... [245.59]
s 42 Rules of construction for instruments concerning property .... [245.60]
s 43 Dispositions depending on date of birth .... [245.61]
s 44 Property devolving with peerages etc .... [245.62]
s 45 Protection of trustees and personal representatives .... [245.63]
s 46 Meaning of 'disposition' .... [245.64]
s 72 Interpretation .... [245.65]
s 73 Transitional provisions .... [245.66]
s 74 Short title, commencement and extent .... [245.67]
Sch 2 Transitional Provisions and Savings .... [245.68]

Family Law Reform Act 1987

s 1 General principle .... [245.70]
s 18 Succession on intestacy .... [245.71]
s 19 Dispositions of property .... [245.72]
s 20 No special protection for trustees and personal representatives .... [245.73]
s 27 Artificial insemination .... [245.74]
s 28 Children of void marriages .... [245.75]
s 30 Orders applying section 1 to other enactments .... [245.76]
s 33 Amendments, transitional provisions, savings and repeals .... [245.77]
s 34 Short title, commencement and extent .... [245.78]

Sch 2 Minor and Consequential Amendments .... [245.79]
Sch 3 Transitional Provisions and Savings .... [245.80]
Sch 4 Repeals .... [245.81]
HUMAN FERTILISATION AND EMBRYOLOGY ACT 1990
s 1 Meaning of 'embryo', 'gamete' and associated expressions .... [245.83]
s 2 Other terms .... [245.84]
s 27 Meaning of 'mother' .... [245.85]
s 28 Meaning of 'father' .... [245.86]
s 29 Effect of sections 27 and 28 .... [245.87]
s 30 Parental orders in favour of gamete donors .... [245.88]
s 47 Index .... [245.89]
s 48 Northern Ireland .... [245.90]
s 49 Short title, commencement, etc .... [245.91]
ADOPTION AND CHILDREN ACT 2002
s 66 Meaning of adoption in Chapter 4 .... [245.93]
s 67 Status conferred by adoption .... [245.94]
s 68 Adoptive relatives .... [245.95]
s 69 Rules of interpretation for instruments concerning property .... [245.96]
s 70 Dispositions depending on date of birth .... [245.97]
s 71 property devolving with peerages etc .... [245.98]
s 72 Protection of trustees and personal representatives .... [245.99]
s 73 Meaning of disposition .... [245.100]
s 139 Amendments, transitional and transitory provisions, savings and repeals .... [245.101]
Sch 4 Transitional and transitory provisions and savings .... [245.102]
GENDER RECOGNITION ACT 2004
s 1 Applications .... [245.104]
s 9 General .... [245.105]
s 12 Parenthood .... [245.106]
s 15 Succession etc .... [245.107]
s 16 Peerages etc .... [245.108]
s 17 Trustees and personal representatives .... [245.109]
s 18 Orders where expectations defeated .... [245.110]
Section 3 – MISCELLANEOUS PROVISIONS RELEVANT TO THE DRAFTING OF WILLS
Note .... [246.1]
APPORTIONMENT ACT 1870
s 1 Short title .... [246.2]
s 2 Rents, etc to be apportionable in respect of time .... [246.3]
s 3 Apportioned part of rent, etc to be payable when the next entire portion shall have become due .... [246.4]
s 4 Persons shall have the same remedies for recovering apportioned parts as for entire portions—Proviso so to rents reserved in certain cases .... [246.5]
s 5 Interpretation .... [246.6]
s 6 Act not to apply to policies of assurance .... [246.7]
s 7 Nor where stipulation made to the contrary .... [246.8]
TRUSTEE ACT 1925
s 12 Power of trustees for sale to sell by auction, etc .... [246.10]
s 13 Power to sell subject to depreciatory conditions .... [246.11]
s 14 Power of trustees to give receipts .... [246.12]
s 15 Power to compound liabilities .... [246.13]
s 16 Power to raise money by sale, mortgage, etc .... [246.14]
s 17 Protection to purchasers and mortgagees dealing with trustees .... [246.15]
s 18 Devolution of powers or trusts .... [246.16]

s 19 Power to insure .... [246.17]
s 20 Application of insurance money where policy kept up under any trust, power or obligation .... [246.18]
s 22 Reversionary interests, valuations, and audit .... [246.20]
s 24 Power to concur with others .... [246.22]
s 25 Delegation of trustee's functions by power of attorney .... [246.23]
s 26 Protection against liability in respect of rents and covenants .... [246.24]
s 27 Protection by means of advertisements .... [246.25]
s 28 Protection in regard to notice .... [246.26]
s 31 Power to apply income for maintenance and to accumulate surplus income during a minority .... [246.29]
s 32 Power of advancement .... [246.30]
s 33 Protective trusts .... [246.31]
s 34 Limitation of the number of trustees .... [246.32]
s 35 Appointments of trustees of settlements and trustees of land .... [246.33]
s 36 Power of appointing new or additional trustees .... [246.34]
s 37 Supplemental provisions as to appointment of trustees .... [246.35]
s 38 Evidence as to a vacancy in a trust .... [246.36]
s 39 Retirement of trustee without a new appointment .... [246.37]
s 40 Vesting of trust property in new or continuing trustees .... [246.38]
s 68 Definitions .... [246.39]
s 69 Application of Act .... [246.40]

LAW OF PROPERTY ACT 1925

s 21 Receipts by married infants .... [246.42]
s 24 Appointment of trustees of land .... [246.44]
s 27 Purchaser not to be concerned with the trusts of the proceeds of sale which are to be paid to two or more trustees or to a trust corporation .... [246.46]
s 31 Trust of mortgaged property where right of redemption is barred .... [246.48]
s 33 Application of Part I to personal representatives .... [246.50]
s 34 Effect of future dispositions to tenants in common .... [246.51]
s 36 Joint tenancies .... [246.53]
s 61 Construction of expressions used in deeds and other instruments .... [246.54]
s 163 Validation of certain gifts void for remoteness .... [246.55]
s 164 General restrictions on accumulation of income .... [246.56]
s 165 Qualification of restrictions on accumulation .... [246.57]
s 166 Restriction on accumulation for the purchase of land .... [246.58]
s 205 General definitions .... [246.59]

ADMINISTRATION OF ESTATES ACT 1925

s 34 Administration of assets .... [246.61]
s 35 Charges on property of deceased to be paid primarily out of the property charged .... [246.62]
s 39 Powers of management .... [246.63]
s 40 Powers of personal representative for raising money, etc .... [246.64]
s 41 Powers of personal representative as to appropriation .... [246.65]
s 42 Power to appoint trustees of infants' property .... [246.66]
s 55 Definitions .... [246.67]
Sch 1 Pt I Rules as to Payment of Debts where the Estate is Insolvent .... [246.68]
Sch 1 Pt II Order of Application of Assets where the Estate is Solvent .... [246.69]

LAW OF PROPERTY (AMENDMENT) ACT 1926

s 3 Meaning of 'trust corporation' .... [246.71]

PUBLIC TRUSTEE RULES 1912

r 30 .... [246.73]

PERPETUITIES AND ACCUMULATIONS ACT 1964

s 1 Power to specify perpetuity period .... [246.74]

s 2 Presumptions and evidence as to future parenthood .... [246.75]
s 3 Uncertainty as to remoteness .... [246.76]
s 4 Reduction of age and exclusion of class members to avoid remoteness .... [246.77]
s 5 Condition relating to death of surviving spouse .... [246.78]
s 6 Saving and acceleration of expectant interests .... [246.79]
s 7 Powers of appointment .... [246.80]
s 8 Administrative powers of trustees .... [246.81]
s 9 Options relating to land .... [246.82]
s 10 Avoidance of contractual and other rights in cases of remoteness .. [246.83]
s 11 Rights for enforcement of rentcharges .... [246.84]
s 12 Possibilities of reverter, conditions subsequent, exceptions and reservations .... [246.85]
s 13 Amendment of s 164 of Law of Property Act 1925 .... [246.86]
s 14 Right to stop accumulations .... [246.87]
s 15 Short title, interpretation and extent .... [246.88]

FAMILY LAW REFORM ACT 1969

s 1 Reduction of age of majority from 21 to 18 .... [246.89]
Sch 1 Statutory Provisions Amended by Substituting 18 for 21 years .... [246.90]
Sch 3 Transitional Provisions and Savings .... [246.91]

INTERPRETATION ACT 1978

s 5 Definitions .... [246.95]
s 17 Repeal and re-enactment .... [246.96]
s 23 Application to other instruments .... [246.97]
Sch 1 Words and expressions defined .... [246.98]

INHERITANCE TAX ACT 1984

s 211 Burden of tax on death .... [246.100]

CHARITIES ACT 1993

s 35 Application of provisions to trust corporations appointed under s 16 or 18 .... [246.101]

TRUSTS OF LAND AND APPOINTMENT OF TRUSTEES ACT 1996

s 1 Meaning of 'trust of land' .... [246.103]
s 2 Trusts in place of settlements .... [246.104]
s 3 Abolition of doctrine of conversion .... [246.105]
s 4 Express trusts for sale as trusts of land .... [246.106]
s 5 Implied trusts for sale as trusts of land .... [246.107]
s 6 General powers of trustees .... [246.108]
s 7 Partition by trustees .... [246.109]
s 8 Exclusion and restriction of powers .... [246.110]
s 9 Delegation by trustees .... [246.111]
s 9A Duties of trustees in connection with delegation etc .... [246.112]
s 10 Consents .... [246.113]
s 11 Consultation with beneficiaries .... [246.114]
s 12 The right to occupy .... [246.115]
s 13 Exclusion and restriction of right to occupy .... [246.116]
s 14 Applications for order .... [246.117]
s 15 Matters relevant in determining applications .... [246.118]
s 16 Protection of purchasers .... [246.119]
s 17 Application of provisions to trusts of proceeds of sale .... [246.120]
s 18 Application of Part to personal representatives .... [246.121]
s 19 Appointment and retirement of trustee at instance of beneficiaries .... [246.122]
s 20 Appointment of substitute for incapable trustee .... [246.123]
s 21 Supplementary .... [246.124]
s 22 Meaning of 'beneficiary' .... [246.125]

s 23 Other interpretation provisions ..... [246.126]
s 24 Application to Crown ..... [246.127]
s 25 Amendments, repeals etc ..... [246.128]
s 26 Power to make consequential provision ..... [246.129]
s 27 Short title, commencement and extent ..... [246.130]
Sch 1 Provisions consequential on section 2 ..... [246.131]

TRUSTEE ACT 2000

s 1 The duty of care ..... [246.133]
s 2 Application of duty of care ..... [246.134]
s 3 General power of investment ..... [246.135]
s 4 Standard investment criteria ..... [246.136]
s 5 Advice ..... [246.137]
s 6 Restriction or exclusion of this Part etc ..... [246.138]
s 7 Existing trusts ..... [246.139]
s 8 Power to acquire freehold and leasehold land ..... [246.140]
s 9 Restriction or exclusion of this Part etc ..... [246.141]
s 10 Existing trusts ..... [246.142]
s 11 Power to employ agents ..... [246.143]
s 12 Persons who may act as agents ..... [246.144]
s 13 Linked functions etc ..... [246.145]
s 14 Terms of agency ..... [246.146]
s 15 Asset management: special restrictions ..... [246.147]
s 16 Power to appoint nominees ..... [246.148]
s 17 Power to appoint custodians ..... [246.149]
s 18 Investment in bearer securities ..... [246.150]
s 19 Persons who may be appointed as nominees or custodians ..... [246.151]
s 20 Terms of appointment of nominees and custodians ..... [246.152]
s 21 Application of sections 22 and 23 ..... [246.153]
s 22 Review of agents, nominees and custodians etc ..... [246.154]
s 23 Liability for agents, nominees and custodians etc ..... [246.155]
s 24 Effect of trustees exceeding their powers ..... [246.156]
s 25 Sole trustees ..... [246.157]
s 26 Restriction or exclusion of this Part etc ..... [246.158]
s 27 Existing trusts ..... [246.159]
s 28 Trustee's entitlement to payment under trust instrument ..... [246.160]
s 29 Remuneration of certain trustees ..... [246.161]
s 30 Remuneration of trustees of charitable trusts ..... [246.162]
s 31 Trustees' expenses ..... [246.163]
s 32 Remuneration and expenses of agents, nominees and custodians ..... [246.164]
s 33 Application ..... [246.1465]
s 34 Power to insure ..... [246.166]
s 35 Personal representatives ..... [246.167]
s 39 Interpretation ..... [246.168]
s 40 Minor and consequential amendments etc ..... [246.169]
s 41 Power to amend other Acts ..... [246.170]
s 42 Commencement and extent ..... [246.171]
s 43 Short title ..... [246.172]
Sch 1 Application of Duty of Care ..... [246.173]

Section 4 – FAMILY PROVISION AND RELIEF FROM FORFEITURE

Note ..... [247.1]

INHERITANCE (PROVISION FOR FAMILY AND DEPENDANTS) ACT 1975

s 1 Application for financial provision from deceased's estate ..... [247.2]
s 2 Powers of court to make orders ..... [247.3]
s 3 Matters to which court is to have regard in exercising powers under s 2 ..... [247.4]

s 4	Time-limit for applications	**[247.5]**
s 5	Interim orders	**[247.6]**
s 6	Variation, discharge etc of orders for periodical payments	**[247.7]**
s 7	Payment of lump sums by instalments	**[247.8]**
s 8	Property treated as part of 'net estate'	**[247.9]**
s 9	Property held on a joint tenancy	**[247.10]**
s 10	Dispositions intended to defeat applications for financial provision	**[247.11]**
s 11	Contracts to leave property by will	**[247.12]**
s 12	Provisions supplementary to ss 10 and 11	**[247.13]**
s 13	Provisions as to trustees in relation to ss 10 and 11	**[247.14]**
s 14	Provision as to cases where no financial relief was granted in divorce proceedings etc	**[247.15]**
s 14A	Provision as to cases where no financial relief was granted in proceedings for the dissolution etc of a civil partnership	**[247.16]**
s 15	Restriction imposed in divorce proceedings, etc on application under this Act	**[247.17]**
s 15ZA	Restriction imposed in proceedings for the dissolution etc of a civil partnership on application under this Act	**[247.18]**
s 15A	Restriction imposed in proceedings under Matrimonial and Family Proceedings Act 1984 on application under this Act	**[247.19]**
s 15B	Restriction imposed in proceedings under Schedule 7 to the Civil Partnership Act 2004 on application under this Act	**[247.20]**
s 16	Variation and discharge of secured periodical payments orders made under Matrimonial Causes Act 1973	**[247.21]**
s 17	Variation and revocation of maintenance agreements	**[247.22]**
s 18	Availability of court's powers under this Act in applications under ss 31 and 36 of the Matrimonial Causes Act 1973	**[247.23]**
s 18A	Availability of court's powers under this Act in applications under paragraphs 60 and 73 of Schedule 5 to the Civil Partnership Act 2004	**[247.24]**
s 19	Effect, duration and form of orders	**[247.25]**
s 20	Provisions as to personal representatives	**[247.26]**
s 21	Admissibility as evidence of statement made by deceased	**[247.27]**
s 22	Jurisdiction of county courts	**[247.28]**
s 23	Determination of date on which representation was first taken out	**[247.29]**
s 24	Effect of this Act on s 46(1)(vi) of Administration of Estates Act 1925	**[247.30]**
s 25	Interpretation	**[247.31]**
s 26	Consequential amendments, repeals and transitional provisions	**[247.32]**
s 27	Short title, commencement and extent	**[247.33]**
FORFEITURE ACT 1982		
s 1	The 'forfeiture rule'	**[247.35]**
s 2	Power to modify the rule	**[247.36]**
s 3	Application for financial provision not affected by the rule	**[247.37]**
s 4	Commissioner to decide whether rule applies to social security benefits	**[247.38]**
s 5	Exclusion of murderers	**[247.39]**
s 6	Corresponding provision for Northern Ireland	**[247.40]**
s 7	Short title, etc	**[247.41]**

SECTION 1

Wills and intestacy

[244.1]

Note. This section contains the Acts of Parliament currently in force concerning wills and intestacy. The only repealed provisions which are included are the more recently repealed provisions of the Wills Act 1837 (WA 1837), the Wills Act Amendment Act 1852, the Wills Act 1861, and the Law of Property Act 1925, s 177.

WILLS ACT 1837

(7 Will 4 & 1 Vict c 26)

[3 July 1837]

[244.2]

Note. The provisions here printed are as amended by the Statute Law Revision (No 2) Act 1888. Further amendments are noted to the specific provisions concerned. Sections 9, 18 and 33 were substituted, and s 18A was inserted, by the Administration of Justice Act 1982 (AJA 1982), ss 17 to 19 (see paras **[244.7]**, **[244.16]**, **[244.36]** and **[244.17]** below). Sections 9 and 33 continue to apply, as originally enacted, to wills of testators dying before 1 January 1983, whereas s 18, as originally enacted, continues to apply to wills made before 1 January 1983, irrespective of the date of the tesator's death. Section 18A applies as respects wills made by persons dying on or after 1 January 1983 and is itself substantively amended by the Law Reform (Succession) Act 1995 (LR(S)A 1995 (see para **[244.18]** below) as respects wills made by persons dying on or after 1 January 1996. Two new sections, ss 18B and 18C, were introduced with effect from 5 December 2005 by CPA 2004, s 71, Sch 4, paras 1 and 2 (see paras **[244.19]**–**[244.20]** below). Section 18B provides for the revocation of a will by the formation of a civil partnership between the testator and another person except where the will is made by a testator who expects to form a civil partnership with a particular person. Section 18C provides for the effects on a testator's will of the dissolution of a civil partnership which has been formed by him.

[244.3]

1. Meaning of certain words in this Act. ... the words and expressions herein-after mentioned, which in their ordinary signification have a more confined or a different meaning, shall in this Act, except where the nature of the provision or the context of the Act shall exclude such construction, be interpreted as follows; (that is to say,) the word 'will' shall extend to a testament, and to a codicil, and to an appointment by will or by writing in the nature of a will in exercise of a power, [and also to an appointment by will of a guardian of a child], ... and to any other testamentary disposition; and the words 'real estate' shall extend to manors, advowsons, messuages, lands, tithes, rents, and hereditaments, ... whether corporeal, incorporeal, or personal, ... and to any estate, right, or interest (other than a chattel interest) therein; and the words 'personal estate' shall extend to leasehold estates and other chattels real, and also to monies, shares of government and other funds, securities for money (not being real estates), debts, choses in action, rights, credits, goods, and all other property whatsoever which by law devolves upon the executor or administrator, and to any share or interest therein; and every word importing the singular number only shall extend and be applied to several persons or things as well as one person or thing; and every word importing the masculine gender only shall extend and be applied to a female as well as a male.[1]

1 Section 1 is printed above in the form currently in force. The omitted words were repealed by the Statute Law Revision Act 1893, the Statute Law (Repeals) Act 1969 (SL(R)A 1969) and the Trusts of Land and Appointment of Trustees Act 1996 (TLATA 1996), s 25(2), Sch 4. The words in square brackets were substituted by the Children Act 1989, s 108(5), Sch 13, para 1 with effect from 11 October 1991 by the Children Act (Commencement and Transitional Provisions) Order 1991 (SI 1991/828).

* * * * *

[244.4]
3. All property may be disposed of by will. … it shall be lawful for every person to devise, bequeath, or dispose of, by his will executed in manner herein-after required, all real estate and all personal estate which he shall be entitled to, either at law or in equity, at the time of his death, and which, if not so devised, bequeathed, or disposed of, would devolve [*upon the heir at law or customary heir of him, or, if he became entitled by descent, of his ancestor, or*] upon his executor or administrator; and … the power hereby given shall extend [*to all real estate of the nature of customary freehold or tenant right, or customary or copyhold, notwithstanding that the testator may not have surrendered the same to the use of his will, or notwithstanding that, being entitled as heir, devisee, or otherwise to be admitted thereto, he shall not have been admitted thereto or notwithstanding that the same, in consequence of the want of a custom to devise or surrender to the use of a will or otherwise, could not at law have been disposed of by will if this Act had not been made or notwithstanding that the same, in consequence of there being a custom that a will or a surrender to the use of a will should continue in force for a limited time only, or any other special custom, could not have been disposed of by will according to the power contained in this Act, if this Act had not been made; and also to estates pur autre vie, whether there shall or shall not by any special occupant thereof, and whether the same shall be freehold, customary freehold, tenant right, customary or copyhold, or of any other tenure, and whether the same shall be a corporeal or an incorporeal hereditament; and also*] to all contingent, executory or other future interests in any real or personal estate, whether the testator may or may not be ascertained as the person or one of the persons in whom the same respectively may become vested, and whether he may be entitled thereto under the instrument by which the same respectively were created, or under any disposition thereof by deed or will; and also to all rights of entry for conditions broken, and other rights of entry; and also to such of the same estates, interests, and rights respectively, and other real and personal estate, as the testator may be entitled to at the time

of his death, notwithstanding that he may become entitled to the same subsequently to the execution of his will.[1]

1 The words in brackets were repealed by the SL(R)A 1969, s 1, Sch, Pt III.

* * * * *

[244.5]
7. No will of a person under age valid. … no will made by any person under the age of [eighteen years] shall be valid.[1]

1 In relation to wills made before the Family Law Reform Act 1969 (FLRA 1969), s 3(1) came into force on 1 January 1970, the age was 21 years.

* * * * *

Deaths before 1 January 1983
(*See note at para* **[244.2] above**)

[244.6]
9. Every will shall be in writing, and signed or acknowledged by the testator in the presence of two witnesses at one time, who shall attest the will. … *no will shall be valid unless it shall be in writing and executed in manner hereinafter mentioned; (that is to say), it shall be signed at the foot or end thereof by the testator, or by some other person in his presence and by his direction;*[1] *and such signature shall be made or acknowledged by the testator in the presence of two or more witnesses present at the same time, and such witnesses shall attest and shall subscribe the will in the presence of the testator, but no form of attestation shall be necessary.*[2]

1 Explained and extended by the Wills Act Amendment Act 1852 (para **[244.40]** ff below).
2 Section 9, as here printed, continues to apply to the will of a testator who died before 1 January 1983. See the Mental Capacity Act 2005, ss 16 and 18 (paras **[244.140]**–**[244.141]** below) for the court's power to direct the execution of a will or codicil on behalf of a person incapable of managing his own affairs.

Deaths on or after 1 January 1983

[244.7]
9. Signing and attestation of wills. No will shall be valid unless—

(a) it is in writing, and signed by the testator, or by some other person in his presence and by his direction; and
(b) it appears that the testator intended by his signature to give effect to the will; and
(c) the signature is made or acknowledged by the testator in the presence of two or more witnesses present at the same time; and
(d) each witness either—
  (i) attests and signs the will; or
  (ii) acknowledges his signature,
  in the presence of the testator (but not necessarily in the presence of any other witness),

but no form of attestation shall be necessary.[1]

1 This section was substituted by the AJA 1982, s 17, in relation to the will of a testator who died on or after 1 January 1983.

[244.8]
10. Appointments by will to be executed like other wills, and to be valid, although other required solemnities are not observed. … no appointment made by will, in exercise of any power, shall be valid, unless the same be executed in manner hereinbefore required; and every will executed in manner hereinbefore required shall, so far as respects the execution and attestation thereof, be a valid execution of a power of appointment by will, notwithstanding it shall have been expressly required that a will made in exercise of such power should be executed with some additional or other form of execution or solemnity.

[244.9]
11. Saving as to wills of soldiers and mariners. Provided always, … that any soldier being in actual military service, or any mariner or seaman being at sea, may dispose of his personal estate as he might have done before the passing of this Act.[1]

1 Explained and extended by the Wills (Soldiers and Sailors) Act 1918 (paras **[244.48]**–**[244.52]** below).

[244.10]
13. Publication not to be requisite. … every will executed in manner hereinbefore required shall be valid without any other publication thereof.

[244.11]
14. Will not to be void on account of incompetency of attesting witness. … if any person who shall attest the execution of a will shall at the time of the execution thereof or at any time afterwards be incompetent to be admitted a witness to prove the execution thereof, such will shall not on that account be invalid.

[244.12]
15. Gifts to an attesting witness to be void.[1] … if any person shall attest the execution of any will to whom or to whose wife or husband any beneficial devise, legacy, estate, interest, gift, or appointment, of or affecting any real or personal estate (other than and except charges and directions for the payment of any debt or debts), shall be thereby given or made, such devise, legacy, estate, interest, gift or appointment shall, so far only as concerns such person attesting the execution of such will, or the wife or husband of such person, or any person claiming under such person or wife or husband, be utterly null and void, and such person so attesting shall be admitted as a witness to prove the execution of such will, or to prove the validity or invalidity thereof, notwithstanding such devise, legacy, estate, interest, gift, or appointment mentioned in such will.[2]

1 With effect from 5 December 2005 this section is extended so as to apply in relation also to the attestation of a will by a person to whose civil partner a disposition is made: CPA 2004, s 71, Sch 4, paras 1 and 3(a) and Civil Partnership Act 2004 (Commencement No 2) Order 2005, SI 2005/3175, These paragraphs are printed in para **[244.133]** below.

2 The attestation of a will by a person to whom, or to whose spouse, there is given or made any such disposition as is described in s 15 is to be disregarded if the will is also attested by at least two 'independent' witnesses: see the Wills Act 1968 (paras **[244.84]**–**[244.85]** below). Section 15 will no longer apply to a charging clause in the will of a testator dying after 1 February 2001 as the right of an executor or trustee to payment in respect of services is treated as remuneration and not as a gift: TrA 2000, ss 28(4) and 35(1), paras **[246.160]**, **[246.167]** below.

[244.13]
16. Creditor attesting to be admitted a witness. … in case by any will any real or personal estate shall be charged with any debt or debts, and any creditor, or the wife or husband [or civil partner][1] of any creditor, whose debt is so charged, shall attest the execution of such will, such creditor, notwithstanding such charge, shall be admitted a witness to prove the execution of such will, or to prove the validity or invalidity thereof.

1 Words added with effect from 5 December 2005 by CPA 2004, s 71, Sch 4, paras 1 and 4 and Civil Partnership Act 2004 (Commencement No 2) Order 2005, SI 2005/3175.

[244.14]
17. Executor to be admitted a witness. … no person shall, on account of his being an executor of a will, be incompetent to be admitted a witness to prove the execution of such will, or a witness to prove the validity or invalidity thereof.
Wills made before 1 January 1983

[244.15]
18. Will to be revoked by marriage. … *every will made by a man or woman shall be revoked by his or her marriage (except a will made in exercise of a power of appointment, when the real or personal estate thereby appointed would not in default of such appointment pass to his or her heir, customary heir, executor, or administrator, or the person entitled as his or her next of kin, under the Statute of Distributions).*[1]

1 The Law of Property Act 1925, s 177 (para **[244.56]** below) excepts from this provision a will made on or after 1 January 1926 and, by virtue of the WA 1837, before 1 January 1983, which is *expressed* to be made in contemplation of a particular marriage. For wills made on or after 1 January 1983, see s 18, as substituted by the AJA 1982, s 18(1): para **[244.16]** below.

Wills made on or after 1 January 1983

[244.16]
18. Wills to be revoked by marriage, except in certain cases.— (1) Subject to subsections (2) to (4) below, a will shall be revoked by the testator's marriage.
(2) A disposition in a will in exercise of a power of appointment shall take effect notwithstanding the testator's subsequent marriage unless the property so appointed would in default of appointment pass to his personal representatives.
(3) Where it appears from a will that at the time it was made the testator was expecting to be married to a particular person and that he intended that the will should not be revoked by the marriage, the will shall not be revoked by his marriage to that person.

(4) Where it appears from a will that at the time it was made the testator was expecting to be married to a particular person and that he intended that a disposition in the will should not be revoked by his marriage to that person,—

(a) that disposition shall take effect notwithstanding the marriage; and
(b) any other disposition in the will shall take effect also, unless it appears from the will that the testator intended the disposition to be revoked by the marriage.[1]

1 See para **[244.15]**, n 1 above.

Deaths on or after 1 January 1983 and before 1 January 1996

[244.17]
18A. Effect of dissolution or annulment of marriage on wills.— (*1*) *Where, after a testator has made a will, a decree of a court [of civil jurisdiction in England and Wales] dissolves or annuls his marriage [or his marriage is dissolved or annulled and the divorce or annulment is entitled to recognition in England and Wales by virtue of Part II of the Family Law Act 1986],—*

(*a*) *the will shall take effect as if any appointment of the former spouse as an executor or as the executor and trustee of the will were omitted; and*
(*b*) *any devise or bequest to the former spouse shall lapse,*

except in so far as a contrary intention appears by the will.[1]
(*2*) *Subsection* (*1*)(*b*) *above is without prejudice to any right of the former spouse to apply for financial provision under the Inheritance* (*Provision for Family and Dependants*) *Act 1975.*
(*3*) *Where—*

(*a*) *by the terms of a will an interest in remainder is subject to a life interest; and*
(*b*) *the life interest lapses by virtue of subsection* (*1*)(*b*) *above,*

the interest in remainder shall be treated as if it had not been subject to the life interest and, if it was contingent upon the termination of the life interest, as if it had not been so contingent.[2]

1 As originally enacted the opening words of s 18A(1) read:
'Where, after a testator has made a will, a decree of a court dissolves or annuls his marriage or declares it void,—'.
The words in square brackets were added or substituted by the Family Law Act 1986, s 53 with effect from 4 April 1988 (SI 1988/375).
2 This section was inserted by the AJA 1982, s 18(2), in relation to the wills (whenever made) of persons dying on or after 1 January 1983. It was substantially amended for deaths on or after 1 January 1996, as set out below.

Deaths on or after 1 January 1996

[244.18]
18A. Effect of dissolution or annulment of marriage on wills.— (1) Where, after a testator has made a will, a decree of a court of civil jurisdiction in England and Wales dissolves or annuls his marriage or his marriage is

dissolved or annulled and the divorce or annulment is entitled to recognition in England and Wales by virtue of Part II of the Family Law Act 1986,—

(a) provisions of the will appointing executors or trustees or conferring a power of appointment, if they appoint or confer the power on the former spouse, shall take effect as if the former spouse had died on the date on which the marriage is dissolved or annulled, and
(b) any property which, or an interest in which, is devised or bequeathed to the former spouse shall pass as if the former spouse had died on that date,

except in so far as a contrary intention appears by the will.
(2) Subsection (1)(b) above is without prejudice to any right of the former spouse to apply for financial provision under the Inheritance (Provision for Family and Dependants) Act 1975.[1]

1 Paragraphs (a) and (b) of s 18A(1) were substituted by the LR(S)A 1995, s 3, as respects a will made by a person dying on or after 1 January 1996 (regardless of the date of the will and the date of the dissolution or annulment) and s 18A(3) was repealed by s 5 of, and the Schedule to, the 1995 Act, as respects a will of a person dying on or after the same date.

[244.19]
[18B Will to be revoked by civil partnership][1] [(1) Subject to subsections (2) to (6), a will is revoked by the formation of a civil partnership between the testator and another person.
(2) A disposition in a will in exercise of a power of appointment takes effect despite the formation of a subsequent civil partnership between the testator and another person unless the property so appointed would in default of appointment pass to the testator's personal representatives.
(3) If it appears from a will—

(a) that at the time it was made the testator was expecting to form a civil partnership with a particular person, and
(b) that he intended that the will should not be revoked by the formation of the civil partnership,

the will is not revoked by its formation.
(4) Subsections (5) and (6) apply if it appears from a will—

(a) that at the time it was made the testator was expecting to form a civil partnership with a particular person, and
(b) that he intended that a disposition in the will should not be revoked by the formation of the civil partnership.

(5) The disposition takes effect despite the formation of the civil partnership.
(6) Any other disposition in the will also takes effect, unless it appears from the will that the testator intended the disposition to be revoked by the formation of the civil partnership.]

1 With effect from 5 December 2005 two new sections, ss 18B and 18C, are inserted immediately after s 18A: CPA 2004, s 71, Sch 4, paras 1 and 2 and Civil Partnership Act 2004 (Commencement No 2) Order 2005, SI 2005/3175. Section 18B provides for the revocation of a will by the formation of a civil partnership between the testator and another person except where the will is made by a testator who expects to form a civil partnership: cf s 18 above.

[244.20]
[18C Effect of dissolution or annulment of civil partnership on wills][1]
[(1) This section applies if, after a testator has made a will—

(a) a court of civil jurisdiction in England and Wales dissolves his civil partnership or makes a nullity order in respect of it, or
(b) his civil partnership is dissolved or annulled and the dissolution or annulment is entitled to recognition in England and Wales by virtue of Chapter 3 of Part 5 of the Civil Partnership Act 2004.

(2) Except in so far as a contrary intention appears by the will—

(a) provisions of the will appointing executors or trustees or conferring a power of appointment, if they appoint or confer the power on the former civil partner, take effect as if the former civil partner had died on the date on which the civil partnership is dissolved or annulled, and
(b) any property which, or an interest in which, is devised or bequeathed to the former civil partner shall pass as if the former civil partner had died on that date.

(3) Subsection (2)(b) does not affect any right of the former civil partner to apply for financial provision under the Inheritance (Provision for Family and Dependants) Act 1975.]

1 See n 1 to s 18B at para **[244.19]** above. The newly inserted s 18C provides for the dissolution or annulment of a civil partnership entered into by a testator to have similar effects on an existing will as the dissolution of a marriage: cf s 18A, printed at para **[244.18]** above.

[244.21]
19. No will to be revoked by presumption. ... no will shall be revoked by any presumption of an intention on the ground of an alteration in circumstances.

[244.22]
20. No will to be revoked otherwise than as aforesaid or by another will or codicil, or by destruction thereof. ... no will or codicil, or any part thereof, shall be revoked otherwise than as aforesaid, or by another will or codicil executed in manner herein-before required, or by some writing declaring an intention to revoke the same and executed in the manner in which a will is herein-before required to be executed, or by the burning, tearing, or otherwise destroying the same by the testator, or by some person in his presence and by his direction, with the intention of revoking the same.

[244.23]
21. No alteration in a will after execution except in certain cases, shall have any effect unless executed as a will. ... no obliteration, interlineation, or other alteration made in any will after the execution thereof shall be valid or have any effect, except so far as the words or effect of the will before such alteration shall not be apparent, unless such alteration shall be executed in like manner as herein-before is required for the execution of the will; but the will, with such alteration as part thereof, shall be deemed to be duly executed

if the signature of the testator and the subscription of the witnesses be made in the margin or on some other part of the will opposite or near to such alteration, or at the foot or end of or opposite to a memorandum referring to such alteration, and written at the end or some other part of the will.

[244.24]
22. No revoked will shall be revived otherwise than by re-execution or a codicil, etc. ... no will or codicil, or any part thereof, which shall be in any manner revoked, shall be revived otherwise than by the re-execution thereof or by a codicil executed in manner herein-before required and showing an intention to revive the same; and when any will or codicil which shall be partly revoked, and afterwards wholly revoked, shall be revived, such revival shall not extend to so much thereof as shall have been revoked before the revocation of the whole thereof, unless an intention to the contrary shall be shown.

[244.25]
23. A devise not to be rendered inoperative by any subsequent conveyance or act. ... no conveyance or other act made or done subsequently to the execution of a will of or relating to any real or personal estate therein comprised, except an act by which such will shall be revoked as aforesaid, shall prevent the operation of the will with respect to such estate or interest in such real or personal estate as the testator shall have power to dispose of by will at the time of his death.

[244.26]
24. A will shall be construed to speak from the death of the testator. ... every will shall be construed, with reference to the real estate and personal estate comprised in it, to speak and take effect as if it had been executed immediately before the death of the testator, unless a contrary intention shall appear by the will.

[244.27]
25. A residuary devise shall include estates comprised in lapsed and void devises. ... unless a contrary intention shall appear by the will, such real estate or interest therein as shall be comprised or intended to be comprised in any devise in such will contained, which shall fail or be void by reason of the death of the devisee in the lifetime of the testator, or by reason of such devise being contrary to law or otherwise incapable of taking effect shall be included in the residuary devise (if any) contained in such will.

[244.28]
26. A general devise of the testator's lands shall include copyhold and leasehold as well as freehold lands. ... a devise of the land of the testator, or of the land of the testator in any place or in the occupation of any person mentioned in his will, or otherwise described in a general manner, and any other general devise which would describe a [*customary, copyhold, or*] leasehold estate if the testator had no freehold estate which could be described by it, shall be construed to include the [*customary, copyhold, and*] leasehold estates of the testator, or his [*customary, copyhold, and*] leasehold

estates, or any of them, to which such description shall extend, as the case may be, as well as freehold estates, unless a contrary intention shall appear by the will.[1]

1 Words in brackets repealed by the SL(R)A 1969, s 1, Sch, Pt III.

[244.29]
27. A general gift shall include estates over which the testator has a general power of appointment. … a general devise of the real estate of the testator, or of the real estate of the testator in any place or in the occupation of any person mentioned in his will, or otherwise described in a general manner, shall be construed to include any real estate, or any real estate to which such description shall extend (as the case may be), which he may have power to appoint in any manner he may think proper, and shall operate as an execution of such power, unless a contrary intention shall appear by the will; and in like manner a bequest of the personal estate of the testator, or any bequest of personal property described in a general manner, shall be construed to include any personal estate, or any personal estate to which such description shall extend (as the case may be), which he may have power to appoint in any manner he may think proper, and shall operate as an execution of such power, unless a contrary intention shall appear by the will.

[244.30]
28. A devise without any words of limitation shall be construed to pass the fee. … where any real estate shall be devised to any person without any words of limitation, such devise shall be construed to pass the fee simple, or other the whole estate or interest which the testator had power to dispose of by will in such real estate, unless a contrary intention shall appear by the will.

[244.31]
29. The words 'die without issue', or 'die without leaving issue', shall be construed to mean die without issue living at the death. … in any devise or bequest of real or personal estate the words 'die without issue,' or 'die without leaving issue,' or 'have no issue,' or any other words which may import either a want or failure of issue of any person in his lifetime or at the time of his death, or an indefinite failure of his issue, shall be construed to mean a want or failure of issue in the lifetime or at the time of the death of such person, and not an indefinite failure of his issue, unless a contrary intention shall appear by the will, by reason of such person having a prior estate tail, or of a preceding gift, being, without any implication arising from such words, a limitation of an estate tail to such person or issue, or otherwise: Provided, that this Act shall not extend to cases where such words as aforesaid import if no issue described in a preceding gift shall be born, or if there shall be no issue who shall live to attain the age or otherwise answer the description required for obtaining a vested estate by a preceding gift to such issue.

[244.32]
30. No devise to trustees or executors, except for a term or a presentation to a church, shall pass a chattel interest. … where any real estate (other than or not being a presentation to a church) shall be devised to any trustee or executor, such devise shall be construed to pass the fee simple or other the whole estate or interest which the testator had power to dispose of by will in such real estate, unless a definite term of years, absolute or determinable, or an estate of freehold, shall thereby be given to him expressly or by implication.

[244.33]
31. Trustees under an unlimited devise, where the trust may endure beyond the life of a person beneficially entitled for life, shall take the fee. … where any real estate shall be devised to a trustee, without any express limitation of the estate to be taken by such trustee, and the beneficial interest in such real estate, or in the surplus rents and profits thereof, shall not be given to any person for life, or such beneficial interest shall be given to any person for life, but the purposes of the trust may continue beyond the life of such person, such devise shall be construed to vest in such trustee the fee simple, or other the whole legal estate which the testator had power to dispose of by will in such real estate, and not an estate determinable when the purposes of the trust shall be satisfied.

[244.34]
32. Devises of estates tail shall not lapse. … where any person to whom any real estate shall be devised for an estate tail or an estate in quasi entail shall die in the lifetime of the testator leaving issue who would be inheritable under such entail, and any such issue shall be living at the time of the death of the testator, such devise shall not lapse, but shall take effect as if the death of such person had happened immediately after the death of the testator, unless a contrary intention shall appear by the will.[1]

1 An entailed interest cannot be created by an instrument coming into operation on or after 1 January 1997, the commencement date of the TLATA 1996; the grant of such an interest by an instrument coming into operation after that date will take effect as the grant of an absolute interest: s 2(6) and Sch 1, para 5 (see paras **[246.104]** and **[246.131]** below). The 1996 Act also repealed the WA 1837, s 32: s 25(2) and Sch 4. The joint effect of these provisions is that the gift of an entailed interest in a will made before 1997 by a testator who dies after 1996 will lapse.

Deaths before 1 January 1983

[244.35]
33. Gifts to children or other issue who leave issue living at the testator's death shall not lapse. *Where any person being a child or other issue of the testator to whom any real or personal estate shall be devised or bequeathed for any estate or interest not determinable at or before the death of such person shall die in the lifetime of the testator leaving issue, and any such issue of such person shall be living at the time of the death of the testator, such devise or bequest shall not lapse, but shall take effect as if the death of such person had happened immediately after the death of the testator, unless a contrary intention shall appear by the will.*[1]

1 Section 33, as here printed, applies in relation to the wills of persons dying before 1 January 1983. In the case of deaths on or after 1 January 1970, the definitions of 'child' and 'issue' are extended so as to include illegitimate children and remoter descendants by the FLRA 1969, s 16, (para **[245.40]** below), and, by virtue of the Adoption and Children Act 2002 (paras **[245.92]** ff below), replacing the Adoption Act 1976, s 39 (para **[245.58]** below), include adopted children and issue in relation to deaths occurring on or after 1 January 1976 (see para **[245.92]**).

Deaths on or after 1 January 1983

[244.36]
33. Gifts to children or other issue who leave issue living at the testator's death shall not lapse.— (1) Where—

(a) a will contains a devise or bequest to a child or remoter descendant of the testator; and
(b) the intended beneficiary dies before the testator, leaving issue; and
(c) issue of the intended beneficiary are living at the testator's death,

then, unless a contrary intention appears by the will, the devise or bequest shall take effect as a devise or bequest to the issue living at the testator's death.
(2) Where—

(a) a will contains a devise or bequest to a class of persons consisting of children or remoter descendants of the testator; and
(b) a member of the class dies before the testator, leaving issue; and
(c) issue of that member are living at the testator's death,

then, unless a contrary intention appears by the will, the devise or bequest shall take effect as if the class included the issue of its deceased member living at the testator's death.
(3) Issue shall take under this section through all degrees, according to their stock, in equal shares if more than one, any gift or share which their parent would have taken and so that no issue shall take whose parent is living at the testator's death and so capable of taking.
(4) For the purposes of this section—

(a) the illegitimacy of any person is to be disregarded; and
(b) a person conceived before the testator's death and born living thereafter is to be taken to have been living at the testator's death.[1]

1 Section 33, as printed here, was substituted by the AJA 1982, s 19 in relation to the wills of persons dying on or after 1 January 1983. By virtue of sub-s (4)(a) references to 'child' and 'issue' include illegitimate children and issue and by virtue of the Adoption and Children Act 2002 (paras **[245.91]** ff below), replacing the Adoption Act 1976, s 39 (para **[245.58]** below), also include adopted children and issue.

[244.37]
34. Act not to extend to wills made before 1838, nor to estates pur autre vie of persons who die before 1838. ... this Act shall not extend to any will made before the first day of January one thousand eight hundred and thirty-eight; and every will re-executed or republished, or revived by any codicil, shall for the purposes of this Act be deemed to have been made at the time at which the same shall be so re-executed, republished or revived; and this Act shall

not extend to any estate pur autre vie of any person who shall die before the first day of January one thousand eight hundred and thirty-eight.

[244.38]
35. Act not to extend to Scotland. ... this Act shall not extend to Scotland.

WILLS ACT AMENDMENT ACT 1852

(15 & 16 Vict c 24)

[17 June 1852]

Lord St Leonards' Act

[244.39]

Note. Although the whole of this Act was repealed by the AJA 1982, s 75 and Sch 9, Pt I, its provisions continue to apply to wills of *testators dying before 1 January 1983*.

[244.40]
1. Position of the testator's signature. *Where by the Wills Act, 1837, it is enacted, that no will shall be valid unless it shall be signed at the foot or end thereof by the testator, or by some other person in his presence, and by his direction: Every will shall, so far only as regards the position of the signature of the testator, or of the person signing for him as aforesaid, be deemed to be valid within the said enactment, as explained by this Act, if the signature shall be so placed at or after, or following, or under, or beside, or opposite to the end of the will, that it shall be apparent on the face of the will that the testator intended to give effect by such his signature to the writing signed as his will; and ... no such will shall be effected by the circumstance that the signature shall not follow or be immediately after the foot or end of the will, or by the circumstance that a blank space shall intervene between the concluding word of the will and the signature, or by the circumstance that the signature shall be placed among the words of the testimonium clause or of the clause of attestation, or shall follow or be after or under the clause of attestation, either with or without a blank space intervening, or shall follow or be after, or under, or beside the names or one of the names of the subscribing witnesses, or by the circumstance that the signature shall be on a side or page or other portion of the paper or papers containing the will whereon no clause or paragraph or disposing part of the will shall be written above the signature, or by the circumstance that there shall appear to be sufficient space on or at the bottom of the preceding side or page or other portion of the same paper on which the will is written to contain the signature; and the enumeration of the above circumstances shall not restrict the generality of the above enactment; but no signature under the said Act or this Act shall be operative to give effect to any disposition or direction which is underneath or which follows it, nor shall it give effect to any disposition or direction inserted after the signature shall be made.*[1]

1 The omitted word was repealed by the Statute Law Revision Act 1893.

[244.41]
2. Act to extend to certain wills already made. *The provisions of this Act shall extend and be applied to every will already made, where administration or probate has not already been granted or ordered by a court of competent*

jurisdiction in consequence of the defective execution of such will, or where the property, not being within the jurisdiction of the ecclesiastical courts, has not been possessed or enjoyed by some person or persons claiming to be entitled thereto in consequence of the defective execution of such will, or the right thereto shall not have been decided to be in some other person or persons than the persons claiming under the will, by a court of competent jurisdiction, in consequence of the defective execution of such will.

[244.42]

3. Interpretation of 'will'. *The word 'will' shall in the construction of this Act be interpreted in like manner as the same is directed to be interpreted under the provisions in this behalf contained in the Wills Act 1837.*

WILLS ACT 1861[1]

(24 & 25 Vict c 114)

Lord Kingsdown's Act

[244.43]

1. Wills of personalty made by British subjects out of the United Kingdom to be admitted, if made according to the forms required by the law of the place where made, or the law of the domicile, or domicile of origin. *Every will and other testamentary instrument made out of the United Kingdom by a British subject (whatever may be the domicile of such person at the time of making the same or at the time of his or her death) shall as regards personal estate be held to be well executed for the purpose of being admitted in England and Ireland*[2] *to probate, and in Scotland to confirmation, if the same be made according to the forms required either by the law of the place where the same was made, or by the law of the place where such person was domiciled when the same was made, or by the laws then in force in that part of Her Majesty's dominions where he had his domicile of origin.*

1 The Wills Act 1861 is repealed with effect from 1 January 1964 (Wills Act 1963, s 7(3)) but the repeal does not invalidate a will executed before that date (Wills Act 1963, s 7(4)). See now the Wills Act 1963 (paras **[244.77]** ff below) which applies to the wills (whenever made) of persons dying on or after 1 January 1964.

2 The expression 'Ireland' used in this Act now excludes the Republic of Ireland (see Art 2 of the Irish Free State (Consequential Adaptation of Enactments) Order 1923).

[244.44]

2. Wills of personalty made in the United Kingdom to be admitted, if made according to the forms required by the law of the place where made. *Every will and other testamentary instrument made within the United Kingdom by any British subject (whatever may be the domicile of such person at the time of making the same or at the time of his or her death) shall as regards personal estate be held to be well executed, and shall be admitted in England and Ireland*[1] *to probate, and in Scotland to confirmation, if the same be executed according to the forms required by the laws for the time being in force in that part of the United Kingdom where the same is made.*

1 The expression 'Ireland' used in this Act now excludes the Republic of Ireland (see Art 2 of the Irish Free State (Consequential Adaptation of Enactments) Order 1923).

[244.45]
3. Change of domicile not to invalidate will. *No will or other testamentary instrument shall be held to be revoked or to have become invalid, nor shall the construction thereof be altered, by reason of any subsequent change of domicile of the person making the same.*

[244.46]
4. Nothing in this Act to invalidate wills of personalty otherwise valid. *Nothing in this Act contained shall invalidate any will or other testamentary instrument as regards personal estate which would have been valid if this Act had not been passed, except as such will or other testamentary instrument may be revoked or altered by any subsequent will or testamentary instrument made valid by this Act.*

[244.47]
5. Application of Act. *This Act shall extend only to wills and other testamentary instruments made by persons who die after the passing of this Act.*[1]

1 The Act is repealed with effect from 1 January 1964: see n 1 to s 1 at para **[244.41]** above.

WILLS (SOLDIERS AND SAILORS) ACT 1918

(7 & 8 Geo 5 c 58)

[6 February 1918]

[244.48]
1. Explanation of s 11 of Wills Act 1837. In order to remove doubts as to the construction of the Wills Act 1837, it is hereby declared and enacted that section eleven of that Act authorises and always has authorised any soldier being in actual military service, or any mariner or seaman being at sea, to dispose of his personal estate as he might have done before the passing of that Act, though under the age of [eighteen years[1]].

1 In relation to wills made before the FLRA 1969, s 3(1) came into force on 1 January 1970, the age was 21 years.

[244.49]
2. Extension of s 11 of Wills Act 1837. Section 11 of the Wills Act 1837 shall extend to any member of His Majesty's naval or marine forces not only when he is at sea but also when he is so circumstanced that if he were a soldier he would be in actual military service within the meaning of that section.

[244.50]
3. Validity of testamentary dispositions of real property made by soldiers and sailors.— (1) A testamentary disposition of any real estate in England or Ireland made by a person to whom section eleven of the Wills Act 1837, applies, and who dies after the passing of this Act, shall, notwithstanding

that the person making the disposition was at the time of making it under [eighteen years[1]] of age or that the disposition has not been made in such manner or form as was at the passing of this Act required by law, be valid in any case where the person making the disposition was of such age and the disposition has been made in such manner and form that if the disposition had been a disposition of personal estate made by such a person domiciled in England or Ireland it would have been valid.

(2) [*Repealed by the Succession (Scotland) Act 1964, s 34(2) and Sch 3.*]

1 In relation to wills made before the FLRA 1969, s 3(1) came into force on 1 January 1970, the age was 21 years.

[244.51]

4. Power to appoint testamentary guardians. Where any person dies after the passing of this Act having made a will which is, or which, if it had been a disposition of property, would have been rendered valid by section eleven of the Wills Act 1837, any appointment contained in that will of any person as guardian of the infant children of the testator shall be of full force and effect.

[244.52]

5. Short title and interpretation. * * * * *

(2) For the purposes of section eleven of the Wills Act 1837 and this Act the expression 'soldier' includes a member of the Air Force, and references in this Act to the said section eleven include a reference to that section as explained and extended by this Act.

LAW OF PROPERTY ACT 1925

(15 & 16 Geo 5 c 20)

[9 April 1925]

[244.53]

Note. This Act came into force on 1 January 1926 (s 209(2) (repealed)).

* * * * *

PART X
WILLS

[244.54]

175. Contingent and future testamentary gifts to carry the intermediate income.— (1) A contingent or future specific devise or bequest of property, whether real or personal, and a contingent residuary devise of freehold land, and a specific or residuary devise of freehold land to trustees upon trust for persons whose interests are contingent or executory shall, subject to the statutory provisions relating to accumulations, carry the intermediate

income of that property from the death of the testator, except so far as such income, or any part thereof, may be otherwise expressly disposed of.
(2) This section applies only to wills coming into operation after the commencement of this Act.

[244.55]
176. Power for tenant in tail in possession to dispose of property by specific devise or bequest.— (1) A tenant in tail of full age shall have power to dispose by will, by means of a devise or bequest referring specifically either to the property or to the instrument under which it was acquired or to entailed property generally—

(a) of all property of which he is tenant in tail in possession at his death; and
(b) of money (including the proceeds of property directed to be sold) subject to be invested in the purchase of property, of which if it had been so invested he would have been tenant in tail in possession at his death;

in like manner as if, after barring the entail, he had been tenant in fee simple or absolute owner thereof for an equitable interest at his death, but, subject to and in default of any such disposition by will, such property shall devolve in the same manner as if this section had not been passed.
(2) This section applies to entailed interests authorised to be created by this Act as well as to estates tail created before the commencement of this Act, but does not extend to a tenant in tail who is by statute restrained from barring or defeating his estate tail, whether the land or property in respect whereof he is so restrained was purchased with money provided by Parliament in consideration of public services or not, or to a tenant in tail after possibility of issue extinct, and does not render any interest which is not disposed of by the will of the tenant in tail liable for his debts or other liabilities.
(3) In this section 'tenant in tail' includes an owner of a base fee in possession who has power to enlarge the base fee into a fee-simple without the concurrence of any other person.
(4) This section only applies to wills executed after the commencement of this Act, or confirmed or republished by codicil executed after such commencement.[1]

1 Note that it has not been possible to create entailed interests since 31 December 1996: TLATA 1996, s 2(6), Sch 1, para 5 (paras **[246.104]** and **[246.131]** above). But this section continues to apply to entailed interests created before 1 January 1997.

Wills made before 1 January 1983

[244.56]
177. Wills in contemplation of marriage.— (*1*) *A will expressed to be made in contemplation of a marriage shall, notwithstanding anything in section eighteen of the Wills Act 1837, or any other statutory provision or rule of law to the contrary, not be revoked by the solemnisation of the marriage contemplated.*
(*2*) *This section only applies to wills made after the commencement of this Act.*[1]

1 Note that s 177 was repealed, with effect from 1 January 1983, by the AJA 1982, s 75, which further substituted replacement provisions in the WA 1837, s 18 (see para **[244.16]** above). Section 177, however, continues to apply to wills made before 1 January 1983 (see s 73(7) of the 1982 Act, para **[244.107]** below).

* * * * *

[244.57]
179. Prescribed forms for reference in wills. The Lord Chancellor may from time to time prescribe and publish forms to which a testator may refer in his will, and give directions as to the manner in which they may be referred to, but, unless so referred to, such forms shall not be deemed to be incorporated in a will.[1]

1 The Statutory Will Forms prescribed pursuant to this section are printed in Part E, paras **[238.7]** ff above.

PART XI
MISCELLANEOUS

* * * * *

[244.58]
184. Presumption of survivorship in regard to claims to property. In all cases where, after the commencement of this Act, two or more persons have died in circumstances rendering it uncertain which of them survived the other or others, such deaths shall (subject to any order of the court), for all purposes affecting the title to property, be presumed to have occurred in order of seniority, and accordingly the younger shall be deemed to have survived the elder.[1]

1 Where an intestate and his or her spouse die on or after 1 January 1953, in circumstances rendering it uncertain which of them survived the other, and the spouse would, by virtue of this section, be deemed to be the survivor, the AEA 1925, s 46, is nevertheless to have effect, as respects the intestate, as if the spouse had not survived him or her (AEA 1925, s 46(3), added in relation to deaths after 1952 by the Intestates' Estates Act 1952 (see para **[244.62]**)).

* * * * *

ADMINISTRATION OF ESTATES ACT 1925

(15 & 16 Geo 5 c 23)

[9 April 1925]

[244.59]

Note. This Act came into force on 1 January 1926 (s 58(2) (repealed)).

* * * * *

PART III
ADMINISTRATION OF ASSETS

[244.60]

33. Trust for sale.— [(1) On the death of a person intestate as to any real or personal estate, that estate shall be held in trust by his personal representatives with the power to sell it.][1]

(2) [The personal representatives shall pay out of

(a) the ready money of the deceased (so far as not disposed of by his will, if any); and

(b) any net money arising from disposing of any other part of his estate (after payment of costs),

all][2] such funeral, testamentary and administration expenses, debts and other liabilities as are properly payable thereout having regard to the rules of administration contained in this Part of this Act, and out of the residue of the said money the personal representative shall set aside a fund sufficient to provide for any pecuniary legacies bequeathed by the will (if any) of the deceased.

(3) During the minority of any beneficiary or the subsistence of any life interest and pending the distribution of the whole or any part of the estate of the deceased, the personal representatives may invest the residue of the said money, or so much thereof as may not have been distributed, [under the Trustee Act 2000][3].

(4) The residue of the said money and any investments for the time being representing the same, [and any part of the estate of the deceased which remains][4] unsold and is not required for the administration purposes aforesaid, is in this Act referred to as the residuary estate of the intestate.

(5) The income (including net rents and profits of real estate and chattels real after payment of rates, taxes, rent, costs of insurance, repairs and other outgoings properly attributable to income) of so much of the real and personal estate of the deceased as may not be disposed of by his will, if any, or may not be required for the administration purposes aforesaid, may, however such estate is invested, as from the death of the deceased, be treated and applied as income, and for that purpose any necessary apportionment may be made between tenant for life and remainderman.

(6) Nothing in this section affects the rights of any creditor of the deceased or the rights of the Crown in respect of death duties.

(7) Where the deceased leaves a will, this section has effect subject to the provisions contained in the will.

1 Sub-s (1): substituted with retrospective effect by the TLATA 1996, s 5, Sch 2, para 5(2), (6).

2 Sub-s (2): words in square brackets substituted with retrospective effect by the TLATA 1996, s 5, Sch 2, para 5(3), (4), (6).

3 Sub-s (3): words in square brackets substituted by the TrA 2000, s 40(1), Sch 2, para 27.

4 Sub-s (4): words in square brackets substituted with retrospective effect by the TLATA 1996, s 5, Sch 2, para 5(3), (4), (6).

* * * * *

PART IV
DISTRIBUTION OF RESIDUARY ESTATE

* * * * *

[244.61]

Note to sections 46 to 49. Sections 46 to 49 of this Act were extensively amended in relation to deaths occurring on or after 1 January 1953 by the Intestates' Estates Act 1952.

They were further amended in relation to deaths on or after 1 January 1967 by the Family Provision Act 1966 (FPA 1966), s 1, and further minor amendments were made by the Administration of Justice Act 1977 (AJA 1977), s 28.

Further amendments as respects intestates dying on or after 1 January 1996 were effected by the Law Reform (Succession) Act 1995, s 1 and are noted to the provisions concerned.

In relation to the estates of persons dying on or after 1 January 1970 and before 4 April 1988 Part IV of the AEA 1925 takes effect subject to the FLRA 1969, s 14 (para **[245.38]** below) and in relation to deaths on or after 4 April 1988 subject to the FLRA 1987, ss 1 and 18 (paras **[245.70]**–**[245.71]** below).

With effect from 5 December 2005 extensive amendments are made to Pt IV of AEA 1925, particularly ss 46 and 47, by CPA 2004, ss 71 and 263(2), Sch 4, paras 7–12 and Civil Partnership Act 2004 (Commencement No 2) Order 2005, SI 2005/3175.

Only the provisions currently applicable are printed below.

[244.62]

46 Succession to real and personal estate on intestacy (1) The residuary estate of an intestate shall be distributed in the manner or be held on the trusts mentioned in this section, namely:—

[(i) If the intestate leaves a [spouse or civil partner][1], then in accordance with the following Table:

TABLE

If the intestate— (1) leaves— (a) no issue, and (b) no parent, or brother or sister of the whole blood, or issue of a brother or sister of the whole blood	the residuary estate shall be held in trust for the surviving [spouse or civil partner][1] absolutely.
(2) leaves issue (whether or not persons mentioned in sub-paragraph (b) above also survive)	the surviving [spouse or civil partner][1] shall take the personal chattels absolutely and, in addition, the residuary estate of the intestate (other than the personal chattels) shall stand charged with the payment of a [fixed net sum][2], free of death duties and costs, to the surviving [spouse or civil partner][1] with interest thereon from the date of the death ... [at such rate as the Lord Chancellor may specify by order][3] until paid or appropriated, and, subject to providing for that sum and the interest thereon, the residuary estate (other than the personal chattels) shall be held—

(a) as to one half upon trust for the surviving [spouse or civil partner][1] during his or her life, and, subject to such life interest, on the statutory trusts for the issue of the intestate, and

(b) as to the other half, on the statutory trusts for the issue of the intestate.

(3) leaves one or more of the following, that is to say, a parent, a brother or sister of the whole blood, or issue of a brother or sister of the whole blood, but leaves no issue

the surviving [spouse or civil partner][1] shall take the personal chattels absolutely and, in addition, the residuary estate of the intestate (other than the personal chattels) shall stand charged with the payment of a [fixed net sum][4], free of death duties and costs, to the surviving [spouse or civil partner][1] with interest thereon from the date of the death ... [at such rate as the Lord Chancellor may specify by order][5] until paid or appropriated, and, subject to providing for that sum and the interest thereon, the residuary estate (other than the personal chattels) shall be held—

(a) as to one half in trust for the surviving [spouse or civil partner][1] absolutely, and

(b) as to the other half—

(i) where the intestate leaves one parent or both parents (whether or not brothers or sisters of the intestate or their issue also survive) in trust for the parent absolutely or, as the case may be, for the two parents in equal shares absolutely

(ii) where the intestate leaves no parent, on the statutory trusts for the brothers and sisters of the whole blood of the intestate.]

[The fixed net sums referred to in paragraphs (2) and (3) of this Table shall be of the amounts provided by or under section 1 of the Family Provision Act 1966]

(ii) If the intestate leaves issue but no [spouse or civil partner][1], the residuary estate of the intestate shall be held on the statutory trusts for the issue of the intestate;

(iii) If the intestate leaves no [spouse or civil partner][1] and no issue but both parents, then ... the residuary estate of the intestate shall be held in trust for the father and mother in equal shares absolutely;

(iv) If the intestate leaves no [spouse or civil partner][1] and no issue but one parent, then ... the residuary estate of the intestate shall be held in trust for the surviving father or mother absolutely;

(v) If the intestate leaves no [spouse or civil partner][1] and no issue and no] parent, then ... the residuary estate of the intestate shall be held in trust for the following persons living at the death of the intestate, and in the following order and manner, namely:—

First, on the statutory trusts for the brothers and sisters of the whole blood of the intestate; but if no person takes an absolutely vested interest under such trusts; then

Second, on the statutory trusts for the brothers and sisters of the half blood of the intestate; but if no person takes an absolutely vested interest under such trusts; then

Third, for the grandparents of the intestate and, if more than one survive the intestate, in equal shares; but if there is no member of this class; then

Fourth, on the statutory trusts for the uncles and aunts of the intestate (being brothers or sisters of the whole blood of a parent of the intestate); but if no person takes an absolutely vested interest under such trusts; then

Fifth, on the statutory trusts for the uncles and aunts of the intestate (being brothers or sisters of the half blood of a parent of the intestate) ...

(vi) In default of any person taking an absolute interest under the foregoing provisions, the residuary estate of the intestate shall belong to the Crown or to the Duchy of Lancaster or to the Duke of Cornwall for the time being, as the case may be, as bona vacantia, and in lieu of any right to escheat.

The Crown or the said Duchy or the said Duke may (without prejudice to the powers reserved by section 9 of the Civil List Act 1910, or any other powers), out of the whole or any part of the property devolving on them respectively, provide, in accordance with the existing practice, for dependents, whether kindred or not, of the intestate, and other persons for whom the intestate might reasonably have been expected to make provision.

[(1A) The power to make orders under subsection (1) above shall be exercisable by statutory instrument subject to annulment in pursuance of a resolution of either House of Parliament; and any such order may be varied or revoked by a subsequent order made under the power.][6]

(2) A husband and wife shall for all purposes of distribution or division under the foregoing provisions of this section be treated as two persons.

[(2A) Where the intestate's [spouse or civil partner][1] survived the intestate but died before the end of the period of 28 days beginning with the day on which the intestate died, this section shall have effect as respects the intestate as if the [spouse or civil partner][1] had not survived the intestate.][7]

[(3) Where the intestate and the intestate's [spouse or civil partner][1] have died in circumstances rendering it uncertain which of them survived the other and the intestate's [spouse or civil partner][1] is by virtue of section one hundred and eighty-four of the Law of Property Act 1925, deemed to have

survived the intestate, this section shall, nevertheless, have effect as respects the intestate as if the [spouse or civil partner][1] had not survived the intestate.
(4) The interest payable on [the fixed net sum][8] payable to a surviving [spouse or civil partner][1] shall be primarily payable out of income.][9]

1 The words 'spouse or civil partner' are substituted throughout s 46 for the words 'husband or wife' by CPA 2004, ss 71 and 263(2). Sch 4, para 7.
2 Words in square brackets substituted by the Family Provisions Act 1966, s 1(2), in relation to persons dying on or after 1 January 1967, for the words 'net sum of five thousand pounds'. The Lord Chancellor has power under s 1(3), (4) of that Act to vary this fixed net sum by statutory instrument. This 'fixed net sum' was £8,750 where the date of death was prior to 1 July 1972 (FPA 1966, s 1(1)) but is £15,000 where the death occurred on or after that date and before 15 March 1977 (Family Provision (Intestate Succession) Order 1977, SI 1977/415); £40,000 where the death occurred on or after 1 March 1981 (the Family Provision (Intestate Succession) Order 1981, SI 1981/255); £75,000 where the death occurred on or after 1 June 1987 (the Family Provision (Intestate Succession) Order 1987, SI 1987/799); and £125,000 where the death occurred on or after 1 December 1993 (the Family Provision (Intestate Succession) Order 1993, SI 1993/2906).
3 Words omitted were repealed by SL(R)A 1981. Words in square brackets substituted by AJA 1977, s 28(1) for the rate of per cent per annum. The rate of interest was 7 per cent per annum from 15 September 1977 to 30 September 1983 and from 1 October 1983 is 6 per cent per annum: see the Intestate Succession (Interest and Capitalisation) Order 1977 (SI 1977/1491), art 2, as amended by SI 1983/1374 (see para **[244.92]** below).
4 Words in square brackets substituted by FPA 1966, s 1(2), in relation to persons dying on or after 1 January 1967, for the words 'net sum of twenty thousand pounds'. The Lord Chancellor has power under s 1(3), (4) to vary this fixed net sum by statutory instrument. This fixed net sum was £30,000 where the death occurred before 1 July 1972, £40,000 for deaths on or after that date and before 15 March 1977, £55,000 for deaths on or after the latter date and before 1 March 1981, and is £85,000 for deaths on or after 1 March 1981 and before 1 June 1987, £125,000 for deaths on or after 1 June 1987 and before 1 December 1993, and is £200,000 for deaths on or after 1 December 1993. The relevant statutory instruments are the same as those relating to the other fixed net sum; see n 2.
5 The words omitted were repealed by SL(R)A 1981. See n 2 for the rates of interest.
6 Sub-s (1A): inserted by AJA 1977, s 28(1).
7 Sub-s (2A): inserted by LR(S)A 1995, s 1(1), as respects an intestate dying on or after 1 January 1996.
8 Words in square brackets substituted by FPA 1966, s 1(2), in relation to persons dying on or after 1 January 1967, for the words 'net sum of five thousand pounds or, as the case may be, twenty thousand pounds'. As to the fixed net sum, see n 2 above.
9 Sub-ss (3) and (4) inserted by the Intestates' Estates Act 1952, s 1(4) and subsequently amended: see nn 1 and 8 above.

[244.63]

47 Statutory trusts in favour of issue and other classes of relatives of intestate (1) Where under this Part of this Act the residuary estate of an intestate, or any part thereof, is directed to be held on the statutory trusts for the issue of the intestate, the same shall be held upon the following trusts, namely:—

(i) In trust, in equal shares if more than one, for all or any the children or child of the intestate, living at the death of the intestate, who attain the age of [eighteen] years[1] or marry under that age [or form a civil partnership under that age], and for all or any of the issue living at the death of the intestate who attain the age of [eighteen] years[1] or marry[, or form a civil partnership,] under that age of any child of the intestate who predeceases the intestate, such issue to take through all degrees, according to their stocks, in equal shares if more than one, the share which their parent would have taken if living at the death of the intestate, and so that no issue shall take whose parent is living at the death of the intestate and so capable of taking;

(ii) The statutory power of advancement, and the statutory provisions which relate to maintenance and accumulation of surplus income, shall apply, but when an infant marries [, or forms a civil partnership,] such infant shall be entitled to give valid receipts for the income of the infant's share or interest;

[*(iii) Where the property held on the statutory trusts for issue is divisible into shares, then any money or property which, by way of advancement or on the marriage of a child of the intestate, has been paid to such child by the intestate or settled by the intestate for the benefit of such child (including any life or less interest and including property covenanted to be paid or settled) shall, subject to any contrary intention expressed or appearing from the circumstances of the case, be taken as being so paid or settled in or towards satisfaction of the share of such child or the share which such child would have taken if living at the death of the intestate, and shall be brought into account, at a valuation (the value to be reckoned as at the death of the intestate), in accordance with the requirements of the personal representatives;*][2]

(iv) The personal representatives may permit any infant contingently interested to have the use and enjoyment of any personal chattels in such manner and subject to such conditions (if any) as the personal representatives may consider reasonable, and without being liable to account for any consequential loss.

(2) If the trusts in favour of the issue of the intestate fail by reason of no child or other issue attaining an absolutely vested interest—

(a) the residuary estate of the intestate and the income thereof and all statutory accumulations, if any, of the income thereof, or so much thereof as may not have been paid or applied under any power affecting the same, shall go, devolve and be held under the provisions of this Part of this Act as if the intestate had died without leaving issue living at the death of the intestate;

(b) references in this Part of this Act to the intestate 'leaving no issue' shall be construed as 'leaving no issue who attain an absolutely vested interest';

(c) references in this Part of this Act to the intestate 'leaving issue' or 'leaving a child or other issue' shall be construed as 'leaving issue who attain an absolutely vested interest.'

(3) Where under this Part of this Act the residuary estate of an intestate or any part thereof is directed to be held on the statutory trusts for any class of relatives of the intestate, other than issue of the intestate, the same shall be held on trusts corresponding to the statutory trusts for the issue of the intestate (other than the provision for bringing any money or property into account) as if such trusts (other than as aforesaid) were repeated with the substitution of references to the members or member of that class for references to the children or child of the intestate.

[(4) References in paragraph (i) of subsection (1) of the last foregoing section to the intestate leaving, or not leaving, a member of the class consisting of brothers or sisters of the whole blood of the intestate and issue of brothers or sisters of the whole blood of the intestate shall be construed as references to the intestate leaving, or not leaving, a member of that class who attains an absolutely vested interest.]
[(5) *Repealed by the Family Provision Act 1966, ss 9, 10, Sch 2.*]

1 In relation to persons dying intestate before FLRA 1969, s 3(2) came into force on 1 January 1970, the age was 21 years.
2 Sub-s (1)(iii): repealed by LR(S)A 1995, ss 1(2)(a), 5, Schedule, as respects persons dying intestate on or after 1 January 1996.

[244.64]
[47A Right of surviving spouse to have his own life interest redeemed]
[(1) Where a surviving [spouse or civil partner] is entitled to the interest in part of the residuary estate, and so elects, the personal representative shall purchase or redeem the life interest by paying the capital value thereof to the tenant for life, or the persons deriving title under the tenant for life, and the costs of the transaction; and thereupon the residuary estate of the intestate may be dealt with and distributed free from the life interest.
(2) [*Repealed by the Administration of Justice Act 1977, s 32, Sch 5, Pt VI.*][1]
(3) An election under this section shall only be exercisable if at the time of the election the whole of the said part of the residuary estate consists of property in possession, but, for the purposes of this section, a life interest in property partly in possession and partly not in possession shall be treated as consisting of two separate life interests in those respective parts of the property.
[(3A) The capital value shall be reckoned in such manner as the Lord Chancellor may by order direct, and an order under this subsection may include transitional provisions.
(3B) The power to make orders under subsection (3A) above shall be exercisable by statutory instrument subject to annulment in pursuance of a resolution of either House of Parliament; and any such order may be varied or revoked by a subsequent order made under the power[2].]
(4) [*Repealed by the Administration of Justice Act 1977, s 32, Sch 5, Pt VI.*]
(5) An election under this section shall be exercisable only within the period of twelve months from the date on which representation with respect to the estate of the intestate is first taken out:
Provided that if the surviving [spouse or civil partner] satisfies the court that the limitation to the said period of twelve months will operate unfairly—

(a) in consequence of the representation first taken out being probate of a will subsequently revoked on the ground that the will was invalid, or
(b) in consequence of a question whether a person had an interest in the estate, or as to the nature of an interest in the estate, not having been determined at the time when representation was first taken out, or
(c) in consequence of some other circumstances affecting the administration or distribution of the estate,

the court may extend the said period.

(6) An election under this section shall be exercisable, except where the tenant for life is the sole personal representative, by notifying the personal representative (or, where there are two or more personal representatives of whom one is the tenant for life, all of them except the tenant for life) in writing; and a notification in writing under this subsection shall not be revocable except with the consent of the personal representative.

(7) Where the tenant for life is the sole personal representative an election under this section shall not be effective unless written notice thereof is given to the [[Senior Registrar] of the Family Division of the High Court][3] within the period within which it must be made; and provision may be made by probate rules for keeping a record of such notices and making that record available to the public.

In this subsection the expression 'probate rules' means rules [of court made under section 127 of the [Supreme Court Act 1981]][4].

(8) An election under this section by a tenant for life who is an infant shall be as valid and binding as it would be if the tenant for life were of age; but the personal representative shall, instead of paying the capital value of the life interest to the tenant for life, deal with it in the same manner as with any other part of the residuary estate to which the tenant for life is absolutely entitled.

(9) In considering for the purposes of the foregoing provisions of this section the question when representation was first taken out, a grant limited to settled land or to trust property shall be left out of account and a grant limited to real estate or to personal estate shall be left out of account unless a grant limited to the remainder of the estate has previously been made or is made at the same time.]

1 Rules (having effect as from 15 September 1977) replacing those formerly enacted by s 47A(2) to calculate the capital value of a life interest in favour of a surviving spouse in the residuary estate are prescribed by the Intestate Succession (Interest and Capitalisation) Order 1977 (SI 1977/1491), art 3 (see para **[244.98]** below).
2 Sub-ss (3A), (3B): inserted by AJA 1977, s 28(3).
3 Words in brackets substituted by AJA 1970, s 1, Sch 2 and SCA 1981, s 152(1), Sch 5.
4 Words in brackets substituted by SCA 1981, s 152(1), Sch 5.

[244.65]

48 Powers of personal representative in respect of interests of surviving spouse (1) [*Repealed by the Intestates' Estates Act 1952, s 2(a).*]

(2) The personal representatives may raise—

- (a) [the fixed net sum][1] or any part thereof and the interest thereon payable to the surviving [spouse or civil partner] of the intestate on the security of the whole or any part of the residuary estate of the intestate (other than the personal chattels), so far as that estate may be sufficient for the purpose of the said sum and interest may not have been satisfied by an appropriation under the statutory power available in that behalf; and
- (b) in like manner the capital sum, if any, required for the purchase or redemption of the life interest of the surviving [spouse or civil partner] of the intestate, or any part thereof not satisfied by the application for that purpose of any part of the residuary estate of the intestate;

and in either case the amount, if any, properly required for the payment of the costs of the transaction.

1 Words in square brackets substituted by FPA 1966, s 1(2), in relation to persons dying on or after 1 January 1967, for the words 'the net sum of five thousand, or as the case may be, twenty thousand pounds'. As to the fixed net sum, see nn 2 and 4 to para **[244.62]** above.

[244.66]

49 Application to cases of partial intestacy [(1)] Where any person dies leaving a will effectively disposing of part of his property, this Part of this Act shall have effect as respects the part of his property not so disposed of subject to the provisions contained in the will and subject to the following modifications:—

(*aa*) *where the deceased leaves a husband or wife who acquires any beneficial interests under the will of the deceased (other than personal chattels specifically bequeathed) the references in this Part of this Act to [the fixed net sum]*[1] *payable to a surviving husband or wife, and to interest on that sum, shall be taken as references to the said sum diminished by the value at the date of death of the said beneficial interests, and to interest on that sum as so diminished, and accordingly, where the said value exceeds the said sum, this Part of this Act shall have effect as if references to the said sum and interest thereon, were omitted;*[2]

(*a*) *the requirements of section forty-seven of this Act as to bringing property into account shall apply to any beneficial interests acquired by any issue of the deceased under the will of the deceased, but not to beneficial interests so acquired by any other persons;*[2]

(b) The personal representative shall, subject to his rights and powers for the purposes of administration, be a trustee for the persons entitled under this Part of this Act in respect of the part of the estate not expressly disposed of unless it appears by the will that the personal representative is intended to take such part beneficially.

(*2*) *References in the foregoing provisions of this section to beneficial interests acquired under a will shall be construed as including a reference to a beneficial interest acquired by virtue of the exercise by the will of a general power of appointment (including the statutory power to dispose of entailed interests), but not of a special power of appointment.*[2]

(*3*) *For the purposes of paragraph (aa) in the foregoing provisions of this section the personal representative shall employ a duly qualified valuer in any case where such employment may be necessary.*[2]

(4) The references in subsection (3) of section 47A of this Act to property are references to property comprised in the residuary estate and, accordingly, where a will of the deceased creates a life interest in property in possession, and the remaining interest in that property forms part of the residuary estate, the said references are references to that remaining interest (which, until the life interest determines, is property not in possession).]

1 In the now repealed sub-s (1)(aa) the words in square brackets were substituted by the FPA 1966, s 1(2), in relation to persons dying on or after 1 January 1967, for the words 'the net sum of five thousand pounds or twenty thousand pounds'. As to the fixed net sum, see nn 2 and 4 to para **[244.62]** above.

1 Sub-ss (1)(aa), (a), (2) and (3) repealed by LR(S)A 1995, ss 1(2)(a), 5, Schedule, as respects persons dying intestate on or after 1 January 1996: see paras **[244.129]**, **[244.132]**, **[244.134]** below.

[244.67]
50 Construction of documents (1) References to any Statutes of Distribution in an instrument inter vivos made or in a will coming into operation after the commencement of this Act, shall be construed as references to this Part of this Act; and references in such an instrument or will to statutory next of kin shall be construed, unless the context otherwise requires, as referring to the persons who would take beneficially on an intestacy under the foregoing provisions of this Part of this Act.[1]
(2) Trusts declared in an instrument inter vivos made, or in a will coming into operation, before the commencement of this Act by reference to the Statutes of Distribution, shall, unless the contrary thereby appears, be construed as referring to the enactments (other than the Intestates' Estates Act 1890) relating to the distribution of effects of intestates which were in force immediately before the commencement of this Act.
[(3) In subsection (1) of this section the reference to this Part of this Act, or the foregoing provisions of this Part of this Act, shall in relation to an instrument inter vivos made, or a will or codicil coming into operation, after the coming into force of section 18 of the Family Law Reform Act 1987 (but not in relation to instruments inter vivos made or wills or codicils coming into operation earlier) be construed as including references to that section.][2]

1 Sub-s (1): modified by IEA 1952, s 6(2) and LR(S)A 1995, s 1(4).
2 Sub-s (3): added by FLRA 1987; in relation to deaths on or after 4 April 1988; cf FLRA 1987, ss 18(3), 33(1), Sch 2.

[244.68]
51 Savings (1) Nothing in this Part of this Act affects the right of any person to take beneficially, by purchase, as heir either general or special.
(2) The foregoing provisions of this Part of this Act do not apply to any beneficial interest in real estate (not including chattels real) to which a [person of unsound mind] or defective living and of full age at the commencement of this Act, and unable, by reason of his incapacity, to make a will, who thereafter dies intestate in respect of such interest without having recovered his testamentary capacity, was entitled at his death, and any such beneficial interest (not being an interest ceasing on his death) shall, without prejudice to any will of the deceased, devolve in accordance with the general law in force before the commencement of this Act applicable to freehold land, and that law shall, notwithstanding any repeal, apply to the case.
For the purposes of this subsection, a [person of unsound mind] or defective who dies intestate as respects any beneficial interest in real estate shall not be deemed to have recovered his testamentary capacity unless his ... receiver has been discharged[1].
(3) Where an infant dies after the commencement of this Act without having been married [or having formed a civil partnership,] [and without issue], and independently of this subsection he would, at his death, have been equitably entitled under a [trust or] settlement (including a will) to a vested estate in fee simple or absolute interest in freehold land, or in any property

... to devolve therewith or as freehold land, such infant shall be deemed to have had [a life interest], and the [trust or] settlement shall be construed accordingly.[2]

(4) [*Repealed by the Trusts of Land and Appointment of Trustees Act 1996, s 25(2), Sch 4.*]

1 Sub-s (2): words in square brackets substituted by Mental Treatment Act 1930, s 20(5); words omitted repealed by MHA 1959, s 149(2), Sch 8.

2 Sub-s (3): first, second and final words in square brackets added, third words in square brackets substituted and words omitted repealed by TLATA 1996, s 25(1), (2), Sch 3, para 6(4), Sch 4.

[244.69]

52 Interpretation of Part IV In this Part of this Act 'real and personal estate' means every beneficial interest (including rights of entry and reverter) of the intestate in real and personal estate which (otherwise than in right of a power of appointment or of the testamentary power conferred by statute to dispose of entailed interests) he could, if of full age and capacity, have disposed of by his will [and references (however expressed) to any relationship between two persons shall be construed in accordance with section 1 of the Family Law Reform Act 1987].[1]

1 The words in brackets were added by FLRA 1987, s 33(1), Sch 2, para 4. For s 55 of this Act (general definitions) see para **[246.67]** below.

PART V
SUPPLEMENTAL

[244.70]

54 Application of Act Save as otherwise expressly provided, this Act does not apply in any case where the death occurred before the commencement of this Act.

* * * * *

INTESTATES' ESTATES ACT 1952

(15 & 16 Geo 6 & 1 Eliz 2 c 64)

[30 October 1952]

[244.71]

Note. The provisions of this Act printed below confer a right on the surviving spouse of an intestate to have the matrimonial home appropriated in or towards satisfaction of his or her share of the intestate's estate.

PART I
AMENDMENTS OF LAW OF INTESTATE SUCCESSION

[244.72]

1. Succession to estate of intestate leaving a surviving spouse.— (1) ... the Administration of Estates Act 1925 (hereafter in this Part of this Act referred to as 'the principal Act') ...

* * * * *

[244.73]
5. Rights of surviving spouse [or civil partner][1] as respects the matrimonial [or civil partnership][1] home. The Second Schedule to this Act shall have effect for enabling the [spouse or civil partner][1] surviving husband or wife of a person dying intestate after the commencement of this Act to acquire the matrimonial home.

1 With effect from 5 December 2005, the heading to this section is amended by the insertion of the words 'or civil partner' after 'spouse' and the words 'or civil partnership' after the word 'matrimonial' and the section itself is amended by the substitution for the words 'husband or wife' the words 'spouse or civil partner': CPA 2004, s 71, Sch 4, para 13 and Civil Partnership Act 2004 (Commencement No 2) Order 2005, SI 2005/3175.

[244.74]
6. Interpretation and construction.— (1) In this Part of this Act the expression 'intestate' has the meaning assigned to it by section fifty-five of the principal Act.
(2) The references in subsection (1) of section fifty of the principal Act (which relates to the construction of documents) to Part IV of that Act, or to the foregoing provisions of that Part, shall in relation to an instrument inter vivos made or a will coming into operation, after the commencement of this Act, but not in relation to instruments inter vivos made or wills coming into operation earlier, be construed as including references to this Part of this Act and the Schedules to be read therewith.

* * * * *

PART III
GENERAL

* * * * *

[244.75]
9. Short title and commencement.— (1) This Act may be cited as the Intestates' Estates Act 1952.
(2) This Act shall come into operation on the first day of January, nineteen hundred and fifty-three.

* * * * *

SECOND SCHEDULE

Section 5

RIGHTS OF SURVIVING SPOUSE [OR CIVIL PARTNER] AS RESPECTS THE MATRIMONIAL [OR CIVIL PARTNERSHIP] HOME

Note. With effect from 5 December 2005, the heading to this Schedule is amended by the insertion of the words 'or civil partner' after 'spouse' and the words 'or civil partnership' after the word 'matrimonial' and the Schedule is amended throughout by the substitution for the words 'husband or wife' the words 'spouse or civil partner': CPA 2004, s 71, Sch 4, para 13 and Civil Partnership Act 2004 (Commencement No 2) Order 2005, SI 2005/3175.

[244.76]

1.— (1) Subject to the provisions of this Schedule, where the residuary estate of the intestate comprises an interest in a dwelling-house in which the surviving [spouse or civil partner][1] was resident at the time of the intestate's death, the surviving [spouse or civil partner][1] may require the personal representative in exercise of the power conferred by section forty-one of the principal Act (and with due regard to the requirements of that section as to valuation) to appropriate the said interest in the dwelling-house in or towards satisfaction of any absolute interest of the surviving [spouse or civil partner][1] in the real and personal estate of the intestate.

(2) The right conferred by this paragraph shall not be exercisable where the interest is—

(a) a tenancy which at the date of the death of the intestate was a tenancy which would determine within the period of two years from that date; or

(b) a tenancy which the landlord by notice given after that date could determine within the remainder of that period.[2]

(3) Nothing in subsection (5) of section forty-one of the principal Act (which requires the personal representative, in making an appropriation to any person under that section, to have regard to the rights of others) shall prevent the personal representative from giving effect to the right conferred by this paragraph.

(4) The reference in this paragraph to an absolute interest in the real and personal estate of the intestate includes a reference to the capital value of a life interest which the surviving [spouse or civil partner][1] has under this Act elected to have redeemed.

(5) Where a part of a building was, at the date of the death of the intestate, occupied as a separate dwelling, that dwelling shall for the purposes of this Schedule be treated as a dwelling-house.

2. Where—

(a) the dwelling-house forms part of a building and an interest in the whole of the building is comprised in the residuary estate; or

(b) the dwelling-house is held with agricultural land and an interest in the agricultural land is comprised in the residuary estate; or

(c) the whole or part of the dwelling-house was at the time of the intestate's death used as a hotel or lodging house; or

(d) a part of the dwelling-house was at the time of the intestate's death used for purposes other than domestic purposes,

the right conferred by paragraph 1 of this Schedule shall not be exercisable unless the court, on being satisifed that the exercise of that right is not likely to diminish the value of assets in the residuary estate (other than the said interest in the dwelling-house) or make them more difficult to dispose of, so orders.

3.— (1) The right conferred by paragraph 1 of this Schedule—

(a) shall not be exercisable after the expiration of twelve months from the first taking out of representation with respect to the intestate's estate;

(b) shall not be exercisable after the death of the surviving [spouse or civil partner][1] ;

(c) shall be exercisable, except where the surviving [spouse or civil partner][1] is the sole personal representative, by notifying the personal representative (or, where there are two or more personal representatives of whom one is the surviving [spouse or civil partner][1] , all of them except the surviving [spouse or civil partner][1]) in writing.

(2) A notification in writing under paragraph (c) of the foregoing subparagraph shall not be revocable except with the consent of the personal representative; but the surviving husband or wife may require the personal representative to have the said interest in the dwelling-house valued in accordance with section forty-one of the principal Act and to inform him or her of the result of that valuation before he or she decides whether to exercise the right.

(3) Subsection (9) of the section forty-seven A added to the principal Act by section two of this Act shall apply for the purposes of the construction of the reference in this paragraph to the first taking out of representation, and the proviso to subsection (5) of that section shall apply for the purpose of enabling the surviving [spouse or civil partner][1] to apply for an extension of the period of twelve months mentioned in this paragraph.

4.— (1) During the period of twelve months mentioned in paragraph 3 of this Schedule the personal representative shall not without the written consent of the surviving [spouse or civil partner][1] sell or otherwise dispose of the said interest in the dwelling-house except in the course of administration owing to want of other assets.

(2) An application to the court under paragraph 2 of this Schedule may be made by the personal representative as well as by the surviving [spouse or civil partner][1] , and if, on an application under that paragraph, the court does not order that the right conferred by paragraph 1 of this Schedule shall be exercisable by the surviving [spouse or civil partner][1] , the court may authorise the personal representative to dispose of the said interest in the dwelling-house within the said period of twelve months.

(3) Where the court under sub-paragraph (3) of paragraph 3 of this Schedule extends the said period of twelve months, the court may direct that this paragraph shall apply in relation to the extended period as it applied in relation to the original period of twelve months.

(4) This paragraph shall not apply where the surviving [spouse or civil partner][1] is the sole personal representative or one of two or more personal representatives.

(5) Nothing in this paragraph shall confer any right on the surviving [spouse or civil partner][1] as against a purchaser from the personal representative.

5.— (1) Where the surviving [spouse or civil partner][1] is one of two or more personal representatives, the rule that a trustee may not be a purchaser of trust property shall not prevent the surviving [spouse or civil partner][1] from purchasing out of the estate of the intestate an interest in a dwelling-house in which the surviving [spouse or civil partner][1] was resident at the time of the intestate's death.

(2) The power of appropriation under section forty-one of the principal Act shall include power to appropriate an interest in a dwelling-house in which the surviving [spouse or civil partner][1] was resident at the time of the intestate's death partly in satisfaction of an interest of the surviving [spouse or civil partner][1] in the real and personal estate of the intestate and partly in return for a payment of money by the surviving [spouse or civil partner][1] to the personal representative.

6.— [(1) Where the surviving spouse or civil partner lacks capacity (within the meaning of the Mental Capacity Act 2005) to make a requirement or give a consent under this Schedule, the requirement or consent may be made or given by a deputy appointed by the Court of Protection with power in that respect or, if no deputy has that power, by that court.][3]

(2) A requirement or consent made or given under this Schedule by a surviving [spouse or civil partner][1] who is an infant shall be as valid and binding as it would be if he or she were of age, and, as respects an appropriation in pursuance of paragraph 1 of this Schedule, the provisions of section forty-one of the principal Act as to obtaining the consent of the infant's parent or guardian, or of the court on behalf of the infant, shall not apply.

7.—

(1) Except where the context otherwise requires, references in this Schedule to a dwelling-house include references to any garden or portion of ground attached to and usually occupied with the dwelling-house or otherwise required for the amenity or convenience of the dwelling-house.

(2) This Schedule shall be construed as one with Part IV of the principal Act.

1 See Note to this Schedule, above.

2 For an exception to this sub-paragraph where the tenancy could give rise to a right to enfranchise, see the Leasehold Reform Act 1967, s 7(8).

3 With effect from 1 October 2007 sub-para (1) substituted by MCA 2005, s 67(1), Sch 6, para 8 for

'(1)Where the surviving husband or wife is a person of unsound mind or a defective, a requirement or consent under this Schedule may be made or given on his or her behalf by the committee or receiver, if any, or, where there is no committee or receiver, by the court.'

* * * * *

WILLS ACT 1963

(1963 c 44)

[31 July 1963]

[244.77]

1. General rule as to formal validity. A will shall be treated as properly executed if its execution conformed to the internal law in force in the territory where it was executed, or in the territory where, at the time of its execution or of the testator's death, he was domiciled or had his habitual residence, or in a state of which, at either of those times, he was a national.

[244.78]
2. Additional rules.— (1) Without prejudice to the preceding section, the following shall be treated as properly executed—

(a) a will executed on board a vessel or aircraft of any description, if the execution of the will conformed to the internal law in force in the territory with which, having regard to its registration (if any) and other relevant circumstances, the vessel or aircraft may be taken to have been most closely connected;
(b) a will so far as it disposes of immovable property, if its execution conformed to the internal law in force in the territory where the property was situated;
(c) a will so far as it revokes a will which under this Act would be treated as properly executed or revokes a provision which under this Act would be treated as comprised in a properly executed will, if the execution of the later will conformed to any law by reference to which the revoked will or provision would be so treated;
(d) a will so far as it exercises a power of appointment, if the execution of the will conformed to the law governing the essential validity of the power.

(2) A will so far as it exercises a power of appointment shall not be treated as improperly executed by reason only that its execution was not in accordance with any formal requirements contained in the instrument creating the power.

[244.79]
3. Certain requirements to be treated as formal. Where (whether in pursuance of this Act or not) a law in force outside the United Kingdom falls to be applied in relation to a will, any requirement of that law whereby special formalities are to be observed by testators answering a particular description, or witnesses to the execution of a will are to possess certain qualifications, shall be treated, notwithstanding any rule of that law to the contrary, as a formal requirement only.

[244.80]
4. Construction of wills. The construction of a will shall not be altered by reason of any change in the testator's domicile after the execution of the will.

[244.81]
5. [*Repealed and replaced by the Succession (Scotland) Act 1964, s 34(2), Sch 3.*]

[244.82]
6. Interpretation.— (1) In this Act—

'internal law' in relation to any territory or state means the law which would apply in a case where no question of the law in force in any other territory or state arose;

'state' means a territory or group of territories having its own law of nationality;

'will' includes any testamentary instrument or act, and 'testator' shall be construed accordingly.

(2) Where under this Act the internal law in force in any territory or state is to be applied in the case of a will, but there are in force in that territory or state two or more systems of internal law relating to the formal validity of wills, the system to be applied shall be ascertained as follows—

(a) if there is in force throughout the territory or state a rule indicating which of those systems can properly be applied in the case in question, that rule shall be followed; or

(b) if there is no such rule, the system shall be that with which the testator was most closely connected at the relevant time, and for this purpose the relevant time is the time of the testator's death where the matter is to be determined by reference to circumstances prevailing at his death, and the time of execution of the will in any other case.

(3) In determining for the purposes of this Act whether or not the execution of a will conformed to a particular law, regard shall be had to the formal requirements of that law at the time of execution, but this shall not prevent account being taken of an alteration of law affecting wills executed at that time if the alteration enables the will to be treated as properly executed.

[244.83]
7. Short title, commencement, repeal and extent.— (1) This Act may be cited as the Wills Act 1963.
(2) This Act shall come into operation on 1 January 1964.
(3) The Wills Act 1861 is hereby repealed.
(4) This Act shall not apply to a will of a testator who died before the time of the commencement of this Act and shall apply to a will of a testator who dies after that time whether the will was executed before or after that time, but so that the repeal of the Wills Act 1861 shall not invalidate a will executed before that time.
(5) It is hereby declared that this Act extends to Northern Ireland [*Remaining words repealed by the Northern Ireland Constitution Act 1973, s 41(1), Sch 6.*]

WILLS ACT 1968

(1968 c 28)

[30 May 1968]

[244.84]
1. Restriction of operation of Wills Act 1837, s 15.—[1] (1) For the purposes of section 15 of the Wills Act 1837 (avoidance of gifts to attesting witnesses and their spouses) the attestation of a will by a person to whom or

to whose spouse there is given or made any such disposition as is described in that section shall be disregarded if the will is duly executed without his attestation and without that of any other such person.
(2) This section applies to the will of any person dying after the passing of this Act, whether executed before or after the passing of this Act.

1 With effect from 5 December 2005, this section is extended so as to apply in relation also to the attestation of a will by a person to whose civil partner a disposition is made: CPA 2004, s 71, Sch 4, para 3(a) and Civil Partnership Act 2004 (Commencement No 2) Order 2005, SI 2005/3175: see paras **[244.132]**–**[244.133]** below.

[244.85]
2. Short title and extent.— (1) This Act may be cited as the Wills Act 1968.
(2) This Act does not extend to Scotland or Northern Ireland.

FAMILY LAW REFORM ACT 1969

(1969 c 46)

[25 July 1969]

[244.86]

Note. This Act, which was brought into force on 1 January 1970, reduced the age of majority from 21 to 18 years. The Act also made provision (since repealed) increasing the property rights of illegitimate children: see paras **[245.37]**–**[245.41]** below.

PART I
REDUCTION OF AGE OF MAJORITY AND RELATED PROVISIONS

* * * * *

[244.87]
3. Provisions relating to wills and intestacy.— (1) [*Amends the Wills Act 1837, s 7,* (para **[244.5]** above) *and the Wills* (*Soldiers and Sailors Act*) *1918, ss 1, 3*(*1*) (paras **[244.48]** and **[244.50]** above).]
(2) [*Amends the Administration of Estates Act 1925, s 47*(*1*)(*i*) (para **[244.61]** above).]
(3) Any will which –

(a) has been made, whether before or after the coming into force of this section, by a person under the age of eighteen; and
(b) is valid by virtue of section 11 of the said Act of 1837 and the said Act of 1918,

may be revoked by that person notwithstanding that he is still under that age whether or not the circumstances are then such that he would be entitled to make a valid will under those provisions.
(4) In this section 'will' has the same meaning as in the said Act of 1837 and 'intestate' has the same meaning as the said Act of 1925.

* * * * *

MATRIMONIAL CAUSES ACT 1973

(1973 c 18)

[23 May 1973]

[244.88]

Note. Section 18(2) of the Matrimonial Causes Act 1973, which deprives the husband or wife of an intestate of any interest in the intestate's estate under the intestacy rules when the parties were judicially separated at the time of the death, replaces the corresponding provisions contained in the Matrimonial Proceedings and Property Act 1970, s 40(1), in relation to deaths on or after 1 August 1970, the commencement date of the earlier Act.

PART I
DIVORCE, NULLITY AND OTHER MATRIMONIAL SUITS

* * * * *

OTHER MATRIMONIAL SUITS

* * * * *

[244.89]

18. Effects of judicial separation * * * * *

(2) If while a decree of judicial separation is in force and the separation is continuing either of the parties to the marriage dies intestate as respects all or any of his or her real or personal property, the property as respects which he or she died intestate shall devolve as if the other party to the marriage had then been dead.

* * * * *

INTESTATE SUCCESSION (INTEREST AND CAPITALISATION) ORDER 1977

SI 1977/1491

[244.90]

Note. This Order was made on 4 September 1977 by the Lord Chancellor under the AEA 1925, s 46(1)(i) (as substituted by the Intestates' Estates Act 1952, s 1, and as amended by the AJA 1977, s 28(1)) and s 47A(3A) of the 1925 Act (as inserted by the AJA 1977, s 28(3)). The Order came into force on 15 September 1977: see article 1(1). The Order is printed below as amended by the Intestate Succession (Interest and Capitalisation) Order 1983, SI 1983/1374.

Article 2 of the Order originally increased the rate of interest payable on the statutory legacy until paid or appropriated to 7 per cent p a (from 4 per cent p a or, in the case of persons dying before 1 January 1953, 8 per cent, p a). Article 2 was amended by the 1983 Order so as to reduce the rate to 6 per cent per annum with effect from 1 October 1983.

Article 3 and the Schedule sets out the formula for calculating the value of the life interest of the surviving spouse of an intestate who elects to capitalise his or her life interest.

[244.91]

1. Citation and Interpretation.— (1) This Order may be cited as the Intestate Succession (Interest and Capitalisation) Order 1977 and shall come into operation on 15th September 1977.

(2) The Interpretation Act 1889 shall apply to the interpretation of this Order as it applies to the interpretation of an Act of Parliament.

[244.92]

2. Interest on Statutory Legacy. For the purposes of section 46(1)(i) of the Administration of Estates Act 1925, as it applies both in respect of persons dying before 1953 and in respect of persons dying after 1952, the specified rate of interest shall be [6] per cent per annum.[1]

1 The figure in square brackets was substituted by SI 1983/1374 with effect from 1 October 1983: see para **[244.90]** above.

[244.93]

3. Capitalisation of Life Interests.— (1) Where after the coming into operation of this Order an election is exercised in accordance with subsection (6) or (7) of section 47A of the Administration of Estates Act 1925, the capital value of the life interest of the surviving spouse shall be reckoned in accordance with the following provisions of this article.

(2) There shall be ascertained, by reference to the index compiled by the Financial Times, The Institute of Actuaries and the Faculty of Actuaries, the average gross redemption yield on medium coupon fifteen-year Government Stocks at the date on which the election was exercised or, if the index was not compiled on that date, by reference to the index on the last date before that date on which it was compiled; and the column which corresponds to that yield in whichever of the Tables set out in the Schedule hereto is applicable to the sex of the surviving spouse shall be the appropriate column for the purposes of paragraph (3) of this article.

(3) The capital value for the purposes of paragraph (1) of this article is the produce of the part of the residuary estate (whether or not yielding income) in respect of which the election was exercised and the multiplier shown in the appropriate column opposite the age which the surviving spouse had attained at the date on which the election was exercised.

Note. The tables printed after LR(S)A 1995 follow Article 3 of this Order.

ADMINISTRATION OF JUSTICE ACT 1982

(1982 c 53)

[28 October 1982]

[244.94]

Note. Part IV of the AJA 1982 effects the most significant changes to the law of wills since the enactment of the WA 1837. With effect from 1 January 1983 the WA 1837, ss 9, 18 and 33 (relating to the signing and attestation of wills, the revocation of wills by marriage and the saving of gifts to children and other issue who predecease a testator in favour of the surviving issue of such children or issue) were replaced (see paras **[244.7]**, **[244.16]** and **[244.36]** above) and a new s 18A (effect of dissolution or annulment of marriage on wills) introduced, which has itself since been replaced (see paras **[244.17]** and **[244.18]** above). Provision is also made by Part IV for the rectification of the wills of testators dying on or after 1 January 1983 and for the admissibility of extrinsic evidence, including evidence of intention, in the interpretation of the wills of testators dying on or after that date. Part IV also makes provision, not yet implemented, for the registration and deposit of wills and for the recognition of international wills by adopting the Annex to the Convention on International Wills (set out in the AJA 1982, Sch 2).

PART IV
WILLS

* * * * *

AMENDMENTS OF WILLS ACT 1837

[244.95]
17. Relaxation of formal requirements for making wills. [*For text, see the Wills Act 1837, s 9 (as substituted) at para* **[244.7]** above.]

[244.96]
18. Effect of marriage or its termination on wills. [*For text, see the Wills Act 1837, ss 18 (as substituted) and 18A as originally introduced by this Act at paras* **[244.16]–[244.17]** above.]

[244.97]
19. Gifts to children etc who predecease testator. [*For text, see the Wills Act 1837, s 33 (as substituted) at para* **[244.36]** above.]

RECTIFICATION AND INTERPRETATION OF WILLS

[244.98]
20. Rectification.— (1) If a court is satisfied that a will is so expressed that it fails to carry out the testator's intentions, in consequence—

(a) of a clerical error; or
(b) of a failure to understand his instructions,

it may order that the will shall be rectified so as to carry out his intentions.
(2) An application for an order under this section shall not, except with the permission of the court, be made after the end of the period of six months from the date on which representation with respect to the estate of the deceased is first taken out.
(3) The provisions of this section shall not render the personal representatives of a deceased person liable for having distributed any part of the estate of the deceased, after the end of the period of six months from the date on which representation with respect to the estate of the deceased is first taken out, on the ground that they ought to have taken into account the possibility that the court might permit the making of an application for an order under this section after the end of that period; but this subsection shall not prejudice any power to recover, by reason of the making of an order under this section, any part of the estate so distributed.
(4) In considering for the purposes of this section when representation with respect to the estate of a deceased person was first taken out, a grant limited to settled land or to trust property shall be left out of account, and a grant

limited to real estate or to personal estate shall be left out of account unless a grant limited to the remainder of the estate has previously been made or is made at the same time.

[244.99]
21. Interpretation of wills—general rules as to evidence.— (1) This section applies to a will—

(a) in so far as any part of it is meaningless;
(b) in so far as the language used in any part of it is ambiguous on the face of it;
(c) in so far as evidence, other than evidence of the testator's intention, shows that the language used in any part of it is ambiguous in the light of surrounding circumstances.

(2) In so far as this section applies to a will extrinsic evidence, including evidence of the testator's intention, may be admitted to assist in its interpretation.

[244.100]
22. Presumption as to effect of gifts to spouses. Except where a contrary intention is shown it shall be presumed that if a testator devises or bequeaths property to his spouse in terms which in themselves would give an absolute interest to the spouse, but by the same instrument purports to give his issue an interest in the same property, the gift to the spouse is absolute notwithstanding the purported gift to the issue.

REGISTRATION OF WILLS

[244.101]
23. Deposit and registration of wills of living persons.[1]— (1) The following, namely—

(a) the Principal Registry of the Family Division of the High Court of Justice;

* * * * *

shall be registering authorities for the purposes of this section.
(2) Each registering authority shall provide and maintain safe and convenient depositories for the custody of the wills of living persons.
(3) Any person may deposit his will in such a depository in accordance with regulations under section 25 below and on payment of the prescribed fee.
(4) It shall be the duty of a registering authority to register in accordance with regulations under section 25 below—

(a) any will deposited in a depository maintained by the authority; and
(b) any other will whose registration is requested under Article 6 of the Registration Convention.

(5) A will deposited in a depository provided—

(a) under section 172 of the Supreme Court of Judicature (Consolidation) Act 1925 or section 126 of the Supreme Court Act 1981; or
(b) under Article 27 of the Administration of Estates (Northern Ireland) Order 1979,

shall be treated for the purposes of this section as if it had been deposited under this section.
(6) In this section 'prescribed' means—

(a) in the application of this section to England and Wales, prescribed by an order under section 130 of the Supreme Court Act 1981;

* * * * *

1 No statutory instrument under s 76(5), (6) (para **[244.108]** below) bringing this section into force has yet been made.

[244.102]
24. Designation of Principal Registry as national body under Registration Convention.[1]— (1) The Principal Registry of the Family Division of the High Court of Justice shall be the national body for the purposes of the Registration Convention, and shall accordingly have the functions assigned to the national body by the Registration Convention including, without prejudice to the general application of the Convention to the Principal Registry by virtue of this section, the functions—

(a) of arranging for the registration of wills in other Contracting States as provided for in Article 6 of the Convention;
(b) of receiving and answering requests for information arising from the national bodies of other Contracting States.

(2) In this Part of this Act 'the Registration Convention' means the Convention on the Establishment of a Scheme of Registration of Wills concluded at Basle on 16th May 1972.

1 No statutory instrument under s 76(5), (6) (para **[244.108]** below) bringing this section into force has yet been made.

[244.103]
25. Regulations as to deposit and registration of wills etc.[1]— (1) Regulations may make provision—

(a) as to the conditions for the deposit of a will;
(b) as to the manner of and procedure for—
   (i) the deposit and registration of a will; and
   (ii) the withdrawal of a will which has been deposited; and
   (iii) the cancellation of the registration of a will; and
(c) as to the manner in which the Principal Registry of the Family Division is to perform its functions as the national body under the Registration Convention.

(2) Regulations under this section may contain such incidental or supplementary provisions as the authority making the regulations considers appropriate.

(3) Any such regulations are to be made—

(a) for England and Wales, by the President of the Family Division of the High Court of Justice, with the concurrence of the Lord Chancellor;

* * * * *

(4) Regulations made by virtue of subsection (1)(c) above shall be made by the Lord Chancellor.
(5) Subject to subsection (6) below, regulations under this section shall be made by statutory instrument and shall be laid before Parliament after being made.

* * * * *

(7) The Statutory Instruments Act 1946 shall apply to a statutory instrument containing regulations made in accordance with subsection (3)(a) ... above as if the regulations had been made by a Minister of the Crown.
(8) Any regulations made under section 172 of the Supreme Court of Judicature (Consolidation) Act 1925 or section 126 of the Supreme Court Act 1981 shall have effect for the purposes of this Part of this Act as they have effect for the purposes of the enactment under which they were made.

1 No statutory instrument under s 76(5), (6) (para **[244.108]**) bringing this section into force has yet been made.

[244.104]
26. [*Fees as to registration in Scotland.*]

[244.105]
27. The form of an international will.[1]— (1) The Annex to the Convention on International Wills shall have the force of law in the United Kingdom.
(2) The Annex is set out in Schedule 2 to this Act.
(3) In this Part of this Act—

'international will' means a will made in accordance with the requirements of the Annex, as set out in Schedule 2 to this Act; and
'the Convention on International Wills' means the Convention providing a Uniform Law on the Form of an International Will concluded at Washington on 26th October 1973.

1 Section 75 effects repeals of previous legislation. No statutory instrument under s 76(5), (6) (para **[244.108]** below) bringing this section into force has yet been made.

[244.106]
28. International wills—procedure.[1]— (1) The persons authorised to act in the United Kingdom in connection with international wills are—

(a) solicitors, and
(b) notaries public.

(2) A person who is authorised under section 6(1) of the Commissioners for Oaths Act 1889 to do notarial acts in any foreign country or place is authorised to act there in connection with international wills.

(3) An international will certified by virtue of subsection (1) or (2) above may be deposited in a depository provided under section 23 above.
(4) Section 23 above shall accordingly have effect in relation to such international wills.
(5) Subject to subsection (6) below, regulations under section 25 above shall have effect in relation to such international wills as they have effect in relation to wills deposited under section 23 above.
(6) Without prejudice to the generality of section 25 above, regulations under that section may make special provision with regard to such international wills.
(7) In section 10 of the Consular Relations Act 1968 (by virtue of which diplomatic agents and consular officials may administer oaths and do notarial acts in certain cases)—

(a) at the end of subsection (1)(b) there shall be added the words 'or (c) in connection with an international will.'; and
(b) at the end of subsection (4) there shall be added the words 'and 'international will' has the meaning assigned to it by section 27 of the Administration of Justice Act 1982'.

1 No statutory instrument under s 76(5), (6) (para **[244.108]** below) bringing this section into force has yet been made.

* * * * *

PART IX
GENERAL AND SUPPLEMENTARY

[244.107]

73. Transitional provisions and savings. * * * * *
(6) Nothing in the following provisions of this Act—

(a) section 17;
(b) section 18(2);
(c) sections 19 to 22;
(d) section 75,[1] so far as it relates—
  (i) to the Wills Act Amendment Act 1852; and
  (ii) to the Family Law Reform Act 1969,

affects the will of a testator who dies before the commencement of the provision in question.
(7) Neither section 18(1) above nor the repeal by this Act of section 177 of the Law of Property Act 1925 affects a will made before the commencement of section 18(1) above.

1 Section 75 effects repeals of previous legislation.

* * * * *

[244.108]
76. Commencement.

* * * * *

(5) The provisions of this Act specified in subsection (6) below shall come into operation on such day as the Lord Chancellor and the Secretary of State may by order jointly appoint.
(6) The provisions of this Act mentioned in subsection (5) above are—

- (a) sections 23 to 25;
- (b) sections 27 and 28;
- (c) section 75, so far as it relates—
  - (i) to section 126 of the Supreme Court Act 1981;[1] and
  - (ii) to Article 27 of the Administration of Estates (Northern Ireland) Order 1979.

(7) Any order under this section shall be made by statutory instrument.
(8) Any such order may appoint different days for different provisions and for different purposes.

* * * * *

(11) Subject to the foregoing provisions of this section, this Act shall come into operation on 1st January 1983.

1 The SCA 1981, s 126 contains the existing provisions for deposit of wills, which will be repealed by s 75, Sch 9, Pt 1, when a commencement order under s 76 is made bringing ss 23 to 25 of the AJA 1982 into force.

[244.109]
77. Extent.— (1) Subject to subsection (6) below, the following provisions of this Act—

* * * * *

(c) sections 17 to 22;

* * * * *

extend to England and Wales only.

* * * * *

(5) The repeal of the Wills Act Amendment Act 1852 by section 75 above does not extend to Northern Ireland.
(6) Subject to subsection (5) above, where any enactment repealed or amended or instrument revoked by this Act extends to any part of the United Kingdom, the repeal, amendment or revocation extends to that part.

[244.110]
78. Citation. This Act may be cited as the Administration of Justice Act 1982.

* * * * *

SCHEDULE 2[1]

Section 27

THE ANNEX TO THE CONVENTION ON INTERNATIONAL WILLS

UNIFORM LAW ON THE FORM OF AN INTERNATIONAL WILL

[244.111]

Article 1

1. A will shall be valid as regards form, irrespective particularly of the place where it is made, of the location of the assets and of the nationality, domicile or residence of the testator, if it is made in the form of an international will complying with the provisions set out in Articles 2 to 5 hereinafter.
2. The invalidity of the will as an international will shall not affect its formal validity as a will of another kind.

1 No statutory instrument under s 76(5), (6) (para **[244.108]** above) bringing s 27, and thus this Schedule, into force has yet been made.

Article 2

This law shall not apply to the form of testamentary dispositions made by two or more persons in one instrument.

Article 3

1. The will shall be made in writing.
2. It need not be written by the testator himself.
3. It may be written in any language, by hand or by any other means.

Article 4

1. The testator shall declare in the presence of two witnesses and of a person authorized to act in connection with international wills that the document is his will and that he knows the contents thereof.
2. The testator need not inform the witnesses, or the authorized person, of the contents of the will.

Article 5

1. In the presence of the witnesses and of the authorized person, the testator shall sign the will or, if he has previously signed it, shall acknowledge his signature.
2. When the testator is unable to sign, he shall indicate the reason therefor to the authorized person who shall make note of this on the will. Moreover, the testator may be authorized by the law under which the authorized person was designated to direct another person to sign on his behalf.

3. The witnesses and the authorized person shall there and then attest the will by signing in the presence of the testator.

Article 6

1. The signatures shall be placed at the end of the will.
2. If the will consists of several sheets, each sheet shall be signed by the testator or, if he is unable to sign, by the person signing on his behalf or, if there is no such person, by the authorized person. In addition, each sheet shall be numbered.

Article 7

1. The date of the will shall be the date of its signature by the authorized person.
2. This date shall be noted at the end of the will by the authorized person.

Article 8

In the absence of any mandatory rule pertaining to the safekeeping of the will, the authorized person shall ask the testator whether he wishes to make a declaration concerning the safekeeping of his will. If so and at the express request of the testator the place where he intends to have his will kept shall be mentioned in the certificate provided for in Article 9.

Article 9

The authorized person shall attach to the will a certificate in the form prescribed in Article 10 establishing that the obligations of this law have been complied with.

Article 10

The certificate drawn up by the authorized person shall be in the following form or in a substantially similar form:

Certificate

(Convention of October 26th, 1973)

1. I, ... (name, address and capacity), a person authorized to act in connection with international wills
2. Certify that on .... (date) at .... (place)
3. (testator) .... (name, address, date and place of birth)
   in my presence and that of the witnesses
4. (a) .... (name, address, date and place of birth)
   (b) .... (name, address, date and place of birth
   has declared that the attached document is his will and that he knows the contents thereof.

5. I furthermore certify that:

6. (a) in my presence and in that of the witnesses

(1) the testator has signed the will or has acknowledged his signature previously affixed.

*(2) following a declaration of the testator stating that he was unable to sign his will for the following reason

....

— I have mentioned this declaration on the will

*— the signature has been affixed by .... (name, address)

7. (b) the witnesses and I have signed the will;

8. *(c) each page of the will has been signed by and numbered:

9. (d) I have satisfied myself as to the identity of the testator and of the witnesses as designated above;

10. (e) the witnesses met the conditions requisite to act as such according to the law under which I am acting;

11. *(f) the testator has requested me to include the following statement concerning the safekeeping of his will:

....

....

12. PLACE

13. DATE

14. SIGNATURE and, if necessary, SEAL

* To be completed if appropriate.

Article 11
The authorised person shall keep a copy of the certificate and deliver another to the testator.

Article 12
In the absence of evidence to the contrary, the certificate of the authorised person shall be conclusive of the formal validity of the instrument as a will under this Law.

Article 13
The absence or irregularity of a certificate shall not affect the formal validity of a will under this Law.

Article 14
The international will shall be subject to the ordinary rules of revocation of wills.

Article 15
In interpreting and applying the provisions of this law, regard shall be had to its international origin and to the need for uniformity in its interpretation.

* * * * *

CHILDREN ACT 1989

(1989 c 41)

[16 November 1989]

[244.112]

Note. The Children Act 1989 (ChA 1989) was brought into force on 14 October 1991 (SI 1991/828). The Act as amended contains comprehensive provisions or the welfare of children, including their guardianship. The powers to appoint guardians are now contained in s 5. A parent with 'parental responsibility' (a term defined by s 3) has power under s 5(3) to appoint an individual to be the child's guardian after his or her death and a guardian is given the like power by s 5(4). The power may be exercised by will or any other writing, subject to the requirement that it be dated and either signed by the person making the appointment or signed at his direction before witnesses; see s 5(5). Sections 2 to 4 prescribe the circumstances in which a parent is deemed to have the parental responsibility which is a prerequisite to the exercise of the power to appoint guardians. Section 4 has been amended with effect from 1 December 2003 by the Adoption and Children Act 2002, s 111. The amendments extend parental responsibility for illegitimate children to fathers registered on the birth certificate, where registration occurs on or after the commencement day. Adoption and children Act 2002, s 112 added with effect from 30 December 2005 a new s 4A providing for the acquisition of parental responsibility by step-parents. Section 6 sets out the circumstances in which the appointment of a guardian may be revoked or disclaimed. One additional important feature of the ChA 1989 is that s 3(3) extends to a parent (and now a step-parent) with parental responsibility the right to call for and deal with all property belonging to his minor child, a right which was formerly available under the Guardianship Act 1973, s 7 only to a guardian.

For a more detailed account of these provisions, and for their practical implications for will drafting, see Vol 1, para **[28.1]** ff and para **[203.47]** ff above.

PART I
INTRODUCTORY

* * * * *

[244.113]
2. Parental responsibility for children.— (1) Where a child's father and mother were married to each other at the time of his birth, they shall each have parental responsibility for the child.
(2) Where a child's father and mother were not married to each other at the time of his birth—

- (a) the mother shall have parental responsibility for the child;
- (b) the father shall not have parental responsibility for the child, unless he acquires it in accordance with the provisions of this Act.

(3) References in this Act to a child whose father and mother were, or (as the case may be) were not, married to each other at the time of his birth must be read with section 1 of the Family Law Reform Act 1987 (which extends their meaning).

(4) The rule of law that a father is the natural guardian of his legitimate child is abolished.
(5) More than one person may have parental responsibility for the same child at the same time.
(6) A person who has parental responsibility for a child at any time shall not cease to have that responsibility solely because some other person subsequently acquires parental responsibility for the child.
(7) Where more than one person has parental responsibility for a child, each of them may act alone and without the other (or others) in meeting that responsibility; but nothing in this Part shall be taken to affect the operation of any enactment which requires the consent of more than one person in a matter affecting the child.
(8) The fact that a person has parental responsibility for a child shall not entitle him to act in any way which would be incompatible with any order made with respect to the child under this Act.
(9) A person who has parental responsibility for a child may not surrender or transfer any part of that responsibility to another but may arrange for some or all of it to be met by one or more persons acting on his behalf.
(10) The person with whom any such arrangement is made may himself be a person who already has parental responsibility for the child concerned.
(11) The making of any such arrangement shall not affect any liability of the person making it which may arise from any failure to meet any part of his parental responsibility for the child concerned.

[244.114]
3. Meaning of 'parental responsibility'.— (1) In this Act 'parental responsibility' means all the rights, duties, powers, responsibilities and authority which by law a parent of a child has in relation to the child and his property.
(2) It also includes the rights, powers and duties which a guardian of the child's estate (appointed, before the commencement of section 5, to act generally) would have had in relation to the child and his property.
(3) The rights referred to in subsection (2) include, in particular, the right of the guardian to receive or recover in his own name, for the benefit of the child, property of whatever description and wherever situated which the child is entitled to receive or recover.
(4) The fact that a person has, or does not have, parental responsibility for a child shall not affect—

(a) any obligation which he may have in relation to the child (such as a statutory duty to maintain the child); or
(b) any rights which, in the event of the child's death, he (or any other person) may have in relation to the child's property.

(5) A person who—

(a) does not have parental responsibility for a particular child; but
(b) has care of the child,

may (subject to the provisions of this Act) do what is reasonable in all the circumstances of the case for the purpose of safeguarding or promoting the child's welfare.

[244.115]
4 Acquisition of parental responsibility by father (1) Where a child's father and mother were not married to each other at the time of his birth([, the father shall acquire parental responsibility for the child if—

(a) he becomes registered as the child's father under any of the enactments specified in subsection (1A);
(b) he and the child's mother make an agreement (a 'parental responsibility agreement') providing for him to have parental responsibility for the child; or
(c) the court, on his application, orders that he shall have parental responsibility for the child.][1]

[(1A) The enactments referred to in subsection (1)(a) are—

(a) paragraphs (a), (b) and (c) of section 10(1) and of section 10A(1) of the Births and Deaths Registration Act 1953;
(b) paragraphs (a), (b)(i) and (c) of section 18(1), and sections 18(2)(b) and 20(1)(a) of the Registration of Births, Deaths and Marriages (Scotland) Act 1965; and
(c) sub-paragraphs (a), (b) and (c) of Article 14(3) of the Births and Deaths Registration (Northern Ireland) Order 1976.

(1B) The [Secretary of State] may by order amend subsection (1A) so as to add further enactments to the list in that subsection.][1]
(2) No parental responsibility agreement shall have effect for the purposes of this Act unless—

(a) it is made in the form prescribed by regulations made by the Lord Chancellor; and
(b) where regulations are made by the Lord Chancellor prescribing the manner in which such agreements must be recorded, it is recorded in the prescribed manner.

[(2A) A person who has acquired parental responsibility under subsection (1) shall cease to have that responsibility only if the court so orders.]
(3) The court may make an order under subsection (2A) on the application—

(a) of any person who has parental responsibility for the child; or
(b) with the leave of the court, of the child himself,

subject, in the case of parental responsibility acquired under subsection (1)(c), to section 12(4).]

(4) The court may only grant leave under subsection (3)(b) if it is satisfied that the child has sufficient understanding to make the proposed application.

[1] Words in square brackets in sub-s (1) substituted and sub-ss (1A), (1B) and (2A) inserted with effect from 1 December 2003 by the Adoption and Children Act 2002, s 111. For the commencement date see SI 2003/3079. The amendments to s 4 do not apply to registrations of births before 1 December 2003: Adoption and Children Act 2002, s111(7).

[244.116]

[4A Acquisition of parental responsibility by step-parent] [(1) Where a child's parent ('parent A') who has parental responsibility for the child is married to[, or a civil partner of,] a person who is not the child's parent ('the step-parent')—

(a) parent A or, if the other parent of the child also has parental responsibility for the child, both parents may by agreement with the step-parent provide for the step-parent to have parental responsibility for the child; or

(b) the court may, on the application of the step-parent, order that the step-parent shall have parental responsibility for the child.

(2) An agreement under subsection (1)(a) is also a 'parental responsibility agreement', and section 4(2) applies in relation to such agreements as it applies in relation to parental responsibility agreements under section 4.

(3) A parental responsibility agreement under subsection (1)(a), or an order under subsection (1)(b), may only be brought to an end by an order of the court made on the application—

(a) of any person who has parental responsibility for the child; or

(b) with the leave of the court, of the child himself.

(4) The court may only grant leave under subsection (3)(b) if it is satisfied that the child has sufficient understanding to make the proposed application.][1]

1 Section 4A inserted with effect from 30 December 2005 by the Adoption and Children Act 2002, s112. For the commencement date see SI 2005/2213. The words 'or a civil partner of' in sub-s (1) were inserted by CPA 2004, s 75(2).

[244.116A]

5. Appointment of guardians.— (1) Where an application with respect to a child is made to the court by any individual, the court may by order appoint that individual to be the child's guardian if—

(a) the child has no parent with parental responsibility for him; or

(b) a residence order has been made with respect to the child in favour of a parent or guardian of his who has died while the order was in force.

(2) The power conferred by subsection (1) may also be exercised in any family proceedings if the court considers that the order should be made even though no application has been made for it.

(3) A parent who has parental responsibility for his child may appoint another individual to be the child's guardian in the event of his death.

(4) A guardian of a child may appoint another individual to take his place as the child's guardian in the event of his death.

(5) An appointment under subsection (3) or (4) shall not have effect unless it is made in writing, is dated and is signed by the person making the appointment or—

(a) in the case of an appointment made by a will which is not signed by the testator, is signed at the direction of the testator in accordance with the requirements of section 9 of the Wills Act 1837; or

(b) in any other case, is signed at the direction of the person making the appointment, in his presence and in the presence of two witnesses who each attest the signature.

(6) A person appointed as a child's guardian under this section shall have parental responsibility for the child concerned.
(7) Where—

(a) on the death of any person making an appointment under subsection (3) or (4), the child concerned has no parent with parental responsibility for him; or
(b) immediately before the death of any person making such an appointment, a residence order in his favour was in force with respect to the child,

the appointment shall take effect on the death of that person.
(8) Where, on the death of any person making an appointment under subsection (3) or (4)—

(a) the child concerned has a parent with parental responsibility for him; and
(b) subsection (7)(b) does not apply,

the appointment shall take effect when the child no longer has a parent who has parental responsibility for him.
(9) Subsections (1) and (7) do not apply if the residence order referred to in paragraph (b) of those subsections was also made in favour of a surviving parent of the child.
(10) Nothing in this section shall be taken to prevent an appointment under subsection (3) or (4) being made by two or more persons acting jointly.
(11) Subject to any provision made by rules of court, no court shall exercise the High Court's inherent jurisdiction to appoint a guardian of the estate of any child.
(12) Where rules of court are made under subsection (11) they may prescribe the circumstances in which, and conditions subject to which, an appointment of such a guardian may be made.
(13) A guardian of a child may only be appointed in accordance with the provisions of this section.

[244.117]
6. Guardians: revocation and disclaimer.— (1) An appointment under section 5(3) or (4) revokes an earlier such appointment (including one made in an unrevoked will or codicil) made by the same person in respect of the same child, unless it is clear (whether as the result of an express provision in the later appointment or by any necessary implication) that the purpose of the later appointment is to appoint an additional guardian.
(2) An appointment under section 5(3) or (4) (including one made in an unrevoked will or codicil) is revoked if the person who made the appointment revokes it by a written and dated instrument which is signed—

(a) by him; or
(b) at his direction, in his presence and in the presence of two witnesses who each attest the signature.

(3) An appointment under section 5(3) or (4) (other than one made in a will or codicil) is revoked if, with the intention of revoking the appointment, the person who made it—

(a) destroys the instrument by which it was made; or
(b) has some other person destroy that instrument in his presence.

[(3A) An appointment under section 5(3) or (4) (including one made in an unrevoked will or codicil) is revoked if the person appointed is the spouse of the person who made the appointment and either—

(a) a decree of a court of civil jurisdiction in England and Wales dissolves or annuls the marriage, or
(b) the marriage is dissolved or annulled and the divorce or annulment is entitled to recognition in England and Wales by virtue of Part II of the Family Law Act 1986,

unless a contrary intention appears by the appointment.][1]
[(3B) An appointment under section 5(3) or (4) (including one made in an unrevoked will or codicil) is revoked if the person appointed is the civil partner of the person who made the appointment and either—

(a) an order of a court of civil jurisdiction in England and Wales dissolves or annuls the civil partnership, or
(b) the civil partnership is dissolved or annulled and the dissolution or annulment is entitled to recognition in England and Wales by virtue of Chapter 3 of Part 5 of the Civil Partnership Act 2004,

unless a contrary intention appears by the appointment.][2]
(4) For the avoidance of doubt, an appointment under section 5(3) or (4) made in a will or codicil is revoked if the will or codicil is revoked.
(5) A person who is appointed as a guardian under section 5(3) or (4) may disclaim his appointment by an instrument in writing signed by him and made within a reasonable time of his first knowing that the appointment has taken effect.
(6) Where regulations are made by the Lord Chancellor prescribing the manner in which such disclaimers must be recorded, no such disclaimer shall have effect unless it is recorded in the prescribed manner.
(7) Any appointment of a guardian under section 5 may be brought to an end at any time by order of the court—

(a) on the application of any person who has parental responsibility for the child;
(b) on the application of the child concerned, with leave of the court; or
(c) in any family proceedings, if the court considers that it should be brought to an end even though no application has been made.

1 Sub-s (3A): inserted by the LR(S)A 1995, s 4(1). Section 4(2) of that Act (para **[244.126]** below) provides that the new subsection is to have effect as regards an appointment made by any person dying on or after 1 January 1996 (regardless of the date of the appointment or the date of the dissolution or annulment).
2 Sub-s (3B): inserted by CPA 2004, s 76 with effect from 5 December 2005 (SI 2005/3175).

* * * * *

PART II
ORDERS WITH RESPECT TO CHILDREN IN
FAMILY PROCEEDINGS

GENERAL

[244.118]
8. Residence, contact and other orders with respect to children.— (1) In this Act—

* * * * *

'a residence order' means an order settling the arrangements to be made as to the person with whom a child is to live; ...

* * * * *

PART XII
MISCELLANEOUS AND GENERAL

* * * * *

GENERAL

* * * * *

[244.119]
105. Interpretation.— (1) In this Act—

* * * * *

'child' means ... a person under the age of eighteen;

* * * * *

'guardian of a child' means a guardian (other than a guardian of the estate of a child) appointed in accordance with the provisions of section 5;

* * * * *

'prescribed' means prescribed by regulations made under this Act;

* * * * *

'residence order' has the meaning given by section 8(1);

* * * * *

(2) References in this Act to a child whose father and mother were, or (as the case may be) were not, married to each other at the time of his birth must be read with section 1 of the Family Law Reform Act 1987 (which extends the meaning of such references).

* * * * *

[244.120]
108. Short title, commencement, extent etc.— (1) This Act may be cited as the Children Act 1989.
(2) Sections 89 and 96(3) to (7), and paragraph 35 of Schedule 12, shall come into force on the passing of this Act and paragraph 36 of Schedule 12 shall come into force at the end of the period of two months beginning with the day on which this Act is passed but otherwise this Act shall come into force on such date as may be appointed by order made by the Lord Chancellor or the Secretary of State, or by both acting jointly.
(3) Different dates may be appointed for different provisions of this Act and in relation to different cases.
(4) The minor amendments set out in Schedule 12 shall have effect.
(5) The consequential amendments set out in Schedule 13 shall have effect.
(6) The transitional provisions and savings set out in Schedule 14 shall have effect.
(7) The repeals set out in Schedule 15 shall have effect.
(8) An order under subsection (2) may make such transitional provisions or savings as appear to the person making the order to be necessary or expedient in connection with the provisions brought into force by the order, including—

(a) provisions adding to or modifying the provisions of Schedule 14; and
(b) such adaptations—
  (i) of the provisions brought into force by the order; and
  (ii) of any provisions of this Act then in force,

as appear to him necessary or expedient in consequence of the partial operation of this Act.
(9) The Lord Chancellor may by order make such amendments or repeals, in such enactments as may be specified in the order, as appear to him to be necessary or expedient in consequence of any provision of this Act.
(10) This Act shall, in its application to the Isles of Scilly, have effect subject to such exceptions, adaptations and modifications as the Secretary of State may by order prescribe.
(11) [*Applies to Scotland only*.]
(12) [*Applies to Northern Ireland only*.]

SCHEDULE 13

Section 108(5)

CONSEQUENTIAL AMENDMENTS

THE WILLS ACT 1837 (C 26)

1. [*Amends the Wills Act 1837, s 1: see para* **[244.3] above**.]

* * * * *

SCHEDULE 14

Section 108(6)

* * * * *

CUSTODY ORDERS, ETC

* * * * *

THE FAMILY LAW REFORM ACT 1987 (C 42)

CONVERSION OF ORDERS UNDER SECTION 4

[244.121]
4. Where, immediately before the day on which Parts I and II come into force, there was in force an order under section 4(1) of the Family Law Reform Act 1987 (order giving father parental rights and duties in relation to a child), then, on and after that day, the order shall be deemed to be an order under section 4 of this Act giving the father parental responsibility for the child.

ORDERS TO WHICH PARAGRAPHS 6 TO 11 APPLY

5.— (1) In paragraphs 6 to 11 'an existing order' means any order which—

- (a) is in force immediately before the commencement of Parts I and II;
- (b) was made under any enactment mentioned in sub-paragraph (2);
- (c) determines all or any of the following—
  - (i) who is to have custody of a child;
  - (ii) who is to have care and control of a child;
  - (iii) who is to have access to a child;
  - (iv) any matter with respect to a child's education or upbringing; and
- (d) is not an order of a kind mentioned in paragraph 15(1).

(2) The enactments are—

- (a) the Domestic Proceedings and Magistrates' Courts Act 1978;
- (b) the Children Act 1975;
- (c) the Matrimonial Causes Act 1973;
- (d) the Guardianship of Minors Acts 1971 and 1973;
- (e) the Matrimonial Causes Act 1965;
- (f) the Matrimonial Proceedings (Magistrates' Courts) Act 1960.

(3) For the purposes of this paragraph and paragraphs 6 to 11 'custody' includes legal custody and joint as well as sole custody but does not include access.

PARENTAL RESPONSIBILITY OF PARENTS

6.— (1) Where—

- (a) a child's father and mother were married to each other at the time of his birth; and

(b) there is an existing order with respect to the child,

each parent shall have parental responsibility for the child in accordance with section 2 as modified by sub-paragraph (3).

(2) Where—

(a) a child's father and mother were not married to each other at the time of his birth; and
(b) there is an existing order with respect to the child,

section 2 shall apply as modified by sub-paragraphs (3) and (4).

(3) The modification is that for section 2(8) there shall be substituted—

'(8) The fact that a person has parental responsibility for a child does not entitle him to act in a way which would be incompatible with any existing order or any order made under this Act with respect to the child'.

(4) The modifications are that—

(a) for the purposes of section 2(2), where the father has custody or care and control of the child by virtue of any existing order, the court shall be deemed to have made (at the commencement of that section) an order under section 4(1) giving him parental responsibility for the child; and
(b) where by virtue of paragraph (a) a court is deemed to have made an order under section 4(1) in favour of a father who has care and control of a child by virtue of an existing order, the court shall not bring the order under section 4(1) to an end at any time while he has care and control of the child by virtue of the order.

* * * * *

GUARDIANS

EXISTING GUARDIANS TO BE GUARDIANS UNDER THIS ACT

[244.122]

12.— (1) Any appointment of a person as guardian of a child which—

(a) was made—
   (i) under sections 3 to 5 of the Guardianship of Minors Act 1971;
   (ii) under section 38(3) of the Sexual Offences Act 1956; or
   (iii) under the High Court's inherent jurisdiction with respect to children; and
(b) has taken effect before the commencement of section 5,

shall (subject to sub-paragraph (2)) be deemed, on and after the commencement of section 5, to be an appointment made and having effect under that section.

(2) Where an appointment of a person as guardian of a child has effect under section 5 by virtue of sub-paragraph (1)(a)(ii), the appointment shall not have effect for a period which is longer than any period specified in the order.

APPOINTMENT OF GUARDIAN NOT YET IN EFFECT

13. Any appointment of a person to be a guardian of a child—

(a) which was made as mentioned in paragraph 12(1)(a)(i); but
(b) which, immediately before the commencement of section 5, had not taken effect,

shall take effect in accordance with section 5 (as modified, where it applies, by paragraph 8(2)).

PERSONS DEEMED TO BE APPOINTED AS GUARDIANS UNDER EXISTING WILLS

14. For the purposes of the Wills Act 1837 and of this Act any disposition by will and testament or devise of the custody and tuition of any child, made before the commencement of section 5 and paragraph 1 of Schedule 13, shall be deemed to be an appointment by will of a guardian of the child.

* * * * *

SCHEDULE 15

Section 108(7)

REPEALS

[244.123]

Note. This Schedule repeals a large number of legislative provisions, including all the extant provisions of the Guardianship of Minors Act 1971 and the Children Act 1975.

LAW REFORM (SUCCESSION) ACT 1995

(1995 c 41)

[8 November 1995]

DISTRIBUTION OF ESTATES

[244.124]

1. Intestacy and partial intestacy.— (1) [*Inserts the Administration of Estates Act 1925, s 46(2A): see para* **[244.62] above**.]

(2) [*Repeals the Administration of Estates Act 1925, ss 47(1)(iii), 49(1)(aa), (a), 49(2), (3): see paras* **[244.63]** *and* **[244.66] above**.]

(3) Subsections (1) and (2) above have effect as respects an intestate dying on or after 1st January 1996.

(4) In section 50 of the 1925 Act (construction of documents), the references in subsection (1) to Part IV of that Act and to the foregoing provisions of that Part shall, in relation to an instrument inter vivos made or a will or codicil coming into operation on or after 1st January 1996 (but not in relation to instruments inter vivos made or wills or codicils coming into operation earlier), be construed as including references to this section.

(5) In this section 'intestate' shall be construed in accordance with section 55(1)(vi) of the 1925 Act.

* * * * *

EFFECT OF DISSOLUTION OR ANNULMENT OF MARRIAGE

[244.125]
3. Effect of dissolution or annulment of marriage on will.— (1) [*Amends the Wills Act 1837, s 18A(1): see para* **[244.18] above**.]
(2) Subsection (1) above has effect as respects a will made by a person dying on or after 1st January 1996 (regardless of the date of the will and the date of the dissolution or annulment).

[244.126]
4. Effect of dissolution or annulment of marriage on appointment of guardian.— (1) [*Amends the Children Act 1989, s 6: see para* **[244.117] above**.]
(2) Subsection (1) above has effect as respects an appointment made by a person dying on or after 1st January 1996 (regardless of the date of the appointment and the date of the dissolution or annulment).

SUPPLEMENTAL

[244.127]
5. Repeals. The enactments mentioned in the Schedule to this Act are repealed in accordance with that Schedule.

[244.128]
6. Citation and extent.— (1) This Act may be cited as the Law Reform (Succession) Act 1995.
(2) This Act extends to England and Wales only.

SCHEDULE

Section 5

REPEALS

[244.129] [*This Schedule repeals (inter alia) the Wills Act 1837, s 18A(3): see para* **[244.18] above**, *as respects the wills of persons dying on or after 1 January 1996 and the Administration of Estates Act 1925, ss 47(1)(iii), 49(1)(aa), (a), (2), (3): see paras* **[244.61]** *and* **[244.64] above**, *as respects intestates (as defined by s 1(5), above) dying on or after that date.*]

Schedule

Table 1 Multiplier to be applied to the part of the residuary estate in respect of which the election is exercised to obtain the capital value of the life interest of a surviving husband when the average gross redemption yield on medium coupon fifteen-year Government Stocks is at the rate shown

Age Last Birthday of Husband	*Less than 8.50%*	*8.50% or between 8.50% and 9.50%*	*9.50% or between 9.50% and 10.50%*	*10.50% or between 10.50% and 11.50%*	*11.50% or between 11.50% and 12.50%*	*12.50% or between 12.50% and 13.50%*	*13.50% or between 13.50% and 14.50%*	*14.50% or between 14.50% and 15.50%*	*15.50% or more*
16	0.882	0.897	0.908	0.917	0.923	0.927	0.931	0.934	0.936
17	0.879	0.895	0.906	0.915	0.921	0.926	0.930	0.933	0.935
18	0.876	0.892	0.904	0.913	0.920	0.925	0.929	0.932	0.934
19	0.873	0.890	0.902	0.911	0.918	0.923	0.928	0.931	0.933
20	0.870	0.887	0.900	0.909	0.917	0.922	0.926	0.930	0.933
21	0.866	0.884	0.897	0.907	0.915	0.921	0.925	0.929	0.932
22	0.863	0.881	0.895	0.905	0.913	0.919	0.924	0.928	0.931
23	0.859	0.878	0.892	0.903	0.911	0.918	0.923	0.927	0.930
24	0.855	0.875	0.890	0.901	0.909	0.916	0.921	0.925	0.929
25	0.852	0.872	0.887	0.898	0.907	0.914	0.920	0.924	0.928
26	0.847	0.868	0.884	0.896	0.905	0.912	0.918	0.923	0.926
27	0.843	0.864	0.880	0.893	0.903	0.910	0.916	0.921	0.925
28	0.838	0.860	0.877	0.890	0.900	0.908	0.914	0.919	0.923
29	0.834	0.856	0.873	0.887	0.897	0.905	0.912	0.917	0.922
30	0.828	0.851	0.869	0.883	0.894	0.903	0.910	0.915	0.920
31	0.823	0.847	0.865	0.879	0.891	0.900	0.907	0.913	0.918
32	0.818	0.842	0.861	0.876	0.887	0.897	0.904	0.911	0.916
33	0.812	0.837	0.856	0.871	0.884	0.893	0.901	0.908	0.913

Age Last Birthday of Husband	*Less than 8.50%*	*8.50% or between 8.50% and 9.50%*	*9.50% or between 9.50% and 10.50%*	*10.50% or between 10.50% and 11.50%*	*11.50% or between 11.50% and 12.50%*	*12.50% or between 12.50% and 13.50%*	*13.50% or between 13.50% and 14.50%*	*14.50% or between 14.50% and 15.50%*	*15.50% or more*
34	0.806	0.831	0.851	0.867	0.880	0.890	0.898	0.905	0.911
35	0.799	0.825	0.846	0.862	0.875	0.886	0.895	0.902	0.908
36	0.792	0.819	0.840	0.857	0.871	0.882	0.891	0.899	0.905
37	0.785	0.813	0.834	0.852	0.866	0.878	0.887	0.895	0.902
38	0.778	0.806	0.828	0.846	0.861	0.873	0.883	0.891	0.898
39	0.771	0.799	0.822	0.840	0.856	0.868	0.879	0.887	0.894
40	0.763	0.792	0.815	0.834	0.850	0.863	0.874	0.883	0.890
41	0.755	0.784	0.808	0.828	0.844	0.857	0.869	0.878	0.886
42	0.746	0.776	0.801	0.821	0.838	0.852	0.863	0.873	0.881
43	0.737	0.768	0.793	0.814	0.831	0.845	0.857	0.868	0.876
44	0.728	0.759	0.785	0.806	0.824	0.839	0.851	0.862	0.871
45	0.719	0.750	0.776	0.798	0.816	0.832	0.845	0.856	0.866
46	0.709	0.741	0.768	0.790	0.809	0.825	0.838	0.850	0.860
47	0.699	0.731	0.758	0.781	0.801	0.817	0.831	0.843	0.853
48	0.688	0.721	0.749	0.772	0.792	0.809	0.823	0.836	0.847
49	0.678	0.711	0.739	0.763	0.783	0.800	0.815	0.828	0.839
50	0.666	0.700	0.729	0.753	0.774	0.791	0.807	0.820	0.832
51	0.655	0.689	0.718	0.743	0.764	0.782	0.798	0.812	0.824
52	0.643	0.678	0.707	0.732	0.754	0.772	0.789	0.803	0.815
53	0.631	0.666	0.695	0.721	0.743	0.762	0.779	0.794	0.807
54	0.619	0.654	0.684	0.710	0.732	0.752	0.769	0.784	0.797
55	0.606	0.641	0.671	0.698	0.721	0.741	0.758	0.774	0.787
56	0.594	0.628	0.659	0.685	0.709	0.729	0.747	0.763	0.777
57	0.580	0.615	0.646	0.673	0.696	0.717	0.735	0.752	0.766

Age Last Birthday of Husband	*Less than 8.50%*	*8.50% or between 8.50% and 9.50%*	*9.50% or between 9.50% and 10.50%*	*10.50% or between 10.50% and 11.50%*	*11.50% or between 11.50% and 12.50%*	*12.50% or between 12.50% and 13.50%*	*13.50% or between 13.50% and 14.50%*	*14.50% or between 14.50% and 15.50%*	*15.50% or more*
58	0.567	0.602	0.633	0.660	0.683	0.705	0.723	0.740	0.755
59	0.553	0.588	0.619	0.646	0.670	0.692	0.711	0.728	0.743
60	0.539	0.574	0.605	0.632	0.657	0.678	0.698	0.715	0.731
61	0.525	0.560	0.590	0.618	0.642	0.664	0.684	0.702	0.718
62	0.510	0.545	0.576	0.603	0.628	0.650	0.670	0.688	0.704
63	0.496	0.530	0.561	0.588	0.613	0.636	0.656	0.674	0.691
64	0.481	0.515	0.546	0.573	0.598	0.621	0.641	0.659	0.676
65	0.466	0.500	0.530	0.558	0.583	0.605	0.626	0.644	0.661
66	0.451	0.485	0.515	0.542	0.567	0.590	0.610	0.629	0.646
67	0.436	0.469	0.499	0.526	0.551	0.574	0.594	0.613	0.631
68	0.421	0.454	0.483	0.510	0.535	0.557	0.578	0.597	0.615
69	0.407	0.438	0.467	0.494	0.518	0.541	0.562	0.581	0.598
70	0.392	0.423	0.452	0.478	0.502	0.524	0.545	0.564	0.582
71	0.377	0.407	0.436	0.462	0.485	0.508	0.528	0.547	0.565
72	0.362	0.392	0.420	0.445	0.469	0.491	0.511	0.530	0.548
73	0.348	0.377	0.404	0.429	0.452	0.474	0.494	0.513	0.531
74	0.333	0.362	0.388	0.413	0.436	0.457	0.477	0.496	0.513
75	0.319	0.347	0.373	0.397	0.419	0.441	0.460	0.479	0.496
76	0.305	0.332	0.357	0.381	0.403	0.424	0.443	0.461	0.479
77	0.292	0.318	0.342	0.365	0.387	0.407	0.426	0.444	0.461
78	0.278	0.304	0.328	0.350	0.371	0.391	0.410	0.427	0.444
79	0.265	0.290	0.313	0.335	0.355	0.375	0.393	0.410	0.427
80	0.253	0.277	0.299	0.320	0.340	0.359	0.377	0.394	0.410
81	0.241	0.264	0.285	0.306	0.325	0.343	0.361	0.377	0.393

Age Last Birthday of Husband	*Less than 8.50%*	*8.50% or between 8.50% and 9.50%*	*9.50% or between 9.50% and 10.50%*	*10.50% or between 10.50% and 11.50%*	*11.50% or between 11.50% and 12.50%*	*12.50% or between 12.50% and 13.50%*	*13.50% or between 13.50% and 14.50%*	*14.50% or between 14.50% and 15.50%*	*15.50% or more*
82	0.229	0.251	0.272	0.292	0.310	0.328	0.345	0.361	0.377
83	0.218	0.239	0.259	0.278	0.296	0.313	0.330	0.346	0.361
84	0.207	0.227	0.246	0.265	0.282	0.299	0.315	0.331	0.345
85	0.196	0.216	0.234	0.252	0.269	0.285	0.301	0.316	0.330
86	0.186	0.205	0.223	0.240	0.256	0.272	0.287	0.302	0.315
87	0.177	0.195	0.212	0.228	0.244	0.259	0.274	0.288	0.301
88	0.168	0.185	0.201	0.217	0.232	0.247	0.261	0.275	0.288
89	0.159	0.176	0.191	0.207	0.221	0.235	0.249	0.262	0.275
90	0.151	0.167	0.182	0.197	0.211	0.224	0.237	0.250	0.262
91	0.144	0.159	0.173	0.187	0.201	0.214	0.227	0.239	0.251
92	0.137	0.151	0.165	0.179	0.192	0.205	0.217	0.229	0.240
93	0.130	0.144	0.158	0.171	0.183	0.196	0.208	0.219	0.230
94	0.124	0.138	0.151	0.163	0.175	0.187	0.199	0.210	0.221
95	0.119	0.132	0.144	0.156	0.168	0.179	0.190	0.201	0.212
96	0.113	0.126	0.138	0.149	0.161	0.172	0.182	0.193	0.203
97	0.108	0.120	0.132	0.143	0.154	0.164	0.175	0.185	0.195
98	0.103	0.115	0.126	0.137	0.147	0.157	0.167	0.177	0.187
99	0.098	0.109	0.119	0.130	0.140	0.150	0.159	0.169	0.178
100 and over	0.093	0.103	0.112	0.123	0.133	0.143	0.151	0.161	0.169

Table 2 Multiplier to be applied to the part or the residuary estate in respect of which the election is exercised to obtain the capital value of the life interest of a surviving wife, when the average gross redemption yield on medium coupon fifteen-year Government Stocks is at the rate shown.

Age Last Birthday of Wife	*Less than 8.50%*	*8.50% or between 8.50% and 9.50%*	*9.50% or between 9.50% and 10.50%*	*10.50% or between 10.50% and 11.50%*	*11.50% or between 11.50% and 12.50%*	*12.50% or between 12.50% and 13.50%*	*13.50% or between 13.50% and 14.50%*	*14.50% or between 14.50% and 15.50%*	*15.50% or more*
16	0.892	0.905	0.915	0.922	0.927	0.930	0.933	0.936	0.937
17	0.889	0.903	0.913	0.920	0.925	0.929	0.933	0.935	0.937
18	0.887	0.901	0.911	0.919	0.924	0.929	0.932	0.934	0.936
19	0.884	0.899	0.910	0.917	0.923	0.928	0.931	0.934	0.936
20	0.882	0.897	0.908	0.916	0.922	0.927	0.930	0.933	0.935
21	0.879	0.895	0.906	0.915	0.921	0.926	0.929	0.932	0.934
22	0.877	0.893	0.904	0.913	0.920	0.925	0.928	0.931	0.934
23	0.874	0.890	0.902	0.911	0.918	0.923	0.927	0.931	0.933
24	0.871	0.888	0.900	0.910	0.917	0.922	0.926	0.930	0.932
25	0.868	0.885	0.898	0.908	0.915	0.921	0.925	0.929	0.932
26	0.864	0.882	0.896	0.906	0.914	0.920	0.924	0.928	0.931
27	0.861	0.879	0.893	0.904	0.912	0.918	0.923	0.927	0.930
28	0.857	0.876	0.891	0.901	0.910	0.916	0.921	0.925	0.929
29	0.853	0.873	0.888	0.899	0.908	0.915	0.920	0.924	0.928
30	0.849	0.869	0.885	0.896	0.906	0.913	0.918	0.923	0.926
31	0.845	0.866	0.882	0.894	0.903	0.911	0.916	0.921	0.925
32	0.840	0.862	0.878	0.891	0.901	0.908	0.914	0.919	0.923
33	0.836	0.858	0.875	0.888	0.898	0.906	0.912	0.918	0.922
34	0.831	0.853	0.871	0.884	0.895	0.903	0.910	0.916	0.920

Age Last Birthday of Wife	*Less than 8.50%*	*8.50% or between 8.50% and 9.50%*	*9.50% or between 9.50% and 10.50%*	*10.50% or between 10.50% and 11.50%*	*11.50% or between 11.50% and 12.50%*	*12.50% or between 12.50% and 13.50%*	*13.50% or between 13.50% and 14.50%*	*14.50% or between 14.50% and 15.50%*	*15.50% or more*
35	0.826	0.849	0.867	0.881	0.892	0.901	0.908	0.913	0.918
36	0.820	0.844	0.863	0.877	0.889	0.898	0.905	0.911	0.916
37	0.815	0.839	0.858	0.873	0.885	0.895	0.902	0.909	0.914
38	0.809	0.834	0.853	0.869	0.881	0.891	0.899	0.906	0.911
39	0.803	0.828	0.848	0.864	0.877	0.888	0.896	0.903	0.909
40	0.796	0.822	0.843	0.860	0.873	0.884	0.893	0.900	0.906
41	0.790	0.816	0.838	0.855	0.869	0.880	0.889	0.897	0.903
42	0.783	0.810	0.832	0.850	0.864	0.876	0.885	0.893	0.900
43	0.775	0.803	0.826	0.844	0.859	0.871	0.881	0.889	0.896
44	0.768	0.796	0.820	0.838	0.854	0.866	0.877	0.885	0.893
45	0.760	0.789	0.813	0.832	0.848	0.861	0.872	0.881	0.889
46	0.752	0.782	0.806	0.826	0.842	0.856	0.867	0.876	0.885
47	0.744	0.774	0.799	0.819	0.836	0.850	0.862	0.872	0.880
48	0.735	0.766	0.791	0.812	0.829	0.844	0.856	0.866	0.875
49	0.726	0.757	0.783	0.804	0.822	0.837	0.850	0.861	0.870
50	0.716	0.748	0.775	0.797	0.815	0.831	0.844	0.855	0.865
51	0.707	0.739	0.766	0.788	0.807	0.823	0.837	0.849	0.859
52	0.697	0.729	0.757	0.780	0.799	0.816	0.830	0.842	0.853
53	0.686	0.719	0.747	0.771	0.791	0.808	0.822	0.835	0.846
54	0.676	0.709	0.737	0.761	0.782	0.799	0.814	0.827	0.839
55	0.664	0.698	0.727	0.751	0.772	0.790	0.806	0.820	0.831
56	0.653	0.687	0.716	0.741	0.763	0.781	0.797	0.811	0.823
57	0.641	0.676	0.705	0.730	0.752	0.771	0.788	0.802	0.815
58	0.629	0.664	0.693	0.719	0.741	0.761	0.778	0.793	0.806

Age Last Birthday of Wife	*Less than 8.50%*	*8.50% or between 8.50% and 9.50%*	*9.50% or between 9.50% and 10.50%*	*10.50% or between 10.50% and 11.50%*	*11.50% or between 11.50% and 12.50%*	*12.50% or between 12.50% and 13.50%*	*13.50% or between 13.50% and 14.50%*	*14.50% or between 14.50% and 15.50%*	*15.50% or more*
59	0.616	0.651	0.681	0.707	0.730	0.750	0.767	0.783	0.796
60	0.603	0.638	0.669	0.695	0.718	0.739	0.757	0.772	0.786
61	0.590	0.625	0.656	0.683	0.706	0.727	0.745	0.761	0.776
62	0.577	0.612	0.643	0.670	0.693	0.715	0.733	0.750	0.764
63	0.563	0.598	0.629	0.656	0.680	0.702	0.721	0.738	0.753
64	0.549	0.584	0.615	0.642	0.667	0.688	0.708	0.725	0.740
65	0.534	0.569	0.600	0.628	0.653	0.674	0.694	0.712	0.728
66	0.520	0.555	0.586	0.613	0.638	0.660	0.680	0.698	0.714
67	0.505	0.540	0.570	0.598	0.623	0.645	0.666	0.684	0.700
68	0.490	0.524	0.555	0.583	0.608	0.630	0.651	0.669	0.686
69	0.475	0.509	0.539	0.567	0.592	0.615	0.635	0.654	0.671
70	0.459	0.493	0.523	0.551	0.576	0.599	0.619	0.638	0.655
71	0.444	0.477	0.507	0.535	0.560	0.582	0.603	0.622	0.640
72	0.428	0.461	0.491	0.518	0.543	0.566	0.586	0.606	0.623
73	0.413	0.445	0.475	0.501	0.526	0.549	0.570	0.589	0.606
74	0.398	0.429	0.458	0.485	0.509	0.532	0.552	0.572	0.589
75	0.382	0.413	0.442	0.468	0.492	0.514	0.535	0.554	0.572
76	0.367	0.397	0.425	0.451	0.475	0.497	0.517	0.536	0.554
77	0.352	0.381	0.408	0.434	0.457	0.479	0.499	0.518	0.536
78	0.337	0.365	0.392	0.417	0.440	0.461	0.482	0.500	0.518
79	0.322	0.350	0.376	0.400	0.423	0.444	0.464	0.482	0.500
80	0.307	0.334	0.360	0.383	0.406	0.426	0.446	0.464	0.482
81	0.293	0.319	0.344	0.367	0.389	0.409	0.428	0.446	0.463
82	0.279	0.304	0.328	0.351	0.372	0.392	0.410	0.428	0.445

Age Last Birthday of Wife	*Less than 8.50%*	*8.50% or between 8.50% and 9.50%*	*9.50% or between 9.50% and 10.50%*	*10.50% or between 10.50% and 11.50%*	*11.50% or between 11.50% and 12.50%*	*12.50% or between 12.50% and 13.50%*	*13.50% or between 13.50% and 14.50%*	*14.50% or between 14.50% and 15.50%*	*15.50% or more*
83	0.265	0.290	0.313	0.335	0.355	0.375	0.393	0.410	0.427
84	0.252	0.276	0.298	0.319	0.339	0.358	0.376	0.393	0.409
85	0.239	0.262	0.284	0.304	0.323	0.342	0.359	0.376	0.392
86	0.227	0.249	0.269	0.289	0.308	0.326	0.343	0.359	0.374
87	0.215	0.236	0.256	0.275	0.293	0.310	0.327	0.342	0.357
88	0.204	0.224	0.243	0.261	0.279	0.295	0.311	0.327	0.341
89	0.193	0.212	0.230	0.248	0.265	0.281	0.296	0.311	0.325
90	0.182	0.201	0.218	0.235	0.251	0.267	0.282	0.296	0.310
91	0.173	0.190	0.207	0.223	0.239	0.254	0.268	0.282	0.296
92	0.164	0.180	0.197	0.212	0.227	0.242	0.256	0.269	0.282
93	0.155	0.171	0.187	0.202	0.216	0.230	0.243	0.256	0.269
94	0.147	0.162	0.177	0.192	0.205	0.219	0.232	0.244	0.256
95	0.139	0.154	0.168	0.182	0.195	0.208	0.221	0.233	0.244
96	0.132	0.146	0.159	0.173	0.185	0.198	0.210	0.222	0.233
97	0.125	0.138	0.151	0.164	0.176	0.188	0.199	0.211	0.222
98	0.118	0.130	0.143	0.155	0.167	0.178	0.189	0.200	0.210
99	0.110	0.122	0.134	0.146	0.157	0.168	0.178	0.189	0.199
100 and over	0.102	0.114	0.125	0.137	0.147	0.158	0.167	0.178	0.188

CIVIL PARTNERSHIP ACT 2004

(2004 c)

[18 November 2004]

[244.130]

Note. This Act, which came into force on 5 December 2005, gives legal recognition to same-sex relationships by permitting two persons of the same sex to register their relationship as a civil partnership and by conferring on civil partnership effectively the same status as marriage. The provisions of the Act relating to the formation, dissolution and annulment of civil partnerships are beyond the scope of this work, but the Act modifies the law of relating to wills, intestate succession and family provision. These changes are effected principally by amending existing legislation, notably WA 1837, AEA 1925 and I(PFD)A 1975. These amendments are noted elsewhere. The Act also contains express provisions concerning succession which are set out below.

PART 1
INTRODUCTION

[244.131]

1 Civil partnership (1) A civil partnership is a relationship between two people of the same sex ('civil partners')—

(a) which is formed when they register as civil partners of each other—
  (i) in England or Wales (under Part 2),
  (ii) in Scotland (under Part 3),
  (iii) in Northern Ireland (under Part 4), or
  (iv) outside the United Kingdom under an Order in Council made under Chapter 1 of Part 5 (registration at British consulates etc or by armed forces personnel), or

(b) which they are treated under Chapter 2 of Part 5 as having formed (at the time determined under that Chapter) by virtue of having registered an overseas relationship.

(2) Subsection (1) is subject to the provisions of this Act under or by virtue of which a civil partnership is void.
(3) A civil partnership ends only on death, dissolution or annulment.
(4) The references in subsection (3) to dissolution and annulment are to dissolution and annulment having effect under or recognised in accordance with this Act.
(5) [*Not reproduced here.*]

PART 2
CIVIL PARTNERSHIP: ENGLAND AND WALES

CHAPTER 3
PROPERTY AND FINANCIAL ARRANGEMENTS

[244.132]

71 Wills, administration of estates and family provision Schedule 4 amends enactments relating to wills, administration of estates and family provision so that they apply in relation to civil partnerships as they apply in relation to marriage.

SCHEDULE 4
WILLS, ADMINISTRATION OF ESTATES AND FAMILY PROVISION

PART 1
WILLS

[244.133]
1 Amend the Wills Act 1837 (c 26) as follows.
2 [*This paragraph inserts ss 18B and 18C after s 18A. For the text of these two new sections see paras* **[244.19]** *and* **[244.20]** *above*].
3 The following provisions—

(a) section 15 of the Wills Act 1837 (c 26) (avoidance of gifts to attesting witnesses and their spouses), and
(b) section 1 of the Wills Act 1968 (c 28) (restriction of operation of section 15),

apply in relation to the attestation of a will by a person to whose civil partner there is given or made any such disposition as is described in section 15 of the 1837 Act as they apply in relation to a person to whose spouse there is given or made any such disposition.

4 [*This paragraph amends s 16 of the Wills Act 1837: see Note to para* **[244.13]** *above.*]
5 Except where a contrary intention is shown, it is presumed that if a testator—

(a) devises or bequeaths property to his civil partner in terms which in themselves would give an absolute interest to the civil partner, but
(b) by the same instrument purports to give his issue an interest in the same property,

the gift to the civil partner is absolute despite the purported gift to the issue.

PART 2
ADMINISTRATION OF ESTATES AND FAMILY PROVISION

[244.134]
7–11 [*These paragraphs amend Part IV of Administration of Estates Act 1925. The relevant sections are reprinted as amended in paras* **[244.62]** ff, *above.*]
12 [*This paragraph amends s 55(1)(xviii) of Administration of Estates Act 1925; see note to para* **[246.67]**, *below.*]
13 [*This paragraph amends Intestates' Estates Act 1952, s 5 and Sch 2: see note to para* **[244.73]**, *above.*]
14 [*This paragraph amends Family Provision Act 1966, s 1(1): see note to para* **[244.62]**, *above.*]
15–27 [*These paragraphs make extensive amendments to Inheritance (Provision for Family and Dependants) Act 1975. The entire Act is reprinted as amended at paras* **[247.1]** ff, *below.*]

MENTAL CAPACITY ACT 2005

(2005 c 9)

[7 April 2005]

[244.135]

Note. This Act, which was brought into force on 1 October 2007, provides for the first time a statutory definition of capacity. The provisions of Part VII of MeHA 1983 which cater for the management of the property and affairs of a patient, and in particular confer power to make a will, are repealed and replaced by the provisions set out below. Section 42 of the 2005 Act gives power to the Lord Chancellor to issue and revise one or more codes of practice. A Code of Practice was issued on 23 April 2007. It is a very lengthy document and, although the Code is of general relevance to questions of testamentary capacity, very little of it is directly concerned with testamentary capacity. The three paragraphs in Chapter 4 of the Code in which testamentary capacity is directly considered are printed in para **[244.146]** below.

PART 1
PERSONS WHO LACK CAPACITY

The principles

[244.136]

1 The principles (1) The following principles apply for the purposes of this Act.

(2) A person must be assumed to have capacity unless it is established that he lacks capacity.

(3) A person is not to be treated as unable to make a decision unless all practicable steps to help him to do so have been taken without success.

(4) A person is not to be treated as unable to make a decision merely because he makes an unwise decision.

(5) An act done, or decision made, under this Act for or on behalf of a person who lacks capacity must be done, or made, in his best interests.

(6) Before the act is done, or the decision is made, regard must be had to whether the purpose for which it is needed can be as effectively achieved in a way that is less restrictive of the person's rights and freedom of action.

Preliminary

[244.137]

2 People who lack capacity (1) For the purposes of this Act, a person lacks capacity in relation to a matter if at the material time he is unable to make a decision for himself in relation to the matter because of an impairment of, or a disturbance in the functioning of, the mind or brain.

(2) It does not matter whether the impairment or disturbance is permanent or temporary.

(3) A lack of capacity cannot be established merely by reference to—

(a) a person's age or appearance, or
(b) a condition of his, or an aspect of his behaviour, which might lead others to make unjustified assumptions about his capacity.

(4) In proceedings under this Act or any other enactment, any question whether a person lacks capacity within the meaning of this Act must be decided on the balance of probabilities.
(5) No power which a person ('D') may exercise under this Act—

(a) in relation to a person who lacks capacity, or
(b) where D reasonably thinks that a person lacks capacity,

is exercisable in relation to a person under 16.
(6) Subsection (5) is subject to section 18(3).

[244.138]
3 Inability to make decisions (1) For the purposes of section 2, a person is unable to make a decision for himself if he is unable—

(a) to understand the information relevant to the decision,
(b) to retain that information,
(c) to use or weigh that information as part of the process of making the decision, or
(d) to communicate his decision (whether by talking, using sign language or any other means).

(2) A person is not to be regarded as unable to understand the information relevant to a decision if he is able to understand an explanation of it given to him in a way that is appropriate to his circumstances (using simple language, visual aids or any other means).
(3) The fact that a person is able to retain the information relevant to a decision for a short period only does not prevent him from being regarded as able to make the decision.
(4) The information relevant to a decision includes information about the reasonably foreseeable consequences of—

(a) deciding one way or another, or
(b) failing to make the decision.

[244.139]
4 Best interests (1) In determining for the purposes of this Act what is in a person's best interests, the person making the determination must not make it merely on the basis of—

(a) the person's age or appearance, or
(b) a condition of his, or an aspect of his behaviour, which might lead others to make unjustified assumptions about what might be in his best interests.

(2) The person making the determination must consider all the relevant circumstances and, in particular, take the following steps.
(3) He must consider—

(a) whether it is likely that the person will at some time have capacity in relation to the matter in question, and
(b) if it appears likely that he will, when that is likely to be.

(4) He must, so far as reasonably practicable, permit and encourage the person to participate, or to improve his ability to participate, as fully as possible in any act done for him and any decision affecting him.

(5) Where the determination relates to life-sustaining treatment he must not, in considering whether the treatment is in the best interests of the person concerned, be motivated by a desire to bring about his death.
(6) He must consider, so far as is reasonably ascertainable—

- (a) the person's past and present wishes and feelings (and, in particular, any relevant written statement made by him when he had capacity),
- (b) the beliefs and values that would be likely to influence his decision if he had capacity, and
- (c) the other factors that he would be likely to consider if he were able to do so.

(7) He must take into account, if it is practicable and appropriate to consult them, the views of—

- (a) anyone named by the person as someone to be consulted on the matter in question or on matters of that kind,
- (b) anyone engaged in caring for the person or interested in his welfare,
- (c) any donee of a lasting power of attorney granted by the person, and
- (d) any deputy appointed for the person by the court,

as to what would be in the person's best interests and, in particular, as to the matters mentioned in subsection (6).
(8) The duties imposed by subsections (1) to (7) also apply in relation to the exercise of any powers which—

- (a) are exercisable under a lasting power of attorney, or
- (b) are exercisable by a person under this Act where he reasonably believes that another person lacks capacity.

(9) In the case of an act done, or a decision made, by a person other than the court, there is sufficient compliance with this section if (having complied with the requirements of subsections (1) to (7)) he reasonably believes that what he does or decides is in the best interests of the person concerned.
(10) 'Life-sustaining treatment' means treatment which in the view of a person providing health care for the person concerned is necessary to sustain life.
(11) 'Relevant circumstances' are those—

- (a) of which the person making the determination is aware, and
- (b) which it would be reasonable to regard as relevant.

* * * * *

[244.140]
16 Powers to make decisions and appoint deputies: general (1) This section applies if a person ('P') lacks capacity in relation to a matter or matters concerning—

- (a) P's personal welfare, or
- (b) P's property and affairs.

(2) The court may—

(a) by making an order, make the decision or decisions on P's behalf in relation to the matter or matters.

* * * * *

(3) The powers of the court under this section are subject to the provisions of this Act and, in particular, to sections 1 (the principles) and 4 (best interests).

* * * * *

(6) Without prejudice to section 4, the court may make the order, give the directions or make the appointment on such terms as it considers are in P's best interests, even though no application is before the court for an order, directions or an appointment on those terms.
(7) An order of the court may be varied or discharged by a subsequent order.

* * * * *

[244.141]
18 Section 16 powers: property and affairs (1) The powers under section 16 as respects P's property and affairs extend in particular to—

* * * * *

(h) the settlement of any of P's property, whether for P's benefit or for the benefit of others;
(i) the execution for P of a will;
(j) the exercise of any power (including a power to consent) vested in P whether beneficially or as trustee or otherwise

* * * * *

(2) No will may be made under subsection (1)(i) at a time when P has not reached 18.

* * * * *

(4) Schedule 2 supplements the provisions of this section.
(5) Section 16(7) (variation and discharge of court orders) is subject to paragraph 6 of Schedule 2.

* * * * *

Miscellaneous and supplementary

[244.142]
42 Codes of practice (1) The Lord Chancellor must prepare and issue one or more codes of practice

(a) for the guidance of persons assessing whether a person has capacity in relation to any matter,
(b) for the guidance of persons acting in connection with the care or treatment of another person (see section 5),

(c) for the guidance of donees of lasting powers of attorney,
(d) for the guidance of deputies appointed by the court,
(e) for the guidance of persons carrying out research in reliance on any provision made by or under this Act (and otherwise with respect to sections 30 to 34),
(f) for the guidance of independent mental capacity advocates,
[(fa) for the guidance of persons exercising functions under Schedule A1,
(fb) for the guidance of representatives appointed under Part 10 of Schedule A1,][1]
(g) with respect to the provisions of sections 24 to 26 (advance decisions and apparent advance decisions), and
(h) with respect to such other matters concerned with this Act as he thinks fit.

(2) The Lord Chancellor may from time to time revise a code.
The Lord Chancellor may delegate the preparation or revision of the whole or any part of a code so far as he considers expedient.
(3) It is the duty of a person to have regard to any relevant code if he is acting in relation to a person who lacks capacity and is doing so in one or more of the following ways —

(a) as the donee of a lasting power of attorney,
(b) as a deputy appointed by the court,
(c) as a person carrying out research in reliance on any provision made by or under this Act (see sections 30 to 34),
(d) as an independent mental capacity advocate,
(e) in a professional capacity,
(f) for remuneration.

(5) If it appears to a court or tribunal conducting any criminal or civil proceedings that

(a) a provision of a code, or
(b) a failure to comply with a code,

is relevant to a question arising in the proceedings, the provision or failure must be taken into account in deciding the question.

(6) A code under subsection (1)(d) may contain separate guidance for deputies appointed by virtue of paragraph 1(2) of Schedule 5 (functions of deputy conferred on receiver appointed under the Mental Health Act).
(7) In this section and in section 43, 'code' means a code prepared or revised under this section.
* * * * *

[1] Sub-s (1): paras (fa), (fb) inserted by the Mental Health Act 2007, s 50(7), Sch 9, Pt 1, paras 1, 8(1), (2) from a date to be appointed.

PART 3
MISCELLANEOUS AND GENERAL

General

[244.143]
64 Interpretation (1) In this Act—

'will' includes codicil.

[244.144]
69 Short title This Act may be cited as the Mental Capacity Act 2005.

SCHEDULE 2
PROPERTY AND AFFAIRS: SUPPLEMENTARY PROVISIONS

Section 18(4)

Wills: general

[244.145]
1 Paragraphs 2 to 4 apply in relation to the execution of a will, by virtue of section 18, on behalf of P.

Provision that may be made in will
2 The will may make any provision (whether by disposing of property or exercising a power or otherwise) which could be made by a will executed by P if he had capacity to make it.

Wills: requirements relating to execution
3 (1) Sub-paragraph (2) applies if under section 16 the court makes an order or gives directions requiring or authorising a person ('the authorised person') to execute a will on behalf of P.
(2) Any will executed in pursuance of the order or direction—

(a) must state that it is signed by P acting by the authorised person,
(b) must be signed by the authorised person with the name of P and his own name, in the presence of two or more witnesses present at the same time,
(c) must be attested and subscribed by those witnesses in the presence of the authorised person, and
(d) must be sealed with the official seal of the court.

Wills: effect of execution

4 (1) This paragraph applies where a will is executed in accordance with paragraph 3.

(2) The Wills Act 1837 (c 26) has effect in relation to the will as if it were signed by P by his own hand, except that—

- (a) s 9 of the 1837 Act (requirements as to signing and attestation) does not apply, and
- (b) in the subsequent provisions of the 1837 Act any reference to execution in the manner required by the previous provisions is to be read as a reference to execution in accordance with paragraph 3.

(3) The will has the same effect for all purposes as if—

- (a) P had had the capacity to make a valid will, and
- (b) the will had been executed by him in the manner required by the 1837 Act.

(4) But sub-paragraph (3) does not have effect in relation to the will—

- (a) in so far as it disposes of immovable property outside England and Wales, or
- (b) in so far as it relates to any other property or matter if, when the will is executed—
  - (i) P is domiciled outside England and Wales, and
  - (ii) the condition in sub-paragraph (5) is met.

(3) The condition is that, under the law of P's domicile, any question of his testamentary capacity would fall to be determined in accordance with the law of a place outside England and Wales.

CODE OF PRACTICE

* * * * *

4. HOW DOES THE ACT DEFINE A PERSON'S CAPACITY AND HOW SHOULD CAPACITY BE ASSESSED?

[244.146]

WHAT OTHER LEGAL TESTS OF CAPACITY ARE THERE?

4.31 The Act makes clear that the definition of 'lack of capacity' and the two-stage test for capacity set out in the Act are 'for the purposes of this Act'. This means that the definition and test are to be used in situations covered by this Act. Schedule 6 of the Act also amends existing laws to ensure that the definition and test are used in other areas of law not covered directly by this Act.

For example, Schedule 6, paragraph 20 allows a person to be disqualified from jury service if they lack the capacity (using this Act's definition) to carry out a juror's tasks.

4.32 There are several tests of capacity that have been produced following judgments in court cases (known as common law tests).[1] These cover:

capacity to make a will[2]
capacity to make a gift
capacity to enter into a contract

capacity to litigate (take part in legal cases), and
capacity to enter into marriage.

4.33 The Act's new definition of capacity is in line with the existing common law tests, and the Act does not replace them. When cases come before the court on the above issues, judges can adopt the new definition if they think it is appropriate. The Act will apply to all other cases relating to financial, healthcare or welfare decisions.

[1] See Note to the Mental Capacity Act 2005 at para **[244.135]** above.

[2] The case cited in the Code in this context is *Banks v Goodfellow* (1870) LR 5 QB 549 CA.

SECTION 2

Succession rights and adoption, legitimation, illegitimacy and change of gender

[245.1]

Note. This Section reproduces in chronological order all the statutory provisions which have governed and now govern the property rights of adopted, legitimated, and illegitimate children under dispositions of property and the rules of intestate succession. They also of course govern the rights of such children's parents and other relatives. We have omitted the Adoption of Children Act 1949, the relevant provisions of which were replaced retrospectively from the same commencement date by the Adoption Act 1950, and the provisions of the Children Act 1975 concerning the effects of legitimation and adoption which were replaced, again with retrospective effect from the same commencement date, by the Legitimacy Act 1976 (LA 1976) and the Adoption Act 1976 (AA 1976).

The main effect of these statutes has been to reverse the common law presumptions as to the meaning of words descriptive of family relationships in dispositions of property, such as wills or settlements (for these presumptions see Vol 1, paras **[72.1]** and **[75.1]** ff) and to enlarge the categories of issue who can take under the intestacy rules. With one exception, each change in the law has only applied to dispositions made after the change in the law has taken effect, and so the repealed statutes included here continue to be relevant to dispositions made when they were in force. The exception is to be found in the Human Fertilisation and Embryology Act 1990 (HFEA 1990), s 29(3) at para **[245.87]** below.

At common law references to children were presumed to be references to legitimate children, i e children born in lawful wedlock, and references to other relationships were likewise confined to persons who were legitimate and who claimed descent or kinship exclusively through persons who were legitimate. Not only were illegitimate persons excluded but also persons who were adopted or legitimated. Statute has made progressive inroads on the austerity of the common law rule. As regards adopted and legitimated children this process culminated in the Children Act 1975 which provided that in relation to instruments made on or after 1 January 1976 (including the wills whenever made of persons dying on or after that date) references to children (or persons related in any other way) were to be deemed in the absence of a contrary intention to include references to adopted and legitimated children (or persons who were adopted or legitimated and claimed descent or kinship through adopted or legitimated persons) and to be deemed to do so whether the adoption or legitimation occurred before or after the date of the instrument or death. The relevant provisions of the Children Act 1975 are not reproduced in this section as they were replaced (with effect from the same commencement date) by the identical provisions of the LA 1976 and the AA 1976.

As regards illegitimate persons the process of development culminated in the comprehensive provisions contained in the Family Law Reform Act 1987 (FLRA 1987) which provides that in relation to instruments made on or after the commencement of the Act (which in the case of wills means wills actually made and not merely confirmed by codicil on or after that time) references to children (or other relatives) are to be deemed to include illegitimate children (or persons claiming kinship through illegitimate persons). This Act (which replaced the more limited provisions of the Family Law Reform Act 1969 (FLRA 1969) was brought into force on 4 April 1988. (For the background to the Act see the Law Commission's Second Report on Illegitimacy, October 1986 (Law Com No 157, Cmnd 9913).)

Mention should also be made of the HFEA 1990 which makes special provision in relation to persons born as a result of artificial insemination, in vitro fertilization or other artificial means.

In relation to older instruments, however, the superseded rules of construction may still be relevant. This section therefore reproduces all the relevant statutory provisions.

For an account of the law governing the property rights of adopted, legitimated and illegimate children see Vol 1, paras **[72.1]** ff and **[75.1]** ff.

Mention should finally be made of the Gender Recognition Act 2004 (paras **[245.102]** ff below) which was brought into force on 4 April 2005. This Act makes provision for changes of gender to be legally recognised, a process which may affect succession rights: see Note at para **[245.102]** below.

ADOPTION OF CHILDREN ACT 1926

(16 & 17 Geo 5 c 29)

[4 August 1926]

[245.2]

Note. Before the passing of this Act adoption had never been recognised by the law, though agreements may have been made which for many purposes placed a stranger in loco parentis. But an adoption order under the Act did not affect rights of succession on an intestacy or the construction of references to children and issue in wills or other dispositions of property.

[245.3]

1. Power to make adoption orders.— (*1*) *Upon an application in the prescribed manner by any person desirous of being authorised to adopt an infant who has never been married, the Court may, subject to the provisions of this Act, make an order (in this Act referred to as 'an adoption order') authorising the applicant to adopt that infant.*

(*2*) *A person so authorised to adopt the infant and an infant authorised to be adopted are in this Act referred to as an 'adopter' and an 'adopted child' respectively, and 'infant' means a person under the age of twenty-one.*

* * * * *

[245.4]

5. Effect of adoption order.

* * * * *

(*2*) *An adoption order shall not deprive the adopted child of any right to or interest in property to which, but for the order, the child would have been entitled under any intestacy or disposition, whether occurring or made before or after the making of the adoption order, or confer on the adopted child any right to or interest in property as a child of the adopter, and the expressions 'child,' 'children' and 'issue' where used in any disposition whether made before or after the making of an adoption order, shall not, unless the contrary intention appears, include an adopted child or children or the issue of an adopted child.*[1]

* * * * *

(*4*) *For the purposes of this section 'disposition' means an assurance of any interest in property by any instrument whether inter vivos or by will including codicil.*

1 Sub-s (2): repealed with effect from 1 January 1950 by the Adoption of Children Act 1949, ss 10(5), 16(3).

* * * * *

[245.5]
12. Short title, commencement and extent.— (*1*) *This Act may be cited as the Adoption of Children Act 1926.*
(*2*) *This Act shall come into operation on the first day of January, nineteen hundred and twenty-seven.*
(*3*) *This Act shall not apply to Scotland or Northern Ireland.*

LEGITIMACY ACT 1926

(16 & 17 Geo 5 c 60)

[15 December 1926]

[245.6]

Note. This Act, which came into force on 1 January 1927, recognised, for the first time in English law, the principle of legitimation by the subsequent marriage of the illegitimate child's parents. Legitimation by subsequent marriage was expressly excluded by this Act in cases where either parent was married to a third person at the date of the child's birth. This bar was removed by the Legitimacy Act 1959, s 1 (para **[245.32]**) with effect from 29 October 1959. The Legitimacy Act 1926, unlike the Adoption of Children Act 1926 (paras **[245.2]**–**[245.5]**) provided for legitimation to confer property rights on legitimated children by deeming the legitimated child to have been born legitimate, but only in relation to intestacies or dispositions (including wills) taking effect after the date of legitimation. These provisions were replaced for most purposes by the FLRA 1969, s 15(4) (para **[245.39]**) and wholly replaced by the Children Act 1975, which was itself replaced by identical provisions in the LA 1976 (paras **[245.43]**–**[245.54]**) and the AA 1976 (paras **[245.55]**–**[245.68]**) in relation to dispositions on or after 1 January 1976.

[245.7]
1. Legitimation by subsequent marriage of parents.— (*1*) *Subject to the provisions of this section, where the parents of an illegitimate person marry or have married one another, whether before or after the commencement of this Act, the marriage shall, if the father of the illegitimate person was or is at the date of the marriage domiciled in England or Wales, render that person, if living, legitimate from the commencement of this Act, or from the date of the marriage, whichever last happens.*[1]
(*2*) *Nothing in this Act shall operate to legitimate a person whose father or mother was married to a third person when the illegitimate person was born.*[2]
(*3*) *The legitimation of a person under this Act does not enable him or his spouse, children or remoter issue to take any interest in real or personal property save as is hereinafter in this Act expressly provided.*[3]

1 Sub-s (1): repealed by the Legitimacy Act 1976, Sch 2.
2 Sub-s (2): repealed with effect from 29 October 1959 by the Legitimacy Act 1959, ss 1(1), 6(3), paras **[245.32]** and **[245.34]**.

3 Sub-s (3): repealed with effect from 1 January 1976 by the Children Act 1975, ss 108(1)(b), (4)(d), Sch 2, Pt II.

* * * * *

[245.8]

3. Rights of legitimated persons, etc, to take interests in property.— (*1*) *Subject to the provisions of this Act, a legitimated person and his spouse, children or more remote issue shall be entitled to take any interest—*

(*a*) *in the estate of an intestate dying after the date of legitimation;*
(*b*) *under any disposition coming into operation after the date of legitimation;*
(*c*) *by descent under an entailed interest created after the date of legitimation;*

in like manner as if the legitimated person had been born legitimate.

(*2*) *Where the right to any property, real or personal, depends on the relative seniority of the children of any person, and those children include one or more legitimated persons, the legitimated person or persons shall rank as if he or they had been born on the day when he or they became legitimated by virtue of this Act, and if more than one such legitimated person became legitimated at the same time, they shall rank as between themselves in order of seniority.*

(*3*) *Where property real or personal or any interest therein is limited in such a way that, if this Act had not been passed, it would (subject or not to any preceding limitations or charges) have devolved (as nearly as the law permits) along with a dignity or title of honour, then nothing in this Act shall operate to sever the property or any interest therein from such dignity, but the same shall go and devolve (without prejudice to the preceding limitations or charges aforesaid) in like manner as if this Act had not been passed. This subsection applies, whether or not there is any express reference to the dignity or title of honour and notwithstanding that in some events the property, or some interest therein, may become severed therefrom.*

(*4*) *This section applies only if and so far as a contrary intention is not expressed in the disposition, and shall have effect subject to the terms of the disposition and to the provisions therein contained.*[1]

1 This section was repealed with effect from 1 January 1976 by the Children Act 1975, s 108(1)(b), (4)(d), Sch 2, Pt II.

[245.9]

4. Succession on intestacy of legitimated persons and their issue. *Where a legitimated person or a child or remoter issue of a legitimated person dies intestate in respect of all or any of his real or personal property, the same persons shall be entitled to take the same interests therein as they would have been entitled to take if the legitimated person had been born legitimate.*[1]

1 This section was repealed with effect from 1 January 1976 by the Children Act 1975, s 108(1)(b), (4)(d), Sch 2, Pt II.

[245.10]

5. Application to illegitimate person dying before marriage of parents. *Where an illegitimate person dies after the commencement of this Act and before the marriage of his parents leaving any spouse, children or remoter issue living at the date of such marriage, then, if that person would, if living at the* *time of the marriage of his parents, have become a legitimated person, the provisions of this Act with respect to the taking of interests in property by, or in succession to, the spouse, children and remoter issue of a legitimated person (including those relating to the rate of death duties) shall apply as if such person as aforesaid had been a legitimated person and the date of the marriage of his parents had been the date of legitimation.*[1]

1 This section was repealed with effect from 1 January 1976 by the Children Act 1975, s 108(1)(b), (4)(d), Sch 2, Pt II.

* * * * *

[245.11]
8. Provisions as to persons legitimated by extraneous law.— (*1*) *Where the parents of an illegitimate person marry or have married one another, whether before or after the commencement of this Act, and the father of the illegitimate person was or is, at the time of the marriage, domiciled in a country, other than England or Wales, by the law of which the illegitimate person became legitimated by virtue of such subsequent marriage, that person, if living, shall in England and Wales be recognised as having been so legitimated from the commencement of this Act or from the date of the marriage, whichever last happens, notwithstanding that his father was not at the time of the birth of such person domiciled in a country in which legitimation by subsequent marriage was permitted by law.*
(*2*) *All the provisions of this Act relating to legitimated persons and to the taking of interests in property by or in succession to a legitimated person and the spouse, children and remoter issue of a legitimated person (including those relating to the rate of death duties) shall apply in the case of a person recognised as having been legitimated under this section, or who would, had he survived the marriage of his parents, have been so recognised; and, accordingly, this Act shall have effect as if references therein to a legitimated person included a person so recognised as having been legitimated.*
(*3*) *For the purposes of this section, the expression 'country' includes Scotland and any other part of His Majesty's Dominions, as well as a foreign country.*[1]

1 This section was repealed with effect from 22 August 1976 by the LA 1976, s 11, Sch 2.

[245.12]
9. Right of illegitimate child and mother of illegitimate child to succeed on intestacy of the other.— (1) *Where, after the commencement of this Act, the mother of an illegitimate child, such child not being a legitimated person, dies intestate as respects all or any of her real or personal property, and does not leave any legitimate issue her surviving, the illegitimate child, or, if he is dead, his issue, shall be entitled to take any interest therein to which he or such issue would have been entitled if he had been born legitimate.*
(*2*) *Where, after the commencement of this Act, an illegitimate child, not being a legitimated person, dies intestate in respect of all or any of his real or personal property, his mother if surviving shall be entitled to take any interest therein to which she would have been entitled if the child had been born legitimate and she had been the only surviving parent.*

(*3*) *This section does not apply to or affect the right of any person to take by purchase or descent any entailed interest in real or personal property.*[1]

1 This section was repealed with effect from 1 January 1970 by the FLRA 1969, s 14(7) (para **[245.38]**).

[245.13]

10. Savings.— (*1*) *Nothing in this Act shall affect the succession to any dignity or title of honour or render any person capable of succeeding to or transmitting a right to succeed to any such dignity or title.*

(*2*) *Nothing in this Act shall affect the operation or construction of any disposition coming into operation before the commencement of this Act, or affect any rights under the intestacy of a person dying before the commencement of this Act.*[1]

1 This section was repealed with effect from 1 January 1976 by the Children Act 1975, s 108(1)(b), (4)(d), Sch 2, Pt II.

[245.14]

11. Interpretation. *For the purposes of this Act, unless the context otherwise requires:—*

The expression 'legitimated person' means a person legitimated by this Act;

The expression 'date of legitimation' means the date of the marriage leading to the legitimation, or where the marriage occurred before the commencement of this Act, the commencement of this Act;

The expression 'disposition' means an assurance of any interest in property by any instrument whether inter vivos or by will;

The expression 'intestate' has the same meaning as in the Administration of Estates Act, 1925, and 'will' includes 'codicil';

The expression 'entailed interest[1]*' has the same meaning as in the Law of Property Act 1925.*[2]

1 See the LPA 1925, s 130(2).

2 This section was repealed with effect from 1 January 1976 by the Children Act 1975, s 108(1)(b), (4)(d), Sch 2, Pt II.

[245.15]

12. Short title and commencement.— (*1*) *This Act may be cited as the Legitimacy Act 1926.*

(*2*) *This Act shall come into operation on the first day of January, nineteen hundred and twenty-seven.*

(*3*) *The provisions of this Act shall, save as therein otherwise expressly provided, extend only to England and Wales.*[1]

1 This section was repealed with effect from 1 January 1976 by the Children Act 1975, s 108(1)(b), (4)(d), Sch 2, Pt II.

* * * * *

ADOPTION ACT 1950

(14 Geo 6 c 26)

[28 July 1950]

[245.16]

Note. This Act came into force on 1 October 1950 but with retrospective effect from 1 January 1950, replacing the similar provisions of the Adoption of Children Act 1949 from the commencement date of that Act. The Act of 1950 gave an adopted child the same rights of succession as a lawful child of the adopter on the death intestate of any person on or after 1 January 1950, provided that the adoption order was made before the death. The Act also reversed the common law rule of construction in relation to dispositions taking effect on or after 1 January 1950 by providing that an adopted child was to be treated as a lawful child of the adopter, provided again that the adoption order was made before the disposition. The Act provided that in the case of a will the date of the disposition was the date on which the will was made, not the date of the testator's death and, further, that a will was not to be treated as made at a later date by reason only of its having been confirmed by a codicil. These provisions were replaced in respect of deaths on or after 1 April 1959 by the very similar provisions contained in the Adoption Act 1958 (paras **[245.24]**–**[245.30]**).

PART I
ADOPTION ORDERS

MAKING OF ADOPTION ORDERS

[245.17]
1. Power to make adoption orders.— (*1*) *Subject to the provisions of this Act, the court may, upon an application made in the prescribed manner by a person domiciled in England or Scotland, make an order (in this Act referred to as an adoption order) authorising the applicant to adopt an infant.*

* * * * *

EFFECTS OF ADOPTION ORDERS

* * * * *

[245.18]
13. English intestacies, wills and settlements.— (*1*) *Where, at any time after the making of an adoption order, the adopter or the adopted person or any other person dies intestate in respect of any real or personal property (other than property subject to an entailed interest under a disposition made before the date of the adoption order), that property shall devolve in all respects as if the adopted person were the child of the adopter born in lawful wedlock and were not the child of any other person.*
(*2*) *In any disposition of real or personal property made, whether by instrument inter vivos or by will (including codicil), after the date of an adoption order—*

(*a*) *any reference (whether express or implied) to the child or children of the adopter shall, unless the contrary intention appears, be construed as, or as including, a reference to the adopted person;*
(*b*) *any reference (whether express or implied) to the child or children of the adopted person's natural parents or either of them shall, unless the contrary intention appears, be construed as not being, or as not including, a reference to the adopted person; and*
(*c*) *any reference (whether express or implied) to a person related to the*

adopted person in any degree shall, unless the contrary intention appears, be construed as a reference to the person who would be related to him in that degree if he were the child of the adopter born in lawful wedlock and were not the child of any other person.

(3) Where under any disposition any real or personal property or any interest in such property is limited (whether subject to any preceding limitation or charge or not) in such a way that would, apart from this section, devolve (as nearly as the law permits) along with a dignity or title of honour, then, whether or not the disposition contains an express reference to the dignity or title of honour, and whether or not the property or some interest in the property may in some event become severed therefrom, nothing in this section shall operate to sever the property or any interest therein from the dignity, but the property or interest shall devolve in all respects as if this section had not been enacted.

* * * * *

[245.19]
14. Provisions supplementary to s 13.— *(1) For the purposes of the application of the Administration of Estates Act 1925, to the devolution of any property in accordance with the provisions of the last foregoing section, and for the purposes of the construction of any such disposition as is mentioned in that section, an adopted person shall be deemed to be related to any other person being the child or adopted child of the adopter or (in the case of a joint adoption) of either of the adopters—*

(a) where he or she was adopted by two spouses jointly, and that other person is the child or adopted child of both of them, as brother or sister of the whole blood;
(b) in any other case, as brother or sister of the half-blood.

(2) Notwithstanding any rule of law, a disposition made by will or codicil executed before the date of an adoption order shall not be treated for the purposes of the last foregoing section as made after that date by reason only that the will or codicil is confirmed by a codicil executed after that date.
(3) Notwithstanding anything in the last foregoing section, trustees or personal representatives may convey or distribute any real or personal property to or among the persons entitled thereto without having ascertained that no adoption order has been made by virtue of which any person is or may be entitled to any interest therein, and shall not be liable to any such person of whose claim they have not had notice at the time of the conveyance or distribution; but nothing in this subsection shall prejudice the right of any such person to follow the property, or any property representing it, into the hands of any person, other than a purchaser, who may have received it.
(4) Where an adoption order is made in respect of a person who has been previously adopted, the previous adoption shall be disregarded for the purposes of the last foregoing section in relation to the devolution of any property on the death of a person dying intestate after the date of the subsequent adoption order and in relation to any disposition of property made after that date.

* * * * *

PART IV
MISCELLANEOUS AND GENERAL

* * * * *

[245.20]

45. Interpretation.— (*1*) *In this Act, unless the context otherwise requires, the following expressions have the meanings hereby respectively assigned to them, that is to say—*

* * * * *

'adoption order' has the meaning assigned to it by section one of this Act,

* * * * *

[245.21]

46. … transitional provisions. * * * * *

(*2*) *Without prejudice to the application of section thirty-eight of the Interpretation Act, 1889* (*which relates to the effect of repeals*)*, the provisions of the Fifth Schedule to this Act shall have effect in relation to the enactments repealed by this section.*

* * * * *

[245.22]

47. Short title … and commencement.— (*1*) *This Act may be cited as the Adoption Act 1950.*

* * * * *

(*3*) *This Act shall come into force on the first day of October, nineteen hundred and fifty.*

* * * * *

FIFTH SCHEDULE

Section 46

TRANSITIONAL PROVISIONS

* * * * *

[245.23]

4. *Sections thirteen to fifteen of this Act shall apply in relation to an adoption order made under the Adoption of Children Act 1926 … as if it were an adoption order within the meaning of those sections respectively:*

Provided that nothing in section thirteen of this Act shall affect the devolution of any property on the intestacy of a person who died before the first day of January, nineteen hundred and fifty, or any disposition made before that date.

* * * * *

ADOPTION ACT 1958

(7 Eliz 2 c 5)

[18 December 1958]

[245.24]

Note. This Act contains very similar provisions governing the rights of adopted children under the intestacy rules and under wills and settlements as the Adoption Act 1950 (paras **[245.16]**–**[245.23]**). The one significant difference is that a disposition by will is treated as made on the testator's death not on the date of the will. A person adopted after the execution of the will but before the testator's death was therefore eligible to take under this Act, though not under the former Act. Sections 16 and 17 of the Act came into force on 1 April 1959 and were repealed as respects things done or events occurring (e g deaths) after 31 December 1975, by the Children Act 1975, s 108, Sch 4, Pt I. Succession rights of adopted persons were regulated by the Children Act 1975, Sch 1. Those provisions were re-enacted by the AA 1976, and are contained in Part IV of that Act (paras **[245.57]**–**[245.64]**) which was brought into force on 1 January 1988 (SI 1987/1242). The AA 1976 has itself been repealed with effect from 30 December 2005 by the Adoption and Children Act 2002 (see paras **[245.92]** ff below) and the succession rights of persons adopted after that date are governed by that Act. The succession rights of persons adopted before that date continue to be governed by the AA 1976.

PART I
ADOPTION ORDERS

MAKING OF ADOPTION ORDERS

[245.25]
1. Power to make adoption orders.— (*1*) *Subject to the provisions of this Act, the court may, upon an application made in the prescribed manner by a person domiciled in England or Scotland, make an order (in this Act referred to as an adoption order) authorising the applicant to adopt an infant.*

* * * * *

EFFECTS OF ADOPTION ORDERS

* * * * *

[245.26]
16. English intestacies, wills and settlements.— (*1*) *Where, at any time after the making of an adoption order, the adopter or the adopted person or any other person dies intestate in respect of any real or personal property (other than property subject to an entailed interest under a disposition to which subsection (2) of this section does not apply), that property shall devolve in all respects as if the adopted person were the child of the adopter born in lawful wedlock and were not the child of any other person.*
(*2*) *In any disposition of real or personal property made, whether by instrument inter vivos or by will (including codicil) after the date of an adoption order—*

(*a*) *any reference (whether express or implied) to the child or children of the adopter shall, unless the contrary intention appears, be construed as, or as including a reference to the adopted person;*

(*b*) *any reference (whether express or implied) to the child or children of the adopted person's natural parents or either of them shall, unless the contrary intention appears, be construed as not being, or as not including, a reference to the adopted person; and*

(*c*) *any reference (whether express or implied) to a person related to the adopted person in any degree shall, unless the contrary intention appears, be construed as a reference to the person who would be related to him in that degree if he were the child of the adopter born in lawful wedlock and were not the child of any other person.*

(*3*) *Where under any disposition any real or personal property or any interest in such property is limited (whether subject to any preceding limitation or charge or not) in such a way that it would, apart from this section, devolve (as nearly as the law permits) along with a dignity or title of honour, then, whether or not the disposition contains an express reference to the dignity or title of honour, and whether or not the property or some interest in the property may in some event become severed therefrom, nothing in this section shall operate to sever the property or any interest therein from the dignity, but the property or interest shall devolve in all respects as if this section had not been enacted.*[1]

1 The repeal of ss 16, 17 by the Children Act 1975, s 108, Sch 4, Pt I, has effect subject to the AA 1976, s 73, Sch 2, para 6(2) (see paras **[244.66]** and **[245.68]**).

* * * * *

[245.27]
17. Provisions supplementary to s 16.— (*1*) *For the purposes of the application of the Administration of Estates Act 1925, to the devolution of any property in accordance with the provisions of the last foregoing section, and for the purposes of the construction of any such disposition as is mentioned in that section, an adopted person shall be deemed to be related to any other person being the child or adopted child of the adopter or (in the case of a joint adoption) of either of the adopters—*

(*a*) *where he or she was adopted by two spouses jointly, and that other person is the child or adopted child of both of them, as brother or sister of the whole blood;*

(*b*) *in any other case, as brother or sister of the half-blood.*

(*2*) *For the purposes of subsection (2) of the last foregoing section, a disposition made by will or codicil shall be treated as made on the date of the death of the testator.*

(*3*) *Notwithstanding anything in the last foregoing section, trustees or personal representatives may convey or distribute any real or personal property to or among the persons entitled thereto without having ascertained that no adoption order has been made by virtue of which any person is or may be entitled to any interest therein, and shall not be liable to any such person of whose claim they have not had notice at the time of the conveyance or distribution; but nothing in this subsection shall prejudice the right of any such person to follow the property, or any property representing it, into the hands of any person, other than a purchaser, who may have received it.*[1]

(*4*) *Where an adoption order is made in respect of a person who has been previously adopted, the previous adoption shall be disregarded for the purposes of the last foregoing section in relation to the devolution of any property on the death of a person dying intestate after the date of the subsequent adoption order, and in relation to any disposition of property made, or taking effect on the death of a person dying, after that date.*[2]

1 Section 17(3) was extended to adoption orders made in the Isle of Man or any of the Channel Islands by the Adoption Act 1964, s 1(1).

2 The repeal of ss 16, 17 by the Children Act 1975, s 108, Sch 4, Pt I, has effect subject to the AA 1976, s 73, Sch 2, para 6(2) (see paras **[244.66]** and **[245.68]**).

* * * * *

PART V
MISCELLANEOUS AND GENERAL

* * * * *

[245.28]

59. Transitional provisions ...— (*1*) *This Act has effect subject to the transitional provisions set out in the Fifth Schedule to this Act.*

* * * * *

[245.29]

60. Short title, extent and commencement.— (*1*) *This Act may be cited as the Adoption Act 1958.*

* * * * *

(*3*) *This Act comes into force on the first day of April, nineteen hundred and fifty-nine.*

FIFTH SCHEDULE

Section 59

TRANSITIONAL PROVISIONS

* * * * *

[245.30]

4.— (*1*) *Subject to the following provisions of this paragraph, sections sixteen to eighteen of this Act apply in relation to an adoption order made under the Adoption Act, 1950, or any enactment repealed by that Act, ... as they apply in relation to an adoption order within the meaning of those sections respectively.*

(*2*) *Nothing in sub-paragraph* (*1*) *of this paragraph affects the devolution of any property on the intestacy of a person who died before the first day of January, nineteen hundred and fifty, or any disposition made before that date.*

(3) Subsection (2) of the said section seventeen does not apply in relation to a disposition made by will or codicil executed before the commencement of this Act unless the will or codicil is confirmed by codicil executed after the commencement of this Act.
(4) Notwithstanding any rule of law, a disposition made by will or codicil executed before the date of an adoption order (within the meaning of section thirteen of the Adoption Act, 1950) shall not be treated for the purposes of section sixteen of this Act as made after that date by reason only that, before the commencement of this Act, the will or codicil was confirmed by a codicil executed after that date.

* * * * *

LEGITIMACY ACT 1959

(7 & 8 Eliz 2 c 73)

[29 July 1959]

[245.31]

Note. The Legitimacy Act 1926, s 1 (para **[245.7]**) established the principle of legitimation by subsequent marriage save in cases where either parent was married to a third person at the date of the illegitimate child's birth. This Act removed that bar. It also extended the principle of legitimacy to cases where the parents or either of them reasonably believed that they were validly married either at the time of conception or by virtue of any subsequent ceremony. These provisions came into force on 29 October 1959 and were repealed by the LA 1976 (paras **[245.43]–[245.54]**).

[245.32]
1. Amendment of Legitimacy Act 1926.— *(1) Subsection (2) of section one of the Legitimacy Act, 1926 (which excludes the operation of that Act in the case of an illegitimate person whose father or mother was married to a third person at the time of the birth) is hereby repealed.*
(2) In relation to an illegitimate person to whom it applies by virtue of this section, the Legitimacy Act 1926, shall have effect as if for references to the commencement of that Act there were substituted references to the commencement of this Act.[1]

1 This section was repealed by the LA 1976, Sch 2.

[245.33]
2. Legitimacy of children of certain void marriages.— *(1) Subject to the provisions of this section, the child of a void marriage, whether born before or after the commencement of this Act, shall be treated as the legitimate child of his parents if at the time of the act of intercourse resulting in the birth (or at the time of the celebration of the marriage if later) both or either of the parties reasonably believed that the marriage was valid.*
(2) This section applies, and applies only, where the father of the child was domiciled in England at the time of the birth or, if he died before the birth, was so domiciled immediately before his death.

(3) This section, so far as it affects the succession to a dignity or title of honour, or the devolution of property settled therewith, applies only to children born after the commencement of this Act.
(4) This section does not affect any rights under the intestacy of a person who died before the commencement of this Act, and does not (except so far as may be necessary to avoid the severance from a dignity or title of honour of property settled therewith) affect the operation or construction of any disposition coming into operation before the commencement of this Act.
(5) In this section the following expressions have the meanings hereby assigned to them, that is to say—

'void marriage' means a marriage, not being voidable only, in respect of which the High Court has or had jurisdiction to grant a decree of nullity, or would have had such jurisdiction if the parties were domiciled in England;
'disposition' has the same meaning as in the Legitimacy Act 1926;

and any reference in this section to property settled with a dignity or title of honour is a reference to any real or personal property, or any interest in such property, which is limited by any disposition (whether subject to a preceding limitation or charge or not) in such a way as to devolve with the dignity or title as nearly as the law permits, whether or not the disposition contains an express reference to the dignity or title and whether or not the property or some interest in the property may in some event become severed from it.[1]

1 Sub-ss (1) to (5): repealed by the LA 1976, Sch 2.

* * * * *

[245.34]
6. Extent, short title, commencement, and saving.— *(1) This Act shall not apply to Scotland or Northern Ireland.*
(2) This Act may be cited as the Legitimacy Act 1959.
(3) This Act shall come into force on the expiration of three months beginning with the day on which it is passed.
(4) It is hereby declared that nothing in this Act affects the Succession to the Throne.[1]

1 Sub-s (4): repealed by the LA 1976, Sch 2.

ADOPTION ACT 1960

(8 & 9 Eliz 2 c 59)

[29 July 1960]

[245.35]

Note. This Act catered for the rather odd situation which arose where an illegitimate child who had been adopted by his natural parents was subsequently legitimated. It will be remembered that under the Legitimacy Act 1926 (paras **[245.6]**–**[245.15]**) an illegitimate child was not legitimated by the subsequent marriage of his parents if at the time of his birth either of his parents was married to a third person. The only step that the parents could take to regularise the position was to adopt the child. However, this bar to legitimation was abolished by the

Legitimacy Act 1959, s 1 (para **[245.32]**). The Adoption Act 1960 provided that in a case of this sort any interested party might apply to revoke the adoption order but expressly provided that such revocation should not affect the rights acquired by the child under the Adoption Act 1958 (paras **[245.24]–[245.30]**) before the revocation of the adoption order. The latter provision was repealed as from 1 January 1976, and the former as from 1 January 1988.

[245.36]
1. Further provision for revocation of adoption orders in cases of legitimation.— (*1*) *Where any person legitimated by virtue of section one of the Legitimacy Act 1959, had been adopted by his father and mother before the commencement of that Act, the court by which the adoption order was made may, on the application of any of the parties concerned, revoke that order.*[1]
(*2*) *The revocation of an adoption order under this section, or under section twenty-six of the Adoption Act 1958, shall not affect the operation of sections sixteen and seventeen of that Act in relation to an intestacy which occurred, or a dispotion which was made, before the revocation.*[2]

1 Sub-s (1): repealed with effect from 1 January 1988 by the AA 1976, s 73(3), Sch 4 (SI 1987/1242).
2 Sub-s (2): repealed with effect from 1 January 1976 by the Children Act 1975, s 108, Sch 4, Pt I.

* * * * *

FAMILY LAW REFORM ACT 1969

(1969 c 46)

[25 July 1969]

[245.37]

Note. Pt II of this Act, which came into force on 1 January 1970, conferred rights of succession on illegitimate children on deaths intestate on or after that date. In relation to dispositions of property made on or after that date, the Act reversed the common law presumptions as to the construction of references to children, issue and other expressions descriptive of relationship. In this context, dispositions by will were treated as made at the date of the will and not on the testator's death and a will was not treated as made at a later date merely because it was confirmed by a codicil. (Compare the similar provisions contained in the Adoption Act 1950, s 14(2) at para **[245.19]** above.) These provisions were replaced as from 4 April 1988 by the more comprehensive provisions contained in the FLRA 1987, ss 1 and 18 to 20 at paras **[245.70]** and **[245.71]–[245.73]** below.

* * * * *

PART II
PROPERTY RIGHTS OF ILLEGITIMATE CHILDREN

[245.38]
14. Right of illegitimate child to succeed on intestacy of parents, and of parents to succeed on intestacy of illegitimate child.— (*1*) *Where either parent of an illegitimate child dies intestate as respects all or any of his or her real or personal property, the illegitimate child or, if he is dead, his issue, shall*

be entitled to take any interest therein to which he or such issue would have been entitled if he had been born legitimate.
(2) *Where an illegitimate child dies intestate in respect of all or any of his real or personal property, each of his parents, if surviving, shall be entitled to take any interest therein to which that parent would have been entitled if the child had been born legitimate.*
(3) *In accordance with the foregoing provisions of this section, Part IV of the Administration of Estates Act 1925 (which deals with the distribution of the estate of an intestate) shall have effect as if—*

(*a*) *any reference to the issue of the intestate included a reference to any illegitimate child of his and to the issue of any such child;*
(*b*) *any reference to the child or children of the intestate included a reference to any illegitimate child or children of his; and*
(*c*) *in relation to an intestate who is an illegitimate child, any reference to the parent, parents, father or mother of the intestate were a reference to his natural parent, parents, father or mother.*

(4) *For the purposes of subsection (2) of this section and of the provisions amended by subsection (3)(c) thereof, an illegitimate child shall be presumed not to have been survived by his father unless the contrary is shown.*
(5) *This section does not apply to or affect the right of any person to take any entailed interest in real or personal property.*
(6) *The reference in section 50 (1) of the said Act of 1925 (which relates to the construction of documents) to Part IV of that Act, or to the foregoing provisions of that Part, shall in relation to an instrument inter vivos made, or a will or codicil coming into operation, after the coming into force of this section (but not in relation to instruments inter vivos made or wills or codicils coming into operation earlier) be construed as including references to this section.*
(7) *Section 9 of the Legitimacy Act 1926 (under which an illegitimate child and his issue are entitled to succeed on the intestacy of his mother if she leaves no legitimate issue, and the mother of an illegitimate child is entitled to succeed on his intestacy as if she were the only surviving parent) is hereby repealed.*
(8) *In this section 'illegitimate child' does not include an illegitimate child who is—*

(*a*) *a legitimated person within the meaning of the said Act of 1926 or a person recognised by virtue of that Act or at common law as having been legitimated; or*
(*b*) *an adopted person under an adoption order made in any part of the United Kingdom, the Isle of Man or the Channel Islands or under an overseas adoption as defined in section 4(3) of the Adoption Act 1968.*

(9) *This section does not affect any rights under the intestacy of a person dying before the coming into force of this section.*[1]

1 Sub-s (8): repealed by the Children Act 1975, s 108(1)(b), (4)(d), Sch 4, Pt II, as from 1 January 1976 and the remainder of s 14 was repealed as from 4 April 1988 by the FLRA 1987, s 33(2), (4), Sch 3, paras 8 to 10 and Sch 4.

[245.39]

15. Presumption that in dispositions of property references to children and other relatives include references to, and to persons related through, illegitimate children.— (*1*) *In any disposition made after the coming into force of this section—*

(*a*) *any reference (whether express or implied) to the child or children of any person shall, unless the contrary intention appears, be construed as, or as including, a reference to any illegitimate child of that person; and*

(*b*) *any reference (whether express or implied) to a person or persons related in some other manner to any person shall, unless the contrary intention appears, be construed as, or as including, a reference to anyone who would be so related if he, or some other person through whom the relationship is deduced, had been born legitimate.*

(*2*) *The foregoing subsection apples only where the reference in question is to a person who is to benefit or to be capable of benefiting under the disposition or, for the purpose of designating such a person, to someone else to or through whom that person is related; but that subsection does not affect the construction of the word 'heir' or 'heirs' or of any expression which is used to create an entailed interest in real or personal property.*

(*3*) *In relation to any disposition made after the coming into force of this section, section 33 of the Trustee Act 1925 (which specifies the trusts implied by a direction that income is to be held on protective trusts for the benefit of any person) shall have effect as if—*

(*a*) *the reference to the children or more remote issue of the principal beneficiary included a reference to any illegitimate child of the principal beneficiary and to anyone who would rank as such issue if he, or some other person through whom he is descended from the principal beneficiary, had been born legitimate; and*

(*b*) *the reference to the issue of the principal beneficiary included a reference to anyone who would rank as such issue if he, or some other person through whom he is descended from the principal beneficiary, had been born legitimate.*

(*4*) *In this section references to an illegitimate child include references to an illegitimate child who is or becomes a legitimated person within the meaning of the Legitimacy Act 1926 or a person recognised by virtue of that Act or at common law as having been legitimated; and in section 3 of that Act—*

(*a*) *subsection (1)(b) (which relates to the effect of dispositions where a person has been legitimated) shall not apply to a disposition made after the coming into force of this section except as respects any interest in relation to which the disposition refers only to persons who are, or whose relationship is deduced through, legitimate persons; and*

(*b*) *subsection (2) (which provides that, where the right to any property depends on the relative seniority of the children of any person, legitimated persons shall rank as if born on the date of legitimation) shall not apply in relation to any right conferred by a disposition made after the coming into force of this section unless the terms of the disposition are such that the children whose relative seniority is in question cannot include any illegitimate children who are not either legitimated persons within the meaning of that Act or persons recognised by virtue of that Act as having been legitimated.*

(*5*) *Where under any disposition any real or personal property or any interest in such property is limited (whether subject to any preceding limitation or charge or not) in such a way that it would, apart from this section, devolve (as nearly as the law permits) along with a dignity or title of honour, then, whether or not the disposition contains an express reference to the dignity or title of honour, and whether or not the property or some interest in the property may in some event become severed therefrom, nothing in this section shall operate to sever the property or any interest therein from the dignity or title, but the property or interest shall devolve in all respects as if this section had not been enacted.*

(*6*) *This section is without prejudice to sections 16 and 17 of the Adoption Act 1958 (which relate to the construction of dispositions in cases of adoption).*

(*7*) *There is hereby abolished, as respects dispositions made after the coming into force of this section, any rule of law that a disposition in favour of illegitimate children not in being when the disposition takes effect is void as contrary to public policy.*

(*8*) *In this section 'disposition' means a disposition, including an oral disposition, of real or personal property whether inter vivos or by will or codicil; and, notwithstanding any rule of law, a disposition made by will or codicil executed before the date on which this section comes into force shall not be treated for the purposes of this section as made on or after that date by reason only that the will or codicil is confirmed by a codicil executed on or after that date.*[1]

1 Sub-ss (4) to (6): repealed by the Children Act 1975, s 108(1)(b), (4)(d), Sch 4, Pt II, as from 1 January 1976; and the remainder of s 15 was repealed as from 4 April 1988 by the FLRA 1987. Section 15 continues to apply to wills made on or after 1 January 1970 and before 4 April 1988.

[245.40]

16. Meaning of 'child' and 'issue' in s 33 of Wills Act 1837.— (*1*) *In relation to a testator who dies after the coming into force of this section, section 33 of the Wills Act 1837 (gift to children or other issue of testator not to lapse if they predecease him but themselves leave issue) shall have effect as if—*

(*a*) *the reference to a child or other issue of the testator (that is, the intended beneficiary) included a reference to any illegitimate child of the testator and to anyone who would rank as such issue if he, or some other person through whom he is descended from the testator, had been born legitimate; and*

(*b*) *the reference to the issue of the intended beneficiary included a reference to anyone who would rank as such issue if he, or some other person through whom he is descended from the intended beneficiary, had been born legitimate.*

(*2*) *In this section 'illegitimate child' includes an illegitimate child who is a legitimated person within the meaning of the Legitimacy Act 1926 or a person recognised by virtue of that Act or at common law as having been legitimated.*[1]

1 Sub-s (2): repealed by the LA 1976, ss 11, Sch 2. Sub-s (1): repealed by the FLRA 1987.

[245.41]
17. Protection of trustees and personal representatives. *Notwithstanding the foregoing provisions of this Part of this Act, trustees or personal representatives may convey or distribute any real or personal property to or among the persons entitled thereto without having ascertained that there is no person who is or may be entitled to any interest therein by virtue of—*

(*a*) *section 14 of this Act so far as it confers any interest on illegimate children or their issue or on the father of an illegitimate child; or*
(*b*) *section 15 or 16 of this Act,*

and shall not be liable to any such person of whose claim they have not had notice at the time of the conveyance or distribution; but nothing in this section shall prejudice the right of any such person to follow the property, or any property representing it, into the hands of any person, other than a purchaser, who may have received it.[1]

1 Repealed by the FLRA 1987, s 20 (para **[245.73]**).

* * * * *

PART IV
MISCELLANEOUS AND GENERAL

[245.42]
28. Short title, interpretation, commencement and extent.— (*1*) *This Act may be cited as the Family Law Reform Act 1969.*
(*2*) *Except where the context otherwise requires, any reference in this Act to any enactment shall be construed as a reference to that enactment as amended, extended or applied by or under any other enactment, including this Act.*
(*3*) *This Act shall come into force on such date as the Lord Chancellor may appoint by order made by statutory instrument, and different dates may be appointed for the coming into force of different provisions.*[1]

1 Pt II of the Act was brought into force on 1 January 1970 (Family Law Reform Act (Commencement No 1) Order 1969, SI 1969/1140).

* * * * *

LEGITIMACY ACT 1976

(1976 c 31)

[22 July 1976]

[245.43]

Note. This Act currently governs the property rights of legitimated children. In effect, the Act protects the rights of legitimated children by treating them as if they had been born legitimate. The rules of construction reflecting this policy are contained in s 5 (para **[245.48]**) and apply to instruments made on or after 1 January 1976, replacing the corresponding rules introduced by the Children Act 1975 from the same commencement date. The new rules apply to a will made before 1 January 1976 if the testator dies on or after that date and apply whether the legitimation takes place before or after the death. The relevant provisions of the Act are printed below, as amended by the AA 1976 and the FLRA 1987.

[245.44]
1. Legitimacy of children of certain void marriages.— (1) The child of a void marriage, whenever born, shall, subject to subsection (2) below and Schedule 1 to this Act, be treated as the legitimate child of his parents if at the time of [the insemination resulting in the birth or, where there was no such act of insemination, the child's conception (or at the time of the celebration of the marriage if later) both or either of the parties reasonably believed that the marriage was valid.
(2) This section only applies where the father of the child was domiciled in England and Wales at the time of the birth, or, if he died before the birth, was so domiciled immediately before his death.
[(3) It is hereby declared for the avoidance of doubt that subsection (1) above applies notwithstanding that the belief that the marriage was valid was due to a mistake as to law.
(4) In relation to a child born after the coming into force of section 28 of the Family Law Reform Act 1987, it shall be presumed for the purposes of subsection (1) above, unless the contrary is shown, that one of the parties to the void marriage reasonably believed at the time of the insemination resulting in the birth or, where there was no such insemination, the child's conception (or at the time of the celebration of the marriage if later) that the marriage was valid.][1]

1 The words in square brackets in sub-s (1) were substituted, and sub-ss (3) and (4) were added, by the FLRA 1987, s 28, with effect from 4 April 1988 (SI 1988/425).

[245.45]
2. Legitimation by subsequent marriage of parents. Subject to the following provisions of this Act, where the parents of an illegitimate person marry one another, the marriage shall, if the father of the illegitimate person is at the date of marriage domiciled in England and Wales, render that person, if living, legitimate from the date of the marriage.

[245.46]
3. Legitimation by extraneous law. Subject to the following provisions of this Act, where the parents of an illegitimate person marry one another and the father of the illegitimate person is not at the time of the marriage domiciled in England and Wales but is domiciled in a country by the law of which the illegitimate person became legitimated by virtue of such subsequent marriage, that person, if living, shall in England and Wales be recognised as having been so legitimated from the date of the marriage notwithstanding that, at the time of his birth, his father was domiciled in a country the law of which did not permit legitimation by subsequent marriage.

[245.47]
4. Legitimation of adopted child.— (1) [Section 39 of the Adoption Act 1976][1] [or section 67 of the Adoption and Children Act 2002][2] does not prevent an adopted child being legitimated under section 2 or 3 above if either natural parent is the sole adoptive parent.

(2) Where an adopted child (with a sole adoptive parent) is legitimated—

(a) [subsection (2) of the said section 39][1] [or subsection 3(b) of the said section 67][2] shall not apply after the legitimation to the natural relationship with the other natural parent, and

(b) revocation of the adoption order in consequence of the legitimation shall not affect [section 39, 41 or 42 of the Adoption Act 1976][1] [or section 67, 68 or 69 of the Adoption and Children Act 2002][2] as it applies to any instrument made before the date of legitimation.

1 The words in the first set of square brackets in sub-ss (1), (2)(a) and (2)(b) were substituted by the AA 1976, s 73(2), Sch 3, para 23 for references to corresponding provisions of the Children Act 1975, as from 1 January 1988 (SI 1987/1242).

2 The words in the second set of square brackets in sub-ss (1), (2)(a) and (2)(b) were inserted with effect from 30 December 2005 by the ACA 2002, s 139(1), Sch 3, paras 16 and 17 and Adoption and Children Act 2002 (Commencement No 9) Order 2005, SI 2005/2213, art 2(o).

[245.48]

5. Rights of legitimated persons and others to take interests in property.—
(1) Subject to any contrary indication, the rules of construction contained in this section apply to any instrument other than an existing instrument, so far as the instrument contains a disposition of property.

(2) For the purposes of this section, provisions of the law of intestate succession applicable to the estate of a deceased person shall be treated as if contained in an instrument executed by him (while of full capacity) immediately before his death.

(3) A legitimated person, and any other person, shall be entitled to take any interest as if the legitimated person had been born legitimate.

(4) A disposition which depends on the date of birth of a child or children of the parent or parents shall be construed as if—

(a) a legitimated child had been born on the date of legitimation,

(b) two or more legitimated children legitimated on the same date had been born on that date in the order of their actual births,

but this does not affect any reference to the age of a child.

(5) Examples of phrases in wills on which subsection (4) above can operate are—

1. Children of A 'living at my death or born afterwards'.
2. Children of A 'living at my death or born afterwards before any one of such children for the time being in existence attains a vested interest, and who attain the age of 21 years'.
3. As in example 1 or 2, but referring to grandchildren of A, instead of children of A.
4. A for life 'until he has a child' and then to his child or children.

Note. Subsection (4) above will not affect the reference to the age of 21 years in example 2.

(6) If an illegitimate person or a person adopted by one of his natural parents dies, or has died before the commencement of this Act, and—

(a) after his death his parents marry or have married; and

(b) the deceased would, if living at the time of the marriage, have become a legitimated person,

this section shall apply for the construction of the instrument so far as it relates to the taking of interests by, or in succession to, his spouse, children and remoter issue as if he had been legitimated by virtue of the marriage.
(7) In this section 'instrument' includes a private Act settling property, but not any other enactment.

[245.49]
6. Dispositions depending on date of birth.— (1) Where a disposition depends on the date of birth of a child who was born illegitimate and who is legitimated (or, if deceased, is treated as legitimated), section 5(4) above does not affect entitlement under Part II of the Family Law Reform Act 1969 (illegitimate children).
(2) Where a disposition depends on the date of birth of an adopted child who is legitimated (or, if deceased, is treated as legitimated) section 5(4) above does not affect entitlement by virtue of [Section 42(2) of the Adoption Act 1976][1] [or section 69(2) of the Adoption and Children Act 2002].[2]
(3) This section applies for example where—

(a) a testator dies in 1976 bequeathing a legacy to his eldest grandchild living at a specified time,
(b) his daughter has an illegitimate child in 1977 who is the first grandchild,
(c) his married son has a child in 1978,
(d) subsequently the illegitimate child is legitimated.

and in all those cases the daughter's child remains the eldest grandchild of the testator throughout.

1 The words in the first set of square brackets in sub-s (2) were substituted by the AA 1976, s 73(2), Sch 3, para 24 for a reference to the corresponding provisions of the Children Act 1975, as from 1 January 1988 (SI 1987/1242).
2 The words in the second set of square brackets in sub-s (2) were inserted with effect from 30 December 2005 by the ACA 2002, s 139(1), Sch 3, paras 16 and 17 and Adoption and Children Act 2002 (Commencement No 9) Order 2005, SI 2005/2213, art 2(o).

[245.50]
7. Protection of trustees and personal representatives.— (1) A trustee or personal representative is not under a duty, by virtue of the law relating to trusts or the administration of estates, to enquire, before conveying or distributing any property, whether any person is illegitimate or has been adopted by one of his natural parents, and could be legitimated (or if deceased be treated as legitimated), if that fact could affect entitlement to the property.
(2) A trustee or personal representative shall not be liable to any person by reason of a conveyance or distribution of the property made without regard to any such fact if he has not received notice of the fact before the conveyance or distribution.
(3) This section does not prejudice the right of a person to follow the property, or any property representing it, into the hands of another person, other than a purchaser, who has received it.

* * * * *

[245.51]
10. Interpretation.— (1) In this Act, except where the context otherwise requires—

'disposition' includes the conferring of a power of appointment and any other disposition of an interest in or right over property;

'existing', in relation to an instrument, means one made before 1st January 1976;

'legitimated person' means a person legitimated or recognised as legitimated—

(a) under section 2 or 3 above;

(b) under section 1 or 8 of the Legitimacy Act 1926; or

(c) except in section 8, by legitimation (whether or not by virtue of the subsequent marriage of his parents) recognised by the law of England and Wales and effected under the law of any other country;

and cognate expressions shall be construed accordingly;

'power of appointment' includes any discretionary power to transfer a beneficial interest in property without the furnishing of valuable consideration;

'void marriage' means a marriage, not being voidable only, in respect of which the High Court has or had jurisdiction to grant a decree of nullity, or would have or would have had such jurisdiction if the parties were domiciled in England and Wales.

(2) For the purposes of this Act 'legitimated person' includes, where the context admits, a person legitimated, or recognised as legitimated, before the passing of the Children Act 1975.
(3) For the purpose of this Act, except where the context otherwise requires—

(a) the death of the testator is the date at which a will or codicil is to be regarded as made;

(b) an oral disposition of property shall be deemed to be contained in an instrument made when the disposition was made.

(4) It is hereby declared that references in this Act to dispositions of property include references to a disposition by the creation of an entailed interest.
(5) Except in so far as the context otherwise requires, any reference in this Act to an enactment shall be construed as a reference to that enactment as amended by or under any other enactment, including this Act.

[245.52]
11. Savings, amendments and repeals.— (1) Schedule 1 to this Act, which contains savings and amendments to enactments consequential upon the provisions of this Act, shall have effect.

* * * * *

[245.53]
12. Short title, commencement and extent.— (1) This Act may be cited as the Legitimacy Act 1976.

(2) This Act shall come into force at the end of the period of one month beginning with the date on which it is passed.
(3) This Act does not extend to Scotland or to Northern Ireland.

SCHEDULE 1

Section 11

SAVINGS

[245.54]
1.— (1) Notwithstanding the repeal by this Act of sections 1 and 8 of the Legitimacy Act 1926 persons legitimated or recognised as legitimated under that Act shall continue to be legitimated or recognised as legitimated by virtue of section 1 or, as the case may be, section 8 of that Act.
(2) In any enactment whether passed before or after this Act references to persons legitimated or recognised as legitimated under section 1 or section 8 of the Legitimacy Act 1926 or under section 2 or section 3 of this Act shall be construed as including references to persons legitimated or recognised as legitimated under section 2 or section 3 of this Act or under section 1 or section 8 of the said Act of 1926 respectively.
2.— (1) The enactments repealed by Part II of Schedule 4 to the Children Act 1975 (which are superseded by section 5 of this Act) shall, notwithstanding those repeals, continue to have effect as respects existing instruments.
In this sub-paragraph 'instrument' has the same meaning as in section 5 of this Act.
(2) Subject to paragraph 3(b) below, nothing in this Act or in the Legitimacy Act 1926 (in so far as the effect of that Act is preserved by sub-paragraph (1) above) shall affect the operation or construction of any disposition coming into operation before 1st January 1927 or affect any rights under the intestacy of a person dying before that date.
(3) Sub-paragraph (2) above shall apply in relation to a person to whom the said Act of 1926 applied by virtue of section 1(1) of the Legitimacy Act 1959 with the substitution for '1st January 1927' of '29th October 1959'.
3. Section 1 does not—

(a) affect any rights under the intestacy of a person who dies before 29th October 1959, or
(b) affect the operation or construction of any disposition coming into operation before 29th October 1959 except so far as may be necessary to avoid the severance from a dignity or title of honour of property limited (expressly or not) to devolve (as nearly as the law permits) along with the dignity or title of honour.

4.— (1) Section 1 of this Act, so far as it affects the succession to a dignity or title of honour, or the devolution of property limited as aforesaid, only applies to children born after 28th October 1959.
(2) Apart from section 1, nothing in this Act shall affect the succession to any dignity or title of honour or render any person capable of succeeding to or transmitting a right to succeed to any such dignity or title.

(3) Apart from section 1, nothing in this Act shall affect the devolution of any property limited (expressly or not) to devolve (as nearly as the law permits) along with any dignity or title of honour.
This sub-paragraph applies only if and so far as a contrary intention is not expressed in the instrument, and shall have effect subject to the instrument.
5. It is hereby declared that nothing in this Act affects the Succession to the Throne.

* * * * *

ADOPTION ACT 1976

(1976 c 36)

[22 July 1976]

[245.55]

Note. This Act governs the property rights of children adopted before 30 December 2005. This Act protects the rights of such adopted children by treating them as if they were the legitimate children of their adoptive parents. The rules of construction embodying this policy are set out in ss 39 to 46 (paras **[245.58]–[245.64]** below). These rules were brought into force as from 1 January 1988 (SI 1987/1242), replacing the corresponding provisions of the Children Act 1975 with effect from the same commencement date. These rules apply to a will made before 1 January 1976 if the testator dies on or after that date and apply whether the adoption takes place before or after the death. The property rights of children adopted on or after 30 December 2005 are governed by the ACA 2002: see paras **[245.92]** ff below.

* * * * *

PART II
ADOPTION ORDERS

THE MAKING OF ADOPTION ORDERS

[245.56]
12. Adoption orders.— (1) An adoption order is an order [giving parental responsibility for a child to][1] the adopters, made on their application by an authorised court.

1 The words in square brackets were substituted by the ChA 1989, s 88(1), Sch 10, Pt I, para 3.

* * * * *

PART IV
STATUS OF ADOPTED CHILDREN

[245.57]
38. Meaning of 'adoption' in Part IV.— (1) In this Part 'adoption' means adoption—

(a) by an adoption order;

(b) by an order made under the Children Act 1975, the Adoption Act 1958, the Adoption Act 1950 or any enactment repealed by the Adoption Act 1950;
(c) by an order made in Scotland, Northern Ireland, the Isle of Man or in any of the Channel Islands;
(d) which is an overseas adoption; or
(e) which is an adoption recognised by the law of England and Wales and effected under the law of any other country,

and cognate expressions shall be construed accordingly.
(2) The definition of adoption includes, where the context admits, an adoption effected before the passing of the Children Act 1975, and the date of an adoption effected by an order is the date of the making of the order.

[245.58]
39. Status conferred by adoption.— (1) An adopted child shall be treated in law—

(a) where the adopters are a married couple, as if he had been born as a child of the marriage (whether or not he was in fact born after the marriage was solemnized);
(b) in any other case, as if he had been born to the adopter in wedlock (but not as a child of any actual marriage of the adopter).

(2) An adopted child shall, subject to subsection (3), be treated in law as if he were not the child of any person other than the adopters or adopter.
(3) In the case of a child adopted by one of its natural parents as sole adoptive parent, subsection (2) has no effect as respects entitlement to property depending on relationship to that parent, or as respects anything else depending on that relationship.
(4) It is hereby declared that this section prevents an adopted child from being illegitimate.
(5) This section has effect—

(a) in the case of an adoption before 1 January 1976, from that date, and
(b) in the case of any other adoption, from the date of the adoption.

(6) Subject to the provisions of this Part, this section—

(a) applies for the construction of enactments or instruments passed or made before the adoption or later, and so applies subject to any contrary indication; and
(b) has effect as respects things done, or events occurring, after the adoption, or after 31st December 1975, whichever is the later.

* * * * *

[245.59]
41. Adoptive relatives. A relationship existing by virtue of section 39 may be referred to as an adoptive relationship, and—

(a) a male adopter may be referred to as the adoptive father;

(b) a female adopter may be referred to as the adoptive mother;
(c) any other relative of any degree under an adoptive relationship may be referred to as an adoptive relative of that degree,

but this section does not prevent the term 'parent', or any other term not qualified by the word 'adoptive' being treated as including an adoptive relative.

[245.60]
42. Rules of construction for instruments concerning property.— (1) Subject to any contrary indication, the rules of construction contained in this section apply to any instrument, other than an existing instrument, so far as it contains a disposition of property.
(2) In applying section 39(1) to a disposition which depends on the date of birth of a child or children of the adoptive parent or parents, the disposition shall be construed as if—

(a) the adopted child had been born on the date of adoption,
(b) two or more children adopted on the same date had been born on that date in the order of their actual births.

but this does not affect any reference to the age of a child.
(3) Examples of phrases in wills on which subsection (2) can operate—

1. Children of A 'living at my death or born afterwards'.
2. Children of A 'living at my death or born afterwards before any one of such children for the time being in existence attains a vested interest and who attain the age of 21 years'.
3. As in example 1 or 2, but referring to grandchildren of A instead of children of A.
4. A for life 'until he has a child', and then to his child or children.

Note. Subsection (2) will not affect the reference to the age of 21 years in example 2.

(4) Section 39(2) does not prejudice any interest vested in possession in the adopted child before the adoption, or any interest expectant (whether immediately or not) upon an interest so vested.[1]
(5) Where it is necessary to determine for the purposes of a disposition of property effected by an instrument whether a woman can have a child, it shall be presumed that once a woman has attained the age of 55 years she will not adopt a child after execution of the instrument, and, notwithstanding section 39, if she does so that child shall not be treated as her child or as the child of her spouse (if any) for the purposes of the instrument.
(6) In this section, 'instrument' includes a private Act settling property, but not any other enactment.

1 In *Staffordshire County Council v B* [1998] 1 FLR 261, [1998] Fam Law 8, Ch D it was held that a child's contingent remainder interest expectant upon his biological mother's life interest was an interest expectant upon an interest vested in possession within this subsection and so was preserved following his adoption. In relation to adoptions made after the coming into force of the ACA 2002 on 30 December 2005 this decision will no longer apply: see ACA 2002, s 69(4) at para **[245.95]** below.

In relation to adoptions made after the coming into force of the ACA 2002 on 30 December 2005, s 69(4) will cease to apply and the decision in *Staffordshire County Council* will no longer be good law.

[245.61]
43. Dispositions depending on date of birth.— (1) Where a disposition depends on the date of birth of a child who was born illegitimate and who is adopted by one of the natural parents as sole adoptive parent, section 42(2) does not affect entitlement under Part II of the Family Law Reform Act 1969 (illegitimate children).
(2) Subsection (1) applies for example where—

- (a) a testator dies in 1976 bequeathing a legacy to his eldest grandchild living at a specified time,
- (b) his daughter has an illegitimate child in 1977 who is the first grandchild,
- (c) his married son has a child in 1978,
- (d) subsequently the illegitimate child is adopted by the mother as sole adoptive parent,

and in all those cases the daughter's child remains the eldest grandchild of the testator throughout.

[245.62]
44. Property devolving with peerages etc.— (1) An adoption does not affect the descent of any peerage or dignity or title of honour.
(2) An adoption shall not affect the devolution of any property limited (expressly or not) to devolve (as nearly as the law permits) along with any peerage or dignity or title of honour.
(3) Subsection (2) applies only if and so far as a contrary intention is not expressed in the instrument, and shall have effect subject to the terms of the instrument.

[245.63]
45. Protection of trustees and personal representatives.— (1) A trustee or personal representative is not under a duty, by virtue of the law relating to trusts or the administration of estates, to enquire, before conveying or distributing any property, whether any adoption has been effected or revoked if that fact could affect entitlement to the property.
(2) A trustee or personal representative shall not be liable to any person by reason of a conveyance or distribution of the property made without regard to any such fact if he has not received notice of the fact before the conveyance or distribution.
(3) This section does not prejudice the right of a person to follow the property, or any property representing it, into the hands of another person, other than a purchaser, who has received it.

[245.64]
46. Meaning of 'disposition'.— (1) In this Part, unless the context otherwise requires,

'disposition' includes the conferring of a power of appointment and any other disposition of an interest in or right over property;
'power of appointment' includes any discretionary power to transfer a beneficial interest in property without the furnishing of valuable consideration.

(2) This Part applies to an oral disposition as if contained in an instrument made when the disposition was made.
(3) For the purposes of this Part, the death of the testator is the date at which a will or codicil is to be regarded as made.
(4) For the purposes of this Part, provisions of the law of intestate succession applicable to the estate of a deceased person shall be treated as if contained in an instrument executed by him (while of full capacity) immediately before his death.
(5) It is hereby declared that references in this Part to dispositions of property include references to a disposition by the creation of an entailed interest.

* * * * *

PART VI
MISCELLANEOUS AND SUPPLEMENTAL

* * * * *

[245.65]
72. Interpretation.— (1) In this Act, unless the context otherwise requires—

* * * * *

['adoption order'—
(a) means an order under section 12(1) …][1]

* * * * *

'existing', in relation to an enactment or other instrument, means one passed or made at any time before 1st January 1976;

1 This definition was substituted by the ChA 1989, s 88(1), Sch 10, Pt I, para 30.

[245.66]
73. Transitional provisions …— (1) The transitional provisions contained in Schedule 2 shall have effect.

* * * * *

[245]
74. Short title commencement and extent.— (1) This Act may be cited as the Adoption Act 1976.
(2) This Act shall come into force on such date as the Secretary of State may by order appoint and different dates may be appointed for different provisions.[1]
[(3) This Act extends to England and Wales only.][2]

1 The foregoing provisions were brought into force on 1 January 1988: see para **[245.55]** above.

2 Sub-s (3): substituted for the original sub-ss (3) and (4) by the ChA 1989, s 88(1), Sch 10, Pt I, para 31.

* * * * *

SCHEDULE 2

Section 73

TRANSITIONAL PROVISIONS AND SAVINGS

* * * * *

RIGHTS RELATING TO PROPERTY

[245.68]

6.— (1) Section 39—

(a) does not apply to an existing instrument or enactment in so far as it contains a disposition of property, and

(b) does not apply to any public general Act in its application to any disposition of property in an existing instrument or enactment.

(2) Sections 16 and 17 of the Adoption Act 1958, and provisions containing references to those sections shall continue to apply in relation to dispositions of property effected by existing instruments notwithstanding the repeal of those sections, and such provisions, by the Children Act 1975.

(3) Section 46 shall apply in relation to this paragraph as if it were contained in Part IV.

* * * * *

FAMILY LAW REFORM ACT 1987

(1987 c 42)

[15 May 1987]

[245.69]

Note. This Act implements a number of Law Commission recommendations for the removal of the legal disadvantages attaching to illegitimacy. The general principle established by s 1 is embodied in the rule of construction set out in sub-s (1) thereof that both in the 1987 Act itself and in all enactments passed and instruments made after the coming into force of the section, references to any relationship between two persons shall, in the absence of a contrary intention, be construed without regard to whether or not the parents of either of them have or had been married to each other at any time. Subsections (2) and (3) exclude the primary rule of construction in relation to any person who is treated as legitimate by statute or who is legitimated or adopted or is otherwise treated in law as legitimate. This qualification of the primary rule of construction preserves the rights of these categories of person, who are otherwise catered for under the general law or under existing legislation (ie the LA 1976 and the AA 1976). Section 1 was brought into force on 4 April 1988 by the Family Law Reform Act 1987 (Commencement No 1) Order 1988 (SI 1988/425).

Part II of the 1987 Act amended, inter alia, the Guardianship of Minors Act 1971, ss 3 and 4; as from 1 April 1989 (SI 1989/382). These provisions were themselves replaced by the ChA 1989, ss 5 and 6, as from 14 October 1991 (ss 5(1) to (10), (13) and 6) and 1 February 1992 (s 5(11), (12)) (SI 1991/828, as amended by SI 1991/1990), which are the provisions currently in force (see paras **[244.116]** ff above).

Part III of the 1987 Act is concerned with property rights. Section 18 (which replaced the more limited provisions of the Family Law Reform Act 1969, s 14) expressly extends the general principle established by s 1 to the rules of intestate succession as they apply to the estates of persons dying after the coming into force of that section. Section 18(2) provides that for the purposes of the intestacy rules an illegitimate person (not being a person treated as legitimate or a legitimated or adopted person) is to be presumed not to have been survived by his father or any person related to him only through his father, unless the contrary is shown. (Compare the more limited presumption contained in s 14(4) of the 1969 Act: para **[245.38]** above). Section 19 (which replaced s 15 of the 1969 Act: para **[245.39]** above) makes more detailed provision for the application of the general principle to inter vivos dispositions and wills and codicils made on or after the date on which that section comes into force. It should be noted that s 19(7) (like s 15(8) of the 1969 Act) provides that a will or codicil made before that date is not to be treated as made on or after that date by reason only that it is confirmed by a codicil made on or after that date. However, the 1987 Act differs from the 1969 Act in the following respects:—

(i) Unlike s 15 of the 1969 Act, it applies to words creating an entailed interest unless a contrary intention appears (see s 19(2) of the 1987 Act, and compare s 15(2) of the 1969 Act). However, like s 15 of the 1969 Act, it does not apply to property limited to devolve with a dignity or title of honour (s 19(4) of the 1987 Act, s 15(5) of the 1969 Act).

(ii) Section 15(1) of the 1969 Act would not have applied if the only illegitimacy causing difficulty was that of the person from whom the relationship had to be traced, e g 'the uncles of R', where R, but not his father, mother or uncles, was illegitimate. The 1987 Act (see in particular s 1(1)) applies to such a case. However, in this type of case the common law presumption that words of relationship were confined to legitimate relations would usually have been displaced because the gift could only have any meaning if the presumption were to be displaced.

(iii) Section 15 of the 1969 Act only applied to references to a relationship where it had the effect of benefiting or rendering capable of benefit someone who was either himself illegitimate or claimed to be related through a person who was illegitimate (s 15(2)); there is no such restriction in the 1987 Act. Thus the descendants of a named monarch for the purposes of a royal lives perpetuity period, in a post-3 April 1988 disposition, will include illegitimate descendants if no contrary intention is shown. To avoid the risk of uncertainty in such a perpetuity period the 1987 Act should be excluded in relation to it. Another example to which the 1987 Act applies but s 15 of the 1969 Act would not have so applied is 'issue' in the precondition of a conditional gift such as 'If X shall predecease me leaving issue', where the gift does not confer any benefit on the issue of X (see e g Form B19.11 at para **[219.24]**).

(iv) Unlike s 15 of the 1969 Act, the general principle embodied in s 1 of the 1987 Act applies in relation to the construction of statutes and statutory instruments passed or made after the coming into force of the section. (See also the corresponding provision added to the Interpretion Act 1978, Sch 1.) Previously specific provision was often made in statutes to cater for illegitimate children. This will no longer be necessary.

Section 20 repeals (without replacing) s 17 of the 1969 Act (para **[245.41]** above) which enabled personal representatives and trustees to distribute property without having ascertained whether or not illegitimate persons were entitled to the property or a share of it under ss 14, 15 or 16 of the 1969 Act (paras **[245.38]**–**[245.40]** above). It should be noted the repeal takes effect in relation to all distributions made after the date on which s 20 of the 1987 Act comes into force, including distributions out of the estates of persons dying before that date and of trust property settled before that date. In all such cases personal representatives and trustees will need to protect themselves by giving notice by advertisement pursuant to the Trustee Act 1925 (TA 1925), s 27 (para **[246.25]** below); see *Re Aldhous* [1955] 2 All ER 80, [1955] 1 WLR 459. The provisions of Pt III of the 1987 Act were bought into force on 4 April 1988 at the same time as s 1 (SI 1988/425).

The 1987 Act also effects certain minor and consequential amendments to other statutory provisions, in particular the TA 1925, s 33 and the AEA 1925, s 50: see paras **[246.31]** below and **[244.67]** above.

PART I
GENERAL PRINCIPLE

[245.70]

1. General principle.— (1) In this Act and enactments passed and instruments made after the coming into force of this section, references (however expressed) to any relationship between two persons shall, unless the contrary intention appears, be construed without regard to whether or not the father and mother of either of them, or the father and mother of any person through whom the relationship is deduced, have or had been married to each other at any time.

(2) In this Act and enactments passed after the coming into force of this section, unless the contrary intention appears—

(a) references to a person whose father and mother were married to each other at the time of his birth include; and

(b) references to a person whose father and mother were not married to each other at the time of his birth do not include,

references to any person to whom subsection (3) below applies, and cognate references shall be construed accordingly.

(3) This subsection applies to any person who—

(a) is treated as legitimate by virtue of section 1 of the Legitimacy Act 1976;

(b) is a legitimated person within the meaning of section 10 of that Act;

[(c) is an adopted child within the meaning of the Adoption and Children Act 2002][1]; or

(d) is otherwise treated in law as legitimate.

(4) For the purpose of construing references falling within subsection (2) above, the time of a person's birth shall be taken to include any time during the period beginning with—

(a) the insemination resulting in his birth; or

(b) where there was no such insemination, his conception,

and (in either case) ending with his birth.

1 Para (c) of sub-s (3) substituted with effect from 30 December 2005: ACA 2002, s 139(1), Sch 3, paras 50 and 51 and Adoption and Children Act 2002 (Commencement No 9) Order 2005, SI 2005/2213, art 2(o).

* * * * *

PART III
PROPERTY RIGHTS

[245.71]
18. Succession on intestacy.— (1) In Part IV of the Administration of Estates Act 1925 (which deals with the distribution of the estate of an intestate), references (however expressed) to any relationship between two persons shall be construed in accordance with section 1 above.
(2) For the purposes of subsection (1) above and that Part of that Act, a person whose father and mother were not married to each other at the time of his birth shall be presumed not to have been survived by his father, or by any person related to him only through his father, unless the contrary is shown.
(3) In section 50(1) of that Act (which relates to the construction of documents), the reference to Part IV of that Act, or to the foregoing provisions of that Part, shall in relation to an instrument inter vivos made, or a will or codicil coming into operation, after the coming into force of this section (but not in relation to instruments inter vivos made or wills or codicils coming into operation earlier) be construed as including references to this section.
(4) This section does not affect any rights under the intestacy of a person dying before the coming into force of this section.

[245.72]
19. Dispositions of property.— (1) In the following dispositions, namely—

(a) dispositions inter vivos made on or after the date on which this section comes into force; and
(b) dispositions by will or codicil where the will or codicil is made on or after that date,

references (whether express or implied) to any relationship between two persons shall be construed in accordance with section 1 above.
(2) It is hereby declared that the use, without more, of the word 'heir' or 'heirs' or any expression which is used to create an entailed interest in real or personal property does not show a contrary intention for the purposes of section 1 as applied by subsection (1) above.
(3) In relation to the dispositions mentioned in subsection (1) above, section 33 of the Trustee Act 1925 (which specifies the trust implied by a direction that income is to be held on protective trusts for the benefit of any person) shall have effect as if any reference (however expressed) to any relationship between two persons were construed in accordance with section 1 above.
(4) Where under any disposition of real or personal property, any interest in such property is limited (whether subject to any preceding limitation or charge or not) in such a way that it would, apart from this section, devolve (as nearly as the law permits) along with a dignity or title of honour, then—

(a) whether or not the disposition contains an express reference to the dignity or title of honour; and
(b) whether or not the property or some interest in the property may in some event become severed from it,

nothing in this section shall operate to sever the property or any interest in it from the dignity or title, but the property or interest shall devolve in all respects as if this section had not been enacted.
(5) This section is without prejudice to section 42 of the Adoption Act 1976 [or section 69 of the Adoption and Children Act 2002][1] (construction of dispositions in cases of adoption).
(6) In this section 'disposition' means a disposition, including an oral disposition, of real or personal property whether inter vivos or by will or codicil.
(7) Notwithstanding any rule of law, a disposition made by will or codicil executed before the date on which this section comes into force shall not be treated for the purposes of this section as made on or after that date by reason only that the will or codicil is confirmed by a codicil executed on or after that date.

1 Words inserted in sub-s (5) with effect from 30 December 2005: ACA 2002, s 139(1), Sch 3, paras 50 and 52 and Adoption and Children Act 2002 (Commencement No 9) Order 2005, SI 2005/2213, art 2(o).

[245.73]
20. No special protection for trustees and personal representatives. Section 17 of the Family Law Reform Act 1969 (which enables trustees and personal representatives to distribute property without having ascertained that no person whose parents were not married to each other at the time of his birth, or who claims through such a person, is or may be entitled to an interest in the property) shall cease to have effect.

* * * * *

PART VI
MISCELLANEOUS AND SUPPLEMENTAL

MISCELLANEOUS

[245.74]
27. Artificial insemination.— (1) Where after the coming into force of this section a child is born in England and Wales as the result of the artificial insemination of a woman who—

(a) was at the time of the insemination a party to a marriage (being a marriage which had not at that time been dissolved or annulled); and
(b) was artificially inseminated with the semen of some person other than the other party to that marriage,

then, unless it is proved to the satisfaction of any court by which the matter has to be determined that the other party to that marriage did not consent to the insemination, the child shall be treated in law as the child of the parties to that marriage and shall not be treated as the child of any person other than the parties to that marriage.
(2) Any reference in this section to a marriage includes a reference to a void marriage if at the time of the insemination resulting in the birth of the child both or either of the parties reasonably believed that the marriage was valid;

and for the purposes of this section it shall be presumed, unless the contrary is shown, that one of the parties so believed at that time that the marriage was valid.

(3) Nothing in this section shall affect the succession to any dignity or title of honour or render any person capable of succeeding to or transmitting a right to succeed to any such dignity or title.[1]

1 Note that this section ceased to have effect in relation to children carried by women as a result of their artificial insemination after the commencement of the HFEA 1990, ss 27 to 29 (paras **[245.85]**–**[245.87]** below); see s 49(4) of the 1990 Act (para **[245.91]** below). These provisions of the 1990 Act commenced on 1 August 1991 (SI 1991/1400).

[245.75]

28. Children of void marriages. ...[1]

1 Note that this section amends the LA 1976, s 1, the text of which (as amended) appears at para **[245.44]** above.

* * * * *

SUPPLEMENTAL

[245.76]

30. Orders applying section 1 to other enactments.— (1) The Lord Chancellor may by order make provision for the construction in accordance with section 1 above of such enactments passed before the coming into force of that section as may be specified in the order.

(2) An order under this section shall so amend the enactments to which it relates as to secure that (so far as practicable) they continue to have the same effect notwithstanding the making of the order.

(3) An order under this section shall be made by statutory instrument which shall be subject to annulment in pursuance of a resolution of either House of Parliament.

* * * * *

[245.77]

33. Amendments, transitional provisions, savings and repeals.— (1) The enactments mentioned in Schedule 2 to this Act shall have effect subject to the amendments there specified, being minor amendments and amendments consequential on the provisions of this Act.

(2) The transitional provisions and savings in Schedule 3 to this Act shall have effect.

(3) The inclusion in this Act of any express saving or amendment shall not be taken as prejudicing the operation of sections 16 and 17 of the Interpretation Act 1978 (which relate to the effect of repeals).

(4) The enactments mentioned in Schedule 4 to this Act are hereby repealed to the extent specified in the third column of that Schedule.

[245.78]

34. Short title, commencement and extent.— (1) This Act may be cited as the Family Law Reform Act 1987.

(2) This Act shall come into force on such day as the Lord Chancellor may by order made by statutory instrument appoint; and different days may be so appointed for different provisions or different purposes.
(3) Without prejudice to the transitional provisions contained in Schedule 3 to this Act, an order under subsection (2) above may make such further transitional provisions as appear to the Lord Chancellor to be necessary or expedient in connection with the provisions brought into force by the order, including—

(a) such adaptations of the provisions so brought into force; and
(b) such adaptations of any provisions of this Act then in force,

as appear to him necessary or expedient in consequence of the partial operation of this Act.

* * * * *

SCHEDULE 2

Section 33(1)

MINOR AND CONSEQUENTIAL AMENDMENTS

[245.79]

Note. Relevant amendments are contained in paras 2, 3 which amend the TA 1925, s 33, and the AEA 1925, s 50 which are printed (as amended) at paras **[246.31]** below and **[244.67]** above.

SCHEDULE 3

Section 33(2)

TRANSITIONAL PROVISIONS AND SAVINGS

* * * * *

PROPERTY RIGHTS

[245.80]
8. The repeal by this Act of section 14 of the Family Law Reform Act 1969 shall not affect any rights arising under the intestacy of a person dying before the coming into force of the repeal.
9. The repeal by this Act of section 15 of the Family Law Reform Act 1969 shall not affect, or affect the operation of section 33 of the Trustee Act 1925 in relation to—

(a) any disposition inter vivos made before the date on which the repeal comes into force; or
(b) any disposition by will or codicil executed before that date.

10. The repeal by this Act of section 17 of the Family Law Reform Act 1969 shall not affect the liability of trustees or personal representatives in respect of any conveyance or distribution made before the coming into force of the repeal.

* * * * *

SCHEDULE 4

Section 33(4)

REPEALS

[245.81]

Note. The provisions repealed include the whole of the Legitimacy Act 1959 and certain provisions of the FLRA 1969. So far as relevant, the repeals are referred to in the notes to each of these statutes.

HUMAN FERTILISATION AND EMBRYOLOGY ACT 1990

(1990 c 37)

[1 November 1990]

[245.82]

Note. This Act introduces a new system of control for the treatment of infertility and for research involving human embryos. It also contains provisions identifying the persons who are to be treated in law as the father (if any) and mother of persons coming into existence as a consequence of artificial insemination or other techniques to deal with infertility that are regulated by the Act (ss 27 and 28). These provisions will affect the construction of wills and other dispositions (even if made before the commencement of the relevant provision), and the operation of the intestacy rules (s 29(3)). There is also provision (s 30) for the courts to make orders, inter alia applying the adoption legislation, in cases of surrogate motherhood. Sections 1, 2, 27 to 29 came into force on 1 August 1991 (SI 1991/1400), and the ancillary provisions in ss 47 to 49 came into force on or before that date. Section 30 was brought into force on dates in 1994 (SI 1994/1776).

PRINCIPAL TERMS USED

[245.83]
1. Meaning of 'embryo', 'gamete' and associated expressions.— (1) In this Act, except where otherwise stated—

(a) embryo means a live human embryo where fertilisation is complete, and

(b) references to an embryo include an egg in the process of fertilisation,

and, for this purpose, fertilisation is not complete until the appearance of a two cell zygote.

(2) This Act, so far as it governs bringing about the creation of an embryo, applies only to bringing about the creation of an embryo outside the human body; and in this Act—

(a) references to embryos the creation of which was brought about *in vitro* (in their application to those where fertilisation is complete) are to those where fertilisation began outside the human body whether or not it was completed there, and

(b) references to embryos taken from a woman do not include embryos whose creation was brought about *in vitro*.

(3) This Act, so far as it governs the keeping or use of an embryo, applies only to keeping or using an embryo outside the human body.
(4) References in this Act to gametes, eggs or sperm, except where otherwise stated, are to live human gametes, eggs or sperm but references below in this Act to gametes or eggs do not include eggs in the process of fertilisation.

[245.84]
2. Other terms.

* * * * *

(3) For the purposes of this Act, a woman is not to be treated as carrying a child until the embryo has become implanted.

* * * * *

STATUS

[245.85]
27. Meaning of 'mother'.— (1) The woman who is carrying or has carried a child as a result of the placing in her of an embryo or of sperm and eggs, and no other woman, is to be treated as the mother of the child.
(2) Subsection (1) above does not apply to any child to the extent that the child is treated by virtue of adoption as not being the [woman's child][1].
(3) Subsection (1) above applies whether the woman was in the United Kingdom or elsewhere at the time of the placing in her of the embryo or the sperm and eggs.

1 Words substituted in sub-s (2) with effect from 30 December 2005: ACA 2002, s 139(1), Sch 3, paras 76 and 77 and Adoption and Children Act 2002 (Commencement No 9) Order 2005, SI 2005/2213, art 2(o).

[245.86]
28. Meaning of 'father'.— (1) This section applies in the case of a child who is being or has been carried by a woman as the result of the placing in her of an embryo or of sperm and eggs or her artificial insemination.
(2) If—

(a) at the time of the placing in her of the embryo or the sperm and eggs or of her insemination, the woman was a party to a marriage, and

(b) the creation of the embryo carried by her was not brought about with the sperm of the other party to the marriage,

then, subject to subsection (5) below, the other party to the marriage shall be treated as the father of the child unless it is shown that he did not consent to the placing in her of the embryo or the sperm and eggs or to her insemination (as the case may be).

(3) If no man is treated, by virtue of subsection (2) above, as the father of the child but—

(a) the embryo or the sperm and eggs were placed in the woman, or she was artificially inseminated, in the course of treatment services provided for her and a man together by a person to whom a licence applies, and
(b) the creation of the embryo carried by her was not brought about with the sperm of that man,

then, subject to subsection (5) below, that man shall be treated as the father of the child.

(4) Where a person is treated as the father of the child by virtue of subsection (2) or (3) above, no other person is to be treated as the father of the child.

(5) Subsections (2) and (3) above do not apply—

(a) in relation to England and Wales and Northern Ireland, to any child who, by virtue of the rules of common law, is treated as the legitimate child of the parties to a marriage,
(b) (*applies to Scotland only*), or
(c) to any child to the extent that the child is treated by virtue of adoption as not being the child of any person other than the adopter or adopters [man's child][1].

(6) Where—

(a) the sperm of a man who had given such consent as is required by paragraph 5 of Schedule 3 to this Act was used for a purpose for which such consent was required, or
(b) the sperm of a man, or any embryo the creation of which was brought about with his sperm, was used after his death,

he is not to be treated as the father of the child.

(7) The references in subsection (2) above to the parties to a marriage at the time there referred to—

(a) are to the parties to a marriage subsisting at that time, unless a judicial separation was then in force, but
(b) include the parties to a void marriage if either or both of them reasonably believed at that time that the marriage was valid; and for the purposes of this subsection it shall be presumed, unless the contrary is shown, that one of them reasonably believed at that time that the marriage was valid.

(8) This section applies whether the woman was in the United Kingdom or elsewhere at the time of the placing in her of the embryo or the sperm and eggs or her artificial insemination.

(9) In subsection (7)(a) above, 'judicial separation' includes a legal separation obtained in a country outside the British Islands and recognised in the United Kingdom.

1 Words substituted in sub-s (5) with effect from 30 December 2005: ACA 2002, s 139(1), Sch 3, paras 76 and 78 and Adoption and Children Act 2002 (Commencement No 9) Order 2005, SI 2005/2213, art 2(o).

[245.87]
29. Effect of sections 27 and 28.— (1) Where by virtue of section 27 or 28 of this Act a person is to be treated as the mother or father of a child, that person is to be treated in law as the mother or, as the case may be, father of the child for all purposes.
(2) Where by virtue of section 27 or 28 of this Act a person is not to be treated as the mother or father of a child, that person is to be treated in law as not being the mother or, as the case may be, father of the child for any purpose.
(3) Where subsection (1) or (2) above has effect, references to any relationship between two people in any enactment, deed or other instrument or document (whenever passed or made) are to be read accordingly.
(4) In relation to England and Wales and Northern Ireland, nothing in the provisions of section 27(1) or 28(2) to (4), read with this section, affects—

(a) the succession to any dignity or title of honour or renders any person capable of succeeding to or transmitting a right to succeed to any such dignity or title, or
(b) the devolution of any property limited (expressly or not) to devolve (as nearly as the law permits) along with any dignity or title of honour.

(5) (*Applies to Scotland only.*)

[245.88]
30. Parental orders in favour of gamete donors.— (1) The court may make an order providing for a child to be treated in law as the child of the parties to a marriage (referred to in this section as 'the husband' and 'the wife') if—

(a) the child has been carried by a woman other than the wife as the result of the placing in her of an embryo or sperm and eggs or her artificial insemination,
(b) the gametes of the husband or the wife, or both, were used to bring about the creation of the embryo, and
(c) the conditions in subsections (2) to (7) below are satisfied.

(2) The husband and the wife must apply for the order within six months of the birth of the child or, in the case of a child born before the coming into force of this Act, within six months of such coming into force.
(3) At the time of the application and of the making of the order—

(a) the child's home must be with the husband and the wife, and
(b) the husband or the wife, of both of them, must be domiciled in a part of the United Kingdom or in the Channel Islands or the Isle of Man.

(4) At the time of the making of the order both the husband and the wife must have attained the age of eighteen.
(5) The court must be satisfied that both the father of the child (including a person who is the father by virtue of section 28 of this Act), where he is not the husband, and the woman who carried the child have freely, and with full understanding of what is involved, agreed unconditionally to the making of the order.
(6) Subsection (5) above does not require the agreement of a person who cannot be found or is incapable of giving agreement and the agreement of the woman who carried the child is ineffective for the purposes of that subsection if given by her less than six weeks after the child's birth.
(7) The court must be satisfied that no money or other benefit (other than for expenses reasonably incurred) has been given or received by the husband or the wife for or in consideration of—

- (a) the making of the order,
- (b) any agreement required by subsection (5) above,
- (c) the handing over of the child to the husband and the wife, or
- (d) the making of any arrangements with a view to the making of the order, unless authorised by the court.

(8) For the purposes of an application under this section—

- (a) in relation to England and Wales, section 92(7) to (10) of, and Part I of Schedule 11 to, the Children Act 1989 (jurisdiction of courts) shall apply for the purposes of this section to determine the meaning of 'the court' as they apply for the purposes of that Act and proceedings on the application shall be 'family proceedings' for the purposes of that Act,
- (b) (*applies to Scotland only*), and
- (c) in relation to Northern Ireland, 'the court' means the High Court or any county court within whose division the child is.

(9) Regulations may provide—

- (a) for any provision of the enactments about adoption to have effect, with such modifications (if any) as may be specified in the regulations, in relation to orders under this section, and applications for such orders, as it has effect in relation to adoption, and applications for adoption orders, and
- (b) for references in any enactment to adoption, an adopted child or an adoptive relationship to be read (respectively) as references to the effect of an order under this section, a child to whom such an order applies and a relationship arising by virtue of the enactments about adoption, as applied by the regulations, and for similar expressions in connection with adoption to be read accordingly,

and the regulations may include such incidental or supplemental provision as appears to the Secretary of State necessary or desirable in consequence of any provision made by virtue of paragraph (a) or (b) above.
(10) In this section 'the enactments about adoption' means the [Adoption and Children Act 2002][1], the Adoption (Scotland) Act 1978 and the Adoption (Northern Ireland) Order 1987.

(11) Subsection (1)(a) above applies whether the woman was in the United Kingdom or elsewhere at the time of the placing in her of the embryo or the sperm and eggs or her artificial insemination.

1 Words substituted in sub-s (10) with effect from 30 December 2005: ACA 2002, s 139(1), Sch 3, paras 76 and 79 and Adoption and Children Act 2002 (Commencement No 9) Order 2005, SI 2005/2213, art 2(o).

* * * * *

MISCELLANEOUS AND GENERAL

* * * * *

[245.89]
47. Index The expressions listed in the left-hand column below are respectively defined or (as the case may be) are to be interpreted in accordance with the provisions of this Act listed in the right-hand column in relation to those expressions.

Expression	*Relevant provision*
Carry, in relation to a child	Section 2(3)
....	....
Embryo	Section 1
Gametes, eggs or sperm	Section 1
....	....

[245.90]
48. Northern Ireland.— (1) This Act (except section 37) extends to Northern Ireland.
(2) Subject to any Order made after the passing of this Act by virtue of subsection (1)(a) of section 3 of the Northern Ireland Constitution Act 1973, the activities governed by this Act shall not be transferred matters for the purposes of that Act, but shall for the purposes of subsection (2) of that section be treated as specified in Schedule 3 to that Act.

[245.91]
49. Short title, commencement, etc.— (1) This Act may be cited as the Human Fertilisation and Embryology Act 1990.
(2) This Act shall come into force on such day as the Secretary of State may by order made by statutory instrument appoint and different days may be appointed for different provisions and for different purposes.
(3) Sections 27 to 29 of this Act shall have effect only in relation to children carried by women as a result of the placing in them of embryos or of sperm and eggs, or of their artificial insemination (as the case may be), after the commencement of those sections.

(4) Section 27 of the Family Law Reform Act 1987 (artificial insemination) does not have effect in relation to children carried by women as the result of their artificial insemination after the commencement of sections 27 to 29 of this Act.

* * * * *

(6) An order under this section may make such transitional provision as the Secretary of State considers necessary or desirable and, in particular, may provide that where activities are carried on under the supervision of a particular individual, being activities which are carried on under the supervision of that individual at the commencement of sections 3 and 4 of this Act, those activities are to be treated, during such period as may be specified in or determined in accordance with the order, as authorised by a licence (having, in addition to the conditions required by this Act, such conditions as may be so specified or determined) under which that individual is the person responsible.
(7) Her Majesty may by Order in Council direct that any of the provisions of this Act shall extend, with such exceptions, adaptations and modifications (if any) as may be specified in the Order, to any of the Channel Islands.

* * * * *

ADOPTION AND CHILDREN ACT 2002

[245.92]

Note. This Act makes amendments to ChA 1989, the relevant sections of which are printed as amended at paras **[244.113]** ff, above. With effect from 30 December 2005, it also repeals the whole of AA 1976, apart from Part IV and para 6 of Sch 2 (which regulate the property and succession rights of adopted children) which continue to apply in relation to persons adopted before 30 December 2005. The corresponding provisions of the 2002 Act set out below, which are in effect identical with the corresponding provisions of AA 1976 save in one minor respect (see note to para **[245.96]** below), apply in relation to persons adopted on or after 30 December 2005: see s 66(2) at para **[245.93]** below.

PART 1
ADOPTION

CHAPTER 4
STATUS OF ADOPTED CHILDREN

[245.93]
66 Meaning of adoption in Chapter 4 (1) In this Chapter 'adoption' means—

(a) adoption by an adoption order or a Scottish or Northern Irish adoption order,
(b) adoption by an order made in the Isle of Man or any of the Channel Islands,
(c) an adoption effected under the law of a Convention country outside

the British Islands, and certified in pursuance of Article 23(1) of the Convention (referred to in this Act as a 'Convention adoption'),
- (d) an overseas adoption, or
- (e) an adoption recognised by the law of England and Wales and effected under the law of any other country;

and related expressions are to be interpreted accordingly.
(2) But references in this Chapter to adoption do not include an adoption effected before the day on which this Chapter comes into force (referred to in this Chapter as 'the appointed day').
(3) Any reference in an enactment to an adopted person within the meaning of this Chapter includes a reference to an adopted child within the meaning of Part 4 of the Adoption Act 1976 (c 36).

[245.94]
67 Status conferred by adoption (1) An adopted person is to be treated in law as if born as the child of the adopters or adopter.
(2) An adopted person is the legitimate child of the adopters or adopter and, if adopted by—

- (a) a couple, or
- (b) one of a couple under section 51(2),

is to be treated as the child of the relationship of the couple in question.
(3) An adopted person—

- (a) if adopted by one of a couple under section 51(2), is to be treated in law as not being the child of any person other than the adopter and the other one of the couple, and
- (b) in any other case, is to be treated in law, subject to subsection (4), as not being the child of any person other than the adopters or adopter;

but this subsection does not affect any reference in this Act to a person's natural parent or to any other natural relationship.
(4) In the case of a person adopted by one of the person's natural parents as sole adoptive parent, subsection (3)(b) has no effect as respects entitlement to property depending on relationship to that parent, or as respects anything else depending on that relationship.
(5) This section has effect from the date of the adoption.
(6) Subject to the provisions of this Chapter and Schedule 4, this section—

- (a) applies for the interpretation of enactments or instruments passed or made before as well as after the adoption, and so applies subject to any contrary indication, and
- (b) has effect as respects things done, or events occurring, on or after the adoption.

[245.95]
68 Adoptive relatives (1) A relationship existing by virtue of section 67 may be referred to as an adoptive relationship, and—

- (a) an adopter may be referred to as an adoptive parent or (as the case may be) as an adoptive father or adoptive mother,

(b) any other relative of any degree under an adoptive relationship may be referred to as an adoptive relative of that degree.

(2) Subsection (1) does not affect the interpretation of any reference, not qualified by the word 'adoptive', to a relationship.
(3) A reference (however expressed) to the adoptive mother and father of a child adopted by—

(a) a couple of the same sex, or
(b) a partner of the child's parent, where the couple are of the same sex,

is to be read as a reference to the child's adoptive parents.

[245.96]
69 Rules of interpretation for instruments concerning property (1) The rules of interpretation contained in this section apply (subject to any contrary indication and to Schedule 4) to any instrument so far as it contains a disposition of property.
(2) In applying section 67(1) and (2) to a disposition which depends on the date of birth of a child or children of the adoptive parent or parents, the disposition is to be interpreted as if—

(a) the adopted person had been born on the date of adoption,
(b) two or more people adopted on the same date had been born on that date in the order of their actual births;

but this does not affect any reference to a person's age.
(3) Examples of phrases in wills on which subsection (2) can operate are—

1 Children of A 'living at my death or born afterwards'.
2 Children of A 'living at my death or born afterwards before any one of such children for the time being in existence attains a vested interest and who attain the age of 21 years'.
3 As in example 1 or 2, but referring to grandchildren of A instead of children of A.
4 A for life 'until he has a child', and then to his child or children.
Note Subsection (2) will not affect the reference to the age of 21 years in example 2.

(4) Section 67(3) does not prejudice—

(a) any qualifying interest, or
(b) any interest expectant (whether immediately or not) upon a qualifying interest.

'Qualifying interest' means an interest vested in possession in the adopted person before the adoption.[1]

(5) Where it is necessary to determine for the purposes of a disposition of property effected by an instrument whether a woman can have a child—

(a) it must be presumed that once a woman has attained the age of 55 years she will not adopt a person after execution of the instrument, and
(b) if she does so, then (in spite of section 67) that person is not to be

treated as her child or (if she does so as one of a couple) as the child of the other one of the couple for the purposes of the instrument.

(6) In this section, 'instrument' includes a private Act settling property, but not any other enactment.

1 Section 69(4) differs from AA 1976, s 42(4), the corresponding provision of the earlier legislation and in effect overrules *Staffordshire County Council v B* [1999] 2 FCR 333, [1998] 1 FLR 261. See note 1 to para **[245.60]** above.

[245.97]
70 Dispositions depending on date of birth (1) Where a disposition depends on the date of birth of a person who was born illegitimate and who is adopted by one of the natural parents as sole adoptive parent, section 69(2) does not affect entitlement by virtue of Part 3 of the Family Law Reform Act 1987 (c 42) (dispositions of property).
(2) Subsection (1) applies for example where—

(a) a testator dies in 2001 bequeathing a legacy to his eldest grandchild living at a specified time,
(b) his unmarried daughter has a child in 2002 who is the first grandchild,
(c) his married son has a child in 2003,
(d) subsequently his unmarried daughter adopts her child as sole adoptive parent.

In that example the status of the daughter's child as the eldest grandchild of the testator is not affected by the events described in paragraphs (c) and (d).

[245.98]
71 Property devolving with peerages etc (1) An adoption does not affect the descent of any peerage or dignity or title of honour.
(2) An adoption does not affect the devolution of any property limited (expressly or not) to devolve (as nearly as the law permits) along with any peerage or dignity or title of honour.
(3) Subsection (2) applies only if and so far as a contrary intention is not expressed in the instrument, and has effect subject to the terms of the instrument.

[245.99]
72 Protection of trustees and personal representatives (1) A trustee or personal representative is not under a duty, by virtue of the law relating to trusts or the administration of estates, to enquire, before conveying or distributing any property, whether any adoption has been effected or revoked if that fact could affect entitlement to the property.
(2) A trustee or personal representative is not liable to any person by reason of a conveyance or distribution of the property made without regard to any such fact if he has not received notice of the fact before the conveyance or distribution.
(3) This section does not prejudice the right of a person to follow the property, or any property representing it, into the hands of another person, other than a purchaser, who has received it.

[245.100]
73 Meaning of disposition (1) This section applies for the purposes of this Chapter.
(2) A disposition includes the conferring of a power of appointment and any other disposition of an interest in or right over property; and in this subsection a power of appointment includes any discretionary power to transfer a beneficial interest in property without the furnishing of valuable consideration.
(3) This Chapter applies to an oral disposition as if contained in an instrument made when the disposition was made.
(4) The date of death of a testator is the date at which a will or codicil is to be regarded as made.
(5) The provisions of the law of intestate succession applicable to the estate of a deceased person are to be treated as if contained in an instrument executed by him (while of full capacity) immediately before his death.

PART 3
MISCELLANEOUS AND FINAL PROVISIONS

CHAPTER 1
MISCELLANEOUS

Amendments etc

[245.101]
139 Amendments, transitional and transitory provisions, savings and repeals
(1) …
(2) Schedule 4 (transitional and transitory provisions and savings) is to have effect.
(3) …

SCHEDULE 4
TRANSITIONAL AND TRANSITORY PROVISIONS AND SAVINGS

Section 139

General rules for continuity

[245.102]

Status
17 (1) Section 67—

(a) does not apply to a pre-1976 instrument or enactment in so far as it contains a disposition of property, and
(b) does not apply to any public general Act in its application to any disposition of property in a pre-1976 instrument or enactment.

(2) Section 73 applies in relation to this paragraph as if this paragraph were contained in Chapter 4 of Part 1; and an instrument or enactment is a pre-1976 instrument or enactment for the purposes of this Schedule if it was passed or made at any time before 1st January 1976.

18 Section 69 does not apply to a pre-1976 instrument.

19 In section 70(1), the reference to Part 3 of the Family Law Reform Act 1987 (c 42) includes Part 2 of the Family Law Reform Act 1969 (c 46).

GENDER RECOGNITION ACT 2004

[245.103]

Note. This Act, which came into force on 4 April 2005 (Gender Recognition Act 2004 (Commencement) Order 2005, SI 2005/54), recognises sex changes by permitting a person who is at least 18 years of age to apply for a gender recognition certificate. If granted, the applicant will be treated as having 'the acquired gender' for all purposes, including succession. The construction of wills or other instruments made before the commencement date is unaffected by the grant of a gender recognition certificate. Otherwise the grant of a certificate has retrospective effect subject to any order which a court may make on the application of a person who is adversely affected.

Applications for gender recognition certificate

[245.104]

1 Applications (1) A person of either gender who is aged at least 18 may make an application for a gender recognition certificate on the basis of—

- (a) living in the other gender, or
- (b) having changed gender under the law of a country or territory outside the United Kingdom.

(2) In this Act 'the acquired gender', in relation to a person by whom an application under subsection (1) is or has been made, means—

- (a) in the case of an application under paragraph (a) of that subsection, the gender in which the person is living, or
- (b) in the case of an application under paragraph (b) of that subsection, the gender to which the person has changed under the law of the country or territory concerned.

Consequences of issue of gender recognition certificate etc

[245.105]

9 General (1) Where a full gender recognition certificate is issued to a person, the person's gender becomes for all purposes the acquired gender (so that, if the acquired gender is the male gender, the person's sex becomes that of a man and, if it is the female gender, the person's sex becomes that of a woman).

(2) Subsection (1) does not affect things done, or events occurring, before the certificate is issued; but it does operate for the interpretation of enactments passed, and instruments and other documents made, before the certificate is issued (as well as those passed or made afterwards).

(3) Subsection (1) is subject to provision made by this Act or any other enactment or any subordinate legislation.

[245.106]
12 Parenthood The fact that a person's gender has become the acquired gender under this Act does not affect the status of the person as the father or mother of a child.

[245.107]
15 Succession etc The fact that a person's gender has become the acquired gender under this Act does not affect the disposal or devolution of property under a will or other instrument made before the appointed day.

[245.108]
16 Peerages etc The fact that a person's gender has become the acquired gender under this Act—

(a) does not affect the descent of any peerage or dignity or title of honour, and

(b) does not affect the devolution of any property limited (expressly or not) by a will or other instrument to devolve (as nearly as the law permits) along with any peerage or dignity or title of honour unless an intention that it should do so is expressed in the will or other instrument.

[245.109]
17 Trustees and personal representatives (1) A trustee or personal representative is not under a duty, by virtue of the law relating to trusts or the administration of estates, to enquire, before conveying or distributing any property, whether a full gender recognition certificate has been issued to any person or revoked (if that fact could affect entitlement to the property).
(2) A trustee or personal representative is not liable to any person by reason of a conveyance or distribution of the property made without regard to whether a full gender recognition certificate has been issued to any person or revoked if the trustee or personal representative has not received notice of the fact before the conveyance or distribution.
(3) This section does not prejudice the right of a person to follow the property, or any property representing it, into the hands of another person who has received it unless that person has purchased it for value in good faith and without notice.

[245.110]
18 Orders where expectations defeated (1) This section applies where the disposition or devolution of any property under a will or other instrument (made on or after the appointed day) is different from what it would be but for the fact that a person's gender has become the acquired gender under this Act.
(2) A person may apply to the High Court or Court of Session for an order on the ground of being adversely affected by the different disposition or devolution of the property.

(3) The court may, if it is satisfied that it is just to do so, make in relation to any person benefiting from the different disposition or devolution of the property such order as it considers appropriate.
(4) An order may, in particular, make provision for—

(a) the payment of a lump sum to the applicant,
(b) the transfer of property to the applicant,
(c) the settlement of property for the benefit of the applicant,
(d) the acquisition of property and either its transfer to the applicant or its settlement for the benefit of the applicant.

(5) An order may contain consequential or supplementary provisions for giving effect to the order or for ensuring that it operates fairly as between the applicant and the other person or persons affected by it; and an order may, in particular, confer powers on trustees.

SECTION 3

Miscellaneous provisions relevant to the drafting of wills

[246.1]

Note. This section does not contain a comprehensive collection of conveyancing statutes, but a selection of statutes which a will draftsman may often have to consider. It includes statutes relating to beneficial interests, administrative powers conferred on personal representatives and trustees and powers to appoint new trustees and trustees' investment powers.

APPORTIONMENT ACT 1870

(33 & 34 Vict c 35)

[1 August 1870]

[246.2]
1. Short title. This Act may be cited for all purposes as 'The Apportionment Act, 1870.'

[246.3]
2. Rents, etc to be apportionable in respect of time. ...
All rents, annuities, dividends, and other periodical payments in the nature of income (whether reserved or made payable under an instrument in writing or otherwise) shall, like interest on money lent, be considered as accruing from day to day, and shall be apportionable in respect of time accordingly.[1]

1 The words omitted from this section were repealed by the Statute Law Revision (No 2) Act 1893.

[246.4]
3. Apportioned part of rent, etc to be payable when the next entire portion shall have become due. The apportioned part of any such rent, annuity, dividend, or other payment shall be payable or recoverable in the case of a continuing rent, annuity, or other such payment when the entire portion of which such apportioned part shall form part shall become due and payable, and not before, and in the case of a rent, annuity, or other such payment determined by re-entry, death, or otherwise when the next entire portion of the same would have been payable if the same had not so determined, and not before.

[246.5]

4. Persons shall have the same remedies for recovering apportioned parts as for entire portions—Proviso as to rents reserved in certain cases. All persons and their respective heirs, executors, administrators, and assigns, and also the executors, administrators, and assigns respectively of persons whose interests determine with their own deaths, shall have such or the same remedies at law and in equity for recovering such apportioned parts as aforesaid when payable (allowing proportionate parts of all just allowances) as they respectively would have had for recovering such entire portions as aforesaid if entitled thereto respectively; provided that persons liable to pay rents reserved out of or charged on lands or other hereditaments of any tenure, and the same lands or other hereditaments, shall not be resorted to for any such apportioned part forming part of an entire or continuing rent as aforesaid specifically, but the entire or continuing rent, including such apportioned part, shall be recovered and received by the heir or other person who, if the rent had not been apportionable under this Act, or otherwise, would have been entitled to such entire or continuing rent, and such apportioned part shall be recoverable from such heir or other person by the executors or other parties entitled under this Act to the same by action at law or suit in equity.

[246.6]

5. Interpretation. In the construction of this Act—

The word 'rents' includes rent service, rentcharge, and rent seck, and also tithes and all periodical payments or renderings in lieu of or in the nature of rent or tithe.

The word 'annuities' includes salaries and pensions.

The word 'dividends' includes (besides dividends strictly so called) all payments made by the name of dividend, bonus, or otherwise out of the revenue of trading or other public companies, divisible between all or any of the members of such respective companies, whether such payments shall be usually made or declared, at any fixed times or otherwise; and all such divisible revenue shall, for the purposes of this Act, be deemed to have accrued by equal daily increment during and within the period for or in respect of which the payment of the same revenue shall be declared or expressed to be made, but the said word 'dividend' does not include payments in the nature of a return or reimbursement of capital.

[246.7]

6. Act not to apply to policies of assurance. Nothing in this Act contained shall render apportionable any annual sums made payable in policies of assurance of any description.

[246.8]

7. Nor where stipulation made to the contrary. The provisions of this Act shall not extend to any case in which it is or shall be expressly stipulated that no apportionment shall take place.

TRUSTEE ACT 1925

(15 & 16 Geo 5 c 19)

[9 April 1925]

[246.9]

Note. The Trustee Act 1925 (TA 1925) came into force on 1 January 1926. The Act is printed as amended by the Trustee Investments Act 1961, the Statute Law Revision Act 1963, the Law of Property (Amendment) Act 1926 (LP(A)A 1926), the Powers of Attorney Act 1971 (PAA 1971), the Statute Law (Repeals) Act 1978, the Trusts of Land and Appointment of Trustees Act 1996 (TLATA 1996) and, more recently, by the Trustee Act 2000 (TrA 2000) which repealed the whole of Part I of the TA 1925 (relating to investments), so far as not already repealed. Other amendments are noted to the provisions concerned.

PART II
GENERAL POWERS OF TRUSTEES AND PERSONAL REPRESENTATIVES

GENERAL POWERS

[246.10]
12. Power of trustees for sale to sell by auction, etc.— (1) Where [a trustee has a duty or power to sell property],[1] he may sell or concur with any other person in selling all or any part of the property, either subject to prior charges or not, and either together or in lots, by public auction or by private contract, subject to any such conditions respecting title or evidence of title or other matter as the trustee thinks fit, with power to vary any contract for sale, and to buy in at any auction, or to rescind any contract for sale and to re-sell, without being answerable for any loss.
(2) A [duty][1] or power to sell or dispose of land includes a [duty][1] or power to sell or dispose of part thereof, whether the division is horizontal, vertical, or made in any other way.
(3) This section does not enable an express power to sell settled land to be exercised where the power is not vested in the tenant for life or statutory owner.

1 Sub-ss (1), (2): words in square brackets substituted by the TLATA 1996, s 25(1), Sch 3, para 3(2).

[246.11]
13. Power to sell subject to depreciatory conditions.— (1) No sale made by a trustee shall be impeached by any beneficiary upon the ground that any of the conditions subject to which the sale was made may have been unnecessarily depreciatory, unless it also appears that the consideration for the sale was thereby rendered inadequate.
(2) No sale made by a trustee shall, after the execution of the conveyance, be impeached as against the purchaser upon the ground that any of the conditions subject to which the sale was made may have been unnecessarily depreciatory, unless it appears that the purchaser was acting in collusion with the trustee at the time when the contract for sale was made.
(3) No purchaser, upon any sale made by a trustee, shall be at liberty to make any objection against the title upon any of the grounds aforesaid.

(4) This section applies to sales made before or after the commencement of this Act.

[246.12]
14. Power of trustees to give receipts.— (1) The receipt in writing of a trustee for any money, securities, [investments][1] or other personal property or effects payable, transferable, or deliverable to him under any trust or power shall be a sufficient discharge to the person paying, transferring, or delivering the same and shall effectually exonerate him from seeing to the application or being answerable for any loss or misapplication thereof.
(2) This section does not, except where the trustee is a trust corporation, enable a sole trustee to give a valid receipt for—

[(a) proceeds of sale or other capital money arising under a trust of land;][2]
(b) capital money arising under the Settled Land Act 1925[3].

(3) This section applies notwithstanding anything to the contrary in the instrument, if any, creating the trust.

1 Word in square brackets added by the TrA 2000, s 40, Sch 2, para 19.
2 Sub-s (2): para (a) substituted by the TLATA 1996, s 25(1), Sch 3, para 3(3).
3 Although it has not been possible to create settlements under the Settled Land Act 1925 (SLA 1925) since 1 January 1997, this reform is without prejudice to existing strict settlements: TLATA 1996, s 2 (para **[246.104]** below). Sub-s (2)(b) therefore continues to apply in relation to such settlements.

[246.13]
15. Power to compound liabilities. A personal representative, or two or more trustees acting together, or, subject to the restrictions imposed in regard to receipts by a sole trustee not being a trust corporation, a sole acting trustee where by the instrument, if any, creating the trust, or by statute, a sole trustee is authorised to execute the trusts and powers reposed in him, may, if and as he or they think fit—

(a) accept any property, real or personal, before the time at which it is made transferable or payable; or
(b) sever and apportion any blended trust funds or property; or
(c) pay or allow any debt or claim on any evidence that he or they think sufficient; or
(d) accept any composition or any security, real or personal, for any debt or for any property, real or personal, claimed; or
(e) allow any time of payment of any debt; or
(f) compromise, compound, abandon, submit to arbitration, or otherwise settle any debt, account, claim, or thing whatever relating to the testator's or intestate's estate or to the trust;

and for any of these purposes may enter into, give, execute, and do such agreements, instruments of composition or arrangement, releases, and other things as to him or them seem expedient, without being responsible for any loss occasioned by any act or thing so done by him or them [if he has or they have discharged the duty of care set out in section 1(1) of the Trustee Act 2000].[1]

1 Words in square brackets substituted by the TrA 2000, s 40, Sch 2, para 20.

[246.14]
16. Power to raise money by sale, mortgage, etc.— (1) Where trustees are authorised by the instrument, if any, creating the trust or by law to pay or apply capital money subject to the trust for any purpose or in any manner, they shall have and shall be deemed always to have had power to raise the money required by sale, conversion, calling in, or mortgage of all or any part of the trust property for the time being in possession.
(2) This section applies notwithstanding anything to the contrary contained in the instrument, if any, creating the trust, but does not apply to trustees of property held for charitable purposes, or to trustees of a settlement for the purposes of the Settled Land Act 1925, not being also the statutory owners.

[246.15]
17. Protection to purchasers and mortgagees dealing with trustees. No purchaser or mortgagee, paying or advancing money on a sale or mortgage purporting to be made under any trust or power vested in trustees, shall be concerned to see that such money is wanted, or that no more than is wanted is raised, or otherwise as to the application thereof.

[246.16]
18. Devolution of powers or trusts.— (1) Where a power or trust is given to or imposed on two or more trustees jointly, the same may be exercised or performed by the survivors or survivor of them for the time being.
(2) Until the appointment of new trustees, the personal representatives or representative for the time being of a sole trustee, or, where there were two or more trustees of the last surviving or continuing trustee, shall be capable of exercising or performing any power or trust which was given to, or capable of being exercised by, the sole or last surviving or continuing trustee, or the other trustees or trustee for the time being of the trust.
(3) This section takes effect subject to the restrictions imposed in regard to receipts by a sole trustee, not being a trust corporation.
(4) In this section 'personal representative' does not include an executor who has renounced or has not proved.

[246.17]
19. Power to insure.— [(1) A trustee may—

(a) insure any property which is subject to the trust against risks of loss or damage due to any event, and
(b) pay the premiums out of the trust funds.

(2) In the case of property held on a bare trust, the power to insure is subject to any direction given by the beneficiary or each of the beneficiaries—

(a) that any property specified in the direction is not to be insured;
(b) that any property specified in the direction is not to be insured except on such conditions as may be so specified.

(3) Property is held on a bare trust if it is held on trust for—

(a) a beneficiary who is of full age and capacity and absolutely entitled to the property subject to the trust, or
(b) beneficiaries each of whom is of full age and capacity and who (taken together) are absolutely entitled to the property subject to the trust.

(4) If a direction under subsection (2) of this section is given, the power to insure, so far as it is subject to the direction, ceases to be a delegable function for the purposes of section 11 of the Trustee Act 2000 (power to employ agents).
(5) In this section 'trust funds' means any income or capital funds of the trust.][1]

1 This section was substituted by the TrA 2000, s 34(1) as from 1 February 2001. Note that the substitution applies to trusts whether created before or after its commencement.

[246.18]
20. Application of insurance money where policy kept up under any trust, power or obligation.— (1) Money receivable by trustees or any beneficiary under a policy of insurance against the loss or damage of any property subject to a trust or to a settlement within the meaning of the Settled Land Act 1925 …[1] shall, where the policy has been kept up under any trust in that behalf or under any power statutory or otherwise, or in performance of any covenant or of any obligation statutory or otherwise, or by a tenant for life impeachable for waste, be capital money for the purposes of the trust or settlement, as the case may be.
(2) If any such money is receivable by any person, other than the trustees of the trust or settlement, that person shall use his best endeavours to recover and receive the money, and shall pay the net residue thereof, after discharging any costs of recovering and receiving it, to the trustees of the trust or settlement, or, if there are no trustees capable of giving a discharge therefor, into court.
(3) Any such money—

(a) if it was receivable in respect of settled land within the meaning of the Settled Land Act 1925, or any building or works thereon, shall be deemed to be capital money arising under that Act from the settled land, and shall be invested or applied by the trustees, or, if in court, under the direction of the court, accordingly;
(b) if it was receivable in respect of personal chattels settled as heirlooms within the meaning of the Settled Land Act, 1925, shall be deemed to be capital money arising under that Act; and shall be applicable by the trustees, or, if in court, under the direction of the court, in like manner as provided by that Act with respect to money arising by sale of chattels as heirlooms as aforesaid;
(c) if it was receivable in respect of [land subject to a trust of land or personal property held on trust for sale],[2] shall be held upon the trusts and subject to the powers and provisions applicable to money arising by a sale under such trust;
(d) in any other case, shall be held upon trusts corresponding as nearly as may be with the trusts affecting the property in respect of which it was payable.

(4) Such money, or any part thereof, may also be applied by the trustees, or, if in court, under the direction of the court, in rebuilding, reinstating, replacing, or replacing the property loss or damaged, but any such application by the trustees shall be subject to the consent of any person whose consent is required by the instrument, if any, creating the trust to the investment of money subject to the trust, and, in the case of money which is deemed to be capital money arising under the Settled Land Act 1925, be subject to the provisions of that Act with respect to the application of capital money by the trustees of the settlement.
(5) Nothing contained in this section prejudices or affects the right of any person to require any such money or any part thereof to be applied in rebuilding reinstating, or repairing the property lost or damaged, or the rights of any mortgagee, lessor, or lessee, whether under any statute or otherwise.
(6) This section applies to policies effected either before or after the commencement of this Act, but only to money received after such commencement.

1 Sub-s (1): words omitted repealed by the TrA 2000, ss 34(2), 40(3), Sch 4, Pt II.
2 Sub-s (3): in para (c) words in square brackets substituted by the TLATA 1996, s 25(1), Sch 3, para 3(5).

[246.19]
21. [*Repealed by the Trustee Act 2000, s 40(1), (3), Sch 2, Pt II, para 21, Sch 4, Pt II.*]

[246.20]
22. Reversionary interests, valuations, and audit.— (1) Where the trust property includes any share or interest in property not vested in the trustees, or the proceeds of the sale of any such property, or any other thing in action, the trustees on the same falling into possession, or becoming payable or transferable may—

(a) agree or ascertain the amount or value thereof or any part thereof in such manner as they may think fit;
(b) accept in or towards satisfaction thereof, at the market or current value, or upon any valuation or estimate of value which they may think fit, any authorised investments;
(c) allow any deductions for duties, costs, charges and expenses which they may think proper or reasonable;
(d) execute any release in respect of the premises so as effectually to discharge all accountable parties from all liability in respect of any matters coming within the scope of such release;

without being responsible in any such case for any loss occasioned by any act or thing so done by them [if they have discharged the duty of care set out in section 1(1) of the Trustee Act 2000].[1]
(2) The trustees shall not be under any obligation and shall not be chargeable with any breach of trust by reason of any omission—

(a) to place any distringas notice or apply for any stop or other like order upon any securities or other property out of or on which such share or interest or other thing in action as aforesaid is derived, payable or charged; or

(b) to take any proceedings on account of any act, default, or neglect on the part of the persons in whom such securities or other property or any of them or any part thereof are for the time being, or had at any time been, vested;

unless and until required in writing so to do by some person, or the guardian of some person, beneficially interested under the trust, and unless also due provision is made to their satisfaction for payment of the costs of any proceedings required to be taken:

Provided that nothing in this subsection shall relieve the trustees of the obligation to get in and obtain payment or transfer of such share or interest or other thing in action on the same falling into possession.

(3) Trustees may, for the purpose of giving effect to the trust, or any of the provisions of the instrument, if any, creating the trust or of any statute, from time to time (by duly qualified agents) ascertain and fix the value of any trust property in such manner as they think proper, and any valuation so made ... shall be binding upon all persons interested under the trust [if the trustees have discharged the duty of care set out in section 1(1) of the Trustee Act 2000].[2]

(4) Trustees may, in their absolute discretion, from time to time, but not more than once in every three years unless the nature of the trust or any special dealings with the trust property make a more frequent exercise of the right reasonable, cause the accounts of the trust property to be examined or audited by an independent accountant, and shall, for that purpose, produce such vouchers and give such information to him as he may require, and the costs of such examination or audit, including the fee of the auditor, shall be paid out of the capital or income of the trust property, or partly in one way and partly in the other as the trustees, in their absolute discretion, think fit, but, in default of any direction by the trustees to the contrary in any special case, costs attributable to capital shall be borne by capital and those attributable to income by income.

1 Words in square brackets in sub-s (1) substituted by the TrA 2000, s 40(1), Sch 2, para 22.
2 Sub-s (3): amended by the TrA 2000, s 40(1), Sch 2, Pt II, para 22.

[246.21]
23. [*Repealed by the Trustee Act 2000, s 40(1), (3), Sch 2, Pt II, para 23, Sch 4, Pt II.*]

[246.22]
24. Power to concur with others. Where an undivided share in [any][1] property, is subject to a trust, or forms part of the estate of a testator or intestate, the trustees or personal representatives may (without prejudice to the [trust][1] affecting the entirety of the land and the powers of the [trustees][1] in reference thereto), execute or exercise any [duty or][1] power vested in them in relation to such share in conjunction with the persons entitled to or having power in that behalf over the other share or shares, and notwithstanding that any one or more of the trustees or personal representatives may be entitled to or interested in any such other share, either in his or their own right or in a fiduciary capacity.

1 Words in square brackets substituted by the TLATA 1996, s 25(1), Sch 3, para 3(6).

[246.23]

[25. Delegation of trustee's functions by power of attorney.]— [(1) Notwithstanding any rule of law or equity to the contrary, a trustee may, by power of attorney, delegate the execution or exercise of all or any of the trusts, powers and discretions vested in him as trustee either alone or jointly with any other person or persons.

(2) A delegation under this section—

(a) commences as provided by the instrument creating the power or, if the instrument makes no provision as to the commencement of the delegation, with the date of the execution of the instrument by the donor; and

(b) continues for a period of twelve months or any shorter period provided by the instrument creating the power.

(3) The persons who may be donees of a power of attorney under this section include a trust corporation.

(4) Before or within seven days after giving a power of attorney under this section the donor shall give written notice of it (specifying the date on which the power comes into operation and its duration, the donee of the power, the reason why the power is given and, where some only are delegated, the trusts, powers and discretions delegated) to—

(a) each person (other than himself), if any, who under any instrument creating the trust has power (whether alone or jointly) to appoint a new trustee; and

(b) each of the other trustees, if any;

but failure to comply with this subsection shall not, in favour of a person dealing with the donee of the power, invalidate any act done or instrument executed by the donee.

(5) A power of attorney given under this section by a single donor—

(a) in the form set out in subsection (6) of this section; or

(b) in a form to the like effect but expressed to be made under this subsection,

shall operate to delegate to the person identified in the form as the single donee of the power the execution and exercise of all the trusts, powers and discretions vested in the donor as trustee (either alone or jointly with any other person or persons) under the single trust so identified.

(6) The form referred to in subsection (5) of this section is as follows—

'THIS GENERAL TRUSTEE POWER OF ATTORNEY is made on [date] by [name of one donor] of [address of donor] as trustee of [name or details of one trust].

I appoint [name of one donee] of [address of donee] to be my attorney [if desired, the date on which the delegation commences or the period for which it continues (or both)] in accordance with section 25(5) of the Trustee Act 1925.

[To be executed as a deed]'.

(7) The donor of a power of attorney given under this section shall be liable for the acts or defaults of the donee in the same manner as if they were the acts or defaults of the donor.

(8) For the purpose of executing or exercising the trusts or powers delegated to him, the donee may exercise any of the powers conferred on the donor as trustee by statute or by the instrument creating the trust, including power, for the purpose of the transfer of any inscribed stock, himself to delegate to an attorney power to transfer, but not including the power of delegation conferred by this section.
(9) The fact that it appears from any power of attorney given under this section, or from any evidence required for the purposes of any such power of attorney or otherwise, that in dealing with any stock the donee of the power is acting in the execution of a trust shall not be deemed for any purpose to affect any person in whose books the stock is inscribed or registered with any notice of the trust.
(10) This section applies to a personal representative, tenant for life and statutory owner as it applies to a trustee except that subsection (4) shall apply as if it required the notice there mentioned to be given—

(a) in the case of a personal representative, to each of the other personal representatives, if any, except any executor who has renounced probate;
(b) in the case of a tenant for life, to the trustees of the settlement and to each person, if any, who together with the person giving the notice constitutes the tenant for life; and
(c) in the case of a statutory owner, to each of the persons, if any, who together with the person giving the notice constitute the statutory owner and, in the case of a statutory owner by virtue of section 23(1)(a) of the Settled Land Act 1925, to the trustees of the settlement.][1]

1 This section was substituted by the Trustee Delegation Act 1999, s 5(1), (2). Note that this section applies to powers of attorney created *after* 1 March 2000.

INDEMNITIES

[246.24]
26. Protection against liability in respect of rents and covenants.—
(1) Where a personal representative or trustee liable as such for—

(a) any rent, covenant, or agreement reserved by or contained in any lease; or
(b) any rent, covenant or agreement payable under or contained in any grant made in consideration of a rentcharge; or
(c) any indemnity given in respect of any rent, covenant or agreement referred to in either of the foregoing paragraphs;

satisfies all liabilities under the lease or grant [which may have accrued and been claimed] up to the date of the conveyance hereinafter mentioned, and, where necessary, sets apart a sufficient fund to answer any future claim that may be made in respect of any fixed and ascertained sum which the lessee or grantee agreed to lay out on the property demised or granted, although the period for laying out the same may not have arrived, then and in any such case the personal representative or trustee may convey the property demised or granted to a purchaser, legatee, devisee, or other person entitled to call for a conveyance thereof and thereafter—

(i) he may distribute the residuary real and personal estate of the deceased testator or intestate, or, as the case may be, the trust estate (other than the fund, if any, set apart as aforesaid) to or amongst the persons entitled thereto, without appropriating any part, or any further part, as the case may be, of the estate of the deceased or of the trust estate to meet any future liability under the said lease or grant;

(ii) notwithstanding such distribution, he shall not be personally liable in respect of any subsequent claim under the said lease or grant.

[(1A) Where a personal representative or trustee has as such entered into, or may as such be required to enter into, an authorised guarantee agreement with respect to any lease comprised in the estate of a deceased testator or intestate or a trust estate (and, in a case where he has entered into such an agreement, he has satisfied all liabilities under it which may have accrued and been claimed up to the date of distribution)—

(a) he may distribute the residuary real and personal estate of the deceased testator or intestate, or the trust estate, to or amongst the persons entitled thereto—

  (i) without appropriating any part of the estate of the deceased, or the trust estate, to meet any future liability (or as the case may be, any liability) under any such agreement, and

  (ii) notwithstanding any potential liability of his to enter into any such agreement; and

(b) notwithstanding such distribution, he shall not be personally liable in respect of any subsequent claim (or, as the case may be, any claim) under any such agreement.

In this subsection 'authorised guarantee agreement' has the same meaning as in the Landlord and Tenant (Covenants) Act 1955.][1]

(2) This section operates without prejudice to the right of the lessor or grantor, or the persons deriving title under the lessor or grantor, to follow the assets of the deceased or the trust property into the hands of the persons amongst whom the same may have been respectively distributed, and applies notwithstanding anything to the contrary in the will or other instrument, if any, creating the trust.

(3) In this section 'lease' includes an underlease and an agreement for a lease or underlease and any instrument giving any such indemnity as aforesaid or varying the liabilities under the lease; 'grant' applies to a grant whether the rent is created by limitation, grant, reservation, or otherwise, and includes an agreement for a grant and any instrument giving any such indemnity as aforesaid or varying the liabilities under the grant; 'lessee' and 'grantee' include persons respectively deriving title under them.

1 Sub-s (1A): inserted by the Landlord and Tenant (Covenants) Act 1995, s 30(1), Sch 1, para 1, and brought into force on 1 January 1996 by the Landlord and Tenant (Covenants) Act 1995 (Commencement) Order 1995, SI 1995/2963.

[246.25]

27. Protection by means of advertisements.— (1) With a view to the conveyance to or distribution among the persons entitled to any real or personal property, the trustees of a settlement [, trustees of land, trustees for sale of personal property][1] or personal representatives, may give notice by advertisement in the Gazette, and in a newspaper circulating in the district in which the land is situated and such other like notices, including notices elsewhere than in England and Wales, as would, in any special case, have been directed by a court of competent jurisdiction in an action for administration, of their intention to make such conveyance or distribution as aforesaid, and requiring any person interested to send to the trustees or personal representatives within the time, not being less than two months, fixed in the notice or, where more than one notice is given, in the last of the notices, particulars of his claim in respect of the property or any part thereof to which the notice relates.

(2) At the expiration of the time fixed by the notice the trustees or personal representatives may convey or distribute the property or any part thereof to which the notice relates, to or among the persons entitled thereto, having regard only to the claims, whether formal or not, of which the trustees or personal representatives then had notice and shall not, as respects the property so conveyed or distributed, be liable to any person of whose claim the trustees or personal representatives have not had notice at the time of conveyance or distribution; but nothing in this section—

(a) prejudices the right of any person to follow the property, or any property representing the same, into the hands of any person, other than a purchaser, who may have received it; or

(b) frees the trustees or personal representatives from any obligation to make searches or obtain official certificates of search similar to those which an intending purchaser would be advised to make or obtain.

(3) This section applies notwithstanding anything to the contrary in the will or other instrument, if any, creating the trust.

1 Sub-s (1): words in square brackets substituted by the TLATA 1996, s 25(1), Sch 3, para 3(7).

[246.26]
28. Protection in regard to notice. A trustee or personal representative acting for the purposes of more than one trust or estate shall not, in the absence of fraud, be affected by notice of any instrument, matter, fact or thing in relation to any particular trust or estate if he has obtained notice thereof merely by reason of his acting or having acted for the purposes of another trust or estate.

[246.27]
29. [*Repealed by the Powers of Attorney Act 1971, s 11(2), (4), Sch 2.*]

[246.28]
30. [*Repealed by the Trustee Act 2000, s 40(1), (3), Sch 2, Pt II, para 24, Sch 4, Pt II.*]

MAINTENANCE, ADVANCEMENT AND PROTECTIVE TRUSTS

[246.29]

31. Power to apply income for maintenance and to accumulate surplus income during a minority.— (1) Where any property is held by trustees in trust for any person for any interest whatsoever, whether vested or contingent, then, subject to any prior interests or charges affecting that property—

- (i) during the infancy of any such person, if his interest so long continues, the trustees may, at their sole discretion, pay to his parent or guardian, if any, or otherwise apply for or towards his maintenance, education, or benefit, the whole or such part, if any, of the income of that property as may, in all the circumstances, be reasonable, whether or not there is—
  - (a) any other fund applicable to the same purpose; or
  - (b) any person bound by law to provide for his maintenance or education; and
- (ii) if such person on attaining the age of [eighteen years][1] has not a vested interest in such income, the trustees shall thenceforth pay the income of that property and of any accretion thereto under subsection (2) of this section to him, until he either attains a vested interest therein or dies, or until failure of his interest:

Provided that, in deciding whether the whole or any part of the income of the property is during a minority to be paid or applied for the purposes aforesaid, the trustees shall have regard to the age of the infant and his requirements and generally to the circumstances of the case, and in particular to what other income, if any, is applicable for the same purposes; and where trustees have notice that the income of more than one fund is applicable for those purposes, then, so far as practicable, unless the entire income of the funds is paid or applied as aforesaid or the court otherwise directs, a proportionate part only of the income of each fund shall be so paid or applied.

(2) During the infancy of any such person, if his interest so long continues, the trustees shall accumulate all the residue of that income [by investing it, and any profits from so investing it][1] from time to time in authorised investments, and shall hold those accumulations as follows—

- (i) If any such person—
  - (a) attains the age of [eighteen years],[2] or marries under that age [or forms a civil partnership][3], and his interest in such income during his infancy [or until his marriage or his formation of a civil partnership][3] is a vested interest; or
  - (b) on attaining the age of [eighteen years][2] or on marriage [or formation of a civil partnership][4] under that age becomes entitled to the property from which such income arose in fee simple, absolute or determinable, or absolutely, or for an entailed interest;

  the trustees shall hold the accumulations in trust for such person absolutely, but without prejudice to any provision with respect thereto contained in any settlement by him made under any statutory powers during his infancy, and so that the receipt of such person after marriage [or formation of a civil partnership][4], and though still an infant, shall be a good discharge; and

(ii) In any other case the trustees shall, notwithstanding that such person had a vested interest in such income, hold the accumulations as an accretion to the capital of the property from which such accumulations arose, and as one fund with such capital for all purposes, and so that, if such property is settled land, such accumulations shall be held upon the same trusts as if the same were capital money arising therefrom;

but the trustees may, at any time during the infancy of such person if his interest so long continues, apply those accumulations, or any part thereof, as if they were income arising in the then current year.

(3) This section applies in the case of a contingent interest only if the limitation or trust carries the intermediate income of the property, but it applies to a future or contingent legacy by the parent of, or a person standing in loco parentis to, the legatee, if and for such period as, under the general law, the legacy carries interest for the maintenance of the legatee, and in any such case as last aforesaid the rate of interest shall (if the income available is sufficient, and subject to any rules of court to the contrary) be five pounds per centum per annum.

(4) This section applies to a vested annuity in like manner as if the annuity were the income of property held by trustees in trust to pay the income thereof to the annuitant for the same period for which the annuity is payable, save that in any case accumulations made during the infancy of the annuitant shall be held in trust for the annuitant or his personal representatives absolutely.

(5) This section does not apply where the instrument, if any, under which the interest arises came into operation before the commencement of this Act.

1 Words substituted by the TrA 2000, s 40(1), Sch 2, para 25.

2 The word 'eighteen' was substituted (twice) by the FLRA, s 1(3), Sch 1, Pt I, for the words 'twenty-one years' but by virtue of s 1(4) of the FLRA 1969 and Sch 3, para 5(1) thereto, the amendment does not affect this section in its application to interests under instruments made before 1970 or, in its application by virtue of the AEA 1925, s 47(1)(ii), to the estate of an intestate dying before 1970 and, by virtue of s 1(4) of, and Sch 3, para 9 to the FLRA 1969, the amendment does not affect the construction of any statutory provision where it is incorporated in and has effect as part of any deed, will or other instrument not otherwise affected by s 1 of the FLRA 1969.

3 Words in second set of square brackets in sub-s (2)(i)(a) added and in third set of square brackets substituted with effect from 5 December 2005: CPA 2004, s 261(1), Sch 27, para 5(1) and (2) and Civil Partnership Act 2004 (Commencement No 2) Order 2005, SI 2005/3175.

4 Words in sub-s (2)(i)(b) and in the following part of sub-s (2)(i) added with effect from 5 December 2005: CPA 2004, s 261(1), Sch 27, para 5(3) and (4) and Civil Partnership Act 2004 (Commencement No 2) Order 2005, SI 2005/3175.

[246.30]

32. Power of advancement.— (1) Trustees may at any time or times pay or apply any capital money subject to a trust, for the advancement or benefit, in such manner as they may, in their absolute discretion, think fit, of any person entitled to the capital of the trust property or of any share thereof, whether absolutely or contingently on his attaining any specified age or on the occurrence of any other event, or subject to a gift over on his death under any specified age or on the occurrence of any other event, and whether in possession or in remainder or reversion, and such payment or application may be made notwithstanding that the interest of such person is liable to be defeated by the exercise of a power of appointment or revocation, or to be diminished by the increase of the class to which he belongs— Provided that—

(a) the money so paid or applied for the advancement or benefit of any person shall not exceed altogether in amount one-half of the presumptive or vested share or interest of that person in the trust property; and

(b) if that person is or becomes absolutely and indefeasibly entitled to a share in the trust property the money so paid or applied shall be brought into account as part of such share; and

(c) no such payment or application shall be made so as to prejudice any person entitled to any prior life or other interest, whether vested or contingent, in the money paid or applied unless such person is in existence and of full age and consents in writing to such payment or application.

[(2) This section does not apply to capital money arising under the Settled Land Act 1925.][1]

(3) This section does not apply to trusts constituted or created before the commencement of this Act.

1 Sub-s (2): substituted by the TLATA 1996, s 25(1), Sch 3, para 3(8).

[246.31]

33. Protective trusts.— (1) Where any income, including an annuity or other periodical income payment, is directed to be held on protective trusts for the benefit of any person (in this section called 'the principal beneficiary') for the period of his life or for any less period, then, during that period (in this section called the 'trust period') the said income shall, without prejudice to any prior interest, be held on the following trusts, namely:—

(i) Upon trust for the principal beneficiary during the trust period or until he, whether before or after the termination of any prior interest, does or attempts to do or suffers any act or thing, or until any event happens, other than an advance under any statutory or express power, whereby, if the said income were payable during the trust period to the principal beneficiary absolutely during that period, he would be deprived of the right to receive the same or any part thereof, in any of which cases, as well as on the termination of the trust period, whichever first happens, this trust of the said income shall fail or determine;

(ii) If the trust aforesaid fails or determines during the subsistence of the trust period, then, during the residue of that period, the said income shall be held upon trust for the application thereof for the maintenance or support, or otherwise for the benefit, of all or any one or more exclusively of the other or others of the following persons (that is to say)—

(a) the principal beneficiary and his or her [spouse or civil partner][1], if any, and his or her children or more remote issue, if any; or
(b) if there is no [spouse or civil partner][1] or issue of the principal beneficiary in existence, the principal beneficiary and the persons who would, if he were actually dead, be entitled to the trust property or the income thereof or to the annuity fund, if any, or arrears of the annuity, as the case may be;

as the trustees in their absolute discretion, without being liable to account for the exercise of such discretion, think fit.
(2) This section does not apply to trusts coming into operation before the commencement of this Act, and has effect subject to any variation of the implied trusts aforesaid contained in the instrument creating the trust.
(3) Nothing in this section operates to validate any trust which would, if contained in the instrument creating the trust, be liable to be set aside.
[(4) In relation to the dispositions mentioned in section 19(1) of the Family Law Reform Act 1987, this section shall have effect as if any reference (however expressed) to any relationship between two persons were construed in accordance with section 1 of that Act.][2]

1 Words in square brackets in sub-s (1)(ii)(a) and (b) substituted with effect from 5 December 2005: CPA 2004 s 261(1), Sch 27, para 6 and Civil Partnership Act 2004 (Commencement No 2) Order 2005, SI 2005/3175.
2 Sub-s (4): added by the Family Law Reform Act 1987, s 33(1), Sch 2, as from 4 April 1988.

PART III
APPOINTMENT AND DISCHARGE OF TRUSTEES

[246.32]
34. Limitation of the number of trustees.— (1) Where, at the commencement of this Act, there are more than four trustees of a settlement of land, or more than four trustees holding land on trust for sale, no new trustees shall (except where as a result of the appointment the number is reduced to four or less) be capable of being appointed until the number is reduced to less than four, and thereafter the number shall not be increased beyond four.
(2) In the case of settlements and dispositions [creating trusts of land][1] made or coming into operation after the commencement of this Act—

(a) the number of trustees thereof shall not in any case exceed four, and where more than four persons are named as such trustees, the four first named (who are able and willing to act) shall alone be the trustees, and the other persons named shall not be trustees unless appointed on the occurrence of a vacancy;
(b) the number of the trustees shall not be increased beyond four.

(3) This section only applies to settlements and dispositions of land, and the restrictions imposed on the number of trustees do not apply—

(a) in the case of land vested in trustees for charitable, ecclesiastical, or public purposes; or
(b) where the net proceeds of the sale of the land are held for like purposes; or

(c) to the trustees of a term of years absolute limited by a settlement on trusts for raising money, or of a like term created under the statutory remedies relating to annual sums charged on land.

1 Sub-s (2): words in square brackets substituted by the TLATA 1996, s 25(1), Sch 3, para 3(9).

[246.33]

35. Appointments of trustees of settlements and [trustees of land].[1]— [(1) Appointments of new trustees of land and of new trustees of any trust of the proceeds of sale of the land shall, subject to any order of the court, be effected by separate instruments, but in such manner as to secure that the same persons become trustees of land and trustees of the trust of the proceeds of sale.][1]

(2) Where new trustees of a settlement are appointed, a memorandum of the names and addresses of the persons who are for the time being the trustees thereof for the purposes of the Settled Land Act 1925, shall be endorsed on or annexed to the last or only principal vesting instrument by or on behalf of the trustees of the settlement, and such vesting instrument shall, for that purpose, be produced by the person having the possession thereof of the trustees of the settlement when so required.

[(3) Where new trustees of land are appointed, a memorandum of the persons who are for the time being the trustees of the land shall be endorsed on or annexed to the conveyance by which the land was vested in trustees of land; and that conveyance shall be produced to the persons who are for the time being the trustees of the land by the person in possession of it in order for that to be done when the trustees require its production.][1]

(4) This section applies only to settlements and dispositions of land.

1 Sub-ss (1), (3) and words in square brackets in heading substituted by the TLATA 1996, s 25(1), Sch 3, para 3(10)(a), (b), (c).

[246.34]

36. Power of appointing new or additional trustees.— (1) Where a trustee, either original or substituted, and whether appointed by a court or otherwise, is dead, or remains out of the United Kingdom for more than twelve months, or desires to be discharged from all or any of the trusts or powers reposed in or conferred on him, or refuses or is unfit to act therein, or is incapable of acting therein, or is an infant, then, subject to the restrictions imposed by this Act on the number of trustees—

(a) the person or persons nominated for the purpose of appointing new trustees by the instrument, if any, creating the trust; or

(b) if there is no such person, or no such person able and willing to act, then the surviving or continuing trustees or trustee for the time being, or the personal representatives of the last surviving or continuing trustee;

may, by writing, appoint one or more other persons (whether or not being the persons exercising the power) to be a trustee or trustees in the place of the trustee so deceased remaining out of the United Kingdom, desiring to be discharged, refusing, or being unfit or being incapable, or being an infant, as aforesaid.

(2) Where a trustee has been removed under a power contained in the instrument creating the trust, a new trustee or new trustees may be appointed in the place of the trustee who is removed, as if he were dead, or, in the case of a corporation, as if the corporation desired to be discharged from the trust, and the provisions of this section shall apply accordingly, but subject to the restrictions imposed by this Act on the number of trustees.
(3) Where a corporation being a trustee is or has been dissolved, either before or after the commencement of this Act, then, for the purposes of this section and of any enactment replaced thereby, the corporation shall be deemed to be and to have been from the date of the dissolution incapable of acting in the trusts or powers reposed in or conferred on the corporation.
(4) The power of appointment given by subsection (1) of this section or any similar previous enactment to the personal representatives of a last surviving or continuing trustee shall be and shall be deemed always to have been exercisable by the executors for the time being (whether original or by representation) of such surviving or continuing trustee who have proved the will of their testator or by the administrators for the time being of such trustee without the concurrence of any executor who has renounced or has not proved.
(5) But a sole or last surviving executor intending to renounce, or all the executors where they all intend to renounce, shall have and shall be deemed always to have had power, at any time before renouncing probate, to exercise the power of appointment given by this section, or by any similar previous enactment, if willing to act for that purpose and without thereby accepting the office of executor.
[(6) Where, in the case of any trust, there are not more than three trustees—][1]

(a) the person or persons nominated for the purpose of appointing new trustees by the instrument, if any, creating the trust; or
(b) if there is no such person, or no such person able and willing to act, then the trustee or trustees for the time being;

may, by writing appoint another person or other persons to be an additional trustee or additional trustees, but it shall not be obligatory to appoint any additional trustee, unless the instrument, if any, creating the trust, or any statutory enactment provides to the contrary, nor shall the number of trustees be increased beyond four by virtue of any such appointment.
[(6A) A person who is either—

(a) both a trustee and attorney for the other trustee (if one other), or for both of the other trustees (if two others), under a registered power; or
(b) attorney under a registered power for the trustee (if one) or for both or each of the trustees (if two or three),

may, if subsection (6B) of this section is satisfied in relation to him, make an appointment under subsection (6)(b) of this section on behalf of the trustee or trustees.
(6B) This subsection is satisfied in relation to an attorney under a registered power for one or more trustees if (as attorney under the power)—

(a) he intends to exercise any function of the trustee or trustees by virtue of section 1(1) of the Trustee Delegation Act 1999; or
(b) he intends to exercise any function of the trustee or trustees in relation to any land, capital proceeds of a conveyance of land or income from land by virtue of its delegation to him under section 25 of this Act or the instrument (if any) creating the trust.

(6C) In subsections (6A) and (6B) of this section 'registered power' means [an enduring power of attorney or lasting power of attorney registered under the Mental Capacity Act 2005][2] a power of attorney created by an instrument which is for the time being registered under section 6 of the Enduring Powers of Attorney Act 1985.
(6D) Subsection (6A) of this section—

(a) applies only if and so far as a contrary intention is not expressed in the instrument creating the power of attorney (or, where more than one, any of them) or the instrument (if any) creating the trust; and
(b) has effect subject to the terms of those instruments.][3]

(7) Every new trustee appointed under this section as well before as after all the trust property becomes by law, or by assurance, or otherwise, vested in him, shall have the same powers, authorities, and discretions, and may in all respects act as if he had been originally appointed a trustee by the instrument, if any, creating the trust.
(8) The provisions of this section relating to a trustee who is dead include the case of a person nominated trustee in a will but dying before the testator, and those relative to a continuing trustee include a refusing or retiring trustee, if willing to act in the execution of the provisions of this section.
[(9) Where a trustee is [lacks capacity to exercise] his functions as trustee and is also entitled in possession to some beneficial interest in the trust property, no appointment of a new trustee in his place shall be made by virtue of paragraph (b) of subsection (1) of this section unless leave to make the appointment has been given by [the Court of Protection].][4]

1 Sub-s (6): words in square brackets substituted by the TLATA 1996, s 25(1), Sch 3, para 3(11).
2 Words in square brackets in sub-s (6C) inserted with effect from 1 October 2007 by the MCA 2005, s 67(1), Sch 6, para 3(1) and (2)(a).
3 Sub-ss (6A)–(6D): inserted by the Trustee Delegation Act 1999, s 8. Note that this applies to powers of attorney created *after* 1 March 2000.
4 Sub-s (9): substituted by the Mental Health Act 1959, s 149(1), Sch 7, Pt I; words in square brackets therein substituted with effect from 1 October 2007 by the MCA 2005, s 67(1), Sch 6, para 3(1) and (2)(b).

[246.35]
37. Supplemental provisions as to appointment of trustees.— (1) On the appointment of a trustee for the whole or any part of trust property—

(a) the number of trustees may, subject to the restrictions imposed by this Act on the number of trustees, be increased; and
(b) a separate set of trustees, not exceeding four, may be appointed for any part of the trust property held on trusts distinct from those relating to any other part or parts of the trust property, notwithstanding that no new trustees or trustee are or is to be appointed for

other parts of the trust property, and any existing trustee may be appointed or remain one of such separate set of trustees, or, if only one trustee was originally appointed, then, save as hereinafter provided, one separate trustee may be so appointed; and

(c) it shall not be obligatory, save as hereinafter provided, to appoint more than one new trustee where only one trustee was originally appointed, or to fill up the original number of trustees where more than two trustees were originally appointed, but, except where only one trustee was originally appointed, and a sole trustee when appointed will be able to give valid receipts for all capital money, a trustee shall not be discharged from his trust unless there will be either a trust corporation or at least two [persons][1] to act as trustees to perform the trust; and

(d) any assurance or thing requisite for vesting the trust property, or any part thereof, in a sole trustee, or jointly in the persons who are the trustees, shall be executed or done.

(2) Nothing in this Act shall authorise the appointment of a sole trustee, not being a trust corporation, where the trustee, when appointed, would not be able to give valid receipts for all capital money arising under the trust.

1 Sub-s (1): in para (c) word in square brackets substituted by the TLATA 1996, s 25(1), Sch 3, para 3(12).

[246.36]
38. Evidence as to a vacancy in a trust.— (1) A statement, contained in any instrument coming into operation after the commencement of this Act by which a new trustee is appointed for any purpose connected with land, to the effect that a trustee has remained out of the United Kingdom for more than twelve months or refuses or is unfit to act, or is incapable of acting, or that he is not entitled to a beneficial interest in the trust property in possession, shall, in favour of a purchaser of a legal estate, be conclusive evidence of the matter stated.
(2) In favour of such purchaser any appointment of a new trustee depending on that statement, and any vesting declaration, express or implied, consequent on the appointment, shall be valid.

[246.37]
39. Retirement of trustee without a new appointment.— (1) Where a trustee is desirous of being discharged from the trust, and after his discharge there will be either a trust corporation or at least two [persons][1] to act as trustees to perform the trust, then, if such trustee as aforesaid by deed declares that he is desirous of being discharged from the trust, and if his co-trustees and such other person, if any, as is empowered to appoint trustees, by deed consent to the discharge of the trustee, and to the vesting in the co-trustees alone of the trust property, the trustee desirous of being discharged shall be deemed to have retired from the trust, and shall, by the deed, be discharged therefrom under this Act, without any new trustee being appointed in his place.
(2) Any assurance or thing requisite for vesting the trust property in the continuing trustees alone shall be excecuted or done.

1 Sub-s (1): word in square brackets substituted by the TLATA 1996, s 25(1), Sch 3, para 3(13).

[246.38]
40. Vesting of trust property in new or continuing trustees.— (1) Where by a deed a new trustee is appointed to perform any trust, then—

(a) if the deed contains a declaration by the appointor to the effect that any estate or interest in any land subject to the trust, or in any chattel so subject, or right to recover or receive any debt or other thing in action so subject, shall vest in the persons who by virtue of the deed become or are the trustees for performing the trust, the deed shall operate, without any conveyance or assignment, to vest in those persons as joint tenants and for the purposes of the trust the estate interest or right to which the declaration relates; and
(b) if the deed is made after the commencement of this Act and does not contain such a declaration, the deed shall, subject to any express provision to the contrary therein contained, operate as if it had contained such a declaration by the appointor extending to all the estates interests and rights with respect to which a declaration could have been made.

(2) Where by a deed a retiring trustee is discharged under [section 39 of this Act or section 19 of the Trusts of Land and Appointment of Trustees Act 1996][1] without a new trustee being appointed, then—

(a) if the deed contains such a declaration as aforesaid by the retiring and continuing trustees, and by the other person, if any, empowered to appoint trustees, the deed shall, without any conveyance or assignment, operate to vest in the continuing trustees alone, as joint tenants, and for the purposes of the trust, the estate, interest, or right to which the declaration relates; and
(b) if the deed is made after the commencement of this Act and does not contain such a declaration, the deed shall, subject to any express provision to the contrary therein contained, operate as if it had contained such a declaration by such persons as aforesaid extending to all the estates, interests and rights with respect to which a declaration could have been made.

(3) An express vesting declaration, whether made before or after the commencement of this Act, shall, notwithstanding that the estate, interest or right to be vested is not expressly referred to, and provided that the other statutory requirements were or are complied with, operate and be deemed always to have operated (but without prejudice to any express provision to the contrary contained in the deed of appointment or discharge) to vest in the persons respectively referred to in subsections (1) and (2) of this section, as the case may require, such estates, interests and rights as are capable of being and ought to be vested in those persons.
(4) This section does not extend—

(a) to land conveyed by way of mortgage for securing money subject to the trust, except land conveyed on trust for securing debentures or debenture stock;

(b) to land held under a lease which contains any covenant, condition or agreement against assignment or disposing of the land without licence or consent, unless, prior to the execution of the deed containing expressly or impliedly the vesting declaration, the requisite licence or consent has been obtained, or unless, by virtue of any statute or rule of law, the vesting declaration, express or implied, would not operate as a breach of covenant or give rise to a forfeiture;

(c) to any share, stock, annuity or property which is only transferable in books kept by a company or other body, or in manner directed by or under an Act of Parliament.

In this subsection lease includes an underlease and an agreement for a lease or underlease.

(5) For purposes of registration of the deed in any registry, the person or persons making the declaration expressly or impliedly, shall be deemed the conveying party or parties, and the conveyance shall be deemed to be made by him or them under a power conferred by this Act.

(6) This section applies to deeds of appointment or discharge executed on or after the first day of January, eighteen hundred and eighty-two.

1 Sub-s (2): words in square brackets substituted by the TLATA 1996, s 25(1), Sch 3, para 3(14).

[246.39]

68. Definitions.— (1) In this Act, unless the context otherwise requires, the following expressions have the meanings hereby assigned to them respectively, that is to say:—

(1) 'Authorised investments' mean investments authorised by the instrument, if any, creating the trust for the investment of money subject to the trust, or by law;

* * * * *

(11) 'Property' includes real and personal property, and any estate share and interest in any property, real or personal, and any debt, and any thing in action, and any other right or interest, whether in possession or not;

(12) 'Rights' include estates and interests;

(13) 'Securities' include stocks, funds, and shares; ... and 'securities payable to bearer' include securities transferable by delivery or by delivery and endorsement;[1]

* * * * *

(17) 'Trust' does not include the duties incident to an estate conveyed by way of mortgage, but with this exception the expressions 'trust' and 'trustee' extend to implied and constructive trusts, and to cases where the trustee has a beneficial interest in the trust property, and to the duties incident to the office of a personal representative, and 'trustee' where the context admits, includes a personal representative, and 'new trustee' includes an additional trustee;

(18) 'Trust corporation' means the Public Trustee or a corporation either appointed by the court in any particular case to be a trustee, or entitled by rules made under subsection (3) of section four of the Public Trustee Act 1906, to act as custodian trustee;[2]

* * * * *

(20) 'United Kingdom' means Great Britain and Northern Ireland.

* * * * *

[(3) Any reference in this Act to a person who lacks capacity in relation to a matter is a
person -

(a) who lacks capacity within the meaning of the Mental Capacity Act 2005 in relation to that matter, or

(b) in respect of whom powers conferred by section 48 of that Act are exercisable and have been exercised in relation to that matter.][3]

1 The words omitted from para (13) were repealed by the Administration of Justice Act 1965, s 17(1), Sch 1.

2 The relevant rule is r 30 of the Public Trustee Rules 1912 (para **[246.73]** below). The definition is enlarged so as to include the Treasury Solicitor, the Official Solicitor, trustees in bankruptcy and certain charitable corporations by the LP(A)A 1926, s 3(1), para **[246.71]** below and is further enlarged by the Charities Act 1993 (CA 1993), s 35 (para **[246.101]** below) so as to include certain corporations appointed by the Charity Commission.

3 Sub-s (3) added with effect from 1 October 2007 by the MCA 2005, s 67(1), Sch 6, para 3(1) and (6).

* * * * *

[246.40]

69. Application of Act.— (1) This Act, except where otherwise expressly provided, applies to trusts including, so far as this Act applies thereto, executorships and administratorships constituted or created either before or after the commencement of this Act.

(2) The powers conferred by this Act on trustees are in addition to the powers conferred by the instrument, if any, creating the trust, but those powers, unless otherwise stated, apply if and so far only as a contrary intention is not expressed in the instrument, if any, creating the trust, and have effect subject to the terms of that instrument.

* * * * *

LAW OF PROPERTY ACT 1925

(15 & 16 Geo 5 c 20)

[9 April 1925]

[246.41]

Note. This Act came into force on 1 January 1926.

PART I
GENERAL PRINCIPLES AS TO LEGAL ESTATES, EQUITABLE INTERESTS AND POWERS

* * * * *

INFANTS AND LUNATICS

* * * * *

[246.42]
21. Receipts by married infants. A married infant shall have power to give valid receipts for all income (including statutory accumulations of income made during the minority) to which the infant may be entitled in like manner as if the infant were of full age.

* * * * *

[246.43] [*Section 23 (duration of trusts for sale) and the heading to it repealed by the Trusts of Land and Appointment of Trustees Act 1996, s 25(2), Sch 4: see now s 16 of the 1996 Act at para* **[246.102]**]

TRUSTS OF LAND[1]

[246.44]
24. Appointment of trustees of land.— (1) The persons having power to appoint new trustees of land shall be bound to appoint the same persons (if any) who are for the time being trustees of any trust of the proceeds of sale of the land.
(2) A purchaser shall not be concerned to see that subsection (1) of this section has been complied with.
(3) This section applies whether the trust of land and the trust of proceeds of sale are created, or arise, before or after the commencement of this Act.[1]

1 The heading and the entire section were substituted by the TLATA 1996, s 25(1), Sch 3, para 4(7).

[246.45] [*Sections 25 (power to postpone sale) and 26 (consents to the execution of a trust for sale) repealed by Trusts of Land and Appointment of Trustees Act* 1996, *s 25(2), Sch 4: see now ss 4 and 10 respectively of the 1996 Act at paras* **[246.106]** *and* **[246.113]** below.]

[246.46]
27. Purchaser not to be concerned with the trusts of the proceeds of sale which are to be paid to two or more trustees or to a trust corporation.—
[(1) A purchaser of a legal estate from trustees of land shall not be concerned with the trusts affecting the land, the net income of the land or the proceeds of sale of the land whether or not those trusts are declared by the same instrument as that by which the trust of land is created.][1]
(2) Notwithstanding anything to the contrary in the instrument (if any) creating a [trust][2] of land or in [any trust affecting the net proceeds of sale of the land if it is sold],[2] the proceeds of sale or other capital money shall not

be paid to or applied by the direction of fewer than two persons as [trustees],[2] except where the trustee is a trust corporation, but this subsection does not affect the right of a sole personal representative as such to give valid receipts for, or direct the application of, proceeds of sale or other capital money, nor, except where capital money arises on the transaction, render it necessary to have more than one trustee.

1 Sub-s (1): substituted by the TLATA 1996, s 25(1), Sch 3, para 4(8)(a).
2 Sub-s (2): words in square brackets substituted by the TLATA 1996, s 25(1), Sch 3, para 4(8)(b).

[246.47] [*Sections 28 (powers of management, &c. conferred on trustees of sale), 29 (delegation of powers of management by trustees for sale), and 30 (powers of court where trustees for sale refuse to exercise powers) repealed by the Trusts of Land and Appointment of Trustees Act 1996, s 25(2), Sch 4: see now ss 6 and 7, 9 and 14 and 15 of the 1996 Act respectively at paras* **[246.108]**, **[246.109]**, **[246.111]**, **[246.117]** *and* **[246.118]** below.]

[246.48]
31. [Trust][1] of mortgaged property where right of redemption is barred.— (1) Where any property, vested in trustees by way of security, becomes, by virtue of the statutes of limitation, or of an order for foreclosure or otherwise, discharged from the right of redemption, it shall be held by them [in trust—

(a) to apply the income from the property in the same manner as interest paid on the mortgage debt would have been applicable; and
(b) if the property is sold, to apply the net proceeds of sale, after payment of costs and expenses, in the same manner as repayment of the mortgage debt would have been applicable.][1]

[(2) Subsection (1) of this section][2] operates without prejudice to any rule of law relating to the apportionment of capital and income between tenant for life and remainderman.
(3) …[3]
[(4) Where—

(a) the mortgage money is capital money for the purposes of the Settled Land Act 1925;
(b) land other than any forming the whole or part of the property mentioned in subsection (1) of this section is, or is deemed to be, subject to the settlement; and
(c) the tenant for life or statutory owner requires the trustees to execute with respect to land forming the whole or part of that property a vesting deed such as would have been required in relation to the land if it had been acquired on a purchase with capital money,

the trustees shall execute such a vesting deed.][4]
(5) This section applies whether the right of redemption was discharged before or after the first day of January, nineteen hundred and twelve, but has effect without prejudice to any dealings or arrangements made before that date.

1 Words in square brackets in section heading and in sub-s (1) substituted by the TLATA 1996, s 5(1), Sch 2, para 1(2), (6).

2 Sub-s (2): words in square brackets substituted by the TLATA 1996, s 5(1), Sch 2, para 1(3).
3 Sub-s (3): repealed by the TLATA 1996, ss 5(1), 25(2), Sch 3, para 1(4), Sch 4.
4 Sub-s (4): substituted by the TLATA 1996, s 5(1), Sch 2, para 1(5).

[246.49] [*Section 32* (*implied trust for sale in personalty settlements*) *repealed in relation to land purchased on or after 1 January 1997 whether trust or will came into operation before or after that date by Trusts of Land and Appointment of Trustees Act 1996, ss 5*(*1*), *25*(*2*), *Sch 2, para 2*(*1*), (*2*), *Sch 4*.]

[246.50]
33. Application of Part I to personal representatives. The provisions of this Part of this Act relating to [trustees of land][1] apply to personal representatives holding [land in trust],[1] but without prejudice to their rights and powers for purposes of administration.

1 Words in square brackets substituted by the TLATA 1996, s 25(1), Sch 3, para 4(9).

UNDIVIDED SHARES AND JOINT OWNERSHIP

[246.51]
34. Effect of future dispositions to tenants in common.— (1) An undivided share in land shall not be capable of being created except as provided by the Settled Land Act 1925 or as hereinafter mentioned.
(2) Where, after the commencement of this Act, land is expressed to be conveyed to any persons in undivided shares and those persons are of full age, the conveyance shall (notwithstanding anything to the contrary in this Act) operate as if the land had been expressed to be conveyed to the grantees, or, if there are more than four grantees, to the four first named in the conveyance, as joint tenants [in trust for the persons interested in the land][1]:
Provided that, where the conveyance is made by way of mortgage the land shall vest in the grantees or such four of them as aforesaid for a term of years absolute (as provided by this Act) as joint tenants subject to cesser on redemption in like manner as if the mortgage money had belonged to them on a joint account, but without prejudice to the beneficial interests in the mortgage money and interest.
(3) A devise bequest or testamentary appointment, coming into operation after the commencement of this Act, of land to two or more persons in undivided shares shall operate as a devise bequest or appointment of the land to …[2] the personal representatives of the testator, and …[2] (but without prejudice to the rights and powers of the personal representatives for purposes of administration) [in trust for the persons interested in the land].[2]
[(3A) In subsections (2) and (3) of this section references to the persons interested in the land include persons interested as trustees or personal representatives (as well as persons beneficially interested).][3]
(4) …[4]

1 Sub-s (2): words in square brackets substituted with retrospective effect by the TLATA 1996, s 5(1), Sch 2, para 3(2), (6).
2 Sub-s (3): words omitted repealed and words in square brackets substituted, in each case with retrospective effect, by the TLATA 1996, ss 591), 25(2), Sch 2, para 3(3), (6), Sch 4.
3 Sub-s (3A): inserted with retrospective effect by the TLATA 1996, s 5(1), Sch 2, para 3(4), (6).

4 Sub-s (4): repealed with retrospective effect by the TLATA 1996, ss 5(1), 25(2), Sch 2, para 3(5), (6), Sch 4.

[246.52] [*Section 35 (meaning of the statutory trusts) repealed by Trusts of Land and Appointment of Trustees Act 1996, s 25(2), Sch 4.*]

[246.53]
36. Joint tenancies.— (1) Where a legal estate (not being settled land) is beneficially limited to or held in trust for any persons as joint tenants, the same shall be held [in trust],[1] in like manner as if the persons beneficially entitled were tenants in common, but not so as to sever their joint tenancy in equity.
(2) No severance of a joint tenancy of a legal estate, so as to create a tenancy in common in land, shall be permissible, whether by operation of law or otherwise, but this subsection does not affect the right of a joint tenant to release his interest to the other joint tenants, or the right to sever a joint tenancy in an equitable interest whether or not the legal estate is vested in the joint tenants:
Provided that, where a legal estate (not being settled land) is vested in joint tenants beneficially, and any tenant desires to sever the joint tenancy in equity, he shall give to the other joint tenants a notice in writing of such desire or do such other acts or things as would, in the case of personal estate, have been effectual to sever the tenancy in equity, and thereupon [the land shall be held in trust on terms][2] which would have been requisite for giving effect to the beneficial interests if there had been an actual severance.
Nothing in this Act affects the right of a survivor of joint tenants, who is solely and beneficially interested, to deal with his legal estate as if it were not held [in trust].[2]
(3) Without prejudice to the right of a joint tenant to release his interest to the other joint tenants no severance of a mortgage term or trust estate, so as to create a tenancy in common, shall be permissible.

1 Sub-s (1): words in square brackets substituted with retrospective effect by the TLATA 1996, s 5(1), Sch 2, para 4(2), (4).
2 Sub-s (2): words in square brackets substituted with retrospective effect by the TLATA 1996, s 5, Sch 2, para 4(3), (4).

* * * * *

PART II
CONTRACTS, CONVEYANCES AND OTHER INSTRUMENTS

* * * * *

CONVEYANCES AND OTHER INSTRUMENTS

* * * * *

[246.54]
61. Construction of expressions used in deeds and other instruments. In all deeds, contracts, wills, orders and other instruments executed, made or coming into operation after the commencement of this Act, unless the context otherwise requires—

(a) 'Month' means calendar month;
(b) 'Person' includes a corporation;
(c) The singular includes the plural and vice versa;
(d) The masculine includes the feminine and vice versa.

* * * * *

PART VII
PERPETUITIES AND ACCUMULATIONS

PERPETUITIES

* * * * *

[246.55]
163. Validation of certain gifts void for remoteness.[1]— (*1*) *Where in a will, settlement or other instrument the absolute vesting either of capital or income of property, or the ascertainment of a beneficiary or class of beneficiaries, is made to depend on the attainment by the beneficiary or members of the class of an age exceeding twenty-one years, and thereby the gift to that beneficiary or class or any member thereof, or any gift over, remainder, executory limitation, or trust arising on the total or partial failure of the original gift, is, or but for this section would be, rendered void for remoteness, the will, settlement, or other instrument shall take effect for the purposes of such gift, gift over, remainder, executory limitation, or trust as if the absolute vesting or ascertainment aforesaid had been made to depend on the beneficiary or member of the class attaining the age of twenty-one years, and that age shall be substituted for the age stated in the will, settlement, or other instrument.*
(*2*) *This section applies to any instrument executed after the commencement of this Act and to any testamentary appointment (whether made in exercise of a general or special power), devise, or bequest contained in the will of a person dying after such commencement, whether the will is made before or after such commencement.*
(*3*) *This section applies without prejudice to any provision whereby the absolute vesting or ascertainment is also made to depend on the marriage of any person, or any other event which may occur before the age stated in the will, settlement, or other instrument is attained.*

1 This section was repealed by the PAA 1964, s 4(6) (para **[246.77]** below) but only as regards instruments taking effect after the commencement of the 1964 Act, ie 16 July 1964 (see s 15(5) of the 1964 Act at para **[246.88]** below).

ACCUMULATIONS

[246.56]
164. General restrictions on accumulation of income.— (1) No person may by any instrument or otherwise settle or dispose of any property in such manner that the income thereof shall, save as hereinafter mentioned, be wholly or partially accumulated for any longer period than one of the following, namely:—

(a) the life of the grantor or settlor; or
(b) a term of twenty-one years from the death of the grantor, settlor or testator; or
(c) the duration of the minority or respective minorities of any person or persons living or en ventre sa mere at the death of the grantor, settlor or testator; or
(d) the duration of the minority or respective minorities only of any person or persons who under the limitations of the instrument directing the accumulations would, for the time being, if of full age, be entitled to the income directed to be accumulated.

In every case where any accumulation is directed otherwise than as aforesaid, the direction shall (save as hereinafter mentioned) be void; and the income of the property directed to be accumulated shall, so long as the same is directed to be accumulated contrary to this section, go to and be received by the person or persons who would have been entitled thereto if such accumulation had not been directed.
(2) This section does not extend to any provision—

(i) for payment of the debts of any grantor, settlor, testator or other person;
(ii) for raising portions for—
    (a) any child, children or remoter issue of any grantor, settlor or testator; or
    (b) any child, children or remoter issue of a person taking any interest under any settlement or other disposition directing the accumulations or to whom any interest is thereby limited;
(iii) respecting the accumulation of the produce of timber or wood;

and accordingly such provisions may be made as if no statutory restrictions on accumulation of income had been imposed.
(3) The restrictions imposed by this section apply to instruments made on or after the twenty-eighth day of July, eighteen hundred, but in the case of wills only where the testator was living and of testamentary capacity after the end of one year from that date.[1]

1 This section has been amended by the PAA 1964, s 13 (para **[246.86]** below) which specifies two further periods of lawful accumulation.

[246.57]
165. Qualification of restrictions on accumulation. Where accumulations of surplus income are made during a minority under any statutory power or under the general law, the period for which such accumulations are made is not (whether the trust was created or the accumulations were made before or

after the commencement of this Act) to be taken into account in determining the periods for which accumulations are permitted to be made by the last preceding section, and accordingly an express trust for accumulation for any other permitted period shall not be deemed to have been invalidated or become invalid, by reason of accumulations also having been made as aforesaid during such minority.

[246.58]
166. Restriction on accumulation for the purchase of land.— (1) No person may settle or dispose of any property in such manner that the income thereof shall be wholly or partially accumulated for the purchase of land only, for any longer period than the duration of the minority or respective minorities of any person or persons who, under the limitations of the instrument directing the accumulation, would for the time being, if of full age, be entitled to the income so directed to be accumulated.
(2) This section does not, nor do the enactments which it replaces, apply to accumulations to be held as capital money for the purposes of the Settled Land Act 1925 or the enactments replaced by that Act, whether or not the accumulations are primarily liable to be laid out in the purchase of land.
(3) This section applies to settlements and dispositions made after the twenty-seventh day of June eighteen hundred and ninety-two.

* * * * *

PART XII
CONSTRUCTION, JURISDICTION, AND GENERAL PROVISIONS

* * * * *

[246.59]
205. General definitions.— (1) In this Act unless the context otherwise requires, the following expressions have the meanings hereby assigned to them respectively, that is to say:—

* * * * *

(ix) 'Land' includes land of any tenure, and mines and minerals, whether or not held apart from the surface, buildings or parts of buildings (whether the division is horizontal, vertical or made in any other way) and other corporeal hereditaments; also a manor, an advowson, and a rent and other incorporeal hereditaments, and an easement, right, privilege, or benefit in, over, or derived from land; [but not an undivided share in land][1]; and 'mines and minerals' include any strata or seam of minerals or substances in or under any land, and powers of working and getting the same [but not an undivided share thereof][1]; and 'manor' includes a lordship, and reputed manor or lordship; and 'hereditament' means any real property which on an intestacy occurring before the commencement of this Act might have devolved upon an heir;

* * * * *

1 The words in square brackets were repealed by the TLATA 1996, s 25(2), Sch 4, presumably on the basis that with the abolition of the doctrine of conversion in relation to land held on trust for sale by s 3 of that Act (para **[246.105]** below), undivided shares in land constitute real property.

ADMINISTRATION OF ESTATES ACT 1925

(15 & 16 Geo 5 c 23)

[9 April 1925]

[246.60]

Note. This Act came into force on 1 January 1926.

* * * * *

[246.61]

34. Administration of assets.— (*1*) *Where the estate of a deceased person is insolvent, his real and personal estate shall be administered in accordance with the rules set out in Part I. of the First Schedule to this Act.*[1]

(2) …[2]

(3) Where the estate of a deceased person is solvent his real and personal estate shall, subject to rules of court and the provisions hereinafter contained as to charges on property of the deceased, and to the provisions, if any, contained in his will, be applicable towards the discharge of the funeral, testamentary and administration expenses, debts and liabilities payable thereout in the order mentioned in Part II of the First Schedule to this Act.

1 Sub-s (1): repealed by the Insolvency Act 1985, s 235(3), Sch 10, Pt III with effect from 29 December 1986. It is replaced by rules under the Insolvency Act 1986, s 421; see the Administration of Insolvent Estates of Deceased Persons Order 1986, SI 1986/1999.

2 Sub-s (2): repealed with savings by the Administration of Estates Act 1971, s 12(2), (4), (6), Sch 2, Pt II.

[246.62]

35. Charges on property of deceased to be paid primarily out of the property charged.— (1) Where a person dies possessed of, or entitled to, or, under a general power of appointment (including the statutory power to dispose of entailed interests) by his will disposes of, an interest in property, which at the time of his death is charged with the payment of money, whether by way of legal mortgage, equitable charge or otherwise (including a lien for unpaid purchase money), and the deceased has not by will deed or other document signified a contrary or other intention, the interest so charged, shall as between the different persons claiming through the deceased, be primarily liable for the payment of the charge; and every part of the said interest, according to its value, shall bear a proportionate part of the charge on the whole thereof.

(2) Such contrary or other intention shall not be deemed to be signified—

(a) by a general direction for the payment of debts or of all the debts of the testator out of his personal estate, or his residuary real and personal estate, or his residuary real estate; or

(b) by a charge of debts upon any such estate;

unless such intention is further signified by words expressly or by necessary implication referring to all or some part of the charge.
(3) Nothing in this section affects the right of a person entitled to the charge to obtain payment or satisfaction thereof either out of the other assets of the deceased or otherwise.

* * * * *

[246.63]
39. Powers of management.— (1) In dealing with the real and personal estate of the deceased his personal representatives shall, for purposes of administration, or during a minority of any beneficiary or the subsistence of any life interest, or until the period of distribution arrives, have—

(i) the same powers and discretions, including power to raise money by mortgage or charge (whether or not by deposit of documents), as a personal representative had before the commencement of this Act, with respect to personal estate vested in him, and such power of raising money by mortgage may in the case of land be exercised by way of legal mortgage; and
(ii) all the powers, discretions and duties conferred or imposed by law on trustees holding land upon an effectual trust for sale (including power to overreach equitable interests and powers as if the same affected the proceeds of sale); and
(iii) all the powers conferred by statute on trustees for sale, and so that every contract entered into by a personal representative shall be binding on and be enforceable against and by the personal representative for the time being of the deceased, and may be carried into effect, or be varied or rescinded by him, and, in the case of a contract entered into by a predecessor, as if it had been entered into by himself.

(2) Nothing in this section shall affect the right of any person to require an assent or conveyance to be made.
(3) This section applies whether the testator or intestate died before or after the commencement of this Act.

[246.64]
40. Powers of personal representative for raising money, etc.— (1) For giving effect to beneficial interests the personal representative may limit or demise land for a term of years absolute, with or without impeachment for waste, to trustees on usual trusts for raising or securing any principal sum and the interest thereon for which the land, or any part thereof, is liable, and may limit or grant a rentcharge for giving effect to an annual or periodical sum for which the land or the income thereof or any part thereof is liable.
(2) This section applies whether the testator or intestate died before or after the commencement of this Act.

[246.65]
41. Powers of personal representative as to appropriation.— (1) The personal representative may appropriate any part of the real or personal estate, including things in action, of the deceased in the actual condition or state of investment thereof at the time of appropriation in or towards satisfaction of any legacy bequeathed by the deceased, or of any other interest or share in his property, whether settled or not, as to the personal representative may seem just and reasonable, according to the respective rights of the persons interested in the property of the deceased:
Provided that—

(i) an appropriation shall not be made under this section so as to affect prejudicially any specific devise or bequest;
(ii) an appropriation of property, whether or not being an investment authorised by law or by the will, if any, of the deceased for the investment of money subject to the trust, shall not (save as hereinafter mentioned) be made under this section except with the following consents:—
(a) when made for the benefit of a person absolutely and beneficially entitled in possession, the consent of that person;
(b) when made in respect of any settled legacy share or interest, the consent of either the trustee thereof, if any (not being also the personal representative), or the person who may for the time being be entitled to the income:

If the person whose consent is so required as aforesaid is an infant or [lacks capacity (within the meaning of the Mental Capacity Act 2005) to give the consent, it][1] shall be given on his behalf by his parents or parent, testamentary or other guardian ... or [a person appointed as deputy for him by the Court of Protection][1], or if, in the case of an infant, there is no such parent or guardian, by the court on the application of his next friend;
(iii) no consent (save of such trustee as aforesaid) shall be required on behalf of a person who may come into existence after the time of appropriation, or who cannot be found or ascertained at that time;
(iv) if no [receiver is acting for a person suffering from mental disorder][1] then, if the appropriation is of an investment authorised by law or by the will, if any, of the deceased for the investment of money subject to the trust, no consent shall be required on behalf of the [said person][1]
(v) if, independently of the personal representative, there is no trustee of a settled legacy share or interest, and no person of full age and capacity entitled to the income thereof, no consent shall be required to an appropriation in respect of such legacy share or interest, provided that the appropriation is of an investment authorised as aforesaid.

[(1A) The county court has jurisdiction under proviso (ii) to subsection (1) of this section where the estate in respect of which the application is made does not exceed in amount or value the county court limit.][2]

(2) Any property duly appropriated under the powers conferred by this section shall thereafter be treated as an authorised investment, and may be retained or dealt with accordingly.

(3) For the purposes of such appropriation, the personal representative may ascertain and fix the value of the respective parts of the real and personal estate and the liabilities of the deceased as he may think fit, and shall for that purpose employ a duly qualified valuer in any case where such employment may be necessary; and may make any conveyance (including an assent) which may be requisite for giving effect to the appropriation.

(4) An appropriation made pursuant to this section shall bind all persons interested in the property of the deceased whose consent is not hereby made requisite.

(5) The personal representative shall, in making the appropriation, have regard to the rights of any person who may thereafter come into existence, or who cannot be found or ascertained at the time of appropriation, and of any other person whose consent is not required by this section.

(6) This section does not prejudice any other power of appropriation conferred by law or by the will (if any) of the deceased, and takes effect with any extended powers conferred by the will (if any) of the deceased, and where an appropriation is made under this section, in respect of a settled legacy, share or interest, the property appropriated shall remain subject to all trusts for sale and powers of leasing, disposition, and management or varying investments which would have been applicable thereto or to the legacy, share or interest in respect of which the appropriation is made, if no such appropriation had been made.

(7) If after any real estate has been appropriated in purported exercise of the powers conferred by this section, the person to whom it was conveyed disposes of it or any interest therein, then, in favour of a purchaser, the appropriation shall be deemed to have been made in accordance with the requirements of this section and after all requisite consents, if any, had been given.

(8) In this section, a settled legacy, share or interest includes any legacy, share or interest to which a person is not absolutely entitled in possession at the date of the appropriation, also an annuity, and 'purchaser' means a purchaser for money or money's worth.

(9) This section applies whether the deceased died intestate or not, and whether before or after the commencement of this Act, and extends to property over which a testator exercises a general power of appointment, including the statutory power to dispose of entailed interests, and authorises the setting apart of a fund to answer an annuity by means of the income of that fund or otherwise.

1 The words in the first (outer) pair of square brackets in sub-s (1)(ii) together with the words in square brackets in sub-s (1)(iv), were substituted, and the words omitted from sub-s (1)(ii) were repealed, by the MHA 1959, s 149(1), Sch 7, Pt I. The words in the second (inner) pair of square brackets at the end of the proviso to sub-s (1) were further substituted with effect from 1 October 2007 by the MCA 2005, s 67(1), Sch 6, para 5(1) and (2).

2 Sub-s (1A): inserted by the CCA 1984, s 148(1), Sch 2, Pt III, para 13.

[246.66]
42. Power to appoint trustees of infants' property.— (1) Where an infant is absolutely entitled under the will or on the intestacy of a person dying before or after the commencement of this Act (in this subsection called 'the deceased') to a devise or legacy, or to the residue of the estate of the deceased, or any share therein, and such devise, legacy, residue or share is not under the will, if any, of the deceased, devised or bequeathed to trustees for the infant, the personal representatives of the deceased may appoint a trust corporation or two or more individuals not exceeding four (whether or not including the personal representatives or one or more of the personal representatives), to be the trustee or trustees of such devise, legacy, residue or share for the infant, and to be trustees of any land devised or any land being or forming part of such residue or share for the purposes of the Settled Land Act 1925, and of the statutory provisions relating to the management of land during a minority, and may execute or do any assurance or thing requisite for vesting such devise, legacy, residue or share in the trustee or trustees so appointed.
On such appointment the personal representatives, as such, shall be discharged from all further liability in respect of such devise, legacy, residue, or share, and the same may be retained in its existing condition or state of investment, or may be converted into money, and such money may be invested in any authorised investment.
(2) Where a personal representative has before the commencement of this Act retained or sold any such devise, legacy, residue or share, and invested the same or the proceeds thereof in any investments in which he was authorised to invest money subject to the trust, then, subject to any order of the court made before such commencement, he shall not be deemed to have incurred any liability on that account, or by reason of not having paid or transferred the money or property into court.

* * * * *

[246.67]
55. Definitions. In this Act, unless the context otherwise requires, the following expressions have the meanings hereby assigned to them respectively, that is to say—
(1)—

(i) 'Administration' means, with reference to the real and personal estate of a deceased person, letters of administration whether general or limited, or with the will annexed or otherwise;
(ii) 'Administrator' means a person to whom administration is granted;
(iii) 'Conveyance includes a mortgage, charge by way of legal mortgage, lease, assent, vesting, declaration, vesting instrument, disclaimer, release and every other assurance of property or of an interest therein by any instrument, except a will, and convey has a corresponding meaning, and disposition includes a conveyance also a devise bequest and an appointment of property contained in a will, and dispose of has a corresponding meaning;

[(iiiA) 'the County Court limit', in relation to any enactment contained in this Act, means the amount for the time being specified by an Order in Council under section 145 of the County Courts Act 1984 as the county court limit for the purposes of that enactment (or, where no such Order in Council has been made, the corresponding limit specified by Order in Council under section 192 of the County Courts Act 1959);][1]

(iv) 'the Court' means the High Court and also the county court, where that court has jurisdiction ...;[2]

(v) 'Income' includes rents and profits;

(vi) 'Intestate' includes a person who leaves a will but dies intestate as to some beneficial interest in his real or personal estate;

[(via) 'Land' has the same meaning as in the Law of Property Act 1925;][3]

(vii) 'Legal estates' mean the estates charges and interests in or over land (subsisting or created at law) which are by statute authorised to subsist or to be created at law; and equitable interests mean all other interests and charges in or over land ... ;[4]

(viii) ... [5]

(ix) 'Pecuniary legacy' includes an annuity, a general legacy, a demonstrative legacy so far as it is not discharged out of the designated property, and any other general direction by a testator for the payment of money, including all death duties free from which any devise, bequest, or payment is made to take effect;

(x) 'Personal chattels' mean carriages, horses, stable furniture and effects (not used for business purposes), motor cars and accessories (not used for business purposes), garden effects, domestic animals, plate, plated articles, linen, china, glass, books, pictures, prints, furniture, jewellery, articles of household or personal use or ornament, musical and scientific instruments and apparatus, wines, liquors and consumable stores, but do not include any chattels used at the death of the intestate for business purposes nor money or securities for money;

(xi) 'Personal representative' means the executor, original or by representation, or administrator for the time being of a deceased person, and as regards any liability for the payment of death duties includes any person who takes possession of or intermeddles with the property of a deceased person without the authority of the personal representatives or the court, and executor includes a person deemed to be appointed executor as respects settled land;

(xii) 'Possession' includes the receipt of rents and profits or the right to receive the same, if any;

(xiii) 'Prescribed' means prescribed by rules of court ... ;[6]

(xiv) 'Probate' means the probate of a will;

(xv) [*Repealed by the Law of Property* (*Miscellaneous Provisions*) *Act 1994, s 21*(*2*), *Sch 2*.]

(xvi) (*Repealed by the Supreme Court Act 1981, s 152*(*4*), *Sch 7*.)

(xvii) 'Property' includes a thing in action and any interest in real or personal property;

(xviii) 'Purchaser' means a lessee, mortgagee, or other person who in good faith acquires an interest in property for valuable consideration, also an intending purchaser and valuable consideration includes marriage [and formation of civil partnership][7] but does not include a nominal consideration in money;

(xix) 'Real estate' save as provided in Part IV of this Act means real estate, including chattels real, which by virtue of Part I of this Act devolves on the personal representative of a deceased person;

(xx) 'Representation means the probate of a will and administration, and the expression taking out representation refers to the obtaining of the probate of a will or of the grant of administration;

(xxi) 'Rent' includes a rent service or a rentcharge, or other rent, toll, duty, or annual or periodical payment in money or moneys worth, issuing out of or charged upon land, but does not include mortgage interest; and rentcharge includes a fee farm rent;

(xxii) [*Repealed by the Supreme Court Act 1981, s 152(4), Sch 7.*]

(xxiii) 'Securities' include stocks, funds, or shares;

(xxiv) 'Tenant for life', 'statutory owner', ...[8] 'settled land', 'settlement', 'trustees of the settlement', 'term of years absolute', 'death duties', and 'legal mortgage', have the same meanings as in the Settled Land Act 1925, and 'entailed interest' and 'charge by way of legal mortgage' have the same meanings as in the Law of Property Act 1925;

(xxv) 'Treasury solicitor' means the solicitor for the affairs of His Majesty's Treasury, and includes the solicitor for the affairs of the Duchy of Lancaster;

(xxvi) 'Trust corporation' means the public trustee or a corporation either appointed by the court in any particular case to be a trustee or entitled by rules made under subsection (3) of section four of the Public Trustee Act 1906, to act as custodian trustee;[9]

(xxvii) [*Repealed by the Trusts of Land and Appointment of Trustees Act 1996, s 25(2), Sch 4.*]

(xxviii) 'Will' includes codicil.

(2) References to a child or issue living at the death of any person include child or issue en ventre sa mère at the death.

(3) References to the estate of a deceased person include property over which the deceased exercises a general power of appointment (including the statutory power to dispose of entailed interests) by his will.

1 Paragraph (iiiA): inserted by the County Courts Act 1984, s 148(1), Sch 2, Pt III, para 15.
2 The remainder of para (iv) was repealed by the Courts Act 1971, s 56(4), Sch 11, Pt II.
3 Paragraph (via): added by the TLATA 1996, s 25(1), Sch 3, para 6(5).
4 The words omitted in para (vii) were repealed by the TLATA 1996, s 25(2), Sch 4.
5 Para (viii) (definitions of 'person of unsound mind' and 'defective') repealed by the MCA 2005, s 67(1), Sch 6, para 5(1) an (3).
6 The words omitted from para (xiii) were repealed by the SCA 1981, s 152(4), Sch 7.

7 Words added with effect from 5 December 2005 by the CPA 2004, s 71, Sch 4, para 12 and Civil Partnership Act 2004 (Commencement No 2) Order 2005, SI 2005/3175.
8 The words omitted from para (xxiv) were repealed by the TLATA 1996, s 25(2), Sch 4.
9 Para (xxvi): see the Public Trustee Rules 1912, r 30: para **[246.73]** below. The definition is enlarged so as to include the Treasury Solicitor, the Official Solicitor, trustees in bankruptcy and certain charitable corporations by the LP(A)A 1926 (para **[246.71]** below) and is further enlarged by the CA 1993, s 35 (para **[246.101]** below) so as to include certain corporations appointed by the Charity Commission.

* * * * *

FIRST SCHEDULE

Section 34

PART 1
RULES AS TO PAYMENT OF DEBTS WHERE THE ESTATE IS INSOLVENT

[246.68]
1. *The funeral, testamentary, and administration expenses have priority.*
2. *Subject as aforesaid, the same rules shall prevail and be observed as to the respective rights of secured and unsecured creditors and as to debts, and liabilities provable and as to the valuation of annuities and future and contingent liabilities respectively, and as to the priorities of debts and liabilities as may be in force for the time being under the law of bankruptcy with respect to the assets of persons adjudged bankrupt.*[1]

1 Pt I was repealed as from 29 December 1986 by the Insolvency Act 1985, s 253(3), Sch 10, Pt III. It is replaced by rules under the Insolvency Act 1986, s 421; see the Administration of Insolvent Estates of Deceased Persons Order 1986, SI 1986/1999.

PART II
ORDER OF APPLICATION OF ASSETS WHERE THE ESTATE IS SOLVENT

[246.69]
1. Property of the deceased undisposed of by will, subject to the retention thereout of a fund sufficient to meet any pecuniary legacies.
2. Property of the deceased not specifically devised or bequeathed but included (either by a specific or general description) in a residuary gift, subject to the retention out of such property of a fund sufficient to meet any pecuniary legacies, so far as not provided for as aforesaid.
3. Property of the deceased specifically appropriated or devised or bequeathed (either by a specific or general description) for the payment of debts.
4. Property of the deceased charged with, or devised or bequeathed (either by a specific or general description) subject to a charge for the payment of debts.
5. The fund, if any, retained to meet pecuniary legacies.
6. Property specifically devised or bequeathed, rateably according to value.

7. Property appointed by will under a general power, including the statutory power to dispose of entailed interests, rateable according to value.
8. The following provisions shall also apply—

(a) The order of application may be varied by the will of the deceased.
(b) ...[1]

1 Paragraph 8(b) (saving for liability of land for its own death duty) was repealed by the Finance (No 2) Act 1983, s 16(4), Sch 2, Pt II, in relation to deaths on or after 26 July 1983, on the introduction of the rules for the incidence of tax now contained in the ITA 1984, s 211: para **[246.100]** below.

LAW OF PROPERTY (AMENDMENT) ACT 1926

(16 & 17 Geo 5 c 11)

[16 June 1926]

[246.70]

Note. Section 3 of this Act, which enlarges the definition of 'trust corporation' contained in the 1925 property legislation, is printed below, as amended by the Supreme Court Act 1981, s 152(1), Sch 5. The definition was further enlarged by the CA 1993, s 35 (para **[246.101]** below) so as to include certain corporations appointed by the Charity Commission.

* * * * *

[246.71]
3. Meaning of 'trust corporation'.— (1) For the purposes of the Law of Property Act 1925, the Settled Land Act 1925, the Trustee Act 1925, the Administration of Estates Act 1925, and the [Supreme Court Act 1981], the expression 'Trust Corporation' includes the Treasury Solicitor, the Official Solicitor and any person holding any other official position prescribed by the Lord Chancellor, and, in relation to the property of a bankrupt and property subject to a deed of arrangement, includes the trustee in bankruptcy and the trustee under the deed respectively, and, in relation to charitable ecclesiastical and public trusts, also includes any local or public authority so prescribed, and any other corporation constituted under the laws of the United Kingdom or any part thereof which satisfies the Lord Chancellor that it undertakes the administration of any such trusts without remuneration, or that by its constitution it is required to apply the whole of its net income after payment of outgoings for charitable, ecclesiastical or public purposes, and is prohibited from distributing, directly or indirectly, any part thereof by way of profits amongst any of its members, and is authorised by him to act in relation to such trusts as a trust corporation.
(2) For the purposes of this provision, the expression 'Treasury Solicitor' means the solicitor for the affairs of His Majesty's Treasury, and includes the solicitor for the affairs of the Duchy of Lancaster.

* * * * *

PUBLIC TRUSTEE RULES 1912

SI 1912/348

[246.72]

Note. Rule 30 of the Public Trustee Rules 1912, SR & O 1912/348, is included as an appendix to the definition of 'trust corporation' contained in the Trustee Act 1925, s 68(18) and the AEA 1925, s 55(1)(xxvi), paras **[246.39]** and **[246.67]** above, (and reproduced in the Settled Land Act 1925, s 117(1)(xxx) and in the Law of Property Act 1925, s 205(1)(xxviii)). The rule is printed here, as substituted by SI 1975/1189 and as further amended by SI 1976/836, SI 1981/358, SI 1984/109, SI 1985/132, SI 1987/1891 and SI 1994/2519. See also the extension of the definition of 'trust corporation' contained in the LP(A)A 1926, s 3 (para **[246.71]** bove). This latter extension is further extended by the CA 1993, s 35 (para **[246.101]** below) so as to include certain corporations appointed by the Charity Commission.

* * * * *

[246.73]

30.— (1) The following corporations shall be entitled to act as custodian trustees:—

(a) the Treasury Solicitor;

(b) any corporation which:—

(i) is constituted under the law of the United Kingdom or of any part thereof, or under the law of any other Member State of the European Economic Community or of any part thereof;

(ii) is empowered by its constitution to undertake trust business (which for the purpose of this rule means the business of acting as trustee under wills and settlements and as executor and administrator) in England and Wales;

(iii) has one or more places of business in the United Kingdom; and

(iv) is—

a company incorporated by special Act of Parliament or Royal Charter, or

a company registered (with or without limited liability) in the United Kingdom under the Companies Act 1948[1] or under the Companies Act (Northern Ireland) 1960 or in another Member State of the European Economic Community and having a capital (in stock or shares) for the time being issued of not less than £250,000 (or its equivalent in the currency of the State where the company is registered), of which not less than £100,000 (or its equivalent) has been paid up in cash, or a company which is registered without limited liability in the United Kingdom under the Companies Act 1948[1] or the Companies Act (Northern Ireland) 1960 or in another Member State of the European Economic Community and of which one of the members is a company within any of the classes defined in this sub-paragraph;

(c) any corporation which is incorporated by special Act or Royal Charter or under the Charitable Trustees Incorporation Act 1872 which is empowered by its constitution to act as a trustee for any charitable purposes, but only in relation to trusts in which its constitution empowers it to act;

(d) any corporation which is constituted under the law of the United Kingdom or of any part thereof and having its place of business there, and which is either:

(i) established for the purpose of undertaking trust business for the benefit of Her Majesty's Navy, Army, Air Force or Civil Service or of any unit, department, member or association of members thereof, and having among its directors or members any persons appointed or nominated by the Defence Council or any Department of State or any one or more of those Departments, or

(ii) authorised by the Lord Chancellor to act in relation to any charitable, ecclesiastical or public trusts as a trust corporation, but only in connection with any such trust as is so authorised;

(e) —

(i) any Regional Health Authority, District Health Authority or special health authority, but only in relation to any trust which the authority is authorised to accept or hold by virtue of section 90 of the National Health Service Act 1977;

(ii) any preserved Board as defined by section 15(6) of the National Health Service Reorganisation Act 1973, but only in relation to any trust which the Board is authorised to accept or hold by virtue of an order made under that section;

(f) the British Gas Corporation, or any subsidiary of the British Gas Corporation, but only in relation to a pension scheme or pension fund established or maintained by the Corporation by virtue of section 36 of the Gas Act 1972;

(g) the London Transport Executive, but only in relation to a pension scheme or pension fund—

(i) which is established or administered by the Executive by virtue of section 6 of the Transport (London) Act 1969, or

(ii) in relation to which rights, liabilities and functions have been transferred to the Executive by an order under section 74 of the Transport Act 1962 as applied by section 18 of the Transport (London) Act 1969;

(h) any of the following, namely:—

(i) the Greater London Council,

(ii) the corporation of any London borough (acting by the council),

(iii) a county council, district council, parish council or community council,

(iv) the Council of the Isles of Scilly,

(v) the Common Council of the City of London,

but only in relation to charitable or public trusts (and not trusts for an ecclesiastical charity or for a charity for the relief of poverty) for the benefit of the inhabitants of the area of the local authority concerned and its neighbourhood, or any part of that area.

(i) any of the following, namely:—
 (i) a metropolitan district council or a non-metropolitan county council,
 (ii) the corporation of any London borough (acting by the council),
 (iii) the Common Council of the City of London,
 (iv) the Council of the Isles of Scilly,

but only in relation to any trust under which property devolves for the sole benefit of a person who occupies residential accommodation provided under section 21(1)(a) of the National Assistance Act 1948 by the local authority concerned or is in the care of that authority; and a corporation acting as a custodian trustee by virtue of this paragraph in relation to any trust shall be entitled to continue so to act in relation to that trust until a new custodian trustee is appointed, notwithstanding that the person concerned ceases to occupy such accommodation or to be in the care of that authority, as the case may be.

(j) the National Coal Board or any subsidiary of the National Coal Board, but only in relation to a scheme or arrangements established under regulations made under section 37 of the Coal Industry Nationalisation Act 1946.

(k) any corporation acting as trustee of the trusts of any pension scheme or pension fund established or maintained by the British Broadcasting Corporation, but only in relation to those trusts.

(l) any corporation appointed by the Secretary of State as a trustee of any scheme having effect by virtue of regulations made under section 37 of the Coal Industry Nationalisation Act 1946 for purposes relating to pensions, gratuities or other like benefits and in relation to which provision is, or has been, made by regulations made under paragraph 2(1) of Schedule 5 to the Coal Industry Act 1994 for the scheme to continue in force notwithstanding the repeal by the Coal Industry Act 1994 of section 37 of the Coal Industry Nationalisation Act 1946 and of the enactments modifying that section, but only in relation to such a scheme.

(2) In this rule 'subsidiary' has the same meaning as in section 154 of the Companies Act 1948.[1]

1 References in sub-rr (1)(b) and (2) to the Companies Act 1948 will now operate as references to the Companies Act 1985, s 736, which re-enacts s 154 of the 1948 Act; see the Interpretation Act 1978, s 17(2) (para **[246.98]** below).

* * * * *

PERPETUITIES AND ACCUMULATIONS ACT 1964

(1964 c 55)

[16 July 1964]

PERPETUITIES

[246.74]
1. Power to specify perpetuity period.— (1) Subject to section 9(2) of this Act and subsection (2) below, where the instrument by which any disposition is made so provides, the perpetuity period applicable to the disposition under the rule against perpetuities, instead of being of any other duration, shall be of a duration equal to such number of years not exceeding eighty as is specified in that behalf in the instrument.
(2) Subsection (1) above shall not have effect where the disposition is made in exercise of a special power of appointment, but where a period is specified under that subsection in the instrument creating such a power the period shall apply in relation to any disposition under the power as it applies in relation to the power itself.

[246.75]
2. Presumptions and evidence as to future parenthood.— (1) Where in any proceedings there arises on the rule against perpetuities a question which turns on the ability of a person to have a child at some future time, then—

(a) subject to paragraph (b) below, it shall be presumed that a male can have a child at the age of fourteen years or over, but not under that age, and that a female can have a child at the age of twelve years or over, but not under that age or over the age of fifty-five years; but
(b) in the case of a living person evidence may be given to show that he or she will or will not be able to have a child at the time in question.

(2) Where any such question is decided by treating a person as unable to have a child at a particular time, and he or she does so, the High Court may make such order as it thinks fit for placing the persons interested in the property comprised in the disposition, so far as may be just, in the position they would have held if the question had not been so decided.
(3) Subject to subsection (2) above, where any such question is decided in relation to a disposition by treating a person as able or unable to have a child at a particular time, then he or she shall be so treated for the purpose of any question which may arise on the rule against perpetuities in relation to the same disposition in any subsequent proceedings.
(4) In the foregoing provisions of this section references to having a child are references to begetting or giving birth to a child, but those provisions (except subsection (1)(b)) shall apply in relation to the possibility that a person will at any time have a child by adoption, legitimation or other means as they apply to his or her ability at that time to beget or give birth to a child.

[246.76]
3. Uncertainty as to remoteness.— (1) Where, apart from the provisions of this section and sections 4 and 5 of this Act, a disposition would be void on the ground that the interest disposed of might not become vested until

too remote a time, the disposition shall be treated, until such time (if any) as it becomes established that the vesting must occur, if at all, after the end of the perpetuity period, as if the disposition were not subject to the rule against perpetuities; and its becoming so established shall not affect the validity of anything previously done in relation to the interest disposed of by way of advancement, application of intermediate income or otherwise.

(2) Where, apart from the said provisions, a disposition consisting of the conferring of a general power of appointment would be void on the ground that the power might not become exercisable until too remote a time, the disposition shall be treated, until such time (if any) as it becomes established that the power will not be exercisable within the perpetuity period, as if the disposition were not subject to the rule against perpetuities.

(3) Where, apart from the said provisions, a disposition consisting of the conferring of any power, option or other right would be void on the ground that the right might be exercised at too remote a time, the disposition shall be treated as regards any exercise of the right within the perpetuity period as if it were not subject to the rule against perpetuities and, subject to the said provisions, shall be treated as void for remoteness only if, and so far as, the right is not fully exercised within that period.

(4) Where this section applies to a disposition and the duration of the perpetuity period is not determined by virtue of section 1 or 9(2) of this Act, it shall be determined as follows:—

(a) where any persons falling within subsection (5) below are individuals in being and ascertainable at the commencement of the perpetuity period the duration of the period shall be determined by reference to their lives and no others, but so that the lives of any description of persons falling within paragraph (b) or (c) of that subsection shall be disregarded if the number of persons of that description is such as to render it impracticable to ascertain the date of death of the survivor;

(b) where there are no lives under paragraph (a) above the period shall be twenty-one years.

(5) The said persons are as follows:—

(a) the person by whom the disposition was made;

(b) a person to whom or in whose favour the disposition was made, that is to say—

(i) in the case of a disposition to a class of persons, any member or potential member of the class;

(ii) in the case of an individual disposition to a person taking only on certain conditions being satisfied, any person as to whom some of the conditions are satisfied and the remainder may in time be satisfied;

(iii) in the case of a special power of appointment exercisable in favour of members of a class, any member or potential member of the class;

(iv) in the case of a special power of appointment exercisable in favour of one person only, that person or, where the object of the power is ascertainable only on certain conditions being satisfied, any person as to whom some of the conditions are satisfied and the remainder may in time be satisfied;

(v) in the case of any power, option or other right, the person on whom the right is conferred;

(c) a person having a child or grandchild within sub-paragraphs (i) to (iv) of paragraph (b) above, or any of whose children or grandchildren, if subsequently born, would by virtue of his or her descent fall within those sub-paragraphs;

(d) any person on the failure or determination of whose prior interest the disposition is limited to take effect.

[246.77]

4. Reduction of age and exclusion of class members to avoid remoteness.—
(1) Where a disposition is limited by reference to the attainment by any person or persons of a specified age exceeding twenty-one years, and it is apparent at the time the disposition is made or becomes apparent at a subsequent time—

(a) that the disposition would, apart from this section, be void for remoteness, but

(b) that it would not be so void if the specified age had been twenty-one years,

the disposition shall be treated for all purposes as if, instead of being limited by reference to the age in fact specified, it had been limited by reference to the age nearest to that age which would, if specified instead, have prevented the disposition from being so void.

(2) Where in the case of any disposition different ages exceeding twenty-one years are specified in relation to different persons—

(a) the reference in paragraph (b) of subsection (1) above to the specified age shall be construed as a reference to all the specified ages, and

(b) that subsection shall operate to reduce each such age so far as is necessary to save the disposition from being void for remoteness.

(3) Where the inclusion of any persons, being potential members of a class or unborn persons who at birth would become members or potential members of the class, prevents the foregoing provisions of this section from operating to save a disposition from being void for remoteness, those persons shall thenceforth be deemed for all the purposes of the disposition to be excluded from the class, and the said provisions shall thereupon have effect accordingly.

(4) Where in the case of a disposition to which subsection (3) above does not apply, it is apparent at the time the disposition is made or becomes apparent at a subsequent time that, apart from this subsection, the inclusion of any persons, being potential members of a class or unborn persons who at birth would become members or potential members of the class, would cause the disposition to be treated as void for remoteness, those persons shall, unless their exclusion would exhaust the class, thenceforth be deemed for all the purposes of the disposition to be excluded from the class.

(5) Where this section has effect in relation to a disposition to which section 3 above applies, the operation of this section shall not affect the validity of anything previously done in relation to the interest disposed of by way of advancement, application of intermediate income or otherwise.
(6) Section 163 of the Law of Property Act 1925 (which saves a disposition from remoteness arising out of a condition requiring the attainment of an age exceeding twenty-one years) is hereby repealed.
[(7) For the avoidance of doubt is is hereby declared that a question arising under section 3 of this Act or subsection (1)(a) above of whether a disposition would be void apart from this section is to be determined as if subsection (6) above had been a separate section of this Act.][1]

1 Sub-s (7): added by the Children Act 1975, s 108, Sch 3, para 43, and preserved from the general repeal of that Act by the ChA 1989, s 108(6), Sch 14, para 38.

[246.78]
5. Condition relating to death of surviving spouse. Where a disposition is limited by reference to the time of death of the survivor of a person in being at the commencement of the perpetuity period and any spouse of that person, and that time has not arrived at the end of the perpetuity period, the disposition shall be treated for all purposes, where to do so would save it from being void for remoteness, as if it had instead been limited by reference to the time immediately before the end of that period.

[246.79]
6. Saving and acceleration of expectant interests. A disposition shall not be treated as void for remoteness by reason only that the interest disposed of is ulterior to and dependent upon an interest under a disposition which is so void, and the vesting of an interest shall not be prevented from being accelerated on the failure of a prior interest by reason only that the failure arises because of remoteness.

[246.80]
7. Powers of appointment. For the purposes of the rule against perpetuities, a power of appointment shall be treated as a special power unless—

(a) in the instrument creating the power it is expressed to be exercisable by one person only, and
(b) it could, at all times during its currency when that person is of full age and capacity, be exercised by him so as immediately to transfer to himself the whole of the interest governed by the power without the consent of any other person or compliance with any other condition, not being a formal condition relating only to the mode of exercise of the power:

Provided that for the purpose of determining whether a disposition made under a power of appointment exercisable by will only is void for remoteness, the power shall be treated as a general power where it would have fallen to be so treated if exercisable by deed.

[246.81]
8. Administrative powers of trustees.— (1) The rule against perpetuities shall not operate to invalidate a power conferred on trustees or other persons to sell, lease, exchange or otherwise dispose of any property for full

consideration, or to do any other act in the administration (as opposed to the distribution) of any property, and shall not prevent the payment to trustees or other persons of reasonable remuneration for their services.
(2) Subsection (1) above shall apply for the purpose of enabling a power to be exercised at any time after the commencement of this Act notwithstanding that the power is conferred by an instrument which took effect before that commencement.

[246.82]
9. Options relating to land.— (1) The rule against perpetuities shall not apply to a disposition consisting of the conferring of an option to acquire for valuable consideration an interest reversionary (whether directly or indirectly) on the term of a lease if—

(a) the option is exercisable only by the lessee or his successors in title, and
(b) it ceases to be exercisable at or before the expiration of one year following the determination of the lease.

This subsection shall apply in relation to an agreement for a lease as it applies in relation to a lease, and 'lessee' shall be construed accordingly.
(2) In the case of a disposition consisting of the conferring of an option to acquire for valuable consideration any interest in land, the perpetuity period under the rule against perpetuities shall be twenty-one years, and section 1 of this Act shall not apply:
Provided that this subsection shall not apply to a right of pre-emption conferred on a public or local authority in respect of land used or to be used for religious purposes where the right becomes exercisable only if the land ceases to be used for such purposes.

[246.83]
10. Avoidance of contractual and other rights in cases of remoteness. Where a disposition inter vivos would fall to be treated as void for remoteness if the rights and duties thereunder were capable of transmission to persons other than the original parties and had been so transmitted, it shall be treated as void as between the person by whom it was made and the person to whom or in whose favour it was made or any successor of his, and no remedy shall lie in contract or otherwise for giving effect to it or making restitution for its lack of effect.

[246.84]
11. Rights for enforcement of rentcharges.— (1) The rule against perpetuities shall not apply to any powers or remedies for recovering or compelling the payment of an annual sum to which section 121 or 122 of the Law of Property Act 1925 applies, or otherwise becoming exercisable or enforceable on the breach of any condition or other requirement relating to that sum.
(2) [*Repeals in part the Law of Property Act 1925, s 121*(*6*).]

[246.85]
12. Possibilities of reverter, conditions subsequent, exceptions and reservations.— (1) In the case of—

(a) a possibility of reverter on the determination of a determinable fee simple, or
(b) a possibility of a resulting trust on the determination of any other determinable interest in property.

the rule against perpetuities shall apply in relation to the provision causing the interest to be determinable as it would apply if that provision were expressed in the form of a condition subsequent giving rise, on breach thereof, to a right of re-entry or an equivalent right in the case of property other than land, and where the provision falls to be treated as void for remoteness the determinable interest shall become an absolute interest.
(2) Where a disposition is subject to any such provision, or to any such condition subsequent, or to any exception or reservation, the disposition shall be treated for the purposes of this Act as including a separate disposition of any rights arising by virtue of the provision, condition subsequent, exception or reservation.

ACCUMULATIONS

[246.86]
13. Amendment of s 164 of Law of Property Act 1925.— (1) The periods for which accumulations of income under a settlement or other disposition are permitted by section 164 of the Law of Property Act 1925 shall include—

(a) a term of twenty-one years from the date of the making of the disposition and
(b) the duration of the minority or respective minorities of any person or persons in being at that date.

(2) It is hereby declared that the restrictions imposed by the said section 164 apply in relation to a power to accumulate income whether or not there is a duty to exercise that power, and that they apply whether or not the power to accumulate extends to income produced by the investment of income previously accumulated.

[246.87]
14. Right to stop accumulations. Section 2 above shall apply to any question as to the right of beneficiaries to put an end to accmulations of income under any disposition as it applies to questions arising on the rule against perpetuities.

SUPPLEMENTAL

[246.88]
15. Short title, interpretation and extent.— (1) This Act may be cited as the Perpetuities and Accumulations Act 1964.
(2) In this Act—

'disposition' includes the conferring of a power of appointment and any other disposition of an interest in or right over property, and references to the interest disposed of shall be construed accordingly;

'in being' means living or en ventre sa mere;
'power of appointment' includes any discretionary power to transfer a beneficial interest in property without the furnishing of valuable consideration;
'will' includes a codicil;

and for the purposes of this Act a disposition contained in a will shall be deemed to be made at the death of the testator.
(3) For the purposes of this Act a person shall be treated as a member of a class if in his case all the conditions identifying a member of the class are satisfied, and shall be treated as a potential member if in his case some only of those conditions are satisfied but there is a possibility that the remainder will in time be satisfied.
(4) Nothing in this Act shall affect the operation of the rule of law rendering void for remoteness certain dispositions under which property is limited to be applied for purposes other than the benefit of any person or class of persons in cases where the property may be so applied after the end of the perpetuity period.
(5) The foregoing sections of this Act shall apply (except as provided in section 8(2) above) only in relation to instruments taking effect after the commencement of this Act, and in the case of an instrument made in the exercise of a special power of appointment shall apply only where the instrument creating the power takes effect after that commencement;
Provided that section 7 above shall apply in all cases for construing the foregoing reference to a special power of appointment.
(6) This Act shall apply in relation to a disposition made otherwise than by an instrument as if the disposition had been contained in an instrument taking effect when the disposition was made.
(7) This Act binds the Crown.

* * * * *

FAMILY LAW REFORM ACT 1969

(1969 c 46)

[25 July 1969]

PART I
REDUCTION OF AGE OF MAJORITY AND RELATED PROVISIONS

[246.89]
1. Reduction of age of majority from 21 to 18.— (1) As from the date on which this section comes into force a person shall attain full age on attaining the age of eighteen instead of on attaining the age of twenty-one; and a person shall attain full age on that date if he has then already attained the age of eighteen but not the age of twenty-one.
(2) The foregoing subsection applies for the purposes of any rule of law, and, in the absence of a definition or of any contrary intention, for the construction of 'full age', 'infant', 'infancy', 'minor', 'minority' and similar expressions in—

(a) any statutory provision, whether passed or made before, on or after the date on which this section comes into force; and
(b) any deed, will or other instrument of whatever nature (not being a statutory provision) made on or after that date.

(3) In the statutory provisions specified in Schedule 1 to this Act for any reference to the age of twenty-one years there shall be substituted a reference to the age of eighteen years; but the amendment by this subsection of the provisions specified in Part II of that Schedule shall be without prejudice to any power of amending or revoking those provisions.
(4) This section does not affect the construction of any such expression as is referred to in subsection (2) of this section in any of the statutory provisions described in Schedule 2 to this Act, and the transitional provisions and savings contained in Schedule 3 to this Act shall have effect in relation to this section.
(5) The Lord Chancellor may by order made by statutory instrument amend any provision in any local enactment passed on or before the date on which this section comes into force (not being a provision described in paragraph 2 of Schedule 2 to this Act) by substituting a reference to the age of eighteen years for any reference therein to the age of twenty-one years; and any statutory instrument containing an order under this subsection shall be subject to annulment in pursuance of a resolution of either House of Parliament.
(6) In this section 'statutory provision' means any enactment (including, except where the context otherwise requires, this Act) and any order, rule, regulation, byelaw or other instrument made in the exercise of a power conferred by any enactment.
(7) Notwithstanding any rule of law, a will or codicil executed before the date on which this section comes into force shall not be treated for the purposes of this section as made on or after that date by reason only that the will or codicil is confirmed by a codicil executed on or after that date.

* * * * *

SCHEDULE 1

Section 1(3)

STATUTORY PROVISIONS AMENDED BY SUBSTITUTING 18 FOR 21 YEARS
Part I

ENACTMENTS

[246.90]

	Short title	*Sections*	*Subject matter*
	...	...	...
c 19	The Trustee Act 1925	Section 31(1)(ii), (2)(i)(a) and (b)	Power to apply income for maintenance and to accumulate surplus income during a minority.

* * * * *

SCHEDULE 3

Section 1(4)

TRANSITIONAL PROVISIONS AND SAVINGS

INTERPRETATION

[246.91]
1.— (1) In this Schedule 'the principal section' means section 1 of this Act and 'the commencement date' means the date on which that section comes into force.
(2) Subsection (7) of the principal section shall apply for the purposes of this Schedule as it applies for the purposes of that section.

* * * * *

POWER OF TRUSTEES TO APPLY INCOME FOR MAINTENANCE OF MINOR

[246.92]
5.— (1) The principal section shall not affect section 31 of the Trustee Act 1925—

(a) in its application to any interest under an instrument made before the commencement date; or
(b) in its application, by virtue of section 47(1)(ii) of the Administration of Estates Act 1925, to the estate of an intestate (within the meaning of that Act) dying before that date.

(2) In any case in which (whether by virtue of this paragraph or paragraph 9 of this Schedule) trustees have power under subsection (1)(i) of the said section 31 to pay income to the parent or guardian of any person who has attained the age eighteen, or to apply it for or towards the maintenance, education or or benefit of any such person, they shall also have power to pay it to that person himself.

* * * * *

ACCUMULATION PERIODS

[246.93]
7. The change, by virtue of the principal section, in the construction of—

(a) sections 164 to 166 of the Law of Property Act 1925;
(b) section 13(1) of the Perpetuities and Accumulations Act 1964,

(which lay down permissible periods for the accumulation of income under settlements and other dispositions) shall not invalidate any direction for accumulation in a settlement or other disposition made by a deed, will or other instrument which was made before the commencement date.

* * * * *

STATUTORY PROVISIONS INCORPORATED IN DEEDS, WILLS ETC

[264.94]
9. The principal section shall not affect the construction of any statutory provision where it is incorporated in and has effect as part of any deed, will or other instrument the construction of which is not affected by that section.

INTERPRETATION ACT 1978

(1978 c 30)

[20 July 1978]

INTERPRETATION AND CONSTRUCTION

[246.95]
5. Definitions. In any Act, unless the contrary intention appears, words and expressions listed in Schedule 1 to this Act are to be construed according to that Schedule.

* * * * *

[246.96]
17. Repeal and re-enactment— …
(2) Where an Act repeals and re-enacts, with or without modification, a previous enactment then, unless the contrary intention appears,—

(a) any reference in any other enactment to the enactment so repealed shall be construed as a reference to the provision re-enacted;

* * * * *

[246.97]
23. Application to other instruments— …
(3) … and in the application to section 17(2)(a) to Acts passed or subordinate legislation made after the commencement of this Act, the reference to any other enactment includes any deed or other instrument or document.

* * * * *

SCHEDULE 1

Section 5

WORDS AND EXPRESSIONS DEFINED

* * * * *

DEFINITIONS

* * * * *

[246.98]
'Land' includes buildings and other structures, land covered with water, and any estate, interest, easement, servitude or right in or over land.
'Writing' includes typing, printing, lithography, photography and other modes of representing or reproducing words in a visible form, and expressions referring to writing are construed accordingly.

* * * * *

INHERITANCE TAX ACT 1984

(1984 c 51)

[31 July 1984]

[246.99]

Note. The original short title of this Act was the Capital Transfer Act 1984. The alternative title was provided by the Finance Act 1986, s 100(1)(a) as from 25 July 1986.

[246.100]
211. Burden of tax on death.— (1) Where personal representatives are liable for tax on the value transferred by a chargeable transfer made on death, the tax shall be treated as part of the general testamentary and administration expenses of the estate, but only so far as it is attributable to the value of property in the United Kingdom which—

(a) vests in the deceased's personal representatives, and
(b) was not immediately before the death comprised in a settlement.

(2) Subsection (1) above shall have effect subject to any contrary intention shown by the deceased in his will.
(3) Where any amount of tax paid by personal representatives on the value transferred by a chargeable transfer made on death does not fall to be borne as part of the general testamentary and administration expenses of the estate, that amount shall, where occasion requires, be repaid to them by the person in whom the property to the value of which the tax is attributable is vested.
(4) References in this section to tax include references to interest on tax.

CHARITIES ACT 1993

(1993 c 10)

[27 May 1993]

PART IV
APPLICATION OF PROPERTY CY-PRÈS AND ASSISTANCE AND SUPERVISION OF CHARITIES BY COURT AND COMMISSIONERS

* * * * *

MEANING OF 'TRUST CORPORATION'

[246.101]
35. Application of provisions to trust corporations appointed under s 16 or 18.— (1) In the definition of 'trust corporation' contained in the following provisions—

(a) section 117(xxx) of the Settled Land Act 1925,
(b) section 68(18) of the Trustee Act 1925,
(c) section 205(xxviii) of the law of Property Act 1925,
(d) section 55(xxvi) of the Administration of Estates Act 1925, and
(e) secion 128 of the Supreme Court Act 1981,

the reference to a corporation appointed by the court in any particular case to be a trustee includes a reference to a corporation appointed by the Commissioners under this Act to be a trustee.
(2) This section shall be deemed always to have had effect; but the reference to section 128 of the Supreme Court Act 1981 shall in relation to any time before 1 January 1982, be construed as a reference to section 175(1) of the Supreme Court of Judicature (Consolidation) Act 1925.[1]

1 Section 175(1) of the Supreme Court (Consolidation) Act 1925 was repealed by the Supreme Court Act 1981, s 152(4), Sch 7 and replaced by s 128 of that Act.

TRUSTS OF LAND AND APPOINTMENT OF TRUSTEES ACT 1996

(1996 c 47)

[24 July 1996]

[246.102]

Note. The TLATA 1996, which came into force on 1 January 1997, makes fundamental changes to the law relating to land held on trust and also effects limited, though significant, changes to the law relating to the appointment and retirement of trustees whether of realty or personalty. The most significant change contained in Part I of the Act (concerning land held on trust) is the introduction of a single system governing land held on trust (the so-called 'trust of land') replacing strict settlements and trusts for sale. The SLA 1925 ceases to apply to newly created trusts, though it continues to apply to existing strict settlements (and strict settlements which derive from existing strict settlements). (Entailed interests have suffered the same fate as strict settlements and can no longer be created either in realty or personalty.) All other forms of trust in relation to land, whether created before or after the coming into force of the Act and whether or not such trusts import a trust for sale, fall within the Act's provisions. It is still possible to create a trust for sale but the doctrine of conversion is abolished in relation to express trusts for sale of land and it now makes no practical difference whether or not land is subjected to a trust for sale.

The Act confers wide administrative powers on trustees of land but imposes a positive (though excludable) duty to consult beneficiaries so far as practicable as to the exercise of their functions in relation to land. The Act confers on beneficiaries with interests in possession rights to occupy land held in trust subject to certain restrictions. The Act confers on the court a wider jurisdiction than it possessed under the Law of Property Act 1925, s 30 (which is repealed) to regulate the exercise by trustees of their functions in relation to land. Part I of the Act applies with appropriate modifications to personal representatives. Part II concerns the appointment and retirement of trustees. This Part gives power to beneficiaries who are sui juris and between them absolutely entitled to property which is held on a trust under which no person is nominated for the purpose of appointing new trustees, to give a unanimous written direction to a trustee to retire, or to the trustees (or the personal representatives of the last surviving trustee) to appoint the person or persons specified in such direction as a new trustee or new trustees. (This provision reverses *Re Brockbank, Ward v Bates* [1948] Ch 206, [1948] 1 All ER 287. A similar power is conferred where a trustee is incapable.

PART I
TRUSTS OF LAND

INTRODUCTORY

[246.103]

1. Meaning of 'trust of land'.— (1) In this Act—

(a) 'trust of land' means (subject to subsection (3)) any trust of property which consists of or includes land, and
(b) 'trustees of land' means trustees of a trust of land.

(2) The reference in subsection (1)(a) to a trust—

(a) is to any description of trust (whether express, implied, resulting or constructive), including a trust for sale and a bare trust, and

(b) includes a trust created, or arising, before the commencement of this Act.

(3) The reference to land in subsection (1)(a) does not include land which (despite section 2) is settled land or which is land to which the Universities and College Estates Act 1925 applies.

SETTLEMENTS AND TRUSTS FOR SALE AS TRUSTS OF LAND

[246.104]
2. Trusts in place of settlements.— (1) No settlement created after the commencement of this Act is a settlement for the purposes of the Settled Land Act 1925; and no settlement shall be deemed to be made under that Act after that commencement.
(2) Subsection (1) does not apply to a settlement created on the occasion of an alteration in any interest in, or of a person becoming entitled under, a settlement which—

(a) is in existence at the commencement of this Act, or
(b) derives from a settlement within paragraph (a) or this paragraph.

(3) But a settlement created as mentioned in subsection (2) is not a settlement for the purposes of the Settled Land Act 1925 if provision to the effect that it is not is made in the instrument, or any of the instruments, by which it is created.
(4) Where at any time after the commencement of this Act there is in the case of any settlement which is a settlement for the purposes of the Settled Land Act 1925 no relevant property which is, or is deemed to be, subject to the settlement, the settlement permanently ceases at that time to be a settlement for the purposes of that Act.
In this subsection 'relevant property' means land and personal chattels to which section 67(1) of the Settled Land Act 1925 (heirlooms) applies.
(5) No land held on charitable, ecclesiastical or public trusts shall be or be deemed to be settled land after the commencement of this Act, even if it was or was deemed to be settled land before that commencement.
(6) Schedule 1 has effect to make provision consequential on this section (including provision to impose a trust in circumstances in which, apart from this section, there would be a settlement for the purposes of the Settled Land Act 1925 (and there would not otherwise be a trust)).

[246.105]
3. Abolition of doctrine of conversion.— (1) Where land is held by trustees subject to a trust for sale, the land is not to be regarded as personal property; and where personal property is subject to a trust for sale in order that the trustees may acquire land, the personal property is not to be regarded as land.
(2) Subsection (1) does not apply to a trust created by a will if the testator died before the commencement of this Act.
(3) Subject to that, subsection (1) applies to a trust whether it is created, or arises, before or after that commencement.

[246.106]
4. Express trusts for sale as trusts of land.— (1) In the case of every trust for sale of land created by a disposition there is to be implied, despite any provision to the contrary made by the disposition, a power for the trustees to postpone sale of the land; and the trustees are not liable in any way for postponing sale of the land, in the exercise of their discretion, for an indefinite period.
(2) Subsection (1) applies to a trust whether it is created, or arises, before or after the commencement of this Act.
(3) Subsection (1) does not affect any liability incurred by trustees before that commencement.

[246.107]
5. Implied trusts for sale as trusts of land.— (1) Schedule 2 has effect in relation to statutory provisions which impose a trust for sale of land in certain circumstances so that in those circumstances there is instead a trust of the land (without a duty to sell).
(2) Section 1 of the Settled Land Act 1925 does not apply to land held on any trust arising by virtue of that Schedule (so that any such land is subject to a trust of land).

FUNCTIONS OF TRUSTEES OF LAND

[246.108]
6. General powers of trustees.— (1) For the purpose of exercising their functions as trustees, the trustees of land have in relation to the land subject to the trust all the powers of an absolute owner.
(2) Where in the case of any land subject to a trust of land each of the beneficiaries interested in the land is a person of full age and capacity who is absolutely entitled to the land, the powers conferred on the trustees by subsection (1) include the power to convey the land to the beneficiaries even though they have not required the trustees to do so; and where land is conveyed by virtue of this subsection—

(a) the beneficiaries shall do whatever is necessary to secure that it vests in them, and
(b) if they fail to do so, the court may make an order requiring them to do so.

(3) The trustees of land have power to [acquire land under the power conferred by section 8 of the Trustee Act 2000].[1]
(4) …
(5) In exercising the powers conferred by this section trustees shall have regard to the rights of the beneficiaries.
(6) The powers conferred by this section shall not be exercised in contravention of, or of any order made in pursuance of, any other enactment or any rule of law or equity.
(7) The reference in subsection (6) to an order includes an order of any court or of the Charity Commissioners.
(8) Where any enactment other than this section confers on trustees authority to act subject to any restriction, limitation or condition, trustees of land may not exercise the powers conferred by this section to do any act

which they are prevented from doing under the other enactment by reason of the restriction, limitation or condition.
[(9) The duty of care under section 1 of the Trustee Act 2000 applies to trustees of land when exercising the powers conferred by this section.][1]

1 Sub-ss (3) amended, (a) repealed and sub-s (9) inserted by the TrA 2000, Sch 2, Pt II, para 45.

[246.109]
7. Partition by trustees.— (1) The trustees of land may, where beneficiaries of full age are absolutely entitled in undivided shares to land subject to the trust, partition the land, or any part of it, and provide (by way of mortgage or otherwise) for the payment of any equality money.
(2) The trustees shall give effect to any such partition by conveying the partitioned land in severalty (whether or not subject to any legal mortgage created for raising equality money), either absolutely or in trust, in accordance with the rights of those beneficiaries.
(3) Before exercising their powers under subsection (2) the trustees shall obtain the consent of each of those beneficiaries.
(4) Where a share in the land is affected by an incumbrance, the trustees may either give effect to it or provide for its discharge from the property allotted to that share as they think fit.
(5) If a share in the land is absolutely vested in a minor, subsections (1) to (4) apply as if he were of full age, except that the trustees may act on his behalf and retain land or other property representing his share in trust for him.

[246.110]
8. Exclusion and restriction of powers.— (1) Sections 6 and 7 do not apply in the case of a trust of land created by a disposition in so far as provision to the effect that they do not apply is made by the disposition.
(2) If the disposition creating such a trust makes provision requiring any consent to be obtained to the exercise of any power conferred by section 6 or 7, the power may not be exercised without that consent.
(3) Subsection (1) does not apply in the case of charitable, ecclesiastical or public trusts.
(4) Subsections (1) and (2) have effect subject to any enactment which prohibits or restricts the effect of provision of the description mentioned in them.

[246.111]
9. Delegation by trustees.— (1) The trustees of land may, by power of attorney, delegate to any beneficiary or beneficiaries of full age and beneficially entitled to an interest in possession in land subject to the trust any of their functions as trustees which relate to the land.
(2) Where trustees purport to delegate to a person by a power of attorney under subsection (1) functions relating to any land and another person in good faith deals with him in relation to the land, he shall be presumed in favour of that other person to have been a person to whom the functions could be delegated unless that other person has knowledge at the time of the transaction that he was not such a person.

And it shall be conclusively presumed in favour of any purchaser whose interest depends on the validity of that transaction that that other person dealt in good faith and did not have such knowledge if that other person makes a statutory declaration to that effect before or within three months after the completion of the purchase.
(3) A power of attorney under subsection (1) shall be given by all the trustees jointly and (unless expressed to be irrevocable and to be given by way of security) may be revoked by any one or more of them; and such a power is revoked by the appointment as a trustee of a person other than those by whom it is given (though not by any of those persons dying or otherwise ceasing to be a trustee).
(4) Where a beneficiary to whom functions are delegated by a power of attorney under subsection (1) ceases to be a person beneficially entitled to an interest in possession in land subject to the trust—

(a) if the functions are delegated to him alone, the power is revoked;
(b) if the functions are delegated to him and to other beneficiaries to be exercised by them jointly (but not separately), the power is revoked if each of the other beneficiaries ceases to be so entitled (but otherwise functions exercisable in accordance with the power are so exercisable by the remaining beneficiary or beneficiaries); and
(c) if the functions are delegated to him and to other beneficiaries to be exercised by them separately (or either separately or jointly), the power is revoked in so far as it relates to him.

(5) A delegation under subsection (1) may be for any period or indefinite.
(6) A power of attorney under subsection (1) cannot be an enduring power within the meaning of the Enduring Powers of Attorney Act 1985.
(7) Beneficiaries to whom functions have been delegated under subsection (1) are, in relation to the exercise of the functions, in the same position as trustees (with the same duties and liabilities); but such beneficiaries shall not be regarded as trustees for any other purposes (including, in particular, the purposes of any enactment permitting the delegation of functions by trustees or imposing requirements relating to the payment of capital money).
(8) …[1]
(9) Neither this section nor the repeal by this Act of section 29 of the Law of Property Act 1925 (which is superseded by this section) affects the operation after the commencement of this Act of any delegation effected before that commencement.[1]

1 Sub-s (8): repealed by the TrA 2000, Sch 2, Pt II, para 46.

[246.112]
[9A. Duties of trustees in connection with delegation etc.—] [(1) The duty of care under section 1 of the Trustee Act 2000 applies to trustees of land in deciding whether to delegate any of their functions under section 9.
(2) Subsection (3) applies if the trustees of land—

(a) delegate any of their functions under section 9, and
(b) the delegation is not irrevocable.

(3) While the delegation continues, the trustees—

(a) must keep the delegation under review,
(b) if circumstances make it appropriate to do so, must consider whether there is a need to exercise any power of intervention that they have, and
(c) if they consider that there is a need to exercise such a power, must do so.

(4) 'Power of intervention' includes—

(a) a power to give directions to the beneficiary;
(b) a power to revoke the delegation.

(5) The duty of care under section 1 of the 2000 Act applies to trustees in carrying out any duty under subsection (3).
(6) A trustee of land is not liable for any act or default of the beneficiary, or beneficiaries, unless the trustee fails to comply with the duty of care in deciding to delegate any of the trustees' functions under section 9 or in carrying out any duty under subsection (3).
(7) Neither this section nor the repeal of section 9(8) by the Trustee Act 2000 affects the operation after the commencement of this section of any delegation effected before that commencement.][1]

1 This section was inserted by the TrA 2000, s 40(1), Sch 2, para 47.

CONSENTS AND CONSULTATION

[246.113]
10. Consents.— (1) If a disposition creating a trust of land requires the consent of more than two persons to the exercise by the trustees of any function relating to the land, the consent of any two of them to the exercise of the function is sufficient in favour of a purchaser.
(2) Subsection (1) does not apply to the exercise of a function by trustees of land held on charitable, ecclesiastical or public trusts.
(3) Where at any time a person whose consent is expressed by a disposition creating a trust of land to be required to the exercise by the trustees of any function relating to the land is not of full age—

(a) his consent is not, in favour of a purchaser, required to the exercise of the function, but
(b) the trustees shall obtain the consent of a parent who has parental responsibility for him (within the meaning of the Children Act 1989) or of a guardian of his.

[246.114]
11. Consultation with beneficiaries.— (1) The trustees of land shall in the exercise of any function relating to land subject to the trust—

(a) so far as practicable, consult the beneficiaries of full age and beneficially entitled to an interest in possession in the land, and
(b) so far as consistent with the general interest of the trust, give effect to the wishes of those beneficiaries, or (in case of dispute) of the majority (according to the value of their combined interests).

(2) Subsection (1) does not apply—

(a) in relation to a trust created by a disposition in so far as provision that it does not apply is made by the disposition,
(b) in relation to a trust created or arising under a will made before the commencement of this Act, or
(c) in relation to the exercise of the power mentioned in section 6(2).

(3) Subsection (1) does not apply to a trust created before the commencement of this Act by a disposition, or a trust created after that commencement by reference to such a trust, unless provision to the effect that it is to apply is made by a deed executed—

(a) in a case in which the trust was created by one person and he is of full capacity, by that person, or
(b) in a case in which the trust was created by more than one person, by such of the persons who created the trust as are alive and of full capacity.

(4) A deed executed for the purposes of subsection (3) is irrevocable.

RIGHT OF BENEFICIARIES TO OCCUPY TRUST LAND

[246.115]
12. The right to occupy.— (1) A beneficiary who is beneficially entitled to an interest in possession in land subject to a trust of land is entitled by reason of his interest to occupy the land at any time if at that time—

(a) the purposes of the trust include making the land available for his occupation (or for the occupation of beneficiaries of a class of which he is a member or of beneficiaries in general), or
(b) the land is held by the trustees so as to be so available.

(2) Subsection (1) does not confer on a beneficiary a right to occupy land if it is either unavailable or unsuitable for occupation by him.
(3) This section is subject to section 13.

[246.116]
13. Exclusion and restriction of right to occupy.— (1) Where two or more beneficiaries are (or apart from this subsection would be) entitled under section 12 to occupy land, the trustees of land may exclude or restrict the entitlement of any one or more (but not all) of them.
(2) Trustees may not under subsection (1)—

(a) unreasonably exclude any beneficiary's entitlement to occupy land, or
(b) restrict any such entitlement to an unreasonable extent.

(3) The trustees of land may from time to time impose reasonable conditions on any beneficiary in relation to his occupation of land by reason of his entitlement under section 12.
(4) The matters to which trustees are to have regard in exercising the powers conferred by this section include—

(a) the intentions of the person or persons (if any) who created the trust,
(b) the purposes for which the land is held, and
(c) the circumstances and wishes of each of the beneficiaries who is (or apart from any previous exercise by the trustees of those powers would be) entitled to occupy the land under section 12.

(5) The conditions which may be imposed on a beneficiary under subsection (3) include, in particular, conditions requiring him—

(a) to pay any outgoings or expenses in respect of the land, or
(b) to assume any other obligation in relation to the land or to any activity which is or is proposed to be conducted there.

(6) Where the entitlement of any beneficiary to occupy land under section 12 has been excluded or restricted, the conditions which may be imposed on any other beneficiary under subsection (3) include, in particular, conditions requiring him to—

(a) make payments by way of compensation to the beneficiary whose entitlement has been excluded or restricted, or
(b) forgo any payment or other benefit to which he would otherwise be entitled under the trust so as to benefit that beneficiary.

(7) The powers conferred on trustees by this section may not be exercised—

(a) so as prevent any person who is in occupation of land (whether or not by reason of an entitlement under section 12) from continuing to occupy the land, or
(b) in a manner likely to result in any such person ceasing to occupy the land,

unless he consents or the court has given approval.
(8) The matters to which the court is to have regard in determining whether to give approval under subsection (7) include the matters mentioned in subsection (4)(a) to (c).

POWERS OF COURT

[246.117]
14. Applications for order.— (1) Any person who is a trustee of land or has an interest in a property subject to a trust of land may make an application to the court for an order under this section.
(2) On an application for an order under this section the court may make any such order—

(a) relating to the exercise by the trustees of any of their functions (including an order relieving them of any obligation to obtain the consent of, or to consult, any person in connection with the exercise of any of their functions), or
(b) declaring the nature or extent of a person's interest in property subject to the trust,

as the court thinks fit.
(3) The court may not under this section make any order as to the appointment or removal of trustees.
(4) The powers conferred on the court by this section are exercisable on an application whether it is made before or after the commencement of this Act.

[246.118]
15. Matters relevant in determining applications.— (1) The matters to which the court is to have regard in determining an application for an order under section 14 include—

(a) the intentions of the person or persons (if any) who created the trust,
(b) the purposes for which the property subject to the trust is held,
(c) the welfare of any minor who occupies or might reasonably be expected to occupy any land subject to the trust as his home, and
(d) the interests of any secured creditor of any beneficiary.

(2) In the case of an application relating to the exercise in relation to any land of the powers conferred on the trustees by section 13, the matters to which the court is to have regard also include the circumstances and wishes of each of the beneficiaries who is (or apart from any previous exercise by the trustees of those powers would be) entitled to occupy the land under section 12.
(3) In the case of any other application, other than one relating to the exercise of the power mentioned in section 6(2), the matters to which the court is to have regard also include the circumstances and wishes of any beneficiaries of full age and entitled to an interest in possession in property subject to the trust or (in case of dispute) of the majority (according to the value of their combined interests).
(4) This section does not apply to an application if section 335A of the Insolvency Act 1986 (which is inserted by Schedule 3 and relates to applications by a trustee of a bankrupt) applies to it.

PURCHASER PROTECTION

[246.119]
16. Protection of purchasers.— (1) A purchaser of land which is or has been subject to a trust need not be concerned to see that any requirement imposed on the trustees by section 6(5), 7(3) or 11(1) has been complied with.
(2) Where—

(a) trustees of land who convey land which (immediately before it is conveyed) is subject to the trust contravene section 6(6) or (8), but
(b) the purchaser of the land from the trustees has no actual notice of the contravention,

the contravention does not invalidate the conveyance.
(3) Where the powers of trustees of land are limited by virtue of section 8—

(a) the trustees shall take all reasonable steps to bring the limitation to the notice of any purchaser of the land from them, but
(b) the limitation does not invalidate any conveyance by the trustees to a purchaser who has no actual notice of the limitation.

(4) Where trustees of land convey land which (immediately before it is conveyed) is subject to the trust to persons believed by them to be beneficiaries absolutely entitled to the land under the trust and of full age and capacity—

(a) the trustees shall execute a deed declaring that they are discharged from the trust in relation to that land, and
(b) if they fail to do so, the court may make an order requiring them to do so.

(5) A purchaser of land to which a deed under subsection (4) relates is entitled to assume that, as from the date of the deed, the land is not subject to the trust unless he has actual notice that the trustees were mistaken in their belief that the land was conveyed to beneficiaries absolutely entitled to the land under the trust and of full age and capacity.
(6) Subsections (2) and (3) do not apply to land held on charitable, ecclesiastical or public trusts.
(7) This section does not apply to registered land.

SUPPLEMENTARY

[246.120]
17. Application of provisions to trusts of proceeds of sale.— (1) [*Repealed by the Trustee Act 2000, Sch 2, Pt II, para 48.*]
(2) Section 14 applies in relation to a trust of proceeds of sale of land and trustees of such a trust as in relation to a trust of land and trustees of land.
(3) In this section 'trust of proceeds of sale of land' means (subject to subsection (5)) any trust of property (other than a trust of land) which consists of or includes—

(a) any proceeds of a disposition of land held in trust (including settled land), or
(b) any property representing any such proceeds.

(4) The references in subsection (3) to a trust—

(a) are to any description of trust (whether express, implied, resulting or constructive), including a trust for sale and a bare trust, and
(b) include a trust created, or arising, before the commencement of this Act.

(5) A trust which (despite section 2) is a settlement for the purposes of the Settled Land Act 1925 cannot be a trust of proceeds of sale of land.
(6) In subsection (3)—

(a) 'disposition' includes any disposition made, or coming into operation, before the commencement of this Act, and
(b) the reference to settled land includes personal chattels to which section 67(1) of the Settled Land Act 1925 (heirlooms) applies.

[246.121]
18. Application of Part to personal representatives.— (1) The provisions of this Part relating to trustees, other than sections 10, 11 and 14, apply to personal representatives, but with appropriate modifications and without prejudice to the functions of personal representatives for the purposes of administration.
(2) The appropriate modifications include—

(a) the substitution of references to persons interested in the due administration of the estate for references to beneficiaries, and
(b) the substitution of references to the will for references to the disposition creating the trust.

(3) Section 3(1) does not apply to personal representatives if the death occurs before the commencement of this Act.

PART II
APPOINTMENT AND RETIREMENT OF TRUSTEES

[246.122]
19. Appointment and retirement of trustee at instance of beneficiaries.—
(1) This section applies in the case of a trust where—

(a) there is no person nominated for the purpose of appointing new trustees by the instrument, if any, creating the trust, and
(b) the beneficiaries under the trust are of full age and capacity and (taken together) are absolutely entitled to the property subject to the trust.

(2) The beneficiaries may give a direction or directions of either or both of the following descriptions—

(a) a written direction to a trustee or trustees to retire from the trust, and
(b) a written direction to the trustees or trustee for the time being (or, if there are none, to the personal representative of the last person who was a trustee) to appoint by writing to be a trustee or trustees the person or persons specified in the direction.

(3) Where—

(a) a trustee has been given a direction under subsection (2)(a),
(b) reasonable arrangements have been made for the protection of any rights of his in connection with the trust,
(c) after he has retired there will be either a trust corporation or at least two persons to act as trustees to perform the trust, and
(d) either another person is to be appointed to be a new trustee on his retirement (whether in compliance with a direction under subsection (2)(b) or otherwise) or the continuing trustees by deed consent to his retirement,

he shall make a deed declaring his retirement and shall be deemed to have retired and be discharged from the trust.

(4) Where a trustee retires under subsection (3) he and the continuing trustees (together with any new trustee) shall (subject to any arrangements for the protection of his rights) do anything necessary to vest the trust property in the continuing trustees (or the continuing and new trustees).
(5) This section has effect subject to the restrictions imposed by the Trustee Act 1925 on the number of trustees.

[246.123]
20. [Appointment of substitute for trustee who lacks capacity].[1]— (1) This section applies where—

- (a) a trustee [lacks capacity (within the meaning of the Mental Capacity Act 2005) to exercise][1] his functions as trustee,
- (b) there is no person who is both entitled and willing and able to appoint a trustee in place of him under section 36(1) of the Trustee Act 1925, and
- (c) the beneficiaries under the trust are of full age and capacity and (taken together) are absolutely entitled to the property subject to the trust.

(2) The beneficiaries may give to—

- [(a) a deputy appointed for the trustee by the Court of Protection,][1]
- (b) an attorney acting for him under the authority of [an enduring power of attorney or lasting power of attorney registered under the Mental Capacity Act 2005][1], or
- (c) a person authorised for the purpose by [the Court of Protection][1],

a written direction to appoint by writing the person or persons specified in the direction to be a trustee or trustees in place of the incapable trustee.

1 With effect from 1 October 2007 heading and passages in square brackets throughout s 20 substituted by the MCA 2005, s 67(1), Sch 6, para 42(1) and (2).

[246.124]
21. Supplementary.— (1) For the purposes of section 19 or 20 a direction is given by beneficiaries if—

- (a) a single direction is jointly given by all of them, or
- (b) (subject to subsection (2)) a direction is given by each of them (whether solely or jointly with one or more, but not all, of the others),

and none of them by writing withdraws the direction given by him before it has been complied with.
(2) Where more than one direction is given each must specify for appointment or retirement the same person or persons.
(3) Subsection (7) of section 36 of the Trustee Act 1925 (powers of trustees appointed under that section) applies to a trustee appointed under section 19 or 20 as if he were appointed under that section.
(4) A direction under section 19 or 20 must not specify a person or persons for appointment if the appointment of that person or those persons would be in contravention of section 35(1) of the Trustee Act 1925 or section 24(1) of the Law of Property Act 1925 (requirements as to identity of trustees).

(5) Sections 19 and 20 do not apply in relation to a trust created by a disposition in so far as provision that they do not apply is made by the disposition.
(6) Sections 19 and 20 do not apply in relation to a trust created before the commencement of this Act by a disposition in so far as provision to the effect that they do not apply is made by a deed executed—

(a) in a case in which the trust was created by one person and he is of full capacity, by that person, or
(b) in a case in which the trust was created by more than one person, by such of the persons who created the trust as are alive and of full capacity.

(7) A deed executed for the purposes of subsection (6) is irrevocable.
(8) Where a deed is executed for the purposes of subsection (6)—

(a) it does not affect anything done before its execution to comply with a direction under section 19 or 20, but
(b) a direction under section 19 or 20 which has been given but not complied with before its execution shall cease to have effect.

PART III
SUPPLEMENTARY

[246.125]
22. Meaning of 'beneficiary'.— (1) In this Act 'beneficiary', in relation to a trust, means any person who under the trust has an interest in property subject to the trust (including a person who has such an interest as a trustee or a personal representative).
(2) In this Act references to a beneficiary who is beneficially entitled do not include a beneficiary who has an interest in property subject to the trust only by reason of being a trustee or personal representative.
(3) For the purposes of this Act a person who is a beneficiary only by reason of being an annuitant is not to be regarded as entitled to an interest in possession in land subject to the trust.

[246.126]
23. Other interpretation provisions.— (1) In this Act 'purchaser' has the same meaning as in Part I of the Law of Property Act 1925.
(2) Subject to that, where an expression used in this Act is given a meaning by the Law of Property Act 1925 it has the same meaning as in that Act unless the context otherwise requires.
(3) In this Act 'the court' means—

(a) the High Court, or
(b) a county court.

[246.127]
24. Application to Crown.— (1) Subject to subsection (2), this Act binds the Crown.
(2) This Act (except so far as it relates to undivided shares and joint ownership) does not affect or alter the descent, devolution or nature of the estates and interests of or in—

(a) land for the time being vested in Her Majesty in right of the Crown or of the Duchy of Lancaster, or
(b) land for the time being belonging to the Duchy of Cornwall and held in right or respect of the Duchy.

[246.128]
25. Amendments, repeals etc.— (1) The enactments mentioned in Schedule 3 have effect subject to the amendments specified in that Schedule (which are minor or consequential on other provisions of this Act).
(2) The enactments mentioned in Schedule 4 are repealed to the extent specified in the third column of that Schedule.
(3) Neither section 2(5) nor the repeal by this Act of section 29 of the Settled Land Act 1925 applies in relation to the deed of settlement set out in the Schedule to the Chequers Estate Act 1917 or the trust instrument set out in the Schedule to the Chevening Estate Act 1959.
(4) The amendments and repeals made by this Act do not affect any entailed interest created before the commencement of this Act.
(5) The amendments and repeals made by this Act in consequence of section 3—

(a) do not affect a trust created by a will if the testator died before the commencement of this Act, and
(b) do not affect personal representatives of a person who died before that commencement;

and the repeal of section 22 of the Partnership Act 1890 does not apply in any circumstances involving the personal representatives of a partner who died before that commencement.

[246.129]
26. Power to make consequential provision.— (1) The Lord Chancellor may by order made by statutory instrument make any such supplementary, transitional or incidental provision as appears to him to be appropriate for any of the purposes of this Act or in consequence of any of the provisions of this Act.
(2) An order under subsection (1) may, in particular, include provision modifying any enactment contained in a public general or local Act which is passed before, or in the same Session as, this Act.
(3) A statutory instrument made in the exercise of the power conferred by this section is subject to annulment in pursuance of a resolution of either House of Parliament.

[246.130]
27. Short title, commencement and extent.— (1) This Act may be cited as the Trusts of Land and Appointment of Trustees Act 1996.
(2) This Act comes into force on such day as the Lord Chancellor appoints by order made by statutory instrument.
(3) Subject to subsection (4), the provisions of this Act extend only to England and Wales.
(4) The repeal in section 30(2) of the Agriculture Act 1970 extends only to Northern Ireland.

SCHEDULE 1

Section 2

PROVISIONS CONSEQUENTIAL ON SECTION 2

MINORS

[246.131]
1.— (1) Where after the commencement of this Act a person purports to convey a legal estate in land to a minor, or two or more minors, alone, the conveyance—

(a) is not effective to pass the legal estate, but
(b) operates as a declaration that the land is held in trust for the minor or minors (or if he purports to convey it to the minor or minors in trust for any persons, for those persons).

(2) Where after the commencement of this Act a person purports to convey a legal estate in land to—

(a) a minor or two or more minors, and
(b) another person who is, or other persons who are, of full age,

the conveyance operates to vest the land in the other person or persons in trust for the minor or minors and the other person or persons (or if he purports to convey it to them in trust for any persons, for those persons).
(3) Where immediately before the commencement of this Act a conveyance is operating (by virtue of section 27 of the Settled Land Act 1925) as an agreement to execute a settlement in favour of a minor or minors—

(a) the agreement ceases to have effect on the commencement of this Act, and
(b) the conveyance subsequently operates instead as a declaration that the land is held in trust for the minor or minors.

2. Where after the commencement of this Act a legal estate in land would, by reason of intestacy or in any other circumstances not dealt with in paragraph 1, vest in a person who is a minor if he were a person of full age, the land is held in trust for the minor.

FAMILY CHARGES
3. Where, by virtue of an instrument coming into operation after the commencement of this Act, land becomes charged voluntarily (or in consideration of marriage [or formation of a civil partnership][1]) or by way of family arrangement, whether immediately or after an interval, with the payment of—

(a) a rentcharge for the life of a person or a shorter period, or
(b) capital, annual or periodical sums for the benefit of a person,

the instrument operates as a declaration that the land is held in trust for giving effect to the charge.

CHARITABLE, ECCLESIASTICAL AND PUBLIC TRUSTS

4.— (1) This paragraph applies in the case of land held on charitable, ecclesiastical or public trusts (other than land to which the Universities and College Estates Act 1925 applies).

(2) Where there is a conveyance of such land—

(a) if neither section 37(1) nor section 39(1) of the Charities Act 1993 applies to the conveyance, it shall state that the land is held on such trusts, and

(b) if neither section 37(2) nor section 39(2) of that Act has been complied with in relation to the conveyance and a purchaser has notice that the land is held on such trusts, he must see that any consents or orders necessary to authorise the transaction have been obtained.

(3) Where any trustees or the majority of any set of trustees have power to transfer or create any legal estate in the land, the estate shall be transferred or created by them in the names and on behalf of the persons in whom it is vested.

ENTAILED INTERESTS

5.— (1) Where a person purports by an instrument coming into operation after the commencement of this Act to grant to another person an entailed interest in real or personal property, the instrument—

(a) is not effective to grant an entailed interest, but

(b) operates instead as a declaration that the property is held in trust absolutely for the person to whom an entailed interest in the property was purportedly granted.

(2) Where a person purports by an instrument coming into operation after the commencement of this Act to declare himself a tenant in tail of real or personal property, the instrument is not effective to create an entailed interest.

PROPERTY HELD ON SETTLEMENT CEASING TO EXIST

6. Where a settlement ceases to be a settlement for the purposes of the Settled Land Act 1925 because no relevant property (within the meaning of section 2(4)) is, or is deemed to be, subject to the settlement, any property which is or later becomes subject to the settlement is held in trust for the persons interested under the settlement.

1 With effect from 5 December 2005 words in square brackets in para 3 inserted by the CPA 2004, s 261(1), Sch 27, para 153 and Civil Partnership Act 2004 (Commencement No 2) Order 2005, SI 2005/3175.

* * * * *

Note. Schedules 2 (Amendment of statutory provisions imposing trust for sale), 3 (Minor and consequential amendments) and 4 (Repeals) are not set out here, but their effect where relevant is mentioned in the notes to the main text.

TRUSTEE ACT 2000

(2000 c 29)

[23 November 2000]

PART I
THE DUTY OF CARE

[246.132]

Note. This Act implements with effect from 1 February 2001 the changes recommended in the joint report of the Law Commission and the Scottish Law Commission *Trustees' Powers and Duties* (1999) Law Com No 260, Scot Law Com 172. Part I introduces a statutory duty of care which applies to trustees in the exercise of the new powers conferred by the Act and in the other circumstances set out in Sch 1. Part II confers a wide new power of investment which gives trustees the same powers of investment as an absolute owner. Part III confers on trustees powers to acquire and manage land similar to those contained in the TLATA 1996, s 6. Part IV provides trustees with wide powers to delegate discretions to agents and to vest trust property in nominees. Part V confers a general power for trust corporations and professional trustees to charge for their services in relation to existing as well as newly created trusts. Part VI contains a number of miscellaneous provisions including a provision conferring a new trustee insurance power (by substituting a new section for the Trustee Act 1925, s 19) and a provision extending the provisions of the Act to personal representatives.

[246.133]
1. The duty of care.— (1) Whenever the duty under this subsection applies to a trustee, he must exercise such care and skill as is reasonable in the circumstances, having regard in particular—

(a) to any special knowledge or experience that he has or holds himself out as having, and
(b) if he acts as trustee in the course of a business or profession, to any special knowledge or experience that it is reasonable to expect of a person acting in the course of that kind of business or profession.

(2) In this Act the duty under subsection (1) is called 'the duty of care'.

[246.134]
2. Application of duty of care. Schedule 1 makes provision about when the duty of care applies to a trustee.

PART II
INVESTMENT

[246.135]
3. General power of investment.— (1) Subject to the provisions of this Part, a trustee may make any kind of investment that he could make if he were absolutely entitled to the assets of the trust.
(2) In this Act the power under subsection (1) is called 'the general power of investment'.
(3) The general power of investment does not permit a trustee to make investments in land other than in loans secured on land (but see also section 8).

(4) A person invests in a loan secured on land if he has rights under any contract under which—

(a) one person provides another with credit, and
(b) the obligation of the borrower to repay is secured on land.

(5) 'Credit' includes any cash loan or other financial accommodation.
(6) 'Cash' includes money in any form.

[246.136]
4. Standard investment criteria.— (1) In exercising any power of investment, whether arising under this Part or otherwise, a trustee must have regard to the standard investment criteria.
(2) A trustee must from time to time review the investments of the trust and consider whether, having regard to the standard investment criteria, they should be varied.
(3) The standard investment criteria, in relation to a trust, are—

(a) the suitability to the trust of investments of the same kind as any particular investment proposed to be made or retained and of that particular investment as an investment of that kind, and
(b) the need for diversification of investments of the trust, in so far as is appropriate to the circumstances of the trust.

[246.137]
5. Advice.— (1) Before exercising any power of investment, whether arising under this Part or otherwise, a trustee must (unless the exception applies) obtain and consider proper advice about the way in which, having regard to the standard investment criteria, the power should be exercised.
(2) When reviewing the investments of the trust, a trustee must (unless the exception applies) obtain and consider proper advice about whether, having regard to the standard investment criteria, the investments should be varied.
(3) The exception is that a trustee need not obtain such advice if he reasonably concludes that in all the circumstances it is unnecessary or inappropriate to do so.
(4) Proper advice is the advice of a person who is reasonably believed by the trustee to be qualified to give it by his ability in and practical experience of financial and other matters relating to the proposed investment.

[246.138]
6. Restriction or exclusion of this Part etc.— (1) The general power of investment is—

(a) in addition to powers conferred on trustees otherwise than by this Act, but
(b) subject to any restriction or exclusion imposed by the trust instrument or by any enactment or any provision of subordinate legislation.

(2) For the purposes of this Act, an enactment or a provision of subordinate legislation is not to be regarded as being, or as being part of, a trust instrument.

(3) In this Act 'subordinate legislation' has the same meaning as in the Interpretation Act 1978.

[246.139]
7. Existing trusts.— (1) This Part applies in relation to trusts whether created before or after its commencement.
(2) No provision relating to the powers of a trustee contained in a trust instrument made before 3rd August 1961 is to be treated (for the purposes of section 6(1)(b)) as restricting or excluding the general power of investment.
(3) A provision contained in a trust instrument made before the commencement of this Part which—

(a) has effect under section 3(2) of the Trustee Investments Act 1961 as a power to invest under that Act, or
(b) confers power to invest under that Act,

is to be treated as conferring the general power of investment on a trustee.

PART III
ACQUISITION OF LAND

[246.140]
8. Power to acquire freehold and leasehold land.— (1) A trustee may acquire freehold or leasehold land in the United Kingdom—

(a) as an investment,
(b) for occupation by a beneficiary, or
(c) for any other reason.

(2) 'Freehold or leasehold land' means—

(a) in relation to England and Wales, a legal estate in land,
(b) in relation to Scotland—
  (i) the estate or interest of the proprietor of the dominium utile or, in the case of land not held on feudal tenure, the estate or interest of the owner, or
  (ii) a tenancy, and
(c) in relation to Northern Ireland, a legal estate in land, including land held under a fee farm grant.

(3) For the purpose of exercising his functions as a trustee, a trustee who acquires land under this section has all the powers of an absolute owner in relation to the land.

[246.141]
9. Restriction or exclusion of this Part etc. The powers conferred by this Part are—

(a) in addition to powers conferred on trustees otherwise than by this Part, but
(b) subject to any restriction or exclusion imposed by the trust instrument or by any enactment or any provision of subordinate legislation.

[246.142]
10. Existing trusts.— (1) This Part does not apply in relation to—

(a) a trust of property which consists of or includes land which (despite section 2 of the Trusts of Land and Appointment of Trustees Act 1996) is settled land, or
(b) a trust to which the Universities and College Estates Act 1925 applies.

(2) Subject to subsection (1), this Part applies in relation to trusts whether created before or after its commencement.

PART IV
AGENTS, NOMINEES AND CUSTODIANS

AGENTS

[246.143]
11. Power to employ agents.— (1) Subject to the provisions of this Part, the trustees of a trust may authorise any person to exercise any or all of their delegable functions as their agent.
(2) In the case of a trust other than a charitable trust, the trustees' delegable functions consist of any function other than—

(a) any function relating to whether or in what way any assets of the trust should be distributed,
(b) any power to decide whether any fees or other payment due to be made out of the trust funds should be made out of income or capital,
(c) any power to appoint a person to be a trustee of the trust, or
(d) any power conferred by any other enactment or the trust instrument which permits the trustees to delegate any of their functions or to appoint a person to act as a nominee or custodian.

(3) In the case of a charitable trust, the trustees' delegable functions are—

(a) any function consisting of carrying out a decision that the trustees have taken;
(b) any function relating to the investment of assets subject to the trust (including, in the case of land held as an investment, managing the land and creating or disposing of an interest in the land);
(c) any function relating to the raising of funds for the trust otherwise than by means of profits of a trade which is an integral part of carrying out the trust's charitable purpose;
(d) any other function prescribed by an order made by the Secretary of State.

(4) For the purposes of subsection (3)(c) a trade is an integral part of carrying out a trust's charitable purpose if, whether carried on in the United Kingdom or elsewhere, the profits are applied solely to the purposes of the trust and either—

(a) the trade is exercised in the course of the actual carrying out of a primary purpose of the trust, or

(b) the work in connection with the trade is mainly carried out by beneficiaries of the trust.

(5) The power to make an order under subsection (3)(d) is exercisable by statutory instrument which shall be subject to annulment in pursuance of a resolution of either House of Parliament.

[246.144]
12. Persons who may act as agents.— (1) Subject to subsection (2), the persons whom the trustees may under section 11 authorise to exercise functions as their agent include one or more of their number.
(2) The trustees may not authorise two (or more) persons to exercise the same function unless they are to exercise the function jointly.
(3) The trustees may not under section 11 authorise a beneficiary to exercise any function as their agent (even if the beneficiary is also a trustee).
(4) The trustees may under section 11 authorise a person to exercise functions as their agent even though he is also appointed to act as their nominee or custodian (whether under section 16, 17 or 18 or any other power).

[246.145]
13. Linked functions etc.— (1) Subject to subsections (2) and (5), a person who is authorised under section 11 to exercise a function is (whatever the terms of the agency) subject to any specific duties or restrictions attached to the function.
For example, a person who is authorised under section 11 to exercise the general power of investment is subject to the duties under section 4 in relation to that power.
(2) A person who is authorised under section 11 to exercise a power which is subject to a requirement to obtain advice is not subject to the requirement if he is the kind of person from whom it would have been proper for the trustees, in compliance with the requirement, to obtain advice.
(3) Subsections (4) and (5) apply to a trust to which section 11(1) of the Trusts of Land and Appointment of Trustees Act 1996 (duties to consult beneficiaries and give effect to their wishes) applies.
(4) The trustees may not under section 11 authorise a person to exercise any of their functions on terms that prevent them from complying with section 11(1) of the 1996 Act.
(5) A person who is authorised under section 11 to exercise any function relating to land subject to the trust is not subject to section 11(1) of the 1996 Act.

[246.146]
14. Terms of agency.— (1) Subject to subsection (2) and sections 15(2) and 29 to 32, the trustees may authorise a person to exercise functions as their agent on such terms as to remuneration and other matters as they may determine.
(2) The trustees may not authorise a person to exercise functions as their agent on any of the terms mentioned in subsection (3) unless it is reasonably necessary for them to do so.

(3) The terms are—

(a) a term permitting the agent to appoint a substitute;
(b) a term restricting the liability of the agent or his substitute to the trustees or any beneficiary;
(c) a term permitting the agent to act in circumstances capable of giving rise to a conflict of interest.

[246.147]
15. Asset management: special restrictions.— (1) The trustees may not authorise a person to exercise any of their asset management functions as their agent except by an agreement which is in or evidenced in writing.
(2) The trustees may not authorise a person to exercise any of their asset management functions as their agent unless—

(a) they have prepared a statement that gives guidance as to how the functions should be exercised ('a policy statement'), and
(b) the agreement under which the agent is to act includes a term to the effect that he will secure compliance with—
    (i) the policy statement, or
    (ii) if the policy statement is revised or replaced under section 22, the revised or replacement policy statement.

(3) The trustees must formulate any guidance given in the policy statement with a view to ensuring that the functions will be exercised in the best interests of the trust.
(4) The policy statement must be in or evidenced in writing.
(5) The asset management functions of trustees are their functions relating to—

(a) the investment of assets subject to the trust,
(b) the acquisition of property which is to be subject to the trust, and
(c) managing property which is subject to the trust and disposing of, or creating or disposing of an interest in, such property.

NOMINEES AND CUSTODIANS

[246.148]
16. Power to appoint nominees.— (1) Subject to the provisions of this Part, the trustees of a trust may—

(a) appoint a person to act as their nominee in relation to such of the assets of the trust as they determine (other than settled land), and
(b) take such steps as are necessary to secure that those assets are vested in a person so appointed.

(2) An appointment under this section must be in or evidenced in writing.
(3) This section does not apply to any trust having a custodian trustee or in relation to any assets vested in the official custodian for charities.

[246.149]
17. Power to appoint custodians.— (1) Subject to the provisions of this Part, the trustees of a trust may appoint a person to act as a custodian in relation to such of the assets of the trust as they may determine.

(2) For the purposes of this Act a person is a custodian in relation to assets if he undertakes the safe custody of the assets or of any documents or records concerning the assets.
(3) An appointment under this section must be in or evidenced in writing.
(4) This section does not apply to any trust having a custodian trustee or in relation to any assets vested in the official custodian for charities.

[246.150]
18. Investment in bearer securities.— (1) If trustees retain or invest in securities payable to bearer, they must appoint a person to act as a custodian of the securities.
(2) Subsection (1) does not apply if the trust instrument or any enactment or provision of subordinate legislation contains provision which (however expressed) permits the trustees to retain or invest in securities payable to bearer without appointing a person to act as a custodian.
(3) An appointment under this section must be in or evidenced in writing.
(4) This section does not apply to any trust having a custodian trustee or in relation to any securities vested in the official custodian for charities.

[246.151]
19. Persons who may be appointed as nominees or custodians.— (1) A person may not be appointed under section 16, 17 or 18 as a nominee or custodian unless one of the relevant conditions is satisfied.
(2) The relevant conditions are that—

(a) the person carries on a business which consists of or includes acting as a nominee or custodian;
(b) the person is a body corporate which is controlled by the trustees;
(c) the person is a body corporate recognised under section 9 of the Administration of Justice Act 1985.

(3) The question whether a body corporate is controlled by trustees is to be determined in accordance with section 840 of the Income and Corporation Taxes Act 1988.
(4) The trustees of a charitable trust which is not an exempt charity must act in accordance with any guidance given by the Charity Commissioners concerning the selection of a person for appointment as a nominee or custodian under section 16, 17 or 18.
(5) Subject to subsections (1) and (4), the persons whom the trustees may under section 16, 17 or 18 appoint as a nominee or custodian include—

(a) one of their number, if that one is a trust corporation, or
(b) two (or more) of their number, if they are to act as joint nominees or joint custodians.

(6) The trustees may under section 16 appoint a person to act as their nominee even though he is also—

(a) appointed to act as their custodian (whether under section 17 or 18 or any other power), or
(b) authorised to exercise functions as their agent (whether under section 11 or any other power).

(7) Likewise, the trustees may under section 17 or 18 appoint a person to act as their custodian even though he is also—

(a) appointed to act as their nominee (whether under section 16 or any other power), or
(b) authorised to exercise functions as their agent (whether under section 11 or any other power).

[246.152]
20. Terms of appointment of nominees and custodians.— (1) Subject to subsection (2) and sections 29 to 32, the trustees may under section 16, 17 or 18 appoint a person to act as a nominee or custodian on such terms as to remuneration and other matters as they may determine.
(2) The trustees may not under section 16, 17 or 18 appoint a person to act as a nominee or custodian on any of the terms mentioned in subsection (3) unless it is reasonably necessary for them to do so.
(3) The terms are—

(a) a term permitting the nominee or custodian to appoint a substitute;
(b) a term restricting the liability of the nominee or custodian or his substitute to the trustees or to any beneficiary;
(c) a term permitting the nominee or custodian to act in circumstances capable of giving rise to a conflict of interest.

REVIEW OF AND LIABILITY FOR AGENTS, NOMINEES AND CUSTODIANS ETC

[246.153]
21. Application of sections 22 and 23.— (1) Sections 22 and 23 apply in a case where trustees have, under section 11, 16, 17 or 18—

(a) authorised a person to exercise functions as their agent, or
(b) appointed a person to act as a nominee or custodian.

(2) Subject to subsection (3), sections 22 and 23 also apply in a case where trustees have, under any power conferred on them by the trust instrument or by any enactment or any provision of subordinate legislation—

(a) authorised a person to exercise functions as their agent, or
(b) appointed a person to act as a nominee or custodian.

(3) If the application of section 22 or 23 is inconsistent with the terms of the trust instrument or the enactment or provision of subordinate legislation, the section in question does not apply.

[246.154]
22. Review of agents, nominees and custodians etc.— (1) While the agent, nominee or custodian continues to act for the trust, the trustees—

(a) must keep under review the arrangements under which the agent, nominee or custodian acts and how those arrangements are being put into effect,

(b) if circumstances make it appropriate to do so, must consider whether there is a need to exercise any power of intervention that they have, and
(c) if they consider that there is a need to exercise such a power, must do so.

(2) If the agent has been authorised to exercise asset management functions, the duty under subsection (1) includes, in particular—

(a) a duty to consider whether there is any need to revise or replace the policy statement made for the purposes of section 15,
(b) if they consider that there is a need to revise or replace the policy statement, a duty to do so, and
(c) a duty to assess whether the policy statement (as it has effect for the time being) is being complied with.

(3) Subsections (3) and (4) of section 15 apply to the revision or replacement of a policy statement under this section as they apply to the making of a policy statement under that section.
(4) 'Power of intervention' includes—

(a) a power to give directions to the agent, nominee or custodian;
(b) a power to revoke the authorisation or appointment.

[246.155]
23. Liability for agents, nominees and custodians etc.— (1) A trustee is not liable for any act or default of the agent, nominee or custodian unless he has failed to comply with the duty of care applicable to him, under paragraph 3 of Schedule 1—

(a) when entering into the arrangements under which the person acts as agent, nominee or custodian, or
(b) when carrying out his duties under section 22.

(2) If a trustee has agreed a term under which the agent, nominee or custodian is permitted to appoint a substitute, the trustee is not liable for any act or default of the substitute unless he has failed to comply with the duty of care applicable to him, under paragraph 3 of Schedule 1—

(a) when agreeing that term, or
(b) when carrying out his duties under section 22 in so far as they relate to the use of the substitute.

SUPPLEMENTARY

[246.156]
24. Effect of trustees exceeding their powers. A failure by the trustees to act within the limits of the powers conferred by this Part—

(a) in authorising a person to exercise a function of theirs as an agent, or
(b) in appointing a person to act as a nominee or custodian,

does not invalidate the authorisation or appointment.

[246.157]
25. Sole trustees.— (1) Subject to subsection (2), this Part applies in relation to a trust having a sole trustee as it applies in relation to other trusts (and references in this Part to trustees—except in sections 12(1) and (3) and 19(5)—are to be read accordingly).
(2) Section 18 does not impose a duty on a sole trustee if that trustee is a trust corporation.

[246.158]
26. Restriction or exclusion of this Part etc. The powers conferred by this Part are—

(a) in addition to powers conferred on trustees otherwise than by this Act, but
(b) subject to any restriction or exclusion imposed by the trust instrument or by any enactment or any provision of subordinate legislation.

[246.159]
27. Existing trusts. This Part applies in relation to trusts whether created before or after its commencement.

PART V
REMUNERATION

[246.160]
28. Trustee's entitlement to payment under trust instrument.— (1) Except to the extent (if any) to which the trust instrument makes inconsistent provision, subsections (2) to (4) apply to a trustee if—

(a) there is a provision in the trust instrument entitling him to receive payment out of trust funds in respect of services provided by him to or on behalf of the trust, and
(b) the trustee is a trust corporation or is acting in a professional capacity.

(2) The trustee is to be treated as entitled under the trust instrument to receive payment in respect of services even if they are services which are capable of being provided by a lay trustee.
(3) Subsection (2) applies to a trustee of a charitable trust who is not a trust corporation only—

(a) if he is not a sole trustee, and
(b) to the extent that a majority of the other trustees have agreed that it should apply to him.

(4) Any payments to which the trustee is entitled in respect of services are to be treated as remuneration for services (and not as a gift) for the purposes of—

(a) section 15 of the Wills Act 1837 (gifts to an attesting witness to be void), and

(b) section 34(3) of the Administration of Estates Act 1925 (order in which estate to be paid out).

(5) For the purposes of this Part, a trustee acts in a professional capacity if he acts in the course of a profession or business which consists of or includes the provision of services in connection with—

(a) the management or administration of trusts generally or a particular kind of trust, or
(b) any particular aspect of the management or administration of trusts generally or a particular kind of trust,

and the services he provides to or on behalf of the trust fall within that description.
(6) For the purposes of this Part, a person acts as a lay trustee if he—

(a) is not a trust corporation, and
(b) does not act in a professional capacity.

[246.161]
29. Remuneration of certain trustees.— (1) Subject to subsection (5), a trustee who—

(a) is a trust corporation, but
(b) is not a trustee of a charitable trust,

is entitled to receive reasonable remuneration out of the trust funds for any services that the trust corporation provides to or on behalf of the trust.
(2) Subject to subsection (5), a trustee who—

(a) acts in a professional capacity, but
(b) is not a trust corporation, a trustee of a charitable trust or a sole trustee,

is entitled to receive reasonable remuneration out of the trust funds for any services that he provides to or on behalf of the trust if each other trustee has agreed in writing that he may be remunerated for the services.
(3) 'Reasonable remuneration' means, in relation to the provision of services by a trustee, such remuneration as is reasonable in the circumstances for the provision of those services to or on behalf of that trust by that trustee and for the purposes of subsection (1) includes, in relation to the provision of services by a trustee who is an authorised institution under the Banking Act 1987 and provides the services in that capacity, the institution's reasonable charges for the provision of such services.
(4) A trustee is entitled to remuneration under this section even if the services in question are capable of being provided by a lay trustee.
(5) A trustee is not entitled to remuneration under this section if any provision about his entitlement to remuneration has been made—

(a) by the trust instrument, or
(b) by any enactment or any provision of subordinate legislation.

(6) This section applies to a trustee who has been authorised under a power conferred by Part IV or the trust instrument—

(a) to exercise functions as an agent of the trustees, or
(b) to act as a nominee or custodian,

as it applies to any other trustee.

[246.162]
30. Remuneration of trustees of charitable trusts.— (1) The Secretary of State may by regulations make provision for the remuneration of trustees of charitable trusts who are trust corporations or act in a professional capacity.
(2) The power under subsection (1) includes power to make provision for the remuneration of a trustee who has been authorised under a power conferred by Part IV or any other enactment or any provision of subordinate legislation, or by the trust instrument—

(a) to exercise functions as an agent of the trustees, or
(b) to act as a nominee or custodian.

(3) Regulations under this section may—

(a) make different provision for different cases;
(b) contain such supplemental, incidental, consequential and transitional provision as the Secretary of State considers appropriate.

(4) The power to make regulations under this section is exercisable by statutory instrument, but no such instrument shall be made unless a draft of it has been laid before Parliament and approved by a resolution of each House of Parliament.

[246.163]
31. Trustees' expenses.— (1) A trustee—

(a) is entitled to be reimbursed from the trust funds, or
(b) may pay out of the trust funds,

expenses properly incurred by him when acting on behalf of the trust.
(2) This section applies to a trustee who has been authorised under a power conferred by Part IV or any other enactment or any provision of subordinate legislation, or by the trust instrument—

(a) to exercise functions as an agent of the trustees, or
(b) to act as a nominee or custodian,

as it applies to any other trustee.

[246.164]
32. Remuneration and expenses of agents, nominees and custodians.—
(1) This section applies if, under a power conferred by Part IV or any other enactment or any provision of subordinate legislation, or by the trust instrument, a person other than a trustee has been—

(a) authorised to exercise functions as an agent of the trustees, or
(b) appointed to act as a nominee or custodian.

(2) The trustees may remunerate the agent, nominee or custodian out of the trust funds for services if—

(a) he is engaged on terms entitling him to be remunerated for those services, and
(b) the amount does not exceed such remuneration as is reasonable in the circumstances for the provision of those services by him to or on behalf of that trust.

(3) The trustees may reimburse the agent, nominee or custodian out of the trust funds for any expenses properly incurred by him in exercising functions as an agent, nominee or custodian.

[246.165]
33. Application.— (1) Subject to subsection (2), sections 28, 29, 31 and 32 apply in relation to services provided to or on behalf of, or (as the case may be) expenses incurred on or after their commencement on behalf of, trusts whenever created.
(2) Nothing in section 28 or 29 is to be treated as affecting the operation of—

(a) section 15 of the Wills Act 1837, or
(b) section 34(3) of the Administration of Estates Act 1925,

in relation to any death occurring before the commencement of section 28 or (as the case may be) section 29.

PART VI
MISCELLANEOUS AND SUPPLEMENTARY

[246.166]
34. Power to insure.— (1) [*This substitutes a new section for s 19 of the Trustee Act 1925: see para* **[246.17]** above.]
(2) In section 20(1) of the Trustee Act 1925 (application of insurance money) omit 'whether by fire or otherwise'.
(3) The amendments made by this section apply in relation to trusts whether created before or after its commencement.

[246.167]
35. Personal representatives.— (1) Subject to the following provisions of this section, this Act applies in relation to a personal representative administering an estate according to the law as it applies to a trustee carrying out a trust for beneficiaries.
(2) For this purpose this Act is to be read with the appropriate modifications and in particular—

(a) references to the trust instrument are to be read as references to the will,
(b) references to a beneficiary or to beneficiaries, apart from the reference to a beneficiary in section 8(1)(b), are to be read as references to a person or the persons interested in the due administration of the estate, and
(c) the reference to a beneficiary in section 8(1)(b) is to be read as a reference to a person who under the will of the deceased or under the law relating to intestacy is beneficially interested in the estate.

(3) Remuneration to which a personal representative is entitled under section 28 or 29 is to be treated as an administration expense for the purposes of—

(a) section 34(3) of the Administration of Estates Act 1925 (order in which estate to be paid out), and

(b) any provision giving reasonable administration expenses priority over the preferential debts listed in Schedule 6 to the Insolvency Act 1986.

(4) Nothing in subsection (3) is to be treated as affecting the operation of the provisions mentioned in paragraphs (a) and (b) of that subsection in relation to any death occurring before the commencement of this section.

* * * * *

[246.168]
39. Interpretation.— (1) In this Act—

'asset' includes any right or interest;

'charitable trust' means a trust under which property is held for charitable purposes and 'charitable purposes' has the same meaning as in the Charities Act 1993;

'custodian trustee' has the same meaning as in the Public Trustee Act 1906;

'enactment' includes any provision of a Measure of the Church Assembly or of the General Synod of the Church of England;

'exempt charity' has the same meaning as in the Charities Act 1993;

'functions' includes powers and duties;

'legal mortgage' has the same meaning as in the Law of Property Act 1925;

'personal representative' has the same meaning as in the Trustee Act 1925;

'settled land' has the same meaning as in the Settled Land Act 1925;

'trust corporation' has the same meaning as in the Trustee Act 1925;

'trust funds' means income or capital funds of the trust.

(2) In this Act the expressions listed below are defined or otherwise explained by the provisions indicated—

asset management functions	section 15(5)
Custodian	section 17(2)
the duty of care	section 1(2)
the general power of investment	section 3(2)
lay trustee	section 28(6)
power of intervention	section 22(4)
the standard investment criteria	section 4(3)
Subordinate legislation	section 6(3)
trustee acting in a professional capacity	section 28(5)
trust instrument	sections 6(2) and 35(2)(a)

[246.169]
40. Minor and consequential amendments etc.— (1) Schedule 2 (minor and consequential amendments) shall have effect.
(2) Schedule 3 (transitional provisions and savings) shall have effect.
(3) Schedule 4 (repeals) shall have effect.

[246.170]
41. Power to amend other Acts.— (1) A Minister of the Crown may by order make such amendments of any Act, including an Act extending to places outside England and Wales, as appear to him appropriate in consequence of or in connection with Part II or III.
(2) Before exercising the power under subsection (1) in relation to a local, personal or private Act, the Minister must consult any person who appears to him to be affected by any proposed amendment.
(3) An order under this section may—

(a) contain such transitional provisions and savings as the Minister thinks fit;
(b) make different provision for different purposes.

(4) The power to make an order under this section is exercisable by statutory instrument which shall be subject to annulment in pursuance of a resolution of either House of Parliament.
(5) 'Minister of the Crown' has the same meaning as in the Ministers of the Crown Act 1975.

[246.171]
42. Commencement and extent.— (1) Section 41, this section and section 43 shall come into force on the day on which this Act is passed.
(2) The remaining provisions of this Act shall come into force on such day as the Lord Chancellor may appoint by order made by statutory instrument; and different days may be so appointed for different purposes.
(3) An order under subsection (2) may contain such transitional provisions and savings as the Lord Chancellor considers appropriate in connection with the order.
(4) Subject to section 41(1) and subsection (5), this Act extends to England and Wales only.
(5) An amendment or repeal in Part II or III of Schedule 2 or Part II of Schedule 4 has the same extent as the provision amended or repealed.

[246.172]
43. Short title. This Act may be cited as the Trustee Act 2000.

SCHEDULE 1

Section 2

APPLICATION OF DUTY OF CARE

INVESTMENT

[246.173]
1. The duty of care applies to a trustee—

(a) when exercising the general power of investment or any other power of investment, however conferred;
(b) when carrying out a duty to which he is subject under section 4 or 5 (duties relating to the exercise of a power of investment or to the review of investments).

ACQUISITION OF LAND

2. The duty of care applies to a trustee—

(a) when exercising the power under section 8 to acquire land;
(b) when exercising any other power to acquire land, however conferred;
(c) when exercising any power in relation to land acquired under a power mentioned in sub-paragraph (a) or (b).

AGENTS, NOMINEES AND CUSTODIANS

3.— (1) The duty of care applies to a trustee—

(a) when entering into arrangements under which a person is authorised under section 11 to exercise functions as an agent;
(b) when entering into arrangements under which a person is appointed under section 16 to act as a nominee;
(c) when entering into arrangements under which a person is appointed under section 17 or 18 to act as a custodian;
(d) when entering into arrangements under which, under any other power, however conferred, a person is authorised to exercise functions as an agent or is appointed to act as a nominee or custodian;
(e) when carrying out his duties under section 22 (review of agent, nominee or custodian, etc).

(2) For the purposes of sub-paragraph (1), entering into arrangements under which a person is authorised to exercise functions or is appointed to act as a nominee or custodian includes, in particular—

(a) selecting the person who is to act,
(b) determining any terms on which he is to act, and
(c) if the person is being authorised to exercise asset management functions, the preparation of a policy statement under section 15.

COMPOUNDING OF LIABILITIES

4. The duty of care applies to a trustee—

(a) when exercising the power under section 15 of the Trustee Act 1925 to do any of the things referred to in that section;
(b) when exercising any corresponding power, however conferred.

INSURANCE

5. The duty of care applies to a trustee—

(a) when exercising the power under section 19 of the Trustee Act 1925 to insure property;

(b) when exercising any corresponding power, however conferred.

REVERSIONARY INTERESTS, VALUATIONS AND AUDIT

6. The duty of care applies to a trustee—

(a) when exercising the power under section 22(1) or (3) of the Trustee Act 1925 to do any of the things referred to there;
(b) when exercising any corresponding power, however conferred.

EXCLUSION OF DUTY OF CARE

7. The duty of care does not apply if or in so far as it appears from the trust instrument that the duty is not meant to apply.

* * * * *

Note. Schedules 2 and 4 contain minor and consequential amendments and repeals of previous statutes which are noted, where relevant, in the earlier pages of this Section. Schedule 3 contains transitional provisions and savings.

SECTION 4

Family provision and relief from forfeiture

INHERITANCE (PROVISION FOR FAMILY AND DEPENDANTS) ACT 1975

(1975 c 63)

[12 November 1975]

[247.1]

Note. For the law of family provision see Vol 1, Chapter 105.

With effect from 5 December 2005 the I(PFD)A 1975 has been substantially amended and four new sections introduced by the CPA 2004, s 71, Sch 4, paras 15–25 and Civil Partnership Act 2004 (Commencement) Order 2005, SI 2005/3175. The Act is printed below as currently in force.

References to capital transfer tax throughout the Inheritance (Provision for Family and Dependants) Act 1975 (I(PFD)A 1975) now have effect as references to inheritance tax: see the Finance Act 1986, s 100(1)(b). For the effect of inheritance tax on an order under the I(PFD)A 1975, see the Inheritance Tax Act 1984 (ITA 1984), s 146; and see further the ITA 1984, s 29A (as inserted by the Finance Act 1989) as to the reduction of the amount of inheritance tax exemption on a deceased person's estate where an exempt beneficiary settles a claim under the I(PFD)A 1975 from his own resources.

[247.2]

1 Application for financial provision from deceased's estate (1) Where after the commencement of this Act a person dies domiciled in England and Wales and is survived by any of the following persons—

[(a) the spouse or civil partner of the deceased;
(b) a former spouse or former civil partner of the deceased, but not one who has formed a subsequent marriage or civil partnership;]
[(ba) any person (not being a person included in paragraph (a) or (b) above) to whom subsection (1A) [or (1B)] below applies;][1]
(c) a child of the deceased;
(d) any person (not being a child of the deceased) who, in the case of any marriage [or civil partnership] to which the deceased was at any time a party, was treated by the deceased as a child of the family in relation to that marriage [or civil partnership];
(e) any person (not being a person included in the foregoing paragraphs of this subsection) who immediately before the death of the deceased was being maintained, either wholly or partly, by the deceased;

that person may apply to the court for an order under section 2 of this Act on the ground that the disposition of the deceased's estate effected by his will or the law relating to intestacy, or the combination of his will and that law, is not such as to make reasonable financial provision for the applicant.

[(1A) This subsection applies to a person if the deceased died on or after 1st January 1996 and, during the whole of the period of two years ending immediately before the date when the deceased died, the person was living—

(a) in the same household as the deceased, and
(b) as the husband or wife of the deceased.][2]

[(1B) This subsection applies to a person if for the whole of the period of two years ending immediately before the date when the deceased died the person was living—

(a) in the same household as the deceased, and
(b) as the civil partner of the deceased.][3]

(2) In this Act 'reasonable financial provision'—

(a) in the case of an application made by virtue of subsection (1)(a) above by the husband or wife of the deceased (except where[, at the date of death, a separation order under the Family Law Act 1996 was in force in relation to the marriage] and the separation was continuing), means such financial provision as it would be reasonable in all the circumstances of the case for a husband or wife to receive, whether or not that provision is required for his or her maintenance;

[(aa) in the case of an application made by virtue of subsection (1)(a) above by the civil partner of the deceased (except where, at the date of death, a separation order under Chapter 2 of Part 2 of the Civil Partnership Act 2004 was in force in relation to the civil partnership and the separation was continuing), means such financial provision as it would be reasonable in all the circumstances of the case for a civil partner to receive, whether or not that provision is required for his or her maintenance;]

(b) in the case of any other application made by virtue of subsection (1) above, means such financial provision as it would be reasonable in all the circumstances of the case for the applicant to receive for his maintenance.

(3) For the purposes of subsection (1)(e) above, a person shall be treated as being maintained by the deceased, either wholly or partly, as the case may be, if the deceased, otherwise than for full valuable consideration, was making a substantial contribution in money or money's worth towards the reasonable needs of that person.

1 Paragraph (ba): inserted by LR(S)A 1995, s 2(2).
2 Sub-s (1A): inserted by LR(S)A 1995, s 2(3).
3 Sub-s (1B) inserted with effect from 5 December 2005 by the Civil Partnership Act 2004, s 71, Sch 4, Pt 2, para 15(1), (5).

[247.3]
2 Powers of court to make orders (1) Subject to the provisions of this Act, where an application is made for an order under this section, the court may, if it is satisfied that the disposition of the deceased's estate effected by

his will or the law relating to intestacy, or the combination of his will and that law, is not such as to make reasonable financial provision for the applicant, make any one or more of the following orders—

(a) an order for the making to the applicant out of the net estate of the deceased of such periodical payments and for such term as may be specified in the order;
(b) an order for the payment to the applicant out of that estate of a lump sum of such amount as may be so specified;
(c) an order for the transfer to the applicant of such property comprised in that estate as may be so specified;
(d) an order for the settlement for the benefit of the applicant of such property comprised in that estate as may be so specified;
(e) an order for the acquisition out of property comprised in that estate of such property as may be so specified and for the transfer of the property so acquired to the applicant or for the settlement thereof for his benefit;
(f) an order varying any ante-nuptial or post-nuptial settlement (including such a settlement made by will) made on the parties to a marriage to which the deceased was one of the parties, the variation being for the benefit of the surviving party to that marriage, or any child of that marriage, or any person who was treated by the deceased as a child of the family in relation to that marriage;
[(g) an order varying any settlement made—
  (i) during the subsistence of a civil partnership formed by the deceased, or
  (ii) in anticipation of the formation of a civil partnership by the deceased,

  on the civil partners (including such a settlement made by will), the variation being for the benefit of the surviving civil partner, or any child of both the civil partners, or any person who was treated by the deceased as a child of the family in relation to that civil partnership].[1]

(2) An order under subsection (1)(a) above providing for the making out of the net estate of the deceased of periodical payments may provide for—

(a) payments of such amount as may be specified in the order,
(b) payments equal to the whole of the income of the net estate or of such portion thereof as may be so specified,
(c) payments equal to the whole of the income of such part of the net estate as the court may direct to be set aside or appropriated for the making out of the income thereof of payments under this section,

or may provide for the amount of the payments or any of them to be determined in any other way the court thinks fit.

(3) Where an order under subsection (1)(a) above provides for the making of payments of an amount specified in the order, the order may direct that such part of the net estate as may be so specified shall be set aside or appropriated for the making out of the income thereof of those payments; but no larger part of the net estate shall be so set aside or appropriated than

is sufficient, at the date of the order, to produce by the income thereof the amount required for the making of those payments.
(4) An order under this section may contain such consequential and supplemental provisions as the court thinks necessary or expedient for the purpose of giving effect to the order or for the purpose of securing that the order operates fairly as between one beneficiary of the estate of the deceased and another and may, in particular, but without prejudice to the generality of this subsection—

(a) order any person who holds any property which forms part of the net estate of the deceased to make such payment or transfer such property as may be specified in the order;
(b) varying the disposition of the deceased's estate effected by the will or the law relating to intestacy, or by both the will and the law relating to intestacy, in such manner as the court thinks fair and reasonable having regard to the provisions of the order and all the circumstances of the case;
(c) confer on the trustees of any property which is the subject of an order under this section such powers as appear to the court to be necessary or expedient.

1 Sub-s (1), para (g) inserted with effect from 5 December 2005 by the Civil Partnership Act 2004, s 71, Sch 4, Pt 2, para 16.

[247.4]
3 Matters to which court is to have regard in exercising powers under section 2 (1) Where an application is made for an order under section 2 of this Act, the court shall, in determining whether the disposition of the deceased's estate effected by his will or the law relating to intestacy, or the combination of his will and that law, is such as to make reasonable financial provision for the applicant and, if the court considers that reasonable financial provision has not been made, in determining whether and in what manner it shall exercise its powers under that section, have regard to the following matters, that is to say—

(a) the financial resources and financial needs which the applicant has or is likely to have in the foreseeable future;
(b) the financial resources and financial needs which any other applicant for an order under section 2 of this Act has or is likely to have in the foreseeable future;
(c) the financial resources and financial needs which any beneficiary of the estate of the deceased has or is likely to have in the foreseeable future;
(d) any obligations and responsibilities which the deceased had towards any applicant for an order under the said section 2 or towards any beneficiary of the estate of the deceased;
(e) the size and nature of the net estate of the deceased;
(f) any physical or mental disability of any applicant for an order under the said section 2 or any beneficiary of the estate of the deceased;
(g) any other matter, including the conduct of the applicant or any other person, which in the circumstances of the case the court may consider relevant.

(2) [This subsection applies, without prejudice to the generality of paragraph (g) of subsection (1) above, where an application for an order under section 2 of this Act is made by virtue of section 1(1)(a) or (b) of this Act.] The court shall, in addition to the matters specifically mentioned in paragraphs (a) to (f) of that subsection, have regard to—

- (a) the age of the applicant and the duration of the marriage [or civil partnership];
- (b) the contribution made by the applicant to the welfare of the family of the deceased, including any contribution made by looking after the home or caring for the family,

[...] in the case of an application by the wife or husband of the deceased, the court shall also, unless at the date of death a [separation order under the Family Law Act 1996] was in force and the separation was continuing, have regard to the provision which the applicant might reasonably have expected to receive if on the day on which the deceased died the marriage, instead of being terminated by death, had been terminated by [a divorce order].
[In the case of an application by the civil partner of the deceased, the court shall also, unless at the date of the death a separation order under Chapter 2 of Part 2 of the Civil Partnership Act 2004 was in force and the separation was continuing, have regard to the provision which the applicant might reasonably have expected to receive if on the day on which the deceased died the civil partnership, instead of being terminated by death, had been terminated by a dissolution order.][1]
[(2A) Without prejudice to the generality of paragraph (g) of subsection (1) above, where an application for an order under section 2 of this Act is made by virtue of s 1(1)(ba) of this Act, the court shall, in addition to the matters specifically mentioned in paragraphs (a) to (f) of that subsection, have regard to—

- (a) the age of the applicant and the length of the period during which the applicant lived as the husband or wife [or civil partner] of the deceased and in the same household as the deceased;
- (b) the contribution made by the applicant to the welfare of the family of the deceased, including any contribution made by looking after the home or caring for the family.][2]

(3) Without prejudice to the generality of paragraph (g) of subsection (1) above, where an application for an order under section 2 of this Act is made by virtue of section 1(1)(c) or 1(1)(d) of this Act, the court shall, in addition to the matters specifically mentioned in paragraphs (a) to (f) of that subsection, have regard to the manner in which the applicant was being or in which he might expect to be educated or trained, and where the application is made by virtue of section 1(1)(d) the court shall also have regard—

- (a) to whether the deceased had assumed any responsibility for the applicant's maintenance and, if so, to the extent to which and the basis upon which the deceased assumed that responsibility and to the length of time for which the deceased discharged that responsibility;
- (b) to whether in assuming and discharging that responsibility the deceased did so knowing that the applicant was not his own child;

(c) to the liability of any other person to maintain the applicant.

(4) Without prejudice to the generality of paragraph (g) of subsection (1) above, where an application for an order under section 2 of this Act is made by virtue of section 1(1)(e) of this Act, the court shall, in addition to the matters specifically mentioned in paragraphs (a) to (f) of that subsection, have regard to the extent to which and the basis upon which the deceased assumed responsibility for the maintenance of the applicant, and to the length of time for which the deceased discharged that responsibility.
(5) In considering the matters to which the court is required to have regard under this section, the court shall take into account the facts as known to the court at the date of the hearing.
(6) In considering the financial resources of any person for the purposes of this section the court shall take into account his earning capacity and in considering the financial needs of any person for the purposes of this section the court shall take into account his financial obligations and responsibilities.

1 Words in first set of square brackets, words in square brackets in para (a) and words in final set of square brackets substituted and word immediately following para (b) omitted with effect from 5 December 2005 by the Civil Partnership Act 2004, s 71, Sch, Pt 2, para 17, Sch 30.
2 Sub-s (2A): inserted by LR(S)A 1995, s 2(1), (4).

[247.5]
4 Time-limit for applications An application for an order under section 2 of this Act shall not, except with the permission of the court, be made after the end of the period of six months from the date on which representation with respect to the estate of the deceased is first taken out.

[247.6]
5 Interim orders (1) Where an application for an order under section 3 of this Act it appears to the court-

(a) that the applicant is in immediate need of financial assistance, but it is not yet possible to determine what order (if any) should be made under that section; and
(b) that property forming part of the net estate of the deceased is or can be made available to meet the need of the applicant;

the court may order that, subject to such conditions or restrictions, if any, as the court may impose and to any further order of the court, there shall be paid to the applicant out of the net estate of the deceased such sum or sums and (if more than one) at such intervals as the court thinks reasonable; and the court may order that, subject to the provisions of this Act, such payments are to be made until such date as the court may specify, not being later than the date on which the court either makes an order under the said section 2 or decides not to exercise its powers under that section.
(2) Subsections (2), (3) and (4) of section 2 of this Act shall apply in relation to an order under this section as they apply in relation to an order under that section.

(3) In determining what order, if any, should be made under this section the court shall, so far as the urgency of the case admits, have regard to the same matters as those to which the court is required to have regard under section 3 of this Act.
(4) An order made under section 2 of this Act may provide that any sum paid to the applicant by virtue of this section shall be treated to such an extent and in such manner as may be provided by that order as having been paid on account of any payment provided for by that order.

[247.7]
6 Variation, discharge, etc of orders for periodical payments (1) Subject to the provisions of this Act, where the court has made an order under section 2(1)(a) of this Act (in this section referred to as 'the original order') for the making of periodical payments to any person (in this section referred to as 'the original recipient'), the court, on an application under this section, shall have power by order to vary or discharge the original order or to suspend any provision of it temporarily and to revive the operation of any provision so suspended.
(2) Without prejudice to the generality of subsection (1) above, an order made on an application for the variation of the original order may—

- (a) provide for the making out of any relevant property of such periodical payments and for such term as may be specified in the order to any person who has applied, or would but for section 4 of this Act be entitled to apply, for an order under section 2 of this Act (whether or not, in the case of any application, an order was made in favour of the applicant);
- (b) provide for the payment out of any relevant property of a lump sum of such amount as may be so specified to the original recipient or to any such person as is mentioned in paragraph (a) above;
- (c) provide for the transfer of the relevant property, or such part thereof as may be so specified, to the original recipient or to any such person as is so mentioned.

(3) Where the original order provides that any periodical payments payable thereunder to the original recipient are to cease on the occurrence of an event specified in the order [(other than the formation of a subsequent marriage or civil partnership by a former spouse or former civil partner)][1] or on the expiration of a period so specified, then, if, before the end of the period of six months from the date of the occurrence of that event or of the expiration of that period, an application is made for an order under this section, the court shall have power to make any order which it would have had power to make if the application had been made before the date (whether in favour of the original recipient or any such person as is mentioned in subsection (2)(a) above and whether having effect from that date or from such later date as the court may specify).
(4) Any reference in this section to the original order shall include a reference to an order made under this section and any reference in this section to the original recipient shall include a reference to any person to whom periodical payments are required to be made by virtue of an order under this section.

(5) An application under this section may be made by any of the following persons, that is to say—

- (a) any person who by virtue of section 1(1) of this Act has applied, or would but for section 4 of this Act be entitled to apply, for an order under section 2 of this Act,
- (b) the personal representatives of the deceased,
- (c) the trustees of any relevant property, and
- (d) any beneficiary of the estate of the deceased.

(6) An order under this section may only affect—

- (a) property the income of which is at the date of the order applicable wholly or in part for the making of periodical payments to any person who has applied for an order under this Act, or
- (b) in the case of an application under subsection (3) above in respect of payments which have ceased to be payable on the occurrence of an event or the expiration of a period, property the income of which was so applicable immediately before the occurrence of that event or the expiration of that period, as the case may be,

and any such property as is mentioned in paragraph (a) or (b) above is in subsections (2) and (5) above referred to as 'relevant property'.
(7) In exercising the powers conferred by this section the court shall have regard to all circumstances of the case, including any change in any of the matters to which the court was required to have regard when making the order to which the application relates.
(8) Where the court makes an order under this section, it may give such consequential directions as it thinks necessary or expedient having regard to the provisions of the order.
(9) No such order as is mentioned in section 2(1)(d), (e) or (f), 9, 10 or 11 of this Act shall be made on an application under this section.
(10) For the avoidance of doubt it is hereby declared that, in relation to an order which provides for the making of periodical payments which are to cease on the occurrence of an event specified in the order [(other than the formation of a subsequent marriage or civil partnership by a former spouse or former civil partner)][1] or on the expiration of a period so specified, the power to vary an order includes power to provide for the making of periodical payments after the expiration of that period or the occurrence of that event.

1 Words in square brackets in sub-ss (3) and (10) substituted with effect from 5 December 2005 by the Civil Partnership Act 2004, s 71, Sch 4, Pt 2, para 19.

[247.8]
7 Payment of lump sums by instalments (1) An order under section 2(1)(b) or 6(2)(b) of this Act for the payment of a lump sum may provide for the payment of that sum by instalments of such amount as may be specified in the order.
(2) Where an order is made by virtue of subsection (1) above, the court shall have power, on an application made by the person to whom the lump sum is payable, by the personal representatives of the deceased or by the trustees of the property out of which the lump sum is payable, to vary that

order by varying the number of instalments payable, the amount of any instalment and the date on which any instalment becomes payable.

Property available for financial provision

[247.9]
8 Property treated as part of 'net estate' (1) Where a deceased person has in accordance with the provisions of any enactment nominated any person to receive any sum of money or other property on his death and that nomination is in force at the time of his death, that sum of money, after deducting therefrom any inheritance tax payable in respect thereof, or that other property, to the extent of the value thereof at the date of the death of the deceased after deducting therefrom any inheritance tax so payable, shall be treated for the purposes of this Act as part of the net estate of the deceased; but this subsection shall not render any person liable for having paid that sum or transferred that other property to the person named in the nomination in accordance with the directions given in the nomination.
(2) Where any sum of money or other property is received by any person as a *donatio mortis causa* made by a deceased person, that sum of money, after deducting therefrom any inheritance tax payable thereon, or that other property, to the extent of the value thereof at the date of the death of the deceased after deducting therefrom any inheritance tax so payable, shall be treated for the purposes of this Act as part of the net estate of the deceased; but this subsection shall not render any person liable for having paid that sum or transferred that other property in order to give effect to that *donatio mortis causa*.
(3) The amount of inheritance tax to be deducted for the purposes of this section shall not exceed the amount of that tax which has been borne by the person nominated by the deceased or, as the case may be, the person who has received a sum of money or other property as a *donatio mortis causa*.

[247.10]
9 Property held on a joint tenancy (1) Where a deceased person was immediately before his death beneficially entitled to a joint tenancy of any property, then, if, before the end of the period of six months from the date on which representation with respect to the estate of the deceased was first taken out, an application is made for an order under section 2 of this Act, the court for the purpose of facilitating the making of financial provision for the applicant under this Act may order that the deceased's severable share of that property, at the value thereof immediately before his death, shall, to such extent as appears to the court to be just in all the circumstances of the case, be treated for the purposes of this Act as part of the net estate of the deceased.
(2) In determining the extent to which any severable share is to be treated as part of the net estate of the deceased by virtue of an order under subsection (1) above, the court shall have regard to any inheritance tax payable in respect of that severable share.
(3) Where an order is made under subsection (1) above, the provisions of this section shall not render any person liable for anything done by him before the order was made.

(4) For the avoidance of doubt it is hereby declared that for the purposes of this section there may be a joint tenancy of a chose in action.

Powers of court in relation to transactions intended to defeat applications for financial provision

[247.11]

10 Dispositions intended to defeat applications for financial provision

(1) Where an application is made to the court for an order under section 2 of this Act, the applicant may, in the proceedings on that application, apply to the court for an order under subsection (2) below.

(2) Where on an application under subsection (1) above the court is satisfied—

(a) that, less than six years before the date of the death of the deceased, the deceased with the intention of defeating an application for financial provision under this Act made a disposition, and

(b) that full valuable consideration for that disposition was not given by the person to whom or for the benefit of whom the disposition was made (in this section referred to as 'the donee') or by any other person, and

(c) that the exercise of the powers conferred by this section would facilitate the making of financial provision for the applicant under this Act,

then, subject to the provisions of this section and of sections 12 and 13 of this Act, the court may order the donee (whether or not at the date of the order he holds any interest in the property disposed of to him or for his benefit by the deceased) to provide, for the purpose of the making of that financial provision, such sum of money or other property as may be specified in the order.

(3) Where an order is made under subsection (2) above as respects any disposition made by the deceased which consisted of the payment of money to or for the benefit of the donee, the amount of any sum of money or the value of any property ordered to be provided under that subsection shall not exceed the amount of the payment made by the deceased after deducting therefrom any inheritance tax borne by the donee in respect of that payment.

(4) Where an order is made under subsection (2) above as respects any disposition made by the deceased which consisted of the transfer of property (other than a sum of money) to or for the benefit of the donee, the amount of any sum of money or the value of any property ordered to be provided under that subsection shall not exceed the value at the date of the death of the deceased of the property disposed of by him to or for the benefit of the donee (or if that property has been disposed of by the person to whom it was transferred by the deceased, the value at the date of that disposal thereof) after deducting therefrom any inheritance tax borne by the donee in respect of the transfer of that property by the deceased.

(5) Where an application (in this subsection referred to as 'the original application') is made for an order under subsection (2) above in relation to any disposition, then, if on an application under this subsection by the donee or by any applicant for an order under section 2 of this Act the court is satisfied—

(a) that, less than six years before the date of the death of the deceased, the deceased with the intention of defeating an application for financial provision under this Act made a disposition other than the disposition which is the subject of the original application, and
(b) that full valuable consideration for that other disposition was not given by the person to whom or for the benefit of whom that other disposition was made or by any other person,

the court may exercise in relation to the person to whom or for the benefit of whom that other disposition was made the powers which the court would have had under subsection (2) above if the original application had been made in respect of that other disposition and the court had been satisfied as to the matters set out in paragraphs (a), (b) and (c) of that subsection; and where any application is made under this subsection, any reference in this section (except in subsection (2)(b)) to the donee shall include a reference to the person to whom or for the benefit of whom that other disposition was made.
(6) In determining whether and in what manner to exercise its powers under this section, the court shall have regard to the circumstances in which any disposition was made and any valuable consideration which was given therefor, the relationship, if any, of the donee to the deceased, the conduct and financial resources of the donee and all the other circumstances of the case.
(7) In this section 'disposition' does not include—

(a) any provision in a will, any such nomination as is mentioned in section 8(1) of this Act or any *donatio mortis causa*, or
(b) any appointment of property made, otherwise than by will, in the exercise of a special power of appointment,

but, subject to these exceptions, includes any payment of money (including the payment of a premium under a policy of assurance) and any conveyance, assurance, appointment or gift of property of any description, whether made by an instrument or otherwise.
(8) The provisions of this section do not apply to any disposition made before the commencement of this Act.

[247.12]
11 Contracts to leave property by will (1) Where an application is made to a court for an order under section 2 of this Act, the applicant may, in the proceedings on that application, apply to the court for an order under this section.
(2) Where on an application under subsection (1) above the court is satisfied—

(a) that the deceased made a contract by which he agreed to leave by his will a sum of money or other property to any person or by which he agreed that a sum of money or other property would be paid or transferred to any person out of his estate, and

(b) that the deceased made that contract with the intention of defeating an application for financial provision under this Act, and

(c) that when the contract was made full valuable consideration for that contract was not given or promised by the person with whom or for the benefit of whom the contract was made (in this section referred to as 'the donee') or by any other person, and

(d) that the exercise of the powers conferred by this section would facilitate the making of financial provision for the applicant under this Act,

then, subject to the provisions of this section and of sections 12 and 13 of this Act, the court may make any one or more of the following orders, that is to say—

(i) if any money has been paid or any other property has been transferred to or for the benefit of the donee in accordance with the contract, an order directing the donee to provide, for the purpose of the making of that financial provision, such sum of money or other property as may be specified in the order;

(ii) if the money or all the money has not been paid or the property or all the property has not been transferred in accordance with the contract, an order directing the personal representatives not to make any payment or transfer any property, or not to make any further payment or transfer any further property, as the case may be, in accordance therewith or directing the personal representatives only to make such payment or transfer such property as may be specified in the order.

(3) Notwithstanding anything in subsection (2) above, the court may exercise its powers thereunder in relation to any contract made by the deceased only to the extent that the court considers that the amount of any sum of money paid or to be paid or the value of any property transferred or to be transferred in accordance with the contract exceeds the value of any valuable consideration given or to be given for that contract, and for this purpose the court shall have regard to the value of property at the date of the hearing.

(4) In determining whether and in what manner to exercise its powers under this section, the court shall have regard to the circumstances in which the contract was made, the relationship, if any, of the donee to the deceased, the conduct and financial resources of the donee and all the other circumstances of the case.

(5) Where an order has been made under subsection (2) above in relation to any contract the rights of any person to enforce that contract or to recover damages or to obtain other relief for the breach thereof shall be subject to any adjustment made by the court under section 12(3) of this Act and shall survive to such extent only as is consistent with giving effect to the terms of that order.

(6) The provisions of this section do not apply to a contract made before the commencement of this Act.

[247.13]

12 Provisions supplementary to sections 10 and 11 (1) Where the exercise of any of the powers conferred by section 10 or 11 of this Act is conditional on the court being satisfied that a disposition or contract was made by a deceased person with the intention of defeating an application for financial provision under this Act, that condition shall be fulfilled if the court is of the opinion that, on a balance of probabilities, the intention of the deceased (though not necessarily his sole intention) in making the disposition or contract was to prevent an order for financial provision being made under this Act or to reduce the amount of the provision which might otherwise be granted by an order thereunder.

(2) Where an application is made under section 11 of this Act with respect to any contract made by the deceased and no valuable consideration was given or promised by any person for that contract then, notwithstanding anything in subsection (1) above, it shall be presumed, unless the contrary is shown, that the deceased made that contract with the intention of defeating an application for financial provision under this Act.

(3) Where the court makes an order under section 10 or 11 of this Act it may give such consequential directions as it thinks fit (including directions requiring the making of any payment or the transfer of any property) for giving effect to the order or for securing a fair adjustment of the rights of the persons affected thereby.

(4) Any power conferred on the court by the said section 10 or 11 to order the donee, in relation to any disposition or contract, to provide any sum of money or other property shall be exercisable in like manner in relation to the personal representative of the donee, and—

(a) any reference in section 10(4) to the disposal of property by the donee shall include a reference to disposal by the personal representative of the donee, and
(b) any reference in section 10(5) to an application by the donee under that subsection shall include a reference to an application by the personal representative of the donee;

but the court shall not have power under the said section 10 or 11 to make an order in respect of any property forming part of the estate of the donee which has been distributed by the personal representative; and the personal representative shall not be liable for having distributed any such property before he has notice of the making of an application under the said section 10 or 11 on the ground that he ought to have taken into account the possibility that such an application would be made.

[247.14]

13 Provisions as to trustees in relation to sections 10 and 11 (1) Where an application is made for—

(a) an order under section 10 of this Act in respect of a disposition made by the deceased to any person as a trustee, or
(b) an order under section 11 of this Act in respect of any payment made or property transferred, in accordance with a contract made by the deceased, to any person as a trustee,

the powers of the court under the said section 10 or 11 to order that trustee to provide a sum of money or other property shall be subject to the following limitation (in addition, in a case of an application under section 10, to any provision regarding the deduction of inheritance tax) namely, that the amount of any sum of money or the value of any property ordered to be provided—

(i) in the case of an application in respect of a disposition which consisted of the payment of money or an application in respect of the payment of money in accordance with a contract, shall not exceed the aggregate of so much of that money as is at the date of the order in the hands of the trustee and the value at that date of any property which represents that money or is derived therefrom and is at that date in the hands of the trustee;

(ii) in the case of an application in respect of a disposition which consisted of the transfer of property (other than a sum of money) or an application in respect of the transfer of property (other than a sum of money) in accordance with a contract, shall not exceed the aggregate of the value at the date of the order of so much of that property as is at that date in the hands of the trustee and the value at that date of any property which represents the first mentioned property or is derived therefrom and is at that date in the hands of the trustee.

(2) Where any such application is made in respect of a disposition made to any person as a trustee or in respect of any payment made or property transferred in pursuance of a contract to any person as a trustee, the trustee shall not be liable for having distributed any money or other property on the ground that he ought to have taken into account the possibility that such an application would be made.

(3) Where any such application is made in respect of a disposition made to any person as a trustee or in respect of any payment made or property transferred in accordance with a contract to any person as a trustee, any reference in the said section 10 or 11 to the donee shall be construed as including a reference to the trustee or trustees for the time being of the trust in question and any reference in subsection (1) or (2) above to a trustee shall be construed in the same way.

Special provisions relating to cases of divorce, separation, etc

[247.15]

14 Provision as to cases where no financial relief was granted in divorce proceedings, etc (1) Where, within twelve months from the date on which [a divorce order or separation order has been made under the Family Law Act 1996 in relation to a marriage or a decree of nullity of marriage has been made absolute], a party to the marriage dies and—

(a) an application for a financial provision order under [s 22A or 23] of the Matrimonial Causes Act 1973 or a property adjustment order under [s 23A or 24] of that Act has not been made by the other party to that marriage, or

(b) such an application has been made but the proceedings thereon have not been determined at the time of the death of the deceased,

then, if an application for an order under section 2 of this Act is made by that other party, the court shall, notwithstanding anything in section 1 or section 3 of this Act, have power, if it thinks it just to do so, to treat that party for the purposes of that application as if[, as the case may be, the divorce order or separation order had not been made or the decree of nullity had not been made absolute].
(2) This section shall not apply in relation to a [separation order] unless at the date of the death of the deceased [the order] was in force and the separation was continuing.

[247.16]
[14A Provision as to cases where no financial relief was granted in proceedings for the dissolution etc of a civil partnership] [(1) Subsection (2) below applies where—

(a) a dissolution order, nullity order, separation order or presumption of death order has been made under Chapter 2 of Part 2 of the Civil Partnership Act 2004 in relation to a civil partnership,
(b) one of the civil partners dies within twelve months from the date on which the order is made, and
(c) either—
  (i) an application for a financial provision order under Part 1 of Schedule 5 to that Act or a property adjustment order under Part 2 of that Schedule has not been made by the other civil partner, or
  (ii) such an application has been made but the proceedings on the application have not been determined at the time of the death of the deceased.

(2) If an application for an order under section 2 of this Act is made by the surviving civil partner, the court shall, notwithstanding anything in section 1 or section 3 of this Act, have power, if it thinks it just to do so, to treat the surviving civil partner as if the order mentioned in subsection (1)(a) above had not been made.
(3) This section shall not apply in relation to a separation order unless at the date of the death of the deceased the separation order was in force and the separation was continuing.]

[247.17]
15 Restriction imposed in divorce proceedings, etc on application under this Act [(1) *On the grant of a decree of divorce, a decree of nullity of marriage or a decree of judicial separation or at any time thereafter* [At any time when the court—

(a) has jurisdiction under section 23A or 24 of the Matrimonial Causes Act 1973 to make a property adjustment order in relation to a marriage; or
(b) would have such jurisdiction if either the jurisdiction had not

already been exercised or an application for such an order were made with the leave of the court,]

the court, if it considers it just to do so, may, on the application of either party to the marriage, order that the other party to the marriage shall not on the death of the applicant be entitled to apply for an order under section 2 of this Act. In this subsection "the court" means the High Court or, where a county court has jurisdiction by virtue of Part V of the Matrimonial and Family Proceedings Act 1984, a county court.]

(2) In the case of a decree of divorce or nullity of marriage an order may be made under subsection (1) above before or after the decree is made absolute, but if it is made before the decree is made absolute it shall not take effect unless the decree is made absolute.

(3) Where an order made under subsection (1) above on the grant of a decree of divorce or nullity of marriage has come into force with respect to a party to a marriage, then, on the death of the other party to that marriage, the court shall not entertain any application for an order under section 2 of this Act made by the first-mentioned party.

(4) Where an order made under subsection (1) above on the grant of a decree of judicial separation has come into force with respect to any party to a marriage, then, if the other party to that marriage dies while the decree is in force and the separation is continuing, the court shall not entertain any application for an order under section 2 of this Act made by the first-mentioned party.

[(2) An order made under subsection (1) above with respect to any party to a marriage has effect in accordance with subsection (3) below at any time—

(a) after the marriage has been dissolved;

(b) after a decree of nullity has been made absolute in relation to the marriage; and

(c) while a separation order under the Family Law Act 1996 is in force in relation to the marriage and the separation is continuing.

(3) If at any time when an order made under subsection (1) above with respect to any party to a marriage has effect the other party to the marriage dies, the court shall not entertain any application made by the surviving party to the marriage for an order under section 2 of this Act.]

1 Sub-s (1): substituted by Matrimonial and Family Proceedings Act 1984, s 8; words in italics prospectively repealed with savings and subsequent words in square brackets prospectively substituted with savings by the Family Law Act 1996, s 66(1), Sch 8, para 27(5), as from a day to be appointed; for savings see s 66(2), Sch 9, para 5.

2 Sub-ss (2)–(4): prospectively substituted, with savings, by subsequent sub-ss (2)–(3), by the Family Law Act 1996,s 66(1), Sch 8, para 27(6), as from a date to be appointed; for savings see s 66(2), Sch 9, para 5.

[247.18]

[15ZA Restriction imposed in proceedings for the dissolution etc of a civil partnership on application under this Act] [(1) On making a dissolution order, nullity order, separation order or presumption of death order under Chapter 2 of Part 2 of the Civil Partnership Act 2004, or at any time after making such an order, the court, if it considers it just to do so, may, on the

application of either of the civil partners, order that the other civil partner shall not on the death of the applicant be entitled to apply for an order under section 2 of this Act.
(2) In subsection (1) above 'the court' means the High Court or, where a county court has jurisdiction by virtue of Part 5 of the Matrimonial and Family Proceedings Act 1984, a county court.
(3) In the case of a dissolution order, nullity order or presumption of death order ('the main order') an order may be made under subsection (1) above before (as well as after) the main order is made final, but if made before the main order is made final it shall not take effect unless the main order is made final.
(4) Where an order under subsection (1) above made in connection with a dissolution order, nullity order or presumption of death order has come into force with respect to a civil partner, then, on the death of the other civil partner, the court shall not entertain any application for an order under section 2 of this Act made by the surviving civil partner.[1]
(5) Where an order under subsection (1) above made in connection with a separation order has come into force with respect to a civil partner, then, if the other civil partner dies while the separation order is in force and the separation is continuing, the court shall not entertain any application for an order under section 2 of this Act made by the surviving civil partner.]

1 Section 15ZA inserted with effect from 5 December 2005 by the Civil Partnership Act 2004, s 71, Sch 4, Pt 2, para 21.

[247.19]

[15A Restriction imposed in proceedings under Matrimonial and Family Proceedings Act 1984 on application under this Act] [(1) On making an order under section 17 of the Matrimonial and Family Proceedings Act 1984 (orders for financial provision and property adjustment following overseas divorces, etc) the court, if it considers it just to do so, may, on the application of either party to the marriage, order that the other party to the marriage shall not on the death of the applicant be entitled to apply for an order under section 2 of this Act.
In this subsection 'the court' means the High Court or, where a county court has jurisdiction by virtue of Part V of the Matrimonial and Family Proceedings Act 1984, a county court.
(2) Where an order under subsection (1) above has been made with respect to a party to a marriage which has been dissolved or annulled, then, on the death of the other party to that marriage, the court shall not entertain an application under section 2 of this Act made by the first-mentioned party.
(3) Where an order under subsection (1) above has been made with respect to a party to a marriage the parties to which have been legally separated, then, if the other party to the marriage dies while the legal separation is in force, the court shall not entertain an application under section 2 of this Act made by the first-mentioned party.][1]

1 Section 15A: inserted by MFPA 1984, s 25(3).

[247.20]

[15B Restriction imposed in proceedings under Schedule 7 to the Civil Partnership Act 2004 on application under this Act] [(1) On making an order under paragraph 9 of Schedule 7 to the Civil Partnership Act 2004 (orders for financial provision, property adjustment and pension-sharing following overseas dissolution etc of civil partnership) the court, if it considers it just to do so, may, on the application of either of the civil partners, order that the other civil partner shall not on the death of the applicant be entitled to apply for an order under section 2 of this Act.

(2) In subsection (1) above 'the court' means the High Court or, where a county court has jurisdiction by virtue of Part 5 of the Matrimonial and Family Proceedings Act 1984, a county court.

(3) Where an order under subsection (1) above has been made with respect to one of the civil partners in a case where a civil partnership has been dissolved or annulled, then, on the death of the other civil partner, the court shall not entertain an application under section 2 of this Act made by the surviving civil partner.

(4) Where an order under subsection (1) above has been made with respect to one of the civil partners in a case where civil partners have been legally separated, then, if the other civil partner dies while the legal separation is in force, the court shall not entertain an application under section 2 of this Act made by the surviving civil partner.][1]

1 Section 15B inserted with effect from 5 December 2005 by the Civil Partnership Act 2004, s 71, Sch 4, Pt 2, para 22.

[247.21]

16 Variation and discharge of secured periodical payments orders made under Matrimonial Causes Act 1973 (1) Where an application for an order under section 2 of this Act is made to the court by any person who was at the time of the death of the deceased entitled to payments from the deceased under a secured periodical payments order made under the Matrimonial Causes Act 1973 [or Schedule 5 to the Civil Partnership Act 2004], then, in the proceedings on that application, the court shall have power, if an application is made under this section by that person or by the personal representative of the deceased, to vary or discharge that periodical payments order or to revive the operation of any provision thereof which has been suspended under section 31 of that Act [of 1973 or Part 11 of that Schedule].[1]

(2) In exercising the powers conferred by this section the court shall have regard to all the circumstances of the case, including any order which the court proposes to make under section 2 or section 5 of this Act and any change (whether resulting from the death of the deceased or otherwise) in any of the matters to which the court was required to have regard when making the secured periodical payments order.

(3) The powers exercisable by the court under this section in relation to an order shall be exercisable also in relation to any instrument executed in pursuance of the order.

1 Words in square brackets in sub-s 91) inserted with effect from 5 December 2005 by the Civil Partnership Act 2004, s 71, Sch 4, Pt 2, para 23.

[247.22]
17 Variation and revocation of maintenance agreements (1) Where an application for an order under section 2 of this Act is made to the court by any person who was at the time of the death of the deceased entitled to payments from the deceased under a maintenance agreement which provided for the continuation of payments under the agreement after the death of the deceased, then, in the proceedings on that application, the court shall have power, if an application is made under this section by that person or by the personal representative of the deceased, to vary or revoke that agreement.
(2) In exercising the powers conferred by this section the court shall have regard to all the circumstances of the case, including any order which the court proposes to make under section 2 or section 5 of this Act and any change (whether resulting from the death of the deceased or otherwise) in any of the circumstances in the light of which the agreement was made.
(3) If a maintenance agreement is varied by the court under this section the like consequences shall ensue as if the variation had been made immediately before the death of the deceased by agreement between the parties and for valuable consideration.
(4) In this section 'maintenance agreement', in relation to a deceased person, means any agreement made, whether in writing or not and whether before or after the commencement of this Act, by the deceased with any person with whom he [formed a marriage or civil partnership], being an agreement which contained provisions governing the rights and liabilities towards one another when living separately of the parties to that marriage [or of the civil partners] (whether or not the marriage [or civil partnership] has been dissolved or annulled) in respect of the making or securing of payments or the disposition or use of any property, including such rights and liabilities with respect to the maintenance or education of any child, whether or not a child of the deceased or a person who was treated by the deceased as a child of the family in relation to that marriage [or civil partnership].[1]

1 Words in first set of square brackets substituted and other words in square brackets inserted with effect from 5 December 2005 by the Civil Partnership Act 2004, s 71, Sch 4, Pt 2, para 24.

[247.23]
18 Availability of court's powers under this Act in applications under sections 31 and 36 of the Matrimonial Causes Act 1973 (1) Where—

(a) a person against whom a secured periodical payments order was made under the Matrimonial Causes Act 1973 has died and an application is made under section 31(6) of that Act for the variation or discharge of that order or for the revival of the operation of any provision thereof which has been suspended, or
(b) a party to a maintenance agreement within the meaning of section 34 of that Act has died, the agreement being one which provides for the continuation of payments thereunder after the death of one of the parties, and an application is made under section 36(1) of that Act for the alteration of the agreement under section 35 thereof.

the court shall have power to direct that the application made under the said section 31(6) or 36(1) shall be deemed to have been accompanied by an application for an order under section 2 of this Act.
(2) Where the court gives a direction under subsection (1) above it shall have power, in the proceedings on the application under the said section 31(6) or 36(1), to make any order which the court would have had power to make under the provisions of this Act if the application under the said section 31(6) or 36(1), as the case may be, had been made jointly with an application for an order under the said section 2; and the court shall have power to give such consequential directions as may be necessary for enabling the court to exercise any of the powers available to the court under this Act in the case of an application for an order under section 2.
(3) Where an order made under section 15(1) of this Act is in force with respect to a party to a marriage, the court shall not give a direction under subsection (1) above with respect to any application made under the said section 31(6) or 36(1) by that party on the death of the other party.

[247.24]
[18A Availability of court's powers under this Act in applications under paragraphs 60 and 73 of Schedule 5 to the Civil Partnership Act 2004]
[(1) Where—

(a) a person against whom a secured periodical payments order was made under Schedule 5 to the Civil Partnership Act 2004 has died and an application is made under paragraph 60 of that Schedule for the variation or discharge of that order or for the revival of the operation of any suspended provision of the order, or
(b) a party to a maintenance agreement within the meaning of Part 13 of that Schedule has died, the agreement being one which provides for the continuation of payments under the agreement after the death of one of the parties, and an application is made under paragraph 73 of that Schedule for the alteration of the agreement under paragraph 69 of that Schedule,

the court shall have power to direct that the application made under paragraph 60 or 73 of that Schedule shall be deemed to have been accompanied by an application for an order under section 2 of this Act.
(2) Where the court gives a direction under subsection (1) above it shall have power, in the proceedings on the application under paragraph 60 or 73 of that Schedule, to make any order which the court would have had power to make under the provisions of this Act if the application under that paragraph had been made jointly with an application for an order under section 2 of this Act; and the court shall have power to give such consequential directions as may be necessary for enabling the court to exercise any of the powers available to the court under this Act in the case of an application for an order under section 2.
(3) Where an order made under section 15ZA(1) of this Act is in force with respect to a civil partner, the court shall not give a direction under subsection (1) above with respect to any application made under paragraph 60 or 73 of that Schedule by that civil partner on the death of the other civil partner.][1]

1 Section 18A inserted with effect from 5 December 2005 by the Civil Partnership Act 2004, s 71, Sch 4, Pt 2, para 25.

Miscellaneous and supplementary provisions

[247.25]
19 Effect, duration and form of orders (1) Where an order is made under section 2 of this Act then for all purposes, including the purposes of the enactments relating to inheritance tax, the will or the law relating to intestacy, or both the will and the law relating to intestacy, as the case may be, shall have effect and be deemed to have had effect as from the deceased's death subject to the provisions of the order.
(2) Any order made under section 2 or 5 of this Act in favour of—

(a) an applicant who was the [former spouse or former civil partner] of the deceased, or
(b) an applicant who was the husband or wife of the deceased in a case where[, at the date of death, a separation order under the Family Law Act 1996 was in force in relation to the marriage with the deceased] and the separation was continuing, [or
(c) an applicant who was the civil partner of the deceased in a case where, at the date of death, a separation order under Chapter 2 of Part 2 of the Civil Partnership Act 2004 was in force in relation to their civil partnership and the separation was continuing,]

shall, in so far as it provides for the making of periodical payments, cease to have effect [on the formation by the applicant of a subsequent marriage or civil partnership, except in relation to any arrears due under the order on the date of the formation of the subsequent marriage or civil partnership].
(3) A copy of every order made under this Act [other than an order made under section 15(1) [or 15ZA(1)] of this Act][1] shall be sent to the principal registry of the Family Division for entry and filing, and a memorandum of the order shall be endorsed on, or permanently annexed to, the probate or letters of administration under which the estate is being administered.

1 Words in square brackets in sub-s (3) inserted by AJA 1982, s 52.

[247.26]
20 Provisions as to personal representatives (1) The provisions of this Act shall not render the personal representative of a deceased person liable for having distributed any part of the estate of the deceased, after the end of the period of six months from the date on which representation with respect to the estate of the deceased is first taken out, on the ground that he ought to have taken into account the possibility—

(a) that the court might permit the making of an application for an order under section 2 of this Act after the end of that period, or
(b) that, where an order has been made under the said section 2, the court might exercise in relation thereto the powers conferred on it by section 6 of this Act,

but this subsection shall not prejudice any power to recover, by reason of the making of an order under this Act, any part of the estate so distributed.

(2) Where the personal representative of a deceased person pays any sum directed by an order under section 5 of this Act to be paid out of the deceased's net estate, he shall not be under any liability by reason of that estate not being sufficient to make the payment, unless at the time of making the payment he has reasonable cause to believe that the estate is not sufficient.

(3) Where a deceased person entered into a contract by which he agreed to leave by his will any sum of money or other property to any person or by which he agreed that a sum of money or other property would be paid or transferred to any person out of his estate, then, if the personal representative of the deceased has reason to believe that the deceased entered into the contract with the intention of defeating an application for financial provision under this Act, he may, notwithstanding anything in that contract, postpone the payment of that sum of money or the transfer of that property until the expiration of the period of six months from the date on which representation with respect to the estate of the deceased is first taken out or, if during that period an application is made for an order under section 2 of this Act, until the determination of the proceedings on that application.

[247.27]
21 Admissibility as evidence of statement made by deceased. [*Repealed by the Civil Evidence Act 1995, s 15(2), Sch 2.*]

[247.28]
22 Jurisdiction of county courts.[1] [*Repealed by AJA 1982, s 75, Sch 9, and replaced by what is now the County Courts Act 1984, s 25 (as amended).*]

1 The jurisdiction of the county court is now unlimited: see CCA 1984, s 25, as amended by CLSA 1990, s 1 and the High Court and County Courts Jurisdiction Order 1991 (SI 1991/724).

[247.29]
23 Determination of date on which representation was first taken out In considering for the purposes of this Act when representation with respect to the estate of a deceased person was first taken out, a grant limited to settled land or to trust property shall be left out of account, and a grant limited to real estate or to personal estate shall be left out of account unless a grant limited to the remainder of the estate has previously been made or is made at the same time.

[247.30]
24 Effect of this Act on section 46(1)(vi) of Administration of Estates Act 1925 Section 46(1)(vi) of the Administration of Estates Act 1925, in so far as it provides for the devolution of property on the Crown, the Duchy of Lancaster or the Duke of Cornwall as bona vacantia, shall have effect subject to the provisions of this Act.

[247.31]
25 Interpretation (1) In this Act—

'beneficiary', in relation to the estate of a deceased person, means—

(a) a person who under the will of the deceased or under the law relating to intestacy is beneficially interested in the estate or would be so interested if an order had not been made under this Act, and
(b) a person who has received any sum of money or other property which by virtue of section 8(1) or 8(2) of this Act is treated as part of the net estate of the deceased or would have received that sum or other property if an order had not been made under this Act;

'child' includes an illegitimate child and a child en ventre sa mere at the death of the deceased;

'the court' [unless the context otherwise requires][1] means the High Court, or where a county court has jurisdiction by virtue of section 22 of this Act[2], a county court;

['former civil partner' means a person whose civil partnership with the deceased was during the lifetime of the deceased either—
(a) dissolved or annulled by an order made under the law of any part of the British Islands, or
(b) dissolved or annulled in any country or territory outside the British Islands by a dissolution or annulment which is entitled to be recognised as valid by the law of England and Wales;][3]

[['former spouse'] means a person whose marriage with the deceased was during the lifetime of the deceased either—
(a) dissolved or annulled by [an order or decree] of divorce or a decree of nullity of marriage granted under the law of any part of the British Islands, or
(b) dissolved or annulled in any country or territory outside the British Islands by a divorce or annulment which is entitled to be recognised as valid by the law of England and Wales;]

'net estate', in relation to a deceased person, means—
(a) all property of which the deceased had power to dispose by his will (otherwise than by virtue of a special power of appointment) less the amount of his funeral, testamentary and administration expenses, debts and liabilities, including any inheritance tax payable out of his estate on his death;
(b) any property in respect of which the deceased held a general power of appointment (not being a power exercisable by will) which has not been exercised;
(c) any sum of money or other property which is treated for the purposes of this Act as part of the net estate of the deceased by virtue of section 8(1) or (2) of this Act;
(d) any property which is treated for the purposes of this Act as part of the net estate of the deceased by virtue of an order made under section 9 of the Act;
(e) any sum of money or other property which is, by reason of a disposition or contract made by the deceased, ordered under section 10 or 11 of this Act to be provided for the purpose of the making of financial provision under this Act;

'property' includes any chose in action;

'reasonable financial provision' has the meaning assigned to it by section 1 of this Act;
'valuable consideration' does not include marriage or a promise of marriage;
'will' includes codicil.

(2) For the purposes of paragraph (a) of the definition of 'net estate' in subsection (1) above a person who is not of full age and capacity shall be treated as having power to dispose by will of all property of which he would have had power to dispose by will if he had been of full age and capacity.
(3) Any reference in this Act to provision out of the net estate of a deceased person includes a reference to provision extending to the whole of that estate.
(4) For the purposes of this Act any reference to a [spouse,] wife or husband shall be treated as including a reference to a person who in good faith entered into a void marriage with the deceased unless either—

(a) the marriage of the deceased and that person was dissolved or annulled during the lifetime of the deceased and the dissolution or annulment is recognised by the law of England and Wales, or
(b) that person has during the lifetime of the deceased [formed a subsequent marriage or civil partnership].

[(4A) For the purposes of this Act any reference to a civil partner shall be treated as including a reference to a person who in good faith formed a void civil partnership with the deceased unless either—

(a) the civil partnership between the deceased and that person was dissolved or annulled during the lifetime of the deceased and the dissolution or annulment is recognised by the law of England and Wales, or
(b) that person has during the lifetime of the deceased formed a subsequent civil partnership or marriage.

(5) Any reference in this Act to the formation of, or to a person who has formed, a subsequent marriage or civil partnership includes (as the case may be) a reference to the formation of, or to a person who has formed, a marriage or civil partnership which is by law void or voidable.
(5A) The formation of a marriage or civil partnership shall be treated for the purposes of this Act as the formation of a subsequent marriage or civil partnership, in relation to either of the spouses or civil partners, notwithstanding that the previous marriage or civil partnership of that spouse or civil partner was void or voidable.]
(6) Any reference in this Act to an order or decree made under the Matrimonial Causes Act 1973 or under any section of that Act shall be construed as including a reference to an order or decree which is deemed to have been made under that Act or under that section thereof, as the case may be.
[(6A) Any reference in this Act to an order made under, or under any provision of, the Civil Partnership Act 2004 shall be construed as including a reference to anything which is deemed to be an order made (as the case may be) under that Act or provision.]

(7) Any reference in this Act to any enactment is a reference to that enactment as amended by or under any subsequent enactment.

1 Words in square brackets inserted by MFPA 1984, s 8(2).
2 The reference to s 22 must be read as a reference to CCA 1984, s 25 (as amended): see IA 1978, s 17(2)(a) at para **[246.96]** above.
3 Definition of 'former wife' or 'former husband' was substituted by MFPA 1984, s 25(2).

[247.32]
26 Consequential amendments, repeals and transitional provisions [*The provisions of this section and the Schedule are omitted.*]

[247.33]
27 Short title, commencement and extent (1) This Act may be cited as the Inheritance (Provision for Family and Dependants) Act 1975.
(2) This Act does not extend to Scotland or Northern Ireland.
(3) This Act shall come into force on 1st April 1976.

FORFEITURE ACT 1982

(1982 c 34)

[13 July 1982]

[247.34]

Note. The Forfeiture Act 1982 (FoA 1982) confers jurisdiction on the court and on the social security commissioners to modify the effect of the forfeiture rule in cases of unlawful killing other than murder, and wholly or partly restore the interest in the victim's estate or the social security benefits of which the offender would otherwise be deprived by the rule. The FoA 1982 also removes any bar to the making of an application for provision under the I(PFD)A 1975 (see paras **[247.1]**–**[247.33]**) or for financial relief under the divorce legislation. For a more detailed account of the operation of the FoA 1982, see Vol 1, paras **[9.20]**–**[9.22]**.

[247.35]
1. The 'forfeiture rule'.— (1) In this Act, the 'forfeiture rule' means the rule of public policy which in certain circumstances precludes a person who has unlawfully killed another from acquiring a benefit in consequence of the killing.
(2) References in this Act to a person who has unlawfully killed another include a reference to a person who has unlawfully aided, abetted, counselled or procured the death of that other and references in this Act to unlawful killing shall be interpreted accordingly.

[247.36]
2. Power to modify the rule.— (1) Where a court determines that the forfeiture rule has precluded a person (in this section referred to as 'the offender') who has unlawfully killed another from acquiring any interest in property mentioned in subsection (4) below, the court may make an order under this section modifying the effect of that rule.
(2) The court shall not make an order under this section modifying the effect of the forfeiture rule in any case unless it is satisfied that, having regard to the conduct of the offender and of the deceased and to such other

circumstances as appear to the court to be material, the justice of the case requires the effect of the rule to be so modified in that case.
(3) In any case where a person stands convicted of an offence of which unlawful killing is an element the court shall not make an order under this section modifying the effect of the forfeiture rule in that case unless proceedings for the purpose are brought before the expiry of the period of three months beginning with his conviction.
(4) The interests in property referred to in subsection (1) above are—

(a) any beneficial interest in property which (apart from the forfeiture rule) the offender would have acquired—
  (i) under the deceased's will (including, as respects Scotland, any writing having testamentary effect) or the law relating to intestacy or by way of ius relicti, ius relictae or legitim;
  (ii) on the nomination of the deceased in accordance with the provisions of any enactment;
  (iii) as a *donatio mortis causa* made by the deceased; or
  (iv) under a special destination (whether relating to heritable or moveable property); or
(b) any beneficial interest in property which (apart from the forfeiture rule) the offender would have acquired in consequence of the death of the deceased, being property which, before the death, was held on trust for any person.

(5) An order under this section may modify the effect of the forfeiture rule in respect of any interest in property to which the determination referred to in subsection (1) above relates and may do so in either or both of the following ways, that is—

(a) where there is more than one such interest, by excluding the application of the rule in respect of any (but not all) of those interests; and
(b) in the case of any such interest in property, by excluding the application of the rule in respect of part of the property.

(6) On the making of an order under this section, the forfeiture rule shall have effect for all purposes (including purposes relating to anything done before the order is made) subject to the modifications made by the order.
(7) The court shall not make an order under this section modifying the effect of the forfeiture rule in respect of any interest in property which, in consequence of the rule, has been acquired before the coming into force of this section by a person other than the offender or a person claiming through him.
(8) In this section—

'property' includes any chose in action or incorporeal moveable property; and 'will' includes codicil.

[247.37]
3. Application for financial provision not affected by the rule.— (1) The forfeiture rule shall not be taken to preclude any person from making any application under a provision mentioned in subsection (2) below or the making of any order on the application.

(2) The provisions referred to in subsection (1) above are—

(a) any provision of the Inheritance (Provision for Family and Dependants) Act 1975;

[(b) sections 31(6) and 36(1) of the Matrimonial Causes Act 1973 (variation by court in England and Wales of periodical payments orders and maintenance agreements in respect of marriages);

(c) paragraphs 60(2) and 73(2) of Schedule 5 to the Civil Partnership Act 2004 (variation by court in England and Wales of periodical payments orders and maintenance agreements in respect of civil partnerships); and

(d) section 13(4) of the Family Law (Scotland) Act 1985 (variation etc. of periodical allowances in respect of marriages and civil partnerships).][1]

1 Paragraphs (b), (c) and (d) substituted with effect from 5 December 2005 by CPA 2004, s 261(1), Sch 27, para 79 and Civil Partnership Act 2004 (Commencement No 2) Order 2005, SI 2005/3175.

[247.38]

4. Commissioner to decide whether rule applies to social security benefits.— (1) Where a question arises as to whether, if a person were otherwise entitled to be eligible for any benefit or advantage under a relevant enactment, he would be precluded by virtue of the forfeiture rule from receiving the whole or part of the benefit or advantage, that question shall (notwithstanding anything in any relevant enactment) be determined by a Commissioner.

[(1A) Where a Commissioner determines that the forfeiture rule has precluded a person (in this section referred to as 'the offender') who has unlawfully killed another from receiving the whole or part of any such benefit or advantage, the Commissioner may make a decision under this subsection modifying the effect of that rule and may do so whether the unlawful killing occurred before or after the coming into force of this subsection.

(1B) The Commissioner shall not make a decision under subsection (1A) above modifying the effect of the forfeiture rule in any case unless he is satisfied that, having regard to the conduct of the offender and of the deceased and to such other circumstances as appear to the Commissioner to be material, the justice of the case requires the effect of the rule to be so modified in that case.

(1C) Subject to subsection (1D) below, a decision under subsection (1A) above may modify the effect of the forfeiture rule in either or both of the following ways—

(a) so that it applies only in respect of a specified proportion of the benefit or advantage;

(b) so that it applies in respect of the benefit or advantage only for a specified period of time.

(1D) Such a decision may not modify the effect of the forfeiture rule so as to allow any person to receive the whole or any part of a benefit or advantage in respect of any period before the commencement of this subsection.

(1E) If the Commissioner thinks it expedient to do so, he may direct that his decision shall apply to any future claim for a benefit or advantage under a relevant enactment, on which a question such as is mentioned in subsection (1) above arises by reason of the same unlawful killing.
(1F) It is immaterial for the purposes of subsection (1E) above whether the claim is in respect of the same or a different benefit or advantage.
(1G) For the purpose of obtaining a decision whether the forfeiture rule should be modified the Secretary of State may refer to a Commissioner for review any determination of a question such as is mentioned in subsection (1) above that was made before the commencement of subsections (1A) to (1F) above (whether by a Commissioner or not) and shall do so if the offender requests him to refer such a determination.
(1H) Subsections (1A) to (1F) above shall have effect on a reference under subsection (1G) above as if in subsection (1A) the words 'it has been determined' were substituted for the words 'a Commissioner determines'.][1]
(2) Regulations under this section may make such provision as appears to the Secretary of State to be necessary or expedient for carrying this section into effect; and (without prejudice to the generality of that) the regulations may, in relation to the question mentioned in subsection (1) above or any determination under that subsection [or any decision under subsection (1A) above][1]—

- (a) apply any provision of any relevant enactment, with or without modifications; or exclude or contain provision corresponding to any such provision; and
- (b) make provision for purposes corresponding to those for which provision may be made by regulations under [section 59 of the Social Security Administration Act 1992][2] (matters relating to adjudication).

(3) The power to make regulations under this section shall be exercisable by statutory instrument which shall be subject to annulment in pursuance of a resolution of either House of Parliament.
(4) [Section 175(3) to (5) of the Social Security Contributions and Benefits Act 1992][2] (provision about extent of power to make regulations) shall apply to the power to make regulations conferred by this section as it applies to the power to make regulations conferred by that Act, but as if for references to that Act there were substituted references to this section.
(5) In this section—

'Commissioner' has the same meaning as in the [Social Security Administration Act 1992]; and
'relevant enactment' means any provision of the following and any instrument made by virtue of such a provision:
the Personal Injuries (Emergency Provisions) Act 1939,
the Pensions (Navy, Army, Air Force and Mercantile Marine) Act 1939,
the Polish Resettlement Act 1947,
. . .
[the Social Security Acts 1975 to 1991,]
[the Social Security Contributions and Benefits Act 1992,]
[the Pension Schemes Act 1993]

and any other enactment relating to pensions or social security prescribed by regulations under this section.[3]

1 Sub-ss (1A) to (1H) and the words in the first pair of square brackets in sub-s (2) were inserted by the Social Security Act 1986, ss 76(1) to (3).
2 The words in the second pair of square brackets in sub-s (2), and the words in square brackets in sub-s (4), were substituted by the Social Security (Consequential Provisions) Act 1992, s 4, Sch 2, para 63(1), (2).
3 In sub-s (5), the words in square brackets in the definition of 'Commissioner' were substituted, and in the definition of 'relevant enactment', the entry omitted (as substituted by the Social Security Act 1986, s 86(1), Sch 10, Pt VI, para 108(b)) was repealed, and the entry relating to the Social Security Contributions and Benefits Act 1992 was added, by the Social Security (Consequential Provisions) Act 1992, ss 3, 4, Sch 1, Sch 2, para 63(3). The entry relating to the Social Security Acts 1975 to 1991 in that definition was substituted by the Statutory Sick Pay Act 1991, s 3(1)(c); and the final entry was added by the Pension Schemes Act 1993, s 190, Sch 8, para 15.

[247.39]
5. Exclusion of murderers. Nothing in this Act or in any order made under section 2 or referred to in section 3(1) of this Act [or in any decision made under section 4(1A) of this Act] shall affect the application of the forfeiture rule in the case of a person who stands convicted of murder.

[247.40]
6. Corresponding provision for Northern Ireland. An Order in Council under paragraph 1(1)(b) of Schedule 1 to the Northern Ireland Act 1974 (legislation for Northern Ireland in the interim period) which contains a statement that it is made only for purposes corresponding to the purposes of this Act—

(a) shall not be subject to paragraph 1(4) and (5) of that Schedule (affirmative resolution of both Houses of Parliament); but
(b) shall be subject to annulment in pursuance of a resolution of either House.

[247.41]
7. Short title, etc.— (1) This Act may be cited as the Forfeiture Act 1982.
(2) Section 4 of this Act shall come into force on such day as the Secretary of State may appoint by order made by statutory instrument; and sections 1 to 3 and 5 of this Act shall come into force on the expiry of the period of three months beginning with the day on which it is passed.
(3) This Act, except section 6, does not extend to Northern Ireland.
(4) Subject to section 2(7) of this Act, an order under section 2 of this Act or an order referred to in section 3(1) of this Act and made in respect of a person who has unlawfully killed another may be made whether the unlawful killing occurred before or after the coming into force of those sections.

Cumulative Index

[References prefixed by an emboldened number up to and including 105 are to entries in volume 1. References prefixed by an emboldened number from 200 onward are to entries in volume 2.]

A

Abatement
annuities, of, **33**.35–**33**.45
legacies, of
demonstrative legacies, **31**.3
general legacies, **31**.1
provision for, **210**.75
satisfaction of debt, in, **31**.2
specific, **31**.4

Absence of attestation clause
generally, **12**.10
presumption of due execution, **13**.2

Absolute gifts
change of words, and, **56**.1–**56**.9
gift over on death, and, **97**.1
precedents
contingent gifts, **215**.1–**215**.8
pecuniary legacies, **210**.9–**210**.14
secret trusts, and
communication of, **36**.6–**36**.7
conditions, **36**.4
generally, **36**.2–**36**.9
tacit acquiescence, **36**.3
superadded powers, and, **83**.9–**83**.10

Absolute interests
generally, **83**.1–**83**.2
gifts by implication, and, **101**.7–**101**.8
gift of annuity, **83**.5
gift of income, **83**.4
gift to executor, **83**.3

Abstraction, fraudulent
revocation of will, and, **18**.30

Acceleration
beneficiary attests will, where, **48**.7
class closing rules, and, **48**.6
disclaimer, on, **48**.8
divorce, on, **48**.14
election under will, and, **48**.12
forfeiture, on, **48**.11
gifts being void for remoteness, on, **48**.13
lapse, on, **48**.10
revocation of gift, on, **48**.9
subsequent interests, of, **48**.5

Acceptance of office
executors, by, **25**.12

Acceptance of secret office
tacit acquiescence, **36**.3

Acceptance of trust
trustees, and, **27**.5

Accessories
description of property, **61**.1

Accretions to shares
generally, **61**.1

Accruer clauses
generally, **90**.1–**90**.6
precedents, **219**.20–**219**.22

Accumulation and maintenance trusts
children's trusts, and, **217**.2
generally, **95**.14
inheritance tax, **218**.69–**218**.70
abolition of privileged status, **200**.19, **200**.107

Accumulation and maintenance trusts – *contd*
permitted periods of, **218**.71–**218**.73
precedent, discretionary trusts, **218**.79–**218**.86
statutory provisions
adaptations and extensions of, **218**.63–**218**.65, **218**.74–**218**.78
generally, **218**.43–**218**.78, **246**.30
Accumulation of income
generally, **61**.1
Accumulations
children, and, **95**.10
generally, **95**.1–**95**.14
minors, and, **95**.6
portions, and, **95**.9
statutory provisions, **246**.86–**246**.87
Accuracy of description
construction of wills, and, **58**.1
Acknowledgement of signature
presence of witnesses, **11**.25
production of signed will, by, **11**.26
second signature, by, **11**.27
sufficiency, **11**.24
Acquisition of dignity
conditions, and, **35**.47
Acquisition of land by trustees
generally, **27**.12
investment powers, and, **220**.17–**220**.19
statutory provisions, **246**.140–**246**.142
Action, rights of
disposable property, **7**.29
Acts before probate
executors, and, **25**.14
Acts of testator
failure of gifts, and, **48**.2
Actual military service
soldiers', etc., wills, and, **16**.2
Additional words
construction of wills, **52**.3
Ademption
advowsons, **41**.13
Ademption – *contd*
change of nature, by
corporate act, by, **41**.14
partnership shares, in, **41**.15
statute, under, **41**.13
codicils, and, **41**.3
conversion, and, **37**.9
exercise of power of appointment, and, **41**.21
generally, **41**.1–**41**.4, **200**.23
gift of freehold land, and, **206**.9
investment of money received, **41**.16
leaseholds, **41**.10
money in bank account, **41**.23
mortgage debt, **41**.9
mortgage of land, **41**.8
nature, **41**.1
options, **41**.20
payment of debt, **41**.19
persons of unsound mind, disposals by, **41**.12
portion, **41**.24
removal of gift, **41**.17
republication of wills, and, **22**.4
sale of land
generally, **41**.5–**41**.6
subject to trust for sale, **41**.7
sale of stocks and shares, **41**.11
transfer into testator's name, **41**.22
undivided shares in land, **41**.18
Administration of Estates Act 1925
amendment, **204**.134
application, **244**.70
definitions, **244**.69, **246**.67
general provisions
administration of assets, **244**.60, **246**.61–**246**.66
distribution of residuary estate, **244**.61–**244**.67
note to provisions, **244**.59
savings, **244**.68
schedule, administration of assets, **246**.68–**246**.69
Administration of Justice Act 1982
amendments
1995, **244**.124

Administration of Justice Act 1982 – *contd*
citation, **244**.119
commencement, **244**.108
extent, **244**.109
general provisions
amendment of Wills Act 1837, **244**.95–**244**.97
interpretation of wills, **244**.99–**244**.100
rectification of wills, **244**.98
registration of wills, **244**.101–**244**.106
note to provisions, **244**.94
schedule, **244**.111
transitional provisions, **244**.107
Administration trusts. *See also* **Residuary gifts**
conversion, and, **214**.2
legacies, and, **214**.9
order of application of assets, and, **214**.4–**214**.8
power of sale, and, **214**.1
power to postpone sale, and, **214**.3
precedents, **214**.10–**214**.26
without trust for sale, **214**.10–**214**.11
Administrative powers. ***See also under individual headings***
appropriation
generally, **220**.70–**220**.71
precedents, **220**.74–**220**.80
taxation, and, **220**.72–**220**.73
borrowing, **220**.69
business, **220**.66–**220**.68
delegation, **220**.35–**220**.36, **220**.38–**220**.39
foreign property, **220**.22, **220**.63–**220**.65
generally, **220**.1–**220**.3
inheritance tax, **220**.4–**220**.10
inheritance tax status, **220**.81
investment powers
advice, **220**.14
company shareholdings, **220**.20
duty of care, **220**.15
enjoyment in kind, **220**.30
land, **220**.17
Administrative powers – *contd*
investment powers – *contd*
loan, **220**.31–**220**.32
mortgages, **220**.16
precedents, **220**.40–**220**.48
preliminary note, **220**.11–**220**.39
sale, **220**.23–**220**.28
standard investment criteria, **220**.13
statutory power
exclusion of, **220**.37
express powers, **220**.18–**220**.19, **220**.29
generally, **220**.12
land, management of
precedents, **220**.59–**220**.62
statutory powers,
consultation, **220**.58
delegation to beneficiary, **220**.54–**220**.57
express powers, **220**.53
generally **220**.49–**220**.50
insurance, **220**.51
limitations, **220**.52
loan guarantees, **220**.81
precedents
appropriation, **220**.74–**220**.80
borrowing, **220**.69
business, **220**.66–**220**.68
foreign property, **220**.63–**220**.65
inheritance tax status, **220**.81
investment powers, **220**.40–**220**.48
loan guarantees, **220**.81
management of land, **220**.59–**220**.62
Admissibility of documents as will
bank mandates, **10**.10
deeds, **10**.5
instructions for will, **10**.7
letters, **10**.8
memoranda, **10**.9
nominations, **10**.11
voluntary settlement, **10**.6
Zavah, **10**.12

Admissibility of documents as will – *contd*
Adopted children
generally, **75**.1–**75**.9, **200**.28, **245**.1
illegitimacy, **72**.11
lapse of gift to, **47**.16
order, meaning, **72**.2
status, **245**.93–**245**.99
statutory provisions
adoption orders, **245**.56
status of adopted children, **245**.57–**245**.64
will, provisions applying to, **237**.10
treatment in law, **72**.3
Adoption Act 1950
citation, **245**.22
commencement, **245**.22
definitions, **245**.20
general provisions, **245**.16, **245**.17–**245**.19
schedule, **245**.23
transitional provisions, **245**.21
Adoption Act 1958
citation, **245**.29
commencement, **245**.29
general provisions, **245**.24, **245**.25–**245**.27
schedule, **245**.30
transitional provisions, **245**.28
Adoption Act 1960
general provisions, **245**.36
introductory note, **245**.35
Adoption Act 1976
application, **245**.67
citation, **245**.67
commencement, **245**.67
definitions, **245**.65
general provisions
adoption orders, **245**.56
introductory note, **245**.55
status of adopted children, **245**.57–**245**.64
schedule, **245**.68
transitional provisions, **245**.66
Adoption and Children Act 2002
disposition, meaning, **245**.99
introductory note, **245**.92
Adoption and Children Act 2002 – *contd*
status of adopted children, **245**.93–**245**.99
transitional and transitory provisions and savings, **245**.101
Adoption of Children Act 1926
application, **245**.5
citation, **245**.5
commencement, **245**.5
general provisions, **245**.2–**245**.4
Advance from bank and undertaking to repay
precedent, **240**.4
Advancement, exercise of powers of
capital gains tax, **218**.102–**218**.103, **242**.3, **242**.5
discretionary trusts, notes and precedents, **218**.87–**218**.108
inheritance tax, **218**.101, **242**.2, **242**.4
precedents, **218**.102–**218**.108, **242**.17–**242**.20
trust for minor children, **242**.19–**242**.20
stamp duty, **242**.6
stamp duty land tax, **242**.6
statutory power
application of, **218**.91–**218**.93
benefit, **218**.94–**218**.98
breach of trust, **218**.100
capital gains tax, **218**.102–**218**.103
extent of, **218**.89
inheritance tax **218**.101
prior interests, and, **218**.90
statutory provisions, **246**.30
vulnerable trusts for, **217**.4
Advantages of wills
generally, **1**.11
Advice, taking of
investment powers, and, **220**.14
Advowsons
ademption, and, **41**.13
Age of majority
introductory note, **200**.27

Age of majority – *contd*
statutory provisions, **244**.87, **246**.89
Aged, relief of
charitable purposes, **102**.5
advancement, **246**.30
Agents, employment of
generally, **246**.143–**246**.147
review of and liability for, **246**.153–**246**.155
supplementary, **246**.156–**246**.159
Agreement for purchase of property
disposable property, **7**.27
Agreement relating to wills
ante-nuptial agreement, and, **3**.5
ascertainable gift, **3**.2
certainty
obligation, of, **3**.3–**3**.4
subject-matter, of, **3**.2
disposition of property, **3**.8
enforcement, **3**.6
exercise of power in particular way
generally, **3**.14
special power, **3**.15
formalities
generally, **3**.3
statutory requirements, **3**.4
generally, **3**.1
inheritance tax, **3**.7
insolvency, **3**.9
intestacy, **3**.11
lapse, **3**.10
mutual wills
effect of first to die abiding, **2**.8
effect of first to die not abiding, 2.7
generally, 2.5
precedents, 201.13
proof, 2.6
obligation, certainty of, **3**.3–**3**.4
proprietary estoppel, and, **3**.1
revocation, **3**.13
subject-matter, certainty of, **3**.2
Agreements to restrict
disposable property, **7**.32
Agricultural business, wills disposing of
agricultural relief
comparison with business relief, **234**.8
conditions, **234**.4
debts charged, **234**.10
farming companies, **234**.6
generally, **234**.1–**234**.3
nature, **234**.7
partially exempt estates, **234**.9
succession, **234**.5
business relief
comparison with agricultural relief, **234**.8
generally, **234**.15
children carrying on business, **234**.15
estate given equally between children, one son having option to purchase farming assets, **234**.17–**234**.30
farming business left to wife or son with residue on trust for wife, **234**.45–**234**.56
farming partnerships with tenancies, **234**.13
legacies to daughters, right of residence to wife, residue to son if farming, **234**.31–**234**.44
nature of assets, **234**.16
precedents, **234**.17–**234**.56
tenant farmers, **234**.12
woodlands, **234**.14
Agricultural tenancies
disposable property, **7**.5
Airmen, wills of
actual military service, meaning, **16**.2
at sea, meaning, **16**.3
exclusion of words, **16**.9
gifts to witnesses, and, **16**.7
introduction, **16**.1
lost will, and, **16**.5
power of appointment, and, **16**.6
proof, **16**.8
revocation, **16**.10
Alienation
conditions, and, **35**.37

Alienation – *contd*
restraints, **99**.1–**99**.10
Aliens
capacity to benefit, **9**.37
capacity to make will, **4**.5
***Allhusen v Whittell*, rule in**
exclusion of, **214**.43–**214**.44
generally, **38**.26–**38**.28
precedents, **214**.45–**214**.47
Alteration of wills
apparent words, and, **14**.2
construction of wills, and, **52**.2
initials of testator and witnesses, **14**.6
interlineations, by, **14**.14
introduction, **14**.1
obliteration, by, **14**.13
pencil, in, **10**.14
presumption as to time of making
evidence of rebuttal, **14**.5–**14**.11
generally, **14**.3
onus of proof, **14**.4
rebuttal of presumption
external evidence, **14**.11
generally, **14**.5
internal evidence, **14**.9–**14**.10
signature of testator and witnesses, **14**.6
subsequent validation, **14**.7–**14**.8
signature of testator and witnesses, **14**.6
subsequent validation, **14**.7–**14**.8
third parties, by, **14**.15
Alteration of words
construction of wills, and, **52**.2
Alternative, donees in the
children, **68**.9
class gifts, **68**.6–**68**.8
concurrent interests, **68**.13
conditions, **68**.11
generally, **68**.1–**68**.15
introduction, **65**.5
parents and issue, **68**.10
substituted gifts, **68**.2
Amalgamated institutions
charitable gifts, and, **103**.9
lapse, and, **212**.31, **232**.68
Ambiguities, construction of
extrinsic evidence
surrounding circumstances, in light of, **57**.26
will, on face of, **57**.25
meaning of words, **50**.4
Anatomical examination and research
generally, **7**.34, **202**.9–**202**.12
precedent, **202**.16
Animals, gifts for upkeep of
capacity to benefit, **9**.31
charitable purposes, **102**.13
generally, **202**.36
precedent, **202**.37–**202**.38
Animus testandi
testamentary intention, and, **10**.4
Annuities
abatement, **33**.35–**33**.45
absolute interests, and, **83**.5
alienation, to cease on, **211**.19–**211**.20
alternatives, **211**.4
capital cost recouped from income, **211**.14
commencement, **33**.11
considerations, **211**.5
creation, **33**.2–**33**.10
deductions, to be paid clear of, **211**.21
definition, **33**.1
description of property, **64**.1
direction to purchase, with, **211**.17
duration, **33**.12–**33**.22
education of children, and, **33**.18
generally, **200**.12
gift of business interests, and, **205**.68
inflationary devaluation, **211**.2
inheritance tax, **33**.32
insertion where residue settled, direction for payment, **211**.25
interest on arrears, **33**.31
investments to answer, power to appropriate, **211**.15–**211**.16
land, charged on, **211**.13
maintenance of animals, and, **33**.16

Annuities – *contd*
maintenance of children, and, **33**.18
means of provision, **211**.6–**211**.7
mentally disabled daughter, in trust for, **211**.23
mitigation of tax, provision for, **211**.18
precedents, **211**.8–**211**.25
priority, **33**.33–**33**.34
reliefs and repayments, liability of annuitant to account for, **211**.10
restraint of marriage, and, **33**.22
several, gift of, **211**.12, **211**.22
simple, gift of, **211**.8
source of money, **33**.23–**33**.32
spendthrift, on trust for, **211**.24
stated sum, amounting to, **211**.11
surplus income, and, **33**.25
taxation, **211**.3
tax-free
generally, **33**.46–**33**.47
precedent, **211**.9
unsatisfactory nature of, **211**.1
vested, treatment for maintenance purposes, **218**.62
Annulment of marriage or civil partnership
failure of gifts on, **47**.2–**47**.4
Ante-nuptial agreement
generally, **3**.5
Anticipated needs
inheritance provision, and, **105**.37
Apparent words
alterations to will, and, **14**.2
Appointment, exercise of power of
ademption, and, **41**.21
capital gains tax, **242**.3, **242**.5
class of persons, among, **40**.2
contemplation of marriage, will made in
introduction, **17**.1
wills after 1982, **17**.8
wills before 1983, **17**.5
contract relating to wills, and
generally, **3**.14
Appointment, exercise of power of – *contd*
contract relating to wills, and – *contd*
special power, **3**.15
covenant against, **40**.11
delegation of power, and, **40**.5
disclaimer of power, and, **40**.12
election, and, **42**.4
foreign element wills, and
capacity of testator, **24**.15
donee domiciled abroad, **24**.12
evidence, **24**.18
immovables, **24**.13
introduction, **24**.11
residuary bequest, **24**.16
revocation, **24**.14
fraudulent appointment
generally, **40**.14
grounds, **40**.15
variation of trusts, **40**.16
general powers
definition, **39**.2
generally, **39**.4–**39**.15
joint will, by, **39**.8
nature, **39**.3
gift of freehold land, and, **206**.29–**206**.30
hybrid powers, **39**.31
inheritance tax, **242**.2, **242**.4
introduction, **39**.1
miscellaneous matters, **40**.1–**40**.21
precedents
age 18-to-25 trust, appointment to, **242**.13–**242**.14
bereaved minor trust , appointment to, **242**.13–**242**.16
discretionary trusts, **242**.7–**242**.11
immediate post-death interests, appointment in residue for grandchildren, **242**.12
release of power, and
generally, **40**.10
implied, **40**.13
severance of appointment, **40**.20
soldiers', etc., wills, and, **16**.6

Appointment, exercise of power of – *contd*
special powers. *See* **Special powers of appointment**
stamp duty, **242**.6
stamp duty land tax, **242**.6
successive instruments, by, **40**.3
Appointment of director
gift of business interests, and, **205**.69
Apportionment Act 1870
citation, **246**.2
definitions, **246**.6
exclusion of,
generally, **214**.48–**214**.52
precedents, **214**.53–**214**.54
general provisions, **246**.3–**246**.8
note to statutory provisions, **246**.1
Apportionment, rules of
adjustment of debts, **38**.26–**38**.28
capital and income, between,
rules, **214**.35
exclusion, **214**.35–**214**.38, **214**.43–**214**.44
precedents, **214**.38–**214**.42, **214**.45–**214**.47
generally, **38**.17–**38**.25, **200**.36
reversionary interests, **38**.22–**38**.23
time apportionment, see Apportionment Act 1870
Apprentices
legacies, and, **30**.27
Approbation
estoppel, and, **43**.4
Appropriation
common law powers
consent, **29**.12
contingent legacies, **29**.3–**29**.4
effect, **29**.14
executor, in favour of, **29**.14
express power, **29**.7
implied power, **29**.8
method, **29**.15
minor's legacies, **29**.5
relevant property, **29**.9
settled shares of residue, **29**.6
stamps, **29**.16
two or more, **29**.10
Appropriation – *contd*
common law powers – *contd*
valuation, **29**.11
vested legacies, **29**.1–**29**.2
consent, **29**.12
contingent legacies, **29**.3–**29**.4
generally, **220**.70–**220**.71
interest on legacies, and, **32**.29
precedents, **220**.74–**220**.80
purchaser protection, **29**.23
resolution of
precedent, **243**.2
preliminary note, **243**.1
self-dealing, **29**.20
statutory powers
effect, **29**.19
extent, **29**.24
introduction, **29**.17
non-existent persons, **29**.21
purchaser protection, **29**.23
self-dealing, **29**.20
valuation, **29**.18
tax aspects, **220**.72–**220**.73
valuation
common law powers, **29**.11
statutory powers, **29**.18
Approval and knowledge. ***See*** **Knowledge and approval**
Appurtenances
generally, **64**.2
introduction, **61**.1
Arrears, payment of
gift of leasehold land, and, **207**.18
Artificial insemination, children born by
capacity to benefit, **9**.27
generally, **74**.3–**74**.5
introduction, **72**.18
introductory note, **200**.28
statutory provisions
consent of married spouse, **245**.74
introductory note, **245**.82
parental orders, **245**.88
status of mother and father, **245**.85–**245**.87
Ascertainable gift
contracts relating to wills, and, **3**.2

Ascertainment of death
disposal of body, and, **202**.6
Assent
exercise of, precedent for, **243**.3
use for successive interests, and, **8**.5
Associated charities
charitable gifts, and, **103**.2
Assumed name
signature of wills, and, **11**.20
At sea
seamen's, etc., wills, meaning, **16**.3
Attesting witnesses
capacity to benefit
charging power, **9**.11
foreign wills, **9**.12
generally, **9**.3–**9**.9
soldiers' wills, **9**.10
generally, **12**.16
professional privilege, and, **12**.17
Attestation
form
generally, **12**.9–**12**.13
notes to precedents, **222**.1–**222**.2
precedents, **222**.3–**222**.16
See also **Attestation clause**
intention
evidence, **12**.15
general rule, **12**.14
introduction, **12**.1–**12**.2
mode
attestation in presence of other witness, **12**.7
attestation in presence of testator, **12**.6
signature in presence of both witnesses, **12**.3
signature must precede attestation, **12**.5
witness must attest will, **12**.4
presumption of due execution, and
absence of attestation clause, **13**.2
general rule, **13**.1
rebuttal, **13**.3
signature affixed by direction of testator, **13**.4
Attestation – *contd*
requirements for execution, **200**.44
superfluous, **12**.8
witnesses, **12**.16–**12**.17
Attestation clause
absence
generally, **12**.10
presumption of due execution, **13**.2
acknowledgment by witness, **12**.13
blind testator, **222**.9
deaf and dumb testator, **222**.10
form, **12**.9
position, **12**.11
precedents, **222**.3–**222**.16
signature
generally, **12**.12
introduction, **11**.6
Avoidance of dispositions
contracts *inter vivos*, **105**.49
discretion, **105**.46
donee, **105**.45
intention to defeat order, **105**.48
inter vivos, **105**.43
introduction, **105**.42
relevant disposition, **105**.47
relevant property, **105**.44

B

Bank account, money in
description of property, **64**.37
Bank, executor and trustee, as
appointment
generally, **25**.6, **203**.26
precedents, **203**.32–**203**.35
charges, **203**.30–**203**.31
Bank mandates
admissibility as will, and, **10**.10
Baptist Union, gifts to
precedent, **212**.17
Bare trust
inheritance tax provisions, **200**.110
Bearer securities
investment powers, and, **220**.21

Begotten children
description of donees, **81**.2
Behaviour of donee
conditions, and, **35**.45
Belongings
description of property, **64**.4
Beneficial interests. *See also* ***under individual headings***
absolute interests, **83**.1–**83**.5
accruer clauses, **90**.1–**90**.6, **219**.20–**219**.22
accumulations, **95**.1–**95**.14, **218**.43–**218**.78
alienation and forfeiture clause, **99**.1–**99**.10, **216**.8 –**216**.9
concurrent gifts, **86**.1–**86**.8
conditional gifts, **91**.1–**91**.6
cumulative gifts, **88**.1–**88**.4
distribution, **87**.1–**87**.4
divesting, **96**.1–**96**.7
entailed interests, **84**.1–**84**.4
failure of issue, **98**.1–**98**.13
gift over on death
contingencies, with, **97**.4–**97**.10
generally, **97**.1–**97**.3
statutory provision, **97**.11
hotchpot clauses, **100**.1–**100**.7, **204**.63–**204**.64, **216**.20, **217**.44–**217**.49
implication, gifts by, **101**.1–**101**.14
joint tenancy, gifts of, **86**.1–**86**.5
life interests, **83**.6–**83**.7, **216**.1–**216**.37
option to purchase, **92**.1–**92**.6, **209**.1–**209**.12
per capita distribution, **87**.1–**87**.4
per stripes distribution, **87**.1–**87**.4
perpetuities, rule against
applicable interests, **94**.33–**94**.40
class gifts, **94**.21–**94**.29
common law, **94**.10–**94**.15, **216**.4
effect of gift being void, **94**.30–**94**.32
period allowed, **94**.1–**94**.9
power of appointment, and, **94**.41–**94**.53
Beneficial interests – *contd*
perpetuities, rule against – *contd*
statute, under, **94**.16–**94**.20, **216**.4
vesting, and, **216**.6–**216**.7
wait and see rule, **216**.5
person and children, gifts to, **85**.1–**85**.3
person and issue, gifts to, **85**.4–**85**.5
quantity of interest given
expression of testator's motive, **82**.5–**82**.6
generally, **82**.1–**82**.4
gifts for particular purposes, **82**.7–**82**.9
substituted gifts, **88**.1–**88**.4
successive interests
cy-près doctrine, **89**.2
generally, **89**.1
superadded powers, gifts with, **83**.8–**83**.20
tenancy in common, gifts of, **86**.6–**86**.8, **204**.69–**204**.70
vesting
affecting circumstances, **93**.4–**93**.9
gift over, effect of, **93**.16–**93**.23
introduction, **93**.1–**93**.3
legacies charged on mixed fund, **93**.45
legacies charged on real property, **93**.44
legacies payable from personal property, **93**.24–**93**.43
remainders, of, **93**.10–**93**.15
Beneficiaries. *See also* **Description of donee**
aliens, **9**.37
animals, **9**.31, **202**.36
attesting witnesses, **9**.3–**9**.12
charities, **9**.28, **212**.1–**212**.2
clubs, **9**.35
companies, **9**.33
corporations, **9**.32
criminals, **9**.44
dead beneficiaries, **9**.2
discrimination, and, **9**.38

Beneficiaries – *contd*
fertilisation, children born by way of, **9**.27, **200**.28–**200**.31
fraud, **9**.23
graves, **9**.29–**9**.30, **202**.18–**202**.26
illegitimate children, **9**.24–**9**.26, **200**.28–**200**.31
institutions, **9**.35
introduction, **9**.1
local authorities, **9**.34
mentally disordered persons, **9**.45
minors, **9**.39–**9**.43
religious disabilities, **9**.36
societies, **9**.35
soundness of mind, and, **9**.45
trade unions, **9**.35
undue influence, **9**.23
unlawful killing, **9**.13–**9**.22
variation of beneficial interests, and, **241**.2

Beneficiary's interest under will
duty of care, and, **1**.14
generally, **1**.8

Benefit of particular property, gift for
generally, **82**.9

Bequests. *See also* **Legacies**
abatement, **31**.1–**31**.5
conditional, **210**.46–**210**.50
debtor, to, **30**.10–**30**.13, **210**.2, **210**.32–**210**.37
debts, **204**.62 –**204**.68
employees, to, **30**.23–**30**.29, **210**.57–**210**.63
executor, to, **30**.14–**30**.18, **210**.51–**210**.53
furniture, of, **204**.37–**204**.50
generally, **30**.1–**30**.7
improvident persons, for, **210**.54–**210**.56
inheritance tax, and, **210**.3–**210**.7, **210**.64–**210**.71
intellectual property, **204**.72–**204**.74
interest and income, **32**.1–**32**.33, **210**.8
meaning, **55**.4

Bequests – *contd*
minors, to, **30**.19–**30**.22, **210**.1, **210**.33–**210**.45
payment or delivery, **30**.30–**30**.43
personal chattels, of, **204**.1–**204**.27
refunding, **31**.6–**31**.21
republication of wills, and, **22**.4
stocks and shares, **30**.8–**30**.9, **204**.51–**204**.61

Bills of exchange
description of property, **64**.53

Blind testator
attestation clause, **222**.9
knowledge and approval, and, **5**.2
signature of wills, and, **11**.22

Blind witness
attestation, and, **12**.16

Blood relationship, donees with
children, **71**.2, **200**.28
cousins, **71**.4, **200**.33
grandchildren, **71**.3, **200**.28
grand-nephews and nieces, **71**.5
half-blood, **71**.1
nephews and nieces, **71**.5, **200**.33

Body of testator, disposal of
anatomical examination and research
  generally, **7**.34, **202**.9–**202**.12
  precedent, **202**.16
ascertainment of death, clause for, **202**.6
cremation, clause for, **202**.4
donor cards, **202**.8
expenses of carrying out directions, clause for, **202**.7
eye hospitals, **202**.14–**202**.15
generally, **7**.33, **202**.2
medical schools, **202**.9–**202**.12
necessary expense only, clause for, **202**.5
organ transplantation, **7**.34, **202**.13–**202**.15
place of burial and tombstone, clause for, **202**.3
therapeutic use
  generally, **202**.13–**202**.15
  precedent, **202**.16–**202**.17

Bona vacantia
total intestacy, and, **104**.10

Bonds
description of property, **64**.5
Bonus on insurance policy
generally, **61**.1
Books
description of property, **64**.6
gift of, **204**.30
***Boraston's case*, rule in**
vesting of remainders, and, **93**.11–**93**.15
Borrowing powers
precedent, **220**.69
Bounty
option to purchase, and, **92**.2
Burden of proof
revocation of will, and
destruction, **18**.24
intention, **18**.7
Burial wishes
generally, **7**.33, **202**.2
precedents, **202**.3
cremation, **202**.4
expenses of carrying out directions, **202**.7
necessary expense only, **202**.5
place of burial and tombstone, **202**.3
Business interests and property, gift of
administrative powers, and, **220**.66–**220**.68
annuity from shares, **205**.68
appointment of director, **205**.69
appointment of executors and trustees, **203**.44
description of property, **64**.7
disposable property, **7**.15
generally, **205**.1–**205**.3
inheritance tax
effect on dispositions, **205**.46–**205**.57
generally, **205**.4–**205**.16
payment by instalments, **205**.17–**205**.20
investment powers, and, **220**.34, **220**.66–**220**.68
land and buildings, **205**.41–**205**.45
Lloyd's underwriting business, **205**.61
Business interests and property, gift of – *contd*
partnership interests, **205**.26–**205**.28
plant and machinery, **205**.41–**205**.45
precedents
annuity from shares, **205**.68
appointment of director, **205**.69
assistance to acquire partnership share, **205**.65
bequest of business, **205**.58
bequest of business to trustees, **205**.59
Lloyd's underwriting business, **205**.61
payment of inheritance tax, **205**.62
share of partnership profits, **205**.64
succession to partnership, **205**.63
trustees' powers, **205**.70–**205**.79
trusts of net profits and sale proceeds, **205**.60
unquoted shares, **205**.66–**205**.67
share of partnership profits, **205**.64
sole traders, **205**.21–**205**.25
succession to partnership, **205**.63
trustees' powers
administrative, **220**.66–**220**.68
generally, **205**.70–**205**.79
trusts of net profits and sale proceeds, **205**.60
unquoted shares
precedents, **205**.66–**205**.67
preliminary note, **205**.29–**205**.40
Business property, wills disposing of
allocation of business and agricultural relief, **233**.2–**233**.7
nil-rate band gifts, and, **233**.8–**233**.10

Business property, wills disposing of – *contd*
one or some of testator's children carrying on business, **233**.12
precedents, **233**.13–**233**.51
private company shares, settlement with top-up legacy on nil-rate band discretionary trust, **233**.13–**233**.35
reciprocal will, spouses having acquired share capital of private trading company, **233**.26–**233**.35
sole trader, business given to sons with legacies to daughters, **233**.36–**233**.51
spouses or civil partners, factors relevant to wills of, **233**.11

C

Cancellation of will
revocation, and, **18**.25
Capacity to benefit
aliens, **9**.37
animals, **9**.31
attesting witnesses, **9**.3–**9**.12
charities, **9**.28
clubs, **9**.35
companies, **9**.33
corporations, **9**.32
criminals, **9**.44
dead beneficiaries, **9**.2
discrimination, and, **9**.38
fertilisation, children born by way of, **9**.27
fraud, **9**.23
graves, **9**.29–**9**.30
illegitimate children, **9**.24–**9**.26
institutions, **9**.35
introduction, **9**.1
local authorities, **9**.34
mentally disordered persons, **9**.45
minors, **9**.39–**9**.43
religious disabilities, **9**.36
societies, **9**.35
soundness of mind, and, **9**.45
Capacity to benefit – *contd*
trade unions, **9**.35
undue influence, **9**.23
unlawful killing, **9**.13–**9**.22
Capacity to make will
aliens, **4**.5
cessation of incapacity to make will, and, **4**.4
criminals, **4**.6
domicile, and, **4**.2, **200**.7
foreign element wills, and, **24**.7, **200**.8
generally, **4**.1, **200**.2–**200**.8
married women, **4**.8
mentally disordered person
examples of exercise of jurisdiction, **4**.24
guidelines as to exercise of jurisdiction, **4**.23
jurisdiction of court, **4**.22
Practice Direction, **4**.25
minors, **4**.7
removal of incapacity to make will, and, **4**.4
soundness of mind. *See* **Soundness of mind**
supervening incapacity to make will, and, **4**.3
Capita, distribution per
generally, **87**.1–**87**.4
Capital gains tax (CGT)
absolute interests or trust interests, treatment of, **200**.127
advancement powers, and, **242**.3
appointment powers, and, **242**.3, **213**.11
appropriations, and, **220**.72
death, and, **200**.39
discretionary distribution of chattels, and, **204**.23–**204**.25
discretionary trusts, and, **218**.27–**218**.28
minors, trusts for, **217**.3
options to purchase property, **209**.4
person with disability, wills providing for, **226**.6–**226**.7
rates, **200**.40

Capital gains tax (CGT) – *contd*
variation of beneficial interests, and, **241**.17
Capriciousness
construction of wills, and, **51**.7–**51**.8
Car
description of property, **64**.8
Carrying on business
conditions, and, **35**.49
powers, **205**.25, **233**.12
precedent, **205**.70
Cash, gift of
description of property, **64**.38
precedent, **204**.81
Cemeteries, gifts for upkeep of
capacity to benefit, **9**.29–**9**.30
churchyards, **202**.20
graves, **202**.19
local authority cemeteries, **202**.22–**202**.27
perpetual gifts from charity to charity, **202**.28
precedents, **202**.31–**202**.35
reverter gifts, **202**.29
value of gifts, **202**.30
Certainty of obligation
contracts relating to wills, and, **3**.3–**3**.4
Certainty of subject-matter
contracts relating to wills, and, **3**.2
creation of interests by will, and, **8**.8
Cessation of incapacity
capacity to make will, and, **4**.4
Cesser of right to prove
executors, of, **25**.11
Chain of office
description of property, **64**.3
Change of circumstances
inaccuracy of description, and, **58**.11
Change of nature of property
corporate act, by, **41**.14
partnership shares, in, **41**.15
statute, under, **41**.13
Change of words
'and' into 'or', **56**.7–**56**.9
generally, **52**.4
Change of words – *contd*
'or' into 'and', **56**.1–**56**.6
Changes in circumstances or wishes
codicils. *See* **Codicils**
Changes in law
codicils. *See* **Codicils**
Charge on rents and profits
unlimited gifts of income, and, **62**.2
Charging powers
banks, **203**.31
limits, **221**.45
nature, **221**.44
precedents, **203**.32–**203**.35, **221**.49–**221**.52
professional trustees providing lay services, **221**.43
statutory and express powers, **221**.42
trust corporations, **203**.30, **221**.47–**221**.48
trustee in professional capacity, **221**.46
Charitable gifts
construction of
amalgamated institutions, **103**.9
associated charities, **103**.2
ceased to exist, **103**.3
charity companies, **103**.4
closing of branch of society, **103**.8
effect of legislation, **103**.10
failure of intention, **103**.6
illegality of purpose, **103**.11
impossibility of purpose, **103**.11
introduction, **103**.1
uncertain description of charity, **103**.7
unincorporated companies, **103**.5
wrongly named charity, **103**.3
delegation of power to determine objects, and, **103**.17
discrimination, and, **103**.12
exhausted income, and, **103**.15
generally, **212**.1–**212**.2
gift of freehold land, and, **206**.26

Charitable gifts – *contd*
lapse
generally, **47**.10
precedent, **212**.31
precedents, **212**.3–**212**.31
surplus income, of
donee charged with payment, to, **103**.14
generally, **103**.13
unexhausted income, and, **103**.16
Charitable purposes
advancement
education, of, **102**.8
religion, of, **102**.9
aged, **102**.5
animals, **102**.13
beneficial to community, **102**.10
charges for services, **102**.18/
community, **102**.10
education, **102**.8
general nature pre-Charities Act 2006, **102**.4
impotence, **102**.6
introduction, **102**.1
meaning, **102**.3
parish work, **102**.17
political purposes, **102**.11
poor
employees, **102**.15
members, **102**.16
relations, **102**.14
poverty, **102**.7
recreation, **102**.12
relief
aged, of, **102**.5
impotent, of, **102**.6
poor persons, of, **102**.14–**102**.16
poverty, of, **102**.7
religion, **102**.9
Charities
accumulations, and, **102**.28
ademption, and, **102**.21
administration and regulation, **103**.23
capacity to benefit, **9**.28
charitable purposes
generally, **102**.4–**102**.18
See also **Charitable purposes**
creation of trust, **102**.19–**102**.25
Charities – *contd*
cy-près doctrine, **103**.18–**103**.22
gifts
construction, **103**.1–**103**.17
lapse, **47**.10
introduction, **102**.1
meaning, **102**.2–**102**.3
rule against perpetuities, and
accumulations, **102**.28
generally, **102**.26
undisposed-of interests, **102**.27
undisposed-of interests, and, **102**.27
Charities Act 1993
general provisions, **246**.101
Charity companies
charitable gifts, and, **103**.4
Chattels
gifts of
collections, **204**.5
consumed in use for successive interests
assent, **8**.5
generally, **8**.4
discretionary distribution
generally, **204**.7–**204**.8
inheritance tax, **204**.9–**204**.10
expenses of transport, **204**.4
generally, **204**.2–**204**.3
not consumed in use for successive interests
assent, **8**.5
generally, **8**.3
precedents, **204**.15 –**204**.34
conditionally exempt gift, **204**.28
clothing, **204**.32
daughter, to, **204**.21–**204**.22
distribution in accordance with testator's wishes, **204**.23
house, **204**.26
letters and papers, **204**.32
library, **204**.30
life interest trusts, **204**.24
nation, gift of work of art to, **204**.29
reference to existing document, **204**.34

Chattels – *contd*
gifts of – *contd*
precedents, **204**.15 –**204**.34 – *contd*
right of selection, **204**.6
short-term discretionary trusts, **204**.25
sports equipment, **204**.31
transport expenses, **204**.27
wife, to, **204**.15–**204**.21
selection, right of
preliminary note, **204**.6
wife, by, **204**.20–**204**.21
transport expenses
precedent, **204**.27
preliminary note, **204**.4
meaning of., **64**.9
personal
description of property, **64**.44
gifts of. *See* gifts, *above*
inheritance tax
discretionary distribution, **204**.9–**204**.10
items of artistic or historic interest given to individuals, **204**.11–**204**.13
items of artistic or historic interest given to museums, **204**.14
meaning, **64**.44
***Chesterfield's Trusts*, rule in**
generally, **38**.22–**38**.23, **214**.35–**214**.38
precedents, excluding, **214**.40–**214**.42
Child-bearing women
description of donees, and, **66**.3
Child of the family
inheritance provision, and
additional considerations, **105**.28
applicant, as, **105**.17
discretion, **105**.208–**105**.25
Childless couples, wills for
default gifts to charity, **231**.4
generally, **231**.1
gifts to take effect after both deaths, **231**.2
gifts to take effect after one death only, **231**.7–**231**.8
Childless couples, wills for – *contd*
inheritance tax, **231**.5
nephews and nieces, gifts to, **231**.9
precedents,
contingent gift of entire estate with alternative gift to nephews and nieces, **231**.14–**231**.29
legacy by survivor to relatives of first to die, **231**.30–**231**.40
life interest for survivor with different ultimate trusts, **231**.41–**231**.51
simple reciprocal wills, **231**.10–**231**.13
survivorship contingencies, **231**.6–**231**.8
Childless individuals, wills for
generally, **232**.1
nephews and nieces with charitable and other legacies to, **232**.64–**232**.79
parents and siblings on discretionary trusts, to, **232**.15–**232**.26
siblings, to
older person for life with remainder to their children, by, **232**.39–**232**.51
older person with substitution for those predeceasing, by, **232**.27–**232**.38
reciprocal wills with ultimate gift to charity, **231**.52–**231**.60
right of residence for sister with ultimate gift to nephews and charity, **231**.61–**231**.76
young person, by, **232**.2–**232**.14
unmarried sister with remainder to siblings, to, **232**.52–**232**.63
Children
accumulations, and, **95**.10

Children – *contd*
adoption, by
generally, **75**.1–**75**.9
illegitimacy, **72**.11
lapse, **47**.16
age of majority, **200**.27
annuities, and, **33**.18
capacity to benefit, **9**.39–**9**.43
capacity to make will, and, **4**.7
charitable purposes, and, **102**.8
description of donees. *See* **Description of donee**
election, and, **42**.14
executors, and, **25**.4
favouring relatives, and, **51**.9
gift of freehold land, and
precedent, **206**.17
preliminary note, **206**.4–**206**.5
illegitimate
capacity to benefit, **9**.24–**9**.26, **200**.32
generally, **72**.1–**72**.14, **200**.28–**200**.29
lapse, **47**.16
inheritance provision, and
additional considerations, **105**.28
applicant, as, **105**.16
child of the family, **105**.17
discretion, **105**.20–**105**.25
will drafting, and, **200**.34
legacies, and
generally, **30**.19–**30**.22
interest, **32**.18–**32**.27
precedents, **210**.33–**210**.45
legitimation, **72**.15–**72**.18, **200**.28–**200**.29
total intestacy, and
generally, **104**.6
statutory trusts, **104**.7
trustees, and, **27**.3
trusts for. *See* **Minors, trusts for**
Children Act 1989
amendments 1995, **244**.126
citation, **244**.120
commencement, **244**.120
definitions, **244**.118–**244**.119
general provisions
appointment of guardians, **244**.116–**244**.117
Children Act 1989 – *contd*
general provisions – *contd*
parental responsibility, **244**.113–**244**.116
residence orders, **244**.118
introductory note, **244**.112
schedules, **244**.120–**244**.123
Choses in action
disposable property, **7**.28
Church of England Board of Finance, gifts to
precedent, **212**.7
Church in Wales, gifts to
precedent, **212**.14
Churches, etc., gifts to
precedents,
Baptist Union, **212**.17
Church of England Board of Finance, to, **212**.7
Church in Wales, to, **212**.14
Congregational Federation, to, **212**.19
Free Christian Church, to, **212**.22–**212**.23
masses, for, **212**.13
Methodist Church, to, **212**.16
Presbyterian Church of Wales, to, **212**.20–**212**.21
religious purposes in a parish, for, **212**.10
Salvation Army, to, **212**.15
Sunday school prizes, for, **212**.11
Synagogue, to, **212**.24
United Reformed Church, to, **212**.18
United Synagogue, to, **212**.24
Unitarian Christian Church, to, **212**.22–**212**.23
vicar of church, to, **212**.8
Churchyards, gifts for upkeep of
capacity to benefit, **9**.29–**9**.30
churchyards, **202**.20
graves, **202**.19
local authority cemeteries, **202**.22–**202**.27
perpetual gifts from charity to charity, **202**.28
precedents, **202**.31–**202**.35
reverter gifts, **202**.29

Churchyards, gifts for upkeep of – *contd*
value of gifts, **202**.30
Civil partnership
appointment of civil partner as sole executor and trustee, **203**.8
dissolution or annulment, effect of, **42**.2–**42**.4
family provision orders, **105**.10–**105**.11, **105**.50
meaning, **244**.131
residence, rights of, **208**.42
revocation of will by, **17**.3
will in contemplation of
commencement, **201**.8, **201**.10
note, **201**.5
wills in favour of partner, introductory note, **200**.24–**200**.26
Civil Partnership Act 2004
general provisions, **244**.131–**244**.132
introductory note, **244**.130
schedule, **244**.133–**244**.134
Claiming bequests
conditions, and, **35**.48
Clarity of words
construction of wills, and, **52**.1
Class gifts
description of donees, and
alternative donees, **68**.6–**68**.8
child-bearing women, **66**.3
generally, **66**.1–**66**.2
introduction, **65**.4
real estate only, of, **66**.22–**66**.23
relevant classes, **66**.19–**66**.21
rules of convenience, **66**.4–**66**.18
gifts to individuals, and, **47**.32
lapse, **47**.29–**47**.35
meaning, **47**.31
rule against perpetuities, and
common law, at, **94**.21
generally, **94**.23–**94**.29
statute, under, **94**.22
time when class ascertained, **47**.34
vesting, **47**.35
Clause headings
precedent concerning, **202**.42
Clerical errors
rectification, and, **6**.2
Closing of branch of society
charitable gifts, and, **103**.8
Clothing
gift of personal chattels, and, **204**.32
Clubs
capacity to benefit, **9**.35
Codicils
ademption, and, **41**.3
changes in circumstances or wishes, precedents for
accounting for advance, **237**.13
alteration of legacies, **237**.21
alteration of trusts of settled share, **237**.15
appointment of guardian, **237**.23
divorce, **237**.18
increase in annuity, **237**.20
marriage settlement brought into hotchpot, **237**.14
protective trusts for insolvent child, **237**.22
reduction of estate, **237**.19
revival of will on remarriage, **237**.16
revocation of legacies, **237**.16
revocation of settlement, **237**.12
sale of specifically devised realty, **237**.17
substitution of executor and trustee, **237**.11
changes in law
adopted persons, as to, **237**.10
bereaved minor, ensuring trust as, **237**.25
capable of being dealt with by codicil, **237**.2–**237**.6
exclusion of provisions of TA 2000, **237**.28
imposition of actual value limit, **237**.31
increasing amount of legacy, **237**.30

Codicils – *contd*
changes in law – *contd*
nil-rate band allowance, carry-forward, **237**.3
nil-rate band legacy, revocation, **237**.24
revisions consequent to TLATA 1996, **237**.4–**237**.5, **237**.27
settled gift, substitution of absolute gift for, **237**.26
variation of appointment of guardian, **237**.29
construction, **20**.3
correcting errors, precedents for
clerical error in will, **237**.32
rendering validity to alterations, **237**.33
effect
confirmation of will, **20**.4
generally, **20**.3
revocation of intermediate codicil, **18**.15
execution, **20**.6
form, **20**.2
generally, **237**.1
gifts by, capacity to benefit, 9.5
introduction, **10**.19
republication
effect, **237**.7–**237**.10
precedent, **237**.34
revival of wills, and
generally, **21**.6
introduction, **20**.9
precedent, **237**.34
reference to will by date, **21**.7
revocation
generally, **20**.7
precedent, **237**.35
revocation of wills, and
generally, **18**.15
share of residue, **20**.5
use, **20**.1

Cohabitees
inheritance provision, and
additional considerations, **105**.27
applicant, as, **105**.14
discretion, **105**.20–**105**.25

Collections
gift of personal chattels, and, **204**.5

College fellowships, gifts to found
precedent, **212**.28

Commencement of will
expectation of civil partnership, **201**.5
expectation of marriage, 201.4
general words, 201.1
precedents
confining will to UK property, **201**.11–**201**.12
expectation of civil partnership, **201**.8, **201**.10
expectation of marriage, **201**.7, **201**.9
mirror will, **201**.14
mutual will, **201**.13
order of Court of Protection, **201**.15
ordinary form, **201**.6
revocation of appointment of guardian, **201**.3
revocation of previous will, **201**.2

Commorientes. *See also* **Survivorship conditions and clauses**
common law, **70**.1
fiscal implications, **219**.5–**219**.11
generally, **200**.17, **219**.1, **219**.12–**219**.13
inheritance tax, **219**.5–**219**.11
practical considerations, **219**.2–**219**.4
precedents, **219**.14–**219**.17
statute, **70**.2–**70**.4
statutory provision, **244**.58

Community benefit
charitable purposes, **102**.10

Companies
capacity to benefit, **9**.33
charitable gifts, and, **103**.4

Company shareholdings
investment powers, and, **220**.20

Compensation
description of property, **61**.1
election, and, **42**.6–**42**.7

Compound liabilities, power to
generally, **246**.13
Compulsory purchase, compensation for
generally, **61**.1
Conditional revocation of will
earlier will, **9**.6
evidence, **19**.6
generally, **19**.1
later will or codicil, **19**.2
Conditional will
extrinsic evidence, **57**.30
generally, **1**.5
Conditionally exempt gift
gift of personal chattels, and, **204**.28
Conditions
acquisition of dignity, against, **35**.47
alienation, against, **35**.37
behaviour of donee, **35**.45
carrying on business, for, **35**.49
claiming bequests, requiring, **35**.48
consent to marriage, for
generally, **35**.9–**35**.17
guardian, by, **35**.13
named person, by, **35**.12
nature, **35**.16
proof, **35**.17
trustee, by, **35**.13
disputing will, not to, **35**.38
effect of invalidity, **34**.17–**34**.20
estoppel, and, **43**.5
execute a release, to, **35**.51
exhibit of art, etc., requiring, **35**.53
generally, **34**.1–**34**.4
HM Forces, against entering, **35**.46
impossible
effect, **34**.8
generally, **34**.7
in terrorem, **34**.13–**34**.16
limitations, and, **34**.3
marriage, requiring
generally, **35**.7
solemnisation, by, **35**.34
miscellaneous, **35**.46–**35**.54
Conditions – *contd*
name and arms clause, **35**.39–**35**.44, **206**.27
performance of
enforcement, **34**.23
excuses for non-performance, **34**.24
substantial, **34**.21
time, **34**.22
perpetuity, against, **35**.52
public policy, against
acquisition of dignity, **35**.47
entering HM Forces, **35**.46
generally, **34**.12
restraint of marriage, **35**.1–**35**.6
relief against, **34**.25
religion, as to
Church of England, **35**.32
Jews, **35**.31
protestants, **35**.23
Roman Catholics, **35**.30
uncertainty, **35**.29
re-marriage, against, **35**.8
repugnant, **34**.5–**34**.6
residence, as to
discharge of, **35**.26
generally, **35**.18–**35**.28
ignorance of, **35**.27
involuntary cesser, **35**.20
provision of home, on, **35**.21
separation of parent and child, **35**.24
separation of spouses, **35**.23
uncertainty, **35**.22
voluntary cesser, **35**.20
restraint of marriage, in
class of persons, with, **35**.4
generally, **35**.2
introduction, **35**.1
particular person, with, **35**.6
particular religion, with person of, **35**.5
specified age, under, **35**.3
rule against perpetuity, offending, **35**.52
separation of parent and child, as to
generally, **35**.36
residence, **35**.24

Conditions – *contd*
separation of spouses, as to
generally, **35**.35
residence, **35**.23
series of gifts, and, **91**.6
settle property, to, **35**.50
solemnisation of marriage, requiring, **35**.34
trusts, and, **34**.4
uncertain, **34**.9–**34**.11
Conditions precedent
generally, **34**.2
in terrorem, **34**.15
vesting, and, **93**.3
Conditions subsequent
certainty, and, **34**.10
generally, **34**.2
in terrorem, **34**.14
Conflict of laws
construction of wills, and, **50**.19
Congregational Federation, gifts to
precedent, **212**.19
Consent
appropriation, and, **29**.12
Consent to marriage, conditions requiring
generally, **35**.9–**35**.17
guardian, by, **35**.13
named person, by, **35**.12
nature, **35**.16
proof, **35**.17
trustee, by, **35**.13
Consideration
variation of beneficial interests, and **241**.7
Construction of wills. ***See also under individual headings***
additional words, **52**.3
admissible evidence
ambiguities
surrounding circumstances, in light of, **57**.26
will, on face of, **57**.25
conditional will, **57**.30
deaths before 1983
ambiguities, **57**.20–**57**.22
general rule, **57**.8–**57**.11
identification of persons or things, **57**.12–**57**.19

Construction of wills – *contd*
admissible evidence – *contd*
difficulty in deciphering words, **57**.6
extrinsic evidence, **57**.23–**57**.27
foreign language will, **57**.6–**57**.7
general rule
ambiguities, **57**.25–**57**.26
introduction, **57**.23
limits, **57**.27
meaninglessness, **57**.24
introduction, **57**.1
meaninglessness, **57**.24
original will, **57**.5
probate copy, **57**.3–**57**.7
rebuttal of presumption, for, **57**.31–**57**.32
rectification, for, **57**.29
secret trusts, of, **57**.28
alterations in words, **52**.2
ambiguous words, **50**.4
application of rules, **50**.21–**50**.22
beneficial interests
absolute interests, **83**.1–**83**.5
accruer clauses, **90**.1–**90**.6
accumulations, **95**.1–**95**.14
alienation and forfeiture clause, **99**.1–**99**.10
concurrent gifts, **86**.1–**86**.8
conditional gifts, **91**.1–**91**.6
cumulative gifts, **88**.1–**88**.4
distribution, **87**.1–**87**.4
divesting, **96**.1–**96**.7
entailed interests, **84**.1–**84**.4
failure of issue, **98**.1–**98**.13
gift over on death, **97**.1–**97**.11
hotchpot clauses, **100**.1–**100**.7
implication, gifts by, **101**.1–**101**.14
joint tenancy, gifts of, **86**.1–**86**.8
life interests, **83**.6–**83**.7
option to purchase, **92**.1–**92**.6
per capita distribution, **87**.1–**87**.4
per stripes distribution, **87**.1–**87**.4
perpetuities, **94**.1–**94**.53

Construction of wills – *contd*
beneficial interests – *contd*
person and children, gifts to, **85**.1–**85**.3
person and issue, gifts to, **85**.4–**85**.5
quantity of interest, **82**.1–**82**.9
substituted gifts, **88**.1–**88**.4
successive interests, **89**.1–**89**.2
superadded powers, gifts with, **83**.8–**83**.20
tenancy in common, gifts of, **86**.1–**86**.8
vesting, **93**.1–**93**.45
capriciousness of will, **51**.7–**51**.8
change of words
'and' into 'or', **56**.7–**56**.9
generally, **52**.4
'or' into 'and', **56**.1–**56**.6
clarity of words, **52**.1
conflict of laws, **50**.19
context of words
generally, **54**.1–**54**.6
introduction, **50**.9–**50**.10
court of construction
duty, **49**.9
generally, **49**.6
ousting jurisdiction, **49**.8
cultural changes, **50**.14
description of donee. *See* **Description of donee**
description of property. *See* **Description of property**
effect to be given to each word, **50**.16–**50**.17
ejusdem generis rule, **54**.3
established rules, **50**.18–**50**.20
etymological meaning, **50**.13
extrinsic evidence
conditional will, **57**.30
deaths before 1983, **57**.8–**57**.22
extrinsic evidence, **57**.23–**57**.27
introduction, **57**.1
probate copy, **57**.3–**57**.7
rebuttal of presumption, for, **57**.31–**57**.32
rectification, for, **57**.29
secret trusts, of, **57**.28

Construction of wills – *contd*
falsa demonstratio, **58**.1–**58**.13
favouring relatives, **51**.9–**51**.12
foreign element wills, and
capacity, **24**.7
debts and gifts, **24**.9
election, **24**.10
governing law, **24**.6
immovable property, **24**.8
knowledge and approval, **24**.7
foreign law, **50**.20
futurity words, **54**.2
general principles
application of rules, **50**.21–**50**.22
effect to be given to each word, **50**.16–**50**.17
established rules, **50**.18–**50**.20
introduction, **50**.2–**50**.3
scope of will, **50**.4–**50**.5
usual meaning of word, **50**.6–**50**.15
whole will, intention collected from, **50**.2
grammatical rules, **50**.8
inaccuracy of description, **58**.1–**58**.13
inconsistency of words
generally, **52**.1–**52**.4
rejection, **52**.6
inference, **50**.5
insertion of words, **52**.3
intention of testator
ascertainment, **49**.2
collation from whole of will, **50**.1
introduction, **49**.1
questions involved, **49**.3
legal documents, **57**.2
legal words, **50**.7
legality of words, **51**.4–**51**.6
meaning of words
bequest, **55**.4
entitled, **55**.3
general rule, **55**.1–**55**.2
introduction, **50**.3
legacy, **55**.4
minority, **55**.5
testamentary expenses, **55**.7
unmarried, **55**.6

Construction of wills – *contd*
meaning of words – *contd*
usual, **50**.6–**50**.15
mistake, and, **5**.8
modern approach, **50**.1
necessity for grant, **49**.7
ordinary meaning, **50**.12
precedent case law, **50**.22
presumptions
against intestacy, **51**.1–**51**.3
favouring relatives, **51**.9–**51**.12
legality of words, **51**.4–**51**.6
rationality of will, **51**.7–**51**.8
unintended life interest, **51**.13
punctuation, **50**.15
rationality of will, **51**.7–**51**.8
recitals, and, **52**.11
rejection of words, **52**.6–**52**.11
repugnance of words, **52**.6
rule against perpetuities, **53**.7
rules
application, **50**.21–**50**.22
appropriate, **50**.18–**50**.20
compliance with, **49**.5
distinction, **49**.4
scope of will, **50**.4–**50**.5
statutory provisions, **244**.99–**244**.100
introductory note, **244**.94
schedule, **244**.111
transitional provisions, **244**.107
surplusage of words, **52**.6
surrounding circumstances, **50**.9–**50**.10
technical terms, **50**.11
technical words, **50**.7
transposition of words, **52**.5
uncertainty, gifts void for
donee, **53**.5
introduction, **53**.1–**53**.2
perpetuity rule, **53**.7
persons to whom fund be appointed, **53**.6
subject-matter of gift, **53**.4
types, **53**.3
unintended life interest, **51**.13
usual meaning of words
context, **50**.9–**50**.10
cultural changes, **50**.14

Construction of wills – *contd*
usual meaning of words – *contd*
etymological meaning, **50**.13
general rule, **50**.6
grammatical rules, **50**.8
legal words, **50**.7
ordinary meaning, **50**.12
punctuation, **50**.15
surrounding circumstances, **50**.9–**50**.10
technical terms, **50**.11
technical words, **50**.7
Consumable stores, gift of
precedent, **204**.36
preliminary note, **204**.35
Contents
description of property, **64**.10
Contents of wills. ***See also under individual headings***
annuities
abatement, **33**.35–**33**.45
commencement, **33**.11
creation, **33**.2–**33**.10
definition, **33**.1
duration, **33**.12–**33**.22
priority, **33**.33–**33**.34
source of money, **33**.23–**33**.32
tax-free, **33**.46–**33**.47
appropriation
common law powers, **29**.1–**29**.16
statutory powers, **29**.17–**29**.24
conditions
alienation, against, **35**.37
behaviour of donee, **35**.45
consent to marriage, for, **35**.9–**35**.17
disputing will, not to, **35**.38
effect of invalidity, **34**.17–**34**.20
generally, **34**.1–**34**.4
impossible, **34**.7–**34**.8
in terrorem, **34**.13–**34**.16
miscellaneous, **35**.46–**35**.54
name and arms clause, **35**.39–**35**.44
performance of, **34**.21–**34**.24
public policy, **34**.12
relief against, **34**.25
religion, as to, **35**.29–**35**.34

Contents of wills – *contd*
conditions – *contd*
repugnant, **34**.5–**34**.6
residence, as to, **35**.18–**35**.28
restraint of marriage, in, **35**.1–**35**.8
separation of parent and child, as to, **35**.36
separation of spouses, as to, **35**.35
uncertain, **34**.9–**34**.11
conversion, **37**.1–**37**.9
exercise of powers of appointment
general powers, **39**.2–**39**.15
hybrid powers, **39**.31
introduction, **39**.1
miscellaneous matters, **40**.1–**40**.21
special powers, **39**.16–**39**.30
legacies
abatement, **31**.1–**31**.5
debtor, to, **30**.10–**30**.13
employees, to, **30**.23–**30**.29
executor, to, **30**.14–**30**.18
generally, **30**.1–**30**.7
interest and income, **32**.1–**32**.33
minors, to, **30**.19–**30**.22
payment or delivery, **30**.30–**30**.43
refunding, **31**.6–**31**.21
stocks and shares, **30**.8–**30**.9
residuary gifts
Allhusen v. Whittell, rule in, **38**.26
Chesterfield's Trusts, rule in, **38**.22–**38**.23
failure of share, **38**.13–**38**.14
Howe v. Dartmouth rule, **38**.17–**38**.28
relevant property, **38**.1–**38**.2
residuary legatee's rights, **38**.15–**38**.16
words required to make, **38**.3–**38**.12
secret trusts
absolute gifts, **36**.2–**36**.9
indefinite trust gifts, **36**.10–**36**.13

Contents of wills – *contd*
secret trusts – *contd*
introduction, **36**.1
Context of words
description of donee, **54**.3
effect, **50**.10
ejusdem generis rule, **54**.6
futurity, of, **54**.2
generally, **54**.1–**54**.4
introduction, **50**.9
same words in different parts of will, **54**.5
Contingent event
survivorship, and, **67**.3
vesting, and, **93**.5–**93**.8
Contingent interests
disposable property, **7**.20
Contingent legacies
appropriation, and, **29**.3–**29**.4
delivery, and, **30**.33
gift of leasehold land, and, **207**.21
interest and income, and, **32**.3
lapse, **47**.18
precedents
simple gifts, **215**.4–**215**.5
pecuniary legacies, **210**.46–**210**.50
predeceasing child, **47**.18
Contingent preference dividend
generally, **61**.1
Contract relating to wills
ante-nuptial agreement, and, **3**.5
ascertainable gift, **3**.2
certainty
obligation, of, **3**.3–**3**.4
subject-matter, of, **3**.2
disposition of property, **3**.8
enforcement, **3**.6
exercise of power in particular way
generally, **3**.14
special power, **3**.15
formalities
generally, **3**.3
statutory requirements, **3**.4
generally, **3**.1
inheritance tax, **3**.7
insolvency, **3**.9
intestacy, **3**.11

Contract relating to wills – *contd*
lapse, **3**.10
mutual wills
effect of first to die abiding, **2**.8
effect of first to die not abiding, 2.7
generally, 2.5
precedent, 201.13
proof, 2.6
obligation, certainty of, **3**.3–**3**.4
proprietary estoppel, and, **3**.1
revocation, **3**.13
subject-matter, certainty of, **3**.2
Contrary intention
description of property, **59**.3
Conversion
ademption, and, **37**.9
date, **37**.6
effect, **37**.5
express direction, **37**.2
failure of purpose, **37**.7
generally, **37**.1
implied, **37**.3
reconversion, **37**.8
request of specified person, at, **37**.4
Co-owned property
disposable property, **7**.31
Copyrights, gift of
generally, **61**.1
precedents, **204**.72–**204**.73
Corporations
appointment of executors and trustees, as
note, **203**.2, **203**.28–**203**.31
precedents, **203**.32–**203**.35
capacity to benefit, **9**.32
executors, and, **25**.6
Correction of errors
precedents
clerical error in will, **237**.32
rendering validity to alterations, **237**.33
rectification, and, **6**.2
Cousins
description of donees, and, **71**.4, **200**.33
County
description of property, **63**.2
Court of construction
duty, **49**.9
generally, **49**.6
ousting jurisdiction, **49**.8
Creation of interests by will
certainty of subject-matter, **8**.8
form, **8**.2
gifts of chattels consumed in use for successive interests
assent, **8**.5
generally, **8**.4
gifts of chattels not consumed in use for successive interests
assent, **8**.5
generally, **8**.3
introduction, **8**.1
option to purchase property, **8**.6, **209**.1–**209**.5
right of selection of one or more properties, **8**.7, **204**.6
Creditors, legacies to
generally, **210**.2
precedents, **210**.28–**210**.32
presumption, **210**.29
Cremation
disposal of body, and, **202**.4
Criminals
capacity to benefit, **9**.44
capacity to make will, **4**.6
Crown
total intestacy, and, **104**.10
Cultural changes
usual meaning of words, effect on, **50**.14
Currency of legacy
generally, **30**.43
interest on legacies, and, **32**.33
precedents, **210**.77–**210**.78
Custodians, employment of
generally, **246**.149–**246**.152
review of and liability for, **246**.153–**246**.155
supplementary, **246**.156–**246**.159
Custody of wills
generally, **10**.20, **200**.46
Customary mourning
legacy for purchase of, **210**.79
Cutting down
clear gifts, and, **82**.2

***Cy-près* doctrine**
charities, and, **103**.18–**103**.21
successive interests, and, **89**.2

D

Daughter
gift of personal chattels to, **204**.21–**204**.22
Dead beneficiaries
capacity to benefit, **9**.2
Deaf and dumb testator
knowledge and approval, and, **5**.2
Dead stock, gift of
precedent, **204**.79
Death of tenant for life
settled land, and, **26**.4
Debentures
description of property, **64**.11
Debtors, legacies to
abatement, **31**.2
generally, **30**.10–**30**.13, **210**.2
precedents, **210**.28–**210**.32
Debts
description of property **64**.12, **64**.39
foreign element wills, and, **24**.9
precedents for gifts of, **204**.62–**204**.68
satisfaction by legacy, and
child from parent, to, **44**.17
generally, **44**.15
parol evidence, **44**.16
Deeds
admissibility as will, and, **10**.5
Deferred legacies
precedents, **210**.20–**210**.24
Definition of will
conditionality, **1**.5
distinguishing features, **1**.2
generally, **1**.1
other documents, **1**.3
revocability, **1**.4
Delegation
investment powers, and, **220**.35–**220**.39
management of land, and, **220**.54–**220**.58
power of appointment, and, **40**.5
Delegation – *contd*
statutory provision, **246**.23
trustees, and, **27**.9
Delivery of legacies
contingent legacies, **30**.33
generally, **30**.30–**30**.43
specific legacies, **30**.34
Delusions of mind
generally, **4**.15
religious belief, **4**.16
Demonstrative legacies
abatement, and, **31**.3
generally, **30**.6
interest and income, and, **32**.4–**32**.17
precedent, **210**.74
Dependants
description of donees, **79**.3
Dependent relative revocation
evidence, **19**.6
examples, **19**.4
generally, **19**.3
Deposit of wills
generally, **10**.20
introductory note, **200**.47
Derivative title
election, and, **42**.8
Descendants
children, **74**.8–**74**.9
issue, **76**.1–**76**.6
Description, designation by
inaccuracy of description, **58**.9
Description of donee. *See also* **Beneficiaries**
adopted children
generally, **75**.1–**75**.9
illegitimacy, **72**.11
alternative, in
children, **68**.9
class gifts, **68**.6–**68**.8
concurrent interests, **68**.13
conditions, **68**.11
generally, **68**.1–**68**.15
introduction, **65**.5
parents and issue, **68**.10
substituted gifts, **68**.2
artificial insemination, children born by
generally, **74**.3–**74**.5
introduction, **72**.18

Description of donee – *contd*
begotten children, **81**.2
blood relationship, by
children, **71**.2
cousins, **71**.4
grandchildren, **71**.3
grand-nephews and nieces, **71**.5
half-blood, **71**.1
nephews and nieces, **71**.5
child-bearing women, **66**.3
children
adoption, by, **75**.1–**75**.9
alternative donees, **68**.9
begotten, **81**.2
blood relationship, **71**.2
en ventre sa mere, **73**.1–**73**.2
fertilisation, by, **74**.3–**74**.5
first son, **81**.3
generally, **74**.1–**74**.9
illegitimacy, **72**.1–**72**.14
issue, as, **76**.3
legitimation, by, **72**.15–**72**.18
meaning, **74**.1
class gifts
alternative donees, **68**.6–**68**.8
child-bearing women, **66**.3
generally, **66**.1–**66**.2
introduction, **65**.4
real estate only, of, **66**.22–**66**.23
relevant classes, **66**.19–**66**.21
rules of convenience, **66**.4–**66**.18
commorientes
common law, **70**.1
statute, **70**.2–**70**.4
context of words
class gifts, **66**.1
generally, **54**.3
contingency, and, **93**.5
cousins, **71**.4
dependants, **79**.3
descendants
children, **74**.8–**74**.9
issue, **76**.1–**76**.6
drafting points, **200**.28–**200**.31
eldest son, **81**.3
employees, **81**.6
en ventre sa mere, **73**.1–**73**.2

Description of donee – *contd*
family
dependants, **79**.3
generally, **79**.1
meaning, **79**.2
first or eldest son, **81**.3
former wife, 80.3
gender recognition, 81.1, 200.28
grandchildren
blood relationship, **71**.3
illegitimacy, **72**.6
grand-nephews and nieces, **71**.5
half-blood relatives, **71**.1
heirs
generally, **78**.1–**78**.7
living person, of, **78**.2
particular character, of, **78**.3
heirs and assigns, **78**.7
heirs and successors, **78**.6
holders of office, **81**.5
husband, **80**.7
illegitimate children
common law, **72**.2–**72**.9
introduction, **72**.1
legitimation, **72**.15–**72**.18
statute, **72**.10–**72**.14
in vitro fertilisation, children born by
generally, **74**.3–**74**.5
introduction, **72**.18
introduction, **54**.3
issue, **76**.1–**76**.6
legitimated children, **72**.15–**72**.18
male descendants
children, **74**.9
issue, **76**.5
nearest relations, **79**.5
nephews and nieces, **71**.5
next of kin
ascertainment of class, **77**.3–**77**.4
excluded persons, **77**.6
executors' discretion, by, **77**.7
generally, **77**.1
rules of distribution, **77**.2
shares, **77**.5
number, by, **69**.1–**69**.2
office holder, **81**.5
offspring, **76**.6
protestants, **81**.4

Description of donee – *contd*
relations, **79**.4–**79**.6
representatives, **79**.7
spouse, **80**.8
surviving spouse, **80**.5
survivors
contingent event, **67**.3
divesting clause, **67**.7
generally, **67**.1–**67**.8
gift over to others, **67**.6
introduction, **65**.5
stirpital, **67**.5
time for ascertainment, **67**.2
time for ascertaining donees
alternative donees, **65**.6
class of persons, **65**.4
generally, **65**.1
groups of individuals, **65**.3
individuals, **65**.2
survivors, **65**.5
widow, **80**.4
wife
divorce, and, **80**.3
invalid marriage, in, **80**.6
subsequent marriage, by, **80**.1
surviving spouse, **80**.5
widowhood, during, **80**.2
will drafting, **200**.30–**200**.31
words descriptive of relationship, **200**.28–**200**.29
younger children, **81**.3
Description of property
accessories, and, **61**.1
annuities, **64**.1
appurtenances, **64**.2
bank account, money in, **64**.37
belongings, **64**.4
bills of exchange, **64**.53
bonds, **64**.5
books, **64**.6
business, **64**.7
car, **64**.8
cash, **64**.38
chain of office, **64**.3
chattels
generally, **64**.9
personal, **64**.44
contents, **64**.10
contrary intention, and, **59**.3
debentures, **64**.11
Description of property – *contd*
debts, **64**.12, **64**.39
devise, **64**.13
dividends, **64**.14
domestic articles, **64**.3
drawings, **64**.3
effects
generally, **64**.15
personal effects, **64**.18
personalty, **64**.17
realty, **64**.16
estate, **64**.19
farm, **64**.20
farm stock, **64**.20
fixtures, **64**.21
freeholds, **64**.22
funds, **64**.23
furniture, **64**.24, **64**.27
generally, **60**.1–**60**.2
generic gifts, and, **59**.2
goods, **64**.25
house, **64**.26
household furniture, **64**.27
household goods, **64**.28
inaccurate description, and, **63**.1
insurance policies, **64**.29
investments, **64**.30
jewellery, **64**.31
land
general devises, **64**.32
tenements, **64**.33
locality, by
county, **63**.2
elsewhere, meaning, **63**.6
estate, **63**.5
generally, **63**.1
occupation, **63**.7
parish, **63**.3
street, **63**.4
messuage, **64**.34
money
bank, at, **64**.37
debts, **64**.39
cash, **64**.38
generally, **64**.35
ready money, **64**.40
wide meaning, **64**.36
money due or owing, **64**.39
motor car, **64**.8, **64**.41
movables, **64**.42

Description of property – *contd*
National Savings Certificates, **64**.58
ornaments, **64**.3
partnership, **64**.43
personal chattels, **64**.44
personal effects, **64**.18
personal estate, **64**.45
pictures, **64**.46
plants, **64**.3
plate, **64**.47
possessions, **64**.48
premises, **64**.49
presents, **64**.50
promissory notes
bonds, and, **64**.5
securities, and, **64**.53
property, **64**.51
real estate, **64**.52
securities, **64**.53
shares, **64**.54
source, by, **63**.8
sporting equipment, **64**.55
stamps, **64**.56
stock, **64**.57
tenements, **64**.33
tenure, by, **63**.9
time of construction, **59**.1–**59**.3
unlimited gifts of income
charge on rents and profits, **62**.2
generally, **62**.1
rent of let property, **62**.4
until marriage, **62**.3
vertu, articles of, **64**.3
war loans and bonds, **64**.58

Destruction, revocation by
burden of proof, **18**.31
codicils, and, **18**.24
duplicate, of, **18**.19
evidence, **18**.26
extent of destruction
generally, **18**.22
partial, **18**.23
foreign element wills, and, **23**.14
incomplete, **18**.20
intention
evidence, **18**.18
generally, **18**.17
presumption, **18**.26–**18**.29

Destruction, revocation by – *contd*
introduction, **18**.17
part, in, **18**.23
presumption of intention
mutilation of will, **18**.27
non-availability, **18**.28
rebuttal of, **18**.29
stranger, by, **18**.21

Devise
description of property, **64**.13

Direction of testator, signature affixed by
attestation, and, **13**.4
precedent, **222**.8

Directions
maintenance, as to, **93**.31–**93**.39
payment, as to, **93**.26–**93**.30
payment of debts, as to, **39**.29

Disability, wills providing for person with
capital gains tax, **226**.6–**226**.7
generally, **226**.1
husband and wife with disabled child and other children
notes to precedent, **226**.13–**226**.21
precedent, **226**.22–**226**.56
income tax, **226**.8
inheritance tax, **226**.3–**226**.5
spouse with mental disorder
note to precedent, **226**.57
precedent, **226**.58–**226**.71
state benefits, **226**.2
vulnerable, trusts for, **226**.9–**226**.12

Disclaimer
beneficial interests, of
effect, **46**.5
generally, **46**.1–**46**.2, **241**.16
onerous property, **46**.3
precedents
gifts, **241**.22–**241**.23
life interest, **241**.24
partial disclaimer, **219**.30
retraction, **46**.4
tax, and, **46**.6
guardians, and, **28**.7
power of appointment, and, **40**.12

Disclaimer – *contd*
precedents
appointment of new trustee, **239**.5
long form, **239**.3
short form, **239**.4
preliminary note, **239**.1
trustees, and, **27**.6
Discretion
inheritance provision, and
additional considerations, **105**.26–**105**.28
financial position of parties, **105**.22
generally, **105**.21
introduction, **105**.20
reasonableness of provision, **105**.23
testator's reasons, **105**.25
testator's state of mind, **105**.24
named person, by, **82**.8
Discretionary grant
settled land, and, **26**.5
Discretionary trusts
accumulation and maintenance
extended provisions, **218**.74–**218**.78
income tax and, **218**.67
inheritance tax and, **218**.69–**218**.70
precedents, **218**.79–**218**.86
Trustee Act 1925, section 31, commentary on, **218**.43–**218**.78. *See also* **Maintenance**
advancement
capital gains tax, and, **218**.102–**218**.103
inheritance tax and, **218**.101
precedents, **218**.104–**218**.108
Trustee Act 1925, section 32, commentary on, **218**.87–**218**.103
capital gains tax, **218**.27–**218**.28
delegation of power of testamentary disposition, and, **218**.3
enjoyment in kind
note, **218**.109
precedents, **218**.110–**218**.112

Discretionary trusts – *contd*
exercise of powers, **218**.117–**218**.118
generally, **218**.1–**218**.2
income tax, **218**.29–**218**.32
inheritance tax
calculation of rate of charge, **218**.11–**218**.14
charge to tax, **218**.8–**218**.10
married couples or civil partners, wills of, **200**.135
nil-rate band
carry-forward, **220**.75, **227**.4, **237**.3
continuing use of, **200**.130
debt or charge schemes, **218**.19–**218**.23
simple, **218**.16–**218**.18
no spouse or civil partner exemption, **218**.24–**218**.25
private company shares, settlement of, **233**.13–**233**.25
tax advantages, **218**.6–**218**.7
trusts created by will, **218**.15
two-year (ITA s 144) trusts, **200**.133, **218**.26, **242**.4
introductory note, **200**.18
loans to beneficiaries, **218**.113–**218**.116
maintenance
extended provisions, **218**.74–**218**.78
income tax and, **218**.67
inheritance tax and, **218**.69–**218**.70
precedents, **218**.79–**218**.86
Trustee Act 1925, section 31, commentary on, **218**.43–**218**.78. *See also* **Maintenance**
powers of appointment, and
capital gains tax, and, **242**.3
generally, **242**.1
inheritance tax, and, **242**.2
precedents, **242**.7–**242**.10
stamp duty, and, **242**.6
stamp duty land tax, **242**.6

Discretionary trusts – *contd*
powers of appointment, and – *contd*
two-year (ITA s 144) trusts, and, **242**.4–**242**.5
precedents
advancement, **218**.104–**218**.108
enjoyment in kind, **218**.110–**218**.112
exercise and release of powers, **218**.117–**218**.119
generally, **218**.33–**218**.36
loans to beneficiaries, **218**.113–**218**.116
maintenance, **218**.79–**218**.86
powers, **218**.37–**218**.42
release of powers, **218**.119
residue, of, for grandchildren, **230**.45–**230**.73
trustees as objects, **218**.4–**218**.5
two-year trusts
generally, **218**.26, **225**.83–**225**.91
precedent, **225**.92–**225**.109

Discrimination
capacity to benefit, and, **9**.38

Disposable property
agreements to restrict, and, **7**.32
agricultural tenancies, **7**.5
body of testator
anatomical examination, **7**.34
generally, **7**.33
transplantation, **7**.34
burial wishes, **7**.33
co-owned property, **7**.31
entailed interests, **7**.2
equitable interests in property
agreements for purchase, **7**.27
choses in action, **7**.28
contingent interests, **7**.20
emblements, **7**.25
estates *pur autre vie*, **7**.19
future interests, **7**.20
generally, **7**.18
gift under will of another, **7**.22
incorporeal heriditaments, **7**.26
leaseholds, **7**.23
possessory title, **7**.30
rent, **7**.24
rights of action, **7**.29

Disposable property – *contd*
equitable interests in property – *contd*
rights of entry, **7**.21
sale proceeds, **7**.27
funeral wishes, **7**.33
generally, **7**.1
insurance policies, **7**.12
joint tenancies, **7**.3
mortgage estates, **7**.16
nomination
friendly society accounts, **7**.10
generally, **7**.9
insurance policies, **7**.12
pension schemes, **7**.13
savings bank accounts, **7**.11
partnership interests, **7**.15
pension schemes, **7**.13
property not belonging to testator, **7**.17
shares in company, **7**.14
statutory tenancies, **7**.4
trust property purchased by trustee, **7**.7
trusts estates, **7**.6
voidable transactions, **7**.8

Disposal of body of testator
anatomical examination and research, for
generally, **7**.34, **202**.9–**202**.12
precedent, **202**.16
ascertainment of death, clause for, **202**.6
cremation, clause for, **202**.4
donor cards, **202**.8
expenses of carrying out directions, clause for, **202**.7
eye hospitals, **202**.14–**202**.15
generally, **7**.33, **202**.2
medical schools, **202**.9–**202**.12
necessary expense only, clause for, **202**.5
organ transplantation
generally, **7**.34, **202**.13–**202**.15
place of burial and tombstone, clause for, **202**.3
therapeutic use
generally, **202**.13–**202**.15
precedent, **202**.16–**202**.17

Disposal of land
settled land, and, **26**.9

Disposition of property
contracts relating to wills, and, **3**.8
other than by will, **1**.9
Dispositive powers created by will, exercise of
authorisation, **242**.1
capital gains tax, and, **242**.3
generally, **242**.1
inheritance tax consequences, **242**.2
precedents
advancement, **242**.17–**242**.20
appointment, **242**.7–**242**.16
stamp duty, **242**.6
stamp duty land tax, **242**.6
two-year (ITA s 144) trusts
capital gains tax, **242**.5
inheritance tax, **200**.133, **242**.4–**242**.4
Disputing will
conditions, and, **35**.38
Dissolution of marriage or civil partnership
failure of gifts on, **47**.2–**47**.4
Distinguishing features of a will
generally, **1**.2–**1**.3
Distribution
generally, **87**.1–**87**.4
Divesting clause
generally, **96**.1–**96**.7
survivorship, and, **67**.7
Divorce
failure of gifts, and, **47**.2–**47**.4
inheritance provision, and, **105**.50
survivorship conditions, and, **224**.16–**224**.23
Domicile
capacity to make will, and, **4**.2
foreign element wills, and, **23**.2
inheritance provision, and, **105**.7
Donatio mortis causa
generally, **1**.15
Donees, description of. ***See* Description of donee**
Donor cards
disposal of body, and, **202**.8
Double death variations
variation of beneficial interests, and, **241**.14
Drawings
description of property, **64**.3
Drunkenness
soundness of mind, and, **4**.19
Dry pen
signature of will with, **11**.18
Due execution, presumption of
absence of attestation clause, and, **13**.2
general rule, **13**.1
generally, **200**.44
rebuttal of, **13**.3
signature affixed by direction of testator, **13**.4
Dumb testator
knowledge and approval, and, **5**.2
attestation clause for deaf and dumb testator, **222**.10
Duplicate will
revocation by destruction, and, **18**.19
Duty of care
investment powers, and, **220**.15
making of will, and
introduction, **1**.14
rectification, and, **6**.4
trustee, and
generally, **27**.8
statutory provisions, **246**.132–**246**.134

E

Eccentricity
soundness of mind, and, **4**.18
Education of children
See also **Maintenance**
annuities, and, **33**.18
charitable purposes, **102**.8
Effects, meaning of
generally, **64**.15
personal effects, **64**.18
personalty, **64**.17
realty, **64**.16
***Ejusdem generis* rule**
context of words, and, **54**.6

Ejusdem generis **rule** – *contd*
residuary gifts, and, **38**.10
satisfaction, and, **44**.11
Eldest son
description of donee, **81**.3
Election
access to information, **42**.9
compensation, **42**.6–**42**.7
derivative title, under, **42**.8
exercise of power of appointment, and, **42**.4
foreign element wills, and
generally, **42**.15
introduction, **24**.10
generally, **42**.1–**42**.4
implication, by, **42**.12
intention to dispose, **42**.5
minors, and, **42**.14
mutual obligation, and, **42**.16
person of unsound mind, by, **42**.13
satisfaction, and, **44**.7
time limits, **42**.11
Emblements
disposable property, **7**.25
Emergency, wills for use in
note, **223**.1
precedents, **223**.2–**223**.13
Employees, legacies to
description of donees, **81**.6
generally, **30**.23–**30**.29
note, **210**.57
precedents, **210**.58–**210**.63
En ventre sa mere
description of donees, and, **73**.1–**73**.2
lapse of gift to child, **47**.17
Enjoyment in kind. *See also* **Residence, rights of**
discretionary trusts
note, **218**.109
precedents, **218**.110–**218**.112
investment powers, exercise of, **220**.30
Enjoyment, rights of
life interests, and, **83**.6
Entailed interests
disposable property, **7**.2
generally, **84**.1–**84**.4
introductory note, **200**.53
Entailed personalty, gift of
precedent, **204**.75
Entailed property, gift of
gift of freehold land, and, **206**.19
Entitled
meaning, **55**.3
Entry, rights of
disposable property, **7**.21
Enumeration of particulars
inaccuracy of description, and, **58**.8
Envelope
signature of wills, and, **11**.7
Equitable interests in property, disposal of
agreements for purchase, **7**.27
choses in action, **7**.28
contingent interests, **7**.20
emblements, **7**.25
estates *pur autre vie*, **7**.19
future interests, **7**.20
generally, **7**.18
gift under will of another, **7**.22
incorporeal heriditaments, **7**.26
leaseholds, **7**.23
possessory title, **7**.30
rent, **7**.24
rights of action, **7**.29
rights of entry, **7**.21
rule against perpetuities, and, **94**.36
sale proceeds, **7**.27
Equity
will taking effect in, **1**.7
Errors, correction of
precedents for codicils
clerical error in will, **237**.32
rendering validity to alterations, **237**.33
rectification, and, **6**.2
Estate
description of property, **63**.5, **64**.19
Estate tail
gifts by implication, and, **101**.11
lapse, and, **47**.20
Estates ***pur autre vie***
disposable property, **7**.19
Estoppel
approbation, and, **43**.4

Estoppel – *contd*
conditions, and, **43**.5
contracts relating to wills, and, **3**.1
generally, **43**.2–**43**.3
hotchpot clause, **43**.6
principles, **43**.1
reprobation, and, **43**.4
Evidence
alterations, and
external, **14**.11
generally, **14**.5
internal, **14**.9–**14**.10
signature of testator and witnesses, **14**.6
subsequent validation, **14**.7–**14**.8
attestation, and, **12**.15
knowledge and approval, and
generally, **5**.2–**5**.3
will prepared by beneficiary, **5**.4–**5**.5
revocation of wills, and
conditional, **19**.6
destruction, **18**.26
soundness of mind, of, **4**.20
Exclusion of time apportionment
note, **214**.48–**214**.52
precedents, **214**.53–**214**.54
Exclusion of words
soldiers', etc., wills, and, **16**.9
Execution of release
conditions, and, **35**.51
Execution of will
form, **12**.9–**12**.13, **200**.44. *See also* **Attestation clause**
intention
evidence, **12**.15
general rule, **12**.14
introduction, **12**.1–**12**.2
mode
attestation in presence of other witness, **12**.7
attestation in presence of testator, **12**.6
signature in presence of both witnesses, **12**.3
signature must precede attestation, **12**.5
witness must attest will, **12**.4
Execution of will – *contd*
presumption of due execution, and
absence of attestation clause, **13**.2
general rule, **13**.1
rebuttal, **13**.3
signature affixed by direction of testator, **13**.4
superfluous, **12**.8
witnesses, **12**.16–**12**.17
Executors
absolute interests, and, **83**.3
acceptance of office, **25**.12
according to tenor, **25**.2
acts before probate, **25**.14
appointees
civil partner, **203**.8
corporations, **25**.6
firms, **25**.5
generally, **25**.4
minors, **25**.4
person of unsound mind, **25**.4
Public Trustee, **25**.8
spouse, **25**.7
appointment. *See* **Executors, appointment of**
cesser of right to prove, **25**.11
corporations, **25**.6
devolution of office, **25**.10
duration of office, **25**.9
estate taken by, **25**.18
firms, **25**.5
legacies to
generally, **30**.14–**30**.18
introduction, **25**.19
precedents, **210**.52–**210**.53
preliminary note, **210**.51
minors, **25**.4
partnerships, **25**.5
person of unsound mind, **25**.4
probate or letters, and
grant, **25**.15
revocation, **25**.16
Public Trustee, **25**.8
renunciation, **25**.13
spouse, **25**.7
Executors, appointment of
acceptance, **25**.12
banks' charges, **203**.31

Executors, appointment of – *contd*
business executors, **203**.44
charging clause
banks, **203**.31
trust corporations, **203**.30
civil partner, **203**.8
conditional, **25**.3
corporations
generally, **203**.2, **203**.28–**203**.31
precedents, **203**.32–**203**.35
duration, **25**.9
foreign property executors, **203**.45
generally, **25**.1
implication, by, **25**.2
individuals
generally, **203**.1–**203**.6
precedents, **203**.7–**203**.13
legacies to
generally, **30**.14–**30**.18, **210**.51
precedents, **210**.52–**210**.53
literary executors, **203**.43
number, **203**.1
precedents
business executors, **203**.44
civil part as executor, **203**.8
corporations, executors as, **203**.32–**203**.35
different persons as trustees, **203**.11
foreign property, executors of, **203**.45
general form, **203**.9
individuals, executors as, **203**.7–**203**.13
literary executors, **203**.43
Public Trustee, executor as, **203**.36–**203**.42
same person as executors and trustees, **203**.10
settled land, executors of, **203**.46
solicitors, executors as, **203**.24–**203**.27
substitution in case of vacancy, provision for, **203**.14
three persons appointed, one abroad, **203**.13

Executors, appointment of – *contd*
precedents – *contd*
wife/civil partner, adult son and infant son when attaining majority, **203**.12
Public Trustee, **203**.36–**203**.42
remuneration clause
banks, **203**.31
trust corporations, **203**.30
renunciation, **25**.13
settled land, **203**.46
solicitors
incorporated practices, **203**.20–**203**.21
limited liability partnerships, **203**.22–**203**.23
partners, **203**.15–**203**.19
precedents, **203**.24–**203**.27
two partners, **203**.16
substituted, **25**.3
trust corporations
generally, **203**.2, **203**.28–**203**.31
precedents, **203**.32–**203**.35

Exercise of power of appointment
ademption, and, **41**.21
capital gains tax, **242**.3
class of persons, among, **40**.2
contemplation of marriage, will made in
introduction, **17**.1
wills after 1982, **17**.6
wills before 1983, **17**.4
contract relating to wills, and
generally, **3**.14
special power, **3**.15
covenant against, **40**.11
delegation of power, and, **40**.5
disclaimer of power, and, **40**.12
election, and, **42**.4
foreign element wills, and
capacity of testator, **24**.15
donee domiciled abroad, **24**.12
evidence, **24**.18
immovables, **24**.13
introduction, **24**.11
residuary bequest, **24**.16
revocation, **24**.14
fraudulent appointment
generally, **40**.14

Exercise of power of appointment – *contd*
fraudulent appointment – *contd*
grounds, **40**.15
variation of trusts, **40**.16
general powers
definition, **39**.2
generally, **39**.4–**39**.15
joint will, by, **39**.8
nature, **39**.3
gift of freehold land, and, **206**.29–**206**.30
hybrid powers, **39**.31
inheritance tax, **242**.2
introduction, **39**.1
miscellaneous matters, **40**.1–**40**.21
precedents
age 18-to-25 trust, appointment to, **242**.13–**242**.14
bereaved minor trust , appointment to, **242**.13–**242**.16
capital gains tax, and, **242**.3
discretionary trusts, **242**.7–**242**.11
generally, **242**.1
immediate post-death interests, appointment in residue for grandchildren, **242**.12inheritance tax, and, **242**.2
stamp duty, and, **242**.6
stamp duty land tax, **242**.8
two-year (ITA s 144) trusts, and, **242**.4–**242**.5
release of power, and
generally, **40**.10
implied, **40**.13
severance of appointment, **40**.20
soldiers', etc., wills, and, **16**.6
special powers, **39**.16–**39**.30
stamp duty, **242**.6
stamp duty land tax, **242**.6
successive instruments, by, **40**.3
Exhausted income
charitable gifts, and, **103**.15
Exhibit of art, etc.
conditions, and, **35**.53
Exoneration of gift from charges
precedent, **204**.78
Eye hospitals
disposal of body, and, **202**.14–**202**.15

F

Failure of gifts
acceleration
beneficiary attests will, where, **48**.7
class closing rules, and, **48**.6
disclaimer, on, **48**.8
divorce, on, **48**.14
election under will, on, **48**.12
forfeiture, on, **48**.11
gifts being void for remoteness, on, **48**.13
lapse, on, **48**.10
revocation of gift, on, **48**.9
subsequent interests, of, **48**.5
acceptance of gift, **45**.1–**45**.2
acts of testator, **48**.2
ademption
generally, **41**.1–**41**.4
particular cases, **41**.5–**41**.24
annulment of marriage or civil partnership, **47**.2–**47**.4
disclaimer of gift, **46**.1–**46**.6
dissolution of marriage or civil partnership, **47**.2–**47**.4
effect
acceleration, **48**.5–**48**.14
contingent gifts over, **48**.15
subject of gift, on, **48**.4
election, **42**.1–**42**.16
estoppel, **43**.1–**43**.6
lapse
application to powers, **47**.36–**47**.39
effect, **47**.5–**47**.10
exceptions, **47**.11–**47**.35
nature, **47**.1
methods, **48**.1–**48**.3
satisfaction, **44**.1–**44**.17
subsequent gifts to donee, by, **48**.3

Failure of issue
generally, **98**.1–**98**.13
Failure of trust, provisions in event of
accruer
generally, **90**.1–**90**.6
precedents, **219**.20–**219**.22
commorientes
fiscal implications, **219**.5–**219**.11
generally, **70**.1 –**70**.4, **200**.17, **219**.1, **219**.12–**219**.13
inheritance tax, **219**.5–**219**.11
practical considerations, **219**.2–**219**.4
precedents, **219**.14–**219**.17
disclaimer
generally, **46**.1–**46**.6
precedent, **219**.30
forfeiture, precedent, **219**.31
lapse
generally, **47**.1–**47**.38
precedents, **219**.23–**219**.29
substitution, precedents, **219**.18–**219**.19
survivorship
divorce, and, **224**.16–**224**.23
generally, **70**.1 –**70**.4, **200**.17, **219**.12–**219**.13, **224**.6–**224**.8
practical considerations, **219**.2–**219**.4
precedents, **219**.14–**219**.17
preliminary note, **219**.1–**219**.13
Falsa demonstratio
change of circumstances, and, **58**.11
description of property, **63**.1
descriptive designation, **58**.9
enumeration of particulars, **58**.8
general rule, **58**.3
generic description, **58**.12
introduction, **58**.2
name and descriptive designation, **58**.10
name designation, **58**.9
partly true as to each subject, **58**.7
partly true as to one subject, **58**.6
Falsa demonstratio – *contd*
partly wrong but applicable to one subject, **58**.5
specific description, **58**.13
wholly true as to one subject, **58**.6
wholly wrong but subject-matter certain, **58**.4
Family
description of donees
dependants, **79**.3
generally, **79**.1
meaning, **79**.2
favouring relatives, and, **51**.10
Family and dependants, provision for
anticipated needs, **105**.37
applicants
child of the family, **105**.17
children, **105**.16
civil partner, **105**.10–**105**.11
cohabitees, **105**.14–**105**.15
former spouse, **105**.11–**105**.13
other persons, **105**.18
spouse, **105**.9
avoidance of dispositions
contracts inter vivos, **105**.49
discretion, **105**.46
donee, **105**.45
intention to defeat order, **105**.48
inter vivos, **105**.43
introduction, **105**.42
relevant disposition, **105**.47
relevant property, **105**.44
child of the family
additional considerations, **105**.28
applicant, as, **105**.17
discretion, **105**.20–**105**.25
children
additional considerations, **105**.28
applicant, as, **105**.16
discretion, **105**.20–**105**.25
civil partner as applicant, **105**.10
cohabitees
additional considerations, **105**.27
applicant, as, **105**.14–**105**.15

Family and dependants, provision for – *contd*
cohabitees – *contd*
different sex couples, **105**.14
discretion, **105**.20–**105**.25
same sex couples, **105**.15
consequential directions, **105**.38
consideration, and, **105**.19
declarations
precedent, **202**.40
preliminary note, **202**.39
discharge, **105**.39
discretion
additional considerations, **105**.26–**105**.28
financial position of parties, **105**.22
generally, **105**.21
introduction, **105**.20
reasonableness of provision, **105**.23
testator's reasons, **105**.25
testator's state of mind, **105**.24
divorce, and, **105**.50
domicile, and, **105**.7
forfeiture, and, **105**.8
former spouse or civil partner
additional considerations, **105**.28
applicant, as, **105**.11–**105**.13
discretion, **105**.20–**105**.25
order relating to, **105**.50
inheritance tax, and, **105**.51
introduction, **105**.1
introductory note, **200**.34
jurisdiction
death of applicant, **105**.6
domicile, **105**.7
generally, **105**.2
intestacy, **105**.3
relevant court, **105**.4
time limits, **105**.5
net estate, **105**.41
orders
interim, **105**.36
introduction, **105**.30
lump sums, **105**.32
periodical payments, **105**.31
purchase of property, **105**.34
settlement of property, **105**.33

Family and dependants, provision for – *contd*
orders – *contd*
transfer of property, **105**.33
variation of marriage or civil partnership settlement, **105**.35
public policy, and, **105**.8
restrictions, **105**.50
spouse
additional considerations, **105**.28
applicant, as, **105**.9
discretion, **105**.20–**105**.25
testamentary power, and, **1**.10
time limits, **105**.5
unlawful killing, and, **9**.22
variation of beneficial interests, and
generally, **105**.39–**105**.40
preliminary note, **241**.20
Family Law Reform Act 1969
citation, **245**.42
commencement, **245**.42
general provisions
age of majority, **244**.87, **246**.89
property rights of illegitimate children, **245**.38–**245**.41
introductory note, **244**.86, **245**.37
transitional provisions, **246**.90–**246**.94
Family Law Reform Act 1987
amendments, **245**.77
citation, **245**.78
commencement, **245**.78
general provisions
artificial insemination, **245**.74
general principle, **245**.70
property rights, **245**.71–**245**.73
introductory note, **245**.69
repeals, **245**.77
savings, **245**.77
schedules, **245**.79–**245**.80
supplemental provisions, **245**.75
transitional provisions, **245**.77
Farm
description of property, **64**.20
Farm stock, gift of
description of property, **64**.20

Farm stock, gift of – *contd*
precedent, **204**.80
Farming business, wills disposing of
agricultural relief
comparison with business relief, **234**.8
conditions, **234**.4
debts charged, **234**.10
farming companies, **234**.6
generally, **234**.1–**234**.3
nature, **234**.7
partially exempt estates, **234**.9
succession, **234**.5
business relief
comparison with agricultural relief, **234**.8
generally, **205**.4–**205**.17, **234**.15
children carrying on business, **234**.15
estate given equally between children, one son having option to purchase farming assets, **234**.17–**234**.30
farming business left to wife or son with residue on trust for wife, **234**.45–**234**.56
farming partnerships with tenancies, **234**.13
legacies to daughters, right of residence to wife, residue to son if farming, **234**.31–**234**.44
nature of assets, **234**.16
precedents, **234**.17–**234**.56
tenant farmers, **234**.12
woodlands, **234**.14
Favouring relatives
children, **51**.9
family, **51**.10
persons entitled on intestacy, **51**.12
relatives of equal degree, **51**.11
Fertilisation, children born by way of
capacity to benefit, **9**.27
generally, **74**.3–**74**.5
introduction, **72**.18
Film rights
generally, **61**.1
Firms
executors, and, **25**.5
First son
description of donees, **81**.3
Fixtures
description of property, **64**.21
Foolishness
soundness of mind, and, **4**.18
Forces, entry into
conditions, and, **35**.46
Foreign currency, legacy in
generally, **30**.43
interest on legacies, and, **32**.33
precedents, **210**.77–**210**.78
Foreign element, wills with
administrative provisions, and, **220**.63–**220**.65
appointment of executors and trustees, **203**.45
capacity, **24**.7
construction
capacity, **24**.7
debts and gifts, **24**.9
election, **24**.10
governing law, **24**.6
immovable property, **24**.8
knowledge and approval, **24**.7
debts and gifts, **24**.9
definitions
domicile, **23**.2
immovables, **23**.3–**23**.4
movables, **23**.5
domicile, **23**.2, **236**.1–**236**.4
election
generally, **42**.15
introduction, **24**.10
essential validity
applicable rules, **24**.2
introduction, **24**.1
legatees, **24**.4
matters, **24**.3
testamentary trusts, **24**.5
exercise of power of appointment
capacity of testator, **24**.15
donee domiciled abroad, **24**.12
evidence, **24**.18
immovables, **24**.13
introduction, **24**.11

Foreign element, wills with – *contd*
exercise of power of appointment – *contd*
residuary bequest, **24**.16
revocation, **24**.14
foreign property
appointment of separate executors to administer, **236**.9–**236**.23
foreign will leaving, **236**.24–**236**.53
formalities
immovables, **23**.11–**23**.12
movables, **23**.6–**23**.10
governing law, **24**.6
immovable property, **24**.8
immovables
definitions, **23**.3–**23**.4
formalities, **23**.11–**23**.12
intestate succession, **23**.17
inheritance tax, **214**.63, **236**.6–**236**.8
international will, **23**.21
intestate succession
immovables, **23**.17
movables, **23**. 16
introduction, **23**.1
knowledge and approval, **24**.7
movables
definitions, **23**.5
formalities, **23**.6–**23**.10
intestate succession, **23**.16
obtaining grants
deceased domiciled in England & Wales, **23**.19
deceased domiciled outside England & Wales, **23**.20
precedents, **236**.9–**236**.53
preparation, **23**.18
revocation
destruction, by, **23**.14
later will, by, **23**.13
marriage, by, **23**.15
trusts, and, **24**.5

Foreign investment
investment powers, **220**.22

Foreign language will
extrinsic evidence, **57**.6–**57**.7

Foreign law
construction of wills, and, **50**.20

Forfeiture
alienation, and, **99**.4
contesting will, and, **219**.31
inheritance provision, and
generally, **105**.8
statutory provisions, **247**.37
intermeddling, and, **219**.31
unlawful killing, and
generally, **9**.13–**9**.22
statutory provisions, **247**.35–**247**.36

Forfeiture Act 1982
citation, **247**.41
commencement, **247**.41
extent, **247**.41
general provisions
financial provision, **247**.37
generally, **247**.35–**247**.36
murderers, **247**.39
Northern Ireland, **247**.40
social security benefits, **247**.38
introductory note, **247**.34

Form of will
admissibility of documents, and
bank mandates, **10**.10
deeds, **10**.5
instructions for will, **10**.7
letters, **10**.8
memoranda, **10**.9
nominations, **10**.11
voluntary settlement, **10**.6
Zavah, **10**.12
codicils, and, **10**.19
date, **10**.2
generally, **200**.9–**200**.26
holograph will, and, **10**.18
international will, and, **10**.3
introduction, **10**.1
printing, **10**.13–**10**.17
testamentary intention, **10**.4
writing, **10**.13–**10**.17

Former spouse
description of donees, and, **80**.3
inheritance provision, and
additional considerations, **105**.28
applicant, as, **105**.11–**105**.13
discretion, **105**.20–**105**.25

Fraud
capacity to benefit, and **9**.23

Fraudulent abstraction
revocation of will, and, **18**.30
Fraudulent appointment
generally, **40**.14
grounds, **40**.15
variation of trusts, **40**.16
Free Christian Church, gifts to
precedent, **212**.22–**212**.23
Free of mortgage, legacies
freehold land, gift, **206**.23
leasehold land, gift of, **207**.17
Free of tax, annuities
generally, **33**.46–**33**.47
precedent, **211**.9
Free of tax, legacies
abatement, **214**.65
general and pecuniary legacies, **214**.64
generally, **200**.37
inheritance tax on events subsequent to death, **214**.66
precedents, **210**.68–**210**.71
variation of beneficial interests, and, **241**.12
works of art, **210**.67–**210**.68
Freedom from influence. ***See also* Undue influence**
generally, **200**.2–**200**.8
Freehold land, gift of
ademption, **206**.9
description of property, **64**.22
generally, **206**.1–**206**.2
inheritance tax, **206**.3
minors, to
precedent, **206**.17
preliminary note, **206**.4–**206**.5
precedents
contracted to purchase, **206**.25
entailed property, **206**.19
exercise of power of appointment, **206**.29–**206**.30
free of mortgage, **206**.23
general gifts, **206**.10–**206**.11
gift over on death without issue, **206**.28
gift to charity, **206**.26
gift to sons with successive gifts over, **206**.33
joint tenancies, **206**.16
Freehold land, gift of – *contd*
precedents – *contd*
minors, **206**.17
proceeds of sale during lifetime, **206**.24
provision against lapse, **206**.35
reference to plan, **206**.37
specific gifts, **206**.12–**206**.15
subject to debts and expenses, **206**.21
subject to inheritance tax, **206**.38–**206**.39
subject to legacies, **206**.20
subject to mortgage, **206**.22
subject to taking name, **206**.27
tenancies in common, **206**.16
tenant in tail, **206**.18
trust for sale, **206**.32
trusts of settlement, **206**.31
repairs, **206**.8
successive interests, **206**.6
Friendly society accounts
nomination, and, **7**.10
Funds
description of property, **64**.23
Funeral wishes
precedent, **202**.3–**202**.6
testator's wishes, and, **7**.33
Furniture, gift of
description of property, **64**.24, **64**.27
generally, **204**.37–**204**.39
precedents, **204**.39–**204**.50
Future interests
disposable property, **7**.20
Futurity, words of
context of words, and, **54**.2

G

Gender recognition
application for certificate, **245**.103
description of donee, **81**.1, **200**.28
Gender Recognition Act 2004
general provisions, **245**.103–**245**.109
introductory note, **245**.102

General power of appointment
definition, **39**.2
generally, **39**.4–**39**.15
joint will, by, **39**.8
nature, **39**.3
Generic description
inaccuracy of description, and, **58**.12
Generic gifts
description of property, **59**.2
Gestation period
rule against perpetuities, and, **94**.4
Gift. *See also subject matter of gift*
acceptance, **45**.1–**45**.2
accordance with testator's wishes, in, **204**.23
clear
cutting down, **82**.2
superadded powers, **83**.9–**83**.11
concurrent, **86**.1–**86**.8
conditional
alteration of conditions, **91**.3
cumulative legacies, and, **91**.6
contingent
leasehold land, **207**.21
precedents, **215**.4–**215**.5
cumulative
conditional gifts, and, **91**.6
generally, **88**.1–**88**.4
generally, **91**.1–**91**.6
executor, to
absolute interests, and, **83**.3
generally, **25**.19
exoneration from charges, **204**.78
failure. *See* **Failure of gift**
implication, by, **101**.1–**101**.14
precedents, **210**.46–**210**.50
subject to payment, **91**.2
substituted
conditional gifts, and, **91**.6
generally, **88**.1–**88**.4
lapse, on
alternative gifts, **47**.23
executor of deceased legatee, legacy to, **47**.24
predeceasing child, **47**.19
substituted legacies, and, **91**.6

Gift – *contd*
under will of another, disposable property, 7.22
witnesses, to, soldiers', etc., wills, and, 16.7
Gift over
change of words, and, **56**.1–**56**.9
contingent, vesting, and, **93**.16
death, on
contingencies, with, **97**.4–**97**.10
generally, **97**.1–**97**.3
statutory provision, **97**.11
vesting, and, **93**.20–**93**.21
divesting, and, **96**.2
failure of issue, and
death of stranger, **98**.5
death without children, **98**.13
death without heir, **98**.12
gift of freehold land, and, **206**.28
implication, by, **101**.5–**101**.7
legacies payable from personal property, and, **93**.41–**93**.43
marriage, on, **93**.20
superadded powers, and
default of exercise of power, **83**.18
executory, **83**.8
survivorship, and, **67**.6
vesting, and, **93**.16–**93**.23
Goods
description of property, **64**.25
Governing law
foreign element wills, and, **24**.6
Grammatical rules
usual meaning of words, and, **50**.8
Grandchildren
blood relationship, **71**.3
illegitimacy, **72**.6
Grand-nephews and nieces
description of donees, and, **71**.5
Grant of lease
residence rights, and, **208**.4
Grants
foreign element wills, and
deceased domiciled in England & Wales, **23**.19
deceased domiciled outside England & Wales, **23**.20

Graves, gifts for upkeep of
capacity to benefit, **9**.29–**9**.30
generally, **202**.18–**202**.30
precedent, **202**.31–**202**.35

Growing crops
generally, **61**.1

Growing crops
generally, **61**.1

Guardians, appointment of
appointees, **28**.3, **203**.57
appointors, **28**.2, **203**.48–**203**.58
before 14 October 1991, **28**.9
conditional, **28**.4
disclaimer, **28**.7
first choice predeceasing testator or disclaiming, alternative on, **203**.63
formalities, **28**.5
former marriage, children of, **203**.65
generally, **203**.47
guardian, by, **203**.66
introduction, **28**.1, **203**.47
mother of illegitimate children, by, **203**.64
number and identity, **203**.57
other parent predeceasing appointer, **203**.60–**203**.61
parental responsibility, **28**.2, **203**.47–**203**.55
precedents, **203**.60–**203**.66
religious education, expression of wishes as to, **203**.62
revocation
commencement of will, **201**.3
generally, **28**.6
previous appointments, of, **203**.59
successive or delegated appointments, **203**.58
statutory provisions, **244**.116–**244**.117
transitional arrangements before 14 October 1991, **28**.8

Guide Association, gifts to
precedent, **212**.30

H

Half-blood relatives
description of donees, and, **71**.1

Heirs
entailed interests, and, **84**.3
generally, **78**.1–**78**.7
living person, of, **78**.2
particular character, of, **78**.3

Heirs and assigns
description of donees, and, **78**.7

Heirs and successors
description of donees, and, **78**.6

HM Forces, entering
conditions, and, **35**.46

Holders of office
description of donees, **81**.5

Holograph will
generally, **10**.18

Hospital supported by public funds, gifts to
precedent, **212**.25

Hotchpot
estoppel, and, **43**.6
generally, **100**.1–**100**.7
partial intestacy, and
death after 1996, **104**.14
death before 1996, **104**.13
precedents
children's trusts, declarations concerning, **217**.44–**217**.49
debt, gift of, **204**.64
debt, release of, **204**.63

House
description of property, **64**.26
gift of personal chattels, **204**.26

Household furniture
description of property, **64**.27

Household goods
description of property, **64**.28

***Howe v. Dartmouth* rule**
adjustment of debts, **38**.26–**38**.28
exclusion of, **214**.29–**214**.38
generally, **38**.17–**38**.25, **200**.36
precedents, **214**.39–**214**.42
reversionary interests, **38**.22–**38**.23

Human Fertilisation and Embryology Act 1990
citation, **245**.91
commencement, **245**.91
definitions, **245**.83–**245**.84
general provisions
parental orders, **245**.88
status of mother and father, **245**.85–**245**.87
introductory note, **245**.82
miscellaneous provisions, **245**.89–**245**.90
Husband. *See also* **Spouse**
description of donee, **80**.7
Hybrid power of appointment
generally, **40**.5

I

Id certum est quod certum redid potest
uncertainty, and, **53**.2
Illegality
charitable gifts, and, **103**.11
creation of interests by will, and, **8**.2
Illegitimate children
capacity to benefit, **9**.24–**9**.26
description of donees
common law, **72**.2–**72**.9
introduction, **72**.1
legitimation, **72**.15–**72**.18
statute, **72**.10–**72**.14
drafting points, **200**.28–**200**.32
lapse of gift to, **47**.16
legitimation
generally, **72**.15–**72**.18
statutory provisions, **245**.44–**245**.50
property rights
statutory provisions, **245**.71–**245**.73
statutory provisions
artificial insemination, **245**.74
general principle, **245**.70
legitimation, **245**.44–**245**.50
property rights, **245**.38–**245**.41, **245**.71–**245**.73
Illiterate testator
signature of wills, and, **11**.22
Immediate needs, legacies for
generally, **210**.15–**210**.18
precedent, **210**.19
Immovable property
foreign element wills
construction, **24**.8
definitions, **23**.3–**23**.4
formalities, **23**.11–**23**.12
intestate succession, **23**.17
Implied election
generally, **42**.12
Impossibility
charitable gifts, and, **103**.11
effect, **34**.8
generally, **34**.7
Impotence, relief of
charitable purposes, **102**.6
Improvident persons, legacies for
note, **210**.54
precedents, **210**.55–**210**.56
***In terrorem* conditions**
generally, **34**.13–**34**.16
In vitro fertilisation, children born by
capacity to benefit, **9**.27
generally, **74**.3–**74**.5
introduction, **72**.18
introductory note, **200**.28
statutory provisions
introductory note, **245**.82
parental orders, **245**.88
status of mother and father, **245**.85–**245**.87
Inaccuracy of description
change of circumstances, and, **58**.11
description of property, **63**.1
descriptive designation, **58**.9
enumeration of particulars, **58**.8
general rule, **58**.3
generic description, **58**.12
introduction, **58**.2
name and descriptive designation, **58**.10
name designation, **58**.9
partly true as to each subject, **58**.7
partly true as to one subject, **58**.6

Inaccuracy of description – *contd*
partly wrong but applicable to one subject, **58**.5
specific description, **58**.13
wholly true as to one subject, **58**.6
wholly wrong but subject-matter certain, **58**.4
Income, gifts of
absolute interests, and, **83**.4
charge on rents and profits, **62**.2
generally, **62**.1
rent of let property, **62**.4
superadded powers, and, **83**.15
until marriage, **62**.3
Income on legacies
class gifts, **32**.28
demonstrative legacies, **32**.4–**32**.17
general legacies, **32**.4–**32**.17
intermediate, **32**.28
introduction, **32**.1
specific legacies, **32**.2–**32**.3
Income tax
discretionary trusts, and, **218**.29–**218**.32
generally, **200**.41–**200**.42
generation skipping, advantages of, **200**.42
minors, trusts for, **217**.3
occupation of previously-disposed of land, on, **241**.19
person with disability, wills providing for, **226**.8
variation of beneficial interests, and, **241**.19
Incomplete destruction
revocation by destruction, and, **18**.20
Inconsistency of words
additional, **52**.3
alterations, **52**.2
change, **52**.4
clarity, **52**.1
insertion, **52**.3
rejection, **52**.6–**52**.11
repugnance, **52**.6
surplusage, **52**.6
transposition, **52**.5
Incorporation in later will
revival of wills, and, **21**.2
Incorporation of unattested documents
coming into existence after will, **15**.2
effect, **15**.3–**15**.4
express declaration, and, **15**.6
introduction, **15**.1
missing document, **15**.5
Incorporeal heriditaments
disposable property, **7**.26
Indemnities
preliminary note, **221**.13–**221**.15
precedents, **221**.16–**221**.26
trustees, for, **246**.24–**246**.26
Indorsement
signature of wills, and, **11**.7
Inference
construction of wills, and **50**.4
cumulative gifts, and, **88**.4
Infertility
statutory provisions
introductory note, **245**.82
parental orders, **245**.88
status of mother and father, **245**.85–**245**.87
Infirmity of mind
soundness of mind, effect on, **4**.17
Inheritance (Provision for Family and Dependants) Act 1975
citation, **247**.33
commencement, **247**.33
definitions, **247**.31
extent, **247**.33
general provisions
divorce and separation cases, **247**.15–**247**.24
generally, **247**.2–**247**.8
property available, **247**.9–**247**.10
transactions intended to defeat applications, **247**.11–**247**.14
introductory note, **247**.1
miscellaneous provisions, **247**.25–**247**.30

Inheritance provision orders. *See* **Family and dependants, provision for**
Inheritance tax
administrative provisions
note, **220**.4–**220**.10
precedent, **220**.81
advancement powers, and, **242**.2
age 18-to-20 trusts, **200**.109, **217**.1, **224**.24–**224**.25
annuities, and, **33**.32
appointment powers, and, **242**.2
bereaved minors, trusts for, **200**.108, **217**.1, **224**.24
business interests, gift of
effect on dispositions, **205**.46–**205**.57
generally, **205**.4–**205**.16
payment by instalments, **205**.17–**205**.20
charge on death
aggregation with lifetime transfers, and, **200**.74
deduction of liabilities on death, **200**.77–**200**.78
generally, **200**.72
gifts with reservation, **200**.76
liability, **200**.79–**200**.80
post death rearrangement, **200**.83
rate of tax, **200**.73
valuation of estate on death, **200**.81–**200**.82
commorientes, and, **219**.5–**219**.11
contracts relating to wills, and, **3**.7
creation of settlements by will
disabled trusts, **200**.105
discretionary trusts, **200**.106
foreign domicile, **200**.103
interests in possession, **200**.93–**200**.102
protective trusts, **200**.104
purposes of trusts, **200**.125
declarations
free of tax only referring to tax on death, **214**.82
generally, **214**.56–**214**.75
Inheritance tax – *contd*
declarations – *contd*
inheritance tax and foreign death duties etc payable out of residue, **214**.76–**214**.77
partial exemption, and, **214**.78–**214**.81
delays in administration, caused by, **200**.123–**200**.124
disabled persons, and, **226**.3–**226**.6
discretionary trusts, and
calculation of rate of charge, **218**.11–**218**.14
charge to tax, **218**.8–**218**.10
charge schemes, **218**.21–**218**.23
nil-rate band, **200**.130, **218**.16–**218**.20
no spouse or civil partner exemption, **218**.24–**218**.25
tax advantages, **218**.6–**218**.7
trusts created by will, **218**.15
two-year trusts, **225**.83–**225**.91
variation of disposition, **218**.26
dispositions by will, effect of, **200**.119–**200**.133
exemptions and reliefs
charities etc, **200**.87–**200**.88
foreign domicile, persons with, **200**.89–**200**.90
particular types of asset, **200**.91
spouses and civil partners, **200**.84–**200**.86
foreign
death duties, legacies, **210**.64–**210**.67
domicile, persons with, **236**.3
incidence, **236**.6
liabilities and expenses, and, **236**.7
property, **214**.63, **236**.5
free of tax, directions concerning, **214**.76–**214**.82
gift with reservation, **200**.76

Inheritance tax – *contd*
incidence of tax
directions as to, **214**.76–**214**.82
generally, **200**.79–**200**.80, **200**.111, **214**.55–**214**.62
interest in possession trust, **200**.102
partially exempt estates, **200**.112–**200**.118
pecuniary legacies, **210**.3–**210**.4
potentially exempt transfers, and, **200**.121, **214**.72
property which bears its own tax, **214**.59–**214**.60
residuary gifts on, **214**.55 –**214**.71
specific bequests, **204**.1, **204**.9–**204**.14
inheritance provision, and, **105**.51
inheritance tax on lifetime gifts, gift of, **210**.66
Inheritance Tax Act 1984
section 39A, **200**.117, **233**.2–**233**.7
section 71, **200**.107
section 89, **226**.3–**226**.5
section 142, **241**.1–**241**.21
section 144, **225**.83–**225**.91
section 211, **214**.55–**214**.71
interest in possession, and
debt and charge schemes, **218**.19–**218**.25
generally, **200**.72, **200**.93–**200**.102, **218**.8–**218**.9
investment powers, **220**.4–**220**.10
meaning, **200**.93– **200**.94
settlements by will, **200**.125
introduction, **1**.12, **200**.68
leasehold land, gift of
note, **207**.14
declaration, **207**.24
legacies, and
generally, **210**.3–**210**.4, **210**.64–**210**.67

Inheritance tax – *contd*
legacies, and – *contd*
precedents concerning, **210**.68–**210**.71
lifetime gifts, **200**.74
main characteristics, **200**.69–**200**.83
nil-rate band
carry-forward, **200**.75, **227**.3, **237**.3
debt or charge schemes, **218**.19–**218**.23
generally, **200**.72, **210**.72, **218**.16–**218**.18, **233**.8–**233**.10
legacy, clause in will, **210**.72, **218**.34, **225**.9–**225**.41, **225**.57–**225**.82, **226**.13, **227**.7 –**227**.38, **233**.17–**233**.35
variation, and, **241**.27
non-exempt beneficiaries, trusts for, **200**.131
options to purchase property, and, **209**.3
partially exempt estates, **200**.112–**200**.118, **214**.72
person with disability, wills providing for, **226**.3–**226**.5
personal chattels, gift of
artistic interest, **204**.11–**204**.14
discretionary distribution, **204**.9–**204**.10
historic interest, **204**.11–**204**.14
potentially exempt transfers
aggregation, **200**.74
generally, **200**.71
liability for, **200**.121
residuary gifts, and
note, **214**.55–**214**.75
precedents, **214**.76–**214**.82
specific gifts, and, **204**.1
spouses and civil partners, gifts to, **200**.84–**200**.86
stocks and shares, gift of
generally, **204**.52–**204**.53
situs of shares, **204**.54
survivorship, and, **200**.134, **219**.5–**219**.11

Inheritance tax – *contd*
trusts created by post-21 March 2006 wills, **200**.126
valuation of estate, **200**.81–**200**.82
variation, and
avoidance, **241**.13
disclaimers, **241**.16
double death variations, **241**.14
multiple variations, **241**.15
subject to tax, **241**.12
will trusts, **200**.92–**200**.106
Inheritance Tax Act 1984
general provisions, **246**.100
introductory note, **246**.99
Initials
alterations to will, and, **14**.6
signature of wills, and, **11**.15
Insertion of words
construction of wills, and, **52**.3
Insolvency
contracts relating to wills, and, **3**.9
Institutions
capacity to benefit, **9**.35
Instructions for will
admissibility as will, and, **10**.7
Insurance policies, gift of
description of property, **64**.29
nomination, and, **7**.12
precedent, **204**.77
Insurance, powers of
generally, **27**.14
management of land, and, **220**.51
statutory provisions, **246**.17–**246**.18
Intellectual property, gift of
precedents, **204**.72–**204**.74
Intention
attestation, and
evidence, **12**.15
general rule, **12**.14
construction of wills, and
ascertainment, **49**.2
collation from whole of will, **50**.2
introduction, **49**.1
meaning of words, **50**.3
questions involved, **49**.3
Intention – *contd*
quantity of interest given, and
expression of testator's motive, **82**.5–**82**.6
generally, **82**.1–**82**.4
gifts for particular purposes, **82**.7–**82**.9
revocation of wills, and
burden of proof, **18**.7
generally, **18**.4–**18**.5
proof, **18**.6
revocation of wills by destruction, and
evidence, **18**.18
generally, **18**.17
presumption, **18**.26–**18**.29
signature of wills, and, **11**.11
testamentary, **10**.4
Intention of testator
ascertainment
collation from whole of will, **50**.2
introduction, **49**.2
meaning of words, **50**.3
expression of, **82**.5–**82**.6
introduction, **49**.1
meaning of words
bequest, **55**.4
entitled, **55**.3
general rule, **55**.1–**55**.2
introduction, **50**.3
legacy, **55**.4
minority, **55**.5
testamentary expenses, **55**.7
unmarried, **55**.6
usual meaning, **50**.6–**50**.15
quantity of interest given, and
clear gifts cut down, **82**.2
expression of motive, **82**.5–**82**.6
generally, **82**.1–**82**.4
gifts for particular purposes, **82**.7–**82**.9
questions involved, **49**.3
Interest on arrears
annuities, and, **33**.31
Interest on legacies
appropriation, and, **32**.29
demonstrative legacies, **32**.4–**32**.17

Interest on legacies – *contd*
foreign currency legacy, **32**.33
general legacies, **32**.4–**32**.17
generally, **210**.8
introduction, **32**.1
minors' legacies, **32**.18–**32**.27
nature of payment, **32**.32
rate, **32**.31
recoverable arrears, **32**.30
specific legacies, **32**.2–**32**.3
Interests created by will
certainty of subject-matter, **8**.8
form, **8**.2
gifts of chattels consumed in use for successive interests
assent, **8**.5
generally, **8**.4
gifts of chattels not consumed in use for successive interests
assent, **8**.5
generally, **8**.3
introduction, **8**.1
option to purchase property, **8**.6
right of selection of one or more properties, **8**.7
Interests in possession
assets in kind, enjoyment of, **200**.95
beneficiary-taxed, **200**.98–**200**.102
capital gains tax, and, **200**.40, **200**.102
deemed, during administration of estate, **200**.97
disabled persons' interests, **200**.99
immediate post-death interests, **200**.98, **200**.126
income tax, and, **200**.41
inheritance tax, and
debt and charge schemes, **218**.19–**218**.25
generally, **200**.72, **200**.93–**200**.102, **218**.8–**218**.9
investment powers, **220**.4–**220**.10
meaning, **200**.93–**208**.94
spouse or civil partner exemption, **200**.84
Interests in possession – *contd*
inheritance tax, and – *contd*
will precedents, status of, **200**.101
overriding powers, **200**.96
rights of occupation, and
generally, **208**.5–**208**.11, **218**.109
meaning **208**.12–**208**.13
variation of beneficial interests, and, **241**.8
Interlineations
alterations to will, and, **14**.14
International will
form, **10**.3
generally, **23**.21
Uniform Law, **244**.111
Interpretation Act 1978
application, **246**.97
definitions, **246**.95
repeals, **246**.96
schedule, **246**.98
Interpretation of wills. *See* **Construction of wills**
Intestacy
contracts relating to wills, and, **3**.11
introduction, **104**.1
partial
generally, **104**.10–**104**.16
See also **Partial intestacy**
presumption against
gap in interests created, **51**.2
introduction, **51**.1
limits, **51**.3
total. *See* **Total intestacy**
wills incorporating rules, **223**.7–**223**.8
Intestate succession
foreign element wills, and
immovables, **23**.17
movables, **23**. 16
interest and capitalisation
citation, **244**.91
general provisions, **244**.92–**244**.93
introductory note, **244**.90
Intestates' Estates Act 1952
citation, **244**.75
commencement, **244**.75

Intestates' Estates Act 1952 – *contd*
definitions, **244**.74
general provisions, **244**.72–**244**.73
introductory note, **244**.71
schedule, **244**.76
Investment of money received
ademption, and, **41**.16
Investment powers
acquisition of land, **220**.17–**220**.19
advice, **220**.14
bearer securities, **220**.21
businesses, **220**.34
company shareholdings, **220**.20
construction of express powers, **220**.29
delegation, **220**.35–**220**.39
duty of care, **220**.15
enjoyment in kind, **220**.30
foreign investment, **220**.22
generally, **27**.11, **220**.11–**220**.12
loans, **220**.31
mortgages, **220**.16
non-income yielding assets, **220**.33
postponement of sale, **220**.28
precedents, **220**.40–**220**.48
sale of land, **220**.23–**220**.27
standard investment criteria, **220**.13
statutory provisions, **246**.135–**246**.139
unsecured personal loans, **220**.32
Investments
description of property, **64**.30
Issue. *See also* **Children**
description of donees, and, **76**.1–**76**.6
drafting points, **200**.28–**200**.32
failure of, **98**.1–**98**.13
total intestacy, and
generally, **104**.6
statutory trusts, **104**.7

J

Jewellery
description of property, **64**.31
Joint property
unlawful killing, and, **9**.19
Joint tenancies
statutory provisions, **246**.53
Joint tenancies, gift of property held on
freehold land, and, **206**.16
disposable property, **7**.3
generally, **86**.1–**86**.5
lapse, **47**.27
precedents, **204**.71
Joint wills
nature, **2**.1
operation, **2**.2

K

Knowledge and approval
blind testator, **5**.2
deaf and dumb testator, **5**.2
evidence
generally, **5**.2–**5**.3
will prepared by beneficiary, **5**.4–**5**.5
foreign element wills, and, **24**.7
introduction, **5**.1
mistake, and
construction of will, **5**.8
omission of words, **5**.7
rectification
clerical errors, **6**.2
failure to understand testator's instructions, **6**.3
introduction, **6**.1
negligence actions, **6**.4
procedure, **6**.5–**6**.6
remedies
introduction, **5**.6
mistake, **5**.7–**5**.8
omission of words, **5**.6
rectification of will, **6**.1–**6**.6
testamentary capacity, **5**.3, **200**.2–**200**.8
undue influence and fraud, **5**.9
will prepared by beneficiary
generally, **5**.4
solicitors, **5**.5
Knowledge of title
election, and, **42**.3

L

Land
general devises, **64**.32
tenements, **64**.33
Lands
freeholds, gifts of
generally, **206**.1–**206**.9
precedents, **206**.10–**206**.31
generally, **60**.1
leaseholds, gifts of
generally, **207**.1–**207**.14
precedents, **207**.15–**207**.26
Lapse
charitable legacies, of
generally, **47**.10
precedent, **212**.31
class gifts, **47**.29–**47**.35
contracts relating to wills, and, **3**.10
divorce, on, **47**.2–**47**.4
effect, **47**.5–**47**.10
exceptions
class gifts, **47**.29–**47**.35
joint tenancy gifts, **47**.27
moral obligation, **47**.21–**47**.22
predeceasing child, **47**.11–**47**.20
settled shares, **47**.25–**47**.26
substituted gifts, **47**.22–**47**.23
tenancy in common gifts, **47**.28
gift of freehold land, and, **206**.35
introductory note, **200**.23
joint tenancy gifts, **47**.27
meaning, **47**.1
moral obligation, **47**.21–**47**.22
powers of appointment, and
generally, **47**.36–**47**.39
special power, **39**.29
precedents, **219**.23–**219**.29
predeceasing child, exception for
adopted children, **47**.16
contingent gifts, **47**.18
death of testator before 1983, **47**.12–**47**.14
en ventre sa mere, **47**.17
estate tail, **47**.20
generally, **47**.15
illegitimate children, **47**.16
Lapse – *contd*
predeceasing child, exception for – *contd*
power of appointment, gift under, **47**.14
statutory provisions, **47**.11–47.12
substituted gifts, **47**.19
settled shares, **47**.25–**47**.26
special power of appointment, and, **39**.29
substituted gifts
alternative, **47**.23
executors of deceased legatee, legacy to, **47**.24
predeceasing child, **47**.19
tenancy in common gifts, **47**.28
***Lassence v. Tierney*, rule in**
intention of testator, and, **82**.4
Later will or codicil, revocation by
codicil, **18**.15
foreign element wills, and, **23**.13
form of instrument, **18**.16
introduction, **18**.8
last will, meaning, **18**.9
lost subsequent will, **18**.13
lost will, **18**.12
partly inconsistent will, **18**.14
same date will, **18**.11
subsequent inconsistent will, **18**.10
undated will, **18**.11
Law of Property Act 1925
amendments, 1926, **246**.70–**246**.71
commencement, **244**.53
definitions
generally, **246**.59
trust corporation, **246**.71
effects of TLATA 1996, **200**.60
general provisions
accumulations, **246**.56–**246**.58
conveyances, **246**.54
joint tenancies, **246**.53
perpetuities, **246**.55
principles as to estates and interests, **246**.42–**246**.50
survivorship, **244**.58
undivided shares, **246**.51

Law of Property Act 1925 – *contd*
general provisions – *contd*
wills, **244**.54–**244**.57
Law Reform (Succession) Act 1995
citation, **244**.128
extent, **244**.128
general provisions, **244**.124–**244**.124
repeals, **244**.127
schedule, **244**.129
Leasehold land, gifts of
ademption, and, **41**.10
disposable property, **7**.23
generally, **207**.1–**207**.14
high value houses, **207**.9–**207**.10
inheritance tax
declaration, **207**.24
generally, **207**.14
low rent flats, **207**.11–**207**.13
precedents
contingent gift, **207**.21
free from mortgage, **207**.17
generally, **207**.15–**207**.26
inheritance tax declaration, **207**.24
payment of arrears, **207**.18
payment of rents and profits, **207**.19
sinking fund policies, **207**.23
undivided share, **207**.22
repairs, **207**.2
settled leaseholds, **207**.6–**207**.8
Leasehold Reform Act 1967
high value houses, **207**.9–**207**.10
Legacies
abatement
demonstrative legacies, **31**.3
general legacies, **31**.1
provision for, **210**.75
satisfaction of debt, in, **31**.2
specific, **31**.4
absolute gifts, **210**.9–**210**.14
apprentices, to, **30**.27
charged on mixed fund, **93**.45
charged on real property, **93**.44
conditional, **210**.46–**210**.50
contingent
delivery, **30**.33
interest and income, **32**.3

Legacies – *contd*
contingent – *contd*
precedents, **210**.46–**210**.50
creditors, to
generally, **210**.2
precedents, **210**.28–**210**.32
currency of
generally, **30**.43
precedents, **210**.77–**210**.78
debtor, to
abatement, **31**.2
generally, **30**.10–**30**.13, **210**.2
precedents, **210**.28–**210**.32
deferred, **210**.20–**210**.24
definition, **30**.1
delivery of, **30**.30–**30**.43
demonstrative
abatement, **31**.3
generally, **30**.6
interest and income, **32**.4–**32**.17
precedent, **210**.74
employees, to
generally, **30**.23–**30**.29 , **210**.57
precedents, **210**.58–**210**.63
executor, to
generally, **30**.14–**30**.18, **210**.51
precedents, **210**.52–**210**.53
failure of, **30**.7
free of tax
generally, **210**.64–**210**.67
precedents, **210**.68–**210**.71
general
abatement, **31**.1
generally, **30**.5
interest and income, **32**.4–**32**.17
immediate needs, for
discussion, **210**.15–**210**.18
precedent, **210**.19
improvident persons
generally, **210**.54
precedents, **210**.55–**210**.56
income
class gifts, **32**.28
demonstrative legacies, **32**.4–**32**.17
general legacies, **32**.4–**32**.17
intermediate, **32**.28

Legacies – *contd*
income – *contd*
introduction, **32**.1
specific legacies, **32**.2–**32**.3
inheritance tax
generally, **210**.64–**210**.67
introductory note, **210**.3–**210**.4
precedents, **210**.68–**210**.71
interest
appropriation, and, **32**.29
demonstrative legacies, **32**.4–**32**.17
foreign currency legacy, **32**.33
general legacies, **32**.4–**32**.17
generally, **32**.1, **210**.8
minors' legacies, **32**.18–**32**.27
nature of payment, **32**.32
rate, **32**.31
recoverable arrears, **32**.30
specific legacies, **32**.2–**32**.3
meaning, **55**.4
minors, to
generally, **30**.19–**30**.22
interest, **32**.18–**32**.27
precedents, **210**.33–**210**.45
nil-rate band legacies, **210**.72
particular property, payable from,. **210**.75
payable from personal property
direction as to maintenance, **93**.31–**93**.39
direction as to payment, **93**.26–**93**.30
generally, **93**.24–**93**.25
gift over, **93**.41–**93**.43
severance from estate, **93**.40
payment of, **30**.30–**30**.43
precedents
absolute gifts, **210**.9–**210**.14
conditional legacies, **210**.46–**210**.50
contingent legacies, **210**.46–**210**.50
currency of legacy, **210**.77–**210**.78
debtors and creditors, **210**.28–**210**.32
deferred legacies, **210**.20–**210**.24
demonstrative legacy, **210**.74

Legacies – *contd*
precedents – *contd*
employees, **210**.58–**210**.63
executors and trustees, **210**.52–**210**.53
immediate needs provision, **210**.19
improvident persons, **210**.55–**210**.56
inheritance tax, **210**.68–**210**.71
legatees cannot be found, **210**.73
minors and children, **210**.33–**210**.45
nil-rate band legacies, **210**.72
prior legacies, **210**.20–**210**.24
purchase of customary mourning, **210**.79
reduction of legacy, **210**.76
substitutional provisions, **210**.25–**210**.26
prior legacies, **210**.20–**210**.24
purchase of customary mourning, **210**.79
reduction of legacy, **210**.76
refunding, **31**.6–**31**.21
release of debt, **30**.4
republication of wills, and, **22**.4
satisfaction by portion, and
different beneficiaries, **44**.13
double portion, **44**.6
ejusdem generis rule, **44**.11
election, **44**.7
gift in nature of portion, **44**.4
introduction, **44**.3
limitations, **44**.12
parol evidence, **44**.14
persons *in loco parentis*, **44**.8
rebuttal of presumption, **44**.9–**44**.10
size of second portion, **44**.5
satisfaction of debt by
child from parent, to, **44**.17
generally, **44**.15
parol evidence, **44**.16
satisfaction of portion by
different beneficiaries, **44**.13
double portion, **44**.6
ejusdem generis rule, **44**.11
election, **44**.7

Legacies – *contd*
satisfaction of portion by – *contd*
gift in nature of portion, **44**.4
introduction, **44**.2
limitations, **44**.12
parol evidence, **44**.14
persons *in loco parentis*, **44**.8
rebuttal of presumption, **44**.9–**44**.10
size of second portion, **44**.5
servants, to, **30**.24
specific
abatement, **31**.4
delivery, **30**.34
generally, **30**.3
interest and income, **32**.2–**32**.3
stocks and shares, of
aliquot share, **30**.9
generally, **30**.8
substitutional provisions, **210**.25–**210**.26
types, **30**.2
Legal documents
construction, modern approach to, **57**.2
Legal words
usual meaning of, **50**.7
Legality of words
presumptions, and, **51**.4–**51**.6
Legitimacy Act 1926
amendments, 1959, **245**.32
application, **245**.15
citation, **245**.15
commencement, **245**.15
definitions, **245**.14
general provisions, **245**.7–**245**.12
introductory note, **245**.6
savings, **245**.13
Legitimacy Act 1959
citation, **245**.34
commencement, **245**.34
general provisions, **245**.32–**245**.33
introductory note, **245**.31
Legitimacy Act 1976
amendments, **245**.52
citation, **245**.53
commencement, **245**.53
definitions, **245**.51
Legitimacy Act 1976 – *contd*
general provisions, **245**.44–**245**.50
introductory note, **245**.43
repeals, **245**.52
savings, **245**.52
schedule, **245**.54
Legitimated children. *See also* **Illegitimate children**
description of donees, and, **72**.15–**72**.18
drafting points, **200**.28
statutory provisions, **245**.44–**245**.50
Letters
admissibility as will, and, **10**.8
Letters and papers
gift of personal chattels, and, **204**.32
Lex domicilii
wills with foreign element, and, **23**.1
Lex situs
wills with foreign element, and, **23**.1
Liability for making of will
introduction, **1**.14
rectification, and, **6**.4
Library
gift of personal chattels, **204**.30
Life interests
determinable interest, **83**.7
generally, **216**.1
gift by implication, and, **101**.4
gift of personal chattels, and, **204**.24
gift over on death, and, **97**.2
immediate post-death, **216**.2
introductory note, **200**.11
immediate post-death, **216**.3
partial intestacy, and, **104**.16
perpetuities, **216**.4–**216**.5
precedents
ancillary provisions, **216**.34–**216**.37
generally, **216**.8–**216**.31
settled legacies, **216**.32–**216**.33
presumptions, and, **51**.13
rights of enjoyment, **83**.6

Life interests – *contd*
superadded powers, and, **83**.11–**83**.14
vesting, **216**.6–**216**.7
Life insurance policy, gift of
precedent, **204**.77
Limitations
conditions, and, **34**.3
Limited companies. *See* **Companies**
Literary executors
appointment, **203**.43
Lithograph
form of will, and, **10**.14
Live stock, gift of
precedent, **204**.79
Lives in being
rule against perpetuities, and, **94**.2
Lloyd's underwriting business
gift of business interests, **205**.61
Loan guarantees
administrative provisions, **220**.81
Loans
investment powers, **220**.31
Loans to beneficiaries
discretionary trusts, and, **218**.113–**218**.116
Local authorities
capacity to benefit, **9**.34
Locality, description by
county, **63**.2
elsewhere, meaning, **63**.6
estate, **63**.5
generally, **63**.1
occupation, **63**.7
parish, **63**.3
street, **63**.4
Lord Kingsdown's Act
application, **244**.47
general provisions, **244**.43–**244**.45
Lost wills
revival of wills, and, **21**.4
revocation by later will or codicil, and
generally, **18**.12
subsequent will, **18**.13
soldiers', etc., wills, and, **16**.5

M

Maintenance. ***See also* Accumulation and maintenance trusts**
discretionary trusts, and
accumulation of surplus income, destination of, **218**.53–**218**.56
adaptation of provisions, **218**.63–**218**.65
annuities, **218**.62
applicable interests, **218**.49
beneficiary, type of, **218**.45
commencement, **218**.46
contingent beneficiaries of full age, income interests of, **218**.52
discussion of statutory provisions, **218**.43–**218**.78
extended provisions, **218**.74–**218**.78
inheritance tax, **218**.69–**218**.70
income of another fund, availability, **218**.50
income tax, **218**.67
intermediate income, interests carrying, **218**.57–**218**.62
permitted periods of accumulation, **218**.71–**218**.73
powers of court, **218**.66
precedents, **218**.79–**218**.86
prior interests, **218**.48
relationship of powers to terms of will, **218**.47
time apportionment of income, **218**.68
trustees' discretion, **218**.51
statutory provisions, **246**.29
Maintenance of animals
annuities, and, **33**.16
generally, **202**.36
precedents, **202**.37–**202**.38
Maintenance of children
annuities, and, **33**.18
Majority, age of
generally, **200**.27

Majority, age of – *contd*
statutory provisions, **244**.87, **246**.89
Making a will
capacity. *See* **Capacity to make will**
introduction, **1**.13
mentally disordered person, for
examples of exercise of jurisdiction, **4**.24
guidelines as to exercise of jurisdiction, **4**.23
jurisdiction of court, **4**.22
Practice Direction, **4**.25
Male descendants
children, and, **74**.9
divesting, and, **96**.3
issue, and, **76**.5
Malum in se
invalidity of conditions, and, **34**.18
Malum prohibitum
invalidity of conditions, and, **34**.18
Management of land, powers of
delegation, **220**.54–**220**.58
express provisions, **220**.53
generally, **220**.49
insurance, **220**.51
limitations on powers, **220**.52
restrictions on powers, **220**.50
Manslaughter
capacity to benefit, and, **9**.13–**9**.22
forfeiture, statutory provisions, **247**.35–**247**.36
Marginal notes
generally, **202**.41
precedent, **202**.42
Mariners, wills of
actual military service, meaning, **16**.2
at sea, meaning, **16**.3
exclusion of words, **16**.9
gifts to witnesses, and, **16**.7
introduction, **16**.1
lost will, and, **16**.5
power of appointment, and, **16**.6
proof, **16**.8
revocation, **16**.10
Marks
signature of wills, and **11**.13
Marriage
conditions in restraint of
class of persons, with, **35**.4
generally, **35**.2
introduction, **35**.1
particular person, with, **35**.6
particular religion, with person of, **35**.5
specified age, under, **35**.3
conditions requiring
generally, **35**.7
solemnisation, by, **35**.34
dissolution or annulment, effect of, **42**.2–**42**.4
effect, **2**.9
gift over, and, **93**.20
unlimited gifts of income, and, **62**.3
Marriage, revocation by
foreign element wills, and, **23**.15
general rule, **17**.2
generally, **17**.1
introduction, **2**.9
wills after 1982
exceptions to rule, **17**.7–**17**.8
general rule, **17**.6
wills before 1983, exceptions to rule, **17**.4–**17**.5
Marriage, will made in contemplation of
introduction, **17**.1
note, **201**.4
precedents, **201**.7, **201**.9
wills after 1982, **17**.6
wills before 1983, **17**.4
Married couples or civil partners with adult children, wills for
destination of property, **225**.7
division of residence between spouse and issue, **225**.42–**225**.56
divorce or dissolution, possibility of, **225**.8
entire estate to spouse absolutely, alternative gift to issue, **225**.110–**225**.123
guardians, **225**.5
introduction, **225**.1–**225**.3

Married couples or civil partners with adult children, wills for – *contd*
mutual wills, **225**.6
nil-rate band legacy to children absolutely
residue to spouse with default gift to children, with, **225**.9–**225**.22
nil-rate band legacy to children on discretionary trust
residue to spouse, with, **225**.57–**225**.67
residue to spouse on protective trusts for life, with, **225**.68–**225**.82
nil-rate band legacy to children on trust
residue to spouse for life with default gift to children on trust, with, **225**.23–**225**.41
reciprocal will, **225**.7
survivorship, **225**.4
two-year discretionary trusts, **225**.83–**225**.109

Married couples or civil partners with young children, wills for
civil partners, **224**.4
divorce or dissolution, **224**.16–**224**.23
estate to spouse absolutely
alternative gift of IPDIs to issue, with, **224**.42–**224**.57
alternative gift to issue, with, **224**.27–**224**.41
estate to spouse for life
power of appointment amongst issue, **224**.73–**224**.85
power to resort to capital with remainder to children, **224**.58–**224**.72
guardians, **224**.11
introduction, **224**.1–**224**.3
mutual wills, **224**.12
reciprocal wills, **224**.12–**224**.15
residence of home for life or until remarriage
income of residue, with, **224**.86–**224**.101

Married couples or civil partners with young children, wills for – *contd*
residence of home for life or until remarriage – *contd*
settled remainders for children, with, **224**.102–**224**.118
survivorship, **224**.6–**224**.10
trusts for children
IHT provisions, **224**.24–**224**.25
income tax and capital gains tax, **224**.26
uncertain order of death, **224**.5

Married women
capacity to make will, **4**.8

Masses, gifts for
precedent, **212**.13

Matrimonial Causes Act 1973
general provisions, **244**.89
introductory note, **244**.87

Medical schools
disposal of body to, **202**.9–**202**.12

Memoranda
admissibility as will, and, **10**.9

Mental Capacity Act 2005
Code of Practice, **244**.142, **244**.146
general provisions, **244**.136–**244**.142
interpretation, **244**.143
introductory note, **244**.135
persons lacking capacity, **244**.136–**244**.142
schedule, **244**.145

Mental disorder
soundness of mind, and, **4**.12

Mentally disordered person
capacity to benefit, **9**.45
power to make will for
attestation, **222**.16
commencement of will, **201**.15
exercise of jurisdiction, **4**.23, **4**,24
jurisdiction of court, **4**.22
Practice Direction, **4**.25

Messuage
description of property, **64**.34

Methodist Church, gifts to
precedent, **212**.16

Mining
rents and royalties, treatment of, **220**.61
Minority
meaning, **55**.5
Minors
capacity to benefit, **9**.39–**9**.43
capacity to make will, **4**.7
election, and, **42**.14
executors, and, **25**.4
favouring relatives, and, **51**.9
gift of freehold land, and
generally, **206**.4–**206**.5
precedent, **206**.17
inheritance provision
additional considerations, **105**.28
applicant, as, **105**.16
child of the family, **105**.17
discretion, **105**.20–**105**.25
legacies
appropriation, **29**.5
generally, **30**.19–**30**.22
interest, **32**.18–**32**.27
precedents, **210**.33–**210**.45
total intestacy
generally, **104**.6
statutory trusts, **104**.7
trusts for. *See* **Minors, trusts for**
trustees, and, 27.3
Minors, trusts for
accumulation and maintenance, **217**.2
age 18-to-25
discretionary trust, appointment from, **242**.13–**242**.14
inheritance tax provisions, **200**.109, **217**.1, **224**.24–**224**.25
parent, creation by, **227**.5
precedents, **217**.9–**217**.33, **217**.43
previous marriage contingency for, **217**.13
bare, **200**.110
bereaved minors
codicil ensuring trust for, **237**.25
Minors, trusts for – *contd*
bereaved minors – *contd*
discretionary trust, appointment from, **242**.13–**242**.14
immediate post-death interest, appointment terminating, **242**.15–**242**.16
inheritance tax provisions, **200**.108, **217**.1, **224**.24
parent, creation by, **227**.5
precedent, **217**.9–**217**.33, **217**.42–**217**.43
capital gains tax, **217**.3
child en ventre, **217**.41
children and issue, meaning, **217**.8
generally, **217**.1–**217**.8
IHT-privileged, **200**.19
income tax, **217**.3
marriage to person not professing certain religion, forfeiture on, **217**.40
nephews and nieces, for, **217**.35–**217**.36
options for, **200**.132
perpetuities, **217**.6
precedents
generally, **217**.9–**217**.41
gifts of land, **217**.42–**217**.43
hotchpot declarations, **217**.44–**217**.49
reference, by, **217**.37–**217**.38
relevant children and issue, **217**.8
revision of will, need for, **200**.138
substitution, **217**.5, **217**.10
vesting, **217**.7
vulnerable, for, **217**.4, **217**.9, **224**.26
wife and children equally, **217**.34
Mirror wills
commencement, **201**.14
Missing document
incorporation of unattested documents, and, **15**.5
Missing wills
revocation by later will or codicil, and
generally, **18**.12

Missing wills – *contd*
revocation by later will or codicil, and – *contd*
subsequent will, **18**.13
soldiers', etc., wills, and, **16**.5
Mistake
construction of will, **5**.8
introductory note, **200**.46
omission of words, **5**.7
revocation of wills, and, **19**.5
Money, meaning of
bank, at, **64**.37
debts, **64**.39
cash, **64**.38
generally, **64**.35
ready money, **64**.40
wide meaning, **64**.36
Money in bank account
ademption, and, **41**.23
description of property, **64**.37
Money due or owing
description of property, **64**.39
More than one family, wills where
children, trusts for, **227**.5
guardianship, **227**.6
married man with adult children and illegitimate child, **227**.50–**227**.62
note, **227**.1–**227**.6
second death, destination of property after, **227**.2
nil-rate band discretionary trusts, **227**.3
survivorship conditions, **227**.4
twice-married spouses each with children from previous marriage, **227**.25–**227**.49
twice-married testator with children from both marriages, **227**.7–**227**.24
Mortgage debt
ademption, and, **41**.9
Mortgage estates
disposable property, **7**.16
Mortgage of land
ademption, and, **41**.8
investment powers, and, **220**.16
Motive of testator. *See also* **Intention of testator**
expression of, **82**.5–**82**.6
Motor car
description of property, **64**.8, **64**.41
Movable property
description of property, **64**.42
foreign element wills, and
definitions, **23**.5
formalities, **23**.6–**23**.10
intestate succession, **23**.16
Murder
capacity to benefit, and, **9**.13–**9**.22
forfeiture, statutory provisions, **247**.35–**247**.36
Mutual obligation
election, and, **42**.16
Mutual wills
agreements relating to
effect of first to die abiding, **2**.8
effect of first to die not abiding, **2**.7
generally, **2**.5
proof, **2**.6
commencement, **201**.13
form, **2**.4
generally, **2**.3
reciprocal wills, and
married couples with adult children, wills for, **225**.7
married couples with young children, wills for, **224**.12
re-marriage, effect of, **2**.9–**2**.10

N

Name and arms clause
conditions, and, **35**.39–**35**.44
precedent, **206**.27
Name, designation by
inaccuracy of description, **58**.9
Named person, gift at discretion of
generally, **82**.8

Nation, gifts of works of art to the
precedent, **204**.29
National Savings Certificates
description of property, **64**.58
Nearest relations
description of donees, and, **79**.5
Negligence action
introduction, **1**.14
rectification, and, **6**.4
Nephews and nieces
description of donees, and, **71**.5, **200**.33
Net estate
inheritance provision, for, **105**.41
Next of kin
ascertainment of class, **77**.3–**77**.4
excluded persons, **77**.6
executors' discretion, by, **77**.7
generally, **77**.1
rules of distribution, **77**.2
shares, **77**.5
Nieces and nephews
description of donees, **71**.5, **200**.33
Nil-rate band legacies
generally, **200**.72, **210**.72, **218**.16–**218**.18, **233**.8–**233**.10
married coupes or civil partners, wills of, **200**.135
precedents, **210**.72, **218**.34, **225**.9–**225**.41, **225**.57–**225**.82, **226**.13, **227**.5 –**227**.38, **233**.17–**233**.35
survivors, provision for, **200**.134
Nil-rate band debt scheme, giving effect to
generally, **218**.19–**218**.23, **243**.1
precedents, **243**.3–**243**.6
Nomination
admissibility as will, and, **10**.11
friendly society accounts, **7**.10
generally, **7**.9
insurance policies, **7**.12
pension schemes, **7**.13
savings bank accounts, **7**.11
Nominees, employment of
generally, **246**.148–**246**.152
Nominees, employment of – *contd*
review of and liability for, **246**.153–**246**.155
supplementary, **246**.156–**246**.159
Non-income yielding assets
investment powers, and, **220**.33
Non-testamentary instruments
advance from bank and undertaking to repay, **240**.4
advancement powers, exercise of
generally, **242**.1–**242**.6
precedents, **242**.17–**242**.20
appointment of partners in solicitors' firm, **240**.3
appointment powers, exercise of
generally, **242**.1–**242**.6
precedents, **242**.7–**242**.16
assent
generally, **243**.1
precedent, **243**.3
declaration of trust of property under secret trust, **240**.5
disclaimer of beneficial interests
generally, **241**.16
precedents, **241**.22–**241**.24
disclaimer of trusteeship
generally, **239**.1
precedents, **239**.3–**239**.5
exercise of dispositive powers created by will
generally, **242**.1–**242**.6
precedents, **242**.7–**242**.16
giving of effect to nil-rate band debt scheme
generally, **243**.1
precedents, **243**.3–**243**.6
notices to Public Trustee, **240**.1–**240**.2
renunciation of probate
generally, **239**.1
precedent, **239**.2
resolution of appropriation
generally, **243**.1
precedent, **243**.2
variation of beneficial interests
generally, **241**.1–**241**.21
precedents, **241**.25–**241**.31
Notice to Public Trustee
precedents, **240**.1–**240**.2

Number of executors
appointment, and, **203**.1
Nuncupative wills
airmen, seamen and soldiers, by, **16**.4

O

Obligation, certainty of
contracts relating to wills, as to, **3**.3–**3**.4
Obliteration
alterations to will, and, **14**.13
Occupation
description of property, **63**.7
Offspring
description of donees, and, **76**.6
Omission of words
knowledge and approval, and, **5**.6
mistake, and, **5**.7
Omnia praesumuntur rite esse acta
absence of attestation clause, and, **13**.2
general rule, **13**.1
rebuttal of, **13**.3
signature affixed by direction of testator, **13**.4
Onerous property
disclaimer of gift, and, **46**.3
Options to purchase property
ademption, and, **41**.20
capital gains tax, **209**.4
creation of interests by will, and, **8**.6
generally, **92**.1–**92**.6
inheritance tax, **209**.3
perpetuities, and, **92**.6
precedents, **209**.6–**209**.12
price, **92**.3
time for exercise, **92**.4
validity, **209**.2
Oral wills
airmen, seamen and soldiers, by, **16**.4
Organ transplantation
generally, **7**.34, **202**.13–**202**.15
precedent, **202**.17
Original will
extrinsic evidence, **57**.5
Ornaments
description of property, **64**.3

P

Parental responsibility
guardians, and, **28**.2
statutory provisions, **244**.113–**244**.117
Parish
description of property, **63**.3
Parish work
charitable purposes, **102**.17
precedents, **212**.8, **212**.10
Parol evidence
debt by legacy, **44**.16
legacies by portion, **44**.14
portion by legacies, **44**.14
Part performance
contracts relating to wills, **3**.4
Partial intestacy
generally, **104**.12
hotchpot
death after 1996, **104**.14
death before 1996, **104**.13
introduction, **104**.10
meaning, **104**.11
surviving spouse or civil partner with life interest, **104**.16
Partial revocation
destruction, and, **18**.23
generally, **18**.32
intention, **18**.33
Partially exempt estates
inheritance tax, **200**.112–**200**.118, **214**.72–**214**.74
Particular manner, gift to benefit in
generally, **82**.7
Partly inconsistent wills
revocation by later will or codicil, and, **18**.14
Partnership interests, gift of. *See also* **Business interests and property, gift of**
disposable property, **7**.15

Partnership interests, gift of – *contd*
generally, **205**.26–**205**.28
introductory note, **200**.15
Partnerships
description of property, **64**.43
executors, and, **25**.5
Patents, gift of
precedents, **204**.74
Payment of debt
ademption, and, **41**.19
Payment of legacies
generally, **30**.30–**30**.43
Pecuniary legacies
abatement
demonstrative legacies, **31**.3
general legacies, **31**.1
provision for, **210**.75
satisfaction of debt, in, **31**.2
specific, **31**.4
absolute gifts, **210**.9–**210**.14
apprentices, to, **30**.27
charged on mixed fund, **93**.45
charged on real property, **93**.44
conditional, **210**.46–**210**.50
contingent
delivery, **30**.33
interest and income, **32**.3
precedents, **210**.46–**210**.50
currency of
generally, **30**.43
precedents, **210**.77–**210**.78
debtor, to
abatement, **31**.2
generally, **30**.10–**30**.13, **210**.2
precedents, **210**.28–**210**.32
deferred, **210**.20–**210**.24
definition, **30**.1
delivery of, **30**.30–**30**.43
demonstrative
abatement, **31**.3
generally, **30**.6
interest and income,
32.4–**32**.17
precedent, **210**.74
employees, to
generally, **30**.23–**30**.29, **210**.57
precedents, **210**.58–**210**.63
executor, to
generally, **30**.14–**30**.18, **210**.51
precedents, **210**.52–**210**.53

Pecuniary legacies – *contd*
failure of, **30**.7
free of tax
generally, **210**.64–**210**.67
precedents, **210**.68–**210**.71
general
abatement, **31**.1
generally, **30**.5
interest and income,
32.4–**32**.17
immediate needs, for
generally, **210**.15–**210**.18
precedent, **210**.19
improvident persons
generally, **210**.54
precedents, **210**.55–**210**.56
income
class gifts, **32**.28
demonstrative legacies,
32.4–**32**.17
general legacies, **32**.4–**32**.17
intermediate, **32**.28
introduction, **32**.1
specific legacies, **32**.2–**32**.3
inheritance tax
introductory note, **210**.3–**210**.4
generally, **210**.64–**210**.67
precedents, **210**.68–**210**.71
interest
appropriation, and, **32**.29
demonstrative legacies,
32.4–**32**.17
foreign currency legacy, **32**.33
general legacies, **32**.4–**32**.17
generally, **32**.1, 210.8
minors' legacies, **32**.18–**32**.27
nature of payment, **32**.32
rate, **32**.31
recoverable arrears, **32**.30
specific legacies, **32**.2–**32**.3
meaning, **55**.4
minors, to
generally, **30**.19–**30**.22
interest, **32**.18–**32**.27
precedents, **210**.33–**210**.45
nil-rate band legacies, **210**.72
payable from personal property
direction as to maintenance,
93.31–**93**.39

Pecuniary legacies – *contd*
payable from personal property – *contd*
direction as to payment, **93**.26–**93**.30
generally, **93**.24–**93**.25
gift over, **93**.41–**93**.43
severance from estate, **93**.40
payment of, **30**.30–**30**.43
precedents
abatement and interest, provision for, **210**.75
absolute gifts, **210**.9–**210**.14
conditional legacies, **210**.46–**210**.50
contingent legacies, **210**.46–**210**.50
currency of legacy, **210**.77–**210**.78
debtors and creditors, **210**.28–**210**.32
deferred legacies, **210**.20–**210**.24
demonstrative legacy, **210**.74
employees, **210**.58–**210**.63
executors and trustees, **210**.52–**210**.53
immediate needs provision, **210**.19
improvident persons, **210**.55–**210**.56
inheritance tax, **210**.68–**210**.71
legatees not able to be found, **210**.73
minors and children, **210**.33–**210**.45
nil-rate band legacies, **210**.72
prior legacies, **210**.20–**210**.24
purchase of customary mourning, **210**.79
reduction of legacy, **210**.76
substitutional provisions, **210**.25–**210**.26
prior legacies, **210**.20–**210**.24
purchase of customary mourning, **210**.79
reduction of legacy, **210**.76
refunding, **31**.6–**31**.21
release of debt, **30**.4
republication of wills, and, **22**.4

Pecuniary legacies – *contd*
satisfaction by portion, and
different beneficiaries, **44**.13
double portion, **44**.6
ejusdem generis rule, **44**.11
election, **44**.7
gift in nature of portion, **44**.4
introduction, **44**.3
limitations, **44**.12
parol evidence, **44**.14
persons *in loco parentis*, **44**.8
rebuttal of presumption, **44**.9–**44**.10
size of second portion, **44**.5
satisfaction of debt by
child from parent, to, **44**.17
generally, **44**.15
parol evidence, **44**.16
satisfaction of portion by
different beneficiaries, **44**.13
double portion, **44**.6
ejusdem generis rule, **44**.11
election, **44**.7
gift in nature of portion, **44**.4
introduction, **44**.2
limitations, **44**.12
parol evidence, **44**.14
persons *in loco parentis*, **44**.8
rebuttal of presumption, **44**.9–**44**.10
size of second portion, **44**.5
servants, to, **30**.24
specific
abatement, **31**.4
delivery, **30**.34
generally, **30**.3
interest and income, **32**.2–**32**.3
stocks and shares, of
aliquot share, **30**.9
generally, **30**.8
substitutional provisions, **210**.25–**210**.26
types, **30**.2
Pencil
alteration of will, and, **10**.14
signature of wills, and, **11**.17
Pension schemes
nomination, and, **7**.13
Per capita distribution
generally, **87**.1–**87**.4

Per stripes distribution
generally, **87**.1–**87**.4
Perpetuities
applicable interests
equitable interests, **94**.36
personal property, **94**.35
real estate, **94**.33
rentcharges, **94**.39
reversion, **94**.40
rights of entry, **94**.34
trusts for sale, **94**.37
trusts of indefinite duration, **94**.38
children's trusts, and, **217**.6
class gifts
common law, at, **94**.21
generally, **94**.23–**94**.29
statute, under, **94**.22
common law, at, **94**.10–**94**.15
conditions, and, **35**.52
creation of interests by will, and, **8**.1
effect of gift being void, **94**.30–**94**.32
gestation period, **94**.4
life interests, and, **216**.4–**216**.5
lives in being, **94**.2
option to purchase, and, **92**.6
period allowed, **94**.1–**94**.9
power of appointment, and
common law, at, **94**.43–**94**.49
generally, **94**.42
remoteness, **94**.41
statute, under, **94**.50–**94**.53
statutory provisions
generally, **246**.74–**246**.85
introduction, **94**.16–**94**.20
pre-PAA 1964, **246**.55
uncertainty, and, **53**.7
wait and see rule
generally, **94**.17
power of appointment, **94**.49, **94**.53
Perpetuities and Accumulations Act 1964
citation, **246**.88
definitions, **246**.88
general provisions
accumulations, **246**.86–**246**.87
perpetuities, **246**.74–**246**.85
Person and children, gifts to
generally, **85**.1–**85**.3
Person and issue, gifts to
generally, **85**.4–**85**.5
Person of unsound mind
ademption, and, **41**.12
election, and, **42**.13
executors, and, **25**.4
Person with disability, wills providing for. ***See* Disability, wills providing for person with**
Personal chattels
description of property, **64**.44
meaning, **200**.14
Personal effects
description of property, **64**.18
Personal estate
generally, **64**.45
introduction, **60**.1
Personal representatives
executors, and, **25**.17
introductory note, **200**.63
trustees, and, **27**.15
Physical infirmity
soundness of mind, effect on, **4**.17
Pictures
description of property, **64**.46
Place of signature
death after 1982, **11**.9–**11**.12
death before 1983, **11**.2–**11**.8
Plants
description of property, **64**.3
Plate
description of property, **64**.47
Playing fields, gifts for provision of
precedent, **212**.26
Political purposes, trusts for
charitable purposes, **102**.11
Poor, relief of
employees, **102**.15
members, **102**.16
relations, **102**.14
Portions
accumulations, and, **95**.9
ademption, and, **41**.24
satisfaction by legacies, and
different beneficiaries, **44**.13

Portions – *contd*
satisfaction by legacies, and – *contd*
double portion, **44**.6
ejusdem generis rule, **44**.11
election, **44**.7
gift in nature of portion, **44**.4
introduction, **44**.2
limitations, **44**.12
parol evidence, **44**.14
persons *in loco parentis*, **44**.8
rebuttal of presumption, **44**.9–**44**.10
size of second portion, **44**.5
satisfaction of legacies by, and
different beneficiaries, **44**.13
double portion, **44**.6
ejusdem generis rule, **44**.11
election, **44**.7
gift in nature of portion, **44**.4
introduction, **44**.3
limitations, **44**.12
parol evidence, **44**.14
persons *in loco parentis*, **44**.8
rebuttal of presumption, **44**.9–**44**.10
size of second portion, **44**.5
Possessions
description of property, **64**.48
Possessory title
disposable property, **7**.30
Postponement
attaining specified age, to, **93**.30
investment powers, and, **220**.28
life interest, to, **93**.29
nature, **93**.4
Poverty, relief of
charitable purposes, **102**.7
Power of appointment
delegation, **40**.5
disclaimer, **40**.12
exercise. *See* **Power of appointment, exercise of**
fraudulent appointment
generally, **40**.14
grounds, **40**.15
variation of trusts, **40**.16
lapse, and, **47**.36–**47**.39
release
generally, **40**.10
implied, **40**.13
Power of appointment – *contd*
rule against perpetuities, and
common law, at, **94**.43–**94**.49
generally, **94**.42
remoteness, **94**.41
statute, under, **94**.50–**94**.53
severance, **40**.20
Power of appointment, exercise of
ademption, and, **41**.21
class of persons, among, **40**.2
contemplation of marriage, will made in
introduction, **17**.1
wills after 1982, **17**.6
wills before 1983, **17**.5
contract relating to wills, and
generally, **3**.14
special power, **3**.15
covenant against, **40**.11
delegation of power, and, **40**.5
disclaimer of power, and, **40**.12
election, and, **42**.4
foreign element wills, and
capacity of testator, **24**.15
donee domiciled abroad, **24**.12
evidence, **24**.18
immovables, **24**.13
introduction, **24**.11
residuary bequest, **24**.16
revocation, **24**.14
fraudulent appointment
generally, **40**.14
grounds, **40**.15
variation of trusts, **40**.16
general powers
definition, **39**.2
generally, **39**.4–**39**.15
joint will, by, **39**.8
nature, **39**.3
hybrid powers, **39**.31
introduction, **39**.1
miscellaneous matters, **40**.1–**40**.21
release of power, and
generally, **40**.10
implied, **40**.13
severance of appointment, **40**.20
soldiers', etc., wills, and, **16**.6
special powers. *See* **Special powers of appointment**

Power of appointment, exercise of – *contd*
successive instruments, by, **40**.3
Precatory words
generally, **82**.5–**82**.6
introductory note, **200**.22
Precedent
construction of wills, and, **50**.22
Predeceased testator
capacity to benefit, **9**.2
Predeceasing child, gifts to
adopted children, **47**.16
contingent gifts, **47**.18
death of testator before 1983, **47**.12–**47**.14
en ventre sa mere, **47**.17
estate tail, **47**.20
generally, **47**.15
illegitimate children, **47**.16
power of appointment, gift under, **47**.14
statutory provisions, **47**.11
substituted gifts, **47**.19
Premises
description of property, **64**.49
Premium bonds, gift of proceeds of
precedent, **204**.82
Presbyterian Church of Wales, gifts to
precedents, **212**.20–**212**.21
Presence of testator
attestation, and, **12**.6
Presence of witness
acknowledgement of signature, and, **11**.25
attestation, and, **12**.7
signature of wills, and, **11**.23, **12**.3
Presents
description of property, **64**.50
Presumptions
due execution
absence of attestation clause, and, **13**.2
general rule, **13**.1
rebuttal of, **13**.3
signature affixed by direction of testator, **13**.4
Presumptions – *contd*
favouring relatives
children, **51**.9
family, **51**.10
persons entitled on intestacy, **51**.12
relatives of equal degree, **51**.11
intestacy, against
gap in interests created, **51**.2
introduction, **51**.1
limits, **51**.3
legality of words, **51**.4–**51**.6
rationality of will, **51**.7–**51**.8
unintended life interest, **51**.13
Printing of will
generally, **10**.13–**10**.17
Prior advance
hotchpot, and, **100**.4–**100**.7
Prior legacies
precedents, **210**.20–**210**.24
Priority
annuities, and, **33**.33–**33**.34
Privileged wills
actual military service, meaning, **16**.2
at sea, meaning, **16**.3
exclusion of words, **16**.9
gifts to witnesses, and, **16**.7
introduction, **16**.1
lost will, and, **16**.5
power of appointment, and, **16**.6
proof, **16**.8
revocation, **16**.10
Probate or letters of administration
executors, and
grant, **25**.15
revocation, **25**.16
evidence, generally, **57**.3–**57**.7
Production of signed will
signature of wills, and, **11**.26
Professional privilege
attesting witnesses, and, **12**.17
Promissory notes
bonds, and, **64**.5
securities, and, **64**.53
Proof of wills
soldiers', etc., wills, **16**.8

Property
description of property, **64**.51
Property not belonging to testator
disposable property, **7**.17
Proprietary estoppel
approbation, and, **43**.4
conditions, and, **43**.5
contracts relating to wills, and, **3**.1
generally, **43**.2–**43**.3
hotchpot clause, **43**.6
principles, **43**.1
reprobation, and, **43**.4
Protective trusts
generally, **200**.20
inheritance tax regime, **200**.104
life interest subject to, **216**.8
statutory provisions, **246**.31
woman for life, to, **216**.9
Protestants
description of donees, **81**.4
capacity to benefit, **9**.13–**9**.22
conditions, and
acquisition of dignity, **35**.47
entering HM Forces, **35**.46
generally, **34**.12
restraint of marriage, **35**.1–**35**.6
creation of interests by will, and, **8**.2
inheritance provision, and, **105**.8
unlawful killings, and, **9**.13–**9**.22
Public Trustee
appointment as executor and trustee, **203**.36–**203**.42
executors, and, **25**.8
notices of death of testator
Trustee appointed executor, **240**.1
Trustee appointed trustee, **240**.2
Public Trustee Rules 1912
general provisions, **246**.73
introductory note, **246**.72
Punctuation
usual meaning of words, and, **50**.15
Purchaser protection
appropriation, and, **29**.23
Purchaser protection – *contd*
trustees, and, **246**.15

Q

Quantity of interest given
clear gifts cut down, **82**.2
expression of testator's motive, **82**.5–**82**.6
generally, **82**.1–**82**.4
gifts for particular purposes, **82**.7–**82**.9
Quasi-inheritable gifts
entailed interests, and, **84**.4

R

Raising money
trustees' powers, and, **246**.14
Rationality of will
presumptions, and, **51**.7–**51**.8
Ready money, gift of
description of property, **64**.38
precedent, **204**.81
Real estate
description of property, **64**.52
rule against perpetuities, and, **94**.33
Reciprocal wills. *See* **Married couples or civil partners with adult children; Married couples or civil partners with young children**
Re-conversion
generally, **37**.8
Recreation
charitable purposes, **102**.12
Rectification
clerical errors, **6**.2
extrinsic evidence, and, **57**.29
failure to understand testator's instructions, **6**.3
introduction, **6**.1
negligence actions, **6**.4
procedure, **6**.5–**6**.6
statutory provisions, **244**.98
Reduction of legacy
precedents, **210**.76

Re-execution
revival of wills, and, **21**.1
Reference to existing document, gifts by
conditional gifts, and, **91**.5
gift of personal chattels, and, **204**.34
Reference to plan, gifts by
gift of freehold land, and, **206**.37
Referential trusts
introductory note, **200**.21
Refunding of legacies
generally, **31**.6–**31**.21
Registration of wills
generally, **10**.20
statutory provisions, **244**.101–**244**.106
Rejection of words
construction of wills, and, **52**.6–**52**.11
Relations
description of donees, **79**.4–**79**.6
Relatives of equal degree
favouring relatives, **51**.11
Release of power of appointment
generally, **40**.10
implied, **40**.13
Release of debt
generally, **30**.4
Religion, advancement of
charitable purposes, **102**.9
Religion, conditions relating to
Church of England, **35**.32
Jews, **35**.31
protestants, **35**.23
Roman Catholics, **35**.30
uncertainty, **35**.29
Religious belief
soundness of mind, and, **4**.16
Religious disabilities
capacity to benefit, and, **9**.36
Religious purposes in a parish, gifts for
precedent, **212**.10
Remainders
vesting, and, **93**.10–**93**.15
Re-marriage
conditions, and, **35**.8
mutual wills, effect on, **2**.9–**2**.10
residence rights, and, **208**.41
Removal of gift
ademption, and, **41**.17
Removal of incapacity
capacity to make will, and, **4**.4
Remuneration clause
banks, **203**.31
trust corporations, **203**.30
Remuneration of trustee
generally, **27**.10
retention of directors' remuneration, **221**.10–**221**.12
statutory provisions, **246**.160–**246**.165
Renewal of lease
generally, **61**.1
Rent
disposable property, **7**.24
unlimited gifts of income, and, **62**.4
Rentcharges
generally, **61**.1
rule against perpetuities, and, **94**.39
Rents and profits, payment of
gift of leasehold land, and, **207**.19
Renunciation
disclaimer of trusteeship
precedents, **239**.3–**239**.5
preliminary note, **239**.1
executors, and, **25**.13
generally, **239**.1
precedent, **239**.2
settled land grant, and, **26**.6
Repairs
freehold land, gift of, **206**.8
leasehold land, gift, **207**.2
right of residence, and, **208**.26–**208**.28
Representatives
description of donees, **79**.7
Reprobation
estoppel, and, **43**.4
Republication of wills
effect
generally, **22**.3
intermediate wills, on, **22**.5
legacies, on, **22**.4
introduction, **22**.1

Republication of wills – *contd*
methods, **22**.2
precedent, **237**.34
Repugnant conditions
generally, **34**.5–**34**.6
Repugnant words
construction of wills, and, **52**.6
Residence, conditions as to
discharge of, **35**.26
generally, **35**.18–**35**.28
ignorance of, **35**.27
involuntary cesser, **35**.20
provision of home, on, **35**.21
separation of parent and child, **35**.24
separation of spouses, **35**.23
uncertainty, **35**.22
voluntary cesser, **35**.20
Residence, rights of
administrative powers, **208**.36
change of residence, **208**.38–**208**.39, **208**.43
children, residence and furniture for, **208**.44
civil partner, of, **208**.42
freedom from liabilities, **208**.29
furniture, use of, **208**.37, **208**.40, **208**.44
generally, **208**.1–**208**.4
grant of lease, by, **208**.4
introductory note, **200**.16
periodic tenancy, **208**.47
personal residence, object of ensuring, **208**.45–**208**.47
precedents, **208**.38–**208**.48
remarriage, **208**.41
rentcharge supporting, **208**.46
short leases, right to, **208**.45
taxation, **208**.30–**208**.35
tenant in common, gift of interest as, **208**.48
trusts of land legislation, under
generally, **208**.5–**208**.18
introduction, **208**.3
wife, to, for life, **208**.43
will, gift by, **208**.19–**208**.28
Residuary gifts
administration trusts
conversion, **214**.2, **214**.16
generally, **214**.1–**214**.9
Residuary gifts – *contd*
administration trusts – *contd*
legacies, **214**.9
order of application of assets, **214**.4–**214**.8
power of sale, **214**.1
power to postpone sale, **214**.3
precedents, **214**.10–**214**.26
without trust for sale, **214**.10–**214**.11
Allhusen v. Whittell, rule in
exclusion, **214**.43–**214**.44
generally, **38**.26–**38**.28
precedents, **214**.45–**214**.47
Chesterfield's Trusts, rule in
exclusion, **214**.29–**214**.38
generally, **38**.22–**38**.23
precedents, **214**.39–**214**.42
ejusdem generis rule, **38**.10
exclusion of time apportionment
generally, **214**.48–**214**.52
precedents, **214**.53–**214**.54
failure of share, **38**.13–**38**.14
Howe v. Dartmouth rule
adjustment of debts, **38**.26–**38**.28
exclusion, **214**.29–**214**.38
generally, **38**.17–**38**.25
precedents, **214**.39–**214**.42
reversionary interests, **38**.22–**38**.23
inheritance tax
directions as to, **214**.17
generally, **214**.55–**214**.75
precedents, **214**.76–**214**.82
precedents
administration trusts, **214**.10–**214**.26
Allhusen v. Whittell, exclusion of rule in, **214**.45–**214**.47
Chesterfield's Trusts, exclusion of rule in, **214**.39–**214**.42
exclusion of time apportionment, **214**.53–**214**.54
Howe v. Dartmouth, exclusion of rule in, **214**.39–**214**.42
inheritance tax, directions as to incidence, **214**.76–**214**.82

Residuary gifts – *contd*
precedents – *contd*
powers and directions for administration of estate, **214**.29–**214**.34
powers and directions for administration of estate, **214**.27–**214**.28
relevant property, **38**.1–**38**.2
residuary legatee's rights, **38**.15–**38**.16
words required to make, **38**.3–**38**.12

Resolution of appropriation
generally, **243**.1
precedent, **243**.2

Restraint of marriage, conditions in
annuities, and, **33**.22
class of persons, with, **35**.4
generally, **35**.2
introduction, **35**.1
particular person, with, **35**.6
particular religion, with person of, **35**.5
specified age, under, **35**.3

Retraction
disclaimer of gift, and, **46**.4

Reversionary interest, gift of
precedent, **204**.76

Review of existing wills
introductory note, **200**.66–**200**.67

Revival of wills
codicils, by
generally, **21**.6
introduction, **20**.9
precedent, **237**.34
reference to will by date, **21**.7
express intention, **21**.5
form, **21**.3
incorporation in later will, by, **21**.2
lost will, and, **21**.4
methods, **21**.1
precedent, **237**.34
re-execution, by, **21**.1
revocation of revoking will, and, **21**.8

Revocability of will
generally, **18**.4

Revocability of will – *contd*
introduction, **1**.4
mutual wills, and, **2**.5

Revocation
guardians, and
commencement of will, **201**.3
generally, **28**.6
settled land grants, **26**.6
will, of. *See* **Revocation of will**

Revocation of will
annulment of marriage, and, **17**.9
cancellation, and, **18**.25
codicil, by
generally, **18**.15
precedent, **237**.35
share of residue, as to, **20**.5
conditional
evidence, **19**.6
generally, **19**.1
later will or codicil, **19**.2
contracts relating to wills, and, **3**.13
delegation of power, and, **18**.3
dependent relative
evidence, **19**.6
examples, **19**.4
generally, **19**.3
destruction, by
burden of proof, **18**.31
codicils, **18**.24
duplicate, of, **18**.19
evidence of intention, **18**.18
extent
generally, **18**.22
partial, **18**.23
foreign element wills, **23**.14
incomplete, **18**.20
intention
evidence, **18**.18
generally, **18**.17
presumption, **18**.26–**18**.29
introduction, **18**.17
part, in, **18**.23
presumption of intention
mutilation of will, **18**.27
non-availability, **18**.28
rebuttal of, **18**.29
stranger, by, **18**.21
divorce, and, **17**.9

Revocation of will – *contd*
foreign element wills, and
destruction, by, **23**.14
later will, by, **23**.13
marriage, by, **23**.15
intention
burden of proof, **18**.7
generally, **18**.4–**18**.5
proof, **18**.6
introductory note, **200**.45
later will or codicil, by
codicil, **18**.15
form of instrument, **18**.16
introduction, **18**.8
last will, meaning, **18**.9
lost subsequent will, **18**.13
lost will, **18**.12
partly inconsistent will, **18**.14
same date will, **18**.11
subsequent inconsistent will, **18**.10
undated will, **18**.11
marriage, by *see* **Marriage, revocation by**
mistake, by, 19.5
partial
destruction, and, **18**.23
generally, **18**.32
intention, **18**.33
precedent, **237**.35
previous will, 201.2
reoking will, 21.8
soldiers', etc., wills, and, **16**.10
voluntary. *See* **Voluntary revocation of will**
Rights of action
disposable property, **7**.29
Rights of enjoyment
life interests, and, **83**.6
Rights of entry
disposable property, **7**.21
rule against perpetuities, and, **94**.34
Rights of selection of one or more properties
creation of interests by will, and, **8**.7
Rule against perpetuities
applicable interests
equitable interests, **94**.36

Rule against perpetuities – *contd*
applicable interests – *contd*
personal property, **94**.35
real estate, **94**.33
rentcharges, **94**.39
reversion, **94**.40
rights of entry, **94**.34
trusts for sale, **94**.37
trusts of indefinite duration, **94**.38
class gifts
common law, at, **94**.21
generally, **94**.23–**94**.29
statute, under, **94**.22
common law, at, **94**.10–**94**.15
conditions, and, **35**.52
creation of interests by will, and, **8**.1
effect of gift being void, **94**.30–**94**.32
gestation period, **94**.4
lives in being, **94**.2
option to purchase, and, **92**.6
period allowed, **94**.1–**94**.9
power of appointment, and
common law, at, **94**.43–**94**.49
generally, **94**.42
remoteness, **94**.41
statute, under, **94**.50–**94**.53
statute, under, **94**.16–**94**.20
uncertainty, and, **53**.7
wait and see rule
generally, **94**.17
power of appointment, **94**.49, **94**.53

S

Sale of land, ademption by
generally, **41**.5–**41**.6
subject to trust for sale, **41**.7
Sale of property
depreciatory conditions, **246**.11
generally, **246**.10
investment powers, and, **220**.23–**220**.27
purchaser protection, **246**.15
receipt for proceeds, **246**.12

Sale of stocks and shares
ademption, and, **41**.11
Sale proceeds
disposable property, **7**.27
Salvation Army, gifts to
precedent, **212**.15
Same date, wills with
revocation by later will or codicil, and, **18**.11
Same words in different parts of will
context of words, and, **54**.5
Satisfaction
debt by legacy, of
child from parent, to, **44**.17
generally, **44**.15
parol evidence, **44**.16
ejusdem generis rule, and, **44**.11
election, and, **44**.7
introduction, **44**.1
legacies by portion, of
different beneficiaries, **44**.13
double portion, **44**.6
ejusdem generis rule, **44**.11
election, **44**.7
gift in nature of portion, **44**.4
introduction, **44**.3
limitations, **44**.12
parol evidence, **44**.14
persons *in loco parentis*, **44**.8
rebuttal of presumption, **44**.9–**44**.10
size of second portion, **44**.5
portion by legacies, of
different beneficiaries, **44**.13
double portion, **44**.6
ejusdem generis rule, **44**.11
election, **44**.7
gift in nature of portion, **44**.4
introduction, **44**.2
limitations, **44**.12
parol evidence, **44**.14
persons *in loco parentis*, **44**.8
rebuttal of presumption, **44**.9–**44**.10
size of second portion, **44**.5
pro tanto, **44**.5
Satisfaction of legacies
republication of wills, and, **22**.4
Satisfaction *pro tanto*
generally **44**.5
Savings bank accounts
nomination, and, **7**.11
Saying of masses, gifts for
capacity to benefit, **9**.36
School, gifts to
precedents
encouragement of sport, **212**.27
provision of playing fields, **212**.26
Scout Association, gifts to
precedent, **212**.29
Seal
signature of wills, and, **11**.19
Seamen, wills of
actual military service, meaning, **16**.2
at sea, meaning, **16**.3
exclusion of words, **16**.9
gifts to witnesses, and, **16**.7
introduction, **16**.1
lost will, and, **16**.5
power of appointment, and, **16**.6
proof, **16**.8
revocation, **16**.10
Second signature
will, of, **11**.27
Secret trusts
absolute gifts
communication of, **36**.6–**36**.7
conditions, **36**.4
generally, **36**.2–**36**.9
tacit acquiescence, **36**.3
declaration of trust of property
precedent, **240**.5
extrinsic evidence of, **57**.28
indefinite trust gifts, **36**.10–**36**.13
introduction, **36**.1
Securities
description of property, **64**.53
Selection of one or more properties
creation of interests by will, and, **8**.7
Selection, right of
gift of personal chattels, and
preliminary note, **204**.6
wife, by, **204**.20–**204**.21

Self-dealing
appropriation, and, **29**.20
generally, **221**.4
precedents, **221**.5–**221**.9
Senility
soundness of mind, effect on, **4**.17
Separation of parent and child, conditions relating to
generally, **35**.36
residence, **35**.24
Separation of spouses, conditions relating to
generally, **35**.35
residence, **35**.23
Series of gifts
conditional gifts, and, **91**.4
Servants
legacies, and, **30**.24
Settled land
appointment of executors and trustees, **203**.46
introductory note, **200**.52
Settled land grant
death of tenant for life, on, **26**.4
devolution of legal estate, **26**.2
discretionary, **26**.5
disposal of settled land, **26**.9
generally, **26**.3
introduction, **26**.1
limitation, **26**.8
renunciation, **26**.6
revocation, **26**.6
special administrators, **26**.7
Settled leaseholds
gift of leasehold land, and, **207**.6–**207**.8
Settled legacies
precedents, **216**.32–**216**.33
Settled shares of residue
appropriation, and, **29**.6
lapse of gift, **47**.25–**47**.26
Settlement of property
conditions, and, **35**.50
Settlements
creation of interests by will, and, **8**.1
introductory note, **200**.21
Several sheets, will over
signature, **11**.4
Severance from estate
vesting, and, **93**.40
Severance of joint tenancy
generally, **86**.5
Severance of power of appointment
generally, **40**.20
Shares in company, gift of
aliquot share, **30**.98
description of property, **64**.54
disposable property, **7**.14
generally, **30**.98, **204**.51–**204**.54
inheritance tax
generally, **204**.52–**204**.53
situs of shares, **204**.54
precedents, **204**.55–**204**.61
Signature affixed by direction of testator
attestation, and, **13**.4
Signature of alterations to will
generally, **14**.6
subsequent validation, **14**.7–**14**.8
third parties, by, **14**.15
Signature of wills
acknowledgement of
presence of witnesses, **11**.25
production of signed will, by, **11**.26
second signature, by, **11**.27
sufficiency, **11**.24
attestation clause, in
generally, **12**.12
introduction, **11**.6
precedents, **222**.3–**222**.16
blind testator, by, **11**.22, **222**.9
deaf and dumb testator, by, **222**.10
envelope, on, **11**.7
form of
assumed name, **11**.20
dry pen, **11**.18
initials, **11**.15
mark, **11**.13
on testator's behalf, **11**.21
pencil, **11**.17
seal, **11**.19
stamp, **11**.16
unfinished signature, **11**.14
wrong name, **11**.20

Signature of wills – *contd*
illiterate testator, by, **11**.22, **222**.7–**222**.8
indorsement, as, **11**.7
intention, and, **11**.11
introduction, **11**.1
place of
death after 1982, **11**.9–**11**.12
death before 1983, **11**.2–**11**.8
presence of witness, in, **11**.23
several sheets, over, **11**.4
testimonium clause, in, **11**.6
unfinished
form, **11**.14
place, **11**.8
words below, **11**.3
Signs
form of will, and, **10**.16
Sinking fund policies
gift of leasehold land, and, **207**.23
Societies
capacity to benefit, **9**.35
Soldiers, wills of
actual military service, meaning, **16**.2
exclusion of words, **16**.9
gifts to witnesses, and, **16**.7
introduction, **16**.1
lost will, and, **16**.5
power of appointment, and, **16**.6
proof, **16**.8
revocation, **16**.10
Sole parents with young children
entire estate willed by mother
minor child, to, **229**.2–**229**.12
sister as executrix and guardian if accepting office, **229**.13–**229**.25
note, **229**.1
Sole traders. *See also* **Business interests and property, gift of**
discussion, **205**.21–**205**.25
Solemnisation of marriage
conditions, and, **35**.34
Solicitors
appointment of executors and trustees, as
incorporated practices, **203**.20–**203**.21
Solicitors – *contd*
appointment of executors and trustees, as – *contd*
limited liability partnerships, **203**.22–**203**.23
partners, **203**.15–**203**.19
precedents, **203**.24–**203**.27
two partners, **203**.16
duties
beneficiaries, to, **1**.14
soundness of mind, as to, **4**.21
Soundness of mind
capacity to benefit, and, **9**.45
criterion, **4**.11
delusions
generally, **4**.15
religious belief, **4**.16
drunkenness, **4**.19
eccentricity, **4**.18
evidence of, **4**.20
foolishness, **4**.18
lucid intervals, **4**.14
mental capacity, test for, **4**.9
mental disorder, **4**.12
presumption, **4**.13
relevant time, **4**.10
religious belief, **4**.16
senility, **4**.17
solicitor's duty, **4**.21, **200**.4–**200**.5
Special administrators. *See also* **Settled land**
generally, **26**.7
Special powers of appointment, exercise of
accumulations, **213**.8
appoint, meaning, **39**.25
authorisation, **242**.1
co-existence with general power, **39**.24
deed, by
generally, **39**.28
with power of revocation, **39**.29
delegation of power, **213**.6
direction to pay debts, **39**.26
essentials
intention to exercise power, **39**.20
introduction, **39**.17

Special powers of appointment, exercise of – *contd*
essentials – *contd*
reference to power, **39**.18
reference to property, **39**.19
failure to, **39**.30
generally, **39**.16–**39**.30, **213**.1–**213**.11
introduction, **213**.1–**213**.2
lapse, **39**.29
objects of power, **213**.3–**213**.5
partial exercise, **39**.21
perpetuities, **213**.7
precedents, **213**.12–**213**.14
residuary gifts, **39**.23
tax considerations, **213**.9–**213**.11
universal gifts, **39**.22
will, by, **39**.27

Specific description
inaccuracy of description, and, **58**.13

Specific legacies
abatement, and, **31**.4
delivery, and, **30**.34
generally, **30**.3, **200**.13
interest and income, and, **32**.2–**32**.3

Specified age, gift at
vesting, and, **93**.6

Sporting equipment
description of property, **64**.55
gift of personal chattels, and, **204**.31

Spouse
description of donees, and, **80**.8
executors, and, **25**.7
gift of personal chattels, and, **204**.15–**204**.21
inheritance provision, and
additional considerations, **105**.28
applicant, as, **105**.9
discretion, **105**.20–**105**.25
total intestacy, and
fixed net sum, **104**.4
generally, **104**.2
personal chattels, **104**.3
redemption and appropriation, **104**.5

Spouse – *contd*
wills in favour of, introductory note, **200**.24–**200**.26

Stamp
appropriation, and, **29**.16
signature of wills, and, **11**.16

Stamp duty
advancement powers, and, **242**.6
appointment powers, and, **242**.6
variation of beneficial interests, and, **241**.18

Stamp duty land tax
advancement powers, and, **242**.6
appointment powers, and, **242**.6
variation of beneficial interests, and, **241**.18

Stamps
description of property, **64**.56

State benefits
person with disability, wills providing for, **226**.2

Statutory tenancies
disposable property, **7**.4

Statutory Will Forms Order 1925
administration trusts, **238**.14
annuity directions, **238**.11
appropriation, power of, **238**.12
charitable legacies, **238**.10
confirmation of settlements, **238**.7
generally, **238**.1–**238**.3
inventory of chattels, **238**.9
personal chattels, meaning of, **238**.8
spouse for life trusts
with power to appoint, **238**.15
without power to appoint, **238**.16
text, **238**.4–**238**.6
trusts of settled legacy, **238**.13

Stripes, distribution per
generally, **87**.1–**87**.4

Stirpital survivorship
generally, **67**.5

Stock
description of property, **64**.57

Stocks and shares, gifts of
aliquot share, **30**.98
description of property, **64**.54
disposable property, **7**.14

Stocks and shares, gifts of – *contd*
generally, **30**.98 , **204**.51–**204**.54
inheritance tax
generally, **204**.52–**204**.53
situs of shares, **204**.54
precedents, **204**.55–**204**.61
Strangers
revocation by destruction, and, **18**.21
Street
description of property, **63**.4
Stud fees
generally, **61**.1
Subject-matter, certainty of
contracts relating to wills, and, **3**.2
Subsequent gifts to donee
failure of gifts, and, **48**.3
Subsequent inconsistent will
revocation by later will or codicil, and, **18**.10
Subsequent marriage of witness
capacity to benefit, and, **9**.7
Subsequent will or codicil, revocation by
codicil, **18**.15
foreign element wills, and, **23**.13
form of instrument, **18**.16
introduction, **18**.8
last will, **18**.9
lost subsequent will, **18**.13
lost will, **18**.12
partly inconsistent will, **18**.14
same date will, **18**.11
subsequent inconsistent will, **18**.10
undated will, **18**.11
Substantial property, wills for owners of
bachelor landowner, settlement of family estate by, **235**.18–**235**.37
controlling shareholding in family company, gift on trusts for employees, residue on charitable trusts, **235**.2–**235**.17
precedents, **235**.2–**235**.37
preliminary note, **235**.1
Substituted gifts
conditional gifts, and, **91**.6
generally, **88**.1–**88**.4
lapse, on
alternative gifts, **47**.23
executor of deceased legatee, legacy to, **47**.24
predeceasing child, **47**.19
Substitution
failure of primary trust, and, **219**.18–**219**.19
legacies, and, **210**.25–**210**.26
Successive gifts
contingencies, and, **93**.6
Successive instruments
power of appointment, and, **40**.3
Successive interests
cy-près doctrine, **89**.2
generally, **89**.1
gift of freehold land, and, **206**.6
Sunday school prizes, gifts to
precedent, **212**.11
Superadded powers, gifts with
generally, **83**.8–**83**.20
Superfluous attestation
capacity to benefit, and, **9**.8
generally, **12**.8
Superstitious uses, gifts for
capacity to benefit, and, **9**.36
Supervening incapacity
capacity to make will, and, **4**.3
Surplus income
annuities, and, **33**.25
charitable gifts, and
donee charged with payment, **103**.14
generally, **103**.13
description of income, and, **61**.1
Surplusage of words
construction of wills, and, **52**.6
Surviving spouse
description of donees, and, **80**.5
partial intestacy, **104**.16
Surviving relatives, gifts to
introductory note, **200**.35
Survivors
contingent event, **67**.3
divesting, and, **67**.7
generally, **67**.1–**67**.8
gift over to others, **67**.6

Survivors – *contd*
introduction, **65**.5
stirpital, **67**.5
time for ascertainment, **67**.2
Survivorship conditions and clauses
common law, **70**.1
divorce or dissolution of civil partnership, possibility of, **224**.16–**224**.23
fiscal implications, **219**.5–**219**.11
generally, **200**.17, **219**.12–**219**.13, **224**.6–**224**.8
gifts other than to spouse or civil partner, **224**.10
guardians, **224**.11
inheritance tax, **219**.5–**219**.11
no longer recommended, **227**.4
order of deaths of spouses uncertain, **224**.5
practical considerations, **219**.2–**219**.4
precedents, **219**.14–**219**.17
reciprocal and mutual wills, **224**.12–**224**.15
statute, **70**.2–**70**.4
statutory provision, **244**.58
Synagogue, gifts to
precedent, **212**.24

T

Tax
disclaimer of gift, and, **46**.6
Tax-free annuities
generally, **33**.46–**33**.47
precedent, **211**.9
Technical terms, meaning of
determination, **50**.11
generally, **50**.7
Tenancy in common
gifts of property subject to
freehold land, **206**.16
generally, **86**.6–**86**.8
lapse, **47**.28
testator's interest, postponed gift of, **208**.48
Tenant in tail
gift of freehold land, and, **206**.18
Tenements
description of property, **64**.33
Tenure
description of property, **63**.9
Testamentary capacity
aliens, **4**.5
cessation of incapacity to make will, and, **4**.4
criminals, **4**.6
domicile, and, **4**.2
generally, **4**.1
knowledge and approval, **5**.3
married women, **4**.8
mentally disordered person
examples of exercise of jurisdiction, **4**.24
guidelines as to exercise of jurisdiction, **4**.23
jurisdiction of court, **4**.22
Practice Direction, **4**.25
minors, **4**.7
removal of incapacity to make will, and, **4**.4
soundness of mind *see* **Soundness of mind**
supervening incapacity to make will, and, **4**.3
Testamentary expenses
meaning, **55**.7
Testamentary intention
form of will, and, **10**.4
Testamentary options
ademption, and, **41**.20
bounty, and, **92**.2
capital gains tax, **209**.4
creation of interests by will, and, **8**.6
generally, **92**.1–**92**.6, **209**.1–**209**.5
inheritance tax, **209**.3
perpetuities, and, **92**.6
precedents, **209**.6–**209**.12
price, **92**.3
time for exercise, **92**.4
validity, **209**.2
Testamentary power
delegation of, **1**.6
generally, **1**.10
Testimonium clause
signature of wills, and, **11**.6

Therapeutic use of body
generally, **7**.34, **202**.13–**202**.15
precedent, **202**.16–**202**.17
Timber
generally, **61**.1
proceeds, treatment of, **220**.61
Time limits
election, and, **42**.11
inheritance provision, and, **105**.5
Tombs, gifts for upkeep of
capacity to benefit, **9**.29–**9**.30
generally, **202**.18–**202**.30
precedent, **202**.31–**202**.35
Tombstone
disposal of body, and, **202**.3
Total intestacy
entitlement of Crown, **104**.10
entitlement of issue
generally, **104**.6
statutory trusts, **104**.7
entitlement of other relatives, **104**.8
entitlement of spouse
fixed net sum, **104**.4
generally, **104**.2
personal chattels, **104**.3
redemption and appropriation, **104**.5
introduction, **104**.1
Trade unions
capacity to benefit, **9**.35
Transfer into testator's name
ademption, and, **41**.22
Transport expenses
gift of personal chattels, and
note, **204**.4
precedent, **204**.27
Transposition of words
construction of wills, and, **52**.5
Trust corporations
appointment as executors and trustees
generally, **203**.2, **203**.28–**203**.31
precedents, **203**.32–**203**.35
meaning, **246**.71, **246**.101
trustees, and, **27**.4
Trust estates
conditions, and, **34**.4
disposable property, **7**.6
Trust estates – *contd*
foreign element wills, and, **24**.5
Trust gifts
capacity to benefit, **9**.4
Trust property purchased by trustee
disposable property, **7**.7
Trustee Act 1925
amendments, 2000, **246**.169
application, **246**.40
definitions, **246**.39
general provisions
accumulation and maintenance, **246**.29
advancement, **246**.30
appointment and discharge of trustees, **246**.32–**246**.38
protective trusts, **246**.31
trustees' powers, **246**.10–**246**.26
introductory note, **246**.9
Trustee Act 2000
amendments, **246**.170
citation, **246**.172
commencement, **246**.171
consequential amendments, **246**.169
definitions, **246**.168
general provisions
acquisition of land powers, **246**.140–**246**.142
agents, **246**.143–**246**.147
custodians, **246**.149–**246**.152
duty of care, **246**.132–**246**.134, **246**.173
investment powers, **246**.135–**246**.139
liability for agents, nominees and custodians, **246**.153–**246**.155
nominees, **246**.148–**246**.152
remuneration of trustee, **246**.160–**246**.165
supplementary, **246**.156–**246**.159
introductory note, **200**.65
miscellaneous provisions, **246**.166–**246**.167
schedule, **246**.173

Trustees
acceptance of trust, **27**.5
appointees
generally, **27**.3
trust corporations, **27**.4
appointment. *See also* **Trustees, appointment of**
generally, **27**.2, **203**.1–**203**.6, **221**.35
precedents, **203**.7–**203**.46, **221**.36–**221**.41
statutory provisions, **246**.32–**246**.35, **246**.122–**246**.124
charging powers
generally, **221**.42–**221**.48
precedents, **221**.49–**221**.52
conduct of trusteeship, **221**.27–**221**.34
delegation, **27**.9
devolution of trust, **27**.7
disclaimer of trust, **27**.6
duty of care
generally, **27**.8
statutory provisions, **246**.143–**246**.134, **246**.173
indemnities, releases and receipts
generally, **221**.13–**221**.15
precedents, **221**.16–**221**.26
introduction, **27**.1
meaning of trustee, **221**.1–**221**.3
minors, and, **27**.3
new or continuing, vesting of trust property in, **246**.38
personal representatives, and, **27**.15
powers, *See* **Trustees, powers of**
precedents
appointment of trustees, **221**.36–**221**.41
charging powers, **221**.49–**221**.52
conduct of trusteeship, **221**.27–**221**.34
indemnities, releases and receipts, **221**.16–**221**.26
meaning of trustee, **221**.1–**221**.3

Trustees – *contd*
precedents – *contd*
retention of directors' remuneration, **221**.10–**221**.12
self-dealing, **221**.5–**221**.9
remuneration
generally, **27**.10
statutory provisions, **246**.160–**246**.165
retention of directors' remuneration, **221**.10–**221**.12
retirement without new appointment, **246**.37
sale of land, for
after 1996, **27**.17
before 1997, **27**.16
self-dealing
generally, **221**.4
precedents, **221**.5–**221**.9
Settled Land Act 1925, under, **27**.18
statutory provisions
appointment of trustee, **246**.32–**246**.35, **246**.122–**246**.124
duty of care, **246**.132–**246**.134, **246**.173
powers of trustee, **246**.10–**246**.26, **246**.135–**246**.159
remuneration of trustee, **246**.160–**246**.165
supplementary, **246**.156–**246**.159
trust corporations, and, **27**.4

Trustees, appointment of
acceptance, **25**.12
banks' charges, **203**.31
business executors, **203**.44
charging clause
banks, **203**.31
trust corporations, **203**.30
conditional, **25**.3
corporations
generally, **203**.2, **203**.28–**203**.31
precedents, **203**.32–**203**.35
duration, **25**.9

Trustees, appointment of – *contd*
foreign property executors, **203**.45
generally, **25**.1
implication, by, **25**.2
individuals
generally, **203**.1–**203**.6
precedents, **203**.7–**203**.13
legacies to
generally, **30**.14–**30**.18, **210**.51
introduction, **25**.19
precedents, **210**.52–**210**.53
literary executors, **203**.43
number
generally, **203**.1
statutory provision, **246**.32
precedents
business executors, **203**.44
civil partner, **203**.8
corporations, **203**.32–**203**.35
executors
different persons as, **203**.11
same persons as, **203**.10
foreign property executors, **203**.45
generally, **221**.36–**221**.41
individuals, **203**.7–**203**.13
literary executors, **203**.43
Public Trustee, **203**.36–**203**.42
settled land executors, **203**.46
solicitors, **203**.24–**203**.27
substitution in case of vacancy, provision for, **203**.14
three persons, one abroad, **203**.13
wife/civil partner, adult son and infant son when attaining majority, **203**.12
Public Trustee, **203**.36–**203**.42
remuneration clause
banks, **203**.31
trust corporations, **203**.30
renunciation, **25**.13
retirement without, **246**.37
settled land, **203**.46
solicitors
incorporated practices, **203**.20–**203**.21
limited liability partnerships, **203**.22–**203**.23

Trustees, appointment of – *contd*
solicitors – *contd*
partners, **203**.15–**203**.19
precedents, **203**.24–**203**.27
two partners, **203**.16
statutory provisions
additional appointments, **246**.34
beneficiaries' appointment, **246**.122
limitation of number, **246**.32
new appointments, **246**.34
substitution for lack of capacity, **246**.123
supplemental provisions, **246**.35, **246**.124
trustees of land, **246**.33
trustees of settlements, **246**.33
substituted, **25**.3
trust corporations
generally, **203**.2, **203**.28–**203**.31
precedents, **203**.32–**203**.35
vacancy, evidence of, **246**.36

Trustees, powers of
accumulation, **246**.29
acquisition of land
generally, **27**.12
statutory provisions, **246**.140–**246**.142
advancement, **246**.30
agents, employment of
generally, **246**.143–**246**.147
review of and liability for, **246**.153–**246**.155
supplementary, **246**.156–**246**.159
compound liabilities, **246**.13
custodians, employment of
generally, **246**.149–**246**.152
review of and liability for, **246**.153–**246**.155
supplementary, **246**.156–**246**.159
delegation
generally, **27**.9
statutory provision, **246**.23
devolution, **246**.16
gift of business interests, and, **205**.70–**205**.79

Trustees, powers of – *contd*
indemnities, **246**.24–**246**.26
insurance
generally, **27**.14
statutory provisions, **246**.17–**246**.18
investment
generally, **27**.11
statutory provisions, **246**.135–**246**.139
land, **27**.13
maintenance, **246**.29
nominees, employment of
generally, **246**.148–**246**.152
review of and liability for, **246**.153–**246**.155
supplementary, **246**.156–**246**.159
preliminary note, **205**.29–**205**.40
purchaser protection, **246**.15
raising money, **246**.14
sale of property
depreciatory conditions, **246**.11
generally, **246**.10
purchaser protection, **246**.15
receipt for proceeds, **246**.12
statutory provisions, **246**.10–**246**.26, **246**.135–**246**.159

Trusts estates
conditions, and, **34**.4
disposable property, **7**.6
foreign element wills, and, **24**.5

Trusts for sale of land
creation of interests by will, and, **8**.2
gift of freehold land, and, **206**.32
introductory note, **200**.54–**200**.60
rule against perpetuities, and, **94**.37
trustees, **27**.16

Trusts of land
creation of interests by will, and, **8**.2
introductory note, **200**.51
meaning, **246**.103
residence rights, and
generally, **208**.5–**208**.18
introduction, **208**.3

Trusts of land – *contd*
statutory provisions
application of proceeds of sale, **246**.120
consents and consultation, **246**.113–**246**.114
introductory note, **246**.102
occupation rights, **246**.115–**246**.116
powers of court, **246**.117–**246**.116
purchaser protection, **246**.119
settlements and trusts for sale, **246**.103–**246**.107
trustees' functions, **246**.108–**246**.112
trustees, **27**.17

Trusts of Land and Appointment of Trustees Act 1996
application, **246**.127
citation, **246**.130
commencement, **246**.130
consequential provisions, **246**.129
definitions, **246**.125–**246**.126
extent, **246**.130
general effect, **200**.48–**200**.64
general provisions
appointment and retirement of trustees, **246**.122–**246**.124
trusts of land, **246**.103–**246**.121
introductory note, **246**.102
repeals, **246**.128
residence rights, **208**.3
schedule, **246**.131

Trusts of net profits and sale proceeds
gift of business interests, and, **205**.60

Trusts of settlement
gift of freehold land, and, **206**.31

Twice-married testators
preliminary note, **227**.1–**227**.6
spouses each with children from previous marriage, **227**.25–**227**.53
testator with children from both marriages, **227**.7–**227**.24

Two-year discretionary trusts
advantages, **225**.90
chattels, **225**.96
disadvantages, **225**.91
exempt distributions, **225**.85–**225**.87
generally, **218**.26
joint property, **225**.93
matrimonial home, **225**.94–**225**.95
precedent, **225**.97–**225**.109
relevant property, **225**.88
relevant trusts, **225**.89

U

Unattested documents, incorporation of
coming into existence after will, **15**.2
effect, **15**.3–**15**.4
express declaration, and, **15**.6
introduction, **15**.1
missing document, **15**.5
Uncertain conditions
generally, **34**.9–**34**.11
religion, and, **35**.29
residence, and, **35**.22
Uncertain description
charitable gifts, and, **103**.7
Uncertainty
donee, as to, **53**.5
introduction, **53**.1–**53**.2
perpetuity rule, and, **53**.7
persons to whom fund be appointed, as to, **53**.6
subject-matter of gift, as to, **53**.4
types, **53**.3
Undated wills
revocation by later will or codicil, and, **18**.11
Undivided shares
statutory provisions, **246**.51
Undivided shares in land, gift of
ademption, and, **41**.18
leasehold land, and, **207**.22
precedents, **204**.69–**204**.70
Undue influence
capacity to benefit, and, **9**.23
Undue influence – *contd*
fraud, **5**.9
introductory note, **200**.2–**200**.8
Unexhausted income
charitable gifts, and, **103**.16
Unfinished signature
form, **11**.14
place, **11**.8
Unincorporated companies
charitable gifts, and, **103**.5
Unintended life interest
presumptions, and, **51**.13
United Reformed Church, gifts to
precedent, **212**.18
United Synagogue, gifts to
precedent, **212**.24
Unitarian Christian Church, gifts to
precedent, **212**.22–**212**.23
Unlawful killing
capacity to benefit, and, **9**.13–**9**.22
forfeiture, statutory provisions, **247**.35–**247**.36
Unlimited gifts of income
charge on rents and profits, **62**.2
generally, **62**.1
rent of let property, **62**.4
until marriage, **62**.3
Unmarried
meaning, **55**.6
Unmarried couples with children, wills for
forms, **228**.4
introduction, **228**.1
lifetime gifts, **228**.3
living together with young children
planning to marry, and, **228**.4–**228**.18
residue on discretionary trusts, with, **228**.19–**228**.32
separated from spouse, where, **228**.33–**228**.43
non-civil partnership, **224**.4
special factors, **228**.2
Unmarried sisters, wills for
inheritance tax, **231**.5
precedent, **231**.52–**231**.60
survivorship, **231**.6–**231**.8

Unmarried testatrix, wills for
inheritance tax, **231**.5
precedent, **231**.61–**231**.76
survivorship, **231**.6–**231**.8
Unquoted shares, gift of
generally, **205**.29–**205**.40
precedents, **205**.66–**205**.67
Unsecured personal loans
investment powers, and, **220**.32
Ut res magis valeat quam pereat
uncertainty, and, **53**.2

V

Valuation
appropriation, and
common law, **29**.11
statutory power, **29**.18
Variation of beneficial interests
beneficiaries, **241**.2
capital gains tax, **241**.17
consideration, **241**.7
double death variations, **241**.14
family provision, and, **105**.39–**105**.40, **241**.20
form, **241**.6
free of tax, **241**.12
income tax, **241**.19
inheritance provision, **105**.39–**105**.40, **241**.20
interests in possession, **241**.8
multiple variations, **241**.15
notice of intention, **241**.3
precedents
creation of nil-rate band non-exempt legacy, **241**.27
death of spouses within two years of each other, **241**.29
disposition, **241**.25
disposition of joint property, **241**.26
short-term interest in possession of survivor, **241**.28
trusts settling life interest, **241**.30–**241**.31
prior to grant of probate, **241**.10
Variation of beneficial interests – *contd*
relevant estate, **241**.5
stamp duty, **241**.18
stamp duty land tax, **241**.18
subject to tax, **241**.12
***Vertu*, articles of**
description of property, **64**.3
Vested legacies
appropriation, and, **29**.1–**29**.2
Vesting
affecting circumstances
contingencies, **93**.5–**93**.8
gift over, **93**.9
postponement, **93**.4
children's trusts, **217**.7
conditions precedent, **93**.3
gift over, effect of
generally, **93**.16–**93**.23
legacies payable from personal property, **93**.41–**93**.43
introduction, **93**.1–**93**.3
legacies charged on mixed fund, **93**.45
legacies charged on real property, **93**.44
legacies payable from personal property
direction as to maintenance, **93**.31–**93**.39
direction as to payment, **93**.26–**93**.30
generally, **93**.24–**93**.25
gift over, **93**.41–**93**.43
severance from estate, **93**.40
life interests, and, **216**.6–**216**.7
meaning, **93**.1
presumption, **93**.2
remainders, of, **93**.10–**93**.15
Vicar of church, gifts to
precedent, **212**.8
Voidable transactions
disposable property, **7**.8
Voluntary revocation of will
codicil, by, **18**.15
destruction, by
burden of proof, **18**.31
codicils, and, **18**.24
duplicate, of, **18**.19
evidence of intention, **18**.18
extent, **18**.22

Voluntary revocation of will – *contd*
destruction, by – *contd*
incomplete, **18**.20
introduction, **18**.17
part, in, **18**.23
presumption, **18**.26–**18**.29
stranger, by, **18**.21
generally, **18**.1
intention
burden of proof, **18**.7
generally, **18**.4–**18**.5
proof, **18**.6
later will or codicil, by
codicil, **18**.15
form of instrument, **18**.16
introduction, **18**.8
last will, meaning, **18**.9
lost subsequent will, **18**.3
lost will, **18**.12
partly inconsistent will, **18**.14
same date will, **18**.11
subsequent inconsistent will, **18**.10
undated will, **18**.11
methods, **18**.2–**18**.3
partial
destruction, and, **18**.23
generally, **18**.32
intention, **18**.33
Voluntary settlement
admissibility as will, and, **10**.6

W

Wait and see rule
generally, **94**.17
power of appointment, and
common law, at, **94**.49
statute, under, **94**.53
War loans and bonds
description of property, **64**.58
Whimsical disposition
presumptions, and, **51**.7–**51**.8
Widowed parent with adult children
entire estate by willed widow
children absolutely, to, **230**.2–**230**.15
Widowed parent with adult children – *contd*
entire estate by willed widow – *contd*
discretionary trusts of residue for grandchildren, **230**.45–**230**.73
division of residue between children on trusts, **230**.16–**230**.29
division of residue between children and grandchildren on trusts, **230**.30–**230**.44
settling residue on children with progressive powers to pay capital, **230**.73–**230**.86
note, **230**.1
Widowed parent with young children
entire estate willed by widow
minor child on contingent trusts, to, **229**.26–**229**.36
settling residue on children with remainder to grandchildren, **229**.37–**229**.50
note, **229**.1
Wife. ***See also*** **Spouse**
divorce, and, **80**.3
gift of personal chattels, and, **204**.15–**204**.21
invalid marriage, in, **80**.6
subsequent marriage, by, **80**.1
surviving spouse, **80**.5
widowhood, during, **80**.2
Wild's case**, rule in**
gift to person and children, and, **85**.2
Will prepared by beneficiary
generally, **5**.4
solicitors, **5**.5
Will trusts
inheritance tax, **200**.92–**200**.106
spouses of civil partners, wills of, **200**.128–**200**.129
Wills Act 1837
amendments
1861, **244**.43–**244**.47
1918, **244**.48–**244**.52

Wills Act 1837 – *contd*
amendments – *contd*
1925, **244**.56
1968, **244**.84
1969, **244**.87
1982, **244**.95–**244**.97
1995, **244**.125, **244**.129
2004, **244**.133
definitions, **244**.3
extent, **244**.37–**244**.38
general provisions, **244**.4–**244**.36
introductory note, **244**.2
Wills Act 1861
application, **244**.47
general provisions, **244**.43–**244**.46
repeal, **244**.83
Wills Act 1963
citation, **244**.83
commencement, **244**.83
definitions, **244**.82
general provisions, **244**.77–**244**.81
Wills Act 1968
citation, **244**.85
general provisions, **244**.84
Wills Act Amendment Act 1852
definitions, **244**.43
general provisions, **244**.40–**244**.42
introductory note, **244**.39
Wills (Soldiers and Sailors) Act 1918
amendments
1969, **244**.87
definitions, **244**.52
general provisions, **244**.48–**244**.51
Witnesses to will
blind person, and, **12**.16
capacity to benefit
charging power, **9**.11
foreign wills, **9**.12
generally, **9**.3–**9**.9
soldiers' wills, **9**.10
generally, **12**.16
professional privilege, and, **12**.17
Wool in store
generally, **61**.1
Words below signature
generally, **11**.3
Written will
form of will, and, **10**.13–**10**.17
Wrong name
charitable gifts, and, **103**.3
signature of wills, and, **11**.20

Z

Zavah
admissibility as will, and, **10**.12

Witnesses of will

Word omitted

Words below signature

Written will

Wrong name

Wills Act Amendment Act 1852

Z

GENERAL TERMS AND CONDITIONS
FOR USE OF THE COMPACT DISC GOODS AND MATERIALS CONTAINED THEREIN

This Licence Agreement is between Reed Elsevier (UK) Limited trading as LexisNexis Butterworths ("we or us") and the individual or company ("you") to whom LexisNexis has agreed to supply the Compact Disc Goods ("the Goods") and the Materials and content contained therein ("the Materials"). The following terms and conditions govern your use of the Goods supplied by LexisNexis and the Materials available therein:

1. LICENCE; RESTRICTIONS ON USE

1.1 You are granted a non-exclusive, non-transferable, limited licence to access and use the Goods and the Materials from time to time made available to you for the purposes only of (i) research or study, (ii) providing professional services to your clients, and (iii) providing academic services to students. This licence is subject to the following limitations:

(a) The right to electronically display the Materials retrieved from the Goods is limited to the display of such Materials primarily to one person at a time;

(b) The right to obtain a printout of the Materials is limited to single printout of the Materials downloaded (collectively, "Authorised Printouts"). You are not permitted to sell these Authorised Printouts; and

(c) The right to retrieve and store machine-readable copies of the Materials is limited to the retrieval of a single copy of the Materials included in the Goods and storage of that copy in machine readable form primarily for one person's exclusive use. You are not permitted to transfer the Goods or the Materials electronically or via any other medium for commercial profit or for resale.

1.2 To the extent expressly permitted by applicable copyright law, you may make copies of Authorised Printouts and distribute Authorised Printouts and copies.

1.3 Except as specifically provided in Sections 1.1 and 1.2, you are otherwise prohibited from downloading, storing, reproducing, transmitting, displaying, printing, copying, distributing, or using the Materials retrieved from the Goods.

1.4 All right, title, and interest (including all copyrights and other intellectual property rights) in the Goods and the Materials (in both print and machine-readable forms) belong to us or our third party suppliers. You acquire no ownership of copyright or other intellectual property rights or proprietary interest in the Goods, the Materials, or copies thereof.

1.5 Except as specifically provided herein, you may not use the Goods or the Materials retrieved from the Goods in any fashion that infringes the copyright or proprietary interests therein.

1.6 You may not remove or obscure the copyright notice or other notices contained in the Materials retrieved from the Goods.

2. ACCESS TO SERVICES

2.1 Only you shall be entitled to access and use the Goods and the Materials ("Authorised Users").

2.2 Except for use incidental to occasional, short-term travel, you may not access the Goods and the Materials from outside the country for which it was issued.

2.3 Materials and features may be added to or withdrawn from the Goods and the Goods otherwise changed without notice.

2.4 You must ensure that each person having access to the Goods and the Materials:

(a) is an Authorised User; and

(b) is using those Goods and the Materials only in accordance with these General Terms and Conditions.

3. LIMITED WARRANTY

3.1 We represent and warrant that we have the right and authority to make the Goods and the Materials available pursuant to these General Terms and Conditions.

3.2 EXCEPT AS OTHERWISE PROVIDED IN SECTION 3.1, THE GOODS AND THE MATERIALS ARE PROVIDED ON AN "AS IS", "AS AVAILABLE" BASIS AND WE MAKE NO EXPRESS WARRANTIES UNDER THIS AGREEMENT, INCLUDING WITHOUT LIMITATION THAT THE GOODS AND THE MATERIALS ARE OR WILL BE COMPLETE OR FREE FROM ERRORS OR THAT INFORMATION WILL CONTINUE TO BE AVAILABLE TO US TO ENABLE US TO KEEP THE GOODS AND THE MATERIALS UP-TO-DATE.

4. LIMITATION OF LIABILITY

4.1 To the maximum extent permitted by law, a Covered Party (as defined below) shall not be liable for any loss, injury, claim, liability, or damage of any kind resulting in any way from (a) any errors in or omissions from the Goods

GENERAL TERMS AND CONDITIONS FOR USE OF THE COMPACT DISC GOODS AND MATERIALS CONTAINED THEREIN - ***continued***

or any Materials available or not included therein, (b) the unavailability or interruption to the supply of the Goods or any features thereof or any Materials, (c) any Authorised Users use or misuse of the Goods or Materials (regardless of whether you received any assistance from a Covered Party in using or misusing the Goods), (d) your use of any equipment in connection with the Goods, (e) the content of Materials, (f) any delay or failure in performance of the Goods, or (g) any negligence of a Covered Party or its employees, contractors or agents in connection with the performance of our obligations under this agreement.

4.2 "Covered Party" means (a) us, our affiliates, and any officer, director, employee, subcontractor, agent, successor, or assign of us or our affiliates; and (b) each third party supplier of the Materials, their affiliates, and any officer, director, employee, subcontractor, agent, successor, or assign of any third party supplier of the Materials or any of their affiliates.

4.3 Our liability to you for breach of any condition or warranty implied under any law which cannot be lawfully modified or excluded by this agreement shall, to the extent permitted by law, be limited at our option to supplying the Goods or the Materials again or paying for their re-supply. Nothing in this Agreement is intended to exclude liability for death or personal injury resulting from any negligence by us.

4.4 Our liability to you for loss or damage of any kind (including loss or damage caused by negligence) is reduced to the extent that you caused or contributed to that loss or damage.

4.5 SUBJECT TO CLAUSE 4.3, THE AGGREGATE LIABILITY OF THE COVERED PARTIES IN CONNECTION WITH ANY OTHER CLAIM ARISING OUT OF OR RELATING TO THE GOODS OR THE MATERIALS SHALL NOT EXCEED THE AMOUNT OF YOUR ACTUAL DIRECT DAMAGES. YOUR RIGHT TO MONETARY DAMAGES IN THAT AMOUNT SHALL BE IN LIEU OF ALL OTHER REMEDIES WHICH YOU MAY HAVE AGAINST ANY COVERED PARTY.

4.6 SUBJECT TO CLAUSE 4.3, THE COVERED PARTIES SHALL NOT BE LIABLE FOR ANY SPECIAL, INDIRECT, INCIDENTAL, OR CONSEQUENTIAL DAMAGES OF ANY KIND WHATSOEVER (INCLUDING, WITHOUT LIMITATION, LEGAL FEES) IN ANY WAY DUE TO, RESULTING FROM, OR ARISING IN CONNECTION WITH THE GOODS, THE MATERIALS, OR THE FAILURE OF ANY COVERED PARTY TO PERFORM ITS OBLIGATIONS, REGARDLESS OF ANY NEGLIGENCE OF ANY COVERED PARTY.

4.7 The Materials are provided for reference purposes only and are not intended, nor should they be used, as a substitute for professional advice or judgement or to provide legal advice with respect to particular circumstances.

4.8 Whilst reasonable efforts are made to make sure the Materials are up to date, you should obtain independent verification or advice before relying upon any piece of information in circumstances where loss or damage may result.

5. MISCELLANEOUS

5.1 These General Terms and Conditions may be changed from time to time as described below or by written agreement.

5.2 The failure of us or any third party supplier of the Materials to enforce any provision hereof shall not constitute or be construed as a waiver of such provision or of the right to enforce it at a later time.

5.3 You may not assign your rights or delegate your duties under these General Terms and Conditions without our prior written consent.

5.4 These General Terms and Conditions shall be governed by and construed in accordance with the laws of England.

5.5 Each third party supplier of the Materials has the right to assert and enforce these provisions directly on its own behalf as a third party beneficiary.

5.6 We will use personal information collected about Authorised Users for the purposes of (a) providing access to and use of the Goods to Authorised Users, (b) providing customer support, billing and other similar activities related to the Goods, and (c) keeping Authorised Users informed about products, services, offers and upcoming events and to improve our services. We may also provide personal information about Authorised Users to third parties for the purpose of providing Authorised Users with direct marketing offers which we think may be of interest. If you do not wish to receive information about other products, services, offers and events, notify us in writing.

5.7 In accordance with the Data Protection Act 1998 we will provide and export personal information about Authorised Users to other members of our company group, including Reed Elsevier Inc. in the United States, for the purposes of (a) providing access to and use of the Goods to Authorised Users, and (b) providing customer support, billing and other similar activities related to the Goods.

5.8 Save for the owners of any intellectual property supplied by us, no third parties shall acquire any rights under this Agreement and the provisions of the Contracts (Rights of Third Parties) Act 1999 are excluded.